Collectible Compact Disc Price Guide 2

Gregory Cooper

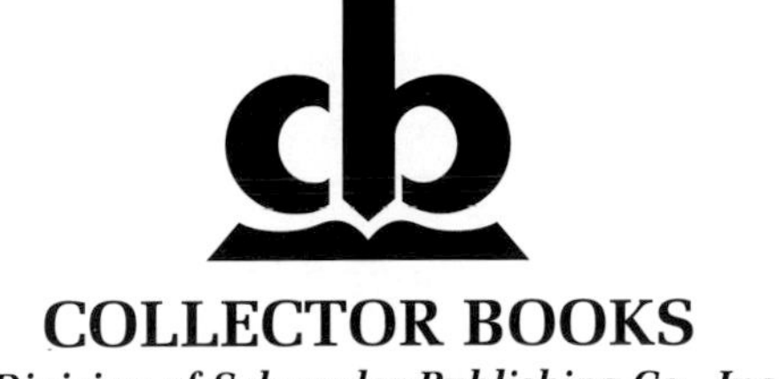

COLLECTOR BOOKS
A Division of Schroeder Publishing Co., Inc.

Contact Us:

CD Specialties, Inc. • P.O. Box 4582 • Pittsburgh, PA 15205 • Fax: 412-787-8532 • email: greg.cooper@cdspec.com

Visit our Website

Join our CD Collectors Club

For more information on updates to this guide, other collectible CDs, CD and laser disc reviews, etc., visit our internet web site at:

http://www.cdspec.com

Contribute

Become a part of history. Let us know about any collectible CD we might have overlooked. If there is any promotional, limited edition, out-of-print, or misprinted CD you don't see in this guide, send us the information. Please include the disc's title, artist, label, catalog number, type of disc, year of release, and country of origin. If you see any discs in the guide missing a catalog number, date of release, or simply a spelling error, tell us. We also want to know what you have paid for your collectible discs so we can update our values.

Please write, fax, or e-mail us. If you want to become a corporate sponsor of compact disc or laser disc collecting, contact us and we will let you know how you can be a part.

Promote your CD or laser disc by featuring it in the next edition of the *Collectible Compact Disc Price Guide (CCDPG)*. Send us a copy of the disc along with any publicity photos and press information. We're looking for anything and everything on optical disc that is limited edition, creatively packaged, a picture disc, or out-of-print, no matter how readily available or unbelievably obscure the disc. We are also looking for any promotional material relating to the CD or laser disc including test discs, prototypes, marketing or advertising kits, mock-ups, and basically anything at all relating to the CD or laser disc.

Advertise

If you wish to advertise your business in the next edition of the *CCDPG*, contact us for an advertising kit. If you have any collectible discs to sell, please send for the list of CDs, CD-ROMs, and laser discs that CD Specialties is looking for. Please note however, that neither CD Specialties nor Collector Books sell CDs or laser discs.

Additional copies of this book may be ordered from:

COLLECTOR BOOKS
P.O. Box 3009
Paducah, Kentucky 42002-3009
or
CD Specialties, Inc.
P.O. Box 4582
Pittsburgh, PA 15205

$17.95. Add $2.00 for postage and handling.

Contents

Dedication

To my family, whose support for so many years has always been an incredible source of inspiration. And, especially to the two most important women in my life, to my wife Carmen and to my mother Carol, but for whose vigilance, patience, and tireless dedication, this book would never have existed.

About the Author

Greg Cooper, the author of the world's first-ever and most respected CD and laser disc collector's guide, has been compiling lists of collectible CDs and tracking their value since 1988. He has scoured the world, consulting regularly with hundreds of collectors, dealers, and manufacturers to create the most complete and accurate data base of CD collectibles ever. Greg has written articles and has consulted on the subject of CD Collecting for numerous magazines and newspapers.

Greg not only enjoys writing about CDs, but he also enjoys creating them. Greg produced, designed, and mastered a special CD sampler for his wedding. The disc boasts a uniquely printed 6-color picture disc packaged in an innovative jewel box packaging design. The disc features officially licensed music contributed by artists such as Queen, Triumph, and Frank Mills, as well as a special wedding greeting by Triumph's Gil Moore.

Greg attends Duquense University's School of Law and plans to pursue a career in Intellectual Property Law (patents, trademarks, and copyrights) upon graduation in 1998. He is also a graduate of Purdue University's School of Materials Engineering, which has enabled him to understand the intricacies of CD technology as well as its relationship to the market place.

Greg currently resides in Pittsburgh, Pennsylvania, with his ever-patient wife Carmen, and their ever-mischievous cats, Sylvester and Brak.

Tommy Steele

Five-time Grammy nominated CD packaging designer, Tommy Steele is the vice president of art & design at Capitol Records in California. He has over twenty years of experience in the music art and design industry, and currently oversees worldwide CD packaging and advertising campaigns. He has also created the cover art for many Capitol records and CDs by such artists as the Beatles, Beach Boys, Eric Johnson, Bob Seger, and Frank Sinatra. Tommy Steele has truly been a pioneer in CD collecting, creating many of the special promotional and limited edition CD packages that have since become collectible. These packages include the famous "Leaning Tower of Pizza" pizza box and picture disc CD package; Tina Turner's "Foreign Affair" passport limited edition CD. Also, he created Capitol's 50th anniversary eight CD boxed set, and Blind Melon's "Soup" menu limited edition CD, just to name a few. Most recently he won the 39th Annual Grammy Award for CD Packaging for his "Ultralounge" design.

Acknowledgments

The *CCDPG #2* was a three-year project and an impossible task for just one person. I am grateful to the following people who believed in the vision of this guide and provided their assistance. Their help was invaluable and made the book that much better.

Wayne Adkins
Judy Anderson
Laurie Anderson
Gail Ashburn
Ken Ayoub
Lisa Bahadoor
Gene Baldwin
Joseph Barton
Chris Baur
James Bell
Colleen Benn
Mike Bessolo
Kevin Beyer
Betty Blank
Paula Bonhomme
Cheryl Botchick
Alain Boucher
Tricia Bowers
Craig Braun
Michelle Brown
Charles Anderson
David Callahan
Allison Cassity
Michael Catpral
Lana Cheek
Laurie Ande Chin
Mario A. Cirillo
David Coffey
Dan Cohen
Carmen Cooper
Carol Cooper
Mark Cooper
T.G. Cooper
Steve Coppel
Scott Cosby
Chris Coult
Leslie Crockett
Stan Cowan
Judy Crowly
Alex Curyea
Josh Danoff
Marlise Dawson
Carlos DeCouto
Galina Dearmin
Frank Deriso
Jim Donio
Paula Donner
David Dorn
Scott Doulas
Spencer Drate
Biji Ebbin
Craig Eggers
Marion Effinger
Loren Eisler
Steve Feldstein
Caroline Fern
Eric Ferris
Marc Finer
Mike Finnegan
John Fitzpatrick
Erik Flannigan
Suzanne Ford
Kim Freeman
Samantha Freeman
James Fries
Beverly Furman
Phil Gambell
Michael Gavner
Renee Geddis
Betsy Gibson
Peter Gidion
Jeff Giltenboth
Michael Goff
Jeff Gold
Barry Goldberg
Margret Goldfarb
Doug Gore
D.R. Goven
Derek Graham
George Grant
Craig Granato
Gene Hall
Lynn Hale
Jeff Hayward
Ginny Herman
John Hertzog
Randi Hill
Terry Hinte
Tim Holt
Horatio
Howie Horowitz
Ray Houle
Peter Howard
Heidi Hudson
Randall Jamail
Nitasha Jarvis
Gordon Jee
Gary Johnson
Wayne Johnson
James Johnston
Michelle Joran
M. Kassem
Shirley Kaye
Dan Kessler
Bill Kim
Chris Kingry
Elise Kingsly
Warren Kolodny
John Kopec
Bruce Kreger
Jim Ladwig
James Lance
Michawl Lang
David Lau
Marie Lawson
Sam Leibowitz
Stewart Levine
Bill Levinson
Janet Levinson
Jeff Lewis
Randy Lovoi
Lorraine Luongo
Sharyon Lynn
Mark Malmut
Rocco Mancini
Tim Mank
Louis Marino
Daniel Marx
Neal May
Darci Mayers
David McDonald
Stephen McGouldrick
Tom McGuiness
Andrea Mclelen
Laurie McManus
Robert McManus
Drew McNally
Joel Miller
Lance Mitzel
Lance Murray
Jeannie Nishida
Neil Norman
Mary-Eileen O'Donnel
John O'Mally
Stephen O'Neal
Shawn O'Sullivan
Cindy Olson
Mike Opelka
Doug Peel
Steven Peeples
Bob Perry
Brent Peterson
Leslie J. Pfenninger
Leslie Philipsen
Tom Philipson
August Polito
Mike Powers
Cherry Pyron
Tom Recchion
Curt Reichwein
Amy Remick
Dave Richards
Lori Rick
Ron Roberg
Tracy Roberson
Julie Robinson
Susan Roth
Tammy Roussin
J.B. Rund
Dan Russo
Stu Sable
Donna Sava
Brian Schantz
Chris Scharf
Joe Schleyhahn
Allen Schluger
Billy Schroeder
Melody Schubert
Jeffrey Schulz
Aida Scorza
Edward Seaman
Greg Seigel
Edward Seaman
Julie Shapiro
Ellen Shea
Barbara Shelly
Bill Shepherd
Ray Slay
Zack Small
Booker Smith
Marcus Sokolski
Louise Spencer
John Sperling
Tommy Steele
Barbara Stockwell
Lisa Stroup
Susan Swan
Laurie Swick
Rick Sylvain
Scott Talbet
Karen Trachtenberg
Heidi Trada
Barry Tucker
Giulio Turturro
Neal Umphred
Gerard Van Der Vorst
Tray Walden
Gina Warren
Tracy Warrington
Lou Warycia
Allen Weinberg
Thad Wharton
Laural Whitcomb
Kat Williams
Phil Zuckerman

Corporate Support

Abbey Road Distributors
AGI
Allan Schluger Company
Alpha Enterprises
American Gramaphone
Ames Specialty Packaging
Angel Records
Applewood Books
Arista Nashville
Around the World Music
Atlantic Records
Aubergine Records
Audio Junction
Azra Records
B&C Connection
Barbara Shelly Public Relations
Billboard Magazine
Blockbuster Music
Blood And Fire
Brouhaha Compact Discs
Buena Vista Television
Calumet Carton Company
Canadian Friends Of Mine
Capital Cities/ ABC, Inc
Capricorn Records
Caroline Records
Castle Communications
CD Collector Newsletter
CD International
CD Review
CEMA Special Products
Central Park West
Charles S. Anderson Design
Chrysalis Records
Cinram
Cleopatra Records
CMC International
CMJ
Cohen Milstein & Hausfeld
Co-Joint Corporation
Communications Research
Contempt Mail Order
Cuba Gmbh
Denon Digital Industries
Denon Records
Digital Audio Disc Corporation
Digital Cafe
Digital Domain
DIR Radio Network
Disc Art
Disc Manufacturing, Inc.
Discolandia
DiscoVision Associates
Dobbin Bolbla Associates
Earwax
EMI Music
Esprit Mail Order
ESX Interactive
Fantasy Records
FedEx
Finest Compact Discs
First Amendment Records
Fox Video
Gelardi Design
General Publishing Company
Giant Records
Gillian and Harris Public Relations
Global Satellite Network
GNP Crescendo
Griffin Music
Harriet Sterling Management
Hasbro Interactive
High Bridge Publishing
Hollywood Records
ICE Newsletter
Image Entertainment
International Packaging Corporation
Invers Ink
Ivy Hill
Jack Wolack's Rare Necessities
JL Records
Judy Anderson Associates
Just Design
Keystone Music Exchange
Kim Freeman & Associates
Kita Group
Knowledge Industry Publications
Laser Exchange
Lasers Edge
Laserfile, Inc.
Lazerla Music Co.
Litzky
London records
Lucasfilm
LucasArts
Lumivision
MacDaddy Entertainment
Manning Selvage & Lee
Max Music
MCA Home Video
MCA Universal
Mercury Records
Mobile Fidelity
Mod Lang
Monster Music
Mosaic Record Company
Music Machine
Music Video Distributors
National Academy of Recording Arts & Sciences, Inc.
National Association of Recording Merchendisers
Nimbus Records
North Georgia Disc
Old Hippie
Optical Disc Association
Opticord
Pacific Microsonics, Inc.
Pendulum Records
Philips Consumer Electronics
Philips Digital Classics
Philips Interactive Media
Pikosso Records
Pilz Records
Pilz Manufacturing
Pinnacle Enterprises
Pioneer Electronics
Pioneer LDCA
Pioneer Video Manufacturing
Allison at Playboy, Inc.
Playmate Toys
Polygram Group Distribution
Pyramid Records
Rand McNally Media Services
Record Rover
Recording Industry Association of America
Reference Recordings
Relative Action
Reprise Records
Republic Pictures
Rhino Records
R.I.P. Records
River North Records
Rock Dreams
Rock Island records
Rockaway Records
Rykodisc
Savoy Records
Schwan
Sega of America
Shape Optimedia
Sight & Sound
Smash Compact Discs
Smogtown Records
Society of Professional Audio Recording Services
Sony Classical
Sony Distribution Services
Sony Electronics
Sony Records
Software Sculptures
Something Special
Sonic Temple
Sonopak
Sound Source Interactive
Southland CD
THX Division, Lucasfilm
Toshiba
Toy Biz
Trek Pak
20th Century Fox Home Video
U.S. Laser Distributors
Varese Sarabande
Verve Records
Viacom Multimedia
Vinyl Vendors
Virgin Records
Voyager
Walt Disney Records
Walt Disney World
Warner Brothers Records
Warner Home Video
Warner Kids
WEA
Westland Graphics
Wiz Technologies
World Wide CD

My sincerest apologies to anyone who was inadvertently omitted. Even as you read this guide, we are working on the next edition. Let us know what collectible discs you have that are not found in this edition.

Cover Design
Beth Summers/Greg Cooper
Layout – Kent Henry
Photography – Charles R. Lynch

Foreword

Is nothing sacred? Is everything collectible? In a word, yes. I am a collector as well, in the process of creating collectibles. But more than that I am involved with teams of people to create art—commercial art, still art nonetheless. The world is awash in a sea of visually stimulating images. The staccato-editing of television commercials and music videos are testimonies to that. My job is to help the consumer find our products by getting good ideas and images translated to the printed medium. The smaller format of CDs is both an opportunity and a challenge. I've always loved books and am an author of a few. The CD format lends itself to good book design in terms of layout, spacing, and typography. It's just smaller — a lot smaller. The reduction of scale dictates stronger, more memorable imagery on covers. Compact disc covers in stores can be likened to mini billboards. Covers have to register quickly to attract buyers.

Which brings us to innovative packaging, both in materials and concept. Every field of commerce tries to push the boundaries of whatever limitations are imposed. That exploration is what has propelled us to find new ways to approach CD packaging. The jewel box format was sold to consumers from the beginning as a fait accompli from the record industry. Album printers have been scurrying ever since to find ways to package CDs utilizing their specialty, board printing and fabrication. The Digi-pak, the Q-pak, the Eco-pak, and various other configurations have emerged as answers to their concerns and have opened the market place to include many new ways to package music. All of these formats have had to fall in line with the size specifications of the standard jewel box.

Making a splash in the hypey world of the record industry and of radio programmers was the instigation of special or limited-edition packaging. Whether a record label was touting their artist roster through a sampler or whether an established artist needed some extra visibility through attention-getting packaging, collectible CDs were bound to happen. Art directors and designers were thrilled to have such an expanded palette available.

Ideas can come from anywhere. And that's where we look for them — anywhere. Execution is king in the final analysis and detail matters. Every aspect is considered, down to the design of the label itself. The questions we like to ask ourselves are "Is the solution unique? Is the solution appropriate? Is the solution affordable?" Our first attempt was a sampler of music now known as the "Capitol Leaning Tower Pizza Box" — a very limited edition. Jim Ladwig of AGI (Album Graphics, Inc.) had shown me a blank box prototype that looked like a pizza box. I've always viewed the historic Capitol Records building in Hollywood, known internally as "The Tower," as the Southern California version of Italy's leaning tower of Pisa. The chef on our box was modeled after our president at the time, Hale Milgrim. We were able to finish this one off with an Italian-colored menu of our sampled artists and their track listing, the imitation grease stain on the bottom of the box, and our first five-color CD label showing the top view of a real pizza pie. Now that's amore!

Our next, more public attempt at a special package, came about in order to showcase our international superstar artist, Tina Turner, to her fans. Her album title provided the immediate concept for this one entitled "Foreign Affair." Tina is a British citizen as it turns out, so we explored a British passport as a way of packaging her new music and highlighting photos. A lot of time and a large team of people went into making this one authentic, including finding the outside material used on genuine British passports. This project had to be completed on a very tight deadline to be released simultaneously with her regular CD and it had to be created to cost consumers not $5 more than her regular CD. Luckily, we got our visas stamped on this one.

I consider music to be one of the world's highest art forms, one that speaks to all cultures about anything and everything — love, money, politics, life — from the profane to the profound. Music is the cheapest form of long-term entertainment that we have. I am proud to assist artists in creating visual art for their music. It is a legacy not to be taken lightly. Music is not a part of our disposable society. I value it as a priceless keepsake available to hear and to look at again and again.

Tommy Steele
Vice-President — Art and Design
Capitol Records

Collectible Compact Discs

Nowadays, virtually any product, a car, a comic book, a baseball card, a Happy Meal toy and yes, even a compact disc (CD), can become collectible. CDs have been around for over 14 and laser discs for almost 20 years. As the *Collectible Compact Disc Price Guide* (*CCDPG*) attests, thousands of discs have come and gone over those years and have become quite rare. Traditionally, music and film memorabilia like records, posters, and advertising materials have been highly collectible. It is logical that the evolution of CDs and laser discs to the collectible plateau would take place.

The fact that this industry is so young only means that there is opportunity. How often will you find that $500 baseball card in a box of commons selling for five cents? Never. How often will you find that $1,000 record in the bargain bin for a buck? Almost never. Well, with the CD, this can happen and will continue to happen for years to come. The *CCDPG* gives you an inside peek into the secrets of the newest collectible craze.

Like almost all collectibles, CDs sell through two markets — a primary market and a secondary market. The primary market is where most CDs start. This is best known as the retail market. Here, discs sell as new for the first time through a retailer like your local Musicland, Camelot, or Tower Record Stores. Manufacturing and distributing costs from the record company plus an added profit margin for the retailer create the base for retail price. The disc's value in the primary market is called its "retail price."

The secondary market in contrast, is a market where the CD has traded hands at least once and is sold as a "used CD." The secondary market comprises record stores that carry used CDs, CD vendors at record shows and in trade papers, and even much of the new "import CD" market. Price in this market is determined by some perceived value that the disc has, either as a valuable commodity or simply as a used product. If the market views the disc as a valuable commodity, the disc's price is set above retail, the amount determined by how much the seller thinks a buyer will be willing to pay. Currently, valuable commodity CDs sell anywhere from $15 to thousands of dollars. If the market views a disc simply as a used product, the disc is valued below retail price. Used discs currently sell anywhere from one $1 to $10. Because CD collecting is new, many discs with potential long time value are being sold today in the secondary market at used CD prices.

Amos, Tori (Y Kan't Tori Read) – Y Kan't Tori Read (Atlantic 81845-2) One of the most highly sought after and popular out-of-print CDs to date. This disc was originally packaged in a long box (not shown). Released in 1988 to little fanfare, in fact *Y Kan't Tori Read* was soon after found in bargain bins from $2.99 to $7.99 still in the long box, until the success of *Little Earthquakes* shot its value peaking at $425.

Collectibility

The secondary market is where you find collectible CDs. Of course the sign of a good collectible is gauged by the strength of this secondary market. The values established in this market are based wholly on the age old laws of supply and demand. The greater the supply and lower the demand, the lower the price. The greater the demand and lower the supply, the greater the price. But what makes a CD collectible? Can we determine the collectibility of a CD that is still at the retail stores? What makes one collectible CD more valuable than another?

The only general characteristics of a collectible CD are that

•it is legitimately manufactured by a record company having copyright ownership over the material on the disc; and

•it is either out-of-print or manufactured in limited quantity.

Since collectibility is defined by the desirability of the CD in the secondary market, the value of a potentially collectible CD might be lower than the original value — at least initially. Consider this opportunity for collectors which, and as we will discuss later, is not so bad.

Once a disc reaches the threshold of being collectible, six factors come into play to determine its degree of collectibility. Those factors are

- popularity and/or demand of the artist on the disc;
- availability of the disc;
- uniqueness of the disc;
- history of the disc;
- retail price of the disc;
- age and preservability of disc; and
- generation and format of music on the disc.

McCartney, Paul – All the Best/New World Sampler (Capitol DPRO-79671)
U.S. 1993 promotional two CD sampler.

Popularity and/or Demand of the Artist

It is important to distinguish between a popular artist and a "collectible" artist. Just because an artist consistently releases number one albums, does not always mean that any collectible discs will result. Of course, the opposite can be true as well. A non-chart topping artist can have such a following that virtually all of their discs become super collectible. For example, artists like Tori Amos whose albums do not race up to the number one Billboard position have such a dedicated following that many of her CDs have become highly collectible and valuable. Some artists like Elvis Presley, Michael Jackson, Madonna, and Pearl Jam enjoy both significant popularity and collectibility. An advantage a highly popular artist does have is high demand. Whether that demand has the wherewithal to pay for a collectible CD is another issue. A disadvantage with a popular artist is that too few CDs by that artist are made in limited quantity. Record companies logically try to make enough product to adequately supply the demand. As a result, discs by popular artists are made in huge quantities, often ranging into the millions.

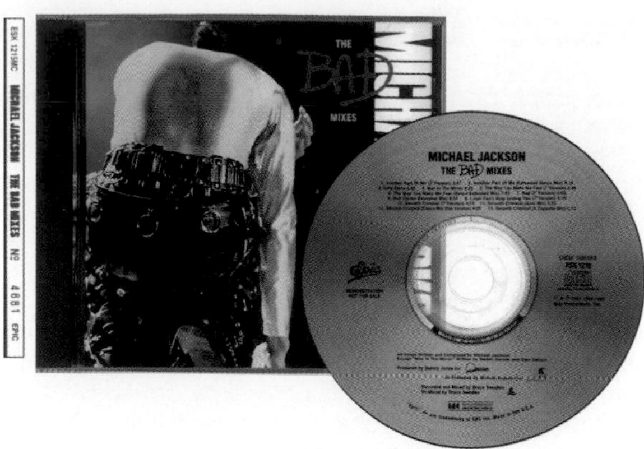

Jackson, Michael (Bad Mixes, The) – (Epic/Monster Music ESK 1215MC) This is probably one of the rarest and most valuable value added CDs. Distributed by Monster Cable as a test disc for their product, the disc is nowhere to be found. Few have turned up but dealers have demanded and collectors have paid between $300 and $500 for this item. The album is a collection of remixed songs from Michael Jackson's *Bad* album.

Availability

Availability relates to the quantity of a particular CD title that makes it to the market place. While the quantity of a title manufactured is a relevant number when gauging availability, it is not totally reliable. In practice, many factors realistically affect — even reduce — the availability of a title in the market place . For instance, CDs that are released for a finite period of time, later recalled and the extras destroyed, as is the case of promotional CDs, will obviously diminish availability. Sometimes a disc is so desirable that even if many copies exist, everyone who has one is reluctant to give it up and thus, very few make it to the secondary market. Sometimes availability is limited in certain geographic areas for various reasons. This was the case when 10,000 copies of the limited edition version of the Rolling Stones' *Steel Wheels* album were released in 1989. It was in such high demand creating such distribution problems that it never made it to the Pittsburgh, Pennsylvania, market. At that time, it was one of the most highly sought collectibles.

These first two categories illustrate the classical doctrine of supply and demand. Obviously the nexus between supply and demand is the most important factor when determining the value of a CD. As previously mentioned, if the demand is high yet supply low, the disc will increase in value. In contrast, if that demand is equal to or falls below the supply, the disc will decrease in value. Keep in mind however, this supply and demand process applied to collectible CDs is very dynamic. The availability of a disc that is currently high to a low demand can, over time, reverse the trend. When the disc supply falls below that demand, look for the disc's value to possibly skyrocket. Being able to predict which CD's supply will fall below its demand is the real trick to collecting potentially valuable CDs.

Grant, Amy – Lead Me On (Myrrh 9016656472) Extremely rare and unique promotional CD. This partial picture disc uses a five color silkscreen process making an impressive combination with the gold reflective layer. Each disc is autographed and individually numbered with black permanent marker.

Uniqueness

These remaining four criteria for collectible CDs are nuances used to determine a more precise value. Some discs, already valuable because of their rarity or artist, become more so because of an additional feature that is unique. This means packaging. Unique packaging makes the disc more valuable because its collectibility transcends merely the collector of that artist to include collectors of any special packaging. This increases the demand for that disc even more. A disc can become valuable strictly on the basis of packaging regardless of the artist.

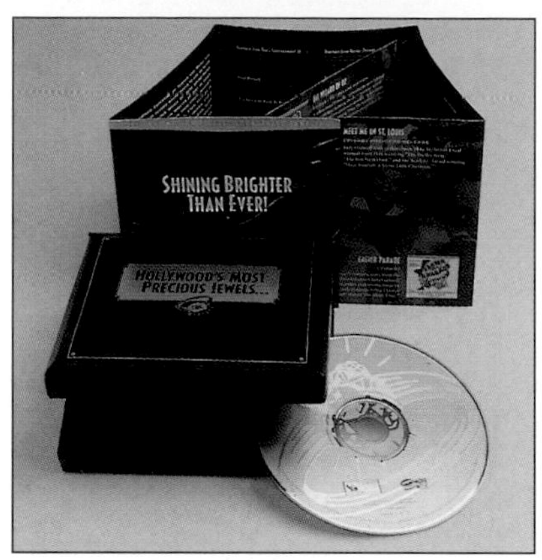

Hollywood's Most Precious Jewels – (Rhino PRCD 7141)

History

A CD having an interesting history always increases its value. This fascination with inside information about a disc eclipses the disc's intrinsic value and gives it a life of its own. Anecdotes about how a CD package was made, or why a particular disc was made, etc., can make the ordinarily mundane collectible CD much more interesting and hence much more valuable.

Library of Congress Presents: Historic Presidential Speeches (Rhino PRCD 7138) Sampler promoting the Rhino boxed set of famous presidential speeches.

Retail Price

It is common knowledge in any collecting community that retail price is generally irrelevant when determining the value of a long established collectible in the secondary market. Because values in the market are based solely on supply and demand, a disc originally retailing for $100 might someday lose value and later sell for only a few dollars. Conversely, a CD retailing for only a few dollars might someday sell for over $100. A caveat however, because CDs are relatively new as collectibles, and CDs are being sold on the secondary market for the first time, the current retail price is often used as an initial guide to establish a basis for worth and will rise or fall depending on the reaction of the market. One also finds used CD stores selling potentially collectible CDs at standard "used CD" prices. This is a great opportunity for us collectors to find valuable CDs at reasonable prices. I have, for example, found rare Elvis Presley reprocessed stereo CDs valued at hundreds of dollars for eight bucks each at such a record store. I am convinced that somewhere out there lies a copy of Tori Amos' *Y Kan't Tori Read* CD lying at the bottom of a $5 bargain bin. In what other collectible market place does there exist this opportunity? None. This is truly one of the advantages of CD collecting.

Costello, Elvis – Taking Liberties (Columbia CK 36839) U.S. 1984 out-of-print CD album.

Age and Preservability

The conventional wisdom that the older a CD is the more valuable it must be is not necessarily a correct assumption. The fact that one CD is older than another does not necessarily make it more valuable. Age of course increases the value of CDs already having potential value. This is not so with CDs in-print for long periods of time. CDs that have been around for years mean more copies are available in the market place. If age was demonstrative to value why are so many old records out-of-print for years still worth almost nothing.

The preservability of CDs and how it relates to value is an interesting issue to collectors. Because CDs are wear resistant and will last for a long time, it is theoretically possible that whatever quantity was available upon release will diminish little over time. This is true except that many valuable discs are housed in elaborate, even fragile, packaging and condition of the package is a big issue. In fact, since minor scratches on the disc do not affect play, those scratches are less likely to affect value then scratches on the package. The more wear and tear a package shows the less valuable it is, even if the disc itself is in perfect condition. Consult the Grading section in this guide to evaluate the condition of your discs.

Preservability is also an issue with different types of CDs. If a disc is of a type that consumers will automatically preserve and take care of, like special limited editions or commemorative CDs, virtually the entire supply of those discs on the collectors' market will be in mint condition. Hence, mint condition will not add to the value of a limited edition CD because it is expected. Poor condition however, will diminish the CD's value dramatically. On the other hand, there is the promotional CD that DJs and reviewers treat as a tool rather than a collectible, often damaging the packaging. Hence, the quantity of promotional CDs available in mint condition diminishes. Finding a promotional disc in mint condition is comparably more valuable than finding a limited edition in mint condition.

Generation and Format of Music

Generation or age of the collector can substantially affect the value of a disc. Often the generation that is most financially secure and can afford to pay the most for a disc will see his or her music becomes more expensive. For example, the prices paid for Beatles collectibles are at an all-time high because the 45 to 55 year old "baby boomer" generation is wealthy enough and willing to pay for these items.

Format of music is also a factor to determine value. The aforementioned generation collects rock and roll rarities from the 50s and 60s, which are currently very hot and very expensive. Other formats of music that are generally collectible are alternative, heavy metal, rhythm & blues, jazz, and country. Other formats like rap, world music, and electronic (new age) music are less collectible. Remember however, these are broad generalizations made over a cross section of artists from each category. Many exceptions to these generalizations exist in every format. Also, those formats that are currently less collectible may become more valuable in the future, and are certainly the formats to watch.

Monkees, The – Then & Now...The Best Of (Arista A2CD 8432) U.S. 1986 out-of-print CD album.

As we look at the various types of collectible CDs, keep these aforementioned value criteria in mind. There is no magic formula in these criteria however, that can produce an exact value. Rather, it is a hodge podge of subjectively applied reasons why a disc receives a certain value. We must each determine for ourselves what a particular disc is worth to us. Time will eventually build a consensus to what a collectible CD is worth just as it has with virtually every other long established collectible.

Fresh Bush And the Invisible Man – Hard Times (IRS DPRO-67104) Promotional CD single depicting President Bush playing guitar.

Out-of-Print Compact Discs

Out-of-print CDs are discs once commonly available, but since deleted and no longer sold at the retail level. But how can any title from media as new as the CD can become out of print, let alone become worth anything? As we know, CDs have been around for over 14 years. Literally thousands of titles have come and gone over that time. While it is true that some titles are deleted because of lackluster sales; they are also deleted because of copyright difficulties, master rights changes, and even errors in the disc or packaging that need correcting. For our purposes, out of print also includes CD-singles and limited editions that appear on the market for only a brief time.

Out-of-print CDs may seem new to the scene. This, however, is a misconception. CDs have been circulating in and out of print since the first CD was released. The first Beatles CD, *Abbey Road*, for example, was deleted immediately after its release in Japan in 1982 due to copyright issues. The rights to David Bowie's CD catalog, released in 1983 by RCA, soon changed hands to Rykodisc. Subsequently, RCA deleted its entire CD catalog. Granted, out-of-print CDs make up only a portion of the listings in this guide, that will change over time. As more titles become deleted, we might see the number of out-of-print titles begin to eclipse other types of collectible CDs.

We have presented for you an extensive listing of out-of-print CDs. The following is a detailed discussion of important distinctions between types of out-of-print CDs.

Green Jello – Cereal Killer Soundtrack (Zoo 72445-11038-2) Original first pressing *Green Jello* version. The disc was repressed under artist *Green Jelly* due to trademark conflicts with Jello brand gelatin by General Foods. The disc was packaged in a generic Zoo Entertainment long box (not shown).

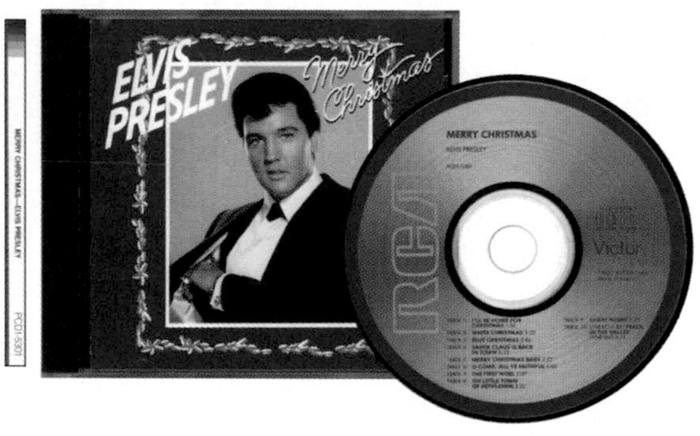

Presley, Elvis – Merry Christmas (RCA PCD1-5301)

Utopia – POV (Passport PBCD 6044)

Beach Boys – Surfin' Sufari and Party/Stack-O-Tracks (Capitol) Rare out-of-print double albums with exclusive bonus tracks. In 1994 the entire Capitol Beach Boys double album series was replaced with single album discs containing no bonus tracks for a mere $3 discount in price.

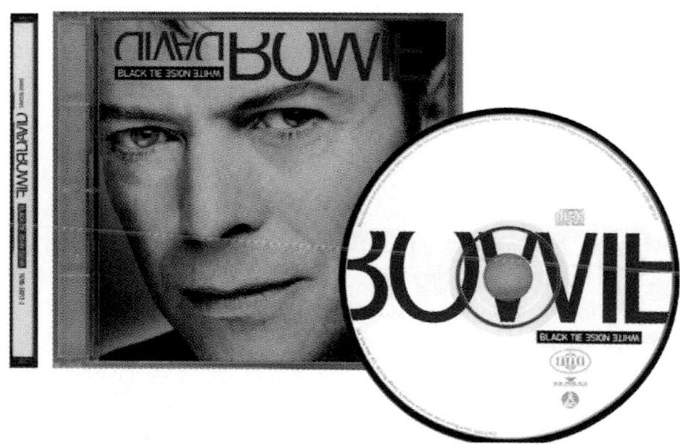

Bowie, David – Black Tie White Noise (Savage 74785-50212-2) First released in 1993 from the now defunct Savage label, the disc has since been reissued by Virgin Records.

Utopia – Trivia (Passport PBCD 6053)

KBC Band – KBC (Arista ARCD 8440)

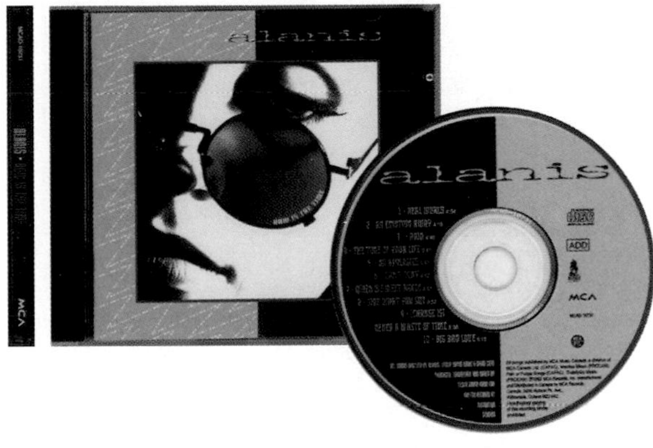

Morissette, Alanis – Now Is the Time (MCA MCAD-101) Sounding more akin to Madonna and Taylor Dane, this long out-of-print CD is a far cry from her most recent work.

Prince – "Black Album" (Warner Brothers) The disc on the left is probably the most infamous reissue. This disc is a quasi reissue, however, because the first issuance never officially occurred though that first disc exists (on the right). The story begins in 1987 when Prince and Warner Brothers, were set to release the album. Prince wanted to release it anonymously. Contrary to Prince's request however, the *Black Album* was advertised as the "new Prince album." Upset by this, Prince scrapped the entire project, buying back all copies of the CD, LP, and cassette to have them destroyed. However, in 1991 a legitimate copy of the *Black Album* on CD sold in an auction for $11,000.

Then in an attempt to fulfill a contract with Warner Brothers, Prince authorized the official release of the *Black Album* on November 22, 1994. The new issue was advertised as "available for a limited time at a 99.99% discount." (Actually a 99.84% discount.)

Regardless of the attempt to replicate the original *Black Album*, the reissue is distinguishable. Most obvious is that the new pressing has a different catalog number (new disc is 45793-2, original disc is 2-45793) and was not packaged in a long box. The original also clocks in one second shorter than the reissue.

Kinks, The – UK Jive (MCA MCAD-6337)

Outlaws – Hurry Sundown (Collector's Pipeline TCP 016CD)

First Issues

First issue CDs are unique to the CD collecting world. These are CDs manufactured in either Japan or Germany for worldwide distribution between 1982 and 1985[1]. The *CCDPG* clearly identifies first issue CDs in the listing by the symbol U.S.† in the country column.

First issues are distinguishable from typical import CDs. Import CDs are made by foreign record companies to be distributed in their respective countries and merely imported into the United States. First issue CDs were manufactured abroad for domestic record companies and distributed exclusively in the United States. If you have any of these first issues, you will notice that the booklet and tray card were printed in the United States and only the disc made in either Germany or Japan.

First issues are rare collectibles because among other reasons, only small numbers of each title were made available. Since there were so few pressing plants to supply the world's demand, everyone received only small shipment of titles. Also, because CD manufacturing was a new process, a plant could only press thousands at a time where today they can press millions at a time.

In today's market first issues have become difficult to distinguish from later common pressings. You can still find first issue CDs in your local record stores selling as used and sprinkled among later pressings. Most stores however, sell used CDs in a closed jewel box sometimes sealed by a plastic keeper or shrink-wrapped. More often, retailers remove the CD from the jewel box altogether leaving the empty box in a bin proving impossible to tell whether it is a first pressing. The only foolproof method to determine if you are buying a first issue is to actually inspect the disc[2].

disc Details

How to Identify A First Issue

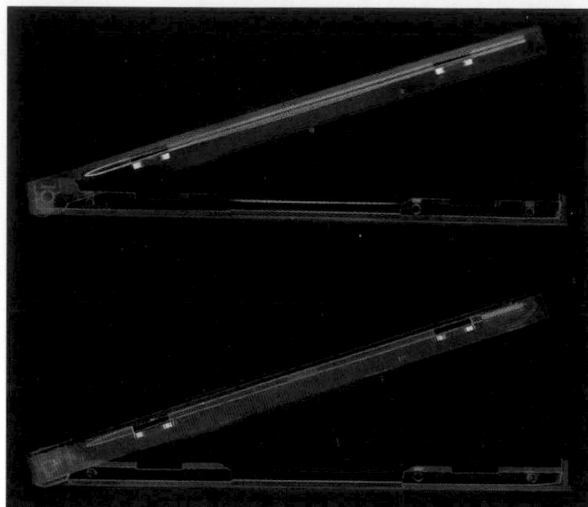

An easy method of identifying a first issue disc from a current disc is to inspect the top and bottom spine of the jewel case lid. On the top is the spine of a first issue door, notice the opaque look. From 1987 on, jewel boxes were manufactured like the box on the bottom having a vertical corrugated look.

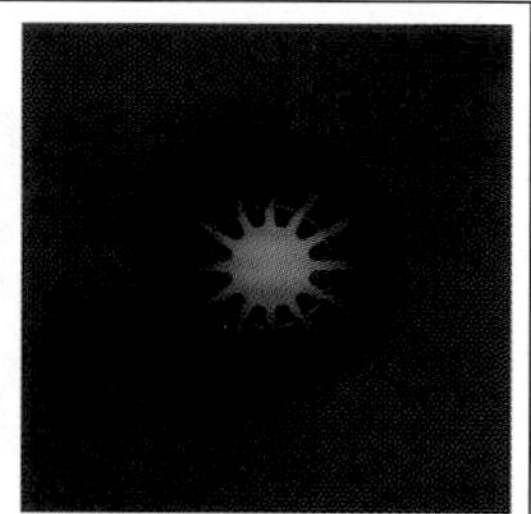

Many have noticed the difference between eight tooth and twelve tooth jewel box trays. The eight tooth is from the original early '80s design of the jewel box. The twelve tooth was created later because it tended to hold the disc a bit more securely than the eight tooth.

Madonna – Like A Virgin (Warner Brothers 9 25157-2) This 1984 first pressing is unique from subsequent pressings in that it has a striking blue base color. This is only available on the first pressing made in Japan for U.S. distribution. All subsequent pressings have one color black title work.

Queen – News of the World (Elektra 112-2) Original Queen CDs on the Elektra label are extremely rare. This original pressing was manufactured in Germany in 1983. Note the two color full printed "cross" graphic indicative of first issue releases manufactured in Hanover. (Some first issues from Japan were printed with this "cross.")

Rolling Stones – Still Life (Atco 39113-2) This rare 1983 album is the first Rolling Stones record on CD. The remaining Rolling Stones catalog was not released until 1986, only *Still Life* and *Rewind Album* from 1984 were available. Notice the trademark "cross logo" indicative of a first issue CD.

Springsteen, Bruce – Nebraska (Columbia CK 38358) This rare version of the album has an extended version of *My Fathers House*, which is four minutes longer than the currently available version. This disc can be identified by the white strip. The rare version **does not** say "Now Made in the U.S.A."

Led Zeppelin IV (Atlantic 19129-2) First Issue Led Zeppelin CD.

Lennon, John – Shaved Fish (EMI CDP 7 46642 2) This first pressing made in Japan for import into the U.S. clocks in at 41:42 as opposed to the current version clocking in at 41:57.

Lennon, John – Double Fantasy (Geffen 2001-2) Original U.S.† 1984 CD album.

disc Details

Made in the U.S.A.?

CDs released by the Columbia family of labels prior to 1984 had a standard format similar to that on the left (i.e. the white vertical bar with the UPC code at the bottom on the back of the tray card). After the opening of the Digital Audio Disc CD manufacturing plant in Terre Haute, Indiana, these same discs were re-released with the same packaging but with "Now Made in the U.S.A." notice in that white space as shown on the right. Discs not containing this notice can be a helpful hint in finding a "first issue" CD by Columbia.

Limited Editions

As the music industry continues to recognize the profitability of the CD collectors' market, more limited editions are accompanying the regular release of many titles. Most limited editions are marketed in elaborate packages, and typically number in quantity from 2,500 to 100,000 copies per title.

The limited edition market is probably the most speculative market in CD collecting. Seasoned collectors in most hobbies live by the adage "if something is sold as limited edition, it isn't, and has little chance of becoming valuable." This rationale is based on collectors' experience with overproduction. The idea of a limited edition should typically conjure up notions of value and rarity. In reality, the term limited edition becomes a code word for manufactured synthetic collectibles. Everyone will be able to buy it at retail price for years thereby causing it to have little secondary market value. This adage, though true, has only limited application toward the CD market. Limited edition CDs have a special attraction because they often contain more extras than the commonly available issue. Additions like elaborate packaging and extra tracks or even bonus discs offering as much as an hour of extra music make limited editions desirable.

The limited edition's only Achilles' heal is the quantity made available. Some record companies are smart and make only enough copies to supply the initial demand. Other record companies have occasionally saturated the market. For example, Rykodisc manufactured only 2,500 limited edition copies of Sugar's *Copper Blue* CD that sold out almost immediately. In contrast, the Rolling Stones limited edition reissues by Virgin Records, manufactured in quantities of about 90,000 copies per title, took some time to evaporate from the market.

As a guideline, limited editions of 2,500 to 10,000 copies can expect to sell out almost immediately. In the current climate, quantities of anything over 10,000 copies, regardless of the artist, will tend to saturate the market. Good news though, 10,000 is the saturation of the current market, not, and I must emphasize not, the future market. As this market expands 10,000 copies will no longer be a saturation point and those limited editions made in larger quantity might substantially increase in value.

Translated, many limited editions manufactured in quantities greater than 10,000 will require time to mature. When limited editions remain on the shelf at the retail level for years, they require time to allow the demand to out weigh the supply. A perfect case illustrating this point is Keith Richards' *Talk Is Cheap* limited edition. It was released in 1988 as one of the first limited edition packages retailing for $19.95. This limited edition took almost three years to completely sell out at the retail level. It was not until four years later in 1992 that the disc matured to the collectors' market where it now fetches up to $40.

Limited editions, by inherence are made to be kept as a collectors' item. They are therefore, preserved so if they do make it to the collectors' market all the available copies are in mint condition. This will create an overabundance of limited editions all in perfect condition thereby lessening potential rarity. This is where the aforementioned preservability criterion becomes a concern.

Many limited editions found in this guide are not elaborate or specially packaged CDs. Instead they are common looking jewel box packaged discs made available for a finite time. In fact, the *CCDPG* contains titles that can still be found at retail, but because they have a finite life span, they qualify for the guide[3]. Classic examples from this category are the Led Zeppelin *Remasters* U.S. two CD pressing marketed through Time/Warner Sound Exchange and Pink Floyd's *The Wall* CD album from Mobile Fidelity. Both were modestly packaged, housed in the standard jewel box, but both were available for just a limited time and are currently unavailable at the retail level.

Costello, Elvis – Kojack Variaty (Warner Brothers 9 45903-2) An unbelievably limited edition of only 200 copies were made available. The disc contains two bonus tracks not available on the regular version – *Step Inside Love* and *Sticks and Stones.*

disc Details

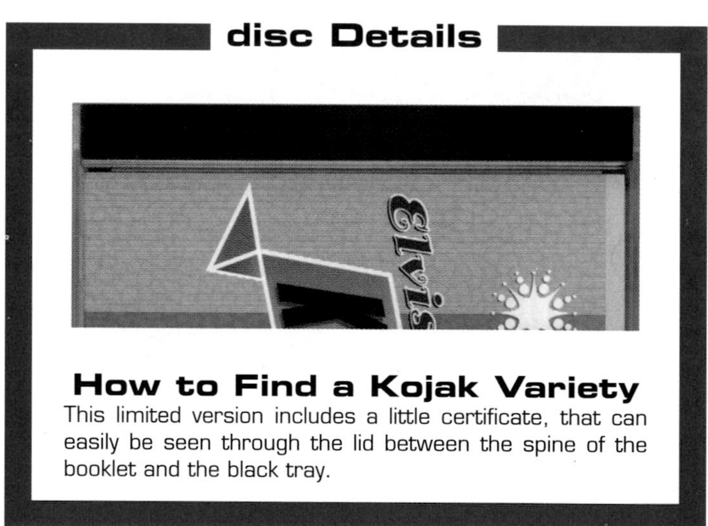

How to Find a Kojak Variety

This limited version includes a little certificate, that can easily be seen through the lid between the spine of the booklet and the black tray.

Richards, Keith and the Expensive Winos – Talk Is Cheap (Virgin 2-9047C) U.S. 1988 limited edition CD. This is one of the first specially packaged CDs ever made.

Presley, Elvis – Legend, The (RCA PD 89000) This 1983 boxed set was the very first Elvis Presley recording available on compact disc. This set was made in a limited edition in Germany. Albums on CD however, became available shortly after in the U.S.

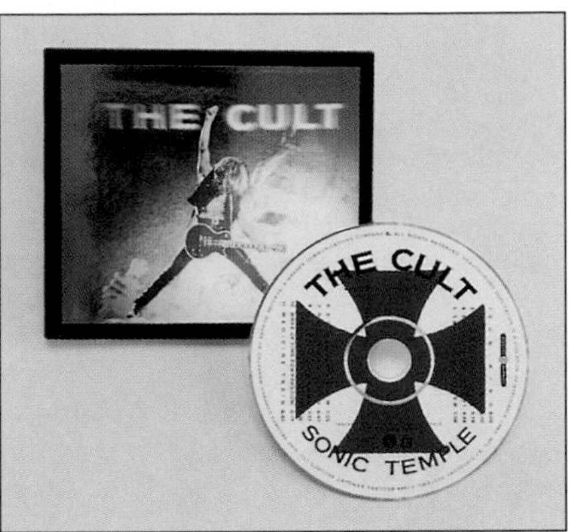

Cult, The – Sonic Temple (Beggars Banquet) First limited edition hologram cover from 1989. The CD mistakenly says "Promotion Only - Not For Sale" even though it was sold at retail. The manufacturer merely neglected to remove the notice from its initial promo-only run.

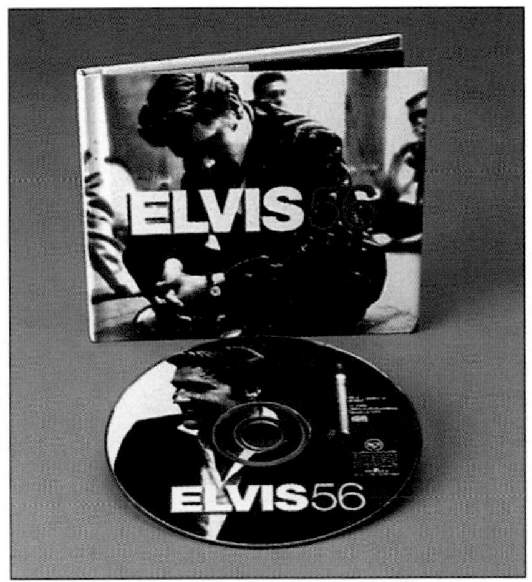

Presley, Elvis – Elvis 56 Collector's Edition (RCA 07863 66817-2) 1995 limited edition version of his Elvis 56 album.

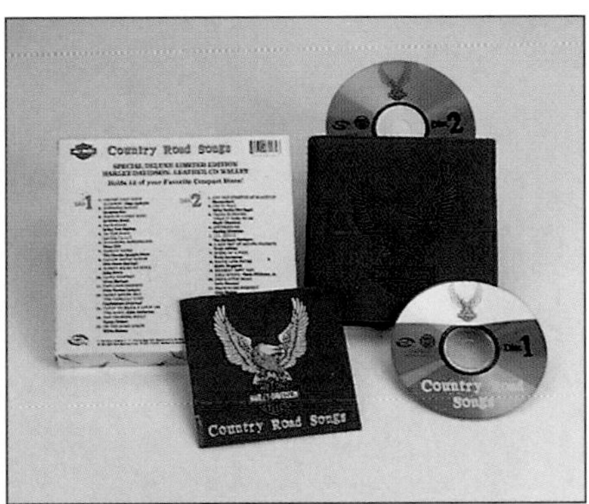

Harley Davidson Country Road Songs – Right Stuff (72438-36448-2-7) U.S. 1996 limited edition CD.

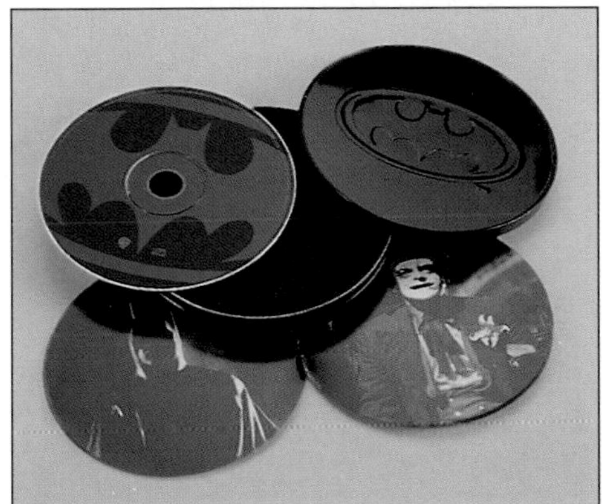

Prince – Batman (Warner 9 25978-2) 1989 limited edition CD soundtrack.

Compact Facts

Limited Editions

To Be or Not to Be

The following are a few limited editions that were planned, but for one reason or another had to be canceled. Michael Jackson's *History 2* CD limited edition in book-type digipak with limited edition coin and booklet. This disc was due for release for the 1995 Christmas season but was canceled because of lackluster sales of the album. *Ozzy Osbourne Live & Loud* limited edition boxed set containing the two CD album and VHS video cassette in special "speaker" box. *Pulp Fiction* laser disc boxed set by Buena Vista Home Video in 1995. An *Evita* limited edition in a special hat box with the Madonna CD soundtrack was scheduled for release in 1996.

First Pressings and Reissues

First pressings is a much broader category than first issues. First pressings encompass all CD titles that have required a subsequent pressing[4]. Currently, most first pressings hold only a "used CD" value. Moreover, the second, third, fourth, and tenth pressings are visually identical to the first. Additional pressings often use the identical master, booklets, print screens, inks, etc. If there is a difference in pressings however, the *CCDPG* makes every effort to note these exceptions.

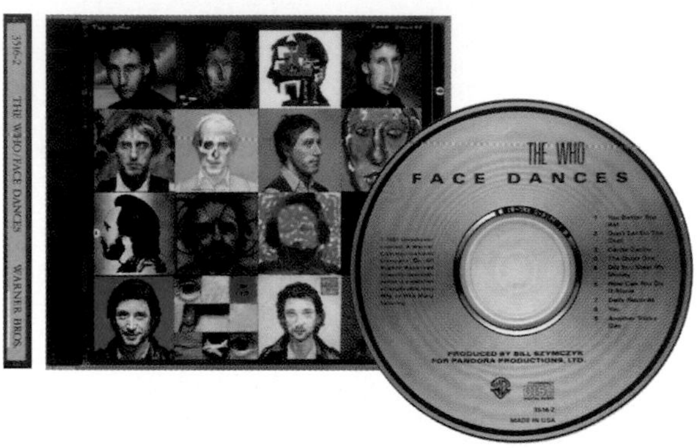

Who, The – Face Dances (Warner Brothers 3516-2)

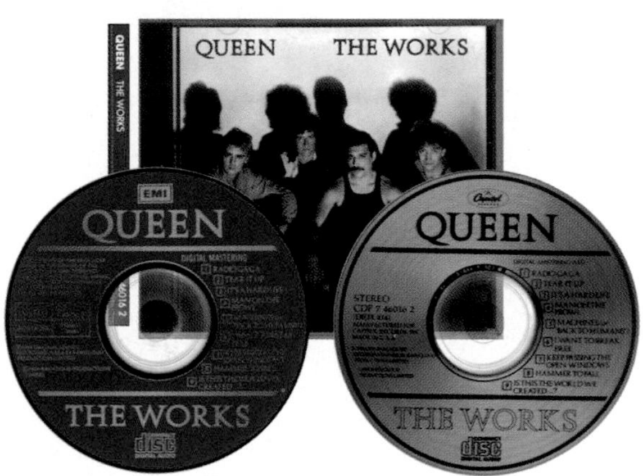

Queen – Works, The (Capitol CDP 7 46016 2) These discs are perfect examples of the distinction between first and subsequent pressings. Notice the disc on the left, this first pressing of the album, made in Japan uses a pink base color with the title work knocked out. The subsequent pressing on the right, made in the U.S. uses black ink for its title work on the plain reflective surface background.

Queen – Greatest Hits (Elektra 5E-564-2) Very rare out-of-print CD. The graphics on this album have yet to be reproduced on any other subsequent domestic release. This cover art does appear inside the booklet of *Hollywood Record's Greatest Hits Volume I & II*, double disc set but not as an original album reissue.

Metallica – Kill 'Em All (Elektra 9 60766-2) This first pressing by Elektra Records, which is in fact a reissue from the same album by Megaforce Records, contains two tracks *Am I Evil?* and *Blitzkrieg*. These tracks are not available on either the prior Megaforce CD or the subsequent Elektra repressings.

10,000 Maniacs – In My Tribe (Elektra 9 608-2) This first release contains the Cat Stevens hit *Peace Train* subsequently removed from the disc.

Chicago – Chicago Transit Authority (Columbia C2K 00008) This first Issue (also a first pressing) is illustrative of how advanced data compression technology has become. This first CD, pressed in 1983, requires two discs to contain the whole album. The version currently found in the record stores contains the entire album on one disc. These two disc versions have become quite desirable to collectors.

CD-Singles

CD-singles are carryovers from the traditional 7" and 12" vinyl singles market. The first documented CD-single was Dire Straits' *Brothers in Arms* from Germany, commemorating the band's 1985 European tour[5]. The arrival of domestic CD-singles did not come until 1986. These first domestic singles were however, promotional issues. 38 Special's *Like No Other Night*, Police's *Don't Stand So Close to Me*, and Orchestral Maneuvers in the Dark *(Forever) Live & Die* were released by A&M Records as the first U.S. CD-singles.

While Europe quickly developed its CD-single catalog starting in 1985, the United States' CD-single market was left exclusively to promotional CDs. In fact, some of the first U.S. commercial CD-singles were the 5" compact disc videos (CDV) issued in 1987 by the Polygram label. From 1988 to 1992 U.S. CD5s trickled out on a limited basis. Not until 1994 did the major record companies commit to issuing a steady stream of CD5s as a counterpart to the common cassette-single.

Dire Straits – Brothers In Arms (Vertigo 884 285-2) World's first CD-single, 1985 German disc.

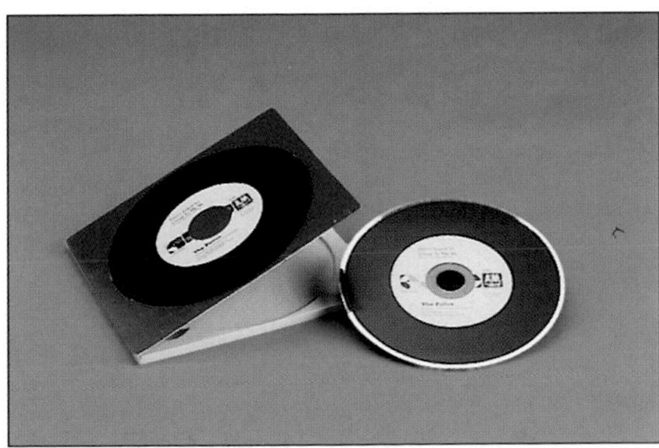

Police – Don't Stand So Close to Me '86 (A&M CD-17435) One of the first U.S. promotional CD-singles. Issued in 1986.

disc Details

All Discs Are Not as Good as Gold

Copper/Aluminum 24 Karat Gold Gold Plastic

Gold discs have become all the rage for manufacturers as for collectors. Though 24 karat gold makes little if no difference in the quality of the CD. However, if the disc advertises that it is made from gold, it should be made of real gold, not merely gold color. Disc manufacturers have developed a new reflective layer comprising a "gold-looking" aluminum/copper composition. This composition produces a layer that looks like gold but this aluminum/copper alloy is much cheaper. How labels are facilitating this scam is by simply labeling the disc as "gold" rather than "24 karat gold." The best way to guard yourself against this is if you have any gold discs made by Mobile Fidelity Sound Lab (MFSL), use it as a reference disc, comparing its color to the color of a suspicious disc. The suspicious disc, if in fact gold, will generally be the same color as the MFSL disc. If aluminum/copper, the disc will look a copper color compared to the MFSL disc. Note that this gold color disc is not bad, and the manufacturers should be commended for developing new ideas with the CD. It is those few labels however, who are trying to exploit this idea to give the impression their disc is something it is not.

CD3 (3" Compact Disc Single)

Sony introduced the first variation to the compact disc format in 1987 with the introduction of the CD3. This was the recording industry's first full fledged effort in the CD-single market. The CD3 format is a small 3" diameter disc. This new size was chosen so consumers could easily distinguish CD-singles from the full length CDs. CD3s held 20 minutes of music containing two to four tracks, and sold for about $3 – 4. Unfortunately, there was little market support for the CD3. It practically became extinct in the U.S. market by 1990. European and Japanese markets took to the CD3 format more than the United States. From 1988 to about 1992 the European market often made a separate 3" and a 5" CD version for the same single. To this day, the Japanese market continues to widely use the CD3 format.

Today, U.S. CD3s are becoming quite a collectible format. Because there are so few titles yet by collectible artists like Bruce Springsteen, Pink Floyd, and the Grateful Dead, look for CD3s to become a super collectible in the next five years.

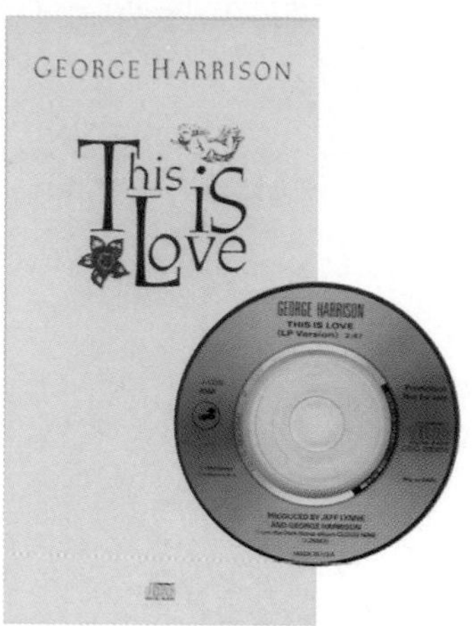

Harrison, George – This Is Love (Dark Horse/Warner Brothers PRO-CD-3068) This rare U.S. promotional CD3 sports the 3" x 6" Japanese "snap-pak" packaging. This is the only known disc to use this packaging.

Compact Discovery DADC Digital Audio Disc Corporation was the first disc manufacturer to produce CD3. These various artist samplers were produced to showcase the CD3 technology.

Springsteen, Bruce – One Step Up (Columbia 38K-7726 – CSIG 000044) Rare promotional CD3.

A&M Presents CD3 (A&M CD 17543) One of the Rarest CD3s to date. This promotional disc was issued in 1987 to promote the soon-to-be-released A&M CD3 catalog. The disc is packaged in a prototype CD3 packaging. This disc comes with a plastic 5" sleeve and adapter. Because most CD player trays were equipped to handle only 5" CDs, an adapter needed to attache to the disc to give it a CD5 size. Most CD trays in players are adapted to handle CD3s without an adapter.

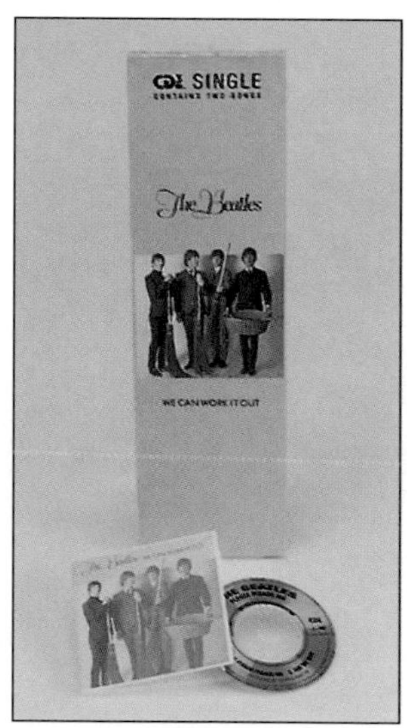

Beatles, The – We Can Work It Out (Capitol)

CD5 (5" Compact Disc Single)

The first proliferation of the commercial CD5 CD-single format in the U.S. market was in 1989. This format has been the standard for promotional CD-singles[6] for years even though no commercial CD5s were available. Replacing the declining CD3, CD5s have become the standard for U.S. CD-singles.

As far as collectibility, CD5s are currently produced in adequate supply. Their value hovers around retail price. Take notice of early CD5s from 1989 to 1992. These discs have come and gone with little notice and are becoming hot collectibles.

For the purposes of the *CCDPG*, all CD-singles are treated as out-of-print discs even if at time of publication, many CD5s are still in print. Because CD-singles by nature, are available for only a finite time, with limited production runs of only one to two pressings they still qualify to list in the *CCDPG*.

Presidents of the United States of America – Peaches (Columbia 44K 78255)

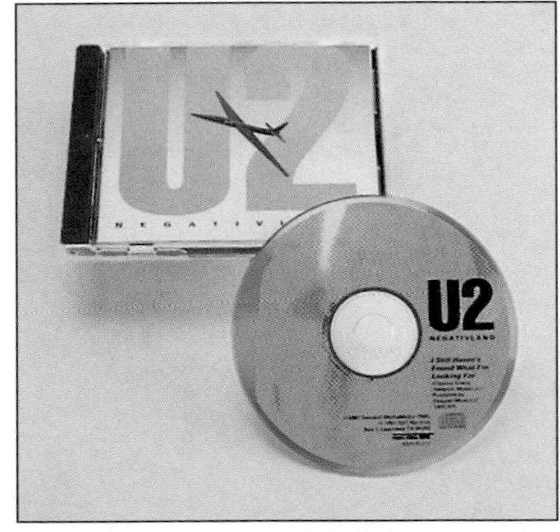

Negativeland – I Still Haven't Found What I'm Looking For (SST CD 272) One of the rarest CD5's to date. And there exists no other disc that had been the subject of as many lawsuits or potential lawsuits as this one. Starting with the cover, Island Records and Warner-Chappel, the group U2's record company and publisher, threatened to sue because the title was deceptively similar to the band U2 and might cause confusion. There were also some trademark issues in the complaint as well. This disc was also the subject of suits. First, there are allegedly illegally lifted samples of the actual song *I Still Haven't Found What I'm Looking For* on the track raising many copyright issues. Second and more interestingly, the disc has a recording of Casey Kasem from his top 40 countdown show explitively referencing the band U2 and their country of origin. Even the band's own record company joined in and sued Negativeland for a whole host of miscellaneous things. Needless to say, the disc was pulled off the shelves, where only 12,000 were made to begin with. This disc is truly a CD rarity.

McCartney, Paul – My Brave Face (Capitol CDP 7 15468 2) Originally not thought to exist, this CD-single does pop-up occasionally on the collectors' market. The disc, scheduled for release in 1989, was canceled shortly before that release. The majority of the discs were destroyed except for a select few.

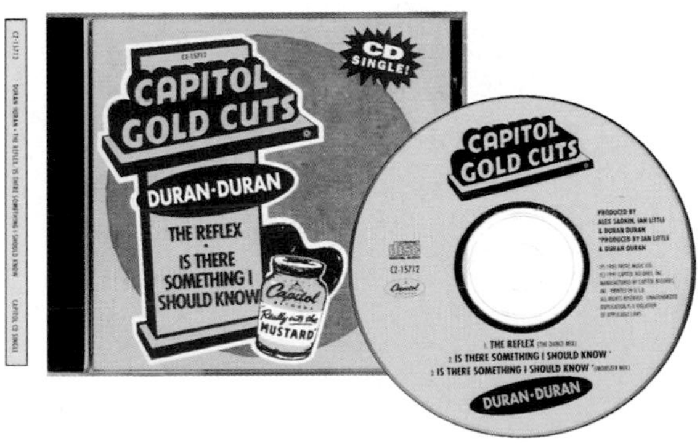

Duran Duran – Reflex, The (Capitol C2-15712) A very early U.S. CD5.

Premiums (Value Added)

CDs sold or given away as premiums or value-added discs are a subset of limited editions. These discs are not distributed through the retail market per se but they are not part of the secondary market either. Value-added CDs are given away free or sold at a special price as part of advertising or direct marketing campaigns by various corporate sponsors. These discs sell or are given away through television, magazines, point-of-purchase displays, and even the back panel of cereal boxes. Most record companies in fact have their own division that specializes in this type of music marketing. They license the music and provide production and manufacturing support. If you notice names on your CDs like CEMA Direct, BMG Direct, or Warner Special Products as the record company, then those CDs are premiums.

Premiums will probably become very collectible in the future because they are manufactured in limited editions, uniquely packaged, and often obscure. The *CCDPG* lists only a small portion of all the premium CDs out there. This is because we have listed only those discs we know about. If you are aware of any we have omitted, let us know[7].

Mattea, Kathy – Special Collection (Mercury DMN 7040 U.S.) 1995 premium CD sampler. Distributed by Kellogs cereals.

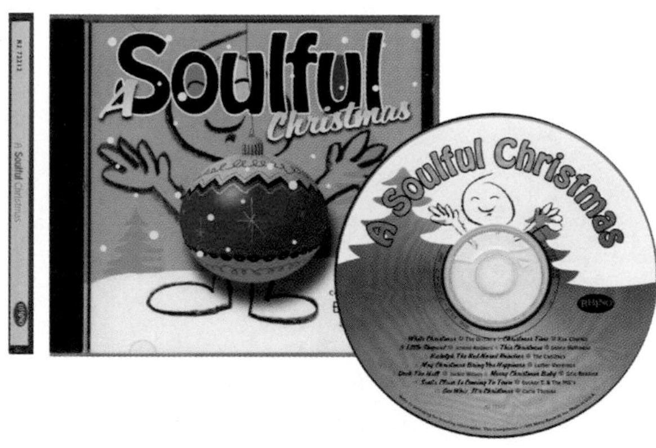

A Soulful Christmas (Rhino/Borders R2 72212) Distributed through Borders Bookstores.

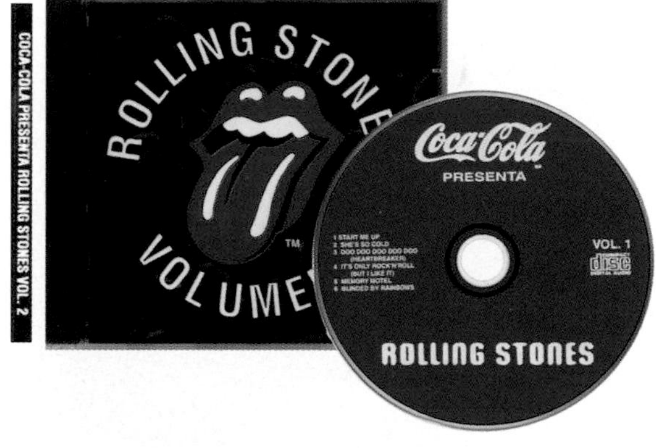

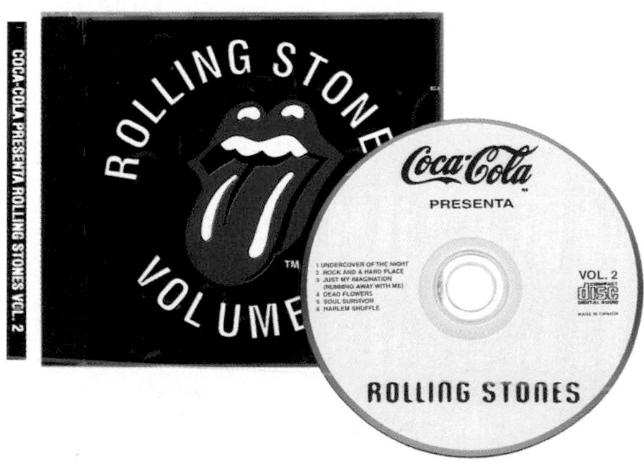

Rolling Stones – Coca Cola Presents Rolling Stones Vol. 1 Rare 1994 Mexican premium given away with proof-of-purchase seals from bottles of Coke.

Braxton, Toni – Secrets (LaFace 008 26020-2) This limited edition CD set was sold exclusively from Best Buy electronics stores. The bonus CD is a special promotional sampler.

Kiss – New York Groove (Mercury MECP 120) This disc is probably the most highly sought after recent value added. Distributed by Blockbuster Music who sponsored the "You Wanted the Best, You Got the Best" tour, to anyone who pre-ordered the album, supplies were depleted almost immediately. Currently, this disc is scarce on the collectors' market at any price.

Modern Rock Live Volume 1 (Sony/ Global Satellite Network) This 1996, two disc set of exclusive live tracks from bands like Blues Traveler, Soul Asylum, and the Dave Matthews Band was given as a premium to anyone who purchased specially marked Sony Discman products.

MTV Replay (Sony Special Products A2 23344/45/46)

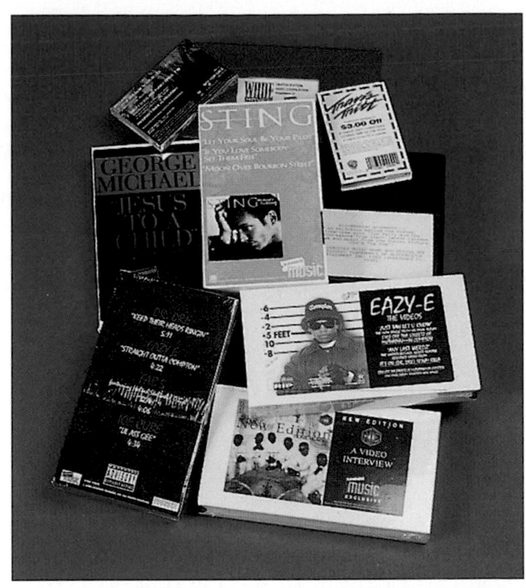

Blockbuster Music Promotions Various premiums offered by Blockbuster Music when you either pre-order or purchase the advertised title at one of their locations. Because these items are very limited in availability, they end up becoming quite rare quite quickly. Make sure you pay attention to the offers your local stores make. A great number of collectible CDs start off by being given away free.

Kiss – You Wanted the Best, You Got the Best (Mercury 314 532 741-2) Limited edition version of the album with free picture phone card. Distributed exclusively by Best Buy.

Long Boxes

The long box appeared in the U.S. market in 1984. These 6" by 12" outer cardboard boxes were made to contain the jewel boxed CD in the bins at the record store. Long boxes were created as a compromise between the retailers and the record companies. Early in the CD's history, retailer bins were made to hold a 12" record; long boxes were designed so that CDs could fit into those existing bins. Two long boxes, standing side-by-side equaled the same dimensions as one vinyl LP. Also, housing the CD in a small jewel box created a fear that theft would become a serious problem. Housing the jewel box in a larger outer long box package quelled those fears.

On April 1, 1993, the recording industry said its final good-bye to the long box as the compact disc's outer packaging. For years, opponents argued long boxes were harmful to the environment because they were discarded after purchase.

In retrospect, throwing away your long box has become the same as throwing away money. The collectibility of long boxes is substantially increasing. Most out-of-print discs still having their long box or blister card[8] are substantially more valuable than those without. It is ever conceivable that long boxes will become even more valuable than the CD it contained. Just looking at availability, assuming most long boxes were destroyed after purchase, there are fewer long boxes of a title existing than the CD.

Because the availability of the long box is so small yet their collectibility so big, this guide offers a separate value for CDs accompanied by their long box as opposed to discs in their jewel box only. Long boxes currently add anywhere from $2 to over $100 onto the value of the CD. I suspect in the next few years, having the long box or blister card with the disc will at least double the value of the CD.

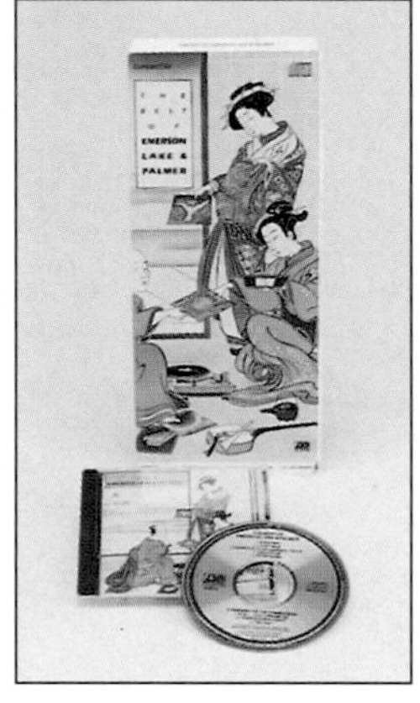

Emerson Lake & Palmer – The Best of (Atlantic 19283-2) Out-of-print CD with original long box by the group's original label Atlantic Records.

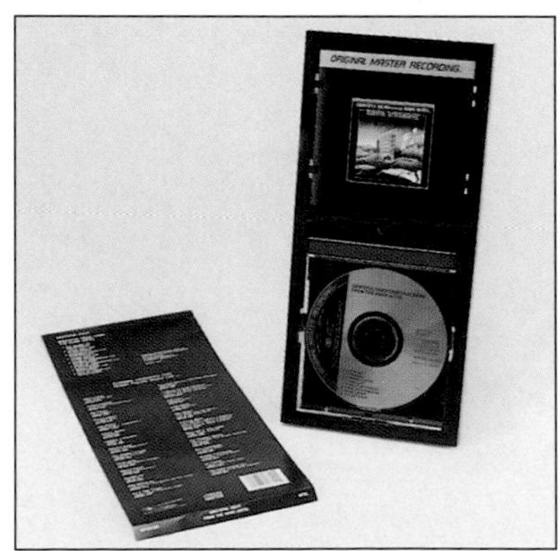

Grateful Dead – From the Mars Hotel (Mobile Fidelity MSFL MFCD 830) Mobile Fidelity for years used a unique plastic skeleton long box. These were advantageous because you could actually see the disc through the packaging. Unfortunately, Mobile fidelity's disc graphics were not that exciting. Mobile Fidelity still offers there discs in a long box, but they now use the traditional cardboard type.

Blister Pack & Blister Card

Many releases before the demise of the long box were house in blister pack plastic clamshell alternative. If the disc was a new release by Mercury or Polygram Records, they also contain blister cards. Having the blister card either with or without the blister pack adds value to the disc.

John, Elton – Goodbye Yellow Brick Road (MCA MCAD2-6894) This original two CD set was housed in separate jewel boxes packaged in a single disc long box. The currently available version of this album is a single disc packaged without the long box. Preserving long boxes will add significant value to your CD.

Soundgarden – Badmotorfinger/Somms (A&M 75021 54001 2) This rare two CD set was inconspicuously released in 1992 months after the release of the single disc version. This is why many collectors might have passed this disc by. Housed in the long box, this limited package looks similar to the single package. The disc is currently very scarce, even more scarce with the long box.

Promotional CDs

Promotional (promo) CDs are issued by record companies for the express purpose of introducing new music and artists to the media. The discs are also used for radio air-play, promotions at record stores, or industry demonstration purposes. Promo CDs are easy to identify. They all have either PROMOTION or DEMONSTRATION ONLY – NOT FOR SALE printed on either the label, the packaging, or both. This notice is necessary because promo CDs are given away by the record companies rather than being sold at retail. Royalties are not paid to the artist since these are essentially marketing tools.

Despite the disc's promotional purpose, they are designed not only as marketing tools but as special collectors' items. Promo CDs are often designed more elaborately than their commercial counterpart with special exterior packaging and interesting four or five color graphics printed on the disc. In addition, many titles contain special cuts not available on the commercially released version.

Promos are also attractive collectibles because there are relatively few made. Promo CDs are usually manufactured in quantities of about 5,000 copies. But as few as 1,000 to as many as 20,000 copies of a promo title have been made. And because many are given away to radio stations and other outlets as a marketing tool, promos tend to show signs of use adversely affecting their condition. This lack of preservation adds to the general value of the promo CD.

Promo CDs, are popular not only because they can be valuable but also because they can be inexpensive. Many promos, especially singles, can in fact be purchased for less than $4.

There are two basic types of promo CDs — Promo-only and Promo-version.

The rarest U2 promotional singles.

Bowie, David – All Saints (Rykodisc) Rare promotional sampler of Christmas music given away to associates of David Bowie. Only a few made it out to the collectors' market.

Promo-only Notices

CD SAMPLER

NOT FOR SALE • PROHIBIDA SU VENTA • 非賣品 • INVENDÂVEL • IKKE FOR SALG • לא למכירה • MÅ IKKE SÆLGES • UNVERKÄUFLICH • NICHT VERKÄUFLICH • SATILIK DEĞILDIR • NO PARA LA VENTA • 비매품 • ΟΧΙ ΠΡΟΣ ΠΩΛΗΣΗ • TIDAK BOLEH DIJUAL • TIDAK UNTUK DIJUAL • NE PEUT ETRE VENDU • NIET VOOR VERKOOP BESTEMD • EJ TILL SALU • ห้ามขาย • EI MYYTÄVÄKSI •

Sade – Interview Deluxe (Epic ESK 4877) U.S. 1992 promotional interview CD.

Yes – An Evening of Yes Music Plus (Herald HER PRO 1)

disc Details

Autographed CDs

The more valuable the disc the less you should autograph it unless it is a real difficult autograph to get. The less the CD is worth like a regular release the more valuable it will be if autographed.

Promo-only

Promo-only discs are manufactured as a unique promotional item. There is no identical standard commercially released equivalent. Even if the promo-only disc's function is to promote a commercial release it is different enough and easily distinguishable from that commercial release. Promo-only CDs often incorporate different disc art work and/or packaging. The disc sometimes contains different edits also distinguishable from the standard commercial release. Promo CD-singles, advance releases, and CD samplers made exclusively for the media and record retailers, found in a simple jewel box also qualify for this category.

An easy way to distinguish between a promo-only disc and a commercial disc is that promo-only, unlike the commercial release, do not have universal price codes (UPC) on the back of the packaging[9]. Promo-only CDs almost always have a special "promotional" catalog number. With a little practice, promotional catalog numbers can be easily differentiated from commercial catalog numbers. Promo-only catalog numbers contain a reference to being promotional such as PRO-CD-#, DPRO-#, or PRCD-#.

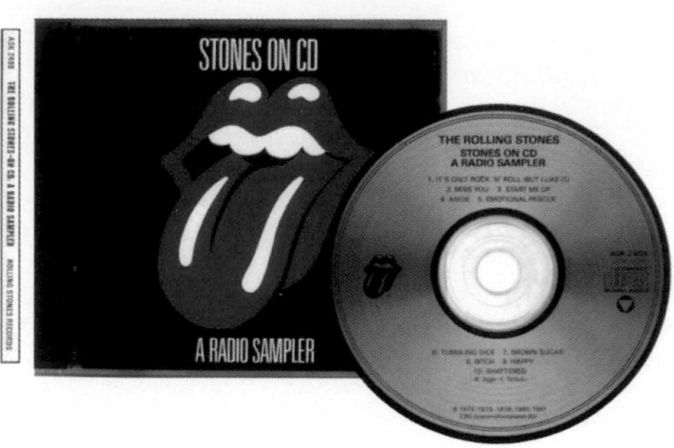

Rolling Stones – Stones on CD (Rolling Stones ASK 2498) This rare 1986 CD is the first promotional Rolling Stones CD in the United States. It was made to promote the upcoming release of the Rolling Stones catalog on CD by Columbia Records.

Rolling Stones – 19 Greatest Radio Hits (Century 21 Programming) Extremely rare promotional radio sampler.

Pink Floyd – Limited Edition Interview Disc (Columbia CSK 6060)

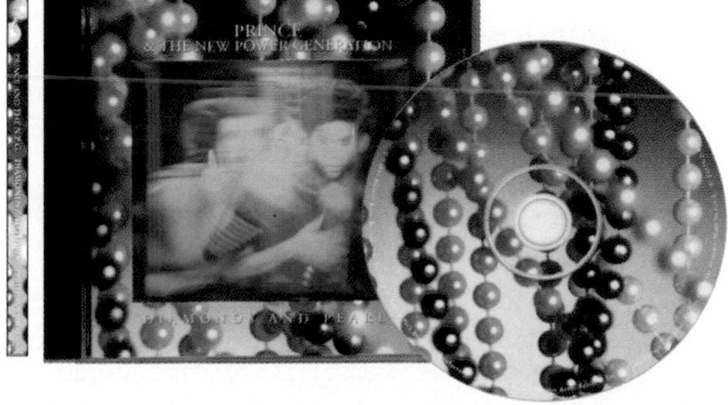

Prince – Diamonds and Pearls (Paisley Park) Two versions of this disc were released. The version on the top is the standard commercial version where the disc on the bottom is the promo-only version. Notice that the standard commercial version has just a one-color printed disc whereas the promo-only version sports a unique full five-color disc.

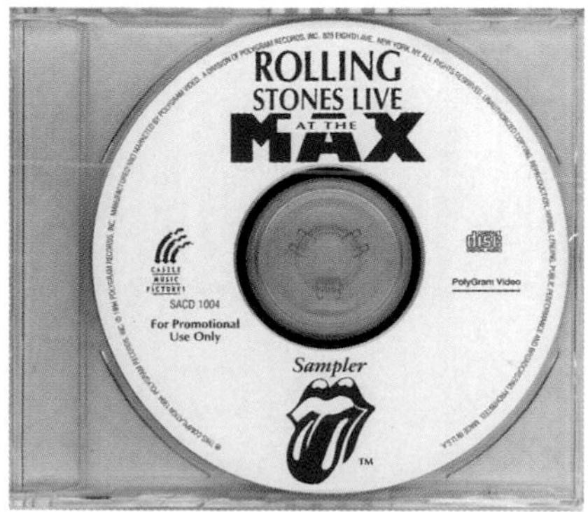

Rolling Stones – Live at the Max (Polygram Video SACD 1004)

Promo-version

Promo-version CDs differ from promo-only CDs. Promo-versions are identical to the standard commercially available version except for some mark on the package to denote promo-version. They are often marked on the print side of an otherwise commercially available CD with the notice "Promotion Only — Not For Sale." Companies like Geffen and Mercury used this practice. Virgin, Warner Brothers, and Capitol would apply a "promotional" notice on either the front booklet or back tray card. As an alternative, either the front, back, or spine of the jewel box including the inserts is purposefully deformed. If you see a drilled hole called a "sunburst," through the UPC code on the back, catalog number on the spine, or somewhere on the front of the jewel box, you have a promo-version CD. Record companies sometimes saw-cut into the spine of the jewel box instead of drilling to also indicate promo-version. These discs go to the music press for review and to the record retailers for play. Sometimes a saw-cut is made to indicate a "cut-out" CD that sells at substantial discount below retail price at record stores.

Virtually all commercial CD and CD-single titles have a promo version counterpart. We have decided at this time not to include promo-versions in this guide, but for a few exceptions. Including promo-versions would increase the guide another 5,000–10,000 titles and probably cause more confusion than information. Anyone with a saw or a drill can make a promo-version.

As far as value goes, these discs often sell as used CDs at used CD prices, rather than as collectibles. Some titles that have the "promotional" label printed on the disc, sell at premium prices, but this is rare. These discs are so uninteresting as promos, especially since they are simply the commercial disc with a different mark or deformation added after manufacture, that they have little collectible value. This is especially true considering all the promo-only CDs and CD samplers available. If you believe however, a promo-version does belong in the listing because of its unique collectibility, let us know and make the argument. We are always willing to be persuaded.

Promo-version disc labels.

Promo-version Marks

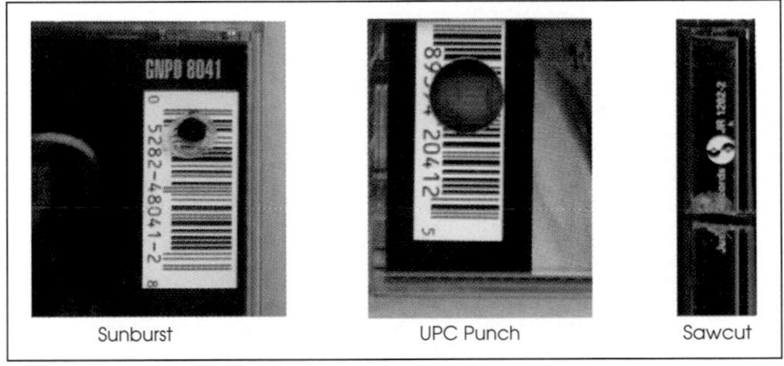

Sunburst UPC Punch Sawcut

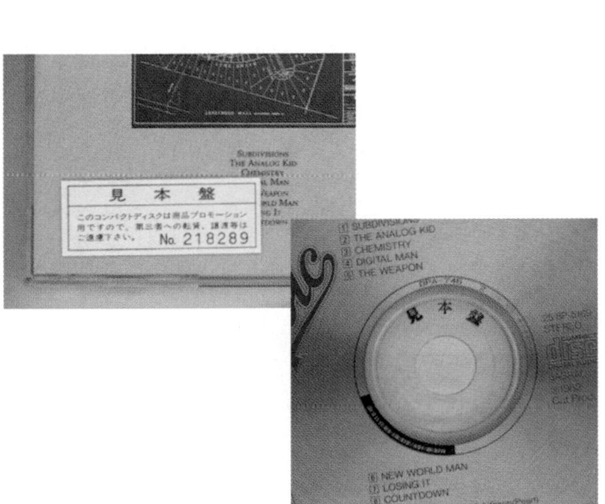

Japanese promo-version CD Most Japanese releases have a promo-version counterpart. These promo-versions can be identified by the labels on the back of the jewel box and the hub of the CD on an otherwise commercial looking CD package.

Sugar – Beaster (Rykodisc RCD50260) Commercial CD and jewel box in book.

Promotional CD-Singles (CDJ)

Promotional CD-singles (CDJ) hold special importance in the *CCDPG* because this format introduced the music collectors' market to collectible CDs. As a consequence, CDJs have become the backbone of the U.S. collectors' market as well as the CD-singles' market.

As previously stated, CDJs were the first U.S. CD-single ever made. Released in 1986, CDJs predate U.S. commercial CD-singles by at least two years. CDJs began to proliferate into the collectors' market in 1987. During these early years of the CDJ, they were quite expensive, starting at around $20 for a common title up to $50 for a more popular title. This was because the CDJ was such a new animal, the market did not know yet how to perceive it. Would they be far and few between, exclusive to special releases or would there be a CDJ made for virtually every single? I think we know the answer to that one. Today, there are practically thousands of CDJs selling as low as four-for-a-dollar. The average price for a CDJ is about $2–3 per disc for a common title. More popular and unusually rare CDJs obviously run more.

The promo CD craze was helped by the fact that it constituted the bulk of the United States CD-single market. Most songs heard on the radio come from a promo CD. Until 1993, the U.S. CD5 market had been sparse, blamed in part on failures of the CD3 and CDV singles market. The domestic CD-single market has only now become viable. As a consequence, there are questions whether new CDJs will become as valuable as those in the past.

Hootie & the Blowfish – Old Man & Me (Atlantic) As you can see there can be significant differences between promotional and commercial CD-singles. On the bottom is the promotional version where the disc above it is the commercially available version.

Soul Asylum – Misery (Columbia CSK 7080) Probably one of the most famous promotional CD-singles. If you've ever seen the video for the song *Misery* where they feature the DADC pressing plant showing the manufacturing process of a compact disc, you might have noticed that the disc they were pressing throughout the video is this very disc.

Young, Neil (and Crazy Horse) – Mansion on the Hill (Reprise) Another example of the differences that can exist between promotional and commercial CD-singles.

Babes and Beavis and Butt-Head in Toyland – Bruise Violet (Reprise PRO-CD-6533-R) This disc is fascinating in that it contains the song surrounding the controversy with the Beavis and Butt-Head television show. In 1993 a 5-year-old from Ohio burned his family's trailer to the ground, killing his 2-year-old sister. The boy said he was inspired to commit this act after watching Beavis and Butt-Head. The controversy surrounded the characters being depicted setting fires. This song was one of those episodes in question. This song along with other episodes were cut from the show and the show moved to a later time slot on MTV. This disc is the only place where this episode is available.

R.E.M. – It's the End of the World as We Know It (IRS CD45-17476) Rare promotional CD-Single from 1987.

Radio Shows

When an artist is interviewed or performs "live" on the radio, the program usually isn't truly live. Rather, these programs have been prerecorded and then syndicated to radio stations. Radio shows are rare commodities because only a single copy is sent to each participating station. Shows like the *King Biscuit Flower Hour*, *Off the Record*, and *In Concert*, around since the days of vinyl and now pressed on CD, are extremely popular with collectors. This popularity is often enhanced if the show has live cuts and interviews exclusive to that disc.

Unlike most promotional CDs, the packaging for radio shows is usually very plain. They are often no more than an unmarked white paper sleeve with a photocopied "cue sheet" listing the program's contents, commercials, and segment times.

The radio show's popularity however, has been taking a beating over the past two years because of the influx of bootleg CDs. The live concert shows, being the most popular type of radio show, are now being bootlegged on CD. A bootleg costs about ½ to ⅓ the price of a radio show and bootlegs do not have pesky commercial breaks like radio shows. Radio shows however, tend to have better sound quality and are an authorized product having value and legitimacy that bootlegs can never attain.

Many collectors are starting to specialize in collecting only CD radio shows. As a guideline, the more the same show is broadcast, the less valuable it will be. Most of the *King Biscuit Flower Hour* shows and *BBC Classic Tracks* listed under the same artist are identical recordings, only distinguishable by airdate and the commercials placed on the disc. Many shows, especially by Westwood One like *In Concert* and *Superstars* are all different. Except for the Pink Floyd versions, *Up Close*, by Media America never repeats a show. Look for the popularity of these shows to rebound over the next several years.

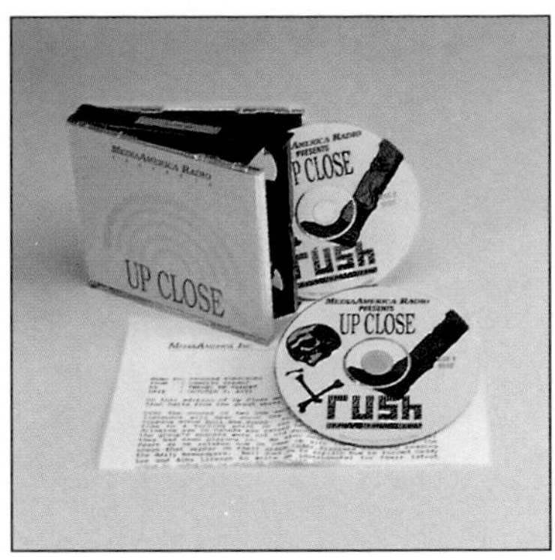

Rush – Up Close (Media America)

Rush – Spirit of Rush, The (Global Satellite Network)

King Biscuit Flower Hour (DIR) The King Biscuit Flower Hour is one of the most famous radio shows in history. It was named after the legendary 1920s "live blues" radio program sponsored by King Biscuit Flour Company. This early show featured live performances by such blues greats as Sonny Boy Williamson. Created by Bob Meyrowitz who got the idea after seeing the Rolling Stones *Gimme Shelter* concert film (and now sponsors the Ultimate Fighting Pay-per-view tournaments), and renamed the show *King Biscuit Flower Hour* (KBFH). Debuting on February 18, 19, with live performances by Blood Sweat and Tears, Mahavishnu, and the then unknown Bruce Springsteen, the KBFH has featured over 450 artists for over 1,000 installments. KBFH debuted on CD on September 6, 1987, with a live concert from Eric Clapton. KBFH, however, has not recorded a new show since 1989. Today, KBFH is syndicated to over 200 radio stations airing reruns of the show.

disc Details

Radio Shows

A Truly Limited Edition

To give you a better appreciation for the rarity of radio shows, the following is a list of shows along with the approximate number of radio stations to which the show is distributed. Because only a portion of those shows ever make it to the collectors' market, they are truly limited editions.

King Biscuit Flower Hour – distributed to 200 to 300 stations

BBC Classic Tracks – distributed to 300 to 350 stations

Superstars – distributed to 275 to 325 stations

In Concert – distributed to 275 to 375 stations

In Concert–Nu Rock – distributed to 75 to 100 stations

Electric Ladyland – distributed to 75 to 100 stations

In the Studio – distributed to 175 to 225 stations

Up Close – distributed to 200 to 250 stations

Import Promotional CDs

The United States is not the only country producing unique promotional CDs. Countries like England, Germany, France, as well as Japan, Canada, and Brazil also produce special promo-only CDs, promo-version CDs, and CDJs. In Japan, just like in the U.S., virtually every CD release is accompanied by a promo-version CD with a promotional notice printed on the stacking ring of the disc and a sticker notice on the back tray card. Note however, that for the same reasons domestic promo-versions are not included in this guide, nor will Japanese or other countries' promo-version CDs be included. As a guideline, the value of foreign promo-version discs can be as high as 25% above the comparable retail version.

As you might expect, foreign promos are priced at a premium compared to domestic promos. However, many of the same rules that govern the value of domestic promos apply to foreign promos as well.

A note about Japanese promo-only releases. While flipping through this guide it is easy to see that there are a lot of Japanese promo-only samplers, and that they are very highly priced, even a 1995 release. This is an interesting aspect of the market because they are considered so rare they command such a high value. This may be true, but take note, considering how rare they may be, Japanese promo-only discs are very common and easily found in the collectors' market. Moreover, their prices, because they are so high, will most likely never change, and if they do it will probably be downward. For example, most promo-only samplers, sold in 1988 for $250, sell today for no more than $250. That is the danger of buying a brand new promo at such a premium price. It is usually a peak and there is no where left to go but down. Now this not true with every disc, but because the market is so new and speculative, be careful.

Interestingly, my favorite promo-only releases from a different country are from our neighbor to the north, Canada. In the promo market, Japanese, English, and German promos have become quite common (relatively speaking). Canadian promos are much rarer. Not only that, but they haven't circulated into the collectors' market like the Japanese or European promos have. If a foreign promo is made in extremely limited quantity, yet the majority of them make it to the collectors' market, they won't be as rare as a disc made in larger quantity that rarely makes it to the collectors' market (that is why quantity made is often not important). Canadian promos follow this scheme and in my opinion are one of the best investments as a category. Canadian promo-only discs are made in significantly fewer numbers than Japanese promo-only but cost a fraction as much. A Canadian promo sampler by a particular artist like Billy Joel may sell for $50 to $100 where a comparable Japanese Billy Joel sampler might sell for $250 to $500. Chances are that the opportunity to buy the Canadian version is much less and because it is valued less, there is room for the value in the Canadian promo to rise whereas the Japanese promo-only will probably remain unchanged.

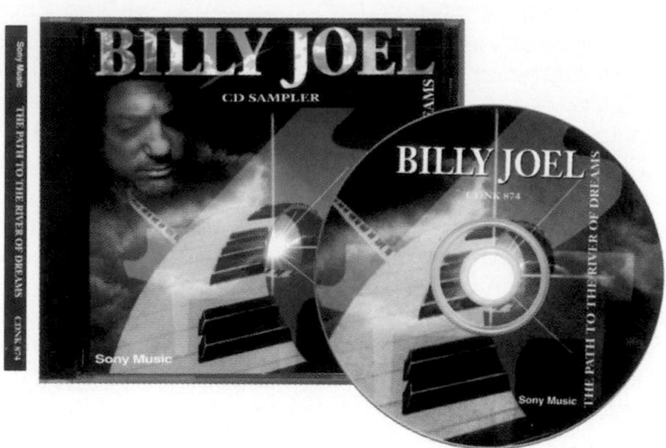

Joel, Billy – Path to the River of Dreams (Sony CDNK 874) Rare 1993 Canadian promotional sampler.

Presley, Elvis – Perfect for Parties (RCA SPA 7-37) Promotional disc from Germany which is actually a reprint of an old 1956 EP promoting various artists like Tito Puente and Tony Scott. The disc also contains an exclusive Elvis Presley interview conducted at the BMG office in Munich.

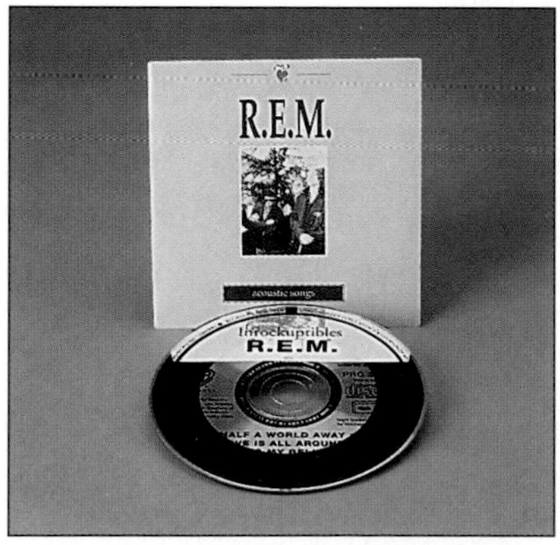

R.E.M. – Les Inrockuptibles (Warner Brothers PRO 2002-2) French promotional sampler.

Promocional (Warner Music CDP0294) Brazilian 1993 promotional sampler.

Promotional Multimedia CD-ROM Press Kits

Traditional paper press kits, including press releases and publicity photos are soon becoming a thing of the past, thanks to the CD. Multimedia CD-ROM press kits are a new application for the CD-ROM technology. CD-ROM press kits are usually formatted for both Apple Macintosh and Windows operating systems and contain everything from press releases and publicity photos like traditional press kits, to film clips and cast interviews.

Traditional press kit information is not the only thing found on these CD-ROMs however. They may also include special information about toy lines, music, and other licensers. This makes the single disc useful, not only to movie and music reviewers, but to sales reps and consumers as well.

Multimedia CD-ROM press kits have only been around since 1992. Television and movie studios like ABC Television, Buena Vista Television, Twentieth-Century Fox, and MGM/UA have issued CD-ROM press kits to reviewers. Because there are currently so few CD-ROM press kits in the market and they contain all sorts of interesting information, usually exclusive to the disc, CD-ROM press kits are naturals for the collector.[10]

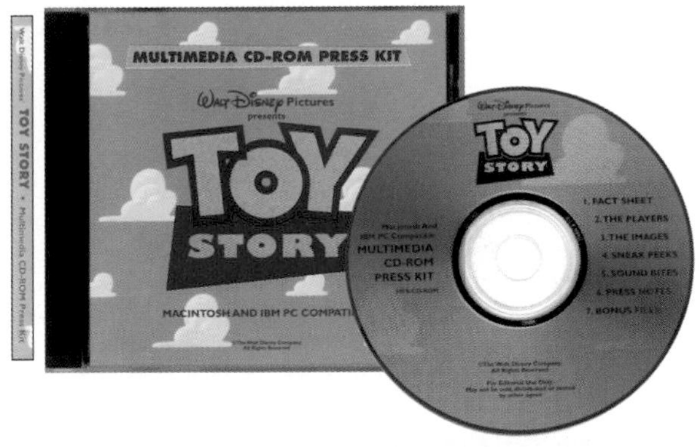

Toy Story: Multimedia CD-ROM Press Kit (Walt Disney)

Stand, The – ABC Public Relations As the first of its kind, this disc introduced the world to the Multimedia CD-ROM press kits. Issued in 1992 and usable on both Apple Macintosh and Windows operating systems, its format is similar and as user friendly as those CD-ROMs made today.

Beatles, The – Anthology 2 Multimedia CD-ROM Press Kit (Apple Corps Ltd.)

Hunchback of Notre Dame: Multimedia CD-ROM Press Kit (Walt Disney Pictures)

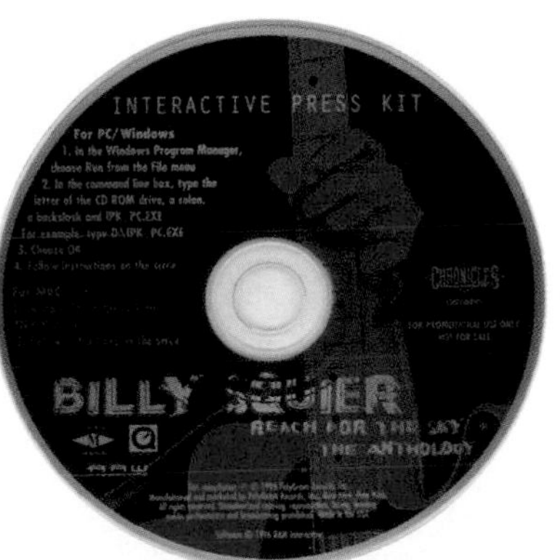

Squire, Billy – Reach for the Sky: Interactive Press Kit (Mercury CHRONIPK1)

Import CDs

Like promos, import CDs played a large part in helping create the collectible CD market. Very few if any domestic music price guide ever mentioned imports. I was asked after the release of the first edition, why I included import CDs since no other record guide has. Just go to any record show or look at any music collector trade paper, or even your own collection and you will see why. Today, imports constitute almost half of all collectible CDs and probably three quarters of all vinyl records.[11] Ignoring imports entirely would be totally ignoring half of the collectible CD market. The *CCDPG* specializes in featuring special import CDs. The pictures illustrating this guide easily demonstrate why imports have become so important to CD collectors and why we should pay more attention to them. Foreign manufacturers brought us the first special edition picture disc CD, special packaging CD, and previously mentioned, CD-single. Foreign manufacturers have also been more daring in producing special edition CDs and CD5s.

Another boost for collectible imports is there are many CD titles released abroad not available in the United States. Special remix CDs as well as albums with bonus tracks or bonus discs have become a staple of the foreign CD catalog and are becoming readily available in the U.S. market. Moreover, because the foreign music industry is structured differently than the United States music industry, foreign CDs often remain in print for only a short time. Obviously this climate significantly contributes to the import's collectibility. Because foreign manufacturers charge more money for a CD, they could afford to take a risk on making a special edition version. That is why foreign limited editions are more prevalent than U.S. limited editions. Another reason is that there are strong collector bases in those respective countries who were willing to pay for limited editions and CD5s. And don't think these companies do not consider the U.S. collectors' market while determining how many of a particular special edition they expect to sell.

Astute collectors have noticed that an import release is often available months in advance of the comparable U.S. release. Surprisingly, it is U.S. CDs exported to foreign countries that cause this phenomenon. U.S. CDs exported to countries like Japan are gray market goods. A gray market good is defined as a foreign manufactured good (in this case the U.S.) bearing a domestic trademark (in this case Japan) imported without the consent of the domestic trademark holder. U.S. exports to Japan are less expensive for the Japanese consumer to buy than the comparable, Japanese-made version. The use of the extra tracks, bonus CDs, and more elaborate packaging makes the Japanese title more attractive. Also there are higher profit margins on Japanese CDs as compared to U.S. CDs.[12] Because U.S. CD exports compete with Japanese CDs, Japanese record companies release titles in advance of the U.S. release helping prevent the U.S. discs from cutting into their sales.

The issue of legality of imports in the U.S. has always been like a cloud hovering over these CDs.[13] Conversely from the example above, Japanese imports are considered gray market goods in the United States. Here gray market goods are goods manufactured and imported from a foreign country like Japan, and bearing a valid U.S. trademark. In practice, the laws concerning gray market goods is very complicated, thus gray, as the name implies. Situations where an American record label being the licenser to foreign record label can sometimes prevent that American label from stopping the importation of foreign CDs. This, along other quirks in the law make this issue unclear. The upshot is that most imports manufactured by the legitimate foreign arm of the American record label, excluding bootlegs and pirated discs as we will examine later, legitimately find their way into the U.S. and do so with little problem. Occasionally, rumors surface that a record company is trying to prevent a particular import CD from reaching the U.S, but this is rare and often just rumor.

However, this has not always been true. Back in 1988, when import CDs started to become popular, the Recording Industry Association of America (RIAA) charged that they were "parallels" of U.S. releases.[14] Importing a CD available on a domestic label was considered a copyright violation. Consequently, one of the largest import distributors at the time, had its stock seized and was forced to close. This action limited the availability of import CDs for several months. Obviously, imports returned in force to not only the CD collectors' market but the consumer market as well.

Metallica – Master of Puppets (Vertigo 838 141-2) Australia has become famous for issuing special edition gold CDs. Such artists as R.E.M., Bryan Adams, Madonna, Guns 'N Roses, and Metallica (shown above) have received this treatment.

Beatles, The – Abbey Road (EMI Odeon CP35-3016) In 1983, this album CD was released in Japan. It was available at a few record stores in the U.S. for about $30. According to *High Fidelity* magazine, however, the disc was pressed without approval from the parent company in England, and it was recalled after a limited run. Because it was the first commercially available Beatles CD and because its availability was limited, Abbey Road is one of the earliest collectible CDs. Above is an original version with the rare obi strip.

Adams, Bryan – Hits on Fire (A&M D50Y3205) One of the earliest limited edition CDs is this 1987 Japanese two CD greatest hits collection. As a unique twist the first disc is a five-color picture disc and the second disc is a "gold" disc.

Import CD-Singles

Import CD-singles have been around since 1985, a year before the first U.S. CD-single. Import CD-singles follow a long tradition from the import vinyl single market. Because they are more exotic than U.S. discs, and there were few domestic CD5s available, import singles gained substantial notoriety. These discs were limited, often creatively packaged, and in the early days of CD-singles (and somewhat today) contained many tracks not available on any comparable U.S. CD. Hence, imports carved their own niche in the market. In the late eighties most import CD-singles were sold exclusively through mail-order or through record show vendors. Only in the past three years have import CD-singles, because of their popularity, filtered through to the major chain stores.

Clapton, Eric – Layla (RSO) Japanese CD3 in the 6"x3" snap pack. Japan is one of the few countries that still market CD3 discs. They are very popular collectibles in the United States.

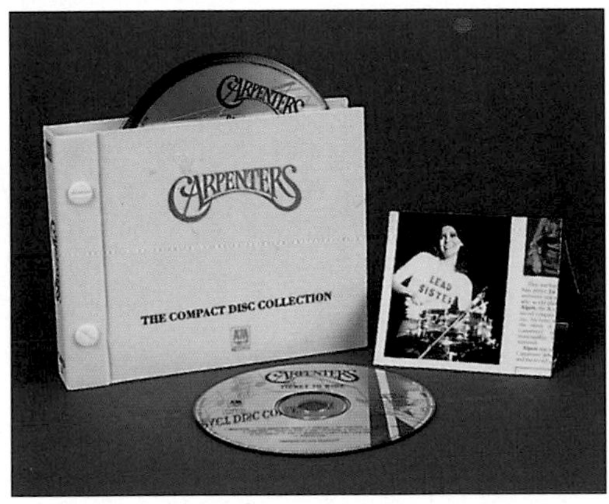

Carpenters, The – Compact Disc Collection, The (A&M CARCD 12) Rare U.K. 1990 12-CD set of all the Carpenters' albums.

Beach Boys, The – Pet Sounds (EMI CP28 1003) One of the oddest import CD stories is that of the first release of this CD album. The domestic re-release of this classic album on CD in 1987 was continually delayed because of creative differences within the band. According to *Rolling Stone* magazine, during one of these arguments the master tapes were "accidentally" sent to Toshiba/EMI in Japan and *Pet Sounds* was mistakenly released. Only a few thousand copies were distributed before it was recalled. The *Pet Sounds* CD was finally reissued in the U.S. about two years later, but in the interim, the Japanese release, which included two bonus tracks not found on the original album, was a highly-sought-after collectible among Beach Boys' fans. The disc contains previously unreleased tracks of *Bkg's* and *Hang on to Your Ego*, later becoming the song *I Know There's an Answer*.

disc Details

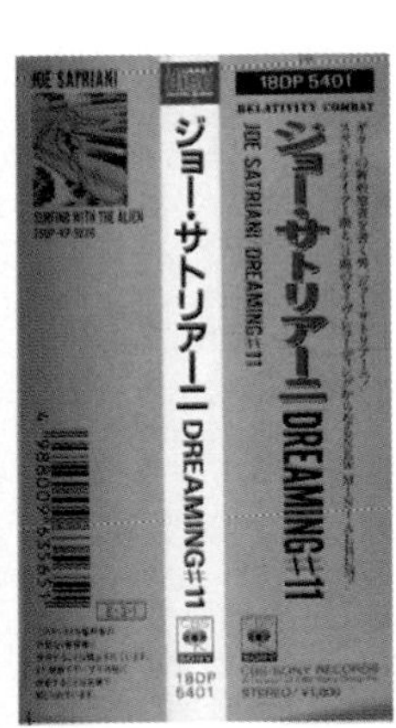

Obi Strips

Ever wonder what those little cardboard strips that fold over the spine of Japanese CDs are for? Well, they are called obi strips and their purpose is to provide Japanese consumers with various information about the disc. These strips, almost always written in Japanese, comprise price of disc, type of music, track listing, discography of other works by that artist, and any bonuses that disc contains. The reason these strips are written in Japanese, where, if you notice, much of the rest of Japanese CDs are written in English, is because much of the music in Japan comes from western countries. These strips are marketing tools so Japanese consumers to learn more about the album.

Obi strips are named after the sash worn around the mid-section with a kimono, traditional Japanese dress. Obi strips have origins all the way back with vinyl records, cassettes, and laser discs. This tradition continues with the CD. Obi strips are very collectible, not so much in and of themselves, but a Japanese CD without the accompanying obi strip is worth substantially less than a disc with the accompanying strip.[15]

Collectible Optical Disc Formats, Applications, and Marketing Technologies

Aside from the traditional digital audio disc, other CD-type formats have become collectible and cause for notice. In fact the most exciting aspect of the CD industry these days is the older optical disc formats as well as new marketing technologies.

Compact Disc Video (CDV)

Introduced in 1988, the CDV appeared in response to the popularity of music videos, thanks in large part to MTV. CDVs offer to the consumer a CD-single worth of music plus a full length video playable on equipped laser disc players. The inner third of the disc held about 20 minutes of digital audio information while the outer two-thirds held about five minutes of laser video data.[16] All of this was accomplished on a standard CD-size disc at a $9.99 price point.

Philips, the inventor of laser disc technology also invented the CDV format. To distinguish CDVs with common CDs, CDVs were molded in a striking gold colored plastic.[17] Polygram Records a subsidiary of Philips, was the first to release a catalog of CDV titles. The discs were packaged in Polygram's signature blister pack and sold through conventional record retailers.

The success of this format was lackluster, mainly because most people who were interested in music videos did not have a laser disc player, thus no way to play the video portion. Few were willing to pay for a CD with video when they had no way to play that video. Over 170 CDV titles in both the American/ Japanese NTSC and the European PAL video formats are known to exist. The CDV began to evaporate from the U.S. and European markets in 1990. CDVs continued to be popular in Japan up through 1992. Today however, CDVs appear only here and there, usually as a novelty, and only distributed as a promotional item.

CDVs have since become quite scarce and as a format, one of today's hottest collectibles. Values ranging from fifteen dollars to a few hundred dollars have collectors scrambling to get almost any CDV they can get their hands on.

Hurricane – I'm on to You (Enigma 72300-2) U.S. 1988 CDV.

R.E.M. – Music from Tourfilm (Warner Brothers PRO-CDV-4460) It was a surprise to see this disc release. Though only a promotional disc, it was released in 1990 years after the CDV stopped being produced.

Bose: Adventures in Surround (Bose) Rare promotional picture disc CDV.

Compact Disc Plus Graphics (CD+G)

A format that has all but disappeared as quietly as it appeared. Debuting in 1988 about the same time, and as a limited alternative to the CDV format, the CD+G lasted almost as long. CD+G is a technology that allowed viewing of basic still pictures and graphics on a television screen hooked up to a specially adapted CD player. In practice, song lyrics or crude graphics scroll down the television screen corresponding to an audio track.

When CD+G was introduced, only the software was available. Though manufacturers were promising players would soon follow. Dedicated CD+G players, however, never materialized. CD+G compatibility did eventually find a home with other digital video format players like compact disc interactive (CD+I) and Sega CD. Today, CD+G has found a particular niche with CD kareoke players where the lyrics appear on the screen in conjunction with the song.

Note that CD+G works differently than CDV and the video will not operate on laser disc/compact disc "combi-players." CD+G, unlike laser disc, produces digitally created video graphics using six bits of video information from a select group of subchannels within the CD coding that regular CD players ignore.[18] Only CD players that recognize these particular digital subcodes can display the graphics. With the advent of DVD, CD+G is a format that is becoming increasingly less necessary.

In late 1996, the Red Book compact disc standard was modified to enable CDs to display titles, not unlike the CD+G data, but on a special screen of your specially adapted CD player. This technology is also an offspring of the same technology used on the minidisc where album and song titles can be shown on a display screen on the player.

As far as collectibility, CD+G has only modest success, due largely to the fact that few discs that use this format exist, and most are still in print. But just as other CD anomalies like CDV and CD3 have become favorites of collectors, CD+G might very well follow.

Super CD System, The (Warner New Media WNM CDV+G PRO #2) Mega-rare U.S. 1995 promotional CD sampler multi-format disc. The first session contians CD+graphics material where the second session is contains CDV material.

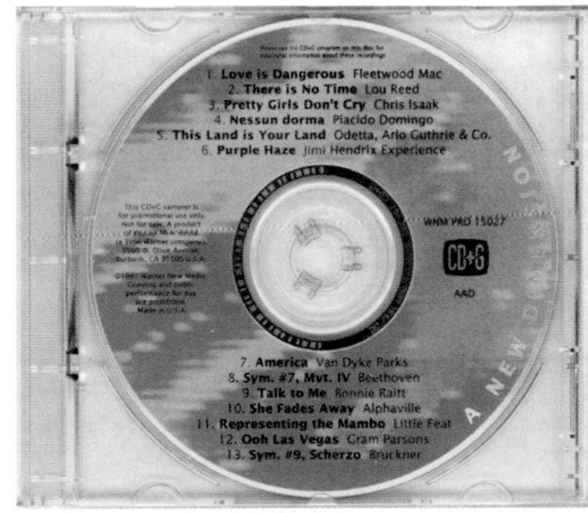

A New Dimension (Warner New Media WMN PRO 15027) Rare promotional CDV given to the first purchasers of Philips CD+I systems in 1992. At the time CD+I players were the only popularly available players compatible with the CD+G encoding.

Compact Disc Interactive (CD+I)

Established in 1989, by Philips Consumer Electronics, CD+I is the format that started the "multimedia revolution" in home consumer electronics. CD+I is a stand alone CD-ROM-type system whose objective is to provide computer-like interaction with a video-game interface. The marketing focus of CD+I during its introduction in 1991 was children's interactive and development, education, and sophisticated games. CD+Is roll out came years before this flurry of CD based multimedia systems. In fact, while CD+I was being marketed in force, other companies were sitting on the sidelines waiting to see how CD+I would fare before releasing their own systems. Once CD+I took off however, everyone joined in. Today, systems like Sega, Nintendo, 3DO, Play Station, and CD-ROM players on personal computers have eclipsed CD+I. These systems however, would not have existed in their current form or grown as fast but for CD+I's contribution.

CD+I is also the forerunner to the new DVD technology. CD+I was the first home electronics format to offer full motion digital video (FMV) on a five inch disc. Using the MPEG-1 system,[19] digital video filled the entire television screen, opposed to those tiny two inch by two inch computer windows offered by traditional CD-ROM. Studios like Paramount and MGM/UA released about 100 films on FMV disc. Picture quality for this first generation digital video however, is only comparable to VHS video tape. How long FMV will last once the higher quality DVD arrives will remain to be seen.

Cool Oldies Jukebox (Philips) This super rare CD+I disc was deleted shortly after release because an unlicensed Janis Ian track had to be removed. The disc was subsequently released without the track.

Compact Disc Read Only Memory (CD-ROM)

The CD-ROM standard was established by Sony and Philips in 1985 as a mass storage carrier, holding up to 650 mega-bytes worth of data. Today, CD-ROMs have become the backbone of the multimedia revolution.

For the collector, CD-ROMs fall into two general categories, either extremely collectible or not collectible at all. CD-ROMs associated with music, movies, and other popular culture having a finite shelf life that are not replaced with update versions have potential to become collectible. CD-ROM data especially in conjunction with audio material is perceived as an added value — offering not only audio music but interactive video as well. CD-ROM companions to current album releases by artists like the Beatles, Prince, Queensryche, and the Replacements fall into this category. Special making of CD-ROMs of movies like *Independence Day* have potential if their availability becomes limited. Other pop culture Icons like comic books have now found their way onto CD-ROM as well, having huge potential for collectibility.

Because CD-ROM game packaging has become more sophisticated and interesting, there is no telling what will happen to their collectibility. There is little evidence yet however, that CD-ROM games will become collectible in the future. These games are usually made in large quantity and their appeal extends to when the next game comes along. But you never know.

Ninety-nine percent of all CD-ROMs will never become collectible. It is inconceivable that your Microsoft Office, Version 4.2 for Macintosh on CD-ROM will ever have collectible value. CD-ROMs that are utilitarian in nature and are updatable with a newer CD-ROM version are less likely to become collectible.

Urotsukidoji III, Volume I (U.S. Magna SSLM-3007) 1996 limited edition CD-ROM film of Japanese anime. Works on both Macintosh and Windows operating systems.

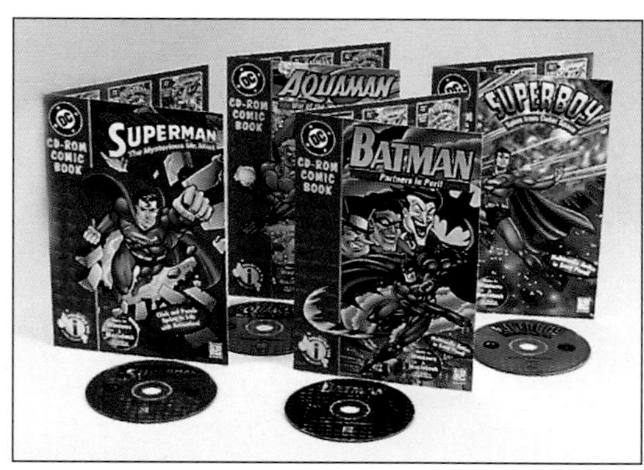

Inverse Ink Comics (Inverse Ink) CD-ROM comics have real potential to become quite collectible. They are very modestly priced limited editions, and contain material not available in print-type comic books. Moreover these can be considered cross collectibles. Both comic book and CD collectors can make up the potential market thus having a larger base than just one.

Woodstock 25th Anniversary CD-ROM (Time Warner) One of the rarest and most elaborate CD-ROMs. This 1994 promotional boxed set was created to promote the release of the Woodstock CD-ROM. It includes a Macintosh and Windows versions of the disc as well as a T-shirt and press materials, all in this large, custom-printed wood box.

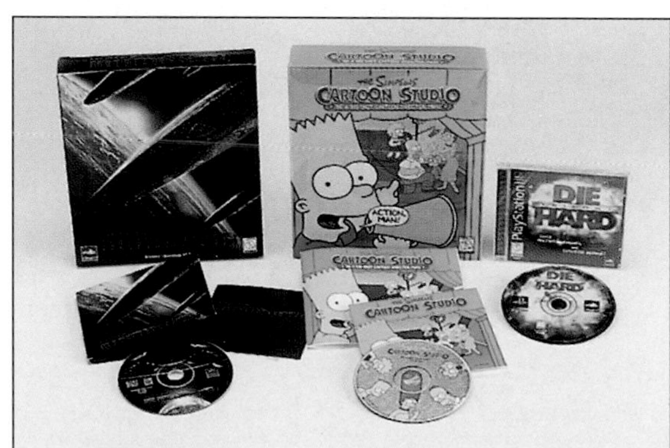

Fox Interactive CD-ROMs (Fox Interactive) CD-ROM packaging designers tend to be a bit more graphically creative than music packaging designers are allowed, even for standard product. (All discs are currently available.)

Star Trek Deep Space Nine: Harbinger (Viacom Newmedia S000801) As an example of special packaging check out Viacom's Star Trek Deep Space Nine Harbinger CD-ROM game. The shelves at electronic stores are quickly replacing record stores in the area of special packaging and graphics. CD-ROM marketers have become much more in-tune than record labels regarding how to use picture disc CDs and CD packaging to get their product sold.

Cyber City Oedo 808, Data 1 (U.S. Magna SSLM-3013) Limited edition comic book with companion CD-ROM. Sold primarily at comic book shops.

Silver Surfer (Toy Biz 48230) Special prototype packaging for yet-to-be released Silver Surfer CD-ROM.

Reboot Action Figures (Irwin 30674) Special, 1996 Canadian edition action figures from the computer animated television series *Reboot*. Each figure features a special 5-color printed CD-ROM game.

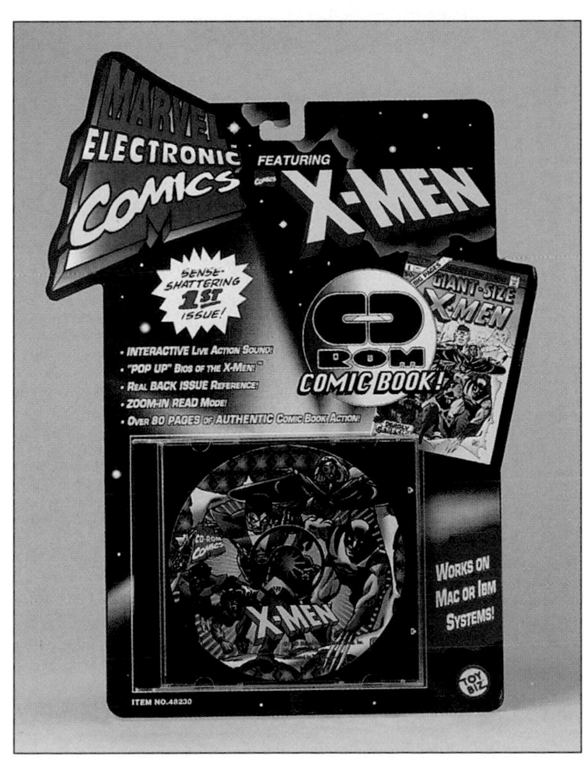

X-Men (Toy Biz 48230) CD-ROM comic in alternative prototype packaging.

Minidiscs (MD)

Introduced by Sony in 1992, minidiscs were developed in response to Philips' digital compact cassette technology. The minidisc is a rewritable optical audio disc format. These miniature, computer diskette-looking discs have become an anomaly to the CD collecting community. The MD format itself has had modest success but that has helped its collectibility because it is perceived as a truly unique item. Many CD collectors purchase promo and out-of-print MDs even without having a MD player.

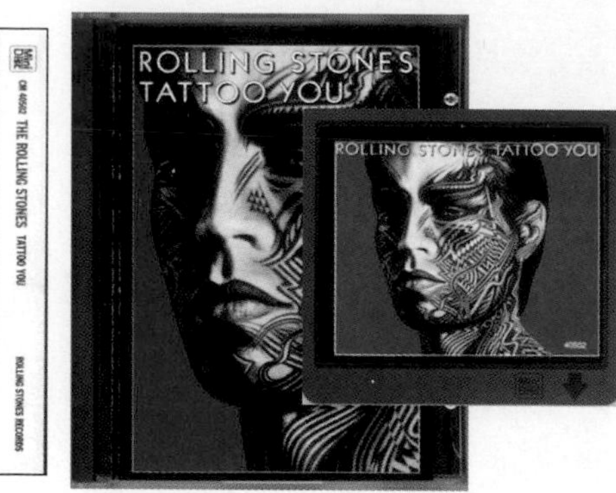

Rolling Stones – Tattoo You (Columbia) These minidiscs were released shortly before the Rolling Stones catalog changed hands from Columbia Records to Virgin Records. The Rolling Stones Records minidiscs as well as the CDs and cassettes were all summarily deleted.

Lwin, Annabella – Car Sex (Sony 660720-2) World's first minidisc single from Germany.

Rolling Stones – Some Girls (Rolling Stones CM 40449)

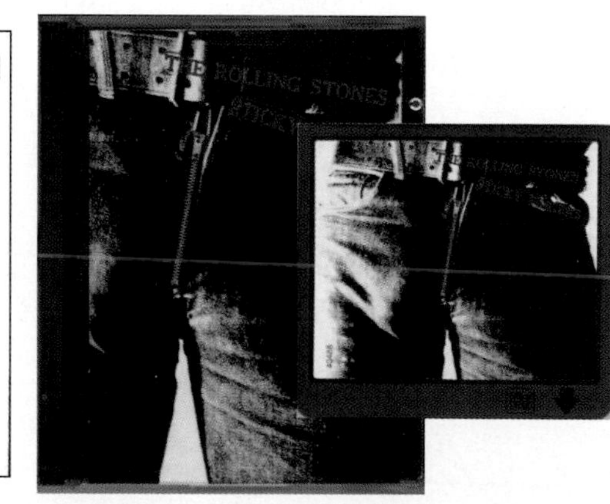

Rolling Stones – Sticky Fingers (Rolling StonesCM 40488)

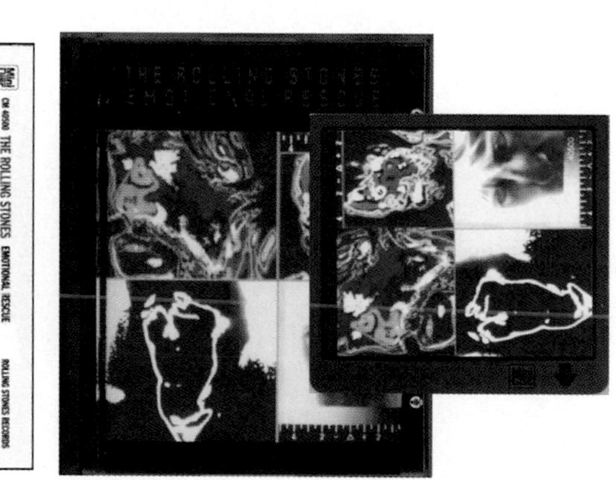

Rolling Stones – Emotional Rescue (Rolling Stones CM 40500)

Audio Book CDs

Audio books are best known to the cassette format, being introduced to the audio CD format in 1991. Commonly released as a companion to both the traditional book and the cassette audio book format, audio book CDs sell in book stores. They are rarely if ever found in record stores.

The collectible outlook of audio book CDs is bright. Because they sell primarily through book stores which stock only one or two copies of a title, audio book CDs are made in relatively small numbers. Book stores also keep stock on the shelf for a limited time. Since the book store industry generally operates on a full return basis, any item may be returned to the publisher or manufacturer for full credit or refund. This is in contrast to the record industry that discourages this practice. Audio book CDs therefore, after selling for a while, might be returned to the publisher. The disc is then deleted with little fanfare or even notice.

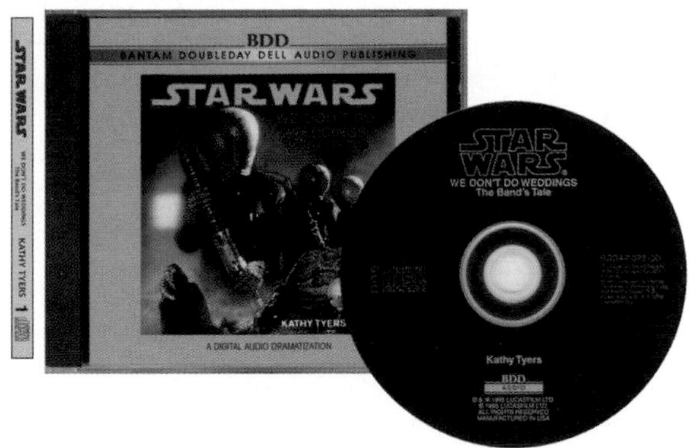

Star Wars: We Don't Do Weddings (BDD 0-553-45540-0)

Star Wars and The Empire Strikes Back: The Complete Original Radio Dramas (High Bridge 1-56511-114-1)

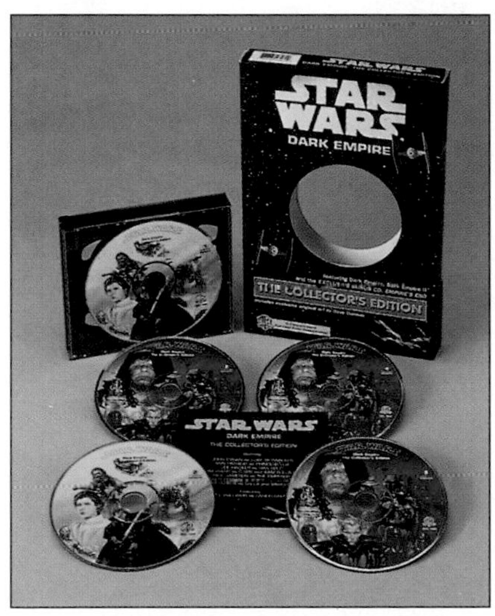

Star Wars: Dark Empire, The Collector's Edition (Warner Brothers Audio Video 2-523474) Audio books like this, having interesting subject matter (anything Star Wars being collectible in an of itself) and great five-color picture disc CDs will certainly be a package to watch.

Recordable CDs (CDR)

Though available since 1990, recordable CDs (CDR) have only been on the collectors' scene since 1994. These discs are usually made in very small quantities of about one to 100 copies. CDRs are usually made to test tape masters,[20] to demo albums or CD-ROMs, and as a quick method of servicing radio stations. CDRs however, are more akin to the cassette tape than to acetate masters, a name mistakenly associated with CDR.[21]

A significant point of confusion with CDRs develops when they are called "gold discs." Though CDRs have a gold reflective layer, do not confuse them with typical gold CDs like the ones from Mobile Fidelity and DCC. When you turn a CDR over you will notice that the read side of the disc is green. This is a dead giveaway that you are holding a CDR. When buying discs especially from record shows or through trade magazines, make sure you distinguish between a CDR and a gold disc.

Another problem with CDRs is that because it is a recordable medium like the cassette tape, it is often a format of choice for bootleggers and pirates. Somebody can record their copy of an out-of-print CD onto a CDR, make multiple copies, and sell them as a limited European gold disc edition to unsuspecting customers.[22] It is therefore, the policy of the *CCDPG* that unless there is some manner of determining the CDRs authenticity, the CDR in question will not be listed in the guide. If you have a question regarding the authority of a particular CDR contact us and we will try to determine its origin.

Jimi Hendrix – Tribute (Warner Brothers) This CDR is unique because the disc is screen printed with the two-color Warner Brothers recording studios logo. Discs with this label are considered to be legitimate over other CDRs without some such label.

disc Details

How to Identify a CD-R

Recordable discs (CDR) come in various sizes from small three inch discs to five and even eight inch recordable video discs. CDRs are easy to identify. Their reflective layer viewed from the print-side is gold and their read-side is a unmistakable dark green. This green color is in fact a dye that when heated creates a simulated pit.

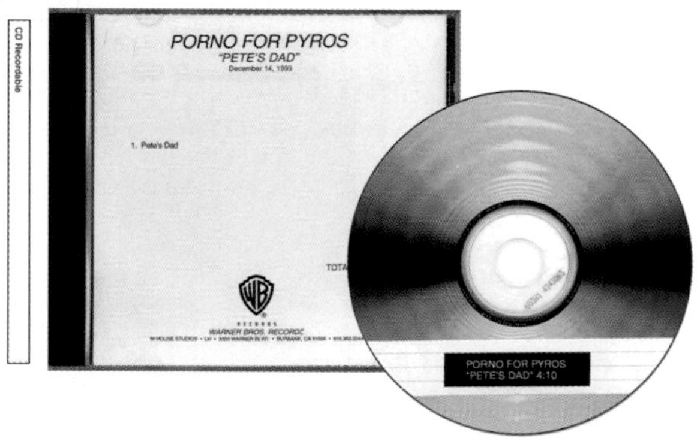

Porno for Pyros – Pete's Dad (Warner Brothers) This is the first known legitimate promotional CDR. Because discs could not be made in time, CDR's were quickly run-off and released to a few radio stations with a letter explaining the song and why a CDR was sent. For a time, this disc was the only available source of the song.

CD-ROM Magazines

Books are not the only paper medium that have found their way to the CD. CD-ROM magazines are quickly becoming a standard in the market place. Targeted predominantly toward entertainment issues and features, CD-ROM magazines contain reviews, video clips, interviews, game previews, and utilities. The collectibility of these CD-ROM magazines will be interesting to watch. Promotional and limited edition CDs become valuable because they are available in limited number and they often contain special interviews or tracks exclusive to that disc. CD-ROM magazines similarly are available only for a limited time, often a two month period per issue. These magazines also have exclusive special video or audio music and interviews by artists like Bush, Soundgarden, Tori Amos, and Metallica.

As mentioned earlier, comic books are joining the CD-ROM revolution. Companies like Marvel and Malibu comics have released CD-ROM versions of some of their most famous comic book titles. These too, like CD-ROM magazines, are available for only a limited time.

Launch (2 Way Media 6) This CD-ROM magazine, introduced in 1995, specializes in exclusive videos and interviews. The disc also usually contains exclusive audio tracks playable in a normal CD player. This, coupled with the fact each issue is available for a limited time gives the disc great potential for collectibility.

Multimedia World – Live (Metatec) This CD-ROM magazine was originally intended to be a stand alone multi-media magazine, but after the first issue combined with *PC World* magazine, it was thus distributed with that magazine. The first issue features a Rolling Stones picture disc CD-ROM from early 1996 that has since become quite rare.

Nautilus CD (Metatec) Promotional CD-ROM distributed free in issues of *MacWorld* Magazine. The disc contains a rare sample of a John Lennon CD-ROM, that as of yet, has never been produced.

Digizine (Ahrens) CD-ROM magazine.

Cybernetics Guardian (U.S. Magna SSLM-3019) 1996 limited edition CD-ROM film of the Japanese anime classic. Works on both Macintosh and Windows operating systems.

Enhanced CD (ECD) & CD Plus (CD+)

Established in 1995, and developed by Philips, Sony, Apple, Microsoft, and the RIAA, the enhanced CD (ECD) is a hybrid of the standard audio CD and the computer data CD-ROM. Often termed a "multimedia format," ECDs are more reminiscent of the CDV rather than a new media carrier breakthrough. Just as the CDV contained laser video data in tandem with audio data, the ECD contains computer data in tandem with audio data.

The ECD, an incarnation of the music industry, is creating "added value" in the ever competitive audio CD market. Liner notes, video clips, and biographies, most often authored in Macromedia Director are usually what is contained in the data portion of the disc. When finished with the audio portion of the disc, the disc can be taken from the CD player to the CD-ROM drive.

There are generally two ECD formats — the mixed mode CD and the stamped multi-session CD. The mixed mode disc contains Red Book audio information placed together with Yellow Book computer data. Mixed mode requires that you skip track one[23] and start audio play on track two. The stamped multi-session disc on the other hand contains all Red Book audio information on the first session of the CD. Your CD player will automatically play this portion of the disc without you having to skip track one. The Yellow Book computer data is then placed in tandem on the second session that your CD-ROM will read. This type of mastering is now designated the Blue Book format (CD+). Be careful with these types however, a few audio CD players might still play the ECD portion of the disc, which if occurs produces a piercing shrill that might damage your speakers.

Another format places the data in a pre-gap area before track one[24] allow the CD audio to begin on track one. This type of disc is called track-zero. This format prevents the potential audio CD problems as mixed mode, but has been discouraged by computer operating systems like Windows 95 and IBM's OS, systems that cannot recognize the track-zero format.

ECD's biggest problem is that these various modes exist. Older CD-ROM drives have trouble reading these discs. The disc often requires special utility software to make it work. The new Blue Book standard will hopefully alleviate most of the current problem with the ECD.

Like the CD+G, ECD rolled out with little fanfare. Most ECD titles are companions to audio-only CDs. ECD, also like CD+G and CDV, does not appear to have been a great sucess. With the myriad of compatability problems with ECD formats and compatability, NEC CD-ROM drives have naggingly been incompatible with ECD. Though many problems have been or are currently being fixed, it may be too late. Trends indicate ECD has the potential to become another fly-by-night technology as CD+G and CDV. As a collector however, never fear. If trends indicate ECD has failed like CD+G or CDV, those trends also indicate they will be highly collectible in a few years. ECDs already have a perceived added value, bringing a premium price as compared to its audio-only counterpart. Also much of the material on ECDs are exclusive, warrenting special significance to the collectors' market. Just as CDVs and formats like CD3s, though failed as a technology, have since become extremely collectible.

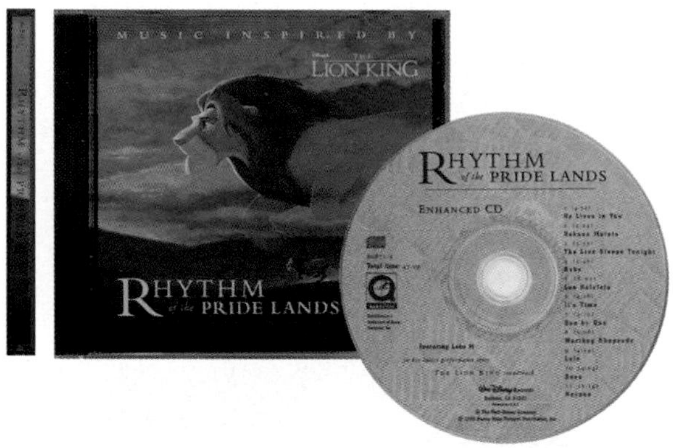

Rhythm Of the Pride Lands (Lion King) (Walt Disney 60871-7) Only 10,000 copies of this disc was ever made. It was sold mostly through computer software outlets usually packaged in Disney's standard blister pack with front blister card (not shown). This identical disc was also pressed under a different catalog number, 608682-2, where only 2,500 copies were made.

Justice Soundboard™

Justice Soundboard is a creative yet simpler CD technology than ECD. Justice Soundboard allows you to play a single track of audio information only when you want. Justice Soundboard is a process whereby a pre-gap is placed at the very beginning of the CD just like the track-zero process described above. The pre-gap is created by placing information before the series of bits on the CD that tells the CD player where the beginning of the disc is. This pre-gap is accessed only by pressing play on your CD player and then hitting the reverse button until you reach the beginning of the pre-gap track. Uses for Justice Soundboard cover anything from interviews and audio liner notes to bonus tracks. The advantage here is that you can hear that track only when you want to hear it. If you want to listen to the album only, the disc will play the album starting from track one by simply pressing the play button.

Justice Soundboard is being used exclusively on Justice label artists. Zoo Entertainment however, uses a variation of the Soundboard technology on their Course of Empire CD.[25] Justice is seeking a declaratory judgment on their Soundboard patents allowing Justice to possibly enjoin Philips from manufacturing a Public Enemy CD that uses a similar technology.[26] In December 1995, Justice Records also filed suit against both Sony and Philips claiming antitrust violations not allowing Soundboard technology to be mastered on discs manufactured inside the United States.

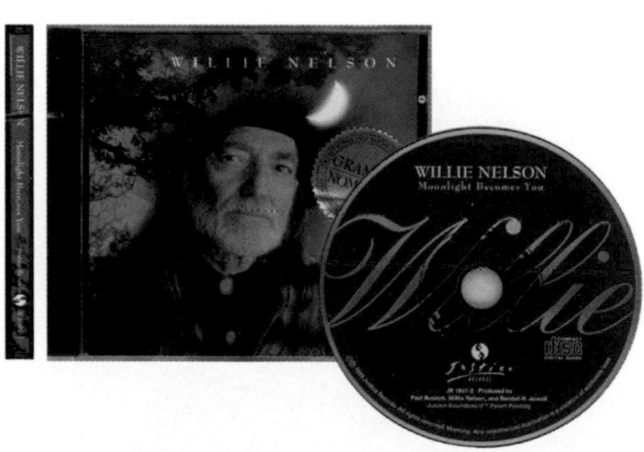

Nelson, Willie – Moonlight Becomes You (Justice Records JR 1601-2) Though still in print, this disc pioneered the Justice Soundboard technology. This pre-gap technology is starting to be used more and more.

Shaped CDs

Vinyl, officially, no longer has anything up on the CD. First, vinyl collectors said LP packaging would always be larger and splashier — now many collector CDs are packed in 12" x 12" sleeves and special three-dimensional packages. Then, vinyl picture discs were a realm unavailable to the CD — now CD picture discs are more common and have reached a level of creativity and sophistication unavailable to vinyl. Shaped vinyl however, was something the CD world could still not touch. Until now! Shaped CDs, first appeared in England in 1990. Currently, there are three major producers of shaped CDs, Pikosso Records in Germany, Disc Art in New York, and Azra Records in California. Today, discs can be cut into virtually any shape.

How can a shaped CD play if you cut into the disc, you may ask? The first part of the answer is to understand that data starts playing at the center of the disc moving outward.[27] As much data as desired can be put onto the disc up to the point where the shape begins. The second part of the answer is shaped CDs, unlike CD3s do not require an adapter to play on most players. The design of a shaped disc usually preserves at least two points of the disc's original edge axially opposite each other. This ensures that the disc will fit into player's standard tray.

Shaped CDs might look great but will they last? This is the number one concern for many collectors. When manufacturing a CD, the metal reflective layer is deposited onto the surface of the disc. An acrylic layer is then applied over the aluminum preventing contaminants from oxidizing and ruining the reflective properties of the layer. Moreover, this acrylic layer flows over the outer edges of the disc fully encapsulating the entire metal layer. After cutting into the disc, the acrylic layer no longer encapsulates the metal. With this protection no longer available, contaminants might be able to propagate into, and oxidize the metal layer affecting its reflective properties. Because shaped CDs are so new, longevity has yet to be scientifically determined. Only time will tell. If the discs do oxidize sometime in the future, an unoxidized disc will certainly be that much more valuable.

Adventures of Pinocchio: Il Colosso (London) Rare Pinocchio shaped CD promoting the 1996 film of the same name.

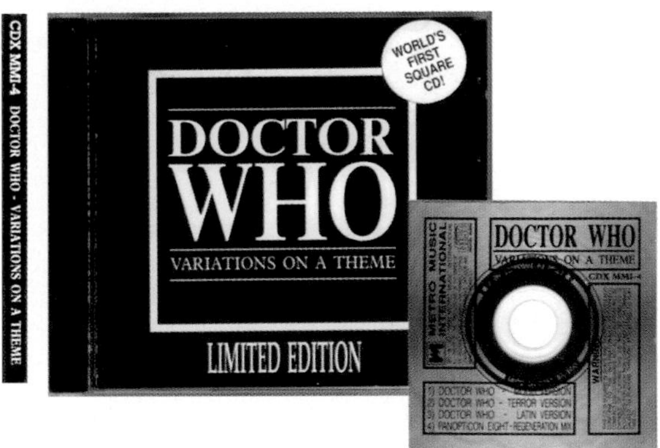

Dr. Who – Variations on a Theme (Metro Music CDX MMI-4) While today, many companies claim theirs was first, this U.K. limited edition distributed by EMI Records is the world's first known shaped CD. This was a clumsy disc because it was too small to fit into a tray-loading CD player, being playable only in a spindle loading CD player (i.e. the disc is placed directly onto the rotating hub of the player).

Bowie, David – Hearts Filthy Lesson (Arista 74321 31807 2) One of the first and rarest shaped CDs made by Pikosso Records by a major recording artist. The disc was made in small quantities and was snatched up from dealers and record stores almost immediately. It was really the disc that introduced the U.S., in a broad sense, to the shaped CD.

AC/DC – Cover You in Oil (Eastwest 7559-64289-2) Shaped disc manufactured by Pikosso Records.

Cool Disc™

Resembling a CD3, Cool Disc is an innovative marketing technology developed by Denon Records. Cool Disc uses a standard twelve centimeter CD but metalizing the surface from the hub to only about one and one-half inch radially from center. When looking at a Cool Disc through a clear jewel box tray, the disc is easily mistaken for a CD3.

The Cool Disc was first manufactured in Japan for a CD video game called *Chun-Chun*. Production is now beginning in the United States but because the process is being patented, exact details of how that process works are not available at this time. Japan didn't pursue the Cool Disc after making the first because some carousel players could not read the disc's existence since the sensors read the outer portion of the disc. Denon USA however, plans to market the Cool Disc to other record companies for any CD application including CD-single, CD-ROM, and ECD.

The small read area can save on licensing fees and the disc's clear portion can employ interesting graphic strategies. Daniel Marx, national media & marketing manager for Denon Records says that the Cool Disc is "a more creative CD format." This "new canvas allows the designer to incorporate full disc printing on the 'see-through' function of the disc expanding graphical possibilities."

Bambi (Walt Disney) Limited edition CD-single "cool-disc." Released in January 1997 and sold exclusively at K-Mart department stores.

Multi-Image™ Compact Disc Jewel Case

Created by the Gelardi Design firm, multi-image is a specially designed jewel box lid having round linear lenses molded onto the face. These lenses, in conjunction with the disc's front booklet, create a "lenticular," producing 3D, animation, and morphing effects. Aside from the specially molded jewel box lid, the technology also includes a special layout design and printed front booklet. The specs on these booklets are tight for both printing and booklet thickness to produce the desired effect.[28] Multi-image covers are unique offering an added value to the jewel box package without straying from the traditional jewel box design. Multi-image cases still meet industry specifications for standard jewel box trays and bases requiring no retooling of the manufacturing line.

The multi-image lid is currently being used with special promotional and limited edition CDs. Be careful, some of these packages are described as 3D, magic-motion, flashing, or given some other similar name. Don't be confused however, these are all multi-image cases.

Emerson Lake & Palmer – Brain Salad Surgery (Rhino) and **Tool – Aenima (Zoo)** Special 1996 collectors edition.

Red Hot Chili Peppers – One Hot Minute (Warner Brothers 9 453-2-DJ)

ImageDisc

ImageDisc is a first generation holographic effect created in the reflective surface of the disc. Glitter effects, title work, and other images refract sparkling around the outer portion of the disc. If you look at the read-side of a normal CD, and move it back and forth, you will notice a rainbow of light appears on the disc. Light refracting off the microscopic pits in the disc creates this rainbow effect. This is exactly how a design in an ImageDisc disc creates its holographic effect.

Developed in 1988 by Disc Manufacturing Inc., ImageDisc is a process whereby an image is engraved into the stamper disc by a cutting laser. After the reflective layer is deposited over the engraved surface, light refracts off the cut grooves bouncing back as a spectrum, or rainbow of light. Like the shaped discs, ImageDiscs are engraved onto an area that does not contain any data so quality of play is unaffected. Image discs are currently being manufactured by Disc Manufacturing, Inc. in the United States and Nimbus Manufacturing in Europe.

DMI ImageDiscs (DMI)

McAuley Shenker Group – Follow the Night (Capitol DPRO-79281) The first known ImageDisc. Manufactured in 1988 by Disc Manufacturing (at that time called Laservideo). The disc is now quite rare.

Rush – Roll the Bones (Atlantic A7524CD 7567-885900-2) Rare 1992 ImageDisc manufactured by Nimbus Manufacturing in Germany.

3-D I•d™

Created by Nimbus, 3-D I•d is a new holographic printing process for the CD. Nimbus developed this process in conjunction with Applied Holographics, a leading design and manufacturing firm of holography packaging, promotional, and security materials. The hologram quality achieved on 3-D I•d is similar to that of holograms printed on traditional paper.

3-D I•d serves dual purposes. The first is to provide counterfeit protection against would-be CD pirates and counterfeiters. A holographic image printed over the CD's mirror band prevents duplication and enhances detection of counterfeit discs at point-of-purchase or at customs. The hologram is then encapsulated to prevent tampering. Corporate logos, title info, trademarks, and inconspicuous holographic features incorporated into the security band allow easy identification.

The second purpose of 3-D I•d is to create high impact three-dimensional holographic images from edge to edge on the print-side surface of the disc. Note that this is a different process than ImageDiscs developed by Disc Manufacturing Inc. Where ImageDiscs are created by engraving the stamper disc, 3-D I•d is printed on the surface of the disc. 3-D I•d's edge-to-edge printing process can create virtually any holographic image to the surface of the disc. The holographic printing process can be used in combination with standard CD printing inks, significantly increasing the marketing ability and expanding the possibilities for CD designers. Nimbus also makes a series of stock holograms available to customers. This allows those customers who do not have access to or funds for making sophisticated holographic images, can still create great holographics on the disc.

Cher – It's a Man's World (Warner Brothers 9 46179-2) The first U.S. limited edition release using the 3d•Id hologram printing.

Compact Disc Problems & Misconceptions

"Laser Rot" (Fade-Out)

First brought to our attention in 1989, the condition known as laser-rot struck fear in all CD owners. Reported as a debilitating digital disease, laser-rot was capable of degenerating your CDs into a worthless piece of plastic in less than 10 years. The cause for laser-rot or technically referred to as fade-out was thought to be from deterioration of the protective acrylic layer applied over the aluminum surface. Once this layer deteriorates, contaminants might cause the reflective layer to oxidize thereby fading out or destroying the layer's reflective properties.

This laser rot hysteria has its roots in England in 1988. A report surfaced claiming this condition arose because of an inherent defect in the compact disc format and manufacturing process. As such, the report stated that all CDs will degrade over a finite period of time, estimated to be eight to fifteen years. This was compounded by a report that came out from the British magazine *Guardian*, about the same time. It was reported, Nimbus Records improperly used solvent-based inks for labeling discs that could "eat" through the acrylic layer, exposing and fading out the aluminum reflective layer. This created a whirlwind of speculation, questioning if we should even buy a CD again.

Stereo Review was first to challenge this laser-rot theory. According to the *Stereo Review*, the Nimbus situation was taken out of context. Nimbus was only saying that their use of improper inks containing certain solvents could cause the CD's protective layer to deteriorate and it was simply a manufacturing flaw that has since been corrected, not a problem with the CD as a format.[29] Reports about discs degenerating in eight to ten years have since been debunked by just about every scientist in the CD industry. The problem with these reports is that the authors confuse isolated manufacturing flaws in the CD with inherent problems in the entire CD format. In accelerated age-testing, CDs have been subjected to extreme temperature and humidity in order to simulate use over long periods of time. There has been no evidence of degradation of a properly made CD as a function of time. In fact, one manufacturer estimated the life span of their optical discs to be over 300 years. Most CD pressing plants have conducted longevity tests and the results have been so conclusive that there is little concern.

Laser-rot or fade-out is probably one of the most talked about non-issues. Most people have no problem whatsoever with this so-called laser-rot. There have been extremely isolated incidents of degradation of the reflective layer on some discs however. Many of these faded discs though were subjected to very extreme handling and environments. On the very few CDs that do have fade-out problems, not due to handling or the environment, most have been determined to be caused from a manufacturing flaw and should have never been allowed to leave the plant. Either contaminated or improper materials used in the manufacturing process tend to be the culprit. After the plastic disc is molded and the metal layer deposited, the acrylic is poured onto the surface of the disc. The disc is then spun rapidly to force the acrylic liquid to coat the entire disc. Occasionally the acrylic layer is not deposited on the disc properly, not covering the entire surface, allowing contaminants to seep through and fade the reflective layer. Alternatively, if there is some foreign particle on the disc's surface during this process, that particle might help contaminants attack and fade-out the reflective layer. With all the safe-guards and quality control measures at modern CD pressing plants, this situation rarely if ever occurs. So even though fade-outs can occur, it is so rare that not much can be done but to simply exchange the disc for a new one.

As a collector, however, it is understandable how this fade-out issue can be of great concern. Even though this condition will most likely never happen to any of your CDs, just the thought makes life uneasy. Moreover, because the problem won't occur until many years down the road, there is no way to tell if the disc you bought will succumb to fade-out. This is especially disconcerting if it happens to a collectible CD. If a commonly available CD fades out, no problem, just return it for a replacement. But if fade out occurs to a collectible CD that might be irreplaceable, what now? That is the collectors' worst fear and is really the reason why this issue won't go away. Take heart though, I have several thousand CDs, most of them collectible and many over 12 years old, and not a single disc has ever faded out.

If, heaven forbid, you think your disc is succumbing to this laser-rot, take it back to the record store where you bought it. If this is not an option because it was purchased too many years ago, my second suggestion is to contact the record company and see if they will exchange the title for a new one.

Laser-rot also affected laser discs during the late 80s. This condition was incurred because of problems with the adhesive that sandwiched between the two disc halves. The problem was generally corrected except for increasing reports of fade-out appearing on certain discs where they have not occured before. Whether this is due to laser-rot or some other condition remains to be seen.

"Pin-Holes"

Hold a CD up to the light and what do you see? Some have found tiny sparkles on the disc that turn out being actual holes in the aluminum reflective layer. Called "Pin-Holes," these tiny areas are unmetalized portions on the surface of the disc. After the plastic substrate of the body is molded, the aluminum reflective layer is made by placing the disc in a chamber where aluminum literally condenses onto the surface of the disc. This process is analogous to water condensation you find on a cold drinking glass on a hot day. Occasionally, the aluminum misses a spot when it is deposited onto the plastic.

Because of all the brouhaha over laser-rot, CDs are heavily scrutinized for quality problems. "Pin-Holes" are an example of this heavy scrutiny. But even more so than laser-rot, "Pin-Holes" are a non-issue with CDs. When the CD was developed, this problem was taken into consideration. That is why Sony developed the Cross Interleave Reed-Solomon Code which is the error correction mechanism all CD players have, to correct for flaws like "Pin-Holes." Detractors speculate than when playing a CD and the laser beam hits the "Pin-Hole" all of those pits are missed affecting play of the disc. In fact the error correction takes care of this problem so that the laser can pass under a "Pin-Hole" and the listener will never know the difference. The error correction works so well in fact, that gaps much larger than "Pin-Holes" containing thousands of pits, can be missed by the laser with no substantial effect in the quality of play.

Pin holes are barely noticeable on a CD, both to the eye and to the laser.

Free BPA Monomer Growth

It is my belief that this is the most common and most significant problem CD owners face. Luckily, it is a curable problem. If you look at the read-side of a compact disc you may perhaps notice some crystalline-looking growth film on the disc. This growth is free Bisphenol A (BPA). BPA is a monomer species used in the polymerization of the polycarbonate plastic disc substrate. This growth is produced by aggressive ink systems that do not fully cure. This happens when a disc is made and printed, the ink is dried using ultraviolet light, the disc then dropped onto a spool stacking one disc on top of another several hundred discs high. Occasionally, the ink does not fully cure and when stacking the disc you have the read-side of a disc stacked on top of the print-side of a disc. Stacking the discs at the manufacturing plant is not a problem. Where the problem lies is when they are shipped to the record company in this stacked position before actual distribution. Often, CDs are shipped to the record company in stacks of about 100 discs. All the discs in the stack literally have the read-side of the disc in contact with the printed print-side of the disc. If these discs are left stacked one on top of another in a warehouse for an extended period of time, the ink from the print side might react with the plastic on the read-side. The BPA is freed and begins to propagate to the disc's read-side surface creating the crystalline growth film. This reaction is very slow, so when you buy a CD, it will appear to be in perfect condition. Then maybe a year later, you might find this mysterious growth on the surface of the disc.

This condition is most prevalent with discs housed in special intricate packages. The reason is these CDs must be inserted into these packages by hand, usually somewhere other than the CD manufacturing plant. So as procedure goes, the disc is block wrapped by the plant, one disc stacked on top of the other, and then shipped to the record company's warehouse or assembler. There, the discs may sit waiting to be inserted into the packages. If the ink is not fully cured and the wait is quite some time, the conditions are ripe for free BPA to react with the ink. This condition is rare in jewel case packaged CDs because the discs usually go right from the printing press to the packing machine that inserts each CD in a jewel box not allowing the CDs to be stacked long enough for the two surfaces to react.

As mentioned at the beginning of this section this condition is curable. The best method to remove the free BPA film is to apply some warm soapy water to the film and wipe clean with a soft cloth. There might be a trace of clouding on the disc but that will not affect the disc's play.

This disc shows an example of free BPA propagating to the surface of the disc. Applying warm soapy water to a cloth and wiping the disc, will remove most of the BPA. The center portion of the disc was cleaned with water and soap.

Up-Cuts

Have you ever put a CD in the player, only wanting to play, track eight, and low and behold, the song actually starts a few seconds after the real beginning of the song? Even stranger, if you play the entire disc, or simply track seven through track eight, there is no problem. This condition, of a track starting after the song actually begins is called an up-cut. The problem that is occurring is that the Lead In/Lead Out times set when the digital coding was placed were too tight. All numbered tracks on a CD are coded with silent markers that tell the CD when a track begins and when it ends. Because of an error when mastering the tape, the begin or end statements are not synchronized with the music and an up-cut occurs. Nothing can be done to fix this problem. The only solution is if the record company provides the disc manufacturer with a corrected master tape. The most infamous case of up-cutting was on the 20-Bit SBM gold disc edition of Bruce Springsteen's *Born to Run*. Track one of the disc would start a few seconds after the song actually started. Sony issued a recall on the disc and reportedly replaced it with a corrected version. If you encounter this situation, contact the record company, report the problem, and see if you can get a replacement or get your money back.

Foam Inserts

Foam inserts have become the most recent concern to CD collectors. Foam inserts are thin foam sheets usually found in two-CD jewel boxes from Germany and England. The foam is used to prevent the discs from popping off the hub of the tray while shipping. It appears that the foam is absorbing some of the chemicals from the disc thus tarnishing said disc. This condition is so new that we have not been able to locate any samples. I have many discs in my collection packaged between these foam inserts, none of them suffering from the described condition. We'll keep you informed if any developments arise.

An example of a CD jewel box with a foam insert included.

Plastic Substrate Flow Swirls

Observe the read-side of a CD and you might notice a series of swirls in the plastic of the disc. Questions arose whether those swirls will affect the ability of the laser to read the disc. Fear not, these patterns in your disc are flow swirls created by the polycarbonate as the disc is being made. When a disc is being pressed, a quantity of liquid polycarbonate plastic is shot through a tube into a disc mold. As the plastic enters the mold it begins to solidify almost immediately. Therefore, the plastic that enters the mold first begins to harden before the last of the plastic enters the mold. Remember, this whole molding and drying process takes about four seconds to complete. The swirls are created by the plastic drying at different rates as it is being injected into the mold. These swirls are a minor consequence of the manufacturing process and have no affect of the playability of the disc.

These flow swirls issustrate how the plastic dried inside the disc mold, but that is about it. These swirls do not impair the laser's ability to read the data in the disc.

Dust and Scratches

Many booklet cards contain a notice informing us to prevent dust and scratches on the read-side of the disc. I think by this time in the CD's evolution, we are all aware that minor dust and scratches don't affect the playability of the disc.

Vinegar Syndrome

This is probably the most ridiculous charge questioning the longevity of the CD. First proposed by the International Council of Archives Conference on Documents proposed that CDs will become unusable in three to five years because the plastic substrate body will turn to acetic acid (common vinegar). They make a bizarre analogy between the degradation of old 20s and 30s movie film to what could happen to compact discs, even though the chemical composition of each medium is completely different. So according to the ICACD if you add a little oil to you CD collection you will have a lifetime supply of salad dressing. I guess it doesn't hurt to prepare. Enough said!

PDO Discs

Philips, one of the inventors of the CD, occasionally has trouble with their discs, unique from other manufacturers because they manufacture a different style of disc. The problem however, has only been at the PDO U.K. plant. PDO also has plants in the United States (now called PMDC) and Germany, both of which have not experienced these problems. Remember, the following problems are very isolated and chances are will have no effect on your PDO discs. Not a single disc from my collection has experienced most of the following problems.

Tarnish and Corrosion

This problem appeared in the late eighties during the height of CD3s. Many of these three inch discs were housed in cheap cardboard sleeves. Apparently, sulfur residue from the inside of the sleeve began to leach into the disc. This sulfur propagated through the acrylic lacquer layer and contaminated the metal reflective surface thereby creating tarnish on the disc. This condition apparently takes years to develop so it wasn't discovered until recently. Still, this is an extremely rare occurrence and is found to be limited to CD3s made in the U.K. only, housed in a cardboard sleeve.

Corrosion on the other hand, another rare occurrence, is a brownish-color degradation. However, this is even more rare because the condition is only created when a PDO disc from the U.K., having a silver, rather than aluminum reflective layer, is used and is placed in an improperly manufactured jewel box (i.e. a box made from impure plastic not made to specification). PDO U.K. has since stopped using silver as the reflective layer and the supplier of the contaminated jewel boxes is no longer being used.

In fact, the lacquer formulation was also changed in 1992 to further prevent this condition.

Plastic Sleeve Bonding

This is the only problem that discs from my collection have experienced, and it occurs with all PDO discs made before 1993 from all countries, not just the U.K. This problem occurs when a PDO disc having printing on a substantial portion of the disc surface is placed into a plastic sleeve. The molecules in the ink and the plastic have a tendency to bond, peeling the ink off onto the plastic.

This problem does not take very long to occur so it is my suggestion that if you have any discs marked PDO from any country, housed in a plastic sleeve, remove it immediately and place into a jewel box. Rykodisc records was one record label that often placed their promo CDs, made at PDO in North Carolina, in such plastic sleeves from 1988 to 1991. Make sure you remove them from the sleeve *immediately*. Value of the disc will be substantially reduced if this condition affects your discs.

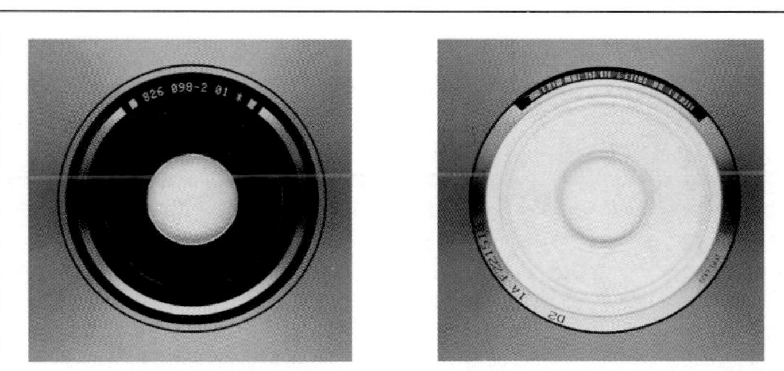

Though both Sony and Philips created the standard for the CD, each had their own idea as to how the CD should be made. Sony's disc was molded with the center hole, Philips center hole is punched. Philips believed that applying a paper label embedded into the print-side of the CD was the way to go. Sony on the other hand believed that silk-screening the disc will produce better results. The disc on the left is made by PDO, now PMDC, notice there is not visible stacking ring. The disc on the right is a Sony-made disc with a clear stacking ring.

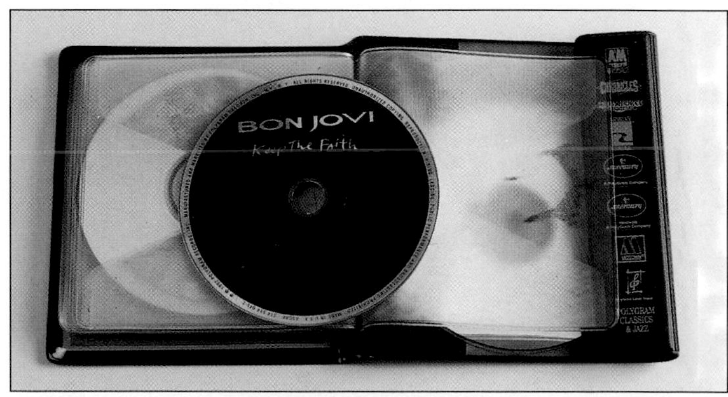

This is an example of what can happen to PDO discs that are stored in plastic sleeves. A portion of the ink bonds to the sleeve. This certainly damages the esthetics and value of the disc, and may in time impair the data stored on the disc since part of the protective layer is removed from the disc.

Laser Discs

Laser discs (LD) are unique collectibles because they are the focus of a very loyal and passionate, yet small group of collectors. LDs are only a modest part of the home video market. However, most home video innovations and trends begin here, then permeate to the rest of the home video market. Surround sound, letter boxing, and supplementary material all first appeared on laser disc.

Laser Disc the Early Years

Battling for a projected $6 billion market, video disc technology was being developed during the late sixties. As the earliest modern optical disc format, the laser disc has been around for nearly 25 years. The laser disc's demonstration to the media was in 1972 at Universal City, California.[30] The disc was originally one-sided, held 40 minutes of video, and cost about $5 per disc.[31] The players were projected to cost about $400 and included a proposal for a 10 disc changer that could play 400 minutes of video. The laser video disc was released to the public as Laser Vision in 1978, four years before the compact disc was introduced to the United States.

Queen – Live In Budapest (Polygram 080 510 1) German 1987 out-of-print laser disc. Notice that these discs were pressed in gold colored plastic like the 5" CDVs.

Terror Train (Fox 1665-80) U.S. 1980 out-of-print laser disc.

Pinocchio (Walt Disney 239 AS) The 1992 release (below) with strikingly different graphics than the original 1985 version (above). Both discs, however have identical catalog numbers.

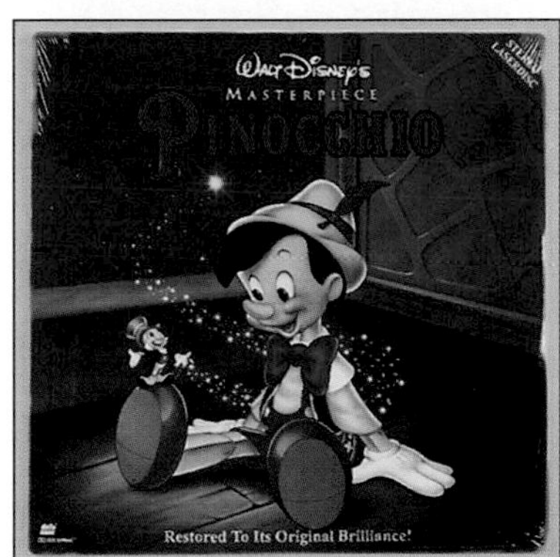

The real battle over a viable home video disc format, however, did not start until the late seventies. In fact, the video disc was considered the most viable video format because all the proposed disc technologies, were at the time, almost half the cost of the video tape format. Various other prototypes emerged during the early seventies, but, most barely reaching the prototype stage. By the late seventies three video disc formats shook-out as finalists to become king of the video disc hill. The first was the laser optical video disc created by MCA, Philips, IBM, and Pioneer. The second was a grooved capacitance system created by RCA, Zenith Radio, and CBS Inc. The third was a grooveless capacitance system created by Matsushita, General Electric, and Thorn EMI. There's no guessing now which format won. Of the many reasons why MCA's optical disc system won was that it was a completely new technology with seemingly infinite possibilities. The capacitance systems were old technologies, literally the home video versions of the vinyl LP. More importantly, tangible features such as perpetual stop motion and huge data storage are available. The capacitance video systems were at the edge of their technological envelope, while optical video discs were just beginning to realize their potential. The ability to store huge amounts of data and interactive multimedia capabilities struck the imagination of the industry in what this disc can do. MCA's laser disc was also helped by the fact that Laser Vision was released more than two years before the capacitance systems.

Another plus for the optical disc format was its software catalog which helped to generate interest in the format. The success of any new home entertainment technology, whether home video, home audio, video game, computer, etc., is software, software, software. No matter what the quality of the hardware, it will live or die by the availability of its software. The Magnavox, Pioneer, and MCA laser disc players and DiscoVision discs controlled the home video market until 1981 while the VHS and Beta video tape wars were going on. When RCA finally released its SelectaVision capacitance driven video disc player that year, it was too late with its obsolete technology and smaller catalog of titles. SelectaVision was not viable against the DiscoVision and Magnetic Video line of around 300 titles, both of which are considered the forefathers of the laser disc. In fact, during these early days of laser disc, only Paramount and UA had yet produced or manufactured any laser disc titles.

DiscoVision

DiscoVision, a subsidiary of MCA (Music Corporation of America), was created in the mid sixties to begin developing video disc technology. DiscoVision accomplished this in large part by buying various companies involved in related technologies. Gauss Electrophysics was one of the first bought. This company invented a technique by which laser-read signals produced from a plastic substrate could detected. The company accumulated more patents for optically based data storage and retrieval technologies. The video disc as we know it was announced in 1974 by MCA.

In the late seventies, MCA and IBM joined forces creating DiscoVision Associates to produce actual laser disc software. A laser disc manufacturing facility was opened in Carson, California. Laser Vision laser discs came to market under the name DiscoVision, first in late 1978 in Atlanta, Georgia, and then in early 1979 in Seattle, Washington. All laser discs brandished a striking silver-colored box or jacket with the DiscoVision trademark at the bottom and the "V" raising up to display the disc's title and graphic. MCA joined with Philips and Pioneer for home and industry applications for the video disc. Discs were not only made for home use but for industry as well. MCA provided over 7,000 industrial LD players to General Motors for showroom applications

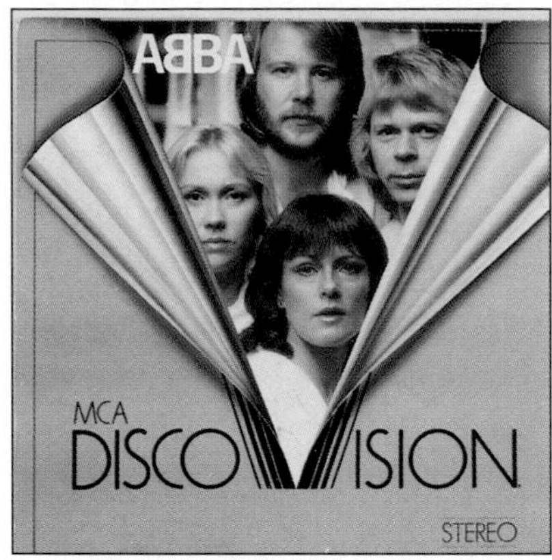

Abba – Abba (Discovision 74-006)

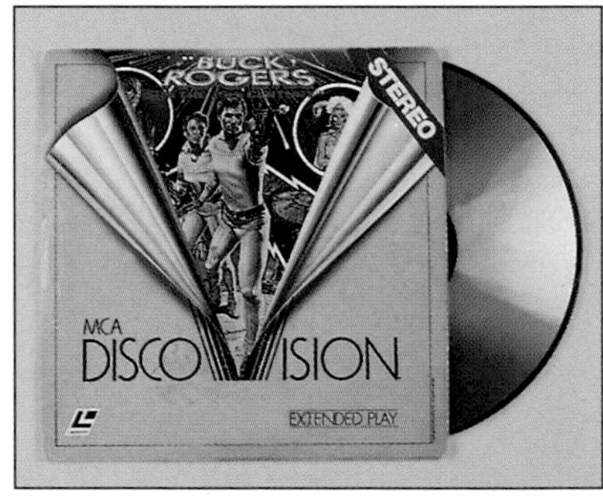

Buck Rogers in the 25th Century (Discovision 13-002) Rare out-of-print DiscoVision laser disc. The DiscoVision lasers that have yet to be remastered and repressed will hold the most value.

disc Details

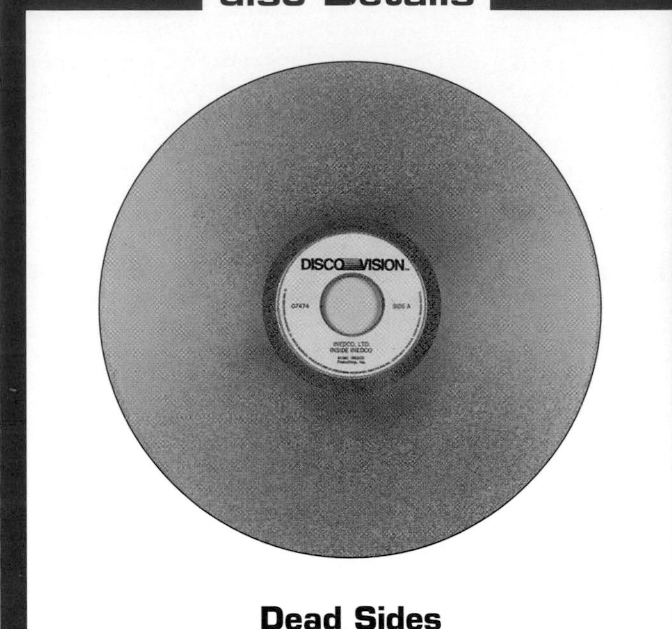

Dead Sides

A curiosity exclusive to DiscoVision discs are dead sides. The standard for 12" laser discs require that they comprise two halves sandwiched together. When a multi disc film only requires an odd number of sides to contain the movie, however, i.e. a five sided movie that requires six discs also require the sixth side be blank. To curb costs, DiscoVision would use halves of either bad or preproduction discs as the dead side. That dead side would be spray coated with an opaque coating to render the dead side unplayable and identifiable. Ingenuitous collectors discovered early on that if removing the coating using rubbing alcohol (alcohol containing about 70% ethyl alcohol by volume) to remove the coating to find an actual full-playing laser disc side. More interesting, some of the uncovered sides were of films never released on DiscoVision laser disc. Those films not available on the DiscoVision label but found on the highly collectible dead sides are:

Andromeda Strain
Anne of the Thousand Days
Bullet
The Monkey's Uncle
Prince And the Pauper
Sugarland Express
Sweet Charity

This $100 million dollar investment by the companies, however, realized severe quality control problems at their newly opened Carson, California plant.[32] While 90% of Japanese-made discs were meeting quality standards, more than 50 percent of DiscoVision discs were defective. In fact, Universal Pioneer Corporation in Japan began supplying discs to DiscoVision because of the quality problems. This problem along with less than projected growth in the market and the complete failure of RCA's SelectaVision, made DiscoVision's future bleak. In 1981, the plant had about 1,000 employees but the operation crashed in March 1982 halting production of DiscoVision discs.[33]

Pioneer came to the rescue in 1982 by buying the Carson plant[34] as well as MCA's entire interest in the Japanese software firm Universal Pioneer Corporation (UPC). UPC was a Tokyo based laser disc player manufacturer and was originally a 50/50 joint venture between Pioneer Electronic Corporation of Tokyo and DiscoVision Associates of the U.S.

During the eighties both Pioneer and Philips created substantial improvements in the laser disc technology. Both quality and digital sound and reliability were vastly improved. The laser disc however, was constantly dogged by VHS video tape which won the video tape wars just as laser disc began to take off. As such, efforts shifted from convincing buyers to chose laser as the video disc of choice to choosing laser video disc over video tape. Laser disc was soon eclipsed by the enormous popularity of VHS video tape. Its primary shortcoming was the lack of recordability.

Pioneer eventually purchased the entire DiscoVision Associates for $200 million dollars in 1989, including the patents. Thought to be too much at the time, it has ended up being a real coup for Pioneer. Because of all the optical disc patents DiscoVision holds, Pioneer reportedly receives royalties of 12 cents per side for every video disc, plus an undisclosed percentage of every laser disc player produced. Pioneer even receives 3 cents per compact disc and CD-ROM as well as 1.5 percent of the manufacturer's cost of every compact disc player.[35] In fact, Philips, purported inventor of the laser disc pays a royalty to Pioneer from the original DiscoVision CD technology patents. With the explosion of CD applications and sales, this risk, has since become a windfall.

DiscoVision currently holds over 1,400 patents related to compact disc and laser disc technologies as well as for the players themselves.[36] DiscoVision has less than 20 employees whose sole job is to oversee the patents and maintain these worldwide license agreements it has with manufacturers of audio discs and audio disc players, video discs and video disc players, as well as all optically based data storage and retrieval devices and media.

Magnetic Video

Starting in 1969 by Andre Blay with five other employees, Magnetic Video Corporation (MVC), based in Farmington Hills, Michigan, began selling industrial training videos. Thanks in part to Sony's release of its first home video tape player/recorder in 1976, Magnetic Video contracted with the 20th Century Fox film studio to begin duplicating and selling theatrical releases in 1977. At the time, Magnetic Video controlled about 40 percent of the home video tape market as the United States' number one producer of video cassettes. In fact, it was so successful that Magnetic Video was bought out by 20th Century Fox in 1979.

In 1980 the UA films, one of the last hold-outs to enter the home video market contracted with MVC. By 1981, MVC was distributing films by Twentieth Century-Fox, Lord Lew Grade's ITC Entertainment, AVCO Embassy, ABC, Viacom International, and Warner Brothers. In 1981 Pioneer contracted with MVC to manufacture MVC laser discs by 20th Century Fox, including the most coveted title at the time, *Star Wars*.

More History

In 1981 MCA along with Pioneer and Magnavox (Philips) created Optical Programming Associates. Their task was to create interactive random-access based discs, particularly for children and educational applications. The first disc was the *First National Kid Disc*. This disc won the first video Grammy award in 1982.

In 1984 Voyager began producing high quality transfers of classic films such as *King Kong* and *Citizen Kane*. These discs were the first to employ the multiple track feature of laser disc to include audio commentaries as well as to include supplementary material including deleted scenes and "Making Of. . ." documentaries. Voyager is also credited with producing the first letter boxed version of a film on laser disc. Max Ophuls' *Lola Montes* led the trend by being the first film to be letterboxed exclusively for laser disc. A trend that has literally become the cornerstone for laser disc format. In December 1988, MGM released *Dr. Zhivago* and *Ben Hur*; they were the first American films to make it to laser disc in letterbox format.

As previously mentioned, the laser disc was originally called Laser Vision. In 1988, through persuasion by Sony and Philips because of too many confusing optical disc acronyms, especially surrounding CD video LDs, which are digital audio LDs, Pioneer changed the name to LD or laser discs.

Currently about 2% of households own laser disc players.

Father of Optical Disc Technology

A little discussed war has been waging since the eighties regarding who should receive credit as the inventor of the optical disc, and for that matter laser disc technology. David Gregg, an engineer from California, invented and patented four patents that create the core of the optical disc technology.

Though the patents were legally assigned to MCA, the name David Gregg receives little recognition as the inventor of the compact disc. Just as other inventions have so changed the American culture like the light bulb or phonograph by Thomas Edison, so has the optically read laser disc by David Gregg. And this is why Mr. Gregg is suing Philips who claimed to be the inventor of the optical disc technology.

Laser Disc Collecting

Out of Print

Laser discs are so collectible because a movie truly isn't on home video until it's on laser disc. The laser disc's quality is unsurpassed, a quality VHS can't touch. As such, when the laser disc's go out of print, which, because of costs and distribution practices, occurs often, those laser discs become quite valuable. Often, as with most everything else, nobody wants a title until the title goes out of print. Once a disc is deleted, there is usually a flurry of interest and a scramble to buy up the remaining copies, even if the disc was available for years, thus driving up its value.

Interestingly, some of the most collectible discs are not out-of-print blockbuster films but rather most are small time cult and horror film classics. But of course the most collectible across the board discs are Disney. But this leads us to collectible longevity. In the music collectible arena, first issues and first pressing CDs are coveted by collectors. Variations in packaging and mastering affect degree of value, but regardless, most have substantial value. Laser discs on the other hand, suffer from a condition where once a new pressing of a particular title is made, the previous title is completely shunned. For example, once Disney's first laser disc release of *Pinocchio* was deleted in the mid-eighties, it was subsequently worth hundred's of dollars. Once the remastered version was released in 1993, sealed copies of the original version sold for less than $20. Be careful though, and don't be too quick to sell off your old titles once the new versions come out, because the trend might change. With all the remastering that studios are doing these days, a trend is setting where material found in the old discs is inadvertently being left out. For instance, when the *Star Wars* Trilogy was remastered and made into a huge $249 mega-boxed set, the previous $69.99 single film versions became worth $25. However, there is a missing audio segment in the *Star Wars* film that is only available on these older pressings. Another aspect largely ignored is cover graphics. Dismissed by many collectors because they claim to be interested only in the movie, not the packaging, there are still those of us who appreciate creative packaging.

Limited Edition Laser Discs

The hottest laser disc collectibles are limited editions. We have talked earlier about the pitfalls of the collectibility of limited editions, but these pitfalls seldom apply to laser discs. The first reason for this is the enormous substance limited edition laser disc packages contain. More than just a remastered movie, laser disc limited editions usually contain exclusive audio commentaries running

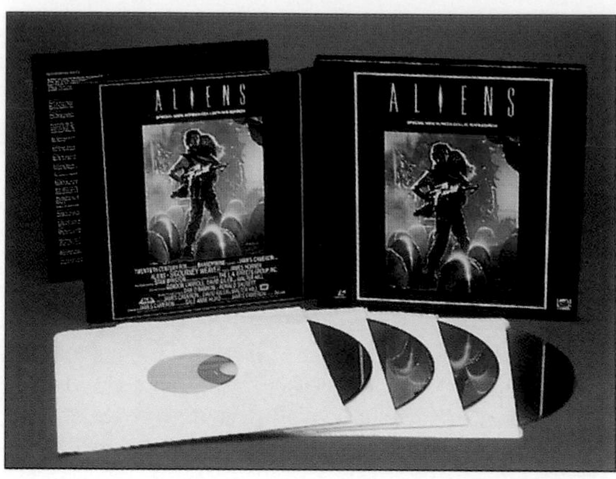

Aliens (Fox 1504-85) U.S. 1991 out-of-print four laser disc boxed set with fifteen minutes of additional footage. This footage will probably not be included on subseqeunt pressings.

Pee-Wee's Playhouse Fun-O-Rama (Image ID6304ME) Rare out-of-print laser disc.

Lady and the Tramp (Walt Disney 582 AS) Super-rare U.S. 1987 out-of-print laser disc.

disc Details

CLV v. CAV

If you are a new collector of laser discs, you might have discovered that often two versions of the same laser disc title may be available. One is usually a single disc version and the other is a multi-disc version. The difference between these two versions is that one is CLV and the other is CAV. But what are the differences, and which one should you buy?

CLV stands for Constant Linear Velocity. This means that the data is passing across the laser beam at the same speed. Because the inner spiral of data is shorter than the outer spiral of data, the disc must be rotated faster (about 1800 revolutions per minute) while the laser is reading data from the inner portion of the disc, and slower (about 600 revolutions per minute) while the laser is reading the outer portion of the disc. CAV stands for Constant Angular Velocity which means that the speed of the data passing the laser fluctuates but the speed of the revolving disc is traveling a constant speed (i.e. constant angular velocity, just like vinyl LP turntables).

All this means to you is what functions the discs will offer. If you own a $1,200 player, it doesn't matter which type of disc you buy. But if you're like me and have an affordable laser disc player, the difference is important. CAV discs allow your player to freeze frame, fast forward, slow motion, and step through the program one frame at a time. If you have a film packed with special effects like *Twister*, you may want to walk through a scene one frame at a time on a CAV disc to see how the special effects develop. CLV discs do not offer these functions. CLV discs offer fast forward but cannot freeze frame, slow motion, or step. The reason this does not matter to more expensive players is those players have a memory chip that stores frames so the aforementioned CAV features can be simulated even on a CLV disc.

The drawback to CAV discs is that they only hold 30 minutes of video per side, where CLV discs hold an entire hour of video. Therefore, CAV versions are most always multi-disc sets, requiring you to change discs part way through the program, and costs about 30 to 50 percent more.

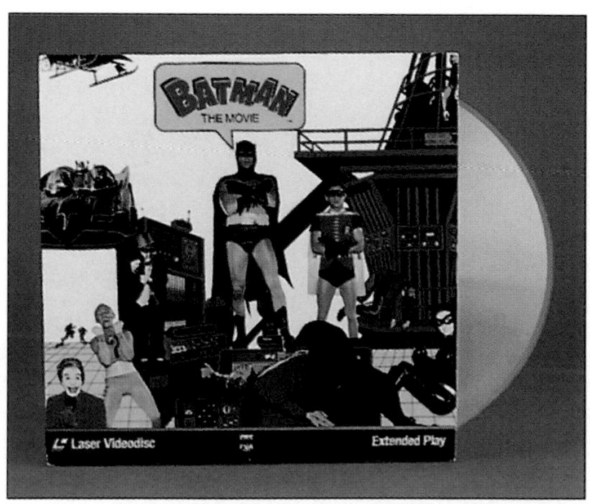

Batman (CBS 1470-80) U.S. 1989 out-of-print laser disc.

through the entire movie on the alternate audio track, special documentaries, interviews, and even deleted scenes. Also, the packaging tends to be outstanding. But the most important aspect of laser disc limited editions is that they are usually truly limited edition. Most quantities never go above 10,000 copies with the average between 5,000 to 8,000. However, Image Entertainment has recently been releasing special limited editions of 2,500 copies. These discs tend to sell out almost immediately and often double in value within the first few months.

Promotional

These lasers, not as prevalent as promotional CDs, are still quite collectible. Most are demonstration discs used to illustrate the capabilities of laser disc players. Most promotional laser discs comprise of snippets from various films. Obviously these are not on the top ten most watched again list, but these discs' value are based on being artifacts. If the promo disc has snippets from an out-of-print and valuable laser disc, however, they become proportionately valuable.

Import Laser Discs

Import laser discs have recently become an important part of CD collecting. Japanese are the most popular because they are in the NSTC format opposed to PAL which is the European format. The Japanese lasers are therefore, compatible with American systems where the European lasers are not. Imports have also become important because there are many titles that are available in Japan but not available in the United States.

Generally, import lasers, especially Japanese, cost about twice to two-and-a-half times that of a domestic laser disc. Also, be careful to inquire whether the foreign lasers have either an English dialog track, or if you are that desperate, have American subtitles.

Eight-Inch laser Disc (8"LD)

Appearing on the scene in 1984 as an EP version of the laser disc, eight-inch laser discs (8"LD) get their name obviously from their eight-inch diameter size. It is estimated that around 200 to 300 titles exist, distributed in the U.S., Japan, and Europe. This format however, like many others, fizzled out by 1991. But just like these defunct optical disc formats, 8"LDs have become quite collectible. A few 8" titles by artists like Bobby Brown and They Might Be Giants can still be found in the laser disc bargain bins. Most however, are scarce.

Aristocats (Walt Disney) This version of Aristocats was made in Taiwan and released months before the American version. Because the soundtrack is in English and the cover is substantially different that the American version, it is quite collectible.

Iron Maiden – Raising Hell (BMG Video) Rare promotional 8" laser disc. What is so curious about this disc is that it was released in 1993 long after the industry had summarily given up on producing 8" LDs. Also, the concert video wasn't even due out on laser disc anyway, just home VHS video.

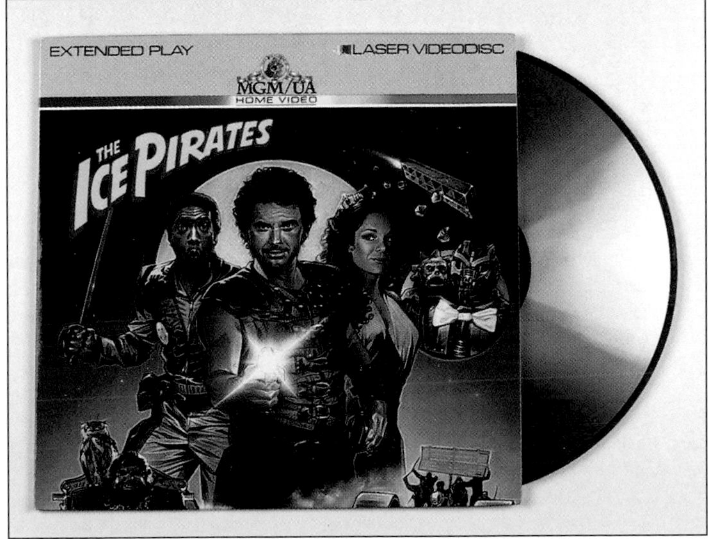

Ice Pirates (MGM/UA ML100427) U.S. 1984 out-of-print laser disc.

Monkees, The (Image ID6267RC) U.S. 1989 out-of-print laser disc.

Aspect Ratios

As laser disc and letterboxing continue to grow in the home video market place, the differences between the various types of letterboxing may be causing unnecessary confusion for consumers and retailers alike. A prime example: both *Ben-Hur* and *E.T. The Extra-Terrestrial* are "letterboxed" on disc, but the black bands above and below the picture on E.T. are almost negligible, while the bands on *Ben-Hur* take up nearly half the available screen space. This all has to do with the theatrical aspect ratios.

1.33 to 1

Known as "Academy Aperture," the numbers refer to width v. height (in this case the picture looks almost square with the image only 33% wider than it is high). This is roughly the same of a frame of 35mm film (fig. 1), as well as a standard video monitor (fig. 2), so virtually no picture information is lost when a film shot in 1.33 is shown on a TV screen. This was the format in which all movies (with very few notable exceptions) were shot prior to 1953 and transition to video poses no problems.

2.35 to 1

In 1953, 20th Century Fox introduced CinemaScope in an attempt to lure the TV happy public (who were transfixed by their newly purchased sets) back to the theaters with the promise of a revolutionary new "Wide Screen" film process. A special lens on the camera would record an image that was nearly two-and-a-half times as wide as it was high and squeeze it onto an ordinary frame of 35mm film, with a similar lens on the projector expanding the picture back to its original panorama (fig. 3).

During the '50s and '60s most moderate and big budget films were shot in the 2.35 to 1 aspect ratio, though often under other names and slightly different aspects. The early '70s saw the fusion of most of these variables into one standard: Panavision. The Panavision company has supplied equipment with which most widescreen movies have been shot during the past two decades. Unfortunately, when a Panavision/CinemaScope film is displayed on video, little more than half of the original image is visible at any given moment, with important characters often missing (fig. 4).

There are two basic solutions to this problem. The most common is to "pan and scan," where a video technician electronically follows the action, panning the film to show the most pertinent information. While accepted as standard operating procedure for years, even the most competent pan/scan job upsets the photographic balance of a film. the other, and arguably the most sensible way to present a 'Scope picture on video is "letterboxing."

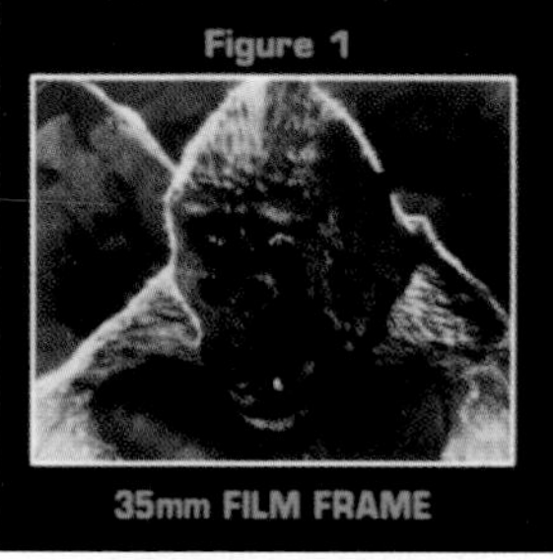

Figure 1
35mm FILM FRAME

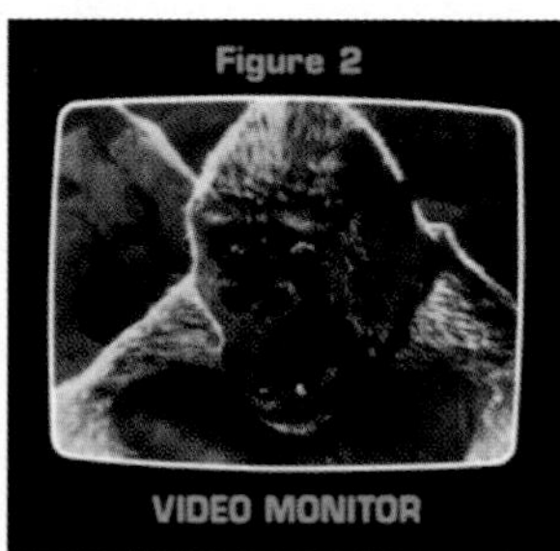

Figure 2
VIDEO MONITOR

Figure 3
THEATER SCREEN

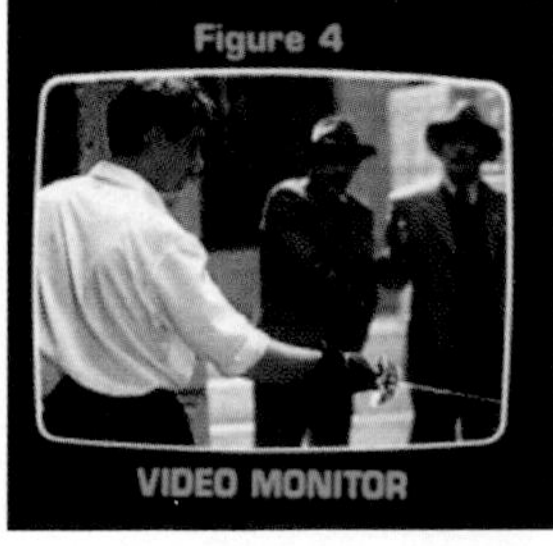

Figure 4
VIDEO MONITOR

Figure 5
VIDEO MONITOR

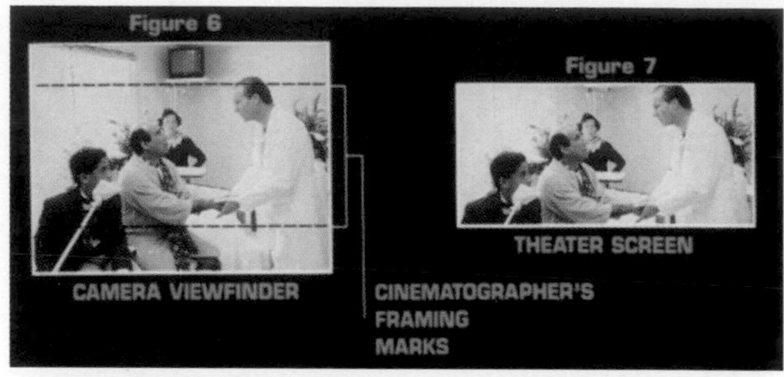

Figure 6
CAMERA VIEWFINDER

Figure 7
THEATER SCREEN

CINEMATOGRAPHER'S FRAMING MARKS

Figure 10
VIDEO MONITOR

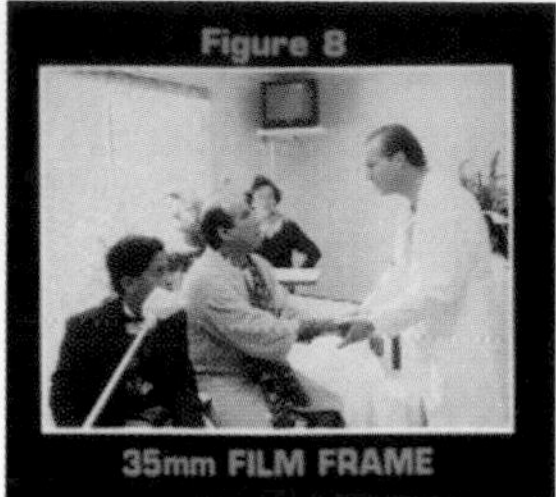

Figure 8
35mm FILM FRAME

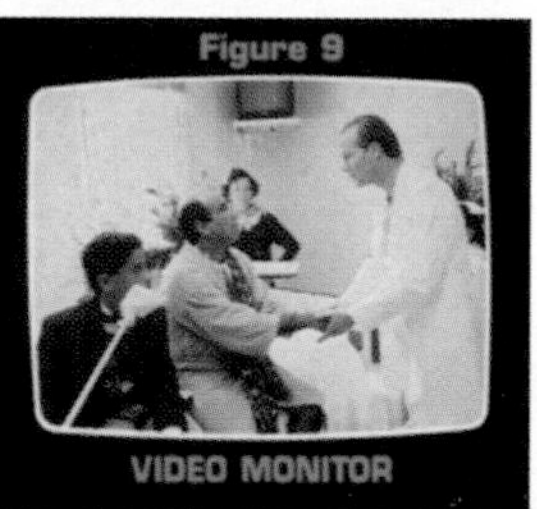

Figure 9
VIDEO MONITOR

Figure 13
VIDEO MONITOR

Figure 14
VIDEO MONITOR

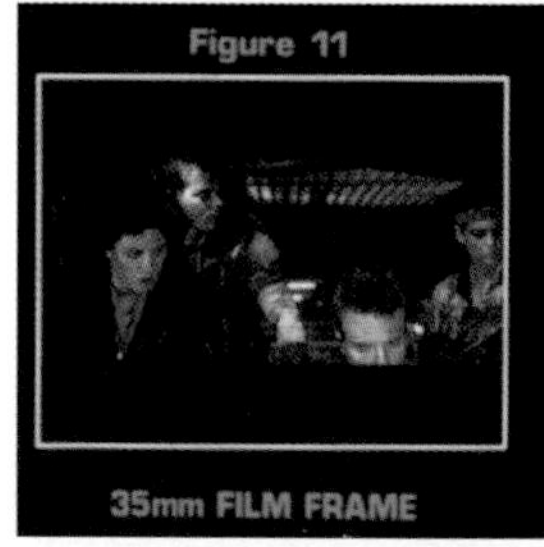

Figure 11
35mm FILM FRAME

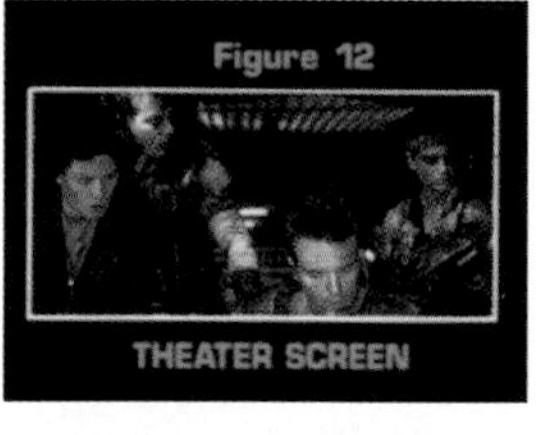

Figure 12
THEATER SCREEN

Instead of panning, scanning, or otherwise altering the original film, letterboxing shows the entire rectangular image across the center of the video screen, with black areas above and below (fig. 5). The only hitch is that the picture is now smaller than a full-screen "cropped" version, but the film image is now complete as photographed, and on laser disc the smallest details are still sharply defined.

1.85 to 1

Here's where things start to get tricky. When CinemaScope proved to be a big box office draw, budget-minded filmmakers began searching a way to make big "widescreen" movies without the expense of using costly CinemaScope cameras and lenses. Various methods were developed and tested, but the most popular way of shooting a film in widescreen without special equipment is the same system used today. The cinematographer uses predetermined framing marks located across the upper and lower sections of the camera's 1.33 viewfinder, composing his shots at an aspect ratio of 1.85 to 1 (fig. 6). While not nearly as wide as CinemaScope or Panavision, 1.85 was deemed the best compromise between shooting in "old-fashioned" 1.33 and shelling out big money for true 'Scope equipment.

Now comes the strange part. While films of this sort are composed for rectangular 1.85 projection (fig. 7) and are indeed seen this way in theaters, the upper and lower portions of the frame, basically dead space, do contain picture information that isn't seen (nor intended to be seen) theatrically (fig. 8). When shown on television though, the shape on the video screen mirrors that which exists on the original film frame, creating a perfect match, with no missing information on the sides of the image. Rather this method gives the viewer more picture at the top and bottom than was seen in theaters (fig. 9). The original composition is thrown off however (i.e. close-ups are no longer close with all the additional picture information above and below), which brings up the subject of "matting." Many films that were shot in 1.33 but composed for 1.85 projection are now frequently matted for laser disc. That is, black bands are stripped in electronically across the top and bottom of the video image so that the same rectangular picture that was seen in theater is duplicated in the home, effectively retaining the original look of the film as intended by the cinematographer and the director (fig. 10).

1.85 to 1 "Hard Matte"

If that isn't enough, a growing number of directors choose to actually matte the film in the camera as it is being shot. The black bands become forever part of the original negative and all subsequent prints (fig. 11). Known as a "hard matte," this is done for a number of reasons, most notably to ensure that the films is always framed correctly (fig. 12). However, hard-matting creates a whole new set of problems when it comes time to transfer the film to video. Since the matte is actually part of the film, the only way to have the image fill the entire video viewing area is to enlarge it until the black bands disappear off the top and bottom of the screen, resulting in soft, grainy pictures with a good amount of information lopped off the sides, creating the unpleasant side effect of now having to pan and scan the image (fig. 13). Fortunately, most hard matte films are now presented on laser with their matte bands in tact (fig. 14).

Source: Image Updates, Issue 13, April 1992, Dennis Rood-Editor.

Discs Not Included in this Guide

Illegally manufactured music has been a serious problem since the beginning of sound recordings. Discs of the type listed in this section, whose origin is not legitimate do not appear or will not appear in the *CCDPG*.

Federal Laws

Provided by the RIAA, the following is a series of laws governing the illegal manufacture and distribution of pirated material.[37]

U.S. Copyright Law {Title 17 U.S.C. Section 101 etseq., Title 18 U.S.C., Section 2319 and Section 2319A}: The federal law protects sound recordings first "fixed" as of February 15, 1972. The law protects copyright owners from the unauthorized reproduction or distribution of sound recordings to the public. Section 2319 applies only to those recordings that are "fixed" with authorization on or after February 15, 1972 (that is, when the performance is put into a tangible form such as a CD).

Those recordings "fixed" prior to February 15, 1972, are protected by criminal law through a state's unauthorized duplication statute. On the civil side, recordings are protected by a state's unfair competition laws. February 15, 1972, is a key date because of changes in copyright laws. Prior to this date there was no federal protection for sound recordings.

Trademark Counterfeiting {Title 18 U.S.C. Section 2320}: This statute deals with sound recordings that also contain the counterfeit trademark of the legitimate manufacturer or artists. The statute covers the "trafficking" as well as attempting to traffick goods containing the counterfeit marks. The penalties imposed by this statute for legal entities, such as corporations, range from $1 million to $5 million. Penalties for individuals range from five years in prison and/or $250,000 in fines to 15 years in prison and/or $1 million in fines.

Anti-Bootleg Statute {Section 2319A}: This federal anti-bootleg statute was created in December 1994. Like the pre-existing state statutes, the new federal statute criminalizes the unauthorized manufacture, distribution, or trafficking in sound recordings and music videos of "live" musical performances. However, the federal statute also provides for the seizure of bootleg recordings or music videos manufactured outside the United States by U.S. Customs at the point of importation. In effect, bootleg recordings are now subject to seizure and forfeiture in the same manner as other property in violation of customs laws.

State Laws

Nearly all states have piracy related laws that make it a criminal offense to pirate, counterfeit, or bootleg audio recordings. The three most commonly used state laws are:

True Name and Address Statute: This statute mandates the actual name and address of the manufacturer of a sound recording be displayed on the packaging. Because pirates, counterfeiters, and bootleggers generally do not display their true name and address on illegal products, they are usually in violation of this statute. All sound recordings, regardless of the date of fixation, are covered under this statute.

Unauthorized Duplication Statute: Pirate and counterfeit sound recordings "fixed" prior to February 15, 1972, are covered by this statute.

Anti-Bootleg Statute: Arenas, promoters, and performers are protected against piracy under this statute, making it a crime to manufacture the sounds of a live performance of an artist and to distribute these reproductions.

Many of these state statutes carry a maximum penalty of up to five years in prison and a $250,000 fine; other state statutes carry misdemeanor penalties.

CD Piracy

The general term "piracy" refers to the illegal duplication and distribution of sound and takes three specific forms: counterfeit, pirate, and bootleg. According to the Recording Industry Association of America, sound recording bootlegging, piracy, and counterfeiting have accounted for almost $300 million in lost record sales annually in the United States.

Bootlegs

Bootlegs are the unauthorized recording of a musical broadcast on radio or television or of a live concert. Bootleg's legality in many countries is unclear due to ambiguous copyright laws, but they are definitely illegal in the United States. Also known as underground recordings, bootlegs usually display the following characteristics:

- ▲ Produced by taping live concerts using a portable cassette recorder, or taping directly by tapping into the venue's sound system or illegally procuring studio outtakes
- ▲ Found primarily on CD, bootlegs are also on vinyl and cassette format
- ▲ Street value ranges from $15 to $100
- ▲ CD packaging usually incorporates a multi-page booklet, and the packaging is becoming increasingly more elaborate with special four-color printed boxes and folders
- ▲ The name or trademark of the performer's legitimate record company is not included, but names of fictitious manufacturers often are.

Counterfeits

Counterfeit recordings are the unauthorized recording of the prerecorded sounds, as well as the unauthorized duplication of original artwork, label, trademark, and packaging of prerecorded music. Counterfeit recordings usually display the following characteristics:[38]

- ▲ Produced by obtaining a legitimate recording and duplicating subsequent counterfeit copies and reproducing artwork and packaging
- ▲ Scale of the reproduction facilities ranges from backroom operations using cheap dual cassette players and rented photocopiers to illegal factories equipped with professional commercial sound reproduction, CD manufacturing and printing equipment
- ▲ Jackets, labels, and insert cards tend to have blurred printing, poorly reproduced colors or photographs
- ▲ Insert cards are sometimes made of paper rather than heavy card stock and usually do not carry liner notes or lyrics, sealed folds from shrink wrapping are often looser or sloppier than the original product

Counterfeit Imports

An increasing problem in this country is counterfeit import CDs. These are CD copies of original albums made in other countries and imported into the United States. What distinguishes these CDs from typical counterfeits however, is that due to different copyright laws these CDs are be manufactured legally abroad but considered illegal in the United States. In Japan for instance, their current copyright laws allow recordings made before 1971 to be copied without acquiring a license or paying royalties. Therefore, many artists like the Beatles, Beach Boys, and Elvis Presley have albums made by record companies other than their official copyright holders. If you see for example, any Beatles CDs especially from Japan, usually a limited edition not made by EMI, that disc is a counterfeit import.[39] Their legality in the States is dubious since the maker is not the original copyright holder nor a foreign subsidiary of that copyright holder. But because these discs enter the country with other legal imports, they are rarely if ever held back by customs. For the purposes of this guide, those imports are not considered collectible and will not be included.

Counterfeit CD Recordables

Another growing problem is CDRs being passed as special or promotional editions of legitimately released albums or singles. CDRs have become an easy way for counterfeiters to manufacture CDs without having to deal with disc makers who often need to see proof of licensing. CDRs are used to counterfeit albums that are otherwise out of print, and are being sold as a limited edition at a premium price. Counterfeiters even learned early to use CDRs from Europe that do not have identification numbers stamped on the hub to prevent the discs from being traced.

Moreover, CDRs are being used to create fraudulent CD singles. Often called "acetates," CDRs are being proffered as special in-house record label promotional sample discs.[40] These CDRs are being sold for up to $250 for a one track single. Because the booklet on a record company's CDR is plain, it is easily forgible by a counterfeiter. This process is analogous to copying a song onto a recordable cassette tape replacing labels with a computer-printed label, then selling that tape for a hundred bucks. Unless promo CDRs are authenticated, they will not be considered for this guide.

Unauthorized Limited Editions

Unauthorized, or third party manufactured limited editions are an enormous problem in the CD collecting community. Typically, unauthorized limited editions consist of a legal CD contained in a package designed to make the disc appear as a special import or limited edition. These packages are made from a variety of materials usually wood or cardboard and often contain trinkets such as bumper stickers, cards, photos, guitar picks, and T-shirts. Unlike bootlegs or counterfeits, the CDs contained in the unauthorized limited edition is usually authentic, typically store-bought CD. Since the packaging comes from third party sources, however, they are not legitimate releases. There is no control over the release, no accounting for the number produced, and no way to authenticate to the package.

Unauthorized limited editions are often hard to differentiate because of their elaborate packaging. Most reach retailers through import distributors and therefore, are difficult to trace. The best way to determine the authenticity of a suspicious package is to ask the retailer about its origin and if it could have been made by a third party rather than the legitimate record company. Simple inspection can also provide an indication of a package's authenticity. If the package has no record company trademark and or catalog number conspicuously visible be suspicious. Also, don't be fooled by certificate of authenticity. Most unauthorized limited editions contain them. Again, look for the record company's name, logo, and copyright information on the certificate. In addition, if you see an advertisement for special limited edition CD boxed sets where the CD is not included, that is a dead give-away that the package is unauthorized.

Pirate Recordings

Pirate recordings are the unauthorized duplication of only the sounds of one or more legitimate recordings. Pirate recordings usually display the following characteristics:[41]

- ▲ Produced by procuring legitimate recordings and duplicating them. Format of choice is audio cassette, occasionally vinyl albums and, increasingly, CDs.

- ▲ Street value is around ten dollars for a ninety-minute compilation tape. Unauthorized compilations (collection of different recordings by one or more artists compiled as a package) of different artists are common on pirate tapes.
- ▲ Cassette packaging is inferior, generally uses only one color, minimal earthwork and a typewritten or crudely printed list of tape contents. Generic earthwork may be used instead of photographs or pictures of the recording group or artist.
- ▲ Unfamiliar or fictitious company names of alleged manufacturers or distributors are often listed or no company names are listed at all.

With the development of tape recording, 8-track cartridge and cassettes, as well as high-speed, relatively low-priced duplicating equipment, the piracy problem began to grow at an alarming rate. Congress responded to the crisis by enacting the Sound Recording Amendment Act of 1971. Today, record, tape, and CD piracy activities encompass crimes punishable on both the federal and state level.

In the last few years, state statutes for piracy have been upgraded to felonies in 33 states/territories. The number of guilty pleas and convictions for sound recording piracy in the United States has increased almost 130 percent since 1991. Anti-piracy statutes generally carry penalties as high as five-year jail terms and $25,000 in fines.

Interview Discs

Throughout this book you will find many promotional interview discs (DJ/ Intvw) released by the artist's record company. There are certain interview disc's however, that are not included in this guide. These interviews, usually coming from Europe, are made by companies that are not that of the interviewed artist. In Europe, interviews are treated differently than other sound recordings. Anyone can put a recorded interview on a CD and sell it under their own label.

Compact Facts

Beethoven's Influence on CD

After Philips' proposal for a eleven and one-half centimeter disc, it was increased to twelve centimeters at the request of Heitaro Nakajimi, then Sony's head of research division. This was so that Beethoven's Ninth Symphony could fit on a single disc holding seventy-four minutes of audio.[42]

1982 CD and Beyond: The History and Future of the Compact Disc

Compact discs did not appear as the foremost standard music and data carrier overnight. Rather, the CD as we know it today was a coordinated effort between technology and marketing. Manufacturers and music labels, all working together, not knowing what would become of the CD, have created what has become the most significant music format in history.[43]

CD Technology

The compact disc was born from a marriage between two different technologies by two different companies. A combination of Sony's digital audio technology and Philips' laser-readable media technology eventually produced the digital audio compact disc. This new technology was created by efforts spanning 60 years.

The origins of digital audio started way back in the 1930s when Bell Laboratory began experimenting with rudimentary digital recording. In May 1967 the NHK Technical Research Institute in Japan successfully created and demonstrated the first digital tape recorder. This early digital-to-analog converter sampled the information using a 12-bit companded system at a frequency of 30kHz.[44] In the mid seventies, digital audio was applied to vinyl LP recordings. Companies like Columbia and Mobile Fidelity Sound Labs began pressing digitally recorded "audiophile" LPs . But these were deficient because the digital part of the process was in the master recording only. The vinyl LP still produced the same old analog sound.

During the late 70s vinyl showed signs of age and obsolescence; focus therefore shifted from a digital recorder to a digital carrier and a digital player. In September 1978, thirty-five Japanese companies organized to create the Digital Audio Disc Convention whose purpose was to recommend, from various proposals within the industry, the best digital audio system.[45]

Philips Consumer Electronics is credited as the first to come up with the idea of the compact disc. Their idea of the compact disc however, was in the form of a laser-read video disc. It was not until Philips teamed up with Sony that the compact disc as we know it began to take shape. Lucky for the CD, much of the "brass" at both Philips and Sony realized the potential of the CD. Individuals like Jan Timmer from Philips and Norio Ohga from Sony were responsible for pushing the technology and bringing these companies together. Granted, skepticism abounded whether this relationship would work because both companies had their own idea of what the CD should be. Both Sony and Philips, however, realized that working together and seeing both efforts potentially succeed was a lesser risk than not working together and seeing both efforts surely fail.

No one could have predicted how symbiotic the relationship between Sony and Philips ended up being. In the United States, Sony was best known for their television electronics, but in Japan, Sony was a leader in digital technology research. Sony contributed their digital audio encoding system as well as the important error correction system. Philips, on the other hand developed the laser-optical pick-ups and the laser-readable data disc. Philips also owned a major record label, Polygram Records. A strong source for catalog proved essential when introducing the new compact disc music carrier. Sony, at that time had no catalog of music to contribute to the effort.[46]

The overall task of the companies was to establish a set of universal standards for the compact disc. It was understood early on in the project that without a universal standard, as existed for the vinyl LP, the CD would have a short future. Exacerbating this task was that both Sony and Philips had decidedly different perceptions of what a CD should be. Philips wanted a disc size of just over 4½" to hold an even 60 minutes of audio. Sony wanted a disc size of 12" reminiscent of the traditional LP. Sony's 12" disc, however, developed in 1977, held 13 hours of audio, decidedly too unwieldy for the market place. Further differences were apparent when it came to sampling rates, Philips lobbied for a 14-bit rate, where Sony wanted a higher quality 16-bit rate.[47]

Once Sony and Philips finally agreed on standards for the digi-

	A Philips/MCA	B Thomson	C JVC	D RCA	E Matsushita	F TED
Signal detection system	Laser system		Capacitance system		Mechanical	
Pick-up	No physical contact		Physical contact			
Signal Recording Surface	one side (buried)	Both sides (surface)				
Cutting	Laser (photo-resistance			Mechanical (Cu)		
Grooves	None (dynamic tracking)			Grooved		
Disc material	Transparent		Added carbon		Optional	
Disc coating	yes (A1)	no	no	no (but surface has foil coating)		
Advantages	Long disc and stylus life			cost		
	High resistant to dirt and scratches Accessibility	Long playing time	Accessibility		Disc material	
			Duct exclusion	Low dropout (mechanical cut)		?
Disadvantages	cost		stylus and disc life			
		low speed revolution difficult	stylus surface?		Stylus construction	
	one side only	subject to scratching				

Courtesy of Sony Electronics

Various Video Disc Systems Proposals

	1	2	3	4	5	6	7	8	9	10	11	12
Manufacturer	Mitsubishi, Teac, etc.	Sony	Hitachi, Nippon, Columbia	Philips	Matsushita	JVC	Pioneer	Hitachi, Nippon, Columbia	Sony	Mitsubishi	Sanyo	Toshiba
Signal detection system	Optical				Mechanical	Capacitance	Optical					Capacitance
Disc diameter (mm)	-300			115	-300							
No. of modulation (rpm)	1800	900	1800	CLV1.5 m/s	450	900	1800	600	450	450	1800	450
Playing time (hours)	0.5	1.0	0.5	10	0.5 x 2	1.0 x 2	0.5	1.5	2.5	2.0	0.5	1.0 x 2
Modulation	Video	MFM	Video	MFM	Video	NRZ-FM	Video	MFM	3PM	MFM	Video	Video
Quantization (bit)	12N	13N	14	14	13N	14	14	16	16	?	13N	14
Channel no.	2											
Sampling frequency (kHz)	46.08	44.056	47.25	44.33	44.056			47.25	44.056			

'77 Aug. – Sept. (1–3) · '78 Mar. (4) · '78 Sept. (5–12)

Courtesy of Sony Electronics

Various Digital Audio Disc Proposals

General Information on Compact Disc Digital Audio
(Sony Corporation/N.V. Philips)

1 Disk

Playing time, single side, 2 channels	Maximum 74 min
Scanning velocity (2 channels)	1.2–1.4 m/s
Sense of rotation seen from reading side	Counterclockwise
Track Pitch	1.6μm
Disc diameter	120mm
Disc thickness	1.2mm[1]
Diameter of center hole	15mm
Starting diameter of program area	50mm

2 Signal Format

Number of channels	2 and/or 4
Quantization, per channel	16 bits linear
Encoding	2's complement
Sampling frequency	44.1 kHz
Error-correction code	CIRC[2]
Channel modulation code	EFM[3]
Channel bit rate	4.3218 Mb/s

[1]Double-sided disc optional
[2]*C*ross *I*nterleave *R*eed *S*olomon *C*ode
[3]*E*ight-to-*F*ourteen Modulation

3 Frame Format

	Data Bits	Channel Bits
Synchronization		24
Control and display	8	14
24 data symbols	192	336
8 error-correction symbols	64	112

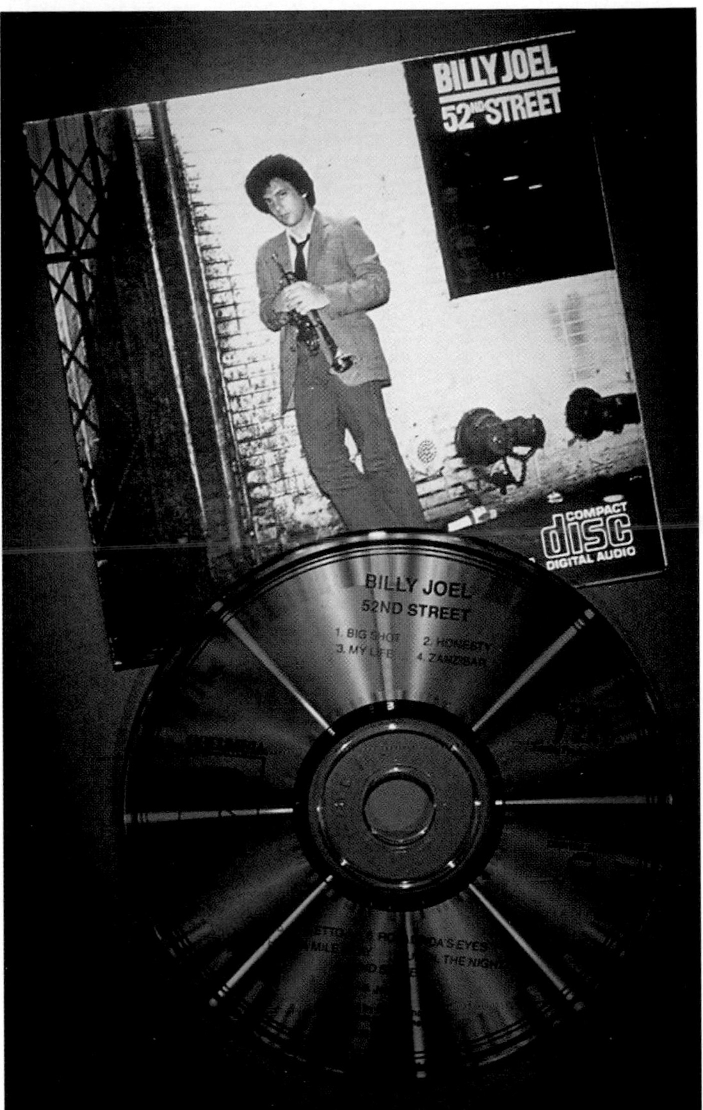

tal audio compact disc and finally proposed them to the industry in 1980. These specs require that all CDs be compatible with all players. The quantization was set at 16-bits per channel, and the sampling frequency was set at 44.1 kilohertz. Optical wavelengths, error correction, and dimensions were also standardized.

On October 1, 1982, the first CD was finally introduced to the consumer market in Japan. Billy Joel's *52nd Street* got the honors. CDs, however, were not introduced to the United States until March 1983. About 35,000 CD players were sold that year. Other milestones in CD technology include the introduction of the first car CD player and the Discman CD player in 1984. In fact, the Discman was the first CD player to sell for less than $300. The first CD changer for car players and first CD player with an outboard digital-to-analog converter were released in 1986. The first carousel tray CD player was released in 1987 and the first 100-CD changer was released in 1993. By 1989 25 million CD players were sold in United States. By 1994, 100 million CD players had been sold in the United States.

CD Pressing Plants

In 1984 the first CD pressing plant, Digital Audio Disc Corporation (DADC) opened in the United States in Terre Haute, Indiana. Founded from a joint venture between Sony and CBS Records, DADC is ironically a converted record manufacturing plant. The DADC plant was in fact, Columbia Records' first vinyl record plant in the United States. The first two CDs to come off the line at DADC were a special promotional CD called the Edison CD Sampler and an appropriately titled disc *Born in the U.S.A.* by Bruce Springsteen. Other plants like Laservideo[48] in Anaheim, California and 3M in Minnesota came on line soon after. Today there are over 100 CD pressing plants around the world.

Springsteen, Bruce – Born In the U.S.A. (Columbia CK 38653) Because of the title, Springsteen's *Born In the U.S.A.* was appropriately the first disc to come off the manufacturing line (along with the Edison CD Sampler) at the first U.S. pressing plant Digital Audio Disc Corporation, just prior to its grand opening in 1984. This disc is unique from every other pressing because of the distinctive red printing on the disc. Termed the red disc, this disc was the only version given this treatment because at the time, the red ink used was very difficult to work with, and in fact, the discs were being worked on up until the night before the plant's inauguration.

Optical Disc Formats & Trademarks

MiniDisc (MD) – 2.5 inch encapsulated recordable disc format.

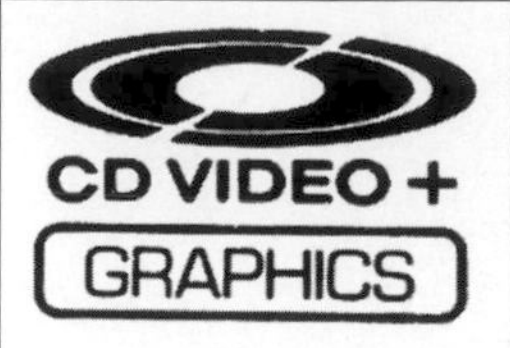

CD Video + Graphics (CDV+G) – Combination of CDV video and red book CD+Graphics.

Compact Disc (CD-ROM) – On all ISO 9660 and other CD-ROM formats.

Compact Disc Digital Audio (CD) – On all digital audio discs.

Laser disc Single (LD Single) – Eight inch laser disc format holding 20 minutes of video.

CD Video LD – Early trademark for digital sound laser discs with multi audio also known as CD video discs. This was designed to indicate discs that contained table of contents, such as track numbers and index numbers. (Most discs today no longer use this trademark.)

CD Video (CDV) – Used on all five inch CDV's. This is also used on early eight and twelve inch video discs, primarily in Europe.

Digital Video Disc (DVD) – Newly released MPEG-2 high definition digital video.

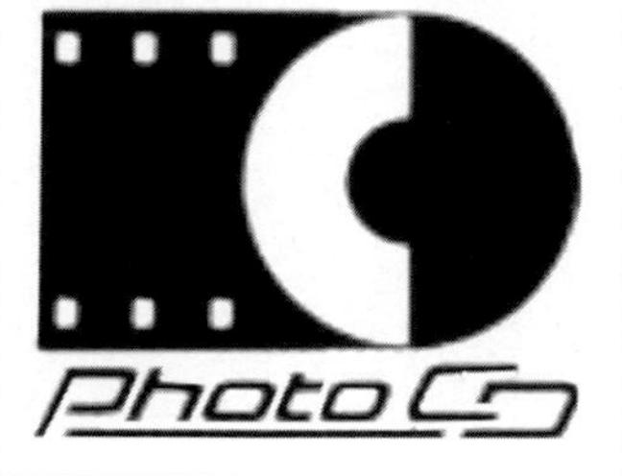

Photo CD – Kodak's Photo CD format.

LaserVision (LV) – Original laser video disc trademark. This mark is found on all laser discs from Discovision and Pioneer discs from 1978 to the mark's phase out in 1988. Laser disc and CD video laser disc for digital audio LDs were the replacement

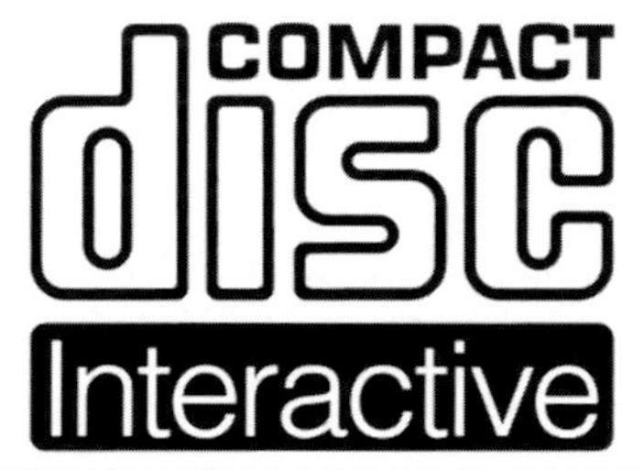

Compact Disc Interactive (CD+I) – Compact disc Interactive full functional specification complying with Green Book specification.

Laser disc (LD) – Pioneer's current trademark for the eight inch and twelve inch video laser disc format.

Compact Disc Digital Video (FMV or Video CD) – All digital video discs. The Video CD is MPEG-1 full screen digital audio and video.

Three Inch CD-Single (CD3, CD single) – This CD Single logo was used predominantly on Japanese CD3s.

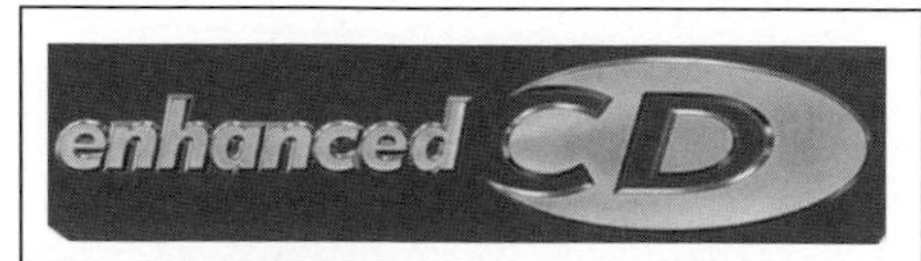

Enhanced CD (ECD or CD+) – Combination CD and computer information.

Compact Disc Digital Audio Graphics (CD+G) – Used on all Red Book digital audio discs that also use the optional TV-Graphics mode as specified for Subcode Channels R-W of the Red Book (Courtesy DMI).

Edison CD Sampler

The Edison CD sampler is a 19 track promotional compilation mastered from original cylinders, diamond discs, and electrical recordings spanning 1877 to 1929. The tracks are a culmination of music from the original Edison record label like John Phillip Sousa's Band playing The Yankee Shuffle recorded in 1906 to Thomas Edison himself playing a piano solo recorded in 1919. There are also many famous speeches like P.T. Barnum's Farewell to the People of Great Britain from 1890, and Theodore Roosevelt's Social and Industrial Justice speech from 1919. To top it off, the sampler also contains the very first words ever recorded into a phonograph — Thomas Edison reciting Mary Had a Little Lamb from 1877, making the disc the most historically significant CD yet created.

The origins of this disc go back to the early 1980s when the Edison Historical site, in West Orange, New Jersey, approached Sony requesting assistance in renovating part of their site. The Edison site wanted to include modern audio technology whose roots were in Edison's inventions. Because Sony was a leader in audio technology, Sony agreed to sponsor an exhibit featuring their first CD player.

From these efforts the idea for the Edison CD Sampler was born. Akira Suzuki and Harry Machida coordinated the efforts on the Sony side deciding this sampler would become an inaugural souvenir for the opening of Digital Audio Disc Corporation's CD plant, soon to come on-line. Edward Jay Pershy, supervisory museum curator of the Edison site at that time, was responsible for providing narration and creating the master. Sony would provide the mechanism for manufacturing the disc.

The disc was manufactured at the Digital Audio Disc Corporation plant in Terre Haute, Indiana, and distributed at the plant's grand opening that September. The disc was given to attendees along with the "red-disc" copy of Bruce Springsteen's *Born in the U.S.A.* Another fascinating aspect of the disc is its front cover. The cover depicts the famous photograph by Matthew Brady of Thomas Edison posed in front of his first cylinder phonograph in 1878. Sony came up with the idea of re-touching the photograph to show Edison holding a compact disc in front of his cylinder player.

A rare 18 track version of the Edison CD Sampler was pressed three years later in Austria for the opening of Digital Audio Disc Corporation's plant in that country on July 29, 1987.

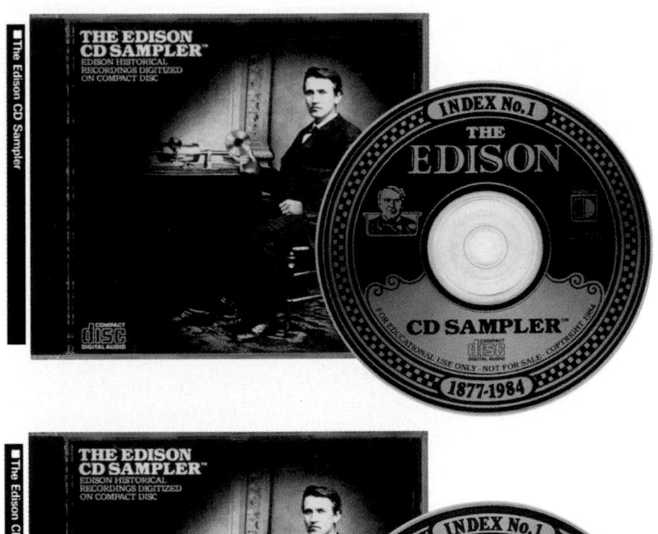

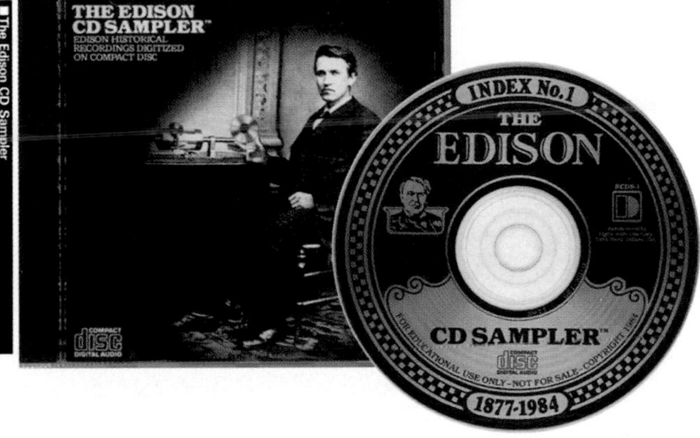

Edison CD Sampler (Sony DADA 1) Both discs look substantially similar, the disc on the bottom is the first, 1984 U.S. pressing comprising 19 tracks. The disc on the top is the second, 1987 Austrian pressing containing 18 tracks. The label on the disc simulates the actual labels from the old Edison Record Company. Notice that on the cover Thomas Edison sitting in front of his first cylinder phonograph is actually holding a CD.

First CD car stereo with the first Discman and first CD player.

First CD boom box.

First CD player.

First CD carousel tray.

First CD changer.

Society of Professional Audio Recording Services (SPARS) Codes

AAD, ADD, and DDD have become familiar sights to all of us over the past 13 years. These letters, usually found on the back tray card of the jewel box, are called SPARS codes. These codes were named after the Society of Professional Audio Recording Services. SPARS is a professional industry association of recording engineers who established the aforementioned codes shortly after the introduction of the compact disc. The codes were subsequently adopted and voluntarily affixed to compact disc packaging by the music industry.

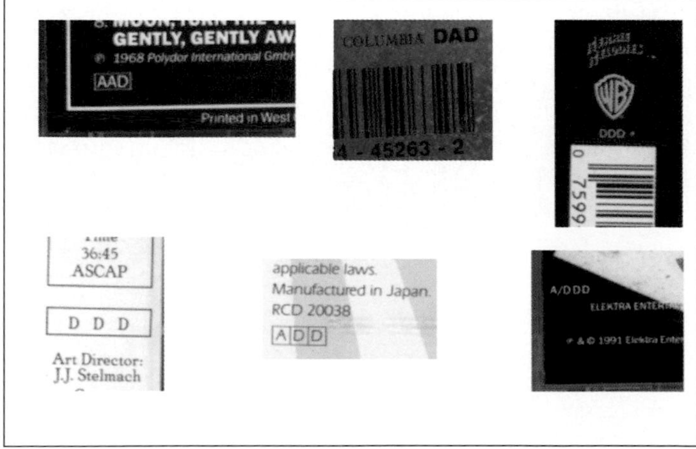

These are the first series of SPARS codes used from 1983 to 1992, along with a standard explanation found in most early CD booklets.

The original purpose of these codes were to distinguish between analog and digital processes used to create the CD as well as to educate the public about the new technology. Each character in the SPARS code three character designation was either an "A" for analog or "D" for digital. The first character in the code represents the "recording" portion of the process. If it were analog, the first character will be A, if digital, obviously it will be D. When the disc is a remaster issue of music recorded prior to the advent of digital audio, this designation will always be A. In 1982, after the proliferation of professional digital recording equipment in studios, this first designation was often D. The second character represented the mixing portion of the process. The third and final character represented the mastering portion of the process. Because the compact disc is a digital data carrier, the last character was always D.[49]

In the late 80s there was some concern from audiophiles that the codes were not entirely accurate. Say you have a song that incorporates many instruments and other effects and the CD's first SPARS code designation was D; audiophiles questioned whether every single Instrument or effect was truly recorded digitally. If the effect was recorded elsewhere and added to the song in the mixing stage, who knows where it came from or how it was recorded. For example, if a speech made by President Kennedy in 1962 was incorporated as background to a song recorded in 1992, the first designation in the SPARS code was D, raising many concerns. The speech track obviously could only have been recorded in analog, so even if the rest of the song was recorded in digital, the entire track your listening to was not recorded in digital. Moreover, if a speech made by President Bush in 1992 were incorporated as background to a song also recorded in 1992, it would still be unclear what source that speech came from, and would raise as many concerns as the Kennedy recording. There were additional

concerns that the codes would be used merely as a marketing tool rather than an informational tool. It was therefore expressed by the audiophile community that SPARS codes were not accurate enough to inform the consumer of the true source of the recordings.

The Compact Disc Digital Audio System offers the best possible sound reproduction—on a small, convenient sound-carrier unit.
The Compact Disc's superior performance is the result of laser-optical scanning combined with digital playback, and is independent of the technology used in making the original recording.
This recording technology is identified on the back cover by a three-letter code:

DDD	Digital tape recorder used during session recording, mixing and/or editing, and mastering (transcription).
ADD	Analog tape recorder used during session recording; digital tape recorder used during subsequent mixing and/or editing and during mastering (transcription).
AAD	Analog tape recorder used during session recording and subsequent mixing and/or editing; digital tape recorder used during mastering (transcription).

In storing and handling the Compact Disc, you should apply the same care as with conventional records.
No further cleaning will be necessary if the Compact Disc is always held by the edges and is replaced in its case directly after playing. Should the Compact Disc become soiled by fingerprints, dust or dirt, it can be wiped (always in a straight line, from centre to edge) with a clean and lint-free, soft, dry cloth. No solvent or abrasive cleaner should ever be used on the disc.
If you follow these suggestions, the Compact Disc will provide a lifetime of pure listening enjoyment.

SPARS notice. To help explain the SPARS codes, many CD booklets contained this notice.

Because of these concerns, SPARS codes were officially retired in 1992. It was decided that the technology was too complex to be accurately represented by a three character code. And because a longer code was too cumbersome and confusing, the SPARS committee voted to retire the codes during their convention in 1991. Since these codes however, were affixed to CD packages voluntarily, discontinuing their use would also have to be made voluntarily. In fact, SPARS codes were found on CD packages through 1993.

The story does not end there, however. Because consumer response was more in favor of the codes than against, SPARS reinstated the codes in April 1995. SPARS reconsidering, determined that the codes served a worthwhile function and generally did reflect the audio recording process. Again, use of these codes are voluntary, so designation will be determined by the powers-that-be behind the production of the CD.

Mirror Bands

All discs have mirror bands of some sort. Mirror bands are the thin reflective bands that round the inside edge of the metalized surface on the disc. These bands are sometimes referred to as inner rings, matrix number bands, etc., but still represent the same thing. There is no industry standard for how the bands should appear so they come in a myriad of sizes.

Mirror bands serve an important function for the manufacturer and record label and usually contain three pieces of information — the manufacturer's work order number in character or bar code form, the customer's catalog or purchase order number, and the pressing plant's name. The manufacturer's work order number or bar code is a quality control device used on the manufacturing line that keeps track of which disc is on which line. The customer number allows the record company to keep track of their discs.

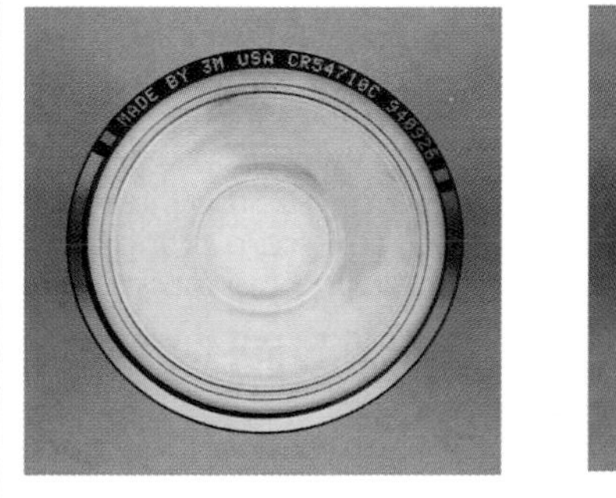

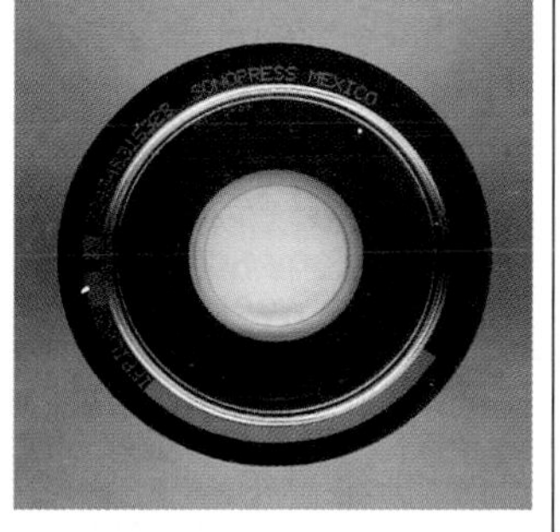

Two types of Mirror Bands.

CD Marketing

No matter how bright an idea we now know CD technology actually is, back in the early 80s the industry knew it was not going to sell itself. Marketing this new music carrier would prove to be quite a task. In fact, marketing the CD ended up revolutionizing music marketing as much as the music itself.

When Sony and Philips joined forces, not only did they contribute different technologies to create the CD, they also contributed their different marketing strengths. As befitting the perspectives of the two different companies, Sony and Philips took two different approaches to bring the CD to market. Sony focused on marketing the compact disc to the consumer market place. In contrast, Philips focused on licensing the CD to the record companies and the manufacturers to produce CDs and CD players.

Digital Discovery (Warner Brothers PRO-CD-2294) An early 1985 sampler promoting compact disc technology.

Sony's objective, independent of Philips's, early on in their campaign was to market the CD as a lifestyle concept. This concept was expressed through the CD's convenience, accessibility, and a greater dynamic range that created better sound quality. One of Sony's first demonstrations of the CD was the first broadcast of CD music at WFMT radio in Chicago, Illinois, in June 1982. In 1982, Sony launched an innovative marketing campaign where 100 radio stations in the top 50 markets in AOR and classical, were given a free CD player and an entire catalog of CD titles in exchange for airplay and acknowledgment that the song was playing from a digital audio compact disc. The difference in sound quality was instantly noticeable. No more scratches or hisses from old vinyl. In fact, so much excitement surrounded the campaign, radio stations began getting requests for songs to be played exclusively from CD.

Another launching pad for the CD, keeping in mind the "lifestyle" concept, was MTV/Sony "Spring Break" promotion in 1984. The program, created by Sony and WEA focused on promoting Sony's new Discman, portable CD player, with college students as the targeted consumer. The program involved a "treasure hunt" where Sony buried CDs in the sand for attendees to find. Participants also won CD players and Discmans while VJ's played music direct from CD. Ironically, although MTV was reluctant first to partic-

special limited-edition CD if you either reserve a copy of a new CD release or purchase the release at that store. In fact, for the collector, these value-added CDs are becoming quite collectible. Chains like Best Buy, Musicland, and Blockbuster Music have all offered special value-added discs to customers.

Blockbuster Music Promotions Display material and premiums offered by Blockbuster Music when you either pre-order or purchase the advertised title at one of their locations. Because these items are very limited in availability, they end up becoming quite rare quite quickly. Make sure you pay attention to the offers your local stores make. A great number of collectible CDs start off by being given away free.

CD Pricing and Anti-Trust Violations

Speaking of prices, have you ever noticed at the record store that all hit titles, regardless of record company, are priced exactly the same? Most catalog titles and mid-line price titles are also priced exactly the same across their respective tiers. Well, some have noticed, and they've filed a class action suit against all the major record companies alleging price fixing. This is the first-ever suit against the record companies by the consumers. Chris Robinson and George Silvey v. EMI Music Distribution was initially filed in Blount County Circuit Court in Maryville, Tennessee, on July 8, 1996. The court granted the suit immediate class-action status, so consumers from other states can join the action.[53] Currently, 14 states have joined the suit. The defendants in this case are EMI Music Distribution Inc., Sony Music Entertainment Inc., WEA Corp., Uni Distribution Corp., Bertelsmann Music Group Inc. (BMG), and Polygram Group Distribution Inc. (PGD). The plaintiffs seek damages up to $5,000 for anybody who purchased CDs from the labels named in the suit beginning June 26, 1992.

According to the complaint, the defendants allegedly engaged in a price-fixing conspiracy. The "(d)efendants have employed a variety of collusive schemes to maintain and increase profit margins on their sale of CDs, much higher than that for vinyl records or cassette tapes, even though the cost of producing a CD has dropped steadily since this new format was introduced in 1983."[54] The record companies allegedly violated "state anti-trust and consumer protection laws by agreeing on the prices they charge retailers for various tiers or categories of their CDs, from front-line releases to budget CDs. (All the record companies) either charge retailers exactly the same price for CDs in these tiers, or are within a few cents of each others' prices. These giant companies are each vertically integrated, so that their complete control over the manufacture and distribution of CDs gives them the power to make these price increases stick." The complaint also alleges that because most consumers are almost finished replacing their vinyl collection with CDs, which created enormous profit, the record companies and distributors have conspired to increase prices to compensate for a drop off in CD sales.

It is a fascinating argument the plaintiffs make regarding CD pricing trends and margins. The plaintiffs argue that as the cost of making a CD decreased, the prices increased. In 1983, the cost to manufacture a CD was $3, now it is between 70¢ to 90¢. In fact, the total cost of bringing a cassette to market is about a dollar less than a CD, but labels charge at least $3.75 or more for a CD than for a cassette. Most interesting, are the plaintiffs' claims regarding production costs and signing bonuses. They contend that with the aid of digital technology, the cost to produce an album has substantially declined. According to the complaint, the album *The Trinity Sessions* by the Cowboy Junkies, which was a million-selling album for BMG Music cost only $250 to record. As far as signing bonuses, the complaint alleges that WEA paid Hootie and the Blowfish only $125,000 as a signing bonus for *Cracked Rear View* which has sold over 13 million units. Now, whether broad characterizations about the industry can be made from these examples is doubtful, but it is still an interesting argument.

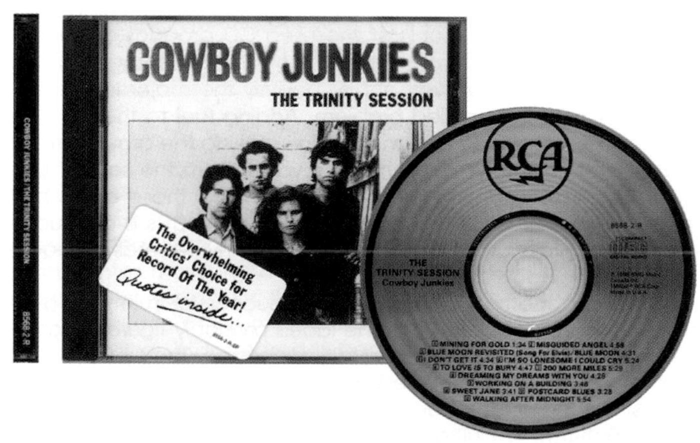

Cowboy Junkies – The Trinity Sessions (RCA 8568-R-SP) Alternate cover version.

Price signaling and minimum advertised prices however, are the crux of the plaintiffs' arguments against the record companies. Plaintiffs contend that the labels make approximately 35% or $4.00

per disc profit. Price signaling is a practice where prices are circulated far in advance of a release to allow time for the other labels to match that price. The complaint alleges that music industry trade papers like *Billboard* are perfect vehicles for this type of activity. In fact, the complaint cites an August 15, 1992, article of *Billboard* where an officer of EMI distribution stated CD prices would increase to $16.98. All other labels immediately raised their prices to identical price points. Minimum advertised prices is a practice where promotions are set so that all the discounts from all the record companies for CDs are the same. In contrast, because many warehouse clubs and electronics stores are using CDs as loss-leaders,[55] pricing is beginning to substantially broaden. In fact, a local Pittsburgh electronics store was selling the new R.E.M. album for less than $8.

The states participating in this class action suit are Alabama, California, District of Columbia, Florida, Illinois, Kansas, Louisiana, Maine, Michigan, Minnesota, Mississippi, New Mexico, North Carolina, North Dakota, Pennsylvania, South Dakota, Tennessee, Washington, West Virginia, and Wisconsin. The action is limited to these states because they are the only states that have laws allowing class action suits by indirect purchasers of goods. In this case the consumers purchase CDs directly from record stores, not distribution companies or record labels directly. In fact, the record stores probably didn't even purchase the CD from the distribution companies or record labels. They probably purchased the discs from independent distributors. It is the independent distributors that purchase directly from the labels. As a result, only those independent distributors, who purchased directly from those companies can have a cause of action. Most states do not allow consumers who purchase goods from a store who purchased them from a distributor, who purchased them from a large distribution company, to sue. As a result, if you do not live in, nor purchased any CDs from, any of the aforementioned states, you will probably not be able to recover from this suit.

This suit, however, is not the first investigation or lawsuit against the major labels. During the seventies, the Department of Justice impaneled a grand jury to investigate price fixing and conspiracy complaints.[56] In 1982, the labels were sued by United National Records which was a class action suit by 4,200 record wholesalers and retailers. This complaint too alleged price fixing and conspiracy. The case however, settled for $26 million in 1985. In 1984, PGD and WEA attempted to merge their distribution companies. This attempt was blocked by the Federal Trade Commission because it would have given the subsequent company control of 25% of the market.[57] In 1993, in England the Heritage Select Committee from Parliament held hearings questioning whether CD prices were artificially kept high. The committee determined however, that the labels committed no wrong doing. Most recently, in 1995, a California store filed a claim against the record labels for price fixing, which is still continuing.[58] The anti-trust division of the Department of Justice is currently investigating the major labels to determine whether they conspired to create a competitor to MTV[59], whether the used CD ban was conspiratorially anticompetitive, and whether anti-trust laws were violated in establishing the technical standards of the DVD.

For those of you who live in any of the aforementioned states, don't be too fast to count your money, however. Litigation like this can take many years unless the labels decide to settle, and if that happens the share per customer might substantially decrease. And remember, because the labels generally have no comment regarding this matter, I can present only one side of the story for you. This may seem to be discouraging evidence for the record companies but it's not fair to be too judgmental until we hear their answer to the complaint. We will probably have an update to this story for you in our next edition.

Resurgence of Vinyl?

Vinyl is being touted as making a comeback. Pearl Jam's *Vitalogy* vinyl version of the album sold 38,000 copies in three weeks putting it 55 on the *Billboard* charts. Proponents cite this example to illustrate the strength and interest of vinyl. What is not disclosed about this example is that this vinyl version of the album was released three weeks before the CD. It actually seems to be a quite poor performance for a band that will certainly sell millions of CDs to sell about 40,000 in three weeks. It is common practice today for record companies to release the vinyl at least a week before the CD, and as a limited edition. It is only logical that vinyl will sell, especially if it is the only format available for new albums.

Compact Facts

Vinyl v. CD

(Millions of Units)

	Vinyl LP	CD
1990	11.7	286.5
1991	4.8	333.4
1992	2.3	407.5
1993	1.2	495.4
1994	1.9	662.1
1995	2.2	727.6

Courtesy of RIAA

CD Packaging

Since 1982, the jewel box compact disc case[60] has been the standard CD packaging world wide. Over the past 15 years however, many challengers have attempted to replace the jewel box, creating much controversy in what the standard packaging should be.

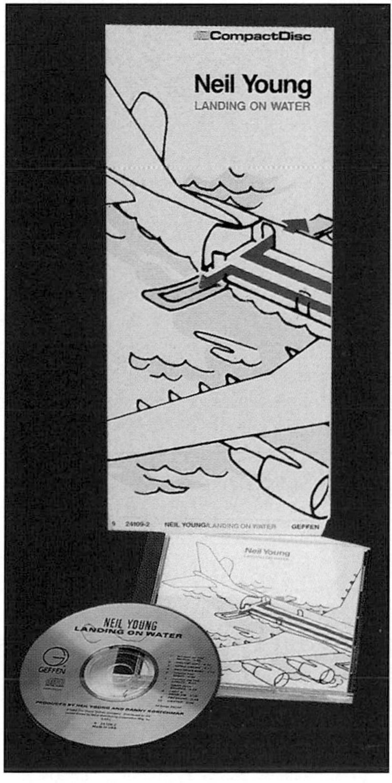

Young, Neil (and Crazy Horse) – Landing on Water (Geffen 9 24109-2) Out-of-print 1986 CD in traditional long box packaging.

The long-running packaging controversy first began in 1985. Record companies were exploring the use of packaging as a marketing tool in order to generate more interest in the CD format. Market research showed that a smaller, streamlined case might have more appeal to consumers than the bulkier jewel box, and still protect the CD just as well. The first commercial attempt was a 6" x 12" fold-open all-paperboard case used for Prince's *Around*

Prince – Around the World in a Day (Warner Brothers 9 25286-2) Original paper board packaging. This disc is only available in the traditional Long box.

the World in a Day and Motley Crue's *Theater of Pain.* Consumers however, rejected the package. The all-paperboard package was dropped four months later and the discs were rereleased in the jewel case/long box configuration.

Undeterred, other new packaging ideas were explored. AGI, a packaging and graphics company, developed the now, well-known digipak — a jewel box-sized cardboard package with a plastic tray securing the disc. In 1986 American Gramophone and A&M Records began packaging CDs in the digipak/long box configuration. Robert Palmer's *Riptide* was one of the first to adopt this packaging. The digipak however, was also initially rejected as a replacement for the jewel box and the titles were returned to the jewel box/long box configuration. It seemed for a time that the alternative CD packaging search was dead.[61]

In 1989 the packaging question returned to life. This time motivated by the alleged waste produced by the CD's long box. The "Ban the Box" organization formed by Robert Simonds of Rykodisc lobbied to eliminate the long box as a part of the CD's regular packaging. Environmental groups joined in the cause claiming that 23 million pounds of extra trash was created from discarded long boxes.[62] However, rather than exploring creative uses for the long box once the disc was removed, efforts began in 1990 to find a new packaging standard. But efforts continued unsuccessfully, the primary obstacle being the cost to refurbish retail store racks to accommodate alternative package sizes and manufacturing retooling.

Smelling the ultimate death of the long box, AGI created the first long box alternative, in early 1991. A&M recording artist Sting released his new CD *Soul Cages* in the "digitrak" CD package. The digitrak is essentially identical to the digipak, except that it is sold in the open, long box-size position stiffened by two plastic rails with a few extra cardboard panels for added graphics. This effort was a compromise between a new non-long box packaging and existing retail fixtures. The digitrak package was able to comfortably fit in the existing 6" x 12" retail bins. Bonnie Raitt, U2, and the Grateful Dead also released new CDs in this configuration. Consumers had mixed reactions, but many retailers disliked the new digitrak package. The major complaints were that the panels on the digitrak could be easily damaged, and, unlike the jewel box, the graphics were not protected by a case that could be replaced.

WEA, owned by Time Warner who also owned Ivy Hill, a major producer of cardboard long boxes, introduced the paper/plastic eco-pak. The eco-pak is similar to the digitrak in that it can be sold in the open, long box-size configuration, it can be broken down into a jewel box size and shape. In contrast however, the eco-pak was essentially a plastic case with a cardboard skin.

Early test eco-pak designs made by Ivy Hill for WEA.

First promotional eco-pak jewel box alternative.

Sony on the other hand, experimented with selling CDs in jewel boxes in the open position secured by brackets. Other alternatives also sprang up. Still none endured as the jewel box, supported heavily by Polygram and Philips, the inventor of the CD and the jewel box. In response to the increased use of the digitrak and other jewel case replacements, a coalition was formed to preserve the use of the jewel box as the CD packaging standard. The group known as J.A.M. (Jewel box Advocates and Manufacturers) was formed in April 1991. This organization ran ads in many of the music industry trade papers touting the advantages of the jewel box and answering the charges from packaging alternative manufacturers.

In March 1992, it became official, the RIAA (Recording Industry Association of America) — a governing body of the recording industry — formally announced that it would adopt the 6" x 5" jewel box size as the standard CD packaging and begin phasing out the long box. The announcement was careful, though, not to formally endorse the jewel box specifically. This opened the door for a flood of packaging alternative proposals. None of these alternatives however, were able to unseat the jewel box as the standard CD package.

The post-long box free world has not been a panacea for marketing disc titles. With a 50 percent reduction in artwork area, graphics needed to be bolder to get attention. Many record stores put the jewel boxes in keepers like cassettes so as to make the presentation of the disc seem larger and prevent theft. Also, in 1994 the first discs by Polygram were packaged with a top-spine edge labeling.

In addition, since the abolition of the long box, a new push has been made to provide an electronic theft protection system standard with the CD package, The National Association of Recording Merchandisers (NARM) has been spearheading the "source-tagging" electronic anti-theft protection system program. Due to the success of various CD package electronic security devices, it does seem that a large long box packaging, as a security device, might be obsolete.

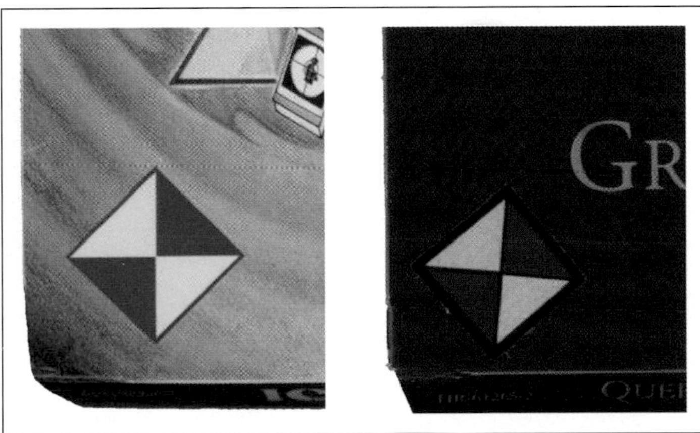

In 1991 and 1992, during the transition from CDs house in long boxes to CDs shrink wrapped in a jewel box only, record companies offered retailers a choice of how they wanted to display the discs. Though all CDs were still housed in long boxes, for those retailers who already redesigned their stores for jewel boxes only, long boxes marked with this sticker can be ripped open and the CD inside is factory shrink wrapped. Those X's with a black boarder (right) are stickers that were placed on existing long boxes. Those X's with no boarder (left) were printed directly on the box denoting the box was much newer.

Williams, Hank Jr. - Monday Night Football Boogie (Warner Brothers PRO-CD-5109) Smart-pak promotional CD packaging, developed by Warner Brothers in 1991, is a combined mailer and CD sleeve. The object was to provide an economical mailing solution for promotional CDs.

Pink Floyd - Animals (Columbia CK 34474) During the early 1990s when as the life of the long box reached its twilight, long box-size alternatives began to be experimented with as a replacement. Sony experimented with packaging the disc in the jewel box only, and then selling it in the open position, held rigid by brackets and having a title bar.

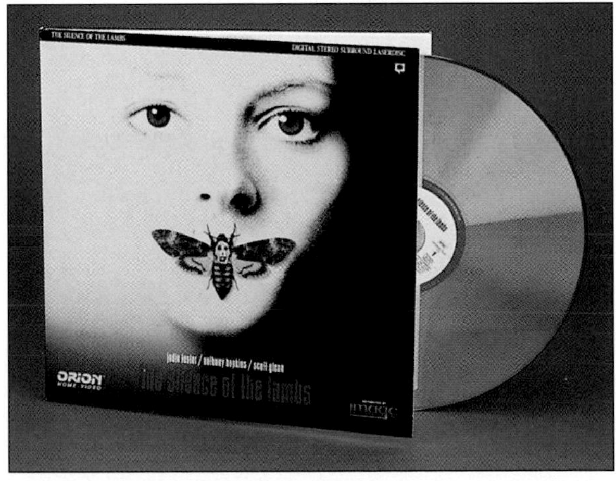

Silence of the Lambs (Orion/Image ID 7434OR) Unique laser disc digi-pak. First tested in 1991 by Image entertainment, it was used for only a few titles. Interestingly, most of discs in LD jewel boxes star Jodi Foster.

Grammy Selection

Though the titles nominated for the best CD packaging are good, they are far from the best packages produced by the record companies. Any special CD package used for promotional purposes or otherwise not generally distributed to the public are ineligible. Most of the special CD packages are specifically created for promotional discs, and therefore, the most creative CD packages end up never being considered by the nominating committee.

Another aspect of CD packaging overlooked by the awards are disc graphics. None of the past winners had very exciting graphics printed on the disc. Arguably, good print work on the disc is more special than special packaging. Usually, packaging design is made well in advance of the pressing of the disc. There is therefore, more time to design the package. On the other hand, the actual CD is often made in a rush, either because the work was just mastered, or available press time was limited. Also, labels are reluctant to produce picture disc CDs, one, because it requires more time to produce,[63] and two, marketing departments at U.S. record labels have yet to learn how to use the picture disc CD as a marketing tool, at least not as effectively as the CD-ROM industry. Picture disc CDs, are therefore a much rarer commodity than even special packaging, when it comes to mass-produced CD albums. A CD picture disc album is indicative of the more detail a record label spends on the presentation of their artist than a CD having no disc graphics. These discs certainly deserve more attention and recognition than they currently receive.

CD Packaging Grammy Award Winners

An award for the "best album package" has been included in the Grammys since 1958. This award was expanded in 1989 to recognize overall packaging designs. The following art directors and CD packages have been nominated and have won Grammys for the "Best Album Package" and "Best Recording Package — Boxed"[64] since the first CD package was nominated in 1989.

1989 — (32nd) Winner for Best Album Package

Roger Gorman for David Bowie *Sound + Vision,* four CD boxed set by Rykodisc.

Nominees for Best Album Package

Tom Recchion for Prince *Batman* (Limited Edition) by Warner Brothers.
Bill Burkes and Tommy Steele for Tina Turner *Foreign Affair* (Special Limited Edition) by Capitol.
Tommy Steele for Fetchin Bones *Monster* by Capitol.
Jimmy Wachtel for Jackson Browne *World in Motion* by Elektra.

1990 (33rd) Winner for Best Album Package

Len Peltier, Jeffrey Gold, and Suzanne Vega for Suzanne Vega *Days of Open Hand* (Limited Edition Hologram Digapak[sic]) by A&M Records.

Nominees for Best Album Package

Jeri Heiden for Fleetwood Mac *Behind the Mask* by Warner Brothers.
Vaughan Oliver for Pixies *Bossanova* by Elektra.
Carol Bobolts, Anita Baker, and Jim Ladwig for Anita Baker *Compositions* (Special Edition Blue Binder Cover) by 4AD/Elektra.
Tom Recchion and Slyvia Reed for Lou Reed and John Cale *Songs for Drella* (Special Edition Black Velvet Cover) by Sire/W.B.

1991 (34th) Winner for Best Album Package

Vartan for Billie Holiday *The Complete Decca Recordings* for GRP Records.

Nominees for Best Album Package

Geoff Gans for Frank Zappa *Beat the Roots* (Limited Edition Box Set) by FOO-EE/Rhino.
Gabrielle Raumberger for Barbra Streisand *Just for the Record* by Columbia.
Steven Baker and Dirk Walter for Elvis Costello *Mighty Like a Rose* (Special Package) by Warner Brothers.
Jeff Gold and Kim Champagne for ZZ Top *Recycler* (Special Package) by Warner Brothers.

1992 (35th) Winner for Best Album Package

Melanie Nissen for Paula Abdul *Spellbound* (Compact Case Limited Edition) by Capitol/ Virgin Records.

Nominees for Best Album Package

Geoff Gans for Aretha Franklin *Queen of Soul — The Atlantic Recordings* by Rhino.
Tommy Steele and Stephan Walker for Hammer *Too Legit to Quit* (Special Package) by Capitol.
Ria Lewerke and Norman Moore for Elvis Presley *Elvis the King of Rock-N-Roll — The Complete 50's Masters* by RCA.
Len Peltier for Suzanne Vega for *99.9°F* (Special Package) by A&M.

1993 (36th) Winner for Best Album Package

David Lau for Billie Holiday *The Complete Billie Holiday On Verve 1945 – 1959* by Verve Records.

Nominees for Best Album Package

David Coleman for Ozzy Osbourne *Live and Loud (Ozzy Osbourne)* by Epic Associated.
Storm Thorgerson and Stylourge for Pink Floyd *Shine On* by Columbia.
Tom Recchion, Michael Stipe, Jeff Gold, and Jim Ladwig for R.E.M. *Automatic for the People* (Second Set) by Reprise.
Kim Champagne and Jeff Gold for Paul Westerberg *14 Songs* by Sire/Reprise.

1994 (37th)
Winner for Best Album Package

Buddy Jackson for Asleep at the Wheel *Tribute to the Music of Bob Wills and the Texas Playboys* by Liberty Records.

Nominees for Best Album Package

Deborah Norcross for *Boingo Boingo* by Giant.
Mary Maurer for Alice in Chains *Jar of Flies* by Columbia.
Michael Coulson & Martha Ladly for Peter Gabriel *Secret World* Live by Geffen.
Mark Farrow, Pet Shop Boys, and Daniel Weil for Pet Shop Boys *Very Relentless* by EMI.

Winner for Best Album Package — Boxed

Chris Thompson for *The Complete Ella Fitzgerald Song Books* by Verve Records.

Nominees for Best Album Package — Boxed

Deborah Norcross for *Boingo Boingo* (limited edition) by Giant.
David Lau for *The Complete Bud Powell* on Verve by Verve.
Chris Bilheimer, Tom Recchion & Michael Stipe for R.E.M. *Monster* (Limited Edition) by Warner Brothers.
Geoff Gans & Coco Shinomiya for *Songs of the Old West* by Rhino.

1995 (38th)
Winner for Best Album Package — Boxed

Robbie Cavolina, Joni Mitchell for Joni Mitchell *Turbulent Indigo* by Reprise.

Nominees for Best Album Package

Gary Burden for Neil Young *Mirror Ball* by Reprise.
Stefan Sagmeister for H.P. Zinker *Mountains of Madness* by Energy.
Tim Stedman for *This Is Fort Apache* by MCA.
Joel Zimmerman for Pearl Jam *Vitalogy* by Epic.

Winner for Best Album Package — Boxed

Frank Zappa, Gail Zappa for Frank Zappa *Civilization Phaze III* by Rykodisc.

Nominees for Best Album Package — Boxed

Blind Melon, Jeffery Fey, Chris Jones, Tommy Steele for Blind Melon *Soup* (Limited Edition) by Capitol.
Mark Farrow for Pet Shop Boys *Alternative* (Limited edition) by EMI.
Storm Thorgerson for Pink Floyd *Pulse* (Limited edition) by Columbia.
Allen Weinberg for Aerosmith *Box of Fire* by Columbia.

1996 (39th)
Winner for Best Album Package

Andy Engel & Tommy Steele for Various Artists (Leopard Skin Sampler) *Ultra–Lounge* by Capitol Records.

Nominees for Best Album Package

Stefan Sagmeister for Lou Reed *Set The Twilight Reeling* by Warner Bros. Records.
Adam Jones & Kevin Willis for Tool *Aenima* by Zoo Entertainment/Volcano Entertainment.
Stefan Sagmeister for Marshall Crenshaw *Miracle of Science* by Razor & Tie Entertainment.
Chika Azuma & Patricia Lie for Stan Getz *East of the Sun: The West Coast Sessions* by Verve Records.

Winner for Best Album Package - Boxed

Chika Azuma & Arnold Levine for Miles Davis & Gil Evans *The Complete Columbia Studio Recordings* by Columbia Records.

Nominees for Best Album Package - Boxed

JoDee Stringham for Frank Sinatra *The Complete Reprise Studio Recordings* by Reprise Records.
Michael Lang, David Lau, & Giulio Turturro for Various Artists *Blues, Boogie, & Bop: The 1940s Mercury Sessions* by Polygram Records.
Giulio Turturro for Antonio Carlos Jobim *The Man From Ipanema* by Verve Records.
Chris Bilheimer & Michael Stipe for R.E.M. *New Adventures In Hi-Fi* by Warner Bros.

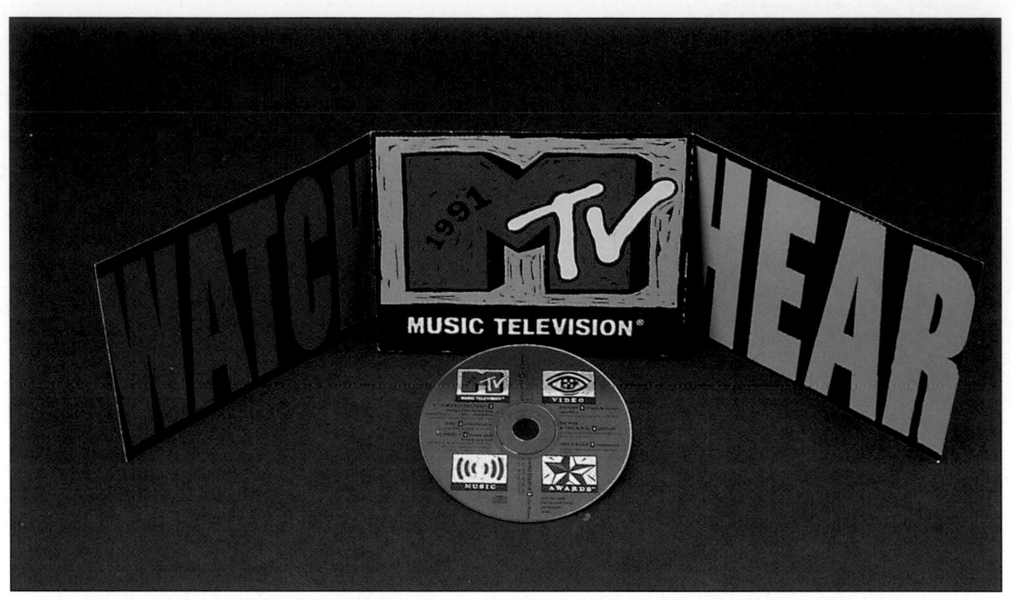

MTV Video Music Awards (MTV Networks) Promotional samplers distributed to promote the MTV music awards.

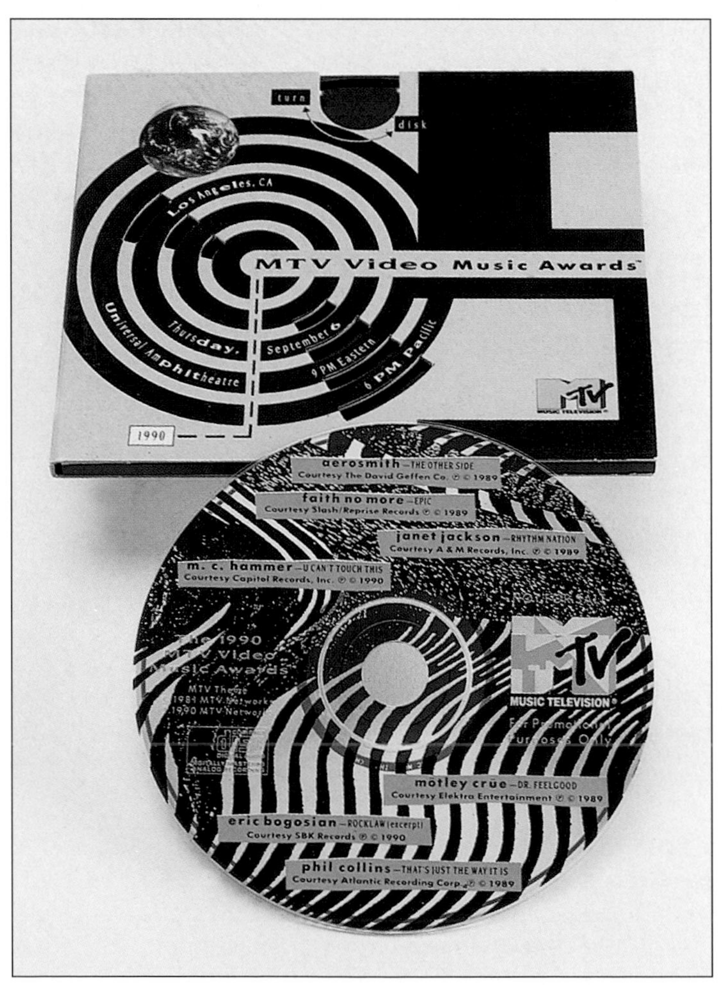

The Compact Distinction: Special Gallery of CD Packaging and Disc Artwork

CDs at the Movies

Crow, The: City Of Angels (Hollywood PRCD 62047-2 DGO1) U.S. 1996 promotional CD album.

Judas Priest – Johnny Be Goode! (Atlantic A9114CD U.K.) 1988 CD5.

Bodyguard, The (Arista 74321-16929-2) U.S. 1993 limited edition CD album.

B-52's – Meet the Flintstones (MCA MAC5P-2998) U.S. 1994 promotional CD-single.

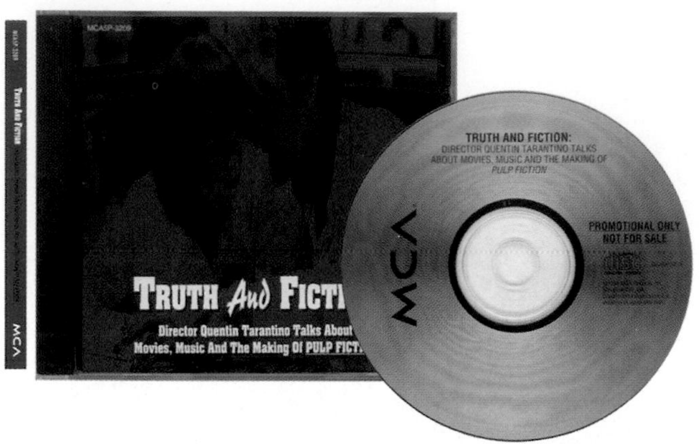

Truth and Fiction (MCA MCA5P-3209) U.S. 1995 promotional CD sampler.

Backbeat (Virgin CDVDJ) U.S. 1994 promotional CD album boxed set.

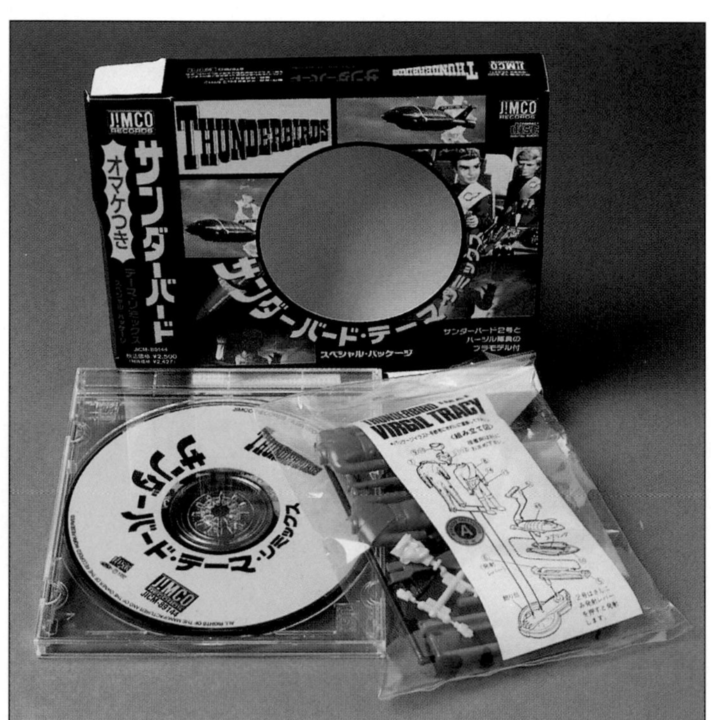

Thunderbirds (Jimco JICM-89144) Japanese 1992 limited edition CD.

Republic Pictures Home Video Catalog: Volume 2 (Republic Pictures) U.S. 1996 promotional CD-ROM sampler.

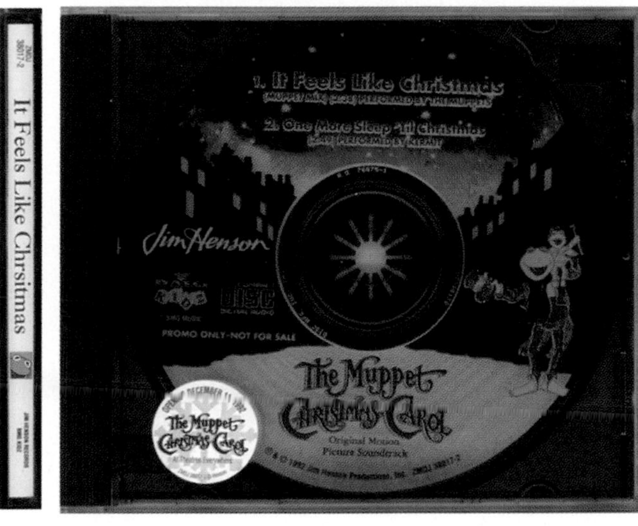

Muppets, The – It Feels Like Christmas (BMG ZMDJ 38017-2) U.S. 1992 promotional CD-single.

Bridges of Madison County (Malpaso 9 45949-2) U.S. 1995 promotional CD album.

Theme from Mission Impossible (Island PRCD 7180-2) Super-rare promotional sampler set with t-shirt and real working camera.

Mortal Kombat (TVT 6110 U.S.) 1995 promotional CD album.

Baerwald, David – Bedtime Stories (A&M 75021 5289 2)
U.S. 1990 promotional CD album.

Harding, John Wesley – Collected Stories 1990–1991 (Sire PRO-CD-4698)
U.S. 1991 promotional CD sampler.

McAnally, Mac – Live and Learn (MCA MCA35-10543)
U.S. 1992 promotional CD album.

Lilliput (4AD LILLIPUT 1/2) U.S. 1992 promotional 2 CD set.

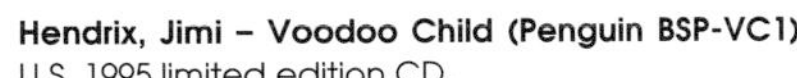

Hendrix, Jimi – Voodoo Child (Penguin BSP-VC1)
U.S. 1995 limited edition CD.

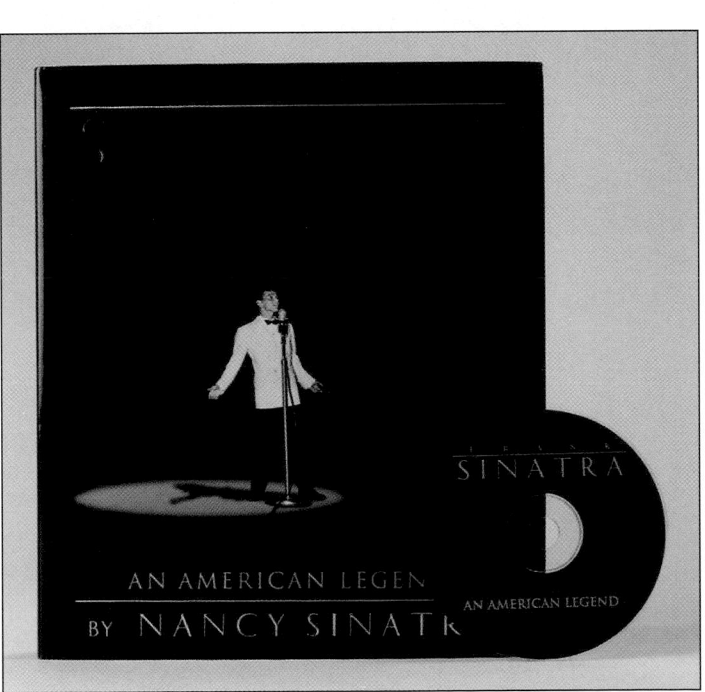

Sinatra, Frank – An American Legend (General Publishing Group)
U.S. 1995 limited edition CD.

Tasty Tower of Treats (Capitol DPRO-79461) Various artist promotional sampler created by Tommy Steele.

Fiesta Delapierre (Max NS 15CD)

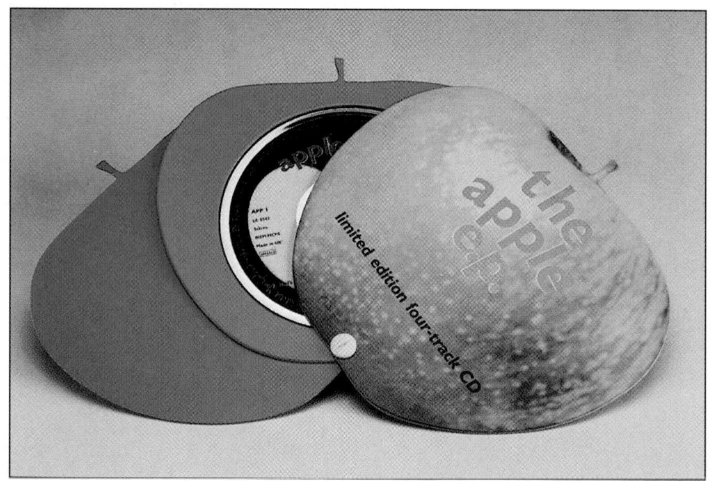

Apple E.P. (EMI CD APPS ICD APPS I)

Rhino's Famous Sweet 16 (Rhino PRCD 7072)

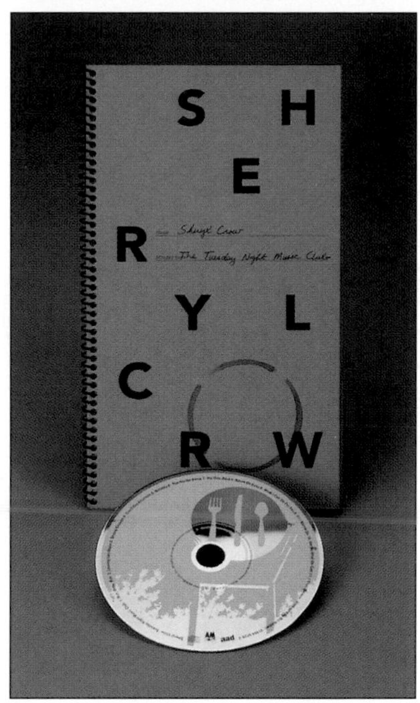

Crow, Sheryl – Tuesday Night Music Club (A&M 31454 0126 2) U.S. 1994 promotional CD album in simulated menu.

Jones, Quincy – Q's Jook Joint (Warner Brothers 9 46109-2) U.S. 1995 limited edition CD.

Filet o' Soul (Right Stuff DPRO-10907) U.S. 1996 promotional CD sampler.

Twin Peaks (Warner Brothers 9 26316-2-DJ) U.S. 1990 promotional CD album.

Dire Straits – Heavy Fuel (Vertigo DSHAM 17)

Pizza World (Mix Max NS 13CD)

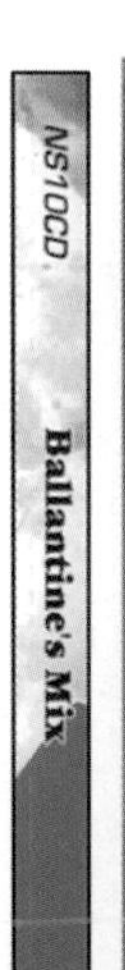

Ballantine's Mix (Max NS10CD)

CD Down on the Farm

Shocked, Michelle – On the Greener Side (Polygram CDP 142) U.S. 1989 promotional CD-single.

Travis, Randy – He Opened the Door (Greatest Hits) (Warner Brothers PRO-CD-5675)

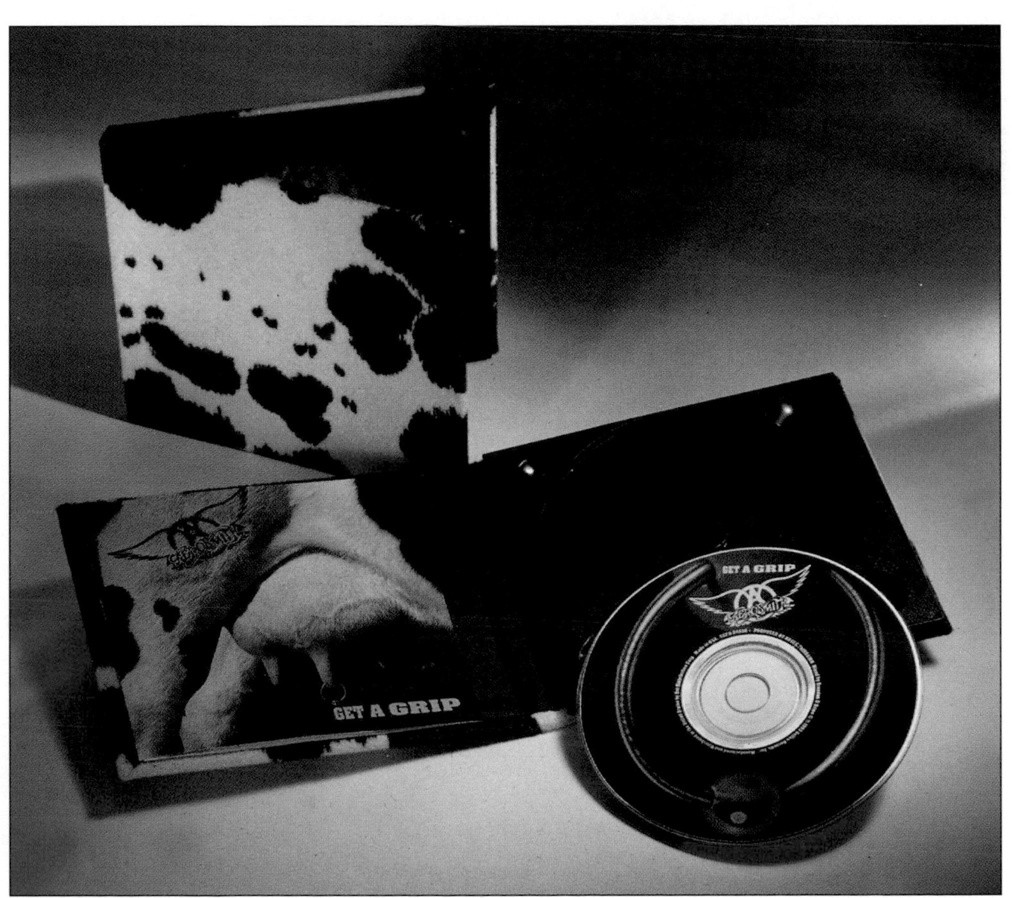

Aerosmith – Get A Grip (Geffen) U.S. 1994 limited edition CD album.

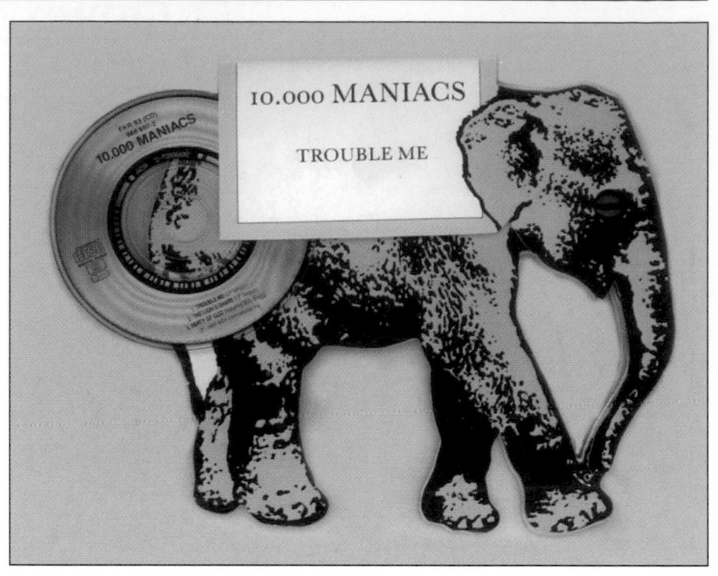

10,000 Maniacs – Trouble Me (Elektra EKR 93(CD) 966 697-2) German 1986 CD3.

Gear Daddy's – Billy's Live Bait (Polydor 847-251-2DJ) U.S. 1990 promotional CD album.

Hatfield, Juliana – Only Everything (Atlantic 92540-2) U.S. 1995 limited edition CD.

CD Golden Gallery

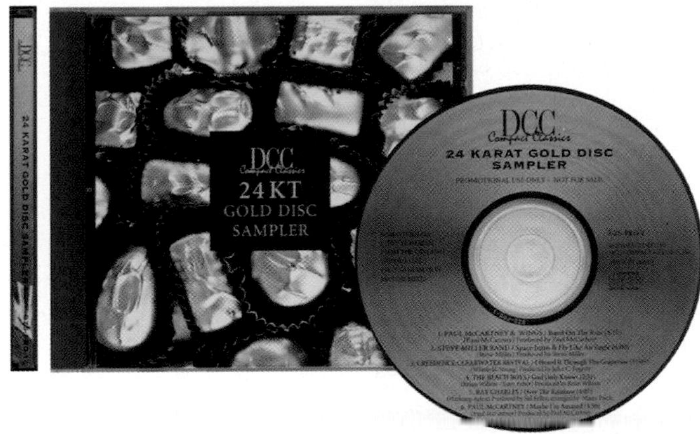

DCC 24 Karat Gold Disc Sampler DCC GZS-PRO-1
U.S. 1993 promotional CD sampler.

Flim & the BB's – Tricycle (dmp GOLD-9000)

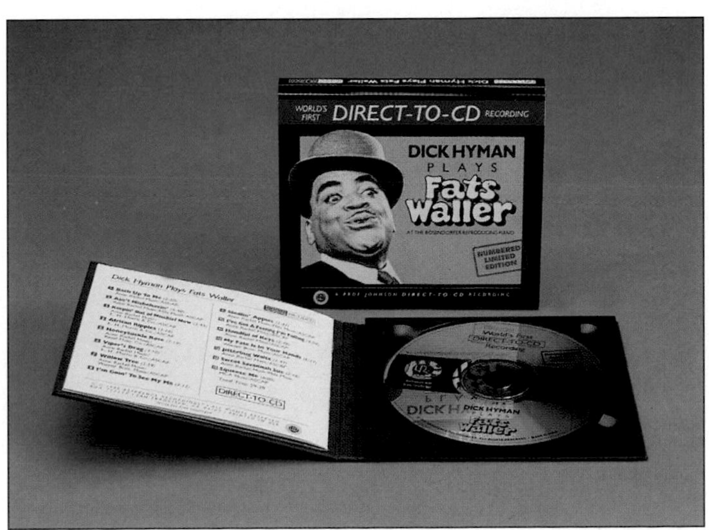

Hyman, Dick – Dick Hyman Plays Fats Waller (Reference Recordings RR-33DCD)
U.S. 1990 limited edition CD.

Mastersound Sampler (Sony CSK 4757) U.S. 1992 promotional CD sampler.

Creedence Clearwater Revival – Chronicle Volumes One and Two (Fantasy) U.S. 1995 limited edition CDs.

Clapton, Eric – Selections from Crossroads 2 (Chronicles PRSAD000182)
U.S. 1995 promotional CD sampler.

Judd, Wynonna – Girls with Guitars (MCA MCA5P-54875)
U.S. 1994 promotional CD-single.

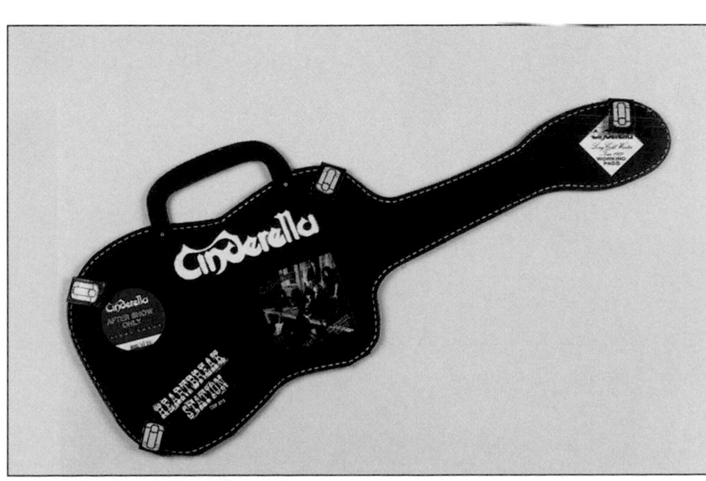

Cinderella – Heartbreak Station (Mercury CDP326)
U.S. 1990 promotional CD-single.

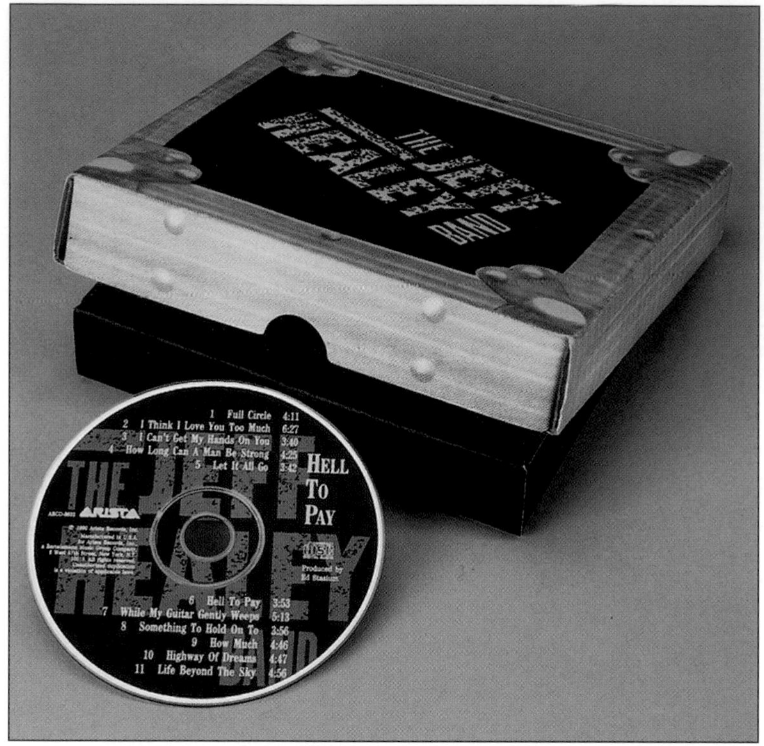

Jeff Healey Band – Hell to Pay (Arista ARCD-8632) U.S. promotional CD album

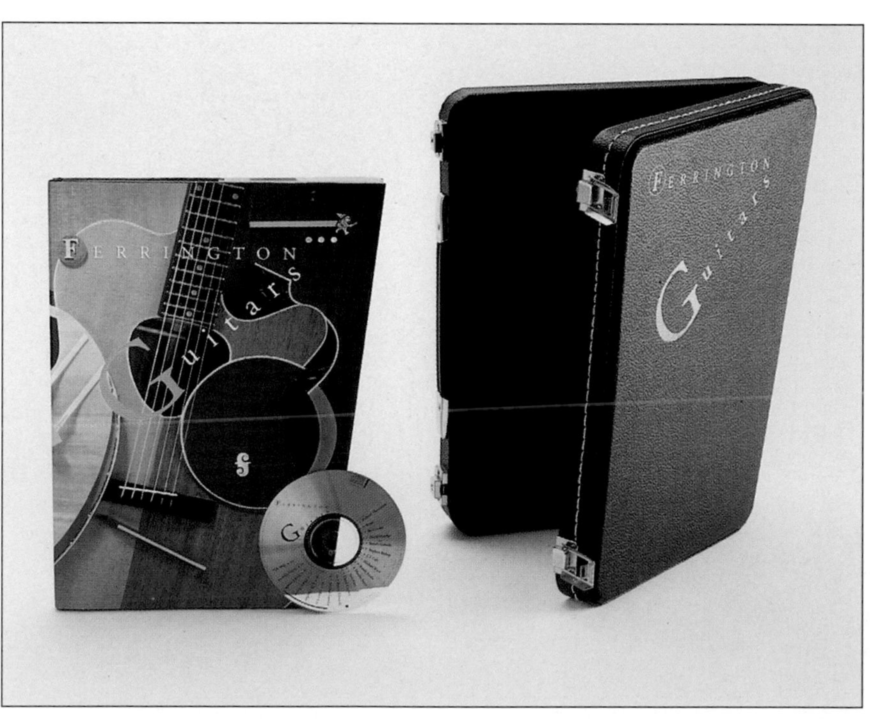

Ferrington Guitars (Harper Collins) U.S. limited edition CD album with book in guitar case.

Hiatt, John – Perfectly Good Guitar (A&M 31454 0135 2) U.S. 1993 promotional CD album in tour crate.

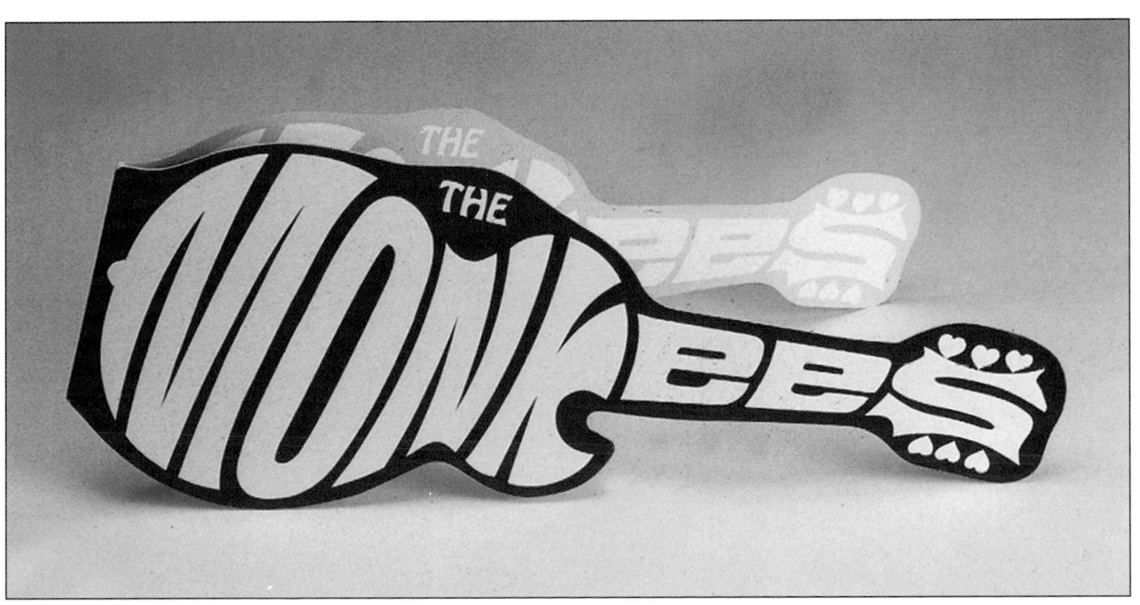

Monkees, The – Sampler (Rhino PRCD 7080) U.S. 1994 promotional CD sampler.

Malmsteen, Yngwie – On Guitar (Polygram SACD 178) U.S. 1990 promotional CD sampler.

Newton-John, Olivia – Warm and Tender (Geffen 9 242572-DJ) U.S. promotional CD album.

E., Sheila – Sex Cymbal (Warner Brothers 26255-2-DJ)
U.S. 1989 promotional CD album.

Rodgers, Paul – Muddy Waters Blues (Victory SACD 679)
U.S. 1993 promotional CD album.

Wakeman, Rick – Wakeman with Wakeman: Official Live Bootleg, The (Griffin GCDRW-156-2) U.S. 1995 limited edition two CD set.

Kravitz, Lenny – Are You Gonna Go My Way (Virgin 724383916900) U.S. 1993 limited edition CD album.

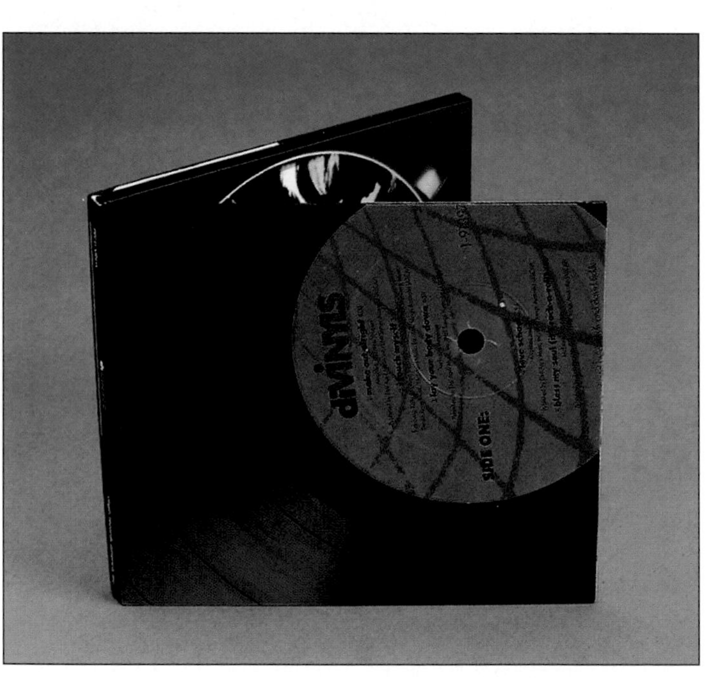

Divinyls – Divinyls (Virgin PRCD VINYL) U.S. 1990 promotional CD album.

I Guess We Didn't Save the LP (Rhino PRO 90045-A/B/C) Three CD sampler set.

Who, The – Live at Leeds (MCA MCAD-11230)
U.S. limited edition CD album.

Luscious Jackson – Deep Shag (Capitol DPRO 79521
U.S. 1994 promotional CD-single.

Stevens, Ray – Breakfast with Ray Stevens (Curb CURBD-1058)
U.S. 1993 promotional CD sampler.

Dramarama – Haven't Got a Clue (Chameleon PR-8435)
U.S. 1993 promotional CDJ.

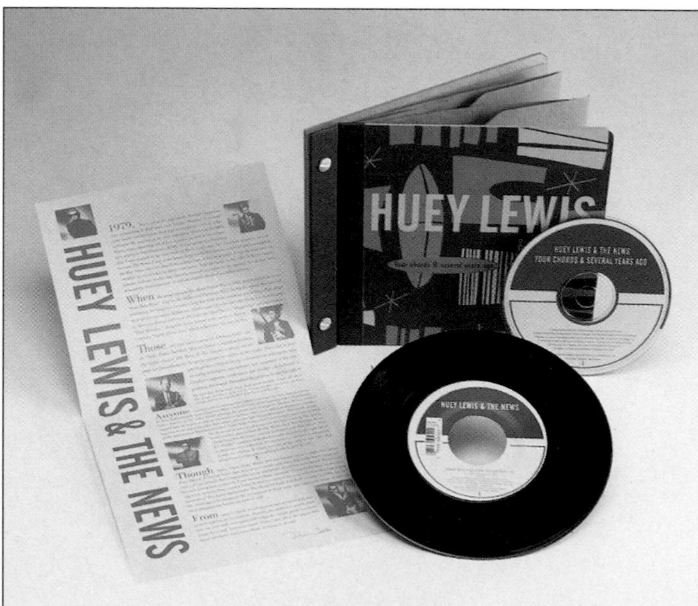

Lewis, Huey & The News – Four Chords & Several Years Ago (Elektra PR 8975) U.S. 1994 promotional CD album.

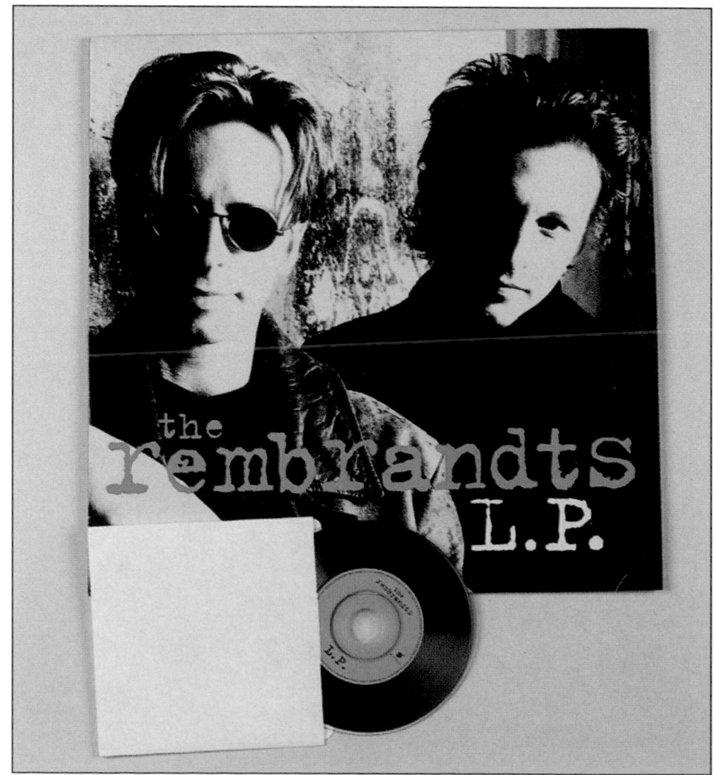

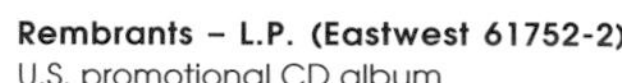
Rembrants – L.P. (Eastwest 61752-2)
U.S. promotional CD album.

Okeh – Rhythm & Blues Story Sampler 1949–1957 (Legacy ESK 5037)
U.S. 1995 promotional CD sampler.

Yes – Yesyears (Sampler Atco PRCD 4009-2)
U.S. 1991 promotional CD sampler.

Bowie, David – Rise and Fall of Ziggy Stardust (Rykodisc 0134-2) U.S. 1990 promotional CD album.

CD Soundtracks

Music of Audrey Hepburn

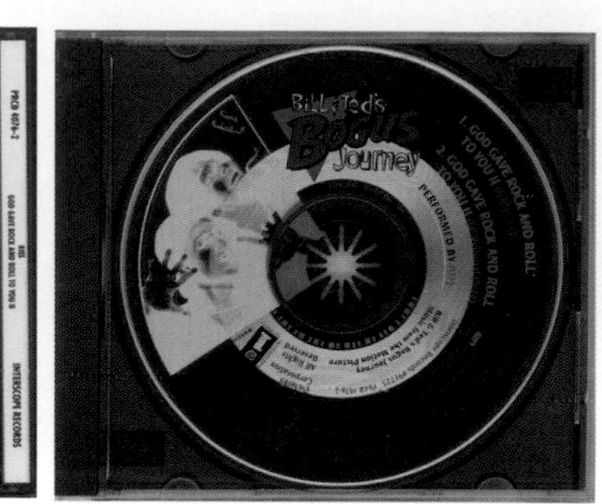

Kiss – God Gave Rock and Roll to You II (Interscope PRCD 4076-2) U.S. 1991 promotional CD-single.

Beauty and the Beast (Walt Disney PCCD-00109)

Batman – Original Television Soundtrack (Casablanca 834 908-2) Out-of-print CD soundtrack of the 1966 television series. Disc was packaged in the typical polygram blister pack.

Mighty Morphin Power Rangers TV Theme & Soundbites (Atlantic PRCD 6019) U.S. 1994 promotional CD sampler.

War of the Worlds – The New Files (X FILE CD) U.S. 1995 promotional CD sampler.

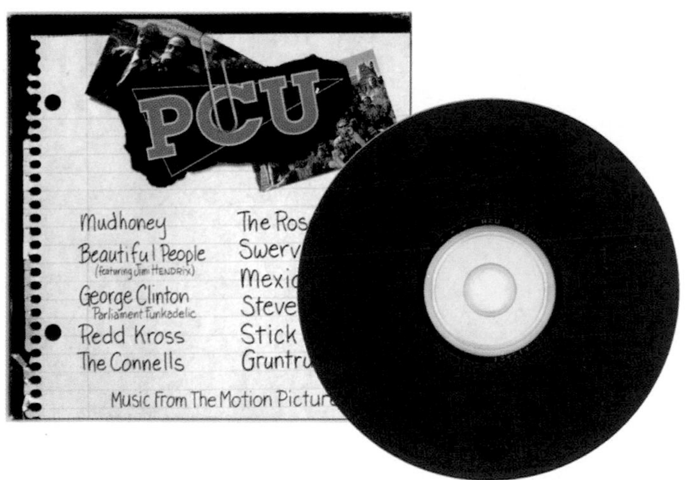

PCU (Fox records) U.S. 1994 promotional CD album.

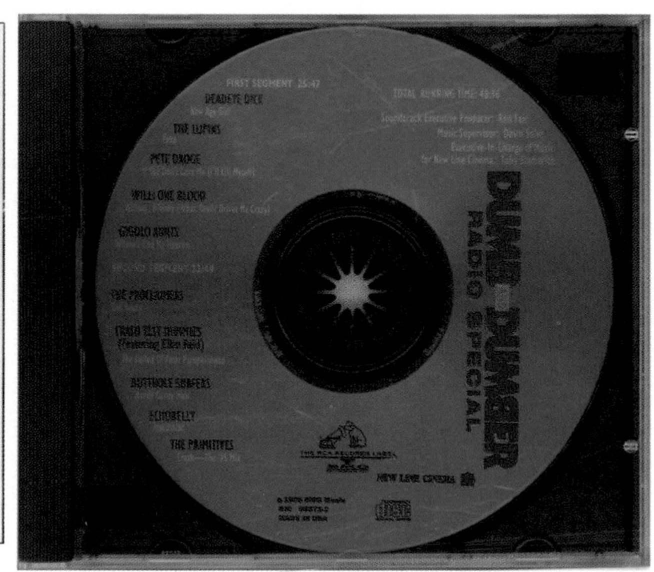

Dumb and Dumber Radio Special (BMG RJC 66572-2) Radio interview disc.

Contact! All-Star Collection (ACDP 1395) Canadian 1994 promotional CD sampler.

NBA Jam Session (MCA MCAD-10786) U.S. promotional CD album.

Sound of the Games, The (Atlanta Olympic Committee) U.S. 1996 limited edition five CD boxed set.

Capitol's Perfect Pitch (Capitol DPRO-79842) U.S. 1991 promotional CD sampler.

Kodak Fun (NS 16CD)

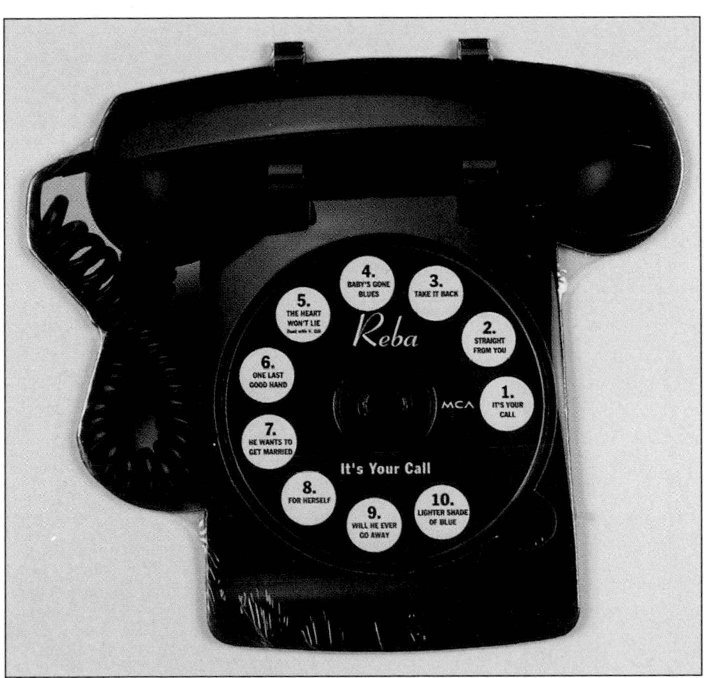

McEntire, Reba – It's Your Call (MCA MCA3P-10673) U.S. 1992 promotional CD album.

Sony Minidisc Sampler

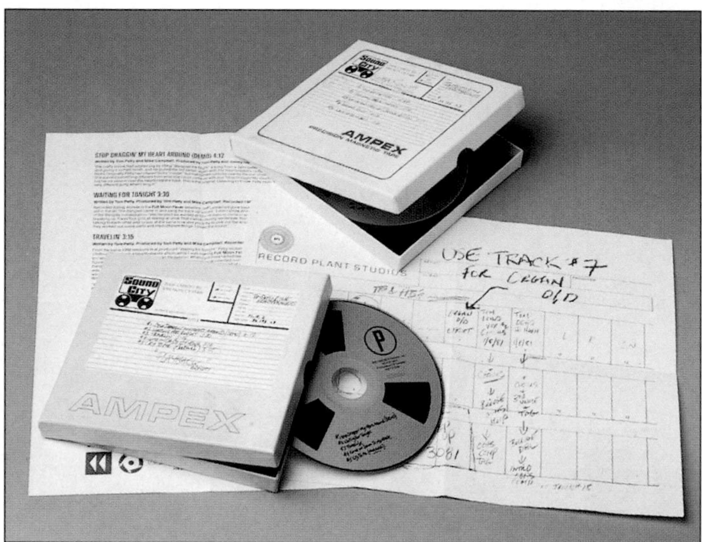

Petty, Tom – Playback Excerpts (MCA)
U.S. promotional CD samplers.

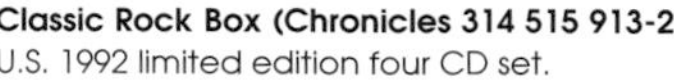

Classic Rock Box (Chronicles 314 515 913-2)
U.S. 1992 limited edition four CD set.

Schoolhouse Rock (Rhino R2B72455)

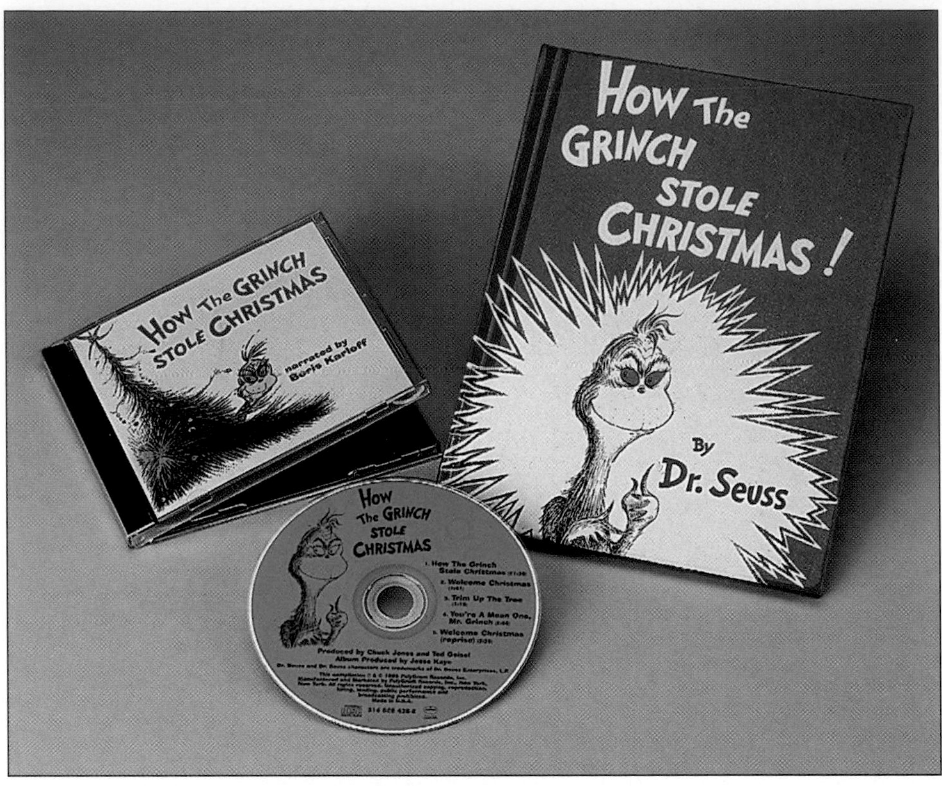

Dr. Seuss – How the Grinch Stole Christmas (Mercury/Nashville 314-528 438-2) Special edition Dr. Seuss CD and book gift set, released for 1995 Christmas season.

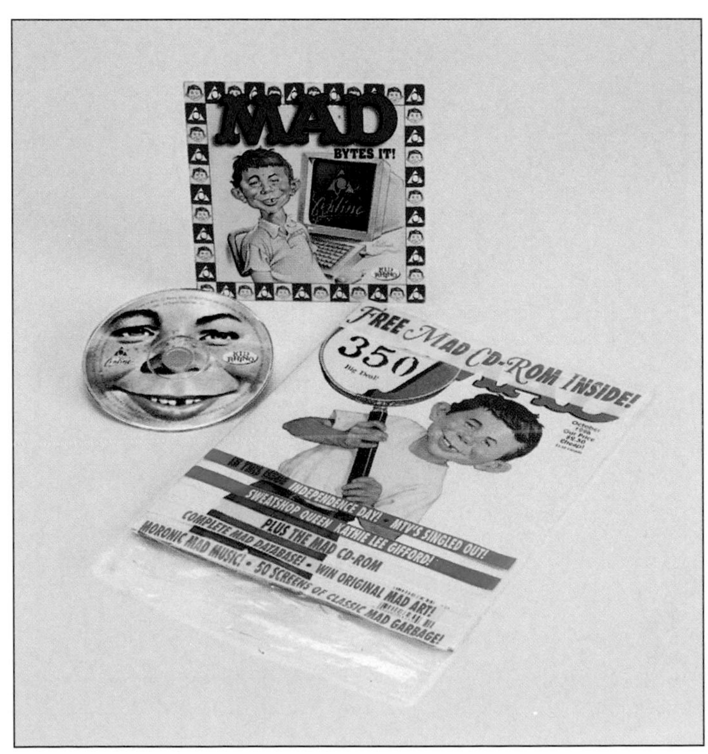

Mad: Bytes It! (Kid Rhino)

Crash Test Dummies – Ghosts That Haunt Me (Arista ARCD-8677)
U.S. 1991 promotional CD album.

Satriani, Joe – Surfing with the Alien (Relativity 88561-8193-2)
U.S. 1987 promotional CD-single.

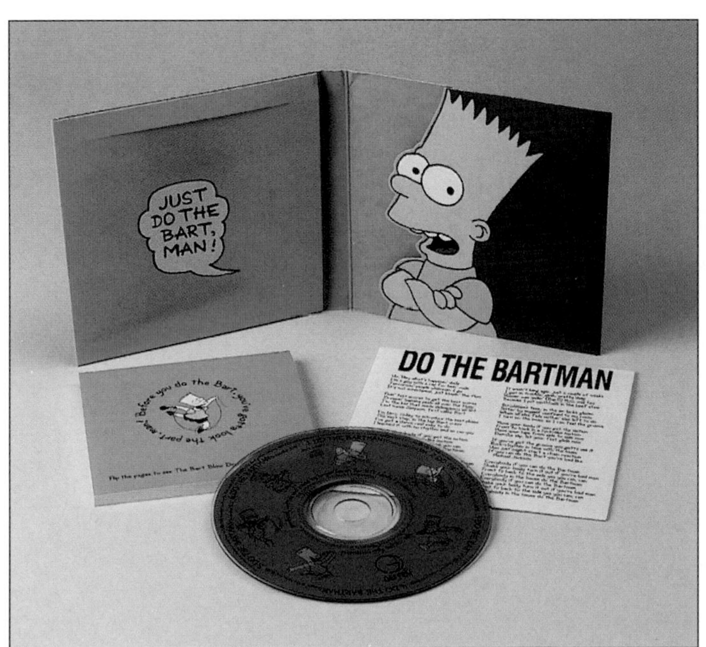

Simpsons, The – Do the Bartman (Geffen PRO-CD-4170)
U.S. 1990 promotional CD-single

Bugs Bunny on Broadway (Warner Brothers 9 26494-2-DJ) U.S. 1990 Promotional CD album.

Carl Stalling Project (Warner Brothers 9 26027-2) Mega-rare U.S. 1990 limited edition CD album. These discs, limited to 6,000 copies, were randomly distributed throughout the retail market. Discs were packaged inside a long box (not shown).

Beavis and Butt-Head With Cher – I Got You Babe (Geffen GFSTD 64)

Entombed – Wolverine Blues (Columbia CK 57742-S1)
U.S. 1994 limited edition CD.

Ren & Stimpy – Little Eediot (Nickelodeon LXK 5473)
U.S. 1993 promotional CD sampler.

Who Framed Roger Rabbit (Disney CD-010)
U.S. 1988 out-of-print CD album.

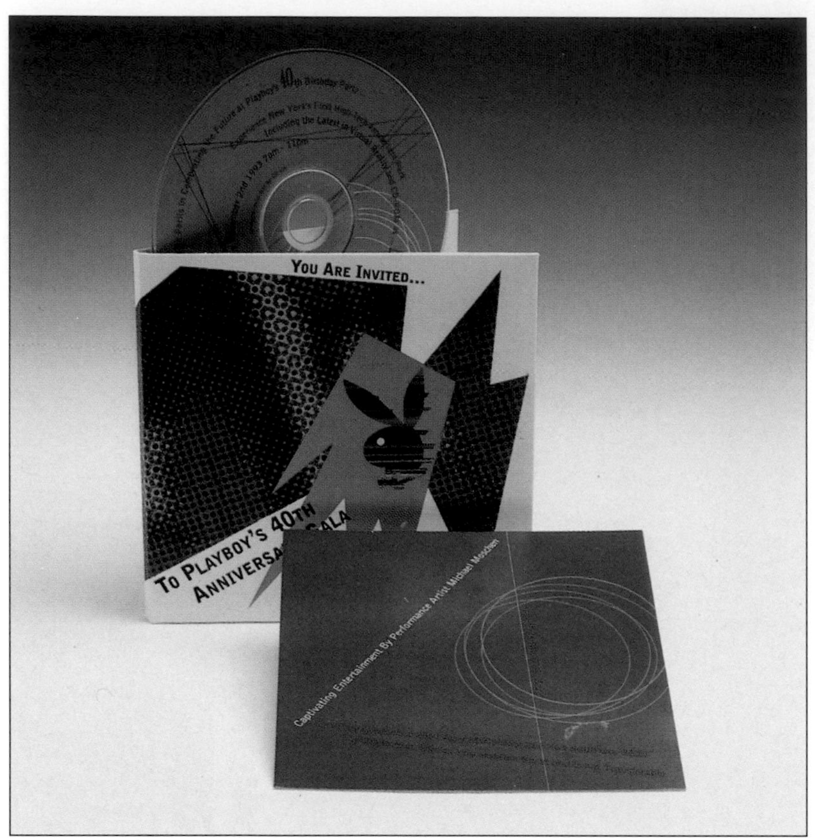

Playboy's 40th Anniversary Gala Invitation (Playboy) Special CD invitation commemorating Playboy's 40th anniversary. The disc however, contains no data.

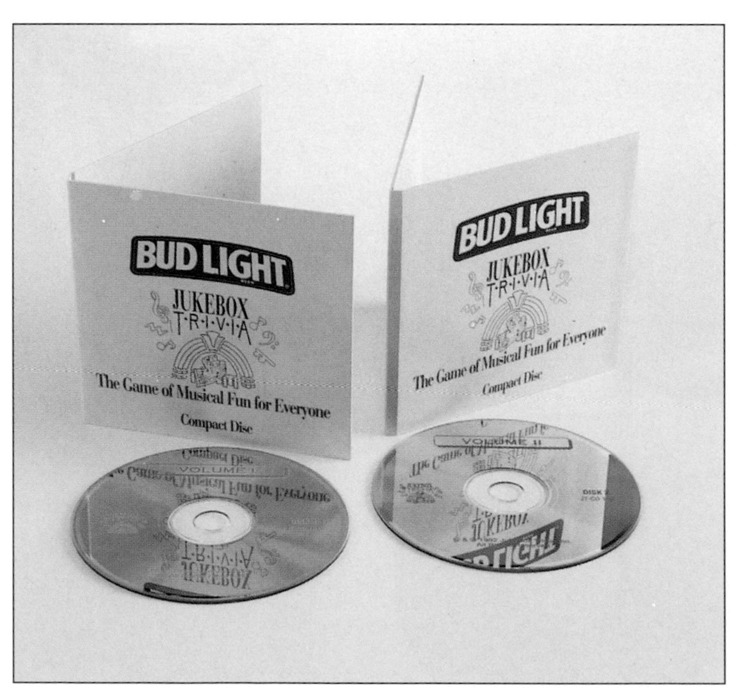

Jukebox Trivia (Bud Light) Prototype packaging for the Jukebox Trivia game. This packaging however, was canceled and never commercially released.

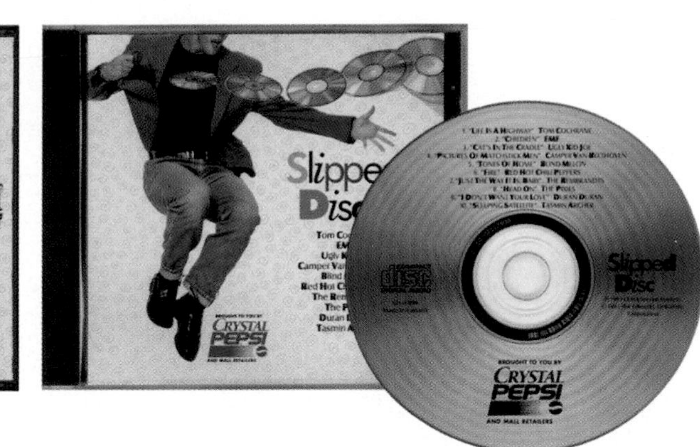

Slipped Disc (CEMA/Crystal Pepsi S21-17499) U.S. 1993 promotional CD sampler sampler given as a value added by CEMA and the now defunct Crystal Pepsi.

Decade of Music (Sony/Billboard A 23565) U.S. 1992 promotional CD sampler.

Canada Dry 80's Encore (CBS A 21426) U.S. 1989 promotional CD sampler.

L'Oreal Studio Line Live! (L'Oreal/Westwood One) 1995 promotional sampler given away free with purchase of L'Oreal hair care products.

Panasonic Power Hits (Panasonic BSD P012/794) U.S. 1994 promotional CD sampler.

Kellogg's Mega Music Mix (RCA/Kellogg's DPC1-1301) U.S. 1996 promotional CD sampler.

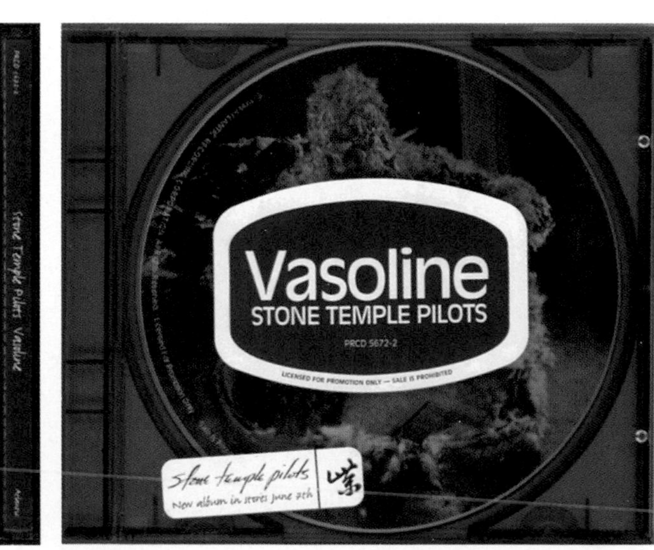

Stone Temple Pilots – Vasoline (Atlantic PRCD 5672-2) U.S. 1994 promotional CD-single.

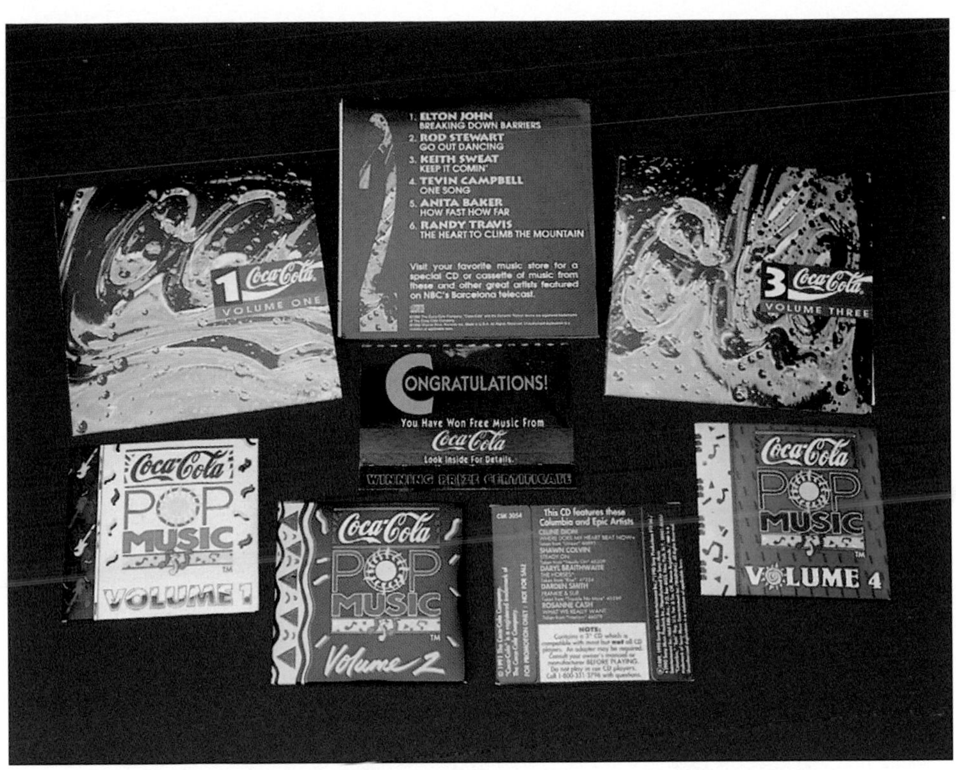

Coca-Cola Volume 1 – 3 (Coca-Cola/Warner Brothers) These CDs were prizes redeemed from winning cards found in 12-packs of Coca-Cola products in the summer of 1992 to commemorate the 1992 Olympics.

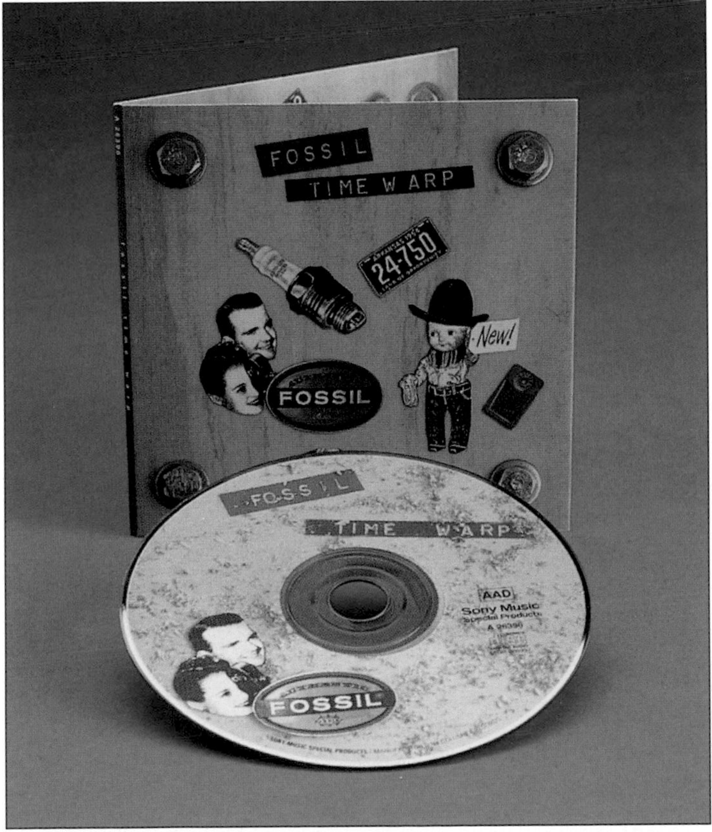

Fossil Time Warp (Fossil/Sony Music Special Products A 26396) U.S. 1995 promotional CD sampler.

Discs in Space

Fantasy Worlds of Irwin Allen (GNP Crescendo) Taking about 15 years to secure licensing, this picture disc CD set is a must for every collector.

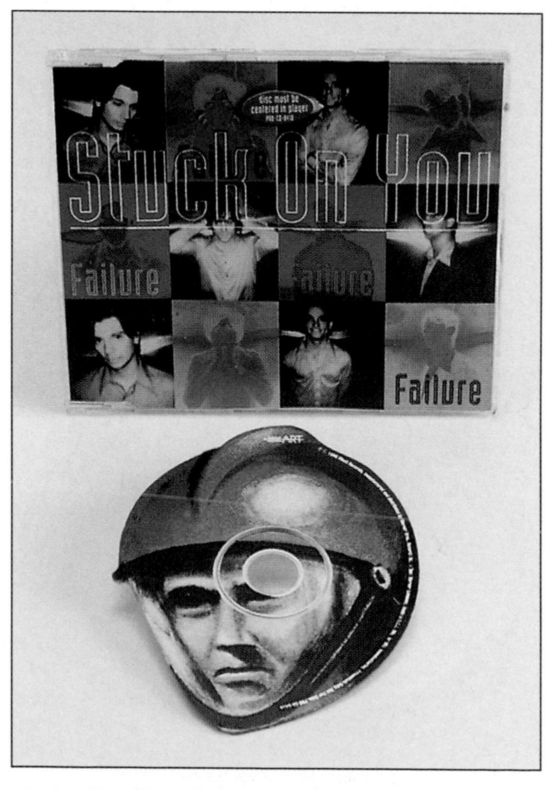

Failure – Stuck on You (Warner Brothers PRO-CD-8410) U.S. promotional shaped CD.

Star Wars (Polydor 800 096-2) U.S. 1985 out-of-print two CD album.

Star Wars Trilogy (BMG Classics) A collection of 1997 limited edition CD album sets. Each set features a unique 3-D l•d hologram printed design.

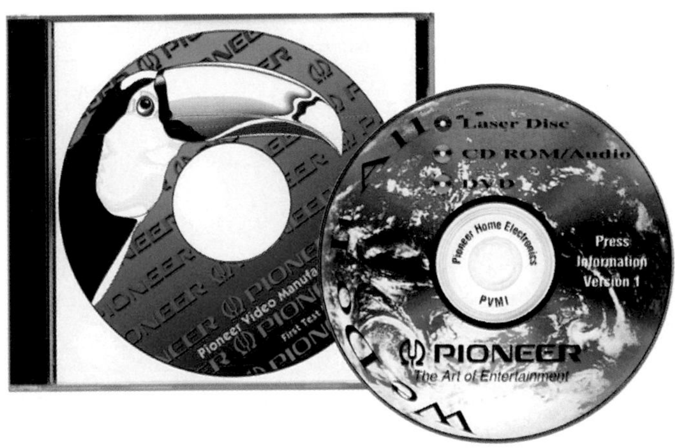

Pioneer Video Manufacturing: Press Information Volume 1 (Pioneer) U.S. 1996 promotional CD-ROM press kit.

Star Trek Picture Disc CDs (GNP Crescendo GNPD 8041) U.S. picture disc CD albums.

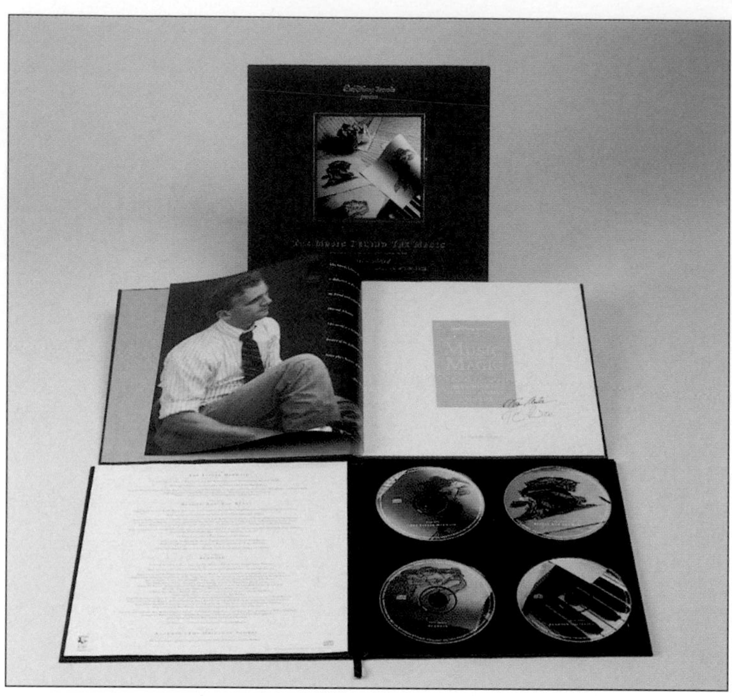

Music Behind the Magic (Walt Disney) U.S. 1995 limited edition picture disc four CD.

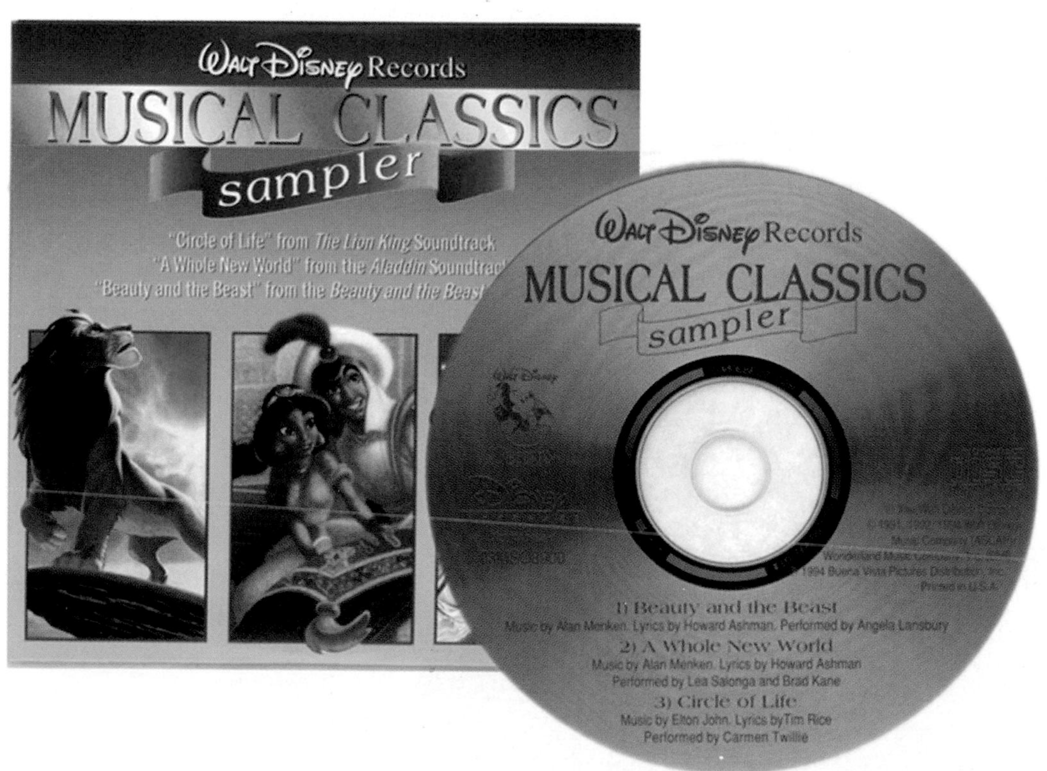

Musical Classics Sampler (Walt Disney 03MSO8900) U.S. 1994 promotional CD sampler.

Walt Disney's Story of...Series (Applewood Books) Rare limited edition picture disc CD audio book series of the original Disney books from the 1930s. Ironically, the reproductions of each book accompanying the disc are the same size as today's jewel boxes. Now that's really planning ahead.

Snow White (Walt Disney) U.S. limited edition CD.

Snow White (Walt Disney CD-004) U.S. 1989 limited edition storybook CD commemorating the 50th anniversary of Snow White.

Hunchback of Notre Dame (Walt Disney 60893-2)

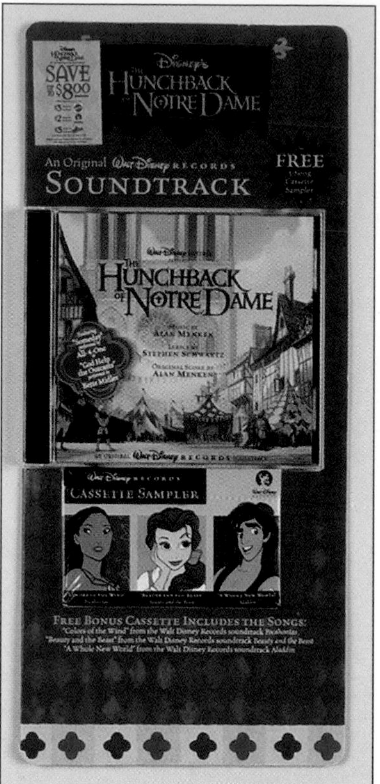

Hunchback of Notre Dame (Walt Disney Records 60893-7)

Aladdin (Walt Disney PCCD-00108) These 1994 Japanese limited edition picture disc Disney CD soundtracks come in an oversized slip case with two figurines from the movie.

Aladdin (Walt Disney 60013-2) Rare 1994 picture disc limited edition CD album with exclusive lenticular. This disc had trouble being noticed because it was marketed through the "childrens' music" section of the record store, remaining largely overlooked.

Pocahontas (Walt Disney 60874-7) Limited edition picture disc version available exclusively at the Musicland family of record stores.

Beauty and the Beast: The Broadway Musical (Walt Disney 60861-7) U.S. 1994 out-of-print picture disc CD album.

John, Elton – Circle of Life (Hollywood PRCD-10448-2) U.S. 1994 promotional CD-single.

Disney: My First Disney CD (Walt Disney PCCD-00135) Japanese 1995 limited edition CD.

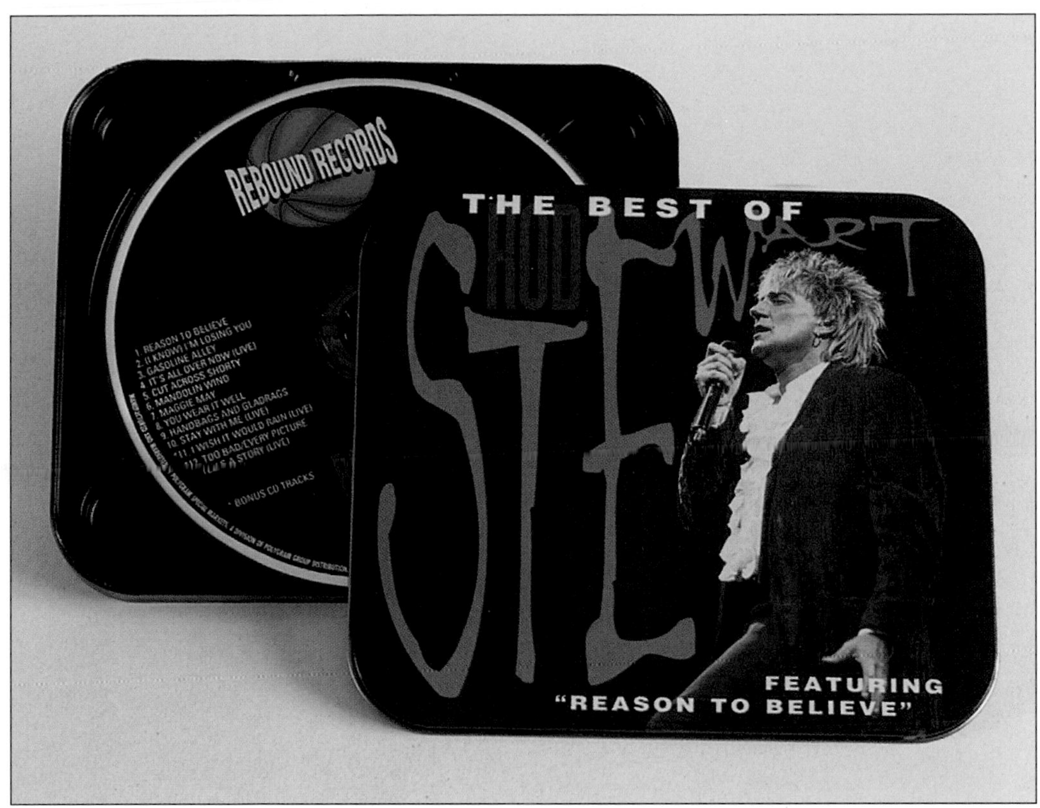

Stewart, Rod – The Best of Rod Stewart (Eclipse 4861-2) U.S. 1996 limited edition CD.

Crash Boom Opera – These Are Crazy Times (Giant 9 26160-2-DJ) U.S. 1990 promotional CD album.

Rollins Band – Weight (Imago IM 21047-2-DJ) U.S. 1994 promotional CD album.

Reel Music (MCA CD33-1256/57) U.S. 1989 promotional CD sampler.

Richie, Lionel – Louder than Words (Mercury 314 532 240-2) U.S. 1996 promotional CD album.

CSA Archive CD-ROM (Charles S. Anderson 100/76) Even utilitarian CD-ROMs can be collectible. This disc, by the Charles S. Anderson design firm, contains a library of custom clip art, but is packaged in this unique tin with a unique pin.

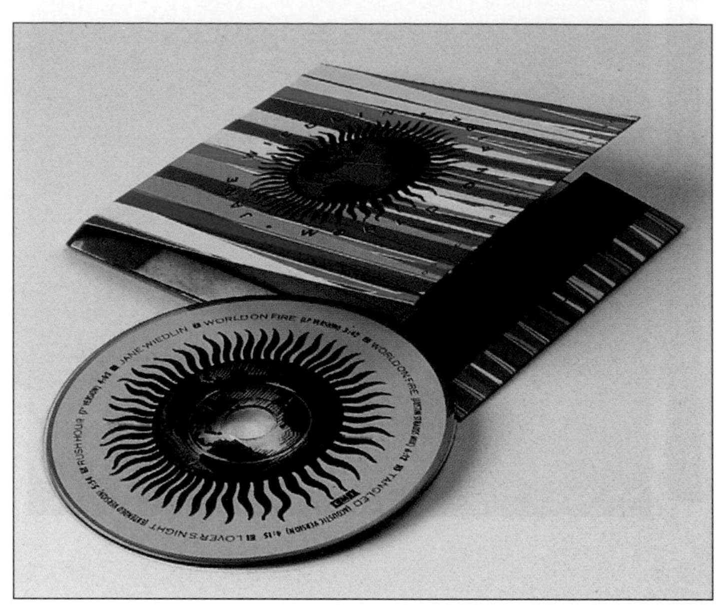

Wiedlin, Jane – World on Fire (EMI E2-56191)
U.S. 1988 CD5. One of the earliest specially packaged U.S. CD-singles.

Red Hot Country (Mercury Nashville 314-522-639-2)
U.S. 1994 promotional CD album.

A Tribute to Sam Sniderman (Caras SAMCD 50)
Canadian 1988 promotional CD sampler.

Mattea, Kathy – Lonesome Standard Time (Mercury CDP 750-P)
U.S. 1992 promotional CD album with greatest hits CD and CDJ.

Cracker – Nothing to Believe In (Virgin DPRO-11511)
U.S. CDJ manufactured by Disc Art. A perfect example of the limitless possibilities of shaped CDs.

3 Inches of the World (Rykodisc RCD3-1009)
Various artist world-music sampler.

Erasure – I Say I Say I Say (Mute Lcd Stumm 115) U.K. 1994 limited edition CD.

Picture Disc Gallery

Carey, Mariah – Mariah Carey (CBS 4668152)

Bad Company – Can't Get Enough (MMG AMCY-95)

Laser Disc Sampler – (Warner Reprise PRO-V-5023) The first ever picture disc laser disc. This 1991 promotional laser disc was designed by Tom Recchion at Warner Brothers Records. Because 8" laser discs can be one sided or two sided, the non-read side of the disc, usually only having a center label, can be printed without any harm to the read side.

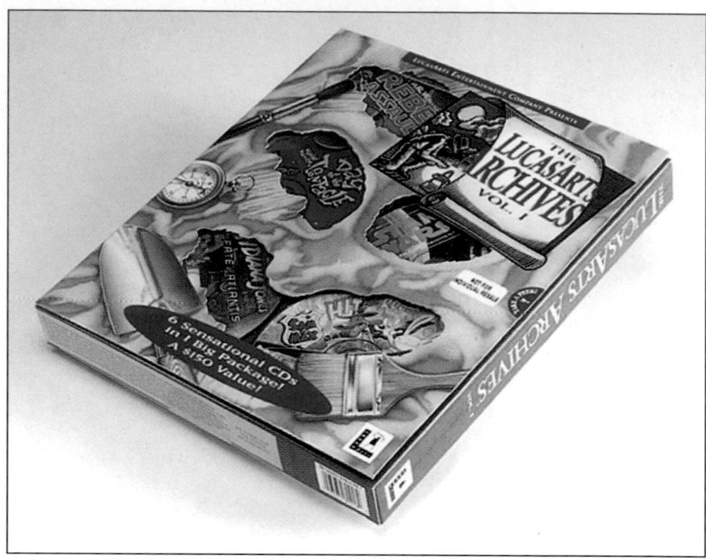

Lucas Arts Samplers (Lucas Arts) Special picture disc version CD-ROMs.

Harding, John Wesley – If You Have Guns (Sire PRO-CD-4498)

Lexis Nexis Online Software

Rush – Roll the Bones (Anthem PRO9) Canadian promotional CD-single.

Rush – Bravado (Atlantic PRCD 4580-2) U.S. promotional CD-single.

Def Leppard – Pyromania (Vertigo 28PD-523) and Def Leppard – Hysteria (Bludgeon Riffola 32PD-1004) Japanese 1988 out-of-print picture disc version CD album.

Iron Maiden – Castle Limited Edition Collection These limited edition sets, issued in 1995 each contain two five-color picture discs. Disc one is a remastered version of the album and disc two is a bonus disc of rare singles tracks. Castle's suggested retail price of $11.98 for each package, makes these titles the best value in the music industry. These editions are selling out fast and being replaced with standard single-disc versions.

Color Me Badd – I Adore Mi Amor (Giant PRO-CD-4943) U.S. promotional CD-single.

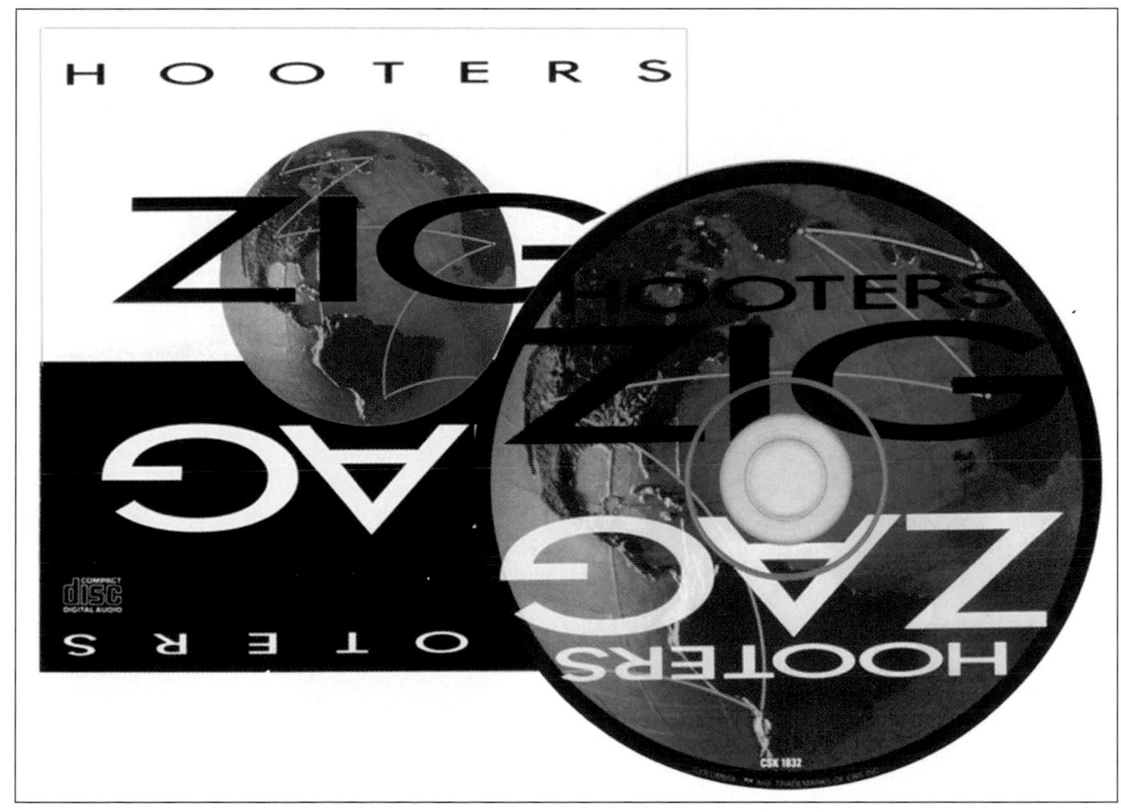

Hooters – Zig Zag (Columbia CSK 1832) U.S. promotional CD album.

John, Elton – Can You Feel the Love Tonight (Hollywood PRCD 10441-2) Promotional picture disc single.

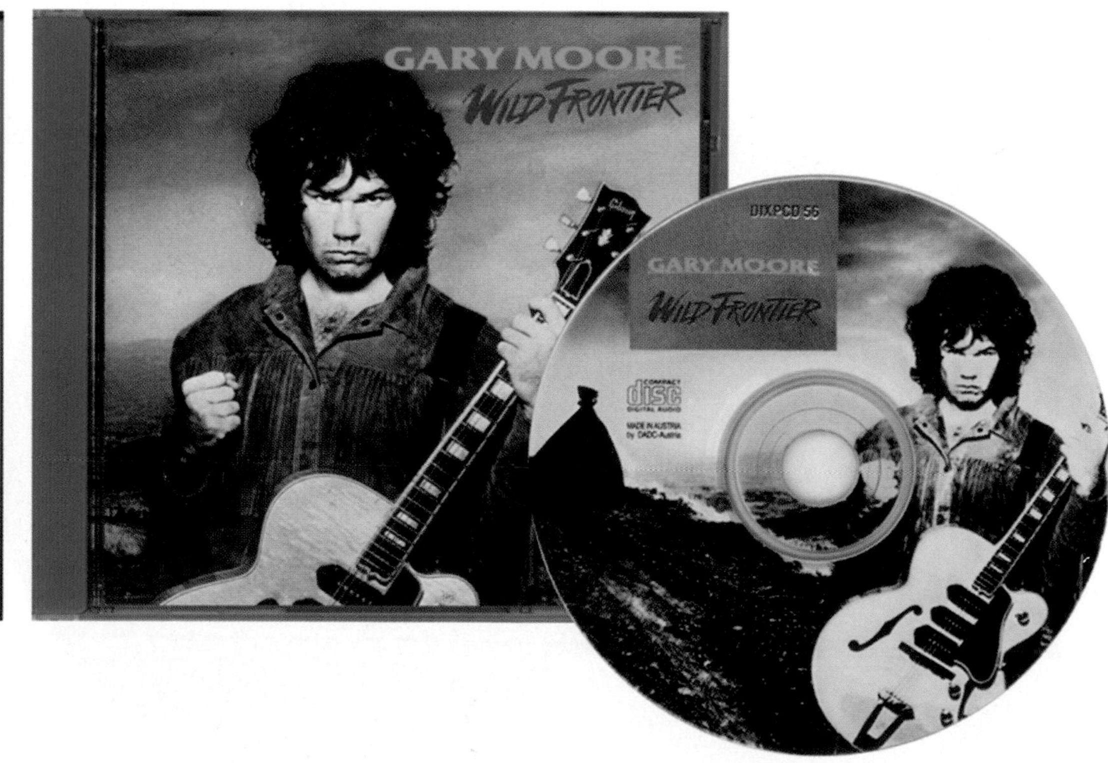

Moore, Gary – Wild Frontier (10 RECORDS DIXCDP 56) German limited edition picture disc CD.

PRO-CD-4038 *JANE'S ADDICTION "STOP"* WARNER BROS.

Jane's Addicton – Stop (Warner Brothers PRO-CD-4038) Promotional CD-single.

PRO-CD-4633 **JANE'S ADDICTION "CLASSIC GIRL"** WARNER BROS.

Jane's Addicton – Classic Girl (Warner Brothers PRO-CD-4633) U.S. 1991 promotional CD-single.

Great White – Once Bitten Twice Shy (Capitol DIDX 004647) U.S. promotional CD-single.

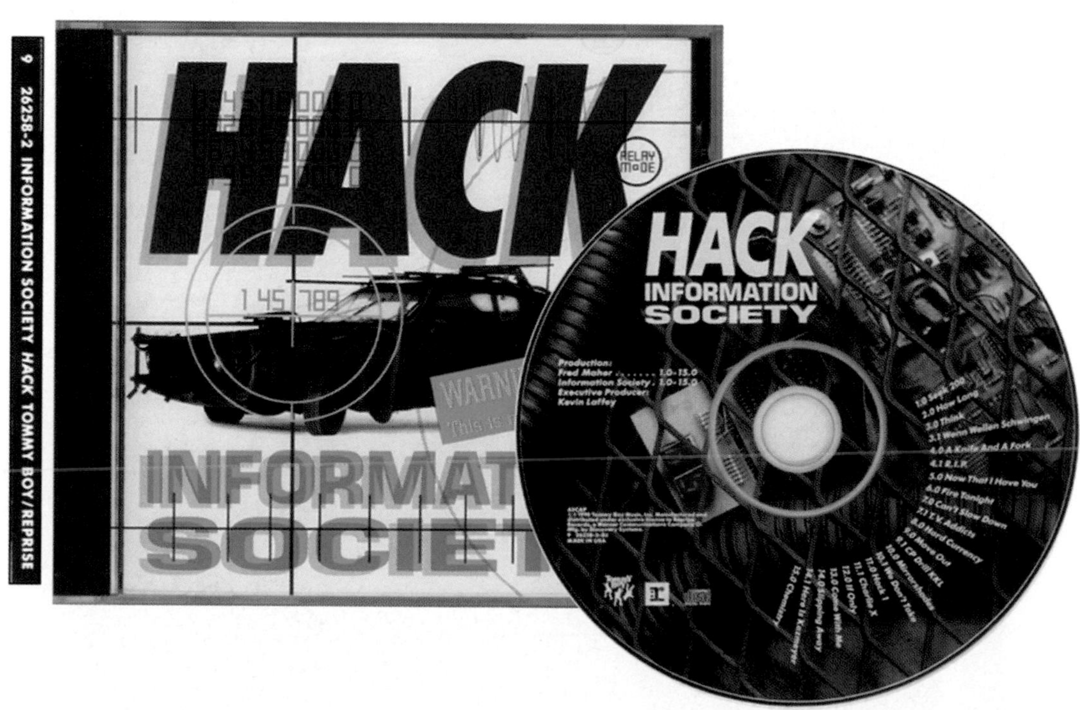

Information Society – Hack (Tommy Boy 9 26258-2-DJ) U.S. promotional picture disc CD album.

Meat Loaf Bat – Out of Hell II (MCA MCAD-104699) These discs are all from the same album and all made less than a year apart. The disc on the far left is the first pressing which is a five-color picture disc CD (white, cyan, yellow, magenta, and black). To cut costs the second pressing was printed in four colors, eliminating the white base layer. Finally, the disc was reduced to a standard two-color title printed disc. Though the album is still in print the first two pressings do have some value.

Meat Loaf – Bat Out of Hell (Epic 90891) Rare Canadian picture disc CD album.

Special Packaging

Motown Sound, The (Motown 37463-1338-2) U.S. 1996 promotional CD sampler.

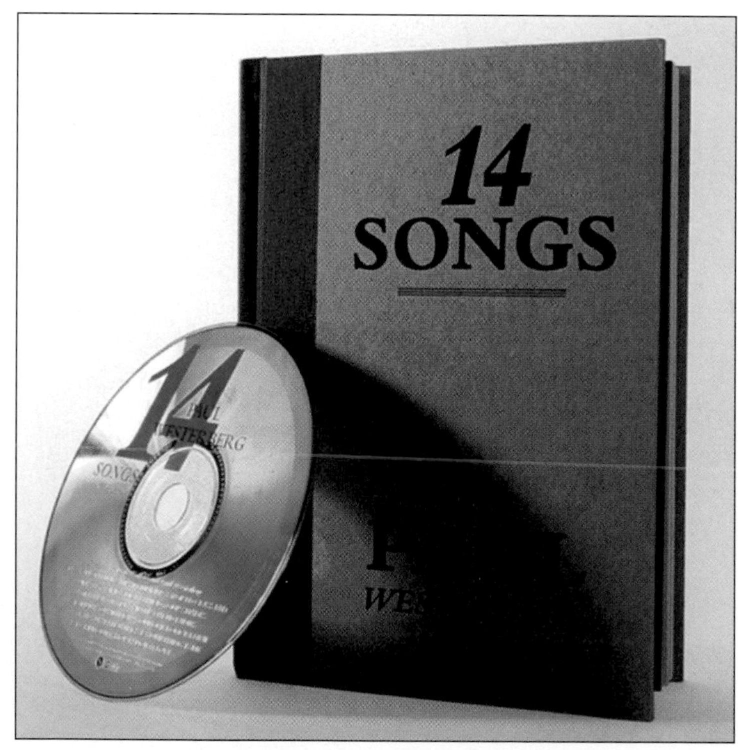

Westerberg, Paul – 14 Songs (Reprise 9 45335-2) U.S. 1993 limited edition CD.

Fitzgerald, Ella – First Lady of Song (Verve 314 517 898-2) Specially packaged CD set.

Bowie, David – Santa Monica '72 (Griffin GCD-392-2) U.S. 1995 limited edition CD album.

Joy to the World: Michael Schulhof Christmas Gift 1991 (Sony) U.S. promotional CD-sampler.

A World in Harmony: Michael Schulhof Christmas Gift 1992 (Sony) U.S. promotional CD-sampler.

Velvet Underground – Live MCMXCIII (Sire 9 45434-2) U.S. 1993 limited edition CD.

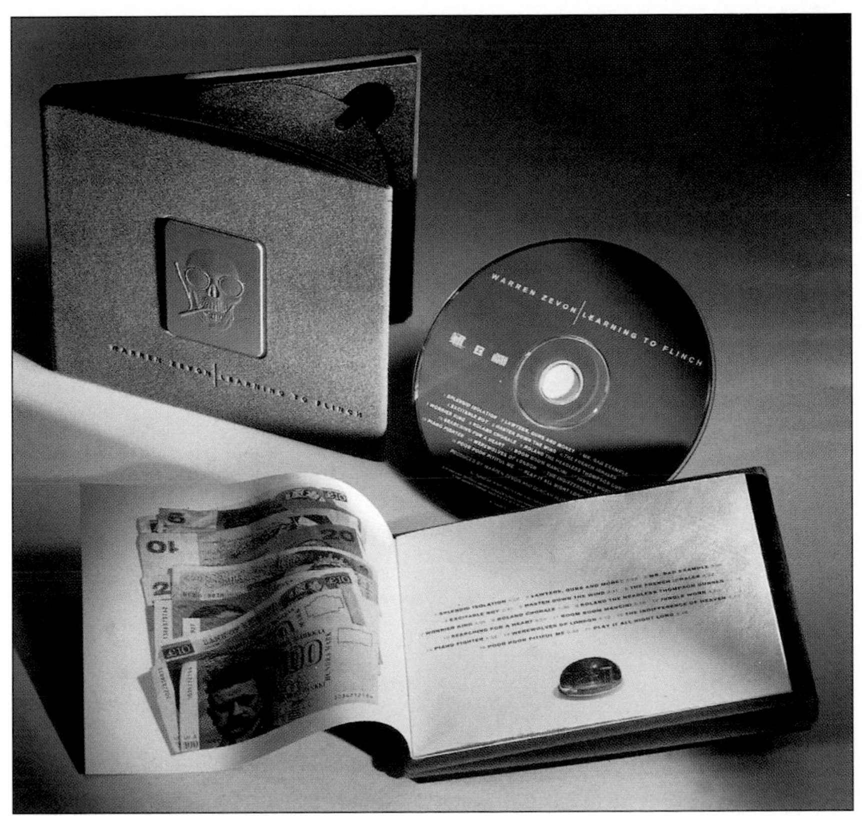

Zevon, Warren – Learning to Flinch (Warner Brothers 2-24496) U.S. limited edition CD.

Crowell, Rodney – Let the Picture Paint Itself (MCA MCAD-11042) U.S. 1994 promotional CD album.

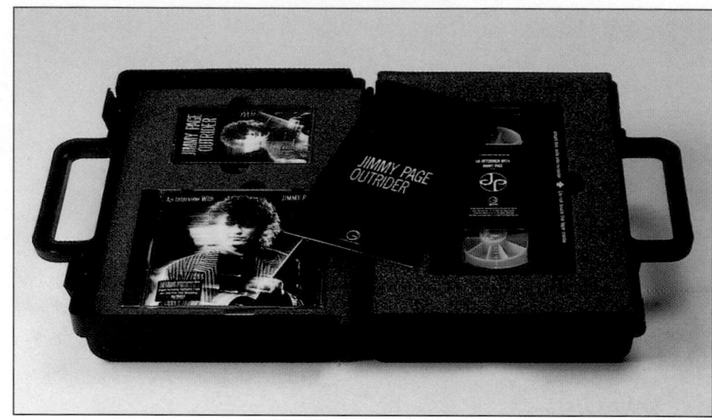

Page, Jimmy – Outrider (Geffen) 1988 promotional edition CD boxed set.

Rondor Music International Music Sampler (Rondor MSPJ 032) Music publishing 12 CD sampler.

Mellencamp, John – Mr. Happy Go Lucky (Mercury 314 532 896-2) Jeffrey Schulz, senior designer at Mercury Records, designed this package for the Mellencamp album. Initial designs were patterned from Bill Levinson's design of Mellencamp's *Dance Naked* special package. Shown are initial drawing and notes along with, print-out designs of the book's contents. Also shown are original prototypes of the books actual design. The first design was spiral-bound book, then came a tape-bound book, until a rivit-bound book was finally agreed upon.

Osbourne, Ozzy – Live & Loud (Epic Z2K 48973) U.S. 1993 limited edition CD album.

Ozzy Osbourne – Live & Loud (Epic) Originally, the *Live & Loud* limited edition created by Jim Ladwig of AGI, Inc., was going to include a special boxed set containing a CD copy of the concert album and a VHS video cassette. This special edition was never produced. Note the prototype version of the digi-pak CD set.

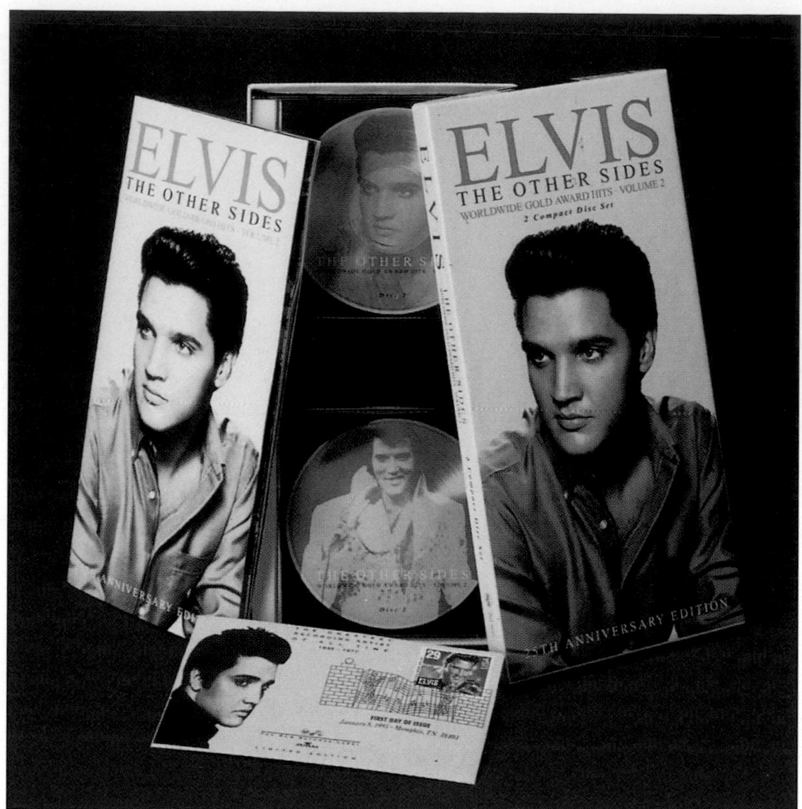

Presley, Elvis – Other Sides: Worldwide Gold Award Hits Volume 2 (RCA 07863 66921-2) U.S. 1996 limited edition CD.

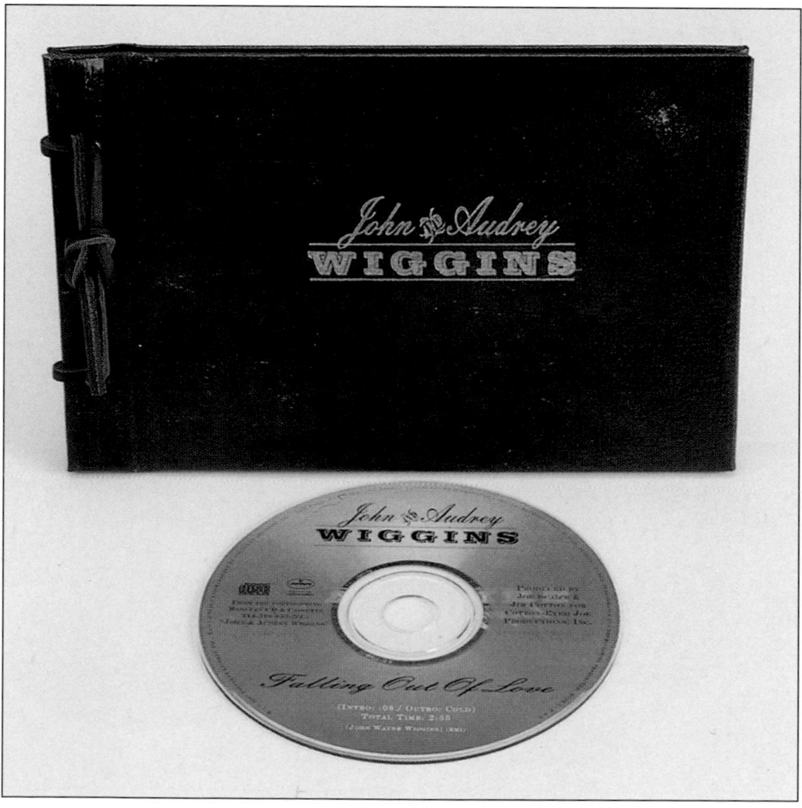

Wiggins, John & Audrey – Falling Out of Love (Mercury CDP 1174) Promotional CD album.

Procol Harum – Chapter One and Chapter Two (Zoo) U.S. promotional CDs.

Sting – The Soul Cages (A&M 75021 7457 2) Rare U.S. 1991 promotional CD album.

Hornsby, Bruce – Harbor Lights (RCA RJC 66230-2) U.S. 1993 promotional CD album.

Costello, Elvis – Mighty Like a Rose (Warner Brothers 9 26593-2) U.S. 1991 limited edition CD.

May, Brian – Driven by You (Hollywood PRCD-10273-2) U.S. 1993 promotional CD-single.

Fordham, Julia – Manhattan Skyline (Virgin PRCDJULIA) U.S. 1989 promotional CD sampler.

Plant, Robert – Ship of Fools (WEA A9281CD 796 611-2) German 1988 CD5 box.

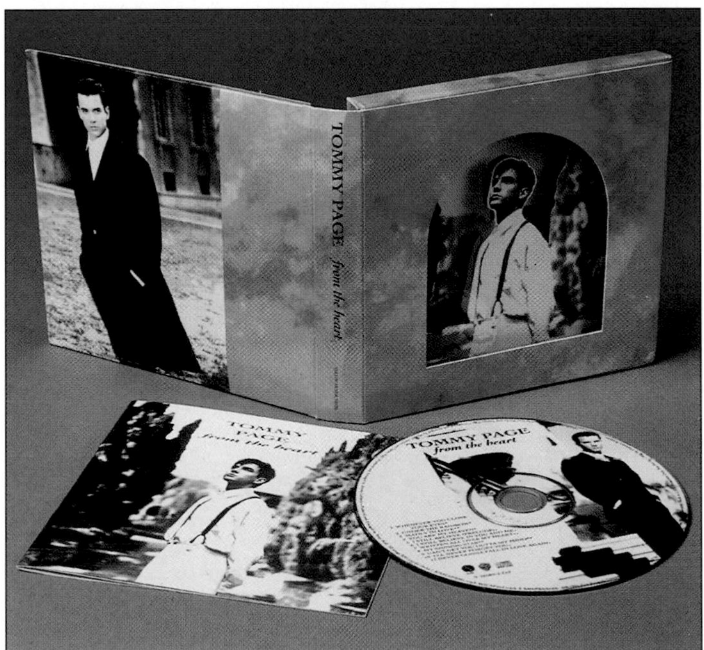

Page, Tommy – From the Heart (Sire 2-26683-2-DJ) U.S. 1991 promotional CD album.

Great White – Hooked (Capitol CDP 7 95330 2) U.S. 1991 promotional CD album.

Rhino Atlantic – Remasters (Rhino/AtlanticPRO2 98120) U.S. 1992 promotional two CD sampler.

Foreigner – Low Down and Dirty (Atlantic PRCD 3999-2) U.S. 1991 promotional CD-single.

Led Zeppelin – Stairway to Heaven 20th Anniversary (Atlantic PRCD 4424-2) U.S. 1992 promotional CD-single.

Church, The – Sometime Anywhere (Arista 18729-2) U.S. 1994 promotional two CD album.

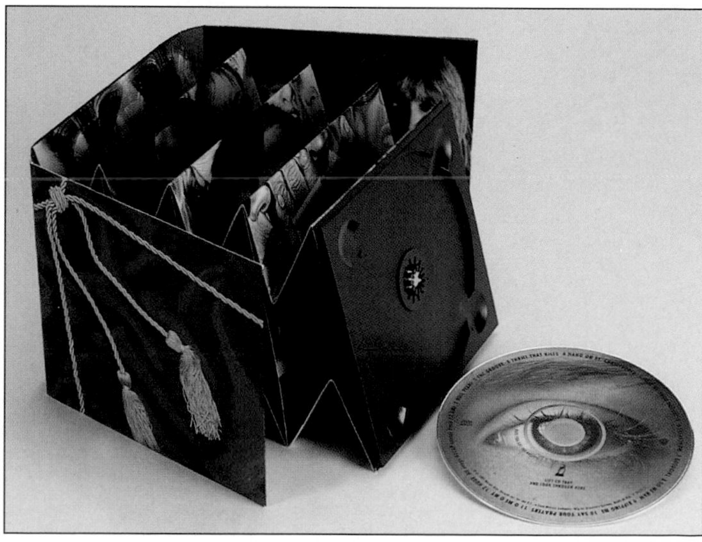

Bullet Boys – Freakshow (Warner Brothers 9 26537-2) U.S. limited edition CD.

Chic – Chic-sm (Warner Brothers 9 26394-2-DJ) U.S. promotional CD album.

Siouxsie and the Banshees – Superstition (Geffen GEFCD-24387DJ) U.S. promotional CD album.

Vixen – How Much Love (EMI DPRO04541) U.S. 1990 promotional CD-single.

Phat Trax (Rhino PRCD 7071) U.S. 1994 promotional CD sampler.

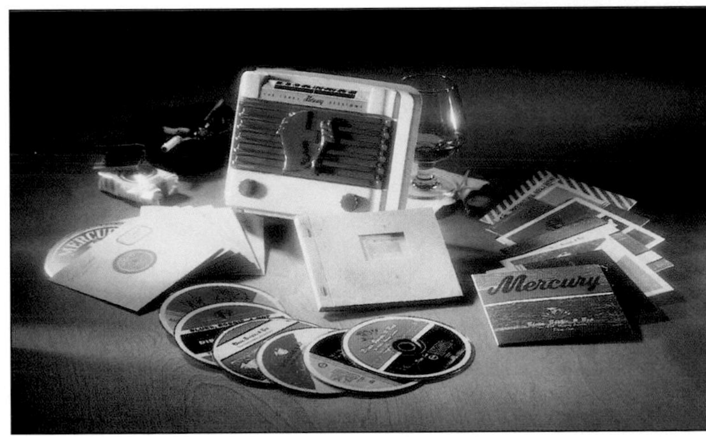

'40s Mercury Sessions: Blues Boogie & Bop (Verve 314 525 609-1) U.S. 1995 limited edition 7 CD package.

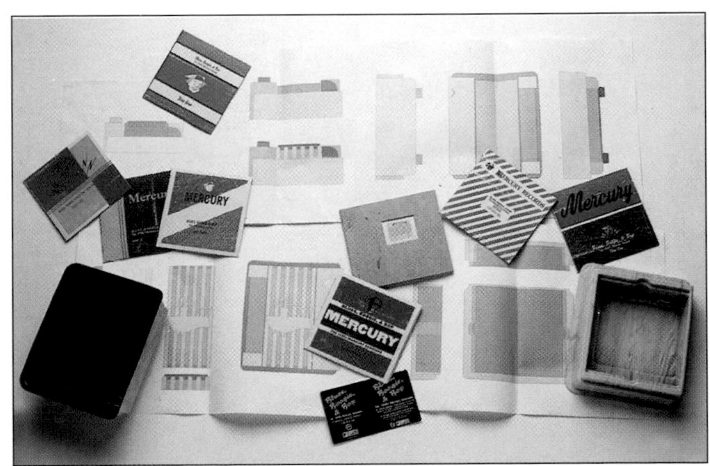

'40s Mercury Sessions: Blues Boogie & Bop (Verve) This ambitious design, created by Giulio Turturro, Michael Lang, and David Lau, was computer created. The designs were then made into molds from which the radio package was formed. Shown are computer-generated layout profiles of the radio package's various components.

Hendrix, Jimi – Lifelines (Reprise 9 26435-2) U.S. 1990 out-of-print four CD boxed set.

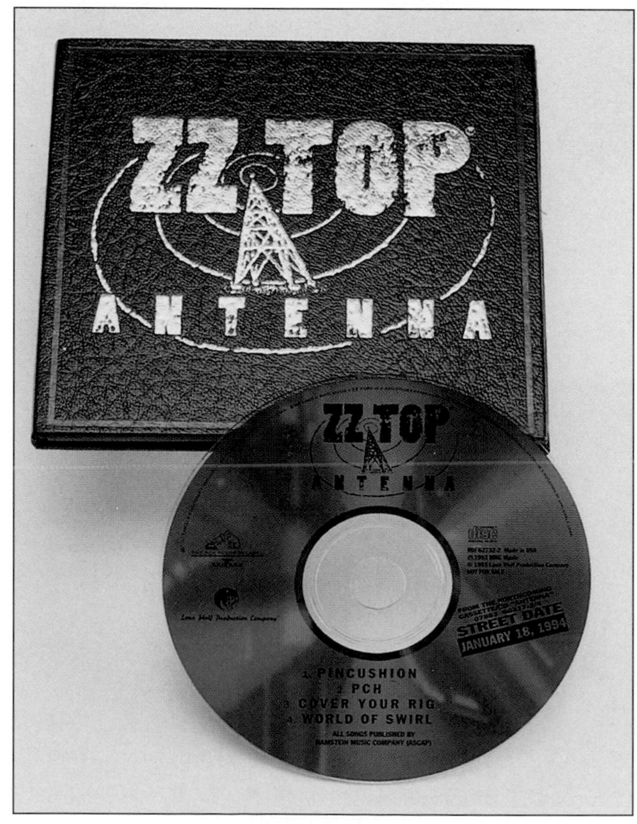

ZZ Top – Antenna (RCA RDJ 62732-2) U.S. 1990 promotional CD sampler.

Jackson, Janet – Rhythm Nation (A&M CD 3920) U.S. 1989 promotional CD album.

Michael, George – Faith (Epic CSK 2850) U.S. 1987 promotional CD album. Any early example of CD special packaging.

Queen – Rocks Volume Box (Hollywood) Rare 1991 promotional four CD boxed set. Each disc was released separately as was the box.

Queensryche – Empire (EMI CDP-7-92806-2) U.S. 1990 promotional CD album.

ZZ Top – Recycler (Warner Brothers 9 26458-2) U.S. 1990 limited edition CD.

Jones, Rickie Lee – Flying Cowboys (Geffen 2-24246-2-DJ) U.S. 1989 promotional CD album.

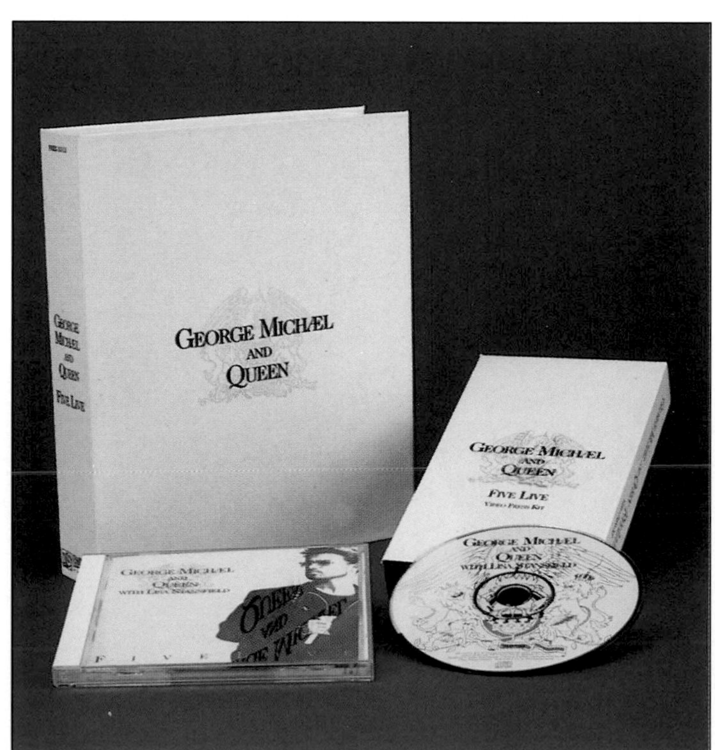

Michael, George and Queen – Five Live (Hollywood PRBX-10313) U.S. 1993 promotional CD album.

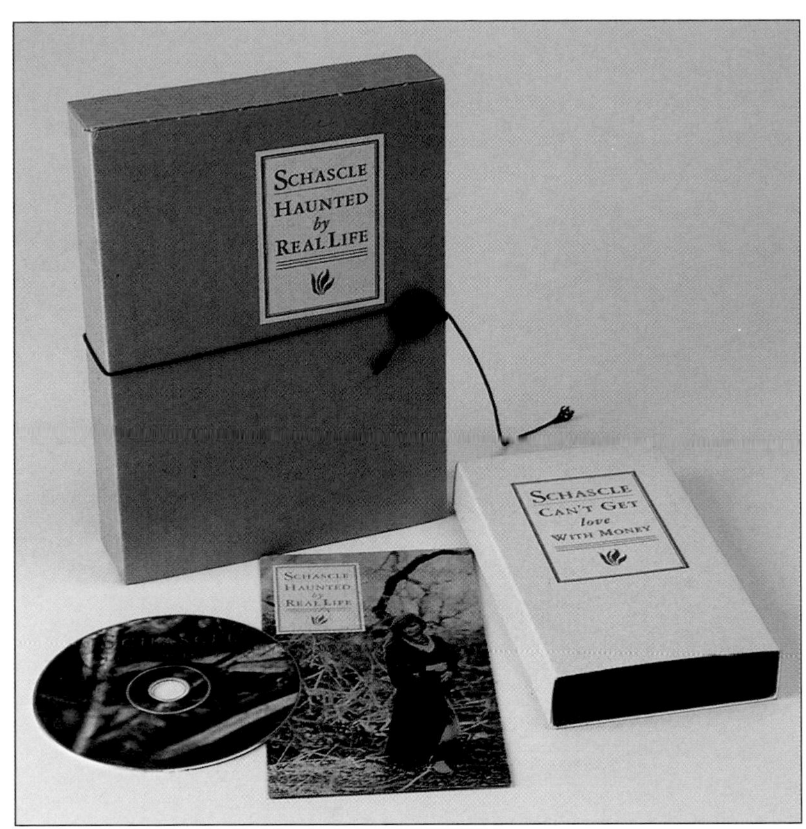

Schascle – Haunted by Real Life (Reprise 9 26510-2-DJ) U.S. 1991 promotional CD album.

Queen – Box of Tricks (Queen Productions Ltd. CDQTEL 0001) U.K. 1992 limited edition CD album. Was sold only via mail order.

Deadicated (Arista ARCD-8669) U.S. 1991 promotional CD album.

Whitesnake – Slip of the Tongue (Geffen 2-24249-DJ) U.S. 1989 promotional CD album.

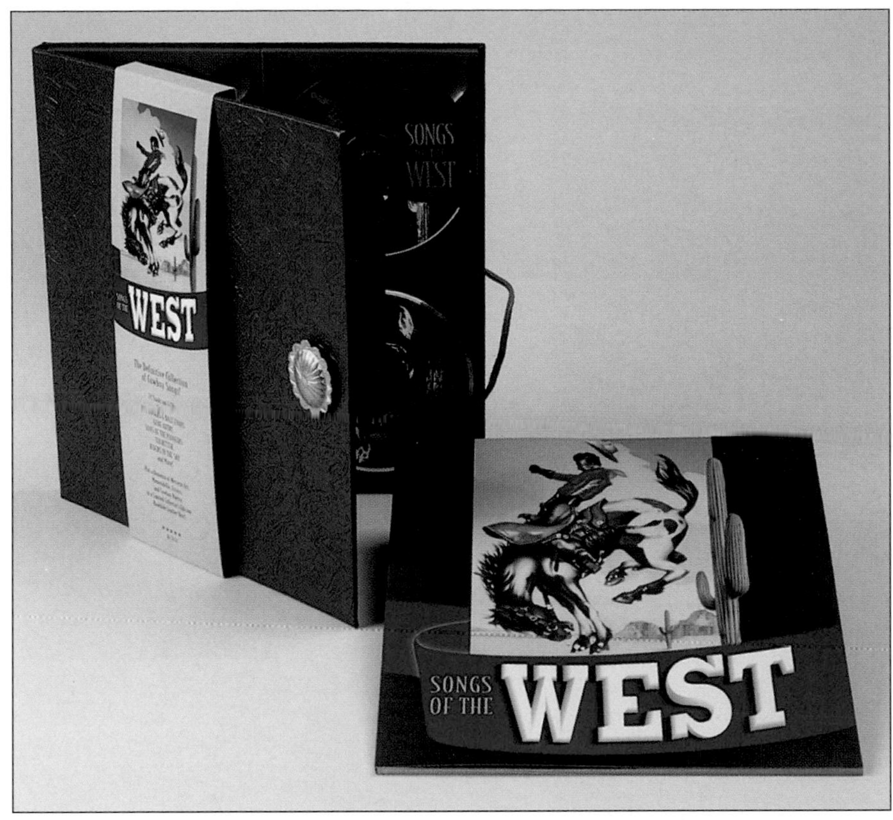

Songs of the Old West (Rhino R2 71451) U.S. 1993 limited edition CD album.

Iron Maiden – The First Ten Years (EMI TOCP-6181-90) Rare Japanese 1990 limited edition 10 CD set.

Hendrix, Jimi – Band of Gypsys (Capitol DPRO-79534) U.S. 1995 promotional CD sampler.

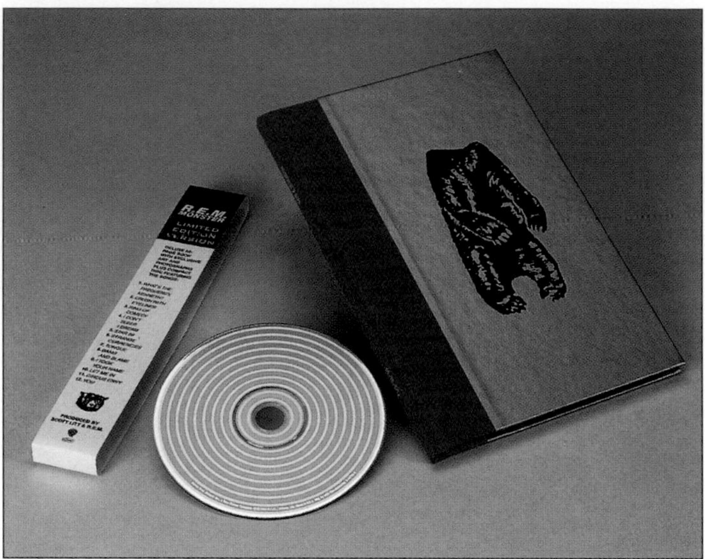

R.E.M. – Monster (Warner Brothers 9 45783-2) U.S. 1994 limited edition CD.

Costello, Elvis – Rykodisc Special Promotional Editions U.S. 1995 promotional CD album.

Browne, Jackson – Retrospective/Three From I'm Alive (Elektra PRCD 8851-2) U.S. 1994 promotional CD sampler.

Zappa, Frank – You Can't Do That On Radio Anymore (Rykodisc) This 1990 promotional sampler is rare because of its packaging. The black digi-pak had problems so very few were made. Many copies of this disc were distributed in plain jewel boxes as well as being reissued in Rykodisc's trademarked green jewel boxes in 1994.

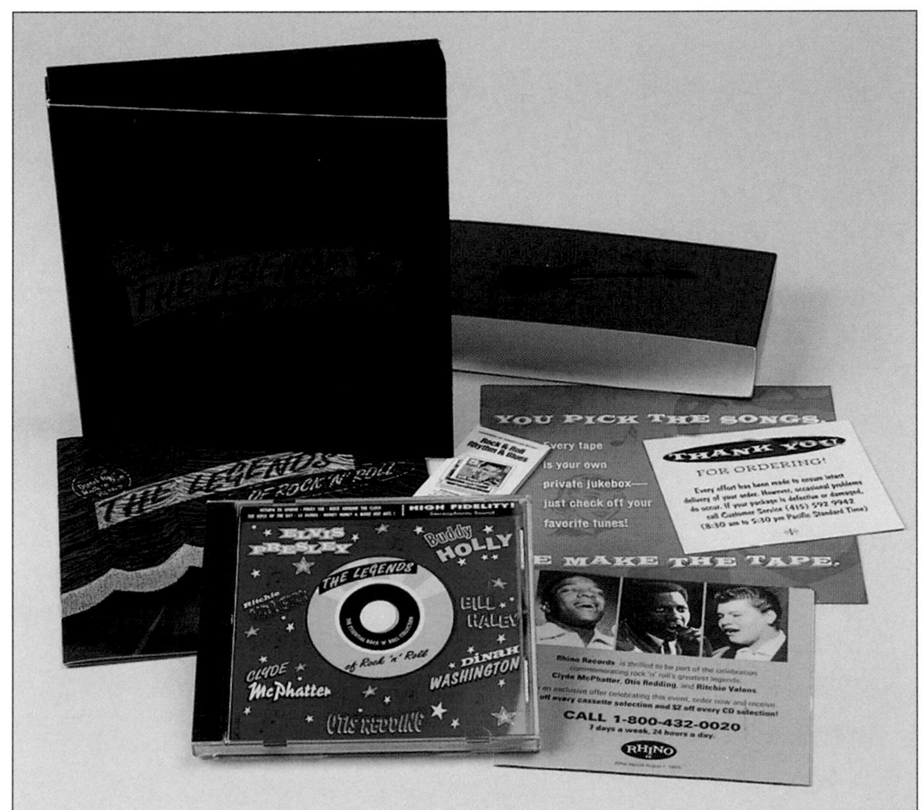

Legends of Rock 'N' Roll (Warner/U.S. Postal Service DMC 1-1100) U.S. 1994 limited edition CD.

Rolling Stones – Collection (Virgin) U.S. 1994 limited edition CD series.

Wood, Ronnie – Like it (Continuum 12211-2) U.S. 1994 promotional CD-single.

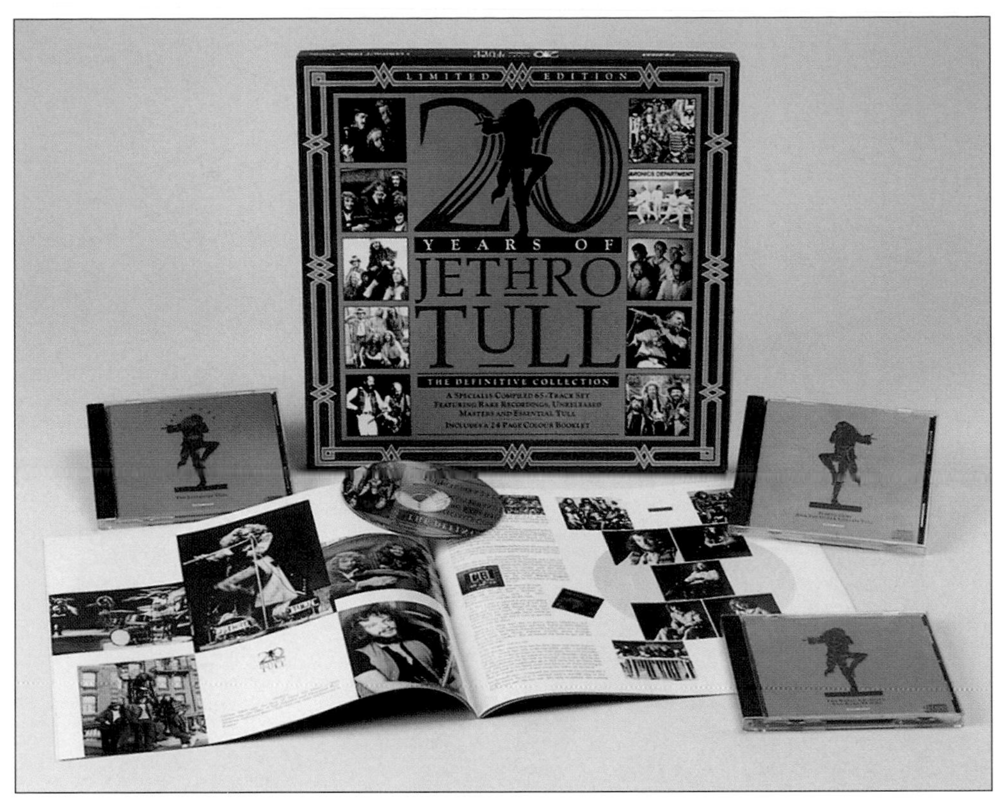

Jethro Tull – 20th Anniversary Box Set (Chrysalis) U.S.† 1993 limited edition four CD boxed set.

Horne, Lena – We'll Be Together Again (Blue Note CDP 7243 8 28974 2 2) U.S. 1994 promotional CD album.

Jobim, Antonio Carlos – The Man from Ipanema (Verve 314 525 880-2)

Bon Jovi – These Days (Mercury 314 528 181-2) U.S. 1995 promotional CD album.

Sinatra, Frank – Complete Reprise Studio Recordings Sampler (Reprise) Super rare promotional CD sampler for the 20 CD limited edition boxed set.

Hammer – Too Legit to Quit (Capitol C2-98083) U.S. 1991 limited edition CD album.

Congos, The – Heart of the Congos (Blood and Fire BAFCD 009) U.S. 1996 limited edition two CD set. The commonly available version contains only one disc.

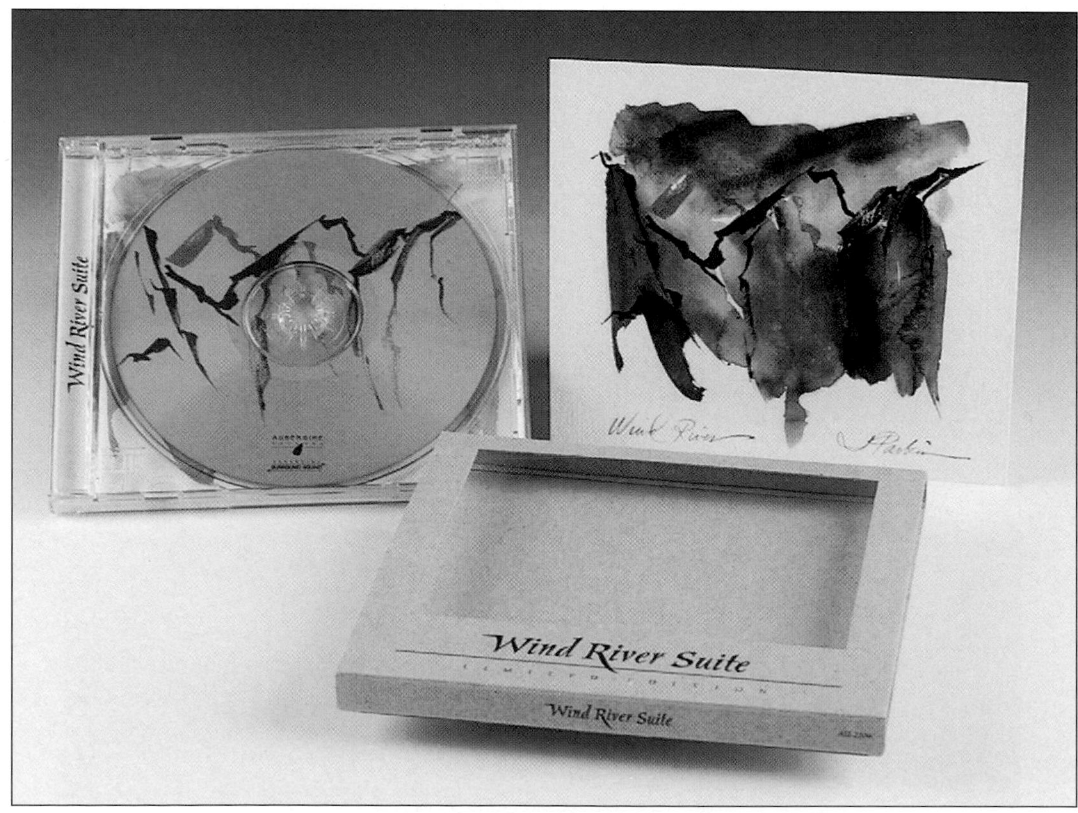

De Azevedo, Lex – Wind River Suite (Aubergine AU2206) U.S. 1995 limited edition CD.

Cheap Trick – Woke Up with a Monster (Warner Brothers 9 45425-2) U.S. 1994 promotional CD album.

McEntire, Reba – Starting Over (MCA MCA3P-3543) U.S. 1995 promotional CD album.

Beatles, The – Anthology Sampler (Capitol DPRO-10289) U.S. 1995 promotional CD sampler.

In Celebration (Warner Music Group) U.S. 1993 promotional two CD sampler.

Savoy Jazz – Limited Edition Series (Savoy Records) U.S. 1996 limited edition CD.

Misfits: Box-Set and Sampler (Caroline) Limited edition boxed set and promotional sampler.

Ryuichi Sakamoto – Playing the Orchestra (Virgin 91002-2) U.S. 1990 limited edition CD.

Guns N' Roses – GN'R Lies (Warner/Pioneer 37PZ-2400) Japanese 1988 limited edition CD album.

Simon, Paul – Rhythm of the Saints (Warner Brothers 9 26098-2-DJ) U.S. 1990 promotional CD album.

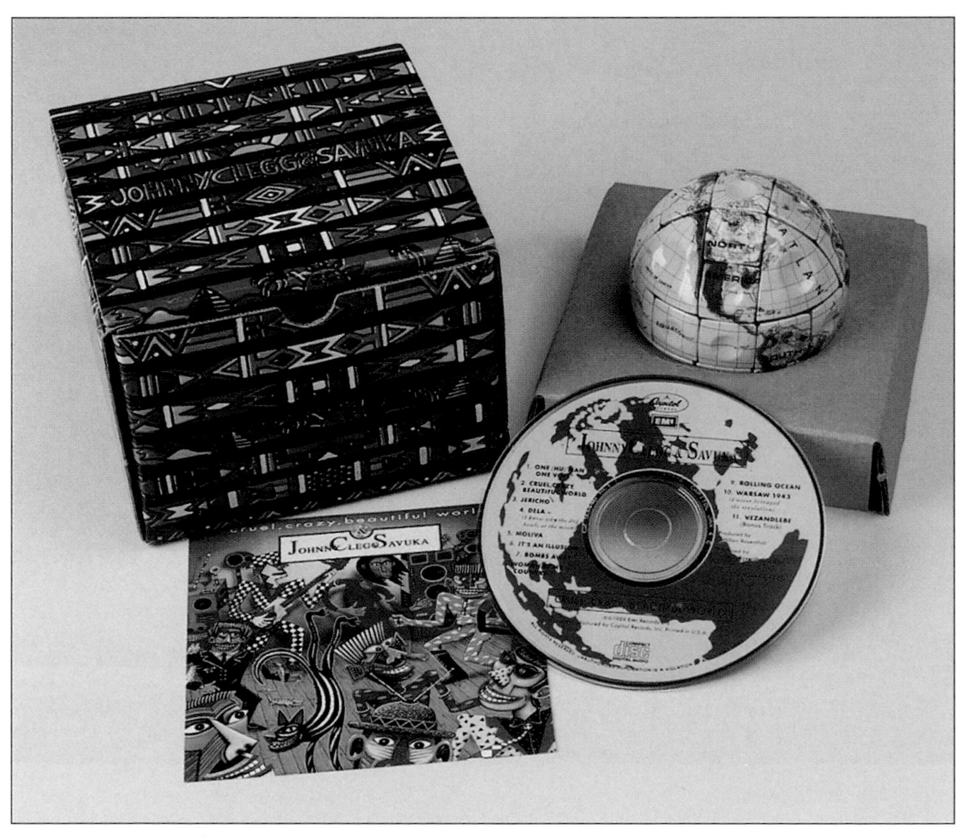

Clegg, Johnny & Savuka – Cruel, Crazy, Beautiful World (Capitol) U.S. 1989 promotional CD album.

Queen – Made in Heaven (Hollywood HR-62017-2) U.S. 1995 promotional CD album with Queen logo on the tray spine.

Queen – The Ultimate Collection (EMI QUEENBOX 20) Rare U.K. 1995 20 picture disc CD set housed in a large wood wall hanging unit. The discs were printed using the high quality off-set printing process attaining paper printing resolution of 150lpi. The pictures on the discs are of the covers of the respective albums. This package was limited to 4800 copies.

Collector's Guide to Buying and Selling Compact Discs

Buying CDs

If you are a new collector, you may be asking yourself, where in the world can I find all these cool CDs. As said before, compact discs are sold through two markets; primary and secondary.

Buying New CDs

The primary market, better known as the retail market is where discs manufactured for retail sale follow the sales chain — manufacturer to distributor to retailer to consumer. This is also the first sale of the disc at a retail price, defined by the mark-up from manufacturing costs, business costs, as well as profit margins. The retail market is important for collectors because many now rare and collectible CDs have their origins there. The retail market might have been where the CD was available at the lowest price.

As discussed, most CDs begin their life at the retail level. Most markets have four types of music stores: retail chain CD stores, independent CD retailers, department stores, and electronic stores. Comparison shopping different records may seem to be a wasted effort, because unless that store carries used or collectible CDs, most record stores all have the same product. But what about price? Granted, the labels are facing a price fixing anti-trust suit, fear not, if you put the effort in, you can get a lot more for your money. The identical CD can be found at different prices. Each store has a unique pricing structure. In fact, a single disc title can have a price difference of as much as $7–8 depending on the store. Research each store and determine which store charges what prices for CDs. You will probably find the most competitive pricing in new, front-line CDs and boxed sets. As previously mentioned, department and electronics stores often carry CDs as loss leaders and can be the best source for new releases at unbelievable prices. Electronics stores however, do not carry a very deep catalog of titles, so if you looking for an old or obscure title, you probably will only find it at a record store. Also, look at used CD stores. Most used CDs sell for $8 or less, making them great values. Chain stores usually have the best price on "budget-line" CDs since they can get larger discounts because they buy more product. If you collect limited editions, check out independent record stores. They tend to be more competitive in these areas than the larger chains who tend to charge full retail price. Remember, the best thing to do is to become familiar with all your local record stores and become familiar with their pricing structure for each tier: front-line, catalog, boxed set, budget-line, and limited edition. If you are savvy enough, you can find many hidden treasures at unbeatable prices.

Buying Collectible CDs

The secondary market, better known as the used or collectors' market, encompass all other types of CD transactions. The secondary market place involves selling used and promo CDs through stores and record conventions or between collectors. The secondary market is where collectors typically conduct most of their business. It is also the market that establishes the value of CDs based solely on worth rather than manufacturing costs and the like.

Collectible CDs are not very difficult to find. Independent record stores that carry used as well as new CDs can be a good source. These stores often carry promos, imports, rare, and out-of-print discs. Even some national chain stores may have a few treasures buried in their racks. For example, I found a rare, out-of-print, sealed copy of Paul McCartney's *Tug of War* on the Columbia label at a large chain store for about $10, now worth about $40. Many chain stores also carry import CDs and CD-singles. Record shows and conventions are usually the best source. These shows usually have many dealers that specialize in such collectible CDs. Trade magazines carry ads for collectible CDs that can be purchased via mail order. In addition, classifieds in these trade papers enable buyers to seek particular items of interest to them.

Selling CDs

Selling CDs is literally an art form. If you are interested in selling a few or all of your discs, there are a few things to keep in mind to get the most out of them. You must weigh the pros and cons from who you want to sell to and what you are willing to trade-off to sell to that group.

There are generally two groups of buyers: resellers and collectors or customers. Resellers are your local record stores or dealers who trade in collectible discs. One reason for selling to resellers is they are generally easy to sell to. Often, they will take your junk as well as your good discs. Also, by selling to a dealer you can get rid of your discs at one time, not wait for customers to come and buy a disc. This certainly saves you time and trouble. Dealers sometimes offer cash, offer trade, or offer both. The rule of thumb however, if you opt for the trade option, you will get about 30% more for your discs than if you want cash. The drawback to selling to a dealer is they will pay at most half of what the disc would be worth to a customer or collector. This is in consideration for the time and effort you save. The reseller must now wait until a customer comes by and purchases a disc. This requires time and effort on the dealer's part. Not to mention, dealers are in this business to make a living and must make some profit off the sale of your traded discs.

One helpful hint in selling your CDs is if you have many discs to sell the conventional wisdom is to sell them all at once to balance the bad with the good. Try instead to unload as much "junk" to as many different dealers that sell used CDs as possible. You will probably get almost nothing for them, but it might be something, and more importantly, you will discover how each dealer buys CDs. Then trade in you best CDs with whatever you have left over. You will probably get the same deal with less junk as with more junk. You will be much farther ahead in terms of knowledge for the next time you want to trade since you are now aware of the buying practices of your local dealers.

Selling CDs directly to consumers or collectors would certainly be the preferred method. This is because customers will pay a much higher price than dealers. Selling CDs to collectors however, takes a lot of time and effort. Most of us are unwilling to put in that time. If you are so inclined, the best way to do it is to either buy a table at your local record convention or to place an ad in one of the music collector's trade papers, like *Goldmine* or *Discoveries* magazines.

Investment

Because collecting CDs is so new, they are probably the world's best current collectible investment. Just about every collectible field, from baseball cards to comic books, is saturated with both product and knowledge. It becomes harder and harder to see huge percentage increases in the value of anything. You will notice that there are many CDs, especially promotional CD-singles that are only worth $2–3. It can be argued that these CDs have little value, which if looking merely at the price is certainly true. However, I like to think of these prices as potential. First of all, its pretty good making $3 from something that cost nothing, because promotional singles are given away free. Second, paying $3 for a CD is certainly a good value. But if that CD increases in value over the next 10 years, even just to $6, you've doubled your money. If the disc increases to $50 or $100, you've hit the jackpot. On the other end, if the disc is eventually worth only $2 or $3, you're not out any substantial investment. Of course the trick is to predict which CDs will become valuable in the next 10 to 20 years. And that of course is anybody's guess.

Also realize, it will take almost 20 years to see how the value of CDs pan out. But I can guarantee, this is the time to buy. Music has always been collectible and CDs are going out of print every day. This is the perfect combination, not to mention the fact that the hobby is so new that not everyone has caught on yet. This is a rare opportunity to literally find gold for pennies. You should take advantage of this because within the next fifteen years this opportunity will be gone.

Condition

Because CDs and their plastic jewel box cases have the perception of being indestructible, the conventional thinking is that they are less susceptible to damage and thus condition not as important. Like everything else, CDs are not indestructible — condition is always of paramount importance when it comes to collectibles. Often times, a collectible that is more susceptible to damage will generally command a higher price than a collectible that is less susceptible to damage. Condition is applied to two aspects of the CD as well as all other optically recorded media. First, condition of the disc itself and second, condition of the disc's packaging.

A CD is certainly a durable media that can resist substantial handling. The most common marks found on the CD are fingerprints and scratches, particularly on the read side of the CD. Most often, these marks do not affect the playability of the disc, but to collectors, it is more aesthetic aspects of the disc that are important. Visible scratches and to a lesser extent fingerprints (because fingerprints can be removed) substantially lessen the value of the disc.

How condition applies to packaging is a very important aspect of CD collecting. There are generally two categories of CD packaging. The first are unique containers like digipak-type packages, or some type of box usually comprising of cardboard or some other material. The second is the traditional jewel box.

Condition, as it relates to unique containers, tends to be obvious. Because of record, comic book, and baseball card collecting, we have a lot of experience with the importance of taking care of paper packaging products as it relates to value. Obviously, when the paper is subjected to physical damage, grease from fingerprints, or environmental exposure like ink fading from the sun or water damage, the value of the product can be substantially impaired. Inspect the package for dented corners, wear on the bottom and sides, creases in the cardboard, and price stickers put directly on a collectible cardboard CD package.

A lesser talked about issue with condition is the jewel box and the paper sleeves contained in the jewel box. Most discussions on condition as it relates to the jewel box has been that condition is not important because the jewel box is replaceable and the paper sleeves are protected by the jewel box. This however is not at all true. Simply take a look at some of the discs in your collection. First, looking at the jewel box itself, it is true that the jewel box is replaceable giving collectors a real advantage, but some forms of the jewel box are not. For instance, today many jewel boxes are embossed or painted with graphics making the jewel box unique to that title and are not replaceable. These boxes should be treated in the same manner as other special packaging made from cardboard. Another aspect of jewel box condition is the rarely talked about "first issue" standard jewel boxes available only from 1982 up to about 1986. These early jewel boxes are easily distinguished from standard jewel boxes available today by examining the top or bottom edge portion of the box's lid. Notice that with all the single disc jewel boxes available today, the edges are "corrugated." Before 1986, these edges were "frosted." It is therefore, easy to determine if those early CDs had their jewel boxes replaced. Often you will find an original issue disc in a corrugated-lid jewel box. As a result, those early discs in the frosted-lid jewel box are more valuable than those same discs replaced by a corrugated-lid jewel box.[66] Also, the condition of the frosted-lid jewel box becomes an issue because they are not replaceable. The fewer scratches, mars, and crazes on the box the more valuable it is.

The second aspect to jewel box condition is the front card or

Starburst (left), UPC punch (center), and Sawcut (right). These markings do not substantially diminish the value of the CD.

booklet and tray card sleeves. Conventional thinking is that because the sleeves are protected behind the plastic of the jewel box, their condition rarely comes into issue. This, however, is far from true. First, the back tray card is where the most hidden damage occurs. In manufacturing, the jewel box tray sandwiches the card between itself and the base, most often done by machine. This process can create folded corners, and crushed lateral edges of the folded over spine portion, occur as a result. Water damage and fading have also been known to appear on the back tray card as well.

Front booklets or card sleeves are another issue. The most frequent damage to these are oil stains from fingerprints on the surface of the sleeve and crimping on the edges. If you find a title having a front booklet that is black with a glossy coating and pull it from the lid with your fingers, you will often find your fingerprints on the booklet created by the oil from your skin. This occurs to some extent to all booklets but it is most apparent on black paper having a gloss coating. The second aspect is crimping to the edge of the front booklet sleeve. Crimping is a type of damage that occurs

Jewel boxes, regardless of how well they protect the disc and booklets, can also do great damage. Inside the lower circles illustrates "crimping" where the booklet does not slide in properly between the tabs and the inside portion of the front lid. When the jewel box is closed an indentation of the tab is crushed into the booklet. Machinery at the pressing plants where the booklet and jewel box is assembled do not allow this to happen. This condition usually occurs when the booklet is pulled in and out carelessly. Always make sure the booklet is properly placed inside the jewel box. Value can be substantially decreased if the booklets have crimps. Also the nodule or bars that prevent the booklet from sliding out of the jewel box lid can also create an indentation if it is allowed to crush against the booklet (see inside ovals at right). Make sure the booklet is slid all the way to the end of the jewel box lid before closing. (But not too far, if the booklet is thin it might slide between the back of the front lid and tray causing the booklet to crease.) The back tray card, though not subject to as much handling as the front tray card, can still suffer damage. Turned-over edged, etc can occur at the spines also substantially affecting value.

when the sleeve is not properly placed in the lid portion of the jewel box. Normally, the sleeve is affixed to the lid of the jewel box by a series of tabs on top and bottom spines of the lid. The sleeve slides between these tabs and the inside face. When the sleeve however, is not inserted properly, it can be crushed by that tab when the jewel box is closed thereby creating a "crimp" in the booklet. These crimps can cause substantial damage to the front sleeve and decrease the value of the disc as a whole.

Other aspects of the paper packaging and sleeve condition are manufacturing flaws like misregistration (color misalignment creating unintentional gaps on the paper). These flaws are outside the control of the collector. However, look for misregistration on the sleeves before purchasing the disc.

I must note that it has been common practice in the CD collecting community not to list condition grading. This is changing however and CD collectors are beginning to appreciate the importance of condition.

Many cardboard sleeve containers suffer from ring wear, a condition that creates an outline of the disc through the sleeve and a wearing away of the ink. Inside the circled areas, you can see the prominence of the disc's outline. On the sides you can see how the black ink is beginning to wear away leaving scratches. This condition is most often caused by many cardboard sleeves being stored next to each other, thereby touching and rubbing up against each other. The pressure and friction between the sleeves causes the cardboard to crease and the ink to be worn away.

Grading Definitions

Condition is generally broken down into five categories: mint, mint minus, very good, good, poor.

Mint (M)

This grade indicates perfect condition.

Disc — No scratches or fingerprints on either the print side or read side of the disc.

Packaging — No crimps, marks, folds, or tears on the front booklet or back tray card. If the disc is contained in a special package, that package must also be in perfect condition — no dented corners, tears, fingerprints, bent edges, scratches, water damage, fading, or sticker price labels. Note that a "sealed" copy does not necessarily mean a "mint" copy. The disc inside may be mint but the outer packaging, especially if cardboard, can suffer damage and wear, regardless of the shrink wrap. Make sure that you inspect the package carefully.

Mint Minus (M-)

Disc — A disc in this condition is nearly mint except for minor wear or bends on the booklet, or one or two very light, subtle scratches on the CD. The difference between mint and mint minus tends to be very gray. The value of a disc in this condition is about 95% of its mint counterpart.

Packaging — Very slight wear on the packaging. No tears, dents, water damage, or fading, and only very slightly dented corners on the packaging or sleeves.

Very Good (VG)

This grade indicates visible wear on both the booklet and the disc.

Disc — Visible scratches on the read side of the disc but not significant enough to hamper play.

Packaging — Visible crimps on the booklet sleeve, slight fading, very minor water damage, and bent or rounded corners with slight tears characterize VG discs. These discs are worth about 50% to 70% of a mint copy. Many times this grade is accompanied by a (+) or (-) further narrowing a disc's condition. Nevertheless, the value is still in the 50% to 70% range. Radio shows especially, that have been aired, tend to show wear indicative of this category.

Good (G)

This is the lowest quality grade that has appreciable value.

Disc — CDs show obvious signs of use and often abuse. The discs have noticeable scratches on the read side but are still playable.

Packaging — Booklets have signs of major wear including crimps, tears, bends, water damage, and fading. These discs are only worth 10% to 20% of their mint value.

Poor (P)

Disc — Discs in this category have deep scratches and other marks making them excellent Frisbees, book marks, and drink coasters. Often times the discs suffer from dropouts and skips when played.

Packaging — The booklets are mangled and torn, if included at all. Significant water damage and fading are also indicative of this condition.

Cleaning and Storing CDs

There are many products on the market for cleaning and storing CDs. While many are good, some may actually be detrimental to your CDs. Rather than reviewing specific products, the following guidelines are provided for keeping CDs looking good and playing well.

• When cleaning CDs, never use an alcohol or other solvent-based cleaner. Solvents can be harmful to the disc and may craze (turn the plastic cloudy white), or dissolve the protective layer.

• Never use any polishes or sand papers that can scratch the disc. The tolerance of a compact disc is very precise and its thickness critical. Polishing the plastic surface with an abrasive to remove a scratch may reduce the thickness and possibly destroy a CD's playability.

• To clean a heavily soiled CD, use mild liquid dish soap, dionized or distilled water, and a soft cloth. Mix a little dish soap with water and apply this solution to the CD using a cloth. Clean off any dirt or fingerprints being careful to wipe outward, perpendicular to the disc's center (never radially around the disc). Rinse with pure water, then carefully pat dry with a clean dry cloth.

The jewel box is currently the best protection for the CD. The teeth on the hub of the tray suspend the disc so there is nothing that touching the read side of the disc preventing scratches. The base and lid help protect the disc. Digipaks and other similar packages having a tray with a hub, can protect in the same manner as the jewel box.

Plastic, paper, or cardboard CD sleeves have an advantage over jewel cases in that they require substantially less space. On the other hand, the CD can get fingerprinted when removed or replaced and this can be detrimental to the surface of the disc. Sleeves certainly won't harm them in terms of playability, but if keeping the surface of the disc in mint condition is of paramount importance, it might be best to remove the disc from its sleeve and place it in a jewel box. Not only will this prevent the disc from becoming increasingly marred when repeatedly removed from the sleeve, but it will also protect the condition of the sleeve itself from ring wear (similar to what occurs with record sleeves over time). Also, because the discs are thicker in relation to the sleeve than records or even laser discs, the CDs tend to crease the sleeve and create ring wear faster than on an LP.

For those of us who do not have the space or resources to place all of your discs that come in cardboard sleeves in plastic jewel boxes, there are some things that can be done to mitigate damage to the discs and the sleeves. First, if you have a disc that you use quite often, you may want to take only that one disc and put it in a jewel box. For the others, put the cardboard sleeves in acid-free plastic protective outer sleeves. This will reduce friction between sleeves, thus reducing wear. Also, store the discs upright keeping minimum pressure on the sides of the sleeve to help prevent creasing a ring on the sleeve from the corners of the disc.

Regardless of packaging, CDs should be stored in a dry place at room temperature. Like most collectibles, it is best to keep discs and their packaging away from direct sunlight to prevent the inks from fading.

How to Use this Guide

The subsequent listing portion of this guide is organized into six sections based on disc content and disc format. Those sections are — Artists, Various Artists, Soundtracks, Series Discs, Theatrical Lasers, and Miscellaneous Discs. The Artist section is comprised of virtually any disc format[67] where the content is identifiable by a particular artist. This includes artists from virtually every audio and video category except for classical. The Various Artists section, like the Artists section, is comprised of all audio and video categories. However, these discs qualify for this section because they cannot be identified by a single artist, rather they are compilations by many artists. The Soundtracks section, as the name implies, consists of soundtracks from movies and television programs, including compilations. This section, however contains more than just soundtracks, there are also audio books and multimedia CD-ROM press kits, usually, but not exclusively, from popular films. The Series Discs section contains discs released periodically having little range in value from discs to disc. Because these discs tend not to be very distinguishable from disc to disc, only the title of an entire series of discs is listed. These discs are most often promo in-store play series, magazine samplers, CD-ROM magazines, and monthly sampler series. The Miscellaneous Discs section is for discs, that by nature of either their format or content, do not easily fit into one of the aforementioned sections. Most often these discs are part of a group of discs that are not necessarily collectible but a particular title is. For example the Miscellaneous titles include CD-ROMs, CD-ROM games, demonstration discs, and cross-collectibles like discs packaged with action figures, toy cars, and comic books.

Valuing Discs

Value can be summed up by the following adage. CDs are only worth what someone is willing to pay for them. The values listed herein are average values for the CD. They are not, and this is important, exact values for a disc. We search all over the world to determine what a particular disc is worth. Then we establish a realistic single value average. We think this is the best way to assign values in a hobby that is so new. The values of discs in the market these days are so volatile that creating an average is very difficult. Values of any particular disc can change dramatically over a six month period — maybe the groups popularity skyrockets or plummets, or maybe some other intangible force drives the prices for a period of time. As a result, the most important thing to understand with these values is do not necessarily expect to see the exact same price on the disc if you see it at a record store or show. Because these values are averages, expect to see prices in the real world either higher or lower than the average in the book. It is your responsibility, by examining the disc, to determine if that value, based the average value paid by other collectors, is what you are willing to pay. No dealer or record store has any obligation to adhere to the values listed in the guide, and in fact, probably won't.

Everything listed in this guide is for discs in mint. And because the market is so new we could literally assign every disc listed herein a rage of $1 to $100, but this won't do anybody any good. So keep in mind the deductions in value noted in the Condition section of this guide. It is up to you to qualitatively examine the item you find, compare its listed price and condition to the value for a mint copy listed in here.

Remember, prices established on the secondary market are based on supply and demand, not manufacturing costs and markups like in the primary market. While this is true, retail price does influence us suggesting a base value when offering the discs for sale for the first time. For example, most CD5s on the secondary market are valued at about $5 to $6 which is about their retail price. This is because the CD5 is so new to the secondary market that retailers use the $5 as an arbitrary point at which to place the CD5 for the first time. You may also notice that many LP CDs are valued at $14 for the disc in its long box and $8 for the disc without long box. As you probably guess, the $14 reflects the cost of the disc new, and $8 reflects the average used CD price. Again, this is because this is the first time these discs have appeared on the secondary market and their value needs to start somewhere. Also, the value of many of these discs are determined at the retail and used CD market. They are so new and many collectors have yet to discover them, that they can still be easily found in these markets (i.e. opportunity for the perceptive collector to find some real treasures).

Laser Discs

Lasers are nothing less of a nightmare to value. Some discs are easy, they are so rare that their substantial value is obvious. However, laser discs, in the current climate are only valuable as long as a subsequent remastered pressing doesn't come along. In that case, the value of the original pressing plummets. Occasionally, the subsequent pressing is missing material from the older pressing. In that case, the first pressing retains some value.

But most often, the range of value is so great that I'm sure there will always be some who will be critical of any value, high or low, from any price guide. As case in point, DiscoVision discs are sold by some dealers as rare collectibles commanding at least $100 for even the most common title. Other, equally knowledgeable dealers believe that because most DiscoVision discs have so many defects and most have been reissued anyway, they should be valued at less than $12. Moreover, equally knowledgeable dealers don't even buy or sell DiscoVision because they are so defective.

Most out-of-print titles average in value around their retail price or double their retail price if a popular film. Disney movies tend to triple in value once the disc has been moratorialized and supply at retail has dwindled. But of course this is only for about seven to nine years until the disc is rereleased. B movies seem to be the laser disc collectors' favorites. And because they are only released for limited periods of time, they always command big bucks. Collectors also love special laser disc editions that contain bonus material that for some reason, had to be recalled. This is what happened to Criterion collection CAV versions of the James Bond films — *Dr. No, From Russia with Love*, and *Goldfinger*. These discs had certain supplementary material that needed to be deleted, so the discs were recalled and replaced with CLV versions, without the supplementary material. Obviously, these discs are quite valuable.

Laser discs, like the other disc collectibles, are valued by taking the average of the real prices. But don't look for dealers to have the exact prices listed in this guide, they will either be a bit higher or a bit lower. With lasers, the spread in values is so great that the buyer must especially evaluate how valuable the disc is to him or her to determine if the price offered is reasonable.

Disc List Legend

The primary method of disc identification for every section is by artist, title, and disc type for the Artist A to Z section, and by title and disc type for all other sections. Other information like label, catalog number, year and notes further identifies the disc to greater precision.

Artist

This entry found only in the Artist A to Z section is the first degree of organization for this section.

Title

Obviously, this entry is the disc title or series title. You will notice that there might be many titles under the same artist with the same name. These are not duplicates but rather they are different discs having the same title. For example, as we examined earlier, many European CD-single releases are issued in two versions. They appear in the listing having the same title. They can be distinguished by their different catalog number, or if the catalog number is not available by the designation (Second version) in the Notes entry below the title entry.

Full Length v. Singles

Under the artist heading in the Artist A to Z, all of the discs are organized as *full length* discs by title A to Z, and *singles* discs by title A to Z. All CD albums, laser discs, 8" laser discs, samplers, and interview discs are *full length*. All CD5, CDJ, CD3, and CDVs are *singles*.

Disc Type

This entry is important because it designates what type of disc. The discs are categorized by the following:

LP ....Long play for CD or any other format
LTD/LP ....Limited edition long play for CD or any other format
LP/LB ....Long play for CD or any other format with long box
LP/BP ....Long play for CD or any other format with blister pack
DJ/LP ....Promotional Long play for CD or any other format
DJ/Smplr ....Promotional long play sampler
DJ/Intvw ....Promotional interview disc
CD5 ....CD-single
CD5/LB ....CD-single with long box
CD3 ....3" CD-single
DJ/CD3 ....Promotional 3" CD-single
CD3/LB ....3" CD-single with long box
CDJ ....Promotional CD-single
CDV ....CD video
DJ/CDV ....Promotional CD video
LD ....Laser disc
DJ/LD ....Promotional laser disc
LTD/LD ....Limited edition laser disc
8" LD ....8" extended play laser disc
RS ....Radio show

Label & Catalog Number

These entries designate the disc's maker (usually a record or studio company) and its individual catalog number. You may see there are occasionally catalog numbers and labels missing from a disc in the listing. This is due to either the disc was never designated a catalog number, or we just did not have the label or catalog number available to us when listing the disc title. If you see any discs missing this information which you might have, please let us know. Your help will certainly make for more complete and accurate listings in the future.

Country

Because the *CCDPG* features collectible discs from all over the world, you will notice discs listed in this guide from more than eleven countries. This entry further identifies the disc. You will notice that many discs with identical titles were released from different countries. Some countries have been abbreviated as follows:

C.S.F.R. ....Former Czechoslovakia
U.S. ....United States
U.S.† ....Discs made in foreign countries for U.S. distribution
U.K. ....United Kingdom

Year

This entry designates the year of release on disc. Note that many CD albums in this guide are reissues of albums created decades before the introduction of digital audio technology. If the date of release on disc is after the original release of the album, only the year the disc version was released is given. You might notice in this section too, that the date might be missing in some title entries. Again, like in the label and catalog number sections, the year information was not available at the time the listing was entered. If you by chance have the year to those disc's missing the same, let us know.

Notes

This entry provides additional detailed information about the disc. Often information about the disc format (CD+I, CD-ROM, etc.), packaging (e.g. size of box or type of packaging, etc.) or what other items are contained in the package, as well as other information is contained in this section. Some standard nomenclature found in this entry are defined as follows:

CAV ....Standard laser disc play
CD+G ....Compact Disc Graphics
CD+I ....Compact Disc Interactive
CD-R ....Recordable CD
CD-ROM ....Read Only Memory CD
CLV ....Extended Laser Disc Play
Distributed by Pioneer ....Indicates that this is an original pressing distributed by Pioneer. The title however, may currently be available through another distributor, with or without significant graphic or disc mastering changes.
Second version ....Second version of disc with same title (used when no catalog number is available to distinguish the two).

Value

There are two possible value entries per title; though most titles will only have one. These two values are for those CDs that were housed in an outer disposable packaging, like the long box (LB) and blister pack (BP). The first value is for a disc that is accompanied by its long box; either sealed inside or carefully removed. For blister packs the disc should either be sealed or, if the disc is a blister card, the first value can also apply to a disc removed from the blister pack but accompanied by the blister card. If there is only one value, that indicates there was not intended outer disposable packaging like the LB or BP.

Japanese CD3 also have two values that distinguished whether the package is still in its complete 3" x 6" package, or whether it has been broken down into a 3" x 3" package. The Japanese manufacturers intend the package to be broken down but as you can see in the listings, the value of the CD3 is diminished by about 75% to 80%.

Also notice that some values are listed as N/A. This means that a reliable value cannot be placed at this time. Remember, this hobby is so new that many collectible discs are just now being discovered. As time goes by values will be assigned to those titles.

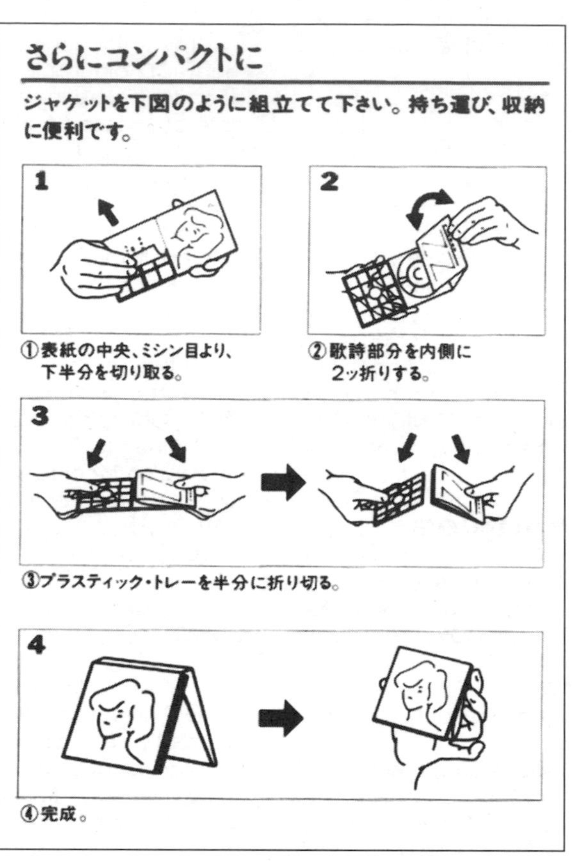

さらにコンパクトに
ジャケットを下図のように組立てて下さい。持ち運び、収納に便利です。
1
①表紙の中央、ミシン目より、下半分を切り取る。
2
②歌詞部分を内側に2ッ折りする。
3
③プラスティック・トレーを半分に折り切る。
4
④完成。

Looking at the list of collectible CDs in this guide, you will notice that for Japanese CD3s there are two values given, the first, greater value is for a Japanese CD3 that retains its entire 6" x 3" packaging as shown above. The second, lesser value is for a Japanese CD3 that does not retain its entire 6" x 3" packaging as shown by the disc below. As shown, the Japanese labels suggest the packaging be broken down to a 3" x 3" size, as the instructions indicate. But if you do, you will destroy the value of the disc by as much as 75%. Never break these packages down as per the instructions, leave the plastic frame intact. (Diagram © Warner-Pioneer Corporation.)

Listing Legend Diagrams

Artist A to Z

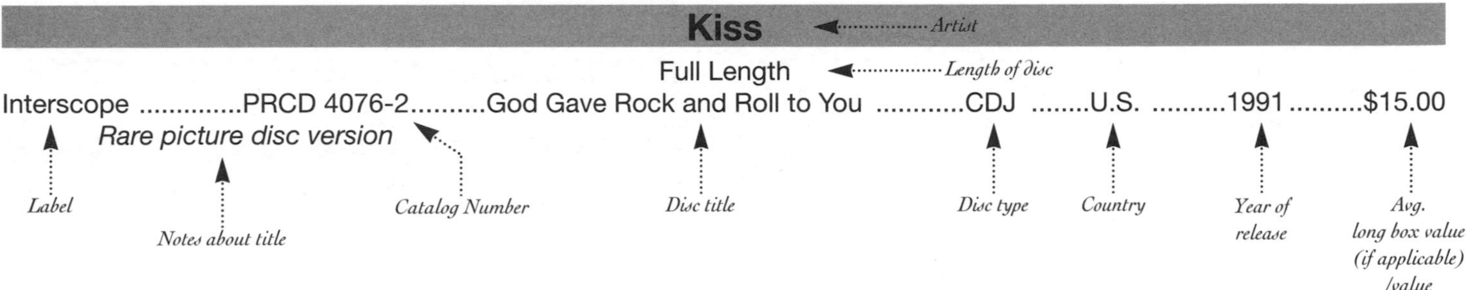

CD Sountracks, Various Artists, and Miscellaneous

Series

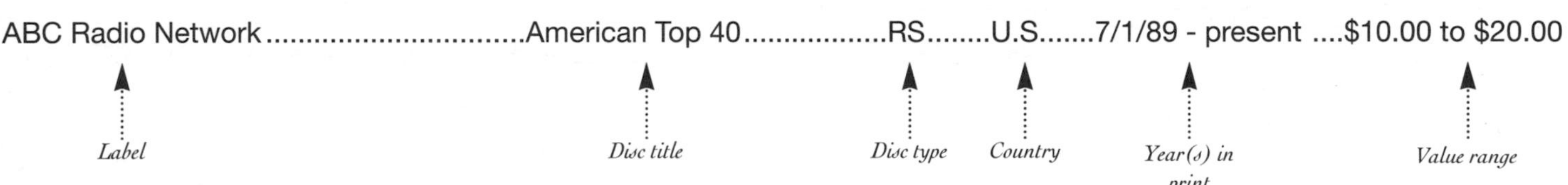

Theatrical Laser Discs

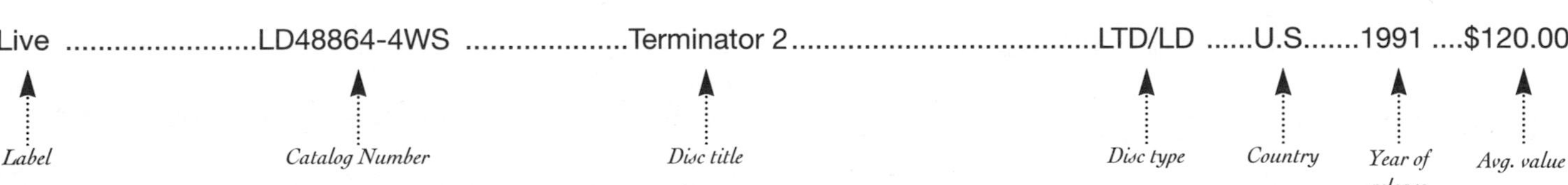

10,000 Maniacs

Full Length

Label	Catalog Number	Title	Type	Country	Year	Longbox Value / Value
Elektra	60962-2	Hope Chest	LP/LB	U.S.		$19.00/$18.00
	Blue sunshine and yellow clouds printed on CD.					
Westwood One		In Concert	RS	U.S.	1993	$80.00
Westwood One		In Concert	RS	U.S.	1994	$80.00
	Airdate: 5/23/94					
Westwood One		In Concert–Nu Rock	RS	U.S.	1995	$100.00
	2 CD set. Airdate: 4/10/95.					
Elektra	9 60738-2	In My Tribe	LP/LB	U.S.	1987	$19.00/$15.00
	Includes withdrawn track "Peace Train".					
Elektra	61593-2	MTV Unplugged	LTD/LP	U.S.	1993	$18.00
	CD in Paper sleeve.					
Elektra		Radio Sampler	DJ/Smplr	U.S.	1994	$18.00
WEA	40115	Time Capsule	LD	U.S.	1991	$25.00
WEA	40115	Time Capsule	LD	U.S.	1991	$25.00
Media America		Up Close	RS	U.S.	1994	$55.00

Singles

Label	Catalog Number	Title	Type	Country	Year	Longbox Value / Value
Elektra		Because the Night	CD5	U.K.	1993	$10.00
Elektra		Because the Night	CD5	U.K.	1993	$10.00
	Second version.					
Elektra		Because the Night	CDJ	U.S.	1993	$3.00
Warner Brothers	22-66342	Candy Everybody Wants	CD5	Canada	1993	$8.00
		Candy Everybody Wants	CD5	U.K.		$10.00
		Candy Everybody Wants	CD5	U.K.		$10.00
	Second version.					
Elektra		Candy Everybody Wants	CD5	U.K.	1993	$10.00
Elektra		Candy Everybody Wants	CD5	U.K.	1993	$10.00
	Second version.					
Elektra		Candy Everybody Wants	CDJ	U.S.	1993	$3.00
Elektra	EKR-100CD	Eat for Two	CD5	U.K.	1989	$10.00
Elektra	PR 8103-2	Eat for Two	CDJ	U.S.	1989	$3.00
Elektra		Eden	CDJ	U.S.		$6.00
Elektra	CD-66296	Few and Far Between	CD5	Canada	1993	$8.00
Elektra	66296-2	Few and Far Between	CD5	U.S.	1993	$5.00
Elektra		Few and Far Between	CDJ	U.S.	1993	$3.00
Elektra		Hey Jack	CDJ	Spain	1993	$25.00
Elektra	966751-2	Like the Weather	CD5	Germany	1988	$10.00
Elektra		Like the Weather	CDJ	U.S.	1988	$3.00
Elektra	PRCD 8259-2	My Mother the War	CDJ	U.S.	1990	$3.00
Elektra	PR 8167-2	Poison in the Well	CDJ	U.S.	1989	$6.00
Elektra		These Are Days	CDJ	U.S.		$3.00
Elektra	09P3-6164	Trouble Me	CD3	Japan	1989	$12.00/$4.00
Elektra		Trouble Me	CDJ	Spain	1993	$25.00
Elektra	EKR 93(CD)	Trouble Me	CD3	U.K.	1989	$15.00
	Elephant-shaped package.					
Elektra	PR 8077-2	Trouble Me	CDJ	U.S.	1989	$3.00
Elektra		What's the Matter Here?	CD5	Germany	1988	$10.00
Elektra	EKR71CD	What's the Matter Here?	CD3	U.K.	1988	$10.00
Elektra	69388-2	What's the Matter Here?	CD3	U.S.	1988	$8.00/$5.00
Elektra	PR 8011-2	What's the Matter Here?	CDJ	U.S.	1988	$3.00
Elektra	66669-2	You Happy Puppet	CD5	U.S.	1989	$8.00
Elektra	PR 8124	You Happy Puppet	CDJ	U.S.	1989	$3.00

101 North

Singles

Label	Catalog Number	Title	Type	Country	Year	Longbox Value / Value
Capitol	DPRO 79824	Trust In Me	CDJ	U.S.	1991	$2.00

12 Gauge

Singles

Label	Catalog Number	Title	Type	Country	Year	Longbox Value / Value
Scotti Brothers	75373	Dunkie Butt	CD5	U.S.	1994	$5.00
Scotti Brothers	75373	Dunkie Butt	CD5	U.S.	1994	$5.00

16 Horsepower

Full Length

Label	Catalog Number	Title	Type	Country	Year	Longbox Value / Value
		Sackcloth 'n Ashes	DJ/LP	U.S.		$7.00
	AMCDP00110	Black Soul Power	CDJ	U.S.		$2.00
		Heel On the Shovel	CDJ	U.S.		$3.00

18th Dye

Singles

Label	Catalog Number	Title	Type	Country	Year	Longbox Value / Value
Matador	118	Crayon	CD5	U.S.	1994	$5.00

2 Bad Boys

Singles

Label	Catalog Number	Title	Type	Country	Year	Longbox Value / Value
		I Totally Miss You	CD5	Germany		$8.00
		Megamix	CD5	Germany		$8.00

2 Bad Mice

Singles

Label	Catalog Number	Title	Type	Country	Year	Longbox Value / Value
	9003	Bombscare	CD5	U.S.	1994	$5.00

2 Dope

Singles

Label	Catalog Number	Title	Type	Country	Year	Longbox Value / Value
Psychotic	1008	Fuck Off	CD5	U.S.	1994	$5.00

2 Pac

Singles

Label	Catalog Number	Title	Type	Country	Year	Longbox Value / Value
		California Love	CDJ	U.S.		$6.00
Atlantic	95774	Dear Mama	CD5	U.S.	1994	$6.00
Atlantic	95724	Temptations	CD5	U.S.	1995	$6.00
		Trapped	CDJ	U.S.		$6.00

2 PM

Singles

Label	Catalog Number	Title	Type	Country	Year	Longbox Value / Value
	1901	Ain't Tryin'	CD5	U.S.	1994	$5.00

20 Fingers

Singles

Label	Catalog Number	Title	Type	Country	Year	Longbox Value / Value
	114	Short Dick Man	CD5	U.S.	1994	$5.00
Zoo	14192	Short Short Man	CD5	U.S.	1994	$5.00

24-K

Singles

Label	Catalog Number	Title	Type	Country	Year	Longbox Value / Value
MCA	MCA5P-3503	Don't Go There	CDJ	U.S.		$2.00

311

Full Length

Label	Catalog Number	Title	Type	Country	Year	Longbox Value / Value
		Do You Right	CDJ	U.S.		$2.00
Capricorn		Enlarged To Show Detail	LTD/LP	U.S.	1996	$20.00
	CD EP and VHS video in box.					

3rd Nation

Singles

Label	Catalog Number	Title	Type	Country	Year	Longbox Value / Value
Atlantic	95810	I Believe	CD5	U.S.	1994	$5.00

3T

Singles

Label	Catalog Number	Title	Type	Country	Year	Longbox Value / Value
		Anything	CDJ	U.K.		$10.00
Epic	77913	Anything	CD5	U.S.	1995	$5.00

49ers

Singles

Label	Catalog Number	Title	Type	Country	Year	Longbox Value / Value
ZYX	6354-8	Die Walkuere	CD5	Germany	1989	$6.00
Alfa	09B3-20	Die Walkuere	CD3	Japan	1989	$13.00/$4.00
BCM	20425	Don't You Love Me	CD5	Germany	1990	$8.00
4th & B'way	BRCD-167	Don't You Love Me	CD5	U.K.	1990	$8.00
BCM	20445	Girl to Girl	CD5	Germany	1990	$8.00
4th & B'way	BRCD-174	Girl to Girl	CD5	U.K.	1990	$8.00
Alfa	ALDB 154	Got to Be Free	CD3	Japan	1992	$13.00/$4.00
Alfa	ALCB-536	Got to Be Free	CD5	Japan	1992	$10.00
Media	BRCD-255	Got to Be Free	CD5	U.K.	1992	$8.00
4th & B'way	BRCD-194	How Longer	CD5	U.K.	1990	$8.00
ZYX	8059-8	Lovin' You	CD5	U.S.	1996	$6.00
4th & B'way	BRCD-257	Message	CD5	U.K.	1992	$8.00
ZYX	6705-8	Move Your Feet	CD5	Germany	1991	$6.00
Alfa	ALCB-424	Move Your Feet	CD5	Japan	1991	$10.00
BCM	20370	Touch Me	CD5	Germany	1990	$8.00
Alfa	ALDB-39	Touch Me	CD3	Japan	1990	$13.00/$4.00
4th & B'way	BRCD-157	Touch Me	CD5	U.K.	1990	$8.00

69 Boyz

Singles

Label	Catalog Number	Title	Type	Country	Year	Longbox Value / Value
Columbia	CSK 6943	Five 0, Five 0	CDJ	U.S.	1995	$3.00
		Hoop In Your Face	CDJ	U.S.		$2.00
	6902	Tootsee Roll	CD5	U.S.	1994	$5.00
	6912	Tootsee Roll (Remix)	CD5	U.S.	1994	$5.00

702

Singles

Label	Catalog Number	Title	Type	Country	Year	Longbox Value / Value
Motown	860612-2	Get It Together	CD5	U.S.	1997	$3.00

808 State

Singles

Label	Catalog Number	Title	Type	Country	Year	Longbox Value / Value
ZTT	ZANG-23CD	Cobra Bora	CD5	U.K.	1990	$8.00
ZTT	9031-72873-2	Cubik Olympic	CD5	Germany	1990	$8.00
ZTT	ZANG-5CD	Cubik Olympic	CD5	U.K.	1990	$8.00
Tommy Boy	959	Cubik Olympic	CD5	U.S.	1989	$4.00
Tommy Boy	TBCD 959	Cubik Olympic	CDJ	U.S.	1989	$2.00
ZTT	ZANG-14CD	In Yer Face	CD5	U.K.	1991	$8.00
ZTT	9031-73577-2	In Yer Face	CD5	U.K.	1991	$8.00
ZTT	WMC5-388	Lift	CD5	Japan	1991	$12.00
ZTT	ZANG-20CD	Lift	CD5	U.K.	1991	$8.00
Tommy Boy	TBCD 549	Moses	CDJ	U.S.	1991	$2.00
		One In Ten	CD5	U.K.		$10.00
ZTT	ZANG-39CD	One In Ten	CD5	U.K.	1991	$8.00
Tommy Boy	533	One In Ten	CD5	U.S.	1991	$4.00
ZZT	9031-74258-2	Oops	CD5	Germany	1991	$8.00
ZTT	WMC5-372	Oops	CD5	Japan	1991	$12.00
ZZT	ZANG-19CD	Oops	CD5	U.K.	1991	$8.00
WEA	2292-46501-2	Pacific 707	CD5	Germany	1989	$8.00
ZZT	ZANG-1CD	Pacific 707	CD5	U.K.	1989	$8.00
ZTT	ZANG-38CD	Plan	CD5	U.K.	1992	$8.00
ZTT	ZANG-33CD	Time Bomb	CD5	U.K.	1992	$8.00

9*1*1*

Singles

Label	Catalog Number	Title	Type	Country	Year	Longbox Value / Value
	9902	Cutie	CD5	U.S.	1994	$5.00

A.B. Logic

Singles

Label	Catalog Number	Title	Type	Country	Year	Longbox Value / Value
WEA	9031-77552-2	Hitman	CD5	Germany	1992	$8.00
WEA	MAG-1004CD	Hitman	CD5	U.K.	1992	$8.00
	Hitman	CDJ	U.S.		1992	$3.00

A.C.E. Project

Singles

Label	Catalog Number	Title	Type	Country	Year	Longbox Value / Value
ZYX	6363-8	Casa Esponalo	CD5	Germany	1990	$6.00

A Certain Ratio

Singles

Label	Catalog Number	Title	Type	Country	Year	Longbox Value / Value
A&M	ACRCD-517	Backs To the Wall	CD5	U.K.	1990	$8.00
A&M	PCDY-10005	Big E, The	CD3	Japan	1989	$13.00/$3.00
A&M	ACRCD-514	Big E, The	CD5	U.K.	1989	$8.00
A&M		Big E, The	CDJ	U.K.	1989	$2.00
A&M	ACRCD-550	Good Together	CD5	U.K.	1990	$8.00
Virgin	CDROB-2	Loosen Up Your Mind	CD5	U.K.	1991	$8.00
Virgin	CDROB-6	Mello M-People	CD5	U.K.	1992	$8.00
A&M	ACRCD-590	Shack Up	CD5	U.K.	1990	$8.00
Virgin	CDROB-5	Twenty Seven Forever	CD5	U.K.	1992	$8.00
A&M	ACRCD-540	Won't Stop Loving You	CD5	U.K.	1990	$8.00
A&M	ACRCD-534	Your Blue Eyes	CD5	U.K.	1989	$8.00

A.D.O.R.

Singles

Label	Catalog Number	Title	Type	Country	Year	Longbox Value / Value
		Let It All Hang Out	CDJ	U.S.		$2.00

A Darker Shade

Singles

Label	Catalog Number	Title	Type	Country	Year	Longbox Value / Value
Mood Indigo	1001	Family	CDJ	U.S.	1991	$3.00

A Few Good Men

Singles

Label	Catalog Number	Title	Type	Country	Year	Longbox Value / Value
LaFace	24079	A Lil Somthin'	CDJ	U.S.	1994	$3.00
LeFace	LEPCD 4135	Have I Never	CDJ	U.S.	1995	$2.00

A.G.A.

Singles

Label	Catalog Number	Title	Type	Country	Year	Longbox Value / Value
BCM	10042	Take Good Care Of My Heart	CD5	Germany	1990	$6.00

A Head

Singles

Label	Catalog Number	Title	CD Type	Country	Year	Longbox Value / Value
Zoth Ommog	21	Deep Down Pressure	CD5	Germany		$10.00

A House

Singles

Label	Catalog Number	Title	CD Type	Country	Year	Longbox Value / Value
Radioactive	3331	360 North Rockingham	CDJ	U.S.	1995	$3.00
Sire	PRO-CD-3321	Call Me Blue	CDJ	U.S.	1988	$2.00
SPV	8769-3	Doodle	CD5	Germany	1990	$8.00
Parlophone	CDAHOU-1	Endless Art	CD5	U.K.	1992	$8.00
Radioactive	PRO-CD-2314	Endless Art	CDJ	U.S.	1992	$2.00
Radioactive	PRO-CD-2199	I Don't Care	CDJ	U.S.	1992	$2.00
WEA	NEG-43CD	I Think I'm Going Mad	CD5	U.K.	1990	$8.00
Radioactive	3354	Strong And the Silent, The	CDJ	U.S.	1995	$3.00
Parlophone	CDAHOU-2	Take It Easy On Me	CD5	U.K.	1992	$8.00
Setanta	344-0336-3	Zop	CD5	Germany	1992	$8.00
Setanta	SET-012CD	Zop	CD5	U.K.	1992	$8.00

A.L.T.

Singles

Label	Catalog Number	Title	CD Type	Country	Year	Longbox Value / Value
	9123	All Nite Long	CDJ	U.S.		$2.00

A.L.T. And The Lost Civilization

Singles

Label	Catalog Number	Title	CD Type	Country	Year	Longbox Value / Value
Atco		Summer Breeze	CDJ	U.S.		$2.00
Atco	PRCD 4632-2	Tequila	CD5	U.S.		$2.00
Atco	PRCD 4632-2	Tequila	CDJ	U.S.		$3.00

A La Carte

Singles

Label	Catalog Number	Title	CD Type	Country	Year	Longbox Value / Value
BMG Ariola	162508	Dancing In Summertime	CD3	Germany	1989	$6.00
BMG Ariola	662508	Dancing In Summertime	CD5	Germany	1989	$6.00

A Lighter Shade Of Brown

Singles

Label	Catalog Number	Title	CD Type	Country	Year	Longbox Value / Value
Pump	19134	Homies With Guitar	CDJ	U.S.	1992	$2.00

A.M. Dre

Singles

Label	Catalog Number	Title	CD Type	Country	Year	Longbox Value / Value
Solar		You Get None	CDJ	U.S.	1994	$2.00

A.M.P.

Singles

Label	Catalog Number	Title	CD Type	Country	Year	Longbox Value / Value
Bellaphon	13007599	Piano In the Dark	CD5	Germany	1991	$6.00

A.R. Kane

Singles

Label	Catalog Number	Title	CD Type	Country	Year	Longbox Value / Value
Luka Bop	PRO-CD-7177	Honey Be	CDJ	U.S.	1994	$2.00
Rough Trade	RTT-239CD	Pop	CD5	U.K.	1989	$6.00

A.S.A.P. (Adrian Smith And Project)

Full Length

Label	Catalog Number	Title	CD Type	Country	Year	Longbox Value / Value
EMI	TOCP-5928	Silver And Gold	LP	Japan	1989	$20.00
Enigma	C2-73572	Silver And Gold	LP	U.S.	1989	$12.00/$7.00

Singles

Label	Catalog Number	Title	CD Type	Country	Year	Longbox Value / Value
EMI	CDEM-131	Down the Wire	CD5	U.K.	1989	$6.00
EMI	203542	Silver & Gold	CD5	Germany	1989	$6.00
EMI	CDEM-107	Silver & Gold	CD5	U.K	1989	$6.00
Enigma		Silver & Gold	CDJ	U.S.	1989	$6.00

A.S.A.P. (As Soon As Possible)

Singles

Label	Catalog Number	Title	CD Type	Country	Year	Longbox Value / Value
Columbia	CODA-38	Cinderella Express	CD3	Japan	1992	$12.00/$3.00
Columbia	CODA-165	Magic In Kobe	CD3	Japan	1993	$12.00/$3.00
Columbia	CODA-8904	Refrain	CD3	Japan	1991	$12.00/$3.00
Columbia	CODA-104	Vacation Hot Lovin'	CD3	Japan	1992	$12.00/$3.00

A.S.K.

Singles

Label	Catalog Number	Title	CD Type	Country	Year	Longbox Value / Value
MCA	MCSTD 1591	Freedom We Cry	CD5	U.K.	1992	$8.00

A Split-Second

Singles

Label	Catalog Number	Title	CD Type	Country	Year	Longbox Value / Value
Caroline	2503	Parallax View, The	CD5	U.S.	1995	$5.00

A.T.E.E.M.

Singles

Label	Catalog Number	Title	CD Type	Country	Year	Longbox Value / Value
Select		Get It On	CDJ	U.S.	1992	$2.00
Select	014	Yeah	CDJ	U.S.	1992	$2.00

A Thousand Points Of Night

Singles

Label	Catalog Number	Title	CD Type	Country	Year	Longbox Value / Value
Polygram	863739	Read My Lips	CD5	U.S.	1992	$4.00
Polygram	CDP767	Read My Lips	CDJ	U.S.	1992	$2.00

A To The D

Singles

Label	Catalog Number	Title	CD Type	Country	Year	Longbox Value / Value
		Renegade Jew	CDJ	U.S.		$2.00

A Tribe Called Quest

Full Length

Label	Catalog Number	Title	CD Type	Country	Year	Longbox Value / Value
Jive	41587-2	Beats, Rhymes And Life	LTD/LP	U.S.	1996	$18.00

Limited edition multi-image cover.

Label	Catalog Number	Title	CD Type	Country	Year	Longbox Value / Value
Jive		Classics	DJ/Smplr	U.S.	1996	$10.00
Jive	42186	Award Tour	CDJ	U.S.	1993	$2.00
Jive	806878	Bonita Applebum	CD5	Germany	1990	$8.00
Jive	JIVECD-256	Bonita Applebum	CD5	U.K.	1990	$8.00
Jive		Bonita Applebum	CDJ	U.S.	1990	$2.00
Jive	JIVECD-265	Can I Kick It?	CD5	U.K.	1990	$8.00
Jive	JIVECD-324	Can I Kick It?	CD5	U.K.	1992	$8.00
Jive		Can I Kick It?	CDJ	U.S.	1992	$2.00
RCA	ZD-4312	Desciption Of A Fool	CD5	Germany	1989	$8.00
Jive	42094	Hot Sex	CDJ	U.S.	1992	$2.00
Jive	JIVCD-270	I Left My Wallet In El Segundo	CD5	U.K.	1991	$8.00
Jive	1300-2 JDJ	I Left My Wallet In El Segundo	CDJ	U.S.	1989	$2.00
Jive	JIVECD-293	Jazz	CD5	U.K.	1992	$8.00
Jive	JIVECD-317	Luck Of Lucien	CD5	U.K.	1992	$8.00
Jive	42211	Oh My God	CD5	U.S.	1994	$5.00
Jive	42211	Oh My God	CDJ	U.S.	1994	$3.00
RCA	ZD-43368	Public Enemy	CD5	Germany	1990	$8.00
Jive	JIVECD-302	Scenario	CD5	U.K.	1992	$8.00
Jive	42056	Scenario	CDJ	U.S.	1992	$2.00

A&A

Singles

Label	Catalog Number	Title	CD Type	Country	Year	Longbox Value / Value
EMI	204403-2	Rockin' To the Beat	CD5	Germany	1991	$6.00

A-Cademix

Singles

Label	Catalog Number	Title	Type	Country	Year	Longbox Value / Value
SPV	0779-2	Come And Make	CD5	Germany	1990	$6.00

A-Chief

Singles

Label	Catalog Number	Title	Type	Country	Year	Longbox Value / Value
Columbia	CODA-8921	Legend Of Love	CD3	Japan	1991	$13.00/$3.00

A-Ha

Full Length

Label	Catalog Number	Title	Type	Country	Year	Longbox Value / Value
Warner Brothers	9 26314-2-DJ	East of the Sun, West Of the Moon	DJ/LP	U.S.	1992	$12.00
Pioneer Artists	CLD-86-004	Hunting Hi And Low	LD	U.S.	1986	$17.00
Warner Brothers	5P2-2131	Road Club	LTD/LP	Japan	1989	$30.00

Picture disc CD.

Label	Catalog Number	Title	Type	Country	Year	Longbox Value / Value
Warner Brothers	9 25501-2	Scoundrel Days	LP/LB	U.S.		$14.00/$8.00
Warner Brothers		Selections '85-'93	DJ/Smplr	Japan	1993	$50.00
Pioneer	43P2-003	Stay On these Roads	LTD/LP	Japan	1988	$20.00

Gold disc.

Label	Catalog Number	Title	Type	Country	Year	Longbox Value / Value
Warner Brothers	925733-6	Stay On these Roads	LTD/LP	U.K.	1988	$35.00

Picture disc CD.

Singles

Label	Catalog Number	Title	Type	Country	Year	Longbox Value / Value
Warner Brothers		Angel	CD5	U.K.	1994	$10.00
Warner Brothers	40400-2	Blood That Moves the Body	CD3	Germany	1988	$6.00
Warner Brothers	920981-2	Blood That Moves the Body	CD3	Germany	1988	$6.00
Warner Brothers	W-7840CD	Blood That Moves the Body	CD3	Japan	1988	$3.00
Warner Brothers	W-0089CD	Blood That Moves the Body	CD3	U.K.	1988	$6.00
WEA	W-7840CD	Blood That Moves the Body	CD5	U.K.	1988	$6.00
Warner Brothers	7599-21768	Crying In the Rain	CD5	Germany	1990	$5.00
Warner Brothers	WPDP-6243	Crying In the Rain	DJ/CD3	Japan	1990	$15.00/$5.00
Warner Brothers	W-954-7CD	Crying In the Rain	CD5	U.K.	1990	$5.00
Warner Brothers	PRO-CD-4462	Crying In the Rain	CDJ	U.S.	1990	$3.00
Warner Brothers	WPDP-6329	Dark Is the Night For All	CD3	Japan	1993	$13.00/$3.00
Warner Brothers		Dark Is the Night For All	CD5	U.K.	1993	$10.00
Warner Brothers		Dark Is the Night For All	CD5	U.K.	1993	$10.00

Second version.

Label	Catalog Number	Title	Type	Country	Year	Longbox Value / Value
Warner Brothers	W-0012CD	Early Morning	CD5	U.K.	1991	$6.00
WEA	7599-21834-2	I Call Your Name	CD5	Germany	1990	$6.00
Warner		Kind Of Xmas Card	CDJ	U.K.	1995	$12.00
Warner Brothers	9362-40246-2	Move To Memphis	CD5	Germany	1991	$8.00
Warner Brothers	WPDP-6291	Move To Memphis	CD3	Japan	1991	$13.00/$4.00
Warner Brothers	W-0070CD	Move To Memphis	CD5	U.K.	1991	$6.00
Warner Brothers		Shapes That Go Together	CD5	U.K.	1994	$10.00

Second version.

Label	Catalog Number	Title	Type	Country	Year	Longbox Value / Value
Warner Brothers	920905-2	Stay On These Roads	CD3	Germany	1988	$8.00
Warner Brothers	10SW-44	Stay On These Roads	CD3	Japan	1988	$13.00/$4.00
Warner Brothers	W-7936CD	Stay On These Roads	CD3	U.K.	1988	$5.00
Warner Brothers	921045-2	Touchy	CD3	Germany	1988	$8.00
Warner Brothers	10P3-6061	Touchy	CD3	Japan	1988	$13.00/$3.00
Warner Brothers	0P3-6061	Touchy	CD3	Japan	1988	$13.00/$4.00
Warner Brothers	W-7749CD	Touchy	CD3	U.K.	1988	$8.00
Pioneer	WPDP-6277	Waiting For Her	CD3	Japan	1991	$13.00/$4.00
WEA	921121-2	You Are the One	CD3	Germany	1988	$7.00
WEA	09P3-6101	You Are the One	CD3	Japan	1988	$13.00/$3.00
WEA	W-7636CD	You Are the One	CD3	U.K.	1988	$7.00
WEA	W-7636CD	You Are the One	CD5	U.K.	1988	$7.00

A-Strings

Singles

Label	Catalog Number	Title	Type	Country	Year	Longbox Value / Value
		A Summer Place	CDJ	U.S.		$2.00

A-Tomiko

Singles

Label	Catalog Number	Title	Type	Country	Year	Longbox Value / Value
ZYX	6243-2	DJ Herbie	CD5	Germany	1989	$6.00

A-Town Players

Singles

Label	Catalog Number	Title	Type	Country	Year	Longbox Value / Value
Life	72007	A Town Drop	CD5	U.S.	1993	$5.00
Warner Brothers	43566	Wassup! Wassup!	CD5	U.S.	1995	$5.00
Premeditated	PRO-CD-7678	Wassup, Wassup	CDJ	U.S.	1995	$3.00

Aaliyah

Singles

Label	Catalog Number	Title	Type	Country	Year	Longbox Value / Value
Rhino	71857	Age Ain't Nothing	CD5	U.S.	1994	$5.00
Jive	42236	At Your Best	CD5	U.S.	1994	$5.00
Jive	42173-2	Back & Forth	CD5	U.S.	1994	$5.00
Jive	42173-2-RDJ	Back & Forth	CDJ	U.S.	1994	$3.00

Aaron, Jay

Full Length

Label	Catalog Number	Title	Type	Country	Year	Longbox Value / Value
Warner Brothers	9 26306-2	Inside Out	LP/LB	U.S.		$10.00/$7.00
Warner Brothers	PRO-CD-4591	Misery's Edge	CDJ	U.S.	1990	$3.00
Warner Brothers	PRO-CD-4482	Rhonda	CDJ	U.S.	1990	$3.00

Aaron, Lee

Full Length

Label	Catalog Number	Title	Type	Country	Year	Longbox Value / Value
Polygram	841387-2	Bodyrock	LP	Germany		$23.00
Attic	ALCB-4	Bodyrock	LP	Japan		$25.00
Attic	841676-2	Call Of the Wild	LP	Germany		$23.00
BMG	258206	Lee Aaron	LP	Germany		$23.00
Virgin	DIXCD-49	Lee Aaron	LP	U.K.		$23.00
Attic	ACD-24104	Lee Aaron/Metal Queen	LP	Germany		$23.00
Polygram	841674-2	Metal Queen	LP	Germany		$23.00
Polygram	511487-2	Some Girls Do	LP	Germany		$23.00

Singles

Label	Catalog Number	Title	Type	Country	Year	Longbox Value / Value
Alfa	ALDB-8	Bodyrock	CD3	Japan	1990	$13.00/$3.00
Polygram	873031-2	Watcha Gonna Do To	CD5	Germany	1989	$5.00

AB Crew

Singles

Label	Catalog Number	Title	Type	Country	Year	Longbox Value / Value
EMI	147503-2	Wo Laufen Sie Denn	CD5	Germany	1990	$5.00

AB Logic

Full Length

Label	Catalog Number	Title	Type	Country	Year	Longbox Value / Value
Eastwest	AMCE-509	AB Logic	LP	Japan		$20.00

Abayale

Singles

Label	Catalog Number	Title	Type	Country	Year	Longbox Value / Value
Sony	657548-5`	Don't Talk About L.O.V.E.	CD5	Germany	1992	$5.00

Abba

Full Length

Label	Catalog Number	Title	Type	Country	Year	Longbox Value / Value
Discovision	74-006	Abba	LD	U.S.	1980	$100.00
Discovision	74-006	Abba	LD	U.S.	1981	$200.00
Pioneer		Abba In Concert	LD	U.S.†	1983	$50.00
Polydor	817352-2	Abba International	LP	Germany		$23.00
		Album, The	LTD/LP	France		N/A

2 CD set.

Abba – Greatest Hits (Atlantic)

Label	Catalog Number	Title	Type	Country	Year	Longbox/Value
CBS	CD32321	Album, The	LP	U.K.		$20.00
Polydor	821217-2	Album, The	LP	U.K.		$20.00
Polydor		Dream World	DJ/Smplr	U.K.	1994	$30.00
Atlantic	19114-2	Greatest Hits	LP/LB	U.S.†	1983	$20.00/$15.00
Atlantic	19114-2	Greatest Hits	LP/LB	U.S.	1986	$20.00/$15.00
Polydor	800012-2	Greatest Hits Vol.2	LP	Germany		$23.00
Polydor	800012-2	Greatest Hits Vol.2	LP	U.K.		$23.00
Atlantic	16009-2	Greatest Hits Vol.2	LP/LB	U.S.†	1983	$20.00/$15.00
Atlantic	16009-2	Greatest Hits Vol.2	LP/LB	U.S.	1986	$20.00/$15.00
Pickwick	50083-2	Hits 1	LP	Germany		$23.00
Pickwick	PWKS-500	Hits 2	LP	U.K.		$23.00
Polydor		Selections From Thank You For the Music	DJ/Smplr	U.S.	1994	$23.00
Atlantic	16023-2	Super Trooper	LP/LB	U.S.		$20.00/$15.00
Polydor	523 472-2	Thank You For the Music	LTD/LP	U.S.	1994	$80.00

4CD set in book #075465

Label	Catalog Number	Title	Type	Country	Year	Longbox/Value
Epic	CD-32322	Voulez-Vous	LP	U.K.		$20.00
		Waterloo	LTD/LP	Australia	1994	$45.00

20th anniversary edition with fan club cover

Singles

Label	Catalog Number	Title	Type	Country	Year	Longbox/Value
Polydor	887215-3	Dancing Queen	CD3	Germany	1989	$12.00
Polygram	PZCD-231	Dancing Queen	CD5	U.K.	1992	$10.00
		Dancing Queen	CDJ	U.S.	1995	$7.00
Polydor	871115-2	Lay All Your Love On Me	CD5	Germany	1988	$10.00
		Medley	CDJ	Spain	1994	$16.00
Polydor		Medley	CDJ	U.S.	1994	$8.00
Polydor		Summer Night City	CD5	Germany	1994	$12.00
Polygram	861213-2	Thank You For the Music	CD5	Germany	1993	$10.00
Polygram	PZCD-250	Thank You For the Music	CD5	U.K.	1993	$10.00
Polygram	863901-2	Voulez-Vous	CD5	Germany	1993	$10.00
Polygram	PZCD-239	Voulez-Vous	CD5	U.K.	1993	$10.00

Abbacadabra

Singles

Label	Catalog Number	Title	Type	Country	Year	Longbox/Value
WEA	PWCD-246	Dancing Queen	CD5	U.K.	1992	$9.00

Abbott, Gregory

Full Length

Label	Catalog Number	Title	Type	Country	Year	Longbox/Value
Columbia	465556-2	I'll Prove It To You	LP	Germany		$15.00
Columbia	460691	I'll Prove It To You	LP	U.K.		$15.00
Columbia	CK-44087	I'll Prove It To You	LP/LB	U.S.		$14.00/$8.00
Columbia	404370-2	Shake You Down	LP	Germany		$15.00
Columbia	450061-2	Shake You Down	LP	U.K.		$15.00

Singles

Label	Catalog Number	Title	Type	Country	Year	Longbox/Value
CBS	10EP-3012	I'll Prove It To You	CD3	Japan	1988	$12.00/$3.00
CBS	38K-7774	I'll Prove It To You	CD3	U.S.	1988	$6.00/$4.00
CBS	44K7809	I'll Prove It To You	CD3	U.S.	1988	$6.00/$4.00
Columbia	CSK 1085	I'll Prove It To You	CDJ	U.S.	1988	$2.00

ABC

Full Length

Label	Catalog Number	Title	Type	Country	Year	Longbox/Value
Pickwick	PWKS-4111P	ABC 1	LP	U.K.		$15.00
MCA	10184	Abracadabra	LP/LB	U.S.		$14.00/$8.00
Mercury	PHCR-2043	Alphabet City	LP	Japan		$20.00
Mercury	832391-2	Alphabet City	LP/LB	U.S.		$14.00/$8.00
Mercury	814661-2	Beauty Stab	LP/LB	U.S.		$14.00/$8.00
Mercury	814661-2	Beauty Stab	LP/BP	U.S.†	1984	$14.00/$8.00
Phonogram	PHCR-2060	How To Be A Zillionaire	LP	Japan		$20.00
Mercury	824904-2	How To Be A Zillionaire	LP/BP	U.S.†	1985	$14.00/$8.00
Mercury	PPD-3041	Lexicon Of Love	LP	Japan		$20.00
Mercury	810003-2	Lexicon Of Love	LP/BP	U.S.†	1984	$14.00/$8.00
IMS	838646-2	Up	LP	Germany		$15.00
Phonogram	PHCR-1061	Up	LP	Japan		$20.00
Mercury	838646	Up	LP/LB	U.S.		$14.00/$8.00

Singles

Label	Catalog Number	Title	Type	Country	Year	Longbox/Value
Polygram	888948-2	King Without A Crown	CD5	Germany	1987	$8.00
Polygram	NTCD-113	King Without A Crown	CD5	U.K.	1987	$8.00
Polygram	875303-2	Look Of Love	CD5	Germany	1990	$8.00
Polygram	NTRCD-116	Look Of Love	CD5	U.K.	1990	$8.00
Polygram	NTCD-116	Look Of Love	CD5	U.K.	1990	$8.00
EMI	204347-2	Love Conquers All	CD5	Germany	1991	$9.00
EMI	CDR-6292	Love Conquers All	CD5	U.K.	1991	$9.00
Polygram	874520-3	One Better World	CD3	Germany	1989	$9.00
Polygram	874289-3	One Better World	CD3	Germany	1989	$9.00
Polygram	874521-2	One Better World	CD5	Germany	1989	$8.00
Polygram	874289-2	One Better World	CD5	Germany	1989	$8.00
Polygram	NTCD-114	One Better World	CD5	U.K.	1989	$8.00
Polygram	876269-2	Real Thing	CD5	Germany	1987	$9.00
Polygram	NTCD-115	Real Thing	CD5	U.K.	1987	$9.00
EMI	204509-2	Say It	CD5	Germany	1991	$8.00
EMI	CDR-6298	Say It	CD5	U.K.	1991	$4.00
MCA	54055	Say It	CD5	U.S.	1991	$4.00
MCA	CD45-1431	Say It	CDJ	U.S.	1991	$6.00
Polygram	888604-2	When Smokey Sings	CD5	Germany	1987	$8.00
Polygram	NTCD-111	When Smokey Sings	CD5	U.K.	1987	$8.00

Abdul, Paula

Full Length

Label	Catalog Number	Title	Type	Country	Year	Longbox/Value
Virgin		Spellbound	LTD/LP	Australia	1991	$30.00
Virgin	2-91753	Spellbound	DJ/LP	U.S.	1991	$30.00

Custom "Compact" case and box.

Label	Catalog Number	Title	Type	Country	Year	Longbox/Value
Unistar		The Paula Abdul Story	RS	U.S.	1991	$12.00

Airdate: 6/14 - 6/16

Company	Disk Number	Title	Type	Country	Year	Longbox/Value
Unistar		Weekly Specials, The	RS	U.S.	1991	$15.00

Airdate: 6/14/91

Singles

Company	Disk Number	Title	Type	Country	Year	Longbox/Value
Virgin		Ain't Ever Gonna Give You Up	CDJ	U.S.		$7.00
Virgin		Blowing Kisses In the Wind	CD5	Australia	1991	$10.00
Virgin	VJDP-10181	Blowing Kisses In the Wind	CD3	Japan	1988	$13.00/$4.00
Virgin		Blowing Kisses In the Wind	CDJ	U.S.	1991	$3.00
Virgin	662549	Cold Hearted	CD5	Germany	1989	$8.00
Siren	VJD-15556	Cold Hearted	CD5	Japan	1989	$16.00
Virgin	VUSCD-27	Cold Hearted	CD5	U.K.	1988	$8.00
Virgin	PRCD 2776	Cold Hearted	CDJ	U.S.	1988	$3.00
Virgin	38510	Crazy Cool	CD5	U.S.	1995	$5.00
Virgin	38512	Crazy Cool	CD5	U.S.	1995	$6.00
Virgin	PRCD 11007	Crazy Cool	CDJ	U.S.	1995	$7.00
Virgin	662244	Forever Your Girl	CD5	Germany	1989	$8.00
Virgin	16244	Forever Your Girl	CD5	Germany	1989	$8.00
Virgin	662516	Forever Your Girl	CD5	Germany	1989	$8.00
Virgin	VJD-10207	Forever Your Girl	CD3	Japan	1989	$13.00/$3.00
Virgin	SRNCD-112	Forever Your Girl	CD3	U.K.	1989	$8.00
Virgin	PRCD 2647	Forever Your Girl	CDJ	U.S.	1989	$3.00
Virgin	SRNCD-101	(It's Just) the Way That You Love Me	CD3	U.K.	1988	$10.00
Virgin	SRNCX-101	(It's Just) the Way That You Love Me	CD3	U.K.	1988	$8.00
Virgin	PRCD 2438	(It's Just) the Way That You Love Me	CDJ	U.S.	1988	$3.00
Virgin	PRCD 2931	(It's Just) the Way That You Love Me	CDJ	U.S.	1988	$3.00
BMG	663436	Knocked Out	CD5	Germany	1990	$8.00
Virgin	VJD-12022	Knocked Out	CD3	Japan	1988	$13.00/$3.00
Siren	SRNCD-92	Knocked Out	CD5	U.K.	1988	$8.00
Virgin	VUSCD-23	Knocked Out	CD5	U.K.	1988	$8.00
Virgin	PRCD 9329	Knocked Out	CDJ	U.S.	1988	$3.00
Virgin	VUSCDJ	My Love Is For Real	CDJ	U.K.	1995	$10.00
Virgin	38493	My Love Is For Real	CD5	U.S.	1995	$5.00
Virgin	38497	My Love Is For Real	CD5	U.S.	1995	$7.00
Virgin	DPRO 12739	My Love Is For Real	CDJ	U.S.	1995	$7.00
Virgin	DPRO-1193	My Love Is For Real	CDJ	U.S.	1995	$7.00
BMG	663023	Opposites Attract	CD5	Germany	1988	$8.00
Japan	VJDP-102	Opposites Attract	CD3	Japan	1988	$13.00/$3.00
Virgin	SRNCD-124	Opposites Attract	CD5	U.K.	1988	$8.00
Virgin		Opposites Attract	CD5	U.S.	1988	$3.00
Virgin		Opposites Attract	CDJ	U.S.	1988	$3.00

Second version.

Company	Disk Number	Title	Type	Country	Year	Longbox/Value
BMG	664680	Promise Of A New Day	CD5	Germany	1991	$8.00
Virgin	VJDP-10172	Promise Of A New Day	CD3	Japan	1988	$13.00/$4.00
Virgin	VUSCD-44	Promise Of A New Day	CD5	U.K.	1991	$8.00
Virgin	PRCD 4043	Promise Of A New Day	CDJ	U.S.	1991	$3.00
BMG	664172	Rush Rush	CD5	Germany	1991	$8.00
Toshiba	VJDP-10157	Rush Rush	CD3	Japan	1991	$13.00/$3.00
Virgin	VUSCD-38	Rush Rush	CD5	U.K.	1991	$8.00
Virgin	PRCD 3815	Rush Rush	CDJ	U.S.	1991	$7.00
Virgin	VJCP-14038	Singles EP, The	CD5	Japan	1992	$25.00
Virgin	161997	Straight Up	CD3	Germany	1988	$8.00
Virgin	661997	Straight Up	CD5	Germany	1989	$8.00
Siren	SRNCD-111	Straight Up	CD3	U.K.	1988	$8.00
Virgin		Vibology	CD5	Australia	1991	$8.00
BMG	664849	Vibology	CD5	Germany	1991	$8.00
Virgin	VJDP-10177	Vibology	CD5	Japan	1991	$8.00
Virgin	PRCD 4098	Vibology	CDJ	U.S.	1991	$3.00
BMG Ariola	662810	Way That You Love Me, The	CD5	Germany	1988	$8.00
Siren	SRNCD-101	Way That You Love Me, The	CD3	U.K.	1988	$8.00
Virgin	VJDP-10192	Will You Marry Me?	CD3	Japan	1992	$13.00/$3.00
Virgin	VUSCD-58	Will You Marry Me?	CD5	U.K.	1992	$8.00
Virgin	PRCD-4471	Will You Marry Me?	CDJ	U.S.	1992	$3.00

Abdul-Malik, Ahmed

Full Length

Company	Disk Number	Title	Type	Country	Year	Longbox/Value
Original Jazz	1820	Jazz Sahara	LP	U.S.		$14.00/$8.00
Original Jazz	1820	Jazz Sahara	LTD/LP	U.S.		$18.00

Abe, Jun

Singles

Company	Disk Number	Title	Type	Country	Year	Longbox/Value
Warner Brothers	WPDL-4328	Be Mine	CD3	Japan	1993	$13.00/$3.00
Warner Brothers	WPDL-4253	Muneippai No Kaze	CD3	Japan	1991	$12.00/$3.00
Warner Brothers	WPDL-4325	One And Only	CD3	Japan	1992	$12.00/$3.00
Warner Brothers	WPDL-4288	Suteki Sai Kimi Wa	CD3	Japan	1992	$12.00/$3.00

Abe, Kimie

Singles

Company	Disk Number	Title	Type	Country	Year	Longbox/Value
Victor	VIDL-10255	Shonan-Sodachi	CD3	Japan	1992	$12.00/$3.00

Abe Midori

Singles

Company	Disk Number	Title	Type	Country	Year	Longbox/Value
Tokuma	TKDA-30716	Nozomizaka	CD3	Japan	1992	$12.00/$3.00

Abercrombie, John

Full Length

Company	Disk Number	Title	Type	Country	Year	Longbox/Value
ECM	841779-2	Animato	LP	Germany		$15.00
ECM	POCJ-1014	Animato	LP	Japan		$20.00
ECM	841779-2	Animato	LP/BP	U.S.		$14.00/$8.00
ECM	829372-2	Characters	LP	Germany		$15.00
ECM	J25J-20315	Characters	LP	Japan		$20.00
Polygram	829372-2	Characters	LP/BP	U.S.		$14.00/$8.00
ECM	J25J-20313	Current Events	LP	Japan		$20.00
ECM	827770-2	Current Events	LP	U.K.		$15.00
ECM	J25J-20316	Gateway	LP	Japan		$20.00
ECM	J25J-20314	Night	LP	Japan	1985	$20.00
ECM	823212-2	Night	LP/BP	U.S.		$14.00/$8.00
ECM	25009-4	Night	LP/LB	U.S.†	1985	$8.00
ECM	837275-2	Works	LP	Germany		$15.00
ECM	837275-2	Works	LP/BP	U.S.		$14.00/$8.00

Singles

Company	Disk Number	Title	Type	Country	Year	Longbox/Value
ECM	JA-2	While We're Young	CDJ	U.S.	1992	$3.00

Abfahrt

Singles

Company	Disk Number	Title	Type	Country	Year	Longbox/Value
ZYX	8-6140	Alone	CD5	Germany	1989	$4.00

Abidul, Noel

Singles

Company	Disk Number	Title	Type	Country	Year	Longbox/Value
ZYX	6276-2	Get Up	CD5	Germany	1990	$4.00

Abigail

Singles

Company	Disk Number	Title	Type	Country	Year	Longbox/Value
ZYX	66042-8	Constant Craving	CD5	U.S.	1996	$6.00
ZYX	7498-8	Don't You Wanna Know?	CD5	U.S.	1994	$7.00
ZYX	7283	Smells Like Teen Spirit	CD5	U.S.	1994	$5.00

Abou-Khalil, Rabih

Label	Catalog Number	Title	Type	Country	Year	Longbox Value/Value
		Full Length				
Enja	6090-2	Al-Jadida	LP/LB	U.S.		$10.00/$6.00
Enja	R2-79048-2	Blue Camel	LP/LB	U.S.		$10.00/$6.00
Polygram	835781-2	Nafas	LP/BP	U.S.		$10.00/$6.00

Above The Law

Label	Catalog Number	Title	Type	Country	Year	Longbox Value/Value
		Singles				
Ruthless	73952	For the Funk Of It	CDJ	U.S.	1991	$2.00
	6324	Kalifornia	CD5	U.S.	1994	$5.00
Ruthless	73230	Murder Rap	CDJ	U.S.	1990	$2.00
Epic	656067-2	Untouchable	CD5	Germany	1990	$8.00
Epic	656067-2	Untouchable	CD5	U.K.	1990	$8.00
Epic	656082-2	Untouchable	CD5	U.K.	1990	$8.00
Epic	ESK 73368	Untouchable	CDJ	U.S.	1990	$2.00
Giant	PRO-CD-5706	V.S.O.P.	CDJ	U.S.	1993	$3.00

Above the Rim

Label	Catalog Number	Title	Type	Country	Year	Longbox Value/Value
		Singles				
Atlantic	95910	I'm Still In Love	CD5	U.S.	1994	$5.00

Abrams, Colonel

Label	Catalog Number	Title	Type	Country	Year	Longbox Value/Value
		Full Length				
MCA	MCAD-42029	You And Me Equals Us	LP/LB	U.S.		$14.00/$8.00

Abrams, Muhal Richard

Label	Catalog Number	Title	Type	Country	Year	Longbox Value/Value
		Full Length				
Black Saint	BSR-0081CD	View From Within	LP/LB	U.S.†	1985	$14.00/$8.00

Absent Friends

Label	Catalog Number	Title	Type	Country	Year	Longbox Value/Value
		Full Length				
rooArt	PHCR-1055	Here's Looking Up Your Dress	LP	Japan		$20.00
rooArt	875 201-2	I Don't Want To Be With Nobody But You	CD5	Australia	1989	$6.00
Polygram	879107 2	I Don't Want To Be With Nobody But You	CD5	Germany	1990	$6.00
Polygram	RARCD-5	I Don't Want To Be With Nobody But You	CD5	U.K.	1990	$6.00

Absolute

Label	Catalog Number	Title	Type	Country	Year	Longbox Value/Value
		Full Length				
Columbia	CK-75313	For All Seasons	LP/LB	U.S.		$14.00/$8.00
Columbia		Cheap Shot	CDJ	U.S.		$2.00
Columbia		Gotta Lambada	CDJ	U.S.		$2.00
Capitol	58381	There Will Come A Day	CD5	U.S.	1995	$5.00

Abstrac

Label	Catalog Number	Title	Type	Country	Year	Longbox Value/Value
		Full Length				
Reprise	92997-2	Abstrac	LP	Germany	1989	$12.00
Reprise	92997-2	Abstrac	LP	U.K.	1989	$12.00
Reprise	9 25997-2	Abstrac	LP/LB	U.S.	1989	$12.00/$8.00
		Singles				
Reprise	PRO-CD-3620	Right And Hype	CDJ	U.S.	1989	$2.00
Reprise		You Are the Party (I Am the Fun)	CDJ	U.S.	1989	$2.00

Abstuerzende Briftauben

Label	Catalog Number	Title	Type	Country	Year	Longbox Value/Value
		Singles				
EMI	203772-2	Im Stradbad	CD5	Germany	1990	$6.00
EMI	2034203-2	Konrad K.	CD5	Germany	1991	$6.00
EMI	204167-2	Mein Kleiner Gruener Kaktus	CD5	Germany	1990	$6.00

Aburd

Label	Catalog Number	Title	Type	Country	Year	Longbox Value/Value
		Singles				
ZYX	BOY-8807-2	Brian	CD5	Germany	1990	$6.00
ZYX	BOY-8836-2	Pure Tribal	CD5	Germany	1992	$6.00

Abwaerts

Label	Catalog Number	Title	Type	Country	Year	Longbox Value/Value
		Singles				
BMG	662660	Die Zeit	CD5	Germany	1990	$4.00
BMG	662660	Sonderug Zur Endstation	CD5	Germany	1990	$4.00

Abyss

Label	Catalog Number	Title	Type	Country	Year	Longbox Value/Value
		Singles				
	U5P1009	Shadow Cast	CDJ	U.S.	1995	$2.00

Abyssinians

Label	Catalog Number	Title	Type	Country	Year	Longbox Value/Value
		Full Length				
Caroline	1686	Arise	LP	U.S.		$14.00/$8.00

AC Black

Label	Catalog Number	Title	Type	Country	Year	Longbox Value/Value
		Full Length				
Motown	R32M-1076	AC Black	LP	Japan		$20.00
Motown	6276	AC Black	LP/BP	U.S.		$12.00/$7.00
		Singles				
RCA	ZD-43090	Funky Situation	CD5	Germany	1989	$7.00

AC/DC

Label	Catalog Number	Title	Type	Country	Year	Longbox Value/Value
		Full Length				
Atlantic	80178-2	'74 Four Jailbreak	LP/LB	U.S.		$14.00/$8.00
	Non-remastered version.					
Album Network		Album Network Special	RS	U.S.	1996	$200.00
	2 CD set. Airdate: 8/17/96.					
Atlantic	16018-2	Back In Black	LP/LB	U.S.		$14.00/$8.00
	Non-remastered version.					
Atlantic	AMCY-888	Ballbreaker	LTD/LP	Japan	1996	$35.00
	First Pressing in slip case.					
Elektra		Ballbreaker	DJ/LP	U.K.	1995	$30.00
Elektra	SAM1693	Ballbreaker	DJ/Smplr	U.K.	1995	$50.00
Westwood One		BBC Classic Tracks	RS	U.S.	1993	$50.00
	2 CD set. Airdate: 11/22/93					
Westwood One		BBC Classic Tracks	RS	U.S.	1993	$50.00
	2 CD set. Airdate: 5/10/93					
Westwood One		BBC Classic Tracks	RS	U.S.	1993	$30.00
	Airdate: 1/18/93					
Westwood One		BBC Classic Tracks	RS	U.S.	1993	$30.00
	Airdate: 4/29/91					
Atlantic	32XD-943	Blow Up your Video	LP	Japan		$25.00
Atlantic	80100-2	Flick Of the Switch	LP/LB	U.S.		$14.00/$8.00
	Non-remastered version.					
Atlantic	81263-2	Fly On the Wall	LP/LB	U.S.†	1985	$14.00/$8.00
Atlantic	11111-2	For Those About To Rock	LP/LB	U.S.		$14.00/$8.00
	Non-remastered version.					
Eastwest	PRCD 116	Hail Caesar	DJ/Smplr	Germany	1995	$38.00
		Hardest Rockin' Halloween	RS	U.S.	1992	$80.00
	2 CD set. Airdate: 10/31/92.					
Atlantic	36142-2	High Voltage	LP/LB	U.S.		$14.00/$8.00
	Non-remastered version.					
Atlantic	18P2-2761	Highway To Hell	LP	Japan		$25.00
Atlantic	19244-2	Highway To Hell	LP/LB	U.S.		$14.00/$8.00
	Non-remastered version.					
Atlantic	19212-2	If You Want Blood You've Got It	LP/LB	U.S.		$14.00/$8.00
	Non-remastered version.					
		In Concert	RS	U.S.	1995	$95.00
	2 CD set. Airdate: 5/10/93					
Album Network		In the Studio (Back In Black)	RS	U.S.		$25.00
Atlantic	36151-2	Let There Be Rock	LP/LB	U.S.		$14.00/$8.00
	Non-remastered version.					
Atco	92212-2	Live	LTD/LP	Canada	1992	$25.00
	2 CD set.					
Atco		Live	DJ/Smplr	U.S.	1992	$25.00
	2 CD set					
Atco	92212-2	Live	LTD/LP	U.S.	1992	$25.00
	2 CD set.					
Atlantic	19180-2	Powerage	LP/LB	U.S.		$14.00/$8.00
	Non-remastered version.					
Atco	SAMP 290	Razors Edge, The	DJ/Intvw	Australia	1992	$50.00
Atco		Razors Edge, The	LTD/LP	Australia	1992	$50.00
	Boxed set with CD and video tape.					
		Riff Contest	DJ/Smplr	Germany	1995	$150.00
	12 track greatest hits CD					
Elektra		Rock Hard Years, The	DJ/Smplr	Australia	1995	$45.00
Atlantic		Rock Hard Years, The	DJ/Smplr	Australia	1995	$45.00
		Superstars	RS	U.S.	1995	$50.00
	Airdate: 2/6/95					
		Superstars	RS	U.S.	1996	$90.00
	2 CD set. Airdate: 2/5/96					
Media America		Up Close	RS	U.S.	1990	$50.00
	2 CD set.					
Media America		Up Close	RS	U.S.	1992	$50.00
	2 CD set.					
Media America		Up Close	RS	U.S.	1993	$50.00
	2 CD set.					
Media America		Up Close	RS	U.S.	1996	$65.00
	2 CD set.					
Atco		Volume 1	LTD/LP	Australia	1995	$110.00
	6 CD album set.					
Atco		Volume 2	LTD/LP	Australia	1995	$100.00
	5 CD album set.					
		Singles				
Alantic	7567-96361-2	Are You Ready	CD5	Germany	1990	$10.00
Atco	PRCD 3746-2	Are You Ready	CDJ	U.S.	1990	$3.00
		Big Gun	CD5	Australia	1992	$10.00
		Big Gun	CD5	U.K.	1992	$10.00
Columbia	CSK 5185	Big Gun	CDJ	U.S.	1992	$7.00
Eastwest		Cover You In Oil	CD5	U.K.	1996	$10.00
Eastwest		Cover You In Oil	CD5	U.K.	1996	$10.00
Atlantic		Cover You In Oil	CDJ	U.S.	1995	$8.00
Atlantic		Dirty Deeds Done Dirt Cheap	CD5	Germany	1993	$9.00
Atlantic		Dirty Deeds Done Dirt Cheap	CD5	U.K	1993	$10.00
Atco	PRCD 4901-2	Dirty Deeds Done Dirt Cheap	CDJ	U.S.	1992	$6.00
		Hard As A Rock	CD5	U.K.		$10.00
Elektra		Hard As A Rock	CD5	U.K.	1995	$10.00
Elektra	64366	Hard As A Rock	CD5	U.S.	1995	$5.00
Elektra	PRCD 9337-2	Hard As A Rock	CDJ	U.S.	1995	$7.00
Atlantic	786617-2	Heatseeker	CD3	Germany	1988	$8.00
Atlantic	10SW-9	Heatseeker	CD3	Japan	1988	$13.00/$3.00
Atlantic	A-9136CD	Heatseeker	CD3	U.K.	1988	$7.00
Atlantic	PR 2208-2	Heatseeker	CDJ	U.S.	1988	$3.00
Atco	CD-96135	Highway To Hell	CD5	Canada	1993	$7.00
Atlantic		Highway To Hell	CD5	U.K.	1992	$8.00
Atco	98491-2	Highway To Hell	CD5	U.S.	1992	$5.00
Atco	CD96135	Highway To Hell	CD5	U.S.	1992	$7.00
Atco	96135-2	Highway To Hell	CD5/LB	U.S.	1992	$7.00/$5.00
Atco	PRCD 4755-2	Highway To Hell	CDJ	U.S.	1992	$7.00
Atco	PRCD 3639-2	Mistress For Christmas	CDJ	U.S.	1990	$6.00
Atlantic	PRCD 3639-2	Mistress For Christmas	CDJ	U.S.	1990	$8.00
		Money Talks	CD5	Australia	1990	$10.00
Atco	7567-96408-2	Money Talks	CD5	Germany	1990	$8.00
Atco	B-8886CD	Money Talks	CD5	U.K.	1990	$8.00
Atco	PRCD 3661-2	Money Talks	CDJ	U.S.	1990	$6.00
Atco	PRCD 3661-2	Money Talks	CDJ	U.S.	1990	$8.00
	With front picture sleeve.					
		Rock Your Heart Out	CD5	Australia	1990	$10.00
Atlantic	786586-2	That's the Way I Wanna Rock 'n Roll	CD3	Germany	1988	$9.00
Atlantic	10SW-49	That's the Way I Wanna Rock 'n Roll	CD3	Japan	1988	$13.00/$3.00
Atlantic	A-9098CD	That's the Way I Wanna Rock 'n Roll	CD3	U.K.	1988	$9.00
Atco	7567-96427-2	Thunderstruck	CD5	Germany	1990	$8.00
Atlantic	AMDY-5031	Thunderstruck	CD3	Japan	1990	$12.00/$4.00
Atco	B-8907CD	Thunderstruck	CD5	U.K.	1990	$8.00
Atco	PRCD 3522-2	Thunderstruck	CDJ	U.S.	1990	$8.00
Atlantic	PRCD 3522-2	Thunderstruck	CDJ	U.S.	1990	$10.00
Atco	7567-96065-2	Whole Lotta Rosie	CD5	Germany	1992	$10.00

Academia, Eleanor

Label	Catalog Number	Title	Type	Country	Year	Longbox Value/Value
		Singles				
Epic	128H-8011	Adventures	CD3	Japan	1988	$8.00/$2.00

Accept

Label	Catalog Number	Title	Type	Country	Year	Longbox Value/Value
		Full Length				
Victor	VICP-8134	Dead On	LTD/LP	Japan		$35.00
Columbia	BEK-44368	Eat the Heat	LP	Canada		$15.00
Castle	2827 023	I'm A Rebel/Breaker	LP	Germany		$20.00
Castle	TFOCD-023	I'm A Rebel/Breaker	LP	U.K.		$20.00
Portrait	RK-39974	Metal Heart	LP/BP	U.S.†	1985	$14.00/$8.00
CBS		No Substitute	LP/LB	U.S.		$12.00/$8.00
		Singles				
RCA	PD-42814	Generation Clash	CD5	Germany	1989	$4.00
RCA	74321 12539	I Don't Wanna Be Like You	CD5	Germany	1993	$10.00

Access

Label	Catalog Number	Title	Type	Country	Year	Longbox Value/Value
		Singles				
Polydor	FHDF-1251	Jewelry Angel	CD3	Japan	1993	$8.00/$2.00
Polydor	FHDF-1283	Naked Desire	CD3	Japan	1993	$8.00/$2.00
Polydor	FHDF-1239	Virgin Emotion	CD3	Japan	1993	$8.00/$2.00

Access Denied

Label	Catalog Number	Title	Type	Country	Year	Longbox Value/Value
		Singles				
ZYX	8-6128	Play This, Play That	CD5	Germany	1989	$4.00

Ace

Label	Catalog Number	Title	Type	Country	Year	Longbox Value/Value
		Full Length				
S-F-Miles	SEECD-214	Best Of	LP	U.S.		$10.00

Ace Cats

Label	Catalog Number	Title	Type	Country	Year	Longbox Value/Value
		Singles				
CBS	654813-3	Sheila	CD3	Germany	1989	$5.00

Ace Juice

Full Length

Label	Catalog Number	Title	Type	Country	Year	Longbox Value / Value
Capitol	C2-90925	Ace Juice	LP/LB	U.S.		$10.00/$6.00

Singles

Label	Catalog Number	Title	Type	Country	Year	Longbox Value / Value
Capitol		Go Go	CDJ	U.S.		$2.00

Ace Of Base

Singles

Label	Catalog Number	Title	Type	Country	Year	Longbox Value / Value
Arista	07822126172	All That She Wants	CD5	Canada	1994	$8.00
Arista	12617	All That She Wants	CD5	U.S.	1994	$5.00
Arista	ASCD 2889	Beautiful Life	CDJ	U.S.		$3.00
Arista		Don't Turn Around	CD5	U.K.	1994	$10.00
Arista		Don't Turn Around	CDJ	U.K.	1994	$12.00
Arista	12692	Don't Turn Around	CD5	U.S.	1994	$6.00
Arista	2691	Don't Turn Around	CDJ	U.S.	1994	$3.00
		Happy Nation	CD5	U.K.		$10.00
	Second version.					
Arista		Happy Nation	CD5	U.K.	1994	$10.00
Arista	12774	Living in Danger	CD5	U.S.	1994	$5.00
Arista	ASCD 2754	Living In Danger	CDJ	U.S.	1995	$3.00
		Lucky Love	CD5	U.K.		$10.00
		Lucky Love	CDJ	U.K.		$10.00
Arista	12673	Sign, The	CD5	U.S.	1994	$5.00
Arista		Sign, The	CD5	Germany	1993	$11.00
Arista	2653	Sign, The	CDJ	U.S.	1993	$3.00
Arista	12673	Sign, The	CD5	U.S.	1994	$6.00

Acetone

Singles

Label	Catalog Number	Title	Type	Country	Year	Longbox Value / Value
Yard	CD2	I'm Gone	CD5	U.S.		$4.00

Acid Horse

Singles

Label	Catalog Number	Title	Type	Country	Year	Longbox Value / Value
SPV	9142-3	No Name, No Slogan	CD5	Germany	1990	$6.00
Wax Trax	WAX-61CD	No Name, No Slogan	CD5	U.K.	1990	$6.00
Devotion	CDDVN-103	No Name, No Slogan	CD5	U.K.	1992	$7.00
Wax Trax	9081	No Name, No Slogan	CD5	U.S.	1989	$5.00

Acid Love

Singles

Label	Catalog Number	Title	Type	Country	Year	Longbox Value / Value
Toshiba	TODT-3048	Love Sensation	CD3	Japan	1993	$13.00/$3.00

Acid Test

Singles

Label	Catalog Number	Title	Type	Country	Year	Longbox Value / Value
Sire	PRO-CD-6645	Blown	CDJ	U.S.	1993	$2.00
Warner Brothers	12-40991	Mr. Skin	CD5	Canada	1993	$8.00

Ackerman, William

Full Length

Label	Catalog Number	Title	Type	Country	Year	Longbox Value / Value
Windam Hill	WD-1014	Passage	LP/LB	U.S.†	1984	$14.00/$8.00
Windam Hill	WD-1028	Past Light	LP/LB	U.S.†	1984	$14.00/$8.00
Windam Hill	17639	Selections From Imaginary Roads	DJ/Smplr	U.S.	1988	$10.00

Singles

Label	Catalog Number	Title	Type	Country	Year	Longbox Value / Value
Windam Hill		Opening Of Doors, The	CDJ	U.S.		$7.00
	Also contains 3 tracks by Andy Narell.					

Acosta, Russell

Singles

Label	Catalog Number	Title	Type	Country	Year	Longbox Value / Value
JRS	822	Deep In My Soul	CDJ	U.S.	1992	$2.00

Acoustic Alchemy

Full Length

Label	Catalog Number	Title	Type	Country	Year	Longbox Value / Value
MCA	MCAD-6291	Blue Chip	LP	U.K.		$18.00
MCA	MCAD-42125	Natural Elements	LP	U.K.		$18.00

Singles

Label	Catalog Number	Title	Type	Country	Year	Longbox Value / Value
		Casino	CDJ	U.S.		$2.00
		Natural Elements	CDJ	U.S.		$2.00

Acrophet

Full Length

Label	Catalog Number	Title	Type	Country	Year	Longbox Value / Value
Triple X	51011	Corrupt Minds	LP/BP	U.S.		$12.00/$7.00
Triple X	51032	Faded Glory	LP/BP	U.S.		$12.00/$7.00

Act

Singles

Label	Catalog Number	Title	Type	Country	Year	Longbox Value / Value
Polygram	CDIMM-2	I Can't Escape From You	CD5	U.K.	1988	$6.00

Act Of State

Singles

Label	Catalog Number	Title	Type	Country	Year	Longbox Value / Value
ZYX	6529-8	Open Doors	CD5	Germany	1991	$5.00

Action

Singles

Label	Catalog Number	Title	Type	Country	Year	Longbox Value / Value
JVC Victor	VDRS-1169	Toki O Koete	CD5	Japan	1989	$8.00
ZYX	6514-2	Zen Eleine Rapperlein	CD5	Germany	1991	$5.00

Action Swingers

Singles

Label	Catalog Number	Title	Type	Country	Year	Longbox Value / Value
SRD	WIJ-14CD	More Fast Numbers	CD5	U.K.	1992	$5.00

Activate

Singles

Label	Catalog Number	Title	Type	Country	Year	Longbox Value / Value
Zyx	1238	Beat Of The Drum	CD5	U.S.	1994	$5.00
		Let the Rhythm Take Control	CD5	U.K.	1994	$8.00
		Let the Rhythm Take Control	CD5	U.K.	1994	$8.00
	Second version.					

Acuff, Roy

Full Length

Label	Catalog Number	Title	Type	Country	Year	Longbox Value / Value
Columbia	CK 48956	Essential Roy Acuff 1936 - 1949	LP/LB	U.S.	1992	$15.00/$10.00
	First page of booklet is misprinted with tribute to Gene Autry.					

Acuna, Alex And The Unknowns

Full Length

Label	Catalog Number	Title	Type	Country	Year	Longbox Value / Value
GRP	3322	Alex Acuna And the Unknowns	LP/LB	U.S.		$12.00/$7.00

Adachi, Kazumi

Singles

Label	Catalog Number	Title	Type	Country	Year	Longbox Value / Value
Victor	VIDL-10268	Al Playoff	CD3	Japan	1992	$13.00/$3.00

Adachi, Yumi

Singles

Label	Catalog Number	Title	Type	Country	Year	Longbox Value / Value
Victor	VIDL-10361	Good Night	CD3	Japan	1993	$8.00/$2.00

Adamo

Full Length

Label	Catalog Number	Title	Type	Country	Year	Longbox Value / Value
Victor	VDP-75	Super Best	LP	Japan		$15.00

Singles

Company	Disk Number	Title	Type	Country	Year	Longbox Value / Value
EMI	147406-2	Es Gibt Noch Engel	CD5	Germany	1988	$5.00

Adams, Bryan

Full Length

Company	Disk Number	Title	Type	Country	Year	Longbox Value / Value
Westwood One		BBC Classic Tracks	RS	U.S.	1994	$20.00
	Airdate: 6/6/94					
A&M		Bryan Adams	LTD/LP	Australia	1994	$25.00
	Gold disc.					
A&M	CD-3100	Bryan Adams	LP/LB	U.S.		$18.00/$12.00
A&M		Cuts Like A Knife	LTD/LP	Australia	1994	$25.00
	Gold disc.					
A&M	CD-4919	Cuts Like A Knife	LP/LB	U.S.†	1994	$14.00/$8.00
A&M	D50Y3205	Hits On Fire	LTD/LP	Japan	1987	$120.00
	One gold disc CD and on picture disc CD.					
A&M	D50Y3205	Hits On Fire	LTD/LP	Japan	1988	$80.00
	2 CD set.					
Westwood One		In Concert	RS	U.S.	1992	$50.00
	2 CD set. With Tom Cochrane, Airdate: 6/8/92					
Westwood One		In Concert	RS	U.S.	1992	$45.00
	Airdate: 7/20/92					
Album Network		In the Studio (Cuts Like A Knife)	RS	U.S.	1988	$20.00
	Airdate: 10/3/88					
Album Network		In the Studio (Cuts Like A Knife)	RS	U.S.	1991	$20.00
	Airdate: 2/18/91					
Album Network		In the Studio (Reckless)	RS	U.S.	1989	$20.00
	Airdate: 11/6/89					
Album Network		In the Studio (Reckless)	RS	U.S.	1993	$20.00
	Airdate: 2/15/93					
A&M		Into the Fire	LTD/LP	Australia	1994	$25.00
	Gold disc.					
DIR		King Biscuit Flour Hour	RS	U.S.	1990	$35.00
	Airdate: 11/25/90					
DIR		King Biscuit Flour Hour	RS	U.S.	1991	$35.00
	Airdate: 10/13/91					
DIR		King Biscuit Flour Hour	RS	U.S.	1992	$35.00
	Airdate: 10/11/92					
DIR		King Biscuit Flour Hour	RS	U.S.	1993	$40.00
	Airdate: 11/21/93					
A&M	PCCY-10080	Live! Live! Live!	LP	Japan	1991	$25.00
A&M		Reckless	LTD/LP	Australia	1994	$25.00
	Gold disc.					
A&M	CD-5013	Reckless	LP/LB	U.S.†	1984	$14.00/$8.00
Pioneer	PA-85-115	Reckless	LD	U.S.	1985	$20.00
A&M	CD-5013	Reckless	LP/LB	U.S.†	1985	$14.00/$8.00
	CD in digipak.					
Pioneer	PA-85-115	Reckless	LD	U.S.	1990	$25.00
	Digital audio					
A&M		So Far So Good	LTD/LP	Australia	1994	$25.00
	Gold disc.					
Westwood One		Superstar Concert	RS	U.S.	1993	$50.00
	2 CD set. Airdate: 11/29/93					
A&M		Waking Up the Neighbors	LTD/LP	Australia	1994	$25.00
	Gold disc.					
A&M		You Want It, You Got It	LTD/LP	Australia	1994	$25.00
	Gold disc.					

Singles

Company	Disk Number	Title	Type	Country	Year	Longbox Value / Value
A&M	580 477	All For Love	CD5	U.K.	1993	$10.00
	With Rod Stewart and Sting					
A&M	31458 0476	All For Love	CD5	U.S.	1993	$5.00
	With Rod Stewart and Sting					
A&M	31458 8243	All For Love	CDJ	U.S.	1993	$7.00
	With Rod Stewart and Sting					
A&M		All I Want Is You	CD5	U.K.	1991	$10.00
A&M	75021 2380-2	All I Want Is You	CDJ	U.S.	1991	$6.00
A&M	75021 5367-2	All I Want Is You	CDJ	U.S.	1991	$6.00
A&M	390812-2	Can't Stop This Thing We Started	CD5	Germany	1991	$10.00
A&M	PCDY-10030	Can't Stop This Thing We Started	CD3	Japan	1991	$12.00/$3.00
A&M	AMCD-812	Can't Stop This Thing We Started	CD5	U.K.	1991	$10.00
A&M	75021 2386 2	Can't Stop This Thing We Started	CD5	U.S.	1991	$5.00
A&M	75021 7276 2	Can't Stop This Thing We Started	CDJ	U.S.	1991	$6.00
A&M	580069-2	Do I Have To Say the Words	CD5	Germany	1992	$10.00
A&M	PODM-1006	Do I Have To Say the Words	CD3	Japan	1992	$3.00
A&M	AMCDR-0068	Do I Have To Say the Words	CD5	U.K.	1992	$10.00
A&M	75021 7384 2	Do I Have To Say the Words	CDJ	U.S.	1991	$3.00
A&M	7031-2370-2	(Everything I Do) I Do It For You	CD5	Canada	1991	$10.00
Polygram	390789-2	(Everything I Do) I Do It For You	CD5	Germany	1991	$10.00
A&M	PCDY-10029	(Everything I Do) I Do It For You	CD3	Japan	1991	$15.00/$4.00
A&M		(Everything I Do) I Do It For You	CD5	U.K.	1991	$10.00
A&M	75021 12380 2	(Everything I Do) I Do It For You	CD5	U.S.	1991	$3.00
A&M	75021 2380 2	(Everything I Do) I Do It For You	CDJ	U.S.	1991	$3.00
A&M	75021 7234 2	(Everything I Do) I Do It For You	CDJ	U.S.	1991	$3.00
A&M		Have You Really Loved A Woman?	CD5	Canada	1995	$10.00
A&M		Have You Really Loved A Woman?	CD5	France	1995	$12.00
A&M	81028-2	Have You Really Loved A Woman?	CD5	U.S.	1995	$6.00
A&M	31458 84282	Have You Really Loved A Woman?	CDJ	U.S.	1995	$6.00
A&M	D15Y-3198	Heat Of the Night	CD3	Japan	1988	$15.00/$4.00
A&M	S12Y-3012	Heaven	CD3	Japan	1988	$13.00/$4.00
A&M		Let's Make A Night To Remember	CDJ	U.S.	1996	$6.00
A&M	580 423	Please Forgive Me	CD5	U.K.	1993	$10.00
A&M		Please Forgive Me	CDJ	U.S.	1993	$3.00
		Rock Steady	CDJ	U.K.	1995	$10.00
	With Bonnie Raitt					
	DPRO10284	Rock Steady	CDJ	U.S.	1995	$7.00
	With Bonnie Raitt					
A&M	S10Y-3102	Run To You	CD3	Japan	1988	$13.00/$4.00
A&M	580545	Run To You	CD5	U.K.	1994	$10.00
A&M	CC-31019	Run To You	CD3	U.S.	1988	$6.00/$4.00
	588320-2	Straight From the Heart	CDJ	Spain	1995	$25.00
	BRYAND2	Summer Of '69	CDJ	Spain	1995	$18.00
	PRO 9002	Tee Live Volume	CDJ	U.S.	1995	$8.00
A&M		The Only Thing That Looks Good To Me Is You	CD5	U.S.	1996	$6.00
A&M		The Only Thing That Looks Good To Me Is You	CDJ	U.S.	1996	$6.00
A&M	PCDY-10031	There Will Never Be Another Tonight	CD3	Japan	1991	$4.00
A&M	AMCD838	There Will Never Be Another Tonight	CD5	U.K.	1992	$10.00
A&M	75021-7315-2	There Will Never Be Another Tonight	CDJ	U.S.	1991	$3.00
A&M	PCDY-10032	Thought I'd Died And Gone To Heaven	CD3	Japan	1992	$13.00/$3.00
A&M		Thought I'd Died And Gone To Heaven	CD5	U.K.	1992	$10.00
A&M	75021 7324-2	Thought I'd Died And Gone To Heaven	CDJ	U.S.	1991	$3.00
A&M	75021 7317-2	Touch the Hand	CDJ	U.S.	1991	$3.00

Adams, Felicia

Singles

Company	Disk Number	Title	Type	Country	Year	Longbox Value / Value
Motown	3746312082	Thinking About You	CDJ	U.S.	1994	$3.00

Adams, George

Full Length

Label	Catalog Number	Title	Type	Country	Year	Longbox Value/Value
Blue Note	CDP-46314	Breakthrough	LP/LB	U.S.		$18.00/$12.00
Timeless	30R2-30	Decisions	LP	Japan		$20.00
Polygram	1004CD	Don't Lose Control	LP/BP	U.S.		$14.00/$8.00
Soul Note	121057-2	Gentlemen's Agreement	LP/LB	U.S.		$14.00/$8.00
Soul Note	SN-1007CD	Hand To Hand	LP/LB	U.S.†	1985	$14.00/$8.00
Timeless	ALCR-48	Life Line	LP	Japan		$20.00
Soul Note	SN-1094CD	Live At the Village Vanguard	LP/LB	U.S.†	1985	$8.00
Timeless	ALCR-49	Melodic Excursions	LP	Japan		$20.00
Blue Note	B2 91984-2	Nightingale	LP/LB	U.S.		$12.00
Blue Note	B2 96689-2	Old Feelings	LP/LB	U.S.		$12.00
Timeless	ALCR-46	Paradise Space Shuttle	LP	Japan		$20.00
Blue Note	CDP-6907	Song Everlasting	LP/LB	U.S.		$12.00
Soul Note	121094-2	Village Vanguard 1	LP/LB	U.S.		$8.00
Soul Note	121044-2	Village Vanguard 2	LP/LB	U.S.		$8.00

Adams, John

Full Length

Label	Catalog Number	Title	Type	Country	Year	Longbox Value/Value
ECM	821465-2	Harmonium	LP	Germany		$15.00
Polygram	821465-2	Harmonium	LP/BP	U.S.		$12.00/$7.00
Nonesuch	79177-2	Nixon In China	LP/BP	U.S.		$12.00/$7.00
Nonesuch		Selections From "Nixon In China"	DJ/Smplr	U.S.		$5.00

Adams, Oleta

Singles

Label	Catalog Number	Title	Type	Country	Year	Longbox Value/Value
Phonogram	PHDR-42	Boku No Hitomki Chisana Taiyo	CD3	Japan	1991	$12.00/$3.00
Polygram	875913-2	Circle Of One	CD5	Germany	1991	$9.00
Phonogram	PHDR-7	Circle Of One	CD3	Japan	1990	$12.00/$3.00
Fontana	PHCR-8011	Circle Of One	CD5	Japan	1991	$15.00
Fontana	OLECD-2	Circle Of One	CD5	U.K.	1991	$6.00
Fontana	CDP 314	Circle Of One	CDJ	U.S.	1990	$3.00
Fontana	CDP 445	Circle Of One	CDJ	U.S.	1991	$3.00
Fontana	CDP 1056	Day I Stop Loving You, The	CDJ	U.S.	1993	$3.00
Polygram	868933-2	Don't Let the Sun Go Down On Me	CD5	Germany	1991	$9.00
Fontana	TRICD-1	Don't Let the Sun Go Down On Me	CD5	U.K.	1991	$9.00
Fontana	CDP-608	Don't Let the Sun Go Down On Me	CDJ	U.S.	1991	$3.00
Polygram	878585-2	Get Here	CD5	Germany	1990	$9.00
Fontana	OLECD 3	Get Here	CD5	U.K.	1990	$9.00
Fontana	CDP 315	Get Here	CDJ	U.S.	1990	$3.00
Fontana	CDP 376	Get Here	CDJ	U.S.	1990	$3.00
Fontana	CDP 945	I Just Had To Hear Your Voice	CDJ	U.S.	1993	$3.00
Polygram	875019-2	Rhythm Of Life	CD5	Germany	1990	$9.00
Fontana	OLECD-1	Rhythm Of Life	CD5	U.K.	1990	$9.00
Fontana	CDP 254	Rhythm Of Life	CDJ	U.S.	1990	$3.00
RCA	62909	We Will Find A Way	CDJ	U.S.	1994	$3.00
Fontana	OLECD-4	You've Got To Give Me Room	CD5	U.K.	1991	$9.00

Adamski

Full Length

Label	Catalog Number	Title	Type	Country	Year	Longbox Value/Value
MCA	2060	Born To Be Alive Sampler	DJ/Smplr	U.S.	1991	$12.00/$7.00
MCA	MCAD-10130	Dr. Adamski's Musical Pharmacy	LP/LB	U.S.	1990	$7.00

Singles

Label	Catalog Number	Title	Type	Country	Year	Longbox Value/Value
MCA	MCSTD-1644	Back To Front	CD5	U.K.	1992	$8.00
MCA	54283	Born To Be Alive	CD5	U.S.	1992	$5.00
MCA	DMCAT-1459	Flashback Jack	CD5	U.K.	1990	$8.00
MCA	DMCAT-1425	Future Freak	CD5	U.K.	1990	$8.00
MCA	MCSTD-1613	Get Your Body	CD5	U.K.	1992	$8.00
MCA	2292-57272-2	Killer	CD5	Germany	1990	$8.00
Pioneer	WMD5-4034	Killer	CD3	Japan	1990	$13.00/$3.00
MCA	DMCAT-1400	Killer	CD5	U.K.	1990	$8.00
MCA		Killer	CDJ	U.S.	1990	$2.00
Eastwest	257305-2	N-R-G	CD5	Germany	1990	$8.00
Pioneer	WMD5-4020	N-R-G	CD3	Japan	1990	$13.00/$3.00
MCA	DMCAT-1386	N-R-G	CD5	U.K.	1990	$8.00
BMG	MCD-18254	Never Goin' Down	CD5	Germany	1991	$8.00
MCA	MCSTD-1578	Never Goin' Down	CD5	U.K.	1991	$8.00
Eastwest	9031-72473-2	Space Jungle (All Shook Up)	CD5	Germany	1990	$8.00
Eastwest	9031-72633-2	Space Jungle (All Shook Up)	CD5	Germany	1990	$8.00
MCA	DMCAT-1435	Space Jungle (All Shook Up)	CD5	U.K.	1990	$8.00
MCA	CD45 53961	Space Jungle (All Shook Up)	CDJ	U.S.	1990	$2.00
MCA	CD45 1261	Space Jungle (All Shook Up)	CDJ	U.S.	1990	$2.00

Adamson, Barry

Full Length

Label	Catalog Number	Title	Type	Country	Year	Longbox Value/Value
Mute	61127	Delusion	LP/LB	U.S.		$12.00/$7.00
Mute	29B2-64	Moss-Side Story	LP	Japan		$20.00

Singles

Label	Catalog Number	Title	Type	Country	Year	Longbox Value/Value
Mute	CDMUTE-149	Cinema Is King	CD5	U.K.	1992	$6.00
Mute	CDMUTE-97	Taming Of the Shrewd	CD5	U.K.	1989	$6.00
Mute	826 963	These Boots Are Made For Walking	CD5	Germany	1991	$6.00
Mute	CDMUTE-119	These Boots Are Made For Walking	CD5	U.K.	1991	$6.00

Addams And Gee

Singles

Label	Catalog Number	Title	Type	Country	Year	Longbox Value/Value
Debut	DEBCD-3108	Chung Kuo	CD5	U.K.	1991	$6.00

Adderley, Cannonball

Full Length

Label	Catalog Number	Title	Type	Country	Year	Longbox Value/Value
Emarcy	834588-2	Cannonball & Coltrane	LP/LB	U.S.		$14.00/$8.00
Phonogram	32JD-118	Cannonball's Sharpshooters	LP	Japan		$20.00
Mercury	EJD-1013	Compact Jazz	LP	Japan		$20.00
Landmark	VDJ-1604	In Europe	LP	Japan		$20.00
Capitol	TOCJ-5313	In Japan	LP	Japan		$20.00
Charly	CD-58	Just Friends	LP	U.S.		$8.00

Adderley, Julian (Cannonball)

Full Length

Label	Catalog Number	Title	Type	Country	Year	Longbox Value/Value
Savoy Records	CY-78989	Presenting Cannonball Adderley	LTD/LP	U.S.	1995	$20.00
CD in miniature repica of original LP sleeve.						

Adeva

Singles

Label	Catalog Number	Title	Type	Country	Year	Longbox Value/Value
Chrysalis	662920	Beautiful Love	CD5	Germany	1990	$8.00
EMI	COOLCD-195	Beautiful Love	CD5	U.K.	1989	$8.00
EMI	COOLCD-248	Don't Let It Show On Your Face	CD5	U.K.	1992	$8.00
Chrysalis	662725	I Thank You	CD5	Germany	1989	$8.00
Cooltempo	COOLCD-192	I Thank You	CD5	U.K.	1989	$8.00
Capitol	DPRO 79356	I Thank You	CDJ	U.S.	1989	$3.00
EMI	COOLCD-264	I'm the One For You	CD5	U.K.	1992	$8.00
Capitol	DPRO-79140	Independent Woman	CDJ	U.S.	1992	$3.00
Chrysalis	323797-2	It Should've Been Me	CD5	Germany	1991	$8.00
EMI	COOLCD-236	It Should've Been Me	CD5	U.K.	1991	$8.00
Capitol	DPRO-79746	It Should've Been Me	CDJ	U.S.	1991	$3.00
Chrysalis	662070	Respect	CD5	Germany	1989	$8.00
EMI	COOLCD-200	Treat Me Right	CD5	U.K.	1990	$8.00
EMI	COOLCD-254	Until You Come Back To Me	CD5	U.K.	1992	$8.00
Chrysalis	662470	Warning	CD5	Germany	1989	$8.00
Cool	COOLCD-185	Warning	CD5	U.K	1989	$8.00
Capitol	DPRO 79981	Warning	CDJ	U.S.	1989	$3.00

Adi

Singles

Label	Catalog Number	Title	Type	Country	Year	Longbox Value/Value
Victor	VICL-2101	Softly	CD3	Japan	1992	$12.00/$3.00

Adioa

Full Length

Label	Catalog Number	Title	Type	Country	Year	Longbox Value/Value
Mango	9857	Soweto Man	LP/LB	U.S.		$14.00/$8.00

Adler, Larry

Singles

Label	Catalog Number	Title	Type	Country	Year	Longbox Value/Value
Mercury	MERCD 408	Man I Love, The	CD5	U.K.	1994	$10.00

Admires

Singles

Label	Catalog Number	Title	Type	Country	Year	Longbox Value/Value
ZYX	6389-8	Out On A Limb	CD5	Germany	1990	$5.00

Adoh, Mitsuko

Singles

Label	Catalog Number	Title	Type	Country	Year	Longbox Value/Value
Victor	VNC-3068	Jinsei-Butai	CD3	Japan	1992	$3.00

Adorable

Singles

Label	Catalog Number	Title	Type	Country	Year	Longbox Value/Value
Creation	CRESCD-140	Homeboy	CD5	U.K.	1992	$8.00
Creation	CRESCD-133	I'll Be Your Saint	CD5	U.K.	1992	$8.00
Creation	CRESCD-153	Sistine Chapel Ceiling	CD5	U.K.	1992	$8.00
Creation	CRESCD-127	Sunshine Smile	CD5	U.K.	1992	$8.00
		Sunshine Smile	CD5	U.S.	1992	$5.00

Adrenalin OD

Singles

Label	Catalog Number	Title	Type	Country	Year	Longbox Value/Value
Buy Our Records	12-018	Cruising With Elvis In Bigfoot's UFO	CDJ	U.S.		$7.00

ADT

Singles

Label	Catalog Number	Title	Type	Country	Year	Longbox Value/Value
	66812	For the Love Of You	CDJ	U.S.	1995	$2.00
	6615	Make A Move	CD5	U.S.	1994	$5.00

Aduc

Singles

Label	Catalog Number	Title	Type	Country	Year	Longbox Value/Value
King	KIDP-45	Rock Me	CD3	Japan	1991	$12.00/$2.00

Adult Net

Full Length

Label	Catalog Number	Title	Type	Country	Year	Longbox Value/Value
Fontana	ADNET-1	Take Me	DJ/Smplr	U.K.	1989	$10.00
Fontana	874238-3	Take Me	CD3	Germany	1989	$8.00
Fontana	874239-2	Take Me	CD5	Germany	1989	$8.00
Fontana	BRXCD-1	Take Me	CD5	U.K.	1989	$8.00
Fontana	874781-2	Waking Up the Sun	CD5	Germany	1989	$8.00
Fontana	BRXCD-3	Waking Up the Sun	CD5	U.K.	1989	$8.00
Fontana	CDP 116	Waking Up the Sun	CDJ	U.S.	1989	$3.00
Fontana	BRXCD-2	Where Were You	CD5	U.K.	1989	$8.00

Adventure Babies

Singles

Label	Catalog Number	Title	Type	Country	Year	Longbox Value/Value
Factory	FACD 347	Barking Man	CD5	U.K.	1992	$10.00

Adventures

Full Length

Label	Catalog Number	Title	Type	Country	Year	Longbox Value/Value
Elektra	9 60772	Sea Of Love	LP/LB	U.S.		$14.00/$8.00
Chrysalis	CCD-1488	Theodore & Friends	LP	U.K.		$15.00
Elektra	9 60772	Trading Secrets With the Moon	LP/LB	U.S.		$14.00/$7.00

Singles

Label	Catalog Number	Title	Type	Country	Year	Longbox Value/Value
Elektra	966773-2	Broken Land	CD3	Germany	1988	$8.00
Elektra	EKR-69CD	Broken Land	CD3	U.K.	1988	$8.00
Elektra	PR 2209-2	Broken Land	CDJ	U.S.	1988	$2.00
Elektra	000046	Broken Land	DJ/CD3	U.S.	1988	$6.00
Elektra	966759-2	Drowning In the Sea Of Love	CD3	Germany	1989	$7.00
Elektra	EKR-76CD	Drowning In the Sea Of Love	CD3	U.K.	1989	$8.00
Elektra	PR 8012-2	Drowning In the Sea Of Love	CDJ	U.S.	1989	$2.00
Polydor	PZCD-238	Monday Monday	CD5	U.K.	1993	$9.00
Elektra	969362-2	One Step From Heaven	CD3	Germany	1989	$8.00
Elektra	EKR-80CD	One Step From Heaven	CD3	U.K.	1989	$8.00
Polydor	PZCD-211	Raining All Over the World	CD5	U.K.	1993	$9.00
Elektra	EKR-98CD	Washington Deceased	CD3	U.K.	1989	$8.00
WEA	966647-2	Your Greatest Shade Of Blue	CD3	Germany	1990	$8.00
Elektra	EKR-106CD	Your Greatest Shade Of Blue	CD3	U.K.	1990	$8.00
Elektra	PR 8147-2	Your Greatest Shade Of Blue	CDJ	U.S.	1990	$2.00

Adventures Of Stevie V

Full Length

Label	Catalog Number	Title	Type	Country	Year	Longbox Value/Value
Mercury	848010	Adventures Of Stevie V	LP/BP	U.S.		$12.00/$7.00

Singles

Label	Catalog Number	Title	Type	Country	Year	Longbox Value/Value
Polygram	878313-2	Body Language	CD5	Germany	1990	$7.00
Mercury	MERCD-331	Body Language	CD5	U.K.	1990	$7.00
Polygram	875637-2	Dirty Cash	CD5	Germany	1990	$7.00
Mercury	MERCD-311	Dirty Cash	CD5	U.K.	1990	$7.00
Polygram	CDP 269	Dirty Cash	CDJ	U.S.	1990	$3.00
Mercury	MERCD-337	Jealousy	CD5	U.K.	1991	$7.00
Polygram	CDP 355	Jealousy	CDJ	U.S.	1991	$3.00

Adverse, Anthony

Singles

Label	Catalog Number	Title	Type	Country	Year	Longbox Value/Value
El	25605-12	Imperial Violets	CD3	Japan	1989	$12.00/$2.00

Aenone

Singles

Label	Catalog Number	Title	Type	Country	Year	Longbox Value/Value
		Saints And Razors	CD5	U.S.		$5.00

Aerosmith

Full Length

Label	Catalog Number	Title	Type	Country	Year	Longbox Value/Value
Sony	SRCS-6951	Aerosmith	LTD/LP	Japan		$40.00
Picture disc CD.						
Columbia	CK-32005	Aerosmith	LP/LB	U.S.		$14.00/$8.00
Non-remastered version.						
Columbia	CK-57360	Aerosmith	LP	U.S.	1992	$12.00
First remastered pressing with expanded booklet.						
Geffen	PRO-CD-3132	Aerosmith/Guns 'n Roses	DJ/Smplr	U.S.	1989	$15.00
With 3 Aerosmith/2 Guns N' Roses tracks						
Def Jam	CSK 2892	Aerosmith/Poison	DJ/Smplr	U.S.	1987	$10.00
1 track by Aerosmith and 1 by Poison.						
Geffen	GEF 245555	Basic Conterto	DJ/Smplr	Spain	1995	$65.00
Westwood One		BBC Classic Tracks	RS	U.S.	1993	$20.00
Airdate: 10/18/93						

Label	Catalog Number	Title	Type	Country	Year	Longbox Value / Value
Westwood One		BBC Classic Tracks	RS	U.S.	1995	$30.00
	Airdate: 1/2/95					
Columbia	CSK 4236	Big Ten Inch Sampler	DJ/Smplr	U.S.	1991	$20.00
Columbia	CXK 66687	Box of Fire	LTD/LP	Canada	1994	$165.00
Sony	SRCS-6960	Classics Live	LTD/LP	Japan		$40.00
	Picture disc CD.					
Columbia	CK-40329	Classics Live	LP/LB	U.S.		$14.00/$8.00
	Non-remastered version.					
Columbia	CK-57369	Classics Live	LP	U.S.	1992	$12.00
	First remastered pressing with expanded booklet.					
Sony	SRCS-6961	Classics Live II	LTD/LP	Japan		$40.00
	Picture disc CD.					
Columbia	CK-40855	Classics Live Vol. 2	LP/LB	U.S.		$14.00/$8.00
	Non-remastered version.					
Columbia	CK-57370	Classics Live Vol. 2	LP	U.S.	1992	$12.00
	Remastered first pressing with expanded booklet.					
Columbia	AEROBOX	Collection	LP	U.K.		$85.00
	4 CD set.					
Geffen	GEFD24SSS	Concerto Basic 40	DJ/Smplr	Spain	1995	$50.00
Geffen	MVCZ-70	Done With Mirrors	LTD/LP	Japan	1995	$65.00
	20 Bit mastered disc.					
Geffen	24091-2	Done With Mirrors	LP/LB	U.S.†	1985	$14.00/$8.00
Sony	SRCS-6955	Draw the Line	LTD/LP	Japan		$40.00
	Picture disc CD.					
Columbia	CK-334856	Draw the Line	LP/LB	U.S.		$14.00/$8.00
	Non-remastered version.					
Columbia	CK-57364	Draw the Line	LP	U.S.	1992	$12.00/$8.00
	Remastered first pressing with expanded booklet.					
Columbia	467385	Draw the Line/Toys In the/Rocks	LP	Germany		$65.00
	3 CD Set					
Global Satellite Network		Dream On Holiday Special	RS	U.S.	1991	$100.00
	3 CD set.					
Westwood One		Fourth Of July Celebration	RS	U.S.	1992	$90.00
	4 CD set. Airdate: 7/4/92.					
Sony	SRCS-6962	Gems	LTD/LP	Japan		$40.00
	Picture disc CD.					
Columbia	CK-44487	Gems	LP/LB	U.S.		$14.00/$8.00
	Non-remastered version.					
Columbia	CK-57371	Gems	LP/LB	U.S.	1992	$12.00/$8.00
	Remastered first pressing with expanded booklet.					
Geffen	GED-24445	Get A Grip	LTD/LP	Germany	1993	$25.00
Geffen	MVCZ-73	Get A Grip	LTD/LP	Japan	1995	$65.00
	20 Bit mastered disc.					
Geffen	GED-24445	Get A Grip	LTD/LP	U.K.	1993	$25.00
Geffen	GEFD-24530	Get A Grip	LTD/LP	U.S.	1993	$30.00
Geffen	GEFD-24530	Get A Grip	LTD/LP	U.S.	1993	$25.00
	Cowhide cover.					
Westwood One		Get A Grip	RS	U.S.	1993	$75.00
	2 CD set.					
Sony	SRCS-6952	Get Your Wings	LTD/LP	Japan		$40.00
	Picture disc CD.					
Columbia	CK-32847	Get Your Wings	LP/LB	U.S.		$8.00
	Non-remastered version.					
Columbia	CK-57369	Get Your Wings	LP/LB	U.S.	1992	$12.00/$8.00
	Remastered first pressing with expanded booklet.					
Sony	SRCS-6958	Greatest Hits	LTD/LP	Japan		$40.00
	Picture disc CD.					
Columbia	CK-36865	Greatest Hits	LP/LB	U.S.		$12.00/$8.00
	Non-remastered version.					
Columbia	CK-57367	Greatest Hits	LP/LB	U.S.	1992	$12.00/$8.00
	Remastered first pressing with expanded booklet.					
Geffen	GRIP 1	Gripping Stuff	DJ/Smplr	U.K.	1994	$35.00
Geffen	GRIP 1	Gripping Stuff	DJ/Smplr	U.K.	1994	$35.00
	Second version.					
Album Network		In the Studio (Get A Grip)	RS	U.S.		$20.00
Album Network		In the Studio (Permenant Vacation)	RS	U.S.		$30.00
Album Network		In the Studio (Pump)	RS	U.S.	1990	$30.00
	Airdate: 12/24/90					
Album Network		In the Studio (Toys In the Attic)	RS	U.S.	1989	$30.00
	Airdate: 10/2/89					
Album Network		In the Studio (Toys In the Attic)	RS	U.S.	1992	$30.00
	Airdate: 11/2/92					
DIR		King Biscuit Flour Hour	RS	U.S.	1988	$50.00
	With Thin Lizzy, Airdate: 9/4/88					
DIR		King Biscuit Flour Hour	RS	U.S.	1989	$40.00
	With Billy Squire, Airdate: 10/16/89					
DIR		King Biscuit Flour Hour	RS	U.S.	1990	$40.00
	With Little Caesar, Airdate: 9/17/90					
DIR		King Biscuit Flour Hour	RS	U.S.	1992	$40.00
	Airdate: 1/12/92					
DIR		King Biscuit Flour Hour	RS	U.S.	1992	$40.00
	Airdate: 12/7/92					
DIR		King Biscuit Flour Hour	RS	U.S.	1995	$30.00
	Airdate: 7/23/95					
Columbia	466733-2	Live Bootleg	DJ/Smplr	Germany	1991	$25.00
	2 CD Set					
Sony	SRCS-6956	Live Bootleg	LTD/LP	Japan		$40.00
	Picture disc CD.					
Westwood One		Livin' & Tourin': On the Edge	RS	U.S.	1993	$30.00
Columbia	A 28478	Made In America	LTD/LP	U.S.	1997	$10.00
	CD sampler available only at WalMart stores.					
Radio Ventures		Masters Of Rock	RS	U.S.	1990	$50.00
	Airdate: 2/12/90					
Sony	SRCS-6957	Night In the Ruts	LTD/LP	Japan		$40.00
	Picture disc CD.					
Columbia	CK-36050	Night In the Ruts	LP/LB	U.S.		$12.00/$8.00
	Non-remastered version.					
Westwood One		Off the Record	RS	U.S.	1994	$30.00
	Airdate: 2/21/94					
Westwood One		Off the Record	RS	U.S.	1994	$30.00
	Airdate: 5/30/94					
Westwood One		Off the Record	RS	U.S.	1994	$20.00
	Airdate: 5/30/94					
Sony	SRCS-5737/9	Pandora's Box	LTD/LP	Japan	1991	$80.00
	3 CD set.					
Columbia	476956 2	Pandora's Toys	LTD/LP	Germany	1994	$80.00
	2 CD album and "Story Of Aerosmith" disc in wood box with patch, sticker, and certificate.					
Columbia	476956-2	Pandora's Toys	LTD/LP	U.K.	1994	$100.00
	Numbered wooden box with second CD "Story Of. . ." sampler.					
Columbia	46209	Pandoras Box	LP	U.S.	1991	$45.00
	3 CD set in 6"x12" box.					
Columbia	476956-9	Pandoras Box (Highlights)	LTD/LP	Canada		$20.00
Geffen	MVCZ71	Permanent Vacation	LTD/LP	Japan	1994	$65.00
	20 Bit mastered disc.					
Geffen	MVCZ-7	Pump	LTD/LP	Japan	1989	$35.00
Pinnacle	MVCZ-7	Pump	DJ/LP	U.K.	1989	$25.00
Geffen	2-24269-Dj	Pump	DJ/LP	U.S.	1989	$30.00

Company	Disk Number	Title	Type	Country	Year	Longbox Value / Value
Geffen	2-24269-2	Pump	LTD/LP	U.S.	1989	$35.00/$25.00
	Limited edition package in long box.					
Sony	SRCS-6959	Rock In A Hard Place	LTD/LP	Japan		$40.00
	Picture disc CD.					
Columbia	CK-38061	Rock In A Hard Place	LP/LB	U.S.		$12.00/$8.00
	Non-remastered version.					
Columbia	CK-57368	Rock In A Hard Place	LP	U.S.	1992	$12.00
	Remastered first pressing with expanded booklet.					
Columbia	CSK 1365	Rock This Way	DJ/Smplr	U.S.	1988	$50.00
Sony	SRCS-6954	Rocks	LTD/LP	Japan		$40.00
	Picture disc CD.					
Columbia	CK-34165	Rocks	LP/LB	U.S.		$12.00/$8.00
	Non-remastered version.					
Columbia	CK-57363	Rocks	LP/LB	U.S.	1992	$12.00/$8.00
	Remastered first pressing with expanded booklet.					
Columbia	SAMP 2195	Story Of Aerosmith, The	DJ/Intvw	U.S.	1994	$25.00
Westwood One		Superstar Concert	RS	U.S.	1994	$90.00
	2 CD set. Airdate: 2/21/94					
Pioneer Artists	PA-90-301	Things That Go Pump	LD	U.S.	1990	
Sony	SRCS-6953	Toys In the Attic	LTD/LP	Japan		$40.00
	Picture disc CD.					
Sony	SRCS-6677	Toys In the Attic	LTDLP/GD	Japan		$40.00
Columbia	CK-33479	Toys In the Attic	LP/LB	U.S.		$12.00/$8.00
	Non-remastered version.					
Columbia	CK-57362	Toys In the Attic	LP	U.S.	1992	$12.00
	Remastered first pressing with expanded booklet.					
Columbia	CK 52857	Toys In the Attic	LTD/LP	U.S.	1992	$30.00/$25.00
	Gold disc with long box.					
Media America		Up Close	RS	U.S.	1989	$55.00
	2 CD set.					
Media America		Up Close	RS	U.S.	1993	$55.00
	3 CD set.					
Media America		Up Close	RS	U.S.	1994	$75.00
	3 CD set.					
Geffen	22P2-2132S	Vacation Club	LP	Japan	1988	$25.00
CBS		Video Scrapbook	LD	U.S.	1990	$30.00
		Singles				
Geffen	PRO-CD-4564	Amazing	CDJ	U.S.	1993	$6.00
Geffen	PRO-CD-4595	Amazing	CDJ	U.S.	1993	$6.00
Geffen	GEF 34CD 920 918-2	Angel	CD3	Germany	1987	$10.00
Geffen	GEF-34CD	Angel	CD3	Japan	1988	$13.00/$5.00
Geffen	PRO-CD-2895	Angel	CDJ	U.S.	1988	$6.00
Geffen	PRO-CD-2871	Angel	DJ/CD3	U.S.	1988	$18.00/$12.00
Geffen	PRO-CD-4692	Blind Man	CDJ	U.S.	1994	$7.00
Geffen	21932	Crazy	CD5	U.S.	1994	$6.00
Geffen	PRO-CD-4624	Crazy	CDJ	U.S.	1994	$7.00
Geffen		Cryin'	CD5	U.K.	1993	$10.00
Geffen		Cryin'	CD5	U.K.	1993	$10.00
	Second version.					
Geffen	PRO-CD-4528	Cryin'	CDJ	U.S.	1993	$7.00
Geffen	PRO-CD-4549	Cryin'	CDJ	U.S.	1993	$7.00
Sony	XEUK11659943	Dream On	CD5	Canada	1990	$10.00
CBS	655575-3	Dream On	CD3	Germany	1990	$10.00
CBS	655575-2	Dream On	CD5	Germany	1990	$10.00
Geffen	GEF 72CD	Dude Looks Like A Lady	CD5	Germany	1988	$10.00
Geffen		Dude Looks Like A Lady	CD3	Japan	1988	$13.00/$5.00
Geffen	GEF72CD	Dude Looks Like A Lady	CD5	U.K.	1990	$10.00
Geffen	DUDE1	Dude Looks Like A Lady	CD5	U.K.	1993	$15.00
Geffen	PRO-CD-2794	Dude Looks Like A Lady	CDJ	U.S.	1987	$10.00
Geffen	GFSTD-46	Eat the Rich	CD5	U.K.	1993	$10.00
Geffen	PRO-CD-4521	Eat the Rich	CDJ	U.S.	1993	$6.00
Geffen	PRO-CD-3806	F.I.N.E.	CDJ	U.S.	1989	$7.00
Geffen	PRO-CD-4552	Fever	CDJ	U.S.	1993	$6.00
Geffen	921416-2	Janie's Got A Gun	CD3	Germany	1989	$10.00
Geffen	09P3-6210	Janie's Got A Gun	CD3	Japan	1989	$13.00/$5.00
Geffen	GEF-68CD	Janie's Got A Gun	CD3	U.K.	1989	$10.00
Geffen	PRO-CD-3794	Janie's Got A Gun	CDJ	U.S.	1989	$8.00
Geffen	GEFDM-21821	Livin' On the Edge	CD5	Canada	1993	$9.00
Geffen	MVCG-13004	Livin' On the Edge	CD3	Japan	1993	$13.00/$5.00
Geffen	GFSXD 35	Livin' On the Edge	CD5	U.K.	1993	$10.00
Geffen		Livin' On the Edge	CD5	U.K.	1993	$10.00
	Second version.					
Geffen	AEROPRO 1	Livin' On the Edge	CDJ	U.K.	1993	$15.00
Geffen	21821	Livin' On the Edge	CD5	U.S.	1993	$5.00
Geffen	PRO-CD-4498	Livin' On the Edge	CDJ	U.S.	1993	$6.00
Geffen	PRO-CD-4515	Livin' On the Edge	CDJ	U.S.	1993	$6.00
Geffen	921333-2	Love In An Elevator	CD3	Germany	1989	$10.00
Geffen	09P3-6190	Love In An Elevator	CD3	Japan	1989	$13.00/$5.00
Geffen	GEF-63CD	Love In An Elevator	CD3	U.K.	1989	$10.00
Geffen	PRO-CD-3645	Love In An Elevator	CDJ	U.S.	1989	$10.00
WEA	7599-21614-2	Other Side, The	CD5	Germany	1990	$10.00
Pioneer	WPDP-6244	Other Side, The	CD3	Japan	1990	$13.00/$5.00
Geffen	GEF-79CD	Other Side, The	CD5	U.K.	1990	$10.00
Geffen	9 21458-2	Other Side, The	CD5	U.S.	1990	$5.00
Geffen	PRO-CD-3918	Other Side, The	CDJ	U.S.	1990	$6.00
Geffen	PRO-CD-4117	Other Side, The	CDJ	U.S.	1990	$8.00
Geffen	10SW-45	Rag Doll	CD3	Japan	1988	$13.00/$5.00
Geffen	GEF-76CD	Rag Doll	CD5	U.K.	1988	$10.00
Geffen	PRO-CD-3089	Rag Doll	CDJ	U.S.	1988	$7.00
Columbia		Shut Up And Dance	CD5	U.K.	1994	$11.00
Columbia		Shut Up And Dance	CD5	U.K.	1994	$11.00
	Second version.					
Columbia	AEROPRO3	Shut Up And Dance	CDJ	U.K.	1994	$15.00
Columbia	660449 5	Sweet Emotion	CDJ	Germany	1994	$10.00
Columbia	657623-2	Sweet Emotion	CD5	Holland	1991	$10.00
Columbia	CSK 4219	Sweet Emotion	CDJ	U.S.	1991	$7.00
Geffen	PRO-CD-4117	Take Me To the Other Side	CDJ	U.S.	1989	$10.00
Geffen	38K-7952	Walk This Way	CD3	U.S.	1987	$8.00/$4.00
Geffen	PRO-CD-3852	What It Takes	CDJ	U.S.	1990	$7.00

Aerzte

Singles

Company	Disk Number	Title	Type	Country	Year	Value
CBS	654772-3	Bitte, Bitte	CD3	Germany	1989	$5.00
CBS	652819-3	Westerland	CD3	Germany	1988	$5.00
CBS	653181-3	Zu Spaet	CD3	Germany	1988	$5.00

Affection

Singles

Company	Disk Number	Title	Type	Country	Year	Value
Hullabaloo	CDHUL-1	Heaven Found	CD5	U.K.	1992	$6.00

Afghan Whigs

Full Length

Company	Disk Number	Title	Type	Country	Year	Value
Elektra	PRCD-8941-2	B-Sides, The	DJ/Intvw	U.S.	1994	$11.00
	261896P	Black Love	DJ/LP	U.S.	1995	$12.00

Singles

Company	Disk Number	Title	Type	Country	Year	Value
Blast First	BFFP95CD	Debonair	CD5	U.K.	1994	$10.00
Blast First	BFFP95CDL	Debonair	CD5	U.K.	1994	$10.00

Label	Catalog Number	Title	Type	Country	Year	Longbox Value / Value
Elektra	PRCD 8831-2	Debonair	CDJ	U.S.	1993	$2.00
Blast First	BFFP89CD	Gentlemen	CD5	U.K.	1993	$10.00
Elektra	PRCD 8880-2	Gentlemen	CDJ	U.S.	1994	$3.00
	PRCD 95402	Going To Town	CDJ	U.S.	1995	$2.00
	PRCD 9442-2	Honky's Ladder	CDJ	U.S.	1995	$2.00
Sub Pop	EFA-08187-03	Turn On the Water	CD5	U.K.	1992	$10.00
Sub Pop	SP133	Turn On the Water	CDJ	U.S.	1992	$6.00
Sub Pop	SPCD-53/215	Uptown Avondale	CD5	U.K.	1992	$10.00
Sub Pop	SP175b	Uptown Avondale	CD5	U.S.	1991	$4.00
Elektra	22-61708	What Jail Is Like	CD5	Canada	1994	$12.00
Elektra	PRCD 8977-2	What Jail Is Like	CDJ	U.S.	1994	$2.00

Africa Djole

Full Length

Label	Catalog Number	Title	Type	Country	Year	Longbox Value / Value
Plane	13401	Live	LP	Germany		$15.00

African Business

Singles

Label	Catalog Number	Title	Type	Country	Year	Longbox Value / Value
ZYX	6383-8	In Zaire	CD5	Germany	1990	$6.00

African Head Charge

Singles

Label	Catalog Number	Title	Type	Country	Year	Longbox Value / Value
Restless	727870	Touch 1	CD5	U.S.	1994	$5.00

African River

Singles

Label	Catalog Number	Title	Type	Country	Year	Longbox Value / Value
		Akill	CDJ	U.S.		$2.00

African Unity

Full Length

Label	Catalog Number	Title	Type	Country	Year	Longbox Value / Value
Zoo	11037	Out Of the Flames	LP/LB	U.S.		$11.00/$6.00

Singles

Label	Catalog Number	Title	Type	Country	Year	Longbox Value / Value
Tabu	28 965 17002	I Love the Way You Make Me Feel	CDJ	U.S.	1991	$2.00

African Warrior

Singles

Label	Catalog Number	Title	Type	Country	Year	Longbox Value / Value
ZYX	6532-8	Scillipap Yo	CD5	Germany	1991	$6.00

Afrika Bambaata

Full Length

Label	Catalog Number	Title	Type	Country	Year	Longbox Value / Value
EMI	CDP-9777-2	Decade Of Darkness	LP/LB	U.S		$14.00/$8.00
Capitol	CDP-90157-2	Light	LP/LB	U.S.		$14.00/$8.00

Singles

Label	Catalog Number	Title	Type	Country	Year	Longbox Value / Value
WEA	ZANG-29CD	Don't Stop…Planet Rock	CD5	U.K.	1992	$7.00
Tonny Boy		Don't Stop…Planet Rock	CD5	U.S.	1992	$5.00
Tonny Boy	538	Don't Stop…Planet Rock	CDJ	U.S.	1992	$3.00
King	KIDP-44	Just Get Up And Dance	CD3	Japan	1991	$15.00/$3.00
EMI	CDMT-100	Just Get Up And Dance	CD5	U.K.	1991	$7.00
EMI	DPRO-56225	Just Get Up And Dance	CDJ	U.S.	1991	$2.00
EMI	12585	Pupunanny	CD5	U.S.	1994	$5.00
Hot Prod.	12585	Pupunanny	CD5	U.S.	1994	$5.00
EMI	202402-2	Reckless	CD5	Germany	1988	$7.00
EMI	CDEM-41	Reckless	CD5	U.K.	1988	$7.00
ZYX	6760-8	Save the World	CD5	Germany	1992	$6.00
Profile	7389	Zulu War Chant	CD5	U.S.	1993	$5.00

Afrikaadelic

Singles

Label	Catalog Number	Title	Type	Country	Year	Longbox Value / Value
BCM	20419	Pita Pata	CD5	Germany	1990	$8.00

Afro-Plane

Singles

Label	Catalog Number	Title	Type	Country	Year	Longbox Value / Value
RCA	62915-RDJ	Shine	CDJ	U.S.	1994	$3.00

Afro-Rican

Singles

Label	Catalog Number	Title	Type	Country	Year	Longbox Value / Value
	DPRO-30057	All Of Puerto Rico	CDJ	U.S.	1995	$2.00
Hot Product	2282	That's What I'm All	CD5	U.S.	1994	$5.00

Afros

Full Length

Label	Catalog Number	Title	Type	Country	Year	Longbox Value / Value
Columbia	CK-46802	Kickin' Afrolistics	LP/LB	U.S.		$12.00/$7.00

Singles

Label	Catalog Number	Title	Type	Country	Year	Longbox Value / Value
Columbia	655257-2	Feel It	CD3	Germany	1990	$8.00
Columbia	656512-2	Feel It	CD5	U.K.	1990	$8.00
Columbia	CSK 73403	Feel It	CDJ	U.S.	1990	$3.00
Columbia		Kickin' Afrolistics	CDJ	U.S.		$3.00

After All

Singles

Label	Catalog Number	Title	Type	Country	Year	Longbox Value / Value
		Bullets	CDJ	Canada		$2.00

After One

Singles

Label	Catalog Number	Title	Type	Country	Year	Longbox Value / Value
ZYX	6437-8	Real Sadness	CD5	Germany	1990	$6.00
ZYX	6391-8	Tom's Dinner Rap	CD5	Germany	1990	$6.00

After Seven

Full Length

Label	Catalog Number	Title	Type	Country	Year	Longbox Value / Value
Virgin	260231	After Seven	LP	U.K.		$18.00
Atlantic	91061	After Seven	LP/LB	U.S.		$12.00/$7.00

Singles

Label	Catalog Number	Title	Type	Country	Year	Longbox Value / Value
Virgin	VJDP-10201	Baby I'm For Real	CD3	Japan	1993	$12.00/$4.00
Virgin	12727	Baby I'm For Real	CDJ	U.S.	1993	$2.00
Virgin	12759	Can He Love U Like This	CDJ	U.S	1992	$2.00
Virgin	663645	Can't Stop	CD5	Germany	1990	$8.00
Virgin	VUSCD-31	Can't Stop	CD5	U.K.	1990	$8.00
Virgin	PRCD 3319	Can't Stop	CDJ	U.S.	1989	$2.00
Virgin	38521	Damn Thing Called Love	CD5	U.S.	1995	$5.00
Virgin	DPRO-11039	Damn Thing Called Love	CDJ	U.S.	1995	$3.00
Virgin	DPRO-11050	Damn Thing Called Love	CDJ	U.S.	1995	$3.00
Virgin	VJCP-1403	Don't Cha' Think	CD3	Japan	1990	$15.00/$4.00
Virgin		Don't Cha' Think	CDJ	U.S.	1990	$3.00
Fox	10006	Gonna Love You Right	CDJ	U.S.	1993	$6.00
Virgin	VUSCD-7	Heat Of the Moment	CD3	U.K.	1990	$8.00
Virgin	VUSCX-7	Heat Of the Moment	CD5	U.K.	1990	$8.00
Virgin	GEMMA	Heat Of the Moment	CDJ	U.S.	1989	$3.00
Virgin	PR 2753	Heat Of the Moment	CDJ	U.S.	1989	$3.00
Virgin	DPRO-11503	How Do You Tell the One	CDJ	U.S.	1995	$3.00
Virgin	VJDP-10199	Kickin' It	CD3	Japan	1992	$15.00/$4.00
Virgin	PRCD12687	Kickin' It	CDJ	U.S.	1992	$3.00
Virgin	3479	My Only Woman	CDJ	U.S.	1989	$3.00
Virgin	PRCD 3882	Nights Like This	CDJ	U.S.	1991	$3.00
Virgin	VUSCD-21	Ready Or Not	CD5	U.K.	1990	$8.00
Virgin	PRCD 3170	Ready Or Not	CDJ	U.S.	1990	$3.00
Virgin	PRCD 3687	Ready Or Not	CDJ	U.S.	1990	$3.00
Virgin	38497	Til You Do Me Right	CD5	U.S.	1995	$5.00
Virgin	DPRO-12744	Til You Do Me Right	CDJ	U.S.	1995	$3.00
Virgin	DPRO-11039	Til You Do Me Right	CDJ	U.S.	1995	$6.00
Virgin	DPRO-11050	Til You Do Me Right	CDJ	U.S.	1995	$6.00
Virgin	12787	Truly Something Special	CDJ	U.S.	1992	$3.00

Aftershock

Singles

Label	Catalog Number	Title	Type	Country	Year	Longbox Value / Value
Virgin	96479	Always Thinking	CD5	U.S.	1990	$5.00
Virgin	PRCD 3226	Always Thinking	CDJ	U.S.	1990	$2.00
Virgin		Cindy Cindy	CDJ	U.S.	1990	$2.00
Virgin	PRCD 3687	Going Through the Motions	CDJ	U.S.	1991	$2.00
Virgin	PRCD 12754	Slave To the Vibe	CDJ	U.S.	1993	$2.00
Virgin		Whenever	CDJ	U.S.		$2.00

AFX

Singles

Label	Catalog Number	Title	Type	Country	Year	Longbox Value / Value
TVT	4810	Analogue Bubble	CD5	U.S.	1994	$4.00

Agaric

Singles

Label	Catalog Number	Title	Type	Country	Year	Longbox Value / Value
SPV	9421	I'm Gonna Beat Dis	CD5	Germany	1989	$2.00

Agawa, Takuo

Singles

Label	Catalog Number	Title	Type	Country	Year	Longbox Value / Value
Canyon	CEDC-1066	Nukumori	CD3	Japan	1991	$12.00/$2.00

Age Of Chance

Full Length

Label	Catalog Number	Title	Type	Country	Year	Longbox Value / Value
Atlantic	91366-2	Mecca	LP/LB	U.S.		$12.00/$7.00

Singles

Label	Catalog Number	Title	Type	Country	Year	Longbox Value / Value
Virgin	CDEP-7	Don't Get Mad Get Even	CD5	Germany	1988	$5.00
Virgin	VSCD-11228	Higher Than Heaven	CD3	U.K.	1990	$5.00
Virgin	VSCDT-1258	Playing With Fire	CD5	U.K.	1990	$5.00
Virgin	VSCD-1133	Times Up	CD3	U.K.	1989	$5.00

Age Of Love

Singles

Label	Catalog Number	Title	Type	Country	Year	Longbox Value / Value
React	CDREACT-9	Age Of Love	CD5	U.K.	1992	$8.00

Agrumh

Singles

Label	Catalog Number	Title	Type	Country	Year	Longbox Value / Value
SPV	9163-3	And Now For Something Completely Different	CD5	Germany	1990	$8.00
APT	BIAS-157CD	And Now For Something Completely Different	CD5	U.K.	1990	$8.00
SPV	9589-3	Price Is	CD5	Germany	1989	$8.00

Ahmad

Singles

Label	Catalog Number	Title	Type	Country	Year	Longbox Value / Value
Giant	9 41416-2	Back In the Day	CD5	U.S.	1994	$5.00
Warner Brothers	41416	Back In The Day	CD5	U.S.	1994	$5.00
Giant	PRO-CD-6799	Back In the Day	CDJ	U.S.	1994	$3.00
Giant	PRO-CD-6901	Back In the Day	CDJ	U.S.	1994	$6.00
Avatar	69712-0064	Only If You Want It	CDJ	U.S.	1995	$6.00
Motown	374631115	Who Can?	CDJ	U.S.	1993	$3.00
Giant	PRO-CD-6896	You Gotta Be	CDJ	U.S.	1994	$3.00
Giant	PRO-CD-7304	You Gotta Be	CDJ	U.S.	1994	$3.00
Motown	374631115	Who Can?	CDJ	U.S.	1993	$2.00

Aion

Singles

Label	Catalog Number	Title	Type	Country	Year	Longbox Value / Value
BMG	BVDR-117	Aion	CD3	Japan	1992	$12.00/$2.00
BMG	BVDR-61	Be Afraid	CD3	Japan	1991	$12.00/$2.00
BMG	BVDR-5020	St. Aion	CD5	Japan	1992	$9.00/$2.00

Air

Full Length

Label	Catalog Number	Title	Type	Country	Year	Longbox Value / Value
Aris	886257	Air Lore	LP	Germany		$12.00
Bluebird	6578-2	Air Lore	LP/BP	U.S.		$12.00/$7.00
Blacksaint	120034-2	Live Air	LP/LB	U.S.		$12.00/$7.00
Blacksaint	BSR004CD	Live at the Montreal Jazz Festival	LP/LB	U.S.†	1985	$12.00/$7.00

Air Miami

Full Length

Label	Catalog Number	Title	Type	Country	Year	Longbox Value / Value
4AD		Me Me Me	DJ/LP	U.S.	1995	$12.00

Singles

Label	Catalog Number	Title	Type	Country	Year	Longbox Value / Value
4AD	BAD 5014	I Hate Milk	CD5	U.K.	1995	$10.00
4AD	PRO-CD-7816	I Hate Milk	CDJ	U.S.	1995	$2.00

Air Project

Singles

Label	Catalog Number	Title	Type	Country	Year	Longbox Value / Value
BCM	20261	Mama	CD5	Germany	1989	$5.00

Air Supply

Full Length

Label	Catalog Number	Title	Type	Country	Year	Longbox Value / Value
Arista	610506	Air Supply	LP	U.K.		$15.00
Arista	ARCD-8283	Air Supply	LP/BP	U.S.†	1985	$14.00/$9.00
Arista	ARCD10-8283	Air Supply	LP/BP	U.S.	1988	$14.00/$9.00
Arista	ARCD-8024	Greatest Hits	LP/BP	U.S.†	1984	$15.00/$10.00
Arista	ARCD 8426	Hearts In Motion	LP/BP	U.S.		$14.00/$9.00
Pioneer	PA-83-058	In Hawaii	LD	U.S.	1984	$30.00
Arista	257891	Lonely Is the Night	LP	U.K.		$15.00
Arista	ARCD-8216	Lost In Love	LP/BP	U.S.†	1985	$14.00/$10.00
Arista	ARCD-8217	One That You Love	LP/BP	U.S.†	1985	$14.00/$10.00
Arista	ARCD10 8217	One That You Love	LP/BP	U.S.	1988	$14.00/$9.00

Singles

Label	Catalog Number	Title	Type	Country	Year	Longbox Value / Value
Giant	PRO-CD-6542	Evidence Of Love	CDJ	U.S.	1993	$6.00
Warner Brothers	WPDP-6323	Goodbye	CD3	Japan	1993	$12.00/$5.00
Warner Brothers	12-41012	It's Never Too Late	CD5	Canada	1993	$8.00
BCM	CD33-3017	Lost In Love	CD3/LB	U.S.	1988	$5.00/$2.00

Airhead

Singles

Label	Catalog Number	Title	Type	Country	Year	Longbox Value / Value
WEA	KDW-48CD	Counting Sheep	CD5	U.K.	1991	$5.00
WEA	KDW-47CD	Funny How	CD5	U.K.	1991	$5.00
WEA	KDW-49CD	Right Now	CD5	U.K.	1991	$5.00

Airkraft

Singles

Label	Catalog Number	Title	Type	Country	Year	Longbox Value / Value
Curb		65 M.P.H.	CDJ	U.S.		$2.00
Curb		Someday You'll Come Runnin'	CD5	U.S.		$2.00
Curb		Somewhere	CDJ	U.S.		$2.00

Airstream

Singles

Label	Catalog Number	Title	Type	Country	Year	Longbox Value / Value
1 L Indian	66-TP7CD	Airstream	CD5	U.K.	1992	$5.00
1 L Indian	96-TP7CD	Crush	CD5	U.K.	1992	$5.00
1 L Indian	56-TP7CD	Follow Through	CD5	U.K.	1991	$5.00

Aizawa, Yuko

Singles

Label	Catalog Number	Title	Type	Country	Year	Longbox Value/Value
Sony	SRDL-3428	Sayonara	CD3	Japan	1992	$12.00/$2.00

Ajax

Full Length

Label	Catalog Number	Title	Type	Country	Year	Longbox Value/Value
Wax Trax	7113	Ajax	LP/BP	U.S.		$12.00/$7.00
Zoo	72445-14224	Ex-Junkie	CD5	U.S.	1995	$5.00
SPV	9199-3	One World	CD5	Germany	1990	$5.00
Wax Trax	WAX-112CD	One World	CD5	U.K.	1990	$5.00

Aka

Singles

Label	Catalog Number	Title	Type	Country	Year	Longbox Value/Value
ZYX	8-6026	Cruel Lovin'	CD5	Germany	1988	$5.00

Akafa Akafa

Singles

Label	Catalog Number	Title	Type	Country	Year	Longbox Value/Value
WEA	YZ-457CD	Sutra/Heaven Upstairs	CD5	U.K.	1990	$5.00

Akasa

Singles

Label	Catalog Number	Title	Type	Country	Year	Longbox Value/Value
WEA	YZ-428CD	Karma Sutra	CD3	U.K.	1989	$5.00
WEA	YZ-405CD	One Night In My Life	CD3	U.K.	1989	$2.00

Akasaka, Akira

Singles

Label	Catalog Number	Title	Type	Country	Year	Longbox Value/Value
Canyon	PCDA-00458	Houki Twist	CD3	Japan	1993	$7.00/$2.00

Akasaka, Taro

Singles

Label	Catalog Number	Title	Type	Country	Year	Longbox Value/Value
King	KIDD-1150	Hyakuju No Michie	CD3	Japan	1992	$7.00/$2.00

Akashi, Mari

Singles

Label	Catalog Number	Title	Type	Country	Year	Longbox Value/Value
King	KIDD-1168	Bungo Ryoshi-Bushi	CD3	Japan	1992	$7.00/$2.00

Akashi, Yuichi

Singles

Label	Catalog Number	Title	Type	Country	Year	Longbox Value/Value
Vap	VPDB-20492	Ima Wa Futari	CD3	Japan	1993	$7.00/$2.00

Akatsuki, Hikari

Singles

Label	Catalog Number	Title	Type	Country	Year	Longbox Value/Value
King	KIDX-41	Koi-Tenjin	CD3	Japan	1991	$7.00/$2.00
King	KIDX-87	Oyako-Gawa	CD3	Japan	1992	$7.00/$2.00

Akatsuki, Miwa

Singles

Label	Catalog Number	Title	Type	Country	Year	Longbox Value/Value
King	KIDD-1152	Shaiwase-Kaikyo	CD3	Japan	1992	$7.00/$2.00

Akemi

Singles

Label	Catalog Number	Title	Type	Country	Year	Longbox Value/Value
Warner Brothers	WPDL-4247	Taiyo No Fumoto	CD3	Japan	1991	$7.00/$2.00

Akiko

Singles

Label	Catalog Number	Title	Type	Country	Year	Longbox Value/Value
Voss	5001	How Could I Ask For More	CDJ	U.S.	1989	$2.00

Akili

Singles

Label	Catalog Number	Title	Type	Country	Year	Longbox Value/Value
		African River	CDJ	U.S.		$2.00

Akim

Singles

Label	Catalog Number	Title	Type	Country	Year	Longbox Value/Value
Victor	VDPS-1032	Unbeatable Dream	CD3	Japan	1989	$7.00/$2.00

Akiyoshi, Toshiko

Full Length

Label	Catalog Number	Title	Type	Country	Year	Longbox Value/Value
Concord	CCD-4069	Finesse	LP/BP	U.S.		$12.00/$7.00
Concord	CCD-4324	Interlude	LP/BP	U.S.		$12.00/$7.00
Columbia	32C38-7874	Toshiko At Top of the Gate	LP	Japan		$18.00
Denon	C38-7874	Toshiko At Top of the Gate	LP/LB	U.S.		$12.00/$7.00

Singles

Label	Catalog Number	Title	Type	Country	Year	Longbox Value/Value
Crown	PAS-1006	Four Seasons	CD3	Japan	1990	$7.00/$2.00

Akkerman, Jan

Full Length

Label	Catalog Number	Title	Type	Country	Year	Longbox Value/Value
Charly	CDCHARLY-17	Complete Guitarist	LP	U.S.		$8.00
Charly	CDCHARLY-90	Pleasure Point	LP	U.S.		$8.00

Singles

Label	Catalog Number	Title	Type	Country	Year	Longbox Value/Value
Sound	CD-4000	Jan Akkerman	CD5	Germany	1988	$7.00
EMI	241065-2	Prima Dona	CD5	Germany	1991	$7.00
EMI	204132-2	Trojan Horse	CD5	Germany	1990	$7.00

Al B. Sure!

Full Length

Label	Catalog Number	Title	Type	Country	Year	Longbox Value/Value
Warner Brothers	26005-2-DJ	Private Times And the Whole 9	DJ/LP	U.S.	1990	$25.00

Picture disc CD in "Black" digipak.

Label	Catalog Number	Title	Type	Country	Year	Longbox Value/Value
Warner Brothers	26005-2-DJ	Private Times And the Whole 9	DJ/LP	U.S.	1990	$17.00

Picture disc CD in "Red" digipak.

Singles

Label	Catalog Number	Title	Type	Country	Year	Longbox Value/Value
Warner Brothers	PRO-CD-4809	Had Enough	CDJ	U.S.	1990	$3.00
Warner Brothers	PRO-CD-4898	Had Enough	CDJ	U.S.	1990	$3.00
Warner Brothers	12-40748	I Don't Wanna Cry	CD5	Canada	1993	$8.00
Warner Brothers	PRO-CD-5580	I'm Still In Love With You	CDJ	U.S.		$2.00
Warner Brothers	W-2980CD	If I'm Not Your Lover	CD3	U.K.	1989	$6.00
Warner Brothers	PRO-CD-3518	If I'm Not Your Lover	CDJ	U.S.	1988	$3.00
Warner Brothers	PRO-CD-3388	Killing Me Softly	CDJ	U.S.	1990	$3.00
WEA	921778-2	Misunderstanding	CD5	Germany	1990	$7.00
WEA	7599-21830-2	Misunderstanding	CD5	Germany	1990	$7.00
Pioneer	WPDP-6256	Misunderstanding	CD3	Japan	1990	$13.00/$3.00
WEA	W-9590CD	Misunderstanding	CD5	U.K.	1990	$7.00
Warner Brothers	21744	Misunderstanding	CD5	U.S.	1990	$4.00
Warner Brothers	PRO-CD-4423	Misunderstanding	CDJ	U.S.	1990	$3.00
Warner Brothers	12-40712	Natalie	CD5	Canada	1993	$8.00
Warner Brothers	9 40712-2	Natalie	CD5	U.S.	1992	$4.00
Warner Brothers	PRO-CD-5785	Natalie	CDJ	U.S.	1992	$2.00
Warner Brothers	10SW-58	Night And Day	CD3	Japan	1988	$13.00/$3.00
Warner Brothers	9 21843-2	No Matter What	CD5	U.S.	1991	$5.00
Warner Brothers	10P3-6043	Off On Your Own	CD3	Japan	1988	$13.00/$2.00
Warner Brothers	27870-2	Off On Your Own	CD3	U.S.	1988	$6.00/$3.00
Warner Brothers		Off On Your Own	CDJ	U.S.	1988	$3.00
Warner Brothers		Rescue Me	CDJ	U.S.		$3.00
Warner Brothers	12-40525	Right Now	CD5	Canada	1993	$8.00
Warner Brothers	9 40525-2	Right Now	CD5	U.S.	1992	$3.00

Alabama

Full Length

Company	Disk Number	Title	Type	Country	Year	Longbox Value/Value
		'90s Country	RS	U.S.	1995	$35.00

Airdate: 11/18/95

Company	Disk Number	Title	Type	Country	Year	Longbox Value/Value
		'90s Country	RS	U.S.	1995	$35.00

Airdate: 6/10/95

Company	Disk Number	Title	Type	Country	Year	Longbox Value/Value
Pioneer Artists	PA-87-185	Alabama	LD	U.S.	1987	$30.00
RCA	PCD1-7014	Alabama Christmas	LP/BP	U.S.†	1985	$15.00/$10.00
Aris	886167	Closer To You	LP	Germany		$15.00
RCA	PCD1-4663	Closer To You	LP/BP	U.S.†	1984	$15.00/$10.00
RCA	PCD1-3930	Feels So Right	LP/BP	U.S.†	1984	$14.00/$10.00
RCA	PD-85339	Forty Hour Week	LP	Germany		$15.00
RCA	PCD1-5339	Forty Hour Week	LP/BP	U.S.†	1985	$14.00/$10.00
RCA	PD-86495	Just Us	LP	Germany		$15.00
RCA	PD-85229	Mountain Music	LP	Germany		$15.00
RCA	PCD1-4229	Mountain Music	LP/BP	U.S.†	1984	$14.00/$10.00
RCA	PCD1-4644	My Home's In Alabama	LP/BP	U.S.†	1984	$14.00/$10.00
		Once Upon A Lifetime	RS	U.S.	1994	$45.00

3 CD set. Airdate: 11/21/94.

Company	Disk Number	Title	Type	Country	Year	Longbox Value/Value
RCA	62636	Reckless	DJ/Intvw	U.S.	1993	$10.00
RCA	PD-84939	Roll On	LP	Germany		$15.00
RCA	PCD1-4939	Roll On	LP/BP	U.S.†	1984	$15.00/$9.00
RCA/Laservideo		Touch, The	DJ/LP	U.S.	1985	$25.00

First CD to be manufactured at DMI Huntsville.

Company	Disk Number	Title	Type	Country	Year	Longbox Value/Value
Heartland	HD1186	Very Best Of Alabama, The	LP	U.S.		$20.00

2 CD set.

Singles

Company	Disk Number	Title	Type	Country	Year	Longbox Value/Value
RCA	62623	Cheap Seats, The	CDJ	U.S.	1994	$6.00
RCA	2706	Forever's As Far As I'll Go	CDJ	U.S.	1990	$6.00
RCA	62428	Once Upon A Lifetime	CDJ	U.S.	1992	$6.00
RCA	62059	Then Again	CDJ	U.S.	1991	$6.00

Alarm

Full Length

Company	Disk Number	Title	Type	Country	Year	Longbox Value/Value
	CDS-43	Alarm, The	DJ/Smplr	Japan	1989	$90.00
IRS	VDP-1507	Change	LP	Japan	1989	$25.00
IRS	IRSD 82018	Change	DJ/LP	U.S.	1989	$15.00
IRS	IRSD 13018	Change	LP/LB	U.S.	1989	$15.00/$10.00
A&M		Curtain Call	DJ/Smplr	Germany		$25.00
IRS	POPPY 1	Curtain Call	DJ/Smplr	U.S.	1988	$25.00
IRS	IRSD-82018-DJ	Curtain Call	DJ/LP	U.S.	1989	$20.00
IRS	IRSD 75050	Declaration	LP/LB	U.S.		$15.00/$10.00
IRS	ICD-70608	Declaration	LP/LB	U.S.†	1984	$15.00/$10.00
IRS	463146-2	Electric Folklore	LP	Germany		$20.00
IRS	VDP-1425	Electric Folklore	LP	Japan		$25.00
Victor	VICP-5054	Raw	LP	Japan		$25.00
Victor	VICP-76	Standards	LP	Japan		$25.00

Singles

Company	Disk Number	Title	Type	Country	Year	Longbox Value/Value
A&M	AMCD-906	Compact Hits	CD5	U.K.	1988	$9.00
EMI	204128-2	Electric Side	CD5	U.K.	1990	$9.00
Victor	VIDP-21	Happy Christmas (War Is Over)	CD3	Japan	1990	$12.00/$3.00
IRS	67040	Happy Christmas (War Is Over)	CDJ	U.S.	1990	$7.00
IRS	241047-2	Love Don't Come Easy	CD5	Germany	1990	$9.00
IRS	EIRSCD 134	Love Don't Come Easy	CD5	U.K.	1990	$9.00
IRS	IRSD 017	Love Don't Come Easy	CDJ	U.S.	1989	$7.00
IRS	241040-3	New South Wales	CD3	Germany	1989	$9.00
IRS	EIRSCD-129	New South Wales	CD5	U.K.	1989	$9.00
IRS	DIRM-155	Presence Of Love	CD5	U.K.	1988	$9.00
IRS		Rain In Summer Time	CD5	U.K.		$9.00
IRS	ALARMCD-3	Raw	CD5	U.K.	1991	$9.00
IRS	67056	Raw	CDJ	U.S.	1991	$7.00
IRS	44797 2377	Save It For Later E.P.	CD5	U.S.	1988	$10.00
A&M	CC-31015	Sixty Eight Guns	CD3	U.S.	1989	$8.00/$5.00
IRS	241030-3	Sold Me Down the River	CD3	Germany	1989	$9.00
IRS	VDPS-1046	Sold Me Down the River	CD3	Japan	1989	$18.00/$5.00
IRS	EIRSD-123	Sold Me Down the River	CD5	U.K.	1989	$9.00
IRS	IRSD 0010	Sold Me Down the River	CDJ	U.S.	1989	$8.00
A&M	CC-31010	Stand	CD3	U.S.	1989	$5.00/$5.00
IRS	ALARMCD-2	Unsafe Building 1990	CD5	U.K.	1990	$9.00

Alaska

Full Length

Company	Disk Number	Title	Type	Country	Year	Longbox Value/Value
Intercord	845-089	Pack, The	LP	Germany		$15.00

Albers Eef

Singles

Company	Disk Number	Title	Type	Country	Year	Longbox Value/Value
Efa	CD-06442	Pyramids	CD5	Germany	1988	$6.00

Albert One

Full Length

Company	Disk Number	Title	Type	Country	Year	Longbox Value/Value
ZYX	CD-9062	Everybody	LP	Germany		$13.00

Singles

Company	Disk Number	Title	Type	Country	Year	Longbox Value/Value
Epic	ESK 7511	Para Que Me Beses	CDJ	U.S.	1995	$2.00

Albertino

Singles

Company	Disk Number	Title	Type	Country	Year	Longbox Value/Value
ZYX	6538-8	Your Love Is Crazy	CD5	Germany	1991	$5.00

Albita

Singles

Company	Disk Number	Title	Type	Country	Year	Longbox Value/Value
Crescent Moon	ESK 6932	No Se Parace	CD5	U.S.	1995	$5.00
Crescent Moon	ESK 6932	No Se Parace	CDJ	U.S.	1995	$3.00

Albright, Gerald

Singles

Company	Disk Number	Title	Type	Country	Year	Longbox Value/Value
Atlantic	PRCD 5463-2	Anniversary	CDJ	U.S.	1994	$2.00
		My, My, My	CDJ	U.S.		$2.00

Albright, William

Full Length

Company	Disk Number	Title	Type	Country	Year	Longbox Value/Value
Music	5004-2	Sweet Sixteens	LP	U.S.		$8.00

Alcatrazz

Full Length

Company	Disk Number	Title	Type	Country	Year	Longbox Value/Value
Grand Slam	12	Live Sentence	LP/BP	U.S.		$14.00/$8.00
Grand Slam	11	No Parole From Rock 'n Roll	LP/BP	U.S.		$12.00/$8.00

Alcohol Funnycar

Singles

Company	Disk Number	Title	Type	Country	Year	Longbox Value/Value
Ruffhouse	6044	Shapes	CDJ	U.S.	1994	$3.00

Aldeanos, Los

Singles

Company	Disk Number	Title	Type	Country	Year	Longbox Value/Value
	113	El Polito	CD5	U.S.	1994	$5.00

Aldrich, Ronnie

Full Length

Label	Catalog Number	Title	Type	Country	Year	Longbox Value / Value
London	820282-2	That Aldrich Feeling	LP/LB	U.S.		$14.00/$8.00

Aleph

Singles

Label	Catalog Number	Title	Type	Country	Year	Longbox Value / Value
Alfa	11B3-30	Bad Power	CD3	Japan	1989	$7.00/$2.00
Alfa	10SR-12	Big Brother	CD3	Japan	1988	$7.00/$2.00
Alfa	ALDB-23	Hero	CD3	Japan	1990	$7.00/$2.00

Alerti

Singles

Label	Catalog Number	Title	Type	Country	Year	Longbox Value / Value
Efa	CD-02817	Are You Hectic	CD5	Germany	1992	$7.00

Alex, Marc

Singles

Label	Catalog Number	Title	Type	Country	Year	Longbox Value / Value
WEA	PWCD-59	Quick, Quick	CDJ	U.K.	1990	$7.00
		Quick, Quick	CDJ	U.S.	1990	$2.00

Alexa

Singles

Label	Catalog Number	Title	Type	Country	Year	Longbox Value / Value
Savage	CDVAG-903	We Don't Remember Why	CD3	U.K.	1989	$5.00

Alexander, Daniele

Singles

Label	Catalog Number	Title	Type	Country	Year	Longbox Value / Value
Mercury	CDP 068	She's There	CDJ	U.S.	1989	$2.00
Mercury	CDP 148	Where Did the Moon Go Wrong	CDJ	U.S.	1989	$2.00
Mercury	CDP 442	Who Can She Turn To	CDJ	U.S.	1991	$2.00

Alexander, Gregg

Singles

Label	Catalog Number	Title	Type	Country	Year	Longbox Value / Value
A&M	S9Y-3105	In the Neighborhood	CD3	Japan	1989	$12.00/$3.00
A&M	CD 17763	In the Neighborhood	CDJ	U.S.	1989	$2.00

Alexander, Monty

Full Length

Label	Catalog Number	Title	Type	Country	Year	Longbox Value / Value
Verve	821 151-2	Duke Ellington Song Book	LP/BP	U.S.†	1984	$14.00/$8.00
Verve	821 151-2	Duke Ellington Song Book	LP/BP	U.S.	1986	$14.00/$8.00
GML	GMLCD-4808	Lil' Darlin'	LTD/LP	Japan		$25.00

Gold disc.

Label	Catalog Number	Title	Type	Country	Year	Longbox Value / Value
MPS	817 487-2	Monteaux Alexander	LP/BP	U.S.		$14.00/$8.00

Alexander, Peter

Singles

Label	Catalog Number	Title	Type	Country	Year	Longbox Value / Value
BMG	664896	Auf Die Liebe Kombat	CD5	Germany	1992	$6.00
BMG	665223	Der Tag DerKleinen Helden	CD5	Germany	1992	$6.00

Alexandria, Lorez

Full Length

Label	Catalog Number	Title	Type	Country	Year	Longbox Value / Value
King	KLP-676	Singing Songs Everyone Knows	LP	U.S.		$8.00
Trend	TRCD-538	Tangerine	LP	U.S.		$8.00
King	KLP-565	Tribute To Lester Young	LP	U.S.		$8.00

Alexis

Singles

Label	Catalog Number	Title	Type	Country	Year	Longbox Value / Value
CBS	655756-3	Close To Heaven	CD3	Germany	1990	$6.00
CBS	656286-3	Lying Eyes	CD3	Germany	1990	$6.00
CBS	C-55720-3	Prisoner Of Love	CD3	Germany	1990	$6.00
CBS	65560-3	Prisoner Of Love	CD3	Germany	1990	$6.00

Alfee

Singles

Label	Catalog Number	Title	Type	Country	Year	Longbox Value / Value
Canyon	PCDA-00405	Believe	CD3	Japan	1993	$8.00/$2.00
Canyon	PCDA-00273	Promised Love	CD3	Japan	1992	$8.00/$2.00
Canyon	PCDA-00429	Victory	CD3	Japan	1993	$8.00/$2.00

Ali Project

Singles

Label	Catalog Number	Title	Type	Country	Year	Longbox Value / Value
Toshiba	TODT-3042	Arashigaoka	CD3	Japan	1993	$2.00

Alias

Full Length

Label	Catalog Number	Title	Type	Country	Year	Longbox Value / Value
Tohiba	TOCP-6444	Alias	LP	Japan	1990	$20.00
EMI	E21S-93908	Alias	DJ/LP	U.S.	1990	$15.00

CD with Video in custom box

Label	Catalog Number	Title	Type	Country	Year	Longbox Value / Value
EMI	203979-2	Haunted Heart	CD5	Germany	1990	$7.00
EMI	DPRO 04358	Haunted Heart	CDJ	U.S.	1990	$2.00
EMI	CDEM-168	More Than Words Can Say	CD5	Germany	1990	$7.00
EMI	CDEM-168	More Than Words Can Say	CD5	U.K.	1990	$7.00
EMI	DPRO 04637	More Than Words Can Say	CDJ	U.S.	1990	$2.00
Giant	PRO-CD-4981	Perfect World	CDJ	U.S.	1991	$2.00
Toshiba	TODP-2286	True Emotion	CD3	Japan	1991	$8.00/$2.00
EMI	CDEM-183	Waiting For Love	CD5	U.K.	1991	$7.00
EMI	DPRO 04707	Waiting For Love	CDJ	U.S.	1990	$2.00
EMI	DPRO 04675	Waiting For Love	CDJ	U.S.	1990	$2.00

Alice

Singles

Label	Catalog Number	Title	Type	Country	Year	Longbox Value / Value
Pinnacle	TOPSCD-005	Giving Our Hearts Away	CD5	U.K.	1990	$7.00
Pinnacle	TOPSCD-006	On My Way Home	CD5	U.K.	1990	$7.00
EMI	118839-3	Visioni	CD5	Germany	1990	$7.00

Alice Donut

Singles

Label	Catalog Number	Title	Type	Country	Year	Longbox Value / Value
Efa	CD-18101	Biggest Ass	CD5	Germany	1992	$6.00
Pinnacle	VIRUS-114CD	Magdaline	CD5	U.K.	1992	$6.00

Alice In Chains

Full Length

Label	Catalog Number	Title	Type	Country	Year	Longbox Value / Value
Columbia	XPCD746	Alice In Chains	DJ/LP	U.K.		$18.00

With 3 plastic flies under clear tray.

Label	Catalog Number	Title	Type	Country	Year	Longbox Value / Value
Columbia	CK-57628	Jar Of Flies	LTD/LP	U.S.	1994	$25.00

With 4 plastic flies under clear tray.

Label	Catalog Number	Title	Type	Country	Year	Longbox Value / Value
Columbia	660047-2	Jar Of Flies/Sap	DJ/Smplr	U.K.	1994	$23.00
Columbia	475713-2	Jar Of Flies/Sap	LTD/LP	U.K.	1994	$20.00

2 CD set.

Label	Catalog Number	Title	Type	Country	Year	Longbox Value / Value
Sony	XPCD 815	MTV Unplugged	DJ/Smplr	U.K.	1996	$20.00
Columbia	660047 2	Sap Jar Of Flies	DJ/Smplr	U.K.	1994	$30.00
Media America		Up Close	RS	U.S.	1995	$45.00
Columbia		Interview	DJ/Intvw	U.S.	1995	$18.00
Columbia		Live At the Moore Theatre	DJ/Smplr	U.S.	1995	$25.00

Singles

Label	Catalog Number	Title	Type	Country	Year	Longbox Value / Value
Columbia	CSK 7656	Again	CDJ	U.S.	1995	$6.00
Columbia	659365	Angry Chair	CD5	U.K.	1992	$11.00
Columbia	CSK 4840	Angry Chair	CDJ	U.S.	1992	$6.00
Columbia		Brother	CD5	U.S.	1992	$5.00
Columbia	659751	Down In A Hole	CD5	U.K.	1993	$11.00
Columbia	CSK 5391	Down In A Hole	CDJ	U.S.	1993	$6.00
Columbia		Grind	CD5	U.K.	1995	$10.00
Columbia	XPCD 743	Grind	CDJ	U.K.	1995	$12.00
Columbia	CSK 7444	Grind	CDJ	U.S.	1995	$6.00
Columbia		Heaven Beside You	CD5	U.K.		$10.00
Columbia		Heaven Beside You	CD5	U.K.		$10.00

Second version.

Label	Catalog Number	Title	Type	Country	Year	Longbox Value / Value
Sony	XPCD 765	Heaven Beside You	CDJ	U.K.	1995	$20.00/$25.00
Columbia	CSK 7598	Heaven Beside You	CDJ	U.S.	1995	$6.00
Columbia	CSK 6056	I Stay Away	CDJ	U.S.	1994	$6.00
Columbia	660047	Jar Of Flies	CD5	U.K.	1994	$12.00
Columbia	CSK 2257	Man In the Box	CDJ	U.S.	1990	$6.00
CBS		No Excuses	CD5	Australia	1994	$12.00
Columbia	660097	No Excuses	CD5	Germany	1994	$11.00
CBS		No Excuses	CD5	Sweden	1994	$12.00
Columbia	CSK 5614	No Excuses	CDJ	U.S.	1994	$6.00
COlumbia	659057	Rooster	CD5	Germany	1992	$11.00
Columbia	CSK 4946	Rooster	CDJ	U.S.	1992	$6.00
Columbia	44K 74182	Sap	CD5	U.S.	1992	$5.00
CBS	74182	Sap	CD5	U.S.	1994	$5.00
Columbia	CSK 4072	Sea Of Sorrow	CDJ	U.S.	1990	$6.00
Columbia		Them Bones	CD5	Australia	1992	$11.00
Columbia	658450	Them Bones	CD5	Germany	1992	$11.00
Columbia	659090	Them Bones	CD5	U.K.	1992	$11.00
Columbia	CSK 4769	Them Bones	CDJ	U.S.	1992	$6.00
Columbia	CSK 2163	We Die Young	CDJ	U.S.	1990	$6.00
Columbia	CSK 5233	What the Hell I Have	CDJ	U.S.	1993	$6.00
Columbia	658328	Would?	CD5	Germany	1992	$11.00
Columbia	65888	Would?	CD5	U.K.	1992	$11.00
Columbia	CSK 4484	Would?	CDJ	U.S.	1992	$6.00

Alie, Marijose

Singles

Label	Catalog Number	Title	Type	Country	Year	Longbox Value / Value
Polydor	PODP-5002	Tou Piti	CD3	Japan	1990	$2.00

Alien

Singles

Label	Catalog Number	Title	Type	Country	Year	Longbox Value / Value
Virgin	VJD-10209	Tears Don't Put Out the Fire	CD3	Japan	1988	$2.00
Virgin	PRCD 2842	Tears Don't Put Out the Fire	CDJ	U.S.	1988	$2.00

Alien Nation

Singles

Label	Catalog Number	Title	Type	Country	Year	Longbox Value / Value
	351160	39	CD5	U.S.	1994	$5.00

Alien Sex Fiend

Full Length

Label	Catalog Number	Title	Type	Country	Year	Longbox Value / Value
Cherry	85044-28	Here Cum Germs	LP	Japan		$18.00
PVC	PVCD-8960	Here Cum Germs	LP/BP	U.S.		$14.00/$8.00
Cherry	CDANA-11	Ignore the Machine	LTD/LP	U.K.		$25.00

Picture disc CD.

Singles

Label	Catalog Number	Title	Type	Country	Year	Longbox Value / Value
SPV	3011	Haunted House	CD3	Germany	1989	$7.00
Cherry	CDANA-46	Haunted House	CD3	U.K.	1989	$7.00
IRS	977 023	I Walk the Line	CD5	Germany	1992	$7.00
SPV	4526-3	Magic	CD5	Germany	1992	$7.00
SPV	3094-3	Now I'm Feeling Zombified	CD5	Germany	1990	$7.00
Anagram	CDANA-52	Now I'm Feeling Zombified	CD5	Germany	1990	$7.00

Alisha

Full Length

Label	Catalog Number	Title	Type	Country	Year	Longbox Value / Value
Vanguard	883661	Alisha	LP	Germany		$12.00
Asmara	ASM-106	Baby Doll Of India	LP/BP	U.S.		$12.00/$8.00
Phonogram	PHCR-1025	Bounce Back	LP	Japan		$18.00
MCA	MCAD-6378	Bounce Back	LP/LB	U.S.		$12.00/$8.00

Singles

Label	Catalog Number	Title	Type	Country	Year	Longbox Value / Value
MCA		Bounce Back	CDJ	U.S.		$2.00
Polygram	870391-2	I Don't Know What Comes Over	CD5	Germany	1988	$4.00
		Wrong Number	CDJ	U.S.		$2.00

Alkaholiks, Tha

Singles

Label	Catalog Number	Title	Type	Country	Year	Longbox Value / Value
RCA	64202	Daaam	CD5	U.S.	1994	$5.00
RCA	62727-2RDJ	Likwit	CDJ	U.S.	1993	$2.00
RCA	62578-2RDJ	Make Room	CDJ	U.S.	1993	$2.00

All

Singles

Label	Catalog Number	Title	Type	Country	Year	Longbox Value / Value
Rough Trade	395 00243	Dot	CD5	Germany	1992	$8.00
Cruz	024	Dot	CD5	U.S.	1992	$4.00
Cruz	033	Guilty	CD5	U.S.	1994	$5.00
Interscope	PRO-CD-6169	Million Bucks	CDJ	U.S.	1995	$3.00
Cruz	030	Shreen	CD5	U.S.	1993	$4.00

All About Eve

Full Length

Label	Catalog Number	Title	Type	Country	Year	Longbox Value / Value
Phonogram	32PD-458	All About Eve	LP	Japan		$25.00
Phonogram	EVCDJ 81	Ballads, The	DJ/Smplr	U.K.	1991	$15.00
Mercury	CDP 018	Every Angel	DJ/Intvw	U.S.	1988	$8.00
Phonogram	PPD-1090	Scarlet And Other Stories	LP	Japan		$25.00
Mercury	838965-2	Scarlet And Other Stories	LP/BP	U.S.		$14.00/$8.00
Polygram	AAECD1	Secret And Other Stories	DJ/Smplr	U.K.	1989	$20.00

Singles

Label	Catalog Number	Title	Type	Country	Year	Longbox Value / Value
Polygram	EVNCD 11	December	CD5	U.K.	1990	$8.00
Mercury	870280-2	Every Angel	CD5	Germany	1988	$8.00
Mercury	EVNCD-7	Every Angel	CD5	U.K.	1988	$8.00
Mercury	868435-2	Farewell Mr. Sorrow	CD5	Germany	1991	$8.00
Mercury	870498-2	Martha's Harbour	CD5	Germany	1990	$8.00
Polygram	EVCDJ 8	Martha's Harbour	CDJ	U.K.	1988	$15.00
Phonogram		Martha's Harbour	CDV	U.K.	1988	$15.00
Mercury	EVNCD-8	Martha's Harbour	CD5	U.K.	1990	$8.00
MCA	MCSTD-1688	Phased	CD5	U.K.	1992	$8.00
Mercury	876245-2	Road To Your Soul	CD5	Germany	1990	$8.00
Phonogram	EVNCD-10	Road To Your Soul	CD5	U.K.	1990	$8.00
Mercury	CDP 150	Road To Your Soul	CDJ	U.S.	1990	$3.00
Mercury	CDP 175	Road To Your Soul	CDJ	U.S.	1990	$3.00
Phonogram	EVECD-12	Scarlet	CD5	U.K.	1990	$8.00
MCA	MCSTD-1706	Some Finer Day	CD5	U.K.	1992	$8.00
Phonogram	PHCR-8010	Thirteen	CD5	Japan	1991	$14.00
Phonogram	EVCDX-13	Thirteen	CD5	U.K.	1991	$8.00
Mercury	872091-2	What Kind Of Fool	CD5	Germany	1990	$8.00
Mercury	EVNCD-9	What Kind Of Fool	CD5	U.K.	1990	$8.00
Mercury	870090-2	Wild Hearted Woman	CD5	Germany	1988	$8.00
Mercury	EVNCD-6	Wild Hearted Woman	CD5	U.K.	1988	$8.00

All, Kyojin

Singles

Label	Catalog Number	Title	Type	Country	Year	Longbox Value / Value
RCA	BVDL-12	Akindo	CD3	Japan	1991	$8.00/$2.00

All Systems Go

Singles

Label	Catalog Number	Title	Type	Country	Year	Longbox Value / Value
BCM	20114	Pop Muzik	CD5	Germany	1989	$7.00

All That Jazz

Singles

Label	Catalog Number	Title	Type	Country	Year	Longbox Value / Value
Virgin	VJD-12007	Even the Trees	CD3	Japan		$7.00/$2.00
Virgin	VJD-15001	Even the Trees	CD3	Japan		$7.00/$2.00

All That & More

Singles

Label	Catalog Number	Title	Type	Country	Year	Longbox Value / Value
	5006	In Da House	CD5	U.S.	1994	$5.00

All-4-One

Singles

Label	Catalog Number	Title	Type	Country	Year	Longbox Value / Value
Atlantic	PRCD 5841-2	Breathless	CDJ	U.S.	1994	$3.00
Atlantic	87134	I Can Love You Like That	CD5	U.S.	1995	$5.00
Atlantic	PRCD 62262	I Can Love You Like That	CDJ	U.S.	1995	$3.00
Atlantic	PRCD 5609-2	I Swear	CDJ	U.S.		$2.00
Atlantic	87097	I'm Your Man	CD5	U.S.	1995	$5.00
Atlantic	PRCD 6423-2	I'm Your Man	CDJ	U.S.	1995	$2.00
Atlantic	85607	Skilz (She's Got)	CD5	U.S.	1994	$5.00
Atlantic	PRCD 5738-2	Skilz (She's Got)	CDJ	U.S.	1994	$3.00
Atlantic	PRCD 5525	So Much Love	CDJ	U.S.	1995	$3.00
Hollywood		Someday	CD5	U.S.	1996	$5.00
Hollywood		Someday	CDJ	U.S.	1996	$6.00
	PRCD6630	These Arms	CDJ	U.S.	1995	$6.00
Atlantic	87098	Yo Te Voy A Querer	CD5	U.S.	1995	$5.00
Atlantic		Yo Te Voy A Querer	CDJ	U.S.	1995	$2.00

Allan, Steve

Singles

Label	Catalog Number	Title	Type	Country	Year	Longbox Value / Value
Da	20492	Letter From My Heart	CD5	Germany	1990	$7.00
Da	20479	Love Is In the Air	CD5	Germany	1990	$7.00

Allen, Donna

Full Length

Label	Catalog Number	Title	Type	Country	Year	Longbox Value / Value
Atlantic	7 91028-2	Heaven On Earth	LP/LB	U.S.		$7.00

Singles

Label	Catalog Number	Title	Type	Country	Year	Longbox Value / Value
BCM	20277	Can We Talk	CD5	Germany	1989	$7.00
BCM	BCM-277CD	Can We Talk	CD5	U.K.	1989	$7.00
BCM	20257	Joy and Pain	CD5	Germany	1989	$7.00
BCM	BCM-257CD	Joy and Pain	CD5	U.K.	1989	$7.00
CBS	77701	Real	CD5	U.S.	1994	$5.00

Allen, Geri

Full Length

Label	Catalog Number	Title	Type	Country	Year	Longbox Value / Value
Plaene	43113	Open On All Sides	LP	Germany		$15.00
IRS	971-501	Printmakers	LP	Germany		$18.00
Polydor	J33J20157	Printmakers	LP	Japan		$25.00
Minor	850001-2	Printmakers	LP/BP	U.S.		$14.00/$8.00
Polydor	J00J-20365	Twylight	LP	Japan		$25.00

Allen, Peter

Full Length

Label	Catalog Number	Title	Type	Country	Year	Longbox Value / Value
Polygram	397077-2	A&M Gold Series	LP	Germany		$18.00
A&M	D25Y-3261	A&M Gold Series	LP	Japan		$25.00
Arista	ARCD-8275	Captured Live At Carnegie Hall	LP/LB	U.S.†	1985	$16.00/$10.00
	2 CD set.					
Arista	ARCD10-8026	Not the Boy Next Door	LP/BP	U.S.		$14.00/$8.00

Singles

Label	Catalog Number	Title	Type	Country	Year	Longbox Value / Value
A&M	PCDY-10022	Don't Cry out Loud	CD3	Japan	1990	$13.00/$3.00
Polygram	390591-2	I Go To Rio	CD5	Germany	1990	$6.00
RCA	60703-2-RDJ	Tonight You Made My Day	CDJ	U.S.	1990	$2.00

Allgood

Singles

Label	Catalog Number	Title	Type	Country	Year	Longbox Value / Value
A&M	31458 8132-2	It's Alright	CDJ	U.S.	1993	$2.00
A&M	31454 0229	Kickin' & Screamin'	CDJ	U.S.	1994	$3.00
A&M	31458 8229-2	Them Changes	CDJ	U.S.	1993	$2.00
A&M	31458 8280	Trilogy	CDJ	U.S.	1994	$3.00

Alliance

Singles

Label	Catalog Number	Title	Type	Country	Year	Longbox Value / Value
ZYX	5956-8	Action	CD5	Germany	1988	$6.00

Alligator

Singles

Label	Catalog Number	Title	Type	Country	Year	Longbox Value / Value
IRS	ISD 009	Sea Of Fire	CDJ	U.S.	1989	$2.00

Allison, Luther

Full Length

Label	Catalog Number	Title	Type	Country	Year	Longbox Value / Value
		House Of Blues	RS	U.S.	1995	$35.00
	Airdate: 8/13/95					
Musidisc	233524	Love Me Papa	LP	Germany		$15.00
Charly	CHAR-254	Power Wire Blues	LP	Germany		$15.00
Aris	883067	Rich Man	LP	Germany		$15.00
Charly	CHAR-201	Rich Man	LP	Germany		$15.00

Allison, Mose

Full Length

Label	Catalog Number	Title	Type	Country	Year	Longbox Value / Value
Blue Note	CJ32-5003	Ever Since the World Ended	LP	Japan		$30.00

Allman Brothers Band

Full Length

Label	Catalog Number	Title	Type	Country	Year	Longbox Value / Value
Album Network		Album Network Special	RS	U.S.	1994	$175.00
	2 CD set. Airdate: 7/1/94					
Epic	ESK 4632	An Acoustic Evening With the Indigo Girls & Allman Brothers Band	DJ/Smplr	U.S.	1992	$75.00
	14 track Live CD with 7 track by each group					
IMS	827588-2	Beginnings	LP	Germany		$20.00
		Ben Manilla	RS	U.S.	1993	$60.00
Pioneer	PA-84-087	Brothers Of the Road	LD	U.S.	1985	$30.00
Pioneer	PA-84-087	Brothers Of the Road	LD	U.S.	1991	$40.00
	Digital version					
Polygram		Dreams	DJ/LP	U.S.	1989	$50.00
	4 CD set in jewel box					
Polygram	CDP 71	Dreams	DJ/Smplr	U.S.	1989	$20.00
Westwood One		In Concert	RS	U.S.	1993	$95.00
	2 CD set. Airdate: 5/24/93					
Westwood One		In Concert	RS	U.S.	1994	$60.00
	Airdate: 1/3/94					
Album Network		In the Studio (Allman Brothers Band)	RS	U.S.		$30.00
Album Network		In the Studio (Allman Brothers Band/Idlewild)	RS	U.S.		$35.00
Album Network		In the Studio (Eat A Peach)	RS	U.S.	1990	$25.00
	Airdate: 2/10/92					

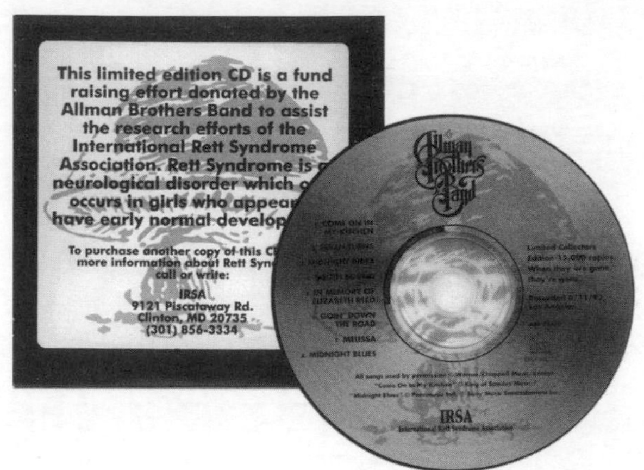

Allman Brothers Band – IRSA Sampler (Sony DISP 002175) U.S. 1994 CD sampler. Proceeeds from the sale of the sampler went to the IRSA.

Company	Disk Number	Title	Type	Country	Year	Longbox Value / Value
Album Network		In the Studio (Eat A Peach)	RS	U.S.	1990	$25.00
	Airdate: 8/13/90					
Album Network		In the Studio (Idlewild South)	RS	U.S.	1989	$25.00
	Airdate: 5/29/89					
Sony	DISP 002175	IRSA Sampler	DJ/Smplr	U.S.	1994	$100.00
DIR		King Biscuit Flour Hour	RS	U.S.	1987	$50.00
	With Crosby Stills & Nash, Airdate: 11/8/87					
DIR		King Biscuit Flour Hour	RS	U.S.	1988	$80.00
	2 CD set. Airdate: 7/23 - 7/30/89					
DIR		King Biscuit Flour Hour	RS	U.S.	1990	$80.00
	2 CD set. Airdate: 6/25 - 7/2/90					
DIR		King Biscuit Flour Hour	RS	U.S.	1990	$40.00
	Airdate: 12/23/90					
DIR		King Biscuit Flour Hour	RS	U.S.	1992	$45.00
	With Blues Traveler, Airdate: 7/6/92					
DIR		King Biscuit Flour Hour	RS	U.S.	1993	$30.00
	Airdate: 5/31/93					
DIR		King Biscuit Flour Hour	RS	U.S.	1994	$35.00
	Airdate: 4/25/94					
Westwood One		Off the Record	RS	U.S.	1993	$30.00
	Airdate: 5/24/93					
Westwood One		Off the Record	RS	U.S.	1994	$25.00
	Airdate: 11/7/94					
Westwood One		Off the Record	RS	U.S.	1994	$25.00
	Airdate: 6/6/94					
Westwood One		Off the Record	RS	U.S.	1995	$25.00
	Airdate: 6/19/95					
Westwood One		Off the Record	RS	U.S.	1996	$25.00
	Airdate: 2/12/96					
Radio Today		Rock Stars	RS	U.S.	1989	$30.00
	2 CD set. Airdate: 7/10/89					
Epic		Seven Turns	DJ/LP	U.S.	1990	$18.00
Westwood One		Super Stars Concert	RS	U.S.	1994	$115.00
	2 CD set. Airdate: 12/12/94					
Westwood One		Super Stars Concert	RS	U.S.	1995	$115.00
	2 CD set. Airdate: 10/2/95					
Media America		Up Close	RS	U.S.	1989	$60.00
	4 CD set.					
Media America		Up Close	RS	U.S.	1990	$60.00
	4 CD set.					
Media America		Up Close	RS	U.S.	1991	$60.00
	4 CD set.					
Media America		Up Close	RS	U.S.	1992	$60.00
	4 CD set.					
Media America		Up Close	RS	U.S.	1994	$60.00
	4 CD set.					
Media America		Up Close	RS	U.S.	1995	$95.00
	3 CD set.					

Singles

Company	Disk Number	Title	Type	Country	Year	Longbox Value / Value
Epic	ESK 6230	Back Where It All Begins	CDJ	U.S.	1994	$6.00
Epic	ESK 4178	Bad Rain	CDJ	U.S.		$6.00
Epic	ESK 4094	End Of the Line	CDJ	U.S.	1991	$6.00
Epic	ESK 2075	Good Clean Fun	CDJ	U.S.	1990	$6.00
Epic	ESK 2258	It Ain't Over Yet	CDJ	U.S.	1990	$6.00
Epic	ESK 4250	Kind Of Bird	CDJ	U.S.	1991	$6.00
Epic	ESK 4609	Melissa	CDJ	U.S.	1992	$6.00
Epic	ESK 6041	No One To Run With	CDJ	U.S.	1994	$6.00
Epic	ESK 4333	Nobody Knows	CDJ	U.S.	1991	$6.00
Epic	ESK 2184	Seven Turns	CDJ	U.S.	1990	$6.00

Allman, Duane

Full Length

Company	Disk Number	Title	Type	Country	Year	Longbox Value / Value
Polydor	P58P-25049	Anthology, Vol. 2	LP	Japan		$25.00

Allman, Greg

Full Length

Company	Disk Number	Title	Type	Country	Year	Longbox Value / Value
Epic	ESK 1183	Just Before the Bullets Fly	DJ/LP	U.S.	1988	$18.00
DIR		King Biscuit Flour Hour	RS	U.S.	1987	$50.00
	Airdate: 12/6/87					
DIR		King Biscuit Flour Hour	RS	U.S.	1988	$50.00
	Airdate: 9/25/88					
DIR		King Biscuit Flour Hour	RS	U.S.	1992	$50.00
	Airdate: 3/8/92					
Polydor	P28P-25074	Laid Back	LP	Japan		$25.00
Media America		Up Close	RS	U.S.	1988	$60.00
	2 CD set.					

Singles

Company	Disk Number	Title	Type	Country	Year	Longbox Value / Value
Virgin	PRCD 3015	I'll Be Holding On	CDJ	U.S.	1989	$6.00
		I'm No Angel	CDJ	U.S.		$6.00

Alloy

Singles

Company	Disk Number	Title	Type	Country	Year	Longbox Value / Value
	11	Paper Thin Front	CD5	U.S.	1994	$5.00

Alma

Singles

Label	Catalog Number	Title	Type	Country	Year	Longbox Value / Value
Original Sound	6596	Make It With You	CD5	U.S.	1993	$3.00

Alma De Noche

Singles

Label	Catalog Number	Title	Type	Country	Year	Longbox Value / Value
Polygram	868441-2	Mama	CD5	Germany	1991	$6.00

Almedia, Laurindo

Full Length

Label	Catalog Number	Title	Type	Country	Year	Longbox Value / Value
Concord	CCD-4150	Brazillian Soul	LP/LB	U.S.†	1985	$13.00/$8.00
East Wind	35JD8	Concierto Aranjuez	LP/BP	U.S.†	1985	$13.00/$8.00

Almighty

Full Length

Label	Catalog Number	Title	Type	Country	Year	Longbox Value / Value
Polydor	841347-2	Blood Fire & Love	LP/BP	U.S.		$14.00/$8.00
Polydor	847961-2	Soul Destruction	LP	Germany		$12.00
Polydor	847961-2	Soul Destruction	LP/BP	U.S.		$14.00/$8.00

Singles

Label	Catalog Number	Title	Type	Country	Year	Longbox Value / Value
Polydor	CDP 624	Devil's Toy	CDJ	U.S.	1992	$3.00
Polydor		Free N' Easy	CDJ	U.S.		$3.00
Polydor	CDP 497	Free 'N' Easy	CDJ	U.S.	1991	$7.00
		Out Of Season	CD5	U.K.		$9.00
		Out Of Season	CD5	U.K.		$9.00
	Second version.					
Polydor	PZCD-66	Power	CD5	U.K.	1990	$9.00
		Wrench	CD5	U.K.		$10.00
		Wrench	CD5	U.K.		$10.00
	Second version.					

Almighty R.S.O.

Singles

Label	Catalog Number	Title	Type	Country	Year	Longbox Value / Value
Epic	ESK 5320	Badd Boyz	CDJ	U.S.	1993	$3.00

Almond, Marc

Full Length

Label	Catalog Number	Title	Type	Country	Year	Longbox Value / Value
Capitol	CDP-94404	Enchanted	LP/LB	U.S.		$14.00/$8.00
Capitol	CDP-91042	Stars We Are	LP/LB	U.S.		$14.00/$8.00
Phonogram	822832-2	Vermin In Ermine	LP	U.K.		$15.00

Singles

Label	Catalog Number	Title	Type	Country	Year	Longbox Value / Value
Parlophone	CDR-6229	A Lover Spurned	CD5	U.K.	1990	$9.00
		Adored and Explored	CD5	U.K.	1995	$10.00
		Adored and Explored	CD5	U.K.	1995	$10.00
	Second version.					
		Adored And Explored	CDJ	U.K.	1995	$10.00
Parlophone	203031-2	Bittersweet	CD5	Germany	1989	$9.00
Parlophone	CDR-6194	Bittersweet	CD5	U.K.	1989	$9.00
EMI		Child Star	CD5	U.K.		$10.00
EMI		Child Star	CDJ	U.K.		$15.00
WEA	9031-76179-2	Days Of Pearly Spencer,The	CD5	Germany	1992	$9.00
		Days Of Pearly Spencer, The	CD5	U.K.		$10.00
	Second version.					
		Days Of Pearly Spencer,The	CD5	U.K.	1992	$9.00
		Days Of Pearly Spencer,The	CDJ	U.K.	1992	$9.00
EMI	203843-2	Desperate Hours, The	CD5	Germany	1990	$9.00
EMI	203949-2	Desperate Hours, The	CD5	Germany	1990	$9.00
EMI	CDR-6252	Desperate Hours, The	CD5	U.K.	1990	$9.00
Capitol	DPRO-79173	Desperate Hours, The	CDJ	U.S.	1990	$2.00
		Idol, The	CD5	U.K.	1995	$10.00
		Idol, The	CD5	U.K.	1995	$10.00
	Second version.					
		Idol, The	CDJ	U.K.	1995	$10.00
Warner Brothers	12-40234	Jacky	CD5	Canada	1993	$8.00
WEA	9031-75442-2	Jacky	CD5	Germany	1991	$9.00
WEA	9031-75497-2	Jacky	CD5	Germany	1991	$9.00
WEA	WMC5-462	Jacky	CD5	Japan	1991	$15.00
WEA	YZ-610CD	Jacky	CD5	U.K.	1991	$9.00
Sire	9 40234-2	Jacky	CD5	U.S.	1991	$4.00
EMI	203665-2	Lover Spurned	CD5	Germany	1990	$9.00
EMI	CDR-6229	Lover Spurned	CD5	U.K.	1990	$9.00
EMI	TODP-2359	Madame De La Luna	CD3	Japan	1992	$15.00/$3.00
Warner Brothers	12-40367	My Hand Over My Heart	CD5	Canada	1993	$8.00
WEA	9031-76027-2	My Hand Over My Heart	CD5	Germany	1992	$9.00
WEA	YZ-633CD	My Hand Over My Heart	CD5	U.K.	1992	$9.00
Warner Brothers	PRO-CD-5332	My Hand Over My Heart	CDJ	U.S.	1991	$2.00
Warner Brothers	9 40367-2	My Hand Over My Heart	CD5	U.S.	1992	$4.00
Parlophone	203289-2	Only the Moment	CD5	Germany	1989	$9.00
Parlophone	CDR-6210	Only the Moment	CD5	U.K.	1989	$9.00
		Out There	CD5	U.K.	1995	$10.00
Parlophone	CDR-6201	Somethings Gotten Hold Of My Heart	CD5	U.K.	1989	$9.00
		Star Child	CD5	U.K.	1995	$10.00
Parlophone	202864-2	Tears Run Rings	CD5	Germany	1989	$9.00
Parlophone	CDR-6186	Tears Run Rings	CD5	U.K.	1989	$9.00
EMI	204002-2	Waifs And Strays	CD5	Germany	1990	$9.00
EMI	CDR-6263	Waifs And Strays	CD5	U.K.	1990	$9.00
Efa	CD-40080	What!	CD3	Germany	1990	$9.00
		What Makes A Man A Man	CD5	U.K.	1993	$9.00
		What Makes A Man A Man	CD5	U.K.	1993	$9.00
	Second version					

Alomar, Carlos

Full Length

Label	Catalog Number	Title	Type	Country	Year	Longbox Value / Value
Private	2019-2	Dream Generator	LP/LB	U.S.		$12.00/$7.00

Alonso, Maria Conchita

Singles

Label	Catalog Number	Title	Type	Country	Year	Longbox Value / Value
Sony Latin	10122	Promesas	CDJ	U.S.	1992	$2.00

Aloof

Singles

Label	Catalog Number	Title	Type	Country	Year	Longbox Value / Value
Ffrr	FCD-150	Never Get Out the Boat	CD3	U.K.	1991	$6.00
Cowboy	RODEOSD-5	On A Mission	CD5	U.K.	1992	$6.00
Cowboy	CDRODEO-12	Purity	CD5	U.K.	1992	$6.00

Alpenwelt Musikanten

Singles

Label	Catalog Number	Title	Type	Country	Year	Longbox Value / Value
BMG	664351	Ich Bin Dein Engel	CD5	Germany	1991	$5.00

Alpert, Herb

Full Length

Label	Catalog Number	Title	Type	Country	Year	Longbox Value / Value
Canyon	D32-Y-3511	A&M Classics	LP	Japan		$25.00
Polygram	394949-2	Blow Your Own Horn	LP	Germany		$15.00
A&M	D32Y-3042	Blow Your Own Horn	LP	Japan		$25.00
A&M	CD-4949	Blow Your Own Horn	LP/LB	U.S.†	1984	$16.00/$10.00
A&M	CD-4949	Blow Your Own Horn	LP/LB	U.S.	1987	$18.00/$10.00
A&M	CD-5022	Bullish	LP/LB	U.S.†	1984	$18.00/$10.00
A&M	CD 17476	Diamonds Remix CD Sampler	DJ/Smplr	U.S.	1987	$18.00
Canyon	PCCY-10006	My Abstract Heart	LP	Japan		$25.00
A&M	CD-5273	My Abstract Heart	LP/LB	U.S.		$18.00/$10.00
A&M	CD-3714	Rise	LP/LB	U.S.†	1984	$18.00/$10.00
	PRO-CD-4876	Sampler	DJ/Smplr	U.S.	1995	$4.00
Polygram	395209-2	Under A Spanish Moon	LP	Germany	1988	$15.00
A&M	D32Y-3244	Under A Spanish Moon	LP	Japan	1988	$20.00
A&M	CD 17593	Under A Spanish Moon	DJ/LP	U.S.	1988	$12.00
	CD in clothbound digipak					
A&M	CD-5209	Under A Spanish Moon	LP/LB	U.S.	1988	$14.00/$8.00
Polygram	396906-2	Very Best Of	LP	Germany		$18.00
Polygram	395082-2	Wild Romance	LP	Germany		$15.00
A&M	D32Y-3043	Wild Romance	LP	Japan		$20.00
A&M	CD-5082	Wild Romance	LP/LB	U.S.†	1985	$15.00/$8.00
A&M	CD-5082	Wild Romance	LP/LB	U.S.	1987	$14.00/$8.00

Singles

Label	Catalog Number	Title	Type	Country	Year	Longbox Value / Value
A&M	390345-2	Compact Hits	CD5	Germany	1988	$10.00
A&M	AMCD-910	Compact Hits	CD5	U.K.	1988	$10.00
A&M	390358-2	I Need You	CD5	Germany	1988	$10.00
A&M	S10Y-3046	I Need You	CD3	Japan	1988	$12.00/$4.00
A&M	75021 7542 2	Jump Street	CDJ	U.S.	1991	$3.00
A&M	CD-17451	Keep Your Eye On Me	CDJ	U.S.	1987	$3.00
A&M	75021 7355-2	Midnight Sun	CDJ	U.S.	1992	$3.00
A&M	75021 7000 2	North On South St.	CDJ	U.S.	1991	$3.00
A&M	S12Y-3029	Rise	CD3	Japan	1988	$15.00/$4.00
A&M	CD-17977	Romance Dance	CDJ	U.S.	1989	$3.00
A&M	S12Y-3028	The Lonely Bull	CD3	Japan	1988	$15.00/$4.00
A&M	AMCD-836	This Guy's In Love With You	CD5	U.K.	1991	$10.00
A&M	CD-17878	Three O'clock Jump	CDJ	U.S.	1989	$3.00

Alpha 1

Singles

Label	Catalog Number	Title	Type	Country	Year	Longbox Value / Value
Strictly Hype	119	Racer X	CD5	U.S.	1994	$5.00

Alpha, Blondy And Solar System

Singles

Label	Catalog Number	Title	Type	Country	Year	Longbox Value / Value
EMI	204656-2	Rendez-Vous	CD5	U.K.	1992	$6.00

Alphabet Soup

Singles

Label	Catalog Number	Title	Type	Country	Year	Longbox Value / Value
Prawn Song	PRCD 5906	Take A Ride	CDJ	U.S.	1995	$3.00

Alphatown

Singles

Label	Catalog Number	Title	Type	Country	Year	Longbox Value / Value
Alphaville		Big In Japan '92	CD5	Germany	1992	$8.00
WEA	246985-2	Forever Young	CD3	Germany	1989	$8.00
Atlantic	PR 24652-2	Forever Young	CDJ	U.S.	1988	$2.00
Alfa	ALDB-16	Hot Stuff	CD3	Japan	1990	$12.00/$2.00
Alfa	ALDB-30	Japan Japan	CD3	Japan	1990	$12.00/$2.00
WEA	246554-2	Mysteries Of Love, The	CD3	Germany	1989	$8.00
Atlantic	PRCD 3187-2	Mysteries Of Love, The	CDJ	U.S.	1989	$2.00
Alfa	11B3-57	Power Of Magic	CD3	Japan		$12.00/$2.00
WEA	247069-2	Romeos	CD3	Germany	1989	$12.00/$8.00
Pioneer	09P3-6145	Romeos	CD3	Japan	1989	$2.00
Atlantic	PR 2681-2	Romeos	CDJ	U.S.	1989	$2.00
WEA	246802-2	Summer Rain	CD3	Germany	1988	$8.00

Alston, Gerald

Full Length

Label	Catalog Number	Title	Type	Country	Year	Longbox Value / Value
Motown	ZD-72651	Gerald Alston	LP	U.K.		$15.00
Motown	MOTD-6298	Open Invitation	LP	Canada		$15.00

Singles

Label	Catalog Number	Title	Type	Country	Year	Longbox Value / Value
RCA	ZD-42624	Activated	CD5	Germany	1989	$8.00
Polygram	ZD-42682	Activated	CD5	U.K.	1989	$8.00
Motown	3746310652	Hell Of A Situation	CDJ	U.S.	1992	$2.00
Motown	374631087	Send For Me	CDJ	U.S.	1992	$2.00
Polygram	ZD-44102	Slow Motion	CD5	U.K.	1991	$8.00
Motown	18269	Slow Motion	CDJ	U.S.	1990	$3.00
Polygram	ZD-43086	Stay A Little While	CD5	U.K.	1989	$8.00
Street Life	75393	Stay the Night	CDJ	U.S.	1994	$3.00

Alston, Jazz Lee

Singles

Label	Catalog Number	Title	Type	Country	Year	Longbox Value / Value
American	6677	Love	CDJ	U.S.	1994	$2.00

Alston, Johnetta

Singles

Label	Catalog Number	Title	Type	Country	Year	Longbox Value / Value
Polygram	NORCD-1	Keep the Fire Burning	CD5	U.K.	1990	$7.00

Alt

Full Length

Label	Catalog Number	Title	Type	Country	Year	Longbox Value / Value
	ALTCD2	Bootleg	LTD/LP	U.S.	1995	$30.00

Alter Boys

Full Length

Label	Catalog Number	Title	Type	Country	Year	Longbox Value / Value
Frontline	CD-9023	Againt the Grain	LP/LB	U.S.		$12.00/$7.00
Aris	880386	Gut Level Music	LP	Germany		$12.00

Altered State

Full Length

Label	Catalog Number	Title	Type	Country	Year	Longbox Value / Value
Warner Brothers	9 26502-2-Dj	Altered State	DJ/LP	U.S.	1991	$10.00

Singles

Label	Catalog Number	Title	Type	Country	Year	Longbox Value / Value
Warner Brothers	9 40155-2	Step into My Groove	CD5	U.S.	1991	$2.00
Warner Brothers	PRO-CD-4876	Step into My Groove	CDJ	U.S.	1991	$2.00

Altern 8

Singles

Label	Catalog Number	Title	Type	Country	Year	Longbox Value / Value
Rough Trade	227 1168 3	Active 8	CD5	Germany	1991	$8.00
Network	NWKCD-34	Active 8	CD5	U.K.	1991	$8.00
Network	NWKCD-59	Brutal 8 E	CD5	U.K.	1992	$8.00
Network	127 1342 3	Evapor 8	CD5	Germany	1991	$8.00
Network	NWK CD38	Evapor 8	CD5	U.K.	1992	$8.00
Network	NWKCD-49	Hynotic St 8	CD5	U.K.	1992	$8.00
ZYX	6555-8	Infiltrate 202	CD5	Germany	1991	$8.00
Network	NWKCD-24	Vertigo EP	CD5	U.K.	1991	$10.00

Altman, Jeff

Full Length

Label	Catalog Number	Title	Type	Country	Year	Longbox Value / Value
Mercury	CDP 138	I'll Flip You Like A Cheese Omelette	DJ/Smplr	U.S.		$8.00

Altschul, Barry

Full Length

Label	Catalog Number	Title	Type	Country	Year	Longbox Value / Value
Polygram	SN-1115CD	That's Nice	LP/BP	U.S.		$8.00

Alvin And The Chipmunks

Singles

Label	Catalog Number	Title	Type	Country	Year	Longbox Value / Value
Epic	ESK 7476	Achy Breaky Heart	CDJ	U.S.	1992	$2.00
Epic	ESK 7779	I Don't Want To Be Alone For Christmas	CDJ	U.S.	1994	$3.00

Label	Catalog Number	Title	Type	Country	Year	Longbox Value / Value
Alvin, Dave						
Singles						
Epic	ESK 2778	Every Night About this Time	CDJ	U.S.	1987	$2.00
Hightone	DAPRO 2	Guilty Man	CDJ	U.S.	1991	$2.00
Alvin, Phil						
Full Length						
WEA	9 25481-2	Unsung Heros	LP/LB	U.S.		$20.00/$16.00
Always						
Singles						
Toshiba	RODT-2851	Itsumo Egao Koishiteru	CD3	Japan	1992	$7.00/$2.00
EL	25610-12	Metroland	CD3	Japan	1989	$12.00/$3.00
Aly-Us						
Singles						
EMI	COOLCD-266	Follow Me	CD5	U.K.	1992	$7.00
Strictly Rhythm	1288	Follow Me	CD5	U.S.	1994	$5.00
Alzo & Udine						
Full Length						
	WCYA-677156	C'mon and Join Us	LP	Japan		$45.00
Amadeus						
Singles						
Continental	1029	La Novia	CD5	U.S.	1994	$5.00
Amazone						
Full Length						
EMI	251360-2	Rough, Tough	LP	Germany		$15.00
Amazons						
Singles						
Canyon	FLDF-10243	Born On the Wind	CD3	Japan	1993	$7.00/$2.00
Sony	SRDL-3345	Door O Akete	CD3	Japan	1991	$7.00/$2.00
Sony	SRDL-3333	Dreamy Sunday	CD3	Japan	1991	$7.00/$2.00
Canyon	FLDF-10216	Oyoge 8 Banme Fushingi	CD3	Japan	1992	$7.00/$2.00
Ambassadors Of Funk						
Singles						
Pinnacle	SMASH-23CD	Super Marioland	CD5	U.K.	1992	$8.00
Ambel, Eric						
Full Length						
Enigma	73329	Roscoe's Gang	LP/LB	U.S.		$12.00/$7.00
Ambitious Lovers						
Full Length						
Virgin	90903-2	Greed	LP	Canada		$12.00
Virgin	259177	Greed	LP	Germany		$12.00
Virgin	86052	Greed	LP/LB	U.S.		$12.00/$7.00
Singles						
Elektra	PRCD 8306-2	Lust	CDJ	U.S.	1990	$2.00
Ambros						
Singles						
Polygram	889416-3	Idealgewicht	CD3	Germany	1989	$6.00
America						
Full Length						
WEA	256169	History	LP	Germany		$18.00
Capitol	CDP-48414	In Concert Live	LP/LB	U.S.		$14.00/$8.00
Capitol		Ventura Highway & Other Favorites	LP/LB	U.S.		$14.00/$8.00
Singles						
WEA	921017-2	Horse With No Name	CD3	Germany	1989	$10.00
WEA	921017-2	Horse With No Name	CD3	U.K.	1989	$10.00
WEA	876772-2	Young Moon	CD5	U.K.	1994	$10.00
American Gramaphone	49451	Young Moon	CDJ	U.S.	1994	$3.00
American Angel						
Singles						
		Grand Theft Ecstasy	CDJ	U.S.		$2.00
American Boys Choir						
Full Length						
Rykodisc	30129	On Christmas Day	LP/BP	U.S.		$12.00/$7.00
American Music Club						
Full Length						
Reprise		Hello Amsterdam	DJ/Smplr	U.S.	1994	$10.00
Reprise		Johnny Mathis Feet	DJ/Smplr	U.S.	1993	$18.00
Reprise	PRO-CD-6527	Johnny Mathis Feet Plus Live Bonus Tracks	DJ/Smplr	U.S.	1994	$30.00
Reprise	PRO-CD-6527	Johnny Mathis Feet Plus Live Tracks	DJ/Smplr	U.S.	1993	$35.00
	CDJ of "Johnny Mathis Feet" and live concert CD.					
Reprise	PRO-CD-6066	Over And Done	DJ/Smplr	U.S.	1993	$20.00
Singles						
Reprise	PRO-CD-7209	Can You Help Me	CDJ	U.S.	1994	$3.00
Reprise		Johnny Mathis Feet	CD5	U.K.	1993	$10.00
Reprise		Johnny Mathis Feet	CD5	U.K.	1993	$10.00
	Second version.					
		Keep Me Around	CD5	U.K.	1993	$10.00
Reprise	PRO-CD-6233	Over And Done	CDJ	U.S.	1993	$7.00
Rough Trade	383 8105 3	Rise	CD5	Germany	1991	$10.00
Rough Trade		Rise	CD5	U.S.	1991	$6.00
Reprise		Wish the World Away	CD5	U.K.	1993	$10.00
Reprise		Wish the World Away	CD5	U.K.	1993	$10.00
	Second version.					
Reprise	PRO-CD-7171	Wish the World Away	CDJ	U.S.	1994	$7.00
AMG						
Singles						
ZYX	6711-8	Bitch Betta Have My Money	CD5	Germany	1992	$5.00
ZYX	6734-8	Jiggable Pie	CD5	Germany	1992	$5.00
Select	009	Jiggable Pie	CDJ	U.S.	1991	$2.00
Amina						
Singles						
Philips	874 433	Belly Dance	CD5	U.K.	1989	$8.00
Polygram	MERCD-322	Belly Dance	CD5	U.K.	1990	$8.00
Mango	7845	Belly Dance	CDJ	U.S.	1990	$2.00
Polygram	868333-2	Le Dernier Qui	CD5	Germany	1990	$8.00
Amir						
Singles						
WEA	171713-2	Rain	CD5	Germany	1990	$6.00

Company	Disk Number	Title	Type	Country	Year	Longbox Value / Value
Ammons, Albert						
Full Length						
Mosaic	MD2-103	Complete Blue Note Recordings	LP	U.S.		$30.00
	2 CD set					
Ammons, Gene						
Full Length						
Teldec	824297	Boogie Woogie And the Blues	LP	Germany		$15.00
Amnesia						
Singles						
BCM	20010	Ibiza	CD5	Germany	1988	$5.00
Amon, Duul II						
Full Length						
Magnum	11	Fool Moon	LP	U.S.		$7.00
Amorphis						
Singles						
Relativity	6918	Black Winter Day	CD5	U.S.	1994	$5.00
Amos, Tori And Tom Jones						
Singles						
ZTT	ZANG 64 CD	I Wanna Get Back With You	CD5	Germany	1995	$10.00
Interscope		I Wanna Get Back With You	CDJ	U.S.	1995	$7.00

Amos, Tori – Precious Things (Atlantic PRCD 4742-2) One of the rarest Tori promotional CDs.

Amos, Tori – Tea With the Waitress (Atlantic PRCD 5498-2) Rare radio interview disc. Most interviews heard on the radio are from these discs. Questions are usually printed in the booklet with the disc only comprising the artist's answers. The dj can therefore read the questions like he is interviewing the artist him or herself.

Company	Disk Number	Title	Type	Country	Year	Longbox Value / Value
Amos, Tori						
Full Length						
Eastwest	PROP100	Boys For Pele	DJ/LP	Germany	1995	$100.00
Atlantic	PRCD 6589-2	Holiday Greetings	DJ/intvw	U.S.	1995	$25.00
Atlantic	PRCD 6536-2	New Music From Tori Amos	DJ/Smplr	U.S.	1995	$34.00
Atlantic		Past the Mission	DJ/Smplr	U.S.	1994	$35.00
Atlantic	PRCD 4742-2	Precious Things	DJ/Smplr	U.S.	1992	$200.00
Atlantic		RAINN PSA's	DJ/Smplr	U.S.	1995	$15.00
Atlantic		Retrospective	DJ/Smplr	U.S.	1997	$50.00
Atlantic	PRCD 5498-2	Tea With the Waitress	DJ/Intvw	U.S.	1994	$50.00
Eastwest	7567806072	Under the Pink	LTD/LP	Australia	1994	$40.00
	2 CD set.					
WEA		Under the Pink	LTD/LP	Australia	1994	$40.00
	CD album plus 4 track VHS video (Pal).					
Atlantic	3 82567-2	Under the Pink	DJ/LP	U.S.	1994	$30.00
	Advance issue					
WEA	81845-2	Y Kant Tori Read	LP	Germany	1988	$300.00
Atlantic	81845-2	Y Kant Tori Read	LP/LB	U.S.	1988	$300.00/$200.00
Singles						
Eastwest		Caught A Little Sneeze	CD5	U.K.	1996	$10.00
Eastwest		Caught A Little Sneeze	CD5	U.K.	1996	$10.00
	Second version.					
Eastwest	A5 52HDJCD	Caught A Little Sneeze	CDJ	U.K.	1996	$25.00
Atlantic	PRCD 6549-2	Caught A Little Sneeze	CDJ	U.S.	1996	$7.00
Eastwest	7567-85905-2	China	CD5	Germany	1992	$12.00
Atlantic	A7531CD	China	CD5	U.K.	1992	$12.00
Eastwest	A 7531CDDJ	China	CDJ	U.K.	1992	$20.00
Atlantic	PR 2452-2	Cool On Your Island	CDJ	U.S.	1988	$50.00
	Also has 2 tracks from Phil Collins.					

Label	Catalog Number	Title	Type	Country	Year	Longbox Value / Value
Eastwest		Cornflake Girl	CD5	Australia	1994	$12.00
Atlantic	CD85693	Cornflake Girl	CD5	Canada	1994	$11.00
Eastwest		Cornflake Girl	CD5	France	1994	$12.00
Eastwest	A 7281CD	Cornflake Girl	CD5	U.K.	1994	$10.00
Eastwest	A 7281CDX	Cornflake Girl	CD5	U.K.	1994	$15.00
Eastwest	A 7281CD-DJ	Cornflake Girl	CDJ	U.K.	1994	$20.00
Atlantic	85655	Cornflake Girl	CD5	U.S.	1994	$5.00
Atlantic		Cornflake Girl	CDJ	U.S.	1994	$10.00
Eastwest		Crucify	CD5	France	1992	$16.00
Eastwest	A 7479CD	Crucify	CD5	U.K.	1992	$15.00
Eastwest	A 7479CDX	Crucify	CD5	U.K.	1992	$30.00
Special edition in box.						
Eastwest	A 7479CDDJ	Crucify	CDJ	U.K.	1992	$20.00
Atlantic	PRCD-4598-2	Crucify	CDJ	U.S.	1992	$10.00
Eastwest	7567856872	God	CD5	Australia	1994	$12.00
Eastwest	A7251CD	God	CD5	U.K.	1994	$10.00
Atlantic	85687-2	God	CD5	U.S.	1994	$6.00
Atlantic	85687	God	CD5	U.S.	1994	$5.00
Atlantic	PRCD5398-2	God	CDJ	U.S.	1994	$7.00
Atlantic	PRCD5408-2	God	CDJ	U.S.	1994	$10.00
Atlantic	85687-2	God	CD5	U.S.	1996	$7.00
Eastwest	A5494CDDJ	Hey Jupiter	CDJ	U.K.	1996	$25.00
Atlantic		Hey Jupiter	CDJ	U.S.	1996	$12.00
Eastwest		Little Drummer Boy	CDJ	U.K.	1992	$50.00
CD-R version.						
Atlantic	PRCD 5409-2	Little Drummer Boy	CDJ	U.S.	1992	$10.00
Eastwest		London Girls	CDJ	France	1996	$50.00
Eastwest	YZ 618CD	Me And A Gun	CD5	U.K.	1991	$40.00
Original issue of "Silent All These Years" with "Me And A Gun" printed on front cover.						
Eastwest		Past the Mission	CD5	Australia	1994	$12.00
Eastwest	A7257CDX	Past the Mission	CD5	U.K.	1994	$15.00
Eastwest	A7257CD	Past the Mission	CD5	U.K.	1994	$10.00
Atlantic		Past the Mission	CDJ	U.S.	1994	$10.00
Eastwest	7567 85677	Pretty Good Year	CD5	Germany	1994	$12.00
Eastwest	A 7263CD	Pretty Good Year	CD5	U.K.	1994	$10.00
Eastwest	A 7263CDX	Pretty Good Year	CD5	U.K.	1994	$10.00
Eastwest	7567-85677-2	Pretty Good Your	CD5	U.K.	1994	$10.00
Atlantic	85499-2	Professional Widow	CDJ	U.S.	1997	$6.00
Eastwest	WMD5-4102	Silent All These Years	CD3	Japan	1992	$18.00/$5.00
Atlantic	YZ-618CD	Silent All These Years	CD5	U.K.	1991	$12.00
Atlantic	YZ-618CD	Silent All These Years	CD5	U.K.	1991	$25.00
Disc has markings of original "Me And A Gun" CD.						
Atlantic	A7433CD	Silent All These Years	CD5	U.K.	1992	$10.00
Atlantic	A7433CDX	Silent All These Years	CD5	U.K.	1992	$12.00
Atlantic	PRCD 4454-2	Silent All These Years	CDJ	U.S.	1992	$10.00
Eastwest		Talulah	CDJ	U.K.	1996	$25.00
Atlantic	PRCD 6720-2	Talulah	CDJ	U.S.	1996	$12.00
Warner Brothers	32-85799	Winter	CD5	Canada	1993	$10.00
WEA	A7504CD	Winter	CD5	U.K.	1992	$12.00
WEA	A7504CDX	Winter	CD5	U.K.	1992	$14.00
WEA	A7504CDDJ	Winter	CDJ	U.K.	1992	$20.00
Atlantic	85799-2	Winter	CD5	U.S.	1992	$7.00
Atlantic	PRCD 4800-2	Winter	CDJ	U.S.	1992	$7.00

Amps

Label	Catalog Number	Title	Type	Country	Year	Longbox Value / Value
Full Length						
4AD		Tipp City	DJ/Smplr	U.S.	1995	$3.00
Singles						
4AD	PRCD 9363-2	Kim Deal's New Band	CDJ	U.S.	1995	$3.00
	PRCD 95172	Pacer	CDJ	U.S.	1995	$6.00
	PRCD 93632	Tripp City	CDJ	U.S.	1995	$6.00

Amre, Diab

Label	Catalog Number	Title	Type	Country	Year	Longbox Value / Value
Singles						
Bellaphon	130 07 350	Mayall-Mayall	CD5	Germany	1990	$6.00

An Emotional Fish

Label	Catalog Number	Title	Type	Country	Year	Longbox Value / Value
Full Length						
Atlantic	7 82150-2	Emotional Fish	LP/LB	U.S.		$14.00/$8.00
Atlantic	PRCD 3828-2	Live Bait	DJ/Smplr	U.S.	1991	$15.00
		Sloper	LP	Ireland	1994	$25.00
Singles						
Eastwest	YZ-539CD	Blue	CD5	U.K.	1990	$9.00
Atlantic	PRCD-5230-2	Careless Child	CDJ	U.S.	1993	$3.00
WEA		Celebratation Live	CD5	U.K.		$10.00
WEA	171794-2	Celebrate	CD5	Germany	1990	$9.00
WEA	9031-71794-2	Celebrate	CD5	Germany	1991	$9.00
WEA	YZ-489CD	Celebrate	CD5	U.K.	1990	$9.00
Atlantic	86136-2	Celebrate	CD5	U.S.	1990	$5.00
Atlantic	PRCD 3520-2	Celebrate	CDJ	U.S.	1990	$3.00
Atlantic		Celebrate	CDJ	U.S.	1990	$3.00
Second version.						
WEA	YZ-613CD	Celebration Live	CD5	U.K.	1990	$9.00
Atlantic	PRCD 3769-2	Grey Matter	CDJ	U.S.	1990	$3.00
WEA	9031-72330-2	Lace Virginia	CD5	Germany	1990	$9.00
WEA	YZ-502CD	Lace Virginia	CD5	U.K.	1990	$9.00
Atlantic	PRCD 5041-2	Rain	CDJ	U.S.	1993	$3.00
		Time Is On the Wall	CD5	Ireland	1994	$10.00

Ana

Label	Catalog Number	Title	Type	Country	Year	Longbox Value / Value
Full Length						
Columbia	CK-45355	Body Language	LP/LB	U.S.		$7.00
Singles						
Epic	CSDS-8151	Angel Of Love	CD3	Japan	1990	$12.00/$3.00
Epic	ZSK 2124	Angel Of Love	CDJ	U.S.	1990	$2.00
Epic	ZSK 73581	Every Time We Say Goodbye	CDJ	U.S.	1990	$2.00
Epic	ZSK 72317	Got To Tell Me Something	CDJ	U.S.	1990	$2.00
CBS	10EP-3006	Shy Boys	CD3	Japan	1988	$2.00

Anaconda

Label	Catalog Number	Title	Type	Country	Year	Longbox Value / Value
Singles						
ZYX	BOY-8825-8	Machine	CD5	Germany	1991	$7.00

Anacrusis

Label	Catalog Number	Title	Type	Country	Year	Longbox Value / Value
Full Length						
Warner Brothers	26616	Manic Impresions	LP/LB	U.S.		$14.00/$8.00
Warner Brothers	45245	Screams & Whispers	LP/LB	U.S.		$14.00/$8.00

Anai, Yuko

Label	Catalog Number	Title	Type	Country	Year	Longbox Value / Value
Singles						
Epic	ESDB-3321	I Want You	CD3	Japan	1992	$12.00/$2.00
Epic	ESDB-3241	Natural Lovers	CD3	Japan	1991	$12.00/$2.00

Anastasia Screamed

Label	Catalog Number	Title	Type	Country	Year	Longbox Value / Value
Singles						
Pinnacle	HYPE-8CD	Fifteen Seconds Or 5 Days	CD5	U.K.	1991	$8.00
Rough Trade	585 0012 3	Tornado	CD5	Germany	1991	$8.00

Anathema

Label	Catalog Number	Title	Type	Country	Year	Longbox Value / Value
Singles						
Pinnacle	VILE-36TCD	Crestfallen	CD5	U.K.	1992	$7.00

And Why Not?

Label	Catalog Number	Title	Type	Country	Year	Longbox Value / Value
Full Length						
Polystar	PSCD-1013	Move Your Skin	LP	Japan		$20.00
Island	842269	Move Your Skin	LP/LB	U.S.		$12.00/$8.00
Singles						
Aris	884696	Cage	CD5	Germany	1990	$8.00
Island	CID-467	Cage	CD5	U.K.	1990	$8.00
BMG	663047	Face, The	CD5	Germany	1990	$8.00
Island	CID-444	Face, The	CD5	U.K.	1990	$8.00
Island	PRCD 6620-2	Face, The	CDJ	U.S.	1990	$2.00
Aris	885592	Restless Days	CD5	Germany	1989	$8.00
Island	CID-426	Restless Days	CD5	U.K.	1989	$8.00
BMG	663299	Something U Got	CD5	Germany	1990	$8.00
Island	CID-452	Something U Got	CD5	U.K.	1990	$8.00

Anders, Thomas

Label	Catalog Number	Title	Type	Country	Year	Longbox Value / Value
Singles						
Eastwest	9031-75026-2	Can't Give You	CD5	Germany	1991	$8.00
Eastwest	246957-2	Love Of My Own	CD5	Germany	1989	$8.00
Eastwest	246575-2	Soldier	CD3	Germany	1989	$8.00
Eastwest	246737-2	Soldier	CD5	Germany	1989	$8.00
Eastwest	9031-74247-2	Sweet Hello, Sad G.	CD5	Germany	1991	$8.00
Eastwest	9031-73757-2	True Love	CD5	Germany	1992	$8.00

Andersen, Bo

Label	Catalog Number	Title	Type	Country	Year	Longbox Value / Value
Singles						
BMG	661842	Reach Out For the Stars	CD5	Germany	1988	$7.00

Andersen, Eric

Label	Catalog Number	Title	Type	Country	Year	Longbox Value / Value
Full Length						
		Exile	LP	Japan		$30.00
		Ghosts Upon the Road	DJ/LP	Japan		$35.00
Advance Issue						
Goldcastle	71327	Ghosts Upon the Road	LP	U.S.		$8.00

Andersen, Gerry

Label	Catalog Number	Title	Type	Country	Year	Longbox Value / Value
Singles						
SPV	8685-3	Project 90	CD5	Germany	1990	$8.00
APT	SPV-1CD	Project 90	CD5	U.K.	1990	$8.00

Anderson, Bruford, Wakeman, Howe

Label	Catalog Number	Title	Type	Country	Year	Longbox Value / Value
Full Length						
Arista	ARCD85-90126	Anderson, Bruford, Wakeman, Howe	DJ/LP	U.S.	1989	$45.00
Picture CD edition.						
DIR		King Biscuit Flour Hour	RS	U.S.	1989	$80.00
2 CD set. Airdate: 1/1 - 1/8/90						
DIR		King Biscuit Flour Hour	RS	U.S.	1990	$45.00
Airdate: 9/24/90						
DIR		King Biscuit Flour Hour	RS	U.S.	1992	$45.00
Airdate: 5/25/92						
DIR		King Biscuit Flour Hour	RS	U.S.	1994	$65.00
Airdate: 11/12/94						
DIR		King Biscuit Flour Hour	RS	U.S.	1995	$65.00
Airdate: 11/26/95						
Radio Ventures		Masters Of Rock	RS	U.S.	1989	$50.00
Airdate: 12/18/89						
Radio Today		Rock Stars	RS	U.S.	1989	$50.00
2 CD set. Airdate: 8/14/89						
Media America		Up Close	RS	U.S.	1989	$70.00
4 CD set.						
Singles						
Arista	162379	Brother Of Mine	CD3	Germany	1989	$10.00
Arista	662379	Brother Of Mine	CD5	Germany	1989	$15.00
Arista	A10D-129	Brother Of Mine	CD3	Japan	1989	$15.00/$4.00
Arista	162379	Brother Of Mine	CD3	U.K.	1989	$10.00
Arista	662379	Brother Of Mine	CD5	U.K.	1989	$12.00
Arista	ASCD-9842	Brother Of Mine	CDJ	U.S.	1989	$6.00
Arista		Brother of Mine + Interview	DJ/CD3	Japan	1989	$25.00
Arista	662618	Order Of the Universe	CD5	Germany	1989	$10.00
Arista	A10D-138	Order Of the Universe	CD3	Japan	1989	$15.00/$4.00
Arista	662618	Order Of the Universe	CD5	U.K.	1989	$10.00
Arista	A10D-150	Quartet (I'm Alive)	CD3	Japan	1989	$15.00/$4.00
Arista	ASCD-9898	Quartet (I'm Alive)	CDJ	U.S.	1989	$10.00

Anderson, Carl

Label	Catalog Number	Title	Type	Country	Year	Longbox Value / Value
Full Length						
GRP	1CD23	Fantasy Hotel	DJ/Smplr	Japan		$35.00
GRP	MVCR-67	Pieces Of A Heart	LP	Japan	1990	$25.00
GRP	MVCZ-13	Pieces Of A Heart	LTD/LP	Japan	1990	$25.00
Gold disc.						
Singles						
GRP	9945	Baby My Heart	CDJ	U.S.	1990	$2.00
GRP		How Deep Does It Go	CDJ	U.S.		$2.00
GRP	9976	Once In A Lifetime	CDJ	U.S.	1992	$2.00
GRP	VIDP-19	Pieces Of A Heart	CD3	Japan	1990	$15.00/$4.00

Anderson, Carleen

Label	Catalog Number	Title	Type	Country	Year	Longbox Value / Value
Singles						
		Mama Said	CD5	U.K.		$10.00
		Mama Said	CD5	U.K.		$10.00
Second version.						
Virgin	14248	Mama Said	CDJ	U.S.	1994	$3.00
		Nervous Breakdown	CD5	U.K.		$8.00
		Nervous Breakdown	CD5	U.K.		$8.00
Second version.						
		True Spirit	CD5	U.K.		$10.00
		True Spirit	CD5	U.K.		$10.00
Second version.						

Anderson, G.G.

Label	Catalog Number	Title	Type	Country	Year	Longbox Value / Value
Singles						
BMG	664124	Engel Von Valparaiso	CD5	Germany	1991	$7.00
BMG	663169	Get the Balance Right	CD5	Germany	1990	$7.00
BMG	662524	Good Bye My Love, Goodbye	CD5	Germany	1989	$7.00
BMG	663723	Heut' Geht's Uns Gut	CD5	Germany	1990	$7.00
BMG	662842	Lady Sunshine	CD5	Germany	1989	$7.00
BMG	665351	Rosalie	CD5	Germany	1992	$7.00
BMG	662224	Sommer, Sonne, Cabrio	CD3	Germany	1989	$7.00
BMG	664475	Sonnenschein Im Blut	CD5	Germany	1991	$7.00
BMG	663369	Uns Geht's Gut	CD5	Germany	1990	$7.00

Anderson, John

Full Length

Label	Catalog Number	Title	Type	Country	Year	Longbox Value / Value
		'90s Country	RS	U.S.	1995	$30.00
	Airdate: 12/9/95					
		'90s Country	RS	U.S.	1995	$30.00
	Airdate: 6/24/95					
MCA	872723	Blue Skies Again	LP	Germany		$15.00
MCA	MCAD-42037	Blue Skies Again	LP/LB	U.S.		$14.00/$8.00
MCA		Christmas Time	DJ/Smplr	U.S.		$15.00
		Country Concert	RS	U.S.	1994	$35.00
	Airdate: 6/4/94					
MCA		Country Till I Die	DJ/Smplr	U.S.		$15.00
MCA	MCAD-42218	Ten	LP/LB	U.S.		$14.00/$8.00

Singles

Label	Catalog Number	Title	Type	Country	Year	Longbox Value / Value
RCA	62443-2-RDJ	Money In the Bank	CDJ	U.S.	1993	$3.00

Anderson, Jon

Full Length

Label	Catalog Number	Title	Type	Country	Year	Longbox Value / Value
		Change We	DJ/LP	U.S.	1994	$25.00
	CD, VHS video, press kit in box.					
		In the City Of Angels	DJ/LP	Japan		$40.00
	Advance issue					
	XDDP93009	In the City Of Angels	DJ/Smplr	Japan		$40.00
		Olias Of Sun Hollow	LP	Japan		$25.00

Singles

Label	Catalog Number	Title	Type	Country	Year	Longbox Value / Value
EMI	203800-2	Far Far Cry	CD5	Germany	1990	$7.00
Enigma	EPRO 255	Far Far Cry	CDJ	U.S.	1989	$2.00
Epic	651514-2	Hold On To Love	CD5	Germany	1988	$8.00
CBS	10EP-3014	Hold On To Love	CD3	Japan	1988	$12.00/$3.00
Epic	651514-2	Hold On To Love	CD5	U.K.	1988	$8.00
Enigma		Hold On To Love	CDJ	U.S.	1988	$2.00
Epic	652947-2	Is It Me	CD5	U.K.	1988	$8.00
Toshiba	TODT-2801	Island Of Life	CD3	Japan	1992	$13.00/$3.00

Anderson, Laurie

Full Length

Label	Catalog Number	Title	Type	Country	Year	Longbox Value / Value
Warner Brothers	2-3674	Big Science	LP/LB	U.S.†	1984	$15.00/$9.00
Warner Brothers		Bright Red Sampler	DJ/Smplr	U.S.	1994	$12.00
Warner Brothers		In Our Sleep	DJ/Smplr	U.S.	1994	$10.00
Warner Brothers	25077-2	Mr. Heartbreak	LP/LB	U.S.†	1984	$15.00/$9.00

Singles

Label	Catalog Number	Title	Type	Country	Year	Longbox Value / Value
Warner Brothers	PRO-CD-3900	Babydoll	CDJ	U.S.	1989	$2.00
Warner Brothers	9 21592-2	Beautiful Red Dress	CD5	U.S.	1990	$35.00
Warner Brothers	PRO-CD-4390	Beautiful Red Dress	CDJ	U.S.	1990	$2.00
Warner	43515	In Our Sleep	CD5	U.S.	1994	$5.00
Warner Brothers		In Our Sleep	CDJ	U.S.	1994	$3.00
Warner Brothers	PRO-CD-3826	Strange Angels	CDJ	U.S.	1989	$2.00

Anderson, Lynn

Full Length

Label	Catalog Number	Title	Type	Country	Year	Longbox Value / Value
Spectrum	CDSREC-85007	Collection	LP	Germany		$15.00
Castle	2610 252	Country Store Collection	LP	Germany		$15.00
Columbia	CK-31641	Greatest Hits	LP/LB	U.S.		$14.00/$8.00

Anderson, Michael

Full Length

Label	Catalog Number	Title	Type	Country	Year	Longbox Value / Value
A&M	CD-5295	Michael Anderson	LP/LB	U.S.		$12.00/$7.00

Singles

Label	Catalog Number	Title	Type	Country	Year	Longbox Value / Value
A&M	CD 17660	I Need You	CDJ	U.S.	1988	$2.00
A&M	390357-2	Sound Alarm	CD5	Germany	1990	$7.00
A&M	CD 17568	Sound Alarm	CDJ	U.S.	1988	$2.00
A&M	CD 18016	True Love	CDJ	U.S.	1990	$2.00
A&M	CD 17621	Until You Love Me	CDJ	U.S.	1988	$2.00

Anderson, Pete

Full Length

Label	Catalog Number	Title	Type	Country	Year	Longbox Value / Value
Entertainment Mgmt	PA-1001	I Don't Have To Work With Your Son, Do I?	DJ/Smplr	U.S.	1993	$35.00
PA	PA1001	I Don't Have To Work With Your Son, Do I?	VA/Smplr	U.S.	1993	$25.00

Anderson, Roshell

Full Length

Label	Catalog Number	Title	Type	Country	Year	Longbox Value / Value
Ichiban	1113	Outlaw Casanova	LP	U.S.		$8.00
Ichiban	1142	Rolling Over	LP	U.S.		$8.00
Ichiban	1053	Stepping Out	LP	U.S.		$8.00
Ichiban	1035	Sweet & Sour	LP	U.S.		$8.00

Anderson, Sharon

Full Length

Label	Catalog Number	Title	Type	Country	Year	Longbox Value / Value
Capitol	CDP-94897	Bottom Line	LP/LB	U.S.		$12.00/$7.00

Andoh, Hideki

Singles

Label	Catalog Number	Title	Type	Country	Year	Longbox Value / Value
Epic	ESDB-3295	Hajimari No Yokan	CD3	Japan	1992	$8.00/$3.00
Epic	ESDB-3334	Kimi Eno Omoi	CD3	Japan	1992	$8.00/$3.00
Epic	ESDB-3385	Moonlight	CD3	Japan	1993	$12.00/$3.00
Epic	ESDB-3243	Odore Odore	CD3	Japan	1991	$12.00/$3.00
Epic	ESDB-3354	Omoi Wa Nami No Youni	CD3	Japan	1992	$12.00/$3.00
Epic	ESDB-3270	Sayonara Itoshi No Baby Blue	CD3	Japan	1991	$12.00/$3.00

Andress, Tuck

Full Length

Label	Catalog Number	Title	Type	Country	Year	Longbox Value / Value
Windham Hill	WD-90-2	Solo Guitar Tracks	DJ/Smplr	U.S.	1990	$8.00

Andrew

Singles

Label	Catalog Number	Title	Type	Country	Year	Longbox Value / Value
Classified	0003	Season For Love	CDJ	U.S.	1993	$2.00

Andrews, Lee

Full Length

Label	Catalog Number	Title	Type	Country	Year	Longbox Value / Value
Point	264023	Best Of	LP	U.S.		$8.00

Andrews, Ruby

Full Length

Label	Catalog Number	Title	Type	Country	Year	Longbox Value / Value
Ichiban	1104	Kiss This	LP	U.S.		$8.00

Andrews Sisters

Full Length

Label	Catalog Number	Title	Type	Country	Year	Longbox Value / Value
Pro Arte	CDD-506	Boogie Woogie Bugle Boy	LP	U.S.		$8.00

Angel

Full Length

Label	Catalog Number	Title	Type	Country	Year	Longbox Value / Value
Virgin	91494	Angel	LP/LB	U.S.		$12.00/$7.00

Singles

Label	Catalog Number	Title	Type	Country	Year	Longbox Value / Value
EMI	203877	Follow Me	CD5	Germany	1990	$6.00
Intercope	PRCD 5301-2	Spirit Of Love	CDJ	U.S.		$2.00
Virgin	VJDP-10168	Your Love Just Ain't Right	CD3	Japan	1991	$13.00/$4.00
Virgin		Your Love Just Ain't Right	CDJ	U.S.	1991	$2.00

Angel, Gabrielle

Singles

Company	Disk Number	Title	Type	Country	Year	Longbox Value / Value
Law	MYCD-310	Wild Woman	CD5	U.K.	1993	$8.00

Angel, Luis

Singles

Company	Disk Number	Title	Type	Country	Year	Longbox Value / Value
Polydor	390315-2	Nadie Mejor Que Tu	CD5	Germany	1989	$6.00

Angel Witch

Full Length

Company	Disk Number	Title	Type	Country	Year	Longbox Value / Value
Roadrunner	9351	Angel Witch	LP	U.S.		$7.00
Enigma	73443	Live	LP/LB	U.S.		$12.00/$7.00

Angela

Singles

Company	Disk Number	Title	Type	Country	Year	Longbox Value / Value
Bellaphon	130 07 337	Dynamite	CD5	Germany	1989	$5.00
Warner Brothers	PRO-CD-3673	Love Me For Being Me	CDJ	U.S.	1990	$2.00

Angelfish

Singles

Company	Disk Number	Title	Type	Country	Year	Longbox Value / Value
Wasteland	9200	Suffocate Me	CDJ	U.S.	1993	$3.00

Angelica

Singles

Company	Disk Number	Title	Type	Country	Year	Longbox Value / Value
Toshiba	TODP-23240	Angel Baby	CD3	Japan	1992	$13.00/$4.00
Quality	15198	Next To You	CDJ	U.S.	1992	$2.00

Angelpie

Singles

Company	Disk Number	Title	Type	Country	Year	Longbox Value / Value
		Tin Foil Valley	CD5	U.K.	1993	$8.00
		Tin Foil Valley	CD5	U.K.	1993	$8.00
	Second version.					

Angels

Full Length

Company	Disk Number	Title	Type	Country	Year	Longbox Value / Value
Chrysalis	21677	Beyond Salvation	LP/LB	U.S.		$12.00/$7.00

Singles

Company	Disk Number	Title	Type	Country	Year	Longbox Value / Value
Chrysalis	DPRO-23470	Dogs are Talking	CDJ	U.S.	1989	$2.00
Chrysalis	DPRO-23495	Let the Night Roll On	CDJ	U.S.	1989	$2.00

Anger, Darol & Barbra Higble Quintet

Full Length

Company	Disk Number	Title	Type	Country	Year	Longbox Value / Value
Windam Hill	WD-1043	Chiaroscuro	LP/LB	U.S.†	1985	$14.00/$8.00
Windam Hill	WD-1036	Live At the Montreaux '84	LP/LB	U.S.†	1985	$14.00/$8.00

Angie And Debbie

Singles

Company	Disk Number	Title	Type	Country	Year	Longbox Value / Value
Capitol	C2 16492-2	Light Of Love	CD5	U.S.	1993	$4.00

Ania, Rosie

Singles

Company	Disk Number	Title	Type	Country	Year	Longbox Value / Value
BMG	663526	Eyes Of A Woman	CD5	Germany	1990	$5.00
Island	CID-461	Eyes Of A Woman	CD5	U.K.	1990	$5.00

Anika

Singles

Company	Disk Number	Title	Type	Country	Year	Longbox Value / Value
Canyon	S9Y-10027	Crazy Lover	CD3	Japan	1989	$12.00/$3.00
Canyon	S9Y-1113	Young Generation	CD3	Japan	1989	$12.00/$3.00

Animal Bag

Singles

Company	Disk Number	Title	Type	Country	Year	Longbox Value / Value
Stardog	CDP 903	Darker Days	CDJ	U.S.	1993	$2.00
Stardog	CDP 821	Everybody	CDJ	U.S.	1992	$2.00
Stardog	CDP 753	Hate St.	CDJ	U.S.	1992	$2.00
Stardog	CDP 886	Hello Bag	CDJ	U.S.	1993	$2.00
Mercury	CDP 1362	Stupidity: For Art's Sake	CDJ	U.S.	1994	$3.00

Animal Logic

Full Length

Company	Disk Number	Title	Type	Country	Year	Longbox Value / Value
Virgin	259928	Animal Logic	LP	Germany		$16.00
IRS	ISD 018	Someday We'll Understand	DJ/Smplr	U.S.	1989	$12.00

Singles

Company	Disk Number	Title	Type	Country	Year	Longbox Value / Value
IRS	ISD 019	As Soon As the Sun Goes Down	CDJ	U.S.	1990	$2.00
IRS	67066	I Won't Be Sleeping Anymore	CDJ	U.S.	1991	$2.00
IRS	13827	Rose Colored Glasses	CD5	U.S.	1991	$4.00
IRS	67059	Rose Colored Glasses	CDJ	U.S.	1991	$2.00
Virgin	162529	Someday We'll Understand	CD3	Germany	1989	$8.00
Virgin	ALSCD-11	Someday We'll Understand	CD3	U.K.	1989	$8.00
IRS	IRSD 018	Someday We'll Understand	CDJ	U.S.	1989	$7.00
Virgin	162167	There's a Spy (In the House of Love)	CD3	Germany	1989	$8.00
Virgin	662167	There's a Spy (In the House of Love)	CD5	Germany	1989	$8.00
Virgin	VJD-10206	There's a Spy (In the House of Love)	CD3	Japan	1989	$12.00/$3.00
Virgin	ALSCD-10	There's a Spy (In the House of Love)	CD3	U.K.	1989	$8.00
IRS	ISD 012	There's a Spy (In the House of Love)	CDJ	U.S.	1989	$6.00

Animal Nightlife

Full Length

Company	Disk Number	Title	Type	Country	Year	Longbox Value / Value
Virgin	259164	Lush Life	LP	Germany		$15.00
Virgin	DIXCD-71	Lush Life	LP	U.K.		$15.00

Singles

Company	Disk Number	Title	Type	Country	Year	Longbox Value / Value
10 Records	TENCD-213	Always Your Humble Slave	CD5	U.K.	1988	$4.00

Animals

Full Length

Company	Disk Number	Title	Type	Country	Year	Longbox Value / Value
BBC Radio		BBC Classic Tracks	RS	U.S.	1991	$25.00
	Airdate: 3/11/91					
BBC Radio		BBC Classic Tracks	RS	U.S.	1991	$25.00
	Airdate: 9/30/91					
BBC Radio		BBC Classic Tracks	RS	U.S.	1992	$25.00
	Airdate: 3/2/92					
SF Miles	SEECD-244	EP Collection	LP	U.S.		$7.00
EMI	CP32-9010	Singles Plus	LP	Japan		$20.00

Singles

Company	Disk Number	Title	Type	Country	Year	Longbox Value / Value
	PIFP-1015	Shake, Rattle & Roll	CDV	Japan		$40.00
EMI	CDEM-154	We've Gotta Get Out Of This Place	CD5	U.K.	1990	$6.00

Animotion

Full Length

Company	Disk Number	Title	Type	Country	Year	Longbox Value / Value
Collector's Pipeline	TCP 018CD	Animotion	LP	U.S.		$16.00
Mercury	822580-2	Animotion	LP/BP	U.S.†	1985	$14.00/$8.00
Polygram	848097-2	Strange Behavior	LP	Germany		$12.00
Phonogram	32PD-105	Strange Behavior	LP	Japan		$20.00
Casablanca	826691-2	Strange Behavior	LP/BP	U.S.		$14.00/$8.00

Singles

Company	Disk Number	Title	Type	Country	Year	Longbox Value / Value
Mercury	MERCD-300	Calling It Love	CD5	U.K.	1989	$6.00
Polydor	CDP 55	Calling It Love	CDJ	U.S.	1989	$2.00
Mercury	871418-3	Room To Move	CD3	Germany	1988	$6.00

Label	Catalog Number	Title	Type	Country	Year	Longbox Value / Value
Mercury	871419-2	Room To Move	CD5	Germany	1988	$6.00
Mercury	PPDS-4	Room To Move	CD3	Japan	1988	$13.00/$4.00
Mercury	MERCD-282	Room To Move	CD5	U.K.	1988	$6.00
Polydor	CDP 40	Room To Move	CDJ	U.S.	1989	$2.00

Anka, Paul

Full Length

Label	Catalog Number	Title	Type	Country	Year	Longbox Value / Value
Chrysalis	DPRO-4737	20 Original Masters	DJ/Smplr	U.S.	1989	$18.00
RCA	PCD1-2691	21 Golden Hits	LP/LB	U.S.†	1984	$15.00/$9.00
Curb	468960-2	Five Decades Of Hits	LP	Germany		$20.00
CBS	450929-2	Greatest Hits	LP	Germany		$20.00
CBS	35DP-104	Walk A Fine Line	LP	Japan		$25.00

Singles

Label	Catalog Number	Title	Type	Country	Year	Longbox Value / Value
Columbia	657385-2	Freedom For the World	CD5	Germany	1992	$7.00
Columbia	ALDB-152	Freedom For the World	CD3	Japan	1992	$12.00/$3.00
Curb	CD45-073	Freedom For the World	CDJ	U.S.	1991	$2.00
Polygram	871107-2	Gimme the Word	CD5	Germany	1988	$7.00
Polygram	889344-3	Steel Guitar and A Glass	CD3	Germany	1989	$8.00

Anna Banana

Singles

Label	Catalog Number	Title	Type	Country	Year	Longbox Value / Value
Warner Brothers	WPDL-4268	Kachikan	CD3	Japan	1991	$8.00/$2.00
Warner Brothers	WPDL-4289	Noroma	CD3	Japan	1992	$8.00/$2.00
Warner Brothers	WPDL-4274	Sayonara Ska	CD3	Japan	1991	$8.00/$2.00

Anna G.

Singles

Label	Catalog Number	Title	Type	Country	Year	Longbox Value / Value
BMG	ANNAGD-1	G'ding G'ding	CD5	U.K.	1990	$6.00

Anna Marie

Singles

Label	Catalog Number	Title	Type	Country	Year	Longbox Value / Value
		Recipe of Love	CDJ	U.S.		$2.00
		This Could Take All Night	CDJ	U.S.		$2.00

Anna-Lucy

Singles

Label	Catalog Number	Title	Type	Country	Year	Longbox Value / Value
Polygram	871626-3	Baby (Your Love)	CD3	Germany	1989	$6.00
Polygram	871627-2	Baby (Your Love)	CD5	Germany	1989	$6.00

Annabella

Full Length

Label	Catalog Number	Title	Type	Country	Year	Longbox Value / Value
RCA	PD-70890	Fever	LP	Germany		$15.00

Annica

Singles

Label	Catalog Number	Title	Type	Country	Year	Longbox Value / Value
CBS	655975-3	Give My Love To You	CD3	Germany	1990	$6.00
Alfa	ALDB-81	Give My Love To You	CD3	Japan	1990	$8.00/$2.00
Alfa	ALDB-82	Give My Love To You	CD3	Japan	1990	$8.00/$2.00
CBS	654961-3	I Can't Deny My Heart	CD3	Germany	1989	$6.00
Alfa	ALDB-62	I Can't Deny My Heart	CD3	Japan	1990	$8.00/$2.00
Alfa	ALDB-63	I Can't Deny My Heart	CD3	Japan	1990	$8.00/$2.00
Alfa	ALDB-101	Naughty, Naughty	CD3	Japan	1991	$8.00/$2.00
Alfa	ALDB-102	Naughty, Naughty	CD3	Japan	1991	$8.00/$2.00

Annihilator

Singles

Label	Catalog Number	Title	Type	Country	Year	Longbox Value / Value
Pinnacle	RR-2425-3	Stonewall	CD5	Gerrmany	1990	$7.00
Apollon	APCY-8044	Stonewall	CD3	Japan	1991	$10.00

Anotha Level

Singles

Label	Catalog Number	Title	Type	Country	Year	Longbox Value / Value
Priority	7087	What's That Cha Say	CDJ	U.S.	1994	$3.00

Another Bad Creation

Singles

Label	Catalog Number	Title	Type	Country	Year	Longbox Value / Value
Motown	374631135	I Don't Wanna 3Be Grown Up	CDJ	U.S.	1993	$2.00
Motown	ZD-44436	Iesha	CD5	U.K.	1991	$8.00
Motown	CD45-1058	Iesha	CDJ	U.S.	1990	$2.00
Motown	BVDM-14	Jealous Girl	CD3	Japan	1991	$12.00/$4.00
Motown	CD45 1576	Jealous Girl	CDJ	U.S.	1991	$2.00
Motown	PRD 90025	Jealous Girl	CDJ	U.S.	1991	$2.00
Motown	PCD 1018	My World	CDJ	U.S.	1991	$2.00
Motown	BVDM-10	Playground	CD3	Japan	1991	$12.00/$4.00
Motown	ZD-45058	Playground	CD5	U.K.	1991	$8.00
Motown	CD45-1249	Playground	CDJ	U.S.	1991	$2.00
Motown	374631151	Where's Ya Little Sista?	CDJ	U.S.	1994	$2.00

Another Class

Singles

Label	Catalog Number	Title	Type	Country	Year	Longbox Value / Value
SPV	0818-3	Ride Like the Wind	CD5	Germany	1992	$6.00

Anquette

Singles

Label	Catalog Number	Title	Type	Country	Year	Longbox Value / Value
BMG	663068	BMG Mix	CD5	Germany	1990	$5.00

Anri

Full Length

Label	Catalog Number	Title	Type	Country	Year	Longbox Value / Value
For Life	FLC-4005	Circuit Of Rainbow	LTD/LP	Japan		$25.00

Gold disc.

Singles

Label	Catalog Number	Title	Type	Country	Year	Longbox Value / Value
Canyon	FLDF-09138	Back To Basic	CD3	Japan	1991	$12.00/$3.00
Canyon	FLDF-10235	Dolphin Ring	CD3	Japan	1993	$12.00/$3.00
Canyon	FLDF-10211	Lani	CD3	Japan	1992	$12.00/$3.00
Canyon	FLDF-09154	Lost Love	CD3	Japan	1991	$12.00/$3.00
Canyon	FLDF-09146	Uso Nara Yasashiku	CD3	Japan	1991	$12.00/$3.00

Ansell, Martin

Full Length

Label	Catalog Number	Title	Type	Country	Year	Longbox Value / Value
Ariola	257631	Englishman	LP	Germany		

Answered Questions

Singles

Label	Catalog Number	Title	Type	Country	Year	Longbox Value / Value
Sentimental	CDJ	U.S.		$2.00		
		What You Deserve	CDJ	U.S.		$2.00

Ant, Adam

Full Length

Label	Catalog Number	Title	Type	Country	Year	Longbox Value / Value
IRS	370330-2	Kings Of the Wild Frontier	LP	Germany		$15.00
Eastwest	2292-56625-2	Manners And Physique	LP	Germany		$14.00
WEA	WMC5-31	Manners And Physique	LP	Japan		$20.00
MCA	DMCG-6068	Manners And Physique	LP	U.K.		$14.00
MCA	MCAD-6315	Manners And Physique	LP/LB	U.S.		$14.00/$8.00
Columbia	CBSCD-25706	Strip	LP	U.K.		$15.00
CBS	EK-39108	Strip	LP/LB	U.S.†	1984	$15.00/$9.00
CBS	CD-26583	Vive Le Rock	LP	Germany		$15.00
EMI		Wonderful	DJ/Smplr	U.K.	1995	$16.00

Singles

Label	Catalog Number	Title	Type	Country	Year	Longbox Value / Value
		Beautiful Dream	CD5	U.K.	1995	$25.00

Withdrawn CD5.

Label	Catalog Number	Title	Type	Country	Year	Longbox Value / Value
		Can't Set Rules About Love	CD5	U.K.		$10.00

Second version.

Label	Catalog Number	Title	Type	Country	Year	Longbox Value / Value
MCA	DMCAT-1404	Can't Set Rules About Love	CD5	U.K.	1990	$9.00
EMI	82178	Gotta Be A Sin	CD5	U.K.	1995	$10.00
EMI		Gotta Be A Sin	CD5	U.K.	1995	$10.00

Second version.

Label	Catalog Number	Title	Type	Country	Year	Longbox Value / Value
EMI		Gotta Be A Sin	CDJ	U.K.	1995	$10.00
EMI		Gotta Be A Sin	CDJ	U.K.	1995	$8.00
EMI		Gotta Be A Sin	CDJ	U.S.	1995	$6.00
MCA		Manners & Physique	CDJ	U.K.	1990	$9.00
Teldec	257424-2	Room At the Top	CD3	Germany	1989	$9.00
MCA	DMCAT-1387	Room At the Top	CD5	U.K.	1990	$9.00
MCA		Room At the Top	CD5	U.S.	1989	$4.00
MCA	CD45 17903	Room At the Top	CDJ	U.S.	1989	$6.00
Eastwest	171969-2	Rough Stuff	CD5	Germany	1990	$9.00
MCA	CD4518375	Rough Stuff	CDJ	U.S.	1990	$7.00
EMI		Wonderful	CD5	U.K.	1995	$8.00
EMI		Wonderful	CD5	U.K.	1995	$8.00

Second version.

Label	Catalog Number	Title	Type	Country	Year	Longbox Value / Value
EMI		Wonderful	CDJ	U.K.	1995	$12.00
Capitol	DPRO-79407	Wonderful	CDJ	U.S.	1995	$3.00

Antena, Isabella

Full Length

Label	Catalog Number	Title	Type	Country	Year	Longbox Value / Value
		Corto Prend Le Large	DJ/Smplr	Japan		$25.00
Interphon	IPCD-2011	Hoping For Love	LP	Germany		$15.00

Singles

Label	Catalog Number	Title	Type	Country	Year	Longbox Value / Value
Victor	VDP-15004	De L'amour Et Des Hommes	CD3	Japan	1990	$13.00/$4.00
Ant	TWI-874-2	De L'amour Et Des Hommes	CD5	U.K.	1990	$8.00

Antenna

Singles

Label	Catalog Number	Title	Type	Country	Year	Longbox Value / Value
Mammoth	MR-0038-2	Sleep	CD5	U.K.	1992	$8.00

Anthem

Full Length

Label	Catalog Number	Title	Type	Country	Year	Longbox Value / Value
Restless	72202-2	Bound To Break	LP/LB	U.S.		$12.00/$7.00

Anthony, Ray

Full Length

Label	Catalog Number	Title	Type	Country	Year	Longbox Value / Value
ASD	CP32-5391	Best 20	LP	Germany		$15.00
Inak	CD-806	In the Groove	LP/LB	U.S.		$14.00/$8.00
Jeton	112	Knock out	LP	U.S.		$8.00
Hindsight	HCD-412	Young Man With A Horn	LP	U.S.		$7.00

Anthrax

Full Length

Label	Catalog Number	Title	Type	Country	Year	Longbox Value / Value
Island	PRCD 6654-2	Free B's	DJ/Smplr	U.S.	1990	$10.00
Foundations	F4	FZ Interview	RS	U.S.	1991	$15.00

Various artist interview show.

Label	Catalog Number	Title	Type	Country	Year	Longbox Value / Value
Island	P22D-20051	I Am the Man	LP	Japan	1987	$20.00
Island	PRCD 6830-2	Live the Island Years Sampler	DJ/Smplr	U.S.	1994	$10.00
WEA	WMC5-601	Sound Of White Noise	LTD/LP	Japan	1993	$45.00

2 CD set.

Label	Catalog Number	Title	Type	Country	Year	Longbox Value / Value
Island	91004-2	State Of Euphoria	LP/LB	U.S.	1988	$14.00/$8.00

With Limited Edition Hologram Sticker.

Singles

Label	Catalog Number	Title	Type	Country	Year	Longbox Value / Value
Island	CDIX 409	Anti-social	CD5	Austria	1989	$10.00
Megaforce	CIDX 409	Anti-social	CD3	Germany	1989	$15.00
Island	PR 2654-2	Anti-social	CDJ	U.S.	1988	$6.00
Island	PR 2654-2	Anti-social	CDJ	U.S.	1988	$8.00
Elektra	PRCD 8821-2	Black Lodge	CDJ	U.S.	1993	$3.00
Island	664 662	Bring On the Noise	CD5	Germany	1991	$12.00
Island	PRCD 6670-2	Bring On the Noise	CDJ	U.S.	1991	$3.00
Elektra		Fueled	CD5	U.K.	1995	$10.00
Elektra	PRCD 9345-2	Fueled	CDJ	U.S.	1995	$6.00
Polydor	PSDD-1006	Got the Time	CD3	Japan	1990	$12.00/$4.00
Polydor	PSCD-1080	Got the Time	CD5	Japan	1991	$15.00
Island	CID-476	Got the Time	CD5	U.K.	1990	$10.00
Island	PRCD 6632-2	Got the Time	CDJ	U.S.	1990	$3.00
Elektra	PRCD 9346-2	High Octane	CDJ	U.S.	1995	$6.00
Island	884702-2	In My World	CD5	Germany	1990	$10.00
Island	CID-470	In My World	CD5	U.K.	1990	$10.00
Island	661738	Make Me Laugh	CD5	Germany	1989	$10.00
Island UK	885066	Make Me Laugh	CD5	Germany	1989	$10.00
Megaforce	P13D-37013	Make Me Laugh	CD3	Japan	1989	$15.00/$4.00
Island	CIDP 379	Make Me Laugh	CD5	U.K.	1989	$15.00
Island	CIDP 379	Make Me Laugh	CD5	U.K.	1989	$30.00

Triangular sleeve

Label	Catalog Number	Title	Type	Country	Year	Longbox Value / Value
Elektra	PRCD 95092	Nothing	CDJ	U.S.	1995	$6.00
Elektra		Only	CD5	Germany	1993	$10.00
Elektra	WMD5-4128	Only	CD3	Japan	1993	$12.00/$4.00
Elektra		Only	CD5	U.K.	1993	$10.00
Elektra		Only	CD5	U.K.	1993	$10.00

Second version.

Label	Catalog Number	Title	Type	Country	Year	Longbox Value / Value
Elektra	PRCD 8755	Only	CDJ	U.S.	1993	$3.00
Elektra	PRCD 8870-2	Room For One More	CDJ	U.S.	1993	$3.00

Anticappella

Singles

Label	Catalog Number	Title	Type	Country	Year	Longbox Value / Value
Columbia	ALCB-469	2 Root 231	CD3	Japan	1992	$13.00/$4.00
WEA	PWCD-205	2 Root 231	CD5	U.K.	1991	$5.00
WEA	PWCD-220	Everyday	CD5	U.K.	1992	$5.00

Antico

Singles

Label	Catalog Number	Title	Type	Country	Year	Longbox Value / Value
Media	ALCB-645	Don't Stop the Rhythm	CD5	Japan	1992	
Adrenalin	9202	Don't Stop the Rhythm	CD5	U.S.	1991	$5.00

Antonella

Singles

Label	Catalog Number	Title	Type	Country	Year	Longbox Value / Value
Canyon	PCDY-00029	Mamma Mia	CD3	Japan	1990	$12.00/$3.00
ZYX	5959-8	Supersonic Level	CD5	Germany	1988	$8.00
Canyon	S10Y-1026	Supersonic Level	CD3	Japan	1988	$12.00/$3.00

Antwort

Singles

Label	Catalog Number	Title	Type	Country	Year	Longbox Value / Value
WEA	9031-74575-2	Meine Jahre	CD5	Germany	1991	$8.00
WEA	9031-72825-2	Sie Haben Alles Verkauft	CD5	Germany	1991	$8.00

Anvil

Full Length

Label	Catalog Number	Title	Type	Country	Year	Longbox Value / Value
Polygram	841869-2	Forged In Fire	LP	Germany		$15.00
Polygram	841870-2	Hard 'n Heavy	LP	Germany		$15.00

Label	Catalog Number	Title	Type	Country	Year	Longbox Value / Value
Roadrunner	RR-3449916	Hard 'n Heavy	LP	U.K.		$15.00
Polygram	841871-2	Metal On Metal	LP	Germany		$15.00
		Anxiety Annie				
		Singles				
Atlantic	A-8967CD	Sugar Bowl	CD5	U.K.	1990	$6.00
		Anything Box				
		Singles				
Epic	ESK 73356	Jubilation	CDJ	U.S.	1990	$2.00
Epic		Living in Oblivion	CDJ	U.S.	1990	$2.00
Epic	ESK 2174	Soul On Fire	CDJ	U.S.	1990	$2.00
		Apache				
		Singles				
Tommy Boy	566	Do Fa Self	CD5	U.S.	1993	$44.00
Isba	IS12K-1054	Gangsta Bitch	CD5	Canada	1993	$7.00
Tommy Boy	541	Gangsta Bitch	CD5	U.S.	1993	$4.00
		Apache Dancers				
		Full Length				
IRS	13034	War Stories	LP/LB	U.S.		$14.00/$8.00
		Apache Indian				
		Singles				
Island	CID-544	Arranged Marriage	CD5	U.K.	1992	$8.00
Mango	857	Chok There	CDJ	U.S.	1993	$2.00
Island	CID 560	Nuff Vibes	CD5	U.K.	1993	$9.00
		Ape Hangers				
		Singles				
A&M	AMSAD00034	I Don't Want To Live Today	CDJ	U.S.	1995	$6.00
A&M	AMSAD00102	Red Hot Rocket	CDJ	U.S.	1995	$6.00
A&M	AMSAD00189	You Don't know What It Takes	CDJ	U.S.	1995	$6.00
AMS	AD00102	Red Hot Rocket	CDJ	U.S.	1995	$2.00
		Apes, Pigs, & Spacemen				
		Singles				
		Safety Net	CD5	U.K.		$10.00
		Safety Net	CD5	U.K.		$10.00
	Second version.					
		Apfelbaum, Peter				
		Singles				
Antillies	6672	World Is Gifted, The	CDJ	U.S.	1991	$2.00
		Aphex Twins				
		Full Length				
Sire		Words & Music	DJ/Intvw	U.S.	1994	$15.00
		Singles				
BMG	RSUK-12CD	Digridoo	CD5	U.K.	1992	$8.00
Sire	66104	Donkey Rhubarb	CD5	U.S.	1995	$5.00
		On	CD5	U.K.		$10.00
	Second version.					
Warner Brothers	12-41217	On	CD5	Canada	1993	$8.00
WEA		On	CD5	U.K.	1993	$9.00
WEA		On	CD5	U.K.	1993	$9.00
	Second version.					
Sire	9 41217-2	On	CD5	U.S.	1993	$4.00
Warner Brothers	41217	On	CD5	U.S.	1994	$5.00
Elektra/Asylum	66143	Ventolin	CD5	U.S.	1994	$5.00
		Aphrodisiac				
		Singles				
BMG	CHAMPCD-238	Song Of the Siren	CD5	U.K.	1990	$6.00
		Apollo 440				
		Singles				
		Liquid Cool	CD5	U.K.		$10.00
		Liquid Cool	CD5	U.K.		$10.00
	Second version.					
		Apollo Smile				
		Full Length				
Geffen	GEFD-24299	Apollo Smile3	LP/LB	U.S.	1991	$14.00/$8.00
Geffen	PRO-CD-4286	Dune Buggy	CDJ	U.S.	1991	$2.00
		Apollonia				
		Full Length				
Warner Brothers	9 25594-2	Apollonia	LP/LB	U.S.		$12.00/$7.00
		Singles				
Warner Brothers	PRO-CD-3394	Mismatch	CDJ	U.S.	1988	$2.00
Warner Brothers	PRO-CD-3573	The Same Dream	CDJ	U.S.	1988	$2.00
		Apostles				
		Singles				
Victory	CDP 687	I Could Be Anything	CDJ	U.S.	1992	$2.00
		Apotheosis				
		Singles				
ZYX	6743-8	O Fortuna	CD5	Germany	1992	$5.00
Hot	12299	O Fortuna	CD5	U.S.	1992	$4.00
		Apple Creation				
		Singles				
Amy	AC-00212CD	Gifthorse	CD5	U.K.	1992	$5.00
		Appleby, Kim				
		Singles				
EMI	204096-2	Don't Worry	CD5	Germany	1990	$8.00
EMI	205206-2	Don't Worry	CD5	Germany	1990	$8.00
EMI	CDR-6272	Don't Worry	CD5	U.K.	1990	$8.00
EMI	CDR-6281	G.L.A.D.	CD5	U.K.	1991	$8.00
EMI	204507-2	If You Cared	CD5	Germany	1991	$8.00
EMI	CDR-6297	If You Cared	CD5	U.K.	1991	$8.00
EMI	204341-2	Mama	CD5	Germany	1991	$8.00
EMI	CDR-6291	Mama	CD5	U.K.	1991	$8.00
		Apples				
		Singles				
Epic	656894-2	Beautiful People	CD5	U.K.	1991	$8.00
Epic	656671-2	Eye Wonder	CD5	U.K.	1991	$8.00
Epic	PROMO CD	Eye Wonder	CDJ	U.K.	1991	$10.00
		Appolo Landing				
		Singles				
Polygram	GOCD-75	Trouble	CD5	U.K.	1992	$6.00

Company	Disk Number	Title	Type	Country	Year	Longbox Value / Value
		April Wine				
		Full Length				
Capitol	CDP-48415-2	Animal Grace	LP/LB	U.S.		$15.00/$9.00
Capitol	CDP-48416-2	First Glance	LP/LB	U.S.		$15.00/$9.00
Capitol	TOCP-6356	Nature Of the Beast	LP	Japan		$20.00
Capitol	CDP-46067	Nature Of the Beast	LP/LB	U.S.†	1985	$14.00/$8.00
Capitol	CDP-48417-2	Power Play	LP/LB	U.S.		$15.00/$9.00
Capitol	CDP-48418-2	Walking Through the Fire	LP/LB	U.S.		$15.00/$9.00
		Singles				
Flood Rosa		Driving With My Eyes Closed	CDJ	U.S.	1994	$7.00
Flood Rosa	CDPRO 0104	Givin' It, Takin' It	CDJ	Canada	1993	$5.00
Flood Rosa	CDPRO 0104	Givin' It, Takin' It	CDJ	U.S.	1993	$6.00
Flood Rosa		Here's looking At You Kid	CDJ	Canada	1993	$5.00
Flood Rosa	CDPRO 005	That's Love	CDJ	Canada	1993	$5.00
Flood Rosa	CDPRO 005	That's Love	CDJ	U.S.	1993	$7.00
		Aprils Motel Room				
		Singles				
		Black 14	CDJ	U.S.	1994	$3.00
		Apsaras				
		Full Length				
CBS	CD-39559	Apsaras	LP	Germany		$15.00
Columbia	CK-39559	Apsaras	LP/LB	U.S.		$12.00/$7.00
		Aquanettas				
		Full Length				
IRS	13033	Love With the Proper Stranger	LP/LB	U.S.	1990	$12.00/$7.00
		Singles				
IRS	ISD 025	Beach Party	CDJ	U.S.	1990	$2.00
		AR Kane				
		Singles				
Luaka Bop	9 40373-2	A Love From Outer Space	CD5	U.S.	1992	$4.00
Luaka Bop	PRO-CD-5261	A Love From Outer Space	CDJ	U.S.	1992	$2.00
		Arabesque				
		Full Length				
Victor	VDP-1130	Best Selection	LP	Japan		$15.00
		ARB				
		Singles				
Motown	CD45-1527	Make You Sweat	CDJ	U.S.	1991	$2.00
		Arc Angels				
		Full Length				
Westwood One		In Concert	RS	U.S.	1993	$30.00
	2 CD set. With Drivin' 'n Cryin', Airdate: 3/1/93					
Westwood One		Off the Record	RS	U.S.	1992	$30.00
	Airdate: 7/27/92					
Geffen		Sampler	DJ/Smplr	U.K.		$8.00
		Singles				
DGC	PRO-CD-4395	Living In A Dream	CDJ	U.S.	1992	$2.00
DGC	PRO-CD-4473	Sent By Angels	CDJ	U.S.	1992	$2.00
DGC	PRO-CD-4496	Shape I'm In	CDJ	U.S.	1992	$2.00
DGC	PRO-CD-4475	Too Many Ways To Fall	CDJ	U.S.	1992	$2.00
		Arcade				
		Singles				
Epic	ESK 6410	Angry	CDJ	U.S.	1994	$2.00
Epic	ESDA-7140	Cry No More	CD3	Japan	1993	$13.00/$4.00
Epic	ESK-5176	Cry No More	CDJ	U.S.	1993	$3.00
Epic	ESDA-7126	Nothin' To Lose	CD3	Japan	1993	$13.00/$4.00
Epic	ESK-5020	Nothin' To Lose	CDJ	U.S.	1993	$3.00
		Arcado				
		Full Length				
Polygram	834441	Behind the Myth	LP/BP	U.S.		$12.00/$7.00
		Arch				
		Full Length				
SPV	0389-2	Messier Album	LP	Germany		
		Singles				
	8266	Only Thing	CD5	Germany	1991	$7.00
Antler	5048	Only Thing	CD5	U.S.	1993	$4.00
		Archangel, Nathalie				
		Full Length				
MCA	MCAD-10021	Owl	LP/LB	U.S.	12	$12.00/$8.00
		Singles				
MCA	MCA5P 2015	I Don't Heal Clean	CDJ	U.S.	1991	$2.00
MCA	MCA5P 2017	I Don't Heal Clean	CDJ	U.S.	1991	$2.00
MCA	MCA5P1427	So Quiet, So Still	CDJ	U.S.	1991	$2.00
		Archer Park				
		Singles				
		Where There's Smoke	CDJ	U.S.	1994	$3.00
		Archer, Tasmin				
		Full Length				
SBK	04550	B-Sides And More	DJ/Smplr	U.S.	1993	$15.00
SBK	04712	Beyond And Back	DJ/Intvw	U.S.	1993	$12.00
EMI	PCD 0358	Special DJ Copy	DJ/Smplr	Japan		$50.00
		Singles				
EMI	CDEM-275	Arienne	CD5	U.K.	1993	$8.00
EMI		In Your Care	CD5	Germany	1993	$8.00
EMI		In Your Care	CD5	U.K.	1993	$8.00
EMI		In Your Care	CD5	U.K.	1993	$8.00
	Second version.					
SBK	04564	In Your Care	CDJ	U.S.	1993	$2.00
EMI		Lords Of the New Church	CD5	U.K.	1993	$8.00
EMI		Lords Of the New Church	CD5	U.K.	1993	$8.00
	Second version.					
SBK	04527	Lords Of the New Church	CDJ	U.S.	1993	$2.00
EMI	81143	Shipbuilding	CD5	U.K.	1994	$9.00
EMI	TODP-2407	Sleeping Satellite	CD3	Japan	1993	$13.00/$4.00
EMI	CDEM-233	Sleeping Satellite	CD5	U.K.	1992	$12.00
SBK	19786	Sleeping Satellite	CDJ	U.S.	1993	$6.00
		Archers Of Loaf				
		Singles				
Alias	064	Harnessed In Slums	CDJ	U.S.	1995	$2.00
Alias		Might	CDJ	U.S.	1996	$2.00
	PROCD0941	What Did You Expect	CDJ	U.S.	1995	$6.00

Archies

Label	Catalog Number	Title	Type	Country	Year	Longbox Value / Value
Singles						
Columbia	CSK 7534	Sugar Sugar	CDJ	U.S.	1995	$6.00

Arden, Jan

Label	Catalog Number	Title	Type	Country	Year	Longbox Value / Value
Singles						
		Could I Be Your Girl	CDJ	U.S.		$2.00
A&M	31458083249	Insensitive	CD5	Canada	1994	$8.00
A&M		Insensitive	CDJ	U.S.	1994	$3.00
		Will You Remember Me	CD5	Canada	1993	$8.00
A&M	31458 8109	Will You Remember Me	CDJ	U.S.	1993	$2.00

Arena, Amy

Label	Catalog Number	Title	Type	Country	Year	Longbox Value / Value
Singles						
	PRO-CD-1005	Excuse Me	CDJ	U.S.		$2.00

Arena, Tina

Label	Catalog Number	Title	Type	Country	Year	Longbox Value / Value
Singles						
Epic	ESK7636	Chains	CDJ	U.S.		$2.00
		Heaven Help My Heart	CDJ	Germany	1995	$10.00
		Heaven Help My Heart	CD5	U.K.		$10.00
Second version.						
		Heaven Help My Heart	CDJ	U.K.	1995	$10.00
		Show Me Heaven	CD5	U.K.		$10.00
		Show Me Heaven	CD5	U.K.		$10.00
Second version.						

Arends, Carolyn

Label	Catalog Number	Title	Type	Country	Year	Longbox Value / Value
Singles						
	KCDP51334	This Is the Stuff	CDJ	U.S.		$2.00

Argent

Label	Catalog Number	Title	Type	Country	Year	Longbox Value / Value
Full Length						
CBS	CD-81202	Greatest Hits	LP	Germany		$15.00
DIR		King Biscuit Flour Hour	RS	U.S.	1988	$35.00
With Mott & the Hopple, Airdate: 7/24/88						

Argent, Rod

Label	Catalog Number	Title	Type	Country	Year	Longbox Value / Value
Full Length						
Relativity	1039	Red House	LP/LB	U.S.		$14.00/$8.00

Ariake, Ichiro

Label	Catalog Number	Title	Type	Country	Year	Longbox Value / Value
Singles						
Crown	CRDW-50036	Takenaka Hanbei	CD3	Japan	1992	$8.00/$2.00

Arichika, Masumi

Label	Catalog Number	Title	Type	Country	Year	Longbox Value / Value
Singles						
Canyon	MRDA-00007	Kimi Wa Boku Ga Suki	CD3	Japan	1992	$12.00/$3.00
Canyon	MRDA-00005	Kiss Kiss Kiss	CD3	Japan	1992	$12.00/$3.00
Canyon	MRDA-00002	True	CD3	Japan	1992	$12.00/$3.00

Ariel

Label	Catalog Number	Title	Type	Country	Year	Longbox Value / Value
Singles						
RCA	PD-44888	Rollercoaster	CD5	U.K.	1991	$8.00

Ariella

Label	Catalog Number	Title	Type	Country	Year	Longbox Value / Value
Singles						
Ariola	BVDP-55	Attention A Lui	CD3	Japan	1992	$12.00/$3.00

Arika

Label	Catalog Number	Title	Type	Country	Year	Longbox Value / Value
Singles						
LDC	PIDL-1044	Megamitachi No Revolution	CD3	Japan	1992	$8.00/$2.00
LDC	PIDL-1029	Rolling Night	CD3	Japan	1991	$8.00/$2.00

Armageddon Dildos

Label	Catalog Number	Title	Type	Country	Year	Longbox Value / Value
Singles						
Warner Brothers	41420	Everyday Is Like Sunday	CD5	U.S.	1994	$5.00
Sire	12-40950	Homicidal Maniac	CD5	Canada	1993	$8.00
Sire	9 40950-2	Homicidal Maniac	CD5	U.S.	1993	$4.00

Armagedon

Label	Catalog Number	Title	Type	Country	Year	Longbox Value / Value
Singles						
Absolute	ABS-008CD	New At Ten	CD5	U.K.	1993	$7.00

Armatrading, Joan

Label	Catalog Number	Title	Type	Country	Year	Longbox Value / Value
Full Length						
IMS	CD-215	A&M Classics	LP	Germany		$18.00
Canyon	D32Y-3510	A&M Classics	LP	Japan		$25.00
Polygram	393141-2	Back To the Night	LP	Germany		$18.00
Polygram	395298-2	Hearts And Flowers	LP	Germany		$18.00
A&M	PCCY-10136	Hearts And Flowers	LP	Japan		$25.00
Polygram	394912-2	Key	LP	Germany	1984	$18.00
A&M	CD-4912	Key	LP/LB	U.S.†	1984	$15.00/$9.00
A&M	CD-3318	Key	LP/LB	U.S.	1987	$14.00/$8.00
Polygram	395040-2	Secret Secrets	LP	Germany		$18.00
A&M	CD-5040	Secret Secrets	LP/LB	U.S.†	1985	$14.00/$8.00
A&M	CD-5040	Secret Secrets	LP/LB	U.S.	1988	$14.00/$8.00
A&M	D25Y-3258	Shouting Stage	LP	Japan		$25.00
A&M	CD-5211	Shouting Stage	LP/LB	U.S.		$14.00/$8.00
Polygram	395130-2	Sleight Of Hand	LP	Germany		$18.00
Canyon	D32Y-3019	Sleight Of Hand	LP	Japan		$25.00
A&M	CD-5130	Sleight Of Hand	LP/LB	U.S.		$14.00/$8.00
Polygram	394732-2	To the Limit	LP	Germany		$18.00
A&M	CD-4732	To the Limit	LP/LB	U.S.		$14.00/$8.00
A&M	CD-4987	Track Record	LP/LB	U.S.†	1984	$15.00/$9.00
Polygram	394876-2	Walk Under Ladders	LP	Germany		$18.00
A&M	CD-3227	Whatever's For Us	LP/LB	U.S.		$14.00/$8.00
Singles						
A&M	75021 7440 2	Always	CDJ	U.S.	1990	$2.00
A&M	390339-2	Compact Hits	CD5	Germany	1988	$8.00
A&M	AMCD-903	Compact Hits	CD5	U.K.	1988	$8.00
A&M	AMCD-595	Free	CD5	U.K.	1990	$8.00
A&M	390361-2	Living For You	CD5	Germany	1988	$8.00
A&M	AMCD-460	Living For You	CD5	U.K.	1988	$8.00
A&M	CC-31009	Living For You	CD3	U.S.	1988	$5.00/$2.00
A&M	CD 17594	Living For You	CDJ	U.S.	1988	$2.00
A&M	AMCD-738	Love And Affection	CD5	U.K.	1991	$8.00
A&M	AMCD-561	More Than One Kind Of Love	CD5	U.K.	1990	$8.00
A&M	75021 8066 2	More Than One Kind Of Love	CD5	U.S.	1990	$2.00
A&M	AMCD-449	Shouting Stage, The	CD5	U.K.	1988	$8.00
A&M	CD 17636-2	Shouting Stage, The	CDJ	U.S.	1988	$2.00
A&M	31458 8001	True Love	CDJ	U.S.	1992	$2.00

Armed Forces

Label	Catalog Number	Title	Type	Country	Year	Longbox Value / Value
Full Length						
Rhino	70368	Take On the Nation	LP/LB	U.S.		$14.00/$8.00

Armored Saint

Label	Catalog Number	Title	Type	Country	Year	Longbox Value / Value
Full Length						
Chrysalis	21516	Delirious Nomad	LP/LB	U.S.		$14.00/$8.00
Chrysalis	21476	March of the Saints	LP/LB	U.S.		$14.00/$8.00
Warner Brothers	26577	Symbol Of Salvation	LP/LB	U.S.		$14.00/$8.00
Singles						
Metal Blade	PRO-CD-4908	Last Train Home	CDJ	U.S.	1991	$2.00
Metal Blade	PRO-CD-5276	Truth Always Hurts, The	CDJ	U.S.	1991	$2.00

Armstrong, Lil Harden

Label	Catalog Number	Title	Type	Country	Year	Longbox Value / Value
Full Length						
Original Jazz	C1823	Chicago Living Legends	LTD/LP	U.S.		$15.00

Armstrong, Louis

Label	Catalog Number	Title	Type	Country	Year	Longbox Value / Value
Full Length						
Affinity	CDAFS-1018-6	And the Blues Singers	LP	Germany		$20.00
Vogue	670501	Beautiful American	LP	Germany		$20.00
Mosaic	MD6-146	Complete Decca Studio Recordings of Louis Armstrong and the All Stars	LTD/LP	U.S.		$90.00
6 CD set.						
Buena Vista	CD006	Disney Songs the Satchmo Way	LP/LB	U.S.		$15.00/$9.00
Vogue	VG-600013	Great Reunion, The	LP	U.S.		$9.00
Moblie Fidelity	MFCD-807	Great Reunion, The	LP/LB	U.S.†	1985	$35.00/$25.00
2CD set with Duke Ellington						
Point	269087	Greatest Hits	LP	U.S.		$9.00
Success	2096CD	Hello Dolly	LP	U.K.		$20.00
Laserlight	15721	Hot Five And Hot Seven	LP	U.S.		$8.00
Mobile Fidelity	BBCCD-597	Jazz Classics, Vol. 4	LP/LB	U.S.		$25.00/$22.00
Bluebird	9759	Laughin' Louie	LP	U.S.		$8.00
WEA	250465-2	Louis And the Good Book	LP	Germany		$20.00
Warner Sound Exchange		Louis And the Good Book	LTD/LP	U.S.	1995	$17.00
Delta	DELT-2007	Louis Armstrong	LP	U.S.		$8.00
Delta	11063	Nineteen Historical Tracks	LP	U.K.		$20.00
Laserlight	15798	On the Road	LP	U.S.		$8.00
King	K28Y-6257	Pasadena Concert	LP	Japan		$25.00
Vogue	VG-600007	Pasadena Concert	LP	U.S.		$9.00
Columbia	CSK 6934	Portrait Of the Artists As a Young Man	DJ/Smplr	U.S.	1995	$20.00
Jazz Up	JU-301	Satchmo	LP	U.S.		$8.00
Verve	823 446-2	Silver Collection	LP/BP	U.S.†	1984	$14.00/$8.00
Point	269087	Super Hits	LP	U.S.		$8.00
Singles						
Polygram	873297-2	Mame	CD5	Germany	1989	$7.00
A&M	390444-2	What A Wonderful World	CD3	Germany	1989	$9.00
A&M	390295-2	What A Wonderful World	CD5	Germany	1989	$9.00
MCA	10SW-41	What A Wonderful World	CD3	Japan	1989	$13.00/$4.00
A&M	S10Y-3006	What A Wonderful World	CD3	Japan	1989	$13.00/$4.00
MCA	MCAD-37287	What A Wonderful World	CD3	U.S.	1989	$6.00/$4.00

Armstrong, Vanessa Bell

Label	Catalog Number	Title	Type	Country	Year	Longbox Value / Value
Singles						
Aris	886783	I'm Coming Back	CD5	Germany	1989	$4.00
Jive	JIVECD-230	I'm Coming Back	CD5	U.K.	1989	$4.00
Jive	JDJ-42129	Something On the Inside	CDJ	U.S.	1993	$3.00

Army Of Lovers

Label	Catalog Number	Title	Type	Country	Year	Longbox Value / Value
Full Length						
		Les Greatest Hits	LTD/LP	Sweden		$30.00
Ultrapop	ULT-9514-2	Massive Luxury Overdose	LTD/LP	Germany		$20.00
Singles						
		Candyman Messiah	CD5	Sweden	1991	$8.00
Warner Brothers	12-40351	Crucified	CD5	Canada	1992	$8.00
King	KIDP-47	Crucified	CD3	Japan	1991	$13.00/$4.00
Pinnacle	WOKCD-2007	Crucified	CD5	U.K.	1991	$8.00
Pinnacle	WOKCD-2017	Crucified	CD5	U.K.	1991	$8.00
Warner Brothers	9 40351-2	Crucified	CD5	U.S.	1991	$2.00
		Give My Life	CD5	U.K.	1995	$10.00
Habana	WOKCD-2023	Judgment Day	CD5	U.K.	1992	$8.00
Warner Brothers	12-40068	My Army Of Lovers	CD5	Canada	1992	$8.00
Giant	9 40068-2	My Army Of Lovers	CD5	U.S.	1991	$8.00
Warner Brothers	12-40545	Obsession	CD5	Canada	1992	$8.00
Pinnacle	WOKCD-2009	Obsession	CD5	U.K.	1991	$8.00
Warner Brothers	9 40545-2	Obsession	CD5	U.S.	1991	$5.00
Intercord	827 042	Ride the Bullet	CD5	Germany	1990	$8.00
Pinnacle	WOKCD-2018	Ride the Bullet	CD5	U.K.	1990	$8.00
Ton Son Ton	SONLCD 12	Ride the Bullet	CD5	U.K.	1990	$12.00
Intercord		Ride the Bullet Remixes	CD5	Germany	1990	$8.00
		Venus & Mars	CD5	Sweden		$10.00
		Venus & Mars	CD5	Sweden		$10.00
Second version.						

Arno

Label	Catalog Number	Title	Type	Country	Year	Longbox Value / Value
Full Length						
BMG	258755	Charlatan	LP	Germany		$15.00

Arnold, Eddy

Label	Catalog Number	Title	Type	Country	Year	Longbox Value / Value
Full Length						
RCA	9963-2	Hand Holdin' Songs	LP/BP	U.S.		$12.00/$7.00
RCA	3020-2	You Don't Miss A Thing	LP/BP	U.S.	1990	$12.00/$7.00
Singles						
RCA	2750-2-RDj	You Don't Miss A Thing	CDJ	U.S.	1990	$2.00

Arnold, Linda

Label	Catalog Number	Title	Type	Country	Year	Longbox Value / Value
Full Length						
A&M	CD-0423	Rainbow Palace	LP/LB	U.S.		$12.00/$7.00

Arnold, P.P.

Label	Catalog Number	Title	Type	Country	Year	Longbox Value / Value
Singles						
BMG	663112	Dynamite	CD5	Germany	1990	$5.00

Around The Way

Label	Catalog Number	Title	Type	Country	Year	Longbox Value / Value
Singles						
		Really Into You	CDJ	U.S.		$2.00
Atlantic	PRCD 4963-2	Way Back When	CDJ	U.S.	1993	$2.00

Arrested Development

Label	Catalog Number	Title	Type	Country	Year	Longbox Value / Value
Full Length						
Chrysalis	TOCP-7989	3 Years, 5 Months And 2 Days	LTD/LP	Japan	1992	$35.00
2 CD set.						
Chrysalis		3 Years, 5 Months And 2 Days	LTD/LP	U.K.	1994	
25th Anniversary edition in 6"x11" longbox.						
Chrysalis		Zingalamaduni	DJ/LP	U.S.	1993	$25.00
CD and press kit in 12"x12" folder						
Singles						
Chrysalis	19942	Africa's Inside Me	CDJ	U.S.	1994	$6.00
Chrysalis	DPRO-58158	Ease My Mind	CDJ	U.S.	1994	$3.00
EMI	323931-2	Mr. Wendal	CD5	Germany	1992	$9.00
Chrysalis	C2 24806-2	Mr. Wendal	CD5	U.S.	1992	$5.00

Label	Catalog Number	Title	Type	Country	Year	Longbox/Value
Chrysalis	DPRO-05498	Mr. Wendal	CDJ	U.S.	1992	$3.00
Chrysalis	DPRO-04684	Natural	CDJ	U.S.	1993	$3.00
EMI	COOLCD-265	People Everyday	CD5	U.K.	1992	$9.00
Cooltempo	239012	People Everyday	CD5	U.K.	1992	$10.00
Chrysalis	DPRO-05466	People Everyday	CDJ	U.S.	1992	$3.00
Chrysalis	C2 24811-2	Revolution	CD5	U.S.	1992	$5.00
Chrysalis	DPRO-04649	Revolution	CDJ	U.S.	1992	$3.00
Chrysalis	F219758	Tennessee	CD5	Canada	1992	$8.00
EMI	COOLCD-253	Tennessee	CD5	U.K.	1992	$9.00
Chrysalis	DPRO-23819	Tennessee	CDJ	U.S.	1992	$3.00
Chrysalis	19851	United Front	CDJ	U.S.	1994	$6.00

Arrington, Steve

Full Length

Label	Catalog Number	Title	Type	Country	Year	Longbox/Value
Manhattan	CDP-46903	Jam Packed	LP/LB	U.S.		$12.00/$7.00

Singles

Label	Catalog Number	Title	Type	Country	Year	Longbox/Value
RCA	62173-2-RDj	No Reason	CDJ	U.S.	1991	$2.00

Arrowknights

Singles

Label	Catalog Number	Title	Type	Country	Year	Longbox/Value
Crown	CRDN-5045	Nakanoshima Blues	CD3	Japan	1992	$8.00/$2.00
Crown	CRDN-142	Ryoshi	CD3	Japan	1992	$8.00/$2.00

Arrows

Full Length

Label	Catalog Number	Title	Type	Country	Year	Longbox/Value
Polygram	395120-2	Lines Are Open	LP	Germany		$15.00

Ars

Singles

Label	Catalog Number	Title	Type	Country	Year	Longbox/Value
CBS-Imagine	CSK 73251	I Want You Here With Me	CDJ	U.S.	1989	$2.00

Arson Garden

Singles

Label	Catalog Number	Title	Type	Country	Year	Longbox/Value
Vertebrae	66014	Drink A Drink Of You	CD5	U.S.	1993	$4.00
Vertebrae	66013	Impossible Space	CDJ	U.S.	1992	$2.00

ART

Singles

Label	Catalog Number	Title	Type	Country	Year	Longbox/Value
	T66182	For the Love Of You	CDJ	U.S.		$3.00

Art Attack

Singles

Label	Catalog Number	Title	Type	Country	Year	Longbox/Value
CBS	657288-2	Also Sprach Zarathustra	CD5	Germany	1991	$6.00

Art Ensemble Of Chicago

Full Length

Label	Catalog Number	Title	Type	Country	Year	Longbox/Value
Disk Union	DIW-09CD	Live in Japan	LP	Japan		$20.00

Art 'n Soul

Singles

Label	Catalog Number	Title	Type	Country	Year	Longbox/Value
	PRCD 6542-2	Ever Since You Went Away	CDJ	U.S.		$2.00

Art Of Noise

Full Length

Label	Catalog Number	Title	Type	Country	Year	Longbox/Value
Polygram	839404-2	Below the Waste	LP/BP	U.S.		$12.00/$7.00
		Best Of	DJ/Smplr	France		$40.00
Polygram	837367-2	Best Of	LP/BP	U.S.		$12.00/$7.00
Polygram	41570	In-No-Sense? Nonsense!	DJ/LP	U.S.		$15.00
Island	842473	Who's Afraid Of	LP/LB	U.S.		$12.00/$7.00

Singles

Label	Catalog Number	Title	Type	Country	Year	Longbox/Value
Polydor	PODP-6001	Art Of Love	CD3	Japan	1990	$8.00/$2.00
China	CHID-23	Art Of Love	CD5	U.K.	1990	$8.00
China	P15D-37009	Close Up	CD3	Japan	1988	$8.00/$2.00
China	CDE-6	Dragnet	CD5	U.K.	1988	$6.00
China	WOKCD-2012	Instruments Of Darkness	CD5	U.K.	1992	$9.00
Island	651757	Moments In Love	CD5	Germany	1989	$6.00
Island	880525	Moments In Love	CD5	Germany	1989	$6.00
Island	P15D-37010	Moments In Love	CD3	Japan	1989	$8.00/$2.00
Island	651757	Moments In Love	CD5	U.K.	1989	$6.00
China	CDP156	Moments In Love	CDJ	U.S.	1989	$2.00
China	889091-2	Paranoimia 89	CD5	Germany	1989	$6.00
China	871773-2	Paranoimia 89	CD5	Germany	1989	$6.00
China	CHICD-14	Paranoimia 89	CD5	U.K.	1989	$6.00
China	WOKCDR-2014	Shades Of Paranoimia	CD5	U.K.	1992	$9.00
China	889684-3	Yebo	CD3	Germany	1989	$7.00
China	889685-2	Yebo	CD5	Germany	1989	$6.00
China	889869-2	Yebo	CD5	Germany	1990	$8.00
China	CHICD-18	Yebo	CD5	U.K.	1989	$6.00

Art Of Noise & Tom Jones

Singles

Label	Catalog Number	Title	Type	Country	Year	Longbox/Value
China	871039-2	Kiss	CD5	Germany	1989	$7.00
China	P13P-37007	Kiss	CD3	Japan	1989	$8.00/$2.00
China	CHICD-11	Kiss	CD5	U.K.	1989	$7.00
China	CDP 32	Kiss	CDJ	U.S.	1989	$3.00

Artch

Full Length

Label	Catalog Number	Title	Type	Country	Year	Longbox/Value
Enigma	73405	Another Return To Church Hill	LP/LB	U.S.		$12.00/$7.00
Metal Blade	26526	For the Sake Of Mankind	LP/LB	U.S.		$12.00/$7.00

Arterberry, Benita

Singles

Label	Catalog Number	Title	Type	Country	Year	Longbox/Value
SBK	05425	Changed	CDJ	U.S.	1991	$2.00

Artful Balance

Full Length

Label	Catalog Number	Title	Type	Country	Year	Longbox/Value
Aris	880352	Artfully Beatles	LP	Germany		$15.00
Aris	880347	Collection	LP	Germany		$15.00

Arthur,Neil

Singles

Label	Catalog Number	Title	Type	Country	Year	Longbox/Value
EMI		I Love I Hate	CD5	U.K.		$8.00
EMI		I Love I Hate	CD5	U.K.		$8.00
Second version.						
EMI	CDCHS-3909	One Day, One Time	CD5	U.K.	1992	$8.00

Artifacts

Singles

Label	Catalog Number	Title	Type	Country	Year	Longbox/Value
Atlantic	95823	C'mon Wit Da Git Do	CD5	U.S.	1994	$5.00

Artists United For Nature

Singles

Label	Catalog Number	Title	Type	Country	Year	Longbox/Value
Virgin	662 764	Yes We Can	CD5	Germany	1989	$12.00

Artman, Gilbert

Full Length

Company	Disk Number	Title	Type	Country	Year	Longbox/Value
Plaene	28006789	Urban Sax	LP	Germany		$15.00

Ash

Singles

Company	Disk Number	Title	Type	Country	Year	Longbox/Value
Reprise	PRO-CD-7644	Jack Names the Plantes	CDJ	U.S.	1995	$2.00
Reprise	PRO-CD-7933	Kung Fu	CDJ	U.S.	1995	$2.00

Ash, Daniel

Full Length

Company	Disk Number	Title	Type	Country	Year	Longbox/Value
RCA	3076-2	Coming Down	LTD/LP	U.S.	1991	$12.00
RCA		Walk This Way	DJ/Intvw	Canada	1991	$15.00
RCA	2831-2-RDj	Walk This Way	DJ/Intvw	U.S.	1991	$8.00

Singles

Company	Disk Number	Title	Type	Country	Year	Longbox/Value
Beggars Banquet	BBQ 9CD	Get Out Of Contol	CD5	U.K.	1992	$9.00
Columbia	CSK 4825	Get Out Of Contol	CDJ	U.S.	1992	$2.00
Columbia	CSK 4872	Get Out Of Contol	CDJ	U.S.	1992	$2.00
Columbia	CSK 4956	Here She Comes	CDJ	U.S.	1993	$2.00
BMG	PD-49222	This Love	CD5	Germany	1991	$9.00
RCA	2754-2-RDJ	This Love	CDJ	U.S.	1991	$2.00
RCA	2789-2-RDJ	This Love	CDJ	U.S.	1991	$2.00
WEA	BEG-246CD	Walk This Way	CD5	U.K.	1991	$9.00

Ash Ra

Full Length

Company	Disk Number	Title	Type	Country	Year	Longbox/Value
Virgin	1668	Belle Alliance	LP/LB	U.S.		$12.00/$7.00
Virgin	1665	Blackouts	LP/LB	U.S.		$12.00/$7.00
Virgin	1666	Correlations	LP/LB	U.S.		$12.00/$7.00

Singles

Company	Disk Number	Title	Type	Country	Year	Longbox/Value
Canyon	PCDY-00063	Take Me	CD3	Japan	1991	$13.00/$4.00

Asha

Singles

Company	Disk Number	Title	Type	Country	Year	Longbox/Value
Zyx	7437	Get U Alone	CD5	U.S.	1994	$5.00

Ashanti

Singles

Company	Disk Number	Title	Type	Country	Year	Longbox/Value
Street Life	72392 78007	Something's Wrong	CD5	U.S.	1994	$5.00

Ashby, Dave

Singles

Company	Disk Number	Title	Type	Country	Year	Longbox/Value
BMG	PD-44692	Alone In the Night	CD5	Germany	1991	$7.00

Ashby, Dorothy

Full Length

Company	Disk Number	Title	Type	Country	Year	Longbox/Value
Philips	814197-2	Concierto De Aranjuez	LP/BP	U.S.†	1985	$14.00/$8.00
Philips	818280-2	Django/Misty	LP/BP	U.S.†	1985	$14.00/$8.00

Ashes & Diamonds

Singles

Company	Disk Number	Title	Type	Country	Year	Longbox/Value
Riverhead	RHCD-1	I Just Want Your Love	CD5	U.K.	1992	$7.00

Ashford & Simpson

Full Length

Company	Disk Number	Title	Type	Country	Year	Longbox/Value
Pioneer Artists	PA-83-041	Ashford & Simpson	LD	U.S.	1983	$25.00
Pioneer	PA85-MO12	Ashford & Simpson	8"LD	U.S.	1985	$7.00
Capitol	CDP-46946	Love Or Physical	LP/LB	U.S.		$14.00/$8.00
EMI	746368-2	Real Love	LP	Germany		$15.00
Capitol	CDP-46368	Real Love	LP/LB	U.S.		$14.00/$8.00
Capitol	CDP-46466	Solid	LP/LB	U.S.		$14.00/$8.00

Singles

Company	Disk Number	Title	Type	Country	Year	Longbox/Value
EMI	203273-2	I'll Be There For You	CD5	Germany	1989	$4.00

Ashida, Shinsuke

Singles

Company	Disk Number	Title	Type	Country	Year	Longbox/Value
Toshiba	TODT-2747	Hohzuri Waltz	CD3	Japan	1991	$8.00/$2.00

Ashikawa, Rui

Singles

Company	Disk Number	Title	Type	Country	Year	Longbox/Value
King	KIDD-1153	Toyohei No Onna	CD3	Japan	1992	$8.00/$2.00

Ashley And Jackson

Singles

Company	Disk Number	Title	Type	Country	Year	Longbox/Value
Polygram	BLR-72	Here I Go Again	CD5	U.K.	1992	$6.00
Polygram	879297-2	Solid Gold	CD5	Germany	1992	$6.00

Ashton, Mark

Singles

Company	Disk Number	Title	Type	Country	Year	Longbox/Value
RCA	8806-2-RDJ	Black and White	CDJ	U.S.	1988	$2.00

Asia

Full Length

Company	Disk Number	Title	Type	Country	Year	Longbox/Value
Geffen	4008-2	Alpha	LP/LB	U.S.†	1984	$14.00/$8.00
Geffen	2008-2	Asia	LP/LB	U.S.†	1984	$14.00/$8.00
Pioneer	PA-84-092	Asia In Asia	LD	U.S.	1991	$35.00
Geffen	GEFD-24072-2	Astra	LP/LB	U.S.		$16.00/$10.00
Album Network		In the Studio (Asia)	RS	U.S.	1990	$20.00
Airdate: 9/17/90						
Album Network		In the Studio (Asia)	RS	U.S.	1994	$20.00
Airdate: 4/4/94						

Singles

Company	Disk Number	Title	Type	Country	Year	Longbox/Value
		Anytime	CD5	U.K.	1994	$10.00
MCA	20851	Astra	CD5	U.S.	1994	$5.00
Geffen	PRO-CD-4141	Days Like These	CDJ	U.S.	1990	$2.00
Geffen	PRO-CD-4144	Days Like These	CDJ	U.S.	1990	$2.00
Grt Pyramid	819	Heaven On Earth	CDJ	U.S.	1992	$2.00
IRS	977 509	Little Rich Boy	CD5	Germany	1993	$8.00
		Military Man	CDJ	Japan		$15.00
Musicdisc	109522	Who Will Stop the Rain?	CD5	U.K.	1992	$2.00
Grt Pyramid	819	Who Will Stop the Rain?	CDJ	U.S.	1992	$2.00

Asia Blue

Singles

Company	Disk Number	Title	Type	Country	Year	Longbox/Value
Polygram	WNRCD-0025	Connect	CD5	U.K.	1992	$7.00
Polygram	WNRCD-882	Escaping	CD5	U.K.	1992	$7.00

Ask

Singles

Company	Disk Number	Title	Type	Country	Year	Longbox/Value
MCA	DMCAT-1430	Dream	CD5	U.K.	1990	$6.00
MCA	MCSTD-1591	Freedom We Cry	CD5	U.K.	1992	$8.00

Aslan

Full Length

Company	Disk Number	Title	Type	Country	Year	Longbox/Value
Capitol	CDP-48989-2	Feel No Shame	LP/LB	U.S.		$12.00/$7.00

Label	Catalog Number	Title	Type	Country	Year	Longbox Value / Value

Asleep At The Wheel

Full Length

Label	Catalog Number	Title	Type	Country	Year	Value
Epic	EK-33097	Asleep At the Wheel	LP/LB	U.S.		$12.00/$7.00

Singles

Label	Catalog Number	Title	Type	Country	Year	Value
MCA	20840	Asleep At The Wheel	CD5	U.S.	1994	$5.00
Liberty	DPRO-79018	Blues For Dixie	CDJ	U.S.	1994	$2.00
Liberty	79038	Blues For Dixie	CDJ	U.S.	1994	$6.00
Arista	ARCD2425	(Get Your Kicks On) Route 66	CDJ	U.S.	1992	$6.00

Asphalt Ballet

Full Length

Label	Catalog Number	Title	Type	Country	Year	Value
Virgin	PR 4408	Blood On the Highway	DJ/Smplr	U.S.	1991	$10.00

Singles

Label	Catalog Number	Title	Type	Country	Year	Value
Virgin	12769	Angry Youth	CDJ	U.S.	1993	$2.00
Virgin	PR 4097	Soul Survive	CDJ	U.S.	1991	$2.00
Virgin	PR 4493	Tuesday's Rain	CDJ	U.S.	1991	$2.00
Virgin	PR 4608	Unlucky Mr. Lucky	CDJ	U.S.	1992	$2.00

Ass Ponys

Singles

Label	Catalog Number	Title	Type	Country	Year	Value
A&M	3145884222	Earth To Grandma	CDJ	U.S.		$2.00
A&M	3145883552	Little Bastard	CDJ	U.S.		$2.00
		Under Cedars And Stars	CDJ	U.S.		$2.00

Associates

Full Length

Label	Catalog Number	Title	Type	Country	Year	Value
WEA	244619-2	Glamour Chase	LP	Germany		$15.00
Virgin	260631-2	Wild And Lonely	LP	Germany	1990	$15.00
Atlantic	7 91389-2	Wild And Lonely	LP/LB	U.S.	1990	$7.00

Associates

Singles

Label	Catalog Number	Title	Type	Country	Year	Value
WEA	YZ-329CD	Country Boy	CD5	U.K.	1988	$7.00
Circa	YRCDT-4649	Fever	CD5	U.K.	1990	$7.00
Circa	YRCD-49	Fire To Ice	CD5	U.K.	1990	$12.00/$7.00
Charisma	PRCD 011	Fire To Ice	CDJ	U.S.	1990	$2.00
WEA	310	Heart Of Glass	CD3	Germany	1989	$7.00
Warner Brothers	YZ-310CD	Heart Of Glass	CD5	U.K.	1989	$7.00
Circa	YRCD-56	Just Can't Say Goodbye	CD5	U.K.	1990	$7.00
Stange Frt	SFPSCD-075	Peel Sessions	CD5	U.K.	1989	$7.00
Circa		Strange Fruit	CD5	U.K.	1990	$7.00

Astaire, Fred

Full Length

Label	Catalog Number	Title	Type	Country	Year	Value
Aris	881009	An Evening With	LP	Germany		$15.00
MCA	MCAD-31175	Best Of	LP/LB	U.S.		$16.00/$10.00
Pro Art	431	Cheek To Cheek	LP	U.S.		$8.00
EMI	TCMFP-5827	Fred Astaire	LP	Germany		$15.00
Nostalgia	244571-2	Puttin' On the Ritz	LP	U.S.		$8.00
RCA	2337	Rarities	LP/LB	U.S.		$16.00/$10.00
Musidisc	192932	Star Forever	LP	Germany		$15.00
Sony	32DP-791	Starring Fred Astaire	LP	Japan		$25.00

Astley, Jon

Full Length

Label	Catalog Number	Title	Type	Country	Year	Value
Atlantic	7 81882	Compleat Angler	LP/LB	U.S.		$12.00/$7.00

Singles

Label	Catalog Number	Title	Type	Country	Year	Value
Atlantic		Been There, Done That	CDJ	U.S.	1988	$2.00
Atlantic	PR 2433-2	Put This Love to the Test	CDJ	U.S.	1988	$2.00

Astley, Rick

Full Length

Label	Catalog Number	Title	Type	Country	Year	Value
RCA	R32P-1173	Hold Me In Your Arms	LP	Japan		$20.00

Singles

Label	Catalog Number	Title	Type	Country	Year	Value
RCA	9030-2-RDJ	Ain't Too Proud To Beg	CDJ	U.S.	1989	$2.00
RCA	PD-44248	Cry For Help	CD5	Germany	1990	$8.00
RCA	PD-44248	Cry For Help	CD5	U.K.	1990	$8.00
RCA	2774-2	Cry For Help	CDJ	U.S.	1991	$2.00
RCA	8872-2-RDJ	Giving Up On Love	CDJ	U.S.	1989	$2.00
RCA	8878-2-RDJ	Giving Up On Love	CDJ	U.S.	1989	$2.00
RCA	PD-42616	Hold Me In Your Arms	CD5	Germany	1989	$8.00
RCA	PD-42616	Hold Me In Your Arms	CD5	U.K.	1989	$8.00
RCA		Hopelessly	CD5	U.K.	1993	$8.00
RCA		Hopelessly	CD5	U.K.	1993	$8.00
Second version.						
RCA	62596	Hopelessly	CDJ	U.S.	1993	$3.00
RCA	PD-4408	Move Right Out	CD5	Germany	1991	$8.00
BMG	BVDP-34	Move Right Out	CD3	Japan	1991	$14.00/$3.00
RCA	PD-4408	Move Right Out	CD5	U.K.	1991	$8.00
RCA	2839-2-RDJ	Move Right Out	CDJ	U.S.	1991	$3.00
RCA	PD-42639	Never Gonna Give You Up	CD3	Germany	1990	$8.00
RCA	R10D-2	Never Gonna Give You Up	CD3	Japan	1990	$14.00/$3.00
RCA	PD-42639	Never Gonna Give You Up	CD3	U.K.	1990	$8.00
RCA	PD-44738	Never Knew Love	CD5	Germany	1991	$8.00
RCA	PD-44738	Never Knew Love	CD5	U.K.	1991	$8.00
RCA	62721	Ones You Love, The	CDJ	U.S.	1993	$2.00
RCA	PD-42190	She Wants To Dance With Me	CD5	Germany	1988	$8.00
RCA	PD-42190	She Wants To Dance With Me	CD5	U.K.	1988	$8.00
RCA		She Wants To Dance With Me	CDJ	U.S.	1988	$2.00
RCA	PD-42574	Take MeTo Your Heart	CD5	Germany	1989	$8.00
RCA	PD-42574	Take MeTo Your Heart	CD5	U.K.	1989	$8.00
RCA	62721	The Ones You Love	CD5	U.S.	1994	$5.00
BMG	BVDP-38	This Must Be Heaven	CD3	Japan	1991	$14.00/$3.00
RCA	PD-41684	When I Fall In Love	CD5	U.K.	1990	$8.00
Old Gold	OG-6197	When I Fall In Love	CD5	U.K.	1993	$8.00
RCA	62068-RDJ	Wonderful You	CDJ	U.S.	1991	$2.00

Astley, Virginia

Full Length

Label	Catalog Number	Title	Type	Country	Year	Value
WEA	242039-2	Hope In A Darkened Heart	LP	Germany		$12.00
WEA	242039-2	Hope In A Darkened Heart	LP	U.K.		$12.00
Geffen	GEFD-24184-2	Hope In A Darkened Heart	LP/LB	U.S.		$14.00/$8.00

Aston, T

Singles

Label	Catalog Number	Title	Type	Country	Year	Value
BCM	20457	Go Get It	CD5	Germany	1990	$7.00

Astor, Tom

Singles

Label	Catalog Number	Title	Type	Country	Year	Value
EMI	147542-2	Hallo Guten Morgen	CD5	Germany	1990	$6.00
EMI	204433-2	Ich Bin Kein Dichter	CD5	Germany	1991	$6.00
EMI	203790-2	Judge Adler	CD5	Germany	1990	$6.00
EMI	147576-2	Take It Easy	CD5	Germany	1991	$6.00
EMI	204633-2	Wo Sind Die Frau'n	CD5	Germany	1992	$6.00

Astor, Willy

Singles

Label	Catalog Number	Title	Type	Country	Year	Value
BMG	664479	Frutti Di Mare	CD5	Germany	1991	$6.00

Aswad

Singles

Label	Catalog Number	Title	Type	Country	Year	Value
Island	162198	Beauty Is Only Skin Deep	CD3	Germany	1989	$8.00
BMG Ariola	662198	Beauty Is Only Skin Deep	CD5	Germany	1989	$8.00
Mango	CIDMX-105	Beauty Is Only Skin Deep	CD3	U.K	1989	$5.00
Island	125	Beauty Is Only Skin Deep	CDJ	U.S.	1989	$2.00
Polydor	PSCD-1084	Best Of My Love	CD3	Japan	1991	$13.00/$4.00
Island	PRCD-7850-2	Best Of My Love	CDJ	U.S.	1990	$2.00
Island	CIDX-341	Don't Turn Around	CD5	U.K.	1988	$8.00
Mango	123	Don't Turn Around	CDJ	U.S.	1988	$2.00
Mango	CIDP-358	Give A Little Love	CD5	U.K.	1991	$8.00
BMG	663558	Next To You	CD5	Germany	1990	$8.00
Polydor	PSDD-1009	Next To You	CD3	Japan	1990	$13.00/$4.00
Island	CIDM-753	Next To You	CD5	U.K.	1990	$8.00
Island	885484	On And On	CD5	Germany	1989	$8.00
Island	CIDM-708	On And On	CD5	U.K.	1989	$8.00
Island	CID-383	Set Them Free	CD5	U.K.	1988	$8.00
Island	CIDP-383	Set Them Free	CD5	U.K.	1988	$8.00
Atlantic	95803	Shine	CD5	U.S.	1994	$5.00
BMG	884967	Smile	CD5	Germany	1990	$8.00
Polydor	PSCD-1077	Smile	CD3	Japan	1990	$13.00/$4.00
Island	CIDM-767	Smile	CD5	U.K.	1990	$8.00
Mango	PSCD-1084	Too Wicked	CD5	Japan	1991	$12.00
Island	CIDM-771	Too Wicked	CD5	U.K.	1991	$8.00
Mesa	6123	You're No Good	CDJ	U.S.		$3.00

Aswan And The Xs

Singles

Label	Catalog Number	Title	Type	Country	Year	Value
ZYX	DST-1054-8	Read In My Mind	CD5	Germany	1991	$5.00

Asylum Party

Singles

Label	Catalog Number	Title	Type	Country	Year	Value
SPV	5363-3	Four Tracks	CD3	Germany	1989	$5.00

Atension

Singles

Label	Catalog Number	Title	Type	Country	Year	Value
		Let Me Push It To Ya	CDJ	U.S		$2.00

Atheist

Full Length

Label	Catalog Number	Title	Type	Country	Year	Value
Warner Brothers	45370	Elements	LP/LB	U.S.		$14.00/$8.00
Warner Brothers	26717	Unquestionable	LP/LB	U.S.		$14.00/$8.00

Atkins, Chet

Full Length

Label	Catalog Number	Title	Type	Country	Year	Value
Aris	886908	Best Selection	LP	Germany		$15.00
Columbia	CSK 6478	Select Cuts	DJ/Smplr	U.S.	1994	$8.00
CBS	CK-39591	Stay Tuned	LP/BP	U.S.†	1985	$15.00/$9.00

Singles

Label	Catalog Number	Title	Type	Country	Year	Value
CBS	656373-3	Poor Boy Blues	CD3	Germany	1990	$10.00
CBS	656373-2	Poor Boy Blues	CD5	U.K.	1990	$10.00
Columbia	CSK 73556	Poor Boy Blues	CDJ	U.S.	1990	$3.00

Atlanta Beat Bo

Singles

Label	Catalog Number	Title	Type	Country	Year	Value
	1901	Cum On Baby	CD5	U.S.	1994	$5.00

Atlanta Rhythm Section

Full Length

Label	Catalog Number	Title	Type	Country	Year	Value
Epic		Truth In A Structured Form	LP/LB	U.S.		$15.00/$10.00

Atlantic Ocean

Singles

Label	Catalog Number	Title	Type	Country	Year	Value
E-Bloc	BLOCCD001	Waterfall	CD5	U.K.	1993	$8.00

Atlantic Starr

Full Length

Label	Catalog Number	Title	Type	Country	Year	Value
Polygram	395019-2	As the Band Turns	LP	Gemany		$12.00
A&M	CD-5019	As the Band Turns	LP/LB	U.S.		$14.00/$8.00
Pioneer	PA87-MO050	As the Band Turns...The Video	8"LD	U.S.	1987	$5.00
Pioneer	PA87-MO050	As the Band Turns...The Video	8"LD	U.S.	1990	$7.00
Digital audio						
Polygram	395141-2	Best Of	LP	Gemany		$12.00
Unistar		Weekly Specials, The	RS	U.S.	1992	$15.00
Airdate: 4/10/92						

Singles

Label	Catalog Number	Title	Type	Country	Year	Value
Warner Brothers	9 21946-2	Always	CD5	U.S.	1992	$4.00
Warner Brothers	PRO-CD-3733	Bring It Back Home Again	CDJ	U.S.	1989	$2.00
A&M	AMCD-907	Compact Hits	CD5	U.K.	1988	$8.00
Arista	ASCD 2749	Everybody's Got Summer	CDJ	U.S.	1994	$3.00
Epic	ESK 73532	Family Of Man	CDJ	U.S.	1990	$3.00
Arista	12709	I'll Remember You	CD5	U.S.	1994	$6.00
Arista	2678	I'll Remember You	CDJ	U.S.	1994	$2.00
Warner Brothers	40203	Love Crazy	CD5	U.S.	1991	$5.00
Warner Brothers	PRO-CD-5036	Love Crazy	CDJ	U.S.	1991	$2.00
Warner Brothers	PRO-CD-5145	Love Crazy	CDJ	U.S.	1991	$2.00
Warner Brothers	PRO-CD-5190	Love Crazy	CDJ	U.S.	1991	$2.00
Warner Brothers	PRO-CD-5243	Love Crazy	CDJ	U.S.	1991	$2.00
Warner Brothers	PRO-CD-5167	Masterpiece	CDJ	U.S.	1991	$6.00
Pioneer	09P3-6119	My First Love	CD3	Japan	1989	$13.00/$4.00
Warner Brothers	PRO-CD-3461	My First Love	CDJ	U.S.	1989	$2.00
Warner Brothers		My Sugar	CDJ	U.S.	1989	$2.00
A&M	390342-2	Secret Lovers	CD5	Germany	1988	$8.00
Warner Brothers	PRO-CD-5156	Unconditional Love	CDJ	U.S.	1991	$2.00
Warner Brothers	PRO-CD-5514	Unconditional Love	CDJ	U.S.	1991	$2.00

Atmosphere

Singles

Label	Catalog Number	Title	Type	Country	Year	Value
CBS	655813-3	Atm-Oz-Fear	CD3	Germany	1990	$14.00/$8.00

Atom Heart

Singles

Label	Catalog Number	Title	Type	Country	Year	Value
SPV	12002-3	Goddamme Drummachine	CD5	Germany	1992	$8.00

Atom Seed

Full Length

Label	Catalog Number	Title	Type	Country	Year	Value
London	828260	Get In Line	LP/LB	U.S.	1991	$8.00
London	LONCD-307	Get In Line	CD5	U.K.	1991	$8.00
London	CDP 615	Get In Line	CDJ	U.S.	1991	$2.00
London	LONCD-3299	Rebel	CD5	U.K.	1991	$8.00
London	CDP 541	Rebel	CDJ	U.S.	1990	$2.00

Atomic Boys

Singles

Label	Catalog Number	Title	Type	Country	Year	Longbox Value / Value
	VMPRO10	Social Misfits	CDJ	U.S.		$2.00

Atomic Opera

Singles

Label	Catalog Number	Title	Type	Country	Year	Longbox Value / Value
	PRO-CD-7054	Joyride	CDJ	U.S.		$2.00

Atoozi

Singles

Label	Catalog Number	Title	Type	Country	Year	Longbox Value / Value
EMI	DPRO-4705	Calling Out Your Name	CDJ	U.S.	1990	$2.00

Atrium

Singles

Label	Catalog Number	Title	Type	Country	Year	Longbox Value / Value
Canyon	PCCY-00112	Jolly Joker	CD5	Japan	1990	$10.00

Attacco, Decente

Singles

Label	Catalog Number	Title	Type	Country	Year	Longbox Value / Value
Pinnacle	AONCD-004	I Don't Care How Long It Takes	CD5	U.K.	1988	$5.00

Attaway, Murray

Singles

Label	Catalog Number	Title	Type	Country	Year	Longbox Value / Value
DGC	PRO-CD-4539	Fall So Far	CDJ	U.S.	1993	$2.00
DGC	PRO-CD-4500	Under Jets	CDJ	U.S.	1993	$2.00

Au Pairs

Full Length

Label	Catalog Number	Title	Type	Country	Year	Longbox Value / Value
SPV	2099	Sense And Sensuality	LP	Germany		$12.00

Audin And Modena

Singles

Label	Catalog Number	Title	Type	Country	Year	Longbox Value / Value
Polygram	867617-2	Song Of Ocardina	CD5	Germany	1991	$5.00

Audio Deluxe

Singles

Label	Catalog Number	Title	Type	Country	Year	Longbox Value / Value
EMI	323794-2	Sixty Seconds	CD5	Germany	1991	$5.00
EMI	FLYRCD-2	Sixty Seconds	CD5	U.K.	1991	$5.00

Audio Sports

Singles

Label	Catalog Number	Title	Type	Country	Year	Longbox Value / Value
All Access	AACD-001	Eat & Buy & Eat	CD5	Japan	1992	$7.00

Audio Two

Full Length

Label	Catalog Number	Title	Type	Country	Year	Longbox Value / Value
Atlantic	7 91358	I Don't Care, The Album	LP/LB	U.S.		$14.00/$8.00
WEA	790907-2	What More Can I Say	LP	Germany		$15.00

Singles

Label	Catalog Number	Title	Type	Country	Year	Longbox Value / Value
		Top Billin'	CDJ	U.S.		$2.00

Aunt Betty's

Singles

Label	Catalog Number	Title	Type	Country	Year	Longbox Value / Value
Eastwest	PRCD 9504-2	Skinny Bone Jones	CDJ	U.S.		$6.00
Eastwest	PRCD 9504-2	Skinny Bone Jones	CDJ	U.S.	1994	$6.00

Aurore

Singles

Label	Catalog Number	Title	Type	Country	Year	Longbox Value / Value
Canyon	CEDC-00087	Lambada	CD3	Japan	1990	$7.00/$2.00

Austin, Bryan

Full Length

Label	Catalog Number	Title	Type	Country	Year	Longbox Value / Value
Patriot	79024	Radio Active	DJ/Intvw	U.S.	1994	$10.00

Austin, Chris

Singles

Label	Catalog Number	Title	Type	Country	Year	Longbox Value / Value
Warner Brothers		Blues Stay Away	CDJ	U.S.		$2.00
Warner Brothers	PRO-CD-3304	Honey I Dare You	CDJ	U.S.	1988	$2.00
Warner Brothers		Lonesome For You	CDJ	U.S.		$2.00

Austin, Patti

Full Length

Label	Catalog Number	Title	Type	Country	Year	Longbox Value / Value
QWest	3591-2	Every Home Should Have One	LP/LB	U.S.†	1984	$15.00/$9.00
King	K20Y-9520	Havana Candy	LP	Japan		$25.00
GRP	MVCZ-14	Love Is Gonna Getcha	LTD/LP	Japan		$30.00
	Gold disc.					
Qwest	923974-2	Patti Austin	LP	U.K.		$18.00
GRP	9984	Patti On Patti	DJ/Intvw	U.S.	1994	$15.00

Singles

Label	Catalog Number	Title	Type	Country	Year	Longbox Value / Value
GRP	9920	Girl Who Used To Be Me	CDJ	U.S.	1989	$2.00
GRP	9967	Givin' In To Love	CDJ	U.S.	1991	$2.00
GRP	9936	Love is Gonna Getcha	CDJ	U.S.	1990	$2.00
	MGDM 3053	Reach	CDJ	U.S.	1995	$3.00
GRP		Smoke Gets In Your Eyes	CDJ	U.S.	1990	$2.00
GRP	9950	Soldier Boy	CDJ	U.S.	1991	$2.00
GRP	9927	Through the Test of Time	CDJ	U.S.	1990	$2.00
GRP	VIDP-17	Together	CD3	Japan	1990	$12.00/$4.00

Austrian Mix Project

Singles

Label	Catalog Number	Title	Type	Country	Year	Longbox Value / Value
BCM	20480	Alle Meine Lieda	CD5	Germany	1990	$8.00

Autechre

Singles

Label	Catalog Number	Title	Type	Country	Year	Longbox Value / Value
TV	8717	Basscard	CD5	U.S.	1994	$5.00

Auteurs

Full Length

Label	Catalog Number	Title	Type	Country	Year	Longbox Value / Value
Delabel	DE3319	Auteurs	DJ/Smplr	U.S.		$15.00
Hut		She Might Take A Train	DJ/Smplr	France	1995	$35.00
	Mail-order only sampler.					

Singles

Label	Catalog Number	Title	Type	Country	Year	Longbox Value / Value
Hut		Back With the Killer Again	CDJ	U.K.	1995	$15.00
Hut	HUTX 41	Chinese Bakery	CD5	U.K.	1994	$8.00
Hut		Chinese Bakery	CD5	U.K.	1994	$8.00
	Second version.					
Hut	HUTCD 36	Lenny Valentino	CD5	U.K.	1994	$8.00
Hut	14135	Lenny Valentino	CDJ	U.S.	1994	$3.00
Hut	HUTCD-24	Showgirl	CD5	U.K.	1992	$8.00

Auto & Cherokee

Singles

Label	Catalog Number	Title	Type	Country	Year	Longbox Value / Value
Morgan Creek	2959 26002	Taste	CD5	U.S.	1992	$4.00

Autograph

Full Length

Label	Catalog Number	Title	Type	Country	Year	Longbox Value / Value
RCA	PCD1-5423	Sign In Please	LP/BP	U.S.†	1985	$15.00/$9.00
Aris	886024	That's the Stuff	LP	Germany		$15.00
RCA	PCD1-7009	That's the Stuff	LP/BP	U.S.		$14.00/$8.00
RCA	PCD1-7009	That's the Stuff	LP/BP	U.S.†	1985	$15.00/$9.00

Autopsy

Singles

Company	Disk Number	Title	Type	Country	Year	Longbox Value / Value
Peaceville	VILE-29TCD	Fiend For Blood	CD5	U.K.	1991	$5.00
Peaceville	29	Fiend For Blood	CD5	U.S.	1992	$4.00
Peaceville	VILE-24TCD	Redistribution For the Dead	CD5	U.K.	1991	$5.00

Autry, Gene

Full Length

Company	Disk Number	Title	Type	Country	Year	Longbox Value / Value
Warner Sound Exchange		22 Legendary Hits	LTD/LP	U.S.	1995	$17.00
Columbia	CK 48957	Essential Gene Autry 1936 - 1946	LP/LB	U.S.	1992	$15.00/$10.00
	First page of booklet is misprinted with tribute to Roy Acuff.					

Auvray, Lydie

Full Length

Company	Disk Number	Title	Type	Country	Year	Longbox Value / Value
Plaene	88431	Ensemble	LP	Germany		$15.00

Singles

Company	Disk Number	Title	Type	Country	Year	Longbox Value / Value
EMI	203585-3	Die Schnelle Gerdi	CD3	Germany	1989	$7.00

Ava

Singles

Company	Disk Number	Title	Type	Country	Year	Longbox Value / Value
Polygram	867111-2	Cry In the Night	CD5	Germany	1991	$5.00
EMI	147477-2	I Want What I Want	CD5	Germany	1990	$5.00
EMI	147457-2	True Love	CD5	Germany	1989	$5.00

Avalance

Singles

Company	Disk Number	Title	Type	Country	Year	Longbox Value / Value
Eastwest	246607-2	I Will Wait	CD3	Germany	1989	$8.00
Eastwest	8 70040	Johnny Come Home	CD3	Germany	1989	$8.00
Eastwest	247000-2	Johnny Come Home	CD3	Germany	1989	$8.00
Eastwest	9031-73816-2	Love Me, Please Love Me	CD5	Germany	1991	$8.00
Eastwest	171122-2	Riding	CD5	Germany	1989	$8.00
Virgin	VSCDT-1452	Walking In the Air	CD3	U.K.	1992	$8.00
Eastwest	9031-75000-2	Young Guns	CD5	Germany	1991	$8.00

Ave, Maria

Singles

Company	Disk Number	Title	Type	Country	Year	Longbox Value / Value
ZYX	6745-8	No Sex 'Til Marriage	CD5	Germany	1992	$7.00

Average White Band

Full Length

Company	Disk Number	Title	Type	Country	Year	Longbox Value / Value
WEA	781515-2	Average White Band	LP	Germany		$18.00
RCD	ND-89091	Best Of	LP	Germany		$23.00

Singles

Company	Disk Number	Title	Type	Country	Year	Longbox Value / Value
Polygram	889308-3	Spirit Of Love	CD3	Germany	1989	$9.00
Polygram	889309-2	Spirit Of Love	CD5	Germany	1989	$9.00
Polygram	8PZCD-56	Spirit Of Love	CD5	U.K.	1989	$9.00

Avila, Bobby Ross

Singles

Company	Disk Number	Title	Type	Country	Year	Longbox Value / Value
Perspective	31458 8179	All That I Do	CDJ	U.S.	1993	$2.00
Perspective	31458 8100	La La Love	CDJ	U.S.	1993	$2.00
RCA	9186-2-RDJ	Merry Go Round	CDJ	U.S.	1990	$2.00
RCA	9072-2-RDJ	Music Man	CDJ	U.S.	1989	$2.00
Perspective	31458 8146	Tu Amor	CDJ	U.S.	1993	$2.00

Awsome 3

Singles

Company	Disk Number	Title	Type	Country	Year	Longbox Value / Value
Citybeat	771CD	Don't Go	CD5	U.K.	1992	$8.00
White Lbl	6491	Don't Go	CDJ	U.S.	1993	$2.00
White Lbl	41040	Don't Go	CDJ	U.S.	1993	$2.00
A&M	AMCD-797	Freedom Of Life	CD5	U.K.	1991	$8.00
A&M	AMCD-591	Hard Up	CD5	U.K.	1991	$8.00

Axelrod, David

Full Length

Company	Disk Number	Title	Type	Country	Year	Longbox Value / Value
Liberty	29970	Big Country, The	DJ/Smplr	U.S.	1995	$12.00

Axodry

Singles

Company	Disk Number	Title	Type	Country	Year	Longbox Value / Value
ZYX	6545-8	Losing You	CD5	Germany	1991	$5.00
ZYX	6002-8	You	CD5	Germany	1991	$5.00

Axton, Hoyt

Full Length

Company	Disk Number	Title	Type	Country	Year	Longbox Value / Value
A&M	3182	Road Songs	LP/LB	U.S.		$8.00

Singles

Company	Disk Number	Title	Type	Country	Year	Longbox Value / Value
DPI	5001	Heartbreak Hotel	CDJ	U.S.	1990	$2.00

Axxis

Full Length

Company	Disk Number	Title	Type	Country	Year	Longbox Value / Value
EMI	TOCP-6446	Axxis II	LP	Japan		$20.00
Captiol	C2-91829	Kingdom Of the Night	LP	Canada		$15.00
Enigma	73568	Kingdom Of the Night	LP/LB	U.S.		$14.00/$8.00

Singles

Company	Disk Number	Title	Type	Country	Year	Longbox Value / Value
EMI	147437-2	Fire And Ice	CD5	Germany	1989	$5.00
EMI	147571-2	Hold You	CD5	Germany	1989	$5.00
EMI	147461-2	Kingdom Of the Night	CD5	Germany	1989	$5.00
EMI	CDR-6225	Kingdom Of the Night	CD5	U.K.	1989	$5.00
EMI	147422-2	Living in the World	CD5	Germany	1989	$5.00
EMI	147528-2	Ships Are Sailing	CD5	Germany	1990	$5.00
EMI	CDR-6225	Touch the Rainbow	CD5	Germany	1990	$5.00
		World Is Looking In Their Eyes	CDJ	U.S.		$2.00

Aya, Yuki

Singles

Company	Disk Number	Title	Type	Country	Year	Longbox Value / Value
Polydor	PODH-1134	Girlfriend	CD3	Japan	1993	$7.00/$2.00

Ayase, Kazumi

Singles

Company	Disk Number	Title	Type	Country	Year	Longbox Value / Value
King	KIDX-51	Michinoku Banka	CD3	Japan	1992	$7.00/$2.00
King	KIDX-111	Noto No Umi	CD3	Japan	1993	$7.00/$2.00
King	KIDX-2072	Otonashigawa	CD3	Japan	1992	$7.00/$2.00
King	KIDX-82	Tamba Koe	CD3	Japan	1992	$7.00/$2.00

Aysha

Singles

Company	Disk Number	Title	Type	Country	Year	Longbox Value / Value
EMI	323564-2	Come On Come On	CD5	Germany	1990	$5.00

Az the Visualiza

Singles

Company	Disk Number	Title	Type	Country	Year	Longbox Value / Value
Capitol	58407	Sugar Hill	CD5	U.S.	1995	$5.00
EMI	58407	Sugar Hill	CD5	U.S.	1995	$5.00

AZ-1

Label	Catalog Number	Title	Type	Country	Year	Longbox Value / Value
		Singles				
Scotti Brothers	75348	Trust In Me	CDJ	U.S.	1992	$3.00
Scotti Brothers	75351	Trust In Time	CD5	U.S.	1992	$4.00
Scotti Brothers	ZSK 75359	With You	CDJ	U.S.	1993	$2.00

Azizi

Label	Catalog Number	Title	Type	Country	Year	Longbox Value / Value
		Singles				
Arista	664444	Don't Say That It's Over	CD5	U.K.	1991	$5.00
Arista	664092	Midnight Lover	CD5	Germany	1991	$5.00
Arista	664092	Midnight Lover	CD5	U.K.	1991	$5.00

Azor, Denis

Label	Catalog Number	Title	Type	Country	Year	Longbox Value / Value
		Singles				
Polygram	867219-2	Ala Li La	CD5	Germany	1991	$5.00
Toshiba	TODP-2325	Ala Li La	CD3	Japan	1991	$7.00/$2.00

Azra

Label	Catalog Number	Title	Type	Country	Year	Longbox Value / Value
		Singles				
BMG	663232	Only Love Can Help	CD5	Germany	1990	$5.00

Aztec Camera

Label	Catalog Number	Title	Type	Country	Year	Longbox Value / Value
		Full Length				
WEA	5CS-67	Best Of, The	DJ/Smplr	Japan		$50.00
Tokuma	32JC-107	High Land, Hard Rain	LP	Japan		$20.00
Sire	9 25646-2	Love	LP/LB	U.S.		$15.00/$9.00
Sire	PRO-CD-5927	Retrospect	DJ/Smplr	U.S.	1993	$15.00
		Singles				
WEA		Birds	CD5	U.S.	1993	$8.00
WEA		Birds	CD5	U.S.	1993	$8.00
Second version.						
WEA	171822-2	Crying Scene	CD5	Germany	1990	$8.00
Pioneer	WMD5-4030	Crying Scene	[illegible]	Japan	[illegible]	$14.00
WEA	YZ-492CD	Crying Scene	CD5	U.K.	1990	$8.00
Sire	9 21591-2	Crying Scene	CD5	U.S.	1990	$2.00
Sire	PRO-CD-4328	Crying Scene	CDJ	U.S.	1990	$2.00
WEA	YZ-154CD	Deep & Wide & Tall	CD3	Germany	1988	$8.00
WEA		Dreams Sweet Dream	CD5	U.K.	1993	$8.00
WEA		Dreams Sweet Dream	CD5	U.K.	1993	$8.00
Second version.						
Warner Brothers	12-21775	Good Morning Britain	CD5	Canada	1992	$8.00
WEA	9031-72592-2	Good Morning Britain	CD5	Germany	1990	$7.00
WEA	YZ-521CD	Good Morning Britain	CD5	U.K.	1990	$8.00
Sire	9 21775-2	Good Morning Britain	CD5	U.S.	1990	$4.00
Sire	PRO-CD-4453	Good Morning Britain	CDJ	U.S.	1990	$2.00
WEA	YZ-168CD	How Men Are	CD3	U.K.	1988	$8.00
WEA	247956-2	Somewhere In My Heart	CD3	Germany	1988	$8.00
WEA	YZ-181CD	Somewhere In My Heart	CD3	U.K.	1988	$8.00
		Sun	CD5	U.K.	1995	$10.00
Warner Brothers	PRO-CD-7922	Sun	CDJ	U.S.	1995	$3.00
WEA	YZ-199CD	Working In A Goldmine	CD3	Germany	1988	$8.00

Azuma

Label	Catalog Number	Title	Type	Country	Year	Longbox Value / Value
		Full Length				
Private	2020-2	Azuma	LP/LB	U.S.		$14.00/$8.00
Private	2037-2	Wanderer	LP/LB	U.S.		$14.00/$8.00
		Singles				
Zyx	7416	No One Breaks My Heart	CD5	U.S.	1994	$5.00
PWL	PWCD-537	Anything For You	CD5	U.K.	1991	$8.00

Azymuth

Label	Catalog Number	Title	Type	Country	Year	Longbox Value / Value
		Full Length				
Milestone	FCD-9101	Telecominication	LP/LB	U.S.†	1985	$8.00

Azzolina

Label	Catalog Number	Title	Type	Country	Year	Longbox Value / Value
		Full Length				
Islan	842650-2	Never Too Late	LP/LB	U.S.		$14.00/$8.00

B#

Label	Catalog Number	Title	Type	Country	Year	Longbox Value / Value
		Singles				
Sony	SRDL-3615	Ichiban Akarui Mado	CD3	Japan	1993	$7.00/$2.00
Sony	SRDL-3329	Natsu No Kanata	CD3	Japan	1991	$7.00/$2.00
Sony	SRDL-3354	Shonen	CD3	Japan	1991	$7.00/$2.00

B 52's

Label	Catalog Number	Title	Type	Country	Year	Longbox Value / Value
		Full Length				
Reprise	26943-2-Dj	Good Stuff	DJ/LP	U.S.	1992	$10.00
Reprise	26995-2	Good Stuff	DP/LB	U.S.	1992	$14.00/$9.00
MCA		Kave Radio Bedrock	DJ/Smplr	U.S.	1994	$8.00
		Singles				
Reprise	921299-2	Channel Z	CD3	Germany	1989	$9.00
Reprise	W2831CD	Channel Z	CD3	U.K.	1989	$9.00
Reprise	W-9737	Channel Z	CD3	U.K.	1989	$9.00
Reprise	921299-2	Channel Z	CD5	U.K.	1989	$9.00
Reprise	W-9526CD	Deadbeat Club	CD3	U.K.	1990	$9.00
Reprise	PRO-CD-3825	Deadbeat Club	CDJ	U.S.	1989	$3.00
Reprise	CD40561	Good Stuff	CD5	Canada	1992	$8.00
Reprise		Good Stuff	CD5	Germany	1992	$9.00
Reprise	W-0109CD	Good Stuff	CD5	U.K.	1992	$9.00
Reprise	PRO-CD-5497	Good Stuff	CDJ	U.S.	1989	$3.00
Reprise	9 40561-2	Good Stuff	CD5	U.S.	1992	$5.00
Reprise	W-0156CDX	Hot Pants Exposion	CD5	U.K.	1993	$9.00
Reprise		Is That You Mo-Dean	CD5	Germany		$10.00
Reprise		Is That You Mo-Dean	CD5	U.S.		$5.00
Reprise		Is That You Mo-Dean	CDJ	U.S.		$7.00
Image disc.						
Warner Brothers	12-21318	Love Shack	CD5	Canada	1990	$8.00
Reprise	921395-2	Love Shack	CD5	Germany	1989	$9.00
Pioneer	WPDP-6212	Love Shack	CD3	Japan	1989	$12.00/$4.00
Reprise	W-9917CD	Love Shack	CD5	U.K.	1989	$9.00
Reprise	9 21318-2	Love Shack	CD5	U.S.	1989	$5.00
Reprise	19430-2	Love Shack	CD5	U.S.	1989	$5.00
Reprise	PRO-CD-3679	Love Shack	CDJ	U.S.	1989	$3.00
MCA		(Meet) the Flintstones	CD5	U.K.	1994	$10.00
MCA	MCA5P-2998	(Meet) the Flintstones	CDJ	U.S.	1994	$7.00
MCA	MCA5P-2998	(Meet) the Flintstones	CDJ	U.S.	1994	$25.00
CD in clamshell package.						
Warner Brothers	12-240642	Revolution Earth	CD5	Canada	1990	$8.00
Reprise	PRO-CD-5677	Revolution Earth	CDJ	U.S.	1992	$2.00
Warner Brothers	12-21441	Roam	CD5	Canada	1990	$8.00
Reprise	W-9827CD	Roam	CD5	U.K.	1990	$9.00
Reprise	9 21441-2	Roam	CD5	U.S.	1989	$5.00
Reprise	PRO-CD-3856	Roam	CDJ	U.S.	1989	$2.00
Warner Brothers	12-40594	Tell It Like It T-I-S	CD5	Canada	1993	$8.00
Reprise	W-0130CD	Tell It Like It T-I-S	CD5	Germany	1992	$9.00
Reprise	W-0130CD	Tell It Like It T-I-S	CD5	U.K.	1992	$11.00
with lie detector						
Reprise	PRO-CD-5663	Tell It Like It T-I-S	CD5	U.S.	1992	$5.00

B Angie B

Label	Catalog Number	Title	Type	Country	Year	Longbox Value / Value
		Full Length				
Capitol	CDP-95236	B Angie B	LP/LB	U.S.		$14.00/$8.00
		Singles				
Capitol		I Don't Want To Lose Your Love	CDJ	U.S.		$2.00
Capitol		So Much Love	CDJ	U.S.		$2.00

B.B.M.

Label	Catalog Number	Title	Type	Country	Year	Longbox Value / Value
		Singles				
		Where In The World	CD5	U.K.		$10.00
		Where In The World	CD5	U.K.		$10.00
Second version.						

B.B. Queen

Label	Catalog Number	Title	Type	Country	Year	Longbox Value / Value
		Singles				
EMI	127530-2	Blueshouse	CD5	Germany	1990	$6.00
EMI	127571-2	Blueshouse	CD5	Germany	1990	$6.00
EMI	127541-2	Blueshouse	CD5	Germany	1990	$6.00
EMI	CDEM-181	Blueshouse	CD5	U.K.	1990	$6.00
EMI	CDEM-199	I Wanna Be Next To You	CD5	U.K.	1990	$6.00

B.C.G.

Label	Catalog Number	Title	Type	Country	Year	Longbox Value / Value
		Singles				
Columbia	ALCA-493	Julianize	CD5	Japan	1993	$8.00
Columbia	ALDA-71	This Is the Joy	CD5	Japan	1993	$8.00

B.E.F.

Label	Catalog Number	Title	Type	Country	Year	Longbox Value / Value
		Singles				
Virgin	TENCD-369	Family Affair	CD5	U.K.	1991	$6.00
Toshiba	VJCP-14035	I Don't Know Why I Love You	CD3	Japan	1991	$7.00
Virgin	TENCD-378	I Don't Know Why I Love You	CD5	U.K.	1991	$6.00

B Factory

Label	Catalog Number	Title	Type	Country	Year	Longbox Value / Value
		Singles				
ZYX	DST-1050-8	People Of All Nations	CD5	Germany	1991	$5.00

B.G. Knoccout & Dresta

Label	Catalog Number	Title	Type	Country	Year	Longbox Value / Value
		Singles				
Polygram	579717	50-50	CD5	U.S.	1995	$5.00
Outburst	314 577 317	Jealousy	CD5	U.S.	1995	$5.00

B.G. Prince Of Rap

Label	Catalog Number	Title	Type	Country	Year	Longbox Value / Value
		Singles				
CBS	657413-5	Give Me the Music	CD5	Germany	1992	$7.00
CBS	657270-3	Rap To the World	CD3	Germany	1992	$7.00
CBS	657270-5	Rap To the World	CD5	Germany	1992	$7.00
CBS	657633-2	Take Control Of the Party	CD5	Germany	1992	$7.00
CBS	657633-5	Take Control Of the Party	CD5	U.K.	1992	$7.00
Epic		Take Control Of the Party	CDJ	U.S.	1991	$2.00
CBS	656585-2	This Beat Is Hot	CD5	Germany	1991	$7.00
Epic	ESK 73842	This Beat Is Hot	CDJ	U.S.	1991	$2.00

B, Heather

Label	Catalog Number	Title	Type	Country	Year	Longbox Value / Value
		Singles				
Capitol	58367	All Glocks Down	CD5	U.S.	1995	$5.00

B.J. Blade

Label	Catalog Number	Title	Type	Country	Year	Longbox Value / Value
		Singles				
ZYX	6355-8	Go Down Rock Yo Body	CD5	Germany	1990	$5.00

B, Jon

Label	Catalog Number	Title	Type	Country	Year	Longbox Value / Value
		Singles				
	BSK 7638	Isn't It Scary	CDJ	U.S.		$3.00
BSK	6838	Pretty Girl	CDJ	U.S.	1995	$2.00
Columbia	77895	Someone To Love	CD5	U.S.	1995	$6.00

B: Love

Label	Catalog Number	Title	Type	Country	Year	Longbox Value / Value
		Singles				
Delabel	DE 035147	Lucy	CD5	France	1992	$8.00

B.N.L.

Label	Catalog Number	Title	Type	Country	Year	Longbox Value / Value
		Singles				
ZYX	6755-8	Electric Salsa	CD5	Germany	1992	$5.00

B.O.X.

Label	Catalog Number	Title	Type	Country	Year	Longbox Value / Value
		Full Length				
Polygram	511375	Beyond Ordinary X-istance	LP/BP	U.S.		$14.00/$8.00
Capitol	CDP-94953	Pleasure And the Pain	LP/LB	U.S.		$14.00/$8.00
		Singles				
Capitol	DPRO-79652	Inside My Heart	CDJ	U.S.	1989	$2.00
Polygram	CDP537	Low Down	CDJ	U.S.	1991	$2.00
Polygram	CDP 617	Rock 'Dat	CDJ	U.S.	1991	$2.00
Capitol	DPRO-79353	Temptation	CDJ	U.S.	1989	$2.00

B.O.Y. El Silencio

Label	Catalog Number	Title	Type	Country	Year	Longbox Value / Value
		Singles				
EMI	204400-2	Because Of You	CD5	Germany	1991	$5.00

B.S.O.G.

Label	Catalog Number	Title	Type	Country	Year	Longbox Value / Value
		Singles				
BMG	PD-44008	Bow Wow Wow	CD5	Germany	1990	$5.00
BMG	PD-44008	Bow Wow Wow	CD5	U.K.	1990	$5.00

B, Sandy

Label	Catalog Number	Title	Type	Country	Year	Longbox Value / Value
		Singles				
Mercury	CDP 848	Feel Like Singin'	CDJ	U.S.	1993	$2.00

B.U.M.S.

Label	Catalog Number	Title	Type	Country	Year	Longbox Value / Value
		Singles				
Priority	53176	Elevation	CD5	U.S.	1994	$5.00

B-Art

Label	Catalog Number	Title	Type	Country	Year	Longbox Value / Value
		Singles				
Sony	654997-2	Streetwise	CD3	Germany	1989	$7.00

B-Code

Label	Catalog Number	Title	Type	Country	Year	Longbox Value / Value
		Singles				
		Feel Good	CDJ	U.S.		$3.00

B-Movie

Label	Catalog Number	Title	Type	Country	Year	Longbox Value / Value
		Singles				
SPV	8784-2	Polar Opposites	CD5	Germany	1991	$6.00

B-Positive

Singles

Label	Catalog Number	Title	Type	Country	Year	Longbox Value / Value
EMI	204399-2	Time Goes By	CD5	Germany	1991	$6.00

B-Tribe

Singles

Label	Catalog Number	Title	Type	Country	Year	Longbox Value / Value
EastWest	1197	Fiesta Fiesta	CD5	Germany		$10.00
Atlantic	85592	Nadie Entiende	CD5	U.S.	1994	$5.00
Atlantic		Nadie Entiende	CDJ	U.S.	1994	$2.00
Atlantic	PRCD 6312-2	Nanita	CDJ	U.S.	1994	$2.00
Alantic	85657-2	You Won't See Me Cry	CDJ	U.S.	1994	$7.00

B4

Singles

Label	Catalog Number	Title	Type	Country	Year	Longbox Value / Value
ZYX	6507-8	What I Am Feeling	CD5	Germany	1991	$5.00

Baad

Singles

Label	Catalog Number	Title	Type	Country	Year	Longbox Value / Value
LDC	ZADL-1009	Aishitai Aisenai	CD3	Japan	1993	$8.00/$2.00

Babayaga

Singles

Label	Catalog Number	Title	Type	Country	Year	Longbox Value / Value
BMG	FLEASC-2	Which Way	CD5	U.K.	1989	$5.00

Babble

Singles

Label	Catalog Number	Title	Type	Country	Year	Longbox Value / Value
Warner Brothers	9 41309-2	Take Me Away	CD5	U.S.	1994	$5.00
Warner Brothers	41309	Take Me Away	CD5	U.S.	1994	$5.00
Warner Brothers	PRO-CD-6476	Take Me Away	CDJ	U.S.	1994	$2.00
Warner Brothers	PRO-CD-6734	Take Me Away	CDJ	U.S.	1994	$2.00
Warner Brothers	PRO-CD-6842	Virtual Audio Words & Music	CDJ	U.S.	1994	$7.00

With Eye Covers

Babes And Beavis And Butthead In Toyland

Singles

Label	Catalog Number	Title	Type	Country	Year	Longbox Value / Value
Reprise	PRO-CD-6533-R	Bruise Violet	CDJ	U.S.	1993	$30.00

Babes In Toyland

Full Length

Label	Catalog Number	Title	Type	Country	Year	Longbox Value / Value
Reprise	PRO-CD-5838	Live At the Academy	DJ/Smplr	U.S.	1992	$12.00
Reprise	2-45339-A	Painkillers	DJ/Smplr	U.S.	1993	$15.00

Singles

Label	Catalog Number	Title	Type	Country	Year	Longbox Value / Value
Reprise	PRO-CD-5612	Bruise Violet	CDJ	U.S.	1992	$3.00
Reprise	PRO-CD-6533-R	Bruise Violet	CDJ	U.S.	1993	$20.00

With censored Beavis and Butthead over-dubs.

Label	Catalog Number	Title	Type	Country	Year	Longbox Value / Value
Reprise	PRO-CD-6272	He's My Thing	CDJ	U.S.	1993	$3.00
Warner Brothers	PRO-CD-7458	Sweet 69	CDJ	U.S.	1994	$3.00
Warner Brothers	17619	We Are Family	CD5	U.S.	1995	$5.00
Warner Brothers	PRO-CD-7642	We Are Family	CDJ	U.S.	1995	$7.00

Babie Love

Singles

Label	Catalog Number	Title	Type	Country	Year	Longbox Value / Value
BMG	663854	Shame, Shame, Shame	CD5	Germany	1991	$5.00

Babooska

Singles

Label	Catalog Number	Title	Type	Country	Year	Longbox Value / Value
Fieldworks	FWCR-39	Babooshka	CD3	Japan	1992	$8.00/$2.00

Baby Animals

Full Length

Label	Catalog Number	Title	Type	Country	Year	Longbox Value / Value
Imago	28004	Baby Animals	DJ/LP	U.S.	1991	$9.00

Singles

Label	Catalog Number	Title	Type	Country	Year	Longbox Value / Value
Imago	28057	Don't Me What To Do	CDJ	U.S.	1993	$3.00
BMG	PD-49156	Early Warning	CD5	U.K.	1991	$8.00
Imago	IM 28005	Early Warning	CDJ	U.S.	1991	$3.00
BMG	PD-49136	One Word	CD5	U.K.	1991	$8.00
Imago	IM 28018	One Word	CDJ	U.S.	1991	$2.00
Imago	IM 28023	One Word	CDJ	U.S.	1992	$2.00
BMG	PD-49118	Painless	CD5	U.K.	1991	$8.00
Imago	IM 28012	Painless	CDJ	U.S.	1991	$3.00
Imago	28073	Stoopid	CDJ	U.S.	1993	$3.00

Baby B

Singles

Label	Catalog Number	Title	Type	Country	Year	Longbox Value / Value
Profile	7410	Let Me Be Your Fantasy	CD5	U.S.	1994	$4.00

Baby Baby

Singles

Label	Catalog Number	Title	Type	Country	Year	Longbox Value / Value
Alfa	11B3-55	Day of Doom Doom	CD3	Japan	1989	$12.00/$3.00
Alfa	ALDB-99	Sex Successes	CD3	Japan	1989	$12.00/$3.00

Baby Chaos

Singles

Label	Catalog Number	Title	Type	Country	Year	Longbox Value / Value
EastWest	9320	Sperm	CDJ	U.S.	1995	$3.00

Baby D

Singles

Label	Catalog Number	Title	Type	Country	Year	Longbox Value / Value
Profile	7410	Let Me Be Your Fantasy	CD5	U.S.	1994	$5.00

Baby Ford

Full Length

Label	Catalog Number	Title	Type	Country	Year	Longbox Value / Value
Warner Brothers	9 26032	OOO	LP/LB	U.S.		$14.00/$8.00

Singles

Label	Catalog Number	Title	Type	Country	Year	Longbox Value / Value
Rough Trade	CD1-334	Beach Bump	CD5	Germany	1990	$8.00
Rough Trade	CD1-125	Beach Bump	CD5	Germany	1990	$8.00
Mute	BFORD 6CD	Beach Bump	CD5	U.K.	1989	$5.00
Pinnacle	BFORD-6CD	Beach Bump	CD5	U.K.	1990	$8.00
Warner Brothers	9 21440-2	Beach Bump	CD5	U.S.	1990	$4.00
Rough Trade	CD1-245	Chikki Chikki Ah Ah	CD5	Germany	1988	$8.00
Pinnacle	BFORD-4CD	Children Of the Revolution	CD5	U.K.	1989	$8.00
Warner Brothers	12-40449	Fetish	CD5	Canada	1992	$8.00
Rough Trade	251 1349 3	Fetish	CD5	Germany	1992	$8.00
Sire	9 40449-2	Fetish	CD5	U.S.	1992	$4.00
Sire	9 21557-2	Let's Talk It Over	CD5	U.S.	1990	$4.00
Warner Brothers	12-40622	Move On	CD5	Canada	1992	$8.00
Warner Brothers	9 40622-2	Move On	CD5	U.S.	1992	$4.00
Pinnacle	BFORD-1CD	Oochy Koochy	CD5	U.K.	1988	$8.00

Baby June

Singles

Label	Catalog Number	Title	Type	Country	Year	Longbox Value / Value
BMG	665271	Hey What's Your Name	CD5	U.K.	1992	$6.00

Babydol

Singles

Label	Catalog Number	Title	Type	Country	Year	Longbox Value / Value
Miracle	2060	I Want You Back	CD5	U.S.	1993	$4.00

Babyface

Full Length

Company	Disk Number	Title	Type	Country	Year	Longbox Value / Value
Pioneer	ID7577CB	Tender Lover The Videos	8"LD	U.S.	1990	$7.00

Singles

Company	Disk Number	Title	Type	Country	Year	Longbox Value / Value
Epic	ESK 77394	And Our Feelings	CDJ	U.S.	1994	$2.00
Epic	34K 77109	For the Cool	CD5	U.S.	1994	$5.00
Epic	ESK 5307	For the Cool	CDJ	U.S.	1994	$2.00
Epic	ESK 5345	For the Cool	CDJ	U.S.	1994	$2.00
Arista	BVDA-45	Give U My Heart	CD3	Japan	1992	$4.00
LaFace	4026	Give U My Heart	CDJ	U.S.	1992	$2.00
Intercord	826 016	It's No Crime	CD3	Germany	1989	$8.00
Intercord	825 016	It's No Crime	CD5	Germany	1989	$8.00
Victor	VDPS-1042	It's No Crime	CD3	Japan	1989	$2.00
		Mary Mack	CDJ	U.S.		$2.00
CBS	656494-3	My Kinda Girl	CD3	Germany	1990	$8.00
Sony	CSDS-8148	My Kinda Girl	CD3	Japan	1990	$13.00/$4.00
Epic	656494-2	My Kinda Girl	CD3	U.K.	1990	$8.00
Epic	ESK 2086	My Kinda Girl	CDJ	U.S.	1990	$2.00
Epic	XEUK11659817	Never Keeping Secrets	CD5	U.K.	1993	$8.00
Epic	ESK 77264	Never Keeping Secrets	CDJ	U.S.		$2.00
Epic	ESK 77217	Rock Bottom	CDJ	U.S.		$2.00
MCA	DMCAT-1389	Tender Lover	CD5	U.K.	1990	$8.00
Epic		Tender Lover	CDJ	U.S.	1990	$2.00
Epic	77550	When Can I See You	CD5	U.S.	1994	$5.00
Epic	ESK 6173	When Can I See You	CDJ	U.S.	1994	$3.00
Solar	74007	Whip Appeal	CDJ	U.S.	1990	$2.00

Babyface & Lisa S.

Singles

Company	Disk Number	Title	Type	Country	Year	Longbox Value / Value
Arista	10022	Dream Away	CD5	U.S.	1994	$5.00

Babylon A.D.

Singles

Company	Disk Number	Title	Type	Country	Year	Longbox Value / Value
Arista	ASCD 2421	Bad Blood	CDJ	U.S.	1992	$3.00
Arista	ASCD 9935	Bang Goes the Bells	CDJ	U.S.	1990	$2.00
Arista	ASCD 3067	Desperate	CDJ	U.S.	1990	$2.00
Arista	A10D-144	Hammer Swings Down	CD3	Japan	1989	$12.00/$4.00
		Hammer Swings Down	CDJ	U.S.	1990	$2.00
Arista	ASCD 2035	Kid Goes Wild, The	CDJ	U.S.	1990	$2.00
Arista	ASCD 2434	So Savage the Heart	CDJ	U.S.	1992	$2.00

Babylon Zoo

Singles

Company	Disk Number	Title	Type	Country	Year	Longbox Value / Value
		Spaceman	CDJ	U.S.		$6.00

Babys

Full Length

Company	Disk Number	Title	Type	Country	Year	Longbox Value / Value
Chrysalis	VK-41351	Anthology	LP/LB	U.S.		$15.00/$9.00
Chrysalis	VK-41129	Babys, The	LP/LB	U.S.		$15.00/$9.00
Chrysalis	VK-41150	Broken Heart	LP/LB	U.S.		$15.00/$9.00
Chrysalis	VK-41195	Head First	LP/LB	U.S.		$15.00/$9.00
Westwood One	VK-41305	On the Edge	LP/LB	U.S.		$15.00/$9.00
Chrysalis	VK-41267	Union Jacks	LP/LB	U.S.		$15.00/$9.00

Babys Breath

Singles

Company	Disk Number	Title	Type	Country	Year	Longbox Value / Value
Sony	SRDL-3407	Sun Goes Down	CD3	Japan	1991	$2.00

Babys Got A Gun

Singles

Company	Disk Number	Title	Type	Country	Year	Longbox Value / Value
No Mercy	NMBSICD	Take the Ride	CD5	U.K.	1990	$5.00

Baccara

Singles

Company	Disk Number	Title	Type	Country	Year	Longbox Value / Value
Teichiku	TEDP-3	Yes Sir I Can Boogie	CD3	Japan	1990	$4.00

Bach, Johnny

Singles

Company	Disk Number	Title	Type	Country	Year	Longbox Value / Value
EMI	203541-3	Buenas Noches	CD3	U.K.	1989	$5.00

Bacharach, Burt

Full Length

Company	Disk Number	Title	Type	Country	Year	Longbox Value / Value
A&M	D32Y-3053	A&M Gold Series	LP	Japan		$20.00
A&M	397072-2	A&M New Gold Series	LP	Germany		$18.00

Singles

Company	Disk Number	Title	Type	Country	Year	Longbox Value / Value
A&M	S12Y-3032	Raindrops Keep Fallin' On My	CD3	Japan	1988	$12.00/$4.00
A&M	CODA-522	With A Smile	CD3	Japan	1988	$12.00/$4.00

Bachman, Randy

Full Length

Company	Disk Number	Title	Type	Country	Year	Longbox Value / Value
	RBSK 1006	Plugged In	DJ/Smplr	Canada		$20.00

Bachman-Turner Overdrive

Full Length

Company	Disk Number	Title	Type	Country	Year	Longbox Value / Value
Mercury	838199-2	Freeways	LP/BP	U.S.		$15.00/$9.00
Album Network		In the Studio Bachman-Turner Overdrive	RS	U.S.		$30.00
Album Network		In the Studio (Not Fragile)	RS	U.S.	1989	$30.00

Airdate: 10/9/89

Singles

Company	Disk Number	Title	Type	Country	Year	Longbox Value / Value
EMI		You Ain't Seen Nothin' Yet	CDV	Japan	1990	$40.00
Polygram	888629-2	You Ain't Seen Nothing Yet	CD5	Germany	1990	$9.00

Back To Fun

Singles

Company	Disk Number	Title	Type	Country	Year	Longbox Value / Value
Polygram	872648-3	Back To Fun Medley	CD3	Germany	1989	$5.00
Polygram	872649-2	Back To Fun Medley	CD5	Germany	1989	$5.00
Polygram	873119-2	Loop Di Love	CD5	Germany	1989	$5.00

Back Up Crew

Singles

Company	Disk Number	Title	Type	Country	Year	Longbox Value / Value
ZYX	8814-8	Take that Ska	CD5	Germany	1990	$5.00

Backbeat (From Motion Picture Of Same Name)

Full Length

Company	Disk Number	Title	Type	Country	Year	Longbox Value / Value
Virgin	CDV DJ-2729	Backbeat	DJ/LP	U.K.	1994	$15.00

Digipak version.

Company	Disk Number	Title	Type	Country	Year	Longbox Value / Value
Virgin	CDVDJ 2729	Backbeat	DJ/LP	U.S.	1994	$15.00
Virgin		Backbeat Box	DJ/LP	U.S.	1994	$120.00

CD album with "Money" CDJ, VHS Video, Cassette, Pin, poster, drum sticks, 3 booklets

Singles

Company	Disk Number	Title	Type	Country	Year	Longbox Value / Value
Virgin	VSCDX 1489	Money	CD5	U.K.	1994	$10.00
Virgin	DPRO-14113	Money	CDJ	U.S.	1994	$7.00
Virgin	VSCDX 1502	Please Mr. Postman	CD5	U.K.	1994	$10.00
VIrgin	VSCDJ B1502	Please Mr. Postman	CDJ	U.K.	1994	$10.00
Virgin		Rock 'N' Roll Music	CD5	U.K.	1994	$10.00

Backstreet

Singles

Label	Catalog Number	Title	Type	Country	Year	Longbox Value/Value
Interscope	PRCD 5861-2	Before I Let You Go	CDJ	U.S.		$2.00
	PRCD 6121	Joy	CDJ	U.S.	1995	$3.00
Jive	JDJ423282	We've Got It Goin' On	CDJ	U.S.	1995	$3.00
Jive	42329-2	We've Got It Goin' On	CD5	U.S.	1996	$4.00

Bad 4 Good

Full Length

Label	Catalog Number	Title	Type	Country	Year	Longbox Value/Value
Interscope	92175-2	Refugee	LP/LB	U.S.		$14.00/$8.00

Singles

Label	Catalog Number	Title	Type	Country	Year	Longbox Value/Value
Atlantic	PRCD 4720-2	Nineteen	CDJ	U.S.		$2.00

Bad Boys Blue

Singles

Label	Catalog Number	Title	Type	Country	Year	Longbox Value/Value
Coconut	661	A World Without You	CD5	U.S.	1988	$4.00
BMG	664721	House Of Silence	CD5	Germany	1991	$8.00
BMG	664721	House Of Silence	CD5	U.K.	1991	$8.00
BMG	663098	How I Need You	CD5	Germany	1990	$8.00
BMG	661953	Hungry For Love	CD5	Germany	1989	$8.00
BMG	661983	Hungry For Love	CD5	Germany	1989	$8.00
BMG	664043	I Don't Know Her Name	CD5	Germany	1989	$8.00
Zoo	17126	I Totally Miss You	CDJ	U.S.	1993	$3.00
BMG	162510	Lady In Black	CD3	Germany	1989	$8.00
BMG	662510	Lady In Black	CD5	Germany	1989	$8.00
BMG	662902	Megamix	CD5	Germany	1989	$8.00
BMG	663654	Queen Of Hearts	CD5	Germany	1990	$8.00
BMG	665110	Save Your Love	CD5	Germany	1992	$8.00
Zoo	17109	Save Your Love	CDJ	U.S.	1992	$3.00
BMG	662766	Train To Knowhere	CD5	Germany	1989	$8.00

Bad Boys, Inc.

Singles

Label	Catalog Number	Title	Type	Country	Year	Longbox Value/Value
		Love Here I Come	CD5	U.K.		$10.00
		Love Here I Come	CD5	U.K.		$10.00
	Second version.					
		More To This World	CD5	U.K.	1993	$8.00
		More To This World	CD5	U.K.	1993	$8.00
	Second version.					
		Take Me Away	CD5	U.K.		$10.00
		Take Me Away	CD5	U.K.		$10.00
	Second version.					
		Walking On Air	CD5	U.K.	1993	$8.00
		Walking On Air	CD5	U.K.	1993	$8.00
	Second version.					

Bad Brains

Full Length

Label	Catalog Number	Title	Type	Country	Year	Longbox Value/Value
Maverick	45882-2-DJ	God Of Love	DJ/LP	U.S.	1995	$8.00

Singles

Label	Catalog Number	Title	Type	Country	Year	Longbox Value/Value
Warner Brothers	PRO-CD-7518	God Of Love	CDJ	U.S.	1995	$2.00
Maverick	PRO-CD-7556	God Of Love	CDJ	U.S.	1995	$2.00
Epic	ESK 5557	Hair	CDJ	U.S.	1993	$2.00
Warner Brothers	PRO-CD-7754-R	Just Keepers	CDJ	U.S.	1995	$2.00
Warner Brothers	PRO-CD-7718	Long Time	CDJ	U.S.	1995	$2.00
Epic	XEUK1166041	Love Is the Answer	CD5	Canada	1993	$9.00
Epic	ESK 5292	Rise	CDJ	U.S.	1993	$2.00

Bad Company

Full Length

Label	Catalog Number	Title	Type	Country	Year	Longbox Value/Value
Atlantic	8501-2	Bad Company	LP/LB	U.S.		$14.00/$8.00
	Non-remastered version.					
BBC Radio		BBC Classic Tracks	RS	U.S.	1991	$25.00
	Airdate: 4/14/92					
BBC Radio		BBC Classic Tracks	RS	U.S.	1991	$25.00
	Airdate: 5/27/91					
BBC Radio		BBC Classic Tracks	RS	U.S.	1992	$25.00
	Airdate: 1/4/92					
Westwood One		BBC Classic Tracks	RS	U.S.	1992	$20.00
	Airdate: 9/14/92					
BBC Radio		BBC Classic Tracks	RS	U.S.	1993	$15.00
	Airdate: 11/10/93					
Atlantic	8500-2	Burnin' Sky	LP/LB	U.S.		$14.00/$8.00
	Non-remastered version.					
Atlantic		Compilation	DJ/Smplr	Japan		N/A
Atlantic	8506-2	Desolation Angels	LP/LB	U.S.		$14.00/$8.00
	Non-remastered version.					
Album Network		In the Studio (Bad Company)	RS	U.S.	1990	$20.00
	Airdate: 7/30/90					
Album Network		In the Studio (Bad Company)	RS	U.S.	1994	$20.00
	Airdate: 6/13/94					
Album Network		In the Studio (Desolation Angel)	RS	U.S.		$20.00
Album Network		In the Studio (Strait Shooter)	RS	U.S.		$20.00
		Live At Electric Ladyland	RS	U.S.	1992	$110.00
	2 CD set. Airdate: 12/13/92					
Westwood One		Off the Record	RS	U.S.	1993	$30.00
	Airdate: 2/1/93					
Westwood One		Off the Record	RS	U.S.	1993	$30.00
	Airdate: 5/31/93					
Westwood One		Off the Record	RS	U.S.	1995	$20.00
	Airdate: 10/16/95					
Westwood One		Off the Record	RS	U.S.	1995	$20.00
	Airdate: 6/26/95					
Radio Today		Rock Stars	RS	U.S.		$65.00
	2 CD set.					
Atlantic	90001-2	Rough Diamonds	LP/LB	U.S.		$14.00/$8.00
	Non-remastered version.					
Westwood One		Superstars	RS	U.S.	1996	$75.00
	2 CD set. Airdate 7/1/96.					
Atlantic	781625-2	Ten From Six	LP	Germany		$18.00
Media America		Up Close	RS	U.S.	1991	$40.00
	2 CD set.					
Media America		Up Close	RS	U.S.	1992	$40.00
	2 CD set.					
Media America		Up Close	RS	U.S.	1995	$50.00
	2 CD set.					

Singles

Label	Catalog Number	Title	Type	Country	Year	Longbox Value/Value
Atlantic	PRCD-92642-2	Abandoned And Alone	CDJ	U.S.	1995	$6.00
Atlantic	PRCD 3487-2	Boys Cry Tough	CDJ	U.S.	1990	$2.00
WEA	A-7954CD	Can't Get Enough	CD3	Japan	1991	$7.00/$2.00
MMG	AMCY-95	Can't Get Enough	CD5	Japan	1991	$25.00
Atlantic	PRCD 9190-2	Down & Dirty	CDJ	U.S.	1995	$3.00
MMG	AMCY-96	Feel Like Makin' Love	CD5	Japan	1990	$15.00
MMG	AMCY-96	Feel Like Makin' Love	CD5	Japan	1991	$25.00
Atlantic	PRCD 9361-2	Gimmie Gimmie	CDJ	U.S.	1995	$3.00
Atlantic	AMDY-5022	Holy Water	CD3	Japan	1990	$12.00/$4.00
Atlantic	PRCD 3316-2	Holy Water	CDJ	U.S.	1990	$2.00
Warner Brothers	32-96141	How About That	CD5	Canada	1992	$8.00
Atco	96141-2	How About That	CD5	U.S.	1992	$6.00/$4.00
Atco	PRCD 4699-2	How About That	CDJ	U.S.	1992	$3.00
Atco	PRCD 3488-2	If You Needed Somebody	CDJ	U.S.	1990	$3.00
Atlantic	7567-96368-2	If You Needed Somebody	CD5	U.S.	1991	$5.00
Atlantic	PRCD 5032	Little Angel	CDJ	U.S.	1993	$3.00
Atlantic	PR 2515-2	No Smoke Without Fire	CDJ	U.S.	1988	$3.00
Atlantic		No Smoke Without Fire	CDJ	U.S.	1988	$3.00
Atco	PRCD 5322-2	Ready For Love	CDJ	U.S.	1993	$3.00
Atlantic	PR 2626-2	Shake It Up	CDJ	U.S.	1988	$3.00
Atco	PRCD 3760-2	Stranger Stranger	CDJ	U.S.	1990	$3.00
Atco	98463-2	This Could Be the One	CD5	U.S.	1992	$4.00
Atco	PRCD 4836-2	This Could Be the One	CDJ	U.S.	1992	$3.00
Atco	PRCD 4053-2	Walk Through Fire	CDJ	U.S.	1991	$3.00
		You're the Only Reason	CDJ	U.S.		$3.00

Bad Dream Fancy Dress

Singles

Label	Catalog Number	Title	Type	Country	Year	Longbox Value/Value
El	25604-12	Supremes	CD3	Japan	1989	$13.00/$4.00

Bad English

Full Length

Label	Catalog Number	Title	Type	Country	Year	Longbox Value/Value
Image	ID7622CB	Bad English	LD	U.S.		$15.00
		Greatest Hits	LTD/LP	U.S.	1995	$30.00
	2CD set.					

Singles

Label	Catalog Number	Title	Type	Country	Year	Longbox Value/Value
Epic		Best Of What I Got	CDJ	U.S.	1989	$2.00
Epic	656113-2	Don't Walk Away	CD5	U.K.	1990	$7.00
Epic	108P-3080	Forget Me Not	CD3	Japan	1989	$13.00/$4.00
CBS	655089-2	Forget Me Not	CD5	U.K.	1989	$5.00
Epic		Forget Me Not	CDJ	U.S.	1989	$2.00
Epic		Heaven Is A Four Letter Word	CDJ	U.S.	1989	$2.00
Epic	ESDA-7042	Possession	CD3	Japan	1990	$13.00/$4.00
Epic	ESK 73398	Possession	CDJ	U.S.	1989	$2.00
Epic	655676-3	Price Of Love	CD5	Germany	1989	$7.00
Epic	ESDA-7023	Price Of Love	CD3	Japan	1989	$13.00/$4.00
Epic	655676-2	Price Of Love	CD5	U.K.	1989	$7.00
Epic	ESK 73094	Price Of Love	CDJ	U.S.	1989	$2.00
Epic		Price Of Love	CDJ	U.S.	1989	$2.00
	Second version.					
Epic	ESK 4269	So This Is Eden	CDJ	U.S.	1991	$2.00
Epic	657420-9	Straight To Your Heart	CD5	U.K.	1991	$6.00
Epic	ESK 73982	Straight To Your Heart	CDJ	U.S.	1991	$2.00
Epic	ESK 74091	Time Alone With You, The	CDJ	U.S.	1991	$2.00
CBS	655347-3	When I See You Smile	CD3	Germany	1989	$6.00
Epic	ESDA-7010	When I See You Smile	CD3	Japan	1989	$12.00/$4.00
CBS	655347-2	When I See You Smile	CD5	U.K.	1989	$6.00
Epic		When I See You Smile	CDJ	U.S.	1989	$2.00

Bad Examples

Singles

Label	Catalog Number	Title	Type	Country	Year	Longbox Value/Value
Jews	5544	Ashes Of My Heart	CD5	Germany	1992	$8.00

Bad Manners

Full Length

Label	Catalog Number	Title	Type	Country	Year	Longbox Value/Value
Relativity	1017	Return Of the Ugly	LP/LB	U.S.		$14.00/$8.00

Bad Messiah

Singles

Label	Catalog Number	Title	Type	Country	Year	Longbox Value/Value
Epic	ESDB-3372	Ai No Okite	CD3	Japan	1993	$13.00/$4.00
Epic	ESDB-3255	Clover	CD3	Japan	1991	$13.00/$4.00
Epic	ESDB-3386	Egoist	CD3	Japan	1993	$13.00/$4.00
Epic	ESDB-3302	Sorya Naize Senorita	CD3	Japan	1992	$13.00/$4.00

Bad Moon Rising

Singles

Label	Catalog Number	Title	Type	Country	Year	Longbox Value/Value
Canyon	PCCY-00425	Blood On the Streets	CD5	Japan	1993	$6.00
Canyon	PCCY-00203	Full Moon Fever	CD5	Japan	1991	$6.00

Bad Mutha Goose And The Brothers Grimm

Singles

Label	Catalog Number	Title	Type	Country	Year	Longbox Value/Value
Alpha	73016	Be Somebody	CD5	U.S.	1991	$4.00

Bad News

Full Length

Label	Catalog Number	Title	Type	Country	Year	Longbox Value/Value
EMI	748310-2	Bad News	LP	Germany		$15.00
EMI	CDEMC-3535	Bad News	LP	U.K.		$15.00
EMI	EMC-3542	Bootleg	LP	U.K.		$15.00

Bad Religion

Full Length

Label	Catalog Number	Title	Type	Country	Year	Longbox Value/Value
Atlantic		Selections From Stranger Than Fiction	DJ/Smplr	U.S.	1994	$7.00

Singles

Label	Catalog Number	Title	Type	Country	Year	Longbox Value/Value
Atlantic	PRCD 5894	21st Century	CDJ	U.S.	1995	$3.00
Atlantic	PRCD 6625-2	A Walk	CDJ	U.S.		$3.00
Atlantic	PRCD-5475-2	American Jesus	CDJ	U.S.	1993	$2.00
Atlantic		Complete	CDJ	U.S.	1995	$6.00
Atlantic		Incomplete	CDJ	U.S.	1995	$3.00
		Infected	CD5	U.K.	1995	$10.00
		Infected	CD5	U.K.	1995	$10.00
	Second version.					
Atlantic	PRCD 5951	Infected	CDJ	U.S.	1995	$3.00
Atlantic	PRCD 6015	Infected	CDJ	U.S.	1995	$6.00
	Second version.					
Atlantic	PRCD-5371-2	Lookin' In	CDJ	U.S.	1993	$2.00
Atlantic	PRCD 6747-2	Punk Rock Song	CDJ	U.S.	1995	$3.00
Atlantic	PRCD 5775	Stranger Than Fiction	CDJ	U.S.	1994	$6.00
Atlantic	PRCD-5277-2	Struck A Nerve	CDJ	U.S.	1993	$2.00

Bad Romance

Full Length

Label	Catalog Number	Title	Type	Country	Year	Longbox Value/Value
Polydor	842746	Code Of Honor	LP/BP	U.S.		$14.00/$8.00

Singles

Label	Catalog Number	Title	Type	Country	Year	Longbox Value/Value
Polydor	CDP 418	House Of My Father, The	CDJ	U.S.	1991	$2.00

Badarou, Wally

Singles

Label	Catalog Number	Title	Type	Country	Year	Longbox Value/Value
Polygram	BRCD-213	Chif Inspector	CD5	U.K.	1991	$6.00
Island	Brw 53	Hi Life	CDV	Germany	1988	$35.00
Island/NTSC	BRW 53	Hi Life	DJ/CDV	U.S.	1988	$15.00

Badd Boyz of the Industry

Singles

Label	Catalog Number	Title	Type	Country	Year	Longbox Value/Value
A&M	31458 8126	One Night Of Freedom	CDJ	U.S.	1993	$2.00
A&M	31458 8186	Where Will You Go	CDJ	U.S.	1993	$2.00

Label	Catalog Number	Title	Type	Country	Year	Longbox Value / Value

Badfinger

Label	Catalog Number	Title	Type	Country	Year	Longbox Value / Value
Full Length						
		Ass	LP	Japan		$75.00
Rykodisc	RCD PRO 9008	Live: Three From Day After Day	DJ/Smplr	U.S.	1990	$20.00
Demon	PEDCD-302	Shine On	LTD/LP	U.K.		$45.00
Picture disc CD.						
Rykodisc		Three From Day After Day	DJ/Smplr	U.S.		$20.00
Singles						
EMI	204652-2	Come And Get It	CD5	Holland	1992	$12.00
EMI	PIFP-1008	Come And Get It	CDV	Japan	1990	$40.00
EMI	TODP-2406	Without You	CD3	Japan	1993	$13.00/$4.00

Badlands

Label	Catalog Number	Title	Type	Country	Year	Longbox Value / Value
Full Length						
Atlantic	7 81966-2	Badlands	LP/LB	U.S.		$14.00/$8.00
Atlantic	7 82251-2	Voodoo Highway	LP/LB	U.S.		$14.00/$8.00
Singles						
Atlantic	PR 2734-2	Dreams In the Dark	CDJ	U.S.	1989	$2.00
Titanium	3992	Joe's Blues	CDJ	U.S.	1991	$2.00
		Last Time, The	CDJ	U.S.		$2.00
Warner Brothers	AMDY-5061	Time Goes By	CD3	Japan	1991	$13.00/$4.00
Atlantic	PRCD 4145-2	Whiskey Dust	CDJ	U.S.	1991	$2.00
Atlantic	PR 2954-2	Winters Call	CDJ	U.S.	1989	$2.00

Badlees

Label	Catalog Number	Title	Type	Country	Year	Longbox Value / Value
Singles						
	ATCD00085	Angeline Is Coming Home	CDJ	U.S.		$3.00
	ATCDP00087	Fear Of Falling	CDJ	U.S.	1995	$2.00

Badman

Label	Catalog Number	Title	Type	Country	Year	Longbox Value / Value
Singles						
SPV	1013-3	Magic Style	CD5	Germany	1990	$6.00
WEA	CBE-759CD	Magic Style	CD5	U.K.	1990	$6.00

Badu, Erykah

Label	Catalog Number	Title	Type	Country	Year	Longbox Value / Value
Singles						
	56002-2	On & On	CD5	U.S.	1996	$4.00

Baerwald, David

Label	Catalog Number	Title	Type	Country	Year	Longbox Value / Value
Full Length						
A&M	31454	Baerwald On Triage	DJ/Smplr	U.S.	1993	$10.00
A&M	PCCY-10130	Bedtime Stories	LP	Japan		$20.00
Custom Book-like box with cassette & Book.						
A&M	75021 5289 2	Bedtime Stories	DJ/LP	U.S.	1990	$18.00
A&M	75021 5289 2	Bedtime Stories	LP/LB	U.S.	1990	$14.00/$8.00
A&M		Introduces Bedtime Stories	DJ/LP	U.S.	1990	$10.00
A&M	75021 5392	Triage	LP/LB	U.S.	1993	$18.00
CD in "file" package.						
Singles						
A&M	CD-18028	All For You	CDJ	U.S.	1990	$2.00
A&M	31458 8049	Brand New Morning	CDJ	U.S.	1992	$2.00
A&M	75021 8104-2	Dance	CDJ	U.S	1990	$2.00
A&M	75021 8086 2	Good Times	CDJ	U.S.	1990	$2.00
A&M	31458 8041	Got No Shotgun Hydrahead Octopus Blues	CDJ	U.S.	1992	$2.00

Baez, Joan

Label	Catalog Number	Title	Type	Country	Year	Longbox Value / Value
Full Length						
Vanguard	VCD-41	Ballad Book	LP	U.S.		$8.00
Guardian	DPRO 7807	Columbia Records Radio Hour	DJ/Smplr	U.S.		$20.00
Goldcastle	71321	Diamonds & Rust	LP	U.S.		$8.00
Polygram	811677-2	Greatest Hits	LP	Germany		$15.00
Vangaurd	811 677-2	Greatest Hits	LP/BP	U.S.†	1984	$15.00/$9.00
Polygram	394603-2	Gulf Wind	LP	Germany		$25.00
Vangaurd		Rare, Live & Classic	DJ/Smplr	U.S.	1993	$20.00
Vangaurd		Rare, Live & Classic	LTD/LP	U.S.	1993	$55.00
3 CD set. Autographed edition version. Limited to 300 copies.						
Goldcastle	71304-2	Recently	LP	U.S.		$8.00
Singles						
		Stones In the Road	CDJ	U.S.		$2.00

Baez, Tony

Label	Catalog Number	Title	Type	Country	Year	Longbox Value / Value
Singles						
WEA	9031-73103-2	Happy	CD5	Germany	1990	$7.00
WEA	171496-2	Nationwide Television	CD5	Germany	1990	$7.00
WEA	9031-72287-2	Perfect World	CD5	Germany	1990	$7.00
WEA	246913-2	Tell Me Why	CD5	Germany	1989	$7.00
WEA	YZ-425CD	Tell Me Why	CD5	Germany	1989	$7.00

Baha Men

Label	Catalog Number	Title	Type	Country	Year	Longbox Value / Value
Singles						
WEA	A-8500CD	Back To the Island	CD5	U.K.	1992	$6.00
Big Beat	4679	Back To the Island	CDJ	U.S.	1992	$2.00
Big Beat	4145	Dancing In the Moonlight	CDJ	U.S.	1994	$3.00

Bailey, Pearl

Label	Catalog Number	Title	Type	Country	Year	Longbox Value / Value
Full Length						
Roulette	SRS9050	Best Of...	LP	U.S.		$10.00

Bailey, Philip

Label	Catalog Number	Title	Type	Country	Year	Longbox Value / Value
Full Length						
Columbia	CK-39542	Chinese Wall	LP/BP	U.S.†	1985	$15.00/$9.00
Columbia	CK-40209	Inside Out	LP/LB	U.S.		$15.00/$9.00
A&M	CD-0754	Triumph	LP/LB	U.S.		$15.00/$9.00
Myrrh	679627-2	Wonders Of Love	LP/LB	U.S.		$15.00/$9.00
Singles						
Zoo	72445-14143	Here With Me	CDJ	U.S.	1994	$3.00
Sony	SRDL-3289	Mid-Summer Blossoms	CD3	Japan	1991	$13.00/$4.00
Epic	654519-3	Twins	CD3	Germany	1989	$3.00
Epic	654519-2	Twins	CD5	Germany	1989	$3.00

Bailter Space

Label	Catalog Number	Title	Type	Country	Year	Longbox Value / Value
Singles						
Matador	41	Aim	CD5	U.S.	1992	$5.00

Band Aid

Label	Catalog Number	Title	Type	Country	Year	Longbox Value / Value
Singles						
Mercury	PHDR-902	Do They Know It's Christmas	CD3	Japan	1992	$13.00/$4.00

Baird, Dan

Label	Catalog Number	Title	Type	Country	Year	Longbox Value / Value
Full Length						
Westwood One		Off the Record	RS	U.S.	1993	$30.00
Airdate: 3/15/93						
Singles						
Polygram	DEFCD-22	I Love You Period	CD5	U.K.	1992	$5.00
Def American	PRO-CD-5661	I Love You Period	CDJ	U.S.	1992	$2.00
Def American	PRO-CD-6142	Look At What You Started	CDJ	U.S.	1993	$2.00
Def American	PRO-CD-6136	Look At What You Started	CDJ	U.S.	1993	$2.00

Bakala

Company	Disk Number	Title	Type	Country	Year	Longbox Value / Value
Singles						
Victor	VDPS-1027	Fantasy Boy	CD3	Japan	1989	$12.00/$3.00

Baker, Anita

Company	Disk Number	Title	Type	Country	Year	Longbox Value / Value
Full Length						
Elektra	60979-2	Compositions	DJ/LP	U.S.	1990	$25.00
2CD set in clothbound book.						
Elektra	60979-2	Compositions	LTD/LP	U.S.	1990	N/A
2 screen printed CD set in clothbound book.						
Pioneer	43P2-0014	Giving You the Best That I've Got	LTD/LP	Japan	1988	$40.00
Gold disc.						
Pioneer	43XD-2004	Rapture	LTD/LP	Japan		$40.00
Gold disc.						
WEA	40105	Rapture	LD	U.S.	1990	$30.00
Elektra	PRCD 9019-2	Retrospective	DJ/Smplr	U.S.	1994	$20.00
		Rhythm Of Love	DJ/LP	U.S.		$20.00
CD in slipcase.						
Singles						
Elektra	PRCD 9008	Body & Soul	CDJ	U.S.	1994	$7.00
Elektra	PR 8277-2	Fairy Tales	CDJ	U.S.	1990	$3.00
Elektra	969367-2	Giving You the Best That I've Got	CD5	Germany	1988	$6.00
Elektra	10P3-6031	Giving You the Best That I've Got	CD3	Japan	1988	$13.00/$4.00
Elektra	EKR-79CD	Giving You the Best That I've Got	CD5	U.K.	1988	$7.00
Elektra	PR 8027-2	Giving You the Best That I've Got	CDJ	U.S.	1988	$3.00
Elektra/Asylum	64497	I Apologize	CD5	U.S.	1994	$5.00
Elektra	PRCD 9069-2	I Apologize	CDJ	U.S.	1995	$3.00
Elektra	PRCD 9147	I Apologize	CDJ	U.S.	1995	$7.00
Elektra	PRCD 9148	It's Been You	CDJ	U.S.	1995	$7.00
Elektra	10P3-6088	Just Because	CD3	Japan	1988	$13.00/$4.00
Elektra	EKR 87CD	Just Because	CD3	U.K.	1988	$9.00
Elektra	PR 8046-2	Just Because	CDJ	U.S.	1988	$3.00
Elektra	09P3-6127	Lead Me Into Love	CD3	Japan	1988	$13.00/$4.00
Elektra	PR 8076-2	Lead Me Into Love	CDJ	U.S.	1988	$2.00
Elektra	PR 8215-2	Soul Inspiration	CDJ	U.S.	1990	$2.00
Elektra	64001-2	Sweet Love	CDV/BP	U.S.	1988	$20.00/$20.00
Elektra	966632-2	Talk To Me	CD5	Germany	1990	$9.00
Elektra	WPDP-6230	Talk To Me	CD3	Japan	1990	$13.00/$4.00
Elektra	EKR-111CD	Talk To Me	CD5	U.K.	1990	$9.00
Elektra	PR 8172-2	Talk To Me	CDJ	U.S.	1990	$3.00
Elektra	PRCD 9221	When You Love Someone	CDJ	U.S.	1995	$7.00

Baker, Arthur

Company	Disk Number	Title	Type	Country	Year	Longbox Value / Value
Full Length						
RCA	CD-61009	Give In To Rhythm	LP/BP	U.S.		$12.00/$7.00
A&M	CD-5262	Merge	LP/LB	U.S.		$12.00/$7.00
Singles						
A&M	CD-17848	2x1	CDJ	U.S.	1989	$3.00
A&M	390463-2	And the Backbeat Disciples	CD5	Germany	1989	$8.00
RCA	62207	IOU	CDJ	U.S.	1992	$2.00
A&M	PCDY-10004	It's Your Time	CD3	Japan	1989	$4.00
A&M	USACD-654	It's Your Time	CD3	U.K.	1989	$8.00
A&M	390494-2	Last Thing On My Mind	CD5	Germany	1990	$8.00
RCA	62073-2-RDJ	Leave the Guns At Home	CDJ	U.S.	1991	$2.00
RCA	62120-2-RDJ	Leave the Guns At Home	CDJ	U.S.	1991	$2.00
A&M	664421	Let There Be Love	CD5	Germany	1990	$8.00
RCA	62035-2-RDJ	Let There Be Love	CDJ	U.S.	1991	$2.00
A&M	US ACD 668	Message Is Love, The	CD5	U.K.	1989	$8.00
A&M	CD-17938	Message Is Love, The	CDJ	U.S.	1989	$3.00
A&M	CD 17890	Mythical Girl	CDJ	U.S.	1989	$3.00
A&M	USACD-655	Talk It Over	CD3	U.K.	1989	$8.00

Baker, Chet

Company	Disk Number	Title	Type	Country	Year	Longbox Value / Value
Full Length						
Blue Note	B2-92932-2	Best Of	LP/LB	U.S.		$16.00/$10.00
A&M	CD-0832	Best Thing For You	LP/LB	U.S.		$14.00/$8.00
IRS	971 946	Candy	LP	Germany		$25.00
Toshiba	CP32-5353	Chet Baker Big Band	LP	Japan		$30.00
Emarcy	837476	Chet In Paris Vol. 3	LP	U.S.		$10.00
Emarcy	837477	Chet In Paris Vol. 4	LP	U.S.		$10.00
Mosaic	MD3-113	Complete Pacific Jazz Live Recordings Of Chet Baker Quartet With Russ Freeman	LP	U.S.		$45.00
3 CD Set						
Mosaic	MD3-122	Complete Pacific Jazz Studio Recordings	LP	U.S.		$45.00
3 CD limited to 7500 copies						
Steeple'se	SCCD-31142	Daybreak	LP	Germany		$25.00
Enja	79600	Last Concert 1	LP	U.S.		$10.00
Enja	79624	Last Concert 2	LP	U.S.		$10.00
Steeple'se	SCCD-31163	No Problem	LP	U.S.		$10.00
Steeple'se	SCCD-31168	This Is Always	LP	Germany		$25.00
Steeple'se	SCCD-31122	Touch Of Your Lips	LP	U.S.		$10.00
A&M	CD-0805	You Can't Go Home Again	LP/LB	U.S.		$14.00/$8.00
Singles						
Alfa	10R3-5	Everything Happens To Me	CD3	Japan	1988	$13.00/$4.00

Baker, George

Company	Disk Number	Title	Type	Country	Year	Longbox Value / Value
Singles						
Polygram	887817-2	Dreamboat	CD5	Germany	1988	$7.00

Baker, Ginger

Company	Disk Number	Title	Type	Country	Year	Longbox Value / Value
Full Length						
Polygram	837 349-2	Ginger Baker's Airforce	LP/BP	U.S.		$15.00/$15.00
		Horse & Trees	LP	Germany		$15.00

Bakers Pink

Company	Disk Number	Title	Type	Country	Year	Longbox Value / Value
Singles						
Epic	ESK 4944	Watercolours	CDJ	U.S.	1993	$2.00

Balaam & The Angel

Company	Disk Number	Title	Type	Country	Year	Longbox Value / Value
Full Length						
Atlantic	7 91287-2	Balaam & The Angel	LP/LB	U.S.		$14.00/$8.00
Atlantic	7 90869-2	Live Free Or Die	LP/LB	U.S.		$14.00/$8.00
Singles						
Virgin	VSCD-1213	I Took A Little	CD5	U.K.	1989	$7.00
Virgin	PR 2963	I Took A Little	CDJ	U.S.	1989	$2.00
Virgin	VSCD-1229	Little Bit Of Love	CD5	U.K.	1990	$2.00
Virgin	PR 3264	Little Bit Of Love	CDJ	U.S.	1989	$2.00
Virgin	1229	Little Bit Of Love	CD3	U.S.	1990	$6.00/$3.00

Balanx

Company	Disk Number	Title	Type	Country	Year	Longbox Value / Value
Full Length						
Ariola	258438	Balanx One	LP	Germany		$15.00

Baldwin And The Whiffles

Company	Disk Number	Title	Type	Country	Year	Longbox Value / Value
Singles						
NCA	17801	Please Mr. Jailor	CDJ	U.S.	1990	$2.00

Label	Catalog Number	Title	Type	Country	Year	Longbox Value / Value

Baldwin, Bob

Singles

Label	Catalog Number	Title	Type	Country	Year	Longbox Value / Value
Atlantic	PR 3105-2	On Our Own	CDJ	U.S.	1990	$2.00

Bali

Singles

Label	Catalog Number	Title	Type	Country	Year	Longbox Value / Value
Virgin	162179	Love To Love	CD3	Germany	1989	$7.00

Balkana

Full Length

Label	Catalog Number	Title	Type	Country	Year	Longbox Value / Value
Atlantic	7 91368-2	Mysterious Voices Of Bulgaria	LP/LB	U.S.		$10.00/$6.00

Ball

Singles

Label	Catalog Number	Title	Type	Country	Year	Longbox Value / Value
Polygram	RURCD-6	First Man You Remember	CD5	U.K.	1989	$6.00
Polygram	PZCD-248	If I Can Dream	CD5	U.K.	1992	$6.00
Polygram	871513-2	It's Still You	CD5	Germany	1991	$6.00
Polygram	PZCD-160	It's Still You	CD5	U.K.	1991	$6.00
Polygram	RURCD-3	It's Still You	CD5	U.K.	1991	$6.00
Polygram	PZCD-206	One Step out Of Time	CD5	U.K.	1992	$6.00

Ball, David

Full Length

Label	Catalog Number	Title	Type	Country	Year	Longbox Value / Value
		Road, The	RS	U.S.	1995	$40.00

2 CD set. Airdate: 2/29/95

Label	Catalog Number	Title	Type	Country	Year	Longbox Value / Value
Warner Brothers	PRO-CD-6706	Thinkin' Problem	DJ/Smplr	U.S.	1993	$5.00

Singles

Label	Catalog Number	Title	Type	Country	Year	Longbox Value / Value
Warner Brothers	PRO-CD-8175-R	Circle Of Friends	CDJ	U.S.	1996	$3.00

Ball, Marcia

Full Length

Label	Catalog Number	Title	Type	Country	Year	Longbox Value / Value
Rounder	PR 1026	A Promotional Interview Disc	DJ/Intvw	U.S.	1994	$12.00

Singles

Label	Catalog Number	Title	Type	Country	Year	Longbox Value / Value
Rounder	1025	Hed Beans	CDJ	U.S.	1994	$2.00

Ball, Michael

Singles

Label	Catalog Number	Title	Type	Country	Year	Longbox Value / Value
		From Here To Eternity	CD5	U.K.		$10.00
		From Here To Eternity	CD5	U.K.		$10.00

Second version.

Label	Catalog Number	Title	Type	Country	Year	Longbox Value / Value
		Lovers We Were	CD5	U.K.		$10.00
		Lovers We Were	CD5	U.K.		$10.00

Second version.

Label	Catalog Number	Title	Type	Country	Year	Longbox Value / Value
		Rose	CD5	U.K.		$10.00
		Rose	CD5	U.K.		$10.00

Second version.

Ball, Patrick

Full Length

Label	Catalog Number	Title	Type	Country	Year	Longbox Value / Value
Fortuna	17005	Music Of Turlough O'Carolan	LP	U.S.		$6.00
Fortuna	17029	Secret isles	LP	U.S.		$6.00

Ballard, Hank

Full Length

Label	Catalog Number	Title	Type	Country	Year	Longbox Value / Value
King	KCD-950	24 Hits Tunes	LP	U.S.		$8.00
King	KCD-541	Greatest Jukebox Hits	LP	U.S.		$8.00
King	KCD-581	Hank Ballard	LP	U.S.		$8.00
Charly	CDCHARLY-88	Live at the Palias	LP	U.S.		$8.00
King	KCD-700	Mr. Rhythm & Blues	LP	U.S.		$8.00
King	KCD-674	One And Only	LP	U.S.		$8.00
King	KCD-618	Singin' & Swingin'	LP	U.S.		$8.00
Charly	CDCHARLY-29	What You Get When the Getting Gets Good	LP	U.S.		$8.00

Ballday, David

Singles

Label	Catalog Number	Title	Type	Country	Year	Longbox Value / Value
Polygram	878189-2	Tear Of the Earth	CD5	Germany	1991	$6.00

Balloon

Singles

Label	Catalog Number	Title	Type	Country	Year	Longbox Value / Value
Balloon	001	Now That the Thrill's Gone	CDJ	U.S.	1992	$2.00
Balloon	BAL 001	Now That the Thrill's Gone	CDJ	U.S.	1992	$2.00
Pinnacle	HENRY-002CD	Tightrope Walker	CD5	U.K.	1991	$6.00

Bam Bam Musique

Singles

Label	Catalog Number	Title	Type	Country	Year	Longbox Value / Value
Splish	SPLISH-4CD	Milk Of Magnesia	CD5	U.K.	1992	$6.00

Bama Band

Full Length

Label	Catalog Number	Title	Type	Country	Year	Longbox Value / Value
Capitol	CDP-9353-2	Takin' Off the Edge	LP/LB	U.S.		$14.00/$8.00

Bambi Slam

Full Length

Label	Catalog Number	Title	Type	Country	Year	Longbox Value / Value
Warner Brothers	9 25852-2	Bambi Slam	LP/LB	U.S.		$6.00

Bamboo Industries

Singles

Label	Catalog Number	Title	Type	Country	Year	Longbox Value / Value
BMG	663128	Catherine Wheel	CD5	Germany	1990	$7.00
BMG	663657	Shake Hands With the Devil	CD5	Germany	1990	$7.00

Bambula

Singles

Label	Catalog Number	Title	Type	Country	Year	Longbox Value / Value
Polygram	867163-2	Lolo Lele	CD5	Grermany	1991	$7.00

Banana Fred

Full Length

Label	Catalog Number	Title	Type	Country	Year	Longbox Value / Value
Polygram	835632-2	Banana Fred	LP	Germany		$15.00
Polygram	887770-2	Stars From Above	CD5	Germany	1988	$7.00

Bananarama

Full Length

Label	Catalog Number	Title	Type	Country	Year	Longbox Value / Value
		12" Mixes	LP	Australia	1990	$35.00
London	820036-2	Bananarama	LP/LB	U.S.†	1984	$14.00/$8.00
London	820036-2	Bananarama	LP/LB	U.S.	1988	$14.00/$8.00
London	810107-2	Deep Sea Diving	LP/LB	U.S.		$14.00/$8.00
Polygram	080631-1	Greatest Hits Collection	LD	U.S.	1986	$25.00
London	828127-2	Greatest Hits Collection	LP/LB	U.S.	1986	$14.00/$8.00
London		Pop Life	LTD/LP	Japan		$35.00

With bandana.

Label	Catalog Number	Title	Type	Country	Year	Longbox Value / Value
London	828013-2	True Confessions	LP/LB	U.S.		$14.00/$8.00
London	828061-2	Wow	LP/LB	U.S.		$14.00/$8.00

Singles

Label	Catalog Number	Title	Type	Country	Year	Longbox Value / Value
London	886630-2	Cruel Summer	CD5	Germany	1989	$6.00
London	8866301-2	Cruel Summer	CD5	Germany	1989	$6.00
London	POOL-37016	Cruel Summer	CD3	Japan	1989	$12.00/$4.00
London	NACD-19	Cruel Summer	CD5	U.K.	1989	$6.00
London	NANCD-19	Cruel Summer	CD5	U.K.	1989	$6.00
ZYX	7810	Every Shade Of Blue	CD5	Germany	1995	$10.00
Curb	1203	Every Shade Of Blue	CDJ	U.S.		$3.00
London	886598-3	Help	CD5	Germany	1989	$6.00
London	P10L-37013	Help	CD3	Japan	1989	$12.00/$4.00
London	POOL-40008	Help	CD3	Japan	1989	$12.00/$4.00
London	LONCD-222	Help	CD5	U.K.	1989	$6.00
London	CDP 222	Help	CDJ	U.S.	1989	$3.00
London	886222-2	I Can't Help It	CD5	Germany	1988	$6.00
London	NANCD-15	I Can't Help It	CD5	U.K.	1988	$6.00
London	P10L-30003	I Heard A Rumour	CD3	Japan	1988	$12.00/$4.00
London	886298-2	I Want You Back	CD5	Germany	1988	$6.00
London	P10L-30007	I Want You Back	CD3	Japan	1988	$12.00/$4.00
London	P10L-30008	I Want You Back	CD3	Japan	1988	$12.00/$4.00
London	NANCD-16	I Want You Back	CD5	U.K.	1988	$6.00
London	886493-2	Lananeeneenoodoo	CD5	Germany	1988	$8.00
London	POCD-1023	Last Thing On My Mind	CD3	Japan	1988	$12.00/$4.00
London		Last Thing On My Mind	CD5	U.K.	1988	$8.00
London		Last Thing On My Mind	CD5	U.K.	1988	$8.00

Second version.

Label	Catalog Number	Title	Type	Country	Year	Longbox Value / Value
London	869395-2	Long Train Running	CD5	Germany	1989	$6.00
Polydor	PODD-1010	Long Train Running	CD3	Japan	1990	$12.00/$4.00
Polydor	POCD-1045	Long Train Running	CD5	Japan	1990	$15.00
London	NACD-24	Long Train Running	CD5	U.K.	1989	$6.00
Polydor	P10L-30002	Love In the First Degree	CD3	Japan	1988	$4.00
London	886362-2	Love, Truth & Honesty	CD3	Germany	1988	$15.00
London	NACD-17	Love, Truth & Honesty	CD5	U.K.	1988	$15.00
London	CDP 31	Love, Truth & Honesty	CDJ	U.S.	1988	$6.00
London	886755-2	Megarama	CD5	Germany	1989	$8.00
London	PODD-1028	More, More, More	CD3	Japan	1993	$13.00/$4.00
London		More, More, More	CD5	U.K.	1993	$9.00
London		More, More, More	CD5	U.K.	1993	$9.00

Second version.

Label	Catalog Number	Title	Type	Country	Year	Longbox Value / Value
London	PODD-1022	Movin' On	CD3	Japan	1992	$12.00/$4.00
London	NANCD-25	Movin' On	CD5	U.K.	1992	$8.00
London	886401-2	Nathan Jones	CD5	Germany	1988	$8.00
London	P10L-4006	Nathan Jones	CD3	Japan	1988	$12.00/$4.00
London	P13-37010	Nathan Jones	CD3	Japan	1988	$12.00/$4.00
London	NACD-18	Nathan Jones	CD5	U.K.	1988	$8.00
London	CDP 46	Nathan Jones	CDJ	U.S.	1989	$3.00
London	869069-2	Only Your Love	CD5	Holland	1990	$12.00
London	PODD-1005	Only Your Love	CD3	Japan	1990	$13.00/$4.00
London	POCD-1015	Only Your Love	CD5	Japan	1990	$15.00
London	NANCD-21	Only Your Love	CD5	U.K.	1990	$12.00
London	869269-2	Preacher Man	CD5	Germany	1991	$8.00
London	POCD-1040	Preacher Man	CD3	Japan	1991	$12.00/$4.00
London	NANCD-23	Preacher Man	CD5	U.K.	1991	$8.00
London	869197-2	Tripping On Your Love	CD5	Germany	1991	$12.00
London	PODD-1013	Tripping On Your Love	CD3	Japan	1991	$13.00/$4.00
London	NANCD-22	Tripping On Your Love	CD5	U.K.	1991	$10.00
London	CDP 568	Tripping On Your Love	CDJ	U.S.	1991	$3.00
London		True Confessions	CDJ	U.S.	1986	$6.00
London	P10L-30006	Venus	CD3	Japan	1987	$12.00/$4.00
London		Venus	CDV	U.K.	1986	$20.00
London	080 027-2	Venus	DJ/CDV	U.S.	1986	$20.00
London	080 027-2	Venus	CDV	U.S.	1988	$35.00

Bananas In The Mood

Singles

Label	Catalog Number	Title	Type	Country	Year	Longbox Value / Value
BMG	663137	Banana Snooke	CD5	Germany	1990	$6.00

Band, The

Full Length

Label	Catalog Number	Title	Type	Country	Year	Longbox Value / Value
Capitol	DPRO-79800	Across the Great Divide	DJ/Smplr	U.S.	1995	$20.00
EMI	748419-2	Anthology, Vol. 1	LP	Germany		$15.00
Capitol	CZ-53	Anthology, Vol. 1	LP	U.K.		$15.00
Capitol	CDP-48419-2	Anthology, Vol. 1	LP/LB	U.S.		$15.00/$9.00
EMI	748986-2	Anthology, Vol. 2	LP	Germany		$15.00
Capitol	CDP-48986-2	Anthology, Vol. 2	LP/LB	U.S.		$15.00/$9.00
		Band Boxed Set Sampler, The	DJ/Smplr	U.S.	1995	$18.00
Pioneer	PA-85-120	Band Is Back, The	LD	U.S.	1985	$20.00
Pioneer	PA-85-120	Band Is Back, The	LD	U.S.	1990	$30.00

Digital audio

Label	Catalog Number	Title	Type	Country	Year	Longbox Value / Value
Capitol	DPRO-79379	Band On CD, The	DJ/Smplr	U.S.	1990	$15.00
Capitol	CDP-46070	Best Of	LP/LB	U.S.†	1985	$15.00/$9.00
EMI	748420-2	Cahoots	LP	Germany		$15.00
Capitol	CZ-138	Cahoots	LP	U.K.		$15.00
Capitol	CDP-48420-2	Cahoots	LP/LB	U.S.		$15.00/$9.00
Album Network		In the Studio (The Band)	RS	U.S.	1988	$20.00

Airdate: 9/5/88

Label	Catalog Number	Title	Type	Country	Year	Longbox Value / Value
Album Network		In the Studio (The Band)	RS	U.S.	1990	$20.00

Airdate: 1/1/90

Label	Catalog Number	Title	Type	Country	Year	Longbox Value / Value
EMI	793591-2	Islands	LP	Germany		$15.00
Capitol	CDP-93591-2	Islands	LP/LB	U.S.		$15.00/$9.00
DIR		King Biscuit Flour Hour	RS	U.S.	1988	$30.00

Airdate: 3/20/88

Label	Catalog Number	Title	Type	Country	Year	Longbox Value / Value
DIR		King Biscuit Flour Hour	RS	U.S.	1990	$30.00

Airdate: 1/29/90

Label	Catalog Number	Title	Type	Country	Year	Longbox Value / Value
DIR		King Biscuit Flour Hour	RS	U.S.	1991	$30.00

With Blues Traveler, Airdate: 4/7/91

Label	Catalog Number	Title	Type	Country	Year	Longbox Value / Value
DIR		King Biscuit Flour Hour	RS	U.S.	1992	$30.00

Airdate: 6/27/92

Label	Catalog Number	Title	Type	Country	Year	Longbox Value / Value
DIR		King Biscuit Flour Hour	RS	U.S.	1994	$40.00

Airdate: 7/24/94

Label	Catalog Number	Title	Type	Country	Year	Longbox Value / Value
EMI	793592-2	Moondog Matinee	LP	Germany		$15.00
Capitol	CDP-93592-2	Moondog Matinee	LP/LB	U.S.		$15.00/$9.00
Mobile Fidelity	UDCD-527	Music From Big Pink	TLD/LP	U.S.		$25.00/$20.00

Gold disc

Label	Catalog Number	Title	Type	Country	Year	Longbox Value / Value
Capitol	CDP-4606	Music From Big Pink	LP/LB	U.S.†	1985	$15.00/$9.00
Capitol	CDP-93592-2	Norther Lights-Southern Cross	LP/LB	U.S.		$15.00/$9.00
Westwood One		Superstars	RS	U.S.	1996	$75.00

2 CD set. Airdate: 7/15/96.

Label	Catalog Number	Title	Type	Country	Year	Longbox Value / Value
Media America		Up Close	RS/1CD	U.S.	1994	$30.00

Singles

Label	Catalog Number	Title	Type	Country	Year	Longbox Value / Value
Pyramid	7031	Atlantic City	CDJ	U.S.	1993	$3.00
Pyramid		Blind Willie Mctell	CDJ	U.S.	1993	$3.00
Pyramid	PRCD 7187	Free Your Mind	CDJ	U.S.	1996	$25.00

3-D ID Hologram printed on the disc.

Label	Catalog Number	Title	Type	Country	Year	Longbox Value / Value
Pyramid	7048	Remedy	CDJ	U.S.	1993	$3.00
Pyramid		Remedy (Live)	CDJ	U.S.	1993	$10.00
Pyramid	PRCD 7172	Stand Up	CDJ	U.S.	1995	$3.00

Band Of Susans

Singles

Label	Catalog Number	Title	Type	Country	Year	Longbox Value / Value
Restless	72722	Now	CD5	U.S.	1992	$5.00

Banda Bahia

Singles

Label	Catalog Number	Title	Type	Country	Year	Longbox Value / Value
Cosmos Records	2003	Chupin Chupon	CD5	U.S.	1994	$5.00

Banda Borracha

Singles

Label	Catalog Number	Title	Type	Country	Year	Longbox Value / Value
	3369	Yo Soy La Nina Fres	CD5	U.S.	1994	$5.00

Banda Del Carro

Singles

Label	Catalog Number	Title	Type	Country	Year	Longbox Value / Value
	1001	Nortenas Al Estilo	CD5	U.S.	1994	$5.00

Banda El Limon

Singles

Label	Catalog Number	Title	Type	Country	Year	Longbox Value / Value
Fonorama	6	15 Exitos Con Sabor	CD5	U.S.	1994	$5.00

Banda Killy's

Singles

Label	Catalog Number	Title	Type	Country	Year	Longbox Value / Value
Joey International	3374	Dejame Comerte A Be	CD5	U.S.	1994	$5.00

Banda La Pinera

Singles

Label	Catalog Number	Title	Type	Country	Year	Longbox Value / Value
	5318	16 Exitos	CD5	U.S.	1994	$5.00

Banda Machos

Singles

Label	Catalog Number	Title	Type	Country	Year	Longbox Value / Value
Eastwest	PRCD 9193	Zappa Mambo	CDJ	U.S.	1995	$3.00

Banda Xochiti

Singles

Label	Catalog Number	Title	Type	Country	Year	Longbox Value / Value
Continental	1030	Si Tu Boquita Fuera	CD5	U.S.	1994	$5.00

Banderas

Full Length

Label	Catalog Number	Title	Type	Country	Year	Longbox Value / Value
Island	7 842474-2	Bandera	LP/LB	U.S.		$14.00/$8.00
London	828247	Ripe	LP/LB	U.S.		$14.00/$8.00

Singles

Label	Catalog Number	Title	Type	Country	Year	Longbox Value / Value
Polygram	869252-2	May This Be Your	CD5	Germany	1991	$7.00
Polygram	869391-2	She Shells	CD5	Germany	1991	$7.00
Aris	885641	Tease	CD5	Germany	1989	$6.00
London	869295-2	This Is Your Life	CD5	Germany	1991	$7.00
Polydor	PODD-1011	This Is Your Life	CD3	Japan	1991	$12.00/$3.00
London	LONCD-290	This Is Your Life	CD5	U.K.	1991	$7.00
London	CDP-419	This Is Your Life	CDJ	U.S.	1991	$2.00
London	CDP 542	Why Aren't You In Love With Me	CDJ	U.S.	1991	$2.00

Bandito Queen

Singles

Label	Catalog Number	Title	Type	Country	Year	Longbox Value / Value
	PRCD 6581	Give It To the Dog	CDJ	U.S.		$2.00

Bandola

Singles

Label	Catalog Number	Title	Type	Country	Year	Longbox Value / Value
Nursery	NYSCD-9	'Til Tuesday	CD5	U.K.	1993	$7.00

Bandy, Moe

Singles

Label	Catalog Number	Title	Type	Country	Year	Longbox Value / Value
	9313	Picture In A Frame	CD5	U.S.	1994	$5.00

Bang

Full Length

Label	Catalog Number	Title	Type	Country	Year	Longbox Value / Value
A&M	75021-5301-2	Clockwise	LP/LB	U.S.		$14.00/$8.00

Singles

Label	Catalog Number	Title	Type	Country	Year	Longbox Value / Value
BMG	663476	Holding My Heart	CD5	Germany	1990	$7.00
Victor	VIDP-15	Holding My Heart	CD3	Japan	1990	$13.00/$4.00
RCA	PD-43882	Holding My Heart	CD5	U.K.	1990	$7.00
A&M	75021 8064 2	Holding My Heart	CDJ	U.S.	1990	$2.00
BMG	662209	You're the One	CD5	Germany	1989	$7.00
RCA	PD-42716	You're the One	CD5	U.K.	1989	$7.00

Bang Bang Machine

Singles

Label	Catalog Number	Title	Type	Country	Year	Longbox Value / Value
Parallel	LLLCD-1	Evil Circus	CD5	U.K.	1992	$7.00

Bang Tango

Singles

Label	Catalog Number	Title	Type	Country	Year	Longbox Value / Value
MCA	10531	Ain't No Jive	CD5	U.S.	1992	$4.00
Mechanic	CD 45 17848	Attack Of Life	CDJ	U.S.	1989	$2.00
MCA	CD45 18062	Breaking My Heart	CDJ	U.S.	1989	$2.00
Mechanic		Breaking Up A Heart Of Stone	CDJ	U.S.	1990	$2.00
Mechanic	CD45-18225	Love Injection	CDJ	U.S.	1990	$2.00
Mechanic	CD45 1652	Midnight Struck	CDJ	U.S.	1991	$2.00
Mechanic	CD45 17853	Someone Like You	CDJ	U.S.	1989	$2.00
Mechanic	CD45 1281	Soul To Soul	CDJ	U.S.	1991	$2.00
Mechanic	CD45-1447	United And True	CDJ	U.S.	1991	$2.00

Bangalore Choir

Singles

Label	Catalog Number	Title	Type	Country	Year	Longbox Value / Value
Giant	PRO-CD-5004	Freight Train Rollin'	CDJ	U.S.	1992	$2.00

Bangles

Full Length

Label	Catalog Number	Title	Type	Country	Year	Longbox Value / Value
Columbia	468330-2	Bangles	LP	U.K.	1991	$45.00

3 CD Set

Label	Catalog Number	Title	Type	Country	Year	Longbox Value / Value
		Definitive Collection	LTD/LP	U.S.	1995	$30.00

2CD set.

Label	Catalog Number	Title	Type	Country	Year	Longbox Value / Value
Columbia		Everything	LTD/LP	Germany	1989	$27.00

2 CD set.

Label	Catalog Number	Title	Type	Country	Year	Longbox Value / Value
Columbia	CSK1520	Everything Tour CD	DJ/LP	U.S.	1989	$25.00
CBS	466769-2	Greatest Hits	LTD/LP	U.K.	1990	$30.00
CBS	466769 2	Greatest Hits	LTD/LP	U.K.	1990	$25.00

Picture disc CD.

Label	Catalog Number	Title	Type	Country	Year	Longbox Value / Value
Sony	SRCS-6895	Starbox	LP	Japan		$35.00
Sony	25 DP-5600	Starbox	LP	Japan		$35.00

Singles

Label	Catalog Number	Title	Type	Country	Year	Longbox Value / Value
CBS	654901-3	Be With You	CD3	Germany	1989	$8.00
CBS	610EP-3084	Be With You	CD3	Japan	1989	$13.00/$4.00
CBS	BANGSC-6	Be With You	CD5	U.K.	1989	$8.00
CBS	BANGSD-6	Be With You	CD5	U.K.	1989	$13.00
Columbia	38K-68744	Be With You	CD3	U.S.	1989	$6.00/$3.00
Columbia	CSK 1569	Be With You	CDJ	U.S.	1989	$3.00
CBS	655155-2	Eternal Flame	CD3	Germany	1988	$8.00
CBS	654550-2	Eternal Flame	CD3	Germany	1989	$8.00
CBS	10EP-3059	Eternal Flame	CD3	Japan	1988	$13.00/$4.00
CBS	BANGSC-5	Eternal Flame	CD5	U.K.	1988	$8.00
Columbia	38K-68533	Eternal Flame	CD3	U.S.	1988	$6.00/$3.00
Columbia	CSK 1417	Eternal Flame	CDJ	U.S.	1988	$3.00
CBS	655988-3	Everything I Wanted	CD5	Germany	1990	$9.00
Def Jam	BANGSC-3	Hazy Shade Of Winter	CD5	U.K.	1988	$9.00
CBS	655313-3	I'll Set You Free	CD3	Germany	1989	$8.00
CBS	BANGSC-7	I'll Set You Free	CD5	U.K.	1989	$8.00
Columbia		I'll Set You Free	CDJ	U.S.	1989	$3.00
CBS	654849-3	In Your Room	CD3	Germany	1988	$8.00
CBS	653081 3	In Your Room	CD3	Germany	1988	$8.00
CBS	10EP-3055	In Your Room	CD3	Japan	1988	$12.00/$4.00
CBS	12EP-3065	In Your Room	CD3	Japan	1988	$13.00/$4.00
		In Your Room	CDV	Japan	1990	$40.00
CBS	654849-3	In Your Room	CD3	U.K.	1988	$8.00
CBS	6BANGSC-4	In Your Room	CD5	U.K.	1988	$8.00
Columbia	38K-8090	In Your Room	CD3	U.S.	1988	$6.00/$3.00
Columbia	CSK 1313	In Your Room	CDJ	U.S.	1988	$3.00
A&M	CC-31011	Real World	CD3	U.S.		$6.00/$3.00
CBS	BANGCD-8	Walk Like An Egyptian	CD5	U.K.	1987	$6.00

Banks, Tony

Full Length

Company	Disk Number	Title	Type	Country	Year	Longbox Value / Value
Giant		Still	LP/LB	U.S.		$14.00/$8.00

Singles

Company	Disk Number	Title	Type	Country	Year	Longbox Value / Value
Giant	PRO-CD-5308	Angel Face	CDJ	U.S.	1992	$2.00
Virgin	VSCDT-1362	Gift, The	CD5	U.K.	1991	$9.00
Virgin	664296	I Wanna Change the Score	CD5	Germany	1991	$9.00
Virgin	VJDP-10160	I Wanna Change the Score	CD3	Japan	1991	$12.00/$4.00
Virgin	VSCDT-1347	I Wanna Change the Score	CD5	U.K.	1991	$9.00
Giant	PRO-CD_5550.	I Wanna Change the Score	CDJ	U.S.	1991	$2.00
Virgin	VSCDT-1406	Still It Takes Me By Suprise	CD5	U.K.	1992	$9.00

Bankstatement

Full Length

Company	Disk Number	Title	Type	Country	Year	Longbox Value / Value
Atlantic		Bankstatement	DJ/LP	U.S.	1989	$15.00

CD in cardboard "Bank Book" with Bio

Company	Disk Number	Title	Type	Country	Year	Longbox Value / Value
Atlantic	7 82007-2	Bankstatement	LP/LB	U.S.	1989	$14.00/$8.00
Atlantic		Sampler	DJ/Smplr	U.K.	1989	$15.00

Singles

Company	Disk Number	Title	Type	Country	Year	Longbox Value / Value
Virgin	VJD-10215	I'll Be Waiting	CD3	Japan	1989	$8.00/$2.00
Virgin	VSCD-1200	I'll Be Waiting	CD3	U.K.	1989	$7.00
Virgin	VSCD-1208	I'll Be Waiting	CD3	U.K.	1989	$7.00
Atlantic	PR 3054-2	Raincloud	CDJ	U.S.	1989	$3.00
BMG	162528	Throwback	CD3	Germany	1989	$7.00
Virgin	VJP-10215	Throwback	CD3	Japan	1989	$8.00/$2.00
Virgin	PRCD 1200	Throwback	CD3	U.K.	1989	$7.00
Atlantic	PR 2804-2	Throwback	CDJ	U.S.	1989	$3.00

Bano, Al

Singles

Company	Disk Number	Title	Type	Country	Year	Longbox Value / Value
WEA	171841-2	Bussa Ancora	CD5	Germany	1990	$7.00
WEA	247004-2	Cara Terra Mia	CD5	Germany	1989	$7.00
WEA	1711992	Donna Per Amore	CD5	Germany	1990	$7.00
WEA	9031-72566-2	Fotografia	CD5	Germany	1990	$7.00
WEA	247644-2	Fragile	CD5	Germany	1990	$7.00
WEA	172899-2	Un Altro Natale	CD5	Germany	1990	$7.00

Banshee

Singles

Company	Disk Number	Title	Type	Country	Year	Longbox Value / Value
		Precious Metal	CDJ	U.S.		$2.00

Banton, Buju

Singles

Company	Disk Number	Title	Type	Country	Year	Longbox Value / Value
		Boom Wa Dis	CDJ	U.S.	1993	$3.00
Loose Cannon	7000	Champion	CDJ	U.S.	1995	$3.00
Mercury	CDP 966	Make My Day	CDJ	U.S.	1993	$2.00

Banton, Mega

Singles

Company	Disk Number	Title	Type	Country	Year	Longbox Value / Value
VP	5382	Daisy	CD5	U.S.	1994	$5.00

Banton, Pato

Singles

Company	Disk Number	Title	Type	Country	Year	Longbox Value / Value
Virgin	92712	Bubbling Hot	CD5	U.K.	1994	$8.00
IRS	IRSD 67102	Bubbling Hot	CDJ	U.S.	1992	$2.00
IRS	IRSD 67034	Wize Up	CDJ	U.S.	1990	$2.00

Bap

Full Length

Company	Disk Number	Title	Type	Country	Year	Longbox Value / Value
EMI	CDP 566-7 91857	Da Capo	LTD/LP	Germany	1989	$15.00

Picture disc CD.

Singles

Company	Disk Number	Title	Type	Country	Year	Longbox Value / Value
EMI	147539-2	Alles Em Lot	CD5	Germany	1990	$8.00
EMI	147425-2	Dat Daeaet Joot	CD5	Germany	1989	$8.00
EMI	147366-3	Fortsetzung Folgt	CD3	Germany	1990	$8.00
EMI	147366-2	Fortsetzung Folgt	CD5	Germany	1990	$8.00
EMI	147399-2	Saison Der Container	CD5	Germany	1988	$8.00
EMI	147445-2	Shanghai	CD3	Germany	1989	$8.00
EMI	147573-2	Sie Maeaet Suechtig	CD5	Germany	1991	$8.00
EMI	147585-2	Verdamp Lang Her	CD5	Germany	1991	$8.00
EMI	147560-2	Vis-A-Vis	CD5	Germany	1991	$8.00

Bar Keys

Singles

Company	Disk Number	Title	Type	Country	Year	Longbox Value / Value
Tavdash	JEA 0100	Tell Me Sumthin' Good	CDJ	U.S.		$2.00

Barbarella

Singles

Company	Disk Number	Title	Type	Country	Year	Longbox Value / Value
Alfa	09B3-69	Sucker For Your Love	CD3	Japan	1989	$13.00/$4.00
Alfa	11B3-70	Sucker For Your Love	CD3	Japan	1989	$13.00/$4.00
EMI	251821-2	We Cheer You Up	CD5	Germany	1989	$8.00

Barber, Billy

Full Length

Company	Disk Number	Title	Type	Country	Year	Longbox Value / Value
Digital Music	CD-445	Shades Of Grey	LP/BP	U.S.†	1985	$8.00

Barber, Chris

Full Length

Company	Disk Number	Title	Type	Country	Year	Longbox Value / Value
Timeless	CDTTD-509	Concert For the BBC	LP	U.S.		$8.00

Barbie

Singles

Company	Disk Number	Title	Type	Country	Year	Longbox Value / Value
Rincon	90062	Together We Can Do It	CDJ	U.S.	1990	$2.00

Barbie Bones

Singles

Company	Disk Number	Title	Type	Country	Year	Longbox Value / Value
Restless	007	Submarine Soul	CDJ	U.S.	1991	$2.00

Barclay, James Harvest

Full Length

Company	Disk Number	Title	Type	Country	Year	Longbox Value / Value
Polygram	831483-2	Face To Face	LP	Germany		$15.00

Label	Catalog Number	Title	Type	Country	Year	Longbox Value / Value
		Sorcerers & Keepers	LP	U.K.		$14.00

Singles

Label	Catalog Number	Title	Type	Country	Year	Longbox Value / Value
Polydor	PZCD-67	Cheap the Bullet	CD5	U.K.	1990	$7.00
Polgram	877255-2	Halfway To Freedom	CD5	Germany	1990	$7.00
Polgram	877877-2	John Lennon's Guitar	CD5	Germany	1990	$7.00
Polygram		Stand Up	CD5	U.K.	1990	$7.00
Polydor	873683-2	Welcome To the Show	CD5	Germany	1990	$7.00

Bardens, Pete

Full Length

Label	Catalog Number	Title	Type	Country	Year	Longbox Value / Value
Capitol	CDP-746868-2	Seen One Earth	LP/LB	U.S.		$14.00/$8.00
Capitol	CDP-748967-2	Speed of the Light	LP/LB	U.S.		$14.00/$8.00

Singles

Label	Catalog Number	Title	Type	Country	Year	Longbox Value / Value
		A Higher Ground	CDJ	U.S.		$2.00
Cinema	78360	Gold	CDJ	U.S.		$2.00
Capitol	DPRO-79418	Whisper In the Wind	CDJ	U.S.	1988	$2.00

Bardeux

Full Length

Label	Catalog Number	Title	Type	Country	Year	Longbox Value / Value
Intercord	848 727	Bold As Love	LP	Germany		$15.00
Enigma	73312	Bold As Love	LP/LB	U.S.		$14.00/$8.00
Enigma	73522	Shangri-La	LP/LB	U.S.		$14.00/$8.00

Singles

Label	Catalog Number	Title	Type	Country	Year	Longbox Value / Value
Alfa	10SR-30	Bleeding Heart	CD3	Japan	1988	$13.00/$4.00
Enigma	EPRO-109	Bleeding Heart	CDJ	U.S.	1988	$2.00
EMI	203631-3	I Love the Bass	CD3	Germany	1989	$7.00
Enigma	EPRO-207	I Love the Bass	CDJ	U.S.	1989	$2.00
Synthicide	71300-2	Three Time Lover	CD3	U.S.	1987	$4.00
Enigma	EPRO-247	Thumbs Up	CDJ	U.S.	1989	$2.00
Alfa	10SR-13	When We Kiss	CD3	Japan	1988	$13.00/$4.00
Enigma	D31C-75018	When We Kiss	CD3	U.S.	1988	$6.00/$4.00

Bardot, Brigitte

Full Length

Label	Catalog Number	Title	Type	Country	Year	Longbox Value / Value
Philips		Brigitte	LTD/LP	France	1994	$100.00

CD in 10"x10" sleeve. French record club release.

Bardots

Singles

Label	Catalog Number	Title	Type	Country	Year	Longbox Value / Value
Rough Trade	381 0099 3	Pretty O	CD5	Germany	1991	$7.00
APT	CHERRE-25CD	Pretty O	CD5	U.K.	1991	$7.00
APT	CHERRE-29CD	Shallow	CD5	U.K.	1991	$7.00

Barefoot Servants

Singles

Label	Catalog Number	Title	Type	Country	Year	Longbox Value / Value
Epic	ESK 5602	Box Of Miracles	CDJ	U.S.	1993	$2.00

Barenaked Ladies

Singles

Label	Catalog Number	Title	Type	Country	Year	Longbox Value / Value
	PRO-CD-7313-R	Alternative Girlfriend	CDJ	U.S.	1995	$3.00
Page	001	Be My Yoko Ono	CDJ	Canada	1992	$10.00
APT	CHERRE-26CD	Be My Yoko Ono	CD5	U.K.	1992	$8.00
Sire	PRO-CD-5616	Be My Yoko Ono	CDJ	U.S.	1992	$2.00
WEA	9362-40750-2	Brian Wilson	CD5	U,K.	1992	$8.00
Reprise	W-0128CD	Enid	CD5	U.K.	1992	$8.00
Sire	PRO-CD-6432	Fight the Power	CDJ	U.S.	1993	$2.00
Sire	PRO-CD-5825	If I Had $1,000,000	CDJ	U.S.	1992	$2.00
Sire	PRO-CD-7145	Jane	CDJ	U.S.	1994	$3.00
		Shoe Box	CDJ	U.S.		$2.00

Barkays

Singles

Label	Catalog Number	Title	Type	Country	Year	Longbox Value / Value
Zoo	17138	Put A Little Nasty On It	CDJ	U.S.	1993	$2.00

Barker, Aaron

Full Length

Label	Catalog Number	Title	Type	Country	Year	Longbox Value / Value
Atlantic	7 82354-2	Taste Of Freedom	LP/LB	U.S.		$12.00/$7.00

Barker, Sally

Singles

Label	Catalog Number	Title	Type	Country	Year	Longbox Value / Value
Aris	883455	Money Is Talking	CD5	U.K.	1990	$7.00

Barkmarket

Full Length

Label	Catalog Number	Title	Type	Country	Year	Longbox Value / Value
	24397-R	L.Ron	DJ/LP	U.S.	1995	$12.00
Def American	PRO-CD-5343	Grinder	CDJ	U.S.	1992	$3.00

Barnes, Jimmy

Full Length

Label	Catalog Number	Title	Type	Country	Year	Longbox Value / Value
		Live '94	DJ/Smplr	U.K.	1995	$70.00
CD in wood box with book						
		Still Got A Long Way To Go	LP	Australia		$18.00
2 CD5 set						
Atlantic	AMCY-188	Two Fries	LP	Japan		$20.00
Atlantic	7 82141-2	Two Fries	LP/LB	U.S.		$14.00/$8.00

Singles

Label	Catalog Number	Title	Type	Country	Year	Longbox Value / Value
		Come Undone	CD5	Australia		$10.00
		Come Undone	CD5	Australia		$10.00
Second version.						
Atlantic	A-7751CD	Good Times	CD5	U.S.	1990	$7.00
Geffen	PRO-CD-3244	I'm Still On Your Side	CDJ	U.S.	1988	$3.00
Geffen	PRO-CD-3285	I'm Still On Your Side	CDJ	U.S.	1988	$2.00
		It Will Be Alright	CD5	Australia	1993	$10.00
Atlantic	PRCD 3673-2	Lay Your Guns Down	CDJ	U.S.	1990	$2.00
Atlantic	A-7722CD	Let's Make It Last All Night	CD5	U.K.	1990	$7.00
Atlantic	PRCD 3510-2	Let's Make It Last All Night	CDJ	U.S.	1990	$2.00
		Still A Long Way To Go	CD5	Australia	1993	$10.00
		Still A Long Way To Go	CD5	Australia	1993	$10.00
Second version.						
Pioneer	10SW61	Too Much Ain't Enough Love	CD3	Japan	1988	$12.00/$4.00
Geffen	PRO-CD-3033	Too Much Ain't Enough Love	CDJ	U.S.	1988	$2.00
Geffen	PRO-CD-3148	Too Much Ain't Enough Love	CDJ	U.S.	1988	$2.00

Barone, Richard

Full Length

Label	Catalog Number	Title	Type	Country	Year	Longbox Value / Value
Passport	PBCD-6058	Cool Blue Halo	LP	U.S.		$12.00
MCA		Primal Dream	DJ/LP	U.S.		$10.00
MCA	MCAD-6370	Primal Dream	LP/LB	U.S.		$14.00/$8.00

Singles

Label	Catalog Number	Title	Type	Country	Year	Longbox Value / Value
Line	LICD-900884	Cry Baby Cry	CD5	Germany	1989	$8.00
Passport	6058	Cry Baby Cry	CDJ	U.S.	1989	$6.00
Mesa	9046	Forbidden	CDJ	U.S.	1993	$2.00
MCA	CD45 18175	I Only Took What I Need	CDJ	U.S.	1990	$2.00
Line	LICD-901003	Primal Cuts	CD5	Germany	1990	$8.00
Line	LICD-900963	River To River	CD5	Germany	1990	$8.00
MCA	CD45 18420	River To River	CDJ	U.S.	1990	$2.00
MCA	CD45 18468	Where the Truth I Lies Need	CDJ	U.S.	1990	$2.00

Barquee, Thomas

Singles

Label	Catalog Number	Title	Type	Country	Year	Longbox Value / Value
CBS	656860-2	Ticket Toulouse	CD5	Germany	1991	$8.00

Barr, Rosanne

Singles

Label	Catalog Number	Title	Type	Country	Year	Longbox Value / Value
		I Enjoy Being A Girl	CDJ	U.S.	1991	$12.00

Barrelhouse Jazzband

Full Length

Label	Catalog Number	Title	Type	Country	Year	Longbox Value / Value
Bellaphon	288 03 001	You Are Driving Me Crazy	LP	Germany		$15.00

Barren Cross

Singles

Label	Catalog Number	Title	Type	Country	Year	Longbox Value / Value
		Cryin' Over You	CDJ	U.S.		$2.00

Barrett, Jimmy "Bee"

Full Length

Label	Catalog Number	Title	Type	Country	Year	Longbox Value / Value
Beeswax		Fact Or Fiction	DJ/LP	U.S.	1991	$8.00

Barrett, John Paul

Singles

Label	Catalog Number	Title	Type	Country	Year	Longbox Value / Value
Radical	CDRAD-2	Move It Better	CD5	U.K.	1989	$7.00
Westside	CDWSR-2	Never Giving Up	CD5	U.K.	1989	$7.00

Barrett, Syd

Singles

Label	Catalog Number	Title	Type	Country	Year	Longbox Value / Value
Sound	883523	Peel Sessions	CD5	Germany	1988	$15.00
Strange Frt	SFPSCD-043	Peel Sessions	CD5	U.K.	1988	$15.00

Barretto, Ray

Full Length

Label	Catalog Number	Title	Type	Country	Year	Longbox Value / Value
Plaene	15950	Tomorrow	LP	Germany		$15.00

Barrio Boyzz

Singles

Label	Catalog Number	Title	Type	Country	Year	Longbox Value / Value
Columbia	CSK 6496	I Like It Like That	CDJ	U.S.	1995	$3.00
	DPRO-10490	I Wish	CDJ	U.S.		$2.00

Barros, Dana

Singles

Label	Catalog Number	Title	Type	Country	Year	Longbox Value / Value
Immortal	6794	Check It	CDJ	U.S.	1994	$3.00

Barrowman, John

Singles

Label	Catalog Number	Title	Type	Country	Year	Longbox Value / Value
Epic	656733-2	I Was Born To Be Me	CD5	U.K.	1991	$7.00

Barry, Alan

Singles

Label	Catalog Number	Title	Type	Country	Year	Longbox Value / Value
Canyon	S9Y-11112	Victim Of Love	CD3	Japan	1989	$13.00/$4.00

Barry, Claudia

Singles

Label	Catalog Number	Title	Type	Country	Year	Longbox Value / Value
ZYX	6583-8	Boogie Woogie Dance	CD5	Germany	1991	$5.00

Barry, John

Singles

Label	Catalog Number	Title	Type	Country	Year	Longbox Value / Value
Epic	656796-2	John Dunbar Theme	CD5	U.K.	1991	$10.00
Epic	ESK 2248	John Dunbar Theme	CDJ	U.S.	1990	$7.00

Barry, Paul

Singles

Label	Catalog Number	Title	Type	Country	Year	Longbox Value / Value
MCA	DMCAT-1394	Letting Go	CD5	U.K.	1990	$7.00

Barsha

Singles

Label	Catalog Number	Title	Type	Country	Year	Longbox Value / Value
Virgin	3490	Who's the Master?	CDJ	U.S.	1990	$2.00

Bart, Lionel

Singles

Label	Catalog Number	Title	Type	Country	Year	Longbox Value / Value
EMI	CDEM-121	Happy Endings	CD5	U.K.	1989	$7.00

Bas Blasta

Singles

Label	Catalog Number	Title	Type	Country	Year	Longbox Value / Value
RCA	62987	Dangerous	CD5	U.S.	1994	$5.00

Bas Noir

Full Length

Label	Catalog Number	Title	Type	Country	Year	Longbox Value / Value
Atlantic	7 82360-2	Ah...Bas Noir	LP/LB	U.S.		$13.00/$7.00
Atlantic	PRCD 4418-2	Superficial Love	CDJ	U.S.	1992	$2.00

Base, Rob

Singles

Label	Catalog Number	Title	Type	Country	Year	Longbox Value / Value
Funky Base	160	Break Of Dawn	CDJ	U.S.	1994	$3.00
		Get Up and Have A Good Time	CDJ	U.S.	1989	$2.00
BCM	20178	It Takes Two	CD5	Geramny	1989	$7.00
BCM	20077	It Takes Two	CD5	Geramny	1989	$7.00
Polygram	874345-2	Joy And Pain	CD5	Canada	1989	$6.00
BCM	20233	Joy And Pain	CD5	Geramny	1989	$7.00
Profile	PCD 7275	Turn It Out	CDJ	U.S.	1989	$2.00
Profile	PCD 7292	Turn It Out	CDJ	U.S.	1990	$2.00

Base Scan

Singles

Label	Catalog Number	Title	Type	Country	Year	Longbox Value / Value
ZYX	6442-8	Disco D.	CD5	Germany	1990	$8.00

Basehead

Singles

Label	Catalog Number	Title	Type	Country	Year	Longbox Value / Value
Imago	72787 25010	2000 B.C.	CDJ	U.S.	1992	$2.00
Imago	72787 28022	2000 B.C.	CDJ	U.S.	1992	$2.00
Imago	28033	Not Over You	CDJ	U.S.	1992	$2.00
Imago	72787 25044	Split Personality	CDJ	U.S.	1992	$2.00

Bash & Pop

Singles

Label	Catalog Number	Title	Type	Country	Year	Longbox Value / Value
Sire	PRO-CD-5941	Loose Ends	CDJ	U.S.	1993	$2.00
Sire	PRO-CD-5976	Never Aim To Please	CDJ	U.S.	1993	$2.00

Basia

Full Length

Label	Catalog Number	Title	Type	Country	Year	Longbox Value / Value
Epic	ESK 1276	Nine Track Sampler	DJ/Smplr	U.S.	1988	$6.00

Singles

Label	Catalog Number	Title	Type	Country	Year	Longbox Value / Value
Epic	655582-3	Baby You're Mind	CD5	Germany	1990	$6.00
Epic	655582-3	Baby You're Mind	CD3	Holland	1990	$6.00
Epic	ESDA-7001	Baby You're Mind	CD3	Japan	1989	$13.00/$4.00
Epic	CDBASH-6	Baby You're Mind	CD5	U.K.	1990	$6.00
Epic	ESK 1961	Baby You're Mind	CDJ	U.S.	1990	$2.00

Label	Catalog Number	Title	Type	Country	Year	Longbox Value / Value
Epic		Baby You're Mine	CD5	U.K.		$10.00
Second version.						
Epic	ESK 73405	Baby You're Mine	CDJ	U.S.	1990	$2.00
Epic	ESCA-5449	Best Remixes	CD3	Japan	1989	$13.00/$4.00
Epic	ESDA-7057	Brave New Hope	CD3	Japan	1990	$13.00/$4.00
Epic	49K 73593	Brave New Hope	CD5	U.S.	1990	$5.00
Epic	655820-3	Cruising For Bruising	CD5	Germany	1990	$6.00
Epic	CDBASH-7	Cruising For Bruising	CD5	U.K.	1990	$6.00
Epic	BASHC-7	Cruising For Bruising	CD5	U.K.	1990	$6.00
Epic	ESK 73239	Cruising For Bruising	CDJ	U.S.	1990	$2.00
Epic	ESK 77573	Drunk On Love	CDJ	U.S.	1994	$3.00
Epic		New Day For You	CDJ	U.S.		$2.00
Epic	660315	On Love	CD5	Germany	1994	$10.00
Epic	CDBASH-3	Prime Time TV	CD5	U.K.	1987	$6.00
Epic	CDBASH-4	Promises	CD5/PD	U.K.	1987	$12.00
Epic		Promises	CDJ	U.S.	1987	$6.00
Epic	ESK 6551	Third Time Lucky	CDJ	U.S.	1994	$3.00
Epic	CDBASH-5	Time And Tide	CD5	U.K.	1987	$6.00
Epic	CPBASH-5	Time And Tide	CD5/PD	U.K.	1987	$12.00
Epic	ESK 1137	Time And Tide	CDJ	U.S.	1987	$2.00
Epic		Until You Come Back To Me	CD3	Holland	1990	$6.00
Epic	ESK-73485	Until You Come Back To Me	CDJ	U.S.	1990	$12.00
Epic		Until You Come Back To Me	CDJ	U.S.	1990	$2.00
Basic Black						
Singles						
Motown	ZD-44058	Nothing But A Party	CD5	U.K.	1990	$7.00
Basic Control						
Singles						
ZYX	6756-8	Basic Control Vol. 2	CD5	Germany	1992	$5.00
Basie, Count						
Full Length						
Verve	825575-2	April In Paris	LP/BP	U.S.†	1985	$14.00/$8.00
Verve	821291-2	Basic Base	LP/BP	U.S.†	1984	$14.00/$8.00
Bluebird	ND-82292-2	Brand New Wagon	LP	U.S.		$12.00/$7.00
Mosaic	MD8-135	Complete Roulette Live Recordings	LTD/LP	U.S.		$120.00
8 CD set. Limited to 7500 copies.						
Emarcy	824867-2	Have A Nice Day	LP/BP	U.S.		$12.00/$7.00
Emarcy	824867-2	Have A Nice Day	LP/BP	U.S.†	1985	$14.00/$8.00
Polygram	825194-2	High Voltage	LP/BP	U.S.		$12.00/$7.00
Polygram	825194-2	High Voltage	LP/BP	U.S.†	1985	$12.00/$7.00
Laserlight	LL-15763	Jazz Collector's Edition	LP	U.S.		$8.00
Pablo	J33J-20007	Kansas City 7	LP	Japan		$20.00
Pablo	J33J-20135	Kansas City 8	LP	Japan		$20.00
Polydor	3112-52	Kansas City Shout	LP	Japan		$20.00
Vogue	CD-600037	Kansas City Suite	LP	U.S.		$8.00
Polygram	821799	L'il Ol' Groovemaker	LP/BP	U.S.	1984	$14.00/$8.00
Polygram	821799	Li'l Ol' Groovemaker	LP/BP	U.S.		$14.00/$8.00
Fantasy	2310928-2	Loose Walk	LP/LB	U.S.		$12.00/$7.00
Pablo	2312112	On the Road Montreux	LP	U.S.		$8.00
Mosaic	MD10-149	Studio Recordings	LTD/LP	U.S.	1994	$150.00
10 CD boxed set.						
Singles						
Polygram	527031	Jazz 'round Midnight	CD5	U.S.	1994	$5.00
	41063	On The Upbeat	CD5	U.S.	1994	$5.00
Basie, Count Orchestra						
Full Length						
Jazz MCG	1002	Count Basie Orchestra With New York Voices Live At MCG	LP	U.S.		$15.00
Bass Bumpers						
Singles						
ZYX	DST-1011-8	Can't Stop Dancing	CD5	Germany	1990	$5.00
Bass Construction						
Singles						
Elicit	CDS-ELIC3	Dance With Power	CD5	U.K.	1992	$6.00
Bass Cube						
Singles						
Pandisc	114	Bad Bass Music	CD5	U.S.	1994	$5.00
Bass Is Bass						
Singles						
	PRED134-2	Hey DJ	CDJ	U.S.		$2.00
Bass Mental						
Singles						
ZYX	DST-1008-8	Three Fourths X-Tasy	CD5	Germany	1990	$5.00
Bass-O-Matic						
Full Length						
Virgin	261948	Science And Melody	LP	Germany		$14.00
Virgin	91616	Set the Controls For the Heart	LP/LB	U.S.		$12.00/$7.00
Virgin	86212	Set the Controls For the Heart Of Bass	LP/LB	U.S.		$12.00/$7.00
Singles						
Virgin	VSCDG-1295	Ease On By	CD5	U.K.	1991	$8.00
BMG	663672	Fascinating Rhythm	CD5	Germany	1990	$8.00
Virgin	VSCDT-1274	Fascinating Rhythm	CD5	U.K.	1990	$8.00
Virgin	PRCD 3712	Fascinating Rhythm	CDJ	U.S.	1990	$2.00
Virgin	VSCDG-1355	Funky Love Vibrations	CD5	U.K.	1991	$8.00
Virgin	VSCDT 1372	Go Getta Nutha Man	CD5	U.K.	1991	$8.00
Virgin	VSCDT-1265	In the Realm Of the Senses	CD5	U.K.	1990	$8.00
Virgin	VSCDG 1392	Science And Melody	CD5	U.K.	1991	$8.00
BMG	664496	Virgin	CD5	Germany	1991	$8.00
Basscut						
Singles						
Virgin	TENCD-342	Say You Love Me	CD5	U.K.	1991	$7.00
Bassey						
Singles						
ZYX	6510-8	How Do You Keep the Music	CD5	Germany	1991	$5.00
Tis	CD-190522	Love Is No Game	CD5	Germany	1988	$6.00
Bassey, Shirley						
Full Length						
Vogue	VG-600021	All By Myself	LP	U.S.		$8.00
Towerbell	CDTOW-7	I Am What I Am	LP	U.K.		$15.00
Vogue	VG-600065	I Am What I Am	LP	U.S.		$8.00
Polygram	838033-2	La Mujer	LP/BP	U.S.		$10.00/$6.00
Bassheads						
Singles						
EMI	CDR-6310	Back To the Old School	CD5	U.K.	1992	$8.00

Company	Disk Number	Title	Type	Country	Year	Longbox Value / Value
EMI	CDR-6303	Is There Anybody Out There	CD5	U.K.	1992	$8.00
Capitol	15829	Is There Anybody Out There	CD5	U.S.	1992	$5.00
EMI	CDR-6326	Who Can Make Me Feel Good	CD5	U.K.	1992	$8.00
Deconstruction	7243 8 80362	Who Can Make Me Feel Good	CDJ	U.S.	1992	$2.00
Bassline						
Singles						
Bellaphon	130 07 598	Maybe This Time	CD5	Germany	1991	$7.00
Bat						
Singles						
Da	FFR-0512	Superlove	CD5	Germany	1989	$7.00
Bat-Maxx						
Singles						
SPV	SPV 55-8436	Fledermaus-House	CD5	Germany	1991	$10.00
Bates						
Singles						
	15546	Hello	CD5	U.S.	1995	$5.00
Bates, Martyn						
Full Length						
SPV	7492	Love Smashed On A Rock	LP	Germany		$15.00
Batfish						
Singles						
RCA	VPCD 0842	All Around the World	CD5	Australia	1991	$8.00
Bathory						
Full Length						
Noise	4827	Hammerheart	LP/BP	U.S.		$12.00/$7.00
Singles						
Noise	4879	Father To Son	CDJ	U.S.	1990	$2.00
Baton Rouge						
Full Length						
Atlantic	7 91661-2	Lights Out On the Playground	LP/LB	U.S.		$14.00/$8.00
Atlantic	7 91661-2	Shake Your Soul	LP/LB	U.S.		$14.00/$8.00
Singles						
		Desperate	CDJ	U.S.		$2.00
		Doctor	CDJ	U.S.		$2.00
		There Was A Time	CDJ	U.S.		$2.00
Atlantic	AMDY-5011	Walks Like A Woman	CD3	Japan	1990	$12.00/$3.00
Atlantic	PR 3198-2	Walks Like A Woman	CDJ	U.S.	1990	$2.00
Bats						
Singles						
Attic	MR00702	Spill The Beans	CD5	Canada	1994	$15.00
Battle, Kathleen						
Full Length						
Grammophon	BP 737	Bach Album Sampler, The	DJ/Smplr	U.S.	1992	$10.00
Bauhaus						
Full Length						
Columbia	35CY-1145	Bauhas 1979-1983, Vol. 1	LP	Japan	1984	$25.00
Beggars Banquet	BEG-0641CD	Bauhas 1979-1983, Vol. 1	LP/BP	U.S		$14.00/$8.00
Beggars Banquet	BEG-0642CD	Bauhas 1979-1983, Vol. 2	LP/BP	U.S		$14.00/$8.00
	TKCB-70474	Bauhaus	DJ/Smplr	Japan		$75.00
Beggars Banquet	18B2-120	Burning From the Inside	LP	Japan		$25.00
Beggars Banquet	18B2-116	In the Flat Field	LP	Japan		$25.00
4AD	CAD-0013CD	In the Flat Field	LP	U.S.		$8.00
Beggars Banquet	18B2-117	Mask	LP	Japan		$25.00
Beggars Banquet	BEG-028CD	Mask	LP/BP	U.S.		$14.00/$8.00
Beggars Banquet	18B2-118	Press the Eject And Give Me the Tape	LP	Japan		$25.00
Beggars Banquet	BEG-038CD	Press the Eject And Give Me the Tape	LP/BP	U.S.		$14.00/$8.00
Beggars Banquet	BEG-004CD	Singles 1981-83	LP/BP	U.S		$14.00/$8.00
Beggars Banquet	18B2-119	Sky's Gone Out	LP	Japan		$25.00
RCA	9804	Swing the Heartache	LP/LB	U.S.		$14.00/$8.00
Singles						
Efa	CD-30159	Bela Lugosi's Dead	CD5	Germany	1988	$8.00
Pinnacle	TEENY-CD	Bela Lugosi's Dead	CD5	U.K.	1988	$8.00
Bay City Rollers						
Singles						
Arista	A10D-118	Saturday Night	CD3	Japan	1989	$13.00/$4.00
Bayernpower						
Singles						
BMG	662458	Funky Cold Medina	CD3	Germany	1989	$7.00
BMG	162458	Funky Cold Medina	CD5	Germany	1989	$7.00
BMG	663251	Looking For Freibier	CD5	Germany	1989	$7.00
BMG	162458	Maedels Traegt's Mich Hoam	CD3	Germany	1990	$7.00
Bayless, John						
Full Length						
Pro Arte	4211	Bach Meets the Beatles	LP	U.S.		$8.00
Pro Arte	346	Bach Meets the Beatles	LP	U.S.		$8.00
Bazooka Joe						
Singles						
SPV	9587-3	Drive	CD3	Germany	1989	$7.00
Apt	BIAS-129CD	Drive	CD3	U.K.	1989	$7.00
SPV	9189-3	Smallville For A Day	CD5	Germany	1989	$7.00
Apt	BIAS-157CD	Smallville For A Day	CD5	U.K.	1989	$7.00
BBM						
Singles						
Virgin		Around the Next Dream	CDJ	U.K.	1995	$12.00
	BBMDJ	Around the World	CDJ	U.K.	1994	$15.00
Virgin	BBM-PRO-201	City Of Gold	CDJ	U.K.	1994	$15.00
Virgin	12687	City Of Gold	CDJ	U.S.	1994	$3.00
Virgin		Waiting In the Wings	CDJ	U.S.	1995	$6.00
Virgin	VSCDG1495	Where In the World	CD5	U.K.	1994	$10.00
Virgin	VSCDX1495	Where In the World	CD5	U.K.	1994	$10.00
Virgin	BBM PRO 2	Where In the World	CDJ	U.K.	1994	$15.00
Be Bop Deluxe						
Full Length						
Capitol	CDP-94733-2	Drastic Plastic	LP/LB	U.S.		$14.00/$7.00
Capitol	CDP-92074-2	Futurama	LP/LB	U.S.		$14.00/$7.00
Beach Boys						
Full Length						
Capitol		All Summer Long	LP/LB	U.S.		$14.00/$8.00
Vestron	LV5080	An American Band	LD	U.S.	1985	$45.00

Label	Catalog Number	Title	Type	Country	Year	Longbox Value / Value
Capitol	CDP 7 93698-2	Beach Boys Party/Stack-O-Track	LP/LB	U.S.		$25.00/$22.00
Capitol	CDP 793694-2	Beach Boys Summer Days And Summer Nights	LP/LB	U.S.		$25.00/$22.00
Columbia	CK-462530-2	Beach Boys, The	LP	Germany		$20.00
Caribou	ZK-39946-2	Beach Boys, The	LP/LB	U.S.†	1985	$15.00/$10.00
Caribou	ZK-39946-2	Beach Boys, The	LP/LB	U.S.	1988	$15.00/$10.00
Bescol	CD-34	Beach Boys vs. Jan & Dean	LP	U.S.		$12.00
	Contains tracks by both artists					
Capitol	CDP 7 48046-2	California Girls	LP/LB	U.S.		$15.00/$10.00
Capitol	XADP-90017	Endless Harmony Golden	DJ/Smplr	Japan		$500.00
	2 CD set					
Capitol	CDP 7 46467-2	Endless Summer	LP	U.K.		$18.00
Columbia	CK-468346	Fifteen Big Ones	LP	Germany		$18.00
Sony	SRCS-6094	Fifteen Big Ones	LP	Japan		$25.00
Caribou	46955-2	Fifteen Big Ones	LP/LB	U.S.		$15.00/$10.00
Capitol	CDP 7 93697-2	Friends/20-20	LP/LB	U.S.		$25.00/$22.00
Columbia		Good Vibrations	LP	U.S.		$14.00
	Distributed by Avon Cosmetics.					
Capitol	DPRO-79728	Good Vibrations	DJ/Smplr	U.S.	1993	$35.00
Capitol		Good Vibrations Session	DJ/Smplr	U.S.	1994	$20.00
Caribou	46952-2	Holland	LP/LB	U.S.		$15.00/$10.00
Caribou	46954-2	In Concert	LP/LB	U.S.		$10.00/$15.00
Capitol	CDP 7 93695-2	In Concert '64/Live In London	LP/LB	U.S.		$25.00/$22.00
Sony	SRCS-6020	Keepin' the Summer Alive	LP	Japan		$25.00
Columbia	CK-36283-2	Keepin' the Summer Alive	LP/LB	U.S.		$15.00/$10.00
Caribou	CK-35752-2	L.A.	LP/LB	U.S.		$15.00/$10.00
Capitol	CDP 7 93693-2	Little Deuce Coupe/All Summer Long	LP/LB	U.S.		$25.00/$22.00
Caribou	46956-2	Love You	LP/LB	U.S.		$15.00/$10.00
Columbia	CK-46957-2	M.I.U. Album	LP/LB	U.S.		$15.00/$10.00
Capitol	CDP 7 93698 2	Party/Stack-O-Tracks	LP/LB	U.S.	1991	$25.00/$22.00
Capitol	CD28-1003	Pet Sounds	LP	Japan	1987	$85.00
	Original version with 15 tracks.					
Capitol		Pet Sounds Sessions	DJ/Smplr	U.S.	1996	N/A
	Special stereo mix versions of songs not available on the boxed set. Limited to 5,000 copies.					
Capitol	CDP 7 93696-2	Smiley Smile/Wild Honey	LP/LB	U.S.	1990	$25.00/$20.00
Capitol	DPRO-79168	Special 14 Track Sampler	DJ/Smplr	U.S.	1989	$25.00
Capitol	PCD-226	Special DJ Copy	DJ/Smplr	Japan		$150.00
	CD in press kit with t-shirt and sticker.					
Capitol		Special DJ Copy II	DJ/Smplr	Japan		$100.00
River North		Stars And Stripes	DJ/Smplr	U.S.	1996	$20.00
Capitol	SPCD-1079	Still Cruisin	DJ/Smplr	Japan		$100.00
Sony	SRCS-6089	Sunflower	LP	Japan		$25.00
Caribou	CK-46950-2	Sunflower	LP/LB	U.S.		$15.00/$10.00
Caribou	CK-46951-2	Surf's Up	LP/LB	U.S.		$15.00/$10.00
Columbia	468326-2	Surf's Up/Holland/Sunflower	LP			$35.00
Capitol	CDP 7 93692-2	Surfer Girl/Surfin' U.S.A.	LP/LB	U.S.		$20.00/$13.00
Mobile Fidelity	UDCD-521	Surfer Girl/Surfin' U.S.A.	LP/LB	U.S.		$25.00/$22.00
Capitol	CDP 7 93691 2	Surfin' Safari/Surfin' U.S.A.	LP/LB	U.S.	1990	$25.00/$22.00
Capitol	CDP 7 48422-2	Surfin' U.S.A.	LP/LB	U.S.		$15.00/$10.00
Capitol		Thirty Years Of Good Vibrations	DJ/LP	U.S.	1993	$100.00
	Advance pressing 5CD set with white silkscreened discs and no boxed set material					
Capitol	DPRO-79728	Thirty Years Of Good Vibrations	DJ/Smplr	U.S.	1993	$25.00
Columbia	465670-2	Twenty Golden Greats	LP	Germany		$20.00
Epic	EK-37445-2	Twenty Golden Greats	LP/LB	U.S.		$15.00/$10.00

Singles

Label	Catalog Number	Title	Type	Country	Year	Longbox Value / Value
EMI	203642-3	California Dreamin'	CD3	Germany	1989	$10.00
Aris	885814	California Dreamin'	CD3	Germany	1990	$10.00
Pioneer	PIFP1026	California Girls	CDV	Japan	1991	$30.00
Phonogram	PHDR-38	Crocodile Rock	CD3	Japan	1991	$13.00/$4.00
Polydor	CDP 581	Crocodile Rock	CDJ	U.S.	1991	$3.00
EMI	CDEMT-1	Do It Again	CD5	U.K.	1991	$10.00
Brother	PROCD-3	Forever	CDJ	U.S.	1992	$3.00
		Fun Fun Fun	CD5	U.K.	1996	$10.00
Jimco	JIDK-29010	Hot Fun In the Summertime	CD3	Japan	1993	$13.00/$4.00
Brother	PROCD-2	Hot Fun In the Summertime	CDJ	U.S.	1992	$3.00
		I Get Around	CD5	Holland	1991	$10.00
Elektra	966743-2	Kokomo	CD3	Germany	1988	$8.00
Elektra	EKR-856D	Kokomo	CD3	U.K.	1988	$8.00
Elektra	PR 8014-2	Kokomo	CDJ	U.S.	1988	$3.00
Rhino	R3 73001	Lil' Bit Of Gold	CD3	U.S.	1989	$6.00/$4.00
	402483-2	Medley	CDJ	Spain	1996	$35.00
RCA	2674-2-RDJ	Problem Child	CDJ	U.S.	1990	$3.00
RCA		Problem Child	CDJ	U.S.	1990	$3.00
	Second version.					
Capitol	DPRO-79823	Somewhere Near Japan	CDJ	U.S.	1989	$3.00
EMI	203518-3	Still Cruisin'	CD3	Germany	1989	$10.00
Toshiba	XP10-2095	Still Cruisin'	CD3	Japan	1989	$13.00/$4.00
Capitol	CDCL-549	Still Cruisin'	CD5	U.K.	1989	$10.00
Capitol	DPRO-79735	Still Cruisin'	CD5	U.S.	1989	$3.00
		Summer Of Love	CDJ	U.S.		$7.00
Aris	885815	Surfin' U.S.A.	CD3	Germany	1990	$10.00
		Under the Boardwalk	CDJ	U.S.		$3.00
EMI	CDCL-579	Wouldn't It Be Nice	CD5	U.K.	1990	$10.00

Beagle

Singles

Label	Catalog Number	Title	Type	Country	Year	Longbox Value / Value
Polygram	863299-2	Things That We Say	CD5	Germany	1992	$7.00
Polygram	PZCD-220	Things That We Say	CD5	U.K.	1992	$7.00

Beal, Jeff

Full Length

Label	Catalog Number	Title	Type	Country	Year	Longbox Value / Value
Island	842651-2	Liberation	LP/LB	U.S.		$14.00/$8.00

Bears

Singles

Label	Catalog Number	Title	Type	Country	Year	Longbox Value / Value
Primitive	17523	Aches & Pains	CDJ	U.S.	1988	$2.00

Beasley, Walter

Full Length

Label	Catalog Number	Title	Type	Country	Year	Longbox Value / Value
Polygram	833866-2	Walter Beasley	LP/LB	U.S.		$14.00/$8.00

Singles

Label	Catalog Number	Title	Type	Country	Year	Longbox Value / Value
Mercury	CDP 920	Don't Say Goodbye	CDJ	U.S.	1993	$2.00
Mercury		Good Love	CDJ	U.S.		$2.00
Mercury	CDP 823	If You Ever Loved Someone And Lost	CDJ	U.S.	1993	$2.00
Mercury	CDP 186	Just Kickin' It	CDJ	U.S.	1989	$2.00
Mercury	CDP 243	You Are the One	CDJ	U.S.	1990	$2.00

Beastie Boys

Full Length

Label	Catalog Number	Title	Type	Country	Year	Longbox Value / Value
Capitol	DPRO-79558	'92 Tour Gratitude	DJ/Smplr	U.S.	1992	$6.00
Capitol		An Exciting Evening At Home	DJ/Smplr	U.S.		$6.00
Capitol	DPRO-79138	Check Your Head	DJ/Smplr	U.S.		$20.00
Capitol	DPRO-79300	Frozen Metal Head	DJ/Smplr	U.S.		$6.00
Capitol		Ill Communication	LTD/LP	Australia	1994	$35.00
	2.CD set.					
Capitol	DPRO-79355	Ill Communication	DJ/LP	U.S.	1994	$12.00
	Clean version.					
		In Sound From Way Out!	DJ/Smplr	France	1994	$50.00
Polygram		In Sound From Way Out!	DJ/Smplr	U.S.	1994	$30.00
Capitol	DPRO-79361	Pretzel Nugget	DJ/Smplr	U.S.	1994	$7.00
EMI	GRAND 1	Sampler	DJ/Smplr	U.K.	1995	$35.00
Capitol	DPRO-79318	Songs From Check Your Head	DJ/Smplr	U.S.		$6.00

Singles

Label	Catalog Number	Title	Type	Country	Year	Longbox Value / Value
		Aglio E Aglio	CD5	U.K.	1995	$10.00
EFA	CD-7092	Cookie Puss	CD5	Germany	1988	$9.00
Rat Cage	MOTR-26CD	Cookie Puss	CD5	U.K.	1993	$9.00
Rat Cage	26	Cookie Puss	CD5	U.S.	1992	$5.00
		Dis Yourself in '89 (Just Do It)	CDJ	U.S.	1989	$9.00
CBS	654847-3	Fight For Your Right	CD3	Germany	1989	$9.00
CBS	654847-3	Fight For Your Right	CD3	U.K.	1989	$7.00
EMI	CDCL-665	Frozen Metal Head	CD5	U.K.	1992	$9.00
Capitol	CD CL 716	Get It Together	CD5	U.K.	1994	$10.00
Capitol		Get It Together	CD5	U.K.	1994	$10.00
	Second version.					
Capital	58171	Get It Together	CD5	U.S.	1994	$5.00
Capitol	DPRO-79359	Get It Together	CDJ	U.S.	1994	$6.00
Capitol	C2 15944	Gratitude	CD5	U.S.	1992	$5.00
Capitol		Gratitude	CDJ	U.S.	1992	$3.00
Capitol	203448-3	Hey Ladies	CD5	Germany	1989	$9.00
Capitol	CDCL-540	Hey Ladies	CD5	U.K.	1989	$5.00
Capitol	DPRO-79699	Hey Ladies	CDJ	U.S.	1989	$3.00
Capitol	C2 15836	Jimmy Jams	CD5	U.S.	1992	$5.00
Capitol	C2 15827	Pass the Mic	CD5	U.S.	1992	$5.00
Capitol	DPRO-79217	Pass the Mic	CDJ	U.S.	1992	$3.00
Capitol	DPRO-79178	Pass the Mic	CDJ	U.S.	1992	$6.00
Capitol	CDCL-21CD	Pass the Mic	CD5	UK.	1992	$9.00
Rat Cage	MOTR-21CD	Polly Wog Stew	CD5	U.K.	1993	$9.00
Rat Cage	21	Polly Wog Stew	CD5	U.S.	1992	$5.00
		Root Down	CD5	U.K.	1995	$10.00
Capitol	33603	Root Down	CD5	U.S.	1995	$5.00
Capitol	DPRO-79628	Root Down	CDJ	U.S.	1995	$7.00
Capitol	DPRO-79357	Sabotoge	CDJ	U.S.	1994	$3.00
Capitol	DPRO-79824	Shadrach	CDJ	U.S.	1989	$3.00
Capitol	C2 15847	So What'cha Want	CDJ	U.S.	1992	$7.00
Capital	COCL7261	Sure Shot	CD5	U.K.	1994	$10.00
Capital		Sure Shot	CD5	U.K.	1994	$10.00
	Second version.					
Capital	58226	Sure Shot	CD5	U.S.	1994	$5.00
Capitol	DPRO-79409	Sure Shot	CDJ	U.S.	1995	$6.00

Beat

Full Length

Label	Catalog Number	Title	Type	Country	Year	Longbox Value / Value
		Fantastic	LTD/LP	U.K.	1994	$30.00

Beat A Max

Full Length

Label	Catalog Number	Title	Type	Country	Year	Longbox Value / Value
SPV	5762	Liason II	LP	Germany		$15.00

Beat Box Clever

Singles

Label	Catalog Number	Title	Type	Country	Year	Longbox Value / Value
Polygram	887741-2	This Contageous	CD5	Germany	1988	$7.00

Beat Club

Singles

Label	Catalog Number	Title	Type	Country	Year	Longbox Value / Value
Robs	CDROB-3	Dreams Were Made To Be Broken	CD5	U.K.	1991	$7.00
ZYX	8-5981	Security	CD5	Germany	1990	$5.00
Robs	CDROB-1	Security	CD5	U.K.	1990	$7.00

Beat Farmers

Full Length

Label	Catalog Number	Title	Type	Country	Year	Longbox Value / Value
Rhino	75887	Tales Of the New West	LP/LB	U.S.		$14.00/$8.00

Singles

Label	Catalog Number	Title	Type	Country	Year	Longbox Value / Value
Sector	2006	Doubts About Love	CDJ	U.S.	1995	$6.00
MCA	CD45 17905	Girl I Almost Married	CDJ	U.S.	1989	$2.00

Beat Pirate

Singles

Label	Catalog Number	Title	Type	Country	Year	Longbox Value / Value
BCM	20142	Are You On 1 Mate	CD5	Germany	1989	$7.00
BCM	20275	Good Times	CD5	Germany	1990	$7.00

Beatles

Full Length

Label	Catalog Number	Title	Type	Country	Year	Longbox Value / Value
Vestron	G88F 5302	A Hard Day's Night	LD	Japan	1985	$80.00
EMI Odeon	CP35-3016	Abbey Road	LP	Japan	1982	$200.00
	Sold without obi stip in generic long box or blister pack.					
EMI Odeon	CP35-3016	Abbey Road	LP	Japan	1982	$450.00
	With obi strip.					
HMV/EMI	BEACD-25/7	Abbey Road	LTD/LP	U.K.	1990	$60.00
	HMV Store boxed set.					
ABC Radio		ABC Radio Special: Beatles '95	RS	U.S.	1996	$250.00
	2 CD set.					
Album Network		Album Network Special: Anthology 3	RS	U.S.	1996	$250.00
	3 CD picture disc set. Airdate: 12/22/96.					
Album Network		Album Network Special: Beatles Anthology II	RS	U.S.	1996	$250.00
	2 CD set. Airdate: 3/17/96					
		All Too Much	RS	Japan	1993	$60.00
	Rarities On Compact Disc Vol.14					
Westwood One		All Too Much	RS	U.S.	1993	$45.00
	Rarities On Compact Disc Vol.14					
Capitol		Anthology I	LP/LB	U.S.	1995	$28.00/$20.00
	Long box version					
Capitol	8 34445 23 6	Anthology I	LTD/LP	U.S.	1995	$35.00
	2CD set with bonus 3rd interview disc. Marketed by Best Buy.					
Capitol	DPRO-10289	Anthology I Sampler	DJ/Smplr	U.S.	1995	$65.00
Parlophone	CDANT2	Anthology II	DJ/Smplr	U.K.	1996	$85.00
Capitol	8-34448-2	Anthology II	LP/LB	U.S.	1996	$28.00/$22.00
	Long box version					
Capitol		Anthology II	LTD/LP	U.S.	1996	$25.00
	Stock CD with interview VHS video. Available only at Musicland Stores.					
Capitol		Anthology II	LTD/LP	U.S.	1996	$30.00
	2 CD set plus bonus interview CD. Available exclusively at Best Buy.					
Album Network		Anthology II	RS	U.S.	1996	$225.00
	2 CD set. Airdate: 3/17/96.					
Apple Corps Ltd.		Anthology II Multimedia CD-ROM Press Kit	DJ/Smplr	U.S.	1996	$175.00
Capitol		Anthology II Sampler	DJ/Smplr	U.S.	1996	$50.00
Apple	ANTH 3	Anthology III	DJ/Smplr	U.K.	1996	$60.00
Capitol		Anthology III	DJ/Smplr	U.S.	1996	$35.00
Capitol		Anthology III	LTD/LP	U.S.	1996	$35.00
	2 CD set with bonus interview CD. Available only through Best Buy stores.					
		At the Beeb	RS	U.S.	1993	$250.00
	6 CD set. Airdate: 5/24/93.					
Parlophone	CDP 7 90045 2	At the Hollywood Bowl	LP	Japan		$150.00
		BBC Beatles Tapes	RS	U.S.	1991	$450.00
	6 CD set. Airdate: 6/10/91					

Label	Catalog Number	Title	Type	Country	Year	Longbox Value / Value
BBC Radio		BBC Clasic Tracks	RS	U.S.	1990	$50.00
	Airdate: 12/24/90					
Westwood One		BBC Classic Tracks	RS	U.S.	1991	$50.00
	Airdate: 1/28/91					
Westwood One		BBC Classic Tracks	RS	U.S.	1991	$50.00
	Airdate: 1/4/91					
Westwood One		BBC Classic Tracks	RS	U.S.	1991	$50.00
	Airdate: 11/4/91					
Westwood One		BBC Classic Tracks	RS	U.S.	1991	$50.00
	Airdate: 5/13/91					
Westwood One		BBC Classic Tracks	RS	U.S.	1991	$50.00
	Airdate: 7/16/91					
Westwood One		BBC Classic Tracks	RS	U.S.	1991	$50.00
	Airdate: 8/26/91					
Westwood One		BBC Classic Tracks	RS	U.S.	1991	$55.00
	Airdate: 4/8/91					
Westwood One		BBC Classic Tracks	RS	U.S.	1992	$50.00
	Airdate: 1/27/92					
Westwood One		BBC Classic Tracks	RS	U.S.	1992	$50.00
	Airdate: 9/28/92					
Westwood One		BBC Classic Tracks	RS	U.S.	1992	$55.00
	Airdate: 3/30/92					
Westwood One		BBC Classic Tracks	RS	U.S.	1993	$30.00
	Airdate: 12/20/93					
Westwood One		BBC Classic Tracks	RS	U.S.	1993	$30.00
	Airdate: 3/8/93					
Westwood One		BBC Classic Tracks	RS	U.S.	1994	$35.00
	Airdate: 2/3/94					
Westwood One		BBC Classic Tracks	RS	U.S.	1994	$35.00
	Airdate: 8/1/94					
Westwood One		BBC Classic Tracks	RS	U.S.	1994	$55.00
	Airdate: 12/19/94					
Westwood One		BBC Master Tapes: Original Masters	RS	U.S.	1990	$600.00
	6 CD set.					
Westwood One		BBC Master Tapes: Original Masters	RS	U.S.	1991	$400.00
	6 CD set. Airdate: 6/10/91.					
Westwood One		BBC Master Tapes: Original Masters	RS	U.S.	1992	$250.00
	6 CD set. Airdate: 5/28/92.					
EMI		BBC Sessions Sampler	DJ/Smplr	France		$120.00
	Sampler CD with french press kit.					
BBC Transcription		BBC Transcription Disc	RS		1993	$800.00
Global Satellite Network		Beatle Breaks Vol. 3	DJ/Intvw	U.S.	1989	$45.00
Westwood One		Beatle Years - Beatles Anthology Vol. 1	RS	U.S.	1996	$50.00
	Airdate: 7/29/96.					
Westwood One		Beatle Years - Beatles Anthology Vol. 2	RS	U.S.	1996	$50.00
	Airdate: 8/5/96.					
Capitol	CDP 97036 2 3	Beatles 1962 - 1966, The	LP	U.S.	1993	$32.00
	1st pressing 2 CD set in red colored jewel box					
Capitol	CDP 97039 2 0	Beatles 1967 - 1970, The	LP	U.S.	1993	$32.00
	1st pressing 2CD seet in Blue colored jewel box					
ABC Radio		Beatles '95	RS	U.S.	1995	$175.00
	2 CD set. Airdate: 11/19/95.					
ABC-Television		Beatles Anthology: Program Information	DJ/Smplr	U.S.	1995	$350.00
	CD-ROm press kit.					
EMI		Beatles At the Beeb	DJ/LP	U.S.		$20.00
Westwood One		Beatles At the Beeb	RS	U.S.	1992	$250.00
	6 CD set.					
Capitol	BBX2-91302	Beatles Deluxe Box Set	LTD/LP	U.S.	1988	$300.00
	Limited edition 14 CD set in numbered roll-top wood box.					
Capitol	BBX2-91302	Beatles Deluxe Box Set	LTD/LP	U.S.	1991	$260.00
	Limited edition 14 CD set in roll-top wood box (not numbered).					
		Beatles I Sverige	LP	Sweden	1994	N/A
	Fan club CD and magazine.					
Polygram	847185-2	Beatles Tapes	LP	U.S.		$15.00
HMV/EMI	BEACD-25/4	Beatles, The (White Album)	LTD/LP	U.K.	1990	$50.00
	HMV Store boxed set.					
Capitol	CDP 7 46443-2	Beatles, The (White Album)	LP	U.S.	1987	$50.00
	2 CD first pressinfg numbered set.					
Capitol	CDP 7 46443-2	Beatles, The (White Album)	LP/LB	U.S.	1987	$40.00/$35.00
	2 CDs in 2 single-CD cases with LB.					
Capitol/Apple	CDP 7 46443-2	Beatles, The (White Album)	LP/LB	U.S.	1991	$28.00/$25.00
	2 CDs in 2 single-CD cases with LB.					
Capitol/Sony		Collection, The	LP	U.S.	1994	$200.00
	4 CD set. Sock coipes of The Beatles 62-70, Beatles Encyclopedia, VHS Video in custom box. Marketed by Sony/Warner Sound Exchange. Limited to 2500 copies.					
MGM	ML100166	Compleat Beatles	LD	U.S.	1982	$20.00
	Non-remastered version.					
MGM/UA	ML100166	Compleat Beatles, The	LD	U.S.	1983	$35.00
Polydor	POCP-1882	Early Tapes	LP	Japan		$30.00
EMI	BCD-20	George Martin Interview	DJ/Intvw	Japan	1994	$75.00
EMI	RNB-1	George Martin Interview	DJ/Intvw	U.K.	1994	$65.00
Century 21 Programming		Gold Disc3	DJ/Smplr	U.S.		$80.00
	Various artist CD. Contains stereo versions of "Day Tripper" and "I Love Her".					
HMV/EMI	BEACD-25/1	HMV Box Vol. 1	LTD/LP	U.K.	1990	$100.00
	4 CD HMV Store boxed set.					
HMV/EMI	BEACD-25/2	HMV Box Vol. 2	LTD/LP	U.K.	1990	$100.00
	4 CD HMV Store boxed set.					
HMV/EMI	BEACDBOX-1	HMV Collection	LTD/LP	U.K.	1990	$350.00
	16CD limited Beatles' CD catalog in hologram box.					
Album Network		In the Studio (1963-1966 "Red Album")	DJ/Smplr	U.S.	1996	$50.00
Album Network		In the Studio (White Album)	RS	U.S.		$80.00
	2 CD set.					
Polydor		Les Beatles	LTD/LP	France	1994	$200.00
	CD in 10"x10" sleeve. French record club release.					
HMV/EMI	BEACD-25/8	Let It Be	LTD/LP	U.K.	1990	$50.00
	HMV Store boxed set.					
EMI/Odeon	TOCP-8401-2	Live At the BBC	DJ/LP	Japan	1994	$200.00
	2 CD set with extra booklet					
EMI	CDPCSPDJ 7261	Live At the BBC Album Sampler	DJ/Smplr	U.S.	1994	$35.00
Spectrum	SPEC-85025	Live At the Star-Club	LP	U.K.		$25.00
Sony	AK 48544	Live At the Star-Club Vol. 1	LP/LB	U.S.	1991	$18.00/$12.00
Columbia	AK 48544	Live At the Star-Club Vol. 1	LP/LB	U.S.	1991	$25.00/$20.00
	First pressing with group photo on front booklet.					
Sony	AK 48604	Live At the Star-Club Vol. 2	LP/LB	U.S.	1991	$18.00/$12.00
Columbia	AK 48604	Live At the Star-Club Vol. 2	LP/LB	U.S.	1991	$25.00/$20.00
	First pressing with group photo on front booklet.					
K-Tel	CD-1473	Live In Hamburg '62	LP	U.S.	1987	$20.00
Westwood One		Long And Winding Road	RS	U.S.	1994	$400.00
	12 CD set. Airdate: 5/30/94					
HMV/EMI	BEACD-25/6	Magical Mystery Tour	LTD/LP	U.K.	1990	$50.00
	HMV Store boxed set.					
Olympia	73K0100A	Olympia Holiday '89	RS	U.S.	1989	$150.00
HMV/EMI	BEACD-25/9	Past Masters, Vol. 1	LTD/LP	U.K.	1990	$50.00
	HMV Store boxed set.					
HMV/EMI	BEACD-25/10	Past Masters, Vol. 2	LTD/LP	U.K.	1990	$50.00
	HMV Store boxed set.					

Company	Disk Number	Title	Type	Country	Year	Longbox Value / Value
Capitol	CDP-746435-2	Please Please Me	LP/LB	U.S.†	1987	$30.00/$30.00
	First pressing with mislabeled SPARS code ADD rather than AAD.					
Westwood One		Rarities On Compact Disc	RS	U.S.	1990	$80.00
	Vol. 2					
Westwood One		Rarities On Compact Disc	RS	U.S.	1992	$35.00
	Vol. 12					
Westwood One		Rarities On Compact Disc	RS	U.S.	1992	$35.00
	Vol. 14					
Romance	SB-18	Raw Energy	LP	U.S.		$40.00
Pioneer Artists	PA-87-M053	Ready Steady Go	LD	U.S.	1990	$17.00
EMI		Red & Blue	DJ/Smplr	France	1994	$45.00
Columbia	A-22131	Rockin' At the Star Club	LP	U.S.	1991	$18.00
	Columbia House CD club issue.					
Columbia	A-22131	Rockin' At the Star Club	LP	U.S.	1991	$25.00
	Columbia House CD club issue, first pressing with group photo on front booklet.					
Sony		Rockin' At the Star Club '62	LP	U.S.	1991	$18.00
DIR		Scott Muni's Ticket to Ride	RS	U.S.	1988	$1,200.00
	52 CD Beatles' music & interview radio show series. Airdates: 5/2/88-4/18/89.					
Capitol	DPRO-79286	Selections From "The Beatles 1962-1966" And "The Beatles 1967-1970"	DJ/Smplr	U.S.	1993	$45.00
		Sgt. Pepper: A Generation Away	RS	U.S.	1994	$85.00
HMV/EMI	BEACD-25/3	Sgt. Pepper's Lonely Hearts Club Band	LTD/LP	U.K.	1990	$50.00
	HMV Store boxed set.					
		Sixties Legends	RS	U.S.	1992	$30.00
	2 CD set. Airdate: 8/29/92					
EMI/Odeon	PCD-29	Toshiba Presents – The Best Of The Beatles 1962-1987	DJ/Smpr	Japan		$500.00
HMV/EMI	BEACD-25/5	Yellow Submarine	LTD/LP	U.K.	1990	$50.00
	HMV Store boxed set.					
		Singles				
Parlophone	203112-3	A Hard Days Night	CD3	Germany	1989	$20.00
EMI Odeon	XP10-2057	A Hard Days Night	CD3	Japan	1989	$25.00/$8.00
Parlophone	CD3R-5160	A Hard Days Night	CD3	U.K.	1989	$20.00
Capitol	C3-44306-2	A Hard Days Night	CD3	U.S.	1989	$8.00/$5.00
EMI		All My Loving	CD5	Sweden	1993	$50.00
Parlophone	201921-3	All You Need	CD3	Germany	1989	$20.00
EMI Odeon	XP2065	All You Need	CD3	Japan	1989	$25.00/$8.00
Parlophone	CD3R-5620	All You Need	CD3	U.K.	1989	$20.00
Capitol	C3-44316-2	All You Need	CD3	U.S.	1989	$8.00/$5.00
Capital		Baby It's You	CD5	Canada	1994	$10.00
Parlophone		Baby It's You	CD5	U.K.	1995	$15.00
Capital	58349	Baby It's You	CD5	U.S.	1994	$7.00
Capitol	DPRO-79553	Baby It's You	CDJ	U.S.	1995	$65.00
Toshiba	XP10-270	Ballad Of John & Yoko	CD3	Japan	1989	$25.00/$8.00
Parlophone	CD3R-5786	Ballad Of John & Yoko	CD3	U.K.	1989	$20.00
Capitol	C3-44313-2	Ballad Of John & Yoko	CD3	U.S.	1989	$8.00/$5.00
Parlophone	203111-3	Can't Buy Me Love	CD3	Germany	1989	$20.00
EMI Odeon	XP10-2056	Can't Buy Me Love	CD3	Japan	1989	$25.00/$8.00
Parlophone	CD3R-5114	Can't Buy Me Love	CD3	U.K.	1989	$20.00
Capitol	C3-44305-2	Can't Buy Me Love	CD3	U.S.	1989	$8.00/$5.00
EMI	CDBSC-1	CD-Singles Collection	CD3	Germany	1989	$130.00
	22 CD boxed set.					
EMI	TODP-2121	CD-Singles Collection	CD3	Japan	1989	$150.00
	22 CD boxed set.					
EMI	203566-0	CD-Singles Collection	CD3	U.K.	1989	$130.00
	22 CD boxed set.					
EMI		Free As A Bird	CD5	France	1995	$20.00
Parlophone		Free As A Bird	CD5	Germany	1995	$15.00
Parlophone		Free As A Bird	CD5	U.K.	1995	$15.00
Parlophone	CDFREEDJ-1	Free As A Bird	CDJ	U.K.	1995	$30.00
Capitol		Free As A Bird	CD5	U.S.	1995	$7.00
Capitol	DPRO-11153	Free As A Bird	CDJ	U.S.	1995	$20.00
Parlophone	203035-3	From Me To You	CD3	Germany	1988	$20.00
EMI Odeon	XP10-2053	From Me To You	CD3	Japan	1988	$25.00/$8.00
Parlophone	CD3R-5015	From Me To You	CD3	U.K.	1988	$20.00
Capitol	C3-44280-2	From Me To You	CD3	U.S.	1988	$8.00/$5.00
Toshiba	XP10-2069	Get Back	CD3	Japan	1989	$25.00/$8.00
Parlophone	CD3R-5777	Get Back	CD3	U.K.	1988	$20.00
Capitol	C3-44320-2	Get Back	CD3	U.S.	1988	$8.00/$5.00
Parlophone	202237-3	Hello, Goodbye	CD3	Germany	1989	$20.00
EMI/Odeon	XP10-2066	Hello, Goodbye	CD3	Japan	1989	$25.00/$8.00
Parlophone	CD3R-5655	Hello, Goodbye	CD3	U.K.	1989	$20.00
Capitol	C3-44317-2	Hello, Goodbye	CD3	U.S.	1989	$8.00/$5.00
EMI	SPCD 16912	Help!	CDJ	France		$90.00
EMI	SPCD 1692	Help!	CDJ	France	1993	$80.00
Parlophone	203115-3	Help!	CD3	Germany	1989	$20.00
EMI/Odeon	XP10-2060	Help!	CD3	Japan	1989	$25.00/$8.00
Parlophone	CD3R-5305	Help!	CD3	U.K.	1989	$20.00
Capitol	C3-44308-2	Help!	CD3	U.S.	1989	$8.00/$5.00
Parlophone	202852-3	Hey Jude	CD3	Germany	1989	$20.00
EMI/Odeon	XP10-2068	Hey Jude	CD3	Japan	1989	$25.00/$8.00
Parlophone	CD3R-5722	Hey Jude	CD3	U.K.	1989	$20.00
Capitol	C3-44319-2	Hey Jude	CD3	U.S.	1989	$8.00/$5.00
Parlophone	203113-3	I Feel Fine	CD3	Germany	1989	$20.00
EMI/Odeon	XP10-2058	I Feel Fine	CD3	Japan	1989	$25.00/$8.00
Parlophone	CD3R-5200	I Feel Fine	CD3	U.K.	1989	$20.00
Capitol	C3-44321-2	I Feel Fine	CD3	U.S.	1989	$8.00/$5.00
Parlophone	203110-3	I Want To Hold Your Hand	CD3	Germany	1989	$20.00
EMI/Odeon	XP10-2055	I Want To Hold Your Hand	CD3	Japan	1989	$25.00/$8.00
Parlophone	CD3R-5084	I Want To Hold Your Hand	CD3	U.K.	1989	$20.00
Capitol	C3-44304-2	I Want To Hold Your Hand	CD3	U.S.	1989	$8.00/$5.00
Capitol	DPRO-79319	I Want To Hold Your Hand	CDJ	U.S.	1994	$65.00
Parlophone	202467-3	Lady Madonna	CD3	Germany	1989	$20.00
EMI/Odeon	XP10-2067	Lady Madonna	CD3	Japan	1989	$25.00/$8.00
Parlophone	CD3R-5675	Lady Madonna	CD3	U.K.	1989	$20.00
Capitol	C3-44318-2	Lady Madonna	CD3	U.S.	1989	$8.00/$5.00
Parlophone	203123-3	Let It Be	CD3	Germany	1989	$20.00
Toshiba	XP10-2072	Let It Be	CD3	Japan	1989	$25.00/$8.00
Parlophone	CD3R-5833	Let It Be	CD3	U.K.	1989	$20.00
Capitol	C3-44315-2	Let It Be	CD3	U.S.	1989	$8.00/$5.00
Capitol	C2-15940-2	Love Me Do	CD5	Canada	1993	$8.00
Parlophone	203034-2	Love Me Do	CD3	Germany	1989	$20.00
EMI/Odeon	XP10-2051	Love Me Do	CD3	Japan	1989	$25.00/$8.00
Parlophone	CD3R-4949	Love Me Do	CD3	U.K.	1989	$20.00
Parlophone	CDRS-4949	Love Me Do	CD5	U.K.	1992	$18.00
Parlophone	CDRX-4949	Love Me Do	CD5	U.K.	1992	$18.00
Capitol	C3-44278-2	Love Me Do	CD3	U.S.	1988	$8.00/$5.00
Capitol	C2-15940-2	Love Me Do	CD5	U.S.	1992	$7.00
Polydor	P10P-30006	My Bonnie	CD3	Japan	1988	$25.00/$8.00
Parlophone	203117-3	Paperback Writer	CD3	Germany	1989	$20.00
EMI/Odeon	XP10-2062	Paperback Writer	CD3	Japan	1989	$25.00/$8.00
Parlophone	CD3R-5452	Paperback Writer	CD3	U.K.	1989	$20.00
Capitol	C3-44310-2	Paperback Writer	CD3	U.S.	1989	$8.00/$5.00
EMI	SPCD 1691	Penny Lane	CDJ	France		$90.00
Parlophone	203033-3	Please Please Me	CD3	Germany	1988	$20.00
EMI/Odeon	XP10-2052	Please Please Me	CD3	Japan	1988	$25.00/$8.00
Parlophone	CD3R-4983	Please Please Me	CD3	U.K.	1988	$20.00
Capitol	C3-44279-2	Please Please Me	CD3	U.S.	1988	$8.00/$5.00

Label	Catalog Number	Title	Type	Country	Year	Longbox Value / Value
Parlophone		Real Love	CD5	U.K.	1996	$15.00
Parlophone	REALDJ 1	Real Love	CDJ	U.K.	1996	$55.00
Capitol		Real Love	CD5	U.S.	1996	$7.00
Capitol	DPRO-11187	Real Love	CDJ	U.S.	1996	$20.00
Parlophone	203036-3	She Loves You	CD3	Germany	1988	$20.00
EMI/Odeon	XP10-2054	She Loves You	CD3	Japan	1988	$25.00/$8.00
Parlophone	CD3R-5055	She Loves You	CD3	U.K.	1988	$20.00
Capitol	C3-44281-2	She Loves You	CD3	U.S.	1988	$8.00/$5.00
Parlophone	203122-3	Something	CD3	Germany	1989	$20.00
Toshiba	XP10-2071	Something	CD3	Japan	1989	$25.00/$8.00
Parlophone	CD3R-5814	Something	CD3	U.K.	1989	$20.00
Capitol	C3-44314-2	Something	CD3	U.S.	1989	$8.00/$5.00
EMI	SPCD 1691	Strawberry Fields Forever	CDJ	France	1993	$80.00
Parlophone	203119-3	Strawberry Fields Forever	CD3	Germany	1989	$20.00
EMI/Odeon	XP-2064	Strawberry Fields Forever	CD3	Japan	1989	$25.00/$8.00
Parlophone	CD3R-5570	Strawberry Fields Forever	CD3	U.K.	1989	$20.00
Capitol	C3-44312-2	Strawberry Fields Forever	CD3	U.S.	1989	$8.00/$5.00
Parlophone	203114-3	Ticket To Ride	CD3	Germany	1989	$20.00
EMI/Odeon	XP10-2059	Ticket To Ride	CD3	Japan	1989	$25.00/$8.00
Parlophone	CD3R-5265	Ticket To Ride	CD3	U.K.	1989	$20.00
Capitol	C3-44307-2	Ticket To Ride	CD3	U.S.	1989	$8.00/$5.00
Parlophone	203116-3	We Can Work It Out	CD3	Germany	1989	$20.00
EMI/Odeon	XP10-2061	We Can Work It Out	CD3	Japan	1989	$25.00/$8.00
Parlophone	CD3R-5839	We Can Work It Out	CD3	U.K.	1989	$20.00
Capitol	C3-44309-2	We Can Work It Out	CD3	U.S.	1989	$8.00/$5.00
Parlophone	203118-3	Yellow Submarine	CD3	Germany	1989	$20.00
EMI/Odeon	XP10-2063	Yellow Submarine	CD3	Japan	1989	$25.00/$8.00
Parlophone	CD3R-5493	Yellow Submarine	CD3	U.K.	1989	$20.00
Capitol	C3-44311-2	Yellow Submarine	CD3	U.S.	1989	$8.00/$5.00

Beatles Revival

Singles

Label	Catalog Number	Title	Type	Country	Year	Longbox Value / Value
RCA	PD-43154	Die Welt [illegible]	CD5	Germany	1989	$7.00

Beatmasters

Singles

Label	Catalog Number	Title	Type	Country	Year	Longbox Value / Value
Rhythm King	4001	Dunno What It Is	CD5	U.S.	1991	$5.00
Sire	9 21739-2	Warm Love	CD5	U.S.	1990	$5.00
Rhythm King	LEFT 31CD	Who's In the House	CD5	U.K.	1989	$10.00

Beatnuts

Full Length

Label	Catalog Number	Title	Type	Country	Year	Longbox Value / Value
Relativity	0185	Intoxicated Dreams–The Radio Friendly EP	DJ/Smplr	U.S.	1993	$7.00

Beats 4 U

Singles

Label	Catalog Number	Title	Type	Country	Year	Longbox Value / Value
EMI	204127-2	I Am Your Punisher	CD5	Germany	1990	$7.00
EMI	203955-2	It's Not Over	CD5	Germany	1990	$7.00
EMI	203883-2	It's Not Over	CD5	Germany	1990	$7.00

Beats International

Full Length

Label	Catalog Number	Title	Type	Country	Year	Longbox Value / Value
Polygram	828306	Excursion Version	LP/BP	U.S.		$14.00/$8.00

Singles

Label	Catalog Number	Title	Type	Country	Year	Longbox Value / Value
Polygram	869171-2	Burundi Blues	CD5	Germany	1990	$7.00
Polygram	GODCD-45	Burundi Blues	CD5	U.K.	1990	$7.00
Polygram	886969-2	Dub Be Good To Me	CD5	Germany	1990	$7.00
GoBeat	GODCD 39	Dub Be Good To Me	CD5	U.K.	1990	$8.00
Elektra	9-66654-2	Dub Be Good To Me	CD5	U.S.	1990	$4.00
Elektra	PRCD 8164-2	Dub Be Good To Me	CDJ	U.S.	1990	$3.00
Polygram	GODCD-51	Echo Chamber	CD5	U.K.	1991	$7.00
		Into the Ghetto	CD5	Australia	[illegible]	$7.00
Polygram	GODCD-64	Into the Ghetto	CD5	U.K.	1990	$7.00
Polygram	869521-2	Sun Doesn't Shine	CD5	Germany	1991	$7.00
Polygram	GODCD-59	Sun Doesn't Shine	CD5	U.K.	1991	$7.00
London	PODD-6002	Thank You Mr. DJ	CD3	Japan	1990	$13.00/$4.00
Polygram	869013-2	Won't Talk About It	CD5	Germany	1990	$7.00
Polygram	GODCD-43	Won't Talk About It	CD5	U.K.	1990	$7.00
Elektra	PRCD 8230-2	Won't Talk About It	CDJ	U.S.	1990	$3.00

Beau Brummels

Singles

Label	Catalog Number	Title	Type	Country	Year	Longbox Value / Value
Aris	885816	Laugh Laugh	CD3	Germany	1990	$8.00

Beau Nasty

Singles

Label	Catalog Number	Title	Type	Country	Year	Longbox Value / Value
		Love Potion No. 9	CDJ	U.S.		$2.00
WTG	PSK 1987	Paradise In the Sand	CDJ	U.S.	1989	$2.00
WTG	PSK 1845	Shake It	CDJ	U.S.	1989	$2.00

Beauties

Full Length

Label	Catalog Number	Title	Type	Country	Year	Longbox Value / Value
Gasoline Alley	54482	Something About the Pain	DJ/Smplr	U.S.	1992	$7.00
Gasoline Alley	54482	Something About the Pain	DJ/Smplr	U.S.	1992	$12.00
	CD and VHS tape in box					

Singles

Label	Catalog Number	Title	Type	Country	Year	Longbox Value / Value
Gasoline Alley	54482	Asses	CD5	U.S.	1992	$5.00

Beautiful

Full Length

Label	Catalog Number	Title	Type	Country	Year	Longbox Value / Value
Giant	PRO-CD-5102	John Doe	DJ/Smplr	U.S.	1992	$6.00

Singles

Label	Catalog Number	Title	Type	Country	Year	Longbox Value / Value
Giant	PRO-CD-4399	Highway	CDJ	U.S.	1991	$2.00
Giant	PRO-CD-5587	Storybook	CDJ	U.S.	1992	$2.00

Beautiful Ballet

Singles

Label	Catalog Number	Title	Type	Country	Year	Longbox Value / Value
ZYX	6463-8	Energy	CD5	U.K.	1991	$6.00

Beautiful Girls

Full Length

Label	Catalog Number	Title	Type	Country	Year	Longbox Value / Value
WEA	PRCD 94162	Sampler	DJ/Smplr	U.S.	1995	$4.00

Beautiful Losers

Singles

Label	Catalog Number	Title	Type	Country	Year	Longbox Value / Value
WEA	NYSCD-10	Be With Me	CD5	U.K.	1992	$7.00

Beautiful People

Full Length

Label	Catalog Number	Title	Type	Country	Year	Longbox Value / Value
Continuum		If '60s Was '90s	DJ/LP	U.S.	1994	$12.00

Singles

Label	Catalog Number	Title	Type	Country	Year	Longbox Value / Value
Continuum	13315	If '60s Was '90s	CDJ	U.S.	1994	$3.00
Continuum	12315	Rilly Groove	CDJ	U.S.	1993	$3.00

Beautiful South

Full Length

Label	Catalog Number	Title	Type	Country	Year	Longbox Value / Value
		Welcome Back	DJ/Smplr	U.S.	1995	$12.00

Singles

Label	Catalog Number	Title	Type	Country	Year	Longbox Value / Value
Go Discs	GOD CD 88	36D	CD5	U.K.	1992	$10.00
Go! Disc	869211-2	A Little Time	CD5	Germany	1990	$8.00
London	POCD-1038	A Little Time	CD5	Japan	1990	$13.00
Go! Disc	GODCD-47	A Little Time	CD5	U.K.	1990	$8.00
Elektra	PRCD 8256-2	A Little Time	CDJ	U.S.	1990	$2.00
Go Disc	GOLCD 78	Bell Bottomed Tear	CD5	U.K.	1992	$8.00
		Everybody's Talkin'	CD5	U.K.		$10.00
		Everybody's Talkin'	CD5	U.K.		$10.00
	Second version.					
		Good As Gold	CD5	U.K.	1994	$9.00
		Good As Gold	CD5	U.K.	1994	$9.00
	Second version.					
Polygram	876681-2	I'll Sail This Ship Alone	CD5	Geramny	1990	$8.00
Elektra	PRCD 8355-2	I've Come For My Award	CDJ	U.S.	1990	$2.00
Go! Disc	GODCD-53	Let Love Speak Up Itself	CD5	U.K.	1990	$8.00
Go! Disc	869253-2	My Book	CD5	Germany	1990	$8.00
Elektra	PRCD 8291-2	My Book	CDJ	U.S.	1990	$2.00
Elektra	9 66578-2	My Book	CDJ	U.S.	1991	$2.00
Polydor	PODD-1017	Old Red Eyes Is Back	CD3	Japan	1992	$13.00/$4.00
Go! Disc	GODCD-66	Old Red Eyes Is Back	CD5	U.K.	1992	$8.00
Elektra	PRCD 8608-2	Old Red Eyes Is Back	CDJ	U.S.	1992	$2.00
		One Last Love Song	CD5	U.K.		$10.00
		One Last Love Song	CD5	U.K.		$10.00
	Second version.					
		Prettiest Eyes	CD5	U.K.	1994	$10.00
		Prettiest Eyes	CD5	U.K.	1994	$10.00
	Second version.					
London	874 486-2D	Song For Whoever	CDJ	Canada	1989	$5.00
Go! Disc	874748-3	Song For Whoever	CD3	Germany	1989	$8.00
Go! Disc	874487-3	Song For Whoever	CD3	Germany	1989	$8.00
Go! Disc	874749-2	Song For Whoever	CD5	Germany	1989	[illegible]
Go! Disc	GODCD-32	Song For Whoever	CD5	U.K.	1989	$8.00
Go! Disc	869689-2	We Are Each Other	CD5	Germany	1992	$8.00
Go! Disc	BPSCD 2	We Are Each Other	CD5	U.K.	1992	$10.00
Go Discs	GOD CD 71	We Are Each Other	CD5	U.K.	1992	$10.00
Elektra	PRCD 8551-2	We Are Each Other	CDJ	U.S.	1992	$2.00
Elektra		Welcome Back	CDJ	U.S.	1995	$8.00
Go! Disc	876068-3	You Keep It All In	CD3	Germany	1989	$8.00
Go! Disc	876069-2	You Keep It All In	CD5	Germany	1989	$8.00
Go! Disc	GODCD-35	You Keep It All In	CD5	U.K.	1990	$8.00
Elektra	PRCD 8154-2	You Keep It All In	CDJ	U.S.	1990	$2.00

Beauvoir, Jean

Full Length

Label	Catalog Number	Title	Type	Country	Year	Longbox Value / Value
Columbia	CK-40403	Drums Along the Mohawk	LP/LB	U.S.		$14.00/$8.00
Columbia	CK-40621	Jacknifed	LP/LB	U.S.		$14.00/$8.00

Singles

Label	Catalog Number	Title	Type	Country	Year	Longbox Value / Value
Virgin	659840	Gamblin' Man	CD5	Germany	1988	$8.00
Virgin	VSCD-1056	Gamblin' Man	CD5	U.K.	1988	$8.00

Beavis And Butt-Head

Full Length

Label	Catalog Number	Title	Type	Country	Year	Longbox Value / Value
Geffen	PRO-CD-4590	Alternative/College Sampler	DJ/Smplr	U.S.	1993	$8.00
Geffen	PRO-CD-4599	Street Sampler	DJ/Smplr	U.S.	1993	$8.00

Singles

Label	Catalog Number	Title	Type	Country	Year	Longbox Value / Value
Geffen	PRO-CD-4580	99 Ways To Die	CDJ	U.S.	1993	$6.00
	With Megadeth					
Geffen		Come To Butt-Head	CDJ	U.S.	1993	$6.00
Geffen	PRO-CD-4589	I Am Hell	CDJ	U.S.	1993	$6.00
	With White Zombie					
Geffen	GFSTD 64	I Got You Babe	CD5	U.K.	1993	$11.00
	With Cher.					
Geffen		I Got You Babe	CD5	U.K.	1993	$12.00
	With Cher. Second version.					
Geffen	PRO-CD-4600	I Got You Babe	CDJ	U.S.	1993	$6.00
	With Cher.					
Geffen	PRO-CD-4600	I Got You Babe	CDJ	U.S.	1993	$10.00

Bechet, Sidney

Full Length

Label	Catalog Number	Title	Type	Country	Year	Longbox Value / Value
Vogue	VG-600122	And His American Friends Vol.1	LP	U.S.		$8.00
Mosaic	MD4-110	Complete Blue Note Recordings	LP	U.S.		$60.00
	4 CD set.					
Vogue	VG-600023	Olympia Concert	LP	U.S.		$8.00
Vogue	VG-600026	Platinum For	LP	U.S.		$8.00

Beck

Full Length

Label	Catalog Number	Title	Type	Country	Year	Longbox Value / Value
DGC	PRO-CD-4653	AAA Sampler	DJ/Smplr	U.S.	1994	$8.00
DGC		Mellow Gold	LTD/LP	Australia	1994	$30.00
	2 CD set.					
DGC	PRO-CD-4633	Mellow Gold	DJ/Smplr	U.S.	1994	$8.00
DGC		Odelay	LTD/LP	Australia	1996	$35.00
	2 CD set.					

Singles

Label	Catalog Number	Title	Type	Country	Year	Longbox Value / Value
DGC	220000	Beercan	CD5	U.S.	1994	$6.00
DGC	DGCDM21930	Loser	CD5	Canada	1994	$7.00
DGC	21930	Loser	CD5	U.S.	1994	$6.00
Geffen		Loser	CDJ	U.S.	1994	$7.00
DGC	PRO-CD-4639	Pay No Mind	CDJ	U.S.	1994	$3.00
DGC		Where It's At	CDJ	U.K.	1996	$10.00

Beck, Jeff

Full Length

Label	Catalog Number	Title	Type	Country	Year	Longbox Value / Value
Epic Legacy	ESK 4275	Beckology: The Sampler	DJ/Smplr	U.S.	1991	$20.00
Epic	ESCA-7601	Blow By Blow	LTD/LP	Japan	1996	$40.00
	20 Bit mastering.					
Epic	EK 33409	Blow By Blow	LP/BP	U.S.†	1984	$15.00/$9.00
Epic	EK53442	Blow By Blow	LP/LB	U.S.	1993	$28.00/$25.00
	20 Bit mastering.					
CBS	ESK 1901	Fire Meets Fury	DJ/Smplr	U.S.	1989	$35.00
CBS/Fender	ESK 1901	Fire Meets Fury	DJ/Smplr	U.S.	1989	$50.00
	Fender guitar cover.					
Epic	EK 39483	Flash	LP/BP	U.S.†	1985	$15.00/$9.00
Westwood One		In Concert	RS	U.S.	1993	$70.00
	Airdate: 3/15/93					
EMI	CP-32-5694	Late '60's	LP	Japan		$25.00
Epic	EK 34433	Live	LP/BP	U.S.†	1985	$15.00/$9.00
	With Jan Hammer Group.					
Epic	ESCA-5865	Star Box	LP	Japan		$30.00
CBS	CD86012	Wired	LP	Germany		$20.00
Epic	EK 33849	Wired	LP/BP	U.S.†	1984	$15.00/$9.00

Singles

Label	Catalog Number	Title	Type	Country	Year	Longbox Value / Value
Sony	XEUK11659733	Crazy Legs	CD5	Canada	1993	$9.00
Epic	CDBECK-1CD	Guitar Shop	CD5	U.K.	1989	$10.00
Reprise	PRO-CD-6614	Manic Depression	CDJ	U.S.	1993	$3.00

Label	Catalog Number	Title	Type	Country	Year	Longbox Value / Value
Reprise	PRO-CD-6726	Manic Depression	CDJ	U.S.	1993	$3.00
Epic	657756-2	People Get Ready	CD5	U.K.	1992	$10.00
Epic	ESK 1930	Riviera Paradise	CDJ	U.S.	1989	$10.00
Epic	108P-3082	Stand On It	CD3	Japan	1989	$13.00/$4.00
Epic	ESK 1812	Stand On It	CDJ	U.S.	1989	$6.00
Epic		Stumble, The	CDJ	U.S.		$6.00
Epic		Train Kept A Rollin	CDJ	U.S.		$6.00

Beck, Joe

Full Length

Label	Catalog Number	Title	Type	Country	Year	Longbox Value / Value
Digital Music	CD-446	Friends	LP/LB	U.S.†	1985	$14.00/$8.00
Digital Music	CD-446	Relaxin'	LP/LB	U.S.†	1985	$14.00/$8.00

Beck, Robin

Full Length

Label	Catalog Number	Title	Type	Country	Year	Longbox Value / Value
Polygram	838768-2	Trouble Or Nothin'	LP/BP	U.S.		$14.00/$8.00

Singles

Label	Catalog Number	Title	Type	Country	Year	Longbox Value / Value
Polygram	876695-2	Don't Lose Any Sleep	CD5	Germany	1990	$8.00
Polygram	872374-3	First Time	CD3	Germany	1989	$8.00
Polygram	872375-2	First Time	CD5	Germany	1989	$8.00
Mercury	CDP 197	First Time	CDJ	U.S.	1989	$2.00
Polygram	872710-3	Save Up All Your Tears	CD3	Germany	1989	$8.00
Polygram	872711-2	Save Up All Your Tears	CD5	Germany	1989	$8.00
Polygram	MERCD-278	Save Up All Your Tears	CD5	U.K.	1989	$8.00
Mercury	CDP 136	Save Up All Your Tears	CDJ	U.S.	1989	$2.00
Polygram	874978-3	Tears In the Rain	CD3	Germany	1989	$8.00
Polygram	874979-2	Tears In the Rain	CD5	Germany	1989	$8.00
Polygram	MERCD-303	Tears In the Rain	CD5	U.K.	1989	$8.00

Becker, Walter

Full Length

Label	Catalog Number	Title	Type	Country	Year	Longbox Value / Value
Giant		Sampler	DJ/Smplr	U.S.	1994	$10.00
Giant	PRO-CD-7144	Words & Music	DJ/Intvw	U.S.	1994	$10.00

Singles

Label	Catalog Number	Title	Type	Country	Year	Longbox Value / Value
Giant		Book Of Liars	CDJ	U.S.		$6.00

Becket, Peter

Singles

Label	Catalog Number	Title	Type	Country	Year	Longbox Value / Value
Alfa	ALDB-151	Hangin' By A Sled	CD3	Japan	1992	$13.00/$4.00

Becketts

Singles

Label	Catalog Number	Title	Type	Country	Year	Longbox Value / Value
Curb	068	Brother Louie	CDJ	U.S.	1991	$2.00
Columbia	657807-2	Everybody You Know	CD5	U.K.	1992	$8.00
Curb	10532	How Can the Girl Refuse	CDJ	U.S.	1989	$2.00
Columbia	658162-2	Summer Song	CD5	U.K.	1992	$8.00
Columbia	657580-2	Teenage Mother Superior	CD5	U.K.	1992	$8.00

Bedhead

Singles

Label	Catalog Number	Title	Type	Country	Year	Longbox Value / Value
Trance	29	Bedhead	CD5	U.S.	1994	$5.00

Bedlam

Full Length

Label	Catalog Number	Title	Type	Country	Year	Longbox Value / Value
MCA	MCAD-10471	Into the Coal	LP/LB	U.S.		$14.00/$8.00

Singles

Label	Catalog Number	Title	Type	Country	Year	Longbox Value / Value
MCA	2115	Carnival Lights	CDJ	U.S.	1992	$2.00

Bee Cee Dee

Singles

Label	Catalog Number	Title	Type	Country	Year	Longbox Value / Value
	1004	Freak Time	CD5	U.S.	1994	$5.00

Bee Gees

Full Length

Label	Catalog Number	Title	Type	Country	Year	Longbox Value / Value
Polydor	825220-2	Bee Bees	LP	Germany		$15.00
Polydor	825220-2	Bee Bees	LP	U.K.		$15.00
Polygram	825220-2	Bee Bees	LP/BP	U.S.		$14.00/$8.00
		Birth of Brilliance	LTD/LP	Australia		N/A
	2CD set.					
RSO	823658-2	Children Of the World	LP/BP	U.S.		$14.00/$8.00
Warner Brothers	9 25441-2	E.S.P.	LP/LB	U.S.		$14.00/$8.00
RSO	825220-2	First	LP/BP	U.S.†	1985	$15.00/$9.00
RSO	800071-2GH	Greatest Hits	LP/LB	U.S.†	1984	$25.00/$18.00
	2 CD set.					
Warner Brothers		High Civilization	LP/LB	U.S.		$14.00/$8.00
Polygram	833659-2	Horizontal	LP/BP	U.S.		$14.00/$8.00
Polygram	833660-2	Idea	LP/BP	U.S.		$14.00/$8.00
Polygram	833788	Life In A Tin Can	LP/BP	U.S.		$14.00/$8.00
RSO	813642-2	Living Eyes	LP	U.K.	1985	$15.00
RSO	813642-2	Living Eyes	LP/BP	U.S.†	1985	$14.00/$8.00
RSO	813642-2	Living Eyes	LP/BP	U.S.	1988	$14.00/$8.00
RSO	833790-2	Main Course	LP/BP	U.S.		$14.00/$8.00
RSO	825451-2	Odessa	LP/BP	U.S.	1985	$14.00/$8.00
Warner Brothers	25887-2-Dj	One	DJ/LP	U.S.	1989	$12.00
Warner Brothers	9 25887-2	One	LP/LB	U.S.	1989	$14.00/$8.00
Polydor	CDP 770	Paying the Price Of Love	DJ/Smplr	U.S.	1993	$20.00
		Size Isn't Everything	DJ/LP	France	1994	$50.00
		Spicks And Specks	LP	U.S.		$10.00
RSO	827335-2	Spirits Having Flown	LP	U.K.		$15.00
Polygram	833786-2	Trafalgar	LP/BP	U.S.		$14.00/$8.00
Polygram	833785-2	Two Years On	LP/BP	U.S.		$14.00/$8.00
IMS	835860-2	Very Best Of	LP	Germany		$25.00

Singles

Label	Catalog Number	Title	Type	Country	Year	Longbox Value / Value
Warner Brothers	920879-2	Angela	CD3	Germany	1988	$8.00
		Blue Island	CDJ	Spain	1994	$25.00
Warner Brothers	PRO-CD-3905	Bodyguard	CDJ	U.S.	1989	$3.00
Warner Brothers	PRO-CD-2902	ESP	CDJ	U.S.	1987	$3.00
	520279	First	CD5	U.S.	1994	$5.00
Polydor	PZCD 299	For Whom the Bell Tolls	CD5	U.K.	1993	$9.00
Polydor		For Whom the Bell Tolls	CDJ	U.K.	1993	$15.00
Polygram	855 332	For Whom The Bell Tolls	CD5	U.S.	1994	$5.00
Polygram	855332	For Whom The Bell Tolls	CD5	U.S.	1994	$5.00
Warner Brothers	PRO-CD-5007	Happy Ever After	CDJ	U.S.	1991	$3.00
IMS	879223-2	How Deep Is Your Love	CD5	Germany	1991	$10.00
RSO	P10W-30002	How Deep Is Your Love	CD3	Japan	1988	$13.00/$4.00
Polygram		How To Fall In Love	CD5	U.K.	1994	$10.00
Polygram		How To Fall In Love	CD5	U.K.	1994	$10.00
	Second version.					
Polygram		How To Fall In Love	CDJ	U.S.	1994	$3.00
Polygram		Kiss Of Life	CDJ	France	1994	$15.00
Polygram		Kiss Of Life	CD5	Germany	1994	$12.00
Pioneer	PIFP-1012	Massachusetts	CDV	Japan		$35.00
Polygram	885871-2	Massachusetts	CD5	Germany	1990	$8.00
RSO	P10W-3003	Night Fever	CD3	Japan	1988	$13.00/$4.00
Warner Brothers	921246-2	One	CD3	Germany	1989	$8.00
Warner Brothers	09D3-6183	One	CD3	Japan	1989	$13.00/$4.00
Warner Brothers	W-2916CD	One	CD3	U.K.	1989	$8.00

Company	Disk Number	Title	Type	Country	Year	Longbox Value / Value
Warner Brothers	PRO-CD-3605	One	CDJ	U.S.	1989	$3.00
Warner Brothers	9362-40093-2	Only Love, The	CD5	Germany	1991	$3.00
Warner Brothers	W-0049CD	Only Love, The	CD5	U.K.	1991	$8.00
Warner Brothers	921175-2	Ordinary Lives	CD3	Germany	1989	$8.00
Pioneer	09P3-6136	Ordinary Lives	CD3	Japan	1989	$13.00/$4.00
Warner Brothers	W-7523CD	Ordinary Lives	CD3	U.K.	1989	$8.00
Polydor	859 165	Paying the Price Of Love	CD5	U.S.	1993	$5.00
Polygram	CDP 1044	Paying the Price Of Love	CDJ	U.S.	1993	$2.00
Warner Brothers	9362-40014-2	Secret Love	CD5	Germany	1991	$8.00
Warner Brothers		Secret Love	CD3	Japan	1991	$13.00/$4.00
Warner Brothers	W-0014CD	Secret Love	CD5	U.K.	1991	$8.00
Warner Brothers		Size isn't Everything	CD5	U.K.		$8.00
Warner Brothers		Staying Alive	CD5	France	1995	$25.00
Warner Brothers	921345-2	Tokyo Nights	CD3	Germany	1989	$8.00
Warner Brothers		Tomorrow the World	CD5	U.K.		$8.00
Warner Brothers	WPDP-6275	True Confessions	CD3	Japan	1991	$13.00/$4.00
Warner Brothers	9362 40088	When He's Gone	CD5	Germany	1991	$8.00
Warner Brothers	W-0029CD	When He's Gone	CD5	U.K.	1991	$8.00
Warner Brothers	PRO-CD-4737	When He's Gone	CDJ	U.S.	1991	$3.00
Warner Brothers	10SW-18	You Win Again	CD3	Japan	1989	$13.00/$4.00
Warner Brothers	PRO-CD-2809	You Win Again	CDJ	U.S.	1987	$3.00
Warner Brothers	PRO-CD-3786	You Win Again	CDJ	U.S.	1989	$3.00

Bee, Robby

Singles

Company	Disk Number	Title	Type	Country	Year	Longbox Value / Value
Warrior	5	Pow Wow Girls	CDJ	U.S.	1991	$2.00

Been, Michael

Singles

Company	Disk Number	Title	Type	Country	Year	Longbox Value / Value
Qwest	PRO-CD-7074-R	Nearly Fell	CDJ	U.S.	1995	$3.00
Red Dot	RDT-3CD	To Feel This Way	CD5	U.K.	1991	$8.00
Qwest	PRO-CD-7056-R	To Feel This Way	CDJ	U.S.	1995	$3.00
Qwest	PRCD 6875-2	Us	CDJ	U.S.	1994	$2.00

Beggars

Singles

Company	Disk Number	Title	Type	Country	Year	Longbox Value / Value
	PRCD 7040-2	Lonely Soul Detonator	CDJ	U.S.		$2.00

Beghe, Francesca

Full Length

Company	Disk Number	Title	Type	Country	Year	Longbox Value / Value
SBK	96206	Heaven Knows	DJ/LP	U.S.	1991	$13.00

Singles

Company	Disk Number	Title	Type	Country	Year	Longbox Value / Value
EMI	TODP-2287	Heaven Knows	CD3	Japan	1991	$13.00/$4.00
SBK	DPRO-05369	Heaven Knows	CDJ	U.S.	1991	$2.00

Beiderbecke, Bix

Singles

Company	Disk Number	Title	Type	Country	Year	Longbox Value / Value
	41065	Singin' The Blues	CD5	U.S.	1994	$5.00

Beijing Spring

Singles

Company	Disk Number	Title	Type	Country	Year	Longbox Value / Value
MCA	MCSTD-1709	I Wanna Be In Love Again	CD5	U.K.	1992	$8.00
BMCA	MCSTD-1633	We Can Keep This Together	CD5	U.K.	1992	$8.00

Beirach, Richard

Full Length

Company	Disk Number	Title	Type	Country	Year	Longbox Value / Value
Owl	380048-2	Common Heart	LP	U.S.		$8.00

Bel Air

Singles

Company	Disk Number	Title	Type	Country	Year	Longbox Value / Value
Polygram	877559-2	Pillow Talk	CD5	Germany	1990	$8.00

Bel Air Strings

Singles

Company	Disk Number	Title	Type	Country	Year	Longbox Value / Value
JVC	VDP-15007	Valentine With Strings	CD5	Japan	1989	$10.00

Bel Canto

Singles

Company	Disk Number	Title	Type	Country	Year	Longbox Value / Value
	PRCD 6649	Rumor	CDJ	U.S.		$3.00
Dali	8740	Shimmering, Warm & Bright	CDJ	U.S.	1993	$2.00
Nettwerk	IRSD 026	Shoulder To the Wheel	CDJ	U.S.	1990	$2.00
Dali	8663	Unicorn	CDJ	U.S.	1992	$2.00

Bel Tane

Singles

Company	Disk Number	Title	Type	Country	Year	Longbox Value / Value
PWL	PWL-231	Solarize	CD5	U.K.	1992	$8.00

Belafonte, Harry

Full Length

Company	Disk Number	Title	Type	Country	Year	Longbox Value / Value
RCA	PD-92247	Belafonte 1989	LP/BP	U.S.		$14.00/$8.00
RCA	886477	Belafonte At Carnegie Hall	LP	Germany		$20.00
RCA	PD-89796	Legend	LP	Germany		$20.00
EMI	46971	Paradise In Gazankulu	LP/BP	U.S.		$14.00/$8.00

Singles

Company	Disk Number	Title	Type	Country	Year	Longbox Value / Value
EMI	203343-2	Island In the Sun	CD5	Germany	1989	$10.00

Belafonte, Shari

Singles

Company	Disk Number	Title	Type	Country	Year	Longbox Value / Value
Polygram	873254-3	Give A Little Love	CD3	Germany	1989	$10.00
Polygram	873255-2	Give A Little Love	CD5	Germany	1989	$10.00
Polygram	887384-2	I Want To Be Needed	CD5	Germany	1988	$10.00
Polygram	887384-2	I Want To Be Needed	CD5	U.K.	1988	$10.00

Belden, Bob

Singles

Company	Disk Number	Title	Type	Country	Year	Longbox Value / Value
Metro Blue	79887	Question Of You, The	CDJ	U.S.	1994	$3.00

Belew, Adrian

Full Length

Company	Disk Number	Title	Type	Country	Year	Longbox Value / Value
Atlantic		Acoustic Adrian	LTD/LP	U.S.	1993	$25.00
	Sold only at concert venues.					
Caroline	CAROLAV1748	Here	DJ/LP	U.S.	1994	$15.00
Atlantic		Inner Revolution	LP/LB	U.S.		$14.00/$8.00
Atlantic		Young Lions	LP/LB	U.S.		$14.00/$8.00

Singles

Company	Disk Number	Title	Type	Country	Year	Longbox Value / Value
		Brave New World	CDJ	Japan		$20.00
Caroline	12	Never Enough	CDJ	U.S.	1994	$8.00
Atlantic	PRCD 3418-2	Not Alone Anymore	CDJ	U.S.	1990	$6.00
Atlantic	PR 2704-2	Oh Daddy	CDJ	U.S.	1989	$6.00
Atlantic	7 86200-2	Oh Daddy	CD5	U.S.	1990	$5.00
Atlantic	AMDY-5017	Pretty Pink Rose	CD3	Japan	1990	$13.00/$4.00
Atlantic	A-7904CD	Pretty Pink Rose	CD5	U.K.	1990	$10.00
Atlantic	7 86200-2	Pretty Pink Rose	CD5	U.S.	1990	$5.00
Atlantic	PRCD 3294-2	Pretty Pink Rose	CDJ	U.S.	1990	$7.00
Atlantic	PRCD 4430-2	Standing In the Shadow	CDJ	U.S.	1992	$6.00

Believers

Label	Catalog Number	Title	Type	Country	Year	Longbox Value / Value
Full Length						
Savage	50202	Extraordinary Life	LP	U.S.		$8.00
Singles						
Savage		Extraordinary Life	CDJ	U.S.		$2.00

Bell Biv Devoe

Label	Catalog Number	Title	Type	Country	Year	Longbox Value / Value
Singles						
MCA	MCA5P-2631	Above the Rim	CDJ	U.S.	1992	$2.00
MCA	CD45 1023	B.B.D.(I Thought It Was Me?)	CDJ	U.S.	1990	$2.00
MCA	CD45 1033	B.B.D.(I Thought It Was Me?)	CDJ	U.S.	1990	$2.00
MCA	9031-72498-2	Do Me!	CD5	Germany	1990	$8.00
Pioneer	WMD5-4033	Do Me!	CD3	Japan	1990	$13.00/$4.00
MCA	DMCAT-1440	Do Me!	CD5	U.K.	1990	$8.00
MCA	CD45-24061	Do Me!	CD5	U.S.	1990	$5.00
MCA	18382	Do Me!	CDJ	U.S.	1990	$2.00
MCA	MCA5P-2317	From the Back	CDJ	U.S.	1992	$2.00
MCA	MVDM-32	Gangsta	CD3	Japan	1992	$13.00/$4.00
MCA	MCA5P-2491	Gangsta	CDJ	U.S.	1992	$2.00
MCA	MCA5P-2538	Gangsta	CDJ	U.S.	1993	$2.00
MCA	53899	I Thought It Was Me	CD5	U.S.	1990	$5.00
MCA	MVDM-38	Lovely	CD3	Japan	1993	$13.00/$4.00
MCA	2292-57258-2	Poison	CD5	Ger many	1990	$8.00
Eastwest	257258-2	Poison	CD5	Germany	1990	$8.00
MCA	WMD5-4028	Poison	CD3	Japan	1990	$13.00/$4.00
MCA	DMCAT-1414	Poison	CD5	U.K.	1990	$8.00
MCA	24056	Poison	CD5	U.S.	1990	$5.00
MCA	CD45 18183	Poison	CDJ	U.S.	1990	$2.00
MCA	CD45 18218	Poison	CDJ	U.S.	1990	$2.00
MCA		Ralph And Johnny	CD3	Japan	1990	$13.00/$4.00
MCA		Ralph And Johnny	CDJ	U.S.	1990	$2.00
MCA	1329	She's Dope	CDJ	U.S.	1990	$6.00
MCA	CD45 1341	She's Dope	CDJ	U.S.	1991	$2.00
MCA	MCA5P-2802	Something In Your Eyes	CDJ	U.S.	1993	$2.00
MCA	CD45 1170	When Will I See You Smile Again	CDJ	U.S.	1990	$2.00
MCA	CD45-1318	When Will I See You Smile Again	CDJ	U.S.	1991	$2.00
MCA	MCD-17850	Word To Mutha	CD5	Germany	1991	$8.00
MCA	MVDM-8	Word To Mutha	CD3	Japan	1991	$13.00/$4.00
MCA	MCSTD-1587	Word To Mutha	CD5	U.K.	1991	$8.00

Bell, Jennifer

Label	Catalog Number	Title	Type	Country	Year	Longbox Value / Value
Singles						
Polygram	887760-2	I Just Can't Get Enough	CD5	Germany	1988	$8.00
Polydor	P13R-37001	I Just Can't Get Enough	CD3	Japan	1988	$13.00/$4.00
Polydor	P10X-30001	Together Forever	CD3	Japan	1988	$13.00/$4.00
Polygram	871698-3	Woman In Love	CD3	Germany	1989	$8.00
Polygram	871699-2	Woman In Love	CD5	Germany	1989	$8.00

Bell, Teja

Label	Catalog Number	Title	Type	Country	Year	Longbox Value / Value
Singles						
		Ukranian Bell Carol	CDJ	U.S.		$2.00

Bellamy Brothers

Label	Catalog Number	Title	Type	Country	Year	Longbox Value / Value
Full Length						
MCA	MCAD-42039	Crazy From the Heart	LP/LB	U.S.		$14.00/$8.00
Atlantic	7 82232-2	Rollin' Thunder	LP/LB	U.S.		$14.00/$8.00
Singles						
BMG	665126	Beggars & Heroes	CD5	Germany	1992	$8.00
BMG	664654	Fly Me To Eden	CD5	Germany	1991	$8.00
		I Could Be Persuaded	CDJ	U.S.		$2.00
BMG	664148	Neon Cowboy	CD5	Germany	1991	$8.00

Bellamy, Lisa

Label	Catalog Number	Title	Type	Country	Year	Longbox Value / Value
Singles						
Sire	9 4001-2	Work It	CD5	U.S.	1991	$5.00
Sire	40010	Work It	CD5	U.S.	1991	$5.00

Belle, Regina

Label	Catalog Number	Title	Type	Country	Year	Longbox Value / Value
Singles						
Sony	SRDS-8254	A Whole New World	CD3	Japan	1993	$13.00/$4.00
	With Peabo Bryson					
Columbia	CSK 74751	A Whole New World	CDJ	U.S.	1992	$6.00
	With Peabo Bryson					
Columbia	655122-5	Baby Come To Me	CD5	Germany	1989	$8.00
Columbia	CSK 1683	Baby Come To Me	CDJ	U.S.	1989	$2.00
Columbia	CSK 7203	Could It Be I'm Falling In Love	CDJ	U.S.	1995	$3.00
Columbia	CSK 5156	Dream In Color	CDJ	U.S.	1993	$2.00
Columbia	655449-2	Good Lovin'	CD5	U.K.	1989	$8.00
Columbia	CSK 1052	How Could You Do It To Me	CDJ	U.S.	1989	$3.00
Columbia	38K 74864	If I Could	CD5	U.S.	1993	$5.00
Columbia	CSK 74864	If I Could	CDJ	U.S.	1993	$3.00
Columbia	44K 77965	Love T.K.O.	CD5	U.S.	1995	$5.00
Columbia	CSK 7252	Love TKO	CDJ	U.S.		$2.00
Columbia	CSK 1946	Make It Like It Was	CDJ	U.S.	1989	$2.00
Columbia	CSK 73022	Make It Like It Was	CDJ	U.S.	1989	$2.00
Columbia	CSK 5155	Quiet Time	CDJ	U.S.	1993	$2.00
Columbia	650938-2	Show Me the Way	CD5	U.K.	1988	$8.00
Columbia	CSK 2818	So Many Tears	CDJ	U.S.	1987	$2.00
Columbia	CSK 73346	This Is Love	CDJ	U.S.	1990	$2.00
Columbia	CSK 73201	What Goes Around	CDJ	U.S.	1990	$2.00
Columbia		You Make Me Feel Brand New	CDJ	U.S.	1995	$2.00

Belle Stars

Label	Catalog Number	Title	Type	Country	Year	Longbox Value / Value
Singles						
EMI	203317-2	Iko Iko	CD5	Germany	1989	$8.00

Bellen, Thomas

Label	Catalog Number	Title	Type	Country	Year	Longbox Value / Value
Singles						
BMG	662819-2	Panama	CD5	Germany	1989	$8.00

Belltower

Label	Catalog Number	Title	Type	Country	Year	Longbox Value / Value
Singles						
Ultimate	TOPP-004CDS	Exploration Day	CD5	U.K.	1991	$8.00
Rough Trade	332 4006-3	In Hollow	CD5	Germany	1991	$8.00
Ultimate	TOPP-006CD	In Hollow	CD5	U.K.	1991	$8.00

Belly

Label	Catalog Number	Title	Type	Country	Year	Longbox Value / Value
Full Length						
Westwood One		In Concert-Nu Rock	RS	U.S.	1994	$50.00
	Airdate: 1/17/94					
Westwood One		In Concert-Nu Rock	RS	U.S.	1995	$50.00
	Airdate: 11/20/95					
Sire		Judas My Heart	DJ/Smplr	U.S.	1995	$15.00
Warner Brothers		King	LTD/LP	U.K.	1995	$22.00
	CD in hardback book package					
Reprise		King	DJ/LP	U.S.		$19.00
Sire	BAD 2009	Star	DJ/LP	U.S.	1993	$20.00
	Special advance issue in U.K. digipak.					
Singles						
Warner	12-41547	Are You Experienced?	CD5	Canada	1994	$8.00
Sire	9 41547-2	Are You Experienced?	CD5	U.S.	1994	$5.00
Sire	PRO-CD-6804	Are You Experienced?	CDJ	U.S.	1994	$7.00
Warner Brothers	12-40868	Feed the Tree	CD5	Canada	1993	$8.00
4AD	BAD-3001CD	Feed the Tree	CD5	U.K.	1993	$11.00
Sire	PRO-CD-5929	Feed the Tree	CDJ	U.S.	1993	$3.00
4AD		Gepetto	CD5	Japan	1993	$20.00
4AD	BAD-2018CD	Gepetto	CD5	U.K.	1993	$11.00
4AD		Gepetto	CD5	U.K.	1993	$11.00
	Second version.					
Sire	PRO-CD-6335	Gepetto	CDJ	U.S.	1994	$6.00
4AD	COCY-75469	Japan Only Special Edition	CD3	Japan	1993	$12.00/$4.00
		King	CD5	U.K.	1995	$10.00
		King	CD5	U.K.	1995	$10.00
	Second version.					
Warner Brothers	41988	Now They'll Sleep	CD5	U.S.	1994	$5.00
Sire	PRO-CD-7383	Now They'll Sleep	CDJ	U.S.	1995	$3.00
Sire		Now They'll Sleep	CDJ	U.S.	1995	$6.00
Sire	PRO-CD-7843	Red	CDJ	U.S.	1995	$6.00
		Seal My Fate	CD5	U.K.	1995	$10.00
		Seal My Fate	CD5	U.K.	1995	$10.00
	Second version.					
Sire	PRO-CD-6131	Slow Dog	CDJ	U.S.	1993	$3.00
4AD	BAD-2009CD	Slow Dog	CD5	U.K.	1993	$11.00
		Super-Connected	CD5	U.K.	1995	$10.00
		Super-Connected	CD5	U.K.	1995	$10.00
	Second version.					
Sire	PRO-CD-7564	Super-Connected	CDJ	U.S.	1995	$6.00

Belouis Some

Label	Catalog Number	Title	Type	Country	Year	Longbox Value / Value
Full Length						
EMI	746701-2	Belouis Some	LP	Germany		$15.00
Collector's Pipeline	TCP 020CD	Some People	LP	U.S.		$16.00
Singles						
EMI	201781-2	Let It Be With You	CD5	Germany	1988	$8.00
EMI	CDR-6154	Let It Be With You	CD5	U.K.	1988	$8.00
EMI	CDR-6176	Some Girls	CD5	U.K.	1988	$8.00

Beloved

Label	Catalog Number	Title	Type	Country	Year	Longbox Value / Value
Full Length						
	PRCD231	Sampler	DJ/Smplr	U.K.		$25.00
Singles						
WEA	170 930-2	Hello	CD5	Germany	1990	$8.00
WEA	YZ-426CD	Hello	CD5	U.K.	1990	$8.00
Atlantic	PR 3163-2	Hello	CDJ	U.S.	1990	$7.00
WEA	9031-72792-2	It's Alright	CD5	Germany	1990	$8.00
WEA	YZ-541CD	It's Alright	CD5	U.K.	1990	$8.00
WEA	YZ-414CD	Loving Feeling	CD5	U.K.	1990	$8.00
WEA	246688-2	Sun Rising	CD5	Germany	1990	$8.00
WEA	YZ-311CD	Sun Rising	CD5	U.K.	1990	$8.00
Warner Brothers	32-85759	Sweet Harmony	CD5	Canada	1992	$8.00
WEA	YZ-3709CD	Sweet Harmony	CD5	U.K.	1990	$8.00
Atlantic		Sweet Harmony	CDJ	U.S.	1992	$2.00
WEA	171470-2	Time After Time	CD5	Germany	1990	$8.00
WEA	YZ-482CD	Time After Time	CD5	U.K.	1990	$8.00
Atlantic	86184-2	Time After Time	CD5	U.S.	1990	$4.00
Atlantic	PRCD 3335-2	Time After Time	CDJ	U.S.	1990	$2.00
WEA	YZ-357CD	Your Love Takes Me Higher	CD5	U.K.	1990	$8.00
WEA	YZ-463CD	Your Love Takes Me Higher	CD5	U.K.	1990	$8.00

Beltram

Label	Catalog Number	Title	Type	Country	Year	Longbox Value / Value
Singles						
BMG	RSUK-3CD	Energy Flash	CD5	U.K.	1991	$8.00

Belva

Label	Catalog Number	Title	Type	Country	Year	Longbox Value / Value
Singles						
EMI	203140-2	Let Me Kiss It	CD5	Germany	1988	$8.00

Bemshi

Label	Catalog Number	Title	Type	Country	Year	Longbox Value / Value
Full Length						
Capitol	CDP 7 91687-2	Womanchild	LP/LB	U.S.		$14.00/$8.00
Singles						
Capitol	DPRO-79388	Where's My Daddy	CDJ	U.S.	1992	$2.00

Ben Folds Five

Label	Catalog Number	Title	Type	Country	Year	Longbox Value / Value
Singles						
	PSRBF5PRO2	Summer	CDJ	U.S.		$3.00
Caroline	BF5PRO1	Underground	CDJ	U.S.	1995	$3.00
		Where's Summer B	CD5	U.K.	1996	$10.00

Benatar, Pat

Label	Catalog Number	Title	Type	Country	Year	Longbox Value / Value
Full Length						
Chrysalis	VK-41275	Crimes Of Passion	LP/LB	U.S.†	1985	$14.00/$8.00
		From 79-93	DJ/Smplr	France	1993	$45.00
Chrysalis	VK-41396	Get Nervous	LP/LB	U.S.†	1985	$14.00/$8.00
Pioneer	PA-85-MO28	Hit Videos	LD	U.S.	1985	$15.00
Pioneer	PA-85-090	In Concert	LD	U.S.	1985	$25.00
Pioneer	PA-85-090	In Concert	LD	U.S.	1990	$35.00
	Digital audio					
Chrysalis	VK-41236	In the Heat Of the Night	LP/LB	U.S.†	1985	$14.00/$8.00
Album Network		In the Studio (Crimes Of Passion)	RS	U.S.	1989	$25.00
	Airdate: 1/9/89					
Album Network		In the Studio (Precious Time)	RS	U.S.	1991	$25.00
	Airdate: 12/2/91					
Album Network		In the Studio (Precious Time)	RS	U.S.	1991	$25.00
	Airdate: 7/1/91					
DIR		King Biscuit Flour Hour	RS	U.S.	1990	$30.00
	Airdate: 1/22/90					
DIR		King Biscuit Flour Hour	RS	U.S.	1991	$30.00
	Airdate: 6/9/91					
DIR		King Biscuit Flour Hour	RS	U.S.	1993	$35.00
	Airdate: 8/8/93					
Chrysalis	VK-41444	Live From Earth	LP/LB	U.S.†	1984	$14.00/$8.00
Album Network		Live From Electric Ladyland	RS	U.S.	1993	$35.00
	Airdate:6-93					
		Live From Electric Ladyland	RS	U.S.	1993	$150.00
	Airdate: 8/15/93					
Westwood One		Off the Record	RS	U.S.	1993	$30.00
	Airdate: 7/12/93					
Westwood One		Off the Record	RS	U.S.	1994	$30.00
	Airdate: 1/31/94					
Vestron	LV1073	Pat Benatar	LD	U.S.	1987	$30.00
Chrysalis	VK-41346	Precious Time	LP/LB	U.S.†	1984	$14.00/$8.00

Label	Catalog Number	Title	Type	Country	Year	Longbox Value / Value
Westwood One		Superstars	RS	U.S.	1996	$90.00
Airdate: 7/22/96.						
Chrysalis	VK-41471	Tropico	LP/LB	U.S.†	1985	$14.00/$8.00
Chrysalis	21805	True Love	DJ/LP	U.S.	1990	$16.00
Media America		Up Close	RS	U.S.	1993	$78.00
2 CD set.						
Chrysalis		Wide Awake In Dreamland	LTD/LP	U.K.	1994	$25.00/$15.00
25th Anniversary edition in 6"x11" longbox						

Singles

Label	Catalog Number	Title	Type	Country	Year	Longbox Value / Value
Chrysalis	XP10-2008	All Fired Up	CD3	Japan	1990	$13.00/$4.00
Chrysalis	PATCD-5	All Fired Up	CD5	U.K.	1990	$9.00
Chrysalis		All Fired Up	CDJ	U.S.	1990	$2.00
Chrysalis	661799	Don't Walk Away	CD5	Germany	1990	$9.00
Chrysalis	PATCD-6	Don't Walk Away	CD3	U.K.	1990	$9.00
Chrysalis	885264	One Love	CD5	Germany	1990	$9.00
Chrysalis	PATCD-7	One Love	CD5	U.K.	1990	$9.00
Chrysalis	DPRO-23428	One Love	CDJ	U.S.	1990	$6.00
Chrysalis	DPRO-23695	Payin' the Cost To Be the Boss	CDJ	U.S.	1991	$2.00
EMI	323753-2	So Long	CD5	Germany	1991	$9.00
Chrysalis	DPRO-23753	So Long	CDJ	U.S.	1991	$2.00
Chrysalis	58001	Somebody's Baby	CD5	U.K.	1993	$10.00
Chrysalis	DPRO-04743	Somebody's Baby	CDJ	U.S.	1993	$3.00
EMI	323718-2	True Love	CD5	Germany	1991	$9.00
EMI	PATCD-8	True Love	CD5	U.K.	1991	$9.00
Chrysalis	DPRO-23696	True Love	CDJ	U.S.	1991	$2.00

Bendik

Full Length

Label	Catalog Number	Title	Type	Country	Year	Longbox Value / Value
Columbia	CK-47458	IX	LP/LB	U.S.		$12.00/$7.00

Bendix, Ralf

Singles

Label	Catalog Number	Title	Type	Country	Year	Longbox Value / Value
EMI	147466-3	Babysitter-Boogie	CD3	Germany	1989	$8.00
EMI	147485-2	Babysitter-Boogie	CD5	Germany	1989	$8.00

Benedictine Monks Of Santo Domingo De Silos

Singles

Label	Catalog Number	Title	Type	Country	Year	Longbox Value / Value
EMI	DPRO-79224	Alleluia	CDJ	U.S.	1994	$6.00

Benito

Singles

Label	Catalog Number	Title	Type	Country	Year	Longbox Value / Value
		Show Me Some Love	CDJ	U.S.		$2.00

Bennett, Tony

Full Length

Label	Catalog Number	Title	Type	Country	Year	Longbox Value / Value
Polydor	J33J-20152	Chicago	LP	Japan		$25.00
Dunhill	DZS-004	Chicago	LP	U.K.		$15.00
Dunhill	DZS-004	Chicago	LP	U.S.		$9.00
Columbia		Forty Years: Selections From the Box	DJ/Smplr	U.S.	1991	$15.00
Columbia		Forty Years: The Artistry Of Tony Bennett	DJ/Smplr	U.S.	1994	$20.00
Columbia	CK-40215	Greatest Hits	LP/LB	U.S.		$15.00/$9.00
CBS	450465-2	Jazz	LP	Germany		$25.00
Laserlight	LL-15722	Jazz Collector Edition	LP	U.S.		$8.00

Singles

Label	Catalog Number	Title	Type	Country	Year	Longbox Value / Value
		Here's To the Ladies	CDJ	U.S.		$6.00
		Moonglow	CDJ	U.S.		$3.00
Atlantic	PRCD 3643-2	Rags To Riches	CDJ	U.S.	1990	$3.00
Columbia	CSK 5603	Steppin' Out With My Baby	CDJ	U.S.	1993	$3.00
Columbia	CSK 77566	Young At Heart	CDJ	U.S.	1995	$7.00

Benoit, David

Full Length

Label	Catalog Number	Title	Type	Country	Year	Longbox Value / Value
		House Of Blues	RS	U.S.	1994	$35.00
2 CD set. Airdate: 9/11/94.						
		World Music	RS	U.S.	1991	$150.00
2 CD set. Airdate: 12/1/91.						

Singles

Label	Catalog Number	Title	Type	Country	Year	Longbox Value / Value
GRP	5134	After the Love Has Gone	CDJ	U.S.	1995	$3.00
GRP	9935	Every Corner Of the World	CDJ	U.S.	1990	$2.00
GRP		Key To You, The	CDJ	U.S.		$2.00
GRP	9942	M.W.A.	CDJ	U.S.	1990	$2.00
GRP	9966	Moments Of Love	CDJ	U.S.	1991	$2.00

Benoit, Tab

Singles

Label	Catalog Number	Title	Type	Country	Year	Longbox Value / Value
Justice	1202	Cross the Line	CDJ	U.S.	1994	$3.00

Benson, George

Full Length

Label	Catalog Number	Title	Type	Country	Year	Longbox Value / Value
A&M	7501-3203-2	Best Of	LP/LB	U.S.		$14.00/$8.00
CBS	450957-2	Beyond the Blue Horizon	LP	Germany		$20.00
Warner Brothers	3111-2	Breezin'	LP/LB	U.S.†	1984	$14.00/$8.00
Intertape	500064	Electrifying	LP	U.K.		$20.00
Warner Brothers	9 23577-2	George Benson Collection	LP/LB	U.S.		$14.00/$8.00
Warner Brothers	03453-2	Give Me the Night	LP/LB	U.S.†	1984	$14.00/$8.00
Warner Brothers	9 2983-2	In Flight	LP/LB	U.S.		$14.00/$8.00
Warner Brothers	PRO-CD-3698	Interview With George Benson	DJ/Intvw	U.S.	1989	$15.00
A&M	7501-0821-2	Other Side Of Abbey Road	LP/LB	U.S.		$14.00/$8.00
A&M	7501-0803-2	Shape of Things To Come	LP/LB	U.S.		$14.00/$8.00
Verve	25178-2	Silver Collection	LP/LB	U.S.†	1984	$14.00/$8.00
A&M	7501-0815-2	Tell It Like It Is	LP/LB	U.S.		$14.00/$8.00
Warner Brothers	9 25907-2	Tenderly	LP/LB	U.S.		$14.00/$8.00
Warner Brothers	9 25178-2	Twenty Twenty	LP/LB	U.S.†	1985	$14.00/$8.00
Warner Brothers	9 25705-2	Twice the Love	LP/LB	U.S.		$14.00/$8.00
Warner Brothers	PRO-CD-3698	Words & Music	DJ/Intvw	U.S.	1989	$7.00
Warner Brothers	PRO-CD-4561	Words & Music	DJ/Intvw	U.S.	1990	$7.00
Warner Brothers	PRO-CD-6486	Words & Music	DJ/Intvw	U.S.	1993	$7.00

Singles

Label	Catalog Number	Title	Type	Country	Year	Longbox Value / Value
Warner Brothers	PRO-CD-4600	Baby Workout	CDJ	U.S.	1990	$3.00
Pioneer	WPDP-6237	Brand New World	CD3	Japan	1990	$13.00/$4.00
Warner Brothers	PRO-CD-2798	Dreamin'	CDJ	U.S.	1987	$3.00
Warner Brothers	PRO-CD-3722	Here There & Everywhere	CDJ	U.S.	1989	$3.00
Warner Brothers	PRO-CD-6365	I'll Be Good To You	CDJ	U.S.	1993	$3.00
BMG	CDAMMI-101	I'll Keep Your Dreams Alive	CD5	U.K.	1992	$10.00
Pyramid	821-2	I'll Keep Your Love Alive	CDJ	U.S.	1992	$3.00
Warner Brothers	921058-2	Let's Do It Again	CD3	Germany	1988	$9.00
Warner Brothers	10P3-6027	Let's Do It Again	CD3	Japan	1988	$13.00/$4.00
Warner Brothers	W-7780CD	Let's Do It Again	CD3	U.K.	1988	$9.00
Warner Brothers	PRO-CD-3209	Let's Do It Again	CDJ	U.S.	1988	$3.00
GRP	5209	Long And Winding Road	CDJ	U.S.	1995	$3.00
Warner Brothers	PRO-CD-6237	Love Of My Life	CDJ	U.S.	1993	$6.00
Warner Brothers	PRO-CD-2982	Since You're Gone	CDJ	U.S.	1988	$3.00
Warner Brothers	921117-2	Twice the Love	CD3	Germany	1988	$9.00
Warner Brothers	W-7665CD	Twice the Love	CD5	U.K.	1988	$9.00
Warner Brothers	PRO-CD-3373	Twice the Love	CDJ	U.S.	1988	$3.00

Benson, Jodi

Singles

Company	Disk Number	Title	Type	Country	Year	Longbox Value / Value
Sparrow	1284	Voice In the Night	CDJ	U.S.	1991	$2.00

Benson & Klugh

Full Length

Company	Disk Number	Title	Type	Country	Year	Longbox Value / Value
Warner Brothers	43P2-0009	Collaboration	LP	Japan		$30.00

Bensusan, Pierre

Full Length

Company	Disk Number	Title	Type	Country	Year	Longbox Value / Value
CBS	4608855-2	Spices	LP	Germany		$15.00

Bentall, Barney

Full Length

Company	Disk Number	Title	Type	Country	Year	Longbox Value / Value
		Ain't Life Strange	DJ/Intvw	Canada		$15.00
Columbia	CK-45193	Barney Bentall & Legendary Hearts	LP/LB	U.S.		$12.00/$7.00

Singles

Company	Disk Number	Title	Type	Country	Year	Longbox Value / Value
		Doin' Fine	CDJ	Canada		$3.00
		Livin' In the '90s	CDJ	Canada		$3.00

Bentall, Barney & The Legendary Hearts

Full Length

Company	Disk Number	Title	Type	Country	Year	Longbox Value / Value
		Ain't Life Strange - Radio Special	DJ/Intvw	Canada	1994	$25.00
		Legendary Hits	DJ/Smplr	Canada	1994	$25.00

Benton, Barbi

Full Length

Company	Disk Number	Title	Type	Country	Year	Longbox Value / Value
Takoma	D272876	Kinetic Voyage	LP	U.S.		$15.00

Benton, Booker

Full Length

Company	Disk Number	Title	Type	Country	Year	Longbox Value / Value
Polygram	836755-2	Forty Greatest Hits	LP/BP	U.S.		$14.00/$8.00

Benton, Fraz

Singles

Company	Disk Number	Title	Type	Country	Year	Longbox Value / Value
BMG	662890	Carry On	CD5	Germany	1989	$8.00

Benz

Singles

Company	Disk Number	Title	Type	Country	Year	Longbox Value / Value
		Boom Rock Soul	CD5	U.K.		$10.00
		Boom Rock Soul	CD5	U.K.		$10.00
Second version.						

Berg, Matraca

Singles

Company	Disk Number	Title	Type	Country	Year	Longbox Value / Value
RCA	PD-49210	Baby, Walk On	CD5	U.K.	1991	$8.00
RCA	PD-49240	I Got It Bad	CD5	U.K.	1991	$8.00

Bergamo, John

Full Length

Company	Disk Number	Title	Type	Country	Year	Longbox Value / Value
Westwood One	42270	On the Edge	LP	Germany		$15.00

Bergman, Bill

Full Length

Company	Disk Number	Title	Type	Country	Year	Longbox Value / Value
Passport	PJCD-88022	Midnight Sax	LP	Germany		$15.00
Passport	PJCD-88022	Midnight Sax	LP	U.K.		$15.00
Passport	PJCD-88022	Midnight Sax	LP/LB	U.S.		$15.00/$10.00

Berkeley, Tyrone

Singles

Company	Disk Number	Title	Type	Country	Year	Longbox Value / Value
		To Touch You LP	CDJ	U.S.		$2.00

Berlin

Full Length

Company	Disk Number	Title	Type	Country	Year	Longbox Value / Value
Pioneer	PA-85-122	Berlin	LD	U.S.	1985	$40.00
Mercury	32PD-117	Count Three And Pray	LP	Japan		$25.00
Mercury	28PD-263	Dancing In Berlin	LP	Japan	1987	$18.00
Polygram	818329-2	Love Life	LP	U.K.		$20.00
Geffen	4025-2	Love Life	LP/LB	U.S.†	1985	$14.00/$8.00

Singles

Company	Disk Number	Title	Type	Country	Year	Longbox Value / Value
Columbia	656361-2	Take My Breath Away	CD5	U.K.	1990	$10.00
DGC	4369	Take My Breath Away '91	CDJ	U.S	1991	$6.00

Berlin, Jeff

Full Length

Company	Disk Number	Title	Type	Country	Year	Longbox Value / Value
Passport	PJCD-88004	Champion	LP	Germany		$15.00
Passport	PJCD-88004	Champion	LP	U.K.		$15.00
Passport	PJCD-88004	Champion	LP/LB	U.S.		$16.00/$10.00
Passport	PJCD-88017	Pump It	LP	Germany		$15.00
Passport	PJCD-88017	Pump It	LP	U.K.		$15.00
Passport	PJCD-88017	Pump It	LP/LB	U.S.		$16.00/$10.00

Berne, Joqui

Singles

Company	Disk Number	Title	Type	Country	Year	Longbox Value / Value
Hi Hat	HYT-2CD	It's Been So Long	CD5	U.K.	1988	$8.00

Berne, Tim

Full Length

Company	Disk Number	Title	Type	Country	Year	Longbox Value / Value
Soul Note	121061-2	Ancestors	LP	U.S.		$9.00
Polygram	834431-2	Fractured Fairy Tales	LP/BP	U.S.		$15.00/$9.00
Polygram	834442-2	Pace Yourself	LP/BP	U.S.		$15.00/$9.00
CBS	460676-2	Sanctified Dreams	LP	Germany		$15.00
Columbia	CK-44073	Sanctified Dreams	LP/LB	U.S.		$15.00/$9.00

Bernhard, Sandra

Singles

Company	Disk Number	Title	Type	Country	Year	Longbox Value / Value
550 Music	6468	Maniac Superstar	CDJ	U.S.	1994	$3.00
Enigma	EPRO-185	Without You I'm Nothing	CDJ	U.S.		$2.00
Columbia	44K 77667	You Make Me Feel	CD5	U.S.	1994	$5.00

Bernhardt, Warren

Full Length

Company	Disk Number	Title	Type	Country	Year	Longbox Value / Value
Digital	CD-441	Trio '83	LP/LB	U.S.†	1985	$14.00/$8.00

Bernie, Paul

Singles

Company	Disk Number	Title	Type	Country	Year	Longbox Value / Value
BMG	663118	Oh No No	CD5	Germany	1990	$8.00
BMG	664495	You For Me, Me For You	CD5	Germany	1990	$8.00

Bernsen, Randy

Singles

Company	Disk Number	Title	Type	Country	Year	Longbox Value / Value
		Be Still And Know	CDJ	U.S.		$2.00

Bernstein, Leonard

Full Length

Company	Disk Number	Title	Type	Country	Year	Longbox Value / Value
Polygram	CAN 734-2	Candide Sampler	DJ/Smplr	U.S.	1991	$15.00

Label	Catalog Number	Title	Type	Country	Year	Longbox Value / Value

Berry, Andrew

Singles

Label	Catalog Number	Title	Type	Country	Year	Longbox Value / Value
Fontana	BERCD-1	Kiss Me I'm Cold	CD5	U.K.	1990	$8.00

Berry, Bill

Full Length

Label	Catalog Number	Title	Type	Country	Year	Longbox Value / Value
Realtime	RT-1001	For Duke	LP/LB	U.S.†	1985	$14.00/$8.00

Berry, Chuck

Full Length

Label	Catalog Number	Title	Type	Country	Year	Longbox Value / Value
Point	262077	Chartbreakers	LP	U.S.		$9.00
Point	262089	Come On	LP	U.S.		$9.00
Polygram	836074-2	Concerto In B Goode	LP/BP	U.S.		$15.00/$9.00
Polygram	836073-2	From St. Louis To Frisco	LP/BP	U.S.		$15.00/$9.00
Teldec	8 24293	Giant Of Tenor Saxofon	LP	Germany		$20.00
Point	262090	Go Go Go	LP	U.S.		$9.00
Chess	9250	Great 28	LP	U.S.		$9.00
Instant	5035	Hail Hail Rock 'N' Roll	LP	U.S.		$9.00
Polygram	836071-2	In Memphis	LP/BP	U.S.		$15.00/$9.00
Polygram	836072-2	Live At the Filmore	LP/BP	U.S.		$15.00/$9.00
Point	262091	Oh Yeah	LP	U.S.		$9.00
Point	269173	Super Hits	LP	U.S.		$9.00

Singles

Label	Catalog Number	Title	Type	Country	Year	Longbox Value / Value
Dino	CDCHUCK-1	Hail Hail Rock 'N' Roll	CD5	U.K.	1991	$9.00
MCA	37280	Maybelline	CD3	U.S.	1988	$6.00/$4.00
Charly	CDS 6	No Particular Place To Go	CD5	France	1989	$9.00
MCA	10P3-6051	No Particular Place To Go	CD3	Japan	1989	$13.00/$4.00
Charly	CDS-6	No Particular Place To Go	CD5	U.K.	1989	$9.00
Old Gold	OG-6143	Roll Over Beethoven	CD3	U.K.	1989	$9.00

Berry, Heidi

Full Length

Label	Catalog Number	Title	Type	Country	Year	Longbox Value / Value
4AD		Heidi Berry	DJ/Smplr	U.K.	1995	$15.00
		Miracle	DJ/LP	U.S.	1996	$15.00

Singles

Label	Catalog Number	Title	Type	Country	Year	Longbox Value / Value
4AD	PRO-CD-6544	Distant Thunder	CDJ	U.S.	1993	$2.00
4AD	PRO-CD-6544	Moon And the Sun, The	CDJ	U.S.	1993	$2.00

Berry, John

Full Length

Label	Catalog Number	Title	Type	Country	Year	Longbox Value / Value
		Country Concert	RS	U.S.	1996	$40.00
Airdate: 8/5/96.						
		Country Edge	RS	U.S.	1994	$20.00
Airdate: 2/19/94						
		Crazy Horse	RS	U.S.	1994	$60.00
Airdate: 9/19/94						
Capitol		Standing On the Edge	DJ/LP	U.S.	1995	$12.00

Singles

Label	Catalog Number	Title	Type	Country	Year	Longbox Value / Value
Capitol	DPRO-79075	Standing On the Edge	CDJ	U.S.	1995	$3.00
Liberty	DPRO-79015	Your Love Amazes Me	CDJ	U.S.	1993	$3.00

Berry, Nick

Singles

Label	Catalog Number	Title	Type	Country	Year	Longbox Value / Value
Columbia	658151-2	Heartbeat	CD5	U.K.	1992	$8.00
Columbia	658759-2	Long Live Love	CD5	U.K.	1992	$8.00

Berryhill, Cindy Lee

Singles

Label	Catalog Number	Title	Type	Country	Year	Longbox Value / Value
Rhino	PRO2 7979	Indirectly Yours	CDJ	U.S.	1988	$2.00
Rhino	PRO2 90022	Supernatural Fact	CDJ	U.S.	1989	$2.00

Bertei, Adele

Singles

Label	Catalog Number	Title	Type	Country	Year	Longbox Value / Value
Imago	72787-25074	Zami Girl	CD5	U.S.	1994	$5.00

Best Kissers In The World

Singles

Label	Catalog Number	Title	Type	Country	Year	Longbox Value / Value
MCA	MCA5P-2897	Bleeder	CDJ	U.S.	1994	$2.00
MCA	MCA5P-2812	Miss Teen U.S.A.	CDJ	U.S.	1993	$2.00
MCA	MCA5P-2561	Pickin' Flowers	CDJ	U.S.	1993	$2.00
MCA	10694	Puddin'	CD5	U.S.	1993	$4.00
Sub Pop	SP 122	Workin' On Donita	CD5	U.S.	1991	$5.00

Better Than Ezra

Full Length

Label	Catalog Number	Title	Type	Country	Year	Longbox Value / Value
Westwood One		In Concert	RS	U.S.		$20.00
Westwood One		In Concert-Nu Rock	RS	U.S.	1996	$75.00
Global Satellite Network		Live Pit	RS	U.S.	1995	$75.00
Airdate: 10/29/95.						

Singles

Label	Catalog Number	Title	Type	Country	Year	Longbox Value / Value
Elektra		Good	CD5	U.K.	1995	$10.00
Elektra		Good	CD5	U.S.	1995	$5.00
Elektra	PRCD 9119-2	Good	CDJ	U.S.	1995	$6.00
Elektra	PRCD 9195-2	In the Blood	CDJ	U.S.	1995	$6.00
Elektra	66065	Rosealia	CD5	U.S.	1995	$5.00
Elektra	PRCD 9362	Rosealia	CDJ	U.S.	1995	$3.00

Bettie Seveert

Full Length

Label	Catalog Number	Title	Type	Country	Year	Longbox Value / Value
Atlantic	7 92285-2	Palomine	LP/LB	U.S.		$12.00/$7.00

Singles

Label	Catalog Number	Title	Type	Country	Year	Longbox Value / Value
Matador	122	Crutches	CD5	U.S.	1994	$5.00
A&M	3458 8324 2	For All We Know	CDJ	U.S.	1994	$7.00
With one track by Sonic Youth						
Matador	5237	Kid's Alright	CDJ	U.S.	1993	$2.00
Matador	PRCD 5327	Palomine	CDJ	U.S.		$6.00
Matador	PRCD 6009-2	Ray Ray Rain	CDJ	U.S.	1995	$3.00
Atlantic	PRCD 6164-2	Something So Wild	CDJ	U.S.	1995	$3.00
Matador	OLE 032	Tom Boy	CD5	U.S.	1993	$4.00

Betts, Dickey Band

Full Length

Label	Catalog Number	Title	Type	Country	Year	Longbox Value / Value
		Live	DJ/Smplr	U.S.		$10.00
Epic		Live	DJ/Smplr	U.S.	1988	$5.00

Beverlee

Singles

Label	Catalog Number	Title	Type	Country	Year	Longbox Value / Value
ZYX	DST-1029-8	Set Me Free	CD5	Germany	1990	$5.00
ZYX	6639-8	Set Me Free	CD5	Germany	1990	$5.00

Beyond

Singles

Label	Catalog Number	Title	Type	Country	Year	Longbox Value / Value
Harvest	CDHAR-5300	Empire	CD5	U.K.	1991	$8.00
Harvest	CONAR 5301	Great Indifference	CD5	U.K.	1991	$8.00
Continuum	19204	Great Indifference	CDJ	U.S.	1992	$3.00
Pinnacle	ABB-22SCD	No Excuse	CD5	U.K.	1990	$8.00
EMI	CDEM-191	One Step Too Far	CD5	U.K.	1991	$8.00

Bi Virtue

Singles

Label	Catalog Number	Title	Type	Country	Year	Longbox Value / Value
Sony	HUG-3CD	Ain't No Sunshine	CD5	U.K.	1992	$8.00

Bianca

Singles

Label	Catalog Number	Title	Type	Country	Year	Longbox Value / Value
Warner Brothers	PRO-CD-3906	My Emotions	CDJ	U.S.	1990	$2.00

Bianco, Bonnie

Full Length

Label	Catalog Number	Title	Type	Country	Year	Longbox Value / Value
Teldec	8 26495	Rhapsody	LP	Germany		$15.00
Teldec	8 26494	Stay	LP	Germany		$15.00
Teldec	8 27493	Too Young	LP	Germany		$15.00
Teldec	8 26209	Un' Americana A Roma	LP	Germany		$15.00

Singles

Label	Catalog Number	Title	Type	Country	Year	Longbox Value / Value
WEA	246881-2	Cry in the Night	CD3	Germany	1989	$8.00
WEA	247111-2	Straight From Your Heart	CD3	Germany	1989	$8.00
WEA	246881-2	When the Price Is Your Love	CD3	Germany	1989	$8.00

Bianco, Lori

Singles

Label	Catalog Number	Title	Type	Country	Year	Longbox Value / Value
WEA	171731-2	Heartbreaker	CD5	Germany	1990	$8.00
WEA	19031-72564-2	Lonely Is the Night	CD5	Germany	1990	$8.00

Bianco, Matt

Full Length

Label	Catalog Number	Title	Type	Country	Year	Longbox Value / Value
		Special Sampler	DJ/Smplr	Japan		$40.00
WEA	247895-2	Don't Blame It On That Girl	CD3	Germany	1988	$8.00
Warner Brothers	10P3 6011	Don't Blame It On That Girl	CD3	Japan	1988	$13.00/$4.00
WEA	YZ-188CD	Don't Blame It On That Girl	CD3	U.K.	1988	$8.00
Atlantic	PR 2620-2	Don't Blame It On That Girl	CDJ	U.S.	1988	$2.00
Eastwest	9031-72559-2	Fire In the Blood	CD5	Germany	1990	$8.00
Eastwest	YZ-532CD	Fire In the Blood	CD5	U.K.	1990	$8.00
WEA	247738-2	Good Times	CD5	Germany	1988	$8.00
WEA	YZ-302CD	Good Times	CD5	U.K.	1988	$8.00
WEA	9031-74997-2	Macumba	CD5	Germany	1991	$8.00
WEA	9031-74997-2	Macumba	CD5	U.K.	1991	$8.00
WEA	247266-2	Nervous	CD5	Germany	1989	$8.00
WEA	YZ-328CD	Nervous	CD5	U.K.	1989	$8.00
WEA	YZ-388CD	Say It's Not Too Late	CD3	U.K.	1989	$8.00
Eastwest	9031-75774-2	What A Fool Believes	CD5	Germany	1991	$8.00
Eastwest	WMC5-487	What A Fool Believes	CD5	Japan	1991	$12.00
WEA	YZ-625CD	What A Fool Believes	CD5	U.K.	1991	$8.00

Bible

Full Length

Label	Catalog Number	Title	Type	Country	Year	Longbox Value / Value
Chrysalis	F2-21613	Eureka	LP/LB	U.S.		$14.00/$8.00

Singles

Label	Catalog Number	Title	Type	Country	Year	Longbox Value / Value
Chrysalis	880876	Crystal Palace	CD5	Germany	1988	$8.00
Chrysalis	BIBCD 2	Crystal Palace	CD5	U.K.	1988	$8.00
EMI	BIBCD-4	Graceland	CD5	U.K.	1989	$8.00
Chrysalis	885043	Honey Be Good	CD5	Germany	1989	$8.00
EMI	BIBCD-5	Honey Be Good	CD5	U.K.	1989	$8.00
EMI	BIBCD-3	Honey Be Good	CD5	U.K.	1989	$8.00

Bid

Singles

Label	Catalog Number	Title	Type	Country	Year	Longbox Value / Value
El	25607-12	Reach For Your Gun	CD3	Japan	1989	$13.00/$4.00

Big

Singles

Label	Catalog Number	Title	Type	Country	Year	Longbox Value / Value
Uptown	2743	Party And Bull	CDJ	U.S.	1993	$2.00

Big Audio Dynamite

Full Length

Label	Catalog Number	Title	Type	Country	Year	Longbox Value / Value
Columbia	CSK 4271	Ally Pally Paradiso	DJ/Smplr	U.S.	1991	$18.00
CBS		Globe, The	LP	Australia	1992	$25.00
2 CD set.						
Columbia		Looking For A Song	DJ/Smplr	U.S.	1995	$12.00
Columbia		Looking For A Song	DJ/Smplr	U.S.	1995	$25.00
2 CD set						
CBS	450137-2	Number 10, Upping Street	LP	Germany		$25.00

Singles

Label	Catalog Number	Title	Type	Country	Year	Longbox Value / Value
Columbia	CSK 6506	6506	CD5	U.K.	1994	$10.00
CBS	CDBAAD-6	Contact	CD5	U.K.	1989	$8.00
Columbia	CSK 73043	Contact	CDJ	U.S.	1989	$3.00
WTG	NSK 1957	Free	CDJ	U.S.	1990	$3.00
Columbia	CSK 4191	Globe, The	CDJ	U.S.	1991	$3.00
	RAR5P3385	I Turned Out Punk	CDJ	U.S.	1995	$7.00
		I Turned Out Punk	CDJ	U.S.	1995	$7.00
Second version.						
Columbia	CSK 4367	Innocent Child	CDJ	U.S.	1992	$3.00
CBS	651621-3	Just Play Music	CD3	Germany	1988	$8.00
CBS	CD BAAD-4	Just Play Music	CD5	U.K.	1988	$8.00
Columbia	CSK 1232	Just Play Music	CDJ	U.S.	1988	$3.00
Columbia	44K 74707	Kool Aid	CD5	U.S.	1992	$5.00
CBS	661018	Looking For A Song	CD5	U.K.	1994	$10.00
CBS		Looking For A Song	CD5	U.K.	1994	$10.00
Second version.						
CBS	77785	Looking For A Song	CD5	U.S.	1994	$5.00
Columbia	CSK 6506	Looking For A Song	CDJ	U.S.	1995	$7.00
CBS	SRCS-6632	On the Road Live '92	CD5	Japan	1992	$16.00
Columbia	44K 74707	On the Road Live '92	CD5	U.S.	1992	$6.00
CBS	CDBAAD-5	Other 99	CD5	U.K.	1988	$6.00
Columbia	CSK 1342	Other 99	CDJ	U.S.	1988	$3.00
Columbia	657640-2	Rush	CD5	U.K.	1991	$10.00
Columbia	44K 73844	Rush	CD5	U.S.	1991	$5.00
Columbia	CSK 4018	Rush	CDJ	U.S.	1991	$6.00
Columbia	85667-2	Should I Stay Or Should I Go	CD5	Germany	1991	$10.00
Also with tracks by The Clash.						
Columbia	85667-2	Should I Stay Or Should I Go	CD5	U.K.	1991	$10.00
Also with tracks by The Clash.						

Big Bam Boo

Full Length

Label	Catalog Number	Title	Type	Country	Year	Longbox Value / Value
Uni		Fun, Faith And Fairplay	LP/LB	U.S.		$9.00/$6.00

Singles

Label	Catalog Number	Title	Type	Country	Year	Longbox Value / Value
MCA	DMCA-1265	Fell Off the Moutain	CD3	U.K.	1988	$8.00
Eastwest	257523-2	If You Could See Me Now	CD3	Germany	1989	$8.00
MCA	DMCAT-1321	If You Could See Me Now	CD5	U.K.	1989	$8.00
Eastwest	8 74002	Shooting From My Heart	CD3	Germany	1989	$8.00
MCA	DMCA-11281	Shooting From My Heart	CD3	U.K.	1989	$8.00
MCA		Shooting From My Heart	CDJ	U.S.	1989	$2.00

Big Big Sun

Full Length

Label	Catalog Number	Title	Type	Country	Year	Longbox Value / Value
Atlantic	7 81964-2	Stop the World	LP/LB	U.S.	1989	$9.00/$6.00

Label	Catalog Number	Title	Type	Country	Year	Longbox/Value
Atlantic	PR 2859-2	Lilacs	CDJ	U.S.	1989	$2.00
Atlantic		Stop the World	CDJ	U.S.	1989	$2.00

Big Country

Full Length

Label	Catalog Number	Title	Type	Country	Year	Longbox/Value
Fox	RDJ 62593-2	Big Sampler	DJ/Smplr	U.S.		$8.00
Mercury	812870-2	Crossing, The	LP/BP	U.S.†	1984	$14.00/$8.00
Warner Brothers	9 25787-2	Peace In Our Time	LP/LB	U.S.		$14.00/$8.00
		Peace In Our Time Album Sampler	DJ/Smplr	U.K.	1988	$10.00
Mercury	826844-2	Seer	LP/BP	U.S.		$14.00/$8.00
Mercury	812870-2	Steeltown	LP/BP	U.S.†	1984	$14.00/$8.00
Mercury	822831-2	Steeltown	LP/BP	U.S.	1986	$14.00/$8.00
		Tracks From Without the Aid	DJ/Smplr	U.K.	1994	$12.00
		Why the Long Face	DJ/Smplr	U.K.	1995	$15.00

Singles

Label	Catalog Number	Title	Type	Country	Year	Longbox/Value
		Alone	CD5	U.K.	1993	$9.00
		Alone	CD5	U.K.	1993	$9.00
Second version.						
Fox	62713	Alone	CDJ	U.S.	1993	$2.00
Mercury	872125-2	Broken Heart	CD5	Germany	1988	$9.00
Mercury	BIGCD-6	Broken Heart	CD5	U.K.	1988	$9.00
Mercury	BIGCD-9	Heart Of the Wild	CD5	U.K.	1990	$9.00
Mercury	870617-2	King Of Emotion	CD5	Germany	1988	$9.00
Mercury	BIGCD-5	King Of Emotion	CD5	U.K.	1988	$9.00
Reprise	PRO-CD-3238	King Of Emotion	CDJ	U.S.	1988	$2.00
		Non (Stop the Test)	CD5	U.K.	1995	$10.00
Fox	62593	One I Love, The	CDJ	U.S.	1993	$2.00
Fox	62654	One I Love, The	CDJ	U.S.	1993	$2.00
Mercury	BIGCD-7	Peace In Our Time	CD5	U.K.	1988	$9.00
Reprise	PRO-CD-3338	Peace In Our Time	CDJ	U.S.	1988	$2.00
Polygram	868921-2	Republican Party Reptile	CD5	Germany	1991	$9.00
		Safety Net	CDJ	U.K.	1993	$20.00
Mercury	875393-2	Save Me	CD5	Germany	1990	$9.00
Mercury	BIGCD-8	Save Me	CD5	U.K.	1990	$9.00
		Ships	CD5	U.K.		$9.00
		Ships	CD5	U.K.		$9.00
Second version.						
Fox	62695	We're Not In Kansas	CDJ	U.S.	1993	$2.00
		You Dreamer	CD5	U.K.	1995	$10.00
		You Dreamer	CD5	U.K.	1995	$10.00
Second version.						

Big Daddy

Singles

Label	Catalog Number	Title	Type	Country	Year	Longbox/Value
Rhino	BOD-2	Like A Virgin	CD5	U.K.	1992	$8.00

Big Daddy Kane

Singles

Label	Catalog Number	Title	Type	Country	Year	Longbox/Value
Cold Chillin'		All of Me	CDJ	U.S.		$2.00
Cold Chillin'	4474	'Cause I Can Do It Right	CDJ	U.S.	1990	$2.00
Cold Chillin'	PRO-CD-5092	Groove With It	CDJ	U.S.	1991	$2.00
Cold Chillin'	PRO-CD-6116	How U Get A Record Deal	CDJ	U.S.	1993	$2.00
Cold Chillin'		I Get the Job Done	CDJ	U.S.		$2.00
Warner Brothers	PRO-CD-3367	I'll Take You There	CDJ	U.S.	1988	$2.00
Cold Chillin'	PRO-CD-4897	It's Hard Being the Kane	CDJ	U.S.	1990	$2.00
Reprise	PRO-CD-4506	It's Hard Being the Kane	CDJ	U.S.	1990	$2.00
Cold Chill	W-0043CD	Keep 'Em On the Floor	CD5	U.K.	1991	$9.00
Cold Chillin	PRO-CD-6610	Looks Like A Job For	CDJ	U.S.	1993	$2.00
Warner Brothers	12-40343	Lover In You, The	CD5	Canada		$8.00
Cold Chillin	9 40149-2	Ooh, Aah, Nah-Nah-Nah	CD5	U.S.	1991	$4.00
Cold Chillin	PRO-CD-4974	Ooh, Aah, Nah-Nah-Nah	CDJ	U.S.	1991	$2.00
WEA	W-2804CD	Smooth Operator	CD5	U.K.	1989	$9.00
Cold Chillin'	PRO-CD-3805	Smooth Operator	CDJ	U.S.	1989	$2.00
Cold Chillin'	PRO-CD-6302	Stop Shammin'	CDJ	U.S.	1993	$2.00
Cold Chillin'	PRO-CD-6375	Very Special	CDJ	U.S.	1993	$2.00

Big Dee, Irwin

Singles

Label	Catalog Number	Title	Type	Country	Year	Longbox/Value
2000AD	IRWNC-1	Slow Dance	CD5	U.K.	1988	$8.00

Big Dipper

Singles

Label	Catalog Number	Title	Type	Country	Year	Longbox/Value
Epic	ESK 2083	Impossible Things	CDJ	U.S.	1990	$2.00
Epic	ESK 2009	Love Barge	CDJ	U.S.	1990	$2.00
Chill	TUV-26CD	Return Of the Living Acid	CD5	U.K.	1993	$9.00

Big Dish

Full Length

Label	Catalog Number	Title	Type	Country	Year	Longbox/Value
Warner Brothers	9 25764-2	Creeping Up On Jesus	LP/LB	U.S.		$12.00/$7.00
Eastwest	7 91636-2	Satellites	LP/LB	U.S.		$12.00/$7.00
Warner Brothers	9 2519-2	Swimmer	LP/LB	U.S.		$12.00/$7.00

Singles

Label	Catalog Number	Title	Type	Country	Year	Longbox/Value
WEA	YZ-563CD	Big Town	CD5	U.K.	1991	$8.00
Virgin	DISH 1	Compact Disc EP	CD5	U.K.	1987	$10.00
Virgin	VSCD 1102	European Rain	CD5	U.K.	1988	$8.00
Virgin	VSCD 1136	Faith Healer	CD5	U.K.	1988	$8.00
Warner Brothers		Life	CDJ	U.S.		$2.00
Eastwest	SAM727	Miss America	CDJ	Germany	1990	$15.00
Eastwest	9031-73153-2	Miss America	CD5	Germany	1991	$8.00
WEA	YZ-529CD	Miss America	CD5	U.K.	1991	$8.00
WEA	YZ-574CD	Twenty-Five Years	CD5	U.K.	1991	$8.00

Big Drill Car

Full Length

Label	Catalog Number	Title	Type	Country	Year	Longbox/Value
Cargo	HED-019	Toured	DJ/Smplr	U.S.	1993	$12.00
Cargo	040	Friend Of Mine	CDJ	U.S.		$2.00

Big F

Full Length

Label	Catalog Number	Title	Type	Country	Year	Longbox/Value
Elektra	7 60886-2	Big F	LP/LB	U.S.		$12.00/$7.00

Singles

Label	Catalog Number	Title	Type	Country	Year	Longbox/Value
Elektra	PR 8145-2	Doctor Vine	CDJ	U.S.	1990	$2.00
Elektra	PR 8179-2	Kill the Cowboy	CDJ	U.S.	1989	$2.00
Chrysalis	26019	Patience Peregrine	CDJ	U.S.	1993	$2.00
Chrysalis	04615	Wicked Thing	CDj	U.S.	1993	$2.00

Big Fun

Singles

Label	Catalog Number	Title	Type	Country	Year	Longbox/Value
RCA	ZD-43062	Blame It On the Boogie	CD5	Germany	1989	$7.00
Jive	11B3-67	Blame It On the Boogie	CD3	Japan	1989	$13.00/$4.00
Jive	JIVECD-217	Blame It On the Boogie	CD5	U.K.	1989	$7.00
RCA	ZD-43328	Can't Shake the Feeling	CD5	Germany	1989	$7.00
Jive	JIVECD-234	Can't Shake the Feeling	CD5	U.K.	1989	$7.00
RCA	ZD-43590	Handful Of Promises	CD5	Germany	1990	$7.00
Jive	JIVECD-243	Handful Of Promises	CD5	U.K.	1990	$7.00
RCA	ZD-435828	Hey There the Lonely	CD5	Germany	1990	$7.00
Jive	JIVECD-204	I Feel the Earth Move	CD5	U.K.	1989	$7.00
Jive	11B3-41	Living For Your Love	CD3	Japan	1989	$13.00/$4.00
RCA	ZD-43886	You've Got A Friend	CD5	Germany	1990	$7.00
Alfa	ALDB-61	You've Got A Friend	CD3	Japan	1989	$13.00/$4.00

Big Hard Excellent Fish

Singles

Company	Disk Number	Title	Type	Country	Year	Longbox/Value
Pinnacle	41TP7-CD	Imperfect List	CD5	U.K.	1990	$7.00

Big Hate

Singles

Company	Disk Number	Title	Type	Country	Year	Longbox/Value
	PROCD7000121	Next Time Around	CDJ	U.S.		$3.00

Big Head Todd And The Monsters

Full Length

Company	Disk Number	Title	Type	Country	Year	Longbox/Value
Westwood One		In Concert	RS	U.S.	1994	$60.00
Airdate: 11/21/94.						
Westwood One		In Concert	RS	U.S.	1994	$60.00
Airdate: 7/18/94						
Westwood One		In Concert	RS	U.S.	1995	$60.00
Airdate: 4/24/95.						

Singles

Company	Disk Number	Title	Type	Country	Year	Longbox/Value
Giant	18381	Bitterweet	CD5	U.S.	1993	$5.00
Giant		Broken Hearted Savior	CDJ	U.S.	1994	$3.00
Giant	PRO-CD-6132	Circle	CDJ	U.S.	1993	$3.00
Giant	PRO-CD-7138	In the Morning	CDJ	U.S.	1994	$3.00
Giant	PRO-CD-7134	In the Morning	CDJ	U.S.	1994	$3.00
Giant	PRO-CD-6541	It's Alright	CDJ	U.S.	1994	$3.00
Giant	PRO-CD-7197	Kensington Line	CDJ	U.S.	1995	$3.00
Giant	9 18381-2	Live	CD5	U.S.	1994	$6.00
Giant	PRO-CD-7407	Wearing Only Flowers	CDJ	U.S.	1995	$3.00

Big Heat

Singles

Company	Disk Number	Title	Type	Country	Year	Longbox/Value
Pinnacle	DRSCD-100	Payday	CD5	U.K.	1989	$7.00

Big House

Full Length

Company	Disk Number	Title	Type	Country	Year	Longbox/Value
RCA	3094	Big House	LP/BP	U.S.		$12.00/$7.00

Singles

Company	Disk Number	Title	Type	Country	Year	Longbox/Value
RCA	74321-107332	All Nite	CD5	U.K.	1992	$8.00
RCA	62040-2-RDJ	Dollar In My Pocket	CDJ	U.S.	1991	$2.00

Big Hunk Of Cheese

Singles

Company	Disk Number	Title	Type	Country	Year	Longbox/Value
		You're Soaking In It	CD5	U.S.		$4.00

Big L

Singles

Company	Disk Number	Title	Type	Country	Year	Longbox/Value
Columbia	77894	MVP	CD5	U.S.	1995	$5.00
CBS	77728	Put It On	CD5	U.S.	1994	$5.00

Big Mountain

Full Length

Company	Disk Number	Title	Type	Country	Year	Longbox/Value
Giant	PRO-CD-7907	Words & Music	DJ/Intvw	U.S.	1995	$10.00

Singles

Company	Disk Number	Title	Type	Country	Year	Longbox/Value
RCA	62847-2	Baby I Love Your Way	CD5	U.S.	1994	$5.00
RCA	62779-2-RDJ	Baby I Love Your Way	CDJ	U.S.	1994	$3.00
RCA		Baby I Love Your Way	CDJ	U.S.	1994	$3.00
Second version.						
RCA		Get Together	CDJ	U.S.	1994	$3.00
Giant	PRO-CD-7288	Strictly Reggae	CDJ	U.S.	1994	$6.00
Giant	41629-2	Sweet Sensual Love	CD5	U.S.	1994	$5.00
Giant	PRO-CD-6998	Sweet Sensual Love	CDJ	U.S.	1994	$3.00
Warner Brothers	24563	Unity	CD5	U.S.	1994	$5.00

Big Mouth

Singles

Company	Disk Number	Title	Type	Country	Year	Longbox/Value
Red Rhino	3SSRR-90	Drop That Ghetto Blaster	CD5	U.K.	1989	$7.00

Big Noise

Singles

Company	Disk Number	Title	Type	Country	Year	Longbox/Value
		I Can't Live Without It	CDJ	U.S.		$2.00
		Name & Number	CDJ	U.S.		$2.00

Big Pig

Full Length

Company	Disk Number	Title	Type	Country	Year	Longbox/Value
A&M	395185-2	Bonk	LP/LB	U.S.		$12.00/$7.00

Singles

Company	Disk Number	Title	Type	Country	Year	Longbox/Value
A&M	S10Y-3008	Breakaway	CD3	Japan	1988	$12.00/$3.00
A&M	392261-2	Hungry Town	CD5	Germany	1987	$7.00
A&M	S10Y-3047	Hungry Town	CD3	Japan	1988	$12.00/$3.00

Big Star

Full Length

Company	Disk Number	Title	Type	Country	Year	Longbox/Value
Rykodisc	VRCD 0222	A Little Big Star	DJ/Smplr	U.S.	1992	$15.00
PVC	PVCD-8933	Sister Lovers	LP	U.S.		$9.00

Big Stick

Singles

Company	Disk Number	Title	Type	Country	Year	Longbox/Value
EMI	CDEM-88	Crack Attack	CD5	U.K.	1989	$7.00

Big Sugar

Singles

Company	Disk Number	Title	Type	Country	Year	Longbox/Value
Jive	JDJ422872	Ride Like Hell	CDJ	U.S.		$3.00

Big Tony

Singles

Company	Disk Number	Title	Type	Country	Year	Longbox/Value
ZYX	6162-8	Let the Music Play	CD5	Germany	1989	$5.00

Big Trouble

Full Length

Company	Disk Number	Title	Type	Country	Year	Longbox/Value
Epic	328P-5012	Big Trouble	LP	Japan	1988	$20.00
Epic	EK-40850	Big Trouble	LP/LB	U.S.	1988	$12.00/$7.00

Singles

Company	Disk Number	Title	Type	Country	Year	Longbox/Value
Epic	651625-2	Crazy World	CD5	U.K.	1988	$7.00

Bigg Ocean Mobb

Singles

Company	Disk Number	Title	Type	Country	Year	Longbox/Value
		Gangster Driven	CDJ	U.S.		$2.00

Bigga Figga

Singles

Company	Disk Number	Title	Type	Country	Year	Longbox/Value
Low	50908	Dwellin' In the Lab	CDJ	U.S.	1995	$2.00

Biggy Smallz

Singles

Company	Disk Number	Title	Type	Country	Year	Longbox/Value
Life	79008	Cruisin'	CD5	U.S.	1993	$4.00

Label	Catalog Number	Title	Type	Country	Year	Longbox Value / Value
Life	9521	Nobody Rides For Free	CD5	U.S.	1994	$4.00
Life	9521	Nobody Rides For Free	CDJ	U.S.	1994	$2.00

Bigod 20

Singles

Label	Catalog Number	Title	Type	Country	Year	Longbox Value / Value
ZYX	6055-8	America	CD5	Germany	1989	$6.00
ZYX	5834-8	Body To Body	CD5	Germany	1989	$6.00
Warner Brothers	12-21755	Bog, the	CD5	Canada		$7.00
Warner Brothers	12-40016	Carpe Denim 2	CD5	Canada		$7.00
Warner Brothers	12-40615	On the Run	CD5	Canada		$7.00
Warner	12-41730	One	CD5	Canada	1994	$8.00
Zoth	123	One Jack Dangers	CD5	U.K.	1994	$8.00

Bigstorm

Singles

Label	Catalog Number	Title	Type	Country	Year	Longbox Value / Value
Sire	PRO-CD-3536	Not Guilty	CDJ	U.S.	1989	$2.00

Bilgeri

Singles

Label	Catalog Number	Title	Type	Country	Year	Longbox Value / Value
WEA	9031-73571-2	In Love With Two Ladies	CD5	Germany	1991	$7.00
WEA	9031-75280-2	Lonely Fighter	CD5	Germany	1991	$7.00

Billy Goat

Singles

Label	Catalog Number	Title	Type	Country	Year	Longbox Value / Value
Third Rail	10214	Ali Rocka	CDJ	U.S.	1992	$2.00
Third Rail	10158	Chef	CDJ	U.S.	1992	$2.00

Billy & The American Suns

Full Length

Label	Catalog Number	Title	Type	Country	Year	Longbox Value / Value
Atlantic	7 82102-2	Thunder In the Valley	LP/LB	U.S.		$14.00/$8.00

Bingo, Bango, B.

Singles

Label	Catalog Number	Title	Type	Country	Year	Longbox Value / Value
Zyx	7501	The Sweat	CD5	U.S.	1994	$5.00

Bingo Boys

Singles

Label	Catalog Number	Title	Type	Country	Year	Longbox Value / Value
Atlantic	PRCD 4054-2	Borrowed Love	CDJ	U.S.	1991	$2.00
Atlantic	PRCD 3947-2	Borrowed Love	CDJ	U.S.	1991	$2.00
Atlantic	7567-86002-2	How To Dance	CD5	Germany	1991	$8.00
Atlantic	A-7756CD	How To Dance	CD5	U.K.	1991	$8.00
Atlantic	PRCD 3759-2	How To Dance	CDJ	U.S.	1991	$2.00
Atlantic	7567-85995-2	No Woman, No Cry	CD5	Germany	1991	$8.00

Biodome

Singles

Label	Catalog Number	Title	Type	Country	Year	Longbox Value / Value
Capitol	DPRO-30025	Saftey Dance	CDJ	U.S.		$2.00

Biohazard

Full Length

Label	Catalog Number	Title	Type	Country	Year	Longbox Value / Value
		Mata Leas	DJ/LP	U.S.	1996	$15.00
Warner Brothers	9 46208-2	Mata Leas	LTD/LP	U.S.	1996	$16.00
CD in limited edition slip case.						
Warner Brothers	9 45595-2	State Of the World Address	LTD/LP	U.S.	1894	$16.00
"LISA" colored plastic jewel case.						
Roadrunner	9002-2	Urban Discipline	LTD/LP	U.S.	1992	$12.00
Digipak version						

Singles

Label	Catalog Number	Title	Type	Country	Year	Longbox Value / Value
Warner Brothers		A Lot To Learn	CDJ	U.S.	1996	$6.00
Warner Brothers	PRO-CD-6698	After Forever	CDJ	U.S.	1994	$6.00
Warner Brothers		Five Blocks To the Subway	CDJ	Australia	1994	$10.00
Warner Brothers	PRO-CD-7055	Five Blocks To the Subway	CDJ	U.S.	1994	$3.00
Warner	12-41683	How It Is	CD5	Canada	1994	$8.00
		How It Is	CD5	U.K.		$10.00
		How It Is	CD5	U.K.		$10.00
Second version.						
Roadrunner	PRO-CD-7024	How It Is	CDJ	U.S.	1995	$3.00
Immortal	5579	Judgment Night	CDJ	U.S.	1993	$6.00
CBS	77429	Judgment Night	CD5	U.S.	1994	$5.00
Roadrunner	065	Punishment	CDJ	U.S.	1992	$2.00
Warner Brothers	PRO-CD-6945	Tales From the Hard Side	CDJ	U.S.	1994	$3.00
Roadrunner	PRO-CD-6945	Tales From the Hard Side	CDJ	U.S.	1995	$3.00
Warner Brothers		This Is How It Is	CDJ	U.S.	1994	$3.00

Bionic Force

Singles

Label	Catalog Number	Title	Type	Country	Year	Longbox Value / Value
EMI	203378-3	Rap Technology	CD3	Germany	1989	$7.00

Birdland

Full Length

Label	Catalog Number	Title	Type	Country	Year	Longbox Value / Value
	SPCD-1163	Birdland	DJ/Smplr	Japan	1994	$40.00

Singles

Label	Catalog Number	Title	Type	Country	Year	Longbox Value / Value
Lazy	LAZY-24CD	Everybody Needs Somebody	CD5	U.K.	1991	$8.00
Lazy	TOCP 6473	Hollow Heart	CD5	Japan	1990	$15.00
Toshiba	TOCP-6573	Shoot You Down	CD3	Japan	1991	$13.00/$4.00
Radio Active	54181	Shoot You Down	CDJ	U.S.	1991	$2.00
Radioactive	1418	Shoot You Down	CDJ	U.S.	1991	$2.00
Lazy	CD40-4	Sleep With Me	CD5	Germany	1991	$8.00
Lazy	LAZY-17CD	Sleep With Me	CD5	U.K.	1991	$8.00
Radioactive	1601	Sleep With Me	CDJ	U.S.	1991	$2.00

Birdology

Full Length

Label	Catalog Number	Title	Type	Country	Year	Longbox Value / Value
Polygram	841133	Live Tribute 1989	LP/BP	U.S.	1989	$14.00/$8.00

Birth Control

Singles

Label	Catalog Number	Title	Type	Country	Year	Longbox Value / Value
Sony	655217-3	Gamma Ray	CD3	Germany	1989	$7.00

Birthday Party

Full Length

Label	Catalog Number	Title	Type	Country	Year	Longbox Value / Value
Suite Beat	SBCD-2017	Collection	LP/LB	U.S.		$14.00/$8.00
4AD	207CD	Junkyard	LP/LB	U.S.		$14.00/$8.00
4AD	104CD	Prayers On Fire	LP/LB	U.S.		$14.00/$8.00

Singles

Label	Catalog Number	Title	Type	Country	Year	Longbox Value / Value
		Drunk On the Pope's Blood	CD5	Australia		$8.00
Sound	2896058	Peel Sessions	CD5	Germany	1990	$7.00
Str Fruit	FPSCD-020	Peel Sessions	CD5	U.K.	1988	$7.00
Rough Trade	609 0419 3	Peel Sessions Vol. 2	CD5	Germany	1990	$7.00

Birthday Suit

Singles

Label	Catalog Number	Title	Type	Country	Year	Longbox Value / Value
Toshiba	TODT-3032	Breathless	CD3	Japan	1993	$13.00/$4.00

Bis

Singles

Label	Catalog Number	Title	Type	Country	Year	Longbox Value / Value
	40-2	This Teen-C Power	CD5	U.S.	1996	$5.00

Biscuit

Singles

Label	Catalog Number	Title	Type	Country	Year	Longbox Value / Value
Sony	656525-5	Biscuit's In the House	CD5	Germany	1991	$8.00
CBS	CSK 73585	Biscuit's In the House	CDJ	U.S.	1991	$2.00

Bishop, Elvin

Full Length

Label	Catalog Number	Title	Type	Country	Year	Longbox Value / Value
		Don't Let the Blossoms Get You Down	LP	U.S.		$10.00
DIR		King Biscuit Flour Hour	RS	U.S.	1988	$35.00
With Alvin Lee, Airdate: 10/23/88						

Bishop, Stephen

Full Length

Label	Catalog Number	Title	Type	Country	Year	Longbox Value / Value
Atlantic	7 81970-2	Bowling In Paris	LP/LB	U.S.		$12.00/$7.00

Singles

Label	Catalog Number	Title	Type	Country	Year	Longbox Value / Value
Atlantic	PR 3110-2	Mr. Heartbreak	CDJ	U.S.	1989	$2.00
Atlantic	PR 2899-2	Walking On Air	CDJ	U.S.	1989	$2.00

Bit Max

Singles

Label	Catalog Number	Title	Type	Country	Year	Longbox Value / Value
ZYX	6509-8	Dance	CD5	Germany	1991	$6.00

Bite The Bullet

Singles

Label	Catalog Number	Title	Type	Country	Year	Longbox Value / Value
Sony	654891-2	Finished With Love	CD5	U.K.	1989	$7.00

Biting Tounges

Singles

Label	Catalog Number	Title	Type	Country	Year	Longbox Value / Value
EFA	CD-17513	Love Out	CD5	Germany	1990	$7.00
Cut Deep	CD-004	Love Out	CD5	U.K.	1990	$7.00

Bitter End

Full Length

Label	Catalog Number	Title	Type	Country	Year	Longbox Value / Value
Warner Brothers	9 26246-2	Harsh Realities	LP/LB	U.S.		$14.00/$8.00

Bivouac

Singles

Label	Catalog Number	Title	Type	Country	Year	Longbox Value / Value
	PRCD 4751	Cynic	CDJ	U.S.		$2.00
EMI	4CD	Slack	CD5	U.K.	1992	$10.00

Biz Markie

Singles

Label	Catalog Number	Title	Type	Country	Year	Longbox Value / Value
Cold Chillin'	3721	Just A Friend	CDJ	U.S.	1989	$3.00
Cold Chillin'	6106	Let Me Turn You On	CDJ	U.S.	1993	$3.00

Bizarre Inc.

Full Length

Label	Catalog Number	Title	Type	Country	Year	Longbox Value / Value
Pinnacle	STEAM-47CL	Energique	LTD/LP	U.K.		$25.00

Singles

Label	Catalog Number	Title	Type	Country	Year	Longbox Value / Value
Crown	AVDD-20039	I'm Gonna Get You	CD3	Japan	1993	$12.00/$3.00
Southern	STORM-46CD	I'm Gonna Get You	CD5	U.K.	1992	$8.00
CBS	44K 74490	I'm Gonna Get You	CD5	U.S.	1992	$4.00
CBS	CSK 74814	I'm Gonna Get You	CDJ	U.S.	1992	$2.00
Southern	STORM-25RCD	Playing With Knives	CD5	U.K.	1991	$8.00
Southern	STORM-36CD	Playing With Knives	CD5	U.K.	1991	$8.00
ZYX	6589-8	Such A Feeling	CD5	Germany	1991	$6.00
Southern	STORM-32CD	Such A Feeling	CD5	U.K.	1991	$8.00
Pinnacle	STORM-60CD	Took My Love	CD5	U.K.	1993	$8.00
Vinyl Solution	BIZ CD2	Took My Love	CD5	U.K.	1993	$8.00
Vinyl Solution	44K 74862	Took My Love	CD5	U.S.	1993	$4.00
Vinyl Solution	CSK 74969	Took My Love	CDJ	U.S.	1993	$2.00

Bizz Nizz

Singles

Label	Catalog Number	Title	Type	Country	Year	Longbox Value / Value
ZYX	6323-8	Don't Miss the Party Line	CD5	Germany	1990	$6.00
Cool Tempo	COOLCD-203	Don't Miss the Party Line	CD5	U.K.	1990	$7.00
ZYX	6394-8	Get Into A Trance	CD5	Germany	1990	$6.00

Bjork

Full Length

Label	Catalog Number	Title	Type	Country	Year	Longbox Value / Value
		As Featured On Songs From the Cold Seas	DJ/Smplr	U.K.	1995	$25.00
CD and custom prints.						
Elektra	PRCD 8914-2	Debut Adult Alternative Sampler	DJ/Smplr	U.S.	1994	$8.00
Westwood One		In Concert-Nu Rock	RS	U.S.	1995	$75.00
Airdate: 6/5/95						
Elektra	61740-2	Post	LP	U.S.	1995	$16.00
First 250,000 copies pressed contained the original version of "Possibly Maybe" which uses unauthorized samples						

Singles

Label	Catalog Number	Title	Type	Country	Year	Longbox Value / Value
		Army Of Me	CD5	U.K.	1995	$10.00
		Army Of Me	CD5	U.K.	1995	$10.00
Second version.						
		Army Of Me	CDJ	U.K.	1995	$12.00
Elektra	PRCD 9152-2	Army Of Me	CDJ	U.S.	1995	$3.00
		Best Of White Labels	CD5	Australia		$10.00
WEA	POCP-1438	Big Time Sensuality	CD5	Japan		$25.00
Ekektra		Big Time Sensuality	CD5	U.K.	1994	$10.00
Ekektra		Big Time Sensuality	CD5	U.K.	1994	$10.00
Second version.						
Elektra	PRCD 8875-2	Big Time Sensuality	CDJ	U.S.	1993	$2.00
Elektra	66242	Big Time Sensuality	CD5	U.S.	1994	$5.00
Elektra	PRCD 8900-2	Big Time Sensuality	CDJ	U.S.	1994	$2.00
Elektra	PRCD 8784-2	Human Behavior	CDJ	U.S.	1993	$2.00
		Hynerballad	CDJ	U.K.	1995	$18.00
Elektra		Isobel	CDJ	U.K.	1995	$12.00
Elektra	PRCD 92362	Isobel	CDJ	U.S.	1995	$6.00
		It's Oh So Quiet	CD5	U.K.		$10.00
Second version.						
		It's Oh So Quiet	CD5	U.K.	1995	$10.00
Elektra	64353	It's Oh So Quiet	CD5	U.S.	1995	$5.00
Elektra	PRCD 9322-2	It's Oh So Quiet	CDJ	U.S.	1995	$6.00
WEA	POCP-7106	It's So Quiet	CD5	Japan	1995	$25.00
Elektra	PRCD 9366-2	Three	CDJ	U.S.	1995	$10.00
Pinnacle	122TP7CD	Venus As A Boy	CD5	U.K.	1993	$10.00
Pinnacle		Venus As A Boy	CD5	U.K.	1993	$10.00
Second version.						
Elektra	PRCD 8835-2	Venus As A Boy	CDJ	U.S.	1993	$2.00
		Violently Happy	CD5	U.K.	1995	$10.00
		Violently Happy	CD5	U.K.	1995	$10.00
Second version.						

Blac Monc

Singles

Label	Catalog Number	Title	Type	Country	Year	Longbox Value / Value
RapALot	7082	Secrets Of the Hidden Temple	CDJ	U.S.	1994	$2.00

Black

Full Length

Label	Catalog Number	Title	Type	Country	Year	Longbox Value / Value
A&M	PCCY-10207	Black	LP	Japan		$20.00
A&M	CD-5365	Black	LP/LB	U.S.		$14.00/$8.00
A&M	D25Y-3271	Comedy	LP	Japan	1988	$20.00
A&M		Comedy	DJ/LP	U.S.	1988	$25.00
	3 CD's					
A&M	CD-5222	Comedy	LP/LB	U.S.	1988	$14.00/$8.00
A&M	PCCY-10208	Wonderful Life	LP	Japan	1987	$20.00
A&M	CD-5165	Wonderful Life	LP/LB	U.S.	1887	$14.00/$8.00

Singles

Label	Catalog Number	Title	Type	Country	Year	Longbox Value / Value
A&M	D15Y-3249	At the Tokyo Power Station	CD3	Japan	1988	$13.00/$4.00
A&M	390365-2	Big One, The	CD5	Germany	1988	$9.00
A&M	D15Y-3055	Big One, The	CD3	Japan	1988	$13.00/$4.00
A&M	AMED 468	Big One, The	CD5	U.K.	1988	$9.00
A&M	CD-17533	Everything Comes Up Roses	CDJ	U.S.	1988	$3.00
A&M	3903780-2	Feel Like Change Nice	CD5	Germany	1991	$9.00
A&M	AMED 4769	Fly Up To the Moon	CD5	U.K.	1991	$9.00
Canyon	PCDY-10026	Here It Comes Again	CD3	Japan	1991	$13.00/$4.00
A&M	75021 7274 2	Here It Comes Again	CDJ	U.S.	1991	$3.00
A&M	CDEE-491	Now You're Gone	CD3	U.K.	1989	$9.00
A&M	AMCD 422	Paradise	CD5	U.K.	1987	$9.00
A&M	392224-2	Sweetest Smile	CD5	Germany	1988	$9.00
A&M	AMCD-394	Sweetest Smile	CD5	U.K.	1987	$9.00
A&M	D12Y-3001	Wonderful Life	CD3	Japan	1987	$13.00/$4.00
A&M	D15Y-3200	Wonderful Life	CD5	Japan	1987	$15.00
A&M	CD 17742	Wonderful Life	CDJ	U.S.	1989	$3.00
A&M	CD-17754	Wonderful Life	CDJ	U.S.	1989	$3.00
A&M	390386-2	You're A Big Girl Now	CD3	Germany	1987	$9.00
A&M	D10Y-3061	You're A Big Girl Now	CD3	Japan	1987	$13.00/$4.00
A&M	CDEE-480	You're A Big Girl Now	CD3	U.K.	1987	$9.00

Black 47

Singles

Label	Catalog Number	Title	Type	Country	Year	Longbox Value / Value
SBK	0777 7 80971	Funky Ceili	CD5	U.S.	1992	$5.00
SBK	19898	Losin' It	CDJ	U.S.	1994	$3.00
SBK	DPRO-04697	Maria's Wedding	CDJ	U.S.	1993	$2.00
SBK	DPRO-0549	Rockin' the Bronx	CDJ	U.S.	1993	$2.00

Black Bambi

Full Length

Label	Catalog Number	Title	Type	Country	Year	Longbox Value / Value
Atlantic	7 82122-2	Black Bambi	LP/LB	U.S.		$9.00/$6.00

Black Beat

Singles

Label	Catalog Number	Title	Type	Country	Year	Longbox Value / Value
EMI	204343-2	Spinning Wheels	CD5	Germany	1991	$8.00

Black & Blue

Singles

Label	Catalog Number	Title	Type	Country	Year	Longbox Value / Value
Geffen	PRO-CD-3034	Live It Up	CDJ	U.S.	1988	$2.00

Black Box

Full Length

Label	Catalog Number	Title	Type	Country	Year	Longbox Value / Value
RCA	61051	Mixed Up	LP/BP	U.S.		$12.00/$7.00

Singles

Label	Catalog Number	Title	Type	Country	Year	Longbox Value / Value
Polygram	879483-2	Bright On Time	CD5	Germany	1991	$8.00
Polygram	877305-2	Everybody Everybody	CD5	Germany	1990	$8.00
Polygram	877423-2	Everybody Everybody	CD5	Germany	1990	$8.00
BMG	BVDP-17	Everybody Everybody	CD3	Japan	1990	$13.00/$4.00
RCA	PD-43716	Everybody Everybody	CD5	U.K.	1990	$8.00
RCA	2628-2-RDJ	Everybody Everybody	CDJ	U.S.	1990	$2.00
Polygram	879089-2	Fantasy	CD5	Germany	1991	$8.00
Polygram	879305-2	Fantasy	CD5	Germany	1991	$8.00
BMG	BVDP-33	Fantasy	CD3	Japan	1991	$13.00/$4.00
RCA	PD-43896	Fantasy	CD5	U.K.	1991	$8.00
RCA	2788-2-RDJ	Fantasy	CDJ	U.S.	1990	$2.00
RCA	62065-2-RDJ	Fantasy	CDJ	U.S.	1991	$2.00
Polygram	877043-2	I Don't Know Anybody Else	CD5	Germany	1990	$8.00
Polygram	873713-2	I Don't Know Anybody Else	CD5	Germany	1990	$8.00
BMG		I Don't Know Anybody Else	CD3	Japan	1990	$13.00/$4.00
RCA	PD-43480	I Don't Know Anybody Else	CD5	U.K.	1990	$8.00
RCA	2735-2-RDJ	I Don't Know Anybody Else	CDJ	U.S.	1990	$2.00
RCA	2756-2-RDJ	I Don't Know Anybody Else	CDJ	U.S.	1990	$2.00
Polygram	879355-2	Megamix	CD5	Germany	1991	$8.00
BMG	BVDCP-9006	Megamix	CD3	Japan	1991	$13.00/$4.00
RCA	PD-45054	Open Your Eyes	CD5	U.K.	1991	$8.00
BMG	BVCP-9012	Party Mix	CD3	Japan	1991	$13.00/$4.00
ZYX	6210-8	Ride On Time	CD5	Germany	1990	$6.00
ZYX	6210R-8	Ride On Time	CD5	Germany	1990	$6.00
ZYX	6210P-8	Ride On Time	CD5	Germany	1990	$6.00
Polydor	879 483-2	Ride On Time	CD5	Germany	1990	$8.00
BMG	B15D-41088	Ride On Time	CD3	Japan	1990	$13.00/$4.00
RCA	PD-43056	Ride On Time	CD5	U.K.	1990	$8.00
RCA	62003-2-RDJ	Ride On Time	CDJ	U.S.	1991	$2.00
Polygram	879823-2	Strike It Up	CD5	Germany	1991	$8.00
RCA	PD-44460	Strike It Up	CD5	U.K.	1991	$8.00
RCA	2799-2-RDJ	Strike It Up	CDJ	U.S.	1990	$2.00
RCA	44236	Total Mix, The	CDJ	U.S.	1990	$12.00

Black Cat Bone

Singles

Label	Catalog Number	Title	Type	Country	Year	Longbox Value / Value
Chameleon	8549	Epic Continues, The	CDJ	U.S.	1992	$2.00

Black, Clint

Full Length

Label	Catalog Number	Title	Type	Country	Year	Longbox Value / Value
		'90s Country	RS	U.S.	1995	$45.00
	Airdate: 5/6/95.					
Unistar		Clint Black Story	RS	U.S.	1993	$30.00
	Airdate: 5/28/93					
RCA		Greatest Hits	DJ/Smplr	U.S.	1996	$20.00
RCA	CLINT1	Hard Way. Open Ended Interview	DJ/Intvw	U.S.	1990	$20.00
		Looking For Christmas	DJ/Intvw	U.S.	1995	$25.00
RCA		One Emotion	DJ/LP	U.S.		$15.00
RCA	237	Put Yourself In My Shoes	DJ/LP	U.S.	1990	$20.00
	CD and cassette in box.					
		Road, The	RS	U.S.	1995	$75.00
	2 CD set. Airdate: 7/28/95					
		Road, The	RS	U.S.	1995	$100.00
	2 CD set. Airdate: 11/17/95					
		Road, The	RS	U.S.	1995	$100.00
	2 CD set. Airdate: 2/24/95					
RCA		State Of Mind	DJ/Smplr	U.S.		$10.00

Singles

Label	Catalog Number	Title	Type	Country	Year	Longbox Value / Value
RCA	RDJ 644412	Christmas For Every Boy And Girl	CDJ	U.S.		$6.00
RCA	62878-2-RDJ	Half the Man	CDJ	U.S.	1994	$3.00
RCA	64451-2-RDJ	Kid, The	CDJ	U.S.	1995	$3.00
RCA	2678-2-RDJ	Put Yourself In My Shoes	CDJ	U.S.	1990	$3.00
RCA	62933-2-RDJ	Untanglin	CDJ	U.S.	1994	$3.00
RCA	62194-2-RDJ	We Tell Ourselves	CDJ	U.S.	1992	$3.00
RCA	62016-2-RDJ	Where Are You Now	CDJ	U.S.	1992	$3.00

Black Crowes – Grits 'N Gravy (Def American PRO-CD-7102) Promotional 1995 greatest hits sampler.

Black Crowes

Full Length

Company	Disk Number	Title	Type	Country	Year	Longbox Value / Value
Def American	PRO-CD-7102	Grits 'N Gravy	DJ/Smplr	U.S.	1995	$30.00
Westwood One		In Concert	RS	U.S.	1995	$85.00
	Airdate: 11/6/95.					
Westwood One		In Concert	RS	U.S.	1995	$85.00
	Airdate: 5/8/95.					
Album Network		In Concert- Live In Houston	RS	U.S.	1994	$55.00
	2 CD set.					
Album Network		In the Studio (Shake Your Money Maker)	RS	U.S.		$35.00
Westwood One		Live At the Greek	RS	U.S.	1991	$50.00
	2 CD set.					
Album Network		Live At the Greek Theater	RS	U.S.	1991	$150.00
	2 CD set. Airdate: 11/18/91.					
Westwood One		Off the Record	RS	U.S.	1992	$40.00
	Airdate: 6/29/92					
Westwood One		Off the Record	RS	U.S.	1992	$40.00
	Airdate: 9/28/92					
Westwood One		Off the Record	RS	U.S.	1993	$40.00
	Airdate: 1/18/93					
Westwood One		Off the Record	RS	U.S.	1995	$35.00
	Airdate: 3/20/95.					
Album Network		Southern Harmony	RS	U.S.	1992	$150.00
	2 CD set. Airdate: 5/7/92.					
Def American	PHCR-16005/6	Southern Harmony & Musical Companion	LTD/LP	Japan	1992	$35.00
	2 CD set.					
Def American		Southern Harmony & Musical Companion	LTD/LP	U.K.	1992	$25.00
	2 CD set.					
Def American	9 26976-2	Southern Harmony & Musical Companion	LP/LB	U.S.	1992	$15.00/$9.00
Album Network		Three Snakes And One Charm World Premiere	RS	U.S.	1996	$100.00
	Airdate: 7/17/96.					
Media America		Up Close	RS	U.S.	1995	$60.00
	2 CD set.					
WEA	38302	Who Killed That Bird	LD	U.S.	1992	$30.00

Singles

Company	Disk Number	Title	Type	Country	Year	Longbox Value / Value
Def American		A Conspiracy	CDJ	U.S.	1994	$7.00
Def American	PRO-CD-7158	A Conspiracy	CDJ	U.S.	1995	$3.00
Def American	PRO-CD-6082	Bad Luck Blue Eyes Goodbye	CDJ	U.S.	1993	$6.00
		Good Friday	CD5	U.K.	1996	$10.00
Geffen		Good Friday	CDJ	U.S.	1996	$6.00
Def American	868839-2	Hard To Handle	CD5	Germany	1991	$10.00
Def American		Hard To Handle	CD3	Japan	1990	$13.00/$4.00
Def American	PHRCR-8004	Hard To Handle	CD5	Japan	1990	$18.00
Def American	DEFAC-6	Hard To Handle	CD5	U.K.	1990	$10.00
Def American	DEFAC-10	Hard To Handle	CD5	U.K.	1991	$10.00
Def American	PRO-CD-4162	Hard To Handle	CDJ	U.S.	1990	$6.00
Def American	PRO-CD-4896	Hard To Handle	CDJ	U.S.	1990	$6.00
Def American		High Head Blues	CDJ	U.K.	1994	$20.00
Def American		High Head Blues	CDJ	U.S.	1994	$7.00
Def American	PRO-CD-7736	High Head Blues	CDJ	U.S.	1995	$3.00
Def American	PHRCR-8025	Hotel Illnes	CD5	Japan	1993	$16.00
Def American	DEFCD 23	Hotel Illness	CD5	U.K.	1992	$10.00
Def American		Hotel Illness	CD5	U.K.	1992	$10.00
	Second version.					
Def American	PRO-CD-5778	Hotel Illness	CDJ	U.S.	1992	$3.00
Def American	DEFAC-4	Jealous Again	CD5	U.K.	1990	$10.00
Def American	PRO-CD-3869	Jealous Again	CDJ	U.S.	1990	$7.00
Def American		Live At Ronnie Scott's	CD5	U.K.	1992	$10.00
Def American		Live At Ronnie Scott's	CD5	U.K.	1992	$10.00
	Second version.					
Def American	DFCDJ121	Live At Ronnie Scott's	CDJ	U.K.	1992	$15.00
Def American		Remedy	CD5	Germany	1992	$10.00
Def American	PHDR-105	Remedy	CD3	Japan	1992	$13.00/$4.00
Def American	DEFCD-16	Remedy	CD5	U.K.	1992	$10.00
Def American	PRO-CD-5406	Remedy	CDJ	U.S.	1992	$6.00
Def American	PRO-CD-5474	Remedy	CDJ	U.S.	1992	$6.00
Def American	DEFAC-13	Seeing Things	CD5	U.K.	1990	$10.00
Def American	DEFAC 13	Seeing Things	CDJ	U.K.	1990	$10.00
Def American	PRO-CD-4810	Seeing Things	CDJ	U.S.	1990	$6.00
Def American		She Talks To Angels	CD5	Australia	1991	$10.00
Def American		She Talks To Angels	CD5	Germany	1991	$10.00
Def American	9 18887-2	She Talks To Angels	CD5	U.S.	1991	$5.00
Def American	PRO-CD-4201	She Talks To Angels	CDJ	U.S.	1991	$6.00
Def American	PRO-CD-4687	She Talks To Angels	CDJ	U.S.	1991	$6.00
Def American	PRO-CD-5916	Sometimes Salvation	CDJ	U.S.	1992	$6.00

Label	Catalog Number	Title	Type	Country	Year	Longbox Value / Value
Def American		Sting Me	CD5	Holland	1992	$10.00
Def American	PHCR-8017	Sting Me	CD5	Japan	1992	$16.00
Geffen		Sting Me	CD5	Japan	1995	$15.00
Def American	PRO-CD-5534	Sting Me	CDJ	U.S.	1992	$6.00
Def American	PRO-CD-5633	Thorn In My Pride	CDJ	U.S.	1992	$6.00
Def American	PRO-CD-5610	Thorn In My Pride	CDJ	U.S.	1992	$6.00
Def American	PHCR-8009	Twice As Hard	CD5	Japan	1991	$3.00
Def American	PRO-CD-4122	Twice As Hard	CDJ	U.S.	1990	$7.00
		Wiser Time	CD5	U.K.	1995	$10.00
Geffen		Wiser Time	CD5	U.K.	1995	$10.00
Second version.						
Geffen		Wiser Time	CDJ	U.S.	1995	$7.00

Black, David

Singles

Label	Catalog Number	Title	Type	Country	Year	Longbox Value / Value
Bust it	79438	Nobody But You	CDJ	U.S.	1992	$2.00

Black Flag

Singles

Label	Catalog Number	Title	Type	Country	Year	Longbox Value / Value
SST	CD-16034	AnnihilateThis Week	CD5	U.K.	1988	$9.00
SST	081	AnnihilateThis Week	CD5	U.S.	1988	$5.00
SST	SSTCD-226	I Can See You	CD5	U.K.	1988	$9.00
SST	226	I Can See You	CD5	U.S.	1988	$5.00
SST	Pinnacle	Jealous Again	CD5	U.K.	1989	$9.00
SST	003	Jealous Again	CD5	U.S.	1989	$5.00
SST	CD-40098	Louie Louie	CD5	U.K.	1991	$9.00
SST	175	Louie Louie	CD5	U.S.	1991	$5.00
SST	CD-40055	Nervous Breakdown	CD3	Germany	1990	$9.00
SST	CD-40063	TV Party	CD5	Germany	1990	$5.00
SST	012	TV Party	CD5	U.S.	1990	$5.00

Black Flames

Full Length

Label	Catalog Number	Title	Type	Country	Year	Longbox Value / Value
Columbia	CK-44030	Black Flames, The	LP/LB	U.S.	1990	$14.00/$8.00

Singles

Label	Catalog Number	Title	Type	Country	Year	Longbox Value / Value
Columbia	CSK 73588	Let Me Show You	CDJ	U.S.	1990	$2.00
Columbai	655819-3	Watching You	CD3	Germany	1990	$7.00
Columbia	CSK 73276	Watching You	CDJ	U.S.	1990	$2.00

Black, Frank

Full Length

Label	Catalog Number	Title	Type	Country	Year	Longbox Value / Value
4AD		Abstract Plain	DJ/Smplr	Australia	1995	$20.00
4AD	8820	Conversation And Music With	DJ/Intvw	U.S.	1994	$10.00
4AD		Cult of Ray	DJ/Smplr	Germany		$20.00
4AD	FB-1	Sampler	DJ/Smplr	U.K.	1994	$15.00
4AD		Sessions	DJ/Smplr	France	1995	$30.00

Singles

Label	Catalog Number	Title	Type	Country	Year	Longbox Value / Value
4AD	4228622192	Hang On To Your Ego	CD5	Canada	1994	$8.00
4AD		Hang On To Your Ego	CDJ	France	1995	$13.00
4AD		Hang On To Your Ego	CDJ	U.S.	1994	$6.00
4AD		Heartache	CD5	U.K.	1994	$10.00
4AD		Heartache	CD5	U.K.	1994	$10.00
Second version.						
4AD	PRCD 8962-2	Heartache	CDJ	U.S.	1994	$6.00
		I Don't Want To Hurt	CD5	U.K.	1996	$10.00
Elektra	PRCD 8816-2	I Heard Ramona Sing	CDJ	U.S.	1993	$3.00
Elektra	PRCD 8731-2	Los Angeles	CDJ	U.S.	1993	$3.00
		Men In Black	CD5	U.K.		$10.00
		Men In Black	CD5	U.K.		$10.00
Second version.						
		Men In Black	CDJ	U.K.	1996	$10.00

Black Girl Rock

Singles

Label	Catalog Number	Title	Type	Country	Year	Longbox Value / Value
Devotion	CDDVND-101	Theme	CD5	U.K.	1993	$8.00

Black Grape

Singles

Label	Catalog Number	Title	Type	Country	Year	Longbox Value / Value
		Fat Neck	CDJ	U.K.	1996	$10.00
		In the Name Of the Father	CD5	U.K.	1995	$10.00
		In the Name Of the Father	CD5	U.K.	1995	$10.00
Second version.						
Radioactive	RARP3545	In the Name Of the Father	CDJ	U.S.	1995	$2.00
Radioactive	RAR5P3680	Kelly's Heroes	CDJ	U.S.		$3.00

Black Kiss

Singles

Label	Catalog Number	Title	Type	Country	Year	Longbox Value / Value
CBS	655745-3	Jump On the Floor	CD3	Germany	1990	$8.00
APT	0385-3	Jump On the Floor	CD5	Germany	1990	$8.00
Alfa	ALDB-59	Jump On the Floor	CD3	Japan	1990	$13.00/$4.00
APT	WHOS-029CD	Jump On the Floor	CD5	U.K.	1990	$8.00

Black Machine

Singles

Label	Catalog Number	Title	Type	Country	Year	Longbox Value / Value
ffrr	023	How Gee	CDJ	U.S.	1994	$3.00
Plateau	697 120 023	How Gee	CDJ	U.S.	1994	$7.00

Black Male

Singles

Label	Catalog Number	Title	Type	Country	Year	Longbox Value / Value
ZYX	DST-1019-8	Get On the Floor	CD5	Germany	1990	$6.00
EMI	204592-2	Ragga Tech	CD5	Germany	1991	$8.00

Black Man's Wagon

Singles

Label	Catalog Number	Title	Type	Country	Year	Longbox Value / Value
Intercord	825 795	Black Beat	CD5	Germany	1990	$8.00

Black Market Flowers

Singles

Label	Catalog Number	Title	Type	Country	Year	Longbox Value / Value
Relativity	0224	Kenny And Cleo	CDJ	U.S.	1993	$2.00

Black, Mary

Singles

Label	Catalog Number	Title	Type	Country	Year	Longbox Value / Value
King	KIDP-17	By the Time It Gets Dark	CD3	Japan	1990	$13.00/$4.00
Gift Horse	79143	Columbus	CDJ	U.S.	1989	$2.00
Polygram	CDGPS-5	Moon And St. Christopher	CD3	U.K.	1992	$8.00
King	KIDP-19	New Frontiers	CD3	Japan	1990	$13.00/$4.00
King	KIDP-43	Thorn Upon the Rose	CD3	Japan	1991	$13.00/$4.00

Black Moon

Singles

Label	Catalog Number	Title	Type	Country	Year	Longbox Value / Value
Wreck		Buck Em Down	CDJ	U.S.	1993	$3.00

Black Riot

Singles

Label	Catalog Number	Title	Type	Country	Year	Longbox Value / Value
Champion	CHAMPCD-75	Day In the Life	CD3	U.K.	1988	$8.00

Black Sabbath

Full Length

Label	Catalog Number	Title	Type	Country	Year	Longbox Value / Value
Castle		1970 - 1987	DJ/Smplr	Japan	1996	$150.00
Phonogram	32PD-489	Best	LP	Japan		$30.00
		Between Heaven & Hell	LTD/LP	U.K.	1995	$28.00
Castle		Black Sabbath	LTD/LP	Austria	1991	$35.00
Picture disc CD.						
Castle	2888 001	Black Sabbath Collection	LTD/LP	U.K.	1988	$110.00
6 CD set in box with book and pin. Limited to 2000 copies.						
Castle	CCSCD-199	Black Sabbath CollectionVol.2	LP	U.K.	1990	$25.00
	TOCP-8128	Cross Purposes	LTD/LP	Japan		$35.00
CD with poster and sticker.						
IRS	DPRO-10744	Cross Purposes	DJ/LP	U.S.	1994	$13.00
EMI		Cross Purposes Live	LTD/LP	U.K.	1994	$35.00
CD with VHS video (PAL).						
IRS		Cross Purposes Live	LTD/LP	U.S.	1994	$25.00
CD and Video in box.						
Reprise		Dehumanizer	LP/LB	U.S.		$14.00/$8.00
Castle		Greatest Hits	LTD/LP	Austria	1991	$35.00
Picture disc CD.						
EMI		Headless Cross, Tyr, Dehumanizer	LTD/LP	U.K.	1994	$35.00
3 CD boxed set.						
Polygram	832704-2	Live At Last	LP	Germany		$25.00
Castle	PACD 002	Paranoid	LTD/LP	Austria	1991	$35.00
Picture disc CD.						
Castle		Sabbath Bloody Sabbath	LTD/LP	Austria	1991	$35.00
Picture disc CD.						
Catle	2827 020	Sabbath Bloody Sabbath/Black Sabbath	LP	U.K.		$30.00
2 CD set						
Polygram	826704-2	Seventh Star	LP	Germany		$25.00
Polygram	826704-2	Seventh Star	LP	U.K.		$25.00
Columbia	2SK 6544	The Bible According To Black Sabbath	DJ/Smplr	U.S.	[illegible]	[illegible]
IRS	713049-2	TYR	LTD/LP	U.K.	1990	$35.00
Picture disc CD.						

Singles

Label	Catalog Number	Title	Type	Country	Year	Longbox Value / Value
IRS	IRSD 002	Black Moon	CDJ	U.S.	1989	$6.00
EMI	241025-3	Call Of the Wild	CD5	Germany	1989	$9.00
IRS	241072-2	Feels Good To Me	CD5	Germany	1990	$9.00
IRS	EIRSCD-148	Feels Good To Me	CD5	U.K.	1990	$9.00
IRS	IRSD-67032	Feels Good To Me	CDJ	U.S.	1990	$6.00
IRS	45-8202	Gates of Hell	CDJ	U.S.	1989	$7.00
IRS	CD-13-8202	Gates of Hell	CDJ	U.S.	1989	$7.00
		Guilty As Hell	CDJ	U.S.		$7.00
EMI	241006-2	Headless Cross	CD5	Germany	1989	$9.00
Warner Brothers	PRO-CD-5704	Iron Man	CDJ	U.S.	1992	$6.00
Pioneer	PIFP-1005	Iron Man	CDV	Japan	1990	$15.00
Old Gold	06-6129	Paranoid	CD3	U.K.	1988	$9.00
Castle	CD3-5	Paranoid	CD3	U.K.	1989	$9.00
Warner Brothers	PRO-CD-5311	Time Machine	CDJ	U.S.	1992	$6.00
IRS	CDEIRS 178	TV Crimes	CD5	U.K.	1992	$9.00
IRS		TV Crimes	CD5	U.K.	1992	$9.00
Second 4version.						
Warner Brothers	PRO-CD-5499	TV Crimes	CDJ	U.S.	1992	$7.00

Black Sheep

Singles

Label	Catalog Number	Title	Type	Country	Year	Longbox Value / Value
Mercury	CDP 416	Flavor Of the Month	CDJ	U.S.	1991	$2.00
Mercury	MERCD-369	Stoblite Honey	CD5	U.S.	1992	$8.00
Mercury	CDP 674	Stoblite Honey	CDJ	U.S.	1992	$2.00
Mercury	CDP 700	Stoblite Honey	CDJ	U.S.	1992	$2.00
Mercury	MERCD-356	Try Counting Sheep	CD5	U.S.	1992	$8.00
Polygram	856171	Without A Doubt	CD5	U.S.	1994	$5.00

Black Slacks

Full Length

Label	Catalog Number	Title	Type	Country	Year	Longbox Value / Value
Bear	BCD15489	Black Slacks	LP	Germany		$25.00
Bear	BCD15446	Is Red Hot	LP	Germany		$25.00

Black Sorrows

Singles

Label	Catalog Number	Title	Type	Country	Year	Longbox Value / Value
CBS	653044-2	Chosen Ones	CD5	U.K.	1989	$8.00
Epic	ESK 1701	Chosen Ones	CDJ	U.S.	1989	$2.00
CBS	653127-2	Harley And Rose	CD5	U.K.	1990	$8.00
Epic	652906 2	Hold On to Me	CD5	U.K.	1988	$8.00
Columbia	659766	Stir It Up	CD5	Australia	1993	$8.00

Black, Stanley

Full Length

Label	Catalog Number	Title	Type	Country	Year	Longbox Value / Value
London	800089-2	Digital Magic	LP	Germany		$15.00
RSO	800089-2	Digital Magic	LP/BP	U.S.		$12.00/$7.00
RSO	800089-2	Digital Magic	LP/BP	U.S.†	1984	$14.00/$8.00
London	K30Y-4032	Latin Best 20	LP	Japan		$20.00
London	820183-2	Russia	LP/BP	U.S.		$12.00/$7.00
London	820183-2	Russia	LP/BP	U.S.†	1985	$14.00/$8.00

Black Tie

Full Length

Label	Catalog Number	Title	Type	Country	Year	Longbox Value / Value
Bench	01	When the Night Falls Radio Sampler	DJ/Smplr	U.S.	1990	$30.00

Black Uhuru

Singles

Label	Catalog Number	Title	Type	Country	Year	Longbox Value / Value
Mesa	76018	One Love	CDJ	U.S.	1993	$3.00
SPV	4968-3	Reggae Rock	CD5	Germany	1990	$8.00
Rhino	76003	Tip Of the Iceberg	CD5	U.S.	1992	$4.00

Black Velvet Band

Full Length

Label	Catalog Number	Title	Type	Country	Year	Longbox Value / Value
Elektra	9 61231-2	King Of Myself	LP/LB	U.S.		$12.00/$7.00
Elektra	9 60885-2	King Of Myself	LP/LB	U.S.		$12.00/$7.00

Singles

Label	Catalog Number	Title	Type	Country	Year	Longbox Value / Value
Elektra	7559-66419-2	Lullaby	CD5	Germany	1989	$2.00
Elektra	EKR-149CD	Lullaby	CD5	U.K.	1989	$2.00
Elektra	PRCD 8560-2	Lullaby	CDJ	U.S.	1989	$2.00
Elektra	PR 8098-2	When Justice Came	CDJ	U.S.	1989	$2.00

Black & White

Full Length

Label	Catalog Number	Title	Type	Country	Year	Longbox Value / Value
Atlantic	7 81967-2	Don't Know Yet	LP/LB	U.S.		$14.00/$8.00

Singles

Label	Catalog Number	Title	Type	Country	Year	Longbox Value / Value
Atlantic	PR 2636-2	Rainbow Bar & Girls	CDJ	U.S.	1989	$2.00

Blackalicious

Singles

Label	Catalog Number	Title	Type	Country	Year	Longbox Value / Value
Sand Castle Records	2	Lyric Fathom-Swan	CD5	U.S.	1994	$5.00

Blackbird

Singles

Label	Catalog Number	Title	Type	Country	Year	Longbox Value / Value
Scotti Brothers	ZSK 75340	Class War	CDJ	U.S.	1992	$3.00
Scotti Brothers	ZSK 75320	Take Me	CDJ	U.S.	1992	$3.00

Blackeyed Susan

Full Length

Label	Catalog Number	Title	Type	Country	Year	Longbox Value / Value
Mercury	848575-2	Electric Rattlebone	LP/BP	U.S.		$14.00/$8.00

Singles

Label	Catalog Number	Title	Type	Country	Year	Longbox Value / Value
Mercury	CDP 431	None Of It Matters	CDJ	U.S.	1991	$2.00
Mercury	CDP 554	Ride With Me	CDJ	U.S.	1991	$2.00
Mercury	CDP 502	Satisfaction	CDJ	U.S.	1991	$2.00

Blackfish

Singles

Label	Catalog Number	Title	Type	Country	Year	Longbox Value / Value
Epic	ESK 5178	Fall, The	CDJ	U.S.	1993	$3.00

Blackfoot

Singles

Label	Catalog Number	Title	Type	Country	Year	Longbox Value / Value
Nalli	N 11347	Doin' My Job	CDJ	U.S.	1991	$2.00
Nalli	1991	Guitar Slingers Song & Dance	CDJ	U.S.	1991	$2.00

Blackgirl

Full Length

Label	Catalog Number	Title	Type	Country	Year	Longbox Value / Value
RCA	RDJ 66384-2	Evolution Of Blackgirl	DJ/Intvw	U.S.	1994	$12.00

Singles

Label	Catalog Number	Title	Type	Country	Year	Longbox Value / Value
Kaper	62882-2-RDJ	90's Girl	CDJ	U.S.	1994	$2.00
RCA	64228	Give Love On Christmas Day	CD5	U.S.	1994	$5.00
RCA	64228-2-RDJ	Give Love On Christmas Day	CDJ	U.S.	1994	$3.00
RCA	62789	Krazy	CD5	U.S.	1994	$5.00
Kaper	62789-2-RDJ	Krazy	CDJ	U.S.	1994	$2.00
RCA	62789-2-RDJ	Krazy	CDJ	U.S.	1994	$3.00
RCA	64309	Let's Do It Again	CD5	U.S.	1994	$5.00
RCA	64309-2-RDJ	Let's Do It Again	CDJ	U.S.	1995	$3.00
		Ninety's Girl	CD5	U.K.		$10.00
		Ninety's Girl	CD5	U.K.		$10.00
	Second version.					
RCA	62910-2-RDJ	Where Did We Go Wrong	CDJ	U.S.	1994	$3.00

Blackhawk

Full Length

Label	Catalog Number	Title	Type	Country	Year	Longbox Value / Value
Westwood One		Country Concert	RS	U.S.	1996	$50.00
	2 CD set. Airdate: 8/19/96.					

Blackjack

Full Length

Label	Catalog Number	Title	Type	Country	Year	Longbox Value / Value
Polygram	843335-2	Blackjack	LP/BP	U.S.		$12.00/$7.00

Blackout Allstars

Singles

Label	Catalog Number	Title	Type	Country	Year	Longbox Value / Value
Sony	42329-2	I Like It	CD5	U.S.	1996	$3.00

Blacksmith

Singles

Label	Catalog Number	Title	Type	Country	Year	Longbox Value / Value
London	886622-3	Get Back To Love	CD3	Germany	1989	$8.00
London	886623-2	Get Back To Love	CD5	Germany	1989	$8.00
Polygram	FCD-111	Get Back To Love	CD5	U.K.	1989	$8.00
Polygram	FCD-130	Hold You Back	CD5	U.K.	1990	$8.00
Warner Brothers	WPCL-729	Hole	CD3	Japan	1993	$13.00/$4.00
Warner Brothers	WPDL-4256	Mama Goes To War	CD3	Japan	1991	$13.00/$4.00

Blackstreet

Singles

Label	Catalog Number	Title	Type	Country	Year	Longbox Value / Value
Atlantic	95805	Before I Let You Go	CD5	U.S.	1994	$5.00
Atlantic	95769	Joy	CD5	U.S.	1994	$5.00
	PRCD 6121	Jury	CDJ	U.S.		$2.00
	PRCD 6311	Tonight's the Night	CDJ	U.S.		$2.00

Blackwell, Alfonso

Singles

Label	Catalog Number	Title	Type	Country	Year	Longbox Value / Value
	SBDJ 78058-2	Free And Easy	CDJ	U.S.		$2.00

Blades, Ruben

Full Length

Label	Catalog Number	Title	Type	Country	Year	Longbox Value / Value
Elektra	9 60754-2	Nothing But the Truth	LP/LB	U.S.		$12.00/$7.00

Singles

Label	Catalog Number	Title	Type	Country	Year	Longbox Value / Value
Elektra		Hit, The	CDJ	U.S.		$2.00
Elektra	PR 2246-2	Hopes On Hold	CDJ	U.S.	1988	$2.00

Blahzay Blahzay

Singles

Label	Catalog Number	Title	Type	Country	Year	Longbox Value / Value
Capitol	DPRO-4092	Danger	CDJ	U.S.		$2.00
	DPRO-4122	Danger	CDJ	U.S.		$3.00

Blaire, Terry

Singles

Label	Catalog Number	Title	Type	Country	Year	Longbox Value / Value
Chrysalis	CHSCD-3478	Ultra Modern Nursery Rhymes	CD5	U.K.	1990	$8.00

Blak Czar

Singles

Label	Catalog Number	Title	Type	Country	Year	Longbox Value / Value
Relativity	0294	Hood, The	CDJ	U.S.	1994	$2.00

Blak Panta

Singles

Label	Catalog Number	Title	Type	Country	Year	Longbox Value / Value
Tommy Boy	680	Do What You Want	CDJ	U.S.	1995	$2.00

Blake Babies

Singles

Label	Catalog Number	Title	Type	Country	Year	Longbox Value / Value
		Lament	CDJ	U.S.	1989	$2.00
Mammoth	378-4025-2	Rosy Jack World	CD5	Germany	1991	$8.00
Mammoth	MR-0025-2	Rosy Jack World	CD5	U.K.	1991	$8.00
Mammoth	25	Rosy Jack World	CD5	U.S.	1991	$5.00

Blake, Ran

Full Length

Label	Catalog Number	Title	Type	Country	Year	Longbox Value / Value
Soul Note	121127-2	Short Life Of Babara Monk	LP	U.S.		$8.00
Soul Note	121077-2	Short Life Of Babara Monk	LP	U.S.		$8.00
Rhino	79238	You Stepped Out Of A Cloud	LP/LB	U.S.		$14.00/$8.00

Blakeley, Peter

Full Length

Label	Catalog Number	Title	Type	Country	Year	Longbox Value / Value
Capitol	CDP 7 90412-2	Harry's Cafe De Wheels	LP/LB	U.S.		$14.00/$8.00

Singles

Label	Catalog Number	Title	Type	Country	Year	Longbox Value / Value
Capitol	203511-2	Crying In the Chapel	CD5	Germany	1990	$8.00
Capitol	204061-2	Crying In the Chapel	CD5	Germany	1990	$8.00
Capitol	CDCL-548	Crying In the Chapel	CD5	U.K.	1990	$8.00
Warner Brothers	41034	I've Been Lonely	CD5	U.S.	1994	$5.00

Company	Disk Number	Title	Type	Country	Year	Longbox Value / Value
Alfa	10R3-2	My Foolish Heart	CD3	Japan	1988	$12.00/$3.00
Alfa	10R3-1	My Funny Valentine	CD3	Japan	1988	$12.00/$3.00
Capitol	204120-2	Quicksand	CD5	Germany	1990	$8.00

Blakey, Art (And Jazz Messengers)

Full Length

Company	Disk Number	Title	Type	Country	Year	Longbox Value / Value
Philips	800064-2	A Night In Tunisia	LP/BP	U.S.†	1984	$14.00/$8.00
Image	ID7166SO	Art Blakely And the Jazz Messengers	LD	U.S.		$25.00
Emarcy	822471-2	Buttercorn Lady	LP/BP	U.S.†	1985	$14.00/$8.00
Mosaic	MD6-141	Complete Blue Note Recording	LTD/LP	U.S.		$90.00
	6 CD set.					
Polygram	834752-2	Des Femmes Disparaissent	LP/BP	U.S.		$14.00/$8.00
Vogue	CD-600107	Drum Night At Birdland	LP	U.S.		$8.00
Bethlehem	6023	Hard Drive	LP/LB	U.S.		$15.00/$10.00
Soul Note	1155	I Get A Kick Out Of You	LP	U.S.		$8.00
Blue Note	CDP 7 46429-2	Indestructible	LP/LB	U.S.		$15.00/$10.00
Blue Note		Indestructible	LTD/LP	U.S.	1995	$19.00
WEA	CD-1578	Jazz Messengers	LP/LB	U.S.		$14.00/$8.00
Polygram	812017	Liasons Dangereuses	LP/BP	U.S.		$14.00/$8.00
Blue Note	CJ28-5075	Like Someone In Love	LP	Japan		$25.00
Blue Note	CDP 7 84245-2	Like Someone In Love	LP/LB	U.S.		$15.00/$10.00
Vogue	CD-600030	Maonin – Blues March	LP	U.S.		$8.00
Blue Note	CJ28-5093	Moaic	LP	Japan		$25.00
Blue Note	CJ28-5121	New Sounds	LP	Japan		$25.00
Blue Note	CDP 7 84436-2	New Sounds	LP/LB	U.S.		$15.00/$10.00
Polygram	800064	Night In Tunisia	LP/BP	U.S.		$14.00/$8.00
Blue Note	CDP 7 86858-2	Ritual	LP/LB	U.S.		$15.00/$10.00
Blue Note	CDP 7 84451-2	Three Blind Mice Vol. 1	LP/LB	U.S.		$15.00/$10.00
Blue Note	CDP 7 84452-2	Three Blind Mice Vol. 2	LP/LB	U.S.		$15.00/$10.00
Atlantic	7 81737-2	With Thelonious Monk	LP/LB	U.S.		$14.00/$8.00

Blame

Singles

Company	Disk Number	Title	Type	Country	Year	Longbox Value / Value
Shadow	SHADOW-11CD	Music Takes You	CD5	U.K.	1992	$7.00

Blameless

Singles

Company	Disk Number	Title	Type	Country	Year	Longbox Value / Value
		Town Clowns	CD5	U.K.		$10.00
		Town Clowns	CD5	U.K.		$10.00
	Second version.					
	PRCD 6187-2	Town Clowns	CDJ	U.S.		$3.00

Blammo

Singles

Company	Disk Number	Title	Type	Country	Year	Longbox Value / Value
APT	MIRACD-038	Magic Pencil	CD5	U.K.	1992	$7.00

Blancmange

Full Length

Company	Disk Number	Title	Type	Country	Year	Longbox Value / Value
London	820301-2	Believe You Me	LP	Germany		$15.00
London	820301-2	Believe You Me	LP	U.K.		$15.00
Pioneer	PA-84-M018	Blancmange	8"LD	U.S.	1985	$8.00
London	810123-2	Happy Families	LP	Germany		$15.00
London	810235-2	Mange Tout	LP	Germany		$15.00

Bland, Bobby Blue

Singles

Company	Disk Number	Title	Type	Country	Year	Longbox Value / Value
Malaco	2303	Double Trouble	CDJ	U.S.	1995	$2.00
Malaco	2199	I Just Tripped On A Piece Of Your Broken Heart	CDJ	U.S.	1995	$2.00

Blando, Deborah

Full Length

Company	Disk Number	Title	Type	Country	Year	Longbox Value / Value
Epic	EK-46883	Different Story	LP/LB	U.S.		$14.00/$8.00

Singles

Company	Disk Number	Title	Type	Country	Year	Longbox Value / Value
Epic	ESDA-7079	Boy (Why You Wanna Make Me Blue)	CD3	Japan	1991	$12.00/$3.00
Epic	ESK 73920	Boy (Why You Wanna Make Me Blue)	CDJ	U.S.	1991	$2.00

Blanke Toto

Full Length

Company	Disk Number	Title	Type	Country	Year	Longbox Value / Value
Aris	883087	Collection	LP	Germany		$15.00
Aris	883071	Tarmontana	LP	Germany		$15.00

Blaque

Singles

Company	Disk Number	Title	Type	Country	Year	Longbox Value / Value
EMI	147582-2	Party Up	CD5	Germany	1991	$7.00

Blaske, Lee

Singles

Company	Disk Number	Title	Type	Country	Year	Longbox Value / Value
	7503	Immortal Kiss Of Th	CD5	U.S.	1994	$5.00

Blast

Singles

Company	Disk Number	Title	Type	Country	Year	Longbox Value / Value
MCA	54913	Crazy Man	CD5	U.S.	1994	$5.00

Blaze

Singles

Company	Disk Number	Title	Type	Country	Year	Longbox Value / Value
Motown	ZD-44056	Get Up	CD5	U.K.	1990	$8.00
RCA	PD-43710	So Special	CD5	Germany	1990	$8.00
RCA	PD-43654	So Special	CD5	U.K.	1990	$8.00
RCA	PD-43710	So Special	CD5	U.K.	1990	$8.00
Motown	CD451024	So Special	CDJ	U.S.	1990	$2.00
RCA	PD-44032	We All Must Live Together	CD5	Germany	1990	$8.00

Bleach

Singles

Company	Disk Number	Title	Type	Country	Year	Longbox Value / Value
APT	10894-2	Shotgun	CD5	U.K.	1992	$8.00
Way Cool	10CD	Snag	CD5	Australia	1991	$8.00
APT	WAY-10CD	Snag	CD5	U.K.	1991	$8.00
Dali	8649	Surround	CDJ	U.S.	1992	$2.00
Dali	8697	Trip And Slide	CDJ	U.S.	1993	$2.00

Blegvad, Peter

Singles

Company	Disk Number	Title	Type	Country	Year	Longbox Value / Value
Silvertone	ORE DJ CD23	Meantime	CD5	Germany	1990	$8.00

Blender, Everton

Singles

Company	Disk Number	Title	Type	Country	Year	Longbox Value / Value
Heartbeat	4604	Lift Up Your Head	CD5	U.S.	1995	$5.00

Blessed Union Of Souls

Singles

Company	Disk Number	Title	Type	Country	Year	Longbox Value / Value
	DPRO-19977	Home	CDJ	U.S.	1995	$3.00
	DPRO-19818	Let Me Be the One	CDJ	U.S.		$3.00
	DPRO-10456	Oh Virginia	CDJ	U.S.		$3.00

Blessing

Full Length

Company	Disk Number	Title	Type	Country	Year	Longbox Value / Value
MCA		Hurricane Room	DJ/Intvw	U.K.	1991	$30.00

Label	Catalog Number	Title	Type	Country	Year	Longbox Value/Value
		Prince Of Deep Water	LP	U.S.		$22.00
MCA	MCAD-10070	Prince Of the Deep Water	LP/LB	U.S.		$14.00/$8.00

Singles

Label	Catalog Number	Title	Type	Country	Year	Value
MCA	MCSTD-1560	Delta Rain	CD5	U.K.	1991	$8.00
MCA	1545	Denial	CDJ	U.S.	1991	$3.00
MCA	MCSTD-1553	Flames	CD5	U.K.	1991	$8.00
MCA	MCD-17552	Highway 52	CD5	Germany	1992	$8.00
MCA	MCSTD-1603	Highway 52	CD5	U.K.	1992	$8.00
MCA	MCSTD-1609	Highway 52	CD5	U.K.	1992	$8.00
MCA	CD45 1337	Highway 52	CDJ	U.S.	1991	$2.00
MCA	MCD-17822	Hurricane Room	CD5	Germany	1992	$8.00
MCA	CD45 1502	Hurricane Room	CDJ	U.S.	1991	$2.00

Bleu, Lundi

Singles

Label	Catalog Number	Title	Type	Country	Year	Value
Epic/Sony	94-5-21	Times, The	CD5	Japan	1992	$15.00

Bleu, Mikki

Full Length

Label	Catalog Number	Title	Type	Country	Year	Longbox Value/Value
EMI	91171-2	I Promise	LP/LB	U.S.	1990	$14.00/$8.00

Singles

Label	Catalog Number	Title	Type	Country	Year	Value
EMI	CDMT-78	I Promise	CD5	U.K.	1990	$8.00

Bley, Carla

Full Length

Label	Catalog Number	Title	Type	Country	Year	Value
ECM	827640	Night Glo	LP	U.S.		$8.00

Bley, Paul

Full Length

Label	Catalog Number	Title	Type	Country	Year	Longbox Value/Value
Soul Note	121140-2	Hot	LP	U.S.		$8.00
Polygram	SN-1090CD	Tango Palace	LP/BP	U.S.		$14.00/$8.00

Blige, Mary J.

Singles

Label	Catalog Number	Title	Type	Country	Year	Value
	UPT5P3529	A Natural Woman	CDJ	U.S.		$3.00
		Be Happy	CD5	U.K.		$10.00
		Be Happy	CD5	U.K.		$10.00

Second version.

Label	Catalog Number	Title	Type	Country	Year	Value
Uptown	MCSXD 2033	Be Happy	CD5	U.K.	1994	$10.00
Uptown	2799	I Don't Want To Do Anything	CDJ	U.S.	1993	$2.00
Uptown	2776	I Don't Want To Do Anything	CDJ	U.S.	1993	$3.00
Uptown	3302	I'm Goin' Down	CDJ	U.S.	1994	$3.00
Uptown	UT5P-3367	I'm Going Down	CDJ	U.S.	1995	$3.00
Uptown	2667	Love No Limit	CDJ	U.S.	1993	$2.00
	ASCD2957	Not Going To Cry	CDJ	U.S.		$3.00
MCA	MCSTD-1721	Real Love	CD5	U.K.	1992	$8.00
MCA	54456	Real Love	CD5	U.S.	1992	$5.00
MCA	MCA5P 2311	Real Love	CDJ	U.S.	1992	$2.00
MCA	MCSTD-1731	Reminisce	CD5	U.K.	1993	$8.00
MCA	54525	Reminisce	CD5	U.S.	1992	$5.00
Uptown	2548	Sweet Thing	CDJ	U.S.	1992	$2.00
Uptown	2581	Sweet Thing	CDJ	U.S.	1992	$3.00
MCA		You Bring Me Joy	CDJ	U.S.		$3.00
Uptown	2760	You Don't Have To Worry	CDJ	U.S.	1993	$6.00
MCA	MCSTD-1683	You Remind Me	CD5	U.K.	1992	$8.00
MCA	54447	You Remind Me	CD5	U.S.	1992	$5.00
MCA	2098	You Remind Me	CDJ	U.S.	1992	$2.00

Blind Melon

Full Length

Label	Catalog Number	Title	Type	Country	Year	Value
Capitol	CDESTX 2188	Blind Melon	LTD/LP	U.K.	1994	$26.00

2 CD set in digipak

Label	Catalog Number	Title	Type	Country	Year	Value
Westwood One		In Concert	RS	U.S.	1993	$50.00

2 CD set. With Spin Doctors. Airdate: 8/16/93

Label	Catalog Number	Title	Type	Country	Year	Value
Westwood One		In Concert	RS	U.S.	1994	$60.00

2 CD set. With New Order, Airdate: 2/14/94

Label	Catalog Number	Title	Type	Country	Year	Value
Westwood One		In Concert-Nu Rock	RS	U.S.	1994	$50.00

Airdate: 2/14/94.

Label	Catalog Number	Title	Type	Country	Year	Value
Westwood One		In Concert-Nu Rock	RS	U.S.	1996	$50.00

Airdate: 2/26/96.

Label	Catalog Number	Title	Type	Country	Year	Value
Capitol	CDP-34615	Soup	LTD/LP	U.S.	1995	$18.00

CD in wallet package.

Singles

Label	Catalog Number	Title	Type	Country	Year	Value
Capitol	DPRO-79491	Bit O' Melon	CDJ	U.S.	1992	$3.00
Capitol	DPRO-79322	Change	CDJ	U.S.	1992	$3.00
Capital	58030	Change	CD5	U.S.	1994	$5.00
Capitol		Galaxie	CD5	U.K.	1995	$10.00
Capitol		Galaxie	CD5	U.K.	1995	$10.00

Second version.

Label	Catalog Number	Title	Type	Country	Year	Value
Capitol	DPRO-79631	Galaxie	CDJ	U.S.	1995	$3.00
Capitol	DPRO-79586	I Wonder	CDJ	U.S.	1992	$3.00
Capitol	DPRO-79397	No Rain	CDJ	U.S.	1992	$3.00
Capitol	C2 15994	No Rain	CD5	U.S.	1993	$6.00
Capital	15994	No Rain	CD5	U.S.	1994	$5.00
	PRCD 6699-2	Three Is A Magic Number	CDJ	U.S.		$3.00
Capitol	DPRO-10276	Toes Across the Water	CDJ	U.S.	1995	$3.00
Capitol		Tones Of Home	CD5	Austalia	1994	$12.00
Capitol	TOCP-7351	Tones Of Home	CD3	Japan	1992	$13.00/$4.00
Capitol	C2 15927	Tones Of Home	CD5	U.S.	1992	$5.00
Capitol	DPRO-79397	Tones Of Home	CDJ	U.S.	1992	$3.00
Capitol	DPRO-79254	Tones Of Home	CDJ	U.S.	1992	$3.00
Capitol	DPRO-79491	Tones Of Home	CDJ	U.S.	1992	$3.00

Blind Mr. Jones

Singles

Label	Catalog Number	Title	Type	Country	Year	Value
Cherry	CDCHERRY-125	Crazy Jazz	CD5	U.K.	1992	$8.00

Blind Tribe

Singles

Label	Catalog Number	Title	Type	Country	Year	Value
Miramar Prod.	8011	Blind Tribe	CD5	U.S.	1994	$5.00

Blink

Singles

Label	Catalog Number	Title	Type	Country	Year	Value
		Cello	CD5	U.K.		$10.00
		Cello	CD5	U.K.		$10.00

Second version.

Label	Catalog Number	Title	Type	Country	Year	Value
Lime		CMJ Seminar	CD5	U.K.	1992	$10.00

Bliss

Singles

Label	Catalog Number	Title	Type	Country	Year	Value
EMI	204371-2	Crash Into the Ocean	CD5	Germany	1991	$8.00
EMI	CDR-6294	Crash Into the Ocean	CD5	U.K.	1991	$8.00
EMI	203435-3	How Does It Feel	CD3	Germany	1989	$8.00
EMI	CDR-6222	How Does It Feel	CD5	U.K.	1989	$8.00
EMI	CDR-6295	I Don't Want To Hurry	CD5	U.K.	1991	$8.00
EMI	203172-2	I Hear You Call	CD5	Germany	1989	$8.00
EMI	CDR-62902	I Hear You Call	CD5	U.K.	1989	$8.00
EMI	CDR-6286	Watching Over Me	CD5	U.K.	1991	$8.00
EMI	203346-2	Won't Let Go	CD5	Germany	1989	$8.00
EMI	CDR-6216	Won't Let Go	CD5	U.K.	1989	$8.00

Blister

Full Length

Label	Catalog Number	Title	Type	Country	Year	Value
		Vigilantes of Love Sampler	DJ/Smplr	U.S.		$10.00

Blitzspeer

Full Length

Label	Catalog Number	Title	Type	Country	Year	Value
Epic	ESK 4461	Man In Black	DJ/Smplr	U.S.	1992	$4.00

Singles

Label	Catalog Number	Title	Type	Country	Year	Value
Epic	ESK 4416	Sonic Glory	CDJ	U.S.	1992	$2.00

Bloc

Full Length

Label	Catalog Number	Title	Type	Country	Year	Longbox Value/Value
A&M	CD53-43	In the Free Zone	LP	U.S.	1991	$14.00/$8.00

Singles

Label	Catalog Number	Title	Type	Country	Year	Value
A&M	75021 7509 2	Speak	CDJ	U.S.	1991	$2.00

Block, Rory

Full Length

Label	Catalog Number	Title	Type	Country	Year	Value
Teldec	8 26955	House Of Hearts	LP	Germany		$15.00
Rounder	1011	Faithless World	CDJ	U.S.	1992	$2.00

Blondie

Full Length

Label	Catalog Number	Title	Type	Country	Year	Longbox Value/Value
Chrysalis	VK-41337	Best Of	LP/LB	U.S.†	1985	$15.00/$10.00
Chrysalis	VK-41384	Hunter	LP/LB	U.S.		$15.00/$10.00
Chrysalis		Parallel Lines	LTD/LP	U.K.	1994	$15.00

25th Anniversary edition in 6"x11" longbox

Singles

Label	Catalog Number	Title	Type	Country	Year	Value
Capitol	[illegible]	Atomic	CD5	U.S.	1994	$5.00
Chrysalis	CHSCD-3342	Call Me	CD5	U.K.	1988	$10.00
Chrysalis	CHSCD-3328	Denis 88 Mix	CD5	U.K.	1988	$9.00
		Heart Of Glass	CDJ	U.K.	1995	$13.00
MCA	58387	Heart Of Glass	CD5	U.S.	1995	$5.00
Capital	58277	Rapture	CD5	U.S.	1994	$5.00
Capitol	58474	Union City Blue	CD5	U.S.	1995	$5.00

Blonker

Singles

Label	Catalog Number	Title	Type	Country	Year	Value
Polygram	874304-3	Blue Carousel	CD3	Germany	1989	$8.00

Blonz

Full Length

Label	Catalog Number	Title	Type	Country	Year	Longbox Value/Value
Imagine	CK 46071	Blonz	LP/LB	U.S.	1990	$14.00/$8.00
Imagine		Blonz/Special Pre-Release	DJ/LP	U.S.	1990	$12.00

Singles

Label	Catalog Number	Title	Type	Country	Year	Value
Imagine	2223	Last Call (For Alcohol)	CDJ	U.S.	1990	$2.00

Blood Feast

Full Length

Label	Catalog Number	Title	Type	Country	Year	Value
Restless	72628	Choppin Block Blues	LP	U.S.		$8.00

Blood & Gasoline

Singles

Label	Catalog Number	Title	Type	Country	Year	Value
Music For Nations	CDKUT-147	FM	CD5	U.K.	1992	$8.00

Blood Of Abraham

Singles

Label	Catalog Number	Title	Type	Country	Year	Value
Ruthless	0222	Stabbed By the Steeple	CDJ	U.S.	1993	$2.00

Blood Sweat & Tears

Full Length

Label	Catalog Number	Title	Type	Country	Year	Longbox Value/Value
Columbia		Found Treasures	LP/LB	U.S.		$14.00/$8.00
CBS	CK-31170	Greatest Hits	LP/BP	U.S.†	1985	$15.00/$9.00

Singles

Label	Catalog Number	Title	Type	Country	Year	Value
CBS	654068-3	Spinning Wheel	CD3	Germany	1989	$8.00
CBS	654068-3	Spinning Wheel	CD3	U.K.	1989	$8.00

Bloodgood

Full Length

Label	Catalog Number	Title	Type	Country	Year	Value
Aris	880384	Bloodgood	LP	Germany		$15.00
Alarma	CDP 70919	Bloodgood	LP	U.S.		$9.00
Aris	880393	Detonation	LP	Germany		$15.00

Bloodhound Gang

Singles

Label	Catalog Number	Title	Type	Country	Year	Value
Columbia	77929	Mama Say	CDJ	U.S.	1995	$3.00

Bloodline

Singles

Label	Catalog Number	Title	Type	Country	Year	Value
EMI	19993	Calling Me Back	CDJ	U.S.	1995	$6.00
EMI	19951	Dixie Peach	CDJ	U.S.	1993	$2.00
	DPRO19870	Stone Cold Hearted	CDJ	U.S.		$3.00

Bloods & Crips

Singles

Label	Catalog Number	Title	Type	Country	Year	Value
Pump	601	Piru Love	CDJ	U.S.	1993	$2.00

Bloom, Luka

Full Length

Label	Catalog Number	Title	Type	Country	Year	Longbox Value/Value
Success		Rx For the Blues	LP/BP	U.S.		$14.00/$8.00
Pulsar		Uncle Bob's Barrelhouse Blues	LP/LB	U.S.		$14.00/$8.00

Singles

Label	Catalog Number	Title	Type	Country	Year	Value
Reprise	PRO-CD-5283	I Need Love	CDJ	U.S.	1992	$2.00
Reprise	PRO-CD-5306	I Need Love	CDJ	U.S.	1992	$2.00
Reprise	PRO-CD-3990	Rescue Mission	CDJ	U.S.	1990	$2.00
Reprise	PRO-CD-6980	Sunny Sailor Boy	CDJ	U.S.	1993	$3.00

Bloomfield, Mike

Full Length

Label	Catalog Number	Title	Type	Country	Year	Longbox Value/Value
		Best Of	LP/LB	U.S.	1987	$14.00/$10.00
		Cruisin' For A Bruisin'	LP/LB	U.S.		$12.00/$10.00
		Rx For the Blues	LP/LB	U.S.		$12.00/$10.00

Bloomsday

Singles

Label	Catalog Number	Title	Type	Country	Year	Value
Island	884970	Strange Honey	CD5	Germany	1990	$8.00
Island	CID-478	Strange Honey	CD5	U.K.	1990	$8.00

Blount, Tanya

Singles

Label	Catalog Number	Title	Type	Country	Year	Value
Polydor	1180	I'm Gonna Make You Mine	CDJ	U.S.	1994	$2.00
Island	PRCD 6898	Remember Love	CDJ	U.S.	1994	$3.00

Label	Catalog Number	Title	Type	Country	Year	Longbox Value / Value

Blow

Singles

Label	Catalog Number	Title	Type	Country	Year	Value
Virgin	TENCD-288	It's Gonna Change	CD3	U.K.	1989	$8.00

Blow, Kurtis

Full Length

Label	Catalog Number	Title	Type	Country	Year	Value
Mercury	830215-2	Kingdom Blow	LP/BP	U.S.		$14.00/$8.00

Singles

Label	Catalog Number	Title	Type	Country	Year	Value
Polygram	874393-2	If I Ruled the World	CD5	Germany	1989	$8.00

Blow Monkeys

Full Length

Label	Catalog Number	Title	Type	Country	Year	Value
RCA	6246-2	She Was Only A Grocer's Daughter	LP/BP	U.S.		$14.00/$8.00

Singles

Label	Catalog Number	Title	Type	Country	Year	Value
RCA	MONK C 6	(Celebrate) the Day After You	CD5	U.K.	1987	$8.00
RCA	PD-42886	Choice	CD5	Germany	1989	$8.00
RCA	R10D-128	Choice	CD3	Japan	1989	$13.00/$4.00
RCA	PD-42886	Choice	CD5	U.K.	1989	$8.00
RCA	42866-2-RDJ	Choice	CDJ	U.S.	1989	$3.00
RCA	PD-4223-2	It Pays To Be Short	CD5	U.K.	1988	$8.00
RCA	PD-43864	La Passionara	CD5	Germany	1990	$8.00
RCA	PD-43864	La Passionara	CD5	U.K.	1990	$8.00
RCA	MONKC-5	Out With Her	CD5	U.K.	1987	$8.00
RCA	PD-43202	Slaves No More	CD5	Germany	1989	$8.00
RCA	PD-43201	Slaves No More	CD5	U.K.	1989	$8.00
RCA	PD-43202	Slaves No More	CD5	U.K.	1989	$8.00
RCA	PD-43624	Springtime For the World	CD5	U.K.	1990	$8.00
RCA	42696	This Is Your Life	CD5	Germany	1989	$8.00
BMG	B15D-41036	This Is Your Life	CD3	Japan	1988	$13.00/$4.00
RCA	42150	This Is Your Life	CD3	U.K.	1989	$8.00
RCA	42696	This Is Your Life	CD5	U.K.	1989	$8.00

Blow Up

Singles

Label	Catalog Number	Title	Type	Country	Year	Value
Pinnacle	CDCHERRY-115	World	CD5	U.K.	1991	$8.00

Blu

Singles

Label	Catalog Number	Title	Type	Country	Year	Value
Motown	860397	Hide & Go Get It	CD5	U.S.	1995	$5.00
Motown	374631289	Hide & Go Get It	CDJ	U.S.	1995	$3.00

Blue

Singles

Label	Catalog Number	Title	Type	Country	Year	Value
Universe	CDUNV-1	Don't Leave Me Standing	CD5	U.K.	1992	$8.00
Polygram	876967-2	Heaven Knows	CD5	Germany	1990	$8.00
Polygram	MERCD-319	Heaven Knows	CD5	U.K.	1990	$8.00
Polygram	MERCD-325	Missing These Kisses	CD5	U.K.	1990	$8.00

Blue Aeroplanes

Full Length

Label	Catalog Number	Title	Type	Country	Year	Value
Chrysalis	21856	Beatsongs	LP/LB	U.S.		$14.00/$8.00
Restless	72314	Friendloverplane	LP/BP	U.S.		$14.00/$8.00
Chrysalis		Swagger	DJ/LP	U.S.	1990	$8.00
Chrysalis	21752	Swagger	LP/LB	U.S.	1990	$14.00/$8.00
Chrysalis	21818	World View Blue	LP/LB	U.S.		$14.00/$8.00

Singles

Label	Catalog Number	Title	Type	Country	Year	Value
BMG	663209-2	And Stones	CD5	Germany	1990	$8.00
BMG	ENYCD-632	And Stones	CD5	U.K.	1990	$8.00
Chrysalis	DPRO-23548	And Stones	CDJ	U.S.	1990	$2.00
EMI	323742-2	Blue Aeroplanes	CD5	Germany	1991	$8.00
Chrysalis	DPRO-23789	Boy In the Bubble, The	CDJ	U.S.	1990	$2.00
EMI	323865-2	Fun	CD5	Germany	1991	$9.00
EMI	ENYCD-628	Jacket Hangs	CD5	U.K.	1990	$8.00
EMI	323602-2	Loved	CD5	Germany	1990	$8.00
EMI	ENYCD 636	Loved	CD5	U.K.	1990	$8.00
EMI	ENYCD-547	Your Own World	CD5	U.K.	1991	$8.00

Blue Angels

Singles

Label	Catalog Number	Title	Type	Country	Year	Value
Solid	ROCD-739	Candy	CD5	U.K.	1992	$8.00

Blue, Barry

Singles

Label	Catalog Number	Title	Type	Country	Year	Value
Sony	655163-3	Dancin' On A Saturday Night	CD3	Germany	1989	$8.00
Supreme	AWOLCD-4	Dancin' On A Saturday Night	CD5	U.K.	1989	$8.00

Blue Blood

Singles

Label	Catalog Number	Title	Type	Country	Year	Value
Sony	CSDS-8183	Say A Prayer	CD3	Japan	1991	$12.00/$3.00

Blue, Buddy

Singles

Label	Catalog Number	Title	Type	Country	Year	Value
RNA	PRO2 90066	Guttersnipes N Zealots	CDJ	U.S.	1991	$2.00

Blue Color

Singles

Label	Catalog Number	Title	Type	Country	Year	Value
Fieldworks	FWCR-52	Blue Color Rocker	CD5	Japan	1992	$10.00

Blue Magic

Full Length

Label	Catalog Number	Title	Type	Country	Year	Value
Columbia	CK-45092	From Out Of the Blue	LP/LB	U.S.		$14.00/$8.00

Singles

Label	Catalog Number	Title	Type	Country	Year	Value
Columbia	654769-2	Romeo & Juliet	CD5	U.K.	1989	$8.00
Def Jam	CSK 1439	Romeo & Juliet	CDJ	U.S.	1989	$2.00

Blue Max

Full Length

Label	Catalog Number	Title	Type	Country	Year	Value
		Strong Emotion	DJ/LP	U.S.		$7.00

Blue Mercedes

Singles

Label	Catalog Number	Title	Type	Country	Year	Value
Pioneer	10SW-30	I Want To Be Your Property	CD3	Japan	1988	$12.00/$3.00
MCA	DBONA 1	I Want To Be Your Property	CD5	U.K.	1988	$7.00
Pioneer	10SW-69	Love Is the Gun	CD3	Japan	1988	$12.00/$3.00
MCA	DBONA-3	Love Is the Gun	CD5	U.K.	1988	$7.00
Pioneer	10SW-55	See Want Must Have	CD3	Japan	1988	$12.00/$3.00
MCA	DBONA -2	See Want Must Have	CD5	U.K.	1988	$7.00
MCA		See Want Must Have	CD5	U.S.	1988	$2.00
MCA	DMCAT-1374	That Beauty Is You	CD5	U.K.	1989	$7.00
MCA	DBONA -4	Tree House	CD5	U.K.	1988	$7.00

Blue Mink

Singles

Label	Catalog Number	Title	Type	Country	Year	Value
Old Gold	DG-6125	Melting Pot	CD3	U.K.	1989	$7.00

Company	Disk Number	Title	Type	Country	Year	Longbox Value / Value

Blue Murder

Full Length

Company	Disk Number	Title	Type	Country	Year	Value
Geffen		Blue Murder	DJ/LP	U.S.	1989	$8.00

Singles

Company	Disk Number	Title	Type	Country	Year	Value
Geffen	PRO-CD-3603	Jellyroll	CDJ	U.S.	1989	$3.00
Geffen	PRO-CD-3407	Valley Of the Kings	CDJ	U.S.	1989	$7.00
Geffen	PRO-CD-4569	We All Fall Down	CDJ	U.S.	1994	$2.00

Blue Nile

Full Length

Company	Disk Number	Title	Type	Country	Year	Value
		Blue Nile, The	DJ/LP	U.S.	1989	$16.00
A&M	CD 5284	Hats	DJ/Smplr	U.S.	1989	$22.00
		Peace At Last	DJ/LP	Germany		$20.00
Virgin	610459	Walk Across the Rooftops	LP	Germany		$20.00

Singles

Company	Disk Number	Title	Type	Country	Year	Value
BMG	159257	Downtown Lights, The	CD5	Germany	1990	$8.00
Virgin	LKSCD-3	Downtown Lights, The	CD5	U.K.	1990	$8.00
A&M	CD 17982	Downtown Lights, The	CDJ	U.S.	1989	$3.00
A&M	2326-2	Downtown Lights, The	CD5	U.S.	1990	$3.00
A&M	CD 18025	Downtown Lights, The	CDJ	U.S.	1990	$3.00
A&M	CD 18032	Downtown Lights, The	CDJ	U.S.	1990	$3.00
Virgin	LKYCD-4	Headlights On the Parade	CD5	U.K.	1990	$8.00
Virgin	LKSCD-4	Headlights On the Parade	CD5	U.K.	1990	$8.00
A&M	CD 18027	Headlights On the Parade	CDJ	U.S.	1989	$3.00
A&M	75021 8079-2	Headlights On the Parade	CDJ	U.S.	1989	$3.00
Virgin	LKSCD-4	Saturday Night	CD5	U.K.	1990	$8.00
Virgin	LKSCX-4	Saturday Night	CD5	U.K.	1990	$8.00

Blue Oyster Cult

Full Length

Company	Disk Number	Title	Type	Country	Year	Value
Columbia	CK-39979	Club Ninja	LP/LB	U.S.		$14.00/$8.00
CBS	CK-37389	Fire Of Unknown Origin	LP/BP	U.S.†	1985	$15.00/$9.00
Columbia		On Flame With Rock And Roll	LP/LB	U.S.		$14.00/$8.00

Singles

Company	Disk Number	Title	Type	Country	Year	Value
CBS	652985-2	Astronomy	CD5	U.K.	1988	$10.00
Columbia	CSK 1218	Astronomy	CDJ	U.S.	1988	$3.00
		Don't Fear the Reaper '94	CD5	U.K.	1994	$10.00
		Don't Fear the Reaper '94	CDJ	U.K.	1994	$15.00
Columbia	CSK 1327	In the Presence of Another World	CDJ	U.S.	1988	$3.00

Blue Pearl

Singles

Company	Disk Number	Title	Type	Country	Year	Value
Big Life	867047-2	Alive	CD5	Germany	1991	$8.00
Big Life	BLRD-44	Alive	CD5	U.K.	1991	$8.00
Big Life	BLRD-67	Can You Feel the Passion	CD5	U.K.	1992	$8.00
Big Life	879145-2	Little Brother	CD5	Germany	1991	$8.00
Big Life	BLR-32CD	Little Brother	CD5	U.K.	1991	$8.00
Big Life	8677497-2	Naked In the Rain	CD5	Germany	1991	$8.00
Big Life	BLR-23CD	Naked In the Rain	CD5	U.K.	1991	$8.00

Blue Rodeo

Full Length

Company	Disk Number	Title	Type	Country	Year	Value
Atlantic	91601-2	Casino	LP/LB	U.S.		$14.00/$8.00
BAtlantic	PRCD 7450-2	Daze In America	DJ/Smplr	U.S.		$15.00
BAtlantic	81971-2	Diamond Mine	LP/LB	U.S.		$14.00/$8.00
BDIR		King Biscuit Flour Hour	RS	U.S.	1991	$30.00
		With Mike & the Mechanics, Airdate: 5/19/91.				
BAtlantic	82412-2	Lost Together	LP/LB	U.S.		$14.00/$8.00
BAtlantic	81832-2	Outskirts	LP/LB	U.S.		$14.00/$8.00

Singles

Company	Disk Number	Title	Type	Country	Year	Value
WEA	BLUE 091	After the Rain	CDJ	Canada	1991	$5.00
Atlantic	PR 2702-2	Diamond Mine	CDJ	U.S.	1989	$2.00
Discovery	77013	Five Days In May	CD5	Germany	1993	$8.00
Discovery	74515	Girl In Green	CDJ	U.S.	1995	$3.00
Atlantic	PRCD 4727-2	Lost Together	CDJ	U.S.	1992	$2.00
Atlantic	PRCD 4727-2	Lost Together	CDJ	U.S.	1992	$3.00
WEA	CD-73969	Til I Am Myself Again	CD5	Canada	1991	$8.00
WEA	BLUE 090	Til I Am Myself Again	CDJ	Canada	1991	$5.00
WEA	YZ-568CD	Til I Am Myself Again	CD5	U.K.	1991	$8.00

Blue Runners

Full Length

Company	Disk Number	Title	Type	Country	Year	Value
Island	848277	Blue Runners, The	LP/LB	U.S.		$12.00/$7.00

Singles

Company	Disk Number	Title	Type	Country	Year	Value
Island	PRCD 8691-2	I Sho Do	CDJ	U.S.	1991	$2.00
Island	PRCD 8691-2	I Sho Do	CDJ	U.S.	1991	$6.00

Blue Shadows

Full Length

Company	Disk Number	Title	Type	Country	Year	Value
		Rockin'	DJ/Smplr	Canada		$20.00

Singles

Company	Disk Number	Title	Type	Country	Year	Value
		If I Were You	CDJ	Canada		$7.00

Blue Sunbeam

Singles

Company	Disk Number	Title	Type	Country	Year	Value
Toshiba	TODP-2183	Dreaming	CD3	Japan	1990	$12.00/$3.00

Blue System

Singles

Company	Disk Number	Title	Type	Country	Year	Value
BMG	664722	Deja Vu	CD5	Germany	1991	$8.00
BMG	663185	Forty-Eight Hours	CD5	Germany	1991	$8.00
BMG	665304	I Will Survive	CD5	Germany	1992	$8.00
BMG	663543	Love Is Such A Lonely Word	CD5	Germany	1991	$8.00
BMG	662843	Love Me On the Rock	CD5	Germany	1991	$8.00
BMG	162138	Love Suite	CD3	Germany	1991	$8.00
BMG	6642138	Love Suite	CD5	Germany	1991	$8.00
BMG	664115	Lucifer	CD5	Germany	1991	$8.00
BMG	162664	Magic Symphony	CD3	Germany	1990	$8.00
BMG	663374	Magic Symphony	CD5	Germany	1990	$8.00
BMG	662664	Magic Symphony	CD5	Germany	1990	$8.00
BMG	PD-43734	Magic Symphony	CD5	U.K.	1990	$8.00
BMG	659918	My Bed Is Too Big	CD5	Germany	1988	$8.00
BMG	665116	Romeo And Juliet	CD5	Germany	1988	$8.00
BMG	661937	Silent Water	CD5	Germany	1988	$8.00
BMG	664450	Testament D'Amelia	CD5	Germany	1991	$8.00
BMG	661699	Under My Skin	CD5	Germany	1988	$8.00
BMG	663815	When Sarah Smiles	CD5	Germany	1990	$8.00

Blue Tattoo

Singles

Company	Disk Number	Title	Type	Country	Year	Value
Alfa	ALDB-52	Love Can Do	CD3	Japan	1990	$13.00/$4.00

Blue Tears

Full Length

Company	Disk Number	Title	Type	Country	Year	Value
MCA	MCAD-6413	Blue Tears	LP/LB	U.S.		$14.00/$8.00

Singles

Company	Disk Number	Title	Type	Country	Year	Value
MCA	CD45 1118	Crush	CDJ	U.S.	1990	$2.00

Label	Catalog Number	Title	Type	Country	Year	Longbox Value / Value
MCA	DMCAT-1458	Rockin' With the Radio	CD5	U.K.	1990	$8.00
MCA	CD45 1827	Rockin' With the Radio	CDJ	U.S.	1990	$2.00

Blue Train

Singles

Label	Catalog Number	Title	Type	Country	Year	Value
BMG	PD-49152	All I Need Is You	CD5	Germany	1991	$8.00
Zoo	ZP 17024	All I Need Is You	CDJ	U.S.	1991	$2.00
Zoo	ZP17034	All I Need Is You	CDJ	U.S.	1991	$3.00
Zoo	ZP 17057	Hardest Thing, The	CDJ	U.S.	1992	$2.00

Blue Up

Singles

Label	Catalog Number	Title	Type	Country	Year	Value
Columbia	CSK 6652	Breathe You Out	CDJ	U.S.	1995	$3.00

Blue Valentine

Full Length

Label	Catalog Number	Title	Type	Country	Year	Value
		House Of Blues	RS	U.S.	1996	$40.00
	2 CD set. Airdate: 2/11/96.					

Blue Vanity

Singles

Label	Catalog Number	Title	Type	Country	Year	Value
Bellaphon	130 07 584	Her Name Is Just Madonna	CD5	Germany	1991	$8.00

Blue Zone

Full Length

Label	Catalog Number	Title	Type	Country	Year	Longbox Value / Value
Arista	ARCD-8552	Big Thing	LP/LB	U.S.		$12.00/$7.00

Singles

Label	Catalog Number	Title	Type	Country	Year	Value
Arista	151548	Jackie	CD3	U.K.	1988	$8.00
Arista	661548	Jackie	CD5	U.K.	1988	$8.00
Arista	ASCD 9725	Jackie	CDJ	U.S.	1988	$2.00
Arista	RHCD-115	Thinking About His Baby	CD3	U.K.	1988	$8.00

Bluebells

Singles

Label	Catalog Number	Title	Type	Country	Year	Value
		Young At Heart	CD5	Germany		$8.00

Blues Brothers

Full Length

Label	Catalog Number	Title	Type	Country	Year	Value
WEA	CD-71613	Live! In Montreax	LP	Canada		$20.00
WEA	WMC5-104	Live! In Montreax	LP	Japan		$20.00

Singles

Label	Catalog Number	Title	Type	Country	Year	Value
Atlantic	A-7912CD	Everybody B	CD5	U.K.	1990	$10.00
Turnstyle	4630-2	Never Found A Girl	CDJ	U.S.	1992	$6.00
Atlantic	786170-2	Soul Man	CD5	Germany	1990	$10.00
Atlantic	A-7897CD	Soul Man	CD5	U.K.	1990	$10.00
Atlantic	7567-86213-2	Think	CD5	Germany	1990	$10.00
Atlantic	A-7951CD	Think	CD5	U.K.	1990	$10.00

Blues Explosion

Full Length

Label	Catalog Number	Title	Type	Country	Year	Value
WEA	780149-2	Blues Explosion	LP	Germany		$15.00

Blues Project

Full Length

Label	Catalog Number	Title	Type	Country	Year	Longbox Value / Value
Polygram	827918	Projections	LP/BP	U.S.		$14.00/$8.00
MCA	MCAD-25984	Reunion In Central Park	LP/LB	U.S.		$14.00/$8.00

Blues Traveler – 1,000,000 People Can't Be Wrong (A&M 31454 8064 2) U.S. 1995 promotional two CD sampler.

Blues Traveler

Full Length

Label	Catalog Number	Title	Type	Country	Year	Value
A&M	31454 8064-2	1,000,000 People Can't Be Wrong	DJ/Smplr	U.S.	1995	$30.00
	2 CD set.					
Westwood One		In Concert	RS	U.S.	1994	$75.00
	Airdate: 11/21/94.					
Westwood One		In Concert	RS	U.S.	1995	$75.00
	Airdate: 8/28/95.					
DIR		King Biscuit Flour Hour	RS	U.S.	1991	$30.00
	With The Band, Airdate: 4/7/91					
DIR		King Biscuit Flour Hour	RS	U.S.	1991	$35.00
	With George Thorogood, Airdate: 4/7/91.					
DIR		King Biscuit Flour Hour	RS	U.S.	1991	$70.00
	With Vaughan Brothers, Airdate: 4/28/91.					
A&M	AMCDP-00035	Live	DJ/Smplr	U.S.	1995	$10.00
Westwood One		Off the Record	RS	U.S.	1996	$30.00
	Interview with Kenny Wayne Sheppard. Airdate 4/22/96.					
A&M	75021 54002 2	On Tour Forever	DJ/Smplr	U.S.	1992	$11.00
Media America		Up Close	RS	U.S.	1995	$25.00

Singles

Label	Catalog Number	Title	Type	Country	Year	Value
A&M	75021 7282 2	All In the Groove	CDJ	U.S.	1991	$3.00
A&M	75021 7405 2	But Anyway	CDJ	U.S.	1990	$3.00
A&M	75021 7508 2	But Anyway	CDJ	U.S.	1991	$3.00
A&M	31458 8117	Conquer Me	CDJ	U.S.	1993	$3.00
A&M	31458 8167	Conquer Me	CDJ	U.S.	1993	$3.00
A&M	31458 8122	Defense & Desire	CDJ	U.S.	1993	$6.00
A&M	581179	Hook	CD5	U.S.	1995	$6.00
A&M	314540265	Hook	CDJ	U.S.	1995	$6.00
A&M	31458 8342	Hook	CDJ	U.S.	1995	$6.00
A&M	75021 7329 2	Mountain Cry	CDJ	U.S.	1991	$3.00
		Mountains Win Again	CDJ	U.S.		$3.00
A&M	31458 8341	Run Around	CDJ	U.S.	1993	$6.00
A & M Records	80983	Run Around	CD5	U.S.	1994	$5.00
A&M	00035	Run Around	CDJ	U.S.	1995	$8.00
A&M	75021 7314 2	Sweet Pain	CDJ	U.S.	1991	$3.00

Bluesbuster

Full Length

Label	Catalog Number	Title	Type	Country	Year	Longbox Value / Value
Landslide		Accept No Substitute	LP/LB	U.S.		$14.00/$8.00

Bluiett Hamiet

Full Length

Label	Catalog Number	Title	Type	Country	Year	Longbox Value / Value
Soul Note	1188	Nali Kola	LP/LB	U.S.		$14.00/$8.00

Blundell, James

Full Length

Label	Catalog Number	Title	Type	Country	Year	Longbox Value / Value
Capital	CDP 96247	Hand It Down	LP/LB	U.S.		$14.00/$8.00

Blur

Full Length

Label	Catalog Number	Title	Type	Country	Year	Value
		Bet Bet Bet: Mark Radcliffe Sessions	DJ/Smplr	France	1992	$25.00
SBK	05455	Blur-To-Go	DJ/Smplr	U.S.	1992	$8.00
SBK	DPRO-05424	Focusing In With Blur	DJ/Intvw	U.S.	1991	$8.00
EMI		Great Escape	LTD/LP	Australia	1995	$32.00
	CD + VHS video					
Westwood One		In Concert-Nu Rock	RS	U.S.	1994	$75.00
	Airdate: 9/12/94.					
EMI	PCD-0476	Parklife	DJ/Smplr	Japan	1994	$100.00
	Cover lights up and "barks" when opened.					
EMI		Parklife	DJ/LP	U.K.	1994	$20.00
EMI		Special Collector's Edition	LTD/LP	U.K.	1995	$45.00
EMI	SPCD-1519	Top Of the U.K.	DJ/Smplr	Japan		$50.00
EMI		Tracy Jack's Bank Holiday	DJ/Smplr	U.S.	1995	$20.00

Singles

Label	Catalog Number	Title	Type	Country	Year	Value
EMI	204412-2	Bang	CD5	Germany	1991	$10.00
EMI	CDFOOD-31	Bang	CD5	U.K.	1991	$10.00
Arista	79016	Big Poppa	CD5	U.S.	1994	$5.00
		Charmless Man	CDJ	France		$15.00
		Charmless Man	CD5	France	1996	$12.00
		Charmless Man	CDJ	U.S.		$6.00
EMI		Chemical World	CD5	U.K.	1993	$10.00
EMI		Chemical World	CD5	U.K.	1993	$10.00
	Second version.					
EMI		Chemical World	CDJ	U.K.	1993	$12.00
SBK	04593	Chemical World	CDJ	U.S.	1993	$2.00
EMI	CDF00D63	Country House	CD5	U.K.	1995	$11.00
EMI	CDF00DS63	Country House	CD5	U.K.	1995	$11.00
EMI		Country House	CDJ	U.K.	1995	$12.00
Virgin	DPRO-11023	Country House	CDJ	U.S.	1995	$12.00
EMI	81823	End Of A Centry	CD5	U.K.	1994	$11.00
EMI	CDFOOD-DJ-56	End Of the Century	CDJ	U.K.	1995	$15.00
EMI		For Tomorrow	CD5	U.K.	1994	$10.00
EMI		For Tomorrow	CD5	U.K.	1994	$10.00
	Second version.					
EMI	82177	Girls & Boys	CD5	U.K.	1994	$10.00
EMI		Girls & Boys	CD5	U.K.	1994	$10.00
	Second version.					
EMI		Girls & Boys	CDJ	U.K.	1994	$13.00
SBK	58155	Girls & Boys	CD5	U.S.	1994	$6.00
SBK	DPRO-19844	Girls & Boys	CDJ	U.S.	1994	$3.00
SBK		Greaty Escape	CDJ	U.S.	1995	$15.00
		It Could Be You	CD5	Australia	1996	$12.00
		Low	CDJ	U.S.		$3.00
EMI		Parklife	CD5	U.K.		$10.00
	Second version.					
EMI	81675	Parklife	CD5	U.K.	1994	$10.00
EMI	CDFOOD-DJ-53	Parklife	CDJ	U.K.	1995	$12.00
EMI	CDFOOD-37	Popscene	CD5	U.K.	1992	$10.00
EMI	204664-2	She's So High	CD5	Germany	1991	$10.00
EMI	CDFOOD-26	She's So High	CD5	U.K.	1991	$10.00
EMI		Sunday Sunday	CD5	U.K.	1994	$10.00
EMI		Sunday Sunday	CD5	U.K.	1994	$10.00
	Second version.					
EMI	204272-2	There's No Other Way	CD5	Germany	1991	$10.00
EMI	CDFOOD-29	There's No Other Way	CD5	U.K.	1991	$10.00
SBK		There's No Other Way	CDJ	U.S.	1991	$3.00
EMI		This Is A Low	CDJ	U.K.	1995	$12.00
EMI	82177	To the End	CD5	U.K.	1995	$10.00
EMI	CDFOOD-DJ-50	To the End	CDJ	U.K.	1995	$12.00
EMI		Universal	CD5	U.K.	1995	$10.00
EMI		Universal	CD5	U.K.	1995	$10.00
	Second version.					
EMI		Universal	CDJ	U.K.	1995	$12.00
EMI		Universal	CDJ	U.K.	1995	$12.00
	Second version.					
EMI	DPRO11516	Universal	CDJ	U.S.		$3.00

BLVD

Singles

Label	Catalog Number	Title	Type	Country	Year	Value
		Never Give Up	CDJ	Canada	1988	$3.00
MCA	CD45 880	Never Give Up	CDJ	U.S.	1988	$2.00

BMG

Singles

Label	Catalog Number	Title	Type	Country	Year	Value
SPV	0777-3	Brother In the Slide	CD5	Germany	1990	$8.00

BMO

Singles

Label	Catalog Number	Title	Type	Country	Year	Value
Hangman	50	Trash Dance	CD5	U.S.	1991	$5.00

BMU

Singles

Label	Catalog Number	Title	Type	Country	Year	Value
Polygram	856200	U Will Know	CD5	U.S.	1994	$5.00

BMX Bandits

Singles

Label	Catalog Number	Title	Type	Country	Year	Value
Creation	CRESCD-131	Serious Drugs	CD5	U.K.	1992	$8.00

Label	Catalog Number	Title	Type	Country	Year	Longbox Value/Value

BND

Singles

Label	Catalog Number	Title	Type	Country	Year	Longbox Value/Value
		Here I Go Again	CD5	U.K.		$10.00
		Here I Go Again	CD5	U.K.		$10.00
	Second version.					

Boa, Philip

Singles

Label	Catalog Number	Title	Type	Country	Year	Longbox Value/Value
Polygram	879503-2	And Then She Kissed Me	CD5	Germany	1991	$8.00
Polygram	887497-2	Annie And the Love Bomber	CD5	Germany	1988	$8.00
Polygram	871448-3	Container Love	CD3	Germany	1988	$8.00
Polygram	877091-2	Ernest Container	CD3	Germany	1988	$8.00
Polygram	873039-2	I Dedicate My Soul	CD5	Germany	1989	$8.00
Polygram	867147-2	Life Long Boardwalk	CD5	Germany	1991	$8.00
Polygram	877169-2	This Is Michael	CD5	Germany	1990	$8.00
Polygram	873559-2	This Is Michael	CD5	Germany	1990	$8.00

Bobby Z

Full Length

Label	Catalog Number	Title	Type	Country	Year	Longbox Value/Value
Atlantic	91288-2	Bobby Z	LP/LB	U.S.		$12.00/$7.00
		Grey Heart	CDJ	U.S.	1990	$2.00
Virgin	PRCD 3037-2	Lie By Lie	CDJ	U.S.	1990	$2.00
Virgin	PRCD 3273-2	You Are Everything	CDJ	U.S.	1990	$2.00

Bobs

Full Length

Label	Catalog Number	Title	Type	Country	Year	Longbox Value/Value
Kaleidisc	K-18	Bobs	LP/LB	U.S.		$14.00/$8.00

Bodeans

Full Length

Label	Catalog Number	Title	Type	Country	Year	Longbox Value/Value
Slash		AOR Sampler	DJ/Smplr	U.S.	1994	$5.00
Slash	9 26487-2-Dj	Black and White	DJ/LP	U.S.	1991	$15.00
Polygram	828161-2	Home	LP	Germany		$23.00
Polygram	P33L-20121	Home	LP	Japan		$25.00
Slash	PRO-CD-7672	Joe Dirt Car Sampler	DJ/Smplr	U.S.	1995	$15.00
Slash		Live At Tower	DJ/Smplr	U.S.	1994	$15.00
Polygram	828112-2	Love & Hope & Sex & Dreams	LP	Germany		$23.00
Polygram	828086-2	Outside Looking In	LP	Germany		$23.00
Polygram	P33L-20062	Outside Looking In	LP	Japan		$25.00
Polygram	833922-2	Players	LP	Germany		$15.00

Singles

Label	Catalog Number	Title	Type	Country	Year	Longbox Value/Value
Slash	PRO-CD-4709	Black, White And Blood Red	CDJ	U.S.	1991	$6.00
		Closer To Free	CD5	Australia	1995	$12.00
Slash	PRO-CD-6594	Closer To Free	CDJ	U.S.	1993	$6.00
Slash	PRO-CD-7979	Closer To Free	CDJ	U.S.	1995	$6.00
Slash		Dreams	CDJ	U.S.		$6.00
Slash	PRO-CD-6557	Feed the Fire	CDJ	U.S.	1993	$6.00
Slash	PRO-CD-6545	Feed the Fire	CDJ	U.S.	1993	$7.00
Slash	PRO-CD-6545	Go Slow Down	CDJ	U.S.	1994	$6.00
Slash	PRO-CD-5139	Good Things	CDJ	U.S.	1991	$6.00
Slash	PRO-CD-7723	Good Things	CDJ	U.S.	1995	$3.00
Slash	PRO-CD-7323	Good Things	CDJ	U.S.	1995	$6.00
Slash	PRO-CD-3757	Good Work	CDJ	U.S.	1989	$6.00
Slash	PRO-CD-6719	Idaho	CDJ	U.S.	1993	$6.00
Slash	PRO-CD-3863	Jing A Bell Rock	CDJ	U.S.	1989	$6.00
Slash	PRO-CD-2825	Only Love	CDJ	U.S.		$6.00
Slash	PRO-CD-4895	Paradise	CDJ	U.S.	1991	$6.00
Slash	PRO-CD-6563	Something's Telling Me	CDJ	U.S.	1993	$6.00
Slash	PRO-CD-3575	You Don't Get Much	CDJ	U.S.	1989	$6.00

Body

Full Length

Label	Catalog Number	Title	Type	Country	Year	Longbox Value/Value
MCA	MCAD-42058	Body	LP	Germany		$15.00

Body 2 Body

Singles

Label	Catalog Number	Title	Type	Country	Year	Longbox Value/Value
ID	658232-2	Let's Get Intimate	CD5	U.K.	1992	$8.00

Body Count

Full Length

Label	Catalog Number	Title	Type	Country	Year	Longbox Value/Value
WEA	CD-26878	Body Count	LP	Canada	1992	$25.00
	With deleted track "Cop Killer."					
WEA	7599-26878-2	Body Count	LP	Germany	1992	$25.00
	With deleted track "Cop Killer."					
WEA	7599-26878-2	Body Count	LP	U.K.	1992	$25.00
	With deleted track "Cop Killer."					
Sire/WB	9 26878-2	Body Count	DJ/LP	U.S.	1992	$25.00
	With deleted track "Cop Killer."					
Sire/Warner Bros.	9 26878-2	Body Count	LP/LB	U.S.	1992	$32.00/$25.00
	With deleted track "Cop Killer."					
		Born Dead	LTD/LP	Australia	1995	$35.00
	2 CD Set					
Foundations		FZ Interview	DJ/Intvw	U.S.	1994	$15.00
Sire	PRO-CD-5492	Radio EP, The	DJ/Smplr	U.S.	1992	$65.00
	With Recalled Body Bag					

Singles

Label	Catalog Number	Title	Type	Country	Year	Longbox Value/Value
		Born Dead	CDJ	U.K.	1994	$10.00
		Born Dead	CDJ	U.K.	1994	$10.00
	Second version.					
		Born Dead Medley	CDJ	U.S.	1994	$6.00
		Hey Joe	CD5	Australia		$10.00
		Necessary Evil	CDJ	U.S.	1994	$6.00
Sire	PRO-CD-5333	There Goes the Neighborhood	CDJ	U.S.	1992	$3.00
Sire	PRO-CD-5647	Winner Loses, The	CDJ	U.S.	1992	$3.00

Body Power

Singles

Label	Catalog Number	Title	Type	Country	Year	Longbox Value/Value
King	091X-18003	It's A Life	CD3	Japan	1989	$12.00/$3.00

Body Rhythm And Soul

Singles

Label	Catalog Number	Title	Type	Country	Year	Longbox Value/Value
Eastwesst	PRCD 5698-2	Bang the Body Goes Boom	CDJ	U.S.	1994	$3.00
Eastwesst	PRCD 5713-2	Bang the Body Goes Boom	CDJ	U.S.	1994	$3.00

Body & Soul

Singles

Label	Catalog Number	Title	Type	Country	Year	Longbox Value/Value
Delicious Vinyl	107	Dance to the Drummer's Beat	CDJ	U.S.	1989	$2.00

Bofill, Angela

Full Length

Label	Catalog Number	Title	Type	Country	Year	Longbox Value/Value
Aris	880736	Angel Of the Night	LP	Germany		$15.00
Aris	880161	Best Of	LP	Germany		$15.00
Capitol	CDP 48335	Intuition	LP/LB	U.S.		$12.00/$7.00
Aris	880058	Let Me Be the One	LP	Germany		$15.00
Aris	880063	Teaser	LP	Germany		$15.00

Singles

Label	Catalog Number	Title	Type	Country	Year	Longbox Value/Value
Jive	42132-2-RDJ	Heavenly Love	CDJ	U.S.	1993	$2.00

Company	Disk Number	Title	Type	Country	Year	Longbox Value/Value
Jive	42124-2-RDJ	I Wanna Love Somebody	CDJ	U.S.	1993	$2.00

Bogaert, Jane

Singles

Company	Disk Number	Title	Type	Country	Year	Longbox Value/Value
BMG	662919	Children Of Love	CD5	U.K.	1989	$8.00

Bogguss, Suzy

Full Length

Company	Disk Number	Title	Type	Country	Year	Longbox Value/Value
		Country Concert	RS	U.S.	1994	$60.00
	Airdate: 7/18/94.					
		Country Concert	RS	U.S.	1995	$60.00
	Airdate: 7/29/95.					
		Give Me Wheels	DJ/LP	U.S.	1996	$15.00

Singles

Company	Disk Number	Title	Type	Country	Year	Longbox Value/Value
Capitol	DPRO-79384	All Things Made New Again	CDJ	U.S.	1990	$2.00
Liberty	DPRO-79636	Heartache	CDJ	U.S.	1993	$3.00
Liberty	CDCL-680	Letting Go	CD5	U.K.	1993	$10.00
Capitol	DPRO-79902	Mr. Santa	CDJ	U.S.	1989	$2.00
Liberty	DPRO-79050	Souvenirs	CDJ	U.S.	1994	$3.00
Liberty	DPRO-79504	Two Step Round the Christmas Tree	CDJ	U.S.	1992	$6.00

Bogmen

Singles

Company	Disk Number	Title	Type	Country	Year	Longbox Value/Value
Arista	2872	Big Burn	CDJ	U.S.	1995	$2.00
		Suddenly	CDJ	U.S.		$3.00

Bogosian, Eric

Full Length

Company	Disk Number	Title	Type	Country	Year	Longbox Value/Value
SBK	53051	If They Ever Knew What I Was Thinking	DJ/Smplr	U.S.	1990	$15.00

Bolan, Marc

Full Length

Company	Disk Number	Title	Type	Country	Year	Longbox Value/Value
	BOLAN CD1	Acoustic Warriors	DJ/Smplr	U.K.	1996	$40.00
Demon		Alternative Bolan Zipgun	LTD/LP	U.K.	1996	$35.00
	Double digipak, limited to 2,000 copies.					
SMS	MP32-5127	Golden Greats	LP	Japan		$30.00

Singles

Company	Disk Number	Title	Type	Country	Year	Longbox Value/Value
Marc On Wax	CDMARC50	Metal Gurn	CD5	U.K.		$8.00
BCherry	CDCHERRY29	You Scare Me To Death	CD5	U.K.	1989	$8.00

Bolin, Tommy

Full Length

Company	Disk Number	Title	Type	Country	Year	Longbox Value/Value
		Fever	LTD/LP	Japan	1996	
	15 CD set.					
		Fever	LTD/LP	Japan	1996	$750.00
	15 CD set. Limited to 500 copies.					
Geffen	PRO-CD-3657	Selections From the Ultimate	DJ/Smplr	U.S.	1989	$8.00
CBS	CD-85274	Teaser	LP	Germany		$20.00
Nemperor	ZK-37534	Teaser	LP/LB	U.S.		$15.00/$9.00

Bolivar, Michael

Full Length

Company	Disk Number	Title	Type	Country	Year	Longbox Value/Value
		Hangin' Out	DJ/LP	U.S.		$20.00
Clarity	CCD-1009	Hangin' Out	LTD/LP	U.S.	1994	$18.00
	Gold disc with multi-image cover.					

Bolland & Bolland

Singles

Company	Disk Number	Title	Type	Country	Year	Longbox Value/Value
Eastwest	9031-75742-2	Lost Boys	CD5	Germany	1991	$8.00
Eastwest	170917-2	Wall Came Tumbling Down	CD5	Germany	1991	$8.00

Bolling, Claude

Full Length

Company	Disk Number	Title	Type	Country	Year	Longbox Value/Value
Columbia	CK-42476	Bolling Plays Ellington, Vol. 2	LP/LB	U.S.		$14.00/$8.00
Columbia	MK-39244	Jazz A La Francaise	LP/LB	U.S.		$14.00/$8.00
Philips	822506-2	Ragtime Boogie Woogie/Jazz Piano	LP/LB	U.S.		$14.00/$8.00
Columbia	CK-33233	Suite For Cello & Jazz Piano	LP/LB	U.S.		$14.00/$8.00
Columbia	CK-39059	Suite For Cello & Jazz Trio	LP/LB	U.S.		$14.00/$8.00
Columbia	CK-35128	Suite For Violin & Jazz Piano	LP/LB	U.S.		$14.00/$8.00
Milan	002	Three Decades Of	DJ/Smplr	U.S.	1993	$8.00

Bollock Brothers

Full Length

Company	Disk Number	Title	Type	Country	Year	Longbox Value/Value
Charly	CD-72	Four Horsemen Of the Apocalypse	LP	U.S.		$8.00

Singles

Company	Disk Number	Title	Type	Country	Year	Longbox Value/Value
JDC		Apocalypse	CD5	U.S.		$5.00
SPV	055-88783	Don't Call Us, We Call You	CD5	Germany	1992	$8.00
JDC	3451	Harley Davidson Of A Bitch	CD5	U.S.		$5.00

Bolshoi

Full Length

Company	Disk Number	Title	Type	Country	Year	Longbox Value/Value
Beggars Banquet	6600	Lindy's Party	LP/LB	U.S.		$14.00/$8.00

Bolt Thrower

Singles

Company	Disk Number	Title	Type	Country	Year	Longbox Value/Value
Earache	MOSH-33CD	Cenotaph	CD5	U.K.	1990	$8.00
Earache	MOSH-73CD	Spearhead	CD5	U.K.	1992	$8.00

Bolton, Michael

Full Length

Company	Disk Number	Title	Type	Country	Year	Longbox Value/Value
Sony	XDDP-93060	Ballad Selection	DJ/Smplr	Japan		$40.00
CBS		Greatest Hits Sampler	DJ/Smplr	U.K.		$30.00
Columbia	CDNK 621	In the Foreground	DJ/Intvw	Canada	1991	$35.00
Columbia		Quiet Storm Sampler	DJ/Smplr	U.S.		$8.00
		Reaching Out	RS	U.S.	1993	$50.00
	2 CD set. Airdate: 8/30/93					
Image	ID7621CB	Soul Provider: The Videos	LD	U.S.		$18.00
Sony	XCDS93136	Sound of Love	DJ/Smplr	Japan	1994	$125.00
Sony		Timeless: The Classics Special Sampler	DJ/Smplr	Japan		$40.00
Unistar		Weekly Specials, The	RS	U.S.	1992	$15.00
	Airdate: 6/12/92					

Singles

Company	Disk Number	Title	Type	Country	Year	Longbox Value/Value
Columbia	CSK 6135	Ain't Got Nothing If You Ain't Got Love	CDJ	U.S.	1994	$2.00
Columbia	CSK 6277	Ain't Got Nothing If You Ain't Got Love	CDJ	U.S.	1994	$3.00
CBS		Can I Touch You There	CDJ	Germany	1995	$12.00
Columbia	CSK 7236	Can I Touch You There	CDJ	U.S.	1995	$3.00
Columbia	CSK 7359	Can I Touch You There	CDJ	U.S.	1995	$3.00
CBS	77376	Completely	CD5	U.S.	1994	$5.00
Columbia	CSK 77376	Completely	CDJ	U.S.	1994	$3.00
CBS	651387-2	Dock Of the Bay	CD5	U.K.	1988	$8.00
Columbia		Dock Of the Bay	CDJ	U.S.	1988	$3.00
CBS		Drift Away	CD5	Germany		$8.00
CBS	656196-3	Georgia On My Mind	CD3	Germany	1990	$8.00
CBS	656196-2	Georgia On My Mind	CD5	Germany	1990	$8.00
CBS	CSDS-8121	Georgia On My Mind	CD3	Japan	1990	$13.00/$4.00
		Georgia On My Mind	CDJ	U.S.	1990	$6.00
	Second version.					

Label	Catalog Number	Title	Type	Country	Year	Longbox Value / Value
Columbia	CSK 73490	Georgia On My Mind	CDJ	U.S.	1990	$7.00
Columbia	6553973-3	How Am I Supposed To Live Without You	CD3	Germany	1989	$8.00
Columbia	655397-5	How Am I Supposed To Live Without You	CD5	U.K.	1989	$8.00
Columbia	CSK 73017	How Am I Supposed To Live Without You	CDJ	U.S.	1989	$3.00
CBS	655836-3	How Can We Be Lovers	CD3	Germany	1989	$8.00
CBS	CSDS-8129	How Can We Be Lovers	CD3	Japan	1989	$13.00/$4.00
CBS	CSDS-8129	How Can We Be Lovers	CD3	Japan	1989	$12.00/$5.00
CBS	655918-2	How Can We Be Lovers	CD5	U.K.	1989	$8.00
CBS	655918-5	How Can We Be Lovers	CD5	U.K.	1989	$8.00
Columbia	CSK 73257	How Can We Be Lovers	CDJ	U.S.	1989	$3.00
CBS	XPCD 423	Lean On Me	CDJ	France	1994	$15.00
CBS		Lean On Me	CD5	U.K.	1994	$10.00
CBS		Lean On Me	CD5	U.K.	1994	$10.00
	Second version.					
CBS	CSDS-8181	Love Is A Wonderful Thing	CD3	Japan	1991	$13.00/$4.00
CBS	656771-2	Love Is A Wonderful Thing	CD5	U.K.	1991	$8.00
Columbia	CSK 4015	Love Is A Wonderful Thing	CDJ	U.S.	1991	$3.00
Columbia	CSK 73719	Love Is A Wonderful Thing	CDJ	U.S.	1991	$3.00
CBS		Love Is So Beautiful	CD5	U.K.	1995	$10.00
CBS		Love Is So Beautiful	CD5	U.K.	1995	$10.00
	Second version.					
Columbia	CSK 7520	Love Is So Beautiful	CDJ	U.S.	1995	$3.00
CBS	SRDS-8223	Missing You Now	CD3	Japan	1992	$13.00/$4.00
CBS		Missing You Now	DJ/CD3	Japan	1992	$20.00
CBS	657991-2	Missing You Now	CD5	U.K.	1992	$8.00
Columbia	CSK 74184	Missing You Now	CDJ	U.S.	1992	$3.00
Columbia	CSK 6497	Once In A Lifetime	CDJ	U.S.	1994	$3.00
Columbia	658897	Reach Out I'll Be There	CD5	Germany	1992	$8.00
CBS	SRDS-8246	Reach Out, I'll Be There	CD3	Japan		$12.00/$4.00
Columbia	CSK 4909	Reach Out I'll Be There	CDJ	U.S.	1992	$3.00
CBS		Said I Loved You But I Lied	CD5	U.K.	1993	$8.00
Columbia	CSK 5508	Said I Loved You But I Lied	CDJ	U.S.	1993	$2.00
CBS	77260	Said I Loved You But I Lied	CD5	U.S.	1994	$5.00
CBS		Soul Of Soul	CD5	U.K.	1993	$8.00
CBS		Soul Of Soul	CD5	U.K.	1993	$8.00
	Second version.					
CBS	654946-3	Soul Provider	CD3	Germany	1989	$8.00
CBS	10EP-3095	Soul Provider	CD3	Japan	1989	$13.00/$4.00
CBS	654946-2	Soul Provider	CD5	U.K.	1989	$8.00
CBS	655877-2	Soul Provider	CD5	U.K.	1990	$8.00
CBS	655877-5	Soul Provider	CD5	U.K.	1990	$8.00
CBS	657725-2	Steel Bars	CD5	Germany	1992	$8.00
CBS	SRDS-8228	Steel Bars	CD3	Japan	1992	$13.00/$4.00
Columbia	CSK 74294	Steel Bars	CDJ	U.S.	1992	$7.00
CBS	651059-2	That's What Love Is All About	CD5	U.K.		$6.00
Columbia		That's What Love Is All About	CDJ	U.S.		$3.00
Columbia	656989-2	Time, Love And Tenderness	CD5	Germany	1991	$8.00
CBS	SRDS-8195	Time, Love And Tenderness	CD3	Japan	1991	$13.00/$4.00
Columbia	656989-2	Time, Love And Tenderness	CD5	U.K.	1991	$8.00
Columbia	CSK 73889	Time, Love And Tenderness	CDJ	U.S.	1991	$3.00
CBS	SRDS-8241	To Love Somebody	CD3	Japan	1992	$13.00/$4.00
CBS		To Love Somebody	CD5	U.K.	1992	$8.00
CBS		To Love Somebody	CD5	U.K.	1992	$8.00
	Second version.					
Columbia	74733	To Love Somebody	CD5	U.S.	1992	$4.00
Columbia	CSK 4806	To Love Somebody	CDJ	U.S.	1992	$3.00
Columbia	38K-7794	Wait On Love	CD3	U.S.	1988	$5.00/$3.00
Columbia	CSK 1072	Wait On Love	CDJ	U.S.	1988	$3.00
Columbia		Walk Away	CDJ	U.S.		$3.00
		When A Man Loves A Woman	CD5	Australia	1996	$12.00
CBS	657488-5	When A Man Loves A Woman	CD5	Germany	1991	$8.00
CBS	SRDS-8211	When A Man Loves A Woman	CD3	Japan	1991	$12.00/$3.00
CBS	657488-2	When A Man Loves A Woman	CD5	U.K.	1991	$8.00
CBS	657488-5	When A Man Loves A Woman	CD5	U.K.	1991	$8.00
Columbia	CSK 74020	When A Man Loves A Woman	CDJ	U.S.	1991	$3.00
CBS	656077-3	When I'm Back on My Feet	CD3	Germany	1990	$8.00
CBS	656077-2	When I'm Back on My Feet	CD5	U.K.	1990	$8.00
CBS	656077-5	When I'm Back on My Feet	CD5	U.K.	1990	$8.00
Columbia	CSK 73342	When I'm Back on My Feet	CDJ	U.S.	1990	$3.00
CBS	SRDS-8253	Yesterday	CD3	Japan	1993	$13.00/$4.00
CBS		Yesterday	DJ/CD3	Japan	1993	$20.00

Bomb, Adam

Singles

Label	Catalog Number	Title	Type	Country	Year	Value
Rock World	5158	Johnny In the Sky	CDJ	U.S.	1993	$2.00

Bomb Party

Singles

Label	Catalog Number	Title	Type	Country	Year	Value
Normal	NORMAL-093CD	Sugar Sugar	CD5	Germany	1989	$8.00

Bomb The Bass

Singles

Label	Catalog Number	Title	Type	Country	Year	Value
Epic	657538-2	Air You Breathe	CD5	Germany	1992	$8.00
Epic	ESCA-5585	Air You Breathe	CD3	Japan	1992	$12.00/$4.00
BCM	20082	Beat Dis	CD5	Germany	1988	$8.00
BCM	BC50-2093-44	Beat Dis	CD5	U.K.	1988	$8.00
4th & B'way	462	Beat Dis	CDJ	U.S.	1988	$2.00
4th & B'way	BRCD 300	Bug Powder Dust	CD5	U.K.	1994	$8.00
		Darkheart	CD5	U.K.		$10.00
		Darkheart	CD5	U.K.		$10.00
	Second version.					
Rough Trade	CD1-84	Don't Make Me Wait	CD5	Germany	1988	$8.00
Pinnacle	DOODCD-124	I Can't Stop	CD5	U.K.	1989	$8.00
Rhythm King 40042		Love So True	CD5	U.S.	1991	$4.00
Pinnacle	DOOD-2CD	Megablast	CD5	U.K.	1988	$8.00
Rough Trade	CD1-235	Say A Little Prayer	CD5	Germany	1988	$8.00
Pinnacle	DOOD-3CD	Say A Little Prayer	CD5	U.K.	1988	$8.00
Epic	657275-2	Winter In July	CD5	Germany	1991	$8.00

Bomb The Bass/Warfield Justin

Singles

Label	Catalog Number	Title	Type	Country	Year	Value
		Bug Powder Dust	CD5	U.K.		$10.00
		Bug Powder Dust	CD5	U.K.		$10.00
	Second version.					

Bomb The Beach

Singles

Label	Catalog Number	Title	Type	Country	Year	Value
Intercord	828 031	Bomb the Beach	CD5	Germany	1988	$8.00

Bombast Broz

Singles

Label	Catalog Number	Title	Type	Country	Year	Value
Polygram	867133-2	Comin' From the	CD5	Germany	1991	$8.00

Bon Jovi

Full Length

Label	Catalog Number	Title	Type	Country	Year	Value
Vertigo		40 Principales	DJ/Smplr	Spain	1995	$35.00

Bon Jovi – Bed Of Roses (Polygram 2801 664) Brazilian 1993 promotional CD-single.

Bon Jovi – Most Requested (Mercury SACD 548) U.S. 1992 promotional CD sampler.

Label	Catalog Number	Title	Type	Country	Year	Value
Vertigo		7800 Fahrenheit	LTD/LP	Australia	1993	$35.00
	Gold disc.					
Mercury	32PD-1003	7800 Fahrenheit	LTD/LP	Japan	1988	$50.00
	Picture disc CD.					
Mercury	PPD-2003	7800 Fahrenheit	LTD/LP	Japan	1990	$35.00
	Special Digipak.					
Mercury	824509-2	7800 Fahrenheit	LP/BP	U.S.†	1985	$15.00/$9.00
Vertigo		Bon Jovi	LTD/LP	Australia	1993	$35.00
	Gold disc					
Mercury	32PD-1002	Bon Jovi	LTD/LP	Japan	1988	$50.00
	Picture disc CD.					
Mercury	PPD-2004	Bon Jovi	LTD/LP	Japan	1990	$35.00
	Special Digipak.					
Mercury	814982-2	Bon Jovi	LP/BP	U.S.†	1984	$15.00/$9.00
Pioneer	PA86-MO35	Breakout!	8"LD	U.S.	1985	$8.00
Pioneer	PA86-MO35	Breakout!	8"LD	U.S.	1989	$12.00
	Digital audio					
Polygram	838605-2	Complete Collection	LP	U.K.	1989	$65.00
	4 CD set.					
Vertigo		Concierto 40	DJ/Smplr	Spain	1995	$85.00
Mercury		Cross Road	DJ/Smplr	U.S.	1994	$20.00
Vertigo		Crossroads	LTD/LP	Australia	1994	$45.00
	Virgin Megastore edition with T-shirt.					
Vertigo	JOVI 1989	Essential	DJ/Smplr	Germany	1989	$50.00
Vertigo	JOVI 1989	Essential	DJ/Smplr	U.K.	1989	$40.00
Vertigo		Good Guys Don't Always Wear White	DJ/Smplr	Austria	1995	$30.00
Vertigo	PCHR-3007	Great Box	LTD/LP	Japan	1991	$100.00
	4 CD boxed set.					
Album Network		In the Studio (Slippery When Wet)	RS	U.S.	1996	$30.00
		Jon Bon Jovi Talks About These Days	DJ/Intvw	Hong Kong	1995	$60.00
Jambco	PHCR-16003/4	Keep the Faith	LTD/LP	Japan	1993	$40.00
	2CD "Mega-Edition" with CD of album and a disc of live material.					
Jambco		Live And Unreleased	DJ/Smplr	U.S.	1993	$40.00
		Live From Pit	RS	U.S.	1996	$75.00
	2 CD set. Airdate 9/1/96.					
Mercury	SACD 548	Most Requested	DJ/Smplr	U.S.	1992	$20.00
Vertigo		New Jersey	LTD/LP	Australia	1993	$35.00
	Gold disc with long box.					
Vertigo	PPD-2001	New Jersey	LTD/LP	Japan	1988	$35.00
	Special Digipak.					
Vertigo	28PD-563	New Jersey	LTD/LP	Japan	1988	$50.00
	Picture disc CD.					
Westwood One		Off the Record	RS	U.S.	1992	$30.00
	Airdate: 12/21/92					
Vertigo		Slippery When Wet	LTD/LP	Australia	1993	$35.00
	Gold disc with long box.					
Mercury	28PD-520	Slippery When Wet	LTD/LP	Japan	1988	$50.00
	Picture disc CD.					
Mercury	PPD-2002	Slippery When Wet	LTD/LP	Japan	1990	$35.00
	Special Digipak.					
Polygram	080-297-1	Slippery When Wet	LD	U.S.	1988	$30.00
Mercury		These Days	LTD/LP	Australia	1995	$40.00
	2 CD set.					
Mercury		These Days	LTD/LP	Canada	1995	$30.00
	CD with two bonus tracks.					
Mercury	4396	These Days	DJ/Smplr	France	1995	$40.00
Mercury	PHCR-1370	These Days	LTD/LP	Japan	1995	$40.00
	CD in hardbound book.					
Mercury	PHCB-1	These Days	LTD/LP	Japan	1996	$70.00
	2 CD set in large book.					
Phonogram		These Days	LTD/LP	U.K.	1996	$35.00
	2 CD set.					

Label	Catalog Number	Title	Type	Country	Year	Longbox Value / Value
Mercury	314 528 181-2	These Days	DJ/LP	U.S.	1995	$65.00
CD and book in box.						
Media America		Up Close	RS	U.S.	1989	$50.00
2 CD set.						
Media America		Up Close	RS	U.S.	1990	$50.00
2 CD set.						
Media America		Up Close	RS	U.S.	1993	$50.00
2 CD set.						
Volkswagon	JOV VW1	Volkswagen Presents Bon Jovi	DJ/Smplr	Germany	1996	$100.00
		Singles				
Vertigo		Always	CD5	Australia	1993	$10.00
Vertigo		Always	CD5	Canada	1993	$10.00
Vertigo		Always	CD5	U.K.		$10.00
Vertigo		Always	CD5	U.K.		$10.00
Second version.						
Polygram	856227	Always	CD5	U.S.	1994	$5.00
Mercury	CDP 1329	Always	CDJ	U.S.	1994	$6.00
Vertigo	872185-2	Bad Medicine	CD5	Germany	1988	$8.00
Mercury	10PD-1	Bad Medicine	CD3	Japan	1988	$13.00/$4.00
Mercury	13PD-1	Bad Medicine	CD3	Japan	1988	$13.00/$4.00
Mercury	PHCR-8029	Bad Medicine	CD5	Japan	1993	$16.00
Vertigo	JOVCD-3	Bad Medicine	CD5	U.K.	1988	$8.00
Mercury	870 657	Bad Medicine	CD3	U.S.	1988	$6.00/$4.00
Mercury	CDP 27	Bad Medicine	CDJ	U.S.	1988	$6.00
Polygram	2801 664	Bed Of Roses	CDJ	Brazil	1993	$100.00
Mercury	PHDR-123	Bed Of Roses	CD3	Japan	1993	$13.00/$4.00
Mercury	PHCR-8023	Bed Of Roses	CD5	Japan	1993	$16.00
Mercury	JOVCD-9	Bed Of Roses	CD5	U.K.	1992	$8.00
Mercury		Bed Of Roses	CD5	U.K.	1992	$8.00
Second version.						
Mercury	CDP 838	Bed Of Roses	CDJ	U.S.	1992	$3.00
Jambco	2801 664	Bed Of Roses (Live)	CDJ	Brazil	1993	$25.00
Mercury	PPDM-1002	Borderline	CD5	Japan	1993	$16.00
Vertigo	872357-2	Born To Be My Baby	CD5	Germany	1988	$9.00
Mercury	13PD-2	Born To Be My Baby	CD3	Japan	1988	$13.00/$4.00
Vertigo	JOVCD-4	Born To Be My Baby	CD5	U.K.	1988	$9.00
Mercury	PHCR-8026	Burning For Love	CD3	Japan	1993	$13.00/$4.00
Mercury	PPDM-1001	Burning For Love	CD5	Japan	1993	$16.00
Mercury		Como Yo Nadie Te Ha Amado	CDJ	U.S.	1995	$10.00
		Dry Country	CDJ	France	1994	$20.00
Mercury	PHCR-3033	Dry Country	CD5	Japan	1994	$30.00
Mercury	PHCR-3033	Dry Country	CD5	Japan	1995	$20.00
Mercury		Dry Country	CD5	U.K.	1994	$10.00
Second version.						
Mercury		Dry Country	CD5	U.K.	1994	$11.00
Gold disc.						
Mercury		Dyin' Ain't Much Of A Livin'	CDJ	France	1995	$45.00
Mercury		Good Guys Always Wear White	CDJ	U.S.	1994	$3.00
Mercury		Hey God	CD5	Germany	1996	$12.00
Mercury		Hey God	CD5	U.K.	1996	$10.00
Mercury		Hey God	CD5	U.K.	1996	$10.00
Second version.						
Mercury		Hey God	CDJ	U.S.	1995	$7.00
Mercury		I Believe	CD5	Japan	1994	$25.00
Mercury		I Believe	CD5	U.K.	1994	$10.00
Mercury		I Believe	CD5	U.K.	1994	$10.00
Second version.						
Mercury	872564-3	I'll Be There For You	CD3	Germnay	1989	$8.00
Mercury	872565-2	I'll Be There For You	CD5	Germnay	1989	$8.00
Mercury	PPDS-1	I'll Be There For You	CD3	Japan	1989	$13.00/$4.00
Mercury	JOVCD-5	I'll Be There For You	CD5	U.K.	1989	$8.00
Mercury	8625502	I'll Sleep When I'm Dead	CD5	Australia	1993	$13.00
Mercury	1690	I'll Sleep When I'm Dead	CDJ	France	1993	$25.00
Jambco	CDP 939	I'll Sleep When I'm Dead	CDJ	U.S.	1993	$3.00
Jamco	PHDR-127	In These Arms	CD3	Japan	1993	$13.00/$4.00
Mercury	CDP 837	In These Arms	CDJ	U.S.	1993	$3.00
Mercury		Keep the Faith	CD5	Germany	1992	$10.00
Mercury	PHDR-115	Keep the Faith	CD3	Japan	1992	$13.00/$4.00
Mercury		Keep the Faith	CD5	U.K.	1992	$10.00
Mercury		Keep the Faith	CD5	U.K.	1992	$10.00
Second version.						
Mercury	864433	Keep the Faith	CD5	U.S.	1992	$5.00
Mercury	CDP 772	Keep the Faith	CDJ	U.S.	1992	$7.00
Mercury	874687-2	Lay Your Hands On Me	CD5	Germany	1989	$9.00
Mercury	JOVCD-6	Lay Your Hands On Me	CD5	U.K.	1989	$9.00
Mercury	CDP 87	Lay Your Hands On Me	CDJ	U.S.	1989	$7.00
Vertigo		Lie To Me	CD5	Canada	1995	$10.00
Mercury	PHCR-8345	Lie To Me	CD5	Japan	1995	$25.00
Mercury		Lie To Me	CD5	U.K.	1995	$10.00
Mercury		Lie To Me	CD5	U.K.	1995	$10.00
Second version.						
Mercury	CDP1510	Lie To Me	CDJ	U.S.	1995	$3.00
Mercury		Lie To Me	CDJ	U.S.	1995	$3.00
Second version.						
Mercury	10PD-2	Livin' On A Prayer	CD3	Japan	1988	$13.00/$4.00
Mercury		Livin' On A Prayer	CDV/BP	Japan	1988	$40.00
Mercury	870 701-2	Livin' On A Prayer	CDV/BP	U.S.	1988	$35.00/$35.00
Mercury	876283-2	Living In Sin	CD5	Canada	1990	$6.00
Mercury	876553-2	Living In Sin	CD5	Germany	1990	$9.00
Mercury	PHCR-8031	Living In Sin	CD3	Japan	1990	$13.00/$4.00
Mercury	876 071-2	Living In Sin	CD5	U.K.	1989	$9.00
Mercury	JOVCD-7	Living In Sin	CD5	U.K.	1990	$9.00
Mercury	CDP 131	Living In Sin	CDJ	U.S.	1989	$7.00
Mercury	876071	Living In Sin	CD5	U.S.	1990	$5.00
Mercury	870 721-2	Never Say Goodbye	CDV/BP	U.S.	1988	$35.00/$35.00
Polygram	PHCR-8343	Please Come Home For Christmas	CD5	Japan	1995	$25.00
CD5 in Christmas card.						
Polygram		Someday I'll Be Saturday Night	CD5	Australia	1995	$11.00
Vertigo		Someday I'll Be Saturday Night	CD5	Canada	1995	$11.00
Mercury	PHCR-8317	Someday I'll Be Saturday Night	CD5	Japan	1995	$25.00
Polygram		Something For the Pain	CD5	Australia	1995	$11.00
Polygram		Something For the Pain	CD5	Australia	1995	$11.00
Second version.						
Vertigo		Something For the Pain	CD5	Canada	1995	$10.00
Mercury	PHDR-920	Something For the Pain	CD5	Japan	1995	$25.00
Mercury		Something For the Pain	CD5	U.K.	1995	$10.00
Mercury		Something For the Pain	CD5	U.K.	1995	$10.00
Second version.						
Mercury		Something For the Pain	CDJ	U.K.	1995	$18.00
Mercury	852296	Something For the Pain	CD5	U.S.	1995	$5.00
Mercury	52387	Something For the Pain	CD5	U.S.	1995	$5.00
Mercury		Something For the Pain	CDJ	U.S.	1995	$6.00
Vertigo		This Ain't A Love Song	CD5	Australia	1995	$11.00
Vertigo		This Ain't A Love Song	CD5	Canada	1995	$11.00
Mercury		This Ain't A Love Song	CDJ	France	1995	$30.00
Mercury		This Ain't A Love Song	CD5	U.K.	1995	$11.00

Company	Disk Number	Title	Type	Country	Year	Longbox Value / Value
Mercury		This Ain't A Love Song	CD5	U.K.	1995	$11.00
Second version.						
Mercury	852059	This Ain't A Love Song	CD5	U.S.	1995	$6.00
Mercury		This Ain't A Love Song	CDJ	U.S.	1995	$7.00
Mercury	PHCR-8330	This Ain't A Love Story	CD5	Japan	1995	$25.00
		Time Of Your Life	CD5	U.K.	1995	$10.00
Mercury	PPDM-1003	Wanted Dead Or Alive	CD5	Japan	1988	$18.00
Vertigo	JOVCD 1	Wanted Dead Or Alive	CDJ	U.K.	1988	$20.00
Mercury	CD7P 01	Wanted Dead Or Alive	CDJ	U.S.	1987	$75.00
Mercury	870 721-2	Wanted Dead Or Alive	CDV	U.S.	1988	$25.00
Mercury	870 721-2	Wanted Dead Or Alive	CDV/BP	U.S.	1988	$35.00/$35.00
Mercury	870 737-2	You Give Love A Bad Name	CDV	U.S.	1988	$25.00
Mercury	870 737-2	You Give Love A Bad Name	CDV/BP	U.S.	1988	$35.00/$35.00

Bon Jovi, Jon

Company	Disk Number	Title	Type	Country	Year	Longbox Value / Value
		Full Length				
Phonogram	PHCR-901	Blaze Of Glory	LTD/LP	Japan	1990	$25.00
Phonogram		Blaze Of Glory	DJ/LP	U.S.	1990	$65.00
CD sountrack plus VHS video of "Young Guns " in box.						
		Singles				
Mercury		Blaze Of Glory	CD3	Japan	1990	$15.00/$4.00
Vertigo		Blaze Of Glory	CD3	U.K.	1990	$8.00
Mercury	875 896-2	Blaze Of Glory	CD5	U.S.	1990	$5.00
Mercury	CDP 279	Blaze Of Glory	CDJ	U.S.	1990	$6.00
Vertigo	878523-2	Miracle	CD5	Germany	1990	$8.00
Murcury	PHCR-8006	Miracle	CD5	Japan	1991	$15.00
Vertigo	JB JCD-2	Miracle	CD5	U.K.	1990	$8.00
Mercury	CDP 331	Miracle	CDJ	U.S.	1990	$7.00
Mercury	868113-2	Never Say Die	CD5	Germany	1991	$9.00

Bond

Company	Disk Number	Title	Type	Country	Year	Longbox Value / Value
		Full Length				
Ariola	258195	Use Me	LP	Germany		$15.00
		Singles				
Polygram	875163-2	Candy-O	CD5	Germany	1990	$8.00

Bond, Graham

Company	Disk Number	Title	Type	Country	Year	Longbox Value / Value
		Full Length				
Repetoire		Holly Magic	LP	Germany		$25.00
Decal		Live With Baker And Bruce	LP	U.K.		$25.00

Bond, Johnny

Company	Disk Number	Title	Type	Country	Year	Longbox Value / Value
		Full Length				
Starday	147	That Wild, Wicked, But Wonderful West	LP	U.S.		$8.00

Bone Club

Company	Disk Number	Title	Type	Country	Year	Longbox Value / Value
		Singles				
Imago	28050	Arrive	CDJ	U.S.	1993	$2.00
Imago	72787 21013	Beautiful	CD5	U.S.	1995	$5.00
Imago	72787 21013	Everything's On Fire	CD5	U.S.	1992	$4.00

Bone Poney

Company	Disk Number	Title	Type	Country	Year	Longbox Value / Value
		Full Length				
Capitol	DPRO-79547	Live From the Southern Belt	DJ/Smplr	U.S.	1995	$10.00
		Singles				
Capitol	DPRO-79581	Where the Water's Deep	CDJ	U.S.	1995	$3.00

Bonedaddys

Company	Disk Number	Title	Type	Country	Year	Longbox Value / Value
		Full Length				
Chameleon	74821	Worldbeatniks	LP/LB	U.S.		$14.00/$8.00
		Singles				
		Hippie Children	CDJ	U.S.	1990	$2.00
Chameleon	CDP 86	Shoorah Shoorah	CDJ	U.S.	1990	$2.00

Bones, Barbie

Company	Disk Number	Title	Type	Country	Year	Longbox Value / Value
		Full Length				
Restless	72535	Brake For Nobody	LP	U.S.		$8.00

Bones Thugs-N-Harmony

Company	Disk Number	Title	Type	Country	Year	Longbox Value / Value
		Singles				
		Crossroads, The	CDJ	U.S.		$3.00
	5540	Foe Tha Love Of	CD5	U.S.	1994	$5.00

Boney James

Company	Disk Number	Title	Type	Country	Year	Longbox Value / Value
		Singles				
Warner Brothers	PRO-CD-7016	Happy Home	CDJ	U.S.	1994	$2.00

Boney M

Company	Disk Number	Title	Type	Country	Year	Longbox Value / Value
		Full Length				
Ariola	610517	Eye Dance	LP	Germany		$25.00
Ariola	610295	Kalimba De Luna	LP	Germany		$25.00
Ariola	610140	Ten Thousand Light Years	LP	Germany		$25.00
		Singles				
Hansa	661973	Megamix	CD5	Germany	1989	$5.00
Hansa	661825	Rivers Of Babylon	CD5	Germany	1988	$5.00
RCA	R10D-110	Rivers Of Babylon	CD3	Japan	1989	$13.00/$4.00
Ariola	662997	Stories	CD5	Germany	1990	$8.00
Ariola	662997	Stories	CD5	U.K.	1990	$8.00
Hansa	162 466	Summer Mega Mix	CD3	Germany	1989	$5.00
Hansa	662 466	Summer Mega Mix	CD5	Germany	1989	$5.00

Boneyard

Company	Disk Number	Title	Type	Country	Year	Longbox Value / Value
		Singles				
Sony	SKCD61	Drop Leaf	CD5	U.K.	1992	$7.00

Bonfire

Company	Disk Number	Title	Type	Country	Year	Longbox Value / Value
		Full Length				
RCA	PCD-6233	Don't Touch the Light	LP/BP	U.S.		$14.00/$8.00
RCA	PCD-6942	Fireworks	LP/BP	U.S.		$14.00/$8.00
		Singles				
RCA	ZD-43082	Hard On Me	CD5	Germany	1989	$7.00
Motown	ZD-43194	Hard On Me	CD5	U.K.	1989	$7.00
RCA	ZD-45088	Rivers Of Glory	CD5	Germany	1991	$7.00
EMI	203889-2	Sword And Stone	CD5	Germany	1990	$7.00
RCA	ZD-43506	Who's Foolin' Who	CD5	Germany	1989	$7.00
Motown	ZD-43506	Who's Foolin' Who	CD5	U.K.	1989	$7.00

Bongiovi, Jodi

Company	Disk Number	Title	Type	Country	Year	Longbox Value / Value
		Singles				
Alpha Int	79838	Keep the Light Burning	CDJ	U.S.	1989	$2.00
Alpha Int	79731	Somebody To Love	CDJ	U.S.	1989	$2.00

Bongo Talk

Company	Disk Number	Title	Type	Country	Year	Longbox Value / Value
		Singles				
Bellaphon	130 07 576	My Girl	CD5	Germany	1991	$7.00

Bonham

Singles

Label	Catalog Number	Title	Type	Country	Year	Longbox Value / Value
WTG	PSK 2005	Bringing Me Down	CDJ	U.S.	1989	$3.00
WTG	PSK 4331	Change of Season	CDJ	U.S.	1992	$3.00
WTG	PSK 1912	Guilty	CDJ	U.S.	1989	$3.00
WTG	PSK 1970	Guilty	CDJ	U.S.	1989	$3.00
Epic	656024-2	Wait For You	CD5	U.K.	1990	$9.00
WTG	PSK 1768	Wait For You	CDJ	U.S.	1989	$6.00
WTG	PSK 1859	Wait For You	CDJ	U.S.	1989	$6.00

Bonham, Tracy

Singles

Label	Catalog Number	Title	Type	Country	Year	Longbox Value / Value
Cherrydisc	384 422-810	Liverpool Sessions	CDJ	U.S.	1995	$2.00
		Mother Mother	CDJ	U.S.		$3.00

Bonilla, Marc

Full Length

Label	Catalog Number	Title	Type	Country	Year	Longbox Value / Value
Reprise	9 26725-2-Dj	EE Ticket	DJ/LP	U.S.	1991	$10.00

Picture disc.

Singles

Label	Catalog Number	Title	Type	Country	Year	Longbox Value / Value
Reprise	PRO-CD-5419	Slaughter On Memory Lane	CDJ	U.S.	1991	$2.00

Bonner, Joe

Full Length

Label	Catalog Number	Title	Type	Country	Year	Longbox Value / Value
IMS	SCCD-31277	Lost Melody	LP	Germany		$15.00

Bonney, Simon

Singles

Label	Catalog Number	Title	Type	Country	Year	Longbox Value / Value
Mute	8588	There Can Only Be One	CDJ	U.S.	1992	$2.00
Mute	8650	There Can Only Be One	CDJ	U.S.	1992	$2.00

Bono

Singles

Label	Catalog Number	Title	Type	Country	Year	Longbox Value / Value
Island	PRCD 6813-2	In the Name Of the Father	CDJ	U.S.	1994	$6.00

Bonoff, Karla

Full Length

Label	Catalog Number	Title	Type	Country	Year	Longbox Value / Value
CBS	35DP-26	Wild Heart Of the Young	LP	Japan		$20.00

Singles

Label	Catalog Number	Title	Type	Country	Year	Longbox Value / Value
MCA	2858	Standing Right Next To Me	CDJ	U.S.	1994	$2.00
MCA		Tell Me Why	CDJ	U.S.		$2.00

Bonzo Dog Band

Full Length

Label	Catalog Number	Title	Type	Country	Year	Longbox Value / Value
Strange Fruit		Peel Sessions	LP/LB	U.S.		$12.00/$7.00
		Let's Make Up And Be Friendly	CDJ	U.S.	1994	$6.00

Boo, Betty

Singles

Label	Catalog Number	Title	Type	Country	Year	Longbox Value / Value
Rough Trade	CD1-85	Burn It Up	CD5	Germany	1988	$7.00
Pinnacle	LEFT-27CD	Burn It Up	CD5	U.K.	1988	$7.00
Warner Brothers	12-40819	Catch Me	CD5	Canada	1993	$7.00
Warner Brothers	9 40819-2	Catch Me	CD5	U.S.	1993	$3.00
Sire		Doin' the Do	CD5	U.S.	1990	$4.00
Sire	PRO-CD-4450	Doin' the Do	CDJ	U.S.	1990	$2.00
Pinnacle	LEFT-44CD	Dunno What It Is (About You)	CD5	U.K.	1991	$7.00
CBS	658001-2	Dunno What It Is (About You)	CD5	U.K.	1992	$7.00
Rhythm King	40041	Dunno What It Is (About You)	CD5	U.S.	1991	$4.00
Pinnacle	YODP-2294	Hey DJ I Can't Dance	CD3	Japan	1989	$13.00/$4.00
Pinnacle	LEFT-34CD	Hey DJ I Can't Dance	CD5	U.K.	1989	$7.00
Sire	PRO-CD-4792	Hey DJ I Can't Dance	CDJ	U.S.	1991	$3.00
WEA	YZ-693	I'm On the Way	CD5	U.K.	1992	$10.00
WEA	WMD5-4120	Let Me Take You There	CD3	Japan	1992	$13.00/$4.00
WEA	YZ-677CD	Let Me Take You There	CD5	U.K.	1992	$7.00
Reprise	12-40639	Things Goin' On	CD5	Canada	1992	$7.00
Reprise	9 40639-2	Things Goin' On	CD5	U.S.	1992	$4.00
Reprise	PRO-CD-5877	Things Goin' On	CDJ	U.S.	1992	$6.00
Reprise	PRO-CD-5882	Things Goin' On	CDJ	U.S.	1992	$6.00
Pinnacle	LEFT-45CD	Twenty-Four Hours	CD5	U.K.	1990	$7.00
Rough Trade	CD1-320	Warm Love	CD5	Germany	1990	$7.00
Pinnacle	LEFT-36CD	Warm Love	CD5	U.K.	1990	$7.00
Sire	9 21739-2	Warm Love	CD5	U.S.	1990	$2.00
Rhythm King	LEFT 43CD	Where Are You Baby?	CD5	U.K.	1991	$7.00
Rhythm King	40181	Where Are You Baby?	CD5	U.K.	1991	$7.00
Pinnacle	LEFT-31CD	Who's In the House	CD5	U.K.	1989	$7.00

Boo Radleys

Full Length

Label	Catalog Number	Title	Type	Country	Year	Longbox Value / Value
		Rarities	DJ/Smplr	France		$22.00

Singles

Label	Catalog Number	Title	Type	Country	Year	Longbox Value / Value
Creation	977 994	Adrenalin	CD5	Germany	1992	$7.00
Creation	CRESCD-124	Adrenalin	CD5	U.K.	1992	$7.00
Columbia	CSK 5505	Barney	CDJ	U.S.	1993	$2.00
Creation	CRESCD 128	Boo Forever	CD5	U.K.	1992	$10.00
Columbia	CSK 4801	Bool Forever	CDJ	U.S.	1992	$2.00
Pinnacle	R-271-3	Every Heaven	CD5	U.K.	1991	$10.00
		Find the Answer Within	CD5	U.K.	1995	$10.00
		Find the Answer Within	CD5	U.K.	1995	$10.00

Second version.

Label	Catalog Number	Title	Type	Country	Year	Longbox Value / Value
Columbia	CDESCD 211X	It's Lulu	CD5	U.K.	1995	$10.00
Columbia	CSK 7312	It's Lulu	CDJ	U.S.	1995	$3.00
Pinnacle	RTD-241CD	Kaleidoscope	CD5	U.K.	1991	$10.00
Ceation	CRESCD-137	Lazarus	CD5	U.K.	1992	$10.00
Creation		Lazarus	CD5	U.K.	1992	$10.00

Second version.

Label	Catalog Number	Title	Type	Country	Year	Longbox Value / Value
Epic	74818	Lazarus	CD5	U.S.	1992	$4.00
Columbia	CSK 5327	Lazarus	CDJ	U.S.	1992	$3.00
Columbia	CSK 6205	Lazarus	CDJ	U.S.	1994	$7.00
Ceation	CRESCD 169	Wish I Was Skinny	CD5	U.K.	1993	$10.00

Boo-Ya T.R.I.B.E.

Full Length

Label	Catalog Number	Title	Type	Country	Year	Longbox Value / Value
4th & B'Way	4017	New Funky Nation	LP/LB	U.S.		$12.00/$7.00

Singles

Label	Catalog Number	Title	Type	Country	Year	Longbox Value / Value
4th & B'Way	BRCD-179	Psyko Funk	CD5	U.K.	1990	$7.00
BMG		Psyko Funk	CD5	U.S.	1990	$7.00
4th & B'Way	510	Psyko Funk	CDJ	U.S.	1990	$2.00
4th & B'Way	BRCD-158	R.A.I.D.	CD5	U.K.	1990	$7.00
BMG	663194	R.A.I.D	CD5	U.S.	1990	$7.00
	3001	Rid Is Coming	CD5	U.S.	1995	$5.00
Warner Brothers	22-66399	Rumors Of A Dead Man	CD5	Canada	1993	$7.00
Elektra	66399	Rumors Of A Dead Man	CD5	U.S.	1992	$4.00
Hollywood	10229	Rumors Of A Dead Man	CDJ	U.S.	1992	$2.00
4th & B'way	518	Walk On the Line	CDJ	U.S.	1990	$2.00

Boogie Box High

Singles

Label	Catalog Number	Title	Type	Country	Year	Longbox Value / Value
SBK	CDSBX-1	Nervous	CD5	U.K.	1989	$7.00

Boogie Boys

Singles

Label	Catalog Number	Title	Type	Country	Year	Longbox Value / Value
SPV	1003-3	Kick the Power	CD5	Germany	1990	$7.00
SPV	1006-3	Love Me Tender	CD5	Germany	1990	$7.00

Boogie Down Productions

Singles

Label	Catalog Number	Title	Type	Country	Year	Longbox Value / Value
Jive	42022-2-RDJ	13 And Good	CDJ	U.S.	1990	$2.00
RCA	ZD-43190	Bo Bo Bo	CD5	Germany	1989	$7.00
Jive	42021	Down Duck	CDJ	U.S.	1992	$7.00
Jive	1367-2-RDJ	Love's Gonna Get 'Cha	CDJ	U.S.	1990	$2.00
Jive	42070-2-RDJ	We In There	CDJ	U.S.	1992	$2.00
Jive	1257-2-RDJ	Why Is That	CDJ	U.S.	1989	$6.00
Jive		Ya Know the Rules	CDJ	U.S.		$2.00

Boogiemonsters

Singles

Label	Catalog Number	Title	Type	Country	Year	Longbox Value / Value
Pendulum	19840	Recognized Thresholds Of Negative Stress	CDJ	U.S.	1994	$3.00

Book Of Love

Full Length

Label	Catalog Number	Title	Type	Country	Year	Longbox Value / Value
Atlantic	925700-2	Lullaby	LP	U.K.		$18.00

Singles

Label	Catalog Number	Title	Type	Country	Year	Longbox Value / Value
Sire	PRO-CD-4479	Alice Everyday	CDJ	U.S.	1991	$2.00
Sire	21767	Alice Everyday	CD5	U.S.	1995	$6.00
Warner Brothers	22-40806	Boy Pop	CD5	Canada	1993	$7.00
Sire	9 41052-2	Hunny Hunny	CD5	U.S.	1993	$4.00
Sire	PRO-CD-6332	Hunny Hunny	CDJ	U.S.	1988	$2.00
Sire		Lullaby	CDJ	U.S.		$2.00
Sire	PRO-CD-3197	Pretty Boys & Pretty Girls	CDJ	U.S.	1988	$2.00
Sire	PRO-CD-4805	Sunny Day	CDJ	U.S.	1991	$2.00

Booker, Chuckii

Singles

Label	Catalog Number	Title	Type	Country	Year	Longbox Value / Value
Atlantic	PRCD 4766-2	Games	CDJ	U.S.	1992	$2.00
Atlantic	PRCD 4912-2	I Should Have Loved You	CDJ	U.S.	1992	$2.00
Atlantic	PRCD 2857-2	Touch	CDJ	U.S.	1989	$2.00
Atlantic	PRCD 5140-2	With All My Heart	CDJ	U.S.		$2.00

Booker, Steve

Singles

Label	Catalog Number	Title	Type	Country	Year	Longbox Value / Value
Parlophone	CDR-6268	Every Time You Walk Away	CD5	U.K.	1990	$7.00
Parlophone	CDR-6280	This Side Of Heaven	CD5	U.K.	1990	$7.00
Parlophone	CDR-6289	Wedding Day	CD5	U.K.	1991	$7.00
Parlophone	CDR-6256	Wedding Day	CD5	U.K.	1991	$7.00

Booker T. And The MGs

Singles

Label	Catalog Number	Title	Type	Country	Year	Longbox Value / Value
MCA	CD45 3014	Cool Dude, The	CDJ	U.S.	1989	$2.00
Columbia	CSK 6026	Cruisin'	CDJ	U.S.	1994	$3.00
Atco	PRCD 3994-2	Green Onions	CDJ	U.S.	1991	$3.00

Boom Crash Opera

Full Length

Label	Catalog Number	Title	Type	Country	Year	Longbox Value / Value
Warner Brothers	9 25636-2	Boom Crash Opera	LP	U.K.		$15.00
Warner Brothers	9 25636-2	Boom Crash Opera	LP/LB	U.S.		$14.00/$8.00
Giant	9 26160-2-Dj	These Are Crazy Times	DJ/LP	U.S.	1990	$10.00

With Jigsaw Puzzle

Label	Catalog Number	Title	Type	Country	Year	Longbox Value / Value
Giant	9 26160-2-Dj	These Are Crazy Times	DJ/LP	U.S.	1990	$15.00

In special octagonal box and cassette

Singles

Label	Catalog Number	Title	Type	Country	Year	Longbox Value / Value
Warner Brothers	PRO-CD-2925	Her Charity	CDJ	U.S.	1990	$2.00
Warner Brothers	PRO-CD-3967	Onion Skins	CDJ	U.S.	1990	$2.00
Warner Brothers	PRO-CD-4481	Talk About It	CDJ	U.S.	1990	$2.00
		Talk About It	CDJ	U.S.	1990	$2.00

Boom Shaka

Singles

Label	Catalog Number	Title	Type	Country	Year	Longbox Value / Value
Liberty	DPRO-79444	Jah Make It Rock	CDJ	U.S.	1992	$2.00

Boom, Taka

Full Length

Label	Catalog Number	Title	Type	Country	Year	Longbox Value / Value
Polygram	827613-2	Middle of the Night	LP	Germany		$15.00

Boomers

Singles

Label	Catalog Number	Title	Type	Country	Year	Longbox Value / Value
WEA	4509 92328	You've Got To Know	CD5	U.K.	1993	$8.00

Boomtown Rats

Full Length

Label	Catalog Number	Title	Type	Country	Year	Longbox Value / Value
		A Tonic For the Troops	LP/LB	U.S.		$12.00/$10.00

Singles

Label	Catalog Number	Title	Type	Country	Year	Longbox Value / Value
Polygram	888975-3	I Don't Like Mondays	CD3	Germany	1989	$8.00
		I Don't Like Mondays	CD5	U.K.		$10.00

Second version.

Label	Catalog Number	Title	Type	Country	Year	Longbox Value / Value
Polygram	688975-3	I Don't Like Mondays	CD3	U.K.	1989	$8.00
Polygram		I Don't Like Mondays	CD5	U.K.	1994	$10.00
Polygram	888975-2	Rat Trap	CD5	Germany	1989	$8.00

Boone, Debbie

Full Length

Label	Catalog Number	Title	Type	Country	Year	Longbox Value / Value
Sparrow	1380	Surrender	LP/LB	U.S.		$12.00/$7.00

Boone, Larry

Full Length

Label	Catalog Number	Title	Type	Country	Year	Longbox Value / Value
Island	842156	Down That River Road	LP/LB	U.S.		$14.00/$8.00
Polygram	836710	Swingin' Doors & Sawdust Floors	LP/BP	U.S.		$14.00/$8.00

Singles

Label	Catalog Number	Title	Type	Country	Year	Longbox Value / Value
Mercury	CDP 169	Everybody Wants Hank Williams	CDJ	U.S.	1990	$2.00
Mercury	CDP 236	Too Blue To Be True	CDJ	U.S.	1990	$2.00

Boone, Pat

Full Length

Label	Catalog Number	Title	Type	Country	Year	Longbox Value / Value
K-Tel	6163	Love Letters	LP	U.S.		$8.00

Singles

Label	Catalog Number	Title	Type	Country	Year	Longbox Value / Value
Laserlight	12384	I Remember Red	CD5	U.S.	1994	$5.00

Boonsquawk

Singles

Label	Catalog Number	Title	Type	Country	Year	Longbox Value / Value
Virgin	TENCD-326	Dirty Games	CD5	U.K.	1990	$7.00

Booth, Tim

Singles

Label	Catalog Number	Title	Type	Country	Year	Value
		Bad Angel	CD5	U.K.	1996	$10.00
		Bad Angel	CD5	U.K.	1996	$10.00
Second version.						

Bootsauce

Singles

Label	Catalog Number	Title	Type	Country	Year	Value
Vertigo	4228668432	Big, Bad & Groovy!	CD5	Canada	1993	$7.00
Vertigo		Love Monkey # 9	CDJ	Canada	1992	$5.00
Island	PRCD 6716-2	Love Monkey # 9	CDJ	U.S.	1992	$2.00
Vertigo	534	Play With Me	CDJ	Canada	1991	$6.00
Vertigo	510 118	Reboot	CD5	Canada	1992	$7.00
Island	PRCD 6734-2	Rollercoaster's Child	CDJ	U.S.	1992	$2.00
Vertigo	875 343 2D	Scratching the Whole	CDJ	Canada	1990	$6.00
Next Plateau	50138	Scratching the Whole	CDJ	U.S.	1990	$2.00

Bordland, Adrian

Singles

Label	Catalog Number	Title	Type	Country	Year	Value
Apt	BIAS-223CD	All the World	CD5	Germany	1991	$7.00
SPV	11030-3	All the World	CD5	Germany	1992	$7.00

Boredome

Singles

Label	Catalog Number	Title	Type	Country	Year	Value
Alternative	41559	Super Roots	CD5	U.S.	1994	$6.00
Warner	12-41559	Pop Kiss	CD5	Canada	1994	$8.00

Borghesia

Singles

Label	Catalog Number	Title	Type	Country	Year	Value
Apt	BIAS-166CD	Message	CD5	U.K.	1990	$7.00
SPV	7388-3	Naked Uniform	CD5	Germany	1990	$7.00
SPV	9140-3	Resistance	CD5	Germany	1990	$7.00
SPV	6733-3	She Is Not Alone	CD5	Germany	1989	$7.00
SPV	8165-3	Surveillance	CD5	Germany	1989	$7.00

Born Jamericans

Singles

Label	Catalog Number	Title	Type	Country	Year	Value
Delicious Vinyl	5427	Boom Shak-A-Tack	CDJ	U.S.		$2.00
Delicious Vinyl	5212	Boom Shak-A-Tak	CDJ	U.S.		$2.00
Delicious Vinyl	5594	Cease 7 Seckle	CDJ	U.S.	1994	$2.00

Boss

Singles

Label	Catalog Number	Title	Type	Country	Year	Value
CBS	11659891	Progress Of Elimination	CD5	Canada	1994	$8.00

Boss Beat

Singles

Label	Catalog Number	Title	Type	Country	Year	Value
Siren	SRNCD-91	Let There Be Drums	CD3	U.K.	1990	$7.00

Boss Hog

Full Length

Label	Catalog Number	Title	Type	Country	Year	Value
Amphetamin	89192	Cold Hands	LP/BP	U.S.		$12.00/$8.00

Singles

Label	Catalog Number	Title	Type	Country	Year	Value
	PRO-CD-4840	I Dig You	CDJ	U.S.		$3.00
DGC	PRO-CD-4872	I Dig You	CDJ	U.S.		$7.00

Boston

Full Length

Label	Catalog Number	Title	Type	Country	Year	Value
Epic	EK 52856	Boston	LTD/LP	U.S.	1992	$29.00/$25.00
Gold disc.						
Epic	EK -35050	Don't Look Back	LP/LB	U.S.†	1985	$15.00/$9.00
Epic		Don't Look Back	LTD/LP	U.S.	1994	$25.00
Gold Disc.						
Album Network		In the Studio (Boston)	RS	U.S.	1988	$25.00
Airdate: 8/29/88						
Album Network		In the Studio (Boston)	RS	U.S.	1990	$25.00
Airdate: 1/15/90						
DIR		King Biscuit Flour Hour	RS	U.S.	1988	$40.00
Airdate: 11/13/88						
DIR		King Biscuit Flour Hour	RS	U.S.	1991	$30.00
With Boston, Airdate: 1/20/91						
DIR		King Biscuit Flour Hour	RS	U.S.	1992	$40.00
Airdate: 4/5/92						
DIR		King Biscuit Flour Hour	RS	U.S.	1995	$60.00
Airdate: 8/6/95.						
Westwood One		Off the Record	RS	U.S.	1995	$25.00
Airdate: 5/22/95.						
Media America		Up Close	RS	U.S.	1994	$60.00
2 CD set.						
MCA		Walk On	LTD/LP	Austalia	1994	$35.00

Singles

Label	Catalog Number	Title	Type	Country	Year	Value
MCA	DMCA-1150	Cant'cha Say	CD5	U.K.	1988	$12.00
		I Need Your Love	CD5	U.K.	1994	$10.00
MCA	MCA5P-2889	I Need Your Love	CDJ	U.S.	1994	$6.00
MCA	MCA5P-3097	I Need Your Love	CDJ	U.S.	1994	$6.00
Epic	654566-3	More Than A Feeling	CD3	Germany	1987	$10.00
Epic	654566-3	More Than A Feeling	CD3	U.K.	1987	$10.00
Epic	34K 02355	More Than A Feeling	CD3	U.S.	1987	$8.00/$5.00
MCA		Star-Spangled Banner	CDJ	U.S.	1995	$8.00
MCA	MCA5P-3110	Walk On	CDJ	U.S.	1994	$3.00
MCA	MCA5P3127	What's Your Name	CDJ	U.S.		$3.00

Boston, Annie Richmond

Singles

Label	Catalog Number	Title	Type	Country	Year	Value
BD	100	Big House Of Time, The	CDJ	Canada	1990	$3.00

Boston Pops

Full Length

Label	Catalog Number	Title	Type	Country	Year	Value
Polygram	411037-2	Aisle Seat	LP	Germany		$20.00
Polygram	412627-2	America, the Dream Goes On	LP	Germany		$20.00
Polygram	411185-2	Out Of This World	LP	Germany		$20.00
Polygram	400071-2	Pops Around the World	LP	Germany		$20.00
Polygram	412884-2	Pops In Space	LP	Germany		$20.00

Botany Five

Singles

Label	Catalog Number	Title	Type	Country	Year	Value
Virgin	VSCDG 1371	Only One In Your Love	CD5	U.K.	1991	$8.00

Bottlerockets

Full Length

Label	Catalog Number	Title	Type	Country	Year	Value
Tag	PRCD 6357-2	Sampler	DJ/Smplr	U.S.		$5.00

Singles

Label	Catalog Number	Title	Type	Country	Year	Value
Eastside	PRCD 6717	1000 Dollar Car	CDJ	U.S.		$3.00
Tag	PRCD 6352-2	I'll Be Comin' Around	CDJ	U.S.		$2.00

Boulevard

Full Length

Company	Disk Number	Title	Type	Country	Year	Value
MCA	42317	Into the Street	LP/LB	U.S.		$12.00/$7.00

Singles

Company	Disk Number	Title	Type	Country	Year	Value
MCA	DMCAT-1308	Dream On	CD5	U.K.	1989	$8.00
MCA	DMCAT-1326	Never Give Up	CD5	U.K.	1989	$8.00

Bounce The Ocean

Full Length

Company	Disk Number	Title	Type	Country	Year	Value
Private	82080	Bounce the Ocean	LP/LB	U.S.		$14.00/$8.00

Singles

Company	Disk Number	Title	Type	Country	Year	Value
Private Msc	81001	Wasting My Time	CDJ	U.S.	1991	$2.00

Bouncer

Singles

Company	Disk Number	Title	Type	Country	Year	Value
Intercord	825 936	Kicks Like A Mule	CD5	Germany	1992	$8.00
Tribalbass	TRIBE-3CD	Kicks Like A Mule	CD5	U.K.	1992	$8.00

Bouncer, Peter

Singles

Company	Disk Number	Title	Type	Country	Year	Value
Pinnacle	SUACD-33	So Here I Come	CD5	U.K.	1991	$8.00

Bouncing Souls

Singles

Company	Disk Number	Title	Type	Country	Year	Value
	BYOO37CD	Maniacal Laughter	CDJ	U.S.		$3.00

Bourbon Club

Singles

Company	Disk Number	Title	Type	Country	Year	Value
BMG	662531	Keeping Your House Together	CD5	Germany	1989	$8.00

Bourbon Tabernacle Choir

Full Length

Company	Disk Number	Title	Type	Country	Year	Value
		Superior Cackling Hen	DJ/Smplr	Canada		$8.00

Bourgeois Braent

Singles

Company	Disk Number	Title	Type	Country	Year	Value
Charisma	CHR PRCD 007	Can't Feel the Pain	CDJ	U.S.	1990	$2.00
Virgin	VJDP-123	Dare To Fall In Love	CD3	Japan	1990	$12.00/$3.00
Charisma	CHR PRCD 001	Dare To Fall In Love	CDJ	U.S.	1990	$7.00
CD in Box						
Charisma	DPRO-14189	Funky Little Nothing	CDJ	U.S.	1992	$2.00
Charisma	CHR PRCD 015	Time Of Season	CDJ	U.S.	1990	$2.00

Bourgeois Tagg

Full Length

Company	Disk Number	Title	Type	Country	Year	Value
Aris	880158	Bourgeois Tagg	LP	Germany		$18.00
DIR		King Biscuit Flour Hour	RS	U.S.	1988	$30.00
Airdate: 1/3/88						
Island	842847-2	Yo Yo	LP/LB	U.S.		$14.00/$8.00

Singles

Company	Disk Number	Title	Type	Country	Year	Value
Island	880791	I Don't Mind At All	CDJ	Germany	1988	$7.00
Island	CID-33	I Don't Mind At All	CDJ	U.K.	1988	$7.00
Island	PR 2103 -2	I Don't Mind At All	CDJ	U.S.	1988	$2.00

Bow Wow Wow

Full Length

Company	Disk Number	Title	Type	Country	Year	Value
		When the Going Gets	LP	U.K.		$14.00

Bowa

Singles

Company	Disk Number	Title	Type	Country	Year	Value
Rough Trade	344 0301 3	Different Story	CD5	Germany	1991	$7.00
Pinnacle	GOOD-8CD	Different Story	CD5	U.K.	1991	$7.00

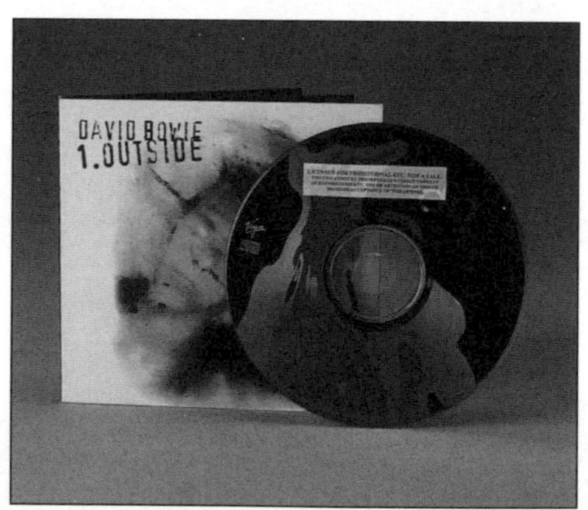

Bowie, David – 1.Outside (Virgin 7243 8 40711 2 7)

Bowie, David

Full Length

Company	Disk Number	Title	Type	Country	Year	Value
Virgin	BVCA 2801/02	1.Outside	LTD/LP	Japan	1995	$35.00
2 CD set.						
Virgin	7243 8 40711 2 7	1.Outside	LTD/LP	U.S.	1995	$18.00
CD in cardboard sleeve.						
Sound	CLACD-154	1966	LP	Germany	1988	$13.00
Garland	GRZ MCD-101	1966	LTD/LP	U.S.	1988	$18.00/$15.00
Picture disc CD.						
Rykodisc	S+V PRO 2	8 From Sound & Vision	DJ/Smplr	U.S.	1989	$35.00
BBC		A Taste of Bowie	DJ/Smplr	U.K.	1995	$21.00
RCA	PD-83890	Aladdin Sane	LP	U.K.	1971	$20.00
RCA	PCD1-4852	Aladdin Sane	LP/BP	U.S.†	1971	$18.00/$15.00
Rykodisc		All Saints	DJ/Smplr	U.S.	1993	$250.00
2 CD set of Christmas music comissioned by Bowie.						
BBC Radio		BBC Classic Tracks	RS	U.S.	1992	$35.00
Airdate: 4/6/92.						
BBC Radio		BBC Classic Tracks	RS	U.S.	1994	$35.00
Airdate: 4/11/94.						
Westwood One		BBC Classic Tracks	RS	U.S.	1995	$40.00
Airdate: 1/23/95.						

Label	Catalog Number	Title	Type	Country	Year	Longbox Value / Value
Savage		Black Tie White Noise	LTD/LP	Australia	1993	$25.00
	Limited edition in jewel box with outer slip case.					
Arista	BVCA-612	Black Tie White Noise	LTD/LP	Japan	1993	$25.00
	Limited edition in jewel box with outer slip case and bonus track.					
Savage		Black Tie White Noise	DJ/Intvw	U.S.	1993	$30.00
	2CD set. CD album plus interview disc.					
Savage		Black Tie White Noise	DJ/LP	U.S.	1993	$15.00
	"Window" Sleeve.					
Savage	74785-50212-2	Black Tie White Noise	LP	U.S.	1993	$15.00
Rykodisc	VRCD 0142	Bowie/Eno Sampler	DJ/Smplr	U.S.	1991	$25.00
Rykodisc	RCD 80171	Changesbowie	LTD/LP	U.S.	1995	$24.00
	20 bit master gold CD.					
RCA	R32P-1040	Changesonebowie	LP	Japan	1976	$30.00
RCA	PD-81732	Changesonebowie	LP	U.K.	1976	$25.00
RCA	PCD1-1732	Changesonebowie	LP/BP	U.S.†	1976	$18.00/$15.00
RCA	PD-84202	Changestwobowie	LP	U.K.		$25.00
RCA	PCD1-4202	Changestwobowie	LP	U.S.†		$25.00
Pioneer	PA84-V02	David Bowie	8"LD	U.S.	1983	$12.00
	Analog audio.					
		David Bowie Collection	DJ/Smplr	Spain	1990	$60.00
	CD sampler with tour shirt and poster.					
RCA	PD-83889	Diamond Dogs	LP	U.K.	1974	$20.00
RCA	PCD1-0576	Diamond Dogs	LP/BP	U.S.†	1974	$18.00/$15.00
Point	438 470-2	Discussions On the Low Symphony	DJ/Smplr	U.K.	1993	$25.00
	With Philip Glass					
BMG	DB001	Excerpts From 1993 Limited Ed.	DJ/Smplr	U.K.	1993	$70.00
	"Window" Sleeve, #'d edition.					
RCA	PD-84919	Fame & Fashion	LP	U.K.	1984	$20.00
RCA	PCD1-4919	Fame & Fashion	LP/BP	U.S.†	1984	$18.00/$15.00
Image	ID6198MP	Glass Spider Tour	LD	U.S.		$40.00
DIR		Glass Spider Tour	RS	U.S.	1987	$600.00
	4 CD set. Airdate: 10/17 - 10/24/87.					
RCA	PD-84792	Golden Years	LP	U.K		[illegible]
RCA	PCD1-4515	Golden Years	LP/BP	U.S.†		$18.00/$15.00
RCA	PD-83867	Heroes	LP	U.K.	1977	$20.00
RCA	PCD1-2522	Heroes	LP/BP	U.S.†	1977	$18.00/$15.00
Rykodisc	rcd pro 9016	High Tech Soul Sampler	DJ/Smplr	U.S.	1991	$25.00
Rykodisc	RYKO RCD 1	High Tech Unit	LTD/LP	U.S.	1991	$75.00
	4 CD set with special metal storage case.					
RCA	PD-84623	Hunky Dory	LP	U.K.	1971	$20.00
RCA	PCD1-4623	Hunky Dory	LP/BP	U.S.†	1971	$18.00/$15.00
Rykodisc	RCD 80133	Hunky Dory	LTD/LP	U.S.	1995	$24.00
	20 bit master gold CD.					
Westwood One		In Concert	RS	U.S.	1993	$85.00
	2 CD set. Airdate: 12/6/93.					
Pioneer	PA-85-113	Jazzin' For Blue Jean	LD	U.S.	1985	$20.00
	Non digital.					
		Jump They Say	DJ/Smplr	France	1993	$50.00
DIR		King Biscuit Flour Hour	RS	U.S.	1988	$140.00
	2 CD set. Airdate: 4/16 - 4/23/88.					
DIR		King Biscuit Flour Hour	RS	U.S.	1989	$140.00
	2 CD set. Airdate: 4/23/89.					
DIR		King Biscuit Flour Hour	RS	U.S.	1994	$145.00
	2 CD set. Airdate: 1/1/94.					
DIR		King Biscuit Flour Hour	RS	U.S.	1995	$145.00
	2 CD set. Airdate: 12/17/95.					
Manhattan	CP43-5772	Let's Dance	LTD/LP	Japan	1987	$50.00
	Gold disc.					
EMI	CDP-46002	Let's Dance	LP/LB	U.S.		$15.00/$8.00
EMI	CDP-46002	Let's Dance	LP/BP	U.S.†	1985	$15.00/$9.00
EMI	CDP-46002	Let's Dance	LP/BP	U.S.	1985	$15.00/$9.00
Griffin		Live At Santa Monica	LTD/LP	U.K.	1994	$25.00
	First pressing with concert ticket replica.					
RCA	PD-84234	Lodger	LP	U.K.	1979	$20.00
RCA	PCD1-3254	Lodger	LP/BP	U.S.†	1979	$18.00/$15.00
Image	ID6307ME	Love You 'Til Tuesday	LD	U.S.		$35.00
RCA	PD-83856	Low	LP	U.K.	1977	$20.00
RCA	PCD1-2030	Low	LP/BP	U.S.†	1977	$18.00/$15.00
Rykodisc	RCD 80142	Low	LTD/LP	U.S.	1995	$24.00
	20 bit master gold CD.					
RCA	PD-84664	Man Who Sold the World	LP	U.K.	1970	$20.00
RCA	PCD1-4816	Man Who Sold the World	LP/BP	U.S.†	1970	$18.00/$15.00
Radio Ventures		Masters Of Rock	RS	U.S.	1990	$50.00
	Airdate: 6/18/90.					
Radio Ventures		Masters Of Rock	RS	U.S.	1990	$50.00
	Airdate: 7/2/90.					
EMI	CDP-46677	Never Let Me Down	LP/LB	U.S.		$15.00/$8.00
Westwood One		Off the Record	RS	U.S.	1993	$40.00
	Airdate: 12/13/93.					
Westwood One		Off the Record	RS	U.S.	1993	$80.00
	2 CD set. Airdate: 4/19/93					
Westwood One		Off the Record	RS	U.S.	1993	$80.00
	2 CD set. Airdate: 9/27/93					
Westwood One		Off the Record	RS	U.S.	1996	$60.00
	2 CD set. Airdate: 1/22/96.					
Westwood One		On the Edge	RS	U.S.	1994	$40.00
		One On One	RS	U.S.	1993	$75.00
	Airdate: 5/10/93.					
Virgin	DPRO-011008	Outside Sampler	DJ/Smplr	U.S.	1995	$15.00
Virgin	SOLO 1	Outside Tour	DJ/Smplr	U.K.	1996	$100.00
		Peace On Earth	LTD/LP	U.S.	1995	$25.00
	With Bing Crosby. Includes a bonus CD-ROM.					
RCA		Peter and the Wolf	LP/BP	U.S.		$35.00/$32.00
RCA	PD-84663	Pinups	LP	U.K.	1973	$20.00
RCA	PCD1-0291	Pinups	LP/BP	U.S.†	1973	$18.00/$15.00
RCA	R32P-1037	Rise And Fall Of Ziggy Stardust	LP	Japan	1972	$30.00
RCA	PD-84702	Rise And Fall Of Ziggy Stardust	LP	U.K.	1972	$20.00
RCA	PCD1-4702	Rise And Fall Of Ziggy Stardust	LP/BP	U.S.†	1972	$18.00/$15.00
Rykodisc	RYKO Analogue RALP 0134-2	Rise And Fall Of Ziggy Stardust	DJ/LP	U.S.	1990	$150.00
	CD and vinyl LP in vinyl LP sleeve with press kit.					
Rykodisc	RCD 10134	Rise And Fall Of Ziggy Stardust	LTD/LP	U.S.	1990	$25.00/$17.00
	CD and boolet in slip case. Includes longbox.					
Griffin	GCD-392-2	Santa Monica '72	LTD/LP	U.S.	1995	$20.00
	CD and 7" record in large sleeve.					
Griffin	GCD-392-2	Santa Monica '72	LTD/LP	U.S.	1995	$60.00
	CD in laser-etched wooden box.					
Griffin		Santa Monica '72	LTD/LP	U.S.	1995	$70.00
	CD in box with T-shirt, VHS video and key chain.					
RCA	PD-83647	Scary Monsters	LP	U.K.	1980	$20.00
RCA	PCD1-3647	Scary Monsters	LP/BP	U.S.†	1980	$15.00
EMI	BOW 90	Selections From Changes Bowie	DJ/Smplr	U.K.	1990	$15.00
Pioneer	PA-84-097	Serious Moonlight	LD	U.S.	1985	$85.00
Pioneer	PA-84-097	Serious Moonlight	LD	U.S.	1989	$85.00
	Digital audio.					
Rykodisc	RCD 10218/19	Singles 1969-1993, The	LTD/LP	U.S.	1993	$35.00
Rykodisc	RCD 10218/9	Singles, The	LTD/LP	U.S.	1993	$28.00
	2 CD set including bonus CD5 of "Little Drummer Boy".					
		So Far 1990	DJ/Smplr	U.K.	1990	$25.00
Rykodisc	RYKO	Soul Period	DJ/Smplr	U.S.	1991	$70.00
	Box set with "High Tech Soul Sampler" and Video Tape.					
Rykodisc	RCD-90120/2	Sound+Vision	LP	U.S.	1989	$50.00
	4 CD set. First issue with CDV.					
Rykodisc	RCD-90120/2	Sound+Vision	LTD/LP	U.S.	1989	$500.00
	4 CD set. Autographed wooden boxed set . Limited to 350 sets.					
Rykodisc	RCD-90120/2	Sound+Vision	LP	U.S.	1994	$50.00
	4 CD set with CD-ROM.					
Rykodisc	RCD PRO 131	Sound & Vision Sampler #1	DJ/Smplr	U.S.	1990	$20.00
Rykodisc		Sound+Vision: The CD Press Release	DJ/Intvw	U.S.	1989	$15.00
RCA	PD-84813	Space Oddity	LP	U.K.	1969	$20.00
RCA	PCD1-4813	Space Oddity	LP/BP	U.S.†	1969	$18.00/$15.00
RCA	PD-89002	Stage	LP	Germany	1983	$20.00
RCA	R32P-1039	Station To Station	LP	Japan	1976	$30.00
RCA	PD-81327	Station To Station	LP	U.K.	1976	$20.00
RCA	PCD1-1327	Station To Station	LP/BP	U.S.†	1976	$20.00
Westwood One		Superstar Concert	RS	U.S.	1992	$70.00
	2 CD set. Airdate: 4/12/92					
Westwood One		Superstars	RS	U.S.	1992	$120.00
	2 CD set. Airdate: 4/12/92.					
Westwood One		Superstars	RS	U.S.	1993	$120.00
	2 CD set. Airdate: 12/13/93.					
EMI	CDP-46047	Tonight	LP/LB	U.S.		$15.00/$8.00
EMI	CDP-46047	Tonight	LP/BP	U.S.†	1985	$15.00/$9.00
EMI	CDP-46047	Tonight	LP/BP	U.S.	1985	$15.00/$9.00
Media America		Up Close	RS	U.S.	1993	$85.00
	2 CD set.					
Media America		Up Close	RS	U.S.	1995	$85.00
	2 CD set.					
RCA	R32P-1038	Young Americans	LP	Japan	1975	$30.00
RCA	PD-80998	Young Americans	LP	U.K.	1975	[illegible]
RCA	PCD1-0998	Young Americans	LP/BP	U.S.†	1975	$18.00/$15.00
Rykodisc	RCD 80134	Ziggy Stardust	LTD/LP	U.S.	1995	$24.00
	20 bit master gold CD.					

Singles

Label	Catalog Number	Title	Type	Country	Year	Longbox Value / Value
Virgin	663264	Absolute Beginners	CD5	Germany	1986	$15.00
Virgin	880996	Absolute Beginners	CD3	Germany	1988	$15.00
Virgin	CDT 20	Absolute Beginners	CD3	U.K.	1986	$15.00
Virgi	CDF-20	Absolute Beginners	CD5	U.K.	1986	$15.00
		Bang Bang	CDJ	U.S.	1987	$25.00
Arista	BVDA-66	Black Tie, White Noise	CD3	Japan	1993	$13.00/$4.00
Arista	74321 148682	Black Tie, White Noise	CD5	U.K.	1993	$10.00
Savage	SADJ-50046-2	Black Tie, White Noise	CDJ	U.S.	1993	$6.00
		Buddha Of Suburbia	CD5	U.K.	1993	$10.00
		Buddha Of Suburbia	CD5	U.K.	1993	$10.00
	Second version.					
		Buddha Of Suburbia	CDJ	U.K.	1993	$15.00
Rykodisc	RCD-51018	Fame '90	CD5	Canada	1990	$7.00
EMI	203805-2	Fame '90	CD5	Germany	1990	$8.00
EMI	CDFAME 90	Fame '90	CD5	U.K.	1990	$8.00
Rykodisc	RCD5 1018	Fame '90	CD5	U.S.	1990	$6.00
Rykodisc	RCD 04580	Fame '90	CDJ	U.S.	1990	$8.00
Rykodisc	RCD PRO 9005	Growin' Up	CDJ	U.S.	1990	$8.00
Virgin		Hearts Filthy Lesson	CD5	Germany	1995	$10.00
Arista	74321 31807 2	Hearts Filthy Lesson	SCD5	Germany	1995	$50.00
	Shaped CD of Bowie's head.					
Arista	BVCA-8806	Hearts Filthy Lesson	CD5	Japan	1995	$20.00
Virgin		Hearts Filthy Lesson	CD5	U.K.	1995	$10.00
Virgin		Hearts Filthy Lesson	CD5	U.K.	1995	$10.00
	Second version.					
Virgin	38518	Hearts Filthy Lesson	CD5	U.S.	1995	$5.00
Virgin		Hearts Filthy Lesson	CD5	U.S.	1995	$5.00
	Second version.					
Virgin	DPRO-11005	Hearts Filthy Lesson	CDJ	U.S.	1995	$6.00
Virgin		Hello Spaceboy	CD5	Japan	1996	$20.00
Virgin	HALLO 1	Hello Spaceboy	CDJ	U.K.	1996	$20.00
	JM038-0018	Jazz For Blue Jean	CDV	Japan		$50.00
Arista	BVDA-64	Jump They Say	CD3	Japan	1993	$13.00/$4.00
Arista	BVCA-612	Jump They Say	DJ/CD3	Japan	1993	$20.00/$20.00
Arista	74321 139422	Jump They Say	CD5	U.K.	1993	$9.00
Arista		Jump They Say	CD5	U.K.	1993	$9.00
	Second version.					
Savage	50034-2	Jump They Say	CD5	U.S.	1993	$5.00
Savage	SADJ-50036-2	Jump They Say	CDJ	U.S.	1993	$7.00
Savage	SADJ-50039-2	Jump They Say	CDJ	U.S.	1993	$7.00
Savage	SADJ-50042-2	Jump They Say	CDJ	U.S.	1993	$7.00
Savage	SADJ-50044-2	Jump They Say	CDJ	U.S.	1993	$7.00
Rykodisc	0218	Little Drummer Boy	CDJ	U.S.	1993	$7.00
		Miracle Goodnight	CDJ	U.S.		$25.00
EMI	31352	Never Let Me Down	CDJ	U.S.	1987	$15.00
Warner Brothers	WPDP-6306	Real Cool World	CD3	Japan	1992	$13.00/$4.00
Warner Brothers	9 40575-2	Real Cool World	CD5	U.S.	1992	$4.00
Warner Brothers	PRO-CD-5600	Real Cool World	CDJ	U.S.	1992	$2.00
Tommy Boy	510	Sound & Vision	CD5	U.S.	1991	$6.00
Rykodisc		Sound & Vision	CD5	U.S.	1994	$6.00
Virgin		Strangers When We Meet	CD5	U.K.	1995	$10.00
		Strangers When We Meet	CDJ	U.K.	1995	$10.00
Virgin	DPRO-11062	Strangers When We Meet	CDJ	U.S.	1995	$3.00
Golden Years	002	Ziggy Stardust	CDJ	U.K.	1994	$15.00
Griffin	382	Ziggy Stardust	CD5	U.S.	1994	$6.00

Bowie, Lester

Full Length

Label	Catalog Number	Title	Type	Country	Year	Longbox Value / Value
Blacksaint	120020-2	Fifth Power	LP	U.S.		$9.00
DIW	821	Great Pretender	LP/BP	U.S.		$14.00/$8.00
DIW	835	My Way	LP/BP	U.S.		$14.00/$8.00
DIW	834	Serious Fun	LP/BP	U.S.		$14.00/$8.00
Atlantic	90650-2	Twilight Dreams	LP/LB	U.S.		$14.00/$8.00

Bowlfish

Singles

Label	Catalog Number	Title	Type	Country	Year	Longbox Value / Value
Roughneck	HYPE-20CD	Mrs. Frank	CD5	U.K.	1993	$8.00

Bowra, Tania

Singles

Label	Catalog Number	Title	Type	Country	Year	Longbox Value / Value
ABC	876 903	No Proposition	CD5	Australia	1989	$8.00

Box

Singles

Label	Catalog Number	Title	Type	Country	Year	Longbox Value / Value
Capitol	DPRO-79353	Temptation	CDJ	U.S.	1989	$3.00

Box The Walls

Full Length

Label	Catalog Number	Title	Type	Country	Year	Longbox Value / Value
	77722PRO	Selections From "Stuff"	DJ/Smplr	U.S.		$6.00

Singles

Label	Catalog Number	Title	Type	Country	Year	Longbox Value / Value
		Like Roses	CDJ	U.S.		$2.00

Box Tops

Singles

Label	Catalog Number	Title	Type	Country	Year	Longbox Value / Value
Arista	162071	Letter, The	CD3	Germany	1989	$8.00
Arista	162071	Letter, The	CD3	U.K.	1989	$8.00
Collectibles	9037	Letter, The	CD5	U.S.	1990	$5.00

Boxcar

Full Length

Label	Catalog Number	Title	Type	Country	Year	Longbox Value / Value
Arista	8610	Vertigo	LP/LB	U.S.		$12.00/$7.00

Singles

Label	Catalog Number	Title	Type	Country	Year	Longbox Value / Value
SPV	9540-3	Freemason	CD3	Germany	1989	$8.00
SPV	662499	Freemason	CD3	U.K.	1989	$8.00
		Gas Stop	CDJ	U.S.		$2.00
Volition	VOLTCD-36	Lolore Remix	CD5	U.K.	1991	$8.00

Boxing Gandhis

Singles

Label	Catalog Number	Title	Type	Country	Year	Longbox Value / Value
Mesa	6147	If You Love Me	CDJ	U.S.		$2.00

Boy Crazy

Singles

Label	Catalog Number	Title	Type	Country	Year	Longbox Value / Value
Polydor	PODP-1073	That's What Love Can Do	CD3	Japan	1993	$13.00/$4.00
Polygram	28403	That's What Love Can Do	CD5	U.S.	1993	$4.00

Boy George (Culture Club)

Full Length

Label	Catalog Number	Title	Type	Country	Year	Longbox Value / Value
Virgin	SA3526	Cheapness And Beauty	DJ/Intvw	France	1994	$100.00
Virgin	VSC-DJ-1490	Devil In Sister George Sampler	DJ/Smplr	U.S.	1994	$12.00
CBS	EK-40345	From Luxury To Heartache	LP/LB	U.S.		$14.00/$8.00
Virgin	PRCD 3557	Generations Of Love	DJ/Smplr	U.S.	1990	$8.00
Virgin	CDV-2546	Tense Nervous Headache	LP	U.K.		$18.00
Virgin	40913	This Time: The First Four Years	LP/LB	U.S.		$14.00/$8.00

Singles

Label	Catalog Number	Title	Type	Country	Year	Longbox Value / Value
Polydor	PODP-1075	Crying Game, The	CD3	Japan	1992	$13.00/$4.00
Spaghetti	CIOCD-6	Crying Game, The	CD5	U.K.	1992	$8.00
Capitol	DPRO-04708	Crying Game, The	CDJ	U.S.	1992	$2.00
SBK	19785	Crying Game, The	CD5	U.S.	1993	$5.00
Capitol	DPRO-04732	Crying Game, The	CDJ	U.S.	1993	$2.00
Capital	58089	Everything I Own	CD5	U.S.	1994	$5.00
Virgin	665 483	Do You Really Want To Hurt Me	CD5	U.S.	1991	$20.00
Virgin	661785	Don't Cry	CD5	Germany		$8.00
Virgin	VJD-12031	Don't Cry	CD3	Japan		$13.00/$4.00
Virgin	BOY 108CD	Don't Take My Mind On A Trip	CD3	U.K.	1989	$8.00
Virgin	662092	Don't Take My Mind On A Trip	CD5	U.K.	1989	$8.00
Virgin	PR 2468	Don't Take My Mind On A Trip	CDJ	U.S.	1989	$3.00
SBK	91596	Everything I Own	CDJ	U.S.	1993	$2.00
Virgin	38505	Funtime	CD5	U.S.	1995	$5.00
Virgin	SPRO-12815	Funtime	CDJ	U.S.	1995	$3.00
Virgin		Future	CDJ	U.K.		$10.00
Virgin		I Adore	CD5	U.K.	1995	$8.00
Virgin		I Adore	CD5	U.K.	1995	$8.00
Second version.						
Virgin		I Adore	CDJ	U.K.	1995	$10.00
Virgin	PR 2139	Live My Life	CDJ	U.S.	1987	$7.00
Virgin	661550	No Clause	CD5	Germany	1988	$8.00
Virgin	VJD-12020	No Clause	CD3	Japan	1988	$13.00/$4.00
Virgin	BOYCD 106	No Clause	CD5	U.K.	1988	$8.00
Virgin	DPRO-12804	Same Thing In Reverse	CDJ	U.S.	1995	$3.00
		These Boots Were Made For Walkin'	CD5	U.K.	1995	$10.00
		These Boots Were Made For Walkin'	CD5	U.K.	1995	$10.00
Second version.						
Virgin	CDEP 9	To Be Reborn	CD5	U.K.		$8.00
Virgin	Boy G	Whisper	CDJ	U.S.	1989	$2.00

Boy Howdy

Full Length

Label	Catalog Number	Title	Type	Country	Year	Longbox Value / Value
Curb		Born That Way	DJ/Intvw	U.S.	1995	$25.00
		Live At the Crazy Horse	RS	U.S.	1994	$40.00
Airdate: 8/15/94.						

Singles

Label	Catalog Number	Title	Type	Country	Year	Longbox Value / Value
Curb	1098	True To His Word	CDJ	U.S.	1994	$3.00

Boy Krazy

Singles

Label	Catalog Number	Title	Type	Country	Year	Longbox Value / Value
London	4228570252	That's What Love Can Do	CD5	Canada	1994	$8.00

Boy Meets Girl

Singles

Label	Catalog Number	Title	Type	Country	Year	Longbox Value / Value
RCA	R10D-116	Bring Down the Moon	CD3	Japan	1988	$12.00/$3.00
RCA	PD-49493	Bring Down the Moon	CD3	U.K.	1988	$7.00
RCA	8807-2-RDJ	Bring Down the Moon	CDJ	U.S.	1988	$2.00
RCA	PD-49398	Stormy Love	CD5	Germany	1989	$7.00
RCA	PD-49398	Stormy Love	CD5	U.K.	1989	$7.00
RCA	PD-49520	Waiting For A Star To Fall	CD5	Germany	1989	$7.00
RCA	R10D-108	Waiting For A Star To Fall	CD3	Japan	1988	$12.00/$3.00
RCA	PD-49520	Waiting For A Star To Fall	CD5	U.K.	1989	$7.00
		Waiting For A Star To Fall	CDJ	U.S.	1989	$2.00

Boy On A Dolphin

Singles

Label	Catalog Number	Title	Type	Country	Year	Longbox Value / Value
Modern	PRCD 5122-2	Nouwe O N'Mazei	CDJ	U.S.		$2.00

Boy Toy

Singles

Label	Catalog Number	Title	Type	Country	Year	Longbox Value / Value
SPV	8198	Touch My Body	CD5	Germany	1989	$7.00
Kaos	KAOS-014CD	Touch My Body	CD5	U.K.	1989	$7.00

Boys

Full Length

Label	Catalog Number	Title	Type	Country	Year	Longbox Value / Value
Pioneer	PA-89-249	Video Message	LD	U.S.	1990	$10.00

Singles

Label	Catalog Number	Title	Type	Country	Year	Longbox Value / Value
Motown	BVDM-3	Crazy	CD3	Japan	1990	$12.00/$3.00
Motown	ZD-44038	Crazy	CD5	U.K.	1990	$8.00
		Crazy	CDJ	U.S.	1990	$2.00
Motown	ZD-42246	Dial My Heart	CD5	Germany	1990	$8.00
Motown	R10M-102	Dial My Heart	CD3	Japan	1990	$12.00/$3.00
Motown	ZD-42246	Dial My Heart	CD5	U.K.	1990	$7.00
Motown	3746310592	Doin' It With the B	CDJ	U.S.	1992	$2.00
Motown	CD45 1308	I Had A Dream	CDJ	U.S.	1991	$2.00
Motown	ZD-42862	Little Romance	CD5	Germany	1989	$8.00
Motown	R10M-104	Lucky Charm	CD3	Japan	1989	$13.00/$3.00
Motown	3746310232	Saga Continues, The	CDJ	U.S.	1992	$2.00
		Thing Called Love	CDJ	U.S.	1990	$2.00

Boys Choir Of Harlem

Singles

Company	Disk Number	Title	Type	Country	Year	Longbox Value / Value
Atlantic	98216-2	Overjoyed	CD5	U.S.	1994	$5.00
Eastwest	PRCD 5865-2	Overjoyed	CDJ	U.S.	1994	$6.00

Boys Club

Full Length

Company	Disk Number	Title	Type	Country	Year	Longbox Value / Value
MCA	42242	Boys Club	LP/LB	U.S.		$12.00/$7.00

Singles

Company	Disk Number	Title	Type	Country	Year	Longbox Value / Value
Pioneer	10P3-6093	I Remember Holding You	CD3	Japan	1989	$12.00/$3.00
MCA	DMCA-1316	I Remember Holding You	CD5	U.K.	1989	$7.00
MCA		I Remember Holding You	CDJ	U.S.	1989	$2.00

Boys Don't Cry

Full Length

Company	Disk Number	Title	Type	Country	Year	Longbox Value / Value
Intercord	845-095	Boys Don't Cry	LP	U.K.		$15.00
BAtlantic	81795-2	Boys Don't Cry	LP/LB	U.S.		$14.00/$8.00

Singles

Company	Disk Number	Title	Type	Country	Year	Longbox Value / Value
ZYX	PE-90103-8	We Got the Magic	CD5	Germany	1991	$6.00
Legacy		We Got the Magic	CDJ	U.S.	1991	$2.00

Boys From Brazil

Singles

Company	Disk Number	Title	Type	Country	Year	Longbox Value / Value
BMG	661983	Getting Hard	CD5	Germany	1989	$7.00

Boys Town Gang

Full Length

Company	Disk Number	Title	Type	Country	Year	Longbox Value / Value
Victor	VDP-102	Cast Of Thousands	LP	Japan		$15.00
Victor	VDP-101	Disc Charge	LP	Japan		$15.00

Boys Voice

Singles

Company	Disk Number	Title	Type	Country	Year	Longbox Value / Value
EMI	147508-2	City Of Your Dreams	CD5	Germany	1990	$7.00
EMI	147530-2	Love Stealer	CD5	Germany	1990	$7.00

Boys Wonder

Singles

Company	Disk Number	Title	Type	Country	Year	Longbox Value / Value
SPV	8690-5	Eat Me Drink Me	CD5	Germany	1990	$7.00

Boytronic

Full Length

Company	Disk Number	Title	Type	Country	Year	Longbox Value / Value
Polygram	824317-2	Continental	LP	Germany		$18.00

Singles

Company	Disk Number	Title	Type	Country	Year	Longbox Value / Value
BCM	20105	Bryllyant You	CD5	Germany	1989	$7.00
BCM	BC50-2132-44	Bryllyant You	CD5	U.K.	1989	$7.00
Polygram	887573-2	Don't Let Me Down	CD5	Germany	1988	$7.00
Polygram	868759-2	Hold On	CD5	Germany	1988	$7.00

Boyz II Men

Singles

Company	Disk Number	Title	Type	Country	Year	Longbox Value / Value
Mowton	LARPRO500	Al Final Del Camino	CDJ	U.S.	1993	$6.00
Motown	PODT-1010	End Of the Road	CD3	Japan	1992	$13.00/$4.00
Motown	TMGCD-1411	End Of the Road	CD5	U.K.	1992	$9.00
Motown	3746313822	I Remember	CDJ	U.S.	1995	$6.00
Motown	4859	I'll Make Love To You	CD5	U.S.	1994	$6.00
Motown	374631216-2	I'll Make Love To You	CDJ	U.S.	1995	$6.00
Motown	PODT-1013	In the Still Of the Night	CD3	Japan	1993	$13.00/$4.00
Motown	TMGCD-1415	In the Still Of the Night	CD5	U.K.	1993	$9.00
Motown	BVDM-16	It's So Hard To Say Goodbye To You	CD3	Japan	1991	$13.00/$4.00
Motown	PODT-1015	It's So Hard To Say Goodbye To You	CD5	Japan	1991	$16.00
Motown	CD45 1641	It's So Hard To Say Goodbye To You	CDJ	U.S.	1991	$2.00
Motown	374634844	Let It Snow	CD5	U.S.	1993	$5.00
Motown	374631129	Let It Snow	CDJ	U.S.	1993	$2.00
Motown	ZD-44438	Motown Philly	CD5	Germany	1991	$10.00
Motown	TMGCD-1402	Motown Philly	CD5	U.K.	1991	$10.00
Motown	ZD-45080	Motown Philly	CD5	U.K.	1991	$10.00
Motown	4779	Motown Philly	CD5	U.S.	1991	$5.00
Motown	CD45 1336	Motown Philly	CDJ	U.S.	1991	$2.00
Motown	90023	Motown Philly	CDJ	U.S.	1991	$2.00
Motown	860245	On Bended Knee	CD5	U.S.	1994	$5.00
Motown	PODT-1005	Please Don't Go	CD3	Japan	1992	$13.00/$4.00
Motown	3746348232	Sympin	CD5	U.S.	1992	$5.00
Motown	3746310552	Sympin	CDJ	U.S.	1992	$2.00
Motown	860275	Thank You	CD5	U.S.	1994	$5.00
Motown	374631270-2	Thank You	CDJ	U.S.	1995	$6.00
Motown	CD45 1006	Uhh Ahh	CDJ	U.S.	1991	$2.00
Motown	860407	Vibin'	CD5	U.S.	1995	$6.00
Motown	3746312772	Vibin'	CDJ	U.S.	1995	$6.00
Motown	374631316-2	Water Runs Dry	CDJ	U.S.	1995	$6.00

Boyz Of Paradise

Singles

Company	Disk Number	Title	Type	Country	Year	Longbox Value / Value
		Runaround, The	CDJ	U.S.		$2.00
	DPRO-50899	Shining Star	CDJ	U.S.		$2.00

Brackeen, Joanne

Full Length

Company	Disk Number	Title	Type	Country	Year	Longbox Value / Value
Concord	CCD-4280	Havin' Fun	LP	U.S.		$8.00
Aris	880110	Special Identity	LP	Germany		$13.00
Polystar	J33D-20005	Special Identity	LP	Japan		$13.00

Brad

Singles

Company	Disk Number	Title	Type	Country	Year	Longbox Value / Value
Epic	659248	20th Century	CD5	U.K.	1993	$10.00

Bradford

Full Length

Company	Disk Number	Title	Type	Country	Year	Longbox Value / Value
Warner Brothers	9 26222	Shouting Quietly	LP/LB	U.S.		$12.00/$7.00

Singles

Company	Disk Number	Title	Type	Country	Year	Longbox Value / Value
Foundation	TFL-4CD	Adrift Again	CD5	U.K.	1989	$8.00
Foundation	TFL-001CD	In Liverpool	CD5	U.K.	1989	$8.00
Village	VILSD-101	Skin Storm	CD5	U.K.	1988	$8.00

Bradshaw, Tiny

Full Length

Company	Disk Number	Title	Type	Country	Year	Longbox Value / Value
Charly	CD-43	Breaking Up the House	LP	U.S.		$8.00

Brady, Paul

Singles

Company	Disk Number	Title	Type	Country	Year	Longbox Value / Value
Fontana	PBCD-3	Blue World	CD5	U.K.	1991	$8.00
Fontana	PBCD 4	Crazy Dreams	CD5	U.K.	1992	$8.00
Mercury	888464-2	Eat the Peach	CD5	U.K.	1987	$9.00
Fontana	PBCD-1	Nobody Knows	CD5	U.K.	1991	$8.00
Fontana	PBCD-12	Soul Child	CD5	U.K.	1991	$8.00
Fontana	CDP 422	Soul Child	CDJ	U.S.	1991	$2.00
Fontana	CDP 425	Soul Child	CDJ	U.S.	1991	$2.00

Bragg, Billy

Full Length

Label	Catalog Number	Title	Type	Country	Year	Longbox Value/Value
Polygram		Accident Waiting To Happen	LTD/LP	Canada	1992	$30.00

2 CD set.

Label	Catalog Number	Title	Type	Country	Year	Longbox Value/Value
	PRCD 9270	Billy Bragg & the Red Stars	DJ/Smplr	U.S.	1993	$45.00
		Live	DJ/Smplr	Canada	1991	$20.00
		Live In Canada	DJ/Smplr	Australia	1991	$20.00
		Still Looking For A New England	DJ/Smplr	U.S.	1996	$22.00

2 CD set.

Singles

Label	Catalog Number	Title	Type	Country	Year	Longbox Value/Value
		Accident Waiting To Happen	CD5	Australia	1992	$8.00
Go! Disc	GOLCD-67	Accident Waiting To Happen	CD5	U.K.	1992	$8.00
Elektra	PRCD 8413-2	Accident Waiting To Happen	CDJ	U.S.	1992	$2.00
Elektra	PRCD 8510-2	Accident Waiting To Happen	CDJ	U.S.	1992	$7.00
Polygram	843664-2	Internationale	CD5	Canada	1991	$7.00
Line	LICD-9 00966	Levi Tubb's Tears	CD5	Germany	1990	$8.00
St. Fruit	SFPSCD-027	Peel Sessions	CD5	U.K.	1988	$8.00
Go Disc	8676652	Sexuality	CD5	Canada	1992	$8.00
Polygram	869437-2	Sexuality	CD5	Germany	1991	$8.00
Elektra	PRCD 8143-2	Sexuality	CDJ	U.S.	1991	$3.00
Go! Disc	869523-2	You Woke Up My Neighborhood	CD5	Germany	1991	$8.00
Go! Disc	GODCD-60	You Woke Up My Neighborhood	CD5	U.K.	1991	$8.00
Elektra	PRCD 8462-2	You Woke Up My Neighborhood	CDJ	U.S.	1991	$3.00

Brain

Singles

Label	Catalog Number	Title	Type	Country	Year	Longbox Value/Value
ZYX	DST-1055-8	Givin' It All	CD5	Germany	1991	$6.00

Brain Child

Singles

Label	Catalog Number	Title	Type	Country	Year	Longbox Value/Value
Feildworks	FWCR-48	Brain Child	CD3	Japan	1992	$13.00/$4.00

Brain Drive

Singles

Label	Catalog Number	Title	Type	Country	Year	Longbox Value/Value
Invitation	VICL-12008	Beauty Blood Monsters	CD5	Japan	1993	$12.00
Xeo	VICL-15020	Realize	CD5	Japan	1993	$12.00

Braithwaite, Daryl

Singles

Label	Catalog Number	Title	Type	Country	Year	Longbox Value/Value
Epic	653029-2	All I Do	CD5	U.K.	1989	$8.00
BEpic	652941-2	As the Days Go By	CD5	U.K.	1989	$8.00
BEpic	658854-2	As the Days Go By	CD5	U.K.	1992	$8.00
BCBS	CSK 1658	As the Days Go By	CDJ	U.S.	1989	$2.00
BCBS	656818-5	Higher Than Hope	CD5	Germany	1991	$8.00
BEpic	658199-2	Higher Than Hope	CD5	U.K.	1992	$8.00
BCBS	654545-5	One Summer	CD3	Germany	1991	$8.00

Bramhall, Doyle

Singles

Label	Catalog Number	Title	Type	Country	Year	Longbox Value/Value
Antones	0027	Change It	CDJ	U.S.	1994	$2.00

Brand, Dollar

Full Length

Label	Catalog Number	Title	Type	Country	Year	Longbox Value/Value
Enja	311210	African Dawn	LP	U.S.†	1984	$15.00/$8.00
Denon	CD-7261	Anthems For the New Nation	LP	U.S.†	1985	$15.00/$8.00
Enja	307902	Live At Montreux	LP	U.S.†	1985	$15.00/$8.00
Enja	311224	Zimbabwe	LP	U.S.†	1984	$15.00/$8.00

Brand New Heavies

Full Length

Label	Catalog Number	Title	Type	Country	Year	Longbox Value/Value
Delicious Vinyl		Brand New Heavies	LP/LB	U.S.		$12.00/$10.00

Singles

Label	Catalog Number	Title	Type	Country	Year	Longbox Value/Value
		Back To Love	CD5	U.K.		$10.00
		Back To Love	CD5	U.K.		$10.00

Second version.

Label	Catalog Number	Title	Type	Country	Year	Longbox Value/Value
Delicious Vinyl	4892	Bonafide Funk	CDJ	U.S.	1992	$2.00
Delicious Vinyl	PRCD 5684-2	Brother Sister	CDJ	U.S.	1994	$2.00
Delicious Vinyl	PRCD 5684	Brother Sister	CDJ	U.S.	1994	$7.00
AcidJazz	BNHCD-1	Don't Let It Go To Your Head	CD5	U.K.	1992	$8.00
AcidJazz	JAZIDCD-25	Dream Come True	CD5	U.K.	1990	$8.00
AcidJazz	FCD-180	Dream Come True	CD5	U.K.	1990	$8.00
Big Beat	10054	Dream Come True	CD5	U.S.	1990	$4.00
Big Beat		Dream Come True	CDJ	U.S.	1990	$2.00
Delicious Vinyl	10054	Dream Come True	CD5	U.S.	1991	$4.00
Delicious Vinyl	869021	Dream On Dreamer	CD5	U.K.	1994	$10.00
Atlantic	95952	Dream On Dreamer	CD5	U.S.	1994	$5.00
Delicious Vinyl	5454	Dream On Dreamer	CDJ	U.S.	1994	$3.00
Delicious Vinyl	4744	Heavy Rhyme Experience	CDJ	U.S.	1992	$2.00
		Midnight At The Oasis	CD5	U.K.		$10.00

Second version.

Label	Catalog Number	Title	Type	Country	Year	Longbox Value/Value
		Midnight At the Oasis	CD5	U.K.	1994	$10.00
Capitol	58491	Mind Trips	CD5	U.S.	1995	$5.00
Delicious Vinyl	10262	Mind Trips	CDJ	U.S.	1995	$6.00
Polygram	869553-2	Never Stop	CD5	Germany	1991	$8.00
Delicious Vinyl	6673	Never Stop	CDJ	U.S.	1991	$2.00
	PRCD 5909	Spend Some Time	CDJ	U.S.	1995	$3.00
AcidJazz	BNHCD-2	Stay This Way	CD5	U.K.	1992	$8.00
AcidJazz	FCD-185	Ultimate Trunk Funk	CD5	U.K.	1992	$8.00

Brand Nubians

Singles

Label	Catalog Number	Title	Type	Country	Year	Longbox Value/Value
Elektra	PRCD 8748-2	Allah U Akbar	CDJ	U.S.	1993	$2.00
Elektra/Asylum	66168	Hold On	CD5	U.S.	1994	$5.00
Elektra	PRCD 8713-2	Love Me Or Leave Me Alone	CDJ	U.S.	1993	$2.00
Elektra	PRCD 8754-2	Love Me Or Leave Me Alone	CDJ	U.S.	1993	$2.00
Elektra	PRCD 8754-2	Punks Jump Up To Get Beat Down	CDJ	U.S.	1993	$2.00
Elektra	PRCD 8658-2	Punks Jump Up To Get Beat Down	CDJ	U.S.	1993	$2.00
Elektra	PR 8313-2	Slow Down	CDJ	U.S.	1990	$2.00
Elektra		Wake Up	CDJ	U.S.		$2.00
Elektra	PRCD 9046-2	Word Is Bond	CDJ	U.S.	1994	$2.00

Brand, Oscar

Full Length

Label	Catalog Number	Title	Type	Country	Year	Longbox Value/Value
	Z-6534	One Hundred Proof Drinking	LP/BP	U.S.	1985	$14.00/$8.00

Brand X

Full Length

Label	Catalog Number	Title	Type	Country	Year	Longbox Value/Value
		Live At the Roxy L.A.	LTD/LP	U.K.	1995	$20.00
Passport	PBCD-9619	Unorthodox Behavior	LP	U.K.		$15.00
Passport	PBCD-9619	Unorthodox Behavior	LP/LB	U.S.		$16.00/$10.00
Passport	PBCD-9054	Xtrax	LP/LB	U.S.		$16.00/$10.00

Brandon

Singles

Label	Catalog Number	Title	Type	Country	Year	Longbox Value/Value
Alpha	79527	Destiny	CDJ	U.S.	1991	$2.00

Brandy

Singles

Label	Catalog Number	Title	Type	Country	Year	Longbox Value/Value
Atlantic	PRCD 6049-2	Baby	CDJ	U.S.	1995	$6.00
Atlantic	85593	Baby (I Wanna Be Down)	CD5	U.S.	1994	$5.00
Atlantic	85577	Best Friend	CD5	U.S.	1995	$5.00
Atlantic	PRCD 6191-2	Best Friend	CDJ	U.S.	1995	$6.00
Atlantic	85551-2	Brokenhearted	CD5	U.S.	1995	$5.00
Atlantic	PRCD 6375-2	Brokenhearted	CDJ	U.S.	1995	$6.00
Atlantic	85640	I Wanna Be Down	CD5	U.S.	1994	$5.00
Atlantic	PRCD 5745-2	I Wanna Be Down	CDJ	U.S.	1995	$6.00
		Sittin' Up In My Room	CD5	U.K.		$10.00
		Sittin' Up In My Room	CD5	U.K.		$10.00

Second version.

Label	Catalog Number	Title	Type	Country	Year	Longbox Value/Value
Arista	ASCD2972	Sittin' Up In My Room	CDJ	U.S.	1995	$2.00

Branigan, Laura

Full Length

Label	Catalog Number	Title	Type	Country	Year	Longbox Value/Value
Atlantic	19289-2	Branigan	LP/LB	U.S.†	1984	$14.00/$8.00
Atlantic	80052-2	Branigan 2	LP/LB	U.S.†	1984	$14.00/$8.00
Atlantic		Hits, The	DJ/Smplr	U.K.		$10.00
Atlantic	81265-2	Hold Me	LP/LB	U.S.†	1985	$14.00/$8.00
Atlantic	81265-2	Hold Me	LP/LB	U.S.	1987	$14.00/$8.00
Pioneer	PA-85-101	Laura Branigan	LD	U.S.	1985	$30.00
Atlantic	80147-2	Self Control	LP/LB	U.S.†	1985	$14.00/$8.00

Singles

Label	Catalog Number	Title	Type	Country	Year	Longbox Value/Value
Atlantic		Come Into My Life	CDJ	U.S.		$2.00
Atlantic	PRCD 5155-2	Didn't We Almost Win It All	CDJ	U.S.	1993	$2.00
		Dim All the Lights	CDJ	U.S.	1995	$3.00
Atlantic	87005	It's Been Hard Enough Getting Over You	CD5	U.S.	1994	$5.00
Atlantic	PRCD 5333-2	It's Been Hard Enough Getting Over You	CDJ	U.S.	1993	$2.00
Atlantic	PRCD 5453-2	It's Been Hard Enough Getting Over You	CDJ	U.S.	1993	$2.00
Atlantic	786182-2	Moonlight On the Water	CD5	Germany	[illegible]	[illegible]
Atlantic	AMDY-5010	Moonlight On the Water	CD3	Japan	1990	$12.00/$3.00
Atlantic	A-7969CD	Moonlight On the Water	CD5	U.K.	1990	$8.00
Atlantic	PRCD 3302-2	Moonlight On the Water	CDJ	U.S.	1990	$2.00
Atlantic	PRCD 3205-2	Moonlight On the Water	CDJ	U.S.	1990	$2.00
Atlantic	PRCD 3355-2	Never In A Million Years	CDJ	U.S.	1990	$2.00
Atlantic	AMDY-5049	Tokio	CD3	Japan	1991	$12.00/$3.00

Brannen, John

Singles

Label	Catalog Number	Title	Type	Country	Year	Longbox Value/Value
Apache	79253	Desolation Angel	CDJ	U.S.	1988	$2.00
Mercury	CDP 1038	Lonesome Side Of Midnight	CDJ	U.S.	1993	$2.00
		Primitive Emotion	CDJ	U.S.		$2.00

Brasa Braza

Singles

Label	Catalog Number	Title	Type	Country	Year	Longbox Value/Value
ZYX	553499-2	Rio Fever	CD5	Germany	1990	$8.00

Brat Pack

Full Length

Label	Catalog Number	Title	Type	Country	Year	Longbox Value/Value
A&M	5296	Brat Pack	LP/LB	U.S.		$12.00/$7.00

Singles

Label	Catalog Number	Title	Type	Country	Year	Longbox Value/Value
A&M	USACD-695	I'm Never Gonna Give You Up	CD5	U.K.	1990	$8.00
A&M		I'm Never Gonna Give You Up	CDJ	U.S.	1989	$2.00
A&M	USACD-6950	You're the Only Woman	CD5	U.K.	1990	$8.00
A&M	CD 17877	You're the Only Woman	CDJ	U.S.	1989	$2.00

Braveros De Pen

Singles

Label	Catalog Number	Title	Type	Country	Year	Longbox Value/Value
Joey International	3375	El Perro	CD5	U.S.	1994	$5.00

Bravo, Jonny

Full Length

Label	Catalog Number	Title	Type	Country	Year	Longbox Value/Value
Arista	ARCD 8820	Then Again, Maybe I Won't	DJ/LP	U.S.	1995	$9.00

Singles

Label	Catalog Number	Title	Type	Country	Year	Longbox Value/Value
Arista	ARCD 2999	Used To Be Cool	CDJ	U.S.	1995	$2.00

Braxton, Toni

Full Length

Label	Catalog Number	Title	Type	Country	Year	Longbox Value/Value
Laface	73008 26020-2	Secrets	LTD/LP	U.S.	1996	$17.00

CD album plus bonus interview CD. Available exclusively at Best Buy.

Singles

Label	Catalog Number	Title	Type	Country	Year	Longbox Value/Value
		Another Sad Song	CD5	U.K.	1993	$10.00
		Another Sad Song	CD5	U.K.	1993	$10.00

Second version.

Label	Catalog Number	Title	Type	Country	Year	Longbox Value/Value
Laface	24049	Another Sad Song	CD5	U.S.	1993	$5.00
Laface	24056	Breathe Again	CD5	U.S.	1994	$5.00
Arista	24056	Breathe Again	CD5	U.S.	1994	$5.00
Arista	24089	How Many Ways	CD5	U.S.	1994	$5.00
Laface	4081	How Many Ways	CDJ	U.S.	1995	$6.00
Laface	4083	I Belong To You	CDJ	U.S.	1995	$6.00
Laface	24041	Love Shoulda Brought You Home	CD5	U.S.	1993	$5.00
Laface	4835	Love Shoulda Brought You Home	CDJ	U.S.	1993	$2.00
		Seven Whole Days	CDJ	U.S.		$6.00
LaFace	24200-2	Unbreak My Heart	CD5	U.S.	1997	$3.50
LaFace	24207-2	Unbreak My Heart	CD5	U.S.	1997	$5.50
Laface	24065	You Mean The World To Me	CD5	U.S.	1994	$5.00
Laface	4064	You Mean the World To Me Home	CDJ	U.S.	1993	$2.00
LaFace	24161-2	You're Making Me High	CD5	U.S.	1996	$5.00

Brazil

Singles

Label	Catalog Number	Title	Type	Country	Year	Longbox Value/Value
Dune	92DD-105	Away	CD5	U.K.	1992	$8.00

Bread

Full Length

Label	Catalog Number	Title	Type	Country	Year	Longbox Value/Value
WEA	960414-2	Anthology	LP	Germany		$15.00

Singles

Label	Catalog Number	Title	Type	Country	Year	Longbox Value/Value
WEA	969343-2	Everything I Own	CD3	Germany	1989	$9.00
WEA	969343-2	Everything I Own	CD3	U.K.	1989	$9.00

Breakdown

Singles

Label	Catalog Number	Title	Type	Country	Year	Longbox Value/Value
Scotti Brothers	78026	Dip Baby Dip	CD5	U.S.	1994	$5.00

Breakfast Club

Full Length

Label	Catalog Number	Title	Type	Country	Year	Longbox Value/Value
MCA		Breakfast Club	DJ/LP	U.S.		$9.00
MCA	MCAD-5821	Breakfast Club	LP/LB	U.S.		$12.00/$7.00

Breathe

Full Length

Label	Catalog Number	Title	Type	Country	Year	Longbox Value/Value
A&M	5320	Peace Of Mind	LP/LB	U.S.		$15.00/$9.00

Singles

Label	Catalog Number	Title	Type	Country	Year	Longbox Value/Value
A&M	CD 17746	All This I Should Have Known	CDJ	U.S.	1988	$3.00
Siren	SRNCD-134	Does She Love That Man	CD5	U.K.	1991	$10.00

Label	Catalog Number	Title	Type	Country	Year	Longbox Value / Value
A&M	75021 7437-2	Does She Love That Man	CDJ	U.S.	1990	$3.00
BMG	16209-3	Don't Tell Me Lies	CD3	Germany	1988	$10.00
BMG	66209-3	Don't Tell Me Lies	CD5	Germany	1988	$10.00
Siren	SRNCD-109	Don't Tell Me Lies	CD3	U.K.	1988	$10.00
A&M		Don't Tell Me Lies	CDJ	U.S.	1988	$3.00
BMG	654687-3	Hands To Heaven	CD3	Germany	1988	$10.00
Siren	SRNCD-68	Hands To Heaven	CD5	U.K.	1988	$10.00
Virgin	161848	How Can I Fall?	CD3	Germany	1988	$10.00
Virgin	VJD 12029	How Can I Fall?	CD3	Japan	1987	$13.00/$4.00
A&M	CD 17590	How Can I Fall?	CDJ	U.S.	1987	$3.00
Siren	SRNCD-95	Jonah	CD5	U.K.	1988	$10.00
Siren	VJDP-133	Say A Prayer	CD3	Japan	1990	$13.00/$4.00
A&M	75021 8108 2	Say A Prayer	CDJ	U.S.	1990	$3.00
BMG	663569	Say Hello	CD5	Germany	1990	$10.00
Siren	SRNCD-131	Say Hello	CD5	U.K.	1990	$10.00
A&M	75021 7517-2	Without Your Love	CDJ	U.S.	1991	$3.00

Breathless

Singles

Label	Catalog Number	Title	Type	Country	Year	Longbox Value / Value
Tenor Vossa	BREATH CD12	Don't Just Disappear	CD5	U.K.	1993	$10.00
Pinnacle	BREATHCD-11	Over & Over	CD5	U.K.	1991	$8.00

Brecker Brothers

Singles

Label	Catalog Number	Title	Type	Country	Year	Longbox Value / Value
GRP	5158	African Skies	CDJ	U.S.	1994	$2.00
MCA	MCSTD-1720	Big Idea	CD5	U.K.	1992	$8.00
GRP	9993	Big Idea	CDJ	U.S.	1992	$2.00

Brecker, Michael

Full Length

Label	Catalog Number	Title	Type	Country	Year	Longbox Value / Value
MCA	MVCM-137	Don't Try This At Home	LP	Japan		$20.00
MCA	MVCM-138	Michael Brecker	LP	Japan		$20.00

Singles

Label	Catalog Number	Title	Type	Country	Year	Longbox Value / Value
Impulse	17730	Suspone	CDJ	U.S.	1988	$2.00

Brecker, Randy

Full Length

Label	Catalog Number	Title	Type	Country	Year	Longbox Value / Value
Passport	PJCD-88013	Amanda	LP	U.K.		$15.00
Passport	PJCD-88013	Amanda	LP/LB	U.S.		$16.00/$10.00

Breeders

Full Length

Label	Catalog Number	Title	Type	Country	Year	Longbox Value / Value
Westwood One		In Concert-Nu Rock	RS	U.S.	1995	$50.00
	Airdate: 1/30/95.					
Westwood One		In Concert-Nu Rock	RS	U.S.	1995	$50.00
	Airdate: 8/14/95.					
Elektra	PRCD 8934-2	Secret History Of	DJ/Intvw	U.S.	1994	$15.00

Singles

Label	Catalog Number	Title	Type	Country	Year	Longbox Value / Value
4AD	4228626892	Cannonball	CD5	Canada	1993	$8.00
Polydor	769743008	Cannonball	CD5	Canada	1994	$23.00
Elektra	66279	Cannonball	CD5	U.S.	1993	$5.00
Elektra	PRCD 8800-2	Cannonball	CDJ	U.S.	1993	$6.00
Elektra/Asylum	66279	Cannonball	CD5	U.S.	1994	$5.00
4AD	BAD3017CD	Divine Hammer	CD5	Canada	1994	$8.00
Elektra	PRCD 8861-2	Divine Hammer	CDJ	U.S.	1993	$6.00
4AD	8666132	Safari	CD5	Canada	1992	$8.00
4AD	120 1318 3	Safari	CD5	Germany	1992	$8.00
4AD	BAD-2003CD	Safari	CD5	U.K.	1992	$8.00
Elektra	66432-2	Safari	CD5	U.S.	1992	$5.00
		Saints	CD5	U.K.	1994	$10.00
Elektra	PRCD 8934	Saints	CDJ	U.S.	1994	$2.00
Elektra	PRCD 8932-2	Saints	CDJ	U.S.	1995	$6.00

Brenda K.

Singles

Label	Catalog Number	Title	Type	Country	Year	Longbox Value / Value
ZYX	553497-2	Fright Night	CD5	Germany	1990	$6.00

Brennan, Marie

Singles

Label	Catalog Number	Title	Type	Country	Year	Longbox Value / Value
RCA	PD-45400	Against the Wind	CD5	U.K.	1992	$7.00
Atlantic	PRCD 5943-2	Big Yellow Taxi	CDJ	U.S.	1991	$7.00
		Big Yellow Taxi	CDJ	U.S.	1995	$3.00

Brewer, Spencer

Singles

Label	Catalog Number	Title	Type	Country	Year	Longbox Value / Value
		Tomorrow's Child	CDJ	U.S.		$2.00

Brewer, Teresa

Full Length

Label	Catalog Number	Title	Type	Country	Year	Longbox Value / Value
Time/Warner Sound Exchange	217778	A Sweet Old-Fashioned Girl	LP	U.S.	1996	$16.00

Brian

Singles

Label	Catalog Number	Title	Type	Country	Year	Longbox Value / Value
Setanta	SET-015CD	Planes	CD5	U.K.	1992	$7.00

Briar

Singles

Label	Catalog Number	Title	Type	Country	Year	Longbox Value / Value
		Frankie	CDJ	U.S.		$2.00

Brick Flower

Singles

Label	Catalog Number	Title	Type	Country	Year	Longbox Value / Value
Canyon	PCCC-00008	Brick Flower	CD5	Japan	1992	$10.00
Canyon	PCDC-00001	Tourists	CD5	Japan	1992	$10.00

Brickell, Edie (And The New Bohemians)

Full Length

Label	Catalog Number	Title	Type	Country	Year	Longbox Value / Value
Geffen	GEF-49CD	What I Am	CD	U.K.	1988	$9.00

Singles

Label	Catalog Number	Title	Type	Country	Year	Longbox Value / Value
MCA	WMD5-4021	A Hard Rain's Gonna Fall	CD3	Japan	1989	$13.00/$4.00
MCA	DMCAT-1397	A Hard Rain's Gonna Fall	CD5	U.K.	1989	$8.00
MCA	CD45 18117	A Hard Rain's Gonna Fall	CDJ	U.S.	1989	$3.00
Geffen	PRO-CD-4175	Black & Blue	CDJ	U.S.	1991	$3.00
Geffen	921207-2	Circle	CD3	Germany	1988	$9.00
Geffen	GEF-51CD	Circle	CD3	U.K.	1988	$9.00
Geffen	PRO-CD-3480	Circle	CDJ	U.S.	1988	$3.00
Geffen	MVCG-13018	Good Times	CD5	Japan	1994	$20.00
DGC		Good Times	CD5	U.K.	1994	$10.00
Geffen	PRO-CD-4661	Good Times	CDJ	U.S.	1994	$3.00
Geffen	GEF-61CD	Love Like We Do	CD3	U.K.	1989	$9.00
Geffen	PRO-CD-3543	Love Like We Do	CDJ	U.S.	1989	$3.00
WEA	7599-21626-2	Mama Help Me	CD5	U.K.	1990	$9.00
Geffen	PRO-CD-4175	Mama Help Me	CDJ	U.S.	1990	$3.00
Geffen	PRO-CD-4667	Tomorrow Comes	CDJ	U.S.	1994	$3.00
Geffen	921153-2	What I Am	CD3	Germany	1988	$9.00
Geffen	10P3-6090	What I Am	CD3	Japan	1988	$12.00/$3.00
Geffen	PRO-CD-3221	What I Am	CDJ	U.S.	1988	$3.00
Geffen	PRO-CD-4697	When the Lights Go Down	CDJ	U.S.	1994	$3.00

Bridewells

Singles

Company	Disk Number	Title	Type	Country	Year	Longbox Value / Value
Expression	EXPEPD-1	Smile	CD5	U.K.	1992	$7.00

Bridge

Singles

Company	Disk Number	Title	Type	Country	Year	Longbox Value / Value
Trattoria	PSCR-1074	Meeting On the Desk	CD3	Japan	1993	$13.00/$4.00
Polydor	PSCR-1065	Windy Afternoon	CD5	Japan	1992	$10.00

Bridge 2 Far

Singles

Company	Disk Number	Title	Type	Country	Year	Longbox Value / Value
WTG	NSK 1940	Heaven On Earth	CDJ	U.S.	1990	$2.00

Bridgewater, Dee Dee

Singles

Company	Disk Number	Title	Type	Country	Year	Longbox Value / Value
Gala	CDGX 1013	Till the Next…Somewhere	CD5	Italy	1989	$12.00
	With Ray Charles.					

Brightman, Sarah

Singles

Company	Disk Number	Title	Type	Country	Year	Longbox Value / Value
Polygram	889542-3	Anything But Lonely	CD3	Germany	1989	$8.00
Polygram	889315-2	Anything But Lonely	CD5	Germany	1989	$8.00
Polygram	RURCD-5	Anything But Lonely	CD5	U.K.	1989	$8.00
A&M	PODM-1012	Captain Nimo	CD3	Japan	1993	$13.00/$4.00
A&M	31458 8114	Captain Nimo	CDJ	U.S.	1993	$2.00
Polydor	CDP 255	Love Changes	CDJ	U.S.	1990	$2.00
Sony	655777-2	Make Believe	CD5	U.K.	1989	$8.00
Polydor	CDP 62	Mr. Monotony	CDJ	U.S.	1989	$2.00
Polydor	P10P-30003	Phantom Of the Opera	CD3	Japan	1988	$13.00/$4.00
A&M	580 307	Second Element	CD5	U.K.	1993	$10.00
Polydor	PZCD-74	Something To Believe In	CD5	U.K.	1990	$2.00

Brik Citi

Singles

Company	Disk Number	Title	Type	Country	Year	Longbox Value / Value
Motown	374631233	Say U Like	CDJ	U.S.	1994	$3.00

Briley, Martin

Full Length

Company	Disk Number	Title	Type	Country	Year	Longbox Value / Value
Pioneer	PA-85-M026	Dangerous Moments	8"LD	U.S.	1985	$10.00
BMercury	822423-2	Dangerous Moments	LP/BP	U.S.	1985	$14.00/$8.00

Brinsley Schwarz

Full Length

Company	Disk Number	Title	Type	Country	Year	Longbox Value / Value
Vivid	VSCD-512	New Favorites	LTD/LP	Japan		$25.00

Brisebois, Danielle

Singles

Company	Disk Number	Title	Type	Country	Year	Longbox Value / Value
Epic	ESK 5905	What If God Fell From the Sky	CDJ	U.S.	1994	$2.00

Britny Fox

Full Length

Company	Disk Number	Title	Type	Country	Year	Longbox Value / Value
Atlantic	91790	Bite Down Hard	LP/LB	U.S.		$12.00/$7.00
Image	ID6959CB	Year Of the Fox	LD	U.S.		$10.00

Singles

Company	Disk Number	Title	Type	Country	Year	Longbox Value / Value
Columbia	CSK 1965	Dream On	CDJ	U.S.	1990	$2.00
Sony	20EP-8015/5	Girlschool	CD3	Japan	1989	$13.00/$4.00
Columbia	653144-2	Girlschool	CD5	U.K.	1988	$8.00
		Girlschool	CDJ	U.S.	1988	$2.00
		Long Way To Love	CDJ	U.S.	1988	$2.00
EastWest	PRCD 4286-2	Louder	CDJ	U.S.	1992	$2.00
EastWest	PRCD 4287-2	Over & Out	CDJ	U.S.	1992	$2.00
Columbia	CSK 1442	Save the Week	CDJ	U.S.	1990	$2.00
Columbia	655499-2	Standing In the Shadows	CD5	U.K.	1990	$8.00

Britton

Singles

Company	Disk Number	Title	Type	Country	Year	Longbox Value / Value
TSR		Hold On	CDJ	U.S.	1988	$2.00

Broadcasters

Singles

Company	Disk Number	Title	Type	Country	Year	Longbox Value / Value
Enigma	EPRO-053	Down In the Trenches	CDJ	U.S.	1987	$2.00

Brockwell, Richard

Singles

Company	Disk Number	Title	Type	Country	Year	Longbox Value / Value
Intercord	825 779	Prayer For Nature	CD5	Germany	1990	$8.00

Brojos

Singles

Company	Disk Number	Title	Type	Country	Year	Longbox Value / Value
Warner Brothers	PRO-CD-4081	Live Like A King	CDJ	U.S.	1990	$2.00
Warner Brothers	PRO-CD-4510	Slow Motion	CDJ	U.S.	1990	$2.00

Broken Bones

Singles

Company	Disk Number	Title	Type	Country	Year	Longbox Value / Value
HMR	HEAVYXD-56	Religion Is Responsible	CD5	U.K.		$8.00

Broken English

Singles

Company	Disk Number	Title	Type	Country	Year	Longbox Value / Value
EMI	CDEM-5	Comin' On Strong	CD5	U.K.	1988	$8.00
EMI	CDEM-69	Do You Really Want Me Back	CD5	U.K.	1988	$8.00
Wild Patch	04688	Hard Core Beats	CDJ	U.S.	1993	$2.00

Broken Glass

Full Length

Company	Disk Number	Title	Type	Country	Year	Longbox Value / Value
Chrysalis	21743	Fast Mean Game	LP/LB	U.S.		$12.00/$7.00

Singles

Company	Disk Number	Title	Type	Country	Year	Longbox Value / Value
Chrysalis	DPRO-23500	Worst Of You Yet	CDJ	U.S.	1990	$2.00

Broken Homes

Full Length

Company	Disk Number	Title	Type	Country	Year	Longbox Value / Value
MCA	MCAD-6384	Wing And A Prayer	LP/LB	U.S.		$14.00/$8.00

Singles

Company	Disk Number	Title	Type	Country	Year	Longbox Value / Value
MCA	CD45 18505	Lock & Key	CDJ	U.S.	1990	$2.00
		Somethin's Gonna Give	CDJ	U.S.		$2.00

Brokop, Lisa

Full Length

Company	Disk Number	Title	Type	Country	Year	Longbox Value / Value
Patriot		Every Little Girl	DJ/LP	U.S.	1995	$18.00
Patriot		Take That	DJ/Smplr	U.S.	1995	$12.00

Singles

Company	Disk Number	Title	Type	Country	Year	Longbox Value / Value
Patriot	79077	One Of Those Nights	CDJ	U.S.	1995	$2.00

Bronco

Singles

Company	Disk Number	Title	Type	Country	Year	Longbox Value / Value
Fonovisa	275	Porque Te Quiero	CDJ	U.S.	1994	$2.00

Label	Catalog Number	Title	Type	Country	Year	Longbox Value / Value
Bronski Beat						
Full Length						
MCA	MCAD-5538	Age Of Consent	LP/LB	U.S.†	1985	$14.00/$8.00
MCA	MCAD-5538	Age Of Consent	LP/LB	U.S.	1988	$14.00/$8.00
		Hundreds & Thousands	LP	Germany		$14.00
MCA	MCAD-5751	Truthdare And Doubledare	LP/LB	U.S.		$14.00/$8.00
MCA	MCAD-5751	Truthdare And Doubledare	LP/LB	U.S.†	1986	$14.00/$8.00
Singles						
BMG	ZD-44100	I'm Gonna Run Away From You	CD5	Germany	1990	$8.00
BMG	ZCD-2	One More Chance	CD5	Germany	1990	$8.00
ZYX	7026-8	Why	CD5	U.S.	1994	$5.00
Bronte Brothers						
Singles						
		Live A Little More	CD5	U.K.		$8.00
		Live A Little More	CD5	U.K.		$8.00
Second version.						
Bronx Male Zystem						
Singles						
SPV	1328-3	Accident - No More	CD5	Germany	1991	$7.00
Bronx Style Bob						
Singles						
Sire	W-0219CD	Forbidden Love	CD5	U.K.	1991	$8.00
Sire	PRO-CD-5361	Forbidden Love	CDJ	U.S.	1991	$2.00
Brood, Herman						
Singles						
Sony	651385-2	Sleeping Bird Cut Me Loose	CD5	Germany	1988	$8.00
Brook, Michael						
Singles						
A&M	709143001	Live At The Aquarium	CD5	Canada	1994	$28.00
Brooke, Jonathan (And The Story)						
Singles						
Blue Thumb	5207	Nothing Sacred	CDJ	U.S.	1995	$2.00
Brooker, Gary						
Full Length						
Mercury	824652-2	Echos In the Night	LP/BP	U.S.		$14.00/$8.00
Brooklyn Funk Essentials						
Singles						
RCA	64298	Creator Has A Master Plan, The	CDJ	U.S.	1995	$6.00
Brooks & Dunn						
Full Length						
		'90s Country	RS	U.S.	1995	$40.00
Airdate: 10/7/95.						
		'90s Country	RS	U.S.	1995	$40.00
Airdate: 4/1/95.						
		'90s Country	RS	U.S.	1995	$40.00
Airdate: 8/19/95.						
Arista	ASCD 2232	Brand New Man	DJ/Intvw	U.S.	1992	$15.00
Singles						
Arista	ASCD-2432	Boot Scootin' Boogie	CDJ	U.S.	1992	$6.00
Arista	ASCD 2460	Lost And Found	CDJ	U.S.	1992	$3.00
		My Maria	CDJ	U.S.		$3.00
Arista	ASCD 2602	She Used To Be Mine	CDJ	U.S.	1993	$3.00
Arista	ASCD 2669	That Ain't No Way To Go	CDJ	U.S.	1994	$3.00
Brooks, Elkie						
Singles						
Legend	CDLM-8	Break the Chain	CD5	U.K.	1986	$8.00
A&M	390348-3	Compact Hits	CD5	Germany	1988	$8.00
A&M	AMCD-913	Compact Hits	CD5	U.K.	1988	$8.00
Brooks, Garth						
Full Length						
Capitol	CDRP243	A New Direction In Music	DJ/Smplr	Australia	1994	$40.00
Capitol		Entertainer Of the Year	DJ/Smplr	U.S.	1995	$25.00
2CD Promo sampler in press kit folder						
Pioneer Artists	PA-92-441	Garth Brooks	LD	U.S.	1992	$25.00
Capitol	S2-17959	Garth Brooks Collection	LP	U.S.	1994	$25.00
		Interview	DJ/Intvw	France	1995	$35.00
Capitol		Last American Hero-Garth Conquers the Earth	DJ/Smplr	Japan	1993	N/A
Liberty	CDPRO 639	Man And His Music, The Record	DJ/Intvw	Canada	1992	$45.00
Capitol		No Fences/Garth Brooks	LTD/LP	Australia	1994	$25.00
Capitol	DPRO-79022	Sampler	DJ/Smplr	U.S.	1993	$20.00
Capitol	DPRO-79070	Zooming CD	DJ/Smplr	U.S.	1995	$30.00
Singles						
Liberty	DPRO-79795	Ain't Going Down	CDJ	U.S.	1993	$6.00
Capitol	CDCL-609	Friends In Low Places	CD5	U.K.	1991	$10.00
Liberty	DPRO-79365	Friends In Low Places (Live)	CDJ	U.S.	1992	$7.00
Capitol	GARTH 1	If Tomorrow Never...	CDJ	U.K.		$15.00
Liberty	DPRO-79540	Old Man's Back In Town, The	CDJ	U.S.	1992	$3.00
Capitol		One Night A Day	CD5	Australia	1993	$10.00
Capitol		Red Strokes	CD5	U.K.	1993	$10.00
Capitol		Red Strokes	CD5	U.K.	1993	$10.00
Second version.						
Capitol	TODP-2361	Shameless	CD3	Japan	1992	$13.00/$4.00
Capitol	CDCL-646	Shameless	CD5	U.K.	1991	$10.00
Capitol		Standing Outside the Fire	CD5	Australia	1994	$12.00
Capitol		Standing Outside the Fire	CD5	U.K.	1994	$10.00
Second version.						
Capitol	CDCLS 712	Standing Outside the Fire	CD5	U.K.	1994	$12.00
Capitol	204506-2	Thunder Rolls	CD5	Germany	1991	$10.00
Liberty	DPRO-79722	Thunder Rolls	CDJ	U.S.	1991	$7.00
Capitol	DPRo-79538	Two Of A Kind	CDJ	U.S.	1991	$3.00
Liberty	DPRO-79382	Unanswered Prayers	CDJ	U.S.	1990	$7.00
Capitol	TODP-2375	We Shall Be Free	CD3	Japan	1992	$13.00/$4.00
Liberty	CDCL-675	We Shall Be Free	CD5	U.K.	1992	$10.00
Liberty	TODP-2410	What She's Doing Now	CD3	Japan	1992	$13.00/$4.00
Liberty	CDCL-656	What She's Doing Now	CD5	U.K.	1992	$10.00
Brooks, Hadda						
Singles						
Classic	11054	La Christmas Blue	CDJ	U.S.	1995	$2.00
Brooks, Karen And Randy Sharp						
Singles						
Mercury	CDP 667	Baby I'm the One	CDJ	U.S.	1992	$2.00
Mercury	CDP 790	That's Another Story	CDJ	U.S.	1992	$2.00
Mercury	CDP 487	That's Another Story	CDJ	U.S.	1992	$6.00
Brooks, Tina						
Full Length						
Blue Note		True Blue	LTD/LP	U.S.	1994	$20.00
Broomfield						
Singles						
Columbia	651629-2	Don't Cover Up Your Feelings	CD5	U.K.	1988	$8.00
Broonzy, Big Bill						
Singles						
Derrick Records	141041	Baby Please Don't Go	CD5	U.S.	1994	$5.00
Bros						
Full Length						
		Are You Mine?	DJ/Smplr	U.S.		$10.00
Columbia	460629-2	Push	LP	U.K.		$13.00
MCA		Push	DJ/LP	U.S.		$7.00
MCA	44285	Push	LP/LB	U.S.		$12.00/$7.00
MCA	45390	Time	LP/LB	U.S.		$12.00/$7.00
Singles						
CBS	656950-2	Are You Mine	CD5	Germany	1991	$8.00
CBS	653166-3	Cat Among the Pigeons	CD3	Germany	1988	$8.00
CBS	653166-2	Cat Among the Pigeons	CD5	Germany	1988	$8.00
CBS	ATOMC-6	Cat Among the Pigeons	CD5	U.K.	1988	$8.00
CBS	655332-3	Chocolate Box	CD3	Germany	1989	$8.00
CBS	CDATOM-8	Chocolate Box	CD5	U.K.	1988	$8.00
CBS	651360-2	Drop the Boy	CD5	Germany	1988	$8.00
CBS	10 8P-3052	Drop the Boy	CD3	Japan	1988	$13.00/$4.00
CBS	12 8P-8014	Drop the Boy	CD3	Japan	1988	$13.00/$4.00
CBS	CDATOM-3	Drop the Boy	CD5	U.K.	1988	$8.00
CBS	651618-2	I Owe You Nothing	CD5	Germany	1988	$8.00
CBS	12 8P-8007	I Owe You Nothing	CD3	Japan	1988	$13.00/$4.00
CBS	12 8P-8008	I Owe You Nothing	CD3	Japan	1988	$13.00/$4.00
CBS	CDATOM-4	I Owe You Nothing	CD5	U.K.	1988	$8.00
Epic		I Owe You Nothing	CDJ	U.S.	1988	$2.00
CBS	653000-3	I'm At the Point Where I Quit	CD3	Germany	1988	$8.00
CBS	CDATOM-5	I'm At the Point Where I Quit	CD5	U.K.	1988	$8.00
Epic	12 8P-8018	Madly In Love	CD3	Japan	1989	$13.00/$4.00
Epic	10 8P-8059	Madly In Love	CD3	Japan	1989	$13.00/$4.00
CBS	CDATOM-10	Madly In Love	CD5	U.K.	1989	$8.00
CBS	10 8P-3056	Silent Night	CD3	Japan	1988	$13.00/$4.00
CBS	CDATOM-6	Silent Night	CD5	U.K.	1988	$8.00
CBS	ESDA-7015	Sister	CD3	Japan	1989	$13.00/$4.00
CBS	CDATOM-9	Sister	CD5	U.K.	1989	$8.00
CBS	654647-2	Too Much	CD5	Germany	1988	$8.00
Epic	12 8P-3078	Too Much	CD3	Japan	1989	$13.00/$4.00
CBS	ATOM C-7	Too Much	CD5	U.K.	1989	$8.00
Epic	ESK 73041	Too Much	CDJ	U.S.	1989	$2.00
CBS	657404-2	Try	CD5	U.K.	1991	$8.00
CBS	651270-2	When Will I Be Famous	CD5	Germany	1988	$8.00
CBS	10 8P-3018	When Will I Be Famous	CD3	Japan	1988	$13.00/$4.00
Epic	12 8P-8001	When Will I Be Famous	CD3	Japan	1988	$13.00/$4.00
Epic	CSK 1161	When Will I Be Famous	CDJ	U.S.	1988	$2.00
Brotha Lynch Hung						
Singles						
Black Market	50854	R.I.P.	CDJ	U.S.	1995	$2.00
Brother						
Singles						
Atlantic	95884	Ghetto	CD5	U.S.	1994	$5.00
Eastwest	PRCD 5717	Ghetto Love	CDJ	U.S.	1994	$3.00
Brother Beyond						
Full Length						
EMI	93940	Trust	LP/LB	U.S.		$14.00/$8.00
Parlophone	203302-2	Be My Twin	CD5	Germany	1989	$8.00
Parlophone	CDR-6195	Be My Twin	CD5	U.K.	1989	$8.00
Capitol	DPRO-79826	Be My Twin	CDJ	U.S.	1989	$2.00
Parlophone	203212-2	Can You Keep A Secret	CD5	Germany	1989	$8.00
Parlophone	CDR 6197	Can You Keep A Secret	CD5	U.K	1989	$8.00
Parlophone	203577-3	Drive On	CD3	Germany	1989	$8.00
Parlophone	CDR-6233	Drive On	CD5	U.K.	1989	$8.00
Parlophone	CDR-6265	Girl I Used To Know, The	CD5	U.K.	1989	$8.00
EMI	DPRO-04521	Girl I Used To Know, The	CDJ	U.S.	1990	$2.00
Parlophone	202789-2	Harder I Try	CD5	Germany	1988	$8.00
Parlophone	CDR-6184	Harder I Try	CD5	U.K.	1988	$8.00
Parlophone	203014-2	He Ain't No Competition	CD5	Germany	1988	$8.00
Toshiba	XP10-2078	He Ain't No Competition	CD3	Japan	1989	$13.00/$4.00
Parlophone	CDR-6194	He Ain't No Competition	CD5	U.K.	1988	$8.00
EMI	DPRO-04656	Just A Heartbeat Away	CDJ	U.S.	1990	$2.00
Parlophone	203769-2	Trust	CD5	Germany	1990	$8.00
Parlophone	CDR-6245	Trust	CD5	U.K.	1990	$8.00
Parlophone	203638-2	When Will I See You Again	CD3	Germany	1988	$8.00
Parlophone	CDR-6239	When Will I See You Again	CD5	U.K.	1988	$8.00
Brother Brother						
Singles						
Chrysalis	CHSCD-3514	All American	CD5	U.K.	1990	$8.00
BMG	664455	If You Did Not	CD5	U.K.	1991	$8.00
Brother Cane						
Full Length						
Westwood One		In Concert	RS	U.S.	1993	$30.00
2 CD set.						
Westwood One		In Concert	RS	U.S.	1994	$30.00
2 CD set. Airdate: 5/9/94.						
Westwood One		In Concert	RS	U.S.	1995	$50.00
Airdate: 2/13/95.						
Singles						
	DPRO-12783	And Fools Shine On	CDJ	U.S.	1995	$2.00
		Breadmaker	CDJ	U.S.	1995	$2.00
		Voice Of Eujena	CDJ	U.S.	1995	$6.00
Brother Phelps						
Full Length						
		Country Edge	RS	U.S.	1993	$20.00
Airdate: 11/15/93.						
Singles						
Asylum	9176	Not So Different After All	CDJ	U.S.	1995	$2.00
Asylum	0005	Were You Really Livin'	CDJ	U.S.	1993	$2.00
Brotherhood Creed						
Singles						
Gasoline Ally	2246	Helluva	CDJ	U.S.	1992	$2.00
Gasoline Ally	2254	Hey Now	CDJ	U.S.	1992	$2.00

Brothers And Systems

Label	Catalog Number	Title	Type	Country	Year	Longbox Value / Value
		Singles				
Nettwerk	13868	½ 4 Me ½ 4 U	CD5	U.S.	1992	$5.00

Brothers Figaro

Label	Catalog Number	Title	Type	Country	Year	Longbox Value / Value
		Full Length				
Geffen	24295	Gypsy Road	LP/LB	U.S.	1990	$12.00/$7.00
Geffen	PRO-CD-4119	Selections From Gypsy Beat	DJ/Smplr	U.S.	1990	$4.00
		Singles				
Geffen		Gold Ring	CDJ	U.S.	1990	$2.00
Geffen		Gypsy Beat	CDJ	U.S.	1990	$2.00

Brothers Four

Label	Catalog Number	Title	Type	Country	Year	Longbox Value / Value
		Full Length				
CBS	35DP-49	Greenfields	LP	Japan		$20.00
Stage Dr	D-112391	In the Name Of Brotherhood	LP/LB	U.S.		$12.00/$7.00

Brothers In Rhythm

Label	Catalog Number	Title	Type	Country	Year	Longbox Value / Value
		Singles				
4th & B'way	BRCD-210	Such A Good Feeling	CD5	U.K.	1991	$7.00

Brothers Johnson

Label	Catalog Number	Title	Type	Country	Year	Longbox Value / Value
		Full Length				
A&M	CD-5162	Kickin'	LP/LB	U.S.		$14.00/$8.00
		Singles				
A&M	S10Y-3021	Kick It To the Curb	CD3	Japan	1988	$13.00/$4.00

Brothers Like Outlaw

Label	Catalog Number	Title	Type	Country	Year	Longbox Value / Value
		Singles				
Island	GESCD-44	Good Vibrations	CD5	U.K.	1992	$7.00
Island	GESCD-42	Trapped Into Darkness	CD5	U.K.	1992	$7.00

Broussard, Jules

Label	Catalog Number	Title	Type	Country	Year	Longbox Value / Value
		Full Length				
Headfirst	A-796-2	Jules Broussard	LP/LB	U.S.		$12.00/$7.00
		Singles				
		Europa	CDJ	U.S.		$2.00

Brown, Arthur

Label	Catalog Number	Title	Type	Country	Year	Longbox Value / Value
		Full Length				
Polydor	833736	Crazy World Of Arther Brown	LP/BP	U.S.		$12.00/$7.00

Brown, Bobby

Label	Catalog Number	Title	Type	Country	Year	Longbox Value / Value
		Full Length				
Pioneer		Humpin'	8"LD	U.S.		$8.00
		Singles				
MCA	10P3-6037	Don't Be Cruel	CD3	Japan	1988	$13.00/$4.00
MCA	DMCA-1310	Don't Be Cruel	CD3	U.K.	1988	$8.00
MCA	MCA5P-2524	Drop It On the One	CDJ	U.S.	1993	$3.00
Eastwest	257562-2	Every Little Step	CD5	Germany	1989	$8.00
MCA	WMD5-4013	Every Little Step	CD3	Japan	1990	$13.00/$4.00
MCA	DMCAT-1338	Every Little Step	CD5	U.K.	1988	$8.00
MCA		Every Little Step	CDJ	U.S.	1988	$3.00
MCA	DMCAT-1421	Freestyle Megamix	CD5	U.K.	1990	$8.00
MCA	WMDM-36	Get Away	CD3	Japan	1993	$13.00/$4.00
MCA	54512	Get Away	CD5	U.S.	1993	$5.00
MCA	MCA5P-2544	Get Away	CDJ	U.S.	1993	$3.00
MCA	WMDM-31	Good Enough	CD3	Japan	1992	$13.00/$4.00
MCA	MCSTD-1704	Good Enough	CD5	U.K.	1992	$8.00
MCA	54521	Good Enough	CD5	U.S.	1992	$5.00
MCA	MCA5P-2439	Good Enough	CDJ	U.S.	1993	$3.00
MCA	MCA5P-2482	Good Enough	CDJ	U.S.	1993	$3.00
MCA	WMDM-312	Humpin' Around	CD3	Japan	1992	$13.00/$4.00
MCA	MCSTD-1680	Humpin' Around	CD5	U.K.	1992	$8.00
MCA	54343	Humpin' Around	CD5	U.S.	1992	$5.00
MCA	MCA5P-2135	Humpin' Around	CDJ	U.S.	1992	$6.00
MCA	10P3-6092	My Perogative	CD3	Japan	1988	$13.00/$4.00
MCA	257702-2	My Perogative	CD3	U.K.	1988	$8.00
MCA	DMCAT-1299	My Perogative	CD5	U.K.	1988	$8.00
MCA		My Perogative	CDJ	U.S.	1988	$3.00
Eastwest	257504-2	On Our Own	CD5	Germany	1989	$8.00
Warner Brothers	09P3-6163	On Our Own	CD3	Japan	1989	$13.00/$4.00
MCA	DMCAT-1350	On Our Own	CD5	U.K.	1989	$8.00
MCA	CD45 17867	On Our Own	CDJ	U.S.	1989	$3.00
Teldec	257410-2	Rock Wit'Cha	CD3	Germany	1988	$8.00
Pioneer	09P3-6186	Rock Wit'Cha	CD3	Japan	1988	$13.00/$4.00
MCA	DMCAT-1367	Rock Wit'Cha	CD5	U.K.	1988	$8.00
WEA	257576-2	Roni	CD3	Germany	1988	$8.00
MCA	09P3-6117	Roni	CD3	Japan	1988	$12.00/$3.00
MCA	DMCAT-1335	Roni	CD5	U.K.	1988	$8.00
MCA	DMCAT-1384	Roni	CD5	U.K.	1988	$8.00
MCA	CD45 17760	Roni	CDJ	U.S.	1988	$3.00
MCA	CD45 18331	She Ain't Worth It	CDJ	U.S.		$3.00
MCA	1957	Something In Common	CD5	U.K.	1993	$10.00
MCA	MCA5P-2752	Something In Common	CDJ	U.S.	1993	$3.00
MCA	MCA5P-2912	Something In Common	CDJ	U.S.	1993	$3.00
MCA	MVDM-41	That's the Way Love Is	CD3	Japan	1993	$13.00/$4.00
MCA	MCA5P-2623	That's the Way Love Is	CDJ	U.S.	1993	$3.00
MCA	MCA5P-2660	That's the Way Love Is	CDJ	U.S.	1993	$3.00
MCA	MCA5P-2682	That's the Way Love Is	CDJ	U.S.	1993	$3.00

Brown, Charles

Label	Catalog Number	Title	Type	Country	Year	Longbox Value / Value
		Singles				
	5006	Blues N Brown	CD5	U.S.	1994	$5.00

Brown, Clifford

Label	Catalog Number	Title	Type	Country	Year	Longbox Value / Value
		Full Length				
EMI	746098-2	Alternate Takes	LP	Germany		$15.00
Emarcy	814648-2	At Basin Street	LP	U.S.†	1985	$15.00/$8.00
Polygram	814647	Best Coast Jazz	LP/BP	U.S.		$14.00/$8.00
Vogue	600025	Big Band	LP	Germany		$15.00
Mo Fi	MFCD-826	Daahoud	LP/LB	U.S.		$18.00/$12.00
Polygram	814640	Jam Session	LP/BP	U.S.		$14.00/$8.00
Polygram	814638	Jams 2	LP/BP	U.S.		$14.00/$8.00
Polygram	814637-2	More Study In Brown	LP	Germany		$15.00
Emarcy	814637-2	More Study In Brown	LP	U.S.†	1985	$15.00/$8.00
Emarcy	814646-2	More Study In Brown	LP	U.S.†	1985	$15.00/$8.00
Vogue	600020	Quartet And Sextet Recordings	LP	Germany		$15.00
Polygram	814646-2	Study In Brown	LP	Germany		$15.00
Polygram	814642-2	With Strings	LP	Germany		$15.00
Emarcy	814642-2	With Strings	LP	U.S.†	1985	$15.00/$8.00

Brown, Clive

Label	Catalog Number	Title	Type	Country	Year	Longbox Value / Value
		Singles				
Mango	CIDM-785	Lorraine	CD5	U.K.	1991	$7.00

Brown, Dennis

Company	Disk Number	Title	Type	Country	Year	Longbox Value / Value
		Full Length				
Rohit	7709	Greatest Hits	LP/BP	U.S.		$12.00/$7.00
		Singles				
Polygram	FXCD-114	Blind Faith	CD5	U.K.	1989	$7.00
Polygram	FCD-152	Love Or Nothing	CD5	U.K.	1991	$7.00
Polygram	869309-2	Love Or Nothing	CD5	U.K.	1991	$7.00
Polygram	FCD-133	Masterplan	CD5	U.K.	1990	$7.00
Polygram	869017-2	Masterplan	CD5	U.K.	1990	$7.00
Polygram	FCD-144	Sun Worshippers	CD5	U.K.	1990	$7.00
Polygram	869155-2	Sun Worshippers	CD5	U.K.	1990	$7.00
FFRR	FCD-190	This Time It's Real	CD5	U.K.	1992	$7.00

Brown, Errol

Company	Disk Number	Title	Type	Country	Year	Longbox Value / Value
		Full Length				
Elektra	60837-2	That's How Love Is	LP/LB	U.S.		$14.00/$8.00
WEA	YZ-162CD	Body Rockin'	CD5	U.K.	1988	$7.00
WEA	YZ-340CD	Love Goes Up And Down	CD3	U.K.	1988	$7.00
WEA	247684	Maya	CD3	Germany	1988	$7.00
WEA	YZ-1313CD	Maya	CD3	U.K.	1988	$7.00
Eastwest	9031-73317-2	Send A Prayer	CD5	Germany	1988	$7.00
Eastwest	4509-90064-2	This Time It's Forever	CD5	Germany	1988	$7.00

Brown, Horace

Company	Disk Number	Title	Type	Country	Year	Longbox Value / Value
		Singles				
		One For the Money	CDJ	U.S.	1995	$3.00
Uptown	3102	Taste Your Love	CDJ	U.S.	1994	$3.00
Uptown	2716	Taste Your Love	CDJ	U.S.	1994	$3.00

Brown, Jack

Company	Disk Number	Title	Type	Country	Year	Longbox Value / Value
		Full Length				
Epic		Question Of Time	LP/LB	U.S.		$14.00/$8.00

Brown, James

Company	Disk Number	Title	Type	Country	Year	Longbox Value / Value
		Full Length				
Polydor Chronicles		40th Anniversary Sampler	DJ/Smplr	U.S.	1996	$20.00
		Can't Get Any Harder	DJ/Smplr	Japan	1993	$75.00
Polygram	825714	CD Of James Brown	LP/BP	U.S.		$14.00/$8.00
Polygram	831700	CD Of James Brown II	LP/BP	U.S.		$14.00/$8.00
Intercord	847-313	Gravity	LP	Germany		$25.00
Scotti Brothers	DSP-1002	J.B. Sampler	DJ/Smplr	Japan	1995	$75.00
Scotti Brothers	ZK-45164	James Brown And Friends	LP/BP	U.S.		$14.00/$8.00
Polygram	847258	Messin' With the Blues	LP/BP	U.S.		$14.00/$8.00
Polygram	825714-2	Sex Machine & Other Soul Classics	LP/BP	U.S.†	1985	$15.00/$9.00
Epic	EK-45164	Soul Session Live	LP/LB	U.S.		$14.00/$8.00
Polydor	SACD 356	Star Time	DJ/Smplr	U.S.	1991	$15.00
Polydor		Star Time	DJ/4CD	U.S.	1991	$35.00
		Singles				
Scotti Brothers	PCCY-00427	Can't Get Any Harder	CD5	Japan	1993	$18.00
Scotti Brothers	75352	Can't Get Any Harder	CD5	U.S.	1992	$5.00
Scotti Brothers	ZSK 75376	Georgia Lina	CDJ	U.S.	1993	$3.00
Polydor	PZCD-185	Get Up..	CD5	U.K.	1991	$10.00
		Gimme Your Love	CDJ	U.S.		$6.00
Scotti Brothers	ZSK 75364	How Long	CDJ	U.S.	1993	$6.00
Polygram	879835-2	I Got You	CD5	Germany	1991	$10.00
BMG	CDFBI-9	I Got You	CD5	U.K.	1992	$10.00
Scotti Brothers	827328	I'm Real	CD3	Germany	1988	$8.00
Scotti Brothers	S10Y-1002	I'm Real	CD3	Japan	1988	$13.00/$4.00
Scotti Brothers	JSBCD-1	I'm Real	CD3	U.K.	1988	$8.00
Scotti Brothers	827328	I'm Real	CD3	U.K.	1988	$8.00
Scotti Brothers	ZSK 1116	I'm Real	CDJ	U.S.	1988	$6.00
Scotti Brothers	ZSK 75295	It's Time To Love	CDJ	U.S.	1991	$6.00
Polygram	868681-2	Move On	CD5	Germany	1991	$10.00
Scotti Brothers	72392 75286	Move On	CD5	U.S.	1991	$5.00
Scotti Brothers	ZSK 75286	Move On	CDJ	U.S.	1991	$3.00
Polygram	889811-2	Papa's Got A Brand New Bag	CD5	Germany	1990	$10.00
Polygram	887604-2	Payback	CD5	Canada	1988	$8.00
Urban	URCD-17	Payback	CD5	U.K.	1988	$10.00
A&M Records	523981	Reality	CD5	U.S.	1994	$5.00
Scotti Brothers	SBDJ 780342	Respect Me	CDJ	U.S.		$6.00
Polydor	CDP454	Say It Loud	CDJ	U.S.		$6.00
Polygram	883923-2	Sex Machine	CD5	Germany	1988	$10.00
Bellaphon	130 07 330	Sex Machine	CD5	Germany	1988	$10.00
Scotti Brothers	PCDY-00114	Sex Machine	CD3	Japan	1993	$13.00/$4.00
Scotti Brothers	827 334	Static	CD5	Germany	1988	$10.00
Scotti Brothers	S10Y-1018	Static	CD3	Japan	1988	$13.00/$4.00
Scotti Brothers	S10Y-1029	Time To Get Busy	CD3	Japan	1988	$13.00/$4.00

Brown, Jocelyn

Company	Disk Number	Title	Type	Country	Year	Longbox Value / Value
		Singles				
Arista		Gimme All Your Lovin'	CD5	U.K.		$10.00
	Second version.					
Arista	74321231312	Gimmie All Your Lovin'	CD5	U.K.	1994	$8.00
Arista		Shot	CD5	U.S.	1994	$6.00

Brown, Julie

Company	Disk Number	Title	Type	Country	Year	Longbox Value / Value
		Full Length				
WEA	9 25634-2	Trapped In the Body of a White Girl	LP	Germany	1988	$15.00
Sire	PRO-CD-3092	Girl Fight Tonight	CDJ	U.S.	1988	$2.00

Brown, Kevin

Company	Disk Number	Title	Type	Country	Year	Longbox Value / Value
		Full Length				
Hanibal	1340	Road Dreams	LP/LB	U.S.		$14.00/$8.00

Brown, Les

Company	Disk Number	Title	Type	Country	Year	Longbox Value / Value
		Full Length				
USA	USACD-685	Anything Goes	LP/LB	U.S.		$14.00/$8.00
Verve	825493-2	Sentimental Journey	LP/LB	U.S.†	1985	$14.00/$8.00

Brown, Mark

Company	Disk Number	Title	Type	Country	Year	Longbox Value / Value
		Singles				
Motown	ZD-43290	Bang Bang	CD5	U.K.	1989	$8.00

Brown, Marty

Company	Disk Number	Title	Type	Country	Year	Longbox Value / Value
		Singles				
MCA	MCA5P-54118	Every Now And Then	CDJ	U.S.	1991	$2.00
MCA	MCA5P-54252	Wildest Dreams	CDJ	U.S.	1991	$2.00

Brown, Michael

Company	Disk Number	Title	Type	Country	Year	Longbox Value / Value
		Singles				
Canyon	S10ED-5067	This Time It's Real	CD3	Japan	1989	$13.00/$4.00

Brown, Miguel

Company	Disk Number	Title	Type	Country	Year	Longbox Value / Value
		Singles				
BMG	662937	I Was Drunk	CD5	Germany	1990	$8.00

Brown, Norman

Label	Catalog Number	Title	Type	Country	Year	Longbox Value / Value
Singles						
Mojazz	374631220	Any Love	CDJ	U.S.	1994	$2.00
Mojazz	374631079	Love's Holiday	CDJ	U.S.	1992	$2.00
Mojazz	374631170	That's the Way Love Is	CDJ	U.S.	1994	$2.00
Mojazz	374631035	Too High	CDJ	U.S.	1992	$2.00

Brown, Oscar Jr.

Label	Catalog Number	Title	Type	Country	Year	Longbox Value / Value
Singles						
Sony	10EP-3037	Work Song	CD3	Japan	1988	$13.00/$4.00

Brown, Ray

Label	Catalog Number	Title	Type	Country	Year	Longbox Value / Value
Full Length						
EMI	90037	Mood For Lovin'	LP/LB	U.S.		$14.00/$8.00
GML	30211	New Two Bass Hits	LTD/LP	Japan		$25.00
	Gold disc.					
East Wind	35JD1 PSI	Tree, The	LP	U.S.†	1985	$15.00/$8.00

Brown, Sam

Label	Catalog Number	Title	Type	Country	Year	Longbox Value / Value
Full Length						
A&M		Stop	LP/LB	U.S.		$14.00/$8.00
A&M	AMCD-705	As One	CD5	U.K.	1990	$8.00
Singles						
A&M	390436-3	Can I Get A Witness	CD3	Germany	1989	$8.00
A&M	390436-2	Can I Get A Witness	CD5	Germany	1989	$8.00
A&M	AMCD-509	Can I Get A Witness	CD5	U.K.	1989	$8.00
A&M	3904537-2	Kissing Gate	CD5	Germany	1989	$8.00
A&M	AMCD-549	Kissing Gate	CD5	U.K.	1989	$8.00
A&M	AMCD-566	Mineworks	CD5	U.K.	1989	$8.00
A&M	390317-2	Stop	CD5	Germany	1988	$8.00
A&M	S10Y-3107	Stop	CD3	Japan	1989	$13.00/$4.00
A&M	AMCD-455	Stop	CD5	U.K.	1988	$8.00
A&M	AMCD-440	Stop	CD5	U.K.	[illegible]	[illegible]
A&M	CD 17042	Stop	CDJ	U.S.	1988	$2.00
A&M	390393-3	Walking Back To Me	CD3	Germany	1989	$8.00
A&M	390290-2	Walking Back To Me	CD5	Germany	1989	$8.00
A&M	390393-2	Walking Back To Me	CD5	Germany	1989	$8.00
A&M	S10Y-3019	Walking Back To Me	CD3	Japan	1988	$13.00/$4.00
A&M	AMCD 432	Walking Back To Me	CD5	U.K.	1988	$8.00
A&M	3902478-2	With A Little Love	CD5	Germany	1989	$8.00
A&M	PCDY-10014	With A Little Love	CD3	Japan	1990	$13.00/$4.00
A&M	AMCD-539	With A Little Love	CD5	U.K.	1988	$8.00

Brown, Shirley

Label	Catalog Number	Title	Type	Country	Year	Longbox Value / Value
Singles						
Malaco	2196	Hearts Are Made To Be Loved	CDJ	U.S.	1994	$2.00
BMalaco	2170	Let's Make Love Tonight	CDJ	U.S.	1992	$2.00

Brown, T. Graham

Label	Catalog Number	Title	Type	Country	Year	Longbox Value / Value
Full Length						
Capitol	CDP 746773	Brilliant Conversationalist	LP/LB	U.S.		$14.00/$8.00
Capitol	CDP 91780	Bumper To Bumper	LP/LB	U.S.		$14.00/$8.00
Capitol	CDP 93547	You Can't Take It With You	LP/LB	U.S.		$14.00/$8.00
Singles						
Capitol	CDCL-494	Power Of Love	CD5	U.K.	1988	$8.00

Brown, Vernell Jr.

Label	Catalog Number	Title	Type	Country	Year	Longbox Value / Value
Full Length						
A&M	CD 5305	Total Eclipse	LP/LB	U.S.		$14.00/$8.00
Singles						
A&M	75021 8092-2	New Shoes	CDJ	U.S.	1990	$2.00

Browne, Duncan

Label	Catalog Number	Title	Type	Country	Year	Longbox Value / Value
Singles						
Line	LICD-9 01130	Wild Places	CD5	Germany	1991	$8.00

Browne, Jackson

Label	Catalog Number	Title	Type	Country	Year	Longbox Value / Value
Full Length						
WEA	PCS-205	History	DJ/Smplr	Japan	1995	$250.00
Album Network		In the Studio (Retrospective)	RS	U.S.	1994	$35.00
Album Network		In the Studio (Running On Empty)	RS	U.S.	1989	$25.00
	Airdate: 7/31/89.					
Album Network		In the Studio (Running On Empty)	RS	U.S.	1993	$25.00
	Airdate: 1/4/93.					
Elektra	60268-2	Lawyers In Love	LP/LB	U.S.†	1984	$14.00/$8.00
Elektra	PRCD 1867-2	Looking East	DJ/LP	U.S.	1996	$14.00
Westwood One		Off the Record	RS	U.S.	1994	$30.00
	Airdate: 3/14/94.					
Westwood One		Off the Record	RS	U.S.	1994	$30.00
	Airdate: 9/5/94.					
Elektra	PRCD 8851-2	Retropective	DJ/Smplr	U.S.	1994	$45.00
Elektra	PRCD 8851-2	Retropective/I'm Alive	DJ/Smplr	U.S.	1994	$125.00
	2CD sampler with booklet in paper sleeve					
Elektra	PRCD 8851-2	Retrospective/Three From I'm Alive	DJ/Smplr	U.S.	1994	$100.00
	2CD in jewel box.					
Elektra	PRCD 8853-2	Three Songs From I'm Alive	DJ/Smplr	U.S.	1993	$10.00
Media America		Up Close	RS	U.S.	1994	$50.00
	2 CD set.					
Singles						
Elektra	PR 8095-2	Anything Can Happen	CDJ	U.S.	1989	$3.00
Elektra	PR 8117-2	Chasing You Into the Light	CDJ	U.S.	1989	$3.00
WEA		Everywhere I Go	CD5	U.K.	1994	$10.00
WEA		Everywhere I Go	CD5	U.K.	1994	$10.00
	Second version.					
Elektra	PRCD 89612	Everywhere I Go	CDJ	U.S.	1994	$6.00
Elektra	EKR176	I'm Alive	CD5	Germany	1993	$10.00
Elektra	PRCD 8854-2	I'm Alive	CDJ	U.S.	1993	$6.00
Elektra	PRCD 8867-2	I'm Alive	CDJ	U.S.	1993	$6.00
		I'm the Cat	CD5	U.K.	1996	$10.00
Elektra	PRCD 9412-2	Looking East	CDJ	U.S.	1996	$6.00
Elektra	PRCD 8895-2	Miles Away	CDJ	U.S.	1993	$6.00
Elektra	PRCD 8896-2	My Problem Is You	CDJ	U.S.	1994	$3.00
WEA	969339-2	Running On Empty	CD3	Germany	1989	$9.00
WEA	969339-2	Running On Empty	CD3	U.K.	1989	$9.00
		Sky Blue And Black	CDJ	Spain	1994	$18.00
Elektra	9042-2	Sky Blue And Black	CDJ	U.S.	1994	$7.00
Elektra	PRCD 9426-2	Some Bridges	CDJ	U.S.	1996	$6.00
Pioneer	09P3-6128	World In Motion	CD3	Japan	1989	$13.00/$4.00
Elektra	PR 8085-2	World In Motion	CDJ	U.S.	1989	$3.00

Browne, Tom

Label	Catalog Number	Title	Type	Country	Year	Longbox Value / Value
Singles						
Arista	664998	Funkin' For Jamaica	CD5	U.K.	1992	$7.00
B	8502	Jam For Real	CD5	U.S.	1994	$5.00

Brownmark

Label	Catalog Number	Title	Type	Country	Year	Longbox Value / Value
Singles						
		Bang Bang	CDJ	U.S.		$2.00

Brownstone

Label	Catalog Number	Title	Type	Country	Year	Longbox Value / Value
Singles						
CBS	77864	Grapevyne	CD5	U.S.	1994	$5.00
Epic	6938	Grapevyne	CDJ	U.S.	1994	$6.00
		I Can't Tell You Why	CD5	U.K.		$10.00
		I Can't Tell You Why	CD5	U.K.		$10.00
	Second version.					
		I You Love Me	CD5	U.K.		$10.00
		I You Love Me	CD5	U.K.		$10.00
	Second version.					
CBS	77733	If You Love Me	CD5	U.S.	1994	$5.00
Epic	6889	If You Love Me	CDJ	U.S.	1994	$6.00
MJJ	77576	Pass the Lovin'	CDJ	U.S.	1994	$2.00

Brubeck, Dave

Label	Catalog Number	Title	Type	Country	Year	Longbox Value / Value
Full Length						
Atlantic	1641-2	All Together Again	LP/LB	U.S.		$12.00/$7.00
Concord	CCD-4299	Reflections	LP/LB	U.S.		$12.00/$7.00
Sony	SRCS-6680	Time Out	LTD/LP	Japan	1993	$35.00
	Gold disc.					
Columbia	CK-52860	Time Out	LP/LB	U.S.	1993	$29.00/$25.00
	Gold disc.					
Sony	SRCS-6680	Time Out	LTD/LP	U.S.	1993	$30.00
	Gold disc.					
CBS	CK-08192	Tme Out	LP/LB	U.S.†	1985	$14.00/$8.00
Singles						
Telarc Jazz	094	Late Night Brubeck	CDJ	U.S.	1994	$7.00

Bruce And Bongo

Label	Catalog Number	Title	Type	Country	Year	Longbox Value / Value
Full Length						
Teldec	8 26372	Geil Album	LP	Germany		$15.00

Bruce And Terry

Label	Catalog Number	Title	Type	Country	Year	Longbox Value / Value
Full Length						
	MMCD-1001	Rare Masters	LP	Japan	1995	$65.00

Bruce, Jack

Label	Catalog Number	Title	Type	Country	Year	Longbox Value / Value
Full Length						
		Cities Of the Heart	LTD/LP	U.S.	1994	$30.00
Polygram	835243	Harmony Row	LP/BP	U.S.		$12.00/$7.00
Polygram	835285	How's Tricks	LP/BP	U.S.		$12.00/$7.00
DIR		King Biscuit Flour Hour	RS	U.S.	1990	$30.00
	With J. Geils Band, Airdate: 3/26/90.					
DIR		King Biscuit Flour Hour	RS	U.S.	1994	$25.00
	With J. Geils Band, Airdate: 1/24/94.					
Polygram	835284	Out Of the Storm	LP/BP	U.S.		$12.00/$7.00
Epic	EK 45279	Question Of Time	LP/LB	U.S.		$12.00/$7.00
Epic		Question Of Time	LP/LB	U.S.		$14.00/$8.00
Polygram	835242	Songs For A Tailor	LP/BP	U.S.		$12.00/$7.00
Polygram	837806	Willpower	LP/BP	U.S.		$12.00/$7.00
Singles						
Epic	ESK 1874	No Surrender!	CDJ	U.S.	1989	$2.00

Brueken, Claudia

Label	Catalog Number	Title	Type	Country	Year	Longbox Value / Value
Singles						
Island	CID-471	Absolute	CD5	U.K.	1990	$12.00
Island	663912	Kiss Like Ether	CD5	Germany	1990	$10.00
Island	CID-479	Kiss Like Ether	CD5	U.K.	1990	$12.00

Bruner, Helen

Label	Catalog Number	Title	Type	Country	Year	Longbox Value / Value
Singles						
		Gimme Real Love	CDJ	U.S.		$2.00
		Missin' You	CDJ	U.S.		$2.00

Brutal Youth

Label	Catalog Number	Title	Type	Country	Year	Longbox Value / Value
Singles						
Earache	EEPK90961	Perpetual Conversation	CD5	Canada	1993	$10.00

Brute

Label	Catalog Number	Title	Type	Country	Year	Longbox Value / Value
Singles						
	DPRO-2030	Good Morning Mr. Hardon	CDJ	U.S.	1994	$2.00

Bryant, Ray

Label	Catalog Number	Title	Type	Country	Year	Longbox Value / Value
Full Length						
Island	842438-2	Blue Moons	LP/LB	U.S.		$14.00/$8.00
Columbia	CK 44058	Con Alma	LP/LB	U.S.		$14.00/$8.00
Polygram	832235	Plays Basie & Ellington	LP/BP	U.S		$14.00/$8.00
Prestige	673	Ray Bryant Trio	LP/BP	U.S.		$14.00/$8.00
Polygram	632589	Today	LP/BP	U.S.		$14.00/$8.00

Bryant, Sharon

Label	Catalog Number	Title	Type	Country	Year	Longbox Value / Value
Singles						
Wing	CDP 187	Body Talk	CDJ	U.S.	1990	$2.00
Wing	CDP 114	Foolish Heart	CDJ	U.S.	1989	$2.00
Wing	CDP 49	Let Go	CDJ	U.S.	1989	$2.00

Bryars, Gavin

Label	Catalog Number	Title	Type	Country	Year	Longbox Value / Value
Full Length						
Polygram	847537	After the Requiem	LP/BP	U.S.		$12.00/$7.00
ECM	829484-2	Three Viennese Dancers	LP	Germany		$15.00
Singles						
		Jesus Blood	CDJ	U.S.		$2.00

Bryson, Peabo

Label	Catalog Number	Title	Type	Country	Year	Longbox Value / Value
Full Length						
Capitol	CDP-46071	Peabo Bryson Collection	LP/LB	U.S.†	1985	$14.00/$8.00
Elektra	60753-2	Positive	LP/LB	U.S.		$14.00/$8.00
Elektra	60484-2	Quiet Storm	LP/LB	U.S.		$14.00/$8.00
Elektra	60362-2	Straight From the Heart	LP/LB	U.S.†	1985	$14.00/$8.00
Elektra	60362-2	Straight From the Heart	LP/LB	U.S.	1987	$14.00/$8.00
Elektra	60427-2	Take No Prisoners	LP/LB	U.S.		$14.00/$8.00
Singles						
Sony	SRDS-8254	A Whole New World	CD3	Japan	1993	$13.00/$4.00
	With Regina Belle.					
Columbia	CSK 74751	A Whole New World	CDJ	U.S.	1992	$6.00
	With Regina Belle.					
Epic	ESDA-7093	Beauty And the Beast	CD3	Japan	1992	$13.00/$3.00
	With Celine Dion.					
Epic	ESK 74090	Beauty And the Beast	CDJ	U.S.	1991	$3.00
	With Celine Dion.					
Columbia	CSK 73745	Can You Stop the Rain	CDJ	U.S.	1991	$2.00
Columbia	CSK 73925	Closer Than Close	CDJ	U.S.	1991	$2.00
Elektra	PR 2252-2	Come On Over Tonight	CDJ	U.S.	1988	$2.00

Label	Catalog Number	Title	Type	Country	Year	Longbox Value / Value
Columbia	CSK 73990	Lost In the Night	CDJ	U.S.	1991	$2.00
Columbia	CSK 74290	Shower With Love	CDJ	U.S.	1991	$2.00
Columbia	CSK 5433	Why Goodbye	CDJ	U.S.	1994	$2.00

Bubble, Puppy

Full Length

Label	Catalog Number	Title	Type	Country	Year	Longbox Value / Value
Collectibles		Gathering Of Promises	LP	U.S.	1994	$10.00

First pressing using falty master.

Buchanan, Catherine

Singles

Label	Catalog Number	Title	Type	Country	Year	Longbox Value / Value
Arista	885000	Love Is	CD5	Germany	1988	$7.00
Arista	661500	Love Is	CD5	U.K.	1988	$7.00

Buchanan, Roy

Full Length

Label	Catalog Number	Title	Type	Country	Year	Longbox Value / Value
Bioya		Buc and the Snake Stretchers	LTD/LP	U.S.	1991	$25.00
Polygram	831838	In the Beginning	LP/BP	U.S.		$12.00/$7.00

Buck-Tick

Singles

Label	Catalog Number	Title	Type	Country	Year	Longbox Value / Value
Invitation	VIDL-131	Dress	CD3	Japan	1993	$13.00/$4.00
Victor	VIDL-77	Jupiter	CD3	Japan	1991	$13.00/$4.00

Buckbeats

Singles

Label	Catalog Number	Title	Type	Country	Year	Longbox Value / Value
Polydor	10GD-5022	Dancing Through the Night	CD3	Japan	1989	$13.00/$4.00
Polydor	10GD-5009	Daydream	CD3	Japan	1989	$13.00/$4.00

Bucketheads

Singles

Label	Catalog Number	Title	Type	Country	Year	Longbox Value / Value
Atlantic	95747	Bomb	CD5	U.S.	1995	$5.00
Atlantic	PRCD 6258-2	Bomb	CDJ	U.S.	1995	$2.00
		Got Myself Together	CDJ	U.S.	1996	$6.00

Buckinghams

Full Length

Label	Catalog Number	Title	Type	Country	Year	Longbox Value / Value
CBS	09812	Greatest Hits	LP/LB	U.S.		$14.00/$8.00

Buckingham, Lindsey

Full Length

Label	Catalog Number	Title	Type	Country	Year	Longbox Value / Value
Polygram	822450-2	Go Insane	LP	Germany		$20.00
Polygram	800045-2	Law And Order	LP	Germany		$20.00
Elektra	561-2	Law And Order	LP/LB	U.S.†	1984	$15.00/$9.00
Westwood One		Off the Record	RS	U.S.	1992	$30.00
	Airdate: 7/13/92.					
Reprise		Out Of the Cradle	LP/LB	U.S.		$14.00/$8.00
Westwood One		Superstars	RS	U.S.	1993	$120.00
	2 CD set. Airdate: 2/28/93.					
Media America		Up Close	RS	U.S.	1992	$30.00
	2 CD set.					
Reprise	PRO-CD-5482	Words & Music	DJ/Intvw	U.S.	1992	$10.00

Singles

Label	Catalog Number	Title	Type	Country	Year	Longbox Value / Value
Mercury		Countdown	CD5	Holland	1992	$8.00
Mercury	MERCD-371	Countdown	CD5	U.K.	1992	$8.00
Reprise	PRO-CD-5526	Countdown	CDJ	U.S.	1992	$3.00
Reprise	PRo-CD-6163	Don't Look Down	CDJ	U.S.	1992	$2.00
Reprise	PRO-CD-5828	Soul Drifter	CDJ	U.S.	1992	$3.00
Reprise	PRO-CD-5450	Wrong	CDJ	U.S.	1992	$3.00

Buckley, Jeff

Full Length

Label	Catalog Number	Title	Type	Country	Year	Longbox Value / Value
Columbia	SAMPCD2281	Album Sampler	DJ/Smplr	U.K.		$30.00
Columbia		Grace	CD5	Australia	1995	$10.00
Columbia		Grace	LTD/LP	Australia	1995	$28.00
	2 CD set.					
Columbia	SAMPCD 2281	Grace	DJ/LP	Holland	1995	$22.00

Singles

Label	Catalog Number	Title	Type	Country	Year	Longbox Value / Value
Columbia		Eternal Life	CD5	Australia	1995	$10.00
Columbia	SAMPCD 28022	Eternal Life	CDJ	Spain	1995	$18.00
Columbia		Eternal Life	CDJ	U.K.	1995	$20.00
Columbia	SAMPCD 2403	Grace	CDJ	Holland	1995	$16.00
Columbia	661107	Grace	CD5	U.K.	1994	$10.00
Columbia		Grace	CDJ	U.K.	1995	$20.00
Columbia	CSK 6453	Grace	CDJ	U.S.	1994	$3.00
Columbia	CSK 6844	Grace	CDJ	U.S.	1995	$3.00
Columbia		Last Goodbye	CD5	U.K.	1994	$10.00
Columbia		Last Goodbye	CD5	U.K.	1994	$10.00
	Second version.					
Columbia	XPCD 639	Last Goodbye	CDJ	U.K.	1994	$12.00
Columbia	CSK 6844	Last Goodbye	CDJ	U.S.	1994	$3.00
Columbia	77296	Live at Sin-E	CDJ	U.S.	1993	$4.00
Columbia		Live From the Bataclan	CD5	U.K.	1995	$10.00
Columbia	SAMPCD 2246	Live From the Bataclan	CDJ	U.K.	1995	$18.00
Columbia	SAMPCD2290	Peyote Radio Theatre	CDJ	Holland	1994	$30.00
Columbia	SAMPCD2290	Peyote Radio Theatre	CDJ	U.K.		$20.00
Columbia	CSK 6206	Peyote Radio Theatre	CDJ	U.S.	1994	$15.00
Columbia	SAMPCD 2960	So Real	CDJ	Holland	1995	$30.00
Columbia		So Real	CD5	U.K.	1995	$10.00
Columbia	SAMPCD 2776	So Real	CDJ	U.K.	1995	$25.00
Columbia	CSK 7197	So Real	CDJ	U.S.	1995	$3.00
Columbia	SAMPCD 2746	Way Young Lovers Do	CDJ	U.K.	1995	$30.00

Buckley, Tim

Full Length

Label	Catalog Number	Title	Type	Country	Year	Longbox Value / Value
		Greetings From L.A.	LP/LB	U.S.		$12.00/$10.00
Str. Fruit	SFPSCD-082	Peel Sessions	CD5	U.K.	1991	$8.00

Bucks Fizz

Full Length

Label	Catalog Number	Title	Type	Country	Year	Longbox Value / Value
RCA	PD-70022	Greatest Hits	LP	Germany		$15.00
Polygram	831424-2	Writing On the Wall	LP	U.K.		$15.00

Buckshot Lefonque

Singles

Label	Catalog Number	Title	Type	Country	Year	Longbox Value / Value
Columbia	77926	Some Cow Lefonque	CD5	U.S.	1995	$5.00

Budd, Harold

Full Length

Label	Catalog Number	Title	Type	Country	Year	Longbox Value / Value
Opal	9 26649-2-Dj	By Dawns Early Light	DJ/LP	U.S.	1991	$17.00
Warner Brothers	9 26025-2	Serpent	LP/LB	U.S.		$12.00/$7.00

Buddah Heads

Singles

Label	Catalog Number	Title	Type	Country	Year	Longbox Value / Value
RCA	66445	Blues Had A Baby	CD5	U.S.	1994	$5.00

Company	Disk Number	Title	Type	Country	Year	Longbox Value / Value
RCA	62924-RDJ	Dodge the Rain	CDJ	U.S.	1994	$2.00

Buddy Rich

Singles

Company	Disk Number	Title	Type	Country	Year	Longbox Value / Value
Atlantic	PRCD 5879	Pick Up the Peices	CDJ	U.S.	1994	$3.00

Budgie

Full Length

Company	Disk Number	Title	Type	Country	Year	Longbox Value / Value
Repertoire	RR 4100-WZ	Bandolier	LTD/LP	Germany	1990	$25.00
	Picture disc CD.					
Repertoire	RR 4012-C	Budgie	LTD/LP	Germany	1989	$25.00
	Picture disc CD.					
Repertoire	RR	Collection	LTD/LP	Germany	1990	$100.00
	5 CD picture disc set.					
Repertoire	RR 4027-C	In For the Kill	LTD/LP	Germany	1989	$50.00
	Picture disc CD.					
Repertoire	RR 4027-C	Never Turn Your Back	LTD/LP	Germany	1989	$50.00
	Picture disc CD.					
Repertoire	RR 4026-C	Squawk	LTD/LP	Germany	1989	$50.00
	Picture disc CD.					

Buehner, Christian

Full Length

Company	Disk Number	Title	Type	Country	Year	Longbox Value / Value
Beyond	CDP-72891	Nightflight	LP/LB	U.S.		$12.00/$7.00

Buffalo Tom

Full Length

Company	Disk Number	Title	Type	Country	Year	Longbox Value / Value
	PCD 402	75 Minutes With	DJ/Smplr	Canada		$35.00
SST	SST-250	Buffalo Tom	LP/BP	U.S.		$14.00/$8.00
		Selected Tracks From Big Red Letter Day	DJ/Smplr	U.S.		$12.00

Singles

Company	Disk Number	Title	Type	Country	Year	Longbox Value / Value
Megadisc	MDC-125276	Crawl	CD5	U.K.	1990	$8.00
Pinnacle	SIT-77CD	Fortune Teller	CD5	U.K.	1991	$8.00
Beggars Banquet	055-31293	I'm Allowed	CD5	U.K.	1994	$10.00
Beggars Banquet	PRO-CD-5448	I'm Allowed	CDJ	U.S.	1993	$2.00
Beggars Banquet	PRO-CD-5451	I'm Allowed	CDJ	U.S.	1993	$2.00
Beggars Banquet	PRO-CD-5214	Sodajerk	CDJ	U.S.	1993	$3.00
Beggars Banquet	PRO-CD-5245	Sodajerk	CDJ	U.S.	1993	$3.00
Eastwest	9231	Summer	CDJ	U.S.	1995	$3.00
Pinnacle	SIT-96CD	Taillights Fade	CD5	U.K.	1991	$8.00
Pinnacle		Tangerine	CD5	U.K.	1995	$9.00
	PRCD 9338-2	Tangerine	CDJ	U.S.	1995	$2.00
Beggars Banquet	5360	Tree House	CDJ	U.S.		$3.00
Beggars Banquet	PRO-CD-5347	Tree House	CDJ	U.S.	1993	$2.00
Beggars Banquet	PRO-CD-5359	Tree House	CDJ	U.S.	1993	$2.00
Pinnacle	0504-3	Velvet Roof	CD5	Germany	1992	$8.00
Pinnacle	SIT-86CD	Velvet Roof	CD5	U.K.	1992	$8.00

Buffett, Jimmy – A1A/Volcano (MCA MCAD-5879) U.S. 1986 out-of-print CD album from MCA's long gone Two-for-One series.

Buffett, Jimmy

Full Length

Company	Disk Number	Title	Type	Country	Year	Longbox Value / Value
MCA	MCAD-5879	A-1-A/Volcano	LP/LB	U.S.	1986	$22.00/$18.00
MCA		Banana Rewind	DJ/LP	U.S.	1996	$13.00
MCA	CD33 3031	Boats, Beaches, Bars & Ballads Sampler	DJ/Smplr	U.S.	1992	$20.00
MCA	MCAD-5875	Changes In Lattitudes/Havana Daydreamin'	LP/LB	U.S.	1986	$22.00/$18.00
Margaritaville		Christmas Island	LTD/LP	U.S.	1996	$17.00
	CD with postcard and ornament. Available exclusively from Camelot Music.					
MCA Special Products	MSD-36031	Great American Summer Fun With	LTD/LP	U.S.	1996	$18.00
	Sold only through select "Target" department stores.					
MCA	MCAD-5923	One Particular Harbour/Riddles In the Sand	LP/LB	U.S.	1986	$22.00/$18.00
MCA	MCAD-5867	Son Of A Son Of A Sailor/Coconut Telegraph	LP/LB	U.S.	1986	$22.00/$18.00

Singles

Company	Disk Number	Title	Type	Country	Year	Longbox Value / Value
MCA	MCA5P-54680	Another Saturday Night	CDJ	U.S.	1993	$3.00
MCA	MCA5P-54408	Bayou Boy	CDJ	U.S.	1992	$3.00
MCA	CD45 18045	Carnival World	CDJ	U.S.	1989	$3.00
MCA	CD45 17897	Take Another Road	CDJ	U.S.	1989	$3.00

Bugnon, Alex

Singles

Company	Disk Number	Title	Type	Country	Year	Longbox Value / Value
Orephus	04220	Piano In the Dark	CDJ	U.S.	1988	$2.00

Bullens, Cindy

Singles

Company	Disk Number	Title	Type	Country	Year	Longbox Value / Value
MCA	CD45 17899	Breakin' the Chain	CDJ	U.S.	1989	$2.00

Bullet Lavolta

Singles

Label	Catalog Number	Title	Type	Country	Year	Longbox Value/Value
RCA	62198-2-RDJ	My Protector	CDJ	U.S.	1992	$2.00
		Swan Dive	CDJ	U.S.		$2.00

Bulletboys

Full Length

Label	Catalog Number	Title	Type	Country	Year	Longbox Value/Value
Warner Brothers	PRO-CD-6224	12 Minute Warning	DJ/Smplr	U.S.	1993	$5.00
Warner Brothers	9 26537-2-DJ	Freakshow	DJ/LP	U.S.	1991	$10.00
Warner Brothers	9 26537-2	Freakshow	LTD/LP	U.S.	1991	$15.00

Singles

Label	Catalog Number	Title	Type	Country	Year	Longbox Value/Value
Warner Brothers	PRO-CD-3393	For the Love of Money	CDJ	U.S.	1988	$3.00
Warner Brothers	PRO-CD-4779	Hang On St. Christopher	CDJ	U.S.	1991	$3.00
Warner Brothers	PRO-CD-6387	Laughing With the Dead	CDJ	U.S.	1994	$3.00
Warner Brothers	PRO-CD-3251	Smooth Up	CDJ	U.S.	1988	$3.00
Waner Brothers	PRO-CD_3251	Smooth Up	CDJ	U.S.	1988	$10.00
Warner Brothers	PRO-CD-4937	Talk To Your Daughter	CDJ	U.S.	1991	$3.00
Warner Brothers	PRO-CD-4695	THC Groove	CDJ	U.S.	1991	$3.00

Bum Bar Bastards

Singles

Label	Catalog Number	Title	Type	Country	Year	Longbox Value/Value
		Tube Bar	CD5	U.S.	1993	$5.00

Bumble

Singles

Label	Catalog Number	Title	Type	Country	Year	Longbox Value/Value
Mother	MUMCD-37	West In Motion	CD5	U.K.	1992	$8.00

Bump

Singles

Label	Catalog Number	Title	Type	Country	Year	Longbox Value/Value
Bood Boy	EDGECD-1	I'm Rushing	CD5	U.K.	1992	$8.00

Bums

Singles

Label	Catalog Number	Title	Type	Country	Year	Longbox Value/Value
Priority	50831	Elevation	CDJ	U.S.	1994	$2.00

Bunburys

Full Length

Label	Catalog Number	Title	Type	Country	Year	Longbox Value/Value
		Bunbury Tales, The	LP	U.K.		$25.00

Singles

Label	Catalog Number	Title	Type	Country	Year	Longbox Value/Value
Arista	A10D-116	Fight	CD3	Japan	1989	$12.00/$3.00

Burch Sisters

Singles

Label	Catalog Number	Title	Type	Country	Year	Longbox Value/Value
Mercury	CDP 216	Honey You Won't Break Me	CDJ	U.S.	1990	$2.00

Burdon, Eric

Full Length

Label	Catalog Number	Title	Type	Country	Year	Longbox Value/Value
Atlantic	8109-2	Best Of	LP/LB	U.S.		$14.00/$8.00
Polygram	835677-2	Good Times	LP	Germany		$25.00
Polygram	825231-2	Starportrait	LP	Germany		$25.00

Singles

Label	Catalog Number	Title	Type	Country	Year	Longbox Value/Value
Polydor	887349-2	Good Times	CD5	Germany	1988	$8.00
Polydor	887349-2	Good Times	CD5	U.K.	1988	$8.00
Polygram	887721-2	Run For Your Life	CD5	Germany	1988	$8.00
Polygram	887721-2	Run For Your Life	CD5	U.K.	1988	$8.00
Striped Horse	615	Run For Your Life	CDJ	U.S.	1988	$2.00
Striped Horse	1215	Run For Your Life	CDJ	U.S.	1988	$2.00
Polygram	8877725-2	Sixteen Tons	CD5	Germany	1988	$8.00

Burell, Kenny

Full Length

Label	Catalog Number	Title	Type	Country	Year	Longbox Value/Value
CBS	450893-2	God Bless the Child	LP	Germany		$15.00

Burke, Solomon

Singles

Label	Catalog Number	Title	Type	Country	Year	Longbox Value/Value
Bizarre Strght 90113		Try A Little Tenderness	CDJ	U.S.	1991	$2.00

Burmer, Richard

Full Length

Label	Catalog Number	Title	Type	Country	Year	Longbox Value/Value
Fortuna	17025	Mosaic	LP/BP	U.S.		$14.00/$8.00

Singles

Label	Catalog Number	Title	Type	Country	Year	Longbox Value/Value
Toshiba	XP10-2046	Across the View	CD3	Japan	1988	$13.00/$4.00

Burn

Singles

Label	Catalog Number	Title	Type	Country	Year	Longbox Value/Value
Revelation	22	Shall Be Judged	CD5	U.S.	1990	$4.00

Burnett, Dorsey

Full Length

Label	Catalog Number	Title	Type	Country	Year	Longbox Value/Value
		Very Best Of	DJ/Smplr	U.S.		$20.00

Burnett, T-Bone

Full Length

Label	Catalog Number	Title	Type	Country	Year	Longbox Value/Value
Uni		T-Bone Burnett	LP/LB	U.S.		$14.00/$8.00
Columbia	CK-40792	Talking Animals	LP/LB	U.S.	1988	$14.00/$8.00

Singles

Label	Catalog Number	Title	Type	Country	Year	Longbox Value/Value
Columbia		Humans From Earth	CDJ	U.S.		$2.00
Columbia	CSK 2908	Killer Moon The	CDJ	U.S.		$2.00
Columbia	CSK 1122	Wild Truth, The	CDJ	U.S.	1988	$2.00

Burnette, Billy

Full Length

Label	Catalog Number	Title	Type	Country	Year	Longbox Value/Value
Capricorn		Very Best Of	DJ/Smplr	U.S.		$20.00

Singles

Label	Catalog Number	Title	Type	Country	Year	Longbox Value/Value
Capricorn	PRO-CD-6322	Bigger the Love, The	CDJ	U.S.	1993	$2.00
Capricorn	PRO-CD-5245	Nothin' To Do	CDJ	U.S.	1992	$2.00
Capricorn	PRO-CD-5931	Tangled Up In Texas	CDJ	U.S.	1992	$2.00

Burning Tree

Full Length

Label	Catalog Number	Title	Type	Country	Year	Longbox Value/Value
Epic	EK 45464	Burning Trees	LP/LB	U.S.		$14.00/$8.00
Epic	ESK 2191	Live From Leeds	DJ/Smplr	U.S.	1990	$15.00

Singles

Label	Catalog Number	Title	Type	Country	Year	Longbox Value/Value
Epic	ESK 2035	Fly On	CDJ	U.S.	1990	$6.00

Burns, George

Full Length

Label	Catalog Number	Title	Type	Country	Year	Longbox Value/Value
Time Warner Sound Exchange		Young At Heart	LP	U.S.	1995	$16.00

Burns, Jerry

Singles

Label	Catalog Number	Title	Type	Country	Year	Longbox Value/Value
Columbia	657946-2	Pale Red	CD5	U.K.	1992	$7.00

Burns, Pete

Singles

Label	Catalog Number	Title	Type	Country	Year	Longbox Value/Value
	DFC 2000	Sex Drive	CD5	Itlay	1994	$12.00

Burrell

Singles

Label	Catalog Number	Title	Type	Country	Year	Longbox Value/Value
Virgin	TENCD-264	Put Your Trust In the Music	CD5	U.K.	1989	$7.00

Burrell, Kenny

Full Length

Label	Catalog Number	Title	Type	Country	Year	Longbox Value/Value
Blue Note	46538	At the Five Spot Cafe	LP/LB	U.S.		$20.00/$15.00
Blue Note	81597	Blue Lights, Vol. 2	LP/LB	U.S.		$20.00/$15.00
Blue Note	46756	Generation	LP/LB	U.S.		$20.00/$15.00
Polygram	825578	Guitar Forms	LP/BP	U.S.		$20.00/$15.00
Verve	825576-2	Guitar Forms	LP/LB	U.S.†	1985	$14.00/$8.00
Blue Note	46399	Midnight Blue	LP/LB	U.S.		$20.00/$15.00
Blue Note		Midnight Blue	LTD/LP	U.S.	1995	$19.00
Blue Note	90260	Pieces Of Blue And the Blue	LP/LB	U.S.		$20.00/$15.00

Burrell, Kenny & Grover Washington

Full Length

Label	Catalog Number	Title	Type	Country	Year	Longbox Value/Value
Capital	CDP-46093	Togethering	LP/LB	U.S.†	1985	$14.00/$8.00

Burroughs, William

Full Length

Label	Catalog Number	Title	Type	Country	Year	Longbox Value/Value
Island	846264-2	Dead City Radio	LP/LB	U.S.		$12.00/$7.00
Warner Brothers	WUCD01	Naked Lunch Excerpt	DJ/Intvw	U.K.		$15.00
Island	PRCD 5003-2	Operators Manual, The	DJ/Intvw	U.S.	1993	$15.00

Burroughs, William and Kurt Cobain

Full Length

Label	Catalog Number	Title	Type	Country	Year	Longbox Value/Value
Tim Ker	92CD044	Priest They Call Him	LP	U.S.	1992	$14.00

Burtnick, Glen

Full Length

Label	Catalog Number	Title	Type	Country	Year	Longbox Value/Value
A&M	CD-5166-2	Heroes And Zeroes	LP/LB	U.S.		$14.00/$8.00

Burton, Ann

Full Length

Label	Catalog Number	Title	Type	Country	Year	Longbox Value/Value
RCA	R32J-1043	It Might As Well Be Love	LP	Japan		$20.00

Burton, Arline

Singles

Label	Catalog Number	Title	Type	Country	Year	Longbox Value/Value
Columbia	44K 77473	Shot In the Dark	CD5	U.S.	1994	$5.00

Burton, Gary

Full Length

Label	Catalog Number	Title	Type	Country	Year	Longbox Value/Value
Bluebird	6280	Artist's Choice	LP/LB	U.S.		$12.00/$7.00
ECM	POCJ-9045	Crystal Silence	LTD/LP	Japan		$30.00
RCA	R32J-1017	Duster	LP	Japan		$23.00
GRP	GRP-3301	Gary Burton & the Berklee All-Stars	LP/LB	U.S.		$12.00/$7.00

Singles

Label	Catalog Number	Title	Type	Country	Year	Longbox Value/Value
		Times Like These	CDJ	U.S.		$2.00

Burton, James

Full Length

Label	Catalog Number	Title	Type	Country	Year	Longbox Value/Value
Canyon	D32-3186	Mr. Telecaster	LP	Japan		$20.00

Busboys

Singles

Label	Catalog Number	Title	Type	Country	Year	Longbox Value/Value
Polydor		Hard Work	CD3	Japan	1988	$12.00/$3.00

Bush

Full Length

Label	Catalog Number	Title	Type	Country	Year	Longbox Value/Value
Westwood One		In Concert	RS	U.S.	1995	$60.00
	Airdate: 7/3/95					
Westwood One		In Concert	RS	U.S.	1996	$60.00
	Airdate: 1/1/96.					
Westwood One		In Concert	RS	U.S.	1996	$60.00
	Airdate: 5/6/96.					
Westwood One		In Concert-Nu Rock	RS	U.S.	1995	$60.00
	Airdate: 11/6/95					
Westwood One		In Concert-Nu Rock	RS	U.S.	1996	$60.00
	Airdate: 6/5/96.					
Global Satellite Network		Live From the Pit	RS	U.S.	1995	$75.00
	Airdate: 9/3/95.					
Interscope	INTD-90091	Razorblade Suitcase	DJ/Smplr	U.S.	1996	$30.00
	CD-ROM sampler. Distributed exclusively at Best Buy and The Warehouse.					

Singles

Label	Catalog Number	Title	Type	Country	Year	Longbox Value/Value
Trauma	85534	Comedown	CD5	U.S.	1995	$5.00
Trauma	PRCD 6297	Comedown	CDJ	U.S.	1995	$7.00
Trauma		Comedown	CDJ	U.S.	1996	$20.00
	CD and VHS video in box.					
Trauma		Everything Zen	CD5	U.K.	1995	$10.00
Trauma	PRCD 6069	Everything Zen	CDJ	U.S.	1995	$6.00
Trauma	PRCD 6524	Glycerine	CDJ	U.S.	1995	$7.00
Trauma		Little Things	CD5	U.K.	1995	$10.00
Trauma		Little Things	CD5	U.S.	1995	$8.00
	Enhanced CD.					
Trauma	PRCD 6137	Little Things	CDJ	U.S.	1995	$7.00
Trauma		Machinehead	CD5	U.K.	1996	$10.00
Trauma		Machinehead	CD5	U.K.	1996	$10.00
	Second version.					
Trauma		Machinehead	CDJ	U.K.	1996	$14.00
Trauma		Machinehead	CDJ	U.K.	1996	$14.00
	Second version.					
Trauma	PRCD 6633	Machinehead	CDJ	U.S.	1996	$6.00
EMI	E280829	Rubberband Girl	CD5	Canada	1993	$10.00

Bush Babies

Singles

Label	Catalog Number	Title	Type	Country	Year	Longbox Value/Value
Virgin	TXC-01	Welcome Home	CD5	U.K.	1992	$7.00

Bush, Kate

Full Length

Label	Catalog Number	Title	Type	Country	Year	Longbox Value/Value
EMI	SPCD-1402-3	Best Works 1978-93	DJ/Smplr	Japan	1993	$275.00
EMI		Dreaming, The	LP/LB	U.S.		$15.00/$9.00
EMI		Hounds Of Love	LP/LB	U.S.†		$15.00/$9.00
EMI	CP35-3045	Kick Inside, The	LP	Japan	1985	$35.00
EMI	CDP-46012	Kick Inside, The	LP/LB	U.S.†	1985	$15.00/$9.00
EMI		Kick Inside, The, Lionheart, Hounds Of Love	LP	France	1993	$100.00
	3 CD Set					
EMI		Live At Hammersmith Odeon	LTD/LP	U.K.	1994	$35.00
	CD and VHS video tape in plastic box.					
EMI		Never Forever	LP/LB	U.S.†		$15.00/$9.00
EMI		Red Shoes	DJ/LP	U.K.	1994	$130.00
	CD album plus promo video, slides, pen and press kit in shoe box.					
EMI		Red Shoes	LTD/LP	U.K.	1994	$40.00
	CD with ballet shoes and certificate in box.					
Capitol	SPRO216	Sampler	DJ/Smplr	Canada		$100.00
Capitol/EMI	C2 93078	Sensual World	LP	Canada	1989	$35.00/$25.00

Label	Catalog Number	Title	Type	Country	Year	Longbox Value / Value
Capitol		Sensual World	DJ/LP	Japan	1989	N/A
Advance issue.						
Image	ID729CB	Sensual World: Kate Bush Videos	8"LD	U.S.	1990	$30.00
EMI		Sensual World, The	DJ/Smplr	Japan		$150.00
		Singles				
EMI	DPRO 855	And So Is Love	CDJ	Canada	1994	$15.00
Columbia	DPRO-855	And So Is Love	CDJ	Canada	1994	$30.00
EMI		And So This Is Love	CD5	U.K.		$10.00
Columbia	44K 73174	Aspects of the Sensual World	CD5	U.S.	1990	$8.00
EMI	DPRO 7 900 2	Cloudbusting	CDJ	U.S.	1986	$65.00
EMI		Eat the Music	CD5	Australia	1994	$12.00
Second version.						
EMI	8814112	Eat the Music	CD5	Australia	1994	$13.00
Scratch And Sniff package.						
EMI		Eat the Music	CDJ	France	1994	$30.00
Columbia	44K 77165	Eat the Music	CD5	U.S.	1994	$6.00
EMI	TOCP-6547	Hounds Of Love	CD5	Japan		$25.00
EMI	203753-2	Love And Anger	CD5	Germany	1989	$10.00
EMI	CDEM-134	Love And Anger	CD5	U.K.	1989	$10.00
Columbia	CSK 1859	Love And Anger	CDJ	U.S.	1989	$20.00
EMI		Man I Love	CDJ	France	1994	$30.00
		Man I Love	CD5	U.K.	1994	$10.00
	LAZA-1	Man I Love	CDJ	U.K.	1994	$35.00
CD with press kit.						
		Man I Love	CDJ	U.S.	1995	$15.00
		Man I Love, The	CD5	Australia	1993	$10.00
EMI	CDEM-279	Moments Of Pleasure	CD5	U.K.	1994	$11.00
EMI	CDEMS-297	Moments Of Pleasure	CD5	U.K.	1994	$14.00
EMI	CDEM-DJ-279	Moments Of Pleasure	CDJ	U.K.	1994	$15.00
EMI		Red Shoes	CD5	U.K.	1994	$11.00
EMI		Red Shoes	CD5	U.K.	1994	$11.00
Second version.						
EMI	CDEM-DJ-1047	Red Shoes	CDJ	U.K.	1994	$15.00
		Rocket Man	CD5	Australia	1992	$12.00
Polygram	866311-2	Rocket Man	CD5	Germany	1992	$13.00
Polygram	866311-2	Rocket Man	CD5	Holland	1992	$12.00
Mercury	PHDR-50	Rocket Man	CD3	Japan	1992	$13.00/$3.00
Mercury	TRICD-2	Rocket Man	CD5	U.K.	1992	$13.00
Polydor	CDP 589	Rocket Man	CDJ	U.S.	1992	$6.00
EMI		Rubberband Girl	CDJ	France	1994	$30.00
EMI		Rubberband Girl	CD5	Japan	1994	$15.00
EMI	CDEMJ 280	Rubberband Girl	CDJ	U.K.	1993	$25.00
EMI	CDEM 280	Rubberband Girl	CD5	U.K.	1994	$11.00
EMI	CDEM-DJ-280	Rubberband Girl	CDJ	U.K.	1994	$15.00
EMI	GIRL1	Rubberband Girl	CDJ	U.K.	1994	$25.00
Advance issue.						
Capitol		Rubberband Girl	CD5	U.S.	1994	$6.00
Capitol	CSK 5504	Rubberband Girl	CDJ	U.S.	1994	$7.00
EMI	203494-3	Sensual World	CD3	Germany	1989	$12.00
Toshiba	TODP-2110	Sensual World	CD3	Japan	1989	$12.00/$4.00
EMI	CDEM 102	Sensual World	CD5	U.K.	1989	$12.00
EMI		Shoe Dance	CD5	U.K.	1994	$10.00
EMI	203612-2	This Woman's Work	CD3	Germany	1989	$10.00
EMI	203612-3	This Woman's Work	CD3	Germany	1989	$10.00
EMI	CDEM 119	This Woman's Work	CD5	U.K.	1989	$10.00
Columbia	CSK 2029	This Woman's Work	CDJ	U.S.	1990	$8.00

Bush, Stan

Label	Catalog Number	Title	Type	Country	Year	Value
		Singles				
Sony	655848-3	Forever	CD3	Germany	1990	$7.00

Bushwacks

Label	Catalog Number	Title	Type	Country	Year	Value
		Singles				
Pallas		Caught Up In the Game	CD5	U.S.	1995	$5.00
Pallas		Rough, Rugg'd & Raw	CD5	U.S.	1995	$5.00

Busta Rhymes

Label	Catalog Number	Title	Type	Country	Year	Value
		Singles				
	PRCD 9419-2	Woo-Hah!	CDJ	U.S.	1995	$2.00

Butcher, Jon

Label	Catalog Number	Title	Type	Country	Year	Value
		Full Length				
Capitol	CDP-790238	Pictures From the Front	LP/LB	U.S.		$12.00/$7.00
		Singles				
Capitol	DPRO-79525	Might As Well Be Free	CDJ	U.S.	1989	$3.00
Capitol	DPRO-79510	Send Me Somebody	CDJ	U.S.	1989	$2.00

Butler, Jerry

Label	Catalog Number	Title	Type	Country	Year	Value
		Full Length				
Charly	CD-54	Soul Workshop	LP/LB	U.S.		$14.00/$8.00
		Singles				
Urgent	269	Angel Flying Too Close To the Ground	CDJ	U.S.	1992	$2.00
Aris	8885817	He Will Break Your Heart	CD3	Germany	1990	$8.00

Butler, Jonathan

Label	Catalog Number	Title	Type	Country	Year	Value
		Singles				
BMG	ZD-44254	All Grow'd Up	CD5	Germany	1990	$8.00
Mercury	CDP-1386	Can We Start All Over Again	CDJ	U.S.	1995	$3.00
BMG	ZD-43970	Heal Our Land	CD5	Germany	1990	$8.00
Jive	JIVECD-258	Heal Our Land	CD5	U.K.	1990	$8.00
		Heal Our Land	CDJ	U.S.	1989	$2.00
Polygram	856277	I'm On My Knees	CD5	U.S.	1994	$5.00
Jive	JIVECD-227	Moonlight	CD5	U.K.	1989	$8.00
Alfa	09B3 26	More Than Friends	CD3	Japan	1988	$13.00/$4.00
RCA	1174 -2-RDJ	More Than Friends	CDJ	U.S.	1988	$2.00
Jive	JIVECD-172	Overflowing	CD5	U.K.	1990	$8.00
RCA	1216-2-RDJ	Sarah, Sarah	CDJ	U.S.	1989	$2.00
		Sing Me Your Love Song	CDJ	U.S.		$2.00
Jive	10SP-5	Take Good Care Of Me	CD3	Japan	1988	$13.00/$4.00
Jive	JIVECD-159	Take Good Care Of Me	CD5	U.K.	1988	$8.00
		Take Good Care Of Me	CDJ	U.S.	1988	$2.00
		Take Me Home	CDJ	U.S.	1988	$2.00
Jive	10SR-42	There's One Born Every Minute	CD3	Japan	1988	$13.00/$4.00
Jive	JIVECD-196	True Love Never Fails	CD5	U.K.	1989	$8.00
Jive	10SR--2	You're the Girl Of My Dreams	CD3	Japan	1988	$13.00/$4.00

Butler, Jonathan & Vincent Henry

Label	Catalog Number	Title	Type	Country	Year	Value
		Full Length				
		Tour Sampler	DJ/Smplr	U.S.		$2.00

Butt Trumpet

Label	Catalog Number	Title	Type	Country	Year	Value
		Singles				
	DPRO-19928	I'm Lonely	CDJ	U.S.		$2.00
	DPRO-19928	I'm Ugly & I don't Know Why	CDJ	U.S.	1995	$6.00

Butterfly Child

Company	Disk Number	Title	Type	Country	Year	Longbox Value / Value
		Singles				
Hark	CDS44-4	Eucalyptus	CD5	U.K.	1991	$7.00

Butterfly, Jonis

Company	Disk Number	Title	Type	Country	Year	Value
		Singles				
Circus	CLOWN-001CD	Happy Love	CD5	U.K.	1992	$7.00

Butthole Surfers

Company	Disk Number	Title	Type	Country	Year	Value
		Full Length				
Capitol	DPRO-79692	Butthole Surfers	DJ/LP	U.S.	1995	$15.00
Capitol	DPRO-79692	Independent Worm Saloon Sampler	DJ/Smplr	U.S.	1993	$20.00
		Singles				
Rough Trade	RTT-240CD	Hurdy Gurdy Man	CD5	U.K.	1990	$9.00
Rough Trade	RUS 97	Hurdy Gurdy Man	CD5	U.S.	1994	$5.00
Capitol	DPRO-79583	Hurdy Gurdy Man	CDJ	U.S.	1994	$3.00
		Pepper	CD5	U.K.	1996	$10.00
		Pepper	CDJ	U.S.		$3.00
Capitol	DPRO-79611	Who Was In My Room Last Night?	CDJ	U.S.	1993	$3.00
Capitol	DPRO-79740	Who Was In My Room Last Night?	CDJ	U.S.	1993	$3.00
Pinnacle	BFFP-41CD	Widow Maker	CD5	U.K.	1989	$9.00
Touch & Go	50	Widow Maker	CD5	U.S.	1989	$5.00
Capitol	DPRO-79299	Wooden Song, The	CDJ	U.S.	1993	$7.00
Capitol	DPRO-79787	You Don't Know Me	CDJ	U.S.	1993	$3.00

Buzon, Pierre

Company	Disk Number	Title	Type	Country	Year	Value
		Full Length				
CBS	00DP-271/4	Piano Ballad	LP	Japan		$15.00

Buzz Stop

Company	Disk Number	Title	Type	Country	Year	Value
		Singles				
Polygram	867159-2	Magic Bus	CD5	Germany	1991	$7.00

Buzzcocks

Company	Disk Number	Title	Type	Country	Year	Value
		Full Length				
		Buzzcocks Live	LD	U.S.		$22.00
EMI	790299-2	Different Kind Of Tension	LP	U.K.		$20.00
Restless	72377	Product	LP/LB	U.S.		$14.00/$8.00
		Singles				
Plantetpac	PPAC-3CD	Alive Tonight	CD5	U.K.	1991	$10.00
Essential	ESSX 2031	Do It	CD5	UK.	1993	$2.00
EMI	CDEM-104	Fab Four	CD5	U.K.	1989	$10.00
Strange Fruit	044	Peel Sessions	CD5	Germany	1989	$10.00
Sound	883524	Peel Sessions	CD5	Germany	1990	$10.00
Str. Fruit	SFRCD-104	Peel Sessions	CD5	U.K.	1990	$10.00
SPV	0959-3	Tomorrow Sunset	CD3	Germany	1989	$10.00

Buzzin' Cousins

Company	Disk Number	Title	Type	Country	Year	Value
		Singles				
Mercury	CDP 626	Sweet Suzanne	CDJ	U.S.	1992	$3.00
Mercury		Sweet Suzanne	CDJ	U.S.	1992	$3.00
Second verse.						

BVSMP

Company	Disk Number	Title	Type	Country	Year	Value
		Singles				
BCM	20019	Anytime	CD5	Germany	1989	$7.00
BCM	BC50-2160-44	Anytime	CD5	U.K.	1989	$7.00
BCM	50-2130-44	Be Gentle	CD5	Germany	1988	$7.00
BCM	BC50-2130-44	Be Gentle	CD5	U.K.	1988	$7.00
BCM	20075	I Need You	CD5	Germany	1988	$7.00
BCM	BC50-2080-44	I Need You	CD5	U.K.	1988	$7.00
BCM	20256	On And On	CD5	Germany	1988	$7.00

By All Means

Company	Disk Number	Title	Type	Country	Year	Value
		Full Length				
Island	842376	Beyond the Dream	LP/LB	U.S.		$12.00/$7.00
Island	842573	By All Means	LP/LB	U.S.		$12.00/$7.00
Motown	6344	It's Real	LP/BP	U.S.		$12.00/$7.00
		Singles				
Island	BRCD 102	I Surrender To Your Love	CD5	U.K.	1988	$8.00
		Let's Get It On	CDJ	1990		$2.00
Aris	884026	Let's Get It On	CD5	Germany	1990	$8.00
Motown	3746310422	Love Lies	CDJ	U.S.	1992	$2.00
Island	BRCD 114	Somebody Save Me	CD5	U.K.	1988	$8.00

Byard, Jaki

Company	Disk Number	Title	Type	Country	Year	Value
		Full Length				
Soul Note	267373	All The Things You Are	LP/LB	U.S.		$12.00/$7.00
Soul Note	1125	Hi Fly	LP/LB	U.S.		$12.00/$7.00
Soul Note	121025-2	To Them, To Us	LP/LB	U.S.		$12.00/$7.00

Byrd, Donald

Company	Disk Number	Title	Type	Country	Year	Value
		Full Length				
Blue Note	46539	At the Half Note Vol. 1	LP/LB	U.S.		$20.00/$15.00
Blue Note	46540	At the Half Note Vol. 2	LP/LB	U.S.		$20.00/$15.00
Blue Note	84019	Byrd In Hand	LP/LB	U.S.		$20.00/$15.00
Blue Note		Byrd In Hand	LTD/LP	U.S.	1995	$19.00
Polygram	833395	Byrd In Paris	LP/BP	U.S.		$14.00/$8.00
Blue Note	84118	Free Form	LP/LB	U.S.		$20.00/$15.00
Blue Note	84188	I'm Trying To Get Home	LP/LB	U.S.		$20.00/$15.00

Byrd, Tracy

Company	Disk Number	Title	Type	Country	Year	Value
		Full Length				
		Country Special	RS	U.S.	1995	$50.00
Airdate: 4/1/95.						
MCA	3428	Love Lessons	DJ/LP	U.S.	1995	$13.00
		Singles				
MCA	MCA5P-54497	Someone To Give My Love To	CDJ	U.S.	1993	$2.00
MCA	MCA5P-54426	That's the Thing About A Memory	CDJ	U.S.	1993	$2.00

Byrds

Company	Disk Number	Title	Type	Country	Year	Value
		Full Length				
Columbia	CSK 2239	1990 Back Pages	DJ/Smplr	U.S.	1990	$25.00
Columbia	CK 9755	Ballad Of Easy Rider	LP/LB	U.S.		$20.00/$15.00
Columbia		Byrds Sampler	DJ/Smplr	U.S.	1996	$20.00
		Definitive Collection	LTD/LP	Germany	1995	$25.00
Columbia	CK 9755	Dr. Byrds & Mr. Hyde	LP/LB	U.S.		$20.00/$15.00
Sony	A 17733	Free Flyte	LP	U.S.	1991	$18.00
Album Network		In the Studio (Original Byrds)	RS	U.S.	1989	$25.00
Airdate: 2/13/89.						
Sony	SRCS-7909	Mr. Tambourine Man	LTD/LP	Japan	1995	$30.00
20 Bit mastering.						
Media America		Up Close	RS	U.S.	1991	$40.00
2 CD set.						
		Singles				
Columbia	CSK 2227	Love That Never Dies	CDJ	U.S.	1990	$6.00

Byrds – Free Flyte (Sony A 17733)

Label	Catalog Number	Title	Type	Country	Year	Longbox Value / Value
CBS	654571-3	Mr. Tambourine Man	CD3	Germany	1990	$10.00
CBS	654571-3	Mr. Tambourine Man	CD3	U.K.	1990	$10.00

Byrne, David

Full Length

Label	Catalog Number	Title	Type	Country	Year	Longbox Value / Value
Sire	PRO-CD-3467	Brazil Classics 1/Beleza Tropical	DJ/Intvw	U.S.	1989	$15.00
WEA	9 256979-2	Catherine Wheel	LP	Germany		$18.00
Sire	2-45666	David Byrne	LTD/LP	U.S.	1994	$26.00

CD in 8.5"x11" book package.

Label	Catalog Number	Title	Type	Country	Year	Longbox Value / Value
Luaka Bop	9 25990-2-Dj	Rei Momo	DJ/LP	U.S.	1989	$18.00
Luaka Bop	PRO-CD-3820	Rei Momo - Words & Music	DJ/Intvw	U.S.	1989	$8.00
Luaka Bop	9 26799-2	Uh-Oh	LTD/LP	U.S.	1992	$15.00

First pressing with translucent red tray .

Singles

Label	Catalog Number	Title	Type	Country	Year	Longbox Value / Value
		Angels	CD5	U.K.	1994	$10.00
Sire	PRO-CD-6965	Angels	CDJ	U.S.	1994	$2.00
Warner Brothers		Ava	CD5	U.S.		$4.00
Warner Brothers	W0263CD	Back In the Box	CD6	U.K.	1004	$10.00
Sire	9 41766-2	Back In the Box	CD5	U.S.	1994	$6.00
Sire	PRO-CD_7058	Back In the Box	CDJ	U.S.	1994	$3.00
Sire	PRO-CD-3929	Dirty Old Town	CDJ	U.S.	1989	$6.00
Chrysalis	DPRO-23626	Don't Fence Me In	CDJ	U.S.	1990	$6.00
Warner Brothers	9 40177-2	Forestry	CD5	U.S.	1991	$5.00
Sire	9031-40383-2	Girl On My Mind	CD5	Germany	1992	$9.00
Sire	W-0086CD	Girl On My Mind	CD5	U.K.	1992	$9.00
Sire	PRO-CD-5347	Girl On My Mind	CDJ	U.S.	1991	$6.00
Luaka Bop	PRO-CD-5530	Hanging Upside Down	CDJ	U.S.	1992	$6.00
Sire	PRO-CD-7160-R	Lilies In the Vally	CDJ	U.S.	1994	$3.00
Sire		Make Believe Mambo	CD5	U.K.	1989	$9.00
Sire	PRO-CD-3800	Make Believe Mambo	CDJ	U.S.	1989	$6.00
Sire	PRO-CD-5920	She's Mad	CDJ	U.S.	1992	$9.00

C.C.C.P.

Singles

Label	Catalog Number	Title	Type	Country	Year	Longbox Value / Value
		Don't Kill the Rain Forest	CD5	Germany		$7.00
		Hallucinogenic Toreador	CD5	Germany		$7.00
MCA	DMCAT-1298	Hard Work	CD5	U.K.	1989	$7.00

C.C. Catch

Full Length

Label	Catalog Number	Title	Type	Country	Year	Longbox Value / Value
Ariola	257707	Catch the Fun	LP	Germany		$20.00
Ariola	258064	Welcome To the Heartbreak Hotel	LP	Germany		$20.00

Singles

Label	Catalog Number	Title	Type	Country	Year	Longbox Value / Value
BMG	162478	Baby I Need Your Love	CD3	Germany	1989	$7.00
BMG	662478	Baby I Need Your Love	CD5	Germany	1989	$7.00
BMG	662478	Back Seat Of Your Cadillac	CD5	Germany	1988	$7.00
RCA	R10D-114	Back Seat Of Your Cadillac	CD3	Japan	1988	$12.00/$3.00
Polygram	889892-3	Big Time	CD3	Geramny	1989	$7.00
Polygram	889893-2	Big Time	CD5	Geramny	1989	$7.00
BMG	662807	Good Guys Only Win In Movies	CD5	Germany	1989	$7.00
Polygram	889893-2	Midnight Hour	CD5	Geramny	1990	$7.00
BMG	652032	Nothing But A Heartache	CD5	Germany	1989	$7.00
BMG	162322	Summer Kisses	CD3	Germany	1989	$7.00
BMG	662322	Summer Kisses	CD5	Germany	1989	$7.00

C.C. Diva

Singles

Label	Catalog Number	Title	Type	Country	Year	Longbox Value / Value
EMI	DPRO-04236	Grazing In the Grass	CDJ	U.S.	1989	$3.00
Manhattan	DPRO-04047	I'll Always Follow You	CDJ	U.S.	1988	$3.00
Toshiba	XP12-5004	Searching For	CD3	Japan	1989	$12.00/$3.00

C & C Music Factory

Full Length

Label	Catalog Number	Title	Type	Country	Year	Longbox Value / Value
Sony/Sega CD		Make Your Own Music Video	LP	U.S.	1993	$10.00

CD-ROM plays only on Sega CD players.

Singles

Label	Catalog Number	Title	Type	Country	Year	Longbox Value / Value
Columbia	CSK 4345	Deeper Love	CDJ	U.S.	1991	$3.00
Columbia	CSK 6220	Do You Wanna Get Funky	CDJ	U.S.	1994	$3.00
CBS	656454-3	Gonna Make You Sweat	CD3	Germany	1990	$8.00
Columbia	44K 73605	Gonna Make You Sweat	CD5	U.S.	1990	$5.00
Columbia	CSK 73604	Gonna Make You Sweat	CDJ	U.S.	1990	$3.00
Columbia	656755-2	Here We Go	CD5	U.K.	1991	$8.00
Columbia	CSK 73690	Here We Go	CDJ	U.S.	1991	$3.00
Columbia		I'll Always Be Around	CDJ	U.S.	1995	$2.00
Sony	SRDS-8208	Just A Touch of Love	CD3	Japan	1991	$13.00/$4.00
Sony	SRCS-5561	Just A Touch of Love	CD5	Japan	1991	$13.00
Columbia	657524-5	Just A Touch of Love	CD5	U.K.	1991	$8.00
Columbia	CSK 74033	Just A Touch of Love	CDJ	U.S.	1991	$3.00
Sony	SRCS-5991	Keep It Comin'	CD5	Japan	1991	$13.00
Columbia	658430-2	Keep It Comin'	CD5	U.K.	1991	$8.00
Columbia	44K 74432	Keep It Comin'	CD5	U.S.	1991	$5.00
Columbia	CSK 74432	Keep It Comin'	CDJ	U.S.	1991	$3.00
Columbia		Robi	CDJ	U.S.	1995	$2.00
Columbia	78048	Robi-Rob's	CD5	U.S.	1995	$5.00
CBS	77742	Take A Toke	CD5	U.S.	1994	$5.00
Columbia	CSK 6631	Take A Toke	CDJ	U.S.	1994	$2.00
Columbia	656690-9	Things That Make You Go Hmm	CD5	Germany	1991	$8.00
Sony	SRCS-5533	Things That Make You Go Hmm	CD5	Japan	1991	$12.00
Columbia	44K 73688	Things That Make You Go Hmm	CD5	U.S.	1991	$5.00
Columbia	CSK 4123	Things That Make You Go Hmm	CDJ	U.S.	1991	$3.00

C'Chantal

Singles

Label	Catalog Number	Title	Type	Country	Year	Longbox Value / Value
BCM	20482	Realm	CD5	Germany	1990	$7.00

C'Est What

Full Length

Label	Catalog Number	Title	Type	Country	Year	Longbox Value / Value
Passport	PJCD-88036	Balance	LP/LB	U.S.		$16.00/$10.00

C'Vello

Singles

Label	Catalog Number	Title	Type	Country	Year	Longbox Value / Value
		This Jam Is Cold	CDJ	U.S.		$2.00
RCA	62148-2-RDJ	Turn You On	CDJ	U.S.	1991	$2.00

C2thype

Singles

Label	Catalog Number	Title	Type	Country	Year	Longbox Value / Value
Griffin	153	Close To the Hype	CD5	Canada	1994	$6.00

Cabaret Voltaire

Full Length

Label	Catalog Number	Title	Type	Country	Year	Longbox Value / Value
EMI	CDP 7-46999	Code	LP/LB	U.S.		$15.00/$10.00
Virgin	610493	Crackdown	LP	Germany		$18.00
Mute	CD-61092	Drain Train/Pressure Company	LP/LB	U.S.		$16.00/$12.00
Efa	CD-5059	Eight Crepuscle Tracks	LP	Germany		$18.00
Mute	CD-61091	Ha	LP/LB	U.S.		$16.00/$12.00
Mute	CD-61004	Johnny Yes No	LP/LB	U.S.		$16.00/$12.00
Mute	CD-61002	Mix-Up	LP/LB	U.S.		$16.00/$12.00
Mute	CD-61003	Two x 45	LP/LB	U.S.		$16.00/$12.00

Singles

Label	Catalog Number	Title	Type	Country	Year	Longbox Value / Value
Parlophone	CDDR-6261	Easy Life	CD5	U.K.	1990	$8.00
Parlophone	CDR 6166	Here To Go	CD5	U.K.	1987	$8.00
Parlophone	CDR6227	Hypnotised	CD5	U.K.	1989	$8.00
Virgin	CVCDT-6	I Want You	CD5	U.K.	1992	$8.00
Parlophone	203829-2	Keep On	CD5	Geramny	1990	$8.00
EMI	203855-2	Keep On	CD5	Geramny	1990	$8.00
Parlophone	CDR 61250	Keep On	CD5	U.K.	1990	$8.00
IRS	972051	Nag Nag Nag	CD5	Germany	1990	$8.00
Grey Area	CABS-1CD	Nag Nag Nag	CD5	U.K.	1990	$8.00
Rough Trade	372 0948-3	What Is Real	CD5	Germany	1991	$8.00
APT	TWI-948-2	What Is Real	CD5	U.K.	1991	$8.00

Cabellos, Cedric

Singles

Label	Catalog Number	Title	Type	Country	Year	Longbox Value / Value
Immortal	6670	Flow On	CDJ	U.S.	1994	$3.00
Immortal	6674	Flow On	CDJ	U.S.	1994	$3.00

Cachet De Vois

Full Length

Label	Catalog Number	Title	Type	Country	Year	Longbox Value / Value
WEA	9 25716-2	Cachet De Vois	LP	U.K.		$15.00

Cactus Rain

Singles

Label	Catalog Number	Title	Type	Country	Year	Longbox Value / Value
Virgin	TENCD-352	Each Day	CD5	U.K.	1991	$8.00
Virgin	TENCD-331	Mystery Train	CD5	U.K.	1991	$8.00
Virgin	663943	Till Comes the Morning	CD5	Geramny	1991	$8.00
Virgin	TENCX-338	Till Comes the Morning	CD5	U.K.	1991	$8.00

Cactus World News

Singles

Label	Catalog Number	Title	Type	Country	Year	Longbox Value / Value
MCA	DMCAT-1340	Rebound	CD5	U.K.	1989	$8.00
MCA	DMCAT-1364	Town Like This	CD5	U.K.	1989	$8.00

Cadell, Merlyn

Singles

Label	Catalog Number	Title	Type	Country	Year	Longbox Value / Value
Sire	PRO-CD-5679	Barbie	CDJ	U.S.	1992	$2.00
Sire	PRO-CD-5379	Sweater, The	CDJ	U.S.	1992	$2.00

Cafferty, John & The Beaver Brown Band

Full Length

Label	Catalog Number	Title	Type	Country	Year	Longbox Value / Value
Scotti Brothers	ZK-39495	Tough All Over	LP/LB	U.S.†	1995	$14.00/$8.00

Singles

Label	Catalog Number	Title	Type	Country	Year	Longbox Value / Value
Canyon	S10Y-1037	Killing Time	CD3	Japan	1989	$13.00/$4.00
Canyon	PCDY-00001	Pride And Passion	CD3	Japan	1989	$12.00/$3.00
Scotti Brothers	ZSK 1662	Pride And Passion	CDJ	U.S.	1989	$2.00
Scotti Brothers	ZSK 1858	Runnin' Thru Fire	CDJ	U.S.		$2.00
Intercord	827-326	Song & Dance	CD5	Germany	1988	$8.00
Canyon	S10Y-1004	Song & Dance	CD3	Japan	1988	$12.00/$3.00
Canyon	S10Y-1023	Victory Dance	CD3	Japan	1988	$12.00/$3.00

Cage, John

Singles

Label	Catalog Number	Title	Type	Country	Year	Longbox Value / Value
Tomato	2696592	Four Walls	CD5	Germany	1989	$8.00

Cage, Nicholas

Singles

Label	Catalog Number	Title	Type	Country	Year	Longbox Value / Value
Polygram	869307-2	Love Me	CD5	Germany	1991	$8.00

Cages

Singles

Label	Catalog Number	Title	Type	Country	Year	Longbox Value / Value
Capitol	DPRO-79550	Hometown	CDJ	U.S.	1992	$2.00
Capitol	DPRO-79427	Too Tired	CDJ	U.S.	1992	$2.00

Cairo

Singles

Label	Catalog Number	Title	Type	Country	Year	Longbox Value / Value
WEA	CBE-1235CD	I Want the Girl	CD5	U.K.	1989	$8.00
Chrysalis	CHSCD-3204	Smokin'	CD5	U.K.	1988	$8.00

Cake

Singles

Label	Catalog Number	Title	Type	Country	Year	Longbox Value / Value
Capricorn	2035	Rock 'n Roll	CDJ	U.S.	1994	$2.00

Calaveri, Nathan

Singles

Label	Catalog Number	Title	Type	Country	Year	Longbox Value / Value
MJJ	6247	Workin' On It	CDJ	U.S.	1994	$2.00

Caldwell, Bobby

Full Length

Label	Catalog Number	Title	Type	Country	Year	Longbox Value / Value
Sin Drome		A Collection Of Songs	DJ/Smplr	U.S.	1991	$12.00
Sindrome	SD2001	Be My Valentine	DJ/Smplr	U.S.	1993	$30.00
	DCI-3093	Special Sampler	DJ/Smplr	Japan		$100.00

Singles

Label	Catalog Number	Title	Type	Country	Year	Longbox Value / Value
Polydor	P10P-40004	Come To Me	CD3	Japan	1988	$13.00/$4.00
Polydor	PODP-1025	Cry	CD3	Japan	1991	$13.00/$4.00
Sin Drome	SDC 4	Don't Lead Me On	CDJ	U.S.	1991	$2.00
Sin Drome	SDC 3	Even Now	CDJ	U.S.	1989	$2.00
Sin Drome	SDC 8	Janet	CDJ	U.S.	1991	$2.00
Sin Drome	1184	Never Take A Chance	CDJ	U.S.	1993	$3.00
Polydor	PODP-1063	One Love	CD3	Japan	1992	$13.00/$4.00

Label	Catalog Number	Title	Type	Country	Year	Longbox Value / Value
Sin Drome	1185	One Love	CDJ	U.S.	1993	$3.00
Sin Drome	SDC	Real Thing	CDJ	U.S.	1990	$2.00
Polydor	PODP-1058	Shape I'm In	CD3	Japan	1992	$13.00/$4.00
Polydor	PODP-40022	Stay With Me	CD3	Japan	1989	$13.00/$4.00
Polydor	PODP-1043	Stuck On You	CD3	Japan	1992	$13.00/$4.00
Polydor	PODP-1016	Without Your Love	CD3	Japan	1991	$13.00/$4.00

Caldwell, Troy

Full Length

Label	Catalog Number	Title	Type	Country	Year	Longbox Value / Value
Cabin Fever	TC-100	Troy Caldwell	DJ/LP	U.S.	1992	$10.00

Cale, J.J.

Full Length

Label	Catalog Number	Title	Type	Country	Year	Longbox Value / Value
Mercury	800038-2	Grasshopper	LP/BP	U.S.†	1984	$14.00/$8.00
		Guitar Man	DJ/LP	France		$25.00
Polygram	811152-2	No. 8	LP	U.K.		$20.00
Mercury	818633-2	Special Edition	LP/BP	U.S.†	1985	$14.00/$8.00
Mercury	801001-2	Troubador	LP/BP	U.S.†	1984	$14.00/$8.00

Singles

Label	Catalog Number	Title	Type	Country	Year	Longbox Value / Value
Silvertone	1319-2-JDJ	Hold On Baby	CDJ	U.S.	1990	$2.00
Silvertone	ORECD-45	Lonesome Train	CD5	U.K.	1992	$8.00
Virgin	14214	Long Way Home	CDJ	U.S.	1994	$3.00
Silvertone	1356-2-JDJ	No Time	CDJ	U.S.	1990	$2.00
Silvertone	ORECD-12	Shanghai'd	CD5	U.K.	1990	$7.00

Cale, John

Full Length

Label	Catalog Number	Title	Type	Country	Year	Longbox Value / Value
Warner Brothers	9 26024-2	Wonder For the Dying	LP/LB	U.S.		$14.00/$8.00

Singles

Label	Catalog Number	Title	Type	Country	Year	Longbox Value / Value
Island	PR 9301-2	Fear	CDJ	U.S.		$3.00
WEA	7599-21826	Spinning Away	CD5	Germany	1990	$10.00

With Brian Eno

California Raisins

Full Length

Label	Catalog Number	Title	Type	Country	Year	Longbox Value / Value
Atlantic	81917-2	Meet the Raisins	LP/LB	U.S.		$12.00/$7.00

Singles

Label	Catalog Number	Title	Type	Country	Year	Longbox Value / Value
Atlantic		Signed, Sealed, Delivered I'm Yours	CDJ	U.S.	1988	$2.00

Call

Full Length

Label	Catalog Number	Title	Type	Country	Year	Longbox Value / Value
MCA	MCAD-6303	Let the Day Begin	LP/LB	U.S.	1989	$12.00/$7.00
MCA	MCAD-1003	Red Moon	LP/LB	U.S.	1989	$12.00/$7.00

Singles

Label	Catalog Number	Title	Type	Country	Year	Longbox Value / Value
Eastwest	257412-2	Let the Day Begin	CD3	Germany	1989	$8.00
Eastwest	DMCAT-1362	Let the Day Begin	CD5	U.K.	1989	$8.00
MCA	CD45 17851	Let the Day Begin	CDJ	U.S.	1989	$2.00
MCA	CD45 1178	Like You've Never Been Loved	CDJ	U.S.	1990	$2.00
MCA	CD45 1008	What's Happened To You	CDJ	U.S.	1989	$2.00
MCA	CD45 1002	When	CDJ	U.S.	1989	$2.00
MCA	DMCAT-1390	You Run	CD5	U.K.	1989	$8.00
MCA	DMCAX-1390	You Run	CD5	U.K.	1989	$10.00
MCA	CD45 18012	You Run	CDJ	U.S.	1989	$2.00

Calloway

Singles

Label	Catalog Number	Title	Type	Country	Year	Longbox Value / Value
Solar	ESK 2110	All the Way	CDJ	U.S.	1990	$2.00
Solar	ESK 74550	I Desire You	CDJ	U.S.	1992	$2.00
Intercord	826-020	I Wanna Be Rich	CD5	Germany	1990	$8.00
Epic	655515-2	I Wanna Be Rich	CDJ	U.K.	1989	$8.00
Epic	ESK 2033	I Wanna Be Rich	CDJ	U.S.	1989	$2.00
Epic	ESK 74541	Let's Get Smooth	CDJ	U.S.	1992	$2.00
Sony	CSDS-8147	Sir Lancelot	CD3	Japan	1990	$12.00/$3.00
Epic	ESK 74008	Sir Lancelot	CDJ	U.S.	1990	$2.00
Epic		Sir Lancelot	CDJ	U.S.	1990	$2.00

Second version.

Calvert, Robert

Full Length

Label	Catalog Number	Title	Type	Country	Year	Longbox Value / Value
Flicknife	SHARP-021CD	Frequency	LP	U.K.		$20.00

Camel

Full Length

Label	Catalog Number	Title	Type	Country	Year	Longbox Value / Value
Polygram	821620-2	Stationary Traveler	LP	Germany		$15.00
Polygram	821620-2	Stationary Traveler	LP	U.K.		$15.00

Cameo

Full Length

Label	Catalog Number	Title	Type	Country	Year	Longbox Value / Value
Pioneer	PA-85-105	Cameo	LD	U.S.	1985	$17.00
Polygram	836002-2	Machismo	LP/BP	U.S.		$12.00/$7.00
Polygram	846 297-2	Real Men Wear Black	DJ/LP	U.S.	1990	$12.00
Atlanta	814-984-2	She's Strange	LP/BP	U.S.†	1984	$14.00/$8.00
Casablanca	824546-2	Single Life	LP/BP	U.S.†	1985	$12.00/$8.00

Singles

Label	Catalog Number	Title	Type	Country	Year	Longbox Value / Value
Polygram	888513-2	Back And Forth	CD5	Germany	1990	$7.00
Atlanta	870 722-2	Candy	CDV/BP	U.S.	1988	$20.00/$20.00
Atlanta	CDP 297	Close Quarters	CDJ	U.S.	1990	$2.00
Reprise	PRO-CD-5224	Emotional Violence	CDJ	U.S.	1992	$2.00
Polygram	875669-2	I Want It Now	CD5	Germany	1990	$7.00
Polygram	875849-2	I Want It Now	CD5	Germany	1990	$7.00
Atlanta	MERCD-327	I Want It Now	CD5	U.K.	1990	$7.00
Atlanta	CDP 262	I Want It Now	CDJ	U.S.	1990	$2.00
Warner	12-40392	Money	CD5	Canada	1993	$10.00
Reprise	9 40392	Money	CD5	U.S.	1992	$2.00
Reprise	PRO-CD-5265	Raw But Nasty	CDJ	U.S.	1992	$2.00
Club	JABCD-77	Skin I'm In	CD5	U.K.	1988	$7.00
Reprise	PRO-CD-5431	That Kind Of Guy	CDJ	U.S.	1992	$2.00
Atlanta	870 703-2	Word Up!	CDV	U.S.	1988	$10.00
Atlanta	870 703-2	Word Up	CDV/BP	U.S.	1988	$20.00/$20.00
Club	872007-2	You Make Me Work	CD5	Germany	1988	$7.00
Club	JABCD-70	You Make Me Work	CD5	U.K.	1988	$7.00

Camero, Robert

Singles

Label	Catalog Number	Title	Type	Country	Year	Longbox Value / Value
Beaver	ALDB-24	Lady Surprise	CD3	Japan	1990	$12.00/$3.00
Alfa	11B3-71	Love Games	CD3	Japan	1990	$12.00/$3.00

Cameron, Steve

Full Length

Label	Catalog Number	Title	Type	Country	Year	Longbox Value / Value
New Age	72207	Titanic Suite	LP/LB	U.S.		$12.00/$7.00

Camouflage

Singles

Label	Catalog Number	Title	Type	Country	Year	Longbox Value / Value
Polygram	885651-2	Great Commandment, The	CD5	Germany	1988	$8.00
Polygram	885651-2	Great Commandment, The	CD5	U.K.	1988	$8.00
Atlantic	PR 2508-2	Great Commandment, The	CDJ	U.S.	1988	$3.00
Polygram	879625-2	Heaven (I Want You)	CD5	Germany	1991	$8.00

Company	Disk Number	Title	Type	Country	Year	Longbox Value / Value
Atlantic	PRCD 3851-2	Heaven (I Want You)	CDJ	U.S.	1991	$2.00
Polygram	871456-3	Love Is A Shield	CD3	Germany	1989	$8.00
Polygram	871457-2	Love Is A Shield	CD5	Germany	1989	$8.00
Polygram	887622-2	Neighbours	CD5	Germany	1988	$8.00
Polygram	887622-2	Neighbours	CD5	U.K.	1988	$8.00
Polygram	873134-3	One Fine Day	CD3	Germany	1989	$8.00
Polygram	873135-2	One Fine Day	CD5	Germany	1989	$8.00
Polygram	887342-2	Stranger Thoughts	CD5	Germany	1988	$8.00
Polygram	887342-2	Stranger Thoughts	CD5	U.K.	1988	$8.00
		That Smiling Face	CDJ	U.S.		$2.00
Atlantic	PRCD 4048-02	This Day	CDJ	U.S.	1991	$2.00

Camp Lo

Singles

Company	Disk Number	Title	Type	Country	Year	Longbox Value / Value
	PRO-CD-74452DJ	Coolie High	CDJ	U.S.		$2.00

Camp, Shawn

Full Length

Company	Disk Number	Title	Type	Country	Year	Longbox Value / Value
		Country Edge	RS	U.S.	1993	$20.00

Airdate: 11/22/93.

Campbell, Ali

Full Length

Company	Disk Number	Title	Type	Country	Year	Longbox Value / Value
Virgin	DPRO-12794	Reggae Sampler	DJ/Smplr	U.S.	1995	$10.00

Singles

Company	Disk Number	Title	Type	Country	Year	Longbox Value / Value
Virgin	38503	That Look In Your Eyes	CD5	U.S.	1995	$5.00

Campbell, Glenn

Full Length

Company	Disk Number	Title	Type	Country	Year	Longbox Value / Value
MCA	MCAD-42210	Light Years	LP/LB	U.S.		$14.00/$8.00
MCA	MCAD-42210	Still Within the Sound Of My Voice	LP/LB	U.S.		$14.00/$8.00
Capitol	CDP 90992	Unconditional Love	LP/LB	U.S.		$14.00/$8.00
Capitol	CDP 93884	Walking In the Sun	LP/LB	U.S.		$14.00/$8.00

Singles

Company	Disk Number	Title	Type	Country	Year	Longbox Value / Value
Capitol	DPRO-79676	Livin' In A House Full Of Love	CDJ	U.S.	1991	$3.00

Campbell, John

Full Length

Company	Disk Number	Title	Type	Country	Year	Longbox Value / Value
Elektra	PRCD 8700-2	Ain't Afraid Of Midnight	DJ/Intvw	U.S.	1993	$10.00

Singles

Company	Disk Number	Title	Type	Country	Year	Longbox Value / Value
Elektra		Devil In My Closet	CDJ	U.S.		$2.00
Elektra	PRCD 8746-2	When the Levee Breaks	CDJ	U.S.	1993	$2.00

Campbell, Mac

Singles

Company	Disk Number	Title	Type	Country	Year	Longbox Value / Value
King	K10Y-20009	Lights In the City	CD3	Japan	1988	$12.00/$3.00

Campbell, Ruth

Singles

Company	Disk Number	Title	Type	Country	Year	Longbox Value / Value
Up Front	UPCD-1	This Is It	CD5	U.K.	1990	$7.00

Campbell, Tevin

Full Length

Company	Disk Number	Title	Type	Country	Year	Longbox Value / Value
QWest	9 26291-2-DJ	T.E.V.I.N.	DJ/LP	U.S.	1991	$15.00

Singles

Company	Disk Number	Title	Type	Country	Year	Longbox Value / Value
QWest	PRO-CD-5484	Alone With You	CDJ	U.S.	1991	$2.00
Qwest	PRO-CD-6701	Always In My Heart	CDJ	U.S.	1993	$2.00
QWest	18260-2	Always In My Heart	CD5	U.S.	1994	$5.00
Qwest	PRO-CD-6975	Always In My Heart	CDJ	U.S.	1994	$2.00
QWest	18346	Can We Talk	CD5	U.S.	1993	$4.00
QWest	PRO-CD-6643	Can We Talk	CDJ	U.S.	1993	$2.00
QWest	PRO-CD-6650	Can We Talk	CDJ	U.S.	1993	$2.00
Warner Brothers	18346	Can We Talk	CD5	U.S.	1994	$5.00
Qwest	PRO-CD-6500	Can We Talk	CDJ	U.S.	1994	$2.00
Warner	12-40756	Confused	CD5	Canada	1993	$10.00
QWest	9 40756-2	Confused	CD5	U.S.	1991	$4.00
QWest	PRO-CD-5743	Confused	CDJ	U.S.	1991	$2.00
QWest	PRO-CD-5922	Confused	CDJ	U.S.	1991	$2.00
Qwest	PRO-CD-6713	Don't Say Goodbye Girl	CDJ	U.S.	1993	$2.00
Warner Brothers	18254	Don't Say Goodbye Girl	CD5	U.S.	1994	$5.00
QWest	PRO-CD-5318	Goodbye	CDJ	U.S.	1991	$2.00
Qwest	18264-2	I'm Ready	CD5	U.S.	1993	$5.00
QWest	PRO-CD-6698	I'm Ready	CDJ	U.S.	1993	$2.00
QWest	PRO-CD-6912	I'm Ready	CDJ	U.S.	1993	$2.00
	5012	I'm Ready	CD5	U.S.	1994	$5.00
QWest	PRO-CD-6854-R	I'm Ready	CDJ	U.S.	1994	$3.00
QWest	PRO-CD-4858	Just Ask Me To	CDJ	U.S.	1991	$2.00
QWest	PRO-CD-5623	One Song	CDJ	U.S.	1991	$2.00
Warner	12-40740	Round And Round	CD5	Canada	1993	$10.00
Warner Brothers	W-0115CD	Round And Round	CD5	U.K.	1990	$8.00
Paisley Park	9 21740-2	Round And Round	CD5	U.S.	1990	$5.00
Paisley Park	PRO-CD-4348	Round And Round	CDJ	U.S.	1990	$2.00
QWest	PRO-CD-6766	Shh	CDJ	U.S.	1993	$2.00
Warner	12-40569	Strawberry Letter 23	CD5	Canada	1993	$10.00
Warner Brothers	PRO-CD-5441	Strawberry Letter 23	CD5	U.S.	1991	$2.00
Warner Brothers	9 40569-2	Strawberry Letter 23	CD5	U.S.	1991	$6.00
Warner Brothers	WPDP-6292	Tell Me Want Me To Do	CD3	Japan	1991	$13.00/$4.00
Warner Brothers	W-0102CD	Tell Me Want Me To Do	CD3	Japan	1992	$13.00/$4.00
QWest	PRO-CD-5070	Tell Me Want Me To Do	CDJ	U.S.	1991	$3.00

Campbell, Trisha

Singles

Company	Disk Number	Title	Type	Country	Year	Longbox Value / Value
Capitol	DPRO-79604	Love Me Down	CDJ	U.S.	1992	$2.00
Capitol	DPRO-79516	Push	CDJ	U.S.	1992	$2.00

Camper Van Beethoven

Full Length

Company	Disk Number	Title	Type	Country	Year	Longbox Value / Value
Virgin		Key Lime Pie	LP/LB	U.S.		$14.00/$8.00
IRS		Vantiques	DJ/Smplr	U.S.		$25.00
Virgin	DPRO-14129	Virgin Years, The	DJ/Smplr	U.S.	1994	$20.00

Features 8 songs by Cracker and 8 by Camper Van Beethoven.

Singles

Company	Disk Number	Title	Type	Country	Year	Longbox Value / Value
Virgin	PRCD 3118	(I Was Born In A) Laundromat	CDJ	U.S.	1989	$2.00
Virgin	VUSCD-8	Pictures Of Matchstick Men	CD3	U.K.	1990	$7.00
Virgin	PRCD 2865	Pictures Of Matchstick Men	CDJ	U.S.	1989	$2.00
Virgin	PRCD 3024	Pictures Of Matchstick Men	CDJ	U.S.	1989	$2.00
Virgin	PRCD 2471	Turquoise Jewelry	CDJ	U.S.	1988	$2.00

Campfire Girls

Singles

Company	Disk Number	Title	Type	Country	Year	Longbox Value / Value
	PRCD 6369	Mood Enhancer	CDJ	U.S.		$2.00

Can

Full Length

Company	Disk Number	Title	Type	Country	Year	Longbox Value / Value
Mute	61073	Can	LP/LB	U.S.		$14.00/$8.00
Restless	71453-2	Cannibalism 1	LP/LB	U.S.		$14.00/$8.00

Label	Catalog Number	Title	Type	Country	Year	Longbox Value / Value
Restless	71441-2	Delay 1968	LP/LB	U.S.		$14.00/$8.00
Restless	71453-2	Edge Bamyasi	LP/LB	U.S.		$14.00/$8.00
Mute	61074	Flow Motion	LP/LB	U.S.		$14.00/$8.00
Restless	71446-2	Future Days	LP/LB	U.S.		$14.00/$8.00
Mute	61076	Landed	LP/LB	U.S.		$14.00/$8.00
Mute	61072	Limited & Unlimited Edition	LP/LB	U.S.		$14.00/$8.00
Restless	71442-2	Monster Movie	LP/LB	U.S.	1990	$14.00/$8.00
Mute	61075	Saw Delight	LP/LB	U.S.		$14.00/$8.00
Restless	71447-2	Soon Over Babaluma	LP/LB	U.S.		$14.00/$8.00
Restless	71443-2	Soundtracks	LP/LB	U.S.		$14.00/$8.00
Restless	71444-2	Tango Mango	LP/LB	U.S.		$14.00/$8.00
		Singles				
Polygram	875751-2	Hoolah Hoolah	CD5	Germany	1990	$9.00
Virgin	2079	Saw Delight	CD5	U.K.		$10.00

Cancioneros Del

Singles

Label	Catalog Number	Title	Type	Country	Year	Value
	1420	Por Los Caminos Del	CD5	U.S.	1994	$5.00

Candee

Singles

Label	Catalog Number	Title	Type	Country	Year	Value
Toshiba	10TX-5010	Get Over You	CD3	Japan		$12.00/$3.00

Candi

Full Length

Label	Catalog Number	Title	Type	Country	Year	Value
IRS	IRSD-42260	Candi	LP/LB	U.S.		$14.00/$8.00
IRS	IRSD-13045	World Keeps On Turnning	LP/LB	U.S.		$14.00/$8.00
		Singles				
Victor	VDPS-1047	Dancing Under A Latin Moon	CD3	Japan	1989	$12.00/$3.00
IRS	EIRSCD-108	Dancing Under A Latin Moon	CD5	U.K.	1989	$8.00
Victor	VDPS-1040	Notice Me	CD3	Japan	1989	$12.00/$3.00
IRS	67049	Saving All In Love	CDJ	U.S.		$2.00
Victor	[illegible]	[illegible]	CD3	Japan	1989	$12.00/$3.00
IRS	241010-2	Under Your Spell	CD5	Germany	1989	$8.00
Victor	VIDP-20	World Just Keeps On Turning	CD3	Japan	1990	$12.00/$3.00
IRS	67031	World Just Keeps On Turning	CDJ	U.S.	1990	$2.00

Candle

Singles

Label	Catalog Number	Title	Type	Country	Year	Value
Lithium	LICD-04	No Eyes	CD5	U.K.	1992	$8.00

Candlebox

Full Length

Label	Catalog Number	Title	Type	Country	Year	Value
Westwood One		In Concert	RS	U.S.	1994	$40.00
Airdate: 8/1/94						
Westwood One		In Concert	RS	U.S.	1994	$50.00
2 CD set. With Guns N' Roses and Cracker, Airdate: 5/23//94.						
Westwood One		In Concert	RS	U.S.	1994	$50.00
Airdate: 10/24/94.						
Westwood One		In Concert	RS	U.S.	1995	$50.00
Airdate: 8/14/95.						
		Singles				
	PRO-CD-8071	Best Friend	CDJ	U.S.	1996	$3.00
Maverick	PRO-CD-6239	Change	CDJ	U.S.	1993	$2.00
Maverick	PRO-CD-6250	Change	CDJ	U.S.	1993	$2.00
Maverick	PRO-CD-7921	Change	CDJ	U.S.	1995	$3.00
Maverick	PRO-CD-7218	Cover Me	CDJ	U.S.	1994	$6.00
	PRO-CD-8218	Cover Me	CDJ	U.S.	1995	$3.00
Maverick	PRO-CD-6770	Far Behind	CDJ	U.S.	1993	$6.00
Maverick	PRO-CD-6999	Far Behind	CDJ	U.S.	1993	$6.00
Warner Brothers		Simple Lessons	CD5	U.K.	1995	$10.00
Maverick	PRO-CD-786	Simple Lessons	CDJ	U.S.	1995	$3.00
	PRO-CD-7977-R	Understanding	CDJ	U.S.	1996	$3.00
Maverick	PRO-CD-6576	You	CDJ	U.S.	1993	$2.00
Maverick	PRO-CD-6802	You	CDJ	U.S.	1993	$2.00
Maverick	18304	You	CD5	U.S.	1994	$6.00

Candlemass

Full Length

Label	Catalog Number	Title	Type	Country	Year	Value
Enigma	73340	Ancient Dreams	LP/BP	U.S.		$12.00/$7.00
Warner Brothers	26444	Double Live	LP/LB	U.S.		$14.00/$8.00
Restless	72241	Nightfall	LP/BP	U.S.		$12.00/$7.00
Enigma	73417	Tales Of Creation	LP/BP	U.S.		$12.00/$7.00

Candy Flip

Full Length

Label	Catalog Number	Title	Type	Country	Year	Value
Atlantic	82264	Madstock	LP/LB	U.S.		$12.00/$7.00
		Singles				
Debut	DEBCD-3106	Redhills Road	CD5	U.K.	1990	$8.00
Atlantic	PRCD 3953-2	Redhills Road	CDJ	U.S.	1990	$2.00
Debut	DEBCD-3102	Space	CD5	U.K.	1990	$8.00
Bellaphon	130-07-356	Strawberry Fields Forever	CD5	Germany	1990	$8.00
Canyon	PCDY-00061	Strawberry Fields Forever	CD3	Japan	1990	$13.00/$4.00
Debut	DEBCD-3092	Strawberry Fields Forever	CD5	U.K.	1990	$8.00
Atlantic	PRCD 3498-2	Strawberry Fields Forever	CDJ	U.S.	1990	$2.00
Atlantic	PRCD 3412-2	Strawberry Fields Forever	CDJ	U.S.	1990	$2.00
Debut	DEBCD-3099	This Can Be Real	CD5	U.K.	1990	$8.00

Candy Harlots

Singles

Label	Catalog Number	Title	Type	Country	Year	Value
Virgin	VOZCD 136	Sister's Crazy	CD5	Austalia	1992	$8.00
Virgin	VOZCD 136	Sister's Crazy	CD5	Germany	1992	$10.00

Candy Shock

Singles

Label	Catalog Number	Title	Type	Country	Year	Value
SPV	1009-3	Rock You Baby	CD5	Germany	1991	$7.00

Candy Skins

Singles

Label	Catalog Number	Title	Type	Country	Year	Value
DGC	PRO-CD-4526	Everybody Loves You	CDJ	U.S.	1993	$3.00
DGC	PRO-CD-4346	For What It's Worth	CDJ	U.S.	1991	$3.00
DGC	DGCTD-3	Submarine Song	CD5	U.K.	1991	$8.00
DGC	PRO-CD-4235	Submarine Song	CDJ	U.S.	1991	$3.00
DGC	PRO-CD-4241	Submarine Song	CDJ	U.S.	1991	$7.00
Geffen	GFSTD-30	Wembley	CD5	U.K.	1993	$8.00
DGC	PRO-CD-4471	Wembley	CDJ	U.S.	1991	$3.00

Candyland

Full Length

Label	Catalog Number	Title	Type	Country	Year	Value
Eastwest	91765-2	Suck It & See	LP/LB	U.S.		$14.00/$8.00
		Singles				
Pinnacle	YESCD-4	Fountain O' Youth	CD5	U.K.	1991	$8.00
Eastwest	PRCD 4066-2	Fountain O' Youth	CDJ	U.K.	1991	$2.00
Pinnacle	YESCD-9	Kingdom	CD5	U.K.	1991	$8.00
Fiction	FICCD-37	Rainbow	CD5	U.K.	1991	$8.00

Candyman

Singles

Label	Catalog Number	Title	Type	Country	Year	Value
Epic	ESK 4104	Candyman Theme	CDJ	U.S.	1991	$2.00
Danzalot		Do Me Right	CDJ	U.S.		$2.00
Epic	656295-3	Knockin' Boots	CD3	Germany	1990	$8.00
Epic	656295-2	Knockin' Boots	CD5	Germany	1990	$8.00
Epic		Knockin' Boots	CDJ	U.S.	1990	$2.00
Epic	656560-5	Melt In Your Mouth	CD5	Germany	1990	$8.00
Sony	ESDA-7069	Nightgown	CD3	Japan	1991	$12.00/$3.00
Epic	ESK 73721	Nightgown	CDJ	U.S.	1991	$2.00
Epic	ESK 4220	Oneighundredskytalkpin-elevenotowosevenine	CDJ	U.S.	1991	$2.00

Canned Heat

Full Length

Label	Catalog Number	Title	Type	Country	Year	Value
Interphon	881059	Canned Heat	LP	Germany		$12.00
		Live!	LP	Germany		$12.00
		One Step Behind the Blues	LP	U.S.		$12.00
Dali	89022	Reheated	LP/BP	U.S.		$14.00/$8.00
		Singles				
River Road	61794	Internal Combustion	CDJ	U.S.	1994	$7.00
Liberty	CDEM-100	Let's Work Together	CD5	U.K.	1989	$10.00

Cantrell, Jerry

Singles

Label	Catalog Number	Title	Type	Country	Year	Value
		Leave Me Alone	CDJ	U.S.		$7.00
	OSK 7966	Leave Me Alone	CDJ	U.S.	1996	$3.00

Capaldi, Jim

Singles

Label	Catalog Number	Title	Type	Country	Year	Value
Island	CID-391	Some Come Running	CD5	U.K.	1988	$8.00
Island	PR 2675-2	Some Come Running	CDJ	U.S.	1988	$2.00
Island	CID 380	[illegible]	[illegible]	U.K.	1988	$8.00
Island	885466	Take Me Home	CD5	Germany	1989	$8.00
Island	CID-419	Take Me Home	CD5	U.K.	1989	$8.00

Capataz

Singles

Label	Catalog Number	Title	Type	Country	Year	Value
Fonorama	4003	"te Quiero"	CD5	U.S.	1994	$5.00

Capelton

Singles

Label	Catalog Number	Title	Type	Country	Year	Value
Polygram	577199	Wings Of the Morning	CD5	U.S.	1995	$5.00

Capercaillie

Singles

Label	Catalog Number	Title	Type	Country	Year	Value
		When You Return	CD5	U.K.		$10.00
		When You Return	CD5	U.K.		$10.00
Second version.						

Capital Tax

Singles

Label	Catalog Number	Title	Type	Country	Year	Value
MCA	2522	I Can't Believe It	CDJ	U.S.	1993	$2.00
MCA	2774	Masha, The	CDJ	U.S.	1993	$2.00

Cappella

Singles

Label	Catalog Number	Title	Type	Country	Year	Value
Cygnet	CDCYG-4	Everybody Listen To It	CD5	U.K.		$8.00
SPV	8410-3	Hel Yom Halib	CD5	Germany	1990	$8.00
Alfa	09B3-21	Hel Yom Halib	CD3	Japan	1990	$12.00/$3.00
		Move On Baby	CD5	U.K.		$8.00
		Move On Baby	CD5	U.K.		$8.00
Second version.						
London	857713	Move On Baby	CD5	U.S.	1994	$5.00
London	6879	Move On Baby	CDJ	U.S.	1994	$3.00
ZYX	6717-8	Take Me Away	CD5	Germany	1992	$6.00
Media	ALCB-448	Take Me Away	CD5	Japan	1992	$13.00
PWL	PWCD-210	Take Me Away	CD5	U.K.	1992	$8.00
		U Got 2 Know	CD5	U.K.		$8.00
		U Got 2 Know	CD5	U.K.		$8.00
Second version.						
Polydor	422857626	U Got 2 Let The Music	CD5	Canada	1994	$23.00

Cappelli, Rachele

Full Length

Label	Catalog Number	Title	Type	Country	Year	Value
Atlantic	81856-2	Rachelle Cappelli	LP/LB	U.S.		$12.00/$7.00
		Singles				
Atlantic		I'm Sorry	CDJ	U.S.		$2.00

Capricorn

Singles

Label	Catalog Number	Title	Type	Country	Year	Value
4th & B'way	BRCD-273	Taste	CD5	U.K.	1992	$8.00

Captain America

Full Length

Label	Catalog Number	Title	Type	Country	Year	Value
Special		At His Best	LP	U.S.		$10.00
		Singles				
Rough Trade	585 0014-3	Bed In	CD5	Germany	1991	$7.00
Rough Trade	585 0016-3	Flame On	CD5	Germany	1991	$7.00
Paperhouse	PAPER-016CD	Flame On	CD5	U.K.	1992	$7.00
Paperhouse	PAPER-016CD	Wow	CD5	U.K.	1991	$7.00

Captain Croon

Singles

Label	Catalog Number	Title	Type	Country	Year	Value
		Judge Ito	CDJ	U.S.	1995	$2.00

Captain George

Singles

Label	Catalog Number	Title	Type	Country	Year	Value
BMG	BVDR-66	Tale Of the Dragon	CD3	Japan	1991	$12.00/$3.00

Captain Hollywood Project

Singles

Label	Catalog Number	Title	Type	Country	Year	Value
Blow Up	825 993	All I Want	CDJ	Germany	1993	$9.00
Imago	72767 25033	All I Want	CDJ	U.S.	1933	$2.00
Debut	DEBCD-3145	More And More	CD5	U.K.	1992	$8.00
Imago	72787-25041	Only With You	CD5	U.S.	1993	$5.00
Imago	28059	Only With You	CDJ	U.S.	1993	$3.00
Imago	72767 25063	Rhythm Of Life	CDJ	U.S.	1994	$2.00
Intercord	825-917	Rock Me	CD5	Germany	1991	$8.00
Bellaphon	130 07-331	Shirley	CD5	Germany	1989	$8.00
Bellaphon	130 07-315	Soul Sister	CD5	Germany	1989	$8.00

Captain Sensible

Full Length

Label	Catalog Number	Title	Type	Country	Year	Value
Collector's Pipeline	TCP 009	Universe Of Geoffrey Brown	LP	U.S.	1992	$16.00

Captain & Tennille

Singles

Label	Catalog Number	Title	Type	Country	Year	Longbox Value/Value
A&M	S12Y-3033	Love Will Keep Us Together	CD3	Japan	1988	$13.00/$4.00

Cara, Irene

Full Length

Label	Catalog Number	Title	Type	Country	Year	Longbox Value/Value
Geffen	4021-2	What A Feeling	LP/LB	U.S.†	1985	$14.00/$8.00
Mercury	P10X-30002	Flashdance	CD3	Japan	1988	$13.00/$4.00

Singles

Label	Catalog Number	Title	Type	Country	Year	Longbox Value/Value
Mercury	PHDR-55	Flashdance	CD3	Japan	1992	$13.00/$4.00
Polygram	887623-2	I Can Fly	CD5	Germany	1988	$7.00
Curb	CD45 10570	Love Survives	CDJ	U.S.	1989	$2.00

Carabba, Tom

Singles

Label	Catalog Number	Title	Type	Country	Year	Longbox Value/Value
BMG	662424	Deliverance	CD5	Germany	1989	$8.00

Caram, Ana

Full Length

Label	Catalog Number	Title	Type	Country	Year	Longbox Value/Value
Chesky	GLD 73	Other Side Of Jobim	LTD/LP	U.S.		N/A
	Gold disc.					

Caravan

Full Length

Label	Catalog Number	Title	Type	Country	Year	Longbox Value/Value
Kingdom	CDKVL-9028	Canterbury Collection	LP	U.K.		$15.00

Caravelli

Full Length

Label	Catalog Number	Title	Type	Country	Year	Longbox Value/Value
Epic	358P-10	Best Of	LP	Japan		$20.00
CBS	CDCBS-86244	Best Of	LP	U.K.		$15.00

Carcass

Singles

Label	Catalog Number	Title	Type	Country	Year	Longbox Value/Value
Columbia	CSK 5542	Buried Dreams	CDJ	U.S.	1993	$2.00
Earache	6274	Embodiment	CDJ	U.S.	1994	$2.00
Earache	MOSH-49CD	Tools Of the Trade	CD5	U.K.	1992	$8.00

Caretaker Race

Singles

Label	Catalog Number	Title	Type	Country	Year	Longbox Value/Value
Foundation	TFL-8CD	Two Steel Rings	CD5	U.K.	1990	$7.00

Carey, Mariah

Full Length

Label	Catalog Number	Title	Type	Country	Year	Longbox Value/Value
Sony	XACS-90023	All I Want For Christmas Is You	DJ/Smplr	Japan	1994	$100.00
Columbia	CSK 7599	In-Store Sampler	DJ/Smplr	U.S.	1996	$15.00
Sony	XACS-90023	Let's Party	DJ/Smplr	Japan	1996	$135.00
Sony	XACS-90032	Love & Dream/Best Collection	DJ/Smplr	Japan		$100.00
CBS	466815 9	Mariah Carey	LTD/LP	Austria	1990	$30.00
	Picture disc CD.					
CBS	4668152	Mariah Carey	LTD/LP	U.K.	1990	$35.00
	Picture disc CD.					
Columbia	CSK 45202	Mariah Carey	DJ/LP	U.S.	1990	$15.00
Columbia		Mariah Carey	LTD/LP	U.S.	1990	$15.00
CBS		Music Box	LTD/LP	Australia	1994	$25.00
	Gold Disc.					
Columbia	474270-2	Music Box	LTD/LP	U.K.	1993	$30.00
Columbia	CSK 3087	Profiled	DJ/Intvw	U.S.	1991	$20.00
Columbia	PCD 187	Unplugged, Radio Special	DJ/Smplr	Canada	1992	$40.00
Unistar		Weekly Specials, The	RS	U.S.	1991	$15.00
	Airdate: 17/26/91					

Single

Label	Catalog Number	Title	Type	Country	Year	Longbox Value/Value
Sony		Special Sampler	DJ/CD3	Japan	1994	$40.00
		All I Want For Christmas	CD5	U.K.		$10.00
	Second version.					
Columbia		All I Want For Christmas	CDJ	U.K.	1994	$15.00
Columbia	CSK 6644	All I Want For Christmas	CDJ	U.S.	1994	$3.00
Sony	SRDS-8291	All I Want For Christmas Is You	CD3	Japan	1993	$13.00/$4.00
Sony	SRDS-8308	Always Be My Baby	CD3	Japan	1996	$13.00/$4.00
Sony		Always Be My Baby	CD5	U.K.	1996	$10.00
Sony		Always Be My Baby	CD5	U.K.	1996	$10.00
	Second version.					
Columbia	CSK 7633	Always Be My Baby	CDJ	U.S.	1996	$3.00
CBS		Anytime U Need A Friend	CD5	U.K.	1994	$11.00
CBS		Anytime U Need A Friend	CD5	U.K.	1994	$11.00
	Second version.					
Columbia	77528	Anytime U Need A Friend	CD5	U.S.	1994	$5.00
Columbia	77543	Anytime U Need A Friend	CD5	U.S.	1994	$5.00
Columbia	CSK 6255	Anytime U Need A Friend	CDJ	U.S.	1994	$3.00
Columbia	SRCS-7451	Anytime You Need A Friend	CD5	Japan		$20.00
Sony	SRDS-8282	Anytime You Need A Friend	CD3	Japan	1993	$13.00/$4.00
Columbia		Anytime You Need A Friend	CDJ	U.K.	1994	$15.00
Columbia	657615-5	Can't Let Go	CD5	Germany	1992	$10.00
Columbia	SRDS-8217	Can't Let Go	CD3	Japan	1991	$15.00/$3.00
Columbia	657662-2	Can't Let Go	CD5	U.K.	1992	$10.00
Columbia	CSK 74088	Can't Let Go	CDJ	U.S.	1991	$3.00
Sony	SRCS 7821	Daydream	CD5	Japan		$20.00
Sony	SRDS-8264	Dream Lover	CD3	Japan	1993	$13.00/$4.00
CBS		Dream Lover	CDJ	U.K.	1993	$12.00
Columbia	44K 77079	Dream Lover	CD5	U.S.	1993	$6.00
Columbia	CSK 5324	Dream Lover	CDJ	U.S.	1993	$2.00
Columbia	CSK 5373	Dream Lover	CDJ	U.S.	1993	$2.00
CBS	77079	Dream Lover	CD5	U.S.	1993	$5.00
CBS	77080	Dream Lover	CD5	U.S.	1994	$5.00
Columbia	SRDS-8203	Emotions	CD3	Japan	1991	$15.00/$3.00
Columbia	657403-2	Emotions	CD5	U.K.	1991	$10.00
Columbia	44K 74037	Emotions	CD5	U.S.	1991	$5.00
Columbia	CSK 73977	Emotions	CDJ	U.S.	1991	$3.00
Columbia	CSK 73977	Emotions	CDJ	U.S.	1991	$3.00
Columbia		Endless Love	CDJ	U.K.	1994	$15.00
Columbia	CSK 6408	Endless Love	CDJ	U.S.	1994	$3.00
Columbia		Endless Love	CDJ	U.S.	1994	$3.00
Sony	SRDS-8303	Fantasy	CD3	Japan	1993	$13.00/$4.00
CBS		Fantasy	CD5	U.K.	1995	$10.00
CBS		Fantasy	CD5	U.K.	1995	$10.00
	Second version.					
Columbia		Fantasy	CDJ	U.K.	1995	$15.00
Columbia	78043	Fantasy	CD5	U.S.	1995	$5.00
Columbia	78044	Fantasy	CD5	U.S.	1995	$6.00
Columbia	CSK 7321	Fantasy	CDJ	U.S.	1995	$6.00
Columbia		Fantasy	CDJ	U.S.	1995	$6.00
	Second version.					
Sony	SRDS-8267	Hero	CD3	Japan	1993	$13.00/$4.00
Sony	SRCS 6969	Hero	CD5	Japan	1993	$20.00
Columbia	CSK 77224	Hero	CDJ	U.S.	1993	$3.00
CBS	77225	Hero	CD5	U.S.	1994	$5.00
Columbia	SRDS-8187	I Don't Wanna Cry	CD3	Japan	1990	$15.00/$3.00
Columbia	CSK 73743	I Don't Wanna Cry	CDJ	U.S.	1991	$3.00
CBS		I'll Be There	CD5	Germany	1991	$8.00
Columbia	SRDS-8232	I'll Be There	CD3	Japan	1991	$15.00/$3.00
Columbia	CSK 74330	I'll Be There	CDJ	U.S.	1991	$7.00
Columbia	SRDS-8249	If It's Over	CD3	Japan	1992	$15.00/$3.00
Columbia		Jesus Born On This Day	CDJ	U.S.	1994	$3.00
CBS		Joy To the World	CD5	Australia	1995	$10.00
Columbia		Joy To the World	CDJ	U.K.	1994	$18.00
Columbia	CSK 6646	Joy To the World	CDJ	U.S.	1994	$3.00
Columbia	656149-3	Love Takes Time	CD3	Gremany	1990	$10.00
Columbia	CSDS-8166	Love Takes Time	CD3	Japan	1994	$15.00/$4.00
Columbia	656364-2	Love Takes Time	CD5	U.K.	1990	$10.00
Columbia	CSK 73455	Love Takes Time	CDJ	U.S.	1990	$3.00
Columbia	657819-2	Make It Happen	CD5	Germany	1992	$15.00
Columbia	SRDS-8222	Make It Happen	CD3	Japan	1991	$15.00/$3.00
Columbia	657941-2	Make It Happen	CD5	U.K.	1992	$15.00
Columbia	44K 74189	Make It Happen	CD5	U.S.	1991	$5.00
Columbia	CSK 74239	Make It Happen	CDJ	U.S.	1991	$6.00
Columbia	CSK 6647	Miss You Most	CDJ	U.S.	1994	$3.00
CBS	77418	Never Forget You	CD5	U.S.	1994	$5.00
Columbia	CSK 5615	Never Forget You	CDJ	U.S.	1994	$3.00
Columbia	CSK 5968	Never Forget You	CDJ	U.S.	1994	$3.00
Columbia	XDCS-93195	One Sweet Day	CDJ	Japan	1995	$65.00
CBS		One Sweet Day	CD5	U.K.	1995	$10.00
CBS		One Sweet Day	CD5	U.K.	1995	$10.00
	Second version.					
CBS		One Sweet Day	CDJ	U.K.	1995	$13.00
Columbia	78074	One Sweet Day	CD5	U.S.	1995	$5.00
Columbia	78075	One Sweet Day	CD5	U.S.	1995	$6.00
Columbia		One Sweet Day	CDJ	U.S.	1995	$3.00
Sony		Open Arms	CD5	Australia	1996	$12.00
Sony		Open Arms	CD5	Australia	1996	$12.00
	Second version.					
Sony		Open Arms	CDJ	Spain	1996	$50.00
Columbia	656538-3	Someday	CD3	Germany	1990	$10.00
Sony		Someday	CD3	Japan	1990	$13.00/$3.00
Sony	CSCS5406	Someday	CD5	Japan	1990	$25.00
Columbia	656583-2	Someday	CD5	U.K.	1990	$10.00
Columbia	CSK 73561	Someday	CDJ	U.S.	1990	$3.00
Columbia	656931-2	There's Got To Be A Way	CD5	Germany	1991	$10.00
Columbia	656931-2	There's Got To Be A Way	CD5	U.K.	1991	$10.00
Columbia	655932-2	Vision Of Love	CD5	Germany	1990	$10.00
Columbia	CSDS-8156	Vision Of Love	CD3	Japan	1990	$13.00/$4.00
Columbia	655932-2	Vision Of Love	CD5	U.K.	1990	$10.00
Columbia	CSK 73346	Vision Of Love	CDJ	U.S.	1990	$8.00
Columbia	CSK 73348	Vision Of Love	CDJ	U.S.	1990	$15.00
	Special digipak package.					
Columbia	SRDS-8271	Without You	CD3	Japan		$13.00/$4.00
Columbia	DP-09	Without You	CD5	Japan		$13.00/$4.00
CBS		Without You	CD5	U.K.	1994	$10.00
CBS		Without You	CD5	U.K.	1994	$10.00
	Second version.					
CBS	XPCD-358	Without You	CDJ	U.K.	1995	$12.00
Columbia	44K 77358	Without You	CD5	U.S.	1994	$5.00
Columbia	CSK 5620	Without You	CDJ	U.S.	1994	$3.00

Carey, Tony

Singles

Company	Disk Number	Title	Type	Country	Year	Longbox Value/Value
Polygram	871634-3	Come To the Flood	CD3	Germany	1989	$7.00
Polygram	871635-2	Come To the Flood	CD5	Germany	1989	$7.00
Polygram	879213-2	Deal	CD5	Germany	1990	$7.00
Polygram	889946-3	I Feel Good	CD3	Germany	1989	$7.00
Polygram	889947-2	I Feel Good	CD5	Germany	1989	$7.00
Polygram	873757-2	No-Man's Land	CD5	Germany	1990	$7.00
Polygram	871387-2	Room With A View	CD5	Germany	1989	$7.00
Polygram	871386-3	Room With A View	CD3	Germany	1989	$7.00
Eastwest	9031-76988-2	Wonderland	CD5	Germany	1992	$7.00

Caribic Girls

Singles

Company	Disk Number	Title	Type	Country	Year	Longbox Value/Value
ZYX	6533-8	Beach Party	CD5	Germany	1991	$6.00

Carina, Molto

Singles

Company	Disk Number	Title	Type	Country	Year	Longbox Value/Value
Alfa	10B3-7	Voice Of the Night	CD3	Japan	1989	$15.00/$3.00

Carlin, George

Full Length

Company	Disk Number	Title	Type	Country	Year	Longbox Value/Value
Vestron	VL3154	George Carlin	LD	U.S.	1987	$30.00

Carlisle, Belinda

Full Length

Company	Disk Number	Title	Type	Country	Year	Longbox Value/Value
Virgin	CDVP-2496	Heaven On Earth	LTD/LP	U.K.	1987	$35.00
	Picture disc CD.					
MCA	MCAD-10446	Live Your Life Be Free	LP/LB	U.S.		$14.00/$8.00
		Real	DJ/LP	U.K.		$20.00
Pioneer Artists	PA-90-023	Runaway Video	LD	U.S.	1990	$25.00

Singles

Company	Disk Number	Title	Type	Country	Year	Longbox Value/Value
		California	CD5	U.K.	1997	$10.00
		California	CD5	U.K.	1997	$10.00
	Second version.					
Virgin	659964	Circle In the Sand	CD5	Germany	1989	$9.00
Virgin	VJD-12012	Circle In the Sand	CD3	Japan	1989	$13.00/$4.00
Virgin	VSCD-1074	Circle In the Sand	CD5	U.K.	1989	$9.00
Virgin	VJDP-10185	Do You Feel Like I Feel?	CD3	Japan	1991	$13.00/$4.00
MCA	CD45 1570	Do You Feel Like I Feel?	CDJ	U.S.	1991	$3.00
BMG	665003	Half the World	CD5	Germany	1992	$9.00
	VSCD-X-1388	Half the World-The Ballads Collection	CD5	U.K.		$15.00
Virgin	659643	Heaven Is A Place	CD5	Germany	1987	$15.00
Virgin	VSCD-1036	Heaven Is A Place	CD5	U.K.	1987	$15.00
Virgin	659785	I Get Weak	CD5	Germany	1989	$9.00
Virgin	VJD-12002	I Get Weak	CD3	Japan	1989	$13.00/$4.00
Virgin	VSCD-1046	I Get Weak	CD5	U.K.	1989	$15.00
		I Get Weak	CDJ	U.S.	1989	$3.00
		In Too Deep	CD5	Germany	1996	$12.00
		In Too Deep	CD5	U.K.	1996	$10.00
Virgin	DPRO-12817	It's Too Real	CDJ	U.S.	1993	$3.00
Germany	662888	La Luna	CD5	Germany	1990	$9.00
Toshiba	VJDP-101	La Luna	CD3	Japan	1990	$13.00/$4.00
Virgin	VSCD-1230	La Luna	CD3	U.K.	1990	$9.00
Virgin	VSCDG 1476	Lay Down Your Arms	CD5	U.K.	1993	$10.00
BMG	662719	Leave A Light On	CD5	Germany	1989	$9.00
Virgin	VJD-10223	Leave A Light On	CD3	Japan	1989	$13.00/$4.00
Virgin	VJD-10221	Leave A Light On	CD3	Japan	1989	$13.00/$4.00
Virgin	VSCD-1210	Leave A Light On	CD3	U.K.	1989	$9.00
Virgin		Leave A Light On	CD5	U.S.	1989	$10.00
MCA	CD45 17984	Leave A Light On	CDJ	U.S.	1989	$3.00
Virgin	VSCDT-1428	Little Black Book	CD5	U.K.	1991	$10.00

Label	Catalog Number	Title	Type	Country	Year	Longbox Value / Value
BMG	664681	Live Your Life Be Free	CD5	Germany	1991	$9.00
Virgin	VJD-110173	Live Your Life Be Free	CD3	Japan	1991	$13.00/$4.00
Virgin	VSCD-1370	Live Your Life Be Free	CD3	U.K.	1991	$9.00
MCA	MCA5P-2087	Live Your Life Be Free	CDJ	U.S.	1991	$3.00
Virgin	VSCD-1150	Love Never Dies	CD5	U.K.	1989	$12.00
IRS	DIRM-118	Mad About You	CD5	U.K.	1988	$9.00
	WDPRO01034	One By One	CDJ	U.S.		$3.00
Virgin	663037	Runaway Horses	CD5	Germany	1990	$9.00
Virgin	VSCD-1244	Runaway Horses	CD5	U.K.	1990	$9.00
BMG	663624	Same Thing	CD5	Germany	1990	$9.00
Virgin	VJD-10224	Same Thing	CD3	Japan	1989	$13.00/$4.00
Virgin	VJD-1415	Same Thing	CD5	Japan	1989	$15.00
BMG	663166	Summer Rain	CD5	Germany	1990	$9.00
Virgin	VSCDT 1323	Summer Rain	CD5	U.K.	1990	$9.00
MCA	18118	Summer Rain	CDJ	U.S.	1989	$3.00
MCA	18171	Summer Rain	CDJ	U.S.	1990	$3.00
Virgin	663295	Vision Of You	CD5	Germany	1990	$9.00
Virgin	VJDP-117	Vision Of You	CD3	Japan	1990	$13.00/$4.00
Virgin	VSCDT 1264	Vision Of You	CD5	U.K.	1990	$9.00
MCA	CD45 18304	Vision Of You	CDJ	U.S.	1989	$3.00
MCA	CD45 1053	(We Want) The Same Thing	CDJ	U.S.	1989	$3.00
Virgin	661719	World Without You	CD5	Germany	1989	$9.00
Virgin	VJD-12025	World Without You	CD3	Japan	1989	$13.00/$4.00
Virgin	VSCD-1114	World Without You	CD5	U.K.	1989	$9.00

Carlos, J

Singles

Label	Catalog Number	Title	Type	Country	Year	Value
Toshiba	TODP-2278	Love Train	CD3	Japan	1991	$13.00/$4.00

Carlos, Roberto

Singles

Label	Catalog Number	Title	Type	Country	Year	Value
Sony Latin	10654	Luz Divina	CDJ	U.S.	1994	$2.00

Carlos, Wendy

Full Length

Label	Catalog Number	Title	Type	Country	Year	Value
CBS	CD-63501	Switched On Bach	LP	Germany		$15.00
Sony	MK-423194	Switched On Bach	LP/LB	U.S.		$14.00/$8.00

Carlson, Paullette

Full Length

Label	Catalog Number	Title	Type	Country	Year	Value
Capitol	CDP 97711	Love Goes On	LP/LB	U.S.		$14.00/$8.00

Carlton

Singles

Label	Catalog Number	Title	Type	Country	Year	Value
Polygram	869133-2	Cool With Nature	CD5	Germany	1990	$7.00
Polygram	SNMCD-1	Do You Dream	CD5	U.K.	1990	$7.00
Polygram	SNMCD-4	Love And Pain	CD5	U.K.	1990	$7.00

Carlton, Larry

Full Length

Label	Catalog Number	Title	Type	Country	Year	Value
MCA	CD33-17344	Discovery And Four Corners Sampler	DJ/Smplr	U.S.	1987	$20.00
		Also with 4 tracks by the Yellow Jackets.				
		Mr. 335 CD Collection	DJ/Smplr	U.S.		N/A

Singles

Label	Catalog Number	Title	Type	Country	Year	Value
MCA	CD45 17812	Josie	CDJ	U.S.	1989	$2.00
MCA	CD45 53119	Minute By Minute	CDJ	U.S.	1987	$2.00
MCA	CD45 17975	On Solid Ground	CDJ	U.S.	1989	$2.00
MCA	CD45 18057	Ringing the Bells Of Christmas	CDJ	U.S.	1989	$2.00

Carman

Singles

Label	Catalog Number	Title	Type	Country	Year	Value
Everland	9012237157	Somewhere Within the Heart	CDJ	U.S.	1996	$3.00

Carmel

Full Length

Label	Catalog Number	Title	Type	Country	Year	Value
London	CARCDS	Set Me Free	DJ/Intvw	U.K.	1990	$25.00

Singles

Label	Catalog Number	Title	Type	Country	Year	Value
Polygram	869235-2	And I Take It For Granted	CD5	Germany	1990	$8.00
London	LONCD-282	And I Take It For Granted	CD5	U.K.	1990	$8.00
London	886672-3	I Have Fallen In Love	CD3	Germany	1989	$8.00
London	886673-2	I Have Fallen In Love	CD5	Germany	1989	$8.00
London	LONCD-227	I Have Fallen In Love	CD5	U.K.	1989	$8.00
London	886925-2	I'm Over You	CD5	Germany	1990	$8.00
London	LONCD-253	I'm Over You	CD5	U.K.	1990	$8.00
Eastwest	Yz873CD	If You Don't Come Back	CD5	Germany	1994	$12.00
Carmel	LONCD 144	It's All In the Game	CD5	U.K.	1987	$8.00
London	886859-2	You Can Have Him	CD5	Germany	1989	$8.00
London	LONCD-248	You Can Have Him	CD5	U.K.	1989	$8.00
WEA	YZ-681CD	You're All I Need	CD5	U.K.	1992	$8.00
WEA	YZ-718CD	You're All I Need	CD5	U.K.	1992	$8.00

Carmen, Eric

Full Length

Label	Catalog Number	Title	Type	Country	Year	Value
Arista	ARCD-8547	Best Of Eric Carmen	LP/LB	U.S.	1988	$15.00/$11.00
CBS	32DP-209	Eric Carmen	LP	Japan		$18.00

Singles

Label	Catalog Number	Title	Type	Country	Year	Value
Arista	BVDA-25	All By Myself	CD3	Japan	1991	$12.00/$3.00
RCA	8917-2-RDJ	Almost Paradise	CDJ	U.S.	1989	$2.00
RCA	PD-49594	Hungry Eyes	CD5	U.K.	1988	$9.00
Arista	661718	Make Me Lose Control	CD5	U.K.	1988	$8.00
		Make Me Lose Control	CDJ	U.S.	1988	$2.00

Carmen, Phil

Singles

Label	Catalog Number	Title	Type	Country	Year	Value
Polygram	867909-2	Borderline	CD5	Germany	1991	$7.00
Polygram	885558-2	City Walls	CD5	Germany	1991	$7.00

Carmichael, Hoagy

Full Length

Label	Catalog Number	Title	Type	Country	Year	Value
Blue Note	46862	Hoagy Sings Carmichael	LP/LB	U.S.		$15.00/$10.00
Blue Note		Hoagy Sings Carmichael	LTD/LP	U.S.	1995	$19.00
Bluebird	8333	Stardust And Much More	LP/LB	U.S.		$15.00/$10.00

Carne, Jean

Full Length

Label	Catalog Number	Title	Type	Country	Year	Value
Atlantic	81811-2	You're Part Of Me	LP/LB	U.S.		$14.00/$8.00

Carnegie, Kim

Singles

Label	Catalog Number	Title	Type	Country	Year	Value
Polygram	ZD-44086	Jazz Rap	CD5	U.K.	1990	$7.00

Carnes, Kim

Full Length

Label	Catalog Number	Title	Type	Country	Year	Value
EMI	CP32-5089	Barking At Airplanes	LP	Germany		$20.00
Toshiba	CP32-5089	Barking At Airplanes	LP	Japan		$25.00
EMI	CDP-46022	Cafe Racer	LP/LB	U.S.†	1985	$14.00/$8.00
Pioneer Artists	PA-84-M010	Kim Carnes	8" LD	U.S.	1985	$11.00
MCA	MCAD-42200	View From the House	LP/LB	U.S.		$14.00/$8.00

Singles

Label	Catalog Number	Title	Type	Country	Year	Value
MCA			CDJ	U.S.	1989	$2.00
MCA	CD45 17670	Crazy in Love	CDJ	U.S.	1988	$2.00
MCA	CD45 17683	Crazy In Love	CDJ	U.S.	1988	$2.00
EMI	DPRO-04655	Gypsy Honeymoon	CDJ	U.S.	1993	$2.00
Zebrazone	TEDP-18	Independent Girl	CD3	Japan	1990	$13.00/$4.00
MCA	DMCA-1290	Just To Spend The Night With You	CD3	U.K.	1989	$9.00

Carnival Art

Full Length

Label	Catalog Number	Title	Type	Country	Year	Value
RCA	66016	Thrumdrone	LP/LB	U.S.		$14.00/$8.00
RCA	66101	Welcome To Vas Legas	LP/LB	U.S.		$14.00/$8.00

Singles

Label	Catalog Number	Title	Type	Country	Year	Value
SPV	0535-3	Blue Food & Black Sparks	CD5	Germany	1991	$8.00
Situation	SIT 93	Holy Smoke	CD5	U.K.		$8.00
WEA	BBQ--8CD	Sucker Punch	CD5	U.K.	1992	$8.00
SPV	0542-3	Wrestling Swamis Vs. Mr. Blue Veins	CD5	Germany	1991	$8.00
Pinnacle	SIT-85CD	Wrestling Swamis Vs. Mr. Blue Veins	CD5	U.K.	1991	$8.00

Carnival Strippers

Singles

Label	Catalog Number	Title	Type	Country	Year	Value
Fox	72445-14127	Shifting Sands	CDJ	U.S.	1994	$2.00

Caro

Singles

Label	Catalog Number	Title	Type	Country	Year	Value
BMG	664903	Volcano	CD5	Germany	1991	$7.00

Carola

Singles

Label	Catalog Number	Title	Type	Country	Year	Value
BMG	PD-44650	Captured By A Lovestorm	CD5	Germany	1991	$7.00
BMG	PD-44650	Captured By A Lovestorm	CD5	U.K.	1991	$7.00

Carpendale, Howard

Full Length

Label	Catalog Number	Title	Type	Country	Year	Value
EMI	746124-2	CD Excluive	LP	Germany		$20.00

Carpenter, Karen

Singles

Label	Catalog Number	Title	Type	Country	Year	Value
A&M	CD 17926	If I Had You	CDJ	U.S.	1989	$6.00

Carpenter, Mary Chapin

Full Length

Label	Catalog Number	Title	Type	Country	Year	Value
		'90s Country	RS	U.S.	1995	$50.00
		Airdate: 12/2/95.				
		'90s Country	RS	U.S.	1995	$50.00
Airdate: 6/3/95.						
		Come On Come On	DJ/Smplr	U.S.	1995	$15.00
Columbia	CSK 1741	State Of the Heart	DJ/LP	U.S.	1989	$10.00

Singles

Label	Catalog Number	Title	Type	Country	Year	Value
Columbia	CSK 77134	Bug, The	CDJ	U.S.	1993	$3.00
Columbia	CSK 2263	Down At the Twist And Shout	CDJ	U.S.	1990	$3.00
Columbia	CSK 73838	Down At the Twist And Shout	CDJ	U.S.	1991	$3.00
Columbia	CSK 74930	Hard Way, The	CDJ	U.S.	1990	$3.00
Columbia		He Thinks He'll Keep Her	CD5	U.K.	1994	$10.00
Columbia	CSK 77316	He Thinks He'll Keep Her	CDJ	U.S.	1994	$3.00
Columbia	CSK 77826	House Of Cards	CDJ	U.S.	1995	$3.00
Columbia	CSK 74345	I Feel Lucky	CDJ	U.S.	1992	$3.00
Columbia	CSK 4916	Passionate Kisses	CDJ	U.S.	1992	$3.00
Columbia		Shut Up And Kiss Me	CD5	U.K.	1995	$10.00
Columbia	CSK 77696	Shut Up And Kiss Me	CDJ	U.S.	1994	$3.00

Carpenter, Richard

Full Length

Label	Catalog Number	Title	Type	Country	Year	Value
A&M	3243178	Time	LP	Japan		$35.00
A&M	CD-5117	Time	LP/LB	U.S.		$25.00/$20.00

Carpenters

Full Length

Label	Catalog Number	Title	Type	Country	Year	Value
A&M	CD-3210	A Christmas Portrait	LP/LB	U.S.†	1985	$14.00/$8.00
A&M		A Song For You	LP/LB	U.S.		$14.00/$8.00
A&M	CD-3270	An Old-Fashioned Christmas	LP/LB	U.S.†	1985	$14.00/$8.00
A&M		Best Of the Best	LTD/LP	Japan		$150.00
	2 CD Set.					
A&M	D300Y-3243	Collected Works	LP	Japan		$40.00
A&M		Collection	LP	Japan	1990	$200.00
	11 CD Set.					
EMI	CDS-260298-2	Collection	LP	U.K.		$100.00
A&M	CARCD 12	Compact Disc Collection, The	LTD/LP	U.K.	1990	$150.00
	12 CD set in book.					
A&M		From the Top	LP	U.S.		$50.00
	4 CD set. First pressing in 12"x12" box.					
A&M	DCI-3068	Karen In My Memories	DJ/Smplr	Japan	1995	$200.00
A&M	CD-3723	Made In America	LP/LB	U.S.		$14.00/$8.00
A&M	CD-3199	Passage	LP/LB	U.S.		$14.00/$8.00
A&M	CD-3601	Singles Collection, The	LP/LB	U.S.†	1984	$14.00/$8.00
		Special Collection	DJ/Smplr	Japan		$75.00
A&M	75021 7246 2	(They Long To Be) Close To You	DJ/Smplr	U.S.	1991	$12.00
	Sampler from boxed set "From the Top."					
A&M	CD-4205	Ticket To Ride	LP/LB	U.S.		$14.00/$8.00
A&M	CD-4954	Voice Of the Heart	LP/LB	U.S.†	1985	$14.00/$8.00
Pioneer	PA-85-123	Yesterday Once More	LD	U.S.	1985	$75.00
A&M	CD-6601	Yesterday Once More	LP/LB	U.S.†	1985	$22.00/$15.00
	2 CD set.					
Pioneer	PA-85-123	Yesterday Once More	LD	U.S.	1989	$75.00

Singles

Label	Catalog Number	Title	Type	Country	Year	Value
A&M	PODM-1059	Christmas Song	CD3	Japan		$17.00/$4.00
A&M	PODM-1028	Close To You	CD3	Japan		$17.00/$4.00
A&M	AMCD 558	Close To You	CD5	U.K.	1990	$10.00
A&M	390337-2	Compact Hits	CD5	Germany	1988	$10.00
A&M	AMCD-901	Compact Hits	CD5	U.K.	1988	$10.00
A&M	PODM-3066	I Need To Be In Love	CD3	Japan		$15.00/$4.00
A&M	PODM-1060	I Need To Be In Love	CD3	Japan		$17.00/$4.00
A&M	PCDY-10007	If I Had You	CD3	Japan	1989	$13.00/$4.00
A&M	75021 7308-2	Let Me Be the One	CDJ	U.S.	1991	$7.00
A&M		Rainy Days And Mondays	CD5	U.K.		$10.00
A&M		Rainy Days And Mondays	CD5	U.K.		$10.00
	Second version.					
	520238	Ticket To Ride	CD5	U.S.	1994	$5.00
A&M		Yesterday Once More	CD5	Australia	1993	$10.00
A&M		Yesterday Once More	CDJ	France	1993	$30.00
A&M	S12Y 3014	Yesterday Once More	CD3	Japan	1988	$15.00/$4.00

Carr, Terri

Full Length

Label	Catalog Number	Title	Type	Country	Year	Value
Mercury		Terri Carr	DJ/LP	U.S.	1995	$18.00
	CD in color press kit					

Carrack, Paul

Full Length

Label	Catalog Number	Title	Type	Country	Year	Longbox Value / Value
Chrysalis	21709	Groove Approved	LP/LB	U.S.		$12.00/$7.00
DIR		King Biscuit Flour Hour	RS	U.S.	1988	$30.00
Airdate: 4/10/88.						
DIR		King Biscuit Flour Hour	RS	U.S.	1989	$30.00
With Squeeze, Airdate: 12/18/89.						
Chrysalis	21578	One Good Reason	LP/LB	U.S.		$12.00/$7.00

Singles

Label	Catalog Number	Title	Type	Country	Year	Longbox Value / Value
EMI	323494-2	Battlefield	CD5	Germany	1990	$8.00
Chrysalis	CHSCD-3494	Battlefield	CD5	U.K.	1989	$8.00
Chrysalis	DPRO-23484	Battlefield	CDJ	U.S.	1989	$2.00
Chrysalis	CHSCD-3164	Don't Shed A Tear	CD5	U.K.	1989	$8.00
Chrysalis	662579	I Live By the Groove	CD5	Germany	1989	$8.00
Chrysalis	CHSCD-3403	I Live By the Groove	CD5	U.K.	1989	$8.00
Chrysalis	DPRO-23427	I Live By the Groove	CDJ	U.S.	1989	$2.00
		In the Time It Takes	CDJ	U.S.		$6.00
Chrysalis	CHSCD-3551	Loveless	CD5	U.K.	1990	$8.00
		Only My Heart Can Tell	CDJ	U.S.		$2.00
Chrysalis	880528	When You Walk In Room	CD5	Germany	1987	$8.00
Chrysalis	CDE-3	When You Walk In Room	CD5	U.K.	1987	$8.00

Carrack, Paul & Terri Nunn

Singles

Label	Catalog Number	Title	Type	Country	Year	Longbox Value / Value
Columbia	CSK 1514	Romance	CDJ	U.S.	1989	$2.00

Carradine, Keith

Singles

Label	Catalog Number	Title	Type	Country	Year	Longbox Value / Value
Columbia	CSK 4225	Look Around	CDJ	U.S.	1991	$2.00

Carreras, Jose

Singles

Label	Catalog Number	Title	Type	Country	Year	Longbox Value / Value
WEA	YZ-438CD	All I Ask Of You	CD3	U.K.	1989	$8.00
		Friends For Life	CDJ	U.S.		$2.00

Carrere, Tia

Singles

Label	Catalog Number	Title	Type	Country	Year	Longbox Value / Value
Warner Brothers	W-0105	Ballroom Blitz	CD5	Germany	1992	$10.00
Warner Brothers	PRO-CD-5313	Ballroom Blitz	CDJ	U.S.	1991	$3.00
Reprise	PRO-CD-6510	I Never Even Told You	CDJ	U.S.	1993	$3.00
Reprise	9 41375-2	State Of Grace	CD5	U.S.	1993	$5.00
Warner Brothers	PRO-CD-5418	Why You Wanna Break My Heart	CDJ	U.S.	1991	$3.00

Carrey, Jim

Singles

Label	Catalog Number	Title	Type	Country	Year	Longbox Value / Value
Columbia	42K 77662	Cuban Pete	CD5	U.S.	1994	$7.00
Chaos	77591	Cuban Pete	CDJ	U.S.	1994	$6.00

Carrington, Terri Lyne

Full Length

Label	Catalog Number	Title	Type	Country	Year	Longbox Value / Value
Verve	Forcast TLC 2	Real Life Story	DJ/Smplr	U.S.	1989	$8.00

Singles

Label	Catalog Number	Title	Type	Country	Year	Longbox Value / Value
Verve Forecast		More Than Woman	CDJ	U.S.	1989	$2.00

Carroll, Dina

Singles

Label	Catalog Number	Title	Type	Country	Year	Longbox Value / Value
A&M	AMCD-0001	Ain't No Man	CD3	Japan	1992	$12.00/$3.00
A&M	314500622	So Close	CD5	Canada	1992	$8.00
A&M	PODM-1009	So Close	CD3	Japan	1993	$12.00/$3.00
A&M	AMCD-0101	So Close	CD5	U.K.	1992	$8.00
A&M	62	So Close	CD5	U.S.	1993	$5.00
A&M	31458 8085	So Close	CDJ	U.S.	1993	$2.00
A&M	31458 8098	So Close	CDJ	U.S.	1993	$2.00
Polygram	AMCD-0088	Special Kind Of Love	CD5	U.K.	1992	$8.00
A&M	31458 8147	Special Kind Of Love	CDJ	U.S.	1993	$2.00
Polygram	AMCD-0184	This Time	CD5	U.K.	1993	$8.00
BMG	ZD-43410	Walk On By	CD5	Germany	1990	$7.00
A&M	PODM-1009	You'll Lose A Good Thing	CD3	Japan	1993	$12.00/$3.00

Cars

Full Length

Label	Catalog Number	Title	Type	Country	Year	Longbox Value / Value
Westwood One		BBC Classic Tracks	RS	U.S.	1994	$20.00
Airdate: 8/22/94.						
Elektra	507-2	Candy-O	LP/LB	U.S.†	1985	$14.00/$8.00
Elektra	135-2	Cars, The	LP/LB	U.S.†	1984	$14.00/$8.00
Elektra	60296-2	Heartbeat City	LP/LB	U.S.†	1984	$14.00/$8.00
Pioneer	PA-85-108	Heartbeat City	LD	U.S.	1985	$20.00
Pioneer	PA-85-108	Heartbeat City	LD	U.S.	1990	$20.00
Digital audio.						
Album Network		In the Studio (Candy-O)	RS	U.S.	1992	$30.00
Airdate: 7/13/92.						
Album Network		In the Studio (Candy-O)	RS	U.S.	1994	$30.00
Airdate: 6/6/94.						
Westwood One		Off the Record	RS	U.S.	1995	$30.00
Airdate: 9/25/95.						
Elektra	567-2	Shake It Up	LP/LB	U.S.†	1984	$14.00/$8.00
Westwood One		Superstar Concert	RS	U.S.	1992	$40.00
2 CD set. Airdate: 8/9/92						

Singles

Label	Catalog Number	Title	Type	Country	Year	Longbox Value / Value
Elektra	PR 2171-2	Coming Up You	CDJ	U.S.	1987	$7.00
Elektra	969342-3	Drive	CD3	Germany	1989	$8.00
Elektra	969342-3	Drive	CD3	U.K.	1989	$8.00

Carson, Jeff

Full Length

Label	Catalog Number	Title	Type	Country	Year	Longbox Value / Value
		Jeff Carson Interview	DJ/Intvw	U.S.	1995	$15.00

Singles

Label	Catalog Number	Title	Type	Country	Year	Longbox Value / Value
Atlantic	76970	Car	CD5	U.S.	1995	$5.00

Carson, Lori

Full Length

Label	Catalog Number	Title	Type	Country	Year	Longbox Value / Value
DGC	7599-24256-2	Shelter	LP	U.K.	1990	$10.00
DGC	2 2456-2-Dj	Shelter	DJ/LP	U.S.	1990	$7.00
DGC	2 2456-2	Shelter	LP/LB	U.S.	1990	$12.00/$7.00

Singles

Label	Catalog Number	Title	Type	Country	Year	Longbox Value / Value
DGC		Every Heartbeat	CDJ	U.S.	1990	$2.00
DGC		Imagine Love	CDJ	U.S.	1990	$2.00

Carter, Benny

Full Length

Label	Catalog Number	Title	Type	Country	Year	Longbox Value / Value
Music	5030	Central City Sketches	LP/BP	U.S.		$14.00/$8.00

Carter, Betty

Singles

Label	Catalog Number	Title	Type	Country	Year	Longbox Value / Value
Verve	BET 2	Droppin' Things	CDJ	U.S.	1990	$2.00

Carter, Carlene

Full Length

Company	Disk Number	Title	Type	Country	Year	Longbox Value / Value
		Live From the Crazy Horse	RS	U.S.	1994	$50.00

Singles

Company	Disk Number	Title	Type	Country	Year	Longbox Value / Value
Reprise	PRO-CD-4459	Come On Back	CDJ	U.S.	1990	$2.00
		Hurricane, The	CDJ	U.S.		$3.00
Reprise	PRO-CD-2932	I Fell In Love	CDJ	U.S.	1990	$2.00
Giant	PRO-CD-6697	I Love You 'Cause I Want To	CDJ	U.S.	1993	$2.00
Reprise	PRO-CD-4886	One In Love	CDJ	U.S.	1990	$2.00
Atlantic	PRCD 5615-2	Something Already Gone	CDJ	U.S.	1993	$3.00
		Sweet Meant To Be	CD5	Germany	1994	$10.00
Reprise	PRO-CD-4701	Sweetest Thing, The	CDJ	U.S.	1990	$2.00
Warner Brothers	PRO-CD-3809	Time's Up	CDJ	U.S.	1989	$2.00
Giant	PRO-CD-6667	Unbreakable Heart	CDJ	U.S.	1993	$2.00
Giant	PRO-CD-6669	Unbreakable Heart	CDJ	U.S.	1993	$2.00

Carter, Chris

Full Length

Company	Disk Number	Title	Type	Country	Year	Longbox Value / Value
Mute	61245	Space Between	LP/LB	U.S.		$14.00/$8.00

Carter, Deana

Full Length

Company	Disk Number	Title	Type	Country	Year	Longbox Value / Value
Capitol		Did I Shave My Legs For This?	LTD/LP	U.S.	1996	$16.00

Carter, Ron

Full Length

Company	Disk Number	Title	Type	Country	Year	Longbox Value / Value
CBS	450556-2	Blues Farm	LP	Germany		$15.00
Fantasy	FCD-9073	Pastels	LP/LB	U.S.†	1985	$14.00/$8.00

Carter, Ron/Herbie Hancock/Tony Williams

Full Length

Company	Disk Number	Title	Type	Country	Year	Longbox Value / Value
Milestone	FCD-9105	Third Plane	LP/LB	U.S.†	1985	$14.00/$8.00

Carter, U.S.M.

Full Length

Company	Disk Number	Title	Type	Country	Year	Longbox Value / Value
Chrysalis		1992 the Love Album	LTD/LP	U.K.	1994	$25.00/$15.00
25th Anniversary edition in 6"x11" longbox.						

Singles

Company	Disk Number	Title	Type	Country	Year	Longbox Value / Value
EMI	323795-2	After the Watershed	CD5	Germany	1991	$8.00
Chrysalis	USMCD-2	After the Watershed	CD5	U.K.	1991	$8.00
Rough Trade	RTT-242CD	Anytime Anyplace	CD5	U.K.	1990	$8.00
Columbia	QTCY-2501	Bloodsport For All	CD3	Japan	1991	$13.00/$4.00
Columbia	QTCY-25012	Bloodsport For All	CD5	Japan	1991	$10.00
Rough Trade	R-268-3	Bloodsport For All	CD5	U.K.	1991	$8.00
Chrysalis	23802	Bloodsport For All	CD5	U.S.	1991	$4.00
Chrysalis	USMCD-5	Do Re Me So Far So Good	CD5	U.K.	1992	$8.00
Pinnacle	TOCP-7882	Everybody's Happy Nowadays	CD5	Japan		$12.00
Chrysalis		Glam Rock Cops	CD5	U.K.		$8.00
Chrysalis		Glam Rock Cops	CD5	U.K.		$8.00
Second version.						
Chrysalis	TOCP-6994	Handbuilt By Perverts	CD3	Japan	1992	$13.00/$4.00
Chrysalis	USMCD-6	Impossible Dream	CD5	U.K.	1992	$8.00
IRS	6728	Lean On Me I Won't Fall Over	CDJ	U.S.	1993	$2.00
		Let's Get Tattoos	CD5	U.K.		$10.00
		Let's Get Tattoos	CD5	U.K.		$10.00
Second version.						
Chrysalis	19757	Only Living Boy In New Cross	CDJ	U.S.	1992	$2.00
Big Cat	USMCD-3	Rubbish	CD5	U.K.	1992	$8.00
Big Cat	ABB-102SCD	Rubbish	CD5	U.K.	1992	$8.00
EMI	323738-2	Sheriff Fatman	CD5	Germany	1991	$8.00
Big Cat	USM CD1	Sheriff Fatman	CD5	U.K.	1989	$8.00

Cartouche

Singles

Company	Disk Number	Title	Type	Country	Year	Longbox Value / Value
ZYX	6421-8	Feel the Groove	CD5	Germany	1990	$6.00
ZYX	6590-8	Let the Music	CD5	Germany	1990	$6.00

Cartwright, Lionel

Singles

Company	Disk Number	Title	Type	Country	Year	Longbox Value / Value
MCA	MCA5P-54440	Be My Angel	CDJ	U.S.	1992	$2.00
MCA	MCA5P-54514	Standing On the Promises	CDJ	U.S.	1992	$2.00

Carvin, Steve

Singles

Company	Disk Number	Title	Type	Country	Year	Longbox Value / Value
BMG	662662	Hungry For Love	CD5	Germany	1989	$7.00

Carwell, Sue Ann

Singles

Company	Disk Number	Title	Type	Country	Year	Longbox Value / Value
MCA	MCA5P-2183	7 Days, 7 Nights	CDJ	U.S.	1992	$2.00
MCA	MCA5P-2344	Sex Or Love	CDJ	U.S.	1992	$2.00

Casa Nero

Singles

Company	Disk Number	Title	Type	Country	Year	Longbox Value / Value
Polygram	390499-2	Dawn	CD5	Germany	1990	$7.00

Cascades

Singles

Company	Disk Number	Title	Type	Country	Year	Longbox Value / Value
Pioneer	10P3-6072	Rhythm Of the Rain	CD3	Japan	1988	$12.00/$3.00

Case, Peter

Singles

Company	Disk Number	Title	Type	Country	Year	Longbox Value / Value
Vangaurd	710	Baltimore	CDJ	U.S.	1995	$3.00
Geffen	PRO-CD-4379	Dream About You	CDJ	U.S.	1989	$2.00
Geffen	PRO-CD-4391	Dream About You	CDJ	U.S.	1989	$7.00
Geffen	PRO-CD-3474	Put Down the Gun	CDJ	U.S.	1989	$2.00

Cash, Andrew

Full Length

Company	Disk Number	Title	Type	Country	Year	Longbox Value / Value
Island	842597	Boomtown	LP/LB	U.S.	1989	$14.00/$8.00
Island	842851	Time And Place	LP/LB	U.S.		$14.00/$8.00

Singles

Company	Disk Number	Title	Type	Country	Year	Longbox Value / Value
Island		A Lot Of Talk	CDJ	Canada		$6.00
Island		Boomtown	CDJ	Canada	1989	$6.00
Island	CID-439	Boomtown	CD5	U.K.	1989	$7.00
Island		Boomtown	CDJ	U.S.	1989	$2.00
Island		Its Over	CDJ	Canada		$2.00
Island		What Am I Gonna Do With These Hands	CDJ	U.S.		$2.00

Cash Crew

Singles

Company	Disk Number	Title	Type	Country	Year	Longbox Value / Value
Scream	WTSCD-4	Back For More	CD5	U.K.	1991	$7.00

Cash, Johnny

Full Length

Company	Disk Number	Title	Type	Country	Year	Longbox Value / Value
Island	842155-2	Boom Chicka Boom	LP/LB	U.S.		$14.00/$8.00
Charly	CD-18	Country Boy	LP	U.S.		$8.00
Polygram	832931	Is Coming To Town	LP/BP	U.S.		$14.00/$8.00

Label	Catalog Number	Title	Type	Country	Year	Longbox Value/Value
Polygram	848051	Mystery Of Life	LP/LB	U.S.		$14.00/$8.00
Polystar	834801-2	One Million Dollars Cash	LP	Germany		$25.00
Columbia		Patriot	LP/LB	U.S.	1990	$14.00/$8.00

Disc lists 10th track as "Rugged Old Flag" rather than "Ragged Old Flag."

Label	Catalog Number	Title	Type	Country	Year	Longbox Value/Value
Bear	BCD-15247	Up Through the Years 1955-1957	LP	U.S.		N/A
Polygram	834778	Water From the Wells Home	LP/BP	U.S.		$14.00/$8.00

Singles

Label	Catalog Number	Title	Type	Country	Year	Longbox Value/Value
Mercury	CDP 170	Farmers Almanac	CDJ	U.S.	1990	$3.00
		Goin' By the Book	CDJ	U.S.		$3.00
Mercury	CDP 360	Greatest Cowboy Of Them All	CDJ	U.S.	1990	$3.00
Aris	885818	I Walk the Line	CD3	Germany	1990	$8.00
Mercury	MERCD-340	Mystery Of Life	CD5	U.K.	1991	$8.00
Mercury	CDP 397	Mystery Of Life	CDJ	U.S.	1991	$3.00
Mercury	CDP 469	Wanted Man	CDJ	U.S.	1991	$3.00

Cash Money Clic

Singles

Label	Catalog Number	Title	Type	Country	Year	Longbox Value/Value
TeeVee Tunes	3911	4 My Click	CD5	U.S.	1994	$5.00

Cash, Rosanne

Full Length

Label	Catalog Number	Title	Type	Country	Year	Longbox Value/Value
		Collectors Item!	DJ/Smplr	U.S.	1994	$15.00
Columbia		Hits 1979 - 1989	DJ/Smplr	U.S.	1989	$15.00
		Interiors: The Full Sessions	DJ/Smplr	U.S.		$12.00
CBS	CK-39463	Rhythm & Romance	LP/LB	U.S.†	1985	$14.00/$8.00
CBS	CK-36965	Seven Year Ache	LP/LB	U.S.†	1984	$14.00/$8.00

Singles

Label	Catalog Number	Title	Type	Country	Year	Longbox Value/Value
Foreward	PRCD 7119-2	I Count the Tears	CDJ	U.S.	1995	$3.00

With Los Lobos.

Singles

Label	Catalog Number	Title	Type	Country	Year	Longbox Value/Value
Columbia	CSK 2299	On the Surface	CDJ	U.S.	1991	$2.00
Columbia	CSK 4063	Real Woman	CDJ	U.S.	1991	$2.00
Columbia	CSK 4953	Seventh Avenue	CDJ	U.S.	1993	$2.00
Columbia	CSK 4919	Wheel, The	CDJ	U.S.	1993	$2.00
Columbia	CSK 5394	You Won't Let Me In	CDJ	U.S.	1993	$2.00
Columbia	CSK 5336	You Won't Let Me In	CDJ	U.S.	1993	$6.00

Cash, Tommy

Singles

Label	Catalog Number	Title	Type	Country	Year	Longbox Value/Value
Laurie	L7CD 142	Hank & George & Lefty & Me	CDJ	U.S.		$3.00

Cashflow

Full Length

Label	Catalog Number	Title	Type	Country	Year	Longbox Value/Value
Atlanta	832187-2	Big Money	LP/BP	U.S.		$12.00/$7.00
Polygram	826028-2	Cashflow	LP/BP	U.S.		$12.00/$7.00

Casper

Singles

Label	Catalog Number	Title	Type	Country	Year	Longbox Value/Value
Capitol	DPRO-79707	War Of Words	CDJ	U.S.	1991	$2.00

Cassandra Complex

Full Length

Label	Catalog Number	Title	Type	Country	Year	Longbox Value/Value
SPV	7194	Grenade	LP	Germany		$15.00

Casserine

Singles

Label	Catalog Number	Title	Type	Country	Year	Longbox Value/Value
Warner Brothers	PRO-CD-7343	Get To Know	CDJ	U.S.	1994	$7.00
Warner Brothers	PRO-CD-7294	We Gotta Run	CDJ	U.S.	1994	$2.00
Warner Brothers	9 41689-2	Why Not Take All Of Me	CD5	U.S.	1994	$5.00

Cassidy, David

Full Length

Label	Catalog Number	Title	Type	Country	Year	Longbox Value/Value
Enigma	73554	David Cassidy '90	LP/LB	U.S.		$12.00/$7.00
		Greatest Hits Live	LP	U.K.		$12.00
Ariola	610454	Romance	LP	Germany		$12.00

Singles

Label	Catalog Number	Title	Type	Country	Year	Longbox Value/Value
Scotti Brothers	ZSK 75337	For All the Lonely	CDJ	U.S.		$2.00
EMI	204060-2	Lyin' To Myself	CD5	Germany	1990	$8.00
Enigma	EPRO-334	Lyin' To Myself	CDJ	U.S.	1990	$2.00

Cassidy, Shaun

Singles

Label	Catalog Number	Title	Type	Country	Year	Longbox Value/Value
Polygram	889864-3	Memory Girl	CD3	Germany	1989	$8.00
Polygram	889865-2	Memory Girl	CD5	Germany	1989	$8.00

Cassiopeia

Singles

Label	Catalog Number	Title	Type	Country	Year	Longbox Value/Value
Polydor	H10P-30002	Bayside Express	CD3	Japan	1988	$12.00/$3.00
Alfa	ALDA-76	Glory	CD3	Japan	1993	$12.00/$3.00

Cast

Singles

Label	Catalog Number	Title	Type	Country	Year	Longbox Value/Value
	PRCD111076	Alright	CDJ	U.S.	1995	$3.00

Castor, Jan

Singles

Label	Catalog Number	Title	Type	Country	Year	Longbox Value/Value
RCA	119	Angel In Me	CDJ	Austrailia	1990	$8.00

Casual

Singles

Label	Catalog Number	Title	Type	Country	Year	Longbox Value/Value
Jive	42189	I Didn't Mean To	CDJ	U.S.	1993	$2.00
Jive	42217	Me-O-Mi-O	CDJ	U.S.	1994	$3.00

Casual Gods

Singles

Label	Catalog Number	Title	Type	Country	Year	Longbox Value/Value
Fontana	JERCD-1	Rev It Up	CD5	U.K.	1988	$8.00

Cat

Singles

Label	Catalog Number	Title	Type	Country	Year	Longbox Value/Value
Red Dot	RDT-1CD	Cat Woman	CD5	U.K.	1989	$7.00
WEA	246516-2	Cat Woman	CD5	U.K.	1989	$7.00

Cat Head

Full Length

Label	Catalog Number	Title	Type	Country	Year	Longbox Value/Value
Restless	72195-2	Hubba	LP/BP	U.S.		$12.00/$7.00

Catch

Full Length

Label	Catalog Number	Title	Type	Country	Year	Longbox Value/Value
Polygram	821359-2	Balance On Wires	LP	Germany		$15.00
Polygram	829014-2	Walk the Water	LP	Germany		$15.00

Singles

Label	Catalog Number	Title	Type	Country	Year	Longbox Value/Value
Polygram	FCD-147	Free	CD5	U.K.	1990	$7.00
BMG	654262	Twenty-Five Years	CD5	Germany	1991	$7.00

Catch My Soul

Singles

Label	Catalog Number	Title	Type	Country	Year	Longbox Value/Value
Vogue	74321173042	Catch My Soul	CD5	France	1993	$10.00

Caterwaul

Full Length

Label	Catalog Number	Title	Type	Country	Year	Longbox Value/Value
IRS	13000	Pin And Web	LP/LB	U.S.		$12.00/$7.00
IRS	13030	Portent Hue	LP/LB	U.S.		$12.00/$7.00

Catfish Hodge

Full Length

Label	Catalog Number	Title	Type	Country	Year	Longbox Value/Value
Hybrid		Down the Road	LP	Japan		$30.00

Cathedral

Singles

Label	Catalog Number	Title	Type	Country	Year	Longbox Value/Value
Columbia	44K 64326	Cosmic Requiem	CD5	U.S.	1994	$5.00
Columbia	CSK 5171	Ride	CDJ	U.S.	1993	$2.00
Columbia	CEPK-53149	Soul Scarface	CD5	Canada	1992	$8.00
Earache	MOSH-40CD	Soul Scarface	CD5	U.K.	1992	$7.00
Earache	44K 53149	Soul Scarface	CD5	U.S.	1992	$5.00

Catherine

Singles

Label	Catalog Number	Title	Type	Country	Year	Longbox Value/Value
TVT	4621	Saint	CDJ	U.S.	1995	$2.00
TVT	4610	Sleepy	CD5	U.S.	1995	$5.00

Catherine, Philip

Full Length

Label	Catalog Number	Title	Type	Country	Year	Longbox Value/Value
Plaene	41100500	Sleep My Love	LP	Germany		$15.00

Catherine Wheel

Full Length

Label	Catalog Number	Title	Type	Country	Year	Longbox Value/Value
Fontana	314518038-2	Chrome	DJ/LP	U.S.		$16.00
Westwood One		In Concert-Nu Rock	RS	U.S.	1995	$45.00

Airdate: 10/9/95.

Singles

Label	Catalog Number	Title	Type	Country	Year	Longbox Value/Value
Fontana	CDP-770	Balloon	CDJ	U.S.	1992	$3.00
		Black Metallic	CDJ	U.S.		$2.00
Fontana	CWCDA5	Crank	CD5	U.K.	1993	$8.00
Fontana		Crank	CD5	U.K.	1993	$8.00

Second version.

Label	Catalog Number	Title	Type	Country	Year	Longbox Value/Value
		Crank	CDJ	U.K.	1995	$15.00
Fontana	CDP 952	Crank	CDJ	U.S.	1993	$2.00
Fontana	CDP 735	I Want To Touch You	CDJ	U.S.	1992	$2.00
Polygram	852430	Judy Staring At the Sun	CD5	U.S.	1995	$5.00
Fontana	CDP 1496	Judy Staring At the Sun	CDJ	U.S.	1995	$3.00
Fontana	CDP 1525	Little Muscle	CDJ	U.S.	1995	$3.00
Fontana	1191	Nude, The	CDJ	U.S.	1994	$3.00
Fontana	CWCDA1	Shallow	CD5	U.K.	1991	$8.00
Fontana	CWCDB 6	Show Me Mary	CD5	U.K.	1993	$12.00
Fontana	CDP 1058	Show Me Mary	CDJ	U.S.		$2.00
Fontana		Waydown	CD5	U.K.	1995	$10.00
Fontana		Waydown	CD5	U.K.	1995	$10.00

Second version.

Label	Catalog Number	Title	Type	Country	Year	Longbox Value/Value
Fontana	1432	Waydown	CDJ	U.S.	1995	$3.00

Catherine/Escoude/Lockwood

Full Length

Label	Catalog Number	Title	Type	Country	Year	Longbox Value/Value
Gramaphone	JMS-031-2	Catherine/Escoude/Lockwood	LP/LB	U.S.†	1985	$14.00/$8.00

Cats

Full Length

Label	Catalog Number	Title	Type	Country	Year	Longbox Value/Value
EMI	CDP-91172	Kicked & Clawed	LP/LB	U.S.		$12.00/$7.00

Cats In Boots

Singles

Label	Catalog Number	Title	Type	Country	Year	Longbox Value/Value
		Her Monkey	CDJ	U.S.		$2.00
EMI	XP10-2100	Shotgun Sally	CD3	Japan	1989	$12.00/$3.00
		Shotgun Sally	CDJ	U.S.	1989	$2.00

Catton, Brian

Full Length

Label	Catalog Number	Title	Type	Country	Year	Longbox Value/Value
Relativity	1051	Spellbound	LP/LB	U.S.		$14.00/$8.00

Catwalk

Singles

Label	Catalog Number	Title	Type	Country	Year	Longbox Value/Value
Zelda	ZELDA-002CD	Bellerina Country	CD5	U.K.	1992	$8.00
Zelda	ZELDA-001CD	Catwalk	CD5	U.K.	1992	$8.00
		Life Is Sweet	CDJ	U.S.	1994	$3.00

Caudel, Stephen

Full Length

Label	Catalog Number	Title	Type	Country	Year	Longbox Value/Value
Polygram	830506-2	Wine Dark Sea	LP	Germany		$15.00

Caufield, Tom

Singles

Label	Catalog Number	Title	Type	Country	Year	Longbox Value/Value
		Long Distance Calling	CDJ	U.S.		$2.00

Caufields

Singles

Label	Catalog Number	Title	Type	Country	Year	Longbox Value/Value
A&M	0027	Day That Came And Went	CDJ	U.S.	1995	$3.00

Caught In The Act

Singles

Label	Catalog Number	Title	Type	Country	Year	Longbox Value/Value
ZYX	66041-8	Love Is Everywhere	CD5	U.S.	1996	$6.00

Cause & Effect

Singles

Label	Catalog Number	Title	Type	Country	Year	Longbox Value/Value
Zoo	14044	Another Minute	CD5	U.S.	1992	$5.00
Zoo	ZP 17065-2	Another Minute	CDJ	U.S.	1992	$2.00
Zoo	ZP 17088-2	What Do You See	CDJ	U.S.	1992	$2.00

Cavaliere, Felix

Singles

Label	Catalog Number	Title	Type	Country	Year	Longbox Value/Value
MCA	3074	If Not For You	CDJ	U.S.	1994	$2.00

Cavallaro, Carmen

Full Length

Label	Catalog Number	Title	Type	Country	Year	Longbox Value/Value
WEA	35XD-506	Best 20	LP	Germany		$15.00

Cave, Nick & The Bad Seeds

Full Length

Label	Catalog Number	Title	Type	Country	Year	Longbox Value/Value
Alfa	50B2-26/9	Crime And Punishment	LP	Japan		$25.00
Mute	ALZB-12	European Tour '92	LTD/LP	Japan		$25.00
Restless	71435	From Here To Eternity	LP/BP	U.S.		$14.00/$8.00
Mute	CD61554	Live Seeds	LTD/LP	Canada	1993	$20.00

CD with extra booklet in box.

Label	Catalog Number	Title	Type	Country	Year	Longbox Value/Value
Alternative	61554	Live Seeds	LTD/LP	U.S.	1993	$18.00

CD with extra booklet in box.

Label	Catalog Number	Title	Type	Country	Year	Longbox Value/Value
		Wonderful World Of Nick Cave	DJ/Smplr	France	1995	$30.00

Singles

Label	Catalog Number	Title	Type	Country	Year	Longbox Value / Value
Intercord	826-896	Deanna	CD5	Germany	1989	$9.00
		Do You Love Me?	CDJ	Australia	1993	$20.00
Elektra	PRCD 8939	Do You Love Me?	CDJ	U.S.	1993	$3.00
		Faraway, So Close	CD5	Australia	1994	$10.00
Elektra	PRCD 8622-2	I Had A Dream	CDJ	U.S.	1992	$6.00
		Loverman	CD5	Australia	1994	$10.00
		Loverman	CD5	U.K.	1994	$10.00
Mute	811-860	Mercy Seat, The	CD5	Germany	1988	$9.00
Mute	CDMUTE-52	Mercy Seat, The	CD5	U.K.	1988	$9.00
Mute	8959	Nobody's Baby Now	CDJ	U.S.	1994	$3.00
		Red Right Hand	CD5	Australia	1993	$10.00
Mute	108	Ship Song, The	CD5	U.K.	1990	$9.00
Intercord	826-998	Straight To You	CD5	Germany	1992	$9.00
Mute	CD MUTE 140	Straight To You	CD5	U.K.	1992	$10.00
Elektra	PRCD 8566-2	Straight To You	CDJ	U.S.	1992	$2.00
Elektra	9 66605-2	Weeping Song	CD5	U.S.	1990	$5.00
Elektra	PRCD 8229-2	Weeping Song	CDJ	U.S.	1990	$2.00
Mute	22-66352	What A Wonderful World	CD5	Canada	1993	$10.00
Mute		What A Wonderful World	CD5	Japan	1992	$15.00
Reprise	PRO-CD-8038	Where the Wild Roses Grow	CDJ	U.S.	1996	$3.00

Cavedogs

Full Length

Label	Catalog Number	Title	Type	Country	Year	Longbox Value / Value
Capitol	CDP-96240	Joyrides For Shut-Ins	LP/LB	U.S.		$12.00/$7.00
Capitol		Rock Takes A Holiday	DJ/Smplr	U.S.		$7.00
Capitol		Six Tender Moments	DJ/Smplr	U.S.	1991	$8.00
Capitol	CDP-97511	Soul Martini	LP/LB	U.S.		$12.00/$7.00

Singles

Label	Catalog Number	Title	Type	Country	Year	Longbox Value / Value
Enigma	EPRO-342	Baba Ghanooj	CDJ	U.S.	1990	$2.00
Enigma	EPRO-337	Bed Of Nails	CDJ	U.S.	1990	$2.00
Capitol	DPRO-79153	Boy In A Plastic Bubble	CDJ	U.S.	1992	$2.00
Enigma	EPRO-320	Leave Me Alone	CDJ	U.S.	1990	$2.00
Capitol	DPRO-79301	Love Grenade	CDJ	U.S.	1991	$2.00
Capitol	DPRO-79096	Rock Takes A Holiday	CDJ	U.S.	1991	$6.00
Restless	72513	Tayter Country	CD5	U.S.	1990	$5.00
Capitol	C2 15706	Tayter Country	CD5	U.S.	1991	$5.00
Capitol	DPRO-79648	Tayter Country	CDJ	U.S.	1991	$6.00

Caveman

Singles

Label	Catalog Number	Title	Type	Country	Year	Longbox Value / Value
IRS	977-580	I'm Ready	CD5	Germany	1991	$8.00
Profile	PROFCD-330	I'm Ready	CD5	U.K.	1991	$8.00
Profile	PROFCD-340	Victory	CD5	U.K.	1991	$8.00

Caymmi, Dori

Full Length

Label	Catalog Number	Title	Type	Country	Year	Longbox Value / Value
Warner Brothers	PRO-CD-7378	Selections From "If Ever"	DJ/Smplr	U.S.	1995	$5.00

Cayne, Carol

Singles

Label	Catalog Number	Title	Type	Country	Year	Longbox Value / Value
EMI	CDSY-12	What My Love Can Bring	CD5	U.K.	1988	$8.00

CD ROM Mickey

Singles

Label	Catalog Number	Title	Type	Country	Year	Longbox Value / Value
	1515	Mouse Pad	CD5	U.S.	1994	$5.00

Ceberano, Kate

Singles

Label	Catalog Number	Title	Type	Country	Year	Longbox Value / Value
Elektra	PRCD-8986-2	Where Has the Soul Gone	CDJ	U.S.	1994	$2.00

Cedell's Colors

Singles

Label	Catalog Number	Title	Type	Country	Year	Longbox Value / Value
Jbr	13002	Spend A Lil Time	CD5	U.S.	1994	$5.00

Celebrate The Nun

Singles

Label	Catalog Number	Title	Type	Country	Year	Longbox Value / Value
EMI	203150-2	Ordinary World	CD5	Germany	1988	$7.00
Polygram	867013-2	Patience	CD5	Germany	1991	$7.00
EMI	203568-3	Will You Be There	CD3	Germany	1990	$7.00
EMI	203521-3	Will You Be There	CD3	Germany	1990	$7.00
EMI	203907-2	Will You Be There	CD5	Germany	1990	$7.00
Parlophone	CDR-6242	Will You Be There	CD3	U.K.	1990	$7.00
		Will You Be There	CDJ	U.S.		$2.00

Celebrity Skins

Singles

Label	Catalog Number	Title	Type	Country	Year	Longbox Value / Value
Triple X	50131	S.O.S.	CD5	U.S.	1990	$5.00

Celestial Navigations

Full Length

Label	Catalog Number	Title	Type	Country	Year	Longbox Value / Value
		Sampler	DJ/Smplr	U.S.		$6.00

Cell

Singles

Label	Catalog Number	Title	Type	Country	Year	Longbox Value / Value
DGC	PRO-CD-4531	Everything Turns	CDJ	U.S.	1993	$2.00
City Slang	EFA-04905-03	Fall	CD5	U.K.	1992	$8.00
DGC	PRO-CD-4492	Fall	CDJ	U.S.	1993	$2.00
DGC	PRO-CD-4659	Milky	CDJ	U.S.	1994	$2.00

Cell Mates

Singles

Label	Catalog Number	Title	Type	Country	Year	Longbox Value / Value
Scotti Brothers	ZSK 75335	Bottle Of Sin	CDJ	U.S.	1992	$2.00

Cella Dwellas

Singles

Label	Catalog Number	Title	Type	Country	Year	Longbox Value / Value
RCA	62962	Land Of The Lost	CD5	U.S.	1994	$5.00

Celli Cel

Singles

Label	Catalog Number	Title	Type	Country	Year	Longbox Value / Value
Jive	JDJ423672	It's Going Down	CDJ	U.S.		$3.00

Cellie, Tom

Singles

Label	Catalog Number	Title	Type	Country	Year	Longbox Value / Value
		Vicki's Song	DJ/CD3	U.S.		$4.00

Celtic Frost

Full Length

Label	Catalog Number	Title	Type	Country	Year	Longbox Value / Value
Noise	4803	Cold Lake	LP/BP	U.S.		$12.00/$7.00
Noise	44842	Into the Pandemonium	LP/BP	U.S.		$12.00/$7.00
Noise	4802	Morbid Tales	LP/BP	U.S.		$12.00/$7.00
Noise	44852	Parched With Thirst	LP/BP	U.S.		$12.00/$7.00
Noise	44841	To Megatherion	LP/BP	U.S.		$12.00/$7.00
Noise	2403	Vanity/Nemesis	LP/BP	U.S.		$12.00/$7.00

Singles

Label	Catalog Number	Title	Type	Country	Year	Longbox Value / Value
Noise	NZCDP 1	Cherry Orchards	CDJ	U.S.	1988	$2.00

Centerfold

Singles

Company	Disk Number	Title	Type	Country	Year	Longbox Value / Value
Epic	XXXC-3	More Money	CD5	U.K.	1989	$8.00

Cerebrano, Kate

Singles

Company	Disk Number	Title	Type	Country	Year	Longbox Value / Value
London	LONCD-236	Bedroom Eyes	CD5	U.K.	1989	$8.00
London	LONCD-2326	Young Boys Are My Weakness	CD5	U.K.	1989	$8.00

Ceremony

Singles

Company	Disk Number	Title	Type	Country	Year	Longbox Value / Value
DGC	PRO-CD-4524	Could've Been Love	CDJ	U.S.	1993	$2.00
DGC	PRO-CD-4524	Ready For Love	CDJ	U.S.	1993	$2.00
DGC	PRO-CD-4605	Ready For Love	CDJ	U.S.	1993	$2.00

Cerrone

Singles

Company	Disk Number	Title	Type	Country	Year	Longbox Value / Value
Hot Prod.	12568	Love & Be Loved	CD5	U.S.	1994	$5.00

Certain Distant Suns

Singles

Company	Disk Number	Title	Type	Country	Year	Longbox Value / Value
Giant	PRO-CD-6997	Bitter	CDJ	U.S.	1994	$2.00
CDM	14343	Dogrocket	CD5	U.S.	1993	$5.00

Cervenka, Exene

Full Length

Company	Disk Number	Title	Type	Country	Year	Longbox Value / Value
Rhino	70913	Old Wives' Tale	LP/LB	U.S.		$12.00/$7.00
Rhino	70757	Running Scared	LP/LB	U.S.		$12.00/$7.00

Singles

Company	Disk Number	Title	Type	Country	Year	Longbox Value / Value
		Just Another Perfect Day	CDJ	U.S.		$2.00

Cetera, Peter

Full Length

Company	Disk Number	Title	Type	Country	Year	Longbox Value / Value
Warner Brothers	2 27712-Dj	One More Story	DJ/LP	U.S.	1988	$10.00
Full Moon	2 27824-2	Peter Cetera	LP/LB	U.S.		$14.00/$8.00

Singles

Company	Disk Number	Title	Type	Country	Year	Longbox Value / Value
Warner Brothers	10P3-6045	Best Of Times	CD3	Japan	1988	$13.00/$4.00
Warner Brothers	2 27712	Best Of Times	CD3	U.S.	1988	$6.00/$3.00
Warner Brothers	PRO-CD-3280	Best Of Times	CDJ	U.S.	1988	$2.00
Warner Brothers	PRO-CD-3325	Best Of Times	CDJ	U.S.	1988	$2.00
Warner Brothers	PRO-CD-3320	Holding Out	CDJ	U.S.	1988	$2.00
River North	51416 4542	(I Wanna Take) Forever Tonight	CDJ	U.S.	1995	$3.00
Warner Brothers	10P3-6005	One Good Woman	CD3	Japan	1988	$13.00/$4.00
Warner Brothers	2 27824	One Good Woman	CD3	U.S.	1988	$6.00/$3.00
Warner Brothers	PRO-CD-3152	One Good Woman	CDJ	U.S.	1988	$2.00
Warner Brothers	27824-2	One More Story	CD3	U.S.	1988	$6.00/$3.00
Warner Brothers	WPDP-6300	Restless Heart	CD3	Japan	1992	$13.00/$4.00
Warner Brothers	PRO-CD-5496	Restless Heart	CDJ	U.S.	1992	$2.00

Ceybil

Singles

Company	Disk Number	Title	Type	Country	Year	Longbox Value / Value
Atlantic	A-7721CD	Love So Special	CD5	U.K.	1991	$7.00

CFM Band

Singles

Company	Disk Number	Title	Type	Country	Year	Longbox Value / Value
4th & B'way	BRCD-216	Jazz It Up	CD5	U.K.	1991	$7.00

Chadbourne, Eugene

Full Length

Company	Disk Number	Title	Type	Country	Year	Longbox Value / Value
Fundamental	SAVE-046CD	Camper Van Chadbourne	LP/BP	U.S.		$12.00/$7.00
Fundamental	SAVE-010CD	Corpses Of Foreign War	LP/BP	U.S.		$12.00/$7.00
Fundamental	SAVE-080CD	Country Music In the World Of Islam	LP/LB	U.S.		$12.00/$7.00
Fundamental	SAVE-007CD	Country Protest	LP/LB	U.S.		$12.00/$7.00
Fundamental	SAVE-069CD	Eddie Chatterbox's Love Trio	LP/LB	U.S.		$12.00/$7.00
Fundamental	SAVE-006CD	There Will Be No Tears Tonight	LP/LB	U.S.		$12.00/$7.00
Fundamental	SAVE-018CD	Vermin Of the Blues	LP/LB	U.S.		$12.00/$7.00

Chagall Guevara

Singles

Company	Disk Number	Title	Type	Country	Year	Longbox Value / Value
		Violent Blue	CDJ	U.S.		$2.00

Chainsaw Daisy

Singles

Company	Disk Number	Title	Type	Country	Year	Longbox Value / Value
Rough Trade	381-0058-3	Love Your Money	CD5	Germany	1992	$8.00
Creation	COCY-5171	Love Your Money	CD5	Japan	1992	$10.00

Chainsaw Kittens

Singles

Company	Disk Number	Title	Type	Country	Year	Longbox Value / Value
Mammoth	MR-0042-2	High In High School	CD5	U.K.	1992	$8.00
Mammoth	42	High In High School	CD5	U.S.	1992	$5.00
Mammoth	5487	Pop Heiress Dies	CDJ	U.S.	1994	$2.00

Chaka Demus & Pliers

Singles

Company	Disk Number	Title	Type	Country	Year	Longbox Value / Value
Mango	CIDM 810	She Don't Let Nobody	CD5	U.K.	1993	$10.00
CMango		Twist & Shout	CDJ	U.S.	1994	$3.00

Chalk Circle

Full Length

Company	Disk Number	Title	Type	Country	Year	Longbox Value / Value
		As the Crow Flies	DJ/Smplr	Canada		$8.00

Singles

Company	Disk Number	Title	Type	Country	Year	Longbox Value / Value
Canyon	S10Y-1024	Out Of Control	CD3	Japan	1988	$12.00/$3.00

Chaloff, Serge

Full Length

Company	Disk Number	Title	Type	Country	Year	Longbox Value / Value
Mosaic	MD4-147	Complete Recordings	LTD/LP	U.S.		$60.00

4 CD set. Limited to 5,000 copies.

Chaloner, Sue

Singles

Company	Disk Number	Title	Type	Country	Year	Longbox Value / Value
Pulse 8	CDLOSE-31	Appreciation	CD5	U.K.	1992	$8.00
Pulse 8	CDLOSE-14	I Wanna Thank You	CD5	U.K.	1992	$8.00
Avex Trax	AVDD-20027	It's Over Now	CD3	Japan	1992	$12.00/$3.00
Pulse 8	CDLOSE-23	It's Over Now	CD5	U.K.	1992	$8.00

Chambers, Paul

Full Length

Company	Disk Number	Title	Type	Country	Year	Longbox Value / Value
Blue Note		Bass On Top	LP	U.K.		$15.00
Blue Note	CDP 46533	Bass On Top	LP/LB	U.S.		$18.00/$12.00
Blue Note		Bass On Top And Chambers Music	LTD/LP	U.S.	1995	$19.00
Blue Note	CDP 84437	Chambers' Music	LP/LB	U.S.		$18.00/$12.00

Champ M.C.

Singles

Company	Disk Number	Title	Type	Country	Year	Longbox Value / Value
Eastwest	PRCD 5656-2	Keep It On the Real	CDJ	U.S.	1994	$2.00
Eastwest	PRCD 5873-2	Sistas Betta Recognize	CDJ	U.S.	1994	$2.00
Polygram	887882-2	Here And Now	CD5	Germany	1989	$8.00

Champaign

Singles

Label	Catalog Number	Title	Type	Country	Year	Longbox Value / Value
Malaco	2180	My Fool	CDJ	U.S.	1992	$2.00

Champlin, Bill

Singles

Label	Catalog Number	Title	Type	Country	Year	Longbox Value / Value
		Burn Down the Night	CD5	U.K.		$10.00
Elektra	WPDP-6219	City	CD3	Japan	1990	$12.00/$3.00
Elektra	WPCP-36454	No Wasted Moments	CD5	Japan	1990	$16.00

Champloos

Singles

Label	Catalog Number	Title	Type	Country	Year	Longbox Value / Value
East World	TODT-2905	Happy Flower	CD3	Japan	1992	$12.00/$3.00

Chance, Jeff

Full Length

Label	Catalog Number	Title	Type	Country	Year	Longbox Value / Value
Mercury	846615	Picture On the Wall	LP/BP	U.S.		$14.00/$8.00

Singles

Label	Catalog Number	Title	Type	Country	Year	Longbox Value / Value
Mercury	CDP 798	A Heartache On Her Hands	CDJ	U.S.	1992	$2.00
Mercury	CDP 443	Thirty Days In Twenty Years	CDJ	U.S.	1990	$2.00

Chandler, Omar

Full Length

Label	Catalog Number	Title	Type	Country	Year	Longbox Value / Value
MCA	MCAD-10057	Omar Chandler	LP/LB	U.S.		$14.00/$8.00

Singles

Label	Catalog Number	Title	Type	Country	Year	Longbox Value / Value
MCA	MCSTD-1543	Better World	CD5	U.K.	1991	$8.00
MCA	CD45-1349	Do You Really Want It	CDJ	U.S.	1991	$2.00
MCA	CD45-1400	This Must Be Heaven	CDJ	U.S.	1991	$2.00
MCA	MCSTD-1561	You Changed For the Better	CD5	U.K.	1991	$8.00

Chanelle

Singles

Label	Catalog Number	Title	Type	Country	Year	Longbox Value / Value
ZYX	6106-8	One Man	CD5	Germany	1989	$6.00
Great Jones	629	Work That Body	CDJ	U.S.	1993	$2.00

Changing Faces

Singles

Label	Catalog Number	Title	Type	Country	Year	Longbox Value / Value
Atlantic	95804	Foolin' Around	CD5	U.S.	1994	$5.00
	PRCD 5929-2	Foolin' Around	CDJ	U.S.	1995	$3.00
Atlantic	95792	Keep It Right There	CD5	U.S.	1994	$5.00
	PRCD 6033-2	Keep It Right There	CDJ	U.S.	1995	$3.00
Atlantic	95909	Stroke You Up	CD5	U.S.	1994	$5.00
	PRCD 5605-2	Stroke You Up	CDJ	U.S.	1995	$3.00
	PRCD 6312-2	We Got It Goin' On	CDJ	U.S.		$3.00

Channel 2

Full Length

Label	Catalog Number	Title	Type	Country	Year	Longbox Value / Value
Polygram	837388	Slammin' At Eleven	LP/BP	U.S.		$14.00/$8.00

Channel Live

Singles

Label	Catalog Number	Title	Type	Country	Year	Longbox Value / Value
Capitol	DPRO-79539	Mad Izm	CDJ	U.S.		$3.00
Capitol	DPRO-79444	Mad Izm	CDJ	U.S.	1994	$2.00

Chaos

Singles

Label	Catalog Number	Title	Type	Country	Year	Longbox Value / Value
Arist	7432111639-2	Farewell My Summer Love	CD5	U.K.	1992	$7.00

Chapin, Tom

Full Length

Label	Catalog Number	Title	Type	Country	Year	Longbox Value / Value
A&M	0402	Family Tree	LP/LB	U.S.		$14.00/$8.00
A&M	0413	Mother Earth	LP/LB	U.S.		$14.00/$8.00

Singles

Label	Catalog Number	Title	Type	Country	Year	Longbox Value / Value
A&M	CD-17672	Shovelling	CDJ	U.S.	1988	$2.00

Chapman, Ben

Singles

Label	Catalog Number	Title	Type	Country	Year	Longbox Value / Value
BMG	PD-44366	Erotic Animals	CD5	U.K.	1991	$7.00
BMG	PD-44002	Summer	CD5	U.K.	1991	$7.00

Chapman, Beth Nielson

Full Length

Label	Catalog Number	Title	Type	Country	Year	Longbox Value / Value
Reprise	PRO-CD-6390	Sampler	DJ/Smplr	U.S.	1993	$7.00
Reprise	2-45233-A	You Hold the Key	DJ/LP	U.S.	1993	$10.00

Advance issue.

Singles

Label	Catalog Number	Title	Type	Country	Year	Longbox Value / Value
Reprise	WPDP-6285	All I Have	CD3	Japan	1991	$13.00/$4.00
Reprise	PRO-CD-4928	All I Have	CDJ	U.S.	1990	$2.00
Reprise	PRO-CD-5223	I Keep Coming Back	CDJ	U.S.	1990	$2.00
Reprise	PRO-CD-6836	In the Time It Takes	CDJ	U.S.	1993	$2.00
Reprise	PRO-CD-5218	Life Holds On	CDJ	U.S.	1990	$2.00
Reprise	PRO-CD-6379	Moment You Were Mine, The	CDJ	U.S.	1993	$2.00
Reprise	PRO-CD-6780	Say It To Me Now	CDJ	U.S.	1993	$3.00
Reprise	PRO-CD-6371	Selections From You Hold the Key	CDJ	U.S.	1993	$6.00
Reprise	WPDP-6270	That's the Easy Part	CD3	Japan	1991	$13.00/$4.00
Reprise	PRO-CD-4812	Walk My Way	CDJ	U.S.	1990	$2.00
Reprise	PRO-CD-7123	When I Feel This Way	CDJ	U.S.	1993	$3.00
Reprise	WPDP-6295	You Light Up My Life	CD3	Japan	1992	$13.00/$4.00

Chapman, Roger

Full Length

Label	Catalog Number	Title	Type	Country	Year	Longbox Value / Value
Polygram	832223-2	Heartbeat/New Age	LP	Germany		$15.00

Chapman, Steven Curtis

Singles

Label	Catalog Number	Title	Type	Country	Year	Longbox Value / Value
Sparrow	79725	Go There With You	CDJ	U.S.	1993	$2.00

Chapman, Tracy

Singles

Label	Catalog Number	Title	Type	Country	Year	Longbox Value / Value
Pioneer	EPDP-6213	All That You Have Is Your Soul	CD3	Japan	1990	$13.00/$4.00
Elektra	EKR-107CD	All That You Have Is Your Soul	CD5	U.K.	1990	$9.00
Elektra	PR 8132-2	All That You Have Is Your Soul	CDJ	U.S.	1989	$2.00
Elektra	969351-2	Baby Can I Hold You	CD5	Germany	1988	$9.00
Elektra	10P3-6081	Baby Can I Hold You	CD3	Japan	1988	$13.00/$4.00
Elektra	EKR-82CD	Baby Can I Hold You	CD5	U.K.	1988	$9.00
Elektra	69356-2	Baby Can I Hold You	CD3	U.S.	1988	$6.00/$3.00
Elektra	PR 8037-2	Baby Can I Hold You	CDJ	U.S.	1988	$2.00
Elektra	WMD5-4078	Bang Bang Bang	CD3	Japan	1992	$13.00/$4.00
Elektra	EKR-144CD	Bang Bang Bang	CD5	U.K.	1992	$9.00
Elektra	PRCD 8555-2	Bang Bang Bang	CDJ	U.S.	1992	$3.00
Elektra	PR 8151-2	Born To Fight	CDJ	U.S.	1989	$2.00
Elektra	966682-2	Crossroads	CD5	Germany	1989	$9.00
Elektra	09P3-6184	Crossroads	CD3	Japan	1989	$13.00/$4.00
Elektra	EKR-95CD	Crossroads	CD5	U.K.	1989	$9.00
Elektra	PR 8106-2	Crossroads	CDJ	U.S.	1989	$2.00
Elektra	WMD5-4110	Dreaming Of A World	CD3	Japan	1992	$13.00/$4.00
Elektra	EKR-152CD	Dreaming Of A World	CD5	U.K.	1992	$9.00
Elektra	PRCD 85252	Dreaming Of A World	CDJ	U.S.	1992	$2.00
Elektra	966758-2	Fast Car	CD3	Germany	1988	$9.00
Elektra	10P3-6022	Fast Car	CD3	Japan	1988	$13.00/$4.00
Elektra	EKR-73CD	Fast Car	CD3	U.K.	1988	$9.00
Elektra	PR 2217-2	Fast Car	CDJ	U.S.	1988	$2.00
Elektra	000047	Fast Car	DJ/CD3	U.S.	1988	$3.00
		Give Me One Reason	CDJ	U.K.	1996	$10.00
Elektra	PRCD 9347-2	Give Me One Reason	CDJ	U.S.		$3.00
Elektra	PRCD 9488-2	Smoke & Ashes	CDJ	U.S.		$3.00
WEA	966645-2	Subcity	CD5	Germany	1990	$9.00
Elektra	966745-2	Talkin' Bout A Revolution	CD3	Germany	1988	$9.00
Elektra	10P3-6032	Talkin' Bout A Revolution	CD3	Japan	1988	$13.00/$4.00
Elektra	EKR-78CD	Talkin' Bout A Revolution	CD3	U.K.	1988	$9.00
Elektra	69383	Talkin' Bout A Revolution	CD3	U.S.	1988	$6.00/$2.00
Elektra	PR 8016-2	Talkin' Bout A Revolution	CDJ	U.S.	1988	$2.00
Elektra	PR 8171-2	This Time	CDJ	U.S.	1989	$2.00

Chappell, Jim

Full Length

Label	Catalog Number	Title	Type	Country	Year	Longbox Value / Value
Real Music	0136	In Search Of the Magic	DJ/LP	U.S.	1992	$8.00
Music West	134	Saturday's Rhapsody	DJ/LP	U.S.	1990	$8.00

Chapter And The Verse

Singles

Label	Catalog Number	Title	Type	Country	Year	Longbox Value / Value
Ten	413	In Another World	CD5	U.K.	1992	$8.00

Chapter Eight

Full Length

Label	Catalog Number	Title	Type	Country	Year	Longbox Value / Value
Capitol	CDP 46947	Forever	LP/LB	U.S.		$14.00/$8.00

Chapterhouse

Full Length

Label	Catalog Number	Title	Type	Country	Year	Longbox Value / Value
Arista	ASCD 18742	Blood Music	LTD/LP	U.S.	1993	$12.00

Includes bonus CD.

Label	Catalog Number	Title	Type	Country	Year	Longbox Value / Value
		Blood Music Sampler	DJ/Smplr	France	1995	$12.00

Singles

Label	Catalog Number	Title	Type	Country	Year	Longbox Value / Value
		Dedicated	CDJ	U.S.		$7.00
3rd Stone	STONE-001CD	Falling Down	CD5	U.K.	1990	$8.00
RCA	62019-2-RDJ	Falling Down	CDJ	U.S.	1990	$2.00
Deadicated	HOUSE-001CD	Mesmerize	CD5	U.K.	1991	$8.00
RCA	62151-2-RDJ	Mesmerize	CDJ	U.S.	1990	$2.00
Dedicated	STONE 003	Pearl	CD5	U.K.	1991	$8.00
3rd Stone	STONE-002CD	Sunburst	CD5	U.K.	1990	$8.00
Deadicated	HOUSE 004	We Are the Beautiful	CD5	U.K.	1993	$10.00
Deadicated	HOUSE 004 CDJ	We Are the Beautiful	CDJ	U.K.	1993	$12.00
Dedicated	2640	We Are the Beautiful	CDJ	U.S.	1993	$2.00

Chaquico, Craig

Full Length

Label	Catalog Number	Title	Type	Country	Year	Longbox Value / Value
Higher Octave	HOMCD 7084	A Thousand Pictures	DJ/LP	U.S.	1996	$20.00

Enhanced CD in press kit folder.

Label	Catalog Number	Title	Type	Country	Year	Longbox Value / Value
Higher Octave		Acoustic Highway	DJ/LP	U.S.	1993	$10.00

Char

Singles

Label	Catalog Number	Title	Type	Country	Year	Longbox Value / Value
Edoya	PSY-4	Black Shoes	CD5	Japan	1989	$10.00
Edoya	PSY-3	When I Wake Up In the Morning	CD5	Japan	1989	$10.00

Charlatans

Full Length

Label	Catalog Number	Title	Type	Country	Year	Longbox Value / Value
Warner Brothers	CB 2CD	Isolation 21.2.91	DJ/Smplr	U.K.	1991	$20.00

Singles

Label	Catalog Number	Title	Type	Country	Year	Longbox Value / Value
RCA	62374-2-RDJ	Can't Even Be Bothered	CDJ	U.S.	1992	$6.00
Beggars Banquet	BBQ27CD	Can't Get Out Of Bed	CD5	U.K.	1994	$10.00
Beggars Banquet	95946	Can't Get Out Of Bed	CD5	U.S.	1994	$5.00
Beggars Banquet	PRO-CD-5450	Can't Get Out Of Bed	CDJ	U.S.	1994	$6.00
Beggars Banquet	PRO-CD-5533	Can't Get Out Of Bed	CDJ	U.S.	1994	$6.00
RCA	62274-2-RDJ	I Don't Want To See the Sights	CDJ	U.S.	1992	$6.00
Dead Good	GOOD-1CD	Indian Rope	CD5	U.K.	1992	$10.00
		Jesus Hairdo	CD5	U.K.	1994	$10.00
		Just When You're Thinkin' Things Over	CD5	U.K.	1995	$11.00
SPV	0546-3	Me In Time	CD5	Germany	1991	$10.00
Pinnacle	SIT-84CD	Me In Time	CD5	U.K.	1991	$10.00
Polygram	875999-2	Only One I Know, The	CD5	Canada	1990	$8.00
SPV	0513-3	Only One I Know, The	CD5	Germany	1990	$10.00
Pinnacle	SIT-70CD	Only One I Know, The	CD5	U.K.	1990	$10.00
Beggars Banquet	2451-2-HDJ	Only One I Know, The	CDJ	U.S.	1990	$2.00
RCA	2690-2-RDJ	Only One I Know, The	CDJ	U.S.	1990	$2.00
Beggars Banquet	ALCB-288	Over Rising	CD5	Japan	1991	$15.00
Pinnacle	SIT-76CD	Over Rising	CD5	U.K.	1991	$10.00
RCA	2832	Over Rising	CD5	U.S.	1991	$5.00
RCA	2777-2-RDJ	Sproston Green	CDJ	U.S.	1991	$2.00
SPV	3092-3	Then	CD5	Germany	1990	$10.00
Pinnacle	SIT-74CD	Then	CD5	U.K.	1990	$10.00
RCA	2451-1-RDJ	Then	CDJ	U.S.	1990	$2.00
Columbia	ALCB-593	Tremolo Song	CD5	Japan	1992	$20.00
Situation	SIT 97CD	Tremolo Song	CD5	U.K.	1992	$10.00
SPV	0506-3	Weirdo	CD5	Germany	1992	$10.00
Pinnacle	SIT-88CD	Weirdo	CD5	U.K.	1992	$10.00
RCA	62264-2-RDJ	Weirdo	CDJ	U.S.	1992	$2.00
Beggars Banquet	62293	Weirdo	CDJ	U.S.	1992	$2.00

Charlatans UK

Full Length

Label	Catalog Number	Title	Type	Country	Year	Longbox Value / Value
Polygram	PCD237	Isolation 12/2/91	DJ/Smplr	Canada	1992	$25.00

Singles

Label	Catalog Number	Title	Type	Country	Year	Longbox Value / Value
	PRCD 6386	Just Lookin'	CDJ	U.S.		$3.00

Charles, Amy Lou

Singles

Label	Catalog Number	Title	Type	Country	Year	Longbox Value / Value
Media	ALCB-574	Weekend	CD5	Japan	1992	$10.00

Charles & Eddie

Singles

Label	Catalog Number	Title	Type	Country	Year	Longbox Value / Value
Capitol	DPRO-79573	Chocolate Milk	CD5	U.S.	1995	$6.00
Capitol	80563	House Is Not A Home	CD5	U.K.	1992	$8.00
Capitol		House Is Not A Home	CD5	U.K.	1992	$8.00

Second version.

Label	Catalog Number	Title	Type	Country	Year	Longbox Value / Value
Capitol	DPRO-79576	House Is Not A Home	CDJ	U.S.	1992	$2.00
Capitol	CDCL-681	N.Y.C.	CD5	U.K.	1993	$8.00
Capitol	DPRO-79478	N.Y.C.	CDJ	U.S.	1992	$2.00
Capitol	C215879	Would I Lie To You	CD5	Canada	1993	$10.00
Capitol	CDCL-673	Would I Lie To You	CD5	U.K.	1992	$8.00

Charles, Kelly

Singles

Label	Catalog Number	Title	Type	Country	Year	Longbox Value / Value
Champion	CHAMPCD-214	Reachin'	CD5	U.K.	1989	$7.00

Charles, Ray

Full Length

Label	Catalog Number	Title	Type	Country	Year	Longbox Value / Value
CBS	CK-39415	Friendship	LP/LB	U.S.		$15.00/$9.00
WEA	38310	Genius Of Soul	LD	U.S.	1993	$30.00
		House Of Blues	RS	U.S.	1994	$60.00

2 CD set. 3/20/94.

Label	Catalog Number	Title	Type	Country	Year	Longbox Value / Value
Pioneer		How Ray Charles Sees Laserdisc	DJ/LD	U.S.		$180.00
WEA	50231	Live 1991	LD	U.S.	1992	$30.00
O.P.A.	OPA-74-612	Ray Charles	LD	U.S.	1985	$45.00
Topline	CD-512	This Love Of Mine	LP/BP	U.S.		$15.00/$9.00
Columbia	CK-38293	Wish You Were Here Tonight	LP/LB	U.S.		$15.00/$9.00

Singles

Label	Catalog Number	Title	Type	Country	Year	Longbox Value / Value
Warner Brothers	PRO-CD-5977	A Song For You	CDJ	U.S.	1993	$3.00
Warner Brothers	PRO-CD-5950	Fresh Out Of Tears	CDJ	U.S.	1993	$3.00
Aris	885820	Georgia On My Mind	CD3	Germany	1990	$10.00
		I Wish I'd Never Loved You At All	CDJ	U.S		$3.00
Warner Brothers	PRO-CD-5978	I'll Be There	CDJ	U.S.	1993	$3.00
Pioneer	WPDP-6248	I'll Take Care Of You	CD3	Japan	1990	$13.00/$4.00
Warner Brothers	PRO-CD-4425	I'll Take Care Of You	CDJ	U.S.	1990	$3.00
Polygram	873130-3	Precious Things	CD3	Germany	1989	$10.00
Warner Brothers	PRO-CD-6215	Still Crazy After All These Years	CDJ	U.S.	1993	$3.00
Gala	CDGX 1013	Till the Next...Somewhere	CD5	Italy	1989	$12.00

With Dee Dee Bridgewater.

Label	Catalog Number	Title	Type	Country	Year	Longbox Value / Value
Aris	885819	Unchain My Heart	CD3	Germany	1990	$10.00
Canyon	PCDY-00032	What'd I Say	CD3	Japan	1990	$13.00/$4.00

Charles, Teddy

Full Length

Label	Catalog Number	Title	Type	Country	Year	Longbox Value / Value
Soul Note	1183	At Verona Jazz Festival '88	LP/BP	U.S.		$12.00/$7.00

Charles, Tina

Full Length

Label	Catalog Number	Title	Type	Country	Year	Longbox Value / Value
Aris	880418	I Love To Love	LP	Germany		$15.00

Singles

Label	Catalog Number	Title	Type	Country	Year	Longbox Value / Value
BMG	662617	Got To Work On Love	CD5	Germany	1989	$7.00

Charleston

Full Length

Label	Catalog Number	Title	Type	Country	Year	Longbox Value / Value
Vogue	600132	Charleston	LP	Germany		$15.00

Charlot

Singles

Label	Catalog Number	Title	Type	Country	Year	Longbox Value / Value
Polygram	871540-3	I Can't Promise You	CD3	Germany	1989	$7.00
Polygram	871541-2	I Can't Promise You	CD5	Germany	1989	$7.00

Charm

Singles

Label	Catalog Number	Title	Type	Country	Year	Longbox Value / Value
Big Beat	A-8464CD	I Love Music	CD5	U.K.	1992	$7.00

Charm Farm

Singles

Label	Catalog Number	Title	Type	Country	Year	Longbox Value / Value
Polygram	CDP 1589	Sick	CDJ	U.S.		$3.00

Charthogs

Singles

Label	Catalog Number	Title	Type	Country	Year	Longbox Value / Value
		Hush Hush Sweet Charlotte	CDJ	U.S.	1994	$3.00

Charvoni

Singles

Label	Catalog Number	Title	Type	Country	Year	Longbox Value / Value
EMI	203366-3	Always There	CD3	Germany	1989	$7.00
EMI	203366-2	Always There	CD5	Germany	1989	$7.00

Chase

Singles

Label	Catalog Number	Title	Type	Country	Year	Longbox Value / Value
Zyx	66018	Love For The Future	CD5	U.S.	1994	$5.00

Chase, Chevy

Full Length

Label	Catalog Number	Title	Type	Country	Year	Longbox Value / Value
Image	ID5162	Best Of Chevy Chase	LD	U.S.		$25.00

Chase The Ace

Singles

Label	Catalog Number	Title	Type	Country	Year	Longbox Value / Value
Da Music	FFR-0504	Let's Do It	CD5	Germany	1989	$7.00

Chava

Singles

Label	Catalog Number	Title	Type	Country	Year	Longbox Value / Value
Spin	ALCA-165	Happy! Happy! Shake	CD5	Japan	1991	$10.00
Spin	ALCA-165	Please Come Home For Christmas	CD5	Japan	1991	$10.00

Chavez, Ingrid

Full Length

Label	Catalog Number	Title	Type	Country	Year	Longbox Value / Value
Warner Brothers	9 40270-2	Hippy Blood	LP/LB	U.S.		$12.00/$7.00
Paisley Park	9 25879-2-Dj	May 19 1990	DJ/LP	U.S.	1991	$10.00

Singles

Label	Catalog Number	Title	Type	Country	Year	Longbox Value / Value
Paisley Park	9 40170 2	Elephant Box	CD5	U.S.	1991	$4.00
Paisley Park	PRO-CD-4929	Elephant Box	CDJ	U.S.	1991	$2.00
Paisley Park	9 40270 2	Hippy Blood	CD5	U.S.	1991	$4.00
Paisley Park	PRO-CD-5155	Hippy Blood	CDJ	U.S.	1991	$2.00

Cheap And Nasty

Singles

Label	Catalog Number	Title	Type	Country	Year	Longbox Value / Value
China	CHICD-34	Beautiful Disaster	CD5	U.K.	1991	$7.00
China	CHICD-31	Mind Across the Ocean	CD5	U.K.	1990	$7.00

Cheap Trick

Full Length

Label	Catalog Number	Title	Type	Country	Year	Longbox Value / Value
Epic	ESK 1012	Best Of Sampler	DJ/Smplr	U.S.	1988	$40.00
Epic		Box Set Sampler	DJ/Smplr	U.S.	1996	$25.00
Epic	ESK 2129	Busted	DJ/LP	U.S.	1990	$18.00
red ant	ADVR 002-2	Cheap Trick	DJ/LP	U.S.	1997	$12.00
Epic Sony	ESCA 5490-1	Greatest Hits, The	LTD/LP	Japan	1991	$50.00

2CD set with outer box and book

Label	Catalog Number	Title	Type	Country	Year	Longbox Value / Value
Album Network		In the Studio (Live At Budokan)	RS	U.S.	1989	$25.00

Airdate: 5/1/89.

Label	Catalog Number	Title	Type	Country	Year	Longbox Value / Value
Album Network		In the Studio (Live At Budokan)	RS	U.S.	1992	$25.00

Airdate: 5/11/92.

Label	Catalog Number	Title	Type	Country	Year	Longbox Value / Value
Epic		Lap Of Luxury	LP/LB	U.S.		$14.00/$8.00
Epic	EK-35795	Live At Budokan	LP/LB	U.S.†	1984	$14.00/$8.00
Epic	ESCA-5861	Starbox	LP	Japan	1993	$30.00
Westwood One		Superstars	RS	U.S.	1996	$80.00

2 CD set. Airdate: 3/4/96.

Label	Catalog Number	Title	Type	Country	Year	Longbox Value / Value
Warner Brothers	PRO-CD-6889	Woke Up With A Monster	DJ/LP	U.S.	1994	$35.00

CD in "file drawer" box

Label	Catalog Number	Title	Type	Country	Year	Longbox Value / Value
Epic Legacy	ESK 8110	You Can Have Sex In America Sampler	DJ/Smplr	U.S.	1996	$22.00

Singles

Label	Catalog Number	Title	Type	Country	Year	Longbox Value / Value
Epic	656148-2	Can't Stop Fallin' In Love	CD5	Germany	1990	$9.00
Epic	ESDA-7021	Can't Stop Fallin' In Love	CD3	Japan	1990	$13.00/$4.00

Cheap Trick – Greatest Hits (Epic Sony ESCA 5490-1)

Company	Disk Number	Title	Type	Country	Year	Longbox Value / Value
Epic	656148-2	Can't Stop Fallin' In Love	CD5	U.K.	1990	$9.00
Epic	ESK 73444	Can't Stop Fallin' In Love	CDJ	U.S.	1990	$3.00
Epic		Cold Turkey	CDJ	U.S.		$3.00
Epic	652896-3	Don't Be Cruel	CD3	Germany	1988	$9.00
Epic/Sony	108P 3038	Don't Be Cruel	CD3	Japan	1988	$13.00/$4.00
Epic	653005-3	Don't Be Cruel	CD3	U.K.	1988	$9.00
Epic	652896-2	Don't Be Cruel	CD5	U.K.	1988	$9.00
Epic	ESK 1216	Don't Be Cruel	CDJ	U.S.	1988	$6.00
Epic	651466-2	Flame, The	CD5	Geramny	1988	$9.00
Epic	654851-3	Flame, The	CD3	Germany	1988	$9.00
Epic	108P-3031	Flame, The	CD3	Japan	1988	$13.00/$4.00
Epic	654851-3	Flame, The	CD3	U.K.	1988	$9.00
Epic	651466-2	Flame, The	CD5	U.K.	1988	$9.00
Epic	ESK 1050	Flame, The	CDJ	U.S.	1988	$7.00
Epic	108P-3055	Ghost Town	CD3	Japan	1988	$13.00/$4.00
Epic	ESK 1326	Ghost Town	CDJ	U.S.	1988	$7.00
Epic		I Want You To Want Me	CD5	Japan	1990	$18.00
Epic	ESK 73566	If You Need Me	CDJ	U.S.	1990	$6.00
Epic	ESK 4206	Magical Mystery Tour	CDJ	U.S.	1991	$6.00
Epic	ESK 1458	Never Had A Lot To Lose	CDJ	U.S.	1988	$3.00
	FCS-136	Never Run Out Of Love	CDJ	Japan	1994	$25.00
Warner Brothers		Never Running Out Of Love	CDJ	Japan	1994	$20.00
Epic	108P-3041	Stop That Thief	CD3	Japan	1988	$13.00/$4.00
Epic	ESDA-7048	Wherever Would I Be	CD3	Japan	1990	$13.00/$4.00
Epic	ESK 73580	Wherever Would I Be	CDJ	U.S.	1990	$3.00
		Woke Up With A Monster	CD5	Australia	1994	$12.00
Warner Brothers	PRO-CD-6814	Woke Up With A Monster	CDJ	U.S.	1994	$3.00
Warner Brothers	FCS-133	You're All I Want To Do	CDJ	Japan	1994	$25.00
Warner Brothers	PRO-CD-6969	You're All I Want To Do	CDJ	U.S.	1994	$3.00
Warner Brothers	PRO-CD-7006	You're All I Want To Do	CDJ	U.S.	1994	$3.00

Cheatham, Jeannie & Jimmy

Full Length

Company	Disk Number	Title	Type	Country	Year	Longbox Value / Value
Concord	CCD-4321	Homeward Bound	LP/LB	U.S.		$12.00/$7.00

Cheatham, Oliver

Singles

Company	Disk Number	Title	Type	Country	Year	Longbox Value / Value
Eastwest	257312-2	Get Down Saturday Night	CD5	U.S.	1990	$7.00
ZYX	5844-8	Go For It	CD5	Germany	1988	$6.00
EMI	204441-2	Put A Little Love In your Heart	CD5	Germany	1991	$7.00

Checker, Chubby

Full Length

Company	Disk Number	Title	Type	Country	Year	Longbox Value / Value
Point	2642026	Twenty Twistin' Hits	LP/LB	U.S.		$12.00/$7.00

Cheek 2 Cheek

Singles

Company	Disk Number	Title	Type	Country	Year	Longbox Value / Value
Bellaphon	130-07-368	You're No Good	CD5	Germany	1990	$7.00

Cheeks, Judy

Singles

Company	Disk Number	Title	Type	Country	Year	Longbox Value / Value
Capitol	58406	As Long As You're Good To Me	CD5	U.S.	1995	$5.00
Polygram	887280-2	I Still Love You	CD5	Germany	1988	$7.00
Polygram	PZCD-11	Just Another Lie	CD5	U.K.	1988	$7.00
Positiva	82604	Reach	CD5	U.K.	1996	$10.00
Capitol	82604	Respect	CD5	U.S.	1994	$5.00
Capital	58341	Respect	CD5	U.S.	1994	$5.00

Chef Raekwon

Singles

Company	Disk Number	Title	Type	Country	Year	Longbox Value / Value
Loud	64418	Ice Cream	CDJ	U.S.	1995	$2.00

Chemical Brothers

Singles

Company	Disk Number	Title	Type	Country	Year	Longbox Value / Value
Virgin	CHEMSD1	Leave Home	CD5	U.K.	1995	$9.00
	6187-2	Setting Sun	CD5	U.S.	1997	$6.00

Chemical People

Singles

Company	Disk Number	Title	Type	Country	Year	Longbox Value / Value
Rough Trade	395-0025-3	Let It Go	CD5	U.K.	1992	$7.00
Cruz	25	Let It Go	CD5	U.S.	1992	$5.00

Chemistry Set

Singles

Company	Disk Number	Title	Type	Country	Year	Longbox Value / Value
Imaginary	MIRACD-026	Don't Turn Away	CD5	U.K.	1991	$7.00

Chemlab

Singles

Company	Disk Number	Title	Type	Country	Year	Longbox Value / Value
Fifth Collumn	001	10 Ton Pressure	CD5	U.S.	1990	$4.00

Chena

Singles

Company	Disk Number	Title	Type	Country	Year	Longbox Value / Value
		Mama Said	CDJ	U.S.		$2.00

Cher

Full Length

Company	Disk Number	Title	Type	Country	Year	Longbox Value / Value
EMI		All I Want, Cher, Sunny Side	LTD/LP	U.K.	1994	$35.00

3 CD boxed set.

Company	Disk Number	Title	Type	Country	Year	Longbox Value / Value
EMI	CDP-92773	Bang Bang	LP/LB	U.S.		$14.00/$8.00
EMI	CDP-91836	Best Of	LP	Canada		$8.00
EMI	CDP-91836	Best Of	LP/LB	U.S.		$14.00/$8.00
Geffen	2 24239-DJ	Heart Of Stone	DJ/LP	U.S.	1989	$20.00
Geffen	M2G 24239	Heart Of Stone	LP/LB	U.S.	1989	$23.00/$20.00
Columbia	CK-38096	I Paralyze	LP/LB	U.S.		$14.00/$8.00
Warner Brothers	PROP 93	It's A Man's World	DJ/LP	Germany	1996	$55.00
Warner Brothers		It's A Man's World	DJ/LP	U.S.	1996	$12.00

Label	Catalog Number	Title	Type	Country	Year	Longbox Value / Value
Reprise	9 46179-2	It's A Man's World	LTD/LP	U.S.	1996	$25.00
	3-Di•d disc.					
Geffen	24421	Love Hurts	DJ/LP	U.S.	1991	$15.00
	CD in wood box with tarrot cards.					
Geffen	GEFD-24421	Love Hurts	LP/LB	U.S.	1991	$20.00/$15.00
	CD in wood box with tarrot cards and custom longbox.					
	CHERCD1	Turning Back the Time	DJ/Smplr	U.K.		$40.00
Unistar		Weekly Specials, The	RS	U.S.	1991	$15.00
	Airdate: 7/19/91.					

Singles

Label	Catalog Number	Title	Type	Country	Year	Longbox Value / Value
Pioneer	09P3-6141	After All	CD3	Japan	1989	$13.00/$4.00
Geffen	GEF-52CD	After All	CD3	U.K.	1989	$9.00
Geffen	GEF-84CD	Baby I'm Yours	CD5	U.K.	1990	$9.00
Geffen	GED-21721	Could've Been You	CD5	Germany	1992	$9.00
Geffen	GFSTD-19	Could've Been You	CD5	U.K.	1992	$9.00
Geffen	GED-19033	Heart In Danger	CD5	Germany	1991	$9.00
Geffen	7599-21517-2	Heart Of Stone	CD5	Germany	1990	$9.00
Geffen	GEF-75CD	Heart Of Stone	CD5	U.K.	1990	$9.00
Geffen	PRO-CD-3822	Heart Of Stone	CDJ	U.S.	1989	$3.00
Geffen	PRO-CD-3989	Heart Of Stone	CDJ	U.S.	1989	$3.00
Geffen	PRO-CD-4005	Heart Of Stone	CDJ	U.S.	1989	$3.00
Geffen		I Got You Babe	CD5	U.K.	1993	$10.00
Geffen	GFSTD 64	I Got You Babe	CD5	U.K.	1993	$11.00
	Limited picture disc CD version, with Beavis and Butt-head.					
Geffen	PRO-CD-4600	I've Got You Babe	CDJ	U.S.	1993	$6.00
	With Beavis and Butt-head.					
Geffen	921306-2	If I Could Turn Back Time	CD5	Germany	1989	$9.00
Geffen	GEF-59CD	If I Could Turn Back Time	CD5	U.K.	1989	$9.00
		If I Could Turn Back Time	CDJ	U.S.	1989	$3.00
		It Ain't Necessarily So	CD5	U.K.	1994	$10.00
Geffen	921425-2	Just Like Jesse James	CD5	Germany	1989	$9.00
Geffen	GEF-69CD	Just Like Jesse James	CD5	U.K.	1989	$9.00
Geffen	PRO-CD-3664	Just Like Jesse James	CDJ	U.S.	1989	$3.00
Geffen	GED-19035	Love And Understanding	CD5	Germany	1991	$8.00
Geffen	MVDG-4	Love And Understanding	CD3	Japan	1991	$13.00/$4.00
Geffen	GFSTD-5	Love And Understanding	CD5	U.K.	1991	$9.00
Geffen	PRO-CD-4296	Love And Understanding	CDJ	U.S.	1991	$3.00
Geffen	GFSTD-16	Love Hurts	CD5	U.K.	1991	$9.00
Geffen	PRO-CD-3284	Main Man	CDJ	U.S.	1987	$6.00
		Many Rivers To Cross	CD5	U.K.		$9.00
		Not Enough Love In the World	CD5	U.K.	1996	$10.00
		Not Enough Time In the World	CD5	U.K.	1995	$12.00
Geffen	GFSTD-29	Oh No Not My Cross Baby	CD5	U.K.	1992	$9.00
Geffen		One By One	CDJ	U.K.		$16.00
Geffen	GED-26676	Save Up All Your Tears	CD5	Germany	1991	$9.00
Geffen	GFSTD-11	Save Up All Your Tears	CD5	U.K.	1991	$9.00
Geffen	PRO-CD-4341	Save Up All Your Tears	CDJ	U.S.	1991	$3.00
Epic	6586673-2	Shoop Shoop Song, The	CD5	U.K.	1991	$9.00
Geffen	PRO-CD-4176	Shoop Shoop Song, The	CDJ	U.S.	1990	$6.00
Geffen	GEF-44CD	Skin Deep	CD5	U.K.	1988	$9.00
Geffen	PRO-CD-3173	Skin Deep	CDJ	U.S.	1988	$3.00
		Walking in Memphis	CD5	U.K.		$10.00
	Second version.					
Geffen		Walking in Memphis	CDJ	U.K.	1995	$16.00
Geffen	920899-2	We All Sleep Alone	CD3	Germany	1988	$9.00
Geffen	10SW-57	We All Sleep Alone	CD3	Japan	1988	$13.00/$4.00
Geffen	GEF-35CD	We All Sleep Alone	CD3	U.K.	1988	$9.00
Geffen	PRO-CD-2971	We All Sleep Alone	CDJ	U.S.	1988	$3.00
Geffen	PRO-CD-4408	When Lovers Become Strangers	CDJ	U.S.	1993	$3.00
Geffen	GFSTD-32	Whenever You're Near	CD5	U.K.	1993	$9.00
Geffen	921605-2	You Wouldn't Know Love	CD5	Germany	1990	$90.00
Geffen	GEF-77CD	You Wouldn't Know Love	CD5	U.K.	1990	$00.00

Cherish

Singles

Label	Catalog Number	Title	Type	Country	Year	Longbox Value / Value
SPV	8444-3	Where Did Our Love Go	CD3	Germany	1990	$7.00

Cherrelle

Full Length

Label	Catalog Number	Title	Type	Country	Year	Longbox Value / Value
Tabu	44148	Affair	LP/LB	U.S.	1989	$14.00/$8.00

Singles

Label	Catalog Number	Title	Type	Country	Year	Longbox Value / Value
Tabu	656202-2	Affair	CD5	U.K.	1990	$8.00
CBS	654673-2	Affair	CD5	U.K.	1990	$8.00
Tabu		Affair	CDJ	U.S.	1989	$2.00
Tabu	653066-2	Everything I Miss At Home	CD5	U.K.	1988	$8.00
Tabu		Everything I Miss At Home	CDJ	U.S.	1989	$2.00
Tabu	28965 1703 2	Never In My Life	CDJ	U.S.	1991	$3.00
Tabu	655800-2	Saturday Love	CD5	Germany	1990	$8.00
Tabu	655800-2	Saturday Love	CD5	U.K.	1990	$8.00
Tabu	28965 1817 2	Still In Love With You	CDj	U.S.	1991	$2.00
A&M	AMCD-861	Tears Of Joy	CD5	U.K.	1992	$8.00
Tabu	28965 1805 2	Tears Of Joy	CDJ	U.S.	1992	$2.00
Tabu	28965 1807 2	Tears Of Joy	CDJ	U.S.	1992	$2.00
Tabu		What More Can I Do For You	CDJ	U.S.		$2.00

Cherry, Ava

Singles

Label	Catalog Number	Title	Type	Country	Year	Longbox Value / Value
Critique	15523	Forget Me Nots	CD5	U.S.	1994	$5.00
Critique	15505	Gimme Gimme	CDJ	U.S.		$2.00

Cherry Coke

Singles

Label	Catalog Number	Title	Type	Country	Year	Longbox Value / Value
Pikosso	872 0009	No hagas el Indio, Haz	SCD5	Germany	1995	$20.00
	"Coke-can" shaped CD.					

Cherry, Don

Full Length

Label	Catalog Number	Title	Type	Country	Year	Longbox Value / Value
A&M	CD-5258	Art Deco	LP/LB	U.S.		$14.00/$8.00
A&M	CD-0809	Brown Rice	LP/LB	U.S.		$14.00/$8.00
Mosaic	MD2-145	Complete Blue Note Recordings	LP	U.S.		$30.00
	2 CD set. Limited to 3500 copies					
Polygram	827488-2	Home Boy, Sister Out	LP	Germany		$15.00
A&M	CD-5323	Multi Kulti	LP/LB	U.S.		$14.00/$8.00
Blue Note		Symphony For Improvisors	LTD/LP	U.S.	1994	$20.00

Cherry, Neneh

Full Length

Label	Catalog Number	Title	Type	Country	Year	Longbox Value / Value
Virgin		Raw Like Sushi	DJ/LP	U.S.	1989	$15.00

Singles

Label	Catalog Number	Title	Type	Country	Year	Longbox Value / Value
Virgin	12782	Buddy X	CDJ	U.S.	1992	$6.00
Virgin	DPRO-12766	Buddy-X	CDJ	U.S.	1992	$3.00
BMG	662105	Buffalo Stance	CD3	Germany	1988	$8.00
BMG	661923	Buffalo Stance	CD5	Germany	1988	$8.00
Virgin	VJD-10216	Buffalo Stance	CD3	Japan	1988	$12.00/$3.00
Circa	YRCD-21	Buffalo Stance	CD3	U.K.	1988	$8.00
Virgin	PRCD 2646	Buffalo Stance	CDJ	U.S.	1988	$3.00
Virgin	PRCD 2989	Heart	CDJ	U.S.	1988	$3.00
BMG	663640	I've Got You Under My Skin	CD5	Germany	1990	$8.00
Toshiba	VJDP-141	I've Got You Under My Skin	CD3	Japan	1990	$12.00/$3.00
Circa	YRCD 53	I've Got You Under My Skin	CD5	U.K.	1990	$8.00
BMG	162795	Inner City Mamma	CD3	Germany	1990	$8.00
BMG	662795	Inner City Mamma	CD5	Germany	1990	$8.00
Circa	YRCD 42	Inner City Mamma	CD5	U.K.	1990	$8.00
BMG	162550	Kisses In the Wind	CD3	Germany	1989	$8.00
BMG	662550	Kisses In the Wind	CD5	Germany	1989	$8.00
Virgin	662603	Kisses In the Wind	CD5	Germany	1989	$8.00
Toshiba	VJCP-1402	Kisses In the Wind	CD3	Japan	1990	$12.00/$3.00
Circa	YRCD-33	Kisses In the Wind	CD3	U.K.	1989	$8.00
Virgin	PRCD 2825	Kisses In the Wind	CDJ	U.S.	1989	$3.00
Virgin	162341	Manchild	CD3	Germany	1989	$8.00
Virgin	662341	Manchild	CD5	Germany	1989	$8.00
Virgin	YRCD-30	Manchild	CD3	U.K.	1989	$8.00
Virgin	PRCD 2988	Manchild	CDJ	U.S.	1988	$3.00
Virgin	PRCD PLEN	Manchild	CDJ	U.S.	1989	$3.00
Virgin	VJDP-10197	Money Love	CD3	Japan	1992	$13.00/$4.00
Circa	YRCDG-83	Money Love	CD5	U.K.	1992	$8.00
Capitol	C2 12610	Money Love	CD5	U.S.	1992	$4.00
Virgin	DPRO-12709	Money Love	CDJ	U.S.	1992	$3.00
		Trouble Man	CDJ	U.S.		$2.00
Motown	860748	Trouble Man	CD5	U.S.	1995	$5.00

Cherry's

Singles

Label	Catalog Number	Title	Type	Country	Year	Longbox Value / Value
Freakin A	FREAK-1CD	Big Fat Kid	CD5	U.K.	1992	$7.00

Cheryl

Singles

Label	Catalog Number	Title	Type	Country	Year	Longbox Value / Value
OTW	CDOTW-14	Sensuality	CD5	U.K.	1992	$7.00

Chesney, Kenny

Full Length

Label	Catalog Number	Title	Type	Country	Year	Longbox Value / Value
Capricorn	6583	An Introduction To Country Radio	DJ/Intvw	U.S.	1993	$12.00

Chester

Singles

Label	Catalog Number	Title	Type	Country	Year	Longbox Value / Value
Canyon	S10Y-1030	Hold the Line	CD3	Japan	1988	$12.00/$3.00

Chestnut, Mark

Full Length

Label	Catalog Number	Title	Type	Country	Year	Longbox Value / Value
		'90s Country	RS	U.S.	1995	$25.00
	Airdate: 7/15/95.					
C		'90s Country	RS	U.S.	1996	$25.00
	Airdate: 1/21/96.					
		Country Concert	RS	U.S.	1996	$50.00
	2 CD set. Airdate: 7/8/96.					

Singles

Label	Catalog Number	Title	Type	Country	Year	Longbox Value / Value
Decca	54941	Goin' Thru the Big D	CDJ	U.S.	1994	$6.00

Chi-Lites

Full Length

Label	Catalog Number	Title	Type	Country	Year	Longbox Value / Value
Ace	CDKEN-911	Best Of	LP/BP	U.S.		$12.00/$7.00
Epic	EK-38627	Greatest Hits	LP/LB	U.S.		$12.00/$7.00

Singles

Label	Catalog Number	Title	Type	Country	Year	Longbox Value / Value
Mar-Ance	72018	Happy Birthday	CD5	U.S.	1994	$5.00
Old Gold	OG-6108	Have You Seen Her	CD3	U.K.	1988	$7.00

Chic

Full Length

Label	Catalog Number	Title	Type	Country	Year	Longbox Value / Value
Warner Brothers	9 26394-2-Dj	Chic-sm	DJ/LP	U.S.	1991	$15.00
	Picture disc.					

Singles

Label	Catalog Number	Title	Type	Country	Year	Longbox Value / Value
Warner Brothers	9362-40364-2	Chic Mystique	CD5	Germany	1991	$8.00
Warner Brothers	WPDP-6297	Chic Mystique	CD3	Japan	1991	$12.00/$3.00
Warner Brothers	9 40225-2	Chic Mystique	CD5	U.S.	1991	$4.00
Warner Brothers	PRO-5069	Chic Mystique	CDJ	U.S.	1991	$2.00
Warner Brothers		Chic Mystique	CDJ/VHS	U.S.	1991	$10.00
Rhino	71851	Everybody Dance	CD5	U.S.	1994	$5.00
WEA	786512-2	Jack Le Freak '88	CD3	Germany	1988	$8.00
Atlantic	10SW-28	Jack Le Freak '88	CD3	Japan	1988	$12.00/$3.00
WEA	786512-2	Jack Le Freak '88	CD3	U.K.	1988	$8.00
Eastwest	170959-2	Megachic	CD5	Germany	1990	$8.00
Atlantic	A-7949CD	Megachic	CD5	U.K.	1990	$8.00
Warner Brothers	W-0107CD	Your Love	CD5	U.K.	1991	$8.00
Warner Brothers	PRO-CD-5658	Your Love	CDJ	U.S.	1992	$2.00

Chicago

Full Length

Label	Catalog Number	Title	Type	Country	Year	Longbox Value / Value
	M/CD 50704	1969-1981	DJ/Smplr	Japan	1995	$150.00
WEA	38338	And The Band Played On	LD	U.S.	1993	$30.00
Columbia	CK 36105	Chicago	LP	U.S.		$14.00/$8.00
CBS	CD-66233	Chicago II	LP	Germany		$25.00
2CD						
Columbia	CK 30110	Chicago II	LP	U.S.		$14.00/$8.00
Columbia	C2K-00024	Chicago II	LP	U.S.		$25.00/$18.00
CBS	CD-69187	Chicago IX	LP	Germany		$20.00
Columbia	CK 33900	Chicago IX	LP	U.S.		$14.00/$8.00
CBS	CD-66221	Chicago Transit Authority	LP	Germany	1984	$25.00
	2CD set					
Columbia	C2K-00008	Chicago Transit Authority	LP/BP	U.S.	1984	$40.00/$35.00
	2CD set					
Columbia	CK 00008	Chicago Transit Authority	LP	U.S.	1987	$14.00/$8.00
	1 CD					
Columbia		Chicago Transit Authority	LP/LB	U.S.	1993	$29.00/$25.00
	Gold disc.					
Columbia	CK 31102	Chicago V	LP	U.S.		$14.00/$8.00
CBS	CD-69041	Chicago VI	LP	Germany		$20.00
Columbia	CK 32400	Chicago VI	LP	U.S.		$14.00/$8.00
Columbia	CK 32810	Chicago VII	LP	U.S.		$14.00/$8.00
Columbia	CK 33100	Chicago VIII	LP	U.S.		$14.00/$8.00
Columbia	CK 34200	Chicago X	LP	U.S.		$14.00/$8.00
Columbia	CK 34860	Chicago XI	LP	U.S.		$14.00/$8.00
Columbia	CK 32810	Chicago XII	LP	U.S.		$14.00/$8.00
Columbia	CK 3517	Chicago XIV	LP	U.S.		$14.00/$8.00
Columbia	CK 37682	Chicago XV	LP	U.S.		$14.00/$8.00
Warner Brothers	23689-2	Chicago XVI	LP/LB	U.S.†	1984	$14.00/$8.00
Warner Brothers	25060-2	Chicago XVII	LP/LB	U.S.†	1985	$14.00/$8.00
Pioneer	CLD-86-005	Chicago XVII	LD	U.S.	1986	$30.00
Columbia	CK-37682	Greatest Hits Vol. 2	LP/LB	U.S.		$14.00/$8.00
Columbia	47416	Group Portrait	LP	U.S.	1991	$60.00
	4CD boxed set					
Columbia	CK-35512	Hot Streets	LP/LB	U.S.		$14.00/$8.00
Columbia	CK 38590	If You Leave Me Now	LP	U.S.		$14.00/$8.00
Album Network		In the Studio (Chicago II)	RS	U.S	1989	$20.00
	Airdate: 2/12/90.					

Label	Catalog Number	Title	Type	Country	Year	Longbox Value / Value
Album Network		In the Studio (Chicago Transit Authority)	RS	U.S.	1989	$20.00
	Airdate: 4/3/89.					
Album Network		In the Studio (Chicago V, VI, VII)	RS	U.S.	1990	$29.00
	Airdate: 7/16/90.					
DIR		King Biscuit Flour Hour	RS	U.S.	1988	$40.00
	Airdate: 7/3/88.					
DIR		King Biscuit Flour Hour	RS	U.S.	1991	$45.00
	Airdate: 9/21/91.					
DIR		King Biscuit Flour Hour	RS	U.S.	1992	$30.00
	Airdate: 6/21/92.					
DIR		King Biscuit Flour Hour	RS	U.S.	1992	$30.00
	Airdate: 9/29/92.					
DIR		King Biscuit Flour Hour	RS	U.S.	1994	$45.00
	Airdate: 11/13/94.					
DIR		King Biscuit Flour Hour	RS	U.S.	1995	$45.00
	Airdate: 11/19/95					
Columbia	C3K 30865	Live At Carnegie Hall	LP	U.S.		$50.00
	3CD boxed set					
Chicago		Night & Day	DJ/Smplr	U.S.	1995	$15.00
CBS	25DP-5206	Star Box	LP	Japan	1988	$35.00
Sony	SRCS-6914	Star Box	LP	Japan	1993	$30.00
Reprise	9 26391-2-Dj	Twenty-1	DJ/LP	U.S.	1991	$15.00
	Picture disc.					

Singles

Label	Catalog Number	Title	Type	Country	Year	Longbox Value / Value
CBS	655570-3	25 or 6 To 4	CD3	Germany	1990	$8.00
Columbia	38K-33193	25 or 6 To 4	CD3	U.S.	1988	$6.00/$2.00
Warner Brothers	WPDP-6255	Chasin' The Wind	CD3	Japan	1990	$15.00/$3.00
Reprise	PRO-CD-4602	Chasin' The Wind	CDJ	U.S.	1991	$7.00
	3003	Chicago III	CD5	U.S.	1994	$5.00
	3001	Chicago Transit Authority	CD5	U.S.	1994	$5.00
	3005	Chicago V	CD5	U.S.	1994	$5.00
	3006	Chicago VI	CD5	U.S.	1994	$5.00
	3007	Chicago VII	CD5	U.S.	1994	$5.00
	3008	Chicago VIII	CD5	U.S.	1994	$5.00
	3010	Chicago X	CD5	U.S.	1994	$5.00
	3013	Chicago XIII	CD5	U.S.	1994	$5.00
	3014	Chicago XIV	CD5	U.S.	1994	$5.00
Chicago	PRO-CD-7601-R	Dream A Little Dream	CDJ	U.S.	1995	$3.00
Warner Brothers	WPDP-6278	Explain It To My Heart	CD3	Japan	1990	$15.00/$3.00
Reprise	PRO-CD-4636	Explain It To My Heart	CDJ	U.S.	1991	$3.00
	3015	Greatest Hits V.2	CD5	U.S.	1994	$5.00
	3009	Greatest Hits Vol. 1	CD5	U.S.	1994	$5.00
CBS	656135-3	Hearts In Trouble	CD3	Germany	1990	$8.00
Sony	CSDS-8155	Hearts In Trouble	CD3	Japan	1990	$15.00/$3.00
CBS	656135-2	Hearts In Trouble	CD5	U.K.	1990	$8.00
DGC	PRO-CD-4133	Hearts In Trouble	CDJ	U.S.	1990	$3.00
Reprise	921003-2	I Don't Wanna Live Without Your Love	CD3	Germany	1988	$8.00
Pioneer	10SW-52	I Don't Wanna Live Without Your Love	CD3	Japan	1988	$15.00/$3.00
Reprise	W-7855CD	I Don't Wanna Live Without Your Love	CD3	U.K.	1988	$8.00
Reprise	PRO-CD-3126	I Don't Wanna Live Without Your Love	CDJ	U.S.	1988	$3.00
	3016	If You Leave Me Now	CD5	U.S.	1994	$5.00
Reprise	921137-2	Look Away	CD3	Germany	1988	$8.00
Pioneer	10P3-6018	Look Away	CD3	Japan	1988	$15.00/$3.00
Reprise	W-7766CD	Look Away	CD3	U.K.	1988	$8.00
Reprise	2 27766	Look Away	CD3	U.S.	1988	$6.00/$2.00
Reprise	PRO-CD-3219	Look Away	CDJ	U.S.	1988	$3.00
Chicago	PRO-CD-7603-R	Night & Day	CDJ	U.S.	1995	$8.00
Reprise	PRO-CD-3487	We Can Last Forever	CDJ	U.S.	1988	$3.00
Warner Brothers	W-2741CD	What Kind Of Man Would I Be?	CD5	U.K.	1990	$8.00
Reprise	PRO-CD-3777	What Kind Of Man Would I Be?	CDJ	U.S.	1989	$3.00
Reprise	PRO-CD-4942	You Come To My Senses	CDJ	U.S.	1991	$3.00
Pioneer	09P3-6123	You're Not Alone	CD3	Japan	1988	$12.00/$3.00
Reprise	2 27757	You're Not Alone	CD3	U.S.	1988	$6.00/$2.00
Reprise	PRO-CD-3233	You're Not Alone	CDJ	U.S.	1988	$3.00

Chicane

Singles

Label	Catalog Number	Title	Type	Country	Year	Longbox Value / Value
Faith	FAIRE-003CD	Wanderlust	CD5	U.K.	1991	$7.00

Chicano, Los

Singles

Label	Catalog Number	Title	Type	Country	Year	Longbox Value / Value
	11428	Serie De Platino	CD5	U.S.	1994	$5.00

Chick

Singles

Label	Catalog Number	Title	Type	Country	Year	Longbox Value / Value
	BSK7250	Malibu	CDJ	U.S.		$2.00

Chickasaw Mudd Puppies

Full Length

Label	Catalog Number	Title	Type	Country	Year	Longbox Value / Value
Wing	843935	Eight Track Stomp	LP/LB	U.S.		$14.00/$8.00
Wing	843 217	White Dirt	DJ/LP	U.S.	1990	$10.00

Singles

Label	Catalog Number	Title	Type	Country	Year	Longbox Value / Value
Wing	233	McIntosh	CDJ	U.S.	1991	$3.00
		White Dirt	CDJ	U.S.	1990	$2.00
Wing	CDP 433	Words & Knives	CDJ	U.S.	1991	$2.00

Chief Obey Commander Ebenezer

Full Length

Label	Catalog Number	Title	Type	Country	Year	Longbox Value / Value
Rykodisc	20111	Get Yer Juju's Out	LP/LB	U.S.		$9.00/$6.00

Chiefs Of Relief

Singles

Label	Catalog Number	Title	Type	Country	Year	Longbox Value / Value
Polygram	887937-2	Freedom To Rock	CD5	Germany	1988	$8.00
Sire	PRO-CD-3030	Freedom To Rock	CDJ	U.S.	1988	$2.00

Chieftains

Full Length

Label	Catalog Number	Title	Type	Country	Year	Longbox Value / Value
Aris	886208	Celtic Wedding	LP	Germany		$18.00

Singles

Label	Catalog Number	Title	Type	Country	Year	Longbox Value / Value
RCA	61039-2-RDJ	Behind Blue Eyes	CDJ	U.S.	1992	$3.00
RCA	61483-2-RDJ	Cotton-Eyed Joe	CDJ	U.S.	1992	$3.00
RCA	68254	Have I Told You Lately	CD5	U.S.	1994	$5.00

Child, Desmond

Full Length

Label	Catalog Number	Title	Type	Country	Year	Longbox Value / Value
EMI	DPRO-05379	Legends-Volume 1	DJ/Smplr	U.S.	1991	$8.00

Singles

Label	Catalog Number	Title	Type	Country	Year	Longbox Value / Value
Elektra	7559-61571-2	Love On A Rooftop	CD5	Germany	1991	$8.00
Elektra	WMD5-4071	Love On A Rooftop	CD3	Japan	1991	$12.00/$3.00
Elektra	EKR-129CD	Love On A Rooftop	CD5	U.K.	1991	$8.00
Elektra	PRCD 8350-2	Love On A Rooftop	CDJ	U.S.	1991	$2.00
WEA	7759-66808-2	Obsession	CD5	Germany	1992	$8.00
Elektra	PRCD 8505-2	Obsession	CDJ	U.S.	1991	$3.00
Elektra	PRCD 8416-2	You're the Story Of My Life	CDJ	U.S.	1991	$2.00

Child, Jane

Full Length

Company	Disk Number	Title	Type	Country	Year	Longbox Value / Value
Elektra	61048-2	Discipline	LP/LB	U.S.		$12.00/$7.00

Singles

Company	Disk Number	Title	Type	Country	Year	Longbox Value / Value
Warner Brothers	9 41372	All I Do	CD5	U.S.	1994	$5.00
Warner Brothers	18174	All I Do	CD5	U.S.	1994	$5.00
Warner Brothers	PRO-CD-6845	All I Do	CDJ	U.S.	1994	$3.00
Warner Brothers	PRO-CD-6553	Do Whatcha Do	CDJ	U.S.	1993	$3.00
WEA	921476-2	Don't Wanna Fall In Love	CD5	Germany	1990	$8.00
Pioneer	WPDP-6222	Don't Wanna Fall In Love	CD3	Japan	1989	$12.00/$3.00
Pioneer	WPCP-3529	Don't Wanna Fall In Love	CD5	Japan	1989	$15.00
WEA	W-9817CD	Don't Wanna Fall In Love	CD5	U.K.	1990	$8.00
Warner Brothers	PRO-CD-3867	Don't Wanna Fall In Love	CDJ	U.S.	1989	$2.00
Warner Brothers	PRO-CD-6462	Here Not There	CDJ	U.S.	1993	$3.00
WEA	921706-2	Welcome To the Real World	CD5	Germany	1990	$8.00
Pioneer	WPDP-6235	Welcome To the Real World	CD3	Japan	1990	$12.00/$3.00
WEA	W-9727CD	Welcome To the Real World	CD5	U.K.	1990	$8.00
Warner Brothers	PRO-CD-3724	Welcome To the Real World	CDJ	U.S.	1989	$2.00
Warner Brothers	9 21537-2	Welcome To the Real World	CD5	U.S.	1990	$4.00

Child, Julia

Full Length

Company	Disk Number	Title	Type	Country	Year	Longbox Value / Value
Discovision		Omelette Show	LD	U.S.	1979	$25.00
Discovision		Quiche Lorraine	LD	U.S.	1979	$25.00
Discovision		To Roast A Chicken	LD	U.S.	1979	$25.00

Child's Play

Full Length

Company	Disk Number	Title	Type	Country	Year	Longbox Value / Value
Chrysalis	21758	Rat Race	LP/LB	U.S.	1990	$9.00/$6.00

Singles

Company	Disk Number	Title	Type	Country	Year	Longbox Value / Value
Chrysalis	DPRO-23572	Day After Night	CDJ	U.S.	1990	$2.00
Chrysalis	DPRO-23586	Rat Race	CDJ	U.S.	1990	$2.00
Chrysalis	DPRO-23673	Wind	CDJ	U.S.	1991	$2.00

Childs, Andy

Full Length

Company	Disk Number	Title	Type	Country	Year	Longbox Value / Value
RCA	66253	Advance Music	DJ/LP	U.S.	1993	$14.00
	CD in digipak.					

Childs, Toni

Full Length

Company	Disk Number	Title	Type	Country	Year	Longbox Value / Value
DGC	PRO-CD-4656	Four Song Sampler	DJ/Smplr	U.S.	1994	$7.00
A&M	75021 5358 2	House Of Hope	DJ/LP	U.S.	1991	$20.00
	CD in box with prints					
DGC	PRO-CD-4655	Words & Music	DJ/Intvw	U.S.	1994	$12.00

Singles

Company	Disk Number	Title	Type	Country	Year	Longbox Value / Value
A&M	390394-3	Don't Walk Away	CD3	Germany	1988	$2.00
A&M	39051-2	Don't Walk Away	CD5	Germany	1988	$8.00
A&M	390394-2	Don't Walk Away	CD5	Germany	1988	$8.00
Canyon	S10Y-3053	Don't Walk Away	CD3	Japan	1988	$12.00/$3.00
A&M	CDEE-462	Don't Walk Away	CD3	U.K.	1988	$8.00
A&M	CD 17605	Don't Walk Away	CDJ	U.S.	1988	$2.00
		House Of Hope	CDJ	U.S.		$2.00
A&M	75021 7316-2	I Want To Walk With You	CDJ	U.S.	1991	$2.00
A&M	390784-2	I've Got To Go Now	CD5	Germany	1991	$8.00
A&M	AMCD-794	I've Got To Go Now	CD5	U.K.	1991	$8.00
A&M	75021 7252-2	I've Got To Go Now	CDJ	U.S.	1991	$2.00
A&M	75021 7470-2	I've Got To Go Now	CDJ	U.S.	1991	$2.00
A&M	75021 7256-2	I've Got To Go Now	CDJ	U.S.	1991	$2.00
A&M	CD 37582	Let The Rain Come Down	DJ/CD3	U.S.	1988	$8.00/$4.00
DGC	PRO-CD-4683	Long Time Coming	CDJ	U.S.	1994	$2.00
Canyon	S9Y-13114	Many Rivers To Cross	CD3	Japan	1989	$12.00/$3.00
A&M	CD 17774	Many Rivers To Cross	CDJ	U.S.	1989	$2.00
A&M	390313-2	Stop Your Fussin'	CD5	Germany	1988	$9.00
A&M	S10-3040	Stop Your Fussin'	CD3	Japan	1988	$12.00/$3.00
A&M	CDEE-508	Stop Your Fussin'	CD3	U.K.	1988	$8.00
A&M	CD 17557	Stop Your Fussin'	CDJ	U.S.	1988	$2.00
A&M	S10Y-3062	Walk And Talk Like Angels	CD3	Japan	1988	$12.00/$3.00
A&M	CD 17615	Walk And Talk Like Angels	CDJ	U.S.	1988	$2.00
A&M	390420-3	Zimbabwae	CD3	Germany	1988	$8.00
A&M	390420-2	Zimbabwae	CD5	Germany	1988	$8.00
A&M	CDEE-492	Zimbabwae	CD3	U.K.	1988	$8.00

Chill, Rob G.

Singles

Company	Disk Number	Title	Type	Country	Year	Longbox Value / Value
Bellaphon	130-07-369	Power	CD5	Germany	1990	$7.00

Chilliwack

Full Length

Company	Disk Number	Title	Type	Country	Year	Longbox Value / Value
		Look In Look Out	LTD/LP	U.K.	1995	$35.00

Chills

Full Length

Company	Disk Number	Title	Type	Country	Year	Longbox Value / Value
Slash	PRO-CD-5479	Soft Bomb	DJ/LP	U.S.	1992	$6.00

Singles

Company	Disk Number	Title	Type	Country	Year	Longbox Value / Value
		Body Reaction	CDJ	U.S.		$2.00
Slash	PRO-CD-5723	Double Summer	CDJ	U.S.	1992	$2.00
Slash	CHICD 1	Heavenly Pop Hit	CD5	U.K.		$9.00
Slash	LASCD-22	Heavenly Pop Hit	CD5	U.K.	1990	$8.00
Slash	PRO-CD-3988	Heavenly Pop Hit	CDJ	U.S.	1990	$2.00
Slash	PRO-CD-5535	Male Monster From ID	CDJ	U.S.	1992	$2.00
Slash	PRO-CD-4330	Oncoming Day, The	CDJ	U.S.	1990	$2.00

Chilly Tee

Singles

Company	Disk Number	Title	Type	Country	Year	Longbox Value / Value
MCA	MCA5P-2665	Get Off Mine	CDJ	U.S.	1993	$2.00
MCA	2791	Get Off Mine	CDJ	U.S.	1993	$3.00

Chilton, Alex

Full Length

Company	Disk Number	Title	Type	Country	Year	Longbox Value / Value
Big Time	6047-2	High Priest	LP/BP	U.S.		$9.00/$6.00

Chimes

Full Length

Company	Disk Number	Title	Type	Country	Year	Longbox Value / Value
Columbia	CK-46008	Chimes	LP/LB	U.S.	1989	$12.00/$7.00

Singles

Company	Disk Number	Title	Type	Country	Year	Longbox Value / Value
Columbia	655166-2	1-2-3	CD5	U.K.	1989	$7.00
Columbia	CSK 73087	1-2-3	CDJ	U.S.	1989	$2.00
CBS	655432-3	Heaven	CD3	Germany	1989	$7.00
CBS	656299-3	Heaven	CD3	Germany	1989	$7.00
Columbia	CHIMC-3	Heaven	CD5	U.K.	1989	$7.00
Columbia	655432-2	Heaven	CD5	U.K.	1989	$7.00
Columbia	655980-3	I Still Haven't Found What I'm Looking For	CD3	Germany	1990	$7.00
Columbia	655980-2	I Still Haven't Found What I'm Looking For	CD5	Germany	1990	$7.00
Columbia	CHIMC-1	I Still Haven't Found What I'm Looking For	CD5	U.K.	1990	$7.00
Columbia	CSK 73310	I Still Haven't Found What I'm Looking For	CDJ	U.S.	1990	$2.00
Columbia	CHIMC-4	Love Comes To Mind	CD5	U.K.	1990	$7.00

Label	Catalog Number	Title	Type	Country	Year	Longbox Value / Value
Columbia	6655851-2	Stronger Together	CD5	U.K.	1990	$7.00
Columbia	656140-3	True Love	CD3	Germany	1990	$7.00
Columbia	CHIMC-2	True Love	CD5	U.K.	1990	$7.00
Columbia	CSK 73538	True Love	CDJ	U.S.	1990	$2.00

China

Singles

Label	Catalog Number	Title	Type	Country	Year	Longbox Value / Value
Street Life	72392 78024	Come And Get It	CD5	U.S.	1995	$5.00
Street Life		Come And Get It	CDJ	U.S.	1995	$2.00
Vertigo	876511-2	In the Middle Of the Night	CD5	Germany	1990	$7.00
Vertigo	875779-2	Sign In the Sky	CD5	Germany	1990	$7.00
Vertigo	866103-2	Slow Dancing	CD5	Germany	1990	$7.00

China Black

Singles

Label	Catalog Number	Title	Type	Country	Year	Longbox Value / Value
Big One	VVBIG-29CD	Searching	CD5	U.K.	1992	$7.00

China Crisis

Full Length

Label	Catalog Number	Title	Type	Country	Year	Longbox Value / Value
A&M	CD-5225	Diary Of A Hollow Horse	LP/LB	U.S.		$14.00/$8.00
A&M	CD-5148	What Price Paradise	LP/LB	U.S.		$14.00/$8.00
Virgin	VSCDT-1297	African And White	CD5	U.K.	1990	$7.00

Singles

Label	Catalog Number	Title	Type	Country	Year	Longbox Value / Value
Virgin	CRIS-92612	Best Kept Secret	CD5	U.K.	1987	$8.00
Virgin	CDT-15	Black May Ray	CD3	U.K.	1988	$7.00
Virgin	VSCD-1188	Red Letter Day	CD3	U.K.	1989	$7.00
Virgin	162080	St. Saviour Square	CD3	Germany	1989	$7.00
Virgin	VJD-10205	St. Saviour Square	CD3	Japan	1989	$12.00/$3.00
Virgin	VSCD-1168	St. Saviour Square	CD3	U.K.	1989	$7.00
A&M	CD 17778	St. Saviour Square	CDJ	U.S.	1989	$2.00

China Drum

Singles

Label	Catalog Number	Title	Type	Country	Year	Longbox Value / Value
MCA	11293	Barrier	CD5	U.S.	1995	$5.00

Chippendales

Singles

Label	Catalog Number	Title	Type	Country	Year	Longbox Value / Value
BMG	CDXRS-3	Give Me Your Body	CD5	U.K.	1992	$7.00

Chita

Singles

Label	Catalog Number	Title	Type	Country	Year	Longbox Value / Value
Crown	CRDN-106	Harmony	CD3	Japan	1991	$12.00/$3.00

Chixdiggit

Full Length

Label	Catalog Number	Title	Type	Country	Year	Longbox Value / Value
Sub Pop	SP355	TBA	DJ/LP	U.S.		$10.00

Chocolate

Singles

Label	Catalog Number	Title	Type	Country	Year	Longbox Value / Value
Eastwest	9031-72509-2	Brazil Brazil	CD5	Germany	1990	$7.00
Eastwest	9031-73295-2	Brazil Brazil	CD5	Germany	1990	$7.00
Eastwest	9031-74526-2	Everybody Salsa	CD5	Germany	1991	$7.00
		Ghetto Holocaust	CDJ	U.S.	1994	$3.00
Eastwest	9031-75784-2	La Ola	CD5	Germany	1992	$7.00
Eastwest	9031-7275-2	Ritmo De La Noche	CD5	Germany	1990	$7.00
Eastwest	171797-2	Ritmo De La Noche	CD5	Germany	1990	$7.00

Chocolate Starfish

Singles

Label	Catalog Number	Title	Type	Country	Year	Longbox Value / Value
EMI	874041	All Over Me	CD5	Australia	1993	$8.00

Choir

Full Length

Label	Catalog Number	Title	Type	Country	Year	Longbox Value / Value
Epic	EK-47734	Circle Slide	LP/LB	U.S.		$14.00/$8.00

Choirboys

Singles

Label	Catalog Number	Title	Type	Country	Year	Longbox Value / Value
WTG	PRO-CD-1800	Boys Will Be Boys	CDJ	U.S.	1989	$2.00
WTG	PRO-CD-1609	Guilty	CDJ	U.S.	1989	$2.00
WTG	PRO-CD-1423	Run To Paradise	CDJ	U.S.	1989	$2.00

Chordettes

Singles

Label	Catalog Number	Title	Type	Country	Year	Longbox Value / Value
Aris	885821	Lollipop	CD3	Germany	1990	$9.00

Chris

Singles

Label	Catalog Number	Title	Type	Country	Year	Longbox Value / Value
Alfa	ALDB-79	Take Me To the Top	CD3	Japan	1990	$12.00/$3.00

Chris, A Lahely

Singles

Label	Catalog Number	Title	Type	Country	Year	Longbox Value / Value
ZYX	6335-8	Give It Up	CD5	Germany	1990	$6.00

Chris And Cosey

Full Length

Label	Catalog Number	Title	Type	Country	Year	Longbox Value / Value
Nettwerk	5017	Exotika & Take Five	LP/BP	U.S.		$14.00/$8.00
Wax Trax	7122	Heartbeat	LP/BP	U.S.		$14.00/$8.00
Wax Trax	7150	Pagan Tango	LP/BP	U.S.		$12.00/$8.00
Wax Trax	7124	Songs Of Love & Lust	LP/BP	U.S.		$14.00/$8.00
Wax Trax	7125	Techno Primitive	LP/BP	U.S.		$14.00/$8.00
Wax Trax	7123	Trance	LP/BP	U.S.		$14.00/$8.00
Relativity	5016	Trust	LP/BP	U.S.		$14.00/$8.00

Chris D

Singles

Label	Catalog Number	Title	Type	Country	Year	Longbox Value / Value
Sympathy	343	Love Cannot Die	CD5	U.S.	1994	$5.00

Christensen, Ana

Singles

Label	Catalog Number	Title	Type	Country	Year	Longbox Value / Value
Columbia	656443	Brave New World	CD5	Australia	1990	$8.00

Christensen, Maria

Singles

Label	Catalog Number	Title	Type	Country	Year	Longbox Value / Value
Atlantic	PRCD 5086-2	I've Got To Find A Way	CDJ	U.S.	1993	$2.00

Christer

Singles

Label	Catalog Number	Title	Type	Country	Year	Longbox Value / Value
Virgin	VSCDT-1387	Jealousy's Kiss	CD5	U.K.	1991	$8.00
Virgin	VSCDT-1366	Red Skies Desert Moon	CD5	U.K.	1991	$8.00
Virgin	VSCDT-1353	Watch Me	CD5	U.K.	1991	$8.00

Christian Death

Full Length

Label	Catalog Number	Title	Type	Country	Year	Longbox Value / Value
Efa	CD-6918	Atrocities	LP	Germany		$18.00
Efa	CD-5056	Only Theatre Of Pain	LP	Germany		$18.00
Efa	CD-5065	Scriptures	LP	Germany		$18.00
Pinnacle	FREUDCD-25P	Sex, Drugs & Jesus Christ	LTD/LP	U.S.		$25.00

Picture disc CD.

Singles

Label	Catalog Number	Title	Type	Country	Year	Longbox Value / Value
Rough Trade	CD5-191	What's the Verdict	CD3	Germany	1988	$8.00
Jungle	JUNGCD-45	What's the Verdict	CD3	U.K.	1988	$8.00
Jungle	JUNGCD-450	Zero Sex	CD3	U.K.	1989	$8.00

Christian, Roger

Singles

Label	Catalog Number	Title	Type	Country	Year	Longbox Value / Value
Island	662606	Take It From Me	CD5	Germany	1989	$7.00
Island	CID-427	Take It From Me	CD5	U.K.	1989	$7.00
Island	CID-442	World Apart	CD5	U.K.	1989	$7.00

Christians

Full Length

Label	Catalog Number	Title	Type	Country	Year	Longbox Value / Value
Island	842451-2	Christians	LP/LB	U.S.		$14.00/$8.00
Island	842268-2	Colour	LP/LB	U.S.		$14.00/$8.00

Singles

Label	Catalog Number	Title	Type	Country	Year	Longbox Value / Value
Island	P10D-30003	Born Again	CD3	Japan	1988	$12.00/$3.00
Island	CIDP-365	Born Again	CD5	U.K.	1988	$8.00
Island	CID 549	Bottle, The	CDJ	U.K.	1993	$10.00
		Father	CD5	U.K.		$8.00
		Father	CD5	U.K.		$8.00

Second version.

Label	Catalog Number	Title	Type	Country	Year	Longbox Value / Value
Eastwest	246855-2	Ferry 'Cross the Mersey	CD5	Germany	1989	$8.00
Island	CID-291	Forgotten Town	CD5	U.K.	1987	$8.00
Island	PR 2184 -2	Forgotten Town	CDJ	U.S.	1987	$2.00
Island	884788	Greenbank Drive	CD5	Germany	1990	$8.00
Island	CIDP-466	Greenbank Drive	CD5	U.K.	1990	$8.00
Island	CID-466	Greenbank Drive	CD5	U.K.	1990	$8.00
Island	661758	Harvest For the World	CD5	Germany	1988	$8.00
Island	CIDP-395	Harvest For the World	CD5	U.K.	1988	$8.00
Island	663091	I Found Out	CD5	Germany	1990	$8.00
Island	PSDD-1005	I Found Out	CD3	Japan	1990	$12.00/$3.00
Island	CIDP-453	I Found Out	CD5	U.K.	1990	$8.00
Island		I Found Out	CDJ	U.S.	1990	$2.00
Island	880728	Ideal World	CD5	Germany	1988	$8.00
Island	CIDX-347	Ideal World	CD3	U.K.	1988	$8.00
Island	CIDP-347	Ideal World	CD5	U.K.	1988	$8.00
Island	10717	What's In A Word	CD5	Germany	1992	$10.00
Island	PHDR-703	What's In A Word	CD3	Japan	1992	$12.00/$3.00
Island	CID-536	What's In A Word	CD5	U.K.	1992	$8.00
Island	880653	When the Fingers Point	CD5	Germany	1988	$8.00
Island	CID-335	When the Fingers Point	CD5	U.K.	1988	$8.00
BMG	662847	Words	CD5	Germany	1990	$8.00
Polydor	PSDD-1002	Words	CD3	Japan	1990	$12.00/$3.00
Island	CIDP-450	Words	CD5	U.K.	1990	$8.00
Island	CIDX-450	Words	CD5	U.K.	1990	$10.00

Christie, David

Singles

Label	Catalog Number	Title	Type	Country	Year	Longbox Value / Value
Intercord	825-778	Saddle Up	CD5	Germany	1990	$8.00

Christie, Tony

Singles

Label	Catalog Number	Title	Type	Country	Year	Longbox Value / Value
BMG	664389	Come With Me To Paradise	CD5	Germany	1991	$8.00
BMG	665051	Going To Havana	CD5	Germany	1992	$8.00
BMG	663365	Kiss In the Night	CD5	Germany	1990	$8.00
BMG	664218	Moonlight & Roses	CD5	Germany	1991	$8.00
BMG	663694	September Love	CD5	Germany	1990	$8.00

Christina

Singles

Label	Catalog Number	Title	Type	Country	Year	Longbox Value / Value
B.M.S.	KIDP-39	Operator	CD3	Japan	1991	$12.00/$3.00

Christopher, Charles

Singles

Label	Catalog Number	Title	Type	Country	Year	Longbox Value / Value
Charisma	12778	Penny For Your Thoughts	CDJ	U.S.	1993	$2.00
Charisma	14190	Think About It	CDJ	U.S.	1993	$2.00

Christopher, Shawn

Singles

Label	Catalog Number	Title	Type	Country	Year	Longbox Value / Value
Arista	664486	Another Sleepless Night	CD5	Germany	1991	$8.00
Arista	664186	Another Sleepless Night	CD5	U.K.	1991	$8.00
Arista	BVDA-41	Don't Lose the Magic	CD3	Japan	1992	$12.00/$3.00
Arista	665097	Don't Lose the Magic	CD5	U.K.	1992	$8.00

Christy

Singles

Label	Catalog Number	Title	Type	Country	Year	Longbox Value / Value
Canyon	S9ED-8008	Somebody	CD3	Japan	1989	$12.00/$3.00

Christy, Lauren

Singles

Label	Catalog Number	Title	Type	Country	Year	Longbox Value / Value
Mercury	856174	Color Of Night	CD5	U.S.	1994	$5.00
Polygram	856174	Color Of Night	CD5	U.S.	1994	$5.00
Mercury	CDP 1027	Steep	CDJ	U.S.	1993	$2.00
Mercury	CDP 884	You Read Me Wrong	CDJ	U.S.	1993	$2.00

Chrome Molly

Full Length

Label	Catalog Number	Title	Type	Country	Year	Longbox Value / Value
CBS	460928-2	Angst	LP	Germany		$15.00

Chroming Rose

Full Length

Label	Catalog Number	Title	Type	Country	Year	Longbox Value / Value
EMI	796248-2	Garden Of Eden	LTD/LP	Germany		$25.00

Picture disc CD.

Singles

Label	Catalog Number	Title	Type	Country	Year	Longbox Value / Value
EMI	147564-2	Hell In His Eyes	CD5	Germany	1991	$8.00

Chubb Rock

Singles

Label	Catalog Number	Title	Type	Country	Year	Longbox Value / Value
Select	8586	Big Man, The	CDJ	U.S.	1992	$2.00
Select	8424	Just the Two Of Us	CDJ	U.S.	1991	$2.00
Select	8696	Yabadabadoo	CDJ	U.S.	1992	$2.00

Chumbawamba

Singles

Label	Catalog Number	Title	Type	Country	Year	Longbox Value / Value
Agit Pop	666	Behave	CD5	France	1992	$10.00

Chunk

Singles

Label	Catalog Number	Title	Type	Country	Year	Longbox Value / Value
Lazy	LAZY-26CD	Chunk	CD5	U.K.	1991	$8.00

Chunky A

Full Length

Label	Catalog Number	Title	Type	Country	Year	Longbox Value / Value
MCA	MCAD-6354	Large And In Charge	LP/LB	U.S.	1989	$12.00/$7.00

Singles

Label	Catalog Number	Title	Type	Country	Year	Longbox Value / Value
MCA	CD45 18080	Owwww	CDJ	U.S.	1989	$7.00
		Sorry	CDJ	U.S.	1989	$2.00

Church, The – Life Before Starfish (Arista APCD-9724)

Church

Full Length

Label	Catalog Number	Title	Type	Country	Year	Longbox Value / Value
Arista		Collection, The	DJ/LP	U.S.	1990	$30.00

Boxed set with CD album, CDJ and Cassette.

Label	Catalog Number	Title	Type	Country	Year	Longbox Value / Value
Arista	BVCA-3	Gold Afternoon Fix	LP	Japan		$25.00
		Hindsight	LTD/LP	Australia		$40.00

2 CD set.

Label	Catalog Number	Title	Type	Country	Year	Longbox Value / Value
Arista	APCD-9724	Life Before Starfish	DJ/Smplr	U.S.	1988	$25.00
Pinnacle	TVD-93356	Priest=Aura	LTD/LP	U.K.		$25.00

Picture disc CD.

Label	Catalog Number	Title	Type	Country	Year	Longbox Value / Value
Arista	18729-2	Sometime Anywhere	DJ/Smplr	U.S.	1994	$30.00

2CD set with patch and press release in large wooden box.

Label	Catalog Number	Title	Type	Country	Year	Longbox Value / Value
Arista	18729-2	Sometime Anywhere	LTD/LP	U.S.	1994	$16.00

2 CD set.

Label	Catalog Number	Title	Type	Country	Year	Longbox Value / Value
Arista	07822187292	Somewhere Else	LTD/LP	Canada	1994	$26.00

2 CD Set

Label	Catalog Number	Title	Type	Country	Year	Longbox Value / Value
Arista	ASCD-9713	Sum Of the Parts	DJ/Smplr	U.S.	1988	$50.00

Singles

Label	Catalog Number	Title	Type	Country	Year	Longbox Value / Value
Arista	885119	Destination	CD5	Germany	1988	$10.00
Arista		Earth Music	CD5	Australia	1994	$10.00
Arista		Feel	CD5	Australia	1992	$10.00
Arista	ASCD-2436	Feel	CDJ	U.S.	1992	$3.00
Arista	2471	Loveblind	CDJ	U.S.	1995	$3.00
Arista	663086	Megalopolis	CD5	U.K.	1990	$10.00
Arista	9944	Megalopolis	CD5	U.S.	1990	$5.00
Arista	ASCD-9950	Megalopolis	CDJ	U.S.	1990	$3.00
Arista		Ripple	CD5	Australia		$10.00
Arista	ASCD-2389	Ripple	CDJ	U.S.	1992	$3.00
Arista	ASCD-2068	Russian Autumm	CDJ	U.S.	1990	$3.00
Arista	ASCD2689	Two Places	CDJ	U.S.	1994	$3.00
Arista		Two Places At Once	CD5	Australia	1994	$12.00
Arista	ASCD-2689	Two Places At Once	CDJ	U.S.	1994	$3.00
Arista	880857	Under the Milkyway	CD5	Germany	1988	$10.00
Arista	659778	Under the Milkyway	CD5	U.K.	1988	$10.00
Arista	ASCD-9669	Under the Milkyway	CDJ	U.S.	1988	$3.00
Arista	ASCD-9687	Under the Milkyway	CDJ	U.S.	1988	$3.00
Arista	ASCD-2042	You're Still Beautiful	CDJ	U.S.	1990	$3.00

Church Of Ecstasy

Singles

Label	Catalog Number	Title	Type	Country	Year	Longbox Value / Value
Sonic	2004	Oowee I Am Ready	CD5	U.S.	1992	$4.00

Chypnotic

Singles

Label	Catalog Number	Title	Type	Country	Year	Longbox Value / Value
BMG	663650	If I Can't Have You	CD5	Germany	1990	$7.00
BMG	663199	Nothing Compares To You	CD5	Germany	1990	$7.00
BMG	664353	Still In Love With You	CD5	Germany	1990	$7.00

Ciaao

Singles

Label	Catalog Number	Title	Type	Country	Year	Longbox Value / Value
Feildworks	FWCR-27	Pop Fight	CD3	Japan	1991	$12.00/$3.00

Cibo Matto

Singles

Label	Catalog Number	Title	Type	Country	Year	Longbox Value / Value
	PRO-CD-8102	Sugar Water	CDJ	U.S.		$2.00

Ciccione Youth

Full Length

Label	Catalog Number	Title	Type	Country	Year	Longbox Value / Value
P&C First Blast	BFUS 28CD	Whitey Album	DJ/Smplr	U.K.	1992	$15.00

Cicero

Singles

Label	Catalog Number	Title	Type	Country	Year	Longbox Value / Value
Polydor	CIOCD-5	Heaven Must Have Sent You Back To Me	CD5	U.K.	1992	$7.00
Polydor	CIOCD-7	Live For Today	CD5	U.K.	1992	$7.00
Polydor	CIOCD-3	Love is Everywhere	CD5	U.K.	1992	$7.00
Polydor	CIOCD-3	That Loving Feeling	CD5	U.K.	1992	$7.00

Cicero, Eugene

Full Length

Label	Catalog Number	Title	Type	Country	Year	Longbox Value / Value
Verve	817924-2	Classics in Rhythm	LP/LB	U.S.†	1985	$14.00/$8.00

Cicone, Don

Singles

Label	Catalog Number	Title	Type	Country	Year	Longbox Value / Value
Polydor	PODP-1041	If I Were You	CD3	Japan	1992	$12.00/$3.00
Polydor	PODP-1051	Lover's Prayer	CD3	Japan	1992	$12.00/$3.00
Polydor	PODP-1036	Mr. Dingley Sad	CD3	Japan	1992	$12.00/$3.00
Polydor	PODP-1023	Nikki I Know	CD3	Japan	1991	$12.00/$3.00
Polydor	PODP-1023	Talk To Me	CD3	Japan	1991	$12.00/$3.00

Cinderella

Full Length

Label	Catalog Number	Title	Type	Country	Year	Longbox Value / Value
Phonogram	28PD-526	Long Cold Winter	LTD/LP	Japan	1988	$40.00

Picture disc CD.

Company	Disk Number	Title	Type	Country	Year	Longbox Value / Value
Phonogram	28PD-527	Night Songs	LTD/LP	Japan	1986	$40.00

Picture disc CD.

Company	Disk Number	Title	Type	Country	Year	Longbox Value / Value
Mercury		Once Around the Ride... Then & Now	DJ/Smplr	Canada	1994	$60.00
Phonogram	CINCDJ 1990	The Story So Far...	DJ/Smplr	Germany	1990	$40.00

Singles

Company	Disk Number	Title	Type	Country	Year	Longbox Value / Value
Mercury	CDP 69	Coming Home	CDJ	U.S.	1988	$8.00
Vertigo	872211-2	Don't Know What You Got	CD5	Germany	1988	$8.00
Vertigo	872639-2	Don't Know What You Got	CD5	Germany	1988	$8.00
Mercury	10PD-3	Don't Know What You Got	CD3	Japan	1988	$13.00/$4.00
Vertigo	VERCD-43	Don't Know What You Got	CD5	U.K.	1988	$8.00
Mercury	CDP 25	Don't Know What You Got	CDJ	U.S.	1988	$6.00
PMV	870 734-2	Don't Know What You Got	CDV/BP	U.S.	1988	$15.00/$12.00
Mercury	CDP 1339	Freewheelin'	CDJ	U.S.	1994	$7.00
Vertigo	VERCD-40	Gypsy Road	CD5	U.K.	1988	$8.00
Mercury	870 725-2	Gypsy Road	CDV/BP	U.S.	1988	$15.00/$12.00
Mercury	870 725-2	Gypsy Road	OS/CDV	U.S.	1988	$20.00
		Heartbreak Station	CD3	Japan	1990	$12.00/$3.00
Polygram	VERCD 53	Heartbreak Station	CD5	U.K.	1990	$15.00
Mercury	CDP 326	Heartbreak Station	CDJ	U.S.	1990	$25.00

Guitar Case Package.

Company	Disk Number	Title	Type	Country	Year	Longbox Value / Value
Reprise	PRO-CD-5309	Hot And Bothered	CDJ	U.S.	1992	$3.00
Mercury	10PD-8	Last Mile, The	CD3	Japan	1988	$13.00/$4.00
Mercury	870 704-2	Last Mile, The	CDV/BP	U.S.	1988	$15.00/$12.00
Mercury	CDP 457	More Things Change, The	CDJ	U.S.	1991	$3.00
Mercury	24VP-3	Nobody's Fool	CDV	Japan	1992	$40.00
Mercury/NTSC	080 047-2	Nobody's Fool	DJ/CDV	U.S.	1986	$35.00
Mercury	080 047-2	Nobody's Fool	CDV	U.S.	1988	$30.00
Mercury	080 047-2	Nobody's Fool	CDV/BP	U.S.	1088	$20.00/$35.00
Polygram	878633-2	Shelter Me	CD5	Germany	1990	$9.00
Phonogram	PHCR-8007	Shelter Me	CD3	Japan	1990	$13.00/$4.00
Mercury	CDP 336	Shelter Me	CDJ	U.S.	1990	$3.00
Mercury	080 705-2	Somebody Save Me	CDV	U.S.	1988	$30.00
Mercury	870 705-2	Somebody Save Me	CDV/BP	U.S.	1988	$35.00

Cinema

Singles

Company	Disk Number	Title	Type	Country	Year	Longbox Value / Value
A&M	S10Y-3003	Put You In My Pocket	CD3	Japan	1988	$12.00/$3.00

Circle C

Full Length

Company	Disk Number	Title	Type	Country	Year	Longbox Value / Value
Geffen	GFD-24319	Circle C	LP/LB	U.S.		$14.00/$8.00

Circle In The Square

Singles

Company	Disk Number	Title	Type	Country	Year	Longbox Value / Value
		Promised Land	CDJ	U.S.		$2.00

Circle Jerks

Singles

Company	Disk Number	Title	Type	Country	Year	Longbox Value / Value
Avenue Records	PRCD 7103	Jerks On 45	CDJ	U.S.	1994	$6.00

Circle of Fear

Singles

Company	Disk Number	Title	Type	Country	Year	Longbox Value / Value
		Dead Souls	CD5	U.S.		$5.00

Circle of Soul

Singles

Company	Disk Number	Title	Type	Country	Year	Longbox Value / Value
Hollywood	PRCD 8397-2	Shattered Faith	CDJ	U.S.	1991	$2.00
Hollywood	8333	Shattered Faith	CDJ	U.S.	1991	$3.00
Hollywood	PRCD 8333-2	Stone In My Shoe	CDJ	U.S.	1991	$2.00
Hollywood	8397	Stone In My Shoe	CDJ	U.S.	1991	$3.00

Circuit

Singles

Company	Disk Number	Title	Type	Country	Year	Longbox Value / Value
Cooltempo	COOLCD-207	Shelter Me	CD5	U.K.	1990	$8.00
Cooltempo	COOLCD-237	Shelter Me	CD5	U.K.	1990	$8.00

Circus

Full Length

Company	Disk Number	Title	Type	Country	Year	Longbox Value / Value
Alfa	ALCA-436/8	Collection	LP	Japan		$0.00

Singles

Company	Disk Number	Title	Type	Country	Year	Longbox Value / Value
Fun House	FHDF-1105	Calender Girl	CD3	Japan	1991	$12.00/$3.00

Circus of Power

Full Length

Company	Disk Number	Title	Type	Country	Year	Longbox Value / Value
RCA	PD-8464	Circus Of Power	LP/BP	U.S.		$14.00/$8.00
Restless	72417	Still Alive	LP/BP	U.S.		$14.00/$8.00
RCA	PD-2022	Vices	LP/BP	U.S.		$14.00/$8.00

Singles

Company	Disk Number	Title	Type	Country	Year	Longbox Value / Value
RCA	BVDP-4	Doctor Potion	CD3	Japan	1990	$13.00/$4.00
RCA	R10D-112	Motor	CD3	Japan	1989	$13.00/$4.00
BMG	PD-49256	Vices	CD5	Germany	1990	$10.00
RCA	2632-2-RDJ	Vices	CDJ	U.S	1990	$2.00
RCA	2632	Vices	CDJ	U.S.	1990	$3.00

Cisco Kid

Singles

Company	Disk Number	Title	Type	Country	Year	Longbox Value / Value
EMI	204595-2	I Like the Way You Move	CD5	Germany	1992	$7.00

Citizen's Utilities

Full Length

Company	Disk Number	Title	Type	Country	Year	Longbox Value / Value
	MUS72	Lost And Foundered	DJ/LP	U.S.		$102.00

City

Full Length

Company	Disk Number	Title	Type	Country	Year	Longbox Value / Value
Teldec	8-26444	Casablanca	LP	Germany		$15.00

CIV

Full Length

Company	Disk Number	Title	Type	Country	Year	Longbox Value / Value
	PRCD 6293-2	Metal Sampler	DJ/Smplr	U.S.		$6.00

Singles

Company	Disk Number	Title	Type	Country	Year	Longbox Value / Value
	PRCD 6284-2	Can't Wait One Minute More	CDJ	U.S.		$2.00
	PRCD 6505-2	Choices Made	CDJ	U.S.		$2.00

CJ's Arrival

Singles

Company	Disk Number	Title	Type	Country	Year	Longbox Value / Value
Intercord	825-902	It Should Have Been Me	CD5	Germany	1991	$7.00

Clail, Gary

Full Length

Company	Disk Number	Title	Type	Country	Year	Longbox Value / Value
RCA	PD-61007	Emotional Hooligan	LP/BP	U.S.		$12.00/$7.00

Singles

Company	Disk Number	Title	Type	Country	Year	Longbox Value / Value
BMG	PD-43846	Beef	CD5	Germany	1990	$8.00
BMG	PD-43844	Beef	CD5	U.K.	1990	$8.00
Perfecto	PD-44952	Emotional Hooligan	CD5	U.K.	1991	$8.00
Perfecto	PD-44564	Escape	CD5	Germany	1991	$8.00
Perfecto	PD-44564	Escape	CD5	U.K.	1991	$8.00
RCA	62147-2	Escape	CD5	U.S.	1991	$5.00

Label	Catalog Number	Title	Type	Country	Year	Longbox Value / Value
Perfecto	PD-44402	Human Nature	CD5	U.K.	1991	$8.00
RCA	2855-2-RDJ	Human Nature	CDJ	U.S.	1991	$2.00
RCA	62066	Human Nature	CDJ	U.S.	1991	$3.00
		These Things Are Worth	CD5	U.K.		$8.00
		These Things Are Worth	CD5	U.K.		$8.00
	Second version.					
RCA	7432111701-2	Who Pays the Piper	CD5	U.K.	1992	$8.00

Clannad – Family Tree Sampler, The (Atlantic PRCD 4945-2)

Clannad

Full Length

Label	Catalog Number	Title	Type	Country	Year	Longbox Value / Value
BBC	BBCCD-727	Atlantic Realm	LP	U.K.		$25.00
TIS	CEFCD-041	Clannad, Vol. 2	LP	Germany		$25.00
Tara	3007	Dulaman	LP/BP	U.S.		$14.00/$8.00
Atlantic	PRCD 4945-2	Family Tree Sampler, The	DJ/Smplr	U.S.	1993	$18.00
Tara	3008	Fuaim	LP/BP	U.S.		$14.00/$8.00
		Lore	LTD/LP	U.K.	1996	$30.00
	2 CD set.					
Atlantic		Sirius Sampler	DJ/Smplr	U.S.	1995	$10.00

Singles

Label	Catalog Number	Title	Type	Country	Year	Longbox Value / Value
MCA	MCD-17571	Both Sides Now	CD5	Germany	1991	$10.00
MCA	MCSTD-1546	Both Sides Now	CD5	U.K.	1991	$10.00
RCA	7432111812-2	Harry's Game	CD5	U.K.	1992	$10.00
Atlantic	PRCD 4675-2	Harry's Game	CDJ	U.S.	1992	$6.00
RCA	PD-43076	Hourglass	CD5	U.K.	1989	$10.00
RCA	PD-42610	Hunter	CD5	Germany	1989	$10.00
RCA	PD-42610	Hunter	CD5	U.K.	1989	$10.00
Atlantic	PRCD 5135-2	I Will Find You	CDJ	U.S.		$2.00
RCA	PD-42874	In A Lifetime	CD5	Germany	1989	$10.00
RCA	PD-42874	In A Lifetime	CD5	U.K.	1989	$10.00
RCA	9171-2-RDJ	In A Lifetime	CDJ	U.S.	1990	$2.00
RCA	PD-43972	In Fortune's Hand	CD5	U.K.	1990	$10.00
		Why Worry	CD5	U.K.		$25.00
	Unissued single.					

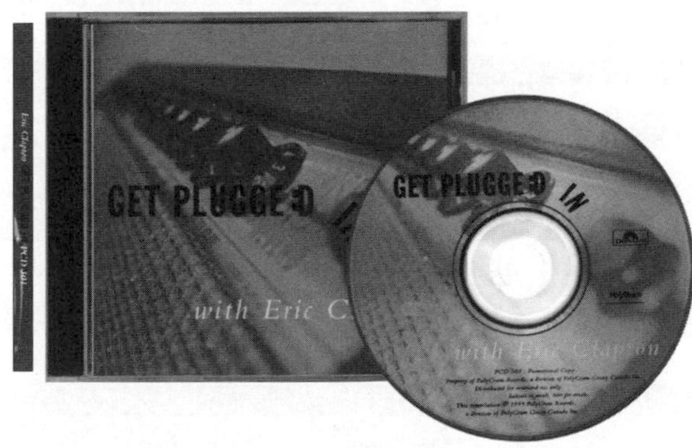

Clapton, Eric – Get Plugged In (Polydor PCD 301) Extremely rare 1993 Canadian promotional sampler. In fact, it is more rare than most of its Clapton Japanese promotional sampler counter-parts.

Clapton, Eric

Full Length

Label	Catalog Number	Title	Type	Country	Year	Longbox Value / Value
WEA	38193	24 Nights	LD	U.S.	1991	$35.00
Album Network		24 Nights	RS	U.S.	1991	$135.00
	2 CD set. Airdate: 11/6/91					
Reprise	PRO-CD-5110	24 Nights Sampler	DJ/Smplr	U.S.	1990	$15.00
RSO	811697-2	461 Ocean Boulevard	LP/BP	U.S.†	1984	$14.00/$8.00
		Blues Concert	RS	U.S.	1995	$135.00
	2 CD set.					
Polydor		Cream Of Clapton	LP	U.K.		$15.00
	Original nonremastered version.					
Global Satellite Network		Cream Of the Crop	RS	U.S.		$100.00
	6 CD set.					
Polydor		Crossroads	DJ/Smplr	U.S.	1988	$200.00
	Andvance issue in 4CD jewel case.					
Polydor	CDP 10	Crossroads	DJ/Smplr	U.S.	1989	$30.00
Polygram	PRSAD00167	Crossroads 2	DJ/LP	U.S.	1996	$55.00
	4 CD set in double jewel box.					
Westwood One		Eric Clapton Story, The	RS	U.S.	1994	$60.00
	2 CD set. Airdate: 10/94.					
Polydor	PCD 301	Get Plugged In	DJ/Smplr	Canada	1993	$150.00
Warner Brothers	PRO 982	Greatest Hits	DJ/Smplr	U.S.	1995	$125.00
Westwood One		History Of Eric Clapton	RS	U.S.	1992	$125.00
	6 CD set. Airdate: 9/4/92.					
		House Of Blues	RS	U.S.	1996	$40.00
	2 CD set. Airdate: 3/31/96.					
Album Network		In the Studio (24 Nights)	RS	U.S.	1991	$40.00
	Airdate: 11/6/91.					
RSO	800 093-2	Just One Night	LP/LB	U.S.†	1984	$22.00/$16.00
	2 CD set.					
DIR		King Biscuit Flour Hour	RS	U.S.	1987	$175.00
	Airdate: 9/6/87, First KBFH show.					
Image	IDML1027	Live	LD	U.S.		$35.00
Vestron	V-1027	Live	LD	U.S.	1986	$35.00
Warner Brothers	23773-2	Money & Cigarettes	LP/LB	U.S.†	1984	$14.00/$8.00
Westwood One		Off the Record	RS	U.S.	1992	$45.00
	Airdate: 6/8/92					
Westwood One		Off the Record	RS	U.S.	1992	$50.00
	Airdate: 12/14/92.					
Westwood One		Off the Record	RS	U.S.	1995	$95.00
	2 CD set. Airdate: 1/23/95.					
Polygram	831320-2	Rainbow Concert	LP	U.S.		$14.00/$10.00
Polydor		Rainbow Concert Sampler, The	DJ/Smplr	U.S.	1995	$20.00
On the Radio		Rarities On Compact Disc	RS	U.S.	1992	$40.00
	Volume11.					
Chronicles	PRSAD000182	Selections From Crossroads 2	DJ/Smplr	U.S.	1995	$25.00
RSO	823 276-2	Slow Hand	LP/BP	U.S.†	1984	$14.00/$8.00
		Still Got Blue	RS	U.S.	1995	$200.00
	6 CD set. Airdate: 5/29/95.					
RSO	800014-2	Time Pieces	LP/BP	U.S.†	1984	$14.00/$8.00
RSO	811835-2	Time Pieces II	LP/BP	U.S.†	1985	$14.00/$8.00
Polydor	PRO-982	Tour Sampler	DJ/Smplr	Germany		$100.00
WEA	38311	Unplugged	LD	U.S.	1992	$30.00
Media America		Up Close	[illegible]	[illegible]	[illegible]	[illegible]
	4 CD set.					
Media America		Up Close	RS	U.S.	1989	$80.00
	4 CD set.					
Media America		Up Close	RS	U.S.	1990	$70.00
	4 CD set.					
Media America		Up Close	RS	U.S.	1992	$60.00
	4 CD set.					
Media America		Up Close	RS	U.S.	1995	$135.00
	3 CD set.					
		Up Close	RS	U.S.	1996	$120.00
	3 CD set.					

Singles

Label	Catalog Number	Title	Type	Country	Year	Longbox Value / Value
Polydor	PZCD-8	After Midnight	CD5	U.K.	1988	$12.00
WEA	921449-2	Bad Love	CD5	Germany	1989	$12.00
Pioneer	WPDP-6218	Bad Love	CD3	Japan	1989	$18.00/$4.00
WEA		Bad Love	CD3	U.K.	1989	$15.00
WEA	W-2644CD	Bad Love	CD5	U.K.	1989	$12.00
Reprise	PRO-CD-3792	Bad Love	CDJ	U.S.	1989	$7.00
Reprise	PRO-CD-4050	Before You Accuse Me	CDJ	U.S.	1989	$7.00
Warner Brothers	PRCD 315	Change the World	CDJ	Germany	1996	$25.00
Warner Brothers		Change the World	CD5	U.K.	1996	$12.00
Reprise		Change the World	CD5	U.S.	1996	$5.00
Reprise		Change the World	CDJ	U.S.	1996	$7.00
		Crossroads	CD3	Japan	1988	$18.00/$4.00
Sound	CDRSL-178	Edge Of Darkness	CD3	Germany	1988	$12.00
Sound	CD-178	Edge Of Darkness	CD3	U.K.	1988	$12.00
Reprise	PRO-CD-7263	Five Long Years	CDJ	U.S.	1994	$7.00
Reprise	PRO-CD-5235	Help Me Up	CDJ	U.S.	1992	$6.00
		Hey Hey	CDJ	Spain	1992	$30.00
WEA		Hoochie Coochie	CDJ	Spain	1995	$40.00
Polygram	889173-2	I Shot the Sheriff	CD5	Germany	1990	$12.00
Warner Brothers		I'm Torn Down	CDJ	Germany	1995	$15.00
Warner Brothers		I'm Torn Down	CDJ	Spain	1995	$28.00
Polydor		I'm Torn Down	CDJ	U.K.		$16.00
Warner Brothers	PRO-CD-7150	I'm Torn Down	CDJ	U.S.	1994	$6.00
WEA	WPCR-440	It Hurts Me Too	CD5	Japan	1995	$25.00
WEA		It Hurts Me Too	CDJ	Spain	1995	$40.00
Warner Brothers		It's Probably Me	CDJ	U.S.		$7.00
Wea	W-0124CD	Layla	CD5	Germany	1992	$12.00
RSO	P10W 30001	Layla	CD3	Japan	1988	$18.00/$4.00
Polydor	PZCD-163	Layla	CD5	U.K.	1991	$12.00
Warner Brothers	9 18787-2	Layla	CD5	U.S.	1992	$5.00
Reprise	PRO-CD-5641	Layla	CDJ	U.S.	1992	$6.00
Reprise	WPDP-6315	Lonely Stranger	CD3	Japan	1992	$13.00/$4.00
WEA	COCD1	Love Can Build A Bridge	CDJ	U.K.	1995	$15.00
	With Chrissie Hynde and Nenah Cherry.					
Reprise	PCS-147	Motherless Child	CDJ	Japan	1992	$50.00
WEA		Motherless Child	CDJ	Spain	1994	$28.00
Reprise		Motherless Child	CD5	U.K.	1994	$10.00
Warner Brothers	18044	Motherless Child	CD5	U.S.	1994	$5.00
Reprise	PRO-CD-7200	Motherless Child	CDJ	U.S.	1994	$7.00
Warner Brothers		Motherless Child	CDJ	U.S.	1994	$7.00
Reprise	7599-21508-2	No Alibis	CD5	Germany	1989	$10.00
Reprise	W-9981CD	No Alibis	CD5	U.K.	1989	$10.00
Reprise	PRO-CD-3797	No Alibis	CDJ	U.S.	1989	$7.00
WEA	921411-2	Pretending	CD5	Germany	1989	$10.00
Reprise	09P3-6203	Pretending	CD3	Japan	1989	$18.00/$4.00
Reprise	W-9770CD	Pretending	CD5	U.K.	1989	$12.00
Reprise	PRO-CD-3789	Pretending	CDJ	U.S.	1989	$15.00
Warner Brothers		Reconsider Baby	CDJ	U.S.		$7.00
Reprise	PRO-CD-4373	Run So Far	CDJ	U.S.	1989	$6.00
Warner Brothers		Running On Faith	CDJ	U.S.	1994	$7.00
Reprise	PRO-CD-6612	Stone Free	CDJ	U.S.	1993	$6.00
		Tear Down	CDJ	U.S.	1994	$7.00
WEA		Tears In Heaven	CDJ	France	1992	$25.00
Reprise	9362-40354-2	Tears In Heaven	CD5	Germany	1992	$10.00
Reprise	WPDP-6325	Tears In Heaven	CD3	Japan	1992	$18.00/$4.00
Reprise	W-0081CD	Tears In Heaven	CD5	U.K.	1992	$10.00
Reprise	PRO-CD-5240	Tears In Heaven	CDJ	U.S.	1992	$7.00
Reprise	PRO-CD-5362	Tears In Heaven	CDJ	U.S.	1992	$7.00
Reprise	PRO-CD-5110	Watch Yourself	CDJ	U.S.	1991	$6.00
WEA	WE 739	Wonderful Tonight	CD5	France	1993	$15.00
WEA		Wonderful Tonight	CDJ	France	1993	$25.00
Reprise	W0069CD	Wonderful Tonight	CD5	Germany	1992	$10.00
Reprise		Wonderful Tonight	CD5	Germany	1992	$10.00
	Second version.					
Reprise	WPDP-6293	Wonderful Tonight	CD3	Japan	1989	$16.00/$4.00
WEA		Wonderful Tonight	CDJ	Spain	1993	$40.00
Reprise	887754-2	Wonderful Tonight	CD5	U.K.	1992	$10.00

Clara

Singles

Label	Catalog Number	Title	Type	Country	Year	Longbox Value / Value
EMI	118834-2	Gimme Little Sign	CD3	Germany	1989	$7.00

Clarissa

Singles

Label	Catalog Number	Title	Type	Country	Year	Longbox Value / Value
	PRCD 6656-2	Sail Away	CDJ	U.S.		$2.00

Clark, Anne

Singles

Label	Catalog Number	Title	Type	Country	Year	Longbox Value / Value
APT	8835-3	Abuse	CD5	Germany	1990	$8.00
APT	558835	Abuse	CD5	U.K.	1990	$8.00
APT	8845-3	Counter Act	CD5	Germany	1991	$8.00
Rough Trade	616-0376-3	Our Darkness	CD5	Germany	1991	$8.00

Clark, Gary

Singles

Label	Catalog Number	Title	Type	Country	Year	Longbox Value / Value
		Freefloating	CD5	U.K.		$8.00
		Freefloating	CD5	U.K.		$8.00

Second version.

Label	Catalog Number	Title	Type	Country	Year	Longbox Value / Value
		Make A Family	CD5	U.K.		$8.00
		Make A Family	CD5	U.K.		$8.00

Second version.

Label	Catalog Number	Title	Type	Country	Year	Longbox Value / Value
		We Sail On the Stormy Waters	CD5	U.K.		$8.00
		We Sail On the Stormy Waters	CD5	U.K.		$8.00

Second version.

Clark, Gene

Singles

Label	Catalog Number	Title	Type	Country	Year	Longbox Value / Value
Demon	GENE 1	I'll Feel A Whole Lot Better	CD5	U.K.		$8.00

Clark, Guy

Singles

Label	Catalog Number	Title	Type	Country	Year	Longbox Value / Value
Mother	MUMCD-11	All Through Throwin' Good Love	CD5	U.K.	1989	$8.00
Asylum	PRCD 8867-2	Baton Rouge	CDJ	U.S.	1992	$2.00

Clark Kit

Singles

Label	Catalog Number	Title	Type	Country	Year	Longbox Value / Value
Reverb	RVBCDS-005	Lovedun	CD5	U.K.	1991	$7.00

Clark, Petula

Full Length

Label	Catalog Number	Title	Type	Country	Year	Longbox Value / Value
S-F Miles	306	EP Collection	LP/LB	U.S.		$14.00/$8.00
GNP	GNPD-2170	Greatest Hits	LP	Germany		$18.00
Teldec	8 26837	Hit Single Collection	LP	Germany		$18.00

Singles

Label	Catalog Number	Title	Type	Country	Year	Longbox Value / Value
Polygram	877019-2	Cheatin' Heart	CD5	Germany	1990	$9.00
Old Gold	DG-6101	Downtown	CD5	U.K.	1988	$9.00
Collectibles	9041	Downtown	CD5	U.S.	1990	$5.00
Pye	PYD-19	Downtown '88	CD5	Germany	1988	$9.00
Eastwest	247171-2	Downtown '88	CD5	Germany	1989	$9.00
Polygram	871663-2	Downtown '88	CD5	Germany	1989	$9.00
Legacy	LGYC-100	I Couldn't Live Without Your Love	CD5	U.K.	1989	$9.00

Clark, Rhonda

Singles

Label	Catalog Number	Title	Type	Country	Year	Longbox Value / Value
Tabu	28965 1804	(If Loving You Is Wrong) I Don't Want To Be Right	CDJ	U.S.	1992	$2.00
Tabu	31458 8004	Must Be Real Live	CDJ	U.S.	1992	$2.00
Tabu	28965 1751	State Of Attraction	CDJ	U.S.	1989	$2.00
Tabu	31458 8026	When the Next Tear Drop Falls	CDJ	U.S.	1992	$2.00

Clark, Susan

Singles

Label	Catalog Number	Title	Type	Country	Year	Longbox Value / Value
ffrr	CDP 637	Deeper	CDJ	U.S.	1992	$2.00

Clark, Terri

Full Length

Label	Catalog Number	Title	Type	Country	Year	Longbox Value / Value
		Country Concert	RS	U.S.	1996	$40.00

Airdate: 8/12/96.

Clark, Will

Singles

Label	Catalog Number	Title	Type	Country	Year	Longbox Value / Value
Laserstar	001	1989 Season Highlights	CDV	U.S.	1989	$25.00

Clarke, Anne

Singles

Label	Catalog Number	Title	Type	Country	Year	Longbox Value / Value
		Elergy For A Lost Summer	CD5	Germany	1991	$8.00

Clarke, Fast Eddie

Full Length

Label	Catalog Number	Title	Type	Country	Year	Longbox Value / Value
		It Ain't Over Till It's Over	LP	U.K.		$12.00

Clarke, Gilby

Singles

Label	Catalog Number	Title	Type	Country	Year	Longbox Value / Value
		Cure Me...Or Kill Me	CDJ	U.K.	1995	$15.00
	DPRO-14186	Cure Me...Or Kill Me	CDJ	U.S.	1994	$3.00

Clarke, Kenny

Full Length

Label	Catalog Number	Title	Type	Country	Year	Longbox Value / Value
Savoy Records	CY-78811	Bohemia After Dark	LTD/LP	U.S.	1996	$20.00

CD in miniature repica of original LP sleeve.

Clarke, Rozlyne

Singles

Label	Catalog Number	Title	Type	Country	Year	Longbox Value / Value
Atlantic	PRCD 3617-2	Eddy Steady Go	CDJ	U.S.	1990	$2.00
Sony	656770-2	Georgeous	CD5	Germany	1991	$8.00

Clarke, Sharon Dee

Singles

Label	Catalog Number	Title	Type	Country	Year	Longbox Value / Value
Bellaphon	130-07-391	Guilty	CD5	Germany	1990	$8.00
Bellaphon	130-07-373	Mr. Right	CD5	Germany	1990	$8.00

Clarke, Sonny

Full Length

Label	Catalog Number	Title	Type	Country	Year	Longbox Value / Value
Blue Note	CDP-46819	Sonny's Crib	LP/LB	U.S.		$20.00/$15.00
Polygram	BSR-0109CD	Voodoo	LP/BP	U.S.		$14.00/$8.00
Blue Note	TOCJ-5663	Cool Struttin'	CD5	Japan	1992	$20.00

Clarke, Stanley

Full Length

Label	Catalog Number	Title	Type	Country	Year	Longbox Value / Value
CBS	CD-82674	Modern Man	LP	Germany		$15.00
CBS	ZK-35303	Modern Man	LP/LB	U.S.		$14.00/$8.00

Singles

Label	Catalog Number	Title	Type	Country	Year	Longbox Value / Value
Epic	ESK 5381	Easy River Drive	CDJ	U.S.	1993	$2.00
Epic	ESK 5311	Fantasy Love	CDJ	U.S.	1993	$2.00
Epic	ESK 2077	Finger Prints	CDJ	U.S.	1990	$2.00
Epic	ESK 77218	Justice Groove	CDJ	U.S.	1993	$2.00
Epic	ESK 73422	Lady	CDJ	U.S.	1990	$2.00
		Learning Curve	CDJ	U.S.		$2.00

Clarke, Stanley & George Duke

Full Length

Company	Disk Number	Title	Type	Country	Year	Longbox Value / Value
Epic	EK-36918	Clark/Duke Project	LP/LB	U.S.†	1985	$14.00/$8.00

Clash

Full Length

Company	Disk Number	Title	Type	Country	Year	Longbox Value / Value
Epic/Legacy	3SK4248	Clash On Broadway, The	DJ/LP	U.S.	1991	$35.00

3CD set in ship case.

Company	Disk Number	Title	Type	Country	Year	Longbox Value / Value
Combat	1036	Crucial Music	LP/LB	U.S.		$14.00/$8.00
Relativity	1022	Crucial Music	LP/LB	U.S.		$14.00/$8.00
Epic/Legacy	ESK 4337	On Broadway: The Interviews	DJ/Intvw	U.S.	1991	$35.00
Epic/Legacy	ESK 4274	On Broadway: The Trailer CD Sampler	DJ/Smplr	U.S.	1991	$17.00
Legacy	53191	Super Black Market	LP	U.S.	1993	$11.00

Songs "Pressure Drop" and "The Prisoner" are listed in reverse order.

Company	Disk Number	Title	Type	Country	Year	Longbox Value / Value
CBS	7098-80	This Is Video Clash	LD	U.S.	1988	$30.00

Singles

Company	Disk Number	Title	Type	Country	Year	Longbox Value / Value
Columbia	CLASHC-1	I Fought the Law	CD5	U.K.	1988	$10.00
		London Calling	CDJ	France	1994	$15.00
Columbia	655170-3	London Calling	CD3	Germany	1989	$10.00
Columbia	656946-2	London Calling	CD5	Germany	1991	$10.00
Columbia	CLASHC-2	London Calling	CD5	U.K.	1988	$10.00
Columbia	651653-3	Radio Clash	CD3	Germany	1989	$10.00
Columbia	651653-3	Radio Clash	CD3	U.K.	1989	$10.00
Columbia	656072-2	Return To Brixton	CD5	U.K.	1990	$10.00
Epic	49K 73516	Return To Brixton	CD5	U.S.	1990	$5.00
Columbia	656814-2	Rock the Casbah	CD5	Germany	1991	$10.00
Columbia	656814-2	Rock the Casbah	CD5	U.K.	1991	$10.00
Epic	ISK 68663	Rock the Casbah	CD3	U.S.	1988	$6.00/$3.00
Columbia	85667-2	Should I Stay Or Should I Go	CD5	Germany	1991	$10.00

Also with tracks by Big Audio Dynamite II.

Company	Disk Number	Title	Type	Country	Year	Longbox Value / Value
Columbia	85667-2	Should I Stay Or Should I Go	CD5	U.K.	1991	$10.00

Also with tracks by Big Audio Dynamite II.

Company	Disk Number	Title	Type	Country	Year	Longbox Value / Value
Columbia	657430-2	Train In Vain	CD5	U.K.	1991	$10.00

Classic Example

Singles

Company	Disk Number	Title	Type	Country	Year	Longbox Value / Value
Boston	10260	Christmas Song	CDJ	U.S.	1992	$2.00
Boston	10275	I Do Care	CDJ	U.S.	1993	$2.00
Hollywood	10201	It's Alright	CDJ	U.S.	1992	$2.00

Clawfinger

Singles

Company	Disk Number	Title	Type	Country	Year	Longbox Value / Value
		Warfair	CD5	U.K.		$8.00
		Warfair	CD5	U.K.		$8.00

Second version.

Clay, Andrew Dice

Full Length

Company	Disk Number	Title	Type	Country	Year	Longbox Value / Value
Def American	PRO-CD-5631	Dice's Greatest (Bleeped) Bits	DJ/Smplr	U.S.	1992	$5.00
		Diceman Cometh	LD	U.S.		$30.00
Def American	CK 3489	O.K. For Radio Play	DJ/Smplr	U.S.	1989	$5.00

Clay, James

Full Length

Company	Disk Number	Title	Type	Country	Year	Longbox Value / Value
Polygram	848279	I Let A Song Go Out	LP/BP	U.S.		$14.00/$8.00

Clayderman, Richard

Full Length

Company	Disk Number	Title	Type	Country	Year	Longbox Value / Value
CBS	CK-40190	A Romantic Christmas	LP/LB	U.S.†	1985	$14.00/$8.00
Columbia	CK-40190	A Romantic Christmas	LP/LB	U.S.	1987	$14.00/$8.00
CBS	CK-39603	Amour	LP/LB	U.S.†	1985	$14.00/$8.00
Columbia	CK-39603	Amour	LP/LB	U.S.	1987	$14.00/$8.00
Delphine	174067-2	France Mon Amour	LP	U.K.		$15.00
CBS	CK-40174	From Paris With Love	LP/LB	U.S.†	1985	$14.00/$8.00
Columbia	CK-40174	From Paris With Love	LP/LB	U.S.	1987	$14.00/$8.00
Columbia	CK-40472	Plays Love Songs of the World	LP/LB	U.S.		$14.00/$8.00
Columbia	CK-44211	Romantic America	LP/LB	U.S.		$14.00/$8.00

Clayton, Buck

Full Length

Company	Disk Number	Title	Type	Country	Year	Longbox Value / Value
Mosaic	MD6-144	Complete CBS Buck Clayton Jam Sessions	LTD/LP	U.S.		$90.00

6 LD boxed set. Limited to 5000 copies.

Company	Disk Number	Title	Type	Country	Year	Longbox Value / Value
Columbia	CK-44291	Jam Sessions From the Vault	LP/LB	U.S.	14	$14.00/$8.00

Singles

Company	Disk Number	Title	Type	Country	Year	Longbox Value / Value
Victor	VIDP-50	Prince Of the Rising Sun	CD3	Japan	1993	$12.00/$3.00

Clayton, Lee

Singles

Company	Disk Number	Title	Type	Country	Year	Longbox Value / Value
Provogue	0716-3	Tequila Is Addictive	CD5	Germany	1990	$7.00
Provogue	PRM-2016-2	Tequila Is Addictive	CD5	U.K.	1990	$7.00

Clayton, Willie

Full Length

Company	Disk Number	Title	Type	Country	Year	Longbox Value / Value
Line	842627	Forever	LP	Germany		$15.00

Clayton-Felt, Josh

Full Length

Company	Disk Number	Title	Type	Country	Year	Longbox Value / Value
		Inarticulate Boy	DJ/LP	U.S.		$8.00

Singles

Company	Disk Number	Title	Type	Country	Year	Longbox Value / Value
	AMCDP00132	Window	CDJ	U.S.		$2.00

Clayton-Thomas, David

Singles

Company	Disk Number	Title	Type	Country	Year	Longbox Value / Value
SRC	17102	Christmas Song, The	CDJ	U.S.	1992	$2.00

Claytown Troupe

Full Length

Company	Disk Number	Title	Type	Country	Year	Longbox Value / Value
Island	842344	Through the Evil	LP/LB	U.S.		$14.00/$8.00

Singles

Company	Disk Number	Title	Type	Country	Year	Longbox Value / Value
Island	885584	Hey Lord	CD5	Germany	1989	$8.00
Island	CID-428	Hey Lord	CD5	U.K.	1989	$8.00
Island	CID-417	Prayer	CD5	U.K.	1989	$8.00
Island	885685	Real Life	CD5	Germany	1990	$8.00
Island	CID-428	Real Life	CD5	U.K.	1990	$8.00
EMI	CDMT-102	Wanted It All	CD5	U.K.	1991	$8.00
EMI	E2 56235	Wanted It All	CD5	U.S.	1991	$5.00
Island	884550	Ways of Love	CD5	Germany	1990	$8.00
Island	CID-464	Ways of Love	CD5	U.K.	1990	$8.00

Cleaners Of Venus

Full Length

Company	Disk Number	Title	Type	Country	Year	Longbox Value / Value
Aris	880185	Under Wartime Conditions	LP	Germany		$15.00

Singles

Company	Disk Number	Title	Type	Country	Year	Longbox Value / Value
Efa	CD-1671	Under Wartime Conditions	CD5	Germany		$7.00

Clegg, Johnny (And Savuka)

Label	Catalog Number	Title	Type	Country	Year	Longbox Value / Value
Full Length						
Capitol	DPRO-790-31	Cruel Crazy Beautiful World	DJ/LP	U.S.	1989	$50.00
Promo CD in box with plastic globe puzzle.						
Capitol	DPRO-79387	Cruel Crazy Beautiful World	DJ/Smplr	U.S.	1990	$4.00
Capitol	CDP-90411	Shadow Man	LP/LB	U.S.		$14.00/$8.00
Singles						
EMI	202389-2	Asimbonanga	CD5	Germany	1989	$9.00
EMI	202948-2	Asimbonanga	CD5	Germany	1989	$9.00
EMI	CDEMI-5603	Asimbonanga	CD5	U.K.	1989	$9.00
EMI	203627-3	Cruel Crazy Beautiful World	CD3	Germany	1989	$9.00
EMI	CDEM-120	Cruel Crazy Beautiful World	CD5	U.K.	1990	$9.00
Capitol	DPRO-79868	Cruel Crazy Beautiful World	CDJ	U.S.	1989	$3.00
EMI	CDEM-56	I Call Your Name	CD5	U.K.	1988	$9.00
Capitol	DPRO-79678	I Can Never Be	CDj	U.S.	1993	$3.00
Capitol	DPRO-79287	Life Is A Magic Thing	CDJ	U.S.	1989	$3.00
EMI	203789-2	One (Hu)man One Vote	CD5	Germany	1990	$9.00
EMI	CDEM-136	One (Hu)man One Vote	CD5	U.K.	1990	$9.00
Capitol	DPRO-79387	One (Hu)man One Vote	CDJ	U.S.	1990	$3.00
EMI	CDEM-5605	Scatterlings Of Africa	CD5	U.K.	1987	$9.00
EMI	CDEM-75	Take My Heart Away	CD5	U.K.	1988	$9.00
EMI	20 2968	Take My Heart Away	CD5	U.K.	1988	$10.00
EMI	2968	Take My Heart Away	CD5	U.K.	1988	$10.00
EMI	DPRO-79673	These Days	CDJ	U.S.	1993	$3.00

Clemons, Clarence

Label	Catalog Number	Title	Type	Country	Year	Longbox Value / Value
Full Length						
CBS	462538-2	Hero	LP	Germany		$15.00
Columbia	CK-40010	Hero	LP/LB	U.S.		$14.00/$8.00
Columbia	CK-40917	Night With Mr. C	LP/LB	U.S.		$14.00/$8.00
Singles						
Columbia	CSK 1772	Quarter To Three	CDJ	U.S.	1989	$7.00

Clergy-Ruami

Label	Catalog Number	Title	Type	Country	Year	Longbox Value / Value
Singles						
Broken	8888	Purity	CDJ	U.S.		$3.00

Cleveland, Ashley

Label	Catalog Number	Title	Type	Country	Year	Longbox Value / Value
Full Length						
Atlantic	AMCY-239	Big Town	LP	U.S.	1991	$15.00
Atlantic	82185-2	Big Town	LP/LB	U.S.	1991	$12.00/$7.00
RCA	62551-2-RDJ	Songs From the Big Town	DJ/Smplr	U.S.		$6.00
Singles						
RCA	62551	Feel Like Failing	CDJ	U.S.	1993	$9.00
		I Could Learn To Love	CDJ	U.S.		$2.00
Atlantic	PRCD 3704-2	Willy	CDJ	U.S.	1991	$2.00

Clever Jeff

Label	Catalog Number	Title	Type	Country	Year	Longbox Value / Value
Singles						
Qwest	PRO-CD-7071	City, The	CDJ	U.S.	1994	$3.00

Cliff, Jimmy

Label	Catalog Number	Title	Type	Country	Year	Longbox Value / Value
Full Length						
CBS	40002	Cliff Hanger	LP/BP	U.S.	1985	$14.00/$8.00
Singles						
Walt Disney Records		Hakuna Matata	CDJ	U.S.	1995	$8.00
Interscope	PRCD 5457-2	Higher And Higher	CDJ	U.S.	1992	$2.00
Chaos	77207	I Can See Clearly Now	CDJ	U.S.	1993	$2.00
JRS	808	I'm A Winner	CDJ	U.S.	1992	$2.00
JRS	808	Peace	CDJ	U.S.	1992	$3.00

Climax Blues Band

Label	Catalog Number	Title	Type	Country	Year	Longbox Value / Value
Full Length						
S-F Miles	222	Couldn't Get It Right	LP/LB	U.S.		$14.00/$8.00
S-F Miles	279	FM Live	LP/LB	U.S.		$14.00/$8.00
S-F Miles	556	Plays On	LP/LB	U.S.		$14.00/$8.00

Climax Chicago Blues Band

Label	Catalog Number	Title	Type	Country	Year	Longbox Value / Value
Full Length						
S-F Miles	555	Climax Chicago Blues Band	LP/LB	U.S.		$14.00/$8.00
S-F Miles	548	Lot Of Bottle	LP/LB	U.S.		$14.00/$8.00
S-F Miles	553	Rich Man	LP/LB	U.S.		$14.00/$8.00
S-F Miles	557	Tightly Knit	LP/LB	U.S.		$14.00/$8.00

Climb

Label	Catalog Number	Title	Type	Country	Year	Longbox Value / Value
Singles						
Toshiba	XP10-2041	Girl Like You	CD3	Japan	1988	$12.00/$3.00
Toshiba	XP10-2076	Try On	CD3	Japan	1989	$12.00/$3.00

Climie, Fisher

Label	Catalog Number	Title	Type	Country	Year	Longbox Value / Value
Full Length						
Capitol	93005	Coming In For the Kill	LP/LB	U.S.		$14.00/$8.00
Capitol	90514	Everything	LP/LB	U.S.		$14.00/$8.00
Singles						
EMI	203505-3	Facts of Love	CD3	Germany	1989	$8.00
Toshiba	TODP-2109	Facts of Love	CD3	Japan	1989	$12.00/$3.00
EMI	CDEM-103	Facts of Love	CD5	U.K.	1989	$8.00
EMI	203584-3	Fire on the Ocean	CD3	Germany	1989	$8.00
EMI	CDEM-112	Fire on the Ocean	CD5	U.K.	1989	$8.00
EMI	CDEM-66	I Won't Bleed For You	CD5	U.K.	1988	$8.00
EMI	CDEM-139	It's Not Supposed To Be That Way	CD5	U.K.	1990	$8.00
EMI	201691-2	Keeping the Mystery Alive	CD5	Germany	1988	$8.00
EMI	202416-2	Love Changes Everything	CD5	Germany	1988	$8.00
Toshiba	XP10-2019	Love Changes Everything	CD3	Japan	1988	$12.00/$3.00
EMI	CDEM-15	Love Changes Everything	CD5	U.K.	1988	$8.00
EMI	CDEM-47	Love Changes Everything	CD5	U.K.	1988	$8.00
EMI	CDEM-81	Love Like A River	CD5	U.K.	1988	$8.00
EMI	CDEM-33	Rise To the Occassion	CD5	U.K.	1988	$8.00
EMI	202597-2	This Is Me	CD5	Germany	1988	$8.00
EMI	CDEM-58	This Is Me	CD5	U.K.	1988	$8.00

Climie, Simon

Label	Catalog Number	Title	Type	Country	Year	Longbox Value / Value
Singles						
Epic	658773-2	Does Your Heart Still Break	CD5	U.K.	1992	$8.00
Epic	658902-2	Oh How the Years Go By	CD5	U.K.	1992	$8.00
Epic	658283-2	Soul Inspiration	CD5	U.K.	1992	$8.00

Cline, Patsy

Label	Catalog Number	Title	Type	Country	Year	Longbox Value / Value
Full Length						
MCA	CD33-3027	Collection Sampler, The	DJ/Smplr	U.S.	1991	$25.00
MCA	MCAD-8925	Commemorative Collection	LP/LB	U.S.		$14.00/$8.00
Eclipse	4865-2	Very Best Of Patsy Cline	LTD/LP	U.S.	1996	$18.00
CD in custom screen-printed square tin.						
Singles						
Eastwest	9031-73659-2	Crazy	CD5	Germany	1991	$10.00
MCA	DMCAT-1465	Crazy	CD5	U.K.	1990	$10.00
	116	Hungry For Love	CD5	U.S.	1994	$5.00
MCA	MCSTD-1465	I Fall To Pieces	CD5	U.K.	1990	$10.00

Clinton, George

Label	Catalog Number	Title	Type	Country	Year	Longbox Value / Value
Full Length						
Capitol	CDP-48424	Best Of	LP/LB	U.S.		$14.00/$8.00
Capitol	CDP-96267	R&B Skeletons	LP/LB	U.S.		$14.00/$8.00
Capitol	CDP-9635	Some Of My Best Jokes Are Friends	LP/LB	U.S.		$14.00/$8.00
Capitol	CDP-9637	You Shouldn't	LP/LB	U.S.		$14.00/$8.00
Singles						
Fox	0014	Erotic City	CDJ	U.S.	1993	$3.00
	BSK7760	If Anybody Gets Funked Up	CDJ	U.S.		$2.00
Paisley Park	PRO-CD-5995	Martial Law	CDJ	U.S.	1993	$2.00
Paisley Park	PRO-CD-5998	Martial Law	CDJ	U.S.	1993	$3.00
Paisley Park	9 41057-2	Paint the White House Black	CD5	U.S.	1993	$5.00
Paisley Park	PRO-CD-6450	Paint the White House Black	CDJ	U.S.	1993	$3.00
Paisley Park	PRO-CD-3717	Tweakin'	CDJ	U.S.	1989	$2.00
WEA	W-7557CD	Why Should I Dog U Out?	CD3	U.S.	1989	$8.00/$4.00
Paisley Park	PRO-CD-3438	Why Should I Dog U Out?	CDJ	U.S.	1989	$2.00

Clinton, Roger

Label	Catalog Number	Title	Type	Country	Year	Longbox Value / Value
Singles						
Pyramid	7085	Fantasy Of Love	CDJ	U.S.	1994	$3.00

Clio & Kay

Label	Catalog Number	Title	Type	Country	Year	Longbox Value / Value
Singles						
Victor	VDPS-1033	Keep On Dancing	CD3	Japan	1989	$12.00/$3.00
Victor	VIDP-39	What Goes Up	CD3	Japan	1991	$12.00/$3.00

Clivilles And Cole

Label	Catalog Number	Title	Type	Country	Year	Longbox Value / Value
Singles						
Columbia	44K 74135	Pride	CD5	U.S.	1991	$4.00

Clock Dva

Label	Catalog Number	Title	Type	Country	Year	Longbox Value / Value
Singles						
Efa	CD-01708	Act	CD5	Germany	1989	$7.00
Contempo	TEMPO-183	Bitstream	CD5	U.K.	1992	$7.00
Contempo	183	Bitstream	CD5	U.S.	1992	$5.00
Contempo	TEMPO-173	Final Program	CD5	U.K.	1991	$7.00
Efa	CD-01701	Hacker	CD5	Germany	1989	$7.00
Wax Trax	68	Hacker	CD5	U.S.	1989	$4.00
Efa	CD-01713	Sound Mirror	CD5	Germany	1990	$7.00
Wax Trax	9105	Sound Mirror	CD5	U.S.	1990	$4.00

Clooney, Rosemary

Label	Catalog Number	Title	Type	Country	Year	Longbox Value / Value
Full Length						
Toshiba	CP35-3078	Aurex Jazz Festival	LP	Japan		$25.00
CBS	32DP-618	Blue Rose	LP	Japan		$25.00
Mobile Fidelity	MFCD-850	Blue Rose	LP/LB	U.S.		$18.00/$15.00
CBS	32DP-671	Ring Around Rosie	LP	Japan		$25.00
Concord	4144	With Love	LP/BP	U.S.		$14.00/$8.00

Clooney, Rosemary, Woody Herman & Woody's Big Band

Label	Catalog Number	Title	Type	Country	Year	Longbox Value / Value
Full Length						
Concord Jazz	CCD-4226	My Buddy	LP/LB	U.S.†	1985	$14.00/$8.00

Close

Label	Catalog Number	Title	Type	Country	Year	Longbox Value / Value
Singles						
MCA	DMCAT-1351	Everytime I Try To Say Goodbye	CD5	U.K.	1989	$7.00

Close, Glenn

Label	Catalog Number	Title	Type	Country	Year	Longbox Value / Value
Singles						
Really Useful	1100	Perfect Year, The	CDJ	U.S.	1993	$2.00

Close Lobsters

Label	Catalog Number	Title	Type	Country	Year	Longbox Value / Value
Full Length						
Enigma	73333	Fox Heads Stalk This Land	LP/LB	U.S.		$12.00/$7.00
Enigma	73521	Headache Rhetoric	LP/LB	U.S.		$12.00/$7.00
Singles						
Fire	BLAZE-25CD	What Is There To Smile About	CD5	U.K.	1988	$7.00

Closer Than Close

Label	Catalog Number	Title	Type	Country	Year	Longbox Value / Value
Singles						
Slam Jam	4509-90283-2	New Life	CD5	U.K.	1992	$7.00
Warner Brothers	9031-76978-2	You Got A Hold On Me	CD5	U.K.	1992	$7.00

Clouds

Label	Catalog Number	Title	Type	Country	Year	Longbox Value / Value
Singles						
Red Eye	859 503	Bower Of Bliss	CD5	Australia	1993	$8.00
Elektra	PRCD 9134	Bower Of Bliss	CDJ	U.S.	1995	$3.00
Rough Trade	344-0369-3	Dude Electric Cell	CD5	Germany	1992	$7.00
Wobble	WOBBCD-002	Dude Electric Cell	CD5	U.K.	1992	$7.00

Clouseau

Label	Catalog Number	Title	Type	Country	Year	Longbox Value / Value
Singles						
		Ana	CD5	Germany		$7.00
Parlophone	119325-2	Close Encounters	CD5	Germany	1992	$7.00
Parlophone	CDR-6300	Close Encounters	CD5	U.K.	1992	$7.00

Club 69

Label	Catalog Number	Title	Type	Country	Year	Longbox Value / Value
Singles						
Capital	58308	Diva	CD5	U.S.	1994	$5.00
Capitol	8308	Diva	CD5	U.S.	1995	$6.00
FFRR	FCD-204	Let Me Be Your Underwear	CD5	U.K.	1992	$7.00
	DPRO 10500	Sugar Pie Guy	CDJ	U.S.		$2.00

Club House

Label	Catalog Number	Title	Type	Country	Year	Longbox Value / Value
Singles						
ZYX	6516-8	Deep In My Heart	CD5	Germany	1991	$6.00
Alfa	ALCB 360	Deep In My Heart	CD5	Japan	1991	$10.00
Atlantic	PRCD 4032-2	Deep In My Heart	CDJ	U.S.	1991	$2.00
Alfa	09B3	I'm A Week	CD3	Japan	1989	$12.00/$3.00
Alfa	ALCB-575	I'm Fallen To	CD5	Japan	1992	$10.00
		Light My Fire	CD5	U.K.		$10.00
		Light My Fire	CD5	U.K.		$10.00
Second version.						
ZYX	7999-8	You And I	CD5	U.S.	1996	$6.00

Club Ice

Label	Catalog Number	Title	Type	Country	Year	Longbox Value / Value
Singles						
Black Mkt.	BMITD-001	Manhassett	CD5	U.K.	1992	$8.00

Club Nouveau

Label	Catalog Number	Title	Type	Country	Year	Longbox Value / Value
Full Length						
Warner Brothers	9 25687-2	Listen To the Message	LP/LB	U.S.		$14.00/$8.00
Singles						
Quality	19116	I Like Your Way	CDJ	U.S.	1992	$2.00
Pioneer	10SW-4	It's A Cold Cold World	CD3	Japan	1988	$12.00/$3.00

Label	Catalog Number	Title	Type	Country	Year	Longbox Value / Value
WEA	920680-2	Lean On Me	CD3	Germany	1989	$8.00
		Let It Go	CDJ	U.S.		$2.00
Warner Brothers	PRO-CD-3736	No Friend of Mine	CDJ	U.S.	1989	$2.00
Quality	19100	Oh Happy Day	CDJ	U.S.	1992	$2.00
Warner Brothers	PRO-CD-3912	Under A Nouveau Groove	CDJ	U.S.	1989	$2.00

Club Z

Singles

Label	Catalog Number	Title	Type	Country	Year	Longbox Value / Value
PWL	PWCD-249	I Wanna Be Someone	CD5	U.K.	1992	$7.00

Clubland

Singles

Label	Catalog Number	Title	Type	Country	Year	Longbox Value / Value
Alfa	ALCB-512	Hold On	CD5	Japan	1992	$10.00
Great Jones	611	Hold On	CDJ	U.S.	1991	$2.00
		Hypnotized	CDJ	U.S.		$2.00
BMG	663480	Let's Get Busy	CD5	Germany	1990	$8.00
Geffen	PRO-CD-4159	Let's Get Busy	CDJ	U.S.	1990	$2.00
Alfa	ALDB-119	Pump the Sound	CD5	Germany	1991	$8.00
ZYX	6461-8	Pump the Sound	CD5	Germnay	1991	$8.00
Alfa	ALCB-576	Set Me Free	CD5	Japan	1992	$10.00
Great Jones	615	Set Me Free	CDJ	U.S.	1991	$2.00

Clubzone

Singles

Label	Catalog Number	Title	Type	Country	Year	Longbox Value / Value
	59006	Hands Up	CD5	U.S.	1994	$5.00

Cluster

Full Length

Label	Catalog Number	Title	Type	Country	Year	Longbox Value / Value
Sky	CD-3005	Sowieso	LP	Germany		$20.00

Clutch

Full Length

Label	Catalog Number	Title	Type	Country	Year	Longbox Value / Value
Eastwest	PRCD 5177-2	A Promo Named Marcus	DJ/Smplr	U.S.	1993	$5.00

Singles

Label	Catalog Number	Title	Type	Country	Year	Longbox Value / Value
	PRCD 9207-2	Escape From the Prison Planet	CDJ	U.S.		$2.00
Earache	MOSH 74CD	Passive Restraints	CD5	U.S.	1993	$5.00
Eastwest	PRCD 9174-2	Songs Of Much Gravity	CDJ	U.S.	1993	$6.00

Co-Jack

Singles

Label	Catalog Number	Title	Type	Country	Year	Longbox Value / Value
Polygram	877491-2	Body Heat	CD5	Germany	1990	$7.00
Polygram	879005-2	Dope Slam-Don't Be Violent	CD5	Germany	1991	$7.00

Coachman

Singles

Label	Catalog Number	Title	Type	Country	Year	Longbox Value / Value
New All.	361-1035-2	Failure To Thrive	CD5	Germany	1991	$7.00
New All.	35	Failure To Thrive	CD5	U.S.	1991	$4.00

Coasters

Full Length

Label	Catalog Number	Title	Type	Country	Year	Longbox Value / Value
Atlantic	33111-2	Greatest Hits	LP/LB	U.S.		$14.00/$8.00

Coats, J.

Singles

Label	Catalog Number	Title	Type	Country	Year	Longbox Value / Value
Smash Box	TEDP-24	You Gotta Go	CD3	Japan	1991	$12.00/$3.00

Cobb, Junie C.

Full Length

Label	Catalog Number	Title	Type	Country	Year	Longbox Value / Value
Original Jazz	1825	Chicago Living Legends	LTD/LP	U.S.		$18.00/$15.00

Cobham, Billy

Singles

Label	Catalog Number	Title	Type	Country	Year	Longbox Value / Value
		Same Ole Love	CDJ	U.S.		$2.00

Cobos, Luis

Singles

Label	Catalog Number	Title	Type	Country	Year	Longbox Value / Value
Epic	656005-2	Turnabout	CD5	U.K.	1990	$7.00

Cobra

Singles

Label	Catalog Number	Title	Type	Country	Year	Longbox Value / Value
ZYX	8005-8	Born 2 Love U	CD5	U.S.	1996	$6.00

Cochran, Brenda

Singles

Label	Catalog Number	Title	Type	Country	Year	Longbox Value / Value
Polydor	PZCD-133	Homeland	CD5	U.K.	1991	$8.00
Polydor	PZCD-73	I Want To Know What Love Is	CD5	U.K.	1990	$8.00

Cochran, Eddie

Full Length

Label	Catalog Number	Title	Type	Country	Year	Longbox Value / Value
EMI	CDP 46580	Best Of	LP/LB	U.S.		$14.00/$8.00
Liberty	791188-2	I'm Ready	LP	Germany		$13.00
Grand Prix	CD-860702	Legend Lives On	LP	Germany		$13.00
Rockstar	RSRCD-001	Rock 'N' Roll Legend	LP	Germany		$13.00
Liberty	791190-2	Somethin' Else	LP	Germany		$13.00
Liberty	791189-2	Summertime Blues	LP	Germany		$13.00
Liberty	791191-2	Three Steps To Heaven	LP	Germany		$13.00

Singles

Label	Catalog Number	Title	Type	Country	Year	Longbox Value / Value
Liberty	202356-2	C'mon Everybody	CD5	Germany	1988	$8.00
Liberty	CDEDDIE-501	C'mon Everybody	CD5	U.K.	1988	$8.00
Old Gold	OG 6183	C'mon Everybody	CD5	U.K.	1992	$10.00
Aris	885823	Summertime Blues	CD3	Germany	1990	$8.00
Old Gold	OG 6179	Three Steps To Heaven	CD5	U.K.	1992	$10.00

Cochrane, Tom (And Red Rider)

Full Length

Label	Catalog Number	Title	Type	Country	Year	Longbox Value / Value
Westwood One		In Concert	RS	U.S.	1992	$50.00
	2 CD set. With Bryan Adams, Airdate: 6/8/92					
Westwood One		In Concert	RS	U.S.	1992	$50.00
	Airdate: 7/20/92.					
		Mad Mad World	DJ/LP	Canada		$25.00
	CD of album plus 2nd interview disc.					
Capitol	CDP 48450	Neruda	LP/LB	U.S.		$14.00/$8.00
EMI	CDP 46432	Tom Cochrane And the Red Rider	LP/LB	U.S.		$14.00/$8.00
RCA		Victory Day	LP/BP	U.S.		$14.00/$8.00

Singles

Label	Catalog Number	Title	Type	Country	Year	Longbox Value / Value
		Big League	CDJ	Canada	1989	$6.00
RCA	PD-49382	Big League	CD5	Germany	1989	$8.00
RCA	8751	Big League	CDJ	U.S.	1988	$2.00
		Calling America	CDJ	U.S.		$2.00
		Good Times	CDJ	Canada		$6.00
		I Wish You Well	CD5	U.K.		$10.00
		I Wish You Well	CD5	U.K.		$10.00
	Second version.					
	DPRO10247	I Wish You Well	CDJ	U.S.		$2.00
Capitol	TODP-2370	Life Is A Highway	CD3	Japan	1991	$13.00/$4.00
Capitol	DPRO-7913	Life Is A Highway	CDJ	U.S.	1991	$3.00
		Mad Mad World	CDJ	Canada		$6.00

Company	Disk Number	Title	Type	Country	Year	Longbox Value / Value
Capitol	DPRO-79212	No Regrets	CDJ	U.S.	1991	$2.00
		Sinking Like the Sunset	CDJ	Canada		$6.00
Capitol		Washed Away	CDJ	Canada	1991	$6.00
Capitol	TODP-2380	Washed Away	CD3	Japan	1991	$12.00/$4.00
Capitol	15938	Washed Away	CD5	U.S.	1991	$5.00
Capitol	DPRO-79441	Washed Away	CDJ	U.S.	1991	$2.00

Cock Robin

Full Length

Company	Disk Number	Title	Type	Country	Year	Longbox Value / Value
Columbia	CK-39582	Cock Robin	LP/BP	U.S.†	1985	$14.00/$8.00
Columbia	CK-45192	First Love Last Rites	LP/LB	U.S.		$14.00/$8.00

Singles

Company	Disk Number	Title	Type	Country	Year	Longbox Value / Value
Columbia	CSK 2849	Biggest Fool of All	CDJ	U.S.	1987	$2.00
Columbia	CSK 73479	It's Only Make Believe	CDJ	U.S.	1990	$2.00
CBS	654848-3	Just Around the Corner	CD3	Germany	1989	$8.00
CBS	655673-3	Manzanar	CD3	Germany	1990	$8.00
CBS	655475-3	Worlds Apart	CD3	Germany	1989	$8.00
Columbia	655808-2	Worlds Apart	CD5	U.K.	1989	$8.00

Cockburn, Bruce

Full Length

Company	Disk Number	Title	Type	Country	Year	Longbox Value / Value
Columbia	CSK 6649	1994 Christmas Sampler	DJ/Smplr	U.S.		$10.00
Gold Castle		Big Circumstance	LP	U.S.		$10.00
		Bruce Cockburn	LD	U.S.		$20.00
Columbia	CSK 4222	Burning Lights/Primer	DJ/LP	U.S.	1991	$20.00
2 CD set.						
Columbia	CSK 6649	Christmas Sampler	DJ/Smplr	U.S.	1994	$12.00
Plaene	PCD-88482	Humans	LP	Germany		$13.00
Columbia		Live	DJ/Smplr	Canada		$20.00
Columbia		Radio Special, The	DJ/Intvw	Canada		$30.00
Plaene	PCD-88406	Rumors Of Glory	LP	Germany		$13.00
Plaene	PCD-88392	Stealing Fire	LP	Germany		$20.00
A&M	CD-80012	Stealing Fire	LP/LB	U.S.†	1985	$14.00/$8.00
Plaene	PCD-88481	Trouble With Normal	LP	Germany		$13.00
Gold Castle		Trouble With Normal	LP/BP	U.S.		$14.00/$8.00
Goldcastle	71305	Waiting For A Miracle	LP/BP	U.S.		$14.00/$8.00
Plaene	PCD-88477	World Of Wonders	LP	Germany		$13.00

Singles

Company	Disk Number	Title	Type	Country	Year	Longbox Value / Value
Columbia	657601-2	A Dream Like Mine	CD5	Germany	1991	$8.00
Columbia	657601-2	A Dream Like Mine	CD5	U.K.	1991	$8.00
Columbia	CSK 4192	A Dream Like Mine	CDJ	U.S.	1991	$2.00
Columbia	CSK 6134	Burton Of the Angel	CDJ	U.S.	1994	$3.00
Columbia		Cry Of A Tiny Babe	CDJ	Canada		$6.00
Columbia		Don't Feel Your Touch	CDJ	Canada		$6.00
Columbia		Great Big Love	CDJ	Canada		$6.00
Columbia	CSK 4413	Great Big Love	CDJ	U.S.	1991	$6.00
Columbia		If A Tree Falls	CDJ	Canada		$6.00
Columbia		If A Tree Falls	CDJ	U.S.		$2.00
Columbia	CSK 5671	Listen For the Laugh	CDJ	U.S.	1994	$7.00
Columbia		Mighty Trucks Of Midnight	CDJ	Canada		$6.00
Columbia		Somebody Touched Me	CDJ	Canada		$6.00
Gold Castle	79623	Where the Death Squad Lives	CDJ	U.S.	1988	$2.00

Cocker, Joe

Full Length

Company	Disk Number	Title	Type	Country	Year	Longbox Value / Value
BBC Radio		BBC Classic Tracks	RS	U.S.	1991	$20.00
	Airdate: 7/11/91.					
BBC Radio		BBC Classic Tracks	RS	U.S.	1991	$20.00
	Airdate: 7/22/91.					
BBC Radio		BBC Classic Tracks	RS	U.S.	1992	$20.00
	Airdate: 8/3/92.					
BBC		BBC Classic Tracks	RS	U.S.	1993	$20.00
	Airdate: 7/26/93.					
Teldec	8 27476	Best Of	LP	Germany		$25.00
EMI		Best Of Live	LP/VHS	U.K.	1994	$35.00
Capitol	CDP-46038	Civilized Man	LP/LB	U.S.†	1985	$14.00/$8.00
A&M	CD-3175	I Can Stand A Little Rain	LP/LB	U.S.		$14.00/$8.00
DIR		King Biscuit Flour Hour	RS	U.S.	1988	$35.00
	Airdate: 12/11/88.					
DIR		King Biscuit Flour Hour	RS	U.S.	1989	$35.00
	Airdate: 8/13/89.					
DIR		King Biscuit Flour Hour	RS	U.S.	1991	$35.00
	Airdate: 7/21/91.					
DIR		King Biscuit Flour Hour	RS	U.S.	1992	$30.00
	Airdate: 8/2/92.					
DIR		King Biscuit Flour Hour	RS	U.S.	1993	$25.00
	Airdate: 4/4/93.					
DIR		King Biscuit Flour Hour	RS	U.S.	1994	$25.00
	Airdate: 7/10/94.					
DIR		King Biscuit Flour Hour	RS	U.S.	1995	$25.00
	Airdate: 5/28/95.					
		Long Voyage Home	DJ/Smplr	U.S.		$15.00
Pioneer	PA-85-133	Mad Dogs & Englishmen	LD	U.S.	1985	$30.00
Mobile Fidelity	MFCD-824	Mad Dogs & Englishmen	LP/LB	U.S.†	1985	$40.00/$35.00
	2 CD set.					
Pioneer	PA-85-133	Mad Dogs & Englishmen	LD	U.S.	1990	$40.00
	Digital audio.					
Radio Today		Rock Stars	RS	U.S.	1989	$30.00
	2 CD set. Airdate: 10/16/89					
Westwood One		Superstar Concert	RS	U.S.	1992	$30.00
	2 CD set. Airdate: 6/28/92					
Westwood One		Superstars	RS	U.S.	1995	$40.00
	2 CD set. Airdate: 5/1/95.					
Media America		Up Close	RS	U.S.	1994	$45.00
	2 CD set.					

Singles

Company	Disk Number	Title	Type	Country	Year	Longbox Value / Value
Capitol	654686-3	Don't You Love Me Anymore	CD3	Germany	1989	$9.00
Capitol	CDCL-493	Don't You Love Me Anymore	CD5	U.K.	1988	$9.00
Capitol	CDCL-645	Feels Like Forever	CD5	U.K.	1992	$9.00
Capitol	DPRO-79256	Feels Like Forever	CDJ	U.S.	1992	$3.00
EMI	203629-3	Fever	CD3	Germany	1989	$9.00
		Have A Little Faith	CD5	U.K.		$10.00
	Second version.					
550 Music	77797	Have A Little Faith In Me	CDJ	U.S.	1994	$6.00
EMI	204619-2	I Can Hear the River	CD5	Germany	1992	$9.00
	520237	I Can Stand A Little	CD5	U.S.	1994	$5.00
EMI	203504-3	I Will Live For You	CD3	Germany	1989	$9.00
		Let The Healing Begin	CD5	U.K.		$10.00
		Let The Healing Begin	CD5	U.K.		$10.00
	Second version.					
EMI	203969-2	Live In the Promised Land	CD5	Germany	1990	$9.00
Capitol	DPRO-79211	Love Is Alive	CDJ	U.S.	1992	$3.00
EMI		Night Calls	CD5	Australia	1991	$10.00
EMI	204523-2	Night Calls	CD5	Germany	1991	$9.00

Label	Catalog Number	Title	Type	Country	Year	Longbox Value / Value
Capitol	DPRO-79584	Night Calls	CDJ	U.S.	1991	$3.00
Capitol	DPRO-79210	Now That the Magic Is Gone	CDJ	U.S.	1992	$3.00
		Simple Things	CD5	U.K.		$10.00
		Simple Things	CD5	U.K.		$10.00
Second version.						
550 Music	77660	Simple Things	CDJ	U.S.	1994	$6.00
EMI	202478-2	Two Wrongs	CD5	Germany	1988	$9.00
Capitol	CDCL-465	Unchain My Heart	CD5	U.K.	1989	$9.00
EMI	203824-2	What Are You Doing With A Fool Like Me	CD5	Germany	1990	$9.00
Capitol	CDCL-572	What Are You Doing With A Fool Like Me	CD5	U.K.	1990	$9.00
Capitol	DPRO-79020	What Are You Doing With A Fool Like Me	CDJ	U.S.	1990	$3.00
EMI	203375-3	When the Night Comes	CD3	Germany	1989	$9.00
Capitol	CDCL-535	When the Night Comes	CD5	U.K.	1989	$9.00
Capitol	DPRO-79898	When the Night Comes	CDJ	U.S.	1989	$3.00
Capitol	DPRO-79710	When the Night Comes	CDJ	U.S.	1989	$3.00
Eastr West	246875-2	With A Little Help From My Friends	CD5	Germany	1989	$9.00
Castle	CD3-8	With A Little Help From My Friends	CD3	U.K.	1988	$9.00
Teichiku	TEDP-4	You Are So Beautiful	CD3	Japan	1990	$13.00/$4.00
Capitol	DPRO-79273	You Can Leave	CDJ	U.S.	1990	$3.00

Cocker, Joe & Bekka Bramlett

Singles

Label	Catalog Number	Title	Type	Country	Year	Longbox Value / Value
		Take Me Home	CD5	U.K.		$10.00
		Take Me Home	CD5	U.K.		$10.00
Second version.						

Cocteau Twins

Full Length

Label	Catalog Number	Title	Type	Country	Year	Longbox Value / Value
Fontana	PCD 436	Canadian Music Sampler	DJ/Smplr	Canada		$40.00
Capitol	DPRO-79065	Cocteau Twins	DJ/Smplr	U.S.	1991	$25.00
Relativity	8040	Pink Opaque	LP/LB	U.S.		$15.00/$10.00
4AD	510	Tiny Dynamite	LP/LB	U.S.		$15.00/$10.00

Singles

Label	Catalog Number	Title	Type	Country	Year	Longbox Value / Value
4AD	BAD-501CD	Aikea-Guinea	CD5	U.K.	1992	$10.00
Creation	COCY-5179	Athol Brose	CD5	Japan	1992	$16.00
Capitol	DPRO-79330	Bluebeard	CDJ	U.S.	1993	$6.00
4AD		Carolyn's Fingers	CDJ	U.S.		$10.00
Capitol	DPRO-79405	Carolyn's Fingers	CDJ	U.S.	1988	$6.00
Fontana	8627172	Evangeline	CD5	Canada	1994	$7.00
Capitol	DPRO-79259	Evangeline	CDJ	U.S.	1993	$6.00
4AD		Heaven Or Las Vegas	CDJ	U.S.		$6.00
Capitol	DPRO-79291	Heaven Or Las Vegas	CDJ	U.S.	1990	$6.00
Capitol	DPRO-79291	Heaven Or Las Vegas	CDJ	U.S.	1990	$7.00
Capitol	DPRO-79498	I Wear Your Ring	CDJ	U.S.	1990	$6.00
4AD	BAD-0011CD	Iceblink Luck	CD5	U.K.	1990	$10.00
Capitol	C2 15626	Iceblink Luck	CD5	U.S.	1990	$5.00
Capitol	DPRO-79686	Iceblink Luck	CDJ	U.S.	1990	$6.00
4AD	BAD-610CD	Love Easy Tears	CD5	U.K.	1992	$10.00
4AD	BAD-213CD	Lullabyes	CD5	U.K.	1992	$10.00
4AD		Milk and Kisses	CDJ	U.S.		$12.00
		Otherness	CD5	U.K.	1995	$10.00
4AD	BAD-303CD	Peppermint	CD5	U.K.	1992	$10.00
4AD	BAD-405CD	Spangle Maker	CD5	U.K.	1992	$10.00
4AD		Summerhead	CDJ	U.S.		$7.00
Capitol	DPRO-79296	Summerhead	CDJ	U.S.	1993	$7.00
Capitol	DPRO-79300	Summerland	CDJ	U.S.	1993	$6.00
4AD	BAD-314CD	Sunburst And Snowblind	CD5	U.K.	1992	$10.00
		Twilights	CD5	U.K.	1995	$10.00
		Twilights	CD5	U.K.	1995	$11.00
		Violaine	CDJ	U.K.		$15.00
		Violaine	CD5	U.K.	1996	$10.00
		Violaine	CD5	U.K.	1996	$10.00
Second version.						

Code 61

Full Length

Label	Catalog Number	Title	Type	Country	Year	Longbox Value / Value
Aris	880881	Drop the Deal	LP	Germany		$15.00

Singles

Label	Catalog Number	Title	Type	Country	Year	Longbox Value / Value
BCM	20184	Drop the Deal	CD5	Germany	1989	$7.00

Code Red

Singles

Label	Catalog Number	Title	Type	Country	Year	Longbox Value / Value
Citybeat	CBE-769CD	Dreamer Dream	CD5	U.K.	1992	$7.00

Cody, Phil

Full Length

Label	Catalog Number	Title	Type	Country	Year	Longbox Value / Value
		Sons Of Intemperance Offering 1995	DJ/Smplr	U.S.	1995	$14.00

Coe, David Allen

Full Length

Label	Catalog Number	Title	Type	Country	Year	Longbox Value / Value
Columbia	CK-40185	17 Greatest Hits	LP/BP	U.S.†	1985	$14.00/$8.00

Coffey, Dennis

Singles

Label	Catalog Number	Title	Type	Country	Year	Longbox Value / Value
Orpheus	4577	Under the Moonlight	CDJ	U.S.	1990	$2.00

Cohen, Leonard

Full Length

Label	Catalog Number	Title	Type	Country	Year	Longbox Value / Value
Columbia	CSK 5249	Live From the Complex L.A.	DJ/Smplr	U.S.	1993	$40.00

Singles

Label	Catalog Number	Title	Type	Country	Year	Longbox Value / Value
Columbia	651599-2	Ain't No Cure For Love	CD5	Germany	1988	$8.00
Columbia	CSK 5607	Be For Real	CDJ	U.S.	1993	$2.00
Columbia	CSK 4932	Closing Time	CDJ	U.S.	1992	$2.00
Columbia	44K 74778	Democracy	CD5	U.S.	1992	$5.00
Columbia	CSK 4867	Democracy	CDJ	U.S.	1992	$2.00
Columbia	654565-3	First We Take Manhattan	CD3	Germany	1988	$8.00
Columbia	654565-3	First We Take Manhattan	CD3	U.K.	1988	$8.00
Columbia	651352-2	First We Take Manhattan	CD5	U.K.	1988	$8.00
Columbia	CSK 5148	Future, The	CDJ	U.S.	1993	$2.00
Columbia	651522-2	I'm Your Man	CD5	U.K.	1988	$8.00

Cohen, Linda

Full Length

Label	Catalog Number	Title	Type	Country	Year	Longbox Value / Value
Tomato	269611	Angel Alley	LP/BP	U.S.		$12.00/$7.00

Cohn, Al and Freddie Green

Full Length

Label	Catalog Number	Title	Type	Country	Year	Longbox Value / Value
Bluebird	6465	Natural Rhythm	LP/BP	U.S.		$12.00/$7.00

Cohn, Marc

Singles

Label	Catalog Number	Title	Type	Country	Year	Longbox Value / Value
Atlantic	PRCD 4102-2	29 Ways	CDJ	U.S.	1991	$2.00
Atlantic	7567-96395-2	Ghost Train	CD5	Germany	1992	$8.00
Atlantic	AMDY-5081	Ghost Train	CD3	Japan	1992	$12.00/$3.00
Atlantic	PRCD 4505-2	Ghost Train	CDJ	U.S.	1992	$2.00
Atlantic	PRCD 5172-2	Paper Walls	CDJ	U.S.	1993	$2.00
Atlantic	PRCD 5251-2	Rainy Season, The	CDJ	U.S.	1993	$2.00
Atlantic	7567-86004-2	Silver Thunderbird	CD5	Germany	1991	$8.00
Atlantic	PRCD 3943-2	Silver Thunderbird	CDJ	U.S.	1991	$2.00
Atlantic	A-7516CD	Strangers In A Car	CD5	U.K.	1992	$8.00
Atlantic	7567-85922-2	True Companion	CD5	Germany	1991	$8.00
Atlantic	7567-85921-2	True Companion	CD5	Germany	1991	$8.00
Atlantic	A-7583CDX	True Companion	CD5	U.K.	1991	$8.00
Atlantic	A-7583CD	True Companion	CD5	U.K.	1991	$8.00
Atlantic	PRCD 4213-2	True Companion	CDJ	U.S.	1991	$2.00
		Turn On Your Radio	CDJ	U.S.	1995	$3.00
Warner	32-84882	Walking In Memphis	CD5	Canada	1994	$6.00
Atlantic	7567-86038-2	Walking In Memphis	CD5	Germany	1991	$8.00
Atlantic	A-7747CD	Walking In Memphis	CD5	U.K.	1991	$8.00
Atlantic		Walking In Memphis	CDJ	U.S.	1991	$2.00
Atlantic		Walking Through the World	CD5	U.K.	1993	$8.00
Atlantic		Walking Through the World	CD5	U.K.	1993	$8.00
Second version.						
Atlantic	PRCD 5066-2	Walking Through the World	CDJ	U.S.	1993	$2.00

Coil

Singles

Label	Catalog Number	Title	Type	Country	Year	Longbox Value / Value
Wax Trax	9144	Snow	CD5	U.S.	1990	$5.00
Wax Trax	13	Tainted Love	CD5	U.S.	1990	$5.00
Efa	CD-1487	Window Pane	CD5	Germany	1990	$5.00
Torso	TORSOCD-174	Window Pane	CD5	U.K.	1990	$8.00
Wax Trax	9142	Window Pane	CD5	U.S.	1990	$5.00

Coil, Pat

Singles

Label	Catalog Number	Title	Type	Country	Year	Longbox Value / Value
Sheffield		Schemes And Dreams	CDJ	U.S.	1994	$2.00

Cola Boy

Singles

Label	Catalog Number	Title	Type	Country	Year	Longbox Value / Value
Arista	664717	He Is Cola	CD5	U.K.	1991	$7.00
Arista	664526	Seven Ways To Love	CD5	Germany	1991	$7.00
Arista	664526	Seven Ways To Love	CD5	U.K.	1991	$7.00

Cold Chisel

Singles

Label	Catalog Number	Title	Type	Country	Year	Longbox Value / Value
		Three Big Hits	CD5	Australia	1994	$14.00
		Three Big Hits	CD5	Australia	1994	$14.00
Second version.						
		Three Big Hits	CD5	Australia	1994	$14.00
Third version.						

Cold Steel

Singles

Label	Catalog Number	Title	Type	Country	Year	Longbox Value / Value
Rough Trade	354-0014-3	Bracing the Fall	CD5	Germany	1992	$7.00

Cold Sweat

Full Length

Label	Catalog Number	Title	Type	Country	Year	Longbox Value / Value
Polygram	834428	Plays J.B.	LP/BP	U.S.		$14.00/$8.00

Singles

Label	Catalog Number	Title	Type	Country	Year	Longbox Value / Value
MCA	CD45 1051	Let's Make Love Tonight	CDJ	U.S.	1990	$2.00

Cold Water Flat

Singles

Label	Catalog Number	Title	Type	Country	Year	Longbox Value / Value
MCA	MCA5P3411	King Of the Underground	CDJ	U.S.		$2.00
Fort Apache	3255	Magnetic North Pole	CDJ	U.S.	1994	$2.00
Fort Apache	3323	Magnetic North Pole	CDJ	U.S.	1995	$2.00

Coldcut

Full Length

Label	Catalog Number	Title	Type	Country	Year	Longbox Value / Value
Warner Brothers	9 25974-2	What's That Noise	LP/LB	U.S.		$14.00/$8.00

Singles

Label	Catalog Number	Title	Type	Country	Year	Longbox Value / Value
Intercord	825-287	Christmas Break	CD5	Germany	1989	$8.00
Big Life	CCUT-7CD	Christmas Break	CD5	U.K.	1989	$8.00
Intercord	825-256	Doctor In the House	CD5	Germany	1988	$8.00
Big Life	CCUT-2CD	Doctor In the House	CD5	U.K.	1988	$8.00
Intercord	825-292	Find A Way	CD5	Germany	1990	$8.00
Big Life	CCUT-8CD	Find A Way	CD5	U.K.	1990	$8.00
Intercord	825-274	My Telephone	CD3	Germany	1989	$8.00
Big Life	CCUT-6CD	My Telephone	CD5	U.K.	1989	$8.00
Intercord	825-271	People Hold On	CD5	Germany	1989	$8.00
Big Life	CCUT-5CD	People Hold On	CD5	U.K.	1989	$8.00
Reprise	PRO-CD-3658	People Hold On	CDJ	U.S.	1989	$2.00
Intercord	825-264	Stop This Crazy Thing	CD5	Germany	1988	$8.00
Big Life	CCUT-4CD	Stop This Crazy Thing	CD3	U.K.	1988	$8.00
Tommy Boy	3849	Stop This Crazy Thing	CDJ	U.S.	1989	$2.00

Coldjam

Singles

Label	Catalog Number	Title	Type	Country	Year	Longbox Value / Value
Intercord	827-203	Last Night A DJ Saved My Life	CD5	Germany	1990	$7.00
Big Wave	BWRCD-39	Last Night A DJ Saved My Life	CD5	U.K.	1990	$7.00

Cole, Debbie

Singles

Label	Catalog Number	Title	Type	Country	Year	Longbox Value / Value
Next Plateau	1078	Could You Be Loved	CDJ	U.S.	1993	$2.00
Night Belle		You Hold the Key	CDJ	U.S.	1993	$2.00

Cole, Freddy

Singles

Label	Catalog Number	Title	Type	Country	Year	Longbox Value / Value
Fantasy	3	Count To Ten	CDJ	U.S.	1995	$3.00

Cole, Gardner

Full Length

Label	Catalog Number	Title	Type	Country	Year	Longbox Value / Value
Warner Brothers		It's Your Life	DJ/LP	U.S.		$8.00
Warner Brothers	9 25739-2	Triangles	LP/LB	U.S.		$14.00/$8.00

Singles

Label	Catalog Number	Title	Type	Country	Year	Longbox Value / Value
		In A Big Way	CDJ	U.S.		$2.00
Warner Brothers	PRO-CD-3192	Live It Up	CDJ	U.S.	1988	$2.00
		Whatever It Takes	CDJ	U.S.		$2.00

Cole, Holly

Full Length

Label	Catalog Number	Title	Type	Country	Year	Longbox Value / Value
		Blame It On My Youth	DJ/Smplr	Canada		$15.00

Singles

Label	Catalog Number	Title	Type	Country	Year	Longbox Value / Value
Toshiba	TODP-2362	Calling You	CD3	Japan	1992	$12.00/$3.00
EMI	DPRO-79209	Calling You	CDJ	U.S.	1991	$2.00
		Cry	CDJ	Canada		$6.00
EMI	DPRO-79844	Don't Smoke In Bed	CDJ	U.S.	1993	$3.00
EMI	TODP-2385	Downtown	CD3	Japan	1992	$12.00/$3.00
EMI	DPRO-79209	God Will	CDJ	U.S.	1992	$2.00
		Talk To Me Baby	CDJ	Canada		$6.00
EMI	DPRO-79370	Trust In Me	CDJ	U.S.	1992	$2.00

Cole, Holly Trio

Label	Catalog Number	Title	Type	Country	Year	Longbox Value / Value
Full Length						
		Musical Truth	DJ/Smplr	Canada	1993	$35.00

Cole, Jude

Label	Catalog Number	Title	Type	Country	Year	Longbox Value / Value
Full Length						
	PRCD 7037	AAA Sampler	DJ/Smplr	U.S.		$7.00
Reprise	PRO-CD-5632	Start the Car	DJ/LP	U.S.	1992	$8.00
Singles						
WEA	921565-2	Baby, It's Tonight	CD5	Germany	1990	$8.00
WEA	W-9869CD	Baby, It's Tonight	CD5	U.K.	1990	$8.00
Reprise	PRO-CD-4013	Baby, It's Tonight	CDJ	U.S.	1990	$2.00
	PRCD 70592	Believe In You	CDJ	U.S.		$2.00
Reprise	PRO-CD-4771	Compared To What	CDJ	U.S.	1991	$2.00
Reprise	PRO-CD-4495	House Full of Reasons	CDJ	U.S.	1991	$2.00
	PRCD 71252	Speed of Life	CDJ	U.S.		$2.00
Reprise	PRO-CD-5629	Start the Car	CDJ	U.S.	1992	$2.00
Reprise	PRO-CD-5642	Start the Car	CDJ	U.S.	1992	$7.00
Reprise	PRO-CD-5842	Tell the Truth	CDJ	U.S.	1992	$2.00
Reprise	PRO-CD-5897	Tell the Truth	CDJ	U.S.	1992	$2.00
Reprise	PRO-CD-4337	Time For Letting Go	CDJ	U.S.	1990	$2.00
Warner Brothers	PRO-CD-2864	You Were In My Heart	CDJ	U.S.		$2.00

Cole, Lloyd

Label	Catalog Number	Title	Type	Country	Year	Longbox Value / Value
Full Length						
Polydor	Weirdone A/B	Don't Get Weird On Me Babe	DJ/LP	U.K.	1991	$20.00
2 CD set.						
		Lloyd Cole	DJ/LP	U.S.		$12.00
Singles						
		Baby	CD5	U.K.	1996	$10.00
		Baby	CD5	U.K.	1996	$10.00
Second version.						
Polydor	COLCD 16	Butterfly	CD5	U.K.	1992	$8.00
Polydor	COLCD-12	Don't Look Back	CD5	U.K.	1990	$8.00
Polydor	COLCD-13	Downtown	CD5	U.K.	1990	$8.00
Capitol	DPRO-79003	Downtown	CDJ	U.S.	1990	$3.00
Polydor	COLCD-10	Forest Fire	CD5	U.K.	1989	$8.00
Polydor	COLCD-9	From the Hip	CD5	U.K.	1988	$8.00
Polydor	887246-2	Jennifer She Said	CD5	Germany	1988	$8.00
Polydor	P13P-30009	Jennifer She Said	CD3	Japan	1988	$15.00/$3.00
Polydor	COLCD-8	Jennifer She Said	CD5	U.K.	1988	$8.00
		Like Lovers Do	CD5	U.K.		$10.00
		Like Lovers Do	CD5	U.K.		$10.00
Second version.						
		Like You'd Like To Save the World	CD5	U.K.		$9.00
		Like You'd Like To Save the World	CD5	U.K.		$9.00
Second version.						
Fontana	VIBES 2	Morning Is Broken	CD5	U.K.	1993	$8.00
Rykodisc	RCD5 1037	Morning Is Broken	CDJ	U.S.	1994	$6.00
Polydor	COLCD-11	No Blue Skies	CD5	U.K.	1990	$8.00
Capitol	DPRO-79944	No Blue Skies	CDJ	U.S.	1990	$3.00
Phonogram	867567-2	She's A Girl And I'm A Man	CD5	Germany	1991	$8.00
Capitol	C2 15753	She's A Girl And I'm A Man	CD5	U.S.	1991	$5.00
Capitol	DPRO-79834	She's A Girl And I'm A Man	CDJ	U.S.	1991	$3.00
		So You'd Like To Save The World	CD5	U.K.		$10.00
		So You'd Like To Save The World	CD5	U.K.		$10.00
Second version.						
Capitol	DPRO-79045	Tell Your Sister	CDJ	U.S.	1991	$3.00
Polydor	COLCD-15	Weeping Wine	CD5	U.K.	1991	$8.00
Capitol	DPRO-79122	Weeping Wine	CDJ	U.S.	1991	$3.00

Cole, Nat King

Label	Catalog Number	Title	Type	Country	Year	Longbox Value / Value
Full Length						
		After Midnight Once More	LD	Japan		$60.00
Topline	CD-508	Body & Soul	LP/BP	U.S.		$14.00/$8.00
Mosaic	MD18-138	Complete Capitol Recording of the Nat King Cole Trio	LP	U.S.		$270.00
18 CD set. Limited to 10,000 copies.						
Decca	25P2-2836	In the Beginning	LP	Germany		$16.00
Delta	11044	Live Vocal Sides 1943-1949	LP	Germany		$16.00
Delta	11044	Live Vocal Sides 1943-1949	LP	U.K.		$16.00
WEA	38266	Nat King Cole: Incomparable	LD	U.S.	1991	$30.00
WEA	38292	Nat King Cole: Incomparable Volume 2	LD	U.S.	1992	$30.00
Capitol	DPRO-79500	Nat King Cole: Selections From…	DJ/Smplr	U.S.	1993	$20.00
		Unforgettable, The	LD	Japan		$60.00
Singles						
Capitol	CDCL-641	Christmas Song, The	CD5	U.K.	1991	$10.00
Capitol	DPRO-79524	Christmas Song, The	CDJ	U.S.	1994	$6.00
EMI	204658-2	More	CD5	Germany	1992	$10.00
Capitol	TODP-2322	Unforgettable	CD3	Japan	1991	$13.00/$4.00
Capitol	CDCL-518	Unforgettable	CD5	U.K.	1988	$10.00
Capitol	CDCL-15975	When I Fall In Love	CD5	U.K.	1987	$10.00

Cole, Natalie

Label	Catalog Number	Title	Type	Country	Year	Longbox Value / Value
Full Length						
		Christmas Special	RS	U.S.	1994	$60.00
Modern	90270-2	Dangerous	LP/LB	U.S.†	1985	$14.00/$8.00
		Music Special	RS	U.S.	1994	$20.00
2 CD set						
Elektra	PRCD 8812-2	Radio Special	RS	U.S.	1993	$18.00
Elektra	61243-2	Unforgettable With Love	LTD/LP	U.S.	1991	$22.00
CD and VHS video in 6"x12" box.						
Singles						
Capitol	DPRO 04443	As A Matter Of Fact	CDJ	U.S.	1989	$3.00
Elektra	PRCD-8473-2	Christmas Song	CDJ	U.S.	1991	$3.00
Elektra	WMC5-569	Christmas Song, The	CD3	Japan	1992	$13.00/$4.00
Elektra	EKR-137CD	Christmas Song, The	CD5	U.K.	1991	$9.00
A&M	CD 17646	Christmas Song, The	CDJ	U.S.	1988	$7.00
With Miles Davis.						
Elektra	PRCD 9015	Did You See Jackie Robinson Hit That Ball?	CDJ	U.S.	1994	$6.00
EMI	202698-2	Everlasting	CD5	Germany	1988	$9.00
EMI	CDMT-46	Everlasting	CD5	U.K	1988	$9.00
Toshiba	XP10-2107	I Do	CD3	Japan	1989	$15.00/$3.00
EMI	DPRO-04330	I Do	CDJ	U.S.	1989	$3.00
EMI	CDMT-57	I Live For Your Love	CDJ	U.S.	1988	$3.00
EMI	202841-2	Jump Start	CD5	Germany	1988	$9.00
EMI	CDMT-50	Jump Start	CD5	U.K.	1988	$9.00
EMI	203321-2	Miss You Like Crazy	CD5	Germany	1989	$9.00
Toshiba	XP10-2084	Miss You Like Crazy	CD3	Japan	1989	$15.00/$3.00
Elektra	WMD5-4101	Mona Lisa	CD3	Japan	1992	$15.00/$3.00
Elektra	PRCD 9044-2	No More Blue Christmas	CDJ	U.S.	1991	$3.00
EMI	202526-2	Pink Cadillac	CD5	Germany	1988	$9.00
Toshiba	XP10-2004	Pink Cadillac	CD3	Japan	1988	$15.00/$3.00
EMI	CDMT-35	Pink Cadillac	CD5	U.K.	1988	$9.00
EMI	DPRO-04020	Pink Cadillac	CDJ	U.S.	1988	$3.00
EMI	203434-3	Rest of the Night	CD3	Germany	1989	$9.00
EMI	CDP 560	Rest of the Night	CD3	U.K.	1989	$12.00
EMI	CDMT-69	Rest of the Night	CD5	U.K.	1989	$9.00

Company	Disk Number	Title	Type	Country	Year	Longbox Value / Value
Elektra	WMD5-4084	Route 66	CD3	Japan	1991	$13.00/$4.00
Elektra	PRCD 8439-2	Route 66	CDJ	U.S.	1991	$3.00
EMI	203611-3	Starting Over Again	CD3	Germany	1989	$9.00
EMI	CDMT-77	Starting Over Again	CD5	U.K.	1989	$9.00
		Starting Over Again	CDJ	U.S.	1989	$3.00
		Take A Look	CD5	U.K.	1993	$10.00
		Take A Look	CD5	U.K.	1993	$10.00
Second version.						
Elektra	8776-2	Take A Look	CDJ	U.S.	1993	$3.00
Capitol	CDCL-629	This Will Be	CD5	U.K.	1991	$9.00
Elektra	7559-66529-2	Unforgettable	CD5	Germany	1991	$10.00
Elektra	WMD5-4070	Unforgettable	CD3	Japan	1991	$13.00/$4.00
Elektra	EKR-128CD	Unforgettable	CD5	U.K.	1991	$10.00
Elektra	PRCD 8374-2	Unforgettable	CDJ	U.S.	1991	$6.00
Elektra	EKR-147CD	Very Thought Of You, The	CD5	U.K.	1992	$9.00
Elektra	PRCD-8521-2	Very Thought Of You, The	CDJ	U.S.	1991	$3.00
Manhattan	DPRO-04083	When I Fall In Love	CDJ	U.S.	1988	$3.00
EMI	203796-2	Wild Women Do	CD5	Germany	1990	$9.00
Toshiba	TOCP-6524	Wild Women Do	CD3	Japan	1990	$13.00/$4.00
EMI	CDMT-81	Wild Women Do	CD5	U.K.	1990	$9.00
EMI	DPRO-04467	Wild Women Do	CDJ	U.S.	1990	$3.00
EMI	DPRO-4559	Wild Women Do	CDJ	U.S.	1990	$3.00

Coleman, Gary

Company	Disk Number	Title	Type	Country	Year	Longbox Value / Value
Full Length						
Ichiban	CDICH-1018	If You Can't Beat Me Rockin'	LP/BP	U.S.		$12.00/$7.00

Coleman, George

Company	Disk Number	Title	Type	Country	Year	Longbox Value / Value
Singles						
Alfa	10R3-11	Autumn In New York	CD3	Japan	1988	$12.00/$3.00

Coleman, Kirby

Company	Disk Number	Title	Type	Country	Year	Longbox Value / Value
Singles						
Intercord	825-758	Hey Toni	CD5	Germany	1989	$9.00

Coleman, Magri

Company	Disk Number	Title	Type	Country	Year	Longbox Value / Value
Singles						
Priority	50799	Let Me Down Gently	CDJ	U.S.	1995	$6.00
Priority	50894	Let Me Down Gently	CDJ	U.S.	1995	$7.00

Coleman, Ornette

Company	Disk Number	Title	Type	Country	Year	Longbox Value / Value
Full Length						
A&M	0807	Dancing In Your Head	LP/LB	U.S.		$14.00/$8.00
Bluebird	6561	Forms & Sounds	LP/LB	U.S.		$14.00/$8.00
Caravan	DREAMS-008	In All Languages	LP/BP	U.S.		$14.00/$8.00
Singles						
		3 Wishes	CDJ	U.S.		$2.00
A&M	0808	Dancing In Your Head	CD5	U.S.		$5.00

Coleman, Steve

Company	Disk Number	Title	Type	Country	Year	Longbox Value / Value
Full Length						
Novus	3119-2	Black Science	LP/BP	U.S.		$14.00/$8.00
Novus	0124163144-2	Drop Kick	LP/BP	U.S.		$14.00/$8.00
Polygram	834401	Motherland Pulse	LP/BP	U.S.		$14.00/$8.00
Polygram	834405	On the Edge Of Tomorrow	LP/BP	U.S.		$14.00/$8.00
Novus	0124163125-2	Rhythm In Mind	LP/BP	U.S.		$14.00/$8.00
Novus	3092-2	Rhythm People	LP/BP	U.S.		$14.00/$8.00
Pangaea	42150	Sine Die	LP/BP	U.S.		$14.00/$8.00
Novus	0124163160-2	Tao Of Mad Phat-Fringe	LP/BP	U.S.		$14.00/$8.00
Polygram	834410	World Expansion	LP/BP	U.S.		$14.00/$8.00

Colina, Michael

Company	Disk Number	Title	Type	Country	Year	Longbox Value / Value
Full Length						
Private Music	2062-2	Rituals	LP/LB	U.S.		$14.00/$8.00
Private Music	2062-2	Shadow of Urbano	LP/LB	U.S.		$14.00/$8.00
Singles						
Private Music		Joy Dancing	CDJ	U.S.		$2.00

Collage

Company	Disk Number	Title	Type	Country	Year	Longbox Value / Value
Singles						
Metropolitan	1035	Diana & I'll Loving	CD5	U.S.	1994	$5.00
Isba	IS12K-1029	Hasta La Vista	CD5	Canada	1993	$6.00

Collapse

Company	Disk Number	Title	Type	Country	Year	Longbox Value / Value
Singles						
City Beat	CBE-761CD	My Love	CD5	U.K.	1991	$8.00

Collapsing Lungs

Company	Disk Number	Title	Type	Country	Year	Longbox Value / Value
Singles						
		Colorblind	CDJ	U.S.	1994	$3.00

Collective Soul

Company	Disk Number	Title	Type	Country	Year	Longbox Value / Value
Full Length						
Album Network		Album Network Special	RS	U.S.	1994	$100.00
Airdate: 10/9/94.						
Atlantic	COLL1	Canadian Tour CD Sampler	DJ/Smplr	Canada	1995	$25.00
Atlantic		Collective Soul	LP	U.S.	1995	$15.00
CD in green colored jewel box with tan tray.						
Westwood One		In Concert	RS	U.S.	1995	$50.00
2 CD set. Airdate: 7/31/95.						
Westwood One		In Concert	RS	U.S.	1996	$50.00
2 CD set. Airdate: 1/1/96.						
Media America		Up Close	RS	U.S.	1995	$35.00
Singles						
Atlantic		Breathe	CDJ	U.S.	1994	$3.00
Atlantic		December	CD5	U.K.	1995	$10.00
Atlantic	PRCD 6158-2	December	CDJ	U.S.	1995	$6.00
Atlantic		Gel	CD5	Australia	1995	$13.00
Atlantic		Gel	CD5	U.K.	1995	$10.00
Atlantic	PRCD 5950-2	Gel	CDJ	U.S.	1995	$6.00
Atlantic		Heaven's Already Here	CDJ	U.S.	1994	$7.00
Atlantic	PRCD 6341-2	Reunion	CDJ	U.S.	1994	$3.00
Atlantic	PRCD 5562-2	Shine	CDJ	U.S.	1994	$3.00
Atlantic	PRCD 5572-2	Shine	CDJ	U.S.	1994	$3.00
Atlantic		Smashing Young Man	CD5	U.K.	1995	$10.00
Atlantic	87088	World I Know	CD5	U.S.	1995	$5.00
Atlantic	PRCD 6479-2	World I Know	CDJ	U.S.	1995	$2.00

College Boyz

Company	Disk Number	Title	Type	Country	Year	Longbox Value / Value
Singles						
Virgin	14154	Rollin'	CDJ	U.S.	1994	$3.00

Collette

Company	Disk Number	Title	Type	Country	Year	Longbox Value / Value
Singles						
Columbia	BELLC-1	Ring My Bell	CD5	U.K.	1989	$7.00

Collie, Mark

Full Length

Label	Catalog Number	Title	Type	Country	Year	Longbox Value/Value
Giant	2-24620-A	Tennessee Plates	DJ/LP	U.S.	1995	$30.00

CD in belt license plate package.

Label	Catalog Number	Title	Type	Country	Year	Longbox Value/Value
Giant		Tennessee Plates	DJ/Smplr	U.S.	1995	$20.00

CD in license plate package.

Singles

Label	Catalog Number	Title	Type	Country	Year	Longbox Value/Value
MCA	MCA5P-54448	Even the Man In the Moon Is Cryin'	CDJ	U.S.	1992	$2.00
Giant	PRO-CD-7794	Lipstick Don't Lie	CDJ	U.S.	1995	$3.00
		Three Words, Two Hearts, One Night	CDJ	U.S.		$3.00

Collins, Albert

Full Length

Label	Catalog Number	Title	Type	Country	Year	Longbox Value/Value
Virgin	86197	Iceman	LP/LB	U.S.		$14.00/$8.00
Alligator	ALCD-4743	Showdown	LP/BP	U.S.		$14.00/$8.00

Singles

Label	Catalog Number	Title	Type	Country	Year	Longbox Value/Value
Virgin	PRCD 031	Travellin' South	CDJ	U.S.	1991	$2.00

Collins, Bootsy

Full Length

Label	Catalog Number	Title	Type	Country	Year	Longbox Value/Value
Rykodisc	RCD 90307/08	Rubber Band Blasters Of the Universe	DJ/Smplr	U.S.	1993	$20.00

2 CD set.

Singles

Label	Catalog Number	Title	Type	Country	Year	Longbox Value/Value
CBS	12EP-3066	First One To the Egg Wins	CD3	Japan	1989	$12.00/$3.00
Lethal Beat	LBR11	Lettin' Ya Know	CD5	U.S.	1990	$4.00
CBS	12EP-8012	Party On Plastic	CD3	Japan	1988	$12.00/$3.00
		Party On Plastic	CDJ	U.S.	1988	$2.00

Collins, Edwyn

Full Length

Label	Catalog Number	Title	Type	Country	Year	Longbox Value/Value
		Hell Bent On Compromise	LTD/LP	U.K.	1995	$45.00

2 CD Set.

Label	Catalog Number	Title	Type	Country	Year	Longbox Value/Value
Westwood One		In Concert	RS	U.S.	1996	$40.00

2 CD set. 1/15/96.

Singles

Label	Catalog Number	Title	Type	Country	Year	Longbox Value/Value
A&M	581235	A Girl Like You	CD5	U.S.	1995	$5.00
Demon	D-1065CD	Fifty Shades Of Blue	CD5	U.K.	1989	$7.00
		Girl Like You	CD5	U.K.		$10.00
		Girl Like You	CD5	U.K.		$10.00

Second version.

Label	Catalog Number	Title	Type	Country	Year	Longbox Value/Value
		If You Could Love Me	CD5	U.K.		$10.00
		If You Could Love Me	CD5	U.K.		$10.00

Second version.

Collins, Jayne

Singles

Label	Catalog Number	Title	Type	Country	Year	Longbox Value/Value
Polydor	10GD-5008	If You Ever Had A Broken Heart	CD3	Japan	1988	$12.00/$3.00

Collins, Jimmy

Singles

Label	Catalog Number	Title	Type	Country	Year	Longbox Value/Value
Platinum		Cowboy Rap	CDJ	U.S.	1990	$2.00
Zoo	14196	Rodeo Rock	CD5	U.S.	1995	$5.00

Collins, Judy

Full Length

Label	Catalog Number	Title	Type	Country	Year	Longbox Value/Value
Elektra	1076-2	Bread And Roses	LP/LB	U.S.		$14.00/$8.00
WEA	252019	Judith	LP	Germany		$13.00
Elektra	111-2	Judith	LP/LB	U.S.†	1984	$14.00/$8.00
Elektra	253	Running For My Life	LP/LB	U.S.		$14.00/$8.00
Goldcastle	71318	Sanity And Grace	LP/BP	U.S.		$12.00/$7.00
Goldcastle	71302	Trust Your Heart	LP/BP	U.S.		$12.00/$7.00

Singles

Label	Catalog Number	Title	Type	Country	Year	Longbox Value/Value
Columbia	CSK 2288	Colorado Song	CDJ	U.S.	1991	$2.00
Columbia	CSK 2164	Fires of Eden	CDJ	U.S.	1990	$2.00

Collins, Michelle

Singles

Label	Catalog Number	Title	Type	Country	Year	Longbox Value/Value
Cherry	CTCD-1	Get Ready	CD5	U.K.	1992	$7.00

Collins, Phil

Full Length

Label	Catalog Number	Title	Type	Country	Year	Longbox Value/Value
		Both Sides	RS	U.S.	1994	$50.00

2 CD set. Airdate: 9/5/94.

Label	Catalog Number	Title	Type	Country	Year	Longbox Value/Value
Pioneer	PCS-6	Buster/The Singles 1981-1988	DJ/Smplr	Japan	1988	$150.00
Pioneer	CS-3	But Seriously 1981-1990	DJ/Smplr	Japan	1990	$150.00
Atlantic		But Seriously...Live	LP/VHS	U.S.	1990	$40.00

CD and VHS video in 12"x12" box.

Label	Catalog Number	Title	Type	Country	Year	Longbox Value/Value
Atlantic	16029-2	Face Value	LP/LB	U.S.†	1984	$14.00/$8.00
		Far Side Of the World	LTD/LP	Australia	1995	$35.00

2 CD set.

Label	Catalog Number	Title	Type	Country	Year	Longbox Value/Value
Atlantic	80035-2	Hello, I Must Be Going	LP/LB	U.S.†	1984	$14.00/$8.00
DIR		King Biscuit Flour Hour	RS	U.S.	1987	$30.00

With Hynde, Gilmour, Airdate: 12/13/87.

Label	Catalog Number	Title	Type	Country	Year	Longbox Value/Value
DIR		King Biscuit Flour Hour	RS	U.S.	1992	$30.00

Airdate: 11/1/92.

Label	Catalog Number	Title	Type	Country	Year	Longbox Value/Value
DIR		King Biscuit Flour Hour	RS	U.S.	1993	$30.00

Airdate: 11/22/93.

Label	Catalog Number	Title	Type	Country	Year	Longbox Value/Value
DIR		King Biscuit Flour Hour	RS	U.S.	1996	$30.00

Airdate: 1/7/96.

Label	Catalog Number	Title	Type	Country	Year	Longbox Value/Value
Pioneer	PA-84-094	Live At Perkins Palace	LD	U.S.	1985	$20.00

Analog audio.

Label	Catalog Number	Title	Type	Country	Year	Longbox Value/Value
Atlantic	81240-2	No Jacket Required	LP/LB	U.S.†	1985	$14.00/$8.00
WEA	50313	No Ticket Required	LD	U.S.	1992	$30.00
Westwood One		Off the Record	RS	U.S.	1993	$20.00

Airdate: 11/29/93.

Label	Catalog Number	Title	Type	Country	Year	Longbox Value/Value
Media America		On Tour	RS	U.S.	1990	$25.00
Pioneer	PA84-M007	Phil Collins	8"LD	U.S.	1984	$15.00

Analog audio.

Label	Catalog Number	Title	Type	Country	Year	Longbox Value/Value
Atlantic	PR 3092-2	Profiled	DJ/Intvw	U.S.	1989	$15.00
Radio Today		Rock Stars	RS	U.S.	1990	$50.00

2 CD set. Airdate: 2/19/90.

Label	Catalog Number	Title	Type	Country	Year	Longbox Value/Value
Atlantic	PHIL 1	Story So Far..., The	DJ/Smplr	Canada	1995	$25.00
Atlantic	PC 001	Story So Far..., The	DJ/Smplr	U.S.†	1993	$25.00
Atlantic	PRCD 5458-2	Story So Far..., The	DJ/Smplr	U.S.	1994	$25.00
Atlantic	PRCD 5370-2	Story (The Interview Disc), The	DJ/Intvw	U.S.	1993	$20.00
Media America		Up Close	RS	U.S.	1989	$40.00

2 CD set.

Label	Catalog Number	Title	Type	Country	Year	Longbox Value/Value
Media America		Up Close	RS	U.S.	1990	$40.00

2 CD set.

Label	Catalog Number	Title	Type	Country	Year	Longbox Value/Value
Media America		Up Close	RS	U.S.	1991	$30.00

2 CD set.

Label	Catalog Number	Title	Type	Country	Year	Longbox Value/Value
Media America		Up Close	RS	U.S.	1993	$40.00

3 CD set.

Singles

Label	Catalog Number	Title	Type	Country	Year	Longbox Value/Value
WEA	257358-2	Another Day in Paradise	CD3	Germany	1989	$10.00
WEA	WMD5-4006	Another Day in Paradise	CD3	Japan	1989	$13.00/$4.00
Virgin	VSCD-1234	Another Day in Paradise	CD3	U.K.	1989	$10.00
Atlantic	86261-2	Another Day in Paradise	CD5	U.S.	1989	$5.00
Atlantic	PR 3048-2	Another Day in Paradise	CDJ	U.S.	1989	$3.00
Atlantic		Both Sides of the Story	CD5	U.K.	1993	$10.00
Atlantic		Both Sides of the Story	CD5	U.K.	1993	$10.00

Second version.

Label	Catalog Number	Title	Type	Country	Year	Longbox Value/Value
Atlantic	PRCD 5310-2	Both Sides of the Story	CDJ	U.S.	1993	$3.00
Atlantic	85714	Both Sides of the Story	CDJ	U.S.	1993	$7.00
WEA		Can't Turn Back the Years	CDJ	Germany	1994	$20.00
Atlantic		Can't Turn Back the Years	CDJ	U.S.	1994	$6.00
WEA	9031-73045-2	Do You Remember	CD5	Germany	1990	$10.00
WEA	173220-2	Do You Remember	CD5	Germany	1990	$10.00
Pioneer	WMD5-4043	Do You Remember	CD3	Japan	1990	$13.00/$4.00
Virgin	VSCD-1305	Do You Remember	CD5	U.K.	1990	$10.00
Virgin	VSCDX 3305	Do You Remember	CD5	U.K.	1990	$20.00

Custom carousel package.

Label	Catalog Number	Title	Type	Country	Year	Longbox Value/Value
Atlantic	PR 3121-2	Do You Remember	CDJ	U.S.	1989	$3.00
Atlantic	VSCDG 1505	Everyday	CD5	U.K.	1994	$10.00
Atlantic		Everyday	CD5	U.K.	1994	$10.00

Second version.

Label	Catalog Number	Title	Type	Country	Year	Longbox Value/Value
Atlantic	PRCD 5300-2	Everyday	CDJ	U.S.	1993	$3.00
Atlantic	PRCD 5406-2	Everyday	CDJ	U.S.	1993	$3.00
Atlantic	85715	Everyday	CD5	U.S.	1994	$6.00
WEA	257845-2	Groovy Kind of Love	CD3	Germany	1988	$10.00
WEA	10P3-6042	Groovy Kind of Love	CD3	Japan	1988	$13.00/$4.00
Virgin	VSCD-1117	Groovy Kind of Love	CD3	U.K.	1988	$10.00
Atlantic	PR 2452-2	Groovy Kind of Love	CDJ	U.S.	1988	$150.00

Also has 2 tracks from Tori Amos' Y Kan't Tori Read.

Label	Catalog Number	Title	Type	Country	Year	Longbox Value/Value
		Hang in Long Enough	CD3	Japan	1989	$13.00/$4.00
Virgin	VSCDT-1300	Hang in Long Enough	CD5	U.K.	1990	$10.00
Atlantic	PRCD 3616-2	Hang in Long Enough	CDJ	U.S.	1989	$3.00
Atlantic	PRCD 5060-2	Hero	CDJ	U.S.	1993	$2.00
WEA	9031-70825-2	I Wish It Would Rain Down	CD3	Germany	1990	$10.00
Pioneer	WMD5-4011	I Wish It Would Rain Down	CD3	Germany	1990	$10.00
Virgin	VSCD-1240	I Wish It Would Rain Down	CD3	U.K.	1990	$10.00
Atlantic	PR 3120-2	I Wish It Would Rain Down	CDJ	U.S.	1990	$3.00
WEA	257672-2	In The Air Tonight	CD3	Germany	1988	$10.00
WEA		In The Air Tonight	CD5	Germany	1988	$10.00
Virgin	VSCD-102	In The Air Tonight	CD5	U.K.	1988	$10.00
Atlantic	PRCD 3642-2	In The Air Tonight	CDJ	U.S.	1990	$18.00
WEA	171448-2	Something Happened on the Way To Heaven	CD5	Germany	1990	$10.00
Pioneer	WMD5-4029	Something Happened on the Way To Heaven	CD3	Japan	1990	$13.00/$4.00
Virgin	VSCD-1251	Something Happened on the Way To Heaven	CD5	U.K.	1990	$10.00
Virgin	VSCDT-1251	Something Happened on the Way To Heaven	CD5	U.K.	1990	$10.00
Atlantic	PR 3392-2	Something Happened on the Way To Heaven	CDJ	U.S.	1990	$3.00
Atlantic	PR 3503-2	Something Happened on the Way To Heaven	CDJ	U.S.	1990	$3.00
WEA	171945-2	That's Just the Way It Is	CD5	Germany	1990	$10.00
Pioneer	WMD5-4039	That's Just the Way It Is	CD3	Japan	1990	$13.00/$4.00
Virgin	VSDT-1277	That's Just the Way It Is	CD5	U.K.	1990	$10.00
Virgin	VSCDX 1277	That's Just the Way It Is	CD5	U.K.	1990	$15.00
Virgin	VS CDJ1277	That's Just the Way It Is	CDJ	U.K.	1990	$11.00
Atlantic	PRCD 3642-2	Three Serious Live Hits	CDJ	U.S.	1990	$3.00
WEA	257739-2	Two Hearts	CD5	Germany	1988	$10.00
Pioneer	WMD5-6086	Two Hearts	CD3	Japan	1988	$13.00/$4.00
Virgin	VSCD-1141	Two Hearts	CD3	U.K.	1988	$10.00
Atlantic	PR 2545-2	Two Hearts	CDJ	U.S.	1988	$3.00
Atlantic		We Wait and We Wonder	CDJ	Germany	1994	$18.00
Atlantic		We Wait and We Wonder	CD5	U.K.	1994	$10.00
Atlantic		We Wait and We Wonder	CD5	U.K.	1994	$10.00

Second version.

Label	Catalog Number	Title	Type	Country	Year	Longbox Value/Value
Atlantic	PRCD 5407-2	We Wait and We Wonder	CDJ	U.S.	1993	$6.00
Atlantic	PRCD 5595-2	We Wait and We Wonder	CDJ	U.S.	1994	$3.00
Pioneer	WMD5-4063	Who Said I Would	CD3	Japan	1990	$13.00/$4.00
Atlantic	PRCD 3758-2	Who Said I Would	CDJ	U.S.	1990	$3.00
Virgin	CDT-1	You Can't Hurry Love	CD3	U.K.	1988	$10.00

Collins, Tyler

Full Length

Label	Catalog Number	Title	Type	Country	Year	Longbox Value/Value
RCA	9642-2	Girls Night Out	LP/BP	U.S.	1990	$14.00/$8.00

Singles

Label	Catalog Number	Title	Type	Country	Year	Longbox Value/Value
RCA	PD-49258	Girls Night Out	CD5	Germany	1990	$8.00
RCA	PD-49260	Girls Night Out	CD5	Germany	1990	$8.00
RCA	PD-49258	Girls Night Out	CD5	U.K.	1990	$8.00
RCA	2558-2-RDJ	Girls Night Out	CDJ	U.S.	1990	$2.00
RCA	BVDP-65	It Doesn't Matter	CD3	Japan	1992	$12.00/$3.00
RCA	62325-2-RDJ	It Doesn't Matter	CDJ	U.S.	1992	$2.00
RCA	BVDP-63	Just Make Me the One	CD3	Japan	1992	$12.00/$3.00
RCA	62203-2-RDJ	Just Make Me the One	CDJ	U.S.	1992	$2.00
		Second Chance	CDJ	U.S.		$2.00
Reprise	7106	Thanks to You	CDJ	U.S.	1994	$3.00
RCA	PD-49306	Whatcha Gonna Do	CD5	Germany	1990	$8.00
		Whatcha Gonna Do	CDJ	U.S.		$2.00

Collinson, Dean

Singles

Label	Catalog Number	Title	Type	Country	Year	Longbox Value/Value
Arista	743113024-2	Runaway	CD5	U.K.	1992	$7.00

Collision

Full Length

Label	Catalog Number	Title	Type	Country	Year	Longbox Value/Value
Columbia	48818	Collision	LTD/LP	U.S.	1993	$16.00

1st pressing in limited Eco-pak.

Label	Catalog Number	Title	Type	Country	Year	Longbox Value/Value
Chaos	CK 4735	Chains	CDJ	U.S.	1992	$2.00
Chaos	CK 4958	Maximum Respect	CDJ	U.S.	1993	$2.00

Colombier, Michael

Full Length

Label	Catalog Number	Title	Type	Country	Year	Longbox Value/Value
A&M	3503	Wings	LP/LB	U.S.		$12.00/$7.00

Colonel Abrams

Singles

Label	Catalog Number	Title	Type	Country	Year	Longbox Value/Value
Scotti Brothers	ZSK 75323	When Somebody Loves	CDJ	U.S.	1992	$2.00
Scotti Brothers	SBDJ 75294	You Don't Know	CDJ	U.S.	1991	$2.00

Color

Singles

Label	Catalog Number	Title	Type	Country	Year	Longbox Value/Value
Crown	JSD-3	Broken Tavern	CD3	Japan	1989	$12.00/$3.00

Color Me Badd

Full Length

Label	Catalog Number	Title	Type	Country	Year	Longbox Value/Value
Giant	9 24429-2-Dj	C.M.B.	DJ/LP	U.S.	1991	$12.00

Picture disc.

Singles

Label	Catalog Number	Title	Type	Country	Year	Longbox Value/Value
Giant	9362-40164-2	All 4 Love	CD5	Germany	1991	$8.00
Giant	W-0053CD	All 4 Love	CD5	U.K.	1991	$8.00
Giant	PRO-CD-4800	All 4 Love	CDJ	U.S.	1991	$3.00
Giant	PRO-CD-6687	Bells, The	CDJ	U.S.	1993	$3.00
Warner Brothers	18268	Bells, The	CD5	U.S.	1994	$5.00
Giant	9 18270-2	Choose	CD5	U.S.	1993	$5.00

Label	Catalog Number	Title	Type	Country	Year	Longbox Value / Value
Giant	PRO-CD-6683	Choose	CDJ	U.S.	1993	$2.00
Giant	PRO-CD-6773	Choose	CDJ	U.S.	1993	$2.00
Giant	9 41348-2	Choose	CD5	U.S.	1994	$5.00
Warner Brothers	18270	Choose	CD5	U.S.	1994	$5.00
Giant	PRO-CD-5111	Color Me Bad	CDJ	U.S.	1991	$3.00
Giant	PRO-CD-6776	Groovy Now	CDJ	U.S.	1993	$2.00
Giant	W-0078CD	Heartbreaker	CD5	U.K.	1992	$8.00
Giant	9362-40227-2	I Adore Mi Amor	CD5	Germany	1991	$8.00
Giant	W-0067CD	I Adore Mi Amor	CD5	U.K.	1991	$8.00
Gaint	PRO-CD-4943	I Adore Mi Amor	CDJ	U.S.	1991	$7.00
Giant	9362-40120-2	I Wanna Sex You Up	CD5	Germany	1991	$8.00
Giant	9362-40095-2	I Wanna Sex You Up	CD5	Germany	1991	$8.00
Giant	W-0036CD	I Wanna Sex You Up	CD5	U.K.	1991	$8.00
Giant	9 40031-2	I Wanna Sex You Up	CD5	U.S.	1991	$4.00
Giant	PRO-CD-4720	I Wanna Sex You Up	CDJ	U.S.	1991	$3.00
Giant	PRO-CD-4916	I Wanna Sex You Up	CDJ	U.S.	1991	$3.00
Giant	PRO-CD-4728	I Wanna Sex You Up	CDJ	U.S.	1991	$3.00
Giant	PRO-CD-6818	Let's Start With Forever	CDJ	U.S.	1993	$2.00
Giant	9 40453-2	Slow Motion	CD5	U.S.	1992	$3.00
Giant	PRO-CD-5446	Slow Motion	CDJ	U.S.	1992	$3.00
Giant	PRO-CD-5169	Thinkin' Back	CDJ	U.S.	1991	$3.00
Giant	PRO-CD-6708	Time and Chance	CDJ	U.S.	1993	$3.00
Giant	9 41147-2	Time and Chance	CD5	U.S.	1993	$6.00

Colorblind, Jam Experience

Singles

Label	Catalog Number	Title	Type	Country	Year	Longbox Value / Value
Str. Fruit	SFPSCD-076	Peel Sessions	CD5	U.K.	1989	$8.00

Colortone

Singles

Label	Catalog Number	Title	Type	Country	Year	Longbox Value / Value
Pash	1086	Nothings Gonna Be Alright	CDJ	U.S.	1988	$2.00

Colour Blue

Singles

Label	Catalog Number	Title	Type	Country	Year	Longbox Value / Value
True Tone	D11059	Rockwell Street	CD5	Australia	1991	$8.00

Colour of Love

Singles

Label	Catalog Number	Title	Type	Country	Year	Longbox Value / Value
Blanco	4509-90567-2	England's Dreaming	CD5	Germany	1992	$7.00
Blanco	NEG-59CD	England's Dreaming	CD5	U.K.	1992	$7.00
Blanco	NEG-58CD	Living Love	CD5	U.K.	1992	$7.00

Colour Zone

Singles

Label	Catalog Number	Title	Type	Country	Year	Longbox Value / Value
Polydor	10GD-5003	Crazy Emotion	CD3	Japan	1988	$12.00/$3.00
CPolydor	15GD-6001	Crazy Emotion	CD3	Japan	1988	$12.00/$3.00

Colourbox

Full Length

Label	Catalog Number	Title	Type	Country	Year	Longbox Value / Value
4AD	508	Colourbox	LP/LB	U.S.		$14.00/$8.00

Colourfield

Full Length

Label	Catalog Number	Title	Type	Country	Year	Longbox Value / Value
Chrysalis	21546	Deception	LP/LB	U.S.		$14.00/$8.00

Colourhaus

Full Length

Label	Catalog Number	Title	Type	Country	Year	Longbox Value / Value
Interscope	92123	Water To the Soul	LP/LB	U.S.		$14.00/$8.00

Singles

Label	Catalog Number	Title	Type	Country	Year	Longbox Value / Value
Atlantic	AMDY-5091	I Would Walk the Earth	CD3	Japan	1992	$12.00/$3.00
Atlantic	AMDY-5084	Innocent Child	CD3	Japan	1992	$12.00/$3.00
Atlantic	A-8553CD	Innocent Child	CD5	U.K.	1992	$8.00
Interscope	PRCD 4409-2	Innocent Child	CDJ	U.S.	1991	$2.00
Atlantic	AMDY-5086	Moving Mountains	CD3	Japan	1992	$12.00/$3.00
		Moving Mountains	CDJ	U.S.	1992	$2.00

Colours

Full Length

Label	Catalog Number	Title	Type	Country	Year	Longbox Value / Value
Atlantic	82089-2	Rules Of Attraction	LP/LB	U.S.		$14.00/$8.00

Singles

Label	Catalog Number	Title	Type	Country	Year	Longbox Value / Value
WEA	YZ-496CD	Don't Stop the Night	CD5	U.K.	1990	$8.00
WEA	YZ-418CD	I Wanna Make Love To You	CD5	U.K.	1990	$8.00
WEA	YZ-460CD	Somebody To Love	CD5	U.K.	1990	$8.00

Colours United

Singles

Label	Catalog Number	Title	Type	Country	Year	Longbox Value / Value
Bellaphon	130-07-593	Legally Dope	CD5	Germany	1991	$8.00

Coltrane, Chi

Singles

Label	Catalog Number	Title	Type	Country	Year	Longbox Value / Value
Polygram	879881-2	I Just Want To Rule My Own	CD5	Germany	1991	$7.00

Coltrane, John

Full Length

Label	Catalog Number	Title	Type	Country	Year	Longbox Value / Value
WEA	30XD-1006	Avant-Garde	LP	Japan		$14.00
Warner Brothers	43P2-0012	Ballads	LTD/LP	Japan		$14.00
Gold disc.						
EMI	746095-2	Blue Train	LP	Germany		$14.00
MCA	MCAD-39103	Coltrane and Ellington	LP	Germany		$14.00
Savoy Jazz	ZD-70529	Countdown	LP	Germany		$14.00
Savoy Jazz	ZD-70529	Countdown	LP/LB	U.S.		$14.00/$8.00
Savoy Jazz	ZD-70818	Dial Africa/Gold Coast	LP	Germany		$14.00
Savoy Jazz	ZD-70818	Dial Africa/Gold Coast	LP/LB	U.S.		$14.00/$8.00
Pioneer	43XD-2009	From Original Master Tapes	LTD/LP	Japan	1988	$20.00
Gold disc.						
Charly	CD-68	Live At Birdland	LP/BP	U.S.		$14.00/$8.00
Pioneer	43P2-0011	Love Supreme	LTD/LP	Japan	1988	$20.00
Gold disc.						
Prestige	60014	With Jazz Giants	LP/BP	U.S.		$14.00/$8.00

Coltrane, Robbie

Singles

Label	Catalog Number	Title	Type	Country	Year	Longbox Value / Value
Pinnacle	POPE-2003	Speedy Gonzalez	CD5	U.K.	1991	$7.00

Colvin, Shawn

Full Length

Label	Catalog Number	Title	Type	Country	Year	Longbox Value / Value
		Steady On	DJ/LP	U.S.	1989	$8.00

Singles

Label	Catalog Number	Title	Type	Country	Year	Longbox Value / Value
Columbia	CSK 74972	Climb On	CDJ	U.S.	1993	$2.00
Columbia	CSK 2057	Diamond In the Rough	CDJ	U.S.	1990	$2.00
Columbia	CSK 73325	Diamond In the Rough	CDJ	U.S.	1990	$2.00
Columbia		Every Little Thing He Does Is Magic	CD5	U.K.	1994	$10.00
Columbia		Every Little Thing He Does Is Magic	CD5	U.K.	1994	$10.00
Second version.						
Columbia		Every Little Thing He Does Is Magic	CDJ	U.K.	1994	$10.00
Columbia	CSK 6266	Every Little Thing He Does Is Magic	CDJ	U.S.	1994	$3.00
		Get Out Of This House	CD5	U.K.	1997	$10.00

Company	Disk Number	Title	Type	Country	Year	Longbox Value / Value
		Get Out Of This House	CD5	U.K.	1997	$10.00
Second version.						
Columbia		I Don't Know Why	CD5	U.K.	1993	$11.00
Columbia		I Don't Know Why	CD5	U.K.	1993	$11.00
Second version.						
Columbia	CSK 4928	I Don't Know Why	CDJ	U.S.	1993	$3.00
Columbia		Lost Soul	CDJ	U.S.		$6.00
Columbia		One Cool Remove	CDJ	U.S.		$6.00
Columbia	CSK 6662	One Cool Remove	CDJ	U.S.	1994	$3.00
Columbia	CSK 4828	Round Of Blues	CDJ	U.S.	1992	$6.00
Columbia	CSK 73061	Steady On	CDJ	U.S.	1989	$2.00
Columbia		Young At Heart	CDJ	U.S.		$6.00

Combined Flavour

Singles

Company	Disk Number	Title	Type	Country	Year	Longbox Value / Value
MCA	MCA5P-2389	Niceness	CDJ	U.S.	1992	$2.00

Coming Of Age

Singles

Company	Disk Number	Title	Type	Country	Year	Longbox Value / Value
Zoo	17135-2	Coming Home To Live	CDJ	U.S.	1993	$2.00
Hdh (fantasy)	103	Compton To Long B	CD5	U.S.	1994	$5.00

Commitments

Singles

Company	Disk Number	Title	Type	Country	Year	Longbox Value / Value
MCA	MCA5P-2107	Medley	CDJ	U.S.	1991	$2.00
MCA	CD45-1625	Mustang Sally	CDJ	U.S.	1991	$2.00
MCA	MCA5P-2180	That's the Way Love Is	CDJ	U.S.	1991	$2.00
MCA	MCSTD-1577	Try A Little Tenderness	CD5	U.K.	1991	$9.00
MCA	CD45-1626	Try A Little Tenderness	CDJ	U.S.	1991	$2.00

Commodores

Full Length

Company	Disk Number	Title	Type	Country	Year	Longbox Value / Value
RCA	ZD-72222	All the Great Love Songs	LP	Germany		$20.00
Motown	MOTD-6107	All the Great Love Songs	LP/BP	U.S.†	1984	$14.00/$8.00
Motown	6068-MD	Compact Command Performances	LP/BP	U.S.†	1984	$14.00/$8.00
RCA	WD-72421	Compact Command Performances	LP	Germany		$20.00
Motown	5353	Heroes	LP/BP	U.S.		$14.00/$8.00
Motown	MOTD-8039	Heroes + Commodores	LP/BP	U.S.		$20.00/$17.00
Motown	ZD-72551	Hot On the Tracks/In the Pocket	LP	Germany		$20.00
Motown	5438	In the Pocket	LP/LB	U.S.		$14.00/$8.00
Motown	5353	Midnight Magic	LP/BP	U.S.		$14.00/$8.00
RCA	ZD-72455	Midnight Magic/Natural High	LP	Germany		$20.00
Motown	5293	Natural High	LP/BP	U.S.		$14.00/$8.00
Motown	MOTD-8014	Natural High + Midnight Magic	LP/BP	U.S.		$20.00/$17.00
Magnum	35	Rise Up	LP/BP	U.S.		$12.00/$7.00
Polydor	835369-2	Rock Solid	LP/BP	U.S.		$14.00/$8.00
Mercury	831194-2	United	LP/BP	U.S.		$14.00/$8.00

Singles

Company	Disk Number	Title	Type	Country	Year	Longbox Value / Value
Canyon	PCDY-00109	Christmas Eve	CD3	Japan	1992	$13.00/$4.00
Motown	R10M-123	Still	CD3	Japan	1989	$13.00/$4.00
Motown	R10M-124	Three Times A Lady	CD3	Japan	1989	$13.00/$4.00

Common Bond

Full Length

Company	Disk Number	Title	Type	Country	Year	Longbox Value / Value
Aris	880392	Anger Into Passion	LP	Germany		$15.00

Common Sense

Singles

Company	Disk Number	Title	Type	Country	Year	Longbox Value / Value
BMG	663079	Danger Waters	CD5	Germany	1990	$8.00
Relativity	0347	Ressurection	CDJ	U.S.	1995	$3.00
Relativity	1250	Resurrection	CD5	U.S.	1994	$5.00

Communards

Full Length

Company	Disk Number	Title	Type	Country	Year	Longbox Value / Value
MCA	MCAD 5794	Communards	LP/LB	U.S.	1986	$14.00/$8.00
MCA	MCAD 42106	Red	LP/LB	U.S.		$14.00/$8.00

Singles

Company	Disk Number	Title	Type	Country	Year	Longbox Value / Value
London	886271-2	For A Friend	CD5	Germany	1988	$8.00
London	LONCD-166	For A Friend	CD5	U.K.	1988	$8.00
London	886206-2	Never Can Say Goodbye	CD5	Germany	1988	$8.00
London	P10L-30004	Never Can Say Goodbye	CD3	Japan	1988	$12.00/$3.00
London	LONCD-158	Never Can Say Goodbye	CD5	U.K.	1988	$8.00
London	8861052	So Cold the Night	CD5	Germany	1988	$8.00
London	886306-2	There's More To Love	CD5	Germany	1988	$8.00
London	LONCD-173	There's More To Love	CD5	U.K.	1988	$8.00
London	8863132-2	You Are My World	CD5	Germany	1988	$8.00

Como, Perry

Full Length

Company	Disk Number	Title	Type	Country	Year	Longbox Value / Value
Aris	886169	Best of Times	LP	Germany		$20.00
RCA	PCD1-0972	Pure Gold	LP/BP	U.S.†	1984	$14.00/$8.00
RCA	CAKD-660	Sings Merry Christmas Songs	LP/LB	U.S.		$12.00/$7.00
Aris	886158	Today	LP	Germany		$20.00

Singles

Company	Disk Number	Title	Type	Country	Year	Longbox Value / Value
RCA	64220	I'll Be Home For Christmas	CD5	U.S.	1994	$5.00
RCA	64221	Silent Night	CD5	U.S.	1994	$5.00

Company

Singles

Company	Disk Number	Title	Type	Country	Year	Longbox Value / Value
Giant	PRO-CD-6434	Angel	CDJ	U.S.	1993	$2.00
Giant	PRO-CD-6686	Love's in Need Of Love	CDJ	U.S.	1993	$2.00

Company B

Full Length

Company	Disk Number	Title	Type	Country	Year	Longbox Value / Value
Atlantic	81983-2	Gotta Dance	LP/LB	U.S.	1989	$14.00/$8.00

Singles

Company	Disk Number	Title	Type	Country	Year	Longbox Value / Value
Atlantic	PR 2999-2	Boogie Woogie Bugle Boy	CDJ	U.S.	1989	$3.00
ZYX	6169-8	Full Circle	CD3	Germany	1989	$8.00
ZYX	6433-8	Goodness Of Love	CD5	Germany	1989	$8.00
ZYX	6044-8	Jam on Me	CD5	Germany	1988	$8.00
ZYX	5970-8	Miami	CD5	Germany	1989	$8.00

Company of Wolves

Full Length

Company	Disk Number	Title	Type	Country	Year	Longbox Value / Value
Island	842184-2	Company of Wolves	LP/LB	U.S.		$14.00/$8.00

Singles

Company	Disk Number	Title	Type	Country	Year	Longbox Value / Value
IMS	876565-2	Call of the Wild	CD5	Germany	1990	$8.00
Mercury	CDP 226	Distance, The	CDJ	U.S.	1990	$2.00

Company She Keeps

Singles

Company	Disk Number	Title	Type	Country	Year	Longbox Value / Value
Bellaphon	130-07-001	What A Girl Wants	CD5	Germany		$7.00

Compton Cartel

Singles

Company	Disk Number	Title	Type	Country	Year	Longbox Value / Value
		So In Love	CDJ	U.S.		$2.00

Label	Catalog Number	Title	Type	Country	Year	Longbox Value / Value
Compton's Most Wanted						
Singles						
QWest	PRO-CD-4901	Growin' Up In the Hood	CDJ	U.S.	1991	$2.00
Orpheus	74447	Hood Took Me Under	CDJ	U.S.	1991	$2.00
Compulsion						
Singles						
Elektra	66228-2	Boogie Woogie	CD5	U.S.	1994	$5.00
		How Do I Breathe	CDJ	U.S.		$3.00
Elektra	PRCD 8947-2	Mall Monarchy	CDJ	U.S.	1994	$3.00
Interscope	PRCD 6125	Mall Monarchy	CDJ	U.S.	1995	$10.00
Enhanced CD.						
Interscope	PRCD 5973	Plan	CDJ	U.S.	1995	$3.00
Comsat Angels						
Full Length						
Island	842850-2	Chasing Shadows	LP/LB	U.S.		$14.00/$8.00
Singles						
Indigo	CSA-001	Driving	CD5	U.K.	1992	$7.00
Con Funk Shun						
Full Length						
Mercury	824345-2	Electric Lady	LP/BP	U.S.	1985	$14.00/$8.00
Conant, Johnathan						
Singles						
		Golden Lies	CDJ	U.S.	1992	$2.00
Concord						
Singles						
BCM	20346	Disco Lambada	CD5	Germany	1989	$7.00
Concrete Blonde						
Full Length						
CBS	450382-2	Concrete Blonde	LP	Germany		$18.00
Capitol	DPRO-79267	Dream 6	DJ/LP		1993	$30.00
Capitol	DPRO 79265	Limited Edition Retail Sampler	DJ/Smplr	U.S.	1994	$10.00
IRS	DPRO-79265	Nuevas Canciones Y Resurr-ecciones	DJ/Smplr	U.S.	1993	$20.00
Singles						
EMI	204131-2	Caroline	CD5	Germany	1990	$9.00
IRS	13811	Caroline	CD5	U.S.	1990	$6.00
IRS	DPRO-67029	Caroline	CDJ	U.S.	1990	$2.00
MCA	CD45 18482	Everybody Knows	CDJ	U.S.	1990	$2.00
IRS	67082	Ghost Of Texas Ladies' Man	CDJ	U.S.	1992	$2.00
EMI	244027-3	God Is a Bullet	CD3	Germany	1989	$9.00
EMI	241027-3	God Is a Bullet	CD3	Germany	1989	$9.00
IRS	DPRO-8201	God Is a Bullet	CDJ	U.S.	1989	$2.00
IRS	EIRSCD-105	Happy Birthday	CD5	U.K.	1989	$9.00
Capitol	DPRO-79268	Heal It Up	CDJ	U.S.	1993	$3.00
Capitol	DPRO-79265	Heal It Up	CDJ	U.S.	1993	$7.00
EMI	241064-2	Joey	CD5	Germany	1989	$9.00
IRS	EIRSCD-143	Joey	CD5	U.K.	1990	$9.00
		Mexican Moon	CD5	U.K.	1994	$10.00
Capitol	DPRO-79311	Mexican Moon	CDJ	U.S.	1993	$3.00
Capital	58120	Mexican Moon	CD5	U.S.	1994	$5.00
IRS	007	Scene Of A Perfect Crime	CDJ	U.S.	1989	$3.00
IRS	80148	Someday	CD5	Austria	1992	$10.00
IRS	80148	Someday	CD5	Austria	1992	$10.00
Second version.						
IRS	DPRO-67092	Someday	CDJ	U.S.	1992	$2.00
IRS		Someday	CDJ	U.S.	1992	$35.00
CD in cardboard "cinderblock" package.						
Capitol	C2 13866	Walking In London	CD5	U.S.	1992	$2.00
IRS	67101	Walking In London	CDJ	U.S.	1992	$2.00
Condemned						
Singles						
		To Protect And To Serve	CDJ	U.S.	1992	$7.00
Condon, Eddie						
Full Length						
Teldec	8 24054	Volume One	LP	Germany		$15.00
Conductor X						
Full Length						
Pioneer	PA86-M030	Coney Hatch	8"LD	U.S.	1985	$8.00
Efa	CD-06302	Conductor X	CD5	Germany	1992	$7.00
Conexion, Latina						
Full Length						
Enja	407201	Calorcito	LP/LB	U.S.†	1985	$14.00/$8.00
Coney Hatch						
Full Length						
Pioneer Artists	PA-86-M030	Coney Hatch	8 "LD	U.S.	1986	$13.00
Confederate Railroad						
Singles						
Atlantic	PRCD 4707-2	Queen Of Memphis	CDJ	U.S.	1994	$2.00
Atlantic	PRCD 5276-2	She Never Cried	CDJ	U.S.	1994	$2.00
Atlantic	PRCD 5363-2	Trashy Woman	CDJ	U.S.	1994	$2.00
Atlantic	PRCD 5006-2	When You Leave Me That Way	CDJ	U.S.	1994	$2.00
Confront James						
Singles						
Sst	309	Just Do It	CD5	U.S.	1994	$5.00
Congo Norvell						
Singles						
Fiasco	106	Lullaby	CD5	U.S.	1992	$5.00
Congos						
Full Length						
Blood And Fire	BAFCD 009	Heart of the Congos	DJ/LP	U.S.	1996	$18.00
Blood And Fire	BAFCD 009	Heart of the Congos	LTD/LP	U.S.	1996	$30.00
2 CD set. in card sleeve.						
Congress						
Singles						
SPV	1023-3	Forty Miles	CD5	Germany	1991	$7.00
SPV	HEART-01CD	Forty Miles	CD5	U.K.	1991	$7.00
Conjunto Bachat						
Singles						
	1414	El Sabor Tropical	CD5	U.S.	1994	$5.00
Conjunto Primav						
Singles						
Joey International	3377	Borracho Y Loco	CD5	U.S.	1994	$5.00
Conlee, John						
Full Length						
MCA	MCAD-31230	Greatest Hits Vol.2	LP/LB	U.S.		$14.00/$8.00
Conley, Earl Thomas						
Full Length						
		Country Star Tracks	RS	U.S.	1991	$15.00
Airdate: 10/12/91.						
RCA	PCD1-4713	Don't Make It Easy For Me	LP/BP	U.S		$14.00/$8.00
RCA	PCD1-4713	Don't Make It Easy For Me	LP/BP	U.S†	1985	$14.00/$8.00
RCA	PCD1-7032	Greatest Hits	LP/BP	U.S†	1985	$14.00/$8.00
RCA	5983-2	Somewhere Between Right and Wrong	LP/BP	U.S.		$14.00/$8.00
RCA	5619-2	Too Many Times	LP/BP	U.S.		$14.00/$8.00
RCA	PCD1-5175	Treadin' Water	LP/BP	U.S†	1985	$14.00/$8.00
Connells						
Singles						
TVT	2592-2	'74-'75	CDJ	U.S.	1993	$2.00
TVT	2593-2P	Connells, The	CDJ	U.S.	1993	$15.00
		Get A Gun	CDJ	U.S.		$2.00
		Hey Wow	CDJ	U.S.	1989	$2.00
TVT	2593	New Boy	CDJ	U.S.	1994	$7.00
		Scotty's Lament	CDJ	U.S.	1989	$2.00
TVT	2591-2	Slackjawed	CDJ	U.S.	1993	$2.00
TVT	2580-2	Stone Cold Yesterday	CDJ	U.S.	1990	$2.00
Connelly, Chris						
Singles						
Devotion	CDDVN 108	Come Down Here	CD5	U.K.	1992	$8.00
Wax Trax	9141	Daredevil	CD5	Canada	1991	$8.00
Wax Trax	89190	July	CD5	U.S.	1992	$8.00
Connelly, John Theory						
Singles						
Relativity	0125	Aggressive	CDJ	U.S.	1991	$2.00
Conners, Stompin' Tom						
Singles						
		Made In the Shade	CDJ	Canada		$5.00
Connick, Harry Jr.						
Full Length						
CBS	XDDP93075	Autumn Selection	DJ/Smplr	Japan	1993	$40.00
Columbia	48808	Blue Light Red Light	LTD/LP	U.S.	1991	$30.00
CD and VHS video in 6"x12" box.						
Columbia	CSK 1504	Everyone's Wild About Harry	DJ/Smplr	U.S.		$10.00
CBS		She	DJ/Smplr	Holland	1995	$18.00
CBS		Star Turtle	DJ/Smplr	U.K.	1995	$18.00
Sony	SRCS-6908	Starbox	LTD/LP	U.S.	1993	$30.00
Singles						
CBS	SRDS-8207	Blue Light, Red Light	CD3	Japan	1991	$13.00/$4.00
Columbia	657536-2	Blue Light, Red Light	CD5	U.K.	1991	$10.00
Columbia	CSK 4207	Blue Light, Red Light	CDJ	U.S.	1991	$3.00
Columbia	CSK 6267	(I Could Only) Whisper Your Name	CDJ	U.S.		$3.00
Columbia	655314-2	It Had To Be You	CD5	U.K.	1989	$10.00
Columbia	CSK 1719	It Had To Be You	CDJ	U.S.	1989	$3.00
Columbia	CSK 1725	It Had To Be You	CDJ	U.S.	1989	$3.00
Columbia	CSK 2289	Promise Me You'll Remember	CDJ	U.S.	1990	$3.00
Columbia	656158-2	Recipe For Love	CD5	U.K.	1991	$10.00
Columbia	656890-2	Recipe For Love	CD5	U.K.	1991	$10.00
Columbia		Recipe For Love	CDJ	U.S.	1991	$3.00
Columbia	CSK 6518	She	CDJ	U.S.	1995	$3.00
Columbia	CSK 4927	Stardust	CDJ	U.S.	1992	$3.00
CBS	SRDS-8186	We Are In Love	CD3	Japan	1991	$13.00/$4.00
Columbia	656468-2	We Are In Love	CD5	U.K.	1991	$10.00
Columbia	657284-2	We Are In Love	CD5	U.K.	1991	$10.00
Columbia	CSK 6267	Whisper Your Name	CDJ	U.S.	1994	$3.00
Conniff, Ray						
Full Length						
Columbia	CK-40167	Christmas Caroling	LP/BP	U.S.†	1985	$14.00/$8.00
Columbia	CK-40499	Here We Come-A-Caroling	LP/LB	U.S.		$12.00/$7.00
Columbia	CK-40214	Sixteen Most Requested	LP/LB	U.S.		$14.00/$8.00
Connolly, Billy						
Singles						
Dover	ROJCD-11	Irish Heartbeat	CD5	U.K.	1990	$7.00
Connors, Bill						
Full Length						
Pathfinder	PTFCD-8707	Assembler	LP/BP	U.S.		$14.00/$8.00
Pathfinder	PTFCD-8620	Double Up	LP/BP	U.S.		$14.00/$8.00
Pathfinder	PTFCD-8503	Step It	LP/BP	U.S.		$14.00/$8.00
Connors, Norman						
Full Length						
Capitol	CDP-48515	Passion	LP/LB	U.S.		$14.00/$8.00
Singles						
Mojazz	374631093	Only When She Cries	CDJ	U.S.	1993	$2.00
Mojazz	374631091	Remember Who You Are	CDJ	U.S.	1993	$2.00
Conquistador						
Singles						
ZYX	CB-508-8	Soledad	CD5	Germany	1990	$7.00
Conscious Daughters						
Singles						
Scarface	7036	Somethin' To Ride On	CDJ	U.S.	1993	$2.00
Scarface	50787	We Roll Deep	CDJ	U.S.	1994	$2.00
Scaarface	50811	We Roll Deep	CDJ	U.S.	1994	$3.00
Consolidated						
Singles						
Nettwerk	6701	Accept Me For What I Am	CDJ	U.S.	1992	$2.00
SPV	8277-3	Brutal Equation	CD5	Germany	1991	$8.00
Nettwerk	Z25G 13822	Brutal Equation	CD5	U.S.	1991	$5.00
		Crackhouse	CD5	U.K.		$10.00
		Crackhouse	CD5	U.K.		$10.00
Second version.						
London	6864	Cutting Alternative	CDJ	U.S.	1994	$3.00
IRS	74006	Dysfunctional	CD5	U.S.	1990	$2.00
Nettwerk	9965-3	This Is Facism	CD5	Germany	1991	$8.00
Nettwerk	NET-036CD	This Is Facism	CD5	U.K.	1991	$8.00

Label	Catalog Number	Title	Type	Country	Year	Longbox Value / Value
Nettwerk	Z25G 113842	This Is Facism	CD5	U.S.	1991	$5.00
Nettwerk	NET-042CD	Tool and Die	CD5	U.K.	1992	$8.00
Capitol	C2 13867	Tool and Die	CD5	U.S.	1992	$5.00
SPV	9955-3	Unity of Oppression	CD5	Germany	1991	$8.00
Nettwerk	Z25G 13828	Unity of Oppression	CD5	U.S.	1991	$2.00

Conspiracy

Singles

Label	Catalog Number	Title	Type	Country	Year	Longbox Value / Value
London	LONCD-263	Everytime You Leave	CD5	U.K.	1990	$8.00
London	869189-2	I Don't Need A Lover	CD5	Germany	1990	$8.00
London	LONCD-277	I Don't Need A Lover	CD5	U.K.	1990	$8.00

Constina

Singles

Label	Catalog Number	Title	Type	Country	Year	Longbox Value / Value
		Are You Lonely Tonight	CDJ	U.S.		$2.00
		Falling Like Rain	CDJ	U.S.		$2.00

Construction

Singles

Label	Catalog Number	Title	Type	Country	Year	Longbox Value / Value
Polygram	879929-2	Oh, Girl	CD5	Germany	1991	$8.00

Consuelo, Ann

Singles

Label	Catalog Number	Title	Type	Country	Year	Longbox Value / Value
Big Beat	10064	See the Day	CD5	U.S.		$5.00

Contagion

Singles

Label	Catalog Number	Title	Type	Country	Year	Longbox Value / Value
Wrld Dmtion	79236	Turn of the Screw	CDJ	U.S.	1993	$2.00

Conte, Paolo

Singles

Label	Catalog Number	Title	Type	Country	Year	Longbox Value / Value
WEA	9031-73254-2	Dragon	CD5	Germany	1991	$8.00

Conti, Robert

Full Length

Label	Catalog Number	Title	Type	Country	Year	Longbox Value / Value
Trend	TRCD-540	Laura	LP/BP	U.S.		$12.00/$7.00

Contours

Singles

Label	Catalog Number	Title	Type	Country	Year	Longbox Value / Value
Private	81020	Do You Love Me	CDJ	U.S.	1994	$3.00

Contraband

Singles

Label	Catalog Number	Title	Type	Country	Year	Longbox Value / Value
Impact	745010-2	All the Way From Memphis	CD5	Germany	1991	$8.00
EMI	TODP-2295	All the Way From Memphis	CD3	Japan	1991	$12.00/$3.00
Impact	CDEM-195	All the Way From Memphis	CD5	U.K.	1991	$8.00
Impact	1393	All the Way From Memphis	CDJ	U.S.	1991	$2.00
Impact	1553	Loud Guitars, Fast Cars	CDJ	U.S.	1991	$2.00
Impact		Tonight You're Mine	CDJ	U.S.	1991	$2.00

Control

Singles

Label	Catalog Number	Title	Type	Country	Year	Longbox Value / Value
BMG	CDGLOBE-105	Dance With Me	CD5	U.K.	1991	$7.00
BMG	CDGLOBE-108	Feel the Music	CD5	U.K.	1991	$7.00
BMG	CDGLOBE-106	Young Hearts	CD5	U.K.	1992	$7.00

Controlled Bleeding

Full Length

Label	Catalog Number	Title	Type	Country	Year	Longbox Value / Value
Wax Trax	7090	Trudge	LP/BP	U.S.		$14.00/$8.00

Singles

Label	Catalog Number	Title	Type	Country	Year	Longbox Value / Value
Wax Trax	9144-3	Fodder Song	CD5	Germany	1989	$7.00
Wax Trax	WAX-91CD	Fodder Song	CD5	U.K.	1989	$7.00
Wax Trax	9091	Fodder Song	CD5	U.S.	1989	$5.00
Waxtrax	WAX 091	Words	CD5	Germany		$10.00

Controllers

Full Length

Label	Catalog Number	Title	Type	Country	Year	Longbox Value / Value
WEA	254989-2	For the Love of My Woman	LP	Germany		$12.00
MCA	MCAD-42043	For the Love of My Woman	LP	U.S.		$14.00/$8.00

Convert

Singles

Label	Catalog Number	Title	Type	Country	Year	Longbox Value / Value
A&M	AMCD-845	Nightbird	CD5	U.K.	1992	$7.00

Conwell, Tommy (& Young Rumblers)

Full Length

Label	Catalog Number	Title	Type	Country	Year	Longbox Value / Value
Columbia	CK-46235	Guitar Trouble	LP/LB	U.S.		$14.00/$8.00

Singles

Label	Catalog Number	Title	Type	Country	Year	Longbox Value / Value
CBS	10EP-3048	I'm Not Your Man	CD3	Japan	1989	$12.00/$3.00
CBS	652933-2	I'm Not Your Man	CD5	U.K.	1989	$8.00
Columbia	CSK1206	I'm Not Your Man	CDJ	U.S.	1988	$2.00
CBS	CSDS-8167	I'm Seventeen	CD3	Japan	1990	$12.00/$3.00
Columbia	CSK 73500	I'm Seventeen	CDJ	U.S.	1990	$2.00
CBS	10EP-3060	If We Never Meet Again	CD3	Japan	1989	$12.00/$3.00
Columbia	654579-2	If We Never Meet Again	CD5	U.K.	1989	$8.00
Columbia	CSK 1399	If We Never Meet Again	CDJ	U.S.	1988	$2.00
Columbia	CSK 2253	Let Me Love You Too	CDJ	U.S.	1990	$2.00
Columbia	CSK 1497	Loves On Fire	CDJ	U.S.	1989	$2.00
		More Than A Kiss	CDJ	U.S.		$2.00

Cony, Chris

Singles

Label	Catalog Number	Title	Type	Country	Year	Longbox Value / Value
Bellaphon	130-07-583	Alone	CD5	Germany	1991	$7.00

Coo Coo

Singles

Label	Catalog Number	Title	Type	Country	Year	Longbox Value / Value
Alfa	11B3-66	All You Need Is Love	CD3	Japan	1989	$12.00/$3.00
Alfa	ALDB-15	Happy Day	CD3	Japan	1989	$12.00/$3.00
Alfa	10SR-23	Upside Down	CD3	Japan	1988	$12.00/$3.00
Alfa	110B3-8	You Can Set Me Free	CD3	Japan	1989	$12.00/$3.00

Cooder, Ry

Full Length

Label	Catalog Number	Title	Type	Country	Year	Longbox Value / Value
Warner Brothers	03358-2	Bop Til You Drop	LP/LB	U.S.†	1984	$14.00/$8.00
Warner Brothers	PCS-40	CD Collection	DJ/Smplr	Japan		$200.00
Warner Brothers		Paradise And Lunch	LP/LB	U.S.		$14.00/$8.00
Warner Brothers		Words & Music	DJ/Intvw	U.S.	1995	$15.00

Singles

Label	Catalog Number	Title	Type	Country	Year	Longbox Value / Value
Warner Brothers	PRO-CD-2873	All Shook Up	CDJ	U.S.	1987	$7.00
WEA	920940-2	Get Rhythm	CD3	Germany	1988	$9.00
WEA	W-8107CD	Get Rhythm	CD3	U.K.	1988	$9.00
Warner Brothers	PRO-CD-2934	Get Rhythm	CDJ	U.S.	1987	$7.00
Sire	PRO-CD-5923	King of the Street	CDJ	U.S.	1992	$2.00

Cook, Betsy

Singles

Company	Disk Number	Title	Type	Country	Year	Longbox Value / Value
Eastwest	YZ-675CD	Docklands	CD5	U.K.	1992	$8.00
Eastwest	9031-77051-2	How Can I Believe	CD5	Germany	1992	$8.00
Eastwest	YZ-658CD	How Can I Believe	CD5	U.K.	1992	$8.00
Eastwest	9031-75734-2	Love Is the Groove	CD5	Germany	1992	$8.00
Eastwest	YZ-621CD	Love Is the Groove	CD5	U.K.	1992	$8.00

Cook, Norman

Singles

Company	Disk Number	Title	Type	Country	Year	Longbox Value / Value
Polygram	874994-3	Don't Talk About It	CD3	Germany	1989	$7.00
Polygram	874995-2	Don't Talk About It	CD5	Germany	1989	$7.00
Go! Discs	GODCD-37	For Spacious Lies	CD5	Germany	1989	$7.00

Cooke, B.

Singles

Company	Disk Number	Title	Type	Country	Year	Longbox Value / Value
BCM	20189	Sharp as a Knife	CD5	Germany	1989	$7.00

Cooke, Sam

Full Length

Company	Disk Number	Title	Type	Country	Year	Longbox Value / Value
RCA	PCD1-5181	Feel It!	LP/BP	U.S.†	1985	$14.00/$8.00
RCA	PCD1-5181	Feel It!	LP/BP	U.S.	1986	$14.00/$8.00

Singles

Company	Disk Number	Title	Type	Country	Year	Longbox Value / Value
RCA	PD-49455	Chain Gang	CD3	Germany	1989	$8.00
RCA	PD-49455	Chain Gang	CD3	U.K.	1989	$8.00
RCA	BVDP-57	(What A) Wonderful World	CD3	Japan	1992	$12.00/$3.00

Cookie Crew

Full Length

Company	Disk Number	Title	Type	Country	Year	Longbox Value / Value
London	828251-2	Fade to Black	LP/BP	U.S.		$12.00/$7.00
London	828134-2	Feelin' Proud	LP/BP	U.S.		$12.00/$7.00

Singles

Company	Disk Number	Title	Type	Country	Year	Longbox Value / Value
London	FFRCD-19	Born This Way	CD5	U.K.	1988	$8.00
ffrr	FCD-110	Come On and Get Some	CD5	U.K.	1989	$8.00
London	886562-3	Got To Keep On	CD3	Germany	1989	$8.00
London	886562-2	Got To Keep On	CD5	Germany	1989	$8.00
London	FFRCD-25	Got To Keep On	CD3	U.K.	1989	$8.00
		Got To Keep On	CDJ	U.S.	1989	$2.00
ffrr	FCD-110	Love Will Bring Us Back Together	CD5	U.K.	1991	$8.00
ffrr	FCD-159	Secret (Of Success)	CD5	U.S.	1991	$8.00
ffrr	CDP 543	Secret (Of Success)	CDJ	U.S.	1991	$2.00

Cool 2

Singles

Company	Disk Number	Title	Type	Country	Year	Longbox Value / Value
ZYX	6553-8	Kinda Groovy	CD5	Germany	1991	$6.00

Cool C

Singles

Company	Disk Number	Title	Type	Country	Year	Longbox Value / Value
Atlantic	7567-86138-2	Life In the Ghetto	CD5	Germany	1990	$7.00

Cool Down Zone

Singles

Company	Disk Number	Title	Type	Country	Year	Longbox Value / Value
Virgin	TENCD-309	Heaven Knows	CD5	U.K.	1990	$7.00
BMG	663584	Waiting For Love	CD5	Germany	1990	$7.00
Virgin	TENCD-318	Waiting For Love	CD5	U.K.	1990	$7.00

Cool, Joe

Full Length

Company	Disk Number	Title	Type	Country	Year	Longbox Value / Value
Canyon	D32Y-0022	Party Animals	LP	Japan		$10.00

Cool Notes

Full Length

Company	Disk Number	Title	Type	Country	Year	Longbox Value / Value
Intercord	845 091	Have A Good Forever	LP	Germany		$15.00

Singles

Company	Disk Number	Title	Type	Country	Year	Longbox Value / Value
Canyon	S9ED-8005	Magic Lover	CD3	Japan	1989	$12.00/$3.00
PWL	ALDB-143	Make This A Special Night	CD3	Japan	1991	$12.00/$3.00
PWL	PWCD-200	Make This A Special Night	CD5	U.K.	1991	$7.00
BMG	CDYD-5	Spend the Night	CD5	U.K.	1990	$7.00

Cool'r

Singles

Company	Disk Number	Title	Type	Country	Year	Longbox Value / Value
A&M	CD 17785	If It Were Me	CDJ	U.S.	1989	$2.00
		Victim	CDJ	U.S.		$2.00

Cooley, Ron

Full Length

Company	Disk Number	Title	Type	Country	Year	Longbox Value / Value
Am Gramm	388	Ancient & the Infant	LP/LB	U.S.		$14.00/$8.00
Am Gramm	368	Daydreams	LP/LB	U.S.		$14.00/$8.00
Am Gramm	378	Rainbows	LP/LB	U.S.		$14.00/$8.00

Coolidge, Rita

Full Length

Company	Disk Number	Title	Type	Country	Year	Longbox Value / Value
		Fire Me Back	DJ/Intvw	Canada		$15.00
Polygram	393238-2	Greatest Hits	LP	Germany		$18.00

Singles

Company	Disk Number	Title	Type	Country	Year	Longbox Value / Value
Attic	ALDB-146	Another Saturday Night	CD3	Japan	1992	$13.00/$4.00
A&M	S12Y-3031	Don't Cry Out Loud	CD3	Japan	1992	$13.00/$4.00
		Fascination	CD3	Japan		$13.00/$4.00
		For You	CDJ	Japan	1994	$15.00
Alfa	ALDB-162	Heart Don't Fall Me Now	CD3	Japan	1992	$13.00/$4.00
		I Just Wanna Be With You	CD3	Japan		$13.00/$4.00
Polygram	879887-2	I'm Still Learning	CD5	Germany	1991	$8.00
Canyon	S9Y-11116	Nice To Meet You	CD3	Japan	1989	$13.00/$4.00
Attic	ALDB-139	Rain	CD3	Japan	1991	$13.00/$4.00
Attic	ALDB-126	Suddenly	CD3	Japan	1991	$13.00/$4.00

Coolio

Singles

Company	Disk Number	Title	Type	Country	Year	Longbox Value / Value
Tommy Boy	608	County Line	CDJ	U.S.	1993	$2.00
Tommy Boy	577	County Line	CD5	U.S.	1994	$5.00
Tommy Boy	TBXCD617	Fantastic Voyage	CD5	Canada	1994	$9.00
Tommy Boy	617	Fantastic Voyage	CD5	U.S.	1994	$5.00
Tommy Boy	620	Fantastic Voyage	CDJ	U.S.	1994	$2.00
MCA	3459	Gangsta's Paradise	CDJ	U.S.	1995	$7.00
Tommy Boy	TBXCD635	I Remember	CD5	Canada	1994	$9.00
Tommy Boy	632	I Remember	CDJ	U.S.	1994	$3.00
Tommy Boy	651	Mama I'm In Love	CDJ	U.S.	1994	$3.00
Tommy Boy	7718	Too Hot	CD5	U.S.	1995	$5.00

Cooly Live

Singles

Company	Disk Number	Title	Type	Country	Year	Longbox Value / Value
RCA	62083-2-RDJ	That's What I Like	CDJ	U.S.	1992	$2.00

Cooper, Alice

Full Length

Company	Disk Number	Title	Type	Country	Year	Longbox Value / Value
Metal Blade	PRO-CD-6454-2	Alice Cooper/Deep Purple-Sampler	DJ/Smplr	U.S.	1990	$15.00
MCA	MCAD-5761	Constrictor	LP/LB	U.S.		$15.00/$9.00
Warner Brothers	9 26445-2	From the Inside	LP/LB	U.S.		$15.00/$9.00
Foundations		FZ Interview	RS	U.S.	1994	$15.00
Epic	ESK 4085	Hey Stupid	DJ/LP	U.S.	1991	$18.00

Cooper, Alice – Stupid News (Epic ESK 4161)

Label	Catalog Number	Title	Type	Country	Year	Longbox Value / Value
		In Concert	RS	U.S.	1992	$50.00
	2 CD set. Airdate: 8/3/92					
Album Network		In the Studio (Billion Dollar Babies)	RS	U.S.	1989	$20.00
	Airdate: 8/14/89.					
Album Network		In the Studio (Killer)	RS	U.S.	1990	$20.00
	Airdate: 2/19/90.					
Album Network		In the Studio (Love It To Death)	RS	U.S.	1991	$20.00
	Airdate: 3/11/91.					
DIR		King Biscuit Flour Hour	RS	U.S.	1988	$35.00
	Airdate: 10/30/88.					
DIR		King Biscuit Flour Hour	RS	U.S.	1990	$35.00
	Airdate: 6/4/90.					
DIR		King Biscuit Flour Hour	RS	U.S.	1991	$35.00
	Airdate: 8/4/91.					
DIR		King Biscuit Flour Hour	RS	U.S.	1993	$25.00
	Airdate: 10/25/93.					
DIR		King Biscuit Flour Hour	RS	U.S.	1993	$25.00
	Airdate: 3/1/93.					
Warner Brothers	26446	Lace & Whiskey	LP/LB	U.S.		$15.00/$9.00
Epic		Last Temptation	LTD/LP	Australia	1994	$40.00
	2 CD set.					
Epic		Last Temptation Box, The	LTD/LP	Japan	1994	$50.00
	CD album plus bonus disc of live tracks and comic book.					
Epic	476594 2	Last Temptation, The	LTD/LP	Germany	1994	$30.00
Epic	476594 2	Last Temptation, The	LTD/LP	U.S.	1994	$20.00
	Limited edition with comic book.					
		Live From Electric Ladyland	RS	U.S.	1991	$50.00
	Airdate: 9/13/91.					
Warner Brothers	26447	Muscle of Love	LP/LB	U.S.		$15.00/$9.00
Epic	ESK 4161	Stupid News	DJ/Intvw	U.S.	1991	$20.00
		Trash	LTD/LP	Australia	1989	$35.00
Epic	EK-45137	Trash	DJ/LP	U.S.	1989	$150.00
	CD, cassette, VHS tape and press kit in large plastic trash can.					
Image	ID7292CB	Video Trash	8"LD	U.S.	1990	$10.00
Image	ID7424RH	Welcome to My Nightmare	LD	U.S.		$85.00
		Singles				
Epic	655318-3	Bed of Nails	CD5	Germany	1989	$10.00
CBS	ALICEC-3	Bed of Nails	CD5	U.K.	1989	$10.00
Epic	657691-2	Burning Our Bed	CD5	Germany	1992	$10.00
Warner Brothers	921132-2	Hello Hooray	CD3	Germany	1989	$10.00
Warner Brothers	921132-2	Hello Hooray	CD3	U.K.	1989	$10.00
Epic	656983-2	Hey Stupid	CD5	Germany	1991	$10.00
Epic	ESDA-7074	Hey Stupid	CD3	Japan	1991	$13.00/$4.00
Epic	656983-2	Hey Stupid	CD5	U.K.	1991	$10.00
Epic	ESK 73835	Hey Stupid	CDJ	U.S.	1991	$6.00
Epic	655472-3	House of Fire	CD3	Germany	1990	$10.00
Epic	ESDA-7013	House of Fire	CD3	Japan	1990	$13.00/$4.00
Epic	ALICEC-4	House of Fire	CD5	U.K.	1989	$10.00
Epic	ESK 73085	House of Fire	CDJ	U.S.	1989	$3.00
Epic	ESK 1355	I Got a Line on You	CDJ	U.S.	1988	$3.00
		It's Me	CD5	Australia	1993	$10.00
Epic	6605632	It's Me	CD5	U.K.	1994	$10.00
Epic		It's Me	CD5	U.K.	1994	$10.00
	Second version.					
Epic		It's Me	CDJ	U.K.	1994	$15.00
Epic		It's Me	CDJ	U.S.	1994	$3.00
Epic		Lost In America	CD5	Australia	1994	$12.00
Epic		Lost In America	CD5	U.K.	1994	$10.00
Epic		Lost In America	CD5	U.K.	1994	$10.00
	Second version.					
Epic	ESK 6045	Lost In America	CDJ	U.S.	1994	$3.00
Epic	657438-2	Love's a Loaded Gun	CD5	Germany	1991	$13.00
	Gun shaped package.					
Epic	ESK 73983	Love's a Loaded Gun	CDJ	U.S.	1991	$3.00
Epic	655758-3	Only My Heart Talkin'	CD3	Germany	1990	$10.00
Epic	ALICEC-5	Only My Heart Talkin'	CD5	U.K.	1990	$10.00
Epic	ESK 73268	Only My Heart Talkin'	CDJ	U.S.	1989	$3.00
CBS	655061-3	Poison	CD3	Germany	1989	$12.00
Epic	655061-2	Poison	CD5	U.K.	1989	$45.00
	CD in cardboard pill bottle package.					
Epic	ESK 1665	Poison	CDJ	U.S.	1989	$6.00
WEA	921132-2	School's Out	CD3	U.K.		$9.00
Epic	ESK 5995	Unholy War	CDJ	U.S.	1994	$3.00

Cooper, Bernadette

Label	Catalog Number	Title	Type	Country	Year	Longbox Value / Value
		Full Length				
MCA	MCAD-10058	Drama According To B.C.	LP/LB	U.S.		$14.00/$8.00

Cooper, Michael

Label	Catalog Number	Title	Type	Country	Year	Longbox Value / Value
		Singles				
		Dinner For Two	CDJ	U.S.		$2.00
		My Baby's House	CDJ	U.S.		$2.00
Reprise	9 40717-2	Shoop Shoop	CD5	U.S.	1992	$4.00
Reprise	PRO-CD-5889	Shoop Shoop	CDJ	U.S.	1992	$2.00
Reprise	PRO-CD-3851	Should Have Been You	CDJ	U.S.	1989	$2.00
		To Prove My Love	CDJ	U.S.		$2.00

Cop Shoot Cop

Label	Catalog Number	Title	Type	Country	Year	Longbox Value / Value
		Singles				
Interscope	PRCD 6307 2	Room 429	CDJ	U.S.	1994	$2.00
Big Cat	ABB-39SCD	Suck City	CD5	U.K.	1992	$7.00
Interscope	PRCD 96116-2	Suck City	CDJ	U.S.	1992	$3.00

Cope, Julian

Label	Catalog Number	Title	Type	Country	Year	Longbox Value / Value
		Full Length				
Island	PRCD 6664-2	Beautiful Love	DJ/Smplr	U.S.	1991	$13.00
Mercury	822832-2	Fried	LP	U.K.		$18.00
		Singles				
Island	885267	5 O'Clock World	CD5	Germany	1989	$9.00
Island	P20D 20089	5 O'Clock World	CD5	Japan	1991	$3.00
Island	CID-399	5 O'Clock World	CD5	U.K.	1989	$9.00
Aris	887072	Beautiful Love	CD5	Germany	1991	$9.00
Island	CID-483	Beautiful Love	CD5	U.K.	1991	$9.00
Island	P15D-37014	Charlotte Anne	CD3	Japan	1988	$13.00/$4.00
Island	CID-380	Charlotte Anne	CD5	U.K.	1988	$9.00
Aris	885467	China Love	CD5	Germany	1991	$9.00
Island	CID-406	China Love	CD5	U.K.	1991	$9.00
Island	868 119-2	East Easy Rider	CD5	U.K.	1991	$9.00
Island	CID-492	East Easy Rider	CD5	U.K.	1991	$9.00
Island	CID-318	Eves Volcano	CD5	U.K.	1987	$10.00
Island		Fear Loves This Place	CD5	U.K.	1992	$10.00
Island		Fear Loves This Place	CD5	U.K.	1992	$10.00
	Second version.					
Island	PRCD 6751-2	Fear Loves This Place	CDJ	U.S.	1992	$3.00
Island	422 868 433	Head	CD5	U.K.	1991	$9.00
Island	422 868 909	Head	CD5	U.K.	1991	$9.00
Island	CID-497	Head	CD5	U.K.	1991	$9.00
		I Come From Another Planet	CD5	U.K.	1996	$10.00
Aris	887308	Island	CD5	Germany	1991	$9.00
		Try, Try, Try	CD5	U.K.	1995	$10.00
American	7729	Try, Try, Try	CDJ	U.S.	1995	$3.00
Island	CID-534	World Shut Your Mouth	CD5	U.K.	1992	$9.00

Copeland, Stewart

Label	Catalog Number	Title	Type	Country	Year	Longbox Value / Value
		Full Length				
IRS		Equalizer, The	LP/LB	U.S.		$14.00/$8.00

Copperhead

Label	Catalog Number	Title	Type	Country	Year	Longbox Value / Value
		Singles				
Mercury	CDP 893	Born Loser	CDJ	U.S.	1993	$2.00
Mercury	CDP 768	Busted	CDJ	U.S.	1992	$2.00

Cora

Label	Catalog Number	Title	Type	Country	Year	Longbox Value / Value
		Singles				
WEA	171967-2	I Call It the Blues	CD5	Germany	1990	$7.00
WEA	246596-2	In the Name of Love	CD5	Germany	1989	$7.00

Corbin/Hanner

Label	Catalog Number	Title	Type	Country	Year	Longbox Value / Value
		Singles				
Mercury	CDP 807	I Will Stand by You	CDJ	U.S.	1992	$2.00
Mercury	CDP 426	One More Night	CDJ	U.S.	1991	$2.00
Mercury		Worksong	CDJ	U.S.		$2.00

Cords

Label	Catalog Number	Title	Type	Country	Year	Longbox Value / Value
		Singles				
TVT	3611	Eat Your Heart Out	CD5	U.S.	1993	$4.00
TVT	3612	Gasping	CDJ	U.S.	1994	$3.00

Corea, Chick

Label	Catalog Number	Title	Type	Country	Year	Longbox Value / Value
		Full Length				
Elektra	60167-2	Again And Again	LP/LB	U.S.		$14.00/$8.00
Elektra/Muse	60167-2	Again And Again	LP/LB	U.S.†	1985	$14.00/$8.00
ECM	25005-2	Children's Songs	LP/LB	U.S.†	1985	$14.00/$8.00
Pioneer	PA-83-037	Live In Tokyo	LD	U.S.	1983	$20.00
Pioneer	PA-83-037	Live In Tokyo	LD	U.S.	1990	$25.00
Philips	410397-2	Meeting	LP/BP	U.S.		$14.00/$8.00
Polygram	825657-2	My Spanish Heart	LP/LB	U.S.†	1985	$14.00/$8.00
ECM	POCJ-9044	Return To Forever	LP	Japan		$25.00
GRP	MVCZ-9	Round Midnight	LTD/LP	Japan		$25.00
	Gold disc.					

Corea, Chick & Friedrich Guida

Label	Catalog Number	Title	Type	Country	Year	Longbox Value / Value
		Full Length				
Philips	410397-2	The Meeting	LP/LB	U.S.†	1985	$14.00/$8.00

Corea, Chick & Gary Burton

Label	Catalog Number	Title	Type	Country	Year	Longbox Value / Value
		Full Length				
ECM	1182-2	In Concert	LP/LB	U.S.†	1985	$14.00/$8.00

Corelli

Label	Catalog Number	Title	Type	Country	Year	Longbox Value / Value
		Singles				
CBS	66722	Concerti Grossi	CD5	U.S.	1994	$5.00

Corina

Label	Catalog Number	Title	Type	Country	Year	Longbox Value / Value
		Singles				
Victor	VICP-15015	Now That You're Gone	CD5	Japan	1992	$13.00
Atco	PRCD 4508-2	Now That You're Gone	CDJ	U.S.	1990	$2.00
Atco	7567-96288	Temptation	CD5	Germany	1991	$7.00
Warner Brothers	AMDY-5058	Temptation	CD3	Japan	1991	$12.00/$3.00
Atco	B-8775CD	Temptation	CD5	U.K.	1991	$7.00
Atco	PRCD 3977-2	Temptation	CDJ	U.S.	1990	$2.00
Victor	VIDP-37	Whispers	CD3	Japan	1991	$12.00/$3.00

Corley, Al

Label	Catalog Number	Title	Type	Country	Year	Longbox Value / Value
		Full Length				
Mercury	822316-2	Square Rooms	LP/BP	U.S.†	1985	$14.00/$8.00
		Singles				
Polygram	872339-2	Land of the Giants	CD5	Germany	1989	$8.00
Polygram	874284-3	Where Are the Children	CD3	Germany	1989	$8.00
Polygram	8874285-2	Where Are the Children	CD5	Germany	1989	$8.00

Corman & Tuscado

Label	Catalog Number	Title	Type	Country	Year	Longbox Value / Value
		Singles				
SPV	8964-2	Leek Shark	CD5	Germany	1992	$7.00

Cornell, Michael

Label	Catalog Number	Title	Type	Country	Year	Longbox Value / Value
		Singles				
Bellaphon	130-07-577	Kiss and Say Goodbye	CD5	Germany	1991	$8.00

Cornershop

Label	Catalog Number	Title	Type	Country	Year	Longbox Value / Value
		Singles				
Wiija	WIJ 33CD	Born Disco: Died Heavy Metal	CD5	U.K.		$10.00
Wiija	WIJ 22CD	Lock Stock & Double Barrel	CD5	U.K.		$10.00
Luka Bop	PRO-CD-7920	Wog	CDJ	U.S.	1995	$3.00

Cornwell, Hugh

Full Length

Label	Catalog Number	Title	Type	Country	Year	Longbox Value / Value
Atlantic	90947-2	Wolf	LP/LB	U.S.		$14.00/$8.00

Singles

Label	Catalog Number	Title	Type	Country	Year	Longbox Value / Value
Virgin	VSCD-945	Another Kind of Love	CD5	U.K.	1988	$8.00
Virgin	VSCD-1093	Another Kind of Love	CD5	U.K.	1988	$8.00

Corona

Singles

Label	Catalog Number	Title	Type	Country	Year	Longbox Value / Value
	PRCD 9171-2	Baby Baby	CDJ	U.S.	1995	$3.00
		Rhythm of The Night	CD5	U.K.		$10.00
		Rhythm of The Night	CD5	U.K.		$10.00
	Second version.					
Atlantic	95808	Rhythm of The Night	CD5	U.S.	1994	$5.00
Elektra	66099	Try Me Out	CD5	U.S.	1995	$5.00

Coroner

Full Length

Label	Catalog Number	Title	Type	Country	Year	Longbox Value / Value
Noise	44836	Mental Vortex	LP/LB	U.S.		$12.00/$7.00
Noise	44811	No More Color	LP/LB	U.S.		$12.00/$7.00
Noise	44802	Punishment For Decadence	LP/LB	U.S.		$12.00/$7.00
Noise	44813	R.I.P.	LP/LB	U.S.		$12.00/$7.00

Singles

Label	Catalog Number	Title	Type	Country	Year	Longbox Value / Value
Noise		About Life	CDJ	U.S.		$2.00
Noise	NZCDP 4	Last Entertainment	CDJ	U.S.	1989	$2.00

Corp

Singles

Label	Catalog Number	Title	Type	Country	Year	Longbox Value / Value
ZYX	7394	On Top of The World	CD5	U.S.	1994	$5.00

Corrosion Of Conformity

Full Length

Label	Catalog Number	Title	Type	Country	Year	Longbox Value / Value
Columbia		Wiseblood	LTD/LP	U.S.	1997	$16.00
	CD with VHS video.					

Singles

Label	Catalog Number	Title	Type	Country	Year	Longbox Value / Value
Columbia	CSK 6525	Albatross	CDJ	U.S.	1994	$3.00
Columbia	CSK 6487	Broken Man	CDJ	U.S.	1994	$7.00
Columbia	CSK 6705	Clean My Wounds	CDJ	U.S.	1994	$3.00
Relativity	0139	Dance Of the Dead	CDJ	U.S.	1992	$3.00
Relativity		Seven Days	CDJ	U.S.	1995	$7.00
IRS	977-601	Vote With A Bullet	CD5	Germany	1992	$8.00
Relativity	RO-2401-3	Vote With A Bullet	CD5	U.K.	1992	$8.00
Relativity	2388-3	Vote With A Bullet	CD5	U.K.	1993	$8.00
Relativity	88561 1081	Vote With A Bullet	CD5	U.S.	1993	$5.00
Relativity	0171	Vote With A Bullet	CDJ	U.S.	1993	$3.00

Corrs

Singles

Label	Catalog Number	Title	Type	Country	Year	Longbox Value / Value
Atlantic	PRCD 6645	Right Time, The	CDJ	U.S.		$3.00
Atlantic	958133	Runaway	CD5	U.S.	1995	$5.00

Corvettes

Singles

Label	Catalog Number	Title	Type	Country	Year	Longbox Value / Value
LDC	HBDL-3007	Dancin'	CD3	Japan	1991	$12.00/$3.00
LDC	HBDL-3302	Danger	CD3	Japan	1992	$12.00/$3.00

Coryell, Larry

Full Length

Label	Catalog Number	Title	Type	Country	Year	Longbox Value / Value
Philips	PHCE-33009	Bolero/Scheherazade	LTD/LP	Japan		$25.00
	Gold disc.					
Verve	810024-2	Bolero/Scheherazade	LP/LB	U.S.†	1985	$14.00/$8.00
Verve	812864-2	L'Oiseau de Feu/Petrouchka	LP/LB	U.S.†	1985	$14.00/$8.00
Polygram	814750-2	Le Sacre du Printemps	LP	Germany		$12.00
Philips	814750-2	Le Sacre du Printemps	LP/LB	U.S.†	1985	$14.00/$8.00
Novus	3072	Tributaries	LP/BP	U.S.		$12.00/$7.00
Keytone	KYTCD-716	With Urszula Dudziak	LP	Germany		$12.00

Singles

Label	Catalog Number	Title	Type	Country	Year	Longbox Value / Value
Concerto	22738	I'll Be Over You	CD5	U.S.	1994	$5.00

Cosby, Bill

Full Length

Label	Catalog Number	Title	Type	Country	Year	Longbox Value / Value
Motown	MOTD-6026	Himself	LP/BP	U.S.		$14.00/$8.00
Capitol	CDP-96678	My Father Confused Me	LP/LB	U.S.		$14.00/$8.00

Cosmic Baby

Singles

Label	Catalog Number	Title	Type	Country	Year	Longbox Value / Value
	59003	Fantasia	CD5	U.S.	1994	$5.00
Logic	74321184322	Loops of Infinity	CD5	U.K.		$10.00

Cosmo Crew

Singles

Label	Catalog Number	Title	Type	Country	Year	Longbox Value / Value
ZYX	6692-8	Back It Up	CD5	U.S.	1994	$5.00
ZYX	DST-1068-8	Groove Is Hypnotising	CD5	Germany	1992	$6.00

Cosmoalpha

Full Length

Label	Catalog Number	Title	Type	Country	Year	Longbox Value / Value
Demon	CD-7207	I Don't Know 30s	LP/BP	U.S.†	1985	$14.00/$8.00

Cossu, Scott

Full Length

Label	Catalog Number	Title	Type	Country	Year	Longbox Value / Value
Windham	WD-1033	Islands	LP/LB	U.S.†	1985	$14.00/$8.00
Windham	371049-2	Reunion	LP	Germany		$15.00

Costa, Nikka

Singles

Label	Catalog Number	Title	Type	Country	Year	Longbox Value / Value
Polygram	889850-3	Renegade	CD3	Germany	1989	$7.00
Polygram	889851-2	Renegade	CD5	Germany	1989	$7.00

Costello, Elvis

Full Length

Label	Catalog Number	Title	Type	Country	Year	Longbox Value / Value
Rykodisc		2½ Years In 31 Minutes	DJ/Smplr	U.K.	1993	$25.00
Rykodisc	VRCD 0271	2½ Years In 31 Minutes	DJ/Smplr	U.S.	1993	$25.00
Columbia	CK 37562	Almost Blue	LP/LB	U.S.		$16.00/$12.00
Rykodisc		Almost Blue/Imperial Bedroom	DJ/LP	U.S.	1994	$35.00
	2 CD set.					
Columbia	CK 35709	Armed Forces	LP/LB	U.S.	1985	$16.00/$12.00
BBC Radio		BBC Classic Tracks	RS	U.S.	1991	$35.00
	Airdate: 10/7/91.					
CBS/Fox	7092-80	Best Of Elvis Costello	LD	U.S.	1988	$35.00
Columbia	CK 40518	Blood And Chocolate	LP/LB	U.S.		$16.00/$12.00
Rykodisc		Blood And Chocolate	LTD/LP	U.S.	1995	$18.00
	2 CD set. 10,000 copies pressed.					
Warner Brothers		Costello & Nieve	DJ/Smplr	U.S.	1996	$50.00
	5 CD-single live set from 1996 concert tour.					
Warner Brothers	46469-2	Costello & Nieve	LTD/LP	U.S.	1996	$50.00
	5 CD-single live set from 1996 concert tour in slip case.					
WEA	38340	Elvis Costello & The Brodsky Quartet	LD	U.S.	1993	$30.00
Warner Brothers		Elvis Costello & the Brodsky Quartet - Live At New York Town Hall	DJ/Smplr	U.S.	1993	$18.00
Warner Brothers	PRO-CD-6018	Excerpts From Juliet Letters	DJ/Smplr	U.S.	1993	$10.00
	6 Tracks.					
Warner Brothers		Excerpts From Juliet Letters	DJ/Smplr	U.S.	1993	$10.00
	7 Tracks.					
Columbia	CK 36347	Get Happy!	LP/LB	U.S.		$16.00/$12.00
Rykodisc	RCD202775	Get Happy!/Trust	DJ/Smplr	U.S.	1994	$40.00
	2CD set with color art, button and custom slip case.					
Rykodisc	VPRCD 275/76	Get Happy!/Trust	DJ/Smplr	U.S.	1994	$70.00
	2CD set with black & white picture sleeves.					
Columbia	CK 39429	Goodbye Cruel World	LP/LB	U.S.†	1985	$16.00/$12.00
Rykodisc		Highlights From Almost Blue	DJ/Smplr	U.K.	1993	$50.00
Columbia	CK 38157	Imperial Bedroom	LP/LB	U.S.		$16.00/$12.00
		Juliet Letters	DJ/Smplr	U.S.	1993	$18.00
	With Brodsky Quartet.					
DIR		King Biscuit Flour Hour	RS	U.S.	1989	$60.00
	Airdate: 3/5/89.					
DIR		King Biscuit Flour Hour	RS	U.S.	1990	$40.00
	Airdate: 8/20/90.					
DIR		King Biscuit Flour Hour	RS	U.S.	1992	$40.00
	Airdate: 8/9/92.					
DIR		King Biscuit Flour Hour	RS	U.S.	1994	$40.00
	Airdate: 2/28/94.					
DIR		King Biscuit Flour Hour	RS	U.S.	1994	$60.00
	Airdate: 3/6/94.					
DIR		King Biscuit Flour Hour	RS	U.S.	1995	$60.00
	Airdate: 7/16/95.					
Demon		King Of America	DJ/LP	U.K.	1995	$40.00
Demon		King Of America	DJ/Smplr	U.K.	1995	$25.00
Columbia	CK 40173	King Of America	LP/LB	U.S.		$16.00/$12.00
Rykodisc		King Of America	LTD/LP	U.S.	1995	$22.00
	2 CD set. 10,000 copies pressed.					
Warner Brothers		Kojak Variety	Dj/LP	U.S.	1995	$300.00
	Special edition with two bonus tracks and certificate, limited to 200 copies.					
	PCS-141	Malice And Magic	DJ/Smplr	Japan	1995	$200.00
Warner Brothers		Malice and Magic	DJ/Smplr	U.S.	1995	$20.00
Columbia	CK 40101	Man	LP/LB	U.S.		$16.00/$12.00
Warner Brothers	9 26593-2	Mighty Like A Rose	LTD/LP	U.S.	1991	$18.00
Columbia	CK 35037	My Aim Is True	LP/LB	U.S.†	1984	$16.00/$12.00
Columbia	CK 38897	Punch Out the Clock	LP/LB	U.S.†	1984	$16.00/$12.00
Columbia	CK 38897	Punch Out the Clock	LP/LB	U.S.	1986	$16.00/$12.00
Rykodisc		Punch the Clock/Goodbye Cruel World	DJ/LP	U.S.	1995	$35.00
	2CD set in slipcase					
Rykodisc	RCD 20279 ADV	Punch the Clock/Goodbye Cruel World	DJ/LP	U.S.	1995	$50.00
Rykodisc		Punch the World	DJ/Smplr	U.S.	1995	$20.00
Demon		Selections From the King Of America	DJ/Smplr	U.K.	1995	$25.00
Warner Brothers	PRO-CD-3426	Spike	DJ/LP	U.S.	1989	$20.00
Columbia	CK 36839	Taking Liberties	LP/LB	U.S.	1986	$25.00/$20.00
		Taking My Life In Your Hands	DJ/Intvw	U.S.	1993	$10.00
Columbia	CK 35331	This Year's Model	LP/LB	U.S.	1978	$16.00/$12.00
Columbia	CK 35331	This Years Model	LP	U.S.		$30.00
Columbia	CK 37051	Trust	LP/LB	U.S.	1978	$16.00/$12.00
	PROP 146	Useless Beauty	DJ/LP	Germany		$40.00
Warner Brothers	PRO-CD-6955	Words & Music (Brutal Youth)	DJ/Intvw	U.S.	1994	$15.00
Warner Brothers		Words & Music: Kojak Variety	DJ/Intvw	U.S.	1995	$20.00

Singles

Label	Catalog Number	Title	Type	Country	Year	Longbox Value / Value
Warner Brothers	W-0245	13 Steps Down	CD5	Germany	1994	$10.00
Warner Brothers		13 Steps Down	CD5	U.K.	1994	$10.00
Warner Brothers	9 18214-2	13 Steps Down	CD5	U.S.	1994	$5.00
Warner Brothers	18214	13 Steps Down	CD5	U.S.	1994	$5.00
Warner Brothers	PRO-CD-6800	13 Steps Down	CDJ	U.S.	1994	$3.00
WEA	W-2949CD	Baby Plays Around	CD3	U.K.	1989	$10.00
Warner Brothers		Clown Strike	CDJ	U.K.	1994	$7.00
		It's Time	CD5	U.K.	1996	$10.00
		It's Time	CD5	U.K.	1996	$10.00
	Second version.					
		Jacksons, Monk & Rowe	CD5	U.K.	1993	$10.00
Warner Brothers	PRO-CD-3720	Let Him Dangle	CDJ	U.S.	1989	$10.00
		Little Atoms	CD5	U.K.	1996	$10.00
		Little Atoms	CD5	U.K.	1996	$10.00
	Fourth version.					
		Little Atoms	CD5	U.K.	1996	$10.00
	Second version.					
		Little Atoms	CD5	U.K.	1996	$10.00
	Third version.					
		London's Brilliant Parade	CD5	U.K.		$10.00
		London's Brilliant Parade	CD5	U.K.		$10.00
	Second version.					
Warner Brothers	9362-40073-2	Other Side Of Summer, The	CD5	Germany	1991	$10.00
Warner Brothers	W-0025CD	Other Side Of Summer, The	CD5	U.K.	1991	$10.00
Warner Brothers	PRO-CD-4781	Other Side Of Summer, The	CDJ	U.S.	1991	$4.00
		Pouring Water On A Drowning Man	CDJ	U.S.	1996	$6.00
Warner Brothers	PRO-CD-7584	Pouring Water On A Drunken Man	CDJ	U.S.	1995	$3.00
		Remove This Doubt	CDJ	Germany		$25.00
Warner Brothers	W-0068CD	So Like Candy	CD5	U.K.	1991	$10.00
		So Like Candy	CDJ	U.S.	1991	$3.00
WEA	93624 15932L	Sulky Girl	CD5	Australia	1994	$12.00
Warner Brothers	W-0234CD	Sulky Girl	CD5	U.K.	1994	$10.00
Warner Brothers	PRO-CD-6907	Sulky Girl	CDJ	U.S.	1994	$3.00
Warner Brothers	PRO-CD-3511	This Town	CDJ	U.S.	1989	$3.00
Warner Brothers	W-758CD	Veronica	CD3	U.K.	1989	$10.00
Warner Brothers	W-7558CDX	Veronica	CD5	U.K.	1989	$13.00
Warner Brothers	PRO-CD-2424	Veronica	CDJ	U.S.	1989	$7.00
		Water On A Drowning Man	CDJ	Spain	1995	$25.00
WEA	W-0251CD	You Tripped At Every Step	CD5	U.K.	1994	$10.00
Warner Brothers		You Tripped At Every Step	CDJ	U.S.	1994	$3.00

Coster, Tom

Full Length

Company	Disk Number	Title	Type	Country	Year	Longbox Value / Value
Headfirst	604	Did Jah Miss Me?	LP/BP	U.S.		$9.00/$6.00
Headfirst	384	From Me To You	LP/BP	U.S.		$9.00/$6.00
Fantasy	FCD-9623	Ivory Exhibition	LP/LB	U.S.†	1985	$14.00/$8.00

Cotton Patch Blues

Full Length

Company	Disk Number	Title	Type	Country	Year	Longbox Value / Value
		Cotton Patch Blues	DJ/Smplr	U.S.		$15.00

Cotton, Paul

Singles

Company	Disk Number	Title	Type	Country	Year	Longbox Value / Value
Sisapa		Changing Horses	CDJ	U.S.	1990	$2.00
		Heart of the Night	CDJ	U.S.		$2.00
		I Can Hear Your Heartbeat	CDJ	U.S.		$2.00

Coughlan, Mary

Full Length

Company	Disk Number	Title	Type	Country	Year	Longbox Value / Value
WEA	MRCD-1	Tired And Emotional	LP	Germany		$15.00

Label	Catalog Number	Title	Type	Country	Year	Longbox Value / Value
WEA	242185-2	Under the Influence	LP	Germany		$15.00

Singles

Label	Catalog Number	Title	Type	Country	Year	Longbox Value / Value
Eastwest	9031 71927-2	A Leaf From A Tree	CD5	Germany	1990	$10.00
Eastwest	YZ-445CD	Invisible To You	CD5	U.K.	1990	$8.00
Eastwest	YZ-497CD	Leaf From A Tree	CD5	U.K.	1990	$8.00
Eastwest	YZ-483CD	Man of the World	CD5	U.K.	1990	$8.00
Eastwest	YZ-651CD	There Is a Bed	CD5	U.K.	1992	$8.00

Count To Twenty

Singles

Label	Catalog Number	Title	Type	Country	Year	Longbox Value / Value
		When You Love Someone	CD5	U.S.	1995	$5.00
	199	You Are the One	CD5	U.S.	1994	$5.00

Countess Vaughn

Singles

Label	Catalog Number	Title	Type	Country	Year	Longbox Value / Value
Charisma	12714	It's A Man's, Man's World	CDJ	U.S.	1992	$2.00

Counting Crows

Full Length

Label	Catalog Number	Title	Type	Country	Year	Longbox Value / Value
Westwood One		In Concert	RS	U.S.	1994	$50.00
	2 CD set. With Jeff Healey, Airdate: 4/11/94					
Westwood One		In Concert	RS	U.S.	1994	$60.00
	Airdate: 12/19/94.					
Westwood One		In Concert	RS	U.S.	1995	$60.00
	2 CD set. Airdate: 6/19/95.					
Westwood One		In Concert -Nu Rock	RS	U.S.	1994	$50.00
	2 CD set. With Squeeze, Airdate: 4/25/94					
Westwood One		In Concert-Nu Rock	RS	U.S.	1995	$60.00
	Airdate: 7/3/95.					

Singles

Label	Catalog Number	Title	Type	Country	Year	Longbox Value / Value
Geffen		Mr. Jones	CD5	U.K.	1994	$10.00
Geffen	PRO-CD-4588	Mr. Jones	CDJ	U.S.	1994	$3.00
Geffen		Omaha	CD5	U.K.	1994	$10.00
Geffen	GFSTD 84	Round Here	CD5	U.K.	1994	$10.00
Geffen	GFSTD 74	Round Here	CD5	U.K.	1994	$10.00
Geffen	PRO-CD-4646	Round Here	CD5	U.S.	1994	$3.00
DGC	PRO-CD-4646	Round Here	CDJ	U.S.	1994	$3.00

Coup

Singles

Label	Catalog Number	Title	Type	Country	Year	Longbox Value / Value
Capitol	58245	Taking These	CD5	U.S.	1994	$5.00

Course Of Empire

Singles

Label	Catalog Number	Title	Type	Country	Year	Longbox Value / Value
Zoo	ZP 17074	Coming of the Century	CDJ	U.S.	1992	$2.00
Zoo	72445 14109	Infested	CD5	U.S.	1992	$4.00

Cover Girls

Full Length

Label	Catalog Number	Title	Type	Country	Year	Longbox Value / Value
Surta	4	Show Me	LP/BP	U.S.		$14.00/$8.00
Capitol	CDP-91041	We Can't Go Wrong	LP/LB	U.S.		$14.00/$8.00

Singles

Label	Catalog Number	Title	Type	Country	Year	Longbox Value / Value
Bellaphon	130-07-364	All That Glitters Isn't Gold	CD5	Germany	1989	$8.00
Victor	VDPS-1029	All That Glitters Isn't Gold	CD3	Japan	1989	$12.00/$3.00
Ryko	VDP-1428	All That Glitters Isn't Gold	CD5	U.K.	1989	$8.00
Capitol	DPRO-79988	All That Glitters Isn't Gold	CDJ	U.S.	1989	$2.00
		Don't Stop Now	CDJ	U.S.		$2.00
CBS	656781-5	Funk Boutique	CD5	Germany	1991	$8.00
Epic	ESK 73698	Funk Boutique	CDJ	U.S.	1990	$2.00
Victor	VDPS-1006	Inside Out	CD3	Japan	1988	$12.00/$3.00
Bellaphon	130-07-322	My Heart Skips A Beat	CD3	Germany	1989	$8.00
Victor	VDPS-1001	Show Me	CD3	Japan	1988	$12.00/$3.00
Epic	ESDA-7117	Thank You	CD3	Japan	1992	$12.00/$3.00
Epic	ESK 74438	Thank You	CDJ	U.S.		$2.00
Bellaphon	130-07-348	We Can't Go Wrong	CD5	Germany	1990	$8.00
Capitol	CDCL-567	We Can't Go Wrong	CD5	U.K.	1990	$8.00
Capitol	DPRO-79883	We Can't Go Wrong	CDJ	U.S.	1989	$2.00
Capitol		We Can't Go Wrong	CDJ	U.S.	1989	$2.00
	Second version.					
Epic	658143-2	Wishing on A Star	CD5	U.K.	1992	$8.00
Columbia	44K 74368	Wishing on A Star	CD5	U.S.	1992	$4.00
Epic	ESK 74343	Wishing on A Star	CDJ	U.S.	1992	$2.00
Epic	ESK 4652	Wishing on A Star	CDJ	U.S.	1992	$2.00

Coverdale, David

Full Length

Label	Catalog Number	Title	Type	Country	Year	Longbox Value / Value
Relativity	1035	Northwinds	LP/LB	U.S.		$14.00/$8.00

Singles

Label	Catalog Number	Title	Type	Country	Year	Longbox Value / Value
CBS	656315-3	Last Note of Freedom	CD3	Germany	1990	$8.00
CBS	CSDS-8154	Last Note of Freedom	CD3	Japan	1990	$13.00/$4.00
Epic	656292-2	Last Note of Freedom	CD5	U.K.	1990	$8.00

Coverdale/Page

Full Length

Label	Catalog Number	Title	Type	Country	Year	Longbox Value / Value
Westwood One		Off the Record	RS	U.S.	1993	$35.00
	Airdate: 8/2/93.					

Singles

Label	Catalog Number	Title	Type	Country	Year	Longbox Value / Value
Geffen	PRO-CD-4529	Over Now	CDJ	U.S.	1993	$6.00
Geffen	XDCS-93108	Pride and Joy	CDJ	Japan	1993	$100.00
Geffen	PRO-CD-4491	Pride and Joy	CDJ	U.S.	1993	$6.00
Geffen	PRO-CD-4504	Shake My Tree	CDJ	U.S.	1993	$6.00
Geffen		Take a Look at Yourself	CDJ	U.S.	1994	$7.00
Geffen		Take Me For A Little While	CD5	U.K.	1993	$10.00
Geffen		Take Me For A Little While	CD5	U.K.	1993	$10.00
	Second version.					
Geffen	PRO-CD-4510	Take Me For A Little While	CDJ	U.S.	1993	$6.00
Geffen	PRO-CD-4535	Take Me For A Little While	CDJ	U.S.	1993	$6.00

Covington, Trisha

Singles

Label	Catalog Number	Title	Type	Country	Year	Longbox Value / Value
Columbia	CSK 6912	Slow Down	CDJ	U.S.	1994	$3.00
Columbia	CSK 5437	Why You Wanna Play Me Out?	CDJ	U.S.	1994	$3.00
Columbia	CSK 6987	Why You Wanna Play Me Out?	CDJ	U.S.	1994	$3.00

Cowboy

Full Length

Label	Catalog Number	Title	Type	Country	Year	Longbox Value / Value
Polygram		Cowboy	LP	Japan		$35.00

Cowboy Copas

Full Length

Label	Catalog Number	Title	Type	Country	Year	Longbox Value / Value
Starday	175	Mister Country Music	LP/BP	U.S.		$12.00/$7.00
Starday	157	Opry Star Spotlight	LP/BP	U.S.		$12.00/$7.00
King	714	Tragic Tales of Love and Life	LP/BP	U.S.		$12.00/$7.00

Cowboy Junkies

Full Length

Label	Catalog Number	Title	Type	Country	Year	Longbox Value / Value
RCA		200 Miles Away	DJ/LP	U.S.		$15.00
RCA	RDJ 66349-2	Collection, The	DJ/5CD	U.S.	1994	$50.00
	5CD albums with front booklets in CD wallet.					
RCA	KCDP 5119	Essential Junk	DJ/Smplr	U.S.	1994	$25.00
RCA	RDJ 62329-2	Live	DJ/Smplr	U.S.	1992	$15.00
RCA	RDJ 66344	Pale Sun, Crescent Moon	DJ/LP	U.S.	1994	$15.00
RCA	DPRO-10744	Pale Sun Crescent Moon	DJ/LP	U.S.	1994	$25.00
RCA	9180-2-RDJ	Sun Comes Up	DJ/Smplr	U.S.	1990	$18.00
RCA	8568-R-SP	Trinity Session, The	DJ/LP	U.S.	1988	$25.00

Singles

Label	Catalog Number	Title	Type	Country	Year	Longbox Value / Value
Geffen	PRo-CD-4841	A Common Disaster	CDJ	U.S.	1996	$3.00
		Angel Mine	CD5	U.K.	1996	$10.00
		Angel Mine	CD5	U.K.	1996	$10.00
RCA	62745-2-RDJ	Anniversary Song	CDJ	U.S.	1993	$3.00
Pinnacle	FRYCD-011	Blue Moon Revisited	CD5	U.K.	1989	$9.00
RCA	64427	Blue Moon Revisited	CDJ	U.S.	1995	$6.00
RCA	PD-49268	'Cause Cheap Is How I Feel	CD5	Germany	1990	$9.00
RCA	PD-49268	'Cause Cheap Is How I Feel	CD5	U.K.	1990	$9.00
RCA	2612-2-RDJ	'Cause Cheap Is How I Feel	CDJ	U.S.	1990	$3.00
BMG	RDJ 62887-2	First Recollection	CDJ	U.S.	1994	$3.00
RCA	62681-2-RDJ	Floorboard Blues	CDJ	U.S.	1993	$3.00
RCA	PD-49110	Horse in the Country	CD5	U.K.	1992	$9.00
RCA	07863623292	Live	CD5	Canada	1992	$7.00
RCA	62329	Live	CD5	U.S.	1992	$5.00
RCA	R10D-122	Misguided Angel	CD3	Japan	1989	$13.00/$4.00
RCA	8958-2-RDJ	Misguided Angel	CDJ	U.S.	1989	$3.00
RCA	8977-2-RDJ	Misguided Angel	CDJ	U.S.	1989	$3.00
RCA	62206-2-RDJ	Murder Tonight, Trailer Park	CDJ	U.S.	1992	$3.00
RCA	62714	Pale Sun	CDJ	U.S.	1994	$6.00
RCA	RDJ 62811	Post, The	CDJ	U.S.	1994	$3.00
RCA	2701-2-RDJ	Rock and Bird	CDJ	U.S.	1990	$3.00
RCA	PD-49138	Southern Rain	CD5	U.K.	1992	$9.00
		Speaking Confidentially	CDJ	U.K.	[illegible]	$10.00
RCA		Sun Comes Up	CD3	Japan	1990	$13.00/$4.00
RCA	PD-49302	Sun Comes Up	CD5	U.K.	1990	$9.00
RCA	8879-2-RDJ	Sweet Jane	CDJ	U.S.	1988	$7.00
RCA	5899-2-RDJ	Sweet Jane	CDJ	U.S.	1994	$3.00
RCA	62310-2-RDJ	This Street, That Man, This Life	CDJ	U.S.		$3.00
RCA		Water Is Wide	CDJ	U.S.		$3.00

Cox, Carl

Singles

Label	Catalog Number	Title	Type	Country	Year	Longbox Value / Value
RCA	74321-102872	Does It Feel Good To You	CD5	U.K.	1992	$8.00

Cox, Deanna

Singles

Label	Catalog Number	Title	Type	Country	Year	Longbox Value / Value
Warner Brothers	PRO-CD-5597	Never Gonna Be Your Fool Again	CDJ	U.S.	1992	$2.00

Cox, Deborah

Singles

Label	Catalog Number	Title	Type	Country	Year	Longbox Value / Value
Arista	12892	Sentimental	CD5	U.S.	1995	$5.00
Arista	ASCD-2852	Sentimental	CDJ	U.S.	1995	$2.00

Cox, Ronny

Singles

Label	Catalog Number	Title	Type	Country	Year	Longbox Value / Value
Mercury	CDP 881	Cowboy Rides, The	CDJ	U.S.	1993	$2.00

Coz

Singles

Label	Catalog Number	Title	Type	Country	Year	Longbox Value / Value
Elektra/Asylum	66140	Keep My Soul	CD5	U.S.	1994	$5.00
Eastwest	PRCD 9169	Keep My Soul	CDJ	U.S.	1995	$3.00
Elektra	66105	No Place Like Tha Hood	CD5	U.S.	1995	$5.00
Eastwest	PRCD 9277	No Place Like Tha Hood	CDJ	U.S.	1995	$3.00

CPO

Singles

Label	Catalog Number	Title	Type	Country	Year	Longbox Value / Value
		This Beat Is Funky	CDJ	U.S.		$2.00

Craaft

Singles

Label	Catalog Number	Title	Type	Country	Year	Longbox Value / Value
BMG	PD-44234	Daytripper	CD5	Germany	1990	$8.00
		Jane	CDJ	U.S.		$2.00

Crack Express

Singles

Label	Catalog Number	Title	Type	Country	Year	Longbox Value / Value
CBS	655286-3	C'est Vogue	CD3	Germany	1989	$7.00
CBS	654788-3	Psycho	CD3	Germany	1989	$7.00

Crack The Sky

Full Length

Label	Catalog Number	Title	Type	Country	Year	Longbox Value / Value
Grudge		Dog City	LP/LB	U.S.		$14.00/$8.00
Grudge	4500`	From the Greenhouse	LP/LB	U.S.	1989	$14.00/$8.00
Grudge		Raw	LP/LB	U.S.		$14.00/$8.00

Singles

Label	Catalog Number	Title	Type	Country	Year	Longbox Value / Value
Grudge	4500	From the Greenhouse	CD5	U.S.	1989	$5.00
Grudge	4752-2-DJ	From the Greenhouse	CDJ	U.S.	1989	$2.00
Grudge	4750-2-DJ	Lost in America	CDJ	U.S.	1989	$2.00
		Love Me Like a Terrorist	CDJ	U.S.		$2.00
Grudge	4768-2-Dj	Mr. President	CDJ	U.S.	1990	$2.00

Cracker

Full Length

Label	Catalog Number	Title	Type	Country	Year	Longbox Value / Value
Album Network		Album Network Special	RS	U.S.	1996	$60.00
	2 CD set. Airdate: 7/7/96.					
Westwood One		In Concert	RS	U.S.	1994	$50.00
	2 CD set. With Guns N' Roses and Candlebox, Airdate: 5/23/94					
Westwood One		In Concert-Nu Rock	RS	U.S.	1994	$60.00
	Airdate: 3/28/94.					
Westwood One		In Concert-Nu Rock	RS	U.S.	1994	$60.00
	Airdate: 9/12/94.					
Virgin	12702	Tuscon	DJ/Smplr	U.S.	1992	$15.00
Virgin	DPRO-14129	Virgin Years, The	DJ/Smplr	U.S.	1994	$20.00
	Features 8 songs by Cracker and 8 by Camper Van Beethoven.					

Singles

Label	Catalog Number	Title	Type	Country	Year	Longbox Value / Value
Capital	38449	Euro-Trash Girl	CD5	U.S.	1994	$5.00
Virgin	DPRO-14209	Euro-Trash Girl	CDJ	U.S.	1994	$6.00
Virgin	VUSAB3	Get Off This Guitar	CD5	U.K.	1994	$10.00
Virgin	VUSDGB3	Get Off This Guitar	CD5	U.K.	1994	$10.00
Virgin		Get Off This Guitar	CDJ	U.K.	1994	$15.00
Virgin	PRCD-14198	Get Off This Guitar	CDJ	U.S.	1993	$2.00
		Get Off This Part	CD5	U.K.		$10.00
		Get Off This Part	CD5	U.K.		$10.00
	Second version.					
Virgin	PRCD-4568	Happy Birthday To Me	CDJ	U.S.	1992	$2.00
Virgin	PRCD-1269	Happy Birthday To Me	CDJ	U.S.	1992	$2.00
		I Hate My Generation	CD5	U.K.	1996	$10.00
		I Hate My Generation	CDJ	U.K.	1996	$10.00
Virgin	PRCD-12736	I Ride My Bike	CDJ	U.S.	1992	$2.00

Label	Catalog Number	Title	Type	Country	Year	Longbox/Value
Virgin	14222	Let's Go For a Ride	CDJ	U.S.	1994	$3.00
Virgin	PRCD-12813	Low	CDJ	U.S.	1993	$2.00
Virgin	14142	Low	CDJ	U.S.	1993	$3.00
Capital	38428	Low	CD5	U.S.	1994	$5.00
Virgin	PRCD-14147	Movie Star	CDJ	U.S.	1994	$2.00
Virgin	DPRO-11530	Nothing To Believe In	CDJ	U.S.	1996	$4.00
Virgin	DPRO-11511	Nothing To Believe In	SCDJ	U.S.	1996	$25.00
Capitol	DPRO-79646	Shake Some Action	CDJ	U.S.	1994	$6.00
Virgin	VUSCD-61	Teen Angst	CD5	U.K.	1991	$8.00
Virgin	PRCD-4380	Teen Angst	CDJ	U.S.	1991	$2.00

Crash & Burn

Singles

Label	Catalog Number	Title	Type	Country	Year	Longbox/Value
RCA	PD-44278	Hot Like This	CD5	U.K.	1991	$8.00

Craig, Robbie

Singles

Label	Catalog Number	Title	Type	Country	Year	Longbox/Value
Polydor	PZCD-226	Magic	CD5	U.K.	1992	$7.00
Polydor	PZCD-209	Nothing I Can't Do	CD5	U.K.	1992	$7.00

Craig, Sara

Singles

Label	Catalog Number	Title	Type	Country	Year	Longbox/Value
Attic	CD447	Thank You	CD5	Canada	1994	$9.00

Cramer, Floyd

Full Length

Label	Catalog Number	Title	Type	Country	Year	Longbox/Value
RCA	CAD1-2508	Almost Persuaded	LP/LB	U.S.		$12.00/$7.00

Cramps

Full Length

Label	Catalog Number	Title	Type	Country	Year	Longbox/Value
Enigma	73617	Creature From Black Leather Lagoon	LP/ LB	U.S.		$12.00/$7.00
Enigma	73579	Date With Elvis	LP/ LB	U.S.		$12.00/$7.00
		Flame Job	DJ/ LP	U.S.		$18.00
Enigma	73578	Smell Of Female	LP/ LB	U.S.		$12.00/$7.00
Enigma	73543	Stay Sick	LP/ LB	U.S.		$12.00/$7.00
SPV	5214	To the Pink	LP	U.K.		$15.00

Singles

Label	Catalog Number	Title	Type	Country	Year	Longbox/Value
Virgin	ENVCD-19	All Women Are Bad	CD5	U.K.	1990	$9.00
Enigma	ENCD 19	All Women Are Bad	CD5	U.K.	1990	$9.00
Enigma	203696-2	Bikini Girls With Machine Guns	CD5	Germany	1990	$9.00
Enigma	ENVCD-17	Bikini Girls With Machine Guns	CD5	U.K.	1990	$9.00
Pinnacle	CDNST-136	Blues Fix	CD5	U.K.	1992	$9.00
Big Beat	136	Blues Fix	CD5	U.K.	1992	$5.00
New Rose	NEAT2 CD	Can Your Pussy Do the Dog	CD3	Germany		$10.00
SPV	5232-3	Can Your Pussy Do the Dog	CD5	Germany	1988	$9.00
Enigma	ENVCD-22	Creature From Black Leather Lagoon	CD5	U.K.	1990	$9.00
Rough Trade	605-3117-3	Eyeball In My Martini	CD5	Germany	1991	$9.00
Pinnacle	CDNST-135	Eyeball In My Martini	CD5	U.K.	1991	$9.00
		Journey To the Center Of Girl	CDJ	U.S.		$7.00
SPV	5233-3	Kizmiaz	CD5	Germany	1988	$9.00
Restless	012	Miniskirt Blues	CDJ	U.S.	1991	$3.00
		Naked Girl Walking Down the Stairs	CDJ	U.S.		$8.00
Medicine Label	7207	Ultra-Twist	CDJ	U.S.	1994	$7.00
medicine	PRO-CD-7207	Ultra-Twist	CDJ	U.S.	1995	$7.00

Cranberries

Full Length

Label	Catalog Number	Title	Type	Country	Year	Longbox/Value
Westwood One		In Concert - Nu Rock	RS	U.S.	1994	$60.00
Island		In Edits	DJ/ Smplr	France		$25.00
Polygram	PL/CRAN01	Live	DJ/ Smplr	U.S.	1995	$80.00
Island/Album Network		Live At the Record Planet	DJ/ Smplr	U.S.	1994	$45.00
Island	CRANCD1	No Need To...	DJ/ Smplr	U.K.		$18.00
		No Need To Argue	LTD/ LP	Australia	1995	$35.00
2 CD set.						
Island		To Faithful	DJ/ Smplr	U.S.	1995	$40.00
CD and VHS video in box.						
Island		To the Faithful Departed	DJ/ Smplr	France	1995	$65.00
Island		To the Faithful Departed	DJ/ Intvw	U.K.	1995	$50.00
Island	CRAN-CD-2	To the Faithful Departed	DJ/ LP	U.K.	1995	$20.00
Island		To the Faithful Departed	DJ/ LP	U.S.	1995	$40.00
CD, VHS video, tree seeds, and scent sticks in box.						
Media America		Up Close	RS	U.S.	1995	$35.00
Media America		Up Close	RS	U.S.	1996	$30.00

Singles

Label	Catalog Number	Title	Type	Country	Year	Longbox/Value
Island		Dreams	CD5	Germany	1994	$10.00
Island	CID-548	Dreams	CD5	U.K.	1992	$10.00
Island		Dreams	CD5	U.K.	1994	$10.00
Island		Dreams	CD5	U.K.	1994	$10.00
Second version.						
Polygram	858487	Dreams What You Are	CD5	U.S.	1994	$5.00
Island	314 514 156	Everybody Else Is Doing It	CD5	U.S.	1993	$5.00
		Free To Decide	CD5	Australia	1996	$12.00
		Free To Decide	CD5	U.K.	1996	$10.00
		Free To Decide	CD5	U.K.	1996	$10.00
Second version.						
		Liar	CDJ	Spain	1995	$25.00
Island		Linger	CD5	France	1992	$15.00
Island	CID-556	Linger	CD5	U.K.	1992	$10.00
		Linger	CD5	U.K.	1995	$11.00
Island	858087	Linger	CD5	U.S.	1994	$5.00
Island		Ode To My Family	CD5	U.K.	1994	$10.00
Island	PRCD 6918-2	Ode to My Family	CDJ	U.S.		$3.00
Polygram	854199	Ode To My Family	CD5	U.S.	1994	$5.00
Island	PRCD 6776-2	Reason	CDJ	U.S.		$7.00
Island		Ridiculous Thoughts	CD5	Australia	1996	$12.00
Island		Ridiculous Thoughts	CD5	U.K.	1995	$10.00
Island	PRCD 6980	Ridiculous Thoughts	CDJ	U.S.	1995	$7.00
Island	PRCD 7011	Ridiculous Thoughts	CDJ	U.S.	1995	$7.00
	CIDX633	Salvation	CD5	U.K.	1995	$12.00
Island		Salvation	CD5	U.K.	1995	$25.00
Island	PRCD 7201-2	Salvation	CDJ	U.S.		$3.00
Island		Salvation	CDJ	U.S.	1995	$6.00
Island	PRCD 6799-2	Still Can't	CDJ	U.S.	1993	$3.00
Island	PRCD 6781	Sunday	CDJ	U.S.	1993	$7.00
Xeric	607-3121-3	Uncertain	CD5	Germany	1991	$20.00
Xeric	XER-014CD	Uncertain	CD5	U.K.	1991	$20.00
Island		Zombie	CD5	U.K.	1994	$10.00
Island		Zombie	CD5	U.K.	1994	$10.00
Second version.						
Island	PRCD 6907-2	Zombie	CDJ	U.S.		$3.00
Island	PRCD 6875-2	Zombie	CDJ	U.S.		$3.00

Cranes

Full Length

Label	Catalog Number	Title	Type	Country	Year	Longbox/Value
Pinnacle	DEDCD-009S	Forever	LTD/ LP	U.S.		$25.00
		Lilies	DJ/ Smplr	U.S.	1995	$10.00
Arista	ASCD 2756	Shining Road	DJ/ Smplr	U.S.	1995	$12.00

Company	Disk Number	Title	Type	Country	Year	Longbox/Value
RCA	62247-2-RDJ	Tomorrow's Tears	DJ/ Intvw	U.S.	1992	$20.00

Singles

Company	Disk Number	Title	Type	Country	Year	Longbox/Value
Dedicated	CRANE-003CD	Adoration	CD5	U.K.	1991	$8.00
Dedicated	CRANE-005	Adrift	CD5	U.K.	1993	$8.00
		Beautiful Friend	CDJ	U.S.	1995	$3.00
Dedicated	CRANE-002CD	Espero	CD5	U.K.	1990	$8.00
RCA	62550-2-RDJ	Everywhere	CDJ	U.S.	1993	$2.00
Dedicated	CRANE-001CD	Inescapable	CD5	U.K.	1990	$8.00
Dedicated	62646	Jewel	CD5	U.S.	1993	$4.00
RCA	62626	Jewel	CDJ	U.S.	1993	$3.00
		Shining Road	CD5	U.K.		$10.00
Arista	ASCD 2767	Shining Road	CDJ	U.S.	1994	$3.00
Dedicated	CRANE-004CD	Tomorrow's Tears	CD5	U.K.	1991	$8.00
		Tomorrow's Tears	CDJ	U.S.	1991	$2.00

Crash, Johnny

Singles

Company	Disk Number	Title	Type	Country	Year	Longbox/Value
WTG	PRO-CD-2112	All the Way In Love	CDJ	U.S.	1990	$2.00
		Hey Kid	CDJ	U.S.		$2.00

Crash Test Dummies

Full Length

Company	Disk Number	Title	Type	Country	Year	Longbox/Value
Arista		A Portrait of an Artist as a Young Dummy	DJ/ Smplr	Canada	1991	$20.00
Arista	ARCD-2131	A Portrait of an Artist as a Young Dummy	DJ/ Smplr	U.S.	1991	$10.00
Arista	ARCD-8677	Ghosts That Haunt Me, The	DJ/ LP	U.S.	1991	$10.00
Oversized "Superman" Card Board Sleeve.						
Arista		Interview	DJ/ Intvw	Canada	1991	$10.00

Singles

Company	Disk Number	Title	Type	Country	Year	Longbox/Value
Arista	74321216882	Afternoons & Coffeespoons	CD5	Canada	1994	$8.00
Arista		Afternoons & Coffeespoons	CD5	U.K.	1994	$10.00
Arista		Afternoons & Coffeespoons	CD5	U.K.	1994	$10.00
Second version.						
Arista	12708	Afternoons & Coffeespoons	CD5	U.S.	1994	$6.00
Arista	ARCD-2706	Afternoons & Coffeespoons	CDJ	U.S.	1994	$3.00
Arista		Androgynous	CDJ	Canada	1991	$5.00
Arista		Androgynous	CDJ	U.S.	1991	$3.00
RCA	642f62	Ballad Of Peter Pumpkinhead	CD5	U.S.	1994	$5.00
RCA	64255-2	Ballad Of Peter Pumpkinhead	CDJ	U.S.	1994	$6.00
Arista		Ghosts That Haunt Me, The	CDJ	Canada	1991	$5.00
Arista	ARCD 2766	God Shuffled	CDJ	U.S.		$3.00
Arista		Mmm Mmm Mmm Mmm	CD5	U.K.	1994	$10.00
Arista		Mmm Mmm Mmm Mmm	CD5	U.K.	1994	$10.00
Second version.						
Arista	ASCD-2654	Mmm Mmm Mmm Mmm	CD5	U.S.	1994	$4.00
Arista	12666	Mmm Mmm Mmm Mmm	CD5	U.S.	1994	$5.00
Arista		Superman's Song	CDJ	U.S.	1991	$3.00

Crash Vegas

Full Length

Company	Disk Number	Title	Type	Country	Year	Longbox/Value
WEA		Crash Into the '90s	DJ/ Smplr	Canada		$10.00
Atlantic	82119-2	Red Earth	LP/ LB	U.S.		$14.00/$8.00

Singles

Company	Disk Number	Title	Type	Country	Year	Longbox/Value
		Inside Out	CDJ	U.S.		$2.00
Atlantic	PRCD 3471-2	Sky	CDJ	U.S.	1989	$2.00
		You and Me	CDJ	Canada		$6.00
London	294	You and Me	CDJ	U.S.	1993	$2.00

Craven, Beverley

Singles

Company	Disk Number	Title	Type	Country	Year	Longbox/Value
Epic	656550-2	Holding On	CD5	U.K.	1991	$8.00
Epic	ESK 73963	Holding On	CDJ	U.K.	1991	$2.00
Epic	659595	Love Shines	CD5	U.K.	1993	$8.00
Epic	657661-2	Memories	CD5	U.K.	1991	$8.00
Epic	657661-5	Memories	CD5	U.K.	1991	$8.00
		Mollie's Song	CD5	U.K.		$9.00
		Mollie's Song	CD5	U.K.		$9.00
Second version.						
Epic	655943-5	Promise Me	CD5	Germany	1990	$8.00
Epic	655943-2	Promise Me	CD5	U.K.	1990	$8.00
		Promise Me	CDJ	U.K.		$2.00
Epic	656234-2	Woman to Woman	CD5	Germany	1990	$8.00
Epic	656234-2	Woman to Woman	CD5	U.K.	1990	$8.00
Epic	657464-2	Woman to Woman	CD5	U.K.	1991	$8.00
Epic	657508-2	You're Not the First	CD5	Germany	1991	$8.00

Crawford, Hank

Full Length

Company	Disk Number	Title	Type	Country	Year	Longbox/Value
Milestone	FCD-9119	Indigo Blue	LP/ LB	U.S.†	1985	$14.00/$8.00
CBS	450958-2	We Got A Good Thing Going	LP	Germany		$15.00
CBS	450566-2	Wildflowers	LP	Germany		$15.00

Crawford, Michael

Full Length

Company	Disk Number	Title	Type	Country	Year	Longbox/Value
Columbia	CK-44321	Songs From the Stage and Screen	LP/ LB	U.S.		$14.00/$8.00

Singles

Company	Disk Number	Title	Type	Country	Year	Longbox/Value
Atlantic	PRCD 5265-2	With Your Hand Upon Your Heart	CDJ	U.S.	1993	$2.00

Crawford, Randy

Full Length

Company	Disk Number	Title	Type	Country	Year	Longbox/Value
		Best	DJ/ Smplr	Japan		N/A
Telstar	TCD-2299	Love Songs	LP	U.K.		$15.00
Warner Brothers	23976-2	Nightline	LP/ LB	U.S.†	1984	$14.00/$8.00

Singles

Company	Disk Number	Title	Type	Country	Year	Longbox/Value
Warner Brothers	PRO-CD-5521	A Lot That You Can Do	CDJ	U.S.	1992	$2.00
Warner Brothers	PRO-CD-5614	A Lot That You Can Do	CDJ	U.S.	1992	$2.00
Pioneer	WPDP-6280	Almaz	CD3	Japan	1991	$12.00/$3.00
		Always	CD3	Japan		$12.00/$3.00
Warner Brothers	PRO-CD-4364	Cigarette in the Rain	CDJ	U.S.	1989	$2.00
WEA	0630 10688	Forget Me Nots	CD5	Germany	1995	$8.00
Warner Brothers	PRO-CD-4031	I Don't Feel Much Like Crying	CDJ	U.S.	1989	$2.00
Pioneer	WPDP-6284	If I Were in Your Shoes	CD3	Japan	1991	$12.00/$3.00
Warner Brothers	PRO-CD-6547	In My Life	CD5	U.S.	1993	$3.00
Warner Brothers	PRO-CD-6581	In My Life	CD5	U.S.	1993	$7.00
WEA	W-2865CD	Knockin' on Heaven's Door	CD3	U.K.	1989	$8.00
Warner Brothers	PRO-CD-3635	Knockin' on Heaven's Door	CD5	U.S.	1989	$3.00
Warner Brothers	PRO-CD-3635	Knockin' on Heaven's Door	CDJ	U.S.	1989	$2.00
Warner Brothers	PRO-CD-6715	Love's Mystery	CDJ	U.S.	1993	$2.00
Warner Brothers	PRO-CD-6884	Mad Over You	CDJ	U.S.	1993	$2.00
		Only You	CDJ	U.S.		$2.00
Warner Brothers	PRO-CD-5580	Rhythm Of Romance	CDJ	U.S.	1992	$2.00
Warner Brothers	PRO-CD-5779	Shine	CDJ	U.S.	1992	$2.00
Warner Brothers	PRO-CD-5351	Shine	CDJ	U.S.	1992	$6.00
Warner Brothers	W-9969CD	Wrap U Up	CD5	U.K.	1990	$8.00
Warner Brothers	PRO-CD-3894	Wrap U Up	CDJ	U.S.	1989	$2.00
Westwood One		In Concert	RS	U.S.	1993	$30.00
Airdate: 3/15/93.						

Cray, Robert

Full Length

Label	Catalog Number	Title	Type	Country	Year	Longbox Value/Value
Westwood One		In Concert	RS	U.S.	1995	$30.00
	Airdate: 5/22/95.					
Mercury	CDP 197	Interview	DJ/Intvw	U.S.	1990	$5.00
DIR		King Biscuit Flour Hour	RS	U.S.	1987	$30.00
	Airdate: 10/25/87.					
DIR		King Biscuit Flour Hour	RS	U.S.	1988	$30.00
	With Fabulous Thunderbirds, Airdate: 3/27/88.					
DIR		King Biscuit Flour Hour	RS	U.S.	1989	$30.00
	Airdate: 5/7/89.					
DIR		King Biscuit Flour Hour	RS	U.S.	1992	$25.00
	Airdate: 11/22/92.					
DIR		King Biscuit Flour Hour	RS	U.S.	1992	$30.00
	Airdate: 3/29/92.					
DIR		King Biscuit Flour Hour	RS	U.S.	1993	$25.00
	Airdate: 11/8/93.					
DIR		King Biscuit Flour Hour	RS	U.S.	1995	$25.00
	Airdate: 1/29/95.					
DIR		King Biscuit Flour Hour	RS	U.S.	1996	$25.00
	Airdate: 3/10/96.					
Mercury	CDP-197	Midnight Stroll	DJ/Smplr	U.S.	1990	$18.00
	Interview CD and CDJ in box.					
Island	81730-2	Who's Been Talkin'	LP/LB	U.S.		$15.00/$9.00

Singles

Label	Catalog Number	Title	Type	Country	Year	Longbox Value/Value
Mercury	CDP-1159	1040 Blues	CDJ	U.S.	1994	$3.00
Mercury	CRACD-7	Acting This Way	CD5	U.K.	1989	$8.00
Mercury	CDP 389	Bouncing Back	CDJ	U.S.	1991	$2.00
Mercury	CRACD-9	Consequences	CD5	U.K.	1990	$8.00
Mercury	CDP 343	Consequences	CDJ	U.S.	1990	$2.00
Mercury	870569-2	Don't Be Afraid of the Dark	CD5	Germany	1988	$8.00
Mercury	CRACD-5	Don't Be Afraid of the Dark	CD5	U.K.	1988	$8.00
Mercury	CDP 21	Don't Be Afraid of the Dark	CDJ	U.S.	1988	$2.00
Mercury	870 741-2	Don't Be Afraid of the Dark	CDV/BP	U.S.	1988	$20.00/$20.00
Mercury	878119-2	Forecast	CD5	Germany	1988	$8.00
Mercury	MERCD-330	Forecast	CD5	U.K.	1988	$8.00
Sound	CD-2000	Four Classic Tracks	CD5	Germany	1988	$8.00
Mercury	CDP 806	I Was Warned	CDJ	U.S.	1992	$2.00
Mercury	CDP 732	Just A Loser	CDJ	U.S.	1992	$2.00
Mercury	SACD 1035	Moan	CDJ	U.S.	1995	$3.00
Mercury	CRACD-6	Night Patrol	CD5	U.K.	1988	$8.00
Mercury	CDP 836	Price I Pay, The	CDJ	U.S.	1992	$8.00
Mercury	080 057-2	Right Next Door	CD5	U.K.	1987	$8.00
Mercury	870 714-2	Right Next Door	CDV/BP	U.S.	1988	$20.00/$20.00
Mercury	080 019-2	Smoking Gun	DJ/CDV	U.S.	1986	$20.00
Hightone Records	080 019-2	Smoking Gun	CDV	U.S.	1987	$20.00
Mercury	870 715-2	Smoking Gun	CDV/BP	U.S.	1987	$20.00/$20.00
Mercury		Some Rainy Morning	CDJ	U.S.	1995	$3.00
Mercury	CDP 381	These Things	CDJ	U.S.		$2.00

Crazy Horse

Full Length

Label	Catalog Number	Title	Type	Country	Year	Longbox Value/Value
Chrysalis	VK-41576	Crazy Horse	LP/LB	U.S.		$14.00/$8.00

Crazy L'eggs

Singles

Label	Catalog Number	Title	Type	Country	Year	Longbox Value/Value
Pandisc	125	Happy And U Know It	CD5	U.S.	1994	$5.00

Crazyhead

Full Length

Label	Catalog Number	Title	Type	Country	Year	Longbox Value/Value
EMI	CDP-91035	Desert Orchid	LP/LB	U.S.		$14.00/$8.00

Singles

Label	Catalog Number	Title	Type	Country	Year	Longbox Value/Value
Aris	884633	Everything's Alright	CD5	Germany	1990	$8.00
Parlophone	CDSGE-2025	Have Love Will Travel	CD5	U.K.	1989	$8.00
EMI	DPRO-04438	Have Love Will Travel	CDJ	U.S.	1989	$2.00
Strange Frt	018	Peel Sessions	CD5	U.K.	1989	$8.00
Food	CDFOOD-14	Rags	CD5	U.K.	1988	$8.00
Food	CDFOOD-12	Time HasTaken Its Toll On Me	CD5	U.K.	1988	$8.00

Cream

Full Length

Label	Catalog Number	Title	Type	Country	Year	Longbox Value/Value
BBC Radio		BBC Classic Tracks	RS	U.S.	1991	$30.00
	Airdate: 1/20/91.					
BBC Radio		BBC Classic Tracks	RS	U.S.	1991	$30.00
	Airdate: 12/2/91.					
BBC Radio		BBC Classic Tracks	RS	U.S.	1991	$30.00
	Airdate: 7/8/91.					
BBC Radio		BBC Classic Tracks	RS	U.S.	1992	$30.00
	Airdate: 1/20/92.					
BBC Radio		BBC Classic Tracks	RS	U.S.	1992	$30.00
	Airdate: 11/30/92.					
BBC Radio		BBC Classic Tracks	RS	U.S.	1992	$30.00
	Airdate: 7/20/92.					
BBC Radio		BBC Classic Tracks	RS	U.S.	1993	$25.00
	Airdate: 1/20/93.					
Westwood One		BBC Classic Tracks	RS	U.S.	1994	$30.00
	Airdate: 11/7/94.					
RSO	823 636-2	Disraeli Gears	LP/BP	U.S.†	1884	$14.00/$8.00
Album Network		In the Studio (Disraeli Gears)	RS	U.S.	1990	$35.00
	Airdate: 3/5/90.					
WEA		Strange Brew	LD	U.S.	1992	$30.00

Singles

Label	Catalog Number	Title	Type	Country	Year	Longbox Value/Value
Polydor	PODP-1033	Crossroads	CD3	Japan	1991	$15.00/$4.00
Pioneer	PIFP-1003	Strange Brew	CDV	Japan	1991	$40.00

Cream De Cocoa

Singles

Label	Catalog Number	Title	Type	Country	Year	Longbox Value/Value
Bob-Ability	B-101	Does Anyone Know Where	CD5	U.S.	1992	$4.00

Cream of Supreme

Full Length

Label	Catalog Number	Title	Type	Country	Year	Longbox Value/Value
Intercord	845 530	Cream of Supreme	LP	Germany		$18.00

Creaming Jesus

Singles

Label	Catalog Number	Title	Type	Country	Year	Longbox Value/Value
Efa	CD-75188	Deadtime	CD5	Germany	1991	$7.00
Jungle	JUNGCD-54	Deadtime	CD5	U.K.	1991	$7.00
Efa	CD-75194	Ditch Dweller	CD5	Germany	1991	$7.00
Jungle	JUNGCD-57	Ditch Dweller	CD5	U.K.	1991	$7.00
Jungle	JUNGCD-58	Headrush	CD5	U.K.	1992	$7.00

Creator

Singles

Label	Catalog Number	Title	Type	Country	Year	Longbox Value/Value
ZYX	6732-8	Creator	CD5	Germany	1992	$7.00

Creatures

Singles

Label	Catalog Number	Title	Type	Country	Year	Longbox Value/Value
Wonderland	SHECD-18	Fury Eyes	CD5	U.K.	1990	$7.00
Wonderland	SHECD-17	Standing There	CD5	U.K.	1990	$7.00

Credit to the Nation

Singles

Label	Catalog Number	Title	Type	Country	Year	Longbox Value/Value
		Teenage Sensation	CD5	U.K.		$8.00
		Teenage Sensation	CD5	U.K.		$8.00
	Second version.					

Creedence Clearwater Revival

Full Length

Label	Catalog Number	Title	Type	Country	Year	Longbox Value/Value
Fantasy	FCD-CCR2	Chronicle	LP/LB	U.S.†	1985	$20.00/$16.00
	2 CD set.					
Fantasy	CCGCD-22-2	Chronicle Volume One	LTD/LP	U.S.	1995	$25.00
Fantasy	CCGCD-23-2	Chronicle Volume Two	LTD/LP	U.S.	1995	$25.00
Fantasy	FCD-8402	Cosmo's Factory	LP/LB	U.S.†	1985	$14.00/$8.00
Fantasy	FCD-4509-2	Country Album	LP	Germany		$23.00
Fantasy	FCD-8393	Green River	LP/LB	U.S.†	1985	$14.00/$8.00
Westwood One		Off the Record	RS	U.S.	1993	$40.00
	Airdate: 3/1/93.					
Westwood One		Off the Record	RS	U.S.	1994	$30.00
	Airdate: 8/15/94.					
Fantasy	FCD-8397	Willie & the Poorboys	LP/LB	U.S.†	1985	$14.00/$8.00

Singles

Label	Catalog Number	Title	Type	Country	Year	Longbox Value/Value
Epic	658004-2	Bad Moon Rising	CD5	U.K.	1992	$10.00
ZYX	6164-8	Hey Tonight	CD5	Germany	1989	$10.00

Creedle

Singles

Label	Catalog Number	Title	Type	Country	Year	Longbox Value/Value
Cargo	022	Half Man, Half Ape	CDJ	U.S.		$2.00

Creeps

Full Length

Label	Catalog Number	Title	Type	Country	Year	Longbox Value/Value
Atlantic	82112-2	Blue Tomato	LP/LB	U.S.		$14.00/$8.00
Skyclad	8	Enjoy the Creeps	LP/BP	U.S.		$14.00/$8.00

Singles

Label	Catalog Number	Title	Type	Country	Year	Longbox Value/Value
Atlantic	PRCD 82112-2	Blue Tomato	CDJ	U.S.	1990	$2.00
WEA	171209-2	Ooh! I Like It!	CD5	Germany	1990	$8.00
WEA	YZ-477CD	Ooh! I Like It!	CD5	U.K.	1990	$8.00
Atlantic	PRCD 3384-2	Ooh! I Like It!	CDJ	U.S.	1990	$2.00

Crenshaw, Marshall

Full Length

Label	Catalog Number	Title	Type	Country	Year	Longbox Value/Value
Paradox	CD45 1343	A Collection	DJ/Smplr	U.S.	1991	$20.00
Warner Brothers	9 25908-2	Good Evening	LP/LB	U.S.		$14.00/$8.00
DIR		King Biscuit Flour Hour	RS	U.S.	1987	$40.00
	With John Hiatt, Airdate: 10/18/87.					
Warner Brothers		Mary Jean	LP/LB	U.S.		$14.00/$8.00

Singles

Label	Catalog Number	Title	Type	Country	Year	Longbox Value/Value
MCA	CD45 1344	Better Back Off	CDJ	U.S.	1991	$2.00
MCA	CD45 1663	Don't Disappear Now	CDJ	U.S.	1991	$2.00
Warner Brothers	PRO-CD-3581	Some Hearts	CDJ	U.S.	1989	$3.00
Sony	SRDS-8242	To Keep Our Alive	CD3	Japan	1992	$15.00/$3.00

Creo-D

Singles

Label	Catalog Number	Title	Type	Country	Year	Longbox Value/Value
Scotti Brothers	78004	Watch Out	CD5	U.S.	1994	$5.00

Crew

Singles

Label	Catalog Number	Title	Type	Country	Year	Longbox Value/Value
A&M	USACD-696	Get Dumb	CD5	U.K.	1990	$8.00

Crew, Jennifer

Singles

Label	Catalog Number	Title	Type	Country	Year	Longbox Value/Value
ZYX	6028-8	Potion Of Love	CD5	Germany	1988	$6.00

Crickets

Singles

Label	Catalog Number	Title	Type	Country	Year	Longbox Value/Value
Sony	CDTSH-1	T-Shirt	CD5	U.K.	1988	$8.00

Crime Fighters

Singles

Label	Catalog Number	Title	Type	Country	Year	Longbox Value/Value
RCA	PD-43136	Bat Attack '89	CD5	Germany	1989	$8.00
RCA	PD-43136	Bat Attack '89	CD5	U.K.	1989	$8.00

Crime & The City Solution

Full Length

Label	Catalog Number	Title	Type	Country	Year	Longbox Value/Value
Restless	71422-2	Bride Ship	LP/LB	U.S.		$14.00/$8.00
Mute	60990	Paradise Discotheque	LP/LB	U.S.		$14.00/$8.00
Restless	71402-2	Shine	LP/LB	U.S.		$14.00/$8.00

Singles

Label	Catalog Number	Title	Type	Country	Year	Longbox Value/Value
Mute	826-953	Dolphins & Sharks	CD5	Germany	1991	$8.00
Mute	CDMUTE-127	Dolphins & Sharks	CD5	U.K.	1991	$8.00
Mute	CDMUTE-114	I Have the Gun	CD5	U.K.	1991	$8.00
Mute	8236	I Have the Gun	CDJ	U.S.	1990	$2.00
Mute	CDMUTE-94	Shadow of No Man	CD5	U.K.		$8.00

Criminal Element Orchestra

Full Length

Label	Catalog Number	Title	Type	Country	Year	Longbox Value/Value
WTG	45233-2	Locked Up	LP/LB	U.S.		$9.00/$6.00

Singles

Label	Catalog Number	Title	Type	Country	Year	Longbox Value/Value
BMG	PD-44072	Everybody	CD5	Germany	1990	$8.00
BMG	PD-44072	Everybody	CD5	U.K.	1990	$8.00
		House Time, Anytime	CDJ	U.S.		$2.00

Criminal Nation

Full Length

Label	Catalog Number	Title	Type	Country	Year	Longbox Value/Value
Nastymix	IGU70240-2	Release the Pressure	DJ/LP	U.S.	1990	$10.00

Singles

Label	Catalog Number	Title	Type	Country	Year	Longbox Value/Value
Nastymix	130	6 Down Deep	CDJ	U.S.	1992	$2.00

Criminal Touch

Singles

Label	Catalog Number	Title	Type	Country	Year	Longbox Value/Value
ZYX	DST-1025-8	Techno Computer One	CD5	Germany	1990	$6.00

Crimson, Glory

Singles

Label	Catalog Number	Title	Type	Country	Year	Longbox Value/Value
Roadrunner	MP10-1	Dream Dancer	CD3	Japan	1988	$12.00/$3.00
Roadrunner	7904-3	Lonely	CD5	Germany	1989	$8.00
Roadrunner	RR-2448-2	Lonely	CD5	Japan	1989	$15.00

Criner, Clyde

Full Length

Label	Catalog Number	Title	Type	Country	Year	Longbox Value/Value
Novus	3029	Behind the Sun	LP/BP	U.S.		$12.00/$7.00
Novus	3066	Colour of the Dark	LP/BP	U.S.		$12.00/$7.00

Cro Mags

Singles

Label	Catalog Number	Title	Type	Country	Year	Longbox Value / Value
Century	7730	See the Signs	CDJ	U.S.		$2.00

Croce, Jim

Full Length

Label	Catalog Number	Title	Type	Country	Year	Longbox Value / Value
Warner Sound Exchange		22 Legendary Hits	LTD/LP	U.S.	1995	$17.00
Atlantic	90469-2	Time in a Bottle	LP/LB	U.S.		$14.00/$8.00
Atlantic	91326-2	Time in a Bottle	LP/LB	U.S.		$14.00/$8.00
Atlantic	90467-2	Time in a Bottle	LP/LB	U.S.		$14.00/$8.00

Croft, Monte

Full Length

Label	Catalog Number	Title	Type	Country	Year	Longbox Value / Value
Columbia	CK-45122	Higher Fire	LP/LB	U.S.		$14.00/$8.00

Croisette

Singles

Label	Catalog Number	Title	Type	Country	Year	Longbox Value / Value
Canyon	13EL-5537	You're a Time Waster	CD3	Japan	1988	$12.00/$3.00

Croker, Brendan & 5 O'Clock Shadows

Full Length

Label	Catalog Number	Title	Type	Country	Year	Longbox Value / Value
Jive	1209-2	Croker, Brendan & 5 O'Clock Shadows	LP/LB	U.S.		$14.00/$8.00

Singles

Label	Catalog Number	Title	Type	Country	Year	Longbox Value / Value
Silvertone	ORECD-8	No Money At All	CD5	U.K.	1989	$7.00
RCA	1252-2-RDJ	No Money At All	CDJ	U.S.	1989	$2.00
Aris	885645	This Kind Of Love	CD5	Germany	1989	$7.00
Silvertone	CLOCK 1	This Man	CD5	U.K.	1989	$7.00
Silvertone	ORECD-5	Wrong Decision	CD5	U.K.	1989	$7.00

Cronin, Kevin & Friends

Singles

Label	Catalog Number	Title	Type	Country	Year	Longbox Value / Value
Epic	ESK 4000	Hard To Believe	CDJ	U.S.	1991	$2.00

Crooklyn Dodgers

Singles

Label	Catalog Number	Title	Type	Country	Year	Longbox Value / Value
		Crooklyn	CDJ	U.S.		$2.00

Cropper, Steve

Full Length

Label	Catalog Number	Title	Type	Country	Year	Longbox Value / Value
		House of Blues	RS	U.S.	1994	$50.00
	2 CD sset. Airdate: 8/14/94.					

Crosby, Bing

Full Length

Label	Catalog Number	Title	Type	Country	Year	Longbox Value / Value
Polygram	824705-2	Bing and Basie	LP	Germany		$14.00
Polygram	824705-2	Bing and Basie	LP/BP	U.S.		$14.00/$8.00
Emarcy	824705-2	Bing and Basie	LP/LB	U.S.†	1985	$14.00/$8.00
Deja Vu	5078	Christmas Collection	LP/BP	U.S.		$14.00/$8.00
MCA	MCAD-25205	Holiday In	LP/LB	U.S.		$14.00/$8.00
Happy Days	HAP-123	Remembering	LP/LB	U.S.		$12.00/$7.00
MCA	MCAD-25205	Sings Christmas Songs	LP/LB	U.S.		$14.00/$8.00

Singles

Label	Catalog Number	Title	Type	Country	Year	Longbox Value / Value
Decca	10P3-6054	White Christmas	CD3	Japan	1988	$12.00/$4.00
MCA	DMCAT-111	White Christmas	CD5	U.K.	1991	$10.00

Crosby, David

Full Length

Label	Catalog Number	Title	Type	Country	Year	Longbox Value / Value
DIR		King Biscuit Flour Hour	RS	U.S.	1989	$30.00
	Airdate: 5/14/89.					
DIR		King Biscuit Flour Hour	RS	U.S.	1989	$40.00
	Airdate: 12/4/89.					
DIR		King Biscuit Flour Hour	RS	U.S.	1991	$30.00
	Airdate: 7/7/91.					
DIR		King Biscuit Flour Hour	RS	U.S.	1992	$40.00
	Airdate: 10/18/92.					
DIR		King Biscuit Flour Hour	RS	U.S.	1994	$30.00
	Airdate: 8/21/94.					
DIR		King Biscuit Flour Hour	RS	U.S.	1995	$30.00
	Airdate: 8/13/95.					
Westwood One		Off the record	RS	U.S.	1993	$20.00
	Airdate: 7/26/93.					
Canyon	D25Y-3303	Oh Yes I Can	LP	Japan		$20.00
A&M	CD-5232	Oh Yes I Can	LP/LB	U.S.		$14.00/$8.00
Radio Today		Rock Stars	RS	U.S.	1989	$35.00
	2 CD set. Airdate: 3/13/89.					

Singles

Label	Catalog Number	Title	Type	Country	Year	Longbox Value / Value
A&M	S10Y-3068	Drive My Car	CD3	Japan	1989	$12.00/$3.00
A&M	CD 17701	Drive My Car	CDJ	U.S.	1989	$2.00
A&M	CD 17720	Drive My Car	CDJ	U.S.	1989	$2.00
Atlantic	PRCD 5060-2	Hero	CDJ	U.S.	1993	$2.00
A&M	CD 17814	In the Wide Ruin	CDJ	U.S.	1989	$2.00
A&M	CD 17758	Lady of the Harbor	CDJ	U.S.	1989	$2.00
Canyon	S10Y-3064	Monkey and the Underdog	CD3	Japan	1989	$12.00/$3.00
A&M	CD 17749	Monkey and the Underdog	CDJ	U.S.	1989	$2.00
Atlantic	PRCD 5179-2	Through Your Hands	CDJ	U.S.	1993	$2.00

Crosby, Rob

Singles

Label	Catalog Number	Title	Type	Country	Year	Longbox Value / Value
		Love Will Bring Her Around	CDJ	U.S.		$2.00

Crosby, Stills & Nash

Full Length

Label	Catalog Number	Title	Type	Country	Year	Longbox Value / Value
		25th Anniversary Special	RS	U.S.	1994	$115.00
	4 CD set. Airdate: 6/26/94.					
WEA	780075-2	Allies	LP	U.K.		$14.00
Atlantic	80075-2	Allies	LP/LB	U.S.†	1985	$14.00/$8.00
Atlantic	80075-2	Allies	LP/LB	U.S.	1987	$14.00/$8.00
Westwood One		BBC Classic Tracks	RS	U.S.	1994	$30.00
	Airdate: 2/26/94.					
Atlantic	19117-2	Crosby, Stills & Nash	LP/LB	U.S.		$14.00/$8.00
	Nonremastered version.					
MCA	74-020	Crosby, Stills & Nash	LD	U.S.	1983	$35.00
Atlantic	19104-2	CSN	LP/LB	U.S.		$14.00/$8.00
	Nonremastered version.					
Atlantic	PRCD 4283-2	CSN	DJ/Smplr	U.S.	1991	$20.00
WEA	250896	Daylight Again	LP	Germany		$15.00
Atlantic	19360-2	Daylight Again	LP/LB	U.S.		$14.00/$8.00
	Nonremastered version.					
Album Network		In the Studio (Crosby Stills & Nash)	RS	U.S.	1988	$25.00
	Airdate: 6/27/88.					
Album Network		In the Studio (Crosby Stills & Nash)	RS	U.S.	1991	$25.00
	Airdate: 2/25/91.					
DIR		King Biscuit Flour Hour	RS	U.S.	1987	$50.00
	With Allman Brothers, Airdate: 11/8/87.					
DIR		King Biscuit Flour Hour	RS	U.S.	1990	$30.00
	Airdate: 6/11/90.					
DIR		King Biscuit Flour Hour	RS	U.S.	1992	$30.00
	Airdate: 2/16/92.					
DIR		King Biscuit Flour Hour	RS	U.S.	1993	$30.00
DIR		King Biscuit Flour Hour	RS	U.S.	1993	$60.00
	Airdate: 10/17/93.					
Atlantic		Live It Up	LP/LB	U.S.		$14.00/$8.00
Westwood One		Off the Record	RS	U.S.	1993	$30.00
	Airdate: 7/26/93.					
Westwood One		Off the Record	RS	U.S.	1994	$20.00
	Airdate: 10/3/94.					
Atlantic	PRCD 3446-2	Profiled	DJ/Intvw	U.S.	1990	$10.00
Westwood One		Superstar Concert	RS	U.S.	1992	$40.00
	2 CD set. Airdate: 10/25/92.					
Media America		Up Close	RS	U.S.	1988	$30.00
	2 CD set.					
Media America		Up Close	RS	U.S.	1989	$30.00
	2 CD set.					
Media America		Up Close	RS	U.S.	1990	$50.00
	4 CD set.					
Media America		Up Close	RS	U.S.	1991	$50.00
	4 CD set.					
Media America		Up Close	RS	U.S.	1994	$70.00
	3 CD set.					

Singles

Label	Catalog Number	Title	Type	Country	Year	Longbox Value / Value
Eastwest	788732-2	Chippin' Away	CD5	Germany	1990	$8.00
Atlantic	AMDY-5004	Chippin' Away	CD3	Japan	1990	$15.00/$3.00
Atlantic	PR 3144-2	Chippin' Away	CDJ	U.S.	1990	$2.00
Atlantic	PRCD 3508-2	(Got To Keep) Open	CDJ	U.S.	1990	$2.00
Atlantic	PR 3492-2	If Anybody Had a Heart	CDJ	U.S.	1990	$2.00
WEA	7567-86144-2	Live It Up	CD5	Germany	1990	$8.00
WEA	A-7909CD	Live It Up	CD5	U.K.	1990	$8.00
Atlantic	PR 3336-2	Live It Up	CDJ	U.S.	1990	$2.00
Atlantic		Only Waiting For You	CDJ	U.S.	1993	$3.00
Atlantic	A-7552CD	Our House	CD5	U.K.	1992	$8.00

Crosby, Stills, Nash & Young

Full Length

Label	Catalog Number	Title	Type	Country	Year	Longbox Value / Value
Atlantic	PR 2552-2	American Dream	DJ/LP	U.S.	1988	$55.00
	Picturedisc CD in digipak.					
Atlantic		American Dream	LP/LB	U.S.	1988	$12.00/$7.00
Atlantic	19118-2	Deja Vu	LP/LB	U.S.		$14.00/$8.00
	Nonremastered version.					
Album Network		In the Studio	RS	U.S.	1988	$35.00
	First "In the Studio Show", Airdate: 6/27/88.					
Album Network		In the Studio (Deja Vu)	RS	U.S.	1989	$25.00
	Airdate: 3/27/89.					
Atlantic	19119-2	So Far	LP/LB	U.S.		$14.00/$8.00
	Nonremastered version.					

Singles

Label	Catalog Number	Title	Type	Country	Year	Longbox Value / Value
Atlantic	786473-2	American Dream	CD3	Germany	1988	$10.00
Atlantic	10P3-6058	American Dream	CD3	Japan	1988	$15.00/$3.00
Atlantic	A-9003CD	American Dream	CD3	U.K.	1988	$10.00
Atlantic	PR 2542-2	American Dream	CDJ	U.S.	1988	$2.00
Atlantic	PR 2497-2	American Dream	CDJ	U.S.	1988	$7.00
Atlantic	PR 2578-2	Got It Made	CDJ	U.S.	1988	$3.00
Atlantic		This Old House	CDJ	U.S.		$3.00
Atlantic	PR 2860-2	Woodstock	CDJ	U.S.	1989	$3.00

Cross

Full Length

Label	Catalog Number	Title	Type	Country	Year	Longbox Value / Value
Virgin	90857-2	Shove It	LP/LB	U.S.		$14.00/$8.00

Singles

Label	Catalog Number	Title	Type	Country	Year	Longbox Value / Value
Virgin	CDEP-10	Cowboys & Indians	CD5	U.K.	1988	$7.00
EMI	147529-2	Final Destination	CD5	Germany	1988	$7.00
Virgin	VJD-12009	Heaven For Everyone	CD3	Japan	1988	$12.00/$3.00
EMI	147516-2	Liar	CD5	Germany	1990	$7.00
EMI	204437-2	New Dark Ages	CD5	Germany	1991	$7.00
EMI	147497-2	Power To Love	CD5	Germany	1990	$7.00
Parlophone	CDR-6251	Power To Love	CD5	U.K.	1990	$7.00
Virgin	CDEP-20	Shove It	CD5	U.K.	1988	$7.00

Cross, Christopher

Full Length

Label	Catalog Number	Title	Type	Country	Year	Longbox Value / Value
Warner Brothers	9 23757-2	Another Page	LP/LB	U.S.†	1984	$14.00/$8.00
Warner Brothers	9 25685-2	Back of My Mind	LP/LB	U.S.		$14.00/$8.00
Warner Brothers	3383-2	Christopher Cross	LP/LB	U.S.†	1984	$14.00/$8.00
Warner Brothers	9 25341-2	Every Turn of the World	LP/LB	U.S.		$14.00/$8.00
Warner Brothers		Serenade 1980-'88	DJ/Smplr	Japan		$40.00

Singles

Label	Catalog Number	Title	Type	Country	Year	Longbox Value / Value
Warner Brothers	10P3-6009	I Will (TakeYou Forever)	CD3	Japan	1988	$12.00/$3.00
		I Will (TakeYou Forever)	CDJ	U.S.	1988	$2.00
Ariola	7432110290-2	In the Blink Of An Eye	CD5	U.K.	1992	$8.00
Geronimo	PSDW-3001	Is There Something	CD3	Japan	1992	$12.00/$3.00
Warner Brothers	921134-2	Ride Like the Wind	CD3	Germany	1989	$8.00
Warner Brothers	921134-2	Ride Like the Wind	CD3	U.K.	1989	$8.00
Warner Brothers	10P3-6048	Swept Away	CD3	Japan	1988	$12.00/$3.00
Warner Brothers	PRO-CD-3319	Swept Away	CDJ	U.S.	1988	$2.00

Cross, Sandra

Singles

Label	Catalog Number	Title	Type	Country	Year	Longbox Value / Value
Ariwa	CEDC-00424	My Guy	CD3	Japan	1992	$12.00/$3.00

Crossfire Choir

Full Length

Label	Catalog Number	Title	Type	Country	Year	Longbox Value / Value
Passport	PBCD-6056	Crossfire Choir	LP	U.K.		$13.00
Passport	PBCD-6056	Crossfire Choir	LP/LB	U.S.		$14.00/$8.00

Crouch, Andrae

Singles

Label	Catalog Number	Title	Type	Country	Year	Longbox Value / Value
Warner Brothers	PRO-CD-6810	Nobody Else Like You	CDJ	U.S.	1994	$2.00
Qwest	PRO-CD-6949	Say So	CDJ	U.S.	1994	$2.00

Crow, Robin

Full Length

Label	Catalog Number	Title	Type	Country	Year	Longbox Value / Value
		Electric Cinema Sampler	DJ/Smplr	U.S.		$6.00

Singles

Label	Catalog Number	Title	Type	Country	Year	Longbox Value / Value
		Sleepwalking	CDJ	U.S.		$2.00

Crow, Sheryl

Full Length

Label	Catalog Number	Title	Type	Country	Year	Longbox Value / Value
A&M		D'yer Maker	DJ/Smplr	U.K.		$16.00
Westwood One		In Concert	RS	U.S.	1994	$120.00
	2 CD set. 12/5/94.					
Westwood One		In Concert	RS	U.S.	1995	$70.00
	Airdate: 8/28/95.					
Westwood One		In Concert-Nu Rock	RS	U.S.	1995	$70.00
	Airdate: 5/22/95.					

Label	Catalog Number	Title	Type	Country	Year	Longbox Value / Value
A&M		Tuesday Night Music Club	LTD/LP	Australia	1995	$35.00
	CD with bonus CD5 of "Can't Cry Anymore."					
A&M		Tuesday Night Music Club	LTD/LP	U.K.	1995	$35.00
	2 CD set.					
A&M	31458 401262	Tuesday Night Music Club	DJ/LP	U.S.	1993	$50.00
	CD in spiral bound book.					
		Singles				
		All I Wanna Do	CD5	U.K.		$10.00
	Second version.					
A&M		All I Wanna Do	CD5	U.K.	1994	$10.00
A&M	31458 8298 2	All I Wanna Do	CDJ	U.K.	1994	$16.00
A&M	31458 8317 2	All I Wanna Do	CDJ	U.S.	1994	$7.00
A&M	31458 8298 2	All I Wanna Do	CDJ	U.S.	1994	$7.00
A&M	PODM-1055	Can't Cry Anymore	CD3	Japan	1995	$17.00/$4.00
A&M		Can't Cry Anymore	CD5	U.K.	1995	$10.00
A&M		Can't Cry Anymore	CD5	U.K.	1995	$10.00
	Second version.					
A&M	581081	Can't Cry Anymore	CD5	U.S.	1995	$6.00
A&M	31458 8284 2	Can't Cry Anymore	CDJ	U.S.	1995	$3.00
A&M		Leaving Las Vegas	CD5	U.K.	1994	$10.00
		Leaving Las Vegas	CD5	U.K.	1994	$10.00
	Second version.					
A&M		Leaving Las Vegas	CDJ	U.K.	1994	$16.00
A&M	31458 8208 2	Leaving Las Vegas	CDJ	U.S.	1993	$2.00
A&M	31458 8261 2	Leaving Las Vegas	CDJ	U.S.	1993	$2.00
A&M	31458 8263 2	Run Baby Run	CDJ	U.K.	1994	$16.00
A&M		Run Baby Run	CD5	U.K.	1995	$10.00
A&M		Run Baby Run	CD5	U.K.	1995	$10.00
A&M		Run Baby Run	CD5	U.K.	1995	$10.00
	Second version.					
A&M		Run Baby Run	CD5	U.K.	1995	$14.00
	Limited edition in box.					
A&M	31458 8263 2	Run Baby Run	CDJ	U.S.	1994	$2.00
A&M	31458 8182 2	Scenes From the Tuesday Night Music Club	CDJ	U.S.	1993	$2.00
		Strong Enough	CD5	U.K.		$10.00
A&M		Strong Enough	CD5	U.K.	1995	$12.00
	Second version.					
A&M	80866	Strong Enough	CD5	U.S.	1994	$5.00
A&M		Strong Enough	CDJ	U.S.	1995	$3.00
A&M		What Can I Do For You	CD5	U.K.	1995	$10.00
A&M		What Can I Do For You	CD5	U.K.	1995	$10.00
	Second version.					
A&M		What Can I Do For You	CDJ	U.K.	1995	$16.00
A&M		What Can I Do For You	CDJ	U.K.	1995	$16.00
	Second version.					
		What I Can Do For You	CD5	U.K.		$10.00

Crowded House

Label	Catalog Number	Title	Type	Country	Year	Longbox Value / Value
		Full Length				
Capitol		104 KRBE	DJ/Smplr	U.S.	1994	$35.00
EMI		An Introduction to Together Alone	DJ/Smplr	U.K.	1995	$20.00
Capitol		Collector's Disc	DJ/Smplr	U.S.	1994	$18.00
	KREE radio sampler.					
EMI		Crowded House, Woodface, Temple	LTD/LP	U.K.	1994	$35.00
	3 CD boxed set.					
Capitol	CD-CD-DJ1	Full House	DJ/Smplr	U.K.	1994	$35.00
Capitol	CD-CD-DJ1	Full House	DJ/Smplr	U.K.	1994	$40.00
	CD with press kit.					
Capitol		Instinct	DJ/Smplr	U.K.	1996	$30.00
DIR		King Biscuit Flour Hour	RS	U.S.	1988	$30.00
	With Squeeze, Airdate: 1/31/88.					
Capitol	CI I1	Live At the Town and Country Club, London	DJ/Smplr	U.K.	1991	$70.00
	2 CD set.					
EMI		Live Eight Miles High	DJ/Smplr	U.S.		$20.00
	With the Byrds.					
Capitol	DPRO-79297	Locked Out	DJ/Smplr	U.S.	1993	$30.00
	CDJ plus "Greatest Hits" sampler.					
Capitol	DPRO-79297	Locked Out	DJ/Smplr	U.S.	1993	$40.00
		Recurring Dream	LTD/LP	U.K.	1996	$35.00
	2 CD set.					
EMI		Woodface	LTD/LP	U.K.	1997	$35.00
	Limited edition centennial CD edition housed in a slip case with a special 100 anniversary booklet.					
Capitol	DPRO-79759	Woodface	DJ/LP	U.S.	1991	$15.00
Capitol		Woodface	LTD/LP	U.S.	1991	$15.00
		Singles				
Capitol	202730-2	Better Be Home Soon	CD5	Germany	1988	$8.00
Toshiba	XP10-2015	Better Be Home Soon	CD3	Japan	1988	$12.00/$3.00
Capitol	CDCL-498	Better Be Home Soon	CD5	U.K.	1988	$10.00
Capitol	DPRO-79341	Better Be Home Soon	CDJ	U.S.	1988	$2.00
Capitol	204351-2	Chocolate Cake	CD5	Germany	1991	$8.00
Tohiba		Chocolate Cake	CD3	Japan	1991	$13.00/$4.00
Capitol	CDCL-618	Chocolate Cake	CD5	U.K.	1991	$8.00
Capitol	C2 15738	Chocolate Cake	CD5	U.S.	1991	$4.00
Capitol	DPRO-79775	Chocolate Cake	CDJ	U.S.	1991	$2.00
		Distant Sun	CD5	U.K.		$10.00
		Distant Sun	CD5	U.K.		$10.00
	Second version.					
Capital	58136	Distant Sun	CD5	U.S.	1994	$5.00
Capitol	DPRO-79333	Distant Sun	CDJ	U.S.	1994	$2.00
Capitol	Cap.5614	Don't Dream It's Over	CDV	U.S.	1987	$20.00
Capitol/NTSC	CAP. 5614	Don't Dream Its Over	DJ/CDV	U.S.	1986	$20.00
		Everything Is Good For You	CD5	Australia	1996	$12.00
		Everything Is Good For You	CDJ	U.K.	1996	$10.00
EMI	204451-2	Fall At Your Feet	CD5	Germany	1991	$8.00
	CDCLX626	Fall At Your Feet	CD5	U.K.		$10.00
Capitol	DPRO-79849	Fall At Your Feet	CDJ	U.S.	1991	$2.00
EMI		Fingers Of Love	CD5	U.K.	1994	$10.00
EMI		Fingers Of Love	CD5	U.K.	1994	$10.00
	Second version.					
EMI	CDCL-DJ-715	Fingers Of Love	CDJ	U.K.	1994	$12.00
Capitol	CDCLS-655	Four Seasons In One Day	CD5	U.K.		$8.00
		Four Seasons In One Day	CD5	U.K.		$8.00
	Second version.					
		Four Seasons In One Day	CDJ	U.S.		$8.00
Capitol	203445-2	I Feel Possessed	CD5	Germany	1989	$8.00
Capitol	C2 15490	I Feel Possessed	CD5	U.S.	1989	$5.00
Capitol	DPRO 15490	I Feel Possessed	CDJ	U.S.	1989	$3.00
		Instinct	CD5	U.K.	1996	$10.00
		Instinct	CD5	U.K.	1996	$10.00
	Second version.					
		Instinct	CDJ	U.K.	1996	$13.00
		It's Only Natural	CD5	U.K.		$10.00
		It's Only Natural	CD5	U.K.		$10.00
	Second version.					
Capitol	DPRO-79738	It's Only Natural	CDJ	U.S.	1991	$2.00
Capitol		Locked Out	CD5	Australia	1993	$12.00
		Locked Out	CD5	Australia	1994	$14.00
Capitol		Locked Out	CD5	U.K.	1993	$10.00
Capitol		Locked Out	CD5	U.K.	1993	$10.00
	Second version.					
Capitol	C2 7243 58088	Locked Out	CD5	U.S.	1993	$5.00
Capitol		Nails in My Feet	CD5	Australia	1993	$12.00
Capitol		Nails in My Feet	CD5	U.K.	1993	$10.00
Capitol		Nails in My Feet	CD5	U.K.	1993	$10.00
	Second version.					
Capitol		Nails in My Feet	CDJ	U.K.	1993	N/A
	CD-R version.					
		Not the Girl You Think	CD5	U.K.	1996	$10.00
		Not the Girl You Think	CD5	U.K.	1996	$10.00
	Second version.					
Capitol		Private Universe	CD5	Australia	1994	$12.00
Capitol		Private Universe	CDJ	France	1994	$25.00
Capitol		Private Universe	CD5	Germany	1994	$10.00
Capitol	CDCL-509	Sister Madly	CD5	U.K.	1988	$8.00
		Suffer Never	CD5	U.K.	1995	$10.00
		Suffer Never	CD5	U.K.	1995	$10.00
	Second version.					
		Weather With You	CDJ	France		$40.00
Capitol	TOCP-7157	Weather With You	CD3	Japan	1992	$12.00/$3.00
Capitol		Weather With You	CD5	U.K.	1992	$8.00
Capitol	DPRO-15734	Weather With You	CDJ	U.S.	1992	$2.00
Capitol	DPRO-9327	Weather With You	CDJ	U.S.	1992	$2.00
Capitol		World Where You Live	CD5	Austria		$8.00
Capitol	DPRO-79070	World Where You Live	CDJ	U.S.		$2.00

Crowell, Rodney

Label	Catalog Number	Title	Type	Country	Year	Longbox Value / Value
		Full Length				
Columbia	CSK 45242	Keys to the Highway	DJ/LP	U.S.	1989	$10.00
MCA	MCAD-11042	Let the Picture Paint Itself	DJ/LP	U.S.	[illegible]	[illegible]
	"Color-seperated" picture digipak.					
Columbia	CSK 4630	Life Is Messy	DJ/LP	U.S.		$10.00
MCA	MCA3P-3004	Sampler	DJ/Smplr	U.S.	1994	$10.00
		Singles				
Columbia	CSK 77240	Even Cowgirls Get the Blues	CDJ	U.S.	1993	$2.00
Columbia	CSK 4642	It's Not For You To Judge	CDJ	U.S.	1993	$2.00
		It's Such A Small World	DJ/CD3	U.S.		$6.00/$3.00
MCA	MCA5P-54821	Let the Picture Paint Itself	CDJ	U.S.	1994	$2.00
Columbia	CSK 4768	Let's Make Trouble	CDJ	U.S.	1992	$2.00
Columbia	CSK 74250	Lovin' All Night	CDJ	U.S.	1992	$2.00
Columbia	CSK 1881	Many a Long Lonesome Highway	CDJ	U.S.	1989	$2.00
Columbia	CSK 73760	Things I Wish I'd Said	CDJ	U.S.	1991	$2.00
Columbia	CSK 4663	What Kind Of Love	CDJ	U.S.	1991	$2.00

Crowface

Label	Catalog Number	Title	Type	Country	Year	Longbox Value / Value
		Singles				
Devotion	CDDVN-101	Don't Look Down	CD5	U.K.	1991	$8.00

Crown Heights Affair

Label	Catalog Number	Title	Type	Country	Year	Longbox Value / Value
		Singles				
SBK	CDSBK-7003	I'll Do Anything	CD5	U.K.	1989	$7.00
		I'll Do Anything	CDJ	U.S.		$2.00

Crown of Thorns

Label	Catalog Number	Title	Type	Country	Year	Longbox Value / Value
		Singles				
	NTHENCDS1	Hike It Up	CD5	U.K.	1994	$10.00

Crucial, Robbie

Label	Catalog Number	Title	Type	Country	Year	Longbox Value / Value
		Singles				
Ariwa	ARICD-056	Crucial View	CD5	U.K.	1990	$7.00

Cruel Sea

Label	Catalog Number	Title	Type	Country	Year	Longbox Value / Value
		Singles				
Polydor	8610372	Black Stick	CD5	Australia	1992	$8.00
Polydor	859291	Honeymoon Is Over, The	CD5	Australia	1993	$8.00
A&M records	851595	Honeymoon Is Over, The	CD5	U.S.	1994	$5.00/$5.00

Cruel Shoes

Label	Catalog Number	Title	Type	Country	Year	Longbox Value / Value
		Full Length				
		Cruel Shoes	LP/LB	U.S.		$12.00/$10.00
		Singles				
Rendezvous	6222	Dancing Shoes	CDJ	U.S.	1992	$2.00
RCA	62353-2-RDJ	Where Are the Angels	CDJ	U.S.	1992	$2.00

Cruel Story of Youth

Label	Catalog Number	Title	Type	Country	Year	Longbox Value / Value
		Full Length				
Columbia	CK-44206	Cruel Story of Youth	LP/LB	U.S.		$14.00/$8.00
		Singles				
Columbia	CSK 1469	You're What You Want to Be	CDJ	U.S.	1989	$2.00

Cruise, Erin

Label	Catalog Number	Title	Type	Country	Year	Longbox Value / Value
		Singles				
		Waiting For You	CDJ	U.S.		$2.00

Cruise, Julee

Label	Catalog Number	Title	Type	Country	Year	Longbox Value / Value
		Full Length				
Warner Brothers	25859-2-Dj	Floating Into the Night	DJ/LP	U.S.	1989	$9.00
	Picture disc.					
		Singles				
WEA	7599-25889-2	Falling	CD5	Germany	1990	$8.00
WEA	921771-2	Falling	CD5	Germany	1990	$8.00
WEA	W-9544CD	Falling	CD5	U.K.	1990	$8.00
Warner Brothers	PRO-CD-4346	Falling	CDJ	U.S.	1990	$2.00
Warner Brothers	W-0004CD	Rockin' Back Inside My Heart	CD5	U.K.	1990	$8.00
Warner Brothers	PRO-CD-3934	Rockin' Back Inside My Heart	CDJ	U.S.	1989	$2.00
Warner Brothers	9 40027-2	Rockin' Back Inside My Heart	CD5	U.S.	1991	$5.00
Warner Brothers	9362-40411-2	Summer Kisses, Winter Tears	CD5	U.K.	1991	$8.00
Warner Brothers	W-0095CD	Summer Kisses, Winter Tears	CD5	U.K.	1991	$8.00

Crumbacher Band

Label	Catalog Number	Title	Type	Country	Year	Longbox Value / Value
		Full Length				
Aris	880385	Escape From the Fallen Planet	LP	Germany		$18.00

Crumbsuckers

Label	Catalog Number	Title	Type	Country	Year	Longbox Value / Value
		Full Length				
IRS	970 954	Life of Dreams	LP	Germany		$18.00

Crunch-O-Matic

Label	Catalog Number	Title	Type	Country	Year	Longbox Value / Value
		Full Length				
Polygram	848139	Caution: Do Not Play	LP/BP	U.S.		$12.00/$7.00

Crusaders

Label	Catalog Number	Title	Type	Country	Year	Longbox Value / Value
		Full Length				
WEA	250776-2	Free as the Wind	LP	Germany		$14.00
MCA	MCAD-42168	Life in the Modern World	LP/LB	U.S.		$14.00/$8.00

Label	Catalog Number	Title	Type	Country	Year	Longbox Value / Value
MCA	MCAD-8017	Royal Jam	LP/LB	U.S.		$14.00/$8.00
MCA	MCAD-3094	Street Life	LP/LB	U.S.†	1985	$14.00/$8.00
MCA	MCAD-42057	Vocal Album	LP/LB	U.S.		$14.00/$8.00
		Singles				
Profile	7371	That's How It Is	CDJ	U.S.	1992	$2.00

Crush

Label	Catalog Number	Title	Type	Country	Year	Longbox Value / Value
		Singles				
Eastwest	PRCD-4970-2	Rain, The	CDJ	U.S.	1993	$2.00
Eastwest	PRCD-5150-2	She Came Down	CDJ	U.S.	1993	$2.00
Eastwest	PRCD-5192-2	She Came Down	CDJ	U.S.	1993	$2.00

Cruzados

Label	Catalog Number	Title	Type	Country	Year	Longbox Value / Value
		Full Length				
Arista	ARCD-8439	After Dark	LP/LB	U.S.		$14.00/$8.00
DIR		King Biscuit Flour Hour	RS	U.S.	1987	$30.00
	Airdate: 11/15/87.					
		Singles				
		Bed Of Lies	CDJ	U.S.		$2.00
MCA	2861	This House	CDJ	U.S.	1993	$2.00

Cry Before Dawn

Label	Catalog Number	Title	Type	Country	Year	Longbox Value / Value
		Singles				
Epic	CDGONE-2	Gone Forever	CD5	U.K.	1988	$8.00
Epic	CDGONE-4	Last of the Sun	CD5	U.K.	1989	$8.00
Epic	655585-2	No Living Without You	CD5	U.K.	1990	$8.00
Epic	654860-2	Witness For the World	CD5	U.K.	1989	$8.00
Epic	CDGONE-3	Witness For the World	CD5	U.K.	1989	$8.00

Cry Charity

Label	Catalog Number	Title	Type	Country	Year	Longbox Value / Value
		Singles				
Morgan Creek	0021	I Want You Back	CDJ	U.S.	1992	$2.00

Cry No More

Label	Catalog Number	Title	Type	Country	Year	Longbox Value / Value
		Singles				
EMI	203703-3	Big Car	CD3	Germany	1990	$7.00
EMI	203817-2	Landslide	CD5	Germany	1990	$7.00
EMI	203492-3	Oh Sharon	CD3	Germany	1989	$7.00

Cry of Love

Label	Catalog Number	Title	Type	Country	Year	Longbox Value / Value
		Full Length				
Columbia	CSK 5594	August 25, 1993	DJ/Smplr	U.S.	1994	$15.00
Westwood One		In Concert	RS	U.S.	1994	$30.00
	2 CD set. Airdate: 1/3/94.					
Westwood One		In Concert	RS	U.S.	1994	$50.00
	Airdate: 10/10/94.					
		Singles				
Columbia		Carnival	CDJ	U.S.	1994	$6.00
Columbia		Too Cold in Winter	CDJ	U.S.	1994	$6.00

Cry Wolf

Label	Catalog Number	Title	Type	Country	Year	Longbox Value / Value
		Full Length				
IRS	13050	Crunch	LP	Canada		$10.00
IRS	13050	Crunch	LP/LB	U.S.		$14.00/$8.00
		Singles				
		Face Down in the Wishing Well	CDJ	U.S.		$2.00
		Pretender	CDJ	U.S.	1990	$2.00

Cryner, Bobbie

Label	Catalog Number	Title	Type	Country	Year	Longbox Value / Value
		Singles				
Epic	ESK 77195	He Feels Guilty	CDJ	U.S.	1993	$2.00

Crypt Keeper

Label	Catalog Number	Title	Type	Country	Year	Longbox Value / Value
		Singles				
Giant	PRO-CD-5577	Crypt Jam, The	CDJ	U.S.	1992	$7.00

Cryptic Slaughter

Label	Catalog Number	Title	Type	Country	Year	Longbox Value / Value
		Full Length				
Restless	72434	Speak Your Peace	LP/BP	U.S.		$12.00/$7.00

Cryptogram

Label	Catalog Number	Title	Type	Country	Year	Longbox Value / Value
		Singles				
Nastymix	76109	Sadness	CDJ	U.S.	1991	$2.00

Crysis

Label	Catalog Number	Title	Type	Country	Year	Longbox Value / Value
		Singles				
Alfa	ALDB-158	I Will Survive	CD3	Japan	1992	$12.00/$3.00

Crystal, Billy

Label	Catalog Number	Title	Type	Country	Year	Longbox Value / Value
		Full Length				
Paramount	LV2329	Billy Crystal	LD	U.S.	1985	$20.00

Crystal Palace

Label	Catalog Number	Title	Type	Country	Year	Longbox Value / Value
		Singles				
EMI	20444-2	Son of Godzilla	CD5	Germany	1991	$8.00

Cua, Rick

Label	Catalog Number	Title	Type	Country	Year	Longbox Value / Value
		Full Length				
Myrrh	24344	Can't Stand Too Tall	LP/LB	U.S.		$14.00/$8.00
Polydor	POCJ-1024	Rhythmystic	LTD/LP	Japan		$20.00
	Gold disc.					

Cud

Label	Catalog Number	Title	Type	Country	Year	Longbox Value / Value
		Full Length				
A&M	5390	Asquarius	LP/LB	U.S.		$12.00/$7.00
A&M	5380	Cud Band	LP/LB	U.S.		$12.00/$7.00
		Singles				
SPV	8675-3	Hey Wire	CD5	Germany	1990	$8.00
Imaginary	MIRACD-018	Hey Wire	CD5	U.K.	1990	$8.00
Imaginary	MIRACD-027	Magic	CD5	U.K.	1991	$8.00
A&M	AMCD-029	Oh No Won't Go	CD5	U.K.	1991	$8.00
A&M	AMCD-0081	Once Again	CD5	U.K.	1991	$8.00
		One Giant Love	CD5	U.K.		$10.00
		One Giant Love	CD5	U.K.		$10.00
	Second version.					
A&M	AMCD-871	Rich & Strange	CD5	U.K.	1992	$8.00
A&M	31458 8043	Rich & Strange	CDJ	U.S.	1992	$2.00
SPV	8761-3	Robinson Crusoe	CD5	Germany	1990	$8.00
Imaginary	MIRCD-021	Robinson Crusoe	CD5	U.K.	1990	$8.00
A&M	AMCD-857	Through the Roof	CD5	U.K.	1992	$8.00
A&M	75021 7345 2	Through the Roof	CDJ	U.S.	1992	$2.00

Cue

Label	Catalog Number	Title	Type	Country	Year	Longbox Value / Value
		Singles				
BCM	20964	Out of the Blue	CD5	Germany	1989	$8.00

Cuevas, Chris

Label	Catalog Number	Title	Type	Country	Year	Longbox Value / Value
		Full Length				
Atlantic	82187-2	Somehow Someday	LP/LB	U.S.		$14.00/$8.00
		Singles				
Atlantic	PRCD 3721-2	Hip Hop	CDJ	U.S.	1991	$2.00
Atlantic	PRCD 4515-2	I Need You	CDJ	U.S.	1991	$2.00
Atlantic	AMDY-5059	Somehow Someday	CD3	Japan	1991	$12.00/$3.00
		You Are the One	CDJ	U.S.		$2.00

Cugny, Laurent

Label	Catalog Number	Title	Type	Country	Year	Longbox Value / Value
		Full Length				
Polygram	848266	Santander	LP/BP	U.S.		$12.00/$7.00

Cult

Label	Catalog Number	Title	Type	Country	Year	Longbox Value / Value
		Full Length				
BBC Transcription		BBC Transcription Disc	RS		1992	$150.00
Vertigo		Classic Cult	DJ/Smplr	Canada	1992	$65.00
Mercury	PCD 133	Classic Cult	DJ/Smplr	Canada	1994	$50.00
Beggars Banquet	57	Dreamtime	LP/LB	U.S.		$14.00/$8.00
Beggars Banquet	BEGA 130CD	For Rockers Ravers, Lovers & Sinners	LP	U.K.	1993	$35.00
	2 CD set.					
Westwood One		In Concert	RS	U.S.	1992	$70.00
	2 CD set. With King's X, Airdate: 9/14/92.					
Westwood One		In Concert	RS	U.S.	1996	$65.00
	Airdate: 2/26/96.					
Vertigo		Live At the Marquee	LTD/LP	Canada		$50.00
	2 CD set.					
Beggars Banquet	2	Love Mixes	LP/LB	U.S.		$14.00/$8.00
Beggars Banquet	1	Manor Sessions	LP/LB	U.S.		$14.00/$8.00
Pinnacle	354619	Pure Cult	LTD/LP	U.K.		$30.00
Sire		Sonic Ceremony	DJ/LP	U.K.	1991	$40.00
	Custom box with CD and VHS tape.					
Sire	9 25871-2	Sonic Temple	LTD/LP	Canada	1989	$20.00
	Hologram cover digipak.					
Pinnacle	354619-2	Sonic Temple	LTD/LP	U.K.	1989	$20.00
	Hologram cover digipak.					
Sire	9 25871-2	Sonic Temple	DJ/LP	U.S.	1989	$20.00
	Hologram cover digipak.					
Sire	9 25871-2	Sonic Temple	LTD/LP	U.S.	1989	$20.00
	Hologram cover digipak.					
		Singles				
Beggars Banquet		Ceremony	CDJ	U.K.	1991	$8.00
		Coming Down	CDJ	Spain	1994	$18.00
Warner Brothers	41803	Coming Down	CD5	U.S.	1994	$5.00
Beggars Banquet	PRO-CD-7091	Coming Down	CDJ	U.S.	1995	$3.00
Vertigo	874669-2	Edie	CD5	Canada	1989	$10.00
BMG	662419	Edie	CD5	Germany	1989	$10.00
Beggars Banquet	BEG 230 CP	Edie	CD3	U.K.	1989	$10.00
Beggars Banquet	BEG 230 CD	Edie	CD5	U.K.	1989	$10.00
Sire	PRO-CD-3631	Edie	CDJ	U.S.	1989	$6.00
Beggars Banquet	BBP 3CD	Electric Mixes, The	CD5	U.K.	1989	$9.00
Vertigo	888 778-2	Fire Woman	CD5	Canada	1989	$10.00
Virgin	662099	Fire Woman	CD5	Germany	1989	$10.00
Beggars Banquet	BEG 228 CD	Fire Woman	CD3	U.K.	1989	$15.00
Sire	PRO-CD-3435	Fire Woman	CDJ	U.S.	1989	$3.00
		Going Down	CD5	U.K.	1994	$10.00
Vertigo		Heart of Soul	CDJ	Canada	1991	$7.00
Vertigo		Heart of Soul	CD5	U.K.	1991	$10.00
Sire	PRO-CD-5187	Heart of Soul	CDJ	U.S.	1991	$2.00
Virgin	659081	Lil' Devil	CD5	Germany		$10.00
Beggars Banquet	BEG-188CD	Lil' Devil	CD5	U.K.		$10.00
Beggars Banquet	BBP 10CD	Live 1986/1987 Wild Flower	CD5	U.K.	1991	$20.00
Beggars Banquet	BBP 1CD	Manor Sessions	CD5	U.K.	1989	$9.00
		Sacred Life	CDJ	Holland		$18.00
Beggars Banquet	4228646372	Sanctuary MCMXCII	CD5	Canada	1993	$10.00
Beggars Banquet	BEG 263CD	Sanctuary MCMXCII	CD5	U.K.	1993	$10.00
Beggars Banquet	BEG 263CD1	Sanctuary MCMXCII	CD5	U.K.	1993	$10.00
Vertigo		She Sells Sanctuary	CDJ	Canada	1991	$7.00
Beggars Banquet	PRO-CD-7290-R	Star	CDJ	U.S.	1995	$3.00
Beggars Banquet	BEG 235 CD	Sun King	CD5	U.K.	1989	$18.00
Sire	PRO-CD-3604	Sun King	CDJ	U.S.	1989	$3.00
Beggars Banquet	842281-2	Sweet Soul Sister	CD5	Canada	1989	$8.00
Beggars Banquet	BEG-241CD	Sweet Soul Sister	CD5	U.K.	1990	$10.00
Sire	PRO-CD-3881	Sweet Soul Sister	CDJ	U.S.	1989	$3.00
Vertigo		Wild Hearted Son	CDJ	Canada	1991	$8.00
BMG	664720	Wild Hearted Son	CD5	Germany	1991	$10.00
Beggars Banquet		Wild Hearted Son	CD5	U.K.	1991	$12.00
Beggars Banquet		Wild Hearted Son	CDJ	U.K.	1991	$8.00
Sire	PRO-CD-5009	Wild Hearted Son	CDJ	U.S.	1991	$3.00
Virgin	VOZCD195T	Wildflower	CD5	Australia	1987	$15.00
Sire	PRO-CD-5708	Witch, The	CDJ	U.S.	1992	$2.00

Cultural Revolution

Label	Catalog Number	Title	Type	Country	Year	Longbox Value / Value
		Singles				
Epic	ESK 77160	Nite & Day	CDJ	U.S.	1993	$2.00

Culture Beat

Label	Catalog Number	Title	Type	Country	Year	Longbox Value / Value
		Full Length				
Epic	EK-47415	Horizon	LP/LB	U.S.		$14.00/$8.00
		Singles				
Epic	49K-73170	Cherry Lips	CD5	U.S.	1989	$4.00
Epic	ESK 1999	Cherry Lips	CDJ	U.S.	1989	$2.00
Epic	655429-3	Der Erdbeermund	CD3	Germany	1990	$9.00
Epic	655726-3	Der Erdbeermund	CD3	Germany	1990	$9.00
Epic	655429-2	Der Erdbeermund	CD5	Germany	1990	$9.00
Epic	655633-2	Der Erdbeermund	CD5	U.K.	1990	$9.00
Epic	46K 77382	Got To Get It	CD5	U.S.	1994	$5.00
Epic	656025-3	I Like You	CD3	Germany	1990	$9.00
Epic	656025-5	I Like You	CD5	Germany	1990	$9.00
Epic	ESCA-5455	I Like You	CD5	Japan	1990	$12.00
Epic	656025-2	I Like You	CD5	U.K.	1990	$9.00
Epic	ESK 73600	I Like You	CDJ	U.S.	1990	$2.00
Epic	46K 77214	Mr. Vain	CD5	U.S.	1993	$5.00
CBS	77214	Mr. Vain	CD5	U.S.	1994	$5.00
Epic	656843-2	No Deeper Meaning	CD5	Germany	1991	$9.00
Epic	656531-3	Tell Me That You Wait	CD3	Germany	1991	$9.00
Epic	656531-2	Tell Me That You Wait	CD5	U.K.	1991	$9.00
Epic	ESK 73762	Tell Me That You Wait	CDJ	U.S.	1991	$2.00

Cummings, Burton

Label	Catalog Number	Title	Type	Country	Year	Longbox Value / Value
		Singles				
Capitol	473	One Day Soon	CDJ	Canada	1990	$5.00

Cure

Label	Catalog Number	Title	Type	Country	Year	Longbox Value / Value
		Full Length				
Fiction	511124-2	Cure	LTD/LP	U.K.	1992	$150.00
	12 CD boxed set.					

Label	Catalog Number	Title	Type	Country	Year	Longbox Value / Value
Fiction	513599-2	Cure	LTD/LP	U.K.	1992	$180.00
15 CD boxed set.						
		Entreat	DJ/Smplr	France		$35.00
Fiction	FIXCD 17	Entreat Live at Wembly	DJ/Smplr	U.K.	1990	$20.00
A&M		Happily Ever After	LP/LB	U.S.		$80.00/$65.00
Westwood One		In Concert-Nu Rock	RS	U.S.	1994	$100.00
2 CD set. Airdate: 11/21/94.						
Westwood One		In Concert-Nu Rock	RS	U.S.	1996	$90.00
2 CD set. Airdate: 5/20/96.						
WEA	40107	In Orange	LD	U.S.	1990	$30.00
		Kiss Me	DJ/Smplr	U.S.		$65.00
WEA	40124	Picture Show	LD	U.S.	1992	$35.00
WEA	40140-6	Play Out	LD	U.S.	1992	$35.00
	Cure1	Pure Cure	DJ/Smplr	Canada	1994	$85.00
		Radio Sampler	DJ/Smplr	U.S.		$30.00
Polygram	DISIN1	Sampler From Disintegration	DJ/Smplr	U.K.		$130.00
		Show	RS	U.S.	1993	$125.00
2 CD set. Airdate: 9/20/93.						
WEA	40101	Staring at the Sea	LD	U.S.	1990	$30.00
		Wild Mood Swings	LTD/LP	Germany	1996	$50.00
2 CD set.						
Fiction		Wild Mood Swings	LTD/LP	U.K.	1996	$35.00
Limited version with book.						
Fiction		Wish	DJ/LP	U.K.		$150.00
Promo box with cassette and CD.						
Fiction	CID 1	Wish Interview '92	DJ/Intvw	U.K.	1992	$25.00
Singles						
Fiction	FICSDJ 51	13th	CDJ	U.K.	1996	$25.00
		13th	CD5	U.S.	1996	$6.00
		13th	CD5	U.S.	1996	$6.00
Second version.						
		13th	CDJ	U.S.	1996	$8.00
Fiction		A Letter to Elsie	CD5	Germany	1993	$15.00
Elektra	PRCD 8627-2	A Letter to Elsie	CDJ	U.S.	1992	$7.00
Elektra	PRCD 8638-2	A Letter to Elsie	CDJ	U.S.	1992	$7.00
Fiction	080 186-2	Catch	CDV	U.K.	1989	$50.00
Fiction	879147-2	Close to Me	CD5	Germany	1990	$15.00
Fiction	FICD-36	Close to Me	CD5	U.K.	1990	$15.00
Fiction	FICDR36	Close to Me	CD5	U.K.	1990	$15.00
Fiction		Close to Me	CDV	U.K.	1990	$60.00
		Close to Me	CDJ	U.S.	1990	$7.00
Fiction	867529-2	Cure	CD5	U.K.	1991	$65.00
5 CD5 boxed set.						
Elektra		Dredd Song	CDJ	U.S.	1995	$8.00
Elektra	66702-2	Fascination Street	CD5	U.S.	1989	$8.00
Elektra	PRCD 8075-2	Fascination Street	CDJ	U.S.	1989	$7.00
	CURE-1	Five Live	CDJ	Australia	1994	$55.00
		Friday I'm in Love	CD5	France	1992	$20.00
Fiction		Friday I'm in Love	CD5	Germany	1992	$18.00
Fiction	POCP-1223	Friday I'm in Love	CD5	Japan	1992	$15.00
Fiction		Friday I'm in Love	CD5	U.K.	1992	$15.00
Elektra	64742-2	Friday I'm in Love	CD5	U.S.	1992	$7.00
Elektra	66416-2	Friday I'm in Love	CD5	U.S.	1992	$7.00
Elektra	PRCD 8578-2	Friday I'm in Love	CDJ	U.S.	1992	$7.00
Fiction		High	CD5	Australia	1992	$15.00
		High	CD5	France	1992	$15.00
Polydor	POCP-1189	High	CD5	Japan	1992	$18.00
Fiction		High	CD5	U.K.	1992	$15.00
Fiction		High	CD5	U.K.	1992	$15.00
Second version.						
Elektra	66437-2	High	CD5	U.S.	1992	$8.00
Elektra	64766-2	High	CD5	U.S.	1992	$8.00
Elektra	PRCD 8547-2	High	CDJ	U.S.	1992	$8.00
Fiction	887330-2	Hot! Hot! Hot!	CD5	Germany	1987	$15.00
Fiction	FIXCD-28	Hot! Hot! Hot!	CD5	U.K.	1987	$15.00
Elektra	PR 2173-2	Hot! Hot! Hot!	CDJ	U.S.	1987	$8.00
Fiction		In Between Days	CDV	U.K.	1990	$60.00
Elektra	PRCD 8382-2	In Between Days	CDJ	U.S.	1990	$8.00
WEA	CD-66633	Integration	CD5	Canada		$15.00
Elektra		Integration	CD5	U.S.		$45.00
4 CD set.						
Fiction	887104-2	Just Like Heaven	CD5	Germany	1988	$15.00
Fiction		Just Like Heaven	CDV	Japan	1989	$70.00
Fiction	POCP-1258	Just Like Heaven	CD5	Japan	1992	$28.00
Fiction	FIXCD-27	Just Like Heaven	CD5	U.K.	1988	$15.00
Elektra	64002-2	Just Like Heaven	CDV/BP	U.S.	1988	$30.00/$30.00
Elektra	PRCD 8825-2	Just Like Heaven	CDJ	U.S.	1990	$8.00
Fiction	889950-3	Love Song	CD3	Germany	1989	$15.00
Fiction	889847-2	Love Song	CD5	Germany	1989	$15.00
Fiction	889950-2	Love Song	CD5	Germany	1989	$15.00
Fiction	FICCD-30	Love Song	CD5	U.K.	1989	$15.00
Elektra	66687-2	Love Song	CD5	U.S.	1989	$8.00
Elektra	PR 8094-2	Love Song	CDJ	U.S.	1989	$8.00
Elektra	PR 8102-2	Love Song	CDJ	U.S.	1989	$8.00
Fiction	889254-3	Lullaby	CD3	Germany	1989	$15.00
Fiction	889255-2	Lullaby	CD5	Germany	1989	$15.00
Fiction	871991-2	Lullaby	CD5	Germany	1989	$15.00
Fiction	FICCD-29	Lullaby	CD3	U.K.	1989	$15.00
Fiction		Lullaby	CDV	U.K.	1990	$60.00
Elektra	66664-2	Lullaby	CD5	U.S.	1989	$8.00
Elektra	PR 8125-2	Lullaby	CDJ	U.S.	1989	$8.00
Fiction		Mint Car	CD5	U.K.	1996	$10.00
Fiction		Mint Car	CDJ	U.S.	1996	$7.00
WEA	CD-66604	Never Enough	CD5	Canada	1990	$14.00
Warner	22-66604	Never Enough	CD5	Canada	1994	$12.00
Fiction	877899-2	Never Enough	CD5	Germany	1990	$15.00
Polydor	PODP-6005	Never Enough	CD5	Japan	1990	$25.00
Fiction	FICD-35	Never Enough	CD5	U.K.	1990	$15.00
Fiction	FICDP-35	Never Enough	CD5	U.K.	1990	$18.00
Elektra	9 66604-2	Never Enough	CD5	U.S.	1990	$7.00
Elektra	PR 8233-2	Never Enough	CDJ	U.S.	1990	$8.00
Elektra	PRCD 82482-2	Never Enough	CDJ	U.S.	1990	$8.00
Fiction	PARISPRO 1	Parispro	CDJ	U.K.	1993	$20.00
Strange Frt	050	Peel Sessions	CD5	U.K.	1988	$15.00
Fiction	873909-2	Pictures of You	CD5	Germany	1990	$15.00
Fiction	873911-2	Pictures of You	CD5	Germany	1990	$15.00
Fiction	FICDA-34	Pictures of You	CD5	U.K.	1990	$15.00
Fiction	FICDB-34	Pictures of You	CD5	U.K.	1990	$15.00
Elektra	66639-2	Pictures of You	CD5	U.S.	1990	$7.00
Elektra	PR 8165-2	Pictures of You	CDJ	U.S.	1990	$8.00
Warner	12-18262	Purple Haze	CD5	Canada	1994	$12.00
Reprise	PRO-CD-6704	Purple Haze	CDJ	U.S.	1993	$8.00
Fiction	SHOWPRO 1	Show	CDJ	U.K.	1993	$20.00
Elektra	66275	Side Show	CD5	U.S.	1993	$86.00
		Wendy Time	CDJ	France		$20.00
Fiction	888454-2	Why Can't I Be You	CD5	Germany	1987	$15.00
Fiction	888454-2	Why Can't I Be You	CD5	U.K.	1987	$15.00

Curio

Label	Catalog Number	Title	Type	Country	Year	Longbox Value / Value
Full Length						
Motown	6299	Special Feeling	LP/LB	U.S.		$14.00/$8.00
Singles						
Canyon	PCDY-00047	I Can't Stay	CD3	Japan	1990	$12.00/$3.00
		I Can't Stay	CDJ	U.S.	1990	$2.00

Curiosity

Label	Catalog Number	Title	Type	Country	Year	Longbox Value / Value
Singles						
Arista	BVDA-46	Hang On In There Baby	CD3	Japan	1992	$15.00/$4.00
RCA	PD-45378	Hang On In There Baby	CD5	U.K.	1992	$7.00
Arista	BVDA-53	I Need Your Lovin'	CD3	Japan	1992	$15.00/$4.00
Arista	74321-111372	I Need Your Lovin'	CD5	U.K.	1992	$7.00

Curiosity Killed the Cat

Label	Catalog Number	Title	Type	Country	Year	Longbox Value / Value
Full Length						
Island	842010-2	Get Ahead	LP/LB	U.S.		$14.00/$8.00
Mercury	832025	Keep Your Distance	LP/BP	U.S.		$14.00/$8.00
Singles						
Mercury	CATCD-7	First Place	CD5	U.K.	1989	$7.00
Mercury	080 113-2	Misfit	CDV	Japan	1987	$30.00
Mercury	24VP-5	Misfit	CDV	Japan	1987	$30.00
Mercury	876203-2	Name And Number	CD5	Germany	1989	$7.00
Mercury	PPDS-15	Name And Number	CD3	Japan	1989	$12.00/$3.00
Mercury	CATCD-6	Name And Number	CD5	U.K.	1989	$7.00
Mercury	CDP 161	Name And Number	CDJ	U.S.	1989	$2.00

Curran, Andy

Label	Catalog Number	Title	Type	Country	Year	Longbox Value / Value
Singles						
		Let Go	CDJ	Canada		$6.00
		License To Love	CDJ	Canada		$6.00

Currie, Billy

Label	Catalog Number	Title	Type	Country	Year	Longbox Value / Value
Full Length						
IRS	42239	Transportation	LP/LB	U.S.		$14.00/$8.00

Curry Gang

Label	Catalog Number	Title	Type	Country	Year	Longbox Value / Value
Singles						
Polygram	873061-2	Get Up, Get Down	CD5	Germany	1989	$7.00

Curry, Mark

Label	Catalog Number	Title	Type	Country	Year	Longbox Value / Value
Full Length						
Virgin	DPRO-12688	It's Only Time	DJ/LP	U.S.	1992	$12.00
Embossed jewel box.						
Virgin		Sampler	DJ/Smplr	U.S.	1995	$6.00
Singles						
	DPRO-14238	Sampler	CDJ	U.S.	1995	$8.00
Virgin	VUSCD-64	Sorry About the Weather	CD5	U.K.	1992	$8.00
Virgin	PRCD 12685	Sorry About the Weather	CDJ	U.S.	1992	$2.00

Curry, Tim

Label	Catalog Number	Title	Type	Country	Year	Longbox Value / Value
Full Length						
A&M	CD-05269	Best Of	LP/LB	U.S.		$14.00/$8.00

Curve

Label	Catalog Number	Title	Type	Country	Year	Longbox Value / Value
Singles						
Anxious	ANXCDS 42	Blacker Three Tacker	CD5	U.K.	1993	$8.00
Anxious	ANXCD 42	Blacker Three Tacker	CD5	U.K.	1993	$8.00
Anxious	ANXCD-27	Blindfold	CD5	U.K.	1991	$8.00
Anxious	ZD-45026	Clipped	CD5	Germany	1991	$8.00
Anxious	ANXCD-35	Clipped	CD5	U.K.	1991	$8.00
SPV	3000-3	Coast Is Clear	CD5	Germany	1991	$8.00
Anxious	ANXCD-30	Coast Is Clear	CD5	U.K.	1991	$8.00
Anxious	ANXCD-36	Fait Accompli	CD5	U.K.	1992	$8.00
Anxious	PRCD -85	Fait Accompli	CDJ	U.S.	1991	$7.00
Charisma	96293	Frozen	CDJ	U.S.	1991	$2.00
Anxious	ANXCD-38	Horror Head	CD5	U.K.	1992	$8.00
Charisma	0100	Horror Head	CDJ	U.S.	1992	$13.00
Charisma	14116	Missing Link	CDJ	U.S.	1994	$7.00
		Pictures of You	CD5	U.K.		$10.00
		Pictures of You	CD5	U.K.		$10.00
Second version.						

Cusato

Label	Catalog Number	Title	Type	Country	Year	Longbox Value / Value
Singles						
ZYX	6344-8	Captain Of Her Heart	CD5	Germany	1990	$6.00

Cussick, Ian

Label	Catalog Number	Title	Type	Country	Year	Longbox Value / Value
Singles						
Line	LICD-9-00874	Love Is the System	CD5	Germany	1989	$7.00
Line	LICD-9-00874	Love Is the System	CD5	U.K.	1989	$7.00
Line	LICD-9-01131	Runaway Train	CD5	Germany	1989	$7.00

Cut 'n Move

Label	Catalog Number	Title	Type	Country	Year	Longbox Value / Value
Full Length						
Epic	EK-47938	Get Serious	LP/LB	U.S.		$14.00/$8.00
Singles						
Epic	ESCA-5497	Get Serious	CD5	Japan	1991	$9.00
Epic	657373-2	Get Serious	CD5	U.K.	1991	$8.00
Epic	ESK 73878	Get Serious	CDJ	U.S.	1991	$2.00
Capitol	58485	I'm Alive	CD5	U.S.	1995	$5.00
Soulpower	74059	Spread Love	CDJ	U.S.	1991	$2.00
Epic	656854-2	Take No Crap	CD5	Germany	1991	$8.00

Cut The Q

Label	Catalog Number	Title	Type	Country	Year	Longbox Value / Value
Singles						
CBS	654764-3	Crackdown	CD3	Germany	1991	$7.00

Cuteman

Label	Catalog Number	Title	Type	Country	Year	Longbox Value / Value
Singles						
Victor	VICL-2065	Age Of "E"	CD5	Japan	1992	$10.00
Victor	VIDL-83	Love Deep Inside	CD3	Japan	1992	$8.00/$2.00
Victor	VIDL-130	Three-D On CD	CD3	Japan	1992	$8.00/$2.00

Cutmaster

Label	Catalog Number	Title	Type	Country	Year	Longbox Value / Value
Singles						
King	K10Y-30002	Rock On	CD3	Japan	1989	$12.00/$3.00

Cutting Crew

Label	Catalog Number	Title	Type	Country	Year	Longbox Value / Value
Full Length						
DIR		King Biscuit Flour Hour	RS	U.S.	1988	$30.00
Airdate: 1/17/88.						
Atlantic		Scattering, The	DJ/LP	U.S.	1989	$10.00
Atlantic	91239-2	Scattering, The	LP/LB	U.S.	1989	$14.00/$8.00
Singles						
Virgin	162155	(Between a) Rock and a Hard Place	CD3	Germany	1989	$8.00
Virgin	662155	(Between a) Rock and a Hard Place	CD5	Germany	1989	$8.00

Label	Catalog Number	Title	Type	Country	Year	Longbox Value/Value
Virgin	VJD-10201	(Between a) Rock and a Hard Place	CD3	Japan	1989	$12.00/$3.00
Siren	SRNCD-108	(Between a) Rock and a Hard Place	CD3	U.K.	1989	$8.00
		(Between a) Rock and a Hard Place	CDJ	U.S.	1989	$2.00
Virgin	PR 2824	Big Noise	CDJ	U.S.	1989	$2.00
BMG	662612	Everything But My Pride	CD5	Germany	1989	$8.00
Virgin	VJD-10127	Everything But My Pride	CD3	Japan	1989	$12.00/$3.00
Siren	CDT-222	Everything But My Pride	CD3	U.K.	1989	$8.00
		Everything But My Pride	CDJ	U.S.	1989	$2.00
Aris	885095	(I Just) Died In Your Arms	CD5	Germany	1988	$8.00
Siren	CDT-25	(I Just) Died In Your Arms	CD3	U.K.	1988	$8.00
Virgin	7 50117-6	(I Just) Died In Your Arms Tonight	DJ/CDV	U.S.	1988	$20.00
Siren	SRNCD-29	I've Been In Love Before	CD5	U.K.	1987	$9.00
Virgin	PRCD 2076	I've Been In Love Before	CDJ	U.S.	1987	$2.00
Virgin	REWD-1	If That's the Way You Want It	CD5	U.K.	1992	$8.00
Virgin	PRCDZAP	Last Thing, The	CD5	U.K.	1989	$9.00
		Last Thing, The	CDJ	U.S.	1989	$2.00
Virgin	658851	One For the Moking-Bird	CD5	Germany	1987	$9.00
Siren	SNIK-4012	One For the Moking-Bird	CD5	U.K.	1987	$9.00
BMG	162637	Scattering, The	CD3	Germany	1989	$8.00
Siren	SRNCD-118	Scattering, The	CD3	U.K.	1989	$8.00
Virgin	PRCD CREW	Scattering, The	CDJ	U.S.	1989	$2.00

Cutting Edge

Singles

Label	Catalog Number	Title	Type	Country	Year	Longbox Value/Value
Columbia	ALDA-38	Hole	CD3	Japan	1991	$12.00/$3.00

Cybex Factor

Singles

Label	Catalog Number	Title	Type	Country	Year	Longbox Value/Value
ZYX	BOY-8840-8	Experiment	CD5	Germany	1992	$6.00

Cycle Sluts From Hell

Singles

Label	Catalog Number	Title	Type	Country	Year	Longbox Value/Value
Epic	ZSK 4006	Speed Queen	CDJ	U.S.	1991	$7.00

Cyclone

Full Length

Label	Catalog Number	Title	Type	Country	Year	Longbox Value/Value
Combat	2016	I Hate Therefore I Am	LP/LB	U.S.		$14.00/$8.00

Singles

Label	Catalog Number	Title	Type	Country	Year	Longbox Value/Value
Pinnacle	NWKCD-28	Sonic Cycology	CD5	U.K.	1991	$6.00

Cynthia

Singles

Label	Catalog Number	Title	Type	Country	Year	Longbox Value/Value
Tommy Boy	656	How I Love Him	CD5	U.S.	1994	$5.00
TBCD 659		How I Love Him	CDJ	U.S.	1995	$3.00

Cypress Hill

Full Length

Label	Catalog Number	Title	Type	Country	Year	Longbox Value/Value
Ruffhouse	4598	Something For the Blunted	DJ/Smplr	U.S.	1992	$10.00

Singles

Label	Catalog Number	Title	Type	Country	Year	Longbox Value/Value
Ruffhouse	4562	Hand on the Clock	CDJ	U.S.	1992	$2.00
Ruffhouse	74105	Hand on the Pump	CDJ	U.S.	1991	$2.00
Ruffhouse	77307	I Ain't Goin' Out Like That	CDJ	U.S.	1993	$2.00
		Insane in the Brain	CD5	U.K.	1992	$10.00
		Insane in the Brain	CD5	U.K.	1992	$10.00
Second version.						
Ruffhouse	44K 77019	Insane in the Brain	CD5	U.S.	1992	$5.00
Ruffhouse	5209	Insane in the Brain	CDJ	U.S.	1992	$2.00
Ruffhouse	44K 74478	Latin Lingo	CD5	U.S.	1992	$5.00
Ruffhouse	4747	Latin Lingo	CDJ	U.S.	1992	$2.00
Ruffhouse		Phunky Feel One, The	CDJ	U.S.		$2.00
		Throw Your Set in the Air	CDJ	U.S.		$3.00
Columbia	78046	Throw Your Set in the Air	CD5	U.S.	1995	$5.00

Cyre

Singles

Label	Catalog Number	Title	Type	Country	Year	Longbox Value/Value
		Life, The	CDJ	U.S.		$2.00

Cyrus, Billy Ray

Full Length

Label	Catalog Number	Title	Type	Country	Year	Longbox Value/Value
Mercury		It Won't Be the Last	DJ/LP	U.S.	1993	$30.00
Mercury	CDP 934	It Won't Be the Last	DJ/Smplr	U.S.	1993	$20.00
CDJ of "In the Heart Of A Woman" with full album in 6"x12" double digipak.						
		It Won't Be the Last	RS	U.S.	1993	$30.00

Singles

Label	Catalog Number	Title	Type	Country	Year	Longbox Value/Value
Mercury	MERCD-373	Achy Breaky Heart	CD5	U.K.	1992	$10.00
Mercury	CDP 638	Achy Breaky Heart	CDJ	U.S.	1992	$3.00
Mercury	MERCD-378	Could've Been Me	CD5	U.K.	1992	$10.00
Polygram	866998	Could've Been Me	CD5	U.S.	1992	$5.00
Mercury	CDP 703	Could've Been Me	CDJ	U.S.	1992	$3.00
Mercury	CDP 775	Could've Been Me	CDJ	U.S.	1992	$3.00
Mercury	CDP 775	Somebody New	CDJ	U.S.	1993	$3.00
Mercury	MERCD-378	These Boots Are Made For Walkin'	CD5	U.K.	1992	$10.00
Mercury	CDP 779	Wher'm I Gonna Live?	CDJ	U.S.	1992	$3.00

D.A.D. (Disneyland After Dark)

Full Length

Label	Catalog Number	Title	Type	Country	Year	Longbox Value/Value
Mega	MRCD 3017	Call Of the Wild	LP	Germany	1989	$20.00
Warner Brothers	25999-2-DJ	No Fuel Left for the Pilgrims	DJ/LP	U.S.	1989	$12.00
Medley	MDCD 6329	No Fuel Left for the Pilgrims	LP	U.S.	1989	$50.00
"Disneyland After Dark" printed on cover.						

Singles

Label	Catalog Number	Title	Type	Country	Year	Longbox Value/Value
Warner Brothers	W-0074CD	Bad Craziness	CD5	U.K.	1991	$8.00
WEA	921489-2	Girl Nation	CD5	Germany	1989	$8.00
Pioneer	WPDP-621	Girl Nation	CD3	Japan	1989	$12.00/$3.00
WEA	W-9887CD	Girl Nation	CD5	U.K.	1989	$8.00
Warner Brothers	PRO-CD-3844	Girl Nation	CDJ	U.S.	1989	$3.00
WEA	9362-40398-2	Grow or Pay	CD5	Germany	1992	$8.00
WEA	W-0092CD	Grow or Pay	CD5	U.K.	1992	$8.00
Warner Brothers	PRO-CD-5254	Grow or Pay	CDJ	U.S.	1992	$3.00
Pioneer	09P3-6205	Sleeping My Day Away	CD3	Japan	1989	$12.00/$3.00
WEA	W-2775CD	Sleeping My Day Away	CD3	U.K.	1989	$8.00
Warner Brothers	PRO-CD-3672	Sleeping My Day Away	CDJ	U.S.	1989	$3.00
Warner Brothers	PRO-CD-3763	Sleeping My Day Away	CDJ	U.S.	1989	$3.00

D Generation

Full Length

Label	Catalog Number	Title	Type	Country	Year	Longbox Value/Value
		No Lunch	DJ/LP	U.S.	1996	$15.00

D.J. Chuck Chill Out

Full Length

Label	Catalog Number	Title	Type	Country	Year	Longbox Value/Value
Polygram	838406-2	Masters of Rhythm	LP/BP	U.S.		$9.00/$6.00

D.J. Jazzy Jeff And The Fresh Prince

Singles

Label	Catalog Number	Title	Type	Country	Year	Longbox Value/Value
Jive		Boom Shake the Room	CD5	U.K.	1993	$10.00
Jive		Boom Shake the Room	CD5	U.K.	1993	$10.00
Second version.						
Jive	42107	Boom Shake the Room	CD5	U.S.	1993	$5.00
Jive		Can't Wait To Be With You	CD5	U.K.		$10.00
Jive		Can't Wait To Be With You	CD5	U.K.		$10.00
Second version.						
Aris	886864	Groove (Jazzy's Groove)	CD5	Germany	1989	$10.00
Jive	1313-2-JDJ	Groove (Jazzy's Groove)	CDJ	U.S.	1989	$2.00
Jive	1278-2-JDJ	I Think I Can Beat Mike Tyson	CDJ	U.S.	1989	$2.00
Jive	42182-2-JDJ	I'm Looking Out For the One	CDJ	U.S.	1993	$2.00
Jive	ALCB-412	Ring My Bell	CD5	Japan	1991	$16.00
Jive	42028-2-JDJ	Ring My Bell	CDJ	U.S.		$2.00
Jive	ZD-44726	Summertime	CD5	Germany	1991	$10.00
Jive	JIVECD-279	Summertime	CD5	U.K.	1991	$10.00
Jive	JIVECD-295	Things That U Do	CD5	U.K.	1992	$10.00
Jive		Twinkle	CD5	U.K.		$10.00
Jive		Twinkle	CD5	U.K.		$10.00
Second version.						

D.J. Kool

Singles

Label	Catalog Number	Title	Type	Country	Year	Longbox Value/Value
Warner Brothers	43764-2	Let Me Clear My Throat	CD5	U.S.	1997	$3.00

D.J. Magic Mike

Singles

Label	Catalog Number	Title	Type	Country	Year	Longbox Value/Value
Magic		Bass the Final Frontier	CDJ	U.S.		$2.00
	9518	Get On It Dog Gon'it	CD5	U.S.	1994	$5.00
	9518	Get On It Dog Gon'it	CD5	U.S.	1994	$5.00
Cheetah		House Of Magic	CDJ	U.S.		$2.00
Magic		This Is How it Should Be	CDJ	U.S.		$2.00

D.J. Massive

Singles

Label	Catalog Number	Title	Type	Country	Year	Longbox Value/Value
Intercord	826-964	Massive Overload	CD5	Germany	1991	$7.00

D.J. Miko

Singles

Label	Catalog Number	Title	Type	Country	Year	Longbox Value/Value
ZYX	6691	What's Up	CD5	U.S.	1994	$6.00

D.J. Morella

Singles

Label	Catalog Number	Title	Type	Country	Year	Longbox Value/Value
Alfa	ALCB-637	Free	CD5	Japan	1992	$10.00
ZYX	6758-8	Revolution	CD5	Germany	1992	$6.00
Alfa	ALCB-516	Revolution	CD5	Japan	1992	$10.00

D.J. Power

Singles

Label	Catalog Number	Title	Type	Country	Year	Longbox Value/Value
Cooltempo	COOLCD-252	Everybody Pump	CD5	U.K.	1992	$6.00

D.J. Professor

Singles

Label	Catalog Number	Title	Type	Country	Year	Longbox Value/Value
ZYX	6472-8	Life Is Life	CD5	Germany	1991	$6.00
PWL	PWCD-219	Rock Me Steady	CD5	U.K.	1992	$7.00
4th & B'way	BRCD-255	We Gotta Do It	CD5	U.K.	1991	$7.00
Alfa	ALCB-449	We Gotta Do It	CD5	U.K.	1992	$10.00

D.J. Quik

Singles

Label	Catalog Number	Title	Type	Country	Year	Longbox Value/Value
Profile	7372	Jus Lyke Compton	CDJ	U.S.	1992	$2.00
Profile	7349	Quik Is the Name	CDJ	U.S.	1991	$2.00
Profile	7384	Way 2 Funky	CDJ	U.S.	1992	$2.00

D.O.

Full Length

Label	Catalog Number	Title	Type	Country	Year	Longbox Value/Value
White Lbl		It	DJ/LP	U.S.	1993	$10.00

D.R.I.

Full Length

Label	Catalog Number	Title	Type	Country	Year	Longbox Value/Value
Restless	72436	Crossover	LP/BP	U.S.		$14.00/$8.00
Image	ID7925EN	Live At the Ritz	LD	U.S.	1987	$15.00

D:Ream

Singles

Label	Catalog Number	Title	Type	Country	Year	Longbox Value/Value
Warner Brothers	41047	Thing Can Only Get	CD5	U.S.	1994	$5.00
		U R the Best Thing	CD5	U.K.		$10.00
		U R the Best Thing	CD5	U.K.		$10.00
Second version.						

D, Schooly

Full Length

Label	Catalog Number	Title	Type	Country	Year	Longbox Value/Value
Rykodisc	RCD 20050	Adventures of Schooly D	LP/LB	U.S.		$12.00/$7.00

D Sign

Singles

Label	Catalog Number	Title	Type	Country	Year	Longbox Value/Value
SPV	8264-3	Burning Cells	CD5	Germany	1991	$7.00
Antler	5047	Burning Cells	CD5	U.S.	1993	$4.00
Polygram	873095-2	In This World	CD5	Germany	1989	$7.00

D&D Project

Singles

Label	Catalog Number	Title	Type	Country	Year	Longbox Value/Value
Arista	12812	Li Unorthodox	CD5	U.S.	1994	$5.00

D'ambrosio, Meredith

Full Length

Label	Catalog Number	Title	Type	Country	Year	Longbox Value/Value
IRS	970 075	It's Your Dance	LP	Germany		$15.00

D'ambrosio, Meredith

Full Length

Label	Catalog Number	Title	Type	Country	Year	Longbox Value/Value
Sunnyside	SSC-1011D	It's Your Dance	LP/LB	U.S.		$14.00/$8.00

D'angelo

Singles

Label	Catalog Number	Title	Type	Country	Year	Longbox Value/Value
Capital	58374	Brown Sugar	CD5	U.S.	1994	$5.00
Capitol	58468	Crusin'	CD5	U.S.	1995	$5.00

D'arby, Terence Trent

Full Length

Label	Catalog Number	Title	Type	Country	Year	Longbox Value/Value
Columbia		Excerpts From...Neither Fish Nor Flesh	DJ/Smplr	Canada	1993	$25.00
CBS	450911-9	Introducing the Hardline	LTD/LP	U.K.	1988	$25.00
Picture disc CD in blister pack.						
Image	ID6331CB	Introducing the Hardline	LD	U.S.	1989	$20.00
CBS	QDCA-93027	T.T.D.	DJ/Smplr	Japan	1993	$75.00
Columbia	CSK 77155	Tour Sampler	DJ/Smplr	U.S.	1993	$8.00

Singles

Label	Catalog Number	Title	Type	Country	Year	Longbox Value/Value
Epic	655100-3	Dance Little Sister	CD3	Germany	1988	$8.00
Epic	108P-3054	Dance Little Sister	CD3	Japan	1988	$12.00/$3.00
Columbia	CSK 1260	Dance Little Sister	CDJ	U.S.	1988	$2.00
Epic	ESCA-5804	Delicate	CD5	Japan		$18.00
Columbia	CSK 77128	Delicate	CDJ	U.S.	1993	$3.00

Label	Catalog Number	Title	Type	Country	Year	Longbox Value / Value
Epic	ESDA-7134	Do You Love Me Like You Say	CD3	Japan	1993	$13.00/$4.00
Columbia	659073	Do You Love Me Like You Say	CD5	U.K.	1993	$9.00
Columbia		Do You Love Me Like You Say	CD5	U.K.	1993	$9.00
Second version.						
Columbia	CSK 74949	Do You Love Me Like You Say	CDJ	U.S.	1993	$3.00
Columbia	CSK 74963	Do You Love Me Like You Say	CDJ	U.S.	1993	$3.00
Columbia	CSK 5133	Do You Love Me Like You Say	CDJ	U.S.	1993	$3.00
		Holding on To You	CD5	U.K.	1995	$10.00
		Holding on To You	CD5	U.K.	1995	$10.00
Second version.						
Columbia	CSK 2812	If You Let Me Stay	CDJ	U.S.		$2.00
Columbia	CSK 77231	Let Her Down Easy	CDJ	U.S.	1993	$3.00
Columbia	CSK 77231	Let Her Down Easy	CDJ	U.S.	1994	$3.00
Columbia	CSK 5132	She Kissed Me	CDJ	U.S.	1993	$3.00
CBS	651315-3	Sign Your Name	CD3	Germany	1988	$9.00
CBS	651315-2	Sign Your Name	CD5	Germany	1988	$9.00
Sony	108P-3030	Sign Your Name	CD3	Japan	1988	$12.00/$3.00
CBS	TRENTC-4	Sign Your Name	CD5	U.K.	1988	$9.00
Columbia	38K-7911	Sign Your Name	CD3	U.S.	1988	$6.00/$3.00
Columbia	CSK 1150	Sign Your Name	CDJ	U.S.	1988	$2.00
CBS	655431	This Side of Love	CD3	Germany	1989	$9.00
Epic	ESDA-7003	This Side of Love	CD3	Japan	1990	$12.00/$4.00
Columbia	TRENTC-5	This Side of Love	CD5	U.K.	1989	$9.00
Columbia	TRENTP-5	This Side of Love	CD5	U.K.	1989	$9.00
Columbia	CSK 73074	This Side of Love	CDJ	U.S.	1989	$2.00
Columbia	CSK 73074	This Side of Love	CDJ	U.S.	1989	$2.00
CBS	655588-3	To Know Someone Deeply	CD3	Germany	1990	$9.00
Epic	ESDA-7016	To Know Someone Deeply	CD3	Japan	1990	$12.00/$3.00
Columbia	TRENTC-6	To Know Someone Deeply	CD5	U.K.	1989	$9.00
Columbia	CSK 73217	To Know Someone Deeply	CDJ	U.S.	1989	$2.00
Columbia		Vibrator	CDJ	U.S.	1995	$6.00
Columbia	44K-7543	Wishing Well	CD3	U.S.	1987	$6.00/$3.00
Columbia	CSK 2882	Wishing Well	CDJ	U.S.	1987	$2.00

D'Influence

Singles

Label	Catalog Number	Title	Type	Country	Year	Longbox Value / Value
EastWest	PRCD 4810-2	Good 4 We	CDJ	U.S.	1992	$3.00
EastWest	PRCD 4831-2	Good 4 We	CDJ	U.S.	1992	$3.00
EastWest	7567-96183-2	Good Lover	CD5	Germany	1992	$8.00
		Good Lover	CD5	U.K.		$10.00
Second version.						
EastWest	A-8573CD	Good Lover	CD5	U.K.	1992	$8.00

D'La Vance

Singles

Label	Catalog Number	Title	Type	Country	Year	Longbox Value / Value
		Itchin' In My Pants	CDJ	U.S.		$2.00

D'Molls

Full Length

Label	Catalog Number	Title	Type	Country	Year	Longbox Value / Value
WEA	781791-2	D'Molls	LP	Germany		$14.00
WEA	782070-2	Warped	LP	Germany		$14.00
Atlantic	82070-2	Warped	LP/LB	U.S.		$14.00/$8.00

D'Nice

Singles

Label	Catalog Number	Title	Type	Country	Year	Longbox Value / Value
		Call Me D'Nice	CDJ	U.S.		$2.00
		Crumbs on the Table	CDJ	U.S.		$2.00
Jive	1335-2-RDJ	Glory	CDJ	U.S.	1990	$2.00
Jive	1435-2-RDJ	Tr 808 is Coming, The	CDJ	U.S.	1991	$2.00

D'Priest

Singles

Label	Catalog Number	Title	Type	Country	Year	Longbox Value / Value
Noise	4878	Heartbeat	CDJ	U.S.	1991	$2.00
		Ride You Through the Night	CDJ	U.S.		$2.00

D'Zyre

Singles

Label	Catalog Number	Title	Type	Country	Year	Longbox Value / Value
		Forever Amo'a	CDJ	U.S.		$2.00

D-Crew

Singles

Label	Catalog Number	Title	Type	Country	Year	Longbox Value / Value
Futureland	TYDY-2037	F1 Starting Grid	CD3	Japan	1992	$12.00/$3.00

D-Dream

Singles

Label	Catalog Number	Title	Type	Country	Year	Longbox Value / Value
Magnet	MAG-101CD	Things Can Only Get Better	CD5	U.K.	1992	$7.00

D-Mob

Singles

Label	Catalog Number	Title	Type	Country	Year	Longbox Value / Value
ffrr	886723-2	C'mon & Get My Love	CD5	Germany	1989	$7.00
ffrr	FCD-117	C'mon & Get My Love	CD5	U.K.	1989	$7.00
ffrr	215	C'mon & Get My Love	CDJ	U.S.	1990	$2.00
ffrr	886607-2	It's Time to Get Funky	CD5	Germany	1989	$7.00
ffrr	FCD-107	It's Time to Get Funky	CD5	U.K.	1989	$7.00
ffrr	ffrr 99	It's Time to Get Funky	CDJ	U.S.	1989	$2.00
		One Day	CD5	U.K.		$10.00
		One Day	CD5	U.K.		$10.00
Second version.						
ffrr	FCD-124	Put Your Hands Together	CD5	U.K.	1989	$7.00
ffrr	886947-2	That's the Way of the World	CD5	Germany	1989	$7.00
London	PODD-6001	That's the Way of the World	CD3	Japan	1990	$12.00/$3.00
ffrr	FCD-132	That's the Way of the World	CD5	U.K.	1989	$7.00
ffrr	229	That's the Way of the World	CDJ	U.S.	1990	$2.00
Polygram	886419-2	We Call It Acieed	CD5	Germany	1988	$7.00
ffrr	ffrr 81	We Call It Acieed	CDJ	U.S.	1989	$2.00

D-Parture

Singles

Label	Catalog Number	Title	Type	Country	Year	Longbox Value / Value
CBS	656793-2	Heartbeat	CD5	Germany	1991	$7.00

D-Shake

Singles

Label	Catalog Number	Title	Type	Country	Year	Longbox Value / Value
Go Bang	CD-13305	Funny Moves	CD5	Germany		$7.00
Go Bang	BANGCDR-0008	Funny Moves	CD5	U.K.		$7.00
Cooltempo	COOLCD-228	My Heart, The Beat	CD5	U.K.	1990	$7.00
BMG	663574	Yaaah	CD5	Germany	1990	$7.00
Cooltempo	COOLCD-213	Yaaah	CD5	U.K.	1990	$7.00

D-Sign

Singles

Label	Catalog Number	Title	Type	Country	Year	Longbox Value / Value
EMI	204706-2	Brainless	CD5	Germany	1992	$7.00

Da

Full Length

Label	Catalog Number	Title	Type	Country	Year	Longbox Value / Value
Aris	881322	Darn Floor-Big Bite	LP	Germany		$18.00

Da Brat

Singles

Label	Catalog Number	Title	Type	Country	Year	Longbox Value / Value
Columbia	77503	Fa All Y'all	CD5	U.S.	1994	$5.00
CBS	77593	Fa All Y'all	CD5	U.S.	1994	$5.00
Columbia	CSK 6877	Give it 2 You	CDJ	U.S.	1994	$3.00

Da Costa, Paulinho

Singles

Label	Catalog Number	Title	Type	Country	Year	Longbox Value / Value
A&M	75021 7231 2	Real Love	CDJ	U.S.	1991	$2.00

Da King And I

Singles

Label	Catalog Number	Title	Type	Country	Year	Longbox Value / Value
RCA	35028	Tears	CD5	U.S.	1994	$5.00

Da Ko Boyz

Singles

Label	Catalog Number	Title	Type	Country	Year	Longbox Value / Value
Maverick	PRO-CD-6872	Da Body Call	CDJ	U.S.	1994	$2.00

Da Lench Mob

Singles

Label	Catalog Number	Title	Type	Country	Year	Longbox Value / Value
Street	5017	Ain't Got No Class	CDJ	U.S.	1993	$2.00
Street	4910	Guerillas in the Store	CDJ	U.S.	1993	$3.00

Da Nayborhoodz

Singles

Label	Catalog Number	Title	Type	Country	Year	Longbox Value / Value
	89402	How We Do It	CD5	U.S.	1994	$5.00

Da Ruffness

Singles

Label	Catalog Number	Title	Type	Country	Year	Longbox Value / Value
Danzalot	72392 75374	1 & 1	CDJ	U.S.	1993	$2.00

Da Youngsta's

Singles

Label	Catalog Number	Title	Type	Country	Year	Longbox Value / Value
EastWest	PRCD 4979-2	Crewz Up	CDJ	U.S.	1992	$2.00
EastWest	95879-2	Hip Hop Ride	CD5	U.S.	1994	$5.00
Electra/Asylum	66174	Mad Props	CD5	U.S.	1994	$5.00
EastWest	PRCD 4421-2	Somethin' 4 Da Youngsta's	CDJ	U.S.	1992	$2.00

Dad Line

Singles

Label	Catalog Number	Title	Type	Country	Year	Longbox Value / Value
Zyx	7532	Broom Base	CD5	U.S.	1994	$5.00
Zyx	7532	Broom Base	CD5	U.S.	1994	$5.00

Dada

Full Length

Label	Catalog Number	Title	Type	Country	Year	Longbox Value / Value
Westwood One		In Concert-Nu Rock	RS	U.S.	1993	$50.00
Airdate: 6/7/93.						

Singles

Label	Catalog Number	Title	Type	Country	Year	Longbox Value / Value
IRS	6702	Dim	CDJ	U.S.	1992	$2.00
Capital	58374	I'm Feeling Nothing	CD5	U.S.	1994	$5.00
IRS	DPRO-6730	My Baby Fell For Ol' St. Nick	CDJ	U.S.	1994	$3.00

Dada Nada

Singles

Label	Catalog Number	Title	Type	Country	Year	Longbox Value / Value
Polygram	IRBCD-53	Deep Love	CD5	U.K.	1990	$8.00

Dada, Sonia

Singles

Label	Catalog Number	Title	Type	Country	Year	Longbox Value / Value
Chameleon	8615	You Ain't Thinking	CDJ	U.S.	1992	$2.00

Daddy Freddy

Full Length

Label	Catalog Number	Title	Type	Country	Year	Longbox Value / Value
Chrysalis	21844	Stress	LP/LB	U.S.		$14.00/$8.00

Singles

Label	Catalog Number	Title	Type	Country	Year	Longbox Value / Value
Pinnacle	NOTE-54CD	Crown, The	CD5	U.K.	1991	$8.00
Chrysalis	23737	Crown, The	CDJ	U.S.	1991	$2.00
BCM	20502	Respect Due	CD5	Germany	1990	$8.00
Chrysalis	04672	Respect Due	CDJ	U.S.	1992	$2.00

Daddy in His Deep Sleep

Full Length

Label	Catalog Number	Title	Type	Country	Year	Longbox Value / Value
Restless	72196-2	Alone With Daddy	LP/BP	U.S.		$9.00/$6.00

Daddy-O

Singles

Label	Catalog Number	Title	Type	Country	Year	Longbox Value / Value
Island	PRCD 6791-2	Brooklyn Bounce	CDJ	U.S.	1993	$2.00

Daddys Of Eden

Singles

Label	Catalog Number	Title	Type	Country	Year	Longbox Value / Value
CBS	ZZK80205	Nobody	CD5	Canada	1994	$8.00

Daffy Duck

Singles

Label	Catalog Number	Title	Type	Country	Year	Longbox Value / Value
WEA	9031-75690-2	Dynamite	CD5	Germany	1991	$8.00
WEA	9031-74793-2	Partyzone	CD5	Germany	1991	$8.00

Dahl, Jeff

Full Length

Label	Catalog Number	Title	Type	Country	Year	Longbox Value / Value
Passport	PVCD-8966	I Kill Me	LP/LB	U.S.		$14.00/$8.00

Daily, E. G.

Full Length

Label	Catalog Number	Title	Type	Country	Year	Longbox Value / Value
A&M	CD-5202	Lace Around the World	LP/LB	U.S.		$14.00/$8.00
A&M	395081-2	Wild Child	LP	Germany		$15.00

Singles

Label	Catalog Number	Title	Type	Country	Year	Longbox Value / Value
A&M	CD 17927	Heart Don't Lie	CDJ	U.S.	1989	$2.00
Canyon	S9Y-13112	Some People	CD3	Japan	1989	$12.00/$3.00
A&M	390435-2	Some People	CD5	U.K.	1989	$8.00
A&M	CD 17829	Some People	CDJ	U.S.	1989	$2.00

Daisy Chainsaw

Singles

Label	Catalog Number	Title	Type	Country	Year	Longbox Value / Value
Pinnacle	92-TP7CD	Hope Your Dreams Come True	CD5	U.K.	1992	$8.00
Diva	DVACD-001	Love Sick Pleasure	CD5	U.K.	1992	$8.00
A&M	75021 2403-2	Love Your Money	CDJ	U.S.	1992	$2.00
Rough Trade	130-1320-3	Pink Flower	CD5	Germany	1992	$8.00
Diva	TPCD-7	Pink Flower	CD5	U.K.	1992	$8.00

Daisy Dee

Singles

Label	Catalog Number	Title	Type	Country	Year	Longbox Value / Value
		Crazy	CDJ	U.S.		$2.00

Dakrash

Singles

Label	Catalog Number	Title	Type	Country	Year	Longbox Value / Value
EMI	202536-2	Wasn't I Good	CD5	Germany	1989	$7.00

Dalbello

Full Length

Label	Catalog Number	Title	Type	Country	Year	Longbox Value / Value
Capitol	CDP 48286	She	LP/LB	U.S.		$14.00/$8.00

Dale

Full Length

Label	Catalog Number	Title	Type	Country	Year	Longbox Value / Value
Paisley Park	9 25599-2	Riot in English	LP/LB	U.S.		$14.00/$8.00

Dali's Car

Full Length

Label	Catalog Number	Title	Type	Country	Year	Longbox Value / Value
Beggars Banquet	52	Walking Hour	LP/LB	U.S.		$14.00/$8.00

Dalton, Lacy J.

Full Length

Label	Catalog Number	Title	Type	Country	Year	Longbox Value / Value
Capitol	CDP-97931	Chains on the Wind	LP/LB	U.S.		$14.00/$8.00
Capitol	CDP-94569	Crazy Love	LP/LB	U.S.		$14.00/$8.00
Capitol	CDP-94059	Survivor	LP/LB	U.S.		$14.00/$8.00

Singles

Label	Catalog Number	Title	Type	Country	Year	Longbox Value / Value
Capitol	DPRO-79550	Forever in My Heart	CDJ	U.S.	1991	$2.00

Daltrey, Roger

Full Length

Label	Catalog Number	Title	Type	Country	Year	Longbox Value / Value
DIR		King Biscuit Flour Hour	RS	U.S.	1988	$40.00
With Pete Townsend, Airdate: 12/18/88.						
DIR		King Biscuit Flour Hour	RS	U.S.	1989	$50.00
Airdate: 10/23/89.						
Westwood One		Off the Record	RS	U.S.	1992	$30.00
Airdate: 11/23/92.						
Westwood One		Off the Record	RS	U.S.	1992	$35.00
Airdate: 8/3/92.						
Westwood One		Off the Record	RS	U.S.	1994	$30.00
Airdate: 5/16/94.						
Atlantic		Rocks in the Head	LP/LB	U.S.		$14.00/$8.00
Atlantic	81269-2	Under A Raging Moon	LP/LB	U.S.†	1985	$14.00/$8.00
Media America		Up Close	RS	U.S.	1992	$40.00
2 CD set.						

Singles

Label	Catalog Number	Title	Type	Country	Year	Longbox Value / Value
		Days of Light	CDJ	U.S.		$7.00
Atlantic	PRCD 4634-2	Days of Light	CDJ	U.S.	1992	$3.00

Dam

Full Length

Label	Catalog Number	Title	Type	Country	Year	Longbox Value / Value
Noise	4840	Inside Out	LP/LB	U.S.		$14.00/$8.00

Dambuilders

Singles

Label	Catalog Number	Title	Type	Country	Year	Longbox Value / Value
	PRCD 9090-2	Slo-Mo Kikaida	CDJ	U.S.	1994	$3.00

Damian

Singles

Label	Catalog Number	Title	Type	Country	Year	Longbox Value / Value
Jive	JIVECD-236	Wig Wam Bam	CD5	U.K.	1989	$7.00

Damian Dame

Full Length

Label	Catalog Number	Title	Type	Country	Year	Longbox Value / Value
LaFace	6000	Damian Dame	LP/LB	U.S.		$14.00/$8.00

Singles

Label	Catalog Number	Title	Type	Country	Year	Longbox Value / Value
Arista	BVDA-21	Exclusivity	CD3	Japan	1991	$12.00/$3.00
LaFace	4000	Exclusivity	CDJ	U.S.	1991	$2.00
Laface	4002	Right Down To It	CDJ	U.S.	1991	$2.00

Damian, Michael

Full Length

Label	Catalog Number	Title	Type	Country	Year	Longbox Value / Value
A&M	CD-5348	Dreams of Summer	LP/LB	U.S.		$14.00/$8.00

Singles

Label	Catalog Number	Title	Type	Country	Year	Longbox Value / Value
A&M	75021 7323 2	Another You	CDJ	U.S.	1991	$2.00
Cypress	YD 17970	Christmas Time Without You	CDJ	U.S.	1987	$2.00
Eastwest	246649-2	Cover of Love	CD5	Germany	1989	$8.00
Alfa	09B3-60	Cover of Love	CD3	Japan	1989	$12.00/$3.00
Cypress	YD 17803	Cover of Love	CDJ	U.S.	1989	$2.00
A&M	75021 7267 2	Let's Get Into This	CDJ	U.S.	1991	$2.00
A&M	75021 7231-2	Real Love	CDJ	U.S.	1991	$2.00
Intercord	828-315	Rock On	CD5	Germany	1989	$8.00
Alfa	09B3-43	Rock On	CD3	Japan	1989	$12.00/$3.00
A&M	CD 17735	Rock On	CDJ	U.S.	1989	$2.00
RCA	ZD-43214	Time Warp	CD5	Germany	1989	$8.00
Cypress	YD 17887	Was It Nothing At All	CDJ	U.S.	1989	$2.00
A&M	75021 7539 2	What a Price to Pay	CDJ	U.S.	1991	$2.00

Damier, Chez

Singles

Label	Catalog Number	Title	Type	Country	Year	Longbox Value / Value
KMS	KUKCD-3	CanYou Feel It	CD5	U.K.	1992	$7.00

Damn

Singles

Label	Catalog Number	Title	Type	Country	Year	Longbox Value / Value
SPV	0732-3	Da Soul's Da Rebel	CD5	Germany	1991	$7.00
Barricade	PRS-1032-2	Da Soul's Da Rebel	CD5	U.K.	1991	$7.00
Barricade	PRM-2015-2	Peace	CD5	Germany	1991	$7.00
SPV	0715-3	Roots	CD5	Germany	1991	$7.00

Damn The Machine

Singles

Label	Catalog Number	Title	Type	Country	Year	Longbox Value / Value
A&M	31458 8133	Lonesome God	CDJ	U.S.	1993	$2.00

Damn Yankees

Full Length

Label	Catalog Number	Title	Type	Country	Year	Longbox Value / Value
Warner Brothers	9 26159-2-Dj	Damn Yankees	DJ/LP	U.S.	1990	$12.00
Warner Brothers	WPZP4958	Don't Tread on Me	LTD/LP	Japan	1992	$30.00
Pinnacle	WPZP4958	Don't Tread on Me	LTD/LP	U.K.	1992	$30.00
Westwood One		Off the Record	RS	U.S.	1992	$20.00
Airdate: 2/15/93.						

Singles

Label	Catalog Number	Title	Type	Country	Year	Longbox Value / Value
Warner Brothers	PRO-CD-4051	Bad Reputation	CDJ	U.S.	1990	$3.00
Warner Brothers	PRO-CD-4321	Come Again	CDJ	U.S.	1990	$3.00
Warner Brothers	PRO-CD-4751	Come Again	CDJ	U.S.	1990	$3.00
Warner Brothers	PRO-CD-4000	Coming of Age	CDJ	U.S.	1990	$3.00
Warner Brothers	PRO-CD-5622	Don't Tread on Me	CDJ	U.S.	1992	$3.00
Warner Brothers	PRO-CD-5870	Fifteen Minutes of Fame	CDJ	U.S.	1992	$3.00
Warner Brothers	7599-21839-2	High Enough	CD5	Germany	1990	$10.00
Warner Brothers	W-0006CD	High Enough	CD5	U.K.	1990	$10.00
Warner Brothers		High Enough	CDJ	U.S.	1990	$3.00
Warner Brothers	PRO-CD-5839	Mister Please	CDJ	U.S.	1992	$3.00
Warner Brothers	PRO-CD-4052	Runaway	CDJ	U.S.	1990	$3.00
Warner Brothers	18612-2	Silence is Broken	CD5	U.S.	1992	$5.00
Warner Brothers	PRO-CD-5962	Silence is Broken	CDJ	U.S.	1992	$3.00
Warner Brothers	PRO-CD-6013	Silence is Broken	CDJ	U.S.	1992	$3.00
Warner Brothers	9362-40646-2	Where You Goin' Now	CD5	U.K.	1992	$10.00
Warner Brothers	9 18728-2	Where You Goin' Now	CD5	U.S.	1992	$4.00
Warner Brothers	PRO-CD-5739	Where You Goin' Now	CDJ	U.S.	1992	$3.00
Warner Brothers	PRO-CD-5774	Where You Goin' Now	CDJ	U.S.	1992	$3.00

Damned

Full Length

Label	Catalog Number	Title	Type	Country	Year	Longbox Value / Value
WEA	254348-2	Anything	LP	Germany		$18.00
Big Beat	CDDAM-1	Best of	LP/LB	U.S.		$14.00/$8.00
Castle	ESPCD-008	Final Damnation	LTD/LP	U.K.		$25.00
Picture disc CD.						
Image	ID7922EN	Final Damnation	LD	U.S.		$20.00
MCA	DMCF-3275	Phantasmagoria	LP	Germany		$18.00

Singles

Label	Catalog Number	Title	Type	Country	Year	Longbox Value / Value
		Final Damnation	CDJ	U.K		$10.00
Deltic	DELT-7C	Fun Factory	CD5	U.K.	1990	$10.00
New Rose	D1	Neat Neat Neat	CD5	France		$11.00
Aris	883512	Peel Sessions	CD5	Germany	1990	$10.00
Strange Fruit	SFPSCD-002	Peel Sessions	CD5	U.K.	1990	$10.00

Dana

Singles

Label	Catalog Number	Title	Type	Country	Year	Longbox Value / Value
ZYX	6005-8	Be My Lover	CD5	Germany	1989	$6.00

Dance Bee

Singles

Label	Catalog Number	Title	Type	Country	Year	Longbox Value / Value
ZYX	6523-8	Party Move	CD5	Germany	1991	$6.00

Dance Conspiracy

Singles

Label	Catalog Number	Title	Type	Country	Year	Longbox Value / Value
WEA	XLS-34CD	Dub War	CD5	U.K.	1992	$8.00

Dance Device

Singles

Label	Catalog Number	Title	Type	Country	Year	Longbox Value / Value
Polygram	867313-2	Don't Go	CD5	Germany	1991	$8.00

Dance With A Stranger

Singles

Label	Catalog Number	Title	Type	Country	Year	Longbox Value / Value
RCA	PD-43604	Invisible Man	CD5	Germany	1990	$8.00
RCA	PD-43604	Invisible Man	CD5	U.K.	1990	$8.00
RCA	PD-44976	Living in the Future Together	CD5	U.K.	1990	$8.00

Dance-O-Rama

Singles

Label	Catalog Number	Title	Type	Country	Year	Longbox Value / Value
ZYX	FR-9241-8	Girl of the Night	CD5	Germany	1991	$6.00

Dancehall Divas

Singles

Label	Catalog Number	Title	Type	Country	Year	Longbox Value / Value
Atlantic	95720	Jamaican Man	CD5	U.S.	1995	$5.00

Dancer

Full Length

Label	Catalog Number	Title	Type	Country	Year	Longbox Value / Value
Arise	CRCR-6036/7	Memorial	LTD/LP	Japan		$35.00
2 CD edition.						

Dancing French

Singles

Label	Catalog Number	Title	Type	Country	Year	Longbox Value / Value
	30	Dancing French Libe	CD5	U.S.	1994	$5.00

Dancing Hoods

Full Length

Label	Catalog Number	Title	Type	Country	Year	Longbox Value / Value
Relativity	88561-8224-2	Hallelujah Anyway	LP/BP	U.S.	1988	$12.00/$7.00

Singles

Label	Catalog Number	Title	Type	Country	Year	Longbox Value / Value
Relativity		Baby's Got Rockets	CDJ	U.S.	1988	$2.00

Dandelion

Singles

Label	Catalog Number	Title	Type	Country	Year	Longbox Value / Value
Ruffhouse	77313	Under My Skin	CDJ	U.S.	1993	$2.00
Ruffhouse	5227	Waiting For A Ride	CDJ	U.S.	1993	$2.00

Dandy

Singles

Label	Catalog Number	Title	Type	Country	Year	Longbox Value / Value
Alfa	10SR-27	I'll Be There	CD3	Japan	1988	$12.00/$3.00

Dane, Dana

Singles

Label	Catalog Number	Title	Type	Country	Year	Longbox Value / Value
Profile	7314	A Little Bit Of Dana Tonight	CDJ	U.S.	1990	$2.00
Warner Brothers	18055	Record Jock	CD5	U.S.	1994	$5.00
Warner Brothers	17907	Rollin Wit Dane	CD5	U.S.	1994	$5.00

Danger Danger

Full Length

Label	Catalog Number	Title	Type	Country	Year	Longbox Value / Value
Epic	ESK 1996	Down Dirty Live	DJ/Smplr	U.S.	1990	$8.00

Singles

Label	Catalog Number	Title	Type	Country	Year	Longbox Value / Value
Epic	ZSK 2003	Bang Bang	CDJ	U.S.	1990	$2.00
Epic	CSDS-8127	Don't Walk Away	CD3	Japan	1990	$12.00/$3.00
Epic	ESK 73606	Don't Walk Away	CDJ	U.S.	1990	$2.00
Sony	SDCD-2	Everybody Wants Some	CD3	Japan	1992	$12.00/$3.00
Sony	SRDS-8216	I Still Think About You	CD3	Japan	1991	$12.00/$3.00
Epic	657838-2	I Still Think About You	CD5	U.K.	1992	$8.00
Epic	ESK 74231	I Still Think About You	CDJ	U.S.	1992	$2.00
		Monkey Business	CD3	Japan	1992	$12.00/$3.00
Epic	657751-2	Monkey Business	CD5	U.K.	1992	$8.00
Epic	ESK 73949	Monkey Business	CDJ	U.S.	1991	$2.00
Sony	CSDS-8103	Naughty Naughty	CD3	Japan	1989	$12.00/$3.00
Epic	ESK 2170	Naughty Naughty	CDJ	U.S.	1990	$2.00
		Think About You	CD3	Japan	1992	$12.00/$3.00
Epic	ZSK 74231	Think About You	CDJ	U.S.	1992	$2.00

Dangerfield, Rodney

Full Length

Label	Catalog Number	Title	Type	Country	Year	Longbox Value / Value
Dove		La Contessa	DJ/Smplr	U.S.	1996	$18.00

Dangerous

Singles

Label	Catalog Number	Title	Type	Country	Year	Longbox Value / Value
Marque	MARQCD-001	Diamonds & Dollars	CD5	U.K.	1990	$8.00

Dangerous Dame

Singles

Label	Catalog Number	Title	Type	Country	Year	Longbox Value / Value
		Far From A Regular	CDJ	U.S.		$2.00

Dangerous Ground

Singles

Label	Catalog Number	Title	Type	Country	Year	Longbox Value / Value
Pinnacle	CDSD-001	Big Fun	CD5	U.K.	1990	$8.00
Pinnacle	CDG-3	Unfaithfully Yours	CD5	U.K.	1990	$8.00

Dangerous Toys

Full Length

Label	Catalog Number	Title	Type	Country	Year	Longbox Value / Value
Columbia	CSK 1703	Dangerous Toys	DJ/LP	U.S.	1989	$15.00

Label	Catalog Number	Title	Type	Country	Year	Longbox Value / Value
		Singles				
Columbia	CSK 4023	Gimme No Lip	CDJ	U.S.	1991	$2.00
Columbia	CSK 4147	Line 'Em Up	CDJ	U.S.	1991	$2.00
Columbia	CSK 1833	Scared	CDJ	U.S.	1989	$2.00
Columbia	CSK 1950	Sport'n a Woody	CDJ	U.S.	1990	$2.00
Dangerous Zone						
		Singles				
ZYX	DST-1061-8	Naughty	CD5	Germany	1991	$6.00
Daniel, Jeffery						
		Full Length				
Columbia	CK 75318	Skinny Boy	LP/LB	U.S.		$14.00/$8.00
		Singles				
Epic	ZSK 74009	She's the Girl	CDJ	U.S.	1990	$2.00
Daniels, Charlie (Band)						
		Full Length				
CBS	7105-80	Charlie Daniels Band	LD	U.S.	1983	$35.00
Epic	ESK 2204	Charlie Daniels Radio Special	DJ/RS	U.S.	1990	$25.00
Epic	EK-36571	Full Moon	LP/LB	U.S.†	1984	$14.00/$8.00
CBS	460034-2	Powder Keg	LP	Germany		$23.00
Epic	ESK 65023	Sampler	DJ/Smplr	U.S.	1996	$8.00
		Singles				
Liberty	DPRO-79739	All Night Long	CDJ	U.S.	1992	$2.00
Liberty	DPRO-74061	Little Folks	CDJ	U.S.	1991	$2.00
Daniels, Chris & Kings						
		Full Length				
Redstone	8901	That's What I Like About the South	LP/BP	U.S.		$14.00/$8.00
Danni						
		Singles				
		Get Into You	CD5	Australia		$10.00
MCA	MCSTD-1600	I Don't Wanna Take the Pain	CD5	U.K.	1991	$8.00
Alfa	ALCB-649	Show You the Way To Go	CD3	Japan	1992	$12.00/$3.00
MCA	MCSTD-1671	Show You the Way To Go	CD5	U.K.	1992	$8.00
Danny and the Juniors						
		Singles				
Old Gold	OG-6148	At the Hop	CD3	U.K.	1989	$10.00
Danny B.						
		Singles				
EMI	323852-2	Heaven	CD5	Germany	1992	$8.00
EMI	323763-2	Life Can Be So Groovy	CD5	Germany	1991	$8.00
Dante, Steven						
		Singles				
Cooltempo	SDCD-1	I'm Too Scared	CD5	U.K.	1988	$8.00
Cooltempo	SDCD-2	Imagination	CD5	U.K.	1988	$8.00
Danzig						
		Full Length				
Def American	PRO-CD-5595	A Taste of Danzig III	DJ/Smplr	U.S.	1992	$10.00
Def American		Danzig	DJ/LP	U.S.	1988	$15.00
		Danzig II Licifage	DJ/LP	U.S.		$15.00
Def American	9 45134-2	Danzig III How the Gods Kill	LTD/LP	U.S.	1992	$28.00
		Singles				
Def American		Can't Speak	CDJ	U.S.	1994	$3.00
Def American	DEFCD-17	Dirty Black Summer	CD5	U.K.	1992	$10.00
Def American	9 40544-2	Dirty Black Summer	CD5	U.S.	1992	$5.00
Def American	PRO-CD-5563	Dirty Black Summer	CDJ	U.S.	1992	$3.00
Def American	PRO-CD-4121	Her Black Wings	CDJ	U.S.	1990	$3.00
Def American		I Don't Mind the Pain	CDJ	U.S.	1994	$3.00
Def American	PRO-CD-4152	Killer Wolf	CDJ	U.S.	1990	$3.00
Def American	PRO-CD-6422	Mother	CDJ	U.S.	1993	$3.00
		Mother '94	CD5	U.K.	1994	$10.00
		Mother '94	CD5	U.K.	1994	$10.00
	Second version.					
Def American	PRO-CD-7083	Until You Call on the Dark	CDJ	U.S.	1994	$3.00
Daou						
		Singles				
Capitol	C2 58142	Are You Satisfied	CD5	U.S.	1994	$6.00
Columbia	CSK 4773	Sympathy Bouquet	CDJ	U.S.	1992	$2.00
Daou, Vanessa						
		Full Length				
		Zipless Airplay Sampler	DJ/Smplr	U.S.	1995	$8.00
Daphne						
		Singles				
Maxi	2019	Change	CD5	U.S.	1994	$5.00
Maxi	01	Mr. Phat	CDJ	U.S.	1994	$2.00
Dare						
		Full Length				
A&M	CD-5221	Out of the Silence	LP/LB	U.S.		$14.00/$8.00
		Singles				
A&M	CDEE-519	Abandon	CD3	U.K.	1988	$8.00
A&M	AMCD-470	Abandon	CD5	U.K.	1988	$8.00
A&M	CD 17622	Abandon	CDJ	U.S.	1988	$2.00
A&M	CDEE-525	Heartbreaker	CD3	U.K.	1988	$8.00
A&M	CDEE-493	Nothing is Stronger Than Love	CD3	U.K.	1988	$8.00
A&M	CD 17731	Nothing is Stronger Than Love	CDJ	U.S.	1988	$2.00
A&M	CDEE-483	Raindance	CD3	U.K.	1988	$8.00
A&M	390824-2	Real Love	CD5	Germany	1991	$8.00
A&M	AMCD-824	Real Love	CD5	U.K.	1991	$8.00
A&M	390824-2	We Don't Need a Reason	CD5	Germany	1991	$8.00
A&M	AMCD-824	We Don't Need a Reason	CD5	U.K.	1991	$8.00
Darin, Bobby						
		Full Length				
Rhino		As Long As I'm Singing	DJ/Smplr	U.S.	1995	$20.00
Motown	9070	Live at the Desert Inn	LP/LB	U.S.		$14.00/$8.00
Dario						
		Singles				
EMI	147555-2	Poison My Heart	CD5	Germany	1991	$8.00
Dark						
		Full Length				
Plaene	42280	Dark	LP	Germany		$15.00
CMP	CMPCD-26	Dark '86	LP/BP	U.S.	1986	$14.00/$8.00
Dark Angel						
		Full Length				
Combat	8114	Darkness Descends	LP/LB	U.S.		$14.00/$8.00
Combat	2013	Live Scars	LP/LB	U.S.		$14.00/$8.00
		Singles				
IRS	977124	Leave Scars	CD5	Germany	1990	$8.00
Darkside						
		Full Length				
RCA	3029	All That Noise	LP/LB	U.S.		$14.00/$8.00
RCA	61121	Mellomania	LP/LB	U.S.		$14.00/$8.00
		Singles				
Pinnacle	SIT-95CD	Mayhem to Meditate	CD5	U.K.	1992	$8.00
SPV	0516-3	Waiting for the Angels	CD5	Germany	1990	$8.00
Pinnacle	SIT-972CD	Waiting for the Angels	CD5	U.K.	1990	$8.00
Darling Buds						
		Full Length				
ECM	843172	Cycles	LP/LB	U.S.		$14.00/$8.00
ECM	827410	Journal October	LP/LB	U.S.		$14.00/$8.00
		Singles				
Epic	BLONDC-1	Burst	CD5	U.K.	1988	$8.00
Epic	BLONDC-6	Crystal Clear	CD5	U.K.	1990	$8.00
Epic	656121	Crystal Clear	CD5	U.K.	1990	$8.00
Columbia	656121	Crystal Clear	CD5	U.S.	1991	$5.00
Columbia	CSK 73662	Crystal Clear	CDJ	U.S.	1991	$2.00
Epic	BLONDC-2	Hit the Ground	CD5	U.K.	1988	$8.00
Epic	656594 2	It Makes No Difference	CD5	U.K.	1990	$8.00
Columbia	CSK 2275	It Makes No Difference	CDJ	U.S.	1990	$2.00
Epic	BLONDC-3	Let's Go Round There	CD5	U.K.	1988	$8.00
Columbia	74446	Pleasure Yourself	CD5	U.S.	1992	$4.00
Epic	658215-2	Sure Thing	CD5	U.K.	1992	$8.00
Epic	BLONDC-5	Tiny Machine	CD5	U.K.	1990	$8.00
Epic	BLONDC-4	You've Got to Choose	CD5	U.K.	1988	$8.00
Darling Cruel						
		Singles				
Polydor	CDP 66	Everything's Over	CDJ	U.S.	1989	$2.00
Darling, Helen						
		Full Length				
Decca/Nashville		Helen Darling	DJ/LP	U.S.	1995	$15.00
Darlow						
		Singles				
Polygram	MAGCD-22	Hot	CD5	U.K.	1992	$7.00
Das Efx						
		Singles				
EastWest	PRCD 5503-2	Baknaffek	CDJ	U.S.	1993	$2.00
EastWest	PRCD 5549-2	Baknaffek	CDJ	U.S.	1993	$2.00
Atlantic	95926	Baknaffek	CD5	U.S.	1994	$5.00
EastWest	PRCD 5326-2	Freakit	CDJ	U.S.	1993	$2.00
EastWest	PRCD 4980-2	If Only	CDJ	U.S.	1993	$2.00
EastWest	PRCD 5654-2	Mic Checka	CDJ	U.S.	1993	$2.00
Elektra	66103	Real Hip-Hop	CD5	U.S.	1995	$5.00
EastWest	PRCD 4854-2	Straight Out the Sewer	CDJ	U.S.	1993	$2.00
EastWest	PRCD 4449-2	They Want Efx	CDJ	U.S.	1992	$2.00
Dash, Sarah						
		Singles				
		You're All I Need	CDJ	U.S.		$2.00
Datcher, Clark						
		Singles				
Virgin	663164	Crown of Thorns	CD5	Germany	1990	$8.00
Virgin	VSCDT-1243	Crown of Thorns	CD5	U.K.	1990	$8.00
Virgin	VSCDP-1243	Crown of Thorns	CD5	U.K.	1990	$8.00
Dattman						
		Singles				
Polygram	TABCD-116	Poor Man's Story	CD5	U.K.	1993	$8.00
Daughter Brite & Soda Pop Mikes						
		Singles				
		Wish We Were Grown	CDJ	U.S.		$2.00
Dave Clark Five						
		Full Length				
Hollywood	10337	55 By Five	DJ/Smplr	U.S.	1993	$12.00
		Singles				
		Glad All Over	CD5	U.K.	1993	$10.00
Davey, Shaun						
		Singles				
Tara	CDS 1	Ripples In Rockpool	CD5	U.K.	1991	$8.00
David and David						
		Singles				
A&M	A&M 003	Welcome To the Boomtown	DJ/CDV	U.S.	1988	$20.00
David, F.R.						
		Full Length				
CBS	460260-2	Reflections	LP	Germany		$18.00
David, Joel						
		Singles				
Old Recds	OLDCD-1	Old Bones	CD5	U.K.	1988	$8.00
David, Michael						
		Singles				
CBS	657485-2	Feelings	CD5	Germany	1992	$8.00
Davies, Debbie						
		Full Length				
		House of Blues	RS	U.S.	1995	$35.00
	2 CD set. Airdate: 1/8/95.					
Davies, Gail						
		Full Length				
Capitol	CDP 94453	Best of	LP/LB	U.S.		$14.00/$8.00
Capitol	CDP 94105	Other Side Of Love	LP/LB	U.S.		$14.00/$8.00
MCA	MCAD-42274	Pretty Words	LP/LB	U.S.		$14.00/$8.00
Davies, Richard						
		Singles				
		Sign Up Maybe For Being	CD5	Australia	1996	$12.00

Davis, Andy

Full Length

Label	Catalog Number	Title	Type	Country	Year	Longbox Value / Value
Relativity	1040	Cleverdon Pier	LP/LB	U.S.		$14.00/$8.00

Davis, Anthony

Full Length

Label	Catalog Number	Title	Type	Country	Year	Longbox Value / Value
Gramaphone	GRCD-8401	Middle Passage	LP/LB	U.S.†	1985	$14.00/$8.00

Davis, Carlene

Singles

Label	Catalog Number	Title	Type	Country	Year	Longbox Value / Value
Gee Street	GESCD-43	Butterflies	CD5	U.K.	1993	$8.00
Gee Street	GESCD-40	Dial by Number	CD5	U.K.	1993	$8.00
Gee Street	422 864 219	Dial by Number	CD5	U.S.	1992	$4.00
Gee Street	559	Dial by Number	CDJ	U.S.	1992	$2.00

Davis, Carole

Full Length

Label	Catalog Number	Title	Type	Country	Year	Longbox Value / Value
Warner Brothers	9 25903-2	Heart of Gold	LP/LB	U.S.		$14.00/$8.00

Singles

Label	Catalog Number	Title	Type	Country	Year	Longbox Value / Value
Atlantic	PRCD 5034-2	J'Aime You	CDJ	U.S.	1993	$2.00

Davis, Chip

Full Length

Label	Catalog Number	Title	Type	Country	Year	Longbox Value / Value
Am Gramm	1	Dinner Music	LTD/LP	U.S.	1991	$15.00

CD sampler, cook book and coffee in wood crate.

Davis, Eddie

Full Length

Label	Catalog Number	Title	Type	Country	Year	Longbox Value / Value
King	506	Modern Jazz	LP/BP	U.S.		$14.00/$8.00
Bluebird	6463	Save Your Love For Me	LP/BP	U.S.		$14.00/$8.00

Davis, Jesse

Singles

Label	Catalog Number	Title	Type	Country	Year	Longbox Value / Value
BMG	PD-44652	Get Up on This	CD5	Germany	1991	$8.00
BMG	PD-45110	Get Up on This	CD5	Germany	1991	$8.00

Davis, John

Singles

Label	Catalog Number	Title	Type	Country	Year	Longbox Value / Value
BMG	664254	Feel the Love Magic	CD5	Germany	1991	$8.00
Polygram	877933-2	Still Be Loving You	CD5	Germany	1990	$8.00
Polygram	873455-2	Who Do You Love	CD5	Germany	1990	$8.00

Davis Jr., Sammy

Full Length

Label	Catalog Number	Title	Type	Country	Year	Longbox Value / Value
Image	ID6671VE	An Evening with Sammy Davis Jr. & Jerry Lewis	LD	U.S.		$25.00
Vogue	600014	Closest of Friends	LP/BP	U.S.		$14.00/$8.00
Capitol	CDP-94071-2	Collector Series	LP/LB	U.S.		$17.00/$13.00
Polygram	837446-2	Our Shining Hour	LP/BP	U.S.		$14.00/$8.00

With Count Basie.

Davis, LJ

Singles

Label	Catalog Number	Title	Type	Country	Year	Longbox Value / Value
Bellaphon	130-07-345	Wake Up and Make Love With Me	CD5	Germany	1990	$8.00

Davis, Mac

Full Length

Label	Catalog Number	Title	Type	Country	Year	Longbox Value / Value
Casablanca	822638-2	Very Best & More	LP/BP	U.S.†	1984	$14.00/$8.00

Singles

Label	Catalog Number	Title	Type	Country	Year	Longbox Value / Value
	117	A Man Don't Cry	CD5	U.S.	1994	$5.00

Davis, Mary

Full Length

Label	Catalog Number	Title	Type	Country	Year	Longbox Value / Value
Epic	EK-40978	Separate Ways	LP/LB	U.S>		$14.00/$8.00

Singles

Label	Catalog Number	Title	Type	Country	Year	Longbox Value / Value
Tabu	655296-2	Don't Wear It Out	CD5	U.K.	1990	$8.00
		Have You Been Loved	CDJ	U.S.		$2.00

Davis, Mike

Singles

Label	Catalog Number	Title	Type	Country	Year	Longbox Value / Value
Jive	JIVECD-311	Ain't No Stoppin' Us Now	CD5	U.K.	1992	$8.00
Jive	42087-2-RDJ	Ain't No Stoppin' Us Now	CDJ	U.S.	1992	$2.00

Davis, Miles

Full Length

Label	Catalog Number	Title	Type	Country	Year	Longbox Value / Value
One Way	AK-21398	Big Fun	LP/LB	U.S.		$14.00/$8.00
EMI		Birth of the Cool, Volume 1, Volume 2	LTD/LP	U.K.	1994	$35.00

3 CD boxed set.

Label	Catalog Number	Title	Type	Country	Year	Longbox Value / Value
Columbia		Columbia Years, The	DJ/Smplr	U.S.		$25.00
CBS		Complete Live at the Plugged	LTD/LP	Japan	1990	N/A

7 CD boxed set.

Label	Catalog Number	Title	Type	Country	Year	Longbox Value / Value
CBS	CK-38991	Decoy	LP/LB	U.S.†	1985	$14.00/$8.00
Philips	822566-2	Elevator to the Scaffold	LP/LB	U.S.†	1985	$14.00/$8.00
Savoy Records	CY-78995	First Miles	LTD/LP	U.S.	1995	$20.00

CD in miniature repica of original LP sleeve.

Label	Catalog Number	Title	Type	Country	Year	Longbox Value / Value
Columbia		Historic Collection	DJ/Intvw	U.S.	1996	$16.00
Columbia	CK-44425	In Person Vol. 2	LP/LB	U.S.		$14.00/$8.00
Sony	SRCS-6681	Kind of Blue	LTD/LP	Japan	1993	$35.00

Gold disc.

Label	Catalog Number	Title	Type	Country	Year	Longbox Value / Value
CBS	CK-08163	Kind of Blue	LP/LB	U.S.†	1985	$14.00/$8.00
Columbia	CK-52861	Kind of Blue	LP/LB	U.S.	1993	$28.00/$24.00

Gold disc.

Label	Catalog Number	Title	Type	Country	Year	Longbox Value / Value
CBS	CK-36790	Man With the Horn	LP/LB	U.S.†	1985	$14.00/$8.00
Warner Brothers	9 25655-2	Music From Siesta	LP/LB	U.S.		$14.00/$8.00
Columbia		Nickel Sessions	DJ/Smplr	U.S.	1995	$25.00
Polygram	822566-2	Nouvelle Vogue	LP	Germany		$15.00
Philips	822566-2	Nouvelle Vogue	LP/LB	U.S.		$14.00/$8.00
CBS	CK-08271	Sketches of Spain	LP/LB	U.S.†	1985	$14.00/$8.00
Mobile	MFCD-828	Someday My Prince Will Come	LP/LB	U.S.†	1985	$14.00/$8.00
CBS	CBSCD-25395	Star People	LP	U.K.		$25.00
CBS	CK-40023	You're Under Arrest	LP/LB	U.S.†	1985	$14.00/$8.00

Singles

Label	Catalog Number	Title	Type	Country	Year	Longbox Value / Value
Warner Brothers	9 40584-2	Blow	CD5	U.S.	1992	$3.00
A&M	CD 17646	Christmas Song	CDJ	U.S.	1988	$7.00

With Natalie Cole.

Label	Catalog Number	Title	Type	Country	Year	Longbox Value / Value
Warner Brothers	WPCP-5066	Doo Bop Song	CD3	Japan	1992	$12.00/$4.00
Warner Brothers	9 40549-2	Doo Bop Song	CD5	U.S.	1992	$6.00
Warner Brothers	PRO-CD-5430	Doo Bop Song	CDJ	U.S.	1992	$3.00
Warner Brothers	PRO-CD-5619	Doo Bop Song	CDJ	U.S.	1992	$3.00
Epic	ESK 1869	Red/Orange/Blue/Violet	CDJ	U.S.	1989	$3.00
Warner Brothers	PRO-CD-3002	Siesta	CDJ	U.S.	1987	$3.00
Columbia	CSK 1376	Summertime	CDJ	U.S.	1988	$3.00

Davis, Nancy

Singles

Label	Catalog Number	Title	Type	Country	Year	Longbox Value / Value
PWL	4509-90709-2	Higher And Higher	CD5	Germany	1992	$8.00
PWL	PWCD-242	Higher And Higher	CD5	U.K.	1992	$8.00
PWL	PWCD-221	If You Belonged to Me	CD5	U.K.	1992	$8.00

Davis, Paul

Singles

Label	Catalog Number	Title	Type	Country	Year	Longbox Value / Value
Arista	CD3-3006	Cool Night	CD3	U.S.	1988	$6.00/$3.00

Davis, Ricky

Singles

Label	Catalog Number	Title	Type	Country	Year	Longbox Value / Value
Alfa	11B3-79	Magic	CD3	Japan	1989	$12.00/$3.00

Davis, Terry

Singles

Label	Catalog Number	Title	Type	Country	Year	Longbox Value / Value
WEA	171961-2	I Really Do Love You	CD5	Germany	1990	$8.00

Davis, Tyrone

Singles

Label	Catalog Number	Title	Type	Country	Year	Longbox Value / Value
	79529	It's So Good	CD5	U.S.	1994	$5.00

Davy Jones' Locker

Singles

Label	Catalog Number	Title	Type	Country	Year	Longbox Value / Value
Efa	CD-13515	Davy Jones' Locker	CD5	Germany	1992	$8.00

Dawn

Singles

Label	Catalog Number	Title	Type	Country	Year	Longbox Value / Value
Arista	162065	Knock Three Times	CD5	Germany	1989	$8.00

Dawson, Dana

Full Length

Label	Catalog Number	Title	Type	Country	Year	Longbox Value / Value
Aris	885030	Ready to Follow You	LP	Germany	1989	$18.00

Singles

Label	Catalog Number	Title	Type	Country	Year	Longbox Value / Value
CBS	652922-3	Ready to Follow You	CD3	Germany	1989	$8.00
CBS	655971-3	Romantic World	CD3	Germany	1991	$8.00
CBS	656817-2-3	Tell Me Bonita	CD5	Germany	1991	$8.00

Dawson, Julian

Singles

Label	Catalog Number	Title	Type	Country	Year	Longbox Value / Value
Polygram	887958-2	Cover to Cover	CD5	Germany	1988	$8.00
BMG	66411	How Can I Sleep Without You	CD5	Germany	1991	$8.00

Dax, Danielle

Singles

Label	Catalog Number	Title	Type	Country	Year	Longbox Value / Value
Sire	9 40047-2	Big Blue '82	CD5	U.S.	1991	$5.00
WEA	W-9529CD	Tomorrow Never Knows	CD5	U.K.	1990	$9.00
Sire	9 21773-2	Tomorrow Never Knows	CD5	U.S.	1990	$4.00

Day, Doris

Full Length

Label	Catalog Number	Title	Type	Country	Year	Longbox Value / Value
Time Warner Sound Exchange		It's Magic - 40 Legendary Hits	LTD/LP	U.S.	1996	$25.00

2 CD set.

Label	Catalog Number	Title	Type	Country	Year	Longbox Value / Value
Columbia	658848-2	Perhaps, Perhaps, Perhaps	CD5	U.K.	1992	$10.00
Columbia	656477-2	Winter Wonderland	CD5	U.K.	1992	$10.00

Day, Morris

Full Length

Label	Catalog Number	Title	Type	Country	Year	Longbox Value / Value
Warner Brothers	9 25651-2	Daydreaming	LP/LB	U.S.		$14.00/$8.00
Pioneer	10SW-34	Fishnet	CD3	Japan	1988	$12.00/$3.00
Reprise	PRO-CD-5879	Gimme Whatcha Got	CDJ	U.S.	1992	$2.00
Reprise	PRO-CD-5782	Gimme Whatcha Got	CDJ	U.S.	1992	$2.00

Day, Patti

Singles

Label	Catalog Number	Title	Type	Country	Year	Longbox Value / Value
		Inch by Inch	CDJ	U.S.		$2.00
BMG	SWRCD-3	Right Before My Eyes	CD5	U.K.	1991	$8.00

Day Z's

Full Length

Label	Catalog Number	Title	Type	Country	Year	Longbox Value / Value
Reprise	9 26128-2	Day Z's	LP/LB	U.S.	1990	$14.00/$8.00

Singles

Label	Catalog Number	Title	Type	Country	Year	Longbox Value / Value
Reprise	PRO-CD-4424	Certainly	CDJ	U.S.	1990	$2.00
Reprise	PRO-CD-4596	Certainly	CDJ	U.S.	1990	$2.00

Dayanti, Chris

Singles

Label	Catalog Number	Title	Type	Country	Year	Longbox Value / Value
Canyon	PCD-00425	Lost in the Storm	CD3	Japan	1993	$13.00/$4.00

Dayeene

Singles

Label	Catalog Number	Title	Type	Country	Year	Longbox Value / Value
Faze 2	CDFAZE-8	Around the World	CD5	U.K.	1992	$8.00

Daylor, Kathy Joe

Singles

Label	Catalog Number	Title	Type	Country	Year	Longbox Value / Value
Polygram	871559-2	Little Witch	CD5	Germany	1989	$8.00
Polygram	877089-2	With Every Beat	CD5	Germany	1989	$8.00

Dayne, Taylor

Singles

Label	Catalog Number	Title	Type	Country	Year	Longbox Value / Value
Arista	BVDA-40	Can't Get Eoungh of Your Love	CD3	Japan	1993	$12.00/$3.00
Arista	12583	Can't Get Eoungh of Your Love	CD5	U.S.	1993	$5.00
Arista	ASCD-2586	Can't Get Eoungh of Your Love	CDJ	U.S.	1993	$2.00
Arista	661687	Don't Rush Me	CD5	Germany	1988	$9.00
Arista	A10D-114	Don't Rush Me	CD3	Japan	1993	$12.00/$3.00
Arista	661687	Don't Rush Me	CD5	U.K.	1988	$9.00
Arista	ARCD 9723	Don't Rush Me	CDJ	U.S.	1988	$2.00
Arista	BVDA-7	Heart of Stone	CD3	Japan	1990	$12.00/$3.00
Arista	ARCD 2057	Heart of Stone	CDJ	U.S.	1990	$2.00
Arista	661536	I'll Aways Love You	CD5	Germany	1988	$9.00
Arista	661536	I'll Aways Love You	CD5	U.K.	1988	$9.00
Arista	662996	I'll Be Your Shelter	CD5	Germany	1990	$9.00
Arista	663211	I'll Be Your Shelter	CD5	U.K.	1990	$9.00
Arista	662996	I'll Be Your Shelter	CD5	U.K.	1990	$9.00
Arista	12659	I'll Wait	CD5	U.S.	1994	$5.00
Arsita	8844277	Love Will Lead You Back	CD5	Germany	1990	$9.00
Arista	A10D-149	Love Will Lead You Back	CD3	Japan	1990	$12.00/$3.00
Arista	663277	Love Will Lead You Back	CD5	U.K.	1990	$9.00
		Love Will Lead You Back	CDJ	U.S.	1990	$2.00
Arista	880858	Prove Your Love	CD5	Germany	1988	$9.00
Arista	659830	Prove Your Love	CD5	U.K.	1988	$9.00
		Say a Prayer	CD5	U.K.		$10.00
		Say a Prayer	CD5	U.K.		$10.00

Second version.

Label	Catalog Number	Title	Type	Country	Year	Longbox Value / Value
Arista	12882	Say a Prayer	CD5	U.S.	1995	$5.00
Arista	12895	Say a Prayer	CD5	U.S.	1995	$2.00
Arista		Send Me A Lover	CDJ	U.S.		$2.00
Arista	662706	With Every Beat of My Heart	CD5	Germany	1989	$9.00
Arista	A10D-126	With Every Beat of My Heart	CD3	Japan	1989	$12.00/$3.00
Arista	662706	With Every Beat of My Heart	CD5	U.K.	1989	$9.00
Arista	ASCD 9895	With Every Beat of My Heart	CDJ	U.S.	1989	$2.00

Label	Catalog Number	Title	Type	Country	Year	Longbox Value / Value
DB's						
Singles						
IRS	17449	Working For Somebody Else	CDJ	U.S.	1987	$2.00
DC Talk						
Singles						
Capitol	25135	Jesus Talk	CD5	U.S.	1995	$5.00
De Angelo, Nino						
Full Length						
Polygram	823716-2	Zeit Fuer Rebellen	LP	Germany		$15.00
Singles						
WEA	247566-3	Baby Jane	CD3	Germany	1988	$8.00
WEA	246941-3	If There is One Thing	CD3	Germany	1988	$8.00
WEA	247087-3	Samuraj	CD3	Germany	1988	$8.00
WEA	9031-72661-2	Vielleicht	CD5	Germany	1990	$8.00
WEA	9031-72660-2	Vielleicht	CD5	Germany	1990	$8.00
WEA	246805-3	Who's Gonna Love You Tonight	CD3	Germany	1989	$8.00
De Azevedo, Lex						
Full Length						
Aubergine	AU2206	Wind River Suite	LTD/LP	U.S.	1995	$18.00
	CD and art print in sleeve.					
De Burgh, Chris						
Full Length						
A&M		Beautiful Dreams	DJ/LP	U.K.		$20.00
A&M	CD-4929	Getaway, The	LP/LB	U.S.†	1984	$14.00/$8.00
A&M	CD-5002	Man in Line	LP/LB	U.S.†	1984	$14.00/$8.00
A&M	AMCD060192	Power of Ten	DJ/Intvw	Canada	1992	$25.00
Telstar	TCD-2248	Very Best of	LP	U.K.		$20.00
Singles						
A&M	390350-2	Compact Hits	CD5	Germany	1988	$9.00
A&M	AMCD-915	Compact Hits	CD5	U.K.	1988	$9.00
A&M	390467-2	Diamond in the Dark	CD5	Germany	1990	$9.00
A&M	AMCD-537	Diamond in the Dark	CD5	U.K.	1990	$9.00
A&M	390418-3	Don't Look Back	CD3	Germany	1989	$9.00
A&M	390419-2	Don't Look Back	CD5	Germany	1989	$9.00
A&M	390565-2	Don't Pay the Ferryman	CD5	Germany	1990	$9.00
A&M	AMCD-581	Don't Pay the Ferryman	CD5	U.K.	1990	$9.00
A&M	S10Y-3051	Love is My Decision	CD3	Japan	1988	$12.00/$3.00
A&M	AMCD-0018	Making the Perfect Man	CD5	U.K.	1992	$9.00
A&M	390367-2	Missing You	CD5	Germany	1988	$9.00
A&M	S10Y3057	Missing You	CD3	Japan	1988	$12.00/$3.00
A&M	CDEE-474	Missing You	CD3	U.K.	1988	$9.00
A&M	CD 17640	Missing You	CDJ	U.S.	1988	$2.00
A&M	390392-3	Sailing Away	CD3	Germany	1989	$9.00
A&M	390405-3	Sailing Away	CD3	Germany	1989	$9.00
A&M	390392-2	Sailing Away	CD5	Germany	1989	$9.00
A&M	390395-2	Sailing Away	CD5	Germany	1989	$9.00
A&M	S10Y-3106	Sailing Away	CD3	Japan	1988	$12.00/$3.00
A&M	CDEE-494	Sailing Away	CD5	U.K.	1989	$9.00
A&M	AMCD-863	Seperate Tables	CD5	U.K.	1992	$9.00
A&M	AMCD-0066	Shine on	CD5	U.K.	1992	$9.00
A&M	390785-2	Simple Truth, The	CD5	Germany	1991	$9.00
A&M	RELCD-1	Simple Truth, The	CD5	U.K.	1991	$9.00
A&M	75021 7258 2	Simple Truth, The	CDJ	U.S.	1991	$2.00
A&M	S10Y-3066	Tender Hands	CD3	Japan	1988	$12.00/$3.00
A&M	CDEE-486	Tender Hands	CD3	U.K.	1988	$9.00
A&M	CD 17676	Tender Hands	CDJ	U.S.	1989	$2.00
A&M	390456-2	This Waiting Heart	CD5	Germany	1988	$9.00
A&M	390456-3	This Waiting Heart	CD3	Germany	1989	$9.00
A&M	390455-2	This Waiting Heart	CD5	Germany	1989	$9.00
A&M	AMCD-528	This Waiting Heart	CD5	U.K.	1988	$9.00
De Danann						
Full Length						
WEA	242205-2	Ballroom	LP	Germany		$15.00
De Grassi, Alex						
Full Length						
Windam Hill	WD-1018	Clockwork	LP/LB	U.S.†	1984	$14.00/$8.00
Windam Hill	WD-1030	Southern Exposure	LP/LB	U.S.†	1984	$14.00/$8.00
De Groot, Connie						
Singles						
BMG	663936	Win It All	CD5	Germany	1990	$9.00
De Havilland, Peter						
Full Length						
Atlantic	90653-2	Bois Du Bologne	LP/LB	U.S.		$14.00/$8.00
De Johnette, Jack						
Full Length						
MCA	42160-2	Zebra	LP/LB	U.S.		$14.00/$8.00
Singles						
MCA	CD45 18312	Jack It	CDJ	U.S.	1990	$2.00
Toshiba	TOCP-7431	Radio Tracks From the 5th World	CD3	Japan	1992	$12.00/$3.00
De La Soul						
Singles						
Eastwest	9031-75574-2	A Roller Skating Jam Named Saturdays	CD5	Germany	1991	$9.00
Tommy Boy	TBCD 990	A Roller Skating Jam Named Saturdays	CDJ	U.S.	1991	$2.00
Tommy Boy	586	Breakdawn	CDJ	U.S.	1993	$2.00
Tommy Boy	595	Ego Trippin	CDJ	U.S.	1993	$2.00
Polygram	876215-2	Eye Know	CD5	Canada	1991	$6.00
Big Life	BLR-13CD	Eye Know	CD5	U.K.	1989	$9.00
Big Life	BLR-64CD	Keepin' the Faith	CD5	U.K.	1991	$9.00
BCM	20387	Magic Number	CD5	Germany	1990	$9.00
Big Life	BLR-14CD	Magic Number	CD5	U.K.	1990	$9.00
BCM	20232	Me Myself and I	CD5	Germany	1989	$9.00
Big Life	BLR-7CD	Me Myself and I	CD5	U.K.	1989	$9.00
CBS	SRCS-5663	Millie Pulled a Pistol on Santa	CD3	Japan	1991	$12.00/$3.00
Tommy Boy	500	Millie Pulled a Pistol on Santa	CDJ	U.S.	1991	$2.00
Eastwest	9031-74416-2	Ring Ring Ring	CD5	Germany	1991	$9.00
Eastwest	9031-74695-2	Ring Ring Ring	CD5	Germany	1991	$9.00
Big Life	BLRD-42	Ring Ring Ring	CD5	U.K.	1991	$9.00
Tommy Boy	964	Ring Ring Ring	CDJ	U.S.	1991	$2.00
Tommy Boy	965	Ring Ring Ring	CDJ	U.S.	1991	$2.00
Tommy Boy	980	Ring Ring Ring	CDJ	U.S.	1991	$2.00
Eastwest	9031-75229-2	Roller Skating Jam Named Saturdays	CD5	Germany	1991	$9.00
Eastwest	9031-75230-2	Roller Skating Jam Named Saturdays	CD5	Germany	1991	$9.00
Tommy Boy	SRCS-5559	Roller Skating Jam Named Saturdays	CD3	Japan	1991	$12.00/$3.00
Big Life	BLRD-55	Roller Skating Jam Named Saturdays	CD5	U.K.	1991	$9.00
Polygram	876195-2	Say No Go	CD5	Canada	1989	$6.00
BCM	20295	Say No Go	CD5	Germany	1989	$9.00
Big Life	BLR-10CD	Say No Go	CD5	U.K.	1989	$9.00
		Say No Go	CDJ	U.S.	1989	$2.00
De Largo, Franco						
Full Length						
Bridge	100 009-2	Accordion Hits Vol.1	LP	Germany		$15.00
Bridge	100 0010-2	Accordion Hits Vol.2	LP	Germany		$15.00
De Lory, Donna						
Full Length						
		Special Sampler	DJ/Smplr	Japan		$30.00
Singles						
	OOGD-4002	Luck is an Angel	CD3	Japan		$13.00/$4.00
De Neufville, Greg						
Singles						
CBS	656916-2	Trust in Prayers	CD5	Germany	1991	$8.00
De Paul, Lindsey						
Singles						
	CEDC-00582	Oh I Do	CD3	Japan		$12.00/$4.00
De Piscopo, Tullio						
Singles						
ZYX	6159-8	Bottle, How Old Are You	CD5	Germany	1989	$6.00
De Shannon, Jackie						
Singles						
Aris	885824	Put a Little Love in Your Heart	CD3	Germany	1990	$9.00
De Versailles, Rene						
Singles						
[illegible]	[illegible]	Top Model	CD5	Germany	1988	$6.00
De Ville, Willy						
Full Length						
A&M	CD-5177	Miracle	LP/LB	U.S.		$14.00/$8.00
De Winkler, Torsten						
Full Length						
Optimism	3212	Mastertouch	LP/BP	U.S.		$12.00/$7.00
De-Lax						
Singles						
For Life	FLDF-10221	Tonight	CD3	Japan	1992	$12.00/$3.00
For Life	FLDF-09144	Voice of Love	CD3	Japan	1991	$12.00/$3.00
Deacon Blue						
Full Length						
Columbia	CK-47937	Fellow Hoodlums	LP/LB	U.S.		$15.00/$9.00
Columbia	CK-40915	Raintown	LP/LB	U.S.		$15.00/$9.00
Columbia	CK-47937	When the World Know's Your Name	LP/LB	U.S.		$14.00/$8.00
Singles						
CBS	CDDEAC-6	Chocolate Girl	CD5	U.K.	1988	$9.00
Columbia	657502-2	Closing Time	CD5	U.K.	1991	$9.00
Columbia	657673-2	Cover From the Sky	CD5	U.K.	1991	$9.00
CBS	CDDEAC-4	Dignity	CD5	U.K.	1988	$9.00
CBS		Dignity	CD5	U.K.	1988	$9.00
Columbia		Dignity	CDJ	U.S.	1988	$2.00
CBS	654912-3	Fergus Sings the Blues	CD3	Germany	1989	$9.00
Columbia	CDDEAC-9	Fergus Sings the Blues	CD5	U.K.	1989	$9.00
CBS		Hang Your Head	CD5	U.K.		$9.00
CBS		Hang Your Head	CD5	U.K.		$9.00
	Second version.					
CBS		I Was Right and You Were Wrong	CD5	U.K.		$9.00
CBS		I Was Right and You Were Wrong	CD5	U.K.		$9.00
	Second version.					
CBS	656169-3	I'll Never Fall in Love Again	CD3	Germany	1990	$9.00
Columbia	CDDEAC-12	I'll Never Fall in Love Again	CD5	U.K.	1990	$9.00
CBS	655212-3	Love and Regret	CD3	Germany	1989	$9.00
Columbia	CDDEAC-10	Love and Regret	CD5	U.K.	1989	$9.00
Columbia	DEACC-10	Love and Regret	CD5	U.K.	1989	$9.00
CBS		Only the Tender	CD5	U.K.	1993	$9.00
CBS	655525-2	Queen of the New Year	CD5	Germany	1990	$9.00
Columbia	CDDEAC-11	Queen of the New Year	CD5	U.K.	1990	$9.00
		Radio On	CDJ	U.K.	1995	$12.00
CBS	653035-3	Real Gone Kid	CD3	Germany	1989	$9.00
Columbia	CDDEAC-7	Real Gone Kid	CD5	U.K.	1989	$9.00
Columbia	CSK 1801	Real Gone Kid	CDJ	U.S.	1989	$2.00
Columbia	657302-2	Twist & Shout	CD5	Germany	1991	$9.00
Columbia	657302-2	Twist & Shout	CD5	U.K.	1991	$9.00
Columbia		Twist & Shout	CDJ	U.S.	1989	$2.00
Columbia	CDDEAC-8	Wages Day	CD5	U.K.	1989	$9.00
CBS	CDDEAC-5	When Will You Make My Telephone Ring	CD5	U.K.	1988	$9.00
CBS	CPDEAC-5	When Will You Make My Telephone Ring	CD5	U.K.	1988	$10.00
Columbia	CSK 1215	When Will You Make My Telephone Ring	CDJ	U.S.	1988	$2.00
Columbia	658973-2	Will We Be Lovers	CD5	U.K.	1993	$9.00
Columbia	656893-2	Your Swaying Arms	CD5	Germany	1991	$9.00
Columbia	656893-2	Your Swaying Arms	CD5	U.K.	1991	$9.00
Columbia	CSK 4070	Your Swaying Arms	CDJ	U.S.	1991	$2.00
Columbia	658786-2	Your Town	CD5	U.K.	1992	$9.00
Columbia	CSK 77067	Your Town	CDJ	U.S.	1993	$2.00
Dead Can Dance						
Full Length						
4AD		Aion	LP/LB	U.S.		$15.00/$10.00
4AD	404	Dead Can Dance	LP/LB	U.S.		$15.00/$10.00
		Into the Labyrinth	DJ/LP	U.S.		$15.00
	CD in special digipak.					
4AD		Reissues	DJ/5CD	U.S.	1994	$55.00
	5 newly reissued CDs in slipcase.					
4AD		Sampler	DJ/Smplr	U.S.	1994	$25.00
4AD	808	Serpent's Egg	LP/LB	U.S.		$15.00/$10.00
		Spirit Chaser	DJ/LP	U.S.	1996	$15.00
4AD	512	Spleen and Ideal	LP/LB	U.S.		$15.00/$10.00
Sony		Starbox	LP	Japan	1993	$30.00
4AD	45769-2	Toward the Within	DJ/LP	U.S.	1994	$15.00
4AD		Within the Realm of a Dying Sun	LP/LB	U.S.		$15.00/$9.00
Singles						
4AD		American Dreaming	CDJ	U.S.	1995	$6.00
4AD	PRO-CD-6700	Carnival is Over	CDJ	U.S.	1994	$6.00
Dead End						
Full Length						
Restless	72334	Shambara	DJ/LP	U.S.		$8.00
Singles						
BMG	B10D-133	So Sweet So Lonely	CD3	Japan	1989	$12.00/$3.00

Label	Catalog Number	Title	Type	Country	Year	Longbox/Value

Dead Horse
Full Length

Label	Catalog Number	Title	Type	Country	Year	Longbox/Value
Warner Brothers	26716	Peaceful Death & Pretty	LP/LB	U.S.		$14.00/$8.00

Dead Hot Workshop
Full Length

Label	Catalog Number	Title	Type	Country	Year	Longbox/Value
		Bottle Rockets, The	DJ/LP	U.S.		$12.00

Singles

Label	Catalog Number	Title	Type	Country	Year	Longbox/Value
Atlantic	92493	River Otis	CD5	U.S.	1994	$5.00

Dead Kennedys
Singles

Label	Catalog Number	Title	Type	Country	Year	Longbox/Value
Efa	CD-30160	Holiday in Cambodia	CD5	Germany	1988	$10.00
Cherry Red	CDCHERRY-13	Holiday in Cambodia	CD5	U.K.	1988	$10.00
Efa	CD-30166	Kill the Poor	CD5	Germany	1988	$10.00
Cherry Red	CDCHERRY-16	Kill the Poor	CD5	U.K.	1988	$10.00
Efa	CD-301601	Too Drunk To F**ck	CD5	Germany	1988	$10.00
Cherry Red	CDCHERRY-14	Too Drunk To F**ck	CD5	U.K.	1988	$10.00

Dead Milkmen
Singles

Label	Catalog Number	Title	Type	Country	Year	Longbox/Value
Hollywood	10191	Conspiracy Song, The	CDJ	U.S.	1992	$2.00
Enigma	EPRO-316	Dollar Signs in Her Eyes	CDJ	U.S.	1990	$3.00
Hollywood	61409-2	If I Had a Gun	CD5	U.S.	1992	$5.00
Hollywood		If I Had a Gun	CDJ	U.S.	1995	$3.00
Enigma	EPRO-282	Methodist Coloring Book	CDJ	U.S.	1990	$3.00
Enigma	EPRO-173	Punk Rock Girl	CDJ	U.S.	1900	$6.00
Hollywood	10141	Secret of Life, The	CDJ	U.S.	1992	$2.00
Enigma	EPRO-180	Smokin' Banana Peels	CDJ	U.S.	1989	$3.00

Dead Moon
Full Length

Label	Catalog Number	Title	Type	Country	Year	Longbox/Value
SBK	93249	Dead On	LP/LB	U.S.		$14.00/$8.00

Dead or Alive
Full Length

Label	Catalog Number	Title	Type	Country	Year	Longbox/Value
		Rip It Up Live	LD	U.S.		$25.00
Epic	ESCA-5864	Starbox	LTD/LP	Japan		$30.00
Columbia	CD-46420	Youthquake	LP	Germany		$25.00
		Youthquake	LD	U.S.		$70.00
Epic	EK-40119	Youthquake	LP/LB	U.S.†	1985	$30.00/$27.00

Singles

Label	Catalog Number	Title	Type	Country	Year	Longbox/Value
Epic	ESDA-7002	Baby Don't Say Goodbye	CD3	Japan	1989	$12.00/$3.00
CBS	BURNSC-6	Baby Don't Say Goodbye	CD5	U.K.	1989	$9.00
CBS	ESDA-7065	Been Gone 2 Long	CD3	Japan	1991	$12.00/$3.00
Epic	108P-3069	Come Home With Me Baby	CD3	Japan	1989	$12.00/$3.00
Epic	128P-3070	Come Home With Me Baby	CD3	Japan	1989	$12.00/$3.00
CBS	BURNSC-5	Come Home With Me Baby	CD5	U.K.	1989	$9.00
Epic	ESK 1637	Come Home With Me Baby	CDJ	U.S.	1989	$2.00
Epic	108P-3056	Give It Back	CD3	Japan	1989	$12.00/$3.00
Epic	128P-8016	Give It Back	CD3	Japan	1989	$12.00/$3.00
Epic	ESCA 6215	Nukleopatra	CD5	Japan		$25.00
Epic	ESCA 7162	Sex Drive	CD3	Japan		$12.00/$4.00
Epic	ESDA-7077	Total Stranger	CD3	Japan	1991	$12.00/$3.00
Epic	108P-3037	Turn Around and Count Ten	CD3	Japan	1988	$12.00/$3.00
Epic	128P-8010	Turn Around and Count Ten	CD3	Japan	1988	$12.00/$3.00
CBS	BURNSC-4	Turn Around and Count Ten	CD5	U.K.	1988	$12.00
		Your Sweetness	DJ/CD3	Japan		$45.00/$25.00

deadBEAT Honeymooners
Singles

Label	Catalog Number	Title	Type	Country	Year	Longbox/Value
Anthem	PR 13	Dial L.O.V.E.	CDJ	Canada		$5.00
Anthem	PR 15	King of the World	CDJ	Canada		$5.00

Deadeye Dick
Singles

Label	Catalog Number	Title	Type	Country	Year	Longbox/Value
Ichiban Records	232	New Age Girl	CD5	U.S.	1994	$5.00

Deadguy
Singles

Label	Catalog Number	Title	Type	Country	Year	Longbox/Value
	12	Work Ethic	CD5	U.S.	1994	$5.00

Dean, Billy
Full Length

Label	Catalog Number	Title	Type	Country	Year	Longbox/Value
		Country Concert	RS	U.S.	1996	$50.00

2 CD set. Airdate: 7/15/96.

Singles

Label	Catalog Number	Title	Type	Country	Year	Longbox/Value
SBK	04627	If There Hadn't Been You	CDJ	U.S.	1992	$2.00

Dean, Hazel
Full Length

Label	Catalog Number	Title	Type	Country	Year	Longbox/Value
Bellaphon	288-07-089	Heart First	LP	Germany		$15.00

Dean, Jimmy
Full Length

Label	Catalog Number	Title	Type	Country	Year	Longbox/Value
Columbia	CK-9285	Greatest Hits	LP/LB	U.S.		$15.00/$9.00

Dean, Paul
Singles

Label	Catalog Number	Title	Type	Country	Year	Longbox/Value
Lisson	DOLED-12	Love Pains	CD5	U.K.	1989	$9.00
EMI	202715-2	Maybe	CD5	Germany	1988	$9.00
EMI	CDEM-62	Maybe	CD5	U.K.	1988	$9.00
Columbia	CSK 1384	Sword & Stone	CDJ	U.S.	1989	$2.00
EMI	202880-2	Turn It Into Love	CD5	Germany	1989	$9.00
EMI	202879-2	Turn It Into Love	CD5	Germany	1989	$9.00
Toshiba	XP10-2047	Turn It Into Love	CD3	Japan	1989	$12.00/$3.00
EMI	CDEM-71	Turn It Into Love	CD5	U.K.	1989	$9.00
EMI	202430-2	Who's Leaving You	CD5	Germany	1988	$9.00
Toshiba	XP10-2017	Who's Leaving You	CD3	Japan	1988	$12.00/$3.00

Dean, Trent
Singles

Label	Catalog Number	Title	Type	Country	Year	Longbox/Value
Chrysalis	DPRO-23655	Livin' It Up	CDJ	U.S.	1991	$2.00

Dear Boy
Singles

Label	Catalog Number	Title	Type	Country	Year	Longbox/Value
Pinnacle	2001-CDS	Grey Clouds	CD5	U.K.	1992	$8.00

Dear Mr. President
Full Length

Label	Catalog Number	Title	Type	Country	Year	Longbox/Value
Atlantic	81880-2	Dear Mr. President	LP/LB	U.S.		$14.00/$8.00

Death Angel
Singles

Label	Catalog Number	Title	Type	Country	Year	Longbox/Value
Geffen	PRO-CD-4171	A Room With a View	CDJ	U.S.	1990	$2.00

Death Row
Full Length

Label	Catalog Number	Title	Type	Country	Year	Longbox/Value
Noise	44453	Deception Ignored	LP/BP	U.S.		$14.00/$8.00

Deb, Debbie
Singles

Label	Catalog Number	Title	Type	Country	Year	Longbox/Value
		There's a Party Goin' on	CD5	U.S.	1995	$5.00

Debarge, El
Full Length

Label	Catalog Number	Title	Type	Country	Year	Longbox/Value
Motown	ZD-72552	All This Love/Special Way	LP	Germany		$12.00
Motown	ZD-72441	El Debarge	LP	Germany		$12.00
Motown	GORD-6181	El Debarge	LP/BP	U.S.		$14.00/$8.00
Motown	GORD-6181	El Debarge	LP/BP	U.S.†		$14.00/$8.00
Motown	WD-72449	Greatest Hits	LP	Germany		$12.00
Motown	GORD-6123	Greatest Hits	LP/BP	U.S.		$14.00/$8.00
Motown	MOTD-6026	Rhythm of the Night	LP/BP	U.S.		$14.00/$8.00
Warner Brothers	PRO-CD-5416	Words And Music	DJ/Intvw	U.S.	1992	$12.00

Singles

Label	Catalog Number	Title	Type	Country	Year	Longbox/Value
King	K10Y-20020	Dance All Night	CD3	Japan	1989	$12.00/$3.00
Warner Brothers	9 40357-2	My Heart Belongs To You	CD5	U.S.	1992	$4.00
Motown	ZD-41696	Real Love	CD5	Germany	1989	$9.00
Motown	R10M-103	Real Love	CD3	Japan	1989	$12.00/$3.00
Motown	ZD-42686	Real Love	CD5	U.K.	1989	$9.00
Motown	R10M-125	Somebody Loves You	CD3	Japan	1989	$12.00/$3.00

Decadance
Singles

Label	Catalog Number	Title	Type	Country	Year	Longbox/Value
BMG	CDGLOBE-117	Decadance	CD5	U.K.	1992	$9.00

Decaro, Nick
Singles

Label	Catalog Number	Title	Type	Country	Year	Longbox/Value
Victor	VIDL-39	Silent Night Lonely Night	CD3	Japan	1990	$12.00/$3.00

Declaration
Singles

Label	Catalog Number	Title	Type	Country	Year	Longbox/Value
Supreme	CDSUPE-183	Declaration	CD5	U.K.	1991	$8.00

Dee, Kiki
Full Length

Label	Catalog Number	Title	Type	Country	Year	Longbox/Value
Columbia	CDSCX-6701	Angel Eyes	LP	U.K.		$20.00

Dee-Lite
Singles

Label	Catalog Number	Title	Type	Country	Year	Longbox/Value
Elektra/Asylum	66172	Call Me	CD5	U.S.	1994	$5.00
Elektra	PRCD 8329-2	E.S.P.	CDJ	U.S.	1990	$2.00
Elektra	7559-66554-2	Good Beat	CD5	Germany	1991	$9.00
Elektra	WMD5-4067	Good Beat	CD3	Japan	1991	$13.00/$4.00
Elektra	EKR-122CD	Good Beat	CD5	U.K.	1991	$9.00
Elektra	PRCD 8363-2	Good Beat	CDJ	U.S.	1991	$2.00
Elektra	7559-66613-2	Grove is in the Heart	CD5	Germany	1990	$10.00
Pioneer	WPDP-6249	Grove is in the Heart	CD3	Japan	1990	$13.00/$4.00
Elektra	EKR-114CD	Grove is in the Heart	CD5	U.K.	1990	$10.00
Elektra	PRCD 8214-2	Grove is in the Heart	CDJ	U.S.	1990	$3.00
Elektra	PR 8198-2-8	Grove is in the Heart	CDJ	U.S.	1990	$6.00

2 CDset with 2nd CD by Heart Throbs.

Label	Catalog Number	Title	Type	Country	Year	Longbox/Value
Elektra	966577-2	How Do You Say Love	CD5	Germany	1991	$9.00
Elektra	EKR-118CD	How Do You Say Love	CD5	U.K.	1991	$9.00
Elektra	PRCD 8575-2	I Had a Dream I Was Falling	CDJ	U.S.	1992	$2.00
		Picnic in the Summertime	CD5	U.K.		$10.00
		Picnic in the Summertime	CD5	U.K.		$10.00

Second version.

Label	Catalog Number	Title	Type	Country	Year	Longbox/Value
Elektra	PRCD 9009-2	Picnic in the Summertime	CDJ	U.S.		$3.00
Elektra	7559-66599-2	Power of Love	CD5	Germany	1990	$9.00
Elektra	EKR-117CD	Power of Love	CD5	U.K.	1990	$9.00
Elektra	66592-2	Power of Love	CD5	U.S.	1990	$5.00
Elektra	PRCD 8275-2	Power of Love	CDJ	U.S.	1990	$2.00
Elektra	WMD5-4106	Runaway	CD3	Japan	1992	$12.00/$3.00
Elektra	EKR-148CD	Runaway	CD5	U.K.	1992	$9.00
Elektra	66422-2	Runaway	CD5	U.S.	1992	$5.00
Elektra	PRCD 8581-2	Runaway	CDJ	U.S.	1992	$2.00
Elektra	66368-2	Thank You Everybody	CD5	U.S.	1992	$2.00

Dee-O
Singles

Label	Catalog Number	Title	Type	Country	Year	Longbox/Value
Capitol	DPRO-79568	Sure Lookin'	CDJ	U.S.	1990	$2.00

Deele
Singles

Label	Catalog Number	Title	Type	Country	Year	Longbox/Value
Solar	70030	Imagination	CDJ	U.S.	1993	$2.00
Victor	VDPS-1012	Two Occasions	CD3	Japan	1988	$12.00/$3.00

Deep
Singles

Label	Catalog Number	Title	Type	Country	Year	Longbox/Value
Intercord	825 786	Hallelujah	CD5	Germany	1990	$8.00
Oval	OVAL-108CD	Pleasure and the Pain	CD5	U.K.	1993	$9.00
Pinnacle	UFO-45004CD	We Came to Love	CD5	U.K.	1992	$8.00

Deep Blue Something
Singles

Label	Catalog Number	Title	Type	Country	Year	Longbox/Value
		Breakfast At Tiffany's	CD5	U.K.	1996	$10.00

Deep C
Singles

Label	Catalog Number	Title	Type	Country	Year	Longbox/Value
Polygram	MAGCD-4	African Reign	CD5	U.K.	1991	$8.00
Polygram	MAGCD-10	Chill to the Panic	CD5	U.K.	1991	$8.00

Deep Forest
Singles

Label	Catalog Number	Title	Type	Country	Year	Longbox/Value
		Boheme	CDJ	France	1995	$15.00
		Bohemian Ballet	CDJ	U.S.		$3.00
		Creation, The	CD5	U.K.	1994	$10.00
		Creation, The	CD5	U.K.	1994	$10.00

Second version.

Label	Catalog Number	Title	Type	Country	Year	Longbox/Value
		Deep Forest	CD5	U.K.		$10.00
		Deep Forest	CD5	U.K.		$10.00

Second version.

Label	Catalog Number	Title	Type	Country	Year	Longbox/Value
Epic		Forest Hymn	CDJ	U.S.	1994	$2.00
Columbia		Forest Hymn	CDJ	U.S.	1995	$3.00
Columbia	77901	Marta's Song	CD5	U.S.	1995	$5.00
		Savanna Dance	CD5	U.K.		$10.00
		Savanna Dance	CD5	U.K.		$10.00

Second version.

Label	Catalog Number	Title	Type	Country	Year	Longbox/Value
Columbia	658877-2	Sweet Lullaby	CD5	U.K.	1992	$8.00
Epic	49K 74919	Sweet Lullaby	CD5	U.S.	1993	$4.00

Label	Catalog Number	Title	Type	Country	Year	Longbox Value / Value

Deep Jam

Singles

Label	Catalog Number	Title	Type	Country	Year	Longbox Value / Value
ZYX	6544-8	When Boys Talk	CD5	Germany	1991	$6.00

Deep, Mobb

Singles

Label	Catalog Number	Title	Type	Country	Year	Longbox Value / Value
RCA	64315	Shook Ones Pt. Ii	CD5	U.S.	1994	$5.00

Deep Purple

Full Length

Label	Catalog Number	Title	Type	Country	Year	Longbox Value / Value
Metal Blade	PRO-CD-6454-2	Alice Cooper/Deep Purple Sampler	DJ/Smplr	U.S.	1990	$15.00
		Battle Rages On, The	LTD/LP	Japan		$25.00
Limited first pressing.						
BBC Radio		BBC Classic Tracks	RS	U.S.	1991	$25.00
Airdate: 11/18/91.						
BBC Radio		BBC Classic Tracks	RS	U.S.	1991	$25.00
Airdate: 2/11/91.						
BBC Radio		BBC Classic Tracks	RS	U.S.	1992	$25.00
Airdate: 4/27/92.						
BBC Radio		BBC Classic Tracks	RS	U.S.	1992	$25.00
Airdate: 9/7/92.						
BBC Radio		BBC Classic Tracks	RS	U.S.	1993	$25.00
Airdate: 8/9/93.						
Passport	PBCD-3607	Book Of Taliesyn	LP/LB	U.S.		$18.00/$14.00
EMI		Book Of Taliesyn, Deep Purple, Shades	LTD/LP	U.K.	1994	$35.00
3 CD boxed set.						
Warner Brothers	26454	Come Taste the Band	LP/LB	U.S.		$15.00/$9.00
Passport	PBCD-3608	Deep Purple	LP/LB	U.S.		$18.00/$14.00
EMI	834019 2 5	Deep Purple in Rock: Anniversary Edition	LTD/LP	U.K.	1995	$23.00
Mercury	831318-2	House Of Blue Light	LP/BP	U.S.		$14.00/$8.00
Westwood One		In Concert	RS	U.S.	1992	$70.00
2 CD set, Airdate: 5/29/92						
Album Network		In the Studio (Machine Head)	RS	U.S.	1988	$25.00
Airdate: 8/22/88.						
Album Network		In the Studio (Machine Head)	RS	U.S.	1991	$20.00
Airdate: 2/11/91.						
EMI		Machine Head	LTD/LP	U.K.	1997	$35.00
Limited edition centennial CD edition housed in a slip case with a special 100 anniversary booklet.						
Warner Brothers	26455	Made in Europe	LP/LB	U.S.		$15.00/$9.00
Westwood One		Off the Record	RS	U.S.	1993	$40.00
Airdate: 10/4/93.						
Polygram	823777-2	Perfect Strangers	LP/BP	U.S.†	1985	$14.00/$8.00
Spectrum		Progression	LP/BP	U.S.		$14.00/$8.00
Passport	PBCD-3606	Shades of	LP/LB	U.S.		$18.00/$14.00
Warner Brothers	26456	Stormbringer	LP/LB	U.S.		$15.00/$9.00
Media America		Up Close	RS	U.S.	1989	$40.00
2 CD set.						
Media America		Up Close	RS	U.S.	1991	$40.00
2 CD set.						
Polygram	080 390-9	Video Singles, The	8"LD	Germany	1987	$15.00

Singles

Label	Catalog Number	Title	Type	Country	Year	Longbox Value / Value
	BVCP-650	Anya	DJ/CD3	Japan		$50.00
Polydor		Anybody's Daughter	CDJ	France	1995	$25.00
Polydor		Anybody's Daughter	CDJ	Germany	1995	$25.00
		Battle Rages on	CDJ	U.K.	1994	$20.00
Warner Brothers	PRO-CD-6359	Battle Rages on	CDJ	U.S.	1994	$3.00
EMI		Black Night	CD5	U.K.	1995	$11.00
RCA	3030-2	Fire in the Basement	CDJ	U.S.	1990	$3.00
	WPDP-6342	Highway Star	DJ/CD3	Japan		$25.00
Polydor	P13P-37002	Hush	CD3	Japan	1988	$13.00/$4.00
Polydor	P10P30015	Hush	CD3	Japan	1988	$13.00/$4.00
Polydor	PZCD-4	Hush	CD5	U.K.	1988	$10.00
Mercury	CDP 16	Hush	CDJ	U.S.	1988	$7.00
RCA	PD-49248	King of Dreams	CD5	Germany	1990	$10.00
RCA	BVDP-23	King of Dreams	CD3	U.K.	1990	$10.00
RCA	PD-49248	King of Dreams	CD5	U.K.	1990	$10.00
RCA	2703-2-RDJ	King of Dreams	CDJ	U.S.	1990	$3.00
RCA	2744-2-RDJ	King of Dreams	CDJ	U.S.	1990	$3.00
RCA	PD-49226	Love Conquers All	CD5	Germany	1991	$10.00
RCA	PD-49226	Love Conquers All	CD5	U.K.	1991	$10.00
RCA	2810-2-RDJ	Love Conquers All	CDJ	U.S.	1991	$3.00
RCA		Smoke on the Water	CD5	U.K.	1993	$10.00
		Sometimes I Feel Like Screaming	CDJ	U.K.		$12.00

Deep Thought

Singles

Label	Catalog Number	Title	Type	Country	Year	Longbox Value / Value
ZYX	8817-8	Kennedy	CD5	Germany	1990	$6.00

Deere, Darren

Singles

Label	Catalog Number	Title	Type	Country	Year	Longbox Value / Value
Eternal	YZ-596CD	Just Watch Me	CD5	U.K.	1991	$8.00

Dees, Sam

Singles

Label	Catalog Number	Title	Type	Country	Year	Longbox Value / Value
RCA	PD-43140	After All	CD5	U.K.	1989	$8.00

Def Boys

Singles

Label	Catalog Number	Title	Type	Country	Year	Longbox Value / Value
ZYX	6364-8	Swing	CD5	Germany	1990	$6.00

Def Con 4

Full Length

Label	Catalog Number	Title	Type	Country	Year	Longbox Value / Value
Warner Brothers	9 26049-2	Def Con 4	LP/LB	U.S.		$14.00/$8.00

Def Fx

Singles

Label	Catalog Number	Title	Type	Country	Year	Longbox Value / Value
Phantom	PHMCD-8	Water	CD5	U.K.	1991	$8.00

Def Jeff

Singles

Label	Catalog Number	Title	Type	Country	Year	Longbox Value / Value
Aris	884024	Dropping Rhythms on	CD5	Germany	1990	$8.00
		Give It Here	CDJ	U.S.		$2.00

Def Leppard

Full Length

Label	Catalog Number	Title	Type	Country	Year	Longbox Value / Value
Phonogram	DEFCD1992	1992 CD Sampler	DJ/Smplr	U.K.	1992	$20.00
Bludgeon Riffola	PHCR-16001/2	Adrenalize	LTD/LP	Japan	1992	$35.00
Special 12 track edition.						
Phonogram		Adrenalize	LTD/LP	U.K.	1992	$20.00
Special Digipak.						
Mercury	838606-2	Collector's Set	LP	U.K.	1989	$70.00
4 CD Set.						
Polygram		Edition Limited Collector	DJ/Smplr	France	1995	$25.00
Phonogram	28PD-524	High 'n Dry	LTD/LP	Japan	1981	$50.00
Picture disc CD.						
Bludgeon Riffola3	2PD-1004	Hysteria	LTD/LP	Japan	1987	$50.00
Picture disc CD.						
Polygram		Hysteria	LD	U.K.	1988	$50.00
Polygram	080359-2	Hysteria	LD	U.S.	1988	$50.00
Westwood One		In Concert	RS	U.S.	1996	$75.00
Airdate: 8/12/96.						
Album Network		In the Studio (Pyromania)	RS	U.S.	1988	$30.00
Airdate: 9/19/88.						
Album Network		In the Studio (Pyromania)	RS	U.S.	1991	$30.00
Airdate: 2/4/91.						
Mercury	SACD 508	Interview With Joe Elliott	DJ/Intvw	U.S.	1992	$15.00
Westwood One		Off the Record	RS	U.S.	1994	$30.00
Airdate: 1/31/94.						
Phonogram	28PD-525	On Through the Night	LTD/LP	U.S.	1980	$35.00
Picture disc CD.						
Vertigo	PPD-2006	Pyromania	LTD/LP	Japan	1983	$35.00
Special Digipak.						
Vertigo	28PD-523	Pyromania	LTD/LP	Japan	1983	$50.00
Picture disc CD.						
Mercury	810308-2	Pyromania	LP/BP	U.S.†	1984	$14.00/$8.00
Bludgeon	DL18	Retroactive	LP	France	1993	$35.00
2 CD set.						
Vertigo		Rock It	DJ/Smplr	Canada	1994	$40.00
Bludgeon Riffola	DL 1989	Rock of Ages Sampler	DJ/Smplr	Germany	1990	$2.00/$25.00
Polygram		Slang	DJ/LP	U.K.	1996	$20.00
Media America		Up Close	RS	U.S.	1989	$50.00
2 CD set.						
Phonogram		Vault	LTD/LP	Canada	1995	$32.00
2 CD set.						
Polygram		Vault	DJ/LP	France	1995	$80.00
Promo CD in plastic sleeve with miniature lock.						
Phonogram		Vault	LTD/LP	U.K.	1995	$32.00
2 CD Set.						
Mercury	528815	Vault	LTD/LP	U.S.	1995	$17.00
CD and jewel box in slipcase.						

Singles

Label	Catalog Number	Title	Type	Country	Year	Longbox Value / Value
		Action	CD5	U.K.	1993	$10.00
	Def Leppard	Action	CD5	U.K.	1993	$10.00
Second version.						
Phonogram	LEPCD-1	Animal	CD5	U.K.	1987	$30.00
Phonogram	870239-2	Armageddon It	CD5	Germany	1988	$15.00
Phonogram	PPDM-1	Armageddon It	CD3	Japan	1988	$15.00/$4.00
Phonogram	LEPCD 4	Armageddon It	CD5	U.K.	1988	$15.00
Bludgeon Riffola	LEPCD-4	Armageddon It	CD5	U.S.	1988	$20.00
Mercury	CDP 1059	Desert Song	CDJ	U.S.	1993	$7.00
Mercury	CDP 765	Elected	CDJ	U.S.	1992	$7.00
Vertigo	4220021512	Have You Ever Needed Someone So Bad	CD5	Canada	1992	$10.00
Phonogram		Have You Ever Needed Someone So Bad	CDJ	France	1992	$20.00
Phonogram	PHDR-121	Have You Ever Needed Someone So Bad	CD3	Japan	1992	$15.00/$4.00
Phonogram	PHCR-8019	Have You Ever Needed Someone So Bad	CD5	Japan	1992	$16.00
Phonogram	LEPCD 8	Have You Ever Needed Someone So Bad	CD5	U.K.	1992	$15.00
Mercury	CDP 722	Have You Ever Needed Someone So Bad	CDJ	U.S.	1992	$3.00
Mercury	PHCR-8022	Heaven Is	CD5	Japan	1992	$16.00
Mercury	LEPCD 9	Heaven Is	CD5	U.K.	1993	$12.00
Polygram		Hysteria	CD5	Canada	1989	$20.00
Bludgeon Riffola	870004-2	Hysteria	CD5	Germany	1988	$25.00
Bludgeon Riffola	LEPCD-3	Hysteria	CD5	U.K.	1988	$25.00
Vertigo		Let's Get Rocked	CD5	Canada	1992	$12.00
Phonogram	PHCR-8013	Let's Get Rocked	CD5	Japan	1992	$16.00
Phonogram	DEF CD-7	Let's Get Rocked	CD5	U.K.	1992	$100.00
Special display box to hold 3 additional CD5's.						
Mercury	CDP 641	Let's Get Rocked	CDJ	U.S.	1992	$6.00
Phonogram	870402-2	Love Bites	CD5	Germany	1988	$10.00
Mercury	10PD-4	Love Bites	CD3	Japan	1988	$15.00/$4.00
Phonogram	LEPCD 5	Love Bites	CD5	U.K.	1988	$10.00
Phonogram	LEPCD 5	Love Bites	CD5	U.K.	1988	$18.00
Vertigo		Make Love Like a Man	CD5	Canada	1992	$12.00
Phonogram		Make Love Like a Man	CDJ	France	1992	$22.00
Phonogram	866991-2	Make Love Like a Man	CD5	Germany	1992	$10.00
Phonogram	PHDR-110	Make Love Like a Man	CD3	Japan	1992	$15.00/$4.00
Phonogram	PHCR-8015	Make Love Like a Man	CD5	Japan	1992	$16.00
Phonogram	LEPCB 7	Make Love Like a Man	CD5	U.K.	1992	$10.00
Mercury	CDP 705	Make Love Like a Man	CDJ	U.S.	1992	$2.00
Mercury		Miss You in a Heartbeat	CD5	U.K.	1994	$13.00
Mercury	CDP 1090	Miss You in a Heartbeat	CDJ	U.S.	1994	$7.00
Phonogram	872595-2	Pour Some Sugar on Me	CD5	Germany	1988	$12.00
Phonogram	872733-2	Pour Some Sugar on Me	CD5	Germany	1988	$12.00
Phonogram		Rock of Ages	CDV	Germany	1988	$45.00
Phonogram	LEPCD 6	Rocket	CD5	Germany	1988	$10.00
Phonogram		Rocket	CDV	Germany	1988	$45.00
Phonogram	PPDM-2	Rocket	CD3	Japan	1988	$15.00/$4.00
Phonogram	LEPCD 6	Rocket	CD5	U.K.	1988	$25.00
Mercury	872 614-2	Rocket	CD3	U.S.	1988	$6.00/$3.00
Mercury	LEPDD15	Slang	CD5	U.K.	1996	$10.00
Mercury		Slang-ROM	CD5	Japan	1996	$27.00
Enhanced CD.						
Phonogram		Tonight	CD5	Germany	1993	$12.00
Phonogram	PHCR-8032	Tonight	CD5	Japan	1992	$16.00
		Tonight	CD5	U.K.		$10.00
		Tonight	CD5	U.K.		$10.00
Second version.						
Mercury	CDP 802	Tonight	CDJ	U.S.	1992	$6.00
Mercury	CDP 858	Tonight	CDJ	U.S.	1992	$6.00
Mercury		Two Steps Behind	CDJ	France	1993	$25.00
With press kit in folder.						
Mercury		Two Steps Behind	CD5	Germany	1994	$20.00
2 CD5 set.						
Mercury		Two Steps Behind	CD5	U.K.	1993	$10.00
Mercury		Two Steps Behind	CD5	U.K.	1993	$12.00
Mercury	CDP 1052	Two Steps Behind	CDJ	U.S.	1993	$6.00
Columbia	CSK 5235	Two Steps Behind	CDJ	U.S.	1993	$6.00
Second version.						
Mercury		When Love and Hate Collide	CDJ	Australia	1995	$18.00
Vertigo		When Love and Hate Collide	CD5	Canada	1995	$10.00
Phonogram	PHCR-8338	When Love and Hate Collide	CD5	Japan		$25.00
Mercury	PHCR-8338	When Love and Hate Collide	CD5	Japan	1995	$22.00
Phonogram		When Love and Hate Collide	CD5	U.K.	1995	$10.00
Phonogram		When Love and Hate Collide	CD5	U.K.	1995	$10.00
Second version.						
Phonogram	LEPCJ 14	When Love and Hate Collide	CDJ	U.K.	1995	$10.00
Mercury	CDP 02	Women	CDJ	U.S.	1987	$75.00
Mercury	CDP 02	Women	CDJ	U.S.	1987	$120.00
Phonogram		Work It Out	CD5	Japan	1996	$20.00
Phonogram		Work It Out	CD5	U.K.	1996	$10.00
Phonogram		Work It Out	CD5	U.K.	1996	$10.00
Second version.						

Def Tones

Singles

Label	Catalog Number	Title	Type	Country	Year	Longbox Value / Value
		Bushwack	CDJ	U.S.	1992	$2.00

Definition FX

Singles

Label	Catalog Number	Title	Type	Country	Year	Longbox Value / Value
RCA	62536-2	Something Inside	CD5	U.S.	1993	$4.00

Definition Of Sound

Full Length

Label	Catalog Number	Title	Type	Country	Year	Longbox Value / Value
		Lick, The	LP/LB	U.S.		$12.00/$8.00
Cardiac	8002	Love & Life	LP/BP	U.S.		$14.00/$8.00

Singles

Label	Catalog Number	Title	Type	Country	Year	Longbox Value / Value
Circa	YRCD-70	Dream Girl	CD5	U.K.	1991	$8.00
Circa	YRCG-80	Moira Jane's Cafe	CD5	U.K.	1992	$8.00
Cardian	4023	Moira Jane's Cafe	CD5	U.S.	1992	$2.00
BMG	663641	Now Is Tomorrow	CD5	Germany	1990	$8.00
Circa	YRCD-54	Now Is Tomorrow	CD5	U.K.	1990	$8.00
Circa	YRCD-61	Wear Your Love Like Heaven	CD5	U.K.	1991	$8.00
Virgin	VJDP-10203	What Are You Under	CD3	Japan	1993	$12.00/$3.00
Circa	YRCD-95	What Are You Under	CD5	U.K.	1992	$8.00
Capitol	C2 12616	What Are You Under	CD5	U.S.	1992	$5.00

Definitive Two

Singles

Label	Catalog Number	Title	Type	Country	Year	Longbox Value / Value
BMG	7432112473-2	I'm Stronger	CD5	U.K.	1992	$8.00

Defrancesco, Joey

Full Length

Label	Catalog Number	Title	Type	Country	Year	Longbox Value / Value
Columbia	CSK 3045	Excerpt From "The Story Thus Far..."	DJ/Smplr	U.S.	1991	$5.00

DeFranco, Buddy

Full Length

Label	Catalog Number	Title	Type	Country	Year	Longbox Value / Value
Mosaic	MD4-117	Complete Verve Recordings	LP	U.S.		$60.00
4 CD set.						

Defunkt

Full Length

Label	Catalog Number	Title	Type	Country	Year	Longbox Value / Value
Aris	881327	Forget the Funk	LP	Germany		$15.00

Singles

Label	Catalog Number	Title	Type	Country	Year	Longbox Value / Value
Enemy	EMY 140	See Through	CD5	Germany	1993	$8.00

Defyer

Singles

Label	Catalog Number	Title	Type	Country	Year	Longbox Value / Value
Toshiba	TODT-2526	Loving Woman	CD3	Japan	1990	$12.00/$3.00

Degrees of Motion

Full Length

Label	Catalog Number	Title	Type	Country	Year	Longbox Value / Value
RCA	74300	Degrees of Motion	LP/BP	U.S.		$14.00/$8.00

Singles

Label	Catalog Number	Title	Type	Country	Year	Longbox Value / Value
Esquire	FCD-184	Do You Want It Right Now	CD5	U.K.	1992	$8.00
Epic	ESDA-7129	Shine On	CD3	Japan	1993	$12.00/$3.00
Capitol	C2 75274	Soul Freedom	CD5	Canada	1992	$7.00
Esquire	FCD-201	Soul Freedom	CD5	U.K.	1992	$8.00

Deice

Singles

Label	Catalog Number	Title	Type	Country	Year	Longbox Value / Value
BMG	663957	What is Sadness?	CD5	Germany	1991	$8.00
Arista	ASCD-2186	What is Sadness?	CDJ	U.S.	1991	$2.00

Deja

Full Length

Label	Catalog Number	Title	Type	Country	Year	Longbox Value / Value
Atlantic	91060-2	Made To Be Together	LP/LB	U.S.		$14.00/$8.00
Atlantic	90601-2	Serious	LP/LB	U.S.		$14.00/$8.00

Singles

Label	Catalog Number	Title	Type	Country	Year	Longbox Value / Value
Virgin	TENCD-275	Goin' Crazy	CD5	U.K.	1989	$8.00
Virgin	TENCD-268	Made To Be Together	CD5	U.K.	1989	$8.00
Virgin	PRCD 2668	Made To Be Together	CDJ	U.S.	1988	$2.00

Dekker, Desmond

Full Length

Label	Catalog Number	Title	Type	Country	Year	Longbox Value / Value
Streetlife	2462515	Israelites, The	LP/BP	U.S.		$14.00/$8.00

Singles

Label	Catalog Number	Title	Type	Country	Year	Longbox Value / Value
Hot	130 07 397	Israelites, The	CD5	Germany	1990	$8.00

Del Amitri

Full Length

Label	Catalog Number	Title	Type	Country	Year	Longbox Value / Value
Chrysalis	21499	Del Amitri	LP/LB	U.S.		$18.00/$15.00
		In-Store Play Sampler	DJ/Smplr	U.S.		$10.00
A&M	AMSAD 00045	In-Store Play Sampler	DJ/Smplr	U.S.		$10.00
		Twisted	LTD/LP	U.S.	1995	$30.00
2CD set.						
A&M	CD 17950	Walkin' Hours	DJ/LP	U.S.	1989	$8.00

Singles

Label	Catalog Number	Title	Type	Country	Year	Longbox Value / Value
A&M	AMCD-870	Always the Last To Know	CD5	U.K.	1989	$9.00
A&M	75021 7385 2	Always the Last To Know	CDJ	U.S.	1989	$2.00
A&M	75021 8072 2	Be My Down Fall	CDJ	U.S.	1989	$2.00
A&M		Here and Now	CDJ	U.S.	1995	$3.00
A&M	5801712	Just Like A Man	CD5	U.K.	1992	$14.00
A&M	31458 8008	Just Like A Man	CDJ	U.S.	1992	$3.00
A&M	CDEE-515	Kiss This Thing Goodbye	CD3	U.K.	1989	$9.00
A&M	AMCD-551	Kiss This Thing Goodbye	CD5	U.K.	1989	$9.00
A&M	AMCDW-551	Kiss This Thing Goodbye	CD5	U.K.	1989	$9.00
A&M	PD 17985	Kiss This Thing Goodbye	CDJ	U.S.	1989	$2.00
A&M	AMCD-555	Move Away Jimmy Blue	CD5	U.K.	1990	$9.00
A&M	390498-2	Nothing Ever Happens	CD5	Germany	1990	$9.00
A&M	AMCD-536	Nothing Ever Happens	CD5	U.K.	1990	$9.00
		Roll To Me	CD5	U.K.	1995	$10.00
		Roll To Me	CD5	U.K.	1995	$10.00
Second version.						
A&M	581115	Roll To Me	CD5	U.S.	1995	$6.00
A&M	314540311	Roll To Me	CDJ	U.S.	1995	$3.00
A&M	31458433	Roll To Me	CDJ	U.S.	1995	$3.00
A&M	390612-2	Spit In the Rain	CD5	Germany	1990	$9.00
A&M	AMCD-589	Spit In the Rain	CD5	U.K.	1990	$9.00
A&M	AMCD-589	Spit In the Rain	CD5	U.K.	1990	$9.00
A&M	CDEE-527	Stone Cold Sober	CD3	U.K.	1989	$9.00
A&M	75021 8065 2	Stone Cold Sober	CDJ	U.S.	1989	$2.00
		Tell Her This	CD5	U.K.		$10.00
		Tell Her This	CD5	U.K.		$10.00
Second version.						
		Tell Her This	CDJ	U.S.		$3.00
A&M		Twisted	CDJ	U.S.	1995	$10.00
A&M	DELSCD1	Twisted	CDJ	U.S.	1995	$12.00
		Walking Hours	CDJ	U.K.	1990	$18.00
A&M	PD 17950	Walking Hours	CDJ	U.S.	1990	$2.00

Del Barrio, Eduardo

Full Length

Label	Catalog Number	Title	Type	Country	Year	Longbox Value / Value
A&M	75021 7468-2	Freeplay	DJ/Smplr	U.S.	1991	$5.00

Del Bloods

Singles

Label	Catalog Number	Title	Type	Country	Year	Longbox Value / Value
Rough Trade	381-0051-3	Black Rabbit	CD5	Germany	1991	$8.00

Del Fuegos

Full Length

Label	Catalog Number	Title	Type	Country	Year	Longbox Value / Value
RCA	9660	Smoking in the Fields	LP/LB	U.S.		$14.00/$8.00

Singles

Label	Catalog Number	Title	Type	Country	Year	Longbox Value / Value
RCA	9161-2-RDJ	Breakaway	CDJ	U.S.	1990	$2.00
RCA	9075-2-RDJ	Move With Me Sister	CDJ	U.S.	1989	$2.00

Del Lords

Full Length

Label	Catalog Number	Title	Type	Country	Year	Longbox Value / Value
Restless	72317	Howlin' At the Halloween Moon	LP/BP	U.S.		$14.00/$8.00
Enigma	73361	Lovers Who Wander	LP/LB	U.S.		$14.00/$8.00

Singles

Label	Catalog Number	Title	Type	Country	Year	Longbox Value / Value
Enigma	EPRO-272	About You	CDJ	U.S.	1990	$2.00
Enigma	ENVCD-14	Poem of the River	CD3	U.K.	1990	$9.00

Del tha Funkee Homosapien

Singles

Label	Catalog Number	Title	Type	Country	Year	Longbox Value / Value
Elektra	PRCD 8795-2	Catch a Bad One	CDJ	U.S.	1993	$2.00
Elektra	PRCD 8779-2	Made in America	CDJ	U.S.	1993	$2.00
Elektra	PRCD 8903-2	Wrongplace	CDJ	U.S.	1993	$2.00

Delage

Singles

Label	Catalog Number	Title	Type	Country	Year	Longbox Value / Value
Polydor	PZCD-148	Running Back For More	CD5	U.K.	1991	$8.00

Delano, Frank

Singles

Label	Catalog Number	Title	Type	Country	Year	Longbox Value / Value
ZYX	6248-8	I Love You, Berlin	CD5	Germany	1989	$6.00

Delegation

Singles

Label	Catalog Number	Title	Type	Country	Year	Longbox Value / Value
BMG	663178	Darlin'	CD5	U.K.	1990	$8.00
ZYX	6252-8	Mix	CD5	Germany	1989	$6.00
ZYX	5998-8	Thanks To You	CD5	Germany	1988	$6.00
ZYX	6368-8	Where's the Love	CD5	Germany	1990	$6.00

Delgado Junior

Full Length

Label	Catalog Number	Title	Type	Country	Year	Longbox Value / Value
Mango	9818	One More Step	LP/BP	U.S.		$12.00/$7.00

Delicious Monster

Singles

Label	Catalog Number	Title	Type	Country	Year	Longbox Value / Value
Apt	EYECD-1	Dull Dull Dull	CD5	U.K.	1992	$8.00
Flute	FLUTE-1CD	Power Missy	CD5	U.K.	1992	$8.00
Flute	FLUTE-2CD	Snuggle	CD5	U.K.	1992	$8.00

Delite

Singles

Label	Catalog Number	Title	Type	Country	Year	Longbox Value / Value
Circa	YRCD-35	Wild Times	CD5	U.K.	1989	$8.00

Dells

Singles

Label	Catalog Number	Title	Type	Country	Year	Longbox Value / Value
Virgin	PRCD 3729	A Heart is a House For Love	CDJ	U.S.	1991	$2.00
Zoo	17071	Come and Get It	CDJ	U.S.	1992	$2.00
Philips	17085	Oh My Love	CDJ	U.S.	1992	$2.00

Delory, Donna

Full Length

Label	Catalog Number	Title	Type	Country	Year	Longbox Value / Value
	ICD-34	Special Sampler	DJ/Smpr	Japan	1994	$35.00

Singles

Label	Catalog Number	Title	Type	Country	Year	Longbox Value / Value
MCA	MVDM-37	Just a Dream	CD3	Japan	1993	$12.00/$3.00
MCA	2291	Just a Dream	CDJ	U.S.	1993	$3.00
MCA	2293	Just a Dream	CDJ	U.S.	1993	$3.00
MCA	MVDM-33	Praying For Love	CD3	Japan	1993	$12.00/$3.00
MCA	2346	Praying For Love	CDJ	U.S.	1993	$3.00

Delta Rebels

Singles

Label	Catalog Number	Title	Type	Country	Year	Longbox Value / Value
Polydor	CDP 70	Tattoo Rosie	CDJ	U.S.	1989	$2.00

Delta Rhythm Boys

Singles

Label	Catalog Number	Title	Type	Country	Year	Longbox Value / Value
EMI	203385-3	Dry Bones	CD3	Germany	1989	$8.00

Dem Boiz

Singles

Label	Catalog Number	Title	Type	Country	Year	Longbox Value / Value
	15561	Body Talk	CD5	U.S.	1995	$5.00

Demus, Chaka And Pliers

Singles

Label	Catalog Number	Title	Type	Country	Year	Longbox Value / Value
Mango	585	I Wanna Be Your Man	CDJ	U.S.	1993	$2.00

Denim

Singles

Label	Catalog Number	Title	Type	Country	Year	Longbox Value / Value
Boy's Own	BOICD-12	Middle of the Road	CD5	U.K.	1993	$8.00

Dennis, Cathy

Singles

Label	Catalog Number	Title	Type	Country	Year	Longbox Value / Value
Polydor	PODP-1019	All Night Long	CD3	Japan	1991	$12.00/$3.00
Polydor	PODP-1068	Baby Are You	CD3	Japan	1992	$12.00/$3.00
Polydor	PODP-1044	Everybody Move	CD3	Japan	1991	$12.00/$3.00
Polydor	CATHD-5	Everybody Move	CD5	U.K.	1991	$8.00
Polydor	CDP 575	Everybody Move	CDJ	U.S.	1991	$2.00
Polydor	CATHD-8	Falling	CD5	U.K.	1993	$8.00
Polydor	CATHD-7	Irresistible	CD5	U.K.	1992	$8.00
Polydor	CDP 816	Irresistible	CDJ	U.S.	1992	$2.00
Polydor	CDP 851	Irresistible	CDJ	U.S.	1992	$2.00
Polydor	877545-2	Just Another Dream	CD5	Germany	1990	$8.00
Polydor	CATHD-2	Just Another Dream	CD5	U.K.	1990	$8.00
Polydor	CDP 322	Just Another Dream	CDJ	U.S.	1990	$2.00
Polydor	867237-2	Too Many Walls	CD5	Germany	1991	$8.00
Polydor	PODP-1030	Too Many Walls	CD3	Japan	1991	$12.00/$3.00
Polydor	CATHD-4	Too Many Walls	CD5	U.K.	1991	$8.00
Polydor	CDP 441	Too Many Walls	CDJ	U.S.	1991	$2.00
Polydor	879971-2	Touch Me	CD5	Germany	1991	$8.00
Polydor	CATHD-3	Touch Me	CD5	U.K.	1991	$8.00
Polydor	PODP-1057	You Lied to Me	CD3	Japan	1992	$12.00/$3.00
Polydor	CATH-6	You Lied to Me	CD5	U.K.	1992	$8.00
Polygram	863453-2	You Lied to Me	CD5	U.S.	1992	$4.00

Label	Catalog Number	Title	Type	Country	Year	Longbox Value / Value
Polygram	CDP 741	You Lied to Me	CDJ	U.S.	1992	$2.00

Dennis, Matt

Singles

Label	Catalog Number	Title	Type	Country	Year	Longbox Value / Value
BMG	BVDP-36	Sweet Joy	CD3	Japan	1991	$12.00/$3.00

Dennis, Stefan

Singles

Label	Catalog Number	Title	Type	Country	Year	Longbox Value / Value
ZYX	6178-8	Don't It Make You	CD5	Germany	1989	$6.00
Sublime	LIMECD-113	This Love Affair	CD5	U.K.	1989	$8.00

Dentists

Full Length

Label	Catalog Number	Title	Type	Country	Year	Longbox Value / Value
Antler	90014	Heads & How to Read Them	LP/BP	U.S.		$14.00/$8.00
EastWest	PRCD 5501-2	Radio Novocaine	DJ/RS	U.S.	1993	$12.00

Singles

Label	Catalog Number	Title	Type	Country	Year	Longbox Value / Value
EastWest	PRCD 5107-2	Gas	CDJ	U.S.	1993	$2.00

Dentz, John

Full Length

Label	Catalog Number	Title	Type	Country	Year	Longbox Value / Value
RealTime	RT-3004	The John Dentz Reunion Band	LP/LB	U.S.†	1985	$14.00/$8.00

Denver, John

Full Length

Label	Catalog Number	Title	Type	Country	Year	Longbox Value / Value
RCA	PCD1-5458	Dreamland Express	LP/BP	U.S.†	1985	$14.00/$8.00
RCA	PCD1-0374	Greatest Hits	LP/BP	U.S.†	1984	$14.00/$8.00
RCA	PCD1-2195	Greatest Hits, Vol. 2	LP/BP	U.S.†	1984	$14.00/$8.00
RCA	PCD1-4740	It's About Time	LP/BP	U.S.†	1984	$14.00/$8.00
RCA	PCD1-4319	Seasons of the Heart	LP/BP	U.S.†	1984	$14.00/$8.00

Singles

Label	Catalog Number	Title	Type	Country	Year	Longbox Value / Value
Windstar	557	Flower That Shattered the Stone	CDJ	U.S.	1990	$2.00

Denys, Rob

Singles

Label	Catalog Number	Title	Type	Country	Year	Longbox Value / Value
EMI	127539-2	Girls For Sale	CD5	Germany	1990	$8.00

Deodato

Full Length

Label	Catalog Number	Title	Type	Country	Year	Longbox Value / Value
CTI	813660-2	Best Of	LP	U.K.		$15.00

Singles

Label	Catalog Number	Title	Type	Country	Year	Longbox Value / Value
Atlantic	PR 3042-2	Everybody Wants My Girl	CDJ	U.S.	1989	$2.00

Depeche Mode

Full Length

Label	Catalog Number	Title	Type	Country	Year	Longbox Value / Value
Sire		101	LP/LB	U.S.		$22.00/$15.00
	2CD set in single jewel boxes with longbox.					
WEA	38155	101	LD	U.S.	1991	$30.00
Sire	PRO-CD-6950	'94 Tour Sampler	DJ/Smplr	U.S.	1994	$15.00
		Can't Get Enough	RS	U.S.	1993	$125.00
	2 CD set. Airdate: 8/29/93.					
Sire	PRO-CD-5192	PRO-CD-5192	DJ/Smplr	U.S.	1991	$25.00
Sire	PRO-CD-5242	PRO-CD-5242	DJ/Smplr	U.S.	1991	$25.00
WEA	38124	Some Great Videos	LD	U.S.	1993	$30.00
		Songs of Faith and Devotion	DJ/LP	U.K.	1993	$35.00
		Songs of Faith and Devotion	LTD/LP	U.K.	1993	$35.00
	2CD set of album plus tour CD of live tracks.					
Sire		Songs of Faith and Devotion	DJ/LP	U.S.	1993	$80.00
	4 CD promotional Boxed set.					
WEA	38181	Strange Too	LD	U.S.	1993	$25.00
Mute	ALCB-33	Violator	LP	Japan	1990	$50.00
	2 CD set.					
Mute		Violator	DJ/LP	U.K.	1990	$50.00
	CD in box.					

Singles

Label	Catalog Number	Title	Type	Country	Year	Longbox Value / Value
Sire	17409-2	Barrel Of A Gun	CD5	U.S.	1996	$4.00
Sire	43828-2	Barrel Of A Gun	CD5	U.S.	1996	$6.00
Mute	811 854	Behind the Wheel	CD3	Germany	1988	$12.00
Mute	826 875	Behind the Wheel	CD5	Germany	1988	$18.00
Mute	CDBONG-15	Behind the Wheel	CD3	U.K.	1988	$12.00
		Behind the Wheel	CDJ	U.K.	1988	$15.00
Sire		Behind the Wheel	CD5	U.S.	1988	$18.00
Sire	PRO-CD-2953	Behind the Wheel	CDJ	U.S.	1988	$25.00
Sire	9 40330-2	Behind the Wheel	CD5	U.S.	1992	$18.00
Mute	826 839	Blasphemous Rumour	CD5	Germany	1989	$18.00
Mute	CDBONG-7	Blasphemous Rumour	CD5	U.K.	1989	$18.00
Warner	12-18380	Condemnation	CD5	Canada	1994	$18.00
Sire	9 41058-2	Condemnation	CD5	U.S.	1993	$18.00
Sire		Condemnation	CDJ	U.S.	1993	$20.00
Mute	811 868	Dreaming of Me	CD3	Germany	1988	$10.00
Mute	CDMUTE 13	Dreaming of Me	CD3	U.K.	1990	$10.00
Sire	9 04289-2	Dreaming of Me	CD5	U.S.	1992	$18.00
Mute	826-922	Enjoy the Silence	CD5	Germany	1990	$18.00
Mute	826-923	Enjoy the Silence	CD5	Germany	1990	$18.00
Mute	826-926	Enjoy the Silence	CD5	Germany	1990	$18.00
Alfa	ALDB-19	Enjoy the Silence	CD3	Japan	1990	$20.00/$8.00
Mute	Y123B	Enjoy the Silence	CDJ	Japan	1990	$25.00
Mute	LCDBONG-18	Enjoy the Silence	CD3	U.K.	1990	$12.00
Mute	CDBONG-18	Enjoy the Silence	CD5	U.K.	1990	$18.00
Sire	9 21490-2	Enjoy the Silence	CD5	U.S.	1990	$18.00
Sire	9 21490 2	Enjoy the Silence	CD5	U.S.	1990	$18.00
Sire	PRO-CD-3976	Enjoy the Silence	CDJ	U.S.	1990	$18.00
Sire	9 18890-2	Enjoy the Silence	CD5	U.S.	1992	$18.00
Mute	826 837	Everything Counts	CD5	Germany	1989	$10.00
Mute	826 813	Everything Counts	CD5	Germany	1989	$18.00
Mute	826 903	Everything Counts	CD5	Germany	1989	$18.00
Mute	CDBONG-16	Everything Counts	CD3	U.K.	1989	$12.00
Mute	CDBONG-3	Everything Counts	CD5	U.K.	1989	$18.00
Sire		Everything Counts	CD5	U.S.	1989	$18.00
Sire	PRO-CD-3485	Everything Counts	CDJ	U.S.	1989	$15.00
Sire	9 40296-2	Everything Counts	CD5	U.S.	1992	$18.00
Sire	9 40331-2	Everything Counts	CD5	U.S.	1992	$18.00
Mute	826 810	Get the Balance Right	CD5	Germany	1989	$18.00
Mute	826 836	Get the Balance Right	CD5	Germany	1989	$18.00
Mute	CDBONG-2	Get the Balance Right	CD5	U.K.	1988	$18.00
Sire	9 40295	Get the Balance Right	CD5	U.S.	1992	$18.00
Sire	PRO-CD-4362	Halo	CDJ	U.S.	1990	$15.00
Reprise	9 40767-2	I Feel You	CD5	Canada	1993	$18.00
Mute	ALCB-721	I Feel You	CD5	Japan	1993	$27.00
Mute	LCD BONG-21	I Feel You	CD5	U.K.	1993	$18.00
Mute		I Feel You	CD5	U.K.	1993	$18.00
	Second version.					
Sire	PRO-CD-6011	I Feel You	CDJ	U.S.	1993	$15.00
Mute	10SP-3	I Want You Now	CD3	Japan	1988	$20.00/$5.00
Warner	12-18241	In Your Room	CD5	Canada	1994	$18.00
Warner Brothers	9 41362-2	In Your Room	CD5	U.S.	1994	$18.00
Warner Brothers	41362	In Your Room	CD5	U.S.	1994	$18.00
Mute	826 832	It's Called a Heart	CD5	Germany	1988	$18.00
Mute	CDBONG-9	It's Called a Heart	CD5	U.K.	1989	$18.00
Mute	826 801	Just Can't Get Enough	CD5	Germany	1988	$18.00
Mute	CDMUTE-16	Just Can't Get Enough	CD5	U.K.	1989	$18.00
Sire	9 40291-2	Just Can't Get Enough	CD5	U.S.	1992	$18.00
Mute	826 807	Leave in Silence	CD5	Germany	1988	$18.00
Mute	CDBONG-1	Leave in Silence	CD5	U.K.	1988	$18.00
Mute	CDLITTLE-15	Leave in Silence	CD5	U.K.	1988	$18.00
Sire	9 40294	Leave in Silence	CD5	U.S.	1992	$18.00
Mute	811 857	Little 15	CD3	Germany	1988	$12.00
Mute	826 880	Little 15	CD5	Germany	1988	$18.00
Mute	CDBONG-4	Love In ILove in Itselfself	CD5	U.K.	1988	$18.00
Mute	826 816	Love in Itself	CD5	Germany	1988	$18.00
Mute	826 838	Love in Itself	CD5	Germany	1988	$18.00
Sire	9 40297	Love in Itself	CD5	U.S.	1992	$18.00
Mute	826-824	Master and Servant	CD5	Germany	1988	$18.00
Mute	CDBONG-6	Master and Servant	CD5	U.K.	1988	$18.00
Mute	826-805	Meaning of Love	CD5	Germany	1988	$18.00
Mute	CDMUTE-22	Meaning of Love	CD5	U.K.	1988	$18.00
Sire	9 40293-2	Meaning of Love	CD5	U.S.	1992	$18.00
Mute	826-868	Never Let Me Down Again	CD5	Germany	1989	$18.00
Sire	PRO-CD-2973	Never Let Me Down Again	CDJ	U.S.	1987	$20.00
Sire	9 40329-2	Never Let Me Down Again	CD5	U.S.	1992	$18.00
Mute	826-800	New Life	CD5	Germany	1988	$18.00
Mute	CDMUTE-14	New Life	CD5	U.K.	1988	$18.00
Sire	9 40290-2	New Life	CD5	U.S.	1992	$18.00
Sire	PRO-CD-6626	One Cares	CDJ	U.S.	1993	$15.00
Sire		One Cares	CDJ	U.S.	1994	$35.00
	CD-R version. Live edit 3:30.					
Sire		One Cares	CDJ	U.S.	1994	$35.00
	CD-R version. Live edit 3:48.					
Mute	826 820	People Are People	CD5	Germany	1989	$18.00
Mute	CDBONG-5	People Are People	CD5	U.K.	1989	$18.00
Mute	826 912	Personal Jesus	CD3	Germany	1990	$12.00
Intercord	826 917	Personal Jesus	CD5	Germany	1990	$18.00
		Personal Jesus	CDJ	Japan	1990	$30.00
Mute	CDBONG 17	Personal Jesus	CD3	U.K.	1990	$12.00
Mute	LCDBONG-17	Personal Jesus	CD3	U.K.	1990	$12.00
Sire	9 21328-2	Personal Jesus	CD5	U.S.	1990	$18.00
Sire	9 18889-2	Personal Jesus	CD5	U.S.	1992	$18.00
Mute	826-933	Policy Of Truth	CD5	Germany	1990	$18.00
Mute	826-934	Policy of Truth	CD5	Germany	1990	$18.00
Mute	LCDBONG -19	Policy of Truth	CD5	U.K.	1990	$18.00
Mute	CDBONG-19	Policy of Truth	CD5	U.K.	1990	$18.00
Mute	CD SBONG-19R	Policy of Truth	CDJ	U.K.	1990	$15.00
Sire	9 21534-2	Policy of Truth	CD5	U.S.	1990	$18.00
Sire	PRO-CD-4027	Policy of Truth	CDJ	U.S.	1990	$15.00
Mute	826 841	Question of Lust	CD5	Germany	1988	$18.00
Mute	826 985	Question of Lust	CD5	Germany	1992	$18.00
Mute	CDBONG-11	Question of Lust	CD5	U.K.	1988	$18.00
Mute	826 850	Question of Time	CD5	Germany	1989	$18.00
Mute	CDBONG-12	Question of Time	CD5	U.K.	1989	$18.00
Mute	826-802	See You	CD5	Germany	1988	$18.00
Mute	CDBONG 18	See You	CD5	U.K.	1988	$18.00
Sire	9 40292-2	See You	CD5	U.S.	1992	$18.00
Mute	826 829	Shake Your Disease	CD5	Germany	1988	$18.00
Mute	CDBONG-8	Shake Your Disease	CD5	U.K.	1988	$18.00
Mute	Y08-2	Single Collection	DJ/CD3	Japan	1990	$75.00
Warner Brothers	40284	Singles 1	CD5	U.S.	1991	$35.00
	6 CD5 set.					
Warner Brothers		Singles 2	CD5	U.S.	1991	$35.00
	6 CD5 set.					
Warner Brothers		Singles 3	CD5	U.S.	1991	$35.00
	6 CD5 set.					
Mute	826-862	Strangelove	CD5	Germany	1989	$18.00
Mute	CD BONG-13	Strangelove	CD5	U.K.	1989	$18.00
Sire	PRO-CD-3213	Strangelove	CDJ	U.S.	1989	$30.00
Sire	9 40326-2	Strangelove	CD5	U.S.	1992	$18.00
Mute	826 835	Stripped	CD5	Germany	1988	$18.00
Mute	CDBONG-10	Stripped	CD5	U.K.	1988	$18.00
Mute	ALCB-772	Walking in My Shoes	CD5	Japan	1993	$25.00
Sire		Walking in My Shoes	CD5	U.K.	1993	$18.00
Sire		Walking in My Shoes	CD5	U.K.	1993	$18.00
	Second version.					
Sire	PRO-CD-6178	Walking in My Shoes	CDJ	U.S.	1993	$15.00
WEA	CD-21735	Word in My Eyes	CD5	Canada	1990	$18.00
Mute	826-945	Word in My Eyes	CD5	Germany	1990	$18.00
Mute	826-946	Word in My Eyes	CD5	Germany	1990	$18.00
Mute	CDBONG-20	Word in My Eyes	CD5	U.K.	1990	$18.00
Mute	LCDBONG-20	Word in My Eyes	CD5	U.K.	1990	$18.00
Sire	9 21735-2	Word in My Eyes	CD5	U.S.	1990	$18.00
Sire	PRO-CD-4531	Word in My Eyes	CDJ	U.S.	1990	$15.00
Sire	PRO-CD-4441	Word in My Eyes	CDJ	U.S.	1990	$18.00
Mute	ALCB-201/4	X1	CD5	Japan	1991	$100.00
	4 CD set.					
Mute	ALCB-205/8	X2	CD5	Japan	1991	$100.00
	4 CD set.					

Deputies Of Love

Singles

Label	Catalog Number	Title	Type	Country	Year	Longbox Value / Value
CBS	657345-2	Deputy of Love	CD5	Germany	1991	$8.00
CBS	657345-5	Deputy of Love	CD5	Germany	1992	$8.00

Derek and the Dominos

Full Length

Label	Catalog Number	Title	Type	Country	Year	Longbox Value / Value
RSO	831416-2	In Concert	LP/BP	U.S.		$15.00/$10.00
RSO	823277-2	Layla and Other Assorted Love Songs	LP/LB	U.S.†	1984	$22.00/$18.00
	2 CD set.					
RSO	823277-2	Layla and Other Assorted Love Songs	LP/LB	U.S.	1988	$22.00/$18.00
	2 CD set.					

Singles

Label	Catalog Number	Title	Type	Country	Year	Longbox Value / Value
Polydor	CDP 298	Little Wing	CDJ	U.S.	1990	$25.00

Derek B

Singles

Label	Catalog Number	Title	Type	Country	Year	Longbox Value / Value
Polygram	870378-2	Bad Young Brothers	CD5	Germany	1988	$8.00
Polygram	DRKCD-112	Bad Young Brothers	CD5	U.K.	1988	$8.00
Polygram	DRKCD-2	We've Got the Justice	CD5	U.K.	1988	$8.00
Hal	HALT-3CD	You've Got to Look Up	CD5	U.K.	1990	$8.00

Derringer, Rick

Full Length

Label	Catalog Number	Title	Type	Country	Year	Longbox Value / Value
Polydor	3112-35	Good Dirty Fun	LP	Japan		$30.00
Pioneer	PA-85-091	Rick Derringer	LD	U.S.	1985	$35.00

Des'ree

Singles

Label	Catalog Number	Title	Type	Country	Year	Longbox Value / Value
Epic	ESCA-5528	Feel So High	CD5	Japan	1992	$12.00

Label	Catalog Number	Title	Type	Country	Year	Longbox Value / Value
CBS	657366-2	Feel So High	CD5	U.K.	1991	$8.00
CBS	657689-2	Feel So High	CD5	U.K.	1991	$8.00
CBS	77693	Feel So High	CD5	U.S.	1994	$5.00
		Little Child	CD5	U.K.		$10.00
		Little Child	CD5	U.K.		$10.00
Second version.						
CBS	657863-2	Miss Adventures	CD5	U.K.	1991	$8.00
CBS	52587	Miss Adventures	CD5	U.S.	1992	$4.00
Epic	BSK 7004	Sampler	CDJ	U.S.	1995	$3.00
Epic	ESCA-5603	Sun Of '79	CD5	Japan	1992	$12.00
Epic	ESCA-5639	Why Should I Love You	CD5	Japan	1992	$12.00
CBS		You Gotta Be	CD5	U.K.		$8.00
CBS		You Gotta Be	CD5	U.K.		$8.00
Second version.						
CBS	77551	You Gotta Be	CD5	U.S.	1994	$5.00

Desert Rose Band

Full Length

Label	Catalog Number	Title	Type	Country	Year	Longbox Value / Value
Curb		Desert Rose Band, The	DJ/Smplr	U.S.		$10.00
Curb	77627	Life Goes On	LP/LB	U.S.		$14.00/$8.00
Curb		Pages of Life	LP/LB	U.S.		$14.00/$8.00

Singles

Label	Catalog Number	Title	Type	Country	Year	Longbox Value / Value
Curb	CD45 54107	Come a Little Closer	CDJ	U.S.	1991	$2.00
Curb	CD45 5 3804	In Another Lifetime	CDJ	U.S.	1990	$2.00
Curb	CD45 1070	Night After Night	CDJ	U.S.	1993	$2.00
MCA	CD45 3004	She Don't Love Nobody	CDJ	U.S.	1988	$3.00
Curb	CD45 53741	Start All Over Again	CDJ	U.S.	1989	$2.00
		Will This Be the Day	CDJ	U.S.		$2.00

Deshay

Full Length

Label	Catalog Number	Title	Type	Country	Year	Longbox Value / Value
A&M	4001	R&B Style	LP/LB	U.S.		$12.00/$7.00

Desire

Singles

Label	Catalog Number	Title	Type	Country	Year	Longbox Value / Value
BMG	664306	This Doub Is Mine	CD5	Germany	1991	$8.00

Desiya

Singles

Label	Catalog Number	Title	Type	Country	Year	Longbox Value / Value
Pinnacle	826-988	Comin' on Strong	CD5	Germany	1992	$8.00
Alfa	ALCB-518	Comin' on Strong	CD3	Japan	1992	$12.00/$3.00
Pinnacle	CDMKT-2	Comin' on Strong	CDJ	U.K.	1992	$8.00
Mute	PRO-CD-8528	Comin' on Strong	CDJ	U.S.	1992	$2.00

Deskee

Full Length

Label	Catalog Number	Title	Type	Country	Year	Longbox Value / Value
RCA	2429-2	No. One is the Number	LP/LB	U.S.		$14.00/$8.00
		Dance, Dance	CDJ	U.S.		$2.00
SPV	0786-2	Kid Get Hyped	CD5	Germany	1990	$8.00
		Kid Get Hyped	CDJ	U.S.	1989	$2.00
SPV	0767-2	Let There Be a House	CD5	Germany	1989	$8.00
SPV	0773-2	Let There Be a House	CD5	Germany	1990	$8.00
		Let There Be a House	CDJ	U.S.	1989	$2.00
SPV	1021-2	Lost In Grove	CD5	Germany	1991	$8.00

Desmond, Paul

Full Length

Label	Catalog Number	Title	Type	Country	Year	Longbox Value / Value
Mosaic	DM4-120	Complete Recordings of the Paul Desmond Quartet	LP	U.S.		$60.00
4 CD set.						
RCA	R32J-1045	Desmond Blue	LP	Japan		$30.00
A&M	0824-2	From the Hot Afternoon	LP/LB	U.S.		$14.00/$8.00
Aris	886213	Late Lament	LP	Germany		$18.00
Bluebird	5778-2	Late Lament	LP	U.S.		$8.00
RCA	R32J-1023	Rossa Antigua	LP	Japan		$30.00

Desolina

Singles

Label	Catalog Number	Title	Type	Country	Year	Longbox Value / Value
Triesca	TRD 0206	You're the Reason	CDJ	U.S.	1992	$7.00

Destruction

Full Length

Label	Catalog Number	Title	Type	Country	Year	Longbox Value / Value
Noise	4823	Cracked Brain	LP/LB	U.S.		$14.00/$8.00
Noise	4807	Live Without Sentence	LP/LB	U.S.		$14.00/$8.00
SPV	85-7535	Mad Butcher/Sentence of Death	LTD/LP	Germany	1988	$10.00
Picture disc CD.						
Steamhammer	SHCD 7005	Mad Butcher/Sentence of Death	LTD/LP	U.S.	1988	$25.00
Picture disc CD.						

Detroit, Marcella

Full Length

Label	Catalog Number	Title	Type	Country	Year	Longbox Value / Value
		Jewel	DJ/LP	Canada	1994	$40.00

Singles

Label	Catalog Number	Title	Type	Country	Year	Longbox Value / Value
Mercury	CDP 1226	I Believe	CDJ	U.S.	1995	$3.00

Detroit, Marcella & John, Elton

Singles

Label	Catalog Number	Title	Type	Country	Year	Longbox Value / Value
		Ain't Nothing Like The Real Thing	CD5	U.K.		$10.00
		Ain't Nothing Like The Real Thing	CD5	U.K.		$10.00
Second version.						

Detroits Most Wanted

Singles

Label	Catalog Number	Title	Type	Country	Year	Longbox Value / Value
Bryant	124	Pop the Trunk	CDJ	U.S.	1992	$2.00

Deuces Wild

Singles

Label	Catalog Number	Title	Type	Country	Year	Longbox Value / Value
CBS	656324-2	Living in the Sun	CD5	Germany	1991	$8.00

Devay

Singles

Label	Catalog Number	Title	Type	Country	Year	Longbox Value / Value
		Rock and a Hard Place	CDJ	Canada		$2.00

Deviation

Singles

Label	Catalog Number	Title	Type	Country	Year	Longbox Value / Value
Dead Good	GOOD-12CD	Hammond Song	CD5	U.K.	1992	$8.00

Devil Dance

Singles

Label	Catalog Number	Title	Type	Country	Year	Longbox Value / Value
ZYX	DST-1083-8	Techno Brett	CD5	Germany	1992	$6.00

Deville, C.C.

Singles

Label	Catalog Number	Title	Type	Country	Year	Longbox Value / Value
Hollywood	PRCD 10331	Hey Good Lookin'	CDJ	U.S.	1993	$2.00

Deville, Willy

Full Length

Label	Catalog Number	Title	Type	Country	Year	Longbox Value / Value
		Backstreets of Desire	LP/LB	U.S.		$12.00/$10.00

Devlins

Singles

Label	Catalog Number	Title	Type	Country	Year	Longbox Value / Value
EMI	CDCL-671	Live Bait	CD5	U.K.	1992	$8.00
		Someone To Talk To	CDJ	Canada		$8.00

Devo

Full Length

Label	Catalog Number	Title	Type	Country	Year	Longbox Value / Value
Elektra	60303-2	Digital Domain	LP/LB	U.S.†	1984	$14.00/$8.00
Warner Brothers	9 3435-2	Freedom of Choice	LP/LB	U.S.†	1984	$14.00/$8.00
Rykodisc	90188 CD (L)	Hardcore Vol.1 1974-1977	LTD/LP	U.S.		$12.00
2CD in blisterpak.						
Enigma	73514	Now It Can Be Told	LP/BP	U.S.		$14.00/$8.00
Enigma	73526	Smooth Noodle Maps	LP/BP	U.S.		$14.00/$8.00
Enigma	73303	Total Devo	LP/BP	U.S.		$14.00/$8.00
Pioneer	PA-84-069	We're All Devo	LD	U.S.	1984	$25.00

Singles

Label	Catalog Number	Title	Type	Country	Year	Longbox Value / Value
Enigma	EPRO-140	Baby Doll	CDJ	U.S.	1988	$3.00
Enigma	75515	Baby Doll	CDJ	U.S.	19988	$7.00
		Disc Dancer	DJ/CD3	U.S.		$2.00
Enigma	203943-2	Post Modern Man (If I Had a Hammer)	CD5	Germany	1990	$9.00
Enigma	CDENV-23	Post Modern Man (If I Had a Hammer)	CD5	U.K.	1990	$9.00
Enigma	EPRO-306	Post Modern Man (If I Had a Hammer)	CDJ	U.S.	1990	$3.00
Enigma	EPRO-307	Post Modern Man (If I Had a Hammer)	CDJ	U.S.	1990	$3.00

Devonsquare

Full Length

Label	Catalog Number	Title	Type	Country	Year	Longbox Value / Value
Atlantic	82343-2	Bye Bye Route 66	LP/LB	U.S.	1992	$12.00/$7.00

Singles

Label	Catalog Number	Title	Type	Country	Year	Longbox Value / Value
Atlantic	PRCD 4295-2	If You Could See Me Now	CDJ	U.S.	1992	$2.00

Dex

Singles

Label	Catalog Number	Title	Type	Country	Year	Longbox Value / Value
Canyon	PCDY-00069	Bang Bang Bang	CD3	Japan	1990	$12.00/$3.00

Dexy's Midnight Runners

Full Length

Label	Catalog Number	Title	Type	Country	Year	Longbox Value / Value
Mercury	822989-2	Don't Stand Me Down	LP	Germany	1985	$14.00
Mercury	822989-2	Don't Stand Me Down	LP/BP	U.S.†	1985	$14.00/$8.00
Mercury	822989-2	Don't Stand Me Down	LP/BP	U.S.	1987	$14.00/$8.00
Mercury	810054-2	Too Rye Eye	LP/BP	U.S.†	1984	$14.00/$8.00
Mercury	810054-2	Too Rye Eye	LP/BP	U.S.	1987	$14.00/$8.00

Singles

Label	Catalog Number	Title	Type	Country	Year	Longbox Value / Value
Mercury	888976-2	Come on Eileen	CD3	Germany	1989	$8.00
Mercury	888976-2	Come on Eileen	CD3	U.K.	1989	$8.00
Mercury	MERCD-347	Come on Eileen	CD5	U.K.	1989	$8.00

DeYoung, Dennis

Full Length

Label	Catalog Number	Title	Type	Country	Year	Longbox Value / Value
Polygram	395109-2	Back to the World	LP	Germany		$15.00
MCA		Boomchild	LP/LB	U.S.		$14.00/$8.00
Polygram	395006-2	Desert Moon	LP	Germany		$15.00
A&M	CD-5006	Desert Moon	LP/LB	U.S.†	1984	$14.00/$8.00
Pioneer	PA87-M051	Three Piece Suit	8"LD	U.S.	1986	$10.00

Singles

Label	Catalog Number	Title	Type	Country	Year	Longbox Value / Value
MCA	10SW-63	Boomchild	CD3	Japan	1988	$13.00/$4.00
		Boomchild	CDJ	U.S.	1988	$2.00
		On the Street Where You Live	CDJ	U.S.	1994	$3.00

DFC

Singles

Label	Catalog Number	Title	Type	Country	Year	Longbox Value / Value
Assult	5410	Caps Get Peeled	CDJ	U.S.		$2.00
Atlantic	95860	Things in tha Hood	CD5	U.S.	1994	$5.00

Di Blasio

Singles

Label	Catalog Number	Title	Type	Country	Year	Longbox Value / Value
BMG	2037-2RLDJ	Hasta Que Te Conoci	CDJ	U.S.	1995	$7.00

Di Meola, Al

Full Length

Label	Catalog Number	Title	Type	Country	Year	Longbox Value / Value
CBS	CK-35277	Casino	LP/LB	U.S.†	1985	$14.00/$8.00
Columbia	CD-82645	Casino	LP	Germany		$15.00
CBS	CK-34461	Elegant Gypsy	LP/LB	U.S.†	1985	$14.00/$8.00
Legacy	CK-53926	Friday Night in San Francisco	LP/LB	U.S.	1993	$29.00/$25.00
CBS	CK-38373	Tour de Force	LP/LB	U.S.†	1985	$14.00/$8.00
Gold disc.						
Columbia	CD-25121	Tour De Force	LP	Germany		$15.00

Singles

Label	Catalog Number	Title	Type	Country	Year	Longbox Value / Value
Tomato	9021	Kiss My Axe	CDJ	U.S.	1991	$2.00

Di Meola, Al/John McLaughlin/Paco De Lucia

Full Length

Label	Catalog Number	Title	Type	Country	Year	Longbox Value / Value
CBS	CK-37152	Friday Night in San Francisco	LP/LB	U.S.†	1985	$14.00/$8.00

Di-Bart, Tony

Singles

Label	Catalog Number	Title	Type	Country	Year	Longbox Value / Value
		Real Thing	CD5	U.K.		$9.00
		Real Thing	CD5	U.K.		$9.00
Second version.						

Diamanda Galas

Singles

Label	Catalog Number	Title	Type	Country	Year	Longbox Value / Value
Restless	7 71419-2	Litanies of Satan, The	CD5	U.S.	1989	$3.00

Diamond

Singles

Label	Catalog Number	Title	Type	Country	Year	Longbox Value / Value
Elektra	66097	Bankhead Bounce	CD5	U.S.	1995	$5.00

Diamond Head

Full Length

Label	Catalog Number	Title	Type	Country	Year	Longbox Value / Value
Metal Blade		Behold the Beginning	LP/LB	U.S.		$14.00/$8.00

Singles

Label	Catalog Number	Title	Type	Country	Year	Longbox Value / Value
Bronze	001	Truckin'	CD5	U.K.	1993	$9.00

Diamond, L.C.

Singles

Label	Catalog Number	Title	Type	Country	Year	Longbox Value / Value
BMG	663515	Girls	CD5	Germany	1990	$7.00

Diamond, Neil

Full Length

Label	Catalog Number	Title	Type	Country	Year	Longbox Value / Value
CBS		Best Years of Our Lives, The	DJ/Smplr	U.K.	1988	$20.00
Columbia	CK-34990	Glad You're Here With Me Tonight	LP/LB	U.S.		$14.00/$8.00
		Greatest Hits 1966 - 1992 Radio Retail Sampler	DJ/Smplr	Canada	1993	$25.00
Columbia	CK-38068	Greatest Hits Vol. 2	LP/LB	U.S.		$14.00/$8.00
Columbia	CK-38068	Greatest Hits Vol. 2	LP/LB	U.S.†	1985	$14.00/$8.00
MCA	MCAD-37252	His 12 Greatest Hits	LP/LB	U.S.†	1985	$14.00/$8.00
MCA	MCAD-37252	Hot August Night	LP/LB	U.S.†	1985	$22.00/$18.00
2 CD set.						

Label	Catalog Number	Title	Type	Country	Year	Longbox Value / Value
Vestron	V-1062	I'm Glad You're Here With Me	LD	U.S.	1986	$35.00
Capitol	CDP-46026	Jazz Singer	LP/LB	U.S.†	1985	$20.00/$16.00
Digipak version.						
Image	IDML1005	Live at the Greek	LD	U.S.		$30.00
MCA	MCAD-37194	Moods	LP/LB	U.S.†	1985	$14.00/$8.00
MCA	MCAD-37196	Taproot Manuscript	LP/LB	U.S.†	1985	$14.00/$8.00
		Tennesse Moon	DJ/Smplr	U.K.	1996	$35.00
Columbia	CSK 1352	This Time & All Time Hits	DJ/Smplr	U.S.	1988	$20.00
Singles						
Columbia	CSK 4665	All I Really Need Is You	CDJ	U.S.	1992	$3.00
Columbia	CSK 1702	Baby Can I Hold You	CDJ	U.S.	1988	$3.00
Old Gold	OG-6149	Cracklin' Rose	CD3	U.K.	1989	$10.00
CBS	657556-2	Don't Turn Around	CD5	Germany	1991	$10.00
Columbia	CSK 4258	Don't Turn Around	CDJ	U.S.	1991	$3.00
Columbia	CSK 4372	Hooked on the Memory of You	CDJ	U.S.	1991	$3.00
CBS	657437-2	If There Were No Dreams	CD5	U.K.	1991	$10.00
Columbia	CSK 4152	If There Were No Dreams	CDJ	U.S.	1991	$3.00
		Marry Me	CD5	Australia	1996	$12.00
CBS	658826-2	Morning Has Broken	CD5	U.K.	1992	$10.00
Columbia	CSK 4837	Morning Has Broken	CDJ	U.S.	1992	$3.00
Columbia	CSK 6268	Play Me	CDJ	U.S.		$3.00
CBS	655451-2	This Time	CD5	U.K.	1989	$10.00
CBS	6554518-2	This Time	CD5	U.K.	1989	$10.00
Columbia	CSK 6268	Will You Love Me Tomorrow	CDJ	U.S.		$3.00
Columbia		You've Lost That Lovin' Feeling	CDJ	U.S.	1993	$3.00

Diamond, Rexx

Label	Catalog Number	Title	Type	Country	Year	Longbox Value / Value
Full Length						
Red Light	8346	Rated Rexx	LP/BP	U.S.		$12.00/$7.00

Diamond Rio

Label	Catalog Number	Title	Type	Country	Year	Longbox Value / Value
Full Length						
		'90s Country	RS	U.S.	1995	$30.00
Airdate: 3/25/95.						
		'90s Country	RS	U.S.	1995	$30.00
Airdate: 9/2/95.						
		'90s Country	RS	U.S.	1996	$30.00
Airdate: 3/2/96.						
		Country Concert	RS	U.S.	1995	$30.00
Airdate: 7/29/95.						
Singles						
		Meet In the Middle Diamond Shell	CDJ	U.S.		$2.00
Arista	2407	Norma Jean Riley	CDJ	U.S.	1992	$2.00
		Oh What a Night	CDJ	U.S.		$2.00

Diamond & the Psychotic Neurotics

Label	Catalog Number	Title	Type	Country	Year	Longbox Value / Value
Singles						
Chemistry	839	Sally Got a One Track Mind	CDJ	U.S.	1993	$2.00

Diana I

Label	Catalog Number	Title	Type	Country	Year	Longbox Value / Value
Singles						
Metropolitan	1035	I'll Be Loving You	CD5	U.S.	1994	$5.00

Diatribe

Label	Catalog Number	Title	Type	Country	Year	Longbox Value / Value
Singles						
Reconstruction	REC-001	Nothing	CD5	U.S.	1992	$5.00

Dibango, Manu

Label	Catalog Number	Title	Type	Country	Year	Longbox Value / Value
Full Length						
Polygram	827014-2	Electric Africa	LP	Germany		$15.00

Dickerson, Walt

Label	Catalog Number	Title	Type	Country	Year	Longbox Value / Value
Full Length						
Original Jazz	1817	This is Walt Dickerson	LTD/LP	U.S.		$13.00

Dickey, Gwen

Label	Catalog Number	Title	Type	Country	Year	Longbox Value / Value
Singles						
Swanyard	SYRCD-7	Car Wash	CD5	U.K.	1990	$8.00

Dickey, Gwen

Label	Catalog Number	Title	Type	Country	Year	Longbox Value / Value
Singles						
Swanyard	CDSYD-21	Don't Stop	CD5	U.K.	1992	$8.00

Dickies

Label	Catalog Number	Title	Type	Country	Year	Longbox Value / Value
Full Length						
A&M		Great Dictations	DJ/Smplr	U.S.		$5.00
A&M	CD-5236	Great Dictations	LP/LB	U.S.		$14.00/$8.00
Singles						
Enigma	EPRO 177	Dummy Up	CDJ	U.S.	1989	$2.00

Dickinson, Bruce

Label	Catalog Number	Title	Type	Country	Year	Longbox Value / Value
Full Length						
CMC International	CMC8203	Alive in Studio A	LTD/LP	U.S.	1995	$26.00
EMI		Balls to Picasso	LTD/LP	U.K.	1994	$25.00
Digipak version.						
Columbia	CK-46139	Tattooed Millionaire	LP/LB	U.S.	1990	$15.00/$10.00
Singles						
EMI	20 3918 2	All the Young Dudes	CD5	Germany	1990	$10.00
EMI	CDEM-142	All the Young Dudes	CD5	U.K.	1990	$10.00
Columbia	CSK 2145	All the Young Dudes	CDJ	U.S.	1990	$3.00
		Back From the Edge	CDJ	U.K.	1995	$12.00
EMI	CDEM-185	Born in '58	CD5	U.K.	1991	$9.00
Jive	1261-2-JDJ	Bring Your Daughter to the Slaughter	CDJ	U.S.	1989	$8.00
Mercury		Cyclops	CDJ	U.S.	1994	$6.00
EMI	CDEM-151	Dive! Dive! Dive!	CD5	U.K.	1990	$11.00
		Shoot All The Clowns	CD5	U.K.		$10.00
		Shoot All The Clowns	CD5	U.K.		$10.00
Second version.						
Mercury	CDP 1290	Shoot All the Clowns	CDJ	U.S.	1994	$7.00
		Skunkworks	CDJ	U.K.	1995	$12.00
EMI	20 3815-2	Tattooed Millionaire	CD5	Germany	1990	$10.00
EMI	CDEM-138	Tattooed Millionaire	CD5	U.K.	1990	$10.00
Columbia	CSK 2050	Tattooed Millionaire	CDJ	U.S.	1990	$6.00
Columbia	CSK 73338	Tattooed Millionaire	CDJ	U.S.	1990	$7.00
EMI		Tears of the Dragon	CD5	U.K.	1994	$10.00
EMI		Tears of the Dragon	CD5	U.K.	1994	$10.00
Second version.						
EMI	CDEM-DJ-32	Tears of the Dragon	CDJ	U.K.	1994	$15.00
Mercury	CDP 1257	Tears of the Dragon	CDJ	U.S.	1994	$3.00

Dickson, Barbara

Label	Catalog Number	Title	Type	Country	Year	Longbox Value / Value
Full Length						
Columbia	463002-2	All For a Song	LP	U.K.		$15.00
Singles						
Columbia	658478-2	Blowin' In the Wind	CD5	U.K.	1992	$8.00
Columbia	658266-2	Don't Think Twice It's Alright	CD5	U.K.	1992	$8.00

Diddley, Bo

Label	Catalog Number	Title	Type	Country	Year	Longbox Value / Value
Full Length						
Point	262092	Bo's a Lumberjack	LP/BP	U.S.		$14.00/$8.00
Point	262094	Bo's Bounce	LP/BP	U.S.		$14.00/$8.00
Point	262093	Bo's Guitar	LP/BP	U.S.		$14.00/$8.00
SF Miles	SEECD-321	EP Collection	LP/BP	U.S.		$14.00/$8.00
		House of Blues	RS	U.S.	1994	$40.00
2 CD set. Airdate: 9/25/94.						
Point	263645	Say Man	LP/BP	U.S.		$14.00/$8.00
Singles						
Charly	CDS 11	Bo Diddley	CD5	France	1989	$10.00
Charly	CDS-11	Bo Diddley	CD5	U.K.	1989	$10.00
MCA	37281	Bo Diddley	CD3	U.S.	1988	$6.00/$3.00
MCA	37326	Who Do You Love	CD3	U.S.	1988	$6.00/$3.00

Die Form

Label	Catalog Number	Title	Type	Country	Year	Longbox Value / Value
Singles						
SPV	1126-3	Savage Logic	CD5	Germany	1991	$8.00

Die In Crisis

Label	Catalog Number	Title	Type	Country	Year	Longbox Value / Value
Singles						
Ariola	BVDR-80	Melodies	CD3	Japan	1992	$12.00/$3.00
Ariola	BVDR-125	My Eyes	CD3	Japan	1992	$12.00/$3.00
Ariola	BVDR-175	Nocturne	CD3	Japan	1992	$12.00/$3.00
Ariola	BVDR-154	To You	CD3	Japan	1992	$12.00/$3.00

Die Krupps

Label	Catalog Number	Title	Type	Country	Year	Longbox Value / Value
Singles						
		Crossfire	CD5	Germany	1994	$11.00
		Enter Sandman	CDJ	Australia	1994	$15.00
Hollywood	66269-2	Enter Sandman	CD5	U.S.	1993	$5.00
Hollywood	10372 0	Enter Sandman	CDJ	U.S.	1993	$3.00

Die Laughing

Label	Catalog Number	Title	Type	Country	Year	Longbox Value / Value
Singles						
Curb	CD45 79087	Humans	CDJ	U.S.	1990	$2.00

Died Pretty

Label	Catalog Number	Title	Type	Country	Year	Longbox Value / Value
Full Length						
Columbia		Caressing Swine...and Some History	DJ/Smplr	U.S.	1994	$12.00
RCA	61106	Doughboy Hollow	LP/LB	U.S.		$14.00/$8.00
Beggars Banquet	2092	Every Brilliant Eye	LP/LB	U.S.		$14.00/$8.00
Singles						
Columbia	6549544	Harness Up	CD5	U.K.	1994	$8.00
Columbia	CSK 5666	Harness Up	CDJ	U.S.	1994	$2.00
SPV	0536-3	Stop Myself	CD5	Germany	1991	$8.00
Beggars Banquet	BEG-238CD	Whitlam Square	CD5	U.K.	1990	$8.00

Diesel

Label	Catalog Number	Title	Type	Country	Year	Longbox Value / Value
Singles						
Parlophone	CDR-6322	Come to Me	CD5	U.K.	1992	$8.00
Giant	PRO-CD-6165	Tip of My Tounge	CDJ	U.S.	1993	$2.00

Diesel, Johnny & The Injectors

Label	Catalog Number	Title	Type	Country	Year	Longbox Value / Value
Full Length						
Chrysalis	41672	Johnny Diesel & The Injectors	DJ/LP	U.S.	1989	$10.00
Chrysalis	21672	Johnny Diesel & The Injectors	LP/LB	U.S.	1989	$14.00/$8.00
Singles						
Chrysalis	CHSCD-3466	Cry In Shame	CD5	U.K.	1989	$8.00
Chrysalis	662136	Don't Need Love	CD5	Germany	1989	$8.00
Chrysalis	CHSCD-3359	Don't Need Love	CD5	U.K.	1989	$8.00
EMI	323621-2	Please Send Me Someone to Love	CD5	Germany	1990	$8.00
Chrysalis	662425	Soul Revival	CD5	Germany	1989	$8.00
Chrysalis	CHSCD-3383	Soul Revival	CD5	U.K.	1989	$8.00

Diesel Park West

Label	Catalog Number	Title	Type	Country	Year	Longbox Value / Value
Full Length						
EMI	CDP-91689	Shakespeare Alabama	LP/LB	U.S.		$14.00/$8.00
Singles						
EMI	203219-2	All the Myths on Sunday	CD5	Germany	1989	$8.00
EMI	CDFOOD-17	All the Myths on Sunday	CD5	U.K.	1989	$8.00
EMI	CDFOOD-36	Boy on Top of the News	CD5	U.K.	1992	$8.00
EMI	CDFOOD-135	Fall in Love	CD5	U.K.	1992	$8.00
EMI	CDFOOD-39	God Only Knows	CD5	U.K.	1992	$8.00
		Here I Stand	CDJ	U.S.		$2.00
EMI	CDFOOD-15	Jackie's Still Sad	CD5	U.K.	1989	$8.00
EMI	203294-2	Like Princes Do	CD5	Germany	1989	$8.00
EMI	CDFOOD-19	Like Princes Do	CD5	U.K.	1989	$8.00
EMI	CDFOOD-20	When the Hoodoo Comes	CD5	U.K.	1989	$8.00
		When the Hoodoo Comes	CDJ	U.S.		$2.00

Dietrich, Marlene

Label	Catalog Number	Title	Type	Country	Year	Longbox Value / Value
Full Length						
Pro Jazz	517	Blue Angel	LP/BP	U.S.		$14.00/$8.00

Dif Juz

Label	Catalog Number	Title	Type	Country	Year	Longbox Value / Value
Full Length						
4AD	CAD-505CD	Extractions	LP/LB	U.S.		$15.00/$9.00

Diffie, Joe

Label	Catalog Number	Title	Type	Country	Year	Longbox Value / Value
Full Length						
		'90s Country	RS	U.S.	1996	$25.00
Airdate: 2/3/96.						
		Country Concert	RS	U.S.	1994	$40.00
Airdate: 8/8/94.						
		Live at the Crazy Horses	RS	U.S.	1994	$50.00
Airdate: 11/14/94.						
Singles						
Epic	ESK 74123	Is It Cold	CDJ	U.S.	1991	$2.00

Difford & Tilbrock

Label	Catalog Number	Title	Type	Country	Year	Longbox Value / Value
Full Length						
A&M	CD-4985	Difford & Tilbrock	LP/LB	U.S.		$14.00/$8.00
A&M	CD-4985	Difford & Tilbrock	LP/LB	U.S.†	1984	$14.00/$8.00

Dig

Label	Catalog Number	Title	Type	Country	Year	Longbox Value / Value
Singles						
Wasteland	2864	Believe	CDJ	U.S.	1993	$2.00
Wasteland	2770	I'll Stay High	CDJ	U.S.	1993	$2.00
Wasteland	10781	Runt	CD5	U.S.	1993	$5.00
		Unlucky Friend	CD5	U.K.		$10.00
		Unlucky Friend	CD5	U.K.		$10.00
Second version.						
Radioactive	3017	Unlucky Friend	CDJ	U.S.	1994	$2.00

Digable Planets

Full Length

Label	Catalog Number	Title	Type	Country	Year	Longbox Value / Value
EMI	DPRO-19937	Dial 7 Interview	DJ/Intvw	U.S.	1995	$10.00
Pendulum	8810	Nickel Bag	CDJ	U.S.	1993	$2.00
Elektra	EKR-159CD	Rebirth Of Slick	CD5	U.K.	1993	$8.00
Pendulum	88643	Rebirth Of Slick	CDJ	U.S.	1993	$2.00
Pendulum	8786	Where I'm From	CDJ	U.S.	1993	$2.00

Digital Excitation

Singles

Label	Catalog Number	Title	Type	Country	Year	Longbox Value / Value
BMG	RSUK-10CD	Pure Pleasure	CD5	U.K.	1992	$8.00

Digital Orgasm

Singles

Label	Catalog Number	Title	Type	Country	Year	Longbox Value / Value
White Lbl	5826	Guilty of Love	CDJ	U.S.	1993	$2.00
Dead Good	GOOD-17CD	Moog Eruption	CD5	U.K.	1992	$8.00
CBS	657706-2	Running Out of Time	CD5	Germany	1992	$8.00
Dead Good	GOOD-9CD	Running Out of Time	CD5	U.K.	1992	$8.00
Dead Good	GOOD-13CD	Startouchers	CD5	U.K.	1992	$8.00

Digital Soul Production

Singles

Label	Catalog Number	Title	Type	Country	Year	Longbox Value / Value
Toshiba	XRCN-1012	Do the Bogle Dance	CD3	Japan	1992	$12.00/$3.00

Digital Underground

Singles

Label	Catalog Number	Title	Type	Country	Year	Longbox Value / Value
BCM	BCM-330CD	Doowutchyalike	CD5	U.K.	1990	$9.00
BCM	BCM-463CD	Doowutchyalike	CD5	U.K.	1990	$9.00
Tommy Boy		Doowutchyalike	CDJ	U.S.	1990	$2.00
BCM	20364	Humpty Dance	CD5	Germany	1990	$10.00
BCM	BCM-364CD	Humpty Dance	CD5	U.K.	1990	$10.00
CBS	SRCS-5604	Kiss You Back	CD5	Japan	1991	$12.00
Big Life	BLRD-63	Kiss You Back	CD5	U.K.	1991	$9.00
Tommy Boy	993	Kiss You Back	CDJ	U.S.	1991	$2.00
Intercord	825 938	No Nose Job	CD5	Germany	1992	$9.00
Big Life	BLRD-71	No Nose Job	CD5	U.K.	1992	$9.00
Tommy Boy	CD513	No Nose Job	CD5	U.S.	1991	$5.00
Tommy Boy	CD525	No Nose Job	CDJ	U.S.	1991	$2.00
BCM	20476	Pocket Man	CD5	Germany	1990	$9.00
BCM	20463	Remix Double	CD5	Germany	1990	$9.00
Tommy Boy	587	Return of the Crazy	CD5	U.S.	1993	$6.00
Big Life	BLR-40CD	Same Song	CD5	U.K.	1991	$9.00
Reprise	PRO-CD-4583	Same Song	CDJ	U.S.	1991	$2.00
Tommy Boy	964	This is an EP	CD5	U.S.	1991	$5.00
Tommy Boy	615	Wussup Eit the Luv	CDJ	U.S.	1994	$2.00

Dillinger

Singles

Label	Catalog Number	Title	Type	Country	Year	Longbox Value / Value
JRS	JSP 5800	Can It Be Love	CDJ	U.S.	1991	$2.00
Black Swan	BSXCD-9	Cokane in My Brain	CD5	U.K.	1992	$8.00
JRS	JSP 800	Home For Better Days	CDJ	U.S.	1991	$2.00

Dillon, Dean

Full Length

Label	Catalog Number	Title	Type	Country	Year	Longbox Value / Value
Atlantic	82183-2	Out of Every Lovin' Mind	LP/LB	U.S.		$14.00/$8.00
Capitol	CDP-48920-2	Slick Nickel	LP/LB	U.S.		$14.00/$8.00

Singles

Label	Catalog Number	Title	Type	Country	Year	Longbox Value / Value
Atlantic	PRCD 5007-2	Hot, Country, and Single	CDJ	U.S.	1993	$2.00

Dillon Fence

Singles

Label	Catalog Number	Title	Type	Country	Year	Longbox Value / Value
Rough Trade	378-4031-3	Christmas	CD5	Germany	1992	$8.00
Rough Trade	MR-0031-2	Christmas	CD5	U.K.	1992	$8.00
Mammoth	0031	Christmas	CD5	U.S.	1991	$4.00

Dim Stars

Singles

Label	Catalog Number	Title	Type	Country	Year	Longbox Value / Value
APT	PAPER-015CD	Plug	CD5	U.K.	1991	$8.00

Dimension

Singles

Label	Catalog Number	Title	Type	Country	Year	Longbox Value / Value
BMG	BMDR-124	Round Trip	CD3	Japan	1992	$12.00/$3.00

Dimples

Singles

Label	Catalog Number	Title	Type	Country	Year	Longbox Value / Value
		Can't Live With or Without You	CDJ	U.S.		$2.00
	7774	Circle You With Love	CD5	U.S.	1994	$5.00

Dink

Singles

Label	Catalog Number	Title	Type	Country	Year	Longbox Value / Value
Capital	58273	Green Mind	CD5	U.S.	1994	$5.00
		Green Mind	CDJ	U.S.	1994	$7.00

Dino

Full Length

Label	Catalog Number	Title	Type	Country	Year	Longbox Value / Value
Island	422 896 481 2	Swingin'	DJ/LP	U.S.	1990	$8.00
	CD and cassette in box.					
Island	846481-2	Swingin'	LP/LB	U.S.	1990	$9.00/$6.00

Singles

Label	Catalog Number	Title	Type	Country	Year	Longbox Value / Value
Island	PRCD 6645-2	Gentle	CDJ	U.S.	1990	$2.00
Island	662619	I Like It	CD5	Germany	1989	$8.00
Island	662781	I Like It	CD5	Germany	1989	$8.00
Polydor	P09D-31006	I Like It	CD3	Japan	1989	$12.00/$3.00
Island	CID-435	I Like It	CD5	U.K.	1989	$8.00
Aris	884892	Romeo	CD3	Germany	1990	$8.00
Polydor	PSDD-1008	Romeo	CD3	Japan	1990	$12.00/$3.00
Island		Romeo	CDJ	U.S.	1990	$2.00
4th & B'way	CCD 7488	Summer Girls	CDJ	U.S.	1988	$2.00
4th & B'way	CCD 7489	Sunshine	CDJ	U.S.	1989	$2.00
Polydor	P09D-31004	Twenty Four	CD3	Japan	1989	$12.00/$3.00

Dinosaur Jr.

Full Length

Label	Catalog Number	Title	Type	Country	Year	Longbox Value / Value
		In A Jar	DJ/Smplr	France		$20.00
Westwood One		In Concert - Nu Rock	RS	U.S.	1994	$65.00
	2 CD set. With James, Airdate: 6/6/94.					
Westwood One		In Concert-Nu Rock	RS	U.S.	1995	$50.00
	Airdate: 2/27/95.					
		Keeblin'	LTD/LP	Australia	1995	$35.00
	2CD set.					
SST	SST-CD-16078	Little Furry Things	LP	Germany		$18.00
Sire	PRO-CD-6143	Out There	DJ/Smplr	U.S.	1993	$15.00

Singles

Label	Catalog Number	Title	Type	Country	Year	Longbox Value / Value
		Feel the Pain	CD5	U.K.	1994	$10.00
Sire	PRO-CD-7087	Feel the Pain	CDJ	U.S.		$3.00
SST	220	Freak Scene	CD5	U.S.	1991	$5.00
Blanco	WMC5-562	Get Me	CD5	Japan	1992	$16.00
Blanco	NEG-60 CD	Get Me	CD5	U.K.	1992	$10.00
Sire	PRO-CD-6328	Goin' Home	CDJ	U.S.	1993	$2.00
Sire	PRO-CD-7541	Grab It	CDJ	U.S.		$3.00
Pinnacle		I Don't Think So	CD5	U.K.	1994	$10.00
Pinnacle	BFFP-47CD	Just Like Heaven	CD5	U.K.	1991	$10.00
SST	SSTCD244	Just Like Heaven	CD5	U.S.	1991	$5.00
		Out There	CD5	U.K.	1992	$10.00
		Out There	CD5	U.K.	1992	$10.00
	Second version.					
Sire		Out There	CDJ	U.S.	1992	$2.00
Blanco	NEG-61CD	Start Coppin'	CD5	U.K.	1992	$10.00
Sire	PRO-CD-5915	Start Coppin'	CDJ	U.S.	1992	$2.00
Blanco	173006-2	Wagon, The	CD5	Germany	1991	$10.00
Blanco	NEG-48CD	Wagon, The	CD5	U.K.	1991	$10.00
Sire	PRO-CD-4704	Wagon, The	CDJ	U.S.	1991	$2.00
Blanco	9031-75390-2	Whatever's Cool With Me	CD5	Germany	1991	$10.00
Blanco	NEG-52CD	Whatever's Cool With Me	CD5	U.K.	1991	$10.00

Dio

Full Length

Label	Catalog Number	Title	Type	Country	Year	Longbox Value / Value
Vertigo		Excerpts From Lock Up the Wolves	DJ/Smplr	U.K.	1990	$15.00
Foundations		FZ	DJ/Intvw	U.S.	1992	$8.00
Vertigo		Great Box	LP	Japan	1990	$65.00
	4 CD set.					
Warner Brothers	9 25100-2	Last in Line	LP/LB	U.S.	1985	$14.00/$8.00
Reprise	9 26212-2-DJ	Lock Up the Wolves	DJ/LP	U.S.	1990	$30.00
	Picture disc CD in Leatherbound digipak.					

Singles

Label	Catalog Number	Title	Type	Country	Year	Longbox Value / Value
Reprise	PRO-CD-4360	Born on the Sun	CDJ	U.S.	1990	$2.00
Reprise	PRO-CD-6760	Evilution	CDJ	U.S.	1994	$2.00
Vertigo	DIOCD-9	Hey Angel	CD5	U.K.	1990	$10.00
Reprise	PRO-CD-4476	Hey Angel	CDJ	U.S.	1990	$2.00
Reprise	PRO-CD-6914	Jesus, Mary & the Holy Ghost	CDJ	U.S.	1994	$2.00
Reprise	PRO-CD-4080	Wild One	CDJ	U.S.	1990	$2.00

Dion (and the Belmonts)

Full Length

Label	Catalog Number	Title	Type	Country	Year	Longbox Value / Value
Ace	CDCH-176	Dion Hits	LP/BP	U.S.		$14.00/$8.00
Columbia	CK-31942	Greatest Hits	LP/LB	U.S.		$14.00/$8.00
Ace	CDCH-915	Runaround Sue	LP/BP	U.S.		$14.00/$8.00
		Unison	DJ/Smplr	U.K.		$25.00
	CD in box.					
Arista		Yo Franki	DJ/Smplr	U.K.		$8.00

Singles

Label	Catalog Number	Title	Type	Country	Year	Longbox Value / Value
Arista	662229	And the Night Stood Still	CD5	Germany	1989	$9.00
Arista	A10D-123	And the Night Stood Still	CD3	Japan	1989	$13.00/$4.00
Arista	662229	And the Night Stood Still	CD5	U.K.	1989	$9.00
Arista	ARCD-9797	And the Night Stood Still	CDJ	U.S.	1989	$2.00
Varese	VSDS-3338	Dream Lover	CD5	U.K.	1991	$11.00
Varese	662556	King of the New York Streets	CD5	U.K.	1989	$9.00
CBS	77230	Power of Love	CD5	U.S.	1994	$5.00
Island	PRCD 6633-2	Romeo	CDJ	U.S.	1990	$2.00
Elektra	PRCD 8191-2	Sea Cruise	CDJ	U.S.	1990	$2.00
Old Gold	OG-6112	Wanderer	CD3	U.K.	1989	$10.00
Arista	662910	Written on the Subway Walls	CD5	U.K.	1990	$9.00

Dion, Celine

Full Length

Label	Catalog Number	Title	Type	Country	Year	Longbox Value / Value
Epic	ESK 4504	Celine Dion	DJ/Smplr	U.S.	1992	$5.00
CBS		Celine/Unison	LTD/LP	Australia		$39.00
	2 CD set.					
Sony	DNK 001133	Collection, The	DJ/Smplr	Canada	1996	$35.00
Epic	ESCA-6340	Colour Of My Love	LTD/LP	Japan		$50.00

Singles

Label	Catalog Number	Title	Type	Country	Year	Longbox Value / Value
	CDP 101	A Quatre pas Dici	CDJ	U.K.		$16.00
CBS	SAMPCD 3437	All By Myself	CDJ	Spain	1996	$30.00
Epic	656160-5	Any Other Way	CD5	Germany	1991	$9.00
Epic	656160-2	Any Other Way	CD5	Germany	1991	$9.00
Epic	ESDA-7070	Any Other Way	CD3	Japan	1991	$13.00/$4.00
Epic	ESK 73665	Any Other Way	CDJ	U.S.	1990	$2.00
Epic	ESDA-7093	Beauty and the Beast	CD3	Japan	1992	$13.00/$3.00
	With Peabo Bryson.					
		Beauty and the Beast	CDJ	U.K.	1993	$25.00
	With Peabo Bryson.					
Epic	ESK 74090	Beauty and the Beast	CDJ	U.S.	1991	$3.00
	With Peabo Bryson.					
Epic	ESDA-7165	Because You Love Me	CD3	Japan	1995	$13.00/$4.00
Epic		Calling You	CDJ	France	1995	$20.00
Epic	ESDA-7095	If You Asked Me To	CD3	Japan	1992	$13.00/$4.00
Epic	658192-2	If You Asked Me To	CD5	U.K.	1992	$9.00
Epic	ESK 74277	If You Asked Me To	CDJ	U.S.	1992	$2.00
CBS	SAMPCD 29841	Just Walk Away	CDJ	Spain	1996	$30.00
Epic	ESDA-7073	Last to Know	CD3	Japan	1991	$13.00/$4.00
Epic	657333-2	Last to Know	CD5	U.K.	1991	$9.00
Epic	ESK 4141	Last To Know	CDJ	U.S.	1991	$2.00
CBS		Le Ballet	CDJ	France	1996	$45.00
Epic	ESDA-7116	Love Can Move Mountains	CD3	Japan	1992	$13.00/$4.00
Epic	658778-2	Love Can Move Mountains	CD5	U.K.	1992	$9.00
Epic	44K 74817	Love Can Move Mountains	CD5	U.S.	1992	$4.00
Epic	ESK 4875	Love Can Move Mountains	CDJ	U.S.	1992	$2.00
Columbia	38K77344	Misled	CD5	Canada	1994	$8.00
Epic	ESCA-5948	Misled	CD5	Japan		$20.00
Epic	ESSA-5948	Misled	CDJ	Japan		$25.00
Epic		Misled	CD5	U.K.	1994	$10.00
Epic		Misled	CD5	U.K.	1994	$10.00
	Second version.					
Epic		Misled	CDJ	U.K.	1994	$12.00
Epic	550 77344	Misled	CDJ	U.S.	1994	$6.00
Epic	ESDA-7104	Nothing Broken But My Heart	CD3	Japan	1992	$13.00/$4.00
Epic	ESK 74336	Nothing Broken But My Heart	CDJ	U.S.	1992	$2.00
		Only One Road	CDJ	U.K.		$10.00
CBS	77230	Power Of Love	CD5	U.S.	1994	$5.00
		Power Of Love, The	CDJ	U.K.	1993	$10.00
550 Music	CSK 5481	Power Of Love, The	CDJ	U.S.	1993	$2.00
		Think Twice	CD5	U.K.		$10.00
		Think Twice	CD5	U.K.		$10.00
	Second version.					
Epic	ESDA-7161	To Love You More	CD3	Japan		$13.00/$4.00
		To M'aimes Encore (To Love Me Again)	CD5	U.K.		$10.00
		To M'aimes Encore (To Love Me Again)	CD5	U.K.		$10.00
	Second version.					
Epic	ESCA-5184	Unison	CD5	Japan	1991	$20.00
Epic	Epic 74809	Water From the Moon	CDJ	U.S.	1992	$2.00
Epic	ESDA-7149	When I Fall in Love	CD3	Japan	1995	$13.00/$4.00
		Where Does My Heart Beat Now	CD5	U.K.		$10.00
Epic	656326-5	Where Does My Heart Beat Now	CD5	U.K.	1991	$9.00
Epic	656326-2	Where Does My Heart Beat Now	CD5	U.K.	1991	$9.00

Label	Catalog Number	Title	Type	Country	Year	Longbox Value / Value
Epic		Ziggy	CDJ	France	1995	$20.00

Dire Straits

Full Length

Label	Catalog Number	Title	Type	Country	Year	Longbox Value / Value
Vertigo	SND-31	1977-1993	DJ/Smplr	Japan	1993	$270.00
Warner Brothers	9 25085-2	Alchemy	LP/LB	U.S.†	1984	$20.00/$15.00
	2 CD set.					
Image	ID6305	Alchemy Live	LD	U.S.		$30.00
BBC Radio		BBC Classic Tracks	RS	U.S.	1991	$45.00
	Airdate: 4/15/91.					
BBC Radio		BBC Classic Tracks	RS	U.S.	1992	$35.00
	Airdate: 6/29/92.					
Warner Brothers	9 25264-2	Brothers in Arms	LP/LB	U.S.†	1985	$14.00/$8.00
		Classic CD (Brothers In Arms)	RS	U.S.	1990	$50.00
	2 CD set. Airdate: 5/28/90.					
Warner Brothers	3330-2	Communique	LP/LB	U.S.†	1984	$14.00/$8.00
Warner Brothers	3266-2	Dire Strait	LP/LB	U.S.†	1984	$14.00/$8.00
Vertigo		Great Box	LTD/LP	Japan	1991	$80.00
	4 CD boxed set.					
Westwood One		In Concert	RS	U.S.	1992	$70.00
	2 CD set. With Police, Airdate: 8/17/92.					
Westwood One		In Concert	RS	U.S.	1993	$50.00
	Airdate: 11/8/93.					
Album Network		In the Studio (Brothers In Arms)	RS	U.S.		$35.00
Album Network		In the Studio (Dire Straits)	RS	U.S.		$35.00
DIR		King Biscuit Flour Hour	RS	U.S.	1987	$50.00
	Airdate: 9/20/87.					
		Live at the BBC	DJ/Smplr	U.K.	1995	$45.00
		Live at the BBC	LTD/LP	U.K.	1995	$25.00
	Digipak version.					
Warner Brothers	23728-2	Love Over Gold	LP/LB	U.S.†	1984	$14.00/$8.00
WEA	38345	On the Night	LD	U.S.	1993	$35.00
WEA	[illegible]	The Videos	LD	U.S.	1993	$35.00
		Timothy White Sessions	RS	U.S.	1992	$150.00
	2 CD set. Airdate: 3/9/92.					
Vertigo	SEPT 1	Until September	DJ/Smplr	U.K.	1991	$20.00
Media America		Up Close	RS	U.S.	1992	$50.00
	2 CD set.					

Singles

Label	Catalog Number	Title	Type	Country	Year	Longbox Value / Value
Vertigo/Philips	884 2852-2	Brothers In Arms	CD5	Germany	1985	$150.00
Warner Brothers	9 25812-2	Brothers In Arms	CDV/BP	U.S.	1988	$20.00/$20.00
Vertigo	DSCD 19	Bug, The	CD5	U.K.		$9.00
		Calling Elvis	CDJ	Canada	1991	$6.00
Vertigo	PHDR-33	Calling Elvis	CD3	Japan	1991	$15.00/$4.00
Vertigo	DSCD-16	Calling Elvis	CD5	U.K.	1991	$10.00
Warner Brothers	PRO-CD-4953	Calling Elvis	CDJ	U.S.	1991	$7.00
Vertigo		Encores	CD5	U.K.	1993	$10.00
Vertigo	886090-2	Heavy Fuel	CD5	Germany	1991	$10.00
Vertigo	DSHAM 17	Heavy Fuel	CD3	U.K.	1991	$10.00
Vertigo	DSHAM 17	Heavy Fuel	CD3	U.K.	1991	$25.00
	Hamburger Package.					
Warner Brothers	PRO-CD-5126	Heavy Fuel	CDJ	U.S.	1991	$3.00
Warner Brothers	PRO-CD-5134	Heavy Fuel	CDJ	U.S.	1991	$3.00
Polygram	CDP 330	I Think I Love You Too Much	CDJ	U.S.	1990	$7.00
Polygram		On Every Street	CD5	France	1991	$12.00
Vertigo	DSCDR--18	On Every Street	CD5	U.K.	1991	$10.00
Warner Brothers	PRO-CD-5394	On Every Street	CDJ	U.S.	1991	$6.00
Vertigo		On the Night	CDJ	U.K.		$20.00
Vertigo	872611-2	Sultans of Swing	CD5	Germany	1988	$11.00
Vertigo	DSCD-15	Sultans of Swing	CD5	U.K.	1988	$11.00
Warner Brothers	9 25814-2	Sultans of Swing	CDV/BP	U.S.	1988	$20.00/$20.00
Vertigo		Ticket to Heaven	CD5	U.K.	1994	$10.00
Warner Brothers	9 25810-2	Twisting by the Pool	CDV/BP	U.S.	1988	$20.00/$20.00
Vertigo		Walk of Life	CDJ	U.K.	1985	N/A
Warner Brothers	9 25811-2	Walk of Life	CDV/BP	U.S.	1988	$20.00/$20.00

Dirt Merchants

Singles

Label	Catalog Number	Title	Type	Country	Year	Longbox Value / Value
Epic	ESK 7734	Love Arena	CDJ	U.S.		$6.00

Dirty Dozen Brass Band

Full Length

Label	Catalog Number	Title	Type	Country	Year	Longbox Value / Value
Concord	43005	My Feet Can't Fail Me Now	LP/BP	U.S.		$14.00/$8.00

Singles

Label	Catalog Number	Title	Type	Country	Year	Longbox Value / Value
Columbia	CSK 2036	That's How You Got Killed Before	CDJ	U.S.	1990	$2.00

Dirty Harry

Singles

Label	Catalog Number	Title	Type	Country	Year	Longbox Value / Value
SPV	7448-3	D'Bop	CD5	Germany	1988	$8.00
Subway	SUBWAY-15CD	D'Bop	CD5	U.K.	1988	$8.00
SPV	9438	Doouble B	CD5	Germany	1988	$8.00

Dirty Looks

Full Length

Label	Catalog Number	Title	Type	Country	Year	Longbox Value / Value
Atlantic	81992-2	Turn of the Screw	LP/LB	U.S.		$14.00/$8.00

Singles

Label	Catalog Number	Title	Type	Country	Year	Longbox Value / Value
Atlantic		Go Away	CDJ	U.S.		$2.00
Atlantic		Nobody Rides For Free	CDJ	U.S.		$2.00
Atlantic		Turn of the Screw	CDJ	U.S.		$2.00

Dirty Rhythm

Singles

Label	Catalog Number	Title	Type	Country	Year	Longbox Value / Value
BFE	852-2	Hot 'n Cold	CDJ	U.S.		$2.00

Dirty Rouge

Singles

Label	Catalog Number	Title	Type	Country	Year	Longbox Value / Value
Rough Trade	331-7001-3	Upstairs To Suzy	CD5	Germany	1992	$8.00

Dirty Water

Singles

Label	Catalog Number	Title	Type	Country	Year	Longbox Value / Value
BMG	664519	Gypsy Woman	CD5	Germany	1991	$8.00

Dirty White Boy

Full Length

Label	Catalog Number	Title	Type	Country	Year	Longbox Value / Value
Polydor	841959-2	Bad Reputation	LP/BP	U.S.		$14.00/$8.00

Singles

Label	Catalog Number	Title	Type	Country	Year	Longbox Value / Value
Polydor	877397-2	Lazy Crazy	CD5	U.K.	1990	$8.00
Polydor	CDP 221	Lazy Crazy	CDJ	U.S.	1990	$2.00
Polydor	PZCD-96	Let's Spend Momma's Money	CD5	U.K.	1990	$8.00
Polydor		Let's Spend Momma's Money	CDJ	U.S.	1990	$2.00

Dis-Dance

Singles

Label	Catalog Number	Title	Type	Country	Year	Longbox Value / Value
EMI	204413-2	Heat It Up	CD5	Germany	1991	$8.00
EMI	204414-2	Heat It Up	CD5	Germany	1991	$8.00

Dis-N-Dat

Singles

Label	Catalog Number	Title	Type	Country	Year	Longbox Value / Value
Epic	ESK 77152	Whoot, Here It Is	CDJ	U.S.	1993	$2.00
Epic	ESK 5452	Whoot, Here It Is	CDJ	U.S.	1993	$2.00

Disco Connection

Singles

Label	Catalog Number	Title	Type	Country	Year	Longbox Value / Value
ZYX	6163-8	Rock Your Baby	CD3	Germany	1989	$8.00

Disco Inferno

Singles

Label	Catalog Number	Title	Type	Country	Year	Longbox Value / Value
Cheree	CHREE-28CD	Summer's Last Sound	CD5	U.K.	1992	$8.00

Dishwalla

Full Length

Label	Catalog Number	Title	Type	Country	Year	Longbox Value / Value
Westwood One		In Concert-Nu Rock	RS	U.S.	1996	$35.00
	Airdate: 8/12/96.					

Singles

Label	Catalog Number	Title	Type	Country	Year	Longbox Value / Value
		Counting Blue Cars	CDJ	U.S.		$3.00

Dismember

Singles

Label	Catalog Number	Title	Type	Country	Year	Longbox Value / Value
SPV	2909-9	Skin Her Alive	CD5	Germany	1991	$8.00

Disposable Heroes of Hiphoprisy

Singles

Label	Catalog Number	Title	Type	Country	Year	Longbox Value / Value
4th & B'way	864287-2	Famous and Dandy Just Like Amos & Andy	CD5	Germany	1992	$9.00
EFA	CD-17641	Famous and Dandy Just Like Amos & Andy	CD5	Germany	1992	$9.00
4th & B'way	BRCD-259	Famous and Dandy Just Like Amos & Andy	CD5	U.K.	1992	$9.00
RTM	PLAY-16CD	Famous and Dandy Just Like Amos & Andy	CD5	U.K.	1992	$9.00
4th & B'way	BRCD-248	Language of Violence	CD5	U.K.	1992	$9.00
4th & B'way	162 440 551	Language of Violence	CD5	U.S.	[illegible]	[illegible]
		Television the Drug of the Nation	CD5	U.K.		$9.00
		Television the Drug of the Nation	CD5	U.K.		$9.00
	Second version.					
		Television the Drug of the Nation	CD5	U.K.		$10.00

Dissidenten

Full Length

Label	Catalog Number	Title	Type	Country	Year	Longbox Value / Value
Warner Brothers	26030-2	Out of This World	LP/LB	U.S.		$14.00/$8.00

Distance

Full Length

Label	Catalog Number	Title	Type	Country	Year	Longbox Value / Value
Reprise	9 26014-2	Under the One Sky	LP/LB	U.S.	1989	$14.00/$8.00

Singles

Label	Catalog Number	Title	Type	Country	Year	Longbox Value / Value
Reprise	PRO-CD-4323	Under the One Sky	CDJ	U.S.	1989	$2.00

Distant Cousins

Singles

Label	Catalog Number	Title	Type	Country	Year	Longbox Value / Value
Ghetto	GTGCD-9	Boo Hoo Hoo	CD5	U.K.	1990	$9.00
Ghetto	GTGC-9CD	I'll Be With You	CD5	U.K.	1990	$9.00
Virgin	VSCDT-1403	My Brother	CD5	U.K.	1990	$9.00
Intercord	827-416	You Used To	CD3	Germany	1989	$9.00
Ghetto	CDGTG-9	You Used To	CD5	U.K.	1990	$9.00
Virgin	VSCDT-1416	You Used To	CD5	U.K.	1992	$9.00

District 6

Full Length

Label	Catalog Number	Title	Type	Country	Year	Longbox Value / Value
		To Be Free	LP/BP	U.S.		$14.00/$8.00

Ditchmaster

Singles

Label	Catalog Number	Title	Type	Country	Year	Longbox Value / Value
Eastwest	9031-7248-2	Turtle Power	CD5	Germany	1990	$8.00

Diverse

Singles

Label	Catalog Number	Title	Type	Country	Year	Longbox Value / Value
Pikosso	872 00028	Hardcoremembranterminator	SCD5	Germany	1995	$20.00
	"Dragon" shaped CD.					
Pikosso	872 00023	In Line Skating	SCD5	Germany	1995	$18.00
	"In Line Skate" shaped CD.					
Pikosso	874 0005	Safari 2002	SCD5	Germany	1995	$18.00
	"Lion" shaped CD.					

Divine

Full Length

Label	Catalog Number	Title	Type	Country	Year	Longbox Value / Value
Aris	883118	Made In England	LP	Germany		$18.00

Singles

Label	Catalog Number	Title	Type	Country	Year	Longbox Value / Value
4th & B'Way	BRCD 296	All I Dream	CD5	U.K.	1993	$8.00
ZYX	5803-8	Hey You!	CD3	Germany	1988	$8.00

Divine Comedy

Singles

Label	Catalog Number	Title	Type	Country	Year	Longbox Value / Value
Rough Trade	344-0330-3	Euro Pop	CD5	Germany	1992	$8.00
Setanta	SET-011CD	Euro Pop	CD5	U.K.	1992	$8.00

Divine Weeks

Singles

Label	Catalog Number	Title	Type	Country	Year	Longbox Value / Value
First Warning	72705-75775	Preachin'	CDJ	U.S.	199	$1.00

Diving For Pearls

Singles

Label	Catalog Number	Title	Type	Country	Year	Longbox Value / Value
Epic	ESK 1696	Gimme Your Good Lovin'	CDJ	U.S.	1989	$2.00
Epic		Have You Forgotten?	CDJ	U.S.	1989	$2.00
Epic		New Moon	CDJ	U.S.	1989	$2.00

Divinyls

Full Length

Label	Catalog Number	Title	Type	Country	Year	Longbox Value / Value
Chrysalis	VK-41404	Desperate	LP/LB	U.S.		$15.00/$9.00
Virgin	PRCD VINYL	Divinyls	DJ/LP	U.S.	1990	$17.00
Chrysalis		Divinyls Live	LTD/LP	Australia	1994	$25.00
Virgin	DIV1	Interview, The	DJ/Intvw	Australia	1994	$25.00
		Live	LTD/LP	Australia	1994	$22.00
Chrysalis	VK-41627	Tempermental	LP/LB	U.S.		$15.00/$9.00
Chrysalis	VK-41511	What A Life	LP/LB	U.S.		$15.00/$9.00

Singles

Label	Catalog Number	Title	Type	Country	Year	Longbox Value / Value
Virgin	PRCD 4134	Bless My Soul	CDJ	U.S.	1991	$8.00
Virgin	663984	I Touch Myself	CD5	Germany	1990	$10.00
Virgin	VJDP 10155	I Touch Myself	CD3	Japan	1991	$12.00/$4.00
Virgin	VUSCD-36	I Touch Myself	CD5	U.K.	1990	$10.00
Virgin	PRCD 3666	I Touch Myself	CDJ	U.S.	1990	$3.00
Virgin	PRCD 4148	I'm On Your Side	CDJ	U.S.	1990	$3.00
Virgin	VJDP-10166	Make Out Alright	CD3	Japan	1991	$13.00/$4.00
Virgin	PRCD 3911	Make Out Alright	CDJ	U.S.	1991	$3.00

Dixie Cups

Singles

Label	Catalog Number	Title	Type	Country	Year	Longbox Value / Value
Aris	885825	Chapel of Love	CD3	Germany	1990	$10.00

Dixie Cups and Shangri-Las

Full Length

Label	Catalog Number	Title	Type	Country	Year	Longbox Value/Value
Charley	CDCHARLEY-38	Dixie Cups Meet Shangri-Las	LP/BP	U.S.		$14.00/$8.00

Dixie Dregs

Full Length

Label	Catalog Number	Title	Type	Country	Year	Longbox Value/Value
Arista	ARCD10-8116	Dregs Of the Eath	LP/LB	U.S.		$15.00/$10.00
		Freefall	LP/LB	U.S.		$12.00/$8.00

Singles

Label	Catalog Number	Title	Type	Country	Year	Longbox Value/Value
Cpricorn	PRO-CD-5540	Bloodsucking Leeches	CDJ	U.S.	1992	$3.00
Capricorn	PRO-CD-5820	Medley	CDJ	U.S.	1992	$3.00

Dixon, Bill

Full Length

Label	Catalog Number	Title	Type	Country	Year	Longbox Value/Value
Soul Note	1138	Son of Sisyphus	LP/BP	U.S.		$15.00/$9.00

Dixon, Don

Full Length

Label	Catalog Number	Title	Type	Country	Year	Longbox Value/Value
Enigma	73356	EEE	LP/LB	U.S.		$14.00/$8.00
		Romeo at Julliard	LP/LB	U.S.		$12.00/$8.00

Singles

Label	Catalog Number	Title	Type	Country	Year	Longbox Value/Value
Enigma	EPRO-226	Bad Reputation	CDJ	U.S.	1989	$2.00
		Gimme Little Sign	CDJ	U.S.		$2.00
Enigma	EPRO-248	Oh Cheap Chatter	CDJ	U.S.	1989	$2.00

Dixon, Willie

Full Length

Label	Catalog Number	Title	Type	Country	Year	Longbox Value/Value
Media America		Hoochie Koochie Mania Tribute	RS	U.S.	1992	$35.00

Airdate: 6/92.

Label	Catalog Number	Title	Type	Country	Year	Longbox Value/Value
MCA/Chess		Original Wang Dang Doodle, The	LP	U.S.	1995	$14.00

First pressing with combined sixth and seventh tracks.

Label	Catalog Number	Title	Type	Country	Year	Longbox Value/Value
Media America		Tribute	RS	U.S.	1992	$25.00

Airdate: 6/23/92.

DJ Miko

Singles

Label	Catalog Number	Title	Type	Country	Year	Longbox Value/Value
ZYX	66026	Hot Stuff	CD5	U.S.	1995	$6.00
ZYX	6691	What's Up	CD5	U.S.	1994	$5.00

Djaimin

Singles

Label	Catalog Number	Title	Type	Country	Year	Longbox Value/Value
Cooltempo	COOLCD-262	Give You	CD5	U.K.	1992	$8.00

Djavan

Full Length

Label	Catalog Number	Title	Type	Country	Year	Longbox Value/Value
Blue Note	CDP-96865-2	Alumbramento	LP/LB	U.S.		$19.00/$12.00

Djura

Singles

Label	Catalog Number	Title	Type	Country	Year	Longbox Value/Value
Luaka Bop	PRO-CD-6512	Adventures in Afropea 2	CDJ	U.S.	1992	$2.00

DMA

Singles

Label	Catalog Number	Title	Type	Country	Year	Longbox Value/Value
ZYX	6531-8	Gypsy Woman	CD5	Germany	1991	$6.00

DNA

Singles

Label	Catalog Number	Title	Type	Country	Year	Longbox Value/Value
EMI	CDEM-226	Blue Love	CD5	U.K.	1992	$10.00

Singles

Label	Catalog Number	Title	Type	Country	Year	Longbox Value/Value
EMI	204661-2	Can You Handle It	CD5	Germany	1992	$10.00
EMI	CDEM-219	Can You Handle It	CD5	U.K.	1992	$10.00
A&M	390564-2	Tom's Diner	CD5	Germany	1990	$11.00
Canyon	PCDY-10018	Tom's Diner	CD3	Japan	1990	$12.00/$4.00
A&M	AMCD-592	Tom's Diner	CD5	U.K.	1990	$11.00

Do

Singles

Label	Catalog Number	Title	Type	Country	Year	Longbox Value/Value
White Lbl	9 40725-2	Guilty of Love	CD5	U.S.	1993	$2.00
White Lbl	9 407934-2	Running Out of Time	CD5	U.S.	1993	$2.00

Do Re Mi

Singles

Label	Catalog Number	Title	Type	Country	Year	Longbox Value/Value
Virgin	VSCD-1005	Adultery	CD5	U.K.	1988	$8.00

Dobbyn, Dave

Full Length

Label	Catalog Number	Title	Type	Country	Year	Longbox Value/Value
Columbia	460655-2	Loyal	LP	Germany		$18.00

Doc

Singles

Label	Catalog Number	Title	Type	Country	Year	Longbox Value/Value
Ruthless	2762	Its Funky Enough	CDJ	U.S.	1989	$2.00
WEA	A-8984CD	Portrait of a Master	CD5	U.K.	1990	$8.00

Doc Box & B Fresh

Singles

Label	Catalog Number	Title	Type	Country	Year	Longbox Value/Value
Motown	ZD-43452	Slow Love	CD5	U.K.	1990	$8.00

Doctor Groove

Singles

Label	Catalog Number	Title	Type	Country	Year	Longbox Value/Value
Alfa	ALDB-114	Kommando	CD3	Japan	1991	$12.00/$3.00

Doctor Ice

Full Length

Label	Catalog Number	Title	Type	Country	Year	Longbox Value/Value
Jive	1280	Mic Stalker	LP/LB	U.S.		$14.00/$8.00

Censored version.

Label	Catalog Number	Title	Type	Country	Year	Longbox Value/Value
Jive	1249	Mic Stalker	LP/LB	U.S.		$14.00/$8.00

Uncensored version.

Doctor Rain

Singles

Label	Catalog Number	Title	Type	Country	Year	Longbox Value/Value
Ghost	GHOST-001CD	Suzanne	CD5	U.K.	1991	$8.00
Imago	28932	Wasted on You	CDJ	U.S.	1992	$2.00

Doctor Spin

Singles

Label	Catalog Number	Title	Type	Country	Year	Longbox Value/Value
Carpet	CRPCD-4	Tetris	CD5	U.K.	1992	$8.00

Doctor & the Medics

Full Length

Label	Catalog Number	Title	Type	Country	Year	Longbox Value/Value
IRS	42026	I Keep Thinking It's Tuesday	LP/LB	U.S.		$14.00/$8.00

Doctors Cat

Singles

Label	Catalog Number	Title	Type	Country	Year	Longbox Value/Value
ZYX	6160-8	Feel	CD5	Germany	1989	$6.00

Dodds, Johnny

Full Length

Label	Catalog Number	Title	Type	Country	Year	Longbox Value/Value
RCA	2293	Blue Clarinet Stomp	LP/BP	U.S.		$14.00/$8.00

Dodge City Productions

Singles

Label	Catalog Number	Title	Type	Country	Year	Longbox Value/Value
4th & B'way	BRCD-261	As Long As We're Around	CD5	U.K.	1993	$8.00
4th & B'way	BRCD-231	Clarity EP	CD5	U.K.	1993	$8.00

Dodgy

Singles

Label	Catalog Number	Title	Type	Country	Year	Longbox Value/Value
		Staying Out For the Summer	CD5	U.K.		$10.00
		Staying Out For the Summer	CD5	U.K.		$10.00

Second version.

Dodo and the Dodos

Singles

Label	Catalog Number	Title	Type	Country	Year	Longbox Value/Value
Polygram	887944-2	Give Me What I Want	CD5	Germany	1989	$8.00

Doe, John

Full Length

Label	Catalog Number	Title	Type	Country	Year	Longbox Value/Value
Geffen		Meet John Doe	LP/LB	U.S.		$14.00/$8.00

Singles

Label	Catalog Number	Title	Type	Country	Year	Longbox Value/Value
DGC	PRO-CD-4155	A Matter of Degrees	CDJ	U.S.	1990	$6.00
DGC	PRO-CD-5698	I Will Always Love You	CDJ	U.S.	1990	$2.00
DGC	PRO-CD-4115	Let's Be Mad	CDJ	U.S.	1990	$2.00

Dog, Tim

Singles

Label	Catalog Number	Title	Type	Country	Year	Longbox Value/Value
Ruffhouse	CSK 4465	Step to Me	CDJ	U.S.	1992	$2.00

Dog's Eye View

Full Length

Label	Catalog Number	Title	Type	Country	Year	Longbox Value/Value
Album Network		Album Network Special	RS	U.S.	1996	$40.00

Airdate: 6/2/96.

Singles

Label	Catalog Number	Title	Type	Country	Year	Longbox Value/Value
Columbia	CSK 7269	Happy Nowhere Sampler	CDJ	U.S.		$7.00

Dogdy

Singles

Label	Catalog Number	Title	Type	Country	Year	Longbox Value/Value
Bostin	BTN-002CDS	Easy Way	CD5	U.K.	1992	$8.00
Bostin	BTN-003CDS	Jungle Dark	CD5	U.K.	1992	$8.00

Dogg, Nate

Singles

Label	Catalog Number	Title	Type	Country	Year	Longbox Value/Value
	PRCD 6110	One More Day	CDJ	U.S.		$3.00

Doggett, Bill

Full Length

Label	Catalog Number	Title	Type	Country	Year	Longbox Value/Value
King	KCD-532	Dame Dreaming	LP/LB	U.S.		$14.00/$8.00
King	KCD-557	Doggett Beat For Dancing	LP/LB	U.S.		$14.00/$8.00

Doggy Stile

Singles

Label	Catalog Number	Title	Type	Country	Year	Longbox Value/Value
	525	Jelly Roll	CD5	U.S.	1994	$5.00

Dogs D'Amour

Full Length

Label	Catalog Number	Title	Type	Country	Year	Longbox Value/Value
China	P25P-20289	Errol Flynn	LTD/LP	Japan		$25.00

Picture disc CD.

Label	Catalog Number	Title	Type	Country	Year	Longbox Value/Value
Polydor	841168-2	Errol Flynn	LP/BP	U.S.		$15.00/$10.00
China	837368-2	In the Dynamite Jet Salon	LP	Germany		$15.00
Polydor	837368-2	In the Dynamite Jet Salon	LP/BP	U.S.		$15.00/$10.00
Polydor		King of Thieves	DJ/LP	U.S.		$13.00
Polydor		King of Thieves	LP/BP	U.S.		$15.00/$1.00
		More Uncharted	LP/VHS	U.K.	1994	$30.00

CD and VHS video in box.

Singles

Label	Catalog Number	Title	Type	Country	Year	Longbox Value/Value
		All or Nothing	CD5	U.K.	1993	$9.00
		All or Nothing	CD5	U.K.	1993	$9.00

Second version.

Label	Catalog Number	Title	Type	Country	Year	Longbox Value/Value
China	CHICD-30	Back on the Juice	CD5	U.K.	1990	$9.00
China	CHICD-27	Empty World	CD5	U.K.	1990	$9.00
China	P13P-37008	How Come It Never Rains	CD3	Japan	1988	$12.00/$4.00
China	CHICD-13	How Come It Never Rains	CD5	U.K.	1988	$9.00
Polydor	CDP 84	How Come It Never Rains	CDJ	U.S.	1988	$3.00
	WOKCDP 2033	No Gypsy Blood '93	CDJ	Austria	1993	$30.00
China	CHICD-17	Satellite Kid	CD5	U.K.	1989	$9.00
China	CHICD-20	Trail of Tears	CD5	U.K.	1988	$9.00
China	CDP 132	Trail of Tears	CDJ	U.S.	1989	$3.00
China	CHICD-24	Victims Of Success	CD5	U.K.	1990	$9.00

Doheny, Ned

Singles

Label	Catalog Number	Title	Type	Country	Year	Longbox Value/Value
Polydor	P10R-30002	Heartbreak In the Making	CD3	Japan	1989	$13.00/$4.00
Polydor	PSDW-1102	Love of Your Own	CD3	Japan	1991	$13.00/$4.00
Polydor	PSDW-1101	Mayo O Sutete	CD3	Japan	1991	$13.00/$4.00
Polydor	PSDW-3002	Two Worlds	CD3	Japan	1992	$13.00/$4.00

Dokken

Full Length

Label	Catalog Number	Title	Type	Country	Year	Longbox Value/Value
WEA	40102	Unchain The Night	LD	U.S.	1990	$25.00

Singles

Label	Catalog Number	Title	Type	Country	Year	Longbox Value/Value
Elektra	10P3-6033	Alone Again	CD3	Japan	1990	$12.00/$3.00
Elektra	PR 8039-2	Alone Again	CDJ	U.S.	1988	$3.00
Elektra	PR 2128-2	Burning Like a Flame	CDJ	U.S.	1988	$3.00
Repertoire	RR-6003	Day After Day	CD5	Germany	1989	$9.00
		Dysfunctional	CDJ	U.S.	1995	$8.00
Elektra	PR 2269-2	Heaven Sent	CDJ	U.S.	1988	$3.00
		Nothing Left To Say	CDJ	U.S.		$3.00
		Shadow of Life	CDJ	U.S.	1995	$3.00
Elektra	PR 8018-2	So Many Tears	CDJ	U.S.	1987	$3.00
		Too High To Fly	CDJ	U.S.	1995	$3.00
Elektra	10P3-6102	Walk Away	CD3	Japan	1988	$12.00/$3.00
Elektra	PR 8048-2	Walk Away	CDJ	U.S.	1988	$3.00

Dokken, Don

Full Length

Label	Catalog Number	Title	Type	Country	Year	Longbox Value/Value
Geffen		Up From the Ashes	LP/LB	U.S.		$12.00/$7.00

Singles

Label	Catalog Number	Title	Type	Country	Year	Longbox Value/Value
Geffen	PRO-CD-4214	Give It Up	CDJ	U.S.	1990	$3.00
Geffen	PRO-CD-4145	Mirror Mirror	CDJ	U.S.	1990	$3.00
Geffen	PRO-CD-4185	Stay	CDJ	U.S.	1990	$3.00

Dolby, Thomas

Full Length

Label	Catalog Number	Title	Type	Country	Year	Longbox Value/Value
EMI	CDP-48075	Aliens Ate My Buick	LP/LB	U.S.	1988	$15.00/$10.00

Label	Catalog Number	Title	Type	Country	Year	Longbox Value / Value
EMI	CDP-46028	Flat Earth, The	LP/LB	U.S.†	1985	$15.00/$10.00
EMI	CDP-46028	Flat Earth, The	LP/LB	U.S.	1988	$15.00/$10.00
EMI	CDP-46009	Golden Age of Wireless	LP/LB	U.S.†	1984	$14.00/$8.00
Pioneer	PA84-M011	Thomas Dolby	8"LD	U.S.	1984	$8.00

Singles

Label	Catalog Number	Title	Type	Country	Year	Longbox Value / Value
Toshiba	XP10-2016	Airhead	CD3	Japan	1988	$13.00/$4.00
EMI	CDMT-38	Airhead	CD5	U.K.	1988	$10.00
EMI	DPRO-04039	Airhead	CDJ	U.S.	1988	$2.00
Virgin	VJDP-10194	Close But No Cigar	CD3	Japan	1992	$13.00/$4.00
Virgin	VSCDJ 141	Close But No Cigar	CDJ	U.K.	1992	$10.00
Giant	PRO-CD-5786	Easteem	CDJ	U.S.	1992	$2.00
EMI	CDMT-59	Hot Sauce	CD5	U.K.	1989	$10.00
EMI		Hot Sauce	CDJ	U.S.	1989	$2.00
		Hyperactive	CD5	U.K.		$10.00
		Hyperactive	CD5	U.K.		$10.00
	Second version.					
Giant	PRO-CD-5958	I Love You Goodbye	CDJ	U.S.	1992	$2.00
EMI	CDMT-71	My Brain Is Like a Sieve	CD5	U.K.	1989	$10.00
Virgin	665478	Silk Pyjamas	CD5	Germany	1992	$10.00
Virgin	665479	Silk Pyjamas	CD5	Germany	1992	$12.00
Virgin	VSCDT-1430	Silk Pyjamas	CD5	U.K.	1992	$10.00
Virgin	VSCDG-1430	Silk Pyjamas	CD5	U.K.	1992	$12.00

Doldinger, Klaus

Full Length

Label	Catalog Number	Title	Type	Country	Year	Longbox Value / Value
Atlantic	82154-2	Balance of Happiness	LP/LB	U.S.		$14.00/$8.00

Dollar

Singles

Label	Catalog Number	Title	Type	Country	Year	Longbox Value / Value
London	886295-2	It's Nature's Way	CD5	Germany	1988	$8.00
London	LONCD-179	It's Nature's Way	CD5	U.K.	1988	$8.00

Dolmen

Singles

Label	Catalog Number	Title	Type	Country	Year	Longbox Value / Value
Polygram	889881-2	In Berlin	CD5	Germany	1989	$8.00

Dolphy, Eric

Full Length

Label	Catalog Number	Title	Type	Country	Year	Longbox Value / Value
Enja	3055-36	Stockholm Sessions	LP	Germany		$15.00
Enja	5045-24	Vintage Dolphy	LP	Germany		$15.00

Domain

Singles

Label	Catalog Number	Title	Type	Country	Year	Longbox Value / Value
Eastwest	170823-2	Edge of the Knife	CD3	Germany	1990	$8.00
Eastwest	247160-2	Heart of Stone	CD5	Germany	1990	$8.00

Domingo, Placido

Singles

Label	Catalog Number	Title	Type	Country	Year	Longbox Value / Value
CBS	CDGOYA-2	I Stand Alone	CD5	U.K.	1989	$10.00
CBS	654843-3	Till I Loved You	CD3	Germany	1989	$10.00
CBS	654843-2	Till I Loved You	CD5	U.K.	1989	$10.00

Dominique, Lisa

Singles

Label	Catalog Number	Title	Type	Country	Year	Longbox Value / Value
Aris	885621	All Fall Down	CD5	Germany	1990	$8.00
BMG	VHFXD-51	All Fall Down	CD5	U.K.	1990	$8.00

Domino

Singles

Label	Catalog Number	Title	Type	Country	Year	Longbox Value / Value
Outburst	77356	Sweet Potato Pie	CD5	U.S.	1994	$6.00
Outburst	77350	Sweet Potato Pie	CDJ	U.S.	1994	$3.00
MCA	MCA5P-3362	Tales From the Hood	CDJ	U.S.	1994	$3.00

Domino, Fats

Full Length

Label	Catalog Number	Title	Type	Country	Year	Longbox Value / Value
Liberty	790294-2	Best Of	LP	Germany		$16.00
EMI	CDP-746581-2	Best Of	LP/LB	U.S.		$15.00/$10.00
Grand Prix	CD-860705	Greatest	LP	Germany		$16.00
Polygram	830767-2	In Concert	LP/BP	U.S.		$15.00/$9.00
		Legendary Imperial Recordings	DJ/Smplr	U.S.	1995	$18.00
EMI		They Call Me the Fat Man	DJ/Smplr	U.S.	1993	$25.00

Singles

Label	Catalog Number	Title	Type	Country	Year	Longbox Value / Value
Aris	885826	Blueberry Hill	CD3	Germany	1990	$10.00
WEA	241605-2	Hello Josephine	CD5	Germany	1989	$10.00
EMI	204648-2	I'm Walkin'	CD5	Germany	1992	$10.00
Liberty	CDCL-596	My Blue Heaven	CD5	U.K.	1990	$10.00
EMI	DPRO-14668	My Blue Heaven	CDJ	U.S.	1990	$3.00

Domino Theory

Singles

Label	Catalog Number	Title	Type	Country	Year	Longbox Value / Value
RCA	9172-2-RDJ	Radio Driver	CDJ	U.S.	1990	$2.00
		Spanish Lullaby	CDJ	U.S.		$2.00

Dominoe

Singles

Label	Catalog Number	Title	Type	Country	Year	Longbox Value / Value
BMG	663056	Angel Don't Cry	CD5	Germany	1990	$8.00
Victor	VDPS-1026	Here I Am	CD3	Japan	1989	$12.00/$3.00
BMG	663532	Keep the Fire Burnin'	CD5	Germany	1990	$8.00

Dominos

Full Length

Label	Catalog Number	Title	Type	Country	Year	Longbox Value / Value
Charly	CD 44	Have Mercy Baby	LP	U.S.		$9.00

Don

Singles

Label	Catalog Number	Title	Type	Country	Year	Longbox Value / Value
Columbia	CSK 73916	Big 12 Inch	CDJ	U.S.	1991	$2.00
Columbia	44K 73727	In There	CDJ	U.S.	1991	$2.00

Don T

Singles

Label	Catalog Number	Title	Type	Country	Year	Longbox Value / Value
Atlantic	92468	Professional Girls	CD5	U.S.	1994	$5.00

Don't Know Yet

Singles

Label	Catalog Number	Title	Type	Country	Year	Longbox Value / Value
		What Time is It?	CDJ	U.S.		$2.00

Don-E

Singles

Label	Catalog Number	Title	Type	Country	Year	Longbox Value / Value
4th & B'way	PHCR-8703	Love Makes the World Go Round	CD3	Japan	1991	$13.00/$4.00
4th & B'way	BRCD-242	Love Makes the World Go Round	CD5	U.K.	1991	$8.00
Island	BRCD-260	Oh My Gosh	CD5	U.K.	1993	$8.00
Island	BRCD-256	Peace in the World	CD5	U.K.	1992	$8.00

Donald D

Singles

Label	Catalog Number	Title	Type	Country	Year	Longbox Value / Value
Sire	PRO-CD-5236	Let the Horns Blow	CDJ	U.S.	1991	$2.00

Donalds, Andre

Singles

Label	Catalog Number	Title	Type	Country	Year	Longbox Value / Value
	DPRO-79879	Mishale	CDJ	U.S.		$3.00

Donaldson, Lou

Full Length

Label	Catalog Number	Title	Type	Country	Year	Longbox Value / Value
Blue Note	CDP-84254-2	Lush Life	LP/LB	U.S.		$20.00/$15.00
Blue Note	CDP-84108-2	Natural Soul	LP/LB	U.S.		$20.00/$15.00
Blue Note	CDP-81537-2	Quartet/Quintet/Sextet	LP/LB	U.S.		$20.00/$15.00

Donheny, Ned

Full Length

Label	Catalog Number	Title	Type	Country	Year	Longbox Value / Value
		Postcards From Hollywood	DJ/LP	Japan	1994	$30.00
	Advance Issue.					

Donna

Singles

Label	Catalog Number	Title	Type	Country	Year	Longbox Value / Value
Canyon	PCDY-00064	Vogue	CD3	Japan	1990	$13.00/$4.00

Donovan

Full Length

Label	Catalog Number	Title	Type	Country	Year	Longbox Value / Value
Trace		Sunshine Superman	LP	Germany		$15.00

Singles

Label	Catalog Number	Title	Type	Country	Year	Longbox Value / Value
		As Time Goes By	CD5	U.K.		$10.00
		As Time Goes By	CD5	U.K.		$10.00
	Second version.					
GNA	61007	Hurdy Gurdy Man	CDJ	U.S.	1991	$3.00
CBS	654852-3	Jennifer Juniper	CD3	Germany	1989	$10.00
Mercury	SYPCD 1	Jennifer Juniper	CD3	U.K.	1990	$10.00
EMI	CDEM-98	Sunshine Superman	CD5	U.K.	1989	$10.00

Donovan, Jason

Full Length

Label	Catalog Number	Title	Type	Country	Year	Longbox Value / Value
Atlantic	82005-2	Ten Good Reasons	LP/LB	U.S.		$15.00/$10.00

Singles

Label	Catalog Number	Title	Type	Country	Year	Longbox Value / Value
PWL	9031-71930-2	Another Night	CD5	Germany	1990	$9.00
PWL	PWCD-58	Another Night	CD5	U.K.	1990	$9.00
Polygram	867317-2	Any Dream Will Do	CD5	Germany	1991	$9.00
Polydor	PODP-1035	Any Dream Will Do	CD3	Japan	1991	$13.00/$4.00
Polydor	POCP-1130	Any Dream Will Do	CD5	Japan	1991	$15.00
Polygram	RURCD-7	Any Dream Will Do	CD5	U.K.	1991	$9.00
PWL	09B3-75	Every Day (I Love You More)	CD3	Japan	1989	$13.00/$4.00
PWL	PWCD-43	Every Day (I Love You More)	CD5	U.K.	1989	$9.00
Atlantic	PR 3027-2	Every Day (I Love You More)	CDJ	U.S.	1989	$2.00
PWL	9031-71378-2	Hang on to Your Love	CD5	Germany	1990	$9.00
Alfa	ALDB-34	Hang on to Your Love	CD3	Japan	1990	$13.00/$4.00
PWL	PWCD-51	Hang on to Your Love	CD5	U.K.	1990	$9.00
PWL	9031-75320-2	Happy Together	CD5	Germany	1991	$9.00
Alfa	ALDB-138	Happy Together	CD3	Japan	1991	$13.00/$4.00
PWL	PWCD-203	Happy Together	CD5	U.K.	1991	$9.00
PWL	9031-72888-2	I'm Doing Fine	CD5	Germany	1990	$9.00
Alfa	ALDB-83	I'm Doing Fine	CD3	Japan	1990	$13.00/$4.00
PWL	PWCD-59	I'm Doing Fine	CD5	U.K.	1990	$9.00
Polydor	RURCD 9	Joseph Mega	CD5	U.K.	1991	$9.00
Polydor	PZCD-222	Mission of Love	CD5	U.K.	1992	$9.00
PWL	8 20948	Nothing Can Divide Us	CD5	Germany	1988	$9.00
PWL	10B3-1	Nothing Can Divide Us	CD3	Japan	1988	$13.00/$4.00
PWL	9031-74694-2	R.S.V.P.	CD5	Germany	1991	$9.00
PWL	ALCB-297	R.S.V.P.	CD5	Japan	1991	$15.00
PWL	PWCD-80	R.S.V.P.	CD5	U.K.	1991	$9.00
PWL	9031-72465-2	Rhythm of the Rain	CD5	Germany	1990	$9.00
Alfa	ALDB-53	Rhythm of the Rain	CD3	Japan	1990	$13.00/$4.00
PWL	PWCD-60	Rhythm of the Rain	CD5	U.K.	1990	$9.00
Eastwest	246899-2	Sealed With a Kiss	CD5	Germany	1989	$9.00
PWL	09B3-63	Sealed With a Kiss	CD3	Japan	1989	$13.00/$4.00
PWL	PWCD-39	Sealed With a Kiss	CD5	U.K.	1989	$9.00
		Sealed With a Kiss	CDJ	U.S.	1989	$2.00
Eastwest	247033-2	Too Many Broken Hearts	CD5	Germany	1989	$9.00
PWL	09B3-35	Too Many Broken Hearts	CD3	Japan	1989	$13.00/$4.00
PWL	11B3-36	Too Many Broken Hearts	CD3	Japan	1989	$13.00/$4.00
PWL	PWCD-32	Too Many Broken Hearts	CD5	U.K.	1989	$9.00
Atlantic	PR 2818-2	Too Many Broken Hearts	CDJ	U.S.	1989	$2.00
Alfa	ALDB-12	When You Come Back to Me	CD3	Japan	1990	$13.00/$4.00
Alfa	ALDB-13	When You Come Back to Me	CD3	Japan	1990	$13.00/$4.00
PWL	PWCD-46	When You Come Back to Me	CD5	U.K.	1990	$9.00

Doobie Brothers

Full Length

Label	Catalog Number	Title	Type	Country	Year	Longbox Value / Value
Westwood One		BBC Classic Tracks	RS	U.S.	1994	$25.00
	Airdate: 5/2/94.					
Warner Brothers	3112-2	Best Of	LP/LB	U.S.†	1985	$14.00/$8.00
Capitol	CDP-94623-2	Brotherhood	LP/LB	U.S.		$15.00/$10.00
		Columbia Records - Rockin' Down the Highway	RS	U.S.	1996	$75.00
	Airdate: 8/12/96.					
EMI		Cycles	DJ/LP	Japan		$40.00
	Advance issue.					
EMI	SPCD-1069	Cycles	DJ/Smpr	Japan	1989	$50.00
Capitol	CDP-90371-2	Cycles	LP/LB	U.S.		$15.00/$10.00
Album Network		In the Studio (Captain & Me)	RS	U.S.	1989	$20.00
	Airdate: 12/4/89.					
Album Network		In the Studio (Doobie Brothers)	RS	U.S.	1993	$20.00
	Airdate: 3/8/93.					
Album Network		In the Studio (Minute By Minute)	RS	U.S.		$20.00
Album Network		In the Studio (Takin' It To the Streets)	RS	U.S.	1990	$20.00
	Airdate: 7/6/90.					
Album Network		In the Studio (Toulouse St)	RS	U.S.	1989	$20.00
	Airdate: 6/12/89.					
DIR		King Biscuit Flour Hour	RS	U.S.	1988	$35.00
	Airdate: 8/14/88.					
DIR		King Biscuit Flour Hour	RS	U.S.	1989	$35.00
	Airdate: 8/21/89.					
DIR		King Biscuit Flour Hour	RS	U.S.	1992	$35.00
	Airdate: 4/12/92.					
DIR		King Biscuit Flour Hour	RS	U.S.	1993	$35.00
	Airdate: 1/24/93.					
DIR		King Biscuit Flour Hour	RS	U.S.	1994	$35.00
	Airdate: 5/18/94.					
DIR		King Biscuit Flour Hour	RS	U.S.	1995	$40.00
	Airdate: 4/23/95.					
Warner Brothers	3193-2	Minute by Minute	LP/LB	U.S.†	1984	$14.00/$8.00
Westwood One		Off the Record	RS	U.S.	1989	$30.00
	Airdate: 6/12/89.					
Radio Today		Rock Stars	RS	U.S.	1989	$30.00
	2 CD set. Airdate: 6/19/89.					
		Rockin' Down	DJ/Smplr	U.S.	1996	$18.00
		Rockin' Down the Highway Sampler	DJ/LP	U.S.	1996	$18.00

Label	Catalog Number	Title	Type	Country	Year	Longbox Value / Value
Westwood One		Superstar Concert	RS	U.S.	1992	$40.00
	2 CD set. Airdate: 6/14/92.					
Westwood One		Superstar Concert	RS	U.S.	1993	$40.00
	2 CD set. Airdate: 1/30/93.					
Westwood One		Superstars	RS	U.S.	1993	$40.00
	2 CD set. Airdate: 8/23/93.					
Media America		Up Close	RS	U.S.	1989	$40.00
	2 CD set.					
		Singles				
Capitol	DPRO-79662	Dangerous	CDJ	U.S.	1991	$3.00
EMI	203400-3	Doctor, The	CD3	Germany	1989	$10.00
Toshiba	XP10-2093	Doctor, The	CD3	Japan	1989	$13.00/$4.00
Capitol	CDCL-536	Doctor, The	CD5	U.K.	1989	$10.00
Capitol	DPRO-79600	Doctor, The	CDJ	U.S.	1989	$3.00
WEA	921133-2	Evil Woman	CD3	Germany	1989	$10.00
WEA	921133-2	Evil Woman	CD3	U.K.	1989	$10.00
		Long Train Runnin'	CD5	U.K.		$10.00
		Long Train Runnin'	CD5	U.K.		$10.00
	Second version.					
Toshiba	XP10-2108	Need a Little Taste of Love	CD3	Japan	1989	$13.00/$4.00
Capitol	CDCL-552	Need a Little Taste of Love	CD5	U.K.	1989	$10.00
Capitol	DPRO-79722	Need a Little Taste of Love	CDJ	U.S.	1989	$3.00
EMI	203722-2	One Chain	CD5	Germany	1989	$10.00
Capitol	DPRO-79786	One Chain	CDJ	U.S.	1989	$3.00
Capitol	DPRO-79820	Rollin' On	CDJ	U.S.	1991	$3.00
Capitol	DPRO-79859	Something You Said	CDJ	U.S.	1991	$3.00

Doop

Singles

Label	Catalog Number	Title	Type	Country	Year	Longbox Value / Value
MCA	54867	Doop	CD5	U.S.	1994	$5.00
	1280	Huckleberry Jam	CD5	U.S.	1994	$5.00

Doors

Full Length

Label	Catalog Number	Title	Type	Country	Year	Longbox Value / Value
Elektra	9 60269-2	Alive, She Cried	LP/LB	U.S.†	1985	$25.00/$22.00
Elektra	9 60269-2	Alive, She Cried	LP/LB	U.S.	1987	$25.00/$22.00
Pioneer	PA-85-126	Dance on Fire	LD	U.S.	1985	$30.00
Pioneer	PA-85-126	Dance on Fire	LD	U.S.	1990	$40.00
	Digital audio.					
Media America		Doors on the Inside, The	RS	U.S.	1988	$250.00
	6 CD set.					
Elektra	9 74007-2	Doors, The	LP/LB	U.S.†	1984	$16.00/$12.00
	Non-remastered version.					
Atlantic	50299-2	In Concert	LP/VHS	U.S.	1991	$35.00
	CD album and VHS Video in box.					
Album Network		In the Studio (Doors, The)	RS	U.S.	1988	$30.00
	Airdate: 8/1/88.					
Album Network		In the Studio (Doors, The)	RS	U.S.	1991	$25.00
	Airdate: 1/21/91.					
Album Network		In the Studio (Doors, The)	RS	U.S.	1992	$25.00
	Airdate: 1/6/92.					
Album Network		In the Studio (L.A. Woman)	RS	U.S.	1989	$35.00
	Airdate: 10/30/89.					
Album Network		In the Studio (Strange Days)	RS	U.S.	1989	$30.00
	Airdate: 1/16/89.					
Album Network		In the Studio (Strange Days)	RS	U.S.	1992	$30.00
	Airdate: 10/12/92.					
Elektra	9 75011-2	L.A. Woman	LP/LB	U.S.	1985	$14.00/$8.00
		Les Doors	DJ/Smplr	France	1991	$40.00
MCA		Live at the Hollywood Bowl	LD	U.S.	1987	$45.00
Elektra	9 60741-2	Live at the Hollywood Bowl	LP/LB	U.S.	1987	$30.00/$25.00
Media America		Media America Special	RS	U.S.	1996	$95.00
	3 CD set.					
		Selection of, The	DJ/Smpr	Japan		$300.00
Westwood One		Setting the Record Straight	RS	U.S.	1991	$350.00
	10 CD set.					
Westwood One		Superstar Concert	RS	U.S.	1992	$90.00
	2 CD set. Airdate: 7/5/92.					
Media America		Up Close	RS	U.S.	1994	$80.00
		Singles				
Elektra	WMC5-351	Break On Through	CD5	Japan	1991	$20.00
Pioneer	PIFF1001	Break On Through	CDV	Japan	1991	$45.00
Elektra	EKR-121CD	Break On Through	CD5	U.K.	1991	$14.00
Elektra	PRCD 8314-2	Break On Through	CDJ	U.S.	1991	$6.00
Elektra		Ghost Song	CDJ	Germany	1995	$20.00
		Light My Fire	CDJ	France	1992	$25.00
Elektra	WMD5-4068	Light My Fire	CD3	Japan	1992	$15.00/$4.00
Elektra	EKR-125CD	Light My Fire	CD5	U.K.	1992	$14.00
Elektra	65927-2	Light My Fire	CD5	U.S.	1992	$5.00
Elektra	969344-2	Riders on the Storm	CD3	Germany	1988	$14.00
Elektra	7559-66509-2	Riders on the Storm	CD5	Germany	1991	$14.00
Elektra	969344-2	Riders on the Storm	CD3	U.K.	1988	$14.00
Elektra	EKR-131CD	Riders on the Storm	CD5	U.K.	1991	$14.00
Elektra	PRCD 8361-2	Roadhouse Blues	CDJ	U.S.	1991	$7.00

Dore, Valerie

Singles

Label	Catalog Number	Title	Type	Country	Year	Longbox Value / Value
ZYX	6158-8	It's So Easy in the Night to Get Closer	CD5	Germany	1989	$8.00

Dorf, Steve & Friends

Singles

Label	Catalog Number	Title	Type	Country	Year	Longbox Value / Value
Warner Brothers		As Long As We Got Each Other	CDJ	U.S.		$2.00
Warner Brothers	PRO-CD-3432	Like the Whole Worlds Watching	CDJ	U.S.		$3.00
Reprise	PRO-CD-3256	Theme From "Growing Pains"	CDJ	U.S.	1988	$3.00

Dorham, Kenny

Full Length

Label	Catalog Number	Title	Type	Country	Year	Longbox Value / Value
Blue Note	CDP-46541-2	Round Midnight	LP/LB	U.S.		$18.00/$15.00
Blue Note	CDP-46542-2	Round Midnight Vol. 2	LP/LB	U.S.		$18.00/$15.00
EMI	B2-84181-2	Trompeta Toccata	LP	Germany		$25.00
Blue Note	CDP-46515-2	Una Mas	LP/LB	U.S.		$18.00/$15.00
Blue Note		Una Mas	LTD/LP	U.S.	1995	$19.00
Blue Note		Whistle Stop	LTD/LP	U.S.	1994	$20.00

Doro

Full Length

Label	Catalog Number	Title	Type	Country	Year	Longbox Value / Value
Mercury	846194-2	Doro	LP/BP	U.S.		$14.00/$8.00
Mercury	838016-2	Force Majeure	LP/BP	U.S.		$14.00/$8.00
		Singles				
Polygram	868975-2	Fall For Me Again	CD5	Germany	1991	$9.00
Polygram	876169-2	Hard Times	CD5	Germany	1989	$9.00
Mercury	CDP 341	Only You	CDJ	U.S.	1990	$2.00
Polygram	875579-2	Unholy Love	CD5	Germany	1990	$9.00
Mercury	CDP 264	Unholy Love	CDJ	U.S.	1990	$2.00
Polygram	872608-3	Whiter Shade of Pale	CD3	Germany	1989	$9.00
Polygram	872609-2	Whiter Shade of Pale	CD5	Germany	1989	$9.00
Mercury	CDP 86	Whiter Shade of Pale	CDJ	U.S.	1989	$2.00

Dorothy

Singles

Label	Catalog Number	Title	Type	Country	Year	Longbox Value / Value
Chrysalis	AZURCD-11	Loving Feeling	CD5	U.K.	1989	$8.00
BMG	611684	Still Waiting	CD5	Germany	1989	$8.00
Chrysalis	AZURCD-8	Still Waiting	CD5	U.K.	1989	$8.00

Dorsey, Gail Ann

Full Length

Label	Catalog Number	Title	Type	Country	Year	Longbox Value / Value
Warner Brothers	25913-2	Corporate World	LP/LB	U.S.		$14.00/$8.00
		Singles				
WEA	YZ-369CD	Just Another Dream	CD3	U.K.	1989	$8.00
WEA	YZ-194CD	Wasted Country	CD3	U.K.	1988	$8.00
WEA	YZ-324CD	Where the Love Is	CD3	U.K.	1989	$8.00

Dorsey, Jimmy

Full Length

Label	Catalog Number	Title	Type	Country	Year	Longbox Value / Value
WEA	781801-2	Then, and Now	LP	Germany		$18.00

Dorsey, Lee

Singles

Label	Catalog Number	Title	Type	Country	Year	Longbox Value / Value
Charly	CDS-5	Working in a Coalmine	CD5	U.K.	1989	$8.00

Dorsey, Tommy

Full Length

Label	Catalog Number	Title	Type	Country	Year	Longbox Value / Value
Curb	77396-2	Best Of	LP/LB	U.S.		$14.00/$8.00
RCA	PD-89810	Legend	LP	Germany		$16.00
Bluebird	3140-2	Music Goes Round & Round	LP	U.S.		$9.00

Double

Singles

Label	Catalog Number	Title	Type	Country	Year	Longbox Value / Value
Polydor	887322-2	Gliding	CD5	Germany	1988	$8.00
Polydor	POCD-903	Gliding	CD5	U.K.	1988	$8.00

Double Action Theater

Full Length

Label	Catalog Number	Title	Type	Country	Year	Longbox Value / Value
Polygram	849289	Double Action Theater	LP/BP	U.S.		$11.00/$7.00

Double Dee

Singles

Label	Catalog Number	Title	Type	Country	Year	Longbox Value / Value
Toshiba	TODP-2333	Don't You Feel	CD3	Japan	1991	$12.00/$3.00
ZYX	6350-8	Found Love	CD5	Germany	1990	$6.00

Double Key

Singles

Label	Catalog Number	Title	Type	Country	Year	Longbox Value / Value
EMI	204434-2	After All This Time	CD5	Germany	1991	$8.00
Polygram	879295-2	Celebrate	CD5	Germany	1991	$8.00
Desire	WANCD-37	Don't Give Up	CD5	U.K.	1990	$8.00
Desire	WANCD-46	Gimme Some More	CD5	U.K.	1990	$8.00
Polygram	889677-2	Just Keep Rockin'	CD5	Germany	1989	$8.00
Desire	WANCD-9	Just Keep Rockin'	CD5	U.K.	1989	$8.00
Polygram	877561-2	Love Don't Live Here Anymore	CD5	Germany	1990	$8.00
Desire	WANCD-32	Love Don't Live Here Anymore	CD5	U.K.	1990	$8.00
Polygram	867171-2	Rub-A-Dub	CD5	Germany	1991	$8.00
Polygram	873233-2	Street Stuff	CD5	Germany	1989	$8.00
Desire	WANCD-18	Street Stuff	CD5	U.K.	1989	$8.00
Polygram	877291-2	Talkback	CD5	Germany	1990	$8.00
Desire	WANTX-27CD	Talkback	CD5	U.K.	1990	$8.00
ZYX	6059-8	Todd Terry	CD5	Germany	1989	$8.00

Double W

Singles

Label	Catalog Number	Title	Type	Country	Year	Longbox Value / Value
RCA	BVCP-9008	Funky Amadeus	CD5	Japan	1991	$10.00

Double X

Singles

Label	Catalog Number	Title	Type	Country	Year	Longbox Value / Value
Atlantic	95861	Money Talks	CD5	U.S.	1994	$5.00
Atlantic	98230	Money Talks	CD5	U.S.	1995	$6.00

Double You

Singles

Label	Catalog Number	Title	Type	Country	Year	Longbox Value / Value
ZYX	8043-8	Because I'm Loving You	CD5	U.S.	1996	$6.00
ZYX	ZYX-6748-8	Please Don't Go	CD5	Germany	1992	$7.00
Victor	VICP-15018	Please Don't Go	CD5	Japan	1992	$12.00
ZYX	ZYX-6748-8	Please Don't Go	CD5	U.K.	1992	$7.00
ZYX	6748-8	Please Don't Go	CD5	U.S.	1993	$8.00
Zyx	7314	Run to Me	CD5	U.S.	1994	$5.00
ZYX	7314-8	Run to Me	CD5	U.S.	1994	$7.00
ZYX	ZYX-6888-8	Who's Foolin' Who	CD5	Germany	1992	$7.00

Doubleplusgood

Singles

Label	Catalog Number	Title	Type	Country	Year	Longbox Value / Value
Sire	9 41038-2	Conga	CD5	U.S.	1993	$4.00

Doug E. Fresh

Singles

Label	Catalog Number	Title	Type	Country	Year	Longbox Value / Value
Bust It	79149	Bustin' Out	CDJ	U.S.	1992	$2.00
Bust It	79361	If I Was Your Man	CDJ	U.S.	1992	$2.00

Doug Lazy

Singles

Label	Catalog Number	Title	Type	Country	Year	Longbox Value / Value
		H.O.U.S.E.	CDJ	U.S.		$2.00

Doughboys

Singles

Label	Catalog Number	Title	Type	Country	Year	Longbox Value / Value
A&M	31458 0339	Shine	CDJ	U.S.	1993	$2.00

Dougie Dee

Singles

Label	Catalog Number	Title	Type	Country	Year	Longbox Value / Value
Mercury	CDP 964	Ain't No Sunshine	CDJ	U.S.	1993	$2.00

Douglas, Mike

Singles

Label	Catalog Number	Title	Type	Country	Year	Longbox Value / Value
CBS	66987	You Don't Have to B	CD5	U.S.	1994	$5.00

Dove Shack

Singles

Label	Catalog Number	Title	Type	Country	Year	Longbox Value / Value
Polygram	579383	Summertime in LBC	CD5	U.S.	1995	$6.00

Doves

Singles

Label	Catalog Number	Title	Type	Country	Year	Longbox Value / Value
Elektra	EKR-138CD	Beaten Up In Love Again	CD5	U.K.	1991	$8.00
Elektra	8432-2	Beaten Up In Love Again	CDJ	U.S.	1991	$2.00
		I Should	CDJ	U.S.	1991	$2.00
Elektra	EKR-132CD	I Wouldn't Know You From the Rest	CDJ	U.K.	1991	$8.00
Elektra	PRCD 8394-2	I Wouldn't Know You From the Rest	CDJ	U.S.	1991	$2.00

Dow Jones

Singles

Label	Catalog Number	Title	Type	Country	Year	Longbox Value / Value
CBS	654998-3	Just A Techno Groove	CD3	Germany	1989	$8.00

Dowie, Ryan

Full Length

Label	Catalog Number	Title	Type	Country	Year	Longbox Value / Value
		Hypocrite	DJ/LP	U.S.	1996	$15.00

Down

Singles

Label	Catalog Number	Title	Type	Country	Year	Longbox Value / Value
		Lifter	CDJ	U.S.		$2.00

Down Town

Singles

Label	Catalog Number	Title	Type	Country	Year	Longbox Value / Value
		One 2 Many	CDJ	U.S.		$2.00
		One 2 Many	CDJ	U.S.		$2.00

Second version.

Down's Family

Singles

Label	Catalog Number	Title	Type	Country	Year	Longbox Value / Value
	69	Beer is Like a Dog	CD5	U.S.	1994	$5.00

Downey, Robert Jr.

Singles

Label	Catalog Number	Title	Type	Country	Year	Longbox Value / Value
Epic	ESDA-7133	Smile	CD3	Japan	1993	$13.00/$4.00
Epic	658905-2	Smile	CD5	U.K.	1992	$10.00
Epic	ESK 74736	Smile	CDJ	U.S.	1993	$2.00

Downing, Will

Singles

Label	Catalog Number	Title	Type	Country	Year	Longbox Value / Value
Mercury	CDP 1189	Break Up Make Up	CDJ	U.S.	1994	$2.00
Island	BRCD-160	Come Together As One	CD5	U.K.	1990	$9.00
4th & B'way	BRCDP-112	Free	CD5	U.K.	1988	$9.00
Island	PR 2174-2	Free	CDJ	U.S.	1988	$2.00
4th & B'way	BRCD-220	I Go Crazy	CD5	U.K.	1991	$9.00
Island	PRCD 6674-2	I Go Crazy	CDJ	U.S.	1991	$2.00
4th & B'way	885025	In My Dreams	CD5	Germany	1988	$9.00
4th & B'way	BRCDP-104	In My Dreams	CD5	U.K.	1988	$9.00
4th & B'way	BRCDX-90	Love Supreme	CD3	U.K.	1988	$9.00
Aris	885594	Test of Time	CD5	Germany	1989	$9.00
4th & B'way	BRCD-146	Test of Time	CD5	U.K.	1989	$9.00
Island	PR 2880-2	Test of Time	CDJ	U.S.	1989	$2.00
4th & B'way	BRCD-211	World is a Ghetto	CD5	U.K.	1991	$9.00

Download

Singles

Label	Catalog Number	Title	Type	Country	Year	Longbox Value / Value
Cleopatra	CLEO 9658-2	Microscopic	CD5	U.S.	1996	$7.00

Downtown Science

Singles

Label	Catalog Number	Title	Type	Country	Year	Longbox Value / Value
		Room Top Breathe	CDJ	U.S.		$2.00

Dozier, Lamont

Full Length

Label	Catalog Number	Title	Type	Country	Year	Longbox Value / Value
Atlantic	PRCD 3924-2	Profiled	DJ/Intvw	U.S.	1991	$8.00
Atlantic	PRCD 3899-2	Love in the Rain	CDJ	U.S.	1991	$2.00
Atlantic	7567-85998-2	Quiet's Too Loud	CD5	U.K.	1991	$8.00

Dozier, Michael

Singles

Label	Catalog Number	Title	Type	Country	Year	Longbox Value / Value
Zyx	66017	Forever	CD5	U.S.	1994	$5.00

Dr. Alban

Singles

Label	Catalog Number	Title	Type	Country	Year	Longbox Value / Value
	59004	Away From Home	CD5	U.S.	1994	$5.00
BMG	663789	Hello Africa	CD5	Germany	1990	$8.00
BMG	663821	Hello Africa	CD5	Germany	1990	$8.00
BMG	663934	Hello Africa	CD5	Germany	1990	$8.00
Arista	665330	It's My Life	CD5	U.K.	1993	$8.00
Arista	12492	It's My Life	CD5	U.S.	1993	$5.00
Arista	18720	It's My Life	CD5	U.S.	1993	$5.00
Arista	2491	It's My Life	CDJ	U.S.	1993	$2.00
	59010	Let the Beat Go on	CD5	U.S.	1994	$5.00
Arista	664194	No Coke	CD5	Germany	1991	$8.00
Arista	664635	No Coke	CD5	U.K.	1991	$8.00
Arista	7432 110872-2	One Love	CD5	U.K.	1992	$8.00
Arista	12597	Sing Hallelujah	CD5	U.S.	1994	$5.00
BMG	664507	Stop the Pollution	CD5	Germany	1991	$8.00
BMG	664414	U & Mi	CD5	Germany	1991	$8.00

Dr. Baker

Singles

Label	Catalog Number	Title	Type	Country	Year	Longbox Value / Value
ZYX	6444-8	Reality	CD5	Germany	1990	$6.00
BMG	665182	Turn Up the Music	CD5	Germany	1992	$8.00

Dr. Dre

Full Length

Label	Catalog Number	Title	Type	Country	Year	Longbox Value / Value
Interscope	P2 57128	Chronic, The	DJ/LP	U.S.	1992	$20.00
Priority	MB 0001-2	Chronic, The	DJ/LP	U.S.	1992	$20.00

CD in fold-open longbox with rolling paper.

Singles

Label	Catalog Number	Title	Type	Country	Year	Longbox Value / Value
Priority	DPRO 6661	Dre Day	CDJ	U.S.		$3.00
Priority Records	53188	Keep Their Heads R	CD5	U.S.	1994	$5.00
Priority	DPRO-7029	Let Me Ride	CDJ	U.S.	1993	$3.00
Priority	DPRO-7034	Let Me Ride	CDJ	U.S.	1993	$3.00
Priority	DPRO-6662	Lil' Ghetto Boy	CDJ	U.S.	1994	$3.00
	PRCD 5963	Natural Born Kilaz	CDJ	U.S.		$3.00
		Nothin' But A "G" Thing	CD5	U.K.		$10.00
		Nothin' But A "G" Thing	CD5	U.K.		$10.00

Second version.

Dr. Feelgood

Singles

Label	Catalog Number	Title	Type	Country	Year	Longbox Value / Value
EMI	202817-2	Break these Chains	CD5	Germany	1988	$8.00
EMI	202523-2	See You Later Alligator	CD5	Germany	1988	$8.00

Dr. Felix

Singles

Label	Catalog Number	Title	Type	Country	Year	Longbox Value / Value
ZYX	5868-8	Patty Time	CD5	Germany		$6.00

Dr. Fink And The Mystery Band

Singles

Label	Catalog Number	Title	Type	Country	Year	Longbox Value / Value
Mysterious	MYSCD-001	Tribute	CD5	U.K.	1992	$8.00

Dr. Hook

Full Length

Label	Catalog Number	Title	Type	Country	Year	Longbox Value / Value
Polygram	80054-2	Players After Dark	LP	Germany		$15.00
Polygram	80054-2	Players After Dark	LP	U.K.		$15.00
Mercury	800054-2	Players After Dark	LP/BP	U.S.†	1984	$14.00/$8.00

Singles

Label	Catalog Number	Title	Type	Country	Year	Longbox Value / Value
EMI	204784-2	Little Bit More	CD5	Germany	1992	$10.00
Capitol	CDEMT-6	Little Bit More	CD5	U.K.	1992	$10.00
Capitol	CDEMT-4	When You're In Love With a Beautiful Woman	CD5	U.K.	1992	$10.00

Dr. John

Full Length

Label	Catalog Number	Title	Type	Country	Year	Longbox Value / Value
Warner Brothers	PRO-CD-5582	Goin' Back To New Orleans	DJ/Smplr	U.S.	1992	$12.00
		House of Blues	RS	U.S.	1994	$40.00

2 CD set. Airdate: 11/13/94.

Singles

Label	Catalog Number	Title	Type	Country	Year	Longbox Value / Value
Warner Brothers	PRO-CD-3815	Candy	CDJ	U.S.	1989	$2.00
Warner Brothers	PRO-CD-3500	Makin' Whoopee!	CDJ	U.S.	1989	$2.00
Warner Brothers	PRO-CD-3784	My Buddy	CDJ	U.S.	1989	$2.00
Warner Brothers	WPDP-6307	When I First Saw Your Face	CD3	Japan	1992	$13.00/$4.00

Dr. Money

Singles

Label	Catalog Number	Title	Type	Country	Year	Longbox Value / Value
Canyon	PCCY-00111	Give Up	CD3	Japan	1990	$12.00/$3.00
Canyon	S10Y-1043	Time After Time	CD3	Japan	1990	$12.00/$3.00

Dr. Mouthquake

Singles

Label	Catalog Number	Title	Type	Country	Year	Longbox Value / Value
Virgin	PROCD-3	Love On Love	CD3	U.K.	1990	$8.00

Dr. Phibes

Singles

Label	Catalog Number	Title	Type	Country	Year	Longbox Value / Value
Rough Trade	344-0275-3	Hazy Lazy	CD5	U.K.	1991	$8.00

Dr. Robert

Singles

Label	Catalog Number	Title	Type	Country	Year	Longbox Value / Value
EMI	CDRZ-3	I've Learnt to Live With Love	CD5	U.K.	1991	$8.00
RCA	R10D-117	Wait	CD3	Japan	1989	$12.00/$3.00
RCA	PD-42569	Wait	CD5	U.K.	1989	$8.00

Dr. Seuss

Full Length

Label	Catalog Number	Title	Type	Country	Year	Longbox Value / Value
RCA	S4D-5194	Dr. Seuss Collection, The	LP	U.S.	1996	$45.00

4 CD set.

Label	Catalog Number	Title	Type	Country	Year	Longbox Value / Value
Mercury Nashville	314-528 438-2	How the Grinch Stole Christmas	LP	U.S.	1995	$20.00

CD and book.

Dr. York

Singles

Label	Catalog Number	Title	Type	Country	Year	Longbox Value / Value
Century	CECD-00209	Let Me Be the One on Christmas	CD3	Japan	1990	$12.00/$3.00

Drake, Nick

Full Length

Label	Catalog Number	Title	Type	Country	Year	Longbox Value / Value
Hannibal	VRCD 4434	Hannibal Sampler, The	DJ/Smplr	U.S.	1993	$13.00
Island	DRAKE-CD-1	Way to Blue Sampler	DJ/Smplr	U.S.		$15.00

Dramacydal

Singles

Label	Catalog Number	Title	Type	Country	Year	Longbox Value / Value
Atlantic	95741	Hard to Imagine	CD5	U.S.	1995	$5.00

Dramarama

Full Length

Label	Catalog Number	Title	Type	Country	Year	Longbox Value / Value
Chameleon	PRCD-8771-8	10 From 5/Hi-Fi Sci-Fi	DJ/Smplr	U.S.	1993	$35.00
Chameleon	PRCD 8771-A/B	Hi-Fi Sci Fi/10 From 5	DJ/Smplr	U.S.	1993	$30.00

2CD sampler plus promo of album.

Label	Catalog Number	Title	Type	Country	Year	Longbox Value / Value
Westwood One		In Concert	RS	U.S.	1992	$50.00

2 CD set. With Drivin' 'N' Cryin', Airdate: 5/11/92.

Label	Catalog Number	Title	Type	Country	Year	Longbox Value / Value
Chameleon		Live In Wanderamaland	DJ/Smplr	U.S.		$10.00
Chameleon		Vinyl EP	DJ/Smplr	U.S.		$10.00

Singles

Label	Catalog Number	Title	Type	Country	Year	Longbox Value / Value
Chameleon	PR 8435	Haven't Got a Clue	CDJ	U.S.	1991	$7.00
Chameleon	PR 8518	Haven't Got a Clue	CDJ	U.S.	1991	$7.00
Chameleon	PR 8559	I've Got Spies	CDJ	U.S.	1992	$7.00
Chameleon	71	Last Cigarette	CDJ	U.S.	1989	$3.00
Chameleon	78	What Are We Gonna Do?	CDJ	U.S.	1990	$3.00
Chameleon	PR 8753	Work For Food	CDJ	U.S.	1993	$3.00

Dread Flimstone

Singles

Label	Catalog Number	Title	Type	Country	Year	Longbox Value / Value
Acid Jazz	ZSK 75298	From the Ghetto	CDJ	U.S.	1991	$2.00
Scotti Brothers	ZSK 75324	Sitting in the Park	CDJ	U.S.	1992	$2.00
Capitol	58492	Trouble in Dub	CD5	U.S.	1995	$5.00

Dread, Mikey

Singles

Label	Catalog Number	Title	Type	Country	Year	Longbox Value / Value
Warner Brothers	PRO-CD-4034	Source (Of Your Divorce), The	CDJ	U.S.	1989	$2.00

Dread Zeppelin

Singles

Label	Catalog Number	Title	Type	Country	Year	Longbox Value / Value
IRS	DPRO-6703 7	Heartbreaker	CDJ	U.S.	1990	$2.00
IRS	204319-2	Stairway to Heaven	CD5	Germany	1990	$10.00
	VIDP-28	Stairway to Heaven	CD3	Japan		$13.00/$4.00
IRS	DREADCD-2	Stairway to Heaven	CD5	U.K.	1990	$10.00
IRS	DPRO-6705 7	Stairway to Heaven	CDJ	U.S.	1990	$4.00
IRS	EIRSCD-154	Your Time Is Gonna Come	CD5	U.K.	1990	$10.00
IRS	DREADCD-1	Your Time Is Gonna Come	CD5	U.K.	1990	$10.00
		Your Time Is Gonna Come	CDJ	U.S.	1990	$4.00

Dreadful Great

Singles

Label	Catalog Number	Title	Type	Country	Year	Longbox Value / Value
BMG	663595	It's All Over Now Baby Blue	CD5	Germany	1990	$8.00

Dream

Singles

Label	Catalog Number	Title	Type	Country	Year	Longbox Value / Value
Magnet	MAG1010	Things Can Only Get Better	CD5	Germany	1993	$8.00
Reprise	9 41047-2	Things Can Only Get Better	CD5	U.S.	1993	$5.00
Reprise	PRO-CD-6609	Things Can Only Get Better	CDJ	U.S.	1993	$2.00
Rhythm King	FXU-3CD	U R the Best Thing	CD5	U.K.	1992	$8.00
Rhythm King		U R the Best Thing	CD5	U.K.	1992	$8.00

Second version.

Dream Academy

Full Length

Label	Catalog Number	Title	Type	Country	Year	Longbox Value / Value
Reprise	9 26307-2-Dj	A Different Kind of Weather	DJ/LP	U.S.	1991	$10.00

Picture disc.

Label	Catalog Number	Title	Type	Country	Year	Longbox Value / Value
Pioneer	CLD-86-003	Dream Academy	LD	U.S.	1986	$25.00

Singles

Label	Catalog Number	Title	Type	Country	Year	Longbox Value / Value
Blanco	NEG-50CD	Angel Of Mercy	CD5	U.K.	1991	$10.00
Reprise	PRO-CD-4892	Angel Of Mercy	CDJ	U.S.	1991	$2.00
Pioneer	10SW-47	In the Heart	CD3	Japan	1988	$13.00/$3.00

Label	Catalog Number	Title	Type	Country	Year	Longbox Value / Value
Reprise	PRO-CD-2841	Indian Summer	CDJ	U.S.		$2.00
WEA	7599-21762-2	Love	CD5	Germany	1990	$10.00
Blanco	NEG-46CD	Love	CD5	U.K.	1990	$10.00
Reprise	9 21738-2	Love	CD5	U.S.	1990	$5.00
Reprise	PRO-CD-4341	Love	CDJ	U.S.	1990	$2.00
Reprise	PRO-CD-4411	Love	CDJ	U.S.	1990	$2.00

Dream Command

Singles

Label	Catalog Number	Title	Type	Country	Year	Longbox Value / Value
		Celestine	CDJ	U.S.		$2.00

Dream Factory

Singles

Label	Catalog Number	Title	Type	Country	Year	Longbox Value / Value
EMI	TODP-2356	Change the World	CD3	Japan	1992	$12.00/$3.00

Dream Frequency

Singles

Label	Catalog Number	Title	Type	Country	Year	Longbox Value / Value
Intercord	825 933	Feel So Real	CD5	Germany	1992	$8.00
City Beat	CBE-763CD	Feel So Real	CD5	U.K.	1992	$8.00
City Beat	CBE-768CD	Take Me	CD5	U.K.	1992	$8.00

Dream Syndicate

Singles

Label	Catalog Number	Title	Type	Country	Year	Longbox Value / Value
Enigma	EPRO-122	I Have Faith	CDJ	U.S.	1988	$2.00

Dream Team

Singles

Label	Catalog Number	Title	Type	Country	Year	Longbox Value / Value
LUM	CDV 8801-2	Flight of the Dream Team	CDV/BP	U.S.	1988	$20.00/$20.00

Dream Theatre

Singles

Label	Catalog Number	Title	Type	Country	Year	Longbox Value / Value
		Silent Man, The	CDJ	U.S.		$3.00
		Status Seeker	CDJ	U.S.		$2.00

Dream Warriors

Singles

Label	Catalog Number	Title	Type	Country	Year	Longbox Value / Value
4th & B'way	CCD 545	Follow Me Not	CDJ	U.S.	1991	$2.00
BMG	664011	Ludi	CD5	Germany	1991	$8.00
4th & B'way	BRCD-206	Ludi	CD5	U.K.	1991	$8.00
BMG	663853	My Definition of Boombastic Jazz Style	CD5	Germany	1991	$8.00
BMG	664159	My Definition of Boombastic Jazz Style	CD5	Germany	1991	$8.00
Island	PSDD-1101	My Definition of Boombastic Jazz Style	CD3	Japan	1991	$13.00/$4.00
4th & B'way	BRCD-197	My Definition of Boombastic Jazz Style	CD5	U.K.	1991	$8.00
4th & B'way	CCD 526	My Definition of Boombastic Jazz Style	CDJ	U.S.	1991	$2.00
BMG	663619	Wash Your Face	CD5	Germany	1990	$10.00
4th & B'way	BRCD-183	Wash Your Face	CD5	U.K.	1990	$10.00

Dreams So Real

Singles

Label	Catalog Number	Title	Type	Country	Year	Longbox Value / Value
Arista	ARCD-9784	Red Lights (Merry Christmas)	CDJ	U.S.	1988	$2.00
BMG	662088	Rough Night in Jericho	CD5	U.K.	1989	$8.00

Dregs

Full Length

Label	Catalog Number	Title	Type	Country	Year	Longbox Value / Value
Arista	ARCD-8116	Dregs of the Earth	LP/LB	U.S.†	1985	$14.00/$8.00

Singles

Label	Catalog Number	Title	Type	Country	Year	Longbox Value / Value
Ensonia	ENS-1000	Off the Record	CD3	U.S.	1988	$6.00/$3.00

Drew, David

Singles

Label	Catalog Number	Title	Type	Country	Year	Longbox Value / Value
		Common Emotion	CDJ	U.S.		$2.00
		Green-Eyed Lady	CDJ	U.S.		$2.00

Drew, Kenny

Full Length

Label	Catalog Number	Title	Type	Country	Year	Longbox Value / Value
Soul Note	SN-1081CD PSI	And Far Away	LP/LB	U.S.†	1985	$14.00/$8.00
Aris	886329	Dream	LP	Germany		$15.00
RCA	CDRJCD-106	Lullaby	LP	Germany		$15.00
GML	CD-4810	Super Gold Sound	LTD/LP	Japan		$25.00
	Gold disc.					
Blue Note	CDP-84059-2	Undercurrent	LP/LB	U.S.		$18.00/$15.00
Blue Note		Undercurrent	LTD/LP	U.S.	1995	$19.00

Singles

Label	Catalog Number	Title	Type	Country	Year	Longbox Value / Value
Alfa	10R3-15	Hush-A-Bye	CD3	Japan	1988	$12.00/$3.00
Alfa	10R3-16	Jingle Bells	CD3	Japan	1988	$12.00/$3.00

Drifters

Full Length

Label	Catalog Number	Title	Type	Country	Year	Longbox Value / Value
Spectrum	CDSPEC-85006	Twenty Greatest Hits	LP	Germany		$18.00

Singles

Label	Catalog Number	Title	Type	Country	Year	Longbox Value / Value
WEA	786511-2	Saturday Night	CD3	Germany	1989	$10.00
WEA	786511-2	Saturday Night	CD3	U.K.	1989	$10.00

Drive

Singles

Label	Catalog Number	Title	Type	Country	Year	Longbox Value / Value
Pinnacle	FST-018CD	Go Out Be Happy	CD5	U.K.	1991	$8.00

Drive Like Jehu

Singles

Label	Catalog Number	Title	Type	Country	Year	Longbox Value / Value
Interscope	CD92363	Yank Crime	CD5	Canada	1994	$14.00

Drive, She Said

Singles

Label	Catalog Number	Title	Type	Country	Year	Longbox Value / Value
CBS	000274	If This Is Love	CDJ	U.S.	1989	$10.00
Intercord	828 511	Think of Love	CD5	Germany	1991	$8.00

Drive Train

Singles

Label	Catalog Number	Title	Type	Country	Year	Longbox Value / Value
ZYX	6582-8	This is the Rhythm	CD5	Germany	1991	$8.00

Drivin 'n Cryin'

Full Length

Label	Catalog Number	Title	Type	Country	Year	Longbox Value / Value
Westwood One		In Concert	RS	U.S.	1992	$50.00
	2 CD set. With Dramarama, Airdate: 5/11/92.					
Westwood One		In Concert	RS	U.S.	1993	$30.00
	2 CD set. With Arc Angels, Airdate: 3/1/93.					
Island	PRCD 6769-2	Oooeee	DJ/Smplr	U.S.	1993	$10.00

Singles

Label	Catalog Number	Title	Type	Country	Year	Longbox Value / Value
Island	PRCD 6703-2	Around the Block	CDJ	U.S.	1991	$2.00
Island	422 868 535-2	Build a Fire	CD5	U.S.	1991	$5.00
Island	PRCD 6668-2	Build a Fire	CDJ	U.S.	1991	$2.00
Island	PRCD 2290-2	Can't Promise You the World	CDJ	U.S.	1988	$2.00
Island	665314	Fly Me Courageous	CD5	Germany	1991	$10.00
Island	CID-523	Fly Me Courageous	CD5	U.K.	1991	$10.00
Island	PRCD 6647-2	Fly Me Courageous	CDJ	U.S.	1991	$6.00
Island	PRCD 2680-2	Honeysuckle Blue	CDJ	U.S.	1989	$2.00
Island	PRCD 6686-2	Innocent, The	CDJ	U.S.	1990	$2.00
Island	PRCD 6771-2	Smoke	CDJ	U.S.	1993	$2.00
Island	PRCD 6771-2	Smoke	CDJ	U.S.	1993	$15.00
	CD packaged with smoke detector.					
Island	PRCD 6758-2	Turn It Up or Turn It Off	CDJ	U.S.	1993	$15.00
Island	PRCD 5787-2	Whiskey Soul Woman	CDJ	U.S.	1993	$2.00

Drizabone

Singles

Label	Catalog Number	Title	Type	Country	Year	Longbox Value / Value
		Brightest Star	CD5	U.K.		$10.00
		Brightest Star	CD5	U.K.		$10.00
	Second version.					
4th & B'way	BRCD-232	Catch the Fire	CD5	U.K.	1991	$8.00
4th & B'way	664584	Real Love	CD5	Germany	1991	$8.00

Droge, Pete

Singles

Label	Catalog Number	Title	Type	Country	Year	Longbox Value / Value
Warner Brothers	PRO-CD-7101	If You Don't Love Me	CDJ	U.S.		$3.00
RCA	64297	If You Don't Love Me	CD5	U.S.	1994	$5.00
Warner Brothers	PRO-CD-7363	Northern Bound Train	CDJ	U.S.		$3.00

Drop

Singles

Label	Catalog Number	Title	Type	Country	Year	Longbox Value / Value
Chapter 22	CHAPCD-57	Mirrored	CD5	U.K.	1991	$8.00

Drop Nineteens

Singles

Label	Catalog Number	Title	Type	Country	Year	Longbox Value / Value
Caroline	1469	Your Aquarium	CD5	U.S.A	1993	$5.00

Dru Down

Singles

Label	Catalog Number	Title	Type	Country	Year	Longbox Value / Value
Relativity	1512	No One Loves You	CD5	U.S.	1994	$5.00

DSK

Singles

Label	Catalog Number	Title	Type	Country	Year	Longbox Value / Value
Bull	CDBBUK-001	Holdin' On	CD5	U.K.	1992	$8.00
ZYX	ZYX-6572-8	What Would We Do	CD5	Germany	1992	$6.00

DTI

Singles

Label	Catalog Number	Title	Type	Country	Year	Longbox Value / Value
Sound	CD-5000	Listen to This	CD5	Germany	1988	$8.00

Dtox

Singles

Label	Catalog Number	Title	Type	Country	Year	Longbox Value / Value
Vitality	CDSVITAL-1	Shattered Glass	CD5	U.K.	1992	$8.00

Duarte, Chris Group

Singles

Label	Catalog Number	Title	Type	Country	Year	Longbox Value / Value
		Scrawl	CDJ	U.S.		$2.00

Dubh Chapter

Singles

Label	Catalog Number	Title	Type	Country	Year	Longbox Value / Value
Virgin	EGOCD-52	Happy is the Bridge	CD5	U.K.	1990	$8.00
Virgin	EGOCD-54	Touch and Go	CD5	U.K.	1990	$8.00

Dudley, Anne

Singles

Label	Catalog Number	Title	Type	Country	Year	Longbox Value / Value
China	CHICD-26	Minarets and Memories	CD5	U.K.	1990	$8.00

Dudley, Dave

Full Length

Label	Catalog Number	Title	Type	Country	Year	Longbox Value / Value
Delta	11040	Here He Is	LP	Germany		$15.00
Delta	11040	Here He Is	LP	U.K.		$15.00

Duel

Singles

Label	Catalog Number	Title	Type	Country	Year	Longbox Value / Value
Virgin	TENTCD-7	Tell Me Why Love Dies	CD5	U.K.	1988	$8.00

Duff

Singles

Label	Catalog Number	Title	Type	Country	Year	Longbox Value / Value
		Believe in Me	CDJ	U.S.		$6.00

Duffy Duck

Singles

Label	Catalog Number	Title	Type	Country	Year	Longbox Value / Value
WEA	9031-74176-2	Party Zone	CD5	Germany	1991	$8.00

Duffy, Stephen

Full Length

Label	Catalog Number	Title	Type	Country	Year	Longbox Value / Value
Virgin	DIXCD29	Because We Love You	LP	U.K.		$15.00
Virgin	610455	Ups and Downs, The	LP	Germany		$15.00

Duke, George

Full Length

Label	Catalog Number	Title	Type	Country	Year	Longbox Value / Value
Columbia	462536-2	Dream on	LP	Germany		$18.00
CBS	EK-37532	Dream on	LP/LB	U.S.†	1985	$14.00/$8.00
Columbia	CD-25262	Guardian of the Light	LP	Germany		$18.00
Polygram	817488-2	I Love the Blues	LP	Germany		$18.00
Verve/MPS	817488-2	I Love the Blues, She Heard Me Cry	LP/LB	U.S.†	1985	$14.00/$8.00
Elektra	960398-2	Thief in the Night	LP	Germany		$18.00
Elektra	60398-2	Thief in the Night	LP/LB	U.S.†	1985	$14.00/$8.00

Singles

Label	Catalog Number	Title	Type	Country	Year	Longbox Value / Value
Elektra	PR 8056-2	Guilty	CDJ	U.S.	1989	$2.00
Elektra	PR 8082-2	Love Ballad	CDJ	U.S.	1989	$2.00

Duke Robillard

Full Length

Label	Catalog Number	Title	Type	Country	Year	Longbox Value / Value
		House of Blues	RS	U.S.	1994	$40.00
	2 CD set. Airdate: 11/20/94.					

Dulfer, Candy

Singles

Label	Catalog Number	Title	Type	Country	Year	Longbox Value / Value
RCA	62627-2-RDJ	2 Funky	CDJ	U.S.	1993	$2.00
RCA	62729-2-RDJ	2 Funky	CDJ	U.S.	1993	$2.00
BMG	663541	Heavenly City	CD5	Germqany	1990	$8.00
RCA	62682-2-RDJ	Mr. Marvin	CDJ	U.S.	1993	$2.00
Ariola	BVDP-83	Pick Up the Pieces	CD3	Japan	1993	$12.00/$3.00
RCA	62805-2-RDJ	Pick Up the Pieces	CDJ	U.S.	1993	$2.00
Ariola	BVDP-75	Sax-a-Go Go	CD3	Japan	1993	$12.00/$3.00
Ariola	7431-11822	Sax-a-Go Go	CD5	U.K.	1993	$8.00
RCA	663176	Sexuality	CD5	Germany	1990	$8.00
RCA	PD-43770	Sexuality	CD5	U.K.	1990	$8.00

Duncan, Carey

Singles

Label	Catalog Number	Title	Type	Country	Year	Longbox Value / Value
Bellaphon	130-07-395	Love and Affection	CD5	Germany	1991	$8.00

Duncan, Celena

Singles

Label	Catalog Number	Title	Type	Country	Year	Longbox Value / Value
Canyon	S13ED-5053	Questions and Answers	CD3	Japan	1988	$12.00/$3.00

Duncan, John

Singles

Label	Catalog Number	Title	Type	Country	Year	Longbox Value / Value
		River of Flames	CD5	Sweden	1991	$8.00

Dunk

Singles

Label	Catalog Number	Title	Type	Country	Year	Longbox Value / Value
ZYX	ZYX-6145-8	Body Control	CD5	Germany	1989	$6.00

Dunn, Holly

Full Length

Label	Catalog Number	Title	Type	Country	Year	Longbox Value / Value
Warner Brothers		Life and Love/All the Stages	DJ/Smplr	U.S.		$40.00
	4 CD set.					

Singles

Label	Catalog Number	Title	Type	Country	Year	Longbox Value / Value
Warner Brothers	PRO-CD-3520	Are You Gonna Love Me	CDJ	U.S.	1989	$2.00
Warner Brothers	PRO-CD-5725	Golden Years	CDJ	U.S.	1992	$2.00
Warner Brothers		Heart Full of Love	CDJ	U.S.		$2.00
Warner Brothers	PRO-CD-5040	No One Takes the Train Anymore	CDJ	U.S.	1991	$2.00

Dunnery, Francis

Singles

Label	Catalog Number	Title	Type	Country	Year	Longbox Value / Value
		American Life in the Summertime	CDJ	U.S.	1994	$3.00
		Homegrown	CDJ	U.S.	1994	$3.00
		What's He Gonna Say?	CD5	U.K.		$10.00
		What's He Gonna Say?	CD5	U.K.		$10.00
	Second version.					

Duo Cabrisas Fa

Singles

Label	Catalog Number	Title	Type	Country	Year	Longbox Value / Value
	11451	Serie De Platino	CD5	U.S.	1994	$5.00

Duran Duran – Decade/Ordinary World (Capitol DPRO-79607)

Duran Duran

Full Length

Label	Catalog Number	Title	Type	Country	Year	Longbox Value / Value
EMI		12" Mixes	LTD/LP	Japan		$50.00
	2 CD set.					
Capitol	CDP-46048	Arena	LP/LB	U.S.†	1985	$14.00/$8.00
EMI	CP18-5769/70	Big Thing	LP	Japan	1988	$30.00
EMI	CD-DDB-33	Big Thing	DJ/LP	U.K.	1988	$40.00
	CD in custom plastic box with press kit.					
Capitol		Big Thing	DJ/LP	U.S.	1988	$50.00
	Custom plastic box with cassette and pin.					
Pioneer	PA84-M013	Dancing on the Valentine	8"LD	U.S.	1984	$8.00
	Analog audio.					
		Decade	LD	U.S.		$32.00
Capitol	DPRO-79235	Decade/Ordinary World	DJ/Smplr	U.S.	1993	$25.00
Capitol	DPRO-79607	Decade/Ordinary World	DJ/Smplr	U.S.	1993	$55.00
	P121-15EM	Duran Duran	LD	Japan		$75.00
EMI		Duran Duran	LTD/LP	U.K.	1993	$30.00
	2 CD set.					
Capitol	CDP-46042	Duran Duran	LP/LB	U.S.†	1985	$14.00/$8.00
EMI	SPCD-1030	I Don't Want Your Love	DJ/Smplr	Japan		N/A
Westwood One		In Concert-Nu Rock	RS	U.S.	1993	$100.00
	2 CD set. Airdate: 7/5/93.					
Westwood One		In Concert-Nu Rock	RS	U.S.	1994	$100.00
	2 CD set. Airdate: 1/17/94.					
EMI	SPCD-1131	Liberty	DJ/LP	Japan	1990	$40.00
EMI		Liberty	DJ/LP	U.K.	1990	N/A
Capitol	7 94241	Liberty	DJ/LP	U.S.	1990	$20.00
	CD in custom box with cassette.					
Capitol	CDP-46003	Rio	LP/LB	U.S.†	1984	$14.00/$8.00
Capitol	CDP-46015	Seven & the Raged Tiger	LP/LB	U.S.†	1984	$14.00/$8.00
Image	I-5031	Sing Blue Silver	LD	U.S.	1985	$35.00
EMI		Thank You	LTD/LP	France	1995	$40.00
	2CD set.					
		Thank You	LTD/LP	Germany	1995	$36.00
	2 CD Set.					
Capitol		Tour Sampler	DJ/Smplr	U.S.	1993	$20.00
EMI		Wedding Album, The	LTD/LP	U.K.	1993	$35.00
	2 CD set.					

Singles

Label	Catalog Number	Title	Type	Country	Year	Longbox Value / Value
EMI	203165-3	All She Wants Is	CD3	Germany	1988	$10.00
EMI	203236-2	All She Wants Is	CD5	Germany	1988	$15.00
Toshiba	XP12-5006	All She Wants Is	CD3	Japan	1988	$15.00/$5.00
EMI	CDDD-11	All She Wants Is	CD3	U.K.	1988	$10.00
Capitol	DPRO-79456	All She Wants Is	CDJ	U.S.	1988	$8.00
EMI	CD-BREATH-1	Breath After Breath	CDJ	U.K.		$30.00
EMI	203651-3	Burning the Ground	CD3	Germany	1989	$10.00
EMI	CDDD-13	Burning the Ground	CD5	U.K.	1989	$18.00
EMI	TOCP-7822	Come Undone	CD3	Japan	1993	$15.00/$5.00
EMI		Come Undone	CD5	U.K.	1993	$18.00
EMI		Come Undone	CD5	U.K.	1993	$18.00
	Second version.					
EMI		Come Undone	CDJ	U.K.	1993	$20.00
Capitol	C2 15969	Come Undone	CD5	U.S.	1993	$6.00
Capitol	C2 15981	Come Undone	CD5	U.S.	1993	$6.00
Capitol	DPRO-79660	Come Undone	CDJ	U.S.	1993	$8.00
Capitol	DPRO-79711	Come Undone	CDJ	U.S.	1993	$8.00
EMI	203320-3	Do You Believe in Shame	CD3	Germany	1988	$10.00
EMI	203320-2	Do You Believe in Shame	CD5	Germany	1988	$18.00
EMI	CDDD-12	Do You Believe in Shame	CD3	U.K.	1988	$10.00
EMI		Femme Fatale	CD5	France	1993	$12.00
EMI	202926-2	I Don't Want Your Love	CD5	Germany	1988	$18.00
EMI	X12P-5002	I Don't Want Your Love	CD3	Japan	1988	$15.00/$5.00
EMI	XP10-2036	I Don't Want Your Love	CD3	Japan	1988	$15.00/$5.00
EMI	CDYOUR-1	I Don't Want Your Love	CD5	U.K.	1988	$18.00
Capitol	DPRO-79246	I Don't Want Your Love	CDJ	U.S.	1988	$8.00
		Lay Lady Lay	CD5	U.K.	1995	$18.00
EMI	201762-2	Meet El Presidente	CD5	Germany	1987	$18.00
EMI	TODP-2368	Ordinary World	CD3	Japan	1993	$16.00/$5.00
Parlophone	CDDDPD16	Ordinary World	CD5	U.K.	1993	$18.00
Parlophone	CDDD17	Ordinary World	CD5	U.K.	1993	$18.00
Capitol	C2 15894	Ordinary World	CD5	U.S.	1993	$5.00
Capitol	DPRO-79588	Ordinary World	CDJ	U.S.	1993	$8.00
EMI	CDDDS20	Perfect Day	CD5	U.K.	1995	$18.00
EMI		Perfect Day	CD5	U.K.	1995	$18.00
	Second version.					
EMI	CDINTPRO1	Perfect Day	CDJ	U.K.	1995	$12.00
Capitol	58393	Perfect Day	CD5	U.S.	1995	$6.00
Capitol	DPRO-79599	Perfect Day	CDJ	U.S.	1995	$8.00
Capitol		Perfect Day	CDJ	U.S.	1995	$8.00
	Second version.					
EMI	CDTOUR-1	Presidential Suite	CD5	U.K.	1987	$18.00
Capitol	C2-15712	Reflex, The	CD5	U.S.	1991	$7.00
EMI	204065-2	Serious	CD5	Germany	1990	$18.00
Parlophone	CDDD-15	Serious	CD5	U.K.	1990	$18.00
Capitol	DPRO-79299	Serious	CDJ	U.S.	1990	$8.00
Parlophone	80839	Too Much Information	CD5	U.K.	1993	$18.00
Parlophone		Too Much Information	CD5	U.K.	1993	$18.00
	Second version.					
Capitol	DPRO-79816	Too Much Information	CDJ	U.S.	1993	$8.00
Capitol	DPRO-79767	Too Much Information	CDJ	U.S.	1993	$10.00
EMI	203960-2	Violence of Summer	CD5	Germany	1990	$18.00
EMI	TODP-2185	Violence of Summer	CD3	Japan	1990	$18.00/$5.00
Parlophone	CDDD-14	Violence of Summer	CD5	U.K.	1990	$18.00
Capitol	C2 15612	Violence of Summer	CD5	U.S.	1990	$5.00
Capitol	DPRO-79288	Violence of Summer	CDJ	U.S.	1990	$8.00
Capitol	DPRO-79235	Violence of Summer	CDJ	U.S.	1990	$8.00
		White Lines	CDJ	France	1995	$20.00
EMI	TOCP-8195	White Lines	CDJ	Japan	1995	$40.00
EMI	CDINTPRO2	White Lines	CDJ	U.K.	1995	$12.00
Capitol	CDDD DJ 007	White Lines	CDJ	U.S.	1995	$8.00
Capitol		White Lines	CDJ	U.S.	1995	$8.00
Capitol		White Lines	CDJ	U.S.	1995	$8.00
	Second version.					

Durutti Column

Singles

Label	Catalog Number	Title	Type	Country	Year	Longbox Value / Value
Rough Trade	410-3063-3	Contra Indications	CD5	Germany	1991	$8.00
Rough Trade	410-0380-3	Live at Womad	CD5	Germany	1991	$8.00
Rough Trade	410-0137-3	When the World	CD5	Germany	1991	$8.00
Factory	FACD-194	When the World	CD5	U.K.	1988	$8.00
Factory	FACD-234	Womad Live	CD5	U.K.	1988	$8.00

Dury, Ian

Full Length

Label	Catalog Number	Title	Type	Country	Year	Longbox Value / Value
		Reasons to Be Cheerful	LTD/LP	U.K.	1996	$35.00
	2 CD set.					

Singles

Label	Catalog Number	Title	Type	Country	Year	Longbox Value / Value
WEA	YZ-437CD	Apples	CD3	U.K.	1989	$8.00
Cooltempo	323739-2	Hit Me With Your Rhythm Stick	CD5	Germany	1991	$8.00
Cooltempo	FLYRCD-1	Hit Me With Your Rhythm Stick	CD5	U.K.	1991	$8.00

Dustin, Alta

Singles

Label	Catalog Number	Title	Type	Country	Year	Longbox Value / Value
Atlantic	PRCD 3843-2	Lookin' For Love	CDJ	U.S.	1991	$2.00
Atlantic	PRCD 3055-2	Tonite	CDJ	U.S.	1989	$2.00

Dutch Swing College Band

Full Length

Label	Catalog Number	Title	Type	Country	Year	Longbox Value / Value
Philips	80006-2	Digital Dixie	LP/LB	U.S.†	1985	$14.00/$8.00
Philips	814068-2	Digital Dutch	LP/LB	U.S.†	1985	$14.00/$8.00
Philips	824256-2	Swinging Studio Sessions	LP/LB	U.S.†	1985	$14.00/$8.00

Duval, Frank

Singles

Label	Catalog Number	Title	Type	Country	Year	Longbox Value / Value
Eastwest	171616-2	Living My Way	CD5	Germany	1990	$8.00
Eastwest	247027-2	Touch My Soul	CD5	Germany	1990	$8.00

Dux Dux

Singles

Label	Catalog Number	Title	Type	Country	Year	Longbox Value / Value
EMI	203935-2	C'mon Boy	CD5	Germany	1990	$8.00
EMI	203351-2	This Is Sound	CD3	Germany	1990	$8.00
EMI	203223-2	This Is Sound	CD5	Germany	1990	$8.00

DWA

Singles

Label	Catalog Number	Title	Type	Country	Year	Longbox Value / Value
Reverb	RVBCDS-018	I Wish I Could Fly	CD5	U.K.	1992	$8.00

Dyal

Singles

Label	Catalog Number	Title	Type	Country	Year	Longbox Value / Value
Canyon	S12Y-3061	More More More	CD3	Japan	1988	$12.00/$3.00

Dylan, Bob

Full Length

Label	Catalog Number	Title	Type	Country	Year	Longbox Value / Value
Columbia	SAMPCD 1476	5 Tracks From the Bootleg Series Volumes 1-3	DJ/Smplr	U.K.	1991	$25.00
Sony	25DP-5284	Another Side of Bob Dylan	LP	Japan		$35.00
Sony	OODP-401/3	Biograph	LTD/LP	Japan		$125.00
	Limited edition 3 CD set.					
Columbia	C3K-38830	Biograph	LP	U.S.†	1985	$50.00
	3CD 12"x12" boxed set.					

Dylan, Bob – Forever Young (Columbia XPCD 116)

Label	Catalog Number	Title	Type	Country	Year	Longbox Value / Value
Sony	SRCS-6682	Blonde on Blonde	LTD/LP	Japan	1992	$35.00
Gold disc.						
Sony	SRCS-7905	Blonde on Blonde	LTD/LP	Japan	1996	$35.00
20 Bit mastering.						
Columbia	CK-53016	Blonde on Blonde	LP/LB	U.S.	1992	$28.00/$25.00
Gold disc.						
CBS	CK-33235	Blood on the Tracks	LP/BP	U.S.†	1984	$14.00/$8.00
Columbia	CSK 3081	Bootleg Sampler, The	DJ/Smplr	U.S.	1991	$25.00
Columbia	46806 2	Bootleg Series: Volumes 1-3	LP	U.S.	1991	$75.00
3 CD set in special 12"x12" boxed set with limited edition T-Shirt and Booklet.						
Westwood One		Bootleg Tapes	RS	U.S.	1991	$350.00
3 CD set. Airdate: 5/13/91.						
CBS	CK-33893	Desire	LP/BP	U.S.†	1985	$14.00/$8.00
Paramount	LV2382	Don't Look Back	LD	U.S.	1986	$40.00
CBS	XCDS 93111-2	Dylan 'n Rock	DJ/Smplr	Japan	1994	$500.00
2 CD set.						
CBS	CK-40110	Empire Burlesque	LP/BP	U.S.†	1984	$14.00/$8.00
Columbia	SAMPCD 1224	Forever Young	DJ/Smplr	Germany	1988	$50.00
Columbia	XPCD 116	Forever Young	DJ/Smplr	U.K.	1990	$50.00
Columbia		Forever Young	DJ/Smplr	U.S.	1990	$40.00
CBS	CK-09463	Greatest Hits	LP/BP	U.S.†	1984	$14.00/$8.00
CBS	3502-80	Hard to Handle	LD	U.S.	1986	$60.00
With Tom Petty.						
Sony	SRCS-7904	Highway 61 Revisited	LTD/LP	Japan	1996	$35.00
20 Bit mastering.						
CBS	CK-9189	Highway 61 Revisited	LP/BP	U.S.†	1984	$14.00/$8.00
CBS	CK-38819	Infidels	LP/BP	U.S.†	1984	$14.00/$8.00
Aris	880883	Live, Vol. 2	LP	Germany		$30.00
Columbia	4624498	Masterpeices	DJ/Smplr	Australia		$180.00
Sony	XDCS-93133	Mr. D's Collection No. 3	DJ/Smplr	Japan	1994	$600.00
CBS	CK-9825	Nashville Skyline	LP/BP	U.S.†	1985	$14.00/$8.00
CBS	CK-39944	Real Live	LP/BP	U.S.†	1985	$14.00/$8.00
Sony	SAMPCD1158	Sampler	DJ/Smplr	Germany	1987	$150.00
Columbia	CSK 4857	Special Advance Sampler	DJ/Smplr	U.S.	1992	$12.00
Columbia	CD-86067	Street-Legal	LP	Germany		$30.00
Sony	SRCS7176	Unplugged	LP	Japan	1995	$125.00
Recalled first pressing includes track "Love Minus Zero/No Limit."						
Media America		Up Close	RS	U.S.	1989	$200.00
2 CD set.						
Media America		Up Close	RS	U.S.	1990	$100.00
2 CD set.						
		Singles				
		Blind Willie McTell	CDJ	U.S.		$7.00
Columbia		Dignity	CD5	U.K.	1994	$12.00
Columbia		Dignity	CD5	U.K.	1994	$12.00
Second version.						
Columbia		Dignity	CDJ	U.K.	1994	$18.00
Columbia	CSK 6595	Dignity	CDJ	U.S.	1994	$8.00
CBS	655358-3	Everything Is Broken	CD3	Germany	1989	$12.00
CBS	655358-2	Everything Is Broken	CD5	Germany	1989	$12.00
Columbia	CSK 1814	Everything Is Broken	CDJ	U.S.	1989	$7.00
Columbia		Knockin' on Heaven's Door	CDJ	U.S.	1995	$12.00
Columbia	CSK 7045	Knockin' on Heaven's Door	CDJ	U.S.	1995	$15.00
CBS		Like a Rolling Stone	CD5	Australia	1991	$20.00
Columbia	CSK 7332	Most of Time	CDJ	U.S.		$6.00
Columbia	CSK 5323	My Back Pages	CDJ	U.S.	1993	$6.00
Columbia		Political World	CD5	U.K.		$12.00
Second version.						
CBS	655643-2	Political World	CD5	U.K.	1990	$13.00
Columbia	CSK 3041	Series of Dreams	CDJ	U.S.	1991	$12.00
Columbia	CSK 4922	Step It Up	CDJ	U.S.	1992	$6.00
CBS	656304-2	Unbelievable	CD5	U.K.	1990	$12.00
Columbia	CSK 2138	Unbelievable	CDJ	U.S.	1990	$6.00

Dylan, Bob & The Grateful Dead

Label	Catalog Number	Title	Type	Country	Year	Value
		Full Length				
Columbia	CSK 1435	Dylan & The Dead	DJ/LP	U.S.	1989	$30.00
Picture disc.						
		Singles				
Columbia		Slow Train	CDJ	Canada	1989	$12.00
Columbia	CSK 1447	Slow Train	CDJ	U.S.	1989	$7.00

Dylans

Label	Catalog Number	Title	Type	Country	Year	Value
		Full Length				
RCA	3029	Dylans, The	LP/LB	U.S.		$14.00/$8.00
RCA		Fruity Sampler	DJ/Smplr	Canada		$15.00
		Singles				
SPV	8231-3	God Like	CD3	Germany	1991	$10.00
RCA	2806-2-RDJ	God Like	CDJ	U.S.	1991	$2.00
Warner Brothers	PRO-CD-5548	Grudge	CDJ	U.S.	1993	$3.00
SPV	0502-3	Mary Quant in Blue	CD5	Germany	1992	$10.00
RCA	62209-2-RDJ	Mary Quant in Blue	CDJ	U.S.	1991	$2.00
SPV	3096-3	My Hands Are Tied	CD3	Germany	1991	$10.00
Pinnacle	SIT-78CD	My Hands Are Tied	CD5	U.K.	1991	$10.00
Pinnacle	SIT-81CD	Planet of Love	CD5	U.K.	1991	$10.00
RCA	62187-2-RDJ	Planet of Love	CDJ	U.S.	1991	$2.00

Dynamite

Label	Catalog Number	Title	Type	Country	Year	Value
		Singles				
Pandisc	110	If You Got a Lotta	CD5	U.S.	1994	$5.00

Dynatones

Label	Catalog Number	Title	Type	Country	Year	Value
		Singles				
		Take the Heart	CDJ	U.S.		$2.00

Dynell, Jonny

Label	Catalog Number	Title	Type	Country	Year	Value
		Singles				
Atlantic	7567-86159-2	Love Find a Way	CD5	Germany	1990	$8.00

Dyson, Gay

Label	Catalog Number	Title	Type	Country	Year	Value
		Singles				
Emir	EMIRCD-1	Pain and Pleasure	CD5	U.K.	1993	$8.00

Dyyva

Label	Catalog Number	Title	Type	Country	Year	Value
		Singles				
Eastwest	9031-73755-2	La Wally	CD5	Germany	1991	$8.00

E

Label	Catalog Number	Title	Type	Country	Year	Value
		Full Length				
Polydor	CDP 454	A Man Called (E)	DJ/LP	U.S.	1992	$8.00
Polydor	CDP 769	Broken Toy Shop	DJ/LP	U.S.	1993	$8.00
		Singles				
Polydor	CDP 743	Are You and Me Gonna Happen	CDJ	U.S.	1992	$2.00
Polygram	CDP 654	Hello Cruel World	CDJ	U.S.	1992	$2.00
Polygram	CDP 690	Nowheresville	CDJ	U.S.	1992	$2.00
Polygram	CDP 1146	Only Thing I Care About, The	CDJ	U.S.	1994	$2.00
Polygram	CDP 772	Shine It All On	CDJ	U.S.	1993	$2.00

E.B. daddy-of-D

Label	Catalog Number	Title	Type	Country	Year	Value
		Singles				
Mobco	1107	I Can Feel The Rage	CD5	U.S.	1994	$5.00

E.M.F.

Label	Catalog Number	Title	Type	Country	Year	Value
		Full Length				
EMI	DPRO-04891	Special Edition	DJ/Smplr	U.S.	1992	$15.00
EMI	DPRO-04891	Special Edition/For In-Store Play	DJ/Smplr	U.S.	1992	$25.00
EMI	TOCP-7397	Stigma	LTD/LP	Japan	1992	$30.00
		Singles				
		Afro King	CD5	U.K.		$10.00
		Afro King	CD5	U.K.		$10.00
Second version.						
Parlophone	CDR 6289	Children	CD5	Austria	1991	$10.00
Parlophone	CDR-6288	Children	CD5	U.K.	1991	$10.00
EMI	204176-2	I Believe	CD5	Germany	1990	$10.00
EMI	204183-2	I Believe	CD5	Germany	1990	$10.00
Parlophone	CDR-6279	I Believe	CD5	U.K.	1990	$10.00
EMI	DPRO-04668	It's You	CDJ	U.S.	1992	$2.00
EMI	204448-2	Lies	CD5	Germany	1991	$10.00
EMI	TODP-2312	Lies	CD3	Japan	1991	$13.00/$4.00
Parlophone	CDR-6296	Lies	CD5	U.K.	1991	$10.00
EMI	DPRO-04816	Lies	CDJ	U.S.	1991	$2.00
EMI	DPRO-04794	Lies	CDJ	U.S.	1991	$2.00
EMI	DPRO-04817	Search & Destroy	CDJ	U.S.	1992	$3.00
Capitol	C2-80209	They're Here	CD5	Canada	1992	$8.00
Parlophone	CDR-6121	They're Here	CD5	U.K.	1992	$10.00
EMI	204098-2	Unbelievable	CD5	Germany	1991	$10.00
EMI	204124-2	Unbelievable	CD5	Germany	1991	$10.00
EMI	TODP-2264	Unbelievable	CD3	Japan	1991	$12.00/$4.00
Parlophone	CDR-6273	Unbelievable	CD5	U.K.	1991	$10.00
EM	56210	Unbelievable	CD5	U.S.	1991	$5.00
EMI		Unbelievable	CDJ	U.S.	1991	$2.00
EMI	TOCP-7354	Unexplained	CD5	Japan	1992	$15.00
Parlophone	CDSGE-2026	Unexplained	CD5	U.K.	1992	$10.00
EMI	DPRO-99401	Unexplained	CDJ	U.S.	1992	$7.00

E.P.O.

Label	Catalog Number	Title	Type	Country	Year	Value
		Singles				
Virgin	VSCDT-1257	Life In Tokyo	CD3	Japan	1990	$12.00/$3.00

E.U.

Label	Catalog Number	Title	Type	Country	Year	Value
		Singles				
Virgin	PR 2645	Buck Wild	CDJ	U.S.	1989	$2.00
Virgin	PRCD 4066	Da Butt	CDJ	U.S.	1988	$2.00
Virgin	PRCD 3477	I Confess	CDJ	U.S.	1990	$2.00
		Livin' Large	CDJ	U.S.		$2.00
		Taste of Your Love	CDJ	U.S.		$2.00

E.Y.C.

Label	Catalog Number	Title	Type	Country	Year	Value
		Singles				
		Black Book	CD5	U.K.		$10.00
		Black Book	CD5	U.K.		$10.00
Second version.						
Gasoline	GAS5P-3237	Black Book	CDJ	U.S.	1995	$2.00
Gasoline	2444	Get Some	CDJ	U.S.	1993	$2.00
		Number One	CD5	U.K.		$8.00
		Number One	CD5	U.K.		$10.00
		Number One	CD5	U.K.		$10.00
Second version.						
		One More Chance	CD5	U.K.		$10.00
		One More Chance	CD5	U.K.		$10.00
Second version.						
Gasoline	2723	One More Chance	CDJ	U.S.	1993	$2.00

E.Y.C.E.Y.C.

Label	Catalog Number	Title	Type	Country	Year	Value
		Singles				
Gasoline	2806	Feelin' Alright	CDJ	U.S.	1993	$2.00

E-Lustrious

Label	Catalog Number	Title	Type	Country	Year	Value
		Singles				
SRD	MOS-001CD	Dance No More	CD5	U.K.	1992	$8.00
SRD	MOS-005CD	On the Ragga Tip	CD5	U.K.	1992	$8.00

E-Zee Bad

Label	Catalog Number	Title	Type	Country	Year	Value
		Singles				
Rock It	ROCL-1004	Club Delicate	CD5	Japan	1993	$12.00
Rock It	RODL-1005	My Girl	CD3	Japan	1993	$12.00/$3.00
Rock It	RODL-1004	Shining Lover	CD3	Japan	1993	$12.00/$3.00
Rock It	RODL-1003	Wow Wow	CD3	Japan	1992	$12.00/$3.00

E-Zee Possee

Label	Catalog Number	Title	Type	Country	Year	Value
		Singles				
Virgin	PROCD-12	Breathing Is E-Zee	CD5	U.K.	1991	$8.00
BMG	663208	Everything Starts With an E	CD5	Germany	1990	$8.00
Virgin	PROCD-1	Everything Starts With an E	CD5	U.K.	1990	$8.00

Label	Catalog Number	Title	Type	Country	Year	Longbox Value / Value
Virgin	PROCD-20	Love on Love	CD5	U.K.	1992	$8.00
BMG	663396	Sun Machine	CD5	Germany	1990	$8.00
Virgin	PROCD-4	Sun Machine	CD5	U.K.	1990	$8.00

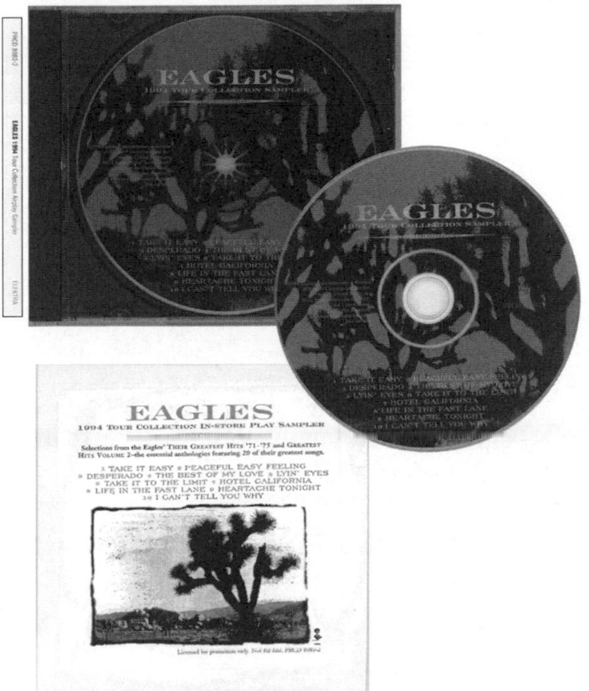

Eagles – 1994 Tour Collection Sampler (Elektra PRCD 8983-2) Identical versions of this promotional sampler were housed in both a jewel box and cardboard sleeve configuration.

Eagles

Full Length

Label	Catalog Number	Title	Type	Country	Year	Longbox Value / Value
Elektra	PRCD 8983-2	1994 Tour Collection Airplay Sampler	DJ/Smplr	U.S.	1994	$25.00
	CD in cardboard sleeve with title sticker.					
Elektra	PRCD 8983-2	1994 Tour Collection Airplay Sampler	DJ/Smplr	U.S.	1994	$25.00
	CD in jewel case with tray card.					
		Classic CD (Hotel California)	RS	U.S.	1990	$80.00
	2 CD set. Airdate: 8/27/90.					
Elektra		Common Thread	DJ/Smplr	Canada	1994	$40.00
	2CD set. Disc One - Eagle Covers, Disc two - originals. Limited to 1000 copies.					
Elektra		Common Thread	LTD/LP	Canada	1994	$35.00
	2CD set. Disc One - Eagle Covers, Disc two - originals. Limited to 20,000 copies.					
		Common Thread Tribute	RS	U.S.	1993	$70.00
	3 CD set. Airdate: 10/16/93.					
Elektra	105-2	Greatest Hits 1971-1975	LP/LB	U.S.†	1984	$14.00/$8.00
Asylum	43P2--0007	Hotel California	LTD/LP	Japan		$50.00
	Gold disc.					
Elektra	103-2	Hotel California	LP/LB	U.S.†	1984	$14.00/$8.00
Album Network		In the Studio (Eagles)	RS	U.S.	1994	$35.00
	Airdate: 5/30/94.					
Album Network		In the Studio (Hotel California)	RS	U.S.	1992	$35.00
	Airdate: 10/19/92.					
Elektra	508-2	Long Run	LP/LB	U.S.†	1984	$14.00/$8.00
Westwood One		Off the Record	RS	U.S.	1994	$75.00
	2 CD set. Airdate: 8/29/94.					
Westwood One		Off the Record	RS	U.S.	1995	$30.00
	Airdate: 4/10/95.					
Global Satellite Network		On the Boarder	RS	U.S.	1991	$80.00
	3 CD set.					
Giant	CD 24531	Originals/Common Threads	DJ/Smplr	Canada	1993	$30.00
	VA album of hits plus second disc of originals by the Eagles.					
Westwood One		Pink Champagne On Ice	RS	U.S.	1990	$100.00
	3 CD set. Airdate: 1/25/90.					
Elektra		Very Best of	LTD/LP	Australia	1995	$35.00
	Gold disc.					
		Very Best of	DJ/Smplr	U.K.	1994	$25.00

Singles

Label	Catalog Number	Title	Type	Country	Year	Longbox Value / Value
Geffen	GEDS004	Get Over It	CDJ	Spain	1995	$12.00
Elektra	PRCD 4679-2	Get Over It	CDJ	U.S.	1995	$7.00
Geffen	GEDS004	Hell and Freeze	CDJ	Spain	1995	$25.00
Asylum	966757-2	Hotel California	CD5	Germany	1988	$13.00
		Hotel California	CD5	Germany	1996	$12.00
Asylum	EKR-10CD	Hotel California	CD5	U.K.	1988	$13.00
Elektra	65926-2	Hotel California	CD5	U.S.	1992	$5.00
Elektra	PRCD 4713	Learn to Be Still	CDJ	U.S.	1995	$7.00
		Love Will Keep Us Alive	CD5	Germany	1996	$12.00
Elektra/Asylum	65922	Please Come Home For	CD5	U.S.	1994	$5.00
Asylum	969341-2	Take It Easy	CD5	Germany	1989	$13.00
Asylum	969341-2	Take It Easy	CD5	U.K.	1989	$13.00

Earle, Stacy

Singles

Label	Catalog Number	Title	Type	Country	Year	Longbox Value / Value
RCA	RDJ 62458-2	Blood From a Stone	CDJ	U.S.	1991	$2.00
RCA	RDJ 62115-2	Love Me All Up	CDJ	U.S.	1991	$2.00
RCA	BVDP-56	Romeo & Juliet	CD3	Japan	1991	$12.00/$3.00
RCA	RDJ 62231-2	Romeo & Juliet	CDJ	U.S.	1991	$2.00
RCA	RDJ 62191-2	Romeo & Juliet	CDJ	U.S.	1992	$2.00
RCA	BVDP-561	Slowly	CD3	Japan	1991	$12.00/$3.00
RCA	RDJ 62271-2	Slowly	CDJ	U.S.	1991	$2.00

Earle, Steve

Singles

Label	Catalog Number	Title	Type	Country	Year	Longbox Value / Value
		Hard Core Troubador	CDJ	U.S.		$5.00
		Johnny Too Bad	CD5	U.K.	1996	$10.00
		More Than I Can Do	CD5	Australia	1996	$12.00

Earle, Steve (and the Dukes)

Full Length

Label	Catalog Number	Title	Type	Country	Year	Longbox Value / Value
MCA	MCAD 9042	An Interview With…	DJ/Intvw	Canada	1990	$12.00
MCA		Hard Way, The	LP/LB	U.S.		$14.00/$8.00
MCA	CD33-1664	Live Sampler	DJ/Smplr	U.S.	1991	$10.00
MCA		Sampler	DJ/Smplr	Canada	1989	$25.00

Singles

Label	Catalog Number	Title	Type	Country	Year	Longbox Value / Value
MCA	CD45 17403	Angry Young Man	CDJ	U.S.	1987	$3.00
MCA	DMCAT-1319	Back to the Wall	CD5	U.K.	1988	$10.00
Uni	CD45 17772	Back to the Wall	CDJ	U.S.	1988	$3.00
MCA	1229	Billy Austin	CDJ	U.S.	1990	$3.00
MCA	DMCA-1280	Copperhead Road	CD5	U.K.	1988	$15.00
Uni	CD45-17681	Copperhead Road	CDJ	U.S.	1988	$7.00
MCA	CD45 17820	Even When I'm Blue	CDJ	U.S.	1989	$3.00
MCA	8 74001	Johnny Come Lately	CD5	Germany	1989	$10.00
MCA	DMCA-1301	Johnny Come Lately	CD5	U.K.	1989	$10.00
MCA	DMCAT-1441	Justice in Ontario	CD5	U.K.	1990	$10.00
Uni	CD45-18077	Nothing But a Child	CDJ	U.S.	1988	$3.00
MCA	DMCAT-1426	Other Kind, The	CD5	U.K.	1990	$10.00
MCA	18399	Other Kind, The	CDJ	U.S.	1990	$3.00
MCA	1019	Promise You Anything	CDJ	U.S.	1990	$3.00

Earth

Singles

Label	Catalog Number	Title	Type	Country	Year	Longbox Value / Value
Sub Pop		Postgraduate Seminars	CD5	U.S.		$10.00
Sub Pop	SPCD 03/252	Seven Angels	CD5	U.K.	1993	$8.00

Earth Eighteen

Singles

Label	Catalog Number	Title	Type	Country	Year	Longbox Value / Value
	41942	Girl of the Downwar	CD5	U.S.	1994	$5.00

Earth People

Singles

Label	Catalog Number	Title	Type	Country	Year	Longbox Value / Value
Champion	CHAMPCD-239	Reach Up To Mars	CD5	U.K.	1990	$8.00

Earth Wind & Fire – Greatest Hits Live Special Radio Sampler (Pyramid PRCD 7212)

Earth Wind & Fire

Full Length

Label	Catalog Number	Title	Type	Country	Year	Longbox Value / Value
CBS	SRCS-7910	All 'n All	LP	Japan		$35.00
CBS	CK-38980	Electric Universe	LP/BP	U.S.†	1984	$14.00/$8.00
Pyramid	PRCD 7212	Greatest Hits Live Special Radio Sampler	DJ/Smplr	U.S.	1996	$15.00
	CD packaged in "laserfile" case.					
CBS		Heritage	DJ/LP	U.S.	1990	$8.00
Pioneer	PA-83-039	In Concert	LD	U.S.	1983	$20.00
	Analog audio.					
Columbia	CSK 4750	Mighty Mighty Sampler	DJ/Smplr	U.S.	1992	$10.00
CBS	CK-38367	Powerlight	LP/BP	U.S.†	1984	$14.00/$8.00
CBS	CK-37548	Raise	LP/BP	U.S.†	1984	$14.00/$8.00
CBS	25DP-5205	Star Box	LP	Japan	1987	$30.00

Singles

Label	Catalog Number	Title	Type	Country	Year	Longbox Value / Value
CBS	654587-3	Boogie Wonderland	CD3	Germany	1989	$10.00
CBS	10EP-3019	Evil Roy	CD3	Japan	1988	$13.00/$4.00
CBS	10EP-3021	Fantasy	CD3	Japan	1988	$13.00/$4.00
Columbia	CSK 73344	For the Love of You	CDJ	U.S.	1990	$2.00
CBS	655580-3	Heritage	CD3	Germany	1990	$10.00
CBS	CSDS-8118	Heritage	CD3	Japan	1990	$13.00/$4.00
Columbia	CDEWF-3	Heritage	CD5	U.K.	1990	$10.00
Columbia	CSK 73205	Heritage	CDJ	U.S.	1990	$2.00
Old Gold	OG-6501	Let's Groove	CD3	Germany	1990	$10.00
Reprise	PRO-CD-6574	Spend the Night	CDJ	U.S.	1993	$2.00
Reprise	18461-2	Sunday Morning	CD5	U.S.	1993	$5.00
CBS	10EP-3004	System of Survival	CD3	Japan	1987	$12.00/$4.00
CBS	CDGWF-1	System of Survival	CD5	U.K.	1987	$10.00
Columbia	CSK 2837	System of Survival	CDJ	U.S.	1987	$7.00
CBS	CSDS-8134	Takin' Chances	CD3	Japan	1990	$13.00/$4.00
CBS	CDEWF-2	Thinking of You	CD5	U.K.	1988	$10.00
Columbia	CSK 1002	Thinking of You	CDJ	U.S.	1988	$2.00
CBS	653048-3	Touch the World	CD3	Germany	1988	$10.00
CBS	12EP-3067	Turn on	CD3	Japan	1989	$13.00/$4.00
Columbia	CSK 1336	Turn on	CDJ	U.S.	1988	$2.00
Reprise	PRO-CD-6723	Two Hearts	CDJ	U.S.	1993	$2.00
Reprise	18249-2	Two Hearts	CD5	U.S.	1994	$5.00
CBS	656132-3	Wanna Be the Man	CD3	Germany	1990	$10.00
CBS	CSDS-8160	Wanna Be the Man	CD3	Japan	1990	$13.00/$4.00
Columbia	CSK 73436	Wanna Be the Man	CDJ	U.S.	1990	$2.00

Earthling

Singles

Label	Catalog Number	Title	Type	Country	Year	Longbox Value / Value
		Echo On My Mind	CD5	U.K.		$10.00
		Echo On My Mind	CD5	U.K.		$10.00
	Second version.					

Earthshaker

Singles

Label	Catalog Number	Title	Type	Country	Year	Longbox Value / Value
WEA	WMD3-3027	Say Goodbye	CD3	Japan	1993	$12.00/$3.00

East 17

Singles

Label	Catalog Number	Title	Type	Country	Year	Longbox Value / Value
London	PODD-1030	Deep Breath	CD3	Japan	1993	$13.00/$4.00
		Deep Breath	CD5	U.K.	1993	$8.00
		Deep Breath	CD5	U.K.	1993	$8.00

Second version.

Label	Catalog Number	Title	Type	Country	Year	Longbox Value / Value
London	CDP 956	Deep Breath	CDJ	U.S.	1993	$2.00
London	LONCD-331	Gold	CD5	U.K.	1992	$10.00
London	PODD-1027	House of Love	CD3	Japan	1993	$13.00/$4.00
London	LONCD-325	House of Love	CD5	U.K.	1993	$10.00
London	CDP 847	House of Love	CDJ	U.S.	1993	$2.00
		Stay Another Day	CD5	U.K.		$10.00
		Stay Another Day	CD5	U.K.		$10.00

Second version.

Label	Catalog Number	Title	Type	Country	Year	Longbox Value / Value
		West End Girls	CD5	U.K.	1993	$8.00
		West End Girls	CD5	U.K.	1993	$8.00

Second version.

East Coast Family

Singles

Label	Catalog Number	Title	Type	Country	Year	Longbox Value / Value
Motown	3746310482	1-4-All-4-1	CDJ	U.S.	1992	$2.00

East Of Eden

Singles

Label	Catalog Number	Title	Type	Country	Year	Longbox Value / Value
Capitol	DPRO-79888	From This World	CDJ	U.S.	1989	$2.00

East Side Beat

Singles

Label	Catalog Number	Title	Type	Country	Year	Longbox Value / Value
ffrr	FCD-206	Alive and Kicking	CD5	U.K.	1992	$8.00
ZYX	ZYX-6522-8	Drivin' in the Beat	CD5	Germany	1992	$6.00
ffrr	869605-2	Ride Like the Wind	CD5	Germany	1991	$8.00
ffrr	FCD-176	Ride Like the Wind	CD5	U.K.	1991	$8.00
ffrr	CDP 633	Ride Like the Wind	CDJ	U.S.	1992	$2.00

Eastbound Expressway

Singles

Label	Catalog Number	Title	Type	Country	Year	Longbox Value / Value
Canyon	S10ED-5072	Whiplash	CD3	Japan	1989	$12.00/$3.00

Easterhouse

Singles

Label	Catalog Number	Title	Type	Country	Year	Longbox Value / Value
Rough Trade	RTT-204CD	Come Out Fighting	CD5	U.K.	1989	$8.00
Columbia	000132	Come Out Fighting	CDJ	U.S.	1989	$2.00

Eastman Jazz Ensemble

Full Length

Label	Catalog Number	Title	Type	Country	Year	Longbox Value / Value
Second Hearing	NGS-9002	Live	LP/LB	U.S.†	1985	$14.00/$8.00

Easton, Sheena

Full Length

Label	Catalog Number	Title	Type	Country	Year	Longbox Value / Value
Pioneer	PA85-M021	A Private Heaven	8"LD	U.S.	1985	$8.00

Analog audio.

Label	Catalog Number	Title	Type	Country	Year	Longbox Value / Value
Capitol	CDP-46054	A Private Heaven	LP/LB	U.S.†	1985	$14.00/$8.00
MCA	ICD-89	In-Store Special	DJ/Smplr	Japan	1994	$80.00
	MP094-15EM	Live at the Palace	LD	Japan		$75.00
EMI	CDP-46417	No Sound But a Heart	LP	U.K.		$20.00
Capitol	CDP-46417	No Sound But a Heart	LP/LB	U.S.		$15.00/$10.00
Pioneer	PA84-M005	Sheena Easton	8"LD	U.S.	1983	$8.00

Analog audio.

Label	Catalog Number	Title	Type	Country	Year	Longbox Value / Value
EMI	CP35-3058	Take My Time	LP	Japan		$23.00
MCA	MVCZ-5	What Comes Naturally	LTD/LP	Japan	1991	$25.00

10"x10" outer package with photocards.

Label	Catalog Number	Title	Type	Country	Year	Longbox Value / Value
EMI	CP32-5039	You Could Have Been With Me	LP	Japan		$23.00

Singles

Label	Catalog Number	Title	Type	Country	Year	Longbox Value / Value
MCA	257558-2	101	CD5	Germany	1989	$10.00
MCA	09P3-6161	101	CD3	Japan	1989	$13.00/$4.00
MCA	DMCA-1348	101	CD3	U.K.	1989	$10.00
MCA	CD45 17807	101	CDJ	U.S.	1989	$2.00
MCA	CD45 17939	101	CDJ	U.S.	1989	$2.00
MCA	2194	A Dream Worth Keeping	CDJ	U.S.	1992	$2.00
MCA	8 20970	Days Like This	CD3	Germany	1989	$10.00
MCA	09P3-6132	Days Like This	CD3	Japan	1989	$13.00/$4.00
MCA	DMCA-1325	Days Like This	CD3	U.K.	1989	$10.00
MCA	CD45 17745	Days Like This	CDJ	U.S.	1989	$2.00
MCA	CD45 18038	Follow My Rainbow	CDJ	U.S.	1988	$2.00
MCA	257742-2	Lover in Me	CD3	Germany	1988	$10.00
MCA	10P3-6066	Lover in Me	CD3	Japan	1988	$13.00/$4.00
MCA	DMCA-1289	Lover in Me	CD3	U.K.	1988	$10.00
MCA	MVDM-50	Miracle of Love	CD3	Japan		$13.00/$4.00
MCA	MVDM-55	My Cherie	CD3	Japan		$13.00/$4.00
MCA	MVDM-50	My Cherie	CDJ	Japan	1995	$17.00/$6.00
MCA		My Cherie	CDJ	U.S.	1995	$3.00
MCA	CD45 17952	No Deposit No Return	CDJ	U.S.	1989	$2.00
MCA	CD45 1616	To Anyone	CDJ	U.S.	1991	$2.00
MCA	MVDM-56	Too Much in Love	CD3	Japan		$13.00/$4.00
MCA	MCD-17733	What Comes Naturally	CD5	Germany	1991	$10.00
MCA	CD45 1134	What Comes Naturally	CDJ	U.S.	1991	$2.00
MCA	CD45 1346	What Comes Naturally	CDJ	U.S.	1991	$2.00
MCA	MCD-17802	You Can Swing It	CD5	Germany	1991	$10.00
MCA	CD45 1493	You Can Swing It	CDJ	U.S.	1991	$2.00

Eastwood, Clint

Full Length

Label	Catalog Number	Title	Type	Country	Year	Longbox Value / Value
Warner Brothers		Bridges of Madison County Interview	DJ/Intvw	U.S.	1995	$12.00
Warner Brothers		Words & Music	DJ/Intvw	U.S.	1995	$15.00

Interview for "Bridges Of Madison County" film.

Easy

Singles

Label	Catalog Number	Title	Type	Country	Year	Longbox Value / Value
Pinnacle	BFFP-61CD	He Brings the Honey	CD5	U.K.	1991	$8.00

Easy Pieces

Singles

Label	Catalog Number	Title	Type	Country	Year	Longbox Value / Value
A&M	CD 17772	Trust One Another	CDJ	U.S.	1988	$2.00
A&M	CD 17618	Whenever You're Ready	CDJ	U.S.	1988	$2.00
A&M	CD 17650	(You're My) Heaven	CDJ	U.S.	1988	$2.00

Easybeats

Full Length

Label	Catalog Number	Title	Type	Country	Year	Longbox Value / Value
EMI	746286-8	Anthology	LP	Germany		$23.00
Aris	885827	Friday on My Mind	CD3	Germany	1990	$10.00

Eazy E

Singles

Label	Catalog Number	Title	Type	Country	Year	Longbox Value / Value
MCA	MCA5P-3054	Luv 4 Dem Gangstaz	CDJ	U.S.	1994	$2.00

Eberhart, Cliff

Singles

Label	Catalog Number	Title	Type	Country	Year	Longbox Value / Value
Windham	90-16	Long Road, The	CDJ	U.S.	1990	$2.00

Echo and the Bunnymen

Full Length

Label	Catalog Number	Title	Type	Country	Year	Longbox Value / Value
WEA	242137-2	Echo & the Bunnymen	LP	Germany		$25.00
Westwood One		In Concert-Nu Rock	RS	U.S.	1993	$50.00

Airdate: 9/13/93.

Singles

Label	Catalog Number	Title	Type	Country	Year	Longbox Value / Value
Sire	PRO-CD-2926	Bedbugs & Ballyhoo	CDJ	U.S.	1988	$2.00
Korova	KOW-44CD	Enlighten Me	CD5	U.K.	1990	$10.00
Sire	PRO-CD-4556	Enlighten Me	CDJ	U.S.	1990	$2.00
Euphoric	381-0089-3	Inside Me, Inside You	CD5	Germany	1991	$10.00
Euphoric	E-002CD	Inside Me, Inside You	CD5	U.K.	1991	$10.00
Sire	PRO-CD-2806	Lips Like Sugar	CDJ	U.S.	1988	$2.00
Strange Fruit	CD-30123	Peel Sessions	CD5	Germany	1988	$9.00
Strange Fruit	SFPSCD-060	Peel Sessions	CD5	U.K.	1988	$9.00
Strange Fruit	60	Peel Sessions	CD5	U.S.	1988	$5.00
Eastwest	WMC5-358	People Are Strange	CD5	Japan	1991	$15.00
Eastwest	YZ-567CD	People Are Strange	CD5	U.K.	1991	$10.00
Document	DC-3	Pictures On My Wall	CD5	U.K.	1990	$10.00
Euphoric	E-001CD	Prove Me Wrong	CD5	U.K.	1991	$10.00

Echobelly

Singles

Label	Catalog Number	Title	Type	Country	Year	Longbox Value / Value
		Great Things	CD5	U.K.	1995	$11.00
		Great Things	CD5	U.K.	1995	$11.00

Second version.

Label	Catalog Number	Title	Type	Country	Year	Longbox Value / Value
		Great Things	CDJ	U.S.	1995	$10.00
		King Of the Kerb	CD5	U.K.		$8.00
		King Of the Kerb	CD5	U.K.		$8.00

Second version.

Echora

Singles

Label	Catalog Number	Title	Type	Country	Year	Longbox Value / Value
Big Beat	500125	Love Is Blind	CD5	U.S.	1993	$4.00
Big Beat	5119	Love Is Blind	CDJ	U.S.	1993	$2.00

Eco

Singles

Label	Catalog Number	Title	Type	Country	Year	Longbox Value / Value
Boy	BOY-8833-8	Geld	CD5	Germany	1991	$8.00
Boy	BOY-8834-8	Geld	CD5	Germany	1991	$8.00

Econoline Crush

Full Length

Label	Catalog Number	Title	Type	Country	Year	Longbox Value / Value
		Purge	DJ/Smplr	Canada		$18.00

Singles

Label	Catalog Number	Title	Type	Country	Year	Longbox Value / Value
EMI	E228989	Purge	CD5	Canada	1994	$13.00

Ecstasy

Singles

Label	Catalog Number	Title	Type	Country	Year	Longbox Value / Value
ZYX	ZYX-6282-8	This Is My House	CD5	Germany	1991	$6.00

Ecstasy Club

Singles

Label	Catalog Number	Title	Type	Country	Year	Longbox Value / Value
Italo-Heat	FFR-0307	Jesus Love the Acid	CD5	Germany	1989	$8.00
Italo-Heat	FFR-0507	Jesus Love the Acid	CD5	Germany	1989	$8.00

Ed

Singles

Label	Catalog Number	Title	Type	Country	Year	Longbox Value / Value
Avex Trax	AVCD-30002	You Really Got Me	CD5	Japan	1992	$10.00

Ed, O.G. and The Bulldogs

Full Length

Label	Catalog Number	Title	Type	Country	Year	Longbox Value / Value
Mercury	CDP 1153	Love Comes and Goes	DJ/Smplr	U.S.	1994	$8.00

Singles

Label	Catalog Number	Title	Type	Country	Year	Longbox Value / Value
PWL	CDP 483	Bug A Boo	CDJ	U.S.	1991	$2.00
Polydor	PZCD-138	I Got to Have It	CD5	U.K.	1991	$8.00

Eddie, John

Singles

Label	Catalog Number	Title	Type	Country	Year	Longbox Value / Value
Elektra	PRCD 8279-2	In Between Days	CDJ	U.S.	1990	$2.00
CBS	1-EP-3088	Swear	CD3	Japan	1989	$13.00/$4.00
Columbia	CSK 1631	Swear	CDJ	U.S.	1989	$2.00
Columbia	CSK 1810	Tough Luck	CDJ	U.S.	1989	$2.00

Edelweiss

Singles

Label	Catalog Number	Title	Type	Country	Year	Longbox Value / Value
WEA	247543-2	Bring Me Edelweiss	CD3	Germany	1988	$8.00
WEA	YZ-353CD	Bring Me Edelweiss	CD3	U.K.	1988	$8.00
		Bring Me Edelweiss	CDJ	U.S.	1988	$2.00
WEA	246656-2	I Can't Get No Satisfaction	CD3	Germany	1989	$8.00
WEA	YZ-442CD	I Can't Get No Satisfaction	CD3	U.K.	1989	$8.00
WEA	WE-739	Starship Edelweiss	CD5	U.K.	1992	$8.00

Eden, Eric

Full Length

Label	Catalog Number	Title	Type	Country	Year	Longbox Value / Value
A&M	75021 7398-2	Eric Eden	DJ/Smplr	U.S.	1992	$6.00
A&M	5395	Grooving Up Slowly	LP/BP	U.S.		$12.00/$7.00

Eder, Linda

Singles

Label	Catalog Number	Title	Type	Country	Year	Longbox Value / Value
RCA	60564-RDJ	A Little Bit of Heaven	CDJ	U.S.	1991	$2.00
Angel	79377	You Are My Home	CDJ	U.S.	1992	$2.00

Edge, Graeme

Full Length

Label	Catalog Number	Title	Type	Country	Year	Longbox Value / Value
Polygram		Kick Off Your Muddy Boots	LP/BP	U.S.		$12.00/$7.00

Edmunds, Dave

Full Length

Label	Catalog Number	Title	Type	Country	Year	Longbox Value / Value
Westwood One		In Concert-Nu Rock	RS	U.S.	1994	$65.00
		Interview	DJ/Intvw	U.S.		$15.00
DIR		King Biscuit Flour Hour	RS	U.S.	1990	$60.00

2 CD set. Airdate: 5/7 – 5/14/90.

Label	Catalog Number	Title	Type	Country	Year	Longbox Value / Value
Atlantic		Tracks On Wax 4	LP/LB	U.S.		$12.00/$7.00
Atlantic		Twangin'	LP/LB	U.S.		$12.00/$7.00

Singles

Label	Catalog Number	Title	Type	Country	Year	Longbox Value / Value
EMI	203771-2	Closer to the Flame	CD5	Germany	1990	$10.00
Capitol	DPRO-79938	Closer to the Flame	CDJ	U.S.	1990	$2.00
Capitol	CDCL-568	King of Love	CD5	U.K.	1990	$10.00
Capitol	DPRO-79773	King of Love	CDJ	U.S.	1989	$2.00

Label	Catalog Number	Title	Type	Country	Year	Longbox Value / Value
		One Step Back	CDJ	U.S.	1995	$6.00

Edsel Auctioneer

Singles

Label	Catalog Number	Title	Type	Country	Year	Longbox Value / Value
Pure Bliss	BLISCDS-2	Dashing Away	CD5	U.K.	1992	$8.00
Toysfactory	TFCK-88703	Voice of Harolds	CD5	Japan	1991	$10.00

Edwards, Charlotte

Singles

Label	Catalog Number	Title	Type	Country	Year	Longbox Value / Value
Mercury	MERCD-297	You Can't Beat the Feeling	CD5	U.K.	1989	$8.00

Edwards, Mark

Full Length

Label	Catalog Number	Title	Type	Country	Year	Longbox Value / Value
R&A	10521-2	Just Having Touched	DJ/Intvw	U.S.	1990	$3.00

Edwards, Michelle

Singles

Label	Catalog Number	Title	Type	Country	Year	Longbox Value / Value
BMG	CDBORG-8	Silent Tear	CD5	U.K.	1990	$8.00

Edwards, Phil

Singles

Label	Catalog Number	Title	Type	Country	Year	Longbox Value / Value
WEA	9031-72638-2	Don't Look Any Further	CD5	Germany	1990	$8.00
WEA	YZ-514CD	La Vie En Vogue	CD5	U.K.	1990	$8.00
WEA	171722-2	Mysterious	CD5	Germany	1990	$8.00

Edwards, Teddy

Singles

Label	Catalog Number	Title	Type	Country	Year	Longbox Value / Value
Verve	4286	Blue Saxaphone	CD5	France	1992	$2.00

Eek-A-Mouse

Singles

Label	Catalog Number	Title	Type	Country	Year	Longbox Value / Value
Island	PRCD 6669-2	Dyer Maker	CDJ	U.S.	1991	$2.00

Eena

Singles

Label	Catalog Number	Title	Type	Country	Year	Longbox Value / Value
BMG	663311	Eighteen So What	CD5	Germany	1990	$8.00
BMG	663928	Gates of Eden	CD5	Germany	1990	$8.00

Efua

Singles

Label	Catalog Number	Title	Type	Country	Year	Longbox Value / Value
Virgin	VSCDT-1438	Down is the Drop	CD5	U.K.	1993	$8.00
Virgin	PRCD 12758	Strawberry Boy	CDJ	U.S.	1993	$2.00

Eg and Alice

Singles

Label	Catalog Number	Title	Type	Country	Year	Longbox Value / Value
Warner Brothers	YZ-627CD	Doesn't Mean That Much to Me	CD5	U.K.	1992	$8.00
Warner Brothers	9031-74952-2	Indian	CD5	U.K.	1991	$8.00

Eggstone

Singles

Label	Catalog Number	Title	Type	Country	Year	Longbox Value / Value
Snap	SNAPC-7	Can't Come Close Enough	CD5	U.K.	1992	$8.00
Snap	SNAPC-2	Shooting Time	CD5	U.K.	1992	$8.00

Egyptian Empire

Singles

Label	Catalog Number	Title	Type	Country	Year	Longbox Value / Value
Polygram	TABCD-115	Horn Track	CD5	U.K.	1992	$8.00

Egyptians

Full Length

Label	Catalog Number	Title	Type	Country	Year	Longbox Value / Value
Rhino		Catalog Sampler	DJ/Smplr	U.S.	1995	$18.00

Eh Dee

Singles

Label	Catalog Number	Title	Type	Country	Year	Longbox Value / Value
Jbr	19001	Total Satisfaction	CD5	U.S.	1994	$5.00

Eighth Wonder

Singles

Label	Catalog Number	Title	Type	Country	Year	Longbox Value / Value
Epic	653006-3	Baby Baby	CD3	Germany	1988	$8.00
Epic	128P-8011	Baby Baby	CD3	Japan	1988	$12.00/$3.00
Epic	108P-3049	Baby Baby	CD3	Japan	1988	$12.00/$3.00
Epic	CDBABE-1	Baby Baby	CD5	U.K.	1988	$8.00
WTG	PSK 1470	Baby Baby	CDJ	U.S.	1988	$2.00
Columbia	651552-9	Cross My Heart	CD5	Germany	1988	$8.00
Epic	108P-3023	Cross My Heart	CD3	Japan	1988	$12.00/$3.00
Columbia	651552-9	Cross My Heart	CD5	U.K.	1988	$8.00
Epic		Cross My Heart	CDJ	U.S.	1988	$2.00
Columbia	651359-8	I'm Not Scared	CD3	Germany	1988	$8.00
Epic	108P-3012	I'm Not Scared	CD3	Japan	1988	$12.00/$3.00
Columbia	651359-8	I'm Not Scared	CD3	U.K.	1988	$8.00
Columbia	SCAREC-1	I'm Not Scared	CD5	U.K.	1988	$8.00
WTG	PSK 1625	I'm Not Scared	CDJ	U.S.	1988	$2.00
Epic	108P-3061	Use Me	CD3	Japan	1989	$12.00/$3.00

Eikhard, Shirley

Singles

Label	Catalog Number	Title	Type	Country	Year	Longbox Value / Value
Cypress	17566	Someone Else	CDJ	U.S.	1988	$2.00

Einstuerzende Neubauten

Full Length

Label	Catalog Number	Title	Type	Country	Year	Longbox Value / Value
Passport	PVCD-9902	Drawings of Ot	LP/LB	U.S.		$14.00/$8.00

El Dogg

Singles

Label	Catalog Number	Title	Type	Country	Year	Longbox Value / Value
Motown	4849	I Gotta Get My Sag on	CD5	U.S.	1994	$5.00

El Magnifico

Singles

Label	Catalog Number	Title	Type	Country	Year	Longbox Value / Value
RCA	62790-2-RDJ	Buzz Kill	CDJ	U.S.	1994	$2.00

Elaine, Terry

Singles

Label	Catalog Number	Title	Type	Country	Year	Longbox Value / Value
EMI	323856-2	You Got Me Turning Around	CD5	Germany	1992	$8.00

Elastica

Full Length

Label	Catalog Number	Title	Type	Country	Year	Longbox Value / Value
Geffen		Elastica	LTD/LP	Australia	1995	$28.00

2 CD set.

Label	Catalog Number	Title	Type	Country	Year	Longbox Value / Value
Geffen		Elastica	DJ/LP	U.S.	1995	$12.00
Westwood One		In Concert-Nu Rock	RS	U.S.	1995	$65.00

Airdate: 11/20/95.

Label	Catalog Number	Title	Type	Country	Year	Longbox Value / Value
		Tour de Force	LTD/LP	Australia	1996	$30.00

2 CD set.

Singles

Label	Catalog Number	Title	Type	Country	Year	Longbox Value / Value
Geffen	PRO-CD-4724	Connection	CDJ	U.S.	1995	$3.00
Geffen		Shutter	CDJ	U.S.	1995	$3.00
Geffen	22001	Stutter	CD5	U.S.	1994	$5.00

Electra

Singles

Label	Catalog Number	Title	Type	Country	Year	Longbox Value / Value
ffrr	FCD-121	Destiny	CD5	U.K.	1989	$8.00
ffrr	868 328-2	Jibaro	CD5	Germany	1988	$8.00

Electra, Carmen

Singles

Label	Catalog Number	Title	Type	Country	Year	Longbox Value / Value
Paisley Park	9 40693-2	Everybody Get On Up	CD5	U.S.	1992	$5.00
Paisley Park	PRO-CD-5933	Everybody Get On Up	CDJ	U.S.	1992	$2.00
Paisley Park	9 40970-2	Fantasia Erotica	CD5	U.S.	1992	$5.00
Paisley Park	W-0114CD	Go Go Dancer	CD5	U.K.	1992	$10.00
Paisley Park	9 40458-2	Go Go Dancer	CD5	U.S.	1992	$5.00

Electrafixion

Singles

Label	Catalog Number	Title	Type	Country	Year	Longbox Value / Value
		Four Song Sampler	CDJ	U.S.		$6.00
		Never	CD5	U.K.		$10.00
		Never	CD5	U.K.		$10.00

Second version.

Electribe 101

Singles

Label	Catalog Number	Title	Type	Country	Year	Longbox Value / Value
Mercury	MERCD-335	Inside Out	CD5	U.K.	1990	$8.00
Club	JABCD-74	Talking With Myself	CD5	U.K.	1988	$8.00
Mercury	MERCD-316	Talking With Myself	CD5	U.K.	1988	$8.00
Mercury	876519-2	Tell Me When the Fever Ended	CD5	Germany	1989	$8.00
Mercury	MERCD-310	Tell Me When the Fever Ended	CD5	U.K.	1989	$8.00
Mercury	MERCD-328	You're Walking	CD5	U.K.	1990	$8.00
Mercury	878001-2	You're Walking	CD5	U.K.	1990	$8.00

Electric Amish

Full Length

Label	Catalog Number	Title	Type	Country	Year	Longbox Value / Value
Donkey Monkey Records	EA1-1995	Barn to Be Wild	LTD/LP	U.S.	1995	$25.00

Electric Angels

Singles

Label	Catalog Number	Title	Type	Country	Year	Longbox Value / Value
Atlantic	PRCD 3400-2	Drinking Song, The	CDJ	U.S.	1990	$2.00
Atlantic		Rattlesnake Kisses	CDJ	U.S.	1990	$2.00

Electric Boy

Full Length

Label	Catalog Number	Title	Type	Country	Year	Longbox Value / Value
		In Concert	RS	U.S.	1992	$35.00

With Mr. Big & Hardline, Airdate: 11/23/92.

Singles

Label	Catalog Number	Title	Type	Country	Year	Longbox Value / Value
Phonogram	PHCR-8005	All Lips 'n Hips	CD3	Japan	1991	$15.00/$4.00
Vertigo	VERCD-48	All Lips 'n Hips	CD5	U.K.	1990	$8.00
Atco	PRCD 3282-2	All Lips 'n Hips	CDJ	U.S.	1990	$2.00
Atco	PRCD 4692-2	Dying To Be Loved	CDJ	U.S.	1992	$2.00
Vertigo	VERCD-50	Electrified	CD5	U.K.	1990	$8.00
		Into the Woods	CDJ	U.S.		$2.00
Vertigo	VERCD-65	Mary in the Mystery World	CD5	U.K.	1992	$8.00
Atco	PRCD 4522-2	Mary in the Mystery World	CDJ	U.S.	1992	$2.00
		Psychedelic Eyes	CDJ	U.S.		$2.00

Electric Glass Ballroom

Singles

Label	Catalog Number	Title	Type	Country	Year	Longbox Value / Value
Midi	MDC2-1181	Beautiful Days	CD5	Japan	1992	$10.00
Midi	MDCL-1213	Cult Star Guidebook	CD5	Japan	1992	$10.00
Midi	MDCL-1206	Speed Freak	CD5	Japan	1992	$10.00

Electric Light Orchestra

Full Length

Label	Catalog Number	Title	Type	Country	Year	Longbox Value / Value
BBC Radio		BBC Classic Tracks	RS	U.S.	1991	$20.00

Airdate: 7/15/91.

Label	Catalog Number	Title	Type	Country	Year	Longbox Value / Value
BBC Radio		BBC Classic Tracks	RS	U.S.	1992	$20.00

Airdate: 7/27/92.

Label	Catalog Number	Title	Type	Country	Year	Longbox Value / Value
BBC Radio		BBC Classic Tracks	RS	U.S.	1993	$20.00

Airdate: 2/22/93.

Label	Catalog Number	Title	Type	Country	Year	Longbox Value / Value
Westwood One		BBC Classic Tracks	RS	U.S.	1993	$30.00

Airdate: 12/6/93.

Label	Catalog Number	Title	Type	Country	Year	Longbox Value / Value
Epic	ZSK 2109	Destination Unknown	DJ/Smplr	U.S.	1990	$20.00
Epic	ZSK 35769	Discovery	LP/BP	U.S.†	1984	$14.00/$8.00
Columbia	64646	Discovery	LTD/LP	U.S.	1995	$26.00

Gold disc.

Label	Catalog Number	Title	Type	Country	Year	Longbox Value / Value
		In Concert	RS	U.S.	1992	$120.00

2 CD set. With Queen, Airdate: 4/27/92.

Label	Catalog Number	Title	Type	Country	Year	Longbox Value / Value
Epic	ZSK 38490	Secret Messages	LP/BP	U.S.†	1984	$14.00/$8.00
Westwood One		Superstars	RS	U.S.	1995	$70.00

Airdate: 6/19/95.

Electric Light Orchestra Part Two

Singles

Label	Catalog Number	Title	Type	Country	Year	Longbox Value / Value
Alfa	ALDB-111	Honest Man	CD3	Japan	1991	$13.00/$4.00
Scotti Brothers	ZSK 75284	Honest Man	CDJ	U.S.	1991	$2.00
Alfa	ALDB-134	Kiss Me Red	CD3	Japan	1991	$13.00/$4.00
Telstar	ELOCD-101	Thousand Eyes	CD5	U.K.	1991	$9.00

Electric Love Hogs

Full Length

Label	Catalog Number	Title	Type	Country	Year	Longbox Value / Value
		Electric Lovehogs	DJ/LP	U.S.		$8.00
London	CDP 704	Mr. Fun	CDJ	U.S.	1992	$2.00
London	LONCD-332	Tribal Monkey	CD5	U.K.	1992	$8.00

Electric Skychu

Singles

Label	Catalog Number	Title	Type	Country	Year	Longbox Value / Value
Moonshine Music	88415	Deus	CD5	U.S.	1994	$5.00

Electronic

Singles

Label	Catalog Number	Title	Type	Country	Year	Longbox Value / Value
Warner Brothers	9 40562-2	Disappointed	CD5	U.S.	1992	$5.00
BMG	664671	Feel Every Beat	CD5	Germany	1991	$10.00
Factory	FACD-328	Feel Every Beat	CD5	U.K.	1991	$10.00
Warner Brothers	9 40159-2	Feel Every Beat	CD5	U.S.	1992	$5.00
Warner Brothers	PRO-CD-5019	Feel Every Beat	CDJ	U.S.	1992	$2.00
		Forbidden	CDJ	U.K.		$12.00
Factory	FACD-287	Get the Message	CD5	U.K.	1991	$10.00
Warner Brothers	9 21832-2	Get the Message	CD5	U.S.	1991	$5.00
Warner Brothers	PRO-CD-4678	Get the Message	CDJ	U.S.	1991	$2.00
BMG	663537	Getting Away With It	CD5	Germany	1990	$10.00
Rough Trade	CD1-124	Getting Away With It	CD5	Germany	1990	$10.00
Factory	FACD-257	Getting Away With It	CD5	U.K.	1990	$10.00
Warner Brothers	9 21498-2	Getting Away With It	CD5	U.S.	1990	$5.00
Warner Brothers	PRO-CD-3987	Getting Away With It	CDJ	U.S.	1990	$2.00

Electroset

Singles

Label	Catalog Number	Title	Type	Country	Year	Longbox Value / Value
ffrr	FCD-203	How Does It Feel	CD5	U.K.	1992	$8.00

Element Of Crime

Singles

Label	Catalog Number	Title	Type	Country	Year	Longbox Value / Value
Polygram	8737649-2	Satelite Town	CD5	Germany	1990	$7.00

Elements

Full Length

Label	Catalog Number	Title	Type	Country	Year	Longbox Value / Value
Passport	PJCD-88029	Blown Away	LP	U.K.		$23.00
Passport	PJCD-88029	Blown Away	LP/LB	U.S.		$14.00/$8.00

Elevation

Singles

Label	Catalog Number	Title	Type	Country	Year	Longbox Value / Value
Mute	CDNOMU-3	Can You Feel It	CD5	U.K.	1992	$8.00

Elevation 4th

Singles

Label	Catalog Number	Title	Type	Country	Year	Longbox Value / Value
ZYX	ZYX-6549-8	Walking	CD5	Germany	1991	$6.00

Eleven

Singles

Label	Catalog Number	Title	Type	Country	Year	Longbox Value / Value
Third Rail	10371	Crash Today	CDJ	U.S.	1993	$2.00
Morgan Creek	PZCD-197	Rainbow's End	CD5	U.K.	1991	$8.00
Morgan Creek	0002	Rainbow's End	CDJ	U.S.	1993	$2.00
Third Rail	10413	Reach Out	CDJ	U.S.	1992	$2.00
Morgan	Creek 0017	Vowel Movement	CDJ	U.S.	1991	$2.00

Eleven Fifty Nine

Singlea

Label	Catalog Number	Title	Type	Country	Year	Longbox Value / Value
Scream	WTSCD-5	Digi	CD5	U.K.	1991	$8.00

Eleventh Dream Day

Singles

Label	Catalog Number	Title	Type	Country	Year	Longbox Value / Value
Atlantic	PRCD 4978-2	Makin' Like aRug	CDJ	U.S.	1993	$3.00
City Slang	EFA-04904-03	Two Sweeties	CD5	U.K.	1992	$8.00

Elfman, Danny

Singles

Label	Catalog Number	Title	Type	Country	Year	Longbox Value / Value
Warner Brothers	PRO-CD-3756	Batman Theme, The	CDJ	U.S.	1989	$2.00

Elias, Elaine

Singles

Label	Catalog Number	Title	Type	Country	Year	Longbox Value / Value
Blue Note	DPRO-79434	Fantasia	CDJ	U.S.	1992	$6.00

Elika

Singles

Label	Catalog Number	Title	Type	Country	Year	Longbox Value / Value
Emotion	APDA-66	Midnight Party	CD3	Japan	1992	$12.00/$3.00

Elisa

Singles

Label	Catalog Number	Title	Type	Country	Year	Longbox Value / Value
ffrr	FCD-200	Love Vibration	CD5	U.K.	1992	$8.00

Elisabetta

Singles

Label	Catalog Number	Title	Type	Country	Year	Longbox Value / Value
Canyon	PCDY-00006	My Sunshine	CD3	Japan	1989	$12.00/$3.00

Elite Club

Singles

Label	Catalog Number	Title	Type	Country	Year	Longbox Value / Value
ZYX	7998-8	Don't Stop the Music	CD5	U.S.	1995	$5.00
Zyx	7516	This Time Baby	CD5	U.S.	1994	$5.00
ZYX	7516-8	This Time Baby	CD5	U.S.	1995	$8.00

Ella Mental

Singles

Label	Catalog Number	Title	Type	Country	Year	Longbox Value / Value
WEA	W-2839CD	You Light up My Life	CD5	U.K.	1989	$8.00

Ellington, All-Stars

Singles

Label	Catalog Number	Title	Type	Country	Year	Longbox Value / Value
Derrick Records	141035	For Duke	CD5	U.S.	1994	$5.00

Ellington, Duke

Full Length

Label	Catalog Number	Title	Type	Country	Year	Longbox Value / Value
Aris	880441	All-Star Road Band	LP	Germany		$25.00
Aris	880442	All-Star Road Band, Vol.2	LP	Germany		$25.00
Moblie Fidelity	MFCD-807	Great Reunion, The	LP/LB	U.S.†	1985	$30.00/$25.00
2CD set with Louis Armstrong.						
Aris	880440	Happy Reunion	LP	Germany		$25.00
RCA	PD-89565	In the Sixties	LP	Germany		$25.00
WEA	250283-2	Meets Coleman Hawkins	LP	Germany		$25.00

Ellington, Duke & Johnny Hodges

Full Length

Label	Catalog Number	Title	Type	Country	Year	Longbox Value / Value
Verve	823637-2	Back to Back	LP/LB	U.S.†	1985	$14.00/$8.00

Ellington, Lance

Singles

Label	Catalog Number	Title	Type	Country	Year	Longbox Value / Value
A&M	AMCD-702	Don't You Ever Leave Me Again	CD5	U.K.	1990	$8.00
Big Beat	10134	Have We Lost Our	CD5	U.S.		$4.00
A&M	AMCD-585	Love Scared	CD5	U.K.	1990	$8.00
A&M	75021 7543 2	Pleasure And Pain	CD5	U.S.	1990	$2.00
A&M	USACD-683	Treat Me Right	CD5	U.K.	1990	$8.00

Elliot, Richard

Full Length

Label	Catalog Number	Title	Type	Country	Year	Longbox Value / Value
		World Music	RS	U.S.	1991	$150.00
Airdate: 10/20/91.						

Singles

Label	Catalog Number	Title	Type	Country	Year	Longbox Value / Value
		Down to the Keys	CDJ	U.S.		$2.00
Enigma	EPRO 309	Movers & Shakers	CDJ	U.S.	1990	$2.00
		Powers Of Suggestion, The	CDJ	U.S.		$2.00
Enigma	EPRO 241	When a Man Loves a Woman	CDJ	U.S.	1989	$2.00

Ellis, Beggs & Howard

Singles

Label	Catalog Number	Title	Type	Country	Year	Longbox Value / Value
RCA	PD-42042	Bad Times	CD5	Germany	1989	$8.00
RCA	PD-42042	Bad Times	CD5	U.K.	1989	$8.00
RCA	PD-42090	Big Bubbles, No Troubles	CD5	Germany	1989	$8.00
RCA	PD-42090	Big Bubbles, No Troubles	CD5	U.K.	1989	$8.00
RCA	PD-42318	Where Did Tomorrow Go?	CD5	Germany	1989	$8.00
RCA	PD-42318	Where Did Tomorrow Go?	CD5	U.K.	1989	$8.00

Ellis, Joey

Singles

Label	Catalog Number	Title	Type	Country	Year	Longbox Value / Value
Capotol	CDCL-814	Thought You Were the One	CD5	U.K.	1991	$8.00
		Thought You Were the One	CDJ	U.S.		$2.00

Ellis, T.C.

Singles

Label	Catalog Number	Title	Type	Country	Year	Longbox Value / Value
Paisley Park	PRO-CD-4471	Miss Thang	CDJ	U.S.	1990	$2.00
Paisley Park	PRO-CD-4909	Pussycat	CDJ	U.S.	1991	$2.00

Ellis, Terry

Singles

Label	Catalog Number	Title	Type	Country	Year	Longbox Value / Value
Elektra	64361	Wherever You Are	CD5	U.S.	1995	$5.00

Elson, Steve

Singles

Label	Catalog Number	Title	Type	Country	Year	Longbox Value / Value
M&G	MAGCD-13	Luna Rosa	CD5	U.K.	1991	$8.00

Ely, Joe

Full Length

Label	Catalog Number	Title	Type	Country	Year	Longbox Value / Value
		Letters	DJ/Smplr	U.S.		$15.00
CD in folder.						

Singles

Label	Catalog Number	Title	Type	Country	Year	Longbox Value / Value
MCA	DMCAT-1453	Row of Dominoes	CD5	U.K.	1990	$8.00
Hightone	001	Settle for Love	CDJ	U.S.		$2.00

Emerson, Keith

Full Length

Label	Catalog Number	Title	Type	Country	Year	Longbox Value / Value
Charly	CDCOLL-1	Collection	LP	Germany		$25.00

Emerson Lake and Palmer

Full Length

Label	Catalog Number	Title	Type	Country	Year	Longbox Value / Value
Album Network		Album Network Special	RS	U.S.	1992	$250.00
Airdate: 7/31/92.						
Atlantic	82403-2	Atlantic Years	LP	U.S.		$23.00
Atlantic	19283-2	Best Of	LP/LB	U.S.†	1984	$14.00/$8.00
Atlantic	19283-2	Best Of	LP/LB	U.S.	1986	$14.00/$8.00
Victory	480003-2	Black Moon	LP	U.S.	1993	$9.00
Atlantic	19124-2	Brain Salad Surgery	LP/LB	U.S.	1985	$14.00/$8.00
Rhino	R2 72459	Brain Salad Surgery	LTD/LP	U.S.	1996	$18.00
Multi-Image cover.						
Victory	480020-2	Brain Salad Surgery	LP	U.S.	1993	$9.00
Victory	383480015-2	Brain Salad Surgery	LTD/LP	U.S.	1993	$17.00
CD in digipak.						
Atlantic	PRCD 4599-2	ELP	DJ/Smplr	U.S.	1992	$10.00
Atlantic	PRCD 4599-2	ELP	DJ/Smplr	U.S.	1992	$18.00
Rare version with front and rear picture sleeves.						
Atlantic	19120-2	Emerson Lake and Palmer	LP/LB	U.S.	1985	$14.00/$8.00
Victory	480016-2	Emerson Lake and Palmer	LP	U.S.	1993	$9.00
		Excerpts From Black Moon	DJ/Smplr	Canada	1992	$25.00
Atlantic	19255-2	In Concert	LP/LB	U.S.		$15.00/$10.00
Victory	480034-2	In the Hot Seat	LP	U.S.	1993	$9.00
Album Network		In the Studio (Trilogy)	RS	U.S.	1992	$25.00
Airdate: 3/23/92.						
DIR		King Biscuit Flour Hour	RS	U.S.	1988	$40.00
Airdate: 3/13/88.						
DIR		King Biscuit Flour Hour	RS	U.S.	1992	$40.00
Airdate: 6/28/92.						
DIR		King Biscuit Flour Hour	RS	U.S.	1993	$35.00
Airdate: 9/27/93.						
DIR		King Biscuit Flour Hour	RS	U.S.	1995	$55.00
Airdate: 9/3/95.						
Victory	480011-2	Live At Royal Albert Hall	LP	U.S.	1993	$9.00
Victory	480028-2	Love Beach	LP	U.S.	1993	$9.00
Victory	VICP-5444	Pictures at an Exhibition	LP	Japan		$65.00
20 Bit master version.						
Atlantic	19283-2	Pictures at an Exhibition	LP/LB	U.S.†	1984	$14.00/$8.00
Atlantic	19283-2	Pictures at an Exhibition	LP/LB	U.S.	1985	$14.00/$8.00
Victory	480018-2	Pictures at an Exhibition	LP	U.S.	1993	$9.00
Victory	484004-2	Return Of the Manticore	LP	U.S.	1993	$60.00
4 CD boxed set.						
Victory	SACD 757	Selections From the Return of Manticore	DJ/Smplr	U.S.	1993	$18.00
Atlantic	19121-2	Tarkus	LP/LB	U.S.	1985	$14.00/$8.00
Victory	480017-2	Tarkus	LP	U.S.	1993	$9.00
Atlantic	19123-2	Trilogy	LP/LB	U.S.	1985	$14.00/$8.00
Victory	480019-2	Trilogy	LP	U.S.	1993	$9.00
Media America		Up Close	RS	U.S.	1992	$50.00
2 CD set.						
Victory	484001-2	Welcome Back My Friends	LP	U.S.	1993	$18.00
2 CD set.						
Victory	484003-2	Works Live	LP	U.S.	1993	$18.00
2 CD set.						
Atlantic	7000-2	Works Volume 1	LP/LB	U.S.	1985	$23.00/$18.00
2 CD set.						
Victory	484002-2	Works Volume 1	LP	U.S.	1993	$18.00
2 CD set.						
Atlantic	19147-2	Works Volume 2	LP/LB	U.S.	1985	$14.00/$8.00
Victory	480025-2	Works Volume 2	LP	U.S.	1993	$9.00

Singles

Label	Catalog Number	Title	Type	Country	Year	Longbox Value / Value
Victory	VICP-15019	Affairs of the Heart	CD5	Japan	1992	$18.00
Victory	CDP 739	Affairs of the Heart	CDJ	U.S.	1992	$2.00
Victory		Black Moon	CD5	Germany	1992	$10.00
Victory	LONCD 320	Black Moon	CD5	U.K.	1992	$10.00
Victory	CDP 694	Black Moon	CDJ	U.S.	1992	$3.00
Victory	VMPR0005	Daddy	CDJ	U.S.	1995	$6.00
Atlantic	A-7393CD	I Believe in Father Christmas	CD5	U.K.	1992	$11.00
Atlantic		I Believe in Father Christmas	CD5	U.S.	1993	$5.00
		Lucky Man	CD5	Germany	1993	$10.00
Victory	VIDP-42	Paper Blood	CD3	Japan	1992	$12.00/$4.00

Emerson, Lake and Powell

Full Length

Label	Catalog Number	Title	Type	Country	Year	Longbox Value / Value
Polydor		Emerson, Lake and Powell	LP/BP	U.S.		$14.00/$9.00

Emery, Ralph

Full Length

Label	Catalog Number	Title	Type	Country	Year	Longbox Value / Value
		Ralph Emery Interviews	RS/VA	U.S.		$10.00

Emil

Singles

Label	Catalog Number	Title	Type	Country	Year	Longbox Value / Value
Arts	HARTLEY-1	My Funny Valentine	CD5	U.K.	1991	$8.00

Emma

Singles

Label	Catalog Number	Title	Type	Country	Year	Longbox Value / Value
Intercord	827-200	Give a Little Love Back to the World	CD5	Germany	1990	$8.00
Big Wave	BWRCD-33	Give a Little Love Back to the World	CD5	U.K.	1990	$8.00

Emmanuel

Singles

Label	Catalog Number	Title	Type	Country	Year	Longbox Value / Value
Polygram	NORCD-5	We Shall Overcome	CD5	U.K.	1991	$8.00

Emmett, Rik

Full Length

Label	Catalog Number	Title	Type	Country	Year	Longbox Value / Value
Charisma		Absolutely	LP/LB	U.S.	1990	$12.00/$7.00
		Straight Up	DJ/Intvw	Canada		$15.00

Label	Catalog Number	Title	Type	Country	Year	Longbox Value / Value
Duke St		When A Heart Breaks	DJ/Intvw	Canada	1990	$10.00

Singles

Label	Catalog Number	Title	Type	Country	Year	Longbox Value / Value
Alert	82002	Bang On	CDJ	Canada	1992	$6.00
Alert	DPRO 226	Bang On	CDJ	Canada	1992	$10.00
Charisma	PRCD 023	Big Lie	CDJ	Canada	1990	$5.00
Charisma	PRCD 023	Big Lie	CDJ	U.S.	1990	$2.00
Duke St.		Saved by Love	CDJ	Canada	1990	$5.00

Empire

Singles

Label	Catalog Number	Title	Type	Country	Year	Longbox Value / Value
Parlophone	CDR-6175	Talk Free	CD5	U.K.	1988	$8.00

Empire Base Building

Singles

Label	Catalog Number	Title	Type	Country	Year	Longbox Value / Value
SPV	11012-3	Feel Melo	CD5	Germany	1992	$8.00

En Vogue

Full Length

Label	Catalog Number	Title	Type	Country	Year	Longbox Value / Value
Pioneer Artists	PA-90-332	Born To Sing	LD	U.S.	1991	$25.00

Singles

Label	Catalog Number	Title	Type	Country	Year	Longbox Value / Value
EastWest	PRCD 5415-2	Desire	CDJ	U.S.	1993	$2.00
Atlantic	PRCD 3829-2	Don't Go	CDJ	U.S.	1991	$2.00
WEA	63987-2	Don't Let Go (Love)	CD5	U.S.	1996	$3.00
WEA	64231-2	Don't Let Go (Love)	CD5	U.S.	1996	$5.00
WEA	AMDY-5090	Free Your Mind	CD3	Japan	1992	$12.00/$4.00
Eastwest	AMCY-504	Free Your Mind	CD3	Japan	1992	$12.00/$4.00
Eastwest	A-8468CD	Free Your Mind	CD5	U.K.	1992	$10.00
Atlantic	96128-2	Free Your Mind	CD5	U.S.	1992	$5.00
Atlantic	98487-2	Free Your Mind	CD5	U.S.	1992	$5.00
Atlantic	PRCD 4791-2	Free Your Mind	CDJ	U.S.	1992	$3.00
Eastwest	A-8445CD	Give It Up, Turn It Loose	CD5	U.K.	1992	$10.00
Atlantic	PRCD 4843-2	Give It Up, Turn It Loose	CDJ	U.S.	1992	$2.00
WEA	AMDY 6000	Giving Him Something He Can Feel	CD3	Japan	1992	$12.00/$4.00
Atlantic	98560-2	Giving Him Something He Can Feel	CD5	U.S.	1992	$5.00
Atlantic	PRCD 4559-2	Giving Him Something He Can Feel	CDJ	U.S.	1992	$2.00
Atlantic	7567-86178-2	Hold On	CD5	Germany	1990	$10.00
Eastwest	786234-2	Hold On	CD5	Germany	1990	$10.00
Atlantic	AMDY-5023	Hold On	CD3	Japan	1990	$12.00/$4.00
Atlantic	A-7908CD	Hold On	CD5	U.K.	1990	$10.00
Atlantic		Hold On	CD5	U.S.	1990	$5.00
Atlantic	PRCD 3386-2	Hold On	CDJ	U.S.	1990	$2.00
Atlantic	7567-86157-2	Lies	CD5	Germany	1990	$10.00
Atlantic	AMDY-5030	Lies	CD3	Japan	1990	$12.00/$4.00
Atlantic	A-7893CD	Lies	CD5	U.K.	1990	$10.00
Atlantic	PRCD 3373-2	Lies	CDJ	U.S.	1990	$2.00
EastWest	PRCD 5011-2	Love Don't Love You	CDJ	U.S.	1993	$2.00
EastWest	AMDY-5068	Mover	CD3	Japan	1990	$12.00/$4.00
WEA	AMDY-5079	My Lovin'	CD3	Japan	1992	$12.00/$4.00
Eastwest	A-8578CD	My Lovin'	CD5	U.K.	1992	$10.00
Atlantic	PRCD 4552-2	My Lovin'	CDJ	U.S.	1992	$3.00
EastWest	PRCD 5225-2	Runaway Love	CDJ	U.S.	1993	$2.00
EastWest	PRCD 5387-2	Runaway Love	CDJ	U.S.	1993	$2.00
Atlantic	7567-86118-2	You Don't Have To Worry	CD5	Germany	1990	$10.00
Atlantic	A-7812CD	You Don't Have To Worry	CD5	U.K.	1990	$10.00
Atlantic	PRCD 3592-2	You Don't Have To Worry	CDJ	U.S.	1990	$2.00

Enchanted

Singles

Label	Catalog Number	Title	Type	Country	Year	Longbox Value / Value
RCA	64219	Enchanted	CD5	U.S.	1994	$5.00

Enea, Laura

Singles

Label	Catalog Number	Title	Type	Country	Year	Longbox Value / Value
Next Plateau	027	Better the Devil You Know	CDJ	U.S.	1993	$2.00

Energy Orchard

Singles

Label	Catalog Number	Title	Type	Country	Year	Longbox Value / Value
Eastwest	257299-2	Belfast	CD5	Germany	1990	$9.00
MCA	DMCAT-1392	Belfast	CD5	U.K.	1990	$9.00
MCA	CD45 18293	Belfast	CDJ	U.S.	1990	$2.00
MCA	MCSTD-1579	Blue Eyed Boy	CD5	U.K.	1990	$9.00
MCA	MCSTD-1605	How the West Was Won	CD5	U.K.	1992	$9.00
		How the West Was Won	CDJ	U.S.	1992	$2.00
MCA	DMCAT-1423	King of Love	CD5	U.K.	1992	$9.00
MCA	DMCAT-1402	Sailortown	CD5	U.K.	1990	$9.00
MCA	CD45 18360	Sailortown	CDJ	U.S.	1990	$2.00
MCA	DMCAT-1445	Somebody's Brother	CD5	U.K.	1990	$9.00
		Somebody's Brother	CDJ	U.S.	1990	$2.00

Engine Alley

Singles

Label	Catalog Number	Title	Type	Country	Year	Longbox Value / Value
Mother	MUMCD 32	Flowerbox	CD5	U.K.	1992	$8.00
Mother	MUMCD-38	Infamy	CD5	U.K.	1992	$8.00

Engineer

Singles

Label	Catalog Number	Title	Type	Country	Year	Longbox Value / Value
ZYX	DST-1091-8	Spiel Mir Das Lied	CD5	Germany	1992	$5.00

Engines Of Aggression

Singles

Label	Catalog Number	Title	Type	Country	Year	Longbox Value / Value
Priority	7030	Illusion Is Real	CDJ	U.S.	1993	$3.00

England, Colin

Singles

Label	Catalog Number	Title	Type	Country	Year	Longbox Value / Value
Motown	3746 310992	Come Over Baby	CDJ	U.S.	1993	$2.00
Motown	CD45 1338	I Got What You Need	CDJ	U.S.	1991	$2.00
Motown	CD45 1370	I Got What You Need	CDJ	U.S.	1991	$2.00
Motown	CD45 1437	I Need Your Love	CDJ	U.S.	1991	$2.00
Motown	3746 31137	Sorry Seems the Hardest Word To Say	CDJ	U.S.	1993	$2.00

English Beat

Full Length

Label	Catalog Number	Title	Type	Country	Year	Longbox Value / Value
IRS	CD-70032	Special Beat Service	LP/LB	U.S.†	1984	$14.00/$8.00
IRS	CD-70040	What Is Beat?	LP/LB	U.S.†	1984	$14.00/$8.00

Singles

Label	Catalog Number	Title	Type	Country	Year	Longbox Value / Value
A&M	CD 31016	I Confess	CD3	U.S.	1988	$6.00/$3.00
A&M	CD 31012	Save It For Later	CD3	U.S.	1988	$6.00/$3.00

Enigma

Full Length

Label	Catalog Number	Title	Type	Country	Year	Longbox Value / Value
Virgin	786423-2	MCMXC A.D	LTD/LP	Germany	1993	$25.00
Virgin		Age of Loneliness	CD5	U.K.	1994	$10.00
Virgin	DPRO-14174	Age of Loneliness	CDJ	U.S.	1994	$3.00
Virgin	DINSD-120	Carly's Song	CD5	U.K.	1994	$10.00
Virgin	DPRO-12749	Carly's Song	CDJ	U.S.	1994	$2.00
Virgin	664040	Mea Culpa Part II	CD5	Germany	1990	$10.00
Virgin	VJCP-14027	Mea Culpa Part II	CD5	Japan	1990	$15.00
Virgin	DINSD-104	Mea Culpa Part II	CD5	U.K.	1990	$10.00
Charisma	PRCD 039	Mea Culpa Part II	CDJ	U.S.	1990	$2.00
Virgin	DPRO-14176	Out From the Deep	CDJ	U.S.	1994	$3.00
Virgin	664391	Principles of Lust	CD5	Germany	1990	$10.00
Virgin	664596	Principles of Lust	CD5	Germany	1990	$10.00
Virgin	VJCP-14030	Principles of Lust	CD5	Japan	1990	$15.00
Virgin	DINSD-110	Principles of Lust	CD5	U.K.	1990	$10.00
Charisma	PRCD 032	Principles of Lust	CDJ	U.S.	1990	$3.00
Charisma	38423	Return to Innocence	CD5	U.S.	1993	$6.00
Charisma	14123	Return to Innocence	CDJ	U.S.	1993	$3.00
Capital	38423	Return to Innocence	CD5	U.S.	1994	$5.00
Virgin	664672	Rivers of Belief	CD5	Germany	1990	$10.00
Virgin	VJDP-10183	Rivers of Belief	CD3	Japan	1992	$13.00/$4.00
Virgin	DINSD-112	Rivers of Belief	CD5	U.K.	1990	$10.00
Charisma	PRCD 078	Rivers of Belief	CDJ	U.S.	1990	$3.00
Virgin		Run to Sun	CD5	U.K.	1994	$10.00
Virgin	032	Sadness	CDJ	U.S.	1990	$2.00
Virgin	663703	Sadness Part 1	CD5	Germany	1990	$10.00
Virgin	VJDP-10152	Sadness Part 1	CD3	Japan	1991	$12.00/$4.00
Virgin	DINSD-101	Sadness Part 1	CD5	U.K.	1990	$10.00
Virgin		Silver and Gold	CDJ	U.S.	1990	$2.00

Eno, Brian

Full Length

Label	Catalog Number	Title	Type	Country	Year	Longbox Value / Value
Virgin	DPRO-14130	1&2 Sampler	DJ/Smplr	U.S.	1994	$25.00
BMG	76896-40005-2	HeadCandy	LP	U.S.	1995	$40.00

CD-ROM

Label	Catalog Number	Title	Type	Country	Year	Longbox Value / Value
Warner Brothers	PRO-CD-5886	Never Net Sampler	DJ/Smplr	U.S.		$12.00
		One/Two	DJ/Smplr	U.S.	1993	$15.00
E'G	EGCD-64	Thursday Afternoon	LP	U.K.		$25.00
Opal	PRO-CD-4691	Words And Music From "Wrong Way Up"	DJ/Intvw	U.S.	1991	$10.00
		Wrong Way Up	DJ/Smplr	U.S.		$10.00

Singles

Label	Catalog Number	Title	Type	Country	Year	Longbox Value / Value
Opal	W-0131CD	Ali Click	CD5	U.K.	1992	$10.00
Warner Brothers	9 40650-2	Ali Click	CD5	U.S.	1992	$5.00
Virgin	CDT-41	Another Green World	CD3	U.K.	1989	$10.00
Warner Brothers	PRO-CD-4493	Been There Done That	CDJ	U.S.	1991	$3.00
Warner Brothers	W-0116CD	Fractal Zoom	CD5	U.K.	1992	$10.00
Warner Brothers	9 40539-2	Fractal Zoom	CD5	U.S.	1992	$5.00
		Lay My Love	CDJ	U.S.		$3.00
Warner Brothers	9 40001-2	One Word	CD5	U.S.	1991	$5.00
Warner Brothers	PRO-CD-4601	One Word	CDJ	U.S.	1991	$3.00
WEA	7599-21826	Spinning Away	CD5	Germany	1990	$10.00

Enos Bunny

Singles

Label	Catalog Number	Title	Type	Country	Year	Longbox Value / Value
CBS	655521-3	Sister	CD3	Germany	1989	$8.00

Enriquez, Jocely

Singles

Label	Catalog Number	Title	Type	Country	Year	Longbox Value / Value
	215	You Are The One	CD5	U.S.	1994	$5.00

Ensonic

Singles

Label	Catalog Number	Title	Type	Country	Year	Longbox Value / Value
BMG	664749	Just A Little Bit	CD5	Germany	1991	$8.00
Chrysalis	23693	No 1 Is 2 Blame	CDJ	U.S.	1991	$2.00
BMG	664321	No One Is to Blame	CD5	Germany	1991	$8.00

Entity

Singles

Label	Catalog Number	Title	Type	Country	Year	Longbox Value / Value
Eastwest	9031-72556-2	This Is a Love Song	CD5	Germany	1990	$8.00

Entombed

Full Length

Label	Catalog Number	Title	Type	Country	Year	Longbox Value / Value
Columbia	CK 57742	Wolverine Blues	LTD/LP	U.S.	1994	$16.00

CD with limited edition comic book.

Singles

Label	Catalog Number	Title	Type	Country	Year	Longbox Value / Value
Earache	322-0038-3	Crawl	CD5	Germany	1991	$8.00
Earache	MOSH-38CD	Crawl	CD5	U.K.	1991	$8.00
Columbia	CSK 6407	Full of Hell	CDJ	U.S.	1994	$3.00
Earache	MOSH-52CD	Stranger Aeons	CD5	U.K.	1991	$8.00

Entouch

Singles

Label	Catalog Number	Title	Type	Country	Year	Longbox Value / Value
Elektra	PR 8134-2	All Night	CDJ	U.S.	1989	$2.00
Elektra	PRCD 8368-2	Drop Dead Gorgegous	CDJ	U.S.	1991	$2.00
Elektra	PR 8084-2	Hype	CDJ	U.S.	1989	$2.00
Elektra	PR 8438-2	She Used To Be My Girl	CDJ	U.S.	1991	$2.00

Enuff Z Nuff

Singles

Label	Catalog Number	Title	Type	Country	Year	Longbox Value / Value
Atco	B-8743CD	Baby Loves You	CD5	U.K.	1991	$9.00
Atco	PRCD 4005-2	Baby Loves You	CDJ	U.S.	1991	$2.00
Atlantic	AMDY-5005	Fly High Michelle	CD3	Japan	1989	$13.00/$4.00
Atco	B-9135CD	Fly High Michelle	CD5	U.K.	1989	$9.00
Atco	PR 3089-2	Fly High Michelle	CDJ	U.S.	1989	$2.00
Arista	ASCD-2569	Innocence	CDJ	U.S.	1993	$2.00
Atco	PRCD 3745-2	Mother's Eyes	CDJ	U.S.	1991	$2.00
Atco	7567 96493-2	New Thing	CD5	Germany	1990	$9.00
Atco	B-8990CD	New Thing	CD5	U.K.	1989	$9.00
Atco	PR 2731-2	New Thing	CDJ	U.S.	1989	$2.00
Arista	ASCD 2468	Right By Your Side	CDJ	U.S.	1993	$2.00

Enya

Full Length

Label	Catalog Number	Title	Type	Country	Year	Longbox Value / Value
Atlantic	81842-2	Enya	LP/LB	U.S.		$14.00/$8.00
Warner Brothers		Many Times, The	DJ/LP	Japan	1995	$150.00

CD and cassette in cloth covered box.

Label	Catalog Number	Title	Type	Country	Year	Longbox Value / Value
Warner Brothers	PROP94	Memory of Trees	DJ/LP	Germany	1995	$50.00
WEA		Memory of Trees	DJ/LP	U.K.	1995	$80.00

CD and Cassette in large "book" package.

Label	Catalog Number	Title	Type	Country	Year	Longbox Value / Value
Reprise		Memory of Trees	DJ/LP	U.S.	1995	$15.00
WEA	38289	Moon Shadows	LD	U.S.	1992	$25.00
WEA		Shepherds Moon	DJ/Smplr	U.K.	1992	$25.00
Geffen		Watermark	LP/LB	U.S.	1988	$19.00/$16.00

Singles

Label	Catalog Number	Title	Type	Country	Year	Longbox Value / Value
WEA		Anywhere Is	CD5	U.K.	1995	$10.00
WEA		Anywhere Is	CD5	U.K.	1995	$10.00

Second version.

Label	Catalog Number	Title	Type	Country	Year	Longbox Value / Value
WEA	WMD5-4098	Book of Days	CD3	Japan	1992	$12.00/$4.00
WEA	WMC5-519	Book of Days	CD5	Japan	1992	$18.00
WEA		Book of Days	CD5	U.K.	1992	$10.00
WEA		Book of Days	CD5	U.K.	1992	$10.00

Second version.

Label	Catalog Number	Title	Type	Country	Year	Longbox Value / Value
Warner Brothers	PRO-CD-5491	Book of Days	CDJ	U.S.	1992	$3.00
WEA	9031-75610-2	Caribbean Blue	CD5	Germany	1992	$10.00
Warner Brothers	WMD5-4080	Caribbean Blue	CD3	Japan	1992	$12.00/$4.00
WEA	YZ-604CD	Caribbean Blue	CD5	U.K.	1992	$10.00

Enya – Watermark (Geffen 9 24233-2)

Label	Catalog Number	Title	Type	Country	Year	Longbox Value / Value
Warner Brothers	PRO-CD-5142	Caribbean Blue	CDJ	U.S.	1992	$3.00
WEA	WMC5-579	Celts	CD5	Japan	1992	$18.00
WEA		Celts	CD5	U.K.	1992	$10.00
WEA		Celts	CD5	U.K.	1992	$10.00
Second version.						
Pioneer	09P3-6126	Evening Falls	CD3	Japan	1988	$12.00/$4.00
WEA	YZ-356CD	Evening Falls	CD3	U.K.	1988	$12.00
Warner Brothers	WMC5-387	Exile	CD5	Japan	1991	$18.00
WEA	YZ580CD	Exile	CD5	U.K.		$12.00
Geffen	PRO-CD-4240	Exile	CDJ	U.S.	1988	$7.00
WEA	YZ-580CD	Exile	CD5	U.S.	1991	$10.00
Warner Brothers	WMD5-4090	How Can I Keep From Singing?	CD3	Japan	1992	$12.00/$4.00
WEA	YZ-635	How Can I Keep From Singing?	CD5	U.K.	1992	$10.00
Edelton	25115	I Want Tomorrow	CD5	Germany	1989	$11.00
Reprise	PRO-CD-6658	Marble Halls	CDJ	U.S.	1993	$8.00
Pioneer	09P3-6204	Oiche Chiun	CD3	Japan	1990	$12.00/$4.00
Reprise	9 40660-2	Oiche Chiun	CD5	U.S.	1992	$5.00
Warner Brothers	PRO-CD-5851	Oiche Chiun	CDJ	U.S.	1992	$6.00
WEA	247607-2	Orinoco Flow (Sail Away)	CD3	Germany	1988	$12.00
Pioneer	10P3-6100	Orinoco Flow (Sail Away)	CD3	Japan	1988	$15.00/$4.00
Pioneer	WMC5-109	Orinoco Flow (Sail Away)	CD5	Japan	1988	$20.00
WEA	YZ-312CD	Orinoco Flow (Sail Away)	CD3	U.K.	1988	$12.00
Geffen	PRO-CD-3389	Orinoco Flow (Sail Away)	CDJ	U.S.	1988	$7.00
Warner Brothers	40660	Silent Night	CD5	U.S.	1994	$5.00
WEA	246903-2	Storms in Africa	CD3	Germany	1988	$12.00
WEA	16P2-2877	Storms in Africa	CD5	Japan		$20.00
WEA	09P3-6153	Storms in Africa	CD3	Japan	1989	$12.00/$4.00
WEA	YZ-368CD	Storms in Africa	CD3	U.K.	1988	$12.00
WEA	YZ-368CDX	Storms in Africa	CD5	U.K.	1988	$18.00
Geffen	PRO-CD-3499	Storms in Africa	CDJ	U.S.	1988	$6.00
Wea	CD98393	The Christmas EP	CD5	U.K.	1994	$11.00

Eon

Singles

Label	Catalog Number	Title	Type	Country	Year	Longbox Value / Value
Columbia	44K-74313	Basket Case	CD5	Canada	1992	$7.00
Vinyl Sol	STORM-39CD	Basket Case	CD5	U.K.	1992	$8.00
Vinyl Sol	CD-18302	Fear: The Mindkiller	CD5	Germany	1991	$8.00
Vinyl Sol	STORM-33CD	Fear: The Mindkiller	CD5	U.K.	1991	$8.00
Vinyl Sol	CD-17190	Inner Mind	CD5	Germany	1991	$8.00
Vinyl Sol	STORM-27CD	Inner Mind	CD5	U.K.	1991	$8.00
Vinyl Sol	STORM-54CD	What Is Music	CD5	U.K.	1992	$8.00

EPMD

Singles

Label	Catalog Number	Title	Type	Country	Year	Longbox Value / Value
Rush	42K 74172	Crossover	CD5	U.S.	1992	$5.00
Def Jam	CSK 73782	Give the People	CDJ	U.S.	1991	$2.00
Def Jam	CSK 73634	Gold Digger	CDJ	U.S.	1990	$2.00
Columbia	42K 74700	Head Banger	CD5	U.S.	1992	$5.00
Columbia	CSK 73701	Rampage	CDJ	U.S.	1990	$2.00
BCM	20307	So Wa'cha Sayin'	CD5	Germany	1989	$8.00
BCM	20122	Strictly Business	CD5	Germany	1989	$8.00

Eq-Laser

Singles

Label	Catalog Number	Title	Type	Country	Year	Longbox Value / Value
SPV	9982-3	Delirium	CD5	Germany	1991	$8.00

Equinox

Singles

Label	Catalog Number	Title	Type	Country	Year	Longbox Value / Value
ZYX	ZYX-6446-8	Amen Part 2	CD5	Germany	1990	$6.00

Erasure

Full Length

Label	Catalog Number	Title	Type	Country	Year	Longbox Value / Value
Mute	ALCB-376	Chorus	LTD/LP	Japan	1991	$35.00
CD in special box with prints.						
Sire/Reprise	9 26668-2	Chorus	DJ/LP	U.S.	1991	$25.00
CD in special box with prints.						
Mute		I Say I Say I Say	DJ/Intvw	U.K.	1994	$40.00
Mute	Lcd Stumm 115	I Say I Say I Say	LTD/LP	U.K.	1994	$40.00
CD in 12"x12" pop up "castle" package.						
Sire		I Say I Say I Say	DJ/Intvw	U.S.	1994	$20.00
Westwood One		In Concert-Nu Rock	RS	U.S.	1994	$90.00
2 CD set. Airdate: 7/18/94.						
Mute	ERAS 5CD	Tour CD	DJ/Smplr	U.K.		$60.00
Mute		Wild	DJ/LP	U.K.		$50.00
Custom printed box with cassette.						
Lumivision	LVD9263	Wild	LD	U.S.	1992	$40.00

Singles

Label	Catalog Number	Title	Type	Country	Year	Longbox Value / Value
		A Little Respect	CD5	Germany		$10.00
		A Little Respect	CD5	U.K.	1988	$10.00
Sire	PRO-CD-3252	A Little Respect	CDJ	U.S.	1988	$10.00
Mute	826 730	Abba-Esque Ep	CD5	Germany	1992	$10.00
Mute	ALCB-557	Abba-Esque Ep	CD5	Japan	1992	$17.00
Mute	CDMUTE-144	Abba-Esque Ep	CD5	U.K.	1992	$10.00
Mute	61386	Abba-Esque Ep	CD5	U.S.	1992	$6.00
Mute	CD66225	Always	CD5	Canada	1994	$8.00
		Always	CDJ	Japan	1994	$30.00
Elektra	66225	Always	CD5	U.K.	1994	$10.00
Mute	LCDMUTE 152	Always	CD5	U.K.	1994	$12.00
Mute		Always	CDJ	U.K.	1994	$70.00
CD in plastic case with combination lock.						

Label | Catalog Number | Title | Type | Country | Year | Longbox Value / Value

Erasure – Chains Of Love (Reprise PRO-CD-3140)

Label	Catalog Number	Title	Type	Country	Year	Longbox Value / Value
Elektra/Asylum	66225	Always	CD5	U.S.	1994	$6.00
Sire	PRO-CD-8945	Always	CDJ	U.S.	1994	$6.00
Mute	826 989	Am I Right?	CD5	Germany	1992	$10.00
Mute	826 990	Am I Right?	CD5	Germany	1992	$10.00
Mute	ALCB-430	Am I Right?	CD5	Japan	1992	$18.00
Mute	CDMUTE-134	Am I Right?	CD5	U.K.	1992	$10.00
Mute	LCDMUTE-134	Am I Right?	CD5	U.K.	1992	$12.00
Mute	826 928	Blue Savannah	CD3	Germany	1989	$10.00
Mute	826 929	Blue Savannah	CD5	Germany	1989	$10.00
Mute	ALDB-9	Blue Savannah	CD3	Japan	1989	$15.00/$4.00
Mute	CDMUTE-109	Blue Savannah	CD5	U.K.	1989	$10.00
Mute	LCDMUTE-109	Blue Savannah	CD5	U.K.	1989	$10.00
Mute	CDMUTE109-R	Blue Savannah	CDJ	U.K.	1989	$15.00
Sire	9-21428-2	Blue Savannah	CD5	U.S.	1989	$5.00
Sire	PRO-CD-3801	Blue Savannah	CDJ	U.S.	1989	$6.00
Mute	826 997	Breath of Life	CD5	Germany	1992	$10.00
Mute	CDMUTE-142	Breath of Life	CD5	U.K.	1992	$10.00
Sire	9 40344-2	Breath of Life	CD5	U.S.	1992	$5.00
Mute INT	826 888	Chains of Love	CD5	Germany	1988	$10.00
Mute INT	826 890	Chains of Love	CD5	Germany	1988	$10.00
Mute	CDMUTE-83	Chains of Love	CD5	U.K.	1988	$10.00
Sire	PRO-CD-3140	Chains of Love	CDJ	U.S.	1988	$20.00
Sire	PRO-CD-4945	Chains of Love	CDJ	U.S.	1991	$6.00
Mute	826 962	Chorus	CD5	Germany	1991	$10.00
Mute	ALCB-319	Chorus	CD5	Japan	1991	$18.00
Mute	CDMUTE-125	Chorus	CD5	U.K.	1991	$10.00
Sire	9 41023-2	Chorus	CD5	U.S.	1991	$5.00
Sire	PRO-CD-5138	Chorus	CDJ	U.S.	1991	$6.00
Mute	CD MUTE-66	Circus, The	CD5	U.K.	1993	$11.00
Intercord	826 901	Crackers International	CD3	Germany	1989	$10.00
Intercord	826 901	Crackers International	CD5	Germany	1989	$10.00
Mute	CDMUTE-93	Crackers International	CD3	U.K.	1989	$11.00
Intercord	826 914	Drama	CD3	Germany	1989	$11.00
Intercord	826 902	Drama	CD3	Germany	1989	$11.00
Intercord	826 916	Drama	CD3	Germany	1989	$11.00
Intercord	826 913	Drama	CD5	Germany	1989	$10.00
Alfa	0983-73	Drama	CD3	Japan	1989	$15.00/$4.00
Mute	CDMUTE-89	Drama	CD5	U.K.	1989	$10.00
Mute	LCDMUTE-89	Drama	CD3	U.K.	1989	$10.00
Sire	9 21356-2	Drama	CD5	U.S.	1989	$5.00
Sire	PRO-CD-3737	Drama	CDJ	U.S.	1989	$6.00
		Fingers And Thumbs	CD5	U.K.	1995	$10.00
		Fingers And Thumbs	CD5	U.K.	1995	$10.00
Second version.						
Elektra	PRCD 9412	Fingers And Thumbs	CDJ	U.S.	1995	$7.00
Mute	826 734	Heveanly Action	CD5	Germany	1988	$10.00
Mute	CD MUTE-42	Heveanly Action	CD5	U.K.	1992	$10.00
Mute	PCD4-00128	I Love Saturday	CD3	Japan		$15.00/$4.00
	PCD4-00128	I Love Saturday	CD3	Japan		$15.00/$5.00
Sire		I Love Saturday	CDJ	U.S.		$10.00
Elektra/Asylum	66171	I Love Saturday	CD5	U.S.	1994	$5.00
Mute		I Say I Say I Say	CD5	U.K.	1995	$15.00
Mute	826 858	It Doesn't Have To Be	CD5	Germany	1988	$10.00
Mute	CDMUTE-56	It Doesn't Have To Be	CD5	U.K.	1988	$10.00
Mute	826 894	Little Respect	CD5	Germany	1988	$10.00
Mute	826 869	Little Respect	CD5	Germany	1988	$10.00
Mute	10SR-33	Little Respect	CD3	Japan	1988	$15.00/$4.00
Mute	CDMUTE 85	Little Respect	CD5	U.K.	1988	$10.00
Mute	826 967	Love to Hate You	CD5	Germany	1991	$10.00
Mute	ALDB-140	Love to Hate You	CD3	Japan	1991	$15.00/$4.00
Mute	CDMUTE-131	Love to Hate You	CD5	U.K.	1991	$10.00
Sire	9 40218-2	Love to Hate You	CD5	U.S.	1991	$5.00
Sire		Love to Hate You	CDJ	U.S.	1991	$6.00
Mute	826 840	Oh L'Amour	CD5	Germany	1988	$10.00
Mute	CD12MUTE-45	Oh L'Amour	CD5	U.K.	1988	$10.00
Mute	CD66208	Run to The Sun	CD5	Canada	1994	$8.00
Mute	PCDY-00125	Run to The Sun	CD3	Japan		$15.00/$4.00
		Run to The Sun	CDJ	U.K.	1994	$15.00
Sire	PRO-CD-8994	Run to The Sun	CDJ	U.S.	1994	$6.00
Mute	826 856	Ship of Fools	CD3	Germany	1988	$10.00
Mute	826 878	Ship of Fools	CD5	Germany	1988	$10.00
Mute	10SR-21	Ship of Fools	CD3	Japan	1988	$15.00/$4.00
Mute	826 854	Sometimes	CD5	Germany	1988	$10.00
Mute	CDMUTE-51	Sometimes	CD5	U.K.	1993	$10.00
Mute	826 935	Star	CD5	Germany	1990	$10.00
Alfa	ALDB-44	Star	CD3	Japan	1990	$15.00/$4.00
Mute	CDMUTE -111	Star	CD5	U.K.	1990	$10.00
Mute	CDMUTE 111CDR	Star	CDJ	U.K.	1990	$15.00
Sire	PRO-CD-4327	Star	CDJ	U.S.	1989	$7.00
Sire	9 21558-2	Star	CD5	U.S.	1990	$5.00
		Stay With Me	CD5	U.K.	1995	$10.00
		Stay With Me	CD5	U.K.	1995	$10.00
Second version.						
Elektra	PRCD 9351	Stay With Me	CDJ	U.S.		$6.00
Elektra	66084	Stay With Me	CD5	U.S.	1995	$5.00
Mute		Take a Chance	CDJ	U.S.	1992	$6.00
		Unconditionally	CD5	U.K.	1995	$10.00
		Unconditionally	CD5	U.K.	1995	$10.00
Second version.						

Label	Catalog Number	Title	Type	Country	Year	Longbox Value / Value
Mute	826 865	Victim of Love	CD5	Germany	1988	$10.00
Mute	826 867	Victim of Love	CD5	Germany	1988	$10.00
Mute	MUTE-61	Victim of Love	CD5	U.K.	1988	$10.00
Mute	826 833	Who Needs Love Like That	CD5	Germany	1988	$10.00
Mute	CDMUTE-40	Who Needs Love Like That	CD5	U.K.	1988	$10.00
Mute	LCD 150	Who Needs Love Like That	CD5	U.K.	1992	$10.00
Mute	9 40721-2	Who Needs Love Like That	CD5	U.S.	1988	$5.00
Mute	826 920	You Surrounded Me	CD5	Germany	1989	$10.00
Mute	826 921	You Surrounded Me	CD5	Germany	1989	$10.00
Mute	CDMUTE-99	You Surrounded Me	CD5	U.K.	1989	$10.00
Mute	LCDMUTE-99	You Surrounded Me	CD5	U.K.	1989	$10.00
Mute	CDMUTE 99R	You Surrounded Me	CDJ	U.K.	1989	$10.00

Erato

Singles

Label	Catalog Number	Title	Type	Country	Year	Value
ZYX	DST-1087-8	French Kiss	CD5	Germany	1992	$6.00

Eric And Good Good Feeling

Singles

Label	Catalog Number	Title	Type	Country	Year	Value
Polygram	889414-3	Good Good Feeling	CD3	Germany	1989	$8.00
Polygram	889415-2	Good Good Feeling	CD5	Germany	1989	$8.00
Equinox	EQNCDS-1	Good Good Feeling	CD5	U.K.	1989	$8.00

Eric B. & Rakim

Singles

Label	Catalog Number	Title	Type	Country	Year	Value
MCA	2509	Casualties Of War	CDJ	U.S.	1992	$2.00
MCA	2385	Casualties Of War	CDJ	U.S.	1992	$2.00
MCA	2267	Don't Sweat the Technique	CDJ	U.S.	1992	$2.00
MCA	2192	Don't Sweat the Technique	CDJ	U.S.	1992	$2.00
MCA	DMCA-1256	Follow the Leader	CD5	U.K.	1988	$8.00
MCA	18499	In the Ghetto	CDJ	U.S.	1990	$2.00
Eastwest	9031-71972-2	Let the Rhythm Hit 'Em	CD5	Germany	1990	$8.00
MCA	DMCAT-1433	Let the Rhythm Hit 'Em	CD5	U.K.	1990	$8.00
MCA	DMCA-1300	Microphone Fiend	CD3	U.K.	1988	$8.00
MCA	DMCA-1272	Put Your Hands Together	CD3	U.K.	1988	$8.00
MCA	DMCA-1303	R (Work, Rest And Play), The	CD3	U.K.	1989	$8.00

Eric the Gardener

Singles

Label	Catalog Number	Title	Type	Country	Year	Value
Mentle	CDMTLE-1	I Live in a Giant Mushroom	CD5	U.K.	1992	$8.00

Eric's Trip

Singles

Label	Catalog Number	Title	Type	Country	Year	Value
SubPop	SP205B	Songs About Chris	CD5	Canada	1994	$16.00
SubPop	SP266B	The Gordon Street Haunting	CD5	Canada	1994	$9.00

Erire

Singles

Label	Catalog Number	Title	Type	Country	Year	Value
Faze 2	CDFAZE-4	I Just Can't Give You Up	CD5	U.K.	1992	$8.00

Erosion

Singles

Label	Catalog Number	Title	Type	Country	Year	Value
SPV	6143-3	Ready For the Gunman	CD5	Germany	1992	$8.00

Erotic Dissidents

Singles

Label	Catalog Number	Title	Type	Country	Year	Value
SPV	7384-3	Move Your Ass and Feel the Beat	CD5	Germany	1999	$8.00
Subway	SUBWAY-101CD	Move Your Ass and Feel the Beat	CD5	U.K.	1988	$8.00
Antler	10	Move Your Ass and Feel the Beat	CD5	U.S.	1993	$4.00
SPV	73872-3	Shake Your Hips	CD5	Germany	1999	$8.00
Subway	SUBWAY-033CD	Shake Your Hips	CD5	U.K.	1988	$8.00
Antler	33	Shake Your Hips	CD5	U.S.	1993	$4.00

Erotic Society

Singles

Label	Catalog Number	Title	Type	Country	Year	Value
BCM	20369	Sex Is Fun	CD5	Germany	1989	$8.00

Erule

Singles

Label	Catalog Number	Title	Type	Country	Year	Value
	351100	Listen Up	CD5	U.S.	1994	$5.00

Escape Club

Full Length

Label	Catalog Number	Title	Type	Country	Year	Value
DIR		King Biscuit Flour Hour	RS	U.S.	1989	$30.00

With Hothouse Flowers, Airdate: 4/2/89.

Singles

Label	Catalog Number	Title	Type	Country	Year	Longbox Value / Value
WEA	9031-73749-2	Call It Poison	CD5	Germany	1991	$10.00
WEA	WMD5-4062	Call It Poison	CD3	Japan	1991	$13.00/$4.00
Atlantic	PR 3753-2	Call It Poison	CDJ	U.S.	1991	$2.00
WEA	9031-74803-2	I'll Be There	CD5	Germany	1991	$10.00
WEA	9031-74804-2	I'll Be There	CD5	Germany	1991	$10.00
WEA	WMC5-443	I'll Be There	CD5	Japan	1991	$15.00
WEA	U-4802CD	I'll Be There	CD5	U.K.	1991	$10.00
Atlantic		I'll Be There	CDJ	U.S.	1991	$2.00
WEA	257676-2	Shake For the Sheik	CD3	Germany	1989	$10.00
Pioneer	10P3-6098	Shake For the Sheik	CD3	Japan	1989	$13.00/$4.00
WEA	U-7723CD	Shake For the Sheik	CD3	U.K.	1989	$10.00
Atlantic	PR 2538-2	Shake For the Sheik	CDJ	U.S.	1988	$2.00
Atlantic	PRCD 4241-2	So Fashionable	CDJ	U.S.	1991	$2.00
Atlantic	PR 2875-2	Twentieth Century Fox	CDJ	U.S.	1989	$2.00
WEA	257590-2	Walking Through Walls	CD3	Germany	1989	$10.00
Atlantic	PR 2606-2	Walking Through Walls	CDJ	U.S.	1988	$2.00
Atlantic	PR 2657-2	Walking Through Walls	CDJ	U.S.	1988	$2.00
Pioneer	10P3-6074	Wild Wild West	CD3	Japan	1988	$13.00/$4.00
Atlantic		Wild Wild West	CDJ	U.S.	1988	$2.00

Escape With Romeo

Singles

Label	Catalog Number	Title	Type	Country	Year	Value
Rough Trade	359-0013-3	Helicopter in the Rain	CD5	Germany	1991	$8.00

Escoffery's

Singles

Label	Catalog Number	Title	Type	Country	Year	Value
Atlantic	PRCD 4132-2	Look Who's Loving Me	CDJ	U.S.	1991	$2.00
Atlantic	PRCD 4356-2	Unobtainable	CDJ	U.S.	1991	$2.00

Escovedo, Alejandro

Singles

Label	Catalog Number	Title	Type	Country	Year	Value
Stony Plain	CDM0017	The End	CD5	Canada	1994	$10.00

Eskimos And Egypt

Singles

Label	Catalog Number	Title	Type	Country	Year	Value
Rough Trade	230-1310-3	Don't You Do It	CD5	Germany	1991	$8.00
Pinnacle	EEF-92CD	Don't You Do It	CD5	U.K.	1991	$8.00
Pinnacle	EEF-96CD	Fall From Grace	CD5	U.K.	1993	$8.00
Pinnacle	EEF-95CD	State of Surrender	CD5	U.K.	1992	$8.00
Rough Trade	230-1312-3	Welcome to the Future	CD5	Germany	1991	$8.00
Pinnacle	EEF-94CD	Welcome to the Future	CD5	U.K.	1991	$8.00

Esperanto

Singles

Label	Catalog Number	Title	Type	Country	Year	Value
M&G	MAGCD-25	Love Is the Answer	CD5	U.K.	1992	$8.00

Espiritu

Singles

Label	Catalog Number	Title	Type	Country	Year	Value
		Bonita Manana	CD5	U.K.		$10.00
		Bonita Manana	CD5	U.K.		$10.00

Second version.

Esposito, Tony

Singles

Label	Catalog Number	Title	Type	Country	Year	Value
BMG	662932	Conga Radio	CD5	Germany	1990	$8.00

Esquire

Singles

Label	Catalog Number	Title	Type	Country	Year	Value
		Sunshine	CDJ	U.S.		$2.00

Esquires

Singles

Label	Catalog Number	Title	Type	Country	Year	Value
Back Track	4	Flashin' Red	CD5	U.S.	1994	$5.00

Essence

Singles

Label	Catalog Number	Title	Type	Country	Year	Value
Midnight	DONG-69CD	Out of Grace	CD5	U.K.	1991	$8.00

Essex

Singles

Label	Catalog Number	Title	Type	Country	Year	Longbox Value / Value
Canyon	PCDA-00236	Lonely Angel	CD3	Japan	1991	$12.00/$3.00

Essex, David

Full Length

Label	Catalog Number	Title	Type	Country	Year	Value
Columbia	CK-465851-2	Rock On	LP	U.K.		$23.00

Singles

Label	Catalog Number	Title	Type	Country	Year	Value
Mercury	SNOWD-91	A Winter's Tale	CD5	U.K.	1991	$9.00
Mercury	MERCD-351	Africa-You Shine	CD5	U.K.	1991	$9.00
Arista	RISCD-11	Myfanwy	CD5	U.K.	1987	$10.00
Columbia	654948-2	Rock On	CD5	U.K.	1989	$8.00

Esta

Singles

Label	Catalog Number	Title	Type	Country	Year	Longbox Value / Value
Polydor	PZCD-227	Desert Sun	CD3	Japan	1993	$12.00/$3.00

Estefan, Gloria (and Miami Sound Machine)

Full Length

Label	Catalog Number	Title	Type	Country	Year	Value
CBS		Abriendo Puertas	DJ/Smplr	U.S.	1996	$165.00

CD album and CD single in wood mini-cabinet with hinged french doors.

Label	Catalog Number	Title	Type	Country	Year	Value
Epic	ESK 1707	Cuts Both Ways Audio Cue Card	DJ/Smplr	U.S.	1989	$22.00
Epic		Hits	DJ/Smplr	U.S.	1988	$22.00
Epic		Hold Me, Thrill Me, Ask Me	DJ/Intvw	U.S.	1995	$15.00
Epic		Into the Night	LTD/LP	Australia		$35.00

2 CD set.

Label	Catalog Number	Title	Type	Country	Year	Value
Columbia	64680	Let It Loose	LTD/LP	U.S.	1995	$26.00

Gold disc.

Label	Catalog Number	Title	Type	Country	Year	Value
Unistar		Unistar Weekly	RS	U.S.	1991	$60.00

Airdate: 8/4/91.

Singles

Label	Catalog Number	Title	Type	Country	Year	Longbox Value / Value
Epic	77977	Abriendo Puertas	CD5	U.S.	1995	$5.00
Epic	ESDA-7114	Always Tomorrow	CD3	Japan	1992	$13.00/$4.00
Epic	658397-2	Always Tomorrow	CD5	U.K.	1992	$10.00
Epic	ESK 74472	Always Tomorrow	CDJ	U.S.	1992	$2.00
Epic	655157-2	Anything For You	CD3	Germany	1989	$10.00

CD in christmas card.

Label	Catalog Number	Title	Type	Country	Year	Longbox Value / Value
Epic	108P-3020	Anything For You	CD3	Japan	1989	$13.00/$4.00
Epic	651673-2	Anything For You	CD5	U.K.	1989	$10.00
Epic	34K-7759	Anything For You	CD3	U.S.	1989	$6.00/$3.00
Epic		Anything For You	CDJ	U.S.	1989	$2.00
		Ayer	CDJ	Spain	1994	$20.00
Epic	ESK 6015	Ayer	CDJ	U.S.	1994	$3.00
Epic	ESK 2789	Betcha Say That	CDJ	U.S.	1987	$6.00
Epic	ESDA-7072	Can't Forget	CD3	Japan	1991	$13.00/$4.00
Epic	ESK 73864	Can't Forget	CDJ	U.S.	1991	$2.00
Epic	651444-2	Can't Stay Away From You	CD3	Germany	1988	$10.00
CBS	654854-3	Can't Stay Away From You	CD3	Germany	1988	$10.00
CBS	654854-3	Can't Stay Away From You	CD3	U.K.	1988	$10.00
Epic	651444-2	Can't Stay Away From You	CD3	U.K.	1988	$10.00
Epic	653195-2	Can't Stay Away From You	CD5	U.K.	1988	$10.00
Epic	44K 73769	Christmas Through Your Eyes	CD5	U.K.		$10.00
Epic	656574-5	Coming Out of the Dark	CD5	Germany	1990	$10.00
Epic	656574-2	Coming Out of the Dark	CD5	U.K.	1990	$10.00
Epic	ESK 73666	Coming Out of the Dark	CDJ	U.S.	1990	$2.00
CBS	654866-3	Conga	CD3	Germany	1989	$10.00
CBS	34K-5457	Conga	CD3	U.S.	1989	$6.00/$3.00
Epic	ESDA-7038	Cuts Both Ways	CD3	Japan	1990	$15.00/$4.00
Epic	655982-2	Cuts Both Ways	CD5	U.K.	1990	$10.00
Epic	ESK 73395	Cuts Both Ways	CDJ	U.S.	1990	$2.00
CBS	77701	Donna Allen/Jambala Real	CD5	U.S.	1994	$5.00
Epic	655054-3	Don't Wanna Lose Your Love	CD3	Germany	1989	$10.00
Epic	108P-3068	Don't Wanna Lose Your Love	CD3	Japan	1989	$13.00/$4.00
Epic	655054-2	Don't Wanna Lose Your Love	CD5	U.K.	1989	$10.00
Epic	ESK 1666	Don't Wanna Lose Your Love	CDJ	U.S.	1989	$2.00
CBS	654556-3	Dr. Beat	CD3	Germany	1989	$10.00
CBS	654557-3	Dr. Beat	CD3	Germany	1989	$10.00
CBS	77775	Everlasting Love	CD5	U.S.	1994	$5.00
Epic		Everlasting Love	CDJ	U.S.	1995	$6.00
Epic	655450-3	Get On Your Feet	CD3	Germany	1989	$10.00
Epic	655450-2	Get On Your Feet	CD5	Germany	1989	$10.00
Epic	108P-3081	Get On Your Feet	CD3	Japan	1989	$15.00/$4.00
Epic	ESK 1808	Get On Your Feet	CDJ	U.S.	1989	$2.00
Epic	ESK 74920	Go Away	CDJ	U.S.	1993	$2.00
Epic	655473-5	Here We Are	CD5	Germany	1990	$10.00
Epic	ESDA-7012	Here We Are	CD3	Japan	1990	$15.00/$4.00
Epic	655473-2	Here We Are	CD5	U.K.	1989	$10.00
Epic	ESK 73084	Here We Are	CDJ	U.S.	1989	$2.00
		Hold Me, Thrill Me, Kiss Me	CDJ	Mexico	1995	$30.00
		Hold Me, Thrill Me, Kiss Me	CD5	U.K.	1995	$10.00
		Hold Me, Thrill Me, Kiss Me	CD5	U.K.	1995	$10.00

Second version.

Label	Catalog Number	Title	Type	Country	Year	Longbox Value / Value
Epic		I Don't Wanna Lose Your Love	CDJ	U.S.		$6.00
Epic	658961-2	I See Your Smile	CD5	U.K.	1993	$10.00
Epic	ESK 74847	I See Your Smile	CDJ	U.S.	1992	$2.00
Epic	ESK 5430	If We Were Lovers	CDJ	U.S.	1993	$3.00
Epic	662044-2	It's Too Late	CD5	U.K.	1995	$20.00
Epic		It's Too Late	CDJ	U.S.	1995	$6.00
Epic	ESDA-7080	Live For Loving You	CD3	Japan	1991	$15.00/$4.00
Epic	657382-5	Live For Loving You	CD5	U.K.	1991	$10.00
Epic	ESK 73962	Live For Loving You	CDJ	U.S.	1991	$2.00

Label	Catalog Number	Title	Type	Country	Year	Longbox Value / Value
	SAMP 3038	Mas Alla	CDJ	Spain		$25.00
Epic	EPC660196	Mi Buen Amor	CDJ	Spain		$18.00
Epic	ESK 5243	Mi Tierra	CDJ	U.S.	1993	$2.00
Epic	658837-2	Miami Hit Mix	CD5	U.K.	1992	$10.00
Epic	657273-2	Nayib's Song	CD5	Germany	1991	$10.00
Epic	652958-3	One Two Three	CD3	Germany	1988	$10.00
Epic	108P3-3032	One Two Three	CD3	Japan	1988	$13.00/$4.00
Epic	652958-2	One Two Three	CD5	U.K.	1988	$10.00
Epic	655280-3	Oye Mi Canto	CD3	Germany	1989	$10.00
Epic	ESDA-7011	Oye Mi Canto	CD3	Japan	1990	$13.00/$4.00
Epic	655287-2	Oye Mi Canto	CD5	U.K.	1989	$10.00
Epic	ESK 73269	Oye Mi Canto	CDJ	U.S.	1990	$2.00
CBS	SAMPCD3278	Reach	CDJ	Spain	1996	$30.00
CBS		Reach	CD5	U.K.	1996	$10.00
CBS		Reach	CD5	U.K.	1996	$10.00
	Second version.					
Epic		Reach	CDJ	U.S.	1996	$3.00
Epic	77707	Real	CD5	U.S.	1994	$5.00
Epic	656968-2	Remember Me With Love	CD5	Germany	1991	$10.00
Epic	656968-2	Remember Me With Love	CD5	U.K.	1991	$10.00
Epic	655094-2	Rhythm is Gonna Get You	CD3	Germany	1989	$10.00
Epic	654514-2	Rhythm is Gonna Get You	CD5	U.K.	1989	$10.00
Epic		Rhythm is Gonna Get You	CDJ	U.S.	1989	$2.00
Epic		Seal Our Fate	CD5	Australia	1991	$12.00
Epic		Seal Our Fate	CDJ	Australia	1991	$14.00
Epic	ESDA-7066	Seal Our Fate	CD3	Japan	1991	$13.00/$4.00
Epic	656773-2	Seal Our Fate	CD5	U.K.	1991	$10.00
Epic	ESK 73769	Seal Our Fate	CDJ	U.S.	1991	$2.00
Epic		Si Señor	CDJ	Spain		$15.00
Epic	44K 77192	Tradicion	CD5	U.S.	1993	$6.00
	SAMP3039	Tres Dejos	CDJ	Spain		$20.00
Epic	ESCA-6381	Tres Deseos	CD3	Japan		$17.00/$4.00
		Turn the Beat Around	CD5	Australia	1994	$10.00
CBS	77631	Turn the Beat Around	CD5	U.S.	1994	$5.00
Epic		Turn the Beat Around	CDJ	U.S.	1995	$6.00
CBS		You'll Be Mine	CD5	U.K.	1996	$10.00
CBS		You'll Be Mine	CD5	U.K.	1996	$10.00
	Second version.					

Estep, Maggie

Singles

Label	Catalog Number	Title	Type	Country	Year	Longbox Value / Value
Imago	28078	Hey Baby	CDJ	U.S.	1994	$2.00

Ester B.

Singles

Label	Catalog Number	Title	Type	Country	Year	Longbox Value / Value
ZYX	6262-8	Pleasure of the Music	CD5	Germany	1989	$6.00
SPV	9104-5	Pleasure of the Music	CD5	Germany	1989	$6.00

Estus, Deon

Polygram

Label	Catalog Number	Title	Type	Country	Year	Longbox Value / Value
889176-3	Heaven Help Me	CD3		Germany	1989	$8.00
Polygram	889177-2	Heaven Help Me	CD5	Germany	1989	$8.00
Polygram	871539-2	Heaven Help Me	CD5	U.K.	1989	$8.00
Polygram	CDP 44	Heaven Help Me	CDJ	U.S.	1989	$2.00
Polygram	871059-2	Me or the Rumours	CD5	U.K.	1989	$8.00
Polydor	CDP 74	Spell	CDJ	U.S.	1989	$2.00

Eternal

Singles

Label	Catalog Number	Title	Type	Country	Year	Longbox Value / Value
	DPRO-19839	Just A Step From Heaven	CDJ	U.S.	1994	$2.00
Warp	WAP-27CD	Mind Odyssey	CD5	U.K.	1992	$8.00
		So Good	CD5	U.K.		$10.00
		So Good	CD5	U.K.		$10.00
	Second version.					
EMI	58113	Stay	CD5	U.S.	1994	$4.00
EMI	19830	Stay	CDJ	U.S.	1994	$2.00

Ether Real

Singles

Label	Catalog Number	Title	Type	Country	Year	Longbox Value / Value
BMG	CDTLOVE-3	Zap	CD5	U.K.	1991	$8.00

Etheridge, Melissa

Full Length

Label	Catalog Number	Title	Type	Country	Year	Longbox Value / Value
Island		Blockbuster Sampler	DJ/Smplr	U.S.	1994	$50.00
Westwood One		In Concert	RS	U.S.	1993	$120.00
	2 CD set. Airdate: 2/1/93.					
Island	PR 2555-2	Live	DJ/Smplr	U.S.	1988	$15.00
Island		Live at the Record Plant	DJ/Smplr	U.S.	1992	$25.00
Westwood One		Off the Record	RS	U.S.	1993	$25.00
	Airdate: 3/8/93.					
Westwood One		Off the Record	RS	U.S.	1994	$50.00
	Airdate: 3/7/94.					
Westwood One		Off the Record	RS	U.S.	1994	$50.00
	Airdate: 9/5/94.					
Westwood One		Off the Record	RS	U.S.	1995	$50.00
	Airdate: 1/2/95.					
Album Network		Record Plant	RS	U.S.	1992	$250.00
	Airdate: 3/26/92.					
		Rock and the Environment	RS	U.S.	1993	$50.00
	2 CD set.					
Island	PRCD 3136-2	Skin Deep	DJ/Smplr	U.S.	1990	$15.00
Media Amereica		Up Close	RS	U.S.	1993	$40.00
Island		Yes I Am	LTD/LP	Australia	1995	$40.00
	2 CD set.					
Island		Your Little Secret	LTD/LP	Australia	1995	$30.00
	2 CD set.					
Island		Your Little Secret	DJ/LP	Canada	1995	$85.00
	2 CD set.					
Island		Your Little Secret	LTD/LP	Germany	1995	$30.00
	2 CD set.					
Island	524154	Your Little Secret	LTD/LP	U.S.	1995	$16.00
	Special jewel box booklet.					

Singles

Label	Catalog Number	Title	Type	Country	Year	Longbox Value / Value
Island	PHDR-701	2001	CD3	Japan	1992	$15.00/$4.00
Island	CID-528	2001	CD5	U.K.	1992	$10.00
Island		2001	CDJ	U.K.	1992	$12.00
Island	8422 866 893	2001	CD5	U.S.	1992	$8.00
Island	PRCD-6730-2	2001	CDJ	U.S.	1992	$6.00
Island	CID-517	Ain't It Heavy	CD5	U.K.	1992	$10.00
Island	PRCD 6700-2	Ain't It Heavy	CDJ	U.S.	1992	$6.00
Island		All American Girl	CD5	Holland	1994	$12.00
Island	PRCD 6819	All American Girl	CDJ	U.S.	1994	$6.00
Aris	885640	Angels, The	CD5	Germany	1989	$10.00
Island	CID-440	Angels, The	CD5	U.K.	1989	$10.00
Island		Angels, The	CDJ	U.K.	1989	$15.00
Island	2-99138	Angels, The	CD5	U.S.	1989	$5.00
Island	PR 3062	Angels, The	CDJ	U.S.	1989	$6.00
Island	661664	Bring Me Some Water	CD5	Germany	1988	$10.00
Island	CID-393	Bring Me Some Water	CD5	U.K.	1988	$10.00
Island	PR 2713-2	Chrome Plated Heart	CDJ	U.S.	1988	$6.00
Island	661928	Chrome Plated Heart (Live)	CD5	Germany	1989	$10.00
Polygram	858029	Come to My Window	CD5	U.S.	1994	$5.00
Island	PRCD 6803-2	Come to My Window	CDJ	U.S.	1994	$3.00
Island	PHCR-8705	Dance Without Sleeping	CD3	Japan	1992	$15.00/$4.00
Island	CID-547	Dance Without Sleeping	CD5	U.K.	1992	$10.00
Island	2-864321	Dance Without Sleeping	CD5	U.S.	1992	$6.00
Island	PRCD 6733-2	Dance Without Sleeping	CDJ	U.S.	1992	$6.00
Island	880951	Don't You Need	CD5	Germany	1988	$10.00
Island	CID-376	Don't You Need	CD5	U.K.	1988	$10.00
Island	CIDP-376	Don't You Need	CD5	U.K.	1988	$10.00
Island		Happy Christmas	CD5	U.S.	1995	$20.00
Island		I Want to Come Over	CDJ	U.S.		$5.00
Island	PRCD 6820-2	I Will Never Be the Same	CDJ	U.S.	1994	$5.00
Island	WOODST4-2	I'm the Only One	CDJ	Spain	1995	$30.00
Island		I'm the Only One	CDJ	U.K.	1993	$15.00
Island	PRCD 6790-2	I'm the Only One	CDJ	U.S.	1993	$5.00
Atlantic		I'm the Only One	CDJ	U.S.	1994	$7.00
Island		If I Wanted To	CD5	U.K.	1995	$10.00
Island		If I Wanted To	CDJ	U.S.	1992	$7.00
	Second version.					
Polygram	854239	If I Wanted To	CD5	U.S.	1994	$5.00
Island		If I Wanted To	CDJ	U.S.	1994	$5.00
Island	2-99127	Let Me Go	CD5	U.S.	1989	$5.00
Island	PR 3109-2	Let Me Go	CDJ	U.S.	1989	$6.00
Island	661733	Live	CD5	Germany	1989	$10.00
Island	662607	No Souvenirs	CD5	Germany	1989	$10.00
Polystar	P09D-31007	No Souvenirs	CD3	Japan	1989	$15.00/$4.00
Island	CID-431	No Souvenirs	CD5	U.K.	1989	$10.00
Island	2-99179	No Souvenirs	CD5	U.S.	1989	$5.00
Island	PR 2879-2	No Souvenirs	CDJ	U.S.	1989	$6.00
Island		Nowhere To Go	CD5	U.K.	1996	$10.00
	Second version.					
Island	854 655-2	Nowhere To Go	CD5	U.K.	1996	$25.00
	Recalled single.					
Island	P10D-30004	Similar Features	CD3	Japan	1988	$15.00/$4.00
Island	CID-356	Similar Features	CD5	U.K.	1988	$10.00
Island	PR 2258-2	Similar Features	CDJ	U.S.	1988	$7.00
Island	663052	You Can Sleep While I Drive	CD5	Germany	1990	$10.00
Island	CID-472	You Can Sleep While I Drive	CD5	U.K.	1990	$10.00
Island		Your Little Secret	CD5	Australia	1995	$10.00
Island		Your Little Secret	CD5	U.K.	1995	$10.00
Island		Your Little Secret	CDJ	U.S.	1996	$5.00

Ethyl Meatplow

Full Length

Label	Catalog Number	Title	Type	Country	Year	Longbox Value / Value
Dali	PRCD 6728	Happy Days Sweetheart	DJ/LP	U.S.	1993	$18.00

Singles

Label	Catalog Number	Title	Type	Country	Year	Longbox Value / Value
Chameleon	8802	Ripened Peach	CDJ	U.S.	1993	$2.00

Etoile, Pierre

Singles

Label	Catalog Number	Title	Type	Country	Year	Longbox Value / Value
Rough Trade	R-272-3	In the Sun	CD5	U.K.	1991	$8.00

Eton

Singles

Label	Catalog Number	Title	Type	Country	Year	Longbox Value / Value
Efa	CD13304	Noisy Town	CD5	Germany	1991	$8.00

Etsel, Roy

Full Length

Label	Catalog Number	Title	Type	Country	Year	Longbox Value / Value
Intercord	860 196	Serenade	LP	Germany		$15.00

Eubanks, Kevin

Full Length

Label	Catalog Number	Title	Type	Country	Year	Longbox Value / Value
GRP	D-9506	Sundance	LP/LB	U.S.†	1985	$14.00/$8.00

Eubanks, Robin

Full Length

Label	Catalog Number	Title	Type	Country	Year	Longbox Value / Value
Polygram	834433	Dedication	LP/BP	U.S.		$12.00/$7.00

Eugenius

Singles

Label	Catalog Number	Title	Type	Country	Year	Longbox Value / Value
Atlantic	PRCD 4848-2	Bed-In	CDJ	U.S.	1992	$2.00
Atlantic	PRCD 5449-2	Blue Above the Rooftops	CDJ	U.S.	1992	$2.00
Atlantic	PRCD 4824-2	Buttermilk	CDJ	U.S.	1992	$2.00
Atlantic	PRCD 4769-2	Flame On	CDJ	U.S.	1992	$2.00
Atlantic	PRCD 4848-2	It Ain't Rocket Science	CDJ	U.S.	1993	$6.00

Euphoria

Singles

Label	Catalog Number	Title	Type	Country	Year	Longbox Value / Value
EMI	TODP-2390	Love You Right	CD3	Japan	1993	$13.00/$4.00
EMI	CDEM-247	Love You Right	CD5	U.K.	1993	$8.00

Eurobeat Connection

Singles

Label	Catalog Number	Title	Type	Country	Year	Longbox Value / Value
Toshiba	XP10-2013	Meet My Friends	CD3	Japan	1988	$13.00/$4.00

Europe

Full Length

Label	Catalog Number	Title	Type	Country	Year	Longbox Value / Value
Victor	VDPB-25001	Out of This Wold	LTD/LP	Japan		$25.00
	Picture disc CD.					
Epic/Sony	468755 2	Prisoners in Paradise	LTD/LP	Austria	1991	$25.00

Singles

Label	Catalog Number	Title	Type	Country	Year	Longbox Value / Value
CBS	654564-3	Carrie	CD3	Germany	1988	$10.00
CBS	654564-3	Carrie	CD3	U.K.	1988	$10.00
CBS	655573-3	Final Countdown, The	CD3	Germany	1988	$10.00
Victor	VDPS-1002	Final Countdown, The	CD3	Japan	1988	$12.00/$4.00
Epic	657851-2	Halfway to Heaven	CD5	U.K.	1992	$9.00
Epic	ESK 74117	Halfway to Heaven	CDJ	U.S.	1991	$2.00
CBS	657630-2	I'll Cry For You	CD5	Germany	1992	$9.00
Epic	ESCA-5628	I'll Cry For You	CD3	Japan	1992	$13.00/$4.00
Epic	ESK 74118	I'll Cry For You	CDJ	U.S.	1991	$2.00
Epic	654573-2	Let the Good Times Rock	CD3	Germany	1988	$10.00
Epic	CDEUR-5	Let the Good Times Rock	CD5	U.K.	1988	$10.00
Epic		Let the Good Times Rock	CDJ	U.S.	1988	$2.00
Victor	VDPS-1031	More Than Meets the Eye	CD3	Japan	1989	$13.00/$4.00
Epic	653097-3	Open Your Heart	CD3	Germany	1988	$9.00
Epic	CDEUR-4	Open Your Heart	CD5	U.K.	1988	$9.00
Epic		Open Your Heart	CDJ	U.S.	1988	$2.00
Epic	657441-2	Prisoners in Paradise	CD5	Germany	19891	$9.00
Epic	ESK 4179	Prisoners in Paradise	CDJ	U.S.	1991	$2.00
Epic	652879-3	Superstitious	CD3	Germany	1988	$10.00
Epic	VDPS-1014	Superstitious	CD3	Japan	1988	$12.00/$4.00
Epic	CDEUR-3	Superstitious	CD5	U.K.	1988	$10.00
Epic	ESK 1225	Superstitious	CDJ	U.S.	1988	$2.00

European Jazz Trio

Singles

Label	Catalog Number	Title	Type	Country	Year	Longbox Value / Value
Alfa	10R3-13	Autumn Leaves	CD3	Japan	1988	$13.00/$4.00
Alfa	ALCR-133	Silent Night	CD3	Japan	19891	$13.00/$4.00

Eurythmics – Live/Rough & Tough At the Roxy (RCA 5629-2-RDJ)

Eurythmics

Full Length

Label	Catalog Number	Title	Type	Country	Year	Longbox Value / Value
RCA	PCD1-5371	1984	LP/BP	U.S.†	1985	$14.00/$8.00
Arista	ASCD-9915	Acoustic Eurythmics	DJ/Smplr	U.S.	1989	$15.00
RCA	PCD1-5429	Be Yourself Tonight	LP/BP	U.S.†	1985	$14.00/$8.00
Polygram	080-221-1	Live	LD	U.S.	1988	$30.00
RCA	LIVE 1	Live 1983-1989 Sampler	DJ/Smplr	U.K.	1994	$25.00
RCA	5629-2-RDJ	Live/Rough & Tough At the Roxy	DJ/Smplr	U.S.	1986	$50.00
Arista	KCDP-51191	Sampled Live	DJ/Smplr	Canada	1994	$50.00
Pioneer	PA-84-078	Sweet Dreams	LD	U.S.	1984	$30.00
RCA	PCD1-4681	Sweet Dreams	LP/BP	U.S.†	1984	$14.00/$8.00
Pioneer	PA-84-078	Sweet Dreams	LD	U.S.	1990	$40.00
Digital audio.						
RCA	PCD1-5429	Touch	LP/BP	U.S.†	1984	$14.00/$8.00
Unistar		Weekly Specials, The	RS	U.S.	1991	$30.00
Airdate: 8/17/91.						

Singles

Label	Catalog Number	Title	Type	Country	Year	Longbox Value / Value
RCA	PD-43266	Angel	CD5	Germany	1989	$10.00
RCA	R10D-138	Angel	CD3	Japan	1989	$15.00/$4.00
RCA	DACD-21	Angel	CD5	U.K.	1989	$10.00
RCA	90875	Angel	CDJ	U.K.	1989	$7.00
RCA	R10D-3	Beethoven (I Love to Listen to)	CD3	Japan	1988	$15.00/$4.00
RCA	DA-16CD	Chill In My Heart	CD5	U.K.	1988	$11.00
RCA	PD-43130	Don't Ask Me Why	CD5	Germany	1989	$10.00
RCA	DACD-19	Don't Ask Me Why	CD5	U.K.	1989	$10.00
RCA	DACD-20	Don't Ask Me Why	CD5	U.K.	1989	$10.00
Arista	ASCD-9880	Don't Ask Me Why	CDJ	U.S.	1989	$2.00
RCA		Don't Ask Me Why (Live)	CDJ	France	1993	$20.00
RCA	886379	I Need a Man	CD5	Germany	1988	$10.00
RCA	DA-15CD	I Need a Man	CD5	U.K.	1988	$10.00
RCA	5361-2-RDJ	I Need a Man	CDJ	U.S.	1988	$2.00
RCA	PD-43402	King and Queen of America	CD5	Germany	1989	$10.00
RCA	BVCP-9002	King and Queen of America	CD5	Japan	1989	$18.00
RCA	DACD-23	King and Queen of America	CD5	U.K.	1989	$15.00
CD5 in wood box.						
RCA	PD-44266	Love Is a Stranger	CD5	Germany	1991	$10.00
BMG	BVDP-32	Love Is a Stranger	CD3	Japan	1991	$13.00/$4.00
RCA	PD-44266	Love Is a Stranger	CD5	U.K.	1991	$10.00
		(My My) Baby's Gonna Cry	CDJ	U.S.		$2.00
RCA	PD-43099	Revival	CD3	Germany	1989	$10.00
RCA	PD-43100	Revival	CD5	Germany	1989	$10.00
RCA	DACD-17	Revival	CD5	U.K.	1989	$10.00
BMG	663275	Sexcrime	CD5	Germany	1990	$10.00
Virgin	CDT-22	Sexcrime	CD3	U.K.	1990	$10.00
Virgin	CDF-22	Sexcrime	CD5	U.K.	1990	$10.00
RCA	886223	Shame	CD5	Germany	1988	$10.00
RCA	DA-14CD	Shame	CD5	U.K.	1988	$10.00
RCA	PD-42651	Sweet Dreams 91	CD3	Germany	1991	$11.00
RCA	PD-45032	Sweet Dreams 91	CD5	Germany	1991	$11.00
RCA	PD-42651	Sweet Dreams 91	CD3	U.K.	1991	$11.00
RCA	PD-45032	Sweet Dreams 91	CD5	U.K.	1991	$11.00
Arista	ASCD-2243	Sweet Dreams 91	CDJ	U.S.	1991	$3.00

Evans, Bill

Full Length

Label	Catalog Number	Title	Type	Country	Year	Longbox Value / Value
Blue Note	CDP 46336-2	Alternative Man	LP/LB	U.S.		$18.00/$15.00
Verve	821983-2	Bill Evans Trio With Symphony Orchestra	LP/LB	U.S.†	1985	$14.00/$8.00
Alfa	56R2-52/3	Consecration the Last	LTD/LP	Japan		$20.00
Gold disc.						
Polygram	821984-2	Conversations With Myself	LP	Germany		$13.00
Verve	821984-2	Conversations With Myself	LP/LB	U.S.†	1985	$14.00/$8.00
Polygram	827844-2	Montreux Jazz Festival	LP	Germany		$13.00
Fantasy	FCD-9529	Quintessence	LP/LB	U.S.†	1985	$14.00/$8.00
Polygram	815057-2	Trio '64	LP	Germany		$13.00
Verve	815057-2	Trio '64	LP/LB	U.S.†	1985	$14.00/$8.00

Singles

Label	Catalog Number	Title	Type	Country	Year	Longbox Value / Value
Lipstick	7450	Push	CD5	U.S.	1994	$5.00

Evans, Faith

Singles

Label	Catalog Number	Title	Type	Country	Year	Longbox Value / Value
	79045	As Soon as I Get Home	CD5	U.S.	1995	$5.00

Evans, Gill

Full Length

Label	Catalog Number	Title	Type	Country	Year	Longbox Value / Value
Blue Note	CDP 46856-2	Great Jazz Standards	LP/LB	U.S.		$18.00/$15.00
Aris	866378	Music Of Jimi Hendrix	LP	Germany		$13.00
Blue Note	CDP 46855-2	New Bottle, Old Wine	LP/LB	U.S.		$18.00/$15.00
Polygram	380049	Paris Blues	LP/BP	U.S.		$12.00/$7.00
Aris	880044	Priestess	LP	Germany		$13.00

Evans, Monette

Singles

Label	Catalog Number	Title	Type	Country	Year	Longbox Value / Value
CBS	656102-3	This Is Time	CD3	Germany	1990	$8.00
CBS	656791-2	Tighten Up Your Thing	CD5	Germany	1990	$8.00

Eve

Singles

Label	Catalog Number	Title	Type	Country	Year	Longbox Value / Value
CBS	SRDL-3596	Freedom For the World	CD3	Japan	1992	$12.00/$3.00

Eve's Plum

Singles

Label	Catalog Number	Title	Type	Country	Year	Longbox Value / Value
Epic	BSK 5642	I Want It All Alive	CDJ	U.S.		$6.00

Everclear

Full Length

Label	Catalog Number	Title	Type	Country	Year	Longbox Value / Value
Westwood One		In Concert	RS	U.S.	1996	$25.00
Westwood One		In Concert	RS	U.S.	1996	$50.00
Airdate: 4/8/96.						
Westwood One		In Concert-Nu Rock	RS	U.S.	1996	$50.00
Airdate: 1/29/96.						
Capitol		In-Store Play	DJ/Smplr	U.S.	1996	$20.00
Capitol	DPRO 79564	Sparkle & Fade	DJ/LP	U.S.		$15.00

Singles

Label	Catalog Number	Title	Type	Country	Year	Longbox Value / Value
Capital	58255	Fire Maple Song	CD5	U.S.	1994	$5.00
EMI		Heart Spark Dollar Sign	CDJ	U.K.	1996	$10.00
EMI		Heart Spark Dollar Sign	CDJ	U.K.	1996	$10.00
Second version.						
Capitol	DPRO 10226	Santa Monica	CDJ	U.S.		$6.00
Capitol		You Make Me Feel Like a Whore	CDJ	U.S.	1996	$6.00

Evergreen

Singles

Label	Catalog Number	Title	Type	Country	Year	Longbox Value / Value
Next Plateau	162 350 036	Tomorrow Never Knows	CDJ	U.S.	1993	$3.00

Everlast

Singles

Label	Catalog Number	Title	Type	Country	Year	Longbox Value / Value
Warner Brothers	9 213230-2	I Got The Knack	CD5	U.S.	1986	$3.00
Warner Brothers	PRO-CD-3779	Never Missin' a Beat	CDJ	U.S.	1989	$2.00
		Rhythm, The	CDJ	U.S.		$2.00

Everly Brothers

Full Length

Label	Catalog Number	Title	Type	Country	Year	Longbox Value / Value
ZYX	CD-9051	Bye Bye Love & Other Hits	LP	Germany		$18.00
Rhino	RNCD-5258	Cadence Classics	LP/LB	U.S.†	1985	$14.00/$8.00
Mercury	822 431-2	EB 84	LP/BP	U.S.†	1984	$14.00/$8.00
Rhino		Headaches And Harmonies	DJ/Smplr	U.S.	1994	$20.00
Spectrum	SPECC-85010	Twenty Greatest Hits	LP	Germany		$18.00

Singles

Label	Catalog Number	Title	Type	Country	Year	Longbox Value / Value
Old Gold	OG-6111	All I Have To Do Is Dream	CD3	U.K.	1989	$10.00
Aris	885829	Bye Bye Love	CD3	Germany	1990	$10.00
EMI	203251-2	Don't Worry Baby	CD5	Germany	1989	$10.00
Mercury	MERCD-280	Don't Worry Baby	CD5	U.K.	1989	$10.00
Warner Brothers	921067-2	Wake Up Little Susie	CD3	Germany	1989	$10.00
Aris	885828	Wake Up Little Susie	CD3	Germany	1990	$10.00
Warner Brothers	921067-2	Wake Up Little Susie	CD3	U.K.	1989	$10.00
Rhino	73008	Wake Up Little Susie	CD3	U.S.	1988	$6.00/$3.00

Every Mother's Nightmare

Singles

Label	Catalog Number	Title	Type	Country	Year	Longbox Value / Value
Arista	ASCD-2509	Already Gone	CDJ	U.S.	1993	$2.00
Arista	ASCD-2489	House of Pain	CDJ	U.S.	1993	$2.00
Arista	ASCD-2559	I Hate Myself	CDJ	U.S.	1993	$2.00
Arista	ASCD-2052	Long Haired Country Boy	CDJ	U.S.	1990	$2.00
Arista	ASCD 2078	Love Can Make You Blind	CDJ	U.S.	1990	$2.00
Arista	ASCD 2012	Walls Come Down	CDJ	U.S.	1990	$2.00

Everyday People

Singles

Label	Catalog Number	Title	Type	Country	Year	Longbox Value / Value
SBK	203777-2	Headline News	CD5	Germany	1990	$9.00
SBK	CDSBK-5	Headline News	CD5	U.K.	1990	$9.00
SBK	DPRO-05345	Headline News	CDJ	U.S.	1990	$2.00
SBK	203982-2	I Guess It Doesn't Matter	CD5	Germany	1990	$9.00
SBK	203983-2	I Guess It Doesn't Matter	CD5	Germany	1990	$9.00
SBK	CDSBK-8	I Guess It Doesn't Matter	CD5	U.K.	1990	$9.00
EMI	204357-2	Place in the Sun	CD5	Germany	1991	$9.00
SBK	CDSBK-14	This Kind of Woman	CD5	U.K.	1990	$9.00

Everything But The Girl

Full Length

Label	Catalog Number	Title	Type	Country	Year	Longbox Value / Value
Atlantic	PR-883	1992 Sampler	DJ/Smplr	Japan	1994	$45.00
Atlantic	PR 5721-2	Interview And Tracks From Amplified Heart	DJ/Smplr	U.S.	1994	$20.00
Atlantic		Sampler	DJ/Smplr	U.S.	1994	$23.00

Singles

Label	Catalog Number	Title	Type	Country	Year	Longbox Value / Value
Atlantic	PRCD 4745-2	Alison	CDJ	U.S.	1992	$2.00
WEA	246623-2	Driving	CD5	Germany	1990	$9.00
Vap	VPCK-82501	Driving	CD5	Japan	1990	$10.00
Blanco	NEG-40CD	Driving	CD5	U.K.	1990	$9.00
Atlantic	PRCD 3173-2	Driving	CDJ	U.S.	1990	$2.00
Atlantic	PRCD 3191-2	Driving	CDJ	U.S.	1990	$2.00
Vap	2550-12	I Don't Wan't to Talk About It	CD3	Japan	1988	$13.00/$4.00
Blanco	NEG-34CD	I Don't Wan't to Talk About It	CD3	U.K.	1988	$9.00
Sire	PRO-CD-3273	I Don't Wan't to Talk About It	CDJ	U.S.	1988	$3.00
Vap	25501-12	I Was Always Your Girl	CD3	Japan	1988	$13.00/$4.00
Blanco	NEG-33CD	I Was Always Your Girl	CD3	U.K.	1988	$9.00
Sire	PRO-CD-3086	I Was Always Your Girl	CDJ	U.S.	1988	$6.00
Blanco	NEG-33CD	Love Is Here Where I Live	CD3	U.K.	1988	$9.00
Toysfactory	TFCK-88830	Love is Strange	CD5	Germany	1992	$9.00
Blanco	NEG-54CD	Love is Strange	CD5	U.K.	1992	$9.00
Atlantic	PRCD 4579-2	Love is Strange	CDJ	U.S.	1992	$2.00
		Missing	CD5	U.K.	1994	$10.00
		Missing	CD5	U.K.	1994	$10.00
Second version.						
Atlantic	85620	Missing	CD5	U.S.	1994	$5.00
Atlantic	PRCD 6442-2	Missing	CDJ	U.S.	1995	$3.00
Cherry Red	CDCHERRY-37	Night and Day	CD5	U.K.	1989	$9.00
Toysfactory	TFCK-88201	Old Friends	CD3	Japan	1991	$13.00/$4.00
Blanco	NEG-51CD	Old Friends	CD5	U.K.	1991	$9.00
VAP	TFCK-88846	Only Living Boy in New York	CD5	Japan	1993	$14.00
		Only Living Boy in New York	CD5	U.K.	1993	$9.00
		Rollercoaster	CDJ	U.S.	1994	$3.00
WEA	171311-2	Take Me	CD5	Germany	1990	$9.00
Blanco	NEG-44CD	Take Me	CD5	U.K.	1990	$9.00
Atlantic	PRCD 3345-2	Take Me	CDJ	U.S.	1990	$2.00
Blanco	NEG-39CD	These Early Days	CD5	U.K.	1988	$9.00
Vap	TFCK-28501	Twin Cities	CD3	Japan	1992	$13.00/$4.00
Blanco	NEG-53CD	Twin Cities	CD5	U.K.	1991	$10.00
Atlantic	PRCD 4362-2	Understanding	CDJ	U.S.	1992	$2.00
		Wrong	CDJ	U.K.		$15.00

Evident

Singles

Label	Catalog Number	Title	Type	Country	Year	Longbox Value/Value
Circa	YRCD-74	Test the Trust	CD5	U.K.	1992	$8.00

Evil Dead

Singles

Label	Catalog Number	Title	Type	Country	Year	Longbox Value/Value
SPV	7590-3	Rise Above	CD5	Germany	1989	$8.00

Evolve Now

Singles

Label	Catalog Number	Title	Type	Country	Year	Longbox Value/Value
Instinct	262	Dream, The	CD5	U.S.	1993	$4.00

Ex-Girlfriend

Full Length

Label	Catalog Number	Title	Type	Country	Year	Longbox Value/Value
Reprise	9 24404-2-Dj	X Marks the Spot	DJ/LP	U.S.	1991	$13.00

Picture disc.

Singles

Label	Catalog Number	Title	Type	Country	Year	Longbox Value/Value
Reprise	PRO-CD-4790	Why Can't You Come Home	CDJ	U.S.	1991	$2.00
Reprise	PRO-CD-4981	You	CDJ	U.S.	1991	$2.00

Ex-Idol

Singles

Label	Catalog Number	Title	Type	Country	Year	Longbox Value/Value
Relativity	1213	Pill Propper	CD5	U.S.	1994	$5.00

Ex-Plain

Singles

Label	Catalog Number	Title	Type	Country	Year	Longbox Value/Value
ZYX	6536-8	Check It Out	CD5	Germany	1991	$6.00

Excess Bleeding Heart

Singles

Label	Catalog Number	Title	Type	Country	Year	Longbox Value/Value
Bubble	BBLCD 300	Dash With Love	CD5	U.K.	1992	$8.00

Excessive Force

Singles

Label	Catalog Number	Title	Type	Country	Year	Longbox Value/Value
Devotion	CDDVN-107	Conquer Your House	CD5	U.K.	1992	$8.00
Wax Trax	9175	Conquer Your House	CD5	U.S.	1992	$5.00

Exciter

Singles

Label	Catalog Number	Title	Type	Country	Year	Longbox Value/Value
Canyon	S9ED-8007	Reaching for the Best	CD3	Japan	1989	$13.00/$4.00

Excused Boots

Singles

Label	Catalog Number	Title	Type	Country	Year	Longbox Value/Value
BMG	FLEASC-1	Just My Luck	CD5	U.K.	1989	$8.00

Exile

Full Length

Label	Catalog Number	Title	Type	Country	Year	Longbox Value/Value
Image	ID6368ME	In Concert	LD	U.S.		$15.00

Singles

Label	Catalog Number	Title	Type	Country	Year	Longbox Value/Value
		Even Now	CDJ	U.S.		$2.00
Epic	ESK 2822	I Can't Get Close Enough	CDJ	U.S.	1987	$2.00

Exit

Singles

Label	Catalog Number	Title	Type	Country	Year	Longbox Value/Value
Media	ALCB-538	Roller Sensation	CD5	Japan	1992	$10.00

Exodus

Full Length

Label	Catalog Number	Title	Type	Country	Year	Longbox Value/Value
		Lesson in Violence	LP	U.S.		$15.00
Combat		Paradise of Flesh	LP/LB	U.S.		$14.00/$8.00

Singles

Label	Catalog Number	Title	Type	Country	Year	Longbox Value/Value
Capitol	DPRO-79406	Lunatic Parade	CDJ	U.S.	1990	$2.00
Capitol	203937-2	Objection Overruled	CD5	Germany	1990	$9.00
Capitol	DPRO-79197	Objection Overruled	CDJ	U.S.	1990	$2.00
Capitol	DPRO-79416	Thorn in My Side	CDJ	U.S.	1990	$2.00

Exotic Birds

Singles

Label	Catalog Number	Title	Type	Country	Year	Longbox Value/Value
Alpha	79482	Imagination	CDJ	U.S.	1990	$2.00

Explorers

Full Length

Label	Catalog Number	Title	Type	Country	Year	Longbox Value/Value
Virgin		Explorers	LP/LB	U.S.		$14.00/$8.00

Expose

Full Length

Label	Catalog Number	Title	Type	Country	Year	Longbox Value/Value
Arista	ASCD-2483	Top Ten Hits of Expose, The	DJ/Smplr	U.S.	1992	$10.00

Singles

Label	Catalog Number	Title	Type	Country	Year	Longbox Value/Value
Arista	ASCD-2600	As Long As I Can	CDJ	U.S.	1993	$2.00
Arista	BVDA-48	I Wish the Phone Would Ring	CD3	Japan	1992	$13.00/$4.00
Arista	12498	I Wish the Phone Would Ring	CD5	U.S.	1992	$4.00
Arista	ASCD-2466	I Wish the Phone Would Ring	CDJ	U.S.	1992	$2.00
Arista	BVDA-60	I'll Never Get Over You	CD3	Japan	1993	$13.00/$4.00
Arista	ASCD-2518	I'll Never Get Over You	CDJ	U.S.	1993	$2.00
Arista	RISCD-45	Let Me Be the One	CD5	U.K.	1988	$9.00
		Serious Change	CDJ	U.S.		$2.00
BMG	BVDA-3	Stop Listen Look And Think	CD3	Japan	1990	$13.00/$4.00
Arista	662928	Tell Me Why	CD5	Germany	1990	$9.00
Arista	A10D-145	Tell Me Why	CD3	Japan	1989	$13.00/$4.00
Arista	663026	Tell Me Why	CD5	U.K.	1990	$9.00
Arista	ASCD 9918	Tell Me Why	CDJ	U.S.	1989	$2.00
Arista	162354	What You Don't Know	CD3	Germany	1989	$9.00
Arista	662354	What You Don't Know	CD5	Germany	1989	$9.00
Arista	A10D-121	What You Don't Know	CD3	Japan	1989	$13.00/$4.00
Arista	A10D-125	What You Don't Know	CD3	Japan	1989	$13.00/$4.00
Arista	662354	What You Don't Know	CD5	U.K.	1989	$9.00
Arista	ASCD 9837	What You Don't Know	CDJ	U.S.	1989	$2.00
Aris	885559	When I Looked at Him	CD5	Germany	1989	$9.00
Arista	A10D-135	When I Looked at Him	CD3	Japan	1989	$13.00/$4.00
Arista	662635	When I Looked at Him	CD5	U.K.	1989	$9.00
Arista	ASCD 2010	Your Baby Never Looked Good in Blue	CDJ	U.S.	1990	$2.00

Exquisite Corpse

Singles

Label	Catalog Number	Title	Type	Country	Year	Longbox Value/Value
WEA	KK-092CD	Resembling Reality	CD5	U.K.	1992	$8.00
WEA	KK-082CD	Strange Attractor	CD5	U.K.	1992	$8.00

Extravaganza

Singles

Label	Catalog Number	Title	Type	Country	Year	Longbox Value/Value
Bellaphon	130 07 309	Boys Do the Boogie	CD5	Germany	1988	$8.00

Extreme

Full Length

Label	Catalog Number	Title	Type	Country	Year	Longbox Value/Value
Canyon		Extreme	DJ/LP	Japan		$40.00
Foundations		FZ Interview	RS/VA	U.S.	1992	$10.00
A&M		III Sides to Every Story	LTD/LP	Japan	1992	$45.00

CD album with bonus CD3, sticker and extra booklet.

Label	Catalog Number	Title	Type	Country	Year	Longbox Value/Value
A&M	31454-0027-2	III Sides To Every Story	LP/LB	U.S.	1992	$15.00/$8.00
Westwood One		Off the Record	RS	U.S.	1992	$30.00

Airdate: 10/5/92.

Label	Catalog Number	Title	Type	Country	Year	Longbox Value/Value
Westwood One		Off the Record	RS	U.S.	1993	$30.00

Airdate: 2/8/93.

Singles

Label	Catalog Number	Title	Type	Country	Year	Longbox Value/Value
A&M	31458 8123	Am I Ever Gonna Change	CDJ	U.S.	1992	$3.00
A&M		Cynical	CDJ	U.S.	1994	$6.00
Canyon	PCDY-10020	Decadance Dance	CD3	Japan	1990	$15.00/$4.00
A&M	AMCD-773	Decadance Dance	CD5	U.K.	1990	$10.00
A&M	75021 8102-2	Decadance Dance	CDJ	U.S.	1990	$3.00
Canyon	DC1-3051	Don't Leave Me Alone	DJ/CD3	Japan		$30.00
A&M	AMCD-737	Get the Funk Out	CD5	U.K.	1991	$10.00
A&M	390 613	Get the Funk Out	CD5	U.S.	1990	$5.00
A&M	75021 7295 2	Get the Funk Out	CDJ	U.S.	1990	$2.00
A&M	75021 7370 2	Get the Funk Out	CDJ	U.S.	1990	$2.00
A&M	75021 7431 2	Get the Funk Out	CDJ	U.S.	1990	$2.00
A&M		Hip Today	CDJ	U.S.	1994	$6.00
A&M	AMCD-839	Hole Hearted	CD5	U.K.	1991	$10.00
A&M	75021 7003 2	Hole Hearted	CDJ	U.S.	1990	$6.00
A&M	S9Y-3103	Kid Ego	CD3	Japan	1989	$13.00/$4.00
A&M	CD-17717	Kid Ego	CDJ	U.S.	1989	$2.00
A&M	S9Y-31309	Little Girls	CD3	Japan	1989	$15.00/$4.00
A&M	CD-17830	Little Girls	CDJ	U.S.	1989	$2.00
A&M	390764-2	More Than Words	CD5	Germany	1991	$10.00
A&M	AMCD 792	More Than Words	CD5	U.K.	1991	$10.00
A&M	75021 7515 2	More Than Words	CDJ	U.S.	1991	$3.00
A&M	CD-17847	Mutha You Don't Wanna Go to School	CDJ	U.S.	1989	$2.00
A&M	PODM-1001	Rest in Peace	CD3	Japan	1992	$13.00/$4.00
A&M	31458 8015 2	Rest in Peace	CDJ	U.S.	1992	$2.00
A&M	31458 8070 2	Rest in Peace	CDJ	U.S.	1992	$2.00
A&M	POCM-1130	Running Gag	CD5	Japan		$20.00
A&M	AMCD-698	Song For Love	CD5	U.K.	1991	$10.00
A&M	PODM-1004	Stop the World	CD3	Japan	1992	$12.00/$4.00
A&M		Stop the World	CD5	U.K.	1992	$10.00
A&M	31458 8030	Stop the World	CDJ	U.S.	1992	$2.00
A&M	31458 8097	Stop the World	CDJ	U.S.	1992	$2.00
A&M		There Is No God	CDJ	France	1994	$15.00
A&M	580 609-2	There Is No God	CD5	Germany	1994	$25.00
A&M		There Is No God	CD5	U.K.	1994	$10.00
A&M	AMCD 0156	Tragic Comic	CD5	U.K.	1993	$10.00
A&M	AMCDR 0156	Tragic Comic	CD5	U.K.	1993	$10.00
A&M	31458 0117	Tragic Comic	CD5	U.S.	1992	$5.00
A&M	31458 8031	Tragic Comic	CDJ	U.S.	1992	$2.00
A&M		Waiting For the Punchline	CDJ	U.S.	1994	$6.00

Extreme Noise Terror

Singles

Label	Catalog Number	Title	Type	Country	Year	Longbox Value/Value
Vinyl	DISC-1X	Phonophobia	CD5	U.K.	1992	$8.00

EYC

Singles

Label	Catalog Number	Title	Type	Country	Year	Longbox Value/Value
		In the Beginning	CD5	U.K.		$10.00
		In the Beginning	CD5	U.K.		$10.00

Second version.

Eye & I

Singles

Label	Catalog Number	Title	Type	Country	Year	Longbox Value/Value
Epic	ESK 74375	Virgin Heart	CDJ	U.S.	1992	$2.00

Eyes

Singles

Label	Catalog Number	Title	Type	Country	Year	Longbox Value/Value
		Callin' All Girls	CDJ	U.S.		$2.00
		Nobody Said It Was Easy	CDJ	U.S.		$2.00

Eyice

Singles

Label	Catalog Number	Title	Type	Country	Year	Longbox Value/Value
Fieldworks	FWCR-51	Standing on the Edge	CD5	Japan	1992	$10.00

EZO

Singles

Label	Catalog Number	Title	Type	Country	Year	Longbox Value/Value
Geffen	PRO-CD-2696	Flash Back Heart Attack	CDJ	U.S.	1987	$2.00
Geffen	PRO-CD-3557	Million Miles Away	CDJ	U.S.	1989	$2.00

F.C.F.

Singles

Label	Catalog Number	Title	Type	Country	Year	Longbox Value/Value
Alfa	ALDB-32	Bad Desire	CD3	Japan	1990	$12.00/$3.00
Alfa	ALCB-328	Bad Desire	CD5	Japan	1990	$10.00
Alfa	ALDB-115	Big Match	CD3	Japan	1990	$12.00/$3.00

F.K.W.

Singles

Label	Catalog Number	Title	Type	Country	Year	Longbox Value/Value
Next Plateau	016	Seize the Day	CDJ	U.S.	1993	$2.00

F.M.

Singles

Label	Catalog Number	Title	Type	Country	Year	Longbox Value/Value
Music For Nations	CDKUT-151	Blues & Soul	CD5	U.K.	1993	$9.00
		Every Time I Think of You	CDJ	U.S.		$2.00
Music For Nations	CDKUT-142	I Heard It Through the Grape Vine	CD5	U.K.	1991	$10.00
Music For Nations	CDKUT-145	Only the Strong Survive	CD5	U.K.	1992	$9.00

F.M. (U.K.)

Singles

Label	Catalog Number	Title	Type	Country	Year	Longbox Value/Value
CBS	655031-2	Bad Luck	CD5	U.K.	1989	$8.00
Epic	CDDINK-2	Every Time I Think of You	CD5	U.K.	1990	$8.00
Epic	DINKC-2	Every Time I Think of You	CD5	U.K.	1990	$8.00
Epic	DINKCD-1	Someday	CD5	U.K.	1989	$8.00

F Machine

Singles

Label	Catalog Number	Title	Type	Country	Year	Longbox Value/Value
Reprise	PRO-CD-3751	Here Comes the 20th Century	CDJ	U.S.	1989	$2.00
Reprise	PRO-CD-3547	Runaway Train	CDJ	U.S.	1989	$2.00

F.O.A.D.

Singles

Label	Catalog Number	Title	Type	Country	Year	Longbox Value/Value
Fieldworks	FWCR-34	R&R Outlaw	CD5	Japan	1992	$10.00

F.O.D.

Singles

Label	Catalog Number	Title	Type	Country	Year	Longbox Value/Value
	55318	All It Takes	CD5	U.S.	1994	$5.00

F.O.M.

Singles

Label	Catalog Number	Title	Type	Country	Year	Longbox Value/Value
SPV	1022-3	Come On Get Up	CD5	Germany	1991	$8.00

F.P.I. Project

Singles

Label	Catalog Number	Title	Type	Country	Year	Longbox Value / Value
ZYX	6256-8	Going Back to My Roots	CD5	Germany	1989	$6.00
ZYX	6290-8	Going Back to My Roots	CD5	Germany	1989	$6.00
BMG	664955	Let's Go	CD5	Germany	1992	$8.00

F.S. Effect

Singles

Label	Catalog Number	Title	Type	Country	Year	Longbox Value / Value
Giant	PRO-CD-4915	I Wanna B Ure Lover	CDJ	U.S.	1991	$2.00

F1 For Help

Singles

Label	Catalog Number	Title	Type	Country	Year	Longbox Value / Value
Pikosso	874 00015	Raumpatrolie	SCD5	Germany	1995	$18.00

"Space ship" shaped CD.

Fab

Full Length

Label	Catalog Number	Title	Type	Country	Year	Longbox Value / Value
Jimco	JIDM-29004/9	Thunderbirds Are Go	LTD/LP	Japan	1992	$75.00

6 CD3 set.

Singles

Label	Catalog Number	Title	Type	Country	Year	Longbox Value / Value
Telstar	FABCD-2	Prisoner Theme	CD5	U.K.	1992	$10.00
Telstar	FABCD-26	Prisoner Theme	CD5	U.K.	1992	$10.00
Jimco	JIDM-29001	Thunderbirds Are Go	CD3	Japan	1992	$12.00/$4.00
Telstar	FABCD-1	Thunderbirds Are Go	CD5	U.K.	1992	$10.00

Faber, Joyce

Singles

Label	Catalog Number	Title	Type	Country	Year	Longbox Value / Value
BMG	663638	You Just Come by Love	CD5	Germany	1990	$8.00

Fabian

Singles

Label	Catalog Number	Title	Type	Country	Year	Longbox Value / Value
Polydor	PODP-1055	Paradiso	CD3	Japan	1992	$12.00/$3.00

Fabu

Singles

Label	Catalog Number	Title	Type	Country	Year	Longbox Value / Value
Atlantic	98175	Just Roll	CD5	U.S.	1994	$5.00
Atlantic	95744	Just Roll	CD5	U.S.	1994	$5.00

Fabulon

Singles

Label	Catalog Number	Title	Type	Country	Year	Longbox Value / Value
Charisma	12695	I'm in a Mood	CDJ	U.S.	1992	$2.00
Charisma	04730	I'm in a Mood	CDJ	U.S.	1992	$2.00

Fabulous Thunderbirds

Full Length

Label	Catalog Number	Title	Type	Country	Year	Longbox Value / Value
		House of Blues	RS	U.S.	1995	$35.00

Airdate: 8/20/95.

Label	Catalog Number	Title	Type	Country	Year	Longbox Value / Value
DIR		King Biscuit Flour Hour	RS	U.S.	1987	$40.00

Airdate: 10/4/87.

Label	Catalog Number	Title	Type	Country	Year	Longbox Value / Value
DIR		King Biscuit Flour Hour	RS	U.S.	1988	$30.00

With Robert Cray, Airdate: 3/27/88.

Label	Catalog Number	Title	Type	Country	Year	Longbox Value / Value
DIR		King Biscuit Flour Hour	RS	U.S.	1991	$35.00

Airdate: 10/21/91.

Label	Catalog Number	Title	Type	Country	Year	Longbox Value / Value
DIR		King Biscuit Flour Hour	RS	U.S.	1992	$35.00

Airdate: 9/13/92.

Label	Catalog Number	Title	Type	Country	Year	Longbox Value / Value
DIR		King Biscuit Flour Hour	RS	U.S.	1993	$35.00

Airdate: 7/25/93.

Label	Catalog Number	Title	Type	Country	Year	Longbox Value / Value
DIR		King Biscuit Flour Hour	RS	U.S.	1994	$35.00

Airdate: 5/29/94.

Label	Catalog Number	Title	Type	Country	Year	Longbox Value / Value
DIR		King Biscuit Flour Hour	RS	U.S.	1995	$35.00

Airdate: 4/16/95.

Singles

Label	Catalog Number	Title	Type	Country	Year	Longbox Value / Value
CBS	CSK 1581	Knock Yourself Out	CDJ	U.S.	1989	$2.00
		Powerful Stuff	CDJ	U.S.		$2.00
CBS	CSK 4203	Roller Coaster	CDJ	U.S.	1991	$2.00
CBS	CSK 2738	Stand Back	CDJ	U.S.	1988	$2.00
CBS	CSK 4124	Twist the Knife	CDJ	U.S.	1991	$2.00

Face Down

Full Length

Label	Catalog Number	Title	Type	Country	Year	Longbox Value / Value
Big Beat	4203	Illegal Drugs Hurt	LP/BP	U.S.		$12.00/$7.00

Face To Face

Full Length

Label	Catalog Number	Title	Type	Country	Year	Longbox Value / Value
Mercury		One Bright Day	DJ/Smplr	U.S.		$5.00

Singles

Label	Catalog Number	Title	Type	Country	Year	Longbox Value / Value
A&M	314589318	A-OK	CDJ	U.S.	1995	$3.00
Mercury	CDP 13	As Forever as You	CDJ	U.S.	1988	$2.00

Faces

Full Length

Label	Catalog Number	Title	Type	Country	Year	Longbox Value / Value
BBC Radio		BBC Classic Tracks	RS	U.S.	1991	$20.00

With Rod Stewart, Airdate: 11/11/91.

Facio, Gianna

Singles

Label	Catalog Number	Title	Type	Country	Year	Longbox Value / Value
BMG	663401	One Two Three Four	CD5	Germany	1990	$8.00

Fact Of Spirit

Singles

Label	Catalog Number	Title	Type	Country	Year	Longbox Value / Value
Italio-Heat	FFR-0515	Ghost in My House	CD5	Germany	1989	$8.00

Fad, J.J.

Singles

Label	Catalog Number	Title	Type	Country	Year	Longbox Value / Value
WEA	796658-3	Supersonic	CD3	Germany	1989	$8.00

Faeltskog, Agnetha

Full Length

Label	Catalog Number	Title	Type	Country	Year	Longbox Value / Value
Polar	825600-2	Eyes of a Woman	LP	Germany		$18.00
Polar	813242-2	Wrap Your Arms Around Me	LP	U.K.		$18.00
Polygram	813242-2	Wrap Your Arms Around Me	LP/BP	U.S.†	1985	$14.00/$8.00

Singles

Label	Catalog Number	Title	Type	Country	Year	Longbox Value / Value
WEA	10SW-6	I Wasn't the One	CD3	Japan	1988	$13.00/$4.00
WEA	248087-2	Last Time	CD5	Germany	1988	$9.00
WEA	10SW-62	Let It Shine	CD3	Japan	1988	$13.00/$4.00

Fagen, Donald

Full Length

Label	Catalog Number	Title	Type	Country	Year	Longbox Value / Value
Reprise	9 45230-2-DJ	Kamakiriad	DJ/LP	U.S.	1993	$30.00

20 SBM gold disc in digipak.

Label	Catalog Number	Title	Type	Country	Year	Longbox Value / Value
Warner Brothers	43XD-2003	Nightfly	LTD/LP	Japan		$40.00

Gold disc.

Label	Catalog Number	Title	Type	Country	Year	Longbox Value / Value
Warner Brothers	9 23696-2	Nightfly	LP/LB	U.S.†	1984	$14.00/$8.00
Media America		Up Close	RS	U.S.	1993	$100.00

3 CD set.

Label	Catalog Number	Title	Type	Country	Year	Longbox Value / Value
Reprise	PRO-CD-6461-R	Words And Music	DJ/Intvw	U.S.	1993	$12.00

Singles

Label	Catalog Number	Title	Type	Country	Year	Longbox Value / Value
WEA	920928-2	Century's End	CD3	Germany	1988	$10.00
Warner Brothers	10SW-22	Century's End	CD3	Japan	1988	$12.00/$4.00
WEA	W-7972CD	Century's End	CD3	U.K.	1988	$10.00
Warner Brothers	CD3 2987	Century's End	CD3	U.S.	1988	$6.00/$3.00
Warner Brothers	PRO-CD-2987	Century's End	CDJ	U.S.	1988	$3.00
Reprise	PRO-CD-6820	Countermoon	CDJ	U.S.	1993	$3.00
Warner/NTSC	2-25679	New Frontier	DJ/CDV	U.S.	1982	$12.00
Warner Brothers	2-25679	New Frontier	DJ/CDV	U.S.	1988	$20.00
Giant	PRO-CD-5186	Pretzel Logic	CDJ	U.S.	1991	$3.00
Reprise	PRO-CD-6592	Snowbound	CDJ	U.S.	1993	$3.00
Reprise	9362 40909	Tomorrow's Girl	CD5	Germany	1993	$10.00
Warner Brothers	WPDP-6320	Tomorrow's Girl	CD3	Japan	1993	$12.00/$4.00
Reprise		Tomorrow's Girl	CD5	U.K.	1993	$10.00
Reprise	PRO-CD-6200	Tomorrow's Girl	CDJ	U.S.	1993	$3.00
Reprise	PRO-CD-6211	Tomorrow's Girl	CDJ	U.S.	1993	$3.00

Failure

Full Length

Label	Catalog Number	Title	Type	Country	Year	Longbox Value / Value
Warner Brothers	PRO-CD-8410	Stuck on You	SCDJ	U.S.	1996	$20.00

Space soldier shaped disc.

Singles

Label	Catalog Number	Title	Type	Country	Year	Longbox Value / Value
Slash	PRO-CD-6788	Moth	CDJ	U.S.	1994	$2.00

Fair Play

Singles

Label	Catalog Number	Title	Type	Country	Year	Longbox Value / Value
Polygram	871211-2	Don't Forget Ben Johnson	CD5	Germany	1988	$8.00
CBS	657799-2	Fighting For Tomorrow	CD5	Germany	1992	$8.00

Fair Sex

Singles

Label	Catalog Number	Title	Type	Country	Year	Longbox Value / Value
Rough Trade	105	Soulspirit	CD5	U.K.	1992	$8.00

Fair Warning

Singles

Label	Catalog Number	Title	Type	Country	Year	Longbox Value / Value
WEA	WMC5-590	In the Ghetto	CD5	Japan	1993	$12.00

Fairground Attraction

Singles

Label	Catalog Number	Title	Type	Country	Year	Longbox Value / Value
RCA	PD-42608	Claire	CD5	Germany	1989	$8.00
RCA	B51D-41002	Claire	CD5	Japan	1989	$10.00
RCA	PD-42608	Claire	CD5	U.K.	1989	$8.00
RCA	PD-42080	Find My Love	CD5	Germany	1988	$8.00
RCA	R15D-2	Find My Love	CD3	Japan	1988	$13.00/$4.00
RCA	PD-42080	Find My Love	CD5	U.K.	1988	$8.00
RCA	PD-42649	Perfect	CD5	Germany	1988	$8.00
RCA	886411	Perfect	CD5	Germany	1988	$8.00
RCA	PD-42649	Perfect	CD3	U.K.	1988	$8.00
RCA	PD-41846	Perfect	CD5	U.K.	1988	$8.00
RCA	74321-134912	Perfect	CD5	U.K.	1993	$9.00
		Perfect	CDJ	U.S.	1988	$2.00
RCA	R10D-107	Smile in a Whisper	CD3	Japan	1989	$13.00/$4.00
RCA	PD-42250	Smile in a Whisper	CD5	U.K.	1988	$8.00
RCA	PD-43654	Walking After Midnight	CD5	Germany	1990	$8.00
RCA	PD-43654	Walking After Midnight	CD5	U.K.	1990	$8.00

Fairport Convention

Full Length

Label	Catalog Number	Title	Type	Country	Year	Longbox Value / Value
SPV	3075	Expletive Delighted	LP	Germany		$18.00
Island	880896	History of	LP	Germany		$18.00
		Red & Gold	LP	U.S.		$10.00

Faith, Adam

Singles

Label	Catalog Number	Title	Type	Country	Year	Longbox Value / Value
		Stuck in the Middle	CD5	U.K.		$10.00

Faith Healers

Singles

Label	Catalog Number	Title	Type	Country	Year	Longbox Value / Value
Elektra	66327-2	Don't Jones Me	CDJ	U.S.	1993	$6.00

Faith Hope Charity

Singles

Label	Catalog Number	Title	Type	Country	Year	Longbox Value / Value
WEA	171586-2	Battle of the Sexes	CD5	Germany	1990	$8.00
WEA	YZ-480CD	Battle of the Sexes	CD5	U.K.	1990	$8.00
WEA	9031-72437-2	Growing Pains	CD5	Germany	1990	$8.00
WEA	YZ-523CD	Growing Pains	CD5	U.K.	1990	$8.00

Faith No More

Full Length

Label	Catalog Number	Title	Type	Country	Year	Longbox Value / Value
Slash	PRO-CD-7496-R	32 Cents For a Postage Stamp?!	DJ/Smplr	U.S.	1995	$20.00
Westwood One		In Concert-Nu Rock	RS	U.S.	1995	$65.00

2 CD set with Stone Temple Pilots. Airdate: 7/17/95.

Label	Catalog Number	Title	Type	Country	Year	Longbox Value / Value
Slash	TVD 93421	King For a Day Fool For a Lifetime	LTD/LP	U.K.	1995	$25.00

2CD set.

Label	Catalog Number	Title	Type	Country	Year	Longbox Value / Value
Slash		King For a Day Sampler	DJ/Smplr	France	1995	$25.00
Slash	PRO-CD-4486	Live From Five Fat B**tards	DJ/Smplr	U.S.	1990	$20.00
Slash	PRO-CD-4486	Live From Five Fat B**tards	DJ/Smplr	U.S.	1990	$25.00

With rubber fish.

Label	Catalog Number	Title	Type	Country	Year	Longbox Value / Value
Westwood One		Superstars	RS	U.S.	1993	$50.00

Airdate: 4/26/93.

Singles

Label	Catalog Number	Title	Type	Country	Year	Longbox Value / Value
Slash	9 40626-2	A Small Victory	CD5	U.S.	1992	$5.00
Slash	PRO-CD-5564	A Small Victory	CDJ	U.S.	1992	$3.00
Immortal	5408	Another Body Murdered	CDJ	U.S.	1993	$3.00
Slash		Digging the Grave	CDJ	U.S.	1995	$3.00
Slash	PRO-CD-6023	Easy Days	CDJ	U.S.	1993	$7.00
Slash	886881-2	Epic	CD5	Germany	1990	$10.00
London	POCD-1021	Epic	CD3	Japan	1990	$12.00/$4.00
Slash	LASCD-21	Epic	CD5	U.K.	1990	$10.00
Slash	LASCD-26	Epic	CD5	U.K.	1990	$10.00
Slash	PRO-CD-3913	Epic	CDJ	U.S.	1989	$3.00
Slash	PRO-CD-4071	Epic	CDJ	U.S.	1989	$3.00
Atlantic	18891-2	Epic	CD5	U.S.	1992	$5.00
London	PODD-1024	Everything's Ruined	CD3	Japan	1992	$12.00/$4.00
London		Everything's Ruined	CD5	U.K.	1992	$10.00
London		Everything's Ruined	CD5	U.K.	1992	$10.00

Second version.

Label	Catalog Number	Title	Type	Country	Year	Longbox Value / Value
		Evidence	CD5	U.K.	1995	$10.00
		Evidence	CD5	U.K.	1995	$10.00

Second version.

Label	Catalog Number	Title	Type	Country	Year	Longbox Value / Value
Slash		Evidence	CDJ	U.S.	1995	$3.00
Polygram	869107-2	Falling To Pieces	CD5	Germany	1990	$10.00
London	POCP-1044	Falling To Pieces	CD5	Japan	1991	$16.00
Slash	PRO-CD-4409	Falling To Pieces	CDJ	U.S.	1990	$2.00
London	886 989-2	From Out Of Nowhere	CD5	U.K.	1990	$10.00
Reprise	PRO-CD-3559	From Out Of Nowhere	CDJ	U.S.	1989	$2.00
London		I'm Easy	CD5	U.K.	1992	$10.00

Label	Catalog Number	Title	Type	Country	Year	Longbox Value / Value
London		I'm Easy	CD5	U.K.	1992	$10.00
Second version.						
Slash	9 40626-2	Land of Sunshine	CD5	U.S.	1992	$5.00
Slash	PRO-CD-5523	Land of Sunshine	CDJ	U.S.	1992	$2.00
Slash	LASCD 37	Midlife Crisis	CD5	U.K.	1992	$10.00
Slash	PRO-CD-5498	Midlife Crisis	CDJ	U.S.	1992	$2.00
		Richochet	CD5	U.K.	1995	$10.00
		Richochet	CD5	U.K.	1995	$10.00
Second version.						
Slash		Ricochet	CDJ	U.S.	1995	$3.00
London	PODD-1020	Small Victory	CD3	Japan	1992	$12.00/$4.00
Slash	LASCD-39	Small Victory	CD5	U.K.	1992	$10.00
Slash	LASCD-40	Small Victory	CD5	U.K.	1992	$10.00
Slash	PRO-CD-5564	Small Victory	CDJ	U.S.	1992	$2.00

Faith Over Reason

Singles

Label	Catalog Number	Title	Type	Country	Year	Longbox Value / Value
Big Cat	ABB-23SCD	Billy Blue	CD5	U.K.	1990	$10.00

Faith, Percy

Full Length

Label	Catalog Number	Title	Type	Country	Year	Longbox Value / Value
CBS	CK-40168	Christmas Melodies	LP/BP	U.S.†	1985	$12.00/$7.00

Faithful, Marianne

Full Length

Label	Catalog Number	Title	Type	Country	Year	Longbox Value / Value
		20th Century Blues	DJ/LP	U.S.	1996	$40.00
Picture disc.						
		Conversation With Paul Gambaccini	DJ/Intvw	U.S.		$5.00
Reddog		Faithless	LP/LB	U.S.		$14.00/$8.00

Falco

Full Length

Label	Catalog Number	Title	Type	Country	Year	Longbox Value / Value
American Sound 79754		Data DeGroove	CDJ	Germany	1991	$6.00
Teldec	8 26380	Falco	LP	Germany		$20.00

Singles

Label	Catalog Number	Title	Type	Country	Year	Longbox Value / Value
Eastwest	9031-71235	Charisma Kommando	CD5	Germany	1990	$10.00
Eastwest	171519-2	Data DeGroove	CD5	Germany	1990	$10.00
Eastwest	9031-76271-2	Der Komissar	CD5	Germany	1992	$10.00
Eastwest	8 20745	Emotional	CD5	Germany		$10.00
Eastwest	246873-2	Komissar	CD5	Germany	1990	$10.00
Eastwest	9031-75223-2	Rock Me Amadeus	CD5	Germany	1991	$10.00
Eastwest	247293-2	Satellite to Satellite	CD5	Germany	1989	$10.00
Teldec	10P3-6075	Satellite to Satellite	CD3	Japan	1988	$12.00/$4.00
Eastwest	247741-2	Wiener Blut	CD5	Germany	1989	$10.00
Waarner	10P3-6041	Wiener Blut	CD3	Japan	1989	$12.00/$4.00

Falcon, Billy

Singles

Label	Catalog Number	Title	Type	Country	Year	Longbox Value / Value
Mercury	CDP 558	Heaven's Highest Hill	CDJ	U.S.	1991	$2.00
Mercury	CDP 636	Married In the Morning	CDJ	U.S.	1991	$2.00
Mercury	MERCD-355	Power Windows	CD5	U.K.	1991	$10.00
Mercury	CDP 465	Power Windows	CDJ	U.S.	1991	$2.00

Falkon Krest

Singles

Label	Catalog Number	Title	Type	Country	Year	Longbox Value / Value
ZYX	7402-8	Western	CD5	U.S.	1995	$5.00

Fall

Full Length

Label	Catalog Number	Title	Type	Country	Year	Longbox Value / Value
		Crash Course '82-'92	DJ/Smplr	U.S.	1993	$10.00
Matador	5094	Extricate	DJ/Smplr	U.S.		$10.00
		Retrospective	DJ/Smplr	U.S.		$8.00
	PRCD 5094	Selections From "Infotainment Scam"	DJ/Smplr	U.S.	1994	$8.00

Singles

Label	Catalog Number	Title	Type	Country	Year	Longbox Value / Value
		Behind the Counter	CD5	U.K.		$10.00
		Behind the Counter	CD5	U.K.		$10.00
Second version.						
Beggars Banquet	BEG-226CD	Cab It Up	CD5	U.K.	1989	$10.00
Polygram	SINCD-8	Free France	CD5	U.K.	1991	$10.00
Beggars Banquet	FALL-2CD	Jerusalem	CD5	U.K.	1988	$10.00
Aris	883518	Peel Sessions	CD5	Germany	1990	$10.00
Polygram	SINCD-5	Popcorn Double Feature	CD5	U.K.	1990	$10.00
IMS	876611-2	Telephone Ring	CD5	Germany	1990	$10.00
Polygram	SINCD-4	Telephone Ring	CD5	U.K.	1990	$10.00
Polygram	SINCD-6	White Lightning	CD5	U.K.	1990	$10.00

Falling Joys

Singles

Label	Catalog Number	Title	Type	Country	Year	Longbox Value / Value
Nettwerk	67095	Black Bandages	CDJ	U.S.	1991	$2.00
Nettwerk	13869	God in a Dustbin	CDJ	U.S.	1992	$2.00
SPV	11000-3	Jennifer	CD5	U.K.	1991	$8.00
Nettwerk	67036	You're in a Mess	CDJ	U.S.	1990	$2.00

Fallon

Singles

Label	Catalog Number	Title	Type	Country	Year	Longbox Value / Value
Swanyard	CDSYD-4	Get On the Move	CD5	U.K.	1990	$8.00

Faltermayer, Harold

Singles

Label	Catalog Number	Title	Type	Country	Year	Longbox Value / Value
BMG	663867	Muscles	CD5	Germany	1990	$10.00
Eastwest	9031-76475-2	Olympic Dreams	CD5	Germany	1992	$10.00

Fam-Lee

Singles

Label	Catalog Number	Title	Type	Country	Year	Longbox Value / Value
Columbia	CSK 73979	Always On My Mind	CDJ	U.S.	1991	$2.00

Fame, Georgie

Full Length

Label	Catalog Number	Title	Type	Country	Year	Longbox Value / Value
Delta	11048	Georgie Fame	LP	Germany		$15.00
Delta	11048	Georgie Fame	LP	U.K.		$15.00

Family

Singles

Label	Catalog Number	Title	Type	Country	Year	Longbox Value / Value
Aris	883529-2	Peel Sessions	CD5	Germany	1990	$8.00
St Fruit	SFPSCD-061	Peel Sessions	CD5	U.K.	1988	$8.00

Family Cat

Singles

Label	Catalog Number	Title	Type	Country	Year	Longbox Value / Value
Bad Girl	BGRL-009SCD	Colour Me Grey	CD5	U.K.	1991	$8.00
Bad Girl	BGRLSCD-4	Nico	CD5	U.K.	1990	$8.00
Bad Girl	BGRLSCD-04	Place With a Name	CD5	U.K.	1990	$8.00
Bad Girl	BGRLSCD-03	Remember What It Is That You Love	CD5	U.K.	1990	$8.00
Dedicated	FCUK-002CD	River of Diamonds	CD5	U.K.	1992	$8.00
Dedicated	FCUK-001CD	Steamroller	CD5	U.K.	1992	$8.00

Family Foundation

Singles

Label	Catalog Number	Title	Type	Country	Year	Longbox Value / Value
PWL	PEWCD-1	Express Yourself	CD5	U.K.	1992	$8.00

Family Go Town

Singles

Label	Catalog Number	Title	Type	Country	Year	Longbox Value / Value
Vertigo	VERCD-66	Box	CD5	U.K.	1992	$8.00
Vertigo	VERCD-70	Turtle	CD5	U.K.	1992	$8.00

Family Stand

Singles

Label	Catalog Number	Title	Type	Country	Year	Longbox Value / Value
Eastwest	786210-2	Ghetto Heaven	CD5	Germany	1990	$8.00
Atlantic	AMDY-5014	Ghetto Heaven	CD3	Japan	1990	$13.00/$4.00
Atlantic	A-7997CD	Ghetto Heaven	CD5	U.K.	1990	$8.00
Atlantic	7567-86149-2	In Summer I Fall	CD5	Germany	1990	$8.00
Atlantic	A-7861CD	In Summer I Fall	CD5	U.K.	1990	$8.00
		In Summer I Fall	CDJ	U.S.	1990	$2.00
Eastwest	7567-97197-2	Shades of Blue	CD5	Germany	1991	$8.00
Eastwest	A-8593CD	Shades of Blue	CD5	U.K.	1991	$8.00

Fan Club

Singles

Label	Catalog Number	Title	Type	Country	Year	Longbox Value / Value
Epic	ESK 73321	Don't Let Me Fall Alone	CDJ	U.S.	1990	$2.00

Fancy

Singles

Label	Catalog Number	Title	Type	Country	Year	Longbox Value / Value
Polygram	873256-3	All My Loving	CD3	Germany	1990	$8.00
Polygram	873257-2	All My Loving	CD5	Germany	1990	$8.00
Polygram	889872-3	Angel Eyes	CD3	Germany	1990	$8.00
Polygram	889873-2	Angel Eyes	CD5	Germany	1990	$8.00
Polygram	887091-2	China Blue	CD5	Germany	1990	$8.00
Polygram	887469-2	Flames of Love	CD5	Germany	1988	$8.00
Polygram	887827-2	Fools Cry	CD5	Germany	1990	$8.00
ZYX	ZYX-3528-8	Fools Cry Rap	CD5	Germany	1990	$6.00
Polygram	885409-2	Lady of Ice	CD5	Germany	1990	$8.00
Polygram	885711-2	Latin Fire	CD5	Germany	1989	$8.00
Polygram	871982-3	No Tears	CD3	Germany	1989	$8.00
Polygram	871983-2	No Tears	CD5	Germany	1989	$8.00
Polygram	889207-2	Slice Me Nice	CD5	Germany	1989	$8.00

Fane, Gary

Singles

Label	Catalog Number	Title	Type	Country	Year	Longbox Value / Value
BMG	PD-43920	Wings of Purity	CD5	Germany	1990	$8.00

Fantasia

Singles

Label	Catalog Number	Title	Type	Country	Year	Longbox Value / Value
Toshiba	XP10-2045	Tonight the Night	CD3	Japan	1988	$13.00/$3.00

Fantastic Planet

Singles

Label	Catalog Number	Title	Type	Country	Year	Longbox Value / Value
A&M	AMCD-0065	Carry on Columbus	CD5	U.K.	1992	$8.00

Fantasy Strings

Full Length

Label	Catalog Number	Title	Type	Country	Year	Longbox Value / Value
Delta	11079	Day by Day	LP	Germany		$18.00
Delta	11079	Day by Day	LP	U.S.		$10.00
Delta	11079	Fantasy Strings	LP	U.K.		$18.00
Delta	11080	In Love	LP	Germany		$18.00
Delta	11080	In Love	LP	U.K.		$18.00
Delta	11080	In Love	LP	U.S.		$10.00
Delta	24031	Sound of Hits	LP	Germany		$18.00

FantasyxUFO

Singles

Label	Catalog Number	Title	Type	Country	Year	Longbox Value / Value
Eastwest	YZ-591CD	Mind, Body, Soul	CD5	U.K.	1991	$8.00

Fardon, Lee

Singles

Label	Catalog Number	Title	Type	Country	Year	Longbox Value / Value
WFT	WFT-5CD	Palestine	CD5	U.K.	1990	$8.00

Farfarello

Singles

Label	Catalog Number	Title	Type	Country	Year	Longbox Value / Value
BMG	663419	Sea of Emotion	CD5	Germany	1990	$8.00

Fargetta

Singles

Label	Catalog Number	Title	Type	Country	Year	Longbox Value / Value
ZYX	6690-8	Your Love	CD5	U.S.	1994	$5.00

Fargo, Donna

Full Length

Label	Catalog Number	Title	Type	Country	Year	Longbox Value / Value
Polygram	830236-2	Winners	LP	Germany		$15.00

Farina, Mark

Singles

Label	Catalog Number	Title	Type	Country	Year	Longbox Value / Value
Alfa	ALDB-41	Gunfire	CD3	Japan	1990	$13.00/$4.00
Alfa	09B3-77	I Love Cha Cha Cha	CD3	Japan	1990	$13.00/$4.00
Alfa	ALDB-106	Rock of Love	CD3	Japan	1991	$13.00/$4.00

Farm

Singles

Label	Catalog Number	Title	Type	Country	Year	Longbox Value / Value
Intercord	825 303	All Together Now	CD5	Germany	1991	$10.00
Produce	CD MILK 103	All Together Now	CD5	U.K.	1991	$10.00
Sire	PRO-CD-4798	All Together Now	CDJ	U.S.	1991	$3.00
		Comfort	CDJ	U.S.	1994	$6.00
Intercord	825 311	Don't Let Me Down	CD5	Germany	1991	$10.00
Produce	CDMILK-104	Don't Let Me Down	CD5	U.K.	1991	$10.00
CBS	658468-2	Don't You Want Me	CD5	U.K.	1992	$10.00
Produce	CDMILK-102	Groovy Train	CD5	U.K.	1991	$10.00
Sire	PRO-CD-4935	Groovy Train	CDJ	U.S.	1991	$3.00
Sire	PRO-CD-5068	Groovy Train	CDJ	U.S.	1991	$3.00
Produce	CDMILK-106	Love See No Color	CD5	U.K.	1992	$10.00
Produce		Love See No Color	CD5	U.K.	1992	$10.00
Second version.						
Sire	PRO-CD-5898	Love See No Color	CDJ	U.S.	1992	$3.00
Warner Brothers	W-0243CD	Messiah	CD5	U.K.	1994	$10.00
Sire	PRO-CD-6906	Messiah	CDJ	U.S.	1994	$3.00
Produce	CDMILK-105	Mind	CD5	U.K.	1991	$10.00
End Product	658173-2	Rising Sun	CD5	U.K.	1992	$10.00
Sire	9 40532-2	Rising Sun	CD5	U.S.	1992	$4.00
Sire	PRO-CD-5594	Rising Sun	CDJ	U.S.	1992	$3.00

Farm Lopez

Singles

Label	Catalog Number	Title	Type	Country	Year	Longbox Value / Value
	2002	LaKabra/Frennetic/	CD5	U.S.	1994	$5.00

Farmer, Art

Full Length

Label	Catalog Number	Title	Type	Country	Year	Longbox Value / Value
Denon	CD-7091	Ambrosia with the Great Jazz Trio	LP/LB	U.S.†	1985	$14.00/$8.00

Label	Catalog Number	Title	Type	Country	Year	Longbox Value / Value
Denon	CD-7071	Maiden Voyage	LP/LB	U.S.†	1985	$14.00/$8.00
Soul Note	CD-7071	Mirage	LP/LB	U.S.†	1985	$14.00/$8.00
East Wind	35-JD5 PSI	The Summer Knows	LP/LB	U.S.†	1985	$14.00/$8.00

Farmer, Mylene

Full Length

Label	Catalog Number	Title	Type	Country	Year	Longbox Value / Value
		California	LTD/LP	France	1995	$25.00

Singles

Label	Catalog Number	Title	Type	Country	Year	Longbox Value / Value
		Beyond My Control	CD5	France		$8.00
		Plus Grandir	CD5	France	1990	$8.00
		Sans Logique	CD5	France		$8.00
	PODP-1121	XXL	CD3	Japan		$13.00/$4.00

Farner, Mark

Full Length

Label	Catalog Number	Title	Type	Country	Year	Longbox Value / Value
		Closer to Home	LP	U.S.	1992	$15.00

Farnham, John

Full Length

Label	Catalog Number	Title	Type	Country	Year	Longbox Value / Value
RCA	3610-2-RDJ	3 Songs From Whispering Jack	DJ/Smplr	U.S.		$4.00
Intercord	847 730	Break the Ice	LP	Germany		$18.00

Singles

Label	Catalog Number	Title	Type	Country	Year	Longbox Value / Value
RCA	PD-42168	Age of Reason	CD5	Germany	1988	$9.00
RCA	R10D-103	Age of Reason	CD3	Japan	1988	$13.00/$4.00
RCA	PD-42168	Age of Reason	CD5	U.K.	1988	$9.00
RCA	CCD003	Beyond the Call	CD5	Autralia	1988	$10.00
RCA	PD-42354	Beyond the Call	CD5	Germany	1988	$9.00
RCA	PD-44216	Burn For You	CD5	Germany	1991	$9.00
RCA	PD-44216	Burn For You	CD5	U.K.	1991	$9.00
RCA	PD-44256	Chain Reaction	CD5	Germany	1990	$9.00
RCA	PD-43986	That's Freedom	CD5	Germany	1990	$9.00
RCA	PD-43986	That's Freedom	CD5	U.K.	1990	$9.00
BMG	002	Two Strong Hearts	CD5	Australia	1988	$10.00
RCA	PD-42304	Two Strong Hearts	CD5	Germany	1988	$9.00
RCA	PD-42304	Two Strong Hearts	CD5	U.K.	1988	$9.00
RCA	8915-2-RDJ	Two Strong Hearts	CDJ	U.S.	1988	$2.00
RCA	9086-2-RDJ	You're the Voice	CDJ	U.S.	1989	$2.00
RCA	2513-2-RDJ	You're the Voice	CDJ	U.S.	1990	$2.00

Farre, Marc

Singles

Label	Catalog Number	Title	Type	Country	Year	Longbox Value / Value
Mode Records	3	Margaret Maybe	CD5	U.S.	1994	$5.00

Farrell, J/Peppe

Singles

Label	Catalog Number	Title	Type	Country	Year	Longbox Value / Value
Derrick Records	141038	Darn That Dream	CD5	U.S.	1994	$5.00

Farrell, Joanne

Singles

Label	Catalog Number	Title	Type	Country	Year	Longbox Value / Value
Atlantic	95766	All I Wanna Do	CD5	U.S.	1994	$5.00

Farrell, Joe

Full Length

Label	Catalog Number	Title	Type	Country	Year	Longbox Value / Value
Columbia	460414-2	Moon Germs	LP	Germany		$15.00

Farris, Dionne

Singles

Label	Catalog Number	Title	Type	Country	Year	Longbox Value / Value
CBS	44K 77810	I Know	CD5	U.S.	1994	$5.00
CBS		I Know	CDJ	U.S.	1994	$7.00

Farrow, Cee

Singles

Label	Catalog Number	Title	Type	Country	Year	Longbox Value / Value
Graphite	1003	Imagination	CDJ	U.S.	1991	$2.00

Fascination

Singles

Label	Catalog Number	Title	Type	Country	Year	Longbox Value / Value
SPV	8412	Serious	CD5	Germany	1989	$8.00

Fashek, Majek

Singles

Label	Catalog Number	Title	Type	Country	Year	Longbox Value / Value
Interscope	PRCD 4186-2	Spirit of Love	CDJ	U.S.	1991	$2.00

Fassie, Brenda

Singles

Label	Catalog Number	Title	Type	Country	Year	Longbox Value / Value
		Black President	CDJ	U.S.		$2.00

Fast Bucks

Singles

Label	Catalog Number	Title	Type	Country	Year	Longbox Value / Value
Sub Pop	8	Gone to the Moon	CDJ	U.S.	1993	$2.00

Fast Eddie

Singles

Label	Catalog Number	Title	Type	Country	Year	Longbox Value / Value
CBS	655366-2	Get On Up	CD5	U.K.	1989	$8.00
ZYX	6081-8	Jack To the Sound	CD5	Germany	1989	$6.00

Fast, Eddie & Dj S

Singles

Label	Catalog Number	Title	Type	Country	Year	Longbox Value / Value
Strictly Hype	120	Body Call	CD5	U.S.	1994	$5.00

Fast Freddie's Fingertips

Singles

Label	Catalog Number	Title	Type	Country	Year	Longbox Value / Value
Phoenix	CHARCD-2	Back On the Tools	CD5	U.K.	1992	$8.00
Phoenix	CHARCD-3	Costa Brava Love	CD5	U.K.	1992	$8.00

Fastbacks

Singles

Label	Catalog Number	Title	Type	Country	Year	Longbox Value / Value
Sub Pop	189	Gone To the Home	CD5	U.S.	1993	$4.00

Faster Pussycat

Full Length

Label	Catalog Number	Title	Type	Country	Year	Longbox Value / Value
Elektra		Wake Me When It's Over	LP/LB	U.S.		$14.00/$8.00
Elektra		Whipped	LP/LB	U.S.		$14.00/$8.00

Singles

Label	Catalog Number	Title	Type	Country	Year	Longbox Value / Value
Elektra	66396-2	Belted Buckled	CD5	U.S.	1992	$8.00
Elektra	PRCD 8661-2	Body Thief, The	CDJ	U.S.	1992	$2.00
WEA	964967-2	House of Pain	CD5	Germany	1989	$10.00
Elektra	EKR-112CD	House of Pain	CD5	U.K.	1989	$10.00
Elektra	PR 8139-2	House of Pain	CDJ	U.S.	1989	$2.00
Elektra	WMD5-4112	Non Stop to Nowhere	CD3	Japan	1992	$12.00/$4.00
Elektra	EKR-153CD	Non Stop to Nowhere	CD5	U.K.	1992	$10.00
Elektra	PRCD 8610-2	Non Stop to Nowhere	CDJ	U.S.	1992	$2.00
Elektra	PR 8105-2	Poison Ivy	CDJ	U.S.	1989	$2.00
Elektra	PR 8213-2	Where There's a Whip There's a Way	CDJ	U.S.	1990	$2.00
Elektra	PRCD 8222-2	You're So Vain	CDJ	U.S.	1990	$3.00

Fastway

Full Length

Label	Catalog Number	Title	Type	Country	Year	Longbox Value / Value
CBS	CK-39373	All Fired Up	LP/BP	U.S.†	1984	$14.00/$8.00

Singles

Label	Catalog Number	Title	Type	Country	Year	Longbox Value / Value
Enigma	EPRO-168	A Fine Line	CDJ	U.S.	1989	$2.00
Legacy	LGYC 104	Bad Bad Girls	CD5	Sweden	1990	$10.00
Enigma		Bad Bad Girls	CDJ	U.S.	1989	$2.00

Fat and Frantic

Singles

Label	Catalog Number	Title	Type	Country	Year	Longbox Value / Value
Icy	FATO-2	I Don't Want to Say Goodbye	CD5	U.K.	1990	$8.00
Icy	FATO-1	Last Night My Wife Hoovered My Head	CD5	U.K.	1990	$8.00

Fat Boys

Singles

Label	Catalog Number	Title	Type	Country	Year	Longbox Value / Value
Urban	URCD-35	Are You Ready	CD5	U.K.	1989	$8.00
Polygram	871525	Baby, You're a Rich Man	CD5	Germany	1989	$8.00
Polygram	873353-2	If It Ain't One Thing It's Another	CD5	Germany	1989	$8.00
Mercury	CDP 106	Lie Z	CDJ	U.S.	1989	$2.00
Polygram	871049-2	Louie, Louie	CD5	Germany	1988	$8.00
Urban	URCDD-26	Louie, Louie	CD5	U.K.	1988	$8.00
Polygram	887638-2	Twist, The	CD5	Germany	1988	$8.00
Urban	URCD-20	Twist, The	CD5	U.K.	1988	$8.00
Mercury	870 742-2	Twist, The	CDV/BP	U.S.	1988	$20.00/$20.00
Emperor	PO86	Whip It On	CDJ	U.S.	1991	$2.00
Polydor	P10P-30014	Wipeout	CD3	Japan	1988	$13.00/$4.00
Polygram	870 706-2	Wipeout	CDV/BP	U.S.	1988	$20.00/$20.00

Fat Lady Sings

Singles

Label	Catalog Number	Title	Type	Country	Year	Longbox Value / Value
Eastwest	YZ-560CD	Arclight	CD5	U.K.	1991	$8.00
Eastwest	[illegible]	Deborah	CD5	U.K.	1991	$8.00
Eastwest	YZ-537CD	Man Scared	CD5	U.K.	1991	$8.00
Atlantic	PRCD 5196-2	Show of Myself	CDJ	U.S.	1993	$2.00
Eastwest	YZ-586CD	Twist	CD5	U.K.	1991	$8.00

Fat Larry's Band

Singles

Label	Catalog Number	Title	Type	Country	Year	Longbox Value / Value
Virgin	CDT-31	Zoom	CD3	U.K.	1988	$8.00

Fat Slags

Singles

Label	Catalog Number	Title	Type	Country	Year	Longbox Value / Value
PWL	4509-90695-2	Summer Holiday	CD5	Germany	1992	$8.00
PWL	PWCD-243	Summer Holiday	CD5	U.K.	1992	$8.00

Fat Tuesday

Singles

Label	Catalog Number	Title	Type	Country	Year	Longbox Value / Value
Columbia	CSK 4823	Califuneral	CDJ	U.S.	1992	$2.00

Fat Tulips

Singles

Label	Catalog Number	Title	Type	Country	Year	Longbox Value / Value
Vinyl	TASK-8	Nostalgia	CD5	U.K.	1992	$8.00

Fatal Attraction

Singles

Label	Catalog Number	Title	Type	Country	Year	Longbox Value / Value
ZYX	6029-8	Music To Be Murdered By	CD5	Germany	1988	$6.00

Fatal Flowers

Singles

Label	Catalog Number	Title	Type	Country	Year	Longbox Value / Value
		Rock & Roll Star	CD5	U.S.		$2.00

Fatback

Singles

Label	Catalog Number	Title	Type	Country	Year	Longbox Value / Value
ZYX	5881-8	All Nite Party	CD5	Germany	1988	$6.00

Fate

Full Length

Label	Catalog Number	Title	Type	Country	Year	Longbox Value / Value
EMI	7 91264 0	Cruisin' For A Bruisin'	LTD/LP	Germany	1988	$15.00

Picture disc CD.

Label	Catalog Number	Title	Type	Country	Year	Longbox Value / Value
EMI	7 46568-2	Matter of Attitude	LP	Germany		$15.00

Singles

Label	Catalog Number	Title	Type	Country	Year	Longbox Value / Value
EMI	138746-2	Lovers	CD5	Germany	1988	$8.00

Fates Warning

Full Length

Label	Catalog Number	Title	Type	Country	Year	Longbox Value / Value
Metal Blade	26698	Parallels	LP/LB	U.S.		$15.00/$9.00

Singles

Label	Catalog Number	Title	Type	Country	Year	Longbox Value / Value
Metal Blade	PROCD-5289	Eye to Eye	CDJ	U.S.	1991	$2.00
Metal Blade	PROCD-4281	Nothing Left to Say	CDJ	U.S.	1990	$2.00
Metal Blade	PROCD-4293	Point Of View	CDJ	U.S.	1991	$2.00

Father Father

Singles

Label	Catalog Number	Title	Type	Country	Year	Longbox Value / Value
Go Discs	GODCD-52	Father Father	CD5	U.K.	1991	$8.00
Polygram	869417-2	Love Life and Love Living	CD5	Germany	1991	$8.00
Polygram	869579-2	Washington Rain	CD5	Germany	1991	$8.00
Polygram	8694393-2	What Is a Soul	CD5	Germany	1991	$8.00

Father M.C.

Singles

Label	Catalog Number	Title	Type	Country	Year	Longbox Value / Value
Uptown	2829	69	CDJ	U.S.	1993	$2.00
MCA	MCA5P-54524	Everything's Gonna Be Alright	CD5	U.S.	1992	$2.00
Uptown	2918	I Beeped You	CDJ	U.S.	1993	$2.00
Uptown	1507	I've Been Watching You	CDJ	U.S.	1993	$2.00
		Lisa Baby	CDJ	U.S.		$2.00
MCA	54446	One Night Stand	CD5	U.S.	1992	$4.00
MCA	MCA5P-2421	One Night Stand	CDJ	U.S.	1992	$2.00
		Treat Them Like They Want To Be Treated	CDJ	U.S.		$2.00

Fatima Mansions

Full Length

Label	Catalog Number	Title	Type	Country	Year	Longbox Value / Value
Album Network		Album Network Special	RS	U.S.	1994	$40.00

Airdate: 11/18/94.

Singles

Label	Catalog Number	Title	Type	Country	Year	Longbox Value / Value
SPV	8689-3	Blues for Causescue	CD5	Germany	1990	$8.00
Radioactive	54152	Blues for Causescue	CD5	U.S.	1991	$4.00
Radioactive	PRO-CD-2029	Blues for Causescue	CDJ	U.S.	1991	$2.00
Radioactive	SKXD 56	Evil Man	CDJ	U.S.	1992	$2.00
Radioactive	SKXD-53	You're a Rose	CD5	U.K.	1991	$8.00

Fatman

Singles

Label	Catalog Number	Title	Type	Country	Year	Longbox Value / Value
ffrr	FCD-140	Release Me	CD5	U.K.	1990	$8.00

Fattburger

Singles

Label	Catalog Number	Title	Type	Country	Year	Longbox Value / Value
		Oh Girl	CDJ	U.S.		$2.00

Fauves

Singles

Label	Catalog Number	Title	Type	Country	Year	Longbox Value/Value
Polydor	8594172	Thin Body Thin Body	CD5	Austalia	1993	$8.00

Favorite Angel

Singles

Label	Catalog Number	Title	Type	Country	Year	Longbox Value/Value
Columbia	CSK 73476	Only Women Bleed	CDJ	U.S.	1990	$2.00

Faze One FM

Singles

Label	Catalog Number	Title	Type	Country	Year	Longbox Value/Value
BMG	663477	Listen to the Band	CD5	U.K.	1990	$8.00

Fazer

Singles

Label	Catalog Number	Title	Type	Country	Year	Longbox Value/Value
Generator	GEN-9102-8	Tekknological Crime	CD5	Germany	1992	$8.00

FCMP

Singles

Label	Catalog Number	Title	Type	Country	Year	Longbox Value/Value
Boy	BOY-8826-8	Demon Dance	CD5	Germany	1991	$8.00

Fear of God

Full Length

Label	Catalog Number	Title	Type	Country	Year	Longbox Value/Value
		Within the Veil	DJ/LP	U.S.		$6.00

Singles

Label	Catalog Number	Title	Type	Country	Year	Longbox Value/Value
Warner Brothers	PRO-CD-4776	Betrayed	CDJ	U.S.	1991	$2.00

Fearing, Stephen

Singles

Label	Catalog Number	Title	Type	Country	Year	Longbox Value/Value
		Race of Fractions	CDJ	Canada		$3.00

Federal Base

Singles

Label	Catalog Number	Title	Type	Country	Year	Longbox Value/Value
ZYX	6779-8	Anybody Out There	CD5	Germany	1992	$6.00

Feelies

Singles

Label	Catalog Number	Title	Type	Country	Year	Longbox Value/Value
Coyote	75021 7537 2	Doin' It Again	CDJ	U.S.	1991	$2.00
A&M	CD 17675	Higher Ground	CDJ	U.S.	1989	$2.00
A&M	CD 17712	Higher Ground	CDJ	U.S.	1989	$6.00
A&M	75021 7225 2	Invitation	CDJ	U.S.	1991	$2.00
A&M	75021 7519 2	Sooner or Later	CDJ	U.S.	1991	$2.00

Feinstein, Michael

Singles

Label	Catalog Number	Title	Type	Country	Year	Longbox Value/Value
Elektra	PRCD 8223-2	Both Sides Now	CDJ	U.S.	1990	$2.00

Feivel & Friends

Singles

Label	Catalog Number	Title	Type	Country	Year	Longbox Value/Value
MCA	MCA 5P-2076	Diddy Diddy Dum Dum	CDJ	U.S.	1991	$2.00

Felder, Wilton

Singles

Label	Catalog Number	Title	Type	Country	Year	Longbox Value/Value
Par	9018	Forever	CDJ	U.S.	1993	$2.00
Par	9007	Since I Fell For You	CDJ	U.S.	1991	$2.00

Feldman, Morton

Singles

Label	Catalog Number	Title	Type	Country	Year	Longbox Value/Value
Elektra	79320-2	Piano & String Quartet	CDJ	U.S.	1993	$3.00
	With Kronos Quartet.					

Felguera, Garcia

Singles

Label	Catalog Number	Title	Type	Country	Year	Longbox Value/Value
CBS	655977-3	Amore	CD3	Germany	1990	$8.00

Feliciano, Jose

Full Length

Label	Catalog Number	Title	Type	Country	Year	Longbox Value/Value
RCA	886210	Feliciano	LP	Germany		$15.00
RCA	66595	Feliciano	LTD/LP	U.S.	1995	$28.00
	Gold disc.					

Singles

Label	Catalog Number	Title	Type	Country	Year	Longbox Value/Value
RCA	64224	Feliz Navidad	CD5	U.S.	1994	$5.00
		Heart Don't Change My Mind	CDJ	U.S.		$2.00
EMI	203430-3	Into the Night	CD3	Germany	1989	$8.00
RCA	PD-49459	Light My Fire	CD3	Germany	1989	$8.00
RCA	PD-49459	Light My Fire	CD3	U.K.	1989	$8.00
EMI	203522-3	Living in a World	CD3	Germany	1989	$8.00
EMI	203247-2	Never Gonna Change	CD5	Germany	1989	$8.00
EMI	204141-2	Solitary Lady	CD5	Germany	1989	$8.00

Felix

Singles

Label	Catalog Number	Title	Type	Country	Year	Longbox Value/Value
RCA	74321-110502	Don't You Want Me	CD5	U.K.	1992	$8.00
RCA	74321-111813	It Will Make Me Crazy	CD5	U.K.	1992	$8.00

Felt

Singles

Label	Catalog Number	Title	Type	Country	Year	Longbox Value/Value
Cherry Red	CDCHERRY-89	Primitive Painters	CD5	U.K.	1988	$8.00
Cherry Red	CDCHERRY-121	Primitive Painters	CD5	U.K.	1988	$8.00

Feltman

Singles

Label	Catalog Number	Title	Type	Country	Year	Longbox Value/Value
EMI	204538-2	Healing	CD5	Germany	1991	$8.00

Fem 2 Fem

Singles

Label	Catalog Number	Title	Type	Country	Year	Longbox Value/Value
'Tique	15503	Switch	CD5	U.S.	1993	$4.00
Critique	15537	Where Did Love Go	CD5	U.S.	1994	$5.00

Femme Fatale

Singles

Label	Catalog Number	Title	Type	Country	Year	Longbox Value/Value
MCA	DMCAT-1309	Falling in and Out of Love	CD5	U.K.	1989	$9.00
MCA	CD45 17700	Falling in and Out of Love	CDJ	U.S.	1988	$3.00
MCA	CD45 17787	Rebel	CDJ	U.S.	1988	$2.00

Fence Of Defense

Singles

Label	Catalog Number	Title	Type	Country	Year	Longbox Value/Value
Epic	ESDB-3299	Don't Look Back	CD3	Japan	1992	$13.00/$4.00
Epic	ESDB-3361	Forever in Love	CD3	Japan	1992	$13.00/$4.00
Epic	ESDB-3374	Mou Ichido Emotion	CD3	Japan	1992	$13.00/$4.00
Epic	ESDB-3217	Toki No Kawa	CD3	Japan	1992	$13.00/$4.00

Fender, Freddy

Singles

Label	Catalog Number	Title	Type	Country	Year	Longbox Value/Value
Reprise	PRO-CD-5049	It's All in the Game	CDJ	U.S.	1991	$2.00

Fender, Jack

Full Length

Label	Catalog Number	Title	Type	Country	Year	Longbox Value/Value
Delta	DELTA-11014	Golden Guitar Tops	LP	Germany		$18.00
Delta	DELTA-11014	Golden Guitar Tops	LP	U.K.		$18.00

Fenton, George

Singles

Label	Catalog Number	Title	Type	Country	Year	Longbox Value/Value
MCA	DMCAT-1228	Cry Freedom	CD5	U.K.	1990	$10.00

Fents

Full Length

Label	Catalog Number	Title	Type	Country	Year	Longbox Value/Value
Passport	PJCD-88031	Other Side	LP	U.K.		$15.00
Passport	PJCD-88031	Other Side	LP	U.S.		$15.00

Ferguson, Maynard

Full Length

Label	Catalog Number	Title	Type	Country	Year	Longbox Value/Value
CBS	36361	Best of	LP/LB	U.S.		$14.00/$8.00
CBS	CK-34457	Conquistador	LP/LB	U.S.†	1985	$14.00/$8.00
Blue Note	CDP 95334-2	Si Si M.F.	LP/LB	U.S.		$18.00/$15.00

Ferguson, Wilson

Singles

Label	Catalog Number	Title	Type	Country	Year	Longbox Value/Value
Canyon	S10Y-1020	I'm Singing Again	CD3	Japan	1988	$12.00/$4.00
Canyon	PCDY-00005	Show Me	CD3	Japan	1988	$12.00/$4.00

Ferrell, Rachelle

Singles

Label	Catalog Number	Title	Type	Country	Year	Longbox Value/Value
Capitol	DPRO 79803	Sentimental	CDJ	U.S.	1992	$2.00
Capitol	DPRO-79603	Welcome to My Love	CDJ	U.S.	1992	$2.00
Capitol	DPRO-79541	Welcome to My Love	CDJ	U.S.	1992	$2.00

Ferrick, Melissa

Singles

Label	Catalog Number	Title	Type	Country	Year	Longbox Value/Value
Atlantic	PRCD 5205-2	Juliana Hatfield Song, The	CDJ	U.S.	1993	$6.00
Atlantic	PRCD 5205-2	Love Song	CDJ	U.S.	1993	$2.00

Ferron

Full Length

Label	Catalog Number	Title	Type	Country	Year	Longbox Value/Value
SPV	3077	Shadows on A Dime	LP	Germany		$15.00

Ferry, Bryan

Full Length

Label	Catalog Number	Title	Type	Country	Year	Longbox Value/Value
Warner Brothers	9 25082-2	Boys and Girls	LP/LB	U.S.†	1985	$14.00/$8.00
Reprise		Bride Stripped Bare	LP/LB	U.S.		$14.00/$8.00
Reprise		In Your Mind	LP/LB	U.S.		$14.00/$8.00
Reprise		Interview	DJ/Intvw	U.S.	1994	$15.00
Reprise		Let's Stick Together	LP/LB	U.S.		$14.00/$8.00
Virgin		Mamouna	DJ/Smplr	U.K.	1994	$25.00
Virgin	DPRO-14227	Mamouna	DJ/Smplr	U.S.	1994	$15.00
		These Foolish Things	LP	U.S.		$12.00

Singles

Label	Catalog Number	Title	Type	Country	Year	Longbox Value/Value
		Are You Lonesome Tonight	CDJ	Canada		$8.00
		Don't Want to Know	CDJ	Japan		$25.00
Virgin	EGOCD-48	He'll Have to Go	CD3	U.K.	1989	$10.00
Virgin	VJDP-10204	I Put a Spell on You	CD3	Japan	1993	$12.00/$4.00
Virgin	VSCDG-1400	I Put a Spell on You	CD5	U.K.	1993	$10.00
Virgin		I Put a Spell on You	CD5	U.K.	1993	$10.00
	Second version.					
Reprise	PRO-CD-6078	I Put a Spell on You	CDJ	U.S.	1993	$3.00
Virgin	659701	Kiss & Tell	CD5	Germany	1987	$10.00
Virgin	VJD-12001	Kiss & Tell	CD3	Japan	1987	$12.00/$4.00
Virgin	CDEP-19	Kiss & Tell	CD5	U.K.	1987	$10.00
Reprise	PRO-CD-2909	Kiss & Tell	CDJ	U.S.	1987	$6.00
Aris	880987	Let's Stick Together	CD3	Germany	1988	$10.00
Virgin	661657	Let's Stick Together	CD5	Germany	1988	$10.00
Virgin	CDT-10	Let's Stick Together	CD3	U.K.	1988	$10.00
Virgin	EGOCD-44	Let's Stick Together	CD5	U.K.	1988	$10.00
Virgin	659986	Limbo	CD5	Germany	1988	$10.00
Virgin	VJD-12023	Limbo	CD3	Japan	1988	$12.00/$4.00
Virgin	VSCD-1066	Limbo	CD5	U.K.	1988	$10.00
Reprise	PRO-CD-2910	Limbo	CDJ	U.S.	1988	$3.00
		Mamouna	CDJ	U.S.		$3.00
Capital	38458	Mamouna	CD3	U.S.	1994	$5.00
Virgin	162164	Price of Love	CD3	Germany	1989	$10.00
Virgin	EGOCD-46	Price of Love	CD3	U.K.	1989	$10.00
Virign	659449	Right Stuff, The	CD5	Germany	1987	$10.00
Virgin	CDEP-8	Right Stuff, The	CD5	U.K.	1987	$10.00
Reprise	PRO-CD-2853	Right Stuff, The	CDJ	U.S.	1987	$6.00
Virgin		Taxi	CDJ	U.K.	1994	$23.00
Virgin	VSCDT 1455	Will You Love Me Tomorrow	CD5	U.K.	1993	$10.00
Virgin		Will You Love Me Tomorrow	CD5	U.K.	1993	$10.00
	Second version.					
Reprise	9 40949-2	Will You Love Me Tomorrow	CD5	U.S.	1993	$5.00
Reprise		Will You Love Me Tomorrow	CDJ	U.S.	1993	$3.00

Festa Mode

Singles

Label	Catalog Number	Title	Type	Country	Year	Longbox Value/Value
Tokuma	TKDA-30751	Season of Glass	CD3	Japan	1992	$13.00/$4.00

Fetchin' Bones

Singles

Label	Catalog Number	Title	Type	Country	Year	Longbox Value/Value
Capitol	DPRO-79684	Love Crushing	CDJ	U.S.	1989	$2.00

FFF

Singles

Label	Catalog Number	Title	Type	Country	Year	Longbox Value/Value
Epic	ESCA-5682	Devil In Me	CD5	Japan	1992	$10.00
Epic	ESCA-5556	New Funk Gerneration	CD5	Japan	1992	$10.00

Fiagbe, Lena

Singles

Label	Catalog Number	Title	Type	Country	Year	Longbox Value/Value
		Gotta Get It Reach	CD5	U.K.		$8.00
		Gotta Get It Reach	CD5	U.K.		$8.00
	Second version.					
		Visions	CD5	U.K.		$10.00
		Visions	CD5	U.K.		$10.00
	Second version.					

Fibbers, Geraldine

Singles

Label	Catalog Number	Title	Type	Country	Year	Longbox Value/Value
		Bitter Honey	CDJ	U.S.		$3.00

Fiction

Singles

Label	Catalog Number	Title	Type	Country	Year	Longbox Value/Value
PWL	PWCD-225	Organomics	CD5	U.K.	1992	$8.00

Fields of the Nephilim

Full Length

Label	Catalog Number	Title	Type	Country	Year	Longbox Value / Value
Vertigo		Elizium	LP	Canada		$10.00
Beggars Banquet		Elizium	LP/LB	U.S.		$12.00/$7.00

Singles

Label	Catalog Number	Title	Type	Country	Year	Longbox Value / Value
SPV	3084-3	For Her Light	CD5	Germany	1990	$8.00
Beggars Banquet	BEG-244CD	For Her Light	CD5	U.K.	1990	$8.00
SPV	3021-3	Psychonaut	CD5	Germany	1989	$8.00
Pinnacle	SIT-57CD	Psychonaut	CD5	U.K.	1989	$8.00
Beggars Banquet	BEG-250CD	Sumerland	CD5	U.K.	1990	$8.00

Fields, Richard "Dimples"

Full Length

Label	Catalog Number	Title	Type	Country	Year	Longbox Value / Value
RCA	PCD1-5169	Mmm...	LP/BP	U.S.†	1984	$12.00/$7.00

Fierce Ruling Diva

Singles

Label	Catalog Number	Title	Type	Country	Year	Longbox Value / Value
Medicine	40828	Get Funky With Me	CD5	U.S.	1993	$4.00
React	CDREACT-3	Rubb It In	CD5	U.K.	1992	$8.00

Fifth Angel

Full Length

Label	Catalog Number	Title	Type	Country	Year	Longbox Value / Value
Epic	EK 44201	Fifth Angel	LP/LB	U.S.		$15.00/$12.00

Fifth Dimension

Singles

Label	Catalog Number	Title	Type	Country	Year	Longbox Value / Value
Columbia	44K 77647	Medley	CD5	U.S.	1994	$5.00
Arista	162064	Up, Up and Away	CD3	Germany	1989	$10.00
Arista	162064	Up, Up and Away	CD3	U.K.	1989	$10.00

Fifth Platoon

Singles

Label	Catalog Number	Title	Type	Country	Year	Longbox Value / Value
SBK	DPRO-05381	Partyline, The	CDJ	U.S.	1991	$2.00

Fifty-Four Forty

Full Length

Label	Catalog Number	Title	Type	Country	Year	Longbox Value / Value
Warner Brothers	9 25961-2	Fight for Love	LP/LB	U.S.		$14.00/$8.00
Warner Brothers	9 25572-2	Show Me	LP/LB	U.S.		$14.00/$8.00
		Smilin' Budda Cabaret	DJ/Smplr	Canada		$15.00

Singles

Label	Catalog Number	Title	Type	Country	Year	Longbox Value / Value
		Blame Your Parents	CDJ	Canada		$8.00
		Music Man	CDJ	Canada		$8.00
Columbia	44K-3188	Music Man	CD5	Canada	1993	$8.00
		Nice to Luv You	CDJ	Canada		$8.00
Warner Brothers	PRO-CD-2912	One Day in Your Life	CDJ	U.S.		$2.00
		She La	CDJ	Canada		$8.00

Fifty-Four Forty-Six

Singles

Label	Catalog Number	Title	Type	Country	Year	Longbox Value / Value
Island	CIDMX-743	You'll Never Get to Heaven	CD5	U.K.	1990	$8.00

Fifty-Second Street

Full Length

Label	Catalog Number	Title	Type	Country	Year	Longbox Value / Value
Ariola	257583	Children of the Night	LP	Germany		$10.00

Fight

Full Length

Label	Catalog Number	Title	Type	Country	Year	Longbox Value / Value
Foundations		FZ Interview	RS/VA	U.S.	1993	$8.00

Singles

Label	Catalog Number	Title	Type	Country	Year	Longbox Value / Value
		Blowout in the Radio Room	CDJ	U.S.		$3.00
		Christmas Ride	CDJ	U.S.		$12.00
Epic	ESK 5599	Immortal Sin	CDJ	U.S.	1994	$3.00
Epic	ESK 5496	Little Crazy	CDJ	U.S.	1994	$3.00
Epic	ESK 5353	Nailed to the Gun	CDJ	U.S.	1993	$3.00

Figures on the Beach

Full Length

Label	Catalog Number	Title	Type	Country	Year	Longbox Value / Value
WEA	925804-1	Figures On The Beach	LP	Germany		$18.00

Singles

Label	Catalog Number	Title	Type	Country	Year	Longbox Value / Value
Sire	PRO-CD-3614	Accidentally 4th Street	CDJ	U.S.	1989	$2.00
Sire	PRO-CD-3486	You Ain't Seen Nothing Yet	CDJ	U.S.	1989	$2.00
Sire	PRO-CD-3523	You Ain't Seen Nothing Yet	CDJ	U.S.	1989	$2.00

Filter

Full Length

Label	Catalog Number	Title	Type	Country	Year	Longbox Value / Value
Westwood One		In Concert	RS	U.S.	1996	$25.00

Singles

Label	Catalog Number	Title	Type	Country	Year	Longbox Value / Value
Warner Brothers	PRO-CD-7456-R	Hey Man Nice Shot	CDJ	U.S.	1995	$3.00
Warner Brothers		Jurassitol	CDJ	U.S.	1995	$6.00

Final Cut

Singles

Label	Catalog Number	Title	Type	Country	Year	Longbox Value / Value
Nettwerk	13864	Testament	CDJ	U.S.	1992	$2.00

Fine Young Cannibals

Singles

Label	Catalog Number	Title	Type	Country	Year	Longbox Value / Value
Polygram	886688-3	Don't Look Back	CD3	Germany	1989	$9.00
London	886689-2	Don't Look Back	CD5	Germany	1989	$9.00
Polydor	POOL-37018	Don't Look Back	CD3	Japan	1989	$13.00/$4.00
Polydor	POOL-40014	Don't Look Back	CD3	Japan	1989	$13.00/$4.00
London	LONCD 220	Don't Look Back	CD5	U.K.	1989	$9.00
IRS	CD45 17895	Don't Look Back	CDJ	U.S.	1989	$2.00
Polygram	88615-2	Ever Fallen in Love	CD5	Germany	1987	$9.00
London	LONCD-121	Ever Fallen in Love	CD5	U.K.	1987	$9.00
Polygram	886558-3	Good Thing	CD3	Germany	1989	$9.00
Polygram	886559-2	Good Thing	CD5	Germany	1989	$9.00
London	POOL-40011	Good Thing	CD3	Japan	1989	$13.00/$4.00
London	POOL-37015	Good Thing	CD3	Japan	1989	$13.00/$4.00
London	LONCD-217	Good Thing	CD5	U.K.	1989	$9.00
London	LONCD-218	Good Thing	CD5	U.K.	1989	$9.00
IRS	CD45 17831	Good Thing	CDJ	U.S.	1989	$2.00
Polygram	886943-2	I'm Not Satisfied	CD5	Germany	1990	$9.00
London	LONCD-252	I'm Not Satisfied	CD5	U.K.	1990	$9.00
MCA	CD45 18142	I'm Not Satisfied	CDJ	U.S.	1988	$2.00
Polygram	886816-3	I'm Not the Man I Used to Be	CD3	Germany	1989	$9.00
Polygram	886817-2	I'm Not the Man I Used to Be	CD5	Germany	1989	$9.00
London	POOL-20131	I'm Not the Man I Used to Be	CD3	Japan	1989	$13.00/$4.00
London	LONCD-244	I'm Not the Man I Used to Be	CD5	U.K.	1989	$9.00
IRS	CD4517957	I'm Not the Man I Used to Be	CDJ	U.S.	1989	$2.00
IRS	CD45 18098	I'm Not the Man I Used to Be	CDJ	U.S.	1989	$2.00
Polygram	869129-2	It's O.K.	CD5	Germany	1990	$9.00
Polygram	869259-2	Johnny Come Home	CD5	Germany	1991	$9.00
Polygram	886361-3	She Drives Me Crazy	CD3	Germany	1988	$9.00
London	886361-2	She Drives Me Crazy	CD5	Germany	1988	$9.00
London	POOL-37012	She Drives Me Crazy	CD3	Japan	1988	$13.00/$4.00
London	LONCD-199	She Drives Me Crazy	CD5	U.K.	1988	$9.00

Finitribe

Singles

Label	Catalog Number	Title	Type	Country	Year	Longbox Value / Value
Rough Trade	230-1150-3	Ace Love Deuce	CD5	Germany	1991	$8.00
Pinnacle	7TP-31CD	Animal Farm	CD5	U.K.	1989	$8.00
Pinnacle	74-TP7CD	Forevergreen	CD5	U.K.	1992	$8.00
Epic	49K 74433	Forevergreen	CD5	U.S.	1993	$5.00
SPV	0515-3	Make It Internal	CD5	Germany	1990	$8.00
Pinnacle	54TP7-CD	One-O-One	CD5	U.K.	1991	$8.00

Fink, Matt

Singles

Label	Catalog Number	Title	Type	Country	Year	Longbox Value / Value
	7501	Music of the Angels	CD5	U.S.	1994	$5.00

Finn

Singles

Label	Catalog Number	Title	Type	Country	Year	Longbox Value / Value
		Angel's Heap	CD5	U.K.		$10.00
		Angel's Heap	CD5	U.K.		$10.00
	Second version.					
		Suffer Never	CD5	U.K.		$10.00
		Suffer Never	CD5	U.K.		$10.00
	Second version.					

Finn Brothers

Singles

Label	Catalog Number	Title	Type	Country	Year	Longbox Value / Value
		Only Talking Sense	CDJ	U.S.	1996	$7.00

Finn, Tim

Full Length

Label	Catalog Number	Title	Type	Country	Year	Longbox Value / Value
EMI		Before and After	DJ/Smplr	U.K.	1994	$15.00
EMI		Live at the Borderline	DJ/Smplr	U.K.		$35.00

Singles

Label	Catalog Number	Title	Type	Country	Year	Longbox Value / Value
Capitol	DPRO-[illegible]	Crescendo	CDJ	U.S.	1989	$2.00
EMI	80892	Hit the Ground	CD5	U.K.	1993	$9.00
EMI		Hit the Ground	CD5	U.K.	1993	$9.00
	Second version.					
Capitol	DPRO-79573	How'm I Gonna Sleep	CDJ	U.S.	1989	$2.00
		Many's the Time	CD5	Australia	1994	$12.00
Capitol	DPRO-79860	Not Even Close	CDJ	U.S.	1990	$2.00
EMI		Persuasion	CD5	U.K.	1993	$10.00
EMI		Persuasion	CD5	U.K.	1993	$10.00
	Second version.					
Capitol	DPRO-79766	Persuasion	CDJ	U.S.	1993	$2.00

Fiona

Full Length

Label	Catalog Number	Title	Type	Country	Year	Longbox Value / Value
WEA	781903-2	Heart Like a Gun	LP	Germany		$23.00

Singles

Label	Catalog Number	Title	Type	Country	Year	Longbox Value / Value
Geffen	PRO-CD-4378	Ain't That Just Like Love	CDJ	U.S.	1991	$2.00
Geffen	PRO-CD-4426	Don't Come Crying	CDJ	U.S.	1992	$2.00
Atlantic	PR 2911-2	Everything You Do	CDJ	U.S.	1989	$2.00
Atlantic	PRCD 3277-2	Little Jeanie	CDJ	U.S.	1989	$2.00
Atlantic	PR 3161-2	Where the Cowboys Go	CDJ	U.S.	1989	$2.00

Fiordaliso

Singles

Label	Catalog Number	Title	Type	Country	Year	Longbox Value / Value
EMI	118861-2	I Love You Man	CD5	Germany	1991	$8.00

Fiorillo, Elisa

Full Length

Label	Catalog Number	Title	Type	Country	Year	Longbox Value / Value
Aris	880970	Elisa Fiorillo	LP	Germany		$18.00

Singles

Label	Catalog Number	Title	Type	Country	Year	Longbox Value / Value
Chrysalis	ELISCD-2	Forgive Me For Dreaming	CD5	U.K.	1988	$8.00
Toshiba	XP10-2006	High Bright Night	CD3	Japan	1988	$13.00/$4.00
Toshiba	XP15-5001	High Bright Night	CD3	Japan	1988	$13.00/$4.00
Chrysalis	ELISCD-1	How Can I Forget You	CD5	U.K.	1988	$8.00
Chrysalis	TOCP-6471	On the Way Up	CD3	Japan	1990	$13.00/$4.00
Chrysalis	TODP-2179	On the Way Up	CD3	Japan	1990	$13.00/$4.00
Chrysalis	CHSCD-3609	On the Way Up	CD5	U.K.	1990	$8.00
Chrysalis	DPRO-23497	On the Way Up	CDJ	U.S.	1990	$2.00
Chrysalis	DPRO-23599	On the Way Up	CDJ	U.S.	1990	$2.00
Chrysalis	DPRO-23670	Ooh This I Need	CDJ	U.S.	1991	$2.00

Fire Engines

Singles

Label	Catalog Number	Title	Type	Country	Year	Longbox Value / Value
Creation	CREV 001	Fond	CD5	France	1992	$8.00

Fire Next Time

Singles

Label	Catalog Number	Title	Type	Country	Year	Longbox Value / Value
Polydor	FNTCD-2	Stay With Me Now	CD5	U.K.	1988	$8.00
Polydor	FNTCD-1	Too Close	CD5	U.K.	1988	$8.00

Fire On Blonde

Singles

Label	Catalog Number	Title	Type	Country	Year	Longbox Value / Value
Pioneer	10P3-6017	Bounce Back	CD3	Japan	1988	$13.00/$4.00

Fire Town

Singles

Label	Catalog Number	Title	Type	Country	Year	Longbox Value / Value
	PR 2767-2	She Reminds Me Of You	CDJ	U.S.	1989	$2.00

Firehose

Full Length

Label	Catalog Number	Title	Type	Country	Year	Longbox Value / Value
Columbia	CSK 5122	Big Bottom Pow Wow	DJ/Intvw	U.S.		$20.00
Columbia	CSK 4947	Blaze	CDJ	U.S.	1993	$3.00
Columbia	CSK 4036	Down With the Bass	CDJ	U.S.	1991	$3.00
Columbia	CSK 4069	Down With the Bass	CDJ	U.S.	1991	$3.00
Columbia	44K 74152	Live Totem Pole	CD5	U.S.	1992	$5.00
CBS	74152	Red and Black	CD5	U.S.	1994	$5.00
Columbia	CSK 5173	Witness	CDJ	U.S.	1993	$3.00

Firehouse

Singles

Label	Catalog Number	Title	Type	Country	Year	Longbox Value / Value
Epic	ESDA-7055	All She Wrote	CD3	Japan	1991	$13.00/$4.00
Epic	ESK 73984	All She Wrote	CDJ	U.S.	1991	$2.00
Epic	656780-2	Don't Treat Me Bad	CD5	Germany	1990	$10.00
Epic	656780-9	Don't Treat Me Bad	CD5	U.K.	1990	$10.00
Epic	ESK 73676	Don't Treat Me Bad	CDJ	U.S.	1990	$3.00
Epic		I Live My Life For You	CDJ	U.S.		$3.00
Epic	656949-2	Love of a Lifetime	CD5	Germany	1990	$9.00
Epic	ESDA-7075	Love of a Lifetime	CD3	Japan	1991	$13.00/$4.00
Epic	ESK 73771	Love of a Lifetime	CDJ	U.S.	1990	$2.00
Epic	ESDA-7098	Reach For the Sky	CD3	Japan	1992	$13.00/$4.00
Epic	ESK 74335	Reach For the Sky	CDJ	U.S.	1992	$2.00
Epic	ESK 2165	Shake & Tumble	CDJ	U.S.	1990	$2.00
Epic	ESDA-7119	Sleeping With You	CD3	Japan	1992	$13.00/$4.00
Epic	ESK 74323	Sleeping With You	CDJ	U.S.	1992	$2.00
Epic	ESK 4874	Sleeping With You	CDJ	U.S.	1992	$2.00
Epic	ESDA-7110	When I Look Into Your Eyes	CD3	Japan	1992	$13.00/$4.00

Label	Catalog Number	Title	Type	Country	Year	Longbox/Value
Epic	658834-2	When I Look Into Your Eyes	CD5	U.K.	1992	$8.00
Epic	ESK 74440	When I Look Into Your Eyes	CDJ	U.S.	1992	$2.00

Firm, The

Full Length

Label	Catalog Number	Title	Type	Country	Year	Longbox/Value
WEA	7 81239-2	Firm, The	LP	Germany		$14.00
Atlantic	7 81239-2	Firm, The	LP/LB	U.S.†	1985	$14.00/$8.00
WEA	7 81628-2	Mean Business	LP	Germany		$14.00

First Cut

Singles

Label	Catalog Number	Title	Type	Country	Year	Longbox/Value
RCA	PD-43068	There's Something in Your Eyes	CD5	Germany	1989	$8.00

First Impact

Singles

Label	Catalog Number	Title	Type	Country	Year	Longbox/Value
World Dance	WDR-1CD	Another One Bites the Dust	CD5	U.K.	1991	$8.00

First Light

Singles

Label	Catalog Number	Title	Type	Country	Year	Longbox/Value
Premiere	CDSGT-1	Loving You	CD5	U.K.	1989	$8.00

First Patrol

Singles

Label	Catalog Number	Title	Type	Country	Year	Longbox/Value
ZYX	6237-8	Nightmare	CD5	Germany	1989	$6.00

First Twins

Singles

Label	Catalog Number	Title	Type	Country	Year	Longbox/Value
ZYX	6557-8	Get It On	CD5	Germany	1991	$6.00

Fischer, Lisa

Singles

Label	Catalog Number	Title	Type	Country	Year	Longbox/Value
Elektra	7559-64535-2	How Can I Ease the Pain	CD5	Germany	1991	$8.00
Elektra	WMD5-4072	How Can I Ease the Pain	CD3	Japan	1991	$13.00/$4.00
Elektra	EKR-127CD	How Can I Ease the Pain	CD5	U.K.	1991	$8.00
Elektra	PRCD 8312-2	How Can I Ease the Pain	CDJ	U.S.	1991	$2.00
Elektra	7559-66503-2	Save Me	CD5	Germany	1991	$8.00
Elektra	WMD5-4076	Save Me	CD3	Japan	1991	$13.00/$4.00
Elektra	EKR-134CD	Save Me	CD5	U.K.	1991	$8.00
Elektra	PRCD 8402-2	Save Me	CDJ	U.S.	1991	$2.00
Elektra	PRCD 8474-2	So Intense	CDJ	U.S.	1991	$2.00

Fischer-Z

Singles

Label	Catalog Number	Title	Type	Country	Year	Longbox/Value
BMG	662506	Masquerade	CD5	Germany	1989	$8.00
BMG	162301	Say No	CD3	Germany	1989	$8.00
BMG	662301	Say No	CD5	Germany	1989	$8.00
BMG	662301	Say No	CD5	U.K.	1989	$8.00

Fischerman's Friend

Singles

Label	Catalog Number	Title	Type	Country	Year	Longbox/Value
Polygram	870399-2	Fischerman's Friend	CD5	Germany	1988	$8.00
Polygram	873153-2	Money	CD5	Germany	1988	$8.00
Polygram	872543-2	Teutonic Beats	CD5	Germany	1988	$8.00

Fish

Full Length

Label	Catalog Number	Title	Type	Country	Year	Longbox/Value
EMI		Acoustic CD	LTD/LP	U.K.	1994	$25.00
EMI		Funny Farm Interview	DJ/Smplr	U.K.		$30.00
Fish & Dick Bros.		Yin & Yang	LTD/LP	U.S.	1995	$30.00

2 CD set. Availble on through fan club.

Singles

Label	Catalog Number	Title	Type	Country	Year	Longbox/Value
EMI	CDP552203562	2 State of Mind	CD5	Germany	1989	$11.00
EMI	CDP552203562	3 State of Mind	CD3	Germany	1989	$11.00
EMI	CDP560-2036552	Big Wedge	CD5	Germany	1989	$11.00
EMI	CDP 560-20 3655 2	Big Wedge	CD5	Germany	1989	$12.00
EMI	CDEM-125	Big Wedge	CD5	U.K.	1989	$11.00
EMI	203946-2	Company	CD5	Germany	1990	$11.00
EMI		Fortunes of War	CD5	U.K.	1994	$10.00
EMI		Fortunes of War	CD5	U.K.	1994	$10.00
	Fourth version.					
EMI		Fortunes of War	CD5	U.K.	1994	$10.00
	Second version.					
EMI		Fortunes of War	CD5	U.K.	1994	$10.00
	Third version.					
EMI	CDEM-135	Gentleman' Excuse Me	CD5	U.K.	1990	$11.00
EMI	203755-2	Gentleman' Excuse Me	CD5	U.K.	1990	$11.00
EMI	867751-2	Internal Exile	CD5	Germany	1991	$11.00
EMI	FISCD-1	Internal Exile	CD5	U.K.	1991	$11.00
		Lady Let It Lie	CD5	U.K.	1994	$11.00
		Lady Let It Lie	CD5	U.K.	1994	$11.00
	Second version.					
Polydor	FISH P#	Something in the Air	CD5	U.K.	1992	$11.00
EMI	CDEM 109	State of Mind	CD5	U.K.	1989	$11.00

Fish Monkey Man

Singles

Label	Catalog Number	Title	Type	Country	Year	Longbox/Value
WEA	FFISH-2CD	Breathing	CD5	U.K.	1991	$8.00
WEA	FFISH-1CD	If I've Told You Once	CD5	U.K.	1991	$8.00

Fishbone

Singles

Label	Catalog Number	Title	Type	Country	Year	Longbox/Value
Columbia	CSK 5280	Black Flowers	CDJ	U.S.	1993	$3.00
Columbia	44K 73549	Bonin' in the Boneyard	CD5	U.S.	1990	$5.00
Columbia	658193-2	Everyday Sunshine	CD5	U.K.	1992	$10.00
Columbia	CSK 73859	Everyday Sunshine	CDJ	U.S.	1991	$3.00
CBS	12EP-8025	Freddie's Dead	CD3	Japan	1989	$13.00/$4.00
Epic	CDFISH-1	Freddie's Dead	CD5	U.K.	1989	$10.00
Sony	SRCS-5741	It's a Wonderful Life	CD5	Japan	1992	$15.00
Columbia	CPFISH-2	Ma and Pa	CD5	U.K.	1991	$10.00
Columbia	CSK 5285	Servitude	CDJ	U.S.	1993	$3.00
Sony	SRD-8194	Sunless Saturday	CD3	Japan	1991	$12.00/$4.00
Columbia	44K 73668	Sunless Saturday	CD5	U.S.	1991	$5.00
Columbia	CSK 3035	Sunless Saturday	CDJ	U.S.	1991	$3.00
Columbia	CSK 5180	Swim	CDJ	U.S.	1993	$3.00

Fisher, Tricia Leigh

Singles

Label	Catalog Number	Title	Type	Country	Year	Longbox/Value
		Empty Beach	CDJ	U.S.		$2.00
		Let's Make the Time	CDJ	U.S.		$2.00

Fit

Singles

Label	Catalog Number	Title	Type	Country	Year	Longbox/Value
A&M	S10Y-3004	Just Havin' Fun	CD3	Japan	1988	$13.00/$4.00

Fitzgerald, Ella

Full Length

Label	Catalog Number	Title	Type	Country	Year	Longbox/Value
Delta	11088	Ella Fitzgerald	LP	Germany	1987	$25.00
IMS	817528-2	Harold Arlen Songbook, Vol.2	LP	Germany	1988	$25.00
Polygram	829534-2	Irving Berlin Songbook, Vol.1	LP	Germany	1985	$25.00
Polygram	829535-2	Irving Berlin Songbook, Vol.2	LP	Germany	1989	$25.00
Polygram	825669-2	Jerome Kern Songbook	LP	Germany	1989	$25.00
Polygram	823247-2	Johnny Mercer Songbook	LP	Germany	1989	$25.00
Verve	825024-2	Sings the George & Ira Gershwin Songbook	LP/LB	U.S.†	1985	$14.00/$8.00
Aris	881008	Star Forever	LP	Germany		$25.00
Verve	821989-2	The Cole Porter Songbook, Volume 1	LP/LB	U.S.†	1985	$14.00/$8.00
Verve	821990-2	The Cole Porter Songbook, Volume 2	LP/LB	U.S.†	1985	$14.00/$8.00
Verve	825669-2	The Jerome Kern Songbook	LP/LB	U.S.†	1985	$14.00/$8.00
Verve	823247-2	The Johnny Mercer Songbook	LP/LB	U.S.†	1985	$14.00/$8.00
Verve	821579-2	The Rodgers & Hart Songbook, Volume 1	LP/LB	U.S.†	1985	$14.00/$8.00
Verve	821580-2	The Rodgers & Hart Songbook, Volume 2	LP/LB	U.S.†	1985	$14.00/$8.00
Verve	823445-2	The Songbooks (Silver Collection)	LP/LB	U.S.†	1985	$14.00/$8.00
Polygram	829536-2	These Are the Blues	LP	Germany	1986	$25.00

Singles

Label	Catalog Number	Title	Type	Country	Year	Longbox/Value
ZYX	5810-8	I Get a Kick Out of You	CD5	Germany	1988	$10.00
Polygram	527032	Jazz 'round Midnight	CD5	U.S.	1994	$5.00

Fitzgerald, Ella & Count Basie

Full Length

Label	Catalog Number	Title	Type	Country	Year	Longbox/Value
Verve	821576-2	On the Sunny Side of the Street	LP/LB	U.S.†	1985	$14.00/$8.00

Fitzgerald, Ella & Louis Armstrong

Full Length

Label	Catalog Number	Title	Type	Country	Year	Longbox/Value
Verve	825373-2	Ella & Louis	LP/LB	U.S.†	1985	$14.00/$8.00
Verve	810049-2	Porgy & Bess	LP/LB	U.S.†	1985	$14.00/$8.00

Five Guys Named Moe

Singles

Label	Catalog Number	Title	Type	Country	Year	Longbox/Value
RCA	PD-44000	If I Were a Man	CD5	U.K.	1990	$8.00
RCA	PD-43502	Selfish Days	CD5	U.K.	1990	$8.00
RCA	PD-43814	She's on the Mountain	CD5	U.K.	1990	$8.00

Five Star

Singles

Label	Catalog Number	Title	Type	Country	Year	Longbox/Value
CBS	656010-3	Hot Love	CD3	Germany	1990	$8.00
CBS	CDFIVE-2	Hot Love	CD5	U.K.	1990	$8.00
		I Give You Give	CD5	U.K.		$10.00
		I Give You Give	CD5	U.K.		$10.00
	Second version.					
Aris	886538	Let Me Be Yours	CD5	Germany	1988	$8.00
RCA	PD-42344	Let Me Be Yours	CD5	U.K.	1988	$8.00
Epic	657480-2	Shine	CD5	U.K.	1991	$8.00
Epic	ESK 4335	Shine	CDJ	U.S.	1991	$2.00
Epic	ESK 74111	Shine	CDJ	U.S.	1991	$2.00
RCA	PD-42647	System Addict	CD5	Germany	1989	$8.00
RCA	PD-42647	System Addict	CD5	U.K.	1989	$8.00
RCA	886417	There's a Brand New World	CD5	Germany	1988	$8.00
RCA	PD-42236	There's a Brand New World	CD5	U.K.	1988	$8.00
CBS	655641-3	Treat Me Like a Lady	CD3	Germany	1990	$8.00
CBS	CDFIVE-1	Treat Me Like a Lady	CD5	U.K.	1990	$8.00
Epic	ESK 73394	Treat Me Like a Lady	CDJ	U.S.	1990	$2.00
RCA	PD-42694	With Every Heartbeat	CD5	U.K.	1989	$8.00

Five Thirty

Singles

Label	Catalog Number	Title	Type	Country	Year	Longbox/Value
Eastwest	YZ-577CD	13th Disciple	CD5	U.K.	1991	$8.00
Atco	PRCD 4159-2	13th Disciple	CDJ	U.S.	1991	$2.00
Eastwest	YZ-530CD	Abstain	CD5	U.K.	1990	$8.00
Eastwest	YZ-594CD	Supernova	CD5	U.K.	1991	$8.00
East Wesr	YZ-624CD	You	CD5	U.K.	1991	$8.00

Five XI

Singles

Label	Catalog Number	Title	Type	Country	Year	Longbox/Value
RCA	62616-2-RDJ	Don't Cry For Me	CDJ	U.S.	1993	$2.00
RCA	62539-2-RDJ	Say It Isn't Over	CDJ	U.S.	1993	$2.00

Fixx

Full Length

Label	Catalog Number	Title	Type	Country	Year	Longbox/Value
Impact	CD45-1287	CD Sampler	DJ/Smplr	U.S.	1991	$5.00
Album Network		In the Studio (Reach the Beach)	RS	U.S.	1989	$20.00
	Airdate: 1/30/89.					
		Live at Electric Ladyland	RS	U.S.	1991	$25.00
	Airdate: 4/29/91.					
MCA	MCAD-5507	Phantoms	LP/LB	U.S.†	1984	$15.00/$10.00
MCA	MCAD-5507	Phantoms	LP/LB	U.S.	1986	$15.00/$10.00
MCA	MCAD-31074	Shuttered Room	LP/LB	U.S.		$15.00/$10.00

Singles

Label	Catalog Number	Title	Type	Country	Year	Longbox/Value
Impact	CD45-1455	All Is Fair	CDJ	U.S.	1991	$2.00
EMI	745020-2	Crucified	CD5	Germany	1991	$10.00
RCA	PD-49496	Driven Out	CD5	Germany	1988	$10.00
RCA	PD-49496	Driven Out	CD5	U.K.	1988	$10.00
RCA	8841-2-RDJ	Driven Out	CDJ	U.S.	1988	$2.00
EMI	745001-2	How Much is Enough	CD5	Germany	1991	$10.00
Toshiba	TODP-2280	How Much is Enough	CD3	Japan	1991	$13.00/$4.00
Impact	CDEM-189	How Much is Enough	CD5	U.K.	1991	$10.00
Impact	CD45 1298	How Much is Enough	CDJ	U.S.	1991	$2.00
Impact	CD45 1331	How Much is Enough	CDJ	U.S.	1991	$2.00
Impact	CD45 1454	No One Has to Cry	CDJ	U.S.	1991	$2.00
RCA	8932-2-RDJ	Precious Stone	CDJ	U.S.	1989	$2.00
Impact	IMPD-1	Shout It Out	CDJ	U.S.	1991	$2.00

Flack, Roberta

Full Length

Label	Catalog Number	Title	Type	Country	Year	Longbox/Value
	ASCD-33	Ballads of, The	DJ/Smplr	Japan		$50.00
Atlantic	19317-2	Best of	LP/LB	U.S.		$16.00/$12.00
Atlantic	19149-2	Blue Lights in the Basement	LP/LB	U.S.		$14.00/$8.00
Atlantic	PRCD 4269-2	Classics, The	DJ/Smplr	U.S.	1991	$12.00
Warner-Pioneer	PCS-78	DJ Promo	DJ/Smplr	Japan		$50.00
Atlantic	8230-2	First Take	LP/LB	U.S.		$14.00/$8.00
Atlantic	19154-2	First Take	LP/LB	U.S.		$14.00/$8.00
Atlantic		Roberta	DJ/Smplr	U.S.		$15.00
Unistar		Story of...	RS	U.S.	1991	$25.00
	Airdate: 11/22/91.					

Singles

Label	Catalog Number	Title	Type	Country	Year	Longbox/Value
Atlantic	PRCD 4484-2	Friend	CDJ	U.S.	1992	$3.00
Atlantic	AMDY-5094	Killing Me Softly	CD3	Japan	1993	$12.00/$4.00
Toshiba	TODT-2967	Last Christmas Eve	CD3	Japan	192	$13.00/$4.00
Pioneer	10P3-6023	Oasis	CD3	Japan	1988	$13.00/$4.00
Atlantic	PR 2510-2	Oasis	CDJ	U.S.	1988	$2.00
Atlantic	7567-85944-2	Set the Night to Music	CD5	Germany	1991	$10.00
Atlantic	AMDY-5071	Set the Night to Music	CD3	Japan	1991	$13.00/$4.00
Atlantic	A-7607CD	Set the Night to Music	CD5	U.K.	1991	$10.00
Atlantic	PRCD 4164-2	Set the Night to Music	CDJ	U.S.	1991	$2.00
Atlantic	PR 2717-2	Shock to My System	CDJ	U.S.	1988	$2.00
Toshiba	TODT-2789	Stop the World	CD3	Japan	1992	$13.00/$4.00

Label	Catalog Number	Title	Type	Country	Year	Longbox Value / Value
Atlantic	A-8941CD	Uh - Uh Ooh - Ooh Look Out	CD5	U.K.	1989	$10.00
Atlantic	PRCD 2624-2	Uh - Uh Ooh - Ooh Look Out	CDJ	U.S.	1989	$2.00
Atlantic	PR 2719-2	Uh - Uh Ooh - Ooh Look Out	CDJ	U.S.	1989	$2.00
Atlantic	PRCD 4614-2	When Someone Tears Your Heart in Two	CDJ	U.S.	1991	$2.00
Atlantic	AMDY-5073	You Make Me Feel Brand New	CD3	Japan	1992	$12.00/$4.00
Atlantic	PRCD 4321-2	You Make Me Feel Brand New	CDJ	U.S.	1991	$2.00

Flack, Roberta & Donny Hathaway

Full Length

Label	Catalog Number	Title	Type	Country	Year	Value
Atlantic	7216-2	Roberta Flack & Donny Hathaway	LP/LB	U.S.		$14.00/$8.00

Flairck

Singles

Label	Catalog Number	Title	Type	Country	Year	Value
ZYX	6185-8	Sofia	CD5	Germany	1989	$6.00

Flame

Singles

Label	Catalog Number	Title	Type	Country	Year	Value
WEA	171480-2	America	CD5	Germany	1990	$9.00
Anxious	CDNERV-11	Move the Moon	CD5	U.K.	1990	$9.00
Epic	655238-2	On the Strength	CD5	U.K.	1989	$9.00
Epic	ESK 73060	One Way Lover	CDJ	U.S.	1989	$2.00
Anxious	CDNERV-8	This Time Tomorrow	CD5	U.K.	1990	$9.00
Giant	PRO-CD-5423	Wild One	CDJ	U.S.	1992	$2.00

Flamin' Grooves

Singles

Label	Catalog Number	Title	Type	Country	Year	Value
National	NAT-031	Sealed With a Kiss	CDJ	U.S.	1992	$2.00
Sire	PRO-CD-3762	Shake Some Action	CDJ	U.S.	1989	$2.00

Flaming Lips

Full Length

Label	Catalog Number	Title	Type	Country	Year	Value
Westwood One		In Concert [illegible]	[illegible]	U.S.	[illegible]	[illegible]
Airdate: 2/12/96.						

Singles

Label	Catalog Number	Title	Type	Country	Year	Value
Warner Brothers	PRO-CD-5401	Everyone Wants To Live Forever	CDJ	U.S.	1992	$2.00
Warner Brothers	PRO-CD-5726	Frogs	CDJ	U.S.	1992	$2.00
		She Don't Use Jelly	CD5	U.K.		$10.00
		She Don't Use Jelly	CD5	U.K.		$10.00
Second version.						
Warner Brothers	9 41102-2	She Don't Use Jelly	CD5	U.S.	1992	$4.00
Warner Brothers	41102	She Don't Use Jelly	CD5	U.S.	1994	$5.00
Warner Brothers	W0335CDX	This Here Giraffe	SCD5	Germany	1996	$25.00
Star Shaped CD.						
Warner Brothers	PRO-CD-6720	Turn It On	CDJ	U.S.	1993	$2.00
Warner Brothers	43509	Turn It On	CD5	U.S.	1994	$5.00
Warner Brothers	9 40244-2	Wastin' Pigs	CD5	U.S.	1991	$4.00

Flamingos

Singles

Label	Catalog Number	Title	Type	Country	Year	Value
Tribecca	77194	I Only Have Eyes for You	CDJ	U.S.	1993	$2.00
Robs	CDROB-8	Reason for Living	CD5	U.K.	1992	$8.00

Flanagan, Tommy

Full Length

Label	Catalog Number	Title	Type	Country	Year	Value
Denon	CD-7260	Alone Too Long	LP/LB	U.S.†	1985	$14.00/$8.00
Enja	CD-4022-41	Giant Steps	LP	Germany		$15.00
Polydor	3112-12	Giant Steps	LP	Japan		$20.00
Enja	311212	Giant Steps	LP/LB	U.S.†	1985	$14.00/$8.00
Enja	311229	Super Session	LP/LB	U.S.†	1985	$14.00/$8.00
Enja	CD-4052-14	Thelonica	LP	Germany		$15.00
Enja	311225	Thelonica	LP/LB	U.S.†	1985	$14.00/$8.00

Singles

Label	Catalog Number	Title	Type	Country	Year	Value
Alfa	10R3-14	My Funny Valentine	CD3	Japan	1988	$12.00/$3.00

Flanagan, Tommy & Hank Jones

Full Length

Label	Catalog Number	Title	Type	Country	Year	Value
Verve	817863-2	I'm All Smiles	LP/LB	U.S.†	1985	$14.00/$8.00
Galaxy	FCD-5113	Our Delights	LP/LB	U.S.†	1985	$14.00/$8.00

Flanagan, Tommy & Kenny Baron

Full Length

Label	Catalog Number	Title	Type	Country	Year	Value
Denon	CD-7263	Together	LP/LB	U.S.†	1985	$14.00/$8.00

Flanery, Sean Patrick

Singles

Label	Catalog Number	Title	Type	Country	Year	Value
Canyon	PCDY-00119	New World Adventure	CD3	Japan	1993	$13.00/$4.00

Flash and The Pan

Singles

Label	Catalog Number	Title	Type	Country	Year	Value
Epic	651120-2	Ayla	CD5	U.K.	1988	$8.00
Epic	65029-3	Something About You	CD3	Germany	1990	$8.00

Flatmates

Singles

Label	Catalog Number	Title	Type	Country	Year	Value
Subway	SUBWAY-021CD	Heaven Knows	CD5	U.K.	1988	$8.00

Flavour

Singles

Label	Catalog Number	Title	Type	Country	Year	Value
		No Matter What You Do	CD5	U.K.		$8.00
		No Matter What You Do	CD5	U.K.		$8.00
Second version.						

Fleck, Bela and The Flecktones

Singles

Label	Catalog Number	Title	Type	Country	Year	Value
Warner Brothers	PRO-CD-5618	Sex in a Pan	CDJ	U.S.	1992	$2.00
Warner Brothers	PRO-CD-3978	Sinister MInister, The	CDJ	U.S.	1990	$2.00

Fleetwood Mac

Full Length

Label	Catalog Number	Title	Type	Country	Year	Value
Warner-Pioneer	PCS-46	1969-1990	DJ/Smplr	Japan	1990	$80.00
Westwood One		BBC Classic Tracks	RS	U.S.	1995	$30.00
Airdate: 10/9/95.						
Warner Brothers	9 26206-2-Dj	Behind the Mask	DJ/LP	U.S.	1990	$18.00
Warner Brothers	9 26206-2	Behind the Mask	LTD/LP	U.S.	1990	$15.00
Warner Brothers	PRO-CD-5905	Chain Sampler	DJ/Smplr	U.S.	1992	$18.00
		Classic CD (Rumors)	RS	U.S.	1990	$80.00
2 CD set. Airdate: 10/29/90.						
Discovision	74-011	Documentary and Live Concert	LD	U.S.	1981	$125.00
MCA	74-011	Documentary and Live Concert	LD	U.S.	1985	$80.00
Reprise	2-2281	Fleetwood Mac	LP/LB	U.S.†	1984	$14.00/$8.00
Album Network		In the Studio (Fleetwood Mac)	RS	U.S.	1989	$25.00
Airdate: 8/7/89.						
Album Network		In the Studio (Rumors)	RS	U.S.	1990	$25.00
Airdate: 10/22/90.						
Album Network		In the Studio (Rumors)	RS	U.S.	1990	$25.00
Airdate: 2/26/90.						

Fleetwood Mac – Documentary And Live Concert (Discovision 74-011)

Label	Catalog Number	Title	Type	Country	Year	Value
DIR		King Biscuit Flour Hour	RS	U.S.	1988	$60.00
Airdate: 9/18/88.						
DIR		King Biscuit Flour Hour	RS	U.S.	1990	$60.00
Airdate: 4/30/90.						
DIR		King Biscuit Flour Hour	RS	U.S.	1992	$60.00
Airdate: 4/19/92.						
DIR		King Biscuit Flour Hour	RS	U.S.	1993	$60.00
Airdate: 12/12/93.						
DIR		King Biscuit Flour Hour	RS	U.S.	1993	$60.00
Airdate: 2/1/93.						
DIR		King Biscuit Flour Hour	RS	U.S.	1995	$40.00
Airdate: 3/26/95.						
DIR		King Biscuit Flour Hour	RS	U.S.	1996	$40.00
Airdate: 3/24/96.						
		Madison Blues Live	LP	U.K.		$13.00
Radio Ventures		Masters of Rock	RS	U.S.	1990	$40.00
Airdate: 7/16/90.						
Warner Brothers	9 23607-2	Mirage	LP/LB	U.S.†	1984	$15.00/$9.00
Pioneer	PA-83-048	Mirage Tour '82	LD	U.S.	1983	$40.00
Pioneer	PA-83-048	Mirage Tour '82	LD	U.S.	1989	$50.00
Digital audio.						
Hypereon		My 25 Years in Fleetwood Mac	LP	U.S.	1992	$25.00
CD in book.						
Radio Today		Rock Stars	RS	U.S.	1989	$50.00
2 CD set. Airdate: 2/20/89.						
HMV		Rumors	LTD/LP	U.K.	1989	$35.00
CD with booklet in 12"x12" box. Manufactered for HMV superstores.						
Warner Brothers	03010-2	Rumors	LP/LB	U.S.†	1984	$14.00/$8.00
Westwood One		Superstars	RS	U.S.	1993	$80.00
2 CD set. Airdate: 5/22/93.						
Westwood One		Superstars	RS	U.S.	1994	$80.00
2 CD set. Airdate: 2/7/94.						
Westwood One		Superstars	RS	U.S.	1995	$80.00
2 CD set. Airdate: 8/7/95.						
		Tango in the Night	LTD/LP	Australia	1995	$45.00
CD album and "PAL" format VHS video i n box.						
Pioneer	43P2-0005	Tango in the Night	LTD/LP	Japan	1989	$50.00
Gold disc.						
Warner Brothers		Time	DJ/LP	U.S.		$10.00
Media America		Up Close	RS	U.S.	1990	$40.00
2 CD set.						

Singles

Label	Catalog Number	Title	Type	Country	Year	Value
CBS	655171-3	Albatross	CD3	Germany	1989	$12.00
CBS	654613-2	Albatross	CD5	U.K.	1989	$12.00
Warner Brothers	921125-2	As Long as You Follow	CD3	Germany	1988	$10.00
Warner Brothers	10P3-6085	As Long as You Follow	CD3	Japan	1988	$12.00/$4.00
Warner Brothers	W-7644CD	As Long as You Follow	CD3	U.K.	1988	$10.00
Warner Brothers	PRO-CD-3351	As Long as You Follow	CDJ	U.S.	1988	$3.00
Warner Brothers	PRO-CD-2170	Big Love	CDJ	U.S.		$3.00
WEA	WE739	Don't Stop	CD5	Germany	1992	$10.00
WEA		Don't Stop	CD5	U.K.	1992	$10.00
Warner Brothers	PRO-CD-5934	Don't Stop	CDJ	U.S.	1992	$3.00
Warner Brothers	920907-2	Everywhere	CD3	Germany	1988	$10.00
Warner Brothers	W-8143CD	Everywhere	CD3	U.K.	1988	$10.00
Warner Brothers	W-8143CD	Everywhere	CD5	U.K.	1988	$10.00
Warner Brothers	PRO-CD-2948	Family Man	CDJ	U.S.	1987	$3.00
Warner Brothers	PRO-CD-4504	Hard Feelings	CDJ	U.S.	1990	$3.00
Warner Brothers	9211171-2	Hold Me	CD3	Germany	1989	$10.00
Warner Brothers	W-7528CD	Hold Me	CD3	U.K.	1989	$10.00
Warner Brothers	17744	I Do	CD5	U.S.	1995	$5.00
Warner Brothers	655491-2	I Need Your Love So Bad	CD3	Germany	1989	$10.00
Warner Brothers	7599-21723-2	In the Back of My Mind	CD5	Germany	1990	$10.00
Warner Brothers	W-9739CD	In the Back of My Mind	CD5	U.K.	1990	$10.00
Warner Brothers	920961-2	Isn't It Midnight	CD3	Germany	1988	$10.00
Warner Brothers	W-7860CD	Isn't It Midnight	CD3	U.K.	1988	$10.00
Warner Brothers	PRO-CD-2821	Little Lies	CDJ	U.S.	1987	$3.00
Warner Brothers	PRO-CDS-2818	Little Lies	DJ/CD3	U.S.	1987	$18.00/$12.00
Warner Brothers	PRO-CD-4302	Love is Dangerous	CDJ	U.S.	1990	$3.00
Warner Brothers		Love Shines	CD5	Germany	1993	$10.00
Warner Brothers	09P3-6118	No Questions Asked	CD3	Japan	1989	$13.00/$4.00
Warner Brothers	9 18661-2	Paper Doll	CD5	U.S.	1992	$5.00
Warner Brothers	PRO-CD-5872	Paper Doll	CDJ	U.S.	1992	$3.00
Warner Brothers	921523-2	Save Me	CD5	Germany	1990	$10.00
Warner Brothers	WPDP-6220	Save Me	CD3	Japan	1990	$13.00/$4.00
Warner Brothers	W-9866CD	Save Me	CD5	U.K.	1990	$10.00
Warner Brothers	PRO-CD-4011	Save Me	CDJ	U.S.	1990	$3.00
Warner Brothers	7599-21709-2	Sky's the Limit	CD5	Germany	1990	$10.00
Warner Brothers	WPDP-6238	Sky's the Limit	CD3	Japan	1990	$13.00/$4.00
Warner Brothers	W-9740CD	Sky's the Limit	CD5	U.K.	1990	$10.00
Warner Brothers	PRO-CD-4010	Sky's the Limit	CDJ	U.S.	1990	$3.00

Fleetwoods

Singles

Label	Catalog Number	Title	Type	Country	Year	Value
ERC	404	Come Softly to Me	CD5	U.S.	1992	$2.00
Aris	885830	Mr. Blue	CD3	Germany	1990	$10.00
Rhino	R3 73009	Mr. Blue	CD3	U.S.	1988	$6.00/$3.00

Flesh + Blood

Singles

Label	Catalog Number	Title	Type	Country	Year	Value
		Fate	CDJ	U.S.		$2.00

Flesh for Lulu

Label	Catalog Number	Title	Type	Country	Year	Longbox Value/Value
		Full Length				
EFA	CD-6361	Long Live the New Flesh	LP	Germany		$20.00
Beggars Banquet	FLESH 1	Decline And Fall	CD5	U.K.	1989	$8.00
Capitol	DPRO-79994	Every Little Word	CDJ	U.S.	1990	$2.00
		Every Little Word	CDJ	U.S.	1990	$2.00
	Second version.					
MCA	MCA5P-2041	She Was	CDJ	U.S.	1991	$2.00
Capitol	DPRO-79293	Siamese Twist	CDJ	U.S.	1987	$3.00
Beggars Banquet	BEG-240CD	Time and Space	CD5	U.K.	1990	$8.00
Capitol	DPRO-79772	Time and Space	CDJ	U.S.	1989	$2.00

Flesheaters

Label	Catalog Number	Title	Type	Country	Year	Longbox Value/Value
		Singles				
SST	292	Sex Diary of Mr. Vampire	CDJ	U.S.	1992	$2.00

Fleshtones

Label	Catalog Number	Title	Type	Country	Year	Longbox Value/Value
		Full Length				
		Laboratory of Sound	DJ/Smplr	U.S.		$20.00
	CD in "lab kit" box.					
		Singles				
Ichiban	202	Beautiful Light	CDJ	U.S.	1993	$2.00

Flies on Fire

Label	Catalog Number	Title	Type	Country	Year	Longbox Value/Value
		Full Length				
Atco	7 91284-2	Flies On Fire	DJ/LP	U.S.	1989	$14.00
	Denim pocket sleeve.					
		Singles				
Atco	PR 3138-2	Baptize Me Over Elvis Presley's Grave	CDJ	U.S.	1989	$2.00
Atco	PR 2898-2	C'mon	CDJ	U.S.	1989	$2.00
Atco	PR 3925-2	Cry to Myself	CDJ	U.S.	1991	$2.00

Flight

Label	Catalog Number	Title	Type	Country	Year	Longbox Value/Value
		Singles				
Butterfly	BFLD-1	Flight by Flight	CD5	U.K.	1993	$8.00

Flim and The BB's

Label	Catalog Number	Title	Type	Country	Year	Longbox Value/Value
		Full Length				
Digital Music	CD-454	Big Notes	LP/LB	U.S.†	1985	$14.00/$8.00
Digital Music	CD-443	Tricycle	LP/LB	U.S.†	1985	$14.00/$8.00
dmp	GOLD-9000	Tricycle	LTD/LP	U.S.	1996	$28.00
	Gold disc.					
Digital Music	CD-447	Tunnel	LP/LB	U.S.†	1985	$14.00/$8.00
		Singles				
Sony/dmp	CSIG 000064	Commemoration of a Decade Of Digital	DJ/CD3	U.S.	1988	$6.00

Flippers

Label	Catalog Number	Title	Type	Country	Year	Longbox Value/Value
		Singles				
		Mona Lisa	CD5	Germany	1991	$8.00

Flock of Seagulls

Label	Catalog Number	Title	Type	Country	Year	Longbox Value/Value
		Full Length				
Jive	CHIP-41	Best of	LP	U.K.		$23.00
Teldec	825100	Flock of Seagulls	LP	U.K.	1984	$23.00
Arista	JRCD-8011	Flock of Seagulls	LP/BP	U.S.†	1984	$18.00/$14.00
Arista	JRCD-8011	Flock of Seagulls	LP/BP	U.S.	1984	$18.00/$14.00
Jive		Listen	LP	U.K.		$23.00
Jive		Same	LP	U.K.		$23.00
CBS	32DP-189	Story of a Young Heart	LP	Japan		$30.00
Jive	CHIP-14	Story of a Young Heart	LP	U.K.		$23.00

Flomasters

Label	Catalog Number	Title	Type	Country	Year	Longbox Value/Value
		Singles				
WEA	XLT-7CD	Let It Take Control	CD5	U.K.	1990	$8.00

Floor Federation

Label	Catalog Number	Title	Type	Country	Year	Longbox Value/Value
		Singles				
One Off	FOFF-003CD	Music for the Masses	CD5	U.K.	1992	$8.00

Flop

Label	Catalog Number	Title	Type	Country	Year	Longbox Value/Value
		Singles				
550 Music	ESK 5646	Great Valedictation	CDJ	U.S.	1994	$2.00
Epic	ESK 5389	Regrets	CDJ	U.S.	1993	$2.00
Epic	ESK 5439	Regrets	CDJ	U.S.	1993	$2.00

Florentines

Label	Catalog Number	Title	Type	Country	Year	Longbox Value/Value
		Singles				
El	25611-12	Man of Mine	CD3	Japan	1989	$13.00/$4.00

Flotsam & Jetsam

Label	Catalog Number	Title	Type	Country	Year	Longbox Value/Value
		Full Length				
MCA	18515	Master Sleeps, The	DJ/Intvw	U.S.	1990	$10.00
		Singles				
SPV	7820-3	Saturday's Night	CD5	Germany	1988	$10.00
Roadrunner	RR-24532	Saturday's Night	CD5	U.K.	1988	$10.00
		Suffer the Masses	CDJ	U.S.		$2.00

Flower Child

Label	Catalog Number	Title	Type	Country	Year	Longbox Value/Value
		Singles				
Fieldworks	FWCR-60	Hey Hey Hey!	CD5	Japan	1992	$10.00

Flowered Up

Label	Catalog Number	Title	Type	Country	Year	Longbox Value/Value
		Full Length				
Polygram	828252-2	A Life With Brian	LP/BP	U.S.		$14.00/$8.00
		Singles				
Heavenly	HVN-3CD	It's On	CD5	U.K.	1990	$8.00
Heavenly	HVN-7CD	Phobia	CD5	U.K.	1990	$8.00
London	FUPCD-1	Take It	CD5	U.K.	1991	$8.00
Epic	ESCA-5621	Weekender	CD5	Japan	1991	$10.00
Heavenly	HVN-16CD	Weekender	CD5	U.K.	1991	$8.00

Flowerhead

Label	Catalog Number	Title	Type	Country	Year	Longbox Value/Value
		Singles				
Zoo	ZP-17095	Acid Rain	CDJ	U.S.	1992	$2.00
Zoo	ZP-17122	All Along the Way	CDJ	U.S.	1992	$2.00
Zoo	ZADV0054	Thunderjeep	CDJ	U.S.	1992	$2.00

Flowers

Label	Catalog Number	Title	Type	Country	Year	Longbox Value/Value
		Singles				
SPV	0766-3	Swinging Thing	CD5	Germany	1989	$8.00

Fluid

Label	Catalog Number	Title	Type	Country	Year	Longbox Value/Value
		Full Length				
Hollywood		Purplemetalflakemusic	LTD/LP	U.S.	1993	$10.00
	Metal flake sticker.					
		Singles				
Hollywood	10309	7/14	CDJ	U.S.	1993	$2.00
Hollywood	10296	Mr. Blameshifter	CDJ	U.S.	1993	$2.00
Hollywood	10328	Pill	CDJ	U.S.	1993	$2.00

Fluke

Label	Catalog Number	Title	Type	Country	Year	Longbox Value/Value
		Singles				
		Bullet	CD5	U.K.		$10.00
		Bullet	CD5	U.K.		$10.00
	Second version.					
Circa	VJCP-14036	Out	CD5	Japan	1991	$10.00
Virgin	FLUKD-1	Out	CD5	U.K.	1991	$8.00
Circa	2-9621	Out	CD5	U.S.	1991	$4.00
Creation	CRESCD-090	Philly	CD5	U.K.	1991	$8.00
		Tosh	CD5	U.K.		$10.00
		Tosh	CD5	U.K.		$10.00
	Second version.					

Flying Burrito Brothers

Label	Catalog Number	Title	Type	Country	Year	Longbox Value/Value
		Full Length				
A&M		Last of the Red Hot Burritos	LP/LB	U.S.		$14.00/$8.00

Flying Elephants

Label	Catalog Number	Title	Type	Country	Year	Longbox Value/Value
		Singles				
EMI	TOCT-8053	Let It Be	CD5	Japan	1993	$12.00
King	KIDS-32	Now My Love	CD3	Japan	1991	$13.00/$4.00
Toshiba	TODT-3053	We Need Peace and Love	CD3	Japan	1993	$13.00/$4.00

Flying Purple People Eaters

Label	Catalog Number	Title	Type	Country	Year	Longbox Value/Value
		Singles				
WEA	9031-73565-2	Purple People Eaters	CD5	Germany	1991	$9.00

Fmob

Label	Catalog Number	Title	Type	Country	Year	Longbox Value/Value
		Singles				
EastWest	PRCD 5610	Pump, Pump	CDJ	U.S.	1994	$2.00

FMT

Label	Catalog Number	Title	Type	Country	Year	Longbox Value/Value
		Singles				
EMI	204324-2	50 Ways to Leave Your Lover	CD5	Germany	1990	$8.00
EMI	204153-2	Suzanne	CD5	Germany	1990	$8.00

Foam

Label	Catalog Number	Title	Type	Country	Year	Longbox Value/Value
		Singles				
UFO	UFO-45007CD	Hinckley Had a Vision	CD5	U.K.	1992	$2.00

Fobidden Fruit

Label	Catalog Number	Title	Type	Country	Year	Longbox Value/Value
		Singles				
Columbia	ALDB-131	How to Keep Your Love	CD3	Japan	1991	$13.00/$4.00
ZYX	6227-8	I'm Satisfied	CD5	Germany	1989	$6.00

Foetus Inc.

Label	Catalog Number	Title	Type	Country	Year	Longbox Value/Value
		Singles				
Big Cat	ABB-16SCD	Butterfly Potion	CD5	U.K.	1990	$8.00

Fog

Label	Catalog Number	Title	Type	Country	Year	Longbox Value/Value
		Singles				
		Been a Long Time	CD5	U.K.	1993	$8.00
		Been a Long Time	CD5	U.K.	1993	$8.00
	Second version.					
Columbia	CSK 5623	Been a Long Time	CDJ	U.S.	1993	$2.00
CBS	77303	Been a Long Time	CD5	U.S.	1994	$5.00

Fogelberg, Dan

Label	Catalog Number	Title	Type	Country	Year	Longbox Value/Value
		Full Length				
Epic	ESK 2728	EP From Exiles	DJ/Smplr	U.S.		$8.00
Epic	EK-38308	Greatest Hits	LP/BP	U.S.†	1984	$14.00/$8.00
Epic	EK-39616	High Country Snows	LP/BP	U.S.†	1985	$14.00/$8.00
Epic	E2K-37393	Innocent Age, The	LP/LB	U.S.†	1985	$20.00/$17.00
	2 CD set.					
Columbia	CD-88533	Netherlands	LP	Germany		$23.00
Epic	EK-34185	Netherlands	LP/BP	U.S.†	1985	$14.00/$8.00
Epic	EK-35634	Phoenix	LP/BP	U.S.†	1984	$14.00/$8.00
Epic	ASK 2728	Selections From the LP Exiles	DJ/Smplr	U.S.	1987	$20.00
Epic	EK-33137	Souvenirs	LP/BP	U.S.†	1984	$14.00/$8.00
Epic	EK-35339	Twin Sons of Mine	LP/BP	U.S.†	1985	$14.00/$8.00
Epic	EK-39004	Windows & Walls	LP/BP	U.S.†	1984	$14.00/$8.00
		Singles				
Epic	ESK 2273	Anastasia's Eyes	CDJ	U.S.	1990	$3.00
Epic	ESK 5435	Magic Every Moment	CDJ	U.S.	1993	$3.00
Epic	ESK 73513	Rhythm of the Rain	CDJ	U.S.	1990	$3.00

Fogerty, John

Label	Catalog Number	Title	Type	Country	Year	Longbox Value/Value
		Full Length				
Warner Brothers	9 25203-2	Centerfield	LP/LB	U.S.†	1985	$65.00/$50.00
	With deleted track "Zonz Kant Dance."					

Foghat

Label	Catalog Number	Title	Type	Country	Year	Longbox Value/Value
		Full Length				
Album Network		In the Studio (Fool for the City)	RS	U.S.		$20.00
DIR		King Biscuit Flour Hour	RS	U.S.	1988	$35.00
	With Poco, Airdate: 10/16/88.					
Westwood One		Superstars	RS	U.S.	1995	$50.00
	Airdate: 2/6/95.					

Foley

Label	Catalog Number	Title	Type	Country	Year	Longbox Value/Value
		Singles				
Mojazz	374631123	Black Rock	CDJ	U.S.	1993	$2.00
Mojazz	374631090	If It's Positive	CDJ	U.S.	1993	$2.00

Foley, Keith

Label	Catalog Number	Title	Type	Country	Year	Longbox Value/Value
		Full Length				
Digital Music	CD-452	Music for Christmas	LP/LB	U.S.†	1985	$14.00/$8.00

Foley, Sub

Label	Catalog Number	Title	Type	Country	Year	Longbox Value/Value
		Full Length				
		House of Blues	RS	U.S.	1995	$30.00
	2 CD set. Airdate: 10/22/95.					

Fonke Socialistiks

Label	Catalog Number	Title	Type	Country	Year	Longbox Value/Value
		Singles				
Priority	07297	You Are My Heaven	CDJ	U.S.	1991	$2.00
Priority	07299	You Are My Heaven	CDJ	U.S.	1991	$2.00

Foo Fighters

Label	Catalog Number	Title	Type	Country	Year	Longbox Value/Value
		Full Length				
Capitol		Foo Fighters	LTD/LP	Australia	1995	$28.00
	2 CD set.					
Capitol		Foo Fighters	LTD/LP	Japan	1995	$36.00
	2 CD set.					

Label	Catalog Number	Title	Type	Country	Year	Longbox/Value
		Singles				
Capitol		Big Me	CDJ	Spain	1995	$30.00
Capitol		Big Me	CDJ	U.S.	1995	$3.00
Capitol		For All the Cows	CD5	U.K.	1995	$10.00
Capitol		For All the Cows	CD5	U.K.	1995	$10.00
Second version.						
Capitol	TOCP-8777	I'll Stick Around	CD5	Japan	1995	$18.00
Capitol		I'll Stick Around	CD5	U.K.	1995	$10.00
Capitol		I'll Stick Around	CDJ	U.S.	1995	$3.00
Capitol	TODP-2524	This Is a Call	CD3	Japan	1995	$13.00/$4.00
Capitol		This Is a Call	CD5	U.K.	1995	$10.00
Capitol		This Is a Call	CDJ	U.S.	1995	$3.00

Fools

Label	Catalog Number	Title	Type	Country	Year	Longbox/Value
		Singles				
Nutmeg	NC-2044	What You Want	CD5	Japan	1991	$10.00

For Carnation

Label	Catalog Number	Title	Type	Country	Year	Longbox/Value
		Singles				
Matador	131	Fight Songs	CD5	U.S.	1994	$5.00

For Love Not Lisa

Label	Catalog Number	Title	Type	Country	Year	Longbox/Value
		Singles				
EastWest	96022	Softhand	CD5	U.S.	1993	$4.00

For Your Nose Only

Label	Catalog Number	Title	Type	Country	Year	Longbox/Value
		Singles				
ZYX	5952-8	Scoobidoo Goes the House	CD5	Germany	1991	$6.00

Forbert, Steve

Label	Catalog Number	Title	Type	Country	Year	Longbox/Value
		Full Length				
		American in Me, The	LP	U.S.		$10.00
		Singles				
Geffen	PRO-CD-4413	American in Me, The	CDJ	U.S.	1992	$2.00
Geffen	PRO-CD-4372	Baby Don't	CDJ	U.S.	1991	$2.00
Geffen	GFSTD-22	Born Too Late	CD5	U.K.	1992	$8.00
Geffen	PRO-CD-3114	Running on Love	CDJ	U.S.		$2.00

Forbidden

Label	Catalog Number	Title	Type	Country	Year	Longbox/Value
		Singles				
Acid Jazz		Candyman	CDJ	U.S.	1992	$2.00

Force Dimension

Label	Catalog Number	Title	Type	Country	Year	Longbox/Value
		Singles				
Rough Trade	390-1048-3	Algorythm	CD5	Germany	1990	$8.00
Force	KK-048	Algorythm	CD5	U.K.	1990	$8.00
Rough Trade	390-1027-3	Dust	CD5	Germany	1990	$8.00
Rough Trade	390-1063-3	New Funk	CD5	Germany	1993	$8.00
Cargo	63	New Funk	CD5	U.S.	1993	$5.00
Rough Trade	390-1028-3	Tension	CD5	Germany	1992	$8.00

Force MDS

Label	Catalog Number	Title	Type	Country	Year	Longbox/Value
		Singles				
Tommy Boy	909	Couldn't Care Less	CDJ	U.S.	1988	$2.00
Tommy Boy	516	Your Love Drives Me Crazy	CDJ	U.S.	1988	$2.00

Force 'n Kozee

Label	Catalog Number	Title	Type	Country	Year	Longbox/Value
		Singles				
Ronin	NINJD-2	Jam	CD5	U.K.	1992	$8.00
Ronin	NINJD-3	Lords Of the Dance	CD5	U.K.	1992	$8.00

Force One Network

Label	Catalog Number	Title	Type	Country	Year	Longbox/Value
		Singles				
Qwest	PRO-CD-5558	Somethin' About You	CDJ	U.S.	1992	$2.00
Qwest	9 40263-2	Spirit	CD5	U.S.	1992	$4.00
Qwest	PRO-CD-5201	Spirit	CDJ	U.S.	1992	$2.00

Force Staccato

Label	Catalog Number	Title	Type	Country	Year	Longbox/Value
		Singles				
ZYX	6459-8	Staccato	CD5	Germany	1991	$6.00

Forcefield

Label	Catalog Number	Title	Type	Country	Year	Longbox/Value
		Full Length				
Aris	880660	Forcefield	LP	Germany		$15.00

Ford, Lita

Label	Catalog Number	Title	Type	Country	Year	Longbox/Value
		Full Length				
RCA		Dangerous Curves	LP/LB	U.S.		$14.00/$8.00
RCA	62164-2-RDJ	Shot of Poison	DJ/Smplr	U.S.	1991	$8.00
		Singles				
RCA		A Future to this Life	CDJ	U.S.		$3.00
RCA	8664-2-RDJ	Back in the Cave	CDJ	U.S.	1988	$3.00
RCA	PD-49409	Close My Eyes Forever	CD3	Germany	1989	$10.00
RCA	PD-49410	Close My Eyes Forever	CD5	Germany	1989	$10.00
RCA	PD-49409	Close My Eyes Forever	CD3	U.K.	1989	$10.00
RCA	8899-2-RDJ	Close My Eyes Forever	CDJ	U.S.	1989	$6.00
RCA	9008-2-RDJ	Falling in and out of Love	CDJ	U.S.	1989	$3.00
RCA	PD-49266	Hungry	CD5	Germany	1990	$10.00
RCA	PD-49266	Hungry	CD5	U.K.	1990	$10.00
RCA	2607-2-RDJ	Hungry	CDJ	U.S.	1990	$3.00
Zyx	7624	Killin' Kind	CD5	U.S.	1994	$5.00
RCA	62097-2-RDJ	Larger Than Life	CDJ	U.S.	1991	$3.00
RCA	PD-49264	Lisa	CD5	U.K.	1990	$10.00
RCA	2673-2-RDJ	Lisa	CDJ	U.S.	1990	$3.00
RCA	62189-2-RDJ	Playing With Fire	CDJ	U.S.	1991	$3.00
RCA	PD-49146	Shot of Poison	CD5	Germany	1991	$10.00
RCA	62074-2-RDJ	Shot of Poison	CDJ	U.S.	1991	$3.00
RCA	62096-2-RDJ	Shot of Poison	CDJ	U.S.	1991	$3.00

Ford, Penny

Label	Catalog Number	Title	Type	Country	Year	Longbox/Value
		Singles				
Columbia	CSK 5315	I'll Be There	CDJ	U.S.	1993	$2.00
Columbia	CSK 87085	I'll Be There	CDJ	U.S.	1993	$2.00
Columbia	CSK 5315	Wherever You Are Tonight	CDJ	U.S.	1993	$2.00

Ford, Rita

Label	Catalog Number	Title	Type	Country	Year	Longbox/Value
		Full Length				
CBS	CK-40171	A Christmas Tree	LP/BP	U.S.†	1985	$12.00/$7.00

Ford, Robben

Label	Catalog Number	Title	Type	Country	Year	Longbox/Value
		Full Length				
		House of Blues	RS	U.S.	1995	$30.00
2 CD set. Airdate: 2/19/95.						
Warner		Inside Story, The	LP	Japan		$35.00
		Singles				
Warner Brothers	PRO-CD-3600	Born Under a Bad Sign	CDJ	U.S.	1989	$2.00
GRP	5126	He Don't Play Nothin' But the Blues	CDJ	U.S.	1993	$2.00
Warner Brothers	PRO-CD-3259	Talk to Your Daughter	CDJ	U.S.	1988	$2.00
Warner Brothers	PRO-CD-3139	Wild About You	CDJ	U.S.	1988	$2.00

Ford, Sir Ted

Label	Catalog Number	Title	Type	Country	Year	Longbox/Value
		Singles				
Stallion		I Found Love	CDJ	U.S.	1994	$2.00

Ford, Tennessee Ernie

Label	Catalog Number	Title	Type	Country	Year	Longbox/Value
		Full Length				
Warner Sound Exchange		40 Legendary Hits	LTD/LP	U.S.	1995	$17.00
EMI	7466210-2	Precious Memories	LP	Germany		$15.00

Ford-Payne, Sheree

Label	Catalog Number	Title	Type	Country	Year	Longbox/Value
		Singles				
	PRO-CD-4828	Love Him Anyway	CDJ	U.S.		$2.00

Fordham, Julia

Label	Catalog Number	Title	Type	Country	Year	Longbox/Value
		Full Length				
Virgin		DJ Copy	DJ/Smplr	Japan		$40.00
Virgin	3514	Genius of Julia Fordham	DJ/Smplr	U.S.	1989	$12.00
Virgin	PRCD JULIA	Manhattan Skyline	DJ/Smplr	U.S.	1989	$18.00
Virgin	JFCD 1	Patches of Happiness	DJ/Smplr	U.S.	1993	$12.00
		Singles				
Virgin		Can't Help Myself	CDJ	Japan		$25.00
Virgin	VJD-12013	Comfort of Strangers	CD3	Japan	1988	$12.00/$4.00
Circa	YRCD-11	Comfort of Strangers	CD5	U.K.	1988	$10.00
Virgin	PR 2669	Comfort of Strangers	CDJ	U.S.	1988	$3.00
		Different Time Different Place	CD5	U.K.		$10.00
		Different Time Different Place	CD5	U.K.		$10.00
Second version.						
Circa	YRCD-39	Genius	CD3	U.K.	1990	$10.00
Circa	YRCD-48	Girlfriend	CD5	U.K.	1990	$10.00
Circa	YRCD-15	Happy Ever After	CD5	U.K.	1988	$10.00
Virgin	PR 2404	Happy Ever After	CDJ	U.S.	1988	$3.00
		I Can't Help Myself	CD5	U.K.		$10.00
		I Can't Help Myself	CD5	U.K.		$10.00
Second version.						
		I Can't Help Myself	CDJ	U.S.	1994	$3.00
Circa	VJDP-10190	I Thought It Was You	CD3	Japan	1992	$12.00/$4.00
		I Thought It Was You	CD5	U.K.		$10.00
		I Thought It Was You	CD5	U.K.		$10.00
Second version.						
Virgin	VJD-120219	Lock and Key	CD3	Japan	1989	$12.00/$4.00
Circa	YRCD-36	Lock and Key	CD3	U.K.	1989	$10.00
Virgin	PRCD 3320	Lock and Key	CDJ	U.S.	1989	$3.00
Virgin	VJDP-10180	(Love Moves in) Mysterious Ways	CD3	Japan	1991	$12.00/$4.00
Circa	YRCD-73	(Love Moves in) Mysterious Ways	CD5	U.K.	1992	$10.00
Virgin	VJDP-103	Manhattan Skyline	CD3	Japan	1990	$12.00/$4.00
Virgin	PRCD 3030	Manhattan Skyline	CDJ	U.S.	1989	$3.00
Circa	VJDP-10162	Melt	CD3	Japan	1991	$12.00/$4.00
Virgin	PR 4195	Mysterious Ways	CDJ	U.S.	1991	$2.00
Virgin	VJDP-119	Porcelain	CD3	Japan	1990	$12.00/$4.00
Virgin	VJDP-10171	Talk Walk Drive	CD3	Japan	1991	$12.00/$4.00
Virgin	4379	Talk Walk Drive	CDJ	U.S.	1991	$2.00
Circa	YRCD-23	Where Does the Time Go	CD3	U.K.	1989	$10.00
Circa	YRCD-17	Woman of the '80s	CD5	U.K.	1988	$10.00

Fore

Label	Catalog Number	Title	Type	Country	Year	Longbox/Value
		Singles				
BMG	663290	Race	CD5	Germany	1990	$10.00

Foreheads In A Fish Tank

Label	Catalog Number	Title	Type	Country	Year	Longbox/Value
		Singles				
APT	SBZCD-014	Haircut	CD5	U.K.	1992	$8.00

Foreign Exchange

Label	Catalog Number	Title	Type	Country	Year	Longbox/Value
		Singles				
	2001	Mystic Dread	CD5	U.S.	1994	$5.00

Foreigner

Label	Catalog Number	Title	Type	Country	Year	Longbox/Value
		Full Length				
Atlantic	81999-2	Agent Provocateur	LP/LB	U.S.†	1985	$14.00/$8.00
Atlantic	81999-2	Agent Provocateur	LP/LB	U.S.	1986	$14.00/$8.00
Atlantic	19999-2	Double Vision	LP/LB	U.S.†	1985	$14.00/$8.00
Atlantic	19999-2	Double Vision	LP/LB	U.S.	1986	$14.00/$8.00
WEA	50177	Feels Like The First Time	LD	U.S.	1992	$30.00
Atlantic	19109-2	Foreigner	LP/LB	U.S.†	1985	$14.00/$8.00
Atlantic	19109-2	Foreigner	LP/LB	U.S.	1986	$14.00/$8.00
Atlantic	81999-2	Foreigner 4	LP/LB	U.S.†	1985	$14.00/$8.00
Atlantic	81999-2	Foreigner 4	LP/LB	U.S.	1986	$14.00/$8.00
Atlantic	29999-2	Head Games	LP/LB	U.S.		$14.00/$8.00
Album Network		In the Studio (Double Vision)	RS	U.S.	1991	$25.00
Airdate: 7/15/91.						
Album Network		In the Studio (Foreigner)	RS	U.S.	1989	$20.00
Airdate: 3/6/89.						
Album Network		In the Studio (Foreigner)	RS	U.S.	1992	$20.00
Airdate: 3/16/92.						
Album Network		In the Studio (Foreigner 4)	RS	U.S.	1989	$20.00
Airdate: 9/11/89.						
Atlantic	43XD-2005	Inside Information	LTD/LP	Japan		$40.00
Gold disc.						
DIR		King Biscuit Flour Hour	RS	U.S.	1991	$30.00
Airdate: 9/22/91.						
DIR		King Biscuit Flour Hour	RS	U.S.	1991	$30.00
With King's X, Airdate: 1/13/91.						
DIR		King Biscuit Flour Hour	RS	U.S.	1992	$30.00
Airdate: 11/15/92.						
DIR		King Biscuit Flour Hour	RS	U.S.	1994	$30.00
Airdate: 4/13/94.						
DIR		King Biscuit Flour Hour	RS	U.S.	1995	$30.00
Airdate: 10/22/95.						
Atlantic	PRCD 5365-2	Live	DJ/Smplr	U.S.	1993	$15.00
		Live at Electric Ladyland	RS	U.S.	1993	$40.00
Airdate: 6/27/93.						
Atlantic		Mr. Moonlight Interview	DJ/Intvw	U.S.	1995	$15.00
Westwood One		Off the Record	RS	U.S.	1992	$25.00
Airdate: 10/26/92.						
Westwood One		Off the Record	RS	U.S.	1993	$30.00
Airdate: 8/9/93.						
Westwood One		Off the Record	RS	U.S.	1995	$25.00
Airdate: 3/13/95.						
Atlantic	PRCD 4007-2	Profiled	DJ/Intvw	U.S.	1991	$8.00
Atlantic	80999-2	Records	LP/LB	U.S.		$14.00/$8.00
Atlantic	80999-2	Records	LP/LB	U.S.†	1984	$14.00/$8.00
Westwood One		Superstar Concert	RS	U.S.	1992	$40.00
2 CD set. Airdate: 10/11/92.						

Label	Catalog Number	Title	Type	Country	Year	Longbox Value / Value
Westwood One		Superstars	RS	U.S.	1995	$50.00
	2 CD set. Airdate: 4/17/95.					
Media America		Up Close	RS	U.S.	1988	$30.00
	2 CD set.					
Media America		Up Close	RS	U.S.	1991	$30.00
	2 CD set.					
Media America		Up Close	RS	U.S.	1992	$30.00
	2 CD set.					
Unistar		Weekly Specials, The	RS	U.S.	1991	$15.00
	Airdate: 8/16/91.					

Singles

Label	Catalog Number	Title	Type	Country	Year	Longbox Value / Value
Atlantic		All I Need To Know	CDJ	U.S.	1995	$6.00
WEA	786537-0	Heart Turns to Stone	CD3	Germany	1987	$10.00
Pioneer	10P3-6001	Heart Turns to Stone	CD3	Japan	1987	$13.00/$4.00
Atlantic	PR 2385-2	Heart Turns to Stone	CDJ	U.S.	1987	$3.00
Atlantic	786569-2	I Don't Want to Live Without You	CD3	Germany	1988	$10.00
Pioneer	10SW-27	I Don't Want to Live Without You	CD3	Japan	1988	$15.00/$4.00
Atlantic	A-9101CD	I Don't Want to Live Without You	CD3	U.K.	1988	$10.00
Atlantic	7567-85962-2	I'll Fight For You	CD5	Germany	1991	$10.00
Atlantic	AMDY-5062	I'll Fight For You	CD3	Japan	1991	$12.00/$4.00
Atlantic	A-7608CD	I'll Fight For You	CD5	U.K.	1991	$10.00
Atlantic	PRCD 4141-2	I'll Fight For You	CDJ	U.S.	1991	$2.00
		Little White Lies	CD5	U.K.	1994	$10.00
Atlantic	7567-86018-2	Low Down and Dirty	CD5	Germany	1991	$10.00
Atlantic	AMDY-5051	Low Down and Dirty	CD3	Japan	1991	$12.00/$4.00
Atlantic	A-7666CD	Low Down and Dirty	CD5	U.K.	1991	$10.00
Atlantic	PRCD 3999-2	Low Down and Dirty	CDJ	U.S.	1991	$3.00
ATLANTIC	PRCD 3999-2	Low Down and Dirty	CDJ	U.S.	1991	$40.00
	CD in simulated car CD player package.					
Atlantic	PRCD 4242-2	Only Heaven Knows	CDJ	U.S.	1991	$2.00
Atlantic	786629-2	Say You Will	CD5	Germany	1988	$10.00
Atlantic	10SW-1	Say You Will	CD3	Japan	1987	$12.00/$4.00
Atlantic	A-9169CD	Say You Will	CD5	U.K.	1987	$10.00
Atlantic	PR 2160-2	Say You Will	CDJ	U.S.	1987	$2.00
Atlantic	PRCD 4786-2	Soul Doctor	CDJ	U.S.	1992	$2.00
Atlantic		Under the Gun	CD5	U.S.	1995	$6.00
Atlantic		Under the Gun	CDJ	U.S.	1995	$6.00
Priority Records	53183	Until the End of Time	CD5	U.S.	1994	$5.00
Atlantic	7567-85877-2	Waiting For a Girl Like You	CD5	Germany	1992	$10.00
Atlantic	A-7493CD	Waiting For a Girl Like You	CD5	U.K.	1992	$10.00
Atlantic	PRCD 4869-2	With Heaven on Our Side	CDJ	U.S.	1992	$2.00

Forester Sisters

Singles

Label	Catalog Number	Title	Type	Country	Year	Longbox Value / Value
Warner Brothers	PRO-CD-3561	Don't You	CDJ	U.S.	1989	$2.00
		Nothing's Gonna Bother Me Tonight	CDJ	U.S.		$2.00
		Old Enough to Know	CDJ	U.S.		$2.00
Warner Brothers	PRO-CD-5123	That Makes One of Us	CDJ	U.S.	1991	$2.00

Forget Me Nots

Singles

Label	Catalog Number	Title	Type	Country	Year	Longbox Value / Value
CBS	657543-2	So Good	CD5	U.K.	1991	$8.00
CBS	658065-2	Soap Singer's Beat	CD5	U.K.	1992	$8.00
CBS	657821-2	Trouble	CD5	U.K.	1992	$8.00

Form

Singles

Label	Catalog Number	Title	Type	Country	Year	Longbox Value / Value
CBS	654762-3	Colors of Ever	CD3	Germany	1989	$8.00
CBS	656020-3	Do You	CD3	Germany	1989	$8.00

Forthcoming Fire

Singles

Label	Catalog Number	Title	Type	Country	Year	Longbox Value / Value
Rough Trade	391-0006-3	Longing for Light	CD5	Germany	1992	$8.00

Fortin, Mark James

Singles

Label	Catalog Number	Title	Type	Country	Year	Longbox Value / Value
		Easy Way Out	CDJ	Canada		$3.00

Fortran 5

Singles

Label	Catalog Number	Title	Type	Country	Year	Longbox Value / Value
Mute	826 965	Groove	CD5	Germany	1991	$8.00
Mute	826 969	Heart on the Line	CD5	Germany	1991	$8.00
Mute	CDMUTE-129	Heart on the Line	CD5	U.K.	1991	$8.00
Mute	66491-2	Heart on the Line	CD5	U.S.	1991	$4.00
Mute	PRCD 8451-2	Heart on the Line	CDJ	U.S.	1991	$2.00
Mute	CDMUTE-135	Look to the Future	CD5	U.K.	1991	$8.00
Mute	66578-2	Love Baby	CD5	U.S.	1990	$4.00

Fortunati, Michael

Singles

Label	Catalog Number	Title	Type	Country	Year	Longbox Value / Value
Now Discs	11B3-24	A.B.C. (It's Called)	CD3	Japan	1989	$13.00/$4.00
Now Discs	10SR-8	Alleluia	CD3	Japan	1989	$13.00/$4.00
Alfa	ALDB-65	Baby You	CD3	Japan	1990	$13.00/$4.00
Alfa	ALDB-145	Big Bang	CD3	Japan	1991	$13.00/$4.00
Now Discs	11B3-56	Danse Avec Moi	CD3	Japan	1989	$13.00/$4.00
Alfa	ALDB-164	Generate	CD3	Japan	1993	$13.00/$4.00
Now Discs	10SR-11	Gioch Di Fortuna	CD3	Japan	1989	$13.00/$4.00
Now Discs	11B3-6	Let Me Down	CD3	Japan	1989	$13.00/$4.00
Alfa	ALDB-157	Take Me Down	CD3	Japan	1992	$13.00/$4.00
Alfa	ALDB-160	Take Me On Up	CD3	Japan	1992	$13.00/$4.00

Foster, David

Singles

Label	Catalog Number	Title	Type	Country	Year	Longbox Value / Value
		And When She Danced	CDJ	U.S.		$2.00
Atlantic	PRCD 3647	Grown-Up Christmas List	CDJ	U.S.	1990	$2.00
		Love Lights the World	CDJ	Japan	1994	$20.00
Atlantic	PRCD 3778	River of Love	CDJ	U.S.	1990	$2.00
Atlantic	PR 2200-2	Winter Games	CDJ	U.S.	1988	$2.00

Foster, Gina

Singles

Label	Catalog Number	Title	Type	Country	Year	Longbox Value / Value
BMG	PD-43484	Cry in Vain	CD5	U.K.	1990	$8.00
BMG	PD-43485	Cry in Vain	CD5	U.K.	1990	$8.00
BMG	PD-43074	Love is a House	CD5	U.K.	1990	$8.00

Foster, Radney

Singles

Label	Catalog Number	Title	Type	Country	Year	Longbox Value / Value
Arista	ASCD 2652	Closing Time	CDJ	U.S.	1994	$2.00

Foster, Vernell

Singles

Label	Catalog Number	Title	Type	Country	Year	Longbox Value / Value
SBK	CDSBK-7005	Love, Joy and Happiness	CD5	U.K.	1990	$8.00

Fountainhead

Singles

Label	Catalog Number	Title	Type	Country	Year	Longbox Value / Value
China	887486-2	Someone Like You	CD5	Germany	1988	$8.00
China	CHICD-2	Someone Like You	CD5	U.K.	1988	$8.00

Four Freshman

Full Length

Label	Catalog Number	Title	Type	Country	Year	Longbox Value / Value
Warner Sound Exchange		22 Legendary Hits	LTD/LP	U.S.	1995	$17.00

Four Fun

Singles

Label	Catalog Number	Title	Type	Country	Year	Longbox Value / Value
		Find a Way	CDJ	U.S.		$2.00

Four Hero

Singles

Label	Catalog Number	Title	Type	Country	Year	Longbox Value / Value
Reinforced	RIVET-1216CD	Where's the Boy	CD5	U.K.	1992	$10.00

Four Horsemen

Full Length

Label	Catalog Number	Title	Type	Country	Year	Longbox Value / Value
Def American	9 26561-2-PR	Nobody Said It Was Easy	DJ/LP	U.S.	1991	$17.00
	Special denim pocket sleeve.					

Singles

Label	Catalog Number	Title	Type	Country	Year	Longbox Value / Value
Def American	DEFCD-12	Nobody Said It Was Easy	CD5	U.K.	1991	$10.00
Def American	PRO-CD-4882	Nobody Said It Was Easy	CDJ	U.S.	1991	$2.00
Def American	DEFAC-15	Rockin' Is My Business	CD5	U.K.	1992	$10.00
Def American	PRO-CD-5059	Rockin' Is My Business	CDJ	U.S.	1991	$2.00
Def American	PRO-CD-5286	Tired Wings	CDJ	U.S.	1991	$2.00

Four Love

Singles

Label	Catalog Number	Title	Type	Country	Year	Longbox Value / Value
Union City	UCRCD-5	Hold Your Head Up High	CD5	U.K.	1992	$8.00

Four Non Blondes

Full Length

Label	Catalog Number	Title	Type	Country	Year	Longbox Value / Value
Westwood One		In Concert	RS	U.S.	1994	$50.00
	Airdate: 4/25/94.					

Singles

Label	Catalog Number	Title	Type	Country	Year	Longbox Value / Value
		Dear Mr. President	CD5	U.K.		$10.00
		Spaceman	CDJ	U.S.		$6.00
		What's Up?	CD5	U.K.		$10.00

Four of Us

Singles

Label	Catalog Number	Title	Type	Country	Year	Longbox Value / Value
CBS	CDFOUR 5	Drag My Bad Name Down	CD5	U.K.	1990	$8.00
CBS	FOURC-2	Drag My Bad Name Down	CD5	U.K.	1990	$8.00
CBS	FOURC-1	I Just Can't Get Enough	CD5	U.K.	1988	$8.00
CBS		I Miss You	CD5	U.K.		$8.00
CBS		I Miss You	CD5	U.K.		$8.00
	Second version.					
Columbia	658329-2	Man Alive	CD5	U.K.	1992	$8.00
CBS	FOURC-3	Mary	CD5	U.K.	1989	$8.00
CBS	CDFOUR 4	Mary	CD5	U.K.	1989	$8.00
CBS	XPCD 124	Mary	CD5	U.K.	1989	$8.00
CBS		She Hits Me	CD5	U.K.		$8.00
CBS		She Hits Me	CD5	U.K.		$8.00
	Second version.					

Four PM

Singles

Label	Catalog Number	Title	Type	Country	Year	Longbox Value / Value
Polygram	857971	Lay Down Your Love	CD5	U.S.	1994	$5.00
Polygram		She's in There	CDJ	U.S.	1994	$2.00
Polygram	857687	Sukiyaki	CD5	U.S.	1994	$5.00

Four Reeves

Singles

Label	Catalog Number	Title	Type	Country	Year	Longbox Value / Value
Eastwest	9031-75447-2	Party	CD5	Germany	1991	$8.00

Four Runner

Full Length

Label	Catalog Number	Title	Type	Country	Year	Longbox Value / Value
		Interview	DJ/intvw	U.S.	1993	$10.00

Four Seasons

Full Length

Label	Catalog Number	Title	Type	Country	Year	Longbox Value / Value
MGM/UA	ML100372	Vivaldi	LD	U.S.	1984	$35.00

Four Seasons (Frankie Valli)

Full Length

Label	Catalog Number	Title	Type	Country	Year	Longbox Value / Value
		Sixties Legends	RS	U.S.	1992	$15.00
	2 CD set. Airdate: 6/19/92.					

Singles

Label	Catalog Number	Title	Type	Country	Year	Longbox Value / Value
Flying	VALCD-1	Can't Take My Eyes off You	CD5	U.K.	1992	$9.00
BCM	20109	December '63 (Oh What a Night)	CD5	Germany	1989	$10.00
Flying	865885-2	December '63 (Oh What a Night)	CD5	Germany	1992	$9.00
BR	CDS-277	December '63 (Oh What a Night)	CD5	U.K.	1988	$10.00
Flying	VALCD-2	December '63 (Oh What a Night)	CD5	U.K.	1992	$9.00
Rhino	885832	Four Seasons	CD3	Germany	1990	$8.00
Aris	885831	Sherry	CD3	Germany	1990	$10.00
Rhino	R3 7373010	Sherry	CD3	U.S.	1988	$6.00/$3.00

Four Sure

Singles

Label	Catalog Number	Title	Type	Country	Year	Longbox Value / Value
Ruffhousse	74871	Innocent Girl	CDJ	U.S.	1993	$2.00
Ruffhousse	77123	Try and Find a Way	CDJ	U.S.	1993	$2.00

Four Tops

Full Length

Label	Catalog Number	Title	Type	Country	Year	Longbox Value / Value
Motown	WD-72220	Compact Command Performance	LP	Germany		$15.00
Aris	886073	Four Tops	LP	Germany		$15.00
Motown	5122	Four Tops	LP/BP	U.S.		$14.00/$8.00
Motown	MOTD-8027	Four Tops + Four Tops Second Album	LP/BP	U.S.†		$14.00/$8.00
Image Entertainment	IG-5003	Four Tops/Live	LD	U.S.	1985	$30.00
Motown	5426	Keeper of the Castle	LP/BP	U.S.		$14.00/$8.00
Motown	5466	Now!	LP/BP	U.S.		$14.00/$8.00
Motown	5444	On Top	LP/BP	U.S.		$14.00/$8.00
Motown	MOTD-8007	Reach Out + Still Waters Run Deep	LP/BP	U.S.†		$14.00/$8.00
Aris	886043	Reach Out/Still Waters Run Deep	LP	Germany		$15.00
		Sixties Legends	RS	U.S.	1992	$15.00
Image	ID64176FR	Temptations and the Four Tops	LD	U.S.		$20.00
Polygram	800049-2	Tonight	LP	Germany		$15.00
Casablanca	800049-2	Tonight	LP/BP	U.S.†	1984	$14.00/$8.00

Singles

Label	Catalog Number	Title	Type	Country	Year	Longbox Value / Value
Aris	886571	Baby I Need Your Loving	CD3	Germany	1989	$10.00
Motown	ZD-41947	Baby I Need Your Loving	CD3	U.K.	1989	$10.00
Arista	162184	Change of Heart	CD3	Germany	1989	$10.00
Arista	662184	Change of Heart	CD5	Germany	1989	$10.00
Arista	162074	Indestructible	CD3	Germany	1988	$10.00
Arista	661510	Indestructible	CD5	Germany	1988	$10.00
Arista		Indestructible	CDJ	U.S.	1988	$3.00
Special Music Co.	8528	It's The Same Old	CD5	U.S.	1994	$5.00
Arista	661850	Loco In Acapulco	CD5	Germany	1988	$10.00
Arista	661850	Loco In Acapulco	CD5	U.K.	1988	$10.00
Arista	662252	Sun Ain't Gonna Shine	CD5	U.K.	1989	$10.00

Label	Catalog Number	Title	Type	Country	Year	Longbox Value/Value

Four Way

Singles

Label	Catalog Number	Title	Type	Country	Year	Longbox Value/Value
		With All My Love	CD5	U.S.		$5.00

Fourplay

Full Length

Label	Catalog Number	Title	Type	Country	Year	Longbox Value/Value
Warner Brothers		Forplay Fourplay	DJ/Smplr	U.S.	1994	$10.00
Warner Brothers	PRO-CD-5140	Words and Music	DJ/Intvw	U.S.	1992	$8.00

Singles

Label	Catalog Number	Title	Type	Country	Year	Longbox Value/Value
Warner Brothers	PRO-CD-4976	After the Dance	CDJ	U.S.	1991	$3.00
Warner Brothers	PRO-CD-6285	Between the Sheets	CDJ	U.S.	1993	$3.00
Warner Brothers	PRO-CD-6444	Between the Sheets	CDJ	U.S.	1993	$3.00
Warner Brothers	PRO-CD-6396	Monterey	CDJ	U.S.	1993	$6.00

Fourteen Karat Soul

Singles

Label	Catalog Number	Title	Type	Country	Year	Longbox Value/Value
Canyon	PCDY-00041	Get Back in Love	CD3	Japan	1990	$13.00/$4.00
Canyon	PCDY-00112	Kierra, For You	CD3	Japan	1992	$13.00/$4.00
Canyon	PCDY-1051	Stand by Me	CD3	Japan	1990	$13.00/$4.00

Fox, Samantha

Full Length

Label	Catalog Number	Title	Type	Country	Year	Longbox Value/Value
Alfa	PACK-1	Megamix Album	LTD/LP	Japan		$30.00

Singles

Label	Catalog Number	Title	Type	Country	Year	Longbox Value/Value
Jive	ZD-44808	Another Woman	CD5	Germany	1991	$10.00
Jive	ALDB-132	Another Woman	CD3	Japan	1991	$13.00/$4.00
Jive	ZZD-44618	(Hurt Me! Hurt Me!) But the Pants Stay On	CD5	Germany	1991	$10.00
Jive	AL08-113	(Hurt Me! Hurt Me!) But the Pants Stay On	CD3	Japan		$13.00/$4.00
Jive	1441-2-JS	(Hurt Me! Hurt Me!) But the Pants Stay On	CD5	U.S.	1991	$5.00
Jive	1441-2-JDJ	(Hurt Me! Hurt Me!) But the Pants Stay On	CDJ	U.S.	1991	$7.00
Jive	8 00009	I Only Wanna Be With You	CD5	Germany	1989	$10.00
Jive	FOXYCD-11	I Only Wanna Be With You	CD5	U.K.	1989	$10.00
RCA	1105-2-RDJ	I Only Wanna Be With You	CDJ	U.S.	1989	$3.00
Jive	10SR-6	I Surrender	CD3	Japan	1988	$13.00/$4.00
Jive	ZD-42954	I Wanna Have Some Fun	CD5	Germany	1989	$10.00
Jive	FOXYCD-12	I Wanna Have Some Fun	CD5	U.K.	1988	$10.00
Jive	1165-2-RDJ	I Wanna Have Some Fun	CDJ	U.S.	1988	$2.00
Jive	4200-2-RDJ	Just One Night	CDJ	U.S.	1991	$2.00
Jive	8 20976	Love House	CD5	Germany	1989	$10.00
Jive	09B3-47	Love House	CD3	Japan	1989	$13.00/$4.00
Jive	1234-2-JDJ	Love House	CDJ	U.S.	1989	$3.00
Jive	247305-2	Naughty Girls (Need Love Too)	CD5	Germany	1989	$12.00
Jive	10SR-10	Naughty Girls (Need Love Too)	CD3	Japan	1989	$13.00/$4.00
Jive	FOXYCD-9	Naughty Girls (Need Love Too)	CD5	U.K.	1989	$12.00
Jive		Naughty Girls (Need Love Too)	CDJ	U.S.	1989	$3.00
Jive	10SR-7	Nothing's Gonna Stop Me Now	CD3	Japan	1988	$13.00/$4.00
Jive	FOXYCD-8	True Devotion	CD5	U.K.	1988	$10.00

Fox, Steve

Singles

Label	Catalog Number	Title	Type	Country	Year	Longbox Value/Value
		Days of my Youth	CDJ	Canada		$3.00
		I Want to Get Old With You	CDJ	Canada		$3.00
		Never Mind	CDJ	Canada		$3.00

Foxworthy, Jeff

Full Length

Label	Catalog Number	Title	Type	Country	Year	Longbox Value/Value
Warner Brothers	PRO-CD-6278	Selections From "You Might Be A Redneck If.."	DJ/Smplr	U.S.	1993	$5.00

Singles

Label	Catalog Number	Title	Type	Country	Year	Longbox Value/Value
	2012	King of the Rednecks	CD5	U.S.	1994	$5.00
	2079	Original	CD5	U.S.	1994	$5.00
	2011	Redneck Test	CD5	U.S.	1994	$5.00
	2043	Redneck Test Vol. 43	CD5	U.S.	1994	$5.00
	2080	Sold Out	CD5	U.S.	1994	$5.00
	2010	You Might Be a Redneck	CD5	U.S.	1994	$5.00

Foxx, Redd

Full Length

Label	Catalog Number	Title	Type	Country	Year	Longbox Value/Value
Vestron Video	VL2008	Redd Foxx/Live	LD	U.S.	1984	$30.00

Fpi Project

Singles

Label	Catalog Number	Title	Type	Country	Year	Longbox Value/Value
Moonshine Music	88042	Come On and Do It	CD5	U.S.	1994	$5.00
ZYX	6428-8	Everybody	CD5	Germany	1990	$6.00
ZYX	6340-8	Risky	CD5	Germany	1990	$6.00
Alfa	ALDB-86	Risky	CD3	Japan	1990	$13.00/$4.00

Fr Connection

Singles

Label	Catalog Number	Title	Type	Country	Year	Longbox Value/Value
Radikal	15514	Listen Up	CDJ	U.S.	1994	$2.00

Fragments

Singles

Label	Catalog Number	Title	Type	Country	Year	Longbox Value/Value
BMG	664567	Love Train	CD5	Germany	1991	$8.00

Frames

Full Length

Label	Catalog Number	Title	Type	Country	Year	Longbox Value/Value
Polygram	512766	Another Love Song	LP/BP	U.S.		$12.00/$7.00

Singles

Label	Catalog Number	Title	Type	Country	Year	Longbox Value/Value
Island	CID-546	Before You Go	CD5	U.K.	1992	$8.00
Island	PRCD 6725-2	Dancer, The	CDJ	U.S.	1992	$2.00
Island	CID-542	Masquerade	CD5	U.K.	1992	$8.00
Island	CID-557	Picture of Love	CD5	U.K.	1992	$8.00

Frampton, Peter

Full Length

Label	Catalog Number	Title	Type	Country	Year	Longbox Value/Value
Westwood One		BBC Classic Tracks	RS	U.S.	1994	$30.00
	Airdate: 4/4/94.					
		Comes Alive II	LTD/LP	U.K.	1995	$28.00
	2 CD set.					
A&M		Frampton Comes Alive	LP/LB	U.S.		$20.00/$17.00
	2CD set in double jewel case with custom longbox.					
Westwood One		In Concert	RS	U.S.	1992	$40.00
	Airdate: 10/26/92.					
Album Network		In the Studio (Best Of)	RS	U.S.	1992	$30.00
	Airdate: 11/23/92.					
Album Network		In the Studio (Comes Alive)	RS	U.S.	1989	$30.00
	Airdate: 10/23/89.					
Virgin		Premonition	LP/LB	U.S.		$14.00/$8.00
Relativity	RRROCD 0245	Seasons Greetings	DJ/Smplr	U.S.	1993	$15.00
Westwood One		Superstars	RS	U.S.	1994	$45.00
	2 CD set. Airdate: 7/25/94.					
Media America		Up Close	RS	U.S.	1994	$45.00

Singles

Label	Catalog Number	Title	Type	Country	Year	Longbox Value/Value
A&M	31458 8059	Bigger They Come, The	CDJ	U.S.	1992	$3.00
Relativity	RPROCD-0283	Day In the Sun	CDJ	U.S.	1993	$3.00
El Dorado	DPRO-10521	For Now	CDJ	U.S.		$3.00
	520289	Frampton	CD5	U.S.	1994	$5.00
Atlantic	PR 2917-2	Holding on to You	CDJ	U.S.	1989	$3.00
Atlantic	PR 3130-2	More Ways Than One	CDJ	U.S.	1989	$3.00
Relativity	RPROCD-0283	You Can Be Sure	CDJ	U.S.	1993	$3.00

Frances, Kay

Singles

Label	Catalog Number	Title	Type	Country	Year	Longbox Value/Value
Polygram	871968-3	I Can Do	CD3	Germany	1989	$8.00
Polygram	871969-2	I Can Do	CD5	Germany	1989	$8.00

Francis, Connie

Full Length

Label	Catalog Number	Title	Type	Country	Year	Longbox Value/Value
Polydor		Box Set Sampler	DJ/Smplr	U.S.	1997	$18.00
Time/Warner Sound Exchange	232538	Who's Sorry Now: 40 Legendary Hits	LP	U.S.	1996	$30.00
	2 CD set.					

Singles

Label	Catalog Number	Title	Type	Country	Year	Longbox Value/Value
Polygram	865385-2	Jive Connie	CD5	Germany	1992	$10.00
Polydor	PODP-1064	Where the Boys Are	CD3	Japan	1992	$13.00/$4.00
Polygram	887183-2	Who's Sorry Now	CD5	Germany	1990	$10.00

Francis, Liz

Singles

Label	Catalog Number	Title	Type	Country	Year	Longbox Value/Value
MCA	MCSTD-1588	Rhythm of Life	CD5	U.K.	1992	$8.00

Francour, Chuck

Singles

Label	Catalog Number	Title	Type	Country	Year	Longbox Value/Value
CBS	651680-3	Dance Dance Dance	CD3	Germany	1988	$8.00

Frank and Walters

Singles

Label	Catalog Number	Title	Type	Country	Year	Longbox Value/Value
		After All	CD5	U.K.		$8.00
		After All	CD5	U.K.		$8.00
	Second version					
		Fashion Crisis Hits New York	CD5	U.K.		$8.00
		Fashion Crisis Hits New York	CD5	U.K.		$8.00
	Second version.					
Go Disc	HOOCD-2	Happy Bushman	CD5	U.K.	1991	$8.00
Go Disc	HOOCD-3	This Is Not a Song	CD5	U.K.	1991	$8.00

Franke

Singles

Label	Catalog Number	Title	Type	Country	Year	Longbox Value/Value
China	WOKCD-2028	Understand This Groove	CD5	U.K.	1992	$8.00

Frankie Goes to Hollywood

Full Length

Label	Catalog Number	Title	Type	Country	Year	Longbox Value/Value
Pioneer	PA-87-189	Frankie Goes to Hollywood	LD	U.S.	1987	$20.00
Pioneer	PA-87-189	Frankie Goes to Hollywood	LD	U.S.	1990	$20.00
	Digital audio.					
Island		Liverpool	LP/LB	U.S.		$14.00/$8.00
Island	90232-2	Welcome to the Pleasuredome	LP/LB	U.S.†	1985	$20.00/$17.00
	2 CD set.					

Singles

Label	Catalog Number	Title	Type	Country	Year	Longbox Value/Value
ZTT	25	Highlights From Warriors Of the Wasteland	CDJ	U.K.	1986	$12.00
ZTT	663874	Power of Love	CD5	U.K.	1990	$10.00
ZTT		Power of Love	CD5	U.K.	1990	$10.00
	Second version.					
ZTT	658434	Rage Hard	CD5	Germany	1989	$10.00
ZTT	651096	Relax	CD5	Germany	1989	$10.00
ZTT	P15D-37007	Relax	CD3	Japan	1989	$12.00/$4.00
Atlantic	85659	Relax	CD5	U.S.	1994	$5.00
ZTT	651325	Two Tribes	CD5	Germany	1989	$10.00
ZTT	P15D-37008	Two Tribes	CD3	Japan	1989	$12.00/$4.00
ZTT	880455	Warriors	CD5	Germany	1988	$10.00
ZTT	ZCID-25	Warriors	CD5	U.K.	1988	$10.00
ZTT	FGTH 2CD	Welcome to the Pleasuredome	CD5	Germany	1993	$10.00

Franklin, Aretha

Full Length

Label	Catalog Number	Title	Type	Country	Year	Longbox Value/Value
Arista	ARCD-8222	Jump to It	LP/LB	U.S.†	1984	$14.00/$8.00
Mobile Fidelity		Live at Filmore West	LP/LB	U.S.		$25.00/$20.00
Rhino	90126	Queen of Soul Sampler	DJ/Smplr	U.S.	1992	$20.00
Chess	CD-600168	Songs of Faith	LP	Germany		$23.00
Arista	ARCD-8222	Who's Zoomin' Who	LP/LB	U.S.†	1985	$14.00/$8.00

Singles

Label	Catalog Number	Title	Type	Country	Year	Longbox Value/Value
Arista		A Deeper Love	CD5	U.K.	1993	$10.00
Arista		A Deeper Love	CD5	U.K.	1993	$10.00
	Second version.					
Arista	12656	A Deeper Love	CD5	U.S.	1993	$5.00
Arista	ASCD-2651	A Deeper Love	CDJ	U.S.	1993	$2.00
Arista	12656	Deeper Love	CD5	U.S.	1994	$5.00
Arista	664420	Every Day People	CD5	Germany	1991	$10.00
Arista	BVDA-22	Every Day People	CD3	Japan	1991	$12.00/$4.00
Arista	664420	Every Day People	CD5	U.K.	1991	$10.00
Arista	ASCD 2239	Every Day People	CDJ	U.S.	1991	$3.00
Arista	162052	Freeway of Love	CD3	Germany	1989	$10.00
Arista	162052	Freeway of Love	CD3	U.K.	1989	$10.00
Arista	662727	Gimme Your Love	CD5	Germany	1989	$10.00
Arista	A10D-139	Gimme Your Love	CD3	Japan	1989	$12.00/$4.00
Arista	662727	Gimme Your Love	CD5	U.K.	1989	$10.00
Arista	ASCD 9906	Gimme Your Love	CDJ	U.S.	1989	$3.00
Arista	12757	Honey	CD5	U.S.	1994	$6.00
WEA	786488-2	I Say a Little Prayer	CD3	Germany	1989	$10.00
WEA	786488-2	I Say a Little Prayer	CD3	U.K.	1989	$10.00
Arista	6162484	It Isn't, It Wasn't	CD3	Germany	1989	$10.00
Arista	662484	It Isn't, It Wasn't	CD5	Germany	1989	$10.00
Arista	662484	It Isn't, It Wasn't	CD5	U.K.	1989	$10.00
Arista	ASCD-9850	It Isn't, It Wasn't	CDJ	U.S.	1989	$3.00
Arista	RICD 6	Jimmy Lee	CD5	Germany	1986	$10.00
Old Gold	OG-6504	Jump to It	CD3	U.K.	1990	$10.00
		Knew You Were Waiting	CDJ	U.S.	1989	$3.00
		Rock-A-Lott	CDJ	U.S.		$3.00
Arista	ASCD 2350	Someone Else's Eyes	CDJ	U.S.	1991	$3.00
Eastwest	9031-74524-2	Think	CD5	Germny	1991	$10.00
Arista	162185	Through the Storm	CD3	Germany	1989	$10.00
Arista	A10D-122	Through the Storm	CD3	Japan	1989	$12.00/$4.00
Arista	162185	Through the Storm	CD3	U.K.	1989	$10.00
Arista	ASCD 9809	Through the Storm	CDJ	U.S.	1989	$3.00
Arista	ASCD 2380	What You See Is What You Sweat	CDJ	U.S.	1991	$3.00

Franklin, Erma

Singles

Label	Catalog Number	Title	Type	Country	Year	Longbox Value/Value
Epic	658384-2	Piece of My Heart	CD5	U.K.	1992	$10.00

Franklin, Rodney

Singles

Label	Catalog Number	Title	Type	Country	Year	Longbox Value/Value
RCA	PD-49476	Gotta Give Up	CD5	Germany	1989	$8.00

Label	Catalog Number	Title	Type	Country	Year	Longbox Value/Value

Franks, Michael

Full Length

Label	Catalog Number	Title	Type	Country	Year	Longbox Value/Value
Reprise	9 2230-2	Art of Love, The	LP/LB	U.S.†	1984	$14.00/$8.00

Singles

Label	Catalog Number	Title	Type	Country	Year	Longbox Value/Value
Reprise	PRO-CD-4084	Art of Love, The	CDJ	U.S.	1990	$2.00
Warner Brothers	PRO-CD-2933	Camera Never Lies, The	CDJ	U.S.	1987	$2.00
Warner Brothers	PRO-CD-2900	Dr. Sax	CDJ	U.S.	1987	$2.00
Warner Brothers	PRO-CD-4564	Speak to Me	CDJ	U.S.	1990	$2.00
Warner Brothers	PRO-CD-4716	Woman in the Waves	CDJ	U.S.	1990	$2.00

Franzisca

Singles

Label	Catalog Number	Title	Type	Country	Year	Longbox Value/Value
BMG	663416	Hold the Dream	CD5	Germany	1990	$8.00

Frazier Chorus

Singles

Label	Catalog Number	Title	Type	Country	Year	Longbox Value/Value
Virgin	VSCDT-1252	Cloud 8	CD5	U.K.	1989	$8.00
Virgin	96378	Cloud 8	CD5	U.S.	1989	$4.00
Charisma	PRCD 030	Cloud 8	CDJ	U.S.	1989	$2.00
Virgin	VSCD-1145	Dream Kitchen	CD3	U.K.	1988	$8.00
Virgin	VSCDT-1284	Nothing	CD5	U.K.	1989	$8.00
Virgin	VSCD-1192	Sloppy Heart	CD3	U.K.	1989	$8.00
Virgin	VSCD-1174	Typical	CD3	U.K.	1989	$8.00
Virgin	VSCDT-1330	Walking on Air	CD5	U.K.	1991	$8.00

Freak Brothers

Singles

Label	Catalog Number	Title	Type	Country	Year	Longbox Value/Value
Subway	SUBWAY-039C	Freak to the Beat	CD5	U.K.	1988	$8.00

Freaked Out Children

Singles

Label	Catalog Number	Title	Type	Country	Year	Longbox Value/Value
Virgin	VOZCD135	Beautiful People	CD5	Australia	1992	$7.00
Virgin	VOZCD128	Spill the Wine	CD5	Australia	1992	$7.00

Freaky Funkin Weirdoz

Singles

Label	Catalog Number	Title	Type	Country	Year	Longbox Value/Value
Arista	12355	Extra Play	CD5	U.S.	1991	$5.00

Freaky Realistic

Singles

Label	Catalog Number	Title	Type	Country	Year	Longbox Value/Value
Polydor		Koochie Ryder	CD5	U.K.		$8.00
Polydor		Koochie Ryder	CD5	U.K.		$8.00
Second version.						
Polydor		Leonard Nimoy	CD5	U.K.		$8.00
Polydor		Leonard Nimoy	CD5	U.K.		$8.00
Second version.						
Polydor	883617-2	Something New	CD5	Germany	1992	$8.00
Polydor	FRECD-1	Something New	CD5	U.K.	1992	$8.00

Fred, Banana

Singles

Label	Catalog Number	Title	Type	Country	Year	Longbox Value/Value
Polygram	887462-2	Time to Cry	CD5	Germany	1988	$8.00

Fredrix, Dee

Singles

Label	Catalog Number	Title	Type	Country	Year	Longbox Value/Value
Eastwest	YZ-725CD	And So I Will Wait For You	CD5	U.K.	1993	$8.00

Free

Full Length

Label	Catalog Number	Title	Type	Country	Year	Longbox Value/Value
BBC Radio		BBC Classic Tracks	RS	U.S.	1992	$40.00
Airdate: 5/18/92.						

Singles

Label	Catalog Number	Title	Type	Country	Year	Longbox Value/Value
Island	664072	All Right Now	CD5	Germany	1991	$11.00
Island	CID-486	All Right Now	CD5	U.K.	1991	$11.00
Island	CIDX-486	All Right Now	CD5	U.K.	1991	$11.00
Island	887227	My Brother Jake	CD5	Germany	1991	$10.00
Island	CID-495	My Brother Jake	CD5	U.K.	1991	$10.00

Free Design

Full Length

Label	Catalog Number	Title	Type	Country	Year	Longbox Value/Value
	HI-5144	15 Tool For Free Design	DJ/Smplr	Japan	1995	$100.00

Free Flight

Singles

Label	Catalog Number	Title	Type	Country	Year	Longbox Value/Value
		Uptown	CDJ	U.S.		$2.00

Free Kitten

Singles

Label	Catalog Number	Title	Type	Country	Year	Longbox Value/Value
Kab N D Records	240	Nice Ass	CD5	U.S.	1994	$5.00

Freedom

Singles

Label	Catalog Number	Title	Type	Country	Year	Longbox Value/Value
Parlophone	CDR-6293	Like It Was Like It Is	CD5	U.K.	1991	$8.00

Freefall

Singles

Label	Catalog Number	Title	Type	Country	Year	Longbox Value/Value
Creation	BFIP-041	Something Pretty Beautiful	CD5	U.K.	1989	$8.00

Freelove, Laurie

Singles

Label	Catalog Number	Title	Type	Country	Year	Longbox Value/Value
Ensign	ENYCD-648	Arms of a Dream	CD5	U.K.	1991	$8.00
Ensign	23720	Smells Like Truth	CDJ	U.S.	1991	$2.00

Freeman, Russ

Full Length

Label	Catalog Number	Title	Type	Country	Year	Longbox Value/Value
Passport	PJCD-88044	Nocturnal Playground	LP	U.S.		$10.00

Freestyle

Singles

Label	Catalog Number	Title	Type	Country	Year	Longbox Value/Value
ZYX	5396-8	Don't Stop	CD5	Germany	1989	$6.00
ZYX	5283-8	In Your Face	CD5	Germany	1990	$6.00

Freestyle Fellowship

Singles

Label	Catalog Number	Title	Type	Country	Year	Longbox Value/Value
4th & B'way	569	Hot Potato	CDJ	U.S.	1993	$2.00

Freeway Philharmonic

Full Length

Label	Catalog Number	Title	Type	Country	Year	Longbox Value/Value
Sheffield Lab	10050-2-F	Sonic Detour	DJ/LP	U.S.	1995	$10.00

Freewheelers

Singles

Label	Catalog Number	Title	Type	Country	Year	Longbox Value/Value
DGC	PRO-CD-4317	No More Booze	CDJ	U.S.	1991	$2.00

Freeze

Singles

Label	Catalog Number	Title	Type	Country	Year	Longbox Value/Value
Profile	7357	Voulez Vous	CDJ	U.S.	1992	$2.00

Freeze Tnt Pres

Singles

Label	Catalog Number	Title	Type	Country	Year	Longbox Value/Value
Tony Nicole Ton	18	The M & J Project	CD5	U.S.	1994	$5.00

Frehley's Comet

Full Length

Label	Catalog Number	Title	Type	Country	Year	Longbox Value/Value
Atlantic	81749-2	Frehley's Comet	LP/LB	U.S.		$18.00/$15.00
Atlantic	781826-2	Live + One	LP/LB	U.S.		$18.00/$15.00
Atlantic	81862-2	Second Sighting	LP/LB	U.S.		$18.00/$15.00
		Trouble Walkin'	LP/LB	U.S.		$14.00/$10.00

Singles

Label	Catalog Number	Title	Type	Country	Year	Longbox Value/Value
Megaforce	3010	Do Ya	CDJ	U.S.	1989	$2.00
Megaforce	2434	It's Over Now	CDJ	U.S.	1988	$2.00

Freiheit

Singles

Label	Catalog Number	Title	Type	Country	Year	Longbox Value/Value
Columbia	652989-2	Keeping the Dream Alive	CD5	U.K.	1988	$8.00
Columbia	652988-2	Kissed You in the Rain	CD5	U.K.	1988	$8.00

French Ecstasy

Singles

Label	Catalog Number	Title	Type	Country	Year	Longbox Value/Value
BMG	662739	Liz and Jack	CD5	Germany	1989	$8.00

French, Nicki

Singles

Label	Catalog Number	Title	Type	Country	Year	Longbox Value/Value
Criterion	15539	Total Eclipse of the Heart	CD5	U.S.	1994	$5.00

Frente

Full Length

Label	Catalog Number	Title	Type	Country	Year	Longbox Value/Value
		Marvin	DJ/Smplr	Canada		$25.00
		Sampler	DJ/Smplr	Canada	1994	$15.00

Singles

Label	Catalog Number	Title	Type	Country	Year	Longbox Value/Value
	PRCD 5623-2	Bizarre Love Triangle	CDJ	U.S.	1994	$2.00
Mushroom	D13025	Goodbye Goodguy	SCD5	Australia	1996	$18.00
"Foot" shaped CD. Part 2 of 3.						
Mushroom	D13026	Jungle	SCD5	Australia	1996	$18.00
"Foot" shaped CD. Part 3 of 3.						
	PRCD 5661-2	Labor of Love	CDJ	U.S.	1994	$2.00
		Ordinary Angels	CDJ	U.S.	1994	$3.00
Mushroom	D13024	What's Come Over Me	SCD5	Australia	1996	$18.00
"Foot" shaped CD. Part 1 of 3.						

Frequency

Singles

Label	Catalog Number	Title	Type	Country	Year	Longbox Value/Value
Invasion	36005	Where Is Your Evidence	CDJ	U.S.	1991	$2.00

Fresh

Singles

Label	Catalog Number	Title	Type	Country	Year	Longbox Value/Value
Magnet	MAG-1008CD	Did I Say "Ti Amo"	CD5	U.K.	1992	$8.00
Eastwest	9031-76408-2	Feel My Rhythm	CD5	Germany	1992	$8.00
Magnet	MAG-100CD	Feel My Rhythm	CD5	U.K.	1992	$8.00

Fresh Bush And The Invisible Man

Singles

Label	Catalog Number	Title	Type	Country	Year	Longbox Value/Value
Capitol	C2 13872	Hard Times	CD5	U.S.	1992	$4.00
IRS	DPRO-67104	Hard Times	CDJ	U.S.	1992	$15.00

Fresh Connection

Singles

Label	Catalog Number	Title	Type	Country	Year	Longbox Value/Value
BMG	663606	Love Don't Live Here Anymore	CD5	Germany	1990	$8.00

Fresh, Doug E

Singles

Label	Catalog Number	Title	Type	Country	Year	Longbox Value/Value
Gee St	591	Freaks	CDJ	U.S.	1993	$2.00
Gee St	583	Light	CDJ	U.S.	1993	$2.00

Fresh & Fly

Singles

Label	Catalog Number	Title	Type	Country	Year	Longbox Value/Value
SPV	1015-3	African Rhythm	CD5	Germany	1991	$8.00
SPV	3547-3	Don't Stop	CD5	Germany	1991	$8.00

Fresh Four

Singles

Label	Catalog Number	Title	Type	Country	Year	Longbox Value/Value
Virgin	TENCD-301	Release Yourself	CD5	U.K.	1990	$8.00
Virgin	TENCD-287	Wishing on a Star	CD5	U.K.	1990	$8.00

Fresh, Sydney

Singles

Label	Catalog Number	Title	Type	Country	Year	Longbox Value/Value
ZYX	DST-1021-8	Feel the Bass	CD5	Germany	1990	$6.00
SPV	2151-3	Party Just Began	CD3	Germany	1989	$8.00
SPV	9110-3	Party Mix	CD5	Germany	1990	$8.00

Frey, Glenn

Full Length

Label	Catalog Number	Title	Type	Country	Year	Longbox Value/Value
MCA	MCAD-5510	Allnighter	LP/LB	U.S.†	1985	$14.00/$8.00
MCA	MCA5P-2469	Live in Dublin	DJ/Smplr	U.S.	1992	$8.00
Westwood One		Off the Record	RS	U.S.	1992	$30.00
Airdate: 7/6/92.						
Media America		Up Close	RS	U.S.	1988	$30.00
2 CD set.						

Singles

Label	Catalog Number	Title	Type	Country	Year	Longbox Value/Value
MCA	MVDM-22	I've Got Mine	CD3	Japan	1992	$12.00/$4.00
MCA	MCSTD-1669	I've Got Mine	CD5	U.K.	1992	$10.00
MCA	54429	I've Got Mine	CD5	U.S.	1992	$5.00
MCA	MCA5P-2276	I've Got Mine	CDJ	U.S.	1992	$3.00
MCA	MCA5P-2300	I've Got Mine	CDJ	U.S.	1992	$3.00
MCA	09P3-6148	Livin' Right	CD3	Japan	1989	$12.00/$4.00
MCA	CD45 17762	Livin' Right	CDJ	U.S.	1989	$3.00
MCA	MCA5P-2266	Love in the 21st Century	CDJ	U.S.	1992	$3.00
MCA	MCD-17565	Part of You, Part of Me	CD5	Germany	1991	$10.00
MCA	MVDM-3	Part of You, Part of Me	CD3	Japan	1991	$12.00/$4.00
MCA	CD45 1358	Part of You, Part of Me	CDJ	U.S.	1991	$6.00
MCA	54461	River of Dreams	CD5	U.S.	1992	$4.00
MCA	MCA5P-2279	River of Dreams	CDJ	U.S.	1992	$3.00
MCA	CD45 17941	Some Kind of Blue	CDJ	U.S.		$3.00
MCA	10P3-6069	Soul Searchin'	CD3	Japan	1988	$12.00/$4.00
MCA	DMCA-1294	Soul Searchin'	CD3	U.K.	1988	$10.00
MCA		Soul Searchin'	CD5	U.S.	1988	$5.00
MCA	2755	Strange Weather	CDJ	U.S.	1993	$2.00
MCA	10P3-6016	True Love	CD3	Japan	1988	$12.00/$4.00
MCA	DMCA-1284	True Love	CD5	U.K.	1988	$10.00
MCA	CD45 17589	True Love	CDJ	U.S.	1988	$3.00

Frey, Kristine

Singles

Label	Catalog Number	Title	Type	Country	Year	Longbox Value/Value
Polygram	865035-2	Fits Like a Glove	CD5	Germany	1991	$8.00

Frida

Full Length

Label	Catalog Number	Title	Type	Country	Year	Longbox Value/Value
Polydor	POLCD-390	Shine	LP	U.K.		$20.00
Polydor	POLCD-355	Something's Going On	LP	U.K.		$20.00

Friday, Gavin

Full Length

Label	Catalog Number	Title	Type	Country	Year	Longbox Value/Value
Island		World According to Me, The	DJ/Smplr	U.K.	1995	$20.00
Island		World According to Me, The	DJ/Smplr	U.S.		$15.00

Singles

Label	Catalog Number	Title	Type	Country	Year	Longbox Value/Value
Aris	885371	Each Man Kills the Thing He Loves	CD5	Germany	1990	$8.00
Island	CID-408	Each Man Kills the Thing He Loves	CD5	U.K.	1990	$8.00
Polygram	842586	Each Man Kills the Thing He Loves	CD5	U.S.	1990	$4.00
Island	CID-533	Falling Off the Edge of the World	CD5	U.K.	1992	$8.00
Rough Trade	604 3129 3	I Want to Live	CD5	Germany	1992	$8.00
Island	CID-506	I Want to Live	CD5	U.K.	1992	$8.00
Island	PRCD 6746-2	I Want to Live	CDJ	U.S.	1992	$2.00
Island	CID-522	King of Trash	CD5	U.K.	1992	$8.00
Island	PRCD 6739-2	King of Trash	CDJ	U.S.	1992	$2.00
Aris	884372	Man of Misfortune	CD5	Germany	1990	$8.00
Island	CID-455	Man of Misfortune	CD5	U.K.	1990	$8.00
Island	CID-430	You Take Away the Sun	CD5	U.K.	1990	$8.00

Friday People

Singles

Label	Catalog Number	Title	Type	Country	Year	Longbox Value/Value
Hansa	663120	Friday People	CD5	Germany	1990	$8.00

Friedmann

Singles

Label	Catalog Number	Title	Type	Country	Year	Longbox Value/Value
Biber	CD-66303	New Moon	CD5	Germany	1988	$8.00

Frieman, David

Full Length

Label	Catalog Number	Title	Type	Country	Year	Longbox Value/Value
Enja	5017-35	Shades of Change	LP	Germany		$10.00

Friends Again

Full Length

Label	Catalog Number	Title	Type	Country	Year	Longbox Value/Value
Mercury	826895-2	Trapped and Unwrapped	LP	U.K.		$15.00

Friends of Carlotta

Singles

Label	Catalog Number	Title	Type	Country	Year	Longbox Value/Value
ZYX	6313-8	Fingerfoc	CD5	Germany	1990	$8.00

Friends of Matthew

Singles

Label	Catalog Number	Title	Type	Country	Year	Longbox Value/Value
Pulse 8	CDLOSE-11	Calling	CD5	U.K.	1991	$8.00

Friends of Mr. Cairo

Singles

Label	Catalog Number	Title	Type	Country	Year	Longbox Value/Value
BCM	20119	Caravan	CD5	Germany	1989	$8.00

Fripp, Robert

Full Length

Label	Catalog Number	Title	Type	Country	Year	Longbox Value/Value
	VPLR-70171	Careful With That Axe	LD	Japan		$75.00

Frisell, Bill

Singles

Label	Catalog Number	Title	Type	Country	Year	Longbox Value/Value
Elektra	PRCD 8710-2	Have a Little Faith	CDJ	U.S.	1993	$6.00

Frisell, Bill & Vernon Reid

Full Length

Label	Catalog Number	Title	Type	Country	Year	Longbox Value/Value
Rykodisc	RCD-10006	Smash & Scatteration	LP/LB	U.S.†	1985	$14.00/$8.00

Frola

Singles

Label	Catalog Number	Title	Type	Country	Year	Longbox Value/Value
Canyon	PCDY-00071	Black is Black	CD3	Japan	1990	$13.00/$3.00

From Good Homes

Full Length

Label	Catalog Number	Title	Type	Country	Year	Longbox Value/Value
RCA	RJC 66586-2	Cool Me Down	DJ/Smplr	U.S.	1995	$10.00

Front

Singles

Label	Catalog Number	Title	Type	Country	Year	Longbox Value/Value
Columbia	655718-2	Fire	CD5	U.K.	1990	$10.00
Columbia		Fire	CDJ	U.S.	1990	$2.00
Columbia	CSK 2925	Le Motion	CDJ	U.S.	1990	$2.00
Columbia	CSK 1915	Pain	CDJ	U.S.	1989	$2.00

Front 242

Full Length

Label	Catalog Number	Title	Type	Country	Year	Longbox Value/Value
Epic		05:22:09:12	LP	U.S.	1994	$15.00
First pressing with limited edition Lalapalooza sticker.						
Epic	ESK 4488	Front 242	DJ/Smplr	U.S.	1992	$15.00
Epic		Tyranny For You	LTD/LP	U.S.	1990	$15.00

Singles

Label	Catalog Number	Title	Type	Country	Year	Longbox Value/Value
APT	MK-4	Commando	CD3	Germany	1989	$9.00
SPV	1387-3	Endless Riddance	CD5	Germany	1989	$9.00
APT	MK-003CD	Endless Riddance	CD5	U.K.	1989	$9.00
Wax Trax	004	Endless Riddance	CD5	U.S.	1989	$5.00
Epic	ESK 2297	Gripped by Fear	CDJ	U.S.	1990	$2.00
SPV	1394-3	Headhunter	CD3	Germany	1988	$10.00
APT	RRECD-6	Headhunter	CD3	U.K.	1988	$10.00
Wax Trax	053	Headhunter	CD5	U.S.	1988	$5.00
SPV	1386-3	Interception	CD5	Germany	1988	$9.00
APT	RRET-003CD	Interception	CD5	U.K.	1988	$9.00
APT	RRECD-9	Master Hits	CD5	U.K.	1989	$9.00
SPV	0375-3	Masterhit	CD3	Germany	1989	$10.00
Wax Trax	036	Masterhit	CD5	U.S.	1989	$5.00
SPV	1346-3	Never Stop	CD5	Germany	1989	$9.00
APT	RRECD-8	Never Stop	CD5	U.K.	1989	$9.00
Wax Trax	9070	Never Stop	CD5	U.S.	1989	$5.00
APT	CD MK-2	No Comment	CD5	Germany	1989	$9.00
SPV	1388-3	Politics of Pressure	CD5	Germany	1988	$9.00
APT	MK-004CD	Politics of Pressure	CD5	U.K.	1988	$9.00
Wax Trax	016	Quite Unusual	CD5	U.S.	1988	$5.00
APT	RRECD-16	Religion	CD5	U.K.	1993	$9.00
APT		Religion	CD5	U.K.	1993	$9.00
Second version.						
Epic	ESK 5146	Religion	CDJ	U.S.	1993	$3.00
SPV	1334-3	Rhythm of Time	CD5	Germany	1991	$9.00
Epic	ESK 73767	Rhythm of Time	CDJ	U.S.	1991	$3.00
APT	MK-003CD	Take On	CD5	U.K.	1988	$9.00
SPV	1337-3	Tragedy For You	CD5	Germany	1990	$9.00
APT	RRECD-10	Tragedy For You	CD5	U.K.	1990	$9.00
SPV	7454-3	Two in One	CD5	Germany	1988	$9.00
APT	MK-009CD	Two in One	CD5	U.K.	1988	$9.00
New Dance	ND-009	U-Men	CD3	Germany		$10.00
New Dance	ND-009	U-Men	CD5	Germany		$10.00

Front Page

Singles

Label	Catalog Number	Title	Type	Country	Year	Longbox Value/Value
Alfa	ALDB-66	Radio Station	CD3	Japan	1990	$12.00/$3.00

Frontier

Singles

Label	Catalog Number	Title	Type	Country	Year	Longbox Value/Value
Vertigo	VERCD-64	Lonely Heart	CD5	U.K.	1991	$8.00

Frontline Assembly

Singles

Label	Catalog Number	Title	Type	Country	Year	Longbox Value/Value
SPV	9557-3	Digital Tension Dementia	CD5	Germany	1989	$8.00
Wax Trax	60	Digital Tension Dementia	CD5	U.S.	1989	$5.00
SPV	4931	Iceolate	CD5	Germany	1990	$8.00
APT	TMSCD-52	Iceolate	CD5	U.K.	1990	$8.00
Wax Trax	9137	Iceolate	CD5	U.S.	1990	$5.00
Intercord	826 237	Mindphaser	CD5	Gerrmany	1992	$8.00
Third Mind	TM-2402-3	Mindphaser	CD5	U.K.	1992	$8.00
SPV	9526-3	No Limit Damaged Goods	CD5	Germany	1989	$8.00
Wax Trax	9087	No Limit Damaged Goods	CD5	U.S.	1989	$5.00
SPV	4984-3	Provision	CD5	Germany	1989	$8.00
Wax Trax	9145	Provision	CD5	U.S.	1989	$5.00
SPV	8240-3	Virus	CD5	Germany	1991	$8.00
Wax Trax	9147	Virus	CD5	U.S.	1991	$5.00

Froon

Full Length

Label	Catalog Number	Title	Type	Country	Year	Longbox Value/Value
Columbia	651561-2	Bobby Mugabe	LP	Germany	1988	$12.00

Singles

Label	Catalog Number	Title	Type	Country	Year	Longbox Value/Value
Columbia	651561-3	Bobby Mugabe	CD3	Germany	1988	$8.00
Columbia	652870-3	Missing Pieces	CD3	Germany	1988	$8.00

Frozen Ghost

Singles

Label	Catalog Number	Title	Type	Country	Year	Longbox Value/Value
Atlantic	PRCD 4422-2	Head Over Heals	CDJ	U.S.		$2.00
Atlantic		Pauper In Paradise	CDJ	U.S.		$2.00
Atlantic		Round And Round	CDJ	U.S.		$2.00

Frumpy

Singles

Label	Catalog Number	Title	Type	Country	Year	Longbox Value/Value
Polygram	876675-2	What It Is	CD5	Germany	1990	$8.00
Polygram	878625-2	When I Fall In Love	CD5	Germany	1990	$8.00

Fryderyk, Jan

Full Length

Label	Catalog Number	Title	Type	Country	Year	Longbox Value/Value
Delta	11058	Works	LP	Germany		$12.00

FSK

Singles

Label	Catalog Number	Title	Type	Country	Year	Longbox Value/Value
Strange Frt	SFPMACD-204	Peel Sessions	CD5	U.K.	1989	$8.00

Fu-Schnickens

Singles

Label	Catalog Number	Title	Type	Country	Year	Longbox Value/Value
Jive	42243	Breakdown	CD5	U.S.	1994	$5.00
Jive	01241-42078	True Fuschnick	CDJ	U.S.	1993	$2.00
Jive	42127	What's Up Doc	CD5	U.S.	1993	$5.00
Jive	42127-2-RDJ	What's Up Doc	CDJ	U.S.	1993	$2.00

Fudge Tunnel

Singles

Label	Catalog Number	Title	Type	Country	Year	Longbox Value/Value
Earach	ESK 5567	10% Changes	CDJ	U.S.	1993	$2.00
Earach	ESK 5362	Grey	CDJ	U.S.	1993	$2.00
Relativity	0131	Sunshine of Your Love	CDJ	U.S.	1991	$2.00
Earache	MOSH-57CD	Teeth	CD5	U.K.	1991	$8.00

Fuel

Singles

Label	Catalog Number	Title	Type	Country	Year	Longbox Value/Value
	47	Monuments to Excess	CD5	U.S.	1994	$5.00

Fugees

Singles

Label	Catalog Number	Title	Type	Country	Year	Longbox Value/Value
Columbia	77633	Vocab	CD5	U.S.	1994	$5.00

Full Force

Singles

Label	Catalog Number	Title	Type	Country	Year	Longbox Value/Value
Columbia	655075-2	Ain't My Type O'Hype	CD5	U.K.	1989	$8.00
Columbia	CSK 1009	All in My Mind	CDJ	U.S.	1988	$2.00
Columbia	CSK 73025	Friend B4 Lovers	CDJ	U.S.	1989	$2.00
Columbia	CSK 73227	Kiss Those Lips	CDJ	U.S.	1989	$2.00
Columbia		Love is For Suckers	CDJ	U.S.		$2.00

Full Moon

Full Length

Label	Catalog Number	Title	Type	Country	Year	Longbox Value/Value
		Full Moon	LP	Japan		$35.00

Full On Sound

Singles

Label	Catalog Number	Title	Type	Country	Year	Longbox Value/Value
ZYX	6747-8	Mayhem	CD5	Germany	1992	$6.00

Full Swing

Singles

Label	Catalog Number	Title	Type	Country	Year	Longbox Value/Value
A&M	CD 17883	End of the Sky	CDJ	U.S.	1989	$2.00

Fuller, Bobby

Singles

Label	Catalog Number	Title	Type	Country	Year	Longbox Value/Value
Aris	885833	I Fought the Law	CD3	Germany	1990	$10.00

Fuller, Curtis

Full Length

Label	Catalog Number	Title	Type	Country	Year	Longbox Value/Value
Savoy Records	CY-78805	Blues-Ette	LTD/LP	U.S.	1996	$20.00
CD in miniature repica of original LP sleeve.						
Savoy Records	CY-78808	Curtis Fuller Jazztet, The	LTD/LP	U.S.	1996	$20.00
CD in miniature repica of original LP sleeve.						
Savoy Records	CY-78806	Images of Curtis Fuller	LTD/LP	U.S.	1996	$20.00
CD in miniature repica of original LP sleeve.						
Savoy Records	CY-78807	Jazz…It's Magic	LTD/LP	U.S.	1996	$20.00
CD in miniature repica of original LP sleeve.						

Fuller, Curtis Sextette

Full Length

Label	Catalog Number	Title	Type	Country	Year	Longbox Value/Value
Savoy Records	CY-78996	Curtis Fuller Sextette, The	LTD/LP	U.S.	1995	$20.00
CD in miniature repica of original LP sleeve.						

Label	Catalog Number	Title	Type	Country	Year	Longbox Value / Value
Fun 4 Fun						
Singles						
Arista	663684	Relax Your Soul	CD5	U.K.	1990	$8.00
Fun Factory						
Singles						
Atlantic	77090	Take Your Chance	CD5	U.S.	1995	$5.00
Fun Fountain						
Singles						
Elektra	7559-66520-2	Masterplan	CD5	Germany	1991	$8.00
Elektra	EKR-130CD	Masterplan	CD5	U.K.	1991	$8.00
Fun Fun						
Singles						
ZYX	6268-8	Give Me Your Love	CD5	Germany	1989	$6.00
Fun To Fun						
Singles						
Polygram	867261-2	Reggae Blue	CD5	Germany	1991	$8.00
Funhouse						
Singles						
BCM	20124	Dancin' Easy	CD5	Germany	1988	$8.00
Funicello, Annette						
Full Length						
	PCCD-00065	Annette	LP	Japan		$40.00
	PCCD-00066	Beach Party	LP	Japan		$40.00
Funk Awlikz						
Singles						
Basix	1307	Don't Stop Hey Ooh	CD5	U.S.	1994	$5.00
Funkdoobiest						
Singles						
Epic	ESK 4969	Bow Wow Wow	CDJ	U.S.	1993	$2.00
Epic	ESK 5240	Freak Mode	CDJ	U.S.	1993	$2.00
Epic	ESK 4240	Funkiest, The	CDJ	U.S.	1993	$2.00
Imortal	ESK 5404	Wopbabalubop	CDJ	U.S.	1993	$2.00
Funkmaster Flex						
Singles						
	20116	Nuttin' But Flavor	CD5	U.S.	1994	$5.00
Funky Bureau						
Singles						
Victor	VICP-15021	Clap Your Hands Together	CD5	Japan	1992	$8.00
Funky Poets						
Singles						
550 Music	77366	Lessons Learned	CDJ	U.S.	1994	$2.00
Funky Sisters						
Singles						
Alfa	ALDB-135	Lovely Feelings	CD3	Japan	1991	$13.00/$4.00
Funky Space Nation						
Singles						
Magnet	MAG-1006CD	Ride the Rocket	CD5	U.K.	1992	$8.00
Funky Stuff						
Full Length						
		Funk Essentials Sampler, The	DJ/Smplr	U.S.	1994	$20.00
Funky Worm						
Singles						
Fon	FON-16CD	Spell	CD5	U.K.	1988	$8.00
Fureys						
Singles						
Ritz	RITZCD-252	Sweet and Gentle Love	CD5	U.K.	1992	$8.00
Furia Grupera						
Singles						
Continental	7026	Tesoros De La Music	CD5	U.S.	1994	$5.00
Furlong, Edward						
Singles						
Canyon	PCDY-00105	Hold On Tight	CD3	Japan	1992	$13.00/$4.00
Canyon	PCDY-00115	I'll Be Waiting	CD3	Japan	1992	$13.00/$4.00
Furniture						
Singles						
Arista	662844	One Step Behind	CD5	U.K.	1990	$8.00
Arista	662648	Slow Motion Kisses	CD5	U.K.	1990	$8.00
Furusawa, Ryojiro						
Full Length						
Denon	CD-7138	Anokoro	LP/LB	U.S.†	1985	$14.00/$8.00
Fury in the Slaughterhouse						
Singles						
RCA	62746-2-RDJ	Every Generation Got It's Own Disease	CDJ	U.S.	1993	$2.00
SPV	9320-3	Kick It Out	CD5	Germany	1990	$8.00
SPV	8838-3	Rain Will Fall	CD5	Germany	1990	$8.00
SPV	8842-3	Trapped Today	CD5	Germany	1990	$8.00
SPV	8831-3	Won't Forget	CD5	Germany	1990	$8.00
Fuse						
Singles						
TVT	8708	Train Tracks	CD5	U.S.	1993	$4.00
Fuzzbox						
Singles						
WEA	09P3-6182	International Rescue	CD3	Japan	1989	$13.00/$4.00
WEA	YZ-347CD	International Rescue	CD3	U.K.	1989	$8.00
WEA	YZ-401CD	Pink Sunshine	CD3	U.K.	1989	$8.00
WEA	246769-2	Self	CD5	Germany	1989	$8.00
WEA	246767-2	Self	CD5	Germany	1989	$8.00
WEA	WMD5-4004	Self	CD3	Japan	1989	$13.00/$4.00
WEA	YZ-408CD	Self	CD3	U.K.	1989	$8.00
Geffen	PRO-CD-3688	Self	CDJ	U.S.	1989	$2.00
WEA	YZ-435CD	Walking on Thin Ice	CD3	U.K.	1989	$8.00
WEA	171708-2	Your Loss, My Gain	CD5	Germany	1989	$8.00
WEA	YZ-486CD	Your Loss, My Gain	CD5	U.K.	1989	$8.00

Label	Catalog Number	Title	Type	Country	Year	Longbox Value / Value
Fuzztones						
Singles						
SPV	0598-8	Action	CD5	Germany	1990	$8.00
Pinnicle	SIT-69CD	Action	CD5	U.K.	1990	$8.00
Fuzzy						
Singles						
	98180	Lemon Rind	CD5	U.S.	1995	$6.00
G.A.T.						
Singles						
MCA	3224	Smiling Faces Sometimes	CDJ	U.S.	1995	$3.00
G Love E						
Singles						
Chrysalis	23485	Dance Baby	CDJ	U.S.	1990	$2.00
G.S.P.						
Singles						
Yo!Yo!	CDYOYO-1	Banana Song	CD5	U.K.	1992	$8.00
G, Warren						
Full Length						
Def Jam	314 537 234-2	Take A Look Over your Shoulder (Reality)	LTD/LP	U.S.	1997	$18.00
	CD album plus bonus CD-single. Available exclusively at Best Buy stores.					
G-Force						
Singles						
SPV	9509-3	Spicy	CD3	Germany	1989	$6.00
G-mo						
Singles						
Zoo	14177	It's an Everyday Thing	CD5	U.S.	1994	$5.00
G-Race						
Singles						
Mercury	PHDA-2	Sherry	CD3	Japan	1991	$12.00/$3.00
G-Wiz						
Singles						
Scotti Brothers	NSK 75360	Teddy Bear	CDJ	U.S.	1993	$2.00
Gable, Eric						
Singles						
Epic	ESK 5990	Driving Me Crazy	CDJ	U.S.	1994	$2.00
Orpus	74160	Straight From the Heart	CDJ	U.S.	1991	$2.00
Gable, Tony						
Singles						
Heads Up	3020	Island Lady	CDJ	U.S.		$2.00
Gabriel, Ana						
Singles						
Sony	CSK 10037	Evidencia	CDJ	U.S.	1992	$2.00
Gabriel, Gunter						
Singles						
ZYX	6353-8	Hey Boss	CD5	Germany	1990	$6.00
Gabriel, Peter						
Full Length						
Geffen	PRO-CD-4412	Before Us: A Brief History	DJ/Smplr	U.S.	1992	$20.00
Virgin		Collection	LTD/LP	U.K.	1988	$175.00
	8 CD set. Limited set of the Gabriel CD catalog plus biography book.					
Virgin	TPAK 9	Collector's Edition	LP	Germany	1991	$45.00
	3 CD Set.					
Geffen/Album Network		From Us to You...	DJ/RS	U.S.	1992	$25.00
Album Network		In the Studio (Us)	RS	U.S.		$35.00
Geffen		in-Store Play Sampler	DJ/Smplr	U.S.	1994	$12.00
DIR		King Biscuit Flour Hour	RS	U.S.	1990	$50.00
	Airdate: 10/9/89.					
DIR		King Biscuit Flour Hour	RS	U.S.	1994	$45.00
	Airdate: 9/18/94.					
Westwood One		Off the Record	RS	U.S.	1993	$30.00
	Airdate: 3/29/93.					
Westwood One		Off the Record	RS	U.S.	1994	$20.00
	Airdate: 7/18/94.					
Westwood One		Off the Record	RS	U.S.	1995	$20.00
	Airdate: 2/6/95.					
Geffen		Secret World Live Radio Sampler	DJ/Smplr	U.S.	1994	$15.00
Geffen	2011-2	Security	LP/LB	U.S.†	1984	$14.00/$8.00
Geffen	PRO-CD-3558	Selections From Passion	DJ/Smplr	U.S.	1989	$8.00
Virgin	PGCDP 5	So	LTD/LP	Austria	1988	$55.00
	Picture disc CD.					
		Special	RS	U.S.	1993	$35.00
	Airdate: 8/29/93.					
Media America		Up Close	RS	U.S.	1991	$50.00
	2 CD set.					
Media America		Up Close	RS	U.S.	1992	$50.00
	2 CD set.					
Media America		Up Close	RS	U.S.	1993	$60.00
	2 CD set.					
Media America		Up Close	RS	U.S.	1994	$45.00
	2 CD set.					
Geffen	VJCP-28125	Us	LP	Japan	1992	$150.00
	Rare 11 track version.					
Interplay		Xploria 1	LTD/LP	U.S.	1993	$45.00
	CD-ROM. Limited edition of CDROM in box with extra booklet.					
Singles						
Virgin	658850	Big Time	CD5	Germany	1987	$11.00
Virgin	GAIL-312	Big Time	CD5	U.K.	1987	$11.00
Virgin	659510	Biko	CD5	Germany	1988	$11.00
Virgin	VJD 12010	Biko	CD3	Japan	1988	$12.00/$5.00
	WOOST3-2	Biko	CDJ	Spain	1995	$40.00
Virgin	CDGS-612	Biko	CD5	U.K.	1988	$11.00
Virgin	VJCP-12009	Blood of Eden	CD5	Japan	1993	$18.00
Virgin	PGSDG 9	Blood of Eden	CD5	U.K.	1993	$11.00
Virgin	PGSDX 9	Blood of Eden	CD5	U.K.	1993	$11.00
Geffen		Come Talk to Me	CDJ	U.S.	1993	$3.00
Virgin	VJDP-10196	Digging in the Dirt	CD3	Japan	1992	$12.00/$5.00
Virgin	VJCP-12001	Digging in the Dirt	CD5	Japan	1992	$18.00
Virgin	PSGDG 7	Digging in the Dirt	CD5	U.K.	1992	$11.00
Virgin	665583	Digging in the Dirt	CD5	U.K.	1992	$11.00
Virgin	PGSDX 7	Digging in the Dirt	CD5	U.K.	1992	$11.00
	Blue Box.					
Virgin	PGSDX 7	Digging in the Dirt	CD5	U.K.	1992	$11.00
	Brown Box.					

Label	Catalog Number	Title	Type	Country	Year	Longbox Value / Value
Virgin		Digging in the Dirt	CDJ	U.K.	1994	$12.00
Geffen	9 21816-2	Digging in the Dirt	CD5	U.S.	1992	$6.00
Geffen	PRO-CD-4446	Digging in the Dirt	CDJ	U.S.	1992	$3.00
Geffen	PRO-CD-2680	Don't Give Up	CDJ	U.S.	1986	$30.00
Geffen	GEFD 9102	Here Comes the Flood	CD5	Canada	1993	$30.00
WTG	PSK 1622	In Your Eyes	CDJ	U.S.	1987	$25.00
Virgin	PGSD 10	Kiss That Frog	CD5	U.K.	1993	$10.00
Virgin	PGSDX 10	Kiss That Frog	CD5	U.K.	1993	$11.00
Geffen	PRO-CD-4495	Kiss That Frog	CDJ	U.S.	1992	$3.00
Virgin	660480	Love Town	CD5	Germany	1994	$10.00
Virgin	XPCD 441	Love Town	CDJ	U.K.	1994	$20.00
Virgin		Red Rain	CD5	U.K.	1994	$10.00
Geffen	PRO-CD-4519	Secret World	CDJ	U.S.	1992	$3.00
Virgin	VSCD 1167	Shaking the Tree	CD5	Germany	1989	$10.00
Virgin	PCD 2789	Shaking the Tree	CDJ	U.S.	1989	$3.00
Geffen	PRO-CD-4217	Shaking the Tree	CDJ	U.S.	1990	$3.00
Virgin	880983	Sledge Hammer	CD3	Germany	1988	$11.00
		Sledge Hammer	CDJ	Holland		$25.00
Virgin	VJD-12010	Sledge Hammer	CD3	Japan	1988	$12.00/$5.00
Virgin	CDT-4	Sledge Hammer	CD3	U.K.	1988	$11.00
Virgin	CDF-4	Sledge Hammer	CD5	U.K.	1990	$11.00
Virgin	885106	Solsbury Hill	CD3	Germany	1989	$11.00
Virgin	CDT-33	Solsbury Hill	CD3	Germany	1989	$11.00
Virgin	CDF-33	Solsbury Hill	CD5	U.K.	1990	$11.00
Virgin	VSCDT-1322	Solsbury Hill	CD5	U.K.	1990	$11.00
Geffen	GEFDM-21820	Steam	CD5	Canada	1993	$8.00
Virgin	VJCP-12007	Steam	CD5	Japan	1993	$18.00
Virgin	PDSDG-8	Steam	CD5	U.K.	1992	$11.00
Virgin	PGSDX 8	Steam	CD5	U.K.	1992	$11.00

CD in black "Church-shaped" box.

Label	Catalog Number	Title	Type	Country	Year	Longbox Value / Value
Geffen	PRO-CD-4479	Steam	CDJ	U.S.	1992	$3.00
Geffen	PRO-CD-4484	Steam	CDJ	U.S.	1992	$3.00
		SW Live	CD5	Australia	1994	$10.00
Epic	ESCA-6321	While the Earth Sleeps	CD5	Japan		$20.00

With Deep Forest.

Gabriel, Tina

Singles

Label	Catalog Number	Title	Type	Country	Year	Longbox Value / Value
King	091X-19009	Boom Boom	CD3	Japan	1989	$13.00/$4.00
King	091X-18010	If You Say Love Me	CD3	Japan	1989	$13.00/$4.00

Gabrielle

Singles

Label	Catalog Number	Title	Type	Country	Year	Longbox Value / Value
Go Discs		Because of You	CD5	U.K.	1993	$8.00
Go Discs		Because of You	CD5	U.K.	1993	$8.00

Second version.

Label	Catalog Number	Title	Type	Country	Year	Longbox Value / Value
Go Discs	GODCD 99	Dreams	CD5	U.K.	1993	$8.00
Go Discs	1011	Dreams	CDJ	U.S.	1993	$2.00
Polygram	857299	Dreams	CD5	U.S.	1994	$5.00

Gadd, Gang

Singles

Label	Catalog Number	Title	Type	Country	Year	Longbox Value / Value
Epic	158H-8007	I Can't Turn You Loose	CD3	Japan	1988	$12.00/$3.00

Gaha, Danni'elle

Singles

Label	Catalog Number	Title	Type	Country	Year	Longbox Value / Value
Epic	658461-2	Do It For Love	CD5	U.K.	1993	$8.00
Epic	658124-2	Stuck in the Middle	CD5	U.K.	1993	$8.00

Gaimboiz

Singles

Label	Catalog Number	Title	Type	Country	Year	Longbox Value / Value
Scotti Brothers	78016	Money	CD5	U.S.	1995	$5.00

Gaines, Jeffrey

Full Length

Label	Catalog Number	Title	Type	Country	Year	Longbox Value / Value
Westwood One		In Concert	RS	U.S.	1995	$50.00

Airdate: 4/24/95.

Singles

Label	Catalog Number	Title	Type	Country	Year	Longbox Value / Value
Capitol	C2 24815	Head Masters Of Mine	CD5	U.S.	1992	$5.00
Chrysalis	CHSCD-3854	Hero in Me	CD5	U.K.	1992	$9.00
Chrysalis	F2 23854	Hero in Me	CD5	U.S.	1992	$4.00
Chrysalis	05472	Hero in Me	CDJ	U.S.	1992	$2.00
Chrysalis	2381	Hero in Me	CDJ	U.S.	1992	$2.00
Chrysalis	05481	Scares Me More	CDJ	U.S.	1992	$2.00

Gaines, Reg E.

Singles

Label	Catalog Number	Title	Type	Country	Year	Longbox Value / Value
Mercury	CDP 1169	Please Don't Take My Air	CDJ	U.S.	1994	$2.00

Gaines, Rosie

Singles

Label	Catalog Number	Title	Type	Country	Year	Longbox Value / Value
Motown	860415	Are You Ready	CD5	U.S.	1995	$6.00
Motown	60323	I Want U	CD5	U.S.	1994	$5.00
Motown	860323	I Want U	CD5	U.S.	1995	$6.00

Galactic Cowboys

Singles

Label	Catalog Number	Title	Type	Country	Year	Longbox Value / Value
DGC	PRO-CD-4517	I Do What I Do	CDJ	U.S.	1993	$2.00
DGC	PRO-CD-4403	I'm Not Amused	CDJ	U.S.	1992	$2.00
DGC	PRO-CD-4514	If I Were a Killer	CDJ	U.S.	1993	$2.00

Galapagos

Singles

Label	Catalog Number	Title	Type	Country	Year	Longbox Value / Value
Toshiba	TODT-2540	Indian Boy	CD3	Japan	1990	$12.00/$3.00
Toshiba	TODT-3002	My Love Again	CD3	Japan	1993	$12.00/$3.00

Galas, Diamanda

Full Length

Label	Catalog Number	Title	Type	Country	Year	Longbox Value / Value
Mute	CDSTUMM-33	Saint of the Pit	LP	U.K.		$15.00

Singles

Label	Catalog Number	Title	Type	Country	Year	Longbox Value / Value
Restless-Mute	7 71423-2	Divine Punishment, The	CD5	U.S.	1989	$2.00

Galaxie 500

Singles

Label	Catalog Number	Title	Type	Country	Year	Longbox Value / Value
Rough Trade	CD1-117	Blue Thunder	CD5	Germany	1990	$8.00
Rough Trade	RTT-246CD	Blue Thunder	CD5	U.K.	1990	$8.00
Rough Trade	246	Blue Thunder	CD5	U.S.	1990	$4.00
Rough Trade	RTT-249CD	Fourth of July	CD5	U.K.	1994	$9.00
Rough Trade	90	Fourth of July	CD5	U.S.	1994	$5.00

Galaxy 2

Singles

Label	Catalog Number	Title	Type	Country	Year	Longbox Value / Value
ZYX	6543-8	Somebody Screams	CD5	Germany	1991	$6.00

Galaxy Trio

Singles

Label	Catalog Number	Title	Type	Country	Year	Longbox Value / Value
Estrus Records	105	Saucers Over Vegas	CD5	U.S.	1994	$5.00

Gales, Eric

Singles

Label	Catalog Number	Title	Type	Country	Year	Longbox Value / Value
Elektra	PRCD 8792-2	Paralyzed	CDJ	U.S.	1993	$2.00
Elektra	PRCD 8434-2	Resurection	CDJ	U.S.	1991	$2.00
Elektra	PRCD 8377-2	Sign Of the Storm	CDJ	U.S.	1991	$2.00

Gallagher

Full Length

Label	Catalog Number	Title	Type	Country	Year	Longbox Value / Value
Paramount	LV2333	Maddist	LD	U.S.	1985	$20.00
Paramount	LV2339	Melon Crazy	LD	U.S.	1985	$20.00
Pioneer	PA-83-046	Uncensored	LD	U.S.	1983	$20.00

Gallagher, Eve

Singles

Label	Catalog Number	Title	Type	Country	Year	Longbox Value / Value
Virgin	PROCD-14	Love Come Down	CD5	U.K.	1991	$8.00
Virgin	664375	Love Is a Master of Disguise	CD5	Germany	1991	$8.00
Virgin	PROCD-11	Love Is a Master of Disguise	CD5	U.K.	1991	$8.00

Galliano

Singles

Label	Catalog Number	Title	Type	Country	Year	Longbox Value / Value
Polygram	866045-2	Jus' Reach	CD5	Germany	1991	$8.00
Polygram	TLKCD-16	Jus' Reach	CD5	U.K.	1991	$8.00
Polygram	TLKCD-29	Jus' Reach	CD5	U.K.	1992	$8.00
Polygram	TLKCS-29	Jus' Reach	CD5	U.K.	1992	$8.00
4th & B'way	162-440 552	Jus' Reach	CD5	U.S.	1991	$4.00
Polygram		Long Time Gone	CD5	U.K.	1992	$8.00
Polygram		Long Time Gone	CD5	U.K.	1992	$8.00

Second version.

Label	Catalog Number	Title	Type	Country	Year	Longbox Value / Value
Polygram	TLKCD-6	Nothing Has Changed	CD5	U.K.	1991	$8.00
Polygram	TLKCD-8	Power and Glory	CD5	U.K.	1991	$8.00
Polygram	TLKCD-24	Prince of Peace	CD5	U.K.	1991	$8.00
Polygram	TLKCD-23	Skunk Funk	CD5	U.K.	1991	$8.00
		Twyford Down	CD5	U.K.		$10.00
		Twyford Down	CD5	U.K.		$10.00

Second version.

Label	Catalog Number	Title	Type	Country	Year	Longbox Value / Value
Polygram	TLKCD-3	Welcome to the Story	CD5	U.K.	1991	$8.00

Gallon Drunk

Singles

Label	Catalog Number	Title	Type	Country	Year	Longbox Value / Value
Clawfist	HUNKACD-011	Bedlam	CD5	U.K.	1992	$8.00
Clawfist	HUNKACD-006	Some Fool's Mess	CD5	U.K.	1992	$8.00

Galloway, Leata

Full Length

Label	Catalog Number	Title	Type	Country	Year	Longbox Value / Value
Columbia		Sampler	DJ/Smplr	U.S.		$5.00

Singles

Label	Catalog Number	Title	Type	Country	Year	Longbox Value / Value
Columbia	652991-2	With Every Beat of My Heart	CD5	U.K.	1988	$8.00
Columbia		With Every Beat of My Heart	CDJ	U.S.	1988	$2.00

Galper, Hal

Full Length

Label	Catalog Number	Title	Type	Country	Year	Longbox Value / Value
Enja	3053-37	Ivory Forest	LP	Germany		$12.00

Galway, James

Full Length

Label	Catalog Number	Title	Type	Country	Year	Longbox Value / Value
RCA	PCD1-5315	In the Pink	LP/BP	U.S.†	1985	$14.00/$8.00
Aris	886170	Song of the Seashore	LP	Germany		$18.00

Singles

Label	Catalog Number	Title	Type	Country	Year	Longbox Value / Value
RCA		Enchanted Forest, The	CDJ	U.S.		$2.00

Gamalon

Singles

Label	Catalog Number	Title	Type	Country	Year	Longbox Value / Value
		Ooh...Babe	CDJ	U.S.		$2.00

Gambale, Frank

Singles

Label	Catalog Number	Title	Type	Country	Year	Longbox Value / Value
JVC	020	Final Frontier	CDJ	U.S.	1993	$2.00

Game

Singles

Label	Catalog Number	Title	Type	Country	Year	Longbox Value / Value
EMI	159979-3	Walkaway	CD3	Germany	1989	$8.00

Gamier Laurent

Singles

Label	Catalog Number	Title	Type	Country	Year	Longbox Value / Value
		Astral Dreams	CD5	U.K.		$10.00
		Astral Dreams	CD5	U.K.		$10.00

Second version.

Gamilah, Shabazz

Singles

Label	Catalog Number	Title	Type	Country	Year	Longbox Value / Value
RCA	62405	America's Living in a War Zone	CDJ	U.S.	1992	$2.00

Gamma Ray

Full Length

Label	Catalog Number	Title	Type	Country	Year	Longbox Value / Value
		Land of the Free	LTD/LP	Japan	1995	$35.00
		Sigh No More	LP/LB	U.S.		$14.00/$10.00

Singles

Label	Catalog Number	Title	Type	Country	Year	Longbox Value / Value
Noise	VICP-15026	Future Madhouse	CD5	Japan	1993	$12.00
Pinnacle	N-02033	Future Madhouse	CD5	U.K.	1993	$8.00
		Heading For Tomorrow	CDJ	U.S.		$2.00
Victor	VICP-15004	Who Do You Think You Are	CD5	Japan	1990	$12.00

Gang of Four

Full Length

Label	Catalog Number	Title	Type	Country	Year	Longbox Value / Value
		Brief History-Greatest Hits	DJ/Smplr	U.S.		$8.00

Singles

Label	Catalog Number	Title	Type	Country	Year	Longbox Value / Value
Warner Brothers	PRO-CD-4547	Damaged Goods	CDJ	U.S.	1990	$2.00
Polydor	CDP 424	Don't Fix What Ain't Broke	CDJ	U.S.	1991	$2.00
Scarlet	SCART-4CD	Money Talks	CD5	U.K.	1990	$8.00
Polydor	867 503	Satellite	CD5	U.S.	1991	$4.00
Polydor	CDP 440	Satellite	CDJ	U.S.	1991	$2.00
Polydor	CDP 500	Satellite	CDJ	U.S.	1991	$2.00
EMI	CDEM-172	To Hell With Poverty	CD5	U.K.	1990	$8.00

Gangstarr

Singles

Label	Catalog Number	Title	Type	Country	Year	Longbox Value / Value
Chrysalis	04685	Gotta Get Over	CDJ	U.S.	1992	$2.00
Columbia	656377-2	Jazz Thing	CD5	U.K.	1990	$8.00
Cooltempo	323706-2	Love Sick	CD5	Germany	1991	$8.00
Cooltempo	COOLCD 234	Love Sick	CD5	U.K.	1991	$8.00
Chrysalis	DPRO-23676	Love Sick	CDJ	U.S.	1991	$2.00
Bellaphon	130 07-328	Manifest	CD5	Germany	1989	$8.00
Capital	58111	Mass Appeal	CD5	U.S.	1994	$5.00
Chrysalis	08727	Mass Appeal	CDJ	U.S.	1994	$2.00
Cooltempo	323667-2	Take a Rest	CD5	Germany	1991	$8.00
Cooltempo	COOLCD 230	Take a Rest	CD5	U.K.	1991	$8.00
Cooltempo	COOLCD-256	Two Deep	CD5	U.K.	1992	$8.00

Gangway

Singles

Label	Catalog Number	Title	Type	Country	Year	Longbox Value / Value
London	LONCD-182	My Girl and Me	CD5	U.K.	1988	$8.00

Ganstas & Thug

Singles

Label	Catalog Number	Title	Type	Country	Year	Longbox Value / Value
MCA	54960	Smiling Faces Somet	CD5	U.S.	1994	$5.00

Gap Band

Full Length

Label	Catalog Number	Title	Type	Country	Year	Longbox Value / Value
RCA	FD-89992	Gap Band 8	LP	Germany		$15.00
Pioneer	PA86-M042	Video Train	8"LD	U.S.	1986	$5.00
Pioneer	PA86-M042	Video Train	8"LD	U.S.	1986	$8.00

Digital audio.

Singles

Label	Catalog Number	Title	Type	Country	Year	Longbox Value / Value
Capitol	DPRO-79942	Addicted To Your Love	CDJ	U.S.	1989	$2.00
EMI	203630-3	All of My Love	CD3	Germany	1989	$9.00
Capitol	CDCL-558	All of My Love	CD5	U.K.	1990	$9.00
		All of My Love	CDJ	U.S.	1989	$2.00
BMG	162016	I'm Gonna Git You Sucka	CD3	U.K.	1989	$9.00
BMG	662016	I'm Gonna Git You Sucka	CD5	U.K.	1989	$9.00
Polygram	874397-2	Party Train	CD5	Germany	1989	$9.00
Capitol	DPRO-79046	We Can Make It Alright	CDJ	U.S.	1990	$2.00

Gappas Gol

Singles

Label	Catalog Number	Title	Type	Country	Year	Longbox Value / Value
El	25615-12	Dinner With Nougat	CD3	Japan	1989	$12.00/$3.00

Garage Project

Singles

Label	Catalog Number	Title	Type	Country	Year	Longbox Value / Value
Toshiba	TOCP-7002	Let the Good Times Roll	CD5	Japan	1992	$10.00
Toshiba	TODP-2328	Turn It Up	CD3	Japan	1992	$13.00/$4.00

Garbage

Full Length

Label	Catalog Number	Title	Type	Country	Year	Longbox Value / Value
Westwood One		In Concert-Nu Rock	RS	U.S.	1996	$90.00

Airdate: 6/17/96.

Singles

Label	Catalog Number	Title	Type	Country	Year	Longbox Value / Value
		Number One Crush	CD5	U.K.	1995	$18.00

CD in plastic sleeve.

Label	Catalog Number	Title	Type	Country	Year	Longbox Value / Value
		Only Happens When It Rains	CDJ	Spain	1995	$30.00
		Queen & Supervixen	CDJ	Spain	1995	$30.00
		Queer	CD5	U.K.	1995	$10.00
		Queer	CD5	U.K.	1995	$10.00

Second version.

Label	Catalog Number	Title	Type	Country	Year	Longbox Value / Value
		Stupid Girl	CD5	Australia	1996	$10.00
		Stupid Girl	CDJ	U.S.	1996	$6.00

Garbarek, Jan

Full Length

Label	Catalog Number	Title	Type	Country	Year	Longbox Value / Value
ECM		Legend of the Seven Dreams	DJ/Smplr	U.S.	1990	$5.00

Singles

Label	Catalog Number	Title	Type	Country	Year	Longbox Value / Value
ECM	JG 2	I Took Up the Runes	CDJ	U.S.	1990	$2.00

Garbarek, Jan, Charlie Haden & Egberto Gismonti

Full Length

Label	Catalog Number	Title	Type	Country	Year	Longbox Value / Value
ECM	1151-2	Magico	LP/LB	U.S.†	1985	$14.00/$8.00

Garcia, Jerry

Singles

Label	Catalog Number	Title	Type	Country	Year	Longbox Value / Value
Arista	ASCD 2343	Deal	CDJ	U.S.	1991	$8.00

Garden of Eden

Singles

Label	Catalog Number	Title	Type	Country	Year	Longbox Value / Value
Intercord	827 040	Garden of Eden	CD5	Germany	1988	$8.00
Sonet	PEPD-2	Garden of Eden	CD5	U.K.	1988	$8.00

Garden of Joy

Singles

Label	Catalog Number	Title	Type	Country	Year	Longbox Value / Value
SBK	DPRO-05487	Eyes of a Child	CDJ	U.S.	1993	$2.00

Gardier, Donna

Singles

Label	Catalog Number	Title	Type	Country	Year	Longbox Value / Value
Virgin	VSCDT-1344	Good Thing	CD5	U.K.	1991	$8.00
Virgin	VSCDT-1307	I'll Be There	CD5	U.K.	1991	$8.00
Virgin	VSCDT-1325	Reach Out	CD5	U.K.	1991	$8.00

Garfunkel, Art

Full Length

Label	Catalog Number	Title	Type	Country	Year	Longbox Value / Value
CBS	32DP-208	Art Garfunkel Album	LP	Japan		$30.00
Columbia	CD-88002	Breakaway	LP	Germany		$15.00
CBS	CK-33700	Breakaway	LP/BP	U.S.†	1985	$14.00/$8.00

Singles

Label	Catalog Number	Title	Type	Country	Year	Longbox Value / Value
Columbia	CSK 5481	Crying in the Rain	CDJ	U.S.	1993	$3.00
Columbia	651450-2	So Much in Love	CD5	Germany	1988	$10.00
CBS	10EP-3013	So Much in Love	CD3	Japan	1988	$13.00/$3.00
Columbia	651450-2	So Much in Love	CD5	U.K.	1988	$10.00

Garland, Judy

Full Length

Label	Catalog Number	Title	Type	Country	Year	Longbox Value / Value
Pioneer	PA-83-040	In Concert	LD	U.S.	1983	$25.00
Pioneer	PA-83-040	In Concert	LD	U.S.	1990	$35.00

Digital audio.

Label	Catalog Number	Title	Type	Country	Year	Longbox Value / Value
WEA	38293	Judy Garland & Friends	LD	U.S.	1992	$30.00
Image	I-5043	Judy's Favorites	LD	U.S.	1986	$35.00

Garner, Erroll

Full Length

Label	Catalog Number	Title	Type	Country	Year	Longbox Value / Value
Columbia	CD-62310	Erroll Garner	LP	Germany		$12.00
Savoy Records	CY-78816	Penthouse Serenade	LTD/LP	U.S.	1996	$20.00

CD in miniature repica of original LP sleeve.

Garrett, Del

Singles

Label	Catalog Number	Title	Type	Country	Year	Longbox Value / Value
Eastwest	170966-2	Hollywood	CD5	Germany	1990	$8.00

Garrett, Kenny

Singles

Label	Catalog Number	Title	Type	Country	Year	Longbox Value / Value
Warner Brothers	PRO-CD-5873	Bone Bop	CDJ	U.S.	1992	$2.00

Garrett, Siedah

Singles

Label	Catalog Number	Title	Type	Country	Year	Longbox Value / Value
WEA	920972-2	K.i.s.s.i.n.g.	CD5	Germany	1988	$8.00
WEA	W-7928CD	K.i.s.s.i.n.g.	CD5	U.K.	1988	$8.00
Qwest	PRO-CD-3123	K.i.s.s.i.n.g.	CDJ	U.S.	1988	$2.00
		Refuse To Be Loose Garyboy	CDJ	U.S.		$2.00
		She's So Fine	CDJ	U.S.		$2.00

Gary's Gang

Singles

Label	Catalog Number	Title	Type	Country	Year	Longbox Value / Value
Zyx	7495	Come Together	CD5	U.S.	1994	$5.00
CBS	651652-3	Keep on Dancing	CD3	Germany	1988	$8.00
BCM	20470	Keep on Dancing	CD5	Germany	1990	$8.00
CBS	651652-3	Keep on Dancing	CD3	U.K.	1988	$8.00
BCM	20470	Keep on Dancing	CD5	U.K.	1990	$8.00

Gas

Singles

Label	Catalog Number	Title	Type	Country	Year	Longbox Value / Value
Alfa	ALDB-25	DJ Play My Beat Now	CD3	Japan	1990	$12.00/$3.00
Alfa	ALDB-98	We Can Make It	CD3	Japan	1990	$12.00/$3.00

Gatlin, Larry

Full Length

Label	Catalog Number	Title	Type	Country	Year	Longbox Value / Value
CBS	CK-40187	17 Greatest Hits	LP/BP	U.S.†	1985	$14.00/$8.00

Gatton, Danny

Full Length

Label	Catalog Number	Title	Type	Country	Year	Longbox Value / Value
Elektra		88 Elmira St.	LP/LB	U.S.		$14.00/$8.00

Singles

Label	Catalog Number	Title	Type	Country	Year	Longbox Value / Value
Elektra	PRCD 8362-2	Funky Man	CDJ	U.S.	1991	$2.00
Elektra	PRCD 8305-2	Funky Man	CDJ	U.S.	1991	$2.00
Elektra	PRCD 8303-2	Simpsons, The	CDJ	U.S.	1990	$2.00

Gaultier, Jean Paul

Singles

Label	Catalog Number	Title	Type	Country	Year	Longbox Value / Value
Mercury	872727-2	How to Do That	CD5	Germany	1989	$10.00

Gauntlet

Singles

Label	Catalog Number	Title	Type	Country	Year	Longbox Value / Value
Generator	GEN-9103-8	Run the Gauntlet	CD5	Germany	1992	$8.00

Gaye, Marvin

Full Length

Label	Catalog Number	Title	Type	Country	Year	Longbox Value / Value
Aris	886041	20 Greatest Hits	LP	Germany		$23.00
Motown	6069-MD	Compact Command Performance	LP/LB	U.S.†	1984	$15.00/$10.00
Motown	ZD-72422	Compact Command Performance Vol. 2	LP	Germany		$23.00
RCA	ZD-72454	Greatest Hits	LP	Germany		$23.00
Motown	TAMD-8010	I Heard It Through the Grapevine + I Want You	LP/LB	U.S.		$20.00/$18.00
RCA	ZD-72457	I Want You/Heard It Through the Grapevine	LP	Germany		$23.00
RCA	WD-72397	Marvin and His Women	LP	Germany		$23.00
Motown	TAMD-8015	Marvin Gaye & Tammi Terrell's Greatest Hits + Diana & Marvin	LP/LB	U.S.		$20.00/$18.00
		Master 1961-1984	LTD/LP	U.S.		$55.00

4 CD boxed set.

Label	Catalog Number	Title	Type	Country	Year	Longbox Value / Value
		Master 1961-1984 Sampler	DJ/Smplr	U.S.		$15.00

4 CD boxed set.

Label	Catalog Number	Title	Type	Country	Year	Longbox Value / Value
		Sixties Legends	RS	U.S.	1992	$15.00

2 CD set. Airdate: 7/24/92.

Label	Catalog Number	Title	Type	Country	Year	Longbox Value / Value
Motown	5218	That Stubborn Kinda Fella	LP/BP	U.S.		$14.00/$8.00
Aris	886096	That Stubborn Kinda Fella/How Sweet It Is to Be Loved By You	LP	Germany		$23.00
Motown	TAMD-8036	Trouble Man + M.P.G.	LP/LB	U.S.		$20.00/$18.00
Aris	886089	United/All I Need	LP	Germany		$23.00
Telstar	TCD-2234	Very Best of	LP	U.K.		$23.00
Motown	314530222	What's Goin' On	LTD/LP	Canada	1994	$18.00
Motown	TAMD-8013	What's Going On + Let's Get It On	LP/LB	U.S.		$20.00/$18.00

Singles

Label	Catalog Number	Title	Type	Country	Year	Longbox Value / Value
Special music co.	8515	I'll Be Doggone	CD5	U.S.	1994	$5.00
Motown	CD45 1169	My Last Chance	CDJ	U.S.	1990	$3.00

Gaye, Nora

Singles

Label	Catalog Number	Title	Type	Country	Year	Longbox Value / Value
Third Stone	4768	I'm Overjoyed	CDJ	U.S.	1992	$2.00
Third Stone	4770	I'm Overjoyed	CDJ	U.S.	1992	$2.00
Third Stone	5221	Love for the Future	CDJ	U.S.	1992	$2.00

Gayle, Crystal

Full Length

Label	Catalog Number	Title	Type	Country	Year	Longbox Value / Value
CBS	CK-38803	Greatest Hits	LP/BP	U.S.†	1995	$14.00/$8.00
Warner Brothers	PRO-CD-3166	Nobody's Angel	CDJ	U.S.	1988	$2.00

Gayle, Michelle

Singles

Label	Catalog Number	Title	Type	Country	Year	Longbox Value / Value
		I'll Find You	CD5	U.K.		$10.00
		I'll Find You	CD5	U.K.		$10.00

Second version.

Gaynor, Gloria

Singles

Label	Catalog Number	Title	Type	Country	Year	Longbox Value / Value
BCM	50-2019-44	Be Soft With Me Tonight	CD5	Germany	1988	$8.00
Fanfare	CDFAN-11	Be Soft With Me Tonight	CD5	U.K.	1988	$8.00
Polygram	887200-3	I Will Survive	CD3	Germany	1989	$9.00
WEA	9031-72653--2	I Will Survive	CD5	Germany	1989	$9.00
Polygram	879827-2	Mega Medley	CD5	Germany	1991	$9.00

Gazebo

Full Length

Label	Catalog Number	Title	Type	Country	Year	Longbox Value / Value
Ariola	610236	Telephone Mama	LP	Germany		$12.00

Singles

Label	Catalog Number	Title	Type	Country	Year	Longbox Value / Value
CBS	10EP-3045	Coincidence	CD3	Japan	1988	$12.00/$3.00

Gazebo and Savage

Singles

Label	Catalog Number	Title	Type	Country	Year	Longbox Value / Value
ZYX	6061-8	I Like Chopin	CD5	Germany	1989	$6.00

Gear Daddy's

Full Length

Label	Catalog Number	Title	Type	Country	Year	Longbox Value / Value
Polydor	847-251-2DJ	Billy's Live Bait	DJ/LP	U.S.	1990	$25.00

CD in "fish package."

Singles

Label	Catalog Number	Title	Type	Country	Year	Longbox Value / Value
Polydor	CDP 346	Color of Her Eyes	CDJ	U.S.	1990	$2.00
Polydor	CDP 253	She's Happy	CDJ	U.S.	1990	$2.00

Gearhead

Singles

Label	Catalog Number	Title	Type	Country	Year	Longbox Value / Value
Wild Boar	930901	Up on Blocks	CD5	U.S.	1993	$4.00

Gedo

Singles

Label	Catalog Number	Title	Type	Country	Year	Longbox Value / Value
Meldac	MEDR-10010	Moonlight Lorita	CD3	Japan	1991	$12.00/$3.00

Geen Apple Quick Step

Singles

Label	Catalog Number	Title	Type	Country	Year	Longbox Value / Value
Warner Brothers	17779	Med	CD5	U.S.	1995	$5.00

Geezinslaws

Label	Catalog Number	Title	Type	Country	Year	Longbox Value / Value
Singles						
Step One	471	I Wish I Had a Job to Shove	CDJ	U.S.	1993	$2.00

Geffries, Evon & The Stand

Label	Catalog Number	Title	Type	Country	Year	Longbox Value / Value
Singles						
		Sex Without Love	CDJ	U.S.		$2.00

Geils, J. Band

Label	Catalog Number	Title	Type	Country	Year	Longbox Value / Value
Full Length						
Album Network		In the Studio (Bloodshot)	RS	U.S.		$20.00
Album Network		In the Studio (Freeze Frame)	RS	U.S.		$20.00
Singles						
Rhino	71875	Must of Got Lost	CD5	U.S.	1994	$5.00

Geldof, Bob

Label	Catalog Number	Title	Type	Country	Year	Longbox Value / Value
Singles						
		Crazy	CD5	U.K.	1994	$10.00
		Crazy	CD5	U.K.	1994	$10.00
Second version.						
Mercury	878519-2	Gospel Song	CD5	Germany	1990	$10.00
Mercury	BOBCD-106	Gospel Song	CD5	U.K.	1990	$10.00
Mercury	875391-2	Great Song of Indifference	CD5	Germany	1990	$10.00
Mercury	BOBCD-104	Great Song of Indifference	CD5	U.K.	1990	$10.00
		Great Song of Indifference	CDJ	U.S.	1990	$3.00
Mercury	BOBCD-1042	Love Like a Rocket	CD5	U.K.	1990	$10.00
Mercury	878079-2	Love or Something Else	CD5	Germany	1990	$10.00
Mercury	BOBCD-105	Love or Something Else	CD5	U.K.	1990	$10.00
Atlantic	PRCD 3507-2	Love or Something Else	CDJ	U.S.	1990	$3.00
Mercury	BOBCD-108	My Happy Angel	CD5	U.K.	1990	$10.00
Mercury	BOBCD-107	Room 19	CD5	U.K.	1992	$10.00
Polydor	CDP 904	Yeah Something	CDJ	U.S.	1992	$3.00

Gemini

Label	Catalog Number	Title	Type	Country	Year	Longbox Value / Value
Full Length						
Polygram	829064-2	Gemini	LP	Germany		$10.00
Singles						
		Even Though You Broke My Heart	CD5	U.K.		$10.00
		Even Though You Broke My Heart	CD5	U.K.		$10.00
Second version.						
		Steal Your Love Away	CD5	U.K.		$10.00
		Steal Your Love Away	CD5	U.K.		$10.00
Second version.						

Gene

Label	Catalog Number	Title	Type	Country	Year	Longbox Value / Value
Full Length						
A&M		For the Dead	DJ/Smplr	U.S.	1995	$5.00
A&M		Olympian	LTD/LP	Australia	1995	$35.00
2CD set.						
A&M	314527662	Olympian	DJ/LP	U.S.	1995	$15.00
Advance pressing.						
A&M		Olympian	DJ/Smplr	U.S.	1995	$12.00
A&M		Sleep Well Tonight	DJ/Smplr	U.S.	1995	$5.00
Singles						
	COST2CD	Be My Light Be My Guide	CD5	U.K.		$25.00
A&M		Olympian	CD5	U.K.	1995	$10.00
A&M		Sick Sober	CDJ	France	1995	$15.00
A&M		Sleep Well Tonight	CDJ	U.S.	1995	$3.00

Gene Loves Jezebel

Label	Catalog Number	Title	Type	Country	Year	Longbox Value / Value
Full Length						
Westwood One		In Concert-Nu Rock	RS	U.S.	1993	$65.00
Airdate: 7/5/93.						
Savage		Remix Sampler	DJ/Smplr	U.S.	1993	$6.00
Singles						
Savage	50040	Break the Chain	CDJ	U.S.	1993	$3.00
Efa	CD-6380	Gorgeous	CD5	Germany	1988	$10.00
Beggars Banquet	BEG-202CD	Gorgeous	CD5	U.K.	1988	$10.00
Savage	50041	Heavenly Body	CDJ	U.S.	1993	$3.00
Alfa	ALDB-60	Jealous	CD3	Japan	1990	$13.00/$3.00
Beggars Banquet	BEG-243CD	Jealous	CD5	U.K.	1990	$10.00
Geffen	PRO-CD-4125	Jealous	CDJ	U.S.	1990	$3.00
Savage	74785 50024	Josephina	CD5	U.S.	1992	$5.00
Savage	50028	Josephina	CDJ	U.S.	1992	$3.00
Geffen	PRO-CD-3051	Suspicion	CDJ	U.S.	1988	$3.00
Geffen	PRO-CD-4173	Tangled Up in You	CDJ	U.S.	1990	$3.00
Geffen	PRO-CD-4157	Tangled Up in You	CDJ	U.S.	1990	$3.00

General Grant

Label	Catalog Number	Title	Type	Country	Year	Longbox Value / Value
Singles						
Ra-Ra	1003	Call Me	CDJ	U.S.	1993	$2.00

General Public

Label	Catalog Number	Title	Type	Country	Year	Longbox Value / Value
Full Length						
Ariola	610242	All the Rage	LP	Germany		$10.00
IRS	CD-70046	All the Rage	LP/BP	U.S.†	1984	$14.00/$8.00
Singles						
CBS	77460	I'll Take You There	CD5	U.S.	1994	$5.00
Epic	ESK 5901	I'll Take You There	CDJ	U.S.	1994	$2.00

Generation

Label	Catalog Number	Title	Type	Country	Year	Longbox Value / Value
Singles						
Polygram	871920-3	Fight for You	CD3	Germany	1989	$10.00
Polygram	871921-2	Fight for You	CD5	Germany	1989	$10.00

Generation X

Label	Catalog Number	Title	Type	Country	Year	Longbox Value / Value
Full Length						
Chrysalis		Generation X	LTD/LP	U.K.	1994	$15.00
25th Anniversary edition in 6"x11" longbox.						
Chrysalis	F2-21169-2	Generation X	LP/LB	U.S.		$18.00/$15.00
Chrysalis	F2-21327-2	Kiss Me Deadly	LP/LB	U.S.		$18.00/$15.00
Chrysalis	F2-21193-2	Vally Of the Dolls	LP/LB	U.S.		$18.00/$15.00

Genesis

Label	Catalog Number	Title	Type	Country	Year	Longbox Value / Value
Full Length						
Atlantic	19313-2	Abacab	LP/LB	U.S.		$14.00/$8.00
Non-remastered version.						
Atlantic	19313-2	Abacab	LP/LB	U.S.†	1984	$14.00/$8.00
Non-remastered version.						
Atlantic	19173-2	And Then There Were Three	LP/LB	U.S.		$14.00/$8.00
Nonremastered version.						
BBC Radio		BBC Classic Tracks	RS	U.S.	1991	$30.00
Airdate: 7/29/91.						
BBC Radio		BBC Classic Tracks	RS	U.S.	1992	$30.00
Airdate: 8/17/92.						
Westwood One		BBC Classic Tracks	RS	U.S.	1993	$40.00
Airdate: 3/29/93.						
BBC Radio		BBC Classic Tracks	RS	U.S.	1994	$30.00
Airdate: 5/2/94.						
Westwood One		BBC Classic Tracks	RS	U.S.	1994	$40.00
Airdate: 5/2/94.						
Virgin	TPAK 1	Collector's Edition	LP	Germany	1990	$45.00
3 CD Set.						
Virgin	16014-2	Duke	LP/LB	U.S.		$14.00/$8.00
Nonremastered version.						
Atlantic	81848-2	Foxtrot	LP/LB	U.S.		$14.00/$8.00
Nonremastered version.						
Jonjo	JMCD 4	From Genesis to Revelation	DJ/Smplr	Canada	1994	$20.00
Atlantic	80116-2	Genesis	LP/LB	U.S.†	1984	$14.00/$8.00
Nonremastered version.						
Unistar		Genesis Story, The	RS	U.S.	1992	$30.00
Polygram	082769	History Of	LD	U.S.		$30.00
Westwood One		In Concert	RS	U.S.	1993	$85.00
2 CD set. Airdate: 4/26/93.						
Album Network		In the Studio (Duke/Abacab)	RS	U.S.	1990	$35.00
Airdate: 1/22/90.						
Album Network		In the Studio (Genesis)	RS	U.S.		$30.00
Virgin	GENPCD 2	Invisible Touch	LTD/LP	Germany	1988	$55.00
Picture disc CD.						
DIR		King Biscuit Flour Hour	RS	U.S.	1988	$40.00
With King Crimson, Airdate: 8/21/88.						
DIR		King Biscuit Flour Hour	RS	U.S.	1988	$50.00
Airdate: 2/14/88.						
DIR		King Biscuit Flour Hour	RS	U.S.	1989	$50.00
Airdate: 4/9/89.						
DIR		King Biscuit Flour Hour	RS	U.S.	1991	$40.00
Airdate: 12/15/91.						
DIR		King Biscuit Flour Hour	RS	U.S.	1992	$40.00
Airdate: 6/14/92						
DIR		King Biscuit Flour Hour	RS	U.S.	1994	$100.00
2 CD set. Airdate: 2/6/94						
DIR		King Biscuit Flour Hour	RS	U.S.	1995	$55.00
2 CD set. Airdate: 2/26/95.						
DIR		King Biscuit Flour Hour	RS	U.S.	1996	$40.00
Airdate: 2/25/96.						
Atlantic	401-2	Lamb Live on Broadway	LP/LB	U.S.		$14.00/$8.00
Nonremastered version.						
Radio Ventures		Masters of Rock	RS	U.S.	1989	$50.00
Airdate: 8/14/89.						
Atlantic	80030-2	Nursery Cryme	LP/LB	U.S.		$14.00/$8.00
Nonremastered version.						
Westwood One		Off the Record	RS	U.S.	1993	$30.00
Airdate: 4/26/93.						
Westwood One		Off the Record	RS	U.S.	1993	$30.00
Airdate: 8/2/93.						
		On Tour 1992	RS	U.S.	1992	$35.00
Atlantic	PRCD 4997	Rarities	DJ/Smplr	U.S.	1993	$20.00
Atlantic	9002-2	Seconds Out	LP/LB	U.S.		$14.00/$8.00
Nonremastered version.						
Atlantic	19277-2	Selling England by the Pound	LP/LB	U.S.		$14.00/$8.00
Nonremastered version.						
Westwood One		Superstars	RS	U.S.	1993	$70.00
2 CD set. Airdate: 11/1/93.						
Westwood One		Superstars	RS	U.S.	1995	$85.00
2 CD set. Airdate: 6/5/95.						
Atlantic	2000-2	Three Sides Live	LP/LB	U.S.†		$14.00/$8.00
Nonremastered version.						
Virgin	38101-2	Trick of the Tail	LP/LB	U.S.		$14.00/$8.00
Nonremastered version.						
Atco	38101-2	Trick of the Tail	LP/LB	U.S.†	1985	$14.00/$8.00
Nonremastered version.						
Media America		Up Close	RS	U.S.	1988	$50.00
2 CD set.						
Media America		Up Close	RS	U.S.	1992	$80.00
4 CD set.						
Atlantic	7 82461-2	Way We Walk Volume II, The	LP/LB	U.S.	1993	$15.00/$10.00
Atlantic	82461-2	Way We Walk Volume Two: The Longs	LTD/LP	U.S.	1993	$20.00
Virgin	VJPR-16	We Know What We Like	DJ/Smplr	Japan	1993	$500.00
2 CD set.						
Unistar		Weekly Specials, The	RS	U.S.	1991	$30.00
Airdate: 1/17/91.						
Razor	MACD-4	Where the Sour Turns Too Sweet	LP	Germany		$25.00
Razor	MACD-4	Where the Sour Turns Too Sweet	LP	U.K.		$25.00
Atlantic	38100-2	Wind and Wuthering	LP/LB	U.S.		$14.00/$8.00
Nonremastered version.						
Singles						
Atlantic	PRCD-4848-2	Domino	CDJ	U.S.	1992	$7.00
Atlantic	PRCD 4616-2	Driving the Last Spike	CDJ	U.S.	1992	$6.00
Virgin	VJDP-10193	Hold on My Heart	CD3	Japan	1992	$12.00/$4.00
Virgin	VJCP-14042	Hold on My Heart	CD5	Japan	1992	$18.00
Virgin	GENSD-8	Hold on My Heart	CD5	U.K.	1991	$11.00
Atlantic	PRCD-4533-2	Hold on My Heart	CDJ	U.S.	1992	$3.00
Virgin	665091	I Can't Dance	CD5	Germany	1992	$10.00
Virgin	VJDP-10184	I Can't Dance	CD3	Japan	1992	$12.00/$4.00
Virgin	VJCP-14040	I Can't Dance	CD5	Japan	1992	$18.00
Atlantic	7 85906-2	I Can't Dance	CD5	U.S.	1991	$5.00
Atlantic	PRCD-4412-2	I Can't Dance	CDJ	U.S.	1991	$3.00
Virgin	GENDX9	Invisible Series (Jesus He Knows Me)	CD5	U.K.	1992	$15.00
In special collector's box.						
Atlantic	VJCP-12002	Jesus He Knows Me	CD5	Japan	1992	$18.00
Atlantic	PRCD-4680-2	Jesus He Knows Me	CDJ	U.S.	1992	$3.00
Virgin	658632	Land of Confusion	CD5	Germany	1987	$10.00
Charisma	SNEG3-12	Land of Confusion	CD5	U.K.	1987	$10.00
Vertigo	866599-2	Mama	CD5	Germany	1991	$10.00
Virgin	CDT-5	Mama	CD3	U.K.	1988	$10.00
Vertigo	866599-2	Mama	CD5	U.K.	1991	$10.00
Virgin	VJCP-12005	Never a Time	CD5	Japan	1992	$18.00
Atlantic	7 87411-2	Never a Time	CD5	U.S.	1992	$5.00
Atlantic	PRCD 4864-2	Never a Time	CDJ	U.S.	1992	$3.00
Virgin	VJDP-10179	No Son of Mine	CD3	Japan	1991	$12.00/$4.00
Virgin	VJCP-14034	No Son of Mine	CD5	Japan	1991	$18.00
Atlantic	7 87571-2	No Son of Mine	CD5	U.S.	1991	$5.00
Atlantic	87571-2	No Son of Mine	CD5	U.S.	1991	$8.00
Atlantic	PRCD 4277-2	No Son of Mine	CDJ	U.S.	1991	$5.00
Aris	885227	Spot the Pigion	CD3	Germany	1989	$10.00
BMG	663280	Spot the Pigion	CD5	Germany	1990	$10.00
Charisma	CDT-412	Spot the Pigion	CD3	U.K.	1989	$10.00
Charisma	CDT-40	Spot the Pigion	CD3	U.K.	1989	$10.00
Virgin	CDF-40	Spot the Pigion	CD5	U.K.	1990	$10.00
Virgin		Tell Me Why	CD5	U.K.		$10.00
Virgin		Tell Me Why	CD5	U.K.		$10.00
Second version.						
Virgin	658888	Tonight, Tonight, Tonight	CD5	Germany	1988	$10.00
Virgin	DRAW-412	Tonight, Tonight, Tonight	CD5	U.K.	1988	$10.00

Geneva

Singles

Label	Catalog Number	Title	Type	Country	Year	Longbox Value / Value
Avex Trax	AVDD-20041	Everytime I See You	CD3	Japan	1993	$13.00/$4.00
Isba	IS12K-1050	Holiday	CD5	Canada	1993	$6.00

Genoa

Singles

Label	Catalog Number	Title	Type	Country	Year	Longbox Value / Value
Vice	DTK-0007	What a Wonderful Life	CD5	Japan	1991	$10.00

Gentlemen Without Weapons

Singles

Label	Catalog Number	Title	Type	Country	Year	Longbox Value / Value
A&M	390363	Unconditional Love	CD5	Germany	1988	$9.00
A&M	AMCD-448	Unconditional Love	CD5	U.K.	1988	$9.00
A&M	CD 17576	Unconditional Love	CDJ	U.S.	1988	$2.00

George, Mona

Singles

Label	Catalog Number	Title	Type	Country	Year	Longbox Value / Value
London	LONCD-271	Just the Way You Like It	CD5	U.K.	1990	$9.00

Georgia Satellites

Full Length

Label	Catalog Number	Title	Type	Country	Year	Longbox Value / Value
TIS	CDSPRAY-301	Keep the Faith	LP	U.K.		$20.00

Singles

Label	Catalog Number	Title	Type	Country	Year	Longbox Value / Value
Elektra		All Over But the Cryin'	CD5	U.S.		$5.00
Elektra	9 66678-2	Another Chance	CD5	U.S.	1989	$5.00
Elektra	PR 8113-2	Another Chance	CDJ	U.S.	1989	$2.00
Elektra	PR 8024-2	Don't Pass Me By	CDJ	U.S.	1988	$2.00
Pioneer	10P3-6079	Hippy Hippy Shake	CD3	Japan	1988	$12.00/$4.00
Elektra	EKR-86CD	Hippy Hippy Shake	CD5	U.K.	1988	$10.00
Elektra	PR 8030-2	Hippy Hippy Shake	CDJ	U.S.	1988	$2.00
Pioneer	10SW-68	Open All Night	CD3	Japan	1988	$12.00/$4.00
Elektra	PR 8007-2	Open All Night	CDJ	U.S.	1988	$2.00
Elektra	PR 8159-2	Shake That Thing	CDJ	U.S.	1990	$2.00
Elektra	EKR-89CD	Sheila	CD3	U.K.	1989	$10.00
Elektra	9 69328-2	Sheila	CD3	U.S.	1988	$6.00/$3.00
Elektra	PR 8045-2	Sheila	CDJ	U.S.	1988	$2.00

Georgio

Singles

Label	Catalog Number	Title	Type	Country	Year	Longbox Value / Value
RCA	62031-2-RDJ	Rollin'	CDJ	U.S.	1991	$2.00

Gerardo

Singles

Label	Catalog Number	Title	Type	Country	Year	Longbox Value / Value
Interscope	AMDY-4088	Here Kitty Kitty	CD3	Japan	1992	$13.00/$4.00
Interscope	PRCD 4711-2	Here Kitty Kitty	CDJ	U.S.	1992	$2.00
Warner Brothers	AMDY-5064	Latin Till I Die	CD3	Japan	1991	$12.00/$3.00
Interscope	PRCD 4253-2	Latin Till I Die	CDJ	U.S.	1991	$2.00
Interscope	96100	Love	CD5	U.S.	1992	$4.00
Interscope	PRCD 4829-2	Love	CDJ	U.S.	1992	$2.00
Atlantic	AMDY-5047	Rico Suave	CD3	Japan	1991	$12.00/$4.00
Atlantic	A-7716CD	Rico Suave	CD5	U.K.	1991	$10.00
Interscope	PRCD 3679-2	Rico Suave	CDJ	U.S.	1990	$3.00
Interscope	AMDY-5053	We Want the Funk	CD3	Japan	1991	$12.00/$4.00
Eastwest	A-8815CD	We Want the Funk	CD5	U.K.	1991	$9.00
Interscope	96357-2	We Want the Funk	CD5	U.S.	1991	$4.00
Interscope	PRCD 3846-2	We Want the Funk	CDJ	U.S.	1991	$2.00
Atlantic	7567-96295-2	When the Lights Go Out	CD5	Germany	1991	$9.00
Warner Brothers	AMDY-5056	When the Lights Go Out	CD3	Japan	1991	$12.00/$4.00
Interscope	PRCD 4103-2	When the Lights Go Out	CDJ	U.S.	1991	$2.00

Germaine, Nikita

Full Length

Label	Catalog Number	Title	Type	Country	Year	Longbox Value / Value
Motown	6345	Sweet as It Comes	LP/LB	U.S.		$14.00/$8.00

Germano, Lisa

Full Length

Label	Catalog Number	Title	Type	Country	Year	Longbox Value / Value
4AD		Geek the Girl	DJ/LP	U.S.	1994	$20.00
		Happiness	DJ/LP	U.K.	1994	$12.00

Singles

Label	Catalog Number	Title	Type	Country	Year	Longbox Value / Value
4AD	PRO-CD-6846	Puppet	CDJ	U.S.	1994	$3.00
Capitol		Stars	CDJ	U.S.	1994	$3.00
Capitol	DPRO-79747	You Make Me Want to Wear Dresses	CDJ	U.S.	1993	$3.00

Germino, Mark

Full Length

Label	Catalog Number	Title	Type	Country	Year	Longbox Value / Value
ZOO	11002	Radartown	LP/LB	U.S.		$12.00/$7.00

Singles

Label	Catalog Number	Title	Type	Country	Year	Longbox Value / Value
RCA	PD-43020	Caught in the Act of Being Ourselves	CD5	U.K.		$8.00
BMG	PD-49216	Let Freedom Ring	CD5	Germany	1991	$8.00
RCA	PD-49166	Rex Bob Lowenstein	CD5	U.K.	1991	$8.00

Gershwin, Dave

Full Length

Label	Catalog Number	Title	Type	Country	Year	Longbox Value / Value
Philips	310690116-2	Gershwin Connection, The	LP	U.S.	1993	$30.00

CD+I

Gershwin, George

Full Length

Label	Catalog Number	Title	Type	Country	Year	Longbox Value / Value
Columbia	CD-76509	Gershwin Plays Gershwin	LP	Germany		$20.00
		Glory of Gershwin	DJ/LP	U.K.	1994	$60.00

Promo sampler with book and press kit.

Get the First Movement

Singles

Label	Catalog Number	Title	Type	Country	Year	Longbox Value / Value
Mercury	CDP 771	Get the First	CDJ	U.S.	1992	$2.00

Get Wild Go Crazy

Singles

Label	Catalog Number	Title	Type	Country	Year	Longbox Value / Value
BMG	664324	Get Wild Go Crazy	CD5	Germany	1991	$8.00

Getz, Mara

Singles

Label	Catalog Number	Title	Type	Country	Year	Longbox Value / Value
Canyon	PCDY-00075	Hello, Full Moon	CD3	Japan	1991	$13.00/$4.00
Canyon	PCDY-00017	In Your Eyes	CD3	Japan	1989	$13.00/$4.00
Canyon	PCDY-00102	World in Her Mind	CD3	Japan	1992	$13.00/$4.00
Canyon	PCDY-00078	You Light the Way	CD3	Japan	1991	$13.00/$4.00

Getz, Stan

Full Length

Label	Catalog Number	Title	Type	Country	Year	Longbox Value / Value
Verve	821725-2	Au Go Go	LP/LB	U.S.†	1985	$14.00/$8.00
Mosaic	MD3-131	Complete Recordings	LTD/LP	U.S.		$45.00

3 CD set. Limited to 7500 copies.

Label	Catalog Number	Title	Type	Country	Year	Longbox Value / Value
Verve	314 531 935-2	East of the Sun-The West Coast Sessions	LTD/LP	U.S.	1996	$40.00
Verve	821982-2	Focus	LP/LB	U.S.†	1985	$14.00/$8.00
Verve	810048-2	Getz/Gilberto with Jobim	LP/LB	U.S.†	1985	$14.00/$8.00
Savoy Records	CY-78993	Opus De Bop	LTD/LP	U.S.	1995	$20.00

CD in miniature repica of original LP sleeve.

Label	Catalog Number	Title	Type	Country	Year	Longbox Value / Value
Concord Jazz	CCD-4188	Pure Getz	LP/LB	U.S.†	1985	$14.00/$8.00
Verve	815054-2	Sweet Rain	LP/LB	U.S.†	1985	$14.00/$8.00

Singles

Label	Catalog Number	Title	Type	Country	Year	Longbox Value / Value
A&M	75021 7430 2	Apasionado	CDJ	U.S.	1990	$2.00

Getz, Stan & Charlie Byrd

Full Length

Label	Catalog Number	Title	Type	Country	Year	Longbox Value / Value
Verve	810061-2GH	Jazz Samba	LP/LB	U.S.†	1985	$14.00/$8.00

Getz, Stan & Laurindo Almeida

Full Length

Label	Catalog Number	Title	Type	Country	Year	Longbox Value / Value
Verve	823149-2	Getz/Almeida	LP/LB	U.S.†	1985	$14.00/$8.00

GGFH

Singles

Label	Catalog Number	Title	Type	Country	Year	Longbox Value / Value
Dreamtime	KTB-9TCD	Reality	CD5	U.K.	1992	$8.00

Ghanai, Dario

Singles

Label	Catalog Number	Title	Type	Country	Year	Longbox Value / Value
EMI	147524-2	Mother Nature	CD5	Germany	1990	$8.00

Ghost III

Singles

Label	Catalog Number	Title	Type	Country	Year	Longbox Value / Value
Canyon	PCDH-00013	Victory	CD3	Japan	1993	$12.00/$3.00

Ghost of an American Airman

Singles

Label	Catalog Number	Title	Type	Country	Year	Longbox Value / Value
Hollywood	8524	Honeychild	CDJ	U.S.	1992	$2.00

Ghostdance

Singles

Label	Catalog Number	Title	Type	Country	Year	Longbox Value / Value
Chrysalis	CHSCD-3402	Celebrate	CD5	U.K.	1989	$8.00
BMG	662500	Down to the Wire	CD5	Germany	1989	$8.00
Chrysalis	CHSCD-3376	Down to the Wire	CD5	U.K.	1989	$8.00
BMG	662501	Introducing Ghostdance	CD5	Germany	1989	$8.00

Ghosttrain

Singles

Label	Catalog Number	Title	Type	Country	Year	Longbox Value / Value
Madcat	MAD-11-3	Ghosttrain	CD5	Germany	1990	$8.00

Giant

Singles

Label	Catalog Number	Title	Type	Country	Year	Longbox Value / Value
Epic	ESK 4433	Chained	CDJ	U.S.	1992	$2.00
A&M	CDEE-562	Double Feature	CD5	U.K.	1990	$8.00
Polygram	390500-2	I'll See You in My Dreams	CD5	U.K.	1989	$8.00
A&M	CD 18010	I'll See You in My Dreams	CDJ	U.S.	1989	$2.00
A&M	PCDY-10006	I'm a Believer	CD3	Japan	1989	$13.00/$4.00
A&M	AMCD-546	I'm a Believer	CD5	U.K.	1989	$8.00
A&M	75021 5272-2	I'm a Believer	CDJ	U.S.	1989	$2.00
A&M	75021 8088-2	I'm a Believer	CDJ	U.S.	1989	$2.00
A&M	CD 17872	I'm a Believer	CDJ	U.S.	1989	$2.00
A&M	CD 17913	Innocent Days	CDJ	U.S.	1989	$2.00
A&M	AMCD-571	It Takes Two	CD5	U.K.	1989	$8.00
A&M	75021 8088 2	It Takes Two	CDJ	U.S.	1989	$2.00
Epic	ESK-4743	Stay	CDJ	U.S.	1992	$2.00
Epic	ESK 4690	Time to Burn	CDj	U.S.	1992	$2.00

Giant Sand

Singles

Label	Catalog Number	Title	Type	Country	Year	Longbox Value / Value
Atlantic	PRCD 3863-2	Shadow To You	CDJ	U.S.	1990	$2.00

Giant Steps

Singles

Label	Catalog Number	Title	Type	Country	Year	Longbox Value / Value
A&M	S9Y-13118	Book of Pride	CD3	Japan	1989	$12.00/$3.00
A&M	S10Y-3058	Into You	CD3	Japan	1988	$12.00/$3.00
A&M	AMCD-451	Into You	CD5	U.K.	1988	$8.00
A&M	CD 17649	Into You	CDJ	U.S.	1988	$2.00
A&M	CD 17597	(The World Don't Need) Another Lover	CDJ	U.S.	1988	$2.00

Giants

Singles

Label	Catalog Number	Title	Type	Country	Year	Longbox Value / Value
ZYX	DST-1071-8	Color Me Badd	CD5	Germany	1992	$6.00

Gibb, Andy

Singles

Label	Catalog Number	Title	Type	Country	Year	Longbox Value / Value
Polygram	889171-2	Too Many	CD5	Germany	1990	$9.00

Gibb, Barry

Full Length

Label	Catalog Number	Title	Type	Country	Year	Longbox Value / Value
MCA	MCAD-5506	Now Voyager	LP/LB	U.S.†	1984	$15.00/$10.00

Singles

Label	Catalog Number	Title	Type	Country	Year	Longbox Value / Value
Polygram	887785-2	Childhood Days	CD5	Germany	1988	$9.00

Gibb, Robin

Full Length

Label	Catalog Number	Title	Type	Country	Year	Longbox Value / Value
Polygram	810896-2	How Old Are You	LP/BP	U.S.†	1984	$15.00/$10.00
Polydor	827592-2	Secret Agent	LP	Germany		$20.00
Polydor	821797-2	Secret Agent	LP	U.K.		$20.00
Polydor	827592-2	Secret Agent	LP	U.K.		$20.00
Atco	810896-2	Secret Agent	LP/LB	U.S.†	1985	$15.00/$10.00

Gibson Brothers

Singles

Label	Catalog Number	Title	Type	Country	Year	Longbox Value / Value
Polygram	887587-2	Cuba	CD5	Germany	1988	$8.00
BCM	20002	Cuba	CD5	Germany	1989	$8.00
Polygram	871605-2	Dancin' the Mambo	CD5	Germany	1989	$8.00
BCM	20417	Megamix	CD5	Germany	1990	$8.00
BCM	20288	Que Sera Mi Vida	CD5	Germany	1989	$8.00

Gibson, Debbie

Full Length

Label	Catalog Number	Title	Type	Country	Year	Longbox Value / Value
Atlantic	50176-2	Anything is Possible	LP/VHS	U.S.	1990	$35.00

CD and VHS video in 12"x12" boxed set.

Label	Catalog Number	Title	Type	Country	Year	Longbox Value / Value
Pioneer Artists	PA-91-336	Around The World	LD	U.S.	1991	$35.00
		Live Out of the Blue	LD	U.S.		$25.00
Atlantic	43P2-0008	Out of the Blue	LTD/LP	Japan	1987	$40.00

Gold disc.

Label	Catalog Number	Title	Type	Country	Year	Longbox Value / Value
Atlantic	PR 2850-2	Profiled!	DJ/Intvw	U.S.	1989	$10.00

Singles

Label	Catalog Number	Title	Type	Country	Year	Longbox Value / Value
Atlantic	7567-86701-2	Anything is Possible	CD5	Germany	1991	$10.00
Atlantic	AMDY-5035	Anything is Possible	CD3	Japan	1990	$13.00/$4.00
Atlantic	A-7735CD	Anything is Possible	CD5	U.K.	1991	$10.00
Atlantic	786424-2	Electric Youth	CD5	Germany	1989	$10.00
Atlantic	09P3-6130	Electric Youth	CD3	Japan	1989	$13.00/$4.00
Atlantic	A-8919CD	Electric Youth	CD5	U.K.	1989	$10.00
Atlantic	A-8919CDP	Electric Youth	CD5	U.K.	1989	$10.00
Atlantic	86427-2	Electric Youth	CD5	U.S.	1989	$5.00

Label	Catalog Number	Title	Type	Country	Year	Longbox Value/Value
Atlantic	PR 2671-2	Electric Youth	CDJ	U.S.	1989	$2.00
Atlantic	PR 2689-2	Electric Youth	CDJ	U.S.	1989	$2.00
Atlantic	PR 8193-2	Electric Youth	CDJ	U.S.	1989	$2.00
Atlantic	AMDY-5106	Eyes of a Child	CD3	Japan	1993	$12.00/$4.00
Atlantic	786556-0	Foolish Beat	CD3	Germany	1988	$10.00
Atlantic	10SW-15	Foolish Beat	CD3	Japan	1988	$12.00/$4.00
Atlantic	A-9059CD	Foolish Beat	CD3	U.K.	1988	$10.00
Atlantic		For Better or For Worse	CDJ	U.S.	1994	$6.00
Atlantic	AMDY-5109	Free Me	CD3	Japan	1993	$12.00/$4.00
Atlantic	AMDY-5076	In His Mind	CD3	Japan	1992	$13.00/$4.00
Atlantic	AMDY-5092	Losin' Myself	CD3	Japan	1993	$12.00/$4.00
Atlantic	PRCD4917-2	Losin' Myself	CDJ	U.S.	1992	$10.00
Atlantic	PRCD 4917-2	Losin' Myself	CDJ	U.S.	1993	$6.00
Atlantic	786457-2	Lost in Your Eyes	CD3	Germany	1989	$10.00
Atlantic	10P3-6057	Lost in Your Eyes	CD3	Japan	1989	$13.00/$4.00
Atlantic	A-8970CD	Lost in Your Eyes	CD3	U.K.	1989	$10.00
Atlantic	PR 2562-2	Lost in Your Eyes	CDJ	U.S.	1989	$2.00
Atlantic	09P3-6165	No More Rhyme	CD3	Japan	1989	$13.00/$4.00
Atlantic	AMDY-5046	One Hand, One Heart	CD3	Japan	1991	$13.00/$4.00
Atlantic	PRCD 3836-2	One Hand, One Heart	CDJ	U.S.	1991	$2.00
Atlantic	AMDY-5054	One Step Ahead	CD3	Japan	1991	$13.00/$4.00
Atlantic	PRCD 3944-2	One Step Ahead	CDJ	U.S.	1991	$2.00
Atlantic	786579-2	Out of the Blue	CD3	Germany	1988	$10.00
Atlantic	A-9091CD	Out of the Blue	CD3	U.K.	1988	$10.00
Atlantic	AMDY-5107	Shock Your Mama	CD3	Japan	1993	$12.00/$4.00
Atlantic	PRCD 5050-2	Shock Your Mama	CDJ	U.S.	1993	$7.00
Atlantic	10P3-5021	Staying Together	CD3	Japan	1988	$13.00/$4.00
Atlantic	A-9020CD	Staying Together	CD3	U.K.	1988	$10.00
Atlantic	AMDY-5042	(This So Called) Miracle	CD3	Japan	1991	$13.00/$4.00
Atlantic	PRCD 3770-2	(This So Called) Miracle	CDJ	U.S.	1990	$2.00
Atlantic	786315-2	We Could Be Together	CD3	Germany	1989	$10.00
Atlantic	09P3-6194	We Could Be Together	CD3	Japan	1989	$13.00/$4.00
Atlantic	A-8896CD	We Could Be Together	CD3	U.K.	1989	$10.00
Atlantic	PR 2724-2	We Could Be Together	CDJ	U.S.	1989	$2.00
Atlantic	AMDY-5034	Without You	CD3	Japan	1990	$13.00/$4.00

Gibson, John

Full Length

Label	Catalog Number	Title	Type	Country	Year	Longbox Value/Value
Aris	881025	Change of Heart	LP	Germany		$10.00
Aris	880390	On the Run	LP	Germany		$10.00

Gibson/Miller Band

Full Length

Label	Catalog Number	Title	Type	Country	Year	Longbox Value/Value
Epic		Where There's Smoke	DJ/LP	U.S.	1993	$15.00

CD in matchbook package.

Singles

Label	Catalog Number	Title	Type	Country	Year	Longbox Value/Value
		Where There's Smoke	CDJ	U.S.		$3.00

CD in Matchbook package.

Gidea Park

Full Length

Label	Catalog Number	Title	Type	Country	Year	Longbox Value/Value
	CEC 00494	California Gold	LP	Japan		$30.00
	CEC00494	California Gold	LP	Japan		$30.00

Advance pressing.

Giggles

Singles

Label	Catalog Number	Title	Type	Country	Year	Longbox Value/Value
EMI	TODP-2355	What Goes Around Comes Around	CD3	Japan	1992	$12.00/$3.00

Gigi on the Beach

Singles

Label	Catalog Number	Title	Type	Country	Year	Longbox Value/Value
A&M	S9Y 1107	Friday Night	CD3	Japan	1989	$12.00/$3.00

Gigolo Aunts

Full Length

Label	Catalog Number	Title	Type	Country	Year	Longbox Value/Value
RCA	RMJ 66392-2	Flippin' Out	DJ/LP	U.S.	1994	$13.00

Singles

Label	Catalog Number	Title	Type	Country	Year	Longbox Value/Value
Fire	BLAZE-58CD	Cope	CD5	U.K.	1992	$8.00
RCA	62802-2-RDJ	Cope	CDJ	U.S.	1992	$2.00

Gilbert, Kevin

Full Length

Label	Catalog Number	Title	Type	Country	Year	Longbox Value/Value
		Thud	LTD/LP	U.S.	1995	$14.00

2 CD set.

Gilberto, Astrud

Full Length

Label	Catalog Number	Title	Type	Country	Year	Longbox Value/Value
Verve	823451-2	Silver Collection: The Astrud Gilberto Album	LP/LB	U.S.†	1985	$14.00/$8.00

Giles, Angie

Singles

Label	Catalog Number	Title	Type	Country	Year	Longbox Value/Value
Island	CID-535	Silent Way	CD5	U.K.	1992	$8.00
Island	CID-513	Submerge	CD5	U.K.	1992	$8.00

Gill, Johnny

Singles

Label	Catalog Number	Title	Type	Country	Year	Longbox Value/Value
Motown	ZD-44104	Fairweather Friend	CD5	Germany	1990	$10.00
Motown	BVDM-5	Fairweather Friend	CD3	Japan	1990	$12.00/$4.00
		Fairweather Friend	CDJ	U.S.	1990	$2.00
Motown	PODY-1016	Floor, The	CD3	Japan	1993	$12.00/$4.00
Motown	374631095	Floor, The	CDJ	U.S.	1993	$2.00
Motown	374631102	Floor, The	CDJ	U.S.	1993	$2.00
Motown	374631110	Floor, The	CDJ	U.S.	1993	$2.00
Motown	BVDM-12	Giving My All To You	CD3	Japan	1991	$12.00/$4.00
Motown	374631119	I Got You	CDJ	U.S.	1993	$2.00
Giant	PRO-CD-4912	I'm Still Walking	CDJ	U.S.	1991	$2.00
Motown	374631132	Long Way From Home	CDJ	U.S.	1993	$2.00
Motown	ZD-44036	My, My, My	CD5	U.K.	1990	$10.00
Motown	374631152	Quiet Time to Play	CDJ	U.S.	1993	$2.00
Motown	ZD-43616	Rub You the Right Way	CD5	Germany	1990	$10.00
Motown	ZD-43702	Rub You the Right Way	CD5	U.K.	1990	$10.00
Motown	374631162	Tell Me How U Want It	CDJ	U.S.	1993	$2.00
Motown	ZD-44272	Wrap My Body Tight	CD5	Germany	1991	$10.00
Motown	BVDM-6	Wrap My Body Tight	CD3	Japan	1991	$12.00/$4.00
Motown	ZD-44272	Wrap My Body Tight	CD5	U.K.	1991	$10.00

Gill, Vince

Full Length

Label	Catalog Number	Title	Type	Country	Year	Longbox Value/Value
		'90s Country	RS	U.S.	1995	$30.00

Airdate: 11/4/95.

Label	Catalog Number	Title	Type	Country	Year	Longbox Value/Value
		'90s Country	RS	U.S.	1995	$30.00

Airdate: 4/22/95.

Label	Catalog Number	Title	Type	Country	Year	Longbox Value/Value
		Christmas Favorites	RS	U.S.	1993	$20.00
		Country Concert	RS	U.S.	1995	$50.00

2 CD set. Airdate: 8/12/95.

Label	Catalog Number	Title	Type	Country	Year	Longbox Value/Value
		Road, The	RS	U.S.	1995	$50.00

2 CD set. Airdate: 4/7/95.

Label	Catalog Number	Title	Type	Country	Year	Longbox Value/Value
Unistar		Vince Gill Story	RS	U.S.	1993	$30.00

Airdate: 6/5/93.

Label	Catalog Number	Title	Type	Country	Year	Longbox Value/Value
		Way Back Home, The	DJ/LP	U.S.		$10.00

Singles

Label	Catalog Number	Title	Type	Country	Year	Longbox Value/Value
MCA	MCA5P-2882	Have Yourself a Merry Little Christmas	CDJ	U.S.	1993	$3.00
MCA	MCA5P-2296	I Still Believe in You	CDJ	U.S.	1992	$2.00
MCA	MCA5P-2366	I Still Believe in You	CDJ	U.S.	1992	$2.00
MCA	MCA5P-54406	I Still Believe in You	CDJ	U.S.	1992	$2.00
MCA	MCA5P-54715	One More Last Chance	CDJ	U.S.	1992	$2.00
MCA	CD45 54026	Pocket Full of Gold	CDJ	U.S.	1991	$2.00
MCA	MCA5P-54706	Tryin' to Get Over You	CDJ	U.S.	1992	$2.00

Gillan

Full Length

Label	Catalog Number	Title	Type	Country	Year	Longbox Value/Value
Metal Blade		Clear Air Turbulence	LP/LB	U.S.		$14.00/$8.00
Metal Blade		Double Agent	LP/LB	U.S.		$14.00/$8.00

Gillan, Andy

Singles

Label	Catalog Number	Title	Type	Country	Year	Longbox Value/Value
CBS	655029-3	Old Flame Burnin'	CD3	Germany	1989	$10.00

Gillan, Ian

Full Length

Label	Catalog Number	Title	Type	Country	Year	Longbox Value/Value
Virgin		Accidentally on Purpose	LP/LB	U.S.		$14.00/$8.00
Griffin		Best of Gillan	LTD/LP	U.S.		$30.00

CD and Book

Label	Catalog Number	Title	Type	Country	Year	Longbox Value/Value
Virgin	DIXDCD-39	What I Did on My Vacation	LP	U.K.		$20.00

Singles

Label	Catalog Number	Title	Type	Country	Year	Longbox Value/Value
Eastwest	172179-2	No Good Luck	CD5	Germany	1990	$10.00
Teldac	YZ-513CD	No Good Luck	CD5	U.K.	1990	$10.00
Eastwest	9031-72041-2	Nothing But the Best	CD5	Germany	1990	$10.00

Gilles, Samantha

Singles

Label	Catalog Number	Title	Type	Country	Year	Longbox Value/Value
Canyon	S10Y-1028	Go Baby Go	CD3	Japan	1988	$12.00/$3.00
Canyon	PCDY-00043	L.O.V.E.	CD3	Japan	1990	$12.00/$3.00
Canyon	S10Y-1015	One-Way Ticket to Heaven	CD3	Japan	1988	$12.00/$3.00
Canyon	PCDY-00021	Perfect Body	CD3	Japan	1989	$12.00/$3.00
Canyon	S10Y-1042	Slow Down	CD3	Japan	1989	$12.00/$3.00

Gillespie, Dizzy

Full Length

Label	Catalog Number	Title	Type	Country	Year	Longbox Value/Value
Image	ID8151VW	A Night In Tunisia	LD	U.S.		$30.00
Savoy Records	CY-78815	Champ, The	LTD/LP	U.S.	1996	$20.00

CD in miniature repica of original LP sleeve.

Label	Catalog Number	Title	Type	Country	Year	Longbox Value/Value
Savoy Records	CY-78814	Groovin' High	LTD/LP	U.S.	1996	$20.00

CD in miniature repica of original LP sleeve.

Label	Catalog Number	Title	Type	Country	Year	Longbox Value/Value
Pablo	CD-311203	Montreux '77	LP	Germany		$25.00
Polygram	817107-2	Portrait of Duke Ellington	LP	Germany		$25.00
Verve	817107-2	Portrait of Duke Ellington	LP/LB	U.S.†	1985	$14.00/$8.00
Polygram	830224-2	With the Double Six Of Paris	LP	Germany		$25.00

Singles

Label	Catalog Number	Title	Type	Country	Year	Longbox Value/Value
BCM	20481	Dance Together	CD5	Germany	1990	$12.00
Alfa	10R3-4	Round Midnight	CD3	Japan	1988	$13.00/$3.00

Gillette

Singles

Label	Catalog Number	Title	Type	Country	Year	Longbox Value/Value
Zoo	14210	Mr. Personality	CD5	U.S.	1994	$5.00

Gilly G

Singles

Label	Catalog Number	Title	Type	Country	Year	Longbox Value/Value
MCA	MCSTD-1572	Racism	CD5	U.K.	1992	$8.00

Gilmore, Jimmie Dale

Singles

Label	Catalog Number	Title	Type	Country	Year	Longbox Value/Value
Elektra	PRCD 8522-2	My Mind's Got a Mind of It's Own	CDJ	U.S.	1992	$2.00

Gilmour, David

Full Length

Label	Catalog Number	Title	Type	Country	Year	Longbox Value/Value
DIR		King Biscuit Flour Hour	RS	U.S.	1987	$30.00

With Hynde, Collins, Airdate: 12/13/87.

Gimix

Singles

Label	Catalog Number	Title	Type	Country	Year	Longbox Value/Value
Vigin	VJDA-00013	Cider	CD3	Japan	1992	$12.00/$3.00

Gin Blossoms

Full Length

Label	Catalog Number	Title	Type	Country	Year	Longbox Value/Value
Album Network		Album Network Special	RS	U.S.		$100.00

2 CD set.

Label	Catalog Number	Title	Type	Country	Year	Longbox Value/Value
	DCI-3156	D.J. Sampler	DJ/Smplr	Japan	1994	$50.00
Westwood One		In Concert	RS	U.S.	1994	$60.00

Airdate: 8/29/94.

Label	Catalog Number	Title	Type	Country	Year	Longbox Value/Value
Westwood One		In Concert	RS	U.S.	1994	$80.00

2 CD set. With Little Feat, Airdate: 10/25/93

Label	Catalog Number	Title	Type	Country	Year	Longbox Value/Value
Westwood One		In Concert	RS	U.S.	1994	$80.00

2 CD set. With Radiohead, Airdate: 11/22/93

Label	Catalog Number	Title	Type	Country	Year	Longbox Value/Value
Westwood One		In Concert	RS	U.S.	1995	$60.00

Airdate: 3/13/95.

Label	Catalog Number	Title	Type	Country	Year	Longbox Value/Value
Westwood One		In Concert	RS	U.S.	1996	$60.00

Airdate: 3/25/96.

Label	Catalog Number	Title	Type	Country	Year	Longbox Value/Value
Westwood One		In Concert-Nu Rock	RS	U.S.	1995	$60.00

Airdate: 1/30/95.

Label	Catalog Number	Title	Type	Country	Year	Longbox Value/Value
Westwood One		In Concert-Nu Rock	RS	U.S.	1995	$60.00

Airdate: 9/11/95.

Label	Catalog Number	Title	Type	Country	Year	Longbox Value/Value
A&M	75021 54032	New Miserable Experience	LP	U.S.	1992	$25.00

Original "desert scene" cover and "basket ball" picture disc.

Label	Catalog Number	Title	Type	Country	Year	Longbox Value/Value
Westwood One		On the Edge	RS	U.S.	1996	$25.00

Airdate: 2/12/96.

Label	Catalog Number	Title	Type	Country	Year	Longbox Value/Value
A&M	31458 8107	Shut Up and Smoke	DJ/Smplr	U.S.	1993	$8.00
A&M		Shut Up and Smoke	DJ/Smplr	U.S.	1995	$12.00
Media America		Up Close	RS	U.S.	1996	$50.00
		Virtuallyalternative	RS	U.S.	1996	$60.00

2 CD set.

Singles

Label	Catalog Number	Title	Type	Country	Year	Longbox Value/Value
A&M	75021 5169-2	Allison Road	CDJ	U.S.	1991	$3.00
A&M	31458 8202 2	Allison Road	CDJ	U.S.	1994	$3.00
		Day Job	CDJ	U.S.		$3.00
		Follow Your Dreams	CD5	U.K.	1996	$10.00
A&M		Found Out About You	CD5	U.K.	1992	$10.00
A&M		Found Out About You	CD5	U.K.	1992	$10.00

Second version.

Label	Catalog Number	Title	Type	Country	Year	Longbox Value/Value
A&M	75021 8055-2	Found Out About You	CDJ	U.S.	1992	$3.00
A&M	75021 7602-2	Hey Jealousy	CDJ	U.S.	1992	$3.00
A&M	75021 8061-2	Lost Horizons	CDJ	U.S.	1992	$3.00
A&M	75021-5403-412	Mrs. Rita	CDJ	U.S.	1992	$6.00
A&M	31458 8107	Until I Fade Away	CDJ	U.S.	1994	$3.00

Label	Catalog Number	Title	Type	Country	Year	Longbox Value / Value

Gina T.

Singles

Label	Catalog Number	Title	Type	Country	Year	Value
Bellaphon	130-07-615	Birds of Paradise	CD5	Germany	1992	$8.00
Bellaphon	130-07-363	Hey Angel	CD5	Germany	1990	$8.00
Bellaphon	130-07-327	In My Fantasy	CD5	Germany	1992	$8.00
Bellaphon	130-07-346	Tokyo By Night	CD5	Germany	1990	$8.00
Bellaphon	130-07-586	You Really Got Me	CD5	Germany	1992	$8.00

Ginn, Greg

Singles

Label	Catalog Number	Title	Type	Country	Year	Value
Cruz	028	Payday	CDJ	U.S.		$2.00

Ginsburg, Allen

Full Length

Label	Catalog Number	Title	Type	Country	Year	Value
Rhino	PRCD 7068-2	Pull My Daisy	DJ/Smplr	U.S.	1994	$8.00

Giovani

Singles

Label	Catalog Number	Title	Type	Country	Year	Value
Elektra	64420	Girl in My Eyes	CD5	U.S.	1995	$5.00

Gipsy and Queen

Singles

Label	Catalog Number	Title	Type	Country	Year	Value
Alfa	11B3-15	Action	CD3	Japan	1989	$12.00/$3.00
Alfa	ALDB-100	Emergency	CD3	Japan	1991	$12.00/$3.00
Alfa	10SR-16	Love	CD3	Japan	1988	$12.00/$3.00

Gipsy Kings

Full Length

Label	Catalog Number	Title	Type	Country	Year	Value
Elektra	60892	Mosaique	LP/LB	U.S.	1989	$12.00/$7.00

Singles

Label	Catalog Number	Title	Type	Country	Year	Value
BMG	CA1-310	A Mi Manera	CD5	U.K.	1988	$8.00
Columbia	657251-2	Baila Me	CD5	Germany	1991	$8.00
Columbia	657251-2	Baila Me	CD5	U.K.	1991	$8.00
Elektra	PRCD 8393-2	Baila Me	CDJ	U.S.	1991	$2.00
Epic	108P-3043	Bamboleo	CD3	Japan	1988	$12.00/$3.00
BMG	CA1-313	Bamboleo	CD5	U.K.	1989	$8.00
Elektra	PR 8041-2	Bamboleo	CDJ	U.S.	1988	$2.00
Elektra	PR 8083-2	Bamboleo	CDJ	U.S.	1988	$2.00
Elektra	PR 8091-2	Djobi Djoba	CDJ	U.S.	1988	$2.00
Elektra	PR 8217-2	Hotel California	CDJ	U.S.	1990	$2.00
Epic	108P-3062	Nina Morena	CD3	Japan	1989	$12.00/$3.00
Columbia	657555	Sin Ella	CD5	Germany	1992	$8.00
Elektra	PRCD 8456-2	Sin Ella	CDJ	U.S.	1991	$3.00
Intercord	825 284	Volare	CD5	Germany	1990	$8.00
BMG	CA1-317	Volare	CD5	U.K.	1989	$8.00
Elektra	PR 8143-2	Volare	CDJ	U.S.	1989	$2.00

Gipsy Queen

Singles

Label	Catalog Number	Title	Type	Country	Year	Value
Alfa	ALDB-77	Call Me	CD3	Japan	1990	$12.00/$3.00

Girl Overboard

Singles

Label	Catalog Number	Title	Type	Country	Year	Value
BMG	BVDP-18	I Can't Believe	CD3	Japan	1990	$12.00/$3.00
BMG	74321 103572	Your Love	CD5	Australia	1992	$8.00

Girl-O-Matic

Singles

Label	Catalog Number	Title	Type	Country	Year	Value
SPV	1010-3	Everybody Dance Now	CD5	Germany	1991	$8.00

Girlfriend

Singles

Label	Catalog Number	Title	Type	Country	Year	Value
RCA	BVCR-9014	Girl's Life	CD5	Japan	1992	$10.00
RCA	BVDR-149	Girl's Life	CD3	Japan	1993	$12.00/$3.00
RCA	BVDR-70	Take It From Me	CD3	Japan	1992	$12.00/$3.00
Arista	7432111425	Take It From Me	CD5	U.K.	1992	$8.00

Girls Against B

Singles

Label	Catalog Number	Title	Type	Country	Year	Value
Touch & Go	140	Kill the Sexplayer	CD5	U.S.	1994	$5.00

Girls Club

Singles

Label	Catalog Number	Title	Type	Country	Year	Value
Sony	SRDL-3379	Celebration	CD3	Japan	1991	$12.00/$3.00

Girls Next Door

Singles

Label	Catalog Number	Title	Type	Country	Year	Value
Atlantic	PR 3001-2	He's Gotta Have Me	CDJ	U.S.	1989	$2.00
Atlantic	PR 3251-2	Maybe You Wouldn't Be Missin' Me Tonight Missin' You Tonight	CDJ	U.S.	1989	$2.00

Girls Talkin'

Singles

Label	Catalog Number	Title	Type	Country	Year	Value
Virgin	TENCD-254	Girls Talkin'	CD3	U.K.		$8.00

Girls Without Boyz

Singles

Label	Catalog Number	Title	Type	Country	Year	Value
EMI	204407-3	I Want You Back	CD5	Germany	1991	$8.00

Girlschool

Singles

Label	Catalog Number	Title	Type	Country	Year	Value
Enigma	EPRO-169	Fox on the Run	CDJ	U.S.	1989	$2.00
Enigma		Head Over Heals	CDJ	U.S.	1989	$2.00

Giuffria

Full Length

Label	Catalog Number	Title	Type	Country	Year	Value
MCA	MCAD-5742	Silk & Steel	LP	Germany		$16.00
MCA	5742	Silk & Steel	LP/LB	U.S.	1986	$15.00/$10.00

Glad

Full Length

Label	Catalog Number	Title	Type	Country	Year	Value
Light Records		A Cappella Gershwin & The A Cappella Project III	DJ/LP	U.S.	1995	$20.00

2 CD in folder.

Singles

Label	Catalog Number	Title	Type	Country	Year	Value
Pump	GLADCD-001	Spaghetti Head	CD5	U.K.	1992	$8.00

Gladys

Singles

Label	Catalog Number	Title	Type	Country	Year	Value
BMG	664829	Made Up Your Mind	CD5	Germany	1989	$8.00

Glamour Camp

Singles

Label	Catalog Number	Title	Type	Country	Year	Value
Toshiba	XP10-2077	She Did It For Love	CD3	Japan	1989	$13.00/$4.00
EMI	DPRO-04272	She Did It For Love	CDJ	U.S.	1989	$2.00

Glasgow

Singles

Label	Catalog Number	Title	Type	Country	Year	Value
Alfa	10SR-45	Secret in the Dark	CD3	Japan	1988	$13.00/$4.00

Glass

Singles

Label	Catalog Number	Title	Type	Country	Year	Value
RCA	PD-43252	It's Amazing	CD5	U.K.	1989	$8.00
RCA	PD-43778	Stop in the Name of Love	CD5	U.K.	1989	$8.00

Glass Hammer

Full Length

Label	Catalog Number	Title	Type	Country	Year	Value
Arion	51111-120	Journey Of the Dunadan	LTD/LP	U.S.	1994	$17.00

Picture disc.

Glass, Philip

Full Length

Label	Catalog Number	Title	Type	Country	Year	Value
		Introduced by Philip Glass	DJ/Smplr	U.S.	1993	$15.00
		Low Symphony	DJ/Smplr	Germany	1993	$30.00
		Powaqqatsi	DJ/Smplr	U.S.		$5.00

Glass Tiger

Singles

Label	Catalog Number	Title	Type	Country	Year	Value
EMI	204298-2	Animal Heart	CD5	Germany	1991	$8.00
Capitol	CDEM-220	Animal Heart	CD5	U.K.	1991	$8.00
Manhattan	202585-2	Diamond Heart	CD5	Germany	1988	$8.00
EMI	CDMT-40	Diamond Heart	CD5	U.K.	1988	$8.00
EMI	DPRO-04103	Far Away From Here	CDJ	U.S.		$2.00
EMI	DPRO-04011	I'm Still Searching	CDJ	U.S.		$2.00
EMI	204489-2	My Town	CD5	Germany	1991	$8.00
EMI	CDEM-212	My Town	CD5	U.K.	1991	$8.00
EMI		My Town	CDJ	U.S.	1990	$2.00

Glasswurk

Singles

Label	Catalog Number	Title	Type	Country	Year	Value
		She Works Her Body Right	CDJ	U.S.		$2.00

Gleason, Jackie

Full Length

Label	Catalog Number	Title	Type	Country	Year	Value
Warner Sound Exchange		22 Melancholy Serenades	LTD/LP	U.S.	1995	$17.00
EMI	484228-2	Music, Martinis & Memories	LP	Germany		$20.00

Glitter, Gary

Singles

Label	Catalog Number	Title	Type	Country	Year	Value
Attitude	CDEM-252	And the Leader Rocks on	CD5	U.K.	1992	$9.00
Old Gold	OG-6128	I Love You Me Love	CD3	U.K.	1990	$8.00
Attitude	OY-1D	Ready To Rock	CD5	U.K.	1991	$8.00
Virgin	VSCDT-1320	Red Hot	CD5	U.K.	1990	$8.00
Old Gold	OG-6132	Rock 'n Roll Part 2	CD3	U.K.	1989	$12.00
		Rock 'n Roll Part 2	CDJ	U.S.	1994	$7.00
Attitude	CDEM-256	Through the Years	CD5	U.K.	1992	$9.00

Global Communication

Singles

Label	Catalog Number	Title	Type	Country	Year	Value
		Maiden Voyage	CD5	U.K.		$10.00
		Maiden Voyage	CD5	U.K.		$10.00

Second version.

Glori, Lori

Singles

Label	Catalog Number	Title	Type	Country	Year	Value
BMG	74321105472	Body-n-Soul	CD5	U.K.	1993	$8.00

Glories

Singles

Label	Catalog Number	Title	Type	Country	Year	Value
Aurora	AU010	Aurora	CDJ	U.S.	1992	$3.00

Glove

Full Length

Label	Catalog Number	Title	Type	Country	Year	Value
Rough Trade	RUS85-2	Blue Sunshine	LP/LB	U.S.	1992	$15.00

Glove E

Singles

Label	Catalog Number	Title	Type	Country	Year	Value
Chrysalis	DPRO-23485	Dance Baby Young	CDJ	U.S.	1990	$2.00

Gloworm

Singles

Label	Catalog Number	Title	Type	Country	Year	Value
Pulse 8	CDLOSE-37	I Lift My Cup	CD5	U.K.	1993	$8.00

GMT

Singles

Label	Catalog Number	Title	Type	Country	Year	Value
MCA	MSCDT-2674	Feel so Good	CD5	U.K.	1992	$8.00

GND

Singles

Label	Catalog Number	Title	Type	Country	Year	Value
ZYX	DST-2089-8	For Fun	CD5	Germany	1992	$6.00

Go

Singles

Label	Catalog Number	Title	Type	Country	Year	Value
Intercord	827 125	Let Your Love Flow	CD5	Germany	1990	$8.00
Alfa	ALDB-26	Let Your Love Flow	CD3	Japan	1990	$12.00/$3.00

Go 101

Singles

Label	Catalog Number	Title	Type	Country	Year	Value
Polydor	PODP-1005	Build It Up	CD3	Japan	1990	$12.00/$3.00

Go West

Full Length

Label	Catalog Number	Title	Type	Country	Year	Value
Chrysalis	880476	Bangs & Crashes	LP	Germany		$20.00
Chrysalis		Go West	LTD/LP	U.K.	1994	$15.00
		25th Anniversary edition in 6"x11" longbox.				
Chrysalis	VK-41495	Go West	LP/LB	U.S.†	1984	$14.00/$8.00

Singles

Label	Catalog Number	Title	Type	Country	Year	Value
Chrysalis		Don't Look Down	DJ/CD3	U.S.		$4.00
Virgin	CDVEE 1	Don't Look Down	CDV	U.S.	1987	$20.00
Chrysalis/NTSC	CDVEE 1	Don't Look Down	DJ/CDV	U.S.	1987	$10.00
Chrysalis		Faithful	CD5	U.K.	1992	$10.00
Chrysalis		Faithful	CD5	U.K.	1992	$10.00
		Second version.				
EMI	C2 56259	Faithful	CD5	U.S.	1992	$5.00
EMI	DPRO-04897	Faithful	CDJ	U.S.	1992	$2.00
Aris	880527	I Want to Hear it From You	CD5	Germany	1988	$9.00
Chrysalis	CDE-5	I Want to Hear it From You	CD5	U.K.	1988	$9.00
EMI	323559-2	King of Wishful Thinking	CD5	Germany	1990	$10.00
Chrysalis	GOWCD-8	King of Wishful Thinking	CD5	U.K.	1990	$10.00
EMI	DPRO-04569	King of Wishful Thinking	CDJ	U.S.	1990	$3.00
Chrysalis		Still in Love	CD5	U.K.	1992	$10.00

Label	Catalog Number	Title	Type	Country	Year	Longbox Value / Value
Chrysalis		Still in Love	CD5	U.K.	1992	$10.00
Second version.						
Chrysalis		Tracks of My Tears	CD5	U.K.	1992	$10.00
Chrysalis		Tracks of My Tears	CD5	U.K.	1992	$10.00
Second version.						
EMI	DPRO-04603	Tracks of My Tears	CDJ	U.S.	1994	$2.00
Chrysalis	CDGOW-13	We Close Our Eyes	CD5	U.K.	1992	$10.00
Chrysalis		We Close Our Eyes	CD5	U.K.	1992	$10.00
Second version.						
Chrysalis	TODP-2411	What You Won't Do For Love	CD3	Japan	1993	$13.00/$4.00
EMI	DPRO-04707	What You Won't Do For Love	CDJ	U.S.	1993	$2.00

Go-Betweens

Singles

Label	Catalog Number	Title	Type	Country	Year	Longbox Value / Value
Strange Frt	SFPSCD-074	Peel Sessions	CD5	U.K.	1989	$8.00
SPV	3017-3	Streets of Your Town	CD5	Germany	1989	$8.00
Beggars Banquet	BEG-218CD	Streets of Your Town	CD5	U.K.	1989	$8.00
Beggars Banquet	BEG-232CD	Streets of Your Town	CD5	U.K.	1989	$8.00
Beggars Banquet	219	Was There Anything I Could Do	CD5	U.K.	1988	$8.00

Go-Go's

Full Length

Label	Catalog Number	Title	Type	Country	Year	Longbox Value / Value
A&M	CD-70021	Beauty and the Beast	LP/LB	U.S.†	1984	$15.00/$10.00
IRS		Return to the Valley	DJ/LP	U.S.	1995	$15.00
A&M	CD-75041	Talk Show	LP/LB	U.S.†	1984	$15.00/$10.00
A&M	CD-75041	Talk Show	LP/LB	U.S.	1986	$15.00/$10.00
Image	ID7416IR	Wild At the Greek	LD	U.S.		$25.00

Singles

Label	Catalog Number	Title	Type	Country	Year	Longbox Value / Value
IRS	AMCD-712	Cool Jerk	CD5	U.K.	1991	$10.00
A&M	75021 7439 2	Cool Jerk	CDJ	U.S.	1990	$2.00
A&M	75021 7478 2	Cool Jerk	CDJ	U.S.	1990	$2.00
A&M	75021 7480 2	Cool Jerk	CDJ	U.S.	1990	$2.00
		Cool Jerk	CDJ	U.S.	1994	$3.00
Capital	58347	Good Girl	CD5	U.S.	1994	$5.00
		Kindered Spirit	CD5	U.K.	1994	$10.00
Capital	58290	Whole World Lost It's Head, The	CD5	U.S.	1994	$5.00
		Whole World Lost It's Head, The	CDJ	U.S.	1994	$3.00

Goat

Singles

Label	Catalog Number	Title	Type	Country	Year	Longbox Value / Value
Beggars Banquet	BEG-256CD	Everybody Wants To Be There	CD5	U.K.	1991	$8.00
SPV	0529-3	Good Times	CD5	Germany	1991	$8.00

Goats

Singles

Label	Catalog Number	Title	Type	Country	Year	Longbox Value / Value
Ruffhouse	CSK 74914	Do the Digs Dug	CDJ	U.S.	1993	$2.00
CBS	77744	Rumblefish	CD5	U.S.	1994	$5.00
Ruffhouse	44K 74726	Typical American	CD5	U.S.	1992	$4.00

Goats Don't Shave

Singles

Label	Catalog Number	Title	Type	Country	Year	Longbox Value / Value
Dino	DINICD-013	Let the World Keep On Turning	CD5	U.K.	1992	$8.00

God Bullies

Singles

Label	Catalog Number	Title	Type	Country	Year	Longbox Value / Value
Altern. Tenacles	152	Kill The King	CD5	U.S.	1994	$5.00

God Machine

Singles

Label	Catalog Number	Title	Type	Country	Year	Longbox Value / Value
Fiction	FICCD-43	Desert Song, The	CD5	U.K.	1992	$8.00
Fiction	FICCD-44	Ego	CD5	U.K.	1992	$8.00
Fiction	FICCD-47	Home	CD5	U.K.	1992	$8.00
Fiction	CDP 941	Home	CDJ	U.S.	1992	$2.00
Fiction	CDP 870	Home	CDJ	U.S.	1992	$6.00

God's Eye

Singles

Label	Catalog Number	Title	Type	Country	Year	Longbox Value / Value
20/20	RUG-2CD	July	CD5	U.K.	1992	$8.00

Goddess

Singles

Label	Catalog Number	Title	Type	Country	Year	Longbox Value / Value
Big Beeat	5054	In My Bed	CDJ	U.S.	1993	$2.00
Epic	658053-2	Sexual	CD5	U.K.	1992	$8.00
Atlantic	96094-2	Sexual	CD5	U.S.	1992	$4.00

Godfathers

Full Length

Label	Catalog Number	Title	Type	Country	Year	Longbox Value / Value
Epic	ESK 2896	Birth, School, Work,Life,Death	DJ/LP	U.S.	1988	$15.00
Epic	ESK 1545	More Songs About Love & Hate	DJ/Smplr	U.S.	1989	$20.00
Epic	ESK 1761	Reverse 2 The Texas Chainsaw Massacre	DJ/Smplr	U.S.	1988	$25.00

Singles

Label	Catalog Number	Title	Type	Country	Year	Longbox Value / Value
Epic	657614	Beats and Pieces	CD5	Australia	1991	$13.00
Epic	CDGFT-2	Cause I Said So	CD5	U.K.	1988	$10.00
Epic	CDGFT-5	I'm Lost, Then I'm Found	CD5	U.K.	1990	$10.00
Epic	CDGFT-3	Love is Dead	CD5	U.K.	1988	$10.00
Epic	CDGFT-2	She Gives Me Love	CD5	U.K.	1989	$10.00
Epic	ESK 1639	She Gives Me Love	CDJ	U.S.	1989	$3.00
Epic	656648-2	Unreal World	CD5	U.K.	1991	$10.00
Epic	ESK 3043	Unreal World	CDJ	U.S.	1991	$3.00

Godflesh

Singles

Label	Catalog Number	Title	Type	Country	Year	Longbox Value / Value
Earache	MOSH-56CD	Cold World	CD5	U.K.	1992	$8.00
Earache	88561-1153	Cold World	CD5	U.S.	1992	$5.00
		Merciless	CDJ	U.S.	1994	$3.00
Relativity	0152	Mothra	CDJ	U.S.	1992	$2.00
Earache	MOSH-47CD	Slateman	CD5	U.K.	1991	$8.00
Columbia	CSK 6824	Xnoybis	CDJ	U.S.		$3.00

Godheadsilo

Singles

Label	Catalog Number	Title	Type	Country	Year	Longbox Value / Value
Kab N D Records	242	Elephantitus of	CD5	U.S.	1994	$5.00

Godley & Creme

Full Length

Label	Catalog Number	Title	Type	Country	Year	Longbox Value / Value
		Freeze Frame	LP/LB	U.S.		$14.00/$10.00
Vestron	ML0753	History	LD	U.S.	1987	$20.00
Polydor	825981-2	History Mix Vol. 1, The	LP/BP	U.S.†	1985	$14.00/$8.00

Singles

Label	Catalog Number	Title	Type	Country	Year	Longbox Value / Value
Polydor	080 011-2	Cry	CDV	U.S.	1987	$15.00
Polydor	080 011-2	Cry	DJ/CDV	U.S.	1987	$14.00
Polygram	871349-2	Golden Boy	CD5	Germany	1989	$8.00
Polygam	887301-2	Little Piece of Heaven	CD5	Germany	1988	$8.00
Polydor	POCD-901	Little Piece of Heaven	CD5	U.K.	1988	$8.00
Polygam	887488-2	Ten Thousand Angels	CD5	Germany	1988	$8.00
Polydor	POCD-913	Ten Thousand Angels	CD5	U.K.	1988	$8.00

Godspeed

Singles

Label	Catalog Number	Title	Type	Country	Year	Longbox Value / Value
		Ride	CDJ	U.S.	1994	$3.00

Godstar

Full Length

Label	Catalog Number	Title	Type	Country	Year	Longbox Value / Value
		Coastal	LTD/LP	U.S.	1995	$30.00
2 CD set.						

Goffin, Louise

Singles

Label	Catalog Number	Title	Type	Country	Year	Longbox Value / Value
Warner Brothers	PRO-CD-3021	Bridge of Sighs	CDJ	U.S.	1988	$2.00
		Never Mind	CDJ	Canada		$3.00

Gogo, David

Singles

Label	Catalog Number	Title	Type	Country	Year	Longbox Value / Value
		Movin' On	CDJ	Canada		$6.00

Gohst

Full Length

Label	Catalog Number	Title	Type	Country	Year	Longbox Value / Value
Hollywood		4	DJ/LP	U.S.		$15.00
CD in digipak						

Gold, Andrew

Singles

Label	Catalog Number	Title	Type	Country	Year	Longbox Value / Value
Canyon	PCDY-00111	Don't Let Life Pass You By	CD3	Japan	1992	$13.00/$4.00
Canyon	PCDY-00081	Home Is Where the Love Is	CD3	Japan	1991	$13.00/$4.00
Canyon	S10Y-1047	Makin' Friends	CD3	Japan	1991	$13.00/$4.00
Canyon	PCDY-00034	Pas O' Mine	CD3	Japan	1991	$13.00/$4.00

Gold, Angie

Singles

Label	Catalog Number	Title	Type	Country	Year	Longbox Value / Value
Alfa	10SR-17	Haunted House	CD3	Japan	1988	$13.00/$4.00
Canyon	S9ED-8010	Right Back in the Middle	CD3	Japan	1989	$13.00/$4.00
Canyon	CEDC-00044	Take My Body	CD3	Japan	1990	$13.00/$4.00

Gold Wings

Singles

Label	Catalog Number	Title	Type	Country	Year	Longbox Value / Value
Victor	VICL-13001	New Japan Rising	CD3	Japan	1990	$13.00/$4.00

Goldberg, Whoopi

Full Length

Label	Catalog Number	Title	Type	Country	Year	Longbox Value / Value
Vestron	VL3112	Whoopi Goldberg	LD	U.S.	1986	$30.00

Singles

Label	Catalog Number	Title	Type	Country	Year	Longbox Value / Value
		Ain't No Mountain High Enough	CDJ	Japan	1994	$30.00

Golden Earring

Full Length

Label	Catalog Number	Title	Type	Country	Year	Longbox Value / Value
Polygram	825371-2	Eight Miles High	LP	U.K.		$20.00
Pioneer	PA-84-139	Live	LD	U.S.	1985	$25.00
Pioneer	PA-85-M022	Notorious Videos	8"LD	U.S.	1985	$12.00

Singles

Label	Catalog Number	Title	Type	Country	Year	Longbox Value / Value
Columbia	656802-2	Going to the Run	CD5	Germany	1991	$10.00
First Quake	4488	I Can't Sleep Without You	CDJ	U.S.	1993	$3.00
21 Records	100 142	My Killer My Shadow	CD5	Germany		$10.00
BMG	162328	Turn the World Around	CD3	Germany	1989	$10.00
BMG	662328	Turn the World Around	CD5	Germany	1989	$10.00

Golden Palominos

Full Length

Label	Catalog Number	Title	Type	Country	Year	Longbox Value / Value
Celluloid		A Dead Horse	LP/LB	U.S.		$14.00/$8.00
Charisma	91745-2	Drunk With Passion	LP/LB	U.S.	1991	$14.00/$8.00
Charisma		Golden Palominos, The	LP/LB	U.S.	1991	$14.00/$8.00

Singles

Label	Catalog Number	Title	Type	Country	Year	Longbox Value / Value
Virgin	PRCD 081	Dying From the Inside	CDJ	U.S.	1991	$2.00
Restless	72786	No Skin	CD5	U.S.	1994	$5.00
Restless	037	These Days	CDJ	U.S.	1993	$2.00

Golden Smog

Full Length

Label	Catalog Number	Title	Type	Country	Year	Longbox Value / Value
Rykodisc		Down By the Old Mainstream	DJ/LP	U.S.	1996	$55.00
Debut CD of album in box titled "35 years of Golden Smog". Limited to 100 copies.						

Singles

Label	Catalog Number	Title	Type	Country	Year	Longbox Value / Value
Rykodisc	VRCD SMOG	Red Headed Stepchild	CDJ	U.S.		$7.00

Golden, William Lee

Singles

Label	Catalog Number	Title	Type	Country	Year	Longbox Value / Value
Mercury	CDP 220	Keep Lookin' Up	CDJ	U.S.	1990	$2.00
Mercury	CDP 275	Louisiana Red Dirt Highway	CDJ	U.S.	1990	$2.00

Goldfinger

Full Length

Label	Catalog Number	Title	Type	Country	Year	Longbox Value / Value
		Goldfinger	DJ/Smplr	U.S.	1996	$12.00

Singles

Label	Catalog Number	Title	Type	Country	Year	Longbox Value / Value
	4001	Freak Nasty	CD5	U.S.	1994	$5.00

Goldings, Larry

Full Length

Label	Catalog Number	Title	Type	Country	Year	Longbox Value / Value
Polygram	511069	Intimacy of the Blues	LP/BP	U.S.		$12.00/$7.00

Goldman, Jean-Jacques

Singles

Label	Catalog Number	Title	Type	Country	Year	Longbox Value / Value
Epic	108P-3084	Jean-Jacques Goldman	CD3	Japan	1989	$13.00/$4.00
Epic	651228-2	La Bas	CD5	U.K.	1989	$8.00

Goldsmith, Glen

Singles

Label	Catalog Number	Title	Type	Country	Year	Longbox Value / Value
RCA	PD-43660	On the One	CD5	U.K.	1990	$8.00
RCA	PD-43180	One Life	CD5	U.K.	1989	$8.00
RCA	886410	Save a Little Bit	CD5	Germany	1988	$8.00
RCA	PD-42148	Save a Little Bit	CD5	U.K.	1988	$8.00
RCA	PD-42076	What You See Is What You Get	CD5	U.K.	1988	$8.00
RCA	886860	You've Got Me Dancin'	CD5	Germany	1990	$8.00
RCA	PD-43314	You've Got Me Dancin'	CD5	U.K.	1990	$8.00

Goldsmith, Jerry

Full Length

Label	Catalog Number	Title	Type	Country	Year	Longbox Value / Value
Varese Sarabande	SRS 2003	Suites & Themes	LTD/LP	U.S.		$20.00

Goldstein, Gil

Full Length

Label	Catalog Number	Title	Type	Country	Year	Longbox Value / Value
Blue Note	CDP-93893-2	City Of Dreams	LP/LB	U.S.		$18.00/$15.00

Singles

Label	Catalog Number	Title	Type	Country	Year	Longbox Value / Value
Big World	2008	My Foolish Heart	CDJ	U.S.	1993	$2.00

Gomez, Daniel

Singles

Label	Catalog Number	Title	Type	Country	Year	Longbox Value / Value
Columbia	656971-2	Dancin' Alone	CD5	Germany	1991	$8.00

Gomez, Eddie

Full Length

Label	Catalog Number	Title	Type	Country	Year	Longbox Value / Value
Denon	CD-7189	With Chick Corea, Steve Gadd	LP/LB	U.S.†	1985	$14.00/$8.00

Singles

Label	Catalog Number	Title	Type	Country	Year	Longbox Value / Value
Epic	158P-8005	Forever	CD3	Japan	1988	$13.00/$3.00

Gonzaguinha

Full Length

Label	Catalog Number	Title	Type	Country	Year	Longbox Value / Value
Blue Note	CDP-91688-2	E.	LP/LB	U.S.		$18.00/$15.00

Gonzales, Babs

Full Length

Label	Catalog Number	Title	Type	Country	Year	Longbox Value / Value
Blue Note	CDP-84464-2	Weird Lullaby	LP/LB	U.S.		$18.00/$15.00

Goo Goo Dolls

Full Length

Label	Catalog Number	Title	Type	Country	Year	Longbox Value / Value
Warner Brothers	26259-2	Hold Me Up	LP/LB	U.S.		$14.00/$8.00

Singles

Label	Catalog Number	Title	Type	Country	Year	Longbox Value / Value
Warner Brothers	PRO-CD-6010	Fallin' Down	CDJ	U.S.	1993	$2.00
Warner Brothers	PRO-CD-7929-R	Long Way Down	CDJ	U.S.	1995	$6.00
		Naked	CDJ	U.S.	1996	$6.00
Warner Brothers	PRO-CD-7389	Only One	CDJ	U.S.	1995	$6.00
Metal Blade	PRO-CD-4711	There You Are	CDJ	U.S.	1990	$2.00
Metal Blade	PRO-CD-4520	There You Are	CDJ	U.S.	1990	$2.00
Warner Brothers	18512-2	We Are the Normal	CD5	U.S.	1993	$5.00
Metal Blade	PRO-CD-6043	We Are the Normal	CDJ	U.S.	1993	$2.00

Good Bad 'n Ugly

Singles

Label	Catalog Number	Title	Type	Country	Year	Longbox Value / Value
Polygram	873401-2	You Better Look Twice	CD5	Germany	1990	$8.00
Polygram	873404-2	You Better Look Twice	CD5	Germany	1990	$8.00

Good Girls

Full Length

Label	Catalog Number	Title	Type	Country	Year	Longbox Value / Value
Motown	6278	All For Your Love	LP/BP	U.S.		$14.00/$8.00
Motown	6347	Just Call Me	LP/BP	U.S.		$14.00/$8.00

Singles

Label	Catalog Number	Title	Type	Country	Year	Longbox Value / Value
Motown		I Need Your Love	CDJ	U.S.		$2.00
Motown	CD45 1083	It Must Be Love	CDJ	U.S.	1992	$2.00
Motown	37431051	Just Call Me	CDJ	U.S.	1992	$2.00

Good Question

Singles

Label	Catalog Number	Title	Type	Country	Year	Longbox Value / Value
Paisley Park	PRO-CD-3119	Got A New Love	CDJ	U.S.	1988	$2.00
Paisley Park	PRO-CD-3545	Listen to Your Heart	CDJ	U.S.	1988	$2.00

Goodbye Hollywood

Singles

Label	Catalog Number	Title	Type	Country	Year	Longbox Value / Value
Polygram	867151-2	Push It Hard Boy	CD5	Germany	1991	$8.00

Goodbye Mr. Mackenzie

Singles

Label	Catalog Number	Title	Type	Country	Year	Longbox Value / Value
BMG	MCD-17795	Blacker Than Black	CD5	Germany	1991	$8.00
Parlophone	CDR-6257	Blacker Than Black	CD5	U.K.	1991	$8.00
Radioactive	1269	Blacker Than Black	CDJ	U.S.	1991	$2.00
Capitol	CDCL-501	Goodbye Mr. Mackenzie	CD5	U.K.	1988	$8.00
Capitol	CDCL-538	Goodwill City	CD5	U.K.	1989	$8.00
Parlophone	CDR-6247	Love Child	CD5	U.K.	1990	$8.00
MCA	MCSTD-1506	Now We Are Married	CD5	U.K.	1990	$8.00
Capitol	CDCL-513	Open Your Arms	CD5	U.K.	1988	$8.00
EMI	203274-2	Rattler	CD5	Germany	1989	$8.00
Capitol	CDCL-522	Rattler	CD5	U.K.	1989	$8.00
Radioactive	54173	Rattler	CD5	U.S.	1991	$5.00

Goodie Mob-Outkast

Singles

Label	Catalog Number	Title	Type	Country	Year	Longbox Value / Value
LaFace	24114	Cell Theory	CD5	U.S.	1995	$5.00
Laface	LFPCD4152	Soul Food	CDJ	U.S.	1995	$2.00

Goodman, Benny

Full Length

Label	Catalog Number	Title	Type	Country	Year	Longbox Value / Value
Aris	880444	Airplay	LP	Germany		$20.00
Mosaic	MD4-148	Complete Capitol Small Group Recordings Of Benny Goodman 1944-45	LTD/LP	U.S.	1994	$60.00
		4 CD set.				
Delta	11042	Famous Works	LP	U.K.		$20.00
London	PPC-820179-2	& Friends	LP/LB	U.S.†	1985	$14.00/$8.00
Bridge	100 021-2	King of Swing	LP	Germany		$20.00

Goodman, Gabrielle

Singles

Label	Catalog Number	Title	Type	Country	Year	Longbox Value / Value
Polydor	CDP 779	Travelin' Light	CDJ	U.S.	1994	$2.00

Goodman, Jerry

Full Length

Label	Catalog Number	Title	Type	Country	Year	Longbox Value / Value
Private Music		It's Alive	LP/LB	U.S.		$14.00/$8.00

Goodmen

Singles

Label	Catalog Number	Title	Type	Country	Year	Longbox Value / Value
ffrr	16235003	Give It Up	CD5	Canada	1994	$9.00
ffrr	162 350 039	Give It Up	CD5	U.S.	1993	$4.00

Goodrum, Randy

Singles

Label	Catalog Number	Title	Type	Country	Year	Longbox Value / Value
Polydor	PODP-1065	Killing Time	CD3	Japan	1992	$13.00/$4.00

Goombas

Singles

Label	Catalog Number	Title	Type	Country	Year	Longbox Value / Value
Capitol	DPRO-79811	Walk the Dinosaur	CDJ	U.S.	1993	$2.00

Goops

Singles

Label	Catalog Number	Title	Type	Country	Year	Longbox Value / Value
	PRO-CD-8013	Vulgar Appetites	CDJ	U.S.	1995	$2.00

Gordon, Dexter

Full Length

Label	Catalog Number	Title	Type	Country	Year	Longbox Value / Value
Blue Note	CDP-84445-2	Clubhouse	LP/LB	U.S.		$18.00/$15.00
Savoy Records	CY-78812	Dexter Rides Again	LTD/LP	U.S.	1996	$20.00
		CD in miniature repica of original LP sleeve.				

Gordon, Lesley

Full Length

Label	Catalog Number	Title	Type	Country	Year	Longbox Value / Value
Polygram	810370-2	Golden Hits	LP	Germany		$15.00

Gordon, Lonnie

Singles

Label	Catalog Number	Title	Type	Country	Year	Longbox Value / Value
Polygram	877735-2	Beyond Your Wildest Dreams	CD5	Germany	1990	$8.00
Supreme	CDSUPE-167	Beyond Your Wildest Dreams	CD5	U.K.	1990	$8.00
Eastwest	9031-74750-2	Gonna Catch You	CD5	Germany	1991	$8.00
Alfa	ALDB-121	Gonna Catch You	CD3	Japan	1991	$12.00/$3.00
Alfa	ALDB-122	Gonna Catch You	CD3	Japan	1991	$12.00/$3.00
Supreme	CDSUPE-185	Gonna Catch You	CD5	U.K.	1991	$8.00
SBK	DPRO-05406	Gonna Catch You	CDJ	U.S.	1991	$2.00
Polygram	873951-2	Happenin' All Over Again	CD5	Germany	1990	$8.00
Alfa	ALDB-1237	Happenin' All Over Again	CD3	Japan	1990	$12.00/$3.00
SBK	DPRO-04570	Happenin' All Over Again	CDJ	U.S.	1993	$2.00
Polygram	879307-2	If I Have to Stand Alone	CD5	Germany	1990	$8.00
Supreme	CDSUPE-151	It's Not Alone	CD5	U.K.	1991	$8.00

Gorky Park

Singles

Label	Catalog Number	Title	Type	Country	Year	Longbox Value / Value
Mercury	PPDS-11	Bang	CD3	Japan	1989	$13.00/$4.00
Mercury	CDP 109	Bang	CDJ	U.S.	1989	$2.00
Mercury	CDP 120	Bang	CDJ	U.S.	1990	$2.00
Crown	CRDP-56	Moscow Calling	CD3	Japan	1992	$13.00/$4.00
Mercury	CDP 173	Peace in Our Time	CDJ	U.S.	1990	$2.00
Mercury	CDP 174	Try to Find Me	CDJ	U.S.	1990	$2.00

Gosdin, Vern

Singles

Label	Catalog Number	Title	Type	Country	Year	Longbox Value / Value
		Is It Raining at Your House	CDJ	U.S.		$2.00

Gota

Singles

Label	Catalog Number	Title	Type	Country	Year	Longbox Value / Value
Sony	SRDL-3591	All Alone	CD3	Japan	1992	$12.00/$3.00
Sony	SRDL-3516	Here We Go	CD3	Japan	1992	$12.00/$3.00
Sony	SRCL-2593	Here We Go	CD5	Japan	1992	$12.00

Gotcha

Singles

Label	Catalog Number	Title	Type	Country	Year	Longbox Value / Value
BMG	664295	Words & Music	CD5	Germany	1991	$8.00

Gothic Slam

Singles

Label	Catalog Number	Title	Type	Country	Year	Longbox Value / Value
Epic	CSK 1843	Who Died and Made You God	CDJ	U.S.	1989	$2.00

Gould, Glen

Full Length

Label	Catalog Number	Title	Type	Country	Year	Longbox Value / Value
CBS	42107	Legacy Vol. 3	LP/LB	U.S.		$14.00/$8.00
CBS	42150	Legacy Vol. 4	LP/LB	U.S.		$14.00/$8.00

Government Issue

Singles

Label	Catalog Number	Title	Type	Country	Year	Longbox Value / Value
Homestead	6033	Strange Wine	CD5	U.S.	1992	$4.00

Gowan

Singles

Label	Catalog Number	Title	Type	Country	Year	Longbox Value / Value
Atlantic	PRCD 3415-2	All the Lovers in the World	CDJ	U.S.		$2.00
Atlantic		Lost Brotherhood	CDJ	U.S.		$2.00
		Out of a Deeper Hunger	CDJ	Canada		$5.00

Gowan, Lawrence

Singles

Label	Catalog Number	Title	Type	Country	Year	Longbox Value / Value
		Dancing on My Own Ground	CDJ	Canada		$3.00
		Soul's Road	CDJ	Canada		$3.00

Grace, Bridget

Singles

Label	Catalog Number	Title	Type	Country	Year	Longbox Value / Value
Polygram	889707-2	Take Me Away	CD5	Germany	1989	$8.00

Grace Mode

Singles

Label	Catalog Number	Title	Type	Country	Year	Longbox Value / Value
Fieldworks	FWCR-50	Modern Jungle	CD5	Japan	1992	$10.00

Grace Pool

Singles

Label	Catalog Number	Title	Type	Country	Year	Longbox Value / Value
		Awake in the Rain	CDJ	U.S.		$2.00
		Stay	CDJ	U.S.		$2.00

Graces

Full Length

Label	Catalog Number	Title	Type	Country	Year	Longbox Value / Value
A&M	CD 17844	Perfect View	DJ/LP	U.S.	1989	$10.00

Singles

Label	Catalog Number	Title	Type	Country	Year	Longbox Value / Value
A&M	CD 17971	50,000 Candles Burning	CDJ	U.S.	1989	$2.00
A&M	390451-2	Lay Down Your Arms	CD5	Germany	1989	$8.00
A&M	PCDY-10002	Lay Down Your Arms	CD3	Japan	1989	$12.00/$3.00
A&M	CDEE-526	Lay Down Your Arms	CD3	U.K.	1989	$8.00
A&M	CD 17822	Lay Down Your Arms	CDJ	U.S.	1989	$2.00
A&M	390503-2	Perfect View	CD5	Germany	1990	$8.00
A&M	PCDY-10010	Perfect View	CD3	Japan	1990	$12.00/$3.00
A&M	CD 17911	Perfect View	CDJ	U.S.	1989	$2.00
A&M	CD 17968	Perfect View	CDJ	U.S.	1989	$2.00

Graham, Bill

Full Length

Label	Catalog Number	Title	Type	Country	Year	Longbox Value / Value
		U.C.	RS	U.S.	1992	$50.00

Graham, Jaki

Singles

Label	Catalog Number	Title	Type	Country	Year	Longbox Value / Value
Critique	15529	Ain't Nobody	CD5	U.S.	1994	$5.00
Essential	ESSX-2015	Band Of Gold	CD5	U.K.	1992	$8.00
EMI	203443-3	Better Part Of Me	CD3	Germany	1989	$8.00
EMI	CDJAKI-16	Better Part Of Me	CD5	U.K.	1989	$8.00
EMI	CDJAKI-17	Every Little Bit Hurts	CD5	U.K.	1989	$8.00
EMI	203402-3	From Now On	CD3	Germany	1989	$8.00
EMI	CDJAKI-15	From Now On	CD5	U.K.	1989	$8.00
EMI	202731-2	No More Tears	CD5	Germany	1988	$8.00
EMI	CDJAKI-12	No More Tears	CD5	U.K.	1988	$8.00
Essential	ESSX-2008	Touch Me	CD5	U.K.	1992	$8.00

Graham, Paul

Singles

Label	Catalog Number	Title	Type	Country	Year	Longbox Value / Value
	ANACAPS101B9	Fly Away	CDJ	U.S.		$2.00

Gramm, Lou

Singles

Label	Catalog Number	Title	Type	Country	Year	Longbox Value / Value
Atlantic	AMDY-5025	Angel With a Dirty Face	CD5	U.K.	1990	$10.00
Atlantic		Angel With a Dirty Face	CDJ	U.S.	1989	$2.00
Atlantic	786252-2	Just Between You and Me	CD5	Germany	1989	$10.00
Atlantic	AMDY-5002	Just Between You and Me	CD3	Japan	1989	$12.00/$4.00
Atlantic	A-8755CD	Just Between You and Me	CD5	U.K.	1989	$10.00

Label	Catalog Number	Title	Type	Country	Year	Longbox Value / Value
Eastwest	786219-2	True Blue Love	CD5	Germany	1990	$10.00
Atlantic	AMDY-5008	True Blue Love	CD3	Japan	1990	$12.00/$4.00
Atlantic	A-7957CD	True Blue Love	CD5	U.K.	1990	$10.00
Atlantic	PR 3059-2	True Blue Love	CDJ	U.S.	1989	$2.00

Granata, Rocco

Singles

Label	Catalog Number	Title	Type	Country	Year	Longbox Value / Value
ZYX	6235-8	Bella Italia	CD5	Germany	1989	$6.00
Bellaphon	130-07-375	Ciao Ciao Bambina	CD5	Germany	1990	$8.00
ZYX	6177-8	Marina	CD5	Germany	1989	$6.00
ZYX	6280-8	Pane, Amore E Cioccolate	CD5	Germany	1989	$6.00

Grand Daddy I.U.

Singles

Label	Catalog Number	Title	Type	Country	Year	Longbox Value / Value
		Something New	CD5	U.S.		$3.00

Grand Funk Railroad

Full Length

Label	Catalog Number	Title	Type	Country	Year	Longbox Value / Value
Collector's Pipeline	TCP 006	Grand Funk Railroad	LP	U.S.		$16.00
Album Network		In the Studio (Closer to Home)	RS	U.S.		$20.00
Album Network		In the Studio (Closer to Home)	RS	U.S.	1989	$20.00
Airdate: 3/13/89.						
Collector's Pipeline	TCP 007	Shine On	LP	U.S.		$16.00

Grand Heights

Singles

Label	Catalog Number	Title	Type	Country	Year	Longbox Value / Value
SPV	1012-3	Fox Bush	CD5	Germany	1991	$8.00

Grand Puba

Singles

Label	Catalog Number	Title	Type	Country	Year	Longbox Value / Value
Elektra	66106	A Little of This	CD5	U.S.	1995	$5.00
Elektra	PRCD 8733-2	Check It Out	CDJ	U.S.	1992	$2.00
Elektra	PRCD 8602-2	What Goes Around	CDJ	U.S.	1992	$2.00

Grand Slam

Singles

Label	Catalog Number	Title	Type	Country	Year	Longbox Value / Value
Dange Crue	ALCA-453	Can't Stop Believin'	CD5	Japan	1993	$12.00
Dange Crue	ALDA-44	Cry Again	CD3	Japan	1993	$12.00/$3.00
Alfa	ALDA-35	Let It Go	CD3	Japan	1991	$12.00/$3.00
Dange Crue	ALDA-70	Song for You	CD3	Japan	1993	$12.00/$3.00

Grandmaster Chicken

Singles

Label	Catalog Number	Title	Type	Country	Year	Longbox Value / Value
Polygram	874087-2	Check Out the Chicken Egg	CD5	Germany	1989	$8.00
Polygram	876087-2	Check Out the Chicken Egg	CD5	Germany	1989	$8.00

Grandmaster Flash

Singles

Label	Catalog Number	Title	Type	Country	Year	Longbox Value / Value
Castle	CD3-2	Adventures of Grandmaster Flash	CD3	U.K.	1988	$8.00
Eastwest	246799-2	Message	CD5	Germany	1989	$8.00
Eastwest	171724-2	White Lines	CD5	Germany	1990	$8.00
Castle	CD3-1	White Lines	CD3	U.K.	1988	$8.00

Grandmaster Slice

Singles

Label	Catalog Number	Title	Type	Country	Year	Longbox Value / Value
Jive	42034-2-RDJ	Thinking of You	CDJ	U.S.	1991	$2.00

Grant, Amy

Full Length

Label	Catalog Number	Title	Type	Country	Year	Longbox Value / Value
IMS	CD-5056	Age to Age	LP	Germany		$18.00
A&M	CD-5056	Age to Age	LP/LB	U.S.		$15.00/$10.00
Reunion	REND-24337	Age to Age	LP/LB	U.S.		$15.00/$10.00
A&M	LV 38400	Age to Age	LD	U.S.	1989	$25.00
A&M	LV38400	Age to Age	LD	U.S.	1996	$35.00
Digital Audio						
IMS	CD-5051	Amy Grant	LP	Germany		$18.00
A&M	CD-5051	Amy Grant	LP/LB	U.S.		$15.00/$10.00
Reunion	REND-24332	Amy Grant	LP/LB	U.S.		$15.00/$10.00
IMS	CD-5057	Christmas Album	LP	Germany		$18.00
A&M	CD-5057	Christmas Album	LP/LB	U.S.		$15.00/$10.00
Reunion	REND-24397	Christmas Album	LP/LB	U.S.		$15.00/$10.00
IMS	CD-3900	Collection	LP	Germany		$18.00
Canyon	D32Y-3073	Collection	LP	Japan		$25.00
A&M	CD-3900	Collection	LP/LB	U.S.		$15.00/$10.00
Reunion	REND-24340	Collection	LP/LB	U.S.		$15.00/$10.00
Pioneer	PA86-M038	Find a Way	8"LD	U.S.	1986	$5.00
Pioneer	PA86-M038	Find a Way	8"LD	U.S.	1989	$10.00
Digital audio.						
A&M		House of Love	DJ/Intvw	U.S.		$30.00
IMS	CD-5054	In Concert, Vol.1	LP	Germany		$18.00
A&M	CD-5054	In Concert, Vol.1	LP/LB	U.S.		$15.00/$10.00
Reunion	REND-24335	In Concert, Vol.1	LP/LB	U.S.		$15.00/$10.00
IMS	CD-5055	In Concert, Vol.2	LP	Germany		$18.00
A&M	CD-5055	In Concert, Vol.2	LP/LB	U.S.		$15.00/$10.00
Reunion	REND-24336	In Concert, Vol.2	LP/LB	U.S.		$15.00/$10.00
		Interview Disc	DJ/Intvw	U.S.	1994	$15.00
A&M	395199-2	Lead Me On	LP	Germany	1988	$20.00
A&M	D32Y-3225	Lead Me On	LP	Japan	1988	$25.00
Myrrh	9016656472	Lead Me On	DJ/LP	U.S.	1988	$175.00
Promo Gold/Picture CD autographed and numbered to on disc.						
IMS	CD-5052	My Father's Eyes	LP	Germany		$18.00
A&M	CD-5052	My Father's Eyes	LP/LB	U.S.		$15.00/$10.00
Reunion	REND-24333	My Father's Eyes	LP/LB	U.S.		$15.00/$10.00
IMS	CD-5053	Never Alone	LP	Germany		$18.00
A&M	CD-5053	Never Alone	LP/LB	U.S.		$15.00/$10.00
Reunion	REND-24334	Never Alone	LP/LB	U.S.		$15.00/$10.00
		Smash Hits	DJ/Smplr	Canada	1992	$30.00
IMS	CD-5058	Straight Ahead	LP	Germany		$18.00
A&M	CD-5058	Straight Ahead	LP/LB	U.S.		$15.00/$10.00
Reunion	REND-24338	Straight Ahead	LP/LB	U.S.		$15.00/$10.00
IMS	CD-5060	Unguarded	LP	Germany		$18.00
Reunion	REND-24339	Unguarded	LP/LB	U.S.		$15.00/$10.00
A&M	CD-5060	Unguarded	LP/LB	U.S.†	1985	$15.00/$10.00
A&M	CD-5060	Unguarded	LP/LB	U.S.	1986	$15.00/$10.00

Singles

Label	Catalog Number	Title	Type	Country	Year	Longbox Value / Value
A&M	390626-2	Baby Baby	CD5	Germany	1991	$10.00
A&M	PCCY-10313	Baby Baby	CD3	Japan	1991	$13.00/$4.00
A&M	AMCD-727	Baby Baby	CD5	U.K.	1991	$10.00
A&M	75021 2397-2	Baby Baby	CD5	U.S.	1991	$5.00
A&M	75021 7512-2	Baby Baby	CDJ	U.S.	1991	$3.00
A&M		Big Yellow Taxi	CDJ	U.S.	1994	$3.00
A&M	390783-2	Every Heartbeat	CD5	Germany	1991	$10.00
A&M	AMCD-783	Every Heartbeat	CD5	U.K.	1991	$10.00
A&M	75021 7541 2	Every Heartbeat	CDJ	U.S.	1991	$3.00
A&M	75021 7264-2	Good For Me	CDJ	U.S.	1991	$3.00
A&M	PODM-1045	House of Love	CD3	Japan		$12.00/$4.00
		House of Love	CD5	U.K.		$10.00
		House of Love	CD5	U.K.		$10.00
Second version.						
A&M Records	80803	House of Love	CD5	U.S.	1994	$5.00
A&M	75021 7339-2	I Will Remember You	CDJ	U.S.	1991	$3.00
A&M	390327-2	Lead Me On	CD5	Germany	1988	$10.00
A&M	S10Y-3018	Lead Me On	CD3	Japan	1988	$12.00/$4.00
A&M	AMCD-453	Lead Me On	CD5	U.K.	1988	$10.00
A&M	CD 17580	Lead Me On	CDJ	U.S.	1988	$3.00
		Lucky One	CD5	U.K.	1994	$10.00
A&M		Lucky One	CD5	U.K.	1994	$10.00
		Lucky One	CD5	U.K.	1994	$10.00
Second version.						
A&M		Lucky One	CDJ	U.S.		$6.00
A&M	5807721	Lucky One	CD5	U.S.	1994	$6.00
A&M	CD 17651	Saved by Love	CDJ	U.S.	1988	$3.00
A&M	75021 7387-2	Smash Hits	CDJ	U.S.	1991	$3.00
A&M	390834-2	That's What Love is For	CD5	Germany	1991	$10.00
A&M	AMCD-666	That's What Love is For	CD5	U.K.	1991	$10.00
A&M	75201 7233 2	That's What Love is For	CDJ	U.S.	1991	$3.00
	PRCD10563-2	Things We Do For Love, The	CDJ	U.S.		$2.00
A&M		Things We Do For Love, The	CDJ	U.S.		$6.00

Grant, David

Singles

Label	Catalog Number	Title	Type	Country	Year	Longbox Value / Value
BMG	662361	Intuition	CD5	Germany	1989	$8.00
4th & B'way	BRCD-169	Keep It Together	CD5	U.K.	1990	$8.00
BMG	885603	Life	CD5	Germany	1989	$8.00
BMG	884703	Life	CD5	Germany	1990	$8.00
4th & B'way	BRCD-145	Life	CD5	U.K.	1989	$8.00
4th & B'way	BRCD-184	Life	CD5	U.K.	1990	$8.00
4th & B'way	546	Wake Up Everybody	CDJ	U.S.	1990	$2.00

Grant, Earl

Singles

Label	Catalog Number	Title	Type	Country	Year	Longbox Value / Value
MCA	MVDM-5	End	CD3	Japan	1991	$13.00/$4.00
Intercord	846 106	All the Hits	LP	Germany		$15.00
Intercord	846 107	Born Tough	LP	Germany		$15.00
Intercord	846 105	Going for Broke	LP	Germany		$15.00
Portrait	RK-39261	Going for Broke	LP/BP	U.S.†	1984	$14.00/$8.00
Intercord	846 104	Killer on the Rampage	LP	Germany		$15.00
CBS	RK-38554	Killer on the Rampage	LP/BP	U.S.†	1984	$14.00/$8.00

Grant, Eddy

Singles

Label	Catalog Number	Title	Type	Country	Year	Longbox Value / Value
EMI	203418-3	Baby Come Back	CD3	Germany	1989	$8.00
Blue Wave	CDR-6224	Baby Come Back	CD5	U.K.	1989	$8.00
EMI	202514-2	Gimme Home Jo'Anna	CD5	Germany	1990	$8.00
EMI	202512-2	Gimme Home Jo'Anna	CD5	Germany	1990	$8.00
Enigma	EPRO-276	Gimme Home Jo'Anna	CDJ	U.S.	1990	$2.00
Blue Wave	CDR-6180	Harmless Piece Of Fun	CD5	U.K.	1988	$8.00
Blue Wave	202981-2	Put a Hold on It	CD5	Germany	1988	$8.00
Blue Wave	CDR-6191	Put a Hold on It	CD5	U.K.	1988	$8.00
EMI	204077-2	Restless World	CD5	Germany	1990	$8.00
Blue Wave	CDR-6217	Walking On Sunshine	CD5	U.K.	1989	$8.00
Pinnacle	92030-2	Welcome To La Tigre	CD5	U.K.	1991	$8.00

Grant Lee Buffalo

Full Length

Label	Catalog Number	Title	Type	Country	Year	Longbox Value / Value
Slash	PRO-CD-6339	Blue Plate Special	DJ/Smplr	U.S.	1993	$13.00
Reprise		Honey I Don't Think Plus Live Tracks	DJ/Smplr	U.S.	1995	$15.00

Singles

Label	Catalog Number	Title	Type	Country	Year	Longbox Value / Value
	LASCDJ 58	2 and 2	CDJ	U.K.	1995	$20.00
Slash	PRO-CD-6030	Fuzzy	CDJ	U.S.	1993	$2.00
Slash	PRO-CD-6152	Fuzzy	CDJ	U.S.	1993	$2.00
Reprise		Fuzzy	CDJ	U.S.	1995	$3.00
		Honey I Don't Think	CD5	U.K.	1995	$10.00
Slash	PRO-CD-6029	Jupiter and Teardrop	CDJ	U.S.	1993	$2.00
Reprise		Lone Star Song	CDJ	U.S.	1995	$3.00
	DPROCD7111	Mockingbirds	CDJ	U.S.	1994	$6.00

Grant, Lisa

Singles

Label	Catalog Number	Title	Type	Country	Year	Longbox Value / Value
King	KIDP-37	Boom Boom Boom	CD3	Japan	1991	$12.00/$3.00

Grant, Tom

Full Length

Label	Catalog Number	Title	Type	Country	Year	Longbox Value / Value
Verve	530	In My Wildest Dreams	DJ/LP	U.S.	1992	$10.00
Verve	543	Monkey Magic	DJ/Smplr	U.S.	1992	$10.00

Singles

Label	Catalog Number	Title	Type	Country	Year	Longbox Value / Value
Verve	555	I've Just Begun To Love You	CDJ	U.S.	1992	$2.00
Canyon	S10Y-1038	If You Were My Girl	CD3	Japan	1989	$12.00/$3.00
Canyon	S9Y-1104	If You Were My Girl	CD3	Japan	1989	$12.00/$3.00

Grapes of Wrath

Singles

Label	Catalog Number	Title	Type	Country	Year	Longbox Value / Value
Capitol	402	All the Things I Wasn't	CDJ	Canada	1989	$6.00
EMI	203774-2	All the Things I Wasn't	CD5	Germany	1990	$8.00
Capitol	DPRO-79937	All the Things I Wasn't	CDJ	U.S.	1989	$2.00
Capitol	CDCL-570	Do You Want To Tell Me	CD5	U.K.	1990	$8.00
Capitol	DPRO-79866	I Am Here	CDJ	U.S.	1988	$2.00
Capitol	DPRO-79881	I Am Here	CDJ	U.S.	1988	$2.00
Capitol	DPRO-79914	Stay	CDJ	U.S.	1989	$2.00
Capitol	DPRO-79047	You May Be Right	CDJ	U.S.	1988	$2.00

Grappelli, Stephan

Full Length

Label	Catalog Number	Title	Type	Country	Year	Longbox Value / Value
Polygram	821865-2	Afternoon In Paris	LP	Germany		$12.00
Verve	821865-2	Afternoon in Paris	LP/LB	U.S.†	1985	$14.00/$8.00
Accord	139004	Plays Music of Gershwin & Porter	LP/LB	U.S.†	1985	$14.00/$8.00
Polygram	825955-2	Shades Of Django	LP	Germany		$12.00
Verve	825955-2	Shades of Django	LP/LB	U.S.†	1985	$14.00/$8.00
Verve	815672-2	Young Django	LP/LB	U.S.†	1985	$14.00/$8.00

Grappelli, Stephan & L. Subramaniam

Full Length

Label	Catalog Number	Title	Type	Country	Year	Longbox Value / Value
Milestone	FCD-9130	Conversations	LP/LB	U.S.†	1985	$14.00/$8.00

Grass Valley

Singles

Label	Catalog Number	Title	Type	Country	Year	Longbox Value / Value
Sony	SRCL-2147	Happiness	CD3	Japan	1991	$12.00/$3.00

Grateful Dead

Full Length

Label	Catalog Number	Title	Type	Country	Year	Longbox Value / Value
Album Network		100 Year Hall	RS	U.S.	1995	$75.00
2 CD set. Airdate: 9/24/95.						
Arista	ASCD-9921	Ante Up - The Built To Last Interview	DJ/Intvw	U.S.	1989	$20.00
WEA	246021	Anthem of the Sun	LP	Germany		$20.00

Label	Catalog Number	Title	Type	Country	Year	Longbox Value/Value
ACE	GDPD-4001	Blues For Allah	LTD/LP	U.K.	1990	$30.00
	Picture disc CD.					
Grateful Dead	GD-4001	Blues For Allah	LP/LB	U.S.		$12.00/$8.00
Arista	ARCD-875-DL	Built To Last	LTD/LP	U.S.	1989	$35.00
Pioneer	PA-82-010	Dead Ahead	LD	U.S.	1982	$75.00
Arista	ACD6-8530	Dead Zone	LTD/LP	U.S.	1987	$100.00
	6 LD boxed set. 12"x12" boxed set with the 6 Arista albums plus large booklet.					
Grateful Dead		Dicks Picks Vol. 1	LP	U.S.		$25.00
	2 CD set.					
Grateful Dead		Dicks Picks Vol. 2	LP	U.S.	1994	$25.00
	2 CD set.					
ACE	GDPD-4007	From the Mars Hotel	LTD/LP	U.K.	1990	$30.00
	Picture disc CD.					
Mobile Fidelity	MFCD 830	From the Mars Hotel	LP/LB	U.S.		$30.00/$25.00
Grateful Dead	4013-2	From the Vault	LP	U.S.		$30.00
	2 CD set in digitrack package.					
Aris	880052	Go to Heaven	LP	Germany	1985	$20.00
Arista	ARCD-8181	Go to Heaven	LP/BP	U.S.†	1985	$15.00/$10.00
DIR		King Biscuit Flour Hour	RS	U.S.	1988	$100.00
	2 CD set. Airdate: 2/21 - 2/28/88					
DIR		King Biscuit Flour Hour	RS	U.S.	1990	$50.00
	Airdate: 12/9/90.					
DIR		King Biscuit Flour Hour	RS	U.S.	1991	$50.00
	Airdate: 12/22/91.					
DIR		King Biscuit Flour Hour	RS	U.S.	1994	$50.00
	Airdate: 6/26/94.					
Radio Today		Rock Stars	RS	U.S.	1989	$60.00
	2 CD set. Airdate: 4/3/89					
Radio Today		Rock Stars	RS	U.S.	1990	$50.00
	2 CD set.					
Arista	ARCD-8228	Shakedown Street	LP/BP	U.S.†	1985	$15.00/$10.00
Grateful Dead	GDPD2-4006	Steel Your Face	LTD/LP	U.K.	1990	$45.00
	2 CD Set					
Arista	ARCD-8065	Tarapin Station	LP/BP	U.S.†	1984	$15.00/$10.00
Arista		The Arista Years	LTD/LP	U.S.	1996	$45.00
	2 CD set with bonus CD sampler "A Glimpse Of the Vault." Available only through Best Buy stores.					
Arista		The Arista Years Radio Sampler	DJ/Smplr	U.S.	1996	$20.00
	CD in cardboard sleeve.					
Arista		The Arista Years Radio Sampler	DJ/Smplr	U.S.	1996	$20.00
	CD in jewel box.					
Media America		Twenty Five Years Playing With the Band	RS	U.S.	1992	$150.00
	4 CD set.					
Media America		Up Close	RS	U.S.	1989	$100.00
	4 CD set.					
Media America		Up Close	RS	U.S.	1992	$150.00
	4 CD set.					
Media America		Up Close (Deadicated)	RS	U.S.	1991	$100.00
	2 CD set.					
ACE	GDPD-4002	Wake The Flood	LTD/LP	U.K.	1990	$30.00
	Picture disc CD.					
Grateful Dead	GD-4002	Wake the Flood	LP/LB	U.S.		$12.00/$8.00
Arista	ACD2-8634DL	Without a Net	LTD/LP	U.S.	1990	$30.00
	2 CD picture disc set in l6"x12" package.					

Singles

Label	Catalog Number	Title	Type	Country	Year	Longbox Value/Value
Arista	CD3-3022	Alabama Getaway	CD3	U.S.	1988	$6.00/$3.00
Arista	A10D-141	Foolish Heart	CD3	Japan	1989	$15.00/$4.00
Arista	ASCD-9899	Foolish Heart	CDJ	U.S.	1989	$7.00
Arista		Throwing Stones	CDJ	U.S.	1987	$7.00
Arista	ASCD-9606	Touch of Grey	CDJ	U.S.	1987	$10.00

Grave Diggers

Full Length

Label	Catalog Number	Title	Type	Country	Year	Longbox Value/Value
BMG		Heart of Darkness	LTD/LP	U.K.	1995	$25.00
	CD with bonus tracks in digipak.					

Gravediggaz

Singles

Label	Catalog Number	Title	Type	Country	Year	Longbox Value/Value
Polygram	854105	Nowhere To Run	CD5	U.S.	1994	$5.00

Graveyard Train

Singles

Label	Catalog Number	Title	Type	Country	Year	Longbox Value/Value
Geffen	PRO-CD-4493	Down the Wire	CDJ	U.S.	1993	$2.00
Geffen	PRO-CD-4541	Reason, The	CDJ	U.S.	1993	$2.00

Gravity

Singles

Label	Catalog Number	Title	Type	Country	Year	Longbox Value/Value
Canyon	PCDY-00008	Music Speaks Louder Than Words	CD3	Japan	1989	$12.00/$3.00

Gravity Kills

Full Length

Label	Catalog Number	Title	Type	Country	Year	Longbox Value/Value
Westwood One		In Concert-Nu Rock	RS	U.S.	1996	$35.00
	Airdate: 8/12/96.					

Gray, David

Singles

Label	Catalog Number	Title	Type	Country	Year	Longbox Value/Value
APT	HUTCD-23	Birds Without Wings	CD5	U.K.	1992	$8.00
	DPRO10486	Faster, Sooner, Now	CDJ	U.S.		$2.00
APT	HUTCD-27	Shine	CD5	U.K.	1992	$8.00

Grays

Singles

Label	Catalog Number	Title	Type	Country	Year	Longbox Value/Value
Epic	ESK 6172	Same Thing	CDJ	U.S.	1993	$6.00
Epic	ESK 5601	Very Best Years	CDJ	U.S.	1993	$7.00

Grayson, Hugh

Singles

Label	Catalog Number	Title	Type	Country	Year	Longbox Value/Value
RCA	PD-49318	Bring It All Back	CD5	Germany	1989	$8.00
RCA	PD-49384	Talk It Over	CD5	Germany	1989	$8.00
RCA	PD-49484	Talk It Over	CD5	Germany	1989	$8.00
RCA	R10D-131	Talk It Over	CD3	Japan	1989	$12.00/$3.00
RCA	PD-49484	Talk It Over	CD5	U.K.	1989	$8.00
		Talk It Over	CDJ	U.S.		$2.00
		Talk It Over	CDJ	U.S.		$2.00

Graystoke

Singles

Label	Catalog Number	Title	Type	Country	Year	Longbox Value/Value
Union	XUNION-3	Every Beat of My Heart	CD5	U.K.	1989	$8.00

Great Big Buildings

Singles

Label	Catalog Number	Title	Type	Country	Year	Longbox Value/Value
SPV	4961-3	Katy Dids	CD5	Germany	1990	$8.00

Great Jazz Trio

Full Length

Label	Catalog Number	Title	Type	Country	Year	Longbox Value/Value
East Wind	35-JjD10 PSI	Chapter II	LP/LB	U.S.†	1985	$14.00/$8.00
East Wind	35-JD3 PSI	I'm Old Fashioned	LP/LB	U.S.†	1985	$14.00/$8.00
East Wind	PHCE-33004	Live at Vanguard	LTD/LP	Japan		$25.00
	Gold disc.					
East Wind	35-JD4 PSI	Love For Sale	LP/LB	U.S.†	1985	$14.00/$8.00
Denon	CD-7097	NY Sophisticate Tribute to Duke Ellington	LP/LB	U.S.†	1985	$14.00/$8.00
Denon	CD-7072	The Club New Yorker	LP/LB	U.S.†	1985	$14.00/$8.00
East Wind	35-JD6 PSI	The Village Vanguard	LP/LB	U.S.†	1985	$14.00/$8.00

Great Northern Electrics

Singles

Label	Catalog Number	Title	Type	Country	Year	Longbox Value/Value
Polydor	PZCD 111	Sunday's Child	CD5	U.K.	1990	$8.00

Great White

Full Length

Label	Catalog Number	Title	Type	Country	Year	Longbox Value/Value
Capitol	DPRO-79286	Back Tracks 1986-1991	DJ/Smplr	U.S.	1992	$15.00
Capitol	DPRO-79017	Great White Blues 'n Boogie Tour	DJ/Smplr	U.S.	1990	$8.00
Capitol	CDP 7 95330 2	Hooked	DJ/LP	U.S.	1991	$35.00
	Promo CD and cassette in custom box wrapped with simulated fishnet.					
Capitol	CDP 7 95330 2	Hooked	LP/LB	U.S.	1991	$17.00/$5.00
Westwood One		In Concert	RS	U.S.	1994	$45.00
	Airdate: 8/1/94.					
Capitol	DPRO-79305	Live at the Ritz	DJ/Smplr	U.S.	1988	$35.00
		Live From Electric Ladyland	RS	U.S.	1991	$35.00
	Airdate: 5/31/91.					
Capitol	DPRO-79034	Live in London	DJ/Smplr	U.S.	1990	$8.00
Westwood One		Off the Record	RS	U.S.	1992	$30.00
	Airdate: 11/2/92.					
Capitol	550	On the Line	DJ/Intvw	Canada	1990	$15.00
Enigma	73295	Recovery	LP	U.S.	1987	$20.00
Enigma	D2-73295	Recovery Live!	LP	U.S.	1987	$25.00
Zoo		Sail Away	DJ/LP	U.S.	1994	$12.00
Zoo	ZADV11080-2	Sail Away	DJ/LP	U.S.	1994	$18.00
Zoo	72445-11080-2	Sail Away	LTD/LP	U.S.	1994	$17.00
	2CD set.					
EMI		Twice Shy/Live at the Ritz	LP	Germany	1989	$25.00
	2 CD set					

Singles

Label	Catalog Number	Title	Type	Country	Year	Longbox Value/Value
EMI	203553-3	Angel Song, The	CD3	Germany	1990	$10.00
Capitol	DPRO-79753	Angel Song, The	CDJ	U.S.	1990	$2.00
		Babe	CDJ	U.S.		$3.00
Capitol		Big Goodbye	CD5	Germany	1992	$10.00
Capitol	DPRO-79433	Big Goodbye	CDJ	U.S.	1992	$2.00
Capitol	204340-2	Call It Rock & Roll	CD5	Germany	1991	$10.00
Toshiba	TODP-2247	Call It Rock & Roll	CD3	Japan	1991	$15.00/$4.00
Toshiba-EMI	TOFF-7505	Call It Rock & Roll	CDV	Japan	1991	$40.00
Capitol	CDCL-625	Call It Rock & Roll	CD5	U.K.	1991	$10.00
Capitol	DPRO-79500	Call It Rock & Roll	CDJ	U.S.	1991	$2.00
Capitol	2043215-2	Congo Square	CD5	Germany	1991	$10.00
Capitol	CDCL-605	Congo Square	CD5	U.K.	1991	$10.00
Odeon	TODP-2285	Desert Moon	CD3	Japan	1991	$13.00/$4.00
Capitol	C2 15744	Desert Moon	CD5	U.S.	1991	$6.00
EMI	203624-3	Heart the Hunter	CD3	Germany	1989	$10.00
Capitol	CDCL-555	Heart the Hunter	CD5	U.K.	1991	$10.00
Capitol	CDCL-562	House Of Broken Love	CD5	U.K.	1989	$10.00
Capitol	DPRO-79784	House Of Broken Love	CDJ	U.S.	1989	$3.00
		Love Is A Lie	CDJ	U.S.		$7.00
Capitol	DPRO-79858	Lovin' Kind	CDJ	U.S.	1991	$3.00
Capitol	DPRO-79682	Mista Bone	CDJ	U.S.	1989	$7.00
Capitol	DPRO-79280	Mistreater	CDJ	U.S.	1987	$6.00
Capitol	DPRO-79017	Move It	CDJ	U.S.	1990	$3.00
Capitol	CDCL-532	Once Bitten Twice Shy	CD5	U.K.	1989	$10.00
Capitol	DIDX 004647	Once Bitten Twice Shy	CDJ	U.S.	1989	$15.00
Capitol	DPRO-79883	Original Queen of Sheba	CDJ	U.S.	1991	$2.00
Capitol	DPRO-79061	Rock Me	CDJ	U.S.	1987	$6.00

Greater Than One

Singles

Label	Catalog Number	Title	Type	Country	Year	Longbox Value/Value
Wax Trax	9078	I Don't Need God	CD5	U.S.	1989	$4.00
EFA	CD-14265	Utopia	CD5	Germany	1989	$8.00
Torso	CD-148	Utopia	CD5	U.K.	1990	$8.00
Wax Trax	9099	Utopia	CD5	U.S.	1989	$4.00

Greaves, Dennis

Singles

Label	Catalog Number	Title	Type	Country	Year	Longbox Value/Value
IRS	241036-3	God Gave Rock and Roll to You	CD3	Germany	1989	$8.00
IRS	EIRSCD-119	God Gave Rock and Roll to You	CD5	U.K.	1989	$8.00
IRS	241015-3	Jealous Man	CD3	Germany	1989	$8.00
IRS	EIRSCD-113	Jealous Man	CD5	U.K.	1989	$8.00

Greed

Singles

Label	Catalog Number	Title	Type	Country	Year	Longbox Value/Value
ZYX	6515-8	Give Me	CD5	Germany	1991	$6.00
Dance Zone	DZONE-001CD	Gonna Let You Go	CD5	U.K.	1991	$8.00
Dance Zone	DANCE-011CD	Love	CD5	U.K.	1991	$8.00

Green, Al

Full Length

Label	Catalog Number	Title	Type	Country	Year	Longbox Value/Value
Motown	5318	Belle Album, The	LP/BP	U.S.		$12.00/$7.00
Motown	5286	Call Me	LP/BP	U.S.		$12.00/$7.00
Motown	MOTD-8040	Call Me + Livin' For You	LP/BP	U.S.		$18.00/$15.00
RCA	ZD-72464	Compact Command Performance	LP	Germany		$18.00
Motown	5432	Explore Your Mind	LP/BP	U.S.		$12.00/$7.00
Motown	5432	Full of Fire	LP/BP	U.S.		$12.00/$7.00
Motown	5283	Greatest Hits Vol. 1	LP/BP	U.S.		$12.00/$7.00
Motown	5432	Greatest Hits Vol. 2	LP/BP	U.S.		$12.00/$7.00
Motown	5284	I'm Still in Love	LP/BP	U.S.		$12.00/$7.00
Motown	5432	Is Love	LP/BP	U.S.		$12.00/$7.00
Motown	MOTD-8018	Let's Stay Together + I'm Still in Love With You	LP/BP	U.S.		$18.00/$15.00
Motown	5290	Lets Stay Together	LP/BP	U.S.		$12.00/$7.00
Motown	5304	Living For You	LP/BP	U.S.		$12.00/$7.00
Motown	5432	Sings the Gospel	LP/BP	U.S.		$12.00/$7.00
Motown	5302	Tokyo Love	LP/BP	U.S.		$12.00/$7.00
Motown	5317	Truth 'n Time	LP/BP	U.S.		$12.00/$7.00

Singles

Label	Catalog Number	Title	Type	Country	Year	Longbox Value/Value
A&M	CD-17784	As Long As We're Together	CDJ	U.S.	1989	$2.00
A&M	390425-2	As Long As Were Together	CD5	Germany	1989	$8.00
Curb	2992	Funny How Times Slip Away	CDJ	U.S.	1992	$7.00
Epic	ESK74232	Love is Reality	CDJ	U.S.		$2.00
MCA	MCA5P3563	Your Heart's in Good Hands	CDJ	U.S.		$2.00

Green Apple Quick Step

Singles

Label	Catalog Number	Title	Type	Country	Year	Longbox Value/Value
Medicine	6524	Dirty Water Ocean	CDJ	U.S.	1993	$2.00
Medicine	6777	Feel My Way	CDJ	U.S.	1994	$7.00

Green, Benny

Full Length

Label	Catalog Number	Title	Type	Country	Year	Longbox Value / Value
Blue Note	CDP-93670-2	Lineage	LP/LB	U.S.		$18.00/$15.00

Green Day

Full Length

Label	Catalog Number	Title	Type	Country	Year	Longbox Value / Value
Reprise	9 45529-A	Dookie	DJ/LP	U.S.	1994	$13.00
Westwood One		In Concert	RS	U.S.	1995	$45.00

Airdate: 8/14/95.

Label	Catalog Number	Title	Type	Country	Year	Longbox Value / Value
Westwood One		In Concert	RS	U.S.	1995	$75.00

2 CD set with the Pretenders. Airdate: 11/7/94.

Label	Catalog Number	Title	Type	Country	Year	Longbox Value / Value
Westwood One		In Concert-Nu Rock	RS	U.S.	1995	$45.00

Airdate: 7/3/95.

Label	Catalog Number	Title	Type	Country	Year	Longbox Value / Value
Warner	PCS-157	Singles	DJ/Smplr	Japan	1994	$100.00

Singles

Label	Catalog Number	Title	Type	Country	Year	Longbox Value / Value
Warner	12-18100	Basket Case	CD5	Canada	1994	$6.00
Warner	PCS-1711	Basket Case	CDJ	Japan	1994	$35.00
		Basket Case	CD5	U.K.	1994	$10.00
Reprise		Basket Case	CDJ	U.S.	1994	$3.00
Reprise	WO339CDX	Brain Stew	SCD5	Germany	1996	$15.00
Reprise		Brain Stew	CDJ	U.S.	1995	$6.00
Warner Brothers	PRO-CD-7866	Geek Stink Breath	CDJ	U.S.	1996	$7.00
Warner Brothers	PRO-CD-7643-R	J.A.R.	CDJ	U.S.	1996	$7.00
Warner	WPCR-204	Live Tracks	CD5	Japan	1995	$26.00
Warner	12-18166	Longview	CD5	Canada	1994	$7.00
Warner Brothers		Longview	CDJ	Spain	1995	$30.00
		Longview	CD5	U.K.	1994	$10.00
Reprise		Longview	CDJ	U.S.	1994	$3.00
Reprise		Longview	CDJ	U.S.	1994	$6.00

Second version.

Label	Catalog Number	Title	Type	Country	Year	Longbox Value / Value
		On the Wagon	CD5	U.K.	1994	$10.00
Warner Brothers	WO327CD1	Stuck With Me	CD5	U.K.	1995	$12.00
		Welcome to Paradise	CD5	U.K.	1994	$10.00
Reprise		Welcome to Paradise	CDJ	U.S.	1994	$6.00
		When I Come Around	CD5	U.K.	1994	$10.00
		When I Come Around	CDJ	U.S.	1994	$8.00

Green, Grant

Full Length

Label	Catalog Number	Title	Type	Country	Year	Longbox Value / Value
Mosaic	MD4-133	Complete Blue Note Recordings	LP	U.S.		$60.00

4 CD set.

Green Jello – Suxx! (Zoo 72445-14057-2)

Green Jelly (Green Jello)

Full Length

Label	Catalog Number	Title	Type	Country	Year	Longbox Value / Value
Zoo	72445-11038	Cereal Killer Soundtrack	LP/LB	U.S.	1992	$18.00/$14.00

Titled "Green Jello")

Label	Catalog Number	Title	Type	Country	Year	Longbox Value / Value
Zoo	72445-11038-2	Cereal Killer Soundtrack	LP	U.S.	1993	$30.00

Singles

Label	Catalog Number	Title	Type	Country	Year	Longbox Value / Value
Zoo	17136	Electric Harley House	CDJ	U.S.	1993	$2.00
Zoo	14057	Suxx!	CD5	U.S.	1992	$6.00
Zoo	72445-14057-2	Suxx!	CD5	U.S.	1992	$10.00
Zoo	ZP1732	Three Little Pigs	CDJ	U.S.		$6.00
Zoo	ZP17111-2	Three Little Pigs	CDJ	U.S.	1992	$3.00

Green Olives

Singles

Label	Catalog Number	Title	Type	Country	Year	Longbox Value / Value
Victor	VDPS-1019	Jive Into the Night	CD3	Japan	1988	$12.00/$3.00
Victor	VDPS-1037	Life is a Bitch	CD3	Japan	1988	$12.00/$3.00
Victor	VICP-15003	Shake My Day	CD5	Japan	1990	$10.00

Green On Red

Full Length

Label	Catalog Number	Title	Type	Country	Year	Longbox Value / Value
Mercury	839122-2	Killer Inside Me	LP	U.K.		$15.00

Singles

Label	Catalog Number	Title	Type	Country	Year	Longbox Value / Value
China	CHICD-16	Keith Can't Read	CD5	U.K.	1989	$8.00
China	WOKCD-2001	Little Things in Life	CD5	U.K.	1991	$8.00
Polydor	CDP 258	Reverend Luther	CDJ	U.S.	1989	$2.00
China	CHICD-21	This Time Around	CD5	U.K.	1989	$8.00
China	873747-2	You Couldn't Get Arrested	CD5	Germany	1990	$8.00
China	CHICD-22	You Couldn't Get Arrested	CD5	U.K.	1990	$8.00

Green, Peter

Full Length

Label	Catalog Number	Title	Type	Country	Year	Longbox Value / Value
		House Of Blues	RS	U.S.	1995	$40.00

2 CD set. Airdate: 8/6/95.

Green String Quartet

Singles

Label	Catalog Number	Title	Type	Country	Year	Longbox Value / Value
Virgin	PRCD 3997	Welcome To the Jungle	CDJ	U.S.	1991	$2.00

Greenberry Woods

Singles

Label	Catalog Number	Title	Type	Country	Year	Longbox Value / Value
Reprise	PRO-CD-6691	Adieu	CDJ	U.S.	1994	$2.00
	PRCD9358-2	Shorty	CDJ	U.S.		$2.00
Reprise	PRO-CD-6731	Trampoline	CDJ	U.S.	1994	$2.00

Greenhouse

Singles

Label	Catalog Number	Title	Type	Country	Year	Longbox Value / Value
Eastwest	9031-72104-2	I Love America	CD5	Germany	1990	$8.00

Greenway

Full Length

Label	Catalog Number	Title	Type	Country	Year	Longbox Value / Value
Atlantic	7 91927-1	Serious Business	LP/LB	U.S.	1986	$15.00/$12.00

Greenwood, Lee

Full Length

Label	Catalog Number	Title	Type	Country	Year	Longbox Value / Value
		Country Star Tracks	RS	U.S.	1991	$20.00

Airdate: 10/19/91.

Label	Catalog Number	Title	Type	Country	Year	Longbox Value / Value
MCA	MCAD-5582	Greatest Hits	LP/LB	U.S.†	1985	$14.00/$8.00
MCA	MCAD-5582	Somebody's Gonna Love You	LP/LB	U.S.†	1985	$14.00/$8.00

Singles

Label	Catalog Number	Title	Type	Country	Year	Longbox Value / Value
MCA	CD45-1335	God Bless the U.S.A.	CDJ	U.S.	1990	$4.00

Gregorian

Singles

Label	Catalog Number	Title	Type	Country	Year	Longbox Value / Value
Polygram	867153-2	Once in a Lifetime	CD5	Germany	1991	$8.00
Metronome	879523-2	So Sad	CD5	Germany	1991	$8.00
Metronome	879523-2	So Sad	CD5	U.K.	1991	$8.00

Gregson, Clive

Singles

Label	Catalog Number	Title	Type	Country	Year	Longbox Value / Value
Rhino	90031	This is a Deal	CDJ	U.S.	1990	$2.00

Gren

Singles

Label	Catalog Number	Title	Type	Country	Year	Longbox Value / Value
	DPRO10513	She Shines	CDJ	U.S.		$2.00
	DPRO10527	Tripping the Life	CDJ	U.S.		$2.00

Greta

Singles

Label	Catalog Number	Title	Type	Country	Year	Longbox Value / Value
Stardog	CDP 978	Fathom	CDJ	U.S.	1993	$2.00
Stardog	862 196	Love is Dead	CD5	U.S.	1993	$5.00
Stardog	CDP 1002	Revolver	CDJ	U.S.	1993	$2.00
Stardog	CDP 885	Rockin' Chair	CDJ	U.S.	1993	$2.00

Grey House

Singles

Label	Catalog Number	Title	Type	Country	Year	Longbox Value / Value
ZYX	6117-8	Move Your Ass	CD5	Germany	1989	$6.00

Grey, Roman

Singles

Label	Catalog Number	Title	Type	Country	Year	Longbox Value / Value
Polygram	871389-2	Ibu	CD5	Germany	1989	$8.00
Polygram	889084-3	Shangri-La	CD3	Germany	1989	$8.00
Polygram	889085-2	Shangri-La	CD5	Germany	1989	$8.00

Grid

Singles

Label	Catalog Number	Title	Type	Country	Year	Longbox Value / Value
WEA	9031-72407-2	Beat Called Love	CD5	Germany	1990	$8.00
Eastwest	YZ-498CD	Beat Called Love	CD5	U.K.	1990	$8.00
Virgin	VSCDT-1421	Figure of Eight	CD5	U.K.	1992	$8.00
Eastwest	YZ-475CD	Flotation	CD5	U.K.	1990	$8.00
Virgin	VSCDT-1427	Heartbeat	CD5	U.K.	1992	$8.00

Griffin, Angee

Singles

Label	Catalog Number	Title	Type	Country	Year	Longbox Value / Value
BMG	663472	Rain	CD5	Germany	1990	$8.00

Griffin, Billy

Singles

Label	Catalog Number	Title	Type	Country	Year	Longbox Value / Value
Motor City	CDMOTCLP-72	Technicolor	CD5	U.K.	1991	$8.00

Griffin, Clive

Singles

Label	Catalog Number	Title	Type	Country	Year	Longbox Value / Value
Mercury	872415-2	Be There	CD5	Germany	1989	$8.00
Mercury	STECD-3	Be There	CD5	U.K.	1989	$8.00
Mercury	STECD-2	Don't Make Me Wait	CD5	U.K.	1989	$8.00
IMS	874463-2	Head Above Water	CD5	Germany	1989	$8.00
Polygram	SILCD-4	Head Above Water	CD5	U.K.	1989	$8.00
Mercury	STECD-6	I'll Be Waiting	CD5	U.K.	1991	$8.00
Mercury	878813-2	Reach For You	CD5	Germany	1991	$8.00
Mercury	STECD-5	Reach For You	CD5	U.K.	1991	$8.00
Mercury	870324-2	Way We Touch	CD5	Germany	1991	$8.00
Mercury	STECD-1	Way We Touch	CD5	U.K.	1991	$8.00

Griffin, Johnny

Full Length

Label	Catalog Number	Title	Type	Country	Year	Longbox Value / Value
EMI	881559-2	Blowing Session	LP	Germany		$12.00
Blue Note		Congregation, The	LTD/LP	U.S.	1994	$20.00
		Dance of Passion Radio Edits	DJ/Smplr	U.S.	1994	$6.00
Blue Note	CDP 46536-2	Introducing	LP/LB	U.S.		$18.00/$15.00
Blue Note		Introducing	LTD/LP	U.S.	1995	$19.00
Sony	J0068DL	Jazz Life of…	LD	U.S.	1986	$30.00
Polygram	821293-2	Tough Tenors	LP	Germany		$12.00

Griffin, Sylvia

Singles

Label	Catalog Number	Title	Type	Country	Year	Longbox Value / Value
Polygram	870377-2	Love's a State of Mind	CD5	Germany	1988	$8.00
Phonogram	BLA3TCD-7	Love's a State of Mind	CD5	U.K.	1988	$8.00

Griffith, Andy

Full Length

Label	Catalog Number	Title	Type	Country	Year	Longbox Value / Value
Warner Sound Exchange		What It Is, Is Andy Griffith	LTD/LP	U.S.	1995	$30.00

2 CD Set.

Griffith, Nanci

Full Length

Label	Catalog Number	Title	Type	Country	Year	Longbox Value / Value
MCA	1693	A Portrait of an Artist	DJ/Smplr	U.S.	1991	$18.00
Elektra	PRCD 9170	AAA Radio Live Sampler	DJ/Smplr	U.S.	1995	$15.00
		Present Echos	DJ/Smplr	U.S.	1993	$25.00
	PRCD93862	Three From "Flyer"	DJ/Smplr	U.S.		$6.00
Elektra	PRCD 9417-2	Time of Inconvenience	DJ/LP	U.S.	1995	$30.00

2 CD set.

Singles

Label	Catalog Number	Title	Type	Country	Year	Longbox Value / Value
Elektra	PRCD 8777-2	Across the Great Divide	CDJ	U.S.	1993	$2.00
MCA	DMCA-1282	From a Distance	CD5	U.K.	1988	$13.00
MCA	MCSTD-1596	Heaven	CD5	U.K.	1991	$10.00
MCA	2069	Heaven	CDJ	U.S.	1991	$2.00
MCA	DCMAT-1358	It's a Hard Life Wherever You Go	CD5	U.K.	1989	$10.00
MCA	CD45 17961	It's a Hard Life Wherever You Go	CDJ	U.S.	1989	$3.00
Elektra	PRCD 8863-2	It's a Hard Life Wherever You Go	CDJ	U.S.	1993	$3.00
MCA	MCSTD-1566	Late Night Grande Hotel	CD5	U.K.	1991	$10.00
MCA	2002	Late Night Grande Hotel	CDJ	U.S.	1991	$2.00
	PRCD93862	On Grafton Street	CDJ	U.S.		$2.00

Label	Catalog Number	Title	Type	Country	Year	Longbox Value / Value
Elektra	PRCD 8714-2	Speed of the Sound of Loneliness	CDJ	U.S.	1993	$3.00
MCA	CD45 18092	Storms	CDJ	U.S.	1989	$3.00
		These Days in an Open Book	CDJ	U.S.		$3.00
Elektra		Time of Inconvenience	CDJ	U.S.	1995	$3.00
MCA	DMCAT-1379	You Made This Love a Teardrop	CD5	U.K.	1989	$10.00

Griffiths, Marcia

Singles

Label	Catalog Number	Title	Type	Country	Year	Value
Aris	884025	Electric Boogie	CD5	Germany	1990	$8.00
Island	CDMNG-726	Electric Boogie	CD5	U.K.	1990	$8.00
Mango	7832	Electric Boogie	CDJ	U.S.	1990	$2.00

Grifters

Singles

Label	Catalog Number	Title	Type	Country	Year	Value
	SUBPROCD43	Last Man Alive	CDJ	U.S.		$3.00

Grimace

Singles

Label	Catalog Number	Title	Type	Country	Year	Value
Gift	003	Tomorrow's Gonna Suck	CD5	U.S.	1992	$4.00

Grimes, Carol

Singles

Label	Catalog Number	Title	Type	Country	Year	Value
Instant	INCD-9 00820	Heart in My Hands	CD5	Germany	1989	$8.00

Grimes, Scott

Singles

Label	Catalog Number	Title	Type	Country	Year	Value
A&M	CD-17762	I Don't Even Mind	CDJ	U.S.	1989	$2.00

Grip

Singles

Label	Catalog Number	Title	Type	Country	Year	Value
Survival	ZD-43750	American Dream	CD5	U.K.	1990	$8.00

Grisman, David

Full Length

Label	Catalog Number	Title	Type	Country	Year	Longbox Value / Value
Mobile Fidelity	UDCD-505	Hot Dawg	LP/LB	U.S.		$30.00/$20.00

Grissom, Rich

Singles

Label	Catalog Number	Title	Type	Country	Year	Value
Mercury	CDP 232	It Must Be Love	CDJ	U.S.	1990	$2.00

Grither

Singles

Label	Catalog Number	Title	Type	Country	Year	Value
MCA	11288	All Smiles	CD5	U.S.	1995	$5.00

Grolnick, Don & Michael Brecker

Full Length

Label	Catalog Number	Title	Type	Country	Year	Longbox Value / Value
Hipp.	HD-106	Hearts and Numbers	LP/LB	U.S.†	1985	$14.00/$8.00

Gronemeyer, Harold

Singles

Label	Catalog Number	Title	Type	Country	Year	Value
SBK	DPRO-05315	Full Moon	CDJ	U.S.	1988	$2.00

Groove '70

Singles

Label	Catalog Number	Title	Type	Country	Year	Value
EMI	323764-2	Get Into the Love Machine	CD5	Germany	1991	$8.00

Groove B Chill

Singles

Label	Catalog Number	Title	Type	Country	Year	Value
A&M	75021 8087 2	Hip Hop Music	CDJ	U.S.	1990	$2.00
A&M	18022	Hip Hop Music	CDJ	U.S.	1990	$2.00
A&M	75021 7412-2	Swingin' Single	CDJ	U.S.	1990	$2.00

Groove Collective

Full Length

Label	Catalog Number	Title	Type	Country	Year	Value
Reprise	PRO-CD-6809	Sampler	DJ/Smplr	U.S.	1994	$7.00

Singles

Label	Catalog Number	Title	Type	Country	Year	Value
Warner Brother	41432	Nerd	CD5	U.S.	1994	$5.00
Warner Brothers	41789	Watchugot	CD5	U.S.	1994	$5.00

Groove Factory

Singles

Label	Catalog Number	Title	Type	Country	Year	Value
WEA	9031-75474-2	Close To Your Heart	CD5	Germany	1991	$8.00
WEA	9031-75438-2	Don't Stop the Music	CD5	Germany	1991	$8.00
WEA	9031-75463-2	Don't Stop the Music	CD5	Germany	1991	$8.00

Groove Theory

Singles

Label	Catalog Number	Title	Type	Country	Year	Value
Epic	ESK 7515	Keep Tryin'	CDJ	U.S.	1995	$3.00
Epic	ESK 7661	Keep Tryin'	CDJ	U.S.	1995	$3.00
Columbia	77961	Tell Me	CD5	U.S.	1995	$5.00

Grotus

Singles

Label	Catalog Number	Title	Type	Country	Year	Value
	PRCD 6986-2	Hand to Mouth	CDJ	U.S.		$2.00

Ground Level

Singles

Label	Catalog Number	Title	Type	Country	Year	Value
Faze 2	CDFAZE-14	Dreams of Heaven	CD5	U.K.	1992	$8.00

Ground Zero

Singles

Label	Catalog Number	Title	Type	Country	Year	Value
Lethal Beat	LBR116	Lettin Ya Know	CDJ	U.S.	1990	$7.00

Group Home

Singles

Label	Catalog Number	Title	Type	Country	Year	Value
Full Frequency	120053	Supa Star	CD5	U.S.	1994	$5.00

Gruesome Twosome

Singles

Label	Catalog Number	Title	Type	Country	Year	Value
Nettwerk	3037	Hallucination Generation	CD5	U.S.	1992	$8.00

Gruntruck

Singles

Label	Catalog Number	Title	Type	Country	Year	Value
Roadrunner	076	Above Me	CDJ	U.S.	1993	$2.00

Grunwalt

Singles

Label	Catalog Number	Title	Type	Country	Year	Value
BMG	662204	Springtime	CD5	Germany	1989	$8.00

Grupo Pegasso

Singles

Label	Catalog Number	Title	Type	Country	Year	Value
	5317	Grupo Pegass	CD5	U.S.	1994	$5.00

Grushecky, Joe and The House Rockers

Singles

Label	Catalog Number	Title	Type	Country	Year	Value
Rounder	1003	How Long	CDJ	U.S.	1989	$2.00

Grusin, Dave

Full Length

Label	Catalog Number	Title	Type	Country	Year	Longbox Value / Value
Sheffield Lab	CD-5	Discovered Again	LP/LB	U.S.†	1985	$14.00/$8.00
GRP	D-8151	Live in Japan	LP/LB	U.S.†	1985	$14.00/$8.00
GRP	D-9507	Mountain Dance	LP/LB	U.S.†	1985	$14.00/$8.00
GRP	D-9507	Night-Lines	LP/LB	U.S.†	1985	$14.00/$8.00
GRP	D-9501	& NY/LA Dream Band	LP/LB	U.S.†	1985	$14.00/$8.00

GSC - Open Universe

Singles

Label	Catalog Number	Title	Type	Country	Year	Value
BMG	663660	Infinity	CD5	Germany	1990	$8.00

GTO

Singles

Label	Catalog Number	Title	Type	Country	Year	Value
Mute	CDNOMU-8	Love is Experience	CD5	U.K	1992	$8.00
Cooltempo	COOLCD-218	Pure	CD5	Germany	1990	$8.00

GTR – GTR (Arista ARCD 8400)

GTR

Full Length

Label	Catalog Number	Title	Type	Country	Year	Longbox Value / Value
Arista	ARCD-88400	GTR	LP/LB	U.S.		$14.00/$8.00
Arista	ARCD-88400	GTR	LP/LB	U.S.†	1986	$14.00/$8.00

Guadacanal Diary

Singles

Label	Catalog Number	Title	Type	Country	Year	Value
Elektra	PR 8055-2	Always Saturday	CDJ	U.S.	1989	$2.00
Elektra	PR 8081-2	Pretty is as Pretty Does	CDJ	U.S.	1989	$2.00

Guaraldi, Vince

Full Length

Label	Catalog Number	Title	Type	Country	Year	Longbox Value / Value
Fantasy	FCD-8089	Cast Your Fate to the Wind	LP/LB	U.S.†	1985	$14.00/$8.00

Guaranteed Raw

Singles

Label	Catalog Number	Title	Type	Country	Year	Value
ZYX	6334-8	Make Your Body Sweat	CD5	Germany	1990	$6.00

Guerra, Jean Luis

Singles

Label	Catalog Number	Title	Type	Country	Year	Value
BMG	664559	Jean Luis Guerra	CD5	Germany	1991	$8.00

Guess Who

Full Length

Label	Catalog Number	Title	Type	Country	Year	Longbox Value / Value
RCA		American Woman	LP/LB	U.S.		$15.00/$12.00
		Canned Heat	LP/LB	U.S.		$15.00/$12.00
Album Network		In the Studio (Guess Who)	RS	U.S.	1992	$20.00
Airdate: 4/6/92.						
RCA		Live at the Paramount	LP/BP	U.S		$14.00/$8.00
Pioneer	PA-85-130	Together Again	LD	U.S.	1990	$30.00
Pioneer	PA-85-130	Together Again	LD	U.S.	1990	$40.00
Digital Audio.						
RCA		Wheatfield Soul	LP/BP	U.S		$14.00/$8.00

Guesss

Singles

Label	Catalog Number	Title	Type	Country	Year	Value
Warner Brothers	PRO-CD-6414	Shu-B	CDJ	U.S.	1993	$2.00
Warner Brothers	PRO-CD-6633	Tell Me Where It Hurts	CDJ	U.S.	1993	$2.00

Gufs

Singles

Label	Catalog Number	Title	Type	Country	Year	Value
	PRCD 6668-2	Crash (Into Me)	CDJ	U.S.		$2.00

Guilty

Singles

Label	Catalog Number	Title	Type	Country	Year	Value
A&M	CD-17905	Tora Tora	CDJ	U.S.	1989	$2.00

Guitar Army

Singles

Label	Catalog Number	Title	Type	Country	Year	Value
BMG	PD-44550	Call Me Up	CD5	Germany	1991	$8.00

Guitar Orchestra

Singles

Label	Catalog Number	Title	Type	Country	Year	Value
Park	PRKCD-5	Pernod for the Bamboo Man	CD5	U.K.	1991	$8.00

Gult Dep

Singles

Label	Catalog Number	Title	Type	Country	Year	Value
Victor	VICL-2068	Flash Back	CD5	Japan	1992	$10.00
Victor	VICL-15016	Walk	CD5	Japan	1993	$10.00

Gumball

Singles

Label	Catalog Number	Title	Type	Country	Year	Value
Columbia	CSK 4960	Accelerator	CDJ	U.S.	1993	$2.00
Columbia	44K 77138	Damage Done	CD5	U.S.	1993	$5.00
APT	PAPER-012CD	Light Shines Through	CD5	U.K.	1991	$8.00
Columbia	CSK 5145	Real Gone Deal	CDJ	U.S.	1993	$2.00
Pinnacle	ABB-41SCD	Wisconsin Hayride	CD5	U.K.	1992	$8.00

Gumbo

Label	Catalog Number	Title	Type	Country	Year	Longbox Value / Value
		Singles				
Chrysalis	04580	A Free Soul	CDJ	U.S.	1993	$2.00
Chrysalis	04737	Basement Magic	CDJ	U.S.	1993	$2.00

Gun

Label	Catalog Number	Title	Type	Country	Year	Longbox Value / Value
		Full Length				
A&M	5383	Gallus	LP/LB	U.S.		$12.00/$7.00
		Singles				
A&M	S9Y-13111	Better Days	CD3	Japan	1989	$12.00/$3.00
A&M	CDEE-505	Better Days	CD3	U.K.	1989	$8.00
A&M	CD 17984	Better Days	CDJ	U.S.	1989	$2.00
		Don't Say It's Over	CD5	U.K.		$10.00
		Don't Say It's Over	CD5	U.K.		$10.00
	Second version.					
A&M	CDEE-531	Inside Out	CD3	U.K.	1989	$8.00
A&M	CDEE-520	Money (Everybody Love Her)	CD3	U.K.	1989	$8.00
A&M	CD-18033	Money (Everybody Love Her)	CDJ	U.S.	1989	$2.00
A&M	AMCD-573	Shame On You	CD5	U.K.	1990	$8.00
A&M	75021 7373-2	Steal Your Fire	CDJ	U.S.	1992	$2.00
A&M	CDEE-541	Taking on the World	CD3	U.K.	1989	$8.00
A&M	75021 7336-2	Welcome to the Real World	CDJ	U.S.	1992	$2.00
		Word Up	CDJ	Spain		$18.00

Gun Club

Label	Catalog Number	Title	Type	Country	Year	Longbox Value / Value
		Full Length				
Efa	CD-2670	Mother Juno	LP	Germany		$15.00
		Singles				
New Rose	143CD	Great Divide, The	CD5	France	1990	$10.00
Efa	CD-02918	Pastoral Hide And Seek	CD5	Germany	1992	$8.00
SPV	5231-3	Sex Beat	CD3	Germany	1988	$8.00
Neat	NEAT-1CD	Sex Beat	CD3	U.K.	1990	$8.00

Gun, Tommy

Label	Catalog Number	Title	Type	Country	Year	Longbox Value / Value
		Full Length				
Thump	THCDPRO 2213	Loco	DJ/Smplr	U.S.	1995	$10.00

Gung-Ho

Label	Catalog Number	Title	Type	Country	Year	Longbox Value / Value
		Singles				
RCA	CDGUN-1	Play to Win	CD5	U.K.	1987	$8.00

Guns 'N Roses – Welcome To the Jungle (Geffen PRO-CD-2668)

Guns 'n Roses

Label	Catalog Number	Title	Type	Country	Year	Longbox Value / Value
		Full Length				
Geffen	PRO-CD-3132	Aerosmith/Guns 'n Roses	DJ/Smplr	U.S.	1989	$15.00
	With 3 Aerosmith/2 Guns N' Roses tracks.					
Geffen		Appetite for Destruction	LTD/LP	Australia	1995	$35.00
	Limited gold disc edition.					
Geffen	WPCD-3690	Appetite for Destruction	LP	Japan	1987	$150.00
	Original cover					
Geffen	MVCZ-6	Appetite for Destruction	LTD/LP	Japan	1991	$35.00
	10"x10" package with cards.					
Geffen	25XD-977	EP	LP	Japan	1989	$75.00
Geffen	37PZ-2400	GN'R Lies	LTD/LP	Japan	1988	$75.00
	CD with "banned" booklet in special box and T-shirt					
Geffen	PRO-CD-4340	Guns 'n Radio	DJ/Smplr	U.S.	1991	$35.00
		In Concert	RS	U.S.	1992	$100.00
	2 CD set.					
Westwood One		In Concert	RS	U.S.	1993	$85.00
	2 CD set. Airdate: 8/2/93.					
Westwood One		In Concert	RS	U.S.	1994	$50.00
	2 CD set. With Candlebox and Cracker, Airdate: 5/23//94					
Westwood One		In Concert-Nu Rock	RS	U.S.	1996	$75.00
	Airdate: 8/12/96.					
Geffen	GED 21825	Interview With Slash	DJ/Intvw	Germany	1993	$35.00
Geffen		Lies	LTD/LP	Australia	1995	$35.00
	Limited gold disc edition.					
Geffen	GED-24450	Making F@*!ing Boxes	LTD/LP	Germany	1993	$90.00
	3CD boxed set with book, pin, and sticker .					
Geffen		Making F@*!ing Boxes	DJ/LP	Holland	1992	$90.00
	"Use Your Illusion" I & II CDs plus interview disc with sticker and patch in 6"x12" box.					
Westwood One		Off the Record	RS	U.S.	1992	$50.00
	Airdate: 8/31/92.					
Westwood One		Off the Record	RS	U.S.	1994	$50.00
	Airdate: 1/24/94.					
Geffen	PRO-CD-4441	On Tour Now	DJ/Smplr	U.S.	1992	$30.00
Geffen	WGNRD 1	Sample Your Illusion	DJ/Smplr	U.K.	1992	$30.00
Geffen	PRO-CD-4328	Selections From Use Your Illusion I and II	DJ/Smplr	U.S.	1991	$18.00
		Slash - Hard Edge Of Rock	RS	U.S.		$120.00
	3 CD set.					
Geffen		Spaghetti Incident?	LTD/LP	Australia	1995	$35.00
	Limited gold disc edition.					
Geffen		Spaghetti Incident?	DJ/LP	Japan	1994	$175.00
	CD, Menu, fork & spoon.					
Westwood One		Superstar Concert	RS	U.S.	1992	$120.00
	2 CD set. Airdate: 8/30/92					
Geffen	GEFD 24415	Use Your Illusion I	LTD/LP	Australia	1992	$50.00
	Limited gold disc edition with custom longbox and T-shirt.					
Geffen		Use Your Illusion I	LTD/LP	Australia	1995	$35.00
	Limited gold disc edition.					
Geffen/MCA	MVCG-43/44	Use Your Illusion I and II	DJ/LP	Japan	1991	$200.00
	2CDs in custom box with press kit.					
Geffen	PRO-CD-4244	Use Your Illusion I and II	DJ/LP	U.S.	1991	$300.00
	Custom 2CD set in oversized double digipak-style package. Limited to 2,000 copies.					
Geffen	GEFD 24420	Use Your Illusion II	LTD/LP	Australia	1992	$50.00
	Limited gold disc edition with custom longbox and T-shirt.					
Geffen		Use Your Illusion II	LTD/LP	Australia	1995	$35.00
	Limited gold disc edition.					
		Singles				
Geffen	PRO-CD-4418	14 Years	CDJ	U.S.	1992	$10.00
Geffen		Ain't It Fun	DJ/CD3	Japan	1993	$20.00
Geffen	GFSTD 62	Ain't It Fun	CD3	U.K.	1993	$10.00
Geffen	FUNCD 1	Ain't It Fun	CDJ	U.K.	1993	$15.00
Geffen	PRO-CD-4579	Ain't It Fun	CDJ	U.S.	1993	$6.00
Geffen	MVCG-13007	Civil War	CD5	Japan	1993	$22.00
Geffen		Civil War	CD5	U.K.	1993	$11.00
Geffen	PRO-CD-4511	Dead Horse	CDJ	U.S.	1993	$7.00
Geffen	GED-21651	Don't Cry	CD5	Germany	1991	$12.00
Geffen	GFSTD 9	Don't Cry	CD5	U.K.	1991	$12.00
Geffen	PRO-CD-4232	Don't Cry	CDJ	U.S.	1991	$15.00
Geffen	PRO-CD-4497	Estranged	CDJ	U.S.	1993	$7.00
Geffen		Estranged	CDJ	U.S.	1993	$65.00
	3 edits, white printed CD in card sleeve.					
Geffen	PRO-CD-4366	Garden of Eden	CDJ	U.S.	1991	$25.00
Geffen		Knockin' on Heaven's Door	CD5	Australia	1992	$15.00
	With poster.					
Geffen	GFSTD 21	Knockin' on Heaven's Door	CD5	U.K.	1992	$10.00
Geffen	PRO-CD-4140	Knockin' on Heaven's Door	CDJ	U.S.	1990	$17.00
Geffen	MVDG-6	Live and Let Die	CD3	Japan	1991	$13.00/$5.00
Geffen	GFSTD 11	Live and Let Die	CD5	U.K.	1991	$20.00
Geffen	PRO-CD-4352	Live and Let Die	CDJ	U.S.	1991	$7.00
Geffen	ROSE CD1	New Rose	CDJ	U.K.		$20.00
Geffen	921316-2	Nightrain	CD3	Germany	1989	$11.00
Geffen	09P3-6178	Nightrain	CD3	Japan	1989	$13.00/$5.00
Geffen	GEF-60CD	Nightrain	CD3	U.K.	1989	$11.00
Geffen	PRO-CD-3625	Nightrain	CDJ	U.S.	1989	$6.00
Geffen		November Rain	CD5	Australia	1992	$15.00
	With poster.					
Geffen		November Rain	CD5	Germany	1992	$10.00
Geffen	MVDG-7	November Rain	CD3	Japan	1992	$13.00/$5.00
Geffen		November Rain	CD5	U.K.	1992	$10.00
Geffen		November Rain	CDJ	U.K.	1992	$25.00
Geffen	PRO-CD-4387	November Rain	CDJ	U.S.	1992	$20.00
Hitmakers	June 19, 1992	November Rain Edits	CDJ	U.S.	1992	$50.00
Geffen	921181-2	Paradise City	CD3	Germany	1989	$12.00
Geffen	10P3-6113	Paradise City	CD3	Japan	1989	$13.00/$5.00
Geffen	GEF 50(CD)	Paradise City	CD3	U.K.	1989	$12.00
Geffen	921271-2	Patience	CD3	Germany	1988	$11.00
Geffen	09P3-6139	Patience	CD3	Japan	1988	$13.00/$5.00
Geffen	GEF-56CD	Patience	CD3	U.K.	1988	$11.00
Geffen	PRO-CD-3437	Patience	CDJ	U.S.	1988	$6.00
Geffen	PRO-CD-4386	Pretty Tied Up	CDJ	U.S.	1992	$15.00
Geffen		Since I Don't Have You	CDJ	Germany	1994	$35.00
Geffen		Since I Don't Have You	CDJ	Japan	1994	$30.00
Geffen	GFSDD 70	Since I Don't Have You	CD5	U.K.	1994	$10.00
Geffen	GFSDXD 70	Since I Don't Have You	CD5	U.K.	1994	$12.00
Geffen	GFSXD 70	Since I Don't Have You	CD5	U.K.	1994	$15.00
Geffen	921243-2	Sweet Child o' Mine	CD3	Germany	1988	$13.00
Geffen	GEF 55CD 921 243-2	Sweet Child o' Mine	CD3	Germany	1989	$15.00
Geffen	10SW-24	Sweet Child o' Mine	CD3	Japan	1988	$13.00/$5.00
Geffen	GEF-55CD	Sweet Child o' Mine	CD3	U.K.	1988	$13.00
Geffen	PRO-CD-3077	Sweet Child o' Mine	CDJ	U.S.	1987	$25.00
Geffen	PRO-CD-3147	Sweet Child o' Mine	CDJ	U.S.	1988	$12.00
		Sympathy for the Devil	CDJ	France	1994	$50.00
Geffen	GEFDS-22005	Sympathy for the Devil	CD5	U.S.	1991	$7.00
Geffen		Sympathy for the Devil	CDJ	U.S.	1994	$35.00
Warner Brothers	WP3 6059	Welcome to the Jungle	CD3	Japan	1987	$13.00/$5.00
Geffen	GEF-47CD	Welcome to the Jungle	CD3	U.K.	1987	$10.00
Geffen	PRO-CD-2668	Welcome to the Jungle	CDJ	U.S.	1987	$15.00
Geffen		Yesterdays	CD5	Australia	1992	$15.00
	With poster.					
Geffen	MVCG-13001	Yesterdays	CD5	Japan	1992	$22.00
Geffen	GFSTD-27	Yesterdays	CD5	U.K.	1992	$10.00
Geffen	PRO-CD-4470	Yesterdays	CDJ	U.S.	1992	$8.00
Geffen	GED-19039	You Could Be Mine	CD5	Germany	1991	$10.00
Geffen	MVDG-3	You Could Be Mine	CD3	Japan	1991	$13.00/$5.00
Geffen	GFSTD 6	You Could Be Mine	CD5	U.K.	1991	$15.00
Geffen	PRO-CD-4235	You Could Be Mine	CDJ	U.S.	1991	$8.00

Gunshot

Label	Catalog Number	Title	Type	Country	Year	Longbox Value / Value
		Singles				
Southern	STORM-40CD	Clear From Present Danger	CD5	U.K.	1991	$8.00

Guru

Label	Catalog Number	Title	Type	Country	Year	Longbox Value / Value
		Singles				
		Feel The Music	CD5	U.K.		$10.00
		Feel The Music	CD5	U.K.		$10.00
	Second version.					
Chrysalis	DPRO-04724	Le Bien, Le Mal	CDJ	U.S.	1993	$2.00
Chrysalis	DPRO-04711	Loungin'	CDJ	U.S.	1993	$2.00
Chrysalis	DPRO-04614	No Time To Play	CDJ	U.S.	1993	$2.00
Capitol	58438	Watch What You Say	CD5	U.S.	1995	$5.00

Guru, Josh

Label	Catalog Number	Title	Type	Country	Year	Longbox Value / Value
		Singles				
BMG	PD-44140	Freaky Dreamer	CD5	Germany	1990	$8.00
ZYX	DST-1057-8	Hallelujah	CD5	Germany	1991	$6.00
RCA	PD-43476	Infinity	CD5	Germany	1990	$8.00
RCA	PD-43476	Infinity	CD5	U.K.	1990	$8.00
RCA	2570-2-RDJ	Infinity	CDJ	U.S.	1990	$2.00
RCA	PD-43648	Who's Law	CD5	Germany	1990	$8.00
RCA	PD-43648	Who's Law	CD5	U.K.	1990	$8.00

Guthrie, Gwen

Label	Catalog Number	Title	Type	Country	Year	Longbox Value / Value
		Singles				
Reprise		Can't Love You Tonight	CDJ	U.S.	1990	$2.00
Reprise	PRO-CD-4332	Miss My Love	CDJ	U.S.	1990	$2.00
Reprise	PRO-CD-4616	Say It Isn't So	CDJ	U.S.	1990	$2.00
Reprise	PRO-CD-4786	Sweet Bitter Love	CDJ	U.S.	1990	$2.00

Gutterball

Label	Catalog Number	Title	Type	Country	Year	Longbox Value / Value
		Full Length				
Mute		Motorcycle Boy	DJ/Smplr	U.S.	1993	$6.00
		Singles				
Mute	8756	Trial Separation Blues	CDJ	U.S.	1993	$2.00

Gutterboy

Singles

Label	Catalog Number	Title	Type	Country	Year	Longbox Value / Value
DGC	PRO-CD-4141	A Rainy Day on Mulberry Street	CDJ	U.S.	1990	$2.00
DGC	PRO-CD-4142	A Rainy Day on Mulberry Street	CDJ	U.S.	1990	$2.00
Mercury	CDP 643	Every Other Night	CDJ	U.S.	1992	$2.00

Guy

Full Length

Label	Catalog Number	Title	Type	Country	Year	Longbox Value / Value
MCA	CD33-1193	Future, The	DJ/LP	U.S.	1990	$8.00

Singles

Label	Catalog Number	Title	Type	Country	Year	Longbox Value / Value
MCA	1542	D-O-G Me Out	CDJ	U.S.	1991	$2.00
MCA	MCSTD-1551	Do Me Right	CD5	U.K.	1991	$8.00
MCA	MCSTD-1528	Her	CD5	U.K.	1991	$8.00
MCA	MCSTD-1575	Her	CD5	U.K.	1991	$8.00
Pioneer	WMD5-4046	I Wanna Get With You	CD3	Japan	1990	$12.00/$3.00
MCA	53931	I Wanna Get With You	CD5	U.S.	1991	$4.00
MCA	1096	I Wanna Get With You	CDJ	U.S.	1991	$2.00
Warner Brothers	WMC5-366	Let's Chill	CD5	Japan	1991	$11.00
MCA	1264	Let's Chill	CDJ	U.S.	1991	$2.00
MCA	MCA5P-2052	Let's Stay Together	CDJ	U.S.	1991	$2.00
	UPT5P35533	Tell Me What You Like	CDJ	U.S.		$2.00

Guy, Buddy

Singles

Label	Catalog Number	Title	Type	Country	Year	Longbox Value / Value
Silvertone	ORECD-25	Damn Right, I've Got the Blues	CD5	U.K.	1991	$10.00
Silvertone	ORECD-30	Mustang Sally	CD5	U.K.	1991	$10.00
Silvertone	ORECD-42	Where Is the Next One	CD5	U.K.	1992	$10.00

Guy Called Gerald

Singles

Label	Catalog Number	Title	Type	Country	Year	Longbox Value / Value
Columbia	AGCGC-2	Automatik	CD5	U.K.	1989	$8.00
Columbia	AGCGC-1	FX	CD5	U.K.	1989	$8.00
Italio-Heat	FFR-0510	Voodoo Ray	CD5	Germany	1989	$8.00
Rham	RCD-8804	Voodoo Ray	CD5	U.K.	1988	$8.00

Guy, Jasmine

Singles

Label	Catalog Number	Title	Type	Country	Year	Longbox Value / Value
Warner Brothers	9 40228-2	Don't Want Money	CD5	U.S.	1990	$4.00
Warner Brothers	PRO-CD-4940	Don't Want Money	CDJ	U.S.	1990	$2.00
Warner Brothers	PRO-CD-4787	Just Want to Hold You	CDJ	U.S.	1990	$2.00
Warner Brothers	9 21597-2	Try Me	CD5	U.S.	1990	$4.00
Warner Brothers	18892-2	Try Me	CD5	U.S.	1990	$4.00
Warner Brothers	PRO-CD-4344	Try Me	CDJ	U.S.	1990	$3.00

Guys Next Door

Singles

Label	Catalog Number	Title	Type	Country	Year	Longbox Value / Value
SBK	05350	I Was Made for You	CDJ	U.S.	1990	$2.00

Gwar

Full Length

Label	Catalog Number	Title	Type	Country	Year	Longbox Value / Value
Metal Blade	26243	America Must Be Destroyed	LP/LB	U.S.		$14.00/$8.00
Metal Blade	45101	Road Behind, The	LP/LB	U.S.		$14.00/$8.00
Metal Blade	26243	Scumdogs of the Earth	LP/LB	U.S.		$14.00/$8.00

Singles

Label	Catalog Number	Title	Type	Country	Year	Longbox Value / Value
Metal Blade	P253905	The Road Behind	CD5	Canada	1994	$15.00

Gypsy Child

Singles

Label	Catalog Number	Title	Type	Country	Year	Longbox Value / Value
King	K12Y-20003	Gypsy Child	CD3	Japan	1988	$12.00/$3.00

Gypsy Rose

Singles

Label	Catalog Number	Title	Type	Country	Year	Longbox Value / Value
RCA	2657-2-RDJ	Poisoned by Love	CDJ	U.S.	1990	$2.00

Gyrl

Singles

Label	Catalog Number	Title	Type	Country	Year	Longbox Value / Value
MCA	55067	Play Another Slow Jam	CD5	U.S.	1995	$5.00

H. Axel

Singles

Label	Catalog Number	Title	Type	Country	Year	Longbox Value / Value
Polygram	873479-2	Oh Well	CD5	Germany	1989	$8.00

H.E.A.L.

Singles

Label	Catalog Number	Title	Type	Country	Year	Longbox Value / Value
Elektra	PRCD 8414-2	Heal Yourself	CDJ	U.S.	1991	$2.00

H.S.A.S.

Full Length

Label	Catalog Number	Title	Type	Country	Year	Longbox Value / Value
Geffen	4023-2	Through the Fire	LP/LB	U.S.		$22.00/$20.00

H Town

Singles

Label	Catalog Number	Title	Type	Country	Year	Longbox Value / Value
Luke	479	Baby I Wanna	CDJ	U.S.	1994	$2.00
Luke	471	Lick U Up	CDJ	U.S.	1993	$2.00

H.W.A.

Singles

Label	Catalog Number	Title	Type	Country	Year	Longbox Value / Value
Jungle	KGBD-008	Supersonic	CD5	U.K.	1992	$8.00

H-Town

Singles

Label	Catalog Number	Title	Type	Country	Year	Longbox Value / Value
	PRO-CD-8005-R	A Thin Line Between Love and Hate	CDJ	U.S.		$2.00

Habit

Singles

Label	Catalog Number	Title	Type	Country	Year	Longbox Value / Value
Virgin	VSCDT-1248	Fly Like an Eagle	CD5	U.K.	1990	$8.00
Virgin	VSCD-1132	Get Back	CD3	U.K.	1990	$8.00
Virgin	VSRCD-1063	Love	CD3	U.K.	1990	$8.00
Virgin	VSCD-1171	Starlight	CD3	U.K.	1990	$8.00

Haddaway

Singles

Label	Catalog Number	Title	Type	Country	Year	Longbox Value / Value
Arista	12648	Life	CD5	U.S.	1994	$5.00
Arista	12576	What is Love	CD5	U.S.	1993	$6.00

Haden, Charlie

Full Length

Label	Catalog Number	Title	Type	Country	Year	Longbox Value / Value
Verve		Quartet West	DJ/Intvw	France	1994	$18.00
Polygram	831673-2	Quartet West	LP	Germany		$12.00

Haden, Charlie & Carla Bley

Full Length

Label	Catalog Number	Title	Type	Country	Year	Longbox Value / Value
ECM	23794-2	Ballad of the Fallen	LP/LB	U.S.†	1985	$14.00/$8.00

Hadley, Tony

Singles

Label	Catalog Number	Title	Type	Country	Year	Longbox Value / Value
EMI	CDEM-234	For Your Blue Eyes Only	CD5	U.K.	1992	$8.00
EMI	CDEM-254	Game of Love	CD5	U.K.	1992	$8.00
EMI	CDEM-222	Lost in Your Love	CD5	U.K.	1992	$8.00

Hagar, Albert

Full Length

Label	Catalog Number	Title	Type	Country	Year	Longbox Value / Value
Star Dust Records		Is This Love	SCDJ	U.S.	1990	$7.00

Hagar, Sammy

Full Length

Label	Catalog Number	Title	Type	Country	Year	Longbox Value / Value
EMI	748431-2	All Night Long	LP	Germany		$20.00
Westwood One		In Concert	RS	U.S.	1994	$50.00
	Airdate: 6/6/94.					
Westwood One		In Concert	RS	U.S.	1995	$50.00
	Airdate: 2/27/95.					
Album Network		In the Studio (Unboxed)	RS	U.S.	1994	$25.00
	Airdate: 4/25/94.					
Capitol	CDP-48432	Live 1980	LP/LB	U.S.		$15.00/$10.00
Capitol	CDP-48434	Musical Chairs	LP/LB	U.S.		$15.00/$10.00
Westwood One		Off the Record	RS	U.S.	1994	$25.00
	Airdate: 5/23/94.					
Capitol	CDP-46471	Rematch & More	LP/LB	U.S.		$15.00/$10.00
Geffen	PRO-CD-2832	Returns Home	DJ/Intvw	U.S.	1987	$16.00
Geffen	GEFD-24144	Sammy Hagar	LP/LB	U.S.	1987	$14.00/$8.00
Capitol	CDP-48433	Street Machine	LP/LB	U.S.		$15.00/$10.00
Geffen	4023-2	Through the Fire	LP/LB	U.S.†	1985	$14.00/$8.00
Geffen	24043-2	VOA	LP/LB	U.S.†	1985	$14.00/$8.00

Singles

Label	Catalog Number	Title	Type	Country	Year	Longbox Value / Value
Geffen	PRO-CD-2750	Give To Live	CDJ	U.S.	1987	$8.00
Geffen	PRO-CD-4616	High Hopes	CDJ	U.S.	1994	$7.00

Hagen, Nina

Singles

Label	Catalog Number	Title	Type	Country	Year	Longbox Value / Value
Mercury	868 625	In My World	CDJ	U.S.	1991	$2.00

Haggard, Merle

Full Length

Label	Catalog Number	Title	Type	Country	Year	Longbox Value / Value
CBS	CK-38203	A Taste of Yesterday's Wine	LP/BP	U.S.†	1985	$14.00/$8.00
Epic		Anthology Sampler	DJ/Smplr	U.S.	1995	$15.00
Epic	EK-37593	Big City	LP/BP	U.S.†	1984	$14.00/$8.00
Epic	EK-39545	His Epic Hits: The First 11	LP/BP	U.S.†	1985	$14.00/$8.00
CBS	CK-37598	Pancho & Lefty	LP/BP	U.S.†	1984	$14.00/$8.00

Singles

Label	Catalog Number	Title	Type	Country	Year	Longbox Value / Value
Epic		When It Rains It Pours	CDJ	U.S.	1995	$2.00

Haig, Paul

Singles

Label	Catalog Number	Title	Type	Country	Year	Longbox Value / Value
Circa	YRCD-47	I Believe in You	CD5	U.K.	1990	$8.00
Circa	YRCD-25	Something Good	CD3	U.K.	1990	$8.00

Hain, Marshall

Singles

Label	Catalog Number	Title	Type	Country	Year	Longbox Value / Value
EMI	CDBET-106	Dancing in the Hall	CD5	U.K.	1992	$8.00

Haindling

Singles

Label	Catalog Number	Title	Type	Country	Year	Longbox Value / Value
Polygramq	867625-2	Liebe	CD5	Germany	1991	$8.00

Hale & Pace

Singles

Label	Catalog Number	Title	Type	Country	Year	Longbox Value / Value
London	LONCD-296	Stonk, The	CD5	U.K.	1991	$8.00

Haley, Bill

Full Length

Label	Catalog Number	Title	Type	Country	Year	Longbox Value / Value
WEA	251722-2	Best of	LP	Germany		$20.00
IMP	PCD-838	Bill Haley and the Comets	LP	U.K.		$20.00
MCA	MCAD-5539	From the Original Master Tapes	LP/LB	U.S.†	1985	$14.00/$8.00
Polygram	821394-2	Rock Around the Clock	LP	Germany		$20.00

Singles

Label	Catalog Number	Title	Type	Country	Year	Longbox Value / Value
WEA	241604-2	Rock Around the Clock	CD5	Germany	1989	$10.00

Half Japanese

Singles

Label	Catalog Number	Title	Type	Country	Year	Longbox Value / Value
APT	TWANG-1CD	Everybody Knows	CD5	U.K.	1991	$8.00

Hall, Aaron

Singles

Label	Catalog Number	Title	Type	Country	Year	Longbox Value / Value
MCA	MCSTD-1632	Don't Be Afraid	CD5	U.K.	1992	$8.00
MCA	54384	Don't Be Afraid	CD5	U.S.	1991	$4.00
MCA	MCA5P-2147	Don't Be Afraid	CDJ	U.S.	1992	$2.00
Salis	2645	Get a Little Funky With Me	CDJ	U.S.	1993	$2.00
Salis	2851	Get a Little Funky With Me	CDJ	U.S.	1993	$2.00
Salis	3014	I Miss You	CDJ	U.S.	1994	$2.00
Salis	2905	Let's Make Love	CDJ	U.S.	1993	$2.00

Hall Aflame

Singles

Label	Catalog Number	Title	Type	Country	Year	Longbox Value / Value
IRS	67061	One Time Winner	CDJ	U.S.	1991	$2.00

Hall, Daryl

Full Length

Label	Catalog Number	Title	Type	Country	Year	Longbox Value / Value
	ODCA-93039	Send Me Soul Power	DJ/Smplr	Japan		$100.00
RCA	886244	Three Hearts in a Happy Ending Machine	LP	Germany	1986	$15.00

Singles

Label	Catalog Number	Title	Type	Country	Year	Longbox Value / Value
RCA	14386-2-RDJ	Dreamtime	CDJ	U.S.	1986	$6.00
		Gloryland	CD5	U.K.	1994	$10.00
		I'm in a Philly Mood	CD5	U.K.	1993	$10.00
		I'm in a Philly Mood	CD5	U.K.	1993	$10.00
	Second version.					
Epic	ESK 5357	I'm in a Philly Mood	CDJ	U.S.	1993	$3.00
Epic	ESCA-5912	Send Me	CDJ	Japan		$20.00

Hall, Jennifer

Singles

Label	Catalog Number	Title	Type	Country	Year	Longbox Value / Value
Warner Brothers	PRO-CD-3071	Ice Cream Days	CDJ	U.S.	1988	$2.00

Hall, Kristen

Singles

Label	Catalog Number	Title	Type	Country	Year	Longbox Value / Value
High St	9313	Empty Promises	CDJ	U.S.	1993	$2.00

Hall, Michael

Singles

Label	Catalog Number	Title	Type	Country	Year	Longbox Value / Value
Dejadisc	72786	Frank Slade's 29th	CD5	U.S.	1994	$5.00

Hall & Oates

Full Length

Label	Catalog Number	Title	Type	Country	Year	Longbox Value / Value
RCA	886326	Along the Red Ledge	LP	Germany		$16.00
RCA	886242	Big Bam Boom	LP	Germany	1985	$16.00

Label	Catalog Number	Title	Type	Country	Year	Longbox Value / Value
RCA	PCD1-5336	Big Bam Boom	LP/BP	U.S.†	1985	$14.00/$8.00
RCA	PCD1-4858	Greatest Hits	LP/BP	U.S.†	1984	$14.00/$8.00
RCA	PCD1-4383	H2O	LP/BP	U.S.†	1984	$14.00/$8.00
RCA	PCD1-7035	Live at the Apollo	LP/BP	U.S.†	1985	$14.00/$8.00
Mobile Fidelity	MFCD-879	Past Times Behind	LP	U.S.		$16.00/$12.00
RCA	886176	Private Eyes	LP	Germany	1984	$16.00
RCA	PCD1-4028	Private Eyes	LP/BP	U.S.†	1984	$14.00/$8.00
Pioneer	PA-8684-077	Rock 'n Soul Live	LD	U.S.	1984	$20.00
Pioneer	PA-8684-077	Rock 'n Soul Live	LD	U.S.	1991	$30.00
	Digital audio.					
Pioneer	PA86-M034	Seven Big Ones	8"LD	U.S.	1984	$10.00
RCA	POTD-1123	Special Sampler	DJ/Smplr	Japan		$100.00
Delta	11094	Together	LP	Germany		$16.00
RCA	886211	Voices	LP	Germany	1985	$16.00
Mobile Fidelity		Voices	LP/LB	U.S.		$25.00/$22.00
RCA	PCD1-3646	Voices	LP/BP	U.S.†	1985	$14.00/$8.00
RCA	886025	X-Static	LP	Germany		$16.00
		Singles				
Arista	663877	Don't Hold Back Your Love	CD5	Germany	1991	$10.00
Arista	ASCD-2151	Don't Hold Back Your Love	CDJ	U.S.	1990	$2.00
Arista	ASCD-2157	Don't Hold Back Your Love	CDJ	U.S.	1990	$2.00
Arista	661730	Downtown Life	CD5	U.K.	1988	$10.00
RCA	B20D 51010	Everything Your Heart Desires	CD5	Japan	1988	$15.00
Arista	659869	Everything Your Heart Desires	CD5	U.K.	1988	$10.00
Arista	663980	Everywhere I Look	CD5	U.K.	1990	$10.00
Pioneer	09P3-6150	Love Train	CD3	Japan	1989	$12.00/$4.00
Sire	PRO-CD-3505	Love Train	CDJ	U.S.	1989	$2.00
RCA	PD-49465	Maneater	CD3	Germany	1989	$10.00
RCA	PD-49465	Maneater	CD3	U.K.	1989	$10.00
Arista	663600	So Close	CD5	Germany	1990	$10.00
Arista	BVDA-2	So Close	CD3	Japan	1990	$12.00/$4.00
Arista	663600	So Close	CD5	U.K.	1990	$10.00
Arista	ASCD-2084	So Close	CDJ	U.S.	1990	$2.00
Arista	663862	Starting All Over Again	CD5	Germany	1991	$10.00
Arista		Starting All Over Again	CD3	Japan	1990	$12.00/$4.00

Hall, Terry

Label	Catalog Number	Title	Type	Country	Year	Longbox Value / Value
		Singles				
Chyrsalis	CHSCD-3381	Missing	CD5	U.K.	1989	$8.00
Chyrsalis	662578	Missing	CD5	U.K.	1989	$8.00

Hall, Tom T.

Label	Catalog Number	Title	Type	Country	Year	Longbox Value / Value
		Full Length				
Polygram	832202-2	Classic	LP	Germany		$10.00

Halliday, Toni

Label	Catalog Number	Title	Type	Country	Year	Longbox Value / Value
		Singles				
Anxious	ANX-005CD	Love Attraction	CD5	U.K.	1988	$8.00
Anxious	ANX-009CD	Time Turns Around	CD5	U.K.	1989	$8.00
Anxious	ANX-003CD	Weekday	CD5	U.K.	1988	$8.00
Anxious	ANX-013CD	Woman in Mind	CD5	U.K.	1989	$8.00

Halligan, Bob

Label	Catalog Number	Title	Type	Country	Year	Longbox Value / Value
		Singles				
Atco	PRCD-3923-2	Could've Been You	CDJ	U.S.	1991	$2.00

Hallyday, David

Label	Catalog Number	Title	Type	Country	Year	Longbox Value / Value
		Singles				
Intercord	827 329	Move	CD5	Germany	1988	$8.00
Canyon	S10Y-1009	Move	CD3	Japan	1988	$12.00/$3.00
Polygram	868291-2	Ooh La La	CD5	Germany	1991	$8.00
Scotti Brothers	PZCD 108	Tears of the Earth	CD5	U.K.	1991	$8.00
Scotti Brothers	NSK 5279	Tears of the Earth	CD5	U.S.	1990	$3.00
Canyon	S10Y-1039	Your Power of Love	CD3	Japan	1989	$12.00/$3.00

Hallyday, Johnny

Label	Catalog Number	Title	Type	Country	Year	Longbox Value / Value
		Full Length				
Vogue	600095	Souvenirs Souvenirs	LP	Germany		$10.00

Halo, James

Label	Catalog Number	Title	Type	Country	Year	Longbox Value / Value
		Singles				
Epic	655730-3	Baby	CD3	Germany	1990	$8.00
Epic	CDHALO-3	Baby	CD5	U.K.	1990	$8.00
Epic	655523-3	Could Have Told You So	CD3	Germany	1990	$8.00
Epic	CDHALO-2	Could Have Told You So	CD5	U.K.	1990	$8.00
Epic	CPHALO-2	Could Have Told You So	CD5	U.K.	1990	$8.00
Epic	CDHALO-4	Magic Hour	CD5	U.K.	1990	$8.00
Epic	CDHALO-1	Wanted	CD5	U.K.	1989	$8.00
Epic	CDHALO-5	Wanted	CD5	U.K.	1990	$8.00

Hamill, Claire

Label	Catalog Number	Title	Type	Country	Year	Longbox Value / Value
		Full Length				
Polygram	830508-2	Voices	LP	Germany		$12.00
Penguin	PENGUINCD-1	Someday We Will All Be Together	CD5	U.K.	1990	$8.00

Hamilton, Scott

Label	Catalog Number	Title	Type	Country	Year	Longbox Value / Value
		Full Length				
Concord Jazz	CCD-4254	The Second Set	LP/LB	U.S.†	1985	$14.00/$8.00

Hamilton, Zemya

Label	Catalog Number	Title	Type	Country	Year	Longbox Value / Value
		Singles				
WEA	9031-71604-2	Going Through	CD5	Germany	1991	$8.00

Hamm, Stuart

Label	Catalog Number	Title	Type	Country	Year	Longbox Value / Value
		Singles				
Relativity	RPROCD-0121	Lone Star	CDJ	U.S.	1991	$15.00
Relativity	PROCD-0121	Lone Star	CDJ	U.S.	1991	$15.00
	With autographed Texas flag.					

Hammer, Jack

Label	Catalog Number	Title	Type	Country	Year	Longbox Value / Value
		Singles				
ZYX	DST-6750-8	Time Is Movin'	CD5	Germany	1992	$6.00

Hammer, Jan

Label	Catalog Number	Title	Type	Country	Year	Longbox Value / Value
		Singles				
MCA	DMCAT-1415	Cancer Theme	CD5	U.K.	1990	$8.00
Eastwest	257398-2	Eurocops	CD5	Germany	1989	$8.00
MCA	DMCA-1305	Runner	CD3	U.K.	1989	$8.00
MCA	257680-2	Too Much To Lose	CD3	Germany	1989	$8.00
MCA	257680-2	Too Much To Lose	CD3	U.K.	1989	$8.00
MCA	DMCA-1200	Tubbs And Valerie	CD3	U.K.	1989	$8.00

Hammer (M.C. Hammer)

Label	Catalog Number	Title	Type	Country	Year	Longbox Value / Value
		Full Length				
Capitol	DPRO-79056	2 Legit 2 Quit	DJ/LP	U.S.	1991	$15.00
Capitol	C2-98083	2 Legit 2 Quit	LTD/LP	U.S.	1991	$15.00
Pioneer Artists	PA-92-430	2 Legit 2 Quit	LD	U.S.	1992	$30.00
Capitol	DPRO-79651	Hits	DJ/Smplr	U.S.	1990	$8.00
	PCD-247	Limited Edition	DJ/Smplr	Japan		$50.00
Pioneer Artists	PA-90-339	Non Stop	LD	U.S.	1991	$30.00
		Singles				
Capitol	TODP-2326	2 Legit 2 Quit	CD3	Japan	1990	$13.00/$4.00
Capitol	TOCP-7070	2 Legit 2 Quit	CD5	Japan	1990	$20.00
Capitol	TOCP-7468	2 Legit 2 Quit	CD5	Japan	1990	$20.00
Capitol	C2 15791	2 Legit 2 Quit	CD5	U.S.	1990	$5.00
Capitol	DPRO-790272	2 Legit 2 Quit	CDJ	U.S.	1991	$3.00
EMI	204631-2	Addams Groove	CD5	Germany	1992	$10.00
Toshiba	TODP-2342	Addams Groove	CD3	Japan	1992	$12.00/$4.00
Capitol	DPRO-79029	Addams Groove	CDJ	U.S.	1991	$3.00
Capitol	CDCL-650	Don't Pass Me By	CD5	U.K.	1992	$10.00
Capitol	DPRO-79196	Don't Pass Me By	CDJ	U.S.	1991	$3.00
Capitol	DPRO-79236	Don't Pass Me By	CDJ	U.S.	1991	$3.00
Wea	CD41473	Don't Stop	CD5	Canada	1994	$8.00
Capitol	DPRO-79093	Gaining Momentum	CDJ	U.S.	1991	$3.00
Capitol	DPRO-79465	Gaining Momentum	CDJ	U.S.	1991	$3.00
	PRO-CD-7981-R	Goin' Up Yonder	CDJ	U.S.	1995	$2.00
Capitol	TODP-2341	Good To Go	CD3	Japan	1992	$12.00/$4.00
Capitol	TODP-2369	Good To Go	CD3	Japan	1992	$13.00/$4.00
Capitol	DPRO-79136	Good To Go	CDJ	U.S.	1990	$3.00
Capitol	204055-2	Have You Seen Her	CD5	Germany	1990	$10.00
Capitol	TODP-2197	Have You Seen Her	CD3	Japan	1990	$12.00/$4.00
Capitol	CDCL-590	Have You Seen Her	CD5	U.K.	1990	$10.00
Capitol	DPRO-79146	Have You Seen Her	CDJ	U.S.	1990	$3.00
Capitol	203804-2	Help the Children	CD5	Germany	1990	$10.00
Capitol	CDCL-564	Help the Children	CD5	U.K.	1990	$10.00
Capitol	DPRO-79892	Help the Children	CDJ	U.S.	1990	$3.00
Capitlol	204200-2	Here Comes the Hammer	CD5	Germany	1990	$10.00
Capitlol	204201-2	Here Comes the Hammer	CD5	Germany	1990	$10.00
Capitol	CDCL-610	Here Comes the Hammer	CD5	U.K.	1990	$10.00
Capitol	C2 15585	Here Comes the Hammer	CD5	U.S.	1990	$5.00
Capitol	DPRO-79445	Here Comes the Hammer	CDJ	U.S.	1990	$3.00
Giant	PRO-CD-6695	It's All Good	CDJ	U.S.	1993	$3.00
Giant	18271	It's All Good	CD5	U.S.	1994	$5.00
Capitol	204021-2	Pray	CD5	Germany	1990	$10.00
Capitol	204015-2	Pray	CD5	Germany	1990	$10.00
Capitol	204151-2	Pray	CD5	Germany	1990	$10.00
Capitol	CDCL-599	Pray	CD5	U.K.	1990	$10.00
Capitol	C2 15661	Pray	CD5	U.S.	1990	$5.00
Capitol	DPRO-79285	Pray	CDJ	U.S.	1990	$3.00
Captiol		Pray	CDJ	U.S.	1990	$3.00
	Second version.					
Warner Brothers	18218	Pumps and a Bump	CD5	U.S.	1994	$5.00
Giant	PRO-CD-6680	Pumps and a Bump	CDJ	U.S.	1994	$3.00
Giant	PRO-CD-6879	Pumps and a Bump	CDJ	U.S.	1994	$3.00
Capitol	204426-2	They Put Me in the Mix	CD5	Germany	1991	$10.00
Capitol	CDCL-607	They Put Me in the Mix	CD5	U.K.	1991	$10.00
Capitol	C2 15749	They Put Me in the Mix	CD5	U.S.	1991	$5.00
Capitol	TODP-2365	This Is the Way We Roll	CD3	Japan	1992	$13.00/$4.00
Capitol	C2 15792	This Is the Way We Roll	CD5	U.S.	1991	$5.00
Capitol	DPRO-79006	This Is the Way We Roll	CDJ	U.S.	1991	$3.00
Capitol	DPRO-79028	This Is the Way We Roll	CDJ	U.S.	1991	$3.00
Capitol	203416-3	Turn This Mutha Out	CD3	Germany	1989	$10.00
Capitol	203925-2	U Can't Touch This	CD5	Germany	1990	$10.00
Capitol	203990-2	U Can't Touch This	CD5	Germany	1990	$10.00
Capitol	TOCP-6642	U Can't Touch This	CD3	Japan	1990	$13.00/$3.00
Capitol	CDCL-578	U Can't Touch This	CD5	U.K.	1990	$10.00
Capitol	DPRO-79071	U Can't Touch This	CDJ	U.S.	1990	$3.00
Capitol	201339-2	Yo! Sweetness	CD5	Germany	1990	$10.00
Capitol	TODP-2284	Yo! Sweetness	CD3	Japan	1990	$12.00/$4.00
Capitol	CDCL-616	Yo! Sweetness	CD5	U.K.	1990	$10.00

Hammer, Mike

Label	Catalog Number	Title	Type	Country	Year	Longbox Value / Value
		Singles				
Canyon	S10Y-1040	Divine	CD3	Japan	1989	$13.00/$4.00

Hammerbox

Label	Catalog Number	Title	Type	Country	Year	Longbox Value / Value
		Singles				
A&M	31458 8119	Hole	CDJ	U.S.	1993	$2.00

Hammond, Albert

Label	Catalog Number	Title	Type	Country	Year	Longbox Value / Value
		Singles				
Columbia	654605-3	It Never Rains in Southern	CD3	Germany	1989	$8.00
Columbia	654605-3	It Never Rains in Southern	CD3	U.K.	1989	$8.00
Epic	655459-3	Under the Christmas Tree	CD3	Germany	1989	$8.00
Epic	655492-2	Under the Christmas Tree	CD5	U.K.	1989	$8.00
Columbia	655394-3	Where You Were	CD3	Germany	1989	$8.00

Hammond, John

Label	Catalog Number	Title	Type	Country	Year	Longbox Value / Value
		Full Length				
		House of Blues	RS	U.S.	1996	$50.00
	2 CD set. Airdate: 1/21/96.					

Hammond, Johnny

Label	Catalog Number	Title	Type	Country	Year	Longbox Value / Value
		Full Length				
Columbia	450560-2	Higher Ground	LP	Germany		$10.00
		Singles				
Charisma	092	I've Got Love If You Want It	CDJ	U.S.	1992	$2.00
Pointblank	14136	Just Your Fool	CDJ	U.S.	1993	$2.00

Hampton, Bruce

Label	Catalog Number	Title	Type	Country	Year	Longbox Value / Value
		Full Length				
Capricorn	5248	A Conversation With	DJ/Intvw	U.S.	1991	$10.00
		Singles				
Capricorn	6472	No Ego's Under Water	CDJ	U.S.	1993	$2.00
Capricorn	5464	Time Is Free	CDJ	U.S.	1992	$2.00
Capricorn	5464	Working On A Building	CDJ	U.S.	1992	$2.00

Hampton, Lionel

Label	Catalog Number	Title	Type	Country	Year	Longbox Value / Value
		Full Length				
GML	CD-5013	Mack the Knife	LTD/LP	Japan		$40.00
	Gold disc.					
Aris	880543	Presents Buddy Rich	LP	Germany		$15.00
Aris	880542	Presents Gerry Mulligan	LP	Germany		$15.00
		Singles				
Alfa	10R3-12	Flying Home	CD3	Japan	1988	$12.00/$3.00

Han-Na

Label	Catalog Number	Title	Type	Country	Year	Longbox Value / Value
		Singles				
Invitation	VICL-12003	Mama	CD5	Japan	1990	$10.00

Hancock, Herbie

Label	Catalog Number	Title	Type	Country	Year	Longbox Value / Value
		Full Length				
Sony	38DP-39	Direct Step	LP	Japan		$30.00
CBS	CD-83491	Feets Don't Fail Me Now	LP	Germany		$20.00

Label	Catalog Number	Title	Type	Country	Year	Longbox Value / Value
CBS	CK-35764	Feets Don't Fail Me Now	LP/LB	U.S.†	1985	$14.00/$8.00
CBS	CK-38814	Future Shock	LP/LB	U.S.†	1985	$14.00/$8.00
CBS	CD-65928	Headhunters	LP	Germany		$20.00
CBS	CK-32731	Headhunters	LP/LB	U.S.†	1985	$14.00/$8.00
CBS	6619-80	Herbie Hancock and the Rocket Band	LD	U.S.	1984	$35.00
		New Standard, The	DJ/Smplr	U.S.		$6.00
Blue Note		Prisoner and My Point of View, The	LTD/LP	U.S.	1995	$19.00
CBS	CK-39478	Sound System	LP/LB	U.S.†	1985	$14.00/$8.00
Sony	38DP-38	VSOP the Quintet	LP	Japan		$30.00

Singles

Label	Catalog Number	Title	Type	Country	Year	Longbox Value / Value
Columbia	CSK 1241	Beat Wise	CDJ	U.S.	1988	$2.00
Columbia	651650-2	Rockit	CD3	Germany	1988	$10.00
Columbia	651650-2	Rockit	CD3	U.K.	1988	$10.00
Old Gold	OG-6502	Rockit	CD5	U.K.	1990	$10.00
	SACD1177	Selections From "New Standard"	CDJ	U.S.		$6.00
Columbia	651432-9	Vibe Alive	CD5	Germany	1988	$10.00
Columbia	12EP-8002	Vibe Alive	CD3	Japan	1988	$12.00/$4.00
Columbia	651432-9	Vibe Alive	CD5	U.K.	1988	$10.00
Columbia	CSK 1079	Vibe Alive	CDJ	U.S.	1988	$2.00

Hand of Fate

Singles

Label	Catalog Number	Title	Type	Country	Year	Longbox Value / Value
		Good Life	CDJ	U.S.		$2.00

Hang Ups

Singles

Label	Catalog Number	Title	Type	Country	Year	Longbox Value / Value
Clean	89250	Comin' Through	CD5	U.S.	1993	$4.00
Clean	036	Waiting	CDJ	U.S.	1993	$2.00

Hangmen

Singles

Label	Catalog Number	Title	Type	Country	Year	Longbox Value / Value
Capitol	DPRO-79718	Rotten Sunday	CDJ	U.S.	1989	$2.00

Hanoi Rocks

Full Length

Label	Catalog Number	Title	Type	Country	Year	Longbox Value / Value
Uzi	PRO-CD-3738	Dim Sum	DJ/Smplr	U.S.	1989	$10.00

Singles

Label	Catalog Number	Title	Type	Country	Year	Longbox Value / Value
Uzi	PRO-CD-3738	Malibu Beach	CDJ	U.S.	1989	$3.00

Hanselmann, David

Singles

Label	Catalog Number	Title	Type	Country	Year	Longbox Value / Value
EMI	203898-2	Go Get the Cup	CD5	Germany	1990	$8.00
Intercord	825 305	Holy Water	CD5	Germany	1991	$8.00
Intercord	810 337	Turn Around	CD5	Germany	1990	$8.00

Hanta, Yo

Singles

Label	Catalog Number	Title	Type	Country	Year	Longbox Value / Value
ZYX	6266-8	Joker	CD5	Germany	1989	$6.00

Happy Mondays

Singles

Label	Catalog Number	Title	Type	Country	Year	Longbox Value / Value
Elektra	PRCD 8671-2	Angel	CDJ	U.S.	1992	$2.00
Factory	FACD-302	Groovy Afro	CD5	U.K.	1990	$9.00
Elektra	60945	Hallelujah	CD5	U.S.	1990	$5.00
Elektra	PRCD 8160-2	Hallelujah	CDJ	U.S.	1990	$2.00
Factory	POCD-1072	Judge Fudge	CD5	Japan	1992	$12.00
Factory	869243-2	Kinky Afro	CD5	Germany	1990	$9.00
London	POCD-1034	Kinky Afro	CD5	Japan	1990	$12.00
Factory	FACD 302	Kinky Afro	CD5	U.K.	1990	$9.00
Elektra	PRCD 8254-2	Kinky Afro	CDJ	U.S.	1990	$2.00
Factory	869319-2	Loose Fit	CD5	Germany	1991	$9.00
Factory	FACD-312	Loose Fit	CD5	U.K.	1991	$9.00
Elektra	PRCD 8382-2	Loose Fit	CDJ	U.S.	1990	$2.00
Elektra	PRCD 8310-2	Loose Fit	CDJ	U.S.	1991	$2.00
Factory	FACD-242R	Madchester	CD5	U.K.	1990	$9.00
Factory	FACD-242	Madchester	CD5	U.K.	1990	$9.00
Strange Frt	SFPSCD-077	Peel Sessions	CD5	U.K.	1990	$9.00
Polygram	869411-2	Step On	CD5	Germany	1990	$9.00
London	POCD-1048	Step On	CD3	Japan	1991	$13.00/$4.00
Factory	FACD-272	Step On	CD5	U.K.	1990	$9.00
Elektra	PRCD 8192-2	Step On	CDJ	U.S.	1991	$2.00
Elektra	PRCD 8309-2	Step On	CDJ	U.S.	1991	$2.00
Factory	FACD-362	Stinkin' Thinkin'	CD5	U.K.	1992	$9.00
Elektra	PRCD 8634-2	Stinkin' Thinkin'	CDJ	U.S.	1992	$2.00
ffrr	FACD-372	Sunshine And Love	CD5	U.K.	1992	$9.00
Elektra	66353	Sunshine And Love	CD5	U.S.	1992	$5.00
Factory	FACD 232	W.F.L.	CD5	U.K.	1989	$9.00
Rough Trade	CD10-264	Wrote for Luck	CD5	Germany	1988	$9.00
Columbia	CY-5027	Wrote for Luck	CD5	Japan	1989	$12.00
Factory	FACD-232	Wrote for Luck	CD5	U.K.	1989	$9.00
Elektra	PRCD 8068-2	Wrote for Luck	CDJ	U.S.	1989	$2.00

Happyhead

Singles

Label	Catalog Number	Title	Type	Country	Year	Longbox Value / Value
EastWest	PRCD 4602-2	Digital Love Thing	CDJ	U.S.	1992	$2.00
EastWest	PRCD 4631-2	Digital Love Thing	CDJ	U.S.	1992	$2.00
Atlantic	7567-96196-2	Fabulous	CD5	Germany	1991	$9.00
EastWest	A-8594	Fabulous	CD5	U.K.	1991	$9.00
EastWest	96196	Fabulous	CD5	U.S.	1992	$4.00
EastWest	PRCD 4433-2	Fabulous	CDJ	U.S.	1992	$2.00

Harajuku

Singles

Label	Catalog Number	Title	Type	Country	Year	Longbox Value / Value
Zyx	66020	Can You Feel the Love	CD5	U.S.	1994	$5.00
ZYX	6677	Phantom of the Opera	CD5	Germany	1993	$6.00
Zyx	6677	Phantom of the Opera	CD5	U.S.	1994	$5.00

Hard Cops

Singles

Label	Catalog Number	Title	Type	Country	Year	Longbox Value / Value
Interscope	A-8608CD	Back in Black	CD5	U.K.	1992	$8.00
Interscope	PRCD 4137-2	Hard Cops	CDJ	U.S.	1991	$2.00

Hardcastle, Paul

Singles

Label	Catalog Number	Title	Type	Country	Year	Longbox Value / Value
Crush	ONE-6905	Are You Ready	CD5	U.K.	1989	$8.00
Victor	VIDP-48	Don't Be Shy	CD3	Japan	1993	$13.00/$4.00
Chrysalis	PAULCD-5	Forty Years	CD5	U.K.	1988	$8.00
ZYX	6434-8	Rainforest '90	CD5	Germany	1990	$8.00
Chrysalis	880859	Walk in the Night	CD5	Germany	1988	$8.00
Chrysalis	PAULCD-4	Walk in the Night	CD5	U.K.	1988	$8.00

Hardford, Chris

Singles

Label	Catalog Number	Title	Type	Country	Year	Longbox Value / Value
Elektra	PRCD 8631-2	Living End	CDJ	U.S.	1992	$2.00
Elektra	PRCD 8644-2	Road With You	CDJ	U.S.	1992	$2.00

Hardin, Eddie

Full Length

Label	Catalog Number	Title	Type	Country	Year	Longbox Value / Value
Polygram	830509-2	Dawn 'Til Dusk	LP	Germany		$12.00

Harding, John Wesley

Full Length

Label	Catalog Number	Title	Type	Country	Year	Longbox Value / Value
Sire	PRO-CD-4698	Collected Stories 1990-1991	DJ/Smplr	U.S.	1991	$15.00
Mod Lang		Dynablob	LTD/LP	U.S.	1995	$18.00
Limited Fan Club release.						
Sire	PRO-CD-5695	Why We Fight	DJ/LP	U.S.	1992	$10.00

Singles

Label	Catalog Number	Title	Type	Country	Year	Longbox Value / Value
Sire	PRO-CD-4087	Cathy's New Clown	CDJ	U.S.	1990	$2.00
Sire	PRO-CD-4773	Crystal Blue Persuasion	CDJ	U.S.	1990	$2.00
WEA	W-9531CD	Dark Dark Heart	CD5	U.K.	1990	$10.00
WEA	W-9749CD	Devil in Me, The	CD5	U.K.	1990	$10.00
Sire	PRO-CD-3893	Devil in Me, The	CDJ	U.S.	1990	$2.00
Sire	PRO-CD-5636	Kill the Messenger	CDJ	U.S.	1992	$2.00
	PRO-CD-7180	Other People's Failure	CDJ	U.S.		$6.00
WEA	W-0007CD	Person You Are, The	CD5	U.K.	1991	$10.00
Sire	PRO-CD-4700	Person You Are, The	CDJ	U.S.	1990	$2.00
Sire	PRO-CD-4498	Sacred Guns/If You Have	CDJ	U.S.	1990	$7.00

Hardline

Full Length

Label	Catalog Number	Title	Type	Country	Year	Longbox Value / Value
		In Concert	RS	U.S.	1992	$35.00
With Electric Boy & Mr. Big, Airdate: 11/23/92.						
MCA	MCD-30094	Can't Find My Way	CD5	U.K.	1992	$8.00
MCA	MVDM-19	Hot Cherie	CD3	Japan	1992	$12.00/$3.00
MCA	MCA5P 2307	Hot Cherie	CDJ	U.S.	1992	$2.00
MCA	MCA5P 2338	Hot Cherie	CDJ	U.S.	1992	$2.00
MCA	MVDM-27	Takin' Me Down	CD3	Japan	1992	$12.00/$3.00
MCA	MCA5P 2207	Takin' Me Down	CDJ	U.S.	1992	$2.00

Hardy, Francoise

Singles

Label	Catalog Number	Title	Type	Country	Year	Longbox Value / Value
Vogue	191045	Suzanne	CD5	Germany	1992	$8.00
Vogue	191044	Tu Verras	CD5	Germany	1992	$8.00

Harket, Morten

Full Length

Label	Catalog Number	Title	Type	Country	Year	Longbox Value / Value
Warner Brothers		Poetenes Evangelium	LTD/LP	Germany	1995	$50.00

Singles

Label	Catalog Number	Title	Type	Country	Year	Longbox Value / Value
Warner Brothers	W0304CD-X	A Kind of Christmas Card	CD5	U.K.	1995	$10.00
		Heaven's Not for Saints	CD5	U.K.	1996	$10.00

Harle, John

Singles

Label	Catalog Number	Title	Type	Country	Year	Longbox Value / Value
Jungle	KGBD-004	Flying	CD5	U.K.	1992	$8.00

Harley, Bill

Full Length

Label	Catalog Number	Title	Type	Country	Year	Longbox Value / Value
A&M	0424	You're in Trouble	LP/LB	U.S.		$12.00/$7.00

Harloff, Fabian

Singles

Label	Catalog Number	Title	Type	Country	Year	Longbox Value / Value
Columbia	655380-3	I Wanna Go Where Love Goes	CD3	Germany	1989	$8.00
WEA	9031-74349-2	Small Town Girl	CD5	Germany	1991	$8.00
Columbia	654582-3	You Light Up My Life	CD3	Germany	1989	$8.00

Harlow

Singles

Label	Catalog Number	Title	Type	Country	Year	Longbox Value / Value
Reprise	PRO-CD-3961	Chain Reaction	CDJ	U.S.	1990	$2.00
Reprise	PRO-CD-4384	When You Love Someone	CDJ	U.S.	1990	$2.00

Harmonicats

Full Length

Label	Catalog Number	Title	Type	Country	Year	Longbox Value / Value
Time Warner Sound Exchange		22 Legendary Hits	LP	U.S.	1995	$16.00

Harmony

Singles

Label	Catalog Number	Title	Type	Country	Year	Longbox Value / Value
Virgin	3727	Your Love Ain't Right	CDJ	U.S.	1991	$2.00

Harmony Innocents

Singles

Label	Catalog Number	Title	Type	Country	Year	Longbox Value / Value
Quality	QALCD626P	That's What I Like	CDJ	U.S.		$3.00

Harnen, Jimmy

Singles

Label	Catalog Number	Title	Type	Country	Year	Longbox Value / Value
Columbia	655026-2	Where Are You Now	CD5	U.K.	1989	$8.00

Harp, Everette

Singles

Label	Catalog Number	Title	Type	Country	Year	Longbox Value / Value
EMI	DPRO-79310	Let's Wait Awhile	CDJ	U.S.	1992	$2.00
EMI	DPRO-79628	More Than You'll Ever Know	CDJ	U.S.	1992	$2.00

Harper, Ben

Full Length

Label	Catalog Number	Title	Type	Country	Year	Longbox Value / Value
	DPRO-12800	Fight for Your Mind	DJ/Smplr	U.S.		$8.00

Singles

Label	Catalog Number	Title	Type	Country	Year	Longbox Value / Value
	DPRO-1410	Don't Take That	CDJ	U.S.		$3.00
Virgin	14096	Four Songs	CDJ	U.S.	1993	$6.00
	DPRO-12814	Ground on Down	CDJ	U.S.		$3.00

Harper, Billie

Full Length

Label	Catalog Number	Title	Type	Country	Year	Longbox Value / Value
Denon	CD-7007	Soran-Bushi	LP/LB	U.S.†	1985	$14.00/$8.00

Harper Brothers

Full Length

Label	Catalog Number	Title	Type	Country	Year	Longbox Value / Value
Vereve	HAR-2	You Can Hide Inside the Music	DJ/LP	U.S.	1992	$12.00

Harper, Roy

Full Length

Label	Catalog Number	Title	Type	Country	Year	Longbox Value / Value
IRS		Once	LP/LB	U.S.		$14.00/$8.00

Harrell, Grady

Singles

Label	Catalog Number	Title	Type	Country	Year	Longbox Value / Value
RCA	9010-2-Dj	Fun	CDJ	U.S.	1989	$2.00

Harriet

Singles

Label	Catalog Number	Title	Type	Country	Year	Longbox Value / Value
Eastwest	9031-73813-2	Temple of Love	CD5	Germany	1989	$9.00
Eastwest	WMC5-393	Temple of Love	CD5	Japan	1989	$10.00
Eastwest	YZ-505CD	Temple of Love	CD5	U.K.	1989	$9.00
Eastwest	PRCD 3701-2	Temple of Love	CDJ	U.S.	1990	$2.00
Eastwest	WMC5-4060	Woman to Man	CD5	Japan	1991	$2.00
Eastwest	YZ-535CD	Woman to Man	CD5	U.K.	1990	$9.00

Harris, Dana

Singles

Label	Catalog Number	Title	Type	Country	Year	Longbox Value / Value
WEA	171425-2	My World Is Empty Without You	CD5	Germany	1991	$8.00

Harris, Emmylou

Full Length

Label	Catalog Number	Title	Type	Country	Year	Longbox Value / Value
Warner Brothers	9 25205-2	Ballad of Sally Rose, The	LP/LB	U.S.†	1985	$14.00/$8.00
WEA	925791-2	Duets	LP	Germany		$25.00
WEA	925791-2	Duets	LP	U.K.		$25.00
WEA	38258	Emmylou Harris & Nashramblers	LD	U.S.	1992	$30.00
Elektra/Asylum		Interview & Music	DJ/Intvw	U.S.	1995	$15.00
Warner Brothers	9 3258-2	Profile	LP/LB	U.S.†	1984	$14.00/$8.00
Warner Brothers	9 25161-2	Profile II	LP/LB	U.S.†	1985	$14.00/$8.00
WEA	925352-2	Thirteen	LP	Germany		$23.00
Warner Brothers	9 23961-2	White Shoes	LP/LB	U.S.†	1984	$14.00/$8.00

Singles

Label	Catalog Number	Title	Type	Country	Year	Longbox Value / Value
Reprise	PRO-CD-4002	Gulf Coast Highway	CDJ	U.S.	1990	$3.00
Reprise	PRO-CD-3370	Heartbreak Hill	CDJ	U.S.	1988	$3.00
Reprise	PRO-CD-4400	Never Be Anyone Else But You	CDJ	U.S.	1990	$3.00
Warner Brothers	WPDP-6299	Slow Dancer	CD3	Japan	1992	$12.00/$4.00
Reprise		Wheels of Love	CDJ	U.S.		$3.00
	PRCD 9505	Wrecking Ball	CDJ	U.S.		$3.00

Harris, Hugh

Singles

Label	Catalog Number	Title	Type	Country	Year	Longbox Value / Value
Capitol	CDCL-541	Alice	CD5	U.K.	1989	$8.00
Capitol	CDCL-563	Mr. Woman Loves Mr. Man	CD5	U.K.	1989	$8.00
Capitol	CDCL-575	Rhythm of Life	CD5	U.K.	1990	$8.00

Harris, Robin

Full Length

Label	Catalog Number	Title	Type	Country	Year	Longbox Value / Value
Wing	SBP 883	Special Radio Edits From Comedy	DJ/Smplr	U.S.	1990	$6.00

Harris, Rolf

Singles

Label	Catalog Number	Title	Type	Country	Year	Longbox Value / Value
EMI	CDEM-210	Sun Arise	CD5	U.K.	1991	$8.00

Harris, Sam

Full Length

Label	Catalog Number	Title	Type	Country	Year	Longbox Value / Value
Motown	6103-MD	Sam Harris	LP/BP	U.S.†	1985	$14.00/$8.00

Harris, Simon

Singles

Label	Catalog Number	Title	Type	Country	Year	Longbox Value / Value
ffrr	FCD-1016	Another Monster Jam	CD5	U.K.	1989	$8.00
Polygram	886294-2	Bass	CD5	Germany	1988	$8.00
Polygram	886294-2	Bass	CD5	U.K.	1988	$8.00
BCM	20473	Don't Stop the Music	CD5	Germany	1990	$8.00
Polygram	886343-2	Here Comes	CD5	Germany	1988	$8.00
ffrr	FCD-106	(I've Got Your) Pleasure Control	CD5	U.K.	1989	$8.00
BCM	20398	Ragga House	CD5	Germany	1990	$8.00
Pinnacle	SMASH-9CD	Ragga House	CD5	U.K.	1990	$8.00
Avex Trax	AVDD-20023	Super Mario Land	CD3	Japan	1992	$13.00/$4.00
BCM	20494	Time	CD5	Germany	1990	$8.00

Harrison, George

Full Length

Label	Catalog Number	Title	Type	Country	Year	Longbox Value / Value
		Bangladesh	DJ/Smplr	Germany	1992	$50.00
Warner Brothers	9 25726-2	Best of Dark Horse 1976 - 1989	DJ/LP	U.S.	1989	$30.00
Dark Horse	9 25643-2	Cloud Nine	DJ/LP	U.S.	1987	$35.00

Picture disc.

Label	Catalog Number	Title	Type	Country	Year	Longbox Value / Value
Dark Horse	43XD-2001	Cloud Nine	LTD/LP	U.S.	1987	$50.00

Gold disc.

Label	Catalog Number	Title	Type	Country	Year	Longbox Value / Value
Album Network		In the Studio (Best of Dark Horse)	RS	U.S.	1990	$50.00

Airdate: 1/8/90.

Label	Catalog Number	Title	Type	Country	Year	Longbox Value / Value
Album Network		In The Studio (Dark Horse)	RS	U.S.		$45.00
Album Network		In the Studio (Live in Japan)	RS	U.S.	1990	$50.00
Dark Horse	PRO-CD-5555	Live in Japan Sampler	DJ/Smplr	U.S.	1992	$25.00
Radio Ventures		Masters of Rock	RS	U.S.	1989	$80.00

Airdate: 7/17/89.

Label	Catalog Number	Title	Type	Country	Year	Longbox Value / Value
Radio Today		Rock Stars	RS	U.S.	1990	$100.00

2 CD set. Airdate: 1/15/90.

Label	Catalog Number	Title	Type	Country	Year	Longbox Value / Value
Media America		Up Close	RS	U.S.	1992	$100.00

2 CD set.

Singles

Label	Catalog Number	Title	Type	Country	Year	Longbox Value / Value
Pioneer	09P3-6191	Cheer Down	CD3	Japan	1989	$18.00/$5.00
WEA	W-2696CD	Cheer Down	CD3	U.K.	1989	$12.00
Dark Horse	PRO-CD-3647	Cheer Down	CDJ	U.S.	1989	$8.00
Dark Horse	PRO-CD-2924	Cloud 9	CDJ	U.S.	1987	$20.00
Dark Horse	10SW-17	Got My Mind Set on You	CD3	Japan	1987	$13.00/$5.00
Dark Horse	PRO-CD-2846	Got My Mind Set on You	CDJ	U.S.	1987	$15.00
Dark Horse	PRO-CD-2846	Got My Mind Set on You	CDJ	U.S.	1987	$60.00

Custom cardboard sleeve.

Label	Catalog Number	Title	Type	Country	Year	Longbox Value / Value
Dark Horse	09P3-6207	Poor Little Girl	CD3	Japan	1989	$18.00/$5.00
WEA	921402-2	Poor Little Girl	CD5	U.K.	1989	$11.00
Dark Horse	PRO-CD-3775	Poor Little Girl	CDJ	U.S.	1989	$7.00
Dark Horse	920959-2	This is Love	CD3	Germany	1988	$11.00
Dark Horse	10SW-59	This is Love	CD3	Japan	1988	$13.00/$5.00
Dark Horse	W-7913CD	This is Love	CD3	U.K.	1988	$11.00
Dark Horse	PRO-CD-3068	This is Love	CDJ	U.S.	1987	$10.00
Dark Horse	PRO-CDS-3068	This is Love	DJ/CD3	U.S.	1987	$20.00
Dark Horse	920860-2	When We Was Fab	CD3	Germany	1988	$10.00
Dark Horse	W-8131CD	When We Was Fab	CD3	U.K.	1988	$10.00

Harrison, Jane

Singles

Label	Catalog Number	Title	Type	Country	Year	Longbox Value / Value
BBC	BBCCDS-227	Ave Maria	CD5	U.K.	1988	$8.00

Harrison, Jerry & Casual Gods

Singles

Label	Catalog Number	Title	Type	Country	Year	Longbox Value / Value
Sire	PRO-CD-3095	Cherokee Chief	CDJ	U.S.	1988	$2.00
Fontana	JERCD-4	Cowboys Got to Go	CD5	U.K.	1990	$9.00
Fontana	878 044-2	Flying Under Radar	CD5	Australia	1990	$9.00
Fontana	JERCD-5	Flying Under Radar	CD5	U.K.	1990	$9.00
Sire	PRO-CD-4067	Flying Under Radar	CDJ	U.S.	1990	$2.00
Fontana	JERCD-3	Kick Start	CD5	U.K.	1990	$9.00
Sire	PRO-CD-4439	Kick Start	CDJ	U.S.	1990	$2.00
Fontana	JERCD-2	Man With a Gun	CD5	U.K.	1988	$9.00
Polygram	88940-2	Rev It Up	CD5	Germany	1988	$9.00
Polygram	88940-2	Rev It Up	CD5	U.K.	1988	$9.00
Sire	PRO-CD-2941	Rev It Up	CDJ	U.S.	1988	$2.00

Harrow, Den

Singles

Label	Catalog Number	Title	Type	Country	Year	Longbox Value / Value
BMG	162409	Holiday Night	CD3	Germany	1989	$8.00
BMG	662409	Holiday Night	CD5	Germany	1989	$8.00
BMG	662884	Take Me Back	CD5	Germany	1989	$8.00
BMG	661726	Yo Have a Way	CD5	Germany	1989	$8.00

Harry, Deborah

Full Length

Label	Catalog Number	Title	Type	Country	Year	Longbox Value / Value
Sire	9 45303-2-DJ	Debravation	DJ/LP	U.S.	1993	$15.00
Sire	9 25938-2	Def Dumb & Blond	DJ/LP	U.S.	1989	$25.00

Lanticular sleeve.

Singles

Label	Catalog Number	Title	Type	Country	Year	Longbox Value / Value
Chrysalis	CHSCD-3452	Brite Side	CD5	U.K.	1989	$10.00
		I Can See Clearly Now	CD5	U.K.	1993	$10.00
		I Can See Clearly Now	CD5	U.K.	1993	$10.00

Second version.

Label	Catalog Number	Title	Type	Country	Year	Longbox Value / Value
Sire	9 41000-2	I Can See Clearly Now	CD5	U.S.	1993	$6.00
Sire	PRO-CD-3636	I Can See Clearly Now	CDJ	U.S.	1993	$3.00
Chrysalis	662567	I Want That Man	CD5	Germany	1988	$10.00
Chrysalis	TODP-2111	I Want That Man	CD3	Japan	1988	$13.00/$4.00
Chrysalis	CHSCD-3369	I Want That Man	CD5	U.K.	1988	$10.00
Sire	9 21322-2	I Want That Man	CD5	U.S.	1988	$5.00
Sire	PRO-CD-3680	I Want That Man	CDJ	U.S.	1988	$3.00
Sire	PRO-CD-3206	Liar Liar	CDJ	U.S.	1988	$3.00
Chrysalis	CHSCD-3537	Maybe For Sure	CD5	U.K.	1990	$10.00
Chrysalis	CHSCD-3491	Sweet and Low	CD5	U.K.	1990	$10.00
Sire	9 21492-2	Sweet and Low	CD5	U.S.	1990	$5.00
Chrysalis	323646-2	Well Did You Evah	CD5	Germany	1990	$10.00
Chrysalis	CHSCD-3646	Well Did You Evah	CD5	U.K.	1990	$10.00

Hart, Corey

Full Length

Label	Catalog Number	Title	Type	Country	Year	Longbox Value / Value
		1984-1987 Special DJ Copy	DJ/Smplr	Japan		$40.00
Capitol	CDP-46077	First Offense	LP/LB	U.S.†	1985	$14.00/$8.00

Singles

Label	Catalog Number	Title	Type	Country	Year	Longbox Value / Value
EMI	4461	A Little Love	CDJ	U.S.	1990	$2.00
Sire	PRO-CD-5662	Always	CDJ	U.S.	1992	$2.00
Sire	W-0099CD	Baby When I Call Your Name	CD5	U.K.	1992	$9.00
Warner Brothers	PRO-CD-5360	Baby When I Call Your Name	CDJ	U.S.	1992	$2.00
EMI	TODP-2176	Can't Stand Losing You	CD3	Japan	1990	$13.00/$4.00
EMI	DPRO-04642	Chase the Sun	CDJ	U.S.	1990	$2.00
EMI	TODP-2394	I Can't Help Falling in Love With You	CD3	Japan	1993	$12.00/$4.00
EMI	XP10-2011	In Your Soul	CD3	Japan	1988	$13.00/$4.00
EMI	DPRO-04076	In Your Soul	CDJ	U.S.	1988	$2.00
EMI	203754-2	Little Love	CD5	Germany	1990	$8.00
EMI	CDMT-83	Little Love	CD5	U.K.	1990	$8.00
EMI	XP10-2040	Spot You in a Coal Mine	CD3	Japan	1988	$13.00/$4.00

Hart, Grant

Singles

Label	Catalog Number	Title	Type	Country	Year	Longbox Value / Value
EFA	CD-16171	2541	CD5	Germany	1988	$8.00
SST	CD 219	2541	CD3	U.S.	1988	$6.00/$3.00
SST	SSTCD-262	All of My Senses	CD5	Germany	1991	$7.00
SST	SSTCD-262	All of My Senses	CD5	U.S.	1991	$5.00

Hart, Mickey

Full Length

Label	Catalog Number	Title	Type	Country	Year	Longbox Value / Value
Rykodisc		Mystery Box	DJ/Smplr	U.S.	1996	$15.00
Rykodisc		Planet Drum	LTD/LP	U.S.	1991	$150.00

CD and autographed book in custom slipcase.

Label	Catalog Number	Title	Type	Country	Year	Longbox Value / Value
Rykodisc	RCD 80206	Planet Drum	LTD/LP	U.S.	1995	$24.00

20 bit master gold CD.

Label	Catalog Number	Title	Type	Country	Year	Longbox Value / Value
Rykodisc		Selections From "At the Edge"	DJ/Smplr	U.S.		$10.00

Singles

Label	Catalog Number	Title	Type	Country	Year	Longbox Value / Value
Rykodisc		# 4 For Gaia	CDJ	U.S.	1990	$3.00
SPV	6845	World	CD3	Germany	1989	$9.00

Hart, Rachel

Singles

Label	Catalog Number	Title	Type	Country	Year	Longbox Value / Value
Canyon	PCDY-00007	One By One	CD3	Japan	1989	$12.00/$3.00

Hart, Robert

Singles

Label	Catalog Number	Title	Type	Country	Year	Longbox Value / Value
Hollywood	HWD-117CD	Angel	CD5	U.K.	1992	$8.00
Hollywood	HWD-126CD	Boys on the Corner	CD5	U.K.	1992	$8.00
Hollywood	HWD-124CD	Fooled Around Again	CD5	U.K.	1992	$8.00
Hollywood	HWD-119CD	Heart and Soul	CD5	U.K.	1992	$8.00

Hartley, Trevor

Singles

Label	Catalog Number	Title	Type	Country	Year	Longbox Value / Value
London	LONCD-216	(No More) Nine Till Five	CD5	U.K.	1989	$8.00

Hartman, Dan

Full Length

Label	Catalog Number	Title	Type	Country	Year	Longbox Value / Value
MCA	MCAD-5525	I Can Dream About You	LP/LB	U.S.†	1985	$14.00/$8.00

Singles

Label	Catalog Number	Title	Type	Country	Year	Longbox Value / Value
CBS	651659-3	Instant Replay	CD3	Columbia	1988	$8.00
CBS	651659-3	Instant Replay	CD3	U.K.	1988	$8.00
A&M	CD-17668	Love You Take, The	CDJ	U.S.	1988	$2.00

Harvey, Dee

Full Length

Label	Catalog Number	Title	Type	Country	Year	Longbox Value / Value
Motown	6330	Just as I Am	LP/BP	U.S.		$14.00/$8.00

Harvey, P.J.

Full Length

Label	Catalog Number	Title	Type	Country	Year	Longbox Value / Value
Island		4-Track Demos	DJ/Smplr	U.S.	1993	$12.00
Westwood One		In Concert-Nu Rock	RS	U.S.	1995	$70.00

Airdate: 10/9/95.

Label	Catalog Number	Title	Type	Country	Year	Longbox Value / Value
		Interview	DJ/Intvw	U.K.	1995	$28.00

Singles

Label	Catalog Number	Title	Type	Country	Year	Longbox Value / Value
Island	PRCD 6770-2	50 Ft. Queenia	CDJ	U.S.	1993	$2.00
		C'mon Billy	CD5	U.K.		$10.00
		C'mon Billy	CD5	U.K.		$10.00

Second version.

Label	Catalog Number	Title	Type	Country	Year	Longbox Value / Value
Island	PRCD 6999-2	C'mon Billy	CDJ	U.S.	1995	$3.00
Island		C'mon Billy	CDJ	U.S.	1995	$3.00

Second version.

Label	Catalog Number	Title	Type	Country	Year	Longbox Value / Value
Island	PRCD 6921-2	Down by the Water	CDJ	U.S.	1995	$3.00
Too Pure	PURECD-5	Dress	CD5	U.K.	1991	$8.00
Island	PRCD 6779-2	Dry	CDJ	U.S.	1993	$2.00
Island	PRCD 6786-2	Man-Size	CDJ	U.S.	1993	$2.00
		Send His Love to Me	CD5	U.K.		$10.00
		Send His Love to Me	CD5	U.K.		$10.00

Second version.

Label	Catalog Number	Title	Type	Country	Year	Longbox Value / Value
Island	PRCD 7097-2	Send His Love To Me	CDJ	U.S.	1995	$7.00

Harvey, Steve

Singles

Label	Catalog Number	Title	Type	Country	Year	Longbox Value / Value
MCA	MCSTD-1678	Body And Soul	CD5	U.K.	1992	$8.00

Hash

Label	Catalog Number	Title	Type	Country	Year	Longbox Value / Value
Full Length						
Elektra	PRCD 8824-2	Five From Hash	DJ/Smplr	U.S.	1993	$9.00
Singles						
Elektra	66286-2	I Forgot My Blanket	CD5	U.S.	1993	$5.00
Elektra	PRCD 8811-2	I Forgot My Blanket	CDJ	U.S.	1993	$2.00

Haslam, Annie

Label	Catalog Number	Title	Type	Country	Year	Longbox Value / Value
Singles						
Epic	ESK 73219	Angels Cry, The	CDJ	U.S.	1989	$2.00

Hasselhoff, David

Label	Catalog Number	Title	Type	Country	Year	Longbox Value / Value
Singles						
BMG	665085	Casablanca	CD5	Germany	1992	$10.00
BMG	663546	Crazy For You	CD5	Germany	1990	$10.00
BMG	664395	Do the Limbo Dance	CD5	Germany	1991	$10.00
BMG	162600	Flying on the Wings	CD3	Germany	1989	$10.00
BMG	662560	Flying on the Wings	CD5	Germany	1989	$10.00
BMG	662600	Flying on the Wings	CD5	Germany	1989	$10.00
BMG	663707	Freedom For the World	CD5	Germany	1990	$10.00
BMG	664791	Gypsy Girl	CD5	Germany	1991	$10.00
BMG	664929	Hands Up For Rock And Roll	CD5	Germany	1991	$10.00
BMG	162388	Is Everbody Happy	CD3	Germany	1989	$10.00
BMG	662388	Is Everbody Happy	CD5	Germany	1989	$10.00
BMG	663234	Je T'aime Means I Love You	CD5	Germany	1990	$10.00
BMG	661936	Looking For Freedom	CD5	Germany	1989	$10.00
CBS	654957-3	Our First Night Together	CD5	Germany	1989	$10.00
BMG	662873	Song of the Night	CD5	Germany	1990	$10.00
		Summer of Love	CD5	U.K.	1994	$10.00

Hassell, Jon

Label	Catalog Number	Title	Type	Country	Year	Longbox Value / Value
Full Length						
		Possible Musics	LP/LB	U.S.		$13.00/$8.00
Singles						
Warner Brothers	41574	Personals	CD5	U.S.	1994	$5.00

Hassles

Label	Catalog Number	Title	Type	Country	Year	Longbox Value / Value
Full Length						
EMI	0777-7-98828-2-3	Hassles, The	LP/LB	U.S.	1992	$30.00/$25.00

Hater

Label	Catalog Number	Title	Type	Country	Year	Longbox Value / Value
Singles						
A&M	31458 8191	Who Do I Kill	CDJ	U.S.	1993	$3.00

Hatfield, Juliana

Label	Catalog Number	Title	Type	Country	Year	Longbox Value / Value
Full Length						
Westwood One		In Concert-Nu Rock	RS	U.S.	1995	$45.00
Airdate: 11/6/95.						
Atlantic	92540-2	Only Everything	LTD/LP	U.S.	1995	$20.00
CD in "buffalo hide" digipak package.						
Singles						
Mammoth	MR-0041-2	Everybody Loves Me But You	CD5	U.K.	1992	$8.00
Mammoth	MR-0045-2	I See You	CD5	U.K.	1992	$8.00
Atlantic	PRCD 5147-2	My Sister	CDJ	U.S.	1993	$2.00
Atlantic	PRCD 5148-2	My Sister	CDJ	U.S.	1993	$2.00
Atlantic		Spin the Bottle	CDJ	U.S.		$3.00
Atlantic	95954	Spin The Bottle	CD5	U.S.	1994	$5.00
Atlantic		Universal Heartbeat	CDJ	U.S.		$3.00
Atlantic	95764	Universal Heartbeat	CD5	U.S.	1994	$5.00
Atlantic		What a Life	CDJ	U.S.		$3.00

Hathaway, Donny

Label	Catalog Number	Title	Type	Country	Year	Longbox Value / Value
Singles						
Warner Brothers	AMDY-5060	Song for You	CD3	Japan	1991	$12.00/$3.00

Hathaway, Lalah

Label	Catalog Number	Title	Type	Country	Year	Longbox Value / Value
Singles						
Virgin	VUSCD-35	Baby Don't Cry	CD5	U.K.	1990	$9.00
Virgin	PRCD 3601	Baby Don't Cry	CDJ	U.S.	1990	$2.00
Virgin	VUSCD-28	Heaven Knows	CD5	U.K.	1990	$9.00
Virgin	HEAVEN	Heaven Knows	CDJ	U.S.	1990	$2.00
Virgin	PRCD 3803	It's Somethin'	CDJ	U.S.	1991	$2.00
Virgin	VJCP-14022	Night & Day	CD5	Japan	1991	$11.00

Hatters

Label	Catalog Number	Title	Type	Country	Year	Longbox Value / Value
Singles						
Atlantic	PRCD 5554-2	Bed Side	CDJ	U.S.	1994	$2.00
		Dig the Rabbit	CDJ	U.S.	1994	$3.00
		Sacrifice	CDJ	U.S.	1994	$3.00

Hatters, David

Label	Catalog Number	Title	Type	Country	Year	Longbox Value / Value
Singles						
King	091X-18011	And Then It Happened	CD3	Japan	1989	$12.00/$3.00

Hatton, Susie

Label	Catalog Number	Title	Type	Country	Year	Longbox Value / Value
Singles						
Giant	PRO-CD-4621	Blue Monday	CDJ	U.S.	1991	$2.00

Haunted Garage

Label	Catalog Number	Title	Type	Country	Year	Longbox Value / Value
Full Length						
Metal Blade	26585	Possession Park	LP/LB	U.S.		$14.00/$8.00
Singles						
Metal Blade	976	976-Kill	CDJ	U.S.	1991	$2.00

Havalinas

Label	Catalog Number	Title	Type	Country	Year	Longbox Value / Value
Singles						
Elektra	PRCD 8153-2	High Hopes	CDJ	U.S.	1990	$2.00
Elektra	PRCD 8181-2	Not Alot to Ask For	CDJ	U.S.	1990	$2.00

Havana 3 A.M.

Label	Catalog Number	Title	Type	Country	Year	Longbox Value / Value
Full Length						
		Havana 3 A.M.	LP/LB	U.S.		$10.00/$6.00
Singles						
	Havana Black	Lone Wolf	CDJ	U.S.		$2.00
IRS	EIRSCD-158	Reach the Rock	CD5	U.K.	1991	$8.00

Havana Black

Label	Catalog Number	Title	Type	Country	Year	Longbox Value / Value
Singles						
Hollywood	8429	Freedom Child	CDJ	U.S.	1991	$2.00
		Hoo Myself	CDJ	U.S.		$2.00

Haven, Miss B.

Label	Catalog Number	Title	Type	Country	Year	Longbox Value / Value
Singles						
WEA	171218-2	Making Love in the Snow	CD5	Germany	1990	$8.00
WEA	YZ-465CD	Making Love in the Snow	CD5	U.K.	1990	$8.00
WEA	YZ-490CD	Nobody's Angel	CD5	U.K.	1990	$8.00

Havens, Richie

Label	Catalog Number	Title	Type	Country	Year	Longbox Value / Value
Full Length						
RBI	RBIC 1400	Simple Things	LP	U.S.	1987	$7.00
CD in fold out package.						
Singles						
Columbia	656833-2	Love Sometimes Says Goodbye	CD5	Germany	1991	$8.00
Solar	4464	Yes	CDJ	U.S.	1994	$2.00

Haverson, Nick

Label	Catalog Number	Title	Type	Country	Year	Longbox Value / Value
Singles						
Telstar	CDHOH-1	Head Over Heals	CD5	U.K.	1992	$8.00

Havoc & Prodeje

Label	Catalog Number	Title	Type	Country	Year	Longbox Value / Value
Singles						
MCA	MCA5P3369	Hood Got Me Feelin' Pain	CDJ	U.S.	1995	$2.00

Hawk And Wonder

Label	Catalog Number	Title	Type	Country	Year	Longbox Value / Value
Singles						
Parlophone	CDHAWK-1	Baby It's You	CD5	U.K.	1991	$8.00

Hawkes, Chesney

Label	Catalog Number	Title	Type	Country	Year	Longbox Value / Value
Singles						
EMI	TODP-2349	Feel So Alive	CD3	Japan	1992	$12.00/$3.00
Chrysalis	23799	Feel So Alive	CDJ	U.S.	1991	$2.00
Chrysalis	TODP-2404	Get the Picture	CD3	Japan	1993	$12.00/$3.00
Chrysalis	323708-2	I'm a Man Not a Boy	CD5	Germany	1991	$8.00
Chrysalis	TOCP-6848	I'm a Man Not a Boy	CD5	Japan	1991	$12.00
Chrysalis	CHSCD-3708	I'm a Man Not a Boy	CD5	U.K.	1991	$8.00
Chrysalis	323627-2	One and Only	CD5	Germany	1991	$8.00
Chrysalis	TODP-2291	One and Only	CD3	Japan	1993	$12.00/$3.00
Chrysalis	CHSCD-3627	One and Only	CD5	U.K.	1991	$8.00
Chrysalis	323681-2	Secrets of the Heart	CD5	Germany	1991	$8.00
Chrysalis	CHSCD-3681	Secrets of the Heart	CD5	U.K.	1991	$8.00

Hawkins, Coleman

Label	Catalog Number	Title	Type	Country	Year	Longbox Value / Value
Full Length						
Teldec	8 24056	And Chocolate Dandies 40-43	LP	Germany		$12.00

Hawkins, Coleman & Ben Webster

Label	Catalog Number	Title	Type	Country	Year	Longbox Value / Value
Full Length						
Verve	823120-2	Hawkins Encounters Webster	LP/LB	U.S.†	1985	$14.00/$8.00

Hawkins, Edwin

Label	Catalog Number	Title	Type	Country	Year	Longbox Value / Value
Singles						
Lection	177	If At First You Don't Succeed	CDJ	U.S.	1990	$2.00
Lection	302	Like Him	CDJ	U.S.	1990	$2.00
Lection	235	Pieces	CDJ	U.S.	1990	$2.00

Hawkins, Ronnie

Label	Catalog Number	Title	Type	Country	Year	Longbox Value / Value
Singles						
Polygram	871739-2	Treasure Chest	CD5	Canada		$7.00

Hawkins, Screamin' Jay

Label	Catalog Number	Title	Type	Country	Year	Longbox Value / Value
Full Length						
Demon	EDCD-104	Frenzy	LP	Germany		$12.00
Singles						
Demon	JAY 1	I Put A Spell On You	CD5	U.K.	1991	$8.00

Hawkins, Sophie B.

Label	Catalog Number	Title	Type	Country	Year	Longbox Value / Value
Full Length						
Sony		In Person	DJ/Intvw	U.S.	1995	$25.00
Sony	SRCS-5875	Tongues And Tails	DJ/LP	Japan	1995	$50.00
CD in press kit.						
Columbia	CSK 4501	Tounges And Tails	DJ/LP	U.S.	1992	$15.00
Singles						
CBS	77801	As I Lay Me Down	CD5	U.S.	1994	$5.00
Columbia	CSK 77801	As I Lay Me Down	CDJ	U.S.	1995	$6.00
Sony	SRDS-8236	California Here I Come	CD3	Japan	1992	$12.00/$4.00
Columbia	CSK 4594	California Here I Come	CDJ	U.S.	1992	$2.00
Sony	SRDS-8230	Damn I Wish I Was Your Lover	CD3	Japan	1992	$12.00/$4.00
Columbia	657735-2	Damn I Wish I Was Your Lover	CD5	U.K.	1993	$10.00
Columbia	658107-2	Damn I Wish I Was Your Lover	CD5	U.K.	1993	$10.00
Columbia	CSK 74164	Damn I Wish I Was Your Lover	CDJ	U.S.	1992	$2.00
		Don't Don't Tell Me No	CD5	U.K.		$10.00
		Don't Don't Tell Me No	CD5	U.K.		$10.00
Second version.						
Sony	SRDS-8244	I Want You	CD3	Japan	1992	$12.00/$4.00
Columbia	658777-2	I Want You	CD5	U.K.	1992	$10.00
Columbia	CSK 4807	I Want You	CDJ	U.S.	1992	$2.00
Columbia	CSK 7693	Only Love	CDJ	U.S.	1995	$3.00
Columbia	SAMP22571	Right Beside You	CDJ	U.K.		$10.00

Hawkins, Ted

Label	Catalog Number	Title	Type	Country	Year	Longbox Value / Value
Singles						
		Strange Conversation	CDJ	U.S.		$7.00

Hawkwind

Label	Catalog Number	Title	Type	Country	Year	Longbox Value / Value
Full Length						
Griffin	GCD 299-0	25 Years On	LTD/LP	U.S.	1994	$65.00
4CD boxed set with book.						
		Alien 4	LTD/LP	U.K.		$25.00
CD in limited digipak.						
Samurai	SAMRCD-039	Anthology, Vol.2	LP	Germany		$20.00
One Way	S21 57660	Hall of the Mountain Grill	LP/LB	U.S.		$15.00/$10.00
One Way	S21 5658	Hawkwind	LP/LB	U.S.		$15.00/$10.00
Video Arts	VALC 3191	Live Legends	LD	Japan		$90.00
One Way	CLEO 57412	Psychedelic Warlords	LTD/LP	U.S.	1992	$18.00
CDin felt bag & button. Limited to 1500 copies						
Griffin	55421 3931-2	Warrior On the Edge Of Time	LTD/LP	U.S.	1993	$30.00
CD in box with book.						
GWR	7762	Xenon Code X	LP	Germany		$20.00
Flicknife	SHARP-014CD	Zones	LP	U.K.		$20.00
Singles						
EMI	805762-2	Gimme Shelter	CD5	U.K.	1993	$10.00
Guitar Recording	1312	Quark Ep	CD5	U.S.	1994	$5.00

Hay, Colin

Label	Catalog Number	Title	Type	Country	Year	Longbox Value / Value
Full Length						
Columbia	450355-2	Looking for Jack	LP	Germany		$12.00
Singles						
MCA	CD45 18373	Help Me	CDJ	U.S.	1990	$2.00
MCA	DMCAT-1408	Into My Life	CD5	U.K.	1990	$8.00
MCA	CD45 18070	Into My Life	CDJ	U.S.	1989	$2.00

Hayes, Hunter

Label	Catalog Number	Title	Type	Country	Year	Longbox Value / Value
Singles						
		What Goes Down	CDJ	U.S.		$2.00

Hayes, Isaac

Full Length

Label	Catalog Number	Title	Type	Country	Year	Longbox Value/Value
		Branded, Raw & Refined Sampler	DJ/Smplr	U.S.		$13.00

Singles

Label	Catalog Number	Title	Type	Country	Year	Longbox Value/Value
	DPRO 11055	Fragile	CDJ	U.S.		$3.00
Virgin	38525	Fragile	CD5	U.S.	1995	$5.00
Columbia	CSK 1250	Showdown	CDJ	U.S.	1988	$2.00
Virgin	38492	Thanks to the Fool	CD5	U.S.	1995	$5.00

Haynes, Warren

Singles

Label	Catalog Number	Title	Type	Country	Year	Longbox Value/Value
Megaforce	888	Fire in the Kitchen	CDJ	u.S.	1993	$2.00

Hayward, Justin

Full Length

Label	Catalog Number	Title	Type	Country	Year	Longbox Value/Value
Towerbell	CDTOW-151	Moving Moutains	LP	U.K.		$15.00
		Night Flight	LP	U.K.		$15.00

Singles

Label	Catalog Number	Title	Type	Country	Year	Longbox Value/Value
		Take Your Chances	CDJ	U.S.	1989	$2.00

Haza, Ofra

Full Length

Label	Catalog Number	Title	Type	Country	Year	Longbox Value/Value
Aris	883024	Broken Dreams	LP	Germany		$12.00

Singles

Label	Catalog Number	Title	Type	Country	Year	Longbox Value/Value
Eastwest	9031-76352-2	Daw Da Hiya	CD5	Germany	1992	$8.00
Eastwest	WMD5-4096	Daw Da Hiya	CD3	Japan	1992	$12.00/$3.00
Eastwest	YZ-662CD	Daw Da Hiya	CD5	U.K.	1992	$8.00
Eastwest	171892-2	Fata Morgana	CD5	Germany	1990	$8.00
Teldec	8 20918	Galbi	CD3	Germany	1988	$8.00
Pioneer	WMD5-4007	I Want To Fly	CD3	Japan	1989	$12.00/$3.00
Eastwest	247771-2	Im Nin' Alu	CD5	Germany	1989	$8.00
Teldec	10P0 0044	Im Nin' Alu	CD3	Japan	1989	$12.00/$3.00
Teldec	20P2-2899	Im Nin' Alu	CD5	Japan	1989	$12.00
Ace	CDSND-1000	Im Nin' Alu	CD5	U.K.	1989	$8.00
Eastwest	8 20982	Shaday	CD5	Germany	1988	$8.00
WEA	W-8326CD	Shaday	CD5	U.K.	1988	$8.00
Eastwest	246651-3	Wish Me Luck	CD3	Germany	1989	$8.00
Eastwest	246652-2	Wish Me Luck	CD5	Germany	1989	$8.00
WEA	W-434CD	Wish Me Luck	CD5	U.K.	1989	$8.00
Eastwest	170964-2	Ya Ba Ye	CD3	Germany	1990	$8.00
Eastwest	170963-3	Ya Ba Ye	CD5	Germany	1990	$8.00
Sire	9 21382-2	Ya Ba Ye	CD5	U.S.	1989	$4.00

Hazard, Mike

Singles

Label	Catalog Number	Title	Type	Country	Year	Longbox Value/Value
Alfa	10SR-44	Stop Me Baby	CD3	Japan	1988	$12.00/$3.00

Hazies

Singles

Label	Catalog Number	Title	Type	Country	Year	Longbox Value/Value
	DPRO 10472	Skin & Bones	CDJ	U.S.		$2.00

He Said

Singles

Label	Catalog Number	Title	Type	Country	Year	Longbox Value/Value
		Could You	CDJ	U.S.		$2.00

Head

Singles

Label	Catalog Number	Title	Type	Country	Year	Longbox Value/Value
		Remedial	CDJ	U.S.		$2.00
Virgin	VSCD-1073	Sinbin	CD5	U.K.	1988	$8.00

Head, Anthony

Singles

Label	Catalog Number	Title	Type	Country	Year	Longbox Value/Value
Chrysalis	CHSCD-3684	Sweet Transvestite	CD5	U.K.	1991	$8.00

Head East

Full Length

Label	Catalog Number	Title	Type	Country	Year	Longbox Value/Value
		Head East	LP/LB	U.S.		$10.00/$6.00

Head Swim

Singles

Label	Catalog Number	Title	Type	Country	Year	Longbox Value/Value
	6606572	Gone to Pot	CD5	U.K.	1994	$10.00

Heads Up

Singles

Label	Catalog Number	Title	Type	Country	Year	Longbox Value/Value
Polygram	873076-2	Don't Ever Let Go	CD5	Germany	1989	$8.00

Headtime

Singles

Label	Catalog Number	Title	Type	Country	Year	Longbox Value/Value
Cherry Red	977 018	I Visualize	CD5	Germany	1991	$8.00
Cherry Red	CDCHERRY-118	I Visualize	CD5	U.K.	1991	$8.00

Healey, Jeff

Full Length

Label	Catalog Number	Title	Type	Country	Year	Longbox Value/Value
Arista	ARCD-8632	Hell to Pay	DJ/LP	U.S.	1990	$18.00
Custom box.						
		House of Blues	RS	U.S.	1995	$40.00
2 CD set. Airdate: 3/12/95.						
		House of Blues	RS	U.S.	1996	$25.00
Airdate: 3/8/96.						
Westwood One		In Concert	RS	U.S.	1992	$50.00
2 CD set. With Chris Whitley, Airdate: 6/8/92						
Westwood One		In Concert	RS	U.S.	1994	$50.00
2 CD set. With Counting Crows, Airdate: 4/11/94						
Westwood One		In Concert	RS	U.S.	1995	$45.00
Airdate: 9/11/95.						
Pioneer Artists	PA-90-020	Jeff Healey Band, The	LD	U.S.	1990	$30.00
Westwood One		Off the Record	RS	U.S.	1993	$30.00
Airdate: 2/22/93.						
Media America		Up Close	RS	U.S.	1993	$30.00

Singles

Label	Catalog Number	Title	Type	Country	Year	Longbox Value/Value
Arista	A10D-124	Angel Eyes	CD3	Japan	1989	$13.00/$4.00
Arista	662210	Angel Eyes	CD5	U.K.	1989	$10.00
Arista	ASCD-9808	Angel Eyes	CDJ	U.S.	1989	$2.00
Arista	885138	Confidence Man	CD5	Germany	1989	$10.00
Arista	661872	Confidence Man	CD5	U.K.	1989	$10.00
Arista	BVDA-54	Cruel Little Number	CD3	Japan	1992	$12.00/$4.00
Arista	74321-11818-2	Cruel Little Number	CD5	U.K.	1992	$10.00
Arista	ASCD-2467	Cruel Little Number	CDJ	U.S.	1992	$2.00
Arista	ASCD 2467	Cruel Little Number	CDJ	U.S.	1992	$2.00
Arista	ASCD-2115	Full Circle	CDJ	U.S.	1990	$2.00
Arista		Heart of an Angel	CDJ	Canada	1992	$8.00
Arista	ARCD 2516	Heart of an Angel	CDJ	U.S.	1992	$2.00
Arista	663901	How Long Can a Man Be Strong	CD5	Germany	1990	$10.00
Arista	ASCD-2116	How Long Can a Man Be Strong	CDJ	U.S.	1990	$2.00
Arista	663280	I Think I Love You Too Much	CD5	Germany	1990	$10.00
Arista	884616	I Think I Love You Too Much	CD5	Germany	1990	$10.00
Arista	663280	I Think I Love You Too Much	CD5	U.K.	1990	$10.00
Arista	ASCD-2031	I Think I Love You Too Much	CDJ	U.S.	1990	$2.00
Arista	ASCD-2521	Lost In Your Eyes	CDJ	U.S.	1992	$2.00
Arista	A10D-133	Roadhouse Blues	CD3	Japan	1989	$12.00/$4.00
Arista		Roadhouse Blues	CDJ	U.S.	1989	$2.00
		Stuck in the Middle With You	CD5	U.K.	1995	$10.00
Arista	ASCD2826	Under Cover	CDJ	U.S.	1994	$6.00
Arista	ASCD2827	Under Cover	CDJ	U.S.	1994	$6.00
Arista	662853	When the Night Comes Falling From the Sky	CD5	U.K.	1989	$10.00
Arista	663622	While My Guitar Gently Weeps	CD5	Germany	1990	$10.00
Arista	663622	While My Guitar Gently Weeps	CD5	U.K.	1990	$10.00
Arista	ASCD-2065	While My Guitar Gently Weeps	CDJ	U.S.	1990	$2.00

Heart

Full Length

Label	Catalog Number	Title	Type	Country	Year	Longbox Value/Value
Capitol	TOCP-6115	Brigade	LTD/LP	Japan	1990	$30.00
CD in felt box with bonus CD3.						
Capitol	DPRO-79967	Brigade	DJ/LP	U.S.	1990	$20.00
EMI		Definitive Collection	LP	U.K.		$30.00
2 CD set.						
Columbia	465222-2	Dog and Butterfly/Little Queen	LP	Germany		$35.00
Capitol		Four for the Road	DJ/Smplr	U.S.	1994	$12.00
Capitol	CDHGFT-1	Heart	LP	U.K.		$65.00
3 CD Set.						
Capitol	CDP 7 46157 2	Heart	LP/LB	U.S.†	1985	$18.00/$15.00
With original versions of "Never" and "Nothin' At All."						
Pioneer	PA86-M046	Heart	8" LD	U.S.	1986	$10.00
Capitol		Hits	DJ/Smplr	Japan		N/A
Album Network		In the Studio (Dog B - Flying Queen)	RS	U.S.		$25.00
Album Network		In the Studio (Dreamboat Annie)	RS	U.S.	1988	$30.00
Airdate: 9/26/88.						
Album Network		In the Studio (Dreamboat Annie)	RS	U.S.	1990	$30.00
Airdate: 6/11/90.						
DIR		King Biscuit Flour Hour	RS	U.S.	1987	$100.00
Airdate: 11/29/87.						
Epic	EK-34799	Little Queen	LP/BP	U.S.†	1985	$14.00/$8.00
Westwood One		Off the Record	RS	U.S.	1992	$35.00
Airdate: 7/20/92.						
Westwood One		Off the Record	RS	U.S.	1994	$30.00
Airdate: 2/28/94.						
Westwood One		Off the Record	RS	U.S.	1995	$35.00
Airdate: 9/11/95.						
Westwood One		Off the Record	RS	U.S.	1996	$35.00
Airdate: 3/4/96.						
Media America		On Tour	RS	U.S.	1990	$25.00
Epic	EK-38800	Passionworks	LP/BP	U.S.†	1984	$14.00/$8.00
Radio Today		Rock Stars	RS	U.S.	1990	$4.00
2 CD set. Airdate: 5/9/90.						
EMI	SPCD-1217	Rock the House Live	DJ/LP	Japan	1993	$60.00
Advance issue.						
Westwood One		Superstars	RS	U.S.	1996	$100.00
2 CD set. Airdate: 1/8/96.						
Media America		Up Close	RS	U.S.	1990	$40.00
2 CD set.						
Media America		Up Close	RS	U.S.	1994	$40.00
EMI	CDLOVE-2	With Love From Heart	LP	U.K.		$35.00
2 CD set.						

Singles

Label	Catalog Number	Title	Type	Country	Year	Longbox Value/Value
Capitol	203775-2	All I Wanna Do Is Make Love To You	CD5	Germany	1990	$10.00
Capitol	CDCL-569	All I Wanna Do Is Make Love To You	CD5	U.K.	1990	$10.00
Capitol	DPRO-79909	All I Wanna Do Is Make Love To You	CDJ	U.S.	1990	$2.00
Capitol	DPRO-79024	Alone	CDJ	U.S.	1989	$3.00
Capitol		Back To Avalon	CDJ	U.S.	1994	$3.00
		Black on Black II	CD5	Australia	1994	$12.00
Capitol		Black on Black II	CDJ	U.S.	1994	$3.00
Capitol	203908-2	I Didn't Want to Need You	CD5	Germany	1990	$10.00
Capitol	CDCL-580	I Didn't Want to Need You	CD5	U.K.	1990	$10.00
Capitol	DPRO-79073	I Didn't Want to Need You	CDJ	U.S.	1990	$3.00
Capitol	CDCL-482	Never	CD5	U.K.	1988	$10.00
Capitol/NTSC	CAP. 5512	Never	DJ/CDV	U.S.	1985	$50.00
Capitol	Cap.5512	Never	CDV	U.S.	1987	$20.00
Capitol	CDCL-507	Nothing at All	CD5	U.K.	1988	$10.00
Capitol	CDCL-595	Secret	CD5	U.K.	1991	$10.00
Capitol	CDCL-603	Secret	CD5	U.K.	1991	$10.00
Capitol	DPRO-79468	Secret	CDJ	U.S.	1990	$3.00
Capitol	C2-15634	Stranded	CD5	U.S.	1990	$6.00
Capitol	DPRO-79270	Stranded	CDJ	U.S.	1990	$3.00
Capitol	CP10-2001	There's the Girl	CD3	Japan	1988	$12.00/$4.00
Capitol	CDCL-473	There's the Girl	CD5	U.K.	1988	$10.00
Capitol	CDCL-487	What About Love	CD5	U.K.	1988	$10.00
Capitol	202070-2	Who Will You Run To	CD5	Germany	1988	$10.00
Capitol	CDCL-457	Who Will You Run To	CD5	U.K.	1988	$10.00
Capitol	7423 8 81049	Will You Be There	CD5	U.K.	1993	$10.00
Capitol	7423 8 81050	Will You Be There	CD5	U.K.	1993	$10.00
Capitol	DPRO-79293	Will You Be There	CDJ	U.S.	1993	$3.00
Capitol	DPRO-79310	Will You Be There	CDJ	U.S.	1993	$3.00
Capitol	DPRO-79298	Woman in Me, The	CDJ	U.S.	1994	$3.00
Capitol	204479-2	You're the Voice	CD5	Germany	1991	$10.00
Capitol	TODP-2297	You're the Voice	CD3	Japan	1991	$12.00/$4.00
Capitol	CDCL-624	You're the Voice	CD5	U.K.	1991	$10.00
Capitol	15748	You're the Voice	CD5	U.S.	1991	$5.00
Capitol	DPRO-79010	You're the Voice	CDJ	U.S.	1991	$3.00

Heart And Fire

Singles

Label	Catalog Number	Title	Type	Country	Year	Longbox Value/Value
Capitol	DPRO-79467	Go For It	CDJ	U.S.	1990	$2.00

Heart, Beau

Singles

Label	Catalog Number	Title	Type	Country	Year	Longbox Value/Value
WEA	246907-2	Dancing on Water	CD3	Germany	1989	$8.00
WEA	246527-2	Deliver Daniel	CD5	Germany	1989	$8.00

Heart Of Gold

Full Length

Label	Catalog Number	Title	Type	Country	Year	Longbox Value/Value
Relix		Double Dose	LP/LB	U.S.		$14.00/$8.00

Singles

Label	Catalog Number	Title	Type	Country	Year	Longbox Value/Value
For Life	FLDF-10219	Twilight Time	CD3	Japan	1992	$12.00/$3.00

Heart Throbs

Full Length

Label	Catalog Number	Title	Type	Country	Year	Longbox Value/Value
A&M	5399	Jubilee Twist	LP/LB	U.S.		$14.00/$8.00
Pinnacle	39TP7-CD	Dreamtime	CD5	U.K.	1990	$10.00
Elektra	PR 8201-2	Dreamtime	CDJ	U.S.	1990	$2.00
Elektra	PR 8198-2-8	Dreamtime	CDJ	U.S.	1990	$6.00
2 CDJ set with 2nd CD by Dee-Lite.						
Rough Trade	CD10-492	I Wonder Why	CD5	Germany	1990	$10.00
Pinnacle	33TP7-CD	I Wonder Why	CD5	U.K.	1990	$10.00
Elektra	PRCD 8302-1	I Wonder Why	CDJ	U.S.	1990	$2.00

Label	Catalog Number	Title	Type	Country	Year	Longbox Value / Value
Elektra	PRCD 8302-2	I Wonder Why	CDJ	U.S.	1990	$2.00
A&M	75021 7390-2	Outside	CDJ	U.S.	1992	$2.00
Pinnacle	70TP7-CD	She's in a Trance	CD5	U.K.	1992	$10.00
Elektra	PRCD 8245-2	She's in a Trance	CDJ	U.S.	1992	$2.00
Rough Trade	230-1182-3	Spongy Thing	CD5	Germany	1992	$10.00
Pinnacle	60TP7-CD	Spongy Thing	CD5	U.K.	1992	$10.00
A&M	CD 17987	Tenderly	CDJ	U.S.	1990	$2.00
Pinnacle	50TP7-CD	Turn Away	CD5	U.K.	1991	$10.00

Heartland

Singles

Label	Catalog Number	Title	Type	Country	Year	Longbox Value / Value
A&M	AMCD-811	Carrie Ann	CD5	U.K.	1991	$8.00
A&M	AMCD-761	Fight Fire With Fire	CD5	U.K.	1991	$8.00

Heat Wave

Singles

Label	Catalog Number	Title	Type	Country	Year	Longbox Value / Value
CBS	651651-3	Boogie Nights	CD3	Germany	1988	$8.00
CBS	651651-3	Boogie Nights	CD3	U.K.	1988	$8.00
Telstar	HWCD-3	Feel Like Making Love	CD5	U.K.	1990	$8.00
Telstar	HWCD-1	Mind Blowing Decisions	CD5	U.K.	1990	$8.00

Heath, Ted

Full Length

Label	Catalog Number	Title	Type	Country	Year	Longbox Value / Value
London	PPC-820180	Fever	LP/LB	U.S.†	1985	$14.00/$8.00

Heaven 17

Singles

Label	Catalog Number	Title	Type	Country	Year	Longbox Value / Value
Virgin	661681	Ballad of Go Go Brown	CD5	Germany	1988	$8.00
Virgin	VSCD-1113	Ballad of Go Go Brown	CD5	U.K.	1988	$8.00
Virgin	CDT-21	Facist Groove Thang	CD5	U.K.	1988	$8.00
Virgin	VSCD-1421	Facist Groove Thang	CD5	U.K.	1993	$8.00
Virgin	880995	Temptation	CD5	Germany	1988	$8.00
Virgin	CDT-19	Temptation	CD5	U.K.	1988	$8.00
Virgin	VSCDT-1446	Temptation	CD5	U.K.	1993	$8.00
Virgin	VSCDT-1134	Train Of Love	CD5	U.K.	1988	$8.00

Heaven on Earth

Singles

Label	Catalog Number	Title	Type	Country	Year	Longbox Value / Value
		On Angel's Wings	CDJ	U.S.		$2.00

Heaven West Eleven

Singles

Label	Catalog Number	Title	Type	Country	Year	Longbox Value / Value
Epic	ESCA-5789	Rivers Run Dry	CD5	Japan	1990	$10.00

Heaven's Edge

Singles

Label	Catalog Number	Title	Type	Country	Year	Longbox Value / Value
Columbia	CSK 2134	Find Another Way	CDJ	U.S.	1990	$2.00
		Skin to Skin	CDJ	U.S.		$2.00

Heaven's Gate

Singles

Label	Catalog Number	Title	Type	Country	Year	Longbox Value / Value
SPV	7640-3	More Hysteria	CD5	Germany	1992	$8.00
Noise	VICP-15013	More Hysteria	CD5	Japan	1991	$10.00

Heavy Bones

Singles

Label	Catalog Number	Title	Type	Country	Year	Longbox Value / Value
Reprise	PRO-CD-5674	Hand That Feeds, The	CDJ	U.S.	1992	$2.00

Heavy D. And The Boyz

Singles

Label	Catalog Number	Title	Type	Country	Year	Longbox Value / Value
Uptown	18300	Big Tyme	CDJ	U.S.	1989	$2.00
MCA	54932	Black Coffee	CD5	U.S.	1994	$5.00
MCA	54420	Don't Cruise	CD5	U.S.	1992	$5.00
MCA		Girlz, They Love Me	CDJ	U.S.		$2.00
Uptown	2969	Got Me Waiting	CDJ	U.S.	1994	$2.00
MCA	MCD-17837	Is It Good to You	CD5	Germany	1991	$9.00
MCA	MVDM-14	Is It Good to You	CD3	Japan	1992	$13.00/$4.00
MCA	MCSTD-1564	Is It Good To You	CD5	U.K.	1991	$9.00
MCA		More Bounce	CDJ	U.S.		$2.00
MCA	MCD-17823	Now That We Found Love	CD5	Germany	1991	$9.00
MCA	MCD-17797	Now That We Found Love	CD5	Germany	1991	$9.00
MCA	MVCM-15001	Now That We Found Love	CD5	Japan	1991	$14.00
MCA	MCSTD-1550	Now That We Found Love	CD5	U.K.	1991	$9.00
MCA	CD45-1479	Now That We Found Love	CDJ	U.S.	1991	$2.00
MCA		Nuttin' But Love	CDJ	U.S.		$2.00
MCA	MCSTD-1589	Peaceful Journey	CD5	U.K.	1991	$9.00
MCA	DMCAT-1370	Somebody For Me	CD5	U.K.	1989	$9.00
MCA	2553	Truthful	CDJ	U.S.	1993	$2.00
Eastwest	257485-2	We Got Our Own Thang	CD5	Germany	1989	$9.00
MCA	DMCAT-1344	We Got Our Own Thang	CD5	U.K.	1989	$9.00
MCA	DMCAX-1344	We Got Our Own Thang	CD5	U.K.	1989	$9.00
MCA	CD45 17976	We Got Our Own Thang	CDJ	U.S.	1989	$2.00
MCA	MVDM-34	Who's the Man?	CD3	Japan	1993	$12.00/$4.00
Uptown	54545	Who's the Man?	CD5	U.S.	1993	$5.00
Uptown	2464	Who's the Man?	CDJ	U.S.	1993	$2.00

Heavy Metal Outlaws

Singles

Label	Catalog Number	Title	Type	Country	Year	Longbox Value / Value
Street Link	HMOSCD-1	Sex for Sexism Sake	CD5	U.K.	1991	$8.00

Heavy's

Singles

Label	Catalog Number	Title	Type	Country	Year	Longbox Value / Value
BMG	162180	Metal Marathon	CD3	Germany	1989	$8.00
BMG	662180	Metal Marathon	CD5	Germany	1989	$8.00

Hed Boys

Singles

Label	Catalog Number	Title	Type	Country	Year	Longbox Value / Value
	59001	Girls and Boys	CD5	U.S.	1994	$5.00

Hedges, Michael

Full Length

Label	Catalog Number	Title	Type	Country	Year	Longbox Value / Value
Windham	WD-1032	Aerial Boundaries	LP/LB	U.S.†	1985	$14.00/$8.00
Open Air	OD-0303	Watching My Life Go By	LP/LB	U.S.†	1985	$14.00/$8.00

Singles

Label	Catalog Number	Title	Type	Country	Year	Longbox Value / Value
Polygram	370003-2	All Along the Watchtower	CD5	Germany	1989	$8.00

Heidi, Berry

Singles

Label	Catalog Number	Title	Type	Country	Year	Longbox Value / Value
4AD	BAD 3010	Moon and the Sun, The	CD5	U.K.	1993	$10.00
4AD	PRO-CD-6321	Moon and the Sun, The	CDJ	U.S.	1993	$2.00

Heights

Singles

Label	Catalog Number	Title	Type	Country	Year	Longbox Value / Value
Capitol	TODP-2386	How Do You Talk to an Angel	CD3	Japan	1992	$12.00/$4.00
Capitol	CDCL-877	How Do You Talk to an Angel	CD5	U.K.	1992	$9.00
Capitol	DPRO-79526	How Do You Talk to an Angel	CDJ	U.S.	1992	$2.00
J&J	79915	How Long	CDJ	U.S.	1991	$2.00
Capitol	DPRO-79560	I'm Still on Your Side	CDJ	U.S.	1992	$2.00

Helga Pictures

Singles

Label	Catalog Number	Title	Type	Country	Year	Longbox Value / Value
intercord	825 321	Love Is a Stranger	CD5	Germany	1992	$8.00

Helix

Full Length

Label	Catalog Number	Title	Type	Country	Year	Longbox Value / Value
Capitol		Back For Another Taste	LP/LB	U.S.		$14.00/$8.00
Pioneer	PA85-M029	Helix	8" LD	U.S.	1984	$10.00
Grudge	4771	Storm, The	CDJ	U.S.	1990	$2.00

Hell Razor

Singles

Label	Catalog Number	Title	Type	Country	Year	Longbox Value / Value
BMG	662740	I Heard It Through the Grape	CD5	Germany	1989	$8.00

Helloween – Master Of the Rings (Castle 101-2)

Helloween

Full Length

Label	Catalog Number	Title	Type	Country	Year	Longbox Value / Value
Victor		Best, the Rest, the Rare	LTD/LP	Japan	1991	$30.00
Victor	VICP-8103	Chameleon	LTD/LP	Japan	1993	$30.00
Victor	VDPG-1	Helloween	LTD/LP	Japan		$35.00
	T-shirt pack.					
RCA		I Want Out Live	LP/LB	U.S.		$12.00/$7.00
RCA	8529-2-R	Keeper of the Seven Keys Part II	DJ/LP	U.S.	1988	$7.00
Victor		Master of the Rings	LTD/LP	Japan	1995	$30.00
	CD and extra booklet in slipcase.					
Castle	101-2	Master of the Rings	LTD/LP	U.S.	1995	$20.00
RCA Victor	VICP-8041/VIZP-1	Pink Bubbles Go Ape	LTD/LP	Japan	1991	$25.00
	T-shirt pack.					
Noise	N-0148-2	Pumpkin Tracks	LP	U.K.	1989	$25.00

Singles

Label	Catalog Number	Title	Type	Country	Year	Longbox Value / Value
Noise	N 0116-3	Dr. Stein	CD3	Germany	1988	$10.00
Victor	VDP-15002	Dr. Stein	CD5	Japan	1988	$15.00
Noise	N 0116-3	Dr. Stein	CD3	U.K.	1988	$10.00
Noise	N 4726	I Want Out	CD3	Germany	1988	$10.00
Noise	N 0126-3	I Want Out	CD3	Germany	1988	$15.00
Noise	N 0216-3	I Want Out	CD3	U.K.	1988	$10.00
Victor	VCP-15009	Judas	CD5	Japan	1991	$15.00
RCA	6399	Keeper of 7 Keys	CD5	U.S.	1994	$5.00
EMI	204220-2	Kids Of the Century	CD5	Germany	1991	$10.00
EMI	CDEM 178	Kids Of the Century	CD5	U.K.	1991	$10.00
EMI		Mr. Ego	CD5	U.K.	1994	$10.00
EMI		Mr. Ego	CD5	U.K.	1994	$10.00
	Second version.					
EMI	7243 8 80146 2 5	Number One	CD5	Holland	1992	$9.00
Victor	VICP-15017	Number One	CD5	Japan	1992	$15.00
EMI	7243 8 80146 2 5	Number One	CD5	U.K.	1992	$15.00
Victor	VICP-15025	When the Sinner	CD5	Japan	1993	$15.00

Hellows

Singles

Label	Catalog Number	Title	Type	Country	Year	Longbox Value / Value
Fieldworks	FWCR-26	Big Mouse Bitch	CD5	Japan	1991	$10.00

Helmet

Full Length

Label	Catalog Number	Title	Type	Country	Year	Longbox Value / Value
Interscope		Betty	LTD/LP	Germany	1994	$32.00
	2 CD set. Blue jewel box.					
Interscope		Betty	LTD/LP	U.K.	1994	$32.00
	2 CD set. Blue jewel box.					
Interscope		Biscuits For Mud	DJ/Smplr	U.S.	1994	$8.00
		Wilma's Rainbow	LTD/LP	Australia	1994	$25.00
	2 CD set.					

Singles

Label	Catalog Number	Title	Type	Country	Year	Longbox Value / Value
Interscope	PRCD-4847-2	Give It	CDJ	U.S.	1992	$3.00
Interscope	PRCD-4592-2	In the Meantime	CDJ	U.S.	1992	$3.00
Immortal	5259	Just Another Victim	CDJ	U.S.	1993	$3.00
Eastwest	A-8484CD	Unsung	CD5	U.K.	1992	$10.00
Interscope	PRCD-4687-2	Unsung	CDJ	U.S.	1992	$3.00
Interscope	PRCD-4788-2	Unsung	CDJ	U.S.	1992	$7.00

Helmsley, Sherman

Singles

Label	Catalog Number	Title	Type	Country	Year	Longbox Value / Value
JRS	815	Everybody Has an Angel	CDJ	U.S.	1992	$2.00

Helter Skelter

Singles

Label	Catalog Number	Title	Type	Country	Year	Longbox Value / Value
Polygram	871121-2	Dr. Jeckyll & Mr. Hyde	CD5	Germany	1988	$8.00

Hemingway Corner

Singles

Label	Catalog Number	Title	Type	Country	Year	Longbox Value / Value
		Man on A Mission	CDJ	Canada		$6.00

Henderson, Joe

Full Length

Label	Catalog Number	Title	Type	Country	Year	Longbox Value / Value
		In and Out	LP/LB	U.S.		$22.00/$18.00
Blue Note		Our Thing	LTD/LP	U.S.	1995	$19.00

Henderson, Scott & Tribal Tech

Full Length

Label	Catalog Number	Title	Type	Country	Year	Longbox Value / Value
Passport	PJCD-88030	Dr. Hee	LP	U.K.		$12.00
Passport	PJCD-88030	Dr. Hee	LP	U.S.		$12.00
Passport	PJCD-88010	Spears	LP	U.K.		$12.00
Passport	PJCD-88010	Spears	LP	U.S.		$12.00

Singles

Label	Catalog Number	Title	Type	Country	Year	Longbox Value / Value
Relativity	0106	Nomad	CDJ	U.S.	1989	$2.00

Hendrix, Jimi

Full Length

Label	Catalog Number	Title	Type	Country	Year	Longbox Value / Value
Reprise	6261-2	Are You Experienced	LP/LB	U.S.		$18.00/$14.00
Capitol	DPRO-79534	Band of Gypsys	DJ/Smplr	U.S.	1995	$25.00
Westwood One		BBC Classic Tracks	RS	U.S.	1991	$35.00
	Airdate: 1/7/91.					
Westwood One		BBC Classic Tracks	RS	U.S.	1991	$35.00
	Airdate: 12/16/91.					
Westwood One		BBC Classic Tracks	RS	U.S.	1991	$35.00
	Airdate: 4/22/91.					
Westwood One		BBC Classic Tracks	RS	U.S.	1992	$35.00
	Airdate: 1/6/92.					
Westwood One		BBC Classic Tracks	RS	U.S.	1992	$35.00
	Airdate: 3/23/92.					
Westwood One		BBC Classic Tracks	RS	U.S.	1992	$50.00
	Airdate: 12/21/92.					
Westwood One		BBC Classic Tracks	RS	U.S.	1993	$35.00
	Airdate: 11/8/93.					
Westwood One		BBC Classic Tracks	RS	U.S.	1993	$35.00
	Airdate: 2/1/93.					
Westwood One		BBC Classic Tracks	RS	U.S.	1993	$50.00
	Airdate: 7/19/93.					
		Before the Experience	LP	U.S.		$12.00
Capitol	CDP 7 46485-2	Best Of	LP	U.K.		$25.00
Reprise	PRO-CD-4541	Between the Lines	DJ/Smplr	U.S.	1990	$15.00
Reprise		Cry of Love	LP/LB	U.S.		$18.00/$15.00
Polydor	823 359-2	Electric Ladyland	LP	Germany	1986	$50.00
	2 CD set with original "nude" cover.					
Reprise		Electric Ladyland	LP/LB	U.S.		$18.00/$15.00
	1 CD version.					
Reprise	6307-2	Electric Ladyland	LP	U.S.	1985	$30.00/$26.00
	2 CD set.					
Reprise		Essential Volume 1	LP/LB	U.S.		$25.00/$20.00
	2 CD version.					
		Guitar Parts	DJ/Smplr	France	1995	$25.00
	Fan magazine promotional CD.					
		Hendrix at the Beeb	RS	U.S.	1992	$120.00
	2 CD set. Airdate: 11/29/92.					
Westwood One		In Concert	RS	U.S.	1994	$75.00
	Airdate: 1/31/94.					
Media America		Inside the Experience	RS	U.S.		$100.00
	3 CD set.					
Image	ID5360VE	Jimi Plays Berkeley	LD	U.S.		$50.00
Reprise	9 25119-2	Kiss the Sky	LP/LB	U.S.†	1985	$15.00/$10.00
Media America		Labor Day 1990	RS	U.S.	1990	$100.00
	3 CD set.					
		Last Experience	LP/LB	U.S.		$14.00/$11.00
Reprise	26435-2	Lifelines	LP	U.S.	1990	$60.00
	4 CD set.					
Castle	HBCD-100	Live and Unreleased	LP	U.K.	1992	$40.00
	3 CD set in limited set with 3 picture discs and T-shirt.					
Rykodisc	90038	Live at Winterland	LTD/LP	U.S.	1987	$35.00
	CD pressed in gold polycarbonate.					
Rykodisc	90038	Live at Winterland	LTD/LP	U.S.	1993	$30.00
	CD album plus bonus CD and t-shirt in 11"x11" box.					
Westwood One		Off the Record	RS	U.S.	1995	$65.00
	2 CD set. Airdate: 11/27/95.					
Westwood One		Off the Record	RS	U.S.	1996	$150.00
	2 CD set.					
Rykodisc	RCD 20078	Radio One	LTD/LP	U.S.	1988	$30.00/$25.00
	Special picture disc version.					
Rykodisc	RCD PRO 0078-5	Radio Radio	DJ/Smplr	U.S.	1989	$45.00
On the Radio		Rarities on Compact Disc	RS	U.S.	1991	$50.00
On the Radio		Rarities on Compact Disc Volume 1	RS	U.S.	1990	$75.00
On the Radio		Rarities on Compact Disc Volume 1	RS	U.S.	1994	$30.00
	Reissue of 1990 disc.					
Westwood One		Setting the Record Straight	RS	U.S.	1992	$120.00
	3 CD set. Airdate: 9/7/92.					
Reprise	2276-2	Smash Hits	LP/LB	U.S.	1989	$15.00/$10.00
	CD+G.					
Reprise		Stages '67-'70	DJ/Smplr	U.S.	1991	$10.00
Album Network		Tribute	RS	U.S.	1993	$75.00
	2 CD set.					
Media America		Up Close	RS	U.S.	1990	$100.00
	2 CD set.					
Kitchen Sink		Voodoo Child	LTD/LP	U.S.	1995	$35.00
	CD in hardbound book.					
Penguin	BSP-VC1	Voodoo Child	LTD/LP	U.S.	1995	$40.00
	CD in Book.					
Kitchen Sink		Voodoo Child	LTD/LP	U.S.	1995	$60.00
	CD in hardbound book and slip case.					

Singles

Label	Catalog Number	Title	Type	Country	Year	Longbox Value / Value
Polydor	PZCD-100	All Along the Watchtower	CD5	U.K.	1990	$11.00
Polydor	873855-2	Crosstown Traffic	CD5	Germany	1990	$11.00
Polydor	PZCD-71	Crosstown Traffic	CD5	U.K.	1990	$11.00
Rykodisc	1008	Day Tripper	CD3	U.S.	1989	$6.00/$3.00
		Gloria	CD5	Australia	1994	$12.00
Polydor	887585-2	Gloria	CD5	Germany	1988	$11.00
Polydor	887585-2	Gloria	CD5	U.K.	1988	$11.00
Rough Trade	CD10-267	Peel Sessions	CD5	Germany	1988	$11.00
Strange Frt	SFPSCD-065	Peel Sessions	CD5	U.K.	1988	$11.00
Polydor	PZCD-33	Purple Haze	CD5	U.K.	1989	$11.00
MCA	MCA5P-3357	Stepping Stone	CDJ	U.S.	1995	$13.00
Polydor	863917-2	Wind Cries Mary	CD5	U.K.	1992	$11.00

Hendryx, Nona

Singles

Label	Catalog Number	Title	Type	Country	Year	Longbox Value / Value
BMG	662645	Women Who Fly	CD5	U.K.	1989	$8.00
Private	2055-2-PP	Women Who Fly	CDJ	U.S.	1989	$2.00

Henley, Don

Full Length

Label	Catalog Number	Title	Type	Country	Year	Longbox Value / Value
Geffen	GHS-24026	Building the Perfect Beast	LP/LB	U.S.†	1985	$14.00/$8.00
Geffen	2-24217	End of the Innocence, The	DJ/LP	U.S.	1989	$25.00
Album Network		In the Studio (Building the Perfect Beast)	RS	U.S.	1990	$20.00
	Airdate: 7/2/90.					
Album Network		In the Studio (End of the Innocence	RS	U.S.		$20.00
Westwood One		Superstar Concert	RS	U.S.	1994	$50.00
	2 CD set. Airdate: 5/16/94.					
Media America		Up Close	RS	U.S.	1990	$30.00
	2 CD set.					

Singles

Label	Catalog Number	Title	Type	Country	Year	Longbox Value / Value
Geffen	921283-2	End of the Innocence, The	CD3	Germany	1989	$10.00
Geffen	09P3-6151	End of the Innocence, The	CD3	Japan	1989	$17.00/$4.00
Geffen	GEF-57CD	End of the Innocence, The	CD3	U.K.	1989	$10.00
Geffen	PRO-CD-3555	End of the Innocence, The	CDJ	U.S.	1989	$7.00
Geffen	PRO-CD-3955	Garden of Allah	CDJ	U.S.	1989	$7.00
Geffen	PRO-CD-3955	Heart of the Matter, The	CDJ	U.S.	1989	$7.00
Geffen	PRO-CD-4103	How Bad Do You Want It?	CDJ	U.S.	1990	$2.00
Geffen	GEF-71CD	Last Worthless Evening	CD5	U.K.	19890	$10.00
Geffen	PRO-CD-3734	Last Worthless Evening	CDJ	U.S.	1989	$7.00
Geffen	GEF 66 CD	New York Minute	CD3	Germany	1989	$12.00
Geffen	PRO-CD-4158	New York Minute	CDJ	U.S.	1990	$7.00
Geffen	PRO-CD-4844	You Don't Know Me At All	CDJ	U.S.		$6.00

Henmi, Mari

Singles

Label	Catalog Number	Title	Type	Country	Year	Longbox Value / Value
Crown	CRDP-43	Victoria Station	CD3	Japan	1992	$13.00/$4.00

Henry, Jay

Singles

Label	Catalog Number	Title	Type	Country	Year	Longbox Value / Value
BMG	CDTMRC-3	If You Love Me	CD5	U.K.	1991	$8.00

Henry, Joe

Full Length

Label	Catalog Number	Title	Type	Country	Year	Longbox Value / Value
	PRCD 5217	Deed To the World	DJ/Smplr	U.S.	1995	$15.00
		Trampoline	DJ/Smplr	U.S.		$8.00

Singles

Label	Catalog Number	Title	Type	Country	Year	Longbox Value / Value
A&M	CD 17716	Here and Gone	CDJ	U.S.	1988	$2.00
A&M	CD 17819	She Is Sleeping	CDJ	U.S.	1989	$2.00

Henry, Pauline

Singles

Label	Catalog Number	Title	Type	Country	Year	Longbox Value / Value
550 Music	6187	Feel Like Making Love	CDJ	U.S.	1994	$3.00

Henry's Dress

Singles

Label	Catalog Number	Title	Type	Country	Year	Longbox Value / Value
Slumberland	34	Henry's Dress	CD5	U.S.	1994	$5.00

Herdon, Ty

Full Length

Label	Catalog Number	Title	Type	Country	Year	Longbox Value / Value
Epic		What Mattered Most	DJ/LP	U.S.	1995	$15.00
	CD in custom envelope.					

Here And Now

Singles

Label	Catalog Number	Title	Type	Country	Year	Longbox Value / Value
Third Stone	5029	Are You Ready	CDJ	U.S.	1993	$2.00
Third Stone	5316	Tastin' Love Again	CDJ	U.S.	1993	$2.00

Heretix

Singles

Label	Catalog Number	Title	Type	Country	Year	Longbox Value / Value
		Heart Attack	CDJ	U.S.		$2.00
		Up and Running	CDJ	U.S.		$2.00

Hericane Alice

Singles

Label	Catalog Number	Title	Type	Country	Year	Longbox Value / Value
Atlantic		Dream Girl	CDJ	U.S.		$2.00
Atlantic		Too Late	CDJ	U.S.		$2.00
Atlantic	PRCD-3122-2	Wild Young and Crazy	CDJ	U.S.	1990	$2.00

Herman, Terry

Full Length

Label	Catalog Number	Title	Type	Country	Year	Longbox Value / Value
Denon	CD-7010	Blue Aranjuez	LP/LB	U.S.†	1985	$14.00/$8.00
Denon	CD-7215	Blue Feeling	LP/LB	U.S.†	1985	$14.00/$8.00
Denon	CD-7130	Blue Michelle	LP/LB	U.S.†	1985	$14.00/$8.00
Denon	CD-7214	Blue Stardust	LP/LB	U.S.†	1985	$14.00/$8.00
Denon	CD-7055	Trio - Begin the Beguine	LP/LB	U.S.†	1985	$14.00/$8.00

Herman, Woody

Full Length

Label	Catalog Number	Title	Type	Country	Year	Longbox Value / Value
Polygram	835319	Walkman Jazz	LP/BP	U.S.		$12.00/$7.00

Herman, Woody & His Big Band

Full Length

Label	Catalog Number	Title	Type	Country	Year	Longbox Value / Value
Fantasy	FCD-9432	Giant Steps	LP/LB	U.S.†	1985	$14.00/$8.00
Concord Jazz	CCD-4240	World Class	LP/LB	U.S.†	1985	$14.00/$8.00

Hermanas Jimene

Singles

Label	Catalog Number	Title	Type	Country	Year	Longbox Value / Value
	1417	Twist Serie De Oro	CD5	U.S.	1994	$5.00

Hernandez

Singles

Label	Catalog Number	Title	Type	Country	Year	Longbox Value / Value
Epic	CDHER-1	All My Love	CD5	U.K.	1989	$8.00
Epic	CDHER-2	I'm Not That Kind of Guy	CD5	U.K.	1989	$8.00

Hernandez, Patrick

Singles

Label	Catalog Number	Title	Type	Country	Year	Longbox Value / Value
ZYX	5987-8	Born To Be Alive	CD5	Germany	1988	$6.00

Hernandez, Wayne

Singles

Label	Catalog Number	Title	Type	Country	Year	Longbox Value / Value
Epic	WAYNEC-4	Bad News	CD5	U.K.	1988	$8.00

Hersh, Kristin

Full Length

Label	Catalog Number	Title	Type	Country	Year	Longbox Value / Value
4AD		Hips And Makers	DJ/LP	U.S.	1994	$12.00
4AD		String	DJ/Smplr	U.S.	1994	$12.00

Singles

Label	Catalog Number	Title	Type	Country	Year	Longbox Value / Value
Sire	CDW45667	Strings	CD5	Canada	1994	$14.00
4AD		Your Ghost	CD5	U.K.	1994	$10.00
4AD	PRO-CD-6714	Your Ghost	CDJ	U.S.	1994	$6.00

Hewerdine, Boo

Singles

Label	Catalog Number	Title	Type	Country	Year	Longbox Value / Value
Ensign	EYNCD-625	All I Want (Is Everything)	CD5	U.K.	1989	$8.00
Ensign	323875-2	Fifty-Nine Yards	CD5	Germany	1992	$8.00
Ensign	EYNCD-654	Fifty-Nine Yards	CD5	U.K.	1992	$8.00
Ensign	EYNCD-653	History	CD5	U.K.	1991	$8.00

Hewett, Howard

Singles

Label	Catalog Number	Title	Type	Country	Year	Longbox Value / Value
Elektra	PR 8032-2	Forever and Ever	CDJ	U.S.	1988	$2.00
		I Can't Tell You Why	CDJ	U.S.		$2.00

Label	Catalog Number	Title	Type	Country	Year	Longbox Value / Value
Elektra	PR 8199-2	If I Could Only Have That Day Back	CDJ	U.S.	1990	$2.00
Elektra	PR 8250-2	Let Me Show You How To Fall	CDJ	U.S.	1990	$2.00
		Once, Twice, Three Times	CDJ	U.S.	1988	$2.00
Elektra	PRCD 8675-2	Save Your Sex For Me	CDJ	U.S.	1992	$2.00
Elektra	PR 8156-2	Show Me	CDJ	U.S.	1990	$2.00
Elektra	PR 2210-2	Strange Relationship	CDJ	U.S.	1988	$2.00
		Strange Relationship	CDJ	U.S.	1988	$2.00

Second version.

Hewitt, Jennifer Love

Singles

Label	Catalog Number	Title	Type	Country	Year	Longbox Value / Value
		Couldn't Find Another Man	CDJ	U.S.		$2.00

Heyman, Richard X.

Singles

Label	Catalog Number	Title	Type	Country	Year	Longbox Value / Value
Cypress	DPRO-79062	Call Out the Military	CDJ	U.S.	1990	$2.00
Sire	PRO-CD-5175	In the Scheme of Things	CDJ	U.S.	1991	$2.00

Heyward, Nick

Full Length

Label	Catalog Number	Title	Type	Country	Year	Longbox Value / Value
WEA		Tangled	DJ/LP	U.K.		$35.00
		Hard Days Nick	CD5	U.K.		$10.00
Epic	ESK 5629	He Doesn't Like It	CDJ	U.S.	1994	$2.00
		Rollerblade	CD5	U.K.		$10.00
WEA	921146-2	Tell Me Why	CD5	Germany	1988	$8.00
WEA	W-7579CD	Tell Me Why	CD5	U.K.	1988	$8.00
		World, The	CD5	U.K.		$10.00
		World, The	CD5	U.K.		$10.00

Second version.

Label	Catalog Number	Title	Type	Country	Year	Longbox Value / Value
WEA		World, The	CDJ	U.K.		$12.00
WEA	921041-2	You're My World	CD5	Germany	1988	$8.00
Warner Brothers	10P3-6060	You're My World	CD3	Japan	1988	$13.00/$4.00
WEA	W-7758CD	You're My World	CD5	U.K.	1988	$8.00
Reprise	PRO-CD-3245	You're My World	CDJ	U.S.	1988	$2.00

Hhead

Singles

Label	Catalog Number	Title	Type	Country	Year	Longbox Value / Value
Capital	30926	Fireman	CD5	U.S.	1994	$5.00

Hi Impact

Singles

Label	Catalog Number	Title	Type	Country	Year	Longbox Value / Value
		Never Stop Loving You	CDJ	U.S.		$2.00

Hi Tek 3

Singles

Label	Catalog Number	Title	Type	Country	Year	Longbox Value / Value
BMG	CDBORG-17	Come On And Dance	CD5	U.K.	1990	$8.00
CBS	656704-3	Spin That Wheel	CD3	Germany	1990	$8.00
CBS	655704-5	Spin That Wheel	CD5	Germany	1990	$8.00
BMG	CDBORG-1	Spin That Wheel	CD5	U.K.	1990	$8.00
BMG	CDBORG-16	Spin That Wheel	CD5	U.K.	1990	$8.00

Hi-C

Singles

Label	Catalog Number	Title	Type	Country	Year	Longbox Value / Value
Hollywood	HWD-105CD	I'm Not Your Puppet	CD5	U.K.	1991	$8.00

Hi-Definition

Singles

Label	Catalog Number	Title	Type	Country	Year	Longbox Value / Value
CBS	656754-2	Saturday	CD5	Germany	1991	$8.00

Hi-Five

Singles

Label	Catalog Number	Title	Type	Country	Year	Longbox Value / Value
Jive	JDJ-42188	Faithful	CDJ	U.S.	1993	$2.00
Jive	JIVECD-283	I Can't Wait Another Minute	CD5	U.K.	1991	$8.00
Jive	JDJ-1445-2	I Can't Wait Another Minute	CDJ	U.S.	1991	$2.00
Jive	JDJ-42012-2	I Can't Wait Another Minute	CDJ	U.S.	1991	$2.00
Jive	ALDB-78	I Just Can't Handle It	CD3	Japan	1990	$13.00/$4.00
Jive	ALCB-454	I Just Can't Handle It	CD5	Japan	1992	$12.00
Jive	1386-2-JDJ	I Just Can't Handle It	CDJ	U.S.	1990	$2.00
Jive	JDJ-42029-2	I Just Can't Handle It	CDJ	U.S.	1992	$2.00
Jive	ZD-44518	I Like the Way (The Kissing Game)	CD5	Germany	1991	$8.00
Jive	JIVECD-271	I Like the Way (The Kissing Game)	CD5	U.K.	1991	$8.00
Jive	1424-2-JDJ	I Like the Way (The Kissing Game)	CDJ	U.S.	1991	$2.00
Jive	ALDB-142	Just Another Girlfriend	CD3	Japan	1991	$13.00/$4.00
Jive	JIVECD-287	Just Another Girlfriend	CD5	U.K.	1991	$8.00
Jive	JDJ-42029-2	Just Another Girlfriend	CDJ	U.S.	1991	$2.00
Jive	JDJ-42041-2	Just Another Girlfriend	CDJ	U.S.	1991	$2.00
Jive	BVDQ-5	Mary Mary	CD3	Japan	1993	$13.00/$4.00
Jive	JDJ-42118-2	Mary Mary	CDJ	U.S.	1992	$2.00
Jive	BVDQ-2	Quality Time	CD3	Japan	1992	$13.00/$4.00
Jive	JDJ-42109-2	Quality Time	CDJ	U.S.	1992	$2.00
Jive	JDJ-42123-2	Quality Time	CDJ	U.S.	1992	$2.00
Jive	BVDQ-1	She's Playing Hard To Get	CD3	Japan	1992	$13.00/$4.00
Jive	CD 316	She's Playing Hard To Get	CD5	U.K.	1992	$8.00
Jive	JIVECD-316	She's Playing Hard To Get	CD5	U.K.	1992	$8.00
Jive	JDJ-42066-2	She's Playing Hard To Get	CDJ	U.S.	1992	$2.00

Hiatt, John

Full Length

Label	Catalog Number	Title	Type	Country	Year	Longbox Value / Value
	DCI-3089	Collection	DJ/Smplr	Japan	1993	$80.00
A&M	31454 80342	In-Store Play Sampler	DJ/Smplr	U.S.	1993	$18.00
A&M	31454 8034 2	In-store Play Sampler	DJ/Smplr	U.S.	1993	$25.00
DIR		King Biscuit Flour Hour	RS	U.S.	1987	$40.00

With Marshall Crenshaw, Airdate: 10/18/87.

Label	Catalog Number	Title	Type	Country	Year	Longbox Value / Value
DIR		King Biscuit Flour Hour	RS	U.S.	1994	$35.00

Airdate: 3/21/94.

Label	Catalog Number	Title	Type	Country	Year	Longbox Value / Value
A&M		Live at the Hiatt	LTD/LP	U.S.	1994	$85.00

Limited to 2,500 copies.

Label	Catalog Number	Title	Type	Country	Year	Longbox Value / Value
A&M	31454 01352	Perfectly Good Guitar	DJ/LP	U.S.	1993	$65.00

CD in "tour case" package with guitar pick and booklet.

Label	Catalog Number	Title	Type	Country	Year	Longbox Value / Value
A&M		Perfectly Good Guitar	LTD/LP	U.S.	1993	$30.00

2 CD set in slip case.

Label	Catalog Number	Title	Type	Country	Year	Longbox Value / Value
Capitol	DPRO-10280	Walk on CD Sampler	DJ/Smplr	U.S.	1995	$30.00

CD-ROM

Singles

Label	Catalog Number	Title	Type	Country	Year	Longbox Value / Value
A&M	31458 8235	Angel	CDJ	U.S.	1993	$6.00
A&M	75021 7415 2	Bring Back Your Love to Me	CDJ	U.S.	1990	$3.00
A&M	31458 8256	Buffalo River	CDJ	U.S.	1993	$7.00
A&M		Buffalo River	CDJ	U.S.	1993	$8.00

Second version.

Label	Catalog Number	Title	Type	Country	Year	Longbox Value / Value
A&M	75021 8078 2	Child of the Wild Blue Yonder	CDJ	U.S.	1990	$3.00
A&M	CD 17707	Drive South	CDJ	U.S.	1989	$3.00
A&M	CD 17495	Have a Little Faith in Me	CDJ	U.S.	1993	$3.00
A&M	CD 17647	Paper Thin	CDJ	U.S.	1988	$3.00
A&M	PODM-1017	Perfectly Good Guitar	CD3	Japan	1994	$13.00/$5.00
A&M	31458 8188	Perfectly Good Guitar	CDJ	U.S.	1993	$3.00
A&M	AMCD-570	Real Fine Love	CD5	U.K.	1990	$10.00
A&M	75021 7420-2	Rest of the Dream	CDJ	U.S.		$3.00
A&M	D13Y-3362	Riot With Hiatt	CD5	Japan	1989	$18.00
Capitol	DPRO11189	Shredding the Document	CDJ	U.S.	1996	$3.00
A&M	390368-2	Slow Turning	CD5	Germany	1988	$10.00
A&M	CD 17611	Slow Turning	CDJ	U.S.	1988	$3.00
A&M	31458 8228	Something Wild	CDJ	U.S.	1993	$3.00
A&M		Stolen Moments	CDJ	U.S.	1994	$25.00

CD single and cassette in press kit.

Label	Catalog Number	Title	Type	Country	Year	Longbox Value / Value
A&M	CD 17645	Thank You Girl	CDJ	U.S.	1987	$6.00
A&M	75021 7415 2	Your Love to Me	CDJ	U.S.	1990	$3.00

Hickman, Sara

Singles

Label	Catalog Number	Title	Type	Country	Year	Longbox Value / Value
Hollywood	HWD-1CD	Blue Eyes Are Sensitive to the Light	CD5	U.K.	1991	$8.00
Hollywood	PRCD 8209-2	Blue Eyes Are Sensitive to the Light	CDJ	U.S.	1990	$2.00
Elektra	PR 8120-2	Equal Scary People	CDJ	U.S.	1989	$2.00
Elektra	PR 8246-2	I Couldn't Help Myself	CDJ	U.S.	1990	$2.00
Elektra	PR 8307-2	In the Fields	CDJ	U.S.	1990	$2.00
Elektra	PR 8335-2	Very Thing, The	CDJ	U.S.	1990	$2.00

Hicks, D'atra

Singles

Label	Catalog Number	Title	Type	Country	Year	Longbox Value / Value
		Heart of Gold	CDJ	U.S.		$2.00
Capitol	CDCL-545	Sweet Talk	CD5	U.K.	1990	$8.00
Capitol		Sweet Talk	CDJ	U.S.	1990	$2.00

Hicks, Marva

Singles

Label	Catalog Number	Title	Type	Country	Year	Longbox Value / Value
Wing	WINCD-11	Got You Where I Want You	CD5	U.K.	1991	$8.00
Polydor	CDP 452	Got You Where I Want You	CDJ	U.S.	1991	$2.00

Hicks, Tina

Singles

Label	Catalog Number	Title	Type	Country	Year	Longbox Value / Value
	15548	Hello	CD5	U.S.	1995	$5.00

High

Singles

Label	Catalog Number	Title	Type	Country	Year	Longbox Value / Value
London	869277-2	Box Set Go	CD5	Germany	1990	$8.00
London	LONCD-261	Box Set Go	CD5	U.K.	1990	$8.00
London	LONCD-286	Box Set Go	CD5	U.K.	1990	$8.00
London	LONCD-297	More	CD5	U.K.	1990	$8.00
London	LONCD-280	Take Your Time	CD5	U.K.	1990	$8.00
London	LONCD-272	Up and Down	CD5	U.K.	1990	$8.00

High Performance

Singles

Label	Catalog Number	Title	Type	Country	Year	Longbox Value / Value
BCM	12452	Here's a Party Jam	CD5	Germany	1990	$8.00

Higher Ground

Singles

Label	Catalog Number	Title	Type	Country	Year	Longbox Value / Value
Cooltempo	COOLCD-246	Higher Ground	CD5	U.K.	1991	$8.00
Cooltempo	COOLCD-239	Somebody	CD5	U.K.	1991	$8.00

Highland Place Mobsters

Singles

Label	Catalog Number	Title	Type	Country	Year	Longbox Value / Value
Arista	BVDA-44	Let's Get Naked	CD3	Japan	1992	$12.00/$3.00

Highlanders

Singles

Label	Catalog Number	Title	Type	Country	Year	Longbox Value / Value
Virgin	VSCD-1217	Children Wonder Why	CD3	U.K.	1989	$8.00
Virgin	VSCD-1155	Never Enough	CD3	U.K.	1989	$8.00

Highway 101

Singles

Label	Catalog Number	Title	Type	Country	Year	Longbox Value / Value
Warner Brothers	PRO-CD-4944	Blame, The	CDJ	U.S.	1991	$2.00
		(Do You Love Me) Just Say Yes	CDJ	U.S.		$2.00
Warner Brothers	PRO-CD-3526	Honky Tonk Heart	CDJ	U.S.	1989	$2.00
Warner Brothers	PRO-CD-3730	Who's the Lonely	CDJ	U.S.	1989	$2.00

Hijack

Singles

Label	Catalog Number	Title	Type	Country	Year	Longbox Value / Value
Epic	655517-2	Badman Is Robbin', The	CD5	Germany	1989	$8.00
Epic	655517-2	Badman Is Robbin', The	CD5	U.K.	1989	$8.00
Epic	ESK 73079	Badman Is Robbin', The	CDJ	U.S.	1989	$2.00
Epic	655787-2	Daddy's Rich	CD5	U.K.	1989	$8.00

Hill, Andrew

Full Length

Label	Catalog Number	Title	Type	Country	Year	Longbox Value / Value
Blue Note		Black Fire	LTD/LP	U.S.	1995	$19.00

Hill, Benny

Singles

Label	Catalog Number	Title	Type	Country	Year	Longbox Value / Value
Continuum	12206	Ernie	CDJ	U.S.	1992	$2.00
Continuum	19206	Ernie	CDJ	U.S.	1992	$10.00

Hill, Billy

Singles

Label	Catalog Number	Title	Type	Country	Year	Longbox Value / Value
		Blue Angel	CDJ	U.S.		$2.00
Reprise	PRO-CD-3842	I Can't Help Myself	CDJ	U.S.	1989	$2.00
Reprise	PRO-CD-3563	Too Much Month at the End of the Money	CDJ	U.S.	1989	$2.00

Hill, Bryan

Singles

Label	Catalog Number	Title	Type	Country	Year	Longbox Value / Value
Sam	5016	Take It Easy	CDJ	U.S.	1991	$2.00

Hill, Dan

Singles

Label	Catalog Number	Title	Type	Country	Year	Longbox Value / Value
DJ	TODP-2367	Hold Me Now	CD3	Japan	1992	$12.00/$3.00
Quality	19107	Hold Me Now	CDJ	U.S.	1992	$2.00
DJ	TODP-2343	I Fall All Over Again	CD3	Japan	1992	$12.00/$3.00

Hill, Faith

Singles

Label	Catalog Number	Title	Type	Country	Year	Longbox Value / Value
Warner Brothers	PRO-CD-6445	Wild One	CDJ	U.S.	1993	$7.00

Hill, Kim

Singles

Label	Catalog Number	Title	Type	Country	Year	Longbox Value / Value
Geffen	PRo-CD-4300	Satisfied	CDJ	U.S.	1991	$2.00

Hill, Malcom J.

Singles

Label	Catalog Number	Title	Type	Country	Year	Longbox Value / Value
Alfa	11B3-16	Come Back and Do It	CD3	Japan	1989	$12.00/$3.00
Alfa	10SR-24	Take A Chance	CD3	Japan	1989	$12.00/$3.00

Hill, Marden

Singles

Label	Catalog Number	Title	Type	Country	Year	Longbox Value / Value
El	25608-12	Robe	CD3	Japan	1989	$12.00/$3.00

Hill, Rocky

Singles

Label	Catalog Number	Title	Type	Country	Year	Longbox Value / Value
		I Won't Be Your Fool	CDJ	U.S.		$2.00

Hill, Warren

Singles

Label	Catalog Number	Title	Type	Country	Year	Longbox Value / Value
RCA	62442	Passion, The	CDJ	U.S.	1992	$2.00

Hilt

Singles

Label	Catalog Number	Title	Type	Country	Year	Longbox Value / Value
Nettwork	W2 3042	Get Stuck	CD5	Canada	1989	$5.00
Nettwork	W2 3042	Get Stuck	CD5	U.S.	1989	$5.00
Nettwork	W2 3045	Stoneman	CD5	Canada	1990	$5.00

Himmelman, Peter

Singles

Label	Catalog Number	Title	Type	Country	Year	Longbox Value / Value
Island	PR 2869-2	245 Days	CDJ	U.S.	1989	$2.00
Epic	ESK 4893	Closer	CDJ	U.S.	1992	$2.00
Epic	ESK 4105	Only Innocent	CDJ	U.S.	1992	$8.00
Island	PR 2120-2	Waning Moon	CDJ	U.S.	1989	$2.00
Epic	ESK 4003	Woman With the Strength Of 10,000 Men	CDJ	U.S.	1991	$2.00
Epic	ESK 5009	You Know Me Better	CDJ	U.S.	1992	$2.00

Hindu Love Gods

Full Length

Label	Catalog Number	Title	Type	Country	Year	Longbox Value / Value
Giant	9 24406-2-Dj	Hindu Love Gods	DJ/LP	U.S.	1990	$10.00

Singles

Label	Catalog Number	Title	Type	Country	Year	Longbox Value / Value
Giant	PRO-CD-4414	Raspberry Beret	CDJ	U.S.	1990	$3.00

Hines, Earl

Singles

Label	Catalog Number	Title	Type	Country	Year	Longbox Value / Value
Derrick Records	141034	Honor Thy Father	CD5	U.S.	1994	$5.00

Hines, Gregory

Singles

Label	Catalog Number	Title	Type	Country	Year	Longbox Value / Value
Epic	652812-2	That Girl Wants to Dance With Me	CD5	U.K.	1988	$8.00
Epic	653109-2	You Need Somebody	CD5	U.K.	1988	$8.00

Hinterland

Singles

Label	Catalog Number	Title	Type	Country	Year	Longbox Value / Value
Island	884023	Dark Hill	CD5	Germany	1989	$8.00
Island	CID-443	Dark Hill	CD5	U.K.	1989	$8.00
Island	884767	Desert Boots	CD5	Germany	1989	$8.00
Island	CID-463	Desert Boots	CD5	U.K.	1989	$8.00

Hip Mens World

Singles

Label	Catalog Number	Title	Type	Country	Year	Longbox Value / Value
ZYX	6324-8	House Factor	CD5	Germany	1990	$6.00

Hip On Ice

Singles

Label	Catalog Number	Title	Type	Country	Year	Longbox Value / Value
Polygram	867141-2	Bend Me Shape Me	CD5	Germany	1991	$8.00
Polygram	877365-2	Sweet Dreams	CD5	Germany	1991	$8.00

Hippie Homeboy

Singles

Label	Catalog Number	Title	Type	Country	Year	Longbox Value / Value
ZYX	6754-8	Start the Panic	CD5	Germany	1992	$6.00

Hippy Chick

Singles

Label	Catalog Number	Title	Type	Country	Year	Longbox Value / Value
Tam Tam	TTT-20CD	Hippy Chick	CD5	U.K.	1990	$8.00

Hipsway

Singles

Label	Catalog Number	Title	Type	Country	Year	Longbox Value / Value
Polygram	87242-3	Your Love	CD3	Germany	1989	$8.00
Polygram	87243-2	Your Love	CD5	Germany	1989	$8.00
Polygram	MERCD-279	Your Love	CD5	U.K.	1989	$8.00

Hiroko

Singles

Label	Catalog Number	Title	Type	Country	Year	Longbox Value / Value
Enigma	EPRO-205	My Love's Wating	CDJ	U.S.	1989	$2.00

Hiroshima

Full Length

Label	Catalog Number	Title	Type	Country	Year	Longbox Value / Value
Epic	ESK 1918	Story Of A Thousand the Cranes	DJ/Smplr	U.S.	1989	$10.00

Singles

Label	Catalog Number	Title	Type	Country	Year	Longbox Value / Value
Epic	000147	Come To Me	CDJ	U.S.	1989	$2.00

Hirt, Al

Full Length

Label	Catalog Number	Title	Type	Country	Year	Longbox Value / Value
Warner Sound Exchange		22 Legendary Hits	LTD/LP	U.S.	1995	$17.00

His Boy Elroy

Singles

Label	Catalog Number	Title	Type	Country	Year	Longbox Value / Value
Immortal	5538	Fade to Black	CDJ	U.S.	1993	$2.00

His Latest Flame

Singles

Label	Catalog Number	Title	Type	Country	Year	Longbox Value / Value
London	LONCD-268	America Blue	CD5	U.K.	1989	$8.00
London	LONCD-240	America Blue	CD5	U.K.	1989	$8.00
London	LONCD-234	Londonderry Road	CD5	U.K.	1989	$8.00
London	886839-2	Love's in the Neighborhood	CD5	Germany	1990	$8.00
London	LONCD-247	Love's in the Neighborhood	CD5	U.K.	1990	$8.00

His Name Is Alive

Singles

Label	Catalog Number	Title	Type	Country	Year	Longbox Value / Value
4AD	PRO-CD-6069	In Every Ford	CDJ	U.S.	1993	$7.00
4AD	BAD-2005CD	Man on the Silver Mountain	CD5	U.K.	1992	$9.00

History

Singles

Label	Catalog Number	Title	Type	Country	Year	Longbox Value / Value
SBK	CDSBK-7008	Afrika	CD5	U.K.	1990	$8.00
SBK	CDSBK-7015	Better World	CD5	U.K.	1990	$8.00

Hit House

Singles

Label	Catalog Number	Title	Type	Country	Year	Longbox Value / Value
Columbia	654771-3	Move Your Feet to the Rhythm	CD3	Germany	1989	$8.00

Hitchcock, Robyn

Full Length

Label	Catalog Number	Title	Type	Country	Year	Longbox Value / Value
A&M	PRCD 7038	Catalog Sampler	DJ/Smplr	U.S.	1995	$15.00
Twin		Eye	LP	U.K.		$12.00
A&M		Globe of Frogs	LP/LB	U.S.		$14.00/$8.00
Midnight		Gotta Let This Hen Out	LP	U.K.		$15.00
Midnight		Groovy Decoy	LP	U.K.		$15.00
Midnight		Invisible Hitchcock	LP	U.K.		$15.00
A&M		Live	DJ/Smplr	U.S.	1993	$15.00
A&M		Spectre	DJ/Intvw	U.S.	1993	$15.00

Singles

Label	Catalog Number	Title	Type	Country	Year	Longbox Value / Value
A&M	S10Y-3009	Balloon Man	CD3	Japan	1988	$13.00/$4.00
A&M	S12Y-3049	Balloon Man	CD3	Japan	1988	$13.00/$4.00
A&M	000052	Balloon Man	CD3	U.S.	1988	$6.00/$3.00
A&M	12374	Balloon Man	CD5	U.S.	1990	$5.00
A&M	75021 7277-2	Dark Green Energy	CDJ	U.S.	1991	$2.00
A&M	31458 8099	Driving Aloud	CDJ	U.S.	1993	$2.00
A&M	31458 8102	Driving Aloud	CDJ	U.S.	1993	$2.00
A&M	CD 17718	Madonna of the Wasps	CDJ	U.S.	1989	$2.00
A&M	CD 17773	Madonna of the Wasps	CDJ	U.S.	1989	$2.00
A&M	75021 7297-2	Oceanside	CDJ	U.S.	1991	$2.00
A&M	CD 17812	One Long Pair of Eyes	CDJ	U.S.	1989	$2.00
A&M	75021 7268 2	So You Think You're in Love	CDJ	U.S.	1991	$2.00
A&M	75021 2392 2	So You Think You're in Love	CDJ	U.S.	1991	$2.00
A&M	75021 7273 2	Ultra Unbelievable Love	CDJ	U.S.	1991	$2.00
A&M	31458 8134	Yip Song	CDJ	U.S.	1993	$2.00

Hitchcock, Russell

Full Length

Label	Catalog Number	Title	Type	Country	Year	Longbox Value / Value
Arista	ARCD-8456	Russell Hitchcock	LP/BP	U.S.	1988	$15.00/$9.00

Hithouse

Singles

Label	Catalog Number	Title	Type	Country	Year	Longbox Value / Value
CBS	656079-3	I've Been Waiting For Your Love	CD3	Germany	1990	$8.00
CBS	656079-5	I've Been Waiting For Your Love	CD5	Germany	1990	$8.00
CBS	CDBORG-5	I've Been Waiting For Your Love	CD5	U.K.	1990	$8.00
CBS	652990-3	Jack to the Sound	CD5	Germany	1988	$8.00
Injection	134870-3	Jack to the Sound	CD5	U.K.	1998	$8.00

Hitmasters

Singles

Label	Catalog Number	Title	Type	Country	Year	Longbox Value / Value
Aris	885172	Sawmix 1	CD5	Germany	1989	$8.00

Hitters, Los

Singles

Label	Catalog Number	Title	Type	Country	Year	Longbox Value / Value
	1418	Rock & Roll	CD5	U.S.	1994	$5.00

Ho-Hum

Singles

Label	Catalog Number	Title	Type	Country	Year	Longbox Value / Value
	U5P1008	One Out of Ten	CDJ	U.S.		$2.00

Hoax

Singles

Label	Catalog Number	Title	Type	Country	Year	Longbox Value / Value
	PRCD6149-2	Scaramouche	CDJ	U.S.		$2.00

Hoax, Terry

Singles

Label	Catalog Number	Title	Type	Country	Year	Longbox Value / Value
Polygram	867839-2	Rubbish Colours	CD5	Germany	1991	$8.00
Polygram	867131-2	Waterland	CD5	Germany	1991	$8.00

Hodes, Art

Full Length

Label	Catalog Number	Title	Type	Country	Year	Longbox Value / Value
Mosaic	MD4-113	Complete Art Hodes Blue Note Sessions	LP	U.S.		$60.00

4 CD set.

Hodgson, Roger

Full Length

Label	Catalog Number	Title	Type	Country	Year	Longbox Value / Value
A&M	CD-5004	In the Eye of the Storm	LP/LB	U.S.†	1984	$8.00/$4.00

Hoffman, Kristin

Singles

Label	Catalog Number	Title	Type	Country	Year	Longbox Value / Value
Eggbert	0100	I Don't Love My Guru Anymore	CDJ	U.S.	1993	$2.00

Hoffman, Peter

Singles

Label	Catalog Number	Title	Type	Country	Year	Longbox Value / Value
Polygram	877369-2	Music of the Night	CD5	Germany	1990	$8.00
Polygram	656367-3	Wild and Lonely Heart	CD3	Germany	1990	$8.00

Hoffner, Helen

Singles

Label	Catalog Number	Title	Type	Country	Year	Longbox Value / Value
Magnet	4509-90507-2	Summer of Love	CD5	U.K.	1992	$8.00
Atlantic	PRCD 4734-2	Summer of Love	CDJ	U.S.	1992	$2.00

Hoffs, Susanna

Full Length

Label	Catalog Number	Title	Type	Country	Year	Longbox Value / Value
		Special 5 Track	DJ/Smplr	U.S.	1996	$10.00
Columbia	CSK 3027	When You're a Boy	DJ/LP	U.S.	1991	$15.00

Special digipak edition.

Singles

Label	Catalog Number	Title	Type	Country	Year	Longbox Value / Value
Columbia	656554-5	My Side of the Bed	CD5	Germany	1991	$9.00
Columbia	CSDS-8158	My Side of the Bed	CD3	Japan	1991	$13.00/$4.00
Columbia	656554-9	My Side of the Bed	CD5	U.K.	1991	$9.00
Columbia	CSK 73529	My Side of the Bed	CDJ	U.S.	1991	$2.00
Columbia	CSK 73899	Only Love	CDJ	U.S.	1991	$2.00
Columbia	656782-2	Unconditional Love	CD5	Germany	1991	$9.00
Columbia	SRDS-8190	Unconditional Love	CD3	Japan	1991	$13.00/$4.00
Columbia	656782-2	Unconditional Love	CD5	U.K.	1991	$9.00
Columbi	CSK 73752	Unconditional Love	CDJ	U.S.	1991	$2.00

Hoggard, Jay

Full Length

Label	Catalog Number	Title	Type	Country	Year	Longbox Value / Value
Gramaphone	GRCD-8204	Love Survives	LP/LB	U.S.†	1985	$14.00/$8.00

Holcomb, Robin

Singles

Label	Catalog Number	Title	Type	Country	Year	Longbox Value / Value
Elektra	PR 8240-2	Nine Lives	CDJ	U.S.	1990	$2.00
Elektra	PRCD 8597-2	One Way	CDJ	U.S.	1992	$10.00

2 CDJ set.

Holdsworth, Allan

Full Length

Label	Catalog Number	Title	Type	Country	Year	Longbox Value / Value
Relativity		Allan Holdsworth	LP/LB	U.S.		$14.00/$8.00
Relativity		Velvet Darkness	LP/LB	U.S.		$14.00/$8.00

Hole

Full Length

Label	Catalog Number	Title	Type	Country	Year	Longbox Value / Value
Westwood One		In Concert-Nu Rock	RS	U.S.	1995	$50.00

Airdate: 8/28/95.

Label	Catalog Number	Title	Type	Country	Year	Longbox Value / Value
Geffen		Live Through This	LTD/LP	Australia	1995	$28.00

2 CD set.

Singles

Label	Catalog Number	Title	Type	Country	Year	Longbox Value / Value
Geffen		Courtney Love MTV Awards Interview	CDJ	U.S.	1994	$18.00
DGC		Doll Parts	CD5	U.K.	1995	$10.00
DGC		Doll Parts	CD5	U.K.	1995	$10.00

Second version.

Label	Catalog Number	Title	Type	Country	Year	Longbox Value / Value
Geffen		Doll Parts	CDJ	U.S.	1994	$7.00

Label	Catalog Number	Title	Type	Country	Year	Longbox Value / Value
DGC		Live Set	CDJ	France	1994	$25.00
DGC		Ms. World	CD5	U.K.	1994	$10.00
DGC	PRO-CD-4636	Ms. World	CDJ	U.S.	1994	$6.00
Geffen		Softer Softest	CDJ	U.S.	1994	$7.00
	SA3408	Violet	CD5	France		$17.00
Geffen		Violet	CDJ	U.S.	1994	$7.00
DGC		Violet Rock Star	CDJ	France	1994	$20.00

Hole, David

Full Length

Label	Catalog Number	Title	Type	Country	Year	Longbox Value / Value
		House of Blues	RS	U.S.	1995	$40.00
2 CD set. Airdate: 11/3/95.						

Singles

Label	Catalog Number	Title	Type	Country	Year	Longbox Value / Value
Alligator		Bottle, The	CDJ	U.S.	1992	$2.00
Alligator		Working Overtime	CDJ	U.S.	1992	$2.00

Holiday, Billie

Full Length

Label	Catalog Number	Title	Type	Country	Year	Longbox Value / Value
Verve	823449-2	Silver Collection	LP/LB	U.S.†	1985	$14.00/$8.00
Verve	815055-2	Songs For Distinguished Lovers	LP/LB	U.S.†	1985	$14.00/$8.00

Singles

Label	Catalog Number	Title	Type	Country	Year	Longbox Value / Value
CBS	SRDS-8185	I'm a Fool to Want You	CD3	Japan	1991	$12.00/$4.00

Holiday Mixers

Singles

Label	Catalog Number	Title	Type	Country	Year	Longbox Value / Value
EMI	203673-2	Merry X-mas	CD5	Germany	1989	$8.00

Holland, Dave

Full Length

Label	Catalog Number	Title	Type	Country	Year	Longbox Value / Value
ECM	25001-2	Jumpin' In	LP/LB	U.S.†	1985	$14.00/$8.00

Holland, Erica

Singles

Label	Catalog Number	Title	Type	Country	Year	Longbox Value / Value
WEA	W-9859CD	I Don't Believe	CD5	U.K.	1990	$8.00

Holland, Jools

Singles

Label	Catalog Number	Title	Type	Country	Year	Longbox Value / Value
IRS	EIRSCD-141	Holy Cow	CD5	U.K.	1990	$8.00
IRS	EIRSCD-145	Maiden's Lament	CD5	U.K.	1990	$8.00
IRS	CDEIRS-170	Together Again	CD5	U.K.	1991	$8.00

Holliday, Jennifer

Full Length

Label	Catalog Number	Title	Type	Country	Year	Longbox Value / Value
Geffen	GHS-2-4014	Feel My Soul	LP/LB	U.S.†	1984	$14.00/$8.00

Singles

Label	Catalog Number	Title	Type	Country	Year	Longbox Value / Value
Arista	2238	I'm on Your Side	CDJ	U.S.	1991	$2.00

Hollies

Singles

Label	Catalog Number	Title	Type	Country	Year	Longbox Value / Value
EMI	CDEM-80	Air That I Breathe	CD5	U.K.	1988	$10.00
WEA	246786-2	Baby Come Back	CD3	Germany	1989	$10.00
EMI	871357-2	He Ain't Heavy, He's My Brother	CD5	Germany	1988	$10.00
EMI	CDEM-74	He Ain't Heavy, He's My Brother	CD5	U.K.	1988	$10.00
EMI	CDEM-264	Woman in Love	CD5	U.K.	1993	$10.00

Hollow Men

Singles

Label	Catalog Number	Title	Type	Country	Year	Longbox Value / Value
BMG	663508	Moon's a Balloon	CD5	U.K.	1990	$8.00
Arista	ASCD-2714	November Comes	CDJ	U.S.	1991	$2.00
BMG	EVNG-605CD	Pantera Rosa	CD5	U.K.	1990	$8.00
BMG	663167	Thanks to the Rolling Sea	CD5	U.K.	1990	$8.00
BMG	EVNG-305CD	White Train	CD5	U.K.	1989	$8.00

Hollow Sunday

Singles

Label	Catalog Number	Title	Type	Country	Year	Longbox Value / Value
Sense	SIGH-1	Wait For It	CD5	U.K.	1991	$8.00

Holloway, Loleatta

Singles

Label	Catalog Number	Title	Type	Country	Year	Longbox Value / Value
Active	8491	Strong Enough	CDJ	U.S.	1992	$2.00
Active	8625	Strong Enough	CDJ	U.S.	1992	$2.00

Holloway, Nancy

Singles

Label	Catalog Number	Title	Type	Country	Year	Longbox Value / Value
Musidisc	CD-190542	You Are My Yesterday	CD5	Germany	1988	$8.00

Holly, Buddy

Full Length

Label	Catalog Number	Title	Type	Country	Year	Longbox Value / Value
MCA	MCAD9603	Not Fade Away	DJ/Smplr	Canada	1995	$30.00

Singles

Label	Catalog Number	Title	Type	Country	Year	Longbox Value / Value
MCA	30124	Jive Buddy	CDJ	Germany	1992	$12.00
MCA	DMCAT-1368	Oh Boy	CD5	U.K.	1989	$11.00
Old Gold	OG-6147	That'll Be the Day	CD3	U.K.	1989	$11.00
MCA	DMCA-1302	True Love Ways	CD3	U.K.	1988	$11.00

Hollywood Bowl Orchestra

Full Length

Label	Catalog Number	Title	Type	Country	Year	Longbox Value / Value
Polygram	HBO 274-2	Gershwins in Hollywood, The	DJ/Smplr	U.S.	1991	$8.00

Hollywood Underground

Singles

Label	Catalog Number	Title	Type	Country	Year	Longbox Value / Value
		Blue Taboo	CDJ	U.S.		$2.00

Holt, John

Singles

Label	Catalog Number	Title	Type	Country	Year	Longbox Value / Value
Quattro	QTCY-1036	Love	CD5	Japan	1992	$10.00

Holy Barbarians

Singles

Label	Catalog Number	Title	Type	Country	Year	Longbox Value / Value
	PRO-CD-8105	Brother Fights	CDJ	U.S.		$2.00

Homeboy

Singles

Label	Catalog Number	Title	Type	Country	Year	Longbox Value / Value
Tam Tam	CDFTTT-051	Work It Out	CD5	U.K.	1991	$8.00

Homework

Singles

Label	Catalog Number	Title	Type	Country	Year	Longbox Value / Value
		Special Kind of Lady	CDJ	U.S.		$2.00

Honesty 69

Singles

Label	Catalog Number	Title	Type	Country	Year	Longbox Value / Value
BCM	20306	French Kiss	CD5	Germany	1989	$8.00
BCM	20373	Rich in Paradise	CD5	Germany	1989	$8.00
BCM	24373	Rich in Paradise	CD5	Germany	1990	$8.00

Honey Smugglers

Singles

Label	Catalog Number	Title	Type	Country	Year	Longbox Value / Value
Ultimate	TOPP-001CDS	Besides Which	CD5	U.K.	1991	$8.00

Honeychild

Singles

Label	Catalog Number	Title	Type	Country	Year	Longbox Value / Value
Virgin	VSCDT-1334	More Than the World	CD5	U.K.	1991	$8.00
Virgin	VSCDT-1364	Smile	CD5	U.K.	1991	$8.00
Virgin	VSCDT-1397	Time	CD5	U.K.	1992	$8.00

Honeychile

Singles

Label	Catalog Number	Title	Type	Country	Year	Longbox Value / Value
CBS	656183-2	Stepping Stone	CD5	U.K.	1990	$5.00

Honeymoon Suite

Singles

Label	Catalog Number	Title	Type	Country	Year	Longbox Value / Value
Warner Brothers		Cold Look	CDJ	U.S.		$2.00
Warner Brothers		Lookin' Out for Number One	CDJ	U.S.		$2.00
WEA	257972-2	Love Changes Everything	CD3	Germany	1988	$9.00
WEA	10SW-36	Love Changes Everything	CD3	Japan	1988	$13.00/$4.00
Warner Brothers	PRO-CD-3039	Love Changes Everything	CDJ	U.S.	1988	$2.00

Hoodoo Gurus

Singles

Label	Catalog Number	Title	Type	Country	Year	Longbox Value / Value
RCA	PD-49196	1000 Miles Away	CD5	U.K.	1991	$10.00
RCA	2854-2-RDJ	1000 Miles Away	CDJ	U.S.	1991	$2.00
BMG	PD-49326	Another World	CD5	U.K.	1990	$10.00
RCA	CCD 005	Come Anytime	CD5	Australia	1989	$10.00
RCA	PD-49350	Come Anytime	CD5	Germany	1989	$10.00
RCA	PD-49350	Come Anytime	CD5	U.K.	1989	$10.00
RCA	8998-2RDJ	Come Anytime	CDJ	U.S.	1989	$2.00
RCA	9082-2-RDJ	Come Anytime	CDJ	U.S.	1989	$2.00
Zoo	ZMJ 11094-2	Crank	CDJ	U.S.	1994	$6.00
RCA	2805-2-RDJ	Miss Freelove	CDJ	U.S.	1991	$2.00
		Nobody	CD5	U.K.	1994	$10.00
Zoo	14169	Right Time	CD5	U.S.	1994	$5.00

Hooker, John Lee

Full Length

Label	Catalog Number	Title	Type	Country	Year	Longbox Value / Value
Vee Jay	81043	Burnin'	LP/LB	U.S.		$15.00/$12.00
Vee Jay	81033	Folklore of	LP/LB	U.S.		$15.00/$12.00
		House of Blues	RS	U.S.	1995	$50.00
2 CD set. Airdate: 3/26/95.						
Vee Jay	81007	I'm John Lee Hooker	LP/LB	U.S.		$15.00/$12.00
Vee Jay	81023	Travelin'	LP/LB	U.S.		$15.00/$12.00

Singles

Label	Catalog Number	Title	Type	Country	Year	Longbox Value / Value
Silvertone	886830	Baby Lee	CD5	Germany	1990	$8.00
Chameleon		Baby Lee	CDJ	U.S.	1990	$2.00
		Boom Boom	CD5	U.K.	1992	$8.00
		Boom Boom	CD5	U.K.	1992	$8.00
Second version.						
Pointblank	12739	Boom Boom	CDJ	U.S.	1992	$2.00
		Chill Out (Things Gonna Change)	CDJ	U.S.		$6.00
Silvertone	886784	Healer, The	CD3	Germany	1990	$9.00
Silvertone	ORECD-10	Healer, The	CD3	U.K.	1990	$9.00
Chameleon	PRCD 69	Healer, The	CDJ	U.S.	1990	$2.00
	5005	I Feel Good	CD5	U.S.	1994	$5.00
Silvertone	ORECD-18	I'm In the Mood	CD5	U.K.	1990	$9.00
Silvertone	ZD-43768	I'm In the Mood	CD5	U.K.	1990	$9.00
Chameleon	PRCD 072	I'm In the Mood	CDJ	U.S.	1990	$2.00
Silvertone	ORECD-29	Mr. Lucky	CD5	U.K.	1991	$8.00
Chameleon	PRCD 061	Mr. Lucky	CDJ	U.S.	1990	$2.00
		One Bourbon, One Scotch, One Beer	CDJ	U.S.		$6.00
Charisma	HOOK1	This Is Hip	CDJ	U.S.	1991	$3.00

Hooters

Full Length

Label	Catalog Number	Title	Type	Country	Year	Longbox Value / Value
DIR		King Biscuit Flour Hour	RS	U.S.	1988	$30.00
With Mr. Mister, Airdate: 1/24/88.						
CBS	CK-39912	Nervous Night	LP/BP	U.S.†	1985	$14.00/$8.00
Sony	SRCS-6897	Starbox	LP	Japan	1993	$30.00
Columbia	CSK 1832	Zig Zag	DJ/LP	U.S.	1989	$18.00
Picturedisc CD.						

Singles

Label	Catalog Number	Title	Type	Country	Year	Longbox Value / Value
CBS	655445-3	500 Miles	CD3	Germany	1990	$10.00
Sony	CSDS-8108	500 Miles	CD3	Japan	1990	$13.00/$4.00
Columbia		500 Miles	CDJ	U.S.	1989	$5.00
CBS	655312-3	Brother, Don't You WalkAway	CD3	Germany	1989	$10.00
Columbia	CSK 7235	Brother, Don't You WalkAway	CDJ	U.S.	1990	$2.00
Columbia	CSK 73320	Heaven Laughs	CDJ	U.S.	1990	$2.00
Sony	15EP-8007	Hooter Mania	CD3	Japan	1988	$13.00/$4.00
CBS	650982-2	Johnny B.	CD5	Germany		$10.00
CBS	655574-3	Johnny B.	CD3	Germany	1990	$10.00
CBS	655574-2	Johnny B.	CD5	Germany	1990	$10.00
Columbia	651302-2	Karla With A K	CD5	U.K.	1990	$10.00
Columbia	657911-2	Karla With A K	CD5	U.K.	1992	$10.00
Sony	CSDS-8119	Man Understands	CD3	Japan	1990	$13.00/$4.00
MCA	MCA5P-2819	Private Emotion	CDJ	U.S.	1993	$2.00
Columbia	651168-2	Satellite	CD5	U.K.	1990	$10.00
MCA	MVDM-40	Twenty-Five Hours a Day	CD3	Japan	1993	$13.00/$4.00
MCA	MCA5P-2657	Twenty-Five Hours a Day	CDJ	U.S.	1993	$2.00

Hootie & The Blowfish

Full Length

Label	Catalog Number	Title	Type	Country	Year	Longbox Value / Value
Westwood One		In Concert	RS	U.S.	1995	$60.00
Airdate: 6/19/95.						
Westwood One		In Concert	RS	U.S.	1996	$60.00
Airdate: 1/15/96.						
Atlantic		Talking With...	DJ/Intvw	U.S.	1996	$20.00

Singles

Label	Catalog Number	Title	Type	Country	Year	Longbox Value / Value
Atlantic		Hold My Hand	CDJ	U.S.	1994	$7.00
Atlantic		I Only Wanna Be With You	CD5	U.K.	1995	$11.00
Atlantic		I Only Wanna Be With You	CD5	U.K.	1995	$11.00
Second version.						
Atlantic	85594	Let Her Cry	CD5	U.S.	1994	$5.00
Atlantic		Let Her Cry	CDJ	U.S.	1995	$7.00
Atlantic	87074-2	Old Man & Me	CD5	U.S.	1996	$5.00
Atlantic	PRCD 6694	Old Man & Me	CDJ	U.S.	1996	$6.00
Atlantic	PRCD6694-2	Old Man & Me	CDJ	U.S.	1996	$7.00
Atlantic	85534	Time	CD5	U.S.	1995	$5.00
Atlantic	87095	Time	CD5	U.S.	1995	$5.00
Atlantic		Tucker's Town	CD5	U.K.	1996	$10.00

Hoovers

Singles

Label	Catalog Number	Title	Type	Country	Year	Longbox Value / Value
Produce	CDHERB-101	Jealous	CD5	U.K.	1991	$8.00
Produce	CDHERB-102	Jealous	CD5	U.K.	1992	$8.00

Label	Catalog Number	Title	Type	Country	Year	Longbox Value / Value

Hope, Bob

Full Length

Label	Catalog Number	Title	Type	Country	Year	Value
		Remembers. . . World War II	LTD/LP	U.S.	1995	$35.00
2 CD set and VHS video in box.						

Horn, Jim

Singles

Label	Catalog Number	Title	Type	Country	Year	Value
Warner Brothers	PRO-CD-3348	Neon Nights	CDJ	U.S.	1988	$2.00
Warner Brothers	PRO-CD-4016	Nightshift	CDJ	U.S.	1990	$2.00
Warner Brothers	PRO-CD-3379	Silver Bells	CDJ	U.S.	1988	$2.00

Horn, Shirley

Full Length

Label	Catalog Number	Title	Type	Country	Year	Value
Verve	HORN 2	Here's to Life	DJ/LP	U.S.	1992	$14.00
Verve	XMAS 2	Secret Of Christmas	CDJ	U.S.	1992	$3.00

Horne, Jimmy Bo

Singles

Label	Catalog Number	Title	Type	Country	Year	Value
Italio-Heat	STH-544CD	Spank '89	CD5	Germany	1989	$8.00

Horne, Lena

Full Length

Label	Catalog Number	Title	Type	Country	Year	Value
Blue Note	DPRo-79873	We'll Be Together Again	DJ/LP	U.S.	1994	$20.00
CD in ribbon-tied box.						
Blue Note	CDP 7243 8 28974 2 2	We'll Be Together Again	DJ/LP	U.S.	1994	$50.00

Hornsby, Bruce – Sony Digital Masters Series (RCA RDJ 61000-2)

Hornsby, Bruce and The Range

Full Length

Label	Catalog Number	Title	Type	Country	Year	Value
RCA	2456-2-DJ	For In-store Play	DJ/Smplr	U.S.	1990	$15.00
RCA	RJC66230-2	Harbor Lights	DJ/LP	U.S.	1993	$25.00
Picturedisc in digipak.						
DIR		King Biscuit Flour Hour	RS	U.S.	1990	$30.00
Airdate: 7/9/90.						
DIR		King Biscuit Flour Hour	RS	U.S.	1992	$30.00
Airdate: 3/22/92.						
DIR		King Biscuit Flour Hour	RS	U.S.	1993	$30.00
Airdate: 1/25/93.						
DIR		King Biscuit Flour Hour	RS	U.S.	1994	$30.00
Airdate: 1/17/94.						
RCA	6275-2-RDJ	Live, The Way It Is Tour 86-87	DJ/Smplr	U.S.	1987	$35.00
Radio Ventures		Masters Of Rock	RS	U.S.	1990	$30.00
Airdate: 11/29/90.						
Westwood One		Off the Record	RS	U.S.	1993	$30.00
Airdate: 5/10/93.						
Sony/RCA	RDJ 61000-2	Sony Digital Masters Series	DJ/Smplr	U.S.	1991	$75.00
RCA	PDTD-1002	Special DJ Copy	DJ/Smplr	Japan	1995	$50.00
Media America		Up Close	RS	U.S.	1993	$20.00

Singles

Label	Catalog Number	Title	Type	Country	Year	Value
RCA	49246	A Night on the Town	CD5	Germany	1990	$10.00
RCA	2686-2-RDJ	A Night on the Town	CDJ	U.S.	1990	$3.00
RCA	PD-49270	Across the River	CD5	Germany	1990	$10.00
BMG	BVDP-3	Across the River	CD3	Japan	1990	$15.00/$4.00
RCA	PD-49270	Across the River	CD5	U.K.	1990	$10.00
RCA	2621-2-RDJ	Across the River	CDJ	U.S.	1990	$3.00
RCA	HORNS-1	Cruise Control	CDJ	U.K.	1995	$12.00
RCA	RDJ643702	Cruise Control	CDJ	U.S.	1995	$3.00
RCA	PD-49512	Defenders of the Flag	CD5	Germany	1988	$10.00
RCA	R10D-111	Defenders of the Flag	CD3	Japan	1988	$15.00/$4.00
RCA	8706-2-RDJ	Defenders of the Flag	CDJ	U.S.	1988	$3.00
RCA	RDJ-62618-2	Fields Of Grey	CDJ	U.S.	1993	$3.00
RCA	2715-2-RDJ	Fire On the Cross	CDJ	U.S.	1990	$7.00
RCA	BVDP-79	Harbor Lights	CD3	Japan	1993	$15.00/$4.00
RCA	PD-49534	Look Out Any Window	CD5	Germany	1988	$10.00
RCA	PD-49534	Look Out Any Window	CD5	U.K.	1988	$10.00
RCA	2704-2-RDJ	Lost Soul	CDJ	U.S.	1990	$3.00
RCA	PD-49770	Mandolin Rain	CD5	U.K.	1990	$10.00
RCA	PD-49296	Night on the Town	CD5	Germany	1990	$10.00
RCA	PD-49296	Night on the Town	CD5	U.K.	1990	$10.00
RCA	RDJ-62570	Passing	CDJ	U.S.	1993	$3.00
RCA		Rainbow's Cadillac	CDJ	U.S.	1993	$3.00
RCA	2846-2-RDJ	Set Me Free	CDJ	U.S.	1991	$3.00
RCA	RDJ644432	Spider Fingers	CDJ	U.S.	1995	$3.00
RCA	RDJ-62580-2	Talk of the Town	CDJ	U.S.	1993	$3.00
RCA	PD-49562	Valley Road, The	CD5	U.K.	1988	$15.00
RCA	PD-49562B	Valley Road, The	CD5	U.K.	1988	$15.00
RCA	7647-2-RDJ	Valley Road, The	CDJ	U.S.	1988	$3.00
RCA	RDJ643692	Walk in the Sun	CDJ	U.S.	1995	$3.00
RCA/NTSC	RCA 002	Way It Is, The	DJ/CDV	U.S.	1987	$50.00

Horse

Singles

Label	Catalog Number	Title	Type	Country	Year	Value
Capitol	CDCL-587	Careful	CD5	U.K.	1990	$8.00
		Celebrate	CD5	U.K.		$8.00
		Celebrate	CD5	U.K.		$8.00
Second version.						
		Home Movies	CD5	U.K.		$8.00
		Home Movies	CD5	U.K.		$8.00
Second version.						
		Shake This Mountain	CD5	U.K.		$8.00
		Shake This Mountain	CD5	U.K.		$8.00
Second version.						
Capitol	CDCL-566	Speed of My Heart	CD5	U.K.	1990	$8.00
EMI	203886-2	Sweet Thing	CD5	Germany	1990	$8.00
Capitol	CDCL-577	Sweet Thing	CD5	U.K.	1990	$8.00
Capitol	CDCL-514	You Could Be Forgiven	CD5	U.K.	1990	$8.00

Horse Flies

Singles

Label	Catalog Number	Title	Type	Country	Year	Value
Polygram	874290-3	Hush	CD3	Germany	1989	$8.00
Polygram	874291-2	Hush	CD5	Germany	1989	$8.00
MCA	1492	Life Is a Rubber Rope	CDJ	U.S.	1991	$2.00
MCA	1351	Sally Ann	CDJ	U.S.	1991	$2.00

Horsepower

Singles

Label	Catalog Number	Title	Type	Country	Year	Value
CBS	EDGECD-2	Bolt	CD5	U.K.	1992	$8.00

Hoskins, Gregory and The Sick People

Singles

Label	Catalog Number	Title	Type	Country	Year	Value
		Dance of the Vulnerable	CDJ	Canada		$3.00
		Let the World Call You Crazy	CDJ	Canada		$3.00
		Marathon Man	CDJ	Canada		$3.00

Hostage Symphony

Singles

Label	Catalog Number	Title	Type	Country	Year	Value
Lemuria	6794	Ugly	CD5	U.S.	1993	$3.00

Hot Chocolate

Singles

Label	Catalog Number	Title	Type	Country	Year	Value
Polygram		It Started With a Kiss	CD5	U.K.		$8.00
Polygram		It Started With a Kiss	CDJ	U.K.		$8.00
Second version.						
Polygram	887918-2	Never Pretend	CD5	Germany	1988	$8.00
Polygram	871764-3	What About You	CD3	Germany	1988	$8.00
Polygram	871765-2	What About You	CD5	Germany	1988	$8.00

Hot House

Singles

Label	Catalog Number	Title	Type	Country	Year	Value
RCA	PD-42114	Crazy	CD5	U.K.	1988	$8.00
RCA	PD-42234	Don't Come to Stay	CD5	U.K.	1988	$8.00
RCA	886445	Don't Come to Stay	CD5	U.K.	1988	$8.00
RCA	PD-42846	Everything You Said	CD5	U.K.	1988	$8.00
RCA	PD-42658	Hard As I Try	CD5	U.K.	1988	$8.00
RCA	PD-43512	Losing the Feeling	CD5	U.K.	1990	$8.00
RCA	PD-43906	Responsible	CD5	U.K.	1990	$8.00

Hot Legs

Singles

Label	Catalog Number	Title	Type	Country	Year	Value
King	KIDS-62	Rockin' Route 16	CD3	Japan	1991	$13.00/$4.00

Hot Tuna

Full Length

Label	Catalog Number	Title	Type	Country	Year	Value
RCA		America's Choice	LP/BP	U.S.		$12.00/$7.00
		House of Blues	RS	U.S.	1994	$35.00
2 CD set. Airdate: 1/23/94.						
RCA		Phosphorescent Rat	LP/BP	U.S.		$12.00/$7.00
RCA		Yellow Fever	LP/BP	U.S.		$12.00/$7.00

Singles

Label	Catalog Number	Title	Type	Country	Year	Value
Epic	ESK 2224	Eve of Destruction	CDJ	U.S.	1990	$2.00

Hotel Hunger

Singles

Label	Catalog Number	Title	Type	Country	Year	Value
		Give Me Love	CDJ	U.S.		$2.00

Hothouse Flowers

Full Length

Label	Catalog Number	Title	Type	Country	Year	Value
Polydor	POCD-9003	Home	LTD/LP	Japan		$40.00
Gold disc.						
DIR		King Biscuit Flour Hour	RS	U.S.	1989	$30.00
With Escape Club, Airdate: 4/2/89.						
Polygram		Live	DJ/Smplr	U.S.		$8.00
Polygram	DCI-3016	Special Compilation	DJ/Smplr	Japan		$50.00

Singles

Label	Catalog Number	Title	Type	Country	Year	Value
London	886301-2	Don't Go	CD5	Germany	1988	$10.00
London	P10L-30011	Don't Go	CD3	Japan	1988	$13.00/$4.00
London	P13L-37004	Don't Go	CD3	Japan	1990	$13.00/$4.00
London	CDP 174	Don't Go	CD5	U.K.	1988	$10.00
London	LONCD-174	Don't Go	CD5	U.K.	1988	$10.00
London	870 720-2	Don't Go	CDV/BP	U.S.	1988	$20.00/$20.00
London	886315-2	Easier in the Morning	CD5	Germany	1988	$10.00
London	LONCD-186	Easier in the Morning	CD5	U.K.	1988	$10.00
London	PODD-1026	Emotional Time	CD3	Japan	1993	$13.00/$4.00
London	LONCD-335	Emotional Time	CD5	U.K.	1993	$10.00
London	869005-2	Give It Up	CD5	Germany	1990	$10.00
London	POCD-1009	Give It Up	CD3	Japan	1990	$15.00/$4.00
London	LONCD-258	Give It Up	CD5	U.K.	1990	$10.00
London	CDP 256	Give It Up	CDJ	U.S.	1990	$2.00
London	869103-2	I Can See Clearly Now	CD5	Germany	1990	$10.00
Polydor	PODD-1007	I Can See Clearly Now	CD3	Japan	1990	$13.00/$4.00
Polydor	POCD-1026	I Can See Clearly Now	CD5	Japan	1990	$15.00
London	LONCD-269	I Can See Clearly Now	CD5	U.K.	1990	$10.00
London	CDP 310	I Can See Clearly Now	CDJ	U.S.	1990	$2.00
London	P10L-40005	I'm Sorry	CD3	Japan	1988	$13.00/$4.00
London	P13L-37007	I'm Sorry	CD3	Japan	1988	$13.00/$4.00
London	LONCD-187	I'm Sorry	CD5	U.K.	1988	$10.00
London	CDP 187	I'm Sorry	CDJ	U.S.	1988	$2.00
London		Isn't It Amazing	CD5	U.K.	1993	$10.00
London		Isn't It Amazing	CD5	U.K.	1993	$10.00
Image disc.						
London	LONCD-276	Movies	CD5	U.K.	1990	$10.00
London	CDP 307	Movies	CDJ	U.S.	1990	$2.00
London		One Tongue	CD5	U.K.	1993	$10.00
London		One Tongue	CD5	U.K.	1993	$10.00
Second version.						
London	CDP 906	One Tongue	CDJ	U.S.	1993	$6.00
London	HOT 1	This Is It	CDJ	U.K.	1993	$12.00

Hound Dog

Singles

Label	Catalog Number	Title	Type	Country	Year	Value
Warner Brothers	AMDX-6048	Bridge	CD3	Japan	1992	$13.00/$4.00
Warner Brothers	AMDX-6037	Fly	CD3	Japan	1991	$13.00/$4.00
Warner Brothers	AMDX-6087	Jealousy	CD3	Japan	1992	$13.00/$4.00
Warner Brothers	AMDX-6085	Sun Also Rises	CD3	Japan	1993	$13.00/$4.00

Label	Catalog Number	Title	Type	Country	Year	Longbox Value / Value

House

Singles

Label	Catalog Number	Title	Type	Country	Year	Longbox Value / Value
		Here Comes The Good Times	CD5	U.K.		$10.00
		Here Comes The Good Times	CD5	U.K.		$10.00

Second version.

House Corporation

Singles

Label	Catalog Number	Title	Type	Country	Year	Longbox Value / Value
ZYX	6502-8	Jammin' on the Dance	CD5	Germany	1991	$6.00

House Crew

Singles

Label	Catalog Number	Title	Type	Country	Year	Longbox Value / Value
Intercord	825 773	All We Wanna Do Is Dance	CD5	Germany	1990	$8.00

House of Freaks

Full Length

Label	Catalog Number	Title	Type	Country	Year	Longbox Value / Value
Giant	9 24417-2-Dj	Cakewalk	DJ/LP	U.S.	1991	$12.00

Picture disc.

Singles

Label	Catalog Number	Title	Type	Country	Year	Longbox Value / Value
Giant	PRO-CD-4815	Rocking Chair	CDJ	U.S.	1991	$2.00

House of Lords

Full Length

Label	Catalog Number	Title	Type	Country	Year	Longbox Value / Value
RCA		Sahara	LP/BP	U.S.		$12.00/$7.00

Singles

Label	Catalog Number	Title	Type	Country	Year	Longbox Value / Value
RCA	PD-49252	Can't Find My Way Home	CD5	Germany	1990	$10.00
RCA	2658-2-RDJ	Can't Find My Way Home	CDJ	U.S.	1990	$2.00
RCA	2804-2-RDJ	Heart on the Line	CDJ	U.S.	1991	$2.00
RCA		I Wanna Be Loved	CDJ	U.S.	1988	$5.00
RCA	8737-2-RDJ	I Wanna Be Loved	CDJ	U.S.	1988	$2.00
RCA	PD-49411	Love Don't Lie	CD5	Germany	1989	$10.00
RCA	8900-2-RDJ	Love Don't Lie	CDJ	U.S.	1989	$2.00
RCA	8900-2-RDJ	Love Don't Lie	CDJ	U.S.	1989	$2.00
Victory	CDP 659	O Father	CDJ	U.S.	1992	$2.00
RCA	2736-2-RDJ	Remember My Name	CDJ	U.S.	1990	$2.00
Victor	VICP-41	What's Forever For	CD3	Japan	1990	$13.00/$4.00
Victor		What's Forever For	DJ/CD3	Japan	1990	$20.00
Victory	383 483 002-2	What's Forever For	CD5	U.S.	1992	$5.00
Victory	CDP 714	What's Forever For	CDJ	U.S.	1992	$2.00

House of Love

Full Length

Label	Catalog Number	Title	Type	Country	Year	Longbox Value / Value
Fontana	CDP 189	Live	DJ/Smplr	U.S.	1990	$10.00

Singles

Label	Catalog Number	Title	Type	Country	Year	Longbox Value / Value
Rough Trade	875283	Beatles & the Stones	CD5	Germany	1990	$9.00
Fontana	HOLCD-42	Beatles & the Stones	CD5	U.K.	1990	$9.00
Fontana	HOLCD-432	Beatles & the Stones	CD5	U.K.	1990	$9.00
Fontana	CDP 270	Beatles & the Stones	CDJ	U.S.	1990	$2.00
Creation	CRESCD-053	Christine	CD5	U.K.	1990	$9.00
Creation	CRESCD-057	Destroy the Heart	CD5	U.K.	1990	$9.00
Fontana	HOLCD-62	Feel	CD5	U.K.	1992	$10.00
Rough Trade	608 5341 3	Girl With the Loneliest Eyes	CD5	Germany	1991	$9.00
Fontana	HOLCD-5	Girl With the Loneliest Eyes	CD5	U.K.	1991	$9.00
Fontana		Honey Honey	CDJ	U.S.		$2.00
Polygram	876315-2	I Don't Know Why I Love You	CD5	Canada	1990	$9.00
Fontana	HOLCD-2	I Don't Know Why I Love You	CD5	U.K.	1989	$9.00
Fontana	CDP 213	I Don't Know Why I Love You	CDJ	U.S.	1989	$2.00
Fontana	CDP 429	Marble	CDJ	U.S.	1991	$2.00
Polygram	874340-3	Never	CD3	Germany	1989	$9.00
Polygram	874341-2	Never	CD5	Germany	1989	$9.00
Fontana	HOLCD-1	Never	CD5	U.K.	1989	$9.00
Fontana	CDP 518	Safe	CDJ	U.S.	1990	$2.00
Polygram	876781-2	Shine On	CD5	Germany	1990	$9.00
Fontana	HOLCD-3	Shine On	CD5	U.K.	1990	$9.00
Fontana		Shine On	CDJ	U.K.	1990	$10.00
Fontana	CDP 731	You Don't Understand	CDJ	U.S.	1992	$2.00

House of Pain

Singles

Label	Catalog Number	Title	Type	Country	Year	Longbox Value / Value
		Greatest Hits	CD5	U.K.		$10.00
WEA	XLS-32CD	Jump Around	CD5	U.K.	1992	$8.00
Tommy Boy	526	Jump Around	CD5	U.S.	1992	$5.00
Tommy Boy	539	Jump Around	CDJ	U.S.	1992	$2.00
Tommy Boy	643	Legend	CD5	U.S.	1994	$5.00
		Over There	CD5	U.K.		$10.00
WEA	XLS-38CD	Shamrocks and Shenanigans	CD5	U.K.	1992	$8.00
Tommy Boy	543	Shamrocks and Shenanigans	CD5	U.S.	1992	$5.00
Tommy Boy	548	Shamrocks and Shenanigans	CDJ	U.S.	1992	$2.00

House of Windsor

Singles

Label	Catalog Number	Title	Type	Country	Year	Longbox Value / Value
Alfa	ALCB-714	Squidgy	CD5	Japan	1992	$12.00
Di-Lema	HRHCD-1	Squidgy	CD5	U.K.	1992	$8.00

Housemartins

Singles

Label	Catalog Number	Title	Type	Country	Year	Longbox Value / Value
Go Discs	GODCD-21	Build	CD5	U.K.	1990	$8.00
Elektra	PR 2162-2	Caravan of Love	CDJ	U.S.	1987	$2.00
Chrysalis	880880	There Is Always Something	CD5	Germany	1988	$8.00
Go Discs	GODCD-22	There Is Always Something	CD5	U.K.	1988	$8.00

Housey, Rachid

Singles

Label	Catalog Number	Title	Type	Country	Year	Longbox Value / Value
ZYX	5533495-2	Harem Party	CD5	Germany	1990	$6.00

Houston, Penelope

Singles

Label	Catalog Number	Title	Type	Country	Year	Longbox Value / Value
	PRO-CD-8014	Sweetheart	CDJ	U.S.	1995	$3.00

Houston, Thelma

Full Length

Label	Catalog Number	Title	Type	Country	Year	Longbox Value / Value
Sheffield	CD-2	I've Got the Music in Me	LP/BP	U.S.†	1985	$14.00/$8.00

Singles

Label	Catalog Number	Title	Type	Country	Year	Longbox Value / Value
Reprise	PRO-CD-4487	Out of My Hands	CDJ	U.S.	1990	$2.00
Reprise	9 40080-2	Throw You Down	CD5	U.S.	1991	$5.00

Houston, Whitney

Full Length

Label	Catalog Number	Title	Type	Country	Year	Longbox Value / Value
Pioneer Artists	PA-86-M044	#1 Video Hit	LD	U.S.	1986	$30.00/$30.00
		All My Love	RS	U.S.	1993	$100.00

2 CD set. Airdate: 8/16/93.

Singles

Label	Catalog Number	Title	Type	Country	Year	Longbox Value / Value
Arista	664000	All the Man I Need	CD5	Germany	1990	$10.00
Arista	ASCD-2156	All the Man I Need	CDJ	U.S.	1990	$2.00
Arista	WHITNEY1	Count on Me	CDJ	U.K.		$20.00
Arista	ASCD2976	Count on Me	CDJ	U.S.	1995	$6.00
Arista	A10D-105	Didn't We Almost Have It All	CD3	Japan	1988	$13.00/$4.00
Arista	RISCD-31	Didn't We Almost Have It All	CD5	U.K.	1988	$10.00
Arista		Exhale	CDJ	U.K.	1995	$15.00
Arista	12917	Exhale	CD5	U.S.	1995	$5.00
Arista	12916	Exhale	CD5	U.S.	1995	$6.00
Arista	ASCD2885	Exhale	CDJ	U.S.	1995	$6.00
Arista	A10D-103	Greatest Love of All	CD3	Japan	1988	$12.00/$4.00
Arista	A10D-102	How Will I Know	CD3	Japan	1988	$12.00/$4.00
Arista	13293-2	I Believe In You & Me	CD5	U.S.	1996	$3.50
Arista	BVDA-32	I Belong to You	CD3	Japan	1991	$13.00/$4.00
Arista	664727	I Belong to You	CD5	U.K.	1991	$10.00
Arista	BVDA-63	I Have Nothing	CD3	Japan	1993	$13.00/$4.00
Arista	ASCD-2527	I Have Nothing	CDJ	U.S.	1992	$2.00
Arista	12527	I Have Nothing	CD5	U.S.	1993	$5.00
Arista	661904	I Know Him So Well	CD5	Germany	1988	$10.00
Arista	A10D-104	I Wanna Dance With Somebody	CD3	Japan	1990	$13.00/$3.00
Arista		I Wanna Dance With Somebody	CDJ	U.S.	1988	$3.00
Arista	BVDA-47	I Will Always Love You	CD3	Japan	1992	$12.00/$4.00
Arista	7432112065-2	I Will Always Love You	CD5	U.K.	1992	$10.00
Arista	12503	I Will Always Love You	CD5	U.S.	1992	$5.00
Arista	ASCD-2490	I Will Always Love You	CDJ	U.S.	1992	$3.00
Arista	BVDA-58	I'm Every Woman	CD3	Japan	1993	$13.00/$4.00
Arista	74321-121502	I'm Every Woman	CD5	U.K.	1993	$10.00
Arista	12520	I'm Every Woman	CD5	U.S.	1992	$6.00
Arista	ASCD-2519	I'm Every Woman	CDJ	U.S.	1992	$6.00
Arista	663594	I'm Your Baby Tonight	CD5	Germany	1990	$10.00
Arista	BVDA-8	I'm Your Baby Tonight	CD3	Japan	1990	$12.00/$4.00
Arita	BVCA-9002	I'm Your Baby Tonight	CD5	Japan	1990	$16.00
Arista	663594	I'm Your Baby Tonight	CD5	U.K.	1990	$10.00
Arista	ASCD-2108	I'm Your Baby Tonight	CDJ	U.S.	1990	$7.00
Arista		It Isn't, It Wasn't	CDJ	U.S.		$2.00
Arista	661516	Love Will Save the Day	CD5	Germany	1988	$10.00
Arista	A10D-108	Love Will Save the Day	CD3	Japan	1988	$13.00/$4.00
Arista	661516	Love Will Save the Day	CD5	U.K.	1988	$10.00
Arista	ASCD-2222	Miracle	CDJ	U.S.	1991	$2.00
Arista	664313	My Name Is Not Susan	CD5	Germany	1991	$10.00
Arista	664659	My Name Is Not Susan	CD5	Germany	1991	$10.00
Arista	BVDA-24	My Name Is Not Susan	CD3	Japan	1991	$13.00/$4.00
Arista	664510	My Name Is Not Susan	CD5	U.K.	1991	$10.00
Arista	ASCD-2259	My Name Is Not Susan	CDJ	U.S.	1991	$2.00
Arista	661725	One Moment In Time	CD5	Germany	1988	$14.00
Arista	661613	One Moment In Time	CD5	U.K.	1988	$12.00
Arista	2650	Queen Of the Night	CDJ	U.S.	1993	$2.00
Arista	74321 1533	Run to You	CD5	U.K.	1992	$8.00
Arista	07822 12581	Run to You	CD5	U.K.	1992	$8.00
Arista	2570	Run to You	CDJ	U.S.	1993	$2.00
Arista	A10D-101	Saving All My Love For You	CD3	Japan	1990	$12.00/$4.00
Arista	A10D-106	So Emotional	CD3	Japan	1988	$12.00/$4.00
Arista		So Emotional	CDJ	U.S.	1988	$2.00
Arista	ASCD 2207	Star Spangled Banner	CD5	U.S.	1991	$5.00
Arista		Star Spangled Banner	CDJ	U.S.	1991	$8.00
Arista	A10D-137	Takin' A Chance	CD3	Japan	1989	$12.00/$4.00
Arista	ASCD-2420	We Didn't Know	CDJ	U.S.		$2.00
Arista	A10D-107	Where Do Broken Hearts Go	CD3	Japan	1988	$12.00/$4.00

Howard, Adina

Singles

Label	Catalog Number	Title	Type	Country	Year	Longbox Value / Value
Elektra/Asylum	66175	Freak Like Me	CD5	U.S.	1994	$5.00
	PRCD 93872	It's All About You	CDJ	U.S.		$3.00
Elektra	66120	Mix Up & Down	CD5	U.S.	1995	$5.00

Howard, Cheryl

Singles

Label	Catalog Number	Title	Type	Country	Year	Longbox Value / Value
Atlantic	PRCD 4465-2	If I Can't Have You	CDJ	U.S.	1992	$2.00

Howard, George

Singles

Label	Catalog Number	Title	Type	Country	Year	Longbox Value / Value
GRP	5117	Grazin' in the Grass	CDJ	U.S.	1993	$2.00
GRP	5127	Only Human	CDJ	U.S.	1993	$2.00

Howard, James Newton

Full Length

Label	Catalog Number	Title	Type	Country	Year	Longbox Value / Value
Sheffield	CD-23	Friends	LP/BP	U.S.†	1985	$14.00/$8.00

Howard, Miki

Full Length

Label	Catalog Number	Title	Type	Country	Year	Longbox Value / Value
Giant	PRO-CD-5682	Femme Fatale Sampler	DJ/Smplr	U.S.	1992	$10.00

Singles

Label	Catalog Number	Title	Type	Country	Year	Longbox Value / Value
Giant	PRO-CD-6033	But I Love You	CDJ	U.S.	1993	$2.00
Atlantic		Come Home to Me	CDJ	U.S.	1989	$2.00
Atlantic	PR 3066-2	Love Under New Management	CDJ	U.S.	1989	$2.00
Giant	PRO-CD-5824	Release Me	CDJ	U.S.	1992	$2.00
Atlantic	A-7935CD	Until You Come Back to Me	CD5	U.K.	1990	$8.00
Atlantic		Until You Come Back to Me	CDJ	U.S.	1989	$2.00

Howard, Robert

Singles

Label	Catalog Number	Title	Type	Country	Year	Longbox Value / Value
RCA	PD-42596	Wait	CD5	U.K.	1989	$8.00

Howard, Tony

Singles

Label	Catalog Number	Title	Type	Country	Year	Longbox Value / Value
Brown Stone	12375	This One's For You	CDJ	U.S.	1993	$2.00

Howe, Steve

Full Length

Label	Catalog Number	Title	Type	Country	Year	Longbox Value / Value
Relativity	1163	Grand Scheme of Things	LP/LB	U.S.		$18.00/$15.00
Relativity	1161	Turbulance	LP/LB	U.S.		$18.00/$15.00

Singles

Label	Catalog Number	Title	Type	Country	Year	Longbox Value / Value
Relativity		Turbulence	CDJ	U.S.	1991	$6.00

Howell, Eddie

Singles

Label	Catalog Number	Title	Type	Country	Year	Longbox Value / Value
		Man From Manhattan	CD5	U.K.	1994	$10.00

Howie, J & Co.

Singles

Label	Catalog Number	Title	Type	Country	Year	Longbox Value / Value
Arista	663750	Come Together	CD5	U.K.	1990	$8.00

Howlin' Maggie

Singles

Label	Catalog Number	Title	Type	Country	Year	Longbox Value / Value
Columbia	CSK 7742	Alcohol	CDJ	U.S.		$3.00

HR

Singles

Label	Catalog Number	Title	Type	Country	Year	Longbox Value / Value
Efa	CD-16137	It's About Luv	CD5	Germany	1989	$8.00
Efa	CD-16136	Keep Out of Reach	CD5	Germany	1989	$8.00

Hubbard, Freddie

Full Length

Label	Catalog Number	Title	Type	Country	Year	Longbox Value / Value
Fantasy	FCD-9626	A Little Night Music	LP/LB	U.S.†	1985	$14.00/$8.00
RealTime	RT-3005	Back To Birdland	LP/LB	U.S.†	1985	$14.00/$8.00
Blue Note		Open Sesame and Hub Cap	LTD/LP	U.S.	1995	$19.00
Enja	311234	Outpost	LP/LB	U.S.†	1985	$14.00/$8.00
Atlantic	80108-2	Sweet Return	LP/LB	U.S.†	1985	$14.00/$8.00
Verve	825956-2	The Hub of Hubbard	LP/LB	U.S.†	1985	$14.00/$8.00

Singles

Label	Catalog Number	Title	Type	Country	Year	Value
Derrick Records	141036	Back to Birdland	CD5	U.S.	1994	$5.00
Blue Note	DPRO-79644	Spanish Rose	CDJ	U.S.	1989	$2.00

Hudson, Elaine

Singles

Label	Catalog Number	Title	Type	Country	Year	Value
RCA	PD-43440	No More the Fool	CD5	U.K.	1990	$8.00
RCA	PD-43488	On a Long Winding Road	CD5	Germany	1990	$8.00
RCA	PD-43488	On a Long Winding Road	CD5	U.K.	1990	$8.00

Hudson, Lavine

Singles

Label	Catalog Number	Title	Type	Country	Year	Value
Virgin	TENCD-390	Abraham, Martin and John	CD5	U.K.	1991	$8.00
Virgin	664185	All I Need	CD5	Germany	1991	$8.00
Virgin	TENCD-339	All I Need	CD5	U.K.	1991	$8.00
Virgin	VSCD-1096	Flesh Of My Flesh	CD5	U.K.	1988	$8.00
Virgin	VSCD-1067	Intervention	CD5	U.K.	1988	$8.00
Virgin	PR 2371	Intervention	CDJ	U.S.	1988	$2.00
Virgin	664483	Little Sensitivity	CD5	Germany	1991	$8.00
Virgin	TENCD-351	Little Sensitivity	CD5	U.K.	1991	$8.00
Virgin	665038	You're Still Loved	CD5	Germany	1991	$8.00

Hue & Cry

Singles

Label	Catalog Number	Title	Type	Country	Year	Value
Circa	YRCD 9	I Refuse	CDJ	U.K.	1988	$9.00
Virgin	PR 2345	Labour of Love	CDJ	U.S.	1988	$2.00
Circa	YRCD 24	Looking For Linda	CD3	U.K.	1989	$9.00
Circa	YRCD 64	My Salt Heart	CD5	U.K.	1988	$9.00
Virgin	YRCD 18	Ordinary Angel	CD5	U.K.	1988	$9.00
Circa	YRCD 41	Peaceful Face	CD3	U.K.	1989	$9.00
Fidelity	CDFIDEL-1	Profoundly Yours	CD5	U.K.	1992	$9.00
Circa	664846	She Makes a Sound	CD5	Germany	1988	$9.00
Circa	YRCDX 79	She Makes a Sound	CD5	U.K.	1988	$9.00
Circa	YRCD 37	Sweet Invisibility	CD3	U.K.	1989	$9.00
Circa	162304	Violently	CD3	Germany	1989	$9.00
Circa	YRCD-29	Violently	CD3	U.K.	1989	$9.00
Circa	YRECD-29	Violently	CD3	U.K.	1989	$9.00

Huggy Bear

Singles

Label	Catalog Number	Title	Type	Country	Year	Value
Kill Rock Stars	236	Weaponry Listens To	CD5	U.S.	1994	$5.00

Hull, Bunny

Singles

Label	Catalog Number	Title	Type	Country	Year	Longbox Value / Value
Canyon	PCDY-00083	Lap of Luxury	CD3	Japan	1991	$12.00/$3.00

Hum

Singles

Label	Catalog Number	Title	Type	Country	Year	Value
	ADL844032	I'd Like Your Hair Long	CDJ	U.S.		$2.00
RCA	RDJ644842	Pod, The	CDJ	U.S.		$2.00
RCA	RDJ643402	Stars	CDJ	U.S.		$2.00
RCA	RDJ643432	Stars	CDJ	U.S.		$2.00

Human League

Full Length

Label	Catalog Number	Title	Type	Country	Year	Longbox Value / Value
A&M	CD-4892	Dare	LP/LB	U.S.†	1984	$14.00/$8.00
A&M	75021 8055 2	Dare to Be Romantic	DJ/Smplr	U.S.	1990	$10.00
Eastwest	PRCD 9185-2	Interview	DJ/Intvw	U.S.		$12.00
A&M	CD-4923	Right	LP/LB	U.S.†	1984	$15.00/$10.00

Singles

Label	Catalog Number	Title	Type	Country	Year	Longbox Value / Value
A&M	75021 8055	Dare To Be Romantic	CDJ	U.S.	1990	$3.00
		Filling Up With Heaven	CD5	U.K.	1995	$10.00
		Filling Up With Heaven	CD5	U.K.	1995	$10.00
Second version.						
Virgin	663520	Heart Like a Wheel	CD5	Germany	1990	$10.00
Toshiba	VJDP-121	Heart Like a Wheel	CD3	Japan	1990	$13.00/$4.00
Virgin	VSCDT-1262	Heart Like a Wheel	CD5	U.K.	1990	$10.00
Virgin	VSCDX-1262	Heart Like a Wheel	CD5	U.K.	1990	$13.00
A&M	75021 7406 2	Heart Like a Wheel	CDJ	U.S.	1990	$2.00
Virgin	CDT-24	(Keep Feeling) Fascination	CD3	U.K.	1988	$10.00
Virgin	880984	Love Action	CD3	Germany	1988	$10.00
Virgin	CDT-6	Love Action	CD3	U.K.	1988	$10.00
Virgin	661788	Love Is All That Matters	CD5	Germany	1988	$10.00
Virgin	VJD-12026	Love Is All That Matters	CD3	Japan	1988	$13.00/$4.00
Virgin	VSCD-1025	Love Is All That Matters	CD5	U.K.	1988	$10.00
	PRCD 9198-2	One Man In My Heart	CDJ	U.S.		$2.00
Virgin		One Man In My Heart	CDJ	U.S.		$3.00
Virgin	VJDP-143	Soundtrack to a Generation	CD3	Japan	1990	$12.00/$4.00
Virgin	VSCDT-1303	Soundtrack to a Generation	CD5	U.K.	1990	$10.00
Elecktra/Asylum	66147	Tell Me When	CD5	U.S.	1994	$5.00
Virgin	PRCD 9155-2	Tell Me When	CDJ	U.S.	1995	$3.00

Human Radio

Singles

Label	Catalog Number	Title	Type	Country	Year	Value
Columbia	CSK 73330	Me & Elvis	CDJ	U.S.	1990	$2.00
Columbia	CSK 2154	My First Million	CDJ	U.S.	1990	$2.00

Human Resource

Singles

Label	Catalog Number	Title	Type	Country	Year	Value
BMG	RSUK-4XCD	Complete Dominator	CD5	U.K.	1991	$8.00
BMG	RSUK 4CD	Dominator	CD5	U.K.	1991	$8.00
Radikal	12321	Dominator	CD5	U.S.	1992	$4.00
ZYX	6738-8	Joke	CD5	Germany	1992	$6.00

Humanoid

Singles

Label	Catalog Number	Title	Type	Country	Year	Longbox Value / Value
ZYX	6135-8	Slam	CD5	Germany	1989	$8.00
ZYX	6047-8	Stakker	CD5	Germany	1989	$8.00
Alfa	11B3-39	Stakker	CD3	Japan	1989	$13.00/$4.00
Passion	CDSTOT-27	Stakker Humanoid	CD5	U.K.	1992	$8.00

Humantronics

Singles

Label	Catalog Number	Title	Type	Country	Year	Value
BMG	664030	Sound of Africa, The	CD5	Germany	1991	$8.00

Humble Pie

Full Length

Label	Catalog Number	Title	Type	Country	Year	Longbox Value / Value
Atco		Go For the Throat	LP/LB	U.S.		$14.00/$8.00
Album Network		In the Studio (Rockin' the Filmore)	RS	U.S.	1991	$25.00
Airdate: 10/21/91.						
DIR		King Biscuit Flour Hour	RS	U.S.	1988	$30.00
Airdate: 9/11/88.						
DIR		King Biscuit Flour Hour	RS	U.S.	1990	$30.00
Airdate: 9/10/90.						
Atco		On To Victory	LP/LB	U.S.		$14.00/$8.00
A&M		Rock On	LP/LB	U.S.		$14.00/$8.00

Singles

Label	Catalog Number	Title	Type	Country	Year	Value
	520240	Rock On	CD5	U.S.	1994	$5.00

Hummel, Mark

Full Length

Label	Catalog Number	Title	Type	Country	Year	Value
		House of Blues	RS	U.S.	1995	$40.00
2 CD set. Airdate: 7/23/95.						

Hummingbirds

Singles

Label	Catalog Number	Title	Type	Country	Year	Value
Polygram	874707-2	Blush	CD5	Germany	1990	$8.00
RooArt	RARCD-3	Blush	CD5	U.K.	1990	$8.00
		Tuesday	CDJ	U.S.		$2.00
Polygram	HARTCD-4	Word Gets Around	CD5	U.K.	1990	$8.00

Humpe, Inga

Singles

Label	Catalog Number	Title	Type	Country	Year	Value
WEA	9031-72552-2	Do I Have To	CD5	Germany	1990	$8.00
WEA	248071-2	No Longer Friends	CD3	Germany	1990	$8.00
WEA	171466-2	Riding Into the Blue	CD5	Germany	1990	$8.00
WEA	246606-2	Something Stupid	CD5	Germany	1989	$8.00

Humperdinck, Englebert

Full Length

Label	Catalog Number	Title	Type	Country	Year	Longbox Value / Value
Polygram	820367	Greatest Hits	LP/BP	U.S.		$14.00/$8.00
Polygram	820459	Release Me	LP/BP	U.S.		$14.00/$8.00

Singles

Label	Catalog Number	Title	Type	Country	Year	Value
BMG	661693	Alone In the Night	CD5	Germany	1988	$9.00
BMG	662760	Angel Heart	CD5	Germany	1989	$9.00
BMG	664010	California Blue	CD5	Germany	1991	$9.00
BMG	661902	Dream With You	CD5	Germany	1989	$9.00
BMG	664705	Dream With You	CD5	Germany	1991	$9.00
BMG	663737	I Wanna Rock You in My Wildest Dreams	CD5	Germany	1990	$9.00
BMG	664040	I Wanna Rock You in My Wildest Dreams	CD5	Germany	1991	$9.00
BMG	664872	Only A Child	CD5	Germany	1989	$9.00
Aris	885670	Red Roses For My Lady	CD3	Germany	1989	$9.00
Polygram	882095-2	Winter World of Love	CD5	Germany	1988	$9.00

Humphrey, Bobbi

Singles

Label	Catalog Number	Title	Type	Country	Year	Value
Warner Brothers	PRO-CD-4354	Let's Get Started	CDJ	U.S.	1990	$2.00

Humphries, Les

Singles

Label	Catalog Number	Title	Type	Country	Year	Value
Eastwest	246711-2	Dance Dance Dance	CD3	Germany	1989	$8.00

Hunger

Singles

Label	Catalog Number	Title	Type	Country	Year	Value
	U5P1007	Vanishing Cream	CDJ	U.S.		$2.00

Hungry I

Singles

Label	Catalog Number	Title	Type	Country	Year	Value
Nursery	NYSCD-6	Sudden Supernature	CD5	U.K.	1991	$8.00

Hunky Dory

Singles

Label	Catalog Number	Title	Type	Country	Year	Longbox Value / Value
El	25606-12	It's Love	CD3	Japan	1989	$13.00/$4.00

Hunniford, Gloria

Singles

Label	Catalog Number	Title	Type	Country	Year	Value
Ocean	CDOCN-6	Give the Children Back Their Childhood	CD5	U.K.	1989	$8.00

Hunter, Ian

Full Length

Label	Catalog Number	Title	Type	Country	Year	Longbox Value / Value
Columbia		All American Boy	LP/LB	U.S.		$14.00/$8.00
Chrysalis	CD25CR13	You're Never Alone With a Schizophrenic	LTD/LP	U.K.	1994	$25.00/$20.00
25th Anniversary edition in 6"x11" longbox.						

Singles

Label	Catalog Number	Title	Type	Country	Year	Value
Polygram	876469-2	American Music	CD5	Germany	1989	$8.00
Mercury	MERCD-315	American Music	CD5	U.K.	1989	$8.00
Mercury	CDP 127	American Music	CDJ	U.S.	1989	$3.00
Mercury	CDP 127	Woman's Intuition	CDJ	U.S.	1989	$3.00

Hunter, Robert

Singles

Label	Catalog Number	Title	Type	Country	Year	Value
		Liberty	CDJ	U.S.	1994	$2.00

Hunter & Roson

Singles

Label	Catalog Number	Title	Type	Country	Year	Value
		Women's Intuition	CDJ	U.S.		$2.00

Hunter, Steve

Full Length

Label	Catalog Number	Title	Type	Country	Year	Longbox Value / Value
		Deacon	LP/LB	U.S.		$12.00/$7.00

Hunters & Collectors

Full Length

Label	Catalog Number	Title	Type	Country	Year	Value
		Demon Flower	LTD/LP	Australia		$25.00
CD with 12 lyric cards.						

Singles

Label	Catalog Number	Title	Type	Country	Year	Value
Atlantic	PRCD 3427-2	Blind Eye	CDJ	U.S.	1990	$2.00
IRS	DIRM-177	Breadline	CD5	U.K.	1988	$10.00
Atlantic	A-7914CD	When the River Runs	CD5	U.K.	1990	$10.00
Atlantic	86202-2	When the River Runs	CD5	U.S.	1989	$5.00
Atlantic	PRCD 3280-2	When the River Runs	CDJ	U.S.	1989	$2.00
Atlantic	PRCD 3328-2	When the River Runs	CDJ	U.S.	1989	$2.00

Huntington, Eddy

Singles

Label	Catalog Number	Title	Type	Country	Year	Longbox Value / Value
Alfa	10B3-5	Bang Bang Baby	CD3	Japan	1989	$12.00/$3.00
Alfa	10SR-31	May Day	CD3	Japan	1989	$12.00/$3.00
Alfa	10SR-15	My Sweet Friend	CD3	Japan	1989	$12.00/$3.00
Alfa	111B3-84	Shock in My Heart	CD3	Japan	1989	$12.00/$3.00
ZYX	6165-8	U.S.S.R.	CD5	Germany	1989	$6.00

Huntsberry, Howard

Singles

Label	Catalog Number	Title	Type	Country	Year	Longbox Value / Value
Pioneer	09P3-6199	Higher and Higher	CD3	Japan	1989	$12.00/$4.00
	80001	Portrait of a Single	CD5	U.S.	1994	$5.00

Hurley, Steve Silk

Singles

Label	Catalog Number	Title	Type	Country	Year	Longbox Value / Value
Atlantic	A-8856CD	Work It Out	CD5	U.K.	1989	$8.00

Hurrah!

Singles

Label	Catalog Number	Title	Type	Country	Year	Longbox Value / Value
Kitchenware	661770	Big Sky	CD3	Germany	1990	$8.00
Kitchenware	SKCD-42	Big Sky	CD3	U.K.	1990	$8.00
Kitchenware	661911	Sweet Sanity	CD5	Germany	1990	$8.00
Kitchenware	SKCD-40	Sweet Sanity	CD5	U.K.	1990	$8.00

Hurricane

Full Length

Label	Catalog Number	Title	Type	Country	Year	Longbox Value / Value
Enigma	2 73511-2	Slave to the Thrill	LP/LB	U.S.	1990	$25.00/$20.00

Banned "nude woman" cover.

Singles

Label	Catalog Number	Title	Type	Country	Year	Longbox Value / Value
Enigma	EPRO-114	I'm On to You	CDJ	U.S.	1988	$2.00
Enigma	72300-2	I'm On to You	CDV	U.S.	1988	$25.00
Enigma	72300-2	I'm On to You	CDV/BP	U.S.	1988	$20.00/$20.00
Enigma	EPRO-267	Little Sister	CDJ	U.S.	1990	$2.00
Alfa	10SR-40	Livin' Over the Edge	CD3	Japan	1988	$13.00/$4.00
Enigma	EPRO-119	Livin' Over the Edge	CDJ	U.S.	1988	$2.00
Enigma		Next to You	CDJ	U.S.	1990	$2.00
Enigma	EPRO-297	Young Man	CDJ	U.S.	1990	$2.00

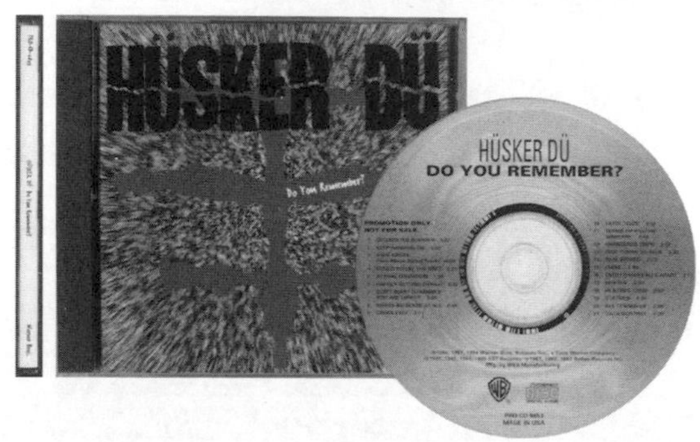

Husker Du – Do You Remember (Warner Brothers PRO-CD-6853)

Hüsker Dü

Full Length

Label	Catalog Number	Title	Type	Country	Year	Longbox Value / Value
Warner Brothers	PRO-CD-6853	Do You Remember?	DJ/Smplr	U.S.	1994	$25.00

Singles

Label	Catalog Number	Title	Type	Country	Year	Longbox Value / Value
Efa	CFD-40065	Eight Miles High	CD5	Germany	1988	$10.00
Pinnacle	SST270CD	Eight Miles High	CD5	U.K.	1990	$10.00
SST	CD 270	Eight Miles High	CD5	U.S.	1990	$10.00
Efa	CD-40066	Makes No Sense at All	CD5	Germany	1989	$10.00
SST	CD-051	Makes No Sense at All	CD5	U.K.	1989	$10.00

Hutch, Willie

Singles

Label	Catalog Number	Title	Type	Country	Year	Longbox Value / Value
Sire	PRO-CD-5345	I Choose You	CDJ	U.S.	1992	$2.00

Hutcherson, Bobby

Full Length

Label	Catalog Number	Title	Type	Country	Year	Longbox Value / Value
Blue Note		Dialogue and Oblique	LTD/LP	U.S.	1995	$19.00

Hutchins, Brent

Singles

Label	Catalog Number	Title	Type	Country	Year	Longbox Value / Value
Hollywood	8210-Dj	Arachnaphobia	CDJ	U.S.	1990	$2.00

Hutton, Tim

Singles

Label	Catalog Number	Title	Type	Country	Year	Longbox Value / Value
Epic	THIEF-2	Prophet	CD5	U.K.	1992	$10.00

Huxley, Parthenon

Singles

Label	Catalog Number	Title	Type	Country	Year	Longbox Value / Value
		Chance to Be Loved	CDJ	U.S.		$2.00
		Double Our Numbers	CDJ	U.S.		$2.00

Hyde, Paul

Singles

Label	Catalog Number	Title	Type	Country	Year	Longbox Value / Value
EMI	203786-2	America Is Sexy	CD5	Germany	1990	$8.00

Hyland, Brian

Singles

Label	Catalog Number	Title	Type	Country	Year	Longbox Value / Value
Old Gold	OG6150	Sealed With a Kiss	CD3	U.K.	1989	$9.00

Hyman, Dick

Full Length

Label	Catalog Number	Title	Type	Country	Year	Longbox Value / Value
Reference	RR-50DCD	Plays Duke Ellington	LTD/LP	U.S.		$28.00
Reference	RR-33DCD	Plays Fats Waller	LTD/LP	U.S.		$28.00

Hyman, Phyllis

Singles

Label	Catalog Number	Title	Type	Country	Year	Longbox Value / Value
Zoo	ZP 17068	I Found Love	CDJ	U.S.	1990	$2.00
Zoo	14238	I Refuse To Be Lonely	CD5	U.S.	1995	$5.00
Zoo	ZP 17040	Living In Confusion	CDJ	U.S.	1990	$2.00
Zoo	ZP 17047	When You Get Right Down To It	CDJ	U.S.	1990	$2.00

Hynde, Chrissie

Full Length

Label	Catalog Number	Title	Type	Country	Year	Longbox Value / Value
DIR		King Biscuit Flour Hour	RS	U.S.	1987	$30.00

With Collins, Gilmour, Airdate: 12/13/87.

Label	Catalog Number	Title	Type	Country	Year	Longbox Value / Value
DIR		King Biscuit Flour Hour	RS	U.S.	1992	$30.00

Airdate: 4/26/92.

Label	Catalog Number	Title	Type	Country	Year	Longbox Value / Value
DIR		King Biscuit Flour Hour	RS	U.S.	1994	$65.00

Airdate: 1/16/94.

Singles

Label	Catalog Number	Title	Type	Country	Year	Longbox Value / Value
Arista	ASCD-2458	Spiritual High	CDJ	U.S.	1992	$2.00

Hyper Go Go

Singles

Label	Catalog Number	Title	Type	Country	Year	Longbox Value / Value
RCA	74321-110492	High	CD5	U.K.	1992	$8.00
CBS	656086-3	This Is Go Go	CD3	Germany	1993	$8.00
CBS	656086-5	This Is Go Go	CD5	Germany	1993	$8.00

Hyperhead

Singles

Label	Catalog Number	Title	Type	Country	Year	Longbox Value / Value
Devotion	CDDVN-109	Teenage Mind	CD5	U.K.	1992	$8.00
Devotion	CDDVN-110	Terminal Fear	CD5	U.K.	1992	$8.00

Hyperstate

Singles

Label	Catalog Number	Title	Type	Country	Year	Longbox Value / Value
Polygram	MAGCD-34	Time After Time	CD5	U.K.	1993	$8.00

Hypnopedia

Singles

Label	Catalog Number	Title	Type	Country	Year	Longbox Value / Value
ZYX	BOY-8823-8	Horror	CD5	Germany	1991	$8.00

Hypnosis

Singles

Label	Catalog Number	Title	Type	Country	Year	Longbox Value / Value
ZYX	5036-8	Pulstar	CD3	Germany	1988	$8.00

Hypnoteck

Singles

Label	Catalog Number	Title	Type	Country	Year	Longbox Value / Value
ZYX	6271-8	Pump Pump It Up	CD5	Germany	1989	$8.00
ZYX	6440-8	Ready Or Not	CD5	Germany	1989	$8.00

Hypnotist

Singles

Label	Catalog Number	Title	Type	Country	Year	Longbox Value / Value
SPV	12001-3	Hardcore	CD5	Germany	1991	$8.00
Rising High	RSN-13CD	Hardcore	CD5	U.K.	1991	$8.00
SPV	1143-3	Rainbows In the Sky	CD5	Germany	1992	$8.00
SPV	12004-3	Remix	CD5	Germany	1992	$8.00
SPV	1134-3	This Is My House	CD5	Germany	1992	$8.00

Hypnotone

Singles

Label	Catalog Number	Title	Type	Country	Year	Longbox Value / Value
Creation	CRESCD-089	Hypnotonic	CD5	U.K.	1991	$8.00

Hysteria

Singles

Label	Catalog Number	Title	Type	Country	Year	Longbox Value / Value
Tam Tam	SAV-107CD	Satisfied	CD5	U.K.	1990	$8.00

Hysterix

Singles

Label	Catalog Number	Title	Type	Country	Year	Longbox Value / Value
		Must Be the Music	CD5	U.K.	1993	$8.00
		Must Be the Music	CD5	U.K.	1993	$8.00

Second version.

I.F.A.

Singles

Label	Catalog Number	Title	Type	Country	Year	Longbox Value / Value
Capitol	58466	Rollin'	CD5	U.S.	1995	$5.00

I Love You

Singles

Label	Catalog Number	Title	Type	Country	Year	Longbox Value / Value
Geffen	PRO-CD-4284	2	CDJ	U.S.	1991	$2.00
Geffen	PRO-CD-4225	Hang Straight Up	CDJ	U.S.	1991	$2.00

I Mother Earth

Singles

Label	Catalog Number	Title	Type	Country	Year	Longbox Value / Value
Capitol	DPRO-79776	Levitate	CDJ	U.S.	1993	$3.00
Capitol	DPRO-79788	Rain Will Fall	CDJ	U.S.	1992	$3.00
Capitol		So Gently We Go	CDJ	Canada	1994	$8.00
Capitol	58249-2	So Gently We Go	CD5	U.S.	1994	$5.00

I, Napoleon

Singles

Label	Catalog Number	Title	Type	Country	Year	Longbox Value / Value
Geffen	PRO-CD-4227	Go To Pieces	CDJ	U.S.	1991	$3.00
Geffen	PRO-CD-4194	Perfect Absolution	CDJ	U.S.	1990	$3.00

I Start Counting

Singles

Label	Catalog Number	Title	Type	Country	Year	Longbox Value / Value
Intercord	826 907	Million Headed Monster	CD5	Germany	1989	$8.00

I've Got The Bullets

Singles

Label	Catalog Number	Title	Type	Country	Year	Longbox Value / Value
CBS	651542	Love Scene	CD5	Holland	1988	$8.00

Ian, Janis

Singles

Label	Catalog Number	Title	Type	Country	Year	Longbox Value / Value
Mercury	CDP 627	Days Like These	CDJ	U.S.	1993	$3.00
Inside Out	TODP-2399	When the Party's Over	CD3	Japan	1993	$13.00/$3.00

Ice Cube

Full Length

Label	Catalog Number	Title	Type	Country	Year	Longbox Value / Value
	DPRO 50873	Radio Sampler	DJ/Smplr	U.S.	1996	$8.00

Singles

Label	Catalog Number	Title	Type	Country	Year	Longbox Value / Value
Aris	884701	Amerikkka's Most Wanted	CD5	Germany	1990	$8.00
Priority	BRCD-192	Amerikkka's Most Wanted	CD5	U.K.	1990	$8.00
Priority Records	53161	Bop Gun	CD5	U.S.	1994	$5.00
		Check Yourself	CD5	U.K.		$8.00
		Check Yourself	CD5	U.K.		$8.00

Second version.

Label	Catalog Number	Title	Type	Country	Year	Longbox Value / Value
	DPRO-50853	Friday	CDJ	U.S.	1995	$2.00
	DPRO-50861	Life as Gee	CDJ	U.S.	1995	$2.00
4th &B'way	BRCD-239	Steady Mobbin'	CD5	U.K.	1991	$8.00
Priority	6610	Steady Mobbin'	CDJ	U.S.	1992	$2.00
Priority	6637	Wicked	CDJ	U.S.	1992	$2.00
		You Know How We Do It	CD5	U.K.		$10.00
		You Know How We Do It	CD5	U.K.		$10.00

Second version.

Label	Catalog Number	Title	Type	Country	Year	Longbox Value / Value
Priority	50786	You Know How We Do It	CDJ	U.S.	1994	$2.00
Priority	7046	You Know How We Do It	CDJ	U.S.	1994	$2.00

Ice M.C.

Singles

Label	Catalog Number	Title	Type	Country	Year	Longbox Value / Value
ZYX	3302-8	CD-Singles Box	CD5	Germany	1991	$25.00

4 CD set.

Label	Catalog Number	Title	Type	Country	Year	Longbox Value / Value
ZYX	6309-8	Cinema	CD5	Germany	1990	$8.00
Alfa	ALCB-29	Easy	CD3	Japan	1990	$12.00/$3.00
Cooltempo	COOLCD-202	Easy	CD5	U.K.	1990	$8.00
ZYX	6215-8	Easy	CD5	U.K.	1990	$8.00
Chrysalis	DPRO-23525	Easy	CDJ	U.S.	1990	$2.00
Polygram	867181-2	Happy Weekend	CD5	Germany	1991	$8.00
ZYX	6425-8	Megamix	CD5	Germany	1990	$8.00
ZYX	6359-8	OK Corral	CD5	Germany	1990	$8.00
Polygram	867971-2	People	CD5	Germany	1991	$8.00
ZYX	6291-8	Scream	CD5	Germany	1990	$8.00
Zyx	66014	Think About the Way	CD5	U.S.	1994	$5.00
ZYX	66014-8	Think About the Way	CD5	U.S.	1995	$6.00

Label	Catalog Number	Title	Type	Country	Year	Longbox Value / Value

ICE T

Label	Catalog Number	Title	Type	Country	Year	Longbox Value / Value
		Full Length				
Sire/Warner Bros.	9 45119-2	Home Invasion	LP/LB	U.S.	1993	$85.00/$70.00
		Singles				
Sire	9 21704-2	Dick Tracy	CD5	U.S.	1989	$5.00
Sire	PRO-CD-3970	Girl Tried to Kill Me, The	CDJ	U.S.	1989	$2.00
		Gotta Lotta Love	CD5	U.K.		$10.00
		Gotta Lotta Love	CD5	U.K.		$10.00
Second version.						
Sire	PRO-CD-3415	High Rollers	CDJ	U.S.	1989	$2.00
Priority	6663	I Ain't New to This	CDJ	U.S.	1993	$2.00
Sire	PRO-CD-3308	I'm Your Pusher	CDJ	U.S.	1988	$2.00
WEA	W-2802CD	Lethal Weapon	CD5	U.K.	1989	$10.00
Sire	PRO-CD-3686	Lethal Weapon	CDJ	U.S.	1989	$2.00
Sire	9 40161-2	Lifestyles of the Rich and Infamous	CD5	U.S.	1991	$5.00
Sire	PRO-CD-4931	Lifestyles of the Rich and Infamous	CDJ	U.S.	1991	$2.00
Sire	PRO-CD-5020	Midnight	CDJ	U.S.	1991	$2.00
Sire	PRO-CD-5392	Mind Over Matter	CDJ	U.S.	1991	$2.00
WEA	7599-21845-2	New Jack Hustler	CD5	Germany	1991	$10.00
Giant	W-0013CD	New Jack Hustler	CD5	U.K.	1991	$10.00
Giant	9 40083-2	New Jack Hustler	CD5	U.S.	1991	$5.00
Giant	PRO-CD-4853	New Jack Hustler	CDJ	U.S.	1991	$2.00
Giant	PRO-CD-4643	New Jack Hustler	CDJ	U.S.	1991	$2.00
Sire	W-0035CD	O.G.	CD5	U.K.	1991	$10.00
Sire	PRO-CD-4761	O.G.	CDJ	U.S.	1991	$2.00
Sire	PRO-CD-4959	O.G.	CDJ	U.S.	1991	$2.00
Sire	PRO-CD-5143	Ricochet	CDJ	U.S.	1991	$2.00
Sire	PRO-CD-3898	What Ya Wanna Do?	CDJ	U.S.	1989	$2.00
Sire	PRO-CD-3865	You Played Yourself	CDJ	U.S.	1989	$2.00

Iceburn/Engine

Label	Catalog Number	Title	Type	Country	Year	Longbox Value / Value
		Singles				
	J4	Split Ep	CD5	U.S.	1994	$5.00

Icehouse

Label	Catalog Number	Title	Type	Country	Year	Longbox Value / Value
		Full Length				
Chrysalis		A Man Of Colours	LP/LB	U.S.	1987	$18.00/$15.00
		Big Wheel	LTD/LP	Australia		$30.00
CD with computer disk in digipak.						
		Play Crazy For Me	DJ/LP	U.S.		$8.00
		Singles				
Chrysalis	DPRO-41592	A Man Of Colours	CDJ	U.S.	1987	$2.00
		Big Wheel	CD5	Austalia		$10.00
Chrysalis	CHSCD-3156	Crazy	CD5	U.K.	1988	$8.00
Aris	880877	Electric Blues	CD5	Germany	1988	$8.00
Chrysalis	CHSCD-3239	Electric Blues	CD5	U.K.	1988	$8.00
		Invisible People	CD5	Australia	1994	$10.00
		Satellite	CD5	Australia	1994	$10.00
BMG	662585	Touch the Fire	CD5	Germany	1989	$8.00
Chrysalis	CHSCD-3472	Touch the Fire	CD5	U.K.	1989	$8.00
Chrysalis	DPRO-23414	Touch the Fire	CDJ	U.S.	1989	$2.00

Icicle Works

Label	Catalog Number	Title	Type	Country	Year	Longbox Value / Value
		Singles				
Efa	CD-6379	High Time	CD5	Germany	1988	$8.00
Beggars Banquet	BEG-203CD	High Time	CD5	U.K.	1988	$8.00
Beggars Banquet	BEG-215CD	Little Girl Lost	CD5	U.K.	1988	$8.00
Epic	WORKSC-101	Melaine Still Hurts	CD5	U.K.	1990	$8.00
Epic	WORKSC-100	Motorcycle Rider	CD5	U.K.	1990	$8.00
Beggars Banquet	0564-2	Numb	CD5	Germany	1988	$8.00
Beggars Banquet	IW-1CD	Numb	CD5	U.K.	1988	$8.00
Beggars Banquet	BEG-262CD	Understanding Jane	CD5	U.K.	1992	$8.00

Icon

Label	Catalog Number	Title	Type	Country	Year	Longbox Value / Value
		Singles				
Megaforce	3201	Forever Young	CDJ	U.S.	1989	$2.00
Atlantic	PR 2889-2	Taking My Breath Away	CDJ	U.S.	1989	$2.00

Icy Blue

Label	Catalog Number	Title	Type	Country	Year	Longbox Value / Value
		Singles				
Giant	9362-40143-2	Pump It	CD5	Germany	1991	$8.00
Jive	WPDP-6287	Pump It	CD3	U.K.	1991	$4.00
Giant	W-0050CD	Pump It	CD5	U.K.	1991	$8.00
Giant	PRO-CD-4725	Pump It	CDJ	U.S.	1991	$2.00

Icy D.

Label	Catalog Number	Title	Type	Country	Year	Longbox Value / Value
		Singles				
BCM	20474	Get On Up and Dance	CD5	Germany	1990	$8.00

Idaho

Label	Catalog Number	Title	Type	Country	Year	Longbox Value / Value
		Singles				
Caroline	1472	Palms	CD5	U.S.	1993	$5.00

Identity Crisis

Label	Catalog Number	Title	Type	Country	Year	Longbox Value / Value
		Singles				
Tabu	374631143	Sing a Simple Song	CDJ	U.S.	1994	$2.00

Ideola

Label	Catalog Number	Title	Type	Country	Year	Longbox Value / Value
		Singles				
A&M	CD 17447	Is It Any Wonder	CDJ	U.S.	1987	$2.00

Idle Threats – Magical Resonant Frequency of the Bowl (Birdman Records IT6969) 1996 out-of-print CD with artwork by Lee Weeks, artist for Marvel Comic's Predator v. Mangus comic book series.

Idle Threats

Label	Catalog Number	Title	Type	Country	Year	Longbox Value / Value
		Full Length				
Birdman Records	IT6969	Magical Resonant Frequency of the Bowl	LTD/LP	U.S.	1996	$15.00
Limited to 1,000 copies.						

Idol, Billy

Label	Catalog Number	Title	Type	Country	Year	Longbox Value / Value
		Full Length				
Chrysalis	VK-41377	Billy Idol	LP/LB	U.S.†	1984	$14.00/$8.00
Vestron	ML1204	Billy Idol	LD	U.S.	1987	$25.00
Chrysalis	F2 21762	Charmed Life	LTD/LP	U.S.	1990	$22.00/$15.00
Chrysalis	094632601827	Cyberpunk	LTD/LP	U.S.	1993	$20.00
CD and 3.5" diskette in digipak.						
Westwood One		In Concert	RS	U.S.	1993	$50.00
2 CD set. With Stone Temple Pilots, Airdate: 11/6/93						
DIR		King Biscuit Flour Hour	RS	U.S.	1987	$30.00
Airdate: 11/22/87.						
DIR		King Biscuit Flour Hour	RS	U.S.	1990	$30.00
Airdate: 12/2/90.						
DIR		King Biscuit Flour Hour	RS	U.S.	1990	$30.00
Airdate: 4/16/90.						
DIR		King Biscuit Flour Hour	RS	U.S.	1992	$30.00
Airdate: 10/25/92.						
DIR		King Biscuit Flour Hour	RS	U.S.	1993	$30.00
Airdate: 8/16/93.						
Westwood One		Off the Record	RS	U.S.	1993	$30.00
Airdate: 6/28/93.						
Westwood One		Off the Record	RS	U.S.	1993	$20.00
Airdate: 6/28/93.						
Westwood One		On the Edge	RS	U.S.	1993	$20.00
Airdate: 6/21/93.						
Chrysalis		Rebel Yell	LTD/LP	U.K.	1994	$25.00/$20.00
25th Anniversary edition in 6"x11" longbox						
Chrysalis	VK-41450	Rebel Yell	LP/LB	U.S.†	1984	$14.00/$8.00
Image	IDVL1204D	Vital Idol	LD	U.S.		$18.00
		Singles				
Chrysalis	IDOLCD-13	Catch My Fall	CD5	U.K.	1988	$10.00
BMG	663123	Cradle of Love	CD5	Germany	1990	$10.00
Chrysalis	IDOLCD-14	Cradle of Love	CD5	U.K.	1990	$10.00
Chrysalis	DPRO-23509	Cradle of Love	CDJ	U.S.	1990	$7.00
EMI	322733-2	Dancing With Myself	CD5	Germany	1990	$10.00
Chrysalis	DPRO-24832	Heroin	CDJ	U.S.	1993	$2.00
Chrysalis	IDOLCD-12	Hot in the City	CD5	U.K.	1990	$10.00
Chrysalis	323578-2	L.A. Woman	CD5	Germany	1990	$10.00
Toshiba	TODP-2212	L.A. Woman	CD3	Japan	1990	$12.00/$4.00
Chrysalis	IDOLCD-15	L.A. Woman	CD5	U.K.	1990	$10.00
Chrysalis	F2 23571	L.A. Woman	CD5	U.S.	1990	$5.00
Chrysalis	DPRO-23571	L.A. Woman	CDJ	U.S.	1990	$2.00
Chrysalis	323603-2	Prodigal Blues	CD5	Germany	1990	$10.00
Chrysalis	TOCP-6570	Prodigal Blues	CD5	Japan	1991	$15.00
Chrysalis	IDOLCD-16	Prodigal Blues	CD5	U.K.	1990	$10.00
Chrysalis	DPRO-23603	Prodigal Blues	CDJ	U.S.	1990	$2.00
EMI	23990	Shock to the System	CD5	Holland	1993	$10.00
Chrysalis	TODP-2412	Shock to the System	CD3	Japan	1993	$12.00/$4.00
EMI		Shock to the System	CD5	U.K.	1993	$10.00
EMI		Shock to the System	CD5	U.K.	1993	$10.00
Second version.						
Chrysalis	DPRO-04718	Shock to the System	CDJ	U.S.	1993	$8.00
CD and 3.5" computer disc.						
		Speed	CD5	U.K.	1994	$10.00
		Speed	CD5	U.K.	1994	$10.00
Second version.						
Chrysalis	DPRO-19867	Speed	CDJ	U.S.	1994	$3.00
Chrysalis	DPRO-04567	Wasteland	CDJ	U.S.	1993	$2.00

Idolls

Label	Catalog Number	Title	Type	Country	Year	Longbox Value / Value
		Singles				
Atlantic	PRCD 3453-2	Give a Dog a Bone	CDJ	U.S.	1990	$2.00

If

Label	Catalog Number	Title	Type	Country	Year	Longbox Value / Value
		Singles				
MCA	MCSTD-1606	Everything and More	CD5	U.K.	1992	$8.00
MCA	MCSTD-1583	Open Up Your Head	CD5	U.K.	1991	$8.00
MCA	DMCAT-1463	Saturday's Angels	CD5	U.K.	1990	$8.00
MCA	MCSTD-1627	Saturday's Angels	CD5	U.K.	1992	$8.00

Ifield, Frank

Label	Catalog Number	Title	Type	Country	Year	Longbox Value / Value
		Singles				
EMI	YODELCD-1	Yodeling Song	CD5	U.K.	1991	$8.00

Iglesias, Julio

Label	Catalog Number	Title	Type	Country	Year	Longbox Value / Value
		Full Length				
CBS	CK-39157	1100 Bell Air Place	LP/BP	U.S.†	1985	$14.00/$8.00
CBS	CK-40180	Libra	LP/BP	U.S.†	1985	$14.00/$8.00
		Singles				
CBS	652928-3	Ae, Ao	CD3	Germany	1988	$8.00
Epic	108P-3040	Ae, Ao	CD3	Japan	1988	$12.00/$3.00
Columbia	JULIOC-3	Ae, Ao	CD5	U.K.	1988	$8.00
Columbia	CSK 1238	Ae, Ao	CDJ	U.S.	1988	$2.00
Columbia	JULIOC-6	Brasilia	CD5	U.K.	1989	$8.00
Epic	10 8P-3066	Caballo Viejo	CD3	Japan	1989	$12.00/$3.00
Columbia	JULIOC-7	Caballo Viejo	CD5	U.K.	1989	$8.00
Columbia	656413-2	Can't Help Falling in Love	CD5	Germany	1990	$8.00
Columbia	JULIOC-8	Can't Help Falling in Love	CD5	U.K.	1990	$8.00
Columbia	CSK 2222	Can't Help Falling in Love	CDJ	U.S.	1990	$2.00
		Crazy	CD5	U.K.		$10.00
		Crazy	CD5	U.K.		$10.00
Second version.						
Columbia	CSK 6005	Crazy	CDJ	U.S.	1994	$2.00
Columbia	CSK 6070	Crazy	CDJ	U.S.	1994	$2.00
Columbia	JULIOC-5	If I Ever Needed You	CD5	U.K.	1989	$8.00
Columbia	JULIOC-4	Love Is On Our Side	CD5	U.K.	1988	$8.00
Columbia	651544-2	My Love	CD5	Germany	1988	$8.00
Epic	108P-3027	My Love	CD3	Japan	1988	$12.00/$3.00
Columbia	JULIOC-2	My Love	CD5	U.K.	1988	$8.00
Columbia	CSK 1102	My Love	CDJ	U.S.	1988	$2.00
Columbia	656928-5	Vincent	CD5	U.K.	1991	$8.00
Columbia	656604-2	When I Need You	CD5	Germany	1991	$8.00
Columbia	656604-2	When I Need You	CD5	U.K.	1991	$8.00

Ignorance

Label	Catalog Number	Title	Type	Country	Year	Longbox Value / Value
		Full Length				
Warner Brothers	26482	Confident Rat, The	LP/LB	U.S.		$14.00/$8.00
Warner Brothers	45039	Positively Shocking	LP/LB	U.S.		$14.00/$8.00

Iguanas

Label	Catalog Number	Title	Type	Country	Year	Longbox Value / Value
		Singles				
MCA	MCA5P-2618	Fortune Teller	CDJ	U.S.	1993	$2.00

Il Close

Singles

Label	Catalog Number	Title	Type	Country	Year	Longbox Value/Value
Tabu	31458 8161	Call Me Up	CDJ	U.S.	1993	$2.00
Tabu	31458 8106	My Conscience	CDJ	U.S.	1993	$2.00
Tabu	31458 8002	So What	CDJ	U.S.	1992	$2.00
Tabu	31458 8084	So What	CDJ	U.S.	1993	$2.00

Il D Extreme

Singles

Label	Catalog Number	Title	Type	Country	Year	Longbox Value/Value
Gasoline Ally	54651	Cry No More	CD5		1993	$5.00
Gasoline Ally	2675	Cry No More	CDJ	U.S.	1993	$2.00
Gasoline Ally	2675	Let Me Love You	CDJ	U.S.	1993	$2.00
Gasoline Ally	2821	Up on the Roof	CDJ	U.S.	1993	$2.00

III

Singles

Label	Catalog Number	Title	Type	Country	Year	Longbox Value/Value
Mercury	1225	Where My Homez	CDJ	U.S.	1994	$2.00

III Al Skratch

Singles

Label	Catalog Number	Title	Type	Country	Year	Longbox Value/Value
Polygram	856125	I'll Take Her	CD5	U.S.	1994	$5.00

Illsley, John

Singles

Label	Catalog Number	Title	Type	Country	Year	Longbox Value/Value
Vertigo	VERCD-39	I Want to See the Man	CD5	U.K.	1988	$8.00
Warner Brothers	PRO-CD-3130	I Want to See the Man	CDJ	U.S.	1988	$2.00

Illusion

Singles

Label	Catalog Number	Title	Type	Country	Year	Longbox Value/Value
		I Want Your Love In Me	CDJ	U.S.		$2.00
ZYX	6170-8	Why Can't We Live	CD5	Germany	1989	$6.00

Imagination

Singles

Label	Catalog Number	Title	Type	Country	Year	Longbox Value/Value
RCA	PD-42660	Love's Taking Over Me	CD5	Germany	1989	$8.00
RCA	PD-42932	Megamix	CD5	Germany	1989	$8.00

Immaculate Fools

Singles

Label	Catalog Number	Title	Type	Country	Year	Longbox Value/Value
		Falling Apart Together	CDJ	U.S.		$2.00
Continuum	13209	Heaven Down Here	CDJ	U.S.	1992	$2.00
CBS	856123-3	Prince, The	CD3	Germany	1990	$8.00
Epic	ESK 2045	Prince, The	CDJ	U.S.	1990	$2.00
CBS	855741-3	Sad	CD3	Germany	1990	$8.00
Continuum	132209	Stand Down	CDJ	U.S.	1992	$2.00

Immature

Singles

Label	Catalog Number	Title	Type	Country	Year	Longbox Value/Value
MCA	54949	Constantly	CD5	U.S.	1994	$5.00
MCA	MCA5P3673	Please Don't Go	CDJ	U.S.		$2.00
Capitol	DPRO-79443	Tear It Up	CDJ	U.S.	1992	$2.00
MCA	MCA5P3584	We Got It	CDJ	U.S.		$2.00

Impala

Singles

Label	Catalog Number	Title	Type	Country	Year	Longbox Value/Value
Estrus Records	106	Kings of the Strip	CD5	U.S.	1994	$5.00

Impedance

Singles

Label	Catalog Number	Title	Type	Country	Year	Longbox Value/Value
Epic	ESK 73206	Tainted Love	CDJ	U.S.	1989	$2.00

Impelletteri

Singles

Label	Catalog Number	Title	Type	Country	Year	Longbox Value/Value
Sony	10EP-3058	Since You've Been Gone	CD3	Japan	1988	$12.00/$4.00

Imperial Drag

Singles

Label	Catalog Number	Title	Type	Country	Year	Longbox Value/Value
	OSK 7920	Boy or a Girl	CDJ	U.S.		$2.00

Imperiet

Singles

Label	Catalog Number	Title	Type	Country	Year	Longbox Value/Value
A&M	390289-2	Be the President	CD5	Germany	1989	$8.00
A&M	390324-2	Peace	CD5	Germany	1988	$8.00

Impertelli

Full Length

Label	Catalog Number	Title	Type	Country	Year	Longbox Value/Value
Relativity	88561-8219-2	Impertelli	LP/LB	U.S.		$15.00/$12.00

Impossibles

Singles

Label	Catalog Number	Title	Type	Country	Year	Longbox Value/Value
Fontana	DELCD-1	Delphis	CD5	U.K.	1991	$8.00
Fontana	DRUCD-12	Drum	CD5	U.K.	1991	$8.00
Fontana	POSCD-1	How Do You Do It	CD5	U.K.	1991	$8.00

Impressions

Singles

Label	Catalog Number	Title	Type	Country	Year	Longbox Value/Value
MCA	22175	It's All Right	CD5	U.S.	1994	$5.00

In House II

Singles

Label	Catalog Number	Title	Type	Country	Year	Longbox Value/Value
Italio-Heat	ffr-0514	Love to Love You Baby	CD5	Germany	1989	$8.00

In Kamoze

Singles

Label	Catalog Number	Title	Type	Country	Year	Longbox Value/Value
	PRCD 9222-2	Listen To Me	CDJ	U.S.		$2.00

In My Head

Singles

Label	Catalog Number	Title	Type	Country	Year	Longbox Value/Value
All Around	CDGLOBE-109	Shine Your Light	CD5	U.K.	1992	$8.00

In & Out of Love

Singles

Label	Catalog Number	Title	Type	Country	Year	Longbox Value/Value
	CRDJ155642	Sergio	CDJ	U.S.		$2.00

In Sotto Voce

Singles

Label	Catalog Number	Title	Type	Country	Year	Longbox Value/Value
Antler	ANT-102CD	Sequence	CD5	U.K.	1993	$5.00
Antler	84	Sequence	CD5	U.S.	1993	$5.00

In the Nusery

Singles

Label	Catalog Number	Title	Type	Country	Year	Longbox Value/Value
SPV	4910-3	Sesudient	CD5	Germany	1990	$8.00
Third Mind	TMSCD-51	Sesudient	CD5	U.K.	1990	$8.00
Wax Trax	9131	Sesudient	CD5	U.S.	1990	$4.00

In Tua Nua

Singles

Label	Catalog Number	Title	Type	Country	Year	Longbox Value/Value
Virgin	VSCD-1072	All I Wanted	CD5	U.K.	1988	$8.00
Virgin	PR 2349	All I Wanted	CDJ	U.S.	1988	$2.00
Virgin	VSCD-1091	Don't Fear Me Now	CD5	U.K.	1988	$8.00
Virgin	PR 2683	Seven Into the Sea	CDJ	U.S.	1989	$2.00
Virgin	VSCD-1118	Wheel of Evil	CD3	U.K.	1990	$8.00

In Vitro

Singles

Label	Catalog Number	Title	Type	Country	Year	Longbox Value/Value
		Man and Woman	CDJ	U.S.		$2.00

Inbreds

Singles

Label	Catalog Number	Title	Type	Country	Year	Longbox Value/Value
	PRCD 6591-2	Amelia Earhart	CDJ	U.S.		$3.00

Incantation

Full Length

Label	Catalog Number	Title	Type	Country	Year	Longbox Value/Value
Passport	PVCD-8945	Music of the Andes	LP	U.S.		$10.00

Incognito

Singles

Label	Catalog Number	Title	Type	Country	Year	Longbox Value/Value
Polygram	868359-2	Always There	CD5	Germany	1991	$8.00
Phonogram	PHCR-8020	Change	CD5	Japan	1992	$10.00
Phonogram	TLKCD-26	Change	CD5	U.K.	1992	$8.00
Phonogram	868923-2	Crazy For You	CD5	Germany	1991	$10.00
Phonogram	TLKCD-14	Crazy For You	CD5	U.K.	1991	$8.00
Phonogram	TPHCR-8016	Don't You Worry About a Thing	CD5	Japan	1991	$8.00
Phonogram	TLKCD-21	Don't You Worry About a Thing	CD5	U.K.	1991	$8.00
Phonogram	TLKCD-7	Inside Life	CD5	U.K.	1991	$8.00
Talkin'Loud	617	Radio Vibes	CDJ	U.S.	1992	$2.00

Incredible Strings Band

Full Length

Label	Catalog Number	Title	Type	Country	Year	Longbox Value/Value
Rykodisc	VRCD 1437	Hannibal Sampler, The	DJ/Smplr	U.S.		$15.00

Indecent Obsession

Singles

Label	Catalog Number	Title	Type	Country	Year	Longbox Value/Value
MCA	MVDM-25	Indio	CD3	Japan	1992	$13.00/$4.00
MCA	MCA5P-2253	Indio	CDJ	U.S.	1992	$2.00
MCA	MVDM-13	Kiss Me	CD3	Japan	1992	$13.00/$4.00
MCA	MCSTD-1615	Kiss Me	CD5	U.K.	192	$8.00
MCA	MVDM-18	Maybe You	CD3	Japan	1992	$13.00/$4.00
MCA	172082-2	Never Gonna Stop	CD5	Germany	1990	$8.00
MCA	WMD5-4049	Never Gonna Stop	CD3	Japan	1990	$13.00/$4.00
MCA	DMCAT-1420	Never Gonna Stop	CD5	U.K.	1990	$8.00
MCA	WMD5-4036	Say Goodbye	CD3	Japan	1990	$13.00/$4.00
Eastwest	257264-2	Tell Me Something	CD5	Germany	1990	$8.00
MCA	WMD5-4025	Tell Me Something	CD3	Japan	1990	$13.00/$4.00
MCA	DMCAT-1406	Tell Me Something	CD5	U.K.	1990	$8.00
MCA		Tell Me Something	CDJ	U.S.	1990	$2.00

India

Singles

Label	Catalog Number	Title	Type	Country	Year	Longbox Value/Value
Reprise	9 21524-2	Love Who Rocks You, The	CD5	U.S.	1990	$4.00
Reprise	9 21280-2	Right From the Start	CD5	U.S.	1989	$2.00
Reprise	PRO-CD-3859	Right From the Start	CDJ	U.S.	1990	$2.00
		You Should Be Loving Me	CDJ	U.S.	1990	$2.00

Indian Summer

Singles

Label	Catalog Number	Title	Type	Country	Year	Longbox Value/Value
Strada	CDSTRAD-1	Just Like Lovers	CD5	U.K.	1989	$8.00

Indians

Singles

Label	Catalog Number	Title	Type	Country	Year	Longbox Value/Value
Polydor	CDP 775	Bed of Roses	CDJ	U.S.	1992	$7.00
		CD in oversized circular cardboard package.				
Polydor	CDP 971	Lock Up the Sky	CDJ	U.S.	1993	$2.00

Indicate

Singles

Label	Catalog Number	Title	Type	Country	Year	Longbox Value/Value
ZYX	6238-8	Latest Idea	CD5	Germany	1989	$6.00

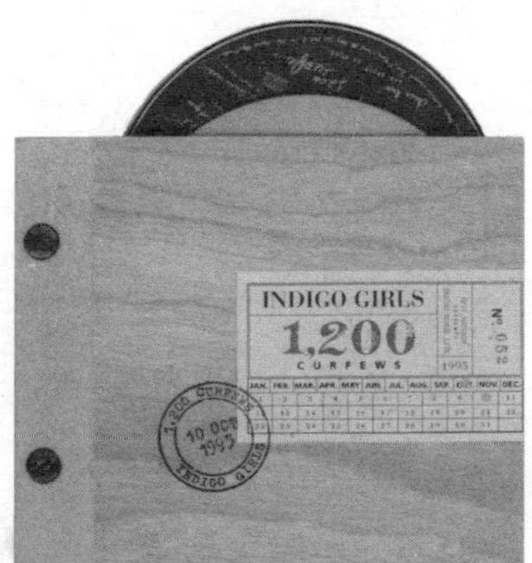

Indigo Girls – 1,200 Curfews (Epic E2K 67229)

Indigo Girls

Full Length

Label	Catalog Number	Title	Type	Country	Year	Longbox Value/Value
Epic	E2K 67229	1,200 Curfews	DJ/LP	U.S.	1995	$75.00
		2 CD set in book with wood panels.				
Epic		1,200 Curfews	LP	U.S.	1995	$25.00
		2 CD set in special digipak.				
Epic	XPCD-650	4.5 The Best of the Indigo Girls	DJ/Smplr	U.K.	1994	$30.00
Epic	ESK 4632	An Acoustic Evening With the Indigo Girls & Allman Brothers Band	DJ/Smplr	U.S.	1992	$75.00
		14 track Live CD with 7 track by each group.				
Epic	ESK 7382	Breaking Curfew	DJ/Smplr	U.S.	1995	$24.00
Epic	ESK 1486	Indigo Girls	DJ/Smplr	U.S.	1989	$15.00

Label	Catalog Number	Title	Type	Country	Year	Longbox Value / Value
Epic		Indigo Girls	LTD/LP	U.S.	1994	$25.00
	Gold disc.					
Image	ID6970CB	Live at the Uptown Lounge	LD	U.S.		$25.00
Epic		Reverse 1-Live	DJ/Smplr	U.S.	1989	$25.00
Epic	ESK 4552	Rites of Passage	DJ/LP	U.S.	1992	$15.00
Epic	ESK 4570	Rites of Passage	DJ/LP	U.S.	1992	$25.00
	Special digipak.					
Epic		Rites of Passage	LP	U.S.	1992	$12.00
	Special digipak.					
Epic	ESK 2201	Shades of Indigo	DJ/Intvw	U.S.	1990	$20.00
Epic		Swamp Ophelia	LP	U.S.	1994	$14.00
	Digipak version.					
Epic	ESK 4864	Three Hits	DJ/Smplr	U.S.	1993	$15.00

Singles

Label	Catalog Number	Title	Type	Country	Year	Longbox Value / Value
Epic	ESK 7382	Breaking Curfew	CDJ	U.S.	1995	$7.00
Epic	ESK 7375	Bury My Heart At Wounded Knee	CDJ	U.S.	1995	$7.00
Epic	654907-2	Closer to Fine	CD5	U.K.	1989	$13.00
Epic	662166-2	Closer to Fine	CD5	U.K.	1989	$13.00
Epic		Closer to Fine	CD5	U.K.	1995	$20.00
Epic		Closer to Fine	CDJ	U.S.	1989	$3.00
Epic	658768-2	Galileo	CD5	U.K.	1992	$11.00
Epic	ESK 74326	Galileo	CDJ	U.S.	1992	$3.00
Epic		Get Together	CDJ	U.S.	1994	$3.00
Epic		Ghost	CDJ	U.S.	1990	$3.00
Epic	ESK 2200	Hammer and a Nail	CDJ	U.S.	1990	$3.00
Epic		Holiday Greeting	CDJ	U.S.		$3.00
Epic	ESK 5657	I Don't Wanna Talk About It	CDJ	U.S.	1994	$3.00
Epic	ESK-4550	Joking	CDJ	U.S.	1992	$3.00
Epic	ESK 73003	Land of Canaan	CDJ	U.S.	1989	$3.00
Epic		Least Complicated	CD5	Australia	1994	$12.00
Epic		Least Complicated	CD5	U.K.	1994	$10.00
Epic	ESK 6081	Least Complicated	CDJ	U.S.	1994	$6.00
Epic	ESK 1490	Love's Recovery	CDJ	U.S.	1989	$3.00
CBS		Power of Two	CD5	Australia	1995	$13.00
CBS	77844	Power of Two	CD5	U.S.	1994	$5.00
		Power of Two	CDJ	U.S.	1994	$6.00
Epic		Reunion	CDJ	U.S.	1994	$6.00
Epic	ESK 6029	Touch Me Fall	CDJ	U.S.	1994	$3.00
Epic	ESK 2284	Watershed	CDJ	U.S.	1990	$3.00

Indio

Singles

Label	Catalog Number	Title	Type	Country	Year	Longbox Value / Value
A&M	CDEE-521	Hard Sun	CD3	U.K.	1989	$8.00
A&M	CD 17808	Hard Sun	CDJ	U.S.	1989	$2.00
A&M	CD 17909	Save for the Memory	CDJ	U.S.	1989	$2.00

Indra

Singles

Label	Catalog Number	Title	Type	Country	Year	Longbox Value / Value
BMG	665354	Misery	CD5	Germany	1992	$8.00

Industrial Strength

Full Length

Label	Catalog Number	Title	Type	Country	Year	Longbox Value / Value
Azra	DD 11591	Industrial Strength	LTD/LP	U.S.	1991	$18.00
	CD in foam rock.					

Infectious Grooves

Full Length

Label	Catalog Number	Title	Type	Country	Year	Longbox Value / Value
Epic	ESK 5004	Busload of Freaks	DJ/Smplr	U.S.	1993	$25.00
	With Suicidal Tendencies.					
Epic	ESK 4979	Sarsippius Ark	DJ/LP	U.S.	1993	$12.00
Epic		Sarsippius Ark	LTD/LP	U.S.	1993	$12.00

Singles

Label	Catalog Number	Title	Type	Country	Year	Longbox Value / Value
Epic	ESK 5142	Great Infectious Cover-Up	CDJ	U.S.	1993	$2.00
Epic	ESK 4432	Infectious Grooves	CDJ	U.S.	1992	$2.00
Epic	ESK 4151	Punk It Up	CDJ	U.S.	1991	$2.00
Epic	ESK 4238	Therapy	CDJ	U.S.	1991	$2.00
Epic	ESK 4949	What's a Party Without Freaks	CDJ	U.S.	1993	$6.00

Infidels

Singles

Label	Catalog Number	Title	Type	Country	Year	Longbox Value / Value
IRS	DPRO-67067	100 Watt Bulb	CDJ	U.S.	1991	$7.00
		Celebrate	CDJ	Canada		$6.00

Information Society

Full Length

Label	Catalog Number	Title	Type	Country	Year	Longbox Value / Value
Tommy Boy	9 26258-2-Dj	Hack	DJ/LP	U.S.	1990	$12.00
	Picture disc.					

Singles

Label	Catalog Number	Title	Type	Country	Year	Longbox Value / Value
Tommy Boy	555	Going, Going, Gone	CDJ	U.S.	1993	$2.00
Tommy Boy	PRO-CD-6012	Going, Going, Gone	CDJ	U.S.	1993	$2.00
Sony	CSDS-8182	How Long	CD3	Japan	1991	$12.00/$4.00
Tommy Boy	PRO-CD-4639	How Long	CDJ	U.S.	1991	$2.00
Sony	10EP-3038	Lay All Your Love on Me	CD3	Japan	1988	$12.00/$4.00
Sony	12EP-8026	Lay All Your Love on Me	CD3	Japan	1988	$12.00/$4.00
Tommy Boy	PRO-CD-3449	Lay All Your Love on Me	CDJ	U.S.	1988	$2.00
Sony	SRDS-8243	Million Watts of Love	CD3	Japan	1992	$12.00/$4.00
Tommy Boy	544	Peace & Love Inc.	CD5	U.S.	1992	$5.00
Tommy Boy	PRO-CD-5686	Peace & Love Inc.	CDJ	U.S.	1992	$2.00
Tommy Boy	PRO-CD-3333	Repetition	CDJ	U.S.	1988	$2.00
Tommy Boy	PRO-CD-4422	Think	CDJ	U.S.	1990	$2.00
Tommy Boy	PRO-CD-3253	Walking Away	CDJ	U.S.	1988	$2.00
Tommy Boy	886421-2	What's on Your Mind	CD5	Germany	1990	$2.00
Tommy Boy	LONCD-211	What's on Your Mind	CD5	U.K.	1990	$2.00
Tommy Boy	PRO-CD-3133	What's on Your Mind	CDJ	U.S.	1988	$2.00

Inga

Singles

Label	Catalog Number	Title	Type	Country	Year	Longbox Value / Value
WEA	YZ-444CD	Riding Into Blue	CD5	U.K.	1990	$8.00

Ingram, Bruce

Singles

Label	Catalog Number	Title	Type	Country	Year	Longbox Value / Value
BMG	663183	Dance With Me	CD5	Germany	1990	$8.00

Ingram, James

Full Length

Label	Catalog Number	Title	Type	Country	Year	Longbox Value / Value
Qwest	23970-2	It's Your Night	LP/LB	U.S.†	1984	$14.00/$8.00

Singles

Label	Catalog Number	Title	Type	Country	Year	Longbox Value / Value
Warner Brothers	WPDP-6312	Always You	CD3	Japan	1992	$12.00/$4.00
WEA	7599-21805-2	I Don't Have the Heart	CD5	Germany	1990	$9.00
Warner Brothers	W-9911CD	I Don't Have the Heart	CD5	U.K.	1990	$9.00
Warner Brothers	PRO-CD-3939	I Don't Have the Heart	CDJ	U.S.	1989	$2.00
Warner Brothers	PRO-CD-3726	I Wanna Come Back	CDJ	U.S.	1989	$2.00
WEA	921258-2	It's Real	CD5	Germany	1989	$9.00
WEA	W-2975CD	It's Real	CD5	U.K.	1989	$9.00
Warner Brothers	PRO-CD-3509	It's Real	CDJ	U.S.	1989	$2.00
QWest	PRO-CD-5607	One More Time	CDJ	U.S.	1992	$2.00
Warner Brothers	PRO-CD-5363	Remember the Dream	CDJ	U.S.	1991	$2.00
Walt Disney	03MS23600	So This Is Love	CD5	U.S.	1995	$7.00
Walt Disney	03MS23600	So This Is Love	CDJ	U.S.	1995	$7.00
Warner Brothers	PRO-CD-6133	Someone Like You	CDJ	U.S.	1993	$2.00
Warner Brothers	PRO-CD-4311	When Was the Last Time Music Made You Cry	CDJ	U.S.	1990	$2.00
Warner Brothers	WPDP-6288	Where Did My Heart Go	CD3	Japan	1991	$12.00/$4.00
Warner Brothers	PRO-CD-4957	Where Did My Heart Go	CDJ	U.S.	1990	$2.00
Warner Brothers	PRO-CD-3638	(You Make Me Feel Like) A Natural Man	CDJ	U.S.	1989	$2.00

Ingry's

Singles

Label	Catalog Number	Title	Type	Country	Year	Longbox Value / Value
Victor	VIDL-10215	1000 Pieces of Jigsaw Puzzle	CD3	Japan	1992	$12.00/$3.00
Invitation	VICL-15013	Flying Christmas	CD5	Japan	1992	$10.00

Inker And Hamilton

Singles

Label	Catalog Number	Title	Type	Country	Year	Longbox Value / Value
WEA	247885-2	Shadow and Light	CD5	Germany	1990	$8.00

Inmates

Singles

Label	Catalog Number	Title	Type	Country	Year	Longbox Value / Value
SPV	8975-3	Rescue Me	CD5	Germany	1992	$8.00

Inner Circle

Singles

Label	Catalog Number	Title	Type	Country	Year	Longbox Value / Value
Eastwest	9031-73424-2	Bad Boys	CD5	Germany	1991	$8.00
Eastwest	YZ-564CD	Bad Boys	CD5	U.K.	1991	$8.00
Atlantic	PRCD 5016-2	Bad Boys	CDJ	U.S.	1991	$2.00
Big Beat	5053	Bad Boys	CDJ	U.S.	1991	$2.00
Atlantic	92261	Bad Boys	CD5	U.S.	1994	$5.00
WEA	9031-77680-2	Sweat	CD5	U.K.	1992	$8.00
Big Beat	PRCD 4996-2	Sweat	CDJ	U.S.	1993	$2.00
Big Beat	5167	Sweat	CDJ	U.S.	1993	$2.00

Inner City

Singles

Label	Catalog Number	Title	Type	Country	Year	Longbox Value / Value
Virgin	162234	Ain't Nothing Better	CD3	Germany	1989	$8.00
Virgin	662234	Ain't Nothing Better	CD5	Germany	1989	$8.00
Virgin	TENCD-252	Ain't Nothing Better	CD3	U.K.	1989	$8.00
Virgin	661749	Big Fun	CD5	Germany	1988	$8.00
CBS	77401	Do Ya	CD5	U.S.	1994	$5.00
Virgin	162428	Do You Love What I Feel	CD3	Germany	1989	$8.00
Virgin	662428	Do You Love What I Feel	CD5	Germany	1989	$8.00
Virgin	TENCD-273	Do You Love What I Feel	CD3	U.K.	1989	$8.00
Virgin	12603	Follow Your Heart	CD5	U.S.	1992	$5.00
Virgin	12719	Follow Your Heart	CDJ	U.S.	1992	$2.00
Virgin	161921	Good Life	CD3	Germany	1988	$8.00
Virgin	661921	Good Life	CD5	Germany	1988	$8.00
Virgin	TENCD-249	Good Life	CD3	U.K.	1988	$8.00
Virgin	PR 2622	Good Life	CDJ	U.S.	1988	$2.00
Virgin	TENCD-365	Hallelujah	CD5	U.K.	1991	$8.00
Virgin	TENCD-398	Hallelujah '92	CD5	U.K.	1992	$8.00
Virgin	TENCD-392	Let It Reign	CD5	U.K.	1991	$8.00
Virgin	TENCD-405	Pennies From Heaven	CD5	U.K.	1992	$8.00
Virgin	TENCD-408	Praise	CD5	U.K.	1992	$8.00
Virgin	663724	That Man	CD5	Germany	1990	$8.00
Virgin	VJCP-1418	That Man	CD5	Japan	1990	$12.00
Virgin	TENCD-334	That Man	CD5	U.K.	1990	$8.00
Virgin	3614	That Man	CD5	U.S.	1990	$2.00
Virgin	663952	Till We Meet Again	CD5	Germany	1991	$8.00
Virgin	TENCD-337	Till We Meet Again	CD5	U.K.	1991	$8.00
Virgin	TENCD-414	Till We Meet Again	CD5	U.K.	1993	$8.00
Virgin	162781	Whatcha Gonna Do With My Lovin	CD3	Germany	1989	$8.00
Virgin	TENCD-290	Whatcha Gonna Do With My Lovin	CD3	U.K.	1989	$8.00
Virgin		Whatcha Gonna Do With My Lovin	CDJ	U.S.	1989	$2.00

Inner Kneipe

Singles

Label	Catalog Number	Title	Type	Country	Year	Longbox Value / Value
Pikosso		Wocha Horst Du Mich	SCD5	Germany	1995	$15.00
	Beer steinshaped disc.					

Inner Light

Singles

Label	Catalog Number	Title	Type	Country	Year	Longbox Value / Value
ZYX	6562-8	Phantasia	CD5	Germany	1991	$8.00

Inner Soul Expression

Singles

Label	Catalog Number	Title	Type	Country	Year	Longbox Value / Value
BMG	664568	Sexy Lady	CD5	Germany	1991	$8.00

Innings

Singles

Label	Catalog Number	Title	Type	Country	Year	Longbox Value / Value
Polygram	867593-2	It's Alright	CD5	Germany	1991	$8.00

Innocence

Singles

Label	Catalog Number	Title	Type	Country	Year	Longbox Value / Value
Cooltempo	COOLCD-267	Build	CD5	U.K.	1992	$8.00
Cooltempo	COOLCD-255	I'll Be There	CD5	U.K.	1992	$8.00
BMG	663379	Innocence	CD5	Germany	1990	$8.00
EMI	323597-2	Let's Push It	CD5	Germany	1990	$8.00
Cooltempo	COOLCD-220	Let's Push It	CD5	U.K.	1990	$8.00
Chrysalis	DPRO-23547	Let's Push It	CDJ	U.S.	1991	$2.00
EMI	323617-2	Matter of Fact	CD5	Germany	1990	$8.00
Cooltempo	COOLCD-233	Matter of Fact	CD5	U.K.	1990	$8.00
EMI	323502-2	Natural Thing	CD5	Germany	1990	$8.00
Cooltempo	COOLCD-201	Natural Thing	CD5	U.K.	1990	$8.00
Cooltempo	COOLCD-263	One Love in My Life	CD5	U.K.	1992	$8.00
Cooltempo	COOLCD-226	Remember the Day	CD5	U.K.	1991	$8.00
EMI	323536-2	Silent Voice	CD5	Germany	1990	$8.00
EMI	323591-2	Silent Voice	CD5	Germany	1990	$8.00
Cooltempo	COOLCD-212	Silent Voice	CD5	U.K.	1990	$8.00

Innocence Mission

Full Length

Label	Catalog Number	Title	Type	Country	Year	Longbox Value / Value
A&M		Glow	DJ/Smplr	U.S.		$13.00
A&M	5274	The Innocence Mission	DJ/LP	U.S.	1991	$20.00

Singles

Label	Catalog Number	Title	Type	Country	Year	Longbox Value / Value
A&M	75021 7260 2	And Hiding Away	CDJ	U.S.	1991	$3.00
A&M	AMCD-563	Black Sheep Wall	CD5	U.K.	1990	$8.00
A&M	CD 17875	Black Sheep Wall	CDJ	U.S.	1989	$2.00
A&M	3145884192	Bright as Yellow	CDJ	U.S.		$3.00
A&M Records	80967	Bright as Yellow	CD5	U.S.	1994	$5.00
A&M		Everything Is Different Now	CDJ	U.S.		$3.00
A&M	CD 17936	I Remember Me	CDJ	U.S.	1989	$2.00
A&M	75021 7293-2	Sorry and Glad Together	CDJ	U.S.	1991	$3.00
A&M	AMCD-543	Wonder of Birds	CD5	U.K.	1990	$8.00
A&M	CD 17932	Wonder of Birds	CD5	U.S.	1989	$5.00

Label	Catalog Number	Title	Type	Country	Year	Longbox Value / Value

Innocent

Singles

Label	Catalog Number	Title	Type	Country	Year	Value
CBS	655197-3	Don't Steal My Heart Away	CD3	Germany	1989	$8.00
CBS	654634-3	Only Answer	CD3	Germany	1989	$8.00

Innocent Obsession

Singles

Label	Catalog Number	Title	Type	Country	Year	Value
Eastwest	172083-2	Say Goodbye	CD5	U.K.	1990	$8.00

Insekt

Singles

Label	Catalog Number	Title	Type	Country	Year	Value
Rough Trade	390 1051-3	Control Your Fear	CD5	Germany	1992	$8.00
Rough Trade	390 1059-3	Stressed	CD5	Germany	1992	$8.00

Insiders

Full Length

Label	Catalog Number	Title	Type	Country	Year	Value
Epic		Ghost on the Beach	DJ/LP	U.S.	1987	$10.00

Singles

Label	Catalog Number	Title	Type	Country	Year	Value
Epic	ESK 2786	Ghost on the Beach	CDJ	U.S.	1987	$2.00

Inspector Morse

Singles

Label	Catalog Number	Title	Type	Country	Year	Value
Virgin	VSCDT-1418	Morse	CD5	U.K.	1992	$8.00

Inspiral Carpets

Full Length

Label	Catalog Number	Title	Type	Country	Year	Value
		1995 Interview	DJ/Intvw	U.K.	1995	$40.00
Westwood One		In Concert-Nu Rock	RS	U.S.	1993	$30.00

Airdate: 5/24/93.

Singles

Label	Catalog Number	Title	Type	Country	Year	Value
		Bitches Brew	CD5	U.K.		$8.00
		Bitches Brew	CD5	U.K.		$8.00
Second version.						
Intercord	826 955	Caravan	CD5	Germany	1991	$8.00
Intercord	826 956	Caravan	CD5	Germany	1991	$8.00
Alfa	ALDB-107	Caravan	CD3	Japan	1991	$12.00/$4.00
Cow	DUNG-13CD	Caravan	CD5	U.K.	1991	$8.00
Elektra	66606-2	Caravan	CD5	U.S.	1991	$5.00
Elektra	PRCD 8352-2	Caravan	CDJ	U.S.	1991	$2.00
Elektra	66606-2	Commercial Rain	CD5	U.S.	1990	$5.00
Elektra	PRCD 8232-2	Commercial Rain	CDJ	U.S.	1990	$2.00
Intercord	826 995	Dressing Me Down	CD5	Germany	1992	$8.00
Cow	DUNG-16CD	Dressing Me Down	CD5	U.K.	1992	$8.00
IRS	977525	Find Out Why	CD5	Germany	1991	$8.00
Cow	DUNG-5CD	Find Out Why	CD5	U.K.	1989	$8.00
Mute	8642	Generations	CDJ	U.S.	1992	$2.00
		I Want You	CD5	U.K.		$8.00
		I Want You	CD5	U.K.		$8.00
Second version.						
Intercord	826 947	Island Head	CD5	Germany	1990	$8.00
Cow	DUNG-11CD	Island Head	CD5	U.K.	1990	$8.00
IRS	977523	Joe	CD5	Germany	1991	$8.00
Cow	DUNG-13CD	Joe	CD5	U.K.	1990	$8.00
IRS	977536	Move	CD5	Germany	1990	$8.00
Cow	DUNG-6CD	Move	CD5	U.K.	1989	$8.00
Elektra	PRCD 8912-2	Party in the Sky	CDJ	U.S.	1994	$2.00
Trang Frt	SSFPSCD-072	Peel Sessions	CD5	U.K.	1989	$8.00
Intercord	826 961	Please Be Cruel	CD5	Germany	1991	$8.00
Mute	ALCB-320	Please Be Cruel	CD5	Japan	1991	$12.00
Cow	DUNG-15CD	Please Be Cruel	CD5	U.K.	1991	$8.00
Elektra	PRCD 8398-2	Please Be Cruel	CDJ	U.S.	1991	$2.00
		Saturn 5	CD5	U.K.		$8.00
		Saturn 5	CD5	U.K.		$8.00
Second version.						
Intercord	826 937	She Comes in the Fall	CD5	Germany	1990	$8.00
Cow	DUNG-10CD	She Comes in the Fall	CD5	U.K.	1990	$8.00
Mute	PRCD 8727-2	Smoking Clothes	CDJ	U.S.	1993	$2.00
Intercord	826 931	This Is How It Feels	CD5	Germany	1990	$8.00
Cow	DUNG-7CD	This Is How It Feels	CD5	U.K.	1990	$8.00
Elektra	PRCD 8281-2	This Is How It Feels	CDJ	U.S.	1990	$2.00
Cow	DUNG-17CD	Two Worlds Collide	CD5	U.K.	1992	$8.00
		Uniform	CD5	U.K.	1994	$10.00
		Uniform	CD5	U.K.	1994	$10.00
Second version.						

Inspiration

Singles

Label	Catalog Number	Title	Type	Country	Year	Value
Polygram	874490-3	Anyway	CD3	Germany	1989	$8.00
Polygram	874491-2	Anyway	CD5	Germany	1989	$8.00
Polygram	868661-2	Mr. Tambourine Man	CD5	Germany	1991	$8.00

Instant Family

Singles

Label	Catalog Number	Title	Type	Country	Year	Value
EMI	204697-2	Hoo Gee	CD5	Germany	1992	$8.00
EMI	204525-2	Night and Day	CD5	Germany	1991	$8.00
EMI	204575-2	White Christmas	CD5	Germany	1991	$8.00

Intact

Singles

Label	Catalog Number	Title	Type	Country	Year	Value
ZYX	BOY-8827-8	Act's of Sensation	CD5	Germany	1990	$8.00

Intastella

Singles

Label	Catalog Number	Title	Type	Country	Year	Value
MCA	MCSTD-1585	Century	CD5	U.K.	1991	$8.00
MCA	MCD-17524	Dream Some Paradise	CD5	Germany	1991	$8.00
MCA	MCSTD-1520	Dream Some Paradise	CD5	U.K.	1991	$8.00
MCA	MCSXD-1559	People	CD5	U.K.	1991	$8.00

Intelligent Hoodlum

Full Length

Label	Catalog Number	Title	Type	Country	Year	Value
A&M	18048	Intelligent Hoodlum	DJ/LP	U.S.	1990	$15.00
CD in custom printed plastic sleeve						
A&M	5311	Intelligent Hoodlum	LP/LB	U.S.	1990	$15.00/$10.00

Singles

Label	Catalog Number	Title	Type	Country	Year	Value
A&M	75021 7497 2	Arrest the President	CDJ	U.S.	1990	$2.00
A&M	AMCD-598	Back to Reality	CD5	U.K.	1990	$8.00
A&M	75021 7424 2	Back to Reality	CDJ	U.S.	1990	$2.00
A&M	75021 8063 2	Black and Proud	CDJ	U.S.	1990	$2.00
A&M	31458 8042	Grand Groove	CDJ	U.S.	1993	$2.00
Tuff Break	311458 8246	Street Life	CDJ	U.S.	1993	$2.00

Interactive

Singles

Label	Catalog Number	Title	Type	Country	Year	Value
ZYX	DST--1031-8	No Control	CD5	Germany	1990	$6.00
ZYX	DST--1077-8	Who Is Elvis	CD5	Germany	1990	$6.00
ZYX	ZYX-6645-BUS	Who Is Elvis	CD5	Germany	1992	$6.00

Interface

Singles

Label	Catalog Number	Title	Type	Country	Year	Value
ZYX	6040-8	Like Puppets	CD5	Germany	19992	$6.00

International Beat

Singles

Label	Catalog Number	Title	Type	Country	Year	Value
Triple X	51097	Hitting Line	CD5	U.S.	1991	$4.00

International Chrysis

Singles

Label	Catalog Number	Title	Type	Country	Year	Value
		Rebel Rebel	CDJ	U.K.		$30.00
CD-R version.						

Interstate 69

Singles

Label	Catalog Number	Title	Type	Country	Year	Value
ZYX	6741-8	Into Trance	CD5	Germany	1992	$6.00

Intime

Singles

Label	Catalog Number	Title	Type	Country	Year	Value
Cooltempo	COOLCD-217	People	CD5	U.K.	1990	$8.00

Into Another

Singles

Label	Catalog Number	Title	Type	Country	Year	Value
	PRCD10549-2	T.A.L.L.	CDJ	U.S.		$2.00

Into Paradise

Singles

Label	Catalog Number	Title	Type	Country	Year	Value
Ensign	EYNCD-644	Angel	CD5	U.K.	1991	$8.00

Intolerator III

Singles

Label	Catalog Number	Title	Type	Country	Year	Value
ZYX	6152-8	Harry's House	CD5	Germany	1989	$8.00

Intrigue

Singles

Label	Catalog Number	Title	Type	Country	Year	Value
	U5P-1000	Dance With Me	CDJ	U.S.		$2.00

Intro

Singles

Label	Catalog Number	Title	Type	Country	Year	Value
	PRCD6444-2	Funny How Time Flies	CDJ	U.S.		$2.00
Atlantic	87183	Never Again	CD5	U.S.	1994	$5.00
	PRCD 5473	Ribbon in the Sky	CDJ	U.S.		$2.00

Intuition

Singles

Label	Catalog Number	Title	Type	Country	Year	Value
Pinnacle	CDFAZE-9	Dance With Me	CD5	U.K.	1992	$8.00
Pulse 8	CDLOSE-20	Greed	CD5	U.K.	1992	$8.00

Intveld, James

Singles

Label	Catalog Number	Title	Type	Country	Year	Value
MCA	CD45 18292	Doin' Time For Bein' Young	CDJ	U.S.	1990	$2.00

Invaderes of the Heart

Singles

Label	Catalog Number	Title	Type	Country	Year	Value
Rough Trade	390 1040-3	Brain That Binds the Body	CD5	Germany	1992	$8.00

Invincible Limit

Singles

Label	Catalog Number	Title	Type	Country	Year	Value
ZYX	5596-8	Push	CD5	Germany	1988	$6.00

Invincible Spirit

Singles

Label	Catalog Number	Title	Type	Country	Year	Value
Lst Chance	036	Take as Normal	CD5	Germany		$8.00

Invisible Limits

Singles

Label	Catalog Number	Title	Type	Country	Year	Value
Rough Trade	350 0037 3	Devil Dance	CD5	Germany	1992	$8.00
Pinnacle	FUNFACD-3917	Golden Dream	CD5	U.K.	1989	$8.00
Rough Trade	CD10-262	Love Is a Kind of Mystery	CD5	Germany	1988	$8.00
Pinnacle	FUN-3909CD	Love Will Tear Us Apart	CD5	Germany	1990	$8.00
Pinnacle	FUNFACD-399	Love Will Tear Us Apart	CD3	U.K.	1990	$8.00

INXS – New Music From (Atlantic PRCD 3416-2)

INXS

Full Length

Label	Catalog Number	Title	Type	Country	Year	Value
Atlantic		Best of...	LTD/LP	Australia	1995	$35.00
Atlantic	PRCD 3416-2	Compilation	DJ/Smplr	U.S.	1990	$30.00
Mercury	838607-2	Complete Collection	LP	U.K.		$70.00
4 CD set.						
Vertigo		Greatest Hits	LTD/LP	U.K.	1994	$30.00
2 CD set.						
Pioneer Artists	PA-90-335	Greatest Video Hits 1980-90	LD	U.S.	1991	$35.00
		House of Blues	RS	U.S.	1994	$35.00
2 CD set. Airdate: 6/12/94.						
Westwood One		In Concert-Nu Rock	RS	U.S.	1993	$80.00
2 CD set. Airdate: 11/8/93.						
Warner Brothers	22P2 2399	Kick (Special Edition)	LP	Japan	1989	$20.00
Atlantic	7 82294-2	Live Baby Live	LTD/LP	U.S.	1991	$15.00

Label	Catalog Number	Title	Type	Country	Year	Longbox/Value
Atlantic		Live Baby Live	LTD/LP	U.S.	1991	$30.00
	Boxed Set with regular issue CD and VHS tape.					
WEA	50284	Live Baby Live	LD	U.S.	1992	$30.00
Sony/Sega CD		Make Your Own Music Video	LP	U.S.	1993	$10.00
	Plays only on Sega CD players.					
Westwood One		Off the Record	RS	U.S.	1992	$30.00
	Airdate: 8/17/92.					
Westwood One		Off the Record	RS	U.S.	1993	$30.00
	Airdate: 11/15/93.					
Westwood One		On the Edge	RS	U.S.	1993	$30.00
	Airdate: 1/11/93.					
Atlantic	PRCD 3675-2	Profiled!	DJ/Intvw	U.S.	1990	$20.00
Vertigo		Samplers	DJ/Smplr	U.K.		$45.00
	3 CD set.					
Atco	90072-2	Shabooh Shoobah	LP/LB	U.S.†	1985	$14.00/$8.00
Vertigo	INCD1	Six of the Best	DJ/Smplr	U.K.	1990	$20.00
Westwood One		Superstars	RS	U.S.	1993	$60.00
	Airdate: 11/8/93.					
Westwood One		Superstars	RS	U.S.	1994	$50.00
	Airdate: 6/20/94.					
Atco	90160-2	Swing	LP/LB	U.S.†	1985	$14.00/$8.00
Media America		Up Close	RS	U.S.	1988	$30.00
	2 CD set.					
Media America		Up Close	RS	U.S.	1989	$30.00
	2 CD set.					
Media America		Up Close	RS	U.S.	1990	$30.00
	2 CD set.					
Media America		Up Close	RS	U.S.	1992	$30.00
	2 CD set.					
Media America		Up Close	RS	U.S.	1993	$60.00
	2 CD set.					
Media America		Up Close	RS	U.S.	1994	[illegible]
	2 CD set.					
WEA	5CS-12	X	DJ/LP	Japan	1990	$45.00
Atlantic	7 82140-2	X	LTD/LP	U.S.	1990	$16.00/$16.00
	Limited edition cardboard sleeve in long box.					
		Singles				
WEA		Beautiful Girl	CD5	U.K.	1992	$10.00
WEA		Beautiful Girl	CD5	U.K.	1992	$10.00
	Second version.					
Atlantic		Beautiful Girl	CD5	U.S.	1992	$5.00
Atlantic	PRCD 4888-2	Beautiful Girl	CDJ	U.S.	1992	$3.00
Polygram	868551-2	Bitter Tears	CD5	Germany	1990	$10.00
WEA	WMD5-4061	Bitter Tears	CD3	Japan	1990	$12.00/$4.00
Atlantic	7 86080 2	Bitter Tears	CD5	U.S.	1990	$5.00
Atlantic	PRCD 3740-2	Bitter Tears	CDJ	U.S.	1990	$3.00
Atlantic	PRCD 3860-2	Bitter Tears	CDJ	U.S.	1990	$3.00
WEA	WMC5-389	By My Side	CD5	Japan	1991	$10.00
Mercury	INXCD-16	By My Side	CD5	U.K.	1991	$10.00
Polygram	870145-2	Devil Inside	CD5	Germany	1987	$10.00
WEA	10SW-33	Devil Inside	CD3	Japan	1987	$12.00/$4.00
Mercury	INXCD-10	Devil Inside	CD5	U.K.	1987	$10.00
Polygram	878647-2	Disappear	CD5	Germany	1990	$10.00
Wea	WMD5-4050	Disappear	CD3	Japan	1990	$12.00/$4.00
Atlantic	86093-2	Disappear	CD5	U.S.	1990	$5.00
Atlantic	PRCD 3655-2	Disappear	CDJ	U.S.	1990	$3.00
		Freedom Deep	CD5	Australia	1994	$12.00
Meercury	INXCT 25	Gift, The	CD5	U.K.	1992	$10.00
Meercur		Gift, The	CD5	U.K.	1992	$10.00
	Second version.					
Atlantic	PRCD 5286-2	Gift, The	CDJ	U.S.	1992	$3.00
WEA	WMD5-4108	Heaven Sent	CD3	Japan	1992	$12.00/$4.00
Atlantic	PRCD-4600-2	Heaven Sent	CDJ	U.S.	1992	$6.00
Polygram	874314-3	Mystify	CD3	Germany	1987	$10.00
Polygram	874315-2	Mystify	CD5	Germany	1987	$10.00
Murcury	INXCD-13	Mystify	CD5	U.K.	1987	$10.00
Atlantic	PR 2549-2	Mystify	CDJ	U.S.	1987	$3.00
Polygram	874314-3	Need You Tonight	CD3	Germany	1987	$10.00
Polygram	872215-2	Need You Tonight	CD5	Germany	1988	$10.00
WEA	10SW-2	Need You Tonight	CD3	Japan	1988	$12.00/$4.00
Mercury	INXCD-8	Need You Tonight	CD5	U.K.	1987	$10.00
Mercury	INXCD-12	Need You Tonight	CD5	U.K.	1988	$10.00
Atlantic	PR 2132-2	Need You Tonight	CDJ	U.S.	1987	$3.00
Polygram	870488-2	Never Tear Us Apart	CD5	Germany	1988	$10.00
WEA	10P3-6019	Never Tear Us Apart	CD3	Japan	1988	$12.00/$4.00
Murcury	INXCD-11	Never Tear Us Apart	CD5	U.K.	1988	$10.00
		Never Tear Us Apart	CDV	U.K.	1989	$25.00
Atlantic	PR 2399-2	Never Tear Us Apart	CDJ	U.S.	1988	$8.00
Polygram	870092-2	New Sensation	CD5	Germany	1988	$10.00
WEA	10SW-37	New Sensation	CD3	Japan	1987	$12.00/$4.00
Mercury	INXCD-9	New Sensation	CD5	U.K.	1987	$10.00
Eastwest	WMD5-4115	Not Enough Time	CD3	Japan	1992	$12.00/$4.00
Mercury		Not Enough Time	CD5	U.K.	1992	$10.00
Atlantic	85819-2	Not Enough Time	CD5	U.S.	1992	$5.00
Atlantic	PRCD 4721-2	Not Enough Time	CDJ	U.S.	1992	$3.00
WEA		Please	CD5	U.K.	1993	$10.00
WEA		Please	CD5	U.K.	1993	$10.00
	Second version.					
Atlantic	PRCD 5369-2	Please	CDJ	U.S.	1993	$3.00
Polygram	866029-2	Shining Star	CD5	Germany	1991	$10.00
Atlantic	5CS-42	Shining Star	CDJ	Japan		$35.00
WEA	WMD5-4085	Shining Star	CD3	Japan	1991	$12.00/$4.00
Mercury	INXCD-18	Shining Star	CD5	U.K.	1991	$10.00
Atlantic	PRCD 4248-2	Shining Star	CDJ	U.S.	1991	$6.00
		Strangest Party	CD5	U.K.		$10.00
		Strangest Party	CD5	U.K.		$10.00
	Second version.					
Atlantic	85609	Strangest Party	CD5	U.S.	1994	$5.00
Mercury	422856311	Strangest Party, The	CD5	Canada	1994	$28.00
polygram	878087-2	Suicide Blonde	CD5	Germany	1990	$10.00
WEA	WMD5-4040	Suicide Blonde	CD3	Japan	1990	$12.00/$4.00
Mercury	INXCD 14	Suicide Blonde	CD5	U.K.	1990	$10.00
Atlantic		Suicide Blonde	CD5	U.S.	1990	$5.00
Atlantic	PR 3460-2	Suicide Blonde	CDJ	U.S.	1990	$6.00
WEA	WMD5-4123	Taste It	CD3	Japan	1992	$12.00/$4.00
WEA		Taste It	CD5	U.K.	1992	$10.00
WEA		Taste It	CD5	U.K.	1992	$10.00
	Second version.					
Atlantic	87409-2	Taste It	CD5	U.S.	1992	$5.00
Atlantic	PRCD 4729-2	Taste It	CDJ	U.S.	1992	$3.00
Atlantic	PRCD 5366-2	Time	CDJ	U.S.	1993	$3.00
Atlantic	PRCD 5367-2	Time	CDJ	U.S.	1993	$3.00

Ioni

Singles

Label	Catalog Number	Title	Type	Country	Year	Longbox/Value
A&M	AMCD-0612	Sentence of Love	CD5	U.K.	1993	$8.00

Iron Butterfly

Full Length

Label	Catalog Number	Title	Type	Country	Year	Longbox/Value
Rhino	R2 72196	In-A-Gadda-Da-Vida	LTD/LP	U.S.	1996	$18.00
	Multi-Image cover in slip case.					
Rhino		In-A-Gadda-Da-Vida	LTD/LP	U.S.	1996	$25.00
	Multi-Image cover, and VHS video in box.					

Iron Maiden – Lord of the Flies (CMC International)

Iron Maiden

Full Length

Label	Catalog Number	Title	Type	Country	Year	Longbox/Value
Pioneer	PA-91-349	12 Wasted Years	LD	U.S.	1991	$35.00
EMI	TOCP-7598	A Real Dead One	LTD/LP	Japan	1993	$28.00
Capitol	CDP 89248 2 1	A Real Dead One	LP	U.S.	1993	$18.00
Castle	113-2	A Real Dead One	LTD/LP	U.S.	1995	$15.00
Capitol		A Real Live One	LP	U.S.	1993	$18.00
Castle	112-2	A Real Live One	LTD/LP	U.S.	1995	$15.00
EMI		Best of the Beast	LTD/LP	U.K.	1996	$36.00
	2 CD picture disc set.					
Castle	124-2	Best of the Beast	LTD/LP	U.S.	1996	$32.00
	2 CD picture disc set.					
EMI		Fear of the Dark	LTD/LP	Australia	1992	$25.00
EMI	TOCP-7155	Fear of the Dark	LTD/LP	Japan	1992	$25.00
EMI		Fear of the Dark	LTD/LP	U.K.	1992	$25.00
EMI	7243 8 35877 2	Fear of the Dark	LTD/LP	U.K.	1995	$25.00
	2 CD set.					
Castle	111-2	Fear of the Dark	LTD/LP	U.S.	1995	$18.00
	2 CD set.					
EMI	TOCP-6181-90	First Ten Years, The	LTD/LP	Japan	1990	$300.00
	10 CD5 boxed set.					
Epic	ESK 4648	Fugitive, The	DJ/Intvw	U.S.	1992	$20.00
EMI	752018-2	Iron Maiden	LP	U.K.	1985	$12.00
EMI	7243 8 35868 2 0	Iron Maiden	LTD/LP	U.K.	1995	$25.00
	2 CD set.					
Capitol	C21Y-91415-2	Iron Maiden	LP/LB	U.S.	1987	$13.00/$8.00
Castle	102-2	Iron Maiden	LTD/LP	U.S.	1995	$18.00
	2 CD set.					
EMI	752019-2	Killers	LP	U.K.	1985	$12.00
EMI	7243 8 35869 2	Killers	LTD/LP	U.K.	1995	$25.00
	2 CD set.					
Capitol	C21Y-91416-2	Killers	LP/LB	U.S.	1987	$13.00/$8.00
Castle	103-2	Killers	LTD/LP	U.S.	1995	$18.00
	2 CD set.					
EMI	746186-2	Live After Death	LP	U.K.	1985	$12.00
EMI	7243 8 35873 2	Live After Death	LTD/LP	U.K.	1995	$25.00
	2 CD set					
Capitol	C21Y-46186	Live After Death	LP/LB	U.S.	1987	$13.00/$8.00
Castle	107-2	Live After Death	LTD/LP	U.S.	1995	$18.00
	2 CD set.					
EMI		Live At Donnington	LP	U.K.	1994	$30.00
	2 CD set.					
EMI		Maiden England	LP/VHS	U.K.	1994	$35.00
Epic		No Prayer for the Dying	DJ/LP	Canada	1990	$50.00
	Promo CD and cassette in custom box.					
EMI	795142-2	No Prayer for the Dying	LP	U.K.	1990	$12.00
EMI	72438358762	No Prayer for the Dying	LTD/LP	U.K.	1995	$25.00
	2 CD set.					
Epic	CK 46905	No Prayer for the Dying	LP/LB	U.S.	1990	$13.00/$8.00
Castle	110-2	No Prayer for the Dying	LTD/LP	U.S.	1995	$18.00
	2 CD set.					
EMI	746364-2	Number of the Beast	LP	U.K.	1985	$12.00
EMI	7243 8 35870 2 0	Number of the Beast	LTD/LP	U.K.	1995	$25.00
	2 CD set.					
Capitol	C21Y-46364	Number of the Beast	LP/LB	U.S.	1987	$13.00/$8.00
Castle	104-2	Number of the Beast	LTD/LP	U.S.	1995	$18.00
	2 CD set.					
EMI	746363-2	Piece of Mind	LP	U.K.	1985	$12.00
EMI	7243 8 35871 2	Piece of Mind	LTD/LP	U.K.	1995	$25.00
	2 CD set.					
Capitol	C21Y-46363	Piece of Mind	LP/LB	U.S.	1987	$13.00/$8.00
Castle	105-2	Piece of Mind	LTD/LP	U.S.	1995	$18.00
	2 CD set.					
EMI	746045-2	Powerslave	LP	U.K.	1985	$12.00
EMI	7243 8 35872 2	Powerslave	LTD/LP	U.K.	1995	$25.00
	2 CD set.					
EMI	7243 8 35872 2 3	Powerslave	LTD/LP	U.K.	1995	$30.00
Capitol	CDP-46045	Powerslave	LP/BP	U.S.†	1985	$14.00/$8.00
Capitol	C21Y-46045	Powerslave	LP/LB	U.S.	1987	$13.00/$8.00
Castle	106-2	Powerslave	LTD/LP	U.S.	1995	$18.00
	2 CD set.					
BMG Video		Raising Hell	DJ/8" LD	U.S.	1993	$75.00
EMI	790258-2	Seventh Son Of A Seventh Son	LP	U.K.	1988	$12.00
EMI	72438358752	Seventh Son of a Seventh Son	LTD/LP	U.K.	1995	$25.00
	2 CD set.					
Capitol	C21Y-90258	Seventh Son of a Seventh Son	LP/LB	U.S.	1988	$13.00/$8.00
Castle	109-2	Seventh Son of a Seventh Son	LTD/LP	U.S.	1995	$18.00
	2 CD set.					
EMI	746341-2	Somewhere in Time	LP	U.K.	1985	$12.00

Label	Catalog Number	Title	Type	Country	Year	Longbox / Value
EMI	7243 8 35874 2	Somewhere in Time	LTD/LP	U.K.	1995	$25.00
	2 CD set.					
Capitol	C21Y-46341	Somewhere in Time	LP/LB	U.S.	1987	$13.00/$8.00
Castle	108-2	Somewhere in Time	LTD/LP	U.S.	1995	$18.00
	2 CD set.					
Pioneer	PA84-M006	Video Pieces	8"LD	U.S.	1983	$25.00
Castle	PROC 6-2	Virus	DJ/Smplr	U.S.	1996	$20.00
EMI	TOCP-8588	X-Factor, The	LTD/LP	Japan	1995	$50.00
	2 CD set.					
		Singles				
EMI	739 992 2	2 Minutes To Midnight	CD5	U.K.	1990	$16.00
EMI	204764-2	Be Quick or Be Dead	CD5	Germany	1992	$10.00
EMI	TOCP-7237	Be Quick or Be Dead	CD5	Japan	1992	$15.00
EMI	CDEM-229	Be Quick or Be Dead	CD5	U.K.	1992	$10.00
Epic	ESK 4551	Be Quick or Be Dead	CDJ	U.S.	1992	$15.00
EMI	204171-2	Bring Your Daughter...to the Slaughter	CD5	Germany	1991	$10.00
EMI	TOCP-6572	Bring Your Daughter...to the Slaughter	CD5	Japan	1990	$15.00
EMI	CDEM-171	Bring Your Daughter...to the Slaughter	CD5	U.K.	1991	$10.00
Epic	ESK 4007	Bring Your Daughter...to the Slaughter	CDJ	U.S.	1991	$20.00
	Picture disc.					
EMI	202460-2	Can I Play With Madness	CD5	Germany	1988	$10.00
Toshiba	XP10-2009	Can I Play With Madness	CD3	Japan	1987	$15.00/$4.00
EMI	CDEM-49	Can I Play With Madness	CD5	U.K.	1987	$10.00
EMI	CDP 79 4001 2	Can I Play With Madness	CD5	U.K.	1990	$16.00
EMI	203048-2	Clairvoyant, The	CD5	Germany	1988	$11.00
EMI	CD EM 79	Clairvoyant, The	CD5	U.K.	1988	$11.00
EMI	CDP 79 4004 2	Clairvoyant, The	CD5	U.K.	1990	$16.00
EMI	202773-2	Evil That Men Do, The	CD5	Germany	1988	$11.00
Toshiba	CP12-5740	Evil That Men Do, The	CD3	Japan	1988	$15.00/$4.00
EMI	CDEM 64	Evil That Men Do, The	CD5	U.K.	1988	$11.00
EMI		Fear of the Dark	CD5	U.K.		$10.00
EMI	CDP 79 3989 2	Flight of Icarus	CD5	U.K.	1990	$16.00
EMI	TOCP-27356	From Here to Eternity	CD5	Japan	1992	$15.00
Epic	ESK 4758	From Here to Eternity	CDJ	U.S.	1992	$10.00
EMI	204028-2	Holy Smoke	CD5	Germany	1990	$10.00
EMI	TOCP-6449	Holy Smoke	CD5	Japan	1990	$15.00
EMI	CDEM 153	Holy Smoke	CD5	U.K.	1990	$10.00
Epic	ESK 2194	Holy Smoke	CDJ	U.S.	1990	$6.00
EMI	CDEM 117	Infinite Dreams	CD5	U.K.	1989	$11.00
CMC International	8 82660 2 4	Lord of Flies	CDJ	U.S.	1996	$14.00
EMI	CDEM 398	Man On the Edge	CD5	U.K.	1995	$15.00
EMI	CDEMS 398	Man On the Edge	CD5	U.K.	1995	$15.00
	CD in box.					
CMC International		Man On the Edge	CDJ	U.S.	1996	$14.00
Epic	ESK 73695	No Prayer For the Dying	CDJ	U.S.	1990	$25.00
EMI	CDP 7939782	Purgatory	CD5	U.K.	1990	$16.00
EMI	CDP 79 3981 2	Run To the Hills	CD5	U.K.	1990	$16.00
EMI	CD IRN 1	Running Free	CD5	U.K.	1990	$16.00
EMI	CDP 79 3995 2	Running Free (Live)	CD5	U.K.	1990	$16.00
Epic	ESK 2233	Tailgunner	CDJ/PD	U.S.	1990	$30.00
EMI	CDP 79 3998 2	Wasted Years	CD5	U.K.	1990	$16.00
EMI	880231-1	Wasting Love	CD5	Germany	1992	$10.00
Epic	ESK 4640	Wasting Love	CDJ	U.S.	1992	$10.00
EMI	CDIRN 2	Women in Uniform	CD5	U.K.	1990	$16.00

Irrwisch

Singles

Label	Catalog Number	Title	Type	Country	Year	Longbox / Value
EMI	176433-2	Living for Love	CD5	Germany	1989	$8.00

Irving, Robert III

Full Length

Label	Catalog Number	Title	Type	Country	Year	Longbox / Value
		Midnight Dream	DJ/Smplr	U.S.		$5.00

Irwin, Russ

Singles

Label	Catalog Number	Title	Type	Country	Year	Longbox / Value
SBK	DPRO-05401	I Need You Now	CDJ	U.S.	1991	$2.00

Isaak, Chris

Full Length

Label	Catalog Number	Title	Type	Country	Year	Longbox / Value
CBS		Forever Blue	LTD/LP	Australia	1995	$30.00
	2 CD set.					
		Singles				
WEA	9362-40003-2	Blue Hotel	CD5	Germany	1990	$10.00
Reprise	W-0005CD	Blue Hotel	CD5	U.K.	1990	$10.00
Reprise	9362 40212	Blue Spanish Sky	CD5	Germany	1991	$10.00
Reprise	W-0062CD	Blue Spanish Sky	CD5	U.K.	1991	$10.00
Reprise	PRO-CD-5035	Blue Spanish Sky	CDJ	U.S.	1990	$2.00
WEA		Can't Do a Thing	CD5	U.S.	1993	$10.00
WEA		Can't Do a Thing	CD5	U.S.	1993	$10.00
	Second version.					
Reprise	PRO-CD-6000	Can't Do a Thing	CDJ	U.S.	1993	$2.00
		Can't Do a Thing (To Stop Me)	CDJ	U.K.		$10.00
		Can't Do a Thing (To Stop Me)	CD5	U.K.		$10.00
	Second version.					
WEA	9362-400058-2	Dancin'	CD5	Germany	1990	$10.00
Reprise	W-0021CD	Dancin'	CD5	U.K.	1991	$10.00
Reprise	PRO-CD-6699	Dark Moon	CDJ	U.S.	1993	$2.00
Reprise	PRO-CD-3567	Don't Make Me Dream About You	CDJ	U.S.	1989	$2.00
Warner Brothers	17761	Go Walking Down There	CD5	U.S.	1995	$5.00
	PRO-CD-7726	Go Walking Down There	CDJ	U.S.	1995	$3.00
	PRO-CD-7953	Graduation Day	CDJ	U.S.	1995	$3.00
WEA	W0182CD2	San Francisco Days	CD5	U.K.	1994	$10.00
WEA		San Francisco Days	CD5	U.K.	1994	$10.00
	Second version.					
Reprise	PRO-CD-6266	San Francisco Days	CDJ	U.S.	1994	$3.00
WEA		Solitary Man	CD5	U.K.	1993	$10.00
Reprise	PRO-CD-6284	Solitary Man	CDJ	U.S.	1993	$3.00
	PRO-CD-7543	Somebody's Crying	CDJ	U.S.	1995	$3.00
Reprise	PRO-CD-6487	Two Hearts	CDJ	U.S.	1993	$3.00
Polygram	869229-2	Wicked Game	CD5	Germany	1990	$10.00
London	LONCD-279	Wicked Game	CD5	U.K.	1990	$10.00

Isham, Mark

Full Length

Label	Catalog Number	Title	Type	Country	Year	Longbox / Value
		Special Edits From Castalia	DJ/Smplr	U.S.		$3.00
Windham	WD-1027	Vapor Drawings	LP/LB	U.S.†	1985	$14.00/$8.00
Windam Hill	WD-1027	Vapor Drawings	LP/LB	U.S.	1987	$14.00/$8.00

Isis

Singles

Label	Catalog Number	Title	Type	Country	Year	Longbox / Value
4th & B'way	BRCD-224	Hail the Word	CD5	U.K.	1991	$8.00
4th & B'way	513-2	Rebel Soul	CDJ	U.S.	1990	$2.00

Island

Singles

Label	Catalog Number	Title	Type	Country	Year	Longbox / Value
EMI	TODT-2814	Stay With Me	CD3	Japan	1992	$13.00/$4.00

Island Inspirational All-Stars

Singles

Label	Catalog Number	Title	Type	Country	Year	Longbox / Value
		Don't Give Up	CDJ	U.S.		$3.00

Isle Of Man

Full Length

Label	Catalog Number	Title	Type	Country	Year	Longbox / Value
		Isle of Man	DJ/LP	U.S.		$4.00

Isley, Alex

Singles

Label	Catalog Number	Title	Type	Country	Year	Longbox / Value
Vam	VMDY-1017	Funny Days	CD3	Japan	1993	$12.00/$3.00

Isley Brothers

Full Length

Label	Catalog Number	Title	Type	Country	Year	Longbox / Value
Motown	5425	Soul on the Rocks	LP/BP	U.S.		$12.00/$7.00
		Singles				
Warner Brothers	PRO-CD-4070	Come Together	CDJ	U.S.	1989	$2.00
Warner Brothers	PRO-CD-6941	I'm So Proud	CDJ	U.S.	1994	$2.00
Old Gold	OG-6506	It's a Disco Night	CD5	Germany	1990	$10.00
Warner Brothers	PRO-CD-5411	Spend the Night Together	CDJ	U.S.	1989	$2.00
Elektra	PRCD 8837-2	Voyage to Atlantis	CDJ	U.S.	1993	$2.00
Warner Brothers	PRO-CD-3771	You'll Never Walk Alone	CDJ	U.S.	1989	$2.00

Isley, Ernest

Singles

Label	Catalog Number	Title	Type	Country	Year	Longbox / Value
Elektra	PR 8184-2	Back to Square One	CDJ	U.S.	1990	$2.00
Elektra	PR 8121-2	High Wire	CDJ	U.S.	1990	$2.00
		Let's Go	CDJ	U.S.		$2.00
Elektra	PR 8163-2	Rising From the Ashes	CDJ	U.S.	1990	$2.00

Isotonik

Singles

Label	Catalog Number	Title	Type	Country	Year	Longbox / Value
ffrr	TABCD-101	Different Strokes	CD5	U.K.	1992	$8.00
ffrr	TABCD-108	Different Strokes	CD5	U.K.	1992	$8.00

Israel Vibratio

Singles

Label	Catalog Number	Title	Type	Country	Year	Longbox / Value
Ras	3175	On the Rock	CD5	U.S.	1994	$5.00

It

Singles

Label	Catalog Number	Title	Type	Country	Year	Longbox / Value
Big Life	BCK-4CD	Rainforest Serenade	CD5	U.K.	1990	$8.00

It Bites

Full Length

Label	Catalog Number	Title	Type	Country	Year	Longbox / Value
Virgin	CDVX-2591	Eat Me in St. Louis	LTD/LP	U.K.		$20.00
		Singles				
Virgin	CDEP-21	Kiss Like Judas	CD5	U.K.	1988	$8.00
		Kiss Like Judas	CDJ	U.S.	1988	$2.00
Virgin	VSCD-1065	Midnight	CD5	U.K.	1988	$8.00
Virgin	MIKE-94112	Old Man and the Angel	CD5	U.K.	1990	$8.00
Virgin	VJD-10208	Sister Sarah	CD3	Japan	1989	$13.00/$3.00
Virgin	VSCD-1202	Sister Sarah	CD3	U.K.	1989	$8.00
Virgin	162254	Still Too Young to Remember	CD3	Germany	1990	$8.00
Virgin	662254	Still Too Young to Remember	CD5	Germany	1990	$8.00
Virgin	VSCD-1238	Still Too Young to Remember	CD3	U.K.	1990	$8.00
Virgin	VSCDX-1184	Still Too Young to Remember	CD3	U.K.	1990	$8.00
Virgin	VSCD-1184	Still Too Young to Remember	CD5	U.K.	1990	$8.00
Virgin	VSCD-1215	Underneath Your Pillow	CD3	U.K.	1990	$8.00
Virgin	VSCD-1263	Underneath Your Pillow	CD5	U.K.	1990	$8.00
Virgin	VSCDT-1263	Underneath Your Pillow	CD5	U.K.	1990	$8.00

It Takes Presidents

Singles

Label	Catalog Number	Title	Type	Country	Year	Longbox / Value
WEA	170980-2	Hey Lord	CD5	Germany	1990	$8.00

It's Immaterial

Singles

Label	Catalog Number	Title	Type	Country	Year	Longbox / Value
Siren	CDT-26	Driving Away From Home	CD3	U.K.	1988	$8.00
Siren	CDT-129	Heaven Knows	CD3	U.K.	1990	$8.00

Itals

Singles

Label	Catalog Number	Title	Type	Country	Year	Longbox / Value
Rhythm	6603	Could You Be Loved	CDJ	U.S.	1991	$2.00

IV Xample

Singles

Label	Catalog Number	Title	Type	Country	Year	Longbox / Value
MCA	MCA5P3271	I'd Rather Be Alone	CDJ	U.S.	1995	$3.00

Ives, Burl

Full Length

Label	Catalog Number	Title	Type	Country	Year	Longbox / Value
Warner Sound Exchange		Sunshine in My Soul	LTD/LP	U.S.	1995	$17.00

Ivory, Steve

Singles

Label	Catalog Number	Title	Type	Country	Year	Longbox / Value
	352180	My Love Song	CD5	U.S.	1994	$5.00

Ivy

Singles

Label	Catalog Number	Title	Type	Country	Year	Longbox / Value
	PRCD6474-2	Beautiful	CDJ	U.S.		$2.00
Seed	95913	Lately	CD5	U.S.	1994	$5.00
Warner	32-95913	Wish It All The Way	CD5	Canada	1994	$8.00

Izzy Ice

Singles

Label	Catalog Number	Title	Type	Country	Year	Longbox / Value
RCA	ZD-43244	Soul Man	CD5	Germany	1989	$8.00

J.

Full Length

Label	Catalog Number	Title	Type	Country	Year	Longbox / Value
A&M	517710	We Are the Majority	LP/BP	U.S.		$12.00/$7.00
		Singles				
A&M	PAMCD-028	Born on the Wrong Side of Bed	CD5	U.K.	1992	$8.00
A&M	42286 1860	Come Over Here	CDJ	U.S.	1992	$2.00
Polydor	42286	Keep the Promise	CD5	U.S.	1992	$3.00

J., David

Full Length

Label	Catalog Number	Title	Type	Country	Year	Longbox / Value
RCA	MCAD-2261	Songs From Another Season	LP/LB	U.S.		$14.00/$8.00
		Singles				
MCA	54424	Candy on the Cross	CD5	U.S.	1992	$4.00
		Fingers in the Grease	CDJ	U.S.		$2.00
MCA	2678-2-RDJ	I'll Be Your Chauffeur	CDJ	U.S.	1990	$2.00
MCA	2613-2-RDJ	I'll Be Your Chauffeur	CDJ	U.S.	1990	$2.00
MCA	2261	Some Big City	CDJ	U.S.	1992	$2.00
MCA	MCA5P-2473	Space Cowboy	CDJ	U.S.	1992	$2.00

J.G.

Singles

Label	Catalog Number	Title	Type	Country	Year	Longbox Value/Value
Gasoline	2873	Put Down the Guns	CDJ	U.S.	1993	$2.00

J. Geils Band

Full Length

Label	Catalog Number	Title	Type	Country	Year	Longbox Value/Value
Atlantic	7260-2	Bloodshot	LP/LB	U.S.		$14.00/$8.00
EMI	CDP-46014	Freeze Frame	LP/LB	U.S.†	1984	$14.00/$8.00
Atlantic	7241-2	Full House Live	LP/LB	U.S.		$14.00/$8.00
Atlantic		Hotline	LP/LB	U.S.		$14.00/$8.00
Album Network		In the Studio (Bloodshot)	RS	U.S.	1990	$20.00
	Airdate: 5/21/90.					
Pioneer Artists	PA-84-M003	J. Geils Band	LD	U.S.	1984	$11.00
DIR		King Biscuit Flour Hour	RS	U.S.	1988	$40.00
	With Slade, Airdate: 6/5/88.					
DIR		King Biscuit Flour Hour	RS	U.S.	1990	$30.00
	With Jack Bruce, Airdate: 3/26/90.					
DIR		King Biscuit Flour Hour	RS	U.S.	1994	$25.00
	With Jack Bruce, Airdate: 1/24/94.					
Atlantic		Ladies Invited	LP/LB	U.S.		$14.00/$8.00
Atlantic	19103-2	Monkey Island	LP/LB	U.S.		$14.00/$8.00
Atlantic	18107-2	Nightmares	LP/LB	U.S.		$14.00/$8.00
EMI	CDP-46080	You're Getting Even	LP/LB	U.S.†	1985	$30.00/$27.00

J.J.

Singles

Label	Catalog Number	Title	Type	Country	Year	Longbox Value/Value
Columbia	656965-2	Crying Over You	CD5	U.K.	1991	$8.00
Columbia	656609-2	If This Is Love	CD5	U.K.	1991	$8.00
Columbia	656322-2	Slide Away	CD5	U.K.	1991	$8.00

J.J. Fad

Singles

Label	Catalog Number	Title	Type	Country	Year	Longbox Value/Value
		Way Out	CDJ	U.S.		$2.00

J.P.S. Experience

Singles

Label	Catalog Number	Title	Type	Country	Year	Longbox Value/Value
Flying Nun	FNCD-212	Precious	CD5	U.K.	1992	$8.00

J.T.

Singles

Label	Catalog Number	Title	Type	Country	Year	Longbox Value/Value
Eastwest	PRCD 3900-2	Swing It	CDJ	U.S.	1991	$2.00

J.T. And The Big Family

Singles

Label	Catalog Number	Title	Type	Country	Year	Longbox Value/Value
ZYX	6361-8	Foreign Affair	CD5	Germany	1990	$8.00
ZYX	6278-8	Moments in Soul	CD5	Germany	1990	$8.00
Champion	CHAMPCD-237	Moments in Soul	CD5	U.K.	1990	$8.00

J.W.P.

Singles

Label	Catalog Number	Title	Type	Country	Year	Longbox Value/Value
EMI	203379-3	Never Again	CD3	Germany	1989	$8.00
EMI	203380-2	Never Again	CD5	Germany	1989	$8.00

J'son

Singles

Label	Catalog Number	Title	Type	Country	Year	Longbox Value/Value
	PRCD105872	I'll Never Stop Loving You	CDJ	U.S.		$2.00
Polygram	64003	Take a Look	CD5	U.S.	1995	$5.00

J-Soul

Singles

Label	Catalog Number	Title	Type	Country	Year	Longbox Value/Value
Toshiba	TODT-2823	Cold Rain	CD3	Japan	1992	$12.00/$3.00
Toshiba	TODT-2824	Dream Play	CD3	Japan	1992	$12.00/$3.00
Toshiba	TODT-2825	Snowy Country	CD3	Japan	1992	$12.00/$3.00

Jabulani

Singles

Label	Catalog Number	Title	Type	Country	Year	Longbox Value/Value
Giant	PRO-CD-5433	Shine Your Light	CDJ	U.S.	1992	$2.00

Jack & Chill

Singles

Label	Catalog Number	Title	Type	Country	Year	Longbox Value/Value
Oval	TENCD-234	Beatin' the Heat	CD5	U.K.	1988	$8.00

Jack D.J.

Singles

Label	Catalog Number	Title	Type	Country	Year	Longbox Value/Value
Intercord	825 740	Hot House	CD5	Germany	1988	$8.00
Intercord	825 032	Turn Me Loose	CD5	Germany	1988	$8.00

Jack MC's

Singles

Label	Catalog Number	Title	Type	Country	Year	Longbox Value/Value
Arista	7432111936-2	Jackie Hustle	CD5	U.K.	1992	$8.00

Jack Rubies

Singles

Label	Catalog Number	Title	Type	Country	Year	Longbox Value/Value
TVT		Book Of Love	CDJ	U.S.	1990	$2.00

Jackers

Singles

Label	Catalog Number	Title	Type	Country	Year	Longbox Value/Value
Epic	ESK7756	Down 4 Life	CDJ	U.S.		$2.00

Jackson, Alan

Full Length

Label	Catalog Number	Title	Type	Country	Year	Longbox Value/Value
		'90s Country	RS	U.S.	1995	$40.00
	Airdate: 10/28/95.					
		'90s Country	RS	U.S.	1995	$40.00
	Airdate: 5/20/95.					
Unistar		Alan Jackson Story	RS	U.S.	1993	$30.00
	Airdate: 7/9/93.					
Westwood One		Country Concert	RS	U.S.	1996	$60.00
	2 CD set. Airdate: 8/26/96.					
		Country Special	RS	U.S.	1994	$40.00
	2 CD set. Airdate: 6/25/94.					
Arista	07822-18801-2	Greatest Hits Collection	DJ/LP	U.S.	1995	$20.00
	CD in 6"x12" package.					
Arista	ASCD-2479	Music Row Theater	DJ/RS	U.S.		$20.00
		Nashville Record Review	RS	U.S.	1993	$40.00
	4 CD set.					
Westwood One		Who I Am	RS	U.S.	1994	$40.00

Singles

Label	Catalog Number	Title	Type	Country	Year	Longbox Value/Value
Arista	ASCD-2220	Don't Rock the Jukebox	CDJ	U.S.	1991	$3.00
Artista	663481	Here In the Real World	CD5	U.K.	1990	$10.00
Arista	ASCD-2166	I'd Love You All Over Again	CDJ	U.S.	1990	$3.00
Arista	ASCD-3048	Little Bitty	CDJ	U.S.	1996	$0.00/$20.00
	Cool Disc.					
Arista	ASCD-2463	She's Got the Rhythm	CDJ	U.S.	1992	$3.00
Arista	ASCD-2697	Summertime Blues	CDJ	U.S.	1994	$3.00
Arista	ASCD-2514	Tonight I Climbed the Wall	CDJ	U.S.	1993	$3.00
Arista	ASCD-2649	You Can't Have It All	CDJ	U.S.	1994	$3.00

Jackson, Chad

Singles

Label	Catalog Number	Title	Type	Country	Year	Longbox Value/Value
Intercord	827 201	Hear the Drummer	CD5	Germany	1990	$8.00

Jackson, Dee D.

Singles

Label	Catalog Number	Title	Type	Country	Year	Longbox Value/Value
Polygram	887807-2	Automatic Lover	CD5	Germany	1989	$8.00
Motown	R10M-120	I Want You Back	CD3	Japan	1989	$13.00/$4.00
Motown	R10M-121	Love You Save	CD3	Japan	1989	$13.00/$4.00
Motown	PODT-1011	Who's Loving You	CD3	Japan	1992	$13.00/$4.00

Jackson, Freddie

Singles

Label	Catalog Number	Title	Type	Country	Year	Longbox Value/Value
Orpheus	4531	All Over You	CDJ	U.S.	1990	$2.00
Capitol	DPRO-79480	Can I Touch You	CDJ	U.S.	1992	$2.00
		Christmas Forever	CDJ	U.S.		$2.00
Capitol	DPRO-79374	Could Use a Little Love Tonight	CDJ	U.S.	1992	$2.00
Capitol	CDCL-510	Crazy	CD5	U.K.	1988	$10.00
Capitol	DPRO-79471	Do Me Again	CDJ	U.S.	1990	$2.00
Capitol	5061	Have You Ever Loved Somebody	DJ/CDV	U.S.	1988	$20.00
Capitol	CDCL-611	Love Me Down	CD5	U.K.	1991	$10.00
Capitol	DPRO-79351	Love Me Down	CDJ	U.S.	1990	$2.00
Curb	10570	Love Survives	CDJ	U.S.	1989	$2.00
Capitol	DPRO-79496	Main Coarse	CDJ	U.S.	1990	$2.00
RCA	62753-2-RDJ	Make Love Easy	CDJ	U.S.	1993	$2.00
Capitol	CDCL-558	Me and Mrs. Jones	CD5	U.K.	1992	$10.00
Capitol	CDCL-502	Nice 'n Slow	CD5	U.K.	1990	$10.00
Capitol	DPRO-79352	Nice 'n Slow	CDJ	U.S.	1990	$2.00
RCA	62782-2-RDJ	Was It Something	CDJ	U.S.	1994	$2.00
RCA	62791-2-RDJ	Was It Something	CDJ	U.S.	1994	$2.00

Jackson, Janet

Full Length

Label	Catalog Number	Title	Type	Country	Year	Longbox Value/Value
A&M		Control	8"LD	Japan		$35.00
A&M	DSP-39	Control	DJ/Smplr	Japan	1988	$120.00
Pioneer	PA-87-195	Control	LD	U.S.	1987	$25.00
A&M	CD-4962	Dream Street	LP/LB	U.S.†	1984	$14.00/$8.00
Virgin		Janet	LTD/LP	Australia	1993	$25.00
	2 CD set.					
Virgin	7243-8-39195-2	Janet	LTD/LP	U.S.	1993	$25.00
	2CD set in book.					
A&M	CD 17966	Remixes	DJ/Smplr	U.S.	1989	$15.00
A&M	AMAD-3920	Rhythm Nation	LTD/LP	U.K.	1989	$30.00
	Picture disc CD.					
A&M	CD 3920	Rhythm Nation	DJ/LP	U.S.	1989	$20.00
	Promo box with CD, cassette, and pin.					
A&M	LV 38408	Rhythm Nation	LD	U.S.	1989	$25.00

Singles

Label	Catalog Number	Title	Type	Country	Year	Longbox Value/Value
Virgin		Again	CD5	U.K.	1993	$15.00
Virgin		Again	CD5	U.K.	1993	$15.00
	Second version.					
Virgin	VSCDJ-1481	Again	CDJ	U.K.	1993	$12.00
Virgin	38411	Again	CD5	U.S.	1993	$9.00
Virgin	12801	Again	CDJ	U.S.	1993	$9.00
A&M	390485-2	Alright	CD5	Germany	1990	$15.00
A&M	USACD-593	Alright	CD5	U.K.	1990	$15.00
A&M	CD 17978	Alright	CDJ	U.S.	1989	$9.00
A&M	CD 17981	Alright	CDJ	U.S.	1990	$9.00
A&M	PCCY-10120	Alright (Remixes)	CD5	Japan	1990	$25.00
Virgin		Anytime, Anyplace	CD5	Germany	1994	$11.00
Virgin		Anytime, Anyplace	CD5	U.K.	1994	$12.00
Virgin		Anytime, Anyplace	CD5	U.K.	1994	$12.00
	Second version.					
Virgin		Anytime, Anyplace	CDJ	U.K.	1994	$15.00
Virgin	38435	Anytime, Anyplace	CD5	U.S.	1994	$8.00
Virgin	DPRO-14151	Anytime, Anyplace	CDJ	U.S.	1994	$9.00
Virgin	38422	Because Of Love	CD5	U.S.	1994	$5.00
Virgin	14111	Because Of Love	CDJ	U.S.	1994	$9.00
		Best Things in Life	CD5	U.K.	1995	$10.00
		Best Things in Life	CD5	U.K.	1995	$10.00
	Second version.					
Perspective	587400-2	Best Things in Life Are Free	CD5	Germany	1992	$9.00
Perspective	PERD-7400	Best Things in Life Are Free	CD5	U.K.	1992	$9.00
A&M	75021 7406 2	Best Things in Life Are Free	CD5	U.S.	1992	$3.00
Perspective	28968 1713	Best Things in Life Are Free	CDJ	U.S.	1992	$9.00
Perspective	28968 1715	Best Things in Life Are Free	CDJ	U.S.	1992	$9.00
A&M	390572-2	Black Cat	CD5	Germany	1990	$11.00
A&M	PCDY-10017	Black Cat	CD3	Japan	1990	$15.00/$5.00
A&M	AMCD-587	Black Cat	CD5	U.K.	1990	$11.00
A&M		Black Cat	CD5	U.S.	1990	$5.00
A&M	75021 7972 2	Black Cat	CDJ	U.S.	1990	$15.00
A&M	397098-2	Black Cat (Remixes)	CD5	Germany	1990	$18.00
A&M	PCCY-10144	Black Cat (Remixes)	CD5	Japan	1989	$20.00
A&M	PCCY-10131	Come Back to Me	CD5	Japan	1990	$20.00
A&M	USACD-581	Come Back to Me	CD5	U.K.	1990	$11.00
A&M	75021 7939-2	Come Back to Me	CDJ	U.S.	1989	$9.00
A&M	D15Y-3199	Control	CD3	Japan	1988	$15.00/$5.00
A&M		Control	DJ/CDV	Japan	1988	$80.00
A&M	396924-2	Control Remixes	CD5	Germany	1986	$20.00
A&M	CDMID-149	Control Remixes	CD5	U.K.	1986	$20.00
A&M	390493-2	Escapade	CD5	Germany	1990	$11.00
A&M	390530-2	Escapade	CD5	Germany	1990	$11.00
A&M	PCDY-10011	Escapade	CD3	Japan	1990	$15.00/$5.00
A&M	USACD-684	Escapade	CD5	U.K.	1990	$11.00
A&M	CD 18002	Escapade	CDJ	U.S.	1989	$9.00
A&M	PCCY-10119	Escapade (Remixes)	CD5	Japan	1989	$20.00
Virgin	12674	If	CD5	U.S.	1993	$6.00
Virgin	12808	If	CDJ	U.S.	1993	$9.00
A&M	390606-2	Love Will Never Do	CD5	Germany	1990	$11.00
A&M	PCDY-10021	Love Will Never Do	CD3	Japan	1990	$15.00/$5.00
A&M	AMCD-700	Love Will Never Do	CD5	U.K.	1990	$11.00
A&M	75021 7444 2	Love Will Never Do	CDJ	U.S.	1990	$9.00
A&M	PCCY-10164	Love Will Never Do (Remixes)	CD5	Japan	1990	$20.00
A&M	390473-2	Miss You Much	CD5	Germany	1989	$11.00
A&M	390452-2	Miss You Much	CD5	Germany	1989	$11.00
A&M	USACD-663	Miss You Much	CD5	U.K.	1989	$11.00
A&M	CD 17917	Miss You Much	CDJ	U.S.	1989	$9.00
A&M	CD 17885	Miss You Much	CDJ	U.S.	1989	$9.00
A&M	PCCY-10083	Miss You Much (Remixes)	CD5	Japan	1989	$20.00
A&M	D22Y-3360	More Control	CD5	Japan	1986	$20.00
A&M	S12Y-3016	Pleasure Principle	CD3	Japan	1988	$15.00/$5.00
A&M	390459-2	Rhythm Nation	CD5	Germany	1989	$11.00
A&M	USACD-673	Rhythm Nation	CD5	U.K.	1989	$11.00
A&M	CD 17915	Rhythm Nation	CDJ	U.S.	1989	$9.00
A&M	CD 17928	Rhythm Nation	CDJ	U.S.	1989	$9.00
A&M	PCCY-10084	Rhythm Nation (Remixes)	CD5	Japan	1989	$20.00
Virgin	PODM-1057	Runaway	CD3	Japan	1995	$13.00/$4.00

Label	Catalog Number	Title	Type	Country	Year	Longbox Value / Value
Virgin	588457-2	Runaway	CDJ	U.K.	1995	$16.00
A&M	581194	Runaway	CD5	U.S.	1995	$6.00
A&M	75021 7514	State of the World	CDJ	U.S.	1990	$9.00
A&M	PCCY-10191	State of the World (Remixes)	CD5	Japan	1991	$20.00
Virgin	VJDP-10207	That's the Way Love Goes	CD3	Japan	1993	$15.00/$5.00
Virgin	DPRO-12773	That's the Way Love Goes	CDJ	U.S.	1993	$9.00
Virgin	DPRO-12795	That's the Way Love Goes	CDJ	U.S.	1993	$9.00
A&M	AMSAD00123	Twenty Foreplay	CDJ	U.S.	1996	$9.00
Virgin	POCM-1153	Twenty-Fourplay	CD5	Japan	1995	$20.00
A&M		Twenty-Fourplay	CD5	U.K.	1995	$11.00
A&M	AMSAD0133	Twenty-Fourplay	CDJ	U.K.	1995	$15.00
Virgin	PCD-0576	What I'll Do	CDJ	Japan	1995	$35.00
Virgin	JJRESP-1	What I'll Do	CDJ	Spain	1995	$18.00
		Whoops Now	CDJ	U.S.		$9.00
		You Want This	CD5	U.K.		$10.00
		You Want This	CD5	U.K.		$10.00
	Second version.					
Virgin	38455	You Want This	CD5	U.S.	1994	$6.00
Virgin		You Want This	CDJ	U.S.	1994	$9.00

Jackson, Jermaine

Full Length

Label	Catalog Number	Title	Type	Country	Year	Longbox Value / Value
Pioneer	PA86-M033	Dynamite Videos	8"LD	U.S.	1986	$10.00
Arista	ARCD-8203	Jermaine Jackson	LP/LB	U.S.†	1984	$14.00/$8.00
Motown	5354	Let's Get Serious	LP/BP	U.S.		$12.00/$7.00

Singles

Label	Catalog Number	Title	Type	Country	Year	Longbox Value / Value
Arista	A10D-136	Don't Take It	CD3	Japan	1989	$12.00/$4.00
Arista	662634	Don't Take It	CD5	U.K.	1989	$10.00
Arista	ASCD-2018	I'd Like to Get to Know You	CDJ	U.S.	1989	$2.00
Arista	A10D-151	Two Ships	CD3	Japan	1990	$12.00/$4.00
Arista	BVDA-36	Word to the Bad	CD3	Japan	1992	$12.00/$4.00
LaFace	4011	Word to the Bad	CDJ	U.S.	1991	$6.00
Laface	BVDA-34	You Said, You Said	CD3	Japan	1991	$12.00/$4.00
LaFace	4003	You Said, You Said	CDJ	U.S.	1991	$6.00
LaFace	4010	You Said, You Said	CDJ	U.S.	1991	$6.00

Jackson, Joe

Full Length

Label	Catalog Number	Title	Type	Country	Year	Longbox Value / Value
Pioneer	PA86-M049	Big World Sessions	8"LD	U.S.	1986	$8.00
Pioneer	PA86-M049	Big World Sessions	8"LD	U.S.	1990	$10.00
	Digital Audio.					
A&M	CD-5000	Body & Soul	LP/LB	U.S.†	1984	$14.00/$8.00
Virgin		Laughter & Lust	LP/LB	U.S.		$14.00/$8.00
A&M	LV38406	Live in Tokyo	LD	U.S.	1989	$35.00
	Digital Audio					
A&M	CD-3187	Look Sharp	LP/LB	U.S.†	1984	$14.00/$8.00
A&M	CD-4906	Night And Day	LP/LB	U.S.†	1984	$14.00/$8.00
Virgin	DPRO 14241	Night Music Sampler	DJ/Smplr	U.S.		$7.00
	DPRO 14241	Sampler	DJ/Smplr	U.S.		$12.00

Singles

Label	Catalog Number	Title	Type	Country	Year	Longbox Value / Value
A&M	CDEE-512	Down to London	CD5	U.K.	1989	$10.00
A&M	CD 17831	Down to London	CDJ	U.S.	1989	$2.00
A&M	390360-2	He's a Shape in a Drape	CD5	Germany	1988	$10.00
A&M	31008C SIG 123	He's a Shape in a Drape	CD3	U.S.	1988	$6.00/$3.00
A&M	CD 17592	He's a Shape in a Drape	CDJ	U.S.	1988	$2.00
A&M	CD 17550	I'm the Man	DJ/CD3	U.S.	1988	$4.00
A&M	S10Y-3039	Jumpin' Jive	CD3	Japan	1988	$13.00/$4.00
A&M	CD 17910	Me and You	CDJ	U.S.	1989	$2.00
A&M	CDEE-506	Nineteen Forever	CD3	U.K.	1989	$10.00
A&M	CD 17766	Nineteen Forever	CDJ	U.S.	1989	$2.00
Virgin	PRCD 3844	Obvious Song	CDJ	U.S.	1991	$2.00
Virgin	PRCD 4015	Oh Well	CDJ	U.S.	1991	$2.00
A&M	AMCD-583	Steppin' Out	CD5	U.K.	1990	$10.00
Toshiba	VJDP-10158	Stranger Than Fiction	CD5	Japan	1991	$4.00
Virgin	VUSCD-40	Stranger Than Fiction	CD5	U.K.	1991	$10.00
Virgin	PRCD 4131	Stranger Than Fiction	CDJ	U.S.	1991	$2.00

Jackson, Keisha

Singles

Label	Catalog Number	Title	Type	Country	Year	Longbox Value / Value
Epic	73260	U Need a Lover	CDJ	U.S.	1990	$2.00

Jackson, Latoya

Full Length

Label	Catalog Number	Title	Type	Country	Year	Longbox Value / Value
Image	ID7770IV	Latoya Jackson	LD	U.S.		$15.00

Singles

Label	Catalog Number	Title	Type	Country	Year	Longbox Value / Value
Eastwest	870071	Bad Girl	CD3	Germany	1989	$8.00
Eastwest	246856-2	Bad Girl	CD5	Germany	1989	$8.00
BCM	20520	Why Don't You Want My Love	CD5	Germany	1990	$8.00
Eastwest	870927	You're Gonna Get Rocked	CD3	Germany	1989	$8.00
Warner Brothers	10P3-6047	You're Gonna Get Rocked	CD3	Japan	1988	$12.00/$4.00

Jackson, Michael

Full Length

Label	Catalog Number	Title	Type	Country	Year	Longbox Value / Value
Epic	450290-9	Bad	LTD/LP	Germany	1987	$45.00/$45.00
	Picture disc version in blister pack.					
Epic	308P-240	Bad	LTD/LP	Japan	1987	$60.00
	Picture disc CD.					
Epic	450290-9	Bad	LTD/LP	U.K.	1987	$45.00/$45.00
	Picture disc version in blister pack.					
Epic		Bad Mixes, The	DJ/Smplr	U.S.		$250.00
	9 Tracks					
Epic/Monster Music	ESK 1215MC	Bad Mixes, The	DJ/Smplr	U.S.	1988	$400.00
	Individually number CD. Limited to 6,000 copies					
Epic	465802 6	Dangerous	LTD/LP	Australia	1993	$35.00
	2 CD set. Bonus remix disc in "Brilliant Box" and slipcase.					
Epic		Dangerous	LTD/LP	Japan	1991	$55.00
	Special edition in 10"x10" "pop-up" book.					
Epic	EK 48900	Dangerous	LTD/LP	U.S.	1991	$20.00
	Special edition in 10"x10" "pop-up" book and copper disc.					
RCA	WD-72630	Farewell My Summer Love	LP	Germany		$27.00
Motown	WD-72630	Farewell My Summer Love	LP	U.K.		$27.00
Motown	MOTD-8000	Got to Be There + Ben	LP/BP	U.S.†		$20.00/$18.00
Epic	ESCA-5030/1	Greatest Hits Decade	LP	Japan		$35.00
Epic	2SK 7122	History	DJ/LP	U.S.	1995	$30.00
	2CD set					
Epic	C2K 59000	History	LP	U.S.	1995	$30.00
	2CD set. First pressing with original lyrics to the song "They Don't Care About Us."					
Epic	C2K 59000	History	LTD/LP	U.S.	1995	$65.00
	2CD set. First 200 copies indiviually numbered.					
Epic	XPCD-656	History Begins	DJ/Smplr	U.K.	1995	$80.00
Epic	Q4-8P90093	History of…, The	DJ/Smplr	Japan		$200.00
	CD in hardbound book cover.					
Epic	K719051	History - The Lifestyle Sampler	DJ/Smplr	U.S.	1995	$50.00
Image	IDVL1000D	Making Michael Jackson's Thriller	LD	U.S.		$35.00
Epic		Megamixes, The	DJ/Smplr	U.S.		$25.00
Epic	EK-35745	Off the Wall	LP/BP	U.S.†	1983	$15.00/$10.00
Epic		Signature Series	DJ/Smplr	U.S.		$20.00
Epic	EK-38112	Thriller	LP/BP	U.S.†	1983	$15.00/$9.00
Unistar		Weekly Specials, The	RS	U.S.	1992	$25.00
	Airdate: 7/24/92.					
Unistar		Weekly Specials, The	RS	U.S.	1992	$25.00
	Airdate: 7/31/92.					

Singles

Label	Catalog Number	Title	Type	Country	Year	Longbox Value / Value
CBS	652844-3	Another Part of Me	CD3	Germany	1988	$18.00
Epic	128P-8009	Another Part of Me	CD3	Japan	1988	$20.00/$5.00
Epic	653004-2	Another Part of Me	CD5	U.K.	1988	$18.00
Epic	652844-2	Another Part of Me	CD5	U.K.	1988	$18.00
CBS	34K-7855	Another Part of Me	CD3	U.S.	1988	$12.00/$5.00
Epic	128P-3002	Bad	CD3	Japan	1987	$20.00/$5.00
Epic	POTC-1838	Bad	CD3	Japan	1987	$35.00
	Deleted "rat" cover.					
Epic	ESK 2808	Bad	CDJ	U.S.	1987	$12.00
Epic	108P-3046	Beat It	CD3	Japan	1989	$18.00/$5.00
CBS	34K-6453	Beat It	CD3	U.S.	1988	$12.00/$5.00
Motown	R10M-122	Ben	CD3	Japan	1989	$18.00/$5.00
Epic	655572-3	Billy Jean	CD3	Germany	1990	$20.00
Epic	655572-2	Billy Jean	CD5	Germany	1990	$20.00
Epic	158P-8017	Billy Jean	CD3	Japan	1990	$20.00/$5.00
Epic	657598-2	Black or White	CD5	Germany	1991	$13.00
		Black or White	CD5	U.K.		$13.00
	Second version.					
Epic	6577731-2	Black or White	CD5	U.K.	1991	$13.00
Epic	34K 74100	Black or White	CD5	U.S.	1991	$13.00
Epic		Black or White Remixes	CDJ	Japan		$35.00
CBS	XPCD-665	Childhood	CDJ	U.K.	1995	$30.00
Epic	651546-2	Dirty Diana	CD5	Germany	1988	$20.00
Epic	108P-3021	Dirty Diana	CD3	Japan	1988	$20.00/$5.00
Epic	651546-9	Dirty Diana	CD5	U.K.	1988	$20.00
CBS	34K-7739	Dirty Diana	CD3	U.S.	1988	$13.00/$5.00
Epic	ESK 1110	Dirty Diana	CDJ	U.S.	1988	$20.00
CBS	651657-3	Don't Stop 'Til You Get Enough	CD3	Germany	1988	$18.00
CBS	651657-3	Don't Stop 'Til You Get Enough	CD3	U.K.	1988	$15.00
Epic	ESCA-6360	Earth Song	CD5	Japan		$25.00
CBS		Earth Song	CD5	U.K.	1995	$18.00
CBS		Earth Song	CD5	U.K.	1995	$20.00
	Second version.					
Epic	ESDA-7125	Give in to Me	CD3	Japan	1993	$20.00/$5.00
Epic	659069-2	Give in to Me	CD5	U.K.	1993	$18.00
Epic		Give in to Me	CDJ	U.K.	1995	$40.00
Epic		Gone Too Soon	CD5	U.K.	1995	$18.00
Epic	ESK 5562	Gone Too Soon	CDJ	U.S.	1993	$15.00
Motown	886595	Got to be There	CD3	Germany	1989	$18.00
Motown	ZD-41951	Got to be There	CD3	U.K.	1989	$18.00
Epic	ESDA-7118	Heal the World	CD3	Japan	1992	$12.00/$5.00
Epic		Heal the World	CD5	U.K.	1992	$18.00
Epic	ESK 74790	Heal the World	CDJ	U.S.	1992	$10.00
Epic	ESK 74708	Heal the World	CDJ	U.S.	1992	$15.00
Epic	108P-3001	I Just Can't Stop Loving You	CD3	Japan	1988	$20.00/$5.00
CBS	34K-7253	I Just Can't Stop Loving You	CD3	U.S.	1988	$12.00/$5.00
Epic	ESK 2750	I Just Can't Stop Loving You	CDJ	U.S.	1988	$3.00
Epic	ESDA-7096	In the Closet	CD3	Japan	1992	$18.00/$5.00
Epic	ESCA-5610	In the Closet	CD5	Japan	1992	$20.00
Epic	ESCA-5611	In the Closet	CD5	Japan	1992	$20.00
Epic	ESCA-5622	In the Closet	CD5	Japan	1992	$20.00
Epic	658018-2	In the Closet	CD5	U.K.	1992	$15.00
Epic	ESK 74266	In the Closet	CDJ	U.S.	1992	$12.00
Epic	ESK 74267	In the Closet	CDJ	U.S.	1992	$12.00
Epic	ESK 4537	In the Closet	CDJ	U.S.	1992	$12.00
Epic	ESDA-7102	Jam	CD3	Japan	1992	$18.00/$5.00
Epic	ESCA-5672	Jam	CD5	Japan	1992	$20.00
Epic	ESCA-5638	Jam	CD5	Japan	1992	$25.00
Epic	658360-2	Jam	CD5	U.K.	1992	$14.00
Epic	34K 74334	Jam	CD5	U.S.	1992	$10.00
Epic	ESK 74333	Jam	CDJ	U.S.	1992	$10.00
CBS	654672-3	Leave Me Alone	CD3	Germany	1988	$18.00
CBS	654672-2	Leave Me Alone	CD5	U.K.	1988	$18.00
CBS	654947-3	Liberian Girl	CD3	Germany	1989	$18.00
CBS	654947-2	Liberian Girl	CD5	Germany	1989	$18.00
Epic	108P-3077	Liberian Girl	CD3	Japan	1989	$20.00/$5.00
Epic	108P-3009	Man In the Mirror	CD3	Germany	1988	$18.00
Epic	651388-2	Man In the Mirror	CD5	U.K.	1988	$18.00
CBS	34K-7668	Man In the Mirror	CD3	U.S.	1988	$15.00/$5.00
Epic	ESK 1006	Man In the Mirror	CDJ	U.S.	1988	$13.00
Sony	MUSAMPDK001	Mega Mix	CDJ	Spain	1988	$35.00
CBS	MUSAPDK001	Megamix	CD5	Holland		$35.00
Epic	108P-3045	Off the Wall	CD3	Japan	1988	$18.00/$5.00
Epic	ESDA-7086	Remember the Time	CD3	Japan	1992	$18.00/$5.00
Epic	ESCA-5582	Remember the Time	CD5	Japan	1992	$20.00
Epic	657774-2	Remember the Time	CD5	U.K.	1992	$18.00
Epic	34K 74201	Remember the Time	CD5	U.S.	1992	$10.00
Epic	ESK 74200	Remember the Time	CDJ	U.S.	1992	$12.00
Epic	ESK 4456	Remember the Time	CDJ	U.S.	1992	$12.00
Epic	ESK 4457	Remember the Time	CDJ	U.S.	1992	$12.00
Epic	78004	Remixes	CD5	U.S.	1995	$15.00
Epic	78005	Remixes	CD5	U.S.	1995	$15.00
Epic	108P-3044	Rock With You	CD3	Japan	1988	$18.00/$5.00
Epic	XPCD722	Rock With You	CDJ	U.K.	1988	$25.00
Epic	ESDA-7159	Scream	CD3	Japan	1995	$18.00/$5.00
Epic	AEK 7123	Scream	CD5	U.K.	1995	$12.00
Epic		Scream	CD5	U.K.	1995	$12.00
	Second version.					
Epic		Scream	CDJ	U.K.	1995	$30.00
Columbia	78000	Scream	CD5	U.S.	1995	$7.00
Epic	78001	Scream	CD5	U.S.	1995	$7.00
Epic		Scream	CDJ	U.S.	1995	$10.00
Epic		Scream	CDJ	U.S.	1995	$10.00
	Second version.					
CBS	653026-3	Smooth Criminal	CD3	Germany	1988	$18.00
Epic	108P-3050	Smooth Criminal	CD3	Japan	1988	$18.00/$5.00
Epic	653026-2	Smooth Criminal	CD5	U.K.	1988	$18.00
Epic	ESK 1274	Smooth Criminal	CDJ	U.S.	1988	$13.00
Epic	TDDD 90052	Someone Put Your Hand Out	DJ/CD3	Japan	1995	$200.00
CBS		Stranger in Moscow	CD5	U.K.	1996	$18.00
Epic		They Don't Care About Us	CD5	Japan	1996	$25.00
Epic		They Don't Care About Us	CD5	U.K.	1996	$12.00
Epic		They Don't Care About Us	CD5	U.K.	1996	$12.00
	Second version.					
Epic	ESK 7723	They Don't Care About Us	CDJ	U.S.	1996	$12.00
Epic	ESK 7251	This Time Around	CDJ	U.S.	1995	$12.00
CBS	654557-3	Thriller	CD3	Germany	1988	$12.00
Epic	108P-3047	Thriller	CD3	Japan	1988	$25.00/$7.00
CBS	654557-2	Thriller	CD5	U.K.	1988	$20.00
CBS	49K-4961	Thriller	CD3	U.S.	1988	$15.00/$6.00

Label	Catalog Number	Title	Type	Country	Year	Longbox Value / Value
Epic	ESCA-5703/7	Tour Souvenir	CD5	Japan	1992	$55.00
	5 CD% picture disc box set.					
Epic	MJ4	Tour Souvenir Pack	CD5	U.K.	1992	$35.00
	4 CD set.					
Epic	108P-3003	Way You Make Me Feel, The	CD3	Japan	1988	$18.00/$5.00
CBS	651275-9	Way You Make Me Feel, The	CD5	U.K.	1988	$18.00
CBS	34K-07645	Way You Make Me Feel, The	CD3	U.S.	1988	$13.00/$4.00
Epic	ESK 2862	Way You Make Me Feel, The	CDJ	U.S.	1988	$10.00
Epic	ESDA-7105	Who Is It	CD3	Japan	1992	$18.00/$5.00
Epic	ESCA-5652	Who Is It	CD5	Japan	1992	$25.00
Epic	658179-5	Who Is It	CD5	U.K.	1992	$12.00
Epic	ESK 74406	Who Is It	CDJ	U.S.	1992	$10.00
Epic		Will You Be There	CDJ	U.S.		$10.00
Epic		Will You Be There	CDJ	U.S.		$10.00
Epic		You Are Not Alone	CD5	Australia	1995	$12.00
Epic		You Are Not Alone	CD5	Australia	1995	$12.00
	Second version.					
Epic	ESCA-6300	You Are Not Alone	CD5	Japan	1995	$18.00
Epic		You Are Not Alone	CD5	U.K.	1995	$11.00
Epic		You Are Not Alone	CD5	U.K.	1995	$11.00
	Second version.					
Epic	XPCD698	You Are Not Alone	CDJ	U.K.	1995	$20.00
Epic	XPCD705	You Are Not Alone	CDJ	U.K.	1995	$20.00
Epic	78002	You Are Not Alone	CD5	U.S.	1995	$5.00
Epic	78003	You Are Not Alone	CD5	U.S.	1995	$6.00
Epic	651661-3	You Can't Win	CD3	Germany	1988	$10.00
Epic	651661-3	You Can't Win	CD3	U.K.	1988	$10.00

Jackson, Millie

Singles

Label	Catalog Number	Title	Type	Country	Year	Longbox Value / Value
	CD34222	Lies That We Live, The	CDJ	U.S.		$2.00
Jive	JIVEC-135	Love is a Dangerous Game	CD5	U.K.	1990	$8.00
Southbound	CDSEWT-702	My Man, a Sweet Man	CD5	U.K.	1989	$8.00
Jive	42016-2-JDJ	Young Man, Older Woman	CDJ	U.S.	1991	$2.00

Jackson, Milt

Full Length

Label	Catalog Number	Title	Type	Country	Year	Longbox Value / Value
Savoy Records	CY-78997	Milt Jackson	LTD/LP	U.S.	1995	$20.00
	CD in miniature repica of original LP sleeve.					
Savoy Records	CY-78804	Opus De Jazz	LTD/LP	U.S.	1996	$20.00
	CD in miniature repica of original LP sleeve.					

Jackson, Paul Jr.

Full Length

Label	Catalog Number	Title	Type	Country	Year	Longbox Value / Value
Atlantic	PRCD 5048-2	Preview of Coming Attractions	DJ/Smplr	U.S.	1992	$8.00

Singles

Label	Catalog Number	Title	Type	Country	Year	Longbox Value / Value
Atlantic	PRCD 3390-2	My Thang	CDJ	U.S.	1990	$2.00

Jackson, Rebbie

Singles

Label	Catalog Number	Title	Type	Country	Year	Longbox Value / Value
Columbia	CSk 2915	Plaything	CDJ	U.S.	1989	$2.00

Jackson, T.J.

Singles

Label	Catalog Number	Title	Type	Country	Year	Longbox Value / Value
Bellaphon	130-07-378	Miss You	CD5	Germany	1990	$8.00

Jacksons

Full Length

Label	Catalog Number	Title	Type	Country	Year	Longbox Value / Value
Motown	6070-MD	Compact Command Performance	LP/BP	U.S.†	1984	$23.00/$18.00
Epic	EK-35552	Destiny	LP/BP	U.S.†	1984	$14.00/$8.00
Motown	MOTD 8019	Diana Ross Presents the Jackson 5 + ABC	LP/BP	U.S.†	1984	$25.00/$22.00
Motown	37463-1347-2	Soulsation	DJ/Smplr	U.S.	1995	$18.00
Motown	MOTD-8011	Third Album + Maybe Tomorrow	LP/BP	U.S.†	1984	$23.00/$20.00
Epic	EK-36424	Triumph	LP/BP	U.S.†	1984	$14.00/$8.00
Epic	EK-38946	Victory	LP/BP	U.S.†	1984	$14.00/$8.00

Singles

Label	Catalog Number	Title	Type	Country	Year	Longbox Value / Value
Epic	108P-3079	2300	CD3	Japan	1989	$12.00/$4.00
Epic	655206-2	2300	CD5	U.K.	1989	$10.00
CBS	654844-3	Art of Madness	CD3	Germany	1989	$10.00
CBS	65455-3	Heartbreak Hotel	CD3	Germany	1989	$10.00
Inverted	705245-1228-2	Jackson Five, The	CD5	U.S.	1995	$10.00
	Limited to 250,000 copies.					
CBS	651660-3	Lovely One	CD3	Germany	1988	$10.00
CBS	651660-3	Lovely One	CD3	U.K.	1988	$10.00
CBS	654808-3	Nothin' (That Compares 2 U)	CD3	Germany	1989	$10.00
Epic	108P-3065	Nothin' (That Compares 2 U)	CD3	Japan	1989	$12.00/$4.00
CBS	654808-2	Nothin' (That Compares 2 U)	CD5	U.K.	1989	$10.00
Epic	ESK 1515	Nothin' (That Compares 2 U)	CDJ	U.S.	1989	$2.00
Epic	ESK 1889	Private Affair	CDJ	U.S.	1989	$2.00
CBS	651656-3	Shake Your Body	CD3	Germany	1988	$10.00
CBS	651656-3	Shake Your Body	CD3	U.K.	1988	$10.00
CBS	654570-3	Show You the Way to Go	CD3	Germany	1989	$10.00
CBS	654570-3	Show You the Way to Go	CD3	U.K.	1989	$10.00
Epic	108P-3048	This Place Hotel	CD3	Japan	1988	$12.00/$4.00
Motown	37463 10662	Who's Lovin' You	CDJ	U.S.	1992	$2.00

Jackyl

Full Length

Label	Catalog Number	Title	Type	Country	Year	Longbox Value / Value
Geffen	PRO-CD-4466	In-Store Sampler	DJ/Smplr	U.S.	1992	$10.00
Geffen	PRO-CD-4466	Sampler	DJ/Smplr	U.S.	1992	$15.00

Singles

Label	Catalog Number	Title	Type	Country	Year	Longbox Value / Value
Geffen	PRO-CD-4505	Dirty Little Mind	CDJ	U.S.	1993	$2.00
Geffen	PRO-CD-4487	Down on Me	CDJ	U.S.	1992	$2.00
Geffen	PRO-CD-4437	I Stand Alone	CDJ	U.S.	1992	$2.00
Geffen	PRO-CD-4478	Lumberjack, The	CDJ	U.S.	1992	$2.00
Geffen		Push Comes To Shove	CD5	U.K.	1994	$10.00
Geffen	21927-2	When Will It Rain	CD5	U.S.	1993	$5.00
Geffen	PRO-CD-4516	When Will It Rain	CDJ	U.S.	1993	$2.00
Geffen	PRO-CD-4534	When Will It Rain	CDJ	U.S.	1993	$2.00

Jaco

Singles

Label	Catalog Number	Title	Type	Country	Year	Longbox Value / Value
Warp	WAP-29CD	Show Some Love	CD5	U.K.	1992	$8.00

Jacob's Mouse

Singles

Label	Catalog Number	Title	Type	Country	Year	Longbox Value / Value
SRD	WIJ-15CD	Ton Up	CD5	U.K.	1992	$8.00

Jade

Singles

Label	Catalog Number	Title	Type	Country	Year	Longbox Value / Value
Warner Brothers	9 41758	5-4-3-2 Yo Time Is	CD5	U.S.	1994	$5.00
Warner Brothers	41758	5-4-3-2 Yo Time Is	CD5	U.S.	1994	$5.00
		Blessed	CDJ	U.S.	1993	$2.00
Warner Brothers	9 40669-2	Don't Walk Away	CD5	U.S.	1993	$4.00
Giant	PRO-CD-5803	Don't Walk Away	CDJ	U.S.	1993	$2.00
Giant	PRO-CD-5926	Don't Walk Away	CDJ	U.S.	1993	$2.00
Giant	W-0140CD	I Wanna Love You	CD5	U.K.	1992	$9.00
Giant	9 40595-2	I Wanna Love You	CD5	U.S.	1992	$4.00
Giant	PRO-CD-5393	I Wanna Love You	CDJ	U.S.	1992	$2.00
Giant	PRO-CD-6352	Looking for Mr. Do Right	CDJ	U.S.	1993	$2.00
Warner	12-40980	One Woman	CD5	U.K.	1994	$8.00
Giant	PRO-CD-6288	One Woman	CDJ	U.S.	1993	$2.00

Jagged Edge

Singles

Label	Catalog Number	Title	Type	Country	Year	Longbox Value / Value
Polydor	PZCD-132	Hell Ain't a Long Way	CD5	U.K.	1991	$8.00
Polydor	CDP 509	Out in the Cold	CDJ	U.S.	1990	$2.00
Polydor	877815-2	You Don't Love Me	CD5	Germany	1991	$8.00
Polydor	PZCD-97	You Don't Love Me	CD5	U.K.	1991	$8.00

Jagger, Mick

Full Length

Label	Catalog Number	Title	Type	Country	Year	Longbox Value / Value
Columbia	460123-2	Primitive Cool	LP	Germany		$14.00
Columbia	460123-9	Primitive Cool	LP/BP	Germany		$25.00/$25.00
	CD picture disc in blister pack.					
Columbia	23DP-5586	Primitive Cool	LP	Japan		$20.00
Columbia	20DP-899	Primitive Cool	LTD/LP	Japan		$35.00
	Picture disc CD.					
Columbia	460123-2	Primitive Cool	LP	U.K.		$14.00
Columbia	460123-9	Primitive Cool	LP/BP	U.K.		$25.00/$25.00
	CD picture disc in blister pack.					
Columbia	CK-40919	Primitive Cool	LP/LB	U.S.		$15.00/$9.00
Columbia	CD-86310	She's the Boss	LP	Germany	1985	$14.00
Columbia	23DP-5585	She's the Boss	LP	Japan	1985	$20.00
Columbia	CD-86310	She's the Boss	LP	U.K.	1985	$14.00
Columbia	CK 39940	She's the Boss	LP	U.S.	1985	$25.00
Columbia	CK-39940	She's the Boss	LP/LB	U.S.†	1985	$15.00/$9.00
Columbia	CK-39940	She's the Boss	LP/LB	U.S.	1987	$15.00/$9.00
DIR		Under Radio Control	RS	U.S.	1987	$200.00
	2 CD set. Airdate: 12/2/87.					
Media America		Up Close	RS	U.S.	1993	$60.00
	2 CD set.					
Atlatnic	PRCD-5002-2	Wandering Spirit	DJ/Intvw	U.S.	1993	$25.00

Singles

Label	Catalog Number	Title	Type	Country	Year	Longbox Value / Value
Atlantic		Angel in My Heart	CD5	Germany	1993	$10.00
Atlantic		Don't Tear Me Up	CD5	Australia	1993	$12.00
Atlantic	AMCY-535	Don't Tear Me Up	CD5	Japan	1993	$20.00
Atlantic	A7368CD	Don't Tear Me Up	CD5	U.K.	1993	$10.00
Atlantic	PRCD-5015-2	Don't Tear Me Up	CDJ	U.S.	1993	$7.00
Atlantic		Evening Gown	CD5	Germany	1993	$11.00
Columbia	CSK 2771	Let's Work	CDJ	U.S.	1987	$7.00
Atlantic		Out of Focus	CD5	Australia	1993	$12.00
Atlantic		Out of Focus	CD5	Germany	1993	$10.00
Atlantic	PRCD 5152-2	Out of Focus	CDJ	U.S.	1993	$7.00
Atlantic		Sweet Thing	CD5	Australia	1993	$12.00
Atlantic		Sweet Thing	CD5	Germany	1993	$10.00
Atlantic	AMDY-5087	Sweet Thing	CD3	Japan	1993	$13.00/$3.00
Atlantic		Sweet Thing	CD5	U.K.	1993	$10.00
Atlantic	87410-2	Sweet Thing	CD5	U.S.	1993	$5.00
Atlantic	PRCD 4800-2	Sweet Thing	CDJ	U.S.	1993	$7.00
Atlantic	PRCD 4939-2	Sweet Thing	CDJ	U.S.	1993	$7.00
CBS	10EP-3003	Throwaway	CD3	Japan	1988	$13.00/$3.00
CBS	THROWC-1	Throwaway	CD5	U.K.	1988	$12.00
Atlantic	PRCD-5020-2	Wired All Night	CDJ	U.S.	1993	$7.00

Jailbox

Singles

Label	Catalog Number	Title	Type	Country	Year	Longbox Value / Value
		Cooling Card	CDJ	U.S.	1994	$3.00

Jaimes, Juliette

Singles

Label	Catalog Number	Title	Type	Country	Year	Longbox Value / Value
Pulse 8	CDLOSE-26	We Got It All	CD5	U.K.	1992	$8.00

Jale

Singles

Label	Catalog Number	Title	Type	Country	Year	Longbox Value / Value
		Dream Cake	CDJ	U.S.	1994	$3.00

Jam

Full Length

Label	Catalog Number	Title	Type	Country	Year	Longbox Value / Value
Polygram	821712-2	Compact Snap	LP/LB	U.S.†	1984	$14.00/$8.00
Polygram	SACD 491	Jam Covers	DJ/Smplr	U.S.	1992	$4.00

Singles

Label	Catalog Number	Title	Type	Country	Year	Longbox Value / Value
Polydor	POCP-1215	Dreams of Children	CD5	Japan	1992	$15.00
Polydor	PZCD-199	Dreams of Children	CD5	U.K.	1992	$9.00
Polygram	887201-2	Going Underground	CD5	Germany	1990	$9.00
Polygram	887926-2	Jam Music	CD5	Germany	1989	$9.00

Jam Champion

Singles

Label	Catalog Number	Title	Type	Country	Year	Longbox Value / Value
	CHAMPCD-236	Don't Look Any Further	CD5	U.K.	1990	$8.00

Jam Crew

Singles

Label	Catalog Number	Title	Type	Country	Year	Longbox Value / Value
ZYX	6556-8	Hi Steppin'	CD5	Germany	1991	$6.00

Jam on the Mutha

Singles

Label	Catalog Number	Title	Type	Country	Year	Longbox Value / Value
BMG	663494	Hotel California	CD5	Germany	1990	$8.00
M&G	MAGCD-3	Hotel California	CD5	U.K.	1990	$8.00

Jam & Spoon

Singles

Label	Catalog Number	Title	Type	Country	Year	Longbox Value / Value
		Complete Stella	CD5	U.K.		$10.00
		Tales From a Danceographic Ocean	CD5	U.K.		$10.00

Jam Tronik

Singles

Label	Catalog Number	Title	Type	Country	Year	Longbox Value / Value
ZYX	6265-8	Another Day in Paradise	CD5	Germany	1989	$6.00
ZYX	6465-8	Another Day in Paradise	CD5	Germany	1989	$6.00
Debut	DEBCD-3093	Another Day in Paradise	CD5	U.K.	1989	$8.00

Jamaica Boys

Singles

Label	Catalog Number	Title	Type	Country	Year	Longbox Value / Value
		Move It	CDJ	U.S.		$2.00
Pioneer	WMD5-4022	Shake It Up	CD3	Japan	1990	$12.00/$4.00

Jamal, Ahmad

Full Length

Label	Catalog Number	Title	Type	Country	Year	Longbox Value / Value
Atlantic	81258-2	Digital Works	LP/LB	U.S.†	1985	$14.00/$8.00

Jamecia

Singles

Label	Catalog Number	Title	Type	Country	Year	Longbox Value / Value
Polygram	52328	Keep It Real	CD5	U.S.	1995	$5.00

James

Full Length

Label	Catalog Number	Title	Type	Country	Year	Longbox Value / Value
Westwood One		In Concert	RS	U.S.	1994	$40.00
Airdate: 11/7/94.						
Westwood One		In Concert - Nu Rock	RS	U.S.	1994	$65.00
2 CD set. With Dinosaur Jr., Airdate: 6/6/94						
Westwood One		In Concert - Nu Rock	RS	U.S.	1994	$70.00
2 CD set with Dinoaur Jr. Airdate: 6/6/94.						
Fontana	CDP 561	Live	DJ/Smplr	U.S.	1992	$25.00
		Live and Acoustic	DJ/Smplr	France	1995	$25.00
Fontana	522827	Wah Wah	LTD/LP	U.S.	1994	$19.00

Singles

Label	Catalog Number	Title	Type	Country	Year	Longbox Value / Value
Fontana	PHDR-104	Born of Frustration	CD3	Japan	1992	$12.00/$3.00
Fontana	JIMCD-10	Born of Frustration	CD5	U.K.	1992	$8.00
Fontana	866 495	Born of Frustration	CD5	U.S.	1992	$4.00
Fontana	CDP 653	Born of Frustration	CDJ	U.S.	1992	$2.00
Polygram	875837-2	Come Home	CD5	Germany	1990	$8.00
Rough Trade	RTT-245CD	Come Home	CD5	U.K.	1989	$8.00
Polygram	875419-2	How Was It For You	CD5	Germany	1990	$8.00
Fontana	JIMCD-5	How Was It For You	CD5	U.K.	1990	$8.00
Fontana	CDP 1010	Laid	CDJ	U.S.	1994	$7.00
Fontana	JIMCD-7	Lose Control	CD5	U.K.	1990	$8.00
Fontana	JIMCD-11	Ring the Bells	CD5	U.K.	1992	$8.00
Fontana	CDP 1222	Say Something	CDJ	U.S.	1994	$2.00
Fontana	JIMCD-12	Seven	CD5	U.K.	1992	$8.00
		She's A Star	CD5	U.K.	1997	$10.00
		She's A Star	CD5	U.K.	1997	$10.00
Second version.						
Polygram	868011-2	Sit Down	CD5	Germany	1991	$8.00
Rough Trade	RTT-225CD	Sit Down	CD3	U.K.	1989	$8.00
Fontana	JIMCD-8	Sit Down	CD5	U.K.	1991	$8.00
Fontana	CDP 510	Sit Down	CDJ	U.S.	1991	$2.00
Fontana	CDP 1089	Sometimes	CDJ	U.S.	1993	$2.00
Fontana	JIMCD-9	Sound	CD5	U.K.	1991	$8.00

James, Bob

Full Length

Label	Catalog Number	Title	Type	Country	Year	Longbox Value / Value
CBS	CGK-36786	All Around the Town	LP/LB	U.S.†	1985	$14.00/$8.00
		Best Collection	DJ/Smplr	Japan		$40.00
WEA	925392-2	Bob James & David Sanborn	LP	Germany		$18.00
Image	ID7737VW	Bob James Live	LD	U.S.		$25.00
WEA	38274-6	For The Record	LD	U.S.	1992	$30.00
Columbia	CD-25546	Foxie	LP	Germany		$18.00
Columbia	CD-84238	Heads	LP	Germany		$18.00
Columbia	CD-82261	Heads	LP	Germany		$18.00
Warner Brothers	PRO-CD-4516	Radio Special	DJ/Intvw	U.S.	1990	$8.00
CBS	CK-35594	Touchdown	LP/LB	U.S.†	1985	$14.00/$8.00

Singles

Label	Catalog Number	Title	Type	Country	Year	Longbox Value / Value
Warner Brothers	PRO-CD-6069	As It Happens	CDJ	U.S.	1992	$2.00
		Ashanti	CDJ	U.S.		$2.00
Warner Brothers	PRO-CD-4333	Bare Bones	CDJ	U.S.	1990	$2.00
Warner Brothers	PRO-CD-6826	Restless	CDJ	U.S.	1994	$2.00
Warner Brothers	PRO-CD-4473	Restoration	CDJ	U.S.	1990	$2.00
Warner Brothers	PRO-CD-3257	Rosalie	CDJ	U.S.	1988	$2.00

James, Bob & Earl Klugh

Full Length

Label	Catalog Number	Title	Type	Country	Year	Longbox Value / Value
CBS	CK-36241	One on One	LP/LB	U.S.†	1985	$14.00/$8.00

James, Colin

Singles

Label	Catalog Number	Title	Type	Country	Year	Longbox Value / Value
		Breakin' Up the House	CDJ	Canada		$6.00
Virgin	PR 2517	Five Long Years	CDJ	U.S.	1988	$2.00
Virgin	VUSCD-33	If You Lean on Me	CD5	U.K.	1990	$8.00
Toshiba	VJDP-127	Just Came Back	CD3	Japan	1990	$12.00/$3.00
Virgin	VUSCD-24	Just Came Back	CD5	U.K.	1990	$8.00
		Just Came Back	CD5	U.S.	1990	$2.00
		Keep on Loving Me Baby	CDJ	U.S.		$2.00
Virgin	PR 2401	Voodoo Thing	CDJ	U.S.	1988	$2.00
		Why'd You Lie?	CDJ	U.S.	1988	$2.00

James, Dexter

Singles

Label	Catalog Number	Title	Type	Country	Year	Longbox Value / Value
Bellaphon	130-07-574	You and Me	CD5	Germany	1991	$8.00

James, Elmore

Full Length

Label	Catalog Number	Title	Type	Country	Year	Longbox Value / Value
Capricorn	5831	King of the Slide Guitar Sampler	DJ/Smplr	U.S.	1992	$14.00

James, Etta

Singles

Label	Catalog Number	Title	Type	Country	Year	Longbox Value / Value
EMI	203315-2	Avenue D	CD5	Germanyu	1989	$10.00
Island	PRCD 6621-2	Beware	CDJ	U.S.	1990	$2.00
Aris	885485	I Got the Will	CD5	Germany	1989	$10.00
Island	CID-418	I Got the Will	CD5	U.K.	1989	$10.00
		Rooftops	CDJ	U.S.		$2.00

James Gang

Full Length

Label	Catalog Number	Title	Type	Country	Year	Longbox Value / Value
Album Network		In the Studio (Rides Again)	RS	U.S.	1989	$20.00
Airdate: 3/20/89.						
Album Network		In the Studio (Rides Again)	RS	U.S.	1992	$20.00
Airdate: 3/30/92.						

James, Harry

Full Length

Label	Catalog Number	Title	Type	Country	Year	Longbox Value / Value
Verve	823229-2	Crazy Rhythm	LP/LB	U.S.†	1985	$14.00/$8.00
London	PPC-820178-2	The Golden Trumpet of	LP/LB	U.S.†	1985	$14.00/$8.00
Sheffield Lab	CD-3	The King James Version	LP/LB	U.S.†	1985	$14.00/$8.00

James, John

Singles

Label	Catalog Number	Title	Type	Country	Year	Longbox Value / Value
Alfa	ALDB-73	I Wanna Know	CD3	Japan	1990	$12.00/$3.00
Polygram	871151-2	She Bought Love	CD5	Germany	1989	$8.00
Big City	69052 9002	Supernatural	CDJ	U.S.	1993	$3.00

James, Michael

Singles

Label	Catalog Number	Title	Type	Country	Year	Longbox Value / Value
Michael James	1034	Bradley	CD5	U.S.	1994	$5.00

James, Rick

Singles

Label	Catalog Number	Title	Type	Country	Year	Longbox Value / Value
Motown	530417	Bustin'out:	CD5	U.S.	1994	$5.00
Special Music Co.	8516	Give It to Me Baby	CD5	U.S.	1994	$5.00
Reprise	PRO-CD-3649	This Magic Moment	CDJ	U.S.	1989	$2.00

James, Tommy (and The Shondells)

Singles

Label	Catalog Number	Title	Type	Country	Year	Longbox Value / Value
Rhino	885835	Crimson and Clover	CD3	Germany	1990	$10.00
Rhino	R3 73046	Crimson and Clover	CD3	U.S.	1988	$6.00/$3.00
Rhino	885834	Hanky Panky	CD3	Germany	1990	$10.00
Polygram	871735-2	Treasure Chest	CD5	Canada	1990	$9.00
Aegis	2	You Take My Breath Away	CDJ	U.S.	1990	$2.00

James, Vinnie

Singles

Label	Catalog Number	Title	Type	Country	Year	Longbox Value / Value
Cypress	DPRO-2387	All American Boys	CDJ	U.S.	1991	$2.00

James, Wendy

Singles

Label	Catalog Number	Title	Type	Country	Year	Longbox Value / Value
MCA	MCSTD 1779	Do You Know What I'm Saying?	CD5	U.K.	1993	$9.00
MCA	MCSTXD 1779	Do You Know What I'm Saying?	CD5	U.K.	1993	$9.00
MCA	MCSTD 1763	London's Brilliant	CD5	U.K.	1993	$9.00
MCA	MCSXD 1763	London's Brilliant	CD5	U.K.	1993	$10.00
MCA	MCSD 1732	Nameless One, The	CD5	U.K.	1993	$8.00
MCA	MCSTD 1732	Nameless One, The	CD5	U.K.	1993	$9.00
MCA	MCSXD 1732	Nameless One, The	CD5	U.K.	1993	$9.00

Jamestown

Singles

Label	Catalog Number	Title	Type	Country	Year	Longbox Value / Value
A&M	390819-2	She Got Soul	CD5	Germany	1991	$8.00
A&M	AMCD-819	She Got Soul	CD5	U.K.	1991	$8.00

Jamiroquai

Full Length

Label	Catalog Number	Title	Type	Country	Year	Longbox Value / Value
550 Music	67903	Travelling Without Moving	LTD/LP	U.S.	1997	$17.00
CD album plus bonus promotional CD-single of "Cosmic Girl."						
Epic	ESCA-5782	Blow Your Mind	CD5	Japan	1993	$12.00
		Half the Man	CD5	U.K.		$10.00
		Half the Man	CD5	U.K.		$10.00
Second version.						
	OSK 7632	Half the Man	CDJ	U.S.		$3.00
	OSK 7651	Light Years	CDJ	U.S.		$3.00
Polygram	77827	Space Cowboy	CD5	U.S.	1995	$6.00
Columbia	77827-2	Space Cowboy	CD5	U.S.	1997	$6.00
Epic	ESCA-5692	When You Gonna Learn?	CD5	Japan	1992	$12.00
Acid Jazz	JAZID-46CD	When You Gonna Learn?	CD5	U.K.	1992	$8.00
Columbia	ESK 5600	When You Gonna Learn?	CD5	U.S.	1993	$2.00
Columbia	44K 74925	When You Gonna Learn?	CD5	U.S.	1993	$5.00

Jamison, Jimi

Singles

Label	Catalog Number	Title	Type	Country	Year	Longbox Value / Value
Intercord	827 336	Ever Since the World Began	CD5	Germany	1989	$8.00
Canyon	PCDY-00020	Ever Since the World Began	CD3	Japan	1989	$12.00/$3.00
Scotti Brothers	ZSK 1782	Ever Since the World Began	CDJ	U.S.	1989	$2.00

Jammy Dee

Singles

Label	Catalog Number	Title	Type	Country	Year	Longbox Value / Value
Avex Trax	AVCD-20032	Special Love	CD3	Japan	1992	$12.00/$3.00

Jan & Dean

Full Length

Label	Catalog Number	Title	Type	Country	Year	Longbox Value / Value
One Way		Golden Hits Vols. 1, 2 & 3	LP	U.S.	1996	$30.00
First pressing 2 CD set with track 11 playing "It's As Easy as 1-2-3" by Jan and Jill Gibson rather than the correct track "1-2-3."						

Singles

Label	Catalog Number	Title	Type	Country	Year	Longbox Value / Value
Rhino	885836	Surf City	CD3	Germany	1990	$8.00

Janata

Singles

Label	Catalog Number	Title	Type	Country	Year	Longbox Value / Value
Mercury	CDP 188	River, The	CDJ	U.S.	1990	$2.00

Jane and Jill

Singles

Label	Catalog Number	Title	Type	Country	Year	Longbox Value / Value
Canyon	PCDY-00024	Lay Lay Baby Lay	CD3	Japan	1989	$12.00/$3.00

Jane Child

Singles

Label	Catalog Number	Title	Type	Country	Year	Longbox Value / Value
Warner Brothers	41372	All I Do	CD5	U.S.	1994	$5.00

Jane's Addiction

Full Length

Label	Catalog Number	Title	Type	Country	Year	Longbox Value / Value
Waarner	W-0031CD	Classic Girl	CD	U.K.	1991	$11.00
Warner Brothers	WPCP-4450	Live and Rare	LP	Japan	1991	$20.00
Warner Brothers	9 25993-2Dj	Ritual De Lo Habitual	DJ/LP	U.S.	1990	$25.00
Warner Brothers	9 25993-2	Ritual De Lo Habitual	DJ/LP	U.S.	1990	$35.00
Warner Brothers	9 26223-2	Ritual De Lo Habitual	LP/LB	U.S.	1990	$14.00/$8.00
White banned cover.						

Singles

Label	Catalog Number	Title	Type	Country	Year	Longbox Value / Value
Warner Brothers	W-0011CD	Been Caught Stealing	CD5	U.K.	1990	$11.00
Warner Brothers	9 21736-2	Been Caught Stealing	CD5	U.S.	1990	$6.00
Warner Brothers	PRO-CD-4039	Been Caught Stealing	CDJ	U.S.	1990	$20.00
Clothbound digipak with mini hand-cuffs attached.						
Warner Brothers	PRO-CD-4523	Been Caught Stealing	CDJ	US.	1990	$3.00
Warner Brothers	9 40129-2	Classic Girl	CD5	U.S.	1991	$5.00
Warner Brothers	PRO-CD-4633	Classic Girl	CDJ	U.S.	1991	$6.00
Warner Brothers	PRO-CD-3324	Had a Dad	CDJ	U.S.	1988	$6.00
		Jane Says	CD5	U.S.	1988	$5.00
Warner Brothers	21559-2	Stop	CD5	U.S.	1990	$5.00
Warner Brothers	PRO-CD-4038	Stop	CDJ	U.S.	1990	$8.00
Warner Brothers	W-9584CD	Three Days	CD5	U.K.	1990	$11.00
Warner Brothers		Three Days	CD5	U.S.	1990	$5.00
Warner Brothers	PRO-CD-4037	Three Days	CDJ	U.S.	1990	$8.00

Janicke

Singles

Label	Catalog Number	Title	Type	Country	Year	Longbox Value / Value
Canyon	S13ED-5055	Say Say Say	CD3	Japan	1988	$12.00/$3.00

Janitor Joe

Singles

Label	Catalog Number	Title	Type	Country	Year	Longbox Value / Value
Reptile	ARRCD-37/245	Boyfriend	CD5	U.K.	1993	$8.00

Jankees

Singles

Label	Catalog Number	Title	Type	Country	Year	Longbox Value / Value
BMG	663578	I Can't Feel It	CD5	Germany	1990	$8.00

Janus, Samantha

Singles

Label	Catalog Number	Title	Type	Country	Year	Longbox Value / Value
Intercord	825 313	Message to Your Heart	CD5	Germany	1991	$8.00

Janz, Paul

Singles

Label	Catalog Number	Title	Type	Country	Year	Longbox Value / Value
A&M	CD 15723	Believe In Me	CDJ	U.S.	1988	$2.00

Label	Catalog Number	Title	Type	Country	Year	Longbox Value / Value
A&M	CD 17989	Every Little Liar	CDJ	U.S.	1990	$2.00
A&M	CD 15723	Send Me a Miracle	CDJ	U.S.	1988	$2.00

Japan

Full Length

Label	Catalog Number	Title	Type	Country	Year	Longbox Value / Value
Caroline		Collector's Edition	LTD/LP	U.K.	1994	$40.00
3 CD picture disc boxed set.						

Singles

Label	Catalog Number	Title	Type	Country	Year	Longbox Value / Value
Virgin	CDT-32	Gentlemen Take Polaroids	CD3	U.K.	1988	$8.00
Virgin	880988	Ghosts	CD3	Germany	1988	$8.00
Virgin	CDT-11	Ghosts	CD3	U.K.	1988	$8.00

Jarboe

Singles

Label	Catalog Number	Title	Type	Country	Year	Longbox Value / Value
Hyperium	5066	Red	CDJ	U.S.	1992	$2.00

Jarre, Jean-Michel

Singles

Label	Catalog Number	Title	Type	Country	Year	Longbox Value / Value
WEA	P-JMJ-0795	14 Julliet 1995 Our La Tolerance Esplinade De Invalidas	CDJ	France	1995	$50.00
Polygram	877391-2	Calypso	CD5	Germany	1990	$8.00
Polygram	877391-2	Calypso	CD5	U.K.	1990	$8.00
Dreyfus	861 905	Chronologie	CD5	Germany	1993	$8.00
		Chronologie	CD5	U.K.	1993	$8.00
		Chronologie	CD5	U.K.	1993	$8.00
Second version.						
Polydor	PZCD-32	London Kid	CD5	U.K.	1988	$8.00
Dreyfus	889921-2	Oxygene IV	CD5	Germany	1989	$8.00
Dreyfus	PZCD-55	Oxygene IV	CD5	U.K.	1989	$8.00
Dreyfus	871027-2	Resolutions	CD5	Germany	1988	$8.00
Dreyfus	PZCD-25	Revolutions	CD5	U.K.	1988	$8.00
Dreyfus	867145-2	Zoolook	CD5	Germny	1991	$8.00

Jarreau, Al

Full Length

Label	Catalog Number	Title	Type	Country	Year	Longbox Value / Value
Warner Brothers	03576-2	Breakin' Away	LP/LB	U.S.†	1984	$14.00/$8.00
Reprise	PRO-CD-5412	Classic Hits	DJ/Smplr	U.S.	1988	$12.00
Warner Brothers	9 25106-2	High Crime	LP/LB	U.S.†	1985	$14.00/$8.00
Pioneer	PA-85-125	In London	LD	U.S.	1985	$30.00
Warner Brothers	9 23801-2	Jarreau	LP/LB	U.S.†	1984	$14.00/$8.00

Singles

Label	Catalog Number	Title	Type	Country	Year	Longbox Value / Value
WEA	257603-2	All or Nothing	CD3	Germany	1989	$10.00
WEA	U7663	All or Nothing	CD3	U.K.	1989	$10.00
Reprise	PRO-CD-3513	All or Nothing	CDJ	U.S.	1989	$2.00
WEA	9031-77569-2	Blue Angel	CD5	U.K.	1992	$10.00
Reprise	PRO-CD-5219	Christmas Song	CDJ	U.S.		$2.00
Reprise	PRO-CD-5322	Heaven on Earth	CDJ	U.S.	1992	$2.00
WEA	257678-2	I Must Have Been a Fool	CD3	Germany	1989	$10.00
WEA	258406-2	Moonlighting	CD5	Germany	1990	$10.00
Reprise	PRO-CD-3429	One Way	CDJ	U.S.	1988	$2.00
MCA	17413	Since I Fell For You	CDJ	U.S.		$2.00
WEA	257762-2	So Good	CD3	Germany	1988	$10.00
		So Good	CDJ	U.S.	1988	$2.00
WEA	U-1810CD	What You Do to Me	CD5	U.K.	1992	$10.00

Jarrett, Keith

Full Length

Label	Catalog Number	Title	Type	Country	Year	Longbox Value / Value
ECM	POCI-1085	Body & Soul	LTD/LP	Japan		$25.00
Gold disc.						
ECM	25007-2	Changes	LP/LB	U.S.†	1985	$14.00/$8.00
ECM	1064-2	Koln Concert	LP/LB	U.S.†	1985	$14.00/$8.00
ECM	23793-2	Standards, Vol. 1	LP/LB	U.S.†	1985	$14.00/$8.00

Singles

Label	Catalog Number	Title	Type	Country	Year	Longbox Value / Value
ECM	CDPROKJ2	Blues	CDJ	U.S.	1990	$2.00

Jarrett, Keith & Jan Garbarek

Full Length

Label	Catalog Number	Title	Type	Country	Year	Longbox Value / Value
ECM	1115-2	My Song	LP/LB	U.S.†	1985	$14.00/$8.00

Jarvic Seven

Singles

Label	Catalog Number	Title	Type	Country	Year	Longbox Value / Value
SPV	8173-3	Bush of Love	CD5	Germany	1988	$8.00

Jasmine

Singles

Label	Catalog Number	Title	Type	Country	Year	Longbox Value / Value
Canyon	PCDY-00028	Running Down	CD3	Japan	1990	$12.00/$3.00

Jason and The Scorchers

Singles

Label	Catalog Number	Title	Type	Country	Year	Longbox Value / Value
A&M	CD 17823	Find You	CDJ	U.S.	1989	$2.00
		Hell's Gates	CD5	U.K.	1995	$10.00
A&M	CDEE-524	Now That You're Gone	CD3	U.K.	1990	$8.00
Liberty	DPRO-79186	Try Me	CDJ	U.S.	1992	$2.00
A&M	CD 17903	When the Angels Cry	CDJ	U.S.	1989	$2.00

Jason, Kenny

Singles

Label	Catalog Number	Title	Type	Country	Year	Longbox Value / Value
Champion	CHAMPCD-41	Can U Dance	CD5	U.K.	1988	$8.00

Jasper, Chris

Singles

Label	Catalog Number	Title	Type	Country	Year	Longbox Value / Value
Gold City	1124	One Time Love	CDJ	U.S.	1988	$2.00

Javanotti

Singles

Label	Catalog Number	Title	Type	Country	Year	Longbox Value / Value
Intercord	825 766	Gimme Five	CD3	Germany	1989	$8.00
WEA	YZ-432CD	Gimme Five	CD3	U.K.	1989	$8.00

Javier

Singles

Label	Catalog Number	Title	Type	Country	Year	Longbox Value / Value
Rampart	80921	Rave It Up	CDJ	U.S.	1992	$2.00

Jawbox

Singles

Label	Catalog Number	Title	Type	Country	Year	Longbox Value / Value
Atlantic	PRCD 5662-2	Calling Card	CDJ	U.S.	1994	$2.00
Atlantic	85700	Savory	CD5	U.S.	1994	$4.00
Atlantic	PRCD 5362-2	Savory	CDJ	U.S.	1994	$2.00
Cruz	85700	Savory + 3	CD5	U.S.	1994	$5.00

Jawbreaker

Singles

Label	Catalog Number	Title	Type	Country	Year	Longbox Value / Value
	PRO-CD-4862	Accident Prone	CDJ	U.S.		$3.00
	PRO-CD-4767	Fireman	CDJ	U.S.		$3.00

Jay and The Americans

Singles

Label	Catalog Number	Title	Type	Country	Year	Longbox Value / Value
Rhino	885837	Come a Little Bit Closer	CD3	Germany	1990	$9.00

Jay Ski

Singles

Label	Catalog Number	Title	Type	Country	Year	Longbox Value / Value
BMG	665039	Going Back to My Roots	CD5	Germay	1991	$8.00
BMG	663603	It's a Family Affair	CD5	Germay	1991	$8.00
BMG	663975	Varwash	CD5	Germany	1991	$8.00

Jaya

Singles

Label	Catalog Number	Title	Type	Country	Year	Longbox Value / Value
		One Kiss Per Minute	CDJ	U.S.		$2.00
		Shadow Love	CDJ	U.S.		$2.00

Jaye

Singles

Label	Catalog Number	Title	Type	Country	Year	Longbox Value / Value
ZYX	DST-1052-8	Move to the Groove	CD5	Germany	1991	$6.00

Jaye, Miles

Singles

Label	Catalog Number	Title	Type	Country	Year	Longbox Value / Value
Aris	885468	Heaven	CD5	Germany	1989	$8.00
4th & B'way	BRCD-133	Heaven	CD5	U.K.	1989	$8.00
Aris	885558	Objective	CD5	Germany	1989	$8.00
4th & B'way	BRCD-142	Objective	CD5	U.K.	1989	$8.00

Jayhawks

Singles

Label	Catalog Number	Title	Type	Country	Year	Longbox Value / Value
		Bad Time	CD5	U.K.	1995	$10.00
		Bad Time	CDJ	U.S.	1995	$3.00
	PRO-CD-7306	Blue	CDJ	U.S.	1995	$3.00
Reprise		Blue Angels	CDJ	U.S.	1994	$6.00
Def American	007	Scrapple	CDJ	U.S.	1993	$2.00
Def American	PRO-CD-6207	Settled Down	CDJ	U.S.	1993	$7.00
Def American	PRO-CD-6040	Take Me With You	CDJ	U.S.	1993	[illegible]
		Waiting for the Sun	CD5	U.K.	1992	$8.00
		Waiting for the Sun	CD5	U.K.	1992	$8.00
Second version.						
Def American	PRO-CD-5867	Waiting for the Sun	CDJ	U.S.	1992	$2.00

Jaymes, Jessie

Singles

Label	Catalog Number	Title	Type	Country	Year	Longbox Value / Value
Delicious Vinyl	6688	Body Heat	CDJ	U.S.	1991	$2.00

Jayne

Singles

Label	Catalog Number	Title	Type	Country	Year	Longbox Value / Value
Polygram	871678-3	In My House	CD3	Germany	1989	$8.00
Polygram	871679-2	In My House	CD5	Germany	1989	$8.00
Polygram	877035-2	There's a Light	CD5	Germany	1989	$8.00

Jayne, Karen

Singles

Label	Catalog Number	Title	Type	Country	Year	Longbox Value / Value
BMG	662042	Between Heaven and Hell	CD5	Germany	1989	$8.00

Jayne, Mari

Singles

Label	Catalog Number	Title	Type	Country	Year	Longbox Value / Value
Kadence	HYDCD-1	Heaven Sent	CD5	U.K.	1992	$8.00

Jaz

Singles

Label	Catalog Number	Title	Type	Country	Year	Longbox Value / Value
EMI	203411--3	Hawaiian Sop	CD3	Germany	1989	$8.00

Jaz A Groove

Singles

Label	Catalog Number	Title	Type	Country	Year	Longbox Value / Value
EMI	DPRO-4770	This Is What U Rap 2	CDJ	U.S.	1991	$2.00

Jazz Butcher

Full Length

Label	Catalog Number	Title	Type	Country	Year	Longbox Value / Value
Polygram	PCD 182	Unconditional	DJ/Smplr	Canada		$20.00

Singles

Label	Catalog Number	Title	Type	Country	Year	Longbox Value / Value
Creation	CRECD-77	Girl Go	CD5	U.K.	1990	$8.00
Sky	7-5081	She's a Yo Yo	CDJ	U.S.		$2.00
Polygram	872183-2	Spooky	CD5	Canada	1990	$8.00

Jazz Club

Full Length

Label	Catalog Number	Title	Type	Country	Year	Longbox Value / Value
Polygram	845147	Drums-Mainstream	LP/BP	U.S.		$12.00/$7.00
Polygram	845147	Guitar/Bass-Mainstream	LP/BP	U.S.		$12.00/$7.00
Polygram	845147	Piano-Mainstream	LP/BP	U.S.		$12.00/$7.00
Polygram	845147	Trombone-Mainstream	LP/BP	U.S.		$12.00/$7.00
Polygram	845147	Trumpet-Mainstream	LP/BP	U.S.		$12.00/$7.00

Jazz Devils

Singles

Label	Catalog Number	Title	Type	Country	Year	Longbox Value / Value
Virgin	VSCD-1108	Back in Town	CD5	U.K.	1988	$8.00
Virgin	VSCD-1138	It's a Crime	CD5	U.K.	1990	$8.00
Virgin	VSCD-1164	Out of the Dark	CD5	U.K.	1990	$8.00
Virgin	VSSCDT-1268	What in the World	CD5	U.K.	1990	$8.00

Jazz & The Brothers Grimm

Singles

Label	Catalog Number	Title	Type	Country	Year	Longbox Value / Value
Intercord	825 776	Casanova	CD5	Germany	1990	$8.00
Tam Tam	CDTT-024	Casanova	CD5	U.K.	1990	$8.00

Jazzhole

Singles

Label	Catalog Number	Title	Type	Country	Year	Longbox Value / Value
Atlantic	95723	Shining Star	CD5	U.S.	1995	$5.00

Jazzi, P

Singles

Label	Catalog Number	Title	Type	Country	Year	Longbox Value / Value
Polygram	390533-2	Feel the Rhythm	CD5	Germany	1990	$8.00
A&M	USACD-691	Feel the Rhythm	CD5	U.K.	1990	$8.00
A&M	75021 7506 2	Feel the Rhythm	CDJ	U.S.	1990	$2.00

Jazzmasters

Singles

Label	Catalog Number	Title	Type	Country	Year	Longbox Value / Value
Victor	VICP-15023	Without You	CD5	Japan	1992	$8.00

Jazztet

Full Length

Label	Catalog Number	Title	Type	Country	Year	Longbox Value / Value
Soul Note	SN-1066CD PSI	Moment to Moment	LP/LB	U.S.†	1985	$14.00/$8.00

JBC

Singles

Label	Catalog Number	Title	Type	Country	Year	Longbox Value / Value
Creation	CRESCD-083	We Love You	CD5	U.K.	1990	$8.00

Jeanne D. And The Force

Singles

Label	Catalog Number	Title	Type	Country	Year	Longbox Value / Value
Intercord	825 780	Shake It Up	CD5	Germany	1990	$8.00

Jefferson Airplane

Full Length

Label	Catalog Number	Title	Type	Country	Year	Longbox Value / Value
DIR		BFH	RS	U.S.	1992	$40.00
Airdate: 2/23/92.						
Album Network		In the Studio (Surrealistic Pillow)	RS	U.S.	1989	$25.00
Airdate: 11/13/89.						
RCA	RDJ 66113-2	Jefferson Airplane Loves You	DJ/Smplr	U.S.	1992	$12.00
Silver disc version.						
RCA	RDJ 66113-2	Jefferson Airplane Loves You	DJ/Smplr	U.S.	1992	$18.00
colored disc version.						
DIR		King Biscuit Flour Hour	RS	U.S.	1989	$40.00
Airdate: 9/11/89.						
DIR		King Biscuit Flour Hour	RS	U.S.	1992	$25.00
Airdate: 2/23/92.						
DIR		King Biscuit Flour Hour	RS	U.S.	1994	$25.00
Airdate: 10/9/94.						
Radio Today		Rock Stars	RS	U.S.	1989	$40.00
2 CD set. Airdate: 9/11/89.						
Mobile Fidelity	UDCD-523	Surrealistic Pillow	LP/BP	U.S.		$30.00/$25.00
RCA	PCD1-3766	Surrealistic Pillow	LP/BP	U.S.†	1984	$14.00/$8.00
RCA	66596	Surrealistic Pillow	LTD/LP	U.S.	1995	$28.00
Gold disc.						
Media America		Up Close	RS	U.S.	1989	$40.00
2 CD set.						

Singles

Label	Catalog Number	Title	Type	Country	Year	Longbox Value / Value
Epic	ESK 1769	Planes	CDJ	U.S.	1989	$2.00
Epic	ESK 73080	True Love	CDJ	U.S.	1989	$2.00
RCA	PD-49463	White Rabbit	CD3	Germany	1990	$10.00
RCA	PD-49463	White Rabbit	CD3	U.K.	1990	$10.00
RCA	2078	White Rabbit	CD3	U.S.	1990	$6.00/$3.00

Jefferson Starship

Full Length

Label	Catalog Number	Title	Type	Country	Year	Longbox Value / Value
Pioneer	PA-84-088	Jefferson Starship	LD	U.S.	1984	$20.00
Pioneer	PA-84-088	Jefferson Starship	LD	U.S.	1990	$30.00
RCA	PCD1-4921	Nuclear Future	LP/BP	U.S.†	1984	$14.00/$8.00
RCA	PCD1-0999	Red Octopus	LP/BP	U.S.†	1984	$14.00/$8.00
RCA	PCD1-4372	Winds of Change	LP/BP	U.S.†	1984	$14.00/$8.00

Jeffreys, Garland

Singles

Label	Catalog Number	Title	Type	Country	Year	Longbox Value / Value
RCA	62295	Answer, The	CDJ	U.S.	1992	$2.00
RCA	PD-49172	Hail Hail Rock 'n Roll	CD5	Germany	1991	$8.00
RCA	PD-49172	Hail Hail Rock 'n Roll	CD5	U.K.	1991	$8.00
RCA	62212	Hail Hail Rock 'n Roll	CD5	U.S.	1990	$5.00
RCA	62175	Hail Hail Rock 'n Roll	CDJ	U.S.	1990	$2.00
RCA	74321-110152	Hail Hail Rock 'n Roll '92	CD5	U.K.	1991	$8.00

Jeffries, Michael

Singles

Label	Catalog Number	Title	Type	Country	Year	Longbox Value / Value
Warner Brothers	W-2797CD	Not Thru Being You	CD5	U.K.	1990	$8.00

Jellybean

Singles

Label	Catalog Number	Title	Type	Country	Year	Longbox Value / Value
Chrysalis	661688	Coming Back For More	CD5	Germany	1988	$9.00
Chrysalis	JELCD-4	Coming Back For More	CD5	U.K.	1988	$9.00
Chrysalis	880863	Just a Mirage	CD5	Germany	1988	$9.00
Chrysalis	JELCD-3	Just a Mirage	CD5	U.K.	1988	$9.00
Atlantic	PRCD 3890-2	Spillin' the Beans	CDJ	U.S.	1991	$2.00
Atlantic	7567-86092-2	What's It Gonna Be	CD5	U.K.	1991	$9.00
Atlantic	PRCD 3668-2	What's It Gonna Be	CDJ	U.S.	1990	$2.00

Jellyfish

Full Length

Label	Catalog Number	Title	Type	Country	Year	Longbox Value / Value
Charisma	PRCD 084	Comes Alive	DJ/Smplr	U.S.	1992	$10.00

Singles

Label	Catalog Number	Title	Type	Country	Year	Longbox Value / Value
Charisma	664267	Baby's Coming Back	CD5	Germany	1990	$10.00
Toshiba	VJDP-135	Baby's Coming Back	CD3	Japan	1990	$13.00/$4.00
Charisma	CUSCD-2	Baby's Coming Back	CD5	U.K.	1990	$10.00
Charisma	PRCD 008	Baby's Coming Back	CD5	U.S.	1990	$7.00
Charisma	PRCD 008	Baby's Coming Back	CDJ	U.S.	1990	$10.00
Charisma		Ghost at Number One, The	CD5	U.K.	1993	$10.00
Charisma		Ghost at Number One, The	CD5	U.K.	1993	$10.00
Second version.						
Charisma	12753	Ghost At Number One, The	CDJ	U.S.	1993	$3.00
Charisma	PRCD 042	I Wanna Stay Home	CDJ	U.S.	1991	$3.00
Charisma	14093	Joining a Fan Club	CDJ	U.S.	1993	$3.00
Charisma	CUSCX 1	King Is Half Undressed, The	CD5	U.K.	1990	$15.00
"Aqua-Pak" package.						
Charisma	PRCD 012	King Is Half Undressed, The	CDJ	U.S.	1990	$3.00
		New Mistake	CD5	Australia		$12.00
Charisma		New Mistake	CD5	U.K.	1993	$10.00
Charisma		New Mistake	CD5	U.K.	1993	$10.00
Second version.						
Charisma	12786	New Mistake	CDJ	U.S.	1993	$3.00
Charisma	CUSCD-3	Scary-Go-Round	CD5	U.K.	1991	$10.00
Charisma	PRCD 019	That Is Why	CDJ	U.S.	1990	$20.00
"Aqua-Pak" package.						

Jenkins, Tomi

Singles

Label	Catalog Number	Title	Type	Country	Year	Longbox Value / Value
Elektra	PR 8074-2	Telling You How It Is	CDJ	U.S.	1989	$2.00

Jennings, Waylon

Full Length

Label	Catalog Number	Title	Type	Country	Year	Longbox Value / Value
		A Man Called Hoss	DJ/Smplr	U.S.		$10.00
RCA	PCD1-3378	Greatest Hits	LP/BP	U.S.†	1983	$14.00/$8.00
RCA	PCD1-2317	Ol' Waylon	LP/BP	U.S.†	1983	$14.00/$8.00
RCA	66299-2	Only Daddy That'll Walk the Line	DJ/Smplr	U.S.	1993	$20.00
2 CD set.						
RCA	PCD1-5325	Vol. 2	LP/BP	U.S.†	1985	$14.00/$8.00
RCA	PCD1-4826	Waylon & Company	LP/BP	U.S.†	1983	$14.00/$8.00
RCA	PCD1-4455	WWII	LP/BP	U.S.†	1983	$14.00/$8.00
With Willie Nelson.						

Singles

Label	Catalog Number	Title	Type	Country	Year	Longbox Value / Value
Epic	ESK 73832	If I Can Find a CLean Shirt	CDJ	U.S.	1991	$2.00
Epic	ESK 74403	Just Talkin'	CDJ	U.S.	1992	$2.00
Epic	ESK 74705	Too Dumb for New York City	CDJ	U.S.	1992	$2.00

Jennings/Nelson

Singles

Label	Catalog Number	Title	Type	Country	Year	Longbox Value / Value
RCA	58401	Waylon & Willie	CD5	U.S.	1994	$5.00

Jennyanykind

Singles

Label	Catalog Number	Title	Type	Country	Year	Longbox Value / Value
Nuage	32	Blues of the Attic	CD5	U.S.	1994	$5.00

Jeremy Days

Singles

Label	Catalog Number	Title	Type	Country	Year	Longbox Value / Value
Polygram	887775-2	Are You Inventive	CD5	Germany	1988	$8.00
Polydor	PODP-37011	Are You Inventive	CD3	Japan	1989	$13.00/$4.00
Polygram	871454-3	Brand New Toy	CD3	Germany	1989	$8.00
Polygram	871455-2	Brand New Toy	CD5	Germany	1989	$8.00
Polygram	PZCD-45	Brand New Toy	CD5	U.K.	1989	$8.00
Polygram	867421-2	Give It a Name	CD5	Germany	1991	$8.00
Polygram	879081-2	History	CD5	Germany	1990	$8.00
Polygram	889478-3	Julie Through the Bunds	CD3	Germany	1989	$8.00
Polygram	889479-2	Julie Through the Bunds	CD5	Germany	1989	$8.00
Polygram	889479-2	Julie Through the Bunds	CD5	U.K.	1989	$8.00
Polygram	873040-3	Rome Wasn't Built in a Day	CD3	Germany	1989	$8.00
Polygram	873041-2	Rome Wasn't Built in a Day	CD5	Germany	1989	$8.00
Polygram	PZCD-59	Rome Wasn't Built in a Day	CD5	U.K.	1989	$8.00
Polygram	879301-2	Sylvia Suddenly	CD5	Germany	1991	$8.00
Polygram	PZCD-124	Sylvia Suddenly	CD5	U.K.	1991	$8.00

Jerky Boys

Full Length

Label	Catalog Number	Title	Type	Country	Year	Longbox Value / Value
Foundations		FZ Interview	DJ/Intvw	U.S.	1994	$15.00
		Jerky Boys 2	DJ/Smplr	U.S.	1995	$18.00

Jerome, B.B.

Singles

Label	Catalog Number	Title	Type	Country	Year	Longbox Value / Value
EMI	204718-2	Shock Rock	CD5	Germany	1992	$8.00
EMI	TODP-2317	Shock Rock	CD3	Japan	1991	$12.00/$3.00
EMI	204315-2	You Can Rock It	CD5	Germany	1991	$8.00

Jesse

Singles

Label	Catalog Number	Title	Type	Country	Year	Longbox Value / Value
		Mother Earth	CD5	U.K.		$8.00
		Mother Earth	CD5	U.K.		$8.00
Second version.						

Jesus Jones

Full Length

Label	Catalog Number	Title	Type	Country	Year	Longbox Value / Value
SBK	DPRO 705	A Perverse Conversation	DJ/Intvw	Canada	1993	$10.00
SBK	DPRO-04704	A Perverse Conversation	DJ/Intvw	U.S.	1993	$8.00
BBC Transcription		BBC Transcription Disc	RS		1991	$250.00
SBK	DPRO-19727	Live	DJ/Smplr	U.S.	1990	$8.00
EMI	TOCP-7170	Perverse	LTD/LP	Japan	1993	$30.00
Extra booklet and slipcase.						

Singles

Label	Catalog Number	Title	Type	Country	Year	Longbox Value / Value
EMI	CDFOOD-22	Bring It Down	CD5	U.K.	1989	$10.00
		Devil You Know	CD5	U.K.		$10.00
Second version.						
Capitol	C2 80450	Devil You Know, The	CD5	Canada	1993	$10.00
EMI	TOCP-7540	Devil You Know, The	CD5	Japan	1993	$15.00
Food	7243 8804 302	Devil You Know, The	CD5	U.K.	1993	$10.00
SBK	DPRO-04677	Devil You Know, The	CDJ	U.S.	1993	$2.00
SBK	DPRO-04548	Don't Believe It	CDJ	U.S.	1993	$2.00
EMI	CDFOOD-18	Info Freako	CD5	U.K.	1989	$10.00
EMI	TOCP-6737	Int'l Bright Young Thing	CD5	Japan	1991	$15.00
SBK	DPRO-19727	Move Mountains	CD5	U.S.	1990	$5.00
EMI	CDFOOD-21	Never Enough	CD5	U.K.	1989	$10.00
EMI	204571-2	Real Real Real	CD5	Germany	1991	$10.00
EMI	TODP 2172	Real Real Real	CD3	Japan	1991	$15.00/$4.00
EMI	TOCP-6877	Real Real Real	CD5	Japan	1991	$15.00
EMI	CDFOOD-24	Real Real Real	CD5	U.K.	1991	$10.00
SBK	DPRO-05402	Real Real Real	CDJ	U.S.	1991	$7.00
SBK	DPRO-05405	Real Real Real	CDJ	U.S.	1991	$7.00
EMI	TODP-2405	Right Decision, The	CD3	Japan	1993	$15.00/$4.00
EMI	7243 8 80528	Right Decision, The	CD5	U.K.	1993	$10.00
SBK	DPRO-04722	Right Decision, The	CDJ	U.S.	1993	$6.00
EMI	204392-2	Right Here, Right Now	CD5	Germany	1991	$10.00
EMI	TOCP-6563	Right Here, Right Now	CD5	Japan	1991	$18.00
EMI	CDFOOD-25	Right Here, Right Now	CD5	U.K.	1991	$10.00
EMI	CDFOOD-30	Right Here, Right Now	CD5	U.K.	1991	$10.00
SBK	K2-19734	Right Here, Right Now	CD5	U.S.	1991	$5.00
SBK	DPRO-05376	Right Here, Right Now	CDJ	U.S.	1991	$6.00
SBK	DPRO-05387	Right Here, Right Now	CDJ	U.S.	1991	$6.00
SBK	DPRO-05423	Welcome Back Victoria	CDJ	U.S.	1991	$2.00
EMI	CDFOOD-28	Who? Where? Why?	CD5	U.K.	1991	$10.00
EMI		Zero's & Ones	CD5	U.K.		$10.00
EMI		Zero's & Ones	CD5	U.K.		$10.00
Second version.						

Jesus Loves You

Singles

Label	Catalog Number	Title	Type	Country	Year	Longbox Value / Value
BMG	162831	After the Love	CD3	Germany	1989	$8.00
BMG	662831	After the Love	CD5	Germany	1989	$8.00
	PROCD2	After the Love	CD3	U.K.		$15.00
	PROCD13	After the Love	CD5	U.K.		$13.00
Virgin	PROCD-2	After the Love	CD3	U.K.	1989	$8.00
Virgin	PROCD-8	Bow Down Mister	CD5	U.K.	1991	$8.00
Virgin	664284	Generations of Love	CD5	Germany	1991	$8.00
Virgin	PROCD-5	Generations of Love	CD5	U.K.	1991	$8.00
Virgin	PROCD-10	Generations of Love	CD5	U.K.	1991	$8.00
Virgin	PRCD 3469	Generations of Love	CDJ	U.S.	1990	$2.00
Virgin	PROCD-57	One on One	CD5	U.K.	1991	$8.00

Jesus & Mary Chain

Full Length

Label	Catalog Number	Title	Type	Country	Year	Longbox Value / Value
Def American	PRO-CD-5336/3340	10 Smash Hits/Reverence	DJ/Smplr	U.S.	1992	$25.00
2 CD set.						
WEA	246283-2	Automatic	LTD/LP	Germany		$25.00
Picture disc CD.						
WEA	WMC5-1	Automatic	LP	Japan		$27.00
WEA	246283-2	Automatic	LTD/LP	U.K.		$25.00
Picture disc CD.						
Westwood One		In Concert-Nu Rock	RS	U.S.	1995	$65.00
Airdate: 3/27/95.						
		Rollercoaster U.S.	DJ/Smplr	U.S.	1992	$10.00

Singles

Label	Catalog Number	Title	Type	Country	Year	Longbox Value / Value
WEA	4509-90232-2	Almost Gold	CD5	Germany	1992	$10.00
WEA	NEG-57CD	Almost Gold	CD5	U.K.	1992	$10.00
Def American	PRO-CD-5606	Almost Gold	CDJ	U.S.	1992	$2.00
Warner Brothers	PRO-CD-2955	April Skies	CDJ	U.S.		$2.00
WEA	NEG-41CD	Blues From a Gun	CD3	U.K.	1989	$10.00
		Come On	CD5	U.K.	1994	$10.00
		Come On	CD5	U.K.	1994	$10.00
Second version.						
WEA	NEG-29CD	Darklands	CD5	U.K.	1988	$10.00
WEA	9031-77054-2	Far Gone and Out	CD5	Germany	1992	$10.00
WEA	NEG-56CD	Far Gone and Out	CD5	U.K.	1992	$10.00
Warner Brothers	9 40422-2	Far Gone and Out	CD5	U.S.	1992	$5.00

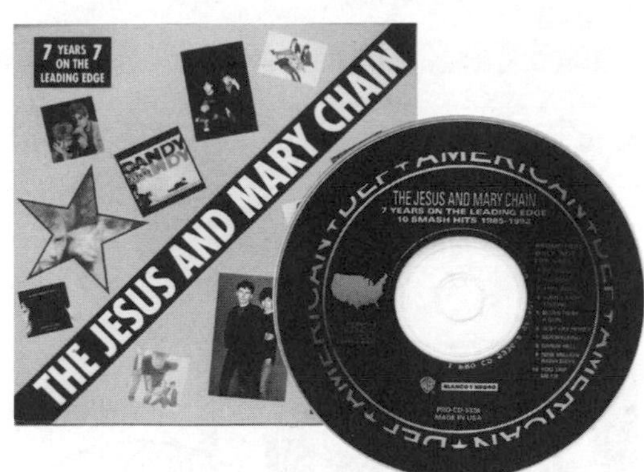

Jesus And Mary Chain – The 7 Years On the Leading Edge 10 Smash Hits 1985–1992 (Def American PRO-CD-5336/3340)

Label	Catalog Number	Title	Type	Country	Year	Longbox Value / Value
Def American	9 40422	Far Gone and Out	CD5	U.S.	1992	$6.00
Def American	PRO-CD-5510	Far Gone and Out	CDJ	U.S.	1992	$2.00
WEA	NEG-42CD	Head On	CD5	U.K.	1989	$10.00
Warner Brothers	PRO-CD-3868	Head On	CDJ	U.S.	1989	$2.00
Warner Brothers	PRO-CD-4058	Her Way o Praying	CDJ	U.S.	1989	$2.00
		I Hate Rock 'n Roll	CD5	U.K.	1995	$10.00
		I Hate Rock 'n Roll	CDJ	U.S.	1995	$6.00
Rough Trade	604-3127-3	Reverence	CD5	Germany	1992	$10.00
WEA	NEG-55CD	Reverence	CD5	U.K.	1992	$10.00
Def American	9 40375-2	Reverence	CD5	U.S.	1992	$4.00
Warner Brothers	PRO-CD-5340	Reverence	CDJ	U.S.	1992	$2.00
WEA	172360-2	Rollercoaster	CD5	U.K.	1990	$10.00
		Sometimes Always	CD5	U.K.	1994	$10.00
		Sometimes Always	CDJ	U.S.	1994	$3.00
WEA	NEG 66CD	Sound of Speed	CD5	U.K.	1993	$10.00
Def American	PRO-CD-5834	Teenage Lust	CDJ	U.S.	1992	$2.00

Jet Red

Singles

Label	Catalog Number	Title	Type	Country	Year	Longbox Value / Value
Relativity	88561-1001	Not the Only One	CDJ	U.S.	1989	$2.00

Jet Vegas

Singles

Label	Catalog Number	Title	Type	Country	Year	Longbox Value / Value
MCA	DMCA-1238	Sex, Power and Fun	CD3	U.K.	1988	$8.00
MCA	DMCAT-1318	You Can't Hold That Against Me	CD5	U.K.	1989	$8.00

Jetboy

Singles

Label	Catalog Number	Title	Type	Country	Year	Longbox Value / Value
MCA	10P3-6068	Feel the Shake	CD3	Japan	1988	$12.00/$3.00
MCA	CD45 18291	Heavy Chevy	CDJ	U.S.	1990	$2.00
MCA		Make Some Noise	CDJ	U.S.		$2.00
MCA	CD45 1067	Stomp on It (Down to the Bricks)	CDJ	U.S.	1990	$2.00

Jethro Tull

Full Length

Label	Catalog Number	Title	Type	Country	Year	Longbox Value / Value
Chrysalis	0946 3 26004	25th Anniversary	LTD/LP	U.S.	1993	$68.00
	4 CD set.					
Chrysalis		Aqualung	LTD/LP	U.K.	1994	$15.00
	25th Anniversary edition in 6"x11" longbox.					
Chrysalis	21044-2	Aqualung	LP/LB	U.S.		$14.00/$8.00
Chrysalis	VK-41044	Aqualung	LP/LB	U.S.†	1984	$14.00/$8.00
Chrysalis	8 52213 2	Aqualung	LTD/LP	U.S.	1996	$17.00
	CD in silver jewel box and slipcase.					
BBC Radio		BBC Classic Tracks	RS	U.S.	1991	$30.00
	Airdate: 3/18/91.					
BBC Radio		BBC Classic Tracks	RS	U.S.	1992	$30.00
	Airdate: 12/14/92.					
BBC Radio		BBC Classic Tracks	RS	U.S.	1993	$20.00
	Airdate: 6/9/93.					
BBC Radio		BBC Classic Tracks	RS	U.S.	1994	$20.00
	Airdate: 2/28/94.					
		Classic CD (Aqualung)	RS	U.S.	1990	$75.00
	Airdate: 11/26/90.					
		Classic CD (Jethro Tull)	RS	U.S.	1990	$100.00
	2 CD set. Airdate: 11/26/90.					
Chrysalis	353406	Definitive Collection, The	LTD/LP	Germany	1988	$65.00
	3 CD set.					
Chrysalis	TBOXCD-1	Definitive Collection, The	LTD/LP	U.K.	1988	$65.00
	3 CD set.					
Chrysalis	F2-21653	Definitive Collection, The	LTD/LP	U.S.	1988	$60.00
	3 CD set.					
Westwood One		In Concert	RS	U.S.	1993	$75.00
	2 CD set. Airdate: 2/15/93.					
Westwood One		In Concert	RS	U.S.	1994	$60.00
	2 CD set. With Raging Slab, Airdate: 2/28/94.					
Album Network		In the Studio (Aqualung)	RS	U.S.	1991	$30.00
	Airdate: 5/27/91.					
Album Network		In the Studio (Benefit)	RS	U.S.	1989	$30.00
	Airdate: 12/18/89.					
Album Network		In the Studio (Thick as a Brick)	RS	U.S.	1991	$30.00
	Airdate: 12/23/91.					
DIR		King Biscuit Flour Hour	RS	U.S.	1988	$50.00
	Airdate: 5/15/88.					
DIR		King Biscuit Flour Hour	RS	U.S.	1988	$100.00
	Airdate: 1/10/88.					
DIR		King Biscuit Flour Hour	RS	U.S.	1989	$40.00
	Airdate: 10/30/89.					
DIR		King Biscuit Flour Hour	RS	U.S.	1991	$30.00
	With King's X, Airdate: 1/6/91.					
DIR		King Biscuit Flour Hour	RS	U.S.	1991	$40.00
	Airdate: 10/6/91.					
DIR		King Biscuit Flour Hour	RS	U.S.	1992	$40.00
	Airdate: 9/27/92.					
DIR		King Biscuit Flour Hour	RS	U.S.	1994	$50.00
	Airdate: 9/11/94.					
Chrysalis	VK-40178	M.U.	LP/LB	U.S.†	1985	$14.00/$8.00

Jethro Tull – Aqualung (Chrysalis 8 52213 2) Special package made in Europe for the U.S. market.

Label	Catalog Number	Title	Type	Country	Year	Longbox Value / Value
Radio Ventures		Masters Of Rock	RS	U.S.	1989	$40.00
	Airdate: 6/12/89.					
Westwood One		Off the Record	RS	U.S.	1995	$35.00
	Airdate: 10/9/95.					
Radio Today		Rock Stars	RS	U.S.	1989	$50.00
	2 CD set. Airdate: 12/3/89.					
Chrysalis		Roots to Branches	DJ/LP	U.S.		$15.00
Chrysalis	DPRO10425	Roots to Branches Sampler	DJ/Smplr	U.S.	1995	$12.00
Image	ID7467PA	Slipstream	LD	U.S.		$35.00
		Source Classic (Aqualung)	RS	U.S.	1990	$50.00
	2 CD set. Airdate: 11/26/90.					
Chrysalis	VK-41003	Thick as a Brick	LP/LB	U.S.†	1985	$14.00/$8.00
Media America		Up Close	RS	U.S.	1989	$50.00
	2 CD set.					
Media America		Up Close	RS	U.S.	1991	$50.00
	2 CD set.					

Singles

Label	Catalog Number	Title	Type	Country	Year	Longbox Value / Value
Chrysalis	DPRO-04657	A Christmas Song	CDJ	U.S.	1989	$6.00
Chrysalis	662575	Another Christmas Song	CD5	Germany	1989	$11.00
Chrysalis	TULLCD-5	Another Christmas Song	CD5	U.K.	1989	$11.00
Chrysalis	DPRO 23471	Another Christmas Song	CDJ	U.S.	1989	$15.00
Chrysalis	DPRO 23801	Doctor My Disease	CDJ	U.S.	1991	$3.00
Chrysalis	DPRO 23418	Kissing Willie	CDJ	U.S.	1989	$3.00
Chrysali	TULPCD1	Part of the Machine	CDJ	U.K.	1988	$30.00
Chrysalis	DPRO 23457	Rattlesnake Trail, The	CDJ	U.S.	1989	$3.00
Chrysalis	TULLCD7	Rocks on the Road	CD5	U.K.	1991	$13.00
	Limited edition box.					
Chrysalis	23818	Rocks on the Road	CD5	U.S.	1991	$6.00
Chrysalis	880790	Said She Was a Dancer	CD5	Germany	1989	$10.00
Chrysalis	TULLCD-4	Said She Was a Dancer	CD5	U.K.	1989	$10.00
Chrysalis	JTPRO 1	Some Day the Sun Won't Shine For You	CDJ	U.K.		$45.00
Chrysalis	323782-2	Still Loving You	CD5	Germany	1991	$10.00
Chrysalis	TULPCD 1	Stormy Monday Blues	CD5	U.K.	1990	$30.00
Chrysalis	323758-2	This Is Not Love	CD5	Germany	1991	$11.00
Chrysalis	TULLCD-6	This Is Not Love	CD5	U.K.	1991	$11.00
Chrysalis	DPRO 23760	This Is Not Love	CDJ	U.S.	1991	$3.00

Jets

Singles

Label	Catalog Number	Title	Type	Country	Year	Longbox Value / Value
		Forever in My Life	CDJ	U.S.		$2.00
Pioneer	10SW-39	Make It Real	CD3	Japan	1988	$12.00/$3.00
Pioneer	09P3-6201	Same Love, The	CD3	Japan	1989	$12.00/$3.00
		Same Love, The	CDJ	U.S.	1988	$2.00
Pioneer	10P3-6025	Sendin' All My Love	CD3	Japan	1988	$12.00/$3.00
		Somebody to Love Me	CDJ	U.S.		$2.00
Pioneer	MVDM-15	Somewhere Out There	CD3	Japan	1992	$13.00/$4.00
Pioneer	WMD5-4044	Special Kind of Love	CD3	Japan	1990	$12.00/$3.00
MCA	1005	Special Kind of Love	CDJ	U.S.	1989	$2.00
Pioneer	09P3-6174	You Better Dance	CD3	Japan	1989	$12.00/$3.00
		You Better Dance	CDJ	U.S.	1989	$2.00

Jett, Joan and The Blackhearts

Full Length

Label	Catalog Number	Title	Type	Country	Year	Longbox Value / Value
Warner Brothers	45567-2	Pure & Simple	DJ/LP	U.S.	1994	$15.00
	Advance Issue.					

Singles

Label	Catalog Number	Title	Type	Country	Year	Longbox Value / Value
		As I Am	CDJ	U.S.		$6.00
Epic	ESK 73985	Backlash	CDJ	U.S.	1991	$2.00
Chrysalis	CHSCD-3518	Dirty Deeds	CD5	U.K.	1990	$10.00
CBS	ZSK 1976	Dirty Deeds	CDJ	U.S.	1990	$2.00
CBS	ZSK 73215	Dirty Deeds	CDJ	U.S.	1990	$2.00
Victor	VIDP-36	Don't Surrender	CD3	Japan	1991	$13.00/$4.00
Epic	ZSK 74067	Don't Surrender	CDJ	U.S.	1991	$2.00
Reprise	PRO-CD-6934	Go Home	CDJ	U.S.	1994	$7.00
Polygram	887644-2	I Hate Myself For Loving You	CD5	Germany	1988	$10.00
Polygram	887644-2	I Hate Myself For Loving You	CD5	U.K.	1988	$10.00
Bellaphon	130-07-329	I Love Rock 'n Roll	CD5	Germany	1989	$10.00
Reprise	PRO-CD-6738	I Love Rock 'n Roll	CDJ	U.S.	1993	$3.00
Reprise	2-18245	I Love Rock 'n Roll	CD5	U.S.	1994	$6.00

Label	Catalog Number	Title	Type	Country	Year	Longbox Value / Value
Victor	VICP-15016	I Love Rock 'n Roll '92	CD5	Japan	1992	$15.00
		Let's Do It	CDJ	U.S.	1994	$6.00
MCA	BH007-2	Light of Day	CDJ	U.S.		$7.00
CBS	ZSK 1324	Little Liar	CDJ	U.S.	1988	$3.00
Chrysalis	CHSCD-3546	Love Hurts	CD5	U.K.	1990	$10.00
Epic	ZSK 2013	Love Hurts	CDJ	U.S.	1989	$3.00
Epic	ZSK 9999	Love Hurts	CDJ	U.S.	1990	$3.00
Epic	ZSK 9999	Love Hurts	CDJ	U.S.	1990	$3.00
	Different mixes.					
Epic	ZSK 73936	Only Good Thing You Ever Said Was Goodbye, The	CDJ	U.S.	1991	$3.00
Bellaphon	130-07-612	Treadin' Water	CD5	Germany	1992	$10.00

Jett, Skyler

Singles

Label	Catalog Number	Title	Type	Country	Year	Longbox Value / Value
Skytime		That's Life	CDJ	U.S.	1991	$3.00

Jewel

Full Length

Label	Catalog Number	Title	Type	Country	Year	Longbox Value / Value
Westwood One		In Concert-Nu Rock	RS	U.S.	1996	$40.00
	Airdate: 7/15/96.					

Singles

Label	Catalog Number	Title	Type	Country	Year	Longbox Value / Value
Atlantic		Who Will Save Your Soul	CDJ	U.K.	1996	$10.00
Atlantic		Who Will Save Your Soul	CD5	U.S.	1995	$4.00
Atlantic	PRCD6585	Who Will Save Your Soul	CDJ	U.S.	1995	$3.00
Atlantic	87021-2	You Were Meant For Me	CD5	U.S.	1996	$3.50
Atlantic	PRCD8416	You Were Meant For Me	CDJ	U.S.	1996	$2.00

Jewelers

Singles

Label	Catalog Number	Title	Type	Country	Year	Longbox Value / Value
Polygram	871426-3	Crying, Hoping	CD3	Germany	1989	$8.00
Polygram	871427-2	Crying, Hoping	CD5	Germany	1989	$8.00

Jeyenne

Singles

Label	Catalog Number	Title	Type	Country	Year	Longbox Value / Value
Bellaphon	130-07-609	Big Confusion	CD5	Germany	1992	$8.00

Jibri Wise One

Singles

Label	Catalog Number	Title	Type	Country	Year	Longbox Value / Value
Ear Candy	38007	I'll Be There For You	CDJ	U.S.	1992	$2.00

Jigsaw

Singles

Label	Catalog Number	Title	Type	Country	Year	Longbox Value / Value
Canyon	S13ED-5064	Let's Not Say Goodbye	CD3	Japan	1988	$12.00/$3.00
Alfa	09B3-27	Sky High	CD3	Japan	1989	$12.00/$3.00
Alfa	11B3-28	Sky High	CD3	Japan	1989	$12.00/$3.00

Jimenez, Flaco

Singles

Label	Catalog Number	Title	Type	Country	Year	Longbox Value / Value
Warner Brothers	PRO-CD-5817	Eres Un Encanto	CDJ	U.S.	1992	$2.00

Jinny

Singles

Label	Catalog Number	Title	Type	Country	Year	Longbox Value / Value
Virgin	VSCDT-1456	Keep Warm	CD5	U.K.	1991	$8.00
Faze 2	CDFAZE-1	Never Give Up	CD5	U.K.	1992	$8.00

Jive Bunny and The Mixmasters

Singles

Label	Catalog Number	Title	Type	Country	Year	Longbox Value / Value
BCM	20500	Can Can You Party	CD5	Germany	1990	$9.00
BMG	MFDCD-007	Can Can You Party	CD5	U.K.	1990	$9.00
BMG	MFDCD-013	Hot Summer Sulsa	CD5	U.K.	1991	$9.00
BCM	20381	Let's Party	CD5	Germany	1989	$9.00
BMG	MFDCD-003	Let's Party	CD5	U.K.	1989	$9.00
BMG	MFDCD-009	Let's Swing Again	CD5	U.K.	1990	$9.00
BMG	MFDCD-012	Over to You John	CD5	U.K.	1991	$9.00
BMG	MFDCD-015	Rock 'n Roll Dance Party	CD5	U.K.	1991	$9.00
BMG	MFDCD-001	Swing the Mood	CD5	Germany	1990	$9.00
BMG	MFDCD-001	Swing the Mood	CD5	U.K.	1990	$9.00
BCM	20430	That Sounds Good to Me	CD5	Germany	1990	$9.00
BMG	MFDCD-004	That Sounds Good to Me	CD5	U.K.	1990	$9.00
BCM	20350	That's the Way I Like It	CD5	Germany	1989	$9.00
BMG	MFDCD-002	That's the Way I Like It	CD5	U.K.	1989	$9.00
		That's the Way I Like It	CDJ	U.S.	1989	$2.00

Jive Five

Singles

Label	Catalog Number	Title	Type	Country	Year	Longbox Value / Value
Rhino	885838	My True Story	CD3	Germany	1990	$8.00

Jive Turkey

Singles

Label	Catalog Number	Title	Type	Country	Year	Longbox Value / Value
Pinnacle	DANCD-062	Fifty Dollar Bill	CD5	U.K.	1991	$8.00

Joao, Maria

Singles

Label	Catalog Number	Title	Type	Country	Year	Longbox Value / Value
Efa	CD-4628	Conversation	CD5	Germany	1987	$8.00

Jobim, Antonio Carlos

Full Length

Label	Catalog Number	Title	Type	Country	Year	Longbox Value / Value
Verve	314 525 880-2	Man From Ipanema, The	LTD/LP	U.S.	1995	$50.00
Verve	823011-2	The Composer Plays	LP/LB	U.S.†	1985	$14.00/$8.00

Jobson, Richard

Singles

Label	Catalog Number	Title	Type	Country	Year	Longbox Value / Value
Parlophone	CDR-6181	Badman	CD5	U.K.	1988	$8.00

Jodeci

Singles

Label	Catalog Number	Title	Type	Country	Year	Longbox Value / Value
MCA	MCSTD-1726	Cherish	CD5	U.K.	1992	$8.00
Uptown	54354	Come and Talk to Me	CD5	U.S.	1992	$4.00
Uptown	1595	Come and Talk to Me	CDJ	U.S.	1992	$2.00
	U5P6585	Freak 'n You	CDJ	U.S.	1995	$2.00
		Get On Up	CDJ	U.S.	1995	$2.00
Uptown	1259	Gotta Love	CDJ	U.S.	1991	$2.00
Uptown	1430	Gotta Love	CDJ	U.S.	1991	$2.00
MCA	MCA5P-2153	I'm Still Waiting	CDJ	U.S.	1992	$2.00
Uptown	2777	Lately	CDJ	U.S.	1993	$2.00
Uptown	2598	Let's Go Through the Motions	CDJ	U.S.	1993	$2.00
Uptown	2732	Let's Go Through the Motions	CDJ	U.S.	1993	$2.00
	UPT5P3524	Love U 4 Life	CDJ	U.S.	1995	$2.00

Joe

Singles

Label	Catalog Number	Title	Type	Country	Year	Longbox Value / Value
		All or Nothing	CD5	U.K.		$10.00
		All or Nothing	CD5	U.K.		$10.00
	Second version.					
	PRCD 7060-2	All the Things	CDJ	U.S.		$2.00
		I'm in Luv	CD5	U.K.		$10.00
		One for Me	CD5	U.K.		$10.00
		One for Me	CD5	U.K.		$10.00
	Second version.					

Joe B & Bad Bro

Singles

Label	Catalog Number	Title	Type	Country	Year	Longbox Value / Value
	79013	Off Da Hook	CD5	U.S.	1994	$5.00

Joe Public

Singles

Label	Catalog Number	Title	Type	Country	Year	Longbox Value / Value
Sony	SRCS-5942	I Miss You	CD5	Japan	1992	$2.00
Columbia	44K 74322	I Miss You	CD5	U.S.	1992	$4.00
Columbia	CSK 74321	I Miss You	CDJ	U.S.	1992	$2.00
Columbia	658765-2	I've Been Watching You	CD5	U.K.	1992	$8.00
Columbia	CSK 4734	I've Been Watching You	CDJ	U.S.	1992	$2.00
Columbia	6657526-2	Live and Learn	CD5	U.K.	1992	$8.00

Joel, Billy – Storm Front Tour CD (Columbia CSK 2127)

Joel, Billy

Full Length

Label	Catalog Number	Title	Type	Country	Year	Longbox Value / Value
Sony	SRCS-6678	52nd Street	LTD/LP	Japan	1992	$35.00
	Gold disc.					
Sony	SRCS-7903	52nd Street	LTD/LP	Japan	1996	$35.00
	20 Bit mastering. CD in Mini-LP sleeve.					
CBS	CK 35609	52nd Street	LP/BP	U.S.†	1982	$35.00/$28.00
	1st commercial CD, manufactured in Japan. Black label on disc.					
Columbia	CK 52858	52nd Street	LP/LB	U.S.	1992	$30.00/$25.00
	Gold disc.					
CBS		A Voyage on the River of Dreams	LTD/LP	Australia	1994	$50.00
	3 CD Set.					
CBS		A Voyage on the River of Dreams	LTD/LP	U.K.	1996	$50.00
	3 CD set.					
CBS	CK-36384	Glass Houses	LP/BP	U.S.†	1983	$14.00/$8.00
Album Network		In the Studio (Glass Houses)	RS	U.S.	1990	$25.00
	Airdate: 8/20/90.					
CBS	CK-38837	Innocent Man	LP/BP	U.S.†	1983	$14.00/$8.00
CBS	SRCS-7598/7600	Journey to the River of Dreams	LTD/LP	Japan	1995	$75.00
	2CD and VHS Video in box.					
CBS	6297-80	Live From Long Island	LD	U.S.	1984	$35.00
CBS	CK-38200	Nylon Curtain	LP/BP	U.S.†	1983	$14.00/$8.00
Sony	CDNK 874	Path to the River of Dreams	DJ/Smplr	Canada	1993	$150.00
CBS	CK-32544	Piano Man	LP/BP	U.S.†	1982	$14.00/$8.00
	First ever CD.					
Westwood One		Piano Men	RS	U.S.	1994	$75.00
	3 CD set. With Elton John, Airdate: 5/30/94.					
CBS	473872	River of Dreams	LTD/LP	U.K.	1994	$35.00
	CD of album plus "live" disc.					
Sony	25DP-5201	Star Box	LTD/LP	Japan		$55.00
Sony		Storm Front Tour '91	DJ/Smplr	Japan	1991	N/A
	2CD set.					
Columbia	CSK 2127	Storm Front Tour, The	DJ/Smplr	U.S.	1990	$20.00
Sony	SRCS-7902	Stranger, The	LTD/LP	Japan	1996	$35.00
	20 Bit mastering. CD in Mini-LP sleeve.					
CBS	CK-34987	Stranger, The	LP/BP	U.S.†	1983	$14.00/$8.00
Media America		Up Close	RS	U.S.	1990	$50.00
	2 CD set.					
Media America		Up Close	RS	U.S.	1994	$50.00
	2 CD set.					
CBS	6297-80	Video Album: Vol. II	LD	U.S.	1987	$25.00
CBS/Sony		When You Wish Upon A Star	DJ/CD3	Japan	1993	$40.00

Singles

Label	Catalog Number	Title	Type	Country	Year	Longbox Value / Value
CBS		All About Soul	CDJ	U.K.	1993	$20.00
Columbia	ESK 5469	All About Soul	CDJ	U.S.	1993	$7.00
Epic	658343	All Shook Up	CD5	U.K.	1992	$15.00
Columbia	ESK 74422	All Shook Up	CDJ	U.S.	1992	$7.00
Columbia	CSK 73602	And So It Goes	CDJ	U.S.	1990	$7.00
Sony	10EP-3002	Back in the U.S.S.R.	CD3	Japan	1989	$18.00/$5.00
Columbia	CSK 2834	Back in the U.S.S.R.	CDJ	U.S.	1989	$12.00
CBS	655903-3	Downeaster Alexa, The	CD5	Germany	1990	$15.00
CBS	CDJOEL-4	Downeaster Alexa, The	CD5	U.K.	1990	$15.00
Columbia	CSK 7333	Downeaster Alexa, The	CDJ	U.S.	1990	$7.00
Sony	CSFM-7708	Honesty	CDV	Japan	1989	$45.00
Columbia	655501-3	I Go to Extremes	CD3	Germany	1990	$11.00
Columbia	655501-5	I Go to Extremes	CD5	Germany	1990	$15.00
Sony	CSDS-8116	I Go to Extremes	CD3	Japan	1990	$18.00/$5.00
Columbia	CDJOEL-2	I Go to Extremes	CD5	U.K.	1990	$15.00
Columbia	JOELCD-2	I Go to Extremes	CD5	U.K.	1990	$15.00
Columbia	ESK 73091	I Go to Extremes	CDJ	U.S.	1990	$7.00
CBS	38K-7950	Just the Way You Are	CD3	U.S.	1988	$7.00/$4.00
Columbia	JOEL-3	Leningrad	CD5	U.K.	1990	$15.00
Columbia	CDJOEL-3	Leningrad	CD5	U.K.	1990	$15.00
CBS		Lullabye	CDJ	U.K.	1994	$14.00
CBS	77363	Lullabye	CD5	U.S.	1994	$7.00
Columbia	CSK 5631	Lullabye	CDJ	U.S.	1994	$7.00
		No Man's Land	CD5	U.K.		$15.00
		No Man's Land	CD5	U.K.		$15.00
	Second version.					
Columbia	CSK 5278	No Man's Land	CDJ	U.S.	1993	$7.00

Label	Catalog Number	Title	Type	Country	Year	Longbox Value / Value
Columbia	CSK 5277	River of Dreams	CDJ	U.S.	1993	$7.00
CBS	CSDS-8175	Special excerpts From "Storm Front"	DJ/CD3	Japan		$35.00
Columbia	656144-3	That's Not Her Style	CD3	Germany	1990	$11.00
Sony	CSDS-8159	That's Not Her Style	CD3	Japan	1990	$18.00/$5.00
Columbia	CDJOEL-5	That's Not Her Style	CD5	U.K.	1990	$15.00
CBS	10EP-3002	Times They Are a Changing	CD3	Japan	1989	$18.00/$5.00
Sony	CSFM-7709	Uptown Girl	CDV	Japan	1989	$45.00
Columbia	655300-3	We Didn't Start the Fire	CD3	Germany	1989	$11.00
Sony	CSDS-8106	We Didn't Start the Fire	CD3	Japan	1989	$18.00/$5.00
Sony	CSFM-7705	We Didn't Start the Fire	CDV	Japan	1989	$45.00
Sony	XDEP 93040	We Didn't Start the Fire	DJ/CD3	Japan	1989	$70.00
Columbia	CDJOEL-1	We Didn't Start the Fire	CD5	U.K.	1989	$15.00
Columbia	CSK73021	We Didn't Start the Fire	CDJ	U.S.	1989	$12.00

Joeski Love

Singles

Label	Catalog Number	Title	Type	Country	Year	Longbox Value / Value
Columbia	CSK 73480	Know She Likes Joe	CDJ	U.S.	1990	$2.00

Johansen, David

Full Length

Label	Catalog Number	Title	Type	Country	Year	Longbox Value / Value
Relativity		Crucial Music	LP/LB	U.S.		$14.00/$8.00
Passport	PRD-6043	Sweet Revenge	LP/LB	U.S.		$14.00/$8.00

John and Julie

Singles

Label	Catalog Number	Title	Type	Country	Year	Longbox Value / Value
WEA	XLS-23CD	Double Happiness	CD5	U.K.	1991	$8.00

John Doe Thing

Full Length

Label	Catalog Number	Title	Type	Country	Year	Longbox Value / Value
		John Doe Thing	DJ/LP	U.S.		$15.00
	CD in file folder press kit.					
Foreward	PRCD 7137	Kissing So Hard	DJ/LP	U.S.	1995	$10.00
Foreward	PRCD 7137	Kissing So Hard	DJ/Smplr	U.S.	1995	$15.00
	CD and Bio in folder.					

John, Elton – Elton John/Bernie Taupin Collection (Polygram Music publishing PIP-CD-002/2)

John, Elton – Ice On Fire (Geffen 9 24077-2)

John, Elton

Full Length

Label	Catalog Number	Title	Type	Country	Year	Longbox Value / Value
Polydor	512738-2	11-17-70	LP	U.S.	1992	$14.00
		25 Years On	DJ/Smplr	U.K.	1995	$80.00
Westwood One		BBC Classic Tracks	RS	U.S.	1991	$35.00
	Airdate: 1/14/91.					
Westwood One		BBC Classic Tracks	RS	U.S.	1991	$35.00
	Airdate: 11/25/91.					
Westwood One		BBC Classic Tracks	RS	U.S.	1991	$35.00
	Airdate: 6/10/91.					
Westwood One		BBC Classic Tracks	RS	U.S.	1992	$35.00
	Airdate: 1/13/92.					
Westwood One		BBC Classic Tracks	RS	U.S.	1992	$35.00
	Airdate: 10/5/92.					
Westwood One		BBC Classic Tracks	RS	U.S.	1992	$35.00
	Airdate: 11/23/92.					
Westwood One		BBC Classic Tracks	RS	U.S.	1993	$35.00
	Airdate: 2/8/93.					
Westwood One		BBC Classic Tracks	RS	U.S.	1993	$35.00
	Airdate: 6/21/93.					
Westwood One		BBC Classic Tracks	RS	U.S.	1993	$35.00
	Airdate: 8/30/93.					
BBC		BBC Classic Tracks	RS	U.S.	1993	$40.00
	Airdate: 12/27/93.					
BBC		BBC Classic Tracks	RS	U.S.	1993	$40.00
	Airdate: 6/21/93.					
Rocket	822818-2	Blue Moves	LP	U.S.		$17.00
Rocket	822888-2	Breaking Hearts	LP	U.S.		$17.00
DJM	821746-2	Breaking Hearts	LP	U.S.		$17.00
Geffen	9 24031-2	Breaking Hearts	LP/LB	U.S.		$20.00/$22.00
Geffen	9 24031-2	Breaking Hearts	LP/LB	U.S.†	1984	$16.00/$11.00
Vestron	ML1024	Breaking Hearts Tour	LD	U.S.	1986	$30.00
Polydor	821746-2	Captian Fantastic & Brown Dirt Cowboy	LP	U.S.	1992	$14.00
Polydor	825488-2	Caribou	LP	U.S.	1992	$14.00
McDonald's		Classic Elton John	LP	U.S.	1994	$8.00
Pickwick	PWKS 551	Collection, The	LP	U.K.	1989	$18.00
DJM	DJMCD10	Don't Shoot Me I'm Only the Piano Player	LP	U.S.		$12.00
Polydor	827690-2	Don't Shoot Me I'm Only the Piano Player	LP	U.S.	1992	$14.00
Polydor	827689-2	Elton John	LP	U.S.	1992	$14.00
Polygram	PIP-CD-002/2	Elton John/Bernie Toupin Collection, The	DJ/Smplr	U.S.	1990	$65.00
	2CD set.					
Polydor	832017-2	Empty Nest	LP	U.S.	1992	$14.00
MCA	MCAD 9070	Excerpts From to Be Continued	DJ/Smplr	U.S.†	1990	$35.00
Geffen	9 24077-2	Fire and Ice	LP/LB	U.S.	1985	$18.00/$15.00
Rocket	800063-2	Fox	LP	U.S.		$30.00
MCA	MCAD2-6894	Goodbye Yellow Brick Road	LP/LB	U.S.†	1983	$45.00/$40.00
	2 CD set.					
MCA	MCAD2-6894	Goodbye Yellow Brick Road	LP/LB	U.S.	1985	$45.00/$40.00
	2 CD set					
Polydor	821747-2	Goodbye Yellow Brick Road	LP	U.S.	1992	$14.00
Vertigo		Great Box	LTD/LP	Japan	1990	$80.00
	4CD set.					
DJM	821750-2	Greatest Hits	LP	Germany	1984	$25.00
	Includes "Candle in the Wind."					
MCA	MCAD 37215	Greatest Hits	LP/LB	U.S.†	1984	$22.00/$18.00
	Includes "Bennie And the Jets."					
Geffen	9 24153-2	Greatest Hits Volume III 1979-1987	LP/LB	U.S.	1987	$18.00/$15.00
Polydor	812739-2	Here and There	LP	U.S.	1992	$14.00
Polygram	829249-2	Honky Chateau	LP	U.S.		$17.00
Polydor	825487-2	Honky Chateau	LP	U.S.	1992	$14.00
Westwood One		I'm Still Standing – Westwood One Special	RS	U.S.	1996	$115.00
	3 CD set. Airdate: 7/7/96.					
Geffen	9 24077-2	Ice on Fire	LP	U.S.	1985	$18.00
Pioneer	PA-83-057	In Central Park	LD	U.S.	1983	$40.00
Pioneer	PA-83-057	In Central Park	LD	U.S.	1990	$50.00
	Digital audio.					
Album Network		In the Studio (Escape)	RS	U.S.	1996	$35.00
Album Network		In the Studio (Goodbye Yellow Brick Road)	RS	U.S.	1988	$35.00
	Airdate: 11/21/88.					
Album Network		In the Studio (Goodbye Yellow Brick Road)	RS	U.S.	1990	$30.00
	Airdate: 12/17/90.					
DIR		King Biscuit Flour Hour	RS	U.S.	1987	$40.00
	Airdate: 12/6/87.					
DIR		King Biscuit Flour Hour	RS	U.S.	1988	$90.00
	Airdate: 11/27 - 12/4/88.					
DIR		King Biscuit Flour Hour	RS	U.S.	1989	$80.00
	2 CD set. Airdate: 5/21 - 5/28/89.					
DIR		King Biscuit Flour Hour	RS	U.S.	1990	$40.00
	Airdate: 3/12/90.					
DIR		King Biscuit Flour Hour	RS	U.S.	1990	$65.00
	Airdate: 10/14/90.					
DIR		King Biscuit Flour Hour	RS	U.S.	1991	$40.00
	Airdate: 8/25/91.					
DIR		King Biscuit Flour Hour	RS/	U.S.	1992	$40.00
	Airdate: 8/23/92.					
DIR		King Biscuit Flour Hour	RS	U.S.	1993	$70.00
	2 CD set.					
DIR		King Biscuit Flour Hour	RS	U.S.	1994	$70.00
	2 CD set. Airdate: 6/12/94.					
DIR		King Biscuit Flour Hour	RS	U.S.	1995	$65.00
	Airdate: 6/11/95.					
Geffen	9 24114-2	Leather Jackets	LP/LB	U.S.	1986	$18.00/$15.00
Discovision		Live	LD	U.S.	1979	$50.00
WEA	50358	Live	LD	U.S.	1992	$35.00
		Live In Australia	LTD/LP	Austalia	1991	$35.00
	Gold disc.					
Rocket		Made in England	DJ/Intvw	U.K.	1995	$30.00
Rocket		Made in England	LTD/LP	U.K.	1995	$25.00
	CD in slip case.					
DJM	DJMCD-5	Madman Across the Water	LP	U.S.		$17.00
Polydor	825487-2	Madman Across the Water	LP	U.S.	1992	$14.00
Image	ID7550VE	Night Time Concert, The	LD	U.S.		$30.00
Westwood One		Off the Record	RS	U.S.	1993	$30.00
	Airdate: 8/16/93.					
Westwood One		Off the Record	RS	U.S.	1994	$30.00
	Airdate: 1/10/94.					
Westwood One		Off the Record	RS	U.S.	1994	$30.00
	Airdate: 4/25/94.					
Westwood One		Off the Record	RS	U.S.	1996	$30.00
	Airdate: 2/26/96.					
Westwood One		Piano Men	RS	U.S.	1994	$75.00
	3 CD set. With Elton John, Airdate: 5/30/94.					
Polydor	SACD 535	Rare Masters/Selections From the Elton John Collection	DJ/Smplr	U.S.	1992	$30.00
	2CD set.					
Rocket	823018-2	Rock of the Westies	LP	U.S.		$17.00
Carrere	CA80196317	Superior Sound Of Elton John	LP	France		$30.00
Westwood One		Superstar Concert	RS	U.S.	1994	$60.00
	2 CD set. Airdate: 1/10/94.					
Westwood One		Superstars	RS	U.S.	1993	$65.00
	2 CD set. Airdate: 8/16/93.					
Rocket	848 236-2	To Be Continued...	LP	U.K.	1991	$125.00
	4CD set.					
MCA	MCAD4-10110	To Be Continued...	LP	U.S.	1990	$100.00
	4CD set.					
CBS	9040-80	To Russia With Elton John	LD	U.S.	1990	$30.00
Geffen	9 4006-2	Too Low For Zero	LP/LB	U.S.†		$18.00/$15.00
Geffen	9 4006-2	Too Low For Zero	LP/LB	U.S.		$18.00/$15.00
MCA	MCAD-37199	Tumbleweed Connection	LP/LB	U.S.	1984	$18.00/$15.00
Polydor	829248-2	Tumbleweed Connection	LP	U.S.	1992	$14.00
MCA		Victim of Love	LP/LB	U.S.		$14.00/$8.00
Unistar		Weekly Specials, The	RS	U.S.	19912	$40.00
	Airdate: 8/7/92.					
Rocket	EJCD 89	World, The	DJ/Smplr	U.K.	1989	$40.00

Label	Catalog Number	Title	Type	Country	Year	Longbox Value / Value
Rocket	SACA 40-41	Your Song	DJ/Smplr	Japan	1993	$300.00
2 CD set.						
		Singles				
		A Woman's Needs	CDJ	Holland		$28.00
MCA	CD4517640	A Word In Spanish	CDJ	U.S.	1988	$8.00
		Ain't Nothin Like the Real Thing	CD5	U.K.	1994	$10.00
		Ain't Nothin Like the Real Thing	CD5	U.K.	1994	$10.00
Second version.						
		Believe	CDJ	Australia	1995	$14.00
Mercury	PHCR-8318	Believe	CDJ	Japan	1995	$20.00
Polygram	856711	Believe	CD5	U.S.	1994	$5.00
		Believe	CDJ	U.S.	1995	$7.00
		Believe	CDJ	U.S.	1995	$7.00
Mercury	PHCR-8340	Blessed	CDJ	Japan	1995	$20.00
Island	852394	Blessed	CD5	U.S.	1995	$5.00
Island	PRCD 7077-2	Blessed	CDJ	U.S.	1995	$7.00
Polygram	64543	Can You Feel	CD5	U.S.	1994	$5.00
		Can You Feel the Love Tonight	CD5	U.K.	1994	$10.00
		Can You Feel the Love Tonight	CD5	U.K.	1994	$10.00
Second version.						
Hollywood		Can You Feel the Love Tonight	CD5	U.S.	1994	$5.00
Hollywood	PRCD 10441-2	Can You Feel the Love Tonight	CDJ	U.S.	1994	$18.00
Polygram	870063-2	Candle in the Wind	CD5	Germany	1988	$12.00
Rocket	EJSCD-15	Candle in the Wind	CD5	U.K.	1988	$12.00
		Circle of Life	CD5	Germany	1994	$10.00
		Circle of Life	CD5	U.K.	1994	$10.00
		Circle of Life	CD5	U.K.	1994	$10.00
Second version.						
Hollywood		Circle of Life	CD5	U.S.	1994	$5.00
Polygram	64516	Circle of Life	CD5	U.S.	1994	$5.00
Hollywood	PRCD 1048-2	Circle of Life	CDJ	U.S.	1994	$15.00
Polygram	875435-2	Club at the End of the Street	CD5	Germany	1990	$12.00
Polygram	878129-2	Club at the End of the Street	CD5	Germany	1990	$12.00
Rocket	EJSCD-21	Club at the End of the Street	CD5	U.K.	1990	$12.00
Rocket	EJSCD-23	Club at the End of the Street	CD5	U.K.	1990	$12.00
MCA	CD45 18303	Club at the End of the Street	CDJ	U.S.	1989	$8.00
Rocket	PHDR-117	Crocodile Rock	CD3	Japan	1992	$15.00/$4.00
MCA	54831	Don't Go Breakin' My Heart	CD5	U.S.	1994	$5.00
		Don't Go Breaking My Heart	CDJ	France	1994	$25.00
CD in "pop-up" cardboard sleeve.						
		Don't Go Breaking My Heart	CD5	U.K.	1994	$10.00
		Don't Go Breaking My Heart	CD5	U.K.	1994	$10.00
Second version.						
MCA	MCA5P-2967	Don't Go Breaking My Heart	CDJ	U.S.	1994	$8.00
Rocket	EJSCD-26	Don't Let the Sun Go Down On Me	CD5	U.K.	1991	$11.00
		Duet For One	CDJ	Spain		$50.00
Polygram	87685-2	Easier to Walk Away	CD5	Germany	1991	$12.00
Rocket	EJSCD-25	Easier to Walk Away	CD5	U.K.	1990	$12.00
Phonogram	PHDR-28	Goodbye Yellow Brick Road	CD3	Japan	1991	$15.00/$5.00
Polygram	874980-3	Healing Hands	CD3	Germany	1988	$12.00
Polygram	874981-2	Healing Hands	CD5	Germany	1988	$12.00
Rocket	PPDS-14	Healing Hands	CD3	Japan	1988	$15.00/$4.00
Rocket	EJSCD-19	Healing Hands	CD5	U.K.	1988	$12.00
Rocket	870325-2	I Don't Wanna Go on With You Like That	CD5	Germany	1988	$12.00
Rocket	EJSCD-16	I Don't Wanna Go on With You Like That	CD5	U.K.	1988	$12.00
MCA	CD45-17535	I Don't Wanna Go on With You Like That	CDJ	U.S.	1988	$18.00
Rocket		Last Song, The	CD5	U.K.	1992	$10.00
Rocket		Last Song, The	CD5	U.K.	1992	$10.00
Second version.						
MCA	MCA5P-2425	Last Song, The	CDJ	U.S.	1992	$8.00
	PHCR-8327	Made in England	CD5	Japan	1995	$18.00
Rocket	EJSDD37	Made in England	CD5	U.K.	1995	$10.00
Rocket	EJSCD37	Made in England	CD5	U.K.	1995	$10.00
Island	ORCD 7014-2	Made in England	CDJ	U.S.	1995	$15.00
Rocket	PRCD 7014-2	Made in England	CD5	U.S.	1995	$4.00
Rocket	852093	Made in England	CD5	U.S.	1995	$5.00
Polydor	CDP 819	Madman Across the Water	CDJ	U.S.	1992	$8.00
Polygram	868257-2	Nikita	CD5	Germany	1991	$11.00
		On Dark Street	CDJ	U.K.		$35.00
Rocket		One, The	CDJ	France	1992	$35.00
Rocket	PHDR-106	One, The	CD3	Japan	1992	$15.00/$4.00
Rocket	866 157-2	One, The	CD5	U.K.	1992	$10.00
Rocket	866 939-2	One, The	CD5	U.K.	1992	$12.00
Phonogram	EJSCR 28	One, The	CD5	U.K.	1992	$15.00
MCA	54435	One, The	CD5	U.S.	1992	$5.00
MCA	MCA5P-2263	One, The	CDJ	U.S.	1992	$7.00
MCA	MCA5P-2302	One, The	CDJ	U.S.	1992	$7.00
		Pain	CDJ	U.S.	1995	$7.00
		Please	CDJ	Spain		$28.00
Rocket	PHDR-118	Runaway Train	CD3	Japan	1992	$15.00/$4.00
Rocket	PHCR-8018	Runaway Train	CD5	Japan	1992	$20.00
		Runaway Train	CD5	U.K.		$10.00
		Runaway Train	CD5	U.K.		$10.00
Second version.						
MCA	54412	Runaway Train	CD5	U.S.	1992	$5.00
MCA	MCA5P-2305	Runaway Train	CDJ	U.S.	1992	$6.00
Polygram	876412-3	Sacrifice	CD3	Germany	1989	$10.00
Polygram	876331-2	Sacrifice	CD5	Germany	1989	$10.00
Polygram	875809-2	Sacrifice	CD5	Germany	1990	$10.00
Rocket	EJSCD 20	Sacrifice	CD5	U.K.	1989	$10.00
Rocket	EJSCD-22	Sacrifice	CD5	U.K.	1990	$10.00
MCA	CD45 18061	Sacrifice	CDJ	U.S.	1989	$6.00
Mercury	PHDE-133	Show Must Go On, The	DJ/CD3	Japan		$25.00
Rocket	862 114-2	Simple Life	CD5	U.K.	1992	$10.00
MCA	MCA5P-2539	Simple Life	CDJ	U.S.	1992	$6.00
Rocket	EJCDS2	Sleeping With the Past	CDJ	U.K.	1994	$12.00
		Through the Storm	CD3	U.K.	1989	$12.00
Polygram	872735-2	Town of Plenty	CD5	Germany	1989	$11.00
Rocket	EJSCD-17	Town of Plenty	CD5	U.K.	1989	$11.00
		True Love	CD5	U.K.	1994	$10.00
		True Love	CD5	U.K.	1994	$10.00
Second version.						
MCA	MCA5P-2875	True Love	CDJ	U.S.	1994	$6.00
Polygram	872015-2	Word in Spanish	CD5	Germany	1988	$11.00
Rocket	EJSCD-18	Word in Spanish	CD5	U.K.	1988	$11.00
Polygram	878425-2	You Gotta Love Someone	CD5	Germany	1990	$11.00
Rocket	EJSCD-24	You Gotta Love Someone	CD5	U.K.	1990	$11.00
MCA	CD45 1135	You Gotta Love Someone	CDJ	U.S.	1990	$6.00
Phonogram	PHDR-119	Your Song	CD3	Japan	1992	$15.00/$4.00

John, Robert

Singles

Label	Catalog Number	Title	Type	Country	Year	Longbox Value / Value
Curb	093	Lion Sleeps Tonight, The	CDJ	U.S.	1992	$2.00
		Lion Sleeps Tonight, The	CDJ	U.S.	1995	$7.00

Johnny Crash

Singles

Label	Catalog Number	Title	Type	Country	Year	Longbox Value / Value
		All the Way in Love	CDJ		U.S.	$2.00
		Hey Kid	CDJ		U.S.	$2.00

Johnny Hates Jazz

Singles

Label	Catalog Number	Title	Type	Country	Year	Longbox Value / Value
Virgin	661577	Don't Say Its Love	CD5	Germany	1988	$10.00
Virgin	VSCD-1081	Don't Say Its Love	CD5	U.K.	1988	$10.00
Virgin	659825	Heart of Gold	CD5	Germany	1988	$10.00
Virgin	VSCD-1045	Heart of Gold	CD5	U.K.	1988	$10.00
Virgin	PR 2367	I Don't Want to be a Hero	CDJ	U.S.	1988	$3.00
Virgin	664653	Last to Know	CD5	Germany	1991	$10.00
Virgin	VSCD-1401	Last to Know	CD5	U.K.	1991	$10.00
Virgin	664250	Let Me Change Your Mind Tonight	CD5	Germany	1991	$10.00
Virgin	VJDP-10159	Let Me Change Your Mind Tonight	CD3	Japan	1991	$12.00/$4.00
Virgin	VSCDT-1220	Let Me Change Your Mind Tonight	CD5	U.K.	1991	$10.00
Virgin	VJDP-12003	Shattered Dreams	CD3	Japan	1988	$12.00/$4.00
Virgin	PR 2177	Shattered Dreams	CDJ	U.S.	1988	$3.00
Virgin	VJD-10001	Turn Back the Clock	CD3	Japan	1989	$12.00/$4.00
Virgin	VSCD1205	Turn Back the Clock	CD3	U.K.	1989	$10.00
Virgin	CDEP-14	Turn Back the Clock	CD5	U.K.	1990	$10.00
Virgin	PR 2348	Turn Back the Clock	CDJ	U.S.	1988	$3.00
Virgin	162601	Turn the Tide	CD3	Germany	1989	$10.00
Virgin	662601	Turn the Tide	CD5	Germany	1989	$10.00
Virgin	VJD-10220	Turn the Tide	CD3	Japan	1989	$12.00/$4.00
Virgin	VSCD-1205	Turn the Tide	CD3	U.K.	1989	$10.00

Johnny O

Singles

Label	Catalog Number	Title	Type	Country	Year	Longbox Value / Value
ZYX	6247-8	Fantasy Girl	CD5	Germany	1989	$6.00
ZYX	6308-8	Memories	CD5	Germany	1989	$6.00
WEA	PWCD-54	Say You'll Be There	CD5	U.K.	1990	$8.00

Johnny P

Singles

Label	Catalog Number	Title	Type	Country	Year	Longbox Value / Value
Relativity	0207	Look Good	CDJ	U.S.	1993	$2.00

Johns, Ethan

Singles

Label	Catalog Number	Title	Type	Country	Year	Longbox Value / Value
Polydor	PZCD-157	This Is Not a Love Song	CD5	U.K.	1991	$8.00

Johnson & Branson

Singles

Label	Catalog Number	Title	Type	Country	Year	Longbox Value / Value
A&M	CD 18006	Jockin' Me	CDJ	U.S.	1990	$2.00
A&M	CD 17906	Let's Get to Know Each Other	CDJ	U.S.	1989	$2.00

Johnson, Brian

Full Length

Label	Catalog Number	Title	Type	Country	Year	Longbox Value / Value
		Keep on Rocking	LP/LB	U.S.		$14.00/$10.00

Johnson, Don

Full Length

Label	Catalog Number	Title	Type	Country	Year	Longbox Value / Value
CBS	3991-80	Heartbeat	LD	U.S.	1987	$20.00
		Singles				
Epic	655234-3	Other People' Lives	CD3	Germany	1989	$8.00
Epic	654976-3	Tell It Like It Is	CD3	Germany	1989	$8.00
Epic	654976-2	Tell It Like It Is	CD5	Germany	1989	$8.00
Epic	655527-3	What If It Takes All Night	CD3	Germany	1989	$8.00

Johnson, Eric

Singles

Label	Catalog Number	Title	Type	Country	Year	Longbox Value / Value
Capitol	DPRO-79159	Cliffs of Dover	CDJ	U.S.	1990	$2.00
Capitol	DPRO-79524	Cliffs of Dover (Live)	CDJ	U.S.	1990	$6.00
Capitol	DPRO-79342	Desert Rose	CDJ	U.S.	1990	$3.00
Capitol	DPRO-79043	Eastwest	CDJ	U.S.	1990	$3.00
Capitol	DPRO-79458	Forty-Mile Town	CDJ	U.S.	1990	$3.00
Capitol	DPRO-79876	High Landrons	CDJ	U.S.	1990	$3.00
Capitol	DPRO-79457	Righteous	CDJ	U.S.	1990	$3.00
Capitol	DPRO-79567	Trademark	CDJ	U.S.	1990	$3.00

Johnson, Holly

Singles

Label	Catalog Number	Title	Type	Country	Year	Longbox Value / Value
MCA	MCD-17548	Across the Universe	CD5	Germany	1991	$9.00
MCA	MCSTD-1513	Across the Universe	CD5	U.K.	1991	$9.00
MCA	257596-2	Americanos	CD3	Germany	1989	$9.00
Pioneer	WMD5-4009	Americanos	CD3	Japan	1990	$13.00/$4.00
MCA	DMCAT-1323	Americanos	CD3	U.K.	1989	$9.00
UNI	CD45-17837	Americanos	CDJ	U.S.	1989	$2.00
UNI	CD45-17986	Americanos	CDJ	U.S.	1989	$2.00
MCA	257512-2	Atomic City	CD3	Germany	1989	$9.00
MCA	DMCAT-1342	Atomic City	CD5	U.K.	1989	$9.00
Eastwest	257405-2	Heaven's Here	CD5	Germany	1989	$9.00
MCA	DMCAT-1365	Heaven's Here	CD5	U.K.	1989	$9.00
MCA	257693-2	Love Train	CD3	Germany	1989	$9.00
Pioneer	09P3-6138	Love Train	CD3	Japan	1989	$13.00/$4.00
MCA	DMCA-1306	Love Train	CD3	U.K.	1989	$9.00
UNI	CD45-17837	Love Train	CDJ	U.S.	1989	$2.00
BMG	MCD-18071	People Want to Dance	CD5	Germany	1991	$9.00
Eastwest	9031-73073-2	Where Has Love Gone	CD5	Germany	1990	$9.00
MCA	DMCAT-1460	Where Has Love Gone	CD5	U.K.	1990	$9.00

Johnson, J.J.

Full Length

Label	Catalog Number	Title	Type	Country	Year	Longbox Value / Value
Savoy Records	CY-78813	J.J. Johnson Jazz Quintet	LTD/LP	U.S.	1996	$20.00
CD in miniature repica of original LP sleeve.						

Johnson, J.J. & Kai Winding

Full Length

Label	Catalog Number	Title	Type	Country	Year	Longbox Value / Value
Savoy Records	CY-78818	Jay And Kai	LTD/LP	U.S.	1996	$20.00
CD in miniature repica of original LP sleeve.						

Johnson, Jesse

Full Length

Label	Catalog Number	Title	Type	Country	Year	Longbox Value / Value
A&M	CD-5024	Jessie Johnson Revue	LP/LB	U.S.†	1985	$14.00/$8.00
		Singles				
A&M	S10Y-3048	Every Shade of Love	CD3	Japan	1988	$13.00/$4.00
A&M	390302-2	Love Struck	CD5	Germany	1989	$9.00
A&M	S10Y-3007	Love Struck	CD3	Japan	1988	$13.00/$4.00
A&M	CD 17547	Love Struck	CDJ	U.S.	1988	$2.00

Johnson, Johnnie

Singles

Label	Catalog Number	Title	Type	Country	Year	Longbox Value / Value
Elektra	PRCD 8826-2	Stumblin'	CDJ	U.S.	1993	$2.00
Elektra	PRCD 8437-2	Tanquerary	CDJ	U.S.	1991	$2.00

Johnson, Lisa

Singles

Label	Catalog Number	Title	Type	Country	Year	Longbox Value/Value
Alfa	ALDB-125	Love	CD3	Japan	1991	$12.00/$3.00
Alfa	ALDB-1041	Say Goodbye	CD3	Japan	1989	$12.00/$3.00

Johnson, Matt

Full Length

Label	Catalog Number	Title	Type	Country	Year	Longbox Value/Value
Critique	15405	Conversations	LP/LB	U.S.		$14.00/$8.00

Johnson, Michael

Singles

Label	Catalog Number	Title	Type	Country	Year	Longbox Value/Value
Atlantic	PRCD 4181-2	One Honest Tear	CDJ	U.S.	1991	$2.00
	PRCD 6575-2	One Way Out	CDJ	U.S.	1995	$2.00

Johnson, Paul

Singles

Label	Catalog Number	Title	Type	Country	Year	Longbox Value/Value
Columbia	PJOHNC-5	Burnin'	CD5	U.K.	1988	$8.00
Columbia	PJOHNC-9	Don't Make Me Wait Too Long	CD5	U.K.	1990	$8.00
CBS	PJOHN C-6	Every Kinda People	CDJ	Germany	1988	$8.00
CBS	PJOHNC6	Every Kinda People	CD5	U.K.	1988	$8.00
CBS	PJOHNC-8	Masquerade	CDJ	U.K.	1989	$8.00
Columbia	654596-3	No More Tomorrows	CD5	Germany	1989	$8.00
CBS	PJOHNC-7	No More Tomorrows	CD5	U.K.	1989	$8.00

Johnson, Puff

Singles

Label	Catalog Number	Title	Type	Country	Year	Longbox Value/Value
	OSK 7655	Forever More	CDJ	U.S.	1995	$2.00

Johnson, Robert

Full Length

Label	Catalog Number	Title	Type	Country	Year	Longbox Value/Value
Media America		Media America Specials	RS	U.S.	1991	$30.00

Airdate: 3/11/01

Johnston, Daniel

Singles

Label	Catalog Number	Title	Type	Country	Year	Longbox Value/Value
APT	TWANG-5CD	Big Big World	CD5	U.K.	1991	$8.00

Johnston, Freedy

Full Length

Label	Catalog Number	Title	Type	Country	Year	Longbox Value/Value
Westwood One		In Concert - Nu Rock	RS	U.S.	1995	$60.00

Airdate: 2/27/95.

Singles

Label	Catalog Number	Title	Type	Country	Year	Longbox Value/Value
	PRCD 8980-2	Bad Reputation	CDJ	U.S.		$2.00

Johnston, Sabrina

Singles

Label	Catalog Number	Title	Type	Country	Year	Longbox Value/Value
Eastwest	9031-76157-2	Friendship	CD5	Germany	1991	$8.00
Eastwest	YZ-637CD	Friendship	CD5	U.K.	1991	$8.00
Eastwest	YZ-661CD	I Wanna Swing	CD5	U.K.	1992	$8.00
Eastwest	WMD5-4099	Peace	CD3	Japan	1992	$13.00/$4.00
Eastwest	YZ-616CD	Peace	CD5	U.K.	1991	$8.00
Eastwest	9031-75403-2	Peace	CD5	U.K.	1991	$8.00

Johnston, Sophie And Peter

Singles

Label	Catalog Number	Title	Type	Country	Year	Longbox Value/Value
Pioneer	10SW-25	Dreams	CD3	Japan	1988	$12.00/$3.00

Joint Venture

Singles

Label	Catalog Number	Title	Type	Country	Year	Longbox Value/Value
Bellaphon	130-18-020	I Want to Thank You	CD5	Germany	1991	$8.00

JoJo

Singles

Label	Catalog Number	Title	Type	Country	Year	Longbox Value/Value
Profile	7406	Itz Da Joint	CDJ	U.S.	1993	$3.00
BMG	661603	Woman's Touch	CD5	Germany	1988	$8.00

Jolene

Singles

Label	Catalog Number	Title	Type	Country	Year	Longbox Value/Value
	7151224	Birdland	CDJ	U.S.		$2.00

Joling, Gerard

Singles

Label	Catalog Number	Title	Type	Country	Year	Longbox Value/Value
Polygram	878201-2	Corazon	CD5	Germany	1991	$8.00
Polygram	875353-2	Let This Night Last Forever	CD5	Germany	1990	$8.00
Polygram	24034-2	Love Is in Your Eyes	CD5	Germany	1990	$8.00
Polygram	874893-2	No More Bolero's	CD5	Germany	1991	$8.00

Jomanda

Full Length

Label	Catalog Number	Title	Type	Country	Year	Longbox Value/Value
Big Beat	4202	Someone to Love Me	LP/BP	U.S.		$14.00/$8.00

Singles

Label	Catalog Number	Title	Type	Country	Year	Longbox Value/Value
BCM	20409	Don't You Want My Love	CD5	Germany	1990	$8.00
RCA	PD-43406	Don't You Want My Love	CD5	U.K.	1990	$8.00
Giant	W-0040CD	Got a Love For You	CD5	U.K.	1991	$8.00
Big Beat	95947	I Cried the Tears	CD5	U.S.	1994	$4.00
Big Beat	5480	I Cried the Tears	CDJ	U.S.	1994	$2.00
Big Beat	5088	I Like It	CDJ	U.S.	1994	$2.00
Big Beat	5113	I Like It	CDJ	U.S.	1994	$2.00
Big Beat	5129	I Like It	CDJ	U.S.	1994	$2.00
BCM	20214	Make My Body Rock	CD5	Germany	1989	$8.00
RCA	PD-42750	Make My Body Rock	CD5	U.K.	1989	$8.00
Big Beat	10034	True Meaning of Love	CD5	U.S.		$4.00

Jon & Vangelis

Full Length

Label	Catalog Number	Title	Type	Country	Year	Longbox Value/Value
Polygram	821929-2	Best Of	LP/BP	U.S.†	1985	$14.00/$8.00
Polygram	800021-2	Friends of Mr. Cairo	LP/BP	U.S.†	1984	$14.00/$8.00
Polygram	813174-2	Private Collection	LP/BP	U.S.†	1984	$14.00/$8.00
Polygram	800027-2	Short Stones	LP/BP	U.S.†	1984	$14.00/$8.00

Jonah, Julian

Singles

Label	Catalog Number	Title	Type	Country	Year	Longbox Value/Value
Cooltempo	COOLCD-208	It's a Jungle Out There	CD5	U.K.	1990	$8.00
		It's a Jungle Out There	CDJ	U.S.	1990	$2.00

Jones, Brian

Full Length

Label	Catalog Number	Title	Type	Country	Year	Longbox Value/Value
Point		Brian Jones Presents the Pipes of Pan at Jajouka	LP	Japan		$30.00
Point	446 612-2	Brian Jones Presents the Pipes of Pan at Jajouka	LTD/LP	U.S.	1995	$40.00

2 CD set in book package.

Singles

Label	Catalog Number	Title	Type	Country	Year	Longbox Value/Value
Point	SACD 1122	Brian Jones Presents the Pipes of Pan at Jajouka	CDJ	U.S.	1995	$8.00

Jones, Brian – Brian Jones Presents the Pipes of Pan at Jajouka (Philips Classics 446 612-2)

Jones, David Lynn

Singles

Label	Catalog Number	Title	Type	Country	Year	Longbox Value/Value
Mercury	CDP 168	Lonely Town	CDJ	U.S.	1990	$2.00

Jones, Depp

Singles

Label	Catalog Number	Title	Type	Country	Year	Longbox Value/Value
CBS	656174-3	Luxury	CD3	Germany	1990	$8.00

Jones, Freddy

Singles

Label	Catalog Number	Title	Type	Country	Year	Longbox Value/Value
Capricorn	6473	Take the Time	CDJ	U.S.	1993	$2.00

Jones, Freddy Band

Singles

Label	Catalog Number	Title	Type	Country	Year	Longbox Value/Value
	PRO42022A	In a Daydream	CDJ	U.S.		$2.00

Jones, Garcia

Singles

Label	Catalog Number	Title	Type	Country	Year	Longbox Value/Value
Mercury	MERCD-323	Let the Music Play	CD5	U.K.	1990	$8.00

Jones, George

Full Length

Label	Catalog Number	Title	Type	Country	Year	Longbox Value/Value
Epic	EGK-38323	Anniversary: Ten Years of Hits	LP/LB	U.S.†	1985	$14.00/$8.00
Heartland	HD 3060	Best of George Jones, The	LP	U.S.		$20.00

2 CD set.

Label	Catalog Number	Title	Type	Country	Year	Longbox Value/Value
Polygram	522635	Collector's Edition	LTD/LP	U.S.	1994	$30.00
		Country Star Tracks	RS	U.S.	1991	$15.00

Airdate: 9/28/91.

Label	Catalog Number	Title	Type	Country	Year	Longbox Value/Value
Epic	EK-36586	I Am What I Am	LP/LB	U.S.†	1985	$14.00/$8.00
Image	ID6367ME	Living Legend in Concert	LD	U.S.		$25.00
Mercury		Original Mercury Masters	LTD/LP	U.S.	1994	$32.00

2CD set.

Singles

Label	Catalog Number	Title	Type	Country	Year	Longbox Value/Value
MCA	MCA5P-54749	High Tech Redneck	CDJ	U.S.	1993	$2.00
MCA	MCA5P-54370	Honky Tonk Myself to Death	CDJ	U.S.	1991	$2.00
MCA	MCA5P-54272	She Loved a Lot in Her Time	CDJ	U.S.	1991	$2.00
Epic	ESK 73424	Six Foot Deep	CDJ	U.S.	1990	$2.00
MCA	MCA5P-54687	Walls Can Fall	CDJ	U.S.	1992	$2.00
MCA	MCA5P-54604	Wrong's What I Do Best	CDJ	U.S.	1992	$2.00
MCA	MCA5P-54187	You Couldn't Get the Picture	CDJ	U.S.	1993	$2.00

Jones, Glenn

Singles

Label	Catalog Number	Title	Type	Country	Year	Longbox Value/Value
		Can We Try Again	CDJ	U.S.		$2.00
Jive	42089-2-JDJ	Every Step of the Way	CDJ	U.S.	1992	$2.00
Aris	886836	Stay	CD5	Germany	1990	$8.00
Jive	JIVECD-247	Stay	CD5	U.K.	1990	$8.00
		Stay	CDJ	U.S.	1990	$2.00

Jones, Grace

Full Length

Label	Catalog Number	Title	Type	Country	Year	Longbox Value/Value
Capitol	CDP-91737	Bulletproof Heart	LP/LB	U.S.	1989	$14.00/$9.00

Singles

Label	Catalog Number	Title	Type	Country	Year	Longbox Value/Value
EMI	203759-2	Amado Mio	CD5	Germany	1990	$8.00
Captiol	CDCL-571	Amado Mio	CD5	U.K.	1990	$8.00
EMI	203549-3	Love on Top of Love	CD3	Germany	1989	$8.00
Capitol	CDCL-557	Love on Top of Love	CD5	U.K.	1989	$8.00
Capitol	DPRO-79759	Love on Top of Love	CDJ	U.S.	1989	$2.00
Island	162-535-500	Sex Drive	CD5	U.S.	1993	$5.00
		Slave to the Rhythm	CD5	U.K.		$8.00
		Slave to the Rhythm	CD5	U.K.		$8.00

Second version.

Jones, Hank

Singles

Label	Catalog Number	Title	Type	Country	Year	Longbox Value/Value
Alfa	10R3-8	My Romance	CD3	Japan	1988	$12.00/$3.00

Jones, Hannah

Singles

Label	Catalog Number	Title	Type	Country	Year	Longbox Value/Value
Love Music	CDTMRC-4	In a Broken Dream	CD5	U.K.	1991	$8.00
Love Music	CDTMRC-7	Keep It On	CD5	U.K.	1992	$8.00
Love Music	CDTMRC-5	Strong Boy	CD5	U.K.	1991	$8.00

Jones, Howard

Full Length

Label	Catalog Number	Title	Type	Country	Year	Longbox Value/Value
Elektra	60390-2	Dream Into Action	LP/LB	U.S.†	1985	$14.00/$8.00

Label	Catalog Number	Title	Type	Country	Year	Longbox Value / Value
Elektra	60346-2	Human's Lib	LP/LB	U.S.†	1984	$14.00/$8.00

Singles

Label	Catalog Number	Title	Type	Country	Year	Longbox Value / Value
WEA	247077-2	Everlasting Love	CD3	Germany	1989	$10.00
Pioneer	09P3-6125	Everlasting Love	CD3	Japan	1989	$12.00/$4.00
Eastwest	HOW-13CD	Everlasting Love	CD3	U.K.	1989	$10.00
		Everlasting Love	CDJ	U.S.		$2.00
Eastwest	4509 92525	I.G.Y.	CD5	U.S.		$10.00
Eastwest	WMD5-4097	Lift Me Up	CD3	Japan	1992	$12.00/$4.00
Eastwest	HOW-15CD	Lift Me Up	CD5	U.K.	1991	$10.00
WEA	246917-2	Prisioner, The	CD3	Germany	1989	$10.00
Eastwest	9031-76516-2	Prisoner, The	CD5	Germany	1992	$10.00
Pioneer	09P3-6154	Prisoner, The	CD3	Japan	1989	$12.00/$4.00
Eastwest	HOW-14CD	Prisoner, The	CD3	U.K.	1989	$10.00
Elektra	66695-2	Prisoner, The	CD5	U.S.	1989	$5.00
Elektra	PRCD 8612-2	Tears to Tell	CDJ	U.S.	1992	$2.00

Jones, J.L.

Full Length

Label	Catalog Number	Title	Type	Country	Year	Longbox Value / Value
		Special Open Ended Conversation	DJ/Intvw	U.S.		$8.00

Jones, Jenny

Singles

Label	Catalog Number	Title	Type	Country	Year	Longbox Value / Value
Go Discs	GODCD-89	Blue	CD5	U.K.	1993	$8.00

Jones, Jo

Full Length

Label	Catalog Number	Title	Type	Country	Year	Longbox Value / Value
Denon	CD-7047	Our Man, Papa Jo	LP/LB	U.S.†	1985	$14.00/$8.00

Jones, Jo Ann

Singles

Label	Catalog Number	Title	Type	Country	Year	Longbox Value / Value
Champion	CHAMPCD-81	I Don't Need Your Love	CD5	U.K.	1988	$8.00
Champion	CHAMPCD-220	I Don't Need Your Love	CD5	U.K.	1989	$8.00

Jones, Karen

Singles

Label	Catalog Number	Title	Type	Country	Year	Longbox Value / Value
Polygram	873887-2	To the Rock	CD5	Germany	1990	$8.00

Jones, Kipper

Singles

Label	Catalog Number	Title	Type	Country	Year	Longbox Value / Value
		Shock Wave	CDJ	U.S.		$2.00

Jones, Marta

Singles

Label	Catalog Number	Title	Type	Country	Year	Longbox Value / Value
Alfa	ALDB-49	Relight My Fire	CD3	Japan	1990	$12.00/$3.00

Jones, Marti

Full Length

Label	Catalog Number	Title	Type	Country	Year	Longbox Value / Value
Polygram	395086-2	Unsophisticated Time	LP	Germany		$15.00

Singles

Label	Catalog Number	Title	Type	Country	Year	Longbox Value / Value
RCA	2545-2-RDJ	Any Kind of Lie	CDJ	U.S.	1990	$2.00
A&M	S10Y-3042	Real One	CD3	Japan	1988	$12.00/$3.00

Jones, Mick

Singles

Label	Catalog Number	Title	Type	Country	Year	Longbox Value / Value
Atlantic	PR 3018-2	4 Wheels Turnin'	CDJ	U.S.	1989	$2.00
Atlanti	PR 2592-2	Everything That Comes Around	CDJ	U.S.	1989	$2.00
WEA	786300-2	Just Wanna Hold	CD5	Germany	1989	$10.00
Pioneer	09P3-6131	Just Wanna Hold	CD3	Japan	1989	$12.00/$4.00
Atlantic	PR 2854-2	Just Wanna Hold	CDJ	U.S.	1989	$2.00

Jones, Quincy

Full Length

Label	Catalog Number	Title	Type	Country	Year	Longbox Value / Value
QWest	9 280202-DJ	Back on the Block	DJ/LP	U.S.	1989	$10.00
A&M	CD-3200	Best of	LP/LB	U.S.†	1985	$14.00/$8.00
Verve	822470-2	Great Wide World of Quincy Jones	LP/LB	U.S.†	1985	$14.00/$8.00
Warner Brothers	9 46109-2	Q's Jook Joint	LTD/LP	U.S.	1995	$10.00/$30.00

CD, booklet, poster, photo, cards, coaster and swizzle stick in box.

Label	Catalog Number	Title	Type	Country	Year	Longbox Value / Value
Warner Brothers	PRO-CD-7997-R	Q's Jook Joint Jazz Sampler	DJ/Smplr	U.S.	1995	$8.00
Emarcy	822469-2	The Birth of a Band	LP/LB	U.S.†	1985	$14.00/$8.00
A&M	CD-3721	The Dude	LP/LB	U.S.†	1985	$14.00/$8.00

Singles

Label	Catalog Number	Title	Type	Country	Year	Longbox Value / Value
A&M	S12Y-3036	Ai No Corrida	CD3	Japan	1988	$15.00/$4.00
WEA	9362-40006-2	Back on the Block	CD5	Germany	1991	$10.00
WEA	W-0047CD	Back on the Block	CD5	U.K.	1991	$10.00
A&M	390343-2	Compact Hits	CD5	Germany	1988	$10.00
A&M	AMCD-908	Compact Hits	CD5	U.K.	1988	$10.00
QWest	PRO-CD-4343	I Don't Go For That	CDJ	U.S.	1989	$2.00
QWest	9 21594-2	I Don't Go For That	CD5	U.S.	1990	$5.00
WEA	921430-2	I'll Be Good to You	CD5	Germany	1989	$10.00
Qwest	09P3-6209	I'll Be Good to You	CD3	Japan	1989	$15.00/$4.00
WEA	W-2697CD	I'll Be Good to You	CD5	U.K.	1989	$10.00
QWest	9 21402-2	I'll Be Good to You	CD5	U.S.	1989	$5.00
QWest	PRO-CD-3832	I'll Be Good to You	CDJ	U.S.	1989	$2.00
Warner Brothers		Introducing Tamia: You Put a Move	CDJ	U.S.	1995	$3.00
QWest	PRO-CD-4496	Jazz Corner Of the World	CDJ	U.S.	1990	$2.00
WEA	7599-2186-2	Listen Up	CD5	Germany	1990	$10.00
Warner Brothers	WPDP-6260	Listen Up	CD3	Japan	1990	$15.00/$4.00
QWest	PRO-CD-4444	Listen Up	CDJ	U.S.	1990	$2.00
Warner Brothers	WPDP-6265	Places You Find Love, The	CD3	Japan	1989	$15.00/$4.00
Qwest	W-0001CD	Places You Find Love, The	CD5	U.K.	1990	$10.00
QWest	PRO-CD-4458	Places You Find Love, The	CDJ	U.S.	1989	$2.00
QWest	PRO-CD-4569	Places You Find Love, The	CDJ	U.S.	1989	$2.00
WEA	WPDP-6215	Secret Garden, The	CD3	Japan	1990	$15.00/$4.00
Qwest	W-9992CD	Secret Garden, The	CD5	U.K.	1990	$10.00
Warner Brothers	9 18893-2	Secret Garden, The	CD5	U.S.	1992	$5.00
Warner Brothers		Secret Garden, The	CDJ	U.S.	1992	$2.00
Warner Brothers	PRO-CD-8104-R	Slow James	CDJ	U.S.	1995	$3.00
WEA	921504-2	Tomorrow	CD5	Germany	1990	$10.00
Warner Brothers	PRO-CD-3986	Tomorrow	CDJ	U.S.	1989	$2.00
Qwest	PRo-CD-4048	Wee B. Dooinit	CDJ	U.S.	1989	$2.00
Warner Brothers	17751	You Put a Move On My Heart	CD5	U.S.	1995	$5.00

Jones, Rickie Lee

Full Length

Label	Catalog Number	Title	Type	Country	Year	Longbox Value / Value
Geffen	PRO-CD-4320	A Special Open Ended Conversation for Radio	DJ/Intvw	U.S.	1991	$13.00
Geffen	2-24246-2-DJ	Flying Cowboys	DJ/LP	U.S.	1989	$50.00

2 CD set.

Label	Catalog Number	Title	Type	Country	Year	Longbox Value / Value
Warner Brothers	25117-2	Magaine, The	LP/LB	U.S.†	1985	$15.00/$9.00
Reprise	PRO-CD-7813	Naked Songs Sampler	DJ/Smplr	U.S.		$10.00
Warner Brothers	3432-2	Pirates	LP/LB	U.S.†	1985	$15.00/$9.00
Warner Brothers	03296-2	Rickie Lee Jones	LP/LB	U.S.†	1984	$15.00/$9.00
Geffen		Traffic From Paradise	LTD/LP	Austalia	1994	$37.00

CD of album plus "live" disc.

Singles

Label	Catalog Number	Title	Type	Country	Year	Longbox Value / Value
Geffen	PRO-CD-3924	Don't Let the Sun Catch You Crying	CDJ	U.S.	1989	$2.00
Geffen	PRO-CD-3956	Don't Let the Sun Catch You Crying	CDJ	U.S.	1989	$2.00
Geffen	PRO-CD-4113	Flying Cowboys	CDJ	U.S.		$2.00
Geffen	PRO-CD-4604	Rebel Rebel	CDJ	U.S.	1993	$2.00
Geffen	GEF-64CD	Satellites	CD3	U.K.	1989	$10.00
Geffen	PRO-CD-3715	Satellites	CDJ	U.S.	1989	$2.00
		Stewart's Coat	CD5	Australia	1994	$12.00
Geffen	PRO-CD-4608	Stewart's Coat	CDJ	U.S.	1993	$2.00

Jones, Spike

Singles

Label	Catalog Number	Title	Type	Country	Year	Longbox Value / Value
RCA	64222	Rudolph the Red Nosed Reindeer	CD5	U.S.	1994	$5.00

Jones, Steve

Singles

Label	Catalog Number	Title	Type	Country	Year	Longbox Value / Value
MCA	CD45 18179	Fire and Gasoline	CDJ	U.S.	1990	$6.00
MCA	DMCAT-1371	Freedom Fighter	CD5	U.K.	1989	$8.00
MCA	CD45 17953	Freedom Fighter	CDJ	U.S.	1989	$2.00
MCA	CD45 17991	Freedom Fighter	CDJ	U.S.	1989	$2.00

Jones, Thad

Full Length

Label	Catalog Number	Title	Type	Country	Year	Longbox Value / Value
Blue Note		Magnificent, The	LTD/LP	U.S.	1995	$19.00

Jones, Tiffany

Singles

Label	Catalog Number	Title	Type	Country	Year	Longbox Value / Value
Toshiba	TODP-2304	Make Me Look	CD3	Japan	1991	$12.00/$3.00

Jones, Tom

Full Length

Label	Catalog Number	Title	Type	Country	Year	Longbox Value / Value
Mercury	818 814-2	Darlin'	LP/BP	U.S.†	1984	$12.00/$7.00
Mercury	810192-2	Golden Hits	LP/BP	U.S.		$12.00/$7.00
London	820 182-2	Love Is on the Radio	LP/BP	U.S.†	1985	$12.00/$7.00
	ASCD-103	Tom Jones	DJ/Smplr	Japan	1995	$50.00
CBS/Fox	4511-80	Tom Jones	LD	U.S.	1985	$35.00
WHV/HBO	90664	Tom Jones	LD	U.S.	1992	$30.00

Singles

Label	Catalog Number	Title	Type	Country	Year	Longbox Value / Value
BMG	CHILDCD-93	All You Need Is Love	CD5	U.K.	1993	$10.00
Jive	ZD-43098	At This Moment	CD5	Germany	1989	$10.00
Jive	JIVECD-219	At This Moment	CD5	U.K.	1989	$10.00
EMI	323698	Carrying a Torch	CD5	Germany	1991	$10.00
Dover	ROJCD-12	Carrying a Torch	CD5	U.K.	1990	$10.00
EMI	323630-2	Couldn't Say Goodbye	CD5	Germany	1991	$10.00
Dover	ROJCD-10	Couldn't Say Goodbye	CD5	U.K.	1990	$10.00
		Delilah	CD5	U.K.		$10.00
		Delilah	CD5	U.K.		$10.00

Second version.

Label	Catalog Number	Title	Type	Country	Year	Longbox Value / Value
Dover	ROJCD 19	I'm Not Feeling It Anymore	CD5	U.K.	1991	$10.00
	PRCD 5926	If I Only Knew	CDJ	U.S.		$2.00
Atlantic	95809	If I Only Knew	CD5	U.S.	1994	$5.00
Jive	246933-2	Move Closer	CD5	Germany	1989	$10.00
Jive	JIVECD-203	Move Closer	CD5	U.K.	1988	$10.00
Jive	1230-2-JDJ	Move Closer	CDJ	U.S.	1989	$2.00

Jones, Tom and Englebert Humperdink

Full Length

Label	Catalog Number	Title	Type	Country	Year	Longbox Value / Value
Eclipse	4864-2	Their Greatest Hits	LTD/LP	U.S.	1996	$18.00

CD in custom screen-printed square tin.

Jones, Tracy

Singles

Label	Catalog Number	Title	Type	Country	Year	Longbox Value / Value
ZYX	6744-8	Promise Me Forever	CD5	Germany	1992	$10.00

Jones, Willi

Singles

Label	Catalog Number	Title	Type	Country	Year	Longbox Value / Value
Geffen	PRO-CD-4124	Love Me Up	CDJ	U.S.	1990	$2.00

Jones, Zeon

Singles

Label	Catalog Number	Title	Type	Country	Year	Longbox Value / Value
Polygram	873091-2	Spin Me Around	CD5	Germany	1989	$8.00

Joneses

Singles

Label	Catalog Number	Title	Type	Country	Year	Longbox Value / Value
Atlantic	PR 3176-2	Don't You Know	CDJ	U.S.	1990	$2.00
Atlantic	PRCD 3421-2	Let's Live Together	CDJ	U.S.	1990	$2.00
Atlantic	PR 3311-2	Steppin' Out	CDJ	U.S.	1990	$2.00

Joplin, Janis – Six Sides of Janis (Columbia CSK 5223)

Joplin, Janis

Full Length

Label	Catalog Number	Title	Type	Country	Year	Longbox Value / Value
Sony	SRCS-7911	Cheap Thrill	LTD/LP	Japan	1995	$35.00

20 Bit Mastering.

Label	Catalog Number	Title	Type	Country	Year	Longbox Value / Value
Sony	SRCS-6255/6	Janis	LP	Japan		$55.00

2 CD set.

Label	Catalog Number	Title	Type	Country	Year	Longbox Value / Value
CBS	CK-30322	Pearl	LP/BP	U.S.†	1984	$14.00/$8.00
Columbia	CSK 5223	Six Sides of Janis	DJ/Smplr	U.S.	1993	$18.00

Jordan, Alison

Singles

Label	Catalog Number	Title	Type	Country	Year	Longbox Value / Value
Arista	74321-100422	Boy From New York City	CD5	U.K.	1992	$9.00

Jordan, Clifford

Full Length

Label	Catalog Number	Title	Type	Country	Year	Longbox Value/Value
Blue Note		Blowing in From Chicago	LTD/LP	U.S.	1994	$20.00

Jordan, Duke

Full Length

Label	Catalog Number	Title	Type	Country	Year	Longbox Value/Value
Blue Note		Flight to Jordan	LTD/LP	U.S.	1995	$19.00

Jordan, Jeremy

Singles

Label	Catalog Number	Title	Type	Country	Year	Longbox Value/Value
Giant	BVDG-1	Wanna Girl	CD5	U.K.	1993	$2.00
Giant	9 40823-2	Wanna Girl	CD5	U.S.	1993	$4.00

Jordan, Kevin

Full Length

Label	Catalog Number	Title	Type	Country	Year	Longbox Value/Value
		No Sign of Rain	DJ/Smplr	Canada		$5.00

Jordan, Louis

Singles

Label	Catalog Number	Title	Type	Country	Year	Longbox Value/Value
MCA	MCSTD-1517	Five Guys Named Moe	CD5	U.K.	1991	$8.00

Jordan, Marc

Full Length

Label	Catalog Number	Title	Type	Country	Year	Longbox Value/Value
RCA	6549-2-RDJ	Catch the Moon	DJ/Smplr	U.S.		$7.00

Singles

Label	Catalog Number	Title	Type	Country	Year	Longbox Value/Value
RCA	6931-2-RDJ	Catch the Moon	CDJ	U.S.	1987	$2.00
RCA	2547-2-RDJ	Edge of the World	CDJ	U.S.	1990	$2.00

Jordan, Michael

Full Length

Label	Catalog Number	Title	Type	Country	Year	Longbox Value/Value
Upper Deck	44456	23 Nights: The Jordan Experience	LTD/LP	U.S.	1996	$25.00
		Interview CD and 23 basketball cards in box.				

Jordan, Montell

Singles

Label	Catalog Number	Title	Type	Country	Year	Longbox Value/Value
	PRCD 7080-2	Daddy's Home	CDJ	U.S.		$2.00
Polygram	851469	This Is How We Do	CD5	U.S.	1995	$6.00

Jordan, Ronny

Singles

Label	Catalog Number	Title	Type	Country	Year	Longbox Value/Value
4th & B'way	536	After Hours	CDJ	U.S.	1992	$2.00
4th & B'way	558	After Hours	CDJ	U.S.	1992	$6.00
4th & B'way	588	After Hours	CDJ	U.S.	1994	$2.00
Island	CID-521	Get To Grips	CD5	U.K.	1992	$8.00
4th & B'way	570	Get To Grips	CDJ	U.S.	1992	$2.00
4th & B'way	586	Silent Night	CDJ	U.S.	1993	$2.00
Antillies	ANNCD-14	So What	CD5	U.K.	1992	$8.00
4th & B'way	554	So What	CDJ	U.S.	1994	$2.00

Jordan, Sass

Full Length

Label	Catalog Number	Title	Type	Country	Year	Longbox Value/Value
Album Network		Album Network Special	RS	U.S.	1994	$80.00
		Airdate: 10/9/94.				
Westwood One		In Concert	RS	U.S.	1995	$80.00
		Airdate: 1/16/95.				
Westwood One		Off the Record	RS	U.S.	1992	$30.00
		Airdate: 7/27/92.				

Singles

Label	Catalog Number	Title	Type	Country	Year	Longbox Value/Value
Impact	2929	High Road Easy	CDJ	U.S.	1994	$2.00
Impact	2193	Make You a Believer	CDJ	U.S.	1992	$2.00
Atlantic	PR 3113-2	So Hard	CDJ	U.S.	1989	$2.00
Atlantic	PR 2892-2	Tell Somebody	CDJ	U.S.	1989	$2.00
IMP	2306	You Don't Have to Remind Me	CDJ	U.S.	1992	$2.00

Jordan, Stanley

Full Length

Label	Catalog Number	Title	Type	Country	Year	Longbox Value/Value
Capital	CDP-46092	Magic Touch	LP/LB	U.S.†	1985	$14.00/$8.00

Singles

Label	Catalog Number	Title	Type	Country	Year	Longbox Value/Value
Arista	ASCD-2655	Bolero	CDJ	U.S.	1994	$2.00

Jordy

Singles

Label	Catalog Number	Title	Type	Country	Year	Longbox Value/Value
Columbia	CSK 5191	Dur Dur D'Etre Bebe	CDJ	U.S.	1993	$2.00

Jose & Luis

Singles

Label	Catalog Number	Title	Type	Country	Year	Longbox Value/Value
Sire	9 40543-2	Queen's English	CD5	U.S.	1993	$4.00

Joseph, Jeff

Singles

Label	Catalog Number	Title	Type	Country	Year	Longbox Value/Value
Polydor	PZCD-51	Big Beat	CD5	U.K.	1989	$8.00

Joseph, Julian

Singles

Label	Catalog Number	Title	Type	Country	Year	Longbox Value/Value
Eastwest	YZ-600CD	Other Side Of Town	CD5	U.K.	1991	$8.00

Joseph, Martyn

Singles

Label	Catalog Number	Title	Type	Country	Year	Longbox Value/Value
Epic	658855-5	Please Sir	CD5	U.K.	1992	$8.00
Epic		Please Sir	CD5	U.K.	1992	$8.00
		Second version.				

Joshua, Maurice

Singles

Label	Catalog Number	Title	Type	Country	Year	Longbox Value/Value
CBS	658101-2	I Gotta Hold On U	CD5	U.K.	1992	$8.00

Joshua Trio

Singles

Label	Catalog Number	Title	Type	Country	Year	Longbox Value/Value
Son	BUACD-192	Fly	CD5	U.K.	1991	$8.00

Journey

Full Length

Label	Catalog Number	Title	Type	Country	Year	Longbox Value/Value
Columbia	CSK 4880	A Test of Time	DJ/Smplr	U.S.	1992	$15.00
CBS	CGK-37016	Captured	LP/BP	U.S.†	1985	$14.00/$8.00
CBS	CK-37406	Escape	LP/BP	U.S.†	1984	$14.00/$8.00
CBS	CK-38504	Frontiers	LP/BP	U.S.†	1984	$14.00/$8.00
Album Network		In the Studio (Escape)	RS	U.S.	1989	$25.00
		Airdate: 9/4/89.				
Album Network		In the Studio (Escape)	RS	U.S.	1991	$25.00
		Airdate: 7/8/91.				
Album Network		In the Studio (Infinity)	RS	U.S.	1988	$25.00
		Airdate: 12/19/88.				
Album Network		In the Studio (Time)	RS	U.S.		$55.00
		2 CD set.				
Sony	SRCS-7912	Infinity	LTD/LP	Japan	1995	$35.00
		20 Bit Mastering.				
DIR		King Biscuit Flour Hour	RS	U.S.	1989	$30.00
		Airdate: 2/26/89.				
DIR		King Biscuit Flour Hour	RS	U.S.	1990	$30.00
		With Michael Penn, Airdate: 10/21/90.				
DIR		King Biscuit Flour Hour	RS	U.S.	1991	$30.00
		Airdate: 12/8/91.				
DIR		King Biscuit Flour Hour	RS	U.S.	1993	$40.00
		Airdate: 2/21/93.				
DIR		King Biscuit Flour Hour	RS	U.S.	1994	$30.00
		Airdate: 2/14/94.				
DIR		King Biscuit Flour Hour	RS	U.S.	1995	$35.00
		Airdate: 3/5/95.				
DIR		King Biscuit Flour Hour	RS	U.S.	1996	$35.00
		Airdate: 2/4/96.				
Columbia	48937	Time 3	LP	U.S.	1992	$45.00
		3 CD set in 6"x12" box.				
Media America		Up Close	RS	U.S.	1989	$30.00
		2 CD set.				

Singles

Label	Catalog Number	Title	Type	Country	Year	Longbox Value/Value
Columbia	38K 07951	Don't Stop Believin'	CD3	U.S.	1988	$7.00/$4.00
Columbia	CSK 4920	Lights	CDJ	U.S.	1992	$7.00
Columbia	38K 78428	When You Love a Woman	CD5	U.S.	1996	$2.00/$4.00
Sony	10EP-3025	Who's Crying Now	CD3	Japan	1988	$12.00/$4.00
Columbia	654541-2	Who's Crying Now	CD5	U.K.	1989	$10.00

Joy

Singles

Label	Catalog Number	Title	Type	Country	Year	Longbox Value/Value
Swanyard	CDSYR-15	I'm Leaving	CD5	U.K.	1990	$8.00
Alfa	ALCB-426	Shine On	CD5	Japan	1992	$12.00

Joy Division

Full Length

Label	Catalog Number	Title	Type	Country	Year	Longbox Value/Value
	DCI-3098	Collection	DJ/Smplr	Japan	1995	$150.00

Singles

Label	Catalog Number	Title	Type	Country	Year	Longbox Value/Value
Factory	FACD-213	Atmosphere	CD5	U.K.	1988	$10.00
		Love Will Tear Us Apart '95	CD5	U.K.	1995	$10.00
Aris	883516	Peel Sessions	CD5	Germany	1990	$10.00
Strange Frt	SFPSCD-013	Peel Sessions	CD5	U.K.	1988	$10.00
Strange Frt	SFPSCD-013	Peel Sessions	CD5	U.S.	1988	$10.00
Aris	883519	Peel Sessions 2	CD5	Germany	1990	$10.00
Strange Frt	SFPSCD-033	Peel Sessions 2	CD5	U.K.	1990	$10.00
Strange Frt	SFPSCD-033	Peel Sessions 2	CD5	U.S.	1990	$10.00

Joy, Jason

Singles

Label	Catalog Number	Title	Type	Country	Year	Longbox Value/Value
Go Discs	GODCD-81	Free Your Body	CD5	U.K.	1992	$8.00

Joy, Ruth

Singles

Label	Catalog Number	Title	Type	Country	Year	Longbox Value/Value
Eastwest	257414-2	Don't Push It	CD3	Germany	1989	$8.00
MCA	MCSTD-1574	Feel	CD5	U.K.	1992	$8.00

Joya

Singles

Label	Catalog Number	Title	Type	Country	Year	Longbox Value/Value
A&M	581167	Gettin' Off on You	CD5	U.S.	1995	$5.00
	ATCD00091	Love U All Ova	CDJ	U.S.		$2.00

Joykiller

Singles

Label	Catalog Number	Title	Type	Country	Year	Longbox Value/Value
	86451S22	Go Bang	CDJ	U.S.		$2.00
	86451S2	Seventeen	CDJ	U.S.		$2.00

Joystick

Singles

Label	Catalog Number	Title	Type	Country	Year	Longbox Value/Value
Polygram	889625-2	My Girl	CD3	Germany	1989	$8.00
Polygram	889624-3	My Girl	CD3	Germany	1989	$8.00

JT Company

Singles

Label	Catalog Number	Title	Type	Country	Year	Longbox Value/Value
WEA	171693-2	Don't Deal With Us	CD5	Germany	1990	$8.00

JTQ & McKoy Noel

Singles

Label	Catalog Number	Title	Type	Country	Year	Longbox Value/Value
		See a Brighter Day	CD5	U.K.		$8.00
		See a Brighter Day	CD5	U.K.		$8.00
		Second version.				

Judas Priest

Full Length

Label	Catalog Number	Title	Type	Country	Year	Longbox Value/Value
RCA	4933	Best of	LP/BP	U.S.		$14.00/$8.00
Gull	GUCD 1026	Best of, The	LP	U.K.	1987	$15.00
CBS	CK-39219	Defenders of the Faith	LP/LB	U.S.†	1984	$14.00/$8.00
CBS	7104-80	Fuel for Life	LD	U.S.	1990	$25.00
DIR		King Biscuit Flour Hour	RS	U.S.	1991	$40.00
		Airdate: 2/17/91.				
CBS	5134-80	Live	LD	U.S.	1990	$25.00
		Metal Works Sampler	DJ/Smplr	U.K.		$25.00
Columbia	C1070013	Priest....Live!	DJ/Smplr	U.S.	1988	$25.00
RCA	5041	Rocka Rolla	LP/BP	U.S.		$12.00/$7.00
RCA	4747	Sad Wings of Destiny	LP/BP	U.S.		$12.00/$7.00
CBS	CK-38160	Screaming for Vengence	LP/LB	U.S.†	1985	$14.00/$8.00
Columbia	CSK 2133	Sharpest Cuts, The	DJ/Smplr	U.S.	1990	$20.00
		9 Track sampler in display card listing 10 tracks.				
Columbia	CSK 2133	Sharpest Cuts, The	DJ/Smplr	U.S.	1990	$30.00
		10 Track sampler housed in slimlne jewel case.				
Epic	ESCA-5858	Star Box	DJ/Smplr	Japan		$35.00

Singles

Label	Catalog Number	Title	Type	Country	Year	Longbox Value/Value
Columbia	656589 2	A Touch of Evil	CD5	U.K.	1991	$10.00
Columbia	CSK 2218	A Touch of Evil	CDJ	U.S.	1990	$2.00
Columbia	CSK 1249	Blood Red Skies	CDJ	U.S.	1988	$2.00
Columbia	CSK1149	I Am a Rocker	CDJ	U.S.	1989	$2.00
Atlantic	A-9114CD	Johnny B. Goode!	CD3	U.K.	1988	$10.00
Atlantic	A9114CD	Johnny B. Goode!	CD5	U.K.	1988	$15.00
Columbia	CSK 3030	Night Crawler	CDJ	U.S.	1991	$2.00
Columbia	CSK 3030	Night Crawler	CDJ	U.S.	1991	$9.00
		With rubber worm.				
Columbia	656273-3	Painkiller	CD3	Germany	1990	$10.00
Columbia	656273-2	Painkiller	CD5	Germany	1990	$10.00
CBS	651689-3	Ram It Down	CD3	Germany	1988	$10.00
CBS	651689-3	Ram It Down	CD3	U.K.	1988	$10.00
Columbia	656589-2	Touch of Evil	CD5	U.K.	1991	$10.00
		'90s Country	RS	U.S.	1996	$40.00
		Airdate: 3/23/96.				

Judd, Wynonna

Full Length

Label	Catalog Number	Title	Type	Country	Year	Longbox Value/Value
Curb	MCA3P-10822	Tell Me Why	DJ/LP	U.S.	1993	$15.00
		Picture disc.				

Label	Catalog Number	Title	Type	Country	Year	Longbox Value / Value
Curb	2171	Wynonna	DJ/LP	U.S.	1992	$35.00
	CD in Guitar-shaped package.					
MCA	MCA3P-3666	Wynonna Sampler	DJ/Smplr	U.S.	1996	$18.00
		Singles				
Curb	MCA5P-54875	Girls With Guitars	CDJ	U.S.	1994	$15.00
	CD in Guitar-shaped package.					
Curb	ALDB-156	I Saw the Light	CD3	Japan	1992	$12.00/$4.00
Curb	MCA5P-54754	Is It Over Yet	CDJ	U.S.	1993	$3.00
Curb	MCA5P-54516	My Strongest Weakness	CDJ	U.S.	1992	$3.00
		No One Else on Earth	CD5	U.K.	1994	$10.00
Curb	MCA5P-2398	No One Else on Earth	CDJ	U.S.	1992	$3.00
Curb	MCA5P-54449	No One Else on Earth	CDJ	U.S.	1992	$3.00
Curb	MCA5P-54689	Only Love	CDJ	U.S.	1993	$3.00
Curb	MCA5P-54809	Rock Bottom	CDJ	U.S.	1994	$3.00
Curb	MCA5P-54320	She Is His Only Need	CDJ	U.S.	1992	$3.00
Curb	MCA5P-54606	Tell Me Why	CDJ	U.S.	1993	$3.00

Judds

Full Length

Label	Catalog Number	Title	Type	Country	Year	Value
Pioneer Artists	PA-89-240	Across The Heartland	LD	U.S.	1989	$30.00
		Judd Music Sampler	DJ/Smplr	U.S.	1992	$15.00
RCA	PCD1-5319	Why Not Me	LP/BP	U.S.†	1985	$14.00/$8.00
		Singles				
RCA	62038-2-RDJ	John Deere Tractor	CDJ	U.S.	1991	$3.00

Judgment Night

Full Length

Label	Catalog Number	Title	Type	Country	Year	Value
		Street Legal Version	DJ/Smplr	U.S.		$15.00

Judybats

Singles

Label	Catalog Number	Title	Type	Country	Year	Value
Sire	PRO-CD-5982	Being Simple	CDJ	U.S.	1993	$2.00
Sire	PRO-CD-6073	Being Simple	CDJ	U.S.	1993	$2.00
Sire	9 40134-2	Daylight	CD5	U.S.	1991	$4.00
Sire	6185	Incredible Bittersweet	CDJ	U.S.	1993	$2.00
Sire	PRO-CD-5439	Is Anything	CDJ	U.S.	1992	$2.00
		Native Son	CDJ	U.S.		$2.00
Warner Brothers	PRO-CD-5265	Saturday	CDJ	U.S.		$2.00
Sire	9 21772-2	She Lives	CD5	U.S.	1990	$4.00
Sire	PRO-CD-6425	Ugly on the Outside	CDJ	U.S.	1993	$2.00

June, Cathaline

Singles

Label	Catalog Number	Title	Type	Country	Year	Value
King	KIDP-34	Destiny	CD3	Japan	1991	$12.00/$3.00

Jungle Brothers

Singles

Label	Catalog Number	Title	Type	Country	Year	Value
Eternal	921598-2	Doin' Our Own Thang	CD5	Germany	1990	$8.00
Eternal	W-9754CD	Doin' Our Own Thang	CD5	U.K.	1990	$8.00
ZYX	6000-8	I'll House You	CD5	Germany	1988	$6.00
ZYX	6000R-8	I'll House You	CD5	U.K.	1988	$6.00
Eternal	921512-2	What U Waiting 4	CD5	Germany	1990	$8.00
Eternal	W-9865CD	What U Waiting 4	CD5	U.K.	1990	$8.00
		What U Waiting 4	CDJ	U.S.	1990	$2.00

Jungle of Trouble

Singles

Label	Catalog Number	Title	Type	Country	Year	Value
Repertoire	RR-6002	Somebody to Love	CD5	Germany	1989	$8.00

Junior

Singles

Label	Catalog Number	Title	Type	Country	Year	Value
MCA	MCSTD-1691	All Over the World	CD5	U.K.	1992	$10.00
MCA	CD45 1262	Better Part of Me	CDJ	U.S.	1991	$2.00
MCA	CD45 1413	Step Off	CDJ	U.S.	1991	$2.00
MCA	MCSTD-1676	Then Came You	CD5	U.K.	1992	$10.00

Junior Mafia

Singles

Label	Catalog Number	Title	Type	Country	Year	Value
	PRCD 6573-2	Get Money	CDJ	U.S.		$2.00
	PRCD 6494-2	I Need You Tonight	CDJ	U.S.		$2.00
	PRCD 6214-2	Player's Anthem	CDJ	U.S.		$2.00

Junior Trucker

Singles

Label	Catalog Number	Title	Type	Country	Year	Value
Virgin	TENCD-299	Don't Test	CD5	U.K.	1990	$8.00
BMG	663427	Sixteen	CD5	Germany	1990	$8.00
Virgin	TENCD-316	Sixteen	CD5	U.K.	1990	$8.00
Virgin	TENCD-382	You Don't Care For Me	CD5	U.K.	1991	$8.00

Junk Monkeys

Full Length

Label	Catalog Number	Title	Type	Country	Year	Value
Metal Blade	45100	Bliss	LP/LB	U.S.		$14.00/$8.00
Metal Blade	26490	Five Star Fling	LP/LB	U.S.		$14.00/$8.00
		Singles				
Metal Blade	PRO-CD-5986	Bliss	CDJ	U.S.	1993	$2.00

Junkhouse

Singles

Label	Catalog Number	Title	Type	Country	Year	Value
Epic		Out of My Head	CDJ	Canada	1994	$5.00
Epic	ESK 5794	Out of My Head	CDJ	U.S.	1994	$2.00

Junkyard

Singles

Label	Catalog Number	Title	Type	Country	Year	Value
Geffen	PRO-CD-4237	All the Time in the World	CDJ	U.S.	1991	$2.00
Geffen	PRO-CD-3514	Hollywood	CDJ	U.S.	1989	$2.00
Geffen	PRO-CD-4303	Nowhere to Go But Down	CDJ	U.S.	1991	$6.00
Geffen	PRO-CD-3858	Simple Man	CDJ	U.S.	1989	$2.00
Geffen	PRO-CD-4339	Slipping Away	CDJ	U.S.	1991	$2.00

Jupiter Project

Singles

Label	Catalog Number	Title	Type	Country	Year	Value
EMI	TODP-2289	Because I Love You	CD3	Japan	1991	$12.00/$3.00
EMI	TOCP-6640	Give	CD5	Japan	1991	$12.00
EMI	TOCP-6742	Nature's Callin'	CD5	Japan	1991	$12.00
EMI	TOCP-7001	Nature's Callin'	CD5	Japan	1991	$12.00

Just Fred

Singles

Label	Catalog Number	Title	Type	Country	Year	Value
	PRO-CD-8091	Bulldozer	CDJ	U.S.	1995	$2.00

Just Seventeen

Singles

Label	Catalog Number	Title	Type	Country	Year	Value
BCM	20517	Miracle of Love	CD5	Germany	1990	$8.00

Juzz Fact

Singles

Label	Catalog Number	Title	Type	Country	Year	Value
ZYX	DMP-22002-8	Feel the Rhythm	CD5	Germany	1991	$8.00

Jv

Singles

Label	Catalog Number	Title	Type	Country	Year	Value
Thump Records	9926	Nayba'hood Queen	CD5	U.S.	1994	$5.00

K.A. Posse

Singles

Label	Catalog Number	Title	Type	Country	Year	Value
CBS	655518-2	Dig This	CD5	U.K.	1990	$8.00

K.C. Flight

Singles

Label	Catalog Number	Title	Type	Country	Year	Value
		Jump for Joy	CDJ	U.S.		$2.00
Popular	PD-49404	Planet E	CD5	U.K.	1989	$8.00
Popular	PD-49336	Summer Madness	CD5	U.K.	1989	$8.00

K.C. & The Sunshine Band

Singles

Label	Catalog Number	Title	Type	Country	Year	Value
BMG	663229	Game of Love	CD5	Germany	1990	$10.00
		Game of Love	CDJ	U.S.		$2.00
Columbia	655103-3	That's the Way I Like It	CD3	Germany	1989	$10.00
Bellaphon	130-21-001	That's the Way I Like It	CD5	Germany	1990	$10.00
Italio-Heat	STH-547CD	That's the Way I Like It	CD5	Germany	1990	$10.00
BMG	MCDFAC-2	That's the Way I Like It	CD5	U.K.	1991	$10.00

K.O.C.

Singles

Label	Catalog Number	Title	Type	Country	Year	Value
SPV	8426-3	Let Your Love Flow	CD5	Germany	1989	$9.00

K.W.S.

Singles

Label	Catalog Number	Title	Type	Country	Year	Value
Pinnacle	NWKCD-65	Hold Back the Night	CD5	U.K.	1992	$8.00
EMI	TODP-2384	Keep It Comin' Love	CD3	Japan	1992	$12.00/$3.00
EMI	TODP-2376	Please Don't Go	CD3	Japan	1992	$12.00/$3.00
Pinnacle	NWKCD-46	Please Don't Go	CD5	U.K.	1992	$8.00
Pinnacle	NWKCD-54	Rock Your Baby	CD5	U.K.	1992	$8.00

K.X.P.

Singles

Label	Catalog Number	Title	Type	Country	Year	Value
Slam Jam	SLAM-11CD	Ain't No Mountain High Enough	CD5	U.K.	1992	$8.00

K-9 Posse

Singles

Label	Catalog Number	Title	Type	Country	Year	Value
Arista	662087	Ain't Nothin' to It	CD5	Germany	1989	$8.00
Arista	ASCD 2196	Get Wild Go Crazy	CDJ	U.S.	1991	$2.00

K-Ci & Jojo The Hailey Bros.

Singles

Label	Catalog Number	Title	Type	Country	Year	Value
Uptown	UPT5P3531	Beautiful	CDJ	U.S.		$2.00

K-Creative

Singles

Label	Catalog Number	Title	Type	Country	Year	Value
Talkin' Loud	TLKCD-32	Stitch in Time	CD5	U.K.	1992	$8.00
Talkin' Loud	TLKCD-27	Summer Breeze	CD5	U.K.	1992	$8.00
Talkin' Loud	TLKCD-20	To Be Free	CD5	U.K.	1992	$8.00

K-Klass

Singles

Label	Catalog Number	Title	Type	Country	Year	Value
Parlophone	CDR-6325	Don't Stop	CD5	U.K.	1992	$8.00
Parlophone	CDR-6302	Rhythm Is a Mystery	CD5	U.K.	1991	$8.00
Parlophone	CDR-6309	So Right	CD5	U.K.	1992	$8.00
Parlophone		What You're Missing	CD5	U.K.	1993	$8.00
Parlophone		What You're Missing	CD5	U.K.	1993	$8.00
	Second version.					

K-sam

Singles

Label	Catalog Number	Title	Type	Country	Year	Value
Youngsta	2473	Infamous Playa	CD5	U.S.	1994	$5.00

K3M

Singles

Label	Catalog Number	Title	Type	Country	Year	Value
PWL	PWCD-214	Listen to the Rhythm	CD5	U.K.	1992	$8.00

K7

Singles

Label	Catalog Number	Title	Type	Country	Year	Value
Tommy Boy	572	Come Baby Come	CD5	U.S.	1993	$5.00
Tommy Boy	607	Come Baby Come	CDJ	U.S.	1993	$2.00
Tommy Boy	572	Come Baby Come	CD5	U.S.	1994	$5.00
Tommy Boy	611	Zunga Zeng	CDJ	U.S.	1993	$2.00

Kadison, Joshua

Full Length

Label	Catalog Number	Title	Type	Country	Year	Value
		Painted Desert Serenade	LTD/LP	U.K.	1996	$35.00
	2 CD set.					
		Singles				
SBK	58099	Beautiful in My Eyes	CD5	U.S.	1993	$5.00
SBK	DPRO-04620	Beautiful in My Eyes	CDJ	U.S.	1993	$2.00

Kage, L.

Singles

Label	Catalog Number	Title	Type	Country	Year	Value
A&M	31458 8165	Freed by Your Love	CDJ	U.S.	1993	$2.00

Kah, Hubert

Singles

Label	Catalog Number	Title	Type	Country	Year	Value
Intercord	825 583	Military Drums	CD5	Germany	1990	$8.00
Intercord	825 763	So Many People	CD3	Germany	1989	$8.00
Intercord	825 722	Welcome, Machine Gun	CD5	Germany	1989	$8.00
CBS	10EP-3261	Welcome, Machine Gun	CD3	Japan	1989	$12.00/$3.00

Kahn, Brenda

Singles

Label	Catalog Number	Title	Type	Country	Year	Value
Chaos	5096	Anesthesia	CDJ	U.S.	1993	$2.00

Kairos, Grace

Singles

Label	Catalog Number	Title	Type	Country	Year	Value
RCA	PD-43152	Carolina	CD5	Germany	1989	$8.00
RCA	PD-43426	I Don't Know What's Going On	CD5	Germany	1989	$8.00

Kaiser, Henry

Full Length

Label	Catalog Number	Title	Type	Country	Year	Value
		Five Heavenly Truths	LP/LB	U.S.		$12.00/$7.00
Reckless		Hope You Like Our New Direction	LP/LB	U.S.		$12.00/$7.00

Kalapana

Singles

Label	Catalog Number	Title	Type	Country	Year	Value
Canyon	PCDY-00046	Back in Your Heart Again	CD3	Japan	1990	$12.00/$3.00

Kam

Singles

Label	Catalog Number	Title	Type	Country	Year	Longbox Value / Value
Eastwest	PRCD 4867-2	Peace Treaty	CDJ	U.S.	1992	$2.00
Elektra/Asylum	66173	Pull Ya Hoe Card	CD5	U.S.	1994	$5.00

Kamen, Michael

Singles

Label	Catalog Number	Title	Type	Country	Year	Longbox Value / Value
Warner Brothers	PRO-CD-4544	Sasha	CDJ	U.S.	1990	$2.00

Kamen, Nick

Singles

Label	Catalog Number	Title	Type	Country	Year	Longbox Value / Value
WEA	247788-2	Bring Me Your Love	CD3	Germany	1988	$8.00
Pioneer	10P3-6063	Bring Me Your Love	CD3	Japan	1988	$12.00/$3.00
WEA	YZ-202CD	Bring Me Your Love	CD3	U.K.	1988	$8.00
WEA	9031-70839-2	I Promised Myself	CD3	Germany	1990	$8.00
WEA	YZ-454CD	I Promised Myself	CD5	U.K.	1990	$8.00
Atlantic	PRCD 3404-2	I Promised Myself	CDJ	U.S.	1990	$2.00
WEA	9031-72958-2	Looking Good Diving	CD5	Germany	1990	$8.00
WEA	172020-2	Oh How Happy	CD5	Germany	1990	$8.00
WEA	YZ-501CD	Oh How Happy	CD5	U.K.	1990	$8.00
WEA	247915-2	Tell Me	CD5	Germany	1988	$8.00
Pioneer	10P3-6020	Tell Me	CD3	Japan	1988	$12.00/$3.00
WEA	YZ-184CD	Tell Me	CD5	U.K.	1988	$8.00
WEA	YZ-672CD	We'll Never Lose What We Have Found	CD5	U.K.	1992	$8.00
WEA	9031-77028-2	You're Not the Only One	CD5	Germany	1992	$8.00
WEA	YZ-655CD	You're Not the Only One	CD5	U.K.	1992	$8.00

Kane, Carmen

Singles

Label	Catalog Number	Title	Type	Country	Year	Longbox Value / Value
CBS	654857-3	Sorry If I Broke Your Heart	CD3	Germany	1989	$8.00

Kane Gang

Singles

Label	Catalog Number	Title	Type	Country	Year	Longbox Value / Value
Capitol	C2 48176	Miracle	CD5	U.S.	1987	$2.00
Kitchenware	080 029-2	Motortown	CDV	U.K.	1988	$10.00

Kanga

Singles

Label	Catalog Number	Title	Type	Country	Year	Longbox Value / Value
Polygram	887695-2	Anything for Kicks	CD5	Germany	1988	$8.00

Kano

Singles

Label	Catalog Number	Title	Type	Country	Year	Longbox Value / Value
Polygram	867429-2	Another Life	CD5	Germany	1991	$8.00

Kansas

Full Length

Label	Catalog Number	Title	Type	Country	Year	Longbox Value / Value
Kirshner	ZK-39283	Best Of	LP/LB	U.S.†	1984	$14.00/$8.00
MCA	MCAD-6254	In the Spirit of Things	LP/LB	U.S.		$14.00/$8.00
Album Network		In the Studio (Leftoverture)	RS	U.S.	1988	$25.00
	Airdate: 11/14/88.					
Album Network		In the Studio (Leftoverture)	RS	U.S.	1992	$25.00
	Airdate: 10/7/92.					
Album Network		In the Studio (Point of No Return)	RS	U.S.	1989	$25.00
	Airdate: 8/21/89.					
DIR		King Biscuit Flour Hour	RS	U.S.	1988	$40.00
	With Queen, Airdate: 8/7/88.					
DIR		King Biscuit Flour Hour	RS	U.S.	1989	$40.00
	Airdate: 6/11/89.					
DIR		King Biscuit Flour Hour	RS	U.S.	1991	$30.00
	With King's X, Airdate: 1/20/91.					
DIR		King Biscuit Flour Hour	RS	U.S.	1992	$40.00
	Airdate: 5/10/92.					
DIR		King Biscuit Flour Hour	RS	U.S.	1993	$40.00
	Airdate: 9/19/93.					
Kirshner	ZK-34929	Point of No Return	LP/LB	U.S.†	1984	$14.00/$8.00
MCA	MCAD-5838	Power	LP/LB	U.S.		$14.00/$8.00
		Power	DJ/Smplr	U.S.	1994	$10.00
Westwood One		Superstars	RS	U.S.	1995	$75.00
	2 CD set. Airdate: 10/16/95.					
		Two for Tuesday	DJ/Smplr	Canada	1995	$15.00

Singles

Label	Catalog Number	Title	Type	Country	Year	Longbox Value / Value
		One Big Sky	CDJ	U.S.		$2.00
MCA	10P3-6053	Stand Beside Me	CD3	Japan	1988	$12.00/$4.00
MCA	CD45 17657	Stand Beside Me	CDJ	U.S.	1988	$2.00
Epic	ZSK 6018-2	Wheels	CDJ	U.S.		$3.00

Kaoma

Full Length

Label	Catalog Number	Title	Type	Country	Year	Longbox Value / Value
Image	ID7398CB	Lambada Videos, The	8"LD	U.S.	1989	$6.00

Singles

Label	Catalog Number	Title	Type	Country	Year	Longbox Value / Value
Columbia	656974-2	Danca Tago Mago	CD5	Germany	1989	$8.00
Columbia	656974-2	Danca Tago Mago	CD5	U.K.	1989	$8.00
Columbia	655235-3	Dancando	CD3	Germany	1990	$8.00
Columbia	655235-5	Dancando	CD5	U.K.	1990	$8.00
Columbia	655011-3	Lambada	CD3	Germany	1989	$8.00
Epic	ESDA-7009	Lambada	CD3	Japan	1989	$12.00/$3.00
Columbia	655011-2	Lambada	CD5	U.K.	1989	$8.00
		Lambada	CDJ	U.S.		$2.00
	Second version.					
Epic	ESK 73090	Lambada	CDJ	U.S.	1989	$2.00
CBS	655637-3	Lambamor	CD3	Germany	1990	$8.00
Epic	ESDA-7041	Lambamor	CD3	Japan	1990	$12.00/$3.00
Epic	ESDA-7020	Melodie D'Amour	CD3	Japan	1990	$12.00/$3.00
CBS	655636-2	Melodie D'Amour	CD5	U.K.	1990	$8.00

Kaos

Singles

Label	Catalog Number	Title	Type	Country	Year	Longbox Value / Value
Kool Kat	KOOL-504CD	Definition of Love	CD5	U.K.	1990	$8.00
Kool Kat	KOOLCD-5042	Gonna Get Over You	CD5	U.K.	1990	$8.00

Kariya

Singles

Label	Catalog Number	Title	Type	Country	Year	Longbox Value / Value
Pinnacle	SBUKSCD-4	Let Me Love You for Tonight	CD5	U.K.	1990	$8.00

Karr, Tim

Singles

Label	Catalog Number	Title	Type	Country	Year	Longbox Value / Value
EMi	203788-2	Rubbin' Me the Right Way	CD5	Germany	1990	$8.00

Kash Da Masta

Singles

Label	Catalog Number	Title	Type	Country	Year	Longbox Value / Value
ZYX	6449-8	Get Ya Yourself Together	CD5	Germany	1990	$8.00

Kashif

Full Length

Label	Catalog Number	Title	Type	Country	Year	Longbox Value / Value
Arista	ARCD-8205	Send Me Your Love	LP/LB	U.S.†	1984	$14.00/$8.00

Singles

Label	Catalog Number	Title	Type	Country	Year	Longbox Value / Value
Arista	ASCD-9626	Love Changes	CDJ	U.S.	1987	$2.00
Arista	A10D-134	Personality	CD3	Japan	1989	$12.00/$3.00

Kastle, Richard

Full Length

Label	Catalog Number	Title	Type	Country	Year	Longbox Value / Value
Virgin	PRCD KASTLE	Streetwise	DJ/LP	U.S.	1991	$12.00

Kat

Singles

Label	Catalog Number	Title	Type	Country	Year	Longbox Value / Value
Life	5	Do You Wanna Party	CDJ	U.S.	1993	$2.00
	79014	Do You Wanna Party	CD5	U.S.	1994	$5.00

Katherine E

Singles

Label	Catalog Number	Title	Type	Country	Year	Longbox Value / Value
WEA	DOOD-2CD	I'm Alright	CD5	U.K.	1991	$8.00
WEA	PWCD-213	Then I Feel Good	CD5	U.K.	1992	$8.00

Kathy And The Tones

Singles

Label	Catalog Number	Title	Type	Country	Year	Longbox Value / Value
Polygram	873087-2	Love Is Not Systematic	CD5	Germany	1989	$8.00

Katmandu

Full Length

Label	Catalog Number	Title	Type	Country	Year	Longbox Value / Value
		A Case for the Blues	LP	U.K.		$12.00
Epic	ESK 2216	Katmandu	DJ/LP	U.S.		$8.00

Singles

Label	Catalog Number	Title	Type	Country	Year	Longbox Value / Value
Epic	ESK 4008	Way You Make Me Feel, The	CDJ	U.S.	1991	$2.00
CBS	ESDA-7062	When the Rain Comes	CD3	Japan	1991	$12.00/$3.00
		When the Rain Comes	CDJ	U.S.		$2.00

Katrina And The Waves

Full Length

Label	Catalog Number	Title	Type	Country	Year	Longbox Value / Value
Fame	CDFA-3204	Katrina and The Waves	LP	U.K.		$15.00
Capitol	CDP 7 46266 2	Waves	LP/LB	U.S.	1986	$15.00/$10.00

Singles

Label	Catalog Number	Title	Type	Country	Year	Longbox Value / Value
Line	9 01137	Brown Eyed Son	CD5	Germany	1991	$8.00
BMG	664685	Pet the Tiger	CD5	Germany	1991	$8.00
EMI	203610-2	Rock & Roll Girl	CD3	Germany	1990	$8.00
SBK	CDSBK-3	Rock & Roll Girl	CD5	U.K.	1989	$8.00
SBK	DPRO-05318	Rock & Roll Girl	CDJ	U.S.	1989	$2.00
BMG	664872	Tears of a Woman	CD5	Germany	1991	$8.00
EMI	203442-3	That's the Way	CD3	Germany	1989	$8.00
Toshiba	XP10-2106	That's the Way	CD3	Japan	1989	$13.00/$3.00
SBK	CDSBK-2	That's the Way	CD5	U.K.	1989	$8.00
SBK	DPRO-06304	That's the Way	CDJ	U.S.	1989	$2.00
		Walking on Sunshine	CD5	U.K.	1996	$10.00
EMI	203878-2	We Got to Get Out of This Place	CD5	Germany	1990	$8.00
SBK	DPRO-05331	We Got to Get Out of This Place	CDJ	U.S.	1990	$2.00

Katt, Jeanette

Full Length

Label	Catalog Number	Title	Type	Country	Year	Longbox Value / Value
A&M	5397	Pink Mischief	LP/LB	U.S.		$12.00/$7.00

Singles

Label	Catalog Number	Title	Type	Country	Year	Longbox Value / Value
A&M	75021 7397-2	Girl Noise	CDJ	U.S.	1992	$2.00
A&M		Girl Noise	CDJ	U.S.	1992	$2.00
	Second version.					
A&M	31458 8066	When I Do Wrong I Do So Right	CDJ	U.S.	1992	$2.00

Katydids

Full Length

Label	Catalog Number	Title	Type	Country	Year	Longbox Value / Value
Reprise	9 26626-2-Dj	Shangri-La	DJ/LP	U.S.	1991	$12.00
	Picture disc.					

Singles

Label	Catalog Number	Title	Type	Country	Year	Longbox Value / Value
Reprise	W-0065CD	Boy Who's Never Found	CD5	U.K.	1991	$9.00
WEA	W-9758CD	Girl In A Jigsaw	CD5	U.K.	1990	$9.00
Reprise	PRO-CD-4094	Heavy Weather Traffic	CDJ	U.S.		$2.00
WEA	W-9852CD	Lights Out	CD5	U.K.	1990	$8.00
Reprise	9 21732-2	Lights Out	CD5	U.S.	1990	$5.00
Reprise	W-0051CD	Seesaw	CD5	U.K.	1991	$8.00
Reprise	W-0082CD	Some Mysterious Sigh	CD5	U.K.	1992	$8.00

Kay, Janet

Singles

Label	Catalog Number	Title	Type	Country	Year	Longbox Value / Value
Sony	SRDS-8210	Imagine	CD3	Japan	1991	$12.00/$3.00
Sony	SRDS-8200	Loving You	CD3	Japan	1991	$12.00/$3.00
Sony	SRDS-8256	Missing You	CD3	Japan	1993	$12.00/$3.00
BMG	MFDCD-006	Silly Games	CD5	U.K.	1990	$2.00

Kayo

Singles

Label	Catalog Number	Title	Type	Country	Year	Longbox Value / Value
BMG	CDBORG-4	Change of Attitude	CD5	U.K.	1990	$8.00

KBC Band

Full Length

Label	Catalog Number	Title	Type	Country	Year	Longbox Value / Value
Arista	ARCD 8440	KBC	LP/LB	U.S.	1986	$18.00/$13.00

KE

Singles

Label	Catalog Number	Title	Type	Country	Year	Longbox Value / Value
RCA	RDJ643712	Strange World	CDJ	U.S.		$2.00
RCA	RDJ643302	Strange World	CDJ	U.S.		$2.00

Keane, Dolores

Singles

Label	Catalog Number	Title	Type	Country	Year	Longbox Value / Value
Pinnacle	DKS-4CD	Lion in a Cage	CD5	U.K.	1989	$8.00

Keaton, Karl

Singles

Label	Catalog Number	Title	Type	Country	Year	Longbox Value / Value
BMG	664383	I Remember	CD5	Germany	1991	$8.00
Arista	563971	Loves Again	CD5	Germany	1991	$8.00
Arista	563971	Loves Again	CD5	U.K.	1991	$8.00
BMG	665082	You Love Me	CD5	Germany	1992	$8.00

Kee, John P.

Singles

Label	Catalog Number	Title	Type	Country	Year	Longbox Value / Value
Verity	43010	I Won't Leave You Anymore	CDJ	U.S.	1994	$2.00

Keedy

Full Length

Label	Catalog Number	Title	Type	Country	Year	Longbox Value / Value
Arista		Chase the Clouds	DJ/LP	U.S.	1991	$30.00
	CD, cassette, VHS video and pin in 12"x12" box.					

Singles

Label	Catalog Number	Title	Type	Country	Year	Longbox Value / Value
Arista	BVDA-23	Always Together	CD3	Japan	1991	$12.00/$3.00
Arista	BVDA-33	Never Neverland	CD3	Japan	1991	$12.00/$3.00
Arista	663991	Save Some Love	CD5	Germany	1991	$8.00
Arista	BVDA-16	Save Some Love	CD3	Japan	1991	$12.00/$3.00
Arista	663991	Save Some Love	CD5	U.K.	1991	$8.00
Arista	BVDA-22	Wishing on the Same Star	CD3	Japan	1991	$12.00/$3.00

Keene, Tommy

Singles

Label	Catalog Number	Title	Type	Country	Year	Longbox Value / Value
Geffen	PRO-CD-3414	Our Car Club	CDJ	U.S.	1989	$2.00
Matador	039	Sleeping on a Rollercoaster	CD5	Canada	1992	$6.00

Keineg, Katell

Singles

Label	Catalog Number	Title	Type	Country	Year	Longbox Value / Value
Elektra	66268	Heslia	CD5	U.S.	1993	$4.00

Keita, Salif

Singles

Label	Catalog Number	Title	Type	Country	Year	Longbox Value / Value
		Cono	CDJ	U.S.		$2.00

Keith, Lisa

Singles

Label	Catalog Number	Title	Type	Country	Year	Longbox Value / Value
Perspective	31458 8178	Better Than You	CDJ	U.S.	1993	$2.00
Perspective	31458 8242	I'm in Love	CDJ	U.S.	1993	$2.00
Perspective	31458 7444	Love Is Alive and Well	CDJ	U.S.	1993	$2.00

Keith, Martin

Singles

Label	Catalog Number	Title	Type	Country	Year	Longbox Value / Value
CBS	77816	Never Find Someone	CD5	U.S.	1994	$5.00

Keith, Toby

Full Length

Label	Catalog Number	Title	Type	Country	Year	Longbox Value / Value
		Big of Truck/Truckload of Hits	DJ/Smplr	U.S.		$18.00
		Blue Moon	DJ/LP	U.S.		$0.00
		Boomtown	DJ/Intvw	U.S.	1994	$12.00
		Christmas to Christmas	DJ/Intvw	U.S.	1995	$12.00

Kelly G

Singles

Label	Catalog Number	Title	Type	Country	Year	Longbox Value / Value
Paparazzi	CLIKCD-1	Teach Me	CD5	U.K.	1992	$8.00

Kelly, Marie

Singles

Label	Catalog Number	Title	Type	Country	Year	Longbox Value / Value
ZYX	DST-1028-8	Feels Like I'm In Love	CD5	Germany	1990	$8.00

Kelly, Paul (and The Messengers)

Singles

Label	Catalog Number	Title	Type	Country	Year	Longbox Value / Value
A&M	CD 17912	Careless	CDJ	U.S.	1989	$2.00
A&M	S10Y-3044	Dumb Things	CD3	Japan	1988	$12.00/$3.00
A&M	CD 17578	Dumb Things	CDJ	U.S.	1988	$2.00
		God's Hotel	CD5	Australia	1994	$10.00
		Love Never Runs on Time	CD5	Australia		$10.00
		Song From the Sixteenth Floor	CD5	Australia		$10.00
A&M	CD 17849	Sweet Guy	CDJ	U.S.	1989	$2.00
A&M	CD 17624	To Her Door	CDJ	U.S.	1988	$2.00
Mushroom	D11060	When I First Met Your Ma	CD5	Australia	1992	$10.00
A&M	390336-2	Won't Get Fooled Again	CD5	Germany	1988	$8.00

Kelly R. and Public Announcement

Full Length

Label	Catalog Number	Title	Type	Country	Year	Longbox Value / Value
Jive	01241-41469	Born into the '90s	DJ/LP	U.S.	1992	$15.00

CD and cassette in bag.

Singles

Label	Catalog Number	Title	Type	Country	Year	Longbox Value / Value
Jive	42206-2	Bump 'n Grind	CD5	U.S.	1994	$5.00
Jive	42206	Bump n Grind	CD5	U.S.	1994	$5.00
Jive	42206-2-JDJ	Bump 'n Grind	CDJ	U.S.	1994	$2.00
Jive	JDJ-42115-2	Dedicated	CDJ	U.S.	1992	$2.00
		Down Low	CDJ	U.S.		$2.00
Jive	JIVECD-306	Honey Love	CD5	U.K.	1992	$8.00
Jive	JDJ-42031-2	Honey Love	CDJ	U.S.	1992	$2.00
Jive	01241-42422-2	I Believe I Can Fly	CD5	U.S.	1996	$5.00
Jive	JDJ-42184-2	Sex Me	CDJ	U.S.	1993	$2.00
Jive	42185	Sex Me	CD5	U.S.	1994	$5.00
Jive	JIVECD-292	She's Got That Vibe	CD5	U.K.	1992	$8.00
Jive	JIVECD-326	She's Got That Vibe	CD5	U.K.	1992	$8.00
Jive	JDJ-42025-2	She's Got That Vibe	CDJ	U.S.	1992	$2.00
Jive	JDJ-42092-2	Slow Dance	CDJ	U.S.	1992	$2.00
		Summer Bunnies	CD5	U.K.		$10.00
		Summer Bunnies	CD5	U.K.		$10.00

Second version.

Label	Catalog Number	Title	Type	Country	Year	Longbox Value / Value
Jive		Your Body's Callin'	CD5	U.K.	1994	$9.00
Jive		Your Body's Callin'	CD5	U.K.	1994	$9.00

Second version.

Label	Catalog Number	Title	Type	Country	Year	Longbox Value / Value
Jive	42221	Your Body's Callin'	CD5	U.S.	1994	$6.00

Kelly, Wynton

Singles

Label	Catalog Number	Title	Type	Country	Year	Longbox Value / Value
Polydor	15YD-6001	Autumn Leaves	CD3	Japan	1988	$12.00/$3.00

Keltner, Lance

Singles

Label	Catalog Number	Title	Type	Country	Year	Longbox Value / Value
Eastwest	PRCD 4477-2	Party's Over	CDJ	U.S.	1992	$2.00

Kemp, Johnny

Singles

Label	Catalog Number	Title	Type	Country	Year	Longbox Value / Value
CBS	654838-3	Birthday Suit	CD3	Germany	1989	$8.00
Sony	10EP-3080	Birthday Suit	CD3	Japan	1989	$12.00/$3.00
Sony	12EP-3068	Dancin' With Myself	CD3	Japan	1989	$12.00/$3.00
Columbia	653020-2	Dancin' With Myself	CD5	U.K.	1988	$8.00
		Dancin' With Myself	CDJ	U.S.	1988	$2.00
CBS	651470-3	Just Got Paid	CD3	Germany	1989	$8.00
Sony	10EP-3041	Just Got Paid	CD3	Japan	1988	$12.00/$3.00
Columbia	651470-2	Just Got Paid	CD5	U.K.	1989	$8.00
		One Thing Leads to Another	CDJ	U.S.		$2.00

Kemp, Tara

Full Length

Label	Catalog Number	Title	Type	Country	Year	Longbox Value / Value
Giant		Tara Kemp	DJ/LP	U.S.		$8.00

Singles

Label	Catalog Number	Title	Type	Country	Year	Longbox Value / Value
Giant	WPDP-6273	Hold You Tonight	CD3	Japan	1991	$12.00/$3.00
Giant	W-0020CD	Hold You Tonight	CD5	U.K.	1991	$8.00
Giant	PRO-CD-4617	Hold You Tonight	CDJ	U.S.	1990	$2.00
Giant	W-0048CD	Piece of My Heart	CD5	U.K.	1991	$8.00
Giant	PRO-CD-4743	Piece of My Heart	CDJ	U.S.	1991	$2.00
Giant	PRO-CD-5006	Too Much	CDJ	U.S.		$2.00

Kennedy, Brian

Singles

Label	Catalog Number	Title	Type	Country	Year	Longbox Value / Value
RCA	PD-43912	Believe It	CD5	U.K.	1990	$8.00
RCA	PD-43418	Captured	CD5	U.K.	1990	$8.00
RCA	PD-43638	Hollow	CD5	U.K.	1990	$8.00

Kennedy, Ray

Singles

Label	Catalog Number	Title	Type	Country	Year	Longbox Value / Value
Sony	SRDS-8238	Just for the Moment	CD3	Japan	1992	$12.00/$3.00
		What a Way to Go	CDJ	U.S.		$2.00

Kennedy, Rose

Singles

Label	Catalog Number	Title	Type	Country	Year	Longbox Value / Value
EMI	241044-2	Love Like This	CD5	Germany	1990	$8.00
IRS	PAND 13	Love Like This	CDJ	U.S.	1990	$2.00
EMI	204106-2	Only Change	CD5	Germany	1991	$8.00

Kenny And Dolly

Full Length

Label	Catalog Number	Title	Type	Country	Year	Longbox Value / Value
Pioneer Artists	PA-86-175	Real Love	LD	U.S.	1987	$25.00

Kenny G.

Full Length

Label	Catalog Number	Title	Type	Country	Year	Longbox Value / Value
Arista	ARCD-8192	G Force	LP/LB	U.S.†	1984	$14.00/$8.00
Arista	ARCD-8282	Gravity	LP/LB	U.S.†	1985	$14.00/$8.00
Image	ID7907VP	Kenny G.	LD	U.S.		$15.00
Pioneer Artists	PA-90-003	Live	LD	U.S.	1990	$30.00

Singles

Label	Catalog Number	Title	Type	Country	Year	Longbox Value / Value
Arista	662293	Against Doctors Orders	CD5	U.K.	1990	$10.00
Arista	BVDA-65	By the Time This Night is Over	CD3	Japan	1993	$13.00/$4.00
Arista		By the Time This Night is Over	CD5	U.K.	1993	$10.00
Arista		By the Time This Night is Over	CD5	U.K.	1993	$10.00

Second version.

Label	Catalog Number	Title	Type	Country	Year	Longbox Value / Value
Arista	12566	By the Time This Night is Over	CD5	U.S.	1993	$4.00
Arista	12707	Even if My Heart	CD5	U.S.	1994	$6.00
Arista	BVDA-38	Forever in Love	CD3	Japan	1992	$12.00/$4.00
Arista	12517	Forever in Love	CD5	U.S.	1992	$5.00
Arista	ASCD-2482	Forever in Love	CDJ	U.S.	1992	$2.00
Arista	ASCD-2618	Sentimental	CDJ	U.S.	1993	$2.00
Arista	A10D-113	Silhouette	CD3	Japan	1989	$12.00/$4.00
Arista		Silhouette	CDJ	U.S.	1988	$2.00
Arista	661832	Silhouettes	CD5	Germany	1988	$10.00
Arista	661832	Silhouettes	CD5	U.K.	1988	$10.00
Arista	BVDA-26	Theme From Dying Young	CD3	Japan	1991	$12.00/$4.00
Arista	664592	Theme From Dying Young	CD5	U.K.	1991	$10.00
Arista	ASCD-2267	Theme From Dying Young	CDJ	U.S.	1991	$2.00
Arista	A10D-117	We've Saved the Best For Last	CD3	Japan	1989	$12.00/$4.00
Arista	161961	We've Saved the Best For Last	CD3	U.K.	1989	$10.00
Arista		We've Saved the Best For Last	CDJ	U.S.	1989	$2.00

Kenton, Stan

Full Length

Label	Catalog Number	Title	Type	Country	Year	Longbox Value / Value
Mosaic	MD4-136	Complete Capitol Recordings	LTD/LP	U.S.		$60.00

4 CD set. Limited to 7500 copies.

Kentucky Headhunters

Singles

Label	Catalog Number	Title	Type	Country	Year	Longbox Value / Value
Mercury	CDP 179	Dumas Walker	CDJ	U.S.	1990	$3.00
Mercury	CDP 524	It's Chillin' Time	CDJ	U.S.	1991	$3.00
Mercury	CDP 553	Let's Work Together	CDJ	U.S.	1991	$3.00
Mercury	CDP 246	Oh Lonesome Me	CDJ	U.S.	1989	$3.00
Mercury	CDP 565	Only Daddy That Will Walk the Line	CDJ	U.S.	1991	$3.00

Kenyatta

Singles

Label	Catalog Number	Title	Type	Country	Year	Longbox Value / Value
Delicious Vinyl	0111	I Wanna Do Something Freaky to You	CDJ	U.S.	1990	$2.00
Delicious Vinyl	BRCD-254	Keep Me Comin'	CD5	U.K.	1992	$8.00
Delicious Vinyl	BRCD-226	Love Again	CD5	U.K.	1992	$8.00

Kenyon, Carol

Singles

Label	Catalog Number	Title	Type	Country	Year	Longbox Value / Value
CBS	654707-3	Fascinating	CD3	Germany	1989	$8.00

Kerbdog

Full Length

Label	Catalog Number	Title	Type	Country	Year	Longbox Value / Value
Mercury		Live at Concrete	DJ/Smplr	U.S.	1995	$10.00

Singles

Label	Catalog Number	Title	Type	Country	Year	Longbox Value / Value
		Dry Riser	CD5	U.K.	1993	$8.00
		Dry Riser	CD5	U.K.	1993	$8.00

Second version.

Label	Catalog Number	Title	Type	Country	Year	Longbox Value / Value
		Dummy Crusher	CD5	U.K.		$10.00
		Dummy Crusher	CD5	U.K.		$10.00

Second version.

Kerosene

Singles

Label	Catalog Number	Title	Type	Country	Year	Longbox Value / Value
Sire	9 40884-2	Got Nothing to Say	CD5	U.S.	1993	$4.00
Dead Good	GOOD-21CD	Sink	CD5	U.K.	1992	$8.00
Sire	PRO-CD-6689	Spring	CDJ	U.S.	1993	$2.00

Kerouac, Jack

Full Length

Label	Catalog Number	Title	Type	Country	Year	Longbox Value / Value
Rhino	90044	Sampler	DJ/Smplr	U.S.	1990	$10.00

Kershaw, Nik

Singles

Label	Catalog Number	Title	Type	Country	Year	Longbox Value / Value
Eastwest	257277-3	Elisabeth Eyes	CD5	Germany	1989	$10.00
MCA	DNIKT-13	Elisabeth Eyes	CD5	U.K.	1989	$10.00
MCA	8 20966	One Step Ahead	CD3	Germany	1988	$10.00
MCA	10P3-6084	One Step Ahead	CD3	Japan	1989	$12.00/$3.00
MCA	DNIK-12	One Step Ahead	CD3	U.K.	1988	$10.00
MCA	MCD-18236	Wouldn't It Be Good	CD5	Germany	1991	$10.00
MCA	NIKTD-14	Wouldn't It Be Good	CD5	U.K.	1991	$10.00

Kershaw, Sammy

Full Length

Label	Catalog Number	Title	Type	Country	Year	Longbox Value / Value
		'90s Country	RS	U.S.	1995	$30.00

Airdate: 9/16/95.

Label	Catalog Number	Title	Type	Country	Year	Longbox Value / Value
		Christmas a Comin'	DJ/Intvw	U.S.	1995	$12.00
		Live at the Crazy Horse	RS	U.S.	1994	$40.00

Airdate: 5/16/94.

Singles

Label	Catalog Number	Title	Type	Country	Year	Longbox Value / Value
Mercury	CDP 749	Anywhere But Here	CDJ	U.S.	1991	$2.00
Mercury	CDP 511	Cadillac Style	CDJ	U.S.	1991	$2.00
Mercury	CDP 598	Don't Go Near the Water	CDJ	U.S.	1991	$2.00
Mercury	CDP 959	I Can't Reach Her Anymore	CDJ	U.S.	1993	$2.00
Mercury	CDP 825	She Don't Know She's Beautiful	CDJ	U.S.	1993	$2.00

Ketchum, Hal

Full Length

Label	Catalog Number	Title	Type	Country	Year	Longbox Value / Value
		Every Little Word	RS	U.S.		$15.00

Key Club

Singles

Label	Catalog Number	Title	Type	Country	Year	Longbox Value / Value
ZYX	DST-1043-8	Just Dance	CD5	Germany	1991	$6.00

Keys, Amy

Singles

Label	Catalog Number	Title	Type	Country	Year	Longbox Value / Value
CBS	655200-2	Good for You	CD5	U.K.	1989	$8.00
CBS	654810-2	Lover's Intuition	CD5	U.K.	1989	$8.00

Khan, Chaka

Full Length

Label	Catalog Number	Title	Type	Country	Year	Longbox Value / Value
Pioneer	PA86-M031	Chaka Khan	8"LD	U.S.	1985	$8.00
Warner Brothers	9 25261-2	I Feel You	LP/LB	U.S.†	1985	$12.00/$7.00
Pioneer	PA-85-129	This is My Night	LD	U.S.	1985	$20.00

Singles

Label	Catalog Number	Title	Type	Country	Year	Longbox Value / Value
WEA	921269-2	Ain't Nobody	CD5	U.K.	1990	$8.00
Warner Brothers	PRO-CD-4742	Don't Look at Me That Way	CDJ	U.S.		$2.00
Warner Brothers	PRO-CD-3439	End of a Love Affair	CDJ	U.S.	1988	$2.00
WEA	921066-2	I Feel for You	CD3	Germany	1989	$8.00
WEA	921358-2	I Feel for You	CD3	Germany	1989	$8.00
WEA	W-2764CD	I Feel for You	CD3	U.K.	1989	$8.00
Warner Brothers	PRO-CD-5783	I Want	CDJ	U.S.	1992	$2.00
WEA	921214-2	I'm Every Woman	CD3	Germany	1989	$8.00
WEA	W-2963CD	I'm Every Woman	CD3	U.K.	1989	$8.00
WEA	921155-2	It's My Party	CD3	Germany	1989	$8.00
Pioneer	10P3-6071	It's My Party	CD3	Japan	1988	$12.00/$3.00
Warner Brothers	PRO-CD-3316	It's My Party	CDJ	U.S.	1988	$2.00
MCA	MCA5P3495	Love Me Still	CDJ	U.S.	1995	$3.00
WEA	9362-40412-2	Love You All My Lifetime	CD5	Germany	1992	$8.00
WEA	W-0087CD	Love You All My Lifetime	CD5	U.K.	1992	$8.00
Warner Brothers	PRO-CD-5338	Love You All My Lifetime	CDJ	U.S.	1992	$2.00
Warner Brothers	PRO-CD-5338	Love You All My Lifetime	CDJ/VHS	U.S.	1992	$15.00
	CDJ plus VHS video in box.					
Lipstick	LIP-80901-2	Take Me Away	CD5	U.K.	1992	$8.00
WEA	W-0120CD	Woman Am I	CD5	U.K.	1992	$8.00
Warner Brothers	PRO-CD-5485	You Can Make the Story Right	CDJ	U.S.	1992	$2.00

Kiara

Full Length

Label	Catalog Number	Title	Type	Country	Year	Longbox Value / Value
Arista		Michigan	DJ/LP	U.S.	1989	$10.00
	CD with fold open license plate					

Singles

Label	Catalog Number	Title	Type	Country	Year	Longbox Value / Value
		Best Of Me, The	CDJ	U.S.		$2.00
Arista	662292	Every Little Thing	CD5	U.K.	1989	$8.00
Arista		Every Little Thing	CDJ	U.S.	1989	$2.00
Arista		Mr. Dee Jay	CDJ	U.S.	1989	$2.00
Arista		Tell Me (Remixes)	CDJ	U.S.	1993	$5.00
	CD-R version.					
Arista	162001	This Time	CD3	U.K.	1989	$8.00

Kicking Back

Singles

Label	Catalog Number	Title	Type	Country	Year	Longbox Value / Value
Virgin	TENCD-297	Devotion	CD3	U.K.	1990	$8.00
Virgin	TENCD-307	Everything	CD3	U.K.	1990	$8.00
Italio-Heat	STH-551CD	Keep on Trying	CD5	Germany	1990	$8.00
APT	SUBCD-014	Keep on Trying	CD5	U.K.	1990	$8.00

Kicks Like a Mule

Singles

Label	Catalog Number	Title	Type	Country	Year	Longbox Value / Value
Tribal	TRIBE-7CD	Number One	CD5	U.K.	1992	$8.00

Kid Can't Dance

Singles

Label	Catalog Number	Title	Type	Country	Year	Longbox Value / Value
Virgin	SRNCD-90	Love Peace & Understanding	CD5	U.K.	1988	$8.00

Kid Capri

Singles

Label	Catalog Number	Title	Type	Country	Year	Longbox Value / Value
		Apollo	CDJ	U.S.		$2.00

Kid Creole And The Coconuts

Singles

Label	Catalog Number	Title	Type	Country	Year	Longbox Value / Value
Sony	CSDS-8144	Dr. Paradise	CD3	Japan	1990	$12.00/$4.00
Sony	656073-3	I Love Girls	CD3	Germany	1990	$9.00
Sony	656073-2	I Love Girls	CD5	U.K.	1990	$9.00
Columbia	CSK 73452	I Love Girls	CDJ	U.S.	1990	$2.00
Musician	PR 8069-2	People Will Talk	CDJ	U.S.	1989	$2.00
Columbia	655698-3	Sex Of It, The	CD3	Germany	1990	$9.00
Sony	CSDS-8128	Sex of It, The	CD3	Japan	1990	$12.00/$4.00
Sony	CSDS-8130	Sex of It, The	CD3	Japan	1990	$12.00/$4.00
Columbia	655698-2	Sex of It, The	CD5	U.K.	1990	$9.00
Columbia	CSK 73256	Sex of It, The	CDJ	U.S.	1990	$2.00

Kid Frost

Singles

Label	Catalog Number	Title	Type	Country	Year	Longbox Value / Value
MCA	MCA5P-2856	Bite the Bullet	CDJ	U.S.	1993	$2.00
Virgin	663484	La Raza	CD5	Germany	1990	$8.00
Virgin	VUSCD-25	La Raza	CD5	U.K.	1990	$8.00
Virgin	GRINGO	La Raza	CDJ	U.S.	1990	$2.00
Virgin	PRCD 3339	La Raza	CDJ	U.S.	1990	$2.00
Virgin	4471	No Sunshine	CDJ	U.S.	1992	$2.00
		That's It	CDJ	U.S.		$2.00
Virgin	VUSCD-52	Thin Line	CD5	U.K.	1992	$8.00

Kid, Joey

Singles

Label	Catalog Number	Title	Type	Country	Year	Longbox Value / Value
Atlantic	AMDY-5028	Counting the Days	CD3	Japan	1990	$12.00/$3.00
		Counting the Days	CDJ	U.S.		$2.00
		Everything I Own	CDJ	U.S.		$2.00
		I'm Not in Love	CDJ	U.S.		$2.00

Kid 'N' Play

Singles

Label	Catalog Number	Title	Type	Country	Year	Longbox Value / Value
WEA	3368-66465-2	Ain't Gonna Hurt Nobody	CD5	Germany	1992	$9.00
Elektra	WMD5-4093	Ain't Gonna Hurt Nobody	CD3	Japan	1992	$12.00/$3.00
BCM	20459	Funhouse	CD5	Germany	1990	$9.00
Select	002	Funhouse	CDJ	U.S.	1990	$2.00
Select	8484	Slippin'	CDJ	U.S.	1991	$2.00

Kid Panic

Singles

Label	Catalog Number	Title	Type	Country	Year	Longbox Value / Value
MCA	MCA5P-54184	We Can Do This	CD5	U.S.		$2.00

Kid, Paul

Singles

Label	Catalog Number	Title	Type	Country	Year	Longbox Value / Value
BCM	20207	Acid in My House	CD5	Germany	1989	$8.00
WEA	172155-2	Take Me Higher	CD5	Germany	1990	$8.00

Kid Rock

Full Length

Label	Catalog Number	Title	Type	Country	Year	Longbox Value / Value
Continuum		Polyfuze Method, The	DJ/LP	U.S.		$15.00

Kid Unknown

Singles

Label	Catalog Number	Title	Type	Country	Year	Longbox Value / Value
Warp	WAP-23CD	Devastating Beat Creator	CD5	U.K.	1992	$8.00
Warp	WAP-20CD	Nightmare	CD5	U.K.	1992	$8.00

Kidd, Carol

Singles

Label	Catalog Number	Title	Type	Country	Year	Longbox Value / Value
Hit	HLC-1	When I Dream	CD5	U.K.	1992	$8.00

Kik Tracee

Singles

Label	Catalog Number	Title	Type	Country	Year	Longbox Value / Value
RCA	2795-2-RDJ	Don't Need Rules	CDJ	U.S.	1991	$2.00
RCA	62023-2-RDJ	Don't Need Rules	CDJ	U.S.	1991	$2.00
RCA	66054-2-RDJ	Field Trip	CDJ	U.S.	1992	$2.00
RCA	2856-2-RDJ	You're So Strange	CDJ	U.S.	1991	$2.00

Kiki

Singles

Label	Catalog Number	Title	Type	Country	Year	Longbox Value / Value
Turnstyle	4541	One Thing	CDJ	U.S.	1992	$2.00

Kill For Thrills

Singles

Label	Catalog Number	Title	Type	Country	Year	Longbox Value / Value
MCA	CD45 17900	Brother's Eyes	CDJ	U.S.	1989	$2.00
MCA	CD4518198	Motorcycle Cowboys	CDJ	U.S.	1989	$2.00

Killer Dwarfs

Singles

Label	Catalog Number	Title	Type	Country	Year	Longbox Value / Value
Epic	ESK 1888	Dirty Weapons	CDJ	U.S.	1990	$2.00
Epic	ESK 2034	Dirty Weapons	CDJ	U.S.	1990	$2.00
		Doesn't Matter	CDJ	U.S.		$2.00
Epic	ESK 4797	Driftin' Back	CDJ	U.S.	1992	$2.00
Epic	ESK 74351	Driftin' Back	CDJ	U.S.	1992	$2.00
Epic	ESK 4608	Hard Luck Town	CDJ	U.S.	1992	$2.00

Killer Ranks

Singles

Label	Catalog Number	Title	Type	Country	Year	Longbox Value / Value
New Creation	1036	Do That to Me One More Time	CDJ	U.S.	1992	$2.00

Killing Joke

Singles

Label	Catalog Number	Title	Type	Country	Year	Longbox Value / Value
Virgin	EGOCD 40	America	CD5	U.K.	1988	$8.00
Zoo	ZP171952	Democracy	CDJ	U.S.		$2.00
		Millenium	CDJ	U.S.	1994	$3.00
Noise	AG-054-3	Money is Not Our God	CD5	U.K.	1990	$8.00
Noise	4877-2-Dj	Money is Not Our God	CDJ	U.S.	1990	$2.00
		Pandemonium	CD5	U.K.		$10.00
		Pandemonium	CD5	U.K.		$10.00
	Second version.					
Zoo	14181	Pandemonium	CD5	U.S.	1994	$5.00

Killing Time

Singles

Label	Catalog Number	Title	Type	Country	Year	Longbox Value / Value
Epic	158H-8009	Bob	CD3	Japan	1988	$12.00/$3.00

Killjoys

Singles

Label	Catalog Number	Title	Type	Country	Year	Longbox Value / Value
MXL		Spin	CD5	Australia	1991	$8.00

Kilo

Singles

Label	Catalog Number	Title	Type	Country	Year	Longbox Value / Value
Cash Money	001	Sleepwalker	CD5	U.S.	1992	$4.00

Kilzer, John

Singles

Label	Catalog Number	Title	Type	Country	Year	Longbox Value / Value
Geffen	PRO-CD-4293	Hands	CDJ	U.S.	1991	$2.00
Geffen	PRO-CD-4349	Marilyn Dean and James Monroe	CDJ	U.S.	1991	$2.00
Geffen	PRO-CD-3302	Memory in the Making	CDJ	U.S.	1988	$2.00
		Red Blue Jeans	CDJ	U.S.		$2.00

Kim, Ranhi

Singles

Label	Catalog Number	Title	Type	Country	Year	Longbox Value / Value
Polydor	PZCD-87	Simple Song	CD5	U.K.	1990	$8.00

Kimmel, Tom

Singles

Label	Catalog Number	Title	Type	Country	Year	Longbox Value / Value
Polydor	CDP 218	A Small Song	CDJ	U.S.	1990	$2.00

Kindred Spirit

Singles

Label	Catalog Number	Title	Type	Country	Year	Longbox Value / Value
IRS	CDEIRS-101	Here in My Eyes	CD5	U.K.	1992	$8.00

King, Akeen

Singles

Label	Catalog Number	Title	Type	Country	Year	Longbox Value / Value
Bellaphon	130-18-018	Let the Rhythm Flow	CD5	Germany	1991	$8.00

King Apparatus

Singles

Label	Catalog Number	Title	Type	Country	Year	Longbox Value / Value
Raw Energy	7424210062	Hospital Waiting Room	CD5	Canada	1993	$8.00

King, B.B.

Full Length

Label	Catalog Number	Title	Type	Country	Year	Longbox Value / Value
Sony	R0194DL	B.B. King	LD	U.S.	1986	$30.00
		House of Blues	RS	U.S.	1995	$40.00
	2 CD set. Airdate: 9/17/95.					
MCA	MCA3P-2428	King of the Blues	DJ/Smplr	U.S.	1992	$15.00

Singles

Label	Catalog Number	Title	Type	Country	Year	Longbox Value / Value
Eastwest	257445-2	Ain't Nobody Home	CD3	Germany	1989	$10.00
MCA	DMCAT-1354	Ain't Nobody Home	CD5	U.K.	1989	$10.00
MCA	MCA5P-2010	Back in LA	CDJ	U.S.	1991	$2.00
MCA	MCA5P-2131	Blues Come Over Me	CDJ	U.S.	1992	$2.00
MCA	20541	Got My Mojo Working	CD5	U.S.	1994	$5.00
GRP	GR2 9925	Joe Cool	CDJ	U.S.	1989	$2.00
MCA	CD45 18450	Peace to the World	CDJ	U.S.	1990	$2.00
MCA	MCA5P-2800	Playin' With My Friends	CDJ	U.S.	1993	$2.00
MCA	MCA5P-2863	Something You Got	CDJ	U.S.	1993	$2.00

King Bee

Singles

Label	Catalog Number	Title	Type	Country	Year	Longbox Value / Value
CBS	656233-3	Back by Dope Demand	CD3	Germany	1990	$8.00
Big One	RUFF-6XCD	Back by Dope Demand	CD3	U.K.	1990	$8.00
Big One	RUFF-6CD	Back by Dope Demand	CD3	U.K.	1990	$8.00
Columbia	655855-2	Cold Slammin'	CD5	Germany	1991	$8.00
Columbia	656552-3	Must Be the Music	CD3	Germany	1990	$8.00

Label	Catalog Number	Title	Type	Country	Year	Longbox Value / Value
Columbia	656552-2	Must Be the Music	CD5	U.K.	1990	$8.00

King, Ben E.

Singles

Label	Catalog Number	Title	Type	Country	Year	Longbox Value / Value
Atlantic	PRCD 3535-2	Book of Love	CDJ	U.S.		$2.00
WEA	786490-2	Stand by Me	CD3	Germany	1989	$10.00
Atlantic	AMDY-5050	Stand by Me	CD3	Japan	1991	$12.00/$4.00
WEA	786490-2	Stand by Me	CD3	U.K.	1989	$10.00
WEA	786489-2	You Don't Know What I Like	CD3	Germany	1989	$10.00
Ichiban	097	You've Got All of Me	CDJ	U.S.	1992	$2.00

King, Bobby and Terry Evans

Singles

Label	Catalog Number	Title	Type	Country	Year	Longbox Value / Value
		Saturday Night	CDJ	U.S.		$2.00
Efa	CD-05755	Seeing Is Believing	CD5	Germany	1988	$9.00

King, Carl

Singles

Label	Catalog Number	Title	Type	Country	Year	Longbox Value / Value
Scotti Brothers	75326	I Love You	CDJ	U.S.	1990	$2.00

King, Carole

Full Length

Label	Catalog Number	Title	Type	Country	Year	Longbox Value / Value
Capitol		City Streets	DJ/LP	U.S.	1989	$16.00
		Masterpiece Vol. 3	LP	Japan		$50.00
Pioneer	PA-83-83	One to One	LD	U.S.	1983	$30.00
Atlantic	80118-2	Speeding Time	LP/LB	U.S.†	1984	$14.00/$8.00
Columbia	66226	Tapestry	LTD/LP	U.S.	1995	$25.00
Gold disc.						

Singles

Label	Catalog Number	Title	Type	Country	Year	Longbox Value / Value
Capitol	203313-2	City Streets	CD5	Germany	1989	$9.00
Capitol	CDCL-527	City Streets	CDJ	U.K.	1989	$9.00
Capitol		City Streets	CDJ	U.S.	1989	$2.00
	7012	Colour of Your Dreams	CDJ	U.S.	1993	$2.00
	6644	Lay Down My Life	CDJ	U.S.	1993	$2.00
		Lovelight	CDJ	U.S.		$2.00
Sony	SRDS-8239	Now and Forever	CD3	Japan	1992	$12.00/$4.00
Columbia	CSK 4667	Now and Forever	CDJ	U.S.	1992	$2.00
Capitol	DPRO-79742	Someone Who Believes in You	CDJ	U.S.	1989	$2.00
		You've Got a Friend	CDJ	U.S.		$6.00

King Cobb Steele

Full Length

Label	Catalog Number	Title	Type	Country	Year	Longbox Value / Value
Raw	PRO CD 01	Sampler & Interview	DJ/Smplr	Canada		$15.00

King Crimson

Full Length

Label	Catalog Number	Title	Type	Country	Year	Longbox Value / Value
Warner Brothers	9 23692-2	Beat	LP/LB	U.S.†	1985	$14.00/$8.00
Caroline		Collector's Edition	LTD/LP	U.K.	1994	$40.00
3 CD picture disc boxed set.						
	DSP-192	Great Deceiver-Live 1973-1974	DJ/Smplr	Japan		N/A
DIR		King Biscuit Flour Hour	RS	U.S.	1988	$40.00
With Genesis, Airdate: 8/21/88.						
		Thrak	LTD/LP	Australia	1995	$25.00
Gold disc.						
		Thrak	LTD/LP	U.K.		$25.00
CD in paper sleeve in metal box with tour book.						
Caroline		Thrak	DJ/Smplr	U.K.	1995	$18.00
Warner Brothers	9 25071-2	Three of a Perfect Pair	LP/LB	U.S.†	1984	$14.00/$8.00
Discipline		Vroom	LTD/LP	U.S.	1995	$20.00
Autographed CD series.						

Singles

Label	Catalog Number	Title	Type	Country	Year	Longbox Value / Value
		21st Century Schizoid Man	CD5	U.K.	1996	$10.00
Capital	38480	Dinosaur	CD5	U.S.	1994	$5.00
		Dinosaur	CDJ	U.S.	1994	$6.00
		People	CDJ	U.S.	1994	$6.00
Virgin	VSCDJ1597	Schizoid Man	CDJ	U.K.		$20.00

King Diamond

Singles

Label	Catalog Number	Title	Type	Country	Year	Longbox Value / Value
Apollon	MP15-5333	Dark Sides	CD3	Japan	1988	$13.00/$4.00

King, Diana

Singles

Label	Catalog Number	Title	Type	Country	Year	Longbox Value / Value
	OSK 77989	Love Triangle	CDJ	U.S.		$2.00
Columbia	78041	Love Triangle	CD5	U.S.	1995	$5.00
Columbia	78025	Love Triangle	CD5	U.S.	1995	$5.00

King, Evelyn Champagne

Full Length

Label	Catalog Number	Title	Type	Country	Year	Longbox Value / Value
RCA	PCD1-5308	So Romantic	LP/BP	U.S.†	1985	$14.00/$8.00

Singles

Label	Catalog Number	Title	Type	Country	Year	Longbox Value / Value
EMI	DPRO-04067	Flirt	CDJ	U.S.	1988	$2.00
		Kisses Don't Lie	CDJ	U.S.		$2.00
RCA	PD-45488	Shame	CD5	U.K.	1992	$9.00
RCA	62350-2-RDJ	Shame '92	CDJ	U.S.	1992	$2.00

King For A Day

Singles

Label	Catalog Number	Title	Type	Country	Year	Longbox Value / Value
Alfa	ALDB-84	Kick That Rhythm	CD3	Japan	1990	$12.00/$3.00

King Kobra

Full Length

Label	Catalog Number	Title	Type	Country	Year	Longbox Value / Value
Rocker		III	LP/LB	U.S.		$14.00/$8.00

King Kong

Singles

Label	Catalog Number	Title	Type	Country	Year	Longbox Value / Value
Alfa	09B3-51	Boom Boom Dollars	CD3	Japan	1989	$12.00/$3.00
Alfa	11B3-52	Boom Boom Dollars	CD3	Japan	1989	$12.00/$3.00
Alfa	ALCB-327	Boom Boom Dollars	CD5	Japan	1989	$10.00
BMG	663425	For a Few Dollars More	CD5	Germany	1990	$8.00
Toshiba	TODP-2263	King Kong	CD3	Japan	1991	$12.00/$3.00
Alfa	09B3-87	Walkie Talkie	CD3	Japan	1991	$12.00/$3.00
Alfa	11B3-88	Walkie Talkie	CD3	Japan	1991	$12.00/$3.00

King Missile

Singles

Label	Catalog Number	Title	Type	Country	Year	Longbox Value / Value
Atlantic	PRCD 5171-2	Martin Scorsese	CDJ	U.S.		$2.00
Atlantic	PRCD 3854-2	My Heart Is a Flower	CDJ	U.S.	1991	$2.00
Atlantic	PRCD 4960-2	Trapped	CDJ	U.S.	1992	$2.00
Atlantic	82208	Way to Salvation, Thes	CD5	U.S.	1991	$5.00
Atlantic	PRCD 5577-2	Love Is...	CDJ	U.S.		$3.00
Atlantic	PRCD 4960-2	Why Are We Trapped	CDJ	U.S.		$3.00

King Of Fools

Full Length

Label	Catalog Number	Title	Type	Country	Year	Longbox Value / Value
Imago	28015-2-DJ	Sad in Wonderland	DJ/Smplr	U.S.	1991	$8.00
Imago	28002-2-DJ	Eat Your Heart	CDJ	U.S.	1991	$2.00
World	WRVD-3	No Man's Land	CD5	U.K.	1990	$8.00
Imago	28015-2-DJ	Sad in Wonderland	CDJ	U.S.	1991	$2.00

King of Kings

Singles

Label	Catalog Number	Title	Type	Country	Year	Longbox Value / Value
DGC	PRO-CD-4224	Burning Home	CDJ	U.S.	1991	$2.00

King of The Hill

Singles

Label	Catalog Number	Title	Type	Country	Year	Longbox Value / Value
SBK	CDKOTH-1	I Do U	CD5	U.K.	1991	$9.00
SBK	CDKOTH-2	If I Say	CD5	U.K.	1991	$9.00
SBK	DPRO-05394	If I Say	CD5	U.S.	1991	$2.00
SBK	DPRO-05415	If I Say	CDJ	U.S.	1991	$2.00

King Sun

Singles

Label	Catalog Number	Title	Type	Country	Year	Longbox Value / Value
Cold Chillin'	7000	Strictly Ghetto	CD5	U.S.	1994	$5.00

King Swamp

Full Length

Label	Catalog Number	Title	Type	Country	Year	Longbox Value / Value
Virgin	696	Interview	DJ/Intvw	U.S.		$8.00
Virgin	2997	One Step Over the Line	DJ/Intvw	U.S.		$8.00

Singles

Label	Catalog Number	Title	Type	Country	Year	Longbox Value / Value
Virgin	KSWCD-2	Blown Away	CD5	U.K.	1989	$9.00
Virgin	PRCD 2839	Blown Away	CDJ	U.S.	1989	$2.00
Virgin	KSWCD 1	Is This Love?	CD3	U.K.	1989	$9.00
Virgin	PRCD 2684	Is This Love?	CDJ	U.S.	1989	$2.00
		Man Behind the Gun	CDJ	U.S.		$2.00
Virgin	PRCD 3515	Wiseblood	CDJ	U.S.	1990	$2.00
Virgin		Wiseblood	CDJ	U.S.	1990	$2.00
Second version.						

King Tee

Singles

Label	Catalog Number	Title	Type	Country	Year	Longbox Value / Value
Capitol	DPRO-79470	At Your Own Risk	CDJ	U.S.	1990	$2.00
MCA	54873	Dippin'	CD5	U.S.	1994	$5.00
Capitol	DPRO-79253	Diss You	CDJ	U.S.	1990	$2.00
		Ruff Ryme	CDJ	U.S.		$2.00

King Tones

Singles

Label	Catalog Number	Title	Type	Country	Year	Longbox Value / Value
Polydor	PODH-1107	Good Night Baby	CD3	Japan	1992	$12.00/$3.00
Victor	VIDL-10244	Wakayama	CD3	Japan	1992	$12.00/$3.00

King's Swingers

Singles

Label	Catalog Number	Title	Type	Country	Year	Longbox Value / Value
Victor	VDCM-12009	Sings Worldwide Pops	CD3	Japan	1988	$12.00/$3.00

King's X

Full Length

Label	Catalog Number	Title	Type	Country	Year	Longbox Value / Value
Atlantic	PRCD 5494-2	Building Blox	DJ/Smplr	U.S.	1994	$18.00
Atlantic	PRCD 5494-2	Building Blox	DJ/Smplr	U.S.	1994	$25.00
Westwood One		In Concert	RS	U.S.	1992	$70.00
2 CD set. With The Cult, Airdate: 9/14/92.						
DIR		King Biscuit Flour Hour	RS	U.S.	1991	$30.00
With Boston, Airdate: 1/27/91.						
DIR		King Biscuit Flour Hour	RS	U.S.	1991	$30.00
With Foreigner, Airdate: 1/13/91.						
DIR		King Biscuit Flour Hour	RS	U.S.	1991	$30.00
With Jethro Tull, Airdate: 1/6/91.						
DIR		King Biscuit Flour Hour	RS	U.S.	1991	$30.00
With Kansas, Airdate: 1/20/91.						

Singles

Label	Catalog Number	Title	Type	Country	Year	Longbox Value / Value
Atlantic	PRCD 4461-2	Black Flag	CDJ	U.S.	1992	$2.00
Atlantic	PRCD 5396-2	Dogman	CDJ	U.S.	1994	$2.00
Atlantic	PRCD 4738-2	Dream in My Life	CDJ	U.S.	1992	$2.00
Atlantic	PRCD 5589-2	Fool You	CDJ	U.S.	1994	$2.00
Megaforce	PRCD 3922-2	I'll Never Get Tired of You	CDJ	U.S.	1990	$2.00
Atlantic	A-7791CD	It's Love	CD5	U.K.	1991	$10.00
Atlantic	PRCD3612-2	It's Love	CDJ	U.S.	1990	$2.00
		Over My Head	CDJ	U.S.		$2.00
		Pillow	CDJ	U.S.	1994	$3.00
		Sometime	CDJ	U.S.		$3.00
		Summerland	CDJ	U.S.		$2.00
Megaforce	PRCD 3765-2	We Are Finding Who We Are	CDJ	U.S.	1990	$2.00

Kingdom Come

Singles

Label	Catalog Number	Title	Type	Country	Year	Longbox Value / Value
Polydor	889225-2	Do You Like It	CD5	Germany	1989	$10.00
Polydor	PODP-40008	Do You Like It	CD3	Japan	1989	$13.00/$4.00
Polydor	KCCDS-3	Do You Like It	CD5	U.K.	1989	$10.00
Polydor	CDP 51	Do You Like It	CDJ	U.S.	1989	$6.00
Polydor	887 436-2	Get It On	CD5	Germany	1988	$10.00
Polydor	P10P-30013	Get It On	CD3	Japan	1988	$13.00/$4.00
Polydor	KCCD-1	Get It On	CD5	U.K.	1988	$10.00
Polygram	870 720-2	Get It On	CDV/BP	U.S.	1988	$20.00/$20.00
Polydor	P13P-37006	Loving You	CD3	Japan	1988	$13.00/$4.00
Polydor	KCCDS-4	Overrated	CD5	U.K.	1988	$10.00
Polydor	CDP 105	Overrated	CDJ	U.S.	1989	$3.00
Polydor	CDP 466	Should I	CDJ	U.S.	1991	$2.00
Polydor	KCCD-2	What Can Love Be	CD5	U.K.	1988	$10.00
Polygram	870 709-2	What Can Love Be	CDV/BP	U.S.	1988	$20.00/$20.00
Polydor	CDP 90	Who Do You Love	CDJ	U.S.	1989	$7.00
Polydor	CDP 526	You're Not the Only...I Know	CDJ	U.S.	1992	$2.00

Kingmaker

Singles

Label	Catalog Number	Title	Type	Country	Year	Longbox Value / Value
Scorch	323912-2	Armchair Anarchist	CD5	U.K.	1992	$8.00
Chrysalis	DPRO-04566	Armchair Anarchist	CDJ	U.S.	1991	$2.00
APT	NONECD-1	Celebrated Working Man	CD5	U.K.	1992	$8.00
EMI	SCORCHCD-3	Idiots at the Wheel	CD5	U.K.	1992	$8.00
EMI	SCORCHCD-5	Killjoy Was Here	CD5	U.K.	1992	$8.00
EMI		Queen Jane	CD5	U.K.		$8.00
EMI		Queen Jane	CD5	U.K.		$8.00
Second version.						
Chrysalis	DPRO-05471	Really Scrape the Sky	CDJ	U.S.	1992	$2.00
EMI		Ten Years Asleep	CD5	U.K.		$8.00
EMI		Ten Years Asleep	CD5	U.K.		$8.00
Second version.						
EMI	SCORCHCD-2	Two Headed	CD5	U.K.	1992	$8.00
EMI	SCORCHCD-1	Waterproof	CD5	U.K.	1992	$8.00
Chrysalis	DPRO094632	When Lucy's Down	CDJ	U.S.	1992	$2.00

Kings Of Swing

Singles

Label	Catalog Number	Title	Type	Country	Year	Longbox Value / Value
Bumrush	3406	Nod Your Head to This	CDJ	U.S.	1990	$2.00
Bumrush	3728	U Know I Love Ya Baby	CDJ	U.S.	1991	$2.00

Kings Of The Sun

Singles

Label	Catalog Number	Title	Type	Country	Year	Longbox Value / Value
RCA	2611-2-RDJ	Drop the Gun	CDJ	U.S.	1990	$2.00
		Lock Me Up	CDJ	U.S.		$2.00
		Serpentine	CDJ	U.S.		$2.00

Kingsbury, Peter

Full Length

Label	Catalog Number	Title	Type	Country	Year	Longbox Value / Value
Polygram	511835-2	A Different Man	LP/BP	U.S.		$12.00/$7.00

Kingston Trio

Full Length

Label	Catalog Number	Title	Type	Country	Year	Longbox Value / Value
Warner Sound Exchange		40 Legendary Hits	LTD/LP	U.S.	1995	$30.00
	2 CD set.					

Singles

Label	Catalog Number	Title	Type	Country	Year	Longbox Value / Value
Rhino	885839	Tom Dooley	CD3	Germany	1990	$10.00

Kinison, Sam

Full Length

Label	Catalog Number	Title	Type	Country	Year	Longbox Value / Value
Warner Brothers	PRO-CD-3327	Wild Thing	DJ/Smplr	U.S.	1988	$20.00

Singles

Label	Catalog Number	Title	Type	Country	Year	Longbox Value / Value
Warner Brothers	PRO-CD-4033	Under My Thumb	CDJ	U.S.	1990	$3.00
Warner Brothers	PRO-CD-3327	Wild Thing	CDJ	U.S.	1988	$7.00

Kinks

Full Length

Label	Catalog Number	Title	Type	Country	Year	Longbox Value / Value
BBC Radio		BBC Classic Tracks	RS	U.S.	1991	$25.00
	Airdate: 2/17/91.					
BBC Radio		BBC Classic Tracks	RS	U.S.	1991	$25.00
	Airdate: 2/25/91.					
BBC Radio		BBC Classic Tracks	RS	U.S.	1991	$25.00
	Airdate: 8/12/91.					
BBC Radio		BBC Classic Tracks	RS	U.S.	1992	$25.00
	Airdate: 8/31/92.					
Westwood One		BBC Classic Tracks	RS	U.S.	1994	$35.00
	Airdate: 3/14/94.					
Westwood One		BBC Classic Tracks	RS	U.S.	1996	$35.00
	Airdate: 2/19/96					
Griffin		Collection, The	LTD/LP	U.S.		$18.00
	Gold disc.					
		Give People What They Want	LP/LB	U.S.		$18.00/$15.00
Aris	880018	Greatest Hits	LP	Germany	1984	$25.00
Compleat	CDKINK-7251	Greatest Hits	LP/LB	U.S.†	1984	$14.00/$8.00
Westwood One		In Concert	RS	U.S.	1994	$65.00
	Airdate: 1/31/94.					
DIR		King Biscuit Flour Hour	RS	U.S.	1987	$40.00
	Airdate: 11/1/87.					
DIR		King Biscuit Flour Hour	RS	U.S.	1989	$40.00
	Airdate: 2/19/89.					
DIR		King Biscuit Flour Hour	RS	U.S.	1989	$40.00
	Airdate: 2/26/89.					
DIR		King Biscuit Flour Hour	RS	U.S.	1990	$40.00
	Airdate: 10/28/90.					
DIR		King Biscuit Flour Hour	RS	U.S.	1992	$40.00
	Airdate: 2/9/92.					
DIR		King Biscuit Flour Hour	RS	U.S.	1993	$40.00
	Airdate: 1/17/93.					
DIR		King Biscuit Flour Hour	RS	U.S.	1994	$40.00
	Airdate: 9/25/94.					
Reprise		Live Kinks, The	LP/LB	U.S.		$14.00/$8.00
MCA		Live the Road	LP/LB	U.S.		$14.00/$8.00
Arista	ARCD-8050	Low Budget	LP/BP	U.S.†	1985	$14.00/$8.00
Radio Ventures		Masters of Rock	RS	U.S.	1990	$50.00
	Airdate: 4/11/90.					
Arista	ARCD-8069	Misfits	LP/BP	U.S.		$14.00/$8.00
Arista	ARCD-8068	Sleepwalker	LP/BP	U.S.		$14.00/$8.00
Arista	ARCD-8018	State of Confusion	LP/BP	U.S.		$14.00/$8.00
Arista	ARCD-8018	State of Confusion	LP/BP	U.S.†	1984	$14.00/$8.00
Westwood One		Superstar Concert	RS	U.S.	1992	$30.00
	2 CD set. Airdate: 8/23/92.					
Westwood One		Superstars	RS	U.S.	1995	$65.00
	Airdate: 6/19/95.					
MCA	MCAD-5822	Think Visual	LP/LB	U.S.	1986	$14.00/$8.00
MCA	MCAD-6337	U.K. Jive	LP/LB	U.S.	1989	$14.00/$8.00
Castle	ESSCP-8	Ultimate Collection, The	LTD/LP	U.K.		$35.00
Media America		Up Close	RS	U.S.	1990	$40.00
	2 CD set.					
Media America		Up Close	RS	U.S.	1993	$60.00
	2 CD set.					
Arista	ARCD 8264	Word of Mouth	LP/LB	U.S.		$14.00/$8.00
Arista	ARCD 8264	Word of Mouth	LP/LB	U.S.†	1985	$14.00/$8.00
Marble		You Really Got Me	LP	U.K.		$15.00

Singles

Label	Catalog Number	Title	Type	Country	Year	Longbox Value / Value
Polygram	886743-2	Down All the Days	CD5	Germany	1989	$11.00
London	LONCD-239	Down All the Days	CD5	U.K.	1989	$11.00
MCA	CD45 18294	Down All the Days	CDJ	U.S.	1989	$3.00
MCA	CD45 18168	Entertainment	CDJ	U.S.	1989	$3.00
Columbia	CSK 5076	Hatred	CDJ	U.S.	1994	$7.00
London	LONCD-250	How Do I Get Close	CD5	U.K.	1989	$8.00
MCA	CD45 17769	How Do I Get Close	CDJ	U.S.	1989	$3.00
Eastwest	246875-2	Lola	CD5	Germany	1989	$11.00
Columbia	CSK 74872	Scattered	CDJ	U.S.	1993	$3.00
Columbia	CSK 5276	Still Searching	CDJ	U.S.	1993	$3.00
Rhino	71849	Tired of Waiting	CD5	U.S.	1994	$5.00
Old Gold	OG-6117	Waterloo Sunset	CD3	U.K.	1989	$10.00
Old Gold	OG-6102	You Really Got Me	CD3	U.K.	1989	$10.00

Kinky Go

Singles

Label	Catalog Number	Title	Type	Country	Year	Longbox Value / Value
Alfa	11B3-33	Kinky Go	CD3	Japan	1989	$12.00/$3.00

Kinky Machine

Singles

Label	Catalog Number	Title	Type	Country	Year	Longbox Value / Value
Lemon	LEMON-3CD	Going Out With God	CD5	U.K.	1992	$8.00
Lemon		Going Out With God	CD5	U.K.	1992	$8.00
	Second version.					
Lemon	LEMON-6CD	Supernatural Giver	CD5	U.K.	1992	$8.00
Oxygen	2758	Supernatural Giver	CDJ	U.S.	1993	$2.00
Lemon	LEMON-4CD	Swivelhead	CD5	U.K.	1992	$8.00

Kinsey Report

Singles

Label	Catalog Number	Title	Type	Country	Year	Longbox Value / Value
Charisma	PRCD 028	Image Maker	CDJ	U.S.	1991	$2.00
Alligator	ALA 10	Midnight Drive	CDJ	U.S.	1989	$2.00
Virgin	12791	Release Yourself	CDJ	U.S.	1993	$2.00

Kirsch, Randell

Singles

Label	Catalog Number	Title	Type	Country	Year	Longbox Value / Value
Pigs On Corn	VS001	Midnight Cowboy	CDJ	U.S.	1992	$2.00

Kiss

Full Length

Label	Catalog Number	Title	Type	Country	Year	Longbox Value / Value
Vertigo		Alive	LTD/LP	Australia		$50.00
	2 CD set.					
Vertigo		Alive II	LTD/LP	Australia		$50.00
	2 CD set.					
Vertigo		Alive III	LTD/LP	Australia		$50.00
	2 CD set.					
Mercury		Alive III, the Trilogy	DJ/LP	U.S.	1993	$80.00
	5 CD set. of "Alive III" plus albums "Alive" and "Alive II."					
Mercury	822495-2	Animalize	LP/BP	U.S.†	1984	$14.00/$8.00
Pioneer	PA-85-141	Animalize Live	LD	U.S.	1985	$40.00
Polystar	P30R-20008	Chikara	LP	Japan	1988	$50.00
PMV	080 373-9	Crazy Nights	8"LD	U.S.	1988	$10.00
TDK	PPD-8003	Dressed to Kill	DJ/Smplr	Japan	1993	$150.00
Polygram	080-101-1	Exposed	LD	U.S.	1988	$35.00
Vertigo		Greatest Kiss	LTD/LP	Australia	1997	$35.00
	Limited edition gold CD with bonus tracks and housed in a slip case.					
TDK	PPD-8001	Kiss	DJ/Smplr	Japan	1993	$150.00
Radio Today		Kiss	RS	U.S.	1993	$125.00
Mercury	PHCR-1245/4213	Kiss My Ass/Double Platinum	DJ/LP	Japan	1994	$400.00
	2 CD set with "kiss my ass" with Japaneese flag as background.					
Mercury	814297-2	Lick It Up	LP/BP	U.S.†	1985	$14.00/$8.00
TDK	PPD-8006	Love Gun	DJ/Smplr	Japan	1993	$150.00
Mercury	PHCR-36	Revenge	LTD/LP	Japan	1992	$27.00
		Strutter	DJ/Smplr	Australia	1994	$25.00
Mercury	800041-2	Unmasked	LP/BP	U.S.†	1985	$14.00/$8.00
Mercury	314 532 741-2	You Wanted the Best, You Got the Best	LTD/LP	U.S.	1996	$17.00
	CD with limited edition phone card.					

Singles

Label	Catalog Number	Title	Type	Country	Year	Longbox Value / Value
Mercury	CDP 04	Crazy Crazy Nights	CDJ	U.S.	1987	$6.00
Mercury	870 750-2	Crazy Crazy Nights	CDV/BP	U.S.	1988	$20.00/$20.00
Mercury	CDP 681	Domino	CDJ	U.S.	1992	$6.00
Mercury		Every Time I Look at You	CDJ	Germany	1996	$20.00
Mercury		Every Time I Look at You	CDJ	U.S.	1992	$6.00
Phonogram	876717-2	Forever	CD5	Canada	1990	$12.00
Vertigo	875173-2	Forever	CD5	Germany	1990	$11.00
Vertigo	KISCD-11	Forever	CD5	U.K.	1990	$11.00
Mercury	CDP 195	Forever	CDJ	U.S.	1989	$6.00
Eastwest	A-8696CD	God Gave Rock and Roll to You	CD5	U.K.	1991	$11.00
Eastwest	7567-96275-2	God Gave Rock and Roll to You	CD5	U.K.	1991	$11.00
Interscope		God Gave Rock and Roll to You	CD5	U.S.	1991	$8.00
	Non PD version with from picture sleeve.					
Interscope	PRCD 4076-2	God Gave Rock and Roll to You	CDJ	U.S.	1991	$15.00
	Rare picture disc version.					
Casablanca	P10X-30005	Hard Luck Woman	CD3	Japan	1988	$12.00/$5.00
Mercury	PPDS-18	Hide Your Heart	CD3	Japan	1989	$18.00/$5.00
Vertigo	KISCD-10	Hide Your Heart	CD5	U.K.	1989	$11.00
Mercury	CDP 140	Hide Your Heart	CDJ	U.S.	1989	$7.00
Mercury	CDP 707	I Just Wanna	CDJ	U.S.	1992	$6.00
Mercury	CDP 882	I Love It Loud	CDJ	U.S.	1992	$7.00
		I Was Made For Lovin' You	CDJ	France	1993	$35.00
Casablanca	874 803-2	I Was Made For Lovin' You	CD5	Germany	1988	$11.00
		I Was Made For Lovin' You	CD5	Holland	1994	$12.00
Casablanca	P10X-30004	I Was Made For Lovin' You	CD3	Japan	1988	$18.00/$5.00
Casablanca	874 803-2	I Was Made For Lovin' You	CD5	U.S.	1988	$15.00
Mercury	870 750 2	Let's Put the X In Sex	CDV	U.S.	1988	$15.00
Mercury	CDP 35	Lets Put the X In Sex	CDJ	U.S.	1988	$6.00
Mercury	870 750-2	Lets Put the X In Sex	CDV/BP	U.S.	1988	$25.00/$25.00
Polydor	080 0452	Lick It Up	DJ/CDV	U.S.	1987	$25.00
Mercury	MECP 120	New York Groove	CDJ	U.S.	1996	$35.00
	Distributed free from Blockbuster Music to purchasers of the Kiss album "You Wanted the Best You Got the Best."					
Vertigo	KISCD-8	Reason to Live	CD5	U.K.	1990	$11.00
		Rise to It	CDJ	U.S.		$7.00
		Strutter	CD3	Australia	1994	$45.00
	5 CD set.					
Mercury	870 710-2	Tears Are Falling	CDV/BP	U.S.	1988	$20.00/$20.00
Vertigo	870 215-2	Turn on the Night	CD5	Germany	1988	$11.00
Casablanca	P10R-30001	Turn on the Night	CD3	Japan	1988	$18.00/$5.00
Vertigo	KISCD-9	Turn on the Night	CD5	U.K.	1988	$11.00
PMV	870 724-2	Turn on the Night	CDV/BP	U.S.	1988	$20.00/$20.00
Mercury	PHDR-107	Unholy	CD3	Japan	1992	$18.00/$5.00
Mercury	KISCD 12	Unholy	CD5	U.K.	1992	$20.00
Mercury	CDP 666	Unholy	CDJ	U.S.	1992	$15.00

Kiss in the Dark

Singles

Label	Catalog Number	Title	Type	Country	Year	Longbox Value / Value
Polygram	874436-3	Backfield in Motion	CD3	Germany	1989	$8.00
Polygram	874437-2	Backfield in Motion	CD5	Germany	1989	$8.00
Polygram	875029-2	Come Back	CD5	Germany	1989	$8.00
Polygram	870337-2	Phone Call	CD5	Germany	1988	$8.00
Polygram	872281-2	Something Special	CD5	Germany	1989	$8.00

Kiss Like This

Singles

Label	Catalog Number	Title	Type	Country	Year	Longbox Value / Value
Chrysalis	KLTCD-1	Faith In You	CD5	U.K.	1990	$8.00
Chrysalis	KLTCD-2	What the World Don't Know	CD5	U.K.	1990	$8.00

Kiss Of The Gypsy

Singles

Label	Catalog Number	Title	Type	Country	Year	Longbox Value / Value
Atlantic	A-7474CD	Take This Old Heart	CD5	U.K.	1992	$8.00
Atlantic	A-5994CD	Whatever It Takes	CD5	U.K.	1992	$8.00
Atlantic	PRCD 4423-2	Whatever It Takes	CDJ	U.S.	1992	$2.00

Kiss The Sky

Singles

Label	Catalog Number	Title	Type	Country	Year	Longbox Value / Value
Victor	VIDP-30	Livin' For You	CD3	Japan	1991	$12.00/$3.00
Motown	3146310312	Livin' For You	CDJ	U.S.	1992	$2.00
Victor	VICP-2064	Voodoo Chile	CD3	Japan	1991	$12.00/$3.00

Kissing The Pink

Singles

Label	Catalog Number	Title	Type	Country	Year	Longbox Value / Value
WEA	YZ-308CD	Stand Up	CD5	U.K.	1989	$8.00

Kita, Tomi

Singles

Label	Catalog Number	Title	Type	Country	Year	Longbox Value / Value
Ra Falcon	20365	Life in Disguise	CDJ	U.S.		$3.00

Kitaro

Full Length

Label	Catalog Number	Title	Type	Country	Year	Longbox Value / Value
Geffen	24087-2	Asia	LP/LB	U.S.†	1985	$14.00/$8.00
Geffen	24082-2	Astral Voyage	LP/LB	U.S.†	1985	$14.00/$8.00

Label	Catalog Number	Title	Type	Country	Year	Longbox Value / Value
Geffen	24083-2	Full Moon Story	LP/LB	U.S.†	1985	$14.00/$8.00
Geffen	24085-2	India	LP/LB	U.S.†	1985	$14.00/$8.00
Geffen	24084-2	Millennia	LP/LB	U.S.†	1985	$14.00/$8.00
Geffen	PRO-CD-4100	Selections From Kojiko	DJ/Smplr	U.S.	1990	$8.00
Am Gramm	187009-2	Silk Road	LP/LB	U.S.†	1985	$14.00/$8.00
Am Gramm	187011-2	Silk Road II	LP/LB	U.S.†	1985	$14.00/$8.00
Geffen	24086-2	Silver Cloud	LP/LB	U.S.†	1985	$14.00/$8.00
Geffen	70XL-2003/4	These Ten Years	LTD/LP	Japan		$40.00

Gold disc.

Singles

Label	Catalog Number	Title	Type	Country	Year	Longbox Value / Value
		Eight Headed Dragon, The	CDJ	U.S.	1990	$2.00
Geffen	PRO-CD-4612	Heaven on Earth	CDJ	U.S.	1993	$2.00
Geffen	PRO-CD-4432	Island of Life	CDJ	U.S.	1992	$2.00
Geffen	PRO-CD-2837	Sundance Moondance	CDJ	U.S.		$2.00

Kitchens of Distinction

Singles

Label	Catalog Number	Title	Type	Country	Year	Longbox Value / Value
A&M	31458 8038	4 Men	CDJ	U.S.	1992	$2.00
Pinnacle	59-TP7CD	Breathing Fear	CD5	U.K.	1992	$8.00
Pinnacle	49-TP7CD	Drive That Fast	CD5	U.K.	1990	$8.00
A&M	75021 7488-2	Drive That Fast	CDJ	U.S.	1990	$2.00
A&M	75021 7494-2	Drive That Fast	CDJ	U.S.	1990	$2.00
Pinnacle	29-TP7CD	Elephantine	CD5	U.K.	1989	$8.00
A&M	75021 7226 2	Gorgeous Love	CDJ	U.S.	1990	$2.00
Pinnacle	43-TP7CD	Quick as Rainbows	CD5	U.K.	1990	$8.00
A&M	75021 7536 2	Quick as Rainbows	CDJ	U.S.	1990	$2.00
A&M	75021 7603-2	Smiling	CDJ	U.S.	1991	$2.00
Pinnacle	69-TP7CD	When in Rome	CD5	U.K.	1992	$8.00

Kite

Singles

Label	Catalog Number	Title	Type	Country	Year	Longbox Value / Value
		Breaking Point	CDJ	Canada		$6.00
		Days of Youth	CDJ	Canada		$6.00

Kitt, Eartha

Singles

Label	Catalog Number	Title	Type	Country	Year	Longbox Value / Value
BMG	162213	Cha-Cha Heels	CD3	Germany	1989	$8.00
BMG	662213	Cha-Cha Heels	CD5	Germany	1989	$8.00
BMG	662213	Cha-Cha Heels	CD3	U.K.	1989	$8.00
BMG	662713	Primitive Man	CD5	Germany	1989	$8.00
BMG	662324	Primitive Man	CD5	U.K.	1989	$8.00
BMG	662713	Primitive Man	CD5	U.K.	1989	$8.00

Kitten

Singles

Label	Catalog Number	Title	Type	Country	Year	Longbox Value / Value
Atlantic	PRCD 4231-2	Dance With Me	CDJ	U.S.	1991	$2.00

Kitty Kat

Singles

Label	Catalog Number	Title	Type	Country	Year	Longbox Value / Value
Great Jonea	623	Rock Me	CDJ	U.S.	1993	$2.00

Kittywinder

Singles

Label	Catalog Number	Title	Type	Country	Year	Longbox Value / Value
	1040	Scream of the Weak	CD5	U.S.	1994	$5.00

Kix

Full Length

Label	Catalog Number	Title	Type	Country	Year	Longbox Value / Value
Atlantic	PRCD 4091-2	Rock Profile	DJ/Intvw	U.S.	1991	$8.00

Singles

Label	Catalog Number	Title	Type	Country	Year	Longbox Value / Value
Atlantic	PR 2573-2	Blow My Fuse	CDJ	U.S.	1988	$2.00
Atlantic	PR 2463-2	Cold Blood	CDJ	U.S.	1988	$2.00
Atlantic	PR 2674-2	Don't Close Your Eyes	CDJ	U.S.	1988	$2.00
Atlantic	PR 2711-2	Get It While It's Hot	CDJ	U.S.	1988	$2.00
Eastwest	PRCD 3988-2	Girl Money	CDJ	U.S.	1991	$2.00
Eastwest	PRCD 4026-2	Girl Money	CDJ	U.S.	1991	$2.00
Eastwest	PRCD 3885-2	Hot Wire	CDJ	U.S.	1991	$2.00
Eastwest	PRCD 4252-2	Same Jane	CDJ	U.S.	1991	$2.00
Eastwest	PRCD 4218-2	Tear Down the Walls	CDJ	U.S.	1991	$3.00

Klause, Bernie

Singles

Label	Catalog Number	Title	Type	Country	Year	Longbox Value / Value
Rykodisc	1005	Jungle Shoes	CDJ	U.S.		$3.00

Klein, Oscar

Singles

Label	Catalog Number	Title	Type	Country	Year	Longbox Value / Value
Intercord	815 232	Swingtime	CD3	Germany	1989	$8.00

Kleo

Singles

Label	Catalog Number	Title	Type	Country	Year	Longbox Value / Value
	1100	Tell Me	CD5	U.S.	1994	$5.00

KLF

Full Length

Label	Catalog Number	Title	Type	Country	Year	Longbox Value / Value
Arista	8657-2403	White Room, The	LP/LB	U.S.	1992	$30.00/$25.00

2CD limited edition.

Singles

Label	Catalog Number	Title	Type	Country	Year	Longbox Value / Value
Intercord	825 797	3 AM Eternal	CD5	Germany	1990	$10.00
Toshiba	TOCP-6744	3 AM Eternal	CD5	Japan	1990	$5.00
APT	KLF-005CD	3 AM Eternal	CD5	U.K.	1990	$10.00
Arista	ASCD-2230	3 AM Eternal	CDJ	U.S.	1990	$3.00
Intercord	825 927	America: What Time is Love?	CD5	Germany	1991	$10.00
APT	KLFUSA-4CD	America: What Time is Love?	CD5	U.K.	1991	$10.00
Toshiba	TODP-2337	Justified And Ancient	CD3	Japan	1991	$13.00/$3.00
Intercord	825 925	Justified And Ancient	CD5	U.K.	1991	$10.00
APT	KLF-010CD	Kylie Said to Jason	CD5	U.K.	1990	$10.00
Intercord	825 907	Last Train To Transcendental	CD5	Germany	1991	$10.00
Intercord	825 9012	Last Train To Transcendental	CD5	Germany	1991	$10.00
Arista	ASCD-2382	Last Train To Transcendental	CDJ	U.S.	1991	$3.00
Arista	ASCD-2403	Stand by the Jams	CDJ	U.S.	1992	$6.00
Arista	07822-12403	Stand by the Jams	CDJ	U.S.	1992	$7.00
Intercord	825 835	This Is What the KLF Is About	CD5	Germany	1992	$10.00
Toshiba	TOCP-7401/3	This Is What the KLF Is About	CD3	Japan	1992	$15.00/$4.00
WEA	9031-72897-2	What Time is Love	CD5	Germany	1991	$10.00
Toshiba	TODP-2332	What Time is Love	CD3	Japan	1991	$15.00/$4.00
Apt	KLF-004CD	What Time is Love	CD5	U.K.	1991	$10.00
Wax Trax	9157	What Time is Love	CD5	U.S.	1990	$5.00
Arista	ASCD-2365	What Time is Love	CDJ	U.S.	1991	$3.00

Klugh, Earl

Full Length

Label	Catalog Number	Title	Type	Country	Year	Longbox Value / Value
EMI	CDP-46007	Low Ride	LP/LB	U.S.†	1985	$14.00/$8.00
Warner	25262-2	Soda Fountain Shuffle	LP/LB	U.S.†	1985	$14.00/$8.00
EMI	CDP-46030	Wishful Thinking	LP/LB	U.S.†	1985	$14.00/$8.00

Singles

Label	Catalog Number	Title	Type	Country	Year	Longbox Value / Value
Warner Brothers	PRO-CD-5189	Days of Wine and Roses	CDJ	U.S.	1991	$2.00
Warner Brothers	PRO-CD-4813	Midnight in San Juan	CDJ	U.S.	1991	$2.00
Warner Brothers	PRO-CD-6064	Prelude	CDJ	U.S.	1993	$2.00

Klugh, Earl & Hiroki Miyano

Full Length

Label	Catalog Number	Title	Type	Country	Year	Longbox Value / Value
Philips	814724-2	Hotel California	LP/LB	U.S.†	1985	$14.00/$8.00

Klymaxx

Singles

Label	Catalog Number	Title	Type	Country	Year	Longbox Value / Value
MCA	DMCAt-1427	Good Love	CD5	U.K.	1990	$8.00
MCA		Good Love	CDJ	U.S.	1990	$2.00
MCA	CD45 1143	When You Kiss Me	CDJ	U.S.	1990	$2.00

KMC Kru

Singles

Label	Catalog Number	Title	Type	Country	Year	Longbox Value / Value
Curb	1015	Nothin' But a Party	CDJ	U.S.	1992	$2.00

KMD

Singles

Label	Catalog Number	Title	Type	Country	Year	Longbox Value / Value
Elektra	PRCD 8336-2	Peachfuzz	CDJ	U.S.	1990	$2.00
Elektra	PRCD 8893-2	Whatniggyknow?	CDJ	U.S.	1994	$2.00
Elektra	PRCD 8338-2	Who Me?	CDJ	U.S.	1991	$2.00

KMFDM

Full Length

Label	Catalog Number	Title	Type	Country	Year	Longbox Value / Value
Wax Trax		Angst	LTD/LP	U.S.	1993	$15.00

CD in digipak with limited edition sticker.

Singles

Label	Catalog Number	Title	Type	Country	Year	Longbox Value / Value
Wax Trax	8707	A Drug Against War	CD5	U.S.	1993	$5.00
SPV	4958-3	Godlike	CD5	Germany	1990	$9.00
Wax Trax	WAX-132CD	Godlike	CD5	U.K.	1990	$9.00
Wax Trax	9132	Godlike	CD5	U.S.	1990	$5.00
TeeVee Tunes	8632	Godlike	CD5	U.S.	1994	$5.00
TeeVee Tunes	8695	Help Us	CD5	U.S.	1994	$5.00
TeeVee	8727	Juke Joint Jezebel	CD5	U.S.	1994	$5.00
Wax Trax	9172	Money	CD5	U.S.	1990	$5.00
TeeVee Tunes	8672	Money	CD5	U.S.	1994	$5.00
Wax Trax	9077	More and Faster	CD5	U.S.	1990	$5.00
Wax Trax	PROMOCD6	Sex on the Flag	CDJ	U.S.	1990	$6.00
TeeVee Records	8723	Sin, Sex & Salvation	CD5	U.S.	1994	$5.00
TeeVee Tunes	8674	Split	CD5	U.S.	1994	$5.00
Big Life	BLRD-87	Sucks	CD5	U.K.	1992	$9.00
TVT	8703	Sucks	CD5	U.S.	1992	$5.00
SPV	4999-3	Thrill Kill Kult	CD5	Germany	1990	$9.00
TeeVee Tunes	8660	Thrill Kill Kult	CD5	U.S.	1994	$5.00
Wax Trax	9108	Virus	CD5	U.S.	1990	$5.00
Wax Trax	9602	Virus	CD5	U.S.	1990	$5.00
TeeVee Tunes	8606	Virus	CD5	U.S.	1994	$5.00
Rough Trade	251-1316-3	Vogue	CD5	Germany	1990	$5.00
Transglobal	TRAN-04CD	Vogue	CD5	U.K.	1990	$9.00
Wax Trax	9178	Vogue	CD5	U.S.	1990	$5.00

Knack

Full Length

Label	Catalog Number	Title	Type	Country	Year	Longbox Value / Value
Pioneer Artists	PA-82-016	At Carnegie Hall	LD	U.S.	1982	$30.00

Singles

Label	Catalog Number	Title	Type	Country	Year	Longbox Value / Value
Charisma	VJCP-10175	One Day at a Time	CD3	Japan	1991	$12.00/$4.00
Charisma	PRCD 043	One Day at a Time	CDJ	U.S.	1991	$2.00
Charisma	VJCP-10154	Rocket o' Love	CD3	Japan	1991	$12.00/$4.00
Charisma	PRCD 025	Rocket o' Love	CDJ	U.S.	1991	$2.00

Knight, Gladys and The Pips

Full Length

Label	Catalog Number	Title	Type	Country	Year	Longbox Value / Value
Motown	5388	If I Were Your Woman	LP/BP	U.S.		$12.00/$7.00
Intertape	500060	Knight, Gladys and The Pips	LP	U.K.		$25.00

Singles

Label	Catalog Number	Title	Type	Country	Year	Longbox Value / Value
Motown	MOTD-70007	I Heard It Through the Grape Vine	CDJ	U.K.		$2.00
MCA	257543-2	License to Kill	CD5	Germany	1989	$10.00
Pioneer	09P3-6'69	License to Kill	CD3	Japan	1989	$12.00/$5.00
MCA	DMCA-1339	License to Kill	CD3	U.K.	1989	$10.00
Eastwest	258114-2	Love Overboard	CD5	Germany	1988	$10.00
MCA	DMCA-1223	Love Overboard	CD5	U.K.	1988	$10.00
		Love Overboard	CDJ	U.S.	1988	$2.00
MCA	1678	Meet Me in the Middle	CDJ	U.S.	1991	$3.00
MCA	2075	Meet Me in the Middle	CDJ	U.S.	1991	$3.00
BMG	MCD-17841	Superwoman	CD5	Germany	1991	$10.00
MCA	CD45 1670	Superwoman	CDJ	U.S.	1991	$3.00
MCA	MCA5P-4639	Where Would I Be	CDJ	U.S.	1991	$2.00

Knight, Holly

Singles

Label	Catalog Number	Title	Type	Country	Year	Longbox Value / Value
Sony	10EP-3057	Heart Don't Fail Me Now	CD3	Japanj	1988	$12.00/$4.00
Columbia	652849-2	Heart Don't Fail Me Now	CD5	U.K.	1988	$10.00
Columbia	CSK 1199	Heart Don't Fail Me Now	CDJ	U.S.	1987	$2.00

Knoer, Joerg

Singles

Label	Catalog Number	Title	Type	Country	Year	Longbox Value / Value
Polygram	873341-2	Gagman	CD5	Germany	1989	$8.00

Knopfler, David

Full Length

Label	Catalog Number	Title	Type	Country	Year	Longbox Value / Value
Radio Ventures		Masters of Rock	RS	U.S.	1990	$50.00

Airdate: 5/21/90.

Singles

Label	Catalog Number	Title	Type	Country	Year	Longbox Value / Value
A&M	CD 17713	Heat Come Down	CDJ	U.S.	1988	$2.00
Polygram	878851-2	Lonely Is the Night	CD5	Germany	1991	$9.00
Cypress	DPRO-17638	Whispers Of Gethsemane	CDJ	U.S.	1988	$2.00
Polygram	868377-2	Yeah...But What Do	CD5	Germany	1991	$9.00

Knopfler, Mark

Full Length

Label	Catalog Number	Title	Type	Country	Year	Longbox Value / Value
Album Network		Album Network Special	RS	U.S.	1996	$130.00

2 CD set. Airdate: 7/23/96.

Label	Catalog Number	Title	Type	Country	Year	Longbox Value / Value
		Golden Heart	DJ/Smplr	U.K.		$80.00

CD boxed set with book, photos, and two Macintosh interactive diskettes.

Label	Catalog Number	Title	Type	Country	Year	Longbox Value / Value
		Golden Heart	DJ/Intvw	U.K.	1996	$65.00
Radio Ventures		Masters of Rock	RS	U.S.	1990	$50.00
Warner Brothers		Words & Music	DJ/Intvw	U.S.	1996	$18.00

Singles

Label	Catalog Number	Title	Type	Country	Year	Longbox Value / Value
		Darling Pretty	CD5	U.K.	1996	$10.00
Vertigo	888989-2	Storybook Love	CD5	Germany	1990	$10.00
Vertigo	VERCD-37	Storybook Love	CD5	U.K.	1990	$10.00

Know How

Singles

Label	Catalog Number	Title	Type	Country	Year	Longbox Value / Value
SPV	8422	Reality	CD5	Germany	1989	$8.00

Knuckles, Frankie

Singles

Label	Catalog Number	Title	Type	Country	Year	Longbox Value / Value
Virgin	VUSCD-52	It's Hard Sometimes	CD5	U.K.	1991	$8.00

Label	Catalog Number	Title	Type	Country	Year	Longbox Value/Value
Virgin	VUSCD-60	Rain Falls	CD5	U.K.	1992	$8.00
Polygram	886660-3	Tears	CD3	Germany	1989	$8.00
Polygram	886661-2	Tears	CD5	Germany	1989	$8.00
Virgin	664564	Whistle Song, The	CD5	Germany	1991	$8.00
Virgin	VUSCD-47	Whistle Song, The	CD5	U.K.	1991	$8.00
Virgin	PRCD 4013	Whistle Song, The	CDJ	U.S.	1991	$2.00

Kohl, Ernest

Singles

Label	Catalog Number	Title	Type	Country	Year	Longbox Value/Value
Zyx	7415	Don't Let Me Down	CD5	U.S.	1994	$5.00

Kold

Singles

Label	Catalog Number	Title	Type	Country	Year	Longbox Value/Value
	79007	Hokeepokee	CD5	U.S.	1994	$5.00

Kon Kan

Singles

Label	Catalog Number	Title	Type	Country	Year	Longbox Value/Value
Atlantic	PRCD 3702-2	(Could've Said) I Told You So	CDJ	U.S.	1990	$2.00
Atlantic		Harry Houdini	CDJ	U.S.		$2.00
Atlantic		I Beg Your Pardon	CDJ	U.S.		$2.00
Atlantic	86121-2	Liberty	CD5	U.S.	1990	$4.00
Atlantic	PRCD 3598-2	Liberty	CDJ	U.S.	1990	$2.00
Atlantic		Puss 'n Boots	CDJ	U.S.		$2.00

Konders, Bobby

Singles

Label	Catalog Number	Title	Type	Country	Year	Longbox Value/Value
Mercury	CDP 717	Rising to the Top	CDJ	U.S.	1992	$2.00

Kongos, John

Singles

Label	Catalog Number	Title	Type	Country	Year	Longbox Value/Value
Eastwest	1717791-2	He's Gonna Step on You Again	CD5	Germany	1990	$8.00

Konitz, Lee

Singles

Label	Catalog Number	Title	Type	Country	Year	Longbox Value/Value
M.A.	737	Ocean Song	CDJ	U.S.	1989	$2.00

Koo

Singles

Label	Catalog Number	Title	Type	Country	Year	Longbox Value/Value
Delta	22 109	Got to Get it Together	CD5	U.S.		$3.00

Kool G Rap

Singles

Label	Catalog Number	Title	Type	Country	Year	Longbox Value/Value
Epic	ESK 7401	Fast Life	CDJ	U.S.		$2.00
Epic	ESK 7162	It's a Shame	CDJ	U.S.		$2.00

Kool G. Rap & D.J. Polo

Singles

Label	Catalog Number	Title	Type	Country	Year	Longbox Value/Value
		Erase Racism	CDJ	U.S.		$2.00

Kool Moe Dee

Singles

Label	Catalog Number	Title	Type	Country	Year	Longbox Value/Value
Jive		All Night Long	CDJ	U.S.		$2.00
Jive	42145-2-JDJ	Can U Feel It	CDJ	U.S.	1993	$2.00
Jive	42015-2-JDJ	Death Blow	CDJ	U.S.	1991	$2.00
Jive	1352-2-JDJ	God Made Me Funke	CDJ	U.S.	1990	$2.00
Alfa	ALDB-110	How Kool Can One Blackman Be	CD3	Japan	1991	$12.00/$3.00
RCA	1453-2-RDJ	How Kool Can One Blackman Be	CDJ	U.S.	1991	$2.00
RCA	ZD-43206	I Got to Work	CD5	Germany	1989	$10.00
Jive		I Got to Work	CDJ	U.S.		$2.00
Jive	ALDB-110	Rise 'n Shine	CD3	Japan	1991	$12.00/$3.00
Jive	1217	They Want Money	CDJ	U.S.	1989	$2.00

Kool Skool

Singles

Label	Catalog Number	Title	Type	Country	Year	Longbox Value/Value
		My Girl	CDJ	U.S.		$2.00
		You Can't Buy My Love	CDJ	U.S.		$2.00

Kool & The Gang

Full Length

Label	Catalog Number	Title	Type	Country	Year	Longbox Value/Value
De-Lite	DECD-9518	Celebrate	LP/BP	U.S.†	1984	$12.00/$7.00
De-Lite	822 943-2	Emergency	LP/BP	U.S.†	1985	$12.00/$7.00
De-Lite	DECD-8505	In the Hart	LP/BP	U.S.†	1984	$12.00/$7.00
Pioneer	PA-85-107	Tonight	LD	U.S.	1985	$20.00

Singles

Label	Catalog Number	Title	Type	Country	Year	Longbox Value/Value
Polygram	874989-2	Celebrate	CD5	Germany	1990	$10.00
Polygram	874829-2	Celebrate	CD5	Germany	1990	$10.00
Polygram	JABCD-78	Celebrate	CD5	U.K.	1990	$10.00
Mercury	MERCD-346	Get Down on It	CD5	U.K.	1991	$10.00
Polygram	879285-2	He's the Boss	CD5	Germany	1990	$10.00
Polygram	873124-3	Never Give Up	CD3	Germany	1989	$10.00
Polygram	873125-2	Never Give Up	CD5	Germany	1989	$10.00
Polygram	888982-2	Peace Meaker	CD5	Germany	1989	$10.00
Polygram	870572-2	Rags to Riches	CD5	Germany	1988	$10.00
Polygram	870572-2	Rags to Riches	CD5	U.K.	1988	$10.00
Mercury	870 738-2	Rags to Riches	CDV/BP	U.S.	1988	$20.00/$20.00
Polygram	889490-3	Raindrops	CD3	Germany	1989	$10.00
Polygram	889491-2	Raindrops	CD5	Germany	1989	$10.00
Polygram	889741-2	Raindrops	CD5	Germany	1989	$10.00
Mercury	MERCD-293	Raindrops	CD5	U.K.	1989	$10.00
Mercury	CDP 85	Raindrops	CDJ	U.S.	1988	$2.00
Curb	D1217	Salute to the Ladies	CDJ	U.S.		$2.00
Polygram	872001-2	Stone Love	CD5	Germany	1988	$10.00
PMV	870 711-2	Stone Love	CDV/BP	U.S.	1988	$20.00/$20.00
Polygram	871341-2	Strong	CD5	Germany	1988	$10.00
Polygram	868259-2	Tonight	CD5	Germany	1988	$10.00
Charly	CDMUTE 1	Unite	CD5	U.K.	1993	$10.00
JRS	820	Unite	CDJ	U.S.	1993	$2.00
Polygram	888074-2	Victory	CD5	Germany	1990	$10.00
Polygram	888074-2	Victory	CD5	U.K.	1990	$10.00
Mercury	080 079-2	Victory	CDV	U.S.	1987	$15.00
Mercury	080 079-2	Victory	DJ/CDV	U.S.	1988	$12.00
Polygram	877009-2	You Are the Meaning of Friend	CD5	Germany	1990	$10.00

Kooper, Al

Full Length

Label	Catalog Number	Title	Type	Country	Year	Longbox Value/Value
		Al's Big Deal/Unclaimed Freight	LP/LB	U.S.		$18.00/$15.00
		House of Blues	RS	U.S.	1995	$40.00

Airdate: 3/19/95.

Label	Catalog Number	Title	Type	Country	Year	Longbox Value/Value
	XDCS-93089	Joy of Flying	DJ/Smplr	Japan	1994	N/A

Koppes, Peter

Singles

Label	Catalog Number	Title	Type	Country	Year	Longbox Value/Value
		Lost Peace, The	CDJ	U.S.	1989	$2.00
Phantom	PHCD12-49	Peak to Peak	CD5	Australia		$8.00

Korda

Singles

Label	Catalog Number	Title	Type	Country	Year	Longbox Value/Value
ZYX	6720-8	Move Your Baby	CD5	Germany	1992	$6.00

Koreana

Singles

Label	Catalog Number	Title	Type	Country	Year	Longbox Value/Value
Polygram	887730-2	Hand in Hand	CD5	Germany	1988	$8.00
Polydor	P10P-30019	Hand in Hand	CD3	Japan	1988	$12.00/$3.00
Polygram	873272-2	Living for Love	CD5	Germany	1990	$8.00
Polygram	873727-2	Living for Love	CD5	Germany	1990	$8.00
Polygram	871313-2	Loving You, Loving Me	CD5	Germany	1988	$8.00

Korgis

Singles

Label	Catalog Number	Title	Type	Country	Year	Longbox Value/Value
Aris	8846475	Everybody's Got to Learn Sometime	CD5	Germany	1990	$8.00
BMG	VHFXD-65	Everybody's Got to Learn Sometime	CD5	U.K.	1990	$8.00

Korn

Full Length

Label	Catalog Number	Title	Type	Country	Year	Longbox Value/Value
Immortal/Epic		Korn	LTD/LP	U.S.	1994	$18.00

CD plus Korn screen saver.

Label	Catalog Number	Title	Type	Country	Year	Longbox Value/Value
Immortal/Epic		Korn	LTD/LP	U.S.	1994	$18.00

CD plus VHS video.

Singles

Label	Catalog Number	Title	Type	Country	Year	Longbox Value/Value
		A.D.I.D.A.S.	CD5	U.K.	1997	$10.00
Immortal/Epic		Clown	CDJ	U.S.		$3.00

Kortez

Singles

Label	Catalog Number	Title	Type	Country	Year	Longbox Value/Value
BCM	20493	Put Your Body on	CD5	Germany	1990	$8.00

Koto

Singles

Label	Catalog Number	Title	Type	Country	Year	Longbox Value/Value
ZYX	6460-8	Acknowledge	CD5	Germany	1991	$8.00
ZYX	6352-8	Champions Cue	CD5	Germany	1990	$8.00
ZYX	6719-8	Mind Machine	CD5	Germany	1990	$8.00

Kottke, Leo

Full Length

Label	Catalog Number	Title	Type	Country	Year	Longbox Value/Value
Takoma		6 & 12 String Guitar	LP/LB	U.S.		$9.00/$6.00
Private Music		Regards From Chuck Pink	LP/LB	Canada		$6.00

Koz, Dave

Full Length

Label	Catalog Number	Title	Type	Country	Year	Longbox Value/Value
Capitol	DPRO-79746	Lucky Man	DJ/Smplr	U.S.	1994	$8.00

Singles

Label	Catalog Number	Title	Type	Country	Year	Longbox Value/Value
Capitol		Castle of Dreams	CDJ	U.S.		$2.00
Capitol	DPRO-79301	Lucky Man	CDJ	U.S.	1994	$2.00
Capitol	DPRO-79731	You Make Me Smile	CDJ	U.S.	1993	$2.00

Kraftwerk

Full Length

Label	Catalog Number	Title	Type	Country	Year	Longbox Value/Value
Warner Brothers	3549-2	Computer World	LP/LB	U.S.†	1985	$14.00/$8.00
EMI		Man-Machine, The	LTD/LP	U.K.	1997	$35.00

Limited edition centennial CD edition housed in a slip case with a special 100 aniversary booklet.

Singles

Label	Catalog Number	Title	Type	Country	Year	Longbox Value/Value
EMI	CDEM-201	Radioactivity	CD5	U.K.	1991	$8.00
Electrola	204516-2	Radioaktivist	CD5	Germany	1991	$8.00
EMI	204325-2	Robot	CD5	Germany	1991	$8.00
EMI	CDEM-192	Robots, The	CD5	U.K.	1991	$8.00
Elektra	9 266526-2	Robots, The	CD5	U.S.	1991	$4.00
Elektra	PRCD 8392-2	Robots, The	CDJ	U.S.	1991	$2.00
Capitol	C2 15620	Trans Europe Express	CD5	U.S.	1990	$5.00

Krause, Bernie

Singles

Label	Catalog Number	Title	Type	Country	Year	Longbox Value/Value
SPV	6850	Jungle Shoes	CD3	Germany	1989	$8.00
		Jungle Shoes	CDJ	U.S.	1988	$2.00

Krauss, Alison

Full Length

Label	Catalog Number	Title	Type	Country	Year	Longbox Value/Value
Rounder		Now That I've Found You: A Collection	DJ/Smplr	U.S.	1995	$13.00
Rounder		So Long So Wrong	LTD/LP	U.S.	1997	$16.00

2 CD set. Sold only at Wal Mart department stores.

Kravitz, Lenny

Full Length

Label	Catalog Number	Title	Type	Country	Year	Longbox Value/Value
Virgin	12803	Any Love in Your Heart	DJ/Smplr	U.S.	1993	$15.00
Virgin	724383916900	Are You Gonna Go My Way	LTD/LP	U.S.	1993	$20.00

CD and Vinyl LP set.

Label	Catalog Number	Title	Type	Country	Year	Longbox Value/Value
Virgin	VJCP-25200	Circus	LTD/LP	Japan	1995	$35.00

Extra Track "Another Life."

Label	Catalog Number	Title	Type	Country	Year	Longbox Value/Value
Virgin	12803	Is There Any Love in Your Heart	DJ/Smplr	U.S.	1993	$18.00
Virgin	3941	Mama Said Sampler	DJ/Smplr	U.S.	1991	$10.00
Westwood One		Off the Record	RS	U.S.	1995	$25.00

Airdate: 9/18/95.

Label	Catalog Number	Title	Type	Country	Year	Longbox Value/Value
Westwood One		Off the Record	RS	U.S.	1996	$25.00

Airdate: 1/15/96.

Label	Catalog Number	Title	Type	Country	Year	Longbox Value/Value
Virgin	3869	Sampler With Soul, The	DJ/Smplr	U.S.	1991	$15.00
Virgin		Universal Love Tour, The	DJ/Smplr	France	1993	$25.00
Media America		Up Close	RS	U.S.	1995	$30.00

Singles

Label	Catalog Number	Title	Type	Country	Year	Longbox Value/Value
Virgin	VJDP-10202	Are You Gonna Go My Way	CD5	Japan	1993	$12.00
Virgin	VUSCD-34	Are You Gonna Go My Way	CD5	U.K.	1991	$10.00
Virgin	DPRO-12755	Are You Gonna Go My Way	CDJ	U.S.	1993	$7.00
	PCD-0368	Believe	CDJ	Japan		$35.00
Virgin	VJCP-20006	Believe	CD5	Japan	1993	$18.00
Virgin	VUSCD 72	Believe	CD5	U.K.	1993	$10.00
Virgin	12781	Believe	CDJ	U.S.	1993	$7.00
Virgin	DPRO11071	Can't Get You Off My Mind	CDJ	U.S.		$2.00
Virgin	11045	Circus	CDJ	U.S.	1995	$7.00
Virgin	PRCD 5981	Fields of Joy	CDJ	U.S.	1991	$7.00
Virgin		Heaven Help	CD5	U.K.	1993	$10.00
Virgin		Heaven Help	CD5	U.K.	1993	$10.00

Second version.

Label	Catalog Number	Title	Type	Country	Year	Longbox Value/Value
Virgin	38412	Heaven Help	CD5	U.S.	1993	$6.00
Virgin	14105	Heaven Help	CDJ	U.S.	1993	$7.00
Virgin	VUSCD-17	I Build this Garden For Us	CD3	U.K.	1990	$10.00
Virgin	PRCD WEED	I Build this Garden For Us	CDJ	U.S.	1990	$7.00
Virgin		Is There Any Love	CD5	Australia		$10.00
Virgin	664397	It Ain't Over Til It's Over	CD5	Germany	1991	$10.00
Virgin	VJCP-14026	It Ain't Over Til It's Over	CD3	Japan	1991	$13.00/$5.00
Virgin	VUSCD-43	It Ain't Over Til It's Over	CD5	U.K.	1991	$10.00
Virgin	PRCD 3883	It Ain't Over Til It's Over	CDJ	U.S.	1991	$7.00
Virgin	VUSCD 26	Let Love Rule	CD5	U.K.	1989	$10.00
Virgin	VUSCD-10	Let Love Rule	CD5	U.K.	1989	$10.00
Virgin	PRCD 2864	Let Love Rule	CDJ	U.S.	1989	$7.00

Label	Catalog Number	Title	Type	Country	Year	Longbox Value / Value
Virgin	VJCP-20002	Live in Japan	CD5	Japan	1991	$20.00
Virgin	VUSCD-20	Mr. Cab Driver	CD5	U.K.	1990	$10.00
Virgin	PRCD 3272	Mr. Cab Driver	CDJ	U.S.	1990	$7.00
Virgin	VJDP-10252	Rock 'n Roll Is Dead	CD3	Japan	1995	$13.00/$5.00
Virgin		Rock 'n Roll Is Dead	CD5	U.K.	1995	$10.00
Virgin	38514	Rock 'n Roll Is Dead	CD5	U.S.		$5.00
Virgin	DPRO-14115	Spinning Around Over You	CDJ	U.S.	1993	$10.00
Virgin	664710	Stand By My Woman	CD5	Germany	1991	$10.00
Virgin	VUSCD-45	Stand By My Woman	CD5	U.K.	1991	$10.00
Virgin	PRCD 4099	Stand By My Woman	CDJ	U.S.	1991	$7.00
Virgin	PRCD 4377	Stop Draggin'	CDJ	U.S.	1991	$10.00
Virgin	665332	What Comes Around Goes Around	CDJ	Germany	1992	$10.00
Virgin	PRCD 4274	What Comes Around Goes Around	CDJ	U.S.	1991	$10.00
		What the F**k Are We Saying?	CD5	Germany		$15.00

Kraze

Singles

Label	Catalog Number	Title	Type	Country	Year	Longbox Value / Value
BCM	20270	Let's Play House	CD5	Germany	1989	$10.00
MCA	DMCAT-1337	Let's Play House	CD5	U.K.	1989	$10.00

Kreator

Singles

Label	Catalog Number	Title	Type	Country	Year	Longbox Value / Value
		People of the Lie	CDJ	U.S.		$2.00

Kreiger, Robby

Full Length

Label	Catalog Number	Title	Type	Country	Year	Longbox Value / Value
		No Habla	LP/LB	U.S.		$13.00/$8.00

Kriss Kross

Full Length

Label	Catalog Number	Title	Type	Country	Year	Longbox Value / Value
Sony/Sega CD		Make Your Own Music Video	LP	U.S.	1993	$10.00

CD-ROM plays only on Sega CD players.

Singles

Label	Catalog Number	Title	Type	Country	Year	Longbox Value / Value
Columbia	CSK 5301	Alright	CDJ	U.S.	1993	$2.00
Columbia	CSK 77397	Da Bomb	CDJ	U.S.		$2.00
CBS	658392-5	I Missed the Bus	CD5	U.K.	1992	$9.00
Columbia	CSK 4761	I Missed the Bus	CDJ	U.S.	1992	$2.00
Columbia	44K 77237	I'm Real	CD5	U.S.	1993	$4.00
Columbia	658858-2	It's A Shame	CD5	U.K.	1992	$9.00
Columbia	CSK 4914	It's A Shame	CDJ	U.S.	1992	$2.00
Sony	SRDS-8233	Jump	CD3	Japan	1992	$12.00/$4.00
Sony	SRCS-5935	Jump	CD5	Japan	1992	$11.00
CBS	657854-2	Jump	CD5	U.K.	1992	$9.00
Columbia	44K 74193	Jump	CD5	U.S.	1992	$5.00
Columbia	CSk 74197	Jump	CDJ	U.S.	1992	$6.00
Columbia	CSK 7721	Live and Die For Hip Hop	CDJ	U.S.		$2.00
Columbia	CSK 7429	Tonight's the Night	CDJ	U.S.		$2.00
Sony	SRCS-5992	Warm It Up	CD5	Japan	1992	$11.00
Columbia	658218-2	Warm It Up	CD5	U.K.	1992	$9.00
Columbia	44K 74377	Warm It Up	CD5	U.S.	1992	$4.00
Columbia	CSK 74376	Warm It Up	CDJ	U.S.	1992	$2.00

Krokus

Full Length

Label	Catalog Number	Title	Type	Country	Year	Longbox Value / Value
Arista	ARCD-8243	Blitz, The	LP/LB	U.S.†	1985	$14.00/$8.00
Arista	ARCD-8005	Headhunter	LP/LB	U.S.†	1985	$14.00/$8.00
MCA	ARCD-42087	Heart Attack	LP/LB	U.S.	1988	$14.00/$8.00
		Metal Rendez-Vous	LP/LB	U.S.		$14.00/$8.00
Pioneer	PA-85-118	Video Blitz, The	LD	U.S.	1985	$25.00

Kronos Quartet

Full Length

Label	Catalog Number	Title	Type	Country	Year	Longbox Value / Value
Nonesuch	79394	Released 1985-1995	LTD/LP	U.S.	1995	$16.00

2 CD set.

Singles

Label	Catalog Number	Title	Type	Country	Year	Longbox Value / Value
Elektra	79255-2	Lutoslawski String Quartet	CD5	U.S.	1991	$5.00
Elektra	79253-2	Piano & String Quartet	CD5	U.S.	1991	$5.00
Elektra	79320-2	Piano & String Quartet	CD5	U.S.	1993	$5.00

With Morton Feldman.

KRS One

Singles

Label	Catalog Number	Title	Type	Country	Year	Longbox Value / Value
Jive	42146-2-JDJ	Outta Here	CDJ	U.S.	1993	$2.00

Krueger, Ulf

Singles

Label	Catalog Number	Title	Type	Country	Year	Longbox Value / Value
Polygram	868265-2	Dr. No	CD5	Germany	1991	$8.00
Polygram	878195-2	Patch Dance	CD5	Germany	1990	$8.00

Krupps

Singles

Label	Catalog Number	Title	Type	Country	Year	Longbox Value / Value
		Bloodsuckers	CD5	U.K.		$10.00
		Bloodsuckers	CD5	U.K.		$10.00

Second version.

Krush

Singles

Label	Catalog Number	Title	Type	Country	Year	Longbox Value / Value
Perspective	31458 8058	Let's Get Together	CDJ	U.S.	1992	$2.00

Krush Brothers

Singles

Label	Catalog Number	Title	Type	Country	Year	Longbox Value / Value
EMI	DPRO-79451	Edge of America, The	CDJ	U.S.		$15.00
Polygram	87007-2	House Arrest	CD5	Germany	1988	$8.00
Polygram	87007-2	House Arrest	CD5	U.K.	1988	$8.00
Pinacle	NWKCD-55	Walking on Sunshine	CD5	U.K.	1988	$8.00

Krush Perpective

Singles

Label	Catalog Number	Title	Type	Country	Year	Longbox Value / Value
A&M	PERD-7416	Let's Get Together	CD5	U.K.	1992	$8.00

Kryzler And Kompany

Singles

Label	Catalog Number	Title	Type	Country	Year	Longbox Value / Value
Epic	ESDB-3394	Moonflower	CD3	Japan	1993	$12.00/$3.00
Epic	ESDB-3331	Steam	CD3	Japan	1993	$12.00/$3.00
Epic	ESDB-3392	Venus Love	CD3	Japan	1993	$12.00/$3.00

Kubota, Toshi

Singles

Label	Catalog Number	Title	Type	Country	Year	Longbox Value / Value
Columbia	77963	Funk It Up	CD5	U.S.	1995	$6.00

Kuepper, Ed

Full Length

Label	Catalog Number	Title	Type	Country	Year	Longbox Value / Value
Dept. Of Foreign Affairs & Trade		Big Backyard, The	RS	Australia	1993	$30.00

Kula Shaker

Full Length

Label	Catalog Number	Title	Type	Country	Year	Longbox Value / Value
Columbia	CK 67822	K	LTD/LP	U.S.	1996	$16.00

Kut Loose

Singles

Label	Catalog Number	Title	Type	Country	Year	Longbox Value / Value
	PRCD 9091-2	I Like	CDJ	U.S.		$2.00
Elektra	66069	Surrender	CD5	U.S.	1995	$5.00

Kwame and The New Beginning

Singles

Label	Catalog Number	Title	Type	Country	Year	Longbox Value / Value
		Oneovdabigboiz	CDJ	U.S.		$2.00

Kyle, Jaime

Singles

Label	Catalog Number	Title	Type	Country	Year	Longbox Value / Value
Atco	PRCD 4544-2	Ragged Heart	CDJ	U.S.	1992	$2.00

Kyper

Singles

Label	Catalog Number	Title	Type	Country	Year	Longbox Value / Value
Atlantic	PRCD 3631-2	Conceited	CDJ	U.S.	1990	$2.00
Atlantic		Spin the Bottle	CDJ	U.S.	1992	$2.00
Atlantic	7567-86183-2	Tic Tac Toe	CD5	Germany	1990	$8.00

Kyuss

Singles

Label	Catalog Number	Title	Type	Country	Year	Longbox Value / Value
WEA	EKR 192 CD2	Deamon Cleaner	CD5	U.K.		$8.00
Dali	8726	Green Machine	CDJ	U.S.	1993	$2.00
	PRCD 9228-2	One Inch Man	CDJ	U.S.		$2.00
Elektra	PRCD 8969-2	Sky Valley Part II	CDJ	U.S.	1993	$2.00
Dali	8693	Thong Song	CDJ	U.S.	1992	$2.00

Kyze

Singles

Label	Catalog Number	Title	Type	Country	Year	Longbox Value / Value
Warner Brothers	PRO-CD-3719	Stomp	CDJ	U.S.	1989	$2.00

L.A.D.

Singles

Label	Catalog Number	Title	Type	Country	Year	Longbox Value / Value
	PRCD 10588-2	Party Nite	CDJ	U.S.		$2.00

L. A. Four

Full Length

Label	Catalog Number	Title	Type	Country	Year	Longbox Value / Value
East Wind	35-JD7 PSI	Going Home	LP/LB	U.S.†	1985	$14.00/$8.00

L.A. Guns

Full Length

Label	Catalog Number	Title	Type	Country	Year	Longbox Value / Value
Vertigo	PPD-1032	Cocked and Loaded	LTD/LP	Japan		$25.00

Picture disc CD.

Label	Catalog Number	Title	Type	Country	Year	Longbox Value / Value
Polydor	CDP 601	Holiday Fourplay	DJ/Smplr	U.S.	1991	$8.00
Vertigo	PPD-1043	L.A. Guns	LTD/LP	Japan		$20.00
Vertigo	28PD-528	L.A. Guns	LTD/LP	Japan		$25.00

Picture disc CD.

Label	Catalog Number	Title	Type	Country	Year	Longbox Value / Value
Polydor		L.A. Guns	DJ/LP	U.S.		$12.00

Singles

Label	Catalog Number	Title	Type	Country	Year	Longbox Value / Value
Mercury	MERCD-361	Ballad of Jane	CD5	U.K.	1991	$10.00
Polygram	CDP 210	Ballad of Jane	CDJ	U.S.	1989	$7.00
Polygram	878006-2	I Wanna Be Your Man	CD5	Canada	1990	$10.00
Polydor	CDP 283	I Wanna Be Your Man	CDJ	U.S.	1990	$2.00
Polydor	CDP 603	It's Over Now	CDJ	U.S.	1991	$2.00
Polydor		Killing Machine	CDJ	U.S.		$3.00
Vertigo	PHDR-36	Kiss My Love Goodbye	CD3	Japan	1991	$12.00/$4.00
Polydor	CDP 490	Kiss My Love Goodbye	CDJ	U.S.	1991	$6.00

With 3D cover and glasses.

Label	Catalog Number	Title	Type	Country	Year	Longbox Value / Value
Polydor		Long Time Dead	CDJ	U.S.		$3.00
Polygram	CDP 165	Never Enough	CDJ	U.S.	1989	$2.00
Polydor	CDP 708	Over the Edge	CDJ	U.S.	1992	$2.00
Vertigo	PPDS-9	Rip & Tear	CD3	Japan	1989	$12.00/$4.00
Polygram	CDP 111	Rip & Tear	CDJ	U.S.	1989	$2.00
Vertigo	870 712-2	Sex Action	CDV/BP	U.S.	1988	$20.00/$20.00
Mercury	865241-2	Some Lie 4 Love	CD5	Germany	1991	$10.00
Mercury	MERCD-358	Some Lie 4 Love	CD5	U.K.	1991	$10.00
Polydor	CDP 436	Some Lie 4 Love	CDJ	U.S.	1991	$2.00
Polydor	CDP 603	There She Goes	CDJ	U.S.	1991	$2.00

L.A. Style

Singles

Label	Catalog Number	Title	Type	Country	Year	Longbox Value / Value
Avex Trax	AVDD-20038	Balloony	CD3	Japan	1993	$12.00/$3.00
ZYX	ZYX-6876-8	I'm Raving	CD5	Germany	1992	$6.00
Avex Trax	AVDD-20033	I'm Raving	CD3	Japan	1992	$12.00/$3.00
ZYX	ZYX-6718-8	James Brown is Dead	CD5	Germany	1992	$8.00
ZYX	ZYX-6586-8	James Brown is Dead	CD5	Germany	1992	$8.00
ZYX	ZYX-6650-8	James Brown is Dead	CD5	Germany	1992	$8.00
Avex Trax	AVDD-20018	James Brown is Dead	CD3	Japan	1992	$12.00/$3.00
ZYX	ZYX-6586-8	James Brown is Dead	CD5	U.K.	1992	$8.00
ZYX	ZYX-6650-8	James Brown is Dead	CD5	U.K.	1992	$8.00
Arista	12387	James Brown is Dead	CD5	U.S.	1992	$4.00

L.B.C. Crew

Singles

Label	Catalog Number	Title	Type	Country	Year	Longbox Value / Value
	PRO-CD-7973	Beware of My Crew	CDJ	U.S.		$2.00

L. Kage

Singles

Label	Catalog Number	Title	Type	Country	Year	Longbox Value / Value
A&M	31458 6116	My Head's on Fire	CDJ	U.S.	1993	$2.00
Pinnacle	51-TP7CD	Passion 91	CD5	U.K.	1991	$8.00

L.L. Cool J.

Singles

Label	Catalog Number	Title	Type	Country	Year	Longbox Value / Value
Def Jam	656961-2	Around the Way Girl	CD5	Germany	1990	$10.00
Def Jam	6566080-5	Around the Way Girl	CD5	U.K.	1990	$10.00
Def Jam	656447-2	Around the Way Girl	CD5	U.K.	1991	$10.00
Def Jam	44K 73610	Around the Way Girl	CD5	U.S.	1990	$5.00
Def Jam	NSK 73609	Around the Way Girl	CDJ	U.S.	1990	$3.00
Def Jam	656133-3	Boomin' System, The	CD3	Germany	1990	$10.00
Def Jam	656133-2	Boomin' System, The	CD5	U.K.	1990	$10.00
Def Jam	NSK 73457	Boomin' System, The	CDJ	U.S.	1990	$3.00
	PRCD 7122-2	Doin' It	CDJ	U.S.		$3.00
Def Jam	NSK 2836	Go Cut Creator Go	CDJ	U.S.	1987	$3.00
Def Jam	NSK 2922	Going Back to Cali	CDJ	U.S.	1987	$3.00
	PRCD 7065-2	Hey Lover	CDJ	U.S.		$3.00
Polygram	577495	Hey Lover	CD5	U.S.	1995	$5.00
Def Jam	NSK 74811	How I'm Comin'	CDJ	U.S.	1993	$3.00
Def Jam	654945-3	I'm That Type of Guy	CD3	Germany	1989	$10.00
Def Jam	CDLLCL-3	I'm That Type of Guy	CD5	U.K.	1989	$10.00
Def Jam	NSK 1605	I'm That Type of Guy	CDJ	U.S.	1989	$3.00
Def Jam	NSK 73207	Jingling Baby	CDJ	U.S.	1990	$3.00
Def Jam	NSK 73706	Mama Said Knock You Out	CDJ	U.S.	1991	$3.00
Def Jam	655243-3	One Shot at Love	CD3	Germany	1989	$10.00
Def Jam	CDLLCJ-4	One Shot at Love	CD5	U.K.	1989	$10.00
Def Jam	NSK 1806	One Shot at Love	CDJ	U.S.	1989	$3.00
Def Jam	44K 74983	Pink Cookies in Plastic Bags	CD5	U.S.	1993	$5.00
Def Jam	NSK 74984	Pink Cookies in Plastic Bags	CDJ	U.S.	1993	$3.00

Label	Catalog Number	Title	Type	Country	Year	Longbox Value / Value
Def Jam	44K 73821	Six Minutes of Pleasure	CD5	U.S.	1991	$5.00
Def Jam	NSK 73820	Six Minutes of Pleasure	CDJ	U.S.	1991	$3.00
Def Jam	NSK 77098	Stand By Your Man	CDJ	U.S.	1993	$3.00
MCA	MCSTD-1594	Strictly Business	CD5	U.K.	1991	$10.00
MCA	2012	Strictly Business	CDJ	U.S.	1991	$3.00
Def Jam	NSK 18376	To Da Breakdown	CDJ	U.S.	1990	$3.00
Def Jam		Who's Afraid of the Big Bad Wolf	CDJ	Canada	1992	$5.00
Def Jam	657592-2	Who's Afraid of the Big Bad Wolf	CD5	Germany	1992	$10.00

L.U.P.O.

Singles

Label	Catalog Number	Title	Type	Country	Year	Longbox Value / Value
Polygram	877981-2	Keep It Up	CD5	Germany	1990	$8.00

L.V.

Singles

Label	Catalog Number	Title	Type	Country	Year	Longbox Value / Value
Tommy Boy	TBCD7723	I Am L.V.	CDJ	U.S.		$3.00
Tommy Boy	TBCD7723	Throw Your Hands Up	CDJ	U.S.		$3.00

L'Trimm

Singles

Label	Catalog Number	Title	Type	Country	Year	Longbox Value / Value
Atlantic		Cars With the Boom	CDJ	U.S.		$2.00
Atlantic	PR 2564-2	Cutie Pie	CDJ	U.S.	1988	$2.00
Atlantic	PRCD 24254-2	Low Rider	CDJ	U.S.	1991	$2.00

L-R

Singles

Label	Catalog Number	Title	Type	Country	Year	Longbox Value / Value
Special	PSDR-3017	Be With You	CD3	Japan	1992	$12.00/$3.00
Polystar	PSCR-1039	L	CD5	Japan	1991	$10.00
Polystar	PSDR-3011	Lazy Girl	CD3	Japan	1992	$12.00/$3.00

L7

Full Length

Label	Catalog Number	Title	Type	Country	Year	Longbox Value / Value
		Hungry for Stink	LTD/LP	Australia	1995	$35.00
	2CD set.					
Slash	PRO-CD-5871	Lose Your Dignity	DJ/Smplr	U.S.	1992	$20.00

Singles

Label	Catalog Number	Title	Type	Country	Year	Longbox Value / Value
Slash		Andres	CD5	Australia	1994	$12.00
Slash	PRO-CD-7017	Andres	CDJ	U.S.	1994	$3.00
Slash	LASCD-36	Everglade	CD5	U.K.	1992	$10.00
Slash	PRO-CD-5371	Everglade	CDJ	U.S.	1992	$3.00
Slash		Hungry for Stink	CDJ	U.S.	1994	$6.00
Slash		Hush Sweet Lover	CD5	Australia	1994	$12.00
Slash		Lose Your Dignity	CDJ	U.S.	1994	$6.00
Slash	LASCD 38	Monster	CD5	U.K.	1992	$10.00
Slash	43834-2	Off the Wagon	CD5	U.S.	1997	$5.00
Slash	PRO-CD-5736	One More Thing	CDJ	U.S.	1992	$3.00
Slash	LASCD-34	Pretend We're Dead	CD5	U.K.	1992	$10.00
Slash		Pretend We're Dead	CD5	U.K.	1992	$10.00
	Second version.					
Slash		Pretend We're Dead	CDJ	U.S.	1992	$3.00
Slash	PRO-CD-7185	Stuck Here Again	CDJ	U.S.	1994	$6.00

LA 800

Singles

Label	Catalog Number	Title	Type	Country	Year	Longbox Value / Value
Polygram	877293-2	Square Dance in the House	CD5	Germany	1990	$8.00

La Mafia

Singles

Label	Catalog Number	Title	Type	Country	Year	Longbox Value / Value
Sony	10311	Gracias	CDJ	U.S.	1993	$2.00
Sony Discos	CDP-12068	Toma Mi Amor	CD5	U.S.	1995	$8.00

LA Mix

Singles

Label	Catalog Number	Title	Type	Country	Year	Longbox Value / Value
BCM	20093	Check This Out	CD5	Germany	1989	$8.00
A&M	USACD-629	Check This Out	CD5	U.K.	1989	$8.00
BCM	390590-2	Coming Back for More	CD5	Germany	1990	$8.00
A&M	USACD-579	Coming Back for More	CD5	U.K.	1990	$8.00
BCM	20283	Get Loose	CD5	Germany	1989	$8.00
A&M	USACD-659	Get Loose	CD3	U.K.	1989	$8.00
A&M	USACD-662	Love Together	CD3	U.K.	1989	$8.00
A&M	USACD-677	Love Together	CD3	U.K.	1989	$8.00
A&M	USACD-707	Mysteries of Love	CD5	U.K.	1990	$8.00
A&M	USACD-755	We Shouldn't Hold Hands in the Dark	CD5	U.K.	1989	$8.00

LA News

Singles

Label	Catalog Number	Title	Type	Country	Year	Longbox Value / Value
Polygram	889178-3	Two of Us	CD3	Germany	1989	$8.00
Polygram	889179-2	Two of Us	CD5	Germany	1989	$8.00

LA Serrena

Singles

Label	Catalog Number	Title	Type	Country	Year	Longbox Value / Value
CBS	657909-2	I'm Free	CD5	Germany	1992	$8.00

LA Tour

Singles

Label	Catalog Number	Title	Type	Country	Year	Longbox Value / Value
Smash	498	Alien's Got a New Hi Fi	CDJ	U.S.	1991	$2.00
Smash	865 525	Cold	CD5	U.S.	1992	$4.00
Smash	009	Craziaskowboi	CDJ	U.S.	1993	$2.00
Smash	162 440 813	E	CD5	U.S.	1993	$4.00
Polygram	867919-2	Involved	CD5	Germany	1991	$8.00
Polygram	879993-2	People Are Still Having Sex	CD5	Germany	1991	$8.00
Polygram	PZCD-147	People Are Still Having Sex	CD5	U.K.	1991	$8.00

LA's

Singles

Label	Catalog Number	Title	Type	Country	Year	Longbox Value / Value
Go Discs	869301-2	Feelin'	CD5	Germany	1991	$8.00
Go Discs	LACD 6	Feelin'	CD5	U.K.	1991	$8.00
Go Discs	869233-2	There She Goes	CD5	Germany	1990	$8.00
London	POCD-1041	There She Goes	CD3	Japan	1991	$12.00/$3.00
Go Discs	LACD 2	There She Goes	CD5	U.K.	1990	$8.00
Go Discs	LASCD-5	There She Goes	CD5	U.K.	1991	$8.00
London	CDP 403	There She Goes	CDJ	U.S.	1990	$2.00
London	CDP 547	There She Goes	CDJ	U.S.	1990	$2.00
Go Discs	LASCD-4	Timeless Melody	CD5	U.K.	1990	$8.00
London	CDP 564	Timeless Melody	CDJ	U.S.	1990	$2.00

Labelle, Patti

Singles

Label	Catalog Number	Title	Type	Country	Year	Longbox Value / Value
MCA	MCA5P-54541	All Right Now	CD5	U.S.	1992	$5.00
MCA	MCA5P-2434	All Right Now	CDJ	U.S.	1992	$3.00
MCA	MCA5P-2535	All Right Now	CDJ	U.S.	1992	$3.00
MCA	MVDM-10	Feels Like Another One	CD3	Japan	1991	$12.00/$4.00
MCA	CD45 1672	Feels Like Another One	CDJ	U.S.	1991	$3.00
MCA	CD45 18298	I Can't Complain	CDJ	U.S.	1990	$3.00
Eastwest	257541-2	If You Asked Me To	CD5	Germany	1989	$10.00
Pioneer	09P3-6067	If You Asked Me To	CD3	Japan	1989	$12.00/$4.00
MCA	DMCA-1357	If You Asked Me To	CD5	U.K.	1989	$10.00
MCA	MCA5P-2072	Somebody Loves You Baby	CDJ	U.S.	1991	$3.00
MCA	MCA5P-2084	Somebody Loves You Baby	CDJ	U.S.	1992	$3.00
MCA	CD45 1120	T'was Love	CDJ	U.S.	1990	$3.00
MCA	55113	Turn It Out	CD5	U.S.	1995	$5.00
		Turn It Out	CDJ	U.S.		$3.00
Virgin	PRCD 3875	We Haven't Finished Yet	CDJ	U.S.	1991	$3.00
MCA	MCA5P-2358	When You Love Somebody	CDJ	U.S.	1992	$3.00
MCA	MCA5P-2157	When You've Been Blessed	CDJ	U.S.	1992	$3.00
Eastwest	257367-2	Yo Mister	CD5	Germany	1989	$10.00
MCA	DMCAT-1376	Yo Mister	CD5	U.K.	1989	$10.00

LaBouche

Singles

Label	Catalog Number	Title	Type	Country	Year	Longbox Value / Value
RCA	64445	Be My Lover	CD5	U.S.	1995	$4.00
RCA		Fallin' in Love	CDJ	U.K.	1995	$8.00
RCA	RDJ64391-2	Fallin' in Love	CDJ	U.S.	1995	$3.00

Lace

Singles

Label	Catalog Number	Title	Type	Country	Year	Longbox Value / Value
Wing	CDP 182	Why It Gotta Be Like That	CDJ	U.S.	1990	$2.00

Ladernacken

Full Length

Label	Catalog Number	Title	Type	Country	Year	Longbox Value / Value
		Boogaloo	LTD/LP	U.S.	1987	$20.00

Ladia

Singles

Label	Catalog Number	Title	Type	Country	Year	Longbox Value / Value
RCA	BVDR-126	Blind	CD3	Japan	1992	$12.00/$3.00

Lady Levi

Singles

Label	Catalog Number	Title	Type	Country	Year	Longbox Value / Value
BMG	ZD-44574	Looking For a Dope Beat	CD5	Germany	1991	$8.00
Motown	1438	Looking For a Dope Beat	CDJ	U.S.	1991	$2.00
Motown	1615	Rude Boys	CDJ	U.S.	1991	$2.00

Lady Lilly

Singles

Label	Catalog Number	Title	Type	Country	Year	Longbox Value / Value
BMG	664243	Morning Evening	CD5	Germany	1991	$8.00

Lady Soul

Singles

Label	Catalog Number	Title	Type	Country	Year	Longbox Value / Value
Boston	8567	Don't Forget About Me	CDJ	U.S.	1992	$2.00
Boston	10198	If My Sister's in Trouble	CDJ	U.S.	1992	$2.00

Laffy, Gerry

Singles

Label	Catalog Number	Title	Type	Country	Year	Longbox Value / Value
Seven Seas	K10Y-20018	Let's Stay Together	CD3	Japan	1989	$12.00/$3.00

Lag Time

Singles

Label	Catalog Number	Title	Type	Country	Year	Longbox Value / Value
Arise	CDR-15	Midnight Driving Rock 'n Roll	CD3	Japan	1992	$12.00/$3.00
Arise	CDR-10	Secret Lover	CD3	Japan	1991	$12.00/$3.00

Lagaylia

Singles

Label	Catalog Number	Title	Type	Country	Year	Longbox Value / Value
CBS	77704	Shower Me	CD5	U.S.	1994	$5.00

Lagrene, Bireli

Singles

Label	Catalog Number	Title	Type	Country	Year	Longbox Value / Value
Blue Note	DPRO-79630	Made in France	CDJ	U.S.	1991	$2.00

Laibach

Singles

Label	Catalog Number	Title	Type	Country	Year	Longbox Value / Value
Restless	71404	Sympathy for the Devil	CD5	U.S.	1988	$4.00

Laid Back

Singles

Label	Catalog Number	Title	Type	Country	Year	Longbox Value / Value
Ariola	662983	Bet It on You	CD5	Germany	1990	$8.00
Ariola	663161	Bet It on You	CD5	Germany	1990	$8.00
Ariola	663281	Highway of Love	CD5	Germany	1990	$8.00
Ariola	162356	Mr. Bakerman	CD3	Germany	1990	$8.00
Ariola	662356	Mr. Bakerman	CD5	Germany	1990	$8.00
Ariola	662356	Mr. Bakerman	CD5	U.K.	1990	$8.00
WEA	W-2836CD	White Horse	CD5	U.K.	1989	$8.00

Laine, Denny

Singles

Label	Catalog Number	Title	Type	Country	Year	Longbox Value / Value
Laserlight	12464	Danger Zone	CD5	U.S.	1994	$5.00

Laine, Paul

Singles

Label	Catalog Number	Title	Type	Country	Year	Longbox Value / Value
Elektra	PRCD 8158-2	Dorianna	CDJ	U.S.	1990	$2.00
Elektra	PRCD 8186-2	We Are the Young	CDJ	U.S.	1990	$2.00

Laing, Shona

Singles

Label	Catalog Number	Title	Type	Country	Year	Longbox Value / Value
Epic	ESK 4834	Fear of Falling	CDJ	U.S.	1992	$2.00

Lake

Singles

Label	Catalog Number	Title	Type	Country	Year	Longbox Value / Value
Polygram	871337-2	In the Midnight	CD5	Germany	1989	$8.00

Lake, Oliver & Jump Up

Full Length

Label	Catalog Number	Title	Type	Country	Year	Longbox Value / Value
Gramaphone	GRCD-8206	Plug It	LP/LB	U.S.†	1985	$14.00/$8.00

Lakeside

Singles

Label	Catalog Number	Title	Type	Country	Year	Longbox Value / Value
CBS	656199-3	Money	CD3	Germany	1990	$8.00
Epic		Money	CDJ	U.S.	1990	$2.00
Epic	ESK 2213	Party Patrol	CDJ	U.S.	1990	$2.00

Lalou

Singles

Label	Catalog Number	Title	Type	Country	Year	Longbox Value / Value
Polygram	867705-2	Facts of Life	CD5	Germany	1991	$8.00
Polygram	867953-2	Facts of Life	CD5	Germany	1991	$8.00

Lamb, Annabel

Singles

Label	Catalog Number	Title	Type	Country	Year	Longbox Value / Value
Polygram	887840-2	Ghosts of You	CD5	Germany	1988	$8.00
Polygram	889082-3	Refugee	CD3	Germany	1989	$8.00
Polygram	889083-2	Refugee	CD5	Germany	1989	$8.00

Lambada

Singles

Label	Catalog Number	Title	Type	Country	Year	Longbox Value / Value
Intercord	825 283	Lambada	CD3	Germany	1989	$7.00

Lambert, Hendricks & Ross

Full Length

Label	Catalog Number	Title	Type	Country	Year	Longbox Value / Value
Blue Note		Swingers, The	LTD/LP	U.S.	1995	$19.00

LaMond, George

Singles

Label	Catalog Number	Title	Type	Country	Year	Longbox Value / Value
Columbia	CSK 74756	Baby, I Believe in You	CDJ	U.S.	1992	$2.00
		Look Into My Eyes	CDJ	U.S.		$2.00
Epic	ESK 73603	No Matter What	CDJ	U.S.	1990	$2.00
Columbia	CSK 74425	Where Does That Leave Love	CDJ	U.S.	1992	$2.00
Columbia	655817-3	Without You	CD3	Germany	1990	$9.00

Landers, Audrey

Singles

Label	Catalog Number	Title	Type	Country	Year	Longbox Value / Value
WEA	246864-2	Gone With the Wild Wind	CD5	Germany	1989	$8.00
WEA	247606-2	Never Wanna Dance	CD5	Germany	1989	$8.00
WEA	867667-2-2	Santa Maria Goodbye	CD5	Germany	1989	$8.00
WEA	171241-2	Shine a Light	CD5	Germany	1989	$8.00
WEA	247233-2	Silverbird	CD5	Germany	1989	$8.00
WEA	246598-2	Sun of Jamaica	CD5	Germany	1989	$8.00
WEA	246599-2	Sun of Jamaica	CD5	Germany	1989	$8.00

Landon Paris

Singles

Label	Catalog Number	Title	Type	Country	Year	Longbox Value / Value
Platz	PLDP-1018	Heat Your Heart	CD3	Japan	1991	$12.00/$3.00

Landreth, Sonny

Full Length

Label	Catalog Number	Title	Type	Country	Year	Longbox Value / Value
		House of Blues	RS	U.S.	1995	$30.00

2 CD set. Airdate: 6/11/95.

Singles

Label	Catalog Number	Title	Type	Country	Year	Longbox Value / Value
		Exit 103A	CDJ	U.S.		$3.00
Praxis	17080	When You're Away	CDJ	U.S.	1992	$2.00

Lane, Shawn

Singles

Label	Catalog Number	Title	Type	Country	Year	Longbox Value / Value
Warner Brothers	PRO-CD-6164	West Side Boogie	CDJ	U.S.	1993	$2.00

Lang, k.d.

Full Length

Label	Catalog Number	Title	Type	Country	Year	Longbox Value / Value
		A Truly Western Experience	LP	Canada		$20.00
Warner Brothers		Ingenue	DJ/LP	U.S.	1993	$15.00

CD in currogated cardboard package.

Label	Catalog Number	Title	Type	Country	Year	Longbox Value / Value
WEA	38234	k.d. Lang	LD	U.S.	1991	$30.00
Sire	PRO-CD-3120	Making Of Shadowland	DJ/Intvw	U.S.		$10.00
Sire		Shadowland	DJ/LP	U.S.	1993	$12.00

Singles

Label	Catalog Number	Title	Type	Country	Year	Longbox Value / Value
Sire	9362-40455-2	Constant Craving	CD5	Germany	1991	$10.00
Sire	WPCP 5505	Constant Craving	CD5	Japan	1992	$18.00
Sire	W-0100CD	Constant Craving	CD5	U.K.	1991	$10.00
Sire	W-0157CD	Constant Craving	CD5	U.K.	1993	$10.00
Sire	PRO-CD-5400	Constant Craving	CDJ	U.S.	1992	$3.00
		Enough Is Enough	CDJ	France		$18.00
Sire		Hush Sweet Lover	CD5	Australia	1994	$12.00
Sire	PRO-CD-6748	Hush Sweet Lover	CDJ	U.S.	1993	$2.00
Sire	PRO-CD-7896-R	If I Were You	CDJ	U.S.		$6.00
Sire	PRO-CD-7859-R	If I Were You	CDJ	U.S.		$6.00
Warner Brothers	17747	If I Were You	CD5	U.S.	1995	$5.00
Sire		Just Keep Me Moving	CDJ	U.K.	1993	$12.00
Sire	9 41197-2	Just Keep Me Moving	CDJ	U.S.	1993	$6.00
Sire	PRO-CD-6600	Just Keep Me Moving	CDJ	U.S.	1993	$6.00
Sire	PRO-CD-6696	Just Keep Me Moving	CDJ	U.S.	1993	$6.00
Sire	PRO-CD-6681	Just Keep Me Moving	CDJ	U.S.	1993	$8.00
Warner Brothers	41197	Just Keep Me Moving	CD5	U.S.	1994	$5.00
Warner	12-41379	Lifted by Love	CD5	Canada	1994	$8.00
Sire	9 41379-2	Lifted by Love	CD5	U.S.	1994	$6.00
Sire		Lifted by Love	CDJ	U.S.	1994	$7.00
Warner Brothers	17999	Love Affair	CD5	U.S.	1994	$5.00
Sire	9362409422	Mind of Love, The	CD5	Australia	1993	$10.00
Sire	W-0170	Mind of Love, The	CD5	Germany	1993	$10.00
Sire	WD170CD	Mind of Love, The	CD5	U.K.	1993	$10.00
Sire	WD170CD2	Mind of Love, The	CD5	U.K.	1993	$10.00

Second version.

Label	Catalog Number	Title	Type	Country	Year	Longbox Value / Value
Sire	PRO-CD-5806	Mind of Love, The	CDJ	U.S.	1993	$6.00
Sire	W-0135CD	Miss Charterlain	CD5	U.K.	1992	$10.00
Sire	9 4079-2	Miss Charterlain	CD5	U.S.	1992	$6.00
Sire	PRO-CD-6002	Miss Charterlain	CDJ	U.S.	1992	$2.00
Sire		Moonglow	CDJ	U.S.		$7.00
		No More Tears	CDJ	France		$30.00
Sire	PRO-CD-3907	Pullin' Back the Reins	CDJ	U.S.	1989	$2.00
Sire	W-9535CD	Ridin' the Rails	CD5	U.K.	1990	$10.00
Sire	PRO-CD-4098	Ridin' the Rails	CDJ	U.S.	1990	$2.00
Sire	PRO-CD-8050-R	Sexuality	CDJ	U.S.		$6.00
Sire	PRO-CD-8147-R	Sexuality	CDJ	U.S.		$6.00
Sire	PRO-CD-3747	Trail of Broken Hearts	CDJ	U.S.	1989	$2.00
Sire	PRO-CD-8033-R	You're OK	CDJ	U.S.		$6.00

Lang, Thomas

Singles

Label	Catalog Number	Title	Type	Country	Year	Longbox Value / Value
BMG	CDDRYC-2	Don't Let Me Be Misunderstood	CD5	U.K.	1992	$8.00
Epic	108P-3083	Fail	CD3	Japan	1989	$12.00/$3.00
BMG	CDDRYC-1	Feels So Right	CD5	U.K.	1992	$8.00
Epic	CDVOW-4	Happy Man	CD5	U.K.	1988	$8.00
Columbia	COCY-5155	I Will	CD5	Japan	1991	$12.00
Epic	655862-2	Longest Song	CD5	U.K.	1990	$8.00

Lang, Zaza

Singles

Label	Catalog Number	Title	Type	Country	Year	Longbox Value / Value
Polygram	874294-3	Catherine Wheel	CD3	Germany	1989	$8.00
Polygram	874295-2	Catherine Wheel	CD5	Germany	1989	$8.00

Lanois, Daniel

Full Length

Label	Catalog Number	Title	Type	Country	Year	Longbox Value / Value
Opal/Warner Bros.	9 25969	Acadie	DJ/LP	U.S.	1989	$12.00

Singles

Label	Catalog Number	Title	Type	Country	Year	Longbox Value / Value
Opal/Warner Bros.	PRO-CD-3948	Jolie Louise	CDJ	U.S.	1989	$3.00
Warner Brothers	PRO-CD-6127	Lotta Love To Give	CDJ	U.S.	1993	$3.00
WEA	921536-2	Maker, The	CD5	Germany	1990	$10.00
Opal	W-9844CD	Maker, The	CD5	U.K.	1990	$10.00
Opal/WB	PRO-CD-3760	Maker, The	CDJ	U.S.	1989	$3.00
Warner Brothers	PRO-CD-6316	Messenger, The	CDJ	U.S.	1993	$6.00
Opal/Warner Bros.	PRO-CD-3942	Still Water	CDJ	U.S.	1989	$3.00

Lanz, David

Singles

Label	Catalog Number	Title	Type	Country	Year	Longbox Value / Value
Narada Lotus	17611	A Whiter Shade of Pale	CDJ	U.S.	1988	$2.00
Narada	ND33 18363	Dark Horse	CDJ	U.S.	1993	$3.00

Laos

Singles

Label	Catalog Number	Title	Type	Country	Year	Longbox Value / Value
Eastwest	171517-2	I Want It	CD5	Germany	1990	$8.00

Laquan

Singles

Label	Catalog Number	Title	Type	Country	Year	Longbox Value / Value
Aris	884705	Now's the B Turn	CD5	Germany	1990	$8.00
4th & B'way	BRCD-180	Now's the B Turn	CD5	U.K.	1990	$8.00
4th & B'way	509	Now's the B Turn	CDJ	U.S.	1990	$2.00
4th & B'way	525	Swing Blue, Sweat Black	CDJ	U.S.	1991	$2.00

Larabell

Singles

Label	Catalog Number	Title	Type	Country	Year	Longbox Value / Value
ZYX	5958-8	You've Got the Power	CD5	Germany	1988	$6.00

Lard

Singles

Label	Catalog Number	Title	Type	Country	Year	Longbox Value / Value
Efa	CD-17612	Power of Lard	CD5	Germany	1990	$8.00
VAP	TFCK-88551	Power of Lard	CD5	Japan	1990	$8.00
Virus	VIRUS-72CD	Power of Lard	CD5	U.K.	1989	$8.00
Virus	72CD	Power of Lard	CD5	U.S.	1989	$4.00

Large Professor

Singles

Label	Catalog Number	Title	Type	Country	Year	Longbox Value / Value
	PRO-CD-4858	Mad Scientist, The	CDJ	U.S.		$2.00

Larin, Liz

Singles

Label	Catalog Number	Title	Type	Country	Year	Longbox Value / Value
Atlantic	PRCD 4919-2	Color Red, The	CDJ	U.S.	1993	$2.00

Larissa

Singles

Label	Catalog Number	Title	Type	Country	Year	Longbox Value / Value
SPV	3740-3	Heaven's Here	CD5	Germany	1990	$8.00

Larr, Larry

Singles

Label	Catalog Number	Title	Type	Country	Year	Longbox Value / Value
Ruffhouse	CSK 73732	Larry, That's What They Call Me	CDJ	U.S.	1993	$2.00

Larson, Anneka

Singles

Label	Catalog Number	Title	Type	Country	Year	Longbox Value / Value
BMG	663386	Heart Of Glass	CD5	Germany	1990	$8.00

Larson, Nicolette

Singles

Label	Catalog Number	Title	Type	Country	Year	Longbox Value / Value
WEA	247936-2	Let Me Be the One	CD5	Germany	1988	$8.00

LaSalle, Denise

Singles

Label	Catalog Number	Title	Type	Country	Year	Longbox Value / Value
Malaco	2181	Don't Jump My Pony	CDJ	U.S.	1992	$2.00

Laser, Mars

Full Length

Label	Catalog Number	Title	Type	Country	Year	Longbox Value / Value
Real Music	RM-0022	Eleventh Hour, The	DJ/LP	U.S.	1993	$8.00

Last Crack

Singles

Label	Catalog Number	Title	Type	Country	Year	Longbox Value / Value
Road Racer	PROMO 30	Energy Mind	CDJ	U.S.	1991	$2.00

Last Exit

Singles

Label	Catalog Number	Title	Type	Country	Year	Longbox Value / Value
Efa	CD-3503	Noise of Trouble	CD5	Germany	1989	$8.00

Last Few Days

Singles

Label	Catalog Number	Title	Type	Country	Year	Longbox Value / Value
Fontana	LFDCD-1	Kicks	CD5	U.K.	1990	$8.00
Fontana	LFDCD-2	Your Love Is Super-Funky	CD5	U.K.	1990	$8.00

Last Gentlemen

Singles

Label	Catalog Number	Title	Type	Country	Year	Longbox Value / Value
Zoo	ZD-17059	Miss Sympathy	CDJ	U.S.	1992	$2.00

Last Tango

Singles

Label	Catalog Number	Title	Type	Country	Year	Longbox Value / Value
Mercury	MERCD-326	City Lights	CD5	U.K.	1990	$8.00

Lather, Barry

Singles

Label	Catalog Number	Title	Type	Country	Year	Longbox Value / Value
		Love in the 3rd Degree	CDJ	U.S.		$2.00

Latimore, Kenny

Singles

Label	Catalog Number	Title	Type	Country	Year	Longbox Value / Value
		Never Too Busy	CDJ	U.S.		$2.00

Latin Alliance

Singles

Label	Catalog Number	Title	Type	Country	Year	Longbox Value / Value
Virgin	VUSCD-48	Low Rider	CD5	U.K.	1991	$8.00
Virgin	PRCD 4044	Low Rider	CDJ	U.S.	1991	$2.00

Latin Prince

Singles

Label	Catalog Number	Title	Type	Country	Year	Longbox Value / Value
Third Stone	5070	With My House	CDJ	U.S.	1993	$2.00

Latin Rascals

Singles

Label	Catalog Number	Title	Type	Country	Year	Longbox Value / Value
		Don't Let Me Be Misunderstood	CDJ	U.S.		$2.00

Latino, Gino

Singles

Label	Catalog Number	Title	Type	Country	Year	Longbox Value / Value
RCA	PD-43042	No Sorry	CD5	U.K.	1989	$8.00
ffrr	FCD-126	Welcome	CD5	U.K.	1990	$8.00
ffrr	886865-2	Welcome	CD5	U.K.	1990	$8.00

Lattisaw, Stacy

Singles

Label	Catalog Number	Title	Type	Country	Year	Longbox Value / Value
Motown	ZD-42264	Call Me	CD5	U.K.	1988	$8.00
Motown	18128	I Don't Have a Heart	CDJ	U.S.	1990	$2.00
Motown	ZD-43174	What You Need	CD5	U.K.	1988	$8.00

Lauper, Cyndi

Full Length

Label	Catalog Number	Title	Type	Country	Year	Longbox Value / Value
CBS	QDCA-93029	Greatest Hits	DJ/Smplr	Japan		$175.00
Epic	SAMP 1776	Hatfull Of Stars	DJ/LP	U.S.†	1993	$30.00
CBS	3570-80	In Paris	LD	U.S.	1988	$35.00
CBS	RK-38930	She's So Unusual	LP/BP	U.S.†	1984	$16.00/$12.00

Singles

Label	Catalog Number	Title	Type	Country	Year	Longbox Value / Value
Epic	ESK 73031	A Night To Remember	CDJ	U.S.	1989	$6.00
Epic		Come on Home	CDJ	Germany	1995	$15.00

Label	Catalog Number	Title	Type	Country	Year	Longbox Value / Value
Epic	ESDA-7160	Come on Home	CD3	Japan	1995	$13.00/$5.00
Epic	ESCA-6297	Come on Home	CD5	Japan	1995	$18.00
		Come on Home	CD5	U.K.		$10.00
Second version.						
Epic		Come on Home	CDJ	U.K.	1995	$15.00
Epic	ESK 1640	First Night With Out You	CDJ	U.S.	1989	$6.00
CBS	655571-3	Girls Just Want to Have Fun	CD3	Germany	1990	$10.00
CBS	655571-2	Girls Just Want to Have Fun	CD5	Germany	1990	$10.00
CBS	34K-5480	Girls Just Want to Have Fun	CD3	U.S.	1990	$6.00/$3.00
Columbia	77968	Girls Just Want to Have Fun	CD5	U.S.	1995	$5.00
Epic		Gonna Be Strong	CDJ	U.K.	1995	$12.00
CBS	6554001-3	Heading West	CD3	Germany	1989	$10.00
Epic	ESDA-7006	Heading West	CD3	Japan	1989	$12.00/$4.00
Epic	CYNCN-6	Heading West	CD5	U.K.	1989	$10.00
Epic	CYNC-6	Heading West	CD5	U.K.	1989	$10.00
		Hey Now (Girls Just Wanna Have Fun)	CDJ	U.S.		$6.00
Epic	654837-3	I Drove All Night	CD3	Germany	1989	$10.00
Epic	108P-3063	I Drove All Night	CD3	Japan	1989	$12.00/$4.00
CBS	CYNCC-4	I Drove All Night	CD5	U.K.	1989	$10.00
CBS	CYNCD-4	I Drove All Night	CD5	U.K.	1989	$12.00
Epic	ESK 1564	I Drove All Night	CDJ	U.S.	1989	$7.00
CBS	652813-3	I Gotta Hole in My Heart	CD3	Germany	1988	$10.00
Epic	108P-3024	I Gotta Hole in My Heart	CD3	Japan	1988	$12.00/$4.00
CBS	652813-3	I Gotta Hole in My Heart	CD3	U.K.	1988	$10.00
CBS	34K-7940	I Gotta Hole in My Heart	CD3	U.S.	1988	$6.00/$3.00
Epic	ESK 1194	I Gotta Hole in My Heart	CDJ	U.S.	1988	$2.00
		I'm Gonna Be Strong	CD5	U.K.		$10.00
		I'm Gonna Be Strong	CD5	U.K.		$10.00
Second version.						
Epic	ESK 7441	I'm Gonna Be Strong	CDJ	U.S.	1995	$3.00
Epic	655091-3	My First Night Without You	CD5	Germany	1989	$10.00
Epic	108P-3074	My First Night Without You	CD3	Japan	1989	$12.00/$4.00
Epic	CDCYN-5	My First Night Without You	CD5	U.K.	1989	$10.00
Epic	ESK 1640	My First Night Without You	CDJ	U.S.	1988	$6.00
CBS	655 6261	Primitive	CD3	Holland		$25.00
Epic		Sallys Pigeons	CD5	Australia	1995	$18.00
Withdrawn single.						
Epic		Sallys Pigeons	CD5	U.K.	1995	$30.00
Withdrawn single.						
Epic	654558-3	She Bop	CD3	Germany	1989	$10.00
Epic	659879	That's What I Think	CD5	U.K.	1993	$10.00
Epic		That's What I Think	CD5	U.K.	1993	$10.00
Second version.						
Epic	49K 77234	That's What I Think	CD5	U.S.	1993	$6.00
Epic	ESK 7723	That's What I Think	CDJ	U.S.	1993	$3.00
Epic		Time After Time	CDJ	U.K.	1995	$25.00
CBS		Who Let in the Rain	CD5	U.K.	1993	$10.00
Epic	34K 74942	Who Let in the Rain	CD5	U.S.	1993	$6.00
Epic	ESK 74942	Who Let in the Rain	CDJ	U.S.	1993	$3.00

Laurel & Hardy

Full Length

Label	Catalog Number	Title	Type	Country	Year	Longbox Value / Value
Mess	MESSCD-1	Another Fine Mess Presents: 1	LTD/LP	U.K.		$25.00
Picture disc CD.						

Laurent

Singles

Label	Catalog Number	Title	Type	Country	Year	Longbox Value / Value
WEA	9031-72731-2	Bad Boys	CD5	Germany	1991	$8.00

Lava, Hay

Singles

Label	Catalog Number	Title	Type	Country	Year	Longbox Value / Value
Nettwerk	3048	Baby	CD5	U.S.	1990	$4.00
Polydor	CDP 303	Baby	CDJ	U.S.	1990	$2.00
Polydor	CDP 219	Won't Matter	CDJ	U.S.	1990	$2.00

LaVerne, Andy

Full Length

Label	Catalog Number	Title	Type	Country	Year	Longbox Value / Value
Digital Music	CD-449	Liquid Silver	LP/LB	U.S.†	1985	$14.00/$8.00

Lavilliers, Bernard

Singles

Label	Catalog Number	Title	Type	Country	Year	Longbox Value / Value
Polygram	889352-3	On the Road Again	CD3	Germany	1989	$8.00
Polygram	889353-2	On the Road Again	CD5	Germany	1989	$8.00

Lavitz T.

Full Length

Label	Catalog Number	Title	Type	Country	Year	Longbox Value / Value
Passport	PJCD-88026	From the West	LP	U.K.		$15.00
Passport	PJCD-88026	From the West	LP/LB	U.S.		$15.00/$10.00
Passport	PJCD-88012	Storytime	LP	U.K.		$15.00
Passport	PJCD-88012	Storytime	LP/LB	U.S.		$15.00/$10.00

Lavoie, Daniel

Singles

Label	Catalog Number	Title	Type	Country	Year	Longbox Value / Value
Curb	1050	Weak For Love	CDJ	U.S.	1993	$2.00

Law

Full Length

Label	Catalog Number	Title	Type	Country	Year	Longbox Value / Value
Atlantic	PRCD 3880-2	Profiled	DJ/Intvw	U.S.	1991	$5.00

Singles

Label	Catalog Number	Title	Type	Country	Year	Longbox Value / Value
Atlantic	AMDY-5043	Laying Down the Law	CD3	Japan	1991	$12.00/$3.00
Atlantic	A-7781CD	Laying Down the Law	CD5	U.K.	1991	$9.00
Atlantic	PRCD 3718-2	Laying Down the Law	CDJ	U.S.	1991	$2.00
Atlantic	PRCD 3933-2	Miss You in a Heartbeat	CDJ	U.S.	1991	$2.00

Law, Joanna

Singles

Label	Catalog Number	Title	Type	Country	Year	Longbox Value / Value
ZYX	6371-8	First Time Ever	CD5	Germany	1990	$6.00

Law, Johnny

Singles

Label	Catalog Number	Title	Type	Country	Year	Longbox Value / Value
Metal Blade	PRO-CD-4754	Too Weak to Fight	CDJ	U.S.	1991	$2.00

Law, Lynda

Singles

Label	Catalog Number	Title	Type	Country	Year	Longbox Value / Value
RCA	PD-43958	I Don't Want Your Love	CD5	U.K.	1990	$8.00

Law, Michelle

Singles

Label	Catalog Number	Title	Type	Country	Year	Longbox Value / Value
BMG	664755	Never Sleep Alone	CD5	Germany	1991	$8.00

Law & Order

Singles

Label	Catalog Number	Title	Type	Country	Year	Longbox Value / Value
MCA	CD45-1565	Plague of Ignorance	CDJ	U.S.	1991	$2.00
MCA		Soul Inside	CDJ	U.S.	1991	$2.00
MCA		We Don't See God	CDJ	U.S.	1991	$2.00
MCA	MCA5P-2129	Why Would You Lie	CDJ	U.S.	1991	$2.00

Lawley, Linda

Singles

Label	Catalog Number	Title	Type	Country	Year	Longbox Value / Value
Line	LICD-900962	Love is Strange	CD5	Germany	1990	$8.00

Lawnmower, Deth

Singles

Label	Catalog Number	Title	Type	Country	Year	Longbox Value / Value
Earache	MOSH-39CD	Kids in America	CD5	U.K.	1991	$8.00

Lawrence, Joey

Singles

Label	Catalog Number	Title	Type	Country	Year	Longbox Value / Value
Impact	2837	I Can't Help Myself	CDJ	U.S.	1993	$2.00
Impact	2674	Stay Forever	CDJ	U.S.	1993	$2.00
Impact	2748	Stay Forever	CDJ	U.S.	1993	$2.00

Lawrence, Martin

Full length

Label	Catalog Number	Title	Type	Country	Year	Longbox Value / Value
	PRCD9333-2	Live! Excerpts From Funk It!	DJ/Smplr	U.S.	1995	$6.00

Singles

Label	Catalog Number	Title	Type	Country	Year	Longbox Value / Value
Eastwest	PRCD 5257-2	Boxin'	CDJ	U.S.	1993	$2.00
Eastwest	PRCD 5259-2	Michael Jackson	CDJ	U.S.	1993	$2.00
Eastwest	PRCD 5258-2	Worrying About Your Weight	CDJ	U.S.	1993	$2.00

Lawrence, Sophie

Singles

Label	Catalog Number	Title	Type	Country	Year	Longbox Value / Value
BMG	ZD-44822	Love's Unkind	CD5	U.K.	1991	$8.00

Lawrence, Syd & Orchestra

Full Length

Label	Catalog Number	Title	Type	Country	Year	Longbox Value / Value
Philips	814356-2	Big Band Swing	LP/LB	U.S.†	1985	$14.00/$8.00
CBS	CK-34330	Romeo & Juliet	LP/LB	U.S.†	1985	$14.00/$8.00
CBS	CK-34330	Romeo & Juliet	LP/LB	U.S.†	1985	$14.00/$8.00

Lawrence, Tracy

Full Length

Label	Catalog Number	Title	Type	Country	Year	Longbox Value / Value
		'90s Country	RS	U.S.	1995	$30.00
Airdate: 7/22/95.						
		'90s Country	RS	U.S.	1996	$30.00
Airdate: 3/9/96.						
		Country Concert	RS	U.S.	1994	$50.00
Airdate: 6/20/94.						
		Road, The	RS	U.S.	1995	$60.00
2 CD set. Airdate: 9/8/95.						

Singles

Label	Catalog Number	Title	Type	Country	Year	Longbox Value / Value
Atlantic	PRCD 5107-2	Can't Break It to My Heart	CDJ	U.S.	1992	$2.00
		I See It Now	CDJ	U.S.	1994	$3.00
Atlantic	PRCD 5466-2	If the Good Die Young	CDJ	U.S.	1992	$2.00
		Renegades, Rebels & Rogues	CDJ	U.S.	1994	$3.00
Atlantic	PRCD 5215-2	Second Home	CDJ	U.S.	1992	$2.00

Laws, Ronnie

Full Length

Label	Catalog Number	Title	Type	Country	Year	Longbox Value / Value
Capitol	CDP 46072	Mr. Nice Guy	LP/LB	U.S.†	1985	$14.00/$8.00

Singles

Label	Catalog Number	Title	Type	Country	Year	Longbox Value / Value
Capitol	58473	Soon As the Posse Rides Out	CD5	U.S.	1995	$5.00

Lay, Sam

Full Length

Label	Catalog Number	Title	Type	Country	Year	Longbox Value / Value
		House of Blues	RS	U.S.	1995	$40.00
2 CD set. Airdate: 2/5/95.						

Layne, Angie

Singles

Label	Catalog Number	Title	Type	Country	Year	Longbox Value / Value
Eastwest	171140-2	Don't Rape My Heart	CD5	Germany	1990	$8.00
Intercord	825 312	Gimme All Your Love	CD5	Germany	1991	$8.00

Layne, Rick

Singles

Label	Catalog Number	Title	Type	Country	Year	Longbox Value / Value
Polygram	887916-3	Like Heaven	CD3	Germany	1989	$8.00
Polygram	887916-2	Like Heaven	CD5	Germany	1989	$8.00

Layton, Lindy

Singles

Label	Catalog Number	Title	Type	Country	Year	Longbox Value / Value
Arista	663845	Echo in My Heart	CD5	Germany	1990	$8.00
Arista	BVDA-20	Echo in My Heart	CD3	Japan	1991	$13.00/$4.00
Arista	663845	Echo in My Heart	CD5	U.K.	1990	$8.00
Pinnacle	DEBCD-3141	I'll Be Frank For You	CD5	U.K.	1992	$8.00
Arista	663452	Silly Games	CD5	Grermany	1990	$8.00
Arista	663452	Silly Games	CD5	U.K.	1990	$8.00
Arista	664174	Wait For Love	CD5	Germany	1991	$8.00
Arista	664174	Wait For Love	CD5	U.K.	1991	$8.00
PWL	PWCD-250	We Got the Love	CD5	U.K.	1992	$8.00
Arista	BVDA-28	Without You	CD3	Japan	1991	$13.00/$3.00

Lazos, Los

Singles

Label	Catalog Number	Title	Type	Country	Year	Longbox Value / Value
	1415	Balada Epoca De Oro	CD5	U.S.	1994	$5.00

Lazy, Doug

Singles

Label	Catalog Number	Title	Type	Country	Year	Longbox Value / Value
ZYX	6319-8	Can't Hold Back (U No)	CD5	Germany	1990	$6.00
		Can't Hold Back (U No)	CDJ	U.S.	1990	$2.00
ZYX	6519-8	H.O.U.S.E.	CD5	Germany	1991	$6.00
		H.O.U.S.E.	CDJ	U.S.	1990	$2.00
ZYX	6184-8	Let It Roll	CD5	Germany	1990	$6.00
Atlantic	PRCD 2891-2	Let It Roll	CDJ	U.S.	1990	$2.00
ZYX	6258-8	Let the Rhythm Pump	CD5	Germany	1990	$6.00
ZYX	6330-8	Megamix	CD5	Germany	1990	$6.00

Le Bon, Simon

Singles

Label	Catalog Number	Title	Type	Country	Year	Longbox Value / Value
		Grey Lady of the Sea	CD3	Japan		$15.00/$4.00

Le Click

Singles

Label	Catalog Number	Title	Type	Country	Year	Longbox Value / Value
	59011	Tonight is the Night	CD5	U.S.	1994	$5.00

Le Freak

Singles

Label	Catalog Number	Title	Type	Country	Year	Longbox Value / Value
BMG	663310	Wild Wild Life	CD5	Germany	1990	$8.00

Leaders of The New School

Singles

Label	Catalog Number	Title	Type	Country	Year	Longbox Value / Value
Elektra	PRCD 8299-2	Case of the PTA	CDJ	U.S.	1991	$2.00

Lear, Amanda

Singles

Label	Catalog Number	Title	Type	Country	Year	Longbox Value / Value
BMG		Fantasy	CD5	U.K.	1989	$10.00

Label	Catalog Number	Title	Type	Country	Year	Longbox Value / Value
BMG	661978	Follow Me	CD5	Germany	1989	$8.00

Leary, Dennis

Full Length

Label	Catalog Number	Title	Type	Country	Year	Longbox Value / Value
A&M	31454 8015 2	No Cure For Cancer	DJ/LP	U.S.	1993	$25.00
A&M	31454 8015-2	No Cure For Cancer Edited For Radio	DJ/LP	U.S.	1993	$15.00

Singles

Label	Catalog Number	Title	Type	Country	Year	Longbox Value / Value
A&M		Asshole	CD5	U.S.	1993	$10.00
A&M	31458 0142	Asshole	CDJ	U.S.	1993	$6.00

Leary, Paul

Full Length

Label	Catalog Number	Title	Type	Country	Year	Longbox Value / Value
Rough Trade		History of Dogs	LP/LB	U.S.		$12.00/$7.00

Leathers

Singles

Label	Catalog Number	Title	Type	Country	Year	Longbox Value / Value
Fieldworks	FWCR-58	Through the Night	CD3	Japan	1992	$13.00/$4.00

Leatherwolf

Full Length

Label	Catalog Number	Title	Type	Country	Year	Longbox Value / Value
Island	90660-2	Leatherwolf	LP/LB	U.S.		$15.00/$12.00

Singles

Label	Catalog Number	Title	Type	Country	Year	Longbox Value / Value
Island	885487	Hideaway	CD5	Germany	1989	$9.00
Island	CID-416	Hideaway	CD5	U.K.	1989	$9.00
Island	PR 2642-2	Hideaway	CDJ	U.S.	1989	$2.00

Led Zeppelin

Full Length

Label	Catalog Number	Title	Type	Country	Year	Longbox Value / Value
Album Network		25th Anniversary	RS	U.S.	1993	$50.00
		2 CD set.				
		25th Anniversary	RS	U.S.	1993	$170.00
6 CD set. Airdate: 7/3/93.						
Album Network		Album Network Special "Led Zeppelin I"	RS	U.S.	1994	$150.00
		2 CD set. 1/30/94.				
Atlantic		Baby Come On Home	DJ/Smplr	France	1994	$75.00
BBC Radio		BBC Classic Tracks	RS	U.S.	1991	$40.00
		Airdate: 12/23/91.				
BBC Radio		BBC Classic Tracks	RS	U.S.	1991	$40.00
		Airdate: 3/25/91.				
Westwood One		BBC Classic Tracks	RS	U.S.	1991	$45.00
		Airdate: 12/31/91.				
Westwood One		BBC Classic Tracks	RS	U.S.	1991	$45.00
		Airdate: 3/25/91.				
BBC Radio		BBC Classic Tracks	RS	U.S.	1992	$40.00
		Airdate: 1/25/93.				
BBC Radio		BBC Classic Tracks	RS	U.S.	1992	$40.00
		Airdate: 12/7/92.				
BBC Radio		BBC Classic Tracks	RS	U.S.	1992	$40.00
		Airdate: 3/9/92.				
Westwood One		BBC Classic Tracks	RS	U.S.	1992	$45.00
		Airdate: 12/7/92.				
Westwood One		BBC Classic Tracks	RS	U.S.	1993	$45.00
		Airdate: 11/1/93.				
Westwood One		BBC Classic Tracks	RS	U.S.	1993	$45.00
		Airdate: 5/31/93.				
Westwood One		BBC Classic Tracks	RS	U.S.	1995	$45.00
		Airdate: 5/8/95.				
Westwood One		BBC Classic Tracks	RS	U.S.	1996	$45.00
		Airdate: 3/11/96.				
Media America		Bring It Home	RS	U.S.	1990	$150.00
		4 CD set. Airdate: 11/9/90.				
		Classic CD (Led Zeppelin IV)	RS	U.S.	1990	$100.00
		2 CD set. Airdate: 10/1/90				
Atlantic	90051-2	Coda	LP/LB	U.S.		$14.00/$8.00
		Nonremastered version.				
Atlantic		Complete Studio Recordings	LTD/LP	U.K.	1993	$165.00
		10 CD set.				
		Final Chapter	RS	U.S.	1991	$250.00
		6 CD set. Airdate: 9/2/91.				
		For Rockers Only	RS	U.S.		$50.00
Atlantic	19130-2	Houses of the Holy	LP/BP	U.S.†	1984	$18.00/$15.00
		In Concert	RS	U.S.	1992	$120.00
		With Nirvana, Airdate: 3/16/92.				
Album Network		In the Studio (Led Zeppelin I)	RS	U.S.	1988	$40.00
		Airdate: 11/7/88.				
Album Network		In the Studio (Led Zeppelin I)	RS	U.S.	1992	$40.00
		Airdate: 11/11/92.				
Album Network		In the Studio (Led Zeppelin IV)	RS	U.S.	1990	$40.00
		Airdate: 9/24/90.				
Atlantic	16002-2	In Through the Out Door	LP/LB	U.S.		$14.00/$8.00
		Nonremastered version.				
		It's Been a Long Time	RS	U.S.	1990	$250.00
		6 CD set. Airdate: 8/90				
Westwood One		Labor Day Special 1990	RS	U.S.	1990	$250.00
		6 CD set.				
Atlantic	7 82144 2	Led Zeppelin	LP	U.S.	1990	$70.00
		4 CD set.				
Global Satellite Network		Led Zeppelin	RS	U.S.	1991	$120.00
		3 CD set.				
Atlantic	19127-2	Led Zeppelin II	LP/LB	U.S.		$18.00/$15.00
		Nonremastered version.				
Atlantic	19128-2	Led Zeppelin III	LP/LB	U.S.		$14.00/$8.00
		Nonremastered version.				
HMV		Led Zeppelin IV	LTD/LP	U.K.	1989	$35.00
		CD with booklet in 12"x12" box. Manufactered for HMV superstores.				
Atlantic	19129-2	Led Zeppelin IV	LP/LB	U.S.		$14.00/$8.00
		Nonremastered version.				
Atlantic	19129-2	Led Zeppelin IV	LP/BP	U.S.†	1984	$17.00/$12.00
Source Classic		Led Zeppelin IV	RS	U.S.	1990	$70.00
		2 CD set.				
		Led Zeppelin - Led Zeptember	RS	U.S.	1993	$135.00
		3 CD set.				
		Ledded/Unledded	RS	U.S.	1995	$180.00
		8 CD set. Airdate: 5/12/95.				
Atlantic	200-2	Physical Graffiti	LP/LB	U.S.		$14.00/$8.00
		Nonremastered version.				
Atlantic	200	Physical Graffiti	LP/LB	U.S.	1986	$25.00/$15.00
		2 CD set in full-size double jewel box				
Atlantic	8416-2	Presence	LP/LB	U.S.		$14.00/$8.00
		Nonremastered version.				
Atlantic	PRCD 3629-2	Profiled	DJ/Intvw	U.S.	1990	$20.00
On the Radio		Rarities on Compact Disc Volume 7	RS	U.S.	1991	$50.00
Atlantic	CD LZ1	Remasters	DJ/Smplr	Germany	1990	$60.00
		Cutom zeppelin shaped box.				
Atlantic	7567 80415-2	Remasters	LP	U.S.	1990	$40.00
		2 CD set.				
Unistar		Showcase of Rock	RS	U.S.	1993	$70.00
		3 CD set. Airdate: 3/20/93.				
Atlantic	ASCD-112	Special Sampler	DJ/Smplr	Japan		$700.00
Atlantic	ASCD-53	Stairway to Heaven 20th Anniversary Edition	DJ/Intvw	Japan	1992	$100.00
		CD single and bonus profiled CD.				
Westwood One		Superstars	RS	U.S.	1993	$85.00
		2 CD set. Airdate: 7/26/93.				
Westwood One		Superstars	RS	U.S.	1994	$85.00
		2 CD set. Airdate: 8/8/94.				
Westwood One		Superstars	RS	U.S.	1995	$85.00
		2 CD set. Airdate: 7/17/95.				
		Tribute To Bonham	RS	U.S.	1990	$275.00
		6 CD set. Airdate: 9/3/90.				
Media America		Up Close	RS	U.S.	1990	$160.00
		4 CD set.				
Media America		Up Close	RS	U.S.	1992	$80.00
		2 CD set.				
Media America		Up Close "Bring It Home"	RS	U.S.	1990	$250.00
		4 CD set.				

Singles

Label	Catalog Number	Title	Type	Country	Year	Longbox Value / Value
Atlantic	PRCD-27	Baby Come On Home	CDJ	Germany	1994	$60.00
Atlantic	PRCD 5255-2	Baby Come On Home	CDJ	U.S.	1993	$10.00
Swan Song	AMCY-97	Hot Dog	CD5	Japan	1990	$20.00
Swan Song	AMCY-98	Immigrant Song	CD5	Japan	1990	$20.00
Atlantic	7567-84909-2	Immigrant Song	CD5	U.S.	1992	$8.00
Atlantic	PRCD 3717 2	Over the Hills and Far Away	CDJ	U.S.	1990	$10.00
Atlantic		Stairway to Heaven	CDJ	France		$75.00
Atlantic	PRCD 4424-2	Stairway to Heaven 20th Anniversary Edition	CDJ	U.S.	1992	$75.00
		CD & 7" vinyl housed in custom pop-up folder with letter.				
Atlantic	PRCD 3627-2	Traveling Riverside Blues	CDJ	U.S.	1990	$10.00

Lee, Alvin

Full Length

Label	Catalog Number	Title	Type	Country	Year	Longbox Value / Value
DIR		King Biscuit Flour Hour	RS	U.S.	1988	$35.00
		With Elvin Bishop, Airdate: 10/23/88.				

Lee, Brenda

Full Length

Label	Catalog Number	Title	Type	Country	Year	Longbox Value / Value
Warner Sound Exchange	217679	22 Legendary Hits	LTD/LP	U.S.	1995	$17.00
MCA	MCSTD-1595	Rockin' Around the Christmas Tree	CD5	U.K.	1991	$8.00
Warner Brothers	PRO-CD-4702	Your One and Only	CDJ	U.S.	1991	$2.00

Lee, Carol

Singles

Label	Catalog Number	Title	Type	Country	Year	Longbox Value / Value
Toshiba	TODP-2182	Mama Girl	CD3	Japan	1990	$12.00/$3.00

Lee, Dana

Singles

Label	Catalog Number	Title	Type	Country	Year	Longbox Value / Value
Hardback	BOSS-10CD	Never Say Forever	CD5	U.K.	1992	$8.00

Lee, Donna

Singles

Label	Catalog Number	Title	Type	Country	Year	Longbox Value / Value
		Do or Die	CDJ	U.S.		$2.00

Lee, Peggy

Singles

Label	Catalog Number	Title	Type	Country	Year	Longbox Value / Value
Capitol	880202-2	Fever	CD5	Germany	1992	$10.00
Capitol	CDPEG-1	Fever	CD5	U.K.	1992	$10.00

Lee, Rory

Singles

Label	Catalog Number	Title	Type	Country	Year	Longbox Value / Value
Shiloh	101	Rory Lee	CD5	U.S.	1994	$5.00

Lee, Spike

Full Length

Label	Catalog Number	Title	Type	Country	Year	Longbox Value / Value
WEA	40116	Spike & Company: Do It Acapella	LD	U.S.	1991	$25.00/$30.00

Lee, Tracy

Singles

Label	Catalog Number	Title	Type	Country	Year	Longbox Value / Value
	85499-2	Theme (It's Party Time)	CD5	U.S.	1997	$3.00

Leeds, Eric

Singles

Label	Catalog Number	Title	Type	Country	Year	Longbox Value / Value
Paisley Park	PRO-CD-4705	Doparmine, The	CDJ	U.S.	1991	$2.00
Paisley Park	PRO-CD-6157	Woman in Chains	CDJ	U.S.	1993	$2.00

Leeds, Jarome

Singles

Label	Catalog Number	Title	Type	Country	Year	Longbox Value / Value
Polygram	877021-2	Lover's Delight	CD5	Germany	1990	$8.00

Leek, Andy

Full Length

Label	Catalog Number	Title	Type	Country	Year	Longbox Value / Value
		Say Something	DJ/Intvw	U.S		$5.00

Singles

Label	Catalog Number	Title	Type	Country	Year	Longbox Value / Value
Atlantic	A-8997CD	Holdin' Onto You	CD5	U.K.	1989	$9.00
		Holdin' Onto You	CDJ	U.S.	1988	$2.00
Atlantic	PR 2359-2	Please Please	CDJ	U.S.	1988	$2.00

Leeway, Daniel

Singles

Label	Catalog Number	Title	Type	Country	Year	Longbox Value / Value
MBI	10	Once Blue Seas	CD5	Sweden	1993	$8.00

Left Wing Facists

Singles

Label	Catalog Number	Title	Type	Country	Year	Longbox Value / Value
Cellar Door	90076	K-Mart Shopper	CDJ	U.S.	1991	$2.00

Leftfield

Singles

Label	Catalog Number	Title	Type	Country	Year	Longbox Value / Value
Columbia	78045	Afro Left	CD5	U.S.	1995	$5.00
Columbia	CSK 7282	Open Up	CDJ	U.S.		$2.00
Hard Hands	HAND-002CD	Song of Life	CD5	U.K.	1992	$8.00

Legacy of Sound

Singles

Label	Catalog Number	Title	Type	Country	Year	Longbox Value / Value
BMG	BVDP-81	Happy	CD3	Japan	1993	$13.00/$4.00

Legend

Singles

Label	Catalog Number	Title	Type	Country	Year	Longbox Value / Value
Champion	CHAMPCD-227	Champion Megamixes	CD5	U.K.	1990	$8.00

Legrand, Michel

Full Length

Label	Catalog Number	Title	Type	Country	Year	Longbox Value / Value
CBS	64367-2	I Love Paris	LTD/LP	U.S.	1994	$25.00
		Gold disc.				

LeMans, Tony

Singles

Label	Catalog Number	Title	Type	Country	Year	Longbox Value / Value
Paisley Park	PRO-CD-3585	Forever More	CDJ	U.S.	1989	$2.00
Paisley Park	PRO-CD-3585	Higher than High	CDJ	U.S.	1989	$2.00
Paisley Park	PRO-CD-3748	Higher than High	CDJ	U.S.	1991	$2.00

Lemon Trees

Singles

Label	Catalog Number	Title	Type	Country	Year	Longbox Value / Value
		Child of Love	CD5	U.K.	1993	$8.00
		Child of Love	CD5	U.K.	1993	$8.00
	Second version.					
		I Can't Face the World	CD5	U.K.	1993	$8.00
		I Can't Face the World	CD5	U.K.	1993	$8.00
	Second version.					
		Let It Loose	CD5	U.K.	1993	$8.00
		Let It Loose	CD5	U.K.	1993	$8.00
	Second version.					
Oxygen	GASPD-1	Love in Your Eyes	CD5	U.K.	1992	$8.00
		Way I Feel	CD5	U.K.	1993	$8.00
		Way I Feel	CD5	U.K.	1993	$8.00
	Second version.					

Lemonheads

Full Length

Label	Catalog Number	Title	Type	Country	Year	Longbox Value / Value
Atlantic	82397-2	It's a Shame About Ray	LP/LB	U.S.		$14.00/$8.00
	First pressing with missing track "Mrs. Robinson."					
Atlantic		It's About Time	DJ/Smplr	U.S.		$10.00

Singles

Label	Catalog Number	Title	Type	Country	Year	Longbox Value / Value
Atlantic	A7259CDX	Big Grey Heart	CD5	U.K.	1993	$10.00
Atlantic	A-7430CD	Confetti	CD5	U.K.	1993	$10.00
Atlantic	PRCD 4743-2	Confetti	CDJ	U.S.	1993	$3.00
Atlantic	PRCD 5421-2	Great Big No, The	CDJ	U.S.	1992	$3.00
Atlantic	PRCD 5423-2	Great Big No, The	CDJ	U.S.	1992	$3.00
Atlantic	PRCD 5424-2	Great Big No, The	CDJ	U.S.	1992	$3.00
Atlantic	PRCD 3500-2	Half the Time	CDJ	U.S.	1990	$3.00
Atlantic	85706-2	Into Your Arms	CD5	U.S.	1993	$6.00
Atlantic	PRCD 5284-2	Into Your Arms	CDJ	U.S.	1993	$3.00
Atlantic		It's a Shame About Ray	CD5	U.K.		$10.00
	Second version.					
Atlantic	A-7423CD	It's a Shame About Ray	CD5	U.K.	1991	$10.00
Atlantic	A-5764CD	It's a Shame About Ray	CD5	U.K.	1992	$10.00
Atlantic	PRCD 4581-2	It's a Shame About Ray	CDJ	U.S.	1991	$3.00
Atlantic	PRCD 4587-2	It's a Shame About Ray	CDJ	U.S.	1991	$3.00
Capitol	DPRO-79693	It's About Time	CDJ	U.S.		$3.00
Atlantic	A-7401CD	Mrs. Robinson	CD5	U.K.	1991	$10.00
Atlantic	PRCD 4862-2	Mrs. Robinson	CDJ	U.S.	1992	$3.00

Lena

Singles

Label	Catalog Number	Title	Type	Country	Year	Longbox Value / Value
		You Come From Earth	CD5	U.K.		$10.00
		You Come From Earth	CD5	U.K.		$10.00
		You Come From Earth	CD5	U.K.		$10.00
	Second version.					

Lennon, John

Full Length

Label	Catalog Number	Title	Type	Country	Year	Longbox Value / Value
ABC		ABC Radio	RS	U.S.	1990	$250.00
	4 CD set.					
EMI	CP32-5750	Double Fantasy	LP	Japan		$55.00
Geffen	2001-2	Double Fantasy	LP	U.S.	1984	$60.00
Geffen	2001-2	Double Fantasy	LP/LB	U.S.†	1984	$100.00/$85.00
EMI	CP43-5773	Imagine	LTD/LP	Japan	1988	$50.00
	Gold disc.					
Pioneer	PA-86-164	Imagine	LD	U.S.	1986	$25.00
	Analog audio.					
DIR		King Biscuit Flour Hour	RS	U.S.	1993	$50.00
	With Warren Zevon, Airdate: 2/14/93.					
DIR		King Biscuit Flour Hour	RS	U.S.	1994	$80.00
	With Warren Zevon. Airdate: 9/4/94.					
DIR		King Biscuit Flour Hour	RS	U.S.	1995	$80.00
	With Warren Zevon. Airdate: 8/20/95.					
Capitol	C2PP-95220	Lennon	LP	U.S.	1990	$70.00
	4 CD set.					
Capitol	C2PP-95220	Lennon	LP	U.S.	1990	$70.00
	4 CD set. First pressing with incorrect track listing.					
Radio Ventures		Masters of Rock	RS	U.S.	1989	$70.00
	Airdate: 9/18/89.					
Polygram	817160-2	Milk & Honey	LP/BP	U.S.†	1984	$14.00/$8.00
ABC		Remember Lennon	RS	U.S.		$200.00
	4 CD set.					
EMI	CDP-7-46642	Shaved Fish	LP/BP	U.S.†	1985	$110.00/$100.00
	First pressing with 11 tracks recalled.					
Capitol		Shaved Fish	LP/LB	U.S.	1987	$15.00/$9.00
	11 Tracks.					
Apple	7-46642-2	Shaved Fish	LP/LB	U.S.	1992	$15.00/$9.00
	11 Track version.					
ABC		Ten Years Later	RS	U.S.	1990	$200.00
	4 CD set. Airdate: 12/9/90.					

Singles

Label	Catalog Number	Title	Type	Country	Year	Longbox Value / Value
EMI	92-6-3	Beautiful Boy	CD3	Japan		$20.00/$8.00
EMI	TODP-2360	Beautiful City	CD3	Japan	1992	$18.00/$2.00
Parlophone	203091-2	Imagine	CD5	Germany	1988	$12.00
Parlophone	CD R6199	Imagine	CD5	U.K.	1988	$12.00
EMI	8800842	Instant Karma	CD5	Australia		$12.00
Capitol	DPRO-79417	Jealous Guy	CDJ	U.S.	1988	$10.00

Lennon, Julian

Full Length

Label	Catalog Number	Title	Type	Country	Year	Longbox Value / Value
Atlantic		Profiled	DJ/Intvw	U.S.		$8.00
Pioneer	PA-86-185	Stand by Me	LD	U.S.	1986	$30.00
Atlantic	80184-2	Valotte	LP/LB	U.S.†	1985	$14.00/$8.00

Singles

Label	Catalog Number	Title	Type	Country	Year	Longbox Value / Value
Virgin	VSCDG-1398	Get A Life	CD5	U.K.	1992	$10.00
Virgin	664824	Help Yourself	CD5	Germany	1991	$10.00
Virgin	VSCDT-1379	Help Yourself	CD5	U.K.	1991	$10.00
Virgin	VSCDG-1379	Help Yourself	CD5	U.K.	1991	$14.00
Atlantic	PRCD 4488-2	Help Yourself	CDJ	U.S.	1991	$6.00
Atlantic	PRCD 4151-2	Listen	CDJ	U.S.	1991	$3.00
Atlantic	PR 2910-2	Mother Mary	CDJ	U.S.	1989	$3.00
Virgin	161822	Now You're in Heaven	CD3	Germany	1989	$10.00
Virgin	661822	Now You're in Heaven	CD5	Germany	1989	$10.00
Virgin	VJD-10011	Now You're in Heaven	CD3	Japan	1989	$12.00/$4.00
Virgin	VSCD-1154	Now You're in Heaven	CD3	U.K.	1989	$10.00
Atlantic	PR 2653-2	Now You're in Heaven	CDJ	U.S.	1989	$6.00
Atlantic	VJDP-10176	Saltwater	CD3	Japan	1991	$12.00/$4.00
Virgin	VSCDT-1361	Saltwater	CD5	U.K.	1991	$10.00
Atlantic	PRCD 4114-2	Saltwater	CDJ	U.S.	1991	$6.00
Atlantic	PRCD 4113-2	Saltwater	CDJ	U.S.	1991	$7.00
Virgin	VJD-10212	You're the One	CD3	Japan	1989	$12.00/$4.00
Virgin	VSCD-1182	You're the One	CD3	U.K.	1989	$10.00
Atlantic	PR 2741-2	You're the One	CDJ	U.S.	1989	$3.00

Lennon, Kipp

Singles

Label	Catalog Number	Title	Type	Country	Year	Longbox Value / Value
Sony	10EP-3047	California Wine	CD3	Japan	1988	$12.00/$3.00

Lennon, Mark

Singles

Label	Catalog Number	Title	Type	Country	Year	Longbox Value / Value
A&M	CD 17667	A Wonderful Life	CDJ	U.S.	1988	$2.00

Lennox, Annie

Full Length

Label	Catalog Number	Title	Type	Country	Year	Longbox Value / Value
		Cold/Colder/Coldest	LP	U.K.	1992	$30.00
	3 CD5 Set.					
Arista	07822 18709-2	Diva	LTD/LP	U.S.	1992	$20.00
	2 picture disc CD set with colored feathers.					
Arista	ASCD2873	In-Store Sampler	DJ/Smplr	U.S.	1995	$12.00
Arista	ASCD-2873	In-Store Sampler	DJ/Smplr	U.S.	1995	$35.00
	2 CD set. Disc one is an Album Network various artist sampler #38. Disc two is a five track live sampler by Annie Lennox.					
		Medusa	DJ/LP	France	1995	$150.00
	Box set with CD, press kit, and rubber stamp.					
		Medusa	DJ/LP	U.K.	1995	$45.00
	CD in press kit.					
	KCDP51079	Why	DJ/Smplr	Canada	1995	$25.00

Singles

Label	Catalog Number	Title	Type	Country	Year	Longbox Value / Value
Arista		A Whiter Shade of Pale	CDJ	U.K.		$10.00
Arista	12884	A Whiter Shade of Pale	CD5	U.S.		$5.00
Arista	ASCD2850	A Whiter Shade of Pale	CDJ	U.S.		$6.00
RCA	74321116902	Cold	CD5	Germany	1992	$10.00
		Little Bird	CDJ	France	1992	$14.00
Arista	07822-12522-2	Little Bird	CD5	U.S.	1992	$5.00
Arista	ASCD-2508	Little Bird	CDJ	U.S.	1992	$3.00
Arista	ASCD-2507	Love Song for a Vampire	CDJ	U.S.	1992	$6.00
Arista	12805	No More I Love You	CD5	U.S.	1994	$5.00
RCA	BVDP-60	Precious	CD3	Japan	1992	$13.00/$3.00
A&M	390382-2	Put A Little Love in Your Heart	CD5	Germany	1988	$10.00
A&M	CDEE-484	Put A Little Love in Your Heart	CD5	U.K.	1988	$10.00
A&M	CD 17645	Put A Little Love in Your Heart	CDJ	U.S.		$3.00
A&M	CD 17645	Put A Little Love in Your Heart	CDJ	U.S.	1988	$3.00
		Something So Right	CD5	U.K.	1995	$10.00
		Something So Right	CD5	U.K.	1995	$10.00
	Second version.					
		Waiting In Vain	CDJ	U.S.		$3.00
Arista	ASCD2914	Waiting In Vain	CDJ	U.S.	1995	$6.00
RCA	BVDP-69	Walking on Broken Glass	CD3	Japan	1992	$12.00/$4.00
		Walking on Broken Glass	CD5	U.K.		$10.00
	Second version.					
Arista		Walking on Broken Glass	CD5	U.K.	1992	$12.00
Arista	07822 12484-2	Walking on Broken Glass	CD5	U.S.	1992	$5.00
Arista	ASCD-2452	Walking on Broken Glass	CDJ	U.S.	1992	$3.00
		Whiter Shade of Pale	CD5	U.K.	1995	$10.00
		Whiter Shade of Pale	CD5	U.K.	1995	$10.00
	Second version.					
RCA	PD-45318	Why	CD5	Germany	1992	$10.00
Arista	BVDP-55	Why	CD3	Japan	1992	$12.00/$4.00
Arista	ASCD-2419	Why	CDJ	U.S.	1992	$3.00

Leno, Jay

Full Length

Label	Catalog Number	Title	Type	Country	Year	Longbox Value / Value
Paramount	LV12547	American Dream	LD	U.S.	1987	$25.00

Leo

Singles

Label	Catalog Number	Title	Type	Country	Year	Longbox Value / Value
Columbia	658876-2	Lookin' Through the Windows	CD5	U.K.	1993	$8.00

Leonhart, Jay

Full Length

Label	Catalog Number	Title	Type	Country	Year	Longbox Value / Value
Digital Music	CD-442	Salamander Pie	LP/LB	U.S.†	1985	$14.00/$8.00

Leotis

Singles

Label	Catalog Number	Title	Type	Country	Year	Longbox Value / Value
Mercury	MERCD-289	On a Mission	CD5	U.K.	1993	$8.00

Leshaun

Singles

Label	Catalog Number	Title	Type	Country	Year	Longbox Value / Value
Tommy Boy	563	Ready or Not	CD5	U.S.	1993	$5.00

Leslie Spit Treeo

Singles

Label	Catalog Number	Title	Type	Country	Year	Longbox Value / Value
		Angel From Montgomery	CDJ	Canada		$3.00
		Sometimes I Wish	CDJ	Canada		$3.00

Less Stress

Singles

Label	Catalog Number	Title	Type	Country	Year	Longbox Value / Value
ffrr	BOICD-4	Don't Dream It's Over	CD5	U.K.	1990	$8.00

Less Than Jake

Singles

Label	Catalog Number	Title	Type	Country	Year	Longbox Value / Value
		Son of Perzore	CDJ	U.S.		$6.00

Leston, Paul

Singles

Label	Catalog Number	Title	Type	Country	Year	Longbox Value / Value
BMG	664700	Get Up and Dance	CD5	Germany	1991	$8.00

Let Loose

Singles

Label	Catalog Number	Title	Type	Country	Year	Longbox Value / Value
		Seventeen	CD5	U.K.		$10.00
		Seventeen	CD5	U.K.		$10.00
	Second version.					

Let's Active

Full Length

Label	Catalog Number	Title	Type	Country	Year	Longbox Value / Value
		Every Dog Has His Day	LP/LB	U.S.		$16.00/$12.00

Lettau, Kevyn

Full Length

Label	Catalog Number	Title	Type	Country	Year	Longbox Value / Value
JVC	016	An Acoustic Sampler	DJ/Smplr	U.S.	1993	$8.00

Letters To Cleo

Singles

Label	Catalog Number	Title	Type	Country	Year	Longbox Value / Value
		Awake	CDJ	U.S.		$3.00
Warner Brothers	17823	Awake	CD5	U.S.	1995	$5.00
	PRO-CD-7868	Demon Rock	CDJ	U.S.		$3.00

Label	Catalog Number	Title	Type	Country	Year	Longbox Value / Value
Warner Brothers	17913	Here & Now	CD5	U.S.	1994	$5.00
Level 42						
		Full Length				
		Level 42	LP/LB	U.S.		$16.00/$12.00
Polygram	810015-2	Pursuit of Accidents	LP/BP	U.S.		$14.00/$8.00
		Singles				
		All Over You	CD5	U.K.		$10.00
		All Over You	CD5	U.K.		$10.00
	Second version.					
Polydor	LEVEL-6	All Over You	CDJ	U.K.		$11.00
Polydor	POCD-911	Children Say	CD5	U.K.	1987	$10.00
RCA	PD-44746	Guaranteed	CD5	Germany	1991	$10.00
RCA	BVDP-47	Guaranteed	CD3	Japan	1991	$12.00/$4.00
RCA	PD-44746	Guaranteed	CD5	U.K.	1991	$10.00
RCA	62178-2-RDJ	Guaranteed	CDJ	U.S.	1991	$2.00
Polydor	P13P 37005	Heaven In My Hands	CD3	Japan	1988	$12.00/$4.00
Polydor	PZCD 14	Heaven In My Hands	CD5	U.K.	1988	$10.00
Polydor	CDP 28	Heaven In My Hands	CDJ	U.S.	1988	$2.00
Polydor	POL 710	Leaving Me Now	CDV	U.K.	1988	$25.00
Polygram	CDP 172	Leaving Me Now	CDJ	U.S.		$2.00
Polydor	P10P-30005	Lessons in Love	CD3	Japan	1988	$12.00/$4.00
		Love in a Peaceful World	CD5	U.K.		$10.00
		Love in a Peaceful World	CD5	U.K.		$10.00
	Second version.					
RCA	PD-44998	Overtime	CD5	U.K.	1991	$10.00
Polydor	885 518-2	Running in the Family	CD5	Germany	1987	$10.00
Polydor	885 518-2	Running in the Family	CD5	U.K.	1987	$10.00
Polygram	870 712-2	Something About You	CDV/BP	U.S.	1988	$14.00/$14.00
Polydor	871033-2	Take a Look	CD5	Germany	1988	$10.00
Polydor	PZCD-24	Take a Look	CD5	U.K.	1988	$10.00
Polydor	873230-3	Take Care of Yourself	CD3	Germany	1989	$10.00
Polydor	POOP-37015	Take Care of Yourself	CD3	Japan	1989	$12.00/$4.00
Polydor	PZCD-58	Take Care of Yourself	CD5	U.K.	1989	$10.00
Polydor	885 694-2	To Be With You Again	CD5	Germany	1987	$8.00
Polydor	871435-2	Tracie	CD5	Germany	1989	$8.00
Polydor	PZCD-34	Tracie	CD5	U.K.	1989	$8.00
Polydor	CDP 42	Tracie	CDJ	U.S.	1989	$2.00
Levellers						
		Full Length				
		Live at the Sheffield Octagon	DJ/Smplr	France		$12.00
Elektra	PRCD 8857-2	Warning	DJ/Smplr	U.S.	1993	$8.00
		Singles				
China	WOKCD-2010	Far From Home	CD5	U.K.	1991	$10.00
China	PCCY-00370	Fifteen Years	CD5	Japan	1992	$13.00
China	WOKCD-2020	Fifteen Years	CD5	U.K.	1991	$10.00
Elektra	PRCD 8680-2	Fifteen Years	CDJ	U.S.	1992	$7.00
Elektra	PRCD 8881-2	Garden, The	CDJ	U.S.	1993	$6.00
	PRCD 9418-2	Hope St.	CDJ	U.S.		$3.00
Elektra	PRCD 8635	Liberty Song	CDJ	U.S.		$2.00
China	WOKCD-2008	One Way	CD5	U.K.	1991	$10.00
Elektra	PRCD 8572-2	One Way	CDJ	U.S.	1991	$7.00
Elektra	PRCD 8937-2	Player, The	CDJ	U.S.	1994	$6.00
APT	10893-2	World Freak Show	CD5	U.K.	1992	$10.00
Levene, Keith						
		Singles				
SPV	6822	If Six Was One	CD5	Germany	1988	$8.00
Rykodisc	1004	If Six Was One	CD3	U.S.	1989	$6.00/$3.00
Levert						
		Singles				
Atlantic	PRCD 5030-2	ABC-123	CDJ	U.S.	1993	$2.00
		Addicted to You	CDJ	U.S.		$2.00
Atlantic	PRCD 3884-2	Baby I'm Ready	CDJ	U.S.	1990	$2.00
Atlanta	81830-2	Casanova	CDV/BP	U.S.	1988	$14.00/$14.00
Atlantic	PRCD 5159-2	Do the Things	CDJ	U.S.	1993	$2.00
Atlantic	PRCD 3990-2	Give a Little Love	CDJ	U.S.	1990	$2.00
		Just Coolin'	CDJ	U.S.		$2.00
		Just Coolin'	CDJ	U.S.		$2.00
	Second version.					
Atlantic	PRCD 3563-2	Rope a Dope Style	CDJ	U.S.	1990	$2.00
Levert, Gerald						
		Singles				
	PRCD 9406-2	Already Missing You	CDJ	U.K.		$3.00
Eastwest	PRCD 4333-2	Baby Hold on to Me	CDJ	U.S.	1991	$2.00
Eastwest	98208	Can't Help Myself	CD5	U.S.	1994	$5.00
Atlantic	98208	Can't Help Myself	CD5	U.S.	1994	$5.00
	PRCD 5725-2	I'd Give Anything	CDJ	U.S.		$3.00
Eastwest	PRCD 4189-2	Private Line	CDJ	U.S.	1991	$2.00
Levitation						
		Singles				
Rough Trade	332-4005-3	After Ever	CD5	Germany	1991	$8.00
APT	TOPP-005CD	After Ever	CD5	U.K.	1991	$8.00
Ultimate	TOPP-003CD	Coppelia	CD5	U.K.	1991	$8.00
Rough Trade	R-285-3	Work Around	CD5	U.K.	1991	$8.00
Capitol	C2 15841	Work Around	CD5	U.S.	1991	$4.00
Levy, Barrington						
		Singles				
MCA	MCA5P-2762	Vice Versa Love	CDJ	U.S.	1993	$2.00
MCA	MCA5P-2838	Work Lipstick	CDJ	U.S.	1993	$2.00
Levy, Kristiana						
		Singles				
EMI	147500-2	Bad Thing	CD5	Germany	1990	$8.00
EMI	147441-2	Influenced	CD5	Germany	1990	$8.00
EMI	147463-2	Love Is a Drug	CD5	Germany	1990	$8.00
EMI	147419-2	Mr. Good Guy	CD5	Germany	1989	$8.00
EMI	147532-2	Rude World	CD5	Germany	1990	$8.00
EMI	147517-2	Sunny Day	CD5	Germany	1990	$8.00
Lewis, Ann						
		Singles				
Victor	VIDL-10294	Lovin' You	CD3	Japan	1992	$12.00/$3.00
Victor	VIDL-10376	Ya! Ya!	CD3	Japan	1993	$12.00/$3.00
Lewis, Charles D.						
		Singles				
Polygram	877777-2	Soca Dance	CD5	Germany	1990	$8.00
Polygram	877777-2	Soca Dance	CD5	U.K.	1990	$8.00

Label	Catalog Number	Title	Type	Country	Year	Longbox Value / Value
Lewis, Dee						
		Singles				
Mercury	DEECD-3	Best of My Love	CD5	U.K.	1990	$8.00
Mercury	DEECD-5	Double Standard	CD5	U.K.	1990	$8.00
Lewis, Donna						
		Singles				
	PRCD 6638-2	I Love You Always Forever	CDJ	U.S.		$2.00
Lewis, Ephraim						
		Singles				
Elektra	7559-66397-2	Drowning Your Eyes	CD5	Germany	1992	$8.00
Elektra	EKR-151CD	Drowning Your Eyes	CD5	U.K.	1992	$8.00
Elektra	PRCD 8656-2	Drowning Your Eyes	CDJ	U.S.	1992	$2.00
Elektra	EKR-146CD	It Can't Be Forever	CD5	U.K.	1992	$8.00
Elektra	PRCD 8580-2	It Can't Be Forever	CDJ	U.S.	1993	$2.00
Lewis, Gary And The Playboys						
		Singles				
Rhino	880840	This Diamond Ring	CD3	Germany	1990	$10.00
Lewis, George						
		Full Length				
Mosaic	MD4-132	Complete Blue Note Recordings	LP	U.S.		$40.00
	4 CD set.					
Lewis, Huey and The News						
		Full Length				
Elektra	PR-8975	Four Chords & Several Years Ago	DJ/LP	U.S.	1994	$15.00
	CD and vinyl 45 in "78 record" book package.					
EMI	CDP-7-93355-2	Hard at Play	DJ/LP	U.S.	1991	$15.00
	CD in full color press kit.					
CBS	6941-80	Hewy Lewis & the News	LD	U.S.	1986	$30.00
Pioneer	PA-86-161	Hewy Lewis & the News	LD	U.S.	1986	$30.00
Album Network		In the Studio (Sports)	RS	U.S.	1988	$15.00
	Airdate: 10/17/88.					
DIR		King Biscuit Flour Hour	RS	U.S.	1991	$30.00
	With Nils Lofgren, Airdate: 5/12/91.					
DIR		King Biscuit Flour Hour	RS	U.S.	1992	$30.00
	Airdate: 5/17/92.					
DIR		King Biscuit Flour Hour	RS	U.S.	1994	$30.00
	Airdate: 6/5/94.					
Chrysalis	VK-41340	Picture This	LP/LB	U.S.†	1985	$14.00/$8.00
		Special DJ Copy On CD	DJ/Smplr	Japan		N/A
Chrysalis		Sports	LTD/LP	U.K.	1994	$25.00/$17.00
	25th Anniversary edition in 6"x11" longbox.					
Chrysalis	VK-41412	Sports	LP/LB	U.S.†	1985	$14.00/$8.00
Media America		Up Close	RS	U.S.	1991	$30.00
	2 CD set.					
		Singles				
EMI	DPRO-04776	Build Me Up	CDJ	U.S.	1991	$3.00
Elektra	EKR 188CD	But It's Alright	CD5	U.K.	1994	$10.00
Chrysalis	HUEYCD-15	Couple Days Off	CD5	U.K.	1991	$10.00
Chrysalis	DPRO-04752	Couple Days Off	CDJ	U.S.	1991	$3.00
EMI	204600-2	He Don't Know	CD5	Germany	1991	$10.00
EMI	DPRO-04807	He Don't Know	CDJ	U.S.	1991	$2.00
Chrysalis	204402-2	Hit Me Like a Hammer	CD5	Germany	1991	$10.00
Chrysalis	TODP-2321	Hit Me Like a Hammer	CD3	Japan	1991	$12.00/$4.00
Chrysalis	HUEYCD-14	Hit Me Like a Hammer	CD5	U.K.	1991	$10.00
EMI	DPRO-04777	Hit Me Like a Hammer	CDJ	U.S.	1991	$2.00
		It's Alright	CD5	U.K.	1994	$10.00
Chrysalis	885044	Perfect World	CD3	Germany	1988	$10.00
Chrysalis	661614	Perfect World	CD5	Germany	1988	$10.00
Chrysalis	XP10-2020	Perfect World	CD3	Japan	1988	$12.00/$4.00
Chrysalis	HUEYCD-10	Perfect World	CD3	U.K.	1988	$10.00
Chrysalis	DPRO-1165	Perfect World	CDJ	U.S.	1988	$3.00
Chrysalis	XP10-2091	Power of Love	CD3	Japan	1989	$12.00/$4.00
Chrysalis	CDE 2	Simple As That	CD5	U.K.	1988	$10.00
Chrysalis	661798	Small World	CD5	Germany	1988	$10.00
Chrysalis	XP10-2037	Small World	CD3	Japan	1988	$12.00/$4.00
Chrysalis	XP10-5003	Small World	CD3	Japan	1988	$12.00/$4.00
Chrysalis	HUEYCD-11	Small World	CD5	U.K.	1988	$10.00
		Some Kind of Wonderful	CD5	U.K.		$10.00
		Some Kind of Wonderful	CD5	U.K.		$10.00
	Second version.					
Elektra	PRCD 8958	Some Kind of Wonderful	CDJ	U.S.	1994	$3.00
Chrysalis	885342	Walking With the Kid	CD5	Germany	1989	$10.00
Chrysalis	HUEYCD-13	Walking With the Kid	CD5	U.K.	1989	$10.00
Chrysalis	HUEYCD-12	World to Me	CD5	U.K.	1988	$10.00
Lewis, Jerry Lee						
		Full Length				
Rhino	RNCD-5255	18 Original Sun Greatest Hits	LP/LB	U.S.†	1984	$14.00/$8.00
Mercury	836935	Killer-Mercury Years Vol. 1	LP/BP	U.S.		$14.00/$8.00
Mercury	836938	Killer-Mercury Years Vol. 2	LP/BP	U.S.		$14.00/$8.00
Mercury	836941	Killer-Mercury Years Vol. 3	LP/BP	U.S.		$14.00/$8.00
Mercury	822 751-2	Session, The	LP/BP	U.S.†	1985	$14.00/$8.00
		Singles				
	PRCD 9187-2	Goosebumps	CDJ	U.S.	1995	$6.00
Polygram	8893212-3	Great Balls of Fire	CD3	Germany	1989	$10.00
Rhino	885842	Great Balls of Fire	CD3	Germany	1990	$10.00
Polydor	PODP-40018	Great Balls of Fire	CD3	Japan	1989	$12.00/$4.00
Old Gold	OG-6115	Great Balls of Fire	CD3	U.K.	1989	$10.00
Charley	CDS-2	Great Balls of Fire	CD5	U.K.	1989	$10.00
Polydor	CDP 76	Great Balls of Fire	CDJ	U.S.	1989	$3.00
Warner Brothers	PRO-CD-4077	It Was the Whiskey	CDJ	U.S.	1990	$3.00
Rhino	885841	Whole Lot of Shakin' Going on	CD3	Germany	1990	$10.00
Lewis, John						
		Full Length				
Philips	824381-2	Plays Bach's "Well-Tempered Clavier"	LP/LB	U.S.†	1985	$14.00/$8.00
Lewis, Marcus						
		Singles				
CBS	854661-3	Club	CD3	Germany	1989	$8.00
CBS	854661-2	Club	CD5	Germany	1989	$8.00
	42427	Last Night	CD5	U.S.	1994	$5.00
Lewis, Ramsey						
		Full Length				
CBS	CK-33194	Sun Goddess	LP/LB	U.S.†	1985	$14.00/$8.00
CBS	CK-35018	Tequila Mockingbird	LP/LB	U.S.†	1985	$14.00/$8.00
		Singles				
Columbia	CSK 1747	Eye on You	CDJ	U.S.	1990	$2.00

Lewis, Ramsey & Nancy Wilson

Full Length

Label	Catalog Number	Title	Type	Country	Year	Longbox Value / Value
CBS	CK-39326	The Two of Us	LP/LB	U.S.†	1985	$14.00/$8.00

Lewis, Shari

Full Length

Label	Catalog Number	Title	Type	Country	Year	Longbox Value / Value
A&M	0422	Lamb Chop in Toyland	LP/LB	U.S.		$12.00/$7.00

Lewis, Shirley

Singles

Label	Catalog Number	Title	Type	Country	Year	Longbox Value / Value
A&M	USACD-675	Boy Meets Girl	CD5	U.K.	1989	$8.00
A&M	USACD-661	Heartbreaker	CD5	U.K.	1989	$8.00
A&M	USACD-660	Realistic	CD5	U.K.	1989	$8.00
A&M	CD 18001	You Can't Hide	CDJ	U.S.	1989	$2.00

Lexi

Singles

Label	Catalog Number	Title	Type	Country	Year	Longbox Value / Value
		Dedicated	CDJ	U.S.		$2.00

Leyton, John

Singles

Label	Catalog Number	Title	Type	Country	Year	Longbox Value / Value
Old Gold	OG-6116	Johnny Remember Me	CD3	U.K.	1989	$8.00

LFO

Singles

Label	Catalog Number	Title	Type	Country	Year	Longbox Value / Value
BMG	663988	Brainstorm	CD5	Germany	1991	$8.00
Warp	WAP-5CD	LFO	CD5	U.K.	1990	$8.00
Tommy Boy	501	Love is the Message	CD5	U.S.	1991	$5.00
Warp	WAP-14CD	We Are Back	CD5	U.K.	1991	$8.00
Tommy Boy	994	We Are Back	CD5	U.S.	1991	$2.00
Warp	WAP-17CD	What is House	CD5	U.K.	1992	$8.00

Lia

Singles

Label	Catalog Number	Title	Type	Country	Year	Longbox Value / Value
Virgin	PR 2453	Tell Me It's Not Too Late	CDJ	U.S.	1988	$2.00

Liaz

Singles

Label	Catalog Number	Title	Type	Country	Year	Longbox Value / Value
Kool Kat	KOOL-512CD	Affection	CD5	U.K.	1990	$8.00

Liberation

Singles

Label	Catalog Number	Title	Type	Country	Year	Longbox Value / Value
ZYX	6865-8	Liberation	CD5	Germany	1992	$6.00

Liberties

Singles

Label	Catalog Number	Title	Type	Country	Year	Longbox Value / Value
Chrysalis	CHSCD-3555	Lonely Tonight	CD5	U.K.	1990	$8.00

Liberty Horses

Singles

Label	Catalog Number	Title	Type	Country	Year	Longbox Value / Value
Rough Trade	R-282-3	Believe	CD5	U.K.	1992	$9.00
Capitol	C2 15926	Shine	CD5	U.S.	1992	$4.00

Liebert, Ottmar

Full Length

Label	Catalog Number	Title	Type	Country	Year	Longbox Value / Value
Epic		Euphoria	LTD/LP	U.S.	1995	$18.00
Epic		Opium Radio Sampler	DJ/Smplr	U.S.		$5.00
Epic		Solo Para Ti	DJ/Smplr	U.S.		$10.00

2 CD set.

Singles

Label	Catalog Number	Title	Type	Country	Year	Longbox Value / Value
CBS	66862	Euphoria E.P.	CD5	U.S.	1994	$5.00

Liebrand, Ben

Singles

Label	Catalog Number	Title	Type	Country	Year	Longbox Value / Value
CBS	655126-3	Eve of the War	CD3	Germany	1989	$8.00
CBS	655126-5	Eve of the War	CD5	Germany	1989	$8.00
CBS	6556175-3	I Wish	CD3	Germany	1989	$8.00
CBS	6556175-2	I Wish	CD5	Germany	1989	$8.00
CBS	6556176-3	Move To the Big Band	CD3	Germany	1989	$8.00
CBS	655854-3	Puls(T)ar	CD3	Germany	1989	$8.00
CBS	655854-5	Puls(T)ar	CD5	Germany	1989	$8.00
CBS	CDLIEB-1	Puls(T)ar	CD5	U.K.	1989	$8.00

Life

Singles

Label	Catalog Number	Title	Type	Country	Year	Longbox Value / Value
Bellaphon	130-07-359	Feel So Good	CD5	Germany	1990	$8.00

Life Is Art

Full Length

Label	Catalog Number	Title	Type	Country	Year	Longbox Value / Value
Gramaphone	GRCD-0001	Sampler	LP/LB	U.S.†	1985	$14.00/$8.00

Life, Sex & Death

Singles

Label	Catalog Number	Title	Type	Country	Year	Longbox Value / Value
Reprise	PRO-CD-5596	Tank	CDJ	U.S.	1992	$2.00
Reprise	PRO-CD-5548	Tank	CDJ	U.S.	1992	$7.00
Reprise	PRO-CD-6149	Telephone Call	CDJ	U.S.	1993	$2.00

Life Unlimited

Singles

Label	Catalog Number	Title	Type	Country	Year	Longbox Value / Value
Pinnacle	PTLCD-1	Sound of Love and Violence	CD5	U.K.	1991	$8.00

Lifter

Singles

Label	Catalog Number	Title	Type	Country	Year	Longbox Value / Value
		Everything Was Beautiful & Nothing Hurt	CDJ	U.S.		$2.00

Light of the World

Singles

Label	Catalog Number	Title	Type	Country	Year	Longbox Value / Value
Cooltempo	COOLCD-232	Keep the Dream Alive	CD5	U.K.	1991	$8.00
Cooltempo	COOLCD-209	One Destination	CD5	U.K.	1991	$8.00

Lighter Shade Of Brown

Singles

Label	Catalog Number	Title	Type	Country	Year	Longbox Value / Value
Polygram	856197	Dip Into My Ride	CD5	U.S.	1994	$5.00
Pump	19105	Spill the Rhyme	CDJ	U.S.	1992	$2.00

Lightning Seeds

Full Length

Label	Catalog Number	Title	Type	Country	Year	Longbox Value / Value
MCA	MCA5P-2262	Sense	DJ/Smplr	U.S.	1992	$12.00

Singles

Label	Catalog Number	Title	Type	Country	Year	Longbox Value / Value
Intercord	827 417	All I Want	CD5	Germany	1990	$10.00
Ghetto	CDGTG-9	All I Want	CD5	U.K.	1990	$10.00
MCA	CD45 18447	All I Want	CDJ	U.S.	1990	$2.00
		All I Want	CDJ	U.S.	1990	$2.00

Second version.

Label	Catalog Number	Title	Type	Country	Year	Longbox Value / Value
MCA	MCA5P-2190	Blowing Bubbles	CDJ	U.S.	1992	$2.00
Intercord	827 415	Joy	CD5	Germany	1989	$10.00
Ghetto	CDGTG-6	Joy	CD5	U.K.	1989	$10.00
MCA	CD 1145	Joy	CDJ	U.S.	1989	$2.00
Ghetto	VSCDG-1402	Life of Riley	CD5	U.K.	1990	$10.00
MCA	54195	Life of Riley	CD5	U.S.	1990	$5.00
MCA	CD45 1584	Life of Riley	CDJ	U.S.	1990	$2.00
		Lucky You	CDJ	U.S.		$3.00
		Perfect	CD5	U.K.	1995	$10.00
		Perfect	CD5	U.K.	1995	$10.00
		Perfect	CD5	U.K.	1995	$10.00
		Perfect	CD5	U.K.	1995	$10.00

Second version.

Label	Catalog Number	Title	Type	Country	Year	Longbox Value / Value
Intercord	825 281	Pure	CD3	Germany	1989	$10.00
Toshiba	TODP-2187	Pure	CD3	Japan	1989	$12.00/$4.00
Ghetto	CDGTG-4	Pure	CD5	U.K.	1989	$10.00
MCA	CD45 1148	Pure	CDJ	U.S.	1990	$2.00
Virgin	VSCDT-1414	Sense	CD5	U.K.	1992	$10.00
MCA	54431	Sense	CD5	U.S.	1992	$5.00
MCA	MCA5P-2278	Sense	CDJ	U.S.	1992	$2.00
Ghetto	CDGTG-8	Sweet Dreams	CD5	U.K.	1990	$10.00
MCA	CD45 1105	Sweet Dreams	CDJ	U.S.	1990	$2.00
Ghetto	CDGTG-7	Upside Down	CD5	U.K.	1990	$10.00

Likkle Wicked

Singles

Label	Catalog Number	Title	Type	Country	Year	Longbox Value / Value
Luke	647	Perfida	CDJ	U.S.	1993	$2.00

Lil Kim

Singles

Label	Catalog Number	Title	Type	Country	Year	Longbox Value / Value
Atlantic	98044-2	No Time	CD5	U.S.	1997	$3.00

Lil Louis And World

Singles

Label	Catalog Number	Title	Type	Country	Year	Longbox Value / Value
Epic	49K 74282	Club Lonely	CD5	U.S.	1992	$5.00
ffrr	886701-2	French Kiss	CD5	Germany	1989	$8.00
London	POOL-37019	French Kiss	CD3	Japan	1989	$13.00/$4.00
ffrr	FCD-115	French Kiss	CD5	U.K.	1989	$8.00
Polygram	886879-2	I Called U	CD5	Germany	1990	$8.00
ffrr	FCD-123	I Called U	CD5	U.K.	1990	$8.00
ffrr	869051-2	Nyce & Slo	CD5	Germany	1990	$8.00
ffrr	FCD-137	Nyce & Slo	CD5	U.K.	1990	$8.00
		Nyce & Slo	CDJ	U.S.	1990	$2.00
ffrr	FCD-197	Saved My Life	CD5	U.K.	1992	$8.00

Lil Suzy

Singles

Label	Catalog Number	Title	Type	Country	Year	Longbox Value / Value
Metropolitan	3001	Promise Me	CD5	U.S.	1994	$5.00

Lilac

Singles

Label	Catalog Number	Title	Type	Country	Year	Longbox Value / Value
Alfa	11B3-85	Bang Bang	CD3	Japan	1989	$12.00/$3.00
Alfa	11B3-17	Come Come Come	CD3	Japan	1989	$12.00/$3.00
Alfa	10SR-29	Jump to the Music	CD3	Japan	1989	$12.00/$3.00

Lilac Time

Full Length

Label	Catalog Number	Title	Type	Country	Year	Longbox Value / Value
		Excerpts From Paradise Circus	DJ/Smplr	U.S.		$6.00

Singles

Label	Catalog Number	Title	Type	Country	Year	Longbox Value / Value
Fontana	876377-2	All For Love and Love For All	CD5	Germany	1990	$8.00
Fontana	LILCD-8	All For Love and Love For All	CD5	U.K.	1990	$8.00
Fontana	LILCD-5	American Eyes	CD5	U.K.	1989	$8.00
Fontana	CDP 149	American Eyes	CDJ	U.S.	1989	$2.00
Fontana	LILCD-4	Black Velvet	CD5	U.K.	1989	$8.00
Fontana	LILCD-6	Days of the Week	CD5	U.K.	1989	$8.00
Creation	CRESCD-104	Dreaming	CD5	U.K.	1991	$8.00
Fontana	LILCD-7	Girl Who Waves at Trains	CD5	U.K.	1989	$8.00
Intercord	828 914	In Inverna Gardens	CD5	Germany	1991	$8.00
Fontana	LILCD-10	Laundry	CD5	U.K.	1990	$8.00
Fontana	LILCD-2	Return to Yesterday	CD5	U.K.	1989	$8.00
Fontana	LILCD-3	You've Gotta Love	CD5	U.K.	1989	$8.00

Lilian, Axe

Singles

Label	Catalog Number	Title	Type	Country	Year	Longbox Value / Value
Music For Nations	CDKUT-152	Here Is Christmas	CD5	U.K.	1992	$8.00
Music For Nations	CDKUT-146	No Matter What	CD5	U.K.	1992	$8.00
IRS	67081	True Believer	CDJ	U.S.	1991	$2.00

Limbomaniacs

Singles

Label	Catalog Number	Title	Type	Country	Year	Longbox Value / Value
In Effect	0619	Butt Funkin'	CDJ	U.S.	1992	$2.00
CBS	657793-2	Shake It	CD5	U.K.	1992	$8.00

Lime

Singles

Label	Catalog Number	Title	Type	Country	Year	Longbox Value / Value
Polygram	887875-2	Your Love	CD5	Germany	1988	$8.00

Limerick, Alison

Singles

Label	Catalog Number	Title	Type	Country	Year	Longbox Value / Value
Arista	74321-102862	Gettin' It Right	CD5	U.K.	1992	$8.00
Arista	664996	Make It on My Own	CD5	U.K.	1992	$8.00
Arista	664208	Where Love Lives	CD5	Germany	1991	$8.00
Arista	663509	Where Love Lives	CD5	U.K.	1990	$8.00
Arista	664208	Where Love Lives	CD5	U.K.	1991	$8.00

Lin Que

Singles

Label	Catalog Number	Title	Type	Country	Year	Longbox Value / Value
	PRCD 9371-2	Let It Fall	CDJ	U.S.		$2.00

Lincke, Susan

Singles

Label	Catalog Number	Title	Type	Country	Year	Longbox Value / Value
King	K10Y-30001	You're My Satisfaction	CD3	Japan	1989	$12.00/$3.00

Lincoln, Abbey

Full Length

Label	Catalog Number	Title	Type	Country	Year	Longbox Value / Value
Enja	311246	Talking to the Sun	LP/LB	U.S.†	1985	$14.00/$8.00
Verve	LIN 2	You Gotta Pay the Band	DJ/LP	U.S.	1991	$15.00

Singles

Label	Catalog Number	Title	Type	Country	Year	Longbox Value / Value
Verve	ABY-2	Devil's Got Your Tounge	CDJ	U.S.	1993	$6.00

Lind, Helena

Singles

Label	Catalog Number	Title	Type	Country	Year	Longbox Value / Value
Polygram	877781-2	Eleni	CD5	Germany	1990	$8.00

Linden, Colin

Full Length

Label	Catalog Number	Title	Type	Country	Year	Longbox Value / Value
A&M		Sampler	DJ/Smplr	Canada	1988	$10.00

Singles

Label	Catalog Number	Title	Type	Country	Year	Longbox Value / Value
A&M		Way Heaven Feels, The	CDJ	Canada		$6.00

Linden, Hal

Singles

Label	Catalog Number	Title	Type	Country	Year	Longbox Value / Value
JP	0001	Meet Me at Jack's	CDJ	U.S.	1993	$2.00

Lindley, David

Singles

Label	Catalog Number	Title	Type	Country	Year	Longbox Value / Value
Elektra	PR 8022-2	Never Know Her	CDJ	U.S.	1988	$2.00

Lindup, Mike

Singles

Label	Catalog Number	Title	Type	Country	Year	Longbox Value / Value
Polygram	PZCD-95	Spirit Is Free, The	CD5	U.K.	1990	$8.00

Line, S.L.

Singles

Label	Catalog Number	Title	Type	Country	Year	Longbox Value / Value
BMG	663111	Another Day In Paradise	CD5	Germany	1990	$8.00

Linear

Singles

Label	Catalog Number	Title	Type	Country	Year	Longbox Value / Value
Atlantic	7567-87877-2	Don't You Come Cryin'	CD5	Germany	1990	$8.00
Atlantic	PRCD 3559-2	Something Going On	CDJ	U.S.	1990	$2.00
Atlantic	AMDY-5013	Spending All My Love	CD3	Japan	1990	$12.00/$3.00
WEA	A-7907CD	Spending All My Love	CD5	U.K.	1990	$8.00
Atlantic	PRCD 4555-2	T.L.C.	CDJ	U.S.	1992	$2.00

Linney, Mike

Singles

Label	Catalog Number	Title	Type	Country	Year	Longbox Value / Value
BMG	664060	Saved Me	CD5	Germany	1991	$8.00
BMG	664642	Shadowland	CD5	Germany	1991	$8.00
BMG	663125	Turn the Music on	CD5	Germany	1990	$8.00
BMG	665017	Woman in Love	CD5	Germany	1992	$8.00

Lins, Ivan

Full Length

Label	Catalog Number	Title	Type	Country	Year	Longbox Value / Value
Polygram	832262-2	Maos	LP/BP	U.S.		$12.00/$7.00

Singles

Label	Catalog Number	Title	Type	Country	Year	Longbox Value / Value
Reprise	PRO-CD-3910	Love Dance	CDJ	U.S.	1989	$2.00
Warner Brothers	W-7151CD	You Moved Me to This	CD5	U.K.	1989	$8.00
Reprise	PRO-CD-3527	You Moved Me to This	CDJ	U.S.	1989	$2.00
Reprise	PRO-CD-3457	You Moved Me to This	CDJ	U.S.	1989	$2.00

Lionrock

Singles

Label	Catalog Number	Title	Type	Country	Year	Longbox Value / Value
BMG	7432112438-2	Lionrock	CD5	U.K.	1992	$8.00

Lions and Ghosts

Singles

Label	Catalog Number	Title	Type	Country	Year	Longbox Value / Value
EMI	DPRO-4248	Arson in Toyland	CDJ	U.S.	1989	$2.00
EMI	DPRO-04363	Too Shy	CDJ	U.S.	1989	$2.00

Lipps Inc.

Singles

Label	Catalog Number	Title	Type	Country	Year	Longbox Value / Value
Polygram	870379-2	Funkytown	CD5	Germany	1989	$8.00

Liquid

Singles

Label	Catalog Number	Title	Type	Country	Year	Longbox Value / Value
WEA	XLS-33CD	Liquid is Liquid	CD5	U.K.	1992	$8.00
WEA	XLS-28CD	Sweet Harmony	CD5	U.K.	1992	$8.00

Liquid Jesus

Singles

Label	Catalog Number	Title	Type	Country	Year	Longbox Value / Value
MCA	MCA5P-2001	Better Or Worse	CDJ	U.S.	1991	$2.00
MCA	1130	Stand	CDJ	U.S.	1990	$2.00

Liquid Oxygen

Singles

Label	Catalog Number	Title	Type	Country	Year	Longbox Value / Value
Champion	CHAMPCD-242	Planet Dance	CD5	U.K.	1990	$8.00

Lisa

Singles

Label	Catalog Number	Title	Type	Country	Year	Longbox Value / Value
King	KIDP-19	I Believe in Music	CD3	Japan	1990	$12.00/$3.00

Lisa Lisa

Singles

Label	Catalog Number	Title	Type	Country	Year	Longbox Value / Value
Pendulum	58094	Skip to My Lu	CD5	U.S.	1993	$4.00
Pendulum	08711	Skip to My Lu	CDJ	U.S.	1993	$2.00
Capital	58094	Skip to My Lu	CD5	U.S.	1994	$5.00

Lisa Lisa & Cult Jam

Full Length

Label	Catalog Number	Title	Type	Country	Year	Longbox Value / Value
CBS	CK-40135	With Full Force	LP/BP	U.S.†	1985	$14.00/$8.00

Singles

Label	Catalog Number	Title	Type	Country	Year	Longbox Value / Value
Columbia	CSK 74096	Forever	CDJ	U.S.		$2.00
Columbia	CSK 1222	Go For Yours	CDJ	U.S.	1988	$2.00
CBS	651670-3	I Wonder If ITake You Home	CD3	Germany	1988	$10.00
CBS	651670-3	I Wonder If ITake You Home	CD3	U.K.	1988	$10.00
CBS	655060-3	Just Git It Together	CD3	Germany	1989	$10.00
CBS	655060-2	Just Git It Together	CD5	U.K.	1989	$10.00
Columbia	CSK 1700	Just Git It Together	CDJ	U.S.	1989	$2.00
Columbia	CSK 1788	Kiss Your Tears Away	CDJ	U.S.	1989	$2.00
CBS	656950-9	Let the Beat Hit 'Em	CD5	Germany	1991	$10.00
Sony	SRCS-5554	Let the Beat Hit 'Em	CD3	Japan	1991	$4.00
CBS	657374-2	Let the Beat Hit 'Em	CD5	U.K.	1991	$10.00
Columbia	44K 73934	Let the Beat Hit 'Em	CD5	U.S.	1991	$5.00
Columbia	CSK 4114	Let the Beat Hit 'Em	CDJ	U.S.	1991	$2.00
Columbia	CSK 4334	Let the Beat Hit 'Em	CDJ	U.S.	1991	$2.00
Columbia	CSK 73847	Let the Beat Hit 'Em	CDJ	U.S.	1991	$2.00
CBS	654781-3	Little Jackie Wants to Be a Star	CD3	Germany	1989	$10.00
CBS	10EP-3082	Little Jackie Wants to Be a Star	CD3	Japan	1989	$12.00/$4.00
CBS	654781-2	Little Jackie Wants to Be a Star	CD5	U.K.	1989	$10.00
Columbia	CSK 1500	Little Jackie Wants to Be a Star	CDJ	U.S.	1989	$2.00
Columbia	CSK 2835	Someone to Love Me for Me	CDJ	U.S.	1987	$2.00
Columbia	CSK 74010	Where Were You When I Needed You	CDJ	U.S.	1990	$2.00

Lisa M

Singles

Label	Catalog Number	Title	Type	Country	Year	Longbox Value / Value
Polydor	PZCD-125	Love's Heartbreak	CD5	U.K.	1991	$8.00

Little America

Singles

Label	Catalog Number	Title	Type	Country	Year	Longbox Value / Value
Geffen	PRO-CD-3430	Where Were You	CDJ	U.S.	1989	$2.00

Little Angels

Full Length

Label	Catalog Number	Title	Type	Country	Year	Longbox Value / Value
Polygram	511060-2	Young Gods	LP/BP	U.S.		$12.00/$7.00

Singles

Label	Catalog Number	Title	Type	Country	Year	Longbox Value / Value
Polydor	LTLCD-1	90 In the Shade	CD5	U.K.	1988	$8.00
Polydor	POCP-1084	Barnyard	CD5	Japan	1991	$3.00
Polydor	LTLCD-3	Do You Wanna Riot	CD5	U.K.	1989	$8.00
Polydor	PRAY 1	Don't Pray for Me	CD5	U.K.	1989	$8.00
		Don't Pray for Me	CDJ	U.S.	1989	$2.00
Polydor	LTLCD-5	Kickin' Up Dust	CD5	U.K.	1990	$8.00
Polydor	CDP 202	Kickin' Up Dust	CDJ	U.S.	1989	$2.00
Polydor	LTLCD-9	Product of the Working Class	CD5	U.K.	1991	$8.00
		Sail Away	CD5	U.K.		$10.00
		Sail Away	CD5	U.K.		$10.00

Second version.

Label	Catalog Number	Title	Type	Country	Year	Longbox Value / Value
Polydor	LTLCD-2	She's a Little Angel	CD5	U.K.	1989	$8.00
Polydor	COCP-1127	She's a Little Angel Live	CD5	Japan	1990	$12.00
Polydor	PODP-1069	Too Much Too Young	CD3	Japan	1993	$13.00/$4.00

Little, Anthony

Singles

Label	Catalog Number	Title	Type	Country	Year	Longbox Value / Value
Rhino	85843	Goin' Out of My Head	CD3	Germany	1990	$10.00

Little Big Band

Singles

Label	Catalog Number	Title	Type	Country	Year	Longbox Value / Value
Factory	FACD-207	Woodland Rock	CD5	U.K.	1989	$8.00

Little Caesar

Full Length

Label	Catalog Number	Title	Type	Country	Year	Longbox Value / Value
DIR		King Biscuit Flour Hour	RS	U.S.	1990	$45.00

Airdate: 9/17/90.

Label	Catalog Number	Title	Type	Country	Year	Longbox Value / Value
DGC	2 24288-Dj	Little Caesar	DJ/LP	U.S.	1990	$10.00

Singles

Label	Catalog Number	Title	Type	Country	Year	Longbox Value / Value
Geffen	7599-21310-2	Chain of Fools	CD5	Germany	1990	$9.00
Geffen	GEF-80CD	Chain of Fools	CD5	U.K.	1990	$9.00
DGC	PRO-CD-4105	Chain of Fools	CDJ	U.S.	1990	$2.00
DGC	PRO-CD-4102	Chain of Fools	CDJ	U.S.	1990	$7.00

Oversized cardboard sleeve.

Label	Catalog Number	Title	Type	Country	Year	Longbox Value / Value
DGC	PRO-CD-4151	From the Start	CDJ	U.S.	1990	$2.00
DGC	PRO-CD-4180	In Your Arms	CDJ	U.S.	1991	$2.00
DGC	PRO-CD-4202	In Your Arms	CDJ	U.S.	1991	$2.00
Metal Blade	72418-2	Name Your Poison	CD5	U.S.	1989	$4.00
DGC	PRO-CD-4442	Slow Ride	CDJ	U.S.	1992	$2.00
DGC	PRO-CD-4424	Stand Up	CDJ	U.S.	1992	$2.00

Little Feat

Full Length

Label	Catalog Number	Title	Type	Country	Year	Longbox Value / Value
Warner Brothers		CD Sampler 1992	DJ/Smplr	U.S.	1992	$8.00
Westwood One		In Concert	RS	U.S.	1994	$80.00

2 CD set. With Gin Blossoms, Airdate: 10/25/93.

Label	Catalog Number	Title	Type	Country	Year	Longbox Value / Value
Album Network		In the Studio (Waiting For Columbus)	RS	U.S.	1988	$25.00

Airdate: 10/10/88.

Label	Catalog Number	Title	Type	Country	Year	Longbox Value / Value
Album Network		In the Studio (Waiting For Columbus)	RS	U.S.	1993	$20.00

Airdate: 2/1/93.

Label	Catalog Number	Title	Type	Country	Year	Longbox Value / Value
DIR		King Biscuit Flour Hour	RS	U.S.	1991	$30.00

Airdate: 11/24/91.

Label	Catalog Number	Title	Type	Country	Year	Longbox Value / Value
DIR		King Biscuit Flour Hour	RS	U.S.	1992	$25.00

Airdate: 7/13/92.

Label	Catalog Number	Title	Type	Country	Year	Longbox Value / Value
		Live From Electric Ladyland	RS	U.S.	1990	$30.00

Airdate: 10/15/90.

Label	Catalog Number	Title	Type	Country	Year	Longbox Value / Value
		Live From the House of Blues	RS	U.S.		$35.00

2 CD set.

Label	Catalog Number	Title	Type	Country	Year	Longbox Value / Value
Warner Brothers		Representing the Mambo	LP/LB	U.S.		$14.00/$8.00
Radio Today		Rock Stars	RS	U.S.	1990	$30.00

2 CD set. Airdate: 5/24/90.

Label	Catalog Number	Title	Type	Country	Year	Longbox Value / Value
Morgan Creek		Shake Me Up	LP/LB	U.S.		$14.00/$8.00
Westwood One		Superstar Concert	RS	U.S.	1992	$40.00

2 CD set. With George Thorogood, Airdate: 11/22/92.

Label	Catalog Number	Title	Type	Country	Year	Longbox Value / Value
Media America		Up Close	RS	U.S.	1988	$30.00

2 CD set.

Label	Catalog Number	Title	Type	Country	Year	Longbox Value / Value
Media America		Up Close	RS	U.S.	1989	$30.00

2 CD set.

Label	Catalog Number	Title	Type	Country	Year	Longbox Value / Value
Media America		Up Close	RS	U.S.	1990	$30.00

2 CD set.

Label	Catalog Number	Title	Type	Country	Year	Longbox Value / Value
Media America		Up Close	RS	U.S.	1991	$30.00

2 CD set.

Singles

Label	Catalog Number	Title	Type	Country	Year	Longbox Value / Value
Morgan Creek	PRO-0008	Fast & Furious	CDJ	U.S.	1991	$2.00
Warner Brothers	PRO-CD-3180	Hate to Lose Your Lovin'	CDJ	U.S.	1988	$2.00
Warner Brothers	PRO-CD-3297	Long Time Till I Get Over You	CDJ	U.S.	1988	$2.00
Warner Brothers	PRO-CD-3296	One Clear Moment	CDJ	U.S.	1988	$2.00
Warner Brothers	PRO-CD-3410	One Clear Moment	CDJ	U.S.	1988	$2.00
Morgan Creek	PRO 0025	Quicksand And Lies	CDJ	U.S.	1992	$2.00
Morgan Creek	PRO 0005	Shake Me Up	CDJ	U.S.	1991	$2.00
Warner Brothers	PRO-CD-4022	Texas Twister	CDJ	U.S.	1990	$2.00
Warner Brothers	PRO-CD-4465	That's Her, She's Mine	CDJ	U.S.	1990	$2.00
Morgan Creek	PZCD-179	Things Happen	CD5	U.K.	1991	$10.00
Morgan Creek	PRO 0007	Things Happen	CDJ	U.S.	1991	$2.00
Morgan Creek	PRO 0015	Things Happen	CDJ	U.S.	1992	$2.00
Warner Brothers	PRO-CD-4307	Woman in Love	CDJ	U.S.	1990	$2.00

Little Indian

Singles

Label	Catalog Number	Title	Type	Country	Year	Longbox Value / Value
Warner Brothers	17754	One Little Indian	CD5	U.S.	1995	$5.00

Little John

Singles

Label	Catalog Number	Title	Type	Country	Year	Longbox Value / Value
	DPRO-10473	Shoelace	CDJ	U.S.		$3.00

Little Milton

Singles

Label	Catalog Number	Title	Type	Country	Year	Longbox Value / Value
Malaco	2189	My Dog and Me	CDJ	U.S.	1993	$2.00

Little Richard

Full Length

Label	Catalog Number	Title	Type	Country	Year	Longbox Value / Value
Delta	11071	Tutti Frutti	LP	U.K.		$15.00
Delta	11071	Tutti Frutti	LP	U.S.		$12.00

Singles

Label	Catalog Number	Title	Type	Country	Year	Longbox Value / Value
Polydor	CDP399	Good Golly Miss Molly	CDJ	U.S.	1991	$2.00
Grudge	4758-2-FDj	Grand Slam	CDJ	U.S.	1989	$2.00
Rhino	885845	Long Tall Sally	CD3	Germany	1990	$10.00
Rhino	885844	Tutti-Frutti	CD3	Germany	1990	$10.00

Little River Band

Full Length

Label	Catalog Number	Title	Type	Country	Year	Longbox Value / Value
MCA		Get Lucky	LP/LB	U.S.		$14.00/$8.00
EMI	CDP-46021	Greatest Hits	LP/LB	U.S.†	1984	$14.00/$8.00
Pioneer Artists	PA-88-038	Live Exposure	LD	U.S.	1983	$25.00
EMI	CDP-46061	Playing to Win	LP/LB	U.S.†	1984	$14.00/$8.00

Singles

Label	Catalog Number	Title	Type	Country	Year	Longbox Value / Value
MCA	CD45 18079	Every Time I Turn Around	CDJ	U.S.	1990	$2.00
MCA	CD45 17894	If I Get Lucky	CDJ	U.S.	1990	$2.00
MCA	09P3-6176	Listen to Your Heart	CD3	Japan	1989	$12.00/$4.00

Label	Catalog Number	Title	Type	Country	Year	Longbox Value / Value
MCA	10P3-6012	Love is a Bridge	CD3	Japan	1988	$12.00/$4.00
MCA	CD45 17576	Love is a Bridge	CDJ	U.S.	1988	$2.00
Curb	059	World Wide Love	CDJ	U.S.	1991	$2.00

Little Seven

Label	Catalog Number	Title	Type	Country	Year	Longbox Value / Value
Singles						
		Time Of Your Life	CD5	U.K.	1995	$10.00

Little, Steven

Label	Catalog Number	Title	Type	Country	Year	Longbox Value / Value
Singles						
EMI	201710-2	Bitter Fruit	CD5	Germany	1990	$8.00
RCA	PD-49394	Love and Forgiveness	CD5	Germany	1989	$8.00
RCA	PD-49444	Revolution	CD5	Germany	1989	$8.00
RCA	PD-49444	Revolution	CD5	U.K.	1989	$8.00

Little Texas

Label	Catalog Number	Title	Type	Country	Year	Longbox Value / Value
Full Length						
Warner Brothers	PRO-CD-6188	What Might Have Been	DJ/LP	U.S.	1993	$20.00
2CD in double digipak.						
Singles						
Warner Brothers	PRO-CD-6632	Big Time	CDJ	U.S.	1993	$2.00

Little Village

Label	Catalog Number	Title	Type	Country	Year	Longbox Value / Value
Full Length						
Westwood One		In Concert	RS	U.S.	1992	$120.00
2 CD set. Airdate: 6/2292.						
Westwood One		Off the Record	RS	U.S.	1992	$40.00
Airdate: 5/25/92.						
Singles						
Reprise	9362-40570-2	Don't Go Away Mad	CD5	Germany	1992	$9.00
Reprise	W-0106CD	Don't Go Away Mad	CD5	U.K.	1992	$9.00
Reprise	PRO-CD-5333	Don't Go Away Mad	CDJ	U.S.	[illegible]	[illegible]
Reprise	PRO-CD-5228	She Runs Hot	CDJ	U.S.	1992	$2.00
Reprise	W-008CD	Solar Sex Panel	CD5	U.K.	1992	$9.00
Reprise	PRO-CD-5222	Solar Sex Panel	CDJ	U.S.	1992	$2.00

Littletown, Rick

Label	Catalog Number	Title	Type	Country	Year	Longbox Value / Value
Singles						
Music	2817	Baby Read My Lips	CD5	U.S.	1993	$2.00

Live

Label	Catalog Number	Title	Type	Country	Year	Longbox Value / Value
Full Length						
Album Network		Live Concert Broadcast	RS	U.S.	1995	$35.00
Radioactive		Throwing Copper	LTD/LP	Australia	1995	$30.00
2 CDset.						
Radioactive		Throwing Copper	DJ/LP	U.S.	1994	$15.00
Promo CD with bonus 14th track.						
Singles						
		All Over You	CD5	U.K.		$10.00
		All Over You	CD5	U.K.		$10.00
Second version.						
Radioactive	RARDM 54442	Beauty of Grey	CD5	U.S.	1992	$5.00
Radioactive		Bi	CD5	Australia	1995	$10.00
Radioactive	RARCD-001	Four Songs	CD5	U.K.	1991	$9.00
Radioactive	RARDS 54236	Four Songs	CD5	U.S.	1992	$5.00
Radioactive		Horse	CDJ	U.S.	1994	$8.00
Radioactive		I Alone	CDJ	U.S.	1994	$8.00
		Lightning Crashes	CD5	U.K.		$10.00
		Lightning Crashes	CD5	U.K.		$10.00
Second version.						
Radioactive		Lightning Crashes	CDJ	U.S.	1994	$8.00
Radioactive	CD45 2320	Mirror Song	CDJ	U.S.	1992	$2.00
Radioactive	RAXTD-1	Operation Spirit	CD5	U.K.	1992	$9.00
Radioactive	CD45 2088	Operation Spirit	CDJ	U.S.	1991	$2.00
Radioactive	54236	Operation Spirit	CD5	U.S.	1994	$6.00
Radioactive	RARDS 54387	Pain Lies on the Riverside	CD5	U.S.	1992	$5.00
Radioactive	CD45 2089	Pain Lies on the Riverside	CDJ	U.S.	1992	$2.00
		Selling the Drama	CD5	U.K.		$10.00
Second version.						
		Selling the Drama	CD5	U.K.	1995	$10.00
Radioactive	CD45 2911	Selling the Drama	CDJ	U.S.	1994	$2.00
Radioactive	RAR5P 2911	Selling the Drama	CDJ	U.S.	1994	$3.00
Radioactive	RAR5P 2979	Selling the Drama	CDJ	U.S.	1994	$3.00
Radioactive		White Discussion	CD5	Australia	1995	$10.00
Radioactive	RAR5P-3083	White Discussion	CDJ	U.S.	1994	$8.00
Radioactive		White Discussion	CDJ	U.S.	1994	$8.00
Second version.						

Live Report

Label	Catalog Number	Title	Type	Country	Year	Longbox Value / Value
Singles						
Cue	662369	Why Do I Always Get It Wrong	CD5	Germany	1989	$8.00
Cue	CDCUE-7	Why Do I Always Get It Wrong	CD5	U.K.	1989	$8.00

Livin' Large

Label	Catalog Number	Title	Type	Country	Year	Longbox Value / Value
Singles						
Virgin	PRCD 3024	Livin' Large	CDJ	U.S.	1989	$2.00
Virgin	PRCD 3029	Livin' Large	CDJ	U.S.	1989	$2.00

Living Colour

Label	Catalog Number	Title	Type	Country	Year	Longbox Value / Value
Full Length						
Epic	ESK 4098	Biscuits	DJ/Smplr	U.S.	1991	$5.00
Epic		Greatest hits	LTD/LP	Japan	1995	$37.00
2 CD Set.						
		Live at Electric Ladyland	RS	U.S.	1990	$35.00
Epic		Live Vivid	DJ/Smplr	Japan	1992	$100.00
Westwood One		Off the Record	RS	U.S.	1993	$30.00
Airdate: 5/3/93.						
Epic	ESK 1491	Open Letter (To a Landlord)	DJ/Smplr	U.S.	1988	$15.00
Epic	ESK 4962	Stain	DJ/Smplr	U.S.	1993	$15.00
With extra track not on commercial version.						
Epic	ESK 2171	Time's Up (Banded Version)	DJLP	U.S.	1990	$15.00
Epic	ESK 2151	Times Up	DJ/LP	U.S.	1990	$8.00
Media America		Up Close	RS	U.S.	1993	$30.00
Singles						
Epic		17 Days	CDJ	Canada		$9.00
Epic	EK 74955	Auslander	CD5	U.S.	1993	$6.00
Epic	653021-3	Cult of Personality	CD5	Germany	1989	$10.00
Epic	CDLCL 5	Cult of Personality	CD5	U.K.	1988	$10.00
Epic	657535-2	Cult of Personality	CD5	U.K.	1991	$10.00
Epic	CSK 1473	Cult of Personality	CDJ	U.S.	1988	$2.00
Epic	ESDA-7047	Elvis is Dead	CD3	Japan	1990	$12.00/$4.00
Epic	ESK 2237	Elvis is Dead	CDJ	U.S.	1990	$2.00
Epic	ESK 5205	End, The	CDJ	U.S.	1993	$7.00
Epic	ESK 73010	Funny Vibe	CDJ	U.S.	1989	$2.00
Epic	CPLCL2	Glamour Boys	CD5	U.K.	1988	$10.00
Epic	LCLC-6	Glamour Boys	CD5	U.K.	1988	$10.00
Epic	CDLCL-6	Glamour Boys	CD5	U.K.	1988	$10.00
Epic	ESK 1746	Glamour Boys	CDJ	U.S.	1988	$15.00
Epic	ESCA-5741	Leave It Alone	CD5	Japan	1993	$15.00
Epic	658976-2	Leave It Alone	CD5	U.K.	1993	$10.00
Epic	ESK 4952	Leave It Alone	CDJ	U.S.	1993	$2.00
Epic	656439-5	Love Rears Its Ugly Head	CD5	Germany	1990	$10.00
Epic	ESDA-7068	Love Rears Its Ugly Head	CD3	Japan	1990	$12.00/$4.00
Epic	656593-2	Love Rears Its Ugly Head	CD5	U.K.	1990	$10.00
Epic	ESK 73660	Love Rears Its Ugly Head	CDJ	U.S.	1990	$2.00
Epic	ESK 73677	Love Rears Its Ugly Head	CDJ	U.S.	1991	$2.00
Epic	CPLCL-1	Middleman	CD5	U.K.	1993	$10.00
Epic	ESK 5151	Nothingness	CDJ	U.S.	1993	$3.00
Epic	ESK 5230	Nothingness	CDJ	U.S.	1993	$3.00
Epic	654729-3	Open Letter (To a Landlord)	CD3	Germany	1989	$10.00
Epic	CDLCL-4	Open Letter (To a Landlord)	CD3	U.K.	1989	$10.00
Epic	ESK 1636	Open Letter (To a Landlord)	CDJ	U.S.	1988	$7.00
Epic	ESK 1685	Open Letter (To a Landlord)	CDJ	U.S.	1988	$7.00
Epic	ESK 2241	Pride	CDJ	U.S.	1990	$3.00
Epic	ESK 2246	Pride	CDJ	U.S.	1990	$3.00
Epic	ESK 2247	Pride	CDJ	U.S.	1990	$6.00
Epic	656908-2	Solace of You	CD5	Germany	1990	$10.00
Epic	656908-9	Solace of You	CD5	U.K.	1990	$10.00
Epic	ESK 73800	Solace of You	CDJ	U.S.	1990	$3.00
Epic		Sunshine of Your Love	CD5	U.S.	1994	$10.00
Epic	LCLC-7	Type	CD5	U.K.	1990	$10.00
Epic	ESK 2147	Type	CDJ	U.S.	1990	$3.00
Epic	ESK 2146	Type	CDJ	U.S.	1990	$3.00
Epic		Type	CDJ	U.S.	1990	$3.00
Second version.						

Living House

Label	Catalog Number	Title	Type	Country	Year	Longbox Value / Value
Singles						
Alfa	ALDB 128	Play the Game	CD3	Japan	1991	$12.00/$3.00

Living in a Box

Label	Catalog Number	Title	Type	Country	Year	Longbox Value / Value
Full Length						
	SPCD-1060	Living in a Box	DJ/Smplr	Japan		$40.00
Singles						
Toshiba	XP10-2003	Bed of Roses	CD3	Japan	1988	$12.00/$3.00
Chrysalis	662012	Blow the House Down	CD5	Germany	1989	$9.00
Toshiba	XP10-5007	Blow the House Down	CD3	Japan	1989	$12.00/$3.00
Chrysalis	LIBCD-5	Blow the House Down	CD5	U.K.	1989	$9.00
Chrysalis	DPRO-23364	Blow the House Down	CDJ	U.S.	1989	$2.00
Chrysalis	885668	Different Air	CD5	Germany	1989	$9.00
Chrysalis	LIBCD-8	Different Air	CD5	U.K.	1989	$9.00
Chrysalis	321676-2	Gatecrashing	CD5	Germany	1989	$9.00
Chrysalis	LIBCD-6	Gatecrashing	CD5	U.K.	1989	$9.00
Chrysalis	880526	Living in a Box	CD5	Germany	1987	$9.00
Chrysalis	CDE-4	Living in a Box	CD5	U.K.	1987	$9.00
Chrysalis	LIBCD-4	Love is the Art	CD5	U.K.	1988	$9.00
Chrysalis	662577	Room in Your Heart	CD5	Germany	1989	$9.00
Chrysalis	LIBCD-7	Room in Your Heart	CD5	U.K.	1989	$9.00
Chrysalis	DPRO-23420	Room in Your Heart	CDJ	U.S.	1989	$2.00

Living Stereo

Label	Catalog Number	Title	Type	Country	Year	Longbox Value / Value
Full Length						
		Living Stereo Story, The	DJ/Smplr	U.S.	1994	$18.00

Lizzy Borden

Label	Catalog Number	Title	Type	Country	Year	Longbox Value / Value
Full Length						
Canyon	D22Y-0346	Master of Disguise	DJ/Smplr	Japan		$35.00
Enigma	CDE-73224	Menace to Society	LP/LB	U.S.		$12.00/[illegible]
Image	ID7924EN	Murderess Metal Road Show	LD	U.S.		$15.00
Restless	72113-2	Murderess Metal Road Show	LP/LB	U.S.		$12.00/$8.00
Enigma	CDE-73254	Terror Rising	LP/LB	U.S.		$12.00/$8.00
Enigma	CDE-73288	Visual Lies	LP/LB	U.S.		$12.00/$8.00
Singles						
Canyon	S9Y-11121	We Got the Power	CD3	Japan	1989	$13.00/$4.00

Lloyd, Charles

Label	Catalog Number	Title	Type	Country	Year	Longbox Value / Value
Singles						
ECM	CHARLES	Notes From Big Sur	CDJ	U.S.	1992	$3.00

Lloyd, Robert

Label	Catalog Number	Title	Type	Country	Year	Longbox Value / Value
Singles						
Virgin	VSSCDT-1196	Funeral Stomp	CD5	U.K.	1990	$8.00
Virgin	VSSCDT-1256	Nothing Matters	CD5	U.K.	1990	$8.00

Lo-Key

Label	Catalog Number	Title	Type	Country	Year	Longbox Value / Value
Singles						
Perspective	28968 1705	Attention: The Shawanda Story	CDJ	U.S.	1992	$2.00
Perspective	31458 8151	Hey There Pretty Lady	CDJ	U.S.	1992	$2.00
Perspective	28968 1712	I Got A Thang 4 Ya	CDJ	U.S.	1992	$2.00
Perspective	31458 8076	I Got A Thang 4 Ya	CDJ	U.S.	1992	$2.00

Lobo Y Melon

Label	Catalog Number	Title	Type	Country	Year	Longbox Value / Value
Singles						
	11423	Serie De Platino	CD5	U.S.	1994	$5.00

Local H

Label	Catalog Number	Title	Type	Country	Year	Longbox Value / Value
Singles						
	PRCD 6976-2	Mayonnaise and Malaise	CDJ	U.S.		$3.00

Lock Up

Label	Catalog Number	Title	Type	Country	Year	Longbox Value / Value
Singles						
Geffen	PRO-CD-4167	24 Hour Man	CDJ	U.S.	1990	$2.00
		Kiss 17 Goodbye	CDJ	U.S.		$2.00
Geffen	PRO-CD-4004	Nothing New	CDJ	U.S.	1990	$2.00

Lode

Label	Catalog Number	Title	Type	Country	Year	Longbox Value / Value
Singles						
	PRO-CD-4881	Legs & Arms	CDJ	U.S.		$3.00

Lodge, J.C.

Label	Catalog Number	Title	Type	Country	Year	Longbox Value / Value
Singles						
Tommy Boy	996	Come Again	CDJ	U.S.	1992	$2.00
Ras	7042	Loving You	CD5	U.S.	1993	$4.00

Loeb, Lisa

Label	Catalog Number	Title	Type	Country	Year	Longbox Value / Value
Singles						
	PRO-CD-4768	Do You Sleep	CDJ	U.S.		$3.00
Geffen	22103	Do You Sleep?	CD5	U.S.	1995	$5.00
RCA	62870	Stay	CD5	U.S.	1994	$6.00
	PRO-CD-4831	Taffy	CDJ	U.S.		$3.00

Lofgren, Nils

Label	Catalog Number	Title	Type	Country	Year	Longbox Value / Value
Full Length						
CBS	CK-39982	Flip	LP/BP	U.S.†	1985	$14.00/$8.00

Label	Catalog Number	Title	Type	Country	Year	Longbox/Value
DIR		King Biscuit Flour Hour	RS	U.S.	1991	$30.00

With Huey Lewis, Airdate: 5/12/91.

Singles

Label	Catalog Number	Title	Type	Country	Year	Longbox/Value
Rykodisc	RCD5 1029	Drunken Driver	CD5	U.S.	1991	$5.00
Rykodisc	RCD5 1026	Just A Little	CD5	U.S.	1992	$5.00
Rykodisc	RCD5 1022	Trouble's Back	CD5	U.S.	1991	$5.00
Intercord	825 310	Valentine	CD5	Germany	1991	$9.00
Alfa	ALDB-147	Valentine	CD3	Japan	1992	$13.00/$4.00
Rykodisc	RCD5 9015	Valentine	CD5	U.S.	1990	$3.00

Logan, Andrew

Full Length

Label	Catalog Number	Title	Type	Country	Year	Longbox/Value
Motown	6337	Show Me Your Heart	LP/BP	U.S.		$12.00/$7.00

Singles

Label	Catalog Number	Title	Type	Country	Year	Longbox/Value
Motown	TMGCD-1410	Living in a World	CD5	U.K.	1992	$8.00
Motown	37463185	Love Can Be Enough	CDJ	U.S.	1992	$2.00

Logan, Jack

Full Length

Label	Catalog Number	Title	Type	Country	Year	Longbox/Value
Cool/Twin Tone		Bulk	LP	U.S.	1994	$25.00

First pressing 2 CD set with disc two that begins with track 25 rather than track one.

Logan, Johnny

Singles

Label	Catalog Number	Title	Type	Country	Year	Longbox/Value
CBS	654977-3	All I Ever Wanted	CD3	Germany	1989	$8.00
CBS	654977-2	All I Ever Wanted	CD5	Germany	1989	$8.00
WEA	9031-75790-2	How About Us	CD5	Germany	1991	$8.00
WEA	9031-77059-2	It's Only Tears	CD5	Germany	1991	$8.00
CBS	655359-3	Lay Down Your Heart	CD3	Germany	1989	$8.00
CBS	652918-3	Lonely Lovers	CD3	Germany	1989	$8.00
CBS	654766-3	Red Lips	CD3	Germany	1989	$8.00

Loggins, Kenny

Full Length

Label	Catalog Number	Title	Type	Country	Year	Longbox/Value
Pioneer	PA-82-019	Alive	LD	U.S.	1982	$35.00
CBS	CK-34388	Best of Friends	LP/BP	U.S.†	1985	$14.00/$8.00
CBS	CK-38127	High Adventure	LP/BP	U.S.†	1984	$14.00/$8.00
CBS	CK-36172	Keep the Fire	LP/BP	U.S.†	1985	$14.00/$8.00
		Return to Pooh Corner	DJ/Intvw	U.S.	1995	$10.00
Mobile Fidelity	MFCD-829	Sittin' In	LP/LB	U.S.†	1985	$16.00/$12.00
CBS	CK-38174	Vox Humana	LP/BP	U.S.†	1985	$14.00/$8.00

Singles

Label	Catalog Number	Title	Type	Country	Year	Longbox/Value
Sony	10EP-3074	Be-Bop-a-Lula	CD3	Japan	1989	$12.00/$4.00
Columbia	CSK 74029	Conviction of the Heart	CDJ	U.S.	1991	$2.00
Columbia	653147-3	I'm Gonna Miss You	CD3	U.K.	1988	$10.00
Sony	SRDS-8205	Leap of Faith	CD3	Japan	1991	$12.00/$4.00
Columbia	CSK 5972	Leap of Faith	CDJ	U.S.	1991	$2.00
Columbia	652867-3	Nobody's Fool	CD3	Germany	1988	$10.00
Sony	10EP-3046	Nobody's Fool	CD3	Japan	1988	$12.00/$4.00
Columbia	CSK 1205	Nobody's Fool	CDJ	U.S.	1988	$2.00
Sony	SRDS-8221	Real Thing, The	CD3	Japan	1992	$12.00/$4.00
Columbia	CSK 74186	Real Thing, The	CDJ	U.S.	1992	$2.00
Columbia	CSK 77196	This Is It	CDJ	U.S.	1993	$2.00

Lois

Singles

Label	Catalog Number	Title	Type	Country	Year	Longbox/Value
Sub Pop	61037	Shy Town	CD5	U.S.	1994	$5.00

Lomax

Singles

Label	Catalog Number	Title	Type	Country	Year	Longbox/Value
ZTT	ZANG-9CD	Waiting In Vain	CD5	U.K.	1991	$8.00

London Boys

Singles

Label	Catalog Number	Title	Type	Country	Year	Longbox/Value
Eastwest	171037-2	Chapel of Love	CD5	Germany	1990	$8.00
Teldec	YZ-458CD	Chapel of Love	CD5	U.K.	1990	$8.00
Pioneer	WMD5-4001	Dance Dance Dance	CD5	U.K.	1989	$8.00
Eastwest	9031-73085-2	Freedom	CD5	Germany	1990	$8.00
Eastwest	246679-2	Harlem Desire	CD5	Germany	1989	$8.00
Teldec	YZ-415CD	Harlem Desire	CD5	U.K.	1989	$8.00
Eastwest	247017-2	London Nights	CD5	Germany	1989	$8.00
EastWest	YZ-393CD	London Nights	CD5	Germany	1989	$8.00
Pioneer	09P3-6180	London Nights	CD3	Japan	1989	$13.00/$4.00
Teldec	870031	London Nights	CD5	U.K.	1989	$8.00
Atlantic	PR 2972-2	London Nights	CDJ	U.S.	1989	$2.00
Eastwest	246524-2	My Love	CD3	Germany	1989	$8.00
Eastwest	170840-2	My Love	CD5	Germany	1989	$8.00
Eastwest	246523-2	My Love	CD5	Germany	1989	$8.00
Teldec	YZ-433CD	My Love	CD3	U.K.	1989	$8.00
Eastwest	247246-2	Requiem	CD3	Germany	1989	$8.00
Pioneer	WMD5-4010	Requiem	CD3	Japan	1989	$15.00/$4.00
Teldec	YZ-345CD	Requiem	CD3	U.K.	1989	$8.00

London, Julie

Singles

Label	Catalog Number	Title	Type	Country	Year	Longbox/Value
Toshiba	TODP-2344	Love Letters	CD3	Japan	1992	$13.00/$4.00

London, Lea

Singles

Label	Catalog Number	Title	Type	Country	Year	Longbox/Value
	1229	Reach Out & Touch	CD5	U.S.	1994	$5.00

London Quireboys

Singles

Label	Catalog Number	Title	Type	Country	Year	Longbox/Value
EMI	203540-3	7 O'Clock	CD3	Germany	1990	$10.00
EMI	TOCP-6099	7 O'Clock	CD5	Japan	1990	$15.00
Parlophone	CDR-6230	7 O'Clock	CD5	U.K.	1990	$10.00
Capitol	DPRO-79910	7 O'Clock	CDJ	U.S.	1990	$3.00
Capitol	DPRO-79016	7 O'Clock	CDJ	U.S.	1990	$25.00

CD housed in special bound "prayer book" package.

Label	Catalog Number	Title	Type	Country	Year	Longbox/Value
EMI	TOCP-7560	Brother Line	CD3	Japan	1993	$15.00/$4.00
Parlophone	203680-2	Hey You	CD5	Germany	1990	$10.00
EMI	TOCP-6143	Hey You	CD5	Japan	1990	$15.00
Parlophone	CDR-6241	Hey You	CD5	U.K.	1990	$10.00
Capitol	DPRO-79271	Hey You	CDJ	U.S.	1990	$2.00
Parlophone	203780-2	I Don't Love You Anymore	CD5	Germany	1990	$10.00
EMI	TOCP-6244	I Don't Love You Anymore	CD5	Japan	1990	$15.00
Parlophone	CDR-6248	I Don't Love You Anymore	CD5	U.K.	1990	$10.00
Capitol		I Don't Love You Anymore	CDJ	U.S.	1990	$2.00
		My Saint Jude	CDJ	Canada		$6.00
EMI	TODP-2213	There She Goes Again	CD3	Japan	1990	$12.00/$4.00
EMI	CDR-6267	There She Goes Again	CD5	U.K.	1990	$10.00

London Suede

Singles

Label	Catalog Number	Title	Type	Country	Year	Longbox/Value
Columbia	CSK 6561	Wild Ones, The	CDJ	U.S.		$3.00

Londonbeat

Singles

Label	Catalog Number	Title	Type	Country	Year	Longbox/Value
RCA	ZD-42292	9:00 AM	CD5	Germany	1988	$9.00
RCA	ANX-008CD	9:00 AM	CD5	U.K.	1988	$9.00
RCA	ZD-44152	A Better Love	CD5	Germany	1990	$9.00
RCA	ANXCD-21	A Better Love	CD5	U.K.	1990	$9.00
RCA	ANXCD-32	A Better Love	CD5	U.K.	1991	$9.00
Radioactive	CD45 1397	A Better Love	CDJ	U.S.	1990	$2.00
	RAR5P3388	Build It With Love	CDJ	U.S.		$3.00
RCA	886427	Falling in Love Again	CD5	Germany	1988	$9.00
RCA	ANX-007CD	Falling in Love Again	CD5	U.K.	1988	$9.00
RCA	ZD-43878	I've Been Thinking About You	CD5	Germany	1990	$9.00
RCA	ANXCD-14	I've Been Thinking About You	CD5	U.K.	1990	$9.00
RCA	BVCP-9011	I've Been Thinking About You	CD5	U.K.	1990	$12.00
Radioactive	CD45 1230	I've Been Thinking About You	CDJ	U.S.	1990	$2.00
Anxious	CD45 1377	I've Been Thinking About You	CDJ	U.S.	1991	$2.00
RCA	ZD-44620	It's in the Blood	CD5	Germany	1991	$9.00
RCA	BVDP-71	Lover You Send Me Colours	CD3	Japan	1992	$13.00/$4.00
RCA	ZD-44126	No Woman No Cry	CD5	Germany	1991	$9.00
RCA	ZD-44124	No Woman No Cry	CD5	Germany	1991	$9.00
RCA	ANXCD-25	No Woman No Cry	CD5	U.K.	1991	$9.00
Radioactive	CD451623	No Woman No Cry	CDJ	U.S.	1991	$2.00
RCA	ANX-011CD	Non-Stop Rock	CD5	U.K.	1989	$9.00
RCA	ANXCD-11	One Blink	CD5	U.K.	1990	$9.00
RCA	886431	There's a Beat Going on	CD5	Germany	1990	$9.00
RCA	ANX-004CD	There's a Beat Going on	CD5	U.K.	1990	$9.00
RCA	BVCP-9011	Thinking About You	CD5	Japan	1991	$14.00
RCA	BVDP-62	You Bring on the Sun	CD3	Japan	1992	$13.00/$4.00
RCA	ANXCD-37	You Bring on the Sun	CD5	U.K.	1992	$9.00

Lonesome Romeos

Singles

Label	Catalog Number	Title	Type	Country	Year	Longbox/Value
Curb	CD45 10533	U.S. Male	CDJ	U.S.	1989	$2.00

Long Vacation

Singles

Label	Catalog Number	Title	Type	Country	Year	Longbox/Value
East World	TODT-3004	Sunday Love	CD3	Japan	1993	$12.00/$3.00
East World	TODT-2975	Tout Tout Pour Ma Cherie	CD3	Japan	1993	$12.00/$3.00

Longet, Claudine

Full Length

Label	Catalog Number	Title	Type	Country	Year	Longbox/Value
	PRAD-0017	Special Sampler	DJ/Smplr	Japan	1995	$40.00

Longhouse

Singles

Label	Catalog Number	Title	Type	Country	Year	Longbox/Value
Warner Brothers	PRO-CD-3115	She Don't Wanna Go Home Tonight	CDJ	U.S.	1988	$2.00

Look People

Singles

Label	Catalog Number	Title	Type	Country	Year	Longbox/Value
Hypnotic		Piece of Egg	CDJ	Canada	1993	$5.00
		Piece of Egg	CDJ	U.S.	1993	$3.00

Look Twice

Singles

Label	Catalog Number	Title	Type	Country	Year	Longbox/Value
Zyx	7396	Move That Body	CD5	U.S.	1994	$5.00

Looking For Adam

Singles

Label	Catalog Number	Title	Type	Country	Year	Longbox/Value
Abstract	ABSCD-092	Carver	CD5	U.K.	1991	$8.00

Loop

Singles

Label	Catalog Number	Title	Type	Country	Year	Longbox/Value
Situation	SIT 64	Arc-Lite	CD5	U.K.	1989	$2.00

Loose Bruce

Singles

Label	Catalog Number	Title	Type	Country	Year	Longbox/Value
Arista	ASCD-2357	Brick House	CDJ	U.S.	1991	$2.00

Loose Ends

Singles

Label	Catalog Number	Title	Type	Country	Year	Longbox/Value
Virgin	TENCD-344	Cheap Talk	CD5	U.K.	1991	$8.00
MCA	1372	Cheap Talk	CDJ	U.S.	1991	$2.00
BMG	663560	Don't Be a Fool	CD5	Germany	1990	$8.00
Virgin	TENCD-312	Don't Be a Fool	CD5	U.K.	1990	$8.00
		Don't Be a Fool	CDJ	U.S.	1990	$2.00
Virgin	CDT-39	Hangin' on a String	CD3	U.K.	1988	$8.00
Virgin	TENCD-406	Hangin' on a String	CD5	U.K.	1992	$8.00
Virgin	TENCD-330	Love's Got Me	CD5	U.K.	1990	$8.00
Virgin	TENCD-409	Magic Touch	CD5	U.K.	1992	$8.00
Virgin	VSCD-1080	Mr. Bachelor	CD5	U.K.	1988	$8.00
Virgin	VSCD-1101	Watching You	CD5	U.K.	1988	$8.00

Lopez, Denise

Singles

Label	Catalog Number	Title	Type	Country	Year	Longbox/Value
A&M	75021 7432-2	Don't You Wanna Be Mine	CDJ	U.S.	1990	$2.00
Canyon	S10Y-3059	If You Feel It	CD3	Japan	1988	$12.00/$3.00
A&M	CD 17635	If You Feel It	CDJ	U.S.	1988	$2.00
A&M	CD 17719	Too Much Too Late	CDJ	U.S.	1989	$2.00

Lorain, A'me

Singles

Label	Catalog Number	Title	Type	Country	Year	Longbox/Value
RCA	BVDP-15	Follow My Heartbeat	CD3	Japan	1990	$12.00/$4.00
RCA	2637-2-RDJ	Follow My Heartbeat	CDJ	U.S.	1990	$2.00
RCA	PD-49294	Whole Wide World	CD5	Germany	1990	$8.00
RCA	PD-49294	Whole Wide World	CD5	U.K.	1990	$8.00
RCA	9099-2-RDJ	Whole Wide World	CDJ	U.S.	1990	$2.00

Lorber, Jeff

Full Length

Label	Catalog Number	Title	Type	Country	Year	Longbox/Value
Verve	701	Coffee Clutch	DJ/Intvw	U.S.	1993	$15.00
Verve	650	Edits Worth Waiting For	DJ/Smplr	U.S.	1993	$8.00
Arista	ARCD-8269	Step by Step	LP/LB	U.S.†	1985	$14.00/$8.00

Lord, Mary Lou

Singles

Label	Catalog Number	Title	Type	Country	Year	Longbox/Value
Kab N Da Records	238	Mary Lou Lord	CD5	U.S.	1994	$5.00

Lords Of Acid

Singles

Label	Catalog Number	Title	Type	Country	Year	Longbox/Value
Caroline	1769	Crablouse	CD5	U.S.	1994	$5.00
Caroline	1769	Crablouse	CD5	U.S.	1994	$6.00
Warner Brothers	43560	Do You Wanna Do	CD5	U.S.	1995	$5.00
SPV	6714-3	Hey Ho	CD5	Germany	1993	$10.00
Antler	3008	Hey Ho	CD5	U.S.	1993	$6.00
Caroline	CAROL 2525	I Must Increase My Bust	CD5	U.S.	1992	$6.00
SPV	8182-3	I Sit On Acid	CD5	Germany	1989	$10.00

Label	Catalog Number	Title	Type	Country	Year	Longbox Value / Value
SPV	9489-3	I Sit On Acid	CD5	Germany	1989	$10.00
Caroline	CAROL 2518	Rough Sex	CD5	U.S.	1992	$6.00
Caroline	CAROL 2512	Take Control	CD5	U.S.	1991	$6.00

Lords Of The Underground

Singles

Label	Catalog Number	Title	Type	Country	Year	Longbox Value / Value
Pendulum	8780	Chief Rocka	CDJ	U.S.	1993	$2.00
		Faith	CDJ	U.S.		$3.00
Capitol	58412	Faith	CD5	U.S.	1995	$5.00

Lords, Traci

Singles

Label	Catalog Number	Title	Type	Country	Year	Longbox Value / Value
MCA	54953	Control	CD5	U.S.	1994	$5.00
	3201	Control	CDJ	U.S.	1995	$6.00
		Foolish Love	CDJ	U.S.		$2.00

Lordz of Brooklyn

Singles

Label	Catalog Number	Title	Type	Country	Year	Longbox Value / Value
Warner Brothers	17966	Saturday Night Fever	CD5	U.S.	1995	$5.00

Lorenz, Trey

Singles

Label	Catalog Number	Title	Type	Country	Year	Longbox Value / Value
Epic	ESDA-7127	Photograph of Mary	CD3	Japan	1993	$12.00/$3.00
Epic	658954-2	Photograph of Mary	CD5	U.K.	1992	$8.00
Epic	ESK 74783	Photograph of Mary	CDJ	U.S.	1992	$2.00
Epic	ESK 4939	Photograph of Mary	CDJ	U.S.	1992	$2.00
Epic	ESDA-123	Someone to Hold	CD3	Japan	1992	$12.00/$3.00
Epic		Someone to Hold	CD5	U.K.		$10.00
	Second version.					
Epic	658785-2	Someone to Hold	CD5	U.K.	1992	$8.00
Epic	ESK 74482	Someone to Hold	CDJ	U.S.	1992	$2.00
Epic	34K 74482	Someone to Hold	CDJ	U.S.	1992	$7.00

Lorenzo

Singles

Label	Catalog Number	Title	Type	Country	Year	Longbox Value / Value
Alpha	79399	Let Me Show You	CDJ	U.S.	1990	$2.00
Alpha	698	Real Love	CDJ	U.S.	1992	$2.00
Alpha	79584	Tik Tok	CDJ	U.S.	1990	$2.00

Loring, Jamie

Full Length

Label	Catalog Number	Title	Type	Country	Year	Longbox Value / Value
Polygram	848324-2	Love or Infatuation	LP/BP	U.S.		$12.00/$7.00

Los Del Rio

Singles

Label	Catalog Number	Title	Type	Country	Year	Longbox Value / Value
RCA	RDJ644082	Macarena	CDJ	U.S.		$3.00

Los Fabulous Cadillacs

Singles

Label	Catalog Number	Title	Type	Country	Year	Longbox Value / Value
Sony	10602	Matador	CDJ	U.S.	1994	$2.00

Los Lobos

Full Length

Label	Catalog Number	Title	Type	Country	Year	Longbox Value / Value
Slash	2-45367-A	Just Another Band From East L.A.	DJ/Smplr	U.S.	1993	$25.00
	Advance issue with second disc of "hits."					
Slash	PRO-CD-6578	World Pack: An AOR Sampler	DJ/Smplr	U.S.	1994	$10.00

Singles

Label	Catalog Number	Title	Type	Country	Year	Longbox Value / Value
Elektra	PRCD 8490-2	Beautiful Maria of My Soul	CDJ	U.S.	1992	$2.00
Elektra	PRCD 8488-2	Bella Maria De Mi Alma	CDJ	U.S.	1992	$2.00
Arista	ASCD-2226	Bertha	CDJ	U.S.	1991	$2.00
Slash	869195-2	Down on the River Bed	CD5	Germany	1990	$10.00
Slash	LASCD-27	Down on the River Bed	CD5	U.K.	1990	$10.00
Slash	PRO-CD-4440	Down on the River Bed	CDJ	U.S.	1990	$2.00
Slash	PRO-CD-5645	Dream in Blue	CDJ	U.S.	1992	$2.00
Slash	PRO-CD-4548	I Can't Understand	CDJ	U.S.	1990	$2.00
London	PODD-1012	Jenny's Got a Pony	CD3	Japan	1990	$12.00/$4.00
Slash	PRO-CD-4443	Jenny's Got a Pony	CDJ	U.S.	1990	$2.00
Warner Brothers	PRO-CD-5789	Kiko and the Lavender Moon	CDJ	U.S.	1992	$2.00
London	P10L-30001	La Bamba	CD3	Japan	1988	$12.00/$4.00
Slash		Lonely Avenue	CDJ	U.S.	1994	$6.00
Warner Brothers	PRO-CD-8125	Mas Y Mas	CDJ	U.S.	1995	$3.00
Slash	PRO-CD-2879	One Time One Night	CDJ	U.S.		$2.00

Los Locos

Singles

Label	Catalog Number	Title	Type	Country	Year	Longbox Value / Value
ZYX	8019-8	El Tiburon	CD5	U.S.	1995	$5.00

Los Manolos

Singles

Label	Catalog Number	Title	Type	Country	Year	Longbox Value / Value
BMG	PD-44616	All My Loving	CD5	Germany	1991	$8.00

Lost

Singles

Label	Catalog Number	Title	Type	Country	Year	Longbox Value / Value
Sony	SRDS-8199	Mindblower	CD3	Japan	1991	$12.00/$3.00

Lost And Profound

Singles

Label	Catalog Number	Title	Type	Country	Year	Longbox Value / Value
		Brand New Set of Lies	CDJ	Canada		$5.00
		Curb the Angels	CDJ	Canada		$5.00
		Winter Raging	CDJ	Canada		$5.00

Lost Soul Band

Singles

Label	Catalog Number	Title	Type	Country	Year	Longbox Value / Value
Silvertone	ORECD-43	Looking Trough the Butcher's Window	CD5	U.K.	1992	$8.00
Silvertone	ORECD-47	Trashscene	CD5	U.K.	1992	$8.00

Lotion

Full Length

Label	Catalog Number	Title	Type	Country	Year	Longbox Value / Value
	246432-2-ADV	Nobody's Fool	DJ/LP	U.S.	1995	$8.00

Singles

Label	Catalog Number	Title	Type	Country	Year	Longbox Value / Value
	PRO-CD-8055	Blind For Now	CDJ	U.S.	1995	$2.00
Kokopop	KOKO-6CD	Head	CD5	U.K.	1992	$9.00
Kokopop	1006	Head	CD5	U.S.	1992	$5.00

Loud

Singles

Label	Catalog Number	Title	Type	Country	Year	Longbox Value / Value
China	CHICD-25	D Generation	CD5	U.K.	1990	$8.00
China	WOKCD-2002	D Generation	CD5	U.K.	1991	$8.00
China	WOKCD-2016	Easy	CD5	U.K.	1992	$8.00
China	CHICD-29	Explosive	CD5	U.K.	1990	$8.00
China	WOKCD-2022	Mary	CD5	U.K.	1992	$8.00
China	CHICD-33	Song For the Lonely	CD5	U.K.	1991	$8.00

Loud Flower

Singles

Label	Catalog Number	Title	Type	Country	Year	Longbox Value / Value
Invasion	INV 36007	Heart to Heart	CD5	U.K.	1991	$2.00

Loud Lucy

Singles

Label	Catalog Number	Title	Type	Country	Year	Longbox Value / Value
	PRO-CD-4870	Down Baby	CDJ	U.S.		$2.00
	PRO-CD-4772	Ticking	CDJ	U.S.		$2.00

Loud Sugar

Singles

Label	Catalog Number	Title	Type	Country	Year	Longbox Value / Value
SBK	DPRO-05428	Faith & Hope & Love	CDJ	U.S.	1991	$2.00
SBK	DPRO-05385	Instant Karma Coffee House	CDJ	U.S.	1991	$2.00

Loudhouse

Singles

Label	Catalog Number	Title	Type	Country	Year	Longbox Value / Value
Virgin	4299	Super Bowl Killer	CDJ	U.S.	1991	$2.00

Loudness

Full Length

Label	Catalog Number	Title	Type	Country	Year	Longbox Value / Value
Atco	PR 2916-2	A Lesson in Loudness	DJ/Smplr	U.S.	1989	$15.00
Denon	CD-7134	Disillusion	LP/BP	U.S.†	1985	$15.00/$9.00
Atco	43XD-2007	Hurricane Eyes	LTD/LP	Japan		$35.00
	Gold disc.					
Atco		On the Prowl	LP/LB	U.S.		$14.00/$8.00
Atco		Soldier of Fortune	LP/LB	U.S.		$14.00/$8.00

Singles

Label	Catalog Number	Title	Type	Country	Year	Longbox Value / Value
Atco	WPDL-4293	Black Widow	CD3	Japan	1992	$12.00/$4.00
Warner Brothers	09P3-6105	Dreamer and Screamer	CD3	Japan	1989	$12.00/$4.00
Atco	WPDL-42278	In the Mirror	CD3	Japan	1989	$12.00/$4.00
Atco	10SW-40	Long Distance Love	CD3	Japan	1988	$12.00/$4.00
Atco	WPCL-551	Slap in the Face	CD3	Japan	1991	$13.00/$4.00
Atco	WPDL-4308	Slaughter House	CD3	Japan	1992	$12.00/$4.00
Atco	PRCD 4119-2	Sleepless Nights	CDJ	U.S.	1991	$2.00
Atco	09P3-6166	You Shook Me	CD3	Japan	1989	$12.00/$4.00

Louie Louie

Singles

Label	Catalog Number	Title	Type	Country	Year	Longbox Value / Value
Hardback	BOSS-12CD	Brother Louie	CD5	U.K.	1993	$8.00
		I Wanna Get Back With You	CDJ	U.S.		$2.00
		Louie "Rap"	CDJ	U.S.		$2.00
		Rodeo Clown	CDJ	U.S.		$2.00
Epic	ESDA-7039	Sittin' in the Lap of Luxury	CD3	Japan	1990	$13.00/$4.00
Epic	655738-3	Sittin' in the Lap of Luxury	CD3	U.K.	1990	$9.00
Epic	655738-2	Sittin' in the Lap of Luxury	CD5	U.K.	1990	$9.00
		Sittin' in the Lap of Luxury	CDJ	U.S.	1990	$2.00
Warner Brothers	Y-2724CD	Thought of It	CD5	U.K.	1993	$9.00
Warner Brothers	PRO-CD-5909	Thought of It	CDJ	U.S.	1992	$2.00
Warner Brothers	9 40745-2	Thought of It	CD5	U.S.	1993	$4.00
Warner Brothers	PRO-CD-6080	Walk With Me	CDJ	U.S.	1993	$2.00

Louise

Singles

Label	Catalog Number	Title	Type	Country	Year	Longbox Value / Value
		Light of My Life	CD5	U.K.		$10.00
		Light of My Life	CD5	U.K.		$10.00
	Second version.					

Love and Laughter

Singles

Label	Catalog Number	Title	Type	Country	Year	Longbox Value / Value
		I Surrender	CDJ	U.S.		$2.00

Love and Money

Full Length

Label	Catalog Number	Title	Type	Country	Year	Longbox Value / Value
Fontana		Strange Kind of Love	DJ/LP	U.S.	1988	$8.00

Singles

Label	Catalog Number	Title	Type	Country	Year	Longbox Value / Value
Fontana	MONCD-5	Hallelujah Man	CD5	U.K.	1988	$8.00
		Hallelujah Man	CDJ	U.S.		$2.00
Fontana	872483-2	Jocelyn Square	CD5	Germany	1989	$8.00
Fontana	MONCD-7	Jocelyn Square	CD5	U.K.	1989	$8.00
Fontana	868563-2	My Love Lives in a Dead House	CD5	Germany	1991	$8.00
Fontana	MONCD-6	Strange Kind of Love	CD5	U.K.	1988	$8.00
Fontana	CDP 56	Strange Kind of Love	CDJ	U.S.	1988	$8.00
Fontana	MONCD-8	Up Escalator	CD5	U.K.	1989	$8.00
Fontana	MONCD-9	Winter	CD5	U.K.	1989	$8.00
Fontana	MONCS-9	Winter	CD5	U.K.	1989	$11.00

Love and Rockets

Full Length

Label	Catalog Number	Title	Type	Country	Year	Longbox Value / Value
Pioneer Artists	PA-89-242	The Haunted Fish	LD	U.S.	1989	$25.00

Love Club

Singles

Label	Catalog Number	Title	Type	Country	Year	Longbox Value / Value
RCA	PD-43463	Das Rote Maar	CD5	Germany	1990	$8.00
		One Last Kiss	CDJ	U.S.		$2.00

Love Corporation

Singles

Label	Catalog Number	Title	Type	Country	Year	Longbox Value / Value
Creation	CRESCD-076	Palatial	CD5	U.K.	1990	$8.00

Love, Darlene

Singles

Label	Catalog Number	Title	Type	Country	Year	Longbox Value / Value
Arista	BVDA-56	All Alone on Christmas	CD3	Japan	1992	$13.00/$4.00
Arista	74321-112476	All Alone on Christmas	CD5	U.K.	1992	$9.00
Columbia	652935-2	He's Sure the Man I Love	CD5	U.K.	1989	$9.00
Columbia	CSK 1259	He's Sure the Man I Love	CDJ	U.S.	1988	$2.00

Love Decade

Singles

Label	Catalog Number	Title	Type	Country	Year	Longbox Value / Value
All Around	CDGLOBE-107	I Feel You	CD5	U.K.	1991	$8.00
Intercord	825 929	So Real	CD5	Germany	1991	$8.00
All Around	CDGLOBE-106	So Real	CD5	U.K.	1991	$8.00
All Around	CDGLOBE-114	When the Morning Comes	CD5	U.K.	1993	$8.00

Love Decree

Singles

Label	Catalog Number	Title	Type	Country	Year	Longbox Value / Value
BMG	662642	Something So Good	CD5	U.K.	1989	$8.00

Love Drops

Singles

Label	Catalog Number	Title	Type	Country	Year	Longbox Value / Value
Warner Brothers	9 40186-2	Feel	CD5	U.S.	1991	$4.00
Warner Brothers	9 40438-2	Feel	CD5	U.S.	1992	$4.00

Love Express

Singles

Label	Catalog Number	Title	Type	Country	Year	Longbox Value / Value
Eastwest	9031-72113-2	Bye Bye Love	CD5	Germany	1990	$8.00

Love, G. (& Special Sauce)

Full Length

Label	Catalog Number	Title	Type	Country	Year	Longbox Value / Value
		Coast to Coast Motel	DJ/LP	U.S.	1994	$8.00

Singles

Label	Catalog Number	Title	Type	Country	Year	Longbox Value / Value
		Cold Beverage	CDJ	U.S.	1994	$3.00

Love/Hate

Singles

Label	Catalog Number	Title	Type	Country	Year	Longbox Value / Value
Columbia	655917-2	Black Out in the Red Room	CD5	U.K.	1990	$10.00
Columbia		Black Out in the Red Room	CDJ	U.S.	1990	$2.00
Columbia	657596-9	Evil Twin	CD5	U.K.	1990	$10.00
Columbia	657596-2	Evil Twin	CD5	U.K.	1990	$10.00
Columbia	CSK 4360	Happy Hour	CDJ	U.S.	1992	$2.00
Columbia	656112-2	She's an Angel	CD5	U.K.	1990	$10.00
Columbia	CSK 2256	She's an Angel	CDJ	U.S.	1990	$2.00
Columbia	657889-2	Wasted in America	CD5	U.K.	1990	$10.00
Columbia	CSK 4529	Wasted in America	CDJ	U.S.	1990	$2.00
Columbia	CSK 2143	Why Do You Think They Call It Dope	CDJ	U.S.	1990	$2.00

Love In Reverse

Singles

Label	Catalog Number	Title	Type	Country	Year	Longbox Value / Value
	PRO-CD-8131A	I Was Dog	CDJ	U.S.	1995	$6.00
	PRO-CD-8094	I'm a Contradiction	CDJ	U.S.	1995	$3.00

Love, Monie

Singles

Label	Catalog Number	Title	Type	Country	Year	Longbox Value / Value
Chrysalis	TODP-2377	Born 2 Breed	CD3	Japan	1993	$12.00/$3.00
Warner Brothers	9 40641-2	Born 2 Breed	CD5	U.S.	1993	$5.00
Warner Brothers	PRO-CD-5801	Born 2 Breed	CDJ	U.S.	1993	$2.00
EMI	323615-2	Down Two Earth	CD5	Germany	1990	$8.00
EMI	323662-2	Down Two Earth	CD5	Germany	1990	$8.00
Warner Brothers	PRO-CD-4862	Down Two Earth	CDJ	U.S.	1990	$2.00
Cooltempo	COOLCD-158	Full Term Love	CD5	U.K.	1992	$0.00
Giant	9 40405-2	Full Term Love	CDJ	U.S.	1992	$2.00
BMG	662344	Grandpa's Party	CD5	Germany	1989	$8.00
Cooltempo	COOLCD-184	Grandpa's Party	CD5	U.K.	1989	$8.00
Warner Brothers	9 40832-2	In a Word	CD5	U.S.	1993	$5.00
EMI	323588-2	It's a Shame	CD5	Germany	1989	$8.00
Cooltempo	COOLCD-219	It's a Shame	CD5	U.K.	1989	$8.00
Warner Brothers	9 21791-2	It's a Shame	CD5	U.S.	1990	$4.00
Warner Brothers	PRO-CD-4528	It's a Shame	CDJ	U.S.	1990	$2.00
Warner Brothers	PRO-CD-4528	It's a Shame	CDJ	U.S.	1990	$2.00
EMI	323534-2	Monie in the Middle	CD5	Germany	1990	$8.00
EMI	663378	Monie in the Middle	CD5	Germany	1990	$8.00
Cooltempo	COOLCD-210	Monie in the Middle	CD5	U.K.	1990	$8.00
Warner Brothers	9 21737-2	Monie in the Middle	CD5	U.S.	1990	$4.00
Warner Brothers	PRO-CD-4415	Monie in the Middle	CDJ	U.S.	1990	$2.00
		Never Give Up	CD5	U.K.		$10.00
		Never Give Up	CD5	U.K.		$10.00

Second version.

Label	Catalog Number	Title	Type	Country	Year	Longbox Value / Value
Cooltempo	COOLCD-224	Ring My Bell	CD5	U.K.	1991	$8.00

Love & Rockets

Full Length

Label	Catalog Number	Title	Type	Country	Year	Longbox Value / Value
Beggars Banquet	9715-2-R	Love & Rockets	DJ/LP	U.S.	1989	$18.00

CD in round tin.

Label	Catalog Number	Title	Type	Country	Year	Longbox Value / Value
RCA	9041-2-DJ	Love & Rockets	DJ/Smplr	U.S.	1990	$18.00
		Sorted Sample	DJ/Smplr	U.K.		$20.00

Singles

Label	Catalog Number	Title	Type	Country	Year	Longbox Value / Value
Warner Brothers	9 41690-2	Body & Soul	CD5	U.S.	1994	$5.00
Polygram	870313-2	Mirror People	CD5	Canada	1988	$10.00
RCA	6072-2-RDJ	Mirror People	CDJ	U.S.	1988	$2.00
Beggars Banquet	BEG-234CD	No Big Deal	CD5	U.K.	1989	$10.00
RCA	9045-2-RDJ	No Big Deal	CDJ	U.S.	1989	$2.00
Beggars Banquet	PD-49400	So Alive	CD5	Germany	1989	$10.00
Beggars Banquet	BEG-494CD	So Alive	CD5	U.K.	1989	$10.00
RCA	8902-2-RDJ	So Alive	CDJ	U.S.	1989	$2.00
	PRO-CD-8129-R	Sweet Love Hangover	CDJ	U.S.	1995	$6.00
Beggars Banquet	PRO-CD-6072	Waiting For Flood	CDJ	U.S.	1989	$2.00

Love & Sas

Singles

Label	Catalog Number	Title	Type	Country	Year	Longbox Value / Value
RCA	PD-49094	Call My Name	CD5	U.K.	1992	$8.00

Love Spit Love

Singles

Label	Catalog Number	Title	Type	Country	Year	Longbox Value / Value
Imago	25090	Change in the Weather	CD5	U.S.	1994	$5.00

Love Station

Singles

Label	Catalog Number	Title	Type	Country	Year	Longbox Value / Value
Pandisc	118	Best of My Love	CD5	U.S.	1994	$5.00

Love Tractor

Singles

Label	Catalog Number	Title	Type	Country	Year	Longbox Value / Value
		Crash	CDJ	U.S.		$2.00

Loveless, Patty

Full Length

Label	Catalog Number	Title	Type	Country	Year	Longbox Value / Value
Epic		When Fallen Angels Cry	DJ/LP	U.S.	1994	$20.00

CD in folder.

Singles

Label	Catalog Number	Title	Type	Country	Year	Longbox Value / Value
MCA	MCA5P-54075	Blue Memories	CDJ	U.S.	1991	$2.00
MCA	CD45 53477	Don't Toss Us Away	CDJ	U.S.	1988	$2.00
Epic	ESK 77416	How Can I Help You Say Goodbye	CDJ	U.S.	1994	$3.00
MCA	CD45 54178	Hurt Me Bad	CDJ	U.S.	1991	$2.00
MCA	MCA5P-53977	I'm That Kind Of Girl	CDJ	U.S.	1990	$2.00
MCA	MCA5P-54271	Jealous Bone	CDJ	U.S.	1991	$2.00

Lovemongers

Singles

Label	Catalog Number	Title	Type	Country	Year	Longbox Value / Value
Capitol	C2 15953	Battle of Evermore	CD5	Canada	1993	$8.00
Capitol	TOCP-7584	Battle of Evermore	CD5	Japan	1993	$12.00

Lover Speaks

Singles

Label	Catalog Number	Title	Type	Country	Year	Longbox Value / Value
A&M	AMCD-438	No More I Love You	CD5	U.K.	1988	$8.00

Loverboy

Full Length

Label	Catalog Number	Title	Type	Country	Year	Longbox Value / Value
CBS	CK-37638	Get Lucky	LP/BP	U.S.	1984	$12.00/$7.00
CBS	CK-38703	Keep It Up	LP/BP	U.S.	1984	$12.00/$7.00
Pioneer	PA-84-071	Live	LD	U.S.	1984	$25.00
CBS	CK-36762	Loverboy	LP/BP	U.S.	1985	$12.00/$7.00
CBS	CK-39953	Lovin' Every Minute	LP/BP	U.S.	1985	$12.00/$7.00

Singles

Label	Catalog Number	Title	Type	Country	Year	Longbox Value / Value
Columbia	851459-2	Break It To Me Gently	CD5	U.K.	1988	$9.00
Columbia	CSK 73066	Too Hot	CDJ	U.S.	1989	$2.00

Lovestation

Singles

Label	Catalog Number	Title	Type	Country	Year	Longbox Value / Value
		Shine On Me	CD5	U.K.		$10.00

Second version.

Lovetrain

Singles

Label	Catalog Number	Title	Type	Country	Year	Longbox Value / Value
Siren	SRNCD-116	Rags To Riches	CD3	U.K.	1989	$8.00
Siren	SRNCD-106	Way of all Flesh	CD5	U.K.	1989	$8.00
Siren	SRNCD-103	Way of all Flesh	CD5	U.K.	1989	$8.00

Lovett, Lyle

Full Length

Label	Catalog Number	Title	Type	Country	Year	Longbox Value / Value
MCA	CD33-18455	Here He Is	DJ/Smplr	U.S.	1990	$18.00
MCA		Songs From I Love Everybody	DJ/Smplr	U.S.	1995	$10.00

Singles

Label	Catalog Number	Title	Type	Country	Year	Longbox Value / Value
MCA	CD45-17815	Here I Am	CDJ	U.S.	1989	$2.00
MCA Curb	CD45-3002	If I Had A Boat	CDJ	U.S.		$2.00
MCA	MCA5P3242	Just the Morning	CDJ	U.S.		$6.00
MCA	CD45-17841	Nobody Knows Me	CDJ	U.S.	1989	$2.00
Curb	2754	North Dakota	CDJ	U.S.	1993	$2.00
MCA	MCA5P-2166	She Already Made Up Her Mind	CDJ	U.S.		$2.00
MCA	MCA5P-2354	She Makes Me Feel Good	CDJ	U.S.	1992	$2.00
MCA		She's No Lady She's My Wife	DJ/CDV	U.S.	1989	$35.00
MCA	DMCAT-1322	Stand By Your Man	CD5	U.K.	1989	$10.00
MCA	MCA5P-2617	Stand By Your Man	CDJ	U.S.	1992	$2.00
MCA	657557-2	You Can't Resist It	CD5	Germany	1992	$10.00
MCA	DMCAT-1355	You Can't Resist It	CD5	U.K.	1992	$10.00
MCA	DMCAT-1651	You Can't Resist It	CD5	U.K.	1992	$10.00
MCA	MCA5P-54153	You Can't Resist It	CDJ	U.S.		$2.00
MCA	CD45-1357	You Can't Resist It	CDJ	U.S.	1991	$2.00
MCA	MCA5P-2319	You've Been Good Up to Now	CDJ	U.S.	1992	$2.00

Lovin' Spoonful

Singles

Label	Catalog Number	Title	Type	Country	Year	Longbox Value / Value
Castle	CD3-11	Summer in the City	CD5	U.K.	1988	$10.00

Low

Singles

Label	Catalog Number	Title	Type	Country	Year	Longbox Value / Value
		Shame	CDJ	U.S.		$2.00
BMG	CDSYD-20	Tearing My Soul Apart	CD5	U.K.	1992	$8.00

Lowe, Nick

Full Length

Label	Catalog Number	Title	Type	Country	Year	Longbox Value / Value
Columbia	CK-37932	Nick the Knife	LP/LB	U.S.		$14.00/$10.00
Upstart	UPST PR1	On Fresh Air	DJ/Smplr	U.S.	1995	$20.00
Reprise		Party of One	LP/LB	U.S.		$12.00/$7.00

Singles

Label	Catalog Number	Title	Type	Country	Year	Longbox Value / Value
WEA	W-9821CD	All Men Are Liars	CD5	U.K.	1990	$8.00
WEA	W-9681CD	All Men Are Liars	CD5	U.K.	1990	$8.00
Reprise	PRO-CD-4057	All Men Are Liars	CDJ	U.S.	1990	$2.00
Reprise	W-9709CD	What's Shaking	CD5	U.K.	1990	$8.00
Reprise	PRO-CD-3975	You Got the Look I Like	CDJ	U.S.	1990	$2.00

Lowe, Paul Alexander

Singles

Label	Catalog Number	Title	Type	Country	Year	Longbox Value / Value
CBS	656758-2	When You Need Me	CD5	Germany	1991	$8.00

Lowen And Navarro

Singles

Label	Catalog Number	Title	Type	Country	Year	Longbox Value / Value
		Walking on a Wire	CDJ	U.S		$2.00

LP/LB

Full Length

Label	Catalog Number	Title	Type	Country	Year	Longbox Value / Value
Aris	880111	80 Below 82	LP	Germany		$15.00

Lso

Singles

Label	Catalog Number	Title	Type	Country	Year	Longbox Value / Value
	72028	Get It Right	CD5	U.S.	1994	$5.00

Luca

Singles

Label	Catalog Number	Title	Type	Country	Year	Longbox Value / Value
Cooltempo	COOLCD-259	Just a Little Bit More	CD5	U.K.	1992	$8.00

Lucas

Singles

Label	Catalog Number	Title	Type	Country	Year	Longbox Value / Value
Warner	32-95842	Lucas With the Lid Off	CD5	Canada	1994	$8.00
Atlantic	95842	Lucas With the Lid Off	CD5	U.S.	1994	$5.00
Uptown	2031	Show Me Your Moves	CDJ	U.S.	1991	$2.00
Polygram	887880-2	Sunshine Dancin'	CD5	Germany	1988	$8.00

Lucas, Dan

Singles

Label	Catalog Number	Title	Type	Country	Year	Longbox Value / Value
BMG	664690	Hold on Me	CD5	Germany	1991	$8.00

Lucien, Jon

Full Length

Label	Catalog Number	Title	Type	Country	Year	Longbox Value / Value
Mercury	CDP 411	Words & Music	DJ/Smplr	U.S.	1991	$10.00

Singles

Label	Catalog Number	Title	Type	Country	Year	Longbox Value / Value
Mercury	CDP 472	Nothin' Lasts Forever	CDJ	U.S.	1991	$2.00
Mercury	CDP 415	Sweet Control	CDJ	U.S.	1991	$2.00

Lucky Dube

Singles

Label	Catalog Number	Title	Type	Country	Year	Longbox Value / Value
Motown	530479	Trinity	CD5	U.S.	1994	$5.00

Lucy

Singles

Label	Catalog Number	Title	Type	Country	Year	Longbox Value / Value
Canyon	PCDY-00070	Tell It to Your Heart	CD3	Japan	1990	$12.00/$3.00

Lucy's Fur Coat

Singles

Label	Catalog Number	Title	Type	Country	Year	Longbox Value / Value
Relativity	0236	Treasure Hands	CDJ	U.S.	1993	$2.00

Lukather, Steve

Singles

Label	Catalog Number	Title	Type	Country	Year	Longbox Value / Value
	10EP-3085	Swear Your Love	CD3	Japan		$12.00/$4.00

Luke

Full Length

Label	Catalog Number	Title	Type	Country	Year	Longbox Value / Value
Luke		Luke's Christmas	DJ/LP	U.S.	1994	$25.00

CD and VHS video in box with press kit.

Singles

Label	Catalog Number	Title	Type	Country	Year	Longbox Value / Value
Luke	PRCD 4397-2	I Wanna Rock	CDJ	U.S.	1992	$2.00
	PRCD7175-2	Scarred	CDJ	U.S.		$3.00
Luke		Work It Out	CDJ	U.S.	1993	$2.00

Lukie D.

Singles

Label	Catalog Number	Title	Type	Country	Year	Longbox Value / Value
Capitol	58493	Oh What Joy You Bring	CD5	U.S.	1995	$5.00

Lukie D-Papa Yaie

Singles

Label	Catalog Number	Title	Type	Country	Year	Longbox Value / Value
Capitol	58480	Used to Be My Girl	CD5	U.S.	1995	$5.00

Lulabox

Singles

Label	Catalog Number	Title	Type	Country	Year	Longbox Value / Value
Radioactive	10703	Full Bleed	CDJ	U.S.	1992	$6.00
Radioactive	2595	I Believe	CDJ	U.S.	1993	$2.00

Lulu

Singles

Label	Catalog Number	Title	Type	Country	Year	Longbox Value / Value
		Every Woman Knows	CD5	U.K.		$10.00
		Every Woman Knows	CD5	U.K.		$10.00
	Second version.					
		Goodbye Baby & Amen	CD5	U.K.	1994	$10.00
SBK	DPRO-04723	I'm Back For More	CDJ	U.S.	1992	$2.00
Dome	CDDOME-1001	Independence	CD5	U.K.	1992	$8.00
SBK	DPRO-19779	Independence	CDJ	U.S.	1992	$2.00

Luna

Singles

Label	Catalog Number	Title	Type	Country	Year	Longbox Value / Value
Elektra	PRCD 8632-2	Anethesia	CDJ	U.S.	1992	$2.00
	PRCD 9373-2	Hedgehog	CDJ	U.S.		$2.00
	PRCD 66738	Season of the Witch	CDJ	U.S.		$2.00
Elektra	PRCD 8686-2	Slash Your Tires	CDJ	U.S.	1992	$2.00
Elektra	EKR-169CD	Slide	CD5	U.K.	1992	$9.00
Elektra	64127-2	Slide	CD5	U.S.	1992	$5.00
Elektra	PRCD 8984-2	This Time Around	CDJ	U.S.	1993	$2.00
Elektra	PRCD 8884-2	Tiger Lily	CDJ	U.S.	1992	$2.00

Lunachicks

Singles

Label	Catalog Number	Title	Type	Country	Year	Longbox Value / Value
Safe House	2105	Apathetic	CD5	U.S.	1992	$4.00

Lungfish

Singles

Label	Catalog Number	Title	Type	Country	Year	Longbox Value / Value
Dischard	92	Pass and Stow	CD5	U.S.	1994	$5.00

Lunz

Singles

Label	Catalog Number	Title	Type	Country	Year	Longbox Value / Value
	DPRO12809	I Got 5 On It	CDJ	U.S.		$2.00
	DPRO11025	Playa Hata	CDJ	U.S.		$2.00

Luscious Jackson

Singles

Label	Catalog Number	Title	Type	Country	Year	Longbox Value / Value
Capitol	DPRO 79380	City Song	CDJ	U.S.	1994	$7.00
Capitol	DPRO 79521	Deep Shag	CDJ	U.S.	1994	$7.00
EMI		Here	CD5	U.K.	1995	$10.00
Capitol	58372	Here	CD5	U.S.	1995	$5.00
Capitol	DPRO 79596	Here	CDJ	U.S.	1995	$7.00

Lush

Full Length

Label	Catalog Number	Title	Type	Country	Year	Longbox Value / Value
Westwood One		In Concert-Nu Rock	RS	U.S.	1996	$60.00
	Airdate: 7/1/96.					
		Last Night	DJ/Smplr	U.S.		$12.00
	LUSH 5CD	Lovelife Sampled	DJ/Smplr	U.K.	1995	$20.00
4AD		Split	DJ/LP	U.K.	194	$15.00
4AD		Split	LTD/LP	U.K.	1994	$30.00
	2CD set.					
4AD/Reprise	9 26798-2-Dj	Spooky	DJ/LP	U.S.	1992	$15.00
	CD in jewel box, housed in custom felt pocket.					
4AD	9 26798-2-DJ	Spooky	DJ/LP	U.S.	1992	$20.00

Singles

Label	Catalog Number	Title	Type	Country	Year	Longbox Value / Value
4AD	JAD 911	Baby Talk	CD5	U.K.	1989	$10.00
4AD	BAD-1016CD	Black Spring	CD5	U.K.	1991	$10.00
4AD		Deluxe	CDJ	U.S.		$6.00
4AD	120 1313 3	For Love	CD5	Germany	1992	$10.00
4AD	BAD-2001CD	For Love	CD5	U.K.	1992	$10.00
4AD	PRO-CD-5299	For Love	CDJ	U.S.	1992	$3.00
4AD		Hypocrite	CDJ	U.S.		$3.00
	PRO-CD-8023	Ladykillers Swirls	CDJ	U.S.		$3.00
4AD	CD10-491	Mad Love	CD5	Germany	1990	$10.00
4AD	BAD 0003	Mad Love	CD5	U.K.	1990	$10.00
4AD	3	Mad Love	CD5	U.S.	1990	$5.00
4AD	9 40231-2	Nothing Natural	CD5	U.S.	1991	$5.00
		Single Girl	CD5	U.K.		$10.00
		Single Girl	CD5	U.K.		$10.00
	Second version.					
Reprise	PRO-CD-5471	Superblast	CDJ	U.S.	1992	$9.00
4AD	BAD 0013	Sweetness and Light	CD5	U.K.	1990	$10.00
Reprise	PRO-CD-4568	Sweetness and Light	CDJ	U.S.	1990	$6.00
Reprise	PRO-CD-7048	When I Die	CDJ	U.S.	1994	$7.00

Lush & Jarvis Cocker

Singles

Label	Catalog Number	Title	Type	Country	Year	Longbox Value / Value
		Ciao	CDJ	U.K.		$15.00

Lustre

Singles

Label	Catalog Number	Title	Type	Country	Year	Longbox Value / Value
	AQMSAD00165	California	CDJ	U.S.		$3.00

Luv

Singles

Label	Catalog Number	Title	Type	Country	Year	Longbox Value / Value
Alfa	ALDB-50	Girl Like Me	CD3	Japan	1990	$12.00/$3.00
RCA	PD-43430	Medley	CD5	Germany	1990	$8.00
Polygram	888635-2	You're the Greatest	CD5	Germany	1990	$8.00

Luv, Ray

Singles

Label	Catalog Number	Title	Type	Country	Year	Longbox Value / Value
Atlantic	85576-2	In the Game	CD5	U.S.	1995	$6.00

Lwin, Annabella

Singles

Label	Catalog Number	Title	Type	Country	Year	Longbox Value / Value
Sony	660720-2	Car Sex	CD5	Germany	1994	$20.00
	Minidisc single.					
		Car Sex	CD5	U.K.		$8.00
		Do What You Do	CD5	U.K.		$8.00
		Do What You Do	CD5	U.K.		$8.00
	Second version.					

Lyle, Bobby

Singles

Label	Catalog Number	Title	Type	Country	Year	Longbox Value / Value
		Love Eyes	CDJ	U.S.		$2.00
		Tropical	CDJ	U.S.		$2.00

Lynch Mob

Full Length

Label	Catalog Number	Title	Type	Country	Year	Longbox Value / Value
Elektra		Lynch Mob	LP/LB	U.S.		$14.00/$8.00
Elektra		Wicked Sensation	LP/LB	U.S.		$14.00/$8.00

Singles

Label	Catalog Number	Title	Type	Country	Year	Longbox Value / Value
Elektra	WMD5-4109	Dream Until Tomorrow	CD3	Japan	1992	$13.00/$4.00
Elektra	PRCD 8616-2	Dream Until Tomorrow	CDJ	U.S.	1992	$2.00
Elektra	PRCD 8356-2	No Bed of Nails	CDJ	U.S.	1990	$2.00
Elektra	PRCD 8301-2	River of Love	CDJ	U.S.	1991	$2.00
Elektra	WMD5-4103	Tangled in the Web	CD3	Japan	1992	$13.00/$4.00
Elektra	PRCD 8558-2	Tangled in the Web	CDJ	U.S.	1992	$2.00
Elektra	PRCD 8582-2	Tangled in the Web	CDJ	U.S.	1992	$2.00
Elektra	PRCD 8284-2	Wicked Sensation	CDJ	U.S.	1992	$2.00

Lynch, Ray

Full Length

Label	Catalog Number	Title	Type	Country	Year	Longbox Value / Value
Ray Lynch	RPLPCD-103	No Blue Thing	LP	U.S.	1989	$15.00
	Original cover.					

Singles

Label	Catalog Number	Title	Type	Country	Year	Longbox Value / Value
Elektra	PRCD 87892	Beast, The	CDJ	U.S.	1993	$2.00
		Rhythm in the Pews	CDJ	U.S.		$2.00

Lynn, Cheryl

Singles

Label	Catalog Number	Title	Type	Country	Year	Longbox Value / Value
Virgin	PRCD 2838	Everytime I Try To Say Goodbye	CDJ	U.S.	1989	$2.00
Sony	SRDS-6213	Got to Be Real	CD3	Japan	1991	$13.00/$4.00
Virgin	PRCD 3238	Upset	CDJ	U.S.	1989	$2.00
Virgin	PRCD 3036	Whatever It Takes	CDJ	U.S.	1989	$2.00

Lynne, Jeff

Full Length

Label	Catalog Number	Title	Type	Country	Year	Longbox Value / Value
Reprise	9 26184-2-Dj	Armchair Theatre	DJ/LP	U.S.	1990	$15.00
Radio Ventures		Masters Of Rock	RS	U.S.	1990	$30.00
	Airdate: 8/16/90.					

Singles

Label	Catalog Number	Title	Type	Country	Year	Longbox Value / Value
WEA	WPDP-6233	Every Little Thing	CD3	Japan	1990	$13.00/$4.00
Reprise	W-9799CD	Every Little Thing	CD5	U.K.	1990	$10.00
Reprise	PRO-CD-4088	Every Little Thing	CDJ	U.S.	1990	$3.00
Reprise	7599-21750-2	Lift Me Up	CD5	Germany	1990	$10.00
WEA	W-9795CD	Lift Me Up	CD5	U.K.	1990	$10.00
Reprise	PRO-CD-4091	Lift Me Up	CDJ	U.S.	1990	$3.00

Lynne, Shelby

Singles

Label	Catalog Number	Title	Type	Country	Year	Longbox Value / Value
Morgan Creek	0034	Feelin' Kind Of Lonely Tonight	CDJ	U.S.	1993	$2.00
Epic	ESK 1060	Hurtin' Side, The	CDJ	U.S.	1989	$2.00
Morgan Creek	0041	Tell Me I'm Crazy	CDJ	U.S.	1993	$2.00
Epic	ESK 73904	Very Last Love, The	CDJ	U.S.	1991	$2.00

Lynyrd Skynyrd

Full Length

Label	Catalog Number	Title	Type	Country	Year	Longbox Value / Value
Album Network		In the Studio (Pronounced)	RS	U.S.	1988	$25.00
	Airdate: 7/11/88.					
Album Network		In the Studio (Pronounced)	RS	U.S.	1990	$20.00
	Airdate: 5/7/90.					
Album Network		In the Studio (Second Helping)	RS	U.S.	1989	$25.00
	Airdate: 1/23/89.					
Album Network		In the Studio (Street Survivors)	RS	U.S.	1989	$25.00
	Airdate: 10/16/89.					
DIR		King Biscuit Flour Hour	RS	U.S.	1988	$50.00
	Airdate: 5/22/88.					
DIR		King Biscuit Flour Hour	RS	U.S.	1989	$35.00
	Airdate: 11/12/89.					
DIR		King Biscuit Flour Hour	RS	U.S.	1991	$35.00
	Airdate: 6/23/91.					
DIR		King Biscuit Flour Hour	RS	U.S.	1992	$35.00
	Airdate: 9/6/92.					
DIR		King Biscuit Flour Hour	RS	U.S.	1994	$35.00
	Airdate: 2/27/94.					
Westwood One		Superstars	RS	U.S.	1996	$90.00
	2 CD set. Airdate: 8/5/96.					
MCA	CD33-2033	Ten From the Swamp	DJ/Smplr	U.S.	1991	$20.00
Media America		Up Close	RS	U.S.	1990	$50.00
	2 CD set.					
Media America		Up Close	RS	U.S.	1991	$50.00
	2 CD set.					

Singles

Label	Catalog Number	Title	Type	Country	Year	Longbox Value / Value
MCA	CD45 1681	All I Can Do Is Write About It	CDJ	U.S.	1991	$6.00
MCA	CD45 17823	Double Trouble	CDJ	U.S.	1989	$6.00
		Down South Dukin'	CDJ	U.S.		$7.00
MCA	DMCA-1251	Freebird	CD3	U.K.	1989	$11.00
Columbia	CSK 78284	White Knuckle Ride	CDJ	U.S.		$7.00

Lynyrd Skynyrd (1991)

Full Length

Label	Catalog Number	Title	Type	Country	Year	Longbox Value / Value
Atlantic		1991	LP/LB	U.S.		$14.00/$8.00
Atlantic		Acoustic Sampler	DJ/Smplr	U.S.	1994	$12.00
Atlantic	PRCD 5078-2	Back to Back: Travis Tritt Interviews Lynyrd Skynyrd	DJ/Intvw	U.S.	1993	$20.00
Atlantic		Last Rebel, The	LP/LB	U.S.		$14.00/$8.00

Singles

Label	Catalog Number	Title	Type	Country	Year	Longbox Value / Value
Atlantic	PRCD 5051-2	Born To Run	CDJ	U.S.	1993	$6.00
Atlantic	PRCD 4953-2	Good Lovin's Hard to Find	CDJ	U.S.	1993	$6.00
Atlantic	PRCD 4117-2	Keeping the Faith	CDJ	U.S.	1991	$6.00
Atlantic	PRCD 5156-2	Last Rebel, The	CDJ	U.S.	1993	$6.00
Atlantic	PRCD 4240-2	Pure & Simple	CDJ	U.S.	1991	$6.00
Atlantic	PRCD 3960-2	Smokestack Lightning	CDJ	U.S.	1991	$6.00

Lyres

Full Length

Label	Catalog Number	Title	Type	Country	Year	Longbox Value / Value
		A Promise of A New Day	LP/LB	U.S.		$14.00/$8.00

M.A.N.I.C.

Singles

Label	Catalog Number	Title	Type	Country	Year	Longbox Value / Value
Union City	UCRCD-2	I'm Comin' Hardcore	CD5	U.K.	1992	$8.00

M Beat Feat Gen

Singles

Label	Catalog Number	Title	Type	Country	Year	Longbox Value / Value
Full Frequency	120057	Incredible	CD5	U.S.	1994	$5.00

M.C. 900 Ft. Jesus

Singles

Label	Catalog Number	Title	Type	Country	Year	Longbox Value / Value
		But If You Go	CDJ	U.S.		$3.00
Warner Brothers	9 41554	If I Only Had A Bra	CD5	U.S.	1994	$5.00
Nettwerk	X25G-13835	Killer Inside	CD5	U.S.	1991	$5.00
Nettwerk	3032	Too Bad	CD5	Canada	1991	$7.00
IRS	74005	Truth Is Out	CDJ	U.S.	1990	$2.00

M.C.B

Singles

Label	Catalog Number	Title	Type	Country	Year	Longbox Value / Value
ZYX	DST-1023-8	Aquarius	CD5	Germany	1990	$6.00

M.C. Brains

Singles

Label	Catalog Number	Title	Type	Country	Year	Longbox Value / Value
Motown	3746310322	Everybody's Talking About M.C.	CDJ	U.S.	1992	$2.00
Motown	1013	Oochie Coochie	CDJ	U.S.	1991	$2.00

M.C. Buzz B

Singles

Label	Catalog Number	Title	Type	Country	Year	Longbox Value / Value
Polydor	PZCD-140	Don't Have the Time	CD5	U.K.	1991	$8.00
Polydor	PZCD-89	Last Tree	CD5	U.K.	1990	$8.00
Polydor	PZCD-121	Never Change	CD5	U.K.	1991	$8.00

M.C. Da Da

Singles

Label	Catalog Number	Title	Type	Country	Year	Longbox Value / Value
Polygram	868063-2	Da Da Da	CD5	Germany	1991	$8.00

M.C. Duke

Singles

Label	Catalog Number	Title	Type	Country	Year	Longbox Value / Value
Pinnacle	NOTE-35CD	Final Conflict	CD5	U.K.	1990	$8.00

M.C. Eiht

Singles

Label	Catalog Number	Title	Type	Country	Year	Longbox Value / Value
Epic	ESK 7600	Thuggin' It Up	CDJ	U.S.		$2.00

M.C. Lethal

Singles

Label	Catalog Number	Title	Type	Country	Year	Longbox Value / Value
Netwerk	NWKCD-60	Rave Digger	CD5	U.K.	1992	$8.00

M.C. Lyte

Singles

Label	Catalog Number	Title	Type	Country	Year	Longbox Value / Value
Atlantic	PRCD 4823-2	Act Like You Know	CDJ	U.S.		$2.00
Elektra	64212-2	Cold Rock A Party	CD5	U.S.	1997	$3.50
Elektra	63985-2	Cold Rock A Party	CD5	U.S.	1997	$5.00
Perspective	PERD-7417	Ice Cream Dream	CD5	U.K.	1993	$8.00
Perspective	31458 8067	Ice Cream Dream	CDJ	U.S.	1993	$2.00
First Priority	5106	Ruffneck	CDJ	U.S.	1993	$2.00
First Priority	5274	Ruffneck	CDJ	U.S.	1993	$2.00

M.C. Mikee Freedom

Singles

Label	Catalog Number	Title	Type	Country	Year	Longbox Value / Value
APT	TEKKCD-12	Set You Free	CD5	U.K.	1992	$8.00

M.C. Sar

Singles

Label	Catalog Number	Title	Type	Country	Year	Longbox Value / Value
ZYX	6289-8	It's On You	CD5	Germany	1990	$6.00
ZYX	6506-8	Make a Move	CD5	Germany	1990	$6.00
ZYX	6250-8	Pump Up the Jam	CD5	Germany	1990	$6.00

M.C. Search

Singles

Label	Catalog Number	Title	Type	Country	Year	Longbox Value / Value
Def Jam	74414	Here It Comes	CDJ	U.S.	1992	$2.00

M.C. Shan

Singles

Label	Catalog Number	Title	Type	Country	Year	Longbox Value / Value
Livin'Large	118	Hip Hop Roughneck	CDJ	U.S.		$2.00
Cold Chillin	3992	It Don't Mean a Thing	CDJ	U.S.	1990	$2.00
Cold Chillin	4550	Time For Us to Defend	CDJ	U.S.	1990	$2.00

M.C. Skat Kat

Singles

Label	Catalog Number	Title	Type	Country	Year	Longbox Value / Value
Virgin	PRCD 3996	Skat Strut	CDJ	U.S.	1991	$7.00
With Paula Abdul.						

M.C. Thick

Full Length

Label	Catalog Number	Title	Type	Country	Year	Longbox Value / Value
Big Beat	14220	Show Ain't Over, The	LP/BP	U.S.		$12.00/$7.00

M.C. Tunes

Singles

Label	Catalog Number	Title	Type	Country	Year	Longbox Value / Value
WEA	1771670-2	Only Rhyme That Bytes	CD5	Germany	1990	$8.00
ZTT	ZANG-3CD	Only Rhyme That Bytes	CD5	U.K.	1990	$8.00
ZTT	ZANG-10CD	Primary Rhyming	CD5	U.K.	1990	$8.00
ZTT	ZANG-6CD	Tunes Split the Atom	CD5	U.K.	1990	$8.00

M.D.C.

Singles

Label	Catalog Number	Title	Type	Country	Year	Longbox Value / Value
WEA	9031-75394-2	You and Me in Ecstasy	CD5	Germany	1991	$8.00

M.Doc

Full Length

Label	Catalog Number	Title	Type	Country	Year	Longbox Value / Value
Polygram	848887	Universal Poet	LP/BP	U.S.		$12.00/$7.00

M People

Singles

Label	Catalog Number	Title	Type	Country	Year	Longbox Value / Value
CBS	77720	Excited	CD5	U.S.	1994	$5.00
		Love Rendevous	CD5	U.K.		$10.00
		Love Rendevous	CD5	U.K.		$10.00
Second version.						
CBS	77417	Moving On Up	CD5	U.S.	1994	$5.00
		Open Your Heart	CDJ	U.S.		$3.00
Columbia	78022	Search For the Hero	CD5	U.S.	1995	$5.00

M&M

Singles

Label	Catalog Number	Title	Type	Country	Year	Longbox Value / Value
Atlantic	PRCD 4691-2	Get To Know Ya	CDJ	U.S.	1992	$2.00

M'Boom

Full Length

Label	Catalog Number	Title	Type	Country	Year	Longbox Value / Value
Soul Note	SN-1059CD PSI	Collage	LP/LB	U.S.†	1985	$14.00/$8.00

M's Queen

Singles

Label	Catalog Number	Title	Type	Country	Year	Longbox Value / Value
Polydor	PSDW-1025	Hello Mr. Monkey	CDJ	Japan	1990	$2.00
Polydor	PSDW-1004	Super Freak	CDJ	Japan	1990	$2.00

M-Beat

Singles

Label	Catalog Number	Title	Type	Country	Year	Longbox Value / Value
		Incredible	CD5	U.K.		$10.00
		Incredible	CD5	U.K.		$10.00
Second version.						
		Sweet Love	CD5	U.K.		$10.00
		Sweet Love	CD5	U.K.		$10.00
Second version.						

M-People

Singles

Label	Catalog Number	Title	Type	Country	Year	Longbox Value / Value
BMG	PD-44440	Colour My Life	CD5	U.K.	1991	$8.00
BMG	74321-11633-2	Excited	CD5	U.K.	1991	$8.00
BMG	PD-44856	How Can I Love You More?	CD5	U.K.	1991	$8.00
BMG	74321-130232	How Can I Love You More?	CD5	U.K.	1993	$8.00
Epic	49K 77417	Moving On Up	CD5	U.S.	1994	$6.00
BMG	PD-45370	Someday	CD5	U.K.	1992	$8.00

Mac Band

Singles

Label	Catalog Number	Title	Type	Country	Year	Longbox Value / Value
MCA	DMCA-1292	Jealous	CD5	U.K.	1988	$9.00
WEA	257859-2	Roses Are Red	CD5	Germany	1988	$9.00
		Someone to Love	CDJ	U.S.		$2.00
MCA	DMCA-1271	Stalemate	CD5	U.K.	1988	$9.00

Mac Machine

Singles

Label	Catalog Number	Title	Type	Country	Year	Longbox Value / Value
ZYX	6331-8	Set It Out	CD5	Germany	1990	$8.00

Mac Sample

Singles

Label	Catalog Number	Title	Type	Country	Year	Longbox Value / Value
SPV	8199-3	House Inspector	CD5	Germany	1989	$8.00

MacAlpine

Singles

Label	Catalog Number	Title	Type	Country	Year	Longbox Value / Value
Squawk	222	World We Live In, The	CDJ	U.S.	1990	$2.00

MacColl, Kristy

Full Length

Label	Catalog Number	Title	Type	Country	Year	Longbox Value / Value
		Advance Music From Titanic Days	DJ/Smplr	U.S.	1994	$8.00
IRS	DPRO-6716	Angel	DJ/Smplr	U.S.	1993	$15.00
		Real MacColl, The	DJ/Smplr	U.S.		$10.00
Charisma	PRCD 3564	Real MacColl, The	DJ/Smplr	U.S.	1990	$8.00

Singles

Label	Catalog Number	Title	Type	Country	Year	Longbox Value / Value
Virgin	VSCDT-1373	All I Ever Wanted	CD5	U.K.	1990	$10.00
Charisma	PRCD 067	All I Ever Wanted	CDJ	U.S.	1990	$2.00
IRS	DPRO-6731	Angel	CDJ	U.S.		$3.00
IRS	6716	Angel	CDJ	U.S.	1993	$2.00
		As Long as You Hold Me	CDJ	U.S.		$3.00
IRS	6719	Can't Stop Killng	CDJ	U.S.	1993	$2.00
		Caroline	CD5	U.K.		$10.00
		Caroline	CD5	U.K.		$10.00
Second version.						
		Caroline	CDJ	U.S.		$3.00
BMG	162465	Days	CD3	Germany	1989	$10.00
Virgin	KMACD-2	Days	CD3	U.K.	1989	$10.00
Virgin	KMACD-4	Don't Come the Cowboy	CD3	U.K.	1990	$10.00
BMG	162253	Free World	CD3	Germany	1989	$10.00
Virgin	KMACD-1	Free World	CD3	U.K.	1989	$10.00
Charisma		Free World	CDJ	U.S.	1989	$2.00
Virgin	KMACD-3	Innocence	CD3	U.K.	1989	$10.00
Charisma		It's a Sin	CDJ	U.S.		$2.00
Chrysalis	323629-2	Miss Otis Regrets	CD5	Germany	1990	$10.00
Chrysalis	CHSCD-3629	Miss Otis Regrets	CD5	U.K.	1990	$10.00
		Titanic Days	CDJ	U.S.	1994	$8.00
BMG	664360	Walking Down Madison	CD5	Germany	1991	$10.00
Charisma	9634-2	Walking Down Madison	CD5	U.S.	1991	$5.00
Charisma	PRCD 062	Walking Down Madison	CDJ	U.S.	1991	$2.00

MacDonald, Ralph

Full Length

Label	Catalog Number	Title	Type	Country	Year	Longbox Value / Value
Polygram	823323-2	Universal Rhythm	LP/BP	U.S.†	1985	$14.00/$8.00

Macgowan, Shane

Singles

Label	Catalog Number	Title	Type	Country	Year	Longbox Value / Value
		Haunted	CD5	U.K.	1995	$10.00
		That Woman's Got Me Drinking	CD5	U.K.		$10.00
		That Woman's Got Me Drinking	CD5	U.K.		$10.00
Second version.						

Machines of Loving Grace

Singles

Label	Catalog Number	Title	Type	Country	Year	Longbox Value / Value
Mammoth	MR-0036-2	Burn Like Brilliant Trash	CD5	U.K.	1992	$8.00
Mammoth	5246	Butterfly Wings	CDJ	U.S.	1993	$2.00
Mammoth	PRCD6363-2	Richest Junkie Still Alive	CDJ	U.S.		$3.00
Mammoth	PRCD 6481-2	Richest Junkie Still Alive	CDJ	U.S.		$3.00
Rough Trade	378 4026 3	Rite Of Shiva	CD5	Germany	1992	$8.00
Mammoth	MR-0026-2	Rite of Shiva	CD5	U.K.	1992	$8.00
Mammoth	0026	Rite of Shiva	CDJ	U.S.	1991	$2.00
Mammoth	PRCD6566-2	Suicide King	CDJ	U.S.		$3.00

Mack 10

Singles

Label	Catalog Number	Title	Type	Country	Year	Longbox Value / Value
	DPRO 30053	Hoo	CDJ	U.S.		$3.00

Mack, Craig

Singles

Label	Catalog Number	Title	Type	Country	Year	Longbox Value / Value
Arista	79002	Flava in Ya Ear	CD5	U.S.	1994	$5.00
Arista	79013	Get Down	CD5	U.S.	1994	$5.00
Arista	9022	Get Down	CD5	U.S.	1994	$5.00

Mack, Jack

Singles

Label	Catalog Number	Title	Type	Country	Year	Longbox Value / Value
Voss	5004	It Don't Bother Me	CDJ	U.S.	1990	$2.00

Mackenzie, Billy

Singles

Label	Catalog Number	Title	Type	Country	Year	Longbox Value / Value
Circa	YRCD-86	Baby	CD5	U.K.	1992	$8.00
Circa	YRCD-91	Colours Will Come	CD5	U.K.	1992	$8.00

MacNeil, Rita

Singles

Label	Catalog Number	Title	Type	Country	Year	Longbox Value / Value
Polydor	PZCD-123	Flying on Your Own	CD5	U.K.	1991	$8.00
Polydor	877949-2	Working Man	CD5	Germany	1991	$8.00
Polydor	PZCD-98	Working Man	CD5	U.K.	1991	$8.00

MacQuire, Sean

Singles

Label	Catalog Number	Title	Type	Country	Year	Longbox Value / Value
		Take This Time	CD5	U.K.		$10.00
		Take This Time	CD5	U.K.		$10.00
Second version.						

Mad

Singles

Label	Catalog Number	Title	Type	Country	Year	Longbox Value / Value
WEA	9031-75555-2	Spy Vs. Spy	CD5	Germany	1991	$8.00
Polygram	879561-2	Thinkin' About You	CD5	Germany	1991	$8.00

Mad Cobra

Singles

Label	Catalog Number	Title	Type	Country	Year	Longbox Value / Value
Columbia	CSK 74917	Legacy	CDJ	U.S.	1993	$2.00

Mad Flava

Singles

Label	Catalog Number	Title	Type	Country	Year	Longbox Value / Value
Priority	7047	Bump Ya Head	CDJ	U.S.	1994	$2.00

Mad Romeo

Singles

Label	Catalog Number	Title	Type	Country	Year	Longbox Value / Value
Polygram	874752-3	I'll Be Good	CD3	Germany	1989	$8.00
Polygram	874753-2	I'll Be Good	CD5	Germany	1989	$8.00
Polygram	CDSYR-11	I'll Be Good	CD5	U.K.	1989	$8.00
Polygram	874140-3	Paradise	CD3	Germany	1989	$8.00
Polygram	874141-2	Paradise	CD5	Germany	1989	$8.00
Polygram	CDSYR-13	Paradise	CD3	U.K.	1989	$8.00

Mad Season

Full Length

Label	Catalog Number	Title	Type	Country	Year	Longbox Value / Value
Sony	CDNK 1089	Live	DJ/Smplr	Canada	1995	$25.00

Singles

Label	Catalog Number	Title	Type	Country	Year	Longbox Value / Value
Columbia	CSK 7145	I Don't Know Anything	CDJ	U.S.	1995	$3.00
		Long Gone Day	CDJ	U.S.		$2.00
Columbia	CSK 7344	Long Gone Day	CDJ	U.S.	1995	$3.00
CBS		River of Deceit	CD5	U.K.	1995	$10.00
Columbia	CSK 6988	River of Deceit	CDJ	U.S.	1995	$3.00

Mad Skillz

Singles

Label	Catalog Number	Title	Type	Country	Year	Longbox Value / Value
Atlantic	95743	Big Beat	CD5	U.S.	1995	$5.00
	D65202	Move Ya Body	CDJ	U.S.		$2.00
	PRCD 6289-2	Nod Factor, The	CDJ	U.S.		$0.00

Madame Star

Singles

Label	Catalog Number	Title	Type	Country	Year	Longbox Value / Value
Cold Chillin'	2035	Looking For a Dame	CD5	U.S.	1994	$5.00

Madame X

Singles

Label	Catalog Number	Title	Type	Country	Year	Longbox Value / Value
Atlantic	81831-2	Just That Kind of Girl	CDV/BP	U.S.	1988	$14.00/$14.00

Madden, Danny

Singles

Label	Catalog Number	Title	Type	Country	Year	Longbox Value / Value
Eternal	YZ-576CD	Facts of Life	CD5	U.K.	1990	$8.00
Eternal	YZ-473CD	Facts of Life	CD5	U.K.	1990	$8.00

Madder Rose

Singles

Label	Catalog Number	Title	Type	Country	Year	Longbox Value / Value
Atlantic	A7256CD	Car Song	CD5	U.K.	1994	$10.00
	95770	Love You Save	CD5	U.S.	1994	$5.00
	95770	Love You Save	CD5	U.S.	1995	$6.00
Atlantic	PRCD 5541-2	Panic on	CDJ	U.S.		$2.00

Madkap

Singles

Label	Catalog Number	Title	Type	Country	Year	Longbox Value / Value
Loud	62445	Da Whole Kit and Kaboodle	CDJ	U.S.	1993	$2.00

Madness

Singles

Label	Catalog Number	Title	Type	Country	Year	Longbox Value / Value
		Harder They Come	CD5	U.K.		$10.00
		Harder They Come	CD5	U.K.		$10.00
Second version.						
Virgin	VSCD-1054	I Pronounce You	CD5	U.K.	1988	$9.00
Virgin	VSCD-1405	It Must Be Love	CD5	U.K.	1992	$9.00
Virgin	VSCD-1477	Night Boat to Cairo	CD5	U.K.	1993	$10.00
Aris	883514	Peel Sessions	CD5	Germany	1990	$9.00
Strange Frt	SFPSCD-007	Peel Sessions	CD5	U.K.	1990	$9.00

Madonna

Full Length

Label	Catalog Number	Title	Type	Country	Year	Longbox Value / Value
Warner Pioneer	PCS 44	1983-1989	DJ/Smplr	Japan	1989	$250.00
Warner Brothers		Bedtime Stories	DJ/LP	U.S.	1994	$30.00
CD in blue velvet digipak. Limited to 2500 copies.						
Warner Pioneer	28XD-456	Dress You up	LP	Japan	1985	$35.00
Sire		Erotica	LTD/LP	Australia	1993	$30.00
Gold disc.						
		Girly Show	DJ/Smplr	Brazil	1993	$60.00
		Girly Show	LTD/LP	France	1994	$0.00
3 track CD with hardbound picture book.						
		Girly Show	LTD/LP	Germany	1994	$0.00
3 track CD with hardbound picture book.						
		Girly Show	LTD/LP	Japan	1994	$0.00
3 track CD with hardbound picture book.						
		Girly Show	LTD/LP	U.K.	1994	$35.00
3 track CD with hardbound picture book.						
Warner Brothers		I'm Breathless	DJ/Smplr	Japan	1990	$40.00
Sire	9 26209-2-Dj	I'm Breathless	DJ/LP	U.S.	1990	$14.00
Picture disc.						
Sire		Immaculate Collection	LTD/LP	Australia	1993	$30.00
Gold disc.						
Sire.	9 26464-2	Immaculate Collection	LTD/LP	U.S.	1990	$35.00
Boxed set including photos and VHS tape.						
WEA	38195	Immaculate Collection	LD	U.S.	1991	$30.00
Sire	9 25844-2-Dj	Like a Prayer	DJ/LP	U.S.	1989	$30.00
Picture disc.						
Sire	9 25844-2	Like a Prayer	DJ/LP	U.S.	1989	$50.00
Warner Pioneer	28XD-455	Like a Virgin	LP	Japan	1985	$35.00
Sire	43P2-0001	Like a Virgin	LTD/LP	Japan	1989	$50.00
Gold disc.						
Warner Brothers		Like a Virgin	DJ/LP	U.S.†		$200.00
Experimental carboard sleeve and outer longbox.						
Warner Brothers	9 25157-2	Like a Virgin	LP	U.S.†	1984	$20.00
Sire	9 25157-2	Like a Virgin	LP/LB	U.S.†	1985	$16.00/$13.00
Pioneer	PA-85-M019	Madonna	8"LD	U.S.	1985	$14.00
Sire	9 23867-2	Madonna	LP/LB	U.S.†	1985	$16.00/$13.00
PMV	080 373-9	Madonna	8"LD	U.S.	1988	$14.00
Pioneer	PA-85-M019	Madonna	8"LD	U.S.	1991	$12.00
Digital audio.						
Warner	PCS-1971	One More Chance	DJ/Smplr	Japan	1995	$200.00
QSOUND	MADONNA	Q Sound Sampler	DJ/Smplr	U.S.	1990	$20.00
		Sex	LP	France	1993	$35.00
Book with CD5.						
Sire	43PD-0002	True Blue	LTD/LP	Japan	1989	$50.00
Gold disc.						
Pioneer	PA-86-160	Virgin Tour	LD	U.S.	1986	$40.00
Sire	43XD-2000	You Can Dance	LTD/LP	Japan	1989	$50.00
Gold disc.						
Sire	PRO-CD-2892	You Can Dance	DJ/Smplr	U.S.	1987	$40.00

Singles

Label	Catalog Number	Title	Type	Country	Year	Longbox Value / Value
Sire	CD-40793	Bad Girl	CD5	Canada	1993	$14.00
Sire	9362-40789-2	Bad Girl	CD5	Germany	1993	$14.00
Maverick	WPDP-6321	Bad Girl	CD3	Japan	1993	$18.00/$4.00
Sire	W-0154CD	Bad Girl	CD5	U.K.	1993	$14.00
Sire	PRO-CD-5888	Bad Girl	CDJ	U.S.	1992	$6.00
Maverick	9 18650	Bad Girl	CD5	U.S.	1993	$6.00
Warner Brothers		Bedtime Stories	CDJ	U.S.	1995	$8.00
2 tracks.						
Warner Brothers		Bedtime Stories	CDJ	U.S.	1995	$8.00
3 tracks.						
Warner Brothers		Bedtime Stories	CDJ	U.S.	1995	$8.00
4 tracks.						
Warner Brothers		Bedtime Story	CD5	Australia	1995	$12.00
Warner Brothers	W0285CDX	Bedtime Story	CD5	U.K.	1995	$12.00
Warner Brothers	W0285CD	Bedtime Story	CD5	U.K.	1995	$12.00
Warner Brothers	W0285CD-DJ-2	Bedtime Story	CDJ	U.K.	1995	$50.00
Warner Brothers	41895	Bedtime Story	CD5	U.S.	1994	$5.00
Warner Brothers	PRO-CD-7444	Bedtime Story	CDJ	U.S.	1994	$7.00
Warner Brothers	17924-2	Bedtime Story	CD5	U.S.	1995	$6.00
		Bye Bye Baby	CD5	Australia	1994	$14.00
		Bye Bye Baby	CD5	U.K.	1994	$14.00
Sire	921326-2	Cherish	CD3	Germany	1989	$14.00
Sire	09P3-6175	Cherish	CD3	Japan	1989	$18.00/$4.00
Sire	PRO-CD-3608	Cherish	CDJ	U.S.	1989	$6.00
Receiver	3000	Cosmic Climb	CD5	France	1993	$13.00
Sire	W-0008	Crazy for You	CD5	Germany	1991	$12.00
Sire	W-0008	Crazy for You	CD5	U.K.	1991	$12.00
Sire	921421-2	Dear Jessie	CD5	Germany	1989	$12.00
Sire	921452-2	Dear Jessie	CD5	Germany	1989	$12.00
Sire	W-2668CD	Dear Jessie	CD5	U.K.	1989	$12.00
Sire	W-2668CDX	Dear Jessie	CD5	U.K.	1989	$12.00
Sire	CD-40722	Deeper and Deeper	CD5	Canada	1992	$8.00
Warner Brothers	WPDP-6316	Deeper and Deeper	CD3	Japan	1993	$18.00/$4.00
Sire	W-0146CD	Deeper and Deeper	CD5	U.K.	1992	$14.00
Sire	9 18639-2	Deeper and Deeper	CD5	U.S.	1992	$5.00
Sire	9 40722-2	Deeper and Deeper	CD5	U.S.	1992	$6.00
Sire	PRO-CD-5896	Deeper and Deeper	CDJ	U.S.	1992	$7.00
Warner Brothers	43809-2	Don't Cry For Me Argentina	CD5	U.S.	1996	$6.00
Sire	CD-40585	Erotic	CD5	Canada	1992	$8.00
Warner Brothers	WPDP-6310	Erotic	CD3	Japan	1992	$18.00/$4.00
Sire	W-0138CD	Erotic	CD5	U.K.	1992	$14.00
Sire	9 18782-2	Erotic	CD5	U.S.	1992	$5.00
Sire	9 40585-2	Erotic	CD5	U.S.	1992	$5.00
Sire	PRO-CD-5648	Erotic	CDJ	U.S.	1992	$6.00
Sire	PRO-CD-5665	Erotic	CDJ	U.S.	1992	$6.00
Sire	921249-2	Express Youself	CD5	Germany	1989	$14.00
Sire	09P3-6147	Express Youself	CD3	Japan	1989	$18.00/$4.00
Sire	W-2948CD	Express Youself	CD5	U.K.	1989	$14.00
Sire	PRO-CD-3541	Express Youself	CDJ	U.S.	1989	$12.00
Sire	7599-21577-2	Hanky Panky	CD5	Germany	1990	$14.00
Sire	WPDP-6235	Hanky Panky	CD3	Japan	1990	$18.00/$4.00
Sire	W-9789CD	Hanky Panky	CD5	U.K.	1990	$14.00
Sire	9 21577-2	Hanky Panky	CD5	U.S.	1990	$5.00
Sire	PRO-CD-4304	Hanky Panky	CDJ	U.S.	1990	$6.00
Sire	7599-21140	Holiday	CD3	Germany	1989	$12.00
Sire		Holiday	CDJ	Germany	1989	$25.00
Sire	7599-21140	Holiday	CD3	U.K.	1989	$12.00
Warner Brothers		Human Nature	CDJ	U.K.	1995	$20.00
Warner Brothers	17882-2	Human Nature	CD5	U.S.	1995	$6.00
Warner Brothers	PRO-CD-7719-R	Human Nature	CDJ	U.S.	1995	$13.00
7 track.						
Warner Brothers		Human Nature	CDJ	U.S.	1995	$14.00
3 track.						
Warner Brothers		Human Nature	CDJ	U.S.	1995	$14.00
4 track.						
Sire	18247-2	I'll Remember	CD5	U.S.	1994	$6.00
Sire		I'll Remember	CD5	Australia	1994	$14.00
Sire		I'll Remember	CD5	U.K.	1994	$14.00
Maverick	PRO-CD-6735	I'll Remember	CDJ	U.S.	1993	$6.00
Warner Brothers	18247	I'll Remember	CD5	U.S.	1994	$5.00
Warner Brothers	41355	I'll Remember	CD5	U.S.	1994	$5.00
		In the Beginning	CD5	France		$25.00
Sire	7599-21141-2	Into the Groove	CD5	Germany	1989	$12.00
Sire	7599-21141-2	Into the Groove	CD5	U.K.	1989	$12.00
Sire	9 21878-2	Into the Groove	CD5	U.S.	1992	$5.00
Sire	CD-21820	Justify My Love	CD5	Canada	1990	$14.00
Warner	12-15988	Justify My Love	CD5	Canada	1994	$6.00
Sire	7599-21851-2	Justify My Love	CD5	Germany	1990	$14.00
Sire	7599-21825-2	Justify My Love	CD5	Germany	1990	$14.00
Sire	WPDP-6261	Justify My Love	CD3	Japan	1990	$18.00/$4.00
Sire	W-9000CD	Justify My Love	CD5	U.K.	1990	$14.00
Sire	9 21820-2	Justify My Love	CD5	U.S.	1990	$5.00
Sire	PRO-CD-4582	Justify My Love	CDJ	U.S.	1990	$7.00
Sire	PRO-CD-4613	Justify My Love	CDJ	U.S.	1990	$7.00
Sire	PRO-CD-3791	Keep It Together	CDJ	U.S.	1989	$14.00
Sire	9 21427-2	Keep It Together	CD5	U.S.	1990	$6.00
Warner	WPDR-3027	La Isa Bonita	CD3	Japan	1995	$17.00/$5.00
Sire	9211191-2	Like a Prayer	CD3	Germany	1989	$14.00
Sire	10P3-6112	Like a Prayer	CD3	Japan	1989	$18.00/$4.00
Sire	20P2-2900	Like a Prayer	CD5	Japan	1989	$25.00
Sire	W-7539CD	Like a Prayer	CD3	U.K.	1989	$14.00
Sire	PRO-CD-3448	Like a Prayer	CDJ	U.S.	1989	$14.00
Sire	WPCP 3437	Like a Virgin	CD5	Japan	1989	$15.00
Warner Brothers	PRO-CD-7934-R	Love Don't Live Here Anymore	CDJ	U.S.	1995	$14.00
Warner Brothers		Love Don't Live Here Anymore	CDJ	U.S.	1995	$14.00
Second version.						
Sire	7599 21139	Lucky Star	CD5	Germany	1989	$14.00
Sire	7599-21139-2	Lucky Star	CD5	U.K.	1989	$14.00
Sire	WPCP-5063	Material Girl	CD5	Japan	1992	$15.00
Sire	09P3-6206	Oh Father	CD3	Japan	1989	$18.00/$4.00
Sire	PRO-CD-3798	Oh Father	CDJ	U.S.	1989	$6.00
Sire	25681-2	Papa Don't Preach	CDV	U.K.	1988	$25.00
Warner Brothers	9 25681-2	Papa Don't Preach	CDV/BP	U.S.	1988	$30.00/$25.00
Sire	PRO CDV 2903	Papa Don't Preach	DJ/CDV	U.S.	1988	$35.00
Sire/Q Sound	MADONNA (V)	Q Sound Experience, The	CDJ	U.S.	1990	$20.00
No Sleeve.						
Sire/Q Sound	MADONNA (V)	Q Sound Experience, The	CDJ	U.S.	1990	$20.00
With sleeve.						
Maverick	18505-2	Rain	CD5	U.S.	1993	$6.00
Maverick	PRO-CD-6182	Rain	CDJ	U.S.	1993	$7.00
Sire	CD-21813	Rescue Me	CD5	Canada	1991	$14.00
Sire	9362 40034-2	Rescue Me	CD5	Germany	1991	$12.00
Sire	9362 40035-2	Rescue Me	CD5	Germany	1991	$12.00
Sire	W-0024CD	Rescue Me	CD5	U.K.	1991	$12.00
Sire	PRO-CD-4577	Rescue Me	CDJ	U.S.	1990	$7.00

Label	Catalog Number	Title	Type	Country	Year	Longbox Value / Value
Sire	PRO-CD-4710	Rescue Me	CDJ	U.S.	1990	$7.00
Sire		Secret	CD5	Australia	1994	$14.00
Sire	CD41772	Secret	CD5	Canada	1994	$8.00
		Secret	CD5	U.K.		$14.00
		Secret	CD5	U.K.		$14.00

Second version.

Label	Catalog Number	Title	Type	Country	Year	Longbox Value / Value
Warner Brothers	41772	Secret	CD5	U.S.	1994	$5.00
Warner Brothers	18035	Secret	CD5	U.S.	1994	$6.00
Sire	PRO-CD-7199	Secret	CDJ	U.S.	1994	$6.00
Sire	10SW-21	Spotlight	CD3	Japan	1988	$18.00/$4.00
		Take a Bow	CD5	U.K.		$14.00
		Take a Bow	CD5	U.K.		$14.00

Second version.

Label	Catalog Number	Title	Type	Country	Year	Longbox Value / Value
Warner Brothers	18000	Take a Bow	CD5	U.S.	1994	$5.00
Warner Brothers	41887	Take a Bow	CD5	U.S.	1994	$5.00
Sire	PRO-CD-7360-R	Take a Bow	CDJ	U.S.	1994	$6.00
Warner Brothers		Take a Bow	CDJ	U.S.	1995	$8.00
Warner	WPCR-191	Take a Bow Remixes	CD5	Japan	1995	$18.00
Warner	12-15987	This Used to be My Playground	CD5	Canada	1994	$6.00
Sire	WPDP-6304	This Used to be My Playground	CD3	Japan	1992	$17.00/$4.00
Sire	W-0122CD	This Used to be My Playground	CD5	U.K.	1992	$14.00
Sire	PRO-CD-5588	This Used to be My Playground	CDJ	U.S.	1992	$8.00
Warner	12-15989	Vogue	CD5	Canada	1994	$6.00
Sire	759 921525	Vogue	CD5	Germany	1990	$14.00
Sire	WPDP-6227	Vogue	CD3	Japan	1990	$12.00/$4.00
Sire	W-9851CD	Vogue	CD5	U.K.	1990	$14.00
Sire	9 21513-2-2	Vogue	CD5	U.S.	1990	$5.00
Sire	9 21513-2-2	Vogue	CD5	U.S.	1990	$5.00

1st pressing in plastic box.

Label	Catalog Number	Title	Type	Country	Year	Longbox Value / Value
Receiver	3006	Wild Dancing	CD5	France	1993	$14.00
Sire	9 25535-2	You Can Dance	CD5	U.S.	1987	$5.00
Warner		You'll See	CDJ	Japan	1995	$40.00
Sire	PRO-CD-7900-R	You'll See	CDJ	U.S.	1995	$6.00
Sire	PRO-CD-8040	You'll See	CDJ	U.S.	1995	$8.00

Maestro

Singles

Label	Catalog Number	Title	Type	Country	Year	Longbox Value / Value
Explicit Records	2	Push	CD5	U.S.	1994	$5.00

Maestro Fresh Wes

Singles

Label	Catalog Number	Title	Type	Country	Year	Longbox Value / Value
Polydor	CDP 649	Another Funky Break	CDJ	U.S.	1992	$2.00
		Drop the Needle	CDJ	U.S.		$2.00
Cypress	DPRO-79064	Louie Rap	CDJ	U.S.	1990	$2.00

Magazine

Full Length

Label	Catalog Number	Title	Type	Country	Year	Longbox Value / Value
		After the Fact	LP/LB	U.S.		$14.00/$8.00

Maggie's Dream

Full Length

Label	Catalog Number	Title	Type	Country	Year	Longbox Value / Value
Capitol	CDP 7 93949 2	Maggie's Dream	DJ/LP	U.S.	1990	$15.00

Special box wih CD and cassette.

Singles

Label	Catalog Number	Title	Type	Country	Year	Longbox Value / Value
Capitol	DPRO-79818	Change For the Better	CDJ	U.S.	1991	$2.00
Capitol	DPRO-79817	Dream Simone	CDJ	U.S.	1991	$2.00
EMI	204214-2	Love & Tears	CD5	Germany	1991	$8.00
Capitol	DPRO-79327	Love & Tears	CDJ	U.S.	1990	$2.00

Maggie's Farm

Singles

Label	Catalog Number	Title	Type	Country	Year	Longbox Value / Value
JRS	807	Glory Road	CDJ	U.S.	1991	$3.00

Magic Affair

Singles

Label	Catalog Number	Title	Type	Country	Year	Longbox Value / Value
Electrola	7243 8 81303 2 5	Give Me All Your Love	CD5	Germany	1994	$15.00

Magic Muscle

Singles

Label	Catalog Number	Title	Type	Country	Year	Longbox Value / Value
Warner Brothers	W-0017CD	Gulp	CD5	U.K.	1991	$8.00

Magma

Singles

Label	Catalog Number	Title	Type	Country	Year	Longbox Value / Value
Seventh	REX VIII	Kohntarkoez	CD5	France	1988	$10.00
Tomato	2696082	Usu Wudu	CD5	Germany	1989	$10.00

Magna Carta

Singles

Label	Catalog Number	Title	Type	Country	Year	Longbox Value / Value
EMI	204165-2	Hymn	CD5	Germany	1990	$8.00
EMI	204225-2	Hymn	CD5	Germany	1990	$8.00

Magnapop

Singles

Label	Catalog Number	Title	Type	Country	Year	Longbox Value / Value
	DPRO 30054	Open the Door	CDJ	U.S.		$2.00
Play It	013	Sugarland	CD5	Germany	1992	$8.00

Magness, Cliff

Singles

Label	Catalog Number	Title	Type	Country	Year	Longbox Value / Value
Warner	PCD-0580	Footprints in the Rain	CDJ	Japan	1995	$20.00

Magnificant Bastards

Singles

Label	Catalog Number	Title	Type	Country	Year	Longbox Value / Value
	PRCD-9216-2	Mockingbird Girl	CDJ	U.S.		$2.00

Magnolias

Singles

Label	Catalog Number	Title	Type	Country	Year	Longbox Value / Value
Alias	A-031D	Hung Up On	CD5	U.K.	1992	$4.00
Alias	31	Hung Up On	CD5	U.S.	1992	$4.00

Magnum

Singles

Label	Catalog Number	Title	Type	Country	Year	Longbox Value / Value
Polydor	887311-2	Days Of No Trust	CD5	Germany	1988	$9.00
Polydor	POCD-910	Days Of No Trust	CD5	U.K.	1988	$9.00
		Days Of No Trust	CDJ	U.S.	1988	$2.00
Polydor	PZCD-94	Heartbroke And Busted	CD5	U.K.	1990	$9.00
Polydor	887666-2	It Must Have Been Love	CD5	Germany	1988	$9.00
Polydor	POCD-930	It Must Have Been Love	CD5	U.K.	1988	$9.00
Castle	CD3-7	Lights Burned Out	CD3	U.K.	1988	$9.00
Music For Nations	CDKUT-148	Only In America	CD5	U.K.	1992	$9.00
Polygram	877455-2	Rockin' Chair	CD5	Germany	1990	$9.00
Polydor	PZCDG-88	Rockin' Chair	CD5	U.K.	1990	$9.00
Polydor	887525-2	Start Talking Love	CD5	Germany	1988	$9.00
Polydor	POCD-920	Start Talking Love	CD5	U.K.	1988	$9.00

Magoo, Polly

Singles

Label	Catalog Number	Title	Type	Country	Year	Longbox Value / Value
BMG	CDTMRC-2	Kiss You Now	CD5	U.K.	1991	$8.00

Maguire, Sean

Singles

Label	Catalog Number	Title	Type	Country	Year	Longbox Value / Value
		You To Me Are Everything	CD5	U.K.		$10.00
		You To Me Are Everything	CD5	U.K.		$10.00

Second version.

Mahall, Taj

Singles

Label	Catalog Number	Title	Type	Country	Year	Longbox Value / Value
Private	81000	Don't Call Us	CDJ	U.S.	1991	$2.00
Private	2086	Love Up	CDJ	U.S.	1991	$7.00

MaHarry, Wendy

Full Length

Label	Catalog Number	Title	Type	Country	Year	Longbox Value / Value
A&M	5370	Fountain Of Youth	LP/BP	U.S.		$12.00/$7.00

Singles

Label	Catalog Number	Title	Type	Country	Year	Longbox Value / Value
A&M	AMCD-575	All That I've Got	CD5	U.K.	1990	$8.00
A&M	CD 17990	All That I've Got	CDJ	U.S.	1990	$2.00
A&M	75021 8103-2	California	CDJ	U.S.	1990	$2.00
A&M	75021 7335-2	How Do I Get Over You	CDJ	U.S.	1991	$2.00

Maher, Ashley

Singles

Label	Catalog Number	Title	Type	Country	Year	Longbox Value / Value
Virgin	VSCDT-1321	Dreaming, Re-Dreaming	CD5	U.K.	1990	$8.00
Virgin	VSCDT-1385	Laughter in the Rain	CD5	U.K.	1992	$8.00
Virgin	VSCDT-1287	So Many Time	CD5	U.K.	1990	$8.00
Virgin	VJDP-124	Step by Step	CD3	Japan	1990	$12.00/$3.00
Virgin	VSCDT-1409	Stumbling Block	CD5	U.K.	1992	$8.00

Mahogany Blue

Singles

Label	Catalog Number	Title	Type	Country	Year	Longbox Value / Value
MCA	MCA5P-2673	Affair	CDJ	U.S.	1993	$2.00

Main Attraction

Singles

Label	Catalog Number	Title	Type	Country	Year	Longbox Value / Value
Satin	1303	I Love You Baby	CD5	U.S.	1992	$2.00
	1303	Sweet Harmony	CD5	U.S.	1994	$5.00

Main Ingredient

Singles

Label	Catalog Number	Title	Type	Country	Year	Longbox Value / Value
Polydor	CDP 190	Nothings Too Good For My Baby	CDJ	U.S.	1990	$2.00

Main Thing

Singles

Label	Catalog Number	Title	Type	Country	Year	Longbox Value / Value
Island	CID-503	My Lover's Keeper	CD5	U.K.	1991	$8.00

Maisonettes

Singles

Label	Catalog Number	Title	Type	Country	Year	Longbox Value / Value
Sound	CD-3000	Heartache Avenue	CD5	Germany	1988	$8.00

Makers

Singles

Label	Catalog Number	Title	Type	Country	Year	Longbox Value / Value
Estrus Records	104	Devil's Nine Question	CD5	U.S.	1994	$5.00

Makin' Spiritual Moves

Full Length

Label	Catalog Number	Title	Type	Country	Year	Longbox Value / Value
		Sampler	DJ/Smplr	U.S.		$6.00

Makowicz, Adam

Full Length

Label	Catalog Number	Title	Type	Country	Year	Longbox Value / Value
Sheffield Lab	CD-21	The Name Is Makowicz	LP/LB	U.S.†	1985	$14.00/$8.00

Malaika

Full Length

Label	Catalog Number	Title	Type	Country	Year	Longbox Value / Value
A&M	31458 8166	Introducing	DJ/Smplr	U.S.	1993	$10.00

Singles

Label	Catalog Number	Title	Type	Country	Year	Longbox Value / Value
A&M	31458 8131	Gotta Know	CDJ	U.S.	1993	$2.00

Malhavoc

Full Length

Label	Catalog Number	Title	Type	Country	Year	Longbox Value / Value
Warner Brothers	45098	Premeditated Murder	LP/LB	U.S.		$12.00/$7.00

Malibu

Singles

Label	Catalog Number	Title	Type	Country	Year	Longbox Value / Value
		I Want Candy	CDJ	U.S.		$2.00

Malloy, Mitch

Singles

Label	Catalog Number	Title	Type	Country	Year	Longbox Value / Value
RCA	62197-2-RDJ	Anything At All	CDJ	U.S.	1991	$2.00

Malmsteen, Yngwie

Full Length

Label	Catalog Number	Title	Type	Country	Year	Longbox Value / Value
Elektra		Fire & Ice	LP/LB	U.S.		$14.00/$8.00
Polygram	CDP 126	Live in Lenningrad	DJ/Smplr	U.S.	1989	$8.00
Polygram	825733-2	Marching Out	LP/BP	U.S.†	1985	$12.00/$7.00
Polygram	SACD 178	On Guitar	DJ/Smplr	U.S.	1990	$45.00

Custum guitar shaped package.

Label	Catalog Number	Title	Type	Country	Year	Longbox Value / Value
Polygram	825324-2	Rising Force	LP/BP	U.S.†	1985	$12.00/$7.00
		Seventh Sign	LTD/LP	Japan		$30.00

CD and jewel box in slipcase.

Singles

Label	Catalog Number	Title	Type	Country	Year	Longbox Value / Value
Polydor	CDP 284	Bedroom Eyes	CDJ	U.S.	1990	$2.00
Elektra	PRCD 8570-2	Dragon Fly	CDJ	U.S.	1992	$2.00
Polydor	YJMCD-1	Heaven Tonight	CD5	U.K.	1988	$10.00
Polygram	870 731-2	Heaven Tonight	CDV/BP	U.S.	1987	$20.00/$20.00
Polydor	422 870 731-2	Heaven Tonight	CDV	U.S.	1988	$15.00
Polydor	PZCD-79	Making Love	CD5	U.K.	1990	$10.00
Polydor	CDP 238	Making Love	CDJ	U.S.	1990	$2.00
Elektra	WMD5-4104	No Mercy	CD3	Japan	1992	$12.00/$4.00
IMS	877599-2	Save Our Love	CD5	Germany	1990	$10.00
Elektra	WMD5-4092	Teaser	CD3	Japan	1992	$12.00/$4.00
Elektra	PRCD 8514-2	Teaser	CDJ	U.S.	1992	$2.00

Malone, Debbie

Singles

Label	Catalog Number	Title	Type	Country	Year	Longbox Value / Value
Pulse 8	CDLOSE-22	Rescue Me	CD5	U.K.	1992	$8.00

Malone, Michelle

Full Length

Label	Catalog Number	Title	Type	Country	Year	Longbox Value / Value
Arista	ASCD-2155	Live Building Fires Over Atlanta	DJ/Smplr	U.S.	1991	$18.00

Singles

Label	Catalog Number	Title	Type	Country	Year	Longbox Value / Value
Arista	ASCD-2043	Big Black Bag	CDJ	U.S.	1990	$2.00
Arista	ASCD-2155	Live Building Over Atlanta	CDJ	U.S.	1991	$2.00

Maloo

Singles

Label	Catalog Number	Title	Type	Country	Year	Longbox Value / Value
Polygram	875509-2	Lovegrow	CD5	Germany	1990	$8.00

Malteze

Singles

Label	Catalog Number	Title	Type	Country	Year	Longbox Value / Value
IRS	977 112	Fountainhead	CD5	Germany	1992	$8.00

Mama's Boys

Singles

Label	Catalog Number	Title	Type	Country	Year	Longbox Value / Value
Jive	MBOYCD-1	Higher Ground	CD5	U.K.	1988	$8.00

Mamas And The Papas

Full Length

Label	Catalog Number	Title	Type	Country	Year	Longbox Value / Value
MCA		Mamas & The Papas	LP/LB	U.S.		$14.00/$8.00

Singles

Label	Catalog Number	Title	Type	Country	Year	Longbox Value / Value
Old Gold	OG-6142	California Dreamin'	CD3	U.K.	1989	$10.00
BMG	MCD-18556	Dream a Little Dream	CD5	Germany	1992	$10.00

Mammoth

Singles

Label	Catalog Number	Title	Type	Country	Year	Longbox Value / Value
Jive	MOTHCD-4	All the Days	CD5	U.K.	1989	$8.00
Jive	MOTHCD-3	Can't Take the Hurt	CD5	U.K.	1989	$8.00
Jive	MOTHCD-1	Fatman	CD5	U.K.	1988	$8.00

Man Called Adam

Singles

Label	Catalog Number	Title	Type	Country	Year	Longbox Value / Value
Big Life	877839-2	Barefoot in the Head	CD5	Germany	1990	$8.00
Big Life	BLR-28CD	Barefoot in the Head	CD5	U.K.	1990	$8.00
Big Life	BLR-59CD	Chrono Psionic Interface	CD5	U.K.	1991	$8.00
Big Life	879633-2	I Want to Know	CD5	Germany	1991	$8.00
Big Life	BLR-38CD	I Want to Know	CD5	U.K.	1991	$8.00

Man Go Fish

Singles

Label	Catalog Number	Title	Type	Country	Year	Longbox Value / Value
Polygram	877269-2	Day by Day	CD5	Germany	1990	$8.00
Polygram	[illegible]	I Do Believe	CD5	Germany	1991	$8.00
Polygram	873461-2	Sentimental Me	CD5	Germany	1990	$8.00

Manchester, Melissa

Full Length

Label	Catalog Number	Title	Type	Country	Year	Longbox Value / Value
Arista	ARCD-8004	Greatest Hits	LP/LB	U.S.†	1984	$14.00/$8.00
Pioneer	PA-82-015	Music of Melissa Manchester	LD	U.S.	1982	$30.00

Singles

Label	Catalog Number	Title	Type	Country	Year	Longbox Value / Value
Arista	CD3-301	Midnight Blue	CD3	U.S.	1989	$6.00/$3.00
Polydor	CDP 130	Walk on By	CDJ	U.S.		$2.00

Manchild

Singles

Label	Catalog Number	Title	Type	Country	Year	Longbox Value / Value
EMI	203798-2	Hypnotized	CD5	Germany	1990	$8.00

Mancini, Henry

Full Length

Label	Catalog Number	Title	Type	Country	Year	Longbox Value / Value
Time Warner Sound Exchange		On the March	LP	U.S.	1995	$16.00
RCA	PCD1-3667	Pure Gold	LP/LB	U.S.†	1984	$14.00/$8.00

Singles

Label	Catalog Number	Title	Type	Country	Year	Longbox Value / Value
RCA	60577-2-RV	Mancini's Monster Hits	CD5	U.S.	1990	$15.00

Glow-in-the-dark CD.

Mandel, Howie

Full Length

Label	Catalog Number	Title	Type	Country	Year	Longbox Value / Value
Paramount	LV12546	Watusi Tour	LD	U.S.	1987	$25.00

Mandera, Freddy

Singles

Label	Catalog Number	Title	Type	Country	Year	Longbox Value / Value
Bellaphon	130-15-001	Mambo	CD5	Germany	1988	$8.00

Mandrell, Barbara

Full Length

Label	Catalog Number	Title	Type	Country	Year	Longbox Value / Value
Warner Sound Exchange		22 Legendary Hits	LTD/LP	U.S.	1995	$17.00

Singles

Label	Catalog Number	Title	Type	Country	Year	Longbox Value / Value
Capitol	DPRO-79475	I'll Leave Something Good Behind	CDJ	U.S.	1990	$2.00

Mandrell, Louise

Full Length

Label	Catalog Number	Title	Type	Country	Year	Longbox Value / Value
RCA	PCD1-5454	Maybe My Baby	LP/BP	U.S.†	1985	$14.00/$8.00
RCA	PCD1-4820	Too Hot Too Sleep	LP/BP	U.S.†	1984	$14.00/$8.00

Mangione, Chuck

Full Length

Label	Catalog Number	Title	Type	Country	Year	Longbox Value / Value
CBS	CK-39479	Disquise	LP/LB	U.S.†	1985	$14.00/$8.00
CBS	CK-38686	Journey to a Rainbow	LP/LB	U.S.†	1985	$14.00/$8.00
Mercury	822539-2	Land of Make Believe	LP/LB	U.S.†	1985	$14.00/$8.00
		Live at the Village Gate	DJ/Smplr	U.S.	1989	$20.00

Singles

Label	Catalog Number	Title	Type	Country	Year	Longbox Value / Value
A&M	S12Y-3037	Feels So Good	CD3	Japan	1988	$12.00/$4.00

Mango Grove

Singles

Label	Catalog Number	Title	Type	Country	Year	Longbox Value / Value
Sony	CSDS-8132	Dance Some More	CD3	Japan	1990	$12.00/$3.00

Manhattan

Singles

Label	Catalog Number	Title	Type	Country	Year	Longbox Value / Value
A&M	CD 17705	Little Calcutta	CDJ	U.S.	1989	$2.00

Manhattan Transfer

Full Length

Label	Catalog Number	Title	Type	Country	Year	Longbox Value / Value
Atlantic	19319-2	Best Of	LP/LB	U.S.†	1984	$14.00/$8.00
Atlantic	80104-2	Bodies & Soul	LP/LB	U.S.†	1984	$14.00/$8.00
Atlantic	90104-2	Bop Doo-Wopp	LP/LB	U.S.†	1985	$14.00/$8.00
Pioneer Artists	PA-83-029	In Concert	LD	U.S.	1983	$25.00
Pioneer Artists	PA-87-020	Live 86	LD	U.S.	1987	$35.00
Atlantic	81266-2	Vocalese	LP/LB	U.S.†	1985	$14.00/$8.00
		World Music	RS	U.S.	1995	$335.00

2 CD set. Airdate: 5/25/95.

Singles

Label	Catalog Number	Title	Type	Country	Year	Longbox Value / Value
Columbia	CSK 4239	A World Apart	CDJ	U.S.	1991	$3.00
Columbia	657321-2	Offbeat of Avenues, The	CD5	Germany	1991	$10.00
Columbia	CSK 4129	Offbeat of Avenues, The	CDJ	U.S.	1991	$7.00

Manhattans

Singles

Label	Catalog Number	Title	Type	Country	Year	Longbox Value / Value
		Why You Wanna Love Me Like That?	CDJ	U.S.		$2.00

Maniac

Singles

Label	Catalog Number	Title	Type	Country	Year	Longbox Value / Value
Motown	860265	2 Deep 2 Deep	CD5	U.S.	1994	$5.00

Manic MC's

Singles

Label	Catalog Number	Title	Type	Country	Year	Longbox Value / Value
MCA	DMCAT-1429	Beat	CD5	U.K.	1990	$8.00
RCA	PD-43038	Mental	CD5	Germany	1989	$8.00

Manic Street Preachers

Singles

Label	Catalog Number	Title	Type	Country	Year	Longbox Value / Value
Epic	ESCA-5773	From Despair to Where	CD3	Japan	1993	$12.00/$3.00
Epic	ESCA-5588	Little Baby Nothing	CD3	Japan	1992	$12.00/$3.00
		Little Baby Nothing	CD5	U.K.		$10.00
		Little Baby Nothing	CD5	U.K.		$10.00

Second version.

Label	Catalog Number	Title	Type	Country	Year	Longbox Value / Value
Columbia	657582-2	Love's Sweet Exile	CD5	Germany	1991	$8.00
Epic	ESCA-5006	Motorcycle Emptiness	CD3	Japan	1992	$12.00/$3.00
Heavenly	HVN-8CD	Motown Junk	CD5	U.K.	1991	$8.00
Damgd Gd	YUBB-4CD	New Art Riot	CD5	U.K.	1992	$8.00
		Revol	CD5	U.K.		$10.00
		Revol	CD5	U.K.		$10.00

Second version.

Label	Catalog Number	Title	Type	Country	Year	Longbox Value / Value
Columbia	CSK 5319	Scream To A Sigh	CDJ	U.S.	1993	$2.00
		She Is Suffering	CD5	U.K.		$10.00
		She Is Suffering	CD5	U.K.		$10.00

Second version.

Label	Catalog Number	Title	Type	Country	Year	Longbox Value / Value
Columbia	657873-2	Slash 'n Burn	CD5	U.K.	1992	$10.00
Columbia	CSK 4506	Slash 'n Burn	CDJ	U.S.	1992	$2.00
Epic	ESCA-5468	Stay Beautiful	CD3	Japan	1992	$12.00/$3.00
Columbia	657337-2	Stay Beautiful	CD5	U.K.	1991	$8.00
Columbia	658382-2	Theme From M.A.S.H.	CD5	Germany	1992	$8.00
Epic	ESCA-5668	Theme From M.A.S.H.	CD5	Japan	1992	$12.00
Epic	ESCA-5580	You Love Us	CD5	Japan	1992	$12.00
Heavenly	HVN-10CD	You Love Us	CD5	U.K.	1991	$8.00

Manifesto

Singles

Label	Catalog Number	Title	Type	Country	Year	Longbox Value / Value
[illegible]	PROB [illegible]	Pattern 26	CDJ	U.S.	1993	$2.00
Rough Trade	585 2050 3	Walking Backwards	CD5	Germany	1992	$8.00

Manilow, Barry

Full Length

Label	Catalog Number	Title	Type	Country	Year	Longbox Value / Value
MGM/UA	ML100148	1st Special	LD	U.S.	1983	$26.00
Arista	ARCD-8254	2:00AM-Paradise Cafe	LP/LB	U.S.†	1984	$14.00/$8.00
Pioneer Artists	PA-84-065	At Greek Theatre	LD	U.S.	1984	$25.00
Pioneer Artists	PA-84-065	At Greek Theatre	LD	U.S.	1990	$40.00
Pioneer Artists	PA-87-181	Barry Manilow	LD	U.S.	1987	$35.00
Arista	ASCD-2092	Christmas Sampler	DJ/Smplr	U.S.	1990	$8.00
Arista	ARCD-8230	Even Now	LP/LB	U.S.†	1984	$14.00/$8.00
Arista	ASCD-2496	Excerpts From the Complete Collection	DJ/Smplr	U.S.	1992	$12.00
Arista	ARCD-8139	Greatest Hits Vol. 1	LP/LB	U.S.†	1985	$14.00/$8.00
Arista	ARCD-8102	Greatest Hits Vol. 2	LP/LB	U.S.†	1984	$14.00/$8.00
RCA	PCD1-7044	In Search of Love	LP/BP	U.S.†	1985	$14.00/$8.00
	LVD-509	Live in Japan	LD	Japan		$70.00
Pioneer Artists	PA-90-022	On Broadway	LD	U.S.	1990	$35.00
Arista	ARCD-8070	Tryin' to Get the Feelin'	LP/LB	U.S.†	1985	$14.00/$8.00

Singles

Label	Catalog Number	Title	Type	Country	Year	Longbox Value / Value
Arista	ASCD-2473	Another Life	CDJ	U.S.	1992	$3.00
Arista	162186	Don't Be Scared	CD3	Germany	1989	$10.00
Arista	662186	Don't Be Scared	CD5	Germany	1989	$10.00
Arista	A10D-120	Don't Be Scared	CD3	Japan	1989	$13.00/$4.00
Arista	662186	Don't Be Scared	CD5	U.K.	1989	$10.00
Arista	A10D-143	Eolia	CD3	Japan	1989	$13.00/$4.00
Arista		Hey Mambo	CDJ	U.S.		$2.00
Arista	663025	If I Can Dream	CD5	U.K.	1990	$10.00
Arista	BVDA-12	Jingle Bells	CD3	Japan	1990	$13.00/$4.00
Arista	665018	Jingle Bells	CD5	U.K.	1990	$10.00
EMI	CDEM336	Let Me Be Your Wings	CD5	U.K.	1994	$10.00
EMI		Let Me Be Your Wings	CD5	U.K.	1994	$10.00
Arista	162051	Mandy	CD3	Germany	1989	$10.00
Arista	162051	Mandy	CD3	U.K.	1989	$10.00
Arista	662652	One That Got Away	CD5	U.K.	1989	$10.00
Arista	663202	Some Good Things Never Last	CD5	U.K.	1990	$10.00
Arista	661938	Swing Step Swing Street	CD5	U.K.	1988	$10.00

Manitoba's Wild Kingdom

Singles

Label	Catalog Number	Title	Type	Country	Year	Longbox Value / Value
MCA	CD45 18180	Fired Up	CDJ	U.S.	1990	$2.00
MCA	CD45 18454	Hair Cut And Attitude	CDJ	U.S.	1990	$2.00
MCA	CD45 18518	New York, New York	CDJ	U.S.	1990	$2.00
MCA	CD45 18347	Party Starts Now, The	CDJ	U.S.	1990	$2.00

Manix

Full Length

Label	Catalog Number	Title	Type	Country	Year	Longbox Value / Value
SPV	1316-3	Oblivion	LP	Germany	1992	$8.00
Reinforced	RIVET-1212CD	Oblivion	LP	U.K.	1992	$8.00
Reinforced	RIVET-1221CD	Rainbow People	LP	U.K.	1992	$8.00

Mann

Singles

Label	Catalog Number	Title	Type	Country	Year	Longbox Value / Value
A&M	AMCD-771	Riders on the Storm	CD5	U.K.	1991	$8.00

Mann, Aimee

Full Length

Label	Catalog Number	Title	Type	Country	Year	Longbox Value / Value
DGC		I'm With Stupid	DJ/Smplr	U.S.		$10.00
Imago		Whatever	DJ/LP	U.S.	1994	$12.00

Advance Issue.

Singles

Label	Catalog Number	Title	Type	Country	Year	Longbox Value / Value
	PRCD 4845	Choice In the Matter	CDJ	U.S.		$2.00
DGC	PRO-CD-4845	Choice In the Matter	CDJ	U.S.		$3.00
Imago		Fourth Of July	CDJ	U.K.	1994	$15.00
		I Should've Known	CD5	U.K.		$10.00
		I Should've Known	CD5	U.K.		$10.00

Second version.

Label	Catalog Number	Title	Type	Country	Year	Longbox Value / Value
Imago	72787-25060	I Should've Known	CD5	U.K.	1993	$10.00
Imago	72787-25032	I Should've Known	CD5	U.S.	1993	$6.00
		Long Shot	CDJ	U.K.		$14.00
		Stupid Thing	CD5	U.K.		$10.00
		Stupid Thing	CD5	U.K.		$10.00

Second version.

Label	Catalog Number	Title	Type	Country	Year	Longbox Value / Value
Imago	72787-25052	Stupid Thing	CD5	U.K.	1993	$10.00
Imago	72787-25053	Stupid Thing	CD5	U.K.	1993	$10.00
Imago	72787-25053	Stupid Thing	CD5	U.S.	1993	$5.00
Imago		That's Just What You	CD5	U.K.	1994	$10.00
Imago	25086	That's Just What You	CD5	U.S.	1994	$5.00
Imago	25086-2	That's Just What You	CD5	U.S.	1994	$6.00
Imago		Whatever	CDJ	U.K.	1994	$18.00
		You Could Make A Killing	CD5	Australia	1996	$12.00
		You Could Make A Killing	CD5	U.K.	1996	$10.00

Mann, Billy

Singles

Label	Catalog Number	Title	Type	Country	Year	Longbox Value / Value
	DVCDP00064	Turn Down the World	CDJ	U.S.		$2.00

Mann, Manfred (Earth Band)

Full Length

Label	Catalog Number	Title	Type	Country	Year	Longbox Value / Value
IRS	977 001	Davy's on the Road	LP	Germany	1991	$10.00

Singles

Label	Catalog Number	Title	Type	Country	Year	Longbox Value / Value
		Nothing Ever Happens	CD5	Germany	1996	$12.00

Manne, Shelly

Full Length

Label	Catalog Number	Title	Type	Country	Year	Longbox Value / Value
Mobile	MFCD-809	My Fair Lady	LP/LB	U.S.†	1985	$14.00/$8.00

Mannheim Steamroller - Christmas In the Aire (American Grammaphone AG-1995-2)
Rare two CD version of three Mannheim Steamroller Christmas albums. The first two albums were compressed onto a single disc.

Mannheim Steamroller

Full length

Label	Catalog Number	Title	Type	Country	Year	Longbox Value / Value
American Grammaphone	AG-1995-2	Christmas in the Air	DJ/LP	U.S.	1995	$20.00

2 CD set.

Label	Catalog Number	Title	Type	Country	Year	Longbox Value / Value
		World Music	RS	U.S.	1991	$335.00

2 CD set. Airdate: 12/2/91.

Singles

Label	Catalog Number	Title	Type	Country	Year	Longbox Value / Value
Am Gramm	AGCD7772	7 Colours of the Rainbow	CDJ	U.S.	1990	$2.00
Am Gramm	AGCD7773	Chakra	CDJ	U.S.	1990	$2.00

Mannsfield, Rodney

Singles

Label	Catalog Number	Title	Type	Country	Year	Longbox Value / Value
A&M	31458 8047	I Found Heaven	CDJ	U.S.	1993	$2.00
A&M	31458 8088	Wanna Make Luv 2 You	CDJ	U.S.	1993	$2.00

Mano Negra

Singles

Label	Catalog Number	Title	Type	Country	Year	Longbox Value / Value
Virgin	663030	King Kong Five	CD5	Germany	1990	$8.00
Virgin	VJCP-1408	King Kong Five	CD5	Japan	1990	$12.00
Virgin	VSCD-1239	King Kong Five	CD3	U.K.	1990	$8.00
Virgin	VSCDT-1239	King Kong Five	CD5	U.K.	1990	$8.00
Virgin	PRCD 3212	King Kong Five	CD5	U.S.	1990	$2.00
Virgin	VJCP-14033	King of Bongo	CD5	Japan	1991	$12.00
Virgin	DINSD-108	King of Bongo	CD5	U.K.	1991	$8.00
Virgin	PR 2468-2	Rock and Roll Band	CDJ	U.S.	1987	$2.00

Manowar

Full Length

Label	Catalog Number	Title	Type	Country	Year	Longbox Value / Value
Atlantic		Hail to England	LP/LB	U.S.		$12.00/$7.00
Atlantic	PRCD 4858-2	Kills	DJ/Smplr	U.S.	1992	$25.00

Singles

Label	Catalog Number	Title	Type	Country	Year	Longbox Value / Value
Atlantic	AMCY-534	Metal Warriors	CD5	Japan	1993	$16.00

Mansfield, Jayne

Full Length

Label	Catalog Number	Title	Type	Country	Year	Longbox Value / Value
		Too Hot to Handle	LTD/LP	U.S.	1994	$22.00

CD in digipak with "pop-up" cover.

Manson, Jono Band

Full Length

Label	Catalog Number	Title	Type	Country	Year	Longbox Value / Value
		Almost Home	DJ/LP	U.S.		$6.00

Singles

Label	Catalog Number	Title	Type	Country	Year	Longbox Value / Value
		Big Daddy Blue	CDJ	U.S.		$2.00

Mantana Blue

Singles

Label	Catalog Number	Title	Type	Country	Year	Longbox Value / Value
BMG	664062	Short Tempers	CD5	Germany	1991	$8.00

Mantera

Singles

Label	Catalog Number	Title	Type	Country	Year	Longbox Value / Value
ZTT	ZANG-34CD	Intensify	CD5	U.K.	1992	$8.00

Mantronix

Singles

Label	Catalog Number	Title	Type	Country	Year	Longbox Value / Value
Capitol	204234-2	Don't Go Messin'	CD5	Germany	1991	$8.00
Capitol	204258-2	Don't Go Messin'	CD5	Germany	1991	$8.00
Capitol	CDCL-608	Don't Go Messin'	CD5	U.K.	1991	$8.00
Capitol	DPRO-79697	Don't Go Messin'	CDJ	U.S.	1991	$2.00
Capitol	203654-2	Got to Have Your Love	CD5	Germany	1990	$8.00
Capitol	203857-2	Got to Have Your Love	CD5	Germany	1990	$8.00
Capitol	CDCL-559	Got to Have Your Love	CD5	U.K.	1990	$8.00
Capitol	DPRO-79946	Got to Have Your Love	CDJ	U.S.	1989	$2.00
Capitol	204365-2	Step to Me	CD5	Germany	1991	$8.00
Capitol	CDCL-513	Step to Me	CD5	U.K.	1991	$8.00
Capitol	DPRO-79499	Step to Me	CDJ	U.S.	1991	$2.00
Capitol	203909-2	Take Your Time	CD5	Germany	1990	$8.00
Capitol	203835-2	Take Your Time	CD5	Germany	1990	$8.00
Capitol	CDCL-573	Take Your Time	CD5	U.K.	1990	$8.00
Capitol	DPRO-79044	Take Your Time	CDJ	U.S.	1990	$2.00

Manuella

Singles

Label	Catalog Number	Title	Type	Country	Year	Longbox Value / Value
Canyon	PCDY-00012	Feel the Action	CD3	Japan	1989	$12.00/$3.00

Manufacture

Singles

Label	Catalog Number	Title	Type	Country	Year	Longbox Value / Value
Nettwerk	NET-029CD	Armed Response	CD5	U.K.	1991	$8.00
SPV	8232-8	Measured Response	CD5	Germany	1991	$8.00

Manyika, Zeke

Singles

Label	Catalog Number	Title	Type	Country	Year	Longbox Value / Value
Parlophone	CDR 6206	Runaway Freedom Train	CD5	U.K.	1989	$8.00

Manzanera & MacKay

Full Length

Label	Catalog Number	Title	Type	Country	Year	Longbox Value / Value
Relativity		Up in Smoke	LP/LB	U.S.		$14.00/$8.00

Manzanera, Phil

Full Length

Label	Catalog Number	Title	Type	Country	Year	Longbox Value / Value
		Southern Cross	DJ/LP	Japan		$25.00

Advance Issue.

Label	Catalog Number	Title	Type	Country	Year	Longbox Value / Value
RCA		Southern Cross	LP/LB	U.S.		$14.00/$8.00
Relativity		Up In Smoke	LP/LB	U.S.		$14.00/$8.00

Singles

Label	Catalog Number	Title	Type	Country	Year	Longbox Value / Value
Agenda	747772	A Million Reasons Why	CDJ	U.S.	1991	$2.00

Maranda, Andree

Singles

Label	Catalog Number	Title	Type	Country	Year	Longbox Value / Value
Polydor	10GD-5006	Itchin' in My Heart	CD3	Japan	1988	$12.00/$3.00

Marathon

Singles

Label	Catalog Number	Title	Type	Country	Year	Longbox Value / Value
Polygram	874385-2	Love Park	CD5	Germany	1989	$8.00
Virgin	TENCD-395	Movin'	CD5	U.K.	1992	$8.00
Polygram	872547-2	So Hard	CD5	Germany	1989	$8.00

Marc V

Singles

Label	Catalog Number	Title	Type	Country	Year	Longbox Value / Value
Elektra	PR 8053-2	Let Them Stare	CDJ	U.S.	1989	$2.00

March On

Singles

Label	Catalog Number	Title	Type	Country	Year	Longbox Value / Value
Reprise	PRO-CD-6421	Dream, The	CDJ	U.S.	1993	$2.00

Marchello

Full Length

Label	Catalog Number	Title	Type	Country	Year	Longbox Value / Value
		Happy Camper Summer Sampler	DJ/Smplr	U.S.		$3.00

Marcus, J.

Singles

Label	Catalog Number	Title	Type	Country	Year	Longbox Value / Value
A&M	390311-2	Liberation Day	CD5	Germany	1988	$8.00

Marcy Brothers

Singles

Label	Catalog Number	Title	Type	Country	Year	Longbox Value / Value
Warner Brothers	PRO-CD-3761	You're Not Even Crying	CDJ	U.S.	1989	$2.00

Mardones, Benny

Singles

Label	Catalog Number	Title	Type	Country	Year	Longbox Value / Value
		For a Little Ride	CDJ	U.S.	1989	$2.00
Curb	CD45 10554	I Never Really Loved You at All	CDJ	U.S.	1989	$2.00
		I'll Be Good to You	CDJ	U.S.	1989	$2.00
Polydor	PODP-40014	Into the Night	CD3	Japan	1989	$13.00/$4.00

Mareen, Mike

Singles

Label	Catalog Number	Title	Type	Country	Year	Longbox Value / Value
ZYX	6168-8	Dancing in the Dark	CD5	Germany	1989	$6.00
ZYX	5985-8	Lady Ecstasy	CD5	Germany	1989	$6.00
ZYX	6115-8	Right Into My Heart	CD5	Germany	1989	$6.00

Margitza, Rick

Singles

Label	Catalog Number	Title	Type	Country	Year	Longbox Value / Value
blue Note	DPRO-79485	Recess	CDJ	U.S.	1990	$7.00

Maria

Singles

Label	Catalog Number	Title	Type	Country	Year	Longbox Value / Value
Polygram	874302-3	Kiss the World	CD3	Germany	1989	$8.00
Polygram	874303-2	Kiss the World	CD5	Germany	1989	$8.00
Polygram	870437-2	Nitetime in the Heart of N.Y.	CD5	Germany	1988	$8.00
Polygram	870631-2	Nitetime in the Heart of N.Y.	CD5	Germany	1988	$8.00

Maria, Tania

Full Length

Label	Catalog Number	Title	Type	Country	Year	Longbox Value / Value
Concord Picante	CCD-4200	Come With Me	LP/LB	U.S.†	1985	$14.00/$8.00
Concord Picante	CCD-4264	The Real Tania Maria: Wild!	LP/LB	U.S.†	1985	$14.00/$8.00

Marie, Teena

Full Length

Label	Catalog Number	Title	Type	Country	Year	Longbox Value / Value
Epic	EK-39479	Starchild	LP/BP	U.S.†	1995	$12.00/$7.00

Singles

Label	Catalog Number	Title	Type	Country	Year	Longbox Value / Value
Epic	ESK 73494	Here's Looking at You	CDJ	U.S.	1990	$2.00
Epic	ESK 2236	If I Were a Bell	CDJ	U.S.	1990	$2.00
Epic	ESK 3049	Just Us Two	CDJ	U.S.	1991	$2.00
Epic	656429-2	Since Day One	CD5	U.K.	1990	$8.00
Epic	ESK 1133	Work It	CDJ	U.S.	1988	$2.00

Marienthal, Eric

Singles

Label	Catalog Number	Title	Type	Country	Year	Longbox Value / Value
GRP	5118	One Touch	CDJ	U.S.	1993	$6.00
GRP	5114	Walk Through the Fire	CDJ	U.S.	1993	$6.00

Marillion

Full Length

Label	Catalog Number	Title	Type	Country	Year	Longbox Value / Value
IRS		Brave	DJ/LP	U.S.	1994	$15.00
Capitol	CDP 46027	Fugazi	LP/LB	U.S.†	1985	$14.00/$8.00

Singles

Label	Catalog Number	Title	Type	Country	Year	Longbox Value / Value
EMI	CDEM-318	Alone Again in the Lap of Luxury	CD5	U.K.	1994	$10.00
EMI		Alone Again in the Lap of Luxury	CD5	U.K.	1994	$10.00

Second version.

Label	Catalog Number	Title	Type	Country	Year	Longbox Value / Value
EMI	CDEM-DJ-318	Alone Again in the Lap of Luxury	CDJ	U.K.	1994	$15.00
EMI		Beautiful	CDJ	Holland		$40.00
EMI		Beautiful	CDJ	U.K.	1994	$12.00
IRS		Cannibal Surf Babe	CDJ	U.S.	1994	$7.00
EMI	204348-2	Cover My Eyes	CD5	Germany	1991	$11.00
EMI	CDMARIL-13	Cover My Eyes	CD5	U.K.	1991	$11.00
IRS	67084	Cover My Eyes	CDJ	U.S.	1991	$6.00
EMI	204517-2	Dry land	CD5	Germany	1991	$11.00
EMI	CDMARIL-15	Dry Land	CD5	U.K.	1991	$11.00

Label	Catalog Number	Title	Type	Country	Year	Longbox Value / Value
EMI	203760-2	Easter	CD5	Germany	1990	$11.00
EMI	CDMARIL-12	Easter	CD5	U.K.	1990	$11.00
EMI	203088-2	Freaks	CD5	Germany	1989	$11.00
EMI	CDMARIL-9	Freaks	CD5	U.K.	1989	$11.00
EMI	CDEM-307	Hollow Man	CD5	U.K.		$10.00
EMI		Hollow Man	CD5	U.K.		$10.00
Second version.						
EMI	203495-3	Hooks in You	CD3	Germany	1989	$11.00
EMI	MARIL-9	Hooks in You	CD5	U.K.	1989	$11.00
EMI	MARIL-10	Hooks in You	CD5	U.K.	1989	$11.00
Capitol	DPRO-79752	Hooks in You	CDJ	U.S.	1989	$6.00
EMI	201816-2	Incommunicado	CD5	Germany	1988	$11.00
EMI	CDMARIL-6	Incommunicado	CD5	U.K.	1988	$11.00
EMI	204409-2	No One Can	CD5	Germany	1991	$11.00
EMI	CDMARIL-14	No One Can	CD5	U.K.	1991	$11.00
IRS	DPRO-67096	No One Can	CDJ	U.S.	1991	$6.00
EMI	CDMARIL-7	Sugar Mice	CD5	U.K	1987	$11.00
EMI	CDMARILS16	Sympathy	CD5	U.K.		$10.00
EMI		Sympathy	CD5	U.K.		$10.00
Second version.						
EMI	203582-3	Uninvited Guest, The	CD3	Germany	1989	$11.00
EMI	CDMARIL-11	Uninvited Guest, The	CD5	U.K.	1989	$11.00
EMI	CDMARIL-8	Uninvited Guest, The	CD5	U.K.	1989	$11.00
Capitol	DPRO-79922	Uninvited Guest, The	CDJ	U.S.	1989	$6.00

Marilyn Manson

Singles

Label	Catalog Number	Title	Type	Country	Year	Longbox Value / Value
Atlantic	PRCD 6517-2	Dope Hat	CDJ	U.S.	1994	$2.00
	95902-2	Get You Gunn	CD5	U.S.	1997	$6.00
Atlantic	95902	Get Your Gun	CD5	U.S.	1994	$5.00
Atlantic	PRCD 5781-2	Get Your Gun	CDJ	U.S.	1994	$2.00
	95806-2	Lunchbox	CD5	U.S.	1997	$6.00
Atlantic	PRCD 6643-2	Sweet Dreams	CDJ	U.S.	1995	$2.00

Marionettes

Singles

Label	Catalog Number	Title	Type	Country	Year	Longbox Value / Value
Efa	Z91004-5	Kisses	CD5	U.K.	1992	$8.00

Mark, Jon

Singles

Label	Catalog Number	Title	Type	Country	Year	Longbox Value / Value
Line	LICD-9 01132	Hot Night	CD5	Germany	1990	$8.00

Markie, Biz

Full Length

Label	Catalog Number	Title	Type	Country	Year	Longbox Value / Value
Warner Brothers	9 26003-2	Biz Never Sleeps	LP/LB	U.S.		$12.00/$7.00

Singles

Label	Catalog Number	Title	Type	Country	Year	Longbox Value / Value
Wea	W-9823CD	Just a Friend	CD5	U.K.	1990	$8.00
Wea	W-2784CD	Just a Friend	CD5	U.K.	1990	$8.00
Cold Chillin	PRO-CD-6106	Let Me Turn You On	CDJ	U.S.	1993	$2.00
Cold Chillin	3911	Spring Again	CDJ	U.S.	1990	$2.00
Cold Chillin	9 40264-2	T.S.R.	CD5	U.S.	1991	$4.00

Marky Mark And The Funky Bunch

Singles

Label	Catalog Number	Title	Type	Country	Year	Longbox Value / Value
Interscope	PRCD 4842-2	Gonna Have a Good Time	CDJ	U.S.	1992	$2.00
Interscope	PRCD 482-2	Gonna Have a Good Time	CDJ	U.S.	1992	$2.00
Interscope	AMDY-5069	Good Vibrations	CD3	Japan	1991	$12.00/$4.00
Interscope	PRCD 4055-2	Good Vibrations	CDJ	U.S.	1991	$6.00
Atlantic	7567-96202-2	I Need Money	CD5	Germany	1992	$8.00
Interscope	AMDY-5078	I Need Money	CD3	Japan	1992	$12.00/$4.00
Interscope	PRCD 4966-2	Loungin'	CDJ	U.S.	1991	$2.00
Interscope	PRCD 4617-2	Peace	CDJ	U.S.	1992	$2.00
Atlantic	7567-96234-2	Wildside	CD5	Germany	1991	$8.00
Interscope	PRCD 4254-2	Wildside	CDJ	U.S.	1991	$2.00
Atlantic	AMDY-5089	You Gotta Believe	CD3	Japan	1992	$12.00/$4.00
Atlantic	A-8480CD	You Gotta Believe	CD5	U.K.	1992	$8.00
Interscope	PRCD 4754-2	You Gotta Believe	CDJ	U.S.	1992	$2.00
Interscope	PRCD 4816-2	You Gotta Believe	CDJ	U.S.	1992	$2.00

Marley, Bob (and The Whalers)

Full Length

Label	Catalog Number	Title	Type	Country	Year	Longbox Value / Value
		Legendary Sampler	DJ/Smplr	Australia	1994	$35.00
Pioneer	PA-82-020	Live at the Santa Barbra Bowl	LD	U.S.	1982	$20.00
Pioneer	PA-82-020	Live at the Santa Barbra Bowl	LD	U.S.	1990	$30.00
Digital audio.						
Island	512280-2	Songs of Freedom	LTD/LP	U.S.	1992	$70.00
4 CD set in special digipak book. Limited to 1,000,000 copies.						
Tuff/Gone	PRCD 6740-2	Songs of Freedom 15 Track Sampler	DJ/Smplr	U.S.	1992	$10.00
Tuff/Gone	PRCD 6740-2	Songs of Freedom 15 Track Sampler	DJ/Smplr	U.S.	1992	$25.00
2 CD set with sampler plus CDJ of I "Iron Lion Zion."						
Radio Today		Songs of Freedom Tribute	RS	U.S.	1992	$75.00
Airdate: 10/26/92.						

Singles

Label	Catalog Number	Title	Type	Country	Year	Longbox Value / Value
BMG	663371	Could You Be Loved	CD5	Germany	1990	$11.00
Tuff/Gone	PRCD 6624-2	Could You Be Loved	CDJ	U.S.	1992	$3.00
Tuff/Gone	PRCD 6651-2	Get Up, Stand Up	CDJ	U.S.	1991	$3.00
Tuff/Gone	PHCR-8704	Iron Lion Zion	CD5	Japan	1992	$18.00
Tuff/Gone	TGXCD-2	Iron Lion Zion	CD5	U.K.	1992	$11.00
Tuff/Gone	PRCD 6749-2	Iron Lion Zion	CDJ	U.S.	1992	$3.00
Island	PSDD-1104	No Woman No Cry	CD3	Japan	1991	$12.00/$4.00
Tuff/Gone	664400	One Love	CD5	Germany	1991	$11.00
Tuff/Gone	TGXCD-1	One Love	CD5	U.K.	1991	$11.00
		What Goes Around Comes Around	CDJ	U.K.	1996	$10.00
Tuff/Gone	PHCR-8709	Why Should I	CD5	Japan	1992	$18.00
Tuff/Gone	TGXCD-3	Why Should I	CD5	U.K.	1991	$11.00

Marley, Marl

Singles

Label	Catalog Number	Title	Type	Country	Year	Longbox Value / Value
Cold Chillin	40310	Check the Mirror	CD5	U.S.	1991	$4.00
Cold Chillin	4919	Symphony Pt. 2, The	CDJ	U.S.	1991	$2.00

Marley, Ziggy (and The Melody Makers)

Full Length

Label	Catalog Number	Title	Type	Country	Year	Longbox Value / Value
Elektra	PRCD 9487-2	Free Like We Want	DJ/Smplr	U.S.	1995	$10.00
		House of Blues	RS	U.S.	1995	$50.00
2 CD set. Airdate: 11/17/95.						
Westwood One		In Concert	RS	U.S.	1993	$80.00
2 CD set. Airdate: 9/13/93.						
Westwood One		In Concert-Nu Rock	RS	U.S.	1993	$80.00
Airdate: 9/13/93.						
Virgin	PROCDZIGGY	One Bright Day	DJ/LP	U.S.	1989	$15.00
CD in oversized fold-open cardboard sleeve.						

Singles

Label	Catalog Number	Title	Type	Country	Year	Longbox Value / Value
Virgin	PRCD 3472	All Love	CDJ	U.S.	1989	$6.00
Virgin	PRCD 3245	Black My Story	CDJ	U.S.	1989	$6.00
Virgin	12804	Brothers And Sisters	CDJ	U.S.	1993	$6.00
Elektra	PRCD 9382-2	Free Like We Want	CDJ	U.S.	1995	$2.00
Virgin	VUSCD-54	Good Time	CD5	U.K.	1991	$10.00
Virgin	PRCD 4100	Good Time	CDJ	U.S.	1991	$6.00
Virgin	14107	Head Top	CDJ	U.S.	1993	$6.00
Virgin	12778	Joy And Blues	CDJ	U.S.	1993	$6.00
Virgin	664349	Kozmik	CD5	Germany	1991	$10.00
Virgin	VUSCD-42	Kozmik	CD5	U.K.	1991	$10.00
Virgin	PRCD 3973	Kozmik	CDJ	U.S.	1991	$6.00
Virgin	162544	Look Who's Dancing	CD3	Germany	1989	$10.00
Virgin	662544	Look Who's Dancing	CD5	Germany	1989	$10.00
Virgin	VUSCD-5	Look Who's Dancing	CD3	U.K.	1989	$10.00
Virgin	96541	Look Who's Dancing	CDJ	U.S.	1989	$6.00
Virgin	PRCD 2826	Look Who's Dancing	CDJ	U.S.	1989	$6.00
Virgin	PRCD 2841	Look Who's Dancing	CDJ	U.S.	1989	$6.00
Virgin	PRCD 3103	One Bright Day	CDJ	U.S.	1989	$6.00
Virgin	VSCD-1049	Tomorrow People	CD5	U.K.	1988	$10.00
Virgin	PRCD 2347	Tomorrow People	CDJ	U.S.	1988	$6.00
Virgin	PRCD 2391	Tumblin' Down	CDJ	U.S.	1988	$6.00
Virgin	PRCD 2494	Tumblin' Down	CDJ	U.S.	1988	$6.00
Virgin	PRCD 2996	Who Will Be There	CDJ	U.S.	1989	$6.00

Marlo, Clair

Singles

Label	Catalog Number	Title	Type	Country	Year	Longbox Value / Value
Sheffield Lab	CDCM3	A Major Technicality	DJ/CD3	U.S.	1988	$5.00
Shefield Lab	T1028-1	Just a Taste From…	DJ/CD3	U.S.	1988	$2.00

Marrow, Lee

Singles

Label	Catalog Number	Title	Type	Country	Year	Longbox Value / Value
Polygram	877479-2	Do You Want Me	CD5	Germany	1990	$8.00
ZYX	6259-8	Lot to Learn	CD5	Germany	1989	$8.00
Champion	[illegible]	Fall	CD5	U.K.	1990	$8.00
ZYX	6464-8	To Go Crazy	CD5	Germany	1991	$8.00

MARRS

Singles

Label	Catalog Number	Title	Type	Country	Year	Longbox Value / Value
4AD	15CY-5012	Pump Up the Volume	CD5	Japan	1987	$15.00
4AD	20CY-2280	Pump Up the Volume	CD5	Japan	1987	$15.00
4AD	BAD-707CD	Pump Up the Volume	CD5	U.K.	1987	$10.00
4th &B'way	452	Pump Up the Volume	CD5	U.S.	1987	$5.00
4th & B'way	452	Pump Up the Volume	CDJ	U.S.	1987	$2.00

Marry Me Jane

Singles

Label	Catalog Number	Title	Type	Country	Year	Longbox Value / Value
	BSK 7640	Twentyone	CDJ	U.S.		$2.00

Mars, Chris

Full Length

Label	Catalog Number	Title	Type	Country	Year	Longbox Value / Value
		75% Less Fact	LP/LB	U.S.		$14.00/$8.00

Singles

Label	Catalog Number	Title	Type	Country	Year	Longbox Value / Value
Smash	6722	Monkey Sees	CDJ	U.S.	1992	$2.00
Smash	650	Popular Creeps	CDJ	U.S.	1992	$2.00

Mars, Gwen

Singles

Label	Catalog Number	Title	Type	Country	Year	Longbox Value / Value
	PRCD106052	Stick	CDJ	U.S.		$2.00

Marsalis, Branford

Singles

Label	Catalog Number	Title	Type	Country	Year	Longbox Value / Value
Columbia	CSK 1654	Housed From Edward	CDJ	U.S.	1989	$7.00
Columbia		Yee and No	CDJ	U.S.		$3.00

Marsalis, Wynton

Full Length

Label	Catalog Number	Title	Type	Country	Year	Longbox Value / Value
CBS	CK-40009	Black Codes (From The Underground)	LP/LB	U.S.†	1985	$14.00/$8.00
CBS	CK-39530	Hot House Flowers	LP/LB	U.S.†	1985	$14.00/$8.00
Columbia	CK-64418	Marsalis, Wynton	LTD/LP	U.S.	1994	$25.00
Gold disc.						
Columbia		Soul Gestures In Southern Blue	DJ/Intvw	U.S.		$15.00
Columbia	CSK 2073	Standard Time Vol.3 Sampler	DJ/Smplr	U.S.	1990	$15.00
CBS	CK-38641	Think of One	LP/LB	U.S.†	1985	$14.00/$8.00
CBS	CK-37574	Wynton Marsalis	LP/LB	U.S.†	1985	$14.00/$8.00

Singles

Label	Catalog Number	Title	Type	Country	Year	Longbox Value / Value
Columbia	CSK 1594	Majesty of the Blues, The	CDJ	U.S.	1989	$3.00
Columbia	CSK 15911	Majesty of the Blues, The	CDJ	U.S.	1989	$3.00

Marscape

Full Length

Label	Catalog Number	Title	Type	Country	Year	Longbox Value / Value
		Marscape	LP/LB	U.S.		$14.00/$8.00

Marsh, Carl

Singles

Label	Catalog Number	Title	Type	Country	Year	Longbox Value / Value
Polygram	CAMCD-1	Every Bone in My Body	CD5	U.K.	1989	$8.00
Polygram	889232-3	Here Comes the Crush	CD3	Germany	1989	$8.00
Polygram	889233-2	Here Comes the Crush	CD5	Germany	1989	$8.00
Polygram	CRUCD-1	Here Comes the Crush	CD3	U.K.	1989	$8.00

Marsh, Hugh

Full Length

Label	Catalog Number	Title	Type	Country	Year	Longbox Value / Value
Duke St	5001	Purple Haze	DJ/Intvw	U.S.	1989	$8.00

Marshall, Amanda

Singles

Label	Catalog Number	Title	Type	Country	Year	Longbox Value / Value
Epic	ESK 7667	Birmingham	CDJ	U.S.		$2.00

Marshall, Jefferson

Singles

Label	Catalog Number	Title	Type	Country	Year	Longbox Value / Value
Polygram	886423-2	Truth	CD5	Germany	1989	$8.00

Marshall, John

Singles

Label	Catalog Number	Title	Type	Country	Year	Longbox Value / Value
WEA	YZ-389CD	Ball Of Confusion	CD5	U.K.	1989	$8.00

Marshall Tucker Band

Full Length

Label	Catalog Number	Title	Type	Country	Year	Longbox Value / Value
Album Network		In the Studio (Best Of)	RS	U.S.	1990	$20.00
Airdate: 11/12/90.						
DIR		King Biscuit Flour Hour	RS	U.S.	1988	$35.00
With New Riders. Airdate: 10/9/88.						
		Southern Spirit	DJ/LP	U.S.	1990	$12.00
Westwood One		Superstars	RS	U.S.	1996	$75.00
2 CD set. Airdate: 6/24/96.						

Singles

Label	Catalog Number	Title	Type	Country	Year	Longbox Value / Value
Cabin Fever	203	Down We Go	CDJ	U.S.	1993	$3.00
Cabin Fever	103	Driving You Out of My Mind	CDJ	U.S.	1993	$3.00
Sisapa		Stay in the Country	CDJ	U.S.	1990	$3.00
Cabin Fever	101	Ten Yard Road	CDJ	U.S.	1992	$3.00

Label	Catalog Number	Title	Type	Country	Year	Longbox Value / Value
	MTB 202	Walk Outside the Lines	CDJ	U.S.		$3.00

Marshall, Wayne

Singles

Label	Catalog Number	Title	Type	Country	Year	Longbox Value / Value
		Ooh Aah	CD5	U.K.		$10.00
		Ooh Aah	CD5	U.K.		$10.00
		Ooh Aah	CD5	U.K.		$10.00
Second version.						

Martha's Vineyard

Singles

Label	Catalog Number	Title	Type	Country	Year	Longbox Value / Value
rooArt	RARCD-1	Old Beach Road	CD5	U.K.	1990	$2.00
rooArt	CDP 240	Old Beach Road	CDJ	U.S.	1989	$2.00
rooArt	CDP 309	Old Beach Road	CDJ	U.S.	1990	$2.00

Martika

Singles

Label	Catalog Number	Title	Type	Country	Year	Longbox Value / Value
Columbia	857709-2	Coloured Kisses	CD5	Germany	1992	$9.00
Columbia	857709-2	Coloured Kisses	CD5	U.K.	1992	$9.00
Columbia	CSK 74194	Coloured Kisses	CDJ	U.S.		$2.00
Columbia	655228-3	I Feel the Earth Move	CD3	Germany	1989	$8.00
Sony	10EP-3094	I Feel the Earth Move	CD3	Japan	1989	$13.00/$4.00
Sony	12EP-3099	I Feel the Earth Move	CD3	Japan	1989	$13.00/$4.00
Columbia	655294-2	I Feel the Earth Move	CD5	U.K.	1989	$8.00
Columbia	656975-5	Love...Thy Will Be Done	CD5	Germany	1991	$8.00
Sony	SRDS-8197	Love...Thy Will Be Done	CD3	Japan	1991	$13.00/$4.00
Columbia	657010-2	Love...Thy Will Be Done	CD5	U.K.	1991	$8.00
Columbia	CSK 73853	Love...Thy Will Be Done	CDJ	U.S.	1991	$2.00
Columbia	657568-2	Martika's Kitchen	CD5	Germany	1991	$8.00
Sony	SRDS-8212	Martika's Kitchen	CD3	Japan	1991	$13.00/$4.00
Columbia	657568-2	Martika's Kitchen	CD5	U.K.	1991	$8.00
Columbia	CSK 74094	Martika's Kitchen	CDJ	U.S.	1991	$2.00
Columbia	655526-3	More Than You Know	CD3	Germany	1989	$8.00
Columbia	654520-2	More Than You Know	CD5	Germany	1989	$8.00
Sony	10EP-3078	More Than You Know	CD3	Japan	1989	$13.00/$4.00
Sony	12EP-3083	More Than You Know	CD3	Japan	1989	$13.00/$4.00
Columbia	655526-2	More Than You Know	CD5	U.K.	1989	$8.00
Columbia	654520-2	More Than You Know	CD5	U.K.	1989	$8.00
		More Than You Know	CDJ	U.S.	1989	$2.00
Columbia	655049-3	Toy Soldiers	CD3	Germany	1989	$8.00
Columbia	650491-3	Toy Soldiers	CD3	Germany	1989	$8.00
Columbia	655049-2	Toy Soldiers	CD5	U.K.	1989	$8.00
Columbia	655731-3	Water	CD3	Germany	1990	$8.00
Columbia	655731-2	Water	CD5	U.K.	1990	$8.00

Martin, Billy Ray

Singles

Label	Catalog Number	Title	Type	Country	Year	Longbox Value / Value
	PRCD 9441-2	Imitation of Life	CDJ	U.S.		$2.00
Elektra	66086	Running Around Town	CD5	U.S.	1995	$5.00
		Your Loving Arms	CDJ	U.S.		$2.00
Elektra/Asylum	66150	Your Loving Arms	CD5	U.S.	1994	$5.00

Martin, Dean

Singles

Label	Catalog Number	Title	Type	Country	Year	Longbox Value / Value
		That's Amore	CD5	U.K.	1996	$10.00

Martin, Eric

Full Length

Label	Catalog Number	Title	Type	Country	Year	Longbox Value / Value
		I'm Only Fooling Myself	LP	U.S.		$15.00

Martin, George And Andy Leek

Full Length

Label	Catalog Number	Title	Type	Country	Year	Longbox Value / Value
Atlantic	PR 2373-2	Say Something	DJ/Intvw	U.S.	1988	$12.00

Martin, Keith

Singles

Label	Catalog Number	Title	Type	Country	Year	Longbox Value / Value
Columbia	CSK 73171	If Love Feels So Good	CDJ	U.S.		$2.00
Columbia	77987	Moment in Time	CD5	U.S.	1995	$5.00

Martin, Linda

Singles

Label	Catalog Number	Title	Type	Country	Year	Longbox Value / Value
Columbia	658131-1	Why Me	CD5	U.K.	1992	$8.00

Martin, Marilyn

Full Length

Label	Catalog Number	Title	Type	Country	Year	Longbox Value / Value
Warner Brothers	32XD-459	Marilyn Martin	LP	Japan	1986	$25.00
With duet with Phil Collins "Separate Lives."						

Singles

Label	Catalog Number	Title	Type	Country	Year	Longbox Value / Value
Atlantic	PR 2421-2	And When She Danced	CDJ	U.S.	1988	$2.00
Pioneer	10SW-26	Possessive Love	CD3	Japan	1988	$13.00/$4.00

Martin, Steve

Full Length

Label	Catalog Number	Title	Type	Country	Year	Longbox Value / Value
Vestron Video	VL3134	Steve Martin	LD	U.S.	1986	$30.00

Martinez, Nancy

Singles

Label	Catalog Number	Title	Type	Country	Year	Longbox Value / Value
A&M	CD 17999	Everlasting	CDJ	U.S.	1987	$2.00
A&M	CD 17962	Save Your Love for Me	CDJ	U.S.	1989	$2.00
A&M	CD 17842	You've Got Me on Fire	CDJ	U.S.	1989	$2.00

Martyn, John

Singles

Label	Catalog Number	Title	Type	Country	Year	Longbox Value / Value
Permenant	CDPERM-1	Deny This Love	CD5	U.K.	1990	$2.00
Permenant	CDPERM-3	Jack the Lad	CD5	U.K.	1991	$2.00
Permenant	CDPERM-6	Sweet Little Mystery	CD5	U.K.	1992	$2.00
Mesa	9047	Sweet Little Mystery	CDJ	U.S.	1992	$3.00

Marvaless

Singles

Label	Catalog Number	Title	Type	Country	Year	Longbox Value / Value
	7198	Just Marvaless	CD5	U.S.	1994	$5.00

Marvin

Full Length

Label	Catalog Number	Title	Type	Country	Year	Longbox Value / Value
Regional	018	Firecracker Sweet, The	DJ/Smplr	U.S.	1992	$8.00

Singles

Label	Catalog Number	Title	Type	Country	Year	Longbox Value / Value
Regional	024	Train of Love	CDJ	U.S.	1992	$2.00
Regional	021	Vanishing Breed	CDJ	U.S.	1992	$2.00

Marx, Richard

Full Length

Label	Catalog Number	Title	Type	Country	Year	Longbox Value / Value
Capitol	DPRO-79956	Marx	DJ/Smplr	U.S.	1991	$10.00
Capitol	DPRO-79942	Marx	DJ/Smplr	U.S.	1991	$10.00
Capitol		Richard Marx	DJ/Smplr	Japan		$40.00
Capitol	DPRO-79961	Richard Marx	DJ/LP	U.S.	1991	$30.00
Capitol	DPRO-79761	Rush St.	DJ/LP	U.S.	1991	$15.00
Picture disc.						
Capitol	C2PM-98036	Rush St.	LTD/LP	U.S.	1991	$12.00
Capitol		Silent Scream	DJ/Smplr	U.S.	1994	$12.00

Singles

Label	Catalog Number	Title	Type	Country	Year	Longbox Value / Value
EMI	203554-3	Angelica	CD3	Germany	1989	$9.00
EMI	203554-2	Angelica	CD5	Germany	1989	$9.00
EMI	CDMT-74	Angelica	CD5	U.K.	1990	$9.00
EMI	DPRO-04426	Angelica	CDJ	U.S.	1990	$2.00
Capitol	TODP-2379	Chains Around My Heart	CD3	Japan	1992	$13.00/$4.00
Capitol	CDCLS 676	Chains Around My Heart	CD5	U.K.	1992	$10.00
Capitol		Chains Around My Heart	CD5	U.K.	1992	$10.00
Second version.						
Capitol	DPRO-79082	Chains Around My Heart	CDJ	U.S.	1992	$2.00
Capitol	DPRO-79085	Chains Around My Heart	CDJ	U.S.	1992	$2.00
EMI	203869-2	Children of the Night	CD5	Germany	1990	$9.00
EMI	CDMT-84	Children of the Night	CD5	U.K.	1990	$9.00
EMI	DPRO-04522	Children of the Night	CDJ	U.S.	1990	$2.00
EMI	CDMT-26	Don't Mean Nothing	CD5	U.K.	1988	$9.00
EMI	CDMT-39	Endless Summer Nights	CD5	U.K.	1988	$9.00
EMI	CDMT-89	Endless Summer Nights	CD5	U.K.	1990	$9.00
EMI	204639-2	Hazard	CD5	Germany	1992	$9.00
EMI	TODP-2347	Hazard	CD3	Japan	1992	$12.00/$3.00
Capitol	DPEO-79095	Hazard	CDJ	U.S.	1991	$2.00
Manhattan	XP10-2021	Hold On To the Night	CD3	Japan	1988	$12.00/$3.00
Capitol	204557-2	Keep Coming Back	CD5	Germany	1991	$9.00
Capitol	TODP-2309	Keep Coming Back	CD3	Japan	1991	$13.00/$4.00
Capitol	CDCLS-634	Keep Coming Back	CD5	U.K.	1992	$9.00
Capitol	C2 15762	Keep Coming Back	CD5	U.S.	1992	$5.00
Capitol	DPRO-79102	Keep Coming Back	CDJ	U.S.	1992	$2.00
Capitol	DPRO-79945	Keep Coming Back	CDJ	U.S.	1992	$2.00
Capitol	DPRO-79957	Keep Coming Back	CDJ	U.S.	1992	$2.00
Capitol		Nothin' You Can Do About It	CDJ	U.S.		$2.00
EMI		Now and Forever	CDJ	Spain		$25.00
		Now and Forever	CD5	U.K.		$10.00
Second version.						
Capitol	DPRO-79240	Now and Forever	CDJ	U.S.	1993	$2.00
Capitol	DPRO-79309	Now and Forever	CDJ	U.S.	1993	$2.00
Capitol	C2 58005	Now and Forever	CD5	U.S.	1994	$5.00
Capitol	DPRO-79958	Playing With Fire	CDJ	U.S.	1991	$2.00
EMI	203475-3	Right Here Waiting	CD3	Germany	1989	$9.00
EMI	CDMT-72	Right Here Waiting	CD3	U.K.	1989	$9.00
EMI	203328-2	Satisfied	CD5	Germany	1989	$9.00
Toshiba	XP10-2050	Satisfied	CD3	Japan	1989	$13.00/$4.00
EMI	CDMT-64	Satisfied	CD5	U.K.	1989	$9.00
EMI	DPRO-04254	Satisfied	CDJ	U.S.	1989	$2.00
EMI	CDMT-32	Should've Known Better	CD5	U.K.	1988	$8.00
EMI		Silent Scream	CD5	U.K.	1994	$10.00
Second version.						
EMI		Silent Scream	CD5	U.K.	1994	$12.00
Capitol		Silent Scream	CDJ	U.S.		$3.00
Capitol	TODP-2364	Take This Heart	CD3	Japan	1992	$13.00/$4.00
Capitol	DPRO-79170	Take This Heart	CDJ	U.S.	1992	$2.00
EMI	203740-2	Too Late to Say Goodbye	CD5	Germany	1990	$9.00
EMI	CDMT-80	Too Late to Say Goodbye	CD5	U.K.	1990	$9.00
EMI	DPRO-04447	Too Late to Say Goodbye	CDJ	U.S.	1990	$2.00
		Way That She Loved Me, The	CD5	U.K.	1994	$10.00
		Way That She Loved Me, The	CD5	U.K.	1994	$10.00
Second version.						
Capitol	DPRO-79376	Way That She Loved Me, The	CDJ	U.S.		$3.00
EMI		Way That She Loves Me	CDJ	U.K.	1994	$12.00

Marxman

Singles

Label	Catalog Number	Title	Type	Country	Year	Longbox Value / Value
Polygram	TLKCD-35	All About Eve	CD5	U.K.	1993	$8.00
Polygram	TLKCD-30	Ship Ahoy	CD5	U.K.	1993	$8.00
A&M	31458 8271	Theme From Marxman	CDJ	U.S.	1994	$6.00

Mary Goes Round

Singles

Label	Catalog Number	Title	Type	Country	Year	Longbox Value / Value
SPV	5431-3	Hot Shot in Space	CD5	Germany	1990	$8.00

Mary Mary

Singles

Label	Catalog Number	Title	Type	Country	Year	Longbox Value / Value
Metrobeat	0005	Everlasting Love	CDJ	U.S.	1993	$2.00

Mary My Hope

Full Length

Label	Catalog Number	Title	Type	Country	Year	Longbox Value / Value
Silvertone	886775	Monster Is Bigger Than the Man	CD5	Germany	1990	$8.00

Singles

Label	Catalog Number	Title	Type	Country	Year	Longbox Value / Value
Silvertone	MMHCD-1	Monster Is Bigger Than the Man	CD5	U.K.	1990	$8.00
Silvertone	1302-2-RDJ	Suicide Kings	CDJ	U.S.	1989	$2.00
RCA	1255-2-RDJ	Wildman Childman	CDJ	U.S.	1989	$2.00

Mary's Danish

Full Length

Label	Catalog Number	Title	Type	Country	Year	Longbox Value / Value
Chameleon	PRCD 81	Live	DJ/Smplr	U.S.	1990	$15.00
Chameleon	PRCD 32	Underwater	DJ/Intvw	U.S.	1992	$15.00

Singles

Label	Catalog Number	Title	Type	Country	Year	Longbox Value / Value
Chameleon	PRCD 66	Don't Crash the Car Tonight	CDJ	U.S.	1989	$2.00
Chameleon	PRCD 89	Foxy Lady	CDJ	U.S.	1989	$2.00
Morgan Creek	PRO 0003	Julies Blanket	CDJ	U.S.	1991	$2.00
Chameleon	PRCD 0004	Yellow Creep Around	CDJ	U.S.	1991	$6.00

Masekela, Hugh

Singles

Label	Catalog Number	Title	Type	Country	Year	Longbox Value / Value
RCA	3081-2-NDJ	If You Don't Know Me By Now	CDJ	U.S.	1989	$2.00

Mason, Dave

Full Length

Label	Catalog Number	Title	Type	Country	Year	Longbox Value / Value
MCA		Dave Mason & Cass Elliot	LP/LB	U.S.		$14.00/$8.00
MCA		Headkeeper	LP/LB	U.S.		$14.00/$8.00
Pioneer	PA-82-021	Live at Perkins Place	LD	U.S.	1982	$25.00
MCA	MCAD-42086	Two Hearts	LP/LB	U.S.	1985	$14.00/$8.00

Singles

Label	Catalog Number	Title	Type	Country	Year	Longbox Value / Value
MCA	CD45 17412	Dreams I Dream	CDJ	U.S.	1987	$2.00

Mason, Jono Band

Singles

Label	Catalog Number	Title	Type	Country	Year	Longbox Value / Value
		Big Daddy Blues	CDJ	U.S.		$3.00

Mass

Singles

Label	Catalog Number	Title	Type	Country	Year	Longbox Value / Value
Abstract	ABCD-093	Godsend	CD5	U.K.	1992	$8.00
		Voices in the Night	CDJ	U.S.		$2.00

Mass Order

Singles

Label	Catalog Number	Title	Type	Country	Year	Longbox Value / Value
Columbia	657748-5	Lift Every Voice	CD5	Germany	1992	$8.00

Label	Catalog Number	Title	Type	Country	Year	Longbox Value / Value
Columbia	657748-5	Lift Every Voice	CD5	U.K.	1992	$8.00

Massacre

Singles

Label	Catalog Number	Title	Type	Country	Year	Longbox Value / Value
Rough Trade	322 0060-3	Inhuman Condition	CD5	Germany	1991	$8.00
Earache	MOSH-60CD	Inhuman Condition	CD5	U.K.	1991	$8.00

Massey, Will T.

Singles

Label	Catalog Number	Title	Type	Country	Year	Longbox Value / Value
MCA	2068	I Ain't Here	CDJ	U.S.	1991	$2.00

Massh

Singles

Label	Catalog Number	Title	Type	Country	Year	Longbox Value / Value
ZYX	B-1080-8	Dance on the Water	CD5	Germany	1991	$8.00

Massive Attack

Singles

Label	Catalog Number	Title	Type	Country	Year	Longbox Value / Value
Virgin	PRCD 4284	Be Thankful For What You Got	CDJ	U.S.	1991	$2.00
Virgin	PRCD 4381	Be Thankful For What You Got	CDJ	U.S.	1991	$3.00
Virgin	WBRX-1	Day Dreaming	CD5	U.K.	1990	$8.00
BMG	663580	Day Dreaming	CD5	U.K.	1990	$8.00
Virgin	WBRDG-4	Hymn Of the Wild Thing	CD5	U.K.	1992	$8.00
		Kharmacoma	CD5	U.K.		$7.00
		Kharmacoma	CD5	U.K.		$7.00

Second version.

Label	Catalog Number	Title	Type	Country	Year	Longbox Value / Value
Capital	38471	Protection	CD5	U.S.	1994	$5.00
Virgin	664346	Safe From Harm	CD5	Germany	1991	$8.00
Virgin	WBRX-3	Safe From Harm	CD5	U.K.	1991	$8.00
Virgin	PRCD 4014	Safe From Harm	CDJ	U.S.	1991	$2.00
	DPRO 12705	Sampler	CDJ	U.S.		$2.00
Capital	38465	Sly	CD5	U.S.	1994	$5.00
Virgin	664035	Unfinished Sympathy	CD5	Germany	1991	$8.00
Virgin	WBRX-2	Unfinished Sympathy	CD5	U.K.	1991	$8.00

Masta Ace Inc.

Singles

Label	Catalog Number	Title	Type	Country	Year	Longbox Value / Value
	DPRO 10206	Sittin' on Chrome	CDJ	U.S.		$2.00
Delicious Vinyl	PRCD 5729	B-Side, The	CDJ	U.S.	1994	$7.00

Mastamind

Singles

Label	Catalog Number	Title	Type	Country	Year	Longbox Value / Value
Reel Life	1027	Lickkuidrano	CD5	U.S.	1994	$5.00

Masterblaster

Singles

Label	Catalog Number	Title	Type	Country	Year	Longbox Value / Value
ZYX	6540-8	Thin Is In	CD5	Germany	1991	$6.00

Masterboy

Singles

Label	Catalog Number	Title	Type	Country	Year	Longbox Value / Value
Polygram	877403-2	Dance to the Beat	CD5	Germany	1990	$8.00
Polygram	867513-2	I Need your Love	CD5	Germany	1991	$8.00
Polygram	879935-2	Shake It Up and Dance	CD5	Germany	1991	$8.00
Polygram	CIOCD-2	Shake It Up and Dance	CD5	U.K.	1991	$8.00

Masters of Reality

Singles

Label	Catalog Number	Title	Type	Country	Year	Longbox Value / Value
Chryalis	DPRO-04728	100 Years	CDJ	U.S.	1993	$2.00
Chryalis	DPRO-04545	Ants in the Kitchen	CDJ	U.S.	1993	$2.00
Def American	PRO-CD-3405	Blue Garden, The	CDJ	U.S.	1988	$3.00
Def American	DEFAC-1	Candy Song, The	CD5	U.K.	1989	$10.00
Delicious Vinyl	6625	Candy Song, The	CDJ	U.S.	1990	$2.00
Delicious Vinyl	6641	Domino	CDJ	U.S.	1990	$2.00
Delicious Vinyl	0001	John Brown	CDJ	U.S.	1991	$2.00

Masterstroke

Singles

Label	Catalog Number	Title	Type	Country	Year	Longbox Value / Value
Mercury	4228649132	Masterstroke	CD5	Canada	1993	$8.00
Mercury	269	Weapon	CD5	Canada	1993	$8.00

Materace

Singles

Label	Catalog Number	Title	Type	Country	Year	Longbox Value / Value
Cold Chillin	4708	Movin' On	CDJ	U.S.	1990	$2.00

Material

Full Length

Label	Catalog Number	Title	Type	Country	Year	Longbox Value / Value
		Seven Souls	LP/LB	U.S.		$14.00/$8.00

Material Issue

Full Length

Label	Catalog Number	Title	Type	Country	Year	Longbox Value / Value
Mercury	CDP 390	Super Hit Explosion	DJ/Smplr	U.S.	1991	$8.00

Singles

Label	Catalog Number	Title	Type	Country	Year	Longbox Value / Value
Mercury	868 165	Diane	CD5	U.S.	1991	$5.00
Mercury	CDP 420	Diane	CDJ	U.S.	1991	$2.00
Mercury	CDP 808	Everything	CDJ	U.S.	1992	$7.00
Mercury	856083-2	Goin' Through Your Purse	CD5	U.S.	1994	$5.00
Mercury	CDP 1161	Kill the Waitress	CDJ	U.S.	1994	$2.00
Mercury	CDP 168	Valerie Loves Me	CDJ	U.S.	1991	$2.00
Polydor	PZCD-254	What Girls Want	CD5	U.K.	1993	$10.00
Mercury	CDP 685	What Girls Want	CDJ	U.S.	1992	$2.00
Mercury	CDP 679	What Girls Want	CDJ	U.S.	1992	$7.00
Mercury	CDP 718	When I Get This Way	CDJ	U.S.	1992	$2.00

Matheson, Andrew

Singles

Label	Catalog Number	Title	Type	Country	Year	Longbox Value / Value
		Crushing the Doll	CDJ	Canada		$6.00

Mathews Southern Comfort

Singles

Label	Catalog Number	Title	Type	Country	Year	Longbox Value / Value
Eastwest	257454-2	Woodstock	CD3	Germany	1989	$8.00

Mathews, Wendy

Singles

Label	Catalog Number	Title	Type	Country	Year	Longbox Value / Value
rooArt	YZ-733CD	Day You Went Away	CD5	U.K.	1993	$8.00

Mathis, Johnny

Full Length

Label	Catalog Number	Title	Type	Country	Year	Longbox Value / Value
Columbia		A Personal Collection	LP	U.S.	1994	$60.00

4 CD set. First pressing with missing second on track 8 on disc 1.

Label	Catalog Number	Title	Type	Country	Year	Longbox Value / Value
CBS	CK-38718	A Special Part of Me	LP/BP	U.S.†	1984	$14.00/$8.00
CBS	CK-36871	Best Of	LP/BP	U.S.†	1985	$14.00/$8.00
CBS	CK-36871	Merry Christmas	LP/BP	U.S.†	1984	$14.00/$8.00
Columbia		Music Of Johnny Mathis: Your Personal Sampler	DJ/Smplr	U.S.		$15.00
CBS	CK-39601	Right From the Heart	LP/BP	U.S.†	1985	$14.00/$8.00
Columbia		Your Personal Sampler	DJ/Smplr	U.S.		$18.00

Singles

Label	Catalog Number	Title	Type	Country	Year	Longbox Value / Value
Columbia	CSK 4286	Better Together	CDJ	U.S.	1991	$2.00
Columbia	654773-2	Daydreamin'	CD5	U.K.	1989	$10.00
Columbia	CSK 69092	In the Still of the Night	CDJ	U.S.	1989	$2.00
Columbia	CSk 4182	You Brought Me Love	CDJ	U.S.	1991	$2.00

Matsui, Keiko

Full Length

Label	Catalog Number	Title	Type	Country	Year	Longbox Value / Value
Passport	PJCD-88024	Drop of Water	LP	U.S.		$15.00
Passport	PJCD-88024	Drop of Water	LP/LB	U.S.		$15.00/$10.00
Passport	PJCD-88043	Under Northern Light	LP/LB	U.S.		$15.00/$10.00

Mattea, Kathy

Full Length

Label	Catalog Number	Title	Type	Country	Year	Longbox Value / Value
Mercury		Good News	DJ/Intvw	U.S.	1994	$20.00
Mercury		Good News Radio Special, The	DJ/Intvw	U.S.	1995	$12.00
		Live From the Crazy Horse	RS	U.S.	1994	$50.00

Airdate: 6/20/94.

Label	Catalog Number	Title	Type	Country	Year	Longbox Value / Value
Mercury	CDP 750-P	Lonesome Standard Time	DJ/LP	U.S.	1992	$50.00

3 CD set in pocket watch package.

Label	Catalog Number	Title	Type	Country	Year	Longbox Value / Value
		Road, The	RS	U.S.	1995	$65.00

2 CD set. Airdate: 5/26/95.

Label	Catalog Number	Title	Type	Country	Year	Longbox Value / Value
Mercury	DMN 7040	Special Collection	DJ/Smplr	U.S.	1995	$30.00
Mercury		Time Pases By	DJ/Intvw	U.S.	1991	$20.00

Singles

Label	Catalog Number	Title	Type	Country	Year	Longbox Value / Value
Mercury	CDP 301	A Few Good Things Remain	CDJ	U.S.	1990	$3.00
Mercury	CDP 525	Asking Us To Dance	CDJ	U.S.	1991	$3.00
Mercury	CDP 268	Battle Hymm Of Love	CDJ	U.S.	1990	$3.00
Mercury	CDP 48	Come From the Heart	CDJ	U.S.	1989	$3.00
Mercury	CDP 879	Listen To the Radio	CDJ	U.S.	1993	$3.00
Mercury	CDP 750	Lonesome Standard Time	CDJ	U.S.	1992	$3.00
Mercury	CDP 876	Seeds	CDJ	U.S.	1993	$3.00
Mercury	CDP 199	She Comes From Fort Worth	CDJ	U.S.	1989	$3.00
Mercury	CDP 826	Standing Knee Deep In A River	CDJ	U.S.	1992	$3.00
Mercury	MERCD-338	Where've You Been	CD5	U.K.	1991	$10.00
Mercury	CDP 444	Whole Lotta Holes	CDJ	U.S.	1991	$3.00

Matthews, Dave Band

Full Length

Label	Catalog Number	Title	Type	Country	Year	Longbox Value / Value
RCA		Crash	DJ/LP	U.S.		$10.00
RCA		Dave Matthews Band	DJ/Smplr	U.S.	1995	$20.00
		House of Blues	RS	U.S.	1995	$100.00

2 CD set. Airdate: 9/8/95.

Label	Catalog Number	Title	Type	Country	Year	Longbox Value / Value
Westwood One		In Concert	RS	U.S.	1995	$65.00

Airdate: 10/9/95.

Label	Catalog Number	Title	Type	Country	Year	Longbox Value / Value
Westwood One		In Concert-Nu Rock	RS	U.S.	1995	$65.00

Airdate: 9/11/95.

Label	Catalog Number	Title	Type	Country	Year	Longbox Value / Value
Westwood One		In Concert-Nu Rock	RS	U.S.	1996	$60.00

Airdate: 8/26/96.

Label	Catalog Number	Title	Type	Country	Year	Longbox Value / Value
RCA	RJC66561-2	Jimi Thing	DJ/Smplr	U.S.	1995	$15.00
		Live From the House of Blues	RS	U.S.	1995	$35.00

2 CD set.

Singles

Label	Catalog Number	Title	Type	Country	Year	Longbox Value / Value
RCA		Ants Marching	CD5	U.S.	1995	$6.00
RCA	RDJ64350-2	Ants Marching	CDJ	U.S.	1995	$6.00
RCA		Recently	CDJ	U.S.	1995	$7.00
RCA	RDJ64453-2	Satellite	CDJ	U.S.	1995	$6.00
		Too Much	CD5	U.K.	1996	$10.00
		Too Much	CDJ	U.K.	1996	$10.00
RCA	RDJ645172	Too Much	CDJ	U.S.	1995	$6.00
RCA	RDJ64324-2	Typical Situation	CDJ	U.S.	1995	$12.00

Matthews, Eric

Singles

Label	Catalog Number	Title	Type	Country	Year	Longbox Value / Value
		Fanfare	CDJ	U.S.	1995	$2.00

Matto, Cibo

Singles

Label	Catalog Number	Title	Type	Country	Year	Longbox Value / Value
	PRO-CD-7987	Know Your Chicken	CDJ	U.S.	1995	$2.00

Maureen

Singles

Label	Catalog Number	Title	Type	Country	Year	Longbox Value / Value
Urban	URBCD-62	It's My Life	CD5	U.K.	1990	$8.00
Urban	URBCD-68	Mesmerise	CD5	U.K.	1991	$8.00

Mauriat, Paul

Full Length

Label	Catalog Number	Title	Type	Country	Year	Longbox Value / Value
Polygram	811170-2	Digital Best	LP/BP	U.S.†	1984	$14.00/$8.00
Polygram	810002-2	Magic	LP/BP	U.S.†	1984	$14.00/$8.00
Pioneer	MP092-U	Melodie	LD	U.S.†	1983	$35.00
Mercury	810 025-2	On Stage	LP/BP	U.S.†	1984	$14.00/$8.00
Pioneer	VAL-3015	Paul Mauriat	LD	U.S.†	1986	$35.00

Maurice and Da Posse

Singles

Label	Catalog Number	Title	Type	Country	Year	Longbox Value / Value
A&M	CD 17929	All Because of You	CDJ	U.S.	1989	$2.00

Mavericks

Full Length

Label	Catalog Number	Title	Type	Country	Year	Longbox Value / Value
		Four Songs	DJ/Smplr	U.S.		$8.00
MCA	MCAD-9591	Sampler	DJ/Smplr	Canada		$20.00

Singles

Label	Catalog Number	Title	Type	Country	Year	Longbox Value / Value
MCA	MCA5P3431	Blue Moon	CDJ	U.S.	1995	$3.00

Mavis Piggott

Singles

Label	Catalog Number	Title	Type	Country	Year	Longbox Value / Value
	9	Late Bloom	CD5	U.S.	1994	$5.00

Maw & Company

Singles

Label	Catalog Number	Title	Type	Country	Year	Longbox Value / Value
Esquire	74347	Gonna Get Back to You	CDJ	U.S.	1992	$2.00

Max

Singles

Label	Catalog Number	Title	Type	Country	Year	Longbox Value / Value
Canyon	PCDY-00019	Day By Day	CD3	Japan	1989	$12.00/$3.00
WEA	246842-2	Dorothy	CD3	Germany	1989	$8.00
Red Dot	RDT-2CD	Hold On	CD5	U.K.	1991	$8.00
Kenedy	KCRCD-2	It's a Hard Life	CD5	U.K.	1993	$8.00
WEA	171348-2	Your Eyes	CD5	Germany	1990	$8.00

Max Headroom

Singles

Label	Catalog Number	Title	Type	Country	Year	Longbox Value / Value
Polydor	889 311-2	Max Headroom Calling	CD3	Germany	1989	$11.00
Polydor	889 310-3	Max Headroom Calling	CD3	Germany	1989	$11.00

Max Q

Singles

Label	Catalog Number	Title	Type	Country	Year	Longbox Value / Value
Mercury	MXQCD-2	Sometimes	CD5	U.K.	1990	$10.00
Atlantic	PR 3086-2	Sometimes	CDJ	U.S.	1989	$3.00

Label	Catalog Number	Title	Type	Country	Year	Longbox Value / Value
Mercury	876051-2	Way of the World	CD5	Germany	1989	$10.00
Alfa	ALDB-21	Way of the World	CD3	Japan	1990	$12.00/$4.00
Mercury	MXQCD-1	Way of the World	CD5	U.K.	1989	$10.00
Atlantic	86317-2	Way of the World	CD5	U.S.	1989	$5.00
Atlantic	PR 2851-2	Way of the World	CDJ	U.S.	1989	$3.00

Max-A-Million

Singles

Label	Catalog Number	Title	Type	Country	Year	Value
Zoo	14216	Fat Boy	CD5	U.S.	1994	$5.00
	1006	Fat Boy	CD5	U.S.	1994	$5.00
Zoo	14239	Sexual Healing	CD5	U.S.	1995	$5.00

Maxi Jazz

Singles

Label	Catalog Number	Title	Type	Country	Year	Value
Tam Tam	CDTT-020	Do You Dance	CD5	U.K.	1990	$10.00

Maxwell

Singles

Label	Catalog Number	Title	Type	Country	Year	Value
Columbia	CSK 7671	Til the Cops Come Knockin'	CDJ	U.S.		$2.00

May, Brian

Full Length

Label	Catalog Number	Title	Type	Country	Year	Value
EMI	898945 2 8	Back to the Light	LTD/LP	Germany	1992	$30.00

Gold disc.

Label	Catalog Number	Title	Type	Country	Year	Value
Westwood One		In Concert	RS	U.S.	1993	$90.00

Airdate: 6/21/93.

Singles

Label	Catalog Number	Title	Type	Country	Year	Value
		Back to the Light	CD5	U.K.		$10.00
		Back to the Light	CD5	U.K.		$10.00

Second version.

Label	Catalog Number	Title	Type	Country	Year	Value
Parlophone		Back to the Light	CDJ	U.K.	1993	$15.00
Parlophone	204586-2	Driven By You	CD5	Germany	1991	$11.00
Parlophone	CDR-6304	Driven By You	CD5	U.K.	1991	$11.00
Hollywood	PRCD-10319	Driven By You	CDJ	U.S.	1992	$6.00
Hollywood	PRCD-10273-2	Driven By You	CDJ	U.S.	1992	$25.00

CD in special hexagonal box with built in working compass.

Label	Catalog Number	Title	Type	Country	Year	Value
		Last Horizon	CD5	U.K.		$10.00

Second version.

Label	Catalog Number	Title	Type	Country	Year	Value
Parlophone	CDR 56371	Last Horizon	CD5	U.K.	1993	$12.00
Parlophone	CDRS 6371	Last Horizon	CD5	U.K.	1993	$20.00
EMI	TOCP-8087	Resurrection	CD5	Japan	1993	$30.00
EMI		Resurrection	CD5	U.K.	1993	$10.00

Second version.

Label	Catalog Number	Title	Type	Country	Year	Value
Hollywood	PRCD-10320	Resurrection	CDJ	U.S.	1993	$6.00
		Resurrection	CDJ	U.S.	1993	$7.00
EMI	TOCP-7436	Too Much Love Will Kill You	CD5	Japan	1991	$16.00
Parlophone	CDR-6320	Too Much Love Will Kill You	CD5	U.K.	1991	$11.00
Hollywood	PRCD-10343	Too Much Love Will Kill You	CDJ	U.S.	1991	$7.00
	SPCD-1705	We Will Rock You	CDJ	France	1993	$30.00

May, Mathilda

Singles

Label	Catalog Number	Title	Type	Country	Year	Value
Epic	ESCA-5762	If You Miss	CD5	Japan	1993	$10.00

May May

Singles

Label	Catalog Number	Title	Type	Country	Year	Value
Scotti Brothers	ZSK 75408	Life's a Test	CDJ	U.S.	1992	$2.00

May, Raymond

Singles

Label	Catalog Number	Title	Type	Country	Year	Value
Elektra	PR 8003-2	Romantic Guy	CDJ	U.S.	1988	$2.00

Mayall, John

Full Length

Label	Catalog Number	Title	Type	Country	Year	Longbox Value / Value
RSO	800086-2	Blues Breakers	LP/BP	U.S.†	1984	$14.00/$8.00
		House of Blues	RS	U.S.	1995	$40.00

2 CD set. Airdate: 1/22/95.

Label	Catalog Number	Title	Type	Country	Year	Value
		House of Blues	RS	U.S.	1995	$40.00

2 CD set. Airdate: 4/7/95.

Label	Catalog Number	Title	Type	Country	Year	Value
		House of Blues	RS	U.S.	1996	$40.00

2 CD set. Airdate: 2/9/96.

Label	Catalog Number	Title	Type	Country	Year	Value
		Live From the House of Blues	RS	U.S.		$35.00

2 CD set.

Singles

Label	Catalog Number	Title	Type	Country	Year	Value
	520206	Bare Wires	CD5	U.S.	1994	$5.00
Island	884700	Sensitive Kind	CD5	Germany	1990	$8.00
Island	CID-474	Sensitive Kind	CD5	U.K.	1990	$8.00

Mayfield, Curtis

Full Length

Label	Catalog Number	Title	Type	Country	Year	Value
Warner Brothers		A Tribute to Curtis Mayfield	DJ/LP	U.S.	1994	$13.00
		House of Blues "Tribute"	RS	U.S.	1996	$40.00

2 CD set. Airdate: 3/4/96.

Label	Catalog Number	Title	Type	Country	Year	Value
		People Get Ready	DJ/Smplr	U.S.		$15.00

Singles

Label	Catalog Number	Title	Type	Country	Year	Value
Ichiban	CDCUR-102	I Mo Git U Succa	CD5	U.K.	1989	$10.00
EMI	204038-2	Superfly	CD5	Germany	1990	$10.00
Capitol	CDCL-586	Superfly 1990	CD5	U.K.	1990	$10.00
Capitol	C2 15614	Superfly 1990	CD5	U.S.	1990	$5.00
Capitol	DPRO-79204	Superfly 1990	CDJ	U.S.	1990	$2.00

Mayorga, Lincoln

Full Length

Label	Catalog Number	Title	Type	Country	Year	Longbox Value / Value
Sheffield Lab	CD-S10	& Distinguished Colleagues Vol. 2: The Missing Linc	LP/LB	U.S.†	1985	$14.00/$8.00

Mays, Lyle

Singles

Label	Catalog Number	Title	Type	Country	Year	Value
Geffen	PRO-CD-3266	Feet First	CDJ	U.S.	1988	$2.00

Maysa

Singles

Label	Catalog Number	Title	Type	Country	Year	Value
MCA	3046	What About Our Love	CD5	U.S.	1995	$6.00

Maze

Singles

Label	Catalog Number	Title	Type	Country	Year	Value
Warner Brothers	W-2895CD	Can't Get Over You	CD5	U.K.	1989	$9.00
Warner Brothers	PRO-CD-3595	Can't Get Over You	CDJ	U.S.	1989	$2.00
Warner Brothers	PRO-CD-3897	Love's on the Run	CDJ	U.S.	1989	$2.00
Warner Brothers	PRO-CD-3780	Silky Soul	CDJ	U.S.	1989	$2.00
Warner Brothers	PRO-CD-6385	Twilight	CDJ	U.S.	1993	$3.00

Mazelle, Kym

Singles

Label	Catalog Number	Title	Type	Country	Year	Value
Capitol	DPRO-79337	Don't Scandalize My Name	CDJ	U.S.	1989	$2.00
EMI	203292-5	Got to Get You Back	CD3	Germany	1989	$8.00
EMI	203292-3	Got to Get You Back	CD3	Germany	1989	$8.00
EMI	203300-3	Got to Get You Back	CD3	Germany	1989	$8.00
EMI	CDSY-25	Got to Get You Back	CD5	U.K.	1989	$8.00
EMI	203534-3	Love Strain	CD3	Germany	1989	$8.00
EMI	203543-3	Love Strain	CD3	Germany	1989	$8.00
EMI	CDSY-30	Love Strain	CD5	U.K.	1989	$8.00
Parlophone	CDR-6287	No One Can Love You More Than Me	CD5	U.K.	1991	$8.00
EMI	203860-2	Useless	CD5	Germany	1988	$8.00
EMI	203861-2	Useless	CD5	Germany	1990	$8.00
EMI	CDSY-18	Useless	CD5	U.K.	1988	$8.00
EMI	CDSY-36	Useless	CD5	U.K.	1988	$8.00
EMI	203622-3	Was That All It Was	CD3	Germany	1990	$8.00
EMI	CDSY-32	Was That All It Was	CD5	U.K.	1990	$8.00
EMI	CDEM-209	Woman of the World	CD5	U.K.	1991	$8.00

Mazzy Star

Full Length

Label	Catalog Number	Title	Type	Country	Year	Value
Capitol	DPRO-79401	Fade Into You	DJ/Smplr	U.S.	1995	$20.00

Singles

Label	Catalog Number	Title	Type	Country	Year	Value
Capitol		Fade Into You	CD5	U.K.	1993	$9.00
Capitol	DPRO-79860	Fade Into You	CDJ	U.S.	1993	$3.00
Capital	58121	Fade Into You	CD5	U.S.	1994	$5.00

MC Spy-D + Friends

Singles

Label	Catalog Number	Title	Type	Country	Year	Value
Parlophone	CDR 6404	Amazing Spiderman, The	CD5	U.S.	1995	$12.00

McAnally, Mac

Full Length

Label	Catalog Number	Title	Type	Country	Year	Value
MCA	MCA35-10543	Live and Learn	DJ/LP	U.S.	1992	$10.00

Promo edition picture disc in simulated hardcover book.

McAuley Schenker Group

Full Length

Label	Catalog Number	Title	Type	Country	Year	Value
Foundations		FZ Interview	RS/VA	U.S.	1993	$10.00
EMI	TOCP-7396	"Unplugged" Live	LTD/LP	Japan	1992	$30.00

Singles

Label	Catalog Number	Title	Type	Country	Year	Value
EMI	147467-2	Anytime	CD5	Germany	1989	$10.00
EMI	147488-2	Anytime	CD5	Germany	1989	$10.00
EMI	CDEM-127	Anytime	CD5	U.K.	1989	$10.00
Capitol	DPRO-79894	Anytime	CDJ	U.S.	1989	$2.00
Capitol		Anytime	CDJ	U.S.	1989	$2.00
IMP	2122	Crazy	CDJ	U.S.	1992	$2.00
Capitol	DRPO-79281	Follow the Night	CDJ	U.S.	1988	$6.00

1st image disc CD.

Label	Catalog Number	Title	Type	Country	Year	Value
Electrola	1C 560 1 47594	Nightmare	CD5	Germany	1991	$10.00
EMI		Save Yourself	CD5	Japan	1989	$15.00
EMI	147510-2	This Is My Heart	CD5	Germany	1990	$10.00
Capitol	DPRO-79975	This Is My Heart	CDJ	U.S.	1989	$2.00
Capitol	DPRO-72122	This Is My Heart	CDJ	U.S.	1989	$2.00
EMI	147603-2	When I'm Gone	CD5	Germany	1992	$10.00
IMP	1682	When I'm Gone	CDJ	U.S.	1992	$2.00

McBride & The Ride

Singles

Label	Catalog Number	Title	Type	Country	Year	Value
MCA	MCA5P-54688	Hurry Sundown	CDJ	U.S.	1993	$2.00

McBroom, Amanda & Lincoln Mayorga

Full Length

Label	Catalog Number	Title	Type	Country	Year	Longbox Value / Value
Sheffield Lab	CD-13	Growing Up in Hollywood Town	LP/LB	U.S.†	1985	$14.00/$8.00
Sheffield Lab	CD-15	West of Oz	LP/LB	U.S.†	1985	$14.00/$8.00

McCain, Edwin

Singles

Label	Catalog Number	Title	Type	Country	Year	Value
	PRCD 6514-2	Alive	CDJ	U.S.		$2.00
Atlantic	98141	Solitude	CD5	U.S.	1995	$5.00
	PRCD 6532-2	Sorry To A Friend	CDJ	U.S.		$2.00

McCall, C.W.

Singles

Label	Catalog Number	Title	Type	Country	Year	Value
		Comin' Back For More	CDJ	U.S.		$2.00

McCarters

Singles

Label	Catalog Number	Title	Type	Country	Year	Value
Warner Brothers	PRO-CD-3743	Quiet While I'm Behind	CDJ	U.S.	1989	$2.00
Warner Brothers	PRO-CD-2911	Timeless and True Love	CDJ	U.S.	1987	$2.00
Warner Brothers	PRO-CD-3433	Up and Gone	CDJ	U.S.	1987	$2.00

McCarthy

Singles

Label	Catalog Number	Title	Type	Country	Year	Value
Midnight	DONG-48CD	Boy Meets Girl	CD5	U.K.	1989	$8.00

McCartney, Paul (and Wings)

Full Length

Label	Catalog Number	Title	Type	Country	Year	Value
Toshiba		1990 World Tour	DJ/Smplr	Japan	1990	$250.00

DJ/CD3, Tour Program, flyer, booklet in custom bag.

Label	Catalog Number	Title	Type	Country	Year	Value
Capitol	DPRO-79671	All the Best/New World Sampler	DJ/Smplr	U.S.	1993	$100.00
EMI/Odeon	TCCP-6117	All the Best!	LTD/LP	Japan	1989	$50.00

Gold disc.

Label	Catalog Number	Title	Type	Country	Year	Value
EMI	SPCD-1330-31	All Time Favorites	DJ/Smplr	Japan	1992	$350.00

2 CD set.

Label	Catalog Number	Title	Type	Country	Year	Value
EMI	DPRO 79044	Angel: Fall/Winter '91 Highlights	DJ/Smplr	U.S.	1991	$15.00
EMI	CDP-748199-2	At the Speed Of Sound	LP	Germany		$12.00

Nonremastered version.

Label	Catalog Number	Title	Type	Country	Year	Value
EMI	CDP-748199-2	At the Speed Of Sound	LP	U.K.		$12.00

Nonremastered version.

Label	Catalog Number	Title	Type	Country	Year	Value
EMI	748200-2	Back to the Egg	LP	Germany		$12.00

Nonremastered version.

Label	Catalog Number	Title	Type	Country	Year	Value
EMI	CZ-218	Back to the Egg	LP	U.K.		$12.00

Nonremastered version.

Label	Catalog Number	Title	Type	Country	Year	Value
EMI	CDP-746055-2	Band on the Run	LP	Germany	1983	$12.00

Nonremastered version.

Label	Catalog Number	Title	Type	Country	Year	Value
EMI/Odeon	CP43-5774	Band on the Run	LTD/LP	Japan	1989	$50.00

Gold disc.

Label	Catalog Number	Title	Type	Country	Year	Value
EMI	CDP-746055-2	Band on the Run	LP	U.K.	1983	$12.00

Nonremastered version.

Label	Catalog Number	Title	Type	Country	Year	Longbox Value / Value
CBS	CK-36482	Band on the Run	LP/LB	U.S.		$30.00/$28.00
CBS	CK-36482	Band on the Run	LP/BP	U.S.†	1983	$30.00/$28.00
EMI		Collection Box	LTD/16CD	Japan	1989	$400.00

McCartney CD catalog in custom presentation box.

Label	Catalog Number	Title	Type	Country	Year	Value
Toshiba		Flowers in the Dirt	DJ/LP	Japan	1989	$300.00

Promo package containing CD with special "Japan-only" messages and custom card.

Label	Catalog Number	Title	Type	Country	Year	Value
Toshiba	TOCP-6118/9	Flowers in the Dirt	LP	Japan	1989	$40.00

2 CD set.

Label	Catalog Number	Title	Type	Country	Year	Value
MPL	CDPCSDX 106	Flowers in the Dirt	LTD/LP	U.S.	1989	$25.00

"Tour Pack" in 12"x12" package with bonus CD3, poster, and stickers.

Label	Catalog Number	Title	Type	Country	Year	Value
Capitol	92213	Gift Box	LP	U.S.	1989	$55.00

4 CD albums in12" x12" boxed set.

Label	Catalog Number	Title	Type	Country	Year	Longbox Value / Value
EMI	CDP-746043-2	Give My Regards to Broadstreet	LP	Germany	1984	$12.00
	Nonremastered version.					
EMI	CDP-746043-2	Give My Regards to Broadstreet	LP	U.K.	1984	$12.00
	Nonremastered version.					
Columbia	CK-39613	Give My Regards to Broadstreet	LP/BP	U.S.†	1984	$23.00/$20.00
Columbia	CK-39613	Give My Regards to Broadstreet	LP/LB	U.S.	1986	$23.00/$20.00
Album Network		In the Studio (Flowers in the Dirt)	RS	U.S.	1990	$40.00
	Airdate: 5/14/90.					
Album Network		In the Studio (Tripping the Live Fantastic, Pt.1)	RS	U.S.	1990	$40.00
	Airdate: 10/29/90.					
Album Network		In the Studio (Tripping the Live Fantastic, Pt.2)	RS	U.S.	1990	$40.00
	Airdate: 11/5/90.					
EMI	CDP-748198-2	London Town	LP	Germany		$12.00
	Nonremastered version.					
Radio Ventures		Masters of Rock	RS	U.S.	1990	$60.00
	Airdate: 3/19/90.					
EMI	CDP-746611-2	McCartney	LP	Germany		$12.00
	Nonremastered version.					
EMI	CDP-746611-2	McCartney	LP	U.K.		$12.00
	Nonremastered version.					
Capitol	PRO-CD-200-277	Michelle	DJ/Smplr	Mexico	1995	$130.00
EMI		New World Collection	LTD/LP	Australia	1995	$50.00
	Limited edition 4 CD boxed set.					
Capitol	DPRO-79671	New World Sampler/All the Best!	DJ/Smplr	U.S.	1993	$45.00
	2 CD set.					
EMI	TOCP-7580	Off the Ground	LTD/LP	Japan	1993	$50.00
	2 CD set.					
Capitol		Off the Ground	DJ/LP	U.S.	1993	$70.00
	CD album and cassette in custom box.					
EMI	TOCP-8207/08	Off the Ground/Complete Works	LTD/LP	Japan	1994	$80.00
Capitol		Off the Ground-The Complete Works	LP	Germany	1993	$40.00
	2 CD set.					
Westwood One		Off the Record	RS	U.S.	1992	$50.00
	Airdate: 1/25/93.					
Westwood One		Off the Record	RS	U.S.	1996	$50.00
	Airdate: 2/19/96.					
Westwood One		Off the Record	RS	U.S.	1993	$50.00
	Airdate: 6/7/93.					
		Oobu Joobu	RS	U.S.	1995	$400.00
	17 CD set.					
EMI	SPCD-1526	Paul Is Cool	DJ/Smplr	Japan	1995	$500.00
Parlophone		Paul Is Live	DJ/Smplr	U.K.	1994	$50.00
Parlophone	COLDJ1LC0299	Paul McCartney Collection, The	DJ/Smplr	U.S.	1993	$50.00
EMI	CDP-74601802	Pipes of Peace	LP	U.K.	1983	$12.00
	Nonremastered version.					
Columbia	CK 39149	Pipes of Peace	LP/BP	U.S.†	1983	$30.00/$28.00
Columbia	CK 39149	Pipes of Peace	LP/LB	U.S.	1983	$30.00/$28.00
EMI	CDP-746612-2	Ram	LP	Germany		$12.00
	Nonremastered version.					
EMI	CZ-29	Ram	LP	U.K.		$12.00
	Nonremastered version.					
EMI	CDP-752026-2	Red Rose Speedway	LP	Germany		$12.00
	Nonremastered version.					
EMI	CDFA-3193	Red Rose Speedway	LP	U.K.		$12.00
	Nonremastered version.					
Capitol	DPRO-79987	Rocks	DJ/Smplr	U.S.	1990	$30.00
Pioneer	PA-82-027	Rockshow	LD	U.S.	1982	$100.00
Pioneer	PA-82-027	Rockshow	LD	U.S.	1989	$100.00
	Digital audio.					
Pioneer	PA86-M037	Rupert And the Frog Song	8"LD	U.S.	1985	$25.00
Westwood One		Superstars	RS	U.S.	1995	$225.00
	Airdate: 7/3/95.					
EMI	CDP-746057-2	Tug of War	LP	Germany	1983	$12.00
	Nonremastered version.					
EMI	CDFA-3210	Tug of War	LP	U.K.	1983	$12.00
	Nonremastered version.					
Columbia	CK 37462	Tug of War	LP/BP	U.S.†	1983	$30.00/$28.00
Columbia	CK 37462	Tug of War	LP/LB	U.S.	1983	$30.00/$28.00
Capitol	C2-96413	Unplugged (The Offical Bootleg)	LP	U.K.	1991	$30.00
Capitol	C2-96413	Unplugged (The Offical Bootleg)	LP/LB	U.S.	1991	$30.00/$28.00
Media America		Up Close	RS	U.S.	1990	$60.00
	2 CD set.					
Media America		Up Close	RS	U.S.	1991	$60.00
	2 CD set.					
Media America		Up Close	RS	U.S.	1993	$145.00
	3 CD set.					
EMI	CDP-746984-2	Venus and Mars	LP	Germany	1984	$12.00
	Nonremastered version.					
EMI	CDFA-3213	Venus and Mars	LP	U.K.	1984	$12.00
	Nonremastered version.					
CBS	CK-36801	Venus and Mars	LP/BP	U.S.†	1984	$30.00/$28.00
CBS	CK-36801	Venus and Mars	LP/LB	U.S.	1984	$30.00/$28.00
Fame	752017-2	Wild Life	LP	Germany		$12.00
	Nonremastered version.					
Fame	CDFA-3101	Wild Life	LP	U.K.		$12.00
	Nonremastered version.					
CBS	C2K-37990	Wings Over America	LP/LB	U.S.†	1984	$100.00/$85.00
	2 CD set.					
CBS	C2K-37990	Wings Over America	LP/LB	U.S.	1984	$100.00/$85.00
	2 CD set.					
Capitol	C2 46715-2	Wings Over America	LP/LB	U.S.	1988	$29.00/$25.00
	2CD set in individual jewel boxes with custom printed longbox.					

Singles

Label	Catalog Number	Title	Type	Country	Year	Longbox Value / Value
EMI	TOCP-6639	All My Trials	CD5	Japan	1990	$25.00
Parlophone	CDR-6278	All My Trials	CD5	U.K.	1990	$18.00
EMI		Biker Like an Icon	CD5	Holland	1993	$10.00
EMI	CDR-DJ-6347	Biker Like an Icon	CDJ	U.K.	1992	$35.00
EMI	204085-2	Birthday	CD5	Germany	1990	$10.00
EMI	TODP-2204	Birthday	CD3	Japan	1990	$15.00/$4.00
EMI	TOFF-7506	Birthday	CDV	Japan	1990	$40.00
Parlophone	CDR-6271	Birthday	CD5	U.K.	1990	$10.00
Capitol	DPRO-79392	Birthday	CDJ	U.S.	1990	$6.00
EMI	TODP-2401	C'mon People	CD3	Japan	1993	$18.00/$5.00
EMI	CDR 6338	C'mon People	CD5	U.K.	1993	$10.00
EMI	CDRS 6338	C'mon People	CD5	U.K.	1993	$10.00
EMI	CDRDJ 6338	C'mon People	CDJ	U.K.	1993	$15.00
Capitol	C2 15988	C'mon People	CD5	U.S.	1993	$6.00
Capitol	DPRO-79743	C'mon People	CDJ	U.S.	1993	$3.00
Parlophone	CDR-6235	Figure of Eight	CD5	U.K.	1989	$25.00
	Includes 1 CD5 and 1 CD3 in booklet-type package.					
EMI	203653-3	Figure of Eight	CD3	Germany	1989	$12.00
Parlophone	CD3R-6235	Figure of Eight	CD3	U.K.	1989	$15.00
Capitol	DPRO-79871	Figure of Eight	CDJ	U.S.	1989	$12.00
EMI	TODP-2397	Hope of Deliverance	CD3	Japan	1993	$18.00/$5.00
Parlophone	CDR 6330	Hope of Deliverance	CD5	U.K.	1993	$12.00
Parlophone	P-MINT-1	Hope of Deliverance	CDJ	U.K.	1993	$12.00
Capitol	C2 15950	Hope of Deliverance	CD5	U.S.	1993	$5.00
Capitol	DPRO-79579	Hope of Deliverance	CDJ	U.S.	1993	$6.00
		It's Now or Never	CDJ	U.K.	1990	$60.00
	With "Viva Las Vegas" by Bruce Springsteen.					
EMI	204174-2	Long and Winding Road	CD5	Germany	1990	$10.00
EMI	TOCP-6638	Long and Winding Road	CD5	Japan	1990	$15.00
		Michelle	CDJ	Mexico		$65.00
Capitol	CDP 7 15468 2	My Brave Face	CD5	U.S.	1989	$300.00
EMI	203358-3	My Brave Face	CD3	Germany	1989	$15.00
EMI	203358-32	My Brave Face	CD5	Germany	1989	$15.00
Toshiba	XP10-2087	My Brave Face	CD3	Japan	1989	$15.00/$4.00
Toshiba	X12P-2088	My Brave Face	CD3	Japan	1989	$15.00/$4.00
Parlophone	CDR-6213	My Brave Face	CD5	U.K.	1989	$15.00
Parlophone	CD-PROMO-PM1	My Brave Face	CDJ	U.K.	1989	$40.00
Capitol	C2 15468-2	My Brave Face	CD5	U.S.	1989	$150.00
	Never officially released CD5.					
Capitol	DPRO-79590	My Brave Face	CDJ	U.S.	1989	$10.00
Capitol	C2 15966-2-9	Off the Ground	CD5	U.S.	1993	$6.00
Capitol	DPRO-79670	Off the Ground	CDJ	U.S.	1993	$7.00
Capitol	DPRO-79792	Off the Ground	CDJ	U.S.	1993	$7.00
Capitol	DPRO-79670	Off the Ground	CDJ	U.S.	1993	$7.00
	Bob Clearmountain remix.					
Capitol	DPRO-79783	Off the Ground	CDJ	U.S.	1993	$7.00
	Keith Cohen remix.					
EMI	202187-2	Once Upon a Long Ago	CD5	Germany	1989	$12.00
EMI		Once Upon a Long Ago	CDV	Japan	1989	$40.00
Parlophone	CDR-6170	Once Upon a Long Ago	CD5	U.K.	1989	$15.00
Capitol	DPRO-79836	Ou Est Le Soleil	CDJ	U.S.	1989	$15.00
Parlophone	203745 2	Put It There	CD5	Germany	1990	$10.00
Parlophone	CDR-6246	Put It There	CD5	U.K.	1990	$10.00
EMI Classics	C2 15796	Save the Child	CD5	U.S.	1991	$5.00
EMI	203448-3	This One	CD3	Japan	1989	$15.00/$4.00
Toshiba	XP12-2103	This One	CD3	Japan	1989	$15.00/$4.00
Parlophone	CDR-6223	This One	CD5	U.K.	1989	$15.00
Capitol	DPRO-79743	This One	CDJ	U.S.	1989	$7.00
Capitol	DPRO-79979	We Got Married	CDJ	U.S.	1989	$7.00

McClinton, Delbert

Singles

Label	Catalog Number	Title	Type	Country	Year	Longbox Value / Value
Curb	101	Every Time I Roll the Dice	CDJ	U.S.		$2.00
Curb	042	I Want to Love You	CDJ	U.S.	1990	$2.00
Curb	015	I'm With You	CDJ	U.S.	1990	$2.00
A&M	CD 17929	Little Bitty Pretty One	CDJ	U.S.	1989	$2.00
Curb	DPRO-79187	My Baby's Lovin'	CDJ	U.S.	1990	$2.00
Curb	079	That's the Way I Feel	CDJ	U.S.		$2.00
Epic	ESK 5028	Weatherman	CDJ	U.S.	1993	$2.00
Curb	1024	Why Me?	CDJ	U.S.	1992	$2.00

McComb, David

Singles

Label	Catalog Number	Title	Type	Country	Year	Longbox Value / Value
Foundation	TFL-11CD	Message	CD5	U.K.	1991	$9.00

McConnell, Rob & Ross Brass

Full Length

Label	Catalog Number	Title	Type	Country	Year	Longbox Value / Value
Verve	823543-2	Present Perfect	LP/LB	U.S.†	1985	$14.00/$8.00

McCoo, Marilyn

Singles

Label	Catalog Number	Title	Type	Country	Year	Longbox Value / Value
Warner Brothers	PRo-CD-5005	Warrior for the Lord	CDJ	U.S.	1991	$2.00

McCoy, Andy

Singles

Label	Catalog Number	Title	Type	Country	Year	Longbox Value / Value
Polydor	10GD-5017	Too Far Gone	CD3	Japan	1988	$13.00/$4.00
Polydor	10GD-5021	Too Much Ain't Enough	CD3	Japan	1988	$13.00/$4.00

McCoy, Neal

Full Length

Label	Catalog Number	Title	Type	Country	Year	Longbox Value / Value
		Country's Cutting Edge	RS	U.S.	1994	$10.00
	Airdate: 1/8/94.					

McCracklin, Jimmy

Singles

Label	Catalog Number	Title	Type	Country	Year	Longbox Value / Value
Charly	CDS-13	Walk	CD5	U.K.	1989	$8.00

McCrae, Gwen

Singles

Label	Catalog Number	Title	Type	Country	Year	Longbox Value / Value
EMI	CDKTDA-2	All This Love I'm Giving	CD5	U.K.	1993	$8.00

McCray, Larry

Singles

Label	Catalog Number	Title	Type	Country	Year	Longbox Value / Value
Pointblank	POBD-1	Ambition	CD5	U.K.	1990	$8.00

McCulloch, Ian

Full Length

Label	Catalog Number	Title	Type	Country	Year	Longbox Value / Value
Sire		Unravelled	DJ/Smplr	U.S.	1992	$10.00

Singles

Label	Catalog Number	Title	Type	Country	Year	Longbox Value / Value
Eastwest	YZ-452CD	Candleland	CD5	U.K.	1990	$10.00
Sire		Candleland	CDJ	U.S.	1989	$2.00
Sire	9 21567-2	Candleland	CD5	U.S.	1990	$5.00
Eastwest	YZ-660CD	Drug For Love	CD5	U.K.	1992	$10.00
Eastwest	YZ-436CD	Faith & Healing	CD5	U.K.	1989	$10.00
Sire	9 21475-2	Faith & Healing	CD5	U.S.	1989	$5.00
Sire	PRO-CD-3793	Faith & Healing	CDJ	U.S.	1989	$2.00
Sire	9 40376-2	Honey Drip	CD5	U.S.	1991	$5.00
Sire	PRO-CD-5323	Honey Drip	CDJ	U.S.	1991	$2.00
Eastwest	9031-76434-2	Lover Lover Lover	CD5	Germany	1991	$10.00
Eastwest	WMD5-4100	Lover Lover Lover	CD3	Japan	1992	$12.00/$4.00
Eastwest	YZ-643CD	Lover Lover Lover	CD5	U.K.	1991	$10.00
Sire	9 40435-2	Lover Lover Lover	CD5	U.S.	1991	$5.00
Sire	PRO-CD-5515	Lover Lover Lover	CDJ	U.S.	1991	$2.00
Eastwest	246718-2	Proud to Fall	CD5	Germany	1989	$10.00
Eastwest	YZ-417CD	Proud to Fall	CD5	U.K.	1989	$10.00
Sire	PRO-CD-3768	Proud to Fall	CDJ	U.S.	1989	$2.00

McDermott, Kevin

Singles

Label	Catalog Number	Title	Type	Country	Year	Longbox Value / Value
Thirteen	KMOCDS-1	Everything Is Over	CD5	U.K.	1991	$9.00
Island	885593	Healing at the Harbour	CD5	Germany	1989	$9.00
Island	CID-437	Healing at the Harbour	CD5	U.K.	1989	$9.00
Island	CID-404	Wheels of Wonder	CD5	U.K.	1989	$9.00
Island	CID-456	Wheels of Wonder	CD5	U.K.	1990	$9.00
Island	885486	Where We Meant to Be	CD5	Germany	1989	$9.00
Island	CID-423	Where We Meant to Be	CD5	U.K.	1989	$9.00

McDermott, Michael

Singles

Label	Catalog Number	Title	Type	Country	Year	Longbox Value / Value
Giant	PRO-CD-4739	A Wall I Must Climb	CDJ	U.S.	1991	$2.00

McDonald, Michael

Label	Catalog Number	Title	Type	Country	Year	Longbox Value / Value
		Full Length				
Reprise	2-45293-A	Blink of an Eye	DJ/LP	U.S.	1993	$10.00
	Advance issue.					
Reprise	PRO-CD-6300	Hits Sampler	DJ/Smplr	U.S.	1993	$10.00
Warner Brothers	23703-2	If That's What It Takes	LP/LB	U.S.†	1984	$14.00/$8.00
Warner Brothers	PRO-CD-6616	Words & Music	DJ/Intvw	U.S.	1993	$15.00
		Singles				
Reprise	9 21734-2	All We Got	CD5	U.S.	1990	$5.00
Reprise	PRO-CD-4395	All We Got	CDJ	U.S.	1990	$3.00
Reprise	PRO-CD-6538	Hey Girl	CDJ	U.S.	1993	$3.00
Reprise	PRO-CD-6264	I Stand For You	CDJ	U.S.	1993	$3.00
Reprise	PRO-CD-6290	I Stand For You	CDJ	U.S.	1993	$3.00
Reprise	PRo-CD-6882	Matters of the Heart	CDJ	U.S.	1993	$3.00
Pioneer	WPDP-6232	Take it to Heart	CD3	Japan	1990	$12.00/$4.00
Reprise	PRO-CD-4054	Take it to Heart	CDJ	U.S.	1990	$3.00
Reprise	W-9769CD	Tear It Up	CD5	U.K.	1990	$10.00
Reprise	PRO-CD-4398	Tear It Up	CDJ	U.S.	1990	$3.00

McDowell, Fred

Label	Catalog Number	Title	Type	Country	Year	Longbox Value / Value
		Singles				
Derrick Records	141040	Ain't Gonna Worry	CD5	U.S.	1994	$5.00

McDowell, Ronnie

Label	Catalog Number	Title	Type	Country	Year	Longbox Value / Value
		Singles				
		Unchained Melody	CDJ	U.S.		$2.00
Curb	DPRO-79124	When a Man Loves a Woman	CDJ	U.S.		$2.00

McEntire, Reba

Label	Catalog Number	Title	Type	Country	Year	Longbox Value / Value
		Full Length				
		'90s Country	RS	U.S.	1995	$40.00
	Airdate: 10/14/95.					
		'90s Country	RS	U.S.	1995	$40.00
	Airdate: 5/13/95.					
MCA		Celebrating 20 Years	DJ/Smplr	U.S.	1996	$20.00
MCA	MCA3P-10673	It's Your Call	DJ/LP	U.S.	1992	$20.00
		Mother's Day Special	RS	U.S.	1994	$30.00
Unistar		Reba McEntire Story	RS	U.S.	1993	$30.00
	Airdate: 6/11/93.					
		Six Pack	RS	U.S.	1995	$30.00
	3 CD set. Airdate: 9/4/95.					
MCA	MCA3P-3543	Starting Over	DJ/LP	U.S.	1995	$28.00
	Picture disc CD in folder.					
		Singles				
MCA	DMCAT-1336	Cathy's Clown	CD5	U.K.	1989	$8.00
MCA	MCA5P-54719	Does He Love You	CDJ	U.S.	1993	$3.00
MCA	MCA5P-54108	Fallin' Out of Love	CDJ	U.S.	1991	$3.00
MCA		Keep Me Hangin' On	CD5	U.S.	1996	$5.00
MCA		Keep Me Hangin' On	CDJ	U.S.	1996	$3.00
MCA	MCA5P-54386	Night the Lights Went Out In Georgia, The	CDJ	U.S.	1992	$3.00
MCA	MCA5P-54769	They Asked About You	CDJ	U.S.	1993	$3.00

McEvoy, Eleanor

Label	Catalog Number	Title	Type	Country	Year	Longbox Value / Value
		Singles				
Geffen	PRO-CD-5462	Apologise	CDJ	U.S.	1993	$2.00
Geffen	PRO-CD-4631	Apologise	CDJ	U.S.	1994	$2.00
Geffen	PRO-CD-4563	Only a Woman's Heart	CDJ	U.S.	1993	$2.00

McFerrin, Bobby

Label	Catalog Number	Title	Type	Country	Year	Longbox Value / Value
		Full Length				
		Medicine Music	DJ/LP	Japan		$30.00
	Advance issue.					
		Singles				
EMI	DPRO-04711	Baby	CDJ	U.S.	1991	$2.00
EMI	202929-2	Don't Worry Be Happy	CD5	Germany	1988	$10.00
EMI	CDMT-56	Don't Worry Be Happy	CD5	U.K.	1988	$10.00
		Don't Worry Be Happy	CDJ	U.S.	1988	$2.00
Blue Note	CDMT-92	Garden, The	CD5	U.K.	1990	$10.00
EMI	203148-2	Good Lovin'	CD3	Germany	1988	$10.00
EMI	203148-3	Good Lovin'	CD3	Germany	1988	$10.00
EMI	CDMT-42	Good Lovin'	CD5	U.K.	1988	$10.00
Manhattan	DPRO-04167	Good Lovin'	CDJ	U.S.	1988	$2.00
		Long and Lasting Love	CDJ	U.S.		$2.00
RCA	62692-2-RDJ	Son of the Pink Panther	CDJ	U.S.	1993	$3.00
Blue Note	DPRo-79223	Spain	CDJ	U.S.	1992	$7.00
EMI	CDBLURE-6	Thinkin' About Your Body	CD5	U.K.	1988	$10.00

McGarrigle, Kate & Ana

Label	Catalog Number	Title	Type	Country	Year	Longbox Value / Value
		Singles				
Private	2070-S1	Heartbeats Accelerating	CDJ	U.S.	1990	$2.00

McGear, Mike

Label	Catalog Number	Title	Type	Country	Year	Longbox Value / Value
		Full Length				
Rykodisc		McGear	LP/LB	U.S.		$14.00/$8.00

McGhee, Brownie

Label	Catalog Number	Title	Type	Country	Year	Longbox Value / Value
		Full Length				
		House of Blues	RS	U.S.	1995	$40.00
	2 CD set. Airdate: 12/1/95.					

McGhee, Jacci

Label	Catalog Number	Title	Type	Country	Year	Longbox Value / Value
		Singles				
MCA	MCA5P-2290	Skeeza	CDJ	U.S.	1992	$2.00
MCA	MCA5P-2559	Something's on My Mind	CDJ	U.S.	1993	$2.00

McGrath, Bob

Label	Catalog Number	Title	Type	Country	Year	Longbox Value / Value
		Full Length				
A&M	0414	Favorite Street Songs	LP/BP	U.S.		$12.00/$7.00

McGraw, Tim

Label	Catalog Number	Title	Type	Country	Year	Longbox Value / Value
		Full Length				
		Not a Moment Too Soon	RS	U.S.	1994	$15.00
		Singles				
Curb	1073	Indian Outlaw	CDJ	U.S.	1994	$2.00

McGraw, Tim/Faith Hill

Label	Catalog Number	Title	Type	Country	Year	Longbox Value / Value
		Full Length				
Curb/Warner Brothers		Tour Sampler	DJ/Smplr	U.S.	1996	$18.00

McGregor, Freddie

Label	Catalog Number	Title	Type	Country	Year	Longbox Value / Value
		Singles				
Polydor	POCD-905	Come To Me	CD5	U.K.	1988	$8.00
Polydor	PZCD-53	Guantanamera	CD5	U.K.	1989	$8.00
Pow Wow	479	(Playing) Hard to Get	CDJ	U.S.	1993	$2.00
Polydor	PZCD-20	So I Will Wait For You	CD5	U.K.	1988	$8.00

McGuinn, Roger

Label	Catalog Number	Title	Type	Country	Year	Longbox Value / Value
		Full Length				
Arista	ASCD-8648	Back From Rio	DJ/LP	U.S.	1990	$18.00
	Picture CD in special box with pull-out tray.					
DIR		King Biscuit Flour Hour	RS	U.S.	1993	$55.00
	Airdate: 10/10/93.					
DIR		King Biscuit Flour Hour	RS	U.S.	1994	$55.00
	Airdate: 12/4/94.					
DIR		King Biscuit Flour Hour	RS	U.S.	1995	$55.00
	Airdate: 12/2/95.					
		Live From Electric Ladyland	RS	U.S.	1991	$40.00
	Airdate: 7/19/91.					
		Singles				
Arista	663993	King of the Hill	CD5	Germany	1991	$10.00
BMG	BVDA-15	King of the Hill	CD3	Japan	1991	$12.00/$4.00
Arista	663993	King of the Hill	CD5	U.K.	1991	$10.00
Arista	ASCD-2154	King of the Hill	CDJ	U.S.	1990	$2.00
Arista	ASCD-2214	Someone to Love	CDJ	U.S.	1990	$2.00

McGuire, Barry

Label	Catalog Number	Title	Type	Country	Year	Longbox Value / Value
		Singles				
Sony	655645-2	Eve of Destruction	CD3	Japan	1990	$13.00/$4.00
Old Gold	OG-6141	Eve of Destruction	CD3	U.K.	1989	$10.00

McKagan, Duff

Label	Catalog Number	Title	Type	Country	Year	Longbox Value / Value
		Singles				
Geffen		Believe in Me	CD5	Japan	1993	$25.00
Geffen	PRO-CD-4559	Believe in Me	CDJ	U.S.	1993	$3.00
Geffen	PRO-CD-4523	Man In the Meadow	CDJ	U.S.	1994	$3.00
Geffen	PRO-CD-4574	Punk Rock	CDJ	U.S.	1993	$3.00

McKay, Kris

Label	Catalog Number	Title	Type	Country	Year	Longbox Value / Value
		Singles				
Arista	ASCD-2062	Any Single Solitary Heart	CDJ	U.S.		$2.00

McKee, Lonette

Label	Catalog Number	Title	Type	Country	Year	Longbox Value / Value
		Singles				
Columbia	CSK 74469	Watch the Birds	CDJ	U.S.	1992	$2.00

McKee, Maria

Label	Catalog Number	Title	Type	Country	Year	Longbox Value / Value
		Full Length				
Geffen	PRO-CD-4570	I Can't Make It Alone	DJ/Smplr	U.S.	1993	$15.00
Geffen		Maria McKee	DJ/LP	U.S.	1989	$20.00
	CD in box with autographed lithograph.					
		Singles				
		Absolutely Barkings Stars	CDJ	U.S.		$3.00
Geffen	PRO-CD-3599	Breathe	CDJ	U.S.	1989	$2.00
		I Can't Make It Alone	CD5	U.K.		$10.00
		I Can't Make It Alone	CD5	U.K.		$10.00
	Second version.					
Geffen	PRO-CD-4512	I'm Gonna Soothe You	CDJ	U.S.	1993	$2.00
Geffen	PRO-CD-3556	I've Forgotten What It Was In You	CDJ	U.S.	1989	$2.00
Geffen	PRO-CD-4156	Show Me Heaven	CDJ	U.S.	1990	$2.00
		That Perfect Dress	CD5	U.K.	1996	$10.00
		That Perfect Dress	CD5	U.K.	1996	$10.00
	Second version.					
		This Perfect Dress	CD5	U.K.	1996	$10.00
		This Perfect Dress	CD5	U.K.	1996	$10.00
	Second version.					
Geffen	PRO-CD-3666	To Miss Someone	CDJ	U.S.	1989	$2.00

McKennitt, Loreena

Label	Catalog Number	Title	Type	Country	Year	Longbox Value / Value
		Full Length				
Warner Brothers		Live In San Francisco	DJ/Smplr	U.S.		$30.00
Warner Brothers		Mask And Mirror, The	LTD/LP	Australia	1994	$30.00
	2 CD set.					
Warner Brothers	PRO-CD-6775	Mask And Mirror, The	DJ/Smplr	U.S.	1994	$12.00
	CDN24	Selections From Loreena McKennitt	DJ/Smplr	Canada	1994	$35.00
		Visit, The	DJ/Smplr	Canada	1992	$30.00
	2 CD sampler and interview discs.					
Warner Brothers	PRO-CD-5809	Visit, The	DJ/Intvw	U.S.	1992	$15.00
		Singles				
		All Souls Night	CDJ	Canada		$6.00
Warner Brothers	PRO-CD-6794	Bonny Swans, The	CDJ	U.S.	1994	$2.00
Warner Brothers	PRO-CD-5671	Lady of Schalott	CDJ	U.S.	1991	$2.00

McKenzie, Scott

Label	Catalog Number	Title	Type	Country	Year	Longbox Value / Value
		Singles				
Columbia	654604-3	San Francisco	CD3	Germany	1989	$9.00
Columbia	655071--3	San Francisco	CD3	Germany	1989	$9.00
Columbia	654604-3	San Francisco	CD3	U.K.	1989	$9.00

McKeown, Les

Label	Catalog Number	Title	Type	Country	Year	Longbox Value / Value
		Singles				
BMG	662041	It's A Game	CD5	Germany	1989	$8.00
BMG	162431	Love Hurts	CD3	Germany	1989	$8.00
BMG	662431	Love Hurts	CD5	Germany	1989	$8.00
BMG	661794	Love Is Just a Breath Away	CD5	Germany	1989	$8.00
BMG	662738	Nobody Makes Me Crazy	CD5	Germany	1989	$8.00
RCA	R10D-133	She's a Lady	CD3	Japan	1989	$13.00/$4.00

McKnight, Brian

Label	Catalog Number	Title	Type	Country	Year	Longbox Value / Value
		Singles				
Polygram	852037	Crazy Love, Love Is	CD5	U.S.	1995	$5.00
Polygram	852226	On the Down Low	CD5	U.S.	1995	$5.00
	CDP1468	On the Low Down	CDJ	U.S.		$2.00
Island	852396	Still in Love	CD5	U.S.	1995	$5.00

McKone, Vivienne

Label	Catalog Number	Title	Type	Country	Year	Longbox Value / Value
		Singles				
ffrr	FCD-202	Beware	CD5	U.K.	1992	$8.00
London	CDP 958	Get To Know You	CDJ	U.S.	1993	$2.00
ffrr	POD-1029	Sing	CD3	Japan	1993	$12.00/$3.00
ffrr	FCD-183	Sing	CD5	U.K.	1992	$8.00
London	CDP 1019	Sing	CDJ	U.S.	1992	$2.00

McKuen, Rod

Label	Catalog Number	Title	Type	Country	Year	Longbox Value / Value
		Singles				
Laserlight	12441	At Carnegie Hall	CD5	U.S.	1994	$5.00
Laserlight	12443	At The Movies	CD5	U.S.	1994	$5.00
Laserlight	12445	Early Harvest	CD5	U.S.	1994	$5.00
Laserlight	12444	French Connection	CD5	U.S.	1994	$5.00
Laserlight	12442	Speaking of Love	CD5	U.S.	1994	$5.00

McLachlan, Craig

Label	Catalog Number	Title	Type	Country	Year	Longbox Value / Value
		Singles				
Columbia	656170-3	Amanda	CD3	Germany	1990	$8.00

Label	Catalog Number	Title	Type	Country	Year	Longbox/Value
Columbia	655784-3	Mona	CD3	Germany	1990	$8.00
Columbia	655784-2	Mona	CD5	Germany	1990	$8.00
Epic	658067-2	One Reason Why	CD5	U.K.	1992	$8.00

McLachlan, Sarah

Full Length

Label	Catalog Number	Title	Type	Country	Year	Longbox/Value
		Album Network Special	RS	U.S.	1995	$200.00
	Airdate: 3/12/95.					
Arista		Fumbling Towards	DJ/Smplr	U.S.	1994	$18.00
Westwood One		In Concert-Nu Rock	RS	U.S.	1996	$100.00
	Airdate: 3/11/96.					
Arista	18631	Solace	DJ/LP	U.S.	1991	$20.00

Singles

Label	Catalog Number	Title	Type	Country	Year	Longbox/Value
Arista	BVDA-11	Ben's Song	CD3	Japan	1990	$12.00/$4.00
Arista		Fumbling Towards Ecstasy	CDJ	Canada		$12.00
Arista	ASCD2690	Good Enough	CDJ	U.S.	1994	$3.00
Arista	ASCD2788	Hold On	CDJ	U.S.		$3.00
Arista		I Will Remember You	CDJ	U.S.		$7.00
Nettwerk	665266	Into the Fire	CD5	U.K.	1992	$10.00
Arista	ASCD-2390	Into the Fire	CDJ	U.S.	1992	$2.00
		Live	CD5	Canada	1994	$10.00
Arista	ASCD 2423	Path of Thorns	CDJ	U.S.	1992	$2.00
Arista	ASCD 2662	Possession	CDJ	U.S.	1992	$2.00

McLaren, Malcom

Singles

Label	Catalog Number	Title	Type	Country	Year	Longbox/Value
Epic	WALTZC-5	Call a Wave	CD5	U.K.	1990	$8.00
Epic	WALTZC-6	Deep in Vogue	CD5	U.K.	1990	$8.00
Epic	655367-3	House of the Blue Danube	CD3	Germany	1990	$8.00
Epic	WALTZC-4	House of the Blue Danube	CD3	U.K.	1990	$8.00
Epic	WALTZP-4	House of the Blue Danube	CD5	U.K.	1990	$8.00
Virgin	CDT-30	Madam Butterfly	CD3	U.K.	1988	$8.00
RCA	PD-49224	Magic's Back	CD5	U.K.	1991	$8.00
Virgin	VSCDT-1273	Opera House	CD5	U.K.	1990	$8.00
	PRCD 6991-2	Revenge of the Flowers	CDJ	U.S.		$2.00
Virgin	PRCD 3667	Romeo and Juliet	CDJ	U.S.	1991	$2.00
Epic	655129-3	Something's Jumping in Your Shorts	CD5	Germany	1989	$8.00
Epic	WALTZC-3	Something's Jumping in Your Shorts	CD5	U.K.	1989	$8.00
Epic	654657-3	Waltz Darling	CD3	Germany	1989	$8.00
Epic	WALTZC-2	Waltz Darling	CD5	U.K.	1989	$8.00

McLaughlin, John

Full Length

Label	Catalog Number	Title	Type	Country	Year	Longbox/Value
		Devotion	LP	Germany		$13.00

McLean, Don

Singles

Label	Catalog Number	Title	Type	Country	Year	Longbox/Value
EMI	CDMCT-3	American Pie	CD5	U.K.	1991	$11.00
Curb	099	American Pie	CDJ	U.S.	1992	$6.00

McLean, Jackie

Full Length

Label	Catalog Number	Title	Type	Country	Year	Longbox/Value
Mosaic	MD4-150	Complete Blue Note 1964-66	LTD/LP	U.S.	1994	$60.00
	4 CD set.					
Blue Note		Jackie's Bag and One Step Beyond	LTD/LP	U.S.	1995	$19.00

McLean, Penny

Singles

Label	Catalog Number	Title	Type	Country	Year	Longbox/Value
Polygram	885878-2	Lady Bump	CD5	Germany	1990	$8.00

McLennan, G.W.

Singles

Label	Catalog Number	Title	Type	Country	Year	Longbox/Value
Beggars Banquet	BEG-254CD	Easy Come Easy Go	CD5	U.K.	1991	$8.00
Beggars Banquet	BEG-247CD	When Word Gets Around	CD5	U.K.	1991	$8.00

McLennan, Grant

Full Length

Label	Catalog Number	Title	Type	Country	Year	Longbox/Value
	PROC60312	Present & Past	DJ/Smplr	U.S.		$15.00
		Present & Past	DJ/Smplr	U.S.		$18.00
		Simone & Perry	CD5	U.K.	1995	$10.00

MCM

Singles

Label	Catalog Number	Title	Type	Country	Year	Longbox/Value
Priority	6611	Xmaz in the Hood	CDJ	U.S.		$7.00

McMurtry, James

Full Length

Label	Catalog Number	Title	Type	Country	Year	Longbox/Value
Columbia	CSK 1734	Too Long in the Wasteland	DJ/LP	U.S.	1989	$5.00
	DJ CD in paper bag with booklet.					

Singles

Label	Catalog Number	Title	Type	Country	Year	Longbox/Value
Columbia	CSK 4589	Where's Johnny	CDJ	U.S.	1992	$2.00

McNabb, Ian

Singles

Label	Catalog Number	Title	Type	Country	Year	Longbox/Value
Way Cool	WAY-14CD	Great Dreams Of Heaven	CD5	U.K.	1991	$8.00
Way Cool	WAY-233	If Love Was Like Guitars	CD5	U.K.	1991	$8.00
Fat Cat	FC-001	These Are the Days	CD5	U.K.	1991	$8.00

McNabb, Michael

Full Length

Label	Catalog Number	Title	Type	Country	Year	Longbox/Value
Mobile Fidelity	MFCD-818	Computer Music	LP/LB	U.S.†	1985	$15.00/$10.00

McNeil, Rita

Singles

Label	Catalog Number	Title	Type	Country	Year	Longbox/Value
Polygram	879949-2	Working Man	CD5	Germany	1990	$8.00

McPillsberry And The 4 Large Crew

Singles

Label	Catalog Number	Title	Type	Country	Year	Longbox/Value
Atlantic	PRCD 3348-2	Me So Hungry	CDJ	U.S.	1990	$2.00

McQueen Street

Singles

Label	Catalog Number	Title	Type	Country	Year	Longbox/Value
SBK	DPRO-05422	In Heaven	CDJ	U.S.	1991	$2.00

Mcrackins

Singles

Label	Catalog Number	Title	Type	Country	Year	Longbox/Value
Shredder Records	26	What Came First	CD5	U.S.	1994	$5.00

McShane, Ian

Singles

Label	Catalog Number	Title	Type	Country	Year	Longbox/Value
Polygram	IANMD-1	Avalon	CD5	U.K.	1992	$8.00

McVie, Christine

Full Length

Label	Catalog Number	Title	Type	Country	Year	Longbox/Value
Pioneer	38XP-75	Christine McVie	LP	Japan	1984	$18.00
Warner Brothers	25059-2	Christine McVie	LP	U.K.	1984	$12.00
Pioneer	PA-84-084	Christine McVie	LD	U.S.	1984	$25.00
Warner Brothers	25059-2	Christine McVie	LP/LB	U.S.†	1984	$15.00/$10.00
Warner Brothers	25059-2	Christine McVie	LP/LB	U.S.	1986	$15.00/$10.00

McVie, John

Full Length

Label	Catalog Number	Title	Type	Country	Year	Longbox/Value
Warner Brothers		McVie's Gotta Band	LP/LB	U.S.		$14.00/$8.00

Singles

Label	Catalog Number	Title	Type	Country	Year	Longbox/Value
Warner Brothers	PRO-CD-5553	Now I Know	CDJ	U.S.	1992	$2.00
Warner Brothers	PRO-CD-5854	One More Feeling	CDJ	U.S.	1992	$2.00

Me

Singles

Label	Catalog Number	Title	Type	Country	Year	Longbox/Value
RCA	62816	Thump	CD5	U.S.	1994	$5.00

Me & My Cousin

Singles

Label	Catalog Number	Title	Type	Country	Year	Longbox/Value
	DPRO-60916	Red Carpet	CDJ	U.S.		$2.00
	DPRO-30032	Smooth	CDJ	U.S.		$2.00

Me Phi Me

Singles

Label	Catalog Number	Title	Type	Country	Year	Longbox/Value
RCA	62369-2-RDJ	Black Sunshine	CDJ	U.S.	1992	$2.00
RCA	62277-2-RDJ	Pu Sho Hands 2 Getha	CDJ	U.S.	1992	$2.00

Meaning

Singles

Label	Catalog Number	Title	Type	Country	Year	Longbox/Value
SPV	9979-3	Showing You the Feeling	CD5	U.K.	1992	$8.00

Meat Beat Manifesto

Singles

Label	Catalog Number	Title	Type	Country	Year	Longbox/Value
Mute	8764	Circles	CDJ	U.S.	1993	$2.00
Pias	BIAS 140CD	Dog Star Man	CDJ	U.K.	1991	$8.00
Pias	142CD	Dog Star Man	CD5	U.S.	1991	$5.00
Pias	BIAS-222CD	Edge Of No Control	CD5	U.K.	1991	$8.00
Sweatbox	SOX-039CD	God O.D.	CD5	U.K.	1990	$8.00
Wax Trax	65	God O.D.	CD5	U.S.	1990	$5.00
SPV	0366-3	Godstar Man	CD3	Germany	1990	$8.00
SPV	9164-3	Helter Skelter	CD5	Germany	1990	$8.00
Pias	BIAS-172CD	Helter Skelter	CD5	U.S.	1991	$8.00
		Midstream	CD5	U.K.		$10.00
	Second version.					
Mute	66343	Midstream	CD5	U.S.	1993	$5.00
Mute	8689	Midstream	CDJ	U.S.	1993	$2.00
SPV	4974-3	Psyche-Out	CD5	Germany	1990	$8.00
Pais	BIAS-182CD	Psyche Out	CD5	U.K.	1990	$8.00
WEA	9 66579-2	Psyche-Out	CD5	U.S.	1990	$5.00
Efa	CD-66608	Strap Down	CD5	Germany	1988	$8.00
Sweatbox	SOX-032CD	Strap Down	CD5	U.K.	1988	$8.00

Meat Loaf

Full Length

Label	Catalog Number	Title	Type	Country	Year	Longbox/Value
Album Network		Album Network Special	RS	U.S.	1993	$150.00
	2 CD set.					
Tommy Boy	1195	Around the World Live	LTD/LP	U.S.	1996	$20.00
	2 CD set in double brilliant box.					
Tommy Boy	1187	Around the World Live	LTD/LP	U.S.	1996	$20.00
	2 CD set in double digi-pak.					
Epic	WEK 90891	Bat Out of Hell	LTD/LP	Canada	1992	$50.00
	Picture disc CD.					
Epic	EK-34974	Bat Out of Hell	LP/BP	U.S.†	1984	$14.00/$8.00
MCA		Bat Out of Hell II: Back Into Hell	LTD/LP	Australia	1994	$35.00
MCA	MCAD-10699	Bat Out of Hell II: Back Into Hell	LP	U.S.	1993	$15.00
	Second pressing 4 color picture disc version.					
MCA	MCAD-10699	Bat Out of Hell II: Back Into Hell	LP	U.S.	1993	$20.00
	First pressing 5 color picture disc version.					
MCA	0881109712	Bat Out of Hell II: Back Into Hell	LTD/LP	U.S.	1993	$27.00
	CD in tire with oversized booklet and box.					
Album Network		In the Studio (Bat Out of Hell)	RS	U.S.	1989	$25.00
	Airdate: 8/28/89.					
MCA	MCA3P3663	Interview (An Instant Classic)	DJ/Intvw	U.S.	1996	$25.00
DIR		King Biscuit Flour Hour	RS	U.S.	1991	$40.00
	Airdate: 11/17/91.					
		Meat Loaf and Friends	LTD/LP	U.K.	1995	$25.00
	2 CD set.					
		Recorded Live at the Hudson Theatre 9/18/93	RS	U.S.	1993	$60.00
Westwood One		Superstars	RS	U.S.	1994	$60.00
	2 CD set. Airdate: 6/6/94.					

Singles

Label	Catalog Number	Title	Type	Country	Year	Longbox/Value
MCA	MCA5P-3576	Amnesty Is Granted	CDJ	U.S.	1995	$6.00
Epic		Bat Out of Hell	CD5	U.K.		$10.00
	Second version.					
Epic	660006	Bat Out of Hell	CD5	U.K.	1993	$10.00
Epic	656982-2	Dead Ringer For Love	CD5	U.K.	1991	$10.00
Epic	654685-3	Heaven Can Wait	CD3	Germany	1989	$10.00
		I'd Do Anything For Love	CD5	U.K.		$10.00
MCA	VJCP-12025	I'd Lie For You	CDJ	Japan	1995	$20.00
MCA	MCA5P3548	I'd Lie For You	CDJ	U.S.	1994	$6.00
MCA		I'd Lie For You	CDJ	U.S.	1994	$6.00
	Second version.					
MCA		I'd Lie For You	CDJ	U.S.	1994	$6.00
	Third version.					
MCA		I'd Lie For You	CD5	U.S.	1995	$5.00
	LEMON-1	Life Is A Lemon and I Want My Money Back	CDJ	U.K.	1994	$15.00
MCA	MCA5P- 2883	Life Is A Lemon and I Want My Money Back	CDJ	U.S.	1994	$7.00
MCA	MCA5P-2883	Life Is A Lemon and I Want My Money Back	CDJ	U.S.	1995	$3.00
MCA		Live Storm	CDJ	U.S.	1994	$7.00
MCA	MCA5P-3641	Not A Dry Eye In the House	CDJ	U.S.	1995	$3.00
		Objects in the Rear View Mirror	CD5	U.K.	1994	$10.00
	Second version.					
	VSCDX1492	Objects in the Rear View Mirror	CD5	U.K.	1994	$12.00
MCA	MCA5P-3016	Objects in the Rear View Mirror	CDJ	U.S.	1994	$3.00
Epic	65467-3	Paradise by the Dashboard Lights	CD3	Germany	1989	$10.00
Epic	65467-3	Paradise by the Dashboard Lights	CD3	U.K.	1989	$10.00
CBS	34K-2371	Paradise by the Dashboard Lights	CD3	U.S.	1989	$7.00/$4.00
MCA	MCAD-2492	Paradise by the Dashboard Lights	CDJ	U.S.	1992	$6.00
		Rock and Roll Dreams Come True	CD5	U.K.		$10.00
		Rock and Roll Dreams Come True	CD5	U.K.		$10.00
	Second version.					
MCA	54797	Rock and Roll Dreams Come True	CD5	U.S.	1994	$5.00
MCA	MCA5P-2884	Rock and Roll Dreams Come True	CDJ	U.S.	1994	$6.00
MCA	MCA5P-2989	Rock and Roll Dreams Come True	CDJ	U.S.	1994	$6.00
Arista	RISCD-14	Special Girl	CD5	U.K.	1987	$11.00
Epic	657491-2	Two Out of Three Ain't Bad	CD3	U.K.	1992	$10.00

Meat Puppets

Full Length

Label	Catalog Number	Title	Type	Country	Year	Longbox Value / Value
London	CDP 481	Forbidden Places	DJ/LP	U.S.	1991	$15.00
London		Tender Cuts	DJ/Smplr	U.S.	1994	$8.00

Singles

Label	Catalog Number	Title	Type	Country	Year	Longbox Value / Value
London	857553	Backwater	CD5	U.S.	1993	$5.00
London	CDP 1116	Backwater	CDJ	U.S.	1993	$2.00
		Lake of Fire	CDJ	U.S.		$3.00
	PRCD 7047-2	Scum	CDJ	U.S.		$3.00
London	CDP 485	Sin	CDJ	U.S.	1991	$2.00
		Tender Cuts	CDJ	U.S.		$6.00
London	CDP 531	Whirlpool	CDJ	U.S.	1991	$2.00

Meatplow, Ethyl

Singles

Label	Catalog Number	Title	Type	Country	Year	Longbox Value / Value
Dali	8770	Devil's Johnson	CDJ	U.S.		$3.00

Medeiros, Glenn

Singles

Label	Catalog Number	Title	Type	Country	Year	Longbox Value / Value
Polygram	878245-2	All I'm Missing Is You	CD5	Germany	1990	$10.00
London	LONCD-275	All I'm Missing Is You	CD5	U.K.	1990	$10.00
MCA	CD45-18507	All I'm Missing Is You	CDJ	U.S.	1990	$2.00
		Doesn't Matter Anymore	CDJ	U.S.		$2.00
Mercury	872337-2	Friend You Give Me a Reason	CD5	Germany	1988	$10.00
Mercury	870583-2	Friend You Give Me a Reason	CD5	U.K.	1990	$10.00
Polygram	870635-2	Long and Lasting Love	CD5	Germany	1988	$10.00
Polygram	LONCD-202	Long and Lasting Love	CD5	U.K.	1988	$10.00
MCA	CD45-1284	Long and Lasting Love	CDJ	U.S.	1988	$2.00
Phonogram	10DP-6	Love Always Finds A Reason	CD3	Japan	1989	$13.00/$4.00
		Me You Blue	CDJ	U.S.		$2.00
		Me You Blue	CDJ	U.S.		$2.00
	Second version.					
MCA	CD45-17780	Never Get Enough of You	CDJ	U.S.		$2.00
Polygram	888610-2	Nothing's Gonna Change My Love	CD5	Germany	1988	$10.00
Polygram	877495-2	She Ain't Worth It	CD5	Germany	1990	$10.00
Phonogram	PHCR-265	She Ain't Worth It	CD5	Japan	1990	$13.00
London	LONCD-265	She Ain't Worth It	CD5	U.K.	1990	$10.00
MCA	CD45-18331	She Ain't Worth It	CDJ	U.S.	1990	$2.00

Medicine

Singles

Label	Catalog Number	Title	Type	Country	Year	Longbox Value / Value
Creation	CRESCD-135	Aruca	CD5	U.K.	1992	$8.00
Creation	CRESCD-141	Five	CD5	U.K.	1992	$8.00
American	6684	Never Click	CDJ	U.S.	1993	$2.00
Wea	CDW45609	The Sounds Of Medicine	CD5	Canada	1994	$14.00

Medicine Wheel

Singles

Label	Catalog Number	Title	Type	Country	Year	Longbox Value / Value
Virgin	VSCDT-1391	Last Emotion	CD5	U.K.	1992	$8.00

Medley, Bill

Singles

Label	Catalog Number	Title	Type	Country	Year	Longbox Value / Value
Curb	072	Don't Let Go	CDJ	U.S.	1991	$2.00
Curb	DPRO-79321	Don't You Love Me Anymore?	CDJ	U.S.	1990	$2.00
Polydor	827 332	He Ain't Heavy, He's My Brother	CD5	Germany	1988	$8.00
Polydor	PZCD-10	He Ain't Heavy, He's My Brother	CD5	U.K.	1988	$8.00
Elektra	PRCD 8101-2	Rude Awakening	CDJ	U.S.	1989	$2.00
RCA	PD-49626	Time of My Life	CD5	U.K.	1991	$8.00
BMG	162169	You've Lost That Lovin' Feeling	CD3	U.K.	1989	$10.00
BMG	662169	You've Lost That Lovin' Feeling	CD5	U.K.	1989	$10.00

Medley, Sue

Full Length

Label	Catalog Number	Title	Type	Country	Year	Longbox Value / Value
		Sue Medley	DJ/LP	Canada		$20.00
	Picture disc.					

Singles

Label	Catalog Number	Title	Type	Country	Year	Longbox Value / Value
Mercury	4228643432	Dangerous Time	CD5	Canada	1991	$7.00
Polygram	868193-2	Dangerous Time	CD5	Germany	1991	$8.00
Mercury	PHDR-27	Dangerous Time	CD3	Japan	1991	$12.00/$3.00

Meet Puppets

Full Length

Label	Catalog Number	Title	Type	Country	Year	Longbox Value / Value
Westwood One		In Concert	RS	U.S.	1994	$60.00
	Airdate: 9/12/94.					
Westwood One		In Concert	RS	U.S.	1995	$60.00
	Airdate: 11/20/95.					

Meg

Singles

Label	Catalog Number	Title	Type	Country	Year	Longbox Value / Value
ZYX	ZYX-6316-8	Lover Girl	CD5	Germany	1990	$8.00

Mega City Four

Singles

Label	Catalog Number	Title	Type	Country	Year	Longbox Value / Value
Big Life	BLA 1	Ticket Collector	CD5	U.K.	1992	$8.00
		Wallflower	CD5	U.K.		$10.00
		Wallflower	CD5	U.K.		$10.00
	Second version.					
Big Life	BLA 2	Words That Say	CD5	U.K.	1992	$8.00

Megadeth

Full Length

Label	Catalog Number	Title	Type	Country	Year	Longbox Value / Value
Foundation		FZ Interview	DJ/Intvw	U.S.	1992	$10.00
Capitol	CDP-33620	Hidden Treasures	LTD/LP	U.S.	1995	$18.00
Capitol	DPRO-79862	Limited Edition! Megadeth Live	DJ/Smplr	U.S.	1992	$12.00
Capitol	DPRO-79757	Maximum Megadeth	DJ/Smplr	U.S.	1991	$20.00
Capitol	DPRO-79396	Megadeth Interview	DJ/Intvw	U.S.	1992	$15.00
Capitol	CDP 7 91935 2	Rust in Peace	DJ/LP	U.S.	1990	$50.00
	CD in custom cofin package with "pop-up" skeleton.					
Pioneer Artists	PA-91-380	Rusted Place	LD	U.S.	1991	$30.00
Capitol	C2 7243 8 30916 2 1	Youthanasia	LTD/LP	Germany	1994	$25.00
	Blue Jewel Box.					
EMI		Youthanasia	DJ/LP	U.K.	1994	$80.00
	CD and press kit in custom box.					
EMI	CDAS100	Youthanasia	DJ/Smplr	U.K.	1994	$16.00
EMI		Youthanasia	LTD/LP	U.K.	1995	$30.00
	Youthanasia CD and Hidden Treasures bonus disc.					
Capitol	30916	Youthanasia	LTD/LP	U.S.	1994	$25.00
	CD and T-shirt in box.					

Singles

Label	Catalog Number	Title	Type	Country	Year	Longbox Value / Value
Geffen	PRO-CD-4580	99 Ways to Die	CDJ	U.S.	1993	$8.00
		A Tout Le Monde	CD5	U.K.	1995	$10.00
Capitol	DPRO79535	A Tout Le Monde	CDJ	U.S.	1994	$6.00
		A Tout Le Monde	CDJ	U.S.	1995	$6.00
Capitol	DPRO-79448	Crown Of Worms	CDJ	U.S.	1994	$15.00
	CD in plastic doll-head package.					
Capitol	8802982	Foreclosure of a Dream	CD5	Germany	1992	$10.00
Capitol	C2 15935	Foreclosure of a Dream	CD5	U.S.	1992	$5.00
Capitol	DPRO-79391	Foreclosure of a Dream	CDJ	U.S.	1992	$3.00
Capitol	204222-2	Hanger 18	CD5	Germany	1990	$10.00
Capitol	TOCP-6667	Hanger 18	CD5	Japan	1990	$18.00
Capitol	CDCL-604	Hanger 18	CD5	U.K.	1990	$10.00
Capitol	C2 15662	Hanger 18	CD5	U.S.	1990	$5.00
Capitol	DPRO-79462	Hanger 18	CDJ	U.S.	1990	$6.00
Capitol	204044-2	Holy Wars...The Punishment Due	CD5	Germany	1990	$10.00
Capitol	CDCL-588	Holy Wars...The Punishment Due	CD5	U.K.	1990	$10.00
Capitol	DPRO-79292	Holy Wars...The Punishment Due	CDJ	U.S.	1990	$7.00
EMI	560-203620 2	No More Mr. Nice Guy	CD5	Germany	1989	$10.00
EMI	CDSBK-2	No More Mr. Nice Guy	CD5	U.K.	1989	$10.00
Capitol	CDCL-669	Skin o' My Teeth	CD5	U.K.	1992	$10.00
Capitol	8802942	Skin o' My Teeth	CD5	U.K.	1992	$10.00
Capitol	8802952	Skin o' My Teeth	CD5	U.K.	1992	$10.00
Capitol	CDCLDJ-669	Skin o' My Teeth	CD5	U.K.	1992	$10.00
Capitol	DPRO-79363	Skin o' My Teeth	CDJ	U.S.	1992	$6.00
Capitol	7234 880492	Sweating Bullets	CD5	Germany	1992	$10.00
		Sweating Bullets	CD5	U.K.		$10.00
		Sweating Bullets	CD5	U.K.		$10.00
	Second version.					
Capitol	DPRO-79592	Sweating Bullets	CDJ	U.S.	1992	$3.00
Capitol	C2 15946	Sweating Bullets	CD5	U.S.	1993	$6.00
Capitol		Symphony of Destruction	CD5	Japan	1992	$18.00
Capitol		Symphony of Destruction	CD5	U.K.	1992	$10.00
Capitol	C2 158702	Symphony of Destruction	CD5	U.S.	1992	$5.00
Capitol	DPRO-79339	Symphony of Destruction	CDJ	U.S.	1992	$7.00
EMI		Train of Consequences	CDJ	Spain	1995	$25.00
EMI	CDCL-DJ-730	Train of Consequences	CDJ	U.K.	1995	$18.00

Meissner, Stan

Singles

Label	Catalog Number	Title	Type	Country	Year	Longbox Value / Value
Duke St.	CRDR-20	It's No Secret	CD3	Japan	1992	$13.00/$4.00

Mekons

Full Length

Label	Catalog Number	Title	Type	Country	Year	Longbox Value / Value
Quarterstick		United	LTD/LP	U.S.	1996	$20.00
	Book and CD set.					

Singles

Label	Catalog Number	Title	Type	Country	Year	Longbox Value / Value
Pinnacle	BFFP-53CD	Amnesia	CD3	U.K.	1989	$8.00
A&M	75021 5325 2	Makes No Difference	CDJ	U.S.	1990	$2.00
Loud	89014	Wicked Midnight	CD5	U.S.	1992	$5.00

Mel-Low

Singles

Label	Catalog Number	Title	Type	Country	Year	Longbox Value / Value
Chaos	77124	Blaze It Up	CDJ	U.S.	1993	$2.00

Melanie

Singles

Label	Catalog Number	Title	Type	Country	Year	Longbox Value / Value
Pinnacle	CDYUM-117	Ruby Tuesday	CD5	U.K.	1989	$8.00

Melendez, Tony

Singles

Label	Catalog Number	Title	Type	Country	Year	Longbox Value / Value
		And the Walls Came Tumblin' Down	CDJ	U.S.		$2.00
Fever	5622	Goody Goody	CDJ	U.S.	1993	$2.00
Fever	77158	Goody Goody	CDJ	U.S.	1993	$2.00
fever	74144	Never Say Never	CDJ	U.S.	1991	$2.00
Fever	73629	Together Forever	CDJ	U.S.	1990	$2.00
Fever	77089	Will You Ever Save Me	CDJ	U.S.	1993	$2.00

Meliah Rage

Singles

Label	Catalog Number	Title	Type	Country	Year	Longbox Value / Value
Epic	ESK 2108	No Mind	CDJ	U.S.	1990	$2.00

Melidian

Full Length

Label	Catalog Number	Title	Type	Country	Year	Longbox Value / Value
CBS	ZSK 1671	Lost in the Wild	DJ/LP	U.S.	1989	$20.00
	Picture disc.					

Singles

Label	Catalog Number	Title	Type	Country	Year	Longbox Value / Value
CBS		Lost in the Wild	CDJ	U.S.	1989	$2.00

Melissa

Singles

Label	Catalog Number	Title	Type	Country	Year	Longbox Value / Value
Sony	656885-2	Focus on the Bass	CD5	Germany	1991	$8.00

Mellencamp, John (Cougar) – Radio's Greatest Hits (Mercury SACD 718)

Mellencamp, John (Cougar)

Full Length

Label	Catalog Number	Title	Type	Country	Year	Longbox Value / Value
Pioneer	PA-85-124	Ain't That America	LD	U.S.	1985	$40.00
Album Network		Album Network Special Sneak Preview	RS	U.S.	1992	$150.00
	2 CD set. Airdate: 1/10/92.					
Riva	RVCD-7501	American Fool	LP/BP	U.S.†	1984	$14.00/$8.00
Mercury	JM-PRO-1	Check It Out - Five Classic Songs	DJ/Smplr	U.K.	1993	$15.00
Mercury		Dance Naked	LTD/LP	Australia	1994	$25.00
	Limited 2 CD set.					
Mercury		Dance Naked	DJ/LP	U.S.	1993	$18.00
Mercury	SACD 885	Dance Naked	DJ/Smplr	U.S.	1994	$125.00
	2 CD sampler housed in book.					
Mercury		Dance Naked Sampler	DJ/Smplr	Germany	1994	$35.00

Label	Catalog Number	Title	Type	Country	Year	Longbox Value / Value
Mercury	PCD 187	Garage Tapes-Live in the Studio	DJ/Smplr	Canada	1992	$125.00
Album Network		In the Studio (Big Daddy)	RS	U.S.	1989	$30.00
Airdate: 7/3/89.						
Album Network		In the Studio (Uh Huh)	RS	U.S.	1989	$30.00
Airdate: 6/26/89.						
Riva	RVCD-7401	John Cougar	LP/BP	U.S.†	1984	$14.00/$8.00
DIR		King Biscuit Flour Hour	RS	U.S.	1989	$45.00
With custom sleeve, Airdate: 7/3/89.						
DIR		King Biscuit Flour Hour	RS	U.S.	1990	$40.00
Airdate: 7/7/90.						
DIR		King Biscuit Flour Hour	RS	U.S.	1991	$40.00
Airdate: 7/28/91.						
DIR		King Biscuit Flour Hour	RS	U.S.	1992	$40.00
Airdate: 5/3/92.						
DIR		King Biscuit Flour Hour	RS	U.S.	1993	$40.00
Airdate: 9/6/93.						
DIR		King Biscuit Flour Hour	RS	U.S.	1994	$40.00
Airdate: 11/16/94.						
DIR		King Biscuit Flour Hour	RS	U.S.	1996	$40.00
Airdate: 4/7/96.						
Mercury		Limited Collector's Edition	DJ/LP	U.S.	1991	$75.00
8 CD set. 8 albums in custom box.						
Mercury	314 532 896-2	Mr. Happy Go Lucky	DJ/LP	U.S.	1996	$100.00
2 CD set in book package.						
Mercury		Mr. Happy Go Lucky (Snippits)	DJ/Smplr	U.S.	1996	$12.00
Riva	RVCD-7403	Nothin' Matters & What If It Did	LP/BP	U.S.†	1984	$14.00/$8.00
Westwood One		Off the Record	RS	U.S.	1994	$30.00
Airdate: 10/31/94.						
Westwood One		Off the Record	RS	U.S.	1995	$20.00
Airdate: 2/20/95.						
Mercury		On Tour	DJ/Smplr	U.S.	1994	$30.00
2 CD set. Disc 1 is a 6 track live sampler with Mellencamp. Disc 2 is the same but of the group Texas.						
Mercury	SACD 923	On Tour Together	DJ/Smplr	U.S.	1994	$30.00
Mercury	SACD 718	Radio's Greatest Hits	DJ/Smplr	U.S.	1993	$125.00
Riva	824865-2	Scarecrow	LP/BP	U.S.†	1985	$14.00/$8.00
Westwood One		Superstar Concert	RS	U.S.	1992	$70.00
2 CD set. Airdate: 9/20/92.						
Westwood One		Superstar Concert	RS	U.S.	1993	$70.00
2 CD set. Airdate: 2/14/93.						
Westwood One		Superstar Concert	RS	U.S.	1994	$70.00
2 CD set. Airdate: 4/18/94.						
Westwood One		Superstars	RS	U.S.	1993	$85.00
2 CDset. Airdate: 8/2/93.						
Westwood One		Superstars	RS	U.S.	1994	$70.00
2 CDset. Airdate: 10/17/94.						
Westwood One		Superstars	RS	U.S.	1995	$70.00
2 CDset. Airdate: 9/4/95.						
		Superstars	RS	U.S.	1996	$90.00
2 CD set. Airdate 4/1/96.						
		Timothy White Sessions	RS	U.S.	1991	$90.00
2 CD set. Airdate: 11/25/91.						
Riva	RVCD-7504	Uh-Huh	LP/BP	U.S.†	1984	$14.00/$8.00
Media America		Up Close	RS	U.S.	1993	$90.00
3 CD set.						

Singles

Label	Catalog Number	Title	Type	Country	Year	Longbox Value / Value
Mercury	PHDR-49	Again Tonight	CD3	Japan	1992	$18.00/$4.00
Mercury	866 415-2	Again Tonight	CD5	U.S.	1992	$6.00
Mercury	CDP 616	Again Tonight	CDJ	U.S.	1992	$5.00
Mercury	MCA5P-2986	Baby, Please Don't Go	CDJ	U.S.	1994	$6.00
Mercury	870125-2	Check It Out	CD5	Canada	1988	$10.00
Mercury	JCMD-10	Check It Out	CD5	U.K.	1988	$10.00
Mercury	CDP 08	Check It Out	CDJ	U.S.	1988	$5.00
Mercury	870 729-2	Check It Out	CDV/BP	U.S.	1988	$20.00/$20.00
Mercury		Cherry Bomb	CD5	Canada	1988	$10.00
Mercury	888934-2	Cherry Bomb	CD5	Germany	1988	$10.00
Mercury	JMCD-9	Cherry Bomb	CD5	U.K.	1988	$10.00
Polygram	856342	Dance Naked	CD5	U.S.	1994	$5.00
Polygram	856353	Dance Naked	CD5	U.S.	1994	$5.00
Mercury		Dance Naked	CDJ	U.S.	1994	$6.00
Mercury	868999-2	Get a Leg Up	CD5	Germany	1991	$10.00
Mercury	MERCD-354	Get a Leg Up	CD5	U.K.	1991	$10.00
Mercury	CDP 546	Get a Leg Up	CDJ	U.S.	1991	$5.00
Mercury	862 771-2	Human Wheels	CD5	Germany	1993	$10.00
Mercury	CDP 997	Human Wheels	CDJ	U.S.	1993	$6.00
Mercury	874793-2	Jackie Brown	CD5	Canada	1910	$10.00
Mercury	CDP 102	Jackie Brown	CDJ	U.S.	1989	$5.00
Mercury		Key West Intermezzo	CD5	U.S.	1996	$5.00
Mercury		Key West Intermezzo	CD5	U.S.	1996	$5.00
Second version.						
Mercury		Key West Intermezzo	CDJ	U.S.	1996	$5.00
Mercury	CDP 709	Last Chance	CD5	U.S.	1992	$5.00
Mercury	870 708-2	Lonely Ol' Night	CDV/BP	U.S.	1988	$20.00/$20.00
Mercury		Love and Happiness	CDJ	Canada	1991	$8.00
Mercury	MERCD 362	Love and Happiness	CD5	U.K.	1992	$10.00
Mercury	CDP 612	Love and Happiness	CDJ	U.S.	1991	$5.00
Mercury	MERCD-368	Now More Than Ever	CD5	U.K.	1992	$10.00
Mercury	CDP 657	Now More Than Ever	CDJ	U.S.	1992	$5.00
Mercury	CDP 691	Now More Than Ever	CDJ	U.S.	1992	$5.00
Mercury	CDP 03	Paper and Fire	CDJ	U.S.	1987	$5.00
Mercury	870 707-2	Paper and Fire	CDV/BP	U.S.	1987	$20.00/$20.00
Mercury	080 213-2	Paper and Fire	DJ/CDV	U.S.	1987	$25.00
Polygram	874423-3	Pop Singer	CD3	Germany	1989	$10.00
Polygram	874422-2	Pop Singer	CD5	Germany	1989	$10.00
Mercury	JMCD-12	Pop Singer	CD5	U.K.	1989	$10.00
Mercury	CDP 52	Pop Singer	CDJ	U.S.	1989	$5.00
Elektra	10P3-6080	Rave On	CD3	Japan	1988	$18.00/$4.00
Elektra	EKR-90CD	Rave On	CD3	U.K.	1988	$10.00
Elektra	PR-69370-2	Rave On	CD3/LB	U.S.	1988	$12.00/$5.00
Elektra	PR 8029-2	Rave On	CDJ	U.S.	1988	$5.00
Elektra	JCMCD-11	Rooty Toot Toot	CD5	U.K	1988	$10.00
Mercury	MRC-DJ-393	What If I Came Knocking	CDJ	U.K.	1993	$15.00
Mercury	CDP 965	What If I Came Knocking	CDJ	U.S.	1993	$5.00
Mercury	CDP 1113	When Jesus Left Birmingham	CDJ	U.S.	1994	$6.00
Mercury		When Jesus Left Birmingham	CDJ	U.S.	1994	$6.00
Second version.						
Polygram		Wild Night	CD5	U.K.	1994	$10.00
Polygram		Wild Night	CD5	U.K.	1994	$10.00
Second version.						
Mercury	858 889-2	Wild Night	CD5	U.S.	1994	$6.00
Mercury		Wild Night	CD5	U.S.	1994	$6.00
Second version.						
Mercury	CDP 1230	Wild Night	CDJ	U.S.	1994	$7.00

Mello Core

Singles

Label	Catalog Number	Title	Type	Country	Year	Longbox Value / Value
PWL	PWCD-247	Good Feeling	CD5	U.K.	1992	$8.00

Mellow Man Ace

Singles

Label	Catalog Number	Title	Type	Country	Year	Longbox Value / Value
Capitol	DPRO-79293	If You Were Mine	CDJ	U.S.	1990	$2.00
Capitol	203806-2	Mentirosa	CD5	Germany	1990	$8.00
Capitol	CDCL-574	Mentirosa	CD5	U.K.	1990	$8.00
Capitol	DPRO-79130	Mentirosa	CDJ	U.S.	1990	$2.00
Capitol	DPRO-79984	What's It Take To Pull a Hottie	CDJ	U.S.	1992	$2.00

Mellow State

Singles

Label	Catalog Number	Title	Type	Country	Year	Longbox Value / Value
Warner Brothers	9031-77037-2	Save Me	CD5	U.K.	1992	$8.00

Melting Hopefuls

Singles

Label	Catalog Number	Title	Type	Country	Year	Longbox Value / Value
		Pulling an Allnighter on Myself	CDJ	U.S.		$2.00

Melvin, Harold

Singles

Label	Catalog Number	Title	Type	Country	Year	Longbox Value / Value
CBS	651662-3	Don't Leave Me This Way	CD3	Germany	1988	$8.00
CBS	651662-3	Don't Leave Me This Way	CD3	U.K.	1988	$8.00
Old Gold	OG-6507	Don't Leave Me This Way	CD3	U.K.	1990	$8.00
CBS	654559-3	Love I Lost	CD3	Germany	1989	$8.00

Melvins

Singles

Label	Catalog Number	Title	Type	Country	Year	Longbox Value / Value
Atlantic	PRCD 5429-2	Lizzy	CDJ	U.S.	1994	$2.00
Atlantic		Revolve	CDJ	U.S.	1994	$7.00

Members of the House

Singles

Label	Catalog Number	Title	Type	Country	Year	Longbox Value / Value
True Love	CDTLOVE-2	These Are My People	CD5	U.K.	1991	$8.00

Men at Large

Singles

Label	Catalog Number	Title	Type	Country	Year	Longbox Value / Value
Eastwest	PRCD 4861-2	So Alone	CDJ	U.S.	1992	$2.00
Eastwest	PRCD 4549-2	Use Me	CDJ	U.S.	1992	$2.00
Eastwest	PRCD 4951-2	Would You Like to Dance	CDJ	U.S.	1992	$2.00

Men at Work

Full Length

Label	Catalog Number	Title	Type	Country	Year	Longbox Value / Value
CBS	CK-37978	Business As Usual	LP/BP	U.S.†	1984	$14.00/$8.00
CBS	CK-38660	Cargo	LP/BP	U.S.†	1984	$14.00/$8.00
Album Network		In the Studio (Business As Usual)	RS	U.S.	1990	$30.00
Airdate: 3/19/90.						
CBS	CK-40078	Two Hearts	LP/BP	U.S.†	1984	$14.00/$8.00

Singles

Label	Catalog Number	Title	Type	Country	Year	Longbox Value / Value
Columbia	654850-3	Down Under	CD3	Germany	1989	$10.00
Columbia	654850-3	Down Under	CD3	U.K.	1989	$10.00

Men of Vision

Singles

Label	Catalog Number	Title	Type	Country	Year	Longbox Value / Value
	BSK 7728	House Keeper	CDJ	U.S.		$2.00

Men They Couldn't Hang

Singles

Label	Catalog Number	Title	Type	Country	Year	Longbox Value / Value
Magnet	CDSELL-5	Colours	CD5	U.K.	1988	$8.00
Magnet	YZ-193CD	Crest	CD3	U.K.	1988	$8.00
Silvertone	ORECD-19	Great Expectations	CD5	U.K.	1990	$8.00
Silvertone	ORECD-46	Great Expectations	CD5	U.K.	1992	$8.00
RCA	1410-2-RDJ	Great Expectations	CDJ	U.S.	1990	$2.00
Silvertone	ORECD-22	Lion and the Unicorn	CD5	U.K.	1990	$8.00
Silvertone	ORECD-14	Map of Morocco	CD5	U.K.	1989	$8.00
Silvertone	ORECD-7	Place in the Sun	CD5	U.K.	1989	$8.00
Silvertone	ORECD-4	Rain, Steam & Speed	CD5	U.K.	1989	$8.00

Men Without Hats

Full Length

Label	Catalog Number	Title	Type	Country	Year	Longbox Value / Value
Mercury	842000-2	In the 21st Century	LP/BP	U.S.		$12.00/$7.00
Mercury		Pop Goes the World	LP/BP	U.S.		$12.00/$7.00
		Rhythm of Youth	LP	U.K.		N/A

Singles

Label	Catalog Number	Title	Type	Country	Year	Longbox Value / Value
Mercury	CDP 151	Hey Man	CDJ	U.S.	1989	$2.00
Mercury	CDP 06	Pop Goes the World	CDJ	U.S.	1987	$2.00
Mercury	870 718-2	Pop Goes the World	CDV/BP	U.S.	1988	$15.00/$15.00

Menace

Singles

Label	Catalog Number	Title	Type	Country	Year	Longbox Value / Value
BMG	663105	Dog House	CD5	Germany	1990	$8.00

Mendelson, Joe

Singles

Label	Catalog Number	Title	Type	Country	Year	Longbox Value / Value
Anthem	PRO 7	Passion	CDJ	Canada		$10.00

Mendes, Sergio

Singles

Label	Catalog Number	Title	Type	Country	Year	Longbox Value / Value
A&M	CD 17817	Mas Que Nada	CDJ	U.S.	1989	$2.00

Menswear

Singles

Label	Catalog Number	Title	Type	Country	Year	Longbox Value / Value
	POCD-9005	Day Dreamer	CD5	Japan	1995	$15.00
	PRCD7957-2	Daydreamer	CDJ	U.S.		$2.00

Mental as Anything

Singles

Label	Catalog Number	Title	Type	Country	Year	Longbox Value / Value
Epic	CDANY-6	Rock and Roll Music	CD5	U.K.	1989	$8.00
Columbia	CSK 1790	Rock and Roll Music	CDJ	U.S.	1989	$2.00

Mental Collapse

Singles

Label	Catalog Number	Title	Type	Country	Year	Longbox Value / Value
Kickin'	KICK-16CDMP	Mental as Anything	CD5	U.K.	1992	$8.00

Mental Generation

Singles

Label	Catalog Number	Title	Type	Country	Year	Longbox Value / Value
Columbia	657388-2	Slam	CD5	Germany	1991	$8.00

Mental Insects

Singles

Label	Catalog Number	Title	Type	Country	Year	Longbox Value / Value
Pteranodon	2048	Skull Tracks	CD5	U.S.	1990	$6.00

Menthol

Singles

Label	Catalog Number	Title	Type	Country	Year	Longbox Value / Value
	DPRO79638	Stress Is Best	CDJ	U.S.		$2.00

Menza, Don & His '80s Big Band

Full Length

Label	Catalog Number	Title	Type	Country	Year	Longbox Value / Value
Realtime	RT-3001	Burnin'	LP/LB	U.S.†	1985	$14.00/$8.00

Merchant, Natalie

Label	Catalog Number	Title	Type	Country	Year	Longbox Value / Value
		Full Length				
	NAT PRO 1	A Companion To Tigerlily	DJ/Smplr	Germany	1995	$35.00
	CD and booklet in slip case.					
Media America		Up Close	RS	U.S.	1995	$30.00
		Singles				
		Carnival	CDJ	Spain	1995	$25.00
Elektra	PRCD 92082	Carnival	CDJ	U.S.	1995	$3.00
		Jealousy	CD5	U.K.	1996	$10.00
		Wonder	CD5	U.K.	1996	$10.00
		Wonder	CD5	U.K.	1996	$10.00
	Second version.					

Merchants Of Venus

Label	Catalog Number	Title	Type	Country	Year	Longbox Value / Value
		Full Length				
Elektra	9 61045-2	Merchants of Venus	LP/LB	U.S.	1991	$15.00/$10.00
		Singles				
Elektra	PRCD 8359-2	Say Ahh	CDJ	U.S.	1991	$2.00

Mercury, Freddie

Label	Catalog Number	Title	Type	Country	Year	Longbox Value / Value
		Full Length				
Columbia	CK 40071	Mr. Bad Guy	LP/LB	U.S.		$40.00/$40.00
Columbia	CK 40071	Mr. Bad Guy	LP/LB	U.S.†	1985	$40.00/$40.00
		Singles				
Polydor	887075-2	Barcelona	CD5	Germany	1988	$12.00
		Barcelona	CDJ	Japan		$20.00
Polydor	POCD-807	Barcelona	CD5	U.K.	1988	$15.00
Polygram	080 548-2	Barcelona	CDV	U.K.	1989	$55.00
Polydor	POL 940	Barcelona	CD5	U.K.	1992	$11.00
Polydor	887787-2	Golden Boy	CD5	Germany	1988	$12.00
Polydor	P10P-40002	Golden Boy	CD3	Japan	1988	$18.00/$4.00
Polydor	PZCD-23	Golden Boy	CD5	U.K.	1988	$12.00
Polygram	080 580-2	Golden Boy	CDV	U.K.	1989	$55.00
EMI	TODP-2396	Great Pretender	CD3	Japan	1993	$18.00/$5.00
Hollywood	PRCD 10202	Great Pretender, the	CDJ	U.S.	1992	$7.00
Polydor	PZCD-29	Guide Me Home	CD5	U.K.	1989	$11.00
Polydor	PZCD-234	How Can I Go On	CD5	U.K.	1992	$11.00
		In My Defense	CD5	U.K.	1992	$12.00
		In My Defense	CD5	U.K.	1992	$12.00
	Second version.					
Parlophone	80767	Living on My Own	CD5	U.K.	1992	$10.00
		Living on My Own	CDJ	U.S.		$10.00
Hollywood	PRCD 10287-2	Living on My Own	CDJ	U.S.	1992	$7.00
Hollywood	PRCD 10235-2	Love Kills	CDJ	U.S.	1992	$7.00
Polygram	080 546-2	Now Can You See the Music	CDV	U.K.	1989	$55.00
		Time	CDJ	U.S.		$10.00
Hollywood	PRCD 10308-2	Time	CDJ	U.S.	1992	$7.00

Mercury Rev

Label	Catalog Number	Title	Type	Country	Year	Longbox Value / Value
		Full Length				
Columbia		Yerself Is Steam	DJ/Smplr	U.S.	1992	$30.00
	2 CD set.					
		Singles				
Columbia	CSK 4948	Car Wash Hair	CDJ	U.S.	1993	$2.00
Columbia	CSK 5532	Somethig For Joey	CDJ	U.S.	1993	$2.00

Mercy Me

Label	Catalog Number	Title	Type	Country	Year	Longbox Value / Value
		Singles				
Cooltempo	COOLCD-221	Don't Wanna Hold On	CD5	U.K.	1990	$8.00

Mercyful Fate

Label	Catalog Number	Title	Type	Country	Year	Longbox Value / Value
		Full Length				
Metal Blade	45318	In the Shadows	LP/LB	U.S.		$12.00/$7.00
		Singles				
Metal Blade	8750	Egypt	CDJ	U.S.	1993	$2.00

Merlin

Label	Catalog Number	Title	Type	Country	Year	Longbox Value / Value
		Singles				
Sire	9 40586-2	You Blow Your Mind	CD5	U.S.	1993	$5.00

Merrill, Helen

Label	Catalog Number	Title	Type	Country	Year	Longbox Value / Value
		Full Length				
Mercury	826340	Complete On Mercury	LP/BP	U.S.		$12.00/$7.00
Emarcy	814643-2	Helen Merrill	LP/LB	U.S.†	1985	$14.00/$8.00

Merritt, Scott

Label	Catalog Number	Title	Type	Country	Year	Longbox Value / Value
		Singles				
IRS	IRSD 020	Are You Sending	CDJ	U.S.	1990	$2.00

Messiah

Label	Catalog Number	Title	Type	Country	Year	Longbox Value / Value
		Singles				
Kickin'	KICK-22CD	I Feel Love	CD5	U.K.	1992	$8.00
Warner Brothers	41827	I Feel Love	CD5	U.S.	1994	$6.00
Noise	0439-2	Psychomorphia	CD5	Germany	1990	$8.00
Pinnacle	N-0180-3	Psychomorphia	CD5	U.K.	1990	$8.00
Kickin'	KICK-12CD	Temple of Dreams	CD5	U.K.	1992	$8.00
Def American	9 40655-2	Temple of Dreams	CDJ	U.S.	1992	$2.00
Kickin'	KICK-10CD	There Is No Law	CD5	U.K.	1992	$8.00
		Thunderdome	CD5	U.K.		$10.00
		Thunderdome	CD5	U.K.		$10.00
	Second version.					
Warner Brothers	41037	Thunderdome	CD5	U.S.	1994	$5.00
White	6789	Thunderdome	CDJ	U.S.	1994	$2.00

Messina, Jim

Label	Catalog Number	Title	Type	Country	Year	Longbox Value / Value
		Full Length				
Warner Brothers		Messina	LP/LB	U.S.		$14.00/$8.00
Warner Brothers		One More Mile	LP/LB	U.S.	14	$8.00

Metal Church

Label	Catalog Number	Title	Type	Country	Year	Longbox Value / Value
		Full Length				
SPV		Hanging in the Balance	LTD/LP	U.S.	1993	$25.00
		Singles				
		Badlands	CDJ	U.S.	1989	$2.00
Epic	ESK 4022	Date With Poverty	CDJ	U.S.	1991	$2.00
		Fake Healer	CDJ	U.S.	1989	$2.00
Epic	ESK 3067	Human Factor, The	CDJ	U.S.	1991	$2.00
Epic	ESK 4212	In Harms Way	CDJ	U.S.	1991	$2.00
Epic	ESK 4133	In Mourning	CDJ	U.S.	1991	$2.00

Metallica

Label	Catalog Number	Title	Type	Country	Year	Longbox Value / Value
		Full Length				
Elektra	PRCD 8879-2	15 Pieces of Live Shit	DJ/Smplr	U.S.	1993	$60.00
	2CD Set in cardboard sleeve.					
Elektra	PRCD 8879-2	15 Pieces of Live Shit	DJ/Smplr	U.S.	1993	$60.00
	2CD Set in Jewel box.					
Sony	25LP 135	2 of One	8"LD	Japan	1989	$35.00

Metallica – CD-Singles Collection (Vertigo) Limited edition U.K. CD-singles boxed set. The singles for this box were released one at a time over a period of over six months.

Label	Catalog Number	Title	Type	Country	Year	Longbox Value / Value
Sony	SRLM 841-3	A Year and A Half In the Life Of Metallica	LTD/LD	Japan	1992	$100.00
	3 LD limited edition boxed set.					
Vertigo	836062-2	And Justice For All	LTD/LP	Australia	1993	$30.00
	Gold disc.					
Vertigo	836062-2	And Justice For All	LTD/LP	Australia	1993	$35.00
	Gold CD with CD5 of "One" in slip case.					
Vertigo		And Justice For All	LTD/LP	U.K.	1993	$30.00
	2 CD set in slip case.					
Music For Nations	977 112	Creeping Death	LP	Germany	1987	$22.00
Music For Nations	CD 12KUT	Creeping Death	LP	U.K.	1987	$22.00
Elektra	9 60757-2	Garage Days Revisited	LP/LB	U.S.	1987	$35.00/$30.00
Vertigo	838 142-2	Kill 'Em All	LTD/LP	Australia	1993	$35.00
	Gold disc.					
Elektra	60766-2	Kill 'Em All	LP/LB	U.S.		$15.00/$9.00
Elektra	60766-2	Kill 'Em All	LP/LB	U.S.		$45.00/$40.00
	12 track CD with additional songs "Am I Evil?" and "Blitzkrieg."					
Megaforce	MRI 069	Kill 'Em All	LP	U.S.	1985	$20.00
Music For Nations	MFN 7	Kill 'Em All	LP	U.S.	1987	$20.00
Elektra	61594-2	Live Shit: Binge & Purge	LTD/LP	U.S.	1992	$120.00
	3CD , 3 VHS video, booklet, and print in tour box.					
Vertigo	MM CJ1	Mandatory Metallica	DJ/Smplr	U.K.	1996	$80.00
Elektra	PR 8071-2	Mandatory Metallica	DJ/Smplr	U.S.	1989	$125.00
	8 track version.					
Elektra	PR 8020-2	Mandatory Metallica	DJ/Smplr	U.S.	1989	$135.00
	7 track version.					
Vertigo	838 141-2	Master of Puppets	LTD/LP	Australia	1993	$30.00
	Gold disc.					
Music For Nations	MFN 60	Master of Puppets	LP	U.S.	1987	$20.00
CBS/Sony	39DP 5176-7	Metalli-Can	LTD/LP	Japan	1987	$400.00
	Limited edition of "And Justic For All" CD with T-shirt in custom paint can.					
Vertigo		Metallica	LTD/LP	Australia	1993	$75.00
	Gold CD in can with T-shirt.					
Vertigo		Metallica	LTD/LP	Germany	1992	$35.00
	CD of album in oversized vinyl pouch.					
Vertigo	838 140-2	Ride the Lightning	LTD/LP	Australia	1993	$30.00
	Gold disc.					
Music For Nations	MFN 27	Ride the Lightning	LP	U.S.	1987	$15.00
Virtigo	METCD 100	Whiplash	DJ/Smplr	Germany	1988	$40.00
		Singles				
Elektra	PR 8099-2	And Justice for All	CDJ	U.S.	1988	$10.00
Elektra	PRCD 8728-2	Don't Tread on Me	CDJ	U.S.	1992	$6.00
Vertigo	868733-2	Enter Sandman	CD5	Germany	1991	$10.00
Sony	SRDS-8204	Enter Sandman	CD3	Japan	1991	$18.00/$5.00
Vertigo	METCD 7	Enter Sandman	CD5	U.K.	1991	$75.00
	Limited withdrawn version CD and title card in 2 drawer box to hold 4 CD singles.					
Vertigo	METCDJ7	Enter Sandman	CDJ	U.K.	1991	$15.00
Vertigo	BOX-DJ1	Enter Sandman	CDJ	U.K.	1993	$25.00
Elektra	PRCD 8407-2	Enter Sandman	CDJ	U.S.	1991	$6.00
Elektra	PRCD 8421-2	Enter Sandman	CDJ	U.S.	1991	$6.00
Elektra	PR 8028-2	Eye of the Beholder	CDJ	U.S.	1988	$6.00
	WOODST2-2	For Whom the Bell Tolls	CDJ	Spain	1996	$65.00
Vertigo	870614-2	Harvester of Sorrow	CD5	Germany	1988	$10.00
Vertigo	METCD-2	Harvester of Sorrow	CD5	U.K.	1988	$10.00
		Hero of the Day	CD5	U.K.	1996	$10.00
		Hero of the Day	CD5	U.K.	1996	$10.00
	Second version.					
Elektra	64248-2	Hero Of the Day	CD5	U.S.	1996	$4.00
Elektra	64197-2	King Of Nothing	CD5	U.S.	1997	$4.00
Vertigo		Mama Said	CD5	Japan	1997	$25.00
Vertigo		Nothing Else Matters	CD5	Germany	1992	$10.00
Sony	SRDS-8225	Nothing Else Matters	CD3	Japan	1992	$18.00/$5.00
Vertigo	METCD 10	Nothing Else Matters	CD5	U.K.	1992	$10.00
Vertigo	METCL 10	Nothing Else Matters	CD5	U.K.	1992	$10.00
Vertigo	METCD 10-DJ	Nothing Else Matters	CDJ	U.K.	1992	$12.00
Elektra	PRCD 8534-2	Nothing Else Matters	CDJ	U.S.	1992	$6.00
Vertigo		One	CD5	Australia	1994	$13.00
Vertigo	874 154-3	One	CD3	Germany	1988	$10.00
Vertigo	874 155-2	One	CD5	Germany	1989	$10.00
Vertigo	874 067-2	One	CD5	Germany	1989	$10.00
Sony	10EP-3077	One	CD3	Japan	1988	$18.00/$5.00
CBS	23DP-5438	One	CD5	Japan	1988	$19.00
	1st issue red screen printed disc.					
CBS	23DP-5438	One	CD5	Japan	1988	$55.00
	Special version with bonus wristband.					
Vertigo	METYCD-5	One	CD5	U.K.	1988	$12.00
Vertigo	METCD-5	One	CD5	U.K.	1994	$10.00
Vertigo		One	CD5	U.K.	1994	$12.00
	Second version.					
Elektra	9 693229-2	One	CD3	U.S.	1988	$20.00/$10.00
Elektra	PR 8044-2	One	CDJ	U.S.	1988	$8.00
Elektra	65920	One	CD5	U.S.	1992	$5.00
Elektra/Asylum	65920	One	CD5	U.S.	1994	$5.00
Vertigo	864 411-2	Sad But True	CD5	Australia	1992	$12.00
Vertigo	METCD-11	Sad But True	CD5	U.K.	1992	$10.00
Vertigo	864 943-2	Sad But True	CD5	U.K.	1992	$10.00
Vertigo	METCH-11	Sad But True	CD5/PD	U.K.	1992	$11.00

Label	Catalog Number	Title	Type	Country	Year	Longbox Value / Value
Elektra	PRCD 8646-2	Sad But True	CDJ	U.S.	1992	$6.00
CBS Sony	SRDS 8204	Stone Cold Crazy	CD3	Japan	1991	$18.00/$5.00
Elektra	PRCD 8224-2	Stone Cold Crazy	CDJ	U.S.	1990	$25.00
Vertigo	866 136	Unforgiven, The	CD5	France	1991	$12.00
Vertigo	866137-2	Unforgiven, The	CD5	Germany	1991	$10.00
Sony	SRDS-8214	Unforgiven, The	CD3	Japan	1991	$18.00/$5.00
Vertigo	METCD 8	Unforgiven, The	CD5	U.K	1991	$10.00
Vertigo	866 139-2	Unforgiven, The	CD5	U.K	1991	$10.00
Elektra	PRCD 8479-2	Unforgiven, The	CDJ	U.S.	1991	$6.00
Elektra		Unforgiven, The	CDJ	U.S.	1991	$6.00
	Second version.					
Vertigo		Until It Sleeps	CD5	Australia	1996	$10.00
Vertigo		Until It Sleeps	CD5	Australia	1996	$10.00
	Second version.					
Elektra		Until It Sleeps	CDJ	France	1996	$65.00
CBS/Sony	SRCS-8062	Until It Sleeps	CD5	Japan	1996	$20.00
Vertigo		Until It Sleeps	CD5	U.K.	1996	$10.00
Vertigo		Until It Sleeps	CD5	U.K.	1996	$10.00
	Second version.					
Elektra	64276-2	Until It Sleeps	CD5	U.S.	1996	$4.00
Elektra		Until It Sleeps	CDJ	U.S.	1996	$7.00
Vertigo		Wherever I May Roam	CD5	Australia	1992	$12.00
Sony	SRCS-6633	Wherever I May Roam	CD5	Japan	1993	$20.00
Vertigo	METCD 9	Wherever I May Roam	CD5	U.K.	1992	$10.00
Vertigo	METCB 9	Wherever I May Roam	CD5	U.K.	1992	$10.00
Vertigo	METCDJ 9	Wherever I May Roam	CDJ	U.K.	1992	$10.00
Elektra		Wherever I May Roam	CDJ	U.S.	1992	$6.00

Metheny, Pat

Full Length

Label	Catalog Number	Title	Type	Country	Year	Longbox Value / Value
ECM	1180-2	80/81	LP/LB	U.S.†	1985	$14.00/$8.00
Geffen		A Special Conversation	DJ/Intvw	U.S.		$12.00
ECM	25008-2	First Circle	LP/LB	U.S.†	1985	$14.00/$8.00
ECM	1216-2	Offramp	LP/LB	U.S.†	1985	$14.00/$8.00

Singles

Label	Catalog Number	Title	Type	Country	Year	Longbox Value / Value
Geffen	PRO-CD-3847	Beat 70	CDJ	U.S.	1989	$2.00
Geffen	PRO-CD-4129	Change of Heart	CDJ	U.S.	1990	$2.00
		Here to Stay	CDJ	U.S.		$3.00
Geffen	PRO-CD-2767	Last Train Home	CDJ	U.S.	1987	$2.00
Geffen	PRO-CD-3617	Slip Away	CDJ	U.S.	1989	$2.00

Metheny, Pat & Lyle Mays

Full Length

Label	Catalog Number	Title	Type	Country	Year	Longbox Value / Value
ECM	1190-2	As Falls Wichita, So Falls Wichita Falls	LP/LB	U.S.†	1985	$14.00/$8.00

Method Man

Singles

Label	Catalog Number	Title	Type	Country	Year	Longbox Value / Value
		I'll Be There For You	CDJ	U.S.		$2.00
Polygram	851879	I'll Be There For You	CD5	U.S.	1995	$6.00
Polygram		I'll Be There For You	CDJ	U.S.	1995	$6.00
Atlantic	87100	Riddler	CD5	U.S.	1995	$5.00
Atlantic	87100-2	Riddler, The	CD5	U.S.	1995	$10.00

Method Of Destruction

Singles

Label	Catalog Number	Title	Type	Country	Year	Longbox Value / Value
Megaforce	818	Intruder	CDJ	U.S.	1992	$2.00

Metrixx

Singles

Label	Catalog Number	Title	Type	Country	Year	Longbox Value / Value
ZYX	ZYX-6537-8	Is It True	CD5	Germany	1991	$6.00

Metropolis

Singles

Label	Catalog Number	Title	Type	Country	Year	Longbox Value / Value
Earth Beat	UCRCD-11	Metropolis	CD5	U.K.	1992	$8.00

Mexakinz

Singles

Label	Catalog Number	Title	Type	Country	Year	Longbox Value / Value
Motown	860478	Confessions: Hell Don't Pay	CD5	U.S.	1995	$5.00

Mic Geronimo

Singles

Label	Catalog Number	Title	Type	Country	Year	Longbox Value / Value
TeeVee	4914	Masta I.C.	CD5	U.S.	1994	$5.00

Michael, Alan

Full Length

Label	Catalog Number	Title	Type	Country	Year	Longbox Value / Value
Pasport	PJCD-88041	Lost In Asia	LP/LB	U.S.		$14.00/$8.00

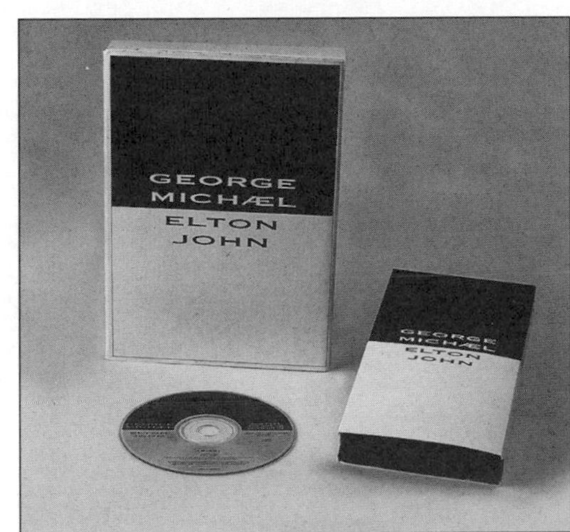

Michael, George & Elton John – Don't Let the Sun Go Down On Me (Columbia CVK 4288)

Michael, George

Full Length

Label	Catalog Number	Title	Type	Country	Year	Longbox Value / Value
Columbia	CVK 4288	Don't Let the Sun Go Down On Me	DJ/LP	U.S.	1991	$30.00
	CDJ and VHS tape press kit in custom box.					
Epic	EPC 460000 9	Faith	LP/BP	Germany	1987	$35.00/$35.00
	Picture disc.					
Epic	308P-241	Faith	LP	Japan	1987	$35.00
	Picture disc.					
Epic	EPC 460000 9	Faith	LP/BP	U.K.	1987	$35.00/$35.00
	Picture disc.					
Columbia	CSK 2850	Faith	DJ/LP	U.S.	1987	$50.00
	CD with hologram front sleeve.					
Epic	CDR-DJ-6340	Five Live	DJ/LP	U.K.	1993	$18.00
Hollywood	PRBX-10313	Five Live	DJ/LP	U.S.	1993	$50.00
	CD in book-type box with promo VHS video.					
Columbia	CSK 2226	Listen Without Preducice: An Interview With...	DJ/Intrvw	U.S.	1990	$10.00
Epic	467295-2	Listen Without Prejudice Volume 1	LP	U.K.	1990	$25.00

Singles

Label	Catalog Number	Title	Type	Country	Year	Longbox Value / Value
Epic	656774-2	Cowboys And Angels	CD5	Germany	1991	$10.00
Epic	656774-2	Cowboys And Angels	CD5	U.K.	1991	$10.00
Epic	657646-2	Don't Let the Sun Go Down On Me	CD5	Germany	1991	$10.00
Epic	ESDA-7087	Don't Let the Sun Go Down On Me	CD3	Japan	1991	$15.00/$5.00
Columbia	44K 74130	Don't Let the Sun Go Down On Me	CD5	U.S.	1991	$5.00
Columbia	CSK 74086	Don't Let the Sun Go Down On Me	CDJ	U.S.	1991	$5.00
CBS		Fast Love	CDJ	U.K.		$20.00
CBS		Fast Love	CDJ	U.K.		$20.00
	Second version.					
Columbia		Fast Love	CDJ	U.S.		$7.00
Epic	651321-2	Father Figure	CD5	Germany	1988	$10.00
Epic	108P-3008	Father Figure	CD3	Japan	1987	$15.00/$5.00
Epic	CDEMU-4	Father Figure	CD5	U.K.	1987	$10.00
Columbia	656390-3	Freedom	CD3	Germany	1990	$10.00
Epic	ESDA-7054	Freedom	CD3	Japan	1990	$15.00/$5.00
Columbia	44K 73584	Freedom	CD5	U.S.	1990	$5.00
Epic	656647-2	Heal the Pain	CD5	Germany	1991	$10.00
Epic	656647-2	Heal the Pain	CD5	U.K.	1991	$10.00
		I Knew You Were Waiting	CDJ	U.S.		$5.00
CBS	654601-3	I Want Your Sex	CDJ	Germany	1987	$10.00
CBS	650783-2	I Want Your Sex	CD5	Germany	1987	$10.00
CBS	654601-3	I Want Your Sex	CD3	U.K.	1987	$10.00
CBS	LUST 1	I Want Your Sex	CD5	U.K.	1987	$10.00
CBS	44K-6814	I Want Your Sex	CD3	U.S.	1987	$7.00/$4.00
CBS	38K-7164	I Want Your Sex	CD3	U.S.	1987	$7.00/$5.00
	VICP-12030	Jesus To A Child	CDJ	Japan	1995	$20.00
CBS		Jesus To A Child	CDJ	U.K.		$20.00
CBS	VSCDXJ1571	Jesus To A Child	CDJ	U.K.		$20.00
CBS		Jesus To A Child	CDJ	U.K.		$20.00
	Second version.					
Columbia		Jesus To A Child	CDJ	U.S.		$7.00
Columbia		Jesus To A Child	CDJ	U.S.		$7.00
	Second version.					
Epic	653049-3	Kissing A Fool	CD3	Germany	1987	$10.00
Epic	108P-3053	Kissing A Fool	CD3	Japan	1987	$15.00/$5.00
Epic	CDEMU-7	Kissing A Fool	CD5	U.K.	1987	$10.00
Columbia	CSK1297	Kissing A Fool	CDJ	U.S.	1987	$6.00
Sony	653185-2	Last Christmas	CD3	Germany	1989	$10.00
CBS	651700-3	Monkey	CD3	Germany	1987	$11.00
Epic	128P-8006	Monkey	CD3	Japan	1987	$15.00/$5.00
CBS	651700-3	Monkey	CD3	U.K.	1987	$11.00
Epic	CDEMU 6	Monkey	CD5	U.K.	1987	$11.00
CBS	38K-7849	Monkey	CD3	U.S.	1987	$7.00/$4.00
CBS	38K-7941	Monkey	CD3	U.S.	1987	$7.00/$4.00
Columbia	CSK 1186	Monkey	CDJ	U.S.	1987	$10.00
Epic	651532-2	One More Try	CD5	Germany	1988	$10.00
Epic	108P-3019	One More Try	CD3	Japan	1988	$15.00/$5.00
Epic	651532-2	One More Try	CD5	U.K.	1988	$10.00
Epic	CDEMU 5	One More Try	CD5	U.K.	1988	$12.00
Columbia	CSK 1091	One More Try	CDJ	U.S.	1987	$6.00
Columbia	656198-3	Praying For Time	CD3	Germany	1990	$10.00
Sony	ESDA-7050	Praying For Time	CD3	Japan	1990	$15.00/$5.00
Epic	GEOC-1	Praying For Time	CD5	U.K.	1990	$11.00
Columbia	CSK 73512	Praying For Time	CDJ	U.S.	1990	$6.00
		Somebody to Love	CD5	U.K.	1993	$10.00
Hollywood	PRCD 10307	Somebody to Love	CDJ	U.S.	1993	$6.00
Hollywood	PRCD-10307-2	Somebody to Love	CDJ	U.S.	1993	$10.00
Hollywood	PRCD 10323	Somebody to Love	CDJ	U.S.	1993	$10.00
	Withdrawn 2 track version.					
Sony	ESDA-7071	Soul Free	CD5	Japan	1991	$5.00
Columbia	CSK 73799	Soul Free	CDJ	U.S.	1991	$5.00
Columbia		Too Funky	CD5	Australia	1992	$10.00
Epic	ESDA-7099	Too Funky	CD3	Japan	1992	$15.00/$5.00
Epic	658058-2	Too Funky	CD5	U.K.	1992	$10.00
Columbia	44K 7452	Too Funky	CD5	U.S.	1992	$5.00
Columbia	CSK 4622	Too Funky	CDJ	U.S.	1992	$5.00
Epic	GEOC 2	Waiting For That Day	CD5	U.K.	1990	$10.00
Columbia	CSK 73663	Waiting For That Day	CDJ	U.S.	1990	$3.00

Michaelis, Lisa

Singles

Label	Catalog Number	Title	Type	Country	Year	Longbox Value / Value
Virgin	PRCD 4609	Rain Falls	CDJ	U.S.	1991	$2.00

Michaels, Lazet

Full Length

Label	Catalog Number	Title	Type	Country	Year	Longbox Value / Value
Zoo	11003	Too Strong	LP/LB	U.S.	1991	$12.00/$7.00

Singles

Label	Catalog Number	Title	Type	Country	Year	Longbox Value / Value
Zoo	ZD-17005	Kraze	CDJ	U.S.	1991	$2.00

Michaels, Robbie

Singles

Label	Catalog Number	Title	Type	Country	Year	Longbox Value / Value
Polydor	PODP-1021	Stay By My Side	CD3	Japan	1991	$12.00/$3.00

Michel'le

Singles

Label	Catalog Number	Title	Type	Country	Year	Longbox Value / Value
Polygram	875133-2	And the World War Four	CD5	Germany	1990	$8.00
Ruthless	3706	If?	CDJ	U.S.	1989	$2.00
Ruthless	3482	Keep Watchin'	CDJ	U.S.	1990	$2.00
Ruthless	3258	Nicety	CDJ	U.S.	1989	$2.00
Atco	796521-2	No More Lies	CD5	Germany	1990	$8.00
Atco	AMDY-5003	No More Lies	CD3	Japan	1990	$13.00/$4.00
Atco	B-9149CD	No More Lies	CD5	U.K.	1990	$8.00
Ruthless	3654	Something In My Heart	CDJ	U.S.	1989	$2.00

Michell, Blue

Full Length

Label	Catalog Number	Title	Type	Country	Year	Longbox Value / Value
Blue Note		Thing To Do, The	LTD/LP	U.S.	1995	$19.00

Midas

Singles

Label	Catalog Number	Title	Type	Country	Year	Longbox Value / Value
King	091X-18001	One on One	CD3	Japan	1989	$12.00/$3.00

Midi Max & Efti

Singles

Label	Catalog Number	Title	Type	Country	Year	Longbox Value / Value
Columbia	44K 74138	Bad Bad Boys	CD5	U.S.	1992	$4.00

Label	Catalog Number	Title	Type	Country	Year	Longbox Value / Value
Columbia	CSK 4584	Bad Bad Boys	CDJ	U.S.	1992	$2.00
Columbia	CSK 4596	Bad Bad Boys	CDJ	U.S.	1992	$2.00
Columbia	CSK 4682	Reggae Steady	CDJ	U.S.	1992	$2.00

Midi Rain

Singles

Label	Catalog Number	Title	Type	Country	Year	Longbox Value / Value
Vinyl	44K 74948	Shine	CDJ	U.S.	1993	$2.00

Midler, Bette

Full Length

Label	Catalog Number	Title	Type	Country	Year	Longbox Value / Value
	VL3080	Art Or Bust	LD	U.S.		$15.00
Atlantic	PRCD 5154-2	Best Bettes	DJ/Smplr	U.S.	1993	$20.00
Atlantic		Best Bettes	DJ/Smplr	U.S.	1994	$10.00
Nelson	12515	Bette Midler Show, The	LD	U.S.	1984	$30.00
Atlantic	7238-2	Divine Miss M., The	LP/LB	U.S.†	1985	$14.00/$8.00
Vestron Video	3080	Midler: Art Or Bust	LD	U.S.	1985	$35.00
Atlantic	80070-2	No Frills	LP/LB	U.S.†	1984	$14.00/$8.00

Singles

Label	Catalog Number	Title	Type	Country	Year	Longbox Value / Value
Atlantic	A-7526CD	Every Road Leads Back to You	CD5	U.K.	1991	$10.00
Atlantic	PRCD 4304-2	Every Road Leads Back to You	CDJ	U.S.	1991	$2.00
Atlantic	7567-78611-2	From a Distance	CD5	Germany	1990	$10.00
Atlantic	AMDY-5032	From a Distance	CD3	Japan	1990	$12.00/$4.00
Atlantic	A-7820CD	From a Distance	CD5	U.K.	1990	$10.00
Atlantic	PRCD 3528-2	From a Distance	CDJ	U.S.	1990	$2.00
Atlantic	7567-85986-2	Gift of Love	CD5	Germany	1991	$10.00
Atlantic	A-7634CD	Gift of Love	CD5	U.K.	1991	$10.00
Atlantic	PRCD 4078-2	Gift of Love	CDJ	U.S.	1991	$2.00
Atlantic	7567-85920-2	In My Life	CD5	Germany	1991	$10.00
Atlantic	AMDY-5070	In My Life	CD3	Japan	1991	$15.00/$4.00
Atlantic	AMDY-5075	In My Life	CD3	Japan	1991	$15.00/$4.00
Atlantic	PRCD 4267-2	In My Life	CDJ	U.S.	1991	$2.00
Atlantic	PRCD 6265-2	In This Life	CDJ	U.S.		$3.00
Atlantic	7567-86027-2	Moonlight Dancing	CD5	Germany	1990	$10.00
Atlantic	AMDY-5048	Moonlight Dancing	CD3	Japan	1990	$15.00/$4.00
Atlantic	PRCD 3879-2	Moonlight Dancing	CDJ	U.S.	1990	$2.00
Atlantic	AMDY-5039	Night and Day	CD3	Japan	1990	$15.00/$4.00
Atlantic	PRCD 3583-2	Night and Day	CDJ	U.S.	1990	$2.00
Atlantic	PRCD 6264-2	To Deserve You	CDJ	U.S.	1994	$6.00
Atlantic	85531	To Deserve You	CD5	U.S.	1995	$5.00
Atlantic	09P3-6171	Under the Boardwalk	CD3	Japan	1989	$15.00/$4.00
Atlantic	A-8976CD	Under the Boardwalk	CD3	U.K.	1989	$10.00
Atlantic	PR 2547-2	Under the Boardwalk	CDJ	U.S.	1988	$2.00
Atlantic	PR 2772-2	Under the Boardwalk	CDJ	U.S.	1988	$2.00
Warner	32-84896	Wind Beneath My Wings	CD5	Canada	1994	$6.00
Atlantic	786405-2	Wind Beneath My Wings	CD3	Germany	1989	$10.00
Atlantic	09P3-6159	Wind Beneath My Wings	CD3	Japan	1991	$15.00/$4.00
Atlantic	A-8972CD	Wind Beneath My Wings	CD3	U.K.	1989	$10.00
Atlantic	PR 2615-2	Wind Beneath My Wings	CDJ	U.S.	1988	$2.00
Atlantic	84896-2	Wind Beneath My Wings	CD5	U.S.	1991	$5.00

Midnight Oil

Full Length

Label	Catalog Number	Title	Type	Country	Year	Longbox Value / Value
CBS	CDOIL-5	Blue Sky Mine	CD	U.K.	1990	$10.00
CBS	SAMP 25800	Blue Sky Mining Interview Disc	DJ/Intvw	Australia	1990	$15.00
Columbia	CK 53793	Earth And Sun And Moon	DJ/LP	U.S.	1993	$20.00
		CD in outer box.				
Columbia	CSK2038	Green Disc, The	DJ/Smplr	U.S.	1990	$20.00
Westwood One		In Concert	RS	U.S.	1993	$50.00
		2 CD set. Airdate: 11/22/93				
Westwood One		In Concert	RS	U.S.	1994	$50.00
		Airdate: 10/24/94.				
Westwood One		In Concert-Nu Rock	RS	U.S.	1994	$50.00
		Airdate: 7/4/94.				
Westwood One		Off the Record	RS	U.S.	1992	$40.00
		Airdate: 6/1/92.				
Westwood One		Off the Record	RS	U.S.	1993	$40.00
		Airdate: 6/14/93.				
Columbia	ESK 4556	Scream in Blue-Live	DJ/LP	U.S.	1992	$16.00

Singles

Label	Catalog Number	Title	Type	Country	Year	Longbox Value / Value
Epic	128P-8012	Beds Are Burning	CD3	Japan	1988	$12.00/$4.00
CBS	CDOIL-1	Beds Are Burning	CD5	U.K.	1988	$10.00
CBS	CDOIL-3	Beds Are Burning	CD5	U.K.	1988	$10.00
Columbia	CSK 1058	Beds Are Burning	CDJ	U.S.	1988	$7.00
CBS	655606-3	Blue Sky Mine	CD3	Germany	1990	$10.00
Epic	ESDA-7022	Blue Sky Mine	CD3	Japan	1990	$12.00/$4.00
Columbia	CSK 73250	Blue Sky Mine	CDJ	U.S.	1990	$6.00
Columbia	CSK 73250	Blue Sky Mine	CDJ	U.S.	1990	$8.00
CBS	651585-2	Dead Heart, The	CD5	Germany	1988	$10.00
CBS	CDOIL-2	Dead Heart, The	CD5	U.K.	1988	$10.00
CBS	CDOIL-4	Dead Heart, The	CD5	U.K.	1988	$10.00
Columbia	CSK 1219	Dead Heart, The	CDJ	U.S.	1988	$3.00
CBS	653051-3	Dreamworld	CD3	Germany	1988	$10.00
Columbia	CSK 5071	Drums of Heaven	CDJ	U.S.	1993	$3.00
Columbia	CSK 5071	Drums of Heaven	CDJ	U.S.	1993	$3.00
CBS	655879-3	Forgotten Years	CD3	Germany	1990	$10.00
CBS	CDOIL-6	Forgotten Years	CD5	U.K.	1990	$13.00
Columbia	44K 73192	Forgotten Years	CD5	U.S.	1990	$5.00
Columbia	CSK 73336	Forgotten Years	CDJ	U.S.	1990	$3.00
CBS	656125-3	King Of the Mountain	CD3	Germany	1990	$10.00
Columbia		King Of the Mountain	CDJ	U.S.	1990	$3.00
Columbia		My Country	CD5	U.K.	1993	$10.00
		Second version.				
Columbia	659370	My County	CD5	U.K.	1993	$10.00
Columbia	CSK 5257	Outbreak	CDJ	U.S.	1993	$2.00
CBS	657899-2	Sometimes	CD5	Germany	1992	$10.00
Columbia	CSK 4560	Sometimes	CDJ	U.S.	1993	$3.00
CBS		Truganini	CD5	U.K.	1993	$10.00
Columbia	CSK 74933	Truganini	CDJ	U.S.	1993	$3.00

Midnight Star

Full Length

Label	Catalog Number	Title	Type	Country	Year	Longbox Value / Value
CBS	75304	Greatest Hits	LP/LB	U.S.		$14.00/$8.00
Solar	60384-2	Planetary Invasion	LP/LB	U.S.†	1985	$14.00/$8.00

Singles

Label	Catalog Number	Title	Type	Country	Year	Longbox Value / Value
Intercord	826 021	Do It (One More Time)	CD5	Germany	1990	$8.00
Epic	ESK 74509	Do It (One More Time)	CDJ	U.S.	1990	$2.00
Epic		Do It (One More Time)	CDJ	U.S.	1990	$2.00
		Second version.				
Intercord	826 013	Don't Rock the Boat	CD5	Germany	1989	$8.00
		Don't Rock the Boat	CDJ	U.S.	1989	$2.00
CBS	656267-3	Luv U Up	CD3	Germany	1990	$8.00
Solar-Epic	ZSK 2156	Luv U Up	CDJ	U.S.	1990	$2.00
Intercord	826 015	Pamper Me	CD3	Germany	1989	$8.00
Epic	ZSK 74530	Red Roses	CDJ	U.S.	1990	$2.00
Intercord	826 014	Snake in the Grass	CD5	Germany	1989	$8.00

Midnight Voices

Singles

Label	Catalog Number	Title	Type	Country	Year	Longbox Value / Value
Monster	7905	Six Bones an Hour	CD5	U.S.	1992	$4.00

Midway Still

Singles

Label	Catalog Number	Title	Type	Country	Year	Longbox Value / Value
Roughneck	585 1015-3	Better Than Before	CD5	Germany	1991	$8.00
Roughneck	HYPE-15CD	Better Than Before	CD5	U.K.	1991	$8.00
Roughneck	HYPE-19CD	Just Get Stuck	CD5	U.K.	1991	$8.00
Roughneck	HYPE-19CD	Just Get Stuck	CD5	U.S.	1991	$5.00
Roughneck	HYPE-13CD	Wish	CD5	U.K.	1991	$8.00

Mighty Lemon Drops

Full Length

Label	Catalog Number	Title	Type	Country	Year	Longbox Value / Value
Sire	26512-Dj	Sound	DJ/LP	U.S.	1991	$10.00
	Picture disc.					

Singles

Label	Catalog Number	Title	Type	Country	Year	Longbox Value / Value
Reprise	PRO-CD-5057	Another Girl	CDJ	U.S.	1991	$6.00
Chrysalis	AZURCD-13	Beautiful Shame	CD5	U.K.	1989	$10.00
Chrysalis	880878	Fall Down	CD5	Germany	1988	$10.00
Chrysalis	AZURCD-9	Fall Down	CD5	U.K.	1988	$10.00
Sire	PRO-CD-3103	Fall Down	CDJ	U.S.	1988	$3.00
Sire	PRO-CD-2963	Inside Out	CDJ	U.S.	1988	$3.00
Chrysalis	AZURCD-12	Into the Heart of Love	CD5	U.K.	1989	$10.00
Reprise	PRO-CD-3751	Into the Heart of Love	CDJ	U.S.	1989	$3.00
Sire	PRO-CD-5574	Into the Sun	CDJ	U.S.	1991	$3.00
Sire	W-0032CD	Too High	CD5	U.K.	1991	$10.00
Sire	PRO-CD-4755	Unkind	CDJ	U.S.	1991	$3.00
Sire	PRO-CD-3880	Where Do We Go From Here?	CDJ	U.S.	1989	$3.00

Mighty Mighty Bosstones, The

Full Length

Label	Catalog Number	Title	Type	Country	Year	Longbox Value / Value
Taang	144	Devil's Night Out	LTD/LP	U.S.	1994	$15.00

Singles

Label	Catalog Number	Title	Type	Country	Year	Longbox Value / Value
Mercury	CDP 983	Don't Know How to Party	CDJ	U.S.	1993	$2.00
Mercury	SACD 1090	Here We Go Again	CDJ	U.S.		$8.00
	CDP1334	Kinder Words	CDJ	U.S.		$2.00
Mercury		Pictures To Prove	CDJ	U.S.	1993	$3.00
Mercury	CDP 1154	Simmer Down	CDJ	U.S.	1993	$2.00
Mercury	CDP 900	Someday I Suppose	CDJ	U.S.	1993	$2.00
Taang	T-48	Where'd You Go	CDJ	U.S.	1993	$7.00

Mijette & Money Mark

Singles

Label	Catalog Number	Title	Type	Country	Year	Longbox Value / Value
London	CDP 692	U Want Me Back	CDJ	U.S.	1992	$2.00

Mike And The Mechanics

Full Length

Label	Catalog Number	Title	Type	Country	Year	Longbox Value / Value
DIR		King Biscuit Flour Hour	RS	U.S.	1989	$30.00
	Airdate: 46/4/89.					
DIR		King Biscuit Flour Hour	RS	U.S.	1991	$30.00
	Airdate: 5/19/91.					
Westwood One		Off the Record	RS	U.S.	1995	$25.00
	Airdate: 4/17/95.					
Radio Today		Rock Stars	RS	U.S.	1989	$30.00
	2 CD set. Airdate: 4/9/89.					

Singles

Label	Catalog Number	Title	Type	Country	Year	Longbox Value / Value
Virgin	664329	A Time and Place	CD5	Germany	1991	$10.00
Virgin	VJDP-10165	A Time and Place	CD3	Japan	1991	$12.00/$4.00
Virgin	VSCDT-1351	A Time and Place	CD5	U.K.	1991	$10.00
		All I Need Is a Miracle	CD5	U.K.	1996	$10.00
Atlantic	PRCD 6427-2	Another Cup of Coffee	CDJ	U.S.		$3.00
Atlantic	PRCD 3930-2	Everybody Get a Second	CDJ	U.S.	1991	$2.00
Virgin	VSCDG-1396	Everybody Get a Second	CD5	U.S.	1992	$10.00
Virgin	VJCP-14031	Get Up	CD3	Japan	1991	$12.00/$4.00
WEA	257710-2	Living Years, The	CD3	Germany	1989	$10.00
Pioneer	09P3-6124	Living Years, The	CD3	Japan	1989	$12.00/$4.00
WEA	U-7717CD	Living Years, The	CD3	U.K.	1988	$10.00
Atlantic	PR 2577-2	Living Years, The	CDJ	U.S.	1988	$3.00
Atlantic		Mea Culpa	CDJ	U.S.		$3.00
		Miracle '96	CDJ	U.K.	1996	$12.00
WEA	U-7602CD	Nobody Knows	CD3	U.K.	1989	$10.00
WEA	257787-2	Nobody's Perfect	CD3	Germany	1988	$10.00
Atlantic	PR 2521-2	Nobody's Perfect	CDJ	U.S.	1988	$2.00
Atlantic	PRCD 6050-2	Over My Shoulder	CDJ	U.S.		$3.00
Atlantic		Revolution	CDJ	U.S.		$2.00
BMG	664699	Second Chance	CD5	Germany	1991	$10.00
Atlantic	PR 2658-2	Seeing Is Believing	CDJ	U.S.	1988	$2.00
		Silent Running	CDJ	France		$20.00
Virgin	VSCDT-1376	Stop Baby	CD5	U.K.	1991	$10.00
Atlantic	PRCD 4177-2	Stop Baby	CDJ	U.S.	1991	$2.00
Virgin	VJDP-10156	Word of Mouth	CD3	Japan	1991	$12.00/$4.00
Atlantic	PRCD 3835-2	Word of Mouth	CDJ	U.S.	1991	$2.00

Miker M.C.

Singles

Label	Catalog Number	Title	Type	Country	Year	Longbox Value / Value
ZYX	DST-5926-8	And the Bite Goes On	CD5	Germany	1988	$6.00
BCM	20396	Show'M the Bass	CD5	Germany	1990	$10.00
Alfa	ALDB-51	Show'M the Bass	CD3	Japan	1990	$13.00/$4.00

Milan

Singles

Label	Catalog Number	Title	Type	Country	Year	Longbox Value / Value
Polydor	PZCD-243	Is It Love You're After	CD5	U.K.	1992	$8.00

Milano, Alyssa

Singles

Label	Catalog Number	Title	Type	Country	Year	Longbox Value / Value
Canyon	PCDY-00030	Best in the World	CD3	Japan	1990	$13.00/$4.00
Canyon	PCDY-00106	Do You See Me?	CD3	Japan	1992	$13.00/$4.00
Canyon	PCDY-00015	Happiness	CD3	Japan	1989	$13.00/$4.00
Canyon	PCDY-00011	I Had a Dream	CD3	Japan	1988	$13.00/$4.00
Canyon	PCDY-00039	I Love When We're Together	CD3	Japan	1990	$13.00/$4.00
Canyon	S10Y-1049	Look In My Heart	CD3	Japan	1989	$13.00/$4.00
Canyon	PCDY-00072	New Sensation	CD3	Japan	1991	$13.00/$4.00
Canyon	S9Y-1103	Straight to the Top	CD3	Japan	1990	$13.00/$4.00
Canyon	S9Y-1106	What a Feeling	CD3	Japan	1990	$13.00/$4.00

Miles, Victoria

Singles

Label	Catalog Number	Title	Type	Country	Year	Longbox Value / Value
Supreme	6755116	Just the Way It Is	CD5	U.K.	1991	$8.00

Milira

Singles

Label	Catalog Number	Title	Type	Country	Year	Longbox Value / Value
Motown	3746310302	One Man Woman	CDJ	U.S.	1992	$2.00
Motown	3746310368	Three's a Crowd	CDJ	U.S.	1992	$2.00

Milkbone

Singles

Label	Catalog Number	Title	Type	Country	Year	Longbox/Value
Capital	58355	Keep It Real	CD5	U.S.	1994	$5.00
	DPRO10201	Where'z Da Party At	CDJ	U.S.		$2.00

Milla

Full Length

Label	Catalog Number	Title	Type	Country	Year	Longbox/Value
Capitol	DPRO-19874	It's Your Life	DJ/Smplr	U.S.	1995	$2.00

Miller, Dennis

Full Length

Label	Catalog Number	Title	Type	Country	Year	Longbox/Value
Columbia	92386	Black & White	LD	U.S.	1992	$30.00
Warner Brothers	PRO-CD-3210	Excerpts From the Off-White Album	DJ/Smplr	U.S.	1988	$4.00
Warner Brothers	PRO-CD-3210	Excerpts From the Off-White Album	DJ/Smplr	U.S.	1988	$15.00

Miller, Frankie

Full Length

Label	Catalog Number	Title	Type	Country	Year	Longbox/Value
Chrysalis		High Life	LTD/LP	U.K.	1994	$30.00
25th Anniversary edition in 6"x11" longbox.						

Miller, Glenn

Full Length

Label	Catalog Number	Title	Type	Country	Year	Longbox/Value
Accord	139201	A Memorial For Glenn Miller	LP/LB	U.S.†	1985	$14.00/$8.00
Accord	139005	A Memorial For Glenn Miller Vol. 2	LP/LB	U.S.†	1985	$14.00/$8.00
GRP	2004	In the Digital Mood	LP/LB	U.S.		$19.00/$15.00
Gold disc.						
GRP	GRP-D-9502	In the Digital Mood	LP/LB	U.S.†	1985	$14.00/$8.00
RCA	PCD1-3666	Pure Gold	LP/BP	U.S.†	1985	$14.00/$8.00
RCA	PCD1-5459	Unforgettable Glenn Miller	LP/BP	U.S.†	1985	$14.00/$8.00

Miller, Steve Band

Full Length

Label	Catalog Number	Title	Type	Country	Year	Longbox/Value
Capitol	CDP-46102	Abracadabra	LP/LB	U.S.†	1985	$14.00/$8.00
Capitol		Born 2 B Blue	DJ/Intvw	U.S.		$8.00
		Brave New World	LP/LB	U.S.		$19.00/$15.00
Capitol	CDP-46103	Built For Speed	LP/LB	U.S.†	1985	$14.00/$8.00
		Children Of the Future	LP/LB	U.S.		$19.00/$15.00
Capitol	CDP-46101	Greatest Hits	LP/LB	U.S.†	1985	$14.00/$8.00
		House of Blues	RS	U.S.	1993	$40.00
2 CD set. Airdate: 9/19/93.						
		House of Blues	RS	U.S.	1996	$40.00
2 CD set. Airdate: 4/21/96.						
Album Network		In the Studio (Book Of Dreams)	RS	U.S.	1989	$20.00
Airdate: 5/15/89.						
Album Network		In the Studio (Book Of Dreams)	RS	U.S.	1992	$20.00
Airdate: 4/27/92.						
Album Network		In the Studio (Fly Like an Eagle)	RS	U.S.	1988	$20.00
Airdate: 9/12/88.						
Album Network		In the Studio (Fly Like an Eagle)	RS	U.S.	1991	$20.00
Airdate: 5/13/91.						
Album Network		In the Studio (Fly Like an Eagle)	RS	U.S.	1996	$20.00
DIR		King Biscuit Flour Hour	RS	U.S.	1989	$35.00
Airdate: 1/8/89.						
DIR		King Biscuit Flour Hour	RS	U.S.	1990	$35.00
Airdate: 7/23/90.						
DIR		King Biscuit Flour Hour	RS	U.S.	1991	$35.00
Airdate: 7/14/91.						
DIR		King Biscuit Flour Hour	RS	U.S.	1992	$35.00
Airdate: 6/29/92.						
DIR		King Biscuit Flour Hour	RS	U.S.	1994	$20.00
Airdate: 7/3/94.						
DIR		King Biscuit Flour Hour	RS	U.S.	1995	$20.00
Airdate: 4/2/95.						
DIR		King Biscuit Flour Hour	RS	U.S.	1996	$20.00
Airdate: 3/17/96.						
Pioneer Artists	PA-83-053	Live	LD	U.S.	1983	$25.00
Westwood One		Off the Record	RS	U.S.	1993	$30.00
Airdate: 9/13/93.						
Westwood One		Off the Record	RS	U.S.	1995	$20.00
Airdate: 8/14/95.						
Westwood One		Off the Record	RS	U.S.	1996	$20.00
Airdate: 1/8/96.						
		Sailor	LP/LB	U.S.		$19.00/$15.00
Capitol	DPRO-5589	Steve Miller Band	DJ/Smplr	U.S.	1994	$18.00
Westwood One		Superstar Concert	RS	U.S.	1992	$40.00
2 CD set. Airdate: 5/31/92						
Media America		Up Close	RS	U.S.	1993	$25.00
2 CD set.						

Singles

Label	Catalog Number	Title	Type	Country	Year	Longbox/Value
Sailor	CDP 979	Blue Eyes	CDJ	U.S.	1993	$3.00
Polydor	CDP 1077	Cry Cry Cry	CDJ	U.S.	1993	$3.00
Arcade	AR-91621-2	Fly Like an Eagle	CD5	U.K.	1991	$11.00
Capitol	203975-2	Joker	CD5	Germany	1990	$11.00
Capitol	CDCL-583	Joker	CD5	U.K.	1990	$11.00
Capitol	DPRO-79439	Just a Little Bit	CDJ	U.S.	1988	$3.00
Polydor	CDP 924	Wild River	CDJ	U.S.	1993	$3.00
Capitol	DPRO-79389	Ya Ya	CDJ	U.S.	1988	$3.00

Milli Vanilli

Full Length

Label	Catalog Number	Title	Type	Country	Year	Longbox/Value
Arista	ASCD 2048	Mega Mix	DJ/Smplr	U.S.	1990	$3.00
Pioneer	PA-90-019	Milli Vanilli	LD	U.S.	1990	$20.00
CAV version.						

Singles

Label	Catalog Number	Title	Type	Country	Year	Longbox/Value
BMG	162870	All or Nothing	CD3	Germany	1989	$4.00
BMG	662225	All or Nothing	CD5	Germany	1989	$4.00
BMG	662870	All or Nothing	CD5	Germany	1989	$4.00
RCA	R10D-142	All or Nothing	CD3	Japan	1989	$9.00/$3.00
Cooltempo	COOLCD-199	All or Nothing	CD5	U.K.	1989	$4.00
BMG	662015	Baby Don't Forget My Number	CD5	Germany	1988	$4
BMG	661841	Baby Don't Forget My Number	CD5	Germany	1988	$4.00
RCA	R10D-121	Baby Don't Forget My Number	CD3	Japan	1989	$5.00
Cooltempo	COOLCD-178	Baby Don't Forget My Number	CD5	U.K.	1988	$4.00
BMG	162364	Blame It on the Rain	CD3	Germany	1989	$4.00
BMG	662364	Blame It on the Rain	CD5	Germany	1989	$4.00
RCA	R10D-136	Blame It on the Rain	CD3	Japan	1989	$9.00/$3.00
Cooltempo	COOLCD-180	Blame It on the Rain	CD5	U.K.	1989	$4.00
BMG	162647	Girl I'm Gonna Miss You	CD3	Germany	1989	$4.00
BMG	662647	Girl I'm Gonna Miss You	CD5	Germany	1989	$4.00
RCA	R10D-127	Girl I'm Gonna Miss You	CD3	Japan	1989	$9.00/$3.00
Cooltempo	COOLCD-191	Girl I'm Gonna Miss You	CD5	U.K.	1989	$4.00
Arista	ASCD 9870	Girl I'm Gonna Miss You	CDJ	U.S.	1989	$2.00
BMG	661589	Girl You Know Its True	CD5	Germany	1989	$4.00
RCA	R15D-4	Girl You Know Its True	CD3	Japan	1989	$9.00/$3.00
Cooltempo	COOLCD-170	Girl You Know Its True	CD5	U.K.	1989	$4.00
Hansa	663813	Keep on Running	CD5	Germany	1990	$4.00
BMG	BVDP-31	Keep on Running	CD3	Japan	1991	$9.00/$3.00
BMG	664539	Nice 'n Easy	CD5	Germany	1991	$4.00
Chrysalis	CHSCD-3686	Too Late	CD5	Germany	1991	$4.00
Hansa	BVDP-40	Too Late	CD3	Japan	1991	$9.00/$3.00

Million Blues

Singles

Label	Catalog Number	Title	Type	Country	Year	Longbox/Value
Arc	CDADQ-1	Living on a Promise	CD5	U.K.	1990	$7.00

Million Dollar Secret

Singles

Label	Catalog Number	Title	Type	Country	Year	Longbox/Value
CBS	655271-3	Cherry	CD3	Germany	1989	$8.00
CBS	654822-3	Don't Think Twice	CD3	Germany	1989	$8.00

Millions

Full Length

Label	Catalog Number	Title	Type	Country	Year	Longbox/Value
Polygram	510108	"M" Is For Millions	LP/BP	U.S.		$13.00/$8.00

Singles

Label	Catalog Number	Title	Type	Country	Year	Longbox/Value
Smash	545	Sometimes	CDJ	U.S.	1991	$2.00

Millions Like Us

Singles

Label	Catalog Number	Title	Type	Country	Year	Longbox/Value
Virgin	PRCD 9412	Guaranteed For Life	CDJ	U.S.		$2.00
Circa	YRCD-9	In Love With Yourself	CD5	U.K.	1988	$8.00

Millionsellers

Singles

Label	Catalog Number	Title	Type	Country	Year	Longbox/Value
Bellaphon	130 07 103	Seventies	CD5	Germany	1991	$9.00
Bellaphon	130 07 104	Sixties	CD5	Germany	1991	$9.00
Bellaphon	130 07 102	Twist	CD5	Germany	1991	$9.00

Mills Brothers

Full Length

Label	Catalog Number	Title	Type	Country	Year	Longbox/Value
Ranwood	R-7035-D	22 Greatest Hits	LP	U.S.†	1985	$8.00
2 CD set.						

Mills, Stephanie

Full Length

Label	Catalog Number	Title	Type	Country	Year	Longbox/Value
Motown	5475	For the First Time	LP/BP	U.S.		$13.00/$8.00
Casablanca	822 421-2	I've Got the Cure	LP/BP	U.S.†	1984	$14.00/$8.00
Pioneer	PA-85-M024	Television Medicine	8"LD	U.S.	1985	$15.00

Singles

Label	Catalog Number	Title	Type	Country	Year	Longbox/Value
MCA	MCA5P-54503	All Day All Night	CD5	U.S.	1993	$5.00
MCA	MCA5P-2345	All Day All Night	CDJ	U.S.	1993	$3.00
MCA	18285	Comfort of a Man	CDJ	U.S.	1989	$2.00
MCA		Home	CDJ	U.S.		$2.00
MCA	MCA5P-54579	Never Do You Wrong	CD5	U.S.	1993	$5.00
MCA	18339	Real Love	CDJ	U.S.	1990	$2.00
Milltown Brothers.						

Singles

Label	Catalog Number	Title	Type	Country	Year	Longbox/Value
A&M	AMCD-704	Apple Green	CD5	Germany	1991	$8.00
A&M	AMCD-704	Apple Green	CD5	U.K.	1991	$8.00
A&M	AMCD-787	Apple Green	CD5	U.K.	1991	$8.00
A&M	75021 7265-2	Apple Green	CDJ	U.S.	1991	$2.00
Big Round	BIRG-101CD	Coming From the Mill	CD5	U.K.	1989	$8.00
A&M	AMCD-758	Here I Stand	CD5	U.K.	1991	$8.00
		It's All Over Now Baby Blue	CD5	U.K.		$10.00
		It's All Over Now Baby Blue	CD5	U.K.		$10.00
Second version.						
A&M	PCCY-10279	Sally Ann	CD5	Japan	1992	$12.00
SPV	8684-3	Seems To Me	CD5	Germany	1990	$8.00
Suburban	MTOWN-0001CD	Seems To Me	CD5	U.K.	1990	$8.00
		Sleepwalking	CD5	U.K.		$10.00
		Sleepwalking	CD5	U.K.		$10.00
Second version.						
		Turnoff	CD5	U.K.		$10.00
		Turnoff	CD5	U.K.		$10.00
Second version.						
A&M	AMCD-711	Which Way Should I Jump?	CD5	U.K.	1991	$8.00
A&M	75021 7004-2	Which Way Should I Jump?	CDJ	U.S.	1991	$2.00

Milner, Joe

Singles

Label	Catalog Number	Title	Type	Country	Year	Longbox/Value
Pioneer	9031-72656-2	Dreams We Dream	CD5	Germany	1990	$8.00
Pioneer	WMD5-4048	Dreams We Dream	CD3	Japan	1990	$12.00/$3.00

Milsap, Ronnie

Full Length

Label	Catalog Number	Title	Type	Country	Year	Longbox/Value
		Country Star Tracks	RS	U.S.	1991	$15.00
Airdate: 10/5/91.						
RCA	PCD1-3772	Greatest Hits	LP/BP	U.S.†	1984	$14.00/$8.00
RCA	PCD1-5425	Greatest Hits Vol. 2	LP/BP	U.S.†	1985	$14.00/$8.00
RCA	PCD1-4311	Inside Ronnie Milsap	LP/BP	U.S.†	1984	$14.00/$8.00
RCA	PCD1-4239	It Was Almost Like a Song	LP/BP	U.S.†	1984	$14.00/$8.00
RCA	PCD1-4670	Keyed Up	LP/BP	U.S.†	1984	$14.00/$8.00
RCA	PCD1-5016	One More Try For Love	LP/BP	U.S.†	1985	$14.00/$8.00
RCA	PCD1-4060	There's No Getting Over Me	LP/BP	U.S.†	1984	$14.00/$8.00

Mind Bomb

Singles

Label	Catalog Number	Title	Type	Country	Year	Longbox/Value
Mercury	862 009	Do You Need Some	CD5	U.S.	1993	$4.00
Mercury	CDP 862	Segue	CDJ	U.S.	1993	$2.00
Mercury	CDP 925	Segue	CDJ	U.S.	1993	$2.00

Mindfunk

Singles

Label	Catalog Number	Title	Type	Country	Year	Longbox/Value
Megaforce	907	Goddess	CDJ	U.S.	1993	$2.00
Epic	ESK 3099	Sugar Ain't So Sweet	CDJ	U.S.	1991	$3.00
Epic	657618-2	Touch You	CD5	U.K.	1991	$8.00

Mindstorm

Singles

Label	Catalog Number	Title	Type	Country	Year	Longbox/Value
Barricade	0721-3	Love Goes Blind	CD5	Germany	1991	$8.00
Barricade	PRS-1029-2	Love Goes Blind	CD5	U.K.	1991	$8.00

Miner, Tim

Full Length

Label	Catalog Number	Title	Type	Country	Year	Longbox/Value
Motown	6350	Tim Miner	LP/BP	U.S.		$12.00/$8.00

Singles

Label	Catalog Number	Title	Type	Country	Year	Longbox/Value
Motown	374631086	Heart	CDJ	U.S.	1992	$2.00

Mingus, Charles

Full Length

Label	Catalog Number	Title	Type	Country	Year	Longbox/Value
Mosaic	MD3-111	Complete Candid Recordings	LP	U.S.	1993	$45.00
3 CD Limited to 7500 copies.						

Ministry

Full Length

Label	Catalog Number	Title	Type	Country	Year	Longbox Value / Value
Lumavision	LVD9104	In Case You Don't Show Up	LD	U.S.	1991	$40.00
Lumivision	LVD9104	Ministry: In Case You Didn't	LD	U.S.	1991	$30.00

Singles

Label	Catalog Number	Title	Type	Country	Year	Longbox Value / Value
		Brick Windows	CDJ	U.S.		$3.00
Sire	9362-40211-2	Jesus Built My Hot Rod	CD5	Germany	1991	$10.00
Sire	9362-40211-2	Jesus Built My Hot Rod	CD5	U.K.	1991	$10.00
Warner Brothers	9 40677-2	Just One Fix	CD5	U.S.		$5.00
Warner Brothers	PRO-CD-6766	Just One Fix	CDJ	U.S.		$3.00
	PRO-CD-7467	Lay Lady Lay	CDJ	U.S.		$2.00
Sire	W-0125CD	N.W.O.	CD5	U.K.	1992	$10.00
Warner Brothers	PRO-CD-5589	N.W.O.	CDJ	U.S.		$3.00

Minnelli, Liza

Full Length

Label	Catalog Number	Title	Type	Country	Year	Longbox Value / Value
		Liza in Concert	LD	U.S.		$50.00
Image	ID7397CB	Visible Results	8" LD	U.S.	1990	$8.00

Singles

Label	Catalog Number	Title	Type	Country	Year	Longbox Value / Value
Teldarc	CD-502S	At Carnegie Hall	DJ/CD3	U.S.	1987	$25.00
Columbia	44K 77189	Day After, The	CD5	U.S.	1993	$6.00
Columbia		Day After, The	CDJ	U.S.	1993	$7.00
CBS	655331-3	Don't Drop Bombs	CD3	Germany	1990	$10.00
Epic	ZEEC-2	Don't Drop Bombs	CD5	U.K.	1989	$10.00
Telarc	CD-502S	Live at Carnegie Hall	DJ/CD3	U.S.	1987	$6.00
CBS	655144-3	Losing My Mind	CD3	Germany	1989	$10.00
Epic	ZEEC-1	Losing My Mind	CD5	U.K.	1989	$10.00
Epic	ESK 73011	Losing My Mind	CDJ	U.S.	1989	$2.00
CBS	655593-3	Love Pains	CD3	Germany	1990	$10.00
CBS	655736-3	Love Pains	CD5	Germany	1990	$10.00
Epic	CDZEE-4	Love Pains	CD5	U.K.	1990	$10.00
Epic	ESK 73355	Love Pains	CDJ	U.S.	1990	$2.00
CBS	655989-3	So Sorry, I Said	CD3	Germany	1990	$10.00
Epic	CPZEE-3	So Sorry, I Said	CD5	U.K.	1990	$12.00

Minogue, Dannii

Full Length

Label	Catalog Number	Title	Type	Country	Year	Longbox Value / Value
PWL		Special Sampler	DJ/Smplr	Japan		$50.00

Singles

Label	Catalog Number	Title	Type	Country	Year	Longbox Value / Value
Alfa	ALCB-409	Baby Love	CD5	Japan	1991	$10.00
		Confide in Me	CD5	U.K.	1994	$10.00
		Confide in Me	CD5	U.K.	1994	$10.00

Second version.

Label	Catalog Number	Title	Type	Country	Year	Longbox Value / Value
		Get Into You	CD5	U.K.	1994	$10.00
Alfa	ALDB-133	Jump to the Beat	CD3	Japan	1991	$12.00/$4.00
MCA	MCA5P-2034	Jump to the Beat	CDJ	U.S.	1991	$2.00
MCA	MCD-17532	Love and Kisses	CD5	Germany	1991	$8.00
MCA	MCSTD-1529	Love and Kisses	CD5	U.K.	1991	$8.00
		Love's on Every Corner	CD5	U.K.		$10.00
		Love's on Every Corner	CD5	U.K.		$10.00

Second version.

Label	Catalog Number	Title	Type	Country	Year	Longbox Value / Value
Alfa	ALDB-127	Success	CD3	Japan	1991	$12.00/$4.00
MCA	MCSTD-1538	Success	CD5	U.K.	1991	$8.00
Savage	2231	Success	CDJ	U.S.	1992	$3.00
MCA	MCSTD 1790	This Is It	CD5	U.K.	1993	$8.00
		This is the Way	CD5	U.K.		$10.00
		This is the Way	CD5	U.K.		$10.00

Second version.

Minogue, Kylie

Full Length

Label	Catalog Number	Title	Type	Country	Year	Longbox Value / Value
		Rhythm of Love	LTD/LP	Australia		$25.00

With bonus tracks in slip case.

Label	Catalog Number	Title	Type	Country	Year	Longbox Value / Value
PWL		Rhythm of Love	DJ/Smplr	Japan		$65.00
PWL	Y12-19	Singles Collection	DJ/Smplr	Japan		$65.00

Singles

Label	Catalog Number	Title	Type	Country	Year	Longbox Value / Value
PWL	ALCB-121	Better the Devil Know You	CD5	Japan	1990	$15.00
PWL	PWCD-56	Better the Devil Know You	CD5	U.K.	1990	$10.00
PWL	171673-2	Better the Devil Know You	CD5	U.S.	1990	$10.00
MCA	CD45 1369	Better the Devil Know You	CDJ	U.S.	1990	$2.00
Alfa	ALCB-692	Celebration	CD5	Japan	1993	$15.00
PWL	PWCD-257	Celebration	CD5	U.K.	1992	$10.00
		Confide In Me	CD5	Australia	1994	$10.00
		Confide In Me	CD5	Australia	1994	$10.00

Second version.

Label	Catalog Number	Title	Type	Country	Year	Longbox Value / Value
Imago		Confide In Me	CD5	U.K.	1994	$10.00
Imago	25083	Confide In Me	CD5	U.S.	1994	$6.00
PWL	HFCD-9	Enjoy Yourself	CD5	U.K.		$10.00
PWL	PWCD-24	Especially For You	CD5	Germany	1989	$10.00
PWL	10B3-12	Especially For You	CD3	Japan	1989	$12.00/$4.00
PWL	PWCD-24	Especially For You	CD5	U.K.	1989	$10.00
PWL	ALCB-503	Finer Feelings	CD5	Japan	1992	$15.00
PWL	PWCD-227	Finer Feelings	CD5	U.K.	1992	$10.00
PWL	99031-76387-2	Give Me Just a Little More Time	CD5	Germany	1992	$10.00
PWL	ALCB-439	Give Me Just a Little More Time	CD5	Japan	1992	$15.00
PWL	PWCD-212	Give Me Just a Little More Time	CD5	U.K.	1992	$10.00
PWL	8 20900	Got To Be Certain	CD5	Germany	1988	$10.00
PWL	10SR-26	Got To Be Certain	CD3	Japan	1988	$12.00/$4.00
PWL	PWCD 12	Got To Be Certain	CD5	U.K.	1988	$10.00
PWL	246935-2	Hand on Your Heart	CD5	Germany	1989	$10.00
Alfa	09B3 44	Hand on Your Heart	CD3	Japan	1989	$12.00/$4.00
Alfa	11B3 45	Hand on Your Heart	CD3	Japan	1989	$12.00/$4.00
PWL	PWCD-35	Hand on Your Heart	CD5	U.K.	1989	$10.00
PWL	10SR-14	I Should Be So Lucky	CD3	Japan	1988	$12.00/$4.00
		I Still Love You	CDJ	U.S.		$2.00
PWL	9031-76002-2	If You Were With Me Now	CD5	Germany	1991	$10.00
PWL	PWCD-208	If You Were With Me Now	CD5	U.K.	1991	$10.00
Teldec	8 70013	It's No Secret	CD5	Germany	1988	$10.00
PWL	10B3-11	It's No Secret	CD3	Japan	1988	$15.00/$4.00
Geffen	PRO-CD-3412	It's No Secret	CDJ	U.S.	1988	$2.00
PWL	2292-47503-2	Je Ne Sais Pas Pourquoi	CD5	Germany	1988	$10.00
PWL	PWCD-21	Je Ne Sais Pas Pourquoi	CD5	U.K.	1988	$10.00
PWL	247648-2	Loco-motion, The	CD5	Germany	1988	$10.00
PWL	10SR-34	Loco-motion, The	CD3	Japan	1988	$15.00/$4.00
PWL	PWCD-14	Loco-motion, The	CD5	U.K.	1988	$10.00
Geffen	PRO-CD-3254	Loco-motion, The	CDJ	U.S.	1988	$2.00
PWL	246561-2	Never Too Late	CD3	Germany	1989	$10.00
PWL	09B3-82	Never Too Late	CD3	Japan	1989	$12.00/$4.00
PWL	PWCD-45	Never Too Late	CD5	U.K.	1989	$10.00
PWL	9031-74737-2	Shocked	CD5	Germany	1991	$10.00
PWL	ALCB-296	Shocked	CD5	Japan	1991	$4.00
PWL	PWCD-81	Shocked	CD5	U.K.	1991	$10.00
PWL	9031-72885-2	Step Back in Time	CD5	Germany	1990	$10.00
Alfa	ALCB-154	Step Back in Time	CD5	Japan	1990	$15.00
PWL	PWCD-64	Step Back in Time	CD5	U.K.	1990	$10.00
PWL	9031-71001-2	Tears on My Pillow	CD5	Germany	1990	$10.00
PWL	ALDB-20	Tears on My Pillow	CD3	Japan	1990	$12.00/$4.00
PWL	PWCD-47	Tears on My Pillow	CD5	U.K.	1990	$10.00
Geffen	PRO-CD-4020	Tears on My Pillow	CDJ	U.S.	1990	$2.00
PWL	10B3-2	Turn It Into Love	CD3	Japan	1988	$12.00/$4.00
PWL	9031-73790-2	What Do I Have To Do	CD5	Germany	1990	$10.00
PWL	ALCB-72	What Do I Have To Do	CD5	Japan	1990	$10.00
PWL	PWCD-72	What Do I Have To Do	CD5	U.K.	1990	$10.00
PWl	ALCB-613	What Kind of Fool	CD5	Japan	1992	$15.00
PWL	PWCD-241	What Kind of Fool	CD5	U.K.	1992	$10.00
PWL		Where Is the Feeling	CD5	U.K.		$10.00
PWL	9031-75452-2	Word Is Out	CD5	Germany	1991	$10.00
PWL	ALCB-371	Word Is Out	CD5	Japan	1991	$10.00
PWL	PWCD-204	Word Is Out	CD5	U.K.	1991	$10.00
PWL	246763-2	Wouldn't Change a Thing	CD5	Germany	1989	$10.00
Alfa	09B3-61	Wouldn't Change a Thing	CD3	Japan	1989	$12.00/$4.00
Alfa	11B3-62	Wouldn't Change a Thing	CD3	Japan	1989	$12.00/$4.00
PWL	PWCD-42	Wouldn't Change a Thing	CD5	U.K.	1989	$10.00
Geffen	PRO-CD-3714	Wouldn't Change a Thing	CDJ	U.S.	1989	$2.00

Mint Condition

Singles

Label	Catalog Number	Title	Type	Country	Year	Longbox Value / Value
Perspective	28968 1703 2	Are You Free	CDJ	U.S.	1991	$2.00
Polygram	PERD-864	Breakin' My Heart	CD5	U.K.	1992	$8.00
Perspective	28968 1711 2	Forever In Your Eyes	CDJ	U.S.	1991	$2.00
Perspective	28968 8201 2	Nobody Does It Betta	CDJ	U.S.	1993	$2.00
Perspective	28968 8073 2	Single To Mingle	CDJ	U.S.	1992	$2.00

Mintzer, Bob

Full Length

Label	Catalog Number	Title	Type	Country	Year	Longbox Value / Value
Digital Music	CD-451	Big Band	LP/LB	U.S.†	1985	$14.00/$8.00

Miracle Legion

Singles

Label	Catalog Number	Title	Type	Country	Year	Longbox Value / Value
Morgan Creek	0012	Snacks & Candy	CDJ	U.S.	1992	$2.00

Mirage

Singles

Label	Catalog Number	Title	Type	Country	Year	Longbox Value / Value
Bellaphon	130 07 582	Everybody Dance Now	CD5	Germany	1991	$8.00
Canyon	S10Y-1050	House Attack	CD3	Japan	1989	$12.00/$3.00
Debut	DEBCD-3062	House Attack	CD5	U.K.	1989	$8.00
Canyon	S10Y-1019	Push the Beat	CD3	Japan	1988	$12.00/$3.00

Miranda

Singles

Label	Catalog Number	Title	Type	Country	Year	Longbox Value / Value
Sunshine	823	Round & Round	CD5	U.S.	1994	$5.00
	822	Your Love Is So Divine	CD5	U.S.	1994	$4.00

Mirillion

Full Length

Label	Catalog Number	Title	Type	Country	Year	Longbox Value / Value
EMI		Script, Fugazi, Misplaced	LTD/LP	U.K.	1994	$35.00

3 CD boxed set.

Misa

Singles

Label	Catalog Number	Title	Type	Country	Year	Longbox Value / Value
RCA	ZD-43460	Shake the House	CD5	Germany	1990	$8.00
		Shake the House	CDJ	U.S.	1990	$2.00

Misbehavin

Singles

Label	Catalog Number	Title	Type	Country	Year	Longbox Value / Value
Capitol	C2 58180	Hot Little Body	CD5	U.S.	1994	$6.00

Misfits

Full Length

Label	Catalog Number	Title	Type	Country	Year	Longbox Value / Value
Plan 9	02/3	Earth A.D. - Wolfsblood	LP/LB	U.S.		$18.00/$15.00

Gold disc.

Label	Catalog Number	Title	Type	Country	Year	Longbox Value / Value
Caroline	CAR7529-2	Misfits	LTD/LP	U.S.	1996	$60.00

4 CD in coffin-shaped boxed set.

Label	Catalog Number	Title	Type	Country	Year	Longbox Value / Value
Caroline	CAR PRCD #17	Misfits: Box-Set Sampler Edition	DJ/Smplr	U.S.	1996	$25.00

Miss World

Singles

Label	Catalog Number	Title	Type	Country	Year	Longbox Value / Value
Atlantic	PRCD 4733-2	First Female Serial Killer	CDJ	U.S.	1992	$2.00

Missing Choir

Singles

Label	Catalog Number	Title	Type	Country	Year	Longbox Value / Value
Polygram	875749-2	Blue State of My Heart	CD5	Germany	1990	$8.00

Missing Persons

Full Length

Label	Catalog Number	Title	Type	Country	Year	Longbox Value / Value
Pioneer	PA84-M015	Surrender Your Heart	8"LD	U.S.	1984	$8.00

Mission

Full Length

Label	Catalog Number	Title	Type	Country	Year	Longbox Value / Value
Mercury		Carved In the Sand	DJ/Intvw	U.S.		$12.00
Polygram	SACD 166	Deliverance Tour 1990, The	DJ/Smplr	U.S.	1990	$15.00
	DRASAMP 2528-2	Neverland	DJ/Smplr	Holland		$25.00
Polygram	SACD 169	Words Upon the Sand	DJ/Intvw	U.S.	1990	$8.00

Singles

Label	Catalog Number	Title	Type	Country	Year	Longbox Value / Value
		Afterglow	CD5	U.K.		$10.00
		Afterglow	CD5	U.K.		$10.00

Second version.

Label	Catalog Number	Title	Type	Country	Year	Longbox Value / Value
Mercury	878 335-2	Amelia	CD5	U.S.	1990	$5.00
Mercury	MTHCD-6	Beyond the Pale	CD5	U.K.	1988	$10.00
Mercury	MTHCD-62	Beyond the Pale	CD5	U.K.	1990	$10.00
Polygram	876491-2	Butterfly on a Wheel	CD5	Canada	1990	$10.00
Polygram		Butterfly on a Wheel	CDJ	Canada	1990	$10.00
Polygram	876779-2	Butterfly on a Wheel	CD5	Germany	1990	$10.00
Mercury	MTHCD-8	Butterfly on a Wheel	CD5	U.K.	1990	$10.00
Mercury	CDP 251	Butterfly on a Wheel	CDJ	U.S.	1990	$7.00
A&M	31458 8155	Damn the Machine	CDJ	U.S.	1993	$2.00
Mercury	876577-2	Deliverance	CD5	Canada	1990	$10.00
Mercury		Deliverance	CDJ	Canada	1990	$10.00
Mercury	876577-2	Deliverance	CD5	Germany	1990	$10.00
Mercury	MTHCD-9	Deliverance	CD5	U.K.	1990	$10.00
Mercury	CDP 203	Deliverance	CDJ	U.S.	1989	$2.00
Mercury	CDP 192	Deliverance	CDJ	U.S.	1990	$2.00
Mercury	MTHCD-11	Hands Across the Ocean	CD5	U.K.	1990	$10.00
Mercury	CDP 354	Hands Across the Ocean	CDJ	U.S.	1990	$2.00
Polygram	87541-2	Into the Blue	CD5	Germany	1990	$10.00
Mercury	MTHCD-10	Into the Blue	CD5	U.K.	1990	$10.00
Mercury	MTYHCD-10	Into the Blue	CD5	U.K.	1990	$10.00
Vertigo	MYTCD 13	Like a Child Again	CD5	U.K.	1992	$10.00
Mercury	864 109	Like a Child Again	CDJ	U.S.	1992	$2.00
Vertigo	866 792	Never Again	CD5	U.K.	1992	$10.00
Vertigo	MYTCB 14	Shades of Greeen	CD5	U.K.	1992	$10.00
Vertigo	MYTCD 14	Shades of Greeen	CD5	U.K.	1992	$12.00
Mercury	870175-2	Tower of Strength	CD5	Germany	1988	$10.00

Label	Catalog Number	Title	Type	Country	Year	Longbox Value / Value
Mercury	MTHCD-4	Tower of Strength	CD5	U.K.	1988	$10.00
		Tower of Strength	CDV	U.K.	1988	$25.00
		Tower of Strength	CD5	U.K.		$10.00

Second version.

Mista

Full Length

Label	Catalog Number	Title	Type	Country	Year	Longbox Value / Value
Eastwest	PRCD-9574-2	Mista	DJ/LP	U.S.	1996	$10.00

CD in digipak.

Mista Grimm

Singles

Label	Catalog Number	Title	Type	Country	Year	Longbox Value / Value
	BSK 6677	Salutation Grimm	CDJ	U.S.		$2.00
	BSK 7067	Steady Gear	CDJ	U.S.		$2.00

Mista Rodd

Singles

Label	Catalog Number	Title	Type	Country	Year	Longbox Value / Value
	1002	Ooh Baby	CD5	U.S.	1994	$5.00

Mitchell

Singles

Label	Catalog Number	Title	Type	Country	Year	Longbox Value / Value
Avex Trax	AVDD-0015	Holy Night	CD3	Japan	1991	$12.00/$3.00

Mitchell, Joni

Full Length

Label	Catalog Number	Title	Type	Country	Year	Longbox Value / Value
Geffen	PRO-CD-3076	A Special Conversation For	DJ/Intvw	U.S.	1988	$12.00
Elektra	1001-2	Court & Spark	LP/LB	U.S.†	1984	$14.00/$8.00
Geffen		Night Ride Home	DJ/Intvw	Canada	1991	$25.00
Geffen	GEFD-24388	Night Ride Home	DJ/LP	U.S.	1991	$15.00
Geffen	GEFD-24388	Night Ride Home	LTD/LP	U.S.	1991	$18.00/$16.00

Limited package in long box.

Label	Catalog Number	Title	Type	Country	Year	Longbox Value / Value
Pioneer	PA-84-100	Refuge of the Road	LD	U.S.	1984	$25.00
Pioneer	PA-84-100	Refuge of the Road	LD	U.S.	1990	$30.00

Digital audio.

Singles

Label	Catalog Number	Title	Type	Country	Year	Longbox Value / Value
Geffen	GED-04236	Come In From the Cold	CD5	Germany	1991	$10.00
Geffen	GFSTD-4	Come In From the Cold	CD5	U.K.	1991	$10.00
Geffen	GFSXD-4	Come In From the Cold	CD5	U.K.	1991	$13.00
Geffen	PRO-CD-4213	Come In From the Cold	CDJ	U.S.	1991	$2.00
Geffen	PRO-CD-3262	Cool Water	CDJ	U.S.	1988	$2.00
Reprise	PRO-CD-8173-R	How Do You Stop	CDJ	U.S.		$3.00
Geffen	920945-2	My Secret Place	CD5	Germany	1988	$10.00
Geffen	GEF-37CD	My Secret Place	CD5	U.K.	1988	$10.00
Geffen	GFSTD-2	Night Ride Home	CD5	U.K.	1991	$10.00
Geffen	PRO-CD-4291	Nothing Can Be Done	CDJ	U.S.	1991	$2.00

Mitchell, Kim

Full Length

Label	Catalog Number	Title	Type	Country	Year	Longbox Value / Value
Atlantic		Rockland	LP/LB	U.S.		$14.00/$8.00

Singles

Label	Catalog Number	Title	Type	Country	Year	Longbox Value / Value
		All We Are	CDJ	Canada		$7.00
		Expedition Sailor	CDJ	Canada		$7.00
		Find the Will	CDJ	Canada		$7.00
		I Am A Wild Party	CDJ	Canada		$7.00
		Lost Lovers Found	CDJ	Canada		$7.00
		Rock & Roll Duty	CDJ	Canada		$7.00
		Rock & Roll Duty	CDJ	U.S.		$2.00
		Rockland Wonderland	CDJ	Canada	1989	$7.00
Atlantic	PR 3043-2	Rockland Wonderland	CDJ	U.S.	1989	$2.00
		Some Folks	CDJ	Canada		$7.00

Mitchell, Yvette

Singles

Label	Catalog Number	Title	Type	Country	Year	Longbox Value / Value
RCA	RDJ644502	Everyday & Everynight	CDJ	U.S.		$2.00

Mitsou

Singles

Label	Catalog Number	Title	Type	Country	Year	Longbox Value / Value
RCA	PD-43396	Bye Bye Mon Cowboy	CD5	Germany	1990	$8.00
RCA	9164-2-RDJ	Bye Bye Mon Cowboy	CDJ	U.S.	1990	$2.00
Atlantic	PRCD 3494-2	In And Out	CDJ	U.S.		$2.00

Mix Factory

Singles

Label	Catalog Number	Title	Type	Country	Year	Longbox Value / Value
All Around	CDGLOBE-113	Burnin' Like Fire	CD5	U.K.	1991	$8.00
All Around	CDGLOBE-120	Take Me Away	CD5	U.K.	1991	$8.00

Mixmaster

Singles

Label	Catalog Number	Title	Type	Country	Year	Longbox Value / Value
BCM	20344	Grand Piano	CD5	Germany	1989	$8.00
BCM	BCM-344CD	Grand Piano	CD5	U.K.	1989	$8.00

Mo

Singles

Label	Catalog Number	Title	Type	Country	Year	Longbox Value / Value
EMI	133451-2	Don't Want To Weep	CD5	Germany	1989	$8.00
EMI	133443-6	Face Of Love	CD5	Germany	1989	$8.00
EMI	133481-2	Sunday Morning	CD5	Germany	1989	$8.00
EMI	133480-2	Wild Wild Wild	CD5	Germany	1989	$8.00

Mo Man

Singles

Label	Catalog Number	Title	Type	Country	Year	Longbox Value / Value
Hollywood	66492	Dis-Moi, Dis-Moi	CD5	U.S.	1991	$4.00

Mobb Deep

Singles

Label	Catalog Number	Title	Type	Country	Year	Longbox Value / Value
4th & B'way	567	Hit It From the Back	CDJ	U.S.	1993	$2.00
RCA	RDJ65428-2	Survival of the Fittest	CDJ	U.S.		$2.00
RCA	64422	Temperature's Rising	CD5	U.S.		$5.00

Mobley, Hank

Full Length

Label	Catalog Number	Title	Type	Country	Year	Longbox Value / Value
Blue Note		Turnaround, The	LTD/LP	U.S.	1995	$19.00

Moby

Full Length

Label	Catalog Number	Title	Type	Country	Year	Longbox Value / Value
Mute		Everything Is Wrong	LTD/LP	U.K.	1995	$30.00

2 CD set.

Singles

Label	Catalog Number	Title	Type	Country	Year	Longbox Value / Value
Elektra		All That I Need Is To Be Loved	CDJ	U.S.		$3.00
	PRCD 9331-2	Bring Back My Hapiness	CDJ	U.S.		$2.00
Elektra	66096	Bring Back My Happiness	CD5	U.S.	1995	$5.00
Instinct	240	Drop a Beat	CD5	U.S.	1992	$4.00
Elektra	PRCD 918-2	Every Time You Touch Me	CDJ	U.S.		$3.00
Elektra/Asylum	66154	Every Time You Touch Me	CD5	U.S.	1994	$5.00
Elektra/Asylum	66180	Feeling So Real	CD5	U.S.	1994	$5.00
		Hymm	CD5	U.K.		$10.00
		Hymm	CD5	U.K.		$10.00

Second version.

Label	Catalog Number	Title	Type	Country	Year	Longbox Value / Value
Elektra	61568	Move	CD5	U.S.		$4.00

Mocca Soul

Full Length

Label	Catalog Number	Title	Type	Country	Year	Longbox Value / Value
Savage	74785 50200	Persistence Of Memory	LP/LB	U.S.	1992	$14.00/$8.00

Singles

Label	Catalog Number	Title	Type	Country	Year	Longbox Value / Value
Savage	50015	Deep Sea So Blue	CDJ	U.S.	1991	$3.00
Savage	2143	Losing You	CDJ	U.S.	1992	$3.00
Intercord	825 775	Rhythm of Love	CD5	Germany	1990	$8.00
Tam Tam	TTT-18CD	Rhythm of Love	CD5	U.K.	1990	$8.00
Tam Tam	TTT-29CD	Why	CD5	U.K.	1990	$8.00

Modern English

Singles

Label	Catalog Number	Title	Type	Country	Year	Longbox Value / Value
TVT	2814-2	Life's Rich Tapestry	CDJ	U.S.	1990	$2.00

Modern Jazz Quartet

Full Length

Label	Catalog Number	Title	Type	Country	Year	Longbox Value / Value
Savoy Records	CY-78986	MJQ	LTD/LP	U.S.	1995	$20.00

CD in miniature repica of original LP sleeve.

Singles

Label	Catalog Number	Title	Type	Country	Year	Longbox Value / Value
Atlantic	PRCD 5547-2	Bags Groove	CDJ	U.S.		$3.00

Moev

Singles

Label	Catalog Number	Title	Type	Country	Year	Longbox Value / Value
Atlantic	PRCD 3494-2	In & Out	CDJ	U.S.	1990	$2.00

Moist

Full Length

Label	Catalog Number	Title	Type	Country	Year	Longbox Value / Value
Chrysalis		Silver	LTD/LP	U.S.	1994	$16.00

CD and VHS Video.

Singles

Label	Catalog Number	Title	Type	Country	Year	Longbox Value / Value
		Push	CDJ	Canada		$5.00
		Push	CD5	U.K.	1995	$10.00
		Push	CD5	U.K.	1995	$10.00

Second version.

Mojave 3

Full Length

Label	Catalog Number	Title	Type	Country	Year	Longbox Value / Value
		Ask Me Tomorrow	DJ/LP	U.S.		$8.00

Mojo Nixon

Singles

Label	Catalog Number	Title	Type	Country	Year	Longbox Value / Value
Enigma	162	(619)239-KING	CDJ	U.S.	1989	$3.00
Enigma	194	Debbie Gibson Is Pregnant	CDJ	U.S.	1989	$3.00
Enigma	336	Destroy All Lawyers	CDJ	U.S.	1990	$3.00

Mokenstef

Singles

Label	Catalog Number	Title	Type	Country	Year	Longbox Value / Value
	PRCD 7118-2	Baby Come Close	CDJ	U.S.		$2.00
	PRCD 6946-2	He's Mine	CDJ	U.S.		$2.00
	PRCD 7023-2	Sex in the Rain	CDJ	U.S.		$2.00

Mollison, Sam

Singles

Label	Catalog Number	Title	Type	Country	Year	Longbox Value / Value
Atomic	WNRCD-003	Will You Love Me in the Morning	CD5	U.K.	1992	$8.00

Molly Hatchet

Full Length

Label	Catalog Number	Title	Type	Country	Year	Longbox Value / Value
CBS		Cut to the Bone	LP/LB	U.S.		$14.00/$8.00
Epic	EK-39621	Deed Is Done, The	LP/LB	U.S.†	1985	$14.00/$8.00
Capitol		Lightning Strikes Twice	LP/LB	U.S.	1989	$14.00/$8.00
Westwood One		Superstars	RS	U.S.	1996	$60.00

Airdate: 6/24/96.

Singles

Label	Catalog Number	Title	Type	Country	Year	Longbox Value / Value
Capitol	DPRO-79879	I Can't Be Watching You	CDJ	U.S.	1989	$2.00
Capitol	DPRO-79765	There Goes the Neigborhood	CDJ	U.S.	1989	$2.00

Mombass

Singles

Label	Catalog Number	Title	Type	Country	Year	Longbox Value / Value
Union City	UCRCD-8	Cry Freedom	CD5	U.K.	1992	$8.00

Moments of Ecstasy

Singles

Label	Catalog Number	Title	Type	Country	Year	Longbox Value / Value
SPV	9487	Wanna Get Out	CD3	Germany	1989	$8.00

Mona Lisa

Singles

Label	Catalog Number	Title	Type	Country	Year	Longbox Value / Value
	PRCD 7119-2	Can't Be Wasting My Time	CDJ	U.S.		$2.00

Money, Eddie

Full Length

Label	Catalog Number	Title	Type	Country	Year	Longbox Value / Value
Album Network		In the Studio (Can't Hold Back)	RS	U.S.	1990	$20.00

Airdate: 6/4/90.

Label	Catalog Number	Title	Type	Country	Year	Longbox Value / Value
Album Network		In the Studio (Eddie Money)	RS	U.S.	1990	$20.00

Airdate: 1/29/90.

Label	Catalog Number	Title	Type	Country	Year	Longbox Value / Value
Album Network		In the Studio (No Control)	RS	U.S.	1992	$20.00

Airdate: 11/9/92.

Label	Catalog Number	Title	Type	Country	Year	Longbox Value / Value
DIR		King Biscuit Flour Hour	RS	U.S.	1989	$30.00

Airdate: 2/5/90.

Label	Catalog Number	Title	Type	Country	Year	Longbox Value / Value
DIR		King Biscuit Flour Hour	RS	U.S.	1989	$30.00

Airdate: 7/2/89.

Label	Catalog Number	Title	Type	Country	Year	Longbox Value / Value
DIR		King Biscuit Flour Hour	RS	U.S.	1990	$30.00

Airdate: 8/13/90.

Label	Catalog Number	Title	Type	Country	Year	Longbox Value / Value
DIR		King Biscuit Flour Hour	RS	U.S.	1992	$30.00

Airdate: 1/19/92.

Label	Catalog Number	Title	Type	Country	Year	Longbox Value / Value
DIR		King Biscuit Flour Hour	RS	U.S.	1993	$30.00

Airdate: 5/24/93.

Label	Catalog Number	Title	Type	Country	Year	Longbox Value / Value
DIR		King Biscuit Flour Hour	RS	U.S.	1996	$25.00

Airdate: 3/31/96.

Label	Catalog Number	Title	Type	Country	Year	Longbox Value / Value
Westwood One		Off the Record	RS	U.S.	1992	$30.00

Airdate: 5/4/92.

Label	Catalog Number	Title	Type	Country	Year	Longbox Value / Value
Westwood One		Off the Record	RS	U.S.	1995	$25.00

Airdate: 9/18/95.

Label	Catalog Number	Title	Type	Country	Year	Longbox Value / Value
Image	ID6967CB	Pictures of Money	LD	U.S.		$30.00
Westwood One		Superstar Concert	RS	U.S.	1992	$30.00

2 CD set. Airdate: 9/27/92.

Label	Catalog Number	Title	Type	Country	Year	Longbox Value / Value
Media America		Up Close	RS	U.S.	1989	$30.00

2 CD set.

Label	Catalog Number	Title	Type	Country	Year	Longbox Value / Value
Media America		Up Close	RS	U.S.	1991	$30.00

2 CD set.

Label	Catalog Number	Title	Type	Country	Year	Longbox Value / Value
Unistar		Weekly Specials, The	RS	U.S.	1992	$15.00

Airdate: 4/3/92.

Label	Catalog Number	Title	Type	Country	Year	Longbox Value / Value
Columbia	CK 38862	Where's the Party	LP/LB	U.S.		$14.00/$8.00

Singles

Label	Catalog Number	Title	Type	Country	Year	Longbox Value / Value
		After This Love	CDJ	U.S.		$2.00
Columbia	CSK 4495	Another Nice Day In L.A.	CDJ	U.S.	1992	$2.00

Label	Catalog Number	Title	Type	Country	Year	Longbox Value / Value
Columbia	CSK 74262	Fall In Love Again	CDJ	U.S.	1991	$2.00
Columbia		Heart For Me	CDJ	U.S.		$3.00
Columbia	CSK 73976	Heaven In the Back Seat	CDJ	U.S.	1991	$2.00
Columbia	CSK 74109	I'll Get By You	CDJ	U.S.	1991	$2.00
Columbia	CSK 1531	Let Me In	CDJ	U.S.	1988	$2.00
Columbia	CSK 73047	Peace in Our Time	CDJ	U.S.	1989	$2.00
Columbia	CSK 4887	Save a Little Room In Your	CDJ	U.S.		$2.00
Sony	10EP-3053	Walk on Water	CD3	Japan	1988	$12.00/$4.00
Columbia	653033-2	Walk on Water	CD5	U.K.	1988	$10.00
Columbia		Walk on Water	CDJ	U.S.	1988	$2.00

Money Talks

Singles

Label	Catalog Number	Title	Type	Country	Year	Longbox Value / Value
BMG	663528	Brave Young Boy	CD5	Germany	1990	$8.00

Monica

Singles

Label	Catalog Number	Title	Type	Country	Year	Longbox Value / Value
	RSCD5040	Don't Take It Personal	CDJ	U.S.		$2.00
Arista	35041	Don't Take It Personal	CD5	U.S.	1994	$5.00

Monifah

Full Length

Label	Catalog Number	Title	Type	Country	Year	Longbox Value / Value
Universal	UPTD-53004	Moods & Moments	LTD/LP	U.S.	1996	$15.00
CD and jewel box in limited edition slip case.						

Monk, Thelonious

Full Length

Label	Catalog Number	Title	Type	Country	Year	Longbox Value / Value
Mosaic	MD3-112	Complete Black Lion and Vogue Recordings	LTD/LP	U.S.		$45.00
3 CD set. Limited to 7500 copies.						

Monkees

Full Length

Label	Catalog Number	Title	Type	Country	Year	Longbox Value / Value
Arista	ARCD-8602	Headquarters	LP/LB	U.S.		$18.00/$15.00
Image	ID6267RC	Monkees, The	LD	U.S.	1985	$25.00
Image	ID6353RC	Monkees, The Vol. 2	LD	U.S.	1985	$25.00
	BVCA-2501	Pisces, Aquarius, Capricorn & Jones	LTD/LP	Japan	1995	$25.00
Arista		Pisces, Aquarius, Capricorn & Jones	LP/LB	U.S.		$18.00/$15.00
Rhino	PRCD 7080	Sampler	DJ/Smplr	U.S.	1994	$30.00
CD in guitar shaped package.						
Arista	A2CD 8432	Then & Now	LP/LB	U.S.	1986	$22.00/$20.00

Singles

Label	Catalog Number	Title	Type	Country	Year	Longbox Value / Value
Arista	A10D-140	Daydream Believer	CD3	Japan	1989	$12.00/$4.00
Rhino		Daydream Believer	CD5	Japan	1996	$18.00
Arista	CD3-3009	Daydream Believer	CD3	U.S.	1989	$7.00/$4.00
Rhino	PRCD 1	Heart And Soul	CDJ	U.S.	1987	$10.00
Arista	CD3-3008	I'm a Believer	CD3	U.S.	1989	$7.00/$4.00
Arista	162053	Last Train to Clarksville	CD3	Germany	1989	$10.00
Arista	662058	Last Train to Clarksville	CD3	U.K.	1989	$10.00
Arista	162053	Last Train to Clarksville	CD3	U.K.	1989	$10.00
Arista	CD3-3007	Last Train to Clarksville	CD3	U.S.	1989	$7.00/$4.00

Monkenstef

Singles

Label	Catalog Number	Title	Type	Country	Year	Longbox Value / Value
Polygram	851706	He's Mine	CD5	U.S.	1995	$6.00

Monroe, Marilyn

Singles

Label	Catalog Number	Title	Type	Country	Year	Longbox Value / Value
ZYX	6080-8	I Wanna Be Loved By You	CD5	Germany	1989	$10.00

Monroe, Michael

Singles

Label	Catalog Number	Title	Type	Country	Year	Longbox Value / Value
Mercury	PHDR-108	Attitude Adjustment	CD3	Japan	1990	$15.00/$4.00
Vertigo	876193-2	Dead, Jail or Rock and Roll	CD5	Germany	1990	$10.00
Mercury	PPDS-15	Dead, Jail or Rock and Roll	CD3	Japan	1990	$15.00/$4.00
Vertigo	VERCD-45	Dead, Jail or Rock and Roll	CD5	U.K.	1990	$10.00
Vertigo	VERCD-46	Man With No Eyes	CD5	U.K.	1990	$10.00
Mercury	CDP 193	Man With No Eyes	CDJ	U.S.	1989	$6.00
Mercury	CDP 107	Not Fakin' It	CDJ	U.S.	1989	$8.00
Mercury		While You Were Looking	CDJ	U.S.		$6.00

Monsoon

Singles

Label	Catalog Number	Title	Type	Country	Year	Longbox Value / Value
Polygram	SOOCD-1	Ever So Lonely	CD5	U.K.	1990	$8.00

Monster Magnet

Full Length

Label	Catalog Number	Title	Type	Country	Year	Longbox Value / Value
Westwood One		In Concert	RS	U.S.	1995	$50.00
Airdate: 11/20/95.						
A&M	AMSAD00096	Interview	DJ/Intvw	U.S.	1993	$15.00

Singles

Label	Catalog Number	Title	Type	Country	Year	Longbox Value / Value
	AMSAD0082	Look Into Your Orb	CDJ	U.S.		$2.00
		Megasonic Teenage Warhead	CDJ	U.S.		$3.00
		Megasonic Teenage Warhead	CD5	U.K.	1995	$10.00
		Megasonic Teenage Warhead	CD5	U.K.	1995	$10.00
Second version.						
A&M	31458 8108	Twin Earth	CDJ	U.S.	1993	$2.00

Monster Voodoo

Singles

Label	Catalog Number	Title	Type	Country	Year	Longbox Value / Value
	62925	Defense Mechanism	CD5	U.S.	1994	$5.00

Montana, June

Singles

Label	Catalog Number	Title	Type	Country	Year	Longbox Value / Value
London	FFRCD-28	I Need Your Love	CD5	U.K.	1989	$8.00

Montez, Chris

Singles

Label	Catalog Number	Title	Type	Country	Year	Longbox Value / Value
Old Gold	OG-6120	Let's Dance	CD3	U.K.	1989	$9.00

Montgomery, John Michael

Full Length

Label	Catalog Number	Title	Type	Country	Year	Longbox Value / Value
Atlantic		What I Do the Best	LTD/LP	U.S.	1996	$18.00
CD and bonus interview CD. Sold exclusively at Blockbuster Music stores.						

Singles

Label	Catalog Number	Title	Type	Country	Year	Longbox Value / Value
		Be My Baby Tonight	CDJ	U.S.	1994	$3.00
Atlantic	PRCD 5108-2	Beer & Bones	CDJ	U.S.	1993	$2.00
Atlantic	PRCD 5551-2	Rope the Moon	CDJ	U.S.	1993	$2.00

Montgomery, Wes

Full Length

Label	Catalog Number	Title	Type	Country	Year	Longbox Value / Value
Verve	821985-2	Bumpin'	LP/LB	U.S.†	1985	$14.00/$8.00
Verve	825676-2	Goin' Out Of My Head	LP/LB	U.S.†	1985	$14.00/$8.00
Verve	810045-2	Movin' Wes	LP/LB	U.S.†	1985	$14.00/$8.00
Verve	823448-2	Wes Montgomery Silver Collection	LP/LB	U.S.†	1985	$14.00/$8.00

Montrose, J.R.

Full Length

Label	Catalog Number	Title	Type	Country	Year	Longbox Value / Value
Blue Note		J.R. Montrose	LTD/LP	U.S.	1994	$20.00

Montrose, Ronnie

Full Length

Label	Catalog Number	Title	Type	Country	Year	Longbox Value / Value
Passport	PJCD-88099	Territory	LP	Germany		$15.00
Passport	PJCD-88099	Territory	LP	U.K.		$15.00
Passport	PJCD-88099	Territory	LP/BP	U.S.		$16.00/$11.00

Singles

Label	Catalog Number	Title	Type	Country	Year	Longbox Value / Value
Enigma	EPRO-110	Tellstar	CDJ	U.S.	1988	$2.00

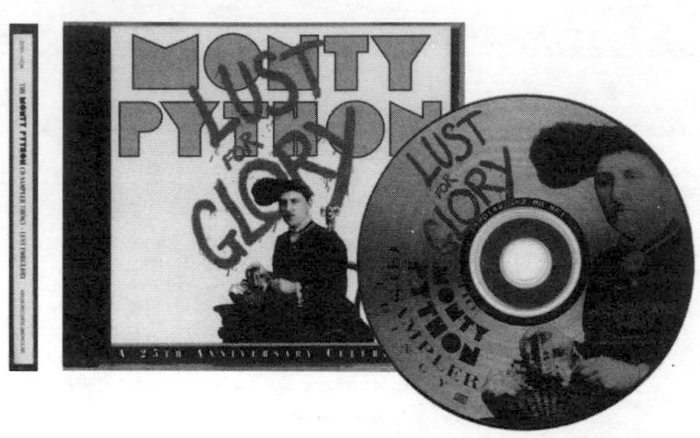

Monty Python – CD Sampler Thingy - Lust For Glory (Virgin DPRO-14236)

Monty Python

Full Length

Label	Catalog Number	Title	Type	Country	Year	Longbox Value / Value
Virgin	DPRO-14236	CD Sampler Thingy - Lust For Glory	DJ/Smplr	U.S.	1994	$25.00

Singles

Label	Catalog Number	Title	Type	Country	Year	Longbox Value / Value
Virgin	664740	Always Look on the Bright Side of Life	CD5	Germany	1991	$10.00
Virgin	PYTHD-1	Always Look on the Bright Side of Life	CD5	U.K.	1991	$10.00
Virgin	PRCD 4160	Always Look on the Bright Side of Life	CDJ	U.S.	1991	$7.00
Virgin	PYTHD-2	Galaxy Song	CD5	U.K.	1991	$10.00
Virgin	665260	I Like Chinese	CD5	Germany	1991	$10.00

Moodswings

Singles

Label	Catalog Number	Title	Type	Country	Year	Longbox Value / Value
Arista	664528	Spiritual High	CD5	U.K.	1991	$10.00
Arista	74321-12771-2	Spiritual High	CD5	U.K.	1991	$10.00
		Taste EP - Rainstorm	CD5	U.K.		$10.00
		Taste EP - Rainstorm	CD5	U.K.		$10.00
Second version.						

Moody Blues

Full Length

Label	Catalog Number	Title	Type	Country	Year	Longbox Value / Value
BBC Radio		BBC Classic Tracks	RS	U.S.	1991	$30.00
Airdate: 9/9/91.						
BBC Radio		BBC Classic Tracks	RS	U.S.	1992	$30.00
Airdate: 11/2/92.						
Westwood One		BBC Classic Tracks	RS	U.S.	1993	$40.00
Airdate: 4/19/93.						
BBC Radio		BBC Classic Tracks	RS	U.S.	1994	$20.00
Airdate: 4/18/92.						
Westwood One		BBC Classic Tracks	RS	U.S.	1994	$40.00
Airdate: 4/18/94.						
Threshold	820155-2	Best of: Voices in the Sky	LP/BP	U.S.†	1985	$14.00/$8.00
Polydor		Highlights From Time Traveler	DJ/Smplr	U.S.	1994	$20.00
Westwood One		In Concert	RS	U.S.	1993	$50.00
Airdate: 1/8/93.						
Album Network		In the Studio (Days of Future Past)	RS	U.S.	1988	$25.00
Airdate: 12/12/88.						
Album Network		In the Studio (Question of Balance)	RS	U.S.	1989	$25.00
Airdate: 11/20/89.						
Album Network		In the Studio (Seventh Sojourn)	RS	U.S.	1991	$25.00
Airdate: 9/30/91.						
DIR		King Biscuit Flour Hour	RS	U.S.	1989	$40.00
Airdate: 8/28/89.						
DIR		King Biscuit Flour Hour	RS	U.S.	1990	$40.00
Airdate: 4/9/90.						
DIR		King Biscuit Flour Hour	RS	U.S.	1991	$40.00
Airdate: 9/15/91.						
DIR		King Biscuit Flour Hour	RS	U.S.	1993	$50.00
Airdate: 4/11/93.						
DIR		King Biscuit Flour Hour	RS	U.S.	1994	$40.00
Airdate: 5/22/94.						
DIR		King Biscuit Flour Hour	RS	U.S.	1995	$50.00
Airdate: 4/30/95.						
		Live From the Whiskey	RS	U.S.	1993	$100.00
Airdate: 8/30/93.						
		Moody Blues Story	RS	U.S.	1994	$30.00
2 CD set. Airdate: 9/18/94.						
Westwood One		Off the Record	RS	U.S.	1993	$30.00
Airdate: 9/6/93.						
Westwood One		Off the Record	RS	U.S.	1994	$30.00
Airdate: 1/24/94.						
Threshold	810119-2	Present	LP/BP	U.S.†	1984	$14.00/$8.00
Westwood One		Superstars	RS	U.S.	1993	$50.00
2 CD set. Airdate: 6/29/93.						
Westwood One		Superstars	RS	U.S.	1993	$80.00
2 CD set. Airdate: 9/6/93.						
Westwood One		Superstars	RS	U.S.	1994	$80.00
2 CD set. Airdate: 11/14/94.						
Westwood One		Superstars	RS	U.S.	1994	$80.00
2 CD set. Airdate: 7/11/94.						
Westwood One		Superstars	RS	U.S.	1995	$80.00
2 CD set. Airdate: 7/24/95.						
Media America		Up Close	RS	U.S.	1988	$40.00
2 CD set.						
Media America		Up Close	RS	U.S.	1992	$40.00
2 CD set.						

Singles

Label	Catalog Number	Title	Type	Country	Year	Longbox Value / Value
Polygram	CDP 529	Bless the Wings	CDJ	U.S.	1991	$2.00

Label	Catalog Number	Title	Type	Country	Year	Longbox Value / Value
Polydor	887600-2	I Know You're Out There Somewhere	CD5	Germany	1988	$10.00
Polydor	POCD-921	I Know You're Out There Somewhere	CD5	U.K.	1988	$10.00
Polydor	422 870 726-2	I Know You're Out There Somewhere	CDV	U.S.	1987	$20.00
Polygram	CDP 15	I Know You're Out There Somewhere	CDJ	U.S.	1988	$2.00
Polygram	870 751-2	I Know You're Out There Somewhere	CDV/BP	U.S.	1988	$20.00/$20.00
Polygram	870 751-2	No More Lies	CDV/BP	U.S.	1988	$20.00/$20.00
Threshold	CDP 154	Question	CDJ	U.S.	1989	$2.00
Polydor	867387-2	Say It With Love	CD5	Germany	1991	$10.00
Polydor	CDP 453	Say It With Love	CDJ	U.S.	1991	$2.00
Polydor	080 023-2	Your Wildest Dreams	CDV	U.S.	1987	$20.00
Polyram	870 713-2	Your Wildest Dreams	CDV/BP	U.S.	1988	$20.00/$20.00
Polydor	080 023-2	Your Wildest Dreams	DJ/CDV	U.S.	1988	$20.00

Moonliters

Singles

Label	Catalog Number	Title	Type	Country	Year	Value
WEA	YZ-327CD	Oh What A Night	CD5	U.K.	1988	$8.00

Moonpools and Caterpillars

Singles

Label	Catalog Number	Title	Type	Country	Year	Value
Elektra	64367	Hear	CD5	U.S.	1995	$5.00
		Little Bird Told Me	CDJ	U.S.		$2.00
	PRCD 9462-2	Ren	CDJ	U.S.		$2.00

Moonshake

Singles

Label	Catalog Number	Title	Type	Country	Year	Value
Matador	5157	Beautiful Pigeon	CDJ	U.S.		$2.00
Creation	CRESCD-101	First	CD5	U.K.	1991	$8.00
Rough Trade	221 1336-3	Secondhand Clothes	CD5	Germany	1991	$8.00
APT	PURECD-9	Secondhand Clothes	CD5	U.K.	1991	$8.00

Moore, Angel

Singles

Label	Catalog Number	Title	Type	Country	Year	Value
Atlantic	85606	Ecstasy	CD5	U.S.	1994	$5.00

Moore, Brian

Singles

Label	Catalog Number	Title	Type	Country	Year	Value
Critique	15531	Stay Awhile	CD5	U.S.	1994	$5.00

Moore, Chante

Full Length

Label	Catalog Number	Title	Type	Country	Year	Value
		A Love	DJ/LP	U.S.	1994	$25.00

CD, VHS video, press kit in box.

Singles

Label	Catalog Number	Title	Type	Country	Year	Value
MCA	2689	As If We Never Met	CDJ	U.S.	1993	$2.00
Salis	2494	It's Alright	CDJ	U.S.	1993	$2.00
Salis	2610	It's Alright	CDJ	U.S.	1993	$2.00
Salis	2091	Love's Taken Over	CDJ	U.S.	1992	$2.00
MCA	54962	Old School Lovin'	CD5	U.S.	1994	$5.00
Salis	2794	Who Do I Turn To	CDJ	U.S.	1993	$2.00
Salis	2810	Who Do I Turn To	CDJ	U.S.	1993	$2.00

Moore, Dorothy

Singles

Label	Catalog Number	Title	Type	Country	Year	Value
Malaco	2172	Be Strong Enough to Hold On	CDJ	U.S.	1991	$2.00
Malaco	2190	Stay Close to Home	CDJ	U.S.	1993	$2.00

Moore, Gary

Full Length

Label	Catalog Number	Title	Type	Country	Year	Value
Virgin	T PAK18	Collector's Edition	LP	Austria	1991	$40.00

3 CD Set

Label	Catalog Number	Title	Type	Country	Year	Value
10 Records	DIXCDP 56	Wild Frontier	LTD/LP	Austria	1988	$35.00

Picture disc CD.

Singles

Label	Catalog Number	Title	Type	Country	Year	Longbox Value / Value
Virgin	GMSCD 1	After the War	CD3	Austria	1988	$10.00
Virgin	GMSCDT-1	After the War	CD5	Austria	1988	$10.00
BMG	161952	After the War	CD3	Germany	1988	$10.00
BMG	661952	After the War	CD5	Germany	1988	$10.00
Virgin	VJD-12033	After the War	CD3	Japan	1988	$12.00/$4.00
BMG	665061	Cold Day in Hell	CD5	Germany	1991	$10.00
Charisma	PRCD 087	Cold Day in Hell	CD5	U.S.	1991	$3.00
Charisma	96199	Cold Day in Hell	CD5	U.S.	1991	$5.00
Castle	CD3-4	Don't Let Me Be Misunderstood	CD3	U.K.	1988	$10.00
Virgin	CDT-35	Empty Rooms	CD3	U.K.	1988	$10.00
Virgin	659080	Friday on My Mind	CD5	Germany	1988	$10.00
Virgin	KERRY-164	Friday on My Mind	CD5	U.K.	1988	$10.00
Virgin	714	Led Clones	CDJ	U.S.	1988	$6.00
Virgin	027	Moving On	CDJ	U.S.	1990	$6.00
Virgin	662962	Oh Pretty Woman	CD5	Germany	1990	$10.00
Virgin	VJCP-1405	Oh Pretty Woman	CD3	Japan	1990	$12.00/$4.00
Virgin	VSCDT-1233	Oh Pretty Woman	CD5	U.K.	1990	$10.00
Charisma	PRCD 003	Oh Pretty Woman	CDJ	U.S.	1990	$6.00
Charisma	DPRO-12707	Only Fuel in Town	CDJ	U.S.		$3.00
Virgin	880992	Over the Hills & Far Away	CD3	Germany	1987	$10.00
Virgin	CDT 16	Over the Hills & Far Away	CD3	U.K.	1987	$10.00
Virgin	VSCDX 1456	Parisienne Walkways	CD5	U.K.	1993	$10.00
Virgin	7432 8 91863-2	Parisienne Walkways	CD5	U.K.	1993	$10.00
Charisma	12789	Parisienne Walkways	CDJ	U.S.	1993	$6.00
Virgin	162081	Ready For Love	CD3	Austria	1989	$10.00
Virgin	662081	Ready For Love	CD3	Austria	1989	$10.00
Virgin	GMSCD 2	Ready For Love	CD3	U.K.	1989	$10.00
Virgin	PRCD 3597	Ready For Love	CDJ	U.S.	1988	$6.00
Virgin	VJCP-20004	Separate Ways	CD5	Japan	1992	$15.00
		Separate Ways	CD5	U.K.		$10.00

Second version.

Label	Catalog Number	Title	Type	Country	Year	Longbox Value / Value
Virgin	VSCDT-1423	Since I Met You Baby	CD5	U.K.	1992	$10.00
Virgin	663246	Still Got the Blues	CD5	Germany	1990	$10.00
Virgin	VJDP-120	Still Got the Blues	CD3	Japan	1990	$12.00/$4.00
Virgin	VJCP-1409	Still Got the Blues	CD5	Japan	1990	$15.00
Virgin	VSCDT-1267	Still Got the Blues	CD5	U.K.	1990	$10.00
Virgin	VSCDX-1267	Still Got the Blues	CD5	U.K.	1990	$10.00
Charisma	PRCD 014	Still Got the Blues	CDJ	U.S.	1990	$6.00
Virgin	VJCP-14046	Story of the Blues	CD5	Japan	1991	$15.00
Virgin	VSCDT-1412	Story of the Blues	CD5	U.K.	1991	$10.00
Charisma	PRCD 099	Story of the Blues	CDJ	U.S.	1991	$3.00
Virgin	VSCDT-1306	Too Tired	CD5	U.K.	1990	$10.00
Virgin	663519	Walking by Myself	CD5	Germany	1990	$10.00
Virgin	VJCP-1413	Walking by Myself	CD5	Japan	1990	$15.00
Virgin	VSCDT-1261	Walking by Myself	CD5	U.K.	1990	$10.00
Virgin	VSCDX-1261	Walking by Myself	CD5	U.K.	1990	$12.00
Virgin	658929	Wild Frontier	CD5	Germany	1988	$10.00
Virgin		Wild Frontier	CD5	U.K.	1988	$10.00

Moore, Ian

Full Length

Label	Catalog Number	Title	Type	Country	Year	Value
Westwood One		In Concert	RS	U.S.	1994	$50.00

2 CD set. Airdate: 6/6/94.

Label	Catalog Number	Title	Type	Country	Year	Value
Westwood One		In Concert	RS	U.S.	1994	$50.00

Airdate: 6/6/94.

Label	Catalog Number	Title	Type	Country	Year	Value
Westwood One		In Concert	RS	U.S.	1995	$50.00

Airdate: 3/13/95.

Label	Catalog Number	Title	Type	Country	Year	Value
Capricorn	6243	Texas Radio Talks to Ian Moore	DJ/Intvw	U.S.	1993	$12.00

Singles

Label	Catalog Number	Title	Type	Country	Year	Value
Capricorn		Barline 99	CDJ	U.S.		$3.00
Capricorn	PRO 6795	Harlem	CDJ	U.S.	1993	$2.00
Capricorn	PRO 6246	How Does It Feel	CDJ	U.S.	1993	$2.00
Capricorn		Society	CDJ	U.S.		$3.00

Moore, Jackie

Singles

Label	Catalog Number	Title	Type	Country	Year	Value
Up Front	UPCD-2	I Wish It Would Rain Down	CD5	U.K.	1990	$8.00

Moore, John

Singles

Label	Catalog Number	Title	Type	Country	Year	Value
Polydor	JMECD-2	Friends	CD5	U.K.	1989	$8.00
Polydor	JMECD-3	Meltdown	CD5	U.K.	1989	$8.00
Polydor	CDP 404	Perfect End	CDJ	U.S.	1991	$2.00
Polydor	JMECD-1	Something About You	CD5	U.K.	1989	$8.00

Moore, Mae

Singles

Label	Catalog Number	Title	Type	Country	Year	Value
		Bohemia	CDJ	Canada	1993	$5.00
Tristar	5577	Bohemia	CDJ	U.S.	1993	$2.00

Moore, Melba

Full Length

Label	Catalog Number	Title	Type	Country	Year	Value
Capitol	DPRO-79364	Moore Love Songs	DJ/Smplr	U.S.		$3.00

Singles

Label	Catalog Number	Title	Type	Country	Year	Value
Capitol	DPRO-79313	I Can't Complain	CDJ	U.S.	1988	$2.00
Capitol	DPRO-79895	Lift Every Voice	CDJ	U.S.	1990	$2.00
Capitol	DPRO-79369	Moore Love Songs	CDJ	U.S.		$10.00
CBS	651663-3	You Stepped Into My Life	CD3	Germany	1988	$8.00
CBS	651663-3	You Stepped Into My Life	CD3	U.K.	1988	$8.00

Moore, Sam

Singles

Label	Catalog Number	Title	Type	Country	Year	Value
MCA	2974	Rainy Night in Georgia	CDJ	U.S.	1994	$2.00

Moore, Thurston

Singles

Label	Catalog Number	Title	Type	Country	Year	Value
		One Soul	CDJ	U.S.		$3.00

Moore, Tina

Singles

Label	Catalog Number	Title	Type	Country	Year	Value
Scotti Brothers	SBDJ78044-2	All I Can	CDJ	U.S.		$2.00
Scotti Brothers	SBDJ75392-2	Color Me Blue	CDJ	U.S.		$2.00

Moorish, Lisa

Singles

Label	Catalog Number	Title	Type	Country	Year	Value
	PRCD 7042-2	I'm Your Man	CDJ	U.S.		$2.00

Moorock, Michael

Full Length

Label	Catalog Number	Title	Type	Country	Year	Value
Griffin	GCD-332-2	New World's Fair	LTD/LP	U.S.	1995	$35.00

CD in box with book.

Moose

Singles

Label	Catalog Number	Title	Type	Country	Year	Value
Hut Records	HUTCD-5	Cool Breeze	CD5	U.K.	1991	$8.00
Hut Records	HUTCD-3	Jack	CD5	U.K.	1991	$8.00
Virgin	PRCD 4319	Jack	CDJ	U.S.	1991	$2.00
Hut Records	HUTCD-20	Little Bird Are You Happy in Your Cage	CD5	U.K.	1992	$8.00
Hut Records	HUTCD-8	Reprise	CD5	U.K.	1991	$8.00
Hut Records	PROMO CD 1	River Will Never Run Dry, The	CDJ	U.K.	1991	$8.00

Morales, Michael

Singles

Label	Catalog Number	Title	Type	Country	Year	Longbox Value / Value
Polydor	PODP-1002	CoolLike the Water	CD3	Japan	1990	$13.00/$4.00
Wing	CDP 155	I Don't Know	CDJ	U.S.	1989	$2.00
Polydor	PODP-1029	I Don't Want to See You	CD3	Japan	1991	$13.00/$4.00
		What I Like About You	CDJ	U.S.	1989	$2.00
		Who Do You Give Your Love To?	CDJ	U.S.	1989	$2.00

More, Kenny

Singles

Label	Catalog Number	Title	Type	Country	Year	Value
Anxious	CDNERV-3	Love Is the Key	CD5	U.K.	1989	$8.00

More Than Paradise

Singles

Label	Catalog Number	Title	Type	Country	Year	Longbox Value / Value
Fun House	FHDF-1187	Love Paradise	CD3	Japan	1992	$12.00/$3.00
Fun House	FHDF-1101	Summer Story	CD3	Japan	1992	$12.00/$3.00

Moreno, Lucha

Singles

Label	Catalog Number	Title	Type	Country	Year	Value
	1412	Cielito Lindo	CD5	U.S.	1994	$5.00

Morgan, Cozette

Singles

Label	Catalog Number	Title	Type	Country	Year	Value
		All Out Of Love	CDJ	U.S.		$2.00

Morgan, George

Full Length

Label	Catalog Number	Title	Type	Country	Year	Value
Bear Family		Candy Kisses	LTD/LP	Germany	1996	$120.00

8 CD set.

Morgan Heritage

Singles

Label	Catalog Number	Title	Type	Country	Year	Value
MCA	54782	Unjust World	CD5	U.S.	1994	$5.00

Morgan, Jamie

Singles

Label	Catalog Number	Title	Type	Country	Year	Value
Tabu	655596	Walk On the Wild Side	CD5	U.K.	1990	$8.00

Morgan, Lee

Full Length

Label	Catalog Number	Title	Type	Country	Year	Value
Blue Note		Delightfulee	LTD/LP	U.S.	1995	$19.00
Savoy Records	CY-78985	Introducing Lee Morgan	LTD/LP	U.S.	1995	$20.00

CD in miniature repica of original LP sleeve.

Morgan, Lorrie

Full Length

Label	Catalog Number	Title	Type	Country	Year	Value
		'90s Country	RS	U.S.	1995	$50.00

Airdate: 8/5/95.

Label	Catalog Number	Title	Type	Country	Year	Longbox Value / Value
		'90s Country	RS	U.S.	1996	$50.00

Airdate: 2/17/96.

Label	Catalog Number	Title	Type	Country	Year	Longbox Value / Value
		Country Special	RS	U.S.	1993	$40.00

Singles

Label	Catalog Number	Title	Type	Country	Year	Longbox Value / Value
RCA	62219-2-RDJ	Something In Red	CDJ	U.S.	1992	$2.00

Morgan, Melissa

Singles

Label	Catalog Number	Title	Type	Country	Year	Longbox Value / Value
Capitol	DPRO-79976	Can You Give Me What I Want	CDJ	U.S.	1990	$2.00
Capitol	DPRO-79211	I Don't Know	CDJ	U.S.	1990	$2.00
Pendulum	8659	I'm Gonna Be Your Lover	CDJ	U.S.	1992	$2.00
		If You Can Do It, I Can Too	CDJ	U.S.		$2.00
Pendulum	8636	Still In Love With You	CDJ	U.S.	1992	$2.00
Pendulum	8600	Through the Years	CDJ	U.S.	1992	$2.00

Morgan, Mike

Full Length

Label	Catalog Number	Title	Type	Country	Year	Longbox Value / Value
		House of Blues	RS	U.S.	1995	$40.00

2 CD set. Airdate: 4/21/95.

Morice, Tara

Singles

Label	Catalog Number	Title	Type	Country	Year	Longbox Value / Value
Columbia	CSK 5106	Time After Time	CDJ	U.S.	1993	$2.00

Morissette, Alanis

Full Length

Label	Catalog Number	Title	Type	Country	Year	Longbox Value / Value
MCA	MCAD-10253	Alanis	LP	Canada	1992	$55.00
Warner Brothers		Jagged Little Pill	DJ/LP	Germany	1995	$50.00
Warner Brothers	PCS-175	Jagged Little Pill	DJ/Smplr	Japan	1995	$35.00
Warner Brothers	SAM1781	Jagged Little Pill	DJ/Smplr	U.K.	1995	$25.00
Maverick	PRO-CD-7744-R	Jagged Little Pill	DJ/LP	U.S.	1995	$15.00
MCA	MCAD-10731	Now Is the Time	LP	Canada	1992	$55.00
Westwood One		Off the Record	RS	U.S.	1995	$25.00

Airdate: 12/4/95.

Singles

Label	Catalog Number	Title	Type	Country	Year	Longbox Value / Value
Warner Brothers		First Ever I Saw Your Face	CD5	Australia	1995	$12.00
Warner Brothers	WPCR-531	Hand in My Pocket	CD5	Japan	1995	$20.00
Warner Brothers		Hand in My Pocket	CD5	U.K.	1995	$11.00
Maverick		Hand in My Pocket	CDJ	U.S.	1995	$6.00
Maverick		Head Over Feet	CD5	U.K.	1996	$10.00
Warner Brothers		Head Over Feet	CDJ	U.K.	1995	$16.00
Warner Brothers	WPCR-757	Ironic	CD5	Japan	1996	$20.00
Maverick	PRO-CD-8035	Ironic	CD5	U.S.	1995	$5.00
Maverick	PRO-CD-8035	Ironic	CDJ	U.S.	1995	$6.00
Maverick	PRCD 0011	Live at the Grammys - You Oughta Know	DJ	U.S.	1996	$28.00
Warner Brothers		Now Is the Time	CD5	U.K.	1995	$11.00
Warner Brothers	WPCR-455	Space Cakes	CD5	Japan	1995	$30.00
Maverick		Space Cakes	CD5	Japan	1996	$25.00
Maverick		You Learn	CD5	Australia	1996	$10.00
Warner Brothers		You Learn	CD5	Japan	1995	$20.00
Maverick		You Learn	CDJ	U.S.	1995	$10.00
Maverick		You Learn	CD5	Germany	1996	$12.00
Warner Brothers	WPCR-300	You Oughta Know	CD5	Japan	1995	$20.00
Maverick	PRO-CD-7732-R	You Oughta Know	CDJ	U.S.	1995	$6.00

1 edit.

Label	Catalog Number	Title	Type	Country	Year	Longbox Value / Value
Maverick	PRO-CD-7732-R	You Oughta Know	CDJ	U.S.	1995	$6.00

2 edits.

Label	Catalog Number	Title	Type	Country	Year	Longbox Value / Value
Maverick		You Oughta Know	CDJ	U.S.	1995	$15.00

Live Grammy Version.

Morphine

Full Length

Label	Catalog Number	Title	Type	Country	Year	Longbox Value / Value
Rykodisc	VRCD 0262	Buena	DJ/Intvw	U.S.		$10.00

Singles

Label	Catalog Number	Title	Type	Country	Year	Longbox Value / Value
Rykodisc	0262	Buena	CDJ	U.S.	1993	$2.00
Rykodisc	1044	Honey White	CD5	U.S.	1994	$5.00
		Supersex	CD5	Australia	1995	$12.00
Rykodisc	1036	Thursday	CDJ	U.S.	1993	$2.00

Morris, Gary

Full Length

Label	Catalog Number	Title	Type	Country	Year	Longbox Value / Value
		Country Star Tracks	RS	U.S.	1991	$15.00

Airdate: 9/21/91.

Singles

Label	Catalog Number	Title	Type	Country	Year	Longbox Value / Value
Capitol	DPRO-79816	Full Moon On An Empty Heart	CDJ	U.S.	1991	$2.00

Morris, Gee

Singles

Label	Catalog Number	Title	Type	Country	Year	Longbox Value / Value
EMI	INDCD-2'	Touch a Hand, Make a Friend	CD5	U.K.	1988	$8.00

Morris, Jenny

Singles

Label	Catalog Number	Title	Type	Country	Year	Longbox Value / Value
Eastwest	9031-75167-2	Break in the Weather	CD5	Germany	1992	$8.00
Eastwest	YZ-649CD	Break in the Weather	CD5	U.K.	1992	$8.00
Eastwest	171820-2	Save Me	CD5	Germany	1990	$8.00
Eastwest	YZ-506CD	Save Me	CD5	U.K.	1990	$8.00
Eastwest	257483-2	She Has To Be Loved	CD5	U.K.	1990	$8.00
Giant	PRO-CD-4387	She Has To Be Loved	CDJ	U.S.	1989	$2.00
Giant	PRO-CD-4508	She Has To Be Loved	CDJ	U.S.	1990	$2.00

Morris, Sarah Jane

Singles

Label	Catalog Number	Title	Type	Country	Year	Longbox Value / Value
Alfa	09B3-13	Can't Get To Sleep Without You	CD3	Japan	1989	$12.00/$3.00
RCA	ZD-42982	Loving a Dream	CD5	Germany	1989	$8.00
Jive	SJMCD-4	Loving a Dream	CD5	U.K.	1989	$8.00
Jive	870006	Me and Mrs. Jones	CD5	Germany	1989	$8.00
Jive	SJMCD-3	Me and Mrs. Jones	CD5	U.K.	1989	$8.00
Factory	FACD-306	World Is In Heaven	CD5	U.K.	1990	$8.00

Morrison, Jim

Full Length

Label	Catalog Number	Title	Type	Country	Year	Longbox Value / Value
Eektra	PRCD 9211-2	Ghost Song	DJ/Intvw	U.S.	1995	$15.00

Singles

Label	Catalog Number	Title	Type	Country	Year	Longbox Value / Value
Efa	CD-40158	Build Me a Woman	CD5	Germany	1990	$15.00
		Ghost Song	CD5	U.K.	1995	$10.00

Morrison, Van

Full Length

Label	Catalog Number	Title	Type	Country	Year	Longbox Value / Value
		Avalon Sunset	DJ/LP	Germany		$25.00

CD, cassette, press kit in special box.

Label	Catalog Number	Title	Type	Country	Year	Longbox Value / Value
HMV		Avalon Sunset	LTD/LP	U.K.	1989	$35.00

CD with booklet in 12"x12" box. Manufactered for HMV superstores.

Label	Catalog Number	Title	Type	Country	Year	Longbox Value / Value
BBC Radio		BBC Classic Tracks	RS	U.S.	1991	$20.00

Airdate: 6/24/91.

Label	Catalog Number	Title	Type	Country	Year	Longbox Value / Value
BBC Radio		BBC Classic Tracks	RS	U.S.	1992	$20.00
Westwood One		BBC Classic Tracks	RS	U.S.	1993	$45.00

Airdate: 5/3/93.

Label	Catalog Number	Title	Type	Country	Year	Longbox Value / Value
Polydor		Collector's Item	DJ/Smplr	U.S.	1994	$12.00
Mercury	PRSAD00117	Days Like These	DJ/Intvw	U.S.	1995	$25.00
Verve	549 949-2	How Long Has This Been Going on Interview	DJ/Intvw	U.S.	1996	$20.00
Polydor	314511 546-2	Hymns to the Silence	LTD/LP	U.S.	1991	$35.00
Polydor		In Celebration of Van Morrison's Mercury Music	DJ/LP	U.S.	1988	$75.00

6 CD set. Six album set in special green promo box.

Label	Catalog Number	Title	Type	Country	Year	Longbox Value / Value
DIR		King Biscuit Flour Hour	RS	U.S.	1989	$40.00

Airdate: 9/18/89.

Label	Catalog Number	Title	Type	Country	Year	Longbox Value / Value
DIR		King Biscuit Flour Hour	RS	U.S.	1990	$40.00

Airdate: 5/21/90.

Label	Catalog Number	Title	Type	Country	Year	Longbox Value / Value
DIR		King Biscuit Flour Hour	RS	U.S.	1991	$40.00

Airdate: 2/3/91.

Label	Catalog Number	Title	Type	Country	Year	Longbox Value / Value
DIR		King Biscuit Flour Hour	RS	U.S.	1992	$40.00

Airdate: 1/26/92.

Label	Catalog Number	Title	Type	Country	Year	Longbox Value / Value
DIR		King Biscuit Flour Hour	RS	U.S.	1993	$45.00

Airdate: 4/18/93.

Label	Catalog Number	Title	Type	Country	Year	Longbox Value / Value
DIR		King Biscuit Flour Hour	RS	U.S.	1994	$45.00

Airdate: 8/7/94.

Label	Catalog Number	Title	Type	Country	Year	Longbox Value / Value
DIR		King Biscuit Flour Hour	RS	U.S.	1995	$45.00

Airdate: 7/30/95.

Label	Catalog Number	Title	Type	Country	Year	Longbox Value / Value
Mercury	818 336-2	Live at Belfast Opera	LP/BP	U.S.†	1984	$14.00/$8.00
Mercury	SAN-FRAN-1	Live Sampler	DJ/Smplr	U.K.		$10.00
Warner Brothers	2-3103	Moondance	LP/LB	U.S.†	1984	$14.00/$8.00
Radio Today		Rock Stars	RS	U.S.	1989	$50.00

2 CD set. Airdate: 3/17/89.

Label	Catalog Number	Title	Type	Country	Year	Longbox Value / Value
Mercury	822 895-2	Sense of Wonder	LP/BP	U.S.†	1984	$14.00/$8.00
Polydor	CDP 560	Songs From Hymns to the Silence	DJ/Smplr	U.S.	1991	$8.00
Polydor		Special In-Store Sampler	DJ/Smplr	U.S.		$5.00
		St. Patrick's Day Special	RS	U.S.	1989	$50.00

2 CD set.

Label	Catalog Number	Title	Type	Country	Year	Longbox Value / Value
		Turn Up Your Radio	RS	U.S.	1989	$50.00

2 CD set. Airdate: 3/15/89.

Label	Catalog Number	Title	Type	Country	Year	Longbox Value / Value
Verve	SACD 1234	Van Live At the Point	DJ/Smplr	U.S.	1996	$20.00

Singles

Label	Catalog Number	Title	Type	Country	Year	Longbox Value / Value
	VAN-1	A Night In San Fancisco	CDJ	Australia		$25.00
Mercury		Ain't That Loving You Baby	CDJ	U.S.	1994	$7.00
Polydor		Ball & Chain	CDJ	U.K.	1993	$10.00
Polydor	CDP 989	Ball & Chain	CDJ	U.S.	1993	$6.00
Polydor	VANCD-4	Coney Island	CD5	U.K.	1990	$10.00
		Days Like These	CD5	U.K.	1995	$10.00
Polydor	VANCD-8	Enlightenment	CD5	U.K.	1990	$10.00
Polydor	VANCD-5	Gloria	CD5	U.K.	1990	$10.00
Polydor		Gloria	CDJ	U.K.	1990	$10.00
Polydor	VANCD-1	Have I Told You Lately	CD5	U.K.	1989	$10.00
Mercury	CDP 108	Have I Told You Lately	CDJ	U.S.	1989	$3.00
Polygram	879959-2	I Can't Stop Loving You	CD5	Germany	1991	$10.00
Polydor	VANCD-9	I Can't Stop Loving You	CD5	U.K.	1991	$10.00
Mercury	MERCD-262	I'll Tell Me Ma	CD5	U.K.	1988	$10.00
		I'm Not Feeling It Anymore	CDJ	Canada	1992	$7.00
Mercury	CDP 623	I'm Not Feeling It Anymore	CDJ	U.S.	1992	$3.00
Polydor	VANCD-3	Orangefield	CD5	U.K.	1989	$10.00
Mercury	CDP 656	Ordinary Life	CDJ	U.S.	1992	$3.00
		Perfect Fit	CDJ	U.S.		$3.00
Polydor	VANCD-6	Real Real Gone	CD5	U.K.	1990	$10.00
Mercury	CDP 340	Real Real Gone	CDJ	U.S.	1990	$3.00
Polydor	889961-2	Whenever God Shines His Light	CD5	Germany	1989	$10.00
Polydor	VANCD-2	Whenever God Shines His Light	CD5	U.K.	1989	$10.00
Mercury	CDP 79	Whenever God Shines His Light	CDJ	U.S.	1989	$3.00
Polydor	VANCD-10	Why Must I Always Explain	CD5	U.K.	1991	$10.00
Polydor	CDP 491	Why Must I Always Explain	CDJ	U.S.	1991	$3.00
		Youth of 1,000 Summers	CDJ	Canada	1991	$7.00
Mercury	CDP 387	Youth of 1,000 Summers	CDJ	U.S.	1991	$3.00

Morrissey

Full Length

Label	Catalog Number	Title	Type	Country	Year	Longbox Value / Value
EMI	SPCD 1740	Family Line	DJ/Smplr	France		$50.00
Westwood One		In Concert-Nu Rock	RS	U.S.	1995	$100.00

Airdate: 9/25/95.

Label	Catalog Number	Title	Type	Country	Year	Longbox Value / Value
EMI		Loop, The	DJ/Smplr	France		$50.00
Warner Brothers	PRO-CD-6778	Now My Heart Is Full	DJ/Smplr	U.S.	1994	$30.00
Reprise	PRO-CD-6778	Now My Heart is Full an Introspective 1984-1994	DJ/Smplr	U.S.	1994	$40.00
Reprise	2-45451-A	Vauxhall and I	DJ/LP	U.S.	1994	$15.00
EMI		Viva Hate	DJ/LP	U.K.		$35.00

CD, cassette, press kit in pecial box.

Singles

Label	Catalog Number	Title	Type	Country	Year	Longbox Value / Value
Warner Brothers	9 40184-2	At Kroq	CD5	U.S.		$7.00
Sire		Billy Bud	CDJ	U.S.		$10.00
WEA	CDR-DJX-6400	Boxers	CDJ	U.K.	1994	$20.00
Warner Brothers	41914	Boxers	CD5	U.S.	1994	$6.00
Warner Brothers	PRO-CD-7372	Boxers	CDJ	U.S.	1994	$8.00
		Boy Racer	CD5	U.K.	1995	$12.00
		Boy Racer	CD5	U.K.	1995	$12.00

Second version.

Label	Catalog Number	Title	Type	Country	Year	Longbox Value / Value
EMI	8803652	Certain People I Know	CD5	Australia	1992	$14.00
EMI	CDPOP-1631	Certain People I Know	CD5	U.K.	1992	$13.00
		Certain People I Know	CD5	U.S.	1992	$7.00
		Dageham Dave	CD5	U.K.	1995	$11.00
	BVCP-8809	Dagehem Dave	CD5	Japan	1995	$20.00
EMI	202605-2	Everyday Is Like Sunday	CD5	Germany	1988	$12.00
EMI	CDPOP-1619	Everyday Is Like Sunday	CD5	U.K.	1988	$12.00
Sire	PRO-CD-3112	Everyday Is Like Sunday	CDJ	U.S.	1988	$10.00
Sire	PRO-CD-5752	Glamourous Glue	CDJ	U.S.		$6.00
Toshiba	TOCP-6164	He Knows I'd Love To See Him	CD3	Japan	1990	$18.00/$4.00
Parlophone		Hold On To Your Friends	CD5	U.K.	1994	$12.00
Parlophone	CDR-DJ-6385	Hold On To Your Friends	CDJ	U.K.	1994	$15.00
EMI	2023301-2	Interesting Drug	CD5	Germany	1989	$12.00
Toshiba	CP15-5889	Interesting Drug	CD5	Japan	1989	$20.00
EMI	CDPOP-1621	Interesting Drug	CD5	U.K.	1989	$12.00
		Interlude	CD5	U.K.	1994	$10.00
	CDPOP-DJ-1632	Jack the Ripper	CDJ	U.K.		$15.00
EMI	203218-2	Last of the International Playboys	CD5	Germany	1989	$10.00
EMI	CDPOP-1620	Last of the International Playboys	CD5	U.K.	1989	$10.00
Parlophone	SPCD 1598	Loop, The	CDJ	France		$20.00
Warner Brothers	41276	More You Ignore Me	CD5	U.S.	1994	$6.00
EMI	CDRDJ6372	More You Ignore Me, The	CDJ	U.K.	1994	$35.00

Recalled due to "Incorrect" graphics on disc.

Label	Catalog Number	Title	Type	Country	Year	Longbox Value / Value
Warner Brothers	PRO-CD-6624	More You Ignore Me, The	CDJ	U.S.	1994	$7.00
EMI	204483-2	My Love of Life	CD5	Germany	1991	$10.00
EMI	CDPOP-1628	My Love of Life	CD5	U.K.	1991	$10.00
Sire	9 40163-2	My Love of Life	CD5	U.S.	1991	$7.00
EMI	203734-2	November Spawned a Monster	CD5	Germany	1990	$10.00
EMI	TOCP-6146	November Spawned a Monster	CD5	Japan	1990	$27.00
EMI	CDPOP-1623	November Spawned a Monster	CD5	U.K.	1990	$10.00

Label	Catalog Number	Title	Type	Country	Year	Longbox Value / Value
Sire	21529-2	November Spawned a Monster	CD5	U.S.	1990	$5.00
Warner	12-41700	Now My Heart Is Full	CD5	Canada	1994	$12.00
Sire		Now My Heart Is Full	CDJ	U.S.	1994	$7.00
EMI	203615-2	Ouija Board	CD5	Germany	1989	$10.00
EMI	TOCP-6145	Ouija Board	CD5	Japan	1989	$15.00
RCA	CDPOP-622	Ouija Board	CD5	U.K.	1989	$10.00
Sire	9 21424-2	Ouija Board	CD5	U.S.	1989	$8.00
EMI	204155-2	Our Frank	CD5	Germany	1991	$13.00
EMI	TOCP-6641	Our Frank	CD5	Japan	1991	$15.00
EMI	CDPOP-1625	Our Frank	CD5	U.K.	1991	$13.00
Sire		Our Frank	CD5	U.S.	1991	$6.00
Sire	PRO-CD-4732	Our Frank	CDJ	U.S.	1991	$6.00
EMI	204054-2	Picadilly Parlare	CD5	Germany	1990	$13.00
EMI	CDPOP-1624	Picadilly Parlare	CD5	U.K.	1990	$13.00
EMI	CDPOP-1627	Pregnant For the Last Time	CD5	U.K.	1991	$13.00
RCA	20 9259 2	Sing Your Life	CD5	Germany	1991	$13.00
RCA	CDPOP-1626	Sing Your Life	CD5	U.K.	1991	$13.00
Sire	9 40084-2	Sing Your Life	CD5	U.S.	1991	$7.00
EMI	202396-2	Suedehead	CD5	Germany	1988	$13.00
Toshiba	XP10-2001	Suedehead	CD3	Japan	1988	$18.00/$4.00
EMI	CDPOP-1618	Suedehead	CD5	U.K.	1988	$13.00
		Suedehead	CDJ	U.S.	1988	$6.00
		Sunny	CD5	U.K.	1995	$12.00
Sire	9 40580-2	Tomorrow	CD5	U.S.	1992	$6.00
Sire	PRO-CD-5637	Tomorrow	CDJ	U.S.	1992	$6.00
EMI	CDPOP-1629	We Hate It When Our Friends Become Successful	CD5	U.K.	1991	$10.00
Sire	9 40560-2	We Hate It When Our Friends Become Successful	CD5	U.S.	1991	$6.00
EMI	CDPOP-1630	You're the One For Me, Fatty	CD5	U.K.	1992	$10.00

Morrissey, Bill

Singles

Label	Catalog Number	Title	Type	Country	Year	Longbox Value / Value
	CDPR 1052	Closed Down Mill	CDJ	U.S.		$2.00

Morro, El

Singles

Label	Catalog Number	Title	Type	Country	Year	Longbox Value / Value
	5322	Rifa	CD5	U.S.	1994	$5.00

Morse, Steve

Full Length

Label	Catalog Number	Title	Type	Country	Year	Longbox Value / Value
Musician	60369-2	Introduction, The	LP/LB	U.S.†	1985	$14.00/$8.00

Singles

Label	Catalog Number	Title	Type	Country	Year	Longbox Value / Value
MCA	CD45-1611	Battle Lines	CDJ	U.S.	1991	$2.00
MCA	CD45-18047	Endless Waves	CDJ	U.S.	1989	$6.00
MCA	MCA5P-2182	Morning Rush Hour	CDJ	U.S.	1992	$2.00
MCA	CD45-1378	Simple Simon	CDJ	U.S.	1991	$2.00
MCA	CD45-17965	Tumeni Notes	CDJ	U.S.	1989	$2.00

Mortal Sin

Singles

Label	Catalog Number	Title	Type	Country	Year	Longbox Value / Value
Vertigo	VERCD-47	I Am Mortal	CD5	U.K.	1990	$8.00

Mosaic

Singles

Label	Catalog Number	Title	Type	Country	Year	Longbox Value / Value
BMG	664512	Dance Now	CD5	Germany	1991	$8.00

Moster Twins

Singles

Label	Catalog Number	Title	Type	Country	Year	Longbox Value / Value
Intercord	825 765	Monster Twins	CD3	Germany	1989	$8.00

Moten

Singles

Label	Catalog Number	Title	Type	Country	Year	Longbox Value / Value
EMI	58004	So Close	CDJ	U.S.	1993	$2.00

Mother Hips

Singles

Label	Catalog Number	Title	Type	Country	Year	Longbox Value / Value
		Shut the Door	CDJ	U.S.		$2.00

Mother Love Bone

Full Length

Label	Catalog Number	Title	Type	Country	Year	Longbox Value / Value
Polydor	843191-2	Apple	LP/BP	U.S.	1990	$23.00/$20.00
Polygram	314 512 884	Mother Love Bone	LP	U.S.	1993	$16.00

2 CD set.

Label	Catalog Number	Title	Type	Country	Year	Longbox Value / Value
Stardog	839011-2	Shine	LP/BP	U.S.	1989	$20.00/$18.00

Singles

Label	Catalog Number	Title	Type	Country	Year	Longbox Value / Value
Polygram	CDP 244	Stardog Champion	CDJ	U.S.	1990	$6.00
Polygram	CDP 763	Stardog Champion	CDJ	U.S.	1992	$6.00
Polygram	CDP 849	Stargazer	CDJ	U.S.	1992	$6.00
Polydor	CDP 348	This Is Shangrila	CDJ	U.S.	1990	$6.00

Mother Station

Singles

Label	Catalog Number	Title	Type	Country	Year	Longbox Value / Value
		Put the Blame On Me	CDJ	U.S.		$2.00

Mother Tongue

Singles

Label	Catalog Number	Title	Type	Country	Year	Longbox Value / Value
		Damage	CDJ	U.S.	1994	$3.00

Mother's Finest

Singles

Label	Catalog Number	Title	Type	Country	Year	Longbox Value / Value
Scotti Brothers	ZSK 75316	Generator	CDJ	U.S.	1992	$2.00
EMI	203625-3	I'm 'n Danger	CD3	Germany	1989	$8.00
EMI	203483-3	Legs and Lipstick	CD3	Germany	1989	$8.00
Scotti Brothers	ZSK 7533	Like a Negro	CDJ	U.S.	1992	$6.00
		Your Wish Is My Command	CDJ	U.S.		$2.00

Mothers

Singles

Label	Catalog Number	Title	Type	Country	Year	Longbox Value / Value
Elektra	EKR-116CD	Even If We Lose	CD5	U.K.	1990	$8.00
Elektra	EKR-119CD	Miracle Man	CD5	U.K.	1991	$8.00
Elektra	PRCD 8331-2	Miracle Man	CDJ	U.S.	1991	$2.00
Isolation	ONLYC-1	Sponge	CD5	U.K.	1990	$8.00
Elektra	EKR-1126CD	Sponge	CD5	U.K.	1991	$8.00

Moti Special

Singles

Label	Catalog Number	Title	Type	Country	Year	Longbox Value / Value
Polygram	877717-2	Behind Closed Doors	CD5	Germany	1990	$8.00
Polygram	873055-2	Dancing For Victory	CD5	Germany	1989	$8.00
Polygram	873955-2	Dancing For Victory	CD5	Germany	1990	$8.00
Polygram	873287-2	In Love We Stand	CD5	Germany	1990	$8.00

Motian, Paul

Full Length

Label	Catalog Number	Title	Type	Country	Year	Longbox Value / Value
ECM	823641-2	It Should've Happened a Long Time Ago	LP/LB	U.S.†	1985	$14.00/$8.00

Motif

Singles

Label	Catalog Number	Title	Type	Country	Year	Longbox Value / Value
Payday	889	Please Me Tonight	CDJ	U.S.	1993	$2.00
Payday	1028	You Hold Me	CDJ	U.S.	1993	$2.00

Motley Crue – Quaternary (Elektra 61664-2) This U.S CD5 was available only through mail order by purchasing a copy of the 1994 Motley Crue album.

Mötley Crüe

Full Length

Label	Catalog Number	Title	Type	Country	Year	Longbox Value / Value
Elektra	PR 8116-2	Crucial Crüe	DJ/Smplr	U.S.	1989	$50.00
Elektra	WMC5-429	Decade of Decadence	LTD/LP	Japan	1991	$30.00
Foundations		FZ Interview	DJ/Intvw	U.S.	1994	$15.00
Westwood One		In Concert	RS	U.S.	1993	$80.00

Airdate: 8/2/93.

Label	Catalog Number	Title	Type	Country	Year	Longbox Value / Value
Elektra	PRCD 8955-2	In-Store Play Sampler	DJ/Smplr	U.S.	1994	$15.00
Elektra	WPZP-5800	Motley Crüe	LTD/LP	Japan	1994	$30.00

CD with extra booklet and outer sleeve.

Label	Catalog Number	Title	Type	Country	Year	Longbox Value / Value
Westwood One		Off the Record	RS	U.S.	1994	$20.00

Airdate: 5/2/94.

Label	Catalog Number	Title	Type	Country	Year	Longbox Value / Value
Elektra	61664-2	Quaternary	Smplr	U.S.	1994	$15.00

Available by mail order only.

Label	Catalog Number	Title	Type	Country	Year	Longbox Value / Value
Elektra	60289-2	Shout at the Devil	LP/LB	U.S.†	1985	$14.00/$8.00
Elektra	60418-2	Theatre of Pain	LP/LB	U.S.†	1985	$25.00/$8.00

Experimental carboard sleeve and outer longbox.

Label	Catalog Number	Title	Type	Country	Year	Longbox Value / Value
WEA	40104	Uncensored	LD	U.S.	1990	$25.00

Singles

Label	Catalog Number	Title	Type	Country	Year	Longbox Value / Value
Elektra	WMD5-4089	Angela	CD3	Japan	1991	$15.00/$4.00
Elektra	PRCD 8513-2	Angela	CDJ	U.S.	1992	$3.00
Elektra	PR 8176-2	Don't Go Away Mad (Just Go Away)	CDJ	U.S.	1989	$6.00
Elektra	9P3 6156	Dr. Feelgood	CD3	Japan	1989	$15.00/$4.00
Elektra	EKR 97CD	Dr. Feelgood	CD3	U.K.	1989	$10.00
Elektra	PR 8108-2	Dr. Feelgood	CDJ	U.S.	1989	$7.00
Elektra	7559-66480	Home Sweet Home	CD5	Germany	1991	$10.00
Elektra	EKR-136CD	Home Sweet Home	CD5	U.K.	1991	$10.00
Elektra	PRCD 8463-2	Home Sweet Home	CDJ	U.S.	1991	$3.00
Elektra	EKR180CD	Hooligan's Holiday	CD5	U.K.	1994	$10.00
Elektra	EKR180CDX	Hooligan's Holiday	CD5	U.K.	1994	$10.00
Elektra	PRCD 8901-2	Hooligan's Holiday	CDJ	U.S.	1994	$6.00
Elektra		Hooligan's Holiday	CDJ	U.S.	1994	$6.00

Second version.

Label	Catalog Number	Title	Type	Country	Year	Longbox Value / Value
Elektra	09P3-6211	Kickstart My Heart	CD3	Japan	1989	$15.00/$4.00
Elektra	PR 8128-2	Kickstart My Heart	CDJ	U.S.	1989	$3.00
Elektra	CD66222	Misunderstood	CD5	Canada	1994	$8.00
Elektra		Misunderstood	CDJ	Germany	1994	$16.00
Elektra	66222-2	Misunderstood	CD5	U.S.	1994	$6.00
Elektra	PRCD 8952-2	Misunderstood	CDJ	U.S.	1994	$3.00
Elektra		Misunderstood	CDJ	U.S.	1994	$3.00

Second version.

Label	Catalog Number	Title	Type	Country	Year	Longbox Value / Value
Elektra	7559-65506-2	Primal Scream	CD5	Germany	1991	$10.00
Elektra	WMD5-4075	Primal Scream	CD3	Japan	1991	$15.00/$4.00
Elektra	EKR-133CD	Primal Scream	CD5	U.K.	1991	$10.00
Elektra	PRCD 8418-2	Primal Scream	CDJ	U.S.	1991	$3.00
Elektra	61664-2	Quaternary	CD5	U.S.	1994	$30.00
Elektra	PR 8204-2	Same Ol' Situation	CDJ	U.S.	1989	$3.00
Elektra		Smoke the Sky	CDJ	U.S.	1994	$6.00
Elektra	PRCD 8990-2	Uncle Jack	CDJ	U.S.	1994	$6.00
Elektra	7559-66638-2	Without You	CD5	Germany	1989	$10.00
Elektra	WPDP-6226	Without You	CD3	Japan	1989	$15.00/$4.00
Elektra	EKR-109CD	Without You	CD5	U.K.	1989	$10.00
Elektra	PR 8152-2	Without You	CDJ	U.S.	1989	$3.00

Motorhead

Full Length

Label	Catalog Number	Title	Type	Country	Year	Longbox Value / Value
Epic	467481 2	1916	LTD/LP	U.K.	1991	$30.00

Picture disc CD.

Label	Catalog Number	Title	Type	Country	Year	Longbox Value / Value
WTG	NSK 4169	Angel City and Other Cities	DJ/Smplr	U.S.	1991	$7.00
Pioneer	PA-87-M0502	Another Perfect Day	8"LD	U.S.	1987	$15.00
Castle	CTVCD 125/1	Best Of Motorhead - All the Aces	LTD/LP	U.K.	1993	$33.00

2CD set.

Label	Catalog Number	Title	Type	Country	Year	Longbox Value / Value
Image	ID7923EN	Birthday Party, The	LD	U.S.		$30.00
Enigma		Birthday Party, The	LP/LB	U.S.		$14.00/$8.00
Foundationa		F16 CD	DJ/Intvw	U.S.	1995	$15.00
Griffin	GCD-219-2	Fistful of Aces: Best of Motorhead	LTD/LP	U.S.	1994	$30.00

CD and book in box.

Label	Catalog Number	Title	Type	Country	Year	Longbox Value / Value
Griffin		Fistful of Aces: Best of Motorhead	LTD/LP	U.S.	1994	$70.00

CD and book in metal box. Limited to 2500 copies.

Label	Catalog Number	Title	Type	Country	Year	Longbox Value / Value
Success		Grind Ya Down	LP	U.K.		$15.00
Griffin	GCD-223-2	Iron Fist	LTD/LP	U.S.	1994	$75.00

CD in metal fist package.

Label	Catalog Number	Title	Type	Country	Year	Longbox Value / Value
Epic	NSK 2295	It's Almost...1916	DJ/Intvw	U.S.	1991	$25.00
WTG	NSK 2295	It's Almost...1916	DJ/Smplr	U.S.	1991	$8.00
Cleopatra	CDLL 57666	On Parole	LP	U.K.	1992	$15.00

Limited edition in felt bag.

Label	Catalog Number	Title	Type	Country	Year	Longbox Value / Value
Dojo		Ultimate Reissue Sampler	DJ/Smplr	U.S.	1996	$15.00

Singles

Label	Catalog Number	Title	Type	Country	Year	Longbox Value / Value
Chocolate	4804	Ace of Spades	CD5	Germany	1993	$10.00
Castle	CD3-10	Ace of Spades	CD3	U.K.	1988	$10.00
WTG	NSK 4903	Bad Religion	CDJ	U.S.	1993	$3.00
		Born to Raise Hell	CD5	U.K.	1994	$10.00

Label	Catalog Number	Title	Type	Country	Year	Longbox Value / Value
		Born to Raise Hell	CDJ	U.S.	1994	$6.00
ZYX		Burner	CD5	Germany	1993	$8.00
ZYX	002-P	Burner	CDJ	Germany	1993	$12.00
Epic	658326-2	Hellraiser	CD5	Germany	1992	$10.00
WTG	NSK 4588	Hellraiser	CDJ	U.S.	1992	$6.00
Reciever	RRSCD 1009	Leaving Here	CD5	U.K.		$12.00
Epic	658809-2	Motorhead '92 Tour E.P.	CD5	U.K.	1992	$10.00
WTG	NSK 4010	No Voices in the Sky	CDJ	U.S.	1991	$7.00
Epic	NSK 4010	No Voices in the Sky	CDJ	U.S.	1991	$15.00
Chiswik	DANMD-92-2	Over the Top	DJ/CD3	Japan		$45.00
		Sacrifice	CDJ	U.S.	1995	$6.00
WTG	NSK 4789	You Better Run	CDJ	U.S.	1992	$2.00

Motorpsycho

Singles

Label	Catalog Number	Title	Type	Country	Year	Longbox Value / Value
Hollywood	10165	Midnite Sun	CDJ	U.S.	1992	$2.00
Hollywood	10108	Truth	CDJ	U.S.	1992	$2.00

Mott the Hoople

Full Length

Label	Catalog Number	Title	Type	Country	Year	Longbox Value / Value
DIR		King Biscuit Flour Hour	RS	U.S.	1988	$35.00

Airdate: 7/24/88.

Label	Catalog Number	Title	Type	Country	Year	Longbox Value / Value
Columbia		London to Memphis	LP/LB	U.S.		$14.00/$8.00

Singles

Label	Catalog Number	Title	Type	Country	Year	Longbox Value / Value
Columbia	654853-3	All the Young Dudes	CD3	Germany	1989	$10.00
Columbia	654853-3	All the Young Dudes	CD3	U.K.	1989	$10.00
Columbia	658177-2	All the Young Dudes	CD5	U.K.	1989	$10.00

Mould, Bob

Full Length

Label	Catalog Number	Title	Type	Country	Year	Longbox Value / Value
Rykodisc		Bob Mould	DJ/LP	U.S.	1996	$12.00
Virgin	PRCD 3513	Rust Bucket Coleseum	DJ/Smplr	U.S.		$15.00
		Wishing Well	DJ/Smplr	U.S.		$15.00
Virgin	PRCD BOB	Workbook	DJ/LP	U.S.	1989	$15.00

Singles

Label	Catalog Number	Title	Type	Country	Year	Longbox Value / Value
		For Knox, King Solomon	CDJ	U.S.	1996	$8.00
Virgin	PRCD 3471	It's Too Late	CDJ	U.S.	1990	$2.00
Virgin	PRCD 3665	Out of Your Life	CDJ	U.S.	1990	$2.00
Virgin	VUSCD-2	See a Little Light	CD5	U.K.	1989	$10.00
Virgin	PR 2685	See a Little Light	CDJ	U.S.	1989	$2.00

Moulin Rouge

Singles

Label	Catalog Number	Title	Type	Country	Year	Longbox Value / Value
Victor	VDPS-1048	Baby I Miss You	CD3	Japan	1989	$12.00/$3.00
Victor	VDPS-1030	Boys Don't Cry	CD3	Japan	1989	$12.00/$3.00
Victor	VDPS-1015	D.J. I Wanna Be Your Record	CD3	Japan	1989	$12.00/$3.00
Victor	VDPS-1027	Tea For Two	CD3	Japan	1989	$12.00/$3.00

Mountain

Full Length

Label	Catalog Number	Title	Type	Country	Year	Longbox Value / Value
Columbia		On Top	LP/LB	U.S.		$14.00/$8.00

Mouskouri, Nana

Full Length

Label	Catalog Number	Title	Type	Country	Year	Longbox Value / Value
Philips	629	Falling in Love Aqain Sampler	DJ/Smplr	U.S.	1991	$8.00

Singles

Label	Catalog Number	Title	Type	Country	Year	Longbox Value / Value
Philips	PRO 2	Even Now	CDJ	U.S.	1991	$2.00

Mouth

Singles

Label	Catalog Number	Title	Type	Country	Year	Longbox Value / Value
		Pure	CDJ	U.S.		$2.00

Mouzon, Alphonse

Full Length

Label	Catalog Number	Title	Type	Country	Year	Longbox Value / Value
Verve	817485-2	By All Means	LP/LB	U.S.†	1985	$14.00/$8.00

Movement

Singles

Label	Catalog Number	Title	Type	Country	Year	Longbox Value / Value
Arista	BVDA-49	Jump	CD3	Germany	1992	$8.00
Arista	74321-11667-2	Jump	CD5	U.K.	1992	$8.00

Moving Target

Singles

Label	Catalog Number	Title	Type	Country	Year	Longbox Value / Value
Taang	72	Last Of the Angels	CD5	U.S.	1993	$4.00

Moyet, Alison

Full Length

Label	Catalog Number	Title	Type	Country	Year	Longbox Value / Value
CBS	CK-39956	Alf	LP/BP	U.S.†	1985	$14.00/$8.00
Columbia		Hoodo	DJ/Smplr	U.S.		$12.00
	XPCD 785	Live No Overdubs	DJ/Smplr	U.K.		$18.00
		Singles Collection	LTD/LP	U.K.	1996	$35.00

2 CD set.

Singles

Label	Catalog Number	Title	Type	Country	Year	Longbox Value / Value
Columbia	654602-3	All Cried Out	CD5	Germany	1989	$9.00
Columbia	654602-3	All Cried Out	CD5	U.K.	1989	$9.00
Columbia	44K 77223	Falling	CD5	U.S.	1994	$6.00
Columbia		Getting Into Something	CD5	U.K.		$9.00
Columbia	656757-2	It Won't Be Long	CD5	U.K.	1991	$9.00
Columbia	CSK 73872	It Won't Be Long	CDJ	U.S.	1991	$2.00
Columbia	MOYETC-5	Love Letters	CD5	U.K.	1990	$9.00
Columbia	657515-2	This House	CD5	Germany	1991	$9.00
Columbia	657515-2	This House	CD5	U.K.	1991	$9.00
Columbia	656939-2	Whispering Your Name	CD5	U.K.	1994	$9.00
Columbia		Whispering Your Name	CD5	U.K.	1994	$10.00

Second version.

Label	Catalog Number	Title	Type	Country	Year	Longbox Value / Value
Columbia	44K 77389	Whispering Your Name	CD5	U.S.	1994	$5.00
CBS	77389	Whispering Your Name	CD5	U.S.	1994	$5.00
Columbia	CSK 6019	Whispering Your Name	CDJ	U.S.	1994	$2.00

Mr. Big

Full Length

Label	Catalog Number	Title	Type	Country	Year	Longbox Value / Value
		Hey Man	LTD/LP	Japan	1996	$30.00
		In Concert	RS	U.S.	1992	$35.00

Airdate: 11/23/92.

Singles

Label	Catalog Number	Title	Type	Country	Year	Longbox Value / Value
Atlantic	PR 2780-2	Addicted To that Rush	CDJ	U.S.	1989	$2.00
Atlantic	PRCD 5422-2	Ain't Seen Love Like That	CDJ	U.S.	1994	$2.00
Atlantic	PR 3080-2	Big Love	CDJ	U.S.	1989	$3.00
Atlantic	PRCD 5279-2	Colorado Bulldog	CDJ	U.S.	1993	$2.00
Atlantic	A-7712CD	Drill Song	CD5	U.K.	1991	$10.00
Atlantic	PRCD 6561-2	Goin' Where the Wind Blows	CDJ	U.S.		$2.00
Atlantic	7567-86040-2	Green Tinted Sixties Mind	CD5	Germany	1991	$10.00
Atlantic	AMDY-5045	Green Tinted Sixties Mind	CD3	Japan	1991	$12.00/$4.00
Atlantic	A-7702CD	Green Tinted Sixties Mind	CD5	U.K.	1991	$10.00
Atlantic	A-7468CD	Green Tinted Sixties Mind	CD5	U.K.	1992	$10.00
Atlantic	PRCD 3796-2	Green Tinted Sixties Mind	CDJ	U.S.	1991	$2.00
Atlantic	AMCY-416	Just Take a Piece of My Heart	CD5	Japan	1992	$15.00
Atlantic	A-7490CD	Just Take a Piece of My Heart	CD5	U.K.	1992	$10.00
Atlantic	PRCD 4445-2	Just Take a Piece of My Heart	CDJ	U.S.	1992	$2.00
Atlantic	PRCD 4022-2	Lucky Strike	CDJ	U.S.	1991	$2.00
Atlantic		Strike Like Lightening	CDJ	U.S.		$2.00
Atlantic	7567-85931-2	To Be With You	CD5	Germany	1991	$10.00
Atlantic	A-7514CD	To Be With You	CD5	U.K.	1991	$10.00
Atlantic	PRCD 4211-2	To Be With You	CDJ	U.S.	1991	$3.00
Atlantic	PRCD 5272-2	Wild World	CDJ	U.S.	1993	$2.00
Atlantic	PRCD 5281-2	Wild World	CDJ	U.S.	1993	$2.00
Elektra	PRCD 2966-2	Wind Me Up	CDJ	U.S.	1989	$2.00

Mr. Big Mouse

Singles

Label	Catalog Number	Title	Type	Country	Year	Longbox Value / Value
SPV	8185-3	Drop That Ghetto Blaster	CD5	Germany	1989	$8.00

Mr. Bungle

Singles

Label	Catalog Number	Title	Type	Country	Year	Longbox Value / Value
Warner Brothers	PRO-CD-4993	Quote Unquote	CDJ	U.S.	1991	$2.00

Mr. Fiddler

Singles

Label	Catalog Number	Title	Type	Country	Year	Longbox Value / Value
		Blackout	CDJ	U.S.		$2.00
Elektra	PRCD 8226-2	Cool About It	CDJ	U.S.	1990	$2.00
Elektra	PRCD 8383-2	So You Wanna Be a Gangster	CDJ	U.S.	1991	$2.00

Mr. Fingers

Singles

Label	Catalog Number	Title	Type	Country	Year	Longbox Value / Value
MCA	MVDM-23	Closer	CD3	Japan	1992	$12.00/$3.00
MCA	MCSTD-1601	Closer	CD5	U.K.	1992	$9.00
MCA	54363	Closer	CD5	U.S.	1992	$5.00
MCA	2435	Closer	CDJ	U.S.	1992	$2.00
MCA	MCSTD-1668	On a Corner Called Jazz	CD5	U.K.	1992	$9.00
MCA	MCSTD-1630	On My Way	CD5	U.K.	1992	$9.00
ffrr	FCD-131	What About This Love	CD5	U.K.	1990	$9.00
MCA	2393	What About This Love	CDJ	U.S.	1992	$2.00

Mr. Lee

Singles

Label	Catalog Number	Title	Type	Country	Year	Longbox Value / Value
RCA	ZD-43326	Get Busy	CD5	Germany	1990	$8.00
Alfa	ALDB-33	Get Busy	CD3	Japan	1990	$12.00/$3.00
Jive	1274-2-JDJ	Get Busy	CDJ	U.S.	1990	$2.00
Jive	JIVECD-330	Hey Love	CD5	U.K.	1993	$8.00
Jive	42017-2-JDJ	Hey Love	CDJ	U.S.	1993	$2.00
RCA	ZD-43822	I Like the Girl	CD5	Germany	1990	$8.00
		I Like the Girl	CDJ	U.S.	1990	$2.00
RCA	ZD-43640	Pump That Body	CD5	Germany	1990	$8.00

Mr. Malik

Singles

Label	Catalog Number	Title	Type	Country	Year	Longbox Value / Value
	SCD5058	Malik Goes On	CDJ	U.S.		$2.00

Mr. Mirainga

Singles

Label	Catalog Number	Title	Type	Country	Year	Longbox Value / Value
MCA	MCA5P3633	Bad Lady	CDJ	U.S.		$2.00
MCA	MCA5P3572	Burnin' Rubber	CDJ	U.S.		$2.00
MCA	MCA5P3572	Burnin' Rubber	CDJ	U.S.		$6.00

Rubber covered package.

Mr. Mister

Full Length

Label	Catalog Number	Title	Type	Country	Year	Longbox Value / Value
DIR		King Biscuit Flour Hour	RS	U.S.	1988	$30.00

Airdate: 1/24/88.

Label	Catalog Number	Title	Type	Country	Year	Longbox Value / Value
Pioneer	CLD-86-002	Welcome	LD	U.S.	1986	$20.00

Singles

Label	Catalog Number	Title	Type	Country	Year	Longbox Value / Value
RCA	PD-49449	Broken Wings	CD3	Germany	1989	$9.00
RCA	PD-49449	Broken Wings	CD3	U.K.	1989	$9.00
RCA/NTSC	RCA 005	Kyrie	DJ/CDV	U.S.	1988	$20.00
RCA	6601-2-RDJ	Something Real	CDJ	U.S.		$2.00
RCA	R10D-9	Stand & Deliver	CD3	Japan	1988	$12.00/$4.00
RCA	7667-2-RDJ	Stand & Deliver	CDJ	U.S.	1987	$2.00

Mr. Reality

Singles

Label	Catalog Number	Title	Type	Country	Year	Longbox Value / Value
SBK	DPRO 04675	Anonymous	CDJ	U.S.	1992	$2.00

Mr. T. Experience

Singles

Label	Catalog Number	Title	Type	Country	Year	Longbox Value / Value
Lookout Records	106	Tapin' Up My Heart	CD5	U.S.	1994	$5.00

Mr. X

Singles

Label	Catalog Number	Title	Type	Country	Year	Longbox Value / Value
	5000	Any Ole Sunday	CD5	U.S.	1994	$5.00

Mr. Zivago

Singles

Label	Catalog Number	Title	Type	Country	Year	Longbox Value / Value
Alfa	ALDB-159	Tell by Your Eyes	CD3	Japan	1992	$12.00/$3.00
Alfa	ALCB-615	Tell by Your Eyes	CD5	Japan	1992	$10.00

Ms. Adventures

Singles

Label	Catalog Number	Title	Type	Country	Year	Longbox Value / Value
Atco	PRCD 3428-2	Undeniable	CDJ	U.S.	1990	$2.00

Mt. Rushmore

Singles

Label	Catalog Number	Title	Type	Country	Year	Longbox Value / Value
Moonshine Music	88400	I've Got the Music	CD5	U.S.	1994	$5.00

MTS

Singles

Label	Catalog Number	Title	Type	Country	Year	Longbox Value / Value
Summit	SCD-5454-2	I'll Be Alright	CD5	U.S.	1996	$5.00

MTV

Full Length

Label	Catalog Number	Title	Type	Country	Year	Longbox Value / Value
Pioneer Artists	PA-91-423	Best of MTV	LD	U.S.	1992	$30.00

Mudhoney

Singles

Label	Catalog Number	Title	Type	Country	Year	Longbox Value / Value
Reprise	9 40741-2	Blinding Sun	CD5	U.S.	1993	$5.00
Tupelo	TUPCD-09	Boiled Beef & Rotting Teeth	CD5	U.K.	1989	$8.00
		Generation Spokesmodel	CD5	U.K.	1995	$10.00
		Generation Spokesmodel	CD5	U.S.	1995	$3.00
Sub Pop		Into the Drink	CDJ	U.S.	1991	$3.00
Sub Pop	SPCD-16/155	Let it Slide	CD5	U.K.	1991	$8.00
Reprise	PRO-CD-6630	No Song II	CDJ	U.S.		$2.00
Reprise	W-0137CD	Suck You Dry	CD5	U.K.	1992	$8.00
Reprise	PRO-CD-5771	Suck You Dry	CDJ	U.S.	1992	$2.00
Efa	11352-03	You Stupid Asshole	CD5	Germany	1992	$8.00
Efa	11352-03	You Stupid Asshole	CD5	U.K.	1992	$8.00

Label	Catalog Number	Title	Type	Country	Year	Longbox Value / Value
Mudhoney/Gilmore						
Singles						
Sub Pop	248	Mudhoney/Gilmore	CD5	U.S.	1994	$5.00
Muffs						
Singles						
	PRO-CD-7760	Agony	CDJ	U.S.		$2.00
Warner Brothers	PRO-CD-6212	Lucky Guy	CDJ	U.S.	1993	$2.00
		Sad Tomorrow	CD5	U.K.	1995	$10.00
Muldar, Jenni						
Singles						
Warner Brothers	PRO-CD-5830	Black Clouds	CDJ	U.S.	1993	$2.00
Muldaur, Maria						
Full Length						
		House of Blues	RS	U.S.	1995	$40.00
2 CD set. Airdate: 4/9/95.						
Mulligan, Gary Quartet						
Full Length						
Mosaic	MD3-102	Complete Pacific Jazz and Capitol Recordings of the Original Gary Mulligan Quartet and Tentette	LP	U.S.		$45.00
3 CD Set.						
Mulligan, Gerry						
Full Length						
GRP	D-9503	Little Big Horn	LP/LB	U.S.†	1985	$14.00/$8.00
Philips	818271-2	Night Lights	LP/LB	U.S.†	1985	$14.00/$8.00
Mulligan, Gerry & Acker Bilk						
Full Length						
Philips	818272-2	Romantic Clarinet for Lovers	LP/LB	U.S.†	1985	$14.00/$8.00
Mungo Jerry						
Singles						
ZYX	6151-8	In the Summertime	CD3	Germany	1989	$8.00
ZYX	6761-8	In the Summertime	CD5	Germany	1989	$8.00
Pikosso	872 0024	In the Summertime	SCD5	Germany	1995	$20.00
"Flower" shaped CD.						
Old Gold	OG-6139	In the Summertime	CD5	U.K.	1989	$10.00
Munks of Funk						
Singles						
Eternal	YZ-471CD	Wonderful Thing	CD5	U.K.	1991	$8.00
Murder Inc.						
Singles						
Devotion	CDDVN-106	Corpuscle	CD5	U.K.	1992	$8.00
Murdersquad						
Singles						
Capitol	DPRO-0404-2	Knock On Wood	CDJ	U.S.	1995	$3.00
Murdock, Shirley						
Singles						
Elektra	PR 8043-2	Found My Way	CDJ	U.S.	1988	$2.00
Elektra		Husband	CDJ	U.S.		$2.00
Elektra	PRCD 8337-2	In Your Eyes	CDJ	U.S.	1991	$2.00
Elektra		Oh What a Feeling	CDJ	U.S.		$2.00
Murmurs						
Singles						
MCA	MCA5P3318	All I Need To Know	CDJ	U.S.		$2.00
Murphey, Michael Martin						
Singles						
Warner Brothers	PRO-CD-6564	Big Iron	CDJ	U.S.	1993	$2.00
Warner Brothers	PRO-CD-3498	Never Givin' Up on Love	CDJ	U.S.	1989	$2.00
Murphy, David Lee						
Full Length						
		Country Edge	RS	U.S.	1995	$40.00
Airdate: 11/25/95.						
Murphy, Eddie						
Full Length						
Paramount	LV2323	Delerious	LD	U.S.	1984	$30.00
Singles						
Motown	3746311212	Desdamona	CDJ	U.S.	1993	$2.00
Motowwn	PODT-1014	I Was a King	CD3	Japan	1993	$13.00/$4.00
Motown	TMGCD-1414	I Was a King	CD5	U.K.	1993	$8.00
Motown	3746311075	I Was a King	CDJ	U.S.	1993	$2.00
		I Was a King	CDJ	U.S.	1995	$15.00
CD and VHS in box with scroll.						
Columbia	655000-3	Put Your Mouth on Me	CD3	Germany	1989	$8.00
Columbia	655262-2	Put Your Mouth on Me	CD5	U.K.	1989	$8.00
Columbia	CSK 1616	Put Your Mouth on Me	CDJ	U.S.	1989	$2.00
Columbia	CSK 1896	Till The Money's Gone	CDJ	U.S.	1989	$2.00
Motown	374631100	Wahtzupwitu	CDJ	U.S.	1993	$2.00
Motown	374631101	Wahtzupwitu	CDJ	U.S.	1993	$2.00
Murphy, Peter						
Full Length						
RCA		Deep	LP/LB	U.S.		$15.00/$12.00
Beggars Banquet	9877	Deep	LP/LB	U.S.	1989	$14.00/$8.00
Beggars Banquet	2174-2-H	Deep	LTD/LP	U.S.	1989	$15.00
RCA	66007	Holy Smoke	LP/LB	U.S.		$18.00/$15.00
Westwood One		In Concert-Nu Rock	RS	U.S.	1993	$50.00
Airdate: 10/11/93.						
RCA	7634	Love Hysteria	LP/LB	U.S.		$12.00/$7.00
		Retrospective	DJ/Smplr	U.S.	1994	$18.00
Singles						
Beggars Banquet	2625-H	A Strange Kind of Love	CDJ	U.S.	1990	$3.00
Polygram	870413-2	All Night Long	CD5	Canada	1988	$10.00
Columbia	10CY-8036	All Night Long	CD3	Japan	1988	$13.00/$4.00
Beggars Banquet	BEG-207CD	All Night Long	CD5	U.K.	1988	$9.00
Vertigo	4228641252	Cuts You Up	CD5	Canada	1992	$10.00
Beggars Banquet	BEG-237CD	Cuts You Up	CD5	U.K.	1990	$8.00
RCA	9140-2-HDJ	Cuts You Up	CDJ	U.S.	1989	$2.00
Beggars Banquet	BEG-261CD	Hit Song	CD5	U.K.	1992	$9.00
RCA	9102-2-HDJ	Line Between the Devil's Teeth	CDJ	U.S.	1989	$2.00
		Scarlet Thing in You	CDJ	U.S.		$3.00
RCA		Strange Kind of Love	CDJ	U.S.		$2.00
RCA	62239-2-RDJ	Sweetest Day, The	CDJ	U.S.	1992	$2.00
RCA	RDJ-6230-2	You're So Close	CD5	U.S.	1992	$5.00
RCA	62302	You're So Close	CDJ	U.S.	1992	$2.00
Murphy's Law						
Singles						
Relativity	1062	Monster Mash	CD5	U.S.	1991	$4.00
Murray, Anne						
Full Length						
Pioneer Artists	PA-92-442	Anne Murray	LD	U.S.	1992	$25.00
Capitol	CDP-46058	Greatest Hits	LP/LB	U.S.†	1985	$14.00/$8.00
Capitol	CDP-4659	Heart Over Mind	LP/LB	U.S.†	1985	$14.00/$8.00
SBK	DPRO-04602	Make Love to Me	DJ/Intvw	U.S.	1993	$15.00
Singles						
		I Can See Arkansas	CDJ	Canada		$10.00
Capitol	DPRO-79747	If I Ever Fall in Love Again	CDJ	U.S.	1989	$2.00
Capitol	DPRO-79600	New Way Out	CDJ	U.S.	1991	$2.00
		Wayward Wind	CDJ	Canada		$5.00
Murray, David						
Full Length						
Black Saint	BSR-0055CD PSI	Home	LP/LB	U.S.†	1985	$14.00/$8.00
Black Saint	BSR-0085CD PSI	Live at Sweet Basil, Vol. 1	LP/LB	U.S.†	1985	$14.00/$8.00
Black Saint	BSR-0045CD PSI	Ming	LP/LB	U.S.†	1985	$14.00/$8.00
Black Saint	BSR-0075CD PSI	Morning Song	LP/LB	U.S.†	1985	$14.00/$8.00
Murray, Keith						
Singles						
Jive	42281	Get Lifted	CD5	U.S.	1994	$5.00
Jive	42248	Most Beautifulest Thing	CD5	U.S.	1994	$5.00
Murray, Phil						
Singles						
Charly	PWM-003CDS	Talk Talk	CD5	U.K.	1991	$8.00
Music of Life						
Singles						
Duke	NOTE 35CD	Final Conflict, The	CD5	U.K.	1990	$8.00
Musicalender						
Full Length						
Atlantic	82839	Rhythms of Time	LP	U.S.		$29.00
Musselwhite, Charlie						
Full Length						
		House of Blues	RS	U.S.	1994	$35.00
2 CD set. Airdate: 2/6/94.						
		House of Blues	RS	U.S.	1996	$35.00
2 CD set. Airdate: 1/12/96.						
Musto & Bones						
Singles						
BCM	20434	All I Want Is To Get Away	CD5	Germany	1990	$8.00
City Beat	CBE-1250CD	All I Want Is To Get Away	CD5	U.K.	1990	$8.00
City Beat	CBE-750CD	All I Want Is To Get Away	CD5	U.K.	1990	$8.00
RCA	62058-2-RDJ	Dangerous on the Dance Floor	CDJ	U.S.	1991	$2.00
Mute America						
Singles						
	MUS82	Toenut	CDJ	U.S.		$2.00
Mwale, Anna						
Singles						
Columbia	656103-3	Get Free	CD3	Germany	1990	$8.00
Columbia	656103-2	Get Free	CD5	U.K.	1990	$8.00
Columbia	654590-3	Touch Sensitive	CD3	Germany	1989	$8.00
My Bloody Valentine						
Singles						
Creation	CRESCD-061	Feed Me With Your Kiss	CD5	U.K.	1990	$8.00
Creation	CRESCD-073	Glider	CD5	U.K.	1990	$8.00
		Only Shallow	CDJ	U.S.		$3.00
Sire	9 26313-2	Soon	CD5	U.S.	1990	$5.00
Creation	CRESCD-085	To Here Knows When	CD5	U.K.	1991	$8.00
Sire	9 40024-2	To Here Knows When	CD5	U.S.	1991	$2.00
Sire	PRO-CD-5303	When You Sleep	CDJ	U.S.	1991	$2.00
Creation	CRESCD-055	You Made Me Realize	CD5	U.K.	1990	$8.00
My Funny Valentine						
Singles						
Polygram	26448	Rodgers & Hart Sngbk.	CD5	U.S.	1994	$5.00
My Jealous God						
Singles						
Fontana	JGCD-1	Easy	CD5	U.K.	1992	$8.00
Rough Trade	RTT-228CD	Everything About You	CD5	U.K.	1990	$8.00
My Little Funhouse						
Singles						
Geffen	21929-2	Destiny	CD5	U.S.	1993	$5.00
Geffen	PRO-CD-4459	I Want Some of That	CDJ	U.S.	1993	$2.00
Geffen	PRO-CD-4499	Wishing Well	CDJ	U.S.	1993	$2.00
My Mine						
Singles						
Intercord	828 034	Hypnotic Tango	CD5	Germany	1988	$8.00
Mychals, Robbie						
Singles						
Alpha	79259	Do You Do For Me	CDJ	U.S.	1990	$2.00
Myer, Billi						
Singles						
BMG	664366	Bad People	CD5	Germany	1991	$8.00
BMG	663986	Send Me an Angel	CD5	Germany	1991	$8.00
Myers, Amina Claudine						
Full Length						
Minor Music	MM-8002 PSI	Jumping in the Sugar Bowl	LP/LB	U.S.†	1985	$14.00/$8.00
Myles, Alannah						
Singles						
Warner	32-84886	Black Velvet	CD5	Canada	1994	$6.00
Atlantic	AMDY-5007	Black Velvet	CD3	Japan	1990	$12.00/$4.00
Atlantic	A-8742CD	Black Velvet	CD5	U.K.	1990	$10.00
Atlantic	PRCD 6409-2	Family Secret	CDJ	U.S.		$2.00
Atlantic	PRCD 4985-2	Living on a Memory	CDJ	U.S.	1992	$2.00
Atlantic	786181-2	Love Is	CD5	Germany	1989	$8.00
Atlantic	AMDY-5020	Love Is	CD3	Japan	1990	$12.00/$4.00
Atlantic	A-8918CD	Love Is	CD5	U.K.	1989	$8.00

Label	Catalog Number	Title	Type	Country	Year	Longbox Value / Value
Atlantic	PR 2673-2	Love Is	CDJ	U.S.	1989	$2.00
Atlantic	786148-2	Lover of Mine	CD5	Germany	1990	$8.00
Atlantic	A-7872CD	Lover of Mine	CD5	U.K.	1990	$8.00
Atlantic	PRCD 3419-2	Lover of Mine	CDJ	U.S.	1990	$2.00
Atlantic	PRCD 4846-2	Our World	CDJ	U.S.	1992	$2.00
Atlantic	7567-858-1	Song Instead of a Kiss	CD5	Germany	1992	$8.00
Atlantic	AMDY-5085	Song Instead of a Kiss	CD3	Japan	1992	$12.00/$4.00
Atlantic		Song Instead of a Kiss	CD5	U.K.	1992	$8.00
Atlantic	PRCD 4775-2	Song Instead of a Kiss	CDJ	U.S.	1992	$2.00
Atlantic	AMDY-5015	Still Got This Thing	CD3	Japan	1990	$12.00/$4.00

Myrrh Metal

Singles

Label	Catalog Number	Title	Type	Country	Year	Longbox Value / Value
		Holy Soldier	CDJ	U.S.		$2.00

Mysidious Misfits

Singles

Label	Catalog Number	Title	Type	Country	Year	Longbox Value / Value
	BSK 7415	Upside Down	CDJ	U.S.		$2.00

Mysteries Of Life

Singles

Label	Catalog Number	Title	Type	Country	Year	Longbox Value / Value
RCA	RDJ 64507-2	Going Through the Motions	CDJ	U.S.		$2.00

Mysterious Art

Singles

Label	Catalog Number	Title	Type	Country	Year	Longbox Value / Value
Columbia	655407-3	Carma	CD3	Germany	1990	$8.00
Columbia	655407-5	Carma	CD5	Germany	1990	$8.00
Columbia	657459-2	High on Mystic Mountain	CD5	Germany	1990	$8.00
Imago	72787 25037	Like a Rolling Stone	CD5	U.S.	1993	$4.00
Columbia	656813-3	Lovin' You	CD3	Germany	1991	$8.00
Columbia	654815-3	Omen	CD3	Germany	1989	$8.00
Columbia	654966-3	Omen	CD3	Germany	1989	$8.00
Columbia	654966-5	Omen	CD5	Germany	1989	$8.00
Columbia	655628-2	Omen	CD3	Germany	1990	$8.00
Columbia	655628-5	Omen	CD5	Germany	1990	$8.00
Columbia	654966-2	Omen	CD5	U.K.	1989	$8.00

Mystery Machine

Singles

Label	Catalog Number	Title	Type	Country	Year	Longbox Value / Value
	DPRO00954	Brand New Song	CDJ	U.S.		$2.00

N.W.A.

Singles

Label	Catalog Number	Title	Type	Country	Year	Longbox Value / Value
Priority	BRCD-238	Alwayz into Somethin'	CD5	U.K.	1991	$10.00
Ruthless	6601	Alwayz into Somethin'	CDJ	U.S.	1991	$3.00
Ruthless	6613	Appetite For Destruction	CDJ	U.S.	1991	$3.00
Aris	884374	Express Yourself	CD5	Germany	1990	$10.00
Priority	BRCD-144	Express Yourself	CD5	U.K.	1990	$10.00
Aris	884704	Gansta Gangsta	CD5	Germany	1990	$10.00
Priority	BRCD-191	Gansta Gangsta	CD5	U.K.	1990	$10.00
Priority	CDS-7224	One Hundred Miles & Runnin'	CD5	Canada	1990	$8.00
Priority	884976	One Hundred Miles & Runnin'	CD5	Germany	1990	$10.00
Priority	BRCD-200	One Hundred Miles & Runnin'	CD5	U.K.	1990	$10.00
Priority	CDS-7224	One Hundred Miles & Runnin'	CD5	U.S.	1990	$5.00

N'Dour, Youssou

Full Length

Label	Catalog Number	Title	Type	Country	Year	Longbox Value / Value
Epic	ESK 4585	Eyes Open	DJ/ Smplr	U.S.	1992	$40.00

Singles

Label	Catalog Number	Title	Type	Country	Year	Longbox Value / Value
Sony	SRDS-8224	Hope	CD3	Japan	1992	$13.00/$4.00
Virgin	VSCD-1207	Lion	CD3	U.K.	1990	$8.00
Columbia		Seven Seconds	CDJ	U.S.	1994	$3.00
BMG	162387	Shakin' the Tree	CD3	Germany	1989	$10.00
BMG	662387	Shakin' the Tree	CD5	Germany	1989	$10.00
Virgin	VSCD-1167	Shakin' the Tree	CD3	Japan	1989	$13.00/$4.00
Virgin	VJD-15553	Shakin' the Tree	CD5	Japan	1989	$15.00

N-Factor

Singles

Label	Catalog Number	Title	Type	Country	Year	Longbox Value / Value
BMG	664481	N-Factor	CD5	Germany	1991	$8.00

N-Joi

Singles

Label	Catalog Number	Title	Type	Country	Year	Longbox Value / Value
RCA	62238-2-RDJ	Mindflux	CDJ	U.S.	1992	$2.00

N-Phase

Singles

Label	Catalog Number	Title	Type	Country	Year	Longbox Value / Value
Warner Brothers	18041	Kiss And Say Goodbye	CD5	U.S.	1994	$5.00

N-Trance

Singles

Label	Catalog Number	Title	Type	Country	Year	Longbox Value / Value
	15547	Set You Free	CD5	U.S.	1995	$5.00

N-Tyce

Singles

Label	Catalog Number	Title	Type	Country	Year	Longbox Value / Value
Capital	58093	Hush Hush Tip	CD5	U.S.	1994	$5.00
Wild Pitch	58093	Hush Hush Tip	CDJ	U.S.	1994	$2.00
Capital	58345	Sure Ya Right	CD5	U.S.	1994	$5.00

Nadja

Singles

Label	Catalog Number	Title	Type	Country	Year	Longbox Value / Value
Polydor	H10R-30001	Stay With Me	CD3	Japan	1988	$12.00/$3.00

Nail, Jimmy

Singles

Label	Catalog Number	Title	Type	Country	Year	Longbox Value / Value
Eastwest	WMD5-4116	Ain't No Doubt	CD3	Japan	1992	$12.00/$3.00
Eastwest	YZ-686CD	Ain't No Doubt	CD5	U.K.	1992	$8.00
Atlantic	PRCD 4736-2	Ain't No Doubt	CDJ	U.S.	1992	$2.00
Eastwest	YZ-721CD	Beautiful	CD5	U.K.	1992	$8.00
Eastwest	AMDE-5093	Laura	CD3	Japan	1993	$12.00/$3.00
Eastwest	YZ-7702CD	Laura	CD5	U.K.	1992	$8.00

Najee

Singles

Label	Catalog Number	Title	Type	Country	Year	Longbox Value / Value
EMI	DPRO-04720	All I Ever Ask	CDJ	U.S.	1993	$2.00
EMI	DPRO-04680	Breezy	CDJ	U.S.	1992	$2.00
EMI	DPRO-04882	I Adore Mi Amor	CDJ	U.S.	1993	$2.00
EMI	DPRO-04612	I'll Be Good To You	CDJ	U.S.	1990	$2.00
EMI	DPRO-04356	Tokyo Blue	CDJ	U.S.	1990	$2.00

Naked

Full Length

Label	Catalog Number	Title	Type	Country	Year	Longbox Value / Value
red ant	ADVR005-2	Naked	DJ/ LP	U.S.	1997	$12.00

Naked Prey

Singles

Label	Catalog Number	Title	Type	Country	Year	Longbox Value / Value
SPV	5125-2	Live in Tucson	CD5	Germany	1990	$8.00
APT	PRAY-10CD	Live in Tucson	CD5	U.K.	1990	$8.00
Fundamental	10CD	Live in Tucson	CD5	U.S.	1990	$4.00

Naked Soul

Singles

Label	Catalog Number	Title	Type	Country	Year	Longbox Value / Value
Scotti Brothers	NSK 75361	Inside Out	CDJ	U.S.	1993	$2.00
Scotti Brothers	NSK 75343	Lonely Me, Lonely You	CDJ	U.S.	1993	$2.00
Scotti Brothers	72392 75270	Seed	CD5	U.S.	1993	$5.00

Naked Sun

Singles

Label	Catalog Number	Title	Type	Country	Year	Longbox Value / Value
SPV	0440-3	Naked Sun	CD5	Germany	1991	$8.00

Naked Truth

Singles

Label	Catalog Number	Title	Type	Country	Year	Longbox Value / Value
Sony	658949-2	Black	CD5	U.K.	1993	$8.00
Sony	658429-2	Read Between the Lines	CD5	U.K.	1993	$8.00

Name

Singles

Label	Catalog Number	Title	Type	Country	Year	Longbox Value / Value
Polygram	889118-3	Last War Song	CD3	Germany	1989	$8.00
Polygram	889119-2	Last War Song	CD5	Germany	1989	$8.00
China	CHICD-15	Last War Song	CD3	U.K.	1989	$8.00
Polygram	873069-2	Runaway	CD5	Germany	1989	$8.00

Nancy Boy

Singles

Label	Catalog Number	Title	Type	Country	Year	Longbox Value / Value
	PRCD 9452-2	Deep Sleep Motel	CDJ	U.S.		$2.00
	PRCD 9457-2	Deep Sleep Motel	CDJ	U.S.		$6.00

Napalm Death

Singles

Label	Catalog Number	Title	Type	Country	Year	Longbox Value / Value
Toysfactory	TFCK-88560	Mass Appeal Madness	CD5	Japan	1991	$12.00
Earache	MOSH-46CD	Mass Appeal Madness	CD5	U.K.	1991	$9.00
Earache	MOSH-14CD	Mentally Murdered	CD5	U.K.	1989	$9.00
Aris	883525	Peel Sessions	CD5	Germany	1990	$9.00
Strange Fruit	DFPSCD-049	Peel Sessions	CD5	U.K.	1990	$9.00
Earache	MOSH-24CD	Suffer the Children	CD5	U.K.	1990	$9.00
Earache	MOSH-65CD	Suffer the Children	CD5	U.K.	1990	$9.00

Narada

Singles

Label	Catalog Number	Title	Type	Country	Year	Longbox Value / Value
Reprise	920955-2	Divine Emotion	CD3	Germany	1988	$8.00
Reprise	W-7967CD	Divine Emotion	CD3	U.K.	1988	$8.00

Narell, Andy

Full Length

Label	Catalog Number	Title	Type	Country	Year	Longbox Value / Value
Hip Pocket	HD-105	Slow Motion	LP/LB	U.S.†	1985	$14.00/$8.00

Singles

Label	Catalog Number	Title	Type	Country	Year	Longbox Value / Value
Windam Hill		Down the Road	CDJ	U.S.		$7.00

Also contains 3 tracks by William Ackerman.

Nas

Singles

Label	Catalog Number	Title	Type	Country	Year	Longbox Value / Value
Columbia	CSK 5686	It Ain't Hard	CDJ	U.S.	1994	$2.00
CBS	77673	One Love	CD5	U.S.	1994	$5.00

NASA

Singles

Label	Catalog Number	Title	Type	Country	Year	Longbox Value / Value
Sire	PRO-CD-4066	Magic Jewelled	CDJ	U.S.	1990	$2.00
Sire	9 21434-2	Shah Shah	CD5	U.S.	1990	$4.00

Nash, Graham

Full Length

Label	Catalog Number	Title	Type	Country	Year	Longbox Value / Value
Atlantic		Innocent Eyes	LP/LB	U.S.	14	$8.00

Nash, Johnny

Singles

Label	Catalog Number	Title	Type	Country	Year	Longbox Value / Value
Columbia	655169-3	I Can See Clearly Now	CD3	Germany	1989	$8.00
Epic	CDJN-1	I Can See Clearly Now	CD5	U.K.	1989	$8.00

Nash, Kenneth

Singles

Label	Catalog Number	Title	Type	Country	Year	Longbox Value / Value
		Fresca	CDJ	U.S.		$2.00

Nashville Children's Chorus

Singles

Label	Catalog Number	Title	Type	Country	Year	Longbox Value / Value
Warner Brothers	PRO-CD-4571	It's Beginning To Look a Lot	CDJ	U.S.	1990	$2.00

Nasty Habits

Singles

Label	Catalog Number	Title	Type	Country	Year	Longbox Value / Value
Reinforced	RIVETCD-33	As Nasty As I Wanna Be	CD5	U.K.	1992	$8.00

Nasty Rox Inc.

Singles

Label	Catalog Number	Title	Type	Country	Year	Longbox Value / Value
WEA	CDNR-1	Escape From New York	CD5	U.K.	1988	$8.00

Natasha's Brother

Singles

Label	Catalog Number	Title	Type	Country	Year	Longbox Value / Value
		Always Come Back To You	CDJ	U.S.		$2.00
		Sara Smile	CDJ	U.S.		$2.00

Nate Dog

Singles

Label	Catalog Number	Title	Type	Country	Year	Longbox Value / Value
	97012-2	Never Leave Me Alone	CD5	U.S.	1996	$3.50

Nath, Pandit Pran

Full Length

Label	Catalog Number	Title	Type	Country	Year	Longbox Value / Value
		Ragas of Morning and Night	LP/LB	U.S.		$18.00/$15.00

National Bass

Singles

Label	Catalog Number	Title	Type	Country	Year	Longbox Value / Value
ZYX	6307-8	Dub Be Good To Me	CD5	Germany	1990	$6.00

National Velvet

Singles

Label	Catalog Number	Title	Type	Country	Year	Longbox Value / Value
		Hysteria	CDJ	Canada		$6.00
		Sex Gorilla	CDJ	Canada		$6.00
		Shine On	CDJ	Canada		$6.00

Natural Life

Singles

Label	Catalog Number	Title	Type	Country	Year	Longbox Value / Value
Intercord	825 325	Natural Life	CD5	Germany	1992	$8.00
CBS	NLIFE-3CD	Natural Life	CD5	U.K.	1992	$8.00
Intercord	977 512	Strange World	CD5	Germany	1992	$8.00
CBS	NLIFE-2CD	Strange World	CD5	U.K.	1992	$8.00

Natural Selection

Singles

Label	Catalog Number	Title	Type	Country	Year	Longbox Value / Value
Eastwest	7567-96282-2	Do Anything	CD5	Germany	1991	$8.00
Eastwest	AMDY-5066	Do Anything	CD3	Japan	1991	$12.00/$3.00
Eastwest	A-8724CD	Do Anything	CD5	U.K.	1991	$8.00
Eastwest	PRCD 4305-2	Hearts Don't Think	CDJ	U.S.	1991	$2.00

Nature

Singles

Label	Catalog Number	Title	Type	Country	Year	Longbox Value / Value
Zoo	ZP171872	Cometh	CDJ	U.S.		$2.00
Zoo		Z-Man's Party	CDJ	U.S.		$2.00

Naughty By Nature

Singles

Label	Catalog Number	Title	Type	Country	Year	Longbox Value / Value
Tommy Boy	TBCD706	Clap Yo Hands	CDJ	U.S.		$2.00
Tommy Boy	670	Craziest	CD5	U.S.	1994	$5.00
Tommy Boy		Craziest	CD5	U.S.	1995	$6.00
Eastwest	9031-76238-2	Everything's Gonna Be Alright	CD5	Germany	1992	$10.00
Big Life	BLRD-65	Everything's Gonna Be Alright	CD5	U.K.	1992	$10.00
Tommy Boy	508	Everything's Gonna Be Alright	CDJ	U.S.	1991	$2.00
Isba	IS12K-1053	Hip Hop Hooray	CD5	Canada	1992	$10.00
Big Life	BLRD-89	Hip Hop Hooray	CD5	U.K.	1992	$10.00
Big Life		Hip Hop Hooray	CD5	U.K.	1992	$10.00

Second version.

Label	Catalog Number	Title	Type	Country	Year	Longbox Value / Value
Tommy Boy	554	Hip Hop Hooray	CD5	U.S.	1992	$5.00
Tommy Boy	569	It's On	CD5	U.S.	1993	$5.00
Tommy Boy	574	It's On	CDJ	U.S.	1993	$2.00
Eastwest	9031-75917-2	O.P.P.	CD5	Germany	1991	$10.00
Big Life	BLRD-74	O.P.P.	CD5	U.K.	1992	$10.00
Tommy Boy	988	O.P.P.	CD5	U.S.	1991	$5.00
Tommy Boy	988	O.P.P.	CDJ	U.S.	1991	$2.00

Naumann, Jeff

Singles

Label	Catalog Number	Title	Type	Country	Year	Longbox Value / Value
POC	003	They're Coming to Take Me Away	CD5	U.S.	1993	$4.00

Navarro, Fats

Full Length

Label	Catalog Number	Title	Type	Country	Year	Longbox Value / Value
Savoy Records	CY-78992	Nostalgia	LTD/LP	U.S.	1995	$20.00

CD in miniature repica of original LP sleeve.

Nayobe

Singles

Label	Catalog Number	Title	Type	Country	Year	Longbox Value / Value
Columbia	656261-2	I'll Be Around	CD3	Germany	1990	$10.00

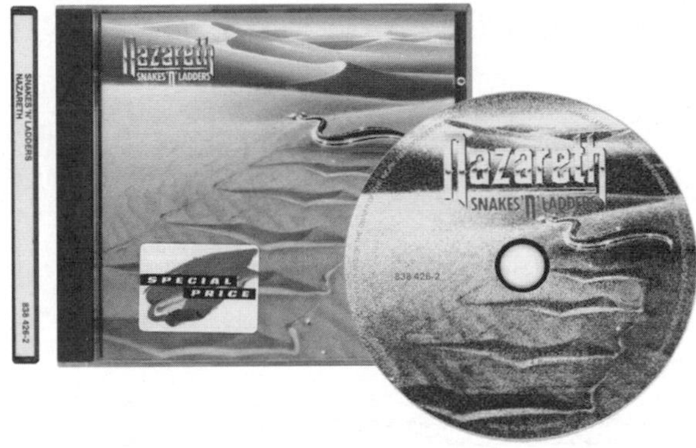

Nazareth – Snakes 'N' Ladders (Vertigo 838 426-2)

Nazareth

Full Length

Label	Catalog Number	Title	Type	Country	Year	Longbox Value / Value
Vertigo		Cinema	LP	Germany		$25.00
A&M		Expect No Mercy	LP/LB	U.S.		$15.00/$10.00
A&M	CD-3225	Hair of the Dog	LP/LB	U.S.	1984	$9.00/$6.00
Image	ID7775EM	Live	LD	U.S.		$25.00
Vertigo	838707-2	Loud 'n Proud	LP	Germany		$25.00
Vertigo	838 426-2	Snakes 'n Ladders	LP	Germany	1989	$25.00

Singles

Label	Catalog Number	Title	Type	Country	Year	Longbox Value / Value
Griffin	6931	Do You Wanna Play House	CD5	Canada	1993	$10.00
Griffin	PR 6931-2	Do You Wanna Play House	CDJ	U.S.	1993	$4.00
IRS	977 450	Every Time It Rains Rock	CD5	Germany	1992	$10.00
Polygram	874326-3	Hang on to a Dream	CD3	Germany	1989	$10.00
Polygram	874327-2	Hang on to a Dream	CD5	Germany	1989	$10.00
A&M		Love Hurts	CD5	U.S.	1996	$6.00
Vertigo	874 732-3	Piece of My Heart	CD3	Germany	1989	$10.00
Vertigo	874 733-2	Piece of My Heart	CD5	Germany	1989	$10.00
MMS	904005-3	Tell Me That You Love Me	CD5	U.K.	1992	$10.00
Castle	CD3-17	This Flight Tonight	CD5	France	1988	$10.00
Polygram	888624-2	This Flight Tonight	CD5	Germany	1990	$10.00
Polygram	876449-2	Water on the Night	CD5	Germany	1989	$10.00

Ndegeocello, Me'shell

Full Length

Label	Catalog Number	Title	Type	Country	Year	Longbox Value / Value
Maverick	9 45333-2	Plantation Lullabies	DJ/LP	U.S.	1993	$15.00

Singles

Label	Catalog Number	Title	Type	Country	Year	Longbox Value / Value
Maverick	9 41039-2	Dread Loc	CD5	U.S.	1993	$5.00
Maverick	PRO-CCD-6485	Dread Loc	CDJ	U.S.	1993	$2.00
		If That's Your Boyfriend	CD5	U.K.		$10.00
		If That's Your Boyfriend	CD5	U.K.		$10.00

Second version.

Label	Catalog Number	Title	Type	Country	Year	Longbox Value / Value
Maverick	9 41316-2	If That's Your Boyfriend	CD5	U.S.	1993	$5.00
Maverick	PRO-CD-6785	If That's Your Boyfriend	CDJ	U.S.	1993	$6.00
Warner Brothers	41316	If That's Your Boyfriend	CD5	U.S.	1994	$5.00
Maverick	PRO-CD-6852	Outside Your Door	CDJ	U.S.	1993	$6.00

Near, Holly

Singles

Label	Catalog Number	Title	Type	Country	Year	Longbox Value / Value
Chameleon	21434	Shah Sha	CD5	U.S.		$4.00
Chameleon	PR 92	Singer In the Storm	CDJ	U.S.	1990	$2.00

Necks

Singles

Label	Catalog Number	Title	Type	Country	Year	Longbox Value / Value
		Sex	CDJ	U.S.		$2.00

Ned's Atomic Dustbin

Full Length

Label	Catalog Number	Title	Type	Country	Year	Longbox Value / Value
Epic/Sony	ESCA 5496	And Besides	LP	Japan	1992	$25.00
Columbia	44K 73991	Grey Cell Green	CD5	U.S.	1991	$5.00
Epic	ESCA-5310	Happy	CD5	Japan	1990	$12.00
Furtive	656680-2	Happy	CD5	U.K.	1990	$9.00
Columbia	CSK 4050	Happy	CDJ	U.S.	1991	$2.00
Epic	ESCA-5708	Intact	CD5	Japan	1992	$12.00
CBS	658816-2	Intact	CD5	U.K.	1992	$9.00
Epic	ESCA-5373	Kill Your Television	CD5	Japan	1992	$12.00
Chapter 22	CHAPCD-48	Kill Your Television	CD5	U.K.	1992	$9.00
Columbia	44K 74202	Kill Your Television	CD5	U.S.	1992	$5.00
Columbia	CSK 4475	Kill Your Television	CDJ	U.S.	1992	$2.00
Epic	ESCA-5657	Not Sleeping Around	CD5	Japan	1992	$12.00
Furtive	658386-2	Not Sleeping Around	CD5	U.K.	1992	$9.00
Columbia	44K-78718	Not Sleeping Around	CD5	U.S.	1992	$5.00
Columbia	CSK 74718	Not Sleeping Around	CDJ	U.S.	1992	$2.00
Chaos	CSK 5239	Saturday Night	CDJ	U.S.	1993	$2.00
		Stuck	CD5	U.K.	1995	$10.00
Columbia		Stuck	CDJ	U.S.	1995	$3.00
Epic	ESCA-5464	Trust	CD5	Japan	1991	$15.00
Columbia	657462-2	Trust	CD5	U.K.	1991	$10.00
Chapter 22	CHAPCD-052	Until You Find Out	CD5	U.K.	1991	$9.00
Columbia		Until You Find Out	CD5	U.S.	1993	$5.00
Columbia	CSK 4931	Walking Through Syrup	CDJ	U.S.	1992	$2.00

Negativeland

Singles

Label	Catalog Number	Title	Type	Country	Year	Longbox Value / Value
Rough Trade	361 0291-3	Guns	CD5	Germany	1992	$10.00
SST	SSTCD 272	I Still Haven't Found What I'm Looking For	CD5	U.S.	1991	$40.00

Recalled CD5.

Label	Catalog Number	Title	Type	Country	Year	Longbox Value / Value
SST	CD 272	I Still Haven't Found What I'm Looking For	CD5	U.S.	1991	$100.00

Negro, Joey

Singles

Label	Catalog Number	Title	Type	Country	Year	Longbox Value / Value
Virgin	TENCD-391	Do What I Feel	CD5	U.K.	1991	$8.00
Virgin	TENCD-397	Enter Your Fantasy	CD5	U.K.	1991	$8.00
Rumour	LICDR-160	Reachin'	CD5	U.K.	1991	$8.00

Neigborhood

Singles

Label	Catalog Number	Title	Type	Country	Year	Longbox Value / Value
Parlophone	CDR-6188	At the Time	CD5	U.K.	1988	$8.00
Parlophone	CDR-6208	Missing Out	CD5	U.K.	1988	$8.00
Third Stone	91723-2	Neigborhoods	LP/LB	U.S.	1991	$14.00/$8.00
Third Stone	4104	Prettiest Girl	CDJ	U.S.	1991	$2.00

Neil, Vince

Full Length

Label	Catalog Number	Title	Type	Country	Year	Longbox Value / Value
Warner Brothers	WPCP-239	Carved In Stone	DJ/LP	Japan		$50.00
Foundations		FZ Interview	RS	U.S.	1992	$10.00

Various artist radio show CD with interviews of Vince Neil.

Singles

Label	Catalog Number	Title	Type	Country	Year	Longbox Value / Value
Warner Brothers	PRO-CD-6275	Can't Change Me	CDJ	U.S.	1993	$2.00
Warner Brothers	9362-40895	Sister of Pain	CD5	Germany	1993	$10.00
		Sister of Pain	CD5	U.K.		$10.00

Second version.

Label	Catalog Number	Title	Type	Country	Year	Longbox Value / Value
Warner Brothers	W-0176CDX	Sister of Pain	CD5	U.K.	1993	$10.00
	PRO-CD-7805-R	Skylar's Song	CDJ	U.S.		$3.00
Hollywood	HWD-123CD	You're Invited	CD5	U.K.	1992	$10.00
Hollywood	10164	You're Invited	CDJ	U.S.	1992	$3.00

Nelson

Singles

Label	Catalog Number	Title	Type	Country	Year	Longbox Value / Value
Geffen	7599-21630-2	After the Rain	CD5	Germany	1990	$9.00
Geffen	GEF-86CD	After the Rain	CD5	U.K.	1990	$9.00
DGC	PRO-CD-4161	After the Rain	CDJ	U.S.	1990	$2.00
Geffen	7599-21617-2	Love and Affection	CD5	Germany	1990	$9.00
Geffen	GEF-82CD	Love and Affection	CD5	U.K.	1990	$9.00
DGC		Love and Affection	CDJ	U.S.	1990	$2.00
DGC	PRO-CD-4200	More Than Ever	CDJ	U.S.	1990	$2.00
DGC	PRO-CD-4210	More Than Ever	CDJ	U.S.	1991	$2.00
Geffen	MVDG-5	Only Time Will Tell	CD3	Japan	1991	$12.00/$4.00
Geffen	GED-21667	Only Time Will Tell	CD5	U.K.	1991	$9.00
DGC	PRO-CD-4229	Only Time Will Tell	CDJ	U.S.	1991	$2.00
Geffen	MVDG-2	Too Many Dreams	CD3	Japan	1991	$12.00/$4.00
Geffen	MVCG-17001	Too Many Dreams	CD5	Japan	1991	$13.00

Nelson, Bill

Full Length

Label	Catalog Number	Title	Type	Country	Year	Longbox Value / Value
Cocteau		Catalogue of Obsessions	LP/LB	U.S.		$12.00/$7.00
Cocteau		Chamber of Dreams	LP/LB	U.S.		$12.00/$7.00
Enigma	73337	Chance Encounters	LP/LB	U.S.		$28.00/$25.00

2 CD set.

Label	Catalog Number	Title	Type	Country	Year	Longbox Value / Value
Cocteau		Das Kabinet & La Bell Et La Bete	LP/LB	U.S.		$12.00/$7.00
Cocteau		Iconography	LP/LB	U.S.		$12.00/$7.00
Cocteau		Map Of Dreams	LP/LB	U.S.		$12.00/$7.00
Enigma	73389	Map Of Dreams	LP/LB	U.S.		$12.00/$7.00
Enigma	73344	Optimism	LP/LB	U.S.		$12.00/$7.00
Cocteau		Pavilions of the Heart and Soul	LP/LB	U.S.		$12.00/$7.00
Cocteau		Quiet Dreaming	LP/LB	U.S.		$12.00/$7.00
Cocteau		Savage Gestures For Charm Sake	LP/LB	U.S.		$12.00/$7.00
Enigma		Sound on Sound	LP/LB	U.S.		$12.00/$7.00
Cocteau		Sounding the Ritual Echo	LP/LB	U.S.		$12.00/$7.00
Cocteau	73372	Strangest Things	LP/LB	U.S.		$12.00/$7.00
Cocteau		Summer of Gods	LP/LB	U.S.		$12.00/$7.00
Cocteau		Twofold Aspect of Everything	LP/LB	U.S.		$28.00/$25.00

2CD Set.

Singles

Label	Catalog Number	Title	Type	Country	Year	Longbox Value / Value
Cocteau	COQTCD-22	Life In Your Hands	CD5	U.K.	1988	$8.00

Nelson, Loey

Full Length

Label	Catalog Number	Title	Type	Country	Year	Longbox Value / Value
Warner Brothers	9 26089-2-Dj	Venus Kissed the Moon	DJ/LP	U.S.	1990	$6.00

Singles

Label	Catalog Number	Title	Type	Country	Year	Longbox Value / Value
Warner Brothers	PRO-CD-4076	Only the Shadows Know	CDJ	U.S.	1990	$2.00
Warner Brothers	PRO-CD-4451	To Stir With Love	CDJ	U.S.	1990	$2.00

Nelson, Ricky

Full Length

Label	Catalog Number	Title	Type	Country	Year	Longbox Value / Value
Image	ID7501RH	A Tribute To Ricky Nelson	LD	U.S.		$20.00

Label	Catalog Number	Title	Type	Country	Year	Longbox Value / Value
		Singles				
EMI	CDEMCT-2	Hello Mary Lou	CD5	U.K.	1991	$10.00
Rhino	885846	Poor Little Fool	CD3	Germany	1990	$10.00

Nelson, Tyka

Label	Catalog Number	Title	Type	Country	Year	Longbox Value / Value
		Singles				
Cooltempo	COOLCD-166	Marc Anthony's Tune	CD5	U.K.	1988	$8.00

Nelson, Willie

Label	Catalog Number	Title	Type	Country	Year	Longbox Value / Value
		Full Length				
Columbia	CSK 45046	A Horse Called Music	DJ/LP	U.S.	1989	$12.00
Columbia		Across the Borderline	DJ/LP	U.S.	1993	$15.00
	CD in digipak.					
CBS	CK-37951	Always on My Mind	LP/BP	U.S.†	1984	$14.00/$8.00
CBS	CK-39145	City of New Orleans	LP/BP	U.S.†	1985	$14.00/$8.00
QVC		Classic Unreleased Collection	LP	U.S.	1994	$45.00
	3 CD Set.					
CBS	CK-39990	Half Nation	LP/BP	U.S.†	1985	$14.00/$8.00
Justice		Night Becomes You	DJ/LP	U.S.	1993	$15.00
	CD in cardboard sleeve.					
CBS	CK-36189	Pretty Paper	LP/BP	U.S.†	1984	$14.00/$8.00
CBS	CK-36883	Somewhere Over the Rainbow	LP/BP	U.S.†	1984	$14.00/$8.00
CBS	CK-35305	Stardust	LP/BP	U.S.†	1984	$14.00/$8.00
CBS	4665-80	Willie Nelson And Friends	LD	U.S.	1985	$30.00
CBS	CK-37951	Without A Song	LP/BP	U.S.†	1984	$14.00/$8.00
		Singles				
Columbia	CSK 73518	Ain't Necessarily So	CDJ	U.S.	1990	$3.00
Columbia	655869-2	Always on My Mimd	CD5	U.K.	1990	$10.00
Columbia	CSK 74993	Graceland	CDJ	U.S.	1993	$3.00
Columbia	CSK 73374	Is the Better Part Over	CDJ	U.S.	1990	$3.00
Columbia	CSK 73655	Piper Came Today	CDJ	U.S.	1990	$3.00
Columbia	CSK 77184	Still Is Still Moving To Me	CDJ	U.S.	1993	$3.00
Columbia	CSK 73749	Ten With a Two	CDJ	U.S.	1991	$3.00
Columbia	CSK 5007	Valentine	CDJ	U.S.	1991	$6.00

Nelsons

Label	Catalog Number	Title	Type	Country	Year	Longbox Value / Value
		Full Length				
Unistar		Unistar Story	RS	U.S.	1991	$50.00
	Airdate: 5/12/91.					

Nemesis

Label	Catalog Number	Title	Type	Country	Year	Longbox Value / Value
		Singles				
Profile	7407	Cantfiguritout	CDJ	U.S.	1993	$2.00
	PRO74312DJ	Drop Tha Bottom	CDJ	U.S.		$2.00
Profile	7341	I Want Your Sex	CDJ	U.S.	1993	$2.00
Profile	7397	Temple of Boom	CDJ	U.S.	1993	$2.00

Nena

Label	Catalog Number	Title	Type	Country	Year	Longbox Value / Value
		Full Length				
CBS	CK-39294	99 Luftballoons	LP/BP	U.S.†	1984	$12.00/$7.00

Nerissa

Label	Catalog Number	Title	Type	Country	Year	Longbox Value / Value
		Singles				
Active	5058	In the Rain	CDJ	U.S.	1993	$2.00
Active	5468	Stars	CDJ	U.S.	1994	$2.00

Nesmith, Michael

Label	Catalog Number	Title	Type	Country	Year	Longbox Value / Value
		Full Length				
		And the Hits Just Keep on Comin'	LP	U.S.		$12.00
Pioneer	PA-81-005	Elephant Parts	LD	U.S.	1982	$50.00
Image	ID6338PA	Nezmusic	LD	U.S.		$30.00
		Tantamount to Treason	LP	U.S.		$12.00

Network

Label	Catalog Number	Title	Type	Country	Year	Longbox Value / Value
		Singles				
CBS	655662-3	Blue Blood Theme	CD3	Germany	1990	$8.00
Chrysalis	CDCHS-3923	Broken Wings	CD5	U.K.	1992	$8.00

Nevada Beach

Label	Catalog Number	Title	Type	Country	Year	Longbox Value / Value
		Singles				
Metal Blade	4427	Waiting for An Angel	CDJ	U.S.	1990	$2.00

Neville, Aaron

Label	Catalog Number	Title	Type	Country	Year	Longbox Value / Value
		Singles				
A&M		Betcha By Golly, Wow	CDJ	U.S.		$2.00
A&M	581077	Can't Stop My Heart From	CD5	U.S.	1995	$6.00
A&M	AMCD-835	Close Your Eyes	CD5	U.K.	1991	$9.00
A&M	75021 7332-2	Close Your Eyes	CDJ	U.S.	1991	$2.00
A&M	PODM-1010	Don't Fall Apart on Me Tonight	CD3	Japan	1993	$12.00/$4.00
A&M	PODM-1019	Don't Fall Apart on Me Tonight	CD3	Japan	1993	$12.00/$4.00
A&M	31458 8169	Don't Fall Apart on Me Tonight	CDJ	U.S.	1993	$2.00
A&M	31458 8118	Don't Fall Apart on Me Tonight	CDJ	U.S.	1993	$2.00
A&M	390762-2	Everybody Plays the Fool	CD5	Germany	1991	$9.00
A&M	AMCD-793	Everybody Plays the Fool	CD5	U.K.	1991	$9.00
A&M	75021 7001 2	Everybody Plays the Fool	CDJ	U.S.	1991	$2.00
A&M	31458 8170	Grand Tour, The	CDJ	U.S.	1993	$3.00
A&M	31458 8150	I Owe You One	CDJ	U.S.	1993	$2.00
A&M	AMCD-841	Louisiana 1927	CD5	U.K.	1992	$9.00
A&M		My Brother, My Brother	CD5	U.K.		$9.00
A&M	31458 8223	Please Come Home For Christmas	CDJ	U.S.	1993	$3.00
A&M	AMCD-798	Somewhere, Somebody	CD5	U.K.	1991	$9.00
A&M	75021 7275-2	Somewhere, Somebody	CDJ	U.S.	1991	$2.00
A&M	581184	Use Me	CD5	U.S.	1995	$6.00

Neville Brothers

Label	Catalog Number	Title	Type	Country	Year	Longbox Value / Value
		Full Length				
A&M	75021 7350-2	Evolution of the Groove 1981 to Now	DJ/Smplr	U.S.	1992	$20.00
		House of Blues	RS	U.S.	1995	$40.00
	2 CD set. Airdate: 2/10/95.					
		House of Blues	RS	U.S.	1996	$40.00
	2 CD set. Airdate: 2/23/96.					
A&M		Mitakuye Oyasin Oyasin	DJ/LP	U.S.		$8.00
Image	ID6939HB	Neville Brothers & Friends: Tell It Like It Is	LD	U.S.		$25.00
		Singles				
A&M	CDEE-548	A Change Is Gonna Come	CD5	U.K.	1990	$9.00
A&M	CD 17931	A Change Is Gonna Come	CDJ	U.S.	1989	$2.00
A&M	CD 18011	A Change Is Gonna Come	CDJ	U.S.	1990	$2.00
A&M	390532-2	Bird on a Wire	CD5	Germany	1990	$9.00
A&M	AMCD-568	Bird on a Wire	CD5	U.K.	1990	$9.00
A&M	CD 18036	Bird on a Wire	CDJ	U.S.	1990	$2.00
A&M	75021 2331	Bird on a Wire	CDJ	U.S.	1990	$2.00
A&M	31458 8275	Congo Square	CDJ	U.S.	1994	$2.00
A&M		Family Groove	CDJ	U.S.		$3.00
A&M	390596-2	Fearless	CD5	Germany	1990	$9.00
A&M	PCCY-10167	Fearless	CD3	Japan	1990	$15.00/$4.00
A&M	75021 7425 2	Fearless	CDJ	U.S.	1990	$2.00
A&M	CD 17739	Fire & Brimstone	CDJ	U.S.	1989	$2.00
A&M	AMCD-872	Fly Like an Eagle	CD5	U.K.	1992	$9.00
A&M	75021 7349-2	Fly Like an Eagle	CDJ	U.S.	1992	$2.00
A&M	75021 7376-2	Fly Like an Eagle	CDJ	U.S.	1992	$2.00
A&M	75021 7445-2	Mystery Train	CDJ	U.S.	1990	$2.00
A&M	580 087	On the Other Side of Paradise	CD5	U.K.	1989	$8.00
A&M	75021 7381 2	One More Day	CDJ	U.S.		$2.00
A&M	AMCD-586	River of Life	CD5	U.K.	1990	$9.00
A&M	75021 7402 2	River of Life	CDJ	U.S.	1989	$2.00
A&M	390427-2	Sister Rosa	CD5	Germany	1989	$9.00
A&M	CD 17732	Sister Rosa	CDJ	U.S.	1989	$2.00
A&M	CD 17769	Sister Rosa	CDJ	U.S.	1989	$2.00
A&M	31458 8035	Take Me To Your Heart	CDJ	U.S.	1992	$2.00
Polydor	4166	Tell It Like It Is	CD5	France	1991	$2.00
A&M	AMCD-545	With God on Our Side	CD5	U.K.	1989	$9.00
A&M	CD 17980	With God on Our Side	CDJ	U.S.	1989	$2.00
A&M	CD 17782	Yellow Moon	CDJ	U.S.	1989	$2.00

Neville, Ivan

Label	Catalog Number	Title	Type	Country	Year	Longbox Value / Value
		Singles				
Polydor	CDP 22	Not Just Another Girl	CDJ	U.S.	1988	$2.00
Polydor	PZCD-50	Primitive Man	CD5	U.K.	1989	$8.00
Polydor	CDP 53	Primitive Man	CDJ	U.S.	1989	$2.00
MCA	CD45 1049	Why Can't I Fall In Love	CDJ	U.S.	1990	$2.00

Neville, Robbie

Label	Catalog Number	Title	Type	Country	Year	Longbox Value / Value
		Singles				
Manhattan	203054-2	Back on Holiday	CD5	Germany	1988	$8.00
Manhattan	CDMT-58	Back on Holiday	CD5	U.K.	1988	$8.00
EMI		Back on Holiday	CDJ	U.S.	1988	$2.00
EMI	DPRO4824	For Your Mind	CDJ	U.S.	11991	$2.00
Manhattan	204430-2	Just Like You	CD5	Germany	1991	$8.00
EMI	DPRO-05757	Just Like You	CDJ	U.S.	1991	$2.00
Manhattan	203267-2	Somebody Like You	CD5	Germany	1991	$8.00
EMI	DPRO-41223	Somebody Like You	CDJ	U.S.	1989	$2.00

New Atlantic

Label	Catalog Number	Title	Type	Country	Year	Longbox Value / Value
		Singles				
Eastwest	9031-76562-2	I Know	CD5	Germany	1992	$8.00
WEA	3BTCD-1	I Know	CD5	U.K.	1992	$8.00
Big Beat	10049	I Know	CD5	U.S.	1992	$4.00
Big Beat	4521	I Know	CDJ	U.S.	1992	$2.00
WEA	3BTCD-2	Into the Future	CD5	U.K.	1992	$8.00
WEA	3BTCD-14	Take Off Some Time	CD5	U.K.	1992	$8.00

New Choice

Label	Catalog Number	Title	Type	Country	Year	Longbox Value / Value
		Singles				
		Funny Feelings	CDJ	U.S.		$2.00

New Edition

Label	Catalog Number	Title	Type	Country	Year	Longbox Value / Value
		Full Length				
MCA	MCAD-5515	New Edition	LP/LB	U.S.†	1985	$14.00/$8.00
		Singles				
MCA	1632	Boys To Men	CDJ	U.S.	1991	$2.00
Warner Brothers	10SW-64	If It Isn't Love	CD3	Japan	1988	$15.00/$4.00
		If It Isn't Love	CDJ	U.S.		$2.00
Warner Brothers	10P3-6039	You're Not My Kind of Girl	CD3	Japan	1988	$15.00/$4.00

New Faith

Label	Catalog Number	Title	Type	Country	Year	Longbox Value / Value
		Singles				
Warner Brothers	PRO-CD-5383	You Were Always There	CDJ	U.S.	1991	$3.00

New Fast Automatic Daffodils

Label	Catalog Number	Title	Type	Country	Year	Longbox Value / Value
		Singles				
APT	BIAS-199CD	All Over My Face	CD5	U.K.	1991	$8.00
SPV	8660-3	Big	CD5	Germany	1990	$8.00
Playtime	AMUSE-7CD	Big	CD5	U.K.	1990	$8.00
Mute	61438	Bong	CD5	U.S.	1992	$5.00
SPV	4998-3	Fishes Eyes	CD5	Germany	1990	$8.00
APT	BIAS-162CD	Fishes Eyes	CD5	U.K.	1990	$8.00
APT	BIAS-139CD	Get Better	CD5	U.K.	1991	$8.00
Mute	8341	Get Better	CDJ	U.S.	1991	$2.00
APT	BIAS-219CD	It's Not What You Know	CD5	U.K.	1992	$8.00
Mute	8759	It's Not What You Know	CDJ	U.S.	1992	$2.00
SPV	0994-3	Music Is Sh*t	CD5	Germany	1990	$8.00
Playtime	AMUSE-6CD	Music Is Sh*t	CD5	U.K.	1989	$8.00
APT	BIAS-229CD	Stockholm	CD5	U.K.	1992	$8.00
Mute	8703	Stockholm	CDJ	U.S.	1992	$2.00

New Frontier

Label	Catalog Number	Title	Type	Country	Year	Longbox Value / Value
		Singles				
Polygram	871179-2	Under Fire	CD5	Germany	1988	$8.00
Polygram	870 740-2	Under Fire	CDV/BP	U.S.	1988	$20.00/$20.00

New Kids On The Block (NKOTB)

Label	Catalog Number	Title	Type	Country	Year	Longbox Value / Value
		Full Length				
CBS	XDDP-93041	Step by Step	DJ/Smplr	Japan		$35.00
Columbia	CK 46767	Step by Step	LTD/LP	U.S.	1990	$10.00
	6"x12" locker style package.					
		Singles				
Sony	SRDS-8189	Call It What You Want	CD3	Japan	1991	$13.00/$4.00
Columbia	CSK 3061	Call It What You Want	CDJ	U.S.	1991	$2.00
Sony	CSDS-8102	Cover Girl	CD3	Japan	1989	$13.00/$4.00
Columbia	BLOCKC-5	Cover Girl	CD5	U.K.	1990	$8.00
Columbia	BLOCKP-5	Cover Girl	CD5	U.K.	1990	$8.00
		Didn't I (Blow Your Mind)	CDJ	U.S.		$2.00
Columbia	44K 77315	Dirty Dawg	CD5	U.S.	1994	$4.00
Columbia	CSK 77293	Dirty Dawg	CDJ	U.S.	1994	$2.00
CBS	77315	Dirty Dawg	CDJ	U.S.	1994	$5.00
CBS	656626-2	Games	CD5	Germany	1991	$8.00
Columbia	CSK 73620	Games	CDJ	U.S.	1990	$2.00
Columbia	655199-3	Hangin' Tough	CD3	Germany	1989	$9.00
Columbia	BLOCKC-1	Hangin' Tough	CD5	U.K.	1989	$9.00
Columbia	BLOCKC-3	Hangin' Tough	CD5	U.K.	1989	$9.00
Sony	SRDS-8215	I Believe in You	CD3	Japan	1991	$13.00/$4.00
Columbia	654863-3	I'll Be Loving You	CD3	Germany	1989	$8.00
Sony	10EP-3079	I'll Be Loving You	CD3	Japan	1989	$13.00/$4.00
Columbia	BLOCKC-4	I'll Be Loving You	CD5	U.K.	1989	$8.00
Columbia	657666-2	If You Go Away	CD5	Germany	1991	$8.00
Columbia	657666-2	If You Go Away	CD5	U.K.	1991	$8.00
Columbia	CSK 4462	If You Go Away	CDJ	U.S.	1991	$2.00
Columbia	656345-3	Let's Try Again	CD3	Germany	1990	$8.00
Sony	CSDS-8165	Let's Try Again	CD3	Japan	1990	$13.00/$4.00
Columbia	CSK 73443	Let's Try Again	CDJ	U.S.	1990	$2.00
Columbia	CSK 77274	Never Let You Go	CDJ	U.S.	1994	$2.00
Columbia	652992-2	Please Don't Go Girl	CD5	Germany	1988	$8.00
Sony	CSFM7701	Please Don't Go Girl	CDV	Japan		$20.00

Label	Catalog Number	Title	Type	Country	Year	Longbox Value / Value
Sony	10EP-3050	Please Don't Go Girl	CD3	Japan	1988	$13.00/$4.00
Columbia		Please Don't Go Girl	CDJ	U.S.	1988	$2.00
Columbia	655905-3	Step by Step	CD3	Germany	1990	$8.00
Sony		Step by Step	CDV	Japan		$20.00
Sony	SRDS-8219	Step by Step	CD3	Japan	1990	$13.00/$4.00
Columbia	CSK 73343	Step by Step	CDJ	U.S.	1990	$6.00
6"x12" locker style package.						
Columbia	656349-3	This One's For the Children	CD3	Germany	1989	$8.00
Sony	CSDS-8109	This One's For the Children	CD3	Japan	1989	$13.00/$4.00
Columbia		This One's For the Children	CDJ	U.S.	1989	$2.00
Columbia	656177-3	Tonight	CD3	Germany	1990	$8.00
Sony	CSDS-8153	Tonight	CD3	Japan	1990	$13.00/$4.00
Columbia	CSK 73461	Tonight	CDJ	U.S.	1990	$2.00
Columbia	653169-3	You Got It (the Right Stuff)	CD3	Germany	1990	$8.00
Sony	10EP-3062	You Got It (the Right Stuff)	CD3	Japan	1990	$13.00/$4.00
Sony	12EP-3069	You Got It (the Right Stuff)	CD3	Japan	1990	$13.00/$4.00
Columbia	BLOCKC-2	You Got It (the Right Stuff)	CD5	U.K.	1989	$8.00
Columbia		You Got It (the Right Stuff)	CDJ	U.S.	1988	$2.00

New Legend

Singles

Label	Catalog Number	Title	Type	Country	Year	Longbox Value / Value
RCA	2622-2-RDJ	Angel of Mercy	CDJ	U.S.	1990	$2.00
BMG	PD-44188	Lonely Thousand Nights	CD5	Germany	1990	$8.00
BMG	PD-43726	No Mercy	CD5	Germany	1990	$8.00
BMG	PD-43634	No More Crazy Nightmares	CD5	Germany	1990	$8.00
RCA		No More Crazy Nightmares	CDJ	U.S.	1990	$2.00

New Mixed Emotions

Singles

Label	Catalog Number	Title	Type	Country	Year	Longbox Value / Value
EMI	147549-2	Sensuality	CD5	Germany	1990	$8.00

New Model Army

Singles

Label	Catalog Number	Title	Type	Country	Year	Longbox Value / Value
EMI	204008-2	Get Me Out	CD5	Germany	1990	$8.00
EMI	CDNMA-10	Get Me Out	CD5	U.K.	1990	$8.00
EMI	203388-3	Green and Grey	CD3	Germany	1989	$8.00
EMI	CDNMA-9	Green and Grey	CD5	U.K.	1989	$8.00
Epic	658935-2	Here Comes the War	CD5	U.K.	1993	$8.00
Epic		Here Comes the War	CDJ	U.S.	1993	$3.00
EMI	204318-2	One Space	CD5	Germany	1991	$8.00
EMI	204086-2	Purity	CD5	Germany	1990	$8.00
EMI	CDNMA-11	Purity	CD5	U.K.	1990	$8.00
EMI	CDNMA-12	Space	CD5	U.K.	1991	$8.00
EMI	203137-2	Stupid Questions	CD5	Germany	1989	$8.00
EMI	CDNMA-7	Stupid Questions	CD5	U.K.	1989	$8.00
EMI	203266-2	Vagabonds	CD5	Germany	1989	$8.00
EMI	CDNMA-8	Vagabonds	CD5	U.K.	1989	$8.00

New Order

Full Length

Label	Catalog Number	Title	Type	Country	Year	Longbox Value / Value
		?	DJ/Smplr	France		$40.00
Westwood One		In Concert	RS	U.S.	1994	$60.00
2 CD set. With Blind Melon, Airdate: 2/14/94						
Qwest	PRO-CD-5970	In Order	DJ/Smplr	U.S.	1993	$18.00
Qwest	PRO-CD-6190	Republic	DJ/LP	U.S.	1993	$15.00
Qwest	9 45311-2	Republic	LTD/LP	U.S.	1993	$25.00
Picture CD in orange digipak.						
		Rest of New Order	LTD/LP	U.K.	1995	$30.00
2 CD set.						

Singles

Label	Catalog Number	Title	Type	Country	Year	Longbox Value / Value
Warner Brothers	PRO-CD-7587	Bizarre Love Triangle	CDJ	U.S.		$3.00
Warner Brothers	20546	Bizarre Love Triangle	CD5	U.S.	1994	$5.00
Warner Brothers	20546-2	Bizarre Love Triangle	CD5	U.S.	1994	$6.00
Polygram	870354-2	Blue Monday	CD5	Canada	1988	$10.00
Rough Trade	CD1-60	Blue Monday	CD5	Germany	1988	$10.00
Factory	10CY-8038	Blue Monday	CD3	Japan	1988	$15.00/$4.00
Factory	FACD-73R	Blue Monday	CD5	U.K.	1988	$10.00
Qwest	PRO-CD-3053	Blue Monday	CDJ	U.S.	1988	$25.00
APT	F8N-8CD	Everything's Gone Green	CD5	U.K.	1990	$10.00
Polygram	827277-2	Fine Time	CD5	Canada	1988	$10.00
Factory	110-0244-3	Fine Time	CD3	Germany	1988	$10.00
CBS	15CY-5022	Fine Time	CD5	Japan	1988	$4.00
Factory	FACD-223	Fine Time	CD5	U.K.	1988	$10.00
Warner Brothers	PRO-CD-7390	Let's Go	CDJ	U.S.	1990	$3.00
Polygram	830408-2	New Order	CD5	Canada	1990	$10.00
Aris	883511	Peel Sessions	CD5	Germany	1990	$10.00
Strange Frt	SFPSCD-001	Peel Sessions	CD5	U.K.	1990	$10.00
Strange Frt	SFPSCD-001	Peel Sessions	CD5	U.S.	1990	$10.00
Aris	883521	Peel Sessions 2	CD5	Germany	1990	$10.00
Strange Frt	SFPSCD-039	Peel Sessions 2	CD5	U.K.	1990	$10.00
Strange Frt	SFPSCD-039	Peel Sessions 2	CD5	U.S.	1990	$10.00
		Regret	CDJ	France	1993	$15.00
London	POCD-1109	Regret	CD5	Japan	1993	$13.00
Qwest	18586-2	Regret	CD5	U.S.	1993	$5.00
Qwest	PRO-CD-6006	Regret	CDJ	U.S.	1993	$3.00
Polygram	874079-2	Round & Round	CD5	Canada	1989	$10.00
Rough Trade	110 0270 3	Round & Round	CD5	Germany	1989	$10.00
Factory	CY-5024	Round & Round	CD3	Japan	1989	$15.00/$4.00
Factory	FACD-263R	Round & Round	CD3	U.K.	1989	$10.00
Factory	FACD-263	Round & Round	CD5	U.K.	1989	$10.00
		Round & Round	CDJ	U.S.	1989	$2.00
London	857219	Ruined in a Day	CD5	U.K.	1993	$10.00
London		Ruined in a Day	CD5	U.K.	1993	$10.00
Second version.						
Qwest	PRO-CD-6318	Ruined in a Day	CDJ	U.S.	1993	$3.00
Factory	FACD-273	Run	CD5	U.K.	1989	$10.00
		Spooky	CD5	Japan	1994	$20.00
		Spooky	CD5	U.K.		$10.00
Second version.						
Warner Brothers	9 41313-2	Spooky	CD5	U.S.	1994	$5.00
Warner Brothers	41313	Spooky	CD5	U.S.	1994	$5.00
Warner Brothers	PRO-CD-6729	Spooky	CDJ	U.S.	1994	$3.00
Factory	10CY-8010	Touched by the Hand of God	CD3	Japan	1988	$15.00/$4.00
Factory	FACD-193	Touched by the Hand of God	CD5	U.K.	1987	$10.00
Qwest	PRO-CD-2899	True Faith	CDJ	U.S.	1987	$2.00
Qwest		True Faith	DJ/CDV	U.S.	1988	$35.00
London	422857402	World	CD5	Canada	1994	$8.00
	POCD-1122	World	CDJ	Japan	1995	$20.00
London	NUOCD3	World	CD5	U.K.	1993	$10.00
Qwest	9 40966-2	World	CDJ	U.S.	1993	$3.00
Factrory	FACD-214	World Cup Single	CD5	U.K.	1990	$10.00
Polygram	846237-2	World in Motion	CD5	Canada	1990	$10.00
Rough Trade	CD1-1006	World in Motion	CD5	Germany	1990	$10.00
Factory	CDCY-5102	World in Motion	CD5	Japan	1990	$13.00
Factory	FACD-293	World in Motion	CD5	U.K.	1990	$10.00
Qwest	21582-2	World in Motion	CD5	U.S.	1990	$5.00
		World (Price of Love)	CD5	U.K.		$10.00
		World (Price of Love)	CD5	U.K.		$10.00
Second version.						

New Power Generation

Singles

Label	Catalog Number	Title	Type	Country	Year	Longbox Value / Value
NPG		Get Wild	CD5	U.K.	1995	$10.00
NPG		Get Wild	CDJ	U.S.	1995	$3.00
Warner Brothers	PRO-CD-8140-R	Girl	CDJ	U.S.	1995	$3.00
NPG		Good Life	CDJ	U.S.	1995	$10.00
NPG		Good Life	CDJ	U.S.	1995	$10.00
Second version.						
		Good Life, The	CD5	Canada	1995	$8.00
		Super Hero	CD5	U.K.		$12.00
NPG		Superhero	CDJ	U.S.	1995	$10.00

New Riders

Full Length

Label	Catalog Number	Title	Type	Country	Year	Longbox Value / Value
DIR		King Biscuit Flour Hour	RS	U.S.	1988	$35.00
Airdate: 10/9/88.						

New Scene

Singles

Label	Catalog Number	Title	Type	Country	Year	Longbox Value / Value
ZYX	8810-8	Out of Control	CD5	Germany	1990	$6.00
Boy	BOY-8834-8	Tonight	CD5	Germany	1990	$6.00
Boy	BOY-8819-8	War In Vietnam	CD5	Germany	1990	$6.00

New Version of Soul

Singles

Label	Catalog Number	Title	Type	Country	Year	Longbox Value / Value
Capitol	DPRO 79846	66 Mello	CDJ	U.S.	1993	$2.00

New York Dolls

Singles

Label	Catalog Number	Title	Type	Country	Year	Longbox Value / Value
Classic	CDEP 14	Personality	CD5	U.K.		$11.00

New York Voices

Singles

Label	Catalog Number	Title	Type	Country	Year	Longbox Value / Value
GRP	VICP-15002	Caravan	CD3	Japan	1990	$12.00/$4.00

Newbury, Mickey

Singles

Label	Catalog Number	Title	Type	Country	Year	Longbox Value / Value
Airborne	0101	An American Trilogy	CDJ	U.S.	1988	$2.00

Newcleus

Singles

Label	Catalog Number	Title	Type	Country	Year	Longbox Value / Value
Bellaphon	130 07 361	Fifty Ways To Get Funky	CD5	Germany	1990	$8.00
Bellaphon	130 07 274	Jam On It	CD5	Germany	1990	$8.00
Bellaphon	130 07 383	Jam On It	CD5	Germany	1990	$8.00

Newell, Martin

Full Length

Label	Catalog Number	Title	Type	Country	Year	Longbox Value / Value
Collector's Pipeline	PIPE CD 002	Greatest Living Englishman, The	LP	U.S.	1993	$16.00

Newkirk

Singles

Label	Catalog Number	Title	Type	Country	Year	Longbox Value / Value
Def Jam	CSK 73849	Small Thing	CDJ	U.S.	1991	$2.00

Newman, Alfred

Full Length

Label	Catalog Number	Title	Type	Country	Year	Longbox Value / Value
Varese Sarabande	9201.11	Film Music of Alfred Newman	LTD/LP	U.S.	1992	$20.00
Limited to 1200 copies.						

Newman, Randy

Full Length

Label	Catalog Number	Title	Type	Country	Year	Longbox Value / Value
Pioneer	PA-85-102	At the Odeon	LD	U.S.	1985	$30.00
Pioneer	PA-85-102	At the Odeon	LD	U.S.	1991	$30.00
Digital audio.						
		Faust	DJ/Intvw	U.S.		$10.00
Reprise		Land of Dreams	LP/LB	U.S.		$14.00/$8.00
Warner Brothers	9 23755-2	Trouble in Paradise	LP/LB	U.S.†	1984	$14.00/$8.00

Singles

Label	Catalog Number	Title	Type	Country	Year	Longbox Value / Value
Warner Brothers	W-7578CD	Falling in Love	CD5	U.K.	1988	$9.00
Reprise	PRO-CD-3397	Falling in Love	CDJ	U.S.	1988	$2.00
Warner Brothers	9 25680-2	I Love L.A.	CDV/BP	U.S.	1988	$20.00/$20.00
Warner/NTSC	2-25680	I Love L.A.	DJ/CDV	U.S.	1988	$20.00
Reprise	PRO-CD-3707	I Love To See You Smile	CDJ	U.S.	1989	$2.00
Warner Brothers	W-7709CD	It's Money That Matters	CD5	U.K.	1988	$9.00
Sire	PRO-CD-3272	It's Money That Matters	CDJ	U.S.	1988	$2.00
Reprise	PRO-CD-6869	Make Up Your Mind	CDJ	U.S.	1994	$3.00
Disney	DSP-1189	You've Got a Friend in Me	CD3	Japan	1995	$15.00/$4.00

Newman, Robert

Singles

Label	Catalog Number	Title	Type	Country	Year	Longbox Value / Value
Canyon	PCDY-00050	Love Me Girl	CD3	Japan	1990	$12.00/$3.00

Newman, Troy

Singles

Label	Catalog Number	Title	Type	Country	Year	Longbox Value / Value
EastWest	PRCD 4074-2	I Can Feel It	CDJ	U.S.	1991	$2.00

Newsboys

Singles

Label	Catalog Number	Title	Type	Country	Year	Longbox Value / Value
	DPRO11507	Take Me To Your Leader	CDJ	U.S.		$6.00

Newsong

Full Length

Label	Catalog Number	Title	Type	Country	Year	Longbox Value / Value
Benson		All Around the World	DJ/LP	U.S.	1991	$15.00
CD in envelope.						

Newton

Singles

Label	Catalog Number	Title	Type	Country	Year	Longbox Value / Value
Critique	15536	Sky High	CD5	U.S.	1994	$5.00

Newton, James

Full Length

Label	Catalog Number	Title	Type	Country	Year	Longbox Value / Value
Celestial Harmonies	CD-012	Echo Canyon	LP/LB	U.S.†	1985	$14.00/$8.00
Gramaphone	GRCD-8205	James Newton	LP/LB	U.S.†	1985	$14.00/$8.00

Newton, Juice

Full Length

Label	Catalog Number	Title	Type	Country	Year	Longbox Value / Value
RCA	8376-2-R	Ain't Gonna Cry	LP/LB	U.S.		$14.00/$8.00
RCA	PCD1-4995	Can't Wait All Night	LP	Germany	1984	$14.00
RCA	PCD1-4995	Can't Wait All Night	LP	U.K.	1984	$14.00
RCA	PCD1-4995	Can't Wait All Night	LP/LB	U.S.		$14.00/$8.00
RCA	PCD1-4995	Can't Wait All Night	LP/LB	U.S.†	1984	$14.00/$8.00
RCA	R32P-1126	Emotion	LP	Japan		$20.00
RCA	6371-2	Emotion	LP/LB	U.S.		$14.00/$8.00
EMI	CDP-746489-2	Greatest Hits	LP	Germany		$14.00
Capitol	CP32-9013	Greatest Hits	LP	Japan		$20.00

Label	Catalog Number	Title	Type	Country	Year	Longbox Value / Value
Capitol	CDP-746489-2	Juice	LP/LB	U.S.		$14.00/$8.00
RCA	PCD1-5493	Old Flame	LP/LB	U.S.†	1984	$14.00/$8.00

Newton, Wayne

Singles

Label	Catalog Number	Title	Type	Country	Year	Longbox Value / Value
Curb	025	At This Moment	CDJ	U.S.	1990	$2.00
		You Don't Know What You've Got	CDJ	U.S.		$2.00

Newton-John, Olivia

Full Length

Label	Catalog Number	Title	Type	Country	Year	Longbox Value / Value
MCA	MCAD-5882	Come on Over/Clearly Love	LP/LB	U.S.	1986	$25.00/$20.00
MCA	MCAD-5878	Don't Stop Believin'/Totally Hot	LP/LB	U.S.	1986	$35.00/$20.00
	HI-5184	GAIA	DJ/Smplr	Japan	1995	$100.00
	2 CD set.					
MCA	MCAD-5226	Greatest Hits	LP/LB	U.S.†	1985	$15.00/$10.00
MCA	MCAD-5226	Greatest Hits	LP/LB	U.S.	1987	$15.00/$10.00
Griffin		Have You Never Been So Mellow	LTD/LP	U.K.	1995	$30.00
	CD and book in box.					
		More Than Physical-Collector's Box	LTD/LP	U.K.	1995	$30.00
MCA	74-005	Oliva	LD	U.S.	1985	$25.00
MCA	74-021	Olivia-In Concert	LD	U.S.	1983	$50.00
Discovision	74-021	Olivia-In Concert	LD	U.S.	1983	$50.00
MCA	74-017	Physical	LD	U.S.	1982	$35.00
MCA	MCAD-5229	Physical	LP/LB	U.S.†	1984	$14.00/$8.00
Geffen	9 242572-Dj	Warm and Tender	DJ/LP	U.S.	1989	$28.00
	CD in cardboard drum and special booklet.					

Singles

Label	Catalog Number	Title	Type	Country	Year	Longbox Value / Value
Geffen	PRO-CD-4449	Deeper Than A River	CDJ	U.S.		$2.00
Polygram	PZCD-136	Grease	CD5	U.K.	1991	$10.00
	With John Travolta.					
Mercury	PHDR-112	I Need Love	CD3	Japan	1992	$15.00/$4.00
		I Need Love	CD5	U.S.	1992	$5.00
	MERCD370	I Need Love	CD5	U.K.	1995	$18.00
Geffen	PRO-CD-4406	I Need Love	CDJ	U.S.	1992	$2.00
		No Matter What You Do	CD5	Australia	1994	$10.00
		No Matter What You Do	CD5	Australia	1994	$10.00
		No Matter What You Do	CDJ	U.K.	1994	$10.00
Geffen	PRO-CD-3782	Reach Out For Me	CDJ	U.S.	1989	$2.00
Mercury	870506-2	Rumour, The	CD5	Germany	1988	$12.00
Polydor	P10C-30001	Rumour, The	CD3	Japan	1988	$15.00/$4.00
Mercury	MERCD-272	Rumour, The	CD5	U.K.	1988	$12.00
MCA	CD 17594	Rumour, The	CDJ	U.S.	1988	$2.00
		Summer Nights	CDJ	France		$30.00
Mercury	MERCD-313	When You Wish Upon a Star	CD5	U.K.	1988	$10.00
Polygram	879411-2	You're the One That I Want	CD5	Germany	1991	$10.00
	With John Travolta.					

Next Issue

Singles

Label	Catalog Number	Title	Type	Country	Year	Longbox Value / Value
Epic	ESK 74397	Dear Mr. President	CDJ	U.S.	1992	$2.00

NFL Goes Motown

Singles

Label	Catalog Number	Title	Type	Country	Year	Longbox Value / Value
Motown	822	Songs From the Big Thrill	CDJ	U.S.	1992	$3.00

Ni Ii U

Singles

Label	Catalog Number	Title	Type	Country	Year	Longbox Value / Value
Arista	12773	I Miss You	CD5	U.S.	1994	$5.00

Nice & Smooth

Singles

Label	Catalog Number	Title	Type	Country	Year	Longbox Value / Value
Columbia	CSK 74365	Cake & Eat It Too	CDJ	U.S.	1992	$2.00

Nichols, Herbie

Full Length

Label	Catalog Number	Title	Type	Country	Year	Longbox Value / Value
Mosaic	MD3-118	Complete Blue Note Recordings	LP	U.S.		$40.00
	3 CD Set					

Nichols, Paula

Singles

Label	Catalog Number	Title	Type	Country	Year	Longbox Value / Value
CBS	651681-3	I've Got This Feeling	CD5	Germany	1988	$8.00
CBS	652845-3	Paris In My Heart	CD5	Germany	1988	$8.00

Nicks, Stevie

Full Length

Label	Catalog Number	Title	Type	Country	Year	Longbox Value / Value
Pioneer Artists	PA-86-M039	8: I Can't Wait	LD	U.S.	1990	$25.00
Modern	38139-2	Bella Donna	LP/LB	U.S.†	1984	$14.00/$8.00
EMI		Best of Stevie Nicks, The	DJ/Smplr	U.K.	1994	$30.00
Pioneer	PA86-M039	I Can't Wait	8"LD	U.S.	1986	$10.00
	MP100-15PA	In Concert	LD	Japan		$80.00
Pioneer	PA-83-033	In Concert	LD	U.S.	1983	$40.00
		Interview	DJ/Intvw	Canada	1990	$40.00
		Live at the Whiskey	RS	U.S.	1993	$150.00
	Airdate: 8/30/93.					
Westwood One		Off the Record	RS	U.S.	1992	$30.00
	Airdate: 8/24/92.					
Westwood One		Off the Record	RS	U.S.	1994	$45.00
	Airdate: 12/19/94.					
Pioneer Artists	PA-88-209	Red Rocks	LD	U.S.	1988	$30.00
EMI	CDEMDDJ 1024	Sample of the Hits So Far	DJ/Smplr	U.K.	1994	$35.00
Modern		Street Angel	DJ/LP	U.S.	1994	$15.00
Westwood One		Superstars	RS	U.S.	1995	$150.00
	2 CD set. Airdate: 1/23/95.					
Media America		Up Close	RS	U.S.	1989	$30.00
	2 CD set.					
Modern	90084-2	Wild Heart	LP/LB	U.S.†	1984	$14.00/$8.00

Singles

Label	Catalog Number	Title	Type	Country	Year	Longbox Value / Value
		Blue Denim	CD5	U.K.	1994	$11.00
	CDDENIM 1	Blue Denim	CDJ	U.K.	1994	$15.00
Modern		Blue Denim	CDJ	U.S.	1994	$6.00
Modern	PRCD 4413	Desiree	CDJ	U.S.	1992	$3.00
EMI	CDEM-214	I Can't Wait	CD5	U.K.	1991	$10.00
EMI	203431-3	Long Way To Go	CD3	Germany	1989	$10.00
EMI	203431-2	Long Way To Go	CD5	Germany	1989	$10.00
Toshiba	X10P-2101	Long Way To Go	CD3	Japan	1989	$15.00/$4.00
Modern	CDEM 97	Long Way To Go	CD5	U.K.	1989	$10.00
Modern	PRCD 4282-2	Love Is A Hard Game To Play	CDJ	U.S.	1991	$6.00
Modern		Maybe Love Will Change Your Mind	CD5	U.K.	1994	$10.00
Modern		Maybe Love Will Change Your Mind	CD5	U.K.	1994	$10.00
	Second version.					
Modern	CDEMDJX 328	Maybe Love Will Change Your Mind	CDJ	U.K.	1994	$15.00
Modern	CDEMDJ 328	Maybe Love Will Change Your Mind	CDJ	U.K.	1994	$40.00
Modern	98270	Maybe Love Will Change Your Mind	CD5	U.S.	1994	$6.00
Modern		Maybe Love Will Change Your Mind	CDJ	U.S.	1994	$3.00
Toshiba	XP10-2089	Rooms on Fire	CD3	Japan	1989	$15.00/$4.00
EMI Modern	CDEM 90	Rooms on Fire	CD5	U.K.	1989	$10.00
Modern	PR 2691-2	Rooms on Fire	CDJ	U.S.	1989	$6.00
Modern	PR 2744-2	Rooms on Fire	CDJ	U.S.	1989	$6.00
Modern	204436-2	Sometimes It's a Bitch	CD5	Germany	1991	$10.00
Modern	CDEM-203	Sometimes It's a Bitch	CD5	U.K.	1991	$10.00
Modern	PRCD 4021-2	Sometimes It's a Bitch	CDJ	U.S.	1991	$3.00
Toshiba	TODP-2313	Time Space	CD3	Japan	1991	$15.00/$4.00
EMI	203569-3	Two Kinds of Love	CD3	U.K.	1989	$10.00
Modern	PR 2875-2	Two Kinds of Love	CDJ	U.S.	1989	$3.00
EMI	CDEM-114	Whole Lotta Trouble	CD5	U.K.	1989	$10.00
Modern	PR 2977-2	Whole Lotta Trouble	CDJ	U.S.	1989	$6.00

Nico

Full Length

Label	Catalog Number	Title	Type	Country	Year	Longbox Value / Value
Restless		Hanging Gardens	LP/LB	U.S.	12	$7.00

Nicole

Singles

Label	Catalog Number	Title	Type	Country	Year	Longbox Value / Value
Atlantic	76027	Runnin' Away	CD5	U.S.	1994	$5.00

Niewood, Gerry

Full Length

Label	Catalog Number	Title	Type	Country	Year	Longbox Value / Value
Digital Music	CD-450	Share My Dream	LP/LB	U.S.†	1985	$14.00/$8.00

Night Ranger

Full Length

Label	Catalog Number	Title	Type	Country	Year	Longbox Value / Value
MCA	MCAD-6238	Big Life	LP/LB	U.S.		$14.00/$8.00
MCA	MCAD-5460	Dawn Patrol	LP/LB	U.S.†	1985	$14.00/$8.00
MCA	MCAD-5839	Man in Motion	LP/LB	U.S.		$14.00/$8.00
MCA	MCAD-5456	Midnight Madness	LP/LB	U.S.†	1985	$14.00/$8.00
MCA	MCAD-5493	Seven Wishes	LP/LB	U.S.†	1985	$14.00/$8.00

Singles

Label	Catalog Number	Title	Type	Country	Year	Longbox Value / Value
MCA	10P3-6094	Don't Start Thinking	CD3	Japan	1989	$12.00/$4.00
		Don't Start Thinking	CDJ	U.S.	1989	$2.00
MCA	10P3-6014	I Did It For Love	CD3	Japan	1988	$12.00/$4.00
		I Did It For Love	CDJ	U.S.	1988	$2.00
		Reason to Be	CDJ	U.S.		$2.00

Nightblooms

Singles

Label	Catalog Number	Title	Type	Country	Year	Longbox Value / Value
Fierce	FRIGHT-057CD	Butterfly Girl	CD5	U.K.	1991	$8.00

Nightcrawlers

Singles

Label	Catalog Number	Title	Type	Country	Year	Longbox Value / Value
4th & B'way	BRCD-250	Living Inside a Dream	CD5	U.K.	1992	$8.00
4th & B'way	BRCD-258	Push the Feeling On	CD5	U.K.	1992	$8.00
Great Jones	530620	Push the Feeling On	CD5	U.S.	1994	$5.00

Nightmares On Wax

Singles

Label	Catalog Number	Title	Type	Country	Year	Longbox Value / Value
Warp	WARP-6CD	Aftermath	CD5	U.K.	1990	$8.00
Warp	WARP-15CD	Biofeedback	CD5	U.K.	1991	$8.00
Warp	WARP-28CD	Happiness	CD5	U.K.	1992	$8.00

Nightwalkers

Singles

Label	Catalog Number	Title	Type	Country	Year	Longbox Value / Value
	1258	Stone Fox Chase	CD5	U.S.	1994	$5.00

Nikita

Singles

Label	Catalog Number	Title	Type	Country	Year	Longbox Value / Value
Motown	374631022	All Over You, All Over Me	CDJ	U.S.	1993	$2.00
Motown	374631088	Sweet As It Comes	CDJ	U.S.	1993	$2.00

Nikki

Singles

Label	Catalog Number	Title	Type	Country	Year	Longbox Value / Value
Geffen	PRO-CD-3549	If You Wanna	CDJ	U.S.	1989	$2.00
Geffen	GEF-78CD	Notice Me	CD5	U.K.	1990	$8.00
Geffen		Notice Me	CDJ	U.S.	1989	$2.00
Geffen		Ooti Ooti	CDJ	U.S.	1989	$2.00

Nikki D

Singles

Label	Catalog Number	Title	Type	Country	Year	Longbox Value / Value
Def Jam	656734	Daddy's Little Girl	CD5	U.K.	1991	$8.00
Epic	ESK 5192	Freak Out	CDJ	U.S.	1993	$2.00
Def Jam	CSK 72811	Hang On Kid	CDJ	U.S.	1991	$2.00

Nil Laura

Singles

Label	Catalog Number	Title	Type	Country	Year	Longbox Value / Value
		Sampler	CDJ	U.S.		$6.00

Nile, Willie

Full Length

Label	Catalog Number	Title	Type	Country	Year	Longbox Value / Value
Columbia		Places I Have Never Been	LP/LB	U.S.		$14.00/$8.00
Columbia	CSK 4055	Everybody Needs A Hammer	CDJ	U.S.	1991	$2.00
Columbia	CSK 73730	Heaven Help the Lonely	CDJ	U.S.	1991	$2.00

Nilsson, Harry (Nilsson)

Full Length

Label	Catalog Number	Title	Type	Country	Year	Longbox Value / Value
RCA	PCD1-4515	Nilsson Schmilsson	LP/BP	U.S.	1984	$15.00/$9.00
RCA	66599	Nilsson Schmilsson	LTD/LP	U.S.	1995	$28.00
	Gold disc.					
RCA	4289-2	Nilsson Sings Newman	LP/BP	U.S.		$15.00/$9.00
RCA		Point, The	LP/BP	U.S.		$15.00/$9.00

Singles

Label	Catalog Number	Title	Type	Country	Year	Longbox Value / Value
RCA	PD-49461	Without You	CD5	Germany	1989	$8.00
RCA	BVDP-77	Without You	CD3	Japan	1993	$12.00/$3.00
RCA	PD-49461	Without You	CD5	U.K.	1989	$8.00

Nine

Singles

Label	Catalog Number	Title	Type	Country	Year	Longbox Value / Value
Profile	7426	Whutcha Want	CD5	U.S.	1994	$5.00

Nine Inch Nails (NIN)

Full Length

Label	Catalog Number	Title	Type	Country	Year	Longbox Value / Value
Interscope		Broken	LP/LB	U.S.	1991	$18.00/$14.00
	Limited edition with bonus CD3.					
Interscope		Closer To God	DJ/Smplr	U.S.	1994	$15.00
		Fixed	LP/LB	U.S.		$15.00/$10.00
Interscope		Halo Ten	DJ/Smplr	U.S.		$18.00
Interscope	PRCD 5519-2	March of the Pigs	DJ/Smplr	U.S.	1993	$15.00

Singles

Label	Catalog Number	Title	Type	Country	Year	Longbox Value / Value
Interscope		Broken	DJ/CD3	U.S.	1991	$7.00
Interscope	PRCD 5868-2	Burn	CDJ	U.S.		$7.00
		Closer to God	CD5	U.K.	1994	$10.00
		Closer to God	CD5	U.K.	1994	$10.00
	Second version.					
Interscope	95905	Closer to God	CD5	U.S.	1994	$6.00
Interscope	PRCD 5664-2	Closer to God	CDJ	U.S.	1994	$6.00
Island	CID-482	Down In It	CD5	U.K.	1991	$10.00

Label	Catalog Number	Title	Type	Country	Year	Longbox Value/Value
Interscope		Down In It	CDJ	U.S.	1991	$7.00
TVT	2611	Down In It	CD5	U.S.	1994	$5.00
TVT	2611	Down In It	CD5	U.S.	1994	$20.00
	Given away at concerts. Disc has custom NIN sticker on front.					
Interscope		Fixed	CD5	U.K.	1992	$10.00
Interscope		Fixed	CD5	U.S.	1992	$6.00
Intercope	95811-2	Further Down the Spiral	CD5	U.S.		$6.00
Interscope	PRCD 4795-2	Happiness Is Slavery	CDJ	U.S.	1992	$6.00
Island	CID-484	Head Like A Hole	CD5	U.K.	1990	$10.00
TVT	2615-2	Head Like A Hole	CD5	U.S.	1990	$6.00
TeeVee Tunes	2615	Head Like A Hole	CD5	U.S.	1994	$5.00
Interscope	PRCD 6179-2	Hurt	CDJ	U.S.	1994	$6.00
		March of The Pigs	CD5	U.K.		$10.00
		March of The Pigs	CD5	U.K.		$10.00
	Second version.					
Interscope		March of the Pigs	CD5	U.K.	1994	$10.00
Interscope		March Of the Pigs	CD5	U.K.	1994	$10.00
	Second version.					
Atlantic	95938	March of the Pigs	CD5	U.S.	1994	$5.00
Interscope	PRCD 5923-2	Piggy	CDJ	U.S.		$6.00
TVT	866151-2	Sin	CD5	U.K.	1990	$10.00
TVT	2617-2	Sin	CD5	U.S.	1990	$5.00
TeeVee Tunes	2617	Sin Long	CD5	U.S.	1994	$5.00
		Suck	CD5	U.K.		$20.00
Interscope		Wish	CDJ	U.S.		$7.00

Nine Ways To Sunday

Full Length

Label	Catalog Number	Title	Type	Country	Year	Longbox Value/Value
Giant	9 24402-2-Dj	Nine Ways To Sunday	DJ/LP	U.S.	1990	$8.00

Singles

Label	Catalog Number	Title	Type	Country	Year	Longbox Value/Value
Giant	PRO-CD-4403	Come Tell Me Now	CDJ	U.S.	1990	$2.00
Giant	PRO-CD-453[illegible]	Come Tell Me N[illegible]	CDJ	U.S.	1990	$2.00

Ninety Five South

Singles

Label	Catalog Number	Title	Type	Country	Year	Longbox Value/Value
	9502	Rodeo	CD5	U.S.	1994	$5.00
		Hump With It	CDJ	U.S.		$2.00

Nirvana – Smells Like Teen Spirit (Geffen PRO-CD-4308)

Nirvana

Full Length

Label	Catalog Number	Title	Type	Country	Year	Longbox Value/Value
Sub Pop		Bleach	LP/BP	U.S.		$15.00/$10.00
	Non-remastered version.					
Geffen		Hormoaning	LP	Australia	1992	$25.00
DGC/Victor	MVCG-17002	Hormoaning	LP	Japan	1992	$25.00
Westwood One		In Concert	RS	U.S.	1992	$80.00
	With Roxy-Blue, Airdate: 10/12/92.					
Westwood One		In Concert	RS	U.S.	1992	$120.00
	With Led Zeppelin, Airdate: 3/16/92.					
Westwood One		In Concert	RS	U.S.	1993	$100.00
	2 CD set. Airdate: 9/6/93.					
Westwood One		In Concert	RS	U.S.	1994	$100.00
	2 CD set. Airdate: 6/20/94.					
Westwood One		In Concert	RS	U.S.	1995	$100.00
	2 CD set. Airdate: 12/4/95.					
DGC	CGCD-24425	Nevermind	LP/LB	U.S.	1991	$18.00/$14.00
	1st Issue without extra Track.					
Geffen		Nevermind & In Utero Singles Box	LP	U.K.	1995	$30.00
	3 CD5 Set.					
DGC	PRO-CD-4382	Nevermind It's An Interview	DJ/Intvw	U.S.	1992	$25.00
Geffen		Nirvana Box	LTD/LP	Germany	1995	$65.00
	Bleach and Hormoaning CDs in 6"x12" box.					

Singles

Label	Catalog Number	Title	Type	Country	Year	Longbox Value/Value
		About a Girl	CD5	Australia	1994	$12.00
Geffen		About a Girl	CDJ	Spanish		$40.00
Geffen		About a Girl	CDJ	U.S.	1994	$6.00
Geffen		All Apologies	CDJ	France		$50.00
Geffen	GFSTD66	All Apologies	CD5	U.K.	1994	$11.00
DGC	PRO-CD-4581	All Apologies	CDJ	U.S.	1993	$6.00
DGC	PRO-CD-4582	All Apologies	CDJ	U.S.	1993	$6.00
DGC	PRO-CD-4583	All Apologies	CDJ	U.S.	1993	$8.00
DGC	PRO-CD-4618	All Apologies	CDJ	U.S.	1994	$8.00
Tupelo	TUPCD 8	Blew	CD5	U.K.	1989	$10.00
Geffen	GED 21745	Come As You Are	CD5	France	1991	$12.00
Geffen	GED 21715	Come As You Are	CD5	Germany	1992	$11.00
Geffen	MVDG-8	Come As You Are	CD3	Japan	1992	$15.00/$4.00
Geffen	PRO-CD-4375	Come As You Are	CDJ	U.S.	1991	$3.00
Geffen	9 21707-2	Come As You Are	CD5	U.S.	1992	$5.00
Geffen	GED21849	Heart Shaped Box	CD5	France	1993	$12.00
Geffen		Heart Shaped Box	CD5	U.K.	1993	$10.00
Geffen	PRO-CD-4545	Heart Shaped Box	CDJ	U.S.	1993	$7.00
Geffen	GED21760	In Bloom	CD5	Germany	1992	$11.00
Geffen	MVCG-13002	In Bloom	CD5	Japan	1992	$18.00
Geffen	GFSTD-34	In Bloom	CD5	U.K.	1992	$11.00
Geffen		In Bloom	CDJ	U.S.		$6.00
Geffen	PRO-CD-4463	In Bloom	CDJ	U.S.	1992	$6.00
Geffen	MVCG-12001	Lithium	CD5	Japan	1992	$18.00
Geffen	9 21815-2	Lithium	CD5	U.S.	1992	$6.00
Geffen	PRO-CD-4429	Lithium	CDJ	U.S.	1992	$6.00
Geffen	21815	Lithium	CD5	U.S.	1994	$5.00
Geffen		Man Who Sold the World	CDJ	U.S.	1994	$6.00
Geffen	PRO-CD-4354	On A Plain	CDJ	U.S.	1991	$6.00
DGC	MVCG-17002	Peel Session and More	CD5	Japan	1992	$18.00
Touch & Go	TG83CD	Puss/Oh the Guilt	CD5	U.S.	1993	$6.00
	With one track by the Jesus Lizard.					
DGC		Rape Me	CDJ	U.K.	1993	$15.00
Tupelo	344 4125 3	Sliver	CD5	Germany	1991	$11.00
Tupelo	TUPCD-25	Sliver	CD5	U.K.	1991	$11.00
Tupelo	TUPCD-25	Sliver	CD5	U.S.	1991	$6.00
DGC	GED 21744	Smells Like Teen Spirit	CD5	France	1991	$12.00
DGC		Smells Like Teen Spirit	CD5	Germany	1991	$11.00
DGC	DGCTD-5	Smells Like Teen Spirit	CD5	U.K.	1991	$11.00
Geffen	9 21673-2	Smells Like Teen Spirit	CD5	U.S.	1991	$6.00
Geffen	PRO-CD-4308	Smells Like Teen Spirit	CDJ	U.S.	1991	$6.00
Geffen	21673	Smells Like Teen Spirit	CD5	U.S.	1994	$5.00
Geffen		Where Did You Sleep Last Night	CDJ	France		$50.00

Nitribit

Singles

Label	Catalog Number	Title	Type	Country	Year	Longbox Value/Value
ZYX	6092-8	Harmonic Drive	CD5	Germany	1989	$6.00
ZYX	6552-8	Savannah	CD5	Germany	1989	$6.00

Nitro

Singles

Label	Catalog Number	Title	Type	Country	Year	Longbox Value/Value
		Long Way From Home	CDJ	U.S.		$2.00
Atomic	WNRCD-788	Who Do You Call?	CD5	U.K.	1991	$8.00

Nits

Singles

Label	Catalog Number	Title	Type	Country	Year	Longbox Value/Value
CBS	655535-3	Home Before Dark	CD3	Germany	1990	$8.00
CBS	654636-3	Train	CD3	Germany	1989	$8.00

Nitty Gritty Dirt Band

Full Length

Label	Catalog Number	Title	Type	Country	Year	Longbox Value/Value
		Country Star Tracks	RS	U.S.	1991	$15.00
	Airdate: 8/10/91.					
Capitol		Live Two Five	LP/LB	U.S.		$16.00/$12.00
MCA		Rest of a Dream	LP/LB	U.S.		$16.00/$12.00
Pioneer	PA-83-034	Tonite	LD	U.S.	1983	$20.00
Warner Brothers		Workin' Band	LP/LB	U.S.		$16.00/$12.00

Singles

Label	Catalog Number	Title	Type	Country	Year	Longbox Value/Value
MCA	CD45 79013	From Small Things	CDJ	U.S.	1990	$2.00
Toshiba	XP10-2022	Mr. Bojangles	CD3	Japan	1988	$15.00/$4.00
Capitol	DPRO-79755	Mr. Bojangles	CDJ	U.S.	1991	$2.00
MCA	53964	Rest of the Dream, The	CDJ	U.S.	1990	$2.00
MCA	CD45 79075	You Made My Life Good Again	CDJ	U.S.	1990	$2.00

Nitzer Ebb

Full Length

Label	Catalog Number	Title	Type	Country	Year	Longbox Value/Value
Geffen	PRO-CD-4374	All States	DJ/Smplr	U.S.	1992	$12.00

Singles

Label	Catalog Number	Title	Type	Country	Year	Longbox Value/Value
Mute	826 957	As Is	CD5	Germany	1991	$9.00
Mute	ALCB-301	As Is	CD5	Japan	1991	$13.00
Mute	CDMUTE-122	As Is	CD5	U.K.	1991	$9.00
Mute	CDMUTE-145	Ascend	CD5	U.K.	1992	$9.00
Intercord	826 874	Control	CD5	Germany	1988	$9.00
Mute	CDMUTE-71	Control	CD5	U.K.	1988	$9.00
Mute	CDMUTE-115	Fun To Be Had	CD5	U.K.	1990	$9.00
Geffen	PRO-CDE-4137	Fun To Be Had	CDJ	U.S.	1990	$2.00
PWR	CDNEB-5	Get Clean	CD5	U.K.	1989	$9.00
Geffen	PRO-CD-4384	Godhead	CDJ	U.S.	1991	$2.00
Geffen	GEFDS 21705	Godhead	CD5	U.S.	1992	$5.00
Intercord	826 881	Hearts And Minds	CD5	Germany	1989	$9.00
Mute	CDMUTE-78	Hearts And Minds	CD5	U.K.	1989	$9.00
Intercord	826 966	I Give To You	CD5	Germany	1991	$9.00
Mute	133	I Give To You	CD5	U.K.	1991	$9.00
Geffen	PRO-CD-4334	I Give To You	CDJ	U.S.	1991	$2.00
PWR	CDNEB-1	Isn't It Funky	CD5	U.K.	1989	$9.00
		Kick It	CDJ	U.S.		$3.00
Intercord	826 924	Lightning Man	CD5	Germany	1990	$9.00
Mute	CDMUTE-106	Lightning Man	CD5	U.K.	1990	$9.00
Geffen	9 21602-2	Lightning Man	CD5	U.S.	1990	$4.00
Intercord	826 909	Shame	CD5	Germany	1989	$9.00
Mute	CDMUTE-96	Shame	CD5	U.K.	1989	$9.00
BCM	50-2016-44	Warsaw Ghetto	CD5	Germany	1988	$9.00
BCM	20037	Warsaw Ghetto	CD5	Germany	1988	$9.00
PWR	CDNEB-2	Warsaw Ghetto	CD5	U.K.	1988	$9.00
PWR	CDNEBX-2	Warsaw Ghetto	CD5	U.K.	1988	$9.00

Nivens

Singles

Label	Catalog Number	Title	Type	Country	Year	Longbox Value/Value
Pinnacle	DANCD-034	Play Blue	CD5	U.K.	1990	$8.00
Pinnacle	DANCD-085	Play Blue	CD5	U.K.	1992	$8.00
Pinnacle	DANCD-060	Recycle	CD5	U.K.	1991	$8.00

Nixon, Mojo

Singles

Label	Catalog Number	Title	Type	Country	Year	Longbox Value/Value
Atlantic		(619) 239–King	CDJ	U.S.	1989	$2.00
Atlantic	PRCD 3494-2	Destroy All Lawyers	CDJ	U.S.	1990	$2.00

Nixons

Full Length

Label	Catalog Number	Title	Type	Country	Year	Longbox Value/Value
MCA	MCAD-11209	Foma	DJ/LP	U.S.	1995	$14.00

Singles

Label	Catalog Number	Title	Type	Country	Year	Longbox Value/Value
MCA	MCA5P3535	Happy Song	CDJ	U.S.		$2.00
		Sister	CDJ	U.K.	1996	$10.00
MCA	MCA5P33700A	Sister	CDJ	U.S.		$2.00
MCA	DNXNT-1	Sweet Temptation	CD5	U.K.	1990	$8.00

No Clue

Singles

Label	Catalog Number	Title	Type	Country	Year	Longbox Value/Value
BMG	664434	Life Is Life	CD5	Germany	1991	$8.00

No Doubt

Full Length

Label	Catalog Number	Title	Type	Country	Year	Longbox Value/Value
Interscope		Live In Los Angeles	DJ/Smplr	U.S.	1996	$20.00
Trauma	PRCD 6667	Live In Los Angeles December 1995	DJ/Smplr	U.S.	1995	$20.00

Singles

Label	Catalog Number	Title	Type	Country	Year	Longbox Value/Value
Trauma	98116-2	Just A Girl	CD5	U.S.	1996	$5.00
Trauma	PRCD 6378	Just A Girl	CDJ	U.S.	1996	$7.00
Interscope		Spider Web	CD5	U.K.	1996	$10.00
	Enhanced CD.					
Trauma	PRCD 6634	Spiderwebs	CDJ	U.S.	1996	$3.00

No Hat Moon

Singles

Label	Catalog Number	Title	Type	Country	Year	Longbox Value/Value
Polydor	PZCD-244	Seasons	CD5	U.K.	1992	$8.00

No Man

Singles

Label	Catalog Number	Title	Type	Country	Year	Longbox Value / Value
Pinnacle	63-TP7CD	Ocean Song	CD5	U.K.	1992	$8.00
CBS	77463	Taking It Like a Man	CD5	U.S.	1994	$5.00
550 Music	5907	Taking It Like a Man	CDJ	U.S.	1994	$2.00

No Sweat

Singles

Label	Catalog Number	Title	Type	Country	Year	Longbox Value / Value
London	LONCD-274	Heart and Soul	CD5	U.K.	1990	$8.00
Polygram	869165-2	Heart and Soul	CD5	U.K.	1990	$8.00
Westwood One	LONCD-270	On the Edge	CD5	U.K.	1990	$8.00
London	LONCD-288	Tear Down the Walls	CD5	U.K.	1990	$8.00

No Two

Singles

Label	Catalog Number	Title	Type	Country	Year	Longbox Value / Value
A&M	CD 17736	Tourist	CDJ	U.S.	1989	$2.00

Noah, Tim

Full Length

Label	Catalog Number	Title	Type	Country	Year	Longbox Value / Value
A&M	0415	Kaddywompas	LP/LB	U.S.		$12.00/$7.00
A&M	0427	Super Tunes	LP/LB	U.S.		$12.00/$7.00

Nobody

Singles

Label	Catalog Number	Title	Type	Country	Year	Longbox Value / Value
WEA	WMD3-3021	Such a Sham	CD3	Japan	1992	$12.00/$3.00

Noel

Singles

Label	Catalog Number	Title	Type	Country	Year	Longbox Value / Value
Polydor	P15D-37001	Like a Child	CD3	Japan	1988	$12.00/$3.00

Noiseworks

Singles

Label	Catalog Number	Title	Type	Country	Year	Longbox Value / Value
Columbia	CSK 4263	Hot Chili Woman	CDJ	U.S.	1991	$2.00
		No Lies	CDJ	U.S.		$2.00
Epic	657371-2	R.I.P.	CD5	U.K.	1991	$8.00
Epic	654845-2	Simple Man	CD5	U.K.	1989	$8.00
Columbia	653010-3	Touch	CD3	Germany	1989	$8.00
Columbia	653010-2	Touch	CD3	U.K.	1989	$8.00
		Touch	CDJ	U.S.	1989	$2.00

Noisy Mama

Full Length

Label	Catalog Number	Title	Type	Country	Year	Longbox Value / Value
Atco	7 91399-2	Everybody Has One	LTD/LP	U.S.	1991	$50.00

Prototype jewel box.

Singles

Label	Catalog Number	Title	Type	Country	Year	Longbox Value / Value
Atco	PRCD 3865-2	Eyes on the Prize	CDJ	U.S.	1991	$2.00
Atco		Heart Of Stone	CDJ	U.S.		$2.00

Nomad

Singles

Label	Catalog Number	Title	Type	Country	Year	Longbox Value / Value
Rumor	RUMCD-60	24 Hours a Day	CD5	U.K.	1992	$8.00
ZYX	6430-8	(I Wanna Give You) Devotion	CD5	Germany	1991	$8.00
Alfa	ALDB-117	(I Wanna Give You) Devotion	CD3	Japan	1991	$13.00/$4.00
Alfa	ALDB-118	(I Wanna Give You) Devotion	CD3	Japan	1991	$13.00/$4.00
Alfa	ALCB-1290	(I Wanna Give You) Devotion	CD5	Japan	1991	$12.00
Rumor	RUMCD-25	(I Wanna Give You) Devotion	CD5	U.K.	1991	$8.00
Capitol	C2 15737	(I Wanna Give You) Devotion	CD5	U.S.	1991	$5.00
Capitol	DPRO-79766	(I Wanna Give You) Devotion	CDJ	U.S.	1991	$2.00
ZYX	6511-8	Just a Groove	CD5	Germany	1991	$8.00
Alfa	ALDB-137	Just a Groove	CD3	Japan	1991	$13.00/$4.00
Alfa	ALCB-359	Just a Groove	CD5	Japan	1991	$12.00
Rumor	RUMCD-33	Just a Groove	CD5	U.K.	1991	$8.00
ZYX	6580-8	Something Special	CD5	Germany	1991	$8.00
Alfa	ALCB-425	Something Special	CD5	Japan	1991	$12.00
Rumor	RUMCD-48	Your Love Is Lifting Me	CD5	U.K.	1991	$8.00

Nomad Soul

Singles

Label	Catalog Number	Title	Type	Country	Year	Longbox Value / Value
Island	CID-505	Candy Mountain	CD5	U.K.	1991	$8.00

Nomeansno

Singles

Label	Catalog Number	Title	Type	Country	Year	Longbox Value / Value
Wrong Stuff	13	Mr. Right & Mr. Wrong	CD5	U.S.	1994	$5.00

Nonce

Singles

Label	Catalog Number	Title	Type	Country	Year	Longbox Value / Value
Warner Brothers	41865	Mix Tapes	CD5	U.S.	1994	$5.00

Nonchalant

Singles

Label	Catalog Number	Title	Type	Country	Year	Longbox Value / Value
MCA	MCA5P3438	5 O'Clock	CDJ	U.S.		$2.00

Nontschew, Mirco

Singles

Label	Catalog Number	Title	Type	Country	Year	Longbox Value / Value
Pikosso	743 213 112 62	Only You	SCD5	Germany	1995	$15.00

Heart shaped disc.

Noone, Peter

Singles

Label	Catalog Number	Title	Type	Country	Year	Longbox Value / Value
Intercord	813 327	I'm Into Something Good	CD3	Germany	1989	$10.00
A&M	YD17714	I'm Into Something Good	CDJ	U.S.	1989	$12.00

Norberg, Erika

Singles

Label	Catalog Number	Title	Type	Country	Year	Longbox Value / Value
BMG	663979	Together We're Lost	CD5	Germany	1991	$8.00

Normal

Singles

Label	Catalog Number	Title	Type	Country	Year	Longbox Value / Value
Mute	71400	TVOD	CD3	U.K.	1988	$8.00
Intercord	826 919	Warm Leatherette	CD5	Germany	1989	$8.00

Norman

Singles

Label	Catalog Number	Title	Type	Country	Year	Longbox Value / Value
Columbia	COCY-5157	Days in the Three	CD3	Japan	1992	$12.00/$3.00

Norman, Chris

Singles

Label	Catalog Number	Title	Type	Country	Year	Longbox Value / Value
Polygram	8809495-2	Back Again	CD3	Germany	1989	$8.00
Polygram	8809494-3	Back Again	CD3	Germany	1989	$8.00
Polygram	867205-2	If You Need My Love Tonight	CD3	Germany	1991	$8.00

Norman, Jessye

Singles

Label	Catalog Number	Title	Type	Country	Year	Longbox Value / Value
Philips	42227-2	Amazing Grace	CD5	U.K.	1988	$8.00
Polygram	422922-2	La Marseilles	CD5	Germany	1989	$8.00

Northern Pikes

Singles

Label	Catalog Number	Title	Type	Country	Year	Longbox Value / Value
Scotti Brothers	ZSK 75301	Dream Away	CDJ	U.S.		$3.00
		Everything	CDJ	Canada		$5.00
Scotti Brothers	ZSK 75311	Girl With a Problem	CDJ	U.S.	1990	$2.00
		One Good Reason	CDJ	U.S.		$7.00
Scotti Brothers	ZSK 75287	She Ain't Pretty	CDJ	U.S.	1990	$2.00
		Teenland	CDJ	Canada		$5.00
		Wait For Me	CDJ	Canada		$5.00

Northside

Singles

Label	Catalog Number	Title	Type	Country	Year	Longbox Value / Value
Factory	FACD-298	My Rising Star	CD5	U.K.	1990	$8.00
Geffen	PRO-CD-4353	My Rising Star	CDJ	U.S.	1991	$2.00
Factory	FACD-308	Take 5	CD5	U.K.	1991	$8.00
Geffen	PRO-CD-4257	Take 5	CDJ	U.S.	1991	$2.00
Factory	FACD-268	Take a Trip	CD5	U.K.	1990	$8.00

Not Drowning, Waiving

Singles

Label	Catalog Number	Title	Type	Country	Year	Longbox Value / Value
Reprise	PRo-CD-6522	Spark	CDJ	U.S.	1993	$2.00

Nothing By Chance

Singles

Label	Catalog Number	Title	Type	Country	Year	Longbox Value / Value
Dover	ROJCD-1	Will Not Shelter	CD5	U.K.	1992	$8.00

Nothing Hillbillies

Singles

Label	Catalog Number	Title	Type	Country	Year	Longbox Value / Value
Warner Brothers	PRO-CD-4340	Bewildered	CDJ	U.S.	1990	$2.00
Polygram	875301-2	Feel Like Going Home	CD5	Germany	1990	$10.00
Vertigo	NHBCD-2	Feel Like Going Home	CD5	U.K.	1990	$10.00
Vertigo	NHBCD-3	Will You Miss Me	CD5	U.K.	1990	$10.00
Warner Brothers	PRO-CD-4092	Will You Miss Me	CDJ	U.S.	1990	$2.00
Polygram	875025-2	Your Own Sweet Way	CD5	Germany	1990	$10.00
Vertigo	NHBCD-1	Your Own Sweet Way	CD5	U.K.	1990	$10.00
Warner Brothers	PRO-CD-3943	Your Own Sweet Way	CDJ	U.S.	1990	$2.00

Notorious

Singles

Label	Catalog Number	Title	Type	Country	Year	Longbox Value / Value
WEA	9031-72418-2	Swalk, The	CD5	Germany	1990	$8.00
Bronze	BYZ-1CD	Swalk, The	CD5	U.K.	1990	$8.00
DGC	PRO-CD-4107	Swalk, The	CDJ	U.S.	1990	$2.00

Notorious Big

Singles

Label	Catalog Number	Title	Type	Country	Year	Longbox Value / Value
Arista	79016	Big Poppa	CD5	U.S.	1994	$5.00
Arista	79020	Big Poppa	CD5	U.S.	1995	$6.00
Arista	9015	Big Poppa	CD5	U.S.	1995	$3.00
Arista	179007	Juicy	CD5	U.S.	1994	$5.00

Nova, Aldo

Full Length

Label	Catalog Number	Title	Type	Country	Year	Longbox Value / Value
Portrait	RK-37498	Aldo Nova	LP/LB	U.S.†	1984	$14.00/$8.00

Singles

Label	Catalog Number	Title	Type	Country	Year	Longbox Value / Value
Mercury	PHDR-26	Blood on the Bricks	CD3	Japan	1991	$12.00/$4.00
Mercury	CDP 436	Blood on the Bricks	CDJ	U.S.	1991	$6.00
Mercury	CDP 571	Someday	CDJ	U.S.	1991	$2.00

Nova, Heather

Full Length

Label	Catalog Number	Title	Type	Country	Year	Longbox Value / Value
		AAA Sampler	DJ/Smplr	U.S.	1996	$8.00

Singles

Label	Catalog Number	Title	Type	Country	Year	Longbox Value / Value
		Maybe an Angel	CDJ	U.S.	1996	$7.00

Nova Mob

Singles

Label	Catalog Number	Title	Type	Country	Year	Longbox Value / Value
Rough Trade	R-267-2	Admiral of the Sea	CD5	U.K.	1994	$6.00
Rough Trade	267-2	Admiral of the Sea	CD5	U.S.	1994	$4.00

Novecento

Singles

Label	Catalog Number	Title	Type	Country	Year	Longbox Value / Value
Alfa	ALDB-40	Come To Me	CD3	Japan	1990	$12.00/$3.00
Zyx	7440	Wait For Me	CD5	U.S.	1994	$5.00

November One

Singles

Label	Catalog Number	Title	Type	Country	Year	Longbox Value / Value
Epic	CDNOV-2	Get Closer	CD5	U.K.	1988	$8.00
Epic	CDNOV-3	Someone Special	CD5	U.K.	1988	$8.00

Noville, John

Singles

Label	Catalog Number	Title	Type	Country	Year	Longbox Value / Value
Eastwest	171258-2	Crime & Passion	CD5	Germany	1990	$8.00
Eastwest	171136-2	I Know	CD5	Germany	1990	$8.00
Eastwest	171260-2	I Know	CD5	Germany	1990	$8.00
Eastwest	9031-73752-2	Politicians	CD5	Germany	1990	$8.00

NRBQ

Full Length

Label	Catalog Number	Title	Type	Country	Year	Longbox Value / Value
Rhino		Message For the Mass Age	DJ/LP	U.S.	1994	$15.00
Virgin	PRCD 2962	One and Only, The	DJ/Smplr	U.S.	1989	$14.00

Singles

Label	Catalog Number	Title	Type	Country	Year	Longbox Value / Value
Virgin		A Little Bit Of Bad Luck	CDJ	U.S.		$6.00
Virgin	PRCD 3115	If I Don't Have You	CDJ	U.S.	1989	$6.00
Virgin	PRCD 2962	It's a Wild Weekend	CDJ	U.S.	1989	$6.00
Rhino	PRCD 7045	Message For the Mass Age	CDJ	U.S.	1994	$8.00
Rhino	PRCD 7065	Over Your Head	CDJ	U.S.	1994	$8.00

NRG

Singles

Label	Catalog Number	Title	Type	Country	Year	Longbox Value / Value
Swanyard	CDSYR-16	Band Of Gold	CD5	U.K.	1990	$9.00
Big Beat	10121	I Need Your Love	CD5	U.S.		$4.00

Nu Colours

Singles

Label	Catalog Number	Title	Type	Country	Year	Longbox Value / Value
Polydor	CDP 896	Fallin' Down	CDJ	U.S.	1993	$2.00
Wildcard	CARDD-3	Power	CD5	U.K.	1992	$8.00
Wildcard	CARDD-1	Tears	CD5	U.K.	1992	$8.00

Nu Girls

Singles

Label	Catalog Number	Title	Type	Country	Year	Longbox Value / Value
Atlantic		Can We Talk About It?	CDJ	U.S.	1989	$2.00
Atlantic	PRCD 2937-2	Rush on Me	CDJ	U.S.	1989	$2.00

Nu Shooz

Singles

Label	Catalog Number	Title	Type	Country	Year	Longbox Value / Value
		Driftin'	CDJ	U.S.		$2.00
Pioneer	10SW-29	Should I Say Yes?	CD3	Japan	1988	$13.00/$4.00

Label	Catalog Number	Title	Type	Country	Year	Longbox Value / Value
		Should I Say Yes?	CDJ	U.S.	1988	$2.00
Atlantic	7567-85827-2	Time Will Tell	CD5	Germany	1992	$8.00
Atlantic	A-7440CD	Time Will Tell	CD5	U.K.	1992	$8.00

Nu Soul Habits

Label	Catalog Number	Title	Type	Country	Year	Longbox Value / Value
Singles						
Motown	3746311	Meant To Be	CDJ	U.S.	1994	$2.00

Nuclear Valdez

Label	Catalog Number	Title	Type	Country	Year	Longbox Value / Value
Full Length						
Epic	ESK 4121	Dream Another Dream	DJ/LP	U.S.	1991	$15.00
Singles						
Epic		Hope	CDJ	U.S.		$2.00
Epic	65741-2	Share a Little Shelter	CD5	Germany	1991	$10.00
Epic	65741-2	Share a Little Shelter	CD5	U.K.	1991	$10.00
Epic	ESK 4112	Share a Little Shelter	CDJ	U.S.	1991	$2.00
Epic	ESK 74159	Share a Little Shelter	CDJ	U.S.	1991	$2.00
Epic	655911-2	Summer	CD5	U.K.	1990	$10.00
Epic		Summer	CDJ	U.S.	1990	$2.00

Nudeswirl

Label	Catalog Number	Title	Type	Country	Year	Longbox Value / Value
Singles						
Megaforce	641	F Sharp	CDJ	U.S.	1993	$2.00
Megaforce	974	F Sharp	CDJ	U.S.	1993	$2.00

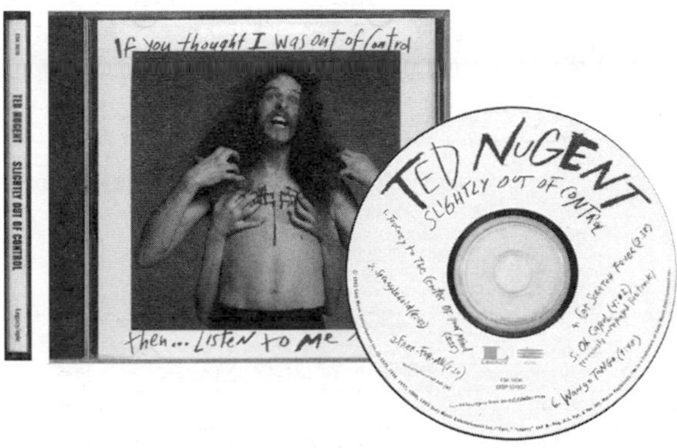

Nugent, Ted – Slightly Out Of Control (Legacy/Epic ESK 5036)

Nugent, Ted

Label	Catalog Number	Title	Type	Country	Year	Longbox Value / Value
Full Length						
		Call of the Wild	LP/LB	U.S.		$14.00/$10.00
		Fixed	LP/LB	U.S.		$15.00/$12.00
Album Network		In the Studio (Cat Scratch Fever)	RS	U.S.		$20.00
Album Network		In the Studio (Free For All/Cat Scratch Fever)	RS	U.S.		$20.00
Album Network		In the Studio (Ted Nugent)	RS	U.S.	1990	$25.00
Airdate: 10/1/90.						
Legacy	ESK 5036	Slightly Out of Control	DJ/Smplr	U.S.	1993	$15.00
Legacy/Epic	ESK 5036	Slightly Out of Control	DJ/Smplr	U.S.	1993	$25.00
		Tooth Fang & Claw	LP/LB	U.S.		$14.00/$10.00
Singles						
		Fred Bear	CDJ	U.S.	1994	$6.00

Numan, Gary

Label	Catalog Number	Title	Type	Country	Year	Longbox Value / Value
Full Length						
		Automatic	LP	U.K.	1989	$25.00
		Skin Mechanic	LP/LB	U.S.		$12.00/$8.00
Singles						
Illegal	ILSCD-1004	America	CD5	U.K.	1988	$10.00
Numa	NUCD-22	Emotion	CD5	U.K.	1991	$10.00
Alfa	ALDB-10	Exhibition	CD3	Japan	1990	$12.00/$4.00
IRS	NUMANCD-1	Heart	CD5	U.K.	1991	$10.00
		Like A Refugee	CD5	U.K.	1994	$10.00
		Like A Refugee	CD5	U.K.	1994	$10.00
Second version.						
Numa	NUCD-124	Machine & Soul	CD5	U.K.	1992	$10.00
Illegal	ILSCD-1003	New Anger	CD5	U.K.	1988	$10.00
Strange Frt	SFPMACD-202	Peel Sessions	CD5	U.K.	1989	$9.00
Numa	NUCD-23	Skin Game	CD5	U.K.	1991	$10.00

Numarx

Label	Catalog Number	Title	Type	Country	Year	Longbox Value / Value
Singles						
ZYX	6380-8	Do It Good	CD5	Germany	1990	$6.00
ZYX	5887-8	Girl You Know It's True	CD5	Germany	1990	$6.00

Nunn, Terri

Label	Catalog Number	Title	Type	Country	Year	Longbox Value / Value
Full Length						
DGC	PRO-CD-4337	Special Sampler	DJ/Smplr	U.S.	1991	$10.00
Singles						
DGC	PRO-CD-4347	89 Lines	CDJ	U.S.	1991	$2.00
DGC	PRO-CD-4428	89 Lines	CDJ	U.S.	1992	$2.00
Mercury	PHDR-56	Let Me Be the One	CD3	Japan	1991	$12.00/$4.00
DGC	PRO-CD-4330	Let Me Be the One	CDJ	U.S.	1991	$2.00
DGC	PRO-CD-4337	Take My Breath Away	CDJ	U.S.	1991	$2.00

Nunnally, Keith

Label	Catalog Number	Title	Type	Country	Year	Longbox Value / Value
Singles						
Giant	W-0079CD	Freedom	CD5	U.K.	1992	$8.00

Nuttin' Nyce

Label	Catalog Number	Title	Type	Country	Year	Longbox Value / Value
Singles						
Jive	42260	Down 4 Whateva	CD5	U.S.	1994	$5.00
		In My Nature	CD5	U.K.		$10.00
		In My Nature	CD5	U.K.		$10.00
Second version.						

Nylons

Label	Catalog Number	Title	Type	Country	Year	Longbox Value / Value
Full Length						
Open Air	OD-0301	One Size Fits All	LP/LB	U.S.†	1985	$14.00/$8.00
Open Air	OD-0304	Seamless	LP/LB	U.S.†	1985	$14.00/$8.00
Singles						
Scotti Brothers	ZSK 75350	Don't Look Any Further	CDJ	U.S.	1992	$2.00
Windham Hill	CD 17898	Drift Away	CDJ	U.S.	1989	$2.00
Windham Hill	WD 17709	Poison Ivy	CDJ	U.S.	1989	$2.00
Alfa	09B3-42	Wildfire	CD3	Japan	1989	$13.00/$4.00
Windham Hill	WD 17807	Wildfire	CDJ	U.S.	1989	$2.00

Nyman, Michael

Label	Catalog Number	Title	Type	Country	Year	Longbox Value / Value
Full Length						
Virgin		Piano, The	LTD/LP	U.S.	1994	$30.00
Gold CD in box with booklet.						
Singles						
		Piano	CD5	U.K.		$10.00
Virgin	14127	Piano, The	CDJ	U.S.	1993	$2.00

Nymphs

Label	Catalog Number	Title	Type	Country	Year	Longbox Value / Value
Singles						
DGC	DGCTD 8	Imitating Angels	CD5	U.S.	1991	$8.00
DGC	PRO-CD-4385	Imitating Angels	CDJ	U.S.	1991	$2.00
DGC	PRO-CD-4342	Sad and Dammed	CDJ	U.S.	1991	$2.00

Nyro, Laura

Label	Catalog Number	Title	Type	Country	Year	Longbox Value / Value
Singles						
Columbia	CSK 5304	A Woman of the World	CDJ	U.S.	1993	$2.00

O.C.

Label	Catalog Number	Title	Type	Country	Year	Longbox Value / Value
Singles						
Capital	58312	Born To Live	CD5	U.S.	1994	$5.00

O.C.P.

Label	Catalog Number	Title	Type	Country	Year	Longbox Value / Value
Singles						
SPV	1014-3	Make It Funny	CD5	Germany	1991	$8.00

O For The

Label	Catalog Number	Title	Type	Country	Year	Longbox Value / Value
Singles						
Vox Box	8778	Wings of Angels	CD5	U.S.	1994	$5.00

O Positive

Label	Catalog Number	Title	Type	Country	Year	Longbox Value / Value
Singles						
Epic	ESK 2032	Back Of My Mind	CDJ	U.S.	1990	$2.00
Epic	ESK 2026	Back Of My Mind	CDJ	U.S.	1990	$6.00
Epic	ESK 2122	Imagine That	CDJ	U.S.	1990	$2.00

O'Connell, Maura

Label	Catalog Number	Title	Type	Country	Year	Longbox Value / Value
Full Length						
Warner Brothers	PRO-CD-4638	A Real Life Story	DJ/LP	U.S.	1991	$10.00
Picture disc.						
Singles						
	VHCD1389	Blue Chalk	CDJ	U.S.		$2.00
Warner Brothers	PRO-CD-4715	Guns of Loves	CDJ	U.S.	1990	$2.00

O'Connor, Hazel

Label	Catalog Number	Title	Type	Country	Year	Longbox Value / Value
Singles						
A&M	390338-2	Compact Hits	CD5	Germany	1988	$8.00
A&M	AMCD-902	Compact Hits	CD5	U.K.	1988	$8.00

O'Connor, Mark

Label	Catalog Number	Title	Type	Country	Year	Longbox Value / Value
Singles						
Warner Brothers	PRo-CD-5103	Bowtie	CDJ	U.S.	1991	$2.00
Warner Brothers	PRO-CD-6202	Devil Comes Back To Georgia	CDJ	U.S.	1994	$2.00
Warner Brothers		Idle Rain	CDJ	U.S.		$2.00

O'Connor, Sinéad

Label	Catalog Number	Title	Type	Country	Year	Longbox Value / Value
Full Length						
Chrysalis	CD25CR13	I Do Not Want What I Have Not Got	LTD/LP	U.K.	1994	$25.00/$15.00
25th Anniversary edition in 6"x11" longbox.						
Chrysalis	SPCD-1112	Special DJ Copy	DJ/Smplr	Japan	1993	$100.00
Chrysalis		Thank You For Hearing Me	DJ/Smplr	U.S.	1994	$30.00
Singles						
Chrysalis	TODP-2374	Am I Not Your Girlfriend?	CD3	Japan	1992	$15.00/$4.00
Chrysalis		Am I Not Your Girlfriend?	CDJ	U.S.	1992	$2.00
Ensign	CDENYS-657	Don't Cry For Me	CD5	U.K.	1991	$10.00
EMI	323547-2	Emperor's New Clothes, The	CD5	Germany	1990	$10.00
Ensign	TOCP-6251	Emperor's New Clothes, The	CD5	Japan	1990	$15.00
Ensign	EYNCD-633	Emperor's New Clothes, The	CD5	U.K.	1990	$10.00
Chrysalis	F2 23585	Emperor's New Clothes, The	CD5	U.S.	1990	$5.00
Charisma	23528	Emperor's New Clothes, The	CDJ	U.S.	1990	$2.00
		Empire	CDJ	U.S.	1996	$7.00
Chrysalis		Fire on Babylon	CDJ	U.S.	1994	$6.00
Aris	880879	I Want Your (Hands on Me)	CD5	Germany	1988	$10.00
Ensign	EYNCD-613	I Want Your (Hands on Me)	CD5	U.K.	1988	$10.00
Ensign	EYNCD-618	Jump in the River	CD5	U.K.	1988	$10.00
BMG	65912	Mandinka	CD5	Germany	1988	$10.00
Ensign	ENY CD611	Mandinka	CD5	U.K.	1987	$10.00
CBS	VKCDS-43733	My Special Child	CD5	Canada	1991	$10.00
EMI	323733-2	My Special Child	CD5	Germany	1991	$10.00
Chrysalis	TODP-2310	My Special Child	CD3	Japan	1991	$15.00/$4.00
Ensign	ENYCD646	My Special Child	CD5	U.K.	1991	$10.00
Chrysalis	F2 23733	My Special Child	CD5	U.S.	1991	$5.00
Chrysalis	323488-2	Nothing Compares 2 U	CD5	Germany	1991	$10.00
Ensign	ENYCD-630	Nothing Compares 2 U	CD5	U.K.	1991	$10.00
Chrysalis		Nothing Compares 2 U	CD5	U.S.	1991	$5.00
Chrysalis	DPRO-23488	Nothing Compares 2 U	CDJ	U.S.	1991	$3.00
Ensign	323839-2	Silent Night	CD5	Germany	1991	$10.00
Ensign	ENYCD-652	Silent Night	CD5	U.K.	1991	$10.00
Ensign	23898-9	Success Has Made a Failure of Our Home	CD5	U.K.	1992	$10.00
Chrysalis		Thank You For Hearing Me	CDJ	U.S.	1994	$6.00
		Thief of Your Heart	CD5	U.K.	1994	$10.00
Ensign	323598-2	Three Babies	CD5	Germany	1990	$10.00
Ensign	ENYCD-635	Three Babies	CD5	U.K.	1990	$10.00
		You Make Me Feel	CDJ	Spain		$20.00

O'Day, Anita

Label	Catalog Number	Title	Type	Country	Year	Longbox Value / Value
Full Length						
GML	GML-30201	Here Is Anita	LTD/LP	Japan		$30.00
Gold disc.						

O'Donnell, Daniel

Label	Catalog Number	Title	Type	Country	Year	Longbox Value / Value
Singles						
Ritz	RITZCD-250	I Just Want To Dance With You	CD5	U.K.	1992	$8.00

O'Hara, Mary Margret

Label	Catalog Number	Title	Type	Country	Year	Longbox Value / Value
Singles						
Virgin	PRCD 2863	Body's In Trouble	CDJ	U.S.	1988	$2.00
Virgin	VSCDG-1395	Christmas	CD5	U.K.	1991	$8.00
Virgin	VSCDG-1225	Ne Day	CD5	U.K.	1989	$8.00

O'Hearn, Patrick

Singles

Label	Catalog Number	Title	Type	Country	Year	Longbox Value / Value
Private	2076	Black Delilah	CDJ	U.S.	1990	$2.00
		Homeward Bound	CDJ	U.S.		$2.00

O'Jays

Singles

Label	Catalog Number	Title	Type	Country	Year	Longbox Value / Value
EMI	DPRO-04665	Don't Let Me Down	CDJ	U.S.	1990	$2.00
EMI	CDMT-96	Emotionally Yours	CD5	U.K.	1991	$8.00
EMI	DPRO-04738	Emotionally Yours	CDJ	U.S.	1991	$2.00
MCA	22137	From The Beginning	CD5	U.S.	1994	$5.00
EMI	DPRO-04273	Have You Had Your Love Today	CDJ	U.S.	1989	$2.00
EMI	DPRO-4828	I Can Hardly Wait Till Christmas	CDJ	U.S.	1991	$2.00
CBS	651664-3	I Love Music	CD5	Germany	1988	$8.00
CBS	651664-3	I Love Music	CD5	U.K.	1988	$8.00
EMI	DPRO 4782	Keep on Lovin' Me	CDJ	U.S.	1991	$2.00
EMI	DPRO-04364	Out of My Mind	CDJ	U.S.	1989	$2.00
Old Gold	OG-6508	Put Our Heads	CD5	U.K.	1990	$10.00
EMI		Reunion	CDJ	U.S.		$2.00
EMI	DPRO-04542	Somebody Else Will	CDJ	U.S.	1993	$2.00

O'Kane, John

Singles

Label	Catalog Number	Title	Type	Country	Year	Longbox Value / Value
Circa	YRCD-75	Dance Goes On	CD5	U.K.	1991	$10.00
Circa	YRCD-88	Stay With Me	CD5	U.K.	1991	$10.00

O'Kanes

Singles

Label	Catalog Number	Title	Type	Country	Year	Longbox Value / Value
Chrysalis		One True Love	CDJ	U.S.		$2.00
Chrysalis	DPRO-73445	Tell Me I Was Dreaming	CDJ	U.S.	1990	$2.00

O'Neal, Alexander

Full Length

Label	Catalog Number	Title	Type	Country	Year	Longbox Value / Value
CBS	40320	Hearsay	LP/LB	U.S.		$12.00/$7.00
Tabu	31458 8149	Love Makes No Sense For	DJ/Smplr	U.S.	1993	$8.00
CBS	45016	My Gift To You	LP/LB	U.S.		$12.00/$7.00

Singles

Label	Catalog Number	Title	Type	Country	Year	Longbox Value / Value
Columbia	656571-2	All True Man	CD5	Germany	1991	$8.00
Tabu	3032	All True Man	CDJ	U.S.	1991	$2.00
Tabu	73626	All True Man	CDJ	U.S.	1991	$2.00
Tabu	31458 8174	Aphrodidia	CDJ	U.S.	1993	$2.00
Tabu	31458 8192	Aphrodidia	CDJ	U.S.	1993	$2.00
Epic	658249-2	Broken Heart Can Mend	CD5	U.K.	1992	$8.00
Columbia	655095-3	Fake	CD3	Germany	1989	$8.00
Tabu	652949-2	Fake	CD5	U.K.	1989	$8.00
Columbia	655049-3	Fake 88	CD3	Germany	1988	$8.00
Columbia	654667-3	Hearsay 89	CD3	Germany	1989	$8.00
Tabu	654667-2	Hearsay 89	CD5	U.K.	1989	$8.00
Columbia	655050-3	Hitmix	CD3	Germany	1989	$8.00
Tabu	655504-2	Hitmix	CD5	U.K.	1989	$8.00
Tabu	31458 8113	In the Middle	CDJ	U.S.	1993	$2.00
Tabu	31458 8154	In the Middle	CDJ	U.S.	1993	$2.00
A&M	AMCD-7708	Love Makes No Sense	CD5	U.K.	1993	$8.00
Tabu	31458 8082	Love Makes No Sense	CDJ	U.S.	1993	$2.00
Tabu	651595-3	Lovers, The	CD3	Germany	1988	$8.00
Tabu	651595-2	Lovers, The	CD5	U.K.	1988	$8.00
Tabu	ZSK 1003	Never Knew Love Like This	CDJ	U.S.	1988	$8.00
Tabu	651382-2	Never Know Love Was Like This	CD5	U.K.	1988	$8.00
Tabu	ZSK 1003	Never Know Love Was Like This	CDJ	U.S.	1988	$3.00
Tabu	654511-3	Our First Christmas	CD5	Germany	1988	$8.00
Epic	658014-2	Sentimental	CD5	U.K.	1992	$8.00
Tabu	656873-2	Shame on Me	CD5	U.K.	1991	$8.00
Tabu	655191-2	Sunshine And Rain	CD5	U.K.	1989	$8.00
Sony	15EP-8022	Tabu Nights	CD3	Japan	1989	$13.00/$4.00
Tabu	653182-2	Thank You For a Good Year	CD5	U.K.	1988	$8.00
Tabu	654533-2	Thank You For a Good Year	CD5	U.K.	1988	$8.00
Tabu	652731-2	What Can I Say To Make You Love Me	CD5	Germany	1988	$8.00
Tabu	652852-2	What Can I Say To Make You Love Me	CD5	U.K.	1988	$8.00
Tabu	656731-2	What Can I Say To Make You Love Me	CD5	U.K.	1988	$8.00
Tabu	73880	What Can I Say To Make You Love Me	CDJ	U.S.	1990	$2.00

O'Neal, De De

Singles

Label	Catalog Number	Title	Type	Country	Year	Longbox Value / Value
Tabu	ZSK 3032	All True Man	CDJ	U.S.	1990	$2.00
Tabu	ZSK 73626	All True Man	CDJ	U.S.	1991	$2.00
Tabu	ZSK 1871	Little Drummer Boy, The	CDJ	U.S.	1989	$2.00
		Vulnerable	CDJ	U.S.		$2.00
Epic	ESK 73810	What Is This Thing Called	CDJ	U.S.	1990	$2.00
Tabu	ZSK 73880	Yoke, The	CDJ	U.S.	1991	$2.00

O'Neal, Shaquille

Singles

Label	Catalog Number	Title	Type	Country	Year	Longbox Value / Value
Jive	42266	Biological Didn't Bother	CD5	U.S.	1994	$5.00
Jive	JDJ 42176-2	(I Know I Got) Skillz	CDJ	U.S.	1993	$3.00
Jive	42200	I'm Outstanding	CD5	U.S.	1993	$5.00
Jive	JDJ 42000-2	I'm Outstanding	CDJ	U.S.	1993	$3.00
Jive	42200	I'm Outstanding	CD5	U.S.	1994	$5.00
Jive	42283	No Hook	CD5	U.S.	1994	$5.00
Jive	42283	No Hook	CD5	U.S.	1994	$5.00

O'Sullivan, Gilbert

Singles

Label	Catalog Number	Title	Type	Country	Year	Longbox Value / Value
Kitty	KTDR-2052	Alone Again	CD3	Japan	1992	$12.00/$3.00
Dover	ROJCD-6	At the Very Mention of Your Name	CD5	U.K.	1990	$8.00
Pinnacle	PRKCD-15	Can't Think Straight	CD5	U.K.	1992	$8.00
Dover	ROJCD-1	Lost a Friend	CD5	U.K.	1990	$8.00
Eastwest	171429-2	So What	CD5	Germany	1990	$8.00
Dover	ROJCD-3	So What	CD5	U.K.	1990	$8.00

O'Williams, Wendy

Full Length

Label	Catalog Number	Title	Type	Country	Year	Longbox Value / Value
Passport	PBCD-6034	W.O.W.	LP/BP	U.S.		$16.00/$12.00

Oak Ridge Boys

Full Length

Label	Catalog Number	Title	Type	Country	Year	Longbox Value / Value
Warner Sound Exchange		40 Legendary Hits	LTD/LP	U.S.	1995	$30.00
	2 CD set.					
MCA	MCAD-5496	Greatest Hits	LP/LB	U.S.†	1985	$14.00/$8.00
MCA		Room Service	LP/LB	U.S.		$14.00/$8.00
MCA		Seasons	LP/LB	U.S.		$14.00/$8.00
MCA	MCAD-5555	Step On Out	LP/LB	U.S.†	1985	$14.00/$8.00
MCA	MCAD-5555	Step On Out	LP/LB	U.S.	1985	$14.00/$8.00
MCA		Together	LP/LB	U.S.		$14.00/$8.00
		Unstoppable	DJ/Intvw	U.S.		$20.00

Singles

Label	Catalog Number	Title	Type	Country	Year	Longbox Value / Value
MCA	CD45 79006	You'll Be My Baby	CDJ	U.S.	1989	$2.00

Oakley, Philip

Full Length

Label	Catalog Number	Title	Type	Country	Year	Longbox Value / Value
A&M	CD-5080	Philip Oakley and Giorgio Moroder	LP/LB	U.S.†	1985	$14.00/$8.00

Oaktown's 357

Singles

Label	Catalog Number	Title	Type	Country	Year	Longbox Value / Value
Capitol	DPRO-79138	Hickeys On Your Chest	CDJ	U.S.	1989	$2.00
Capitol	C2 15776	Honey	CD5	U.S.	1991	$5.00
Capitol	DPRO-79928	Honey	CDJ	U.S.	1991	$2.00
Capitol	DPRO-79021	It's Not Your Money	CDJ	U.S.	1991	$2.00
Capitol		Juicy Gotcha Krazy	CDJ	U.S.		$2.00
Capitol	C2 15729	Turn It Up	CD5	U.S.	1991	$5.00
Capitol	DPRO-79744	Turn It Up	CDJ	U.S.	1991	$2.00
Capitol	DPRO-79172	We Like It	CDJ	U.S.	1990	$2.00

Oasis

Full Length

Label	Catalog Number	Title	Type	Country	Year	Longbox Value / Value
CBS		Definitely Maybe	DJ/Smplr	Australia	1994	$22.00
CBS		Definitely Maybe	LTD/LP	Australia	1994	$35.00
	2 CD set.					
CBS		Definitely Maybe	DJ/Smplr	U.K.	1994	$18.00
Epic		Definitely Maybe	DJ/Smplr	U.S.	1994	$18.00
Westwood One		In Concert	RS	U.S.	1995	$60.00
	Airdate: 6/5/95.					
Westwood One		In Concert-Nu Rock	RS	U.S.	1995	$60.00
	Airdate: 10/23/95.					
Westwood One		In Concert-Nu Rock	RS	U.S.	1996	$60.00
	Airdate: 3/11/96.					
Epic		Live at the Caberet Metro	DJ/Smplr	U.S.	1994	$75.00
	CD sampler in paper sleeve.					
CBS		Live Footage	DJ/Smplr	France	1994	$60.00
Westwood One		Live From Knebworth	RS	U.S.	1996	$80.00
	2 CD set. Airdate: 8/17/96.					
Media America		Up Close	RS	U.S.	1995	$35.00
Epic		What's the Story	DJ/LP	U.S.	1994	$18.00

Singles

Label	Catalog Number	Title	Type	Country	Year	Longbox Value / Value
Sony		CD Singles Collection	CD5	Australia	1996	$35.00
	4 CD set.					
Sony		CD Singles Collection Volume 1	CD5	Canada	1996	$40.00
	4 CD set.					
Sony		CD Singles Collection Volume 2	CD5	Canada	1996	$40.00
	4 CD set.					
Epic	ESK 7719	Champagne Supernova	CDJ	U.S.	1994	$6.00
Sony	XEUK11660729	Cigarettes & Alcohol	CD5	U.K.	1994	$9.00
Creation		Come On Feel the Noize	CDJ	U.K.	1995	$15.00
CBS		Don't Look Back in Anger	CD5	U.K.	1994	$10.00
Epic		Don't Look Back in Anger	CDJ	U.S.	1994	$10.00
CBS		Live Forever	CD5	U.K.	1994	$10.00
CBS	77830	Live Forever	CD5	U.S.	1994	$5.00
Epic		Live Forever	CDJ	U.S.	1994	$6.00
Epic	ESCA-6392	Look Back In Anger	CD5	Japan	1995	$20.00
Epic	ESK 7302	Morning Glory	CDJ	U.S.		$6.00
Epic	ESK 7042	Rock 'n Roll Star	CDJ	U.S.	1994	$6.00
CBS		Roll With It	CD5	U.K.	1995	$11.00
CBS		Roll With It	CDJ	U.K.	1995	$12.00
CBS		Some Might Say	CD5	U.K.	1995	$10.00
CBS		Some Might Say	CDJ	U.K.	1995	$12.00
CBS		Some Might Say	CDJ	U.K.	1995	$12.00
	Second version.					
Epic	ESK 7440	Supersonic	CDJ	U.S.	1994	$6.00
Epic		Whatever	CDJ	U.K.	1994	$12.00
Epic	ESCA-6378	Wonderwall	CD5	Japan	1995	$20.00
CBS		Wonderwall	CD5	U.K.	1995	$10.00
Epic	ESK 7440	Wonderwall	CDJ	U.S.	1995	$6.00

Object

Singles

Label	Catalog Number	Title	Type	Country	Year	Longbox Value / Value
SPV	0813-3	Terminator 2	CD3	Germany	1991	$8.00
OSPV	0813-3R	Terminator 2	CD5	Germany	1991	$8.00

Obsessed

Singles

Label	Catalog Number	Title	Type	Country	Year	Longbox Value / Value
Columbia	CSK 5693	Streetside	CDJ	U.S.	1994	$2.00

Obsession

Full Length

Label	Catalog Number	Title	Type	Country	Year	Longbox Value / Value
Enigma	32XB-194	Methods of Madness	LP	Japan		$35.00
Enigma	CDE-73262	Methods of Madness	LP/LB	U.S.		$25.00/$23.00

Ocasek, Ric

Full Length

Label	Catalog Number	Title	Type	Country	Year	Longbox Value / Value
Reprise	9 26552-2-Dj	Fireball Zone	DJ/LP	U.S.	1991	$10.00
Warner Brothers	CDW 45248	Negative Theatre	LP	Canada	1993	$65.00
	Never offically released.					

Singles

Label	Catalog Number	Title	Type	Country	Year	Longbox Value / Value
Reprise	PRO-CD-6530	Don't Let Go	CDJ	U.S.	1993	$2.00
Reprise	PRO-CD-4833	Rockaway	CDJ	U.S.	1991	$3.00
Reprise	PRO-CD-5100	Way You Look Tonight	CDJ	U.S.	1991	$3.00

Ocean, Billy

Full Length

Label	Catalog Number	Title	Type	Country	Year	Longbox Value / Value
	PDTD-1062	Special Sampler	DJ/Smplr	Japan		$35.00
Jive	JRCD-8213	Suddenly	LP/BP	U.S.†	1985	$14.00/$8.00

Singles

Label	Catalog Number	Title	Type	Country	Year	Longbox Value / Value
Eastwest	247304-2	Calypso Crazy	CD5	Germany	1989	$10.00
Jive	BOSCD-2	Calypso Crazy	CD5	U.K.	1989	$10.00
Jive	BOSCD-3	Colour of Love	CD5	U.K.	1988	$10.00
Jive	BVDQ-4	Everything's So Different Without You	CD3	Japan	1993	$12.00/$4.00
Jive	JDJ 42135-2	Everything's So Different Without You	CD5	U.S.	1993	$2.00
Alfa	10SP-1	Get Outa My Dreams	CD3	Japan	1988	$12.00/$4.00
Jive	BOSCD-1	Get Outa My Dreams	CD5	U.K.	1988	$10.00
Jive	9678-2	Get Outa My Dreams	CDJ	US.	1988	$2.00
		Get Outta My Dreams, Get Into My Car	CDJ	U.S.		$2.00
		I Sleep Much Better	CDJ	U.S.		$2.00
Jive	1311-2-JDJ	I Sleep Much Better	CDJ	U.S.	1989	$2.00
RCA	ZD-43126	License to Chill	CD5	Germany	1989	$10.00
Alfa	09B3-74	License to Chill	CD3	Japan	1989	$12.00/$4.00
Jive	BOSCD-5	License to Chill	CD5	U.K.	1989	$10.00
RCA	1279-2-RDj	License to Chill	CDJ	U.S.	1989	$2.00
Jive	BVDQ-3	Pressure	CD3	Japan	1993	$12.00/$4.00
Jive	BOSCD-6	Pressure	CD5	U.K.	1993	$10.00
Eastwest	247571-2	Stand and Deliver	CD5	Germany	1993	$10.00
Jive	BOSCD-4	Stand and Deliver	CD5	U.K.	1993	$10.00
Alfa	10SP-19	Tear Down These Walls	CD3	Japan	1988	$12.00/$4.00

Ocean Blue

Full Length

Label	Catalog Number	Title	Type	Country	Year	Longbox Value/Value
Westwood One		In Concert-Nu Rock	RS	U.S.	1994	$70.00
Airdate: 6/20/94.						

Singles

Label	Catalog Number	Title	Type	Country	Year	Longbox Value/Value
Sire	PRO-CD-5106	Ballerina Out of Control	CDJ	U.S.		$2.00
		Between Something And Nothing	CDJ	U.S.		$2.00
Sire	PRO-CD-3963	Drifting, Falling	CDJ	U.S.	1989	$2.00
Sire	PRO-CD-5257	Mercury	CDJ	U.S.	1990	$2.00
Sire	PRO-CD-6384	Sublime	CDJ	U.S.	1993	$2.00

Ocean Bluff

Singles

Label	Catalog Number	Title	Type	Country	Year	Longbox Value/Value
	DPRO 10419	Save Me	CDJ	U.S.		$2.00

Ocean Colour Scene

Singles

Label	Catalog Number	Title	Type	Country	Year	Longbox Value/Value
Fontana	OSCD-3	DoYourself a Favor	CD5	U.K.	1992	$8.00
Fontana	CDP 859	DoYourself a Favor	CDJ	US.	1992	$5.00
Fontana	OSCD-2	Giving It All Away	CD5	U.K.	1992	$8.00
Fontana	OSCD-1	Sway	CD5	U.K.	1992	$8.00
Fontana	CDP 738	Sway	CDJ	U.S.	1992	$2.00
Polygram	PHCR-8012	Yesterday Today	CD5	Japan	1991	$12.00
Polygram	FITCD-002	Yesterday Today	CD5	U.K.	1991	$8.00

Oceanic

Singles

Label	Catalog Number	Title	Type	Country	Year	Longbox Value/Value
Dead Good	GOOD-14CD	Controlling Me	CD5	U.K.	1992	$8.00
Dead Good	GOOD-22CD	Ignorance	CD5	U.K.	1992	$8.00
Eastwest	9031-75568-2	Insanity	CD5	Germany	1992	$8.00
Dead Good	GOOD-4CD	Insanity	CD5	U.K.	1992	$8.00
Rough Trade	244 0209 2	Wished Love	CD5	Germany	1991	$8.00
Dead Good	GOOD-5CD	Wicked Love	CD5	U.K.	1991	$8.00

Ochs, Phil

Full Length

Label	Catalog Number	Title	Type	Country	Year	Longbox Value/Value
Mobile Fidelity		Gunfight At Carnegie Hall	LP/LB	U.S.		$23.00/$20.00

October Project

Full Length

Label	Catalog Number	Title	Type	Country	Year	Longbox Value/Value
Epic	ESK 5413	October Project	DJ/LP	U.S.	1993	$10.00

Singles

Label	Catalog Number	Title	Type	Country	Year	Longbox Value/Value
Epic	ESK 5652	Be My Hero	CDJ	U.S.	1994	$2.00
Epic	ESK 5451	Bury My Love	CDJ	U.S.	1993	$2.00
Epic	ESK 5662	Return to Me	CDJ	U.S.		$2.00
Epic	77562	Return to Me	CD5	U.S.	1994	$6.00

Odds

Full Length

Label	Catalog Number	Title	Type	Country	Year	Longbox Value/Value
	PRCD 95822	Special AAA Sampler	DJ/Smplr	U.S.		$8.00

Singles

Label	Catalog Number	Title	Type	Country	Year	Longbox Value/Value
Zoo	ZD-17127	Heterosexual Man	CDJ	U.S.	1993	$3.00
Zoo	ZD-17028	Love Is the Subject	CDJ	U.S.	1991	$3.00
	PRCD 92822	Truth Untold	CDJ	U.S.		$2.00

Off Shore

Singles

Label	Catalog Number	Title	Type	Country	Year	Longbox Value/Value
Epic	657638-2	Got To Get Away	CD5	Germany	1992	$10.00
Epic	656034-3	I Can't Take the Power	CD3	Germany	1990	$10.00
Epic	656034-5	I Can't Take the Power	CD5	Germany	1990	$10.00
Epic	ESK 73751	I Can't Take the Power	CDJ	U.S.	1990	$2.00
Epic	656825-2	I Got a Little Song	CD3	Germany	1990	$10.00

Offspring

Singles

Label	Catalog Number	Title	Type	Country	Year	Longbox Value/Value
		Come Out and Play	CD5	U.K.	1994	$10.00
	864248	Kick Him He's Down	CDJ	U.S.	1994	$6.00
	86432	Self Esteem	CDJ	U.S.	1994	$6.00

Oh Well

Singles

Label	Catalog Number	Title	Type	Country	Year	Longbox Value/Value
Polygram	867587-2	Dance To the Music	CD5	Germany	1991	$8.00
EMI	203707-2	I'll Be Forever Your Man	CD5	Germany	1990	$8.00
EMI	202993-2	Oh Well	CD5	Germany	1988	$8.00
EMI	203600-2	Oh Well	CD5	Germany	1988	$8.00
Parlophone	CDR-6235	Oh Well	CD5	U.K.	1988	$8.00
EMI	203741-2	Radar Love	CD5	Germany	1990	$8.00
Parlophone	CDR-6244	Radar Love	CD5	U.K.	1990	$8.00

Ohno, Eri

Full Length

Label	Catalog Number	Title	Type	Country	Year	Longbox Value/Value
Denon	CD-7085	Easy To Love	LP/LB	U.S.†	1985	$14.00/$8.00
Denon	CD-7016	Eri, My Dear	LP/LB	U.S.†	1985	$14.00/$8.00

Oiler

Singles

Label	Catalog Number	Title	Type	Country	Year	Longbox Value/Value
Sympathy	263	Missing Part One	CD5	U.S.	1994	$5.00

Oingo Boingo

Full Length

Label	Catalog Number	Title	Type	Country	Year	Longbox Value/Value
A&M	AMSAD00187	Selections From "Farewell"	DJ/Smplr	U.S.	1995	$15.00
Reprise	24568-2	Boingo	LTD/LP	U.S.	1994	$25.00
		Boingo Jr.	DJ/Smplr	U.S.		$8.00
MCA	CD33-17671	Winning Side	DJ/Smplr	U.S.	1988	$8.00

Singles

Label	Catalog Number	Title	Type	Country	Year	Longbox Value/Value
Reprise	PRO-CD-6891	Hey	CDJ	U.S.	1994	$3.00
MCA	CD45 18147	Out of Control	CDJ	U.S.	1990	$2.00
MCA	CD45 18250	Out of Control	CDJ	U.S.	1990	$2.00
MCA	CD45 18385	Skin	CDJ	U.S.	1990	$2.00
MCA	CD45 18112	When the Lights Go Out	CDJ	U.S.	1990	$2.00

Olvis

Singles

Label	Catalog Number	Title	Type	Country	Year	Longbox Value/Value
Restless	033	Regular Thang	CDJ	U.S.	1993	$2.00

Okeh Lateral Cut

Singles

Label	Catalog Number	Title	Type	Country	Year	Longbox Value/Value
		Keh' Mo'	CDJ	U.S.		$2.00

Old Dirty Bastard

Singles

Label	Catalog Number	Title	Type	Country	Year	Longbox Value/Value
Elektra/Asylum	66166	Brooklyn Zoo	CD5	U.S.	1994	$5.00
Elektra	PRCD 9108-2	Brooklyn Zoo	CDJ	U.S.	1995	$3.00
	PRCD 9380-2	Rawhide	CDJ	U.S.		$2.00
	PRCD 9276-2	Shimmy Shimmy	CDJ	U.S.		$2.00
Elektra	66128	Shimmy Shimmy	CD5	U.S.	1995	$6.00
Elektra	PRCD 9112-2	Shimmy Shimmy	CDJ	U.S.	1995	$3.00

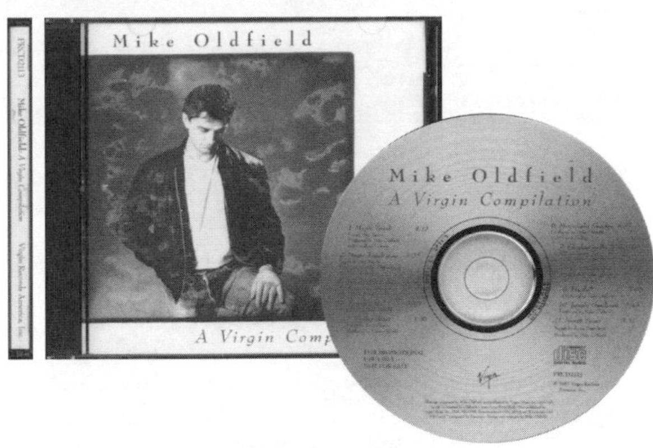

Oldfield, Mike – A Vrgin Compilation (Virgin PRCD2113)

Oldfield, Mike

Full Length

Label	Catalog Number	Title	Type	Country	Year	Longbox Value/Value
Virgin	PRCD2113	A Virgin Compilation	DJ/Smplr	U.S.	1987	$75.00
Caroline		Collector's Edition	LTD/LP	U.K.	1994	$45.00
3 CD picture disc boxed set.						
Virgin		Islands	DJ/Smplr	U.K.		$15.00
		Songs Of Distant Earth	DJ/LP	U.S.		$8.00
Warner Brothers	PRO-CD-5705	Tubular Bells II	DJ/LP	U.S.	1992	$10.00

Singles

Label	Catalog Number	Title	Type	Country	Year	Longbox Value/Value
		Bell	CD5	U.K.		$10.00
		Bell	CD5	U.K.		$10.00
Second version.						
Virgin	VSCD-1189	Earthmoving	CD3	U.K.	1989	$10.00
Virgin	664430	Gimme Back	CD5	Germany	1991	$10.00
Virgin	663951	Heaven's Open	CD5	Germany	1991	$10.00
Virgin	VSCDT-1341	Heaven's Open	CD5	U.K.	1991	$10.00
WEA	YZ871CDX	Hibernaculum	CD5	U.K.	1995	$10.00
WEA	YZ871CD-DJ	Hibernaculum	CDJ	U.K.	1995	$15.00
Virgin	662761	Holy	CD5	Germany	1989	$10.00
Virgin	PRCD 3208	Hostage	CDJ	U.S.	1989	$3.00
Virgin	162383	Innocent	CD3	Germany	1989	$10.00
Virgin	662383	Innocent	CD5	Germany	1989	$10.00
Virgin	VSCD-1214	Innocent	CD3	U.K.	1989	$10.00
Virgin	CDEP-6	Islands	CD5	U.K.	1988	$10.00
Virgin	880985	Moonlight Shadow	CD3	Germany	1988	$10.00
Virgin	883273	Moonlight Shadow	CD5	Germany	1988	$10.00
Virgin	CDF-7	Moonlight Shadow	CD5	U.K.	1988	$10.00
Virgin	CDT-7	Moonlight Shadow	CD3	U.K.	1990	$10.00
Reprise	PRO-CD-5800	Sentinel	CDJ	U.S.	1992	$6.00
		Tattoo	CD5	U.K.		$10.00
Virgin	PRCD 3572	Tubular Bells	CDJ	U.S.	1989	$7.00

Olivares, David

Singles

Label	Catalog Number	Title	Type	Country	Year	Longbox Value/Value
Cema Latino	31826	Tu Y Yo	CD5	U.S.	1994	$5.00

Oliver, Jane

Full Length

Label	Catalog Number	Title	Type	Country	Year	Longbox Value/Value
CBS	CK-35437	Stay the Night	LP/BP	U.S.†	1984	$12.00/$7.00

Oliver Who?

Singles

Label	Catalog Number	Title	Type	Country	Year	Longbox Value/Value
Zoo	ZD-17086	Clever	CDJ	U.S.	1992	$2.00

Omar And The Howlers

Singles

Label	Catalog Number	Title	Type	Country	Year	Longbox Value/Value
Provogue	PRM-20412	Born On the Bayou	CD5	U.K.	1992	$8.00
Talkin' Loud	TLKCD-13	Don't Mean a Thing	CD5	U.K.	1991	$8.00
Talkin' Loud	TLKCD-28	Music	CD5	U.K.	1991	$8.00
Columbia	CSK 1223	Rattlesnake Shake	CDJ	U.S.	1988	$2.00
RCA	RDJ64316-2	Saturday	CDJ	U.S.		$2.00
RCA	RDJ64432-2	There's Nothing Like This	CDJ	U.S.		$2.00
Talkin' Loud	868289-2	There's Nothing Like This	CD5	Germany	1991	$8.00
Talkin' Loud	TLKCD-9	There's Nothing Like This	CD5	U.K.	1991	$8.00
Talkin' Loud	TLKCD-22	Your Loss My Gain	CD5	U.K.	1991	$8.00

Omartain, Michael

Singles

Label	Catalog Number	Title	Type	Country	Year	Longbox Value/Value
Epic	ESK 4167	Let My Heart Be the First To Know	CDJ	U.S.	1991	$2.00

One

Singles

Label	Catalog Number	Title	Type	Country	Year	Longbox Value/Value
Virgin	V292500	Wide Load	CD5	Canada	1994	$7.00

One 2 Many

Singles

Label	Catalog Number	Title	Type	Country	Year	Longbox Value/Value
A&M	CDEE-490	Another Man	CD3	U.K.	1989	$8.00
A&M	390377-2	Down Town	CD5	Germany	1989	$8.00
A&M	S10Y-3067	Down Town	CD3	Japan	1989	$13.00/$4.00
A&M	CDEE-476	Down Town	CD3	U.K.	1989	$8.00
A&M	CD 17708	Down Town	CDJ	U.S.	1989	$2.00
A&M	CD 17743	Down Town	CDJ	U.S.	1989	$2.00
A&M	CDEE-496	Nearly There	CD3	U.K.	1989	$8.00
A&M	75021 7952-2	Peace of Mind	CDJ	U.S.	1992	$2.00
A&M	CDEE-518	Writing on the Wall	CD3	U.K.	1989	$8.00

One 2 One

Singles

Label	Catalog Number	Title	Type	Country	Year	Longbox Value/Value
A&M	75021 7344	Memory Lane	CDJ	U.S.	1992	$2.00
A&M	75021 7325	Peace of Mind	CDJ	U.S.	1992	$2.00
A&M	75021 7952	Peace of Mind	CDJ	U.S.	1992	$2.00
A&M		Peace of Mind (Love Goes On)	CDJ	U.S.	1991	$3.00

One Cause One Effect

Singles

Label	Catalog Number	Title	Type	Country	Year	Longbox Value/Value
Capitol		Midnight Lover	CDJ	U.S.		$2.00
Capitol	DPRO-79288	Up With Hope, Down With Dope	CDJ	U.S.	1990	$2.00

One Dove

Singles

Label	Catalog Number	Title	Type	Country	Year	Longbox Value / Value
ffrr	015	Breakdown	CDJ	U.S.	1993	$2.00
ffrr	044	White Love	CDJ	U.S.	1993	$2.00
ffrr	100	White Love	CDJ	U.S.	1993	$2.00

One Drops

Singles

Label	Catalog Number	Title	Type	Country	Year	Longbox Value / Value
Nutmeg	NC-2042	Don't Worry	CD5	Japan	1991	$10.00

One Hand One Heart

Singles

Label	Catalog Number	Title	Type	Country	Year	Longbox Value / Value
Epic	CDWUN-1	Miracle Heart	CD5	U.K.	1988	$8.00
Epic	CDWUN-2	One Step Closer	CD5	U.K.	1988	$8.00

One More Time

Singles

Label	Catalog Number	Title	Type	Country	Year	Longbox Value / Value
PWL	PWCD-251	Highland	CD5	U.K.	1992	$8.00

One Nation

Singles

Label	Catalog Number	Title	Type	Country	Year	Longbox Value / Value
IRS	EIRSCD-151	How Long	CD5	U.K.	1990	$8.00
		My Commitment	CDJ	U.S.		$2.00
IRS	EIRSCD-112	What You See	CD5	U.K.	1989	$8.00

One On One

Singles

Label	Catalog Number	Title	Type	Country	Year	Longbox Value / Value
BMG	162882	You're My Type	CD3	Germany	1989	$8.00

One Thousand Mona Lisas

Full Length

Label	Catalog Number	Title	Type	Country	Year	Longbox Value / Value
RCA	RDJ6678-2	Sampler, The	DJ/Smplr	U.S.		$5.00

Singles

Label	Catalog Number	Title	Type	Country	Year	Longbox Value / Value
RCA	RDJ64501-2	Girlfriendly	CDJ	U.S.		$2.00
RCA	RDJ64452-2	How Would You Know	CDJ	U.S.		$2.00

One World

Singles

Label	Catalog Number	Title	Type	Country	Year	Longbox Value / Value
ffrr	886901-2	Down on Love	CD5	Germany	1990	$8.00
ffrr	FCD-129	Down on Love	CD5	U.K.	1990	$8.00

Only Child

Singles

Label	Catalog Number	Title	Type	Country	Year	Longbox Value / Value
Rampage	70835	I Believe in You	CDJ	U.S.	1988	$2.00

Ono, Yoko

Full Length

Label	Catalog Number	Title	Type	Country	Year	Longbox Value / Value
Rykodisc	RCD 10224 29	Onobox Ultracase	LTD/LP	U.S.	1992	$250.00
7 CD set in "Anvil" Case with glass key and bonus CD sampler. Limited to 350 sets.						
Polydor	827530-2	Starpeace	LP	U.K.		$15.00
Pioneer	PA-85-116	Then & Now	LD	U.S.	1985	$25.00
	PCD-0296	Walking on Thin Ice	DJ/Smplr	Japan	1992	$120.00
Rykodisc	RCD 20230	Walking on Thin Ice	DJ/Smplr	U.S.	1992	$35.00

Singles

Label	Catalog Number	Title	Type	Country	Year	Longbox Value / Value
Rykodisc	VRCD ONO	An Xmas Message From Yoko	CDJ	U.S.	1991	$40.00
EMI	TODP-2360	Beautiful Boy	CD3	Japan	1992	$13.00/$4.00
Rykodisc		Never Say Goodbye	CDJ	U.S.	1995	$10.00

Onyx

Singles

Label	Catalog Number	Title	Type	Country	Year	Longbox Value / Value
Polygram	577115	Last Dayz, All We Got Iz Us	CD5	U.S.	1995	$5.00
CBS	74982	Shifflee	CD5	U.S.	1993	$6.00
JML	77163	Shifflee	CDJ	U.S.	1993	$2.00
CBS	77039	Slam	CD5	U.S.	1993	$6.00
Chaos	CSK 4856	Throw Ya Gunz	CDJ	U.S.	1992	$2.00

Open Skies

Singles

Label	Catalog Number	Title	Type	Country	Year	Longbox Value / Value
Reinforced	RIVET-1231CD	Deep in Your Skies	CD5	U.K.	1992	$8.00

Opus

Singles

Label	Catalog Number	Title	Type	Country	Year	Longbox Value / Value
Polygram	871237-2	Live Is Life	CD5	Germany	1989	$8.00
Polygram	873463-2	When the Night Comes	CD5	Germany	1989	$8.00
Polygram	873487-2	When the Night Comes	CD5	Germany	1989	$8.00

Opus 3

Singles

Label	Catalog Number	Title	Type	Country	Year	Longbox Value / Value
Eastwest	PRCD 4832-2	I Talk to the Wind	CDJ	U.S.	1992	$2.00
Eastwest	PRCD 4498-2	It's a Fine Day	CDJ	U.S.	1992	$2.00
Eastwest	PRCD 5629-2	When You Made the Mountain	CDJ	U.S.	1994	$2.00

Or-N-More

Singles

Label	Catalog Number	Title	Type	Country	Year	Longbox Value / Value
EMI	DPRO 4764	Every Other Day	CDJ	U.S.	1991	$2.00

Oracle

Singles

Label	Catalog Number	Title	Type	Country	Year	Longbox Value / Value
RCA	68117	Kilamanjaro	CD5	U.S.	1994	$5.00

Orb

Full Length

Label	Catalog Number	Title	Type	Country	Year	Longbox Value / Value
Mercury		An Introduction	DJ/Smplr	U.S.	1992	$12.00

Singles

Label	Catalog Number	Title	Type	Country	Year	Longbox Value / Value
Mercury	CDP 804	Blue Room	CDJ	U.S.	1992	$2.00
Vertigo		Towers of Dub	CDJ	U.K.	1992	$10.00

Orbison, Roy

Full Length

Label	Catalog Number	Title	Type	Country	Year	Longbox Value / Value
		A Black 'n White Night	DJ/LP	U.S.		$35.00
CD and VHS video in box.						
Virgin	PRCD Parlaroy	Black And White Night	DJ/LP	U.S.	1989	$25.00
Orbison Records	ROBW2000-2	Black & White Night	LTD/LP	U.S.	1997	$18.00
Limited edition CD in "pop-up" packaging.						
		Mystery Girl	LTD/LP	Australia	1989	$30.00
Gold disc.						
Virgin	PROCD-ROY	Mystery Girl	DJ/LP	U.S.	1989	$25.00
		Original, The	LP	U.S.		$10.00
Virgin	PRCDPolary	Polaroy	DJ/Smplr	U.S.	1989	$30.00

Singles

Label	Catalog Number	Title	Type	Country	Year	Longbox Value / Value
Virgin	662389	California Blue	CD5	Germany	1989	$10.00
Virgin	VSCD-1193	California Blue	CD3	U.K.	1989	$10.00
Virgin	2756	California Blue	CDJ	U.S.	1989	$6.00
Virgin	VJDP-10198	Crying	CD3	Japan	1992	$15.00/$4.00
Virgin	VUSCD 63	Crying	CD5	U.K.	1992	$10.00
		Heartbreak Radio	CD5	U.K.		$10.00
		Heartbreak Radio	CD5	U.K.		$10.00
Second version.						
Virgin	DPRO-12731	Heartbreak Radio	CDJ	U.S.	1992	$3.00
MCA	MCD-17859	I Drove All Night	CD5	Germany	1992	$10.00
MCA	MCSTD-1652	I Drove All Night	CD5	U.K.	1992	$10.00
MCA	54419	I Drove All Night	CD5	U.S.	1992	$5.00
MCA	2025	I Drove All Night	CDJ	U.S.	1992	$2.00
Virgin	PRCD 2044	In Dreams	CDJ	U.S.	1987	$3.00
Virgin	655578-3	Oh Pretty Woman	CD3	Germany	1990	$10.00
Virgin	655578-2	Oh Pretty Woman	CD5	Germany	1990	$10.00
Virgin	662772-2	Oh Pretty Woman	CD5	Germany	1990	$10.00
Virgin	VJDP-104	Oh Pretty Woman	CD3	Japan	1990	$15.00/$4.00
Virgin	VSCD-1224	Oh Pretty Woman	CD5	U.K.	1989	$10.00
Virgin	PRCD 2964	Oh Pretty Woman	CDJ	U.S.	1989	$3.00
Virgin	VSDS-3324	Only the Lonely	CDJ	U.S.		$3.00
Virgin	162150	She's a Mystery To Me	CD3	Germany	1989	$10.00
Virgin	VJD-10211	She's a Mystery To Me	CD3	Japan	1989	$12.00/$4.00
Virgin	VSCD-1173	She's a Mystery To Me	CD3	U.K.	1989	$10.00
Virgin	PRCD 2667	She's a Mystery To Me	CDJ	U.S.	1989	$3.00
BMG	663423	Windsurfer	CD5	Germany	1990	$10.00
Virgin	162000	You Got It	CD3	Germany	1989	$10.00
Virgin	VJD-15502	You Got It	CD3	Japan	1989	$15.00
Virgin	VSCD-1166	You Got It	CD3	U.K.	1989	$10.00
Virgin	PRCD 2593	You Got It	CDJ	U.S.	1989	$3.00

Orbison, Roy And k.d. Lang

Singles

Label	Catalog Number	Title	Type	Country	Year	Longbox Value / Value
		Crying	CD5	U.K.		$10.00
Second version.						

Orbita

Singles

Label	Catalog Number	Title	Type	Country	Year	Longbox Value / Value
Pikosso	872 0025	Call Me Misha	SCD5	Germany	1995	$15.00
"Telephone" shaped CD.						
Full Frequency	120047	Are We Here	CD5	U.S.	1994	$5.00
ffrr	886977-2	Crime	CD5	Germany	1990	$8.00
ffrr	FCD-135	Crime	CD5	U.K.	1990	$8.00
ffrr	162 350 009	Halcyon	CD5	U.S.	1992	$5.00
ffrr	869515-2	Midnight	CD5	Germany	1990	$8.00
ffrr	869649-2	Munitions	CD5	U.K.	1992	$8.00
ffrr	FCD-145	Omen	CD5	U.K.	1990	$8.00
ffrr	FCD-149	Satan	CD5	U.K.	1990	$8.00

Orchestral Maneuvres in the Dark (O.M.D.)

Singles

Label	Catalog Number	Title	Type	Country	Year	Longbox Value / Value
BMG	665004	Call My Name	CD5	Germany	1991	$9.00
		Dream of Me	CD5	U.K.		$10.00
		Dream of Me	CD5	U.K.		$10.00
Second version.						
Virgin	PRCD 14097	Dream Of Me	CDJ	U.S.	1993	$3.00
Virgin	659702	Dreaming	CD5	Germany	1988	$9.00
Virgin	VJD-12002	Dreaming	CD3	Japan	1988	$15.00/$4.00
Virgin	VJD-1503	Dreaming	CD3	Japan	1988	$15.00/$4.00
Virgin	VSCD-987	Dreaming	CD5	U.K.	1988	$9.00
A&M	312004	Dreaming	CD3	U.S.	1988	$6.00/$4.00
A&M	CD 17541	Dreaming	CDJ	U.S.	1988	$2.00
A&M	75021 2373-2	Dreaming	CD5	U.S.	1993	$5.00
Virgin	VSCDG 1471	Everyday	CD5	U.K.	1993	$10.00
A&M	CD 17422	(Forever) Live & Die	CDJ	U.S.	1986	$7.00
Virgin	CDV-DJ-2715	Liberator	CDJ	U.K.	1994	$12.00
Virgin		Live	CDJ	France		$20.00
Virgin	880909	Locomotion	CD3	Germany	1988	$9.00
Virgin	CDT-12	Locomotion	CD3	U.K.	1988	$9.00
Virgin	CDT-27	Maid Of Orleans	CD3	U.K.	1988	$9.00
Virgin	VSCDX 1331	Pandora's Box	CD5	U.K.	1991	$11.00
CD in custom wooden box.						
Virgin	2-96338	Pandora's Box	CD5	U.S.	1991	$5.00
Virgin	PRCD 3949	Pandora's Box	CDJ	U.S.	1991	$6.00
Virgin	663790	Sailing on the Seven Seas	CD5	Germany	1991	$9.00
Virgin	VJCP-14023	Sailing on the Seven Seas	CD5	Japan	1991	$13.00
Virgin	VSCDT 1310	Sailing on the Seven Seas	CD5	U.K.	1991	$9.00
Virgin	659000	Shame	CD5	Germany	1990	$9.00
Virgin	MIKE-93813	Shame	CD5	U.K.	1990	$9.00
Virgin	PRCD 12668	Stand Above Me	CDJ	U.S.	1993	$3.00
Virgin	PRCD 12777	Stand Above Me	CDJ	U.S.	1993	$3.00
Virgin	664670	Then You Turn Away	CD5	Germany	1991	$9.00
Virgin	VSCDT-1368	Then You Turn Away	CD5	U.K.	1991	$9.00

Oregon

Full Length

Label	Catalog Number	Title	Type	Country	Year	Longbox Value / Value
ECM	23796-2	Oregon	LP/LB	U.S.†	1985	$14.00/$8.00

Orellana, Raul

Singles

Label	Catalog Number	Title	Type	Country	Year	Longbox Value / Value
Parlophone	CDR-6328	My Sun Will Get You	CD5	U.K.	1992	$8.00
Alfa	ALDB-28	Real Wild House, The	CD3	Japan	1990	$12.00/$3.00
BCM	BCM-322CD	Real Wild House, The	CD5	U.K.	1989	$8.00
		Real Wild House, The	CDJ	U.S.		$2.00
BCM	20418	Toros	CD5	Germany	1990	$8.00

Organized Konfusion

Singles

Label	Catalog Number	Title	Type	Country	Year	Longbox Value / Value
Hollywood	PRCD 8384-2	Who Stole My Last Piece of	CDJ	U.S.	1991	$2.00

Origin

Singles

Label	Catalog Number	Title	Type	Country	Year	Longbox Value / Value
Virgin	PRCD 3263	Growing Old	CDJ	U.S.	1990	$2.00
Hut	HUTCD-4	Set Sails Free	CD5	U.K.	1991	$8.00
		Set Sails Free	CDJ	U.S.		$2.00

Originals

Full Length

Label	Catalog Number	Title	Type	Country	Year	Longbox Value / Value
Motown	5462	Baby I'm For Real	LP/BP	U.S.		$12.00/$7.00
Motown	5462	Portrait of the	LP/BP	U.S.		$12.00/$7.00

Orion The Hunter

Full Length

Label	Catalog Number	Title	Type	Country	Year	Longbox Value / Value
Portrait	RK-39239	Orion the Hunter	LP/LB	U.S.†	1984	$14.00/$8.00

Orlando, Tony

Singles

Label	Catalog Number	Title	Type	Country	Year	Longbox Value / Value
Quality	15159	With Every Yellow Ribbon	CDJ	U.S.	1991	$2.00

Orleans, Joan

Singles

Label	Catalog Number	Title	Type	Country	Year	Longbox Value / Value
Intercord	825 756	I Don't Wanna Be Lonely	CD5	Germany	1989	$8.00

Orquesta De La Luz

Singles

Label	Catalog Number	Title	Type	Country	Year	Longbox Value / Value
Sony	10400	Mambo De La Luz	CDJ	U.S.	1993	$2.00

Orrall, Robert Ellis

Singles

Label	Catalog Number	Title	Type	Country	Year	Longbox Value / Value
RCA	RDJ 62335-2	Boom! It Was Over	CDJ	U.S.	1992	$2.00

Osborne, Jeffrey

Full Length

Label	Catalog Number	Title	Type	Country	Year	Longbox Value / Value
A&M	CD-5017	Don't Stop	LP/LB	U.S.†	1985	$12.00/$7.00
A&M	CD-4940	Stay With Me Tonight	LP/LB	U.S.†	1984	$12.00/$7.00

Singles

Label	Catalog Number	Title	Type	Country	Year	Longbox Value / Value
A&M	CD 17670	All Because Of You	CDJ	U.S.	1988	$2.00
A&M	CD 17616	Can't Go Back On A Promise	CDJ	U.S.	1988	$2.00
Arista	663992	If My Brother's in Trouble	CD5	Germany	1991	$9.00
Arista	663992	If My Brother's in Trouble	CD5	U.K.	1991	$9.00
Arista	ASCD-2212	If My Brother's in Trouble	CDJ	U.S.	1991	$2.00
Arista	ASCD-2236	Morning After, The	CDJ	U.S.	1991	$2.00
Arista	ASCD-2127	Only Human	CDJ	U.S.	1990	$2.00
A&M	S10Y-3045	She's Only the Left	CD3	Japan	1988	$13.00/$4.00
A&M	CD 17596	She's Only the Left	CDJ	U.S.	1988	$2.00

Osborne, Joan

Full Length

Label	Catalog Number	Title	Type	Country	Year	Longbox Value / Value
Womanly Hips		Blue Million Miles	LP	U.S.	1993	$35.00
Westwood One		In Concert	RS	U.S.	1996	$50.00
Airdate: 5/6/96.						
Womanly Hips		Soul Show	LP	U.S.	1991	$35.00

Singles

Label	Catalog Number	Title	Type	Country	Year	Longbox Value / Value
		Blue Million Miles	CDJ	U.S.	1993	$2.00
		One of Us	CDJ	U.K.	1995	$15.00
Polygram	852366	One of Us	CD5	U.S.	1995	$5.00
		One of Us	CDJ	U.S.	1995	$7.00
		Right Hand Man	CDJ	U.K.	1995	$15.00
		Spoonful of…	CDJ	U.K.	1995	$25.00
	JOCD13	St. Teresa	CDJ	U.K.	1995	$15.00
		St. Teresa	CD5	U.K.	1996	$10.00
		St. Teresa	CD5	U.K.	1996	$10.00
Second version.						

Osbourne, Anders

Singles

Label	Catalog Number	Title	Type	Country	Year	Longbox Value / Value
	BSK 7845	What's Going On Here	CDJ	U.S.		$3.00

Osbourne, Ozzy – No More Tears Demo Sessions (Epic ZSK 4643) Limited numbered promotional edition CD with unreleased demo versions of the tracks from the *No More Tears* album.

Osbourne, Ozzy

Full Length

Label	Catalog Number	Title	Type	Country	Year	Longbox Value / Value
CBS	SAMP 3143	Ballads of Oz	DJ/Smplr	Holland	1996	$40.00
CBS		Ballads of Oz	DJ/Smplr	U.K.	1996	$25.00
Jet	ZK-38987	Bark at the Moon	LP/LB	U.S.†	1984	$14.00/$8.00
Jet	ZK-38987	Bark at the Moon	LP/LB	U.S.	1987	$14.00/$8.00
Columbia	465211-1	Bark at the Moon/Blizzard of Ozz	LP	Germany		$25.00
2 CD set.						
Epic	465211-1	Bark at the Moon/Blizzard of Ozz	LP	U.K.		$25.00
2 CD set.						
CBS/Sony	49DP5210-2	Bible of Ozz	LTD/LP	Japan	1988	$200.00
CD of "No Rest For the Wicked" in bound book, slipcover, patch and belt buckle.						
Jet	EK-36812	Blizzard of Ozz	LP/LB	U.S.		$14.00/$8.00
Jet	ZK-37492	Diary of a Madman	LP/LB	U.S.†	1985	$14.00/$8.00
Jet	ZK-37492	Diary of a Madman	LP/LB	U.S.	1987	$14.00/$8.00
Album Network		In the Studio (Blizzard Of Ozz)	RS	U.S.		$30.00
Album Network		In the Studio (No More Tears)	RS	U.S.		$30.00
Jet	ZK-45451	Just Say Ozzy	LP/LB	U.S.		$14.00/$8.00
DIR		King Biscuit Flour Hour	RS	U.S.	1992	$35.00
Airdate: 1/27/92.						
DIR		King Biscuit Flour Hour	RS	U.S.	1992	$35.00
Airdate: 11/30/92.						
Sony	473798-9	Live & Loud	LTD/LP	Germany	1993	$40.00
2CD set						
Sony	SRCS-6763/4	Live & Loud	LTD/LP	Germany	1993	$40.00
2CD set						
Epic	473798-9	Live & Loud	LTD/LP	U.K.	1993	$40.00
2CD set						
Epic	Z2K 48973	Live & Loud	LTD/LP	U.S.	1993	$28.00
2CD set in double digipak with speaker grill on cover.						
Epic	ZSK 5247	Live & Loud Sampler	DJ/Smplr	U.S.	1993	$18.00
Epic	EK-46795	No More Tears	LP/LB	U.S.		$14.00/$8.00
Epic	ZSK 4643	No More Tears Demo Sessions	DJ/Smplr	U.S.	1992	$125.00
Jet	ZK-44245	No Rest For the Wicked	LP/LB	U.S.	1988	$14.00/$8.00
Columbia	468334-2	No Rest For the Wicked/Bark at the Moon/Ultimate Sin, The	LP	Germany		$25.00
3 CD set.						
Columbia	468334-2	No Rest For the Wicked/Bark at the Moon/Ultimate Sin, The	LP	U.K.		$25.00
3 CD set.						
Columbia	471606-2	No Rest For the Wicked/Ultimate Sin, The	LP	Germany		$25.00
2 CD set.						
Westwood One		Off the Record	RS	U.S.	1992	$40.00
Airdate: 10/19/92.						
Westwood One		Off the Record	RS	U.S.	1992	$40.00
Airdate: 6/15/92.						
Epic	XDGS-93190	Ozztory	DJ/Smplr	Japan	1996	$150.00
CBS	ASK-2699	Sampler from Tribute	DJ/Smplr	U.S.	1987	$30.00
Jet	CK-38350	Speak of the Devil	LP/LB	U.S.		$14.00/$8.00
		Special	RS	U.S.	1993	$100.00
3 CD set.						
Sony	SRCS-6911	Starbox	LTD/LP	Japan		$30.00
CBS	CDL 57129/A-21852	Ten Commandments	LP/LB	U.S.	1990	$35.00
Jet	ZGK-40714	Tribute	LP/LB	U.S.		$14.00/$8.00
CBS	6199-80	Ultimate Ozzy, The	LD	U.S.	1990	$25.00
Jet	ZK-40026	Ultimate Sin	LP/LB	U.S.		$14.00/$8.00
Media America		Up Close	RS	U.S.	1992	$45.00
2 CD set.						
Media America		Up Close	RS	U.S.	1993	$45.00
2 CD set.						
Media America		Up Close	RS	U.S.	1996	$50.00
2 CD set.						
Sony	27LP 131	Wicked Videos	8"LD	Japan	1988	$35.00
Image	ID6335CB	Wicked Videos	LD	U.S.		$30.00

Singles

Label	Catalog Number	Title	Type	Country	Year	Longbox Value / Value
Epic	652875-2	Back To Ozz	CD5	U.K.	1988	$10.00
Epic		Breaking All the Rules	CDJ	U.S.	1988	$10.00
CBS	659340	Changes	CD5	U.K.	1993	$10.00
CBS	XPCD282	Changes	CDJ	U.K.	1993	$15.00
Epic	ZSK 74986	Changes	CDJ	U.S.	1993	$6.00
Epic	ZSK 74986	Changes	CDJ	U.S.	1993	$10.00
CBS	ZSK 1345	Crazy Babies	CDJ	U.S.	1988	$10.00
CBS	ZSK 1426	Crazy Babies	CDJ	U.S.	1989	$10.00
CBS		I Just Want You	CD5	U.K.	1996	$10.00
CBS		I Just Want You	CD5	U.K.	1996	$10.00
Second version.						
CBS	XPCD 2060	I Just Want You	CDJ	U.K.	1996	$16.00
CBS	ZSK 1948	Live Pigs	CDJ	U.S.	1988	$10.00
CBS		Mama, I'm Coming Home	CD5	Australia	1992	$12.00
CBS	657617-5	Mama, I'm Coming Home	CD5	Germany	1992	$10.00
Epic	45K 74265	Mama, I'm Coming Home	CD5	U.S.	1992	$5.00
Epic	ZSK 74093	Mama, I'm Coming Home	CDJ	U.S.	1992	$3.00
Sony	10EP-3051	Miracle Man	CD3	Japan	1988	$18.00/$4.00
Epic	653063-2	Miracle Man	CD5	U.K.	1988	$10.00
CBS	ZSK 1344	Miracle Man	CDJ	U.S.	1988	$3.00
Epic	ESK 4605	Mr. Tinkertrain	CDJ	U.S.	1992	$3.00
Epic	657440-2	No More Tears	CD5	U.K.	1991	$15.00
Wallet pack.						
Epic	ESK 73973	No More Tears	CDJ	U.S.	1991	$3.00
Epic		Perry Mason	CDJ	U.S.	1996	$3.00
Epic	ZSK 4493	Road to Nowhere	CDJ	U.S.	1992	$2.00
Epic		See You on the Other Side	CDJ	U.S.	1996	$6.00
Epic	ZSK 4742	Time After Time	CDJ	U.S.	1992	$2.00

Osby, Greg

Singles

Label	Catalog Number	Title	Type	Country	Year	Longbox Value / Value
Blue Note	DPRO-79626	Mr. Gutterman	CDJ	U.S.	1993	$7.00

Oscar

Singles

Label	Catalog Number	Title	Type	Country	Year	Longbox Value / Value
Epic	ESK 74732	I'm Calling You	CDJ	U.S.	1992	$2.00
Epic	ESK 74732	Keep Touching Me	CDJ	U.S.	1993	$2.00

Oslin, K.T.

Full Length

Label	Catalog Number	Title	Type	Country	Year	Longbox Value / Value
		Country Star Tracks	RS	U.S.	1991	$15.00
Airdate: 8/17/91.						

Singles

Label	Catalog Number	Title	Type	Country	Year	Longbox Value / Value
		All I Need	CDJ	U.S.		$2.00
RCA	RDJ 62053	Cornell Crawford	CDJ	U.S.	1991	$2.00
RCA	RDJ 62751	Feeding the hungry	CDJ	U.S.	1993	$2.00
RCA	RDJ 62561	Hold Me	CDJ	U.S.	1993	$2.00
RCA	RDJ 62499	No Way Home	CDJ	U.S.	1991	$2.00
RCA	2567-2-RDJ	Two Hearts	CDJ	U.S.	1990	$2.00

Osmond Boys

Singles

Label	Catalog Number	Title	Type	Country	Year	Longbox Value / Value
Curb	CD45 79140	Hey Girl	CDJ	U.S.	1990	$2.00
Curb	657567-2	I Can't Help Myself	CD5	Germany	1991	$8.00
Curb	657722-2	Show Me the Way	CD5	Germany	1992	$8.00
Curb	657722-2	Show Me the Way	CD5	U.K.	1992	$8.00

Singles

Label	Catalog Number	Title	Type	Country	Year	Longbox Value / Value
Virgin	CDEP-15	Groove	CD5	U.K.	1988	$9.00
Capitol	DPRO-79752	Hold On	CDJ	U.S.	1989	$2.00
Capitol	DPRO-79863	Hold On	CDJ	U.S.	1989	$2.00
Capitol	DPRO-79885	I'll Be Good to You	CDJ	U.S.	1989	$2.00
Capitol	DPRO-79689	Love Will Survive	CDJ	U.S.	1990	$2.00
EMI	204182-2	My Love Is a Fire	CD5	Germany	1990	$9.00
EMI	204186-2	My Love Is a Fire	CD5	Germany	1990	$9.00
Capitol	CDCL-600	My Love Is a Fire	CD5	U.K.	1991	$9.00
Capitol	DPRO-79332	My Love Is a Fire	CDJ	U.S.	1990	$2.00
BMG	662405	Soldier of Love	CD5	Germany	1989	$9.00
Virgin	VJD-10213	Soldier of Love	CD3	Japan	1989	$12.00/$4.00
Virgin	VSCD-1094	Soldier of Love	CD5	U.K.	1989	$9.00

Ostin, Mo

Full Length

Label	Catalog Number	Title	Type	Country	Year	Longbox Value / Value
Warner Brothers	PRO-MO1994	Mo's Songs	DJ/Smplr	U.S.	1994	$300.00
6 CD set in box with rare George Harrison tracks.						

Other Ones

Singles

Label	Catalog Number	Title	Type	Country	Year	Longbox Value / Value
BMG	664572	Another Holiday	CD5	Germany	1991	$8.00
Virgin	661746	Emotional Baby	CD5	Germany	1988	$8.00
Virgin	661751	Emotional Baby	CD5	Germany	1988	$8.00
Virgin	6691801	Holiday	CD5	Germany	1988	$8.00
Virgin	661969	Money and Gold	CD5	Germany	1988	$8.00

Other Two

Singles

Label	Catalog Number	Title	Type	Country	Year	Longbox Value / Value
Qwest	9 41155-2	Selfish	CDJ	U.S.	1993	$3.00
Factory	FACD-329	Tasty Fish	CD5	U.K.	1991	$8.00

Otis, Johnny

Singles

Label	Catalog Number	Title	Type	Country	Year	Longbox Value / Value
	8002	Otisology	CD5	U.S.	1994	$5.00

Otte, Hans

Full Length

Label	Catalog Number	Title	Type	Country	Year	Longbox Value / Value
Kuckuck	CD-069/70	Das Buch der Klange	LP/LB	U.S.†	1985	$14.00/$8.00

Ottmar, Liebert

Full Length

Label	Catalog Number	Title	Type	Country	Year	Longbox Value / Value
Epic	ESK 5299	Special 4 Track Sampler	DJ/Smplr	U.S.	1993	$5.00

Ouch

Singles

Label	Catalog Number	Title	Type	Country	Year	Longbox Value / Value
Cavell	CDS1	I Need You More	CDJ	U.K.	1992	$8.00

Oui 3

Singles

Label	Catalog Number	Title	Type	Country	Year	Longbox Value / Value
MCA	MCSXD 1736	For What It's Worth	CDJ	U.K.	1993	$8.00

Our House

Singles

Label	Catalog Number	Title	Type	Country	Year	Longbox Value / Value
Turnstyle	4741	Our House	CDJ	U.S.	1992	$3.00

Our Lady Of Peace

Full Length

Label	Catalog Number	Title	Type	Country	Year	Longbox Value / Value
		Live 95	DJ/Smplr	U.S.		$8.00

Singles

Label	Catalog Number	Title	Type	Country	Year	Longbox Value / Value
		Birdman, The	CDJ	Canada		$5.00

Out of The Ordinary

Singles

Label	Catalog Number	Title	Type	Country	Year	Longbox Value / Value
ZYX	5978-8	Dream	CD5	Germany	1988	$6.00
ZYX	5978R-8	Dream	CD5	Germany	1988	$6.00
ZYX	6314-8	Play It Again	CD5	Germany	1990	$6.00

Outfield

Full Length

Label	Catalog Number	Title	Type	Country	Year	Longbox Value / Value
DIR		King Biscuit Flour Hour	RS	U.S.	1991	$30.00
	With Styx, Airdate: 3/24/91.					
CBS	CK-40027	Play Deep	LP/BP	U.S.†	1985	$12.00/$7.00

Singles

Label	Catalog Number	Title	Type	Country	Year	Longbox Value / Value
MCA	MCSTD-1639	Closer to Me	CD5	U.K.	1992	$9.00
MCA	MCA5P- 2168	Closer to Me	CDJ	U.S.	1992	$2.00
MCA	MCSTD-1501	For You	CD5	U.K.	1990	$9.00
MCA	CD45 1138	For You	CDJ	U.S.	1990	$2.00
MCA	MCSTD-1593	Going Back	CD5	U.K.	1991	$9.00
Columbia	655059-3	My Paradise	CD3	Germany	1989	$9.00
Sony	10EP-3097	My Paradise	CD3	Japan	1989	$13.00/$4.00
Columbia	CSK 1669	My Paradise	CDJ	U.S.	1989	$2.00
MCA	MCSTD-1536	Take It All	CD5	U.K.	1991	$8.00
MCA	CD45-1250	Take It All	CDJ	U.S.	1990	$2.00
Columbia	654739-3	Voices of Babylon	CD3	Germany	1989	$9.00
Sony	10EP-3081	Voices of Babylon	CD3	Japan	1989	$13.00/$3.00
Columbia	654739-2	Voices of Babylon	CD5	U.K.	1989	$9.00
Columbia	CSK 1493	Voices of Babylon	CDJ	U.S.	1989	$2.00
MCA	MCA5P-2277	Winning It All	CDJ	U.S.	1992	$2.00

Outkast

Singles

Label	Catalog Number	Title	Type	Country	Year	Longbox Value / Value
Arista	24086	Git Up, Git Out	CD5	U.S.	1994	$5.00
Laface	24066	Player's Ball	CD5	U.S.	1994	$5.00
Arista	24061	Player's Ball	CD5	U.S.	1994	$5.00
Arista	24071	Southernplaya	CD5	U.S.	1994	$5.00

Outlaws

Full Length

Label	Catalog Number	Title	Type	Country	Year	Longbox Value / Value
Collector's Pipeline	TCP 012CD	Ghost Riders	LP	U.S.	1993	$16.00
Collector's Pipeline	TCP 016CD	Hurry Sundown	LP	U.S.	1994	$16.00
Collector's Pipeline	TCP 011CD	Lady in Waiting	LP	U.S.	1993	$16.00
Collector's Pipeline	TCP 010CD	Outlaws	LP	U.S.	1993	$16.00
RCA	PCD1-1321	Outlaws, The	LP/BP	U.S.†	1984	$14.00/$8.00

Outrider

Full Length

Label	Catalog Number	Title	Type	Country	Year	Longbox Value / Value
Prestige		No Way Out	LP	U.S.	1991	$15.00

Overkill

Singles

Label	Catalog Number	Title	Type	Country	Year	Longbox Value / Value
Atlantic	PRCD 4977-2	I Hear Black	CDJ	U.S.	1993	$3.00
Atlantic	PRCD 5064-2	Spiritual Void	CDJ	U.S.	1993	$3.00

Overweight Pooch

Singles

Label	Catalog Number	Title	Type	Country	Year	Longbox Value / Value
A&M	75021 7544 2	Ace Is A Spade	CDJ	U.S	1991	$2.00
A&M	AMCD-847	I Like It	CD5	U.K.	1992	$8.00

Overwhelming Colorfast

Singles

Label	Catalog Number	Title	Type	Country	Year	Longbox Value / Value
Relativity	0178	Bender	CDJ	U.S.	1992	$6.00
Relativity	0160	It's Tomorrow	CDJ	U.S.	1992	$2.00

Ovis

Singles

Label	Catalog Number	Title	Type	Country	Year	Longbox Value / Value
Restless	72760	Regular Thang	CD5	U.S.	1994	$5.00

Owens, Buck

Full Length

Label	Catalog Number	Title	Type	Country	Year	Longbox Value / Value
Curb		Collection 1959 - 1990	DJ/Smplr	U.S.		$20.00

Singles

Label	Catalog Number	Title	Type	Country	Year	Longbox Value / Value
Curb	DPRO-79396	Kickin' In	CDJ	U.S.	1990	$6.00

Owens, Darnell

Singles

Label	Catalog Number	Title	Type	Country	Year	Longbox Value / Value
MCA	MCA5P-2656	Since You Want Away	CDJ	U.S.	1993	$2.00

Owens, Jessy

Singles

Label	Catalog Number	Title	Type	Country	Year	Longbox Value / Value
Polygram	867905-2	You Were on My Mind	CD5	Germany	1991	$8.00

Owens, Robert

Singles

Label	Catalog Number	Title	Type	Country	Year	Longbox Value / Value
Freetown	FTI-10CD	Gotta Work	CD5	U.K.	1992	$8.00

Oyster Band

Singles

Label	Catalog Number	Title	Type	Country	Year	Longbox Value / Value
Rykodisc	RCD5 1034	Cry Cry	CD5	U.S.	1994	$5.00

Ozric Tentacles

Full Length

Label	Catalog Number	Title	Type	Country	Year	Longbox Value / Value
IRS		Strangeitude	DJ/LP	U.S.		$20.00

P.O.V.

Singles

Label	Catalog Number	Title	Type	Country	Year	Longbox Value / Value
Giant	9 40987-2	All Thru the Nite	CD5	U.S.	1993	$5.00
Giant	PRO-CD-6382	All Thru the Nite	CDJ	U.S.	1993	$2.00
Giant	PRO-CD-6003	Anutha Luv	CDJ	U.S.	1993	$2.00

P.T.P.

Singles

Label	Catalog Number	Title	Type	Country	Year	Longbox Value / Value
SPV	9165-3	Rubber Glove Seduction	CD5	Germany	1989	$8.00
Devotion	CDDVN-104	Rubber Glove Seduction	CD5	U.K.	1989	$8.00
Wax Trax	9073	Rubber Glove Seduction	CD5	U.S.	1989	$5.00

P W O G

Singles

Label	Catalog Number	Title	Type	Country	Year	Longbox Value / Value
Restless	72817	Peel Session	CD5	U.S.	1994	$5.00

P-Smoke

Singles

Label	Catalog Number	Title	Type	Country	Year	Longbox Value / Value
Sony	SRCS-5631	Mild & Wild	CD3	Japan	1991	$13.00/$3.00

Pace, Tom

Singles

Label	Catalog Number	Title	Type	Country	Year	Longbox Value / Value
Polygram	885872-3	Maybe	CD3	Germany	1989	$8.00
Polygram	885872-2	Maybe	CD5	Germany	1989	$8.00

Page, Jimmy

Full Length

Label	Catalog Number	Title	Type	Country	Year	Longbox Value / Value
Sony	AK 52428	Jimmy's Back Pages	LP/LB	U.S.	1992	$18.00/$15.00
Geffen		Outrider	DJ/Intvw	U.S.	1988	$150.00
	Interview CD, Cassette, VHS video and poster in plastic "lunch box."					
Geffen		Outrider	LP/LB	U.S.	1988	$14.00/$8.00
Geffen	PRO-CD-3099	Outrider: An Interview With...	DJ/Intvw	U.S.	1988	$20.00
Media America		Up Close	RS	U.S.	1988	$40.00
	2 CD set.					
Media America		Up Close	RS	U.S.	1989	$40.00
	2 CD set.					

Singles

Label	Catalog Number	Title	Type	Country	Year	Longbox Value / Value
Geffen	PRO-CD-3286	Prison Blues	CDJ	U.S.	1988	$6.00
Pioneer	10SW-60	Wasting My Time	CD3	Japan	1988	$12.00/$4.00
Geffen	PRO-CD-3083	Wasting My Time	CDJ	U.S.	1988	$6.00

Page, Martin

Singles

Label	Catalog Number	Title	Type	Country	Year	Longbox Value / Value
Polygram	856674	In The House of Stone	CD5	U.S.	1994	$5.00
	CDP 1444	Keeper of the Flame	CDJ	U.S.		$2.00

Page, Tommy

Full Length

Label	Catalog Number	Title	Type	Country	Year	Longbox Value / Value
Sire	PRO-CD-3616	23 Interview	DJ/Intvw	U.S.	1989	$5.00
Sire	2-26683-2-Dj	From the Heart	DJ/LP	U.S.	1991	$9.00
	Promo album in custom 3D-box.					

Singles

Label	Catalog Number	Title	Type	Country	Year	Longbox Value / Value
Sire	PRO-CD-3350	A Shoulder to Cry on	CDJ	U.S.	1988	$2.00
Sire	PRO-CD-3566	A Zillion Kisses	CDJ	U.S.	1988	$2.00
WEA	921532-2	I'll Be Your Everything	CD5	Germany	1990	$8.00
Sire	WPDP-6223	I'll Be Your Everything	CD3	Japan	1990	$12.00/$3.00
WEA	W-9959CD	I'll Be Your Everything	CD5	U.K.	1990	$8.00
Sire	PRO-CD-3908	I'll Be Your Everything	CDJ	U.S.	1990	$2.00
Sire	PRO-CD-5054	My Shining Star	CDJ	U.S.		$2.00
Sire	09P3-6120	Republic of Idols	CD3	Japan	1989	$12.00/$3.00
Warner Brothers	10P3-6046	Shag	CD3	Japan	1988	$12.00/$3.00
Warner Brothers	W-2999CD	Shoulder to Cry on	CD5	U.K.	1989	$8.00
WEA	7599-21754-2	Turn on the Radio	CD5	Germany	1990	$8.00
Sire	PRO-CD-4383	Turn on the Radio	CDJ	U.S.	1990	$2.00
Sire	PRO-CD-4461	Turn on the Radio	CDJ	U.S.	1990	$2.00
Sire	10P3-6003	Turning Me On	CD3	Japan	1988	$12.00/$3.00
WEA	9362-40127-2	Under the Rainbow	CD5	Germany	1991	$8.00
WEA	W-0044CD	Under the Rainbow	CD5	U.K.	1991	$8.00
Sire	WPDP-6234	When I Dream of You	CD3	Japan	1990	$12.00/$3.00
Sire		When I Dream of You	CDJ	U.S.		$2.00
WEA	9362-40122-2	Whenever You Close Your Eyes	CD5	Germany	1991	$8.00
Sire	WPDP-6281	Whenever You Close Your Eyes	CD3	Japan	1991	$12.00/$3.00
Sire	PRO-CD-4797	Whenever You Close Your Eyes	CDJ	U.S.	1991	$2.00
Sire	WPDP-6263	You Make Christmas Feel Like Heaven	CD3	Japan	1991	$12.00/$3.00
Sire	PRO-CD-4524	You Make Christmas Feel Like Heaven	CDJ	U.S.	1991	$2.00
Sire	W-2866CD	Zillion Kisses	CD3	U.K.	1989	$8.00

Paige, Elaine

Singles

Label	Catalog Number	Title	Type	Country	Year	Longbox Value / Value
RCA	PD-44392	Heart Don't Change My Mind	CD5	U.K.	1991	$8.00
Siren	SRNCD-110	Radio Ga-Ga	CD5	U.K.	1989	$8.00
RCA	PD-44450	Well Almost	CD5	U.K.	1991	$8.00

Paige, Kevin

Singles

Label	Catalog Number	Title	Type	Country	Year	Longbox Value / Value
		A Touch of Paradise	CDJ	U.S.		$2.00
Chrysalis	CHSCD-3444	Anything I Want	CD5	U.K.	1990	$8.00
		Anything I Want	CDJ	U.S.	1990	$2.00
Chrysalis	662678	Don't Shut Me Out	CD5	Germany	1990	$8.00
Chrysalis	CHSCD-3389	Don't Shut Me Out	CD5	U.K.	1990	$8.00
Chrysalis	TODP-2178	Touch of Paradise	CD3	Japan	1990	$13.00/$4.00

Paige, Raiana

Singles

Label	Catalog Number	Title	Type	Country	Year	Longbox Value / Value
Intercord	826 120	Open Up Your Heart	CD5	Germany	1989	$8.00
Pinnacle	SBUKSCD-10	Open Up Your Heart	CD5	U.K.	1989	$8.00

Paint The World

Singles

Label	Catalog Number	Title	Type	Country	Year	Longbox Value / Value
RCA	PD-42918	That's the Reason I'm Alive	CD5	U.K.	1989	$8.00
RCA	PD-42704	Worldwide	CD5	U.K.	1989	$8.00

Pajama Party

Singles

Label	Catalog Number	Title	Type	Country	Year	Longbox Value / Value
Atlantic	PRCD 3768-2	Got My Eye on You	CDJ	U.S.	1991	$2.00
Atlantic	AMDY-5019	Hide and Seek	CD3	Japan	1989	$12.00/$3.00
Atlantic	PR 3196-2	Hide and Seek	CDJ	U.S.	1989	$2.00
		Living Inside Your Love	CDJ	U.S.		$2.00
Atlantic	PR 2986-2	Over and Over	CDJ	U.S.	1989	$2.00

Palace Brothers

Singles

Label	Catalog Number	Title	Type	Country	Year	Longbox Value / Value
Caroline	37	Come In	CD5	U.S.	1994	$5.00

Paladins

Singles

Label	Catalog Number	Title	Type	Country	Year	Longbox Value / Value
Alligator	13	Follow Your Heart	CDJ	U.S.	1990	$2.00

Pale Divine

Singles

Label	Catalog Number	Title	Type	Country	Year	Longbox Value / Value
Atco	PRCD 4158-2	Something About Me	CDJ	U.S.	1991	$2.00

Pale Saints

Singles

Label	Catalog Number	Title	Type	Country	Year	Longbox Value / Value
4AD		Angel	CDJ	U.S.	1994	$6.00
4AD	5546	Blue Flower	CD5	U.K.	1992	$3.00
4AD		Fine Friend	CDJ	U.S.	1994	$9.00
4AD	BAD4013CD	Fine Friends	CD5	Canada	1994	$8.00
4AD	COCY-5136	Flesh Balloon	CD3	Japan	1989	$12.00/$3.00
4AD	BAD-1009CD	Flesh Balloon	CD5	U.K.	1989	$8.00
4AD	BAD-0015CD	Half the Life	CD5	U.K.	1989	$8.00
4AD		Henry	CDJ	U.S.	1994	$6.00
4AD	BAD-0015CD	Sight of You	CD5	U.K.	1989	$8.00
4AD	BAD-2008CD	Throwing Back the Apple	CD5	U.K.	1989	$8.00

Paleface

Singles

Label	Catalog Number	Title	Type	Country	Year	Longbox Value / Value
Polydor	CDP 528	Bum And Rob	CDJ	U.S.	1991	$2.00

Palmer, Holly

Full Length

Label	Catalog Number	Title	Type	Country	Year	Longbox Value / Value
Reprise	PRO-CD-8365	Different Languages	DJ/Smplr	U.S.	1996	$0.00/$10.00

Palmer, Keith

Singles

Label	Catalog Number	Title	Type	Country	Year	Longbox Value / Value
Epic	ESK 73988	Don't Throw Me in the Briar Patch	CDJ	U.S.	1991	$2.00

Palmer, Robert

Full Length

Label	Catalog Number	Title	Type	Country	Year	Longbox Value / Value
BBC Radio		BBC Classic Tracks	RS	U.S.	1991	$20.00
	Airdate: 2/18/91.					
BBC Radio		BBC Classic Tracks	RS	U.S.	1992	$20.00
	Airdate: 2/10/92.					
Westwood One		BBC Classic Tracks	RS	U.S.	1995	$20.00
	Airdate: 3/20/95.					
DIR		King Biscuit Flour Hour	RS	U.S.	1988	$30.00
	Airdate: 4/3/88.					
DIR		King Biscuit Flour Hour	RS	U.S.	1990	$30.00
	Airdate: 1/15/90.					
DIR		King Biscuit Flour Hour	RS	U.S.	1991	$30.00
	Airdate: 3/3/91.					
DIR		King Biscuit Flour Hour	RS	U.S.	1994	$15.00
	Airdate: 10/23/94.					
DIR		King Biscuit Flour Hour	RS	U.S.	1995	$15.00
	Airdate: 12/3/95.					
Island	A2-90471	Riptide	LP	U.S.	1985	$10.00
	Columbia House Record Club digipak version.					
Island	A2-90471	Riptide	LP	U.S.	1985	$15.00/$10.00
	Digipak version.					
Manhattan	DPRO-04121	Simply Palmer-A Special Interview Compact Disc	DJ/Intvw	U.S.	1988	$5.00
Media America		Up Close	RS	U.S.	1988	$30.00
	2 CD set.					
Media America		Up Close	RS	U.S.	1991	$30.00
	2 CD set.					

Singles

Label	Catalog Number	Title	Type	Country	Year	Longbox Value / Value
Island	P15D37004	Addicted to Love	CD3	Japan	1988	$13.00/$4.00
Island/NTSC	IS 270	Addicted to Love	DJ/CDV	U.S.	1988	$20.00
Island	885633	Bad Case of Loving You	CD5	Germany	1989	$9.00
Island	CID-438	Bad Case of Loving You	CD5	U.K.	1989	$9.00
Island	PR 3045-2	Bad Case of Loving You	CDJ	U.S.	1989	$2.00
Island	PRCD 6741-2	Can We Still Be Friends	CDJ	U.S.	1992	$2.00
EMI	CDEM-85	Change His Ways	CD5	U.K.	1989	$9.00
EMI	204350-2	Dreams to Remember	CD5	Germany	1991	$9.00
EMI	CDEM-193	Dreams to Remember	CD5	U.K.	1991	$9.00
Toshiba	XP10-2039	Early in the Morning	CD3	Japan	1988	$13.00/$4.00
EMI	DPRO-04153	Early in the Morning	CDJ	U.S.	1988	$2.00
EMI	DPRO-04211	Early in the Morning	CDJ	U.S.	1988	$2.00
Island	887296	Every Kinda People	CD5	Germany	1991	$9.00
Island	CID-498	Every Kinda People	CD5	U.K.	1991	$9.00
Island	PRCD 6714-2	Every Kinda People	CDJ	U.S.	1992	$2.00
EMI		Girl You Want	CD5	U.K.	1994	$10.00
	Second version.					
EMI	CDEM-186	Happiness	CD5	U.K.	1991	$9.00
Island	204110-2	I'll Be Your Baby Tonight	CD5	Germany	1991	$9.00
EMI	CDEM-167	I'll Be Your Baby Tonight	CD5	U.K.	1991	$9.00
EMI	DPRO-04747	I'll Be Your Baby Tonight	CDJ	U.S.	1991	$2.00
EMI	CDEM-99	It Could Happen to You	CD5	U.K.	1989	$9.00
EMI	DPRO-04514	Life in Detail	CDJ	U.S.	1990	$2.00
EMI	DPRO-04742	Life in Detail	CDJ	U.S.	1990	$2.00
EMI	204180-2	Mercy Mercy Me	CD5	Germany	1991	$9.00
Toshiba	TODP-2268	Mercy Mercy Me	CD3	Japan	1991	$13.00/$4.00
EMI	DPRO-4742	Mercy Mercy Me	CDJ	U.S.	1991	$2.00
EMI	DPRO-04193	More Than Ever	CDJ	U.S.	1988	$2.00
		Nightcraft	CD5	U.K.		$10.00
		Nightcraft	CD5	U.K.		$10.00
	Second version.					
Island	P15D-37005	Riptide	CD3	Japan	1988	$13.00/$4.00
Toshiba	XP10-2074	She Makes My Day	CD3	Japan	1988	$13.00/$4.00
EMI	CDEM-65	She Makes My Day	CD5	U.K.	1988	$9.00
EMI		She Makes My Day	CDJ	U.S.	1988	$2.00
EMI	202691-3	Simply Irresistable	CD3	Germany	1988	$9.00
EMI	202692-2	Simply Irresistible	CD5	Germany	1988	$9.00
Toshiba	XP10-2010	Simply Irresistible	CD3	Japan	1988	$13.00/$4.00
EMI	CDEM-61	Simply Irresistible	CD5	U.K.	1988	$9.00
EMI	DPRO 04075	Simply Irresistible	CDJ	U.S.	1988	$2.00
Polystar	P51D-37006	Sweet Lies	CD3	Japan	1988	$13.00/$4.00
Island	CIDX-352	Sweet Lies	CD3	U.K.	1988	$9.00
Island	PR 2190-2	Sweet Lies	CDJ	U.S.	1988	$2.00
EMI	DPRO 04307	Tell Me I'm Not Dreaming	CDJ	U.S.	1989	$2.00
EMI	DPRO 4743	You Can't Get Enough Of A Good Thing	CDJ	U.S.	1991	$2.00
EMI	DPRO 4651	You're Amazing	CDJ	U.S.	1990	$2.00
EMI	DPRO 4699	You're Amazing	CDJ	U.S.	1990	$2.00

Palumbo, John

Singles

Label	Catalog Number	Title	Type	Country	Year	Longbox Value / Value
Grudge	4762-2-RDj	Drifting Back to Motown	CDJ	U.S.	1989	$2.00
Grudge	4760-2-RDj	Walk on the Wild Side	CDJ	U.S.	1989	$2.00

Pandora's Box

Singles

Label	Catalog Number	Title	Type	Country	Year	Longbox Value / Value
Virgin	VSCD-1227	Good Girls Go to Heaven	CD3	U.K.	1990	$8.00
Virgin	162703	It's All Coming Back to Me Now	CD3	Germany	1990	$8.00
Virgin	VSCD-1216	It's All Coming Back to Me Now	CD3	U.K.	1990	$8.00
Virgin	VSCDX-1216	It's All Coming Back to Me Now	CD3	U.K.	1990	$8.00
Virgin	VSCD-1275	Safe Sex	CD3	U.K.	1990	$8.00

Panic

Full Length

Label	Catalog Number	Title	Type	Country	Year	Longbox Value / Value
Warner Brothers	26576	Epidemic	LP/LB	U.S.		$12.00/$8.00
Warner Brothers	45215	Fact	LP/LB	U.S.		$12.00/$8.00

Panic Zone

Singles

Label	Catalog Number	Title	Type	Country	Year	Longbox Value / Value
ZYX	6504-8	We Will Rock You	CD5	Germany	1991	$6.00

Pantera

Full Length

Label	Catalog Number	Title	Type	Country	Year	Longbox Value / Value
Atco	PRCD 4538-2	A Not So Vulgar Display of Power	DJ/Smplr	U.S.	1992	$10.00
		Driven Down Under '94 Souvenir Collection	LTD/LP	Australia	1995	$60.00
	3 CD set.					
		Far Beyond Driven	LTD/LP	Australia	1994	$35.00
	3 CD set.					
Atco		Hostile Mixes	DJ/Smplr	U.S.	1994	$10.00
Atco		In-Store Play Sampler	DJ/Smplr	U.S.	1994	$10.00
		Tour Souvenir	LTD/LP	Japan	1994	$50.00
	3 CD set.					

Singles

Label	Catalog Number	Title	Type	Country	Year	Longbox Value / Value
Atco	PRCD 3965-2	Cemetery Gates	CDJ	U.S.	1990	$3.00
	PRCD 9543-2	Drag the Waters	CDJ	U.S.		$2.00
Atco	PRCD 4990-2	F**king Hostile	CDJ	U.S.	1992	$3.00
Atco		Five Minutes Alone	CDJ	U.S.	1994	$3.00
Atco		Hollow	CDJ	U.S.	1994	$3.00
Eastwest	PRCD 5511-2	I'm Broken	CDJ	U.S.	1994	$3.00
Eastwest	PRCD 5528-2	I'm Broken	CDJ	U.S.	1994	$3.00
Eastwest	PRCD 5555-2	I'm Broken	CDJ	U.S.	1994	$6.00
		I'm Broken/Slaughtered	CD5	U.K.		$10.00
	AMCY-870	Live	CD5	Japan	1995	$20.00
Atco	A-5845CD	Mouth for War	CD5	U.K.	1992	$10.00
Atco	PRCD 4414-2	Mouth for War	CDJ	U.S.	1992	$3.00
Atco		Planet Caravan	CDJ	U.S.	1994	$3.00
Atco		Planet Caravan	CDJ	U.S.	1994	$3.00
	Second version.					
Atco	PRCD 3871-2	Psycho Holiday	CDJ	U.S.	1990	$3.00
Atco	PRCD 4651-2	This Love	CDJ	U.S.	1992	$3.00
Atco	PRCD 4866-2	Walk	CDJ	U.S.	1992	$3.00

Papa's Culture

Singles

Label	Catalog Number	Title	Type	Country	Year	Longbox Value / Value
Elektra	PRCD 8719-2	Swim	CDJ	U.S.	1993	$2.00

Paperboy

Singles

Label	Catalog Number	Title	Type	Country	Year	Longbox Value / Value
Next Plateau	021	Bumpin'	CDJ	U.S.	1993	$2.00
ffrr	4228570592	Ditty	CD5	U.K.	1993	$8.00
Full Frequency	50012	Ditty	CD5	U.S.	1993	$4.00

Papillon

Singles

Label	Catalog Number	Title	Type	Country	Year	Longbox Value / Value
Polygram	390768-2	Different World	CD5	Germany	1991	$8.00

Paradis, Vanessa

Full Length

Label	Catalog Number	Title	Type	Country	Year	Longbox Value / Value
	POCP-1403	Live	LP	Japan		$40.00
	DC1-3106	Works	DJ/Smplr	Japan		$100.00

Singles

Label	Catalog Number	Title	Type	Country	Year	Longbox Value / Value
Remark	863781-2	Be My Baby	CD5	Germany	1992	$8.00
Remark	861169-2	Be My Baby	CD5	Germany	1992	$8.00
Remark	PODP-1061	Be My Baby	CD3	Japan	1992	$12.00/$3.00
Remark	PZCD-235	Be My Baby	CD5	U.K.	1992	$8.00
Remark	PZCDD-235	Be My Baby	CD5	U.K.	1992	$8.00
Polydor	CDP 784	Be My Baby	CDJ	U.S.	1992	$2.00
	PODP-1094	Gotta Have It	CD3	Japan		$12.00/$4.00
Polydor	P10P-3004	Joe Le Taxi	CD3	Japan	1988	$12.00/$3.00
		Joe Le Taxi	CDJ	U.S.	1988	$2.00
	PODP-1079	Just As Long as You Are There	CD3	Japan		$12.00/$4.00
		Just As Long as You Are There	CD5	U.K.		$10.00
		Just As Long as You Are There	CD5	U.K.		$10.00
	Second version.					
Polydor	PODP-1022	L'Amour Anne Sour	CD3	Japan	1991	$12.00/$3.00
Polygram	887308-2	Manolo Manolete	CD5	Germany	1987	$8.00
Polydor	P10P-30012	Manolo Manolete	CD3	Japan	1988	$12.00/$3.00
Polygram	887640-2	Marilyn and John	CD5	Germany	1988	$8.00
Polydor	P10P-30017	Marilyn and John	CD3	Japan	1988	$12.00/$3.00
Polydor	P10P-37003	Marilyn and John	CD3	Japan	1988	$12.00/$3.00
Polygram	871224-3	Maxou	CD3	Germany	1989	$8.00
Polygram	871225-2	Maxou	CD5	Germany	1989	$8.00
Remark	PZCD-38	Maxou	CD5	U.K.	1989	$8.00
	PODP-1088	Natural High	CD3	Japan		$12.00/$4.00
Remark	PODP-1070	Sunday Mondays	CD3	Japan	1993	$12.00/$3.00
Remark	PZCDD-251-DJ	Sunday Mondays	CDJ	U.K.	1993	$15.00
		Sunday Mornings	CD5	U.K.		$10.00
		Sunday Mornings	CD5	U.K.		$10.00
	Second version.					

Paradise Lost

Singles

Label	Catalog Number	Title	Type	Country	Year	Longbox Value / Value
Pinnacle	CDKUT-150	As I Die	CD5	U.K.	1993	$8.00
Metal Blade	14012-2	As I Die	CD5	U.S.	1993	$5.00

Paradise Programme

Singles

Label	Catalog Number	Title	Type	Country	Year	Longbox Value / Value
CBS	657903-2	Deep Green	CD5	Germany	1992	$8.00
CBS	656545-2	Rain	CD5	Germany	1992	$8.00

Paranoid

Singles

Label	Catalog Number	Title	Type	Country	Year	Longbox Value / Value
SPV	1333-3	I Dominate You	CD5	Germany	1991	$8.00
SPV	1327-3	Vicious Circle	CD5	Germany	1991	$8.00

Parental Advisory

Singles

Label	Catalog Number	Title	Type	Country	Year	Longbox Value / Value
MCA	MCA5P-2503	Lifeline	CDJ	U.S.	1993	$2.00
MCA	MCA5P-2757	Manic	CDJ	U.S.	1993	$2.00

Pariah

Singles

Label	Catalog Number	Title	Type	Country	Year	Longbox Value / Value
Scarface	101	Assata's Song	CD5	U.S.	1992	$2.00
Scarface	102	Assata's Song	CD5	U.S.	1993	$4.00
Geffen	PRO-CD-4547	Make Believe	CDJ	U.S.	1993	$2.00
Geffen	PRO-CD-4532	Powerless	CDJ	U.S.	1993	$2.00

Paris Angels

Label	Catalog Number	Title	Type	Country	Year	Longbox Value / Value
		Singles				
Virgin	VSCDG-1365	Fade	CD5	U.K.	1991	$8.00
Sheer Joy	SHEER-005CD	Oh Yes	CD5	U.K.	1991	$8.00
SPV	8751-3	Perfume	CD5	Germany	1990	$8.00
Virgin	VSCDT-1360	Perfume	CD5	U.K.	1990	$8.00
SPV	8766-3	Scope	CD5	Germany	1990	$8.00
Sheer Joy	SHEER-006CD	Scope	CD5	U.K.	1991	$8.00

Paris by Air

Label	Catalog Number	Title	Type	Country	Year	Longbox Value / Value
		Singles				
Columbia	CSK 73261	C'mon and Dance With Me	CDJ	U.S.	1990	$2.00
Columbia	CSK 1886	Voices in Your Hand	CDJ	U.S.	1989	$2.00

Paris, Mica

Label	Catalog Number	Title	Type	Country	Year	Longbox Value / Value
		Full Length				
Island	PRCD 6801-2	Wait Baby Love Interview, The	DJ/Intvw	U.S.	1993	$15.00
		Singles				
BMG	861773	Breathe Life Into Me	CD5	Germany	1989	$8.00
4th & B'way	BRCD-115	Breathe Life Into Me	CD5	U.K.	1989	$8.00
Island	PR 2870-2	Breathe Life Into Me	CDJ	U.S.	1989	$2.00
BMG	663461	Contribution	CD5	Germany	1990	$8.00
4th & B'way	BRCD-188	Contribution	CD5	U.K.	1990	$8.00
Island	PRCD 6652	Contribution	CDJ	U.S.	1991	$2.00
Island	PRCD 6666	Contribution	CDJ	U.S.	1991	$2.00
Island	PHDR-126	I Wanna Hold on to You	CD3	Japan	1993	$13.00/$4.00
Island	PRCD 6774	I Wanna Hold on to You	CDJ	U.S.	1993	$2.00
4th & B'way	BRCD-207	If I Love U 2 Nite	CD5	U.K.	1991	$8.00
BMG	661643	Like Dreamers Do	CD5	Germany	1988	$8.00
4th & B'way	BRCDP-108	Like Dreamers Do	CD5	U.K.	1988	$8.00
BMG	665024	My One Temptation	CD5	Germany	1988	$8.00
Polydor	P10D-30005	My One Temptation	CD3	Japan	1988	$12.00/$3.00
4th & B'way	BRCD-85	My One Temptation	CD5	U.K.	1988	$8.00
Island	PR 2567-2	My One Temptation	CDJ	U.S.	1988	$2.00
Island	BRCD-199	South of the River	CD5	U.K.	1990	$8.00
Island	BRCD-122	Where is the Love	CD5	U.K.	1989	$8.00
		Whisper a Prayer	CD5	U.K.		$10.00
		Whisper a Prayer	CD5	U.K.		$10.00
	Second version.					
Island	PRCD 6789-2	Whisper a Prayer	CDJ	U.S.	1993	$2.00
Big Life	867741-2	Young Soul Rebel	CD5	Germany	1991	$8.00
Big Life	BLRD-57	Young Soul Rebel	CD5	U.K.	1991	$8.00
Scotti Brothers	ZSK 75305	Young Soul Rebel	CDJ	U.S.	1991	$2.00

Paris, Twila

Label	Catalog Number	Title	Type	Country	Year	Longbox Value / Value
		Full Length				
		Where I Stand	DJ/LP	U.S.		$12.00
	Advance release.					

Parker, Charlie

Label	Catalog Number	Title	Type	Country	Year	Longbox Value / Value
		Full Length				
Savoy Records	CY-78810	Bird Returns, The	LTD/LP	U.S.	1996	$20.00
	CD in miniature repica of original LP sleeve.					
Savoy Records	CY-78982	Charlie Parker Memorial Vol. 1	LTD/LP	U.S.	1995	$20.00
	CD in miniature repica of original LP sleeve.					
Savoy Records	CY-78984	Charlie Parker Memorial Vol. 2	LTD/LP	U.S.	1995	$20.00
	CD in miniature repica of original LP sleeve.					
Savoy Records	CY-78990	Charlie Parker Story, The	LTD/LP	U.S.	1995	$20.00
	CD in miniature repica of original LP sleeve.					
		Complete Savoy Years	LTD/LP	Japan	1995	$150.00
	8 CD boxed set.					
Savoy Records	CY-78991	Genius of Charlie Parker	LTD/LP	U.S.	1995	$20.00
	CD in miniature repica of original LP sleeve.					
Savoy Records	CY-78983	Immortal Charlie Parker Story, The	LTD/LP	U.S.	1995	$20.00
	CD in miniature repica of original LP sleeve.					
Savoy Records	CY-78809	Newly Discovered Sides of Charlie Parker	LTD/LP	U.S.	1996	$20.00
	CD in miniature repica ozzf original LP sleeve.					
Verve	825671-2	Now's The Time	LP/LB	U.S.†	1985	$14.00/$8.00

Parker, Graham

Label	Catalog Number	Title	Type	Country	Year	Longbox Value / Value
		Full Length				
Arista	ASCD-8234	Another Grey Area	LP/LB	U.S.†	1985	$14.00/$8.00
Arista		Best of 1988-1991	LP/LB	U.S.†	1991	$14.00/$8.00
Demon		Human Soul	LP	U.K.		$15.00
		Mona Lisa's Sister	LP	U.S.		$10.00
Elektra	60388-2	Steady Nerves	LP/LB	U.S.†	1985	$14.00/$8.00
RCA		Struck by Lightning	LP/BP	U.S.		$14.00/$8.00
		Singles				
RCA	9114-2-RDj	Big Man on Paper	CDJ	U.S.	1989	$2.00
RCA	9178-2-RDj	Everything Goes	CDJ	U.S.	1990	$2.00
		Haunted Episodes	CDJ	U.S.		$3.00
Capitol	C2 15939	Here It Comes Again	CD5	U.S.	1992	$5.00
Capitol	DPRO-79390	Release Me	CDJ	U.S.	1992	$2.00

Parker, Gregg

Label	Catalog Number	Title	Type	Country	Year	Longbox Value / Value
		Singles				
Line	UBCD-900849	Black Dog	CD5	Germany	1989	$8.00

Parker, Gwen

Label	Catalog Number	Title	Type	Country	Year	Longbox Value / Value
		Singles				
Columbia	654696-3	My Mama Always Told Me	CD3	Germany	1989	$8.00

Parker, Maceo

Label	Catalog Number	Title	Type	Country	Year	Longbox Value / Value
		Full Length				
Verve	PAR-2	Galactic Grooves	DJ/Smplr	U.S.	1992	$10.00
Polygram	MAC-2	Mo' Roots	DJ/LP	U.S.	1991	$15.00
	Picture disc.					
		Singles				
4th & B'way	515	Let 'Em Out	CDJ	U.S.	1990	$2.00

Parker, Ray Jr.

Label	Catalog Number	Title	Type	Country	Year	Longbox Value / Value
		Singles				
Arista	A10D-142	Ghostbusters	CD3	Japan	1989	$12.00/$4.00
MCA	CD45 1683	Girl I Saw You	CDJ	U.S.	1991	$2.00
MCA	CD45 1464	She Needs to Get Some	CDJ	U.S.	1991	$2.00
MCA	CD45 1646	She Needs to Get Some	CDJ	U.S.	1991	$2.00

Parker, Rick

Label	Catalog Number	Title	Type	Country	Year	Longbox Value / Value
		Singles				
Geffen	PRO-CD-4313	Salesgirl	CDJ	U.S.	1991	$2.00
Geffen	PRO-CD-4367	Salesgirl	CDJ	U.S.	1992	$2.00

Parkhill International

Label	Catalog Number	Title	Type	Country	Year	Longbox Value / Value
		Singles				
Jive	KGBD-001	I Want to Be Together	CD5	U.K.	1992	$8.00

Parks, John Andrew

Label	Catalog Number	Title	Type	Country	Year	Longbox Value / Value
		Singles				
Capitol	DPRO 79110	Ten Gallon Dreams	CDJ	U.S.	1990	$2.00

Parks, Van Dyke

Label	Catalog Number	Title	Type	Country	Year	Longbox Value / Value
		Full Length				
Warner Brothers	23829-2	Jump!	LP/LB	U.S.†	1984	$14.00/$8.00

Parlan, Horace

Label	Catalog Number	Title	Type	Country	Year	Longbox Value / Value
		Full Length				
Blue Note		Happy Frame of Mind	LTD/LP	U.S.	1995	$19.00

Parnell, Lee Roy

Label	Catalog Number	Title	Type	Country	Year	Longbox Value / Value
		Singles				
Arista	ASCD-2400	Rock, The	CDJ	U.S.	1991	$2.00
Arista	ASCD-2523	Tender Moment	CDJ	U.S.	1993	$6.00
Arista	ASCD-2523	What Kind of Fool Do You Think I Am	CDJ	U.S.	1992	$2.00

Parr, John

Label	Catalog Number	Title	Type	Country	Year	Longbox Value / Value
		Singles				
Music For Nations	CDKUT-144	Man With A Vision	CD5	U.K.	1992	$9.00
Columbia	652886-3	Restless Heart	CD3	Germany	1988	$9.00
Trax	CDTX-2	Restless Heart	CD5	U.K.	1988	$9.00
BMG	663927	West Ward	CD5	Germany	1990	$9.00

Parsons, Alan

Label	Catalog Number	Title	Type	Country	Year	Longbox Value / Value
		Full Length				
Album Network		In the Studio (I, Robot)	RS	U.S.		$30.00
Westwood One		Superstars	RS	U.S.	1996	$50.00
	2 CD set. Airdate: 2/19/96.					

Parsons, Alan Project

Label	Catalog Number	Title	Type	Country	Year	Longbox Value / Value
		Full Length				
Arista	ARCD-8204	Ammonia Avenue	LP/LB	U.S.†	1984	$14.00/$8.00
Arista	ARCD-8193	Best of	LP/LB	U.S.†	1984	$14.00/$8.00
Arista	ARCD-8062	Eve	LP/LB	U.S.†	1985	$14.00/$8.00
Arista	ARCD-8033	I In the Sky	LP/LB	U.S.†	1984	$14.00/$8.00
Mobile Fidelity	MFCD-804	I Robot	LP/LB	U.S.†	1984	$28.00/$25.00
Arista	ARCD-8040	I Robot	LP/LB	U.S.†	1985	$14.00/$8.00
Arista	ARCD-8225	Pyramid	LP/LB	U.S.†	1985	$14.00/$8.00
Arista	07822-18744-2	Try Anything Once	LTD/LP	U.S.	1993	$25.00
	Limited edition gold disc of album in digipak.					
Arista	07822-18744-2	Try Anything Once	LTD/LP	U.S.	1993	$30.00
Arista	ARCD-8226	Turn of a Friendly Card	LP/LB	U.S.†	1985	$14.00/$8.00
Arista	ARCD-8263	Vulture Culture	LP/LB	U.S.†	1984	$14.00/$8.00
		Singles				
Arista	ASCD-2660	One Life	CDJ	U.S.	1994	$3.00
Arista	ASCD-2623	Turn It Up	CDJ	U.S.	1993	$3.00
Arista		Wine From the Water	CD5	U.K.		$10.00

Parsons, Steve

Label	Catalog Number	Title	Type	Country	Year	Longbox Value / Value
		Full Length				
		Colors: Dream of Gold	LP/LB	U.S.		$18.00/$15.00

Partland Brothers

Label	Catalog Number	Title	Type	Country	Year	Longbox Value / Value
		Singles				
		Soul City	CDJ	Canada		$3.00

Partners Crime Syndicate

Label	Catalog Number	Title	Type	Country	Year	Longbox Value / Value
		Singles				
Columbia	655826-3	54-56	CD3	Germany	1990	$8.00

Partners in Kryme

Label	Catalog Number	Title	Type	Country	Year	Longbox Value / Value
		Singles				
EMI	203933-2	Turtle Power	CD5	Germany	1990	$8.00
		Turtle Power	CDJ	U.S.	1990	$2.00
EMI	204102-2	Undercover	CD5	Germany	1990	$8.00
SBK	CDSBK-15	Undercover	CD5	U.K.	1990	$8.00
		Undercover	CDJ	U.S.	1990	$2.00

Parton, Dolly

Label	Catalog Number	Title	Type	Country	Year	Longbox Value / Value
		Full Length				
RCA	PCD1-4940	Great Pretender, The	LP/BP	U.S.†	1984	$14.00/$8.00
RCA	PCD1-4422	Greatest Hits	LP/BP	U.S.†	1985	$14.00/$8.00
Columbia	CSK 2159	Home for Christmas	DJ/RS	U.S.	1990	$15.00
Pioneer	PA-84-068	In London	LD	U.S.	1984	$20.00
Pioneer	PA-84-068	In London	LD	U.S.	1990	$20.00
	Digital audio.					
RCA	PCD1-5414	Real Love	LP/BP	U.S.†	1985	$15.00/$10.00
RCA	PCD1-5414	Real Love	LP/BP	U.S.	1985	$15.00/$10.00
Columbia	CSK 53199	Slow Dancing With the Moon	DJ/LP	U.S.	1992	$20.00
	CD in digipak.					
		Singles				
RCA	PD-49447	9 To 5	CD3	Germany	1989	$10.00
RCA	PD-49447	9 To 5	CD3	U.K.	1989	$10.00
Columbia	CSK 5590	Day I Fall in Love	CDJ	U.S.	1993	$6.00
Columbia	651434-2	I Know You by Heart	CD5	U.K.	1988	$10.00
Columbia	CSK 6256	When You Tell Me	CDJ	U.S.	1995	$6.00
Columbia	DOLLYC-2	Why'd You Come in Here Lookin' Like That	CD5	U.K.	1989	$10.00
Columbia	CSK 1588	Why'd You Come in Here Lookin' Like That	CDJ	U.S.	1989	$7.00

Parton, Dolly/Ronstadt, Linda/Harris, Emmy Lou

Label	Catalog Number	Title	Type	Country	Year	Longbox Value / Value
		Singles				
		Telling Me Lies	CDJ	U.S.		$7.00

Party

Label	Catalog Number	Title	Type	Country	Year	Longbox Value / Value
		Singles				
Hollywood	PCDY-00107	Free	CD3	Japan	1992	$12.00/$3.00
Hollywood	HWD-1122CD	Free	CD5	U.K.	1992	$8.00
Hollywood	PRCD 8231-2	I Found Love	CDJ	U.S.	1990	$2.00
Intercord	825 934	In My Dreams	CD5	Germany	1992	$9.00
Hollywood	HWD-113CD	Peace, Love & Understanding	CD5	U.K.	1991	$9.00
Hollywood	PRCD 8498-2	Private Affair	CDJ	U.S.	1992	$2.00
Intercord	825 914	Summer Vacation	CD5	Germany	1991	$9.00
Hollywood	HWD-106CD	Summer Vacation	CD5	U.K.	1991	$9.00
Hollywood	PRCD 8208-2	Summer Vacation	CDJ	U.S.	1990	$2.00
Hollywood	PRCD 8366-2	Summer Vacation	CDJ	U.S.	1991	$2.00
Hollywood	PRCD 8293-2	That's Why	CDJ	U.S.	1991	$2.00

Pasadenas

Label	Catalog Number	Title	Type	Country	Year	Longbox Value / Value
		Singles				
Columbia	656845-2	Another Lover	CD5	Germany	1991	$9.00
Columbia	656845-2	Another Lover	CD5	U.K.	1991	$9.00
Columbia	653155-3	Enchanted Lady	CD3	U.K.	1988	$9.00
Columbia	CDPASA-3	Enchanted Lady	CD5	U.K.	1988	$9.00

Label	Catalog Number	Title	Type	Country	Year	Longbox Value / Value
Columbia	654768-3	Funny Feeling	CD3	Germany	1989	$9.00
Columbia	658056-2	I Believe in You	CD5	U.K.	1992	$9.00
Columbia	657718-2	I'm Doing Fine	CD5	Germany	1992	$9.00
Columbia	658774-2	Let's Stay Together	CD5	U.K.	1992	$9.00
Columbia	655937-2	Love Thing	CD5	Germany	1990	$9.00
Columbia	CDPASA-4	Love Thing	CD5	U.K.	1990	$9.00
Columbia	657925-2	Make It With You	CD5	Germany	1992	$9.00
Columbia	657925-2	Make It With You	CD5	U.K.	1992	$9.00
Columbia	658341-2	Moving In the Right Direction	CD5	U.K.	1992	$9.00
Columbia	656087-3	Reeling	CD3	Germany	1990	$9.00
Columbia	ESDA-7046	Reeling	CD3	Japan	1990	$13.00/$4.00
Columbia	PASAC-5	Reeling	CD5	U.K.	1990	$9.00
Columbia	CDPASA-2	Riding in a Train	CD5	U.K.	1988	$9.00
Columbia		Riding in a Train	CDJ	U.S.	1988	$2.00
Columbia	651594-2	Tribute (Right on)	CD5	Germany	1988	$9.00
Columbia	PASAC-1	Tribute (Right on)	CD5	U.K.	1988	$9.00
Columbia	CSK 1438	Tribute (Right on)	CDJ	U.S.	1989	$2.00

Passengers – Original Sound Chats (Island OST2)

Passengers

Full Length

Label	Catalog Number	Title	Type	Country	Year	Longbox Value / Value
Island	OST2	Original SoundChats	DJ/Intvw	U.K.	1995	$85.00
	2 CD set.					

Singles

Label	Catalog Number	Title	Type	Country	Year	Longbox Value / Value
Island		Bosnia	CDJ	U.S.	1995	$35.00
	CDJ and VHS in box.					
Island		Miss Sarajevo	CD5	U.K.	1995	$12.00
Island		Miss Sarajevo	CDJ	U.K.	1995	$18.00
Island		Miss Sarajevo	CDJ	U.S.	1995	$10.00

Passion

Singles

Label	Catalog Number	Title	Type	Country	Year	Longbox Value / Value
MCA	MCA5P3472	Where I'm From	CDJ	U.S.		$2.00

Pastels

Singles

Label	Catalog Number	Title	Type	Country	Year	Longbox Value / Value
Paperhouse	PAPER 008	Speeding Motorcycle	CD5	U.K.	1991	$8.00
Paperhouse	PAPER 011	Thru Your Heart	CD5	U.K.	1991	$8.00
Matador	114	Yoga	CD5	U.S.	1994	$5.00

Pat & Mick

Singles

Label	Catalog Number	Title	Type	Country	Year	Longbox Value / Value
PWL	PWCD-75	Gimme Some	CD5	U.K.	1991	$8.00
Eastwest	246974-2	I Haven't Stopped Dancing Yet	CD5	Germany	1989	$8.00
Alfa	11B3-37	I Haven't Stopped Dancing Yet	CD3	Japan	1989	$13.00/$4.00
PWL	PWCD-33	I Haven't Stopped Dancing Yet	CD5	U.K.	1989	$8.00
Alfa	11B3-37	Let's All Chant	CD3	Japan	1988	$13.00/$4.00
PWL	PWCD-233	Shake Your Groove Thing	CD5	U.K.	1992	$8.00
East Wet	9031-7168-2	Use It Up and Wear It Out	CD5	Germany	1990	$8.00
Alfa	ALDB-47	Use It Up and Wear It Out	CD3	Japan	1990	$13.00/$4.00
PWL	PWCD-55	Use It Up and Wear It Out	CD5	U.K.	1990	$8.00
		Use It Up and Wear It Out	CDJ	U.S.	1990	$2.00

Patra

Singles

Label	Catalog Number	Title	Type	Country	Year	Longbox Value / Value
Columbia	77970	Pull Up to the Bumper	CD5	U.S.	1995	$5.00
	BSK 7615	Scent of Attraction	CDJ	U.S.		$2.00
Epic	ESK 77289	Worker Man	CDJ	U.S.	1994	$2.00

Patti, Sandi

Singles

Label	Catalog Number	Title	Type	Country	Year	Longbox Value / Value
Word	9011095154	Another Time, Another Place	CDJ	U.S.	1990	$3.00
Epic	ESK 4420	Another Time, Another Place	CDJ	U.S.	1991	$2.00
Word	9016450157	Exalt Thy Name	CDJ	U.S.	1989	$3.00

Patton, John

Full Length

Label	Catalog Number	Title	Type	Country	Year	Longbox Value / Value
Blue Note		Blue John	LTD/LP	U.S.	1995	$19.00

Paul Bley

Full Length

Label	Catalog Number	Title	Type	Country	Year	Longbox Value / Value
Savoy Records	CY-78987	Footloose	LTD/LP	U.S.	1995	$20.00
	CD in miniature repica of original LP sleeve.					

Paul, Chris

Singles

Label	Catalog Number	Title	Type	Country	Year	Longbox Value / Value
EMI	202462-2	Back in My Arms	CD5	Germany	1988	$8.00

Paul, Les

Full Length

Label	Catalog Number	Title	Type	Country	Year	Longbox Value / Value
Image	ID7236HB	He Changed the Music	LD	U.S.		$25.00

Singles

Label	Catalog Number	Title	Type	Country	Year	Longbox Value / Value
Rhino	R3 73039	How High the Moon	CD3	U.S.	1988	$5.00/$2.00

Pavarotti, Luciano

Full Length

Label	Catalog Number	Title	Type	Country	Year	Longbox Value / Value
Castle	CMM CD 103	Nessun Dorma	LP	U.K.	1994	$25.00
	CD+I.					
London	PAV-1	Songbook	DJ/Smplr	U.S.	1991	$20.00

Pavement

Singles

Label	Catalog Number	Title	Type	Country	Year	Longbox Value / Value
	PRO-CD-7469R	AT&T	CDJ	U.S.		$2.00
		Gold Soundz	CD5	U.K.	1994	$10.00
		Gold Soundz	CDJ	U.S.	1994	$3.00
	PRO-CD-7499R	Rattled by the Rush	CDJ	U.S.		$2.00
Matador	134	Rattled by the Rush	CD5	U.S.	1994	$5.00

Paw

Singles

Label	Catalog Number	Title	Type	Country	Year	Longbox Value / Value
A&M	31458 8171	Couldn't Know	CDJ	U.S.	1993	$2.00
		Jessie	CD5	U.K.		$10.00
		Jessie	CD5	U.K.		$10.00
	Second version.					
A&M	31458 8129	Jessie	CDJ	U.S.	1993	$2.00

Pawlak, Andy

Singles

Label	Catalog Number	Title	Type	Country	Year	Longbox Value / Value
Fontana	PAWCD-1	Mermaids	CD5	U.K.	1988	$8.00
Fontana	PAWCD-2	Secrets	CD5	U.K.	1988	$8.00
Fontana	PAWCD-3	She Kept Ahold of Love	CD5	U.K.	1988	$8.00

Paycheck, Johnny

Singles

Label	Catalog Number	Title	Type	Country	Year	Longbox Value / Value
Playback	20	Next of Kin	CDJ	U.S.	1993	$2.00

PC Quest

Singles

Label	Catalog Number	Title	Type	Country	Year	Longbox Value / Value
RCA	RDJ-62075-2	After the Summer's Gone	CDJ	U.S.	1991	$2.00

Peacetime

Singles

Label	Catalog Number	Title	Type	Country	Year	Longbox Value / Value
RCA	PD 49988	Truth Will Set You Free	CD5	U.K.	1992	$8.00

Peacock Palace

Singles

Label	Catalog Number	Title	Type	Country	Year	Longbox Value / Value
Columbia	657779-2	Henry's Song	CD5	Germany	1992	$8.00
Columbia	657397-2	Like a Snake	CD5	Germany	1992	$8.00

Pearl Jam

Full Length

Label	Catalog Number	Title	Type	Country	Year	Longbox Value / Value
Epic		Cultivate the Tour	DJ/Smplr	U.S.	1992	$25.00
Epic	XPCD337	Five Tracks From the New Album	DJ/Smplr	U.K.	1993	$30.00
Z100 Radio		Fox Theatre, Atlanta, Georgia 4/3/94	DJ/Smplr	U.S.	1994	$35.00
	2 CD set.					
98 ROCK Radio		Fox Theatre, Atlanta, Georgia 4/3/94	DJ/Smplr	U.S.	1994	$35.00
	2 CD set.					
KROQ		Fox Theatre, Atlanta, Georgia 4/3/94	RS	U.S.	1994	$30.00
Epic	XACS90025/6	Freak	DJ/Smplr	Japan	1996	$200.00
	2 CD set.					
Westwood One		In Concert	RS	U.S.	1992	$70.00
	2 CD set. With Richie Sambora, Airdate: 9/28/92.					
Westwood One		In Concert	RS	U.S.	1992	$120.00
	2 CD set. With Smithereens, Airdate: 4/13/92.					
Westwood One		In Concert	RS	U.S.	1994	$90.00
	2 CD set. Airdate: 7/4/94.					
Westwood One		In Concert	RS	U.S.	1995	$90.00
	2 CD set. Airdate: 10/23/95.					
Westwood One		In Concert	RS	U.S.	1995	$90.00
	2 CD set. Airdate: 4/10/95.					
Westwood One		In Concert-Nu Rock	RS	U.S.	1993	$55.00
	Airdate: 8/16/93.					
Westwood One		In Concert-Nu Rock	RS	U.S.	1994	$90.00
	2 CD set. Airdate: 8/29/94.					
Q-101 Chicago		Live at Soldier Field	LTD/LP	U.S.	1995	$35.00
	2 CD Set.					
KOME San Jose		Live at Spartan Stadium	LTD/LP	U.S.	1995	$35.00
	2 CD Set.					
CBS		Monkey Wrenched Radio	DJ/Smplr	Germany	1995	$500.00
	4 CD set in digipak.					
CBS		No Code	LTD/LP	Australia	1996	$335.00
	CD with VHS video tape.					
Westwood One		Off the Record	RS	U.S.	1992	$40.00
	With Social Distortion, Airdate: 4/27/92.					
Z-100 New York		Self Pollution	RS	U.S.	1995	$125.00
	4 CD picture discs.					
KPNT Chicago		Spin the Black Circle: Live At Soldier Field	DJ/Smplr	U.S.	1996	$50.00
	Radio station sponsord 2 CD live concert.					
Westwood One		Superstars	RS	U.S.	1993	$60.00
	Airdate: 3/28/93.					
Epic	EPC468884	Ten	LP	Germany	1991	$25.00
	14 track version.					
Epic	468884 5	Ten	LTD/LP	U.K.	1992	$25.00
Epic	ZK-53136	Vs	LTD/LP	U.S.	1993	$16.00
	CD in ecopak with different booklet from jewel box version.					

Singles

Label	Catalog Number	Title	Type	Country	Year	Longbox Value / Value
Epic	657572	Alive	CD5	Australia	1991	$12.00
Epic	657572-2	Alive	CD5	Germany	1991	$10.00
Sony	SRCS-5884	Alive	CD5	Japan	1991	$15.00
Epic	657572-2	Alive	CD5	U.K.	1991	$12.00
Epic	ZSK 4166	Alive	CDJ	U.S.	1991	$7.00
Epic	ZSK 4041	Alive	CDJ	U.S.	1991	$15.00
Epic	77933	Alive	CD5	U.S.	1995	$5.00
Epic	660338	Animal	CD5	Australia	1994	$12.00
Epic	66519	Animal	CD5	Australia	1994	$12.00
Epic	XPCD378	Animal	CDJ	U.K	1994	$25.00
Epic	77948	Animal	CD5	U.S.	1995	$5.00
Epic	660020	Daughter	CD5	Australia	1994	$12.00
Epic	EPC 660020	Daughter	CD5	Germany	1994	$10.00
Epic	SAMP 2036	Daughter	CDJ	Germany	1994	$18.00
Epic	SRDS-8273	Daughter	CD3	Japan	1994	$17.00/$4.00
Epic	XDCS-93143	Daughter	CDJ	Japan	1994	$25.00
Epic	77938	Daughter	CD5	U.S.	1995	$5.00
Epic	EPC 660291 2	Dissident	CD5	Germany	1994	$12.00
Epic	EPC 660291-5	Dissident	CD5	Germany	1994	$12.00

Label	Catalog Number	Title	Type	Country	Year	Longbox Value / Value
Epic	EPC 66105529	Dissident	CD5	Germany	1994	$12.00
Epic	EPC 66105528	Dissident	CD5	Germany	1994	$12.00
Epic	SRCS-7777	Dissident	CD5	Japan	1995	$27.00
Epic	660441 2	Dissident	CD5	U.K.	1994	$15.00
Epic	660441 5	Dissident	CD5	U.K.	1994	$15.00
Epic	XPCD427	Dissident	CDJ	U.K.	1994	$15.00
Epic		Dissident	CDJ	U.S.	1994	$7.00
Epic	77939	Dissident	CD5	U.S.	1995	$5.00
Epic		Dissident (Live)	CDJ	U.S.	1994	$15.00
Epic	657857	Even Flow	CD5	Australia	1992	$12.00
Epic		Even Flow	CDJ	Canada	1992	$7.00
Epic	657857-2	Even Flow	CD5	U.K.	1992	$10.00
Epic		Even Flow	CDJ	U.K.	1992	$25.00
Epic	ZSK 4469	Even Flow	CDJ	U.S.	1992	$7.00
Epic	77934	Even Flow	CD5	U.S.	1995	$5.00
Epic	659795	Go	CD5	Germany	1993	$10.00
Epic	SAMOCD 1956	Go	CD5	Germany	1993	$10.00
Epic		Go	CDJ	Germany	1993	$14.00
Epic	659795	Go	CD5	U.K.	1993	$15.00

With bonus cassette single.

Label	Catalog Number	Title	Type	Country	Year	Longbox Value / Value
Epic	ZSK 5487	Go	CDJ	U.S.	1993	$6.00
Epic	77937	Go	CD5	U.S.	1995	$5.00
Epic	77873	Immortality	CD5	U.S.	1995	$6.00
Epic		Immortality	CDJ	U.S.	1995	$7.00
Epic	658180	Jeremy	CD5	Australia	1992	$12.00
Epic	658180	Jeremy	CD5	Germany	1992	$10.00
Epic	658258 2	Jeremy	CD5	U.K.	1992	$10.00
Epic	ESK 4606	Jeremy	CDJ	U.S.	1992	$7.00
Epic	77935	Jeremy	CD5	U.S.	1995	$5.00
Epic	660291 5	Live in Atlanta	CD5	Germany	1994	$15.00

Limited edition CD5 with 7 tracks in tri-fold digipak.

Label	Catalog Number	Title	Type	Country	Year	Longbox Value / Value
Epic	XPCD 2003	Merkinball	CDJ	U.K.	1995	$18.00
Epic		Merkinball	CD5	U.S.	1995	$5.00
Epic		Merkinball	CDJ	U.S.	1995	$7.00
Epic	SRDS-8292	Not for You	CD3	Japan	1995	$15.00/$4.00
Epic		Not for You	CDJ	U.K.	1995	$12.00
Epic		Not For You	CDJ	U.S.	1995	$7.00
Epic	658472	Oceans	CD5	Australia	1992	$12.00
Epic	658472 2	Oceans	CD5	Germany	1992	$10.00
Epic	658472 2	Oceans	CD5	Germany	1992	$13.00

Limited edition picture disc in digipak.

Label	Catalog Number	Title	Type	Country	Year	Longbox Value / Value
Epic	77936	Oceans	CD5	U.S.	1995	$5.00
Epic		Rearview Mirror	CDJ	Australia	1994	$50.00
Epic	34K77771	Spin the Black Circle	CD5	Canada	1994	$8.00
Epic		Spin the Black Circle	CDJ	Germany	1994	$14.00
Epic		Spin the Black Circle	CD5	U.S.	1994	$5.00
CBS	77771	Spin the Black Circle	CD5	U.S.	1994	$5.00
Epic	SAMP 3615	Who Are You	CDJ	Holland	1996	$20.00

Pearson, Duke

Full Length

Label	Catalog Number	Title	Type	Country	Year	Longbox Value / Value
Blue Note		Wahoo	LTD/LP	U.S.	1995	$19.00

Peaston, David

Singles

Label	Catalog Number	Title	Type	Country	Year	Longbox Value / Value
MCA	CD45 1659	String	CDJ	U.S.	1991	$2.00
Geffen	PRO-CD-3504	Two Wrongs (Don't Make a Right)	CDJ	U.S.	1989	$2.00
Geffen	GEF-70CD	We're All in This Together	CD5	U.K.	1990	$8.00
Geffen	PRO-CD-3964	We're All in This Together	CDJ	U.S.	1989	$2.00

Pebbles

Singles

Label	Catalog Number	Title	Type	Country	Year	Longbox Value / Value
MCA	MCA5P3273	Are You Ready?	CDJ	U.S.		$2.00
MCA	55074	Are You Ready?	CD5	U.S.	1995	$5.00
MCA	CD45 1182	Backyard	CDJ	U.S.	1990	$2.00
MCA	10P3-6040	Do Me Right	CD3	Japan	1988	$13.00/$4.00
WEA	258083-2	Girlfriend	CD3	Germany	1988	$8.00
WEA	10SW-31	Girlfriend	CD3	Japan	1988	$13.00/$4.00
MCA	DMCA-1233	Girlfriend	CD5	U.k.	1988	$8.00
Eastwest	9031-72477-2	Giving You the Benefit	CD5	Germany	1990	$8.00
WEA	WMD5-4032	Giving You the Benefit	CD3	Japan	1990	$13.00/$4.00
MCA	DMCAT-1440	Giving You the Benefit	CD5	U.K.	1990	$8.00
WEA	WMD5-4052	Love Makes Things Happen	CD3	Japan	1990	$13.00/$4.00
MCA	CD45 1151	Love Makes Things Happen	CDJ	U.S.	1990	$2.00
WEA	258027-2	Mercedes Boy	CD3	Germany	1988	$8.00
MCA	10SW-51	Mercedes Boy	CD3	Japan	1988	$13.00/$4.00
MCA	DMCA-1248	Mercedes Boy	CD5	U.K.	1988	$8.00
MCA	10P3-6013	Take Your Time	CD3	Japan	1988	$13.00/$4.00
MCA	DMCA-1273	Take Your Time	CD5	U.K.	1988	$8.00

Peeples, Nia

Singles

Label	Catalog Number	Title	Type	Country	Year	Longbox Value / Value
Charisma	PRCD 093	Faces of Love	CDJ	U.S.	1992	$2.00
BMG	665205	Kissing the Wind	CD5	Germany	1992	$8.00
Charisma	VJDP-10188	Kissing the Wind	CD3	Japan	1992	$13.00/$4.00
Charisma	CUSCD-7	Kissing the Wind	CD5	U.K.	1992	$8.00
Charisma	PRCD 088	Kissing the Wind	CDJ	U.S.	1992	$2.00
BMG	664905	Street of Dreams	CD5	Germany	1991	$8.00
Charisma	CUSCD-6	Street of Dreams	CD5	U.K.	1991	$8.00
Charisma	96269-2	Street of Dreams	CD5	U.S.	1991	$5.00
Charisma	PRCD 063	Street of Dreams	CDJ	U.S.	1991	$2.00
Mercury	870447-2	Trouble	CD5	Germany	1988	$8.00
Mercury	CDP 11	Trouble	CDJ	U.S.	1988	$2.00

Pekadores, Los

Singles

Label	Catalog Number	Title	Type	Country	Year	Longbox Value / Value
Cema Latino	31518	Firma Este Papel	CD5	U.S.	1994	$5.00

Pele

Singles

Label	Catalog Number	Title	Type	Country	Year	Longbox Value / Value
		Don't Worship Me	CD5	U.K.		$10.00
		Don't Worship Me	CD5	U.K.		$10.00

Second version.

Label	Catalog Number	Title	Type	Country	Year	Longbox Value / Value
Polydor	POL-940	Fair Blows in the Wind	CD5	U.K.	1992	$8.00
		Fireworks	CD5	U.K.		$10.00
		Fireworks	CD5	U.K.		$10.00

Second version.

Label	Catalog Number	Title	Type	Country	Year	Longbox Value / Value
M&G	MAGCD-20	Megalomania	CD5	U.K.	1992	$8.00
M&G	MAGCD-16	Raid the Palace	CD5	U.K.	1992	$8.00

Pendergrass, Teddy

Full Length

Label	Catalog Number	Title	Type	Country	Year	Longbox Value / Value
Asylum	60317-2	Love Language	LP/LB	U.S.†	1985	$14.00/$8.00
Asylum	60447-2	Working It Black	LP/LB	U.S.†	1985	$14.00/$8.00

Singles

Label	Catalog Number	Title	Type	Country	Year	Longbox Value / Value
		2 A.M.	CDJ	U.S.		$3.00
Elektra	PRCD 8178-2	Glad to Be Alive	CDJ	U.S.	1990	$2.00
Elektra	PRCD 8257-2	How Can You Mend a Broken	CDJ	U.S.	1990	$2.00
Elektra	PRCD 8357-2	I Find Everything in You	CDJ	U.S.	1991	$3.00
Elektra	PRCD 8300-2	It Should've Been You	CDJ	U.S.	1990	$3.00
Elektra	PRCD 8323-2	It Should've Been You	CDJ	U.S.	1990	$3.00
Elektra	PR 1001-2	Joy	CDJ	U.S.	1988	$3.00
Elektra	PR 8035-2	Love is the Power	CDJ	U.S.	1988	$3.00
Elektra	PRCD 8218-2	Make It With You	CDJ	U.S.	1990	$3.00
Elektra	PR 8062-2	This is the Last Time	CDJ	U.S.	1988	$3.00
Elektra	PRCD 8822-2	Voodoo	CDJ	U.S.	1993	$3.00

Pendragon

Singles

Label	Catalog Number	Title	Type	Country	Year	Longbox Value / Value
Bellaphon	130-07-569	Saved by You	CD5	Germany	1991	$8.00

Peniston, Ce Ce

Full Length

Label	Catalog Number	Title	Type	Country	Year	Longbox Value / Value
A&M		Four Selections From Finally	DJ/Smplr	U.S.	1992	$6.00

Singles

Label	Catalog Number	Title	Type	Country	Year	Longbox Value / Value
A&M	31458 8017	Crazy Love	CDJ	U.S.	1992	$2.00
A&M	75021 7281-2	Finally	CDJ	U.S.	1991	$3.00
A&M	75021 7385-2	Finally	CDJ	U.S.	1991	$3.00
A&M	580769	Hit by Love	CD5	U.S.	1994	$5.00
A&M Records	80843	I'm in The Mood	CD5	U.S.	1994	$5.00
A&M	31458 8020	Inside That I Cried	CDJ	U.S.	1992	$2.00
A&M	75021 7337 2	Keep on Walkin'	CDJ	U.S.	1992	$3.00
A&M	75021 2395-2	We Got a Love Thang	CDJ	U.S.	1992	$3.00
A&M	75021 7330-2	We Got a Love Thang	CDJ	U.S.	1992	$3.00

Penn, Michael

Full Length

Label	Catalog Number	Title	Type	Country	Year	Longbox Value / Value
DIR		King Biscuit Flour Hour	RS	U.S.	1990	$30.00

With Journey, Airdate: 10/21/90.

Singles

Label	Catalog Number	Title	Type	Country	Year	Longbox Value / Value
RCA	2647-2-RDj	Brave New World	CDJ	U.S.	1990	$2.00
RCA	62457-2	Free Time	CD5	U.S.	1993	$5.00
RCA	RDJ 62456-2	Free Time	CDJ	U.S.	1993	$2.00
RCA		Long Way Down	CDJ	U.S.		$2.00
RCA	PD-49322	No Myth	CD5	Germany	1990	$8.00
RCA	PD-49322	No Myth	CD5	U.K.	1990	$8.00
RCA	9111-2-RDj	No Myth	CDJ	U.S.	1990	$2.00
RCA		No Myth	CDJ	U.S.	1990	$2.00

Second version.

Label	Catalog Number	Title	Type	Country	Year	Longbox Value / Value
RCA	BVDP-68	Seen the Doctor	CD3	Japan	1992	$13.00/$4.00
RCA	RDJ 62339-2	Seen the Doctor	CDJ	U.S.	1992	$2.00
RCA	RJD-62340-2	Strange Seasons	CDJ	U.S.		$2.00
RCA	92001-2-RDj	This & That	CDJ	U.S.	1990	$2.00
RCA		This & That	CDJ	U.S.	1990	$2.00

Second version.

Pennywise

Singles

Label	Catalog Number	Title	Type	Country	Year	Longbox Value / Value
	EP186429	Dying To Know	CDJ	U.S.		$2.00
		Searchin'	CDJ	U.S.		$2.00

Penthouse Four

Singles

Label	Catalog Number	Title	Type	Country	Year	Longbox Value / Value
SPV	8414-3	Slave of Love	CD5	Germany	1988	$8.00

People Get Ready

Singles

Label	Catalog Number	Title	Type	Country	Year	Longbox Value / Value
Produce	CDBUMP-101	Be My Friend	CD5	U.K.	1992	$8.00
Produce	CDBUMP-102	Natural High	CD5	U.K.	1992	$8.00

People People

Singles

Label	Catalog Number	Title	Type	Country	Year	Longbox Value / Value
Cooltempo	663297	Are You Spoken For	CD5	Germany	1990	$8.00
Cooltempo	COOLCD-205	Are You Spoken For	CD5	U.K.	1990	$8.00

Pepper, Art

Full Length

Label	Catalog Number	Title	Type	Country	Year	Longbox Value / Value
RealTime	RT-3009	Darn That Dream	LP/LB	U.S.†	1985	$14.00/$8.00
Mobile	MFCD-805	Modern Jazz Classics	LP/LB	U.S.†	1985	$14.00/$8.00
Savoy Records	CY-78819	Surf Ride	LTD/LP	U.S.	1996	$20.00

CD in miniature repica of original LP sleeve.

Label	Catalog Number	Title	Type	Country	Year	Longbox Value / Value
Galaxy	FCD-5140	Winter Moon	LP/LB	U.S.†	1985	$14.00/$8.00

Pepper, Art/John Klemmer/Joe Henderson/Johnny Griffin

Full Length

Label	Catalog Number	Title	Type	Country	Year	Longbox Value / Value
Galaxy	FCD-5133	Ballads by Four	LP/LB	U.S.†	1985	$14.00/$8.00

Pepper, Jim

Full Length

Label	Catalog Number	Title	Type	Country	Year	Longbox Value / Value
Rykodisc	RCD-10001	Comin' and Goin'	LP/LB	U.S.†	1985	$14.00/$8.00

Perception

Singles

Label	Catalog Number	Title	Type	Country	Year	Longbox Value / Value
Talkin'Loud	TLKCD 33	Take U Higher	CD5	U.K.	1993	$8.00

Percewood

Singles

Label	Catalog Number	Title	Type	Country	Year	Longbox Value / Value
Polygram	876741-2	Dancin' on the Edge	CD5	Germany	1990	$8.00

Pere Ubu

Full Length

Label	Catalog Number	Title	Type	Country	Year	Longbox Value / Value
Geffen		Datapanik in the Year Zero	LTD/LP	U.S.	1996	$60.00

Limited edition 5 CD set.

Label	Catalog Number	Title	Type	Country	Year	Longbox Value / Value
Imago	28058	Kathleen	DJ/Intvw	U.S.	1993	$12.00
Fontana	CDP 514	Worlds in Collision	DJ/Smplr	U.S.	1991	$12.00

Singles

Label	Catalog Number	Title	Type	Country	Year	Longbox Value / Value
Fontana	UBUCD-4	Breath	CD5	U.K.	1989	$10.00
Fontana		Breath	CDJ	U.K.	1989	$10.00
Fontana	CDP 125	Breath	CDJ	U.S.	1989	$2.00
Fontana	UBUCD-5	I Hear They Smoke the Barbecue	CD5	U.K.	1989	$10.00
IMS	874469-2	Love Love Love	CD5	Germany	1989	$10.00
Fontana	UBUCD-33	Love Love Love	CD5	U.K.	1989	$10.00
Fontana	UBUCD-6	Oh Catherine	CD5	U.K.	1991	$10.00
Imago	28045	Sleep Walk	CDJ	U.S.		$2.00
Fontana	874240-3	Waiting for Mary	CD3	Germany	1989	$10.00
Fontana	874241-2	Waiting for Mary	CD5	Germany	1989	$10.00
Fontana	UBUCD-2	Waiting for Mary	CD5	U.K.	1989	$10.00
Fontana	CDP 98	Waiting for Mary	CDJ	U.S.	1989	$2.00
Fontana	UBUCD-1	We Have the Technology	CD5	Germany	1988	$10.00
Restless	7 72340-2	We Have the Technology	CD3	U.S.	1988	$6.00/$4.00

Peregrins

Singles

Label	Catalog Number	Title	Type	Country	Year	Longbox Value / Value
MCA	CD45 17862	True Believer	CDJ	U.S.	1989	$2.00

Perfect Day

Singles

Label	Catalog Number	Title	Type	Country	Year	Longbox Value/Value
London	LONCD-188	Jane	CD5	U.K.	1988	$8.00
London	LONCD-242	King of Fools	CD5	U.K.	1990	$8.00
London	886449-2	Liberty Town	CD5	Germany	1989	$8.00
London	LONCD-214	Liberty Town	CD5	U.K.	1989	$8.00
London	LONCD-207	This Is America	CD5	U.K.	1988	$8.00

Perfect Gentlemen

Singles

Label	Catalog Number	Title	Type	Country	Year	Longbox Value/Value
Columbia	656008-2	Ooh La La	CD3	Germany	1990	$8.00
Sony	CSDS-8146	Ooh La La	CD3	Japan	1990	$12.00/$3.00
Columbia	CSK 73211	Ooh La La	CDJ	U.S.	1990	$2.00

Perfect Stranger

Label	Catalog Number	Title	Type	Country	Year	Longbox Value/Value
Full Length						
Passport	PVCD-8964	Chasing the Heart	LP/BP	U.S.		$12.00/$7.00
Singles						
Atlantic	76969	I'm A Stranger Here	CD5	U.S.	1995	$5.00

Performance Guaranteed

Singles

Label	Catalog Number	Title	Type	Country	Year	Longbox Value/Value
Hollywood	PRCD 8342	Peace	CDJ	U.S.	1991	$2.00

Perkins, Carl

Singles

Label	Catalog Number	Title	Type	Country	Year	Longbox Value/Value
Rhino	885847	Blue Suede Shoes	CD3	Germany	1989	$10.00
Charly	CDS-9	Blue Suede Shoes	CD5	U.K.	1989	$10.00

Perkins, Johnathan

Singles

Label	Catalog Number	Title	Type	Country	Year	Longbox Value/Value
Anxious	ANXCD-16	I Can't Say No	CD5	U.K.	1990	$8.00
BMG	ZD-44178	Makes Love Much Better	CD5	Germany	1990	[illegible]

Perri

Singles

Label	Catalog Number	Title	Type	Country	Year	Longbox Value/Value
MCA	DMCA-1293	Fall in Love	CD5	U.K.	1988	$8.00
Motown	ZD-43084	Feel So Good	CD5	U.K.	1989	$8.00
MCA	DMCA-1311	I'm the One	CD5	U.K.	1989	$8.00
		It's Been You	CDJ	U.S.		$2.00

Perry, Linda

Singles

Label	Catalog Number	Title	Type	Country	Year	Longbox Value/Value
		Fill Me Up	CD5	U.K.	1996	$10.00

Perry, Phil

Singles

Label	Catalog Number	Title	Type	Country	Year	Longbox Value/Value
Capitol	CDCL-615	Amazing Love	CD5	U.K.	1991	$8.00
Capitol	DPRO 79706	Amazing Love	CDJ	U.S.	1991	$2.00
Capitol	DPRO 79552	Call Me	CDJ	U.S.	1991	$2.00

Perry, Steve

Label	Catalog Number	Title	Type	Country	Year	Longbox Value/Value
Full Length						
Westwood One		Off the Record	RS	U.S.	1994	$35.00
Airdate: 8/8/94.						
Westwood One		Off the Record	RS	U.S.	1995	$35.00
Airdate: 1/2/95.						
	XDCS-93148	Sound Sampler	DJ/Smplr	Japan	1994	$75.00
CBS	CK-39334	Street Talk	LP/BP	U.S.†	1994	$14.00/$8.00
Singles						
Columbia	CSK 7088	Donna Please	CDJ	U.S.		$3.00
		Missing You	CDJ	U.S.		$3.00
CBS	77761	Missing You	CD5	U.S.	1994	$5.00
Columbia	6606012	You Better Wait	CD5	U.K.	1994	$10.00
Columbia	44K77669	You Better Wait	CD5	U.S.		$5.00
Columbia		You Better Wait	CDJ	U.S.		$3.00

Persia

Full Length

Label	Catalog Number	Title	Type	Country	Year	Longbox Value/Value
Azra	IW 1034	First Strike	LTD/LP	U.S.	1991	$10.00
CD in "matchbook" sleeve.						

Pesco, Paul

Singles

Label	Catalog Number	Title	Type	Country	Year	Longbox Value/Value
Sire	PRO-CD-3678	Black is Black	CDJ	U.S.	1989	$2.00

Pet Shop Boys

Label	Catalog Number	Title	Type	Country	Year	Longbox Value/Value
Full Length						
EMI	CP32-5507	Actually	LP	Japan		$40.00
First pressing.						
EMI	90263	Actually	LP/LB	U.S.		$23.00/$20.00
2 CD set.						
EMI	CDPCSD166	Alternative	LTD/LP	U.K.	1995	$35.00
2 CD set in lenticular sleeve. Limited to 20,000 copies.						
EMI	34353	Alternative	LTD/LP	U.S.	1995	$25.00
2 CD set in lenticular sleeve. Limited to 20,000 copies.						
EMI		Behaviour	DJ/LP	Canada		$50.00
CD and press kit in custom box.						
Toshiba	TOCP-6440	Behaviour	LTD/LP	Japan		$35.00
Capitol	30852-2	Disco 2	LTD/LP	U.S.	1994	$17.00
2 CD set in brilliant box.						
EMI	PSBCDMTV1	Discography	DJ/Smplr	U.K.		$50.00
Toshiba		Pet Shop Boys	DJ/Smplr	Japan	1990	$300.00
Toshiba	PCD-0399	Promotion	DJ/Smplr	Japan	1993	$300.00
	CDPCSDX143	Very Relentless	LTD/LP	U.K.	1995	$30.00
2 CD set.						
Capitol	27010	Very Relentless	LTD/LP	U.S.†	1994	$29.00
2 CD set.						
EMI	E2-27171	Very Relentless	LTD/LP	U.S.	1994	$30.00
2 CD set.						
Singles						
EMI		Absolutely Fabulous	CD5	Australia	1994	$15.00
EMI	CDR 6382	Absolutely Fabulous	CD5	U.K.	1994	$20.00
Toshiba	XP10-2002	Always on My Mind	CD3	Japan	1988	$15.00/$4.00
Parlophone	CDR-6171	Always on My Mind	CD5	U.K.	1988	$10.00
Manhattan	DPRO-04058	Always on My Mind	CDJ	U.S.	1988	$12.00
		Before	CDJ	U.S.		$18.00
EMI	204125-2	Being Boring	CD5	Germany	1990	$10.00
EMI	204126-2	Being Boring	CD5	Germany	1990	$10.00
Parlophone	CDR-6275	Being Boring	CD5	U.K.	1990	$10.00
		Can You Forgive Her	CD5	U.K.		$10.00
		Can You Forgive Her	CD5	U.K.		$10.00
Second version.						
Parlophone	CDR-6348	Can You Forgive Her	CD5	U.K.	1993	$10.00
Parlophone	CDRS-6348	Can You Forgive Her	CD5	U.K.	1993	$10.00
EMI	56281	Can You Forgive Her	CD5	U.S.	1993	$6.00
Parlophone	CDR-198	Devices	CD5	U.K.	1989	$10.00
Toshiba	TODP-2323	DJ Culture	CD3	Japan	1991	$15.00/$4.00
Parlophone	CDR-6301	DJ Culture	CD5	U.K.	1991	$10.00
Parlophone	CDRX-6301	DJ Culture	CD5	U.K.	1991	$10.00
EMI	202927-3	Domino Dancing	CD3	Germany	1988	$12.00
EMI	202917-2	Domino Dancing	CD5	Germany	1988	$12.00
Toshiba	XP10-2024	Domino Dancing	CD3	Japan	1988	$13.00/$3.00
Parlophone	CDR-6190	Domino Dancing	CD5	U.K.	1988	$10.00
		Domino Dancing	CDJ	U.S.	1988	$6.00
Parlophone	CDR-6356	Go West	CD5	U.K.	1993	$10.00
Parlophone	80848	Go West	CD5	U.K.	1993	$10.00
EMI	58084	Go West	CD5	U.S.	1993	$6.00
EMI	DPRO-04519	Go West	CDJ	U.S.	1993	$8.00
EMI	202471-2	Heart	CD5	Germany	1988	$10.00
Parlophone	CDR-6177	Heart	CD5	U.K.	1988	$10.00
		How Can You Expect Me to Be Taken Seriously	CDJ	U.S.	1994	$6.00
EMI	DPRO 4698	How Can You Explain	CDJ	U.S.	1991	$6.00
EMI	56205	How Can You Explain	CD5	U.S.	1992	$5.00
Capital	58122	I Wouldn't Normally	CD5	U.S.	1994	$5.00
		I Wouldn't Normally Do This Kind of Thing	CD5	U.K.		$10.00
Capitol		I Wouldn't Normally Do This Kind of Thing	CDJ	U.S.	1995	$8.00
EMI	201889-2	It's a Sin	CD5	Germany	1992	$10.00
Parlophone	CDR-6158	It's a Sin	CD5	U.K.	1992	$10.00
EMI	203420-3	It's Alright	CD3	Germany	1989	$10.00
EMI	203450-3	It's Alright	CD3	Germany	1989	$10.00
EMI	203450-2	It's Alright	CD5	Germany	1989	$10.00
Parlophone	CDR-6220	It's Alright	CD5	U.K.	1989	$10.00
EMI	204224-2	Jealousy	CD5	Germany	1991	$10.00
EMI	204372-2	Jealousy	CD5	Germany	1991	$10.00
Parlophone	CDR-6283	Jealousy	CD5	U.K.	1991	$10.00
Parlophone	CDRS-6283	Jealousy	CD5	U.K.	1991	$10.00
EMI	203081-3	Left to My Own Devices	CD3	Germany	1989	$10.00
EMI	203081-2	Left to My Own Devices	CD5	Germany	1989	$10.00
Toshiba	XP12-5005	Left to My Own Devices	CD3	Japan	1989	$13.00/$3.00
EMI	CDR-6190	Left to My Own Devices	CD5	U.K.	1989	$10.00
EMI		Liberation	CD5	Australia	1994	$15.00
EMI		Liberation	CD5	Australia	1994	$15.00
Second version.						
		Liberation	CD5	U.K.		$10.00
		Liberation	CD5	U.K.		$10.00
Second version.						
ZYX	ZYX-5995-8	Megamix	CD5	Germany	1988	$10.00
ZYX	ZYX-5401-8	One More Chance	CD3	Germany	1988	$10.00
EMI		Paninaro	CD5	Germany	1995	$10.00
EMI	CDRS6414	Paninaro	CD5	U.K.	1995	$10.00
EMI	CDR6414	Paninaro	CD5	U.K.	1995	$10.00
Capitol	38369	Paninaro	CD5	U.S.	1995	$5.00
EMI	58370	Paninaro	CD5	U.S.	1995	$6.00
EMI		Paninaro '95	CDJ	U.K.	1995	$25.00
Capitol		Paninaro '95	CDJ	U.S.	1995	$14.00
EMI	202152-2	Rent	CD5	Germany	1990	$10.00
Parlophone	CDR-6168	Rent	CD5	U.K.	1990	$10.00
		Se a Vide E	CD5	U.K.	1996	$10.00
		Se a Vide E	CD5	U.K.	1996	$10.00
Second version.						
EMI	204062-2	So Hard	CD5	Germany	1990	$10.00
EMI	204092-2	So Hard	CD5	Germany	1990	$10.00
Toshiba	TODP-2203	So Hard	CD3	Japan	1990	$15.00/$5.00
Parlophone	CDR-6269	So Hard	CD5	U.K.	1990	$10.00
Parlophone	CDRX-6269	So Hard	CD5	U.K.	1990	$10.00
EMI	DPRO 4650	So Hard	CDJ	U.S.	1990	$10.00
ZYX	6016-8	Ultimate Mix	CD5	Germany	1988	$10.00
EMI	204617-2	Was It Worth It	CD5	Germany	1991	$10.00
Parlophone	CDR-6306	Was It Worth It	CD5	U.K.	1991	$10.00
EMI	56244	Was It Worth It	CD5	U.S.	1991	$6.00
ZYX	ZYX-3301-8	West End Girls	CD5	Germany	1990	$10.00
ZYX	ZYX-5196-8	West End Sunglasses	CD3	Germany	1989	$10.00
Parlophone	CDR-6163	What Have I Done to Deserve This	CD5	U.K.	1990	$10.00
Toshiba	TODP-2273	Where the Streets Have No Name	CD3	Japan	1991	$15.00/$5.00
Parlophone	CDR-6285	Where the Streets Have No Name	CD5	U.K.	1991	$10.00
EMI	56217	Where the Streets Have No Name	CD5	U.S.	1991	$6.00
EMI	DPRO 04753	Where the Streets Have No Name	CDJ	U.S.	1991	$6.00
Capital	58319	Yesterday When I Was	CD5	U.S.	1994	$5.00
		Yesterday When I Was Mad	CD5	Australia	1994	$10.00
		Yesterday When I Was Mad	CD5	U.K.	1994	$10.00
		Yesterday When I Was Mad	CD5	U.K.	1994	$10.00
Second version.						

Petak, Michael

Full Length

Label	Catalog Number	Title	Type	Country	Year	Longbox Value/Value
Slash		Pretty Little Lonely	LTD/LP	U.S.	1994	$16.00
CD shrink-wrapped with a VHS video tape.						

Peter, Paul & Mary

Label	Catalog Number	Title	Type	Country	Year	Longbox Value/Value
Full Length						
Warner Brothers	PRO-CD-6386	Selections From Peter, Paul & Mommy, Too	DJ/Smplr	U.S.	1994	$8.00
Singles						
Warner Brothers	PRO-CD-7853-R	Kid, The	CDJ	U.S.		$3.00

Peters, Bernadette

Full Length

Label	Catalog Number	Title	Type	Country	Year	Longbox Value/Value
Discovision	74-008	Bernadette Peters	LD	U.S.	1981	$25.00

Peters, Mike

Singles

Label	Catalog Number	Title	Type	Country	Year	Longbox Value/Value
		Back Into the System	CD5	U.K.		$10.00
		Back Into the System	CD5	U.K.		$10.00
Second version.						

Peterson, Lucky

Singles

Label	Catalog Number	Title	Type	Country	Year	Longbox Value/Value
Verve	730	Don't Cloud Up on Me	CDJ	U.S.	1993	$2.00

Peterson, Oscar

Full Length

Label	Catalog Number	Title	Type	Country	Year	Longbox Value/Value
Verve	825769-2	A Jazz Portrait of Frank Sinatra	LP/LB	U.S.†	1985	$14.00/$8.00
Verve	821724-2	Night Train	LP/LB	U.S.†	1985	$14.00/$8.00
Verve	817490-2	Reunion Blues	LP/LB	U.S.†	1985	$14.00/$8.00
Verve	823447-2D	Silver Collection	LP/LB	U.S.†	1985	$14.00/$8.00
Verve	817489-2	Tristeza on Piano	LP/LB	U.S.†	1985	$14.00/$8.00
Verve	810047-2	We Get Requests	LP/LB	U.S.†	1985	$14.00/$8.00
Verve	821575-2	West Side Story	LP/LB	U.S.†	1985	$14.00/$8.00

Peterson, Oscar & Clark Terry

Full Length

Label	Catalog Number	Title	Type	Country	Year	Longbox Value/Value
Emarcy	818840-2	Trio + One	LP/LB	U.S.†	1985	$14.00/$8.00

Label	Catalog Number	Title	Type	Country	Year	Longbox Value / Value

Peterson, Oscar Trio

Full Length

Label	Catalog Number	Title	Type	Country	Year	Longbox Value / Value
Verve	314 531 766 2BK01	London House Sessions, The	LTD/LP	U.S.	1996	$65.00

Peterson, Ricky

Singles

Label	Catalog Number	Title	Type	Country	Year	Longbox Value / Value
Warner Brothers	PRO-CD-4045	Livin' It Up	CDJ	U.S.	1990	$2.00

Petra

Singles

Label	Catalog Number	Title	Type	Country	Year	Longbox Value / Value
BMG	663344	Here and When	CD5	Germany	1990	$8.00
BCM	20371	Just Let Go	CD5	Germany	1989	$8.00

Petrucciani, Michael

Full Length

Label	Catalog Number	Title	Type	Country	Year	Longbox Value / Value
Polygram	380025-2	Michael Petrucciani	LP/BP	U.S.		$12.00/$7.00

Petty, Tom (and The Heartbreakers)

Full Length

Label	Catalog Number	Title	Type	Country	Year	Longbox Value / Value
MCA	TOM 2	1991 Tom Petty Interview	DJ/Intvw	U.S.	1991	$15.00
MCA	DMCA 1190	All Mixed	DJ/Smplr	U.K.	1990	$15.00
Global Satellite Network		American Rebel	RS	U.S.	1991	$80.00
	3 CD set.					
Westwood One		BBC Classic Tracks	RS	U.S.	1993	$50.00
	Airdate: 10/25/93.					
Westwood One		BBC Classic Tracks	RS	U.S.	1994	$50.00
	Airdate: 10/25/94.					
MCA	MCAD-5105	Damn the Torpedoes	LP/LB	U.S.†	1985	$14.00/$8.00
MCA	MCAD-6253-P	Full Moon Fever	DJ/LP	U.S.	1989	$15.00
MCA	CD33-1478	Gone Gator Sampler	DJ/Smplr	U.S.	1991	$15.00
MCA	MCAD-37239	Hard Promises	LP/LB	U.S.†	1985	$14.00/$8.00
CBS	3502-80	Hard to Handle	LD	U.S.	1986	$60.00
	With Bob Dylan.					
Album Network		In the Studio (Damn the Torpedos)	RS	U.S.	1988	$25.00
	Airdate: 8/15/88.					
Album Network		In the Studio (Full Moon Fever)	RS	U.S.	1989	$25.00
	Airdate: 12/25/89.					
Album Network		In the Studio (Full Moon Fever)	RS	U.S.	1989	$25.00
	Airdate: 4/24/89.					
Album Network		In the Studio (Into the Great Wide Open)	RS	U.S.		$20.00
DIR		King Biscuit Flour Hour	RS	U.S.	1990	$40.00
	Airdate: 8/6/90.					
DIR		King Biscuit Flour Hour	RS	U.S.	1991	$40.00
	Airdate: 6/16/91.					
DIR		King Biscuit Flour Hour	RS	U.S.	1992	$40.00
	Airdate: 9/28/92.					
DIR		King Biscuit Flour Hour	RS	U.S.	1993	$40.00
	Airdate: 12/26/93.					
DIR		King Biscuit Flour Hour	RS	U.S.	1993	$40.00
	Airdate: 4/19/93.					
DIR		King Biscuit Flour Hour	RS	U.S.	1994	$40.00
	Airdate: 12/18/94.					
DIR		King Biscuit Flour Hour	RS	U.S.	1996	$40.00
	Airdate: 3/3/96.					
MCA	MCAD-5360	Long After Dark	LP/LB	U.S.†	1985	$14.00/$8.00
Westwood One		Off the Record	RS	U.S.	1993	$30.00
	Airdate: 10/25/93.					
Westwood One		Off the Record	RS	U.S.	1993	$30.00
	Airdate: 10/25/93.					
Westwood One		Off the Record	RS	U.S.	1993	$30.00
	Airdate: 6/28/93.					
Westwood One		Off the Record	RS	U.S.	1994	$30.00
	Airdate: 12/18/94.					
Westwood One		Off the Record	RS	U.S.	1994	$30.00
	Airdate: 3/21/94.					
Westwood One		Off the Record	RS	U.S.	1994	$30.00
	Airdate: 3/21/94.					
Westwood One		Off the Record	RS	U.S.	1995	$30.00
	Airdate: 4/3/95.					
Westwood One		Off the Record	RS	U.S.	1995	$30.00
	Airdate: 7/31/95.					
MCA	MCA3P-3624	Playback Excerpts	DJ/Smplr	U.S.	1995	$35.00
MCA	MCA3P-3604	Playback Excerpts	DJ/Smplr	U.S.	1995	$35.00
Radio Today		Rock Stars	RS	U.S.	1989	$40.00
	2 CD set. Airdate: 5/22/89.					
MCA	MCAD 95102	Selections From Playback	DJ/Smplr	Canada	1995	$45.00
MCA	MCAD-5486	Southern Accents	LP/LB	U.S.†	1985	$14.00/$8.00
Westwood One		Superstar Concert	RS	U.S.	1992	$70.00
	2 CD set. Airdate: 3/29/92.					
Westwood One		Superstar Concert	RS	U.S.	1992	$70.00
	2 CD set. Airdate: 9/13/92.					
Westwood One		Superstar Concert	RS	U.S.	1993	$70.00
	2 CD set. Airdate: 3/14/93.					
Westwood One		Superstar Concert	RS	U.S.	1994	$60.00
	2 CD set. Airdate: 3/21/94.					
Westwood One		Superstars	RS	U.S.	1994	$85.00
	2 CD set. Airdate: 8/22/94.					
Global Satellite Network		Tom Petty & American Rebels	RS	U.S.	1990	$80.00
	3 CD set.					
MCA	MCAD-37143	Tom Petty and The Heartbreakers	LP/LB	U.S.		$18.00/$14.00
MCA	MCAD-31085	Tom Petty and The Heartbreakers	LP/LB	U.S.		$18.00/$14.00
MCA	MCAD-31085	Tom Petty And The Heartbreakers	LP/LB	U.S.†	1985	$18.00/$14.00
MCA	1CD-1	Tom Petty Special	DJ/Smplr	Japan		$100.00
Media America		Up Close	RS	U.S.	1989	$40.00
	2 CD set.					
Media America		Up Close	RS	U.S.	1995	$75.00
	3 CD set.					
Media America		Up Close	RS	U.S.	1996	$75.00
	3 CD set.					
		Wildflower Weekend	RS	U.S.	1994	$25.00
Warner Brothers		Wildflowers	LTD/LP	U.S.	1994	$17.00
	CD with special booklet, slipcase, and clear tray. Limited to 500,000 copies.					
Warner Brothers		Wildflowers	LTD/LP	U.S.	1994	$30.00
	Limited edition version randomly autographed by Tom Petty. Limited to 200 copies.					

Singles

Label	Catalog Number	Title	Type	Country	Year	Longbox Value / Value
MCA	9031-71924	A Face in the Crowd	CD5	Germany	1990	$10.00
MCA	DMCAT-1449	A Face in the Crowd	CD5	U.K.	1990	$10.00
MCA	CD45 18813	A Face in the Crowd	CDJ	U.S.	1989	$2.00
MCA	MCA5P-3008	American Girl	CDJ	U.S.	1994	$7.00
Warner Brothers	PRO-CD-7893-R	Cabin Down Below	CDJ	U.S.	1995	$3.00
		Christmas All Over Again	CDJ	Germany	1993	$27.00
Eastwest	257308-2	Free Fallin'	CD5	Germany	1989	$10.00
MCA	DMCAT-1381	Free Fallin'	CD5	U.K.	1989	$10.00
MCA	DMCAX 1381	Free Fallin'	CD5	U.K.	1989	$12.00
MCA	CD45 18056	Free Fallin'	CDJ	U.S.	1989	$2.00
MCA	CD45 18073	Free Fallin'	CDJ	U.S.	1989	$3.00
Warner Brothers	18026	Higher Place	CD5	U.S.	1995	$5.00
Warner Brothers	PRO-CD-7230	Higher Place	CDJ	U.S.	1995	$3.00
Eastwest	257579-2	I Won't Back Down	CD5	Germany	1989	$10.00
Pioneer	09P3-6038	I Won't Back Down	CD3	Japan	1989	$15.00/$5.00
MCA	DMACT-1334	I Won't Back Down	CD5	U.K.	1989	$10.00
MCA	CD45 17622	I Won't Back Down	CDJ	U.S.	1989	$2.00
MCA	MCSTD-1570	Into the Great Wide Open	CD5	U.K.	1991	$10.00
MCA	CD45-1485	Into the Great Wide Open	CDJ	U.S.	1991	$7.00
Warner Brothers		It's Good to Be King	CD5	U.K.	1995	$10.00
Warner Brothers	17925-2	It's Good to Be King	CD5	U.S.	1995	$6.00
Warner Brothers	PRO-CD-7475	It's Good to Be King	CDJ	U.S.	1995	$6.00
MCA	MCSTD-1610	Kings Highway	CD5	U.K.	1991	$10.00
MCA	CD45-2067	Kings Highway	CDJ	U.S.	1991	$2.00
MCA	MCD-17798	Learning to Fly	CD5	Germany	1991	$10.00
MCA	MCSTD 1555	Learning to Fly	CD5	U.K.	1991	$10.00
MCA	MCXTD 1555	Learning to Fly	CD5	U.K.	1991	$12.00
MCA	CD45-1482	Learning to Fly	CDJ	U.S.	1991	$7.00
MCA	MCA5P-2110	Makin' Some Noise	CDJ	U.S.	1991	$3.00
MCA		Mary Jane's Last Dance	CD5	U.K.	1993	$10.00
MCA		Mary Jane's Last Dance	CD5	U.K.	1993	$10.00
	Second version.					
MCA	MCA5P-2813	Mary Jane's Last Dance	CDJ	U.S.	1993	$6.00
MCA	CD45 1627	Out In the Cold	CDJ	U.S.	1989	$3.00
MCA		Peace in L.A.	CD5	U.S.	1992	$4.00
MCA	MCA5P-2286	Peace in L.A.	CDJ	U.S.	1992	$2.00
Eastwest	257463-2	Runnin' Down a Dream	CD5	Germany	1989	$10.00
MCA	DMCAT-1359	Runnin' Down a Dream	CD5	U.K.	1989	$10.00
MCA	CD45 17938	Runnin' Down a Dream	CDJ	U.S.	1989	$6.00
MCA	MCA5P-2879	Something In the Air	CDJ	U.S.	1994	$6.00
MCA	MCD-17870	Too Good to Be True	CD5	U.K.	1992	$10.00
MCA		Too Good to Be True	CD5	U.K.	1992	$10.00
	Second version.					
MCA	DMCAT-1428	Yer So Bad	CD5	U.K.	1989	$10.00
MCA	CD45 18335	Yer So Bad	CDJ	U.S.	1989	$2.00
Warner Brothers	18030	You Don't Know How It Feels	CD5	U.S.	1994	$5.00
Warner Brothers	PRO-CD-7250	You Don't Know How It Feels	CDJ	U.S.	1994	$6.00
Warner Brothers	PRO-CD-7222	You Don't Know How It Feels	CDJ	U.S.	1994	$6.00
Warner Brothers	PRO-CD-7226	You Wreck Me	CDJ	U.S.	1995	$6.00

Pfeifer, Bob

Full Length

Label	Catalog Number	Title	Type	Country	Year	Longbox Value / Value
Passport	PBCD-6057	After Words	LP/LB	U.K.		$12.00
Passport	PBCD-6057	After Words	LP/LB	U.S.		$16.00/$12.00

Phair, Liz

Full Length

Label	Catalog Number	Title	Type	Country	Year	Longbox Value / Value
Atlantic		Whip-Smart	DJ/LP	U.S.	1994	$18.00

Singles

Label	Catalog Number	Title	Type	Country	Year	Longbox Value / Value
Atlantic	PRCD 6199-2	Jealousy	CDJ	U.S.		$3.00
Atlantic		Supernova	CDJ	U.S.	1994	$3.00
MCA	MCA5P3645	Tra La La La (Theme From the Banana Splits Show)	CDJ	U.S.	1995	$6.00
Atlantic	PRCD 6037-2	Whip Smart	CDJ	U.S.	1994	$6.00

Phalon

Singles

Label	Catalog Number	Title	Type	Country	Year	Longbox Value / Value
Elektra	PRCD 8207-2	Dance Floor of Life	CDJ	U.S.	1990	$2.00
Elektra	PRCD 8272-2	Don't Cha Wanna	CDJ	U.S.	1990	$2.00
Elektra	PRCD 8315-2	Ready or Not	CDJ	U.S.	1990	$2.00
Elektra	PRCD 8189-2	Rising to the Top	CDJ	U.S.	1990	$2.00

Phantom Chords

Singles

Label	Catalog Number	Title	Type	Country	Year	Longbox Value / Value
Polygram	MAGCD-1	Johnny Remember Me	CD5	U.K.	1990	$8.00

Pharao

Singles

Label	Catalog Number	Title	Type	Country	Year	Longbox Value / Value
CBS	77774	I Show You Secrets	CD5	U.S.	1994	$5.00

Pharaoh

Singles

Label	Catalog Number	Title	Type	Country	Year	Longbox Value / Value
ZYX	6723-8	Dance Like An Egyptian	CD5	Germany	1992	$6.00

Pharcyde

Singles

Label	Catalog Number	Title	Type	Country	Year	Longbox Value / Value
Delicious Vinyl	4987	Passin' Me By	CDJ	U.S.		$2.00
	DPRO 10238	Runnin'	CDJ	U.S.		$2.00
Capitol	58483	Runnin	CD5	U.S.	1995	$5.00
Delicious Vinyl	4987	Ya Mama	CDJ	U.S.	1992	$2.00

Phil and The Noise

Singles

Label	Catalog Number	Title	Type	Country	Year	Longbox Value / Value
BMG	663019	On My Own Tonight	CD5	Germany	1990	$8.00
BMG	663019	Second Chance	CD5	Germany	1990	$8.00

Phillips, Anthony

Full Length

Label	Catalog Number	Title	Type	Country	Year	Longbox Value / Value
Progress		Finger Painting	LP	Canada		$12.00

Singles

Label	Catalog Number	Title	Type	Country	Year	Longbox Value / Value
Pye	PYD-18	Anthem From Tarka	CD5	U.K.	1988	$8.00
Virgin	CDV 2638	Slow Dance	CD5	U.K.	1990	$8.00

Phillips, Chynna

Singles

Label	Catalog Number	Title	Type	Country	Year	Longbox Value / Value
	DPRO 1414	Naked And Scared	CDJ	U.S.		$2.00

Phillips, Dewayne

Singles

Label	Catalog Number	Title	Type	Country	Year	Longbox Value / Value
		I Don't Want to Know Your Name	CDJ	U.S.		$2.00

Phillips, Phil And Twilights

Singles

Label	Catalog Number	Title	Type	Country	Year	Longbox Value / Value
Mercury	CDP 158	Sea of Love	CDJ	U.S.	1989	$2.00

Phillips, Sam

Full Length

Label	Catalog Number	Title	Type	Country	Year	Longbox Value / Value
Virgin	DPRO-14202	Love and Kisses	DJ/Smplr	U.S.		$6.00
		Love and Kisses	DJ/Smplr	U.S.		$6.00

Singles

Label	Catalog Number	Title	Type	Country	Year	Longbox Value / Value
Virgin	PRCD 14131	Baby I Can't Please You	CDJ	U.S.	1994	$2.00
		Flame	CDJ	U.S.		$2.00
		Holding on to the Earth	CDJ	U.S.		$2.00
Virgin	PRCD 2378	I Don't Know How to Say Goodbye to You	CDJ	U.S.	1988	$2.00
Virgin	VUSCD-50	Where the Colors Don't Go	CD5	U.K.	1991	$8.00
Virgin	PRCD 4135	Where the Colors Don't Go	CDJ	U.S.	1991	$2.00

Label	Catalog Number	Title	Type	Country	Year	Longbox Value / Value
Philosopher Kings						
Full Length						
Columbia		We're the...Album Sampler	DJ/Smplr	U.S.		$4.00
Singles						
Columbia	CSK 7454	Charms	CDJ	U.S.		$2.00
Phish						
Full Length						
Elektra		Hoist	DJ/LP	U.S.	1994	$15.00
	Stock CD in bag with metal hoist.					
Elektra		Sampler	DJ/Smplr	U.S.		$15.00
Singles						
	PRCD 9229-2	Bouncing Around the Room	CDJ	U.S.		$3.00
Elektra	PRCD 8511-2	Chalk Dust Torture	CDJ	U.S.	1992	$2.00
Elektra	PRCD 8915-2	Down With Disease	CDJ	U.S.	1994	$2.00
Elektra	PRCD 8707-2	Fast Enough For You	CDJ	U.S.	1993	$2.00
	PRCD 9364-2	Gumbo	CDJ	U.S.		$3.00
	PRCD 9012-2	Julius	CDJ	U.S.		$3.00
Elektra	PRCD 8768-2	Wedge, The	CDJ	U.S.	1993	$2.00
Phlegma						
Singles						
ZYX	6452-8	Madness	CD5	Germany	1991	$8.00
Phranc						
Singles						
Island	PRCD 6675-2	'64 Ford	CDJ	U.S.	1991	$2.00
Island	PR 2944-2	Blood Bath	CDJ	U.S.	1989	$2.00
Island	CID-501	I'm Not Romantic	CD5	U.K.	1991	$8.00
Island	PRCD 6656-2	I'm Not Romantic	CDJ	U.S.	1991	$2.00
Physical Motion						
Singles						
ZYX	DST-1024-8	Video Killed the Radio Star	CD5	Germany	1990	$8.00
Piaf, Edith						
Full Length						
Time Warner Sound Exchange		40 Legendary Hits	LP	U.S.	1995	$29.00
	2 CD set.					
Piano, The						
Singles						
	DPRO 14127	Heart Awks Pleasure First	CDJ	U.S.		$2.00
Piazza, Rod						
Full Length						
		House of Blues	RS	U.S.	1994	$40.00
	2 CD set. Airdate: 12/11/94.					
Picasso Trigger						
Singles						
Alias	77	Ain't	CD5	U.S.	1994	$5.00
Pickett, Wilson						
Full Length						
Motown	6244	American Soul Man	LP/BP	U.S.		$12.00/$7.00
		House Of Blues	RS	U.S.	1996	$40.00
	2 CD set. Airdate: 2/4/96.					
Singles						
WEA	786495-2	Funky Broadway	CD3	Germany	1989	$8.00
WEA	786495-2	Funky Broadway	CD3	U.K.	1989	$8.00
WEA	786494-2	Six-Three-Four-Five-Seven-Eight-Nine	CD3	Germany	1989	$8.00
WEA	786494-2	Six-Three-Four-Five-Seven-Eight-Nine	CD3	U.K.	1989	$8.00
Piece Dogs						
Singles						
Energy	PRO 3	Devil Dog	CDJ	U.S.	1992	$2.00
Pierre, D.J.						
Singles						
Capital	58234	Muzik Set You Free	CD5	U.S.	1994	$5.00
Pilgrim, Billy						
Singles						
		Insomnia	CDJ	U.S.	1994	$3.00
	PRCD 6167-2	Sweet Louisiana	CDJ	U.S.	1994	$3.00
Pine Country						
Singles						
Mango	CIDM-749	I'm Still Waiting	CD5	U.K.	1990	$8.00
4th & B'way	571	Psalm	CDJ	U.S.	1992	$2.00
Island	CID-562	Redemption Song	CD5	U.K.	1992	$8.00
Antilles	ANNCD-4	Traditions Beckoning	CD5	U.K.	1990	$8.00
Pink Floyd						
Full Length						
CBS/Sony		A Momentary Lapse of Reason	DJ/LP	Japan	1987	$200.00
	Advance issue in custom sleeve.					
CBS/Sony	32DP 820	A Momentary Lapse of Reason	DJ/LP	Japan	1987	$200.00
	CD in custom clip case and special promo booklet.					
Columbia	CSK 1100	A Momentary Lapse of Reason Tour CD	DJ/Smplr	U.S.	1988	$20.00
Capitol	CDP 46383	A Saucerful Of Secrets	LP/LB	U.S.		$14.00/$8.00
	Non-remastered version.					
CBS	CK-34474	Animals	LP/BP	U.S.†	1985	$14.00/$8.00
Westwood One		BBC Classic Tracks	RS	U.S.	1992	$50.00
	Airdate: 10/26/92.					
BBC Radio		BBC Classic Tracks	RS	U.S.	1992	$60.00
	Airdate: 10/26/92.					
Westwood One		BBC Classic Tracks	RS	U.S.	1993	$50.00
	Airdate: 6/7/93.					
		Classic CD (Dark Side of the Moon)	RS	U.S.	1990	$50.00
	2 CD set. Airdate: 4/30/90.					
EMI	CP35-3017	Dark Side of the Moon	LP	Japan	1982	$70.00
Harvest	CP43-5771	Dark Side of the Moon	LTD/LP	Japan	1988	$60.00
	Gold disc.					
Harvest	CDP 7 46001 2	Dark Side of the Moon	LP/BP	U.S.†	1983	$75.00/$70.00
Capitol	46001	Dark Side of the Moon	LP/LB	U.S.	1986	$15.00/$9.00
	Non-remastered version.					
Mobile Fidelity	517	Dark Side of the Moon	LP/LB	U.S.	1989	$30.00/$20.00
EMI	0777 7 81479 2 3	Dark Side of the Moon 20th Anniversary Edition	LTD/LP	U.K.	1993	$18.00
EMI	81479 2 3	Dark Side of the Moon 20th Anniversary Edition	DJ/LP	U.S.	1993	$100.00
	Press kit box with CD, photo, press release, and 3 slides.					
EMI	0777 7 81479 2 3	Dark Side of the Moon 20th Anniversary Edition	LTD/LP	U.S.	1993	$18.00
EMI		Delicate Sound of Thunder	DJ/Smplr	U.K.	1988	$30.00

Pink Floyd – Rarities: A CD Full Of Secrets (Westwood One Vol. 10)

Label	Catalog Number	Title	Type	Country	Year	Longbox Value / Value
CBS		Division Bell	LTD/LP	Australia	1994	$40.00
	CD in numbered slip case.					
CBS		Division Bell	DJ/LP	France	1994	$130.00
	CD, cassette, and press kit in 12"X12" embossed box.					
		Division Bell	DJ/LP	U.K.	1994	$100.00
	CD, tape and press kit in box.					
		Echoes	RS	U.S.	1995	$250.00
	6 CD set. Airdat: 9/4/95.					
EMI		European Tour '89	DJ/Smplr	U.K.	1989	$25.00
BBC Classic Tracks		Family Tree	RS	U.S.	1995	$50.00
	Airdate: 12/18/95.					
Sony	XDCS-93138	Fate of Circles	DJ/Smplr	Japan	1995	$500.00
	2 CD set.					
CBS	CK-38243	Final Cut, The	LP/BP	U.S.†	1985	$14.00/$8.00
Capitol	91340	Gift Set	LP	U.S.	1989	$50.00
	4 CD set of Dark Side of the Moon, Meddle +.					
CBS/Sony		Great Day For Freedom	LP	Japan	1994	$25.00
Album Network		In the Studio (Best of)	RS	U.S.		$100.00
	2 CD set.					
Album Network		In the Studio (Dark Side of the Moon)	RS	U.S.	1988	$40.00
	Airdate: 8/8/88.					
Album Network		In the Studio (Dark Side of the Moon)	RS	U.S.	1990	$40.00
	Airdate: 3/12/90.					
Album Network		In the Studio (Division Bell)	RS	U.S.		$100.00
	2 CD set.					
Album Network		In the Studio (Shine On)	RS	U.S.	1989	$40.00
	Airdate: 2/1/92.					
Album Network		In the Studio (Wall, The Pt1 & 2)	RS	U.S.	1989	$120.00
	Airdate: 7/10 to 7/17/89.					
Album Network		In the Studio (Wall, The Pt1 & 2)	RS	U.S.	1990	$120.00
	Airdate: 7/9 to 7/16/90.					
Album Network		In the Studio (Wish You We Here)	RS	U.S.		$100.00
	2 CD set.					
Columbia	CSK 6060	Limited Edition Interview Disc	DJ/Intvw	U.S.	1994	$35.00
Polygram	080731-1	Live at Pompeii	LD	U.S.	1989	$35.00
Capitol	CDP 46034	Meddle	LP/BP	U.S.†		$14.00/$8.00
	Non-remastered version.					
Capitol	CDP 46034	Meddle	LP/LB	U.S.		$14.00/$8.00
	Non-remastered version.					
EMI	746386-2	More	LP	U.K.	1985	$20.00
	Early non-remastered version.					
EMI	746385-2	Obscured by Clouds	LP	U.K.	1985	$20.00
	Early non-remastered version.					
EMI		Pulse	LTD/LP	U.K.	1995	$50.00
	2 CD set.					
Columbia	67063	Pulse	LP	U.S.	1995	$25.00
	Lighted double slipcase.					
Columbia	67063	Pulse	LP/LB	U.S.	1995	$35.00/$25.00
	Lighted double slipcase with longbox.					
On the Radio		Rarities on Compact Disc- A CD Full of Secrets	RS	U.S.	1992	$45.00
EMI	SHINE 1	Selected Tracks From Shine on	DJ/Smplr	U.K.	1992	$40.00
Columbia	CSK 4848	Selections From the Box	DJ/Smplr	U.S.	1992	$20.00
Columbia	CXK 53180	Shine on	LTD/LP	U.S.	1992	$160.00
	9 CD boxed set. First pressing having "Columbia" printed on all discs including those which should have "Capitol" printed on the disc.					
Westwood One		Show Goes on, The	RS	U.S.	1994	$150.00
	3 CD set. Airdate: 7/4/94.					
		Show Goes on, The	RS	U.S.	1994	$150.00
	3 CD set. Airdate: 7/4/94.					
Westwood One		Superstar Concert	RS	U.S.	1992	$120.00
	2 CD set. Airdate: 6/7/92.					
Westwood One		Superstar Concert	RS	U.S.	1993	$95.00
	2 CD set. Airdate: 9/20/93.					
Westwood One		Superstar Concert	RS	U.S.	1994	$120.00
	2 CD set. Airdate: 5/2/94.					
		Twenty Fifth Anniversary	RS	U.S.	1992	$300.00
	6 CD set. Airdate: 5/25/92.					
MCA Radio		Up Close	RS	U.S.	1988	$100.00
	2 CD set. First "Up Close" radio show.					
Media America		Up Close	RS	U.S.	1989	$80.00
	2 CD set.					
Media America		Up Close	RS	U.S.	1990	$70.00
	2 CD set.					
Media America		Up Close	RS	U.S.	1995	$145.00
	4 CD set.					
Point	SACD 1125	Us & Them Symphonic Pink Floyd	DJ/Smplr	U.S.	1995	$10.00
CBS	C2K-36183	Wall, The	LP/LB	U.S.†	1985	$25.00/$20.00
	2 CD set.					
Mobile Fidelity	UDCD 2-537	Wall, The	LP/LB	U.S.	1990	$75.00/$60.00
	2 CD set.					
CBS	CK-33453	Wish You Were Here	LP/BP	U.S.†	1985	$14.00/$8.00
Global Satellite Network		Wish You Were Here	RS	U.S.	1991	$150.00
	3 CD set.					
Columbia	CK-53753	Wish You Were Here	LP/LB	U.S.	1993	$30.00/$25.00
	Gold disc.					
Singles						
Columbia	38K-03118	Another Brick in the Wall	CD3	U.S.	1987	$18.00/$12.00
Columbia	CSK 1375	Comfortably Numb	CDJ	U.S.	1988	$25.00

Label	Catalog Number	Title	Type	Country	Year	Longbox Value/Value
EMI	SPCD 1760	High Hopes	CDJ	France	1994	$40.00
EMI		High Hopes	CD5	U.K.	1994	$12.00
Columbia		High Hopes	CDJ	U.S.	1994	$8.00
S-F- Miles	SEACD-4	Interstellar Overdrive	CD5	U.K.	1991	$12.00
EMI	SPCD 1809	Keep Talking	CDJ	France	1994	$45.00
EMI	PINK 1	Keep Talking	CDJ	Germany	1994	$20.00
EMI	PINK 1	Keep Talking	CDJ	U.K.	1994	$25.00
Columbia	CSK 6007	Keep Talking	CDJ	U.S.	1994	$8.00
EMI	202048-2	Learning to Fly	CD5	Germany	1988	$20.00
EMI	CD EM 26	Learning to Fly	CD5	U.K.	1987	$20.00
Columbia	CSK 2775	Learning to Fly	CDJ	U.S.	1987	$20.00
EMI	MONEY-1	Money	CDJ	Germany	1994	$40.00
CBS	10EP-3005	On the Turning Away	CD3	Japan	1987	$18.00/$4.00
EMI	CD EM 14	On the Turning Away	CD5	U.K.	1987	$18.00
EMI	CD EM 52	One Slip	CD5	U.K.	1987	$15.00
EMI		Take It Back	CDJ	Australia	1994	$12.00
EMI		Take It Back	CDJ	Australia	1994	$12.00
	Second version.					
EMI	SPCD 1733	Take It Back	CDJ	France	1994	$30.00
EMI		Take It Back	CDJ	France	1994	$30.00
	Second version.					
EMI		Take It Back	CD5	U.K.	1994	$13.00
EMI		Take It Back	CD5	U.K.	1994	$13.00
	Second version.					
EMI	CDEM-DJ-309	Take It Back	CDJ	U.K.	1994	$11.00
Columbia	44K 77493	Take It Back	CD5	U.S.	1994	$6.00
Columbia	CSK 6069	Take It Back	CDJ	U.S.	1994	$8.00
Columbia		What Do You Want With Me	CDJ	U.S.	1995	$10.00
CBS		Wish You Were Here	CD5	France	1995	$60.00
CBS		Wish You Were Here	CD5	Germany	1995	$16.00
CBS		Wish You Were Here	CD5	U.K.	1995	$16.00

Pirates of The Mississippi

Label	Catalog Number	Title	Type	Country	Year	Longbox Value/Value
		Full Length				
Capitol		Dreams	DJ/LP	U.S.	1993	$15.00
		Singles				
Capitol		Feed Jake	CDJ	U.S.	1993	$15.00
	CD and VHS video in 10"x15" box with press kit.					
Capitol	DPRO-79067	Georgia Peaches	CDJ	U.S.	1991	$3.00
Pikosso		Sun Side	SCD5	Germany	1995	$15.00
	Sawbladeshaped disc.					

Pitney, Gene

Label	Catalog Number	Title	Type	Country	Year	Longbox Value/Value
		Singles				
Old Gold	OG-6107	24 Hours From Tulsa	CD3	U.K.	1988	$10.00
Rhino	885848	(I Wanna) Love My Life Away	CD3	Germany	1990	$10.00
Rhino	885849	It Hurts to Be in Love	CD3	Germany	1990	$10.00
Columbia	654749-2	It's Over It's Over	CD5	U.K.	1989	$10.00
Polygram	PZCD-134	Let the Heartaches Begin	CD5	U.K.	1991	$10.00

Pitt, William

Label	Catalog Number	Title	Type	Country	Year	Longbox Value/Value
		Singles				
Polygram	885590-2	City Lights	CD5	Germany	1988	$8.00
Polygram	877275-2	Such a Lonely Night	CD5	Germany	1988	$8.00

Pixies

Label	Catalog Number	Title	Type	Country	Year	Longbox Value/Value
		Full Length				
		Live	DJ/Smplr	France		$45.00
		Singles				
4AD	PIX-1999CD	Alec Eiffel	CD5	U.K.	1992	$10.00
Elektra	66444-2	Alec Eiffel	CD5	U.S.	1992	$5.00
Elektra	PRCD 8519-2	Alec Eiffel	CDJ	U.S.	1992	$2.00
Elektra	PRCD 8287-2	Allison	CDJ	U.S.	1990	$2.00
4AD	848027-2	Dig for Fire	CD5	Canada	1990	$10.00
4AD	BAD-0014CD	Dig for Fire	CD5	U.K.	1990	$10.00
Elektra	66596 2	Dig for Fire	CD5	U.S.	1990	$5.00
Elektra	PRCD 82151-2	Dig for Fire	CDJ	U.S.	1991	$2.00
4AD	BAD-805CD	Gigantic	CD5	U.K.	1990	$10.00
		Head On	CD5	Canada		$10.00
4AD	COCY-5172	Head On	CD3	Japan	1992	$12.00/$5.00
Elektra	PRCD 8476-2	Head On	CDJ	U.S.	1992	$2.00
Elektra	PRCD 8535-2	Head On	CDJ	U.S.	1992	$2.00
4AD	874755-2	Here Comes Your Man	CD5	Canada	1989	$10.00
4AD	BAD-909CD	Here Comes Your Man	CD5	U.K.	1989	$10.00
Elektra	66694-2	Here Comes Your Man	CD5	U.S.	1989	$5.00
Elektra	PR 8090-2	Here Comes Your Man	CDJ	U.S.	1989	$2.00
Elektra	PRCD 8441-2	Letter to Memphis	CDJ	U.S.	1991	$2.00
4AD	BAD-904CD	Monkey Gone to Heaven	CD5	U.K.	1989	$10.00
Elektra	66707 2	Monkey Gone to Heaven	CD5	U.S.	1989	$5.00
Elektra	PR 8073-2	Monkey Gone to Heaven	CDJ	U.S.	1989	$2.00
4AD	BAD-1008CD	Planet of Sound	CD5	U.K.	1991	$10.00
4AD	846552-2	Velouria	CD5	Canada	1990	$10.00
4AD	BAD-0009	Velouria	CD5	U.K.	1990	$10.00
Elektra	PRCD 8202-2	Velouria	CDJ	U.S.	1990	$2.00
Elektra	66616-2	Velouria	CD5	U.S.	1992	$5.00

Pizzicato Five

Label	Catalog Number	Title	Type	Country	Year	Longbox Value/Value
		Full Length				
Matador	PRCD 6374-2	Happy Sad		U.S.	1995	$3.00
		Singles				
Atlantic	95725	Happy Sad	CD5	U.S.	1995	$5.00
Matador	128	Quickie	CD5	U.S.	1995	$6.00

Plan B

Label	Catalog Number	Title	Type	Country	Year	Longbox Value/Value
		Singles				
BMG	662530	Beam Me Up, Scotty	CD5	Germany	1989	$8.00
BMG	663881	Discontentment	CD5	Germany	1989	$8.00
		Run for Cover	CDJ	U.S.		$2.00
		Run for Cover	CDJ	U.S.		$2.00
	Second version.					

Planet D

Label	Catalog Number	Title	Type	Country	Year	Longbox Value/Value
		Singles				
Eastwest	9031-74936-2	Caravan at Night	CD5	Germany	1991	$8.00

Plant, Robert

Label	Catalog Number	Title	Type	Country	Year	Longbox Value/Value
		Full Length				
Atlantic		Excerpts From Manic Nirvana	DJ/Smplr	U.K.	1990	$15.00
Album Network		In the Studio (Now and Zen)	RS	U.S.	1988	$35.00
	Airdate: 10/31/88.					
DIR		King Biscuit Flour Hour	RS	U.S.	1990	$50.00
	Airdate:3/5/90.					
Esparanza	7 91361-2	Manic Nirvana	LTD/LP	U.S.	1990	$25.00/$15.00
	CD in digipak and banner housed in custom longbox.					
Westwood One		Off the Record	RS	U.S.	1993	$30.00
	Airdate: 11/22/93.					
Westwood One		Off the Record	RS	U.S.	1993	$30.00
	Airdate: 7/5/93.					
Westwood One		Off the Record	RS	U.S.	1994	$30.00
	Airdate: 4/11/94.					
Media America		On Tour	RS	U.S.	1990	$25.00
Swan Song	90101-2	Principle of Moments	LP/LB	U.S.†	1984	$14.00/$8.00
Esparanza	PRCD 3297-2	Profiled	DJ/Intvw	U.S.	1990	$15.00
Esparanza	90265-2	Shakin' Not Stirred	LP/LB	U.S.†	1985	$14.00/$8.00
Media America		Up Close	RS	U.S.	1990	$70.00
	4 CD set.					
Esparanza	PRCD 3301-2	World Premiere Broadcast	DJ/RS	U.S.	1990	$15.00
	Manic Nirvana.					
		Singles				
Atlantic		29 Palms	CD5	U.K.	1993	$11.00
	CD in custom digipak.					
Atlantic		29 Palms	CD5	U.K.	1993	$12.00
	Second version.					
Esparanza	PRCD 5097-2	29 Palms	CDJ	U.S.	1993	$6.00
		Calling to You	CD5	U.K.		$12.00
	Second version.					
Fontana	FATEX 3	Calling to You	CD5	U.K.	1993	$12.00
Esperanza	PRCD 5082-2	Calling to You	CDJ	U.S.	1993	$6.00
Atlantic	796716-2	Heaven Knows	CD5	Germany	1988	$12.00
Atlantic	10SW-10	Heaven Knows	CD3	Japan	1988	$18.00/$5.00
Atlantic	A-9373CD	Heaven Knows	CD5	U.K.	1988	$12.00
Esperanza	PR 2221-2	Heaven Knows	CDJ	U.S.	1988	$6.00
Atlantic	7567-96473-2	Hurting Kind	CD5	Germany	1990	$12.00
Atlantic	AMDY 5000	Hurting Kind	CD3	Japan	1990	$18.00/$5.00
Atlantic	A-8985CD	Hurting Kind	CD5	U.K.	1990	$12.00
Esperanza	96483-2	Hurting Kind	CD5	U.S.	1990	$5.00
Esperanza	PRCD 3186-2	Hurting Kind	CDJ	U.S.	1990	$6.00
Fontana		I Believe	CD5	U.K.	1993	$12.00
Fontana	FATEX 2	I Believe	CD5	U.K.	1993	$12.00
Atlantic	PRCD 5273-2	I Believe	CDJ	U.S.	1993	$6.00
Atlantic	PRCD 5302-2	I Believe	CDJ	U.S.	1993	$6.00
		If I Was a Carpenter	CD5	U.K.		$12.00
		If I Was a Carpenter	CD5	U.K.		$12.00
	Second version.					
Atlantic		If I Were a Carpenter	CDJ	Germany	1993	$15.00
Esperasa		If I Were a Carpenter	CDJ	U.K.	1993	$12.00
Esperasa	PRCD 5393-2	If I Were a Carpenter	CDJ	U.S.	1993	$3.00
Esparanza	PRCD 3636-2	Nirvana	CDJ	U.S.	1990	$3.00
WEA	796 611-2	Ship of Fools	CD3	Germany	1988	$15.00
	CD in special collectors' box.					
Pioneer	10P3-6002	Ship of Fools	CD3	Japan	1988	$18.00/$5.00
Atlantic	A-9281CD	Ship of Fools	CD3	U.K.	1988	$12.00
Mute	CDMUTE-74	Ship of Fools	CD5	U.K.	1988	$12.00
Atlantic	PR 2436-2	Ship of Fools	CDJ	U.S.	1988	$7.00
	Also contains a track by Debbie Gibson.					
Esparanza	PRCD 3449-2	SSS & Q	CDJ	U.S.	1990	$3.00
Atlantic	796666-2	Tall Cool One	CD3	Germany	1989	$15.00
Pioneer	10SW-48	Tall Cool One	CD3	Japan	1989	$12.00/$5.00
Atlantic	A-9348CD	Tall Cool One	CD3	U.K.	1989	$12.00
Atlantic		Walking Towards Paradise	CDJ	U.S.		$3.00
Esparanza	A-8945CD	Your Ma Said You Cried in Your Sleep Last Night	CD5	U.K.	1990	$12.00
Esparanza	PRCD 3349-2	Your Ma Said You Cried in Your Sleep Last Night	CDJ	U.S.	1990	$3.00

Plant, Robert/Page, Jimmy

Label	Catalog Number	Title	Type	Country	Year	Longbox Value/Value
		Full Length				
Atlantic		A Songwriting Legacy	DJ/Smplr	U.S.	1994	$30.00
	10 Track sampler.					
Atlantic	PRCD 6095-2	A Songwriting Legacy	DJ/Smplr	U.S.	1994	$35.00
	12 Track sampler.					
Atlantic	PRCDD 6094-2	A Songwriting Legacy	DJ/Smplr	U.S.	1996	$45.00
	"Miller Genuine Draft" beer promotional sampler.					
Atlantic	PRCD 5987-2	Conversations With	DJ/Intvw	U.S.	1995	$35.00
		Singles				
Atlantic		Battle of Evermore	CDJ	U.K.	1994	$35.00
Atlantic		Gallows Pole	CD5	U.K.	1994	$12.00
Atlantic		Gallows Pole	CDJ	U.K.	1994	$25.00
Atlantic	PRCD 5921-2	Gallows Pole	CDJ	U.S.	1994	$12.00
Atlantic		Kashmir	CD5	France	1994	$12.00
Atlantic		Nobody's Fault But Mine	CDJ	U.S.	1994	$12.00
Atlantic	PRCD 6017-2	Thank You	CDJ	U.S.	1994	$12.00
Atlantic	85591-2	Wonderful One	CD5	U.S.	1995	$6.00
Atlantic		Wonderful One	CDJ	U.S.	1995	$15.00

Plastique

Label	Catalog Number	Title	Type	Country	Year	Longbox Value/Value
		Singles				
		Touch Someone	CDJ	U.S.		$2.00

Platinum Blonde

Label	Catalog Number	Title	Type	Country	Year	Longbox Value/Value
		Singles				
Epic	ESK 368	Contact	CDJ	U.S.	1987	$3.00

Platters

Label	Catalog Number	Title	Type	Country	Year	Longbox Value/Value
		Full Length				
Polygram	826447-2	Golden Hits	LP/BP	U.S.		$12.00/$7.00
Time/Warner Sound Exchange	232512	Twilight Time	LP	U.S.	1996	$30.00
	2 CD set.					
		Singles				
	7515	Great Pretender	CD5	U.S.	1994	$5.00
Polygram	888968-2	Great Pretenders	CD5	Germany	1990	$10.00
Philips	PHDR-29	Only You	CD3	Japan	1991	$12.00/$5.00
Mercury	PHDR-35	Twilight Time	CD3	Japan	1991	$12.00/$4.00

Playa Pancho & La Sno

Label	Catalog Number	Title	Type	Country	Year	Longbox Value/Value
		Singles				
Columbia	77957	Whatz Up, Whatz Up	CD5	U.S.	1995	$5.00

Playa Poncho

Label	Catalog Number	Title	Type	Country	Year	Longbox Value/Value
		Singles				
Columbia	CSK 7743	Koochie Kuterz	CDJ	U.S.		$2.00

Players

Label	Catalog Number	Title	Type	Country	Year	Longbox Value/Value
		Full Length				
Passport	PJCD-88040	Dream Come True	LP/BP	U.S.		$12.00/$7.00
Passport	PJCD-88014	Players Live	LP	U.K.		$15.00
Passport	PJCD-88014	Players Live	LP/BP	U.S.		$12.00/$7.00

Pleasure

Label	Catalog Number	Title	Type	Country	Year	Longbox Value/Value
		Singles				
ZYX	GDC 2095-8	Glide	CD5	U.S.	1995	$8.00

Pleasure Bombs

Singles

Label	Catalog Number	Title	Type	Country	Year	Longbox Value/Value
Atco	PRCD 3968-2	Love Takes a Walk	CDJ	U.S.	1991	$2.00

Pleasure Fucker

Singles

Label	Catalog Number	Title	Type	Country	Year	Longbox Value/Value
Sympathy	359	Ripped to the Tits	CD5	U.S.	1994	$5.00

Pleasure Principle

Singles

Label	Catalog Number	Title	Type	Country	Year	Longbox Value/Value
EMI	204016-2	Shake Your Body	CD5	Germany	1990	$8.00
EMI	203830-2	Trip to My Soul	CD5	Germany	1990	$8.00

Pleasure Thieves

Singles

Label	Catalog Number	Title	Type	Country	Year	Longbox Value/Value
Hollywood	PRCD 10151	Blue Flowers	CDJ	U.S.	1992	$2.00

Plexi

Singles

Label	Catalog Number	Title	Type	Country	Year	Longbox Value/Value
	95771	Plexi	CD5	U.S.	1994	$5.00

PM

Singles

Label	Catalog Number	Title	Type	Country	Year	Longbox Value/Value
Warner Brothers	PRO-CD-3218	Piece of Paradise	CDJ	U.S.	1988	$2.00
Warner Brothers	PRO-CD-3452	Say It Again	CDJ	U.S.	1988	$2.00
	8909	You	CD5	U.S.	1994	$5.00

PM Dawn

Singles

Label	Catalog Number	Title	Type	Country	Year	Longbox Value/Value
Island	PRCD 6671-2	A Watcher's Point of View	CDJ	U.S.	1991	$2.00
Gee Street	PRCD 6712-2	Comatose	CDJ	U.S.	1991	$2.00
	[illegible]	Downtown Venus	CDJ	U.S.		[illegible]
	PRCD70682	Downtown Venus	CDJ	U.S.		$6.00
Polygram	854409	Downtown Venus	CD5	U.S.	1995	$5.00
Polygram	GESCD-39	I'd Die Without You	CD5	U.K.	1992	$9.00
Laface	73008 24039	I'd Die Without You	CD5	U.S.	1992	$5.00
Laface	4034	I'd Die Without You	CDJ	U.S.	1992	$2.00
Laface	4036	I'd Die Without You	CDJ	U.S.	1992	$2.00
Phonogram	PHCR-8712	Looking Through Patient Eyes	CD5	Japan	1993	$15.00
Gee Street	422-862 025	Looking Through Patient Eyes	CD5	U.S.	1991	$5.00
Gee Street	PRCD 6765-2	Looking Through Patient Eyes	CDJ	U.S.	1991	$2.00
Gee Street	GESCD 49	More Than Likely	CD5	U.K.	1993	$9.00
Gee Street		More Than Likely	CD5	U.K.	1993	$9.00
Second version.						
BMG	664860	Paper Doll	CD5	Germany	1991	$9.00
Island	PSCD-1193	Paper Doll	CD5	Japan	1991	$15.00
Island	PSDD-3003	Paper Doll	CD3	Japan	1992	$12.00/$4.00
Island	422 866 375	Paper Doll	CD5	U.S.	1992	$5.00
Island	PRCD-6699-2	Paper Doll	CDJ	U.S.	1992	$3.00
Gee Street	PRCD 6766-2	Plastic	CDJ	U.S.	1993	$2.00
Polygram	665163	Reality Used to Be a Friend	CD5	Germany	1992	$9.00
Polygram	GESCD-37	Reality Used to Be a Friend	CD5	U.K.	1992	$9.00
Island	PRCD-6711-2	Reality Used to Be a Friend	CDJ	U.S.	1992	$2.00
Polygram	664619	Set Adrift on Memory Bliss	CD5	Germany	1991	$9.00
Polygram	GESCD-33	Set Adrift on Memory Bliss	CD5	U.K.	1991	$9.00
Island	866095	Set Adrift on Memory Bliss	CD5	U.S.	1991	$5.00
Island	PRD 6690	Set Adrift on Memory Bliss	CDJ	U.S.	1991	$2.00
	PRCD70992	Sometimes I Miss You So Much	CDJ	U.S.		$6.00
Polygram	664401	Watcher's Point of View	CD5	Germany	1991	$9.00
Polygram	GESCD-32	Watcher's Point of View	CD5	U.K.	1991	$9.00
Gee Street	422 862 475	Ways of the Wind, The	CD5	U.S.	1993	$5.00
Gee Street	PRC 6778-2	Ways of the Wind, The	CDJ	U.S.	1993	$3.00
Gee Street	422 858 057	You Got Me Floatin'	CD5	U.S.	1993	$5.00
Gee Street	PRCD 6808	You Got Me Floatin'	CDJ	U.S.	1993	$3.00
Gee Street	PRCD 6809	You Got Me Floatin'	CDJ	U.S.	1993	$3.00

Pocket Change

Full Length

Label	Catalog Number	Title	Type	Country	Year	Longbox Value/Value
Passport	PJCD-88018	Random Aces	LP	U.K.		$15.00
Passport	PJCD-88018	Random Aces	LP/BP	U.S.		$12.00/$7.00

Poco

Full Length

Label	Catalog Number	Title	Type	Country	Year	Longbox Value/Value
DIR		King Biscuit Flour Hour	RS	U.S.	1988	$35.00
Airdate: 10/16/88.						
RCA		Legacy	DJ/LP	U.S.		$15.00
RCA	9183-2-RDj	Nature of Love, The	DJ/Intvw	U.S.	1990	$10.00
RCA	7135	Radio Special	DJ/Intvw	Canada	1989	$25.00

Singles

Label	Catalog Number	Title	Type	Country	Year	Longbox Value/Value
RCA	PD-49340	Call It Love	CD5	Germany	1989	$10.00
RCA	R10D-130	Call It Love	CD3	Japan	1989	$12.00/$5.00
RCA	PD-49340	Call It Love	CD5	U.K.	1989	$10.00
RCA	9039-2-RDj	Call It Love	CDJ	U.S.	1989	$7.00
Stallion		I Found Love	CDJ	U.S.	1994	$10.00
RCA	PD-49314	Nothin' to Hide	CD5	Germany	1989	$10.00
RCA	R10D-141	Nothin' to Hide	CD3	Japan	1989	$15.00/$4.00
RCA	9131-2-RDj	Nothin' to Hide	CDJ	U.S.	1989	$2.00
RCA	2623-2-RDj	What Do People Know	CDJ	U.S.	1990	$2.00

Poe

Full Length

Label	Catalog Number	Title	Type	Country	Year	Longbox Value/Value
Westwood One		In Concert-Nu Rock	RS	U.S.	1996	$40.00
Airdate: 8/26/96.						
Atlantic	PRCD 6635-2	Trigger Happy Jack		U.S.		$3.00

Singles

Label	Catalog Number	Title	Type	Country	Year	Longbox Value/Value
	PRCD 6660	Angry Johnny	CDJ	U.S.		$2.00
	PRCD 6392-2	Trigger Happy Jack	CDJ	U.S.		$2.00
Atlantic	95722	Trigger Happy Jack	CD5	U.S.	1995	$5.00

Poetess

Singles

Label	Catalog Number	Title	Type	Country	Year	Longbox Value/Value
Poetic	4556	Making Some Change	CDJ	U.S.	1992	$2.00

Poets

Singles

Label	Catalog Number	Title	Type	Country	Year	Longbox Value/Value
RCA	2726-2-RDj	Subversive	CDJ	U.S.	1990	$2.00

Pogues

Singles

Label	Catalog Number	Title	Type	Country	Year	Longbox Value/Value
EMI	CDNY-1	Fairytale of New York	CD5	U.K.	1988	$12.00
Warner Brothers	YZ-628CD	Fairytale of New York	CD5	U.K.	1991	$10.00
Eastwest	9031-77488-2	Honky Tonk Woman	CD5	Germany	1992	$10.00
Warner Brothers	YZ-673CD	Honky Tonk Woman	CD5	U.K.	1992	$10.00
Stiff	CDFG-1	If I Should Fall From Grace	CD5	U.K.	1988	$12.00
East Wet	9031-71861-2	Jack's Heroe's	CD5	Germany	1990	$10.00
Warner Brothers	YZ-500CD	Jack's Heroe's	CD5	U.K.	1990	$10.00
Warner Brothers	870085	Misty Morning, Albert Bridge	CD5	Germany	1989	$10.00
Eastwest	246804-2	Misty Morning, Albert Bridge	CD5	Germany	1989	$10.00
Warner Brothers	YZ-407CD	Misty Morning, Albert Bridge	CD5	U.K.	1989	$10.00
Elektra	PRCD 8887-2	Once Upon a Time	CDJ	U.S.	1993	$2.00
Eastwest	9031-75475-2	Poguetry in Motion	CD5	Germany	1991	$10.00
Warner Brothers	YZ-603CD	Poguetry in Motion	CD5	U.K.	1991	$10.00
Eastwest	9031-73075-2	Sayonara	CD5	Germany	1991	$10.00
Eastwest	9031-72402-2	Summer Rrain	CD5	Germany	1990	$10.00
Warner Brothers	YZ-519CD	Summer Rrain	CD5	U.K.	1990	$10.00
		Tuesday Morning	CD5	U.K.		$10.00
		Tuesday Morning	CD5	U.K.		$10.00
Second version.						
Elektra	PRCD 8849-2	Tuesday Morning	CDJ	U.S.	1993	$2.00
Warner Brothers	YZ-409CD	White City	CD5	U.K.	1989	$10.00
Eastwest	820999	Yeah, Yeah, Yeah, Yeah, Yeah	CD5	Germany	1988	$10.00
Warner Brothers	YZ-355CD	Yeah, Yeah, Yeah, Yeah, Yeah	CD5	U.K.	1988	$10.00

Poi Dog Pondering

Singles

Label	Catalog Number	Title	Type	Country	Year	Longbox Value/Value
Columbia	CSK 74203	Be the One	CDJ	U.S.	1992	$2.00
Columbia	CSK 2093	Everybody's Trying	CDJ	U.S.	1990	$7.00
Columbia	44K-73733	Fruitless	CD5	U.S.	1990	$4.00
Columbia	CSK 4610	Get Me On	CDJ	U.S.	1992	$2.00
Columbia	44K 74083	Jack Ass Ginger	CD5	U.S.	1990	$4.00
Columbia	655395-2	Living With the Dreaming Body	CD5	U.K.	1990	$9.00
Columbia	655996-2	U Li L Lu	CD5	U.K.	1990	$9.00

Poindexter, Buster

Full Length

Label	Catalog Number	Title	Type	Country	Year	Longbox Value/Value
		House of Blues	RS	U.S.	1994	$40.00
2 CD set. Airdate: 7/17/94.						

Singles

Label	Catalog Number	Title	Type	Country	Year	Longbox Value/Value
RCA	[illegible]	All Night Party	[illegible]	U.K.	[illegible]	[illegible]
RCA	9007-2-RDj	All Night Party	CDJ	U.S.	1989	$2.00
Forward	7060	Breakin' Up the House	CDJ	U.S.	1994	$2.00
RCA	PD-49408	Hit the Road Jack	CD5	U.K.	1989	$8.00
RCA	8914-2-RDJ	Hit the Road Jack	CDJ	U.S.	1989	$2.00
RCA	9195-2-RDj	Under the Sea	CDJ	U.S.	1990	$2.00

Point of Grace

Full Length

Label	Catalog Number	Title	Type	Country	Year	Longbox Value/Value
		Radio Hits	DJ/Smplr	U.S.	1996	$15.00

Pointer, June

Singles

Label	Catalog Number	Title	Type	Country	Year	Longbox Value/Value
Columbia	000145	Right on Time	CDJ	U.S.	1989	$2.00

Pointer Sisters

Full Length

Label	Catalog Number	Title	Type	Country	Year	Longbox Value/Value
RCA	PCD1-4705	Break Out	LP/BP	U.S.†	1984	$14.00/$8.00
RCA	PCD1-5487	Contact	LP/BP	U.S.†	1985	$14.00/$8.00
Image	ID7239HB	Live in Africa	LD	U.S.		$20.00
Pioneer	PA86-M047	So Excited	8"LD	U.S.	1986	$7.00

Singles

Label	Catalog Number	Title	Type	Country	Year	Longbox Value/Value
Motown		After You	CDJ	U.S.		$2.00
RCA	PD-49469	Automatic	CD3	Germany	1989	$9.00
RCA	PD-49469	Automatic	CD3	U.K.	1989	$9.00
RCA	PD-43036	Automatic	CD5	U.K.	1989	$9.00
SBK	DPRO-04572	Don't Walk Away	CDJ	U.S.	1993	$2.00
RCA	ZD-43678	Friend's Advice	CD5	Germany	1990	$9.00
RCA	ZD-43678	Friend's Advice	CD5	U.K.	1990	$9.00
Motown	90003	Friend's Advice	CDJ	U.S.	1990	$3.00
Motown	CD45 1035	Insanity	CDJ	U.S.		$2.00
Sony	10EP-3049	Power of Persuasion	CD3	Japan	1988	$12.00/$4.00

Poison

Full Length

Label	Catalog Number	Title	Type	Country	Year	Longbox Value/Value
Def Jam	CSK 2892	Aerosmith/Poison	DJ/Smplr	U.S.	1987	$10.00
1 track by Aerosmith and 1 by Poison.						
Capitol	CDEST 2126	Flesh & Blood	DJ/LP	U.K.	1990	$100.00
CD, cassette housed in First-Aid box with bandages, pins, and press kit.						
Capitol	CDP 7 91813 2	Flesh & Blood	LP/LB	U.S.	1990	$16.00/$12.00
CBS	38DP-5024/5	Open Up and Say...Ahh!	LTD/LP	Japan	1988	$40.00
T-shirt pack.						
Capitol	CDP 548493	Open Up and Say...Ahh!	LP/LB	U.S.	1988	$16.00/$13.00
Banned cover.						
Image	ID7916EN	Sight For Sore Ears!	LD	U.S.		$25.00

Singles

Label	Catalog Number	Title	Type	Country	Year	Longbox Value/Value
EMI	203174-2	Every Rose Has Its Thorn	CD5	Germany	1988	$10.00
Enigma	10EP-3056	Every Rose Has Its Thorn	CD3	Japan	1988	$12.00/$4.00
Enigma	CDCL-520	Every Rose Has Its Thorn	CD5	U.K.	1988	$10.00
Capitol	C3-44203-2	Every Rose Has Its Thorn	CD3	U.S.	1988	$7.00/$4.00
Sony	12EP-8008	Fallen Angel	CD3	Japan	1990	$12.00/$4.00
Capitol	CDCL-500	Fallen Angel	CD5	U.K.	1990	$10.00
Capitol	DPRO-79995	Life Goes On	CDJ	U.S.	1991	$2.00
Sony	10EP-3016	Nothin' But a Good Time	CD3	Japan	1988	$12.00/$4.00
Capitol	CDCL-539	Nothin' But a Good Time	CD5	U.K.	1988	$10.00
Capitol	DPRO 79301	Nothin' But a Good Time	CDJ	U.S.	1988	$2.00
Sony	CSDS-8178	Ride the Wind	CD3	Japan	1991	$12.00/$4.00
Capitol	DPRO-79275	Ride the Wind	CDJ	U.S.	1991	$2.00
Capitol		Rough Mixes, The	CDJ	U.S.	1993	$7.00
Capitol	DPRO-79815	Sacrifice	CDJ	U.S.	1990	$3.00
Capitol	204599-2	So Tell Me Why	CD5	Germany	1991	$10.00
Capitol	TODP-2329	So Tell Me Why	CD3	Japan	1991	$12.00/$4.00
Capitol	CDCL-640	So Tell Me Why	CD5	U.K.	1991	$10.00
Capitol	DPRO-79007	So Tell Me Why	CDJ	U.S.	1991	$3.00
Capitol	204074-2	Something to Believe in	CD5	Germany	1990	$10.00
Sony	CSDS-8169	Something to Believe in	CD3	Japan	1990	$12.00/$4.00
Capitol	CDCL-594	Something to Believe in	CD5	U.K.	1990	$10.00
Capitol	DPRO-79272	Something to Believe in	CDJ	U.S.	1990	$6.00
Capitol	TODP-2392	Stand	CD3	Japan	1993	$12.00/$4.00
		Stand	CD5	U.K.		$10.00
		Stand	CD5	U.K.		$10.00
Second version.						
Capitol	DPRO-79585	Stand	CDJ	U.S.	1993	$3.00
Capitol/NTSC	CAP.5686	Talk Dirty to Me	DJ/CDV	U.S.	1988	$30.00
Capitol	203923-2	Unskinny Bop	CD5	Germany	1990	$10.00
Capitol	CDCL-582	Unskinny Bop	CD5	U.K.	1990	$10.00
Capitol	DPRO-79133	Unskinny Bop	CDJ	U.S.	1990	$3.00
Capitol	DPRO-79658	Until You Suffer Some	CDJ	U.S.	1993	$3.00
Capitol	DPRO-79710	Until You Suffer Some	CDJ	U.S.	1993	$3.00
Enigma	203264-2	Your Mama Don't Dance	CD5	Germany	1989	$10.00
CBS/Sony	10EP 3071	Your Mama Don't Dance	CD3	Japan	1988	$12.00/$4.00
Enigma	CDCL-523	Your Mama Don't Dance	CD5	U.K.	1989	$10.00

Poison Clan

Singles

Label	Catalog Number	Title	Type	Country	Year	Longbox Value/Value
Luke		Dance All Night	CDJ	U.S.	1993	$2.00

Label	Catalog Number	Title	Type	Country	Year	Longbox Value / Value
Luke	470	Don't Sleep on a Hizzo	CDJ	U.S.	1993	$2.00
	185	Fire Up This Funk	CD5	U.S.	1995	$5.00
BMG	6638605	Girl That I Hate	CD5	Germany	1990	$8.00

Pol

Singles

Label	Catalog Number	Title	Type	Country	Year	Longbox Value / Value
	PRCD 7394	Stupid	CDJ	U.S.		$2.00
	PRCD 7656	White Punks on Dope	CDJ	U.S.		$2.00

Polara

Singles

Label	Catalog Number	Title	Type	Country	Year	Longbox Value / Value
Twin/Tone	RPRO-066	Counting Down	CDJ	U.S.	1995	$7.00

Polaro

Singles

Label	Catalog Number	Title	Type	Country	Year	Longbox Value / Value
	PRCD 6593	Source of Light	CDJ	U.S.		$2.00

Police

Full Length

Label	Catalog Number	Title	Type	Country	Year	Longbox Value / Value
A&M	CD-3902	BBC Classic Tracks	LP/LB	U.S.		$14.00/$9.00
BBC Radio		BBC Classic Tracks	RS	U.S.	1991	$20.00
Airdate: 5/20/91.						
BBC Radio		BBC Classic Tracks	RS	U.S.	1992	$20.00
Airdate: 5/4/92.						
BBC Radio		BBC Classic Tracks	RS	U.S.	1993	$20.00
Airdate: 2/15/93.						
BBC Radio		BBC Classic Tracks	RS	U.S.	1994	$20.00
Airdate: 2/14/94.						
A&M	CD-3902	Every Breath You Take	LP/LB	U.S.		$14.00/$8.00
Pioneer	PA-87-196	Every Breath You Take	LD	U.S.	1987	$45.00
Pioneer	PA-87-196	Every Breath You Take	LD	U.S.	1990	$40.00
Digital audio.						
Pioneer		Every Breath You Take - The Videos	LD	U.S.	1986	$35.00
A&M	CD-3730	Ghost in the Machine	LP/LB	U.S.		$14.00/$8.00
A&M	CD-3730	Ghost in the Machine	LP/LB	U.S.†	1984	$14.00/$8.00
A&M		Greatest Hits	DJ/Smplr	U.K.	1995	$25.00
A&M		Greatest Hits Sampler	DJ/Smplr	U.K.	1992	$25.00
Westwood One		In Concert	RS	U.S.	1992	$70.00
2 CD set. With Dire Straits, Airdate: 8/17/92.						
Westwood One		In Concert	RS	U.S.	1994	$50.00
2 CD set. Airdate: 3/14/94.						
Album Network		In the Studio (Synchronicity)	RS	U.S.		$20.00
Album Network		In the Studio (Zenyatta Mondatta)	RS	U.S.	1990	$30.00
Airdate: 12/3/90.						
A&M		Live!	DJ/Smplr	U.K.	1995	$25.00
A&M		Live!	DJ/Smplr	U.S.	1995	$30.00
		Message in a Box	RS	U.S.	1993	$100.00
3 CD set.						
Westwood One		Off the Record	RS	U.S.	1993	$60.00
2 CD set. Airdate: 12/27/93.						
Westwood One		Off the Record	RS	U.S.	1994	$50.00
2 CD set. Airdate: 6/27/94.						
A&M	CD-4753	Outlandos d'Amour	LP/LB	U.S.†	1984	$14.00/$8.00
Radio Today		Outlandos To Synchro	RS	U.S.	1995	$60.00
A&M	CD-3311	Outlands D'Amour	LP/LB	U.S.		$14.00/$9.00
A&M	CD-3312	Reggatta De Blanc	LP/LB	U.S.		$14.00/$9.00
A&M	CD-4792	Reggatta De Blanc	LP/LB	U.S.†	1984	$14.00/$8.00
A&M		Selections From Message in a Box	DJ/Smplr	U.S.	1993	$18.00
Westwood One		Superstars	RS	U.S.	1993	$60.00
Airdate: 3/28/93.						
Westwood One		Superstars	RS	U.S.	1995	$60.00
Airdate: 4/3/95.						
A&M	CD-3735	Synchronicity	LP/LB	U.S.		$14.00/$9.00
A&M	CD-3735	Synchronicity	LP/LB	U.S.†	1984	$14.00/$8.00
Pioneeer	PA-84-096	Synchronicity Concert	LD	U.S.	1984	$40.00
Pioneeer	PA-84-096	Synchronicity Concert	LD	U.S.	1984	$40.00
Digital audio.						
A&M	CD-3720	Zenyatta Mondatta	LP/LB	U.S.†	1984	$14.00/$8.00

Singles

Label	Catalog Number	Title	Type	Country	Year	Longbox Value / Value
A&M	390341-2	Compact Hits	CD5	Germany	1988	$10.00
A&M	AMCD-905	Compact Hits	CD5	U.K.	1988	$10.00
A&M	S12Y-3011	De Do Do Do, De Da, Da, Da	CD3	Japan	1988	$18.00/$5.00
A&M	CD-17435	Don't Stand So Close to Me '86	CDJ	U.S.	1986	$25.00
A&M/NTSC	A & M 002	Don't Stand So Close to Me '86	DJ/CDV	U.S.	1988	$50.00
A&M		Every Breath You Take	CDV	Japan	1989	$30.00

Polyphemus

Singles

Label	Catalog Number	Title	Type	Country	Year	Longbox Value / Value
Beggars Banquet	BBQ 12CD	Masses of Tiny Dots	CD5	U.K.	1993	$8.00

Pomeranz, David

Singles

Label	Catalog Number	Title	Type	Country	Year	Longbox Value / Value
		Far Away Lands (From the Summit)	CDJ	U.S.		$2.00

Pond

Singles

Label	Catalog Number	Title	Type	Country	Year	Longbox Value / Value
Sub Pop	SPCD-59/222	Wheel	CD5	U.K.	1992	$8.00

Ponty, Jean-Luc

Full Length

Label	Catalog Number	Title	Type	Country	Year	Longbox Value / Value
Atlantic	80098-2	Individual Choice	LP/LB	U.S.†	1985	$14.00/$8.00
Atlantic	19333-2	Mystical Adventures	LP/LB	U.S.†	1985	$14.00/$8.00
Atlantic	80185-2	Open Mind	LP/LB	U.S.†	1985	$14.00/$8.00
Columbia		Storytelling	DJ/Smplr	U.S.	1989	$4.00

Singles

Label	Catalog Number	Title	Type	Country	Year	Longbox Value / Value
Columbia	CSK 1835	In the Fast Lane	CDJ	U.S.	1989	$2.00

Pooh Sticks

Singles

Label	Catalog Number	Title	Type	Country	Year	Longbox Value / Value
	98178	Cool In A Crisis	CD5	U.S.	1994	$5.00

Pool, Grace

Singles

Label	Catalog Number	Title	Type	Country	Year	Longbox Value / Value
Reprise	PRO-CD-3398	Stay	CDJ	U.S.	1988	$2.00

Poorboys

Singles

Label	Catalog Number	Title	Type	Country	Year	Longbox Value / Value
Hollywood	HWD-121CD	Brand New Amerika	CD5	U.K.	1992	$8.00
Hollywood	PRCD 8221-2	Spider and the Fly, The	CDJ	U.S.	1990	$2.00

Pop, Iggy

Full Length

Label	Catalog Number	Title	Type	Country	Year	Longbox Value / Value
DIR		King Biscuit Flour Hour	RS	U.S.	1988	$50.00
Airdate: 8/28/88.						
DIR		King Biscuit Flour Hour	RS	U.S.	1989	$50.00
Airdate: 2/12/89.						
DIR		King Biscuit Flour Hour	RS	U.S.	1991	$40.00
Airdate: 2/10/91.						
DIR		King Biscuit Flour Hour	RS	U.S.	1994	$50.00
Airdate: 10/16/94.						
A&M	CD17641	Live at Channel 7-19-88	DJ/Smplr	U.S.	1988	$30.00
Virgin	DPRO1267	Naughty Little Doggie Droppings	DJ/Smplr	Canada	1995	$25.00
Virgin	PRCD 3365	Raw Traxx	DJ/Smplr	U.S.	1990	$15.00

Singles

Label	Catalog Number	Title	Type	Country	Year	Longbox Value / Value
Virgin	VUSCD77	Beside You	CD5	Holland	1993	$10.00
Virgin	DPRO-14195	Beside You	CDJ	U.S.	1993	$6.00
Virgin	PRCD BUTT	Butt Town	CDJ	U.S.	1990	$20.00
Virgin	663634	Candy	CD5	Germany	1990	$11.00
Toshiba	VJDP-137	Candy	CD3	Japan	1990	$12.00/$5.00
Virgin	VUSCD-29	Candy	CD5	U.K.	1990	$11.00
Virgin	PRCD IGGY	Candy	CDJ	U.S.	1990	$3.00
A&M	S10Y-3017	Cold Metal	CD3	Japan	1988	$12.00/$4.00
A&M	390356-2	Cold Metal	CD5	U.K.	1988	$10.00
A&M	CD 17573	Cold Metal	CDJ	U.S.	1988	$6.00
A&M	AMCD-909	Compact Hits	CD5	U.K.	1988	$10.00
Virgin	DPRO11084	Heart is Save	CDJ	U.S.		$7.00
A&M	AMCD-475	High on You	CD5	U.K.	1988	$10.00
A&M	CD 17632	High on You	CDJ	U.S.	1988	$6.00
BMG	663440	Home	CD5	Germany	1990	$10.00
Virgin	VUSCD-22	Home	CD5	U.K.	1990	$10.00
Virgin	PRCD 3364	Home	CDJ	U.S.	1990	$3.00
Virgin	VOZEP CDO2	Livin' on the Edge of Night	CD5	Australia	1990	$12.00
BMG	662988	Livin' on the Edge of Night	CD5	Germany	1990	$10.00
Virgin	VUSCD-18	Livin' on the Edge of Night	CD5	U.K.	1990	$10.00
Virgin	96497	Livin' on the Edge of Night	CD5	U.S.	1990	$5.00
Virgin	PRCD 3072	Livin' on the Edge of Night	CDJ	U.S.	1990	$3.00
Virgin	PRCD 3204	Livin' on the Edge of Night	CDJ	U.S.	1990	$3.00
Virgin	LLCD1	Louie Louie	CD5	Holland	1993	$10.00
Virgin	LLCE1	Louie Louie	CD5	Holland	1993	$10.00
Virgin	IGWEI	Louie Louie	CD5	Holland	1993	$40.00
		Mixin' In the Colours	CDJ	Spain		$20.00
A&M	390344-2	Real World	CD5	Germany	1988	$10.00
		To Belong	CDJ	France		$28.00
Virgin	VUSCD-37	Undefeated	CD5	U.K.	1991	$10.00
Virgin	PRCD 12816	Wild America	CDJ	U.S.	1993	$3.00

Pop Poppins

Singles

Label	Catalog Number	Title	Type	Country	Year	Longbox Value / Value
Carpe	31006	Epitome of a Simplicity	CD5	U.S.	1992	$4.00

Pop Will Eat Itself

Full Length

Label	Catalog Number	Title	Type	Country	Year	Longbox Value / Value
		Amalgamation	DJ/Smplr	U.S.	1994	$8.00

Singles

Label	Catalog Number	Title	Type	Country	Year	Longbox Value / Value
RCA	PD-44556	92F Boilerhouse	CD5	U.K.	1991	$9.00
Warner	32-95887	Amalgamation	CD5	Canada	1994	$8.00
RCA	2834-2-RDJ	Another Man's Rhubarb	CDJ	U.S.	1992	$3.00
RCA	74321-110132	Bulletproof	CD5	U.K.	1992	$9.00
RCA	PD-49620	Can U Dig It?	CD5	Germany	1989	$9.00
RCA	PD-49620	Can U Dig It?	CD5	U.K.	1989	$9.00
RCA	9087-2-RDJ	Can U Dig It?	CDJ	U.S.	1989	$2.00
RCA	PD-44024	Dance of the Mad	CD5	U.K.	1990	$9.00
RCA	2732-2-RDJ	Dance of the Mad	CDJ	U.S.	1990	$2.00
RCA	PD-42884	Def Con 001	CD5	U.K.	1989	$9.00
		Familus Horribilus	CD5	U.K.		$10.00
		Familus Horribilus	CD5	U.K.		$10.00
Second version.						
RCA	74321 128812	Get the Girl	CD5	U.K.	1992	$9.00
		Get The Girl! Kill The Baddies!	CD5	U.K.		$10.00
		Get The Girl! Kill The Baddies!	CD5	U.K.		$10.00
Second version.						
RCA	RDJ-62416-2	I've Always Been a Coward	CDJ	U.S.	1992	$2.00
RCA	PD-45468	Karmadrome	CD5	U.K.	1992	$9.00
RCA	62321	Karmadrome	CD5	U.S.	1992	$5.00
		RSVP	CDJ	U.S.	1994	$7.00
RCA	PD-43736	Touched by the Hand of Cicciolina	CD5	U.K.	1990	$9.00
RCA	PD-42894	Very Metal Noise Pollution	CD5	U.K.	1989	$9.00
RCA	PD-42762	Wise Up Sucker	CD5	U.K.	1989	$9.00
RCA	PD-44244	X, Y, & Zee	CD5	Germany	1990	$9.00
RCA	PD-44244	X, Y, & Zee	CD5	U.K.	1990	$9.00
RCA	2763-2-RDJ	X, Y, & Zee	CDJ	U.S.	1990	$2.00

Pop's Cool Love

Singles

Label	Catalog Number	Title	Type	Country	Year	Longbox Value / Value
		Buzz	CDJ	U.S.	1991	$2.00
Elektra	PRCD 8388-2	Buzz	CDJ	U.S.	1991	$2.00
Elektra	PRCD 8486-2	Free Love	CDJ	U.S.	1991	$2.00
Elektra	PRCD 8486-2	Free Me	CDJ	U.S.	1991	$2.00

Pope, Raul and Robbie Rist

Singles

Label	Catalog Number	Title	Type	Country	Year	Longbox Value / Value
		Life After Stacy	CDJ	U.S.		$2.00

Popinjays

Singles

Label	Catalog Number	Title	Type	Country	Year	Longbox Value / Value
Epic	ESK 4672	Monster Mouth	CDJ	U.S.	1992	$2.00
Epic	ESK 4879	Too Jung	CDJ	U.S.	1992	$2.00
Alfa	D2 73021	Vote Elvis	CD5	U.K.	1991	$8.00

Popper, John

Full Length

Label	Catalog Number	Title	Type	Country	Year	Longbox Value / Value
		House of Blues	RS	U.S.	1996	$40.00
2 CD set. Airdate: 4/14/96.						

Poppy Factory

Singles

Label	Catalog Number	Title	Type	Country	Year	Longbox Value / Value
Chrysalis	POPPYCD-4	Fabulous Breakfast	CD5	U.K.	1991	$9.00
Chrysalis	POPPYCD-2	Seven X Seven	CD5	U.K.	1991	$9.00
Chrysalis	POPPYCD-3	Stars	CD5	U.K.	1991	$9.00

Porno for Pyros

Singles

Label	Catalog Number	Title	Type	Country	Year	Longbox Value / Value
Warner Brothers	PRO-CD-6120	Cursed Female	CDJ	U.S.	1993	$7.00
Warner Brothers	PRO-CD-6277	Meija	CDJ	U.S.	1993	$6.00
Warner Brothers		Pete's Dad	CDJ	U.S.	1993	$50.00
CD-R version.						
Warner Brothers	PRO-CD-8019-R	Pete's Dad	CDJ	U.S.	1995	$6.00
Warner Brothers	9 184880-2	Pets	CD5	U.S.	1993	$6.00
Warner Brothers	PRO-CD-6167	Pets	CDJ	U.S.	1993	$6.00
Warner Brothers	41449-2	Sadness	CD5	U.S.	1993	$6.00
Warner Brothers	PRO-CD-6575	Sadness	CDJ	U.S.	1993	$6.00
Warner Brothers	41449	Sadness	CD5	U.S.	1994	$5.00
Warner Borthers		Tahitian Moon	CDJ	U.K.	1996	$10.00

Label	Catalog Number	Title	Type	Country	Year	Longbox Value/Value
Warner Borthers		Tahitian Moon	CDJ	U.S.	1996	$6.00
Porsha						
Singles						
Bellaphon	130-18-022	Say Goodbye	CD5	Germany	1991	$8.00
Portastatic						
Singles						
Merge Records	80	Scrapbook Ep	CD5	U.S.	1994	$5.00
Porter, Art						
Singles						
Verve	686	Straight to the Point	CDJ	U.S.	1993	$2.00
Porter, Cole						
Singles						
Polygram	16986	Cole in Concert: Jus	CD5	U.S.	1994	$5.00
Porter, Dexter						
Singles						
BMG	662931	Fiesta	CD5	Germany	1990	$8.00
Portishead						
Singles						
	PRCD 6958-2	Glory Box	CDJ	U.S.		$2.00
		Numb	CD5	U.K.	1995	$11.00
		Sour Times	CDJ	U.S.		$6.00
Polygram	857817	Sour, Times N. In. M	CD5	U.S.	1994	$5.00
Portnoy, Jerry						
Full Length						
		House of Blues	RS	U.S.	1995	$40.00
2 CD set. Airdate: 11/12/95.						
Portrait						
Singles						
	DPRO10235	All That Matters	CDJ	U.S.		$2.00
Atlas	1168	Be Thankful For What You Got	CDJ	U.S.	1994	$2.00
Capitol	DPRO-79714	Day by Day	CDJ	U.S.	1992	$2.00
Capitol	DPRO-79392	Here We Go Again	CDJ	U.S.	1992	$2.00
	DPRO 79612	How Deep is Your Love	CDJ	U.S.		$2.00
Posies						
Full Length						
		CD Sampler	DJ/Smplr	U.S.	1996	$15.00
Westwood One		In Concert-Nu Rock	RS	U.S.	1993	$70.00
Airdate: 10/11/93.						
Singles						
DGC	PRO-CD-4548	Definite Door	CDJ	U.S.	1993	$2.00
DGC	62815-2	Going Going Gone	CD5	U.S.	1993	$5.00
DGC	PRO-CD-4154	Golden Blunders, The	CDJ	U.S.	1990	$2.00
DGC	PRO-CD-4551	Solar Sister	CDJ	U.S.	1993	$2.00
DGC	9 21631-2	Suddenly Mary	CD5	U.S.	1991	$5.00
DGC	PRO-CD-4205	Suddenly Mary	CDJ	U.S.	1991	$2.00
DGC	PRO-CD-4206	Suddenly Mary	CDJ	U.S.	1991	$2.00
Positive Energy						
Singles						
ZYX	DST-1017-8	Wade in the Water	CD5	Germany	1990	$6.00
Positive Gang						
Singles						
		Sweet Freedom	CD5	U.K.		$10.00
		Sweet Freedom	CD5	U.K.		$10.00
Second version.						
Positive K						
Singles						
Island	PRCD 6761	Ain't No Crime	CDJ	U.S.	1993	$2.00
Island	PRCD 6802	Carhoppers	CDJ	U.S.	1993	$2.00
Island	PRCD 6764	I Got a Man	CDJ	U.S.	1993	$2.00
Positivity						
Singles						
Cooltempo	COOLCD-240	Positivity	CD5	U.K.	1991	$8.00
Possum Dixon						
Full Length						
		Extra Tracks	DJ/Smplr	U.S.		$8.00
Singles						
	PRCD 6673	Emergency's About to End	CDJ	U.S.		$2.00
Interscope	PRCD 5385	Watch the Girl Destroy Me	CDJ	U.S.	1993	$2.00
Interscope	PRCD 5364	Watch the Girl Destroy Me	CDJ	U.S.	1993	$2.00
Poster Children						
Full Length						
	245737A	Junior Citizens Sampler	DJ/Smplr	U.S.		$8.00
Singles						
Creation	CREASCD 152	Clock Street	CD5	U.K.	1993	$8.00
Sire	PRO-CD-5969	Clock Street	CDJ	U.S.	1993	$2.00
Sire	PRO-CD-6034	Clock Street	CDJ	U.S.	1993	$2.00
Potatomen						
Singles						
Lookout Records	101	Now	CD5	U.S.	1994	$5.00
Pourcel, Frank						
Full Length						
EMI	CDP 46017	In A Nostalgic Mood	LP/LB	U.S.†	1984	$14.00/$8.00
Poverty Stinks						
Singles						
Poko	12	It's Not That Easy	CD5	U.S.	1992	$8.00
Powell, Andrew and The Philharmonic Orchestra						
Full Length						
EMI	CDP-46006	Best of the Alan Parsons Project	LP/LB	U.S.†	1984	$14.00/$8.00
Mobile Fidelity	MFCD-806	Best of the Alan Parsons Project	LP/LB	U.S.†	1984	$25.00/$20.00
Powell, Baden						
Full Length						
Verve	821855-2	Estudos	LP/LB	U.S.†	1985	$14.00/$8.00
Verve	817491-2	Tristeza on Guitar	LP/LB	U.S.†	1985	$14.00/$8.00
Powell, Jesse						
Singles						
	LSI53665	All I Need	CDJ	U.S.		$2.00
Power Of Dreams						
Singles						
Polydor	PZCD-80	100 Ways to Kill a Love	CD5	U.K.	1990	$8.00
Polydor	PZCD-117	American Dream	CD5	U.K.	1990	$8.00
Polydor	PZCD-90	Joke's on Me	CD5	U.K.	1990	$8.00
Polydor	PZCD-93	Never Been to Texas	CD5	U.K.	1990	$8.00
Polydor	PZCD-137	Power of Dreams	CD5	U.K.	1990	$8.00
Lemon	LEMON-005CD	Second Son	CD5	U.K.	1992	$8.00
Polydor	PZCD-193	Slowdown	CD5	U.K.	1992	$8.00
Polydor	PZCD-137	Stay	CD5	U.K.	1991	$8.00
Polydor	PZCD-200	There I Go Again	CD5	U.K.	1992	$8.00
Power Trio From Hell, The						
Singles						
Reprise	PRO-CD-6038	Go to Hell	CDJ	U.S.	1993	$6.00
Powermad						
Full Length						
Reprise		Madness Begins, The	DJ/Smplr	U.S.		$7.00
Singles						
Reprise	PRO-CD-4431	Slaughterhouse	CDJ	U.S.	1989	$2.00
Reprise	PRO-CD-3345	Terminator	CDJ	U.S.		$2.00
Powerrule						
Singles						
Interscope	PRCD 4426	Pass the Vide	CDJ	U.S.	1992	$2.00
Interscope	PRCD 4090	That's the Way It Is	CDJ	U.S.	1992	$2.00
Prairie Oyster						
Full Length						
		Complete Prairie Oyster Radio Show	DJ/Intvw	Canada		$16.00
Praise						
Singles						
WEA	YZ-670CD	Dream On	CD5	U.K.	1992	$8.00
WEA	4509-90624-2	Easy Way Out	CD5	Germany	1993	$8.00
WEA	WMD5-4124	Easy Way Out	CD3	Japan	1993	$13.00/$4.00
WEA	YZ-687CD	Easy Way Out	CD5	U.K.	1993	$8.00
Giant	40536-2	Easy Way Out	CD5	U.S.	1992	$5.00
Giant	PRO-CD-5627	Easy Way Out	CDJ	U.S.	1992	$2.00
MPM	655821-2	Love Without Reason	CD5	U.K.	1991	$8.00
Columbia	656611-5	Only You	CD5	Germany	1991	$8.00
Praxis						
Singles						
Axiom	6726	Animal Behavior	CDJ	U.S.	1992	$2.00
Pray TV						
Singles						
Wasteland	9203	Aftermath	CD5	U.S.	1993	$4.00
Prayers						
Singles						
Warner Brothers	9 40040-2	Alleluia	CD5	U.S.	1990	$4.00
Precious						
Full Length						
Big Beat	4201	Soft But Hard	LP/BP	U.S.		$14.00/$8.00
Singles						
MCA	DMCA-1349	In Motion	CD3	U.K.	1989	$8.00
Precious Metal						
Singles						
Chameleon	PRCD 96	Downhill Dreamer	CDJ	U.S.	1990	$6.00
Chameleon	PRCD 95	Mr. Big Stuff	CDJ	U.S.	1990	$2.00
Prefab Sprout						
Full Length						
		Jordan: The Highlights	DJ/Smplr	Japan		N/A
Singles						
Kitchenware	SKCD 62	All the World Lovers	CD5	U.K.	1992	$9.00
Epic	ESK 2187	All the World Lovers	CDJ	U.S.	1990	$2.00
CBS	651378-2	Cars and Girls	CD5	Germany	1988	$9.00
CBS	SDSK-35	Cars and Girls	CD5	U.K.	1988	$9.00
CBS	SDDSK-35	Cars and Girls	CD5	U.K.	1988	$9.00
CBS	SDSK-41	Golden Calf	CD5	U.K.	1989	$9.00
CBS	SDSK-38	Hey Manhattan	CD5	U.K.	1988	$9.00
Epic	ESK 1145	I Remember That	CDJ	U.S.	1988	$2.00
Kitchenware	SKCD 60	If You Don't Love Me	CD5	U.K.	1992	$9.00
CBS	SDSK-49	Jordan	CD5	U.K.	1990	$9.00
CBS	651536-2	King of Rock 'n Roll	CD5	Germany	1988	$9.00
CBS	SDSK-37	King of Rock 'n Roll	CD5	U.K.	1988	$9.00
CBS	656141-3	Looking for Atlantis	CD3	Germany	1990	$9.00
CBS	SDSK-47	Looking for Atlantis	CD5	U.K.	1990	$9.00
CBS	SKQ-47	Looking for Atlantis	CD5	U.K.	1990	$9.00
Epic	ESK 2196	Looking For Atlantis	CDJ	U.S.	1990	$8.00
Epic	ESK 2276	Machine Gun Ibiza	CDJ	U.S.	1990	$2.00
CBS	SDSK-39	Nothingales	CD5	U.K.	1989	$9.00
CBS	SDSK-48	We Let the Stars Go	CD5	U.K.	1990	$9.00
Epic	ESK 2271	We Let the Stars Go	CDJ	U.S.	1990	$2.00
Prescott, Tracey						
Full Length						
		If You Only Knew	DJ/Intvw	Canada		$10.00
Presence						
Singles						
Reality	LOLCD-3	Act of Faith	CD5	U.K.	1992	$8.00
Reality	LOLCD-2	All I See	CD5	U.K.	1992	$8.00
Reality	LOLCD-1	In Wonder	CD5	U.K.	1991	$8.00
Smash	004	Never	CDJ	U.S.	1993	$2.00
King	091X-10004	Tenderness	CD3	Japan	1989	$13.00/$4.00
Presidents of the United States of America						
Full Length						
Columbia		II	LTD/LP	U.S.	1997	$18.00
CD album plus bonus CD sampler. Sold exclusively at Best Buy stores.						
		Presidents of The United States of America	LTD/LP	U.K.	1996	$35.00
2 CD set.						
Columbia	CSK 7224	Presidents of The United States of America	DJ/LP	U.S.	1995	$12.00
Singles						
CBS		Lump	CD5	U.K.	1995	$10.00
Columbia		Lump	CDJ	U.S.	1995	$3.00
CBS		Peaches	CD5	Germany	1995	$10.00
Sony		Peaches	CD5	Japan	1995	$18.00
CBS	SAMPCD3191	Peaches	CDJ	U.K.	1995	$15.00
Columbia	44K 78255	Peaches	CD5	U.S.	1995	$6.00

Label	Catalog Number	Title	Type	Country	Year	Longbox Value / Value
Columbia	CSK 7404	Peaches	CDJ	U.S.	1995	$7.00

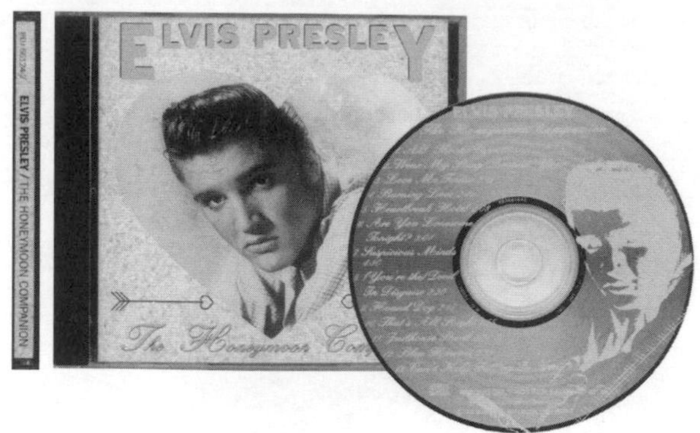

Presley, Elvis – Honeymoon Companion (RCA RDJ 66124-2)

Presley, Elvis – Shake, Rattle & Roll (RCA 6382-2-RDJ)

Presley, Elvis

Full Length

Label	Catalog Number	Title	Type	Country	Year	Longbox Value / Value
RCA	PCD1-5197	50,000,000 Elvis Fans Can't Be Wrong	LP/BP	U.S.†	1984	$14.00/$8.00
RCA	PCD1-2075	50,000,000 Elvis Fans Can't Be Wrong	LP/BP	U.S.†	1984	$300.00/$280.00
		Reprocessed stereo version.				
RCA		A Celebration	LTD/LP	Australia	1994	$35.00
Aris	886569	All Time Greatest Hits	LP	Germany		$15.00
RCA	R32P-1155	Alternate Aloha, The	LP	Japan		$20.00
RCA	6985-2-R	Alternate Aloha, The	LP/BP	U.S.	1988	$22.00/$20.00
		Picture disc version.				
RCA	PD-85430	Always on My Mind	LP	Germany		$20.00
Aris		As Recorded at Madison Square Garden	LP	Germany		$20.00
RCA	886495	As Recorded Live on Stage in Memphis	LP	Germany		$20.00
BBC Transcription		BBC Transcription Disc	RS		1993	$800.00
RCA	CAD1-2595	Burning Love & Hits From His Movies Vol. 2	LP	U.S.		$18.00
RCA	886486-2	By Request Best 20	LP	Germany		$18.00
RCA	CD-90112	CD Siamond Series	LP	U.K.	1985	$23.00
RCA	PCD1-5486	Christmas Album	LP/BP	U.S.†	1985	$15.00/$10.00
Special	CAKD-2428	Christmas Album	LP/BP	U.S.	1985	$15.00/$10.00
RCA	ATCD 2107-2	Christmas Favorites: Elvis Presley & Jim Reeves	LP	U.S.	1991	$25.00
RCA	ATCD 2106-2	Christmas Memories: From Elvis & Alabama	LP	U.S.	1991	$25.00
RCA	PD-89248	Collection Vol. 1	LP	Germany		$20.00
RCA	PD-89249	Collection Vol. 2	LP	Germany		$20.00
RCA		Double Features	LP	U.S.	1993	$100.00
		4 CD picture discs in film can with large booket and pin.				
RCA	PCD1-5199	Elvis	LP/BP	U.S.†	1984	$14.00/$8.00
RCA	PCD1-1382	Elvis	LP/BP	U.S.†	1984	$300.00/$280.00
		Reprocessed stereo version.				
RCA	PCD1-5199	Elvis	LP/BP	U.S.	1986	$14.00/$8.00
RCA	07863 66817-2	Elvis 56 Collector's Edition	LTD/LP	U.S.	1996	$20.00
		Limited edition picture disc CD in bound "book" package.				
Pioneer	PA-85-145	Elvis Aloha	LD	U.S.	1985	$20.00
		Analog audio.				
RCA	DPC10984	Elvis at His Romantic Best	LP	U.S.	1991	$15.00
		Distributed by Avon.				
Pioneer	PA-85-146	Elvis Comeback Special	LD	U.S.	1985	$20.00
		Analog audio.				
RCA		Elvis En Los '90	DJ/Smplr	Argentina	1995	$125.00
RCA	3450-2	Elvis For Everyone	LP/BP	U.S.		$15.00/$10.00
RCA	ND-89004	Elvis For Everyone, Vol. 1	LP	U.S.		$20.00
Freedman/Fairfax		Elvis: His Life and Music	LTD/LP	U.S.	1994	$70.00
		4 CD set and book in 12"x12" box.				
		Elvis in Hollywood	Intvw/Box	U.S.	1994	$45.00
		Interview CD with VHS video and book in custom box.				
RCA	8468-2	Elvis in Nashville	LP/BP	U.S.		$15.00/$10.00
Image	IDVL1054	Elvis Memories	LD	U.S.		$25.00
Vestron	VL1054	Elvis Memories	LD	U.S.	1987	$25.00
RCA	886480	Elvis in Concert	LP	Germany		$25.00
		2 CD set.				
RCA	R25P-1010/2	Elvis in Concert	LP	Japan		$35.00
		2 CD set.				
MGM/UA	ML100153	Elvis on Tour	LD	U.S.	1984	$35.00
RCA	PCD1-5198	Elvis Presley	LP/BP	U.S.†	1984	$14.00/$8.00
RCA	PCD1-1254	Elvis Presley	LP/BP	U.S.†	1984	$300.00/$280.00
		Reprocessed stereo version.				
RCA	PCD1-5198	Elvis Presley	LP/BP	U.S.	1986	$14.00/$8.00
RCA	TCD 106	Elvis Presley: 1954-1961	LP	U.S.		$35.00
RCA	66121-2	Elvis Presley Radio Special	DJ/RS	U.S.	1992	$50.00
RCA/Time	TCD 126	Elvis, The King: 1954-1965	LP	U.S.		$35.00
Walt Disney	1032	Elvis Vol.1: Great Performance	LD	U.S.	1990	$40.00
Walt Disney	1033	Elvis Vol. 2: Great Performance	LD	U.S.	1990	$40.00
RCA	6738-2	Essential 1	LP/BP	U.S.		$15.00/$10.00
RCA		Essential '60s Master	DJ/Smplr	Germany	1993	$120.00
RCA		Essential Collection	LTD/LP	Australia	1994	$25.00
		Jewel box version.				
RCA		Essential Collection	LTD/LP	Australia	1994	$30.00
		CD in digipak with EMS phone card.				
RCA		Essential Collection	LTD/LP	Canada	1995	$28.00
Aris	886347	Fifteen Queens for a King	LP	Germany		$20.00
RCA	SVC2-0710	Fifty Years, Fifty Hits	LP	U.S.	1990	$25.00
		2 CD set				
RCA		From Memphis to Austria	DJ/Smplr	Austria	1995	$150.00
RCA		From Memphis to Venice	DJ/Smplr	Germany	1994	$150.00
RCA	SRCA EP0012	From Nashville to Memphis	DJ/Smplr	France	1993	$100.00
RCA	PCD1-5196	Golden Records Volume 1	LP/BP	U.S.†	1984	$15.00/$10.00
RCA	PCD1-1707	Golden Records Volume 1	LP/BP	U.S.†	1984	$300.00/$280.00
		Reprocessed stereo version.				
RCA	PD-84941	Golden Records Volume 5	LP	Germany	1984	$20.00
RCA	PCD1-4941	Golden Records Volume 5	LP/BP	U.S.†	1984	$15.00/$10.00
RCA	SVC2-0824	Good Rockin' Tonight	LP	U.S.	1988	$30.00
		2 CD set.				
RCA	RDJ 66124-2	Honeymoon Companion, The	DJ/Smplr	U.S.	1992	$50.00
RCA	ND-89474	I Wish You a Merry Christmas	LP	Germany		$18.00
RCA	66506-2	If Every Day Was Like Christmas	LTD/LP	U.S.	1994	$20.00
RCA	R25P-1006	King Creole	LP	Japan		$25.00
RCA	KCDP 51310	King of Rock and Roll II Eatons Sampler	DJ/Smplr	Canada	1995	$100.00
RCA	66050 2	King of Rock 'n Roll: Complete '50s Masters	LTD/LP	U.S.	1992	$70.00
		5 CD boxed set.				
RCA	KCDP-51096	King of Rock 'n Roll Eatons Sampler	DJ/Smplr	Canada	1992	$75.00
BMG	74321102022	King of Rock 'n Roll Sampler	DJ/Smplr	Germany	1992	$50.00
RCA	19531	King-The Legend-The Man And the Legend	DJ/Smplr	Isreal	1992	$70.00
Aris	886386	La Legende, Vol. 1	LP	Germany		$20.00
BMG	74321103432	La Voix Du Rock	LTD/LP	France	1992	$60.00
		2 CD set.				
RCA	PD-8900	Legend, The	LTD/LP	Germany	1983	$250.00
		3 CD set. First Elvis CDs, 60 song best of with certificate of authenticity. Limited to 5000 copies.				
RCA	CAD1-2650	Love Me Tender	LD	U.S.	1987	$15.00
BMG	CAD1-2650	Love Me Tender	LP	U.S.	1987	$20.00
RCA	ND-90302	Memories of Christmas	LP	Germany		$15.00
Motown	B19D-41087	Memories of Christmas	LP	Japan		$25.00
RCA	PCD1-5301	Merry Christmas	LP/BP	U.S.	1984	$400.00/$400.00
RCA	2023-2	Million Dollar Quartet	LP/LB	U.S.		$15.00/$10.00
RCA	BVCP-2060	NBC TV Special	LP	Japan		$25.00
RCA	07863 66921-2	Other Sides: Worldwide Gold Award Hits Volume 2	LTD/LP	U.S.	1996	$0.00/$30.00
RCA	RDJ 62328-2	Out of the Box	DJ/Smplr	U.S.	1992	$30.00
RCA	RDJ 62624-2	Out of the Box: 6 From the '60s	DJ/Smplr	Canada	1993	$25.00
RCA	RDJ 62624-2	Out of the Box: 6 From the '60s	DJ/Smplr	U.S.	1993	$25.00
RCA	RDJ 66765-2	Out of the Box: 6 From the '70s	DJ/Smplr	U.S.	1995	$25.00
RCA	SPA 7-37	Perfect For Parties	DJ/Smplr	Germany	1993	$325.00
RCA	R25P-1008	Pot Luck	LP	Japan		$25.00
		Private Presley: The Missing Years	LTD/LP	U.S.	1993	$25.00
		Biography book with CD of interviews and performance.				
RCA	PD-89003	Rare Elvis Vol. 1	LP	Germany		$18.00
RCA	PD-5418	Reconsider Baby	LP	Germany	1985	$12.00
RCA	R32P-1080	Reconsider Baby	LP	Japan		$25.00
RCA	PCD1-5418	Reconsider Baby	LP/BP	U.S.†	1985	$14.00/$8.00
Aris	886493	Return of the Rocker	LP	Germany		$15.00
RCA	R32P-1073	Return of the Rocker	LP	Japan		$25.00
RCA	PCD-5600-2	Return of the Rocker	LP/LB	U.S.		$15.00/$10.00
RCA	PCD1-5182	Rocker	LP/BP	U.S.†	1985	$14.00/$8.00
RCA		Selections From Amazing Grace	DJ/Smplr	Germany	1994	$100.00
RCA		Selections From Amazing Grace	DJ/Smplr	U.S.	1994	$40.00
RCA	6382-2-RDj	Shake, Rattle & Roll	DJ/Smplr	U.S.	1992	$80.00
BMG	297508	Sixteen Top Tracks	LP	Germany		$18.00
RCA	PCD2-1250	Speedway/Clambake	LP/BP	U.S.		$22.00/$18.00
HMV		Sun Collection	LTD/LP	U.K.	1989	$40.00
		CD with booklet in 12"x12" box. Manufactered for HMV superstores.				
RCA	PD-89388	Thrity-Two Film Hits Vol. 1	LP	Germany		$20.00
RCA	PD-89388	Thrity-Two Film Hits Vol. 1	LP	U.K.		$20.00
RCA	PD-89550	Thrity-Two Film Hits Vol. 2	LP	Germany		$20.00
RCA	PD-89550	Thrity-Two Film Hits Vol. 2	LP	U.K.		$20.00
RCA		Uddrag Fra the Essential Collection	DJ/Smplr	Denmark	1995	$150.00
RCA	PD-89535	Valentine Gift for You	LP	Germany		$15.00
RCA	PCD1-5353	Valentine Gift for You	LP/LB	U.S.		$27.00/$25.00
RCA		Walk a Mile in My Shoes	DJ/Smplr	U.S.	1995	$50.00

Singles

Label	Catalog Number	Title	Type	Country	Year	Longbox Value / Value
RCA	PD-49178	Are You Lonesome Tonight	CD5	Germany	1991	$12.00
RCA	PD-49178	Are You Lonesome Tonight	CD5	U.K.	1991	$12.00
RCA	8994-2-RH	Are You Lonesome Tonight	CD5	U.S.	1989	$30.00
		Juke box version.				
RCA	8993-2-RH	Blue Suede Shoes	CD5	U.S.	1989	$30.00
		Juke box version.				
RCA	8991-2-RH	Can't Help Falling in Love	CD5	U.S.	1989	$30.00
		Juke box version.				
RCA		Don't Be Cruel	CDJ	Japan	1994	$150.00
		Feature track "Don't Be Cruel" by both Elvis and Ringo Star.				
RCA	62404	Don't Be Cruel	CD5	U.S.	1992	$6.00
RCA	62404-2	Don't Be Cruel	CD5	U.S.	1992	$20.00
		Juke box version.				
RCA	PD-49467	Heartbreak Hotel	CD5	Germany	1989	$12.00
RCA	PD-49467	Heartbreak Hotel	CD5	U.K.	1989	$12.00
RCA	8989-2-RH	Hound Dog	CD5	U.S.	1989	$30.00
		Juke box version.				
RCA	8992-2-RH	Jailhouse Rock	CD5	U.S.	1989	$30.00
		Juke box version.				
RCA	ELVIS58	Love Letters	CDJ	U.K.	1993	$75.00
RCA	PD-49474	Mean Woman Blues	CD5	U.K.	1989	$12.00
RCA	2654-2-RDj	My Happiness	CDJ	U.S.	1990	$50.00
RCA	R10D-1034	Mystery Train	CD3	Japan	1989	$15.00/$4.00
RCA	PD-49596	Stuck on You	CD5	U.K.	1990	$12.00
RCA		Twelfth of Never, The	CD5	U.K.	1995	$14.00

Pressure Drop

Singles

Label	Catalog Number	Title	Type	Country	Year	Longbox Value / Value
BCM	20428	Feeling Good	CD5	Germany	1990	$8.00
Arista	74321-12622-2	You're Mine	CD5	U.K.	1992	$8.00

Preston, Billy

Full Length

Label	Catalog Number	Title	Type	Country	Year	Longbox Value / Value
Capitol		That's the Way God Planned It	LP/LB	U.S.		$15.00/$9.00

Label	Catalog Number	Title	Type	Country	Year	Longbox/ Value

Pretenders

Full Length

Label	Catalog Number	Title	Type	Country	Year	Value
BBC Radio		BBC Classic Tracks	RS	U.S.	1991	$20.00
	Airdate: 4/1/91.					
Westwood One		BBC Classic Tracks	RS	U.S.	1992	$40.00
	Airdate: 3/16/92.					
Westwood One		BBC Classic Tracks	RS	U.S.	1993	$40.00
	Airdate: 8/2/93.					
Westwood One		BBC Classic Tracks	RS	U.S.	1994	$40.00
	Airdate: 1/31/94.					
		Don't Get Me Wrong	DJ/Smplr	Germany	1994	$25.00
Westwood One		In Concert	RS	U.S.	1994	$50.00
	2 CD set. Airdate: 4/25/94.					
Westwood One		In Concert	RS	U.S.	1995	$75.00
	2 CD set with the Green Day. Airdate: 11/7/94.					
Westwood One		In Concert	RS	U.S.	1996	$50.00
	Airdate: 1/29/96.					
Westwood One		In Concert - Nu Rock	RS	U.S.	1994	$50.00
	2 CD set. Airdate: 6/20/94.					
Westwood One		In Concert - Nu Rock	RS	U.S.	1994	$85.00
	Airdate: 10/24/94.					
DIR		King Biscuit Flour Hour	RS	U.S.	1990	$30.00
	Airdate: 6/18/90.					
Sire	9 45572	Last of the Ingredients	DJ/LP	U.S.	1994	$10.00
Sire	9 23980-3	Learning to Crawl	LP/LB	U.S.†	1984	$14.00/$8.00
Westwood One		Off the Record	RS	U.S.	1994	$25.00
	Airdate: 12/5/94.					
Westwood One		Off the Record	RS	U.S.	1994	$25.00
	Airdate: 7/25/94.					
Westwood One		Off the Record	RS	U.S.	1995	$25.00
	Airdate: 12/4/95.					
Westwood One		Off the Record	RS	U.S.	1995	$25.00
	Airdate: 6/21/95.					
Westwood One		Off the Record	RS	U.S.	1996	$25.00
	Airdate: 3/11/96.					
Sire	9 26219-2	Packed	DJ/LP	U.S.	1990	$15.00
	CD in carton with title sticker.					
Sire	6083-2	Pretenders	LP/LB	U.S.†	1984	$14.00/$8.00
Westwood One		Superstars	RS	U.S.	1994	$85.00
	2 CD set. Airdate: 9/19/94.					
Media America		Up Close	RS	U.S.	1994	$50.00
	2 CD set.					
Media America		Up Close	RS	U.S.	1995	$65.00
	2 CD set.					

Singles

Label	Catalog Number	Title	Type	Country	Year	Value
Reprise	PRO-CD-7892	2000 Miles	CDJ	U.S.		$3.00
		997	CD5	U.K.	1994	$10.00
		997	CD5	U.K.	1994	$10.00
	Second version.					
Reprise	PRO-CD-8118-R	Angel of the Morning	CDJ	U.S.		$3.00
Sire		Bold as Love	CDJ	U.S.		$2.00
Sire		Everyday Is Like Sunday	CDJ	U.S.	1995	$3.00
Sire	PRO-CD-4072	Hold a Candle to This	CDJ	U.S.	1990	$2.00
Warner	12-18160	I'll Stand by You	CD5	Canada	1994	$6.00
		I'll Stand by You	CDJ	Spain		$28.00
WEA		I'll Stand by You	CD5	U.K.	1994	$10.00
WEA	YZ815CD	I'll Stand by You	CD5	U.K.	1994	$10.00
	Second version.					
Sire	PRO-CD-6903	I'll Stand by You	CDJ	U.S.	1994	$3.00
MCA	MCA5P-2625	I'm Not in Love	CDJ	U.S.	1993	$3.00
WEA	YZ-156CD	Kid	CD5	U.K.	1990	$10.00
Reprise	PRO-CD-7021	Money Talks	CDJ	U.S.		$3.00
WEA	9031-71697-2	Never Do That	CD5	Germany	1990	$10.00
Pioneer	WMD5-4026	Never Do That	CD3	Japan	1990	$15.00/$4.00
WEA	YZ-469CD	Never Do That	CD5	U.K.	1990	$10.00
Sire	PRO-CD-4061	Never Do That	CDJ	U.S.	1990	$2.00
Warner	12-18163	Right in My Veins	CD5	Canada	1994	$6.00
		Right in My Veins	CD5	U.K.	1994	$10.00
		Right in My Veins	CD5	U.K.	1994	$10.00
	Second version.					
Sire	PRO-CD-6880	Right in My Veins	CDJ	U.S.	1994	$7.00
WEA	9031-72494-2	Sense of Purpose	CD5	Germany	1990	$10.00
WEA	YZ-507CD	Sense of Purpose	CD5	U.K.	1990	$10.00
WEA	YZ-507CDX	Sense of Purpose	CD5	U.K.	1990	$12.00
Reprise	PRO-CD-7964	Sense of Purpose	CDJ	U.S.		$3.00
Sire	PRO-CD-4089	Sense of Purpose	CDJ	U.S.	1990	$2.00
Polydor	P10P-40003	Windows of the World	CD3	Japan	1988	$15.00/$4.00
Polydor	PRECD-69	Windows of the World	CD3	U.K.	1989	$10.00

Pretty Boy Floyd

Singles

Label	Catalog Number	Title	Type	Country	Year	Value
MCA		I Wanna Be With You	CDJ	U.S.	1989	$2.00
MCA		Leather Boyz With Electric Toys	CDJ	U.S.	1989	$2.00
MCA	DMCAT-1393	Rock and Roll	CD5	U.K.	1990	$8.00
MCA	DMCAP-1393	Rock and Roll	CD5	U.K.	1990	$8.00
MCA	CD45-78017	Rock and Roll	CDJ	U.S.	1989	$3.00

Pretty In Pink

Full Length

Label	Catalog Number	Title	Type	Country	Year	Value
Motown	6317	Wake Up	LP/BP	U.S.	1991	$12.00/$7.00

Singles

Label	Catalog Number	Title	Type	Country	Year	Value
Motown	1005	Dreams	CDJ	U.S.	1991	$2.00

Pretty Maids

Singles

Label	Catalog Number	Title	Type	Country	Year	Value
Epic	ESDA-7122	In the Minds of the Young	CD3	Japan	1992	$13.00/$4.00
Epic	ESCA-5644	Offside	CD5	Japan	1992	$12.00
Epic	ESDA-7097	Please Don't Leave Me	CD3	Japan	1992	$13.00/$4.00
Epic	655884-3	Savage Heart	CD3	Germany	1990	$8.00

Pretty Poison

Singles

Label	Catalog Number	Title	Type	Country	Year	Value
Warlok	400	Better Be Good to Me	CD5	U.S.	1992	$5.00
Virgin	VJD-10002	Nightime	CD3	Japan	1988	$13.00/$4.00
Virgin	PRCD 8350	Nightime	CDJ	U.S.	1988	$2.00
Virgin	PR 2346	When I Look in Your Eyes	CDJ	U.S.	1988	$2.00

Pretty Tone Capone

Singles

Label	Catalog Number	Title	Type	Country	Year	Value
III	119	Across 10th St.	CD5	U.S.		$2.00

Pretty & Twisted

Singles

Label	Catalog Number	Title	Type	Country	Year	Value
	PRO-CD-7701	Ride	CDJ	U.S.		$2.00

Price, Alan

Singles

Label	Catalog Number	Title	Type	Country	Year	Value
Ariola	659911	Changes	CD5	U.K.	1988	$10.00
Old Gold	OG-6127	Simon Smith and the Amazing Dancing Bear	CD3	U.K.	1989	$10.00

Price, Rick

Singles

Label	Catalog Number	Title	Type	Country	Year	Value
Columbia	657798	Not a Day Goes by	CD5	Australia	1992	$12.00

Prick

Singles

Label	Catalog Number	Title	Type	Country	Year	Value
	PRCD 6240	Animal	CDJ	U.S.		$2.00

Pride, Charley

Full Length

Label	Catalog Number	Title	Type	Country	Year	Value
RCA	PRCD1-4151	Greatest Hits	LP/BP	U.S.†	1984	$14.00/$8.00
RCA	PRCD1-4822	Night Games	LP/BP	U.S.†	1984	$14.00/$8.00

Pride & Glory

Singles

Label	Catalog Number	Title	Type	Country	Year	Value
Geffen		Horse Called War	CDJ	U.S.		$7.00
Geffen	PRO-CD-4641	Losin' Your Mind	CDJ	U.S.	1994	$2.00

Priest, Maxi

Singles

Label	Catalog Number	Title	Type	Country	Year	Value
BMG	663249	Close to You	CD5	Germany	1990	$10.00
Virgin	VJDP-12002	Close to You	CD3	Japan	1990	$15.00/$4.00
Virgin	TENCD-294	Close to You	CD5	U.K.	1990	$10.00
Charisma	PRCD 006	Close to You	CDJ	U.S.	1990	$3.00
Virgin	TENCD-238	Goodbye to Love Again	CD5	U.K.	1989	$10.00
Virgin	PRCD 2623	Goodbye to Love Again	CDJ	U.S.	1989	$3.00
Virgin	VJDP-12004	Groovin' in the Night	CD3	Japan	1990	$15.00/$4.00
Virgin	TENCD-412	Groovin' in the Night	CD5	U.K.	1992	$10.00
Charisma	C2 12619	Groovin' in the Night	CD5	U.S.	1992	$5.00
Charisma	PRCD 12721	Groovin' in the Night	CDJ	U.S.	1992	$3.00
Charisma	PRCD 12740	Groovin' in the Night	CDJ	U.S.	1992	$3.00
Virgin	TENCD-207	How Can We Ease the Pain	CD5	U.K.	1988	$10.00
Virgin	VJDP-14019	Human Work of Art	CD3	Japan	1990	$15.00/$4.00
Virgin	TENCD-328	Human Work of Art	CD5	U.K.	1990	$10.00
BMG	663782	Human Work of Art	CD5	U.K.	1990	$10.00
Virgin	TENCD-343	Just a Little Bit Longer	CD5	U.K.	1991	$10.00
Charisma	PRCD 021	Just a Little Bit Longer	CDJ	U.S.	1990	$3.00
Virgin	VJCP-12006	Just Wanna Know	CD5	Japan	1993	$15.00
Virgin	TENCD-416	Just Wanna Know	CD5	U.K.	1992	$10.00
Virgin	VJCP-12010	One More Chance	CD5	Japan	1992	$15.00
Charisma	PRCD 12757	One More Chance	CDJ	U.S.	1992	$3.00
Virgin	VJCP-1414	Peace Throughout the World	CD5	Japan	1990	$15.00
Virgin	TENCD-317	Peace Throughout the World	CD5	U.K.	1990	$10.00
Virgin	VJCP-14032	Searching	CD5	Japan	1990	$15.00
Virgin	GUYSCD-198	Some Guys Have All the Luck	CD5	U.K.	1988	$10.00
Charisma	PRCD 074	Some Guys Have All the Luck	CDJ	U.S.	1988	$3.00
Virgin	659953	Wild World	CD5	Germany	1988	$10.00
Virgin	TENCD-221	Wild World	CD5	U.K.	1988	$10.00
		Wild World	CDJ	U.S.	1988	$3.00

Prima, Louis

Full Length

Label	Catalog Number	Title	Type	Country	Year	Value
Bear Family		Complete Sun Singles, Vol. 1	LTD/LP	Germany	1994	$120.00
	8 CD set.					

Primal Scream

Full Length

Label	Catalog Number	Title	Type	Country	Year	Value
	ESCA-5944	Give Out but Don't Give Up	DJ/Smplr	Japan	1994	$225.00
	2CD set with press kit and booklet.					
Westwood One		In Concert-Nu Rock	RS	U.S.	1994	$65.00
	Airdate: 7/4/94.					
Sire	9 26714-2	Screamadelica	DJ/LP	U.S.	1991	$12.00
	Picture disc.					
	QDCA-93041	Souls	DJ/Smplr	Japan	1994	$100.00

Singles

Label	Catalog Number	Title	Type	Country	Year	Value
Creation	COCY-6986	Come Together	CD5	Japan	1990	$14.00
Creation	COCY-7986	Come Together	CD5	Japan	1991	$14.00
Creation	CRESCD-078	Come Together	CD5	U.K.	1990	$9.00
		Cry Myself Blind	CD5	U.K.	1994	$10.00
		Cry Myself Blind	CD5	U.K.	1994	$10.00
	Second version.					
Creation	COCY-5181	Damaged	CD5	Japan	1991	$14.00
Sire	PRO-CD-5278	Damaged	CDJ	U.S.	1991	$2.00
Intercord	828 912	Don't Fight It, Feel It	CD5	Germany	1992	$9.00
Creation	110	Don't Fight It, Feel It	CD5	U.K.	1991	$9.00
Intercord	828 910	Higher Than the Sun	CD5	Germany	1991	$9.00
Creation	CRESCD-096	Higher Than the Sun	CD5	U.K.	1991	$9.00
Creation	CRESCD-067	Ivy Ivy Ivy	CD5	U.K.	1989	$9.00
		Jailbird	CD5	U.K.	1994	$10.00
Creation	CRESCD-070	Loaded	CD5	U.K.	1990	$9.00
Intercord	828 915	Movin' on Up	CD5	Germany	1991	$9.00
Intercord	828 916	Movin' on Up	CD5	Germany	1991	$9.00
Creation	COCY-5156	Movin' on Up	CD5	Japan	1991	$14.00
Creation	CRESCD-117	Movin' on Up	CD5	U.K.	1991	$9.00
Sire	9 40193-2	Movin' on Up	CD5	U.S.	1991	$5.00
Sire	PRO-CD-5063	Movin' on Up	CDJ	U.S.	1991	$2.00
Sire	6846-2	Rocks	CD5	U.S.	1994	$5.00
Warner Brothers	18189	Rocks	CD5	U.S.	1994	$5.00
Sire	PRO-CD-6262	Slip Inside This House	CDJ	U.S.	1991	$2.00

Prime Minister Pete Nice & Daddy Rich

Singles

Label	Catalog Number	Title	Type	Country	Year	Value
Def Jam	CSK 4966	Kick the Bobo	CDJ	U.S.	1993	$2.00

Primitive Radio Gods

Singles

Label	Catalog Number	Title	Type	Country	Year	Value
		Standing Outside a Broken Phone Booth	CDJ	U.S.	1996	$6.00
	From the "Cable Guy" movie Soundtrack.					

Primitives

Singles

Label	Catalog Number	Title	Type	Country	Year	Value
RCA	9187-2-RDj	All the Way	CDJ	U.S.	1990	$2.00
RCA	R10D-10	Crash	CD3	Japan	1988	$13.00/$4.00
RCA	PD-44978	Earth Thing	CD5	U.K.	1991	$9.00
RCA	PD-45346	Lead Me Astray	CD5	U.K.	1992	$9.00
Aris	886412	Out of Reach	CD5	Germany	1988	$9.00
RCA	PD-42012	Out of Reach	CD5	U.K.	1988	$9.00
RCA	PD-43173	Secrets	CD5	Germany	1989	$9.00
RCA	PD-43173	Secrets	CD5	U.K.	1989	$9.00
RCA	9135-2-RDj	Secrets	CDJ	U.S.	1989	$2.00
RCA	PD-429438	Sick of It	CD5	Germany	1989	$9.00
RCA	R10D-129	Sick of It	CD3	Japan	1989	$13.00/$4.00

Label	Catalog Number	Title	Type	Country	Year	Longbox Value / Value
RCA	PD-42948	Sick of It	CD5	U.K.	1989	$9.00
RCA	9088-2-RDj	Sick of It	CDJ	U.S.	1989	$2.00
RCA	PD-44978	Spells	CD5	U.K.	1991	$9.00
RCA	PD-44482	You Are the Way	CD5	U.K.	1991	$9.00

Primus

Full Length

Label	Catalog Number	Title	Type	Country	Year	Longbox Value / Value
Interscope	792257-2	Pork Soda	LP	U.S.	1993	$14.00
	CD club version in jewelbox.					
Interscope	PRCD 6242-2	Sampler	DJ/Smplr	U.S.	1994	$8.00

Singles

Label	Catalog Number	Title	Type	Country	Year	Longbox Value / Value
Interscope	PRCD 4376-2	Jerry Was a Race Car Driver	CDJ	U.S.	1994	$6.00
Atlantic	9 6208-2	Miscellaneous Debris	CD5	U.S.	1992	$5.00
Interscope	PRCD 5170	Mr. Krinkle	CDJ	U.S.	1994	$3.00
Intercope	PRCD 6483-2	Mrs. Blainleen	CDJ	U.S.	1995	$3.00
Intercope	PRCD 3881-2	Seas of Cheese	CDJ	U.S.	1991	$2.00
Intercope	PRCD 4340-2	Seas of Cheese	CDJ	U.S.	1991	$8.00
Intercope		Southbound Pachyderm	CDJ	U.S.	1995	$8.00
Interscope	PRCD 6242	Wynona's Big Brown Beaver	CDJ	U.S.	1994	$3.00

Prince

Full Length

Label	Catalog Number	Title	Type	Country	Year	Longbox Value / Value
Warner/BMG	9 23720-2	1999	LP	U.S.†	1982	$14.00
	BMG CD Club version with10 Tracks.					
Warner Brothers	9 23720-2	1999	LP/LB	U.S.†	1982	$17.00/$14.00
	10 Track version. Missing track "D.M.S.R."					
Warner Brothers		Around the World in a Day	LTD/LP	Germany	1994	$30.00
	Gold CD.					
Warner Brothers	9 25286-2	Around the World in a Day	LP/LB	U.S.†	1985	$23.00/$20.00
	Experimental carboard sleeve and outer longbox.					
Warner Brothers	33PZ-2870	Batcan (Soundtrack)	LTD/LP	Japan	1989	$25.00
	CD in can.					
Warner Brothers	9 25978-2	Batcan (Soundtrack)	LTD/LP	U.K.	1989	$15.00
	CD in can.					
Warner Brothers	9 25978-2	Batcan (Soundtrack)	LTD/LP	U.S.	1989	$15.00
	CD in can.					
Warner Brothers		Batman	LTD/LP	U.K.	1989	$25.00
	Picture disc CD.					
Warner Brothers		"Black Album"	LP	Australia	1994	$25.00
Warner Brothers	9362-45793-2	"Black Album"	LTD/LP	Germany	1994	$19.00
Warner Brothers	25677-2	"Black Album"	LP/LB	U.S.	1987	$3,000.00/$2,000.00
Warner Brothers	3601-2	Controversy	LP/LB	U.S.†	1984	$14.00/$8.00
Warner Brothers	SAM 1037	Crown Jewels	DJ/Smplr	U.K.	1992	$65.00
Paisley Park	9 25379-2-Dj	Diamonds and Pearls	DJ/LP	U.S.	1991	$25.00
	Picture disc.					
Warner Brothers	3478-2	Dirty Mind	LP/LB	U.S.†	1985	$14.00/$8.00
Warner Brothers	PCS-186	Endorphinmachine	DJ/Smplr	Japan	1995	$100.00
Warner Brothers	PCS-14	Forever Young	DJ/Smplr	Japan	1995	$100.00
Pioneer	PCS-55	Graffiti Bridge	DJ/LP	Japan	1990	$150.00
Paisley Park	9 27493-2-Dj	Graffiti Bridge	DJ/LP	U.S.	1990	$25.00
	Picture disc.					
Paisley Park	PRCD2	Hits, The	DJ/Smplr	U.K.	1993	$50.00
Pioneer	PA-86-183	Live	LD	U.S.	1986	$40.00
Pioneer	PA-86-183	Live	LD	U.S.	1989	$40.00
	Digital audio.					
Paisley Park	9 27493-2-Dj	Love Sexy	DJ/LP	U.S.	1988	$15.00
Warner Brothers	PCS-124	My Name Was Prince	DJ/Smplr	Japan	1995	$200.00
WEA	38291	Prince & The New Power Generation	LD	U.S.	1992	$30.00
Warner	43P2-0004	Purple Rain	LTD/LP	Japan	1988	$50.00
	Gold disc.					
Warner Brothers		Purple Rain	DJ/LP	U.S.†		$200.00
	Experimental carboard sleeve and outer longbox.					
Warner Brothers	25110-2	Purple Rain	LP/LB	U.S.†	1985	$14.00/$8.00
Paisley Park	9 45121-2-Dj	"Symbol"	DJ/LP	U.S.	1992	$35.00
	Picture disc in gold bound digipak.					
Paisley Park	9 45121-2	"Symbol"	LTD/LP	U.S.	1992	$25.00
	Goldbound digipak.					

Singles

Label	Catalog Number	Title	Type	Country	Year	Longbox Value / Value
Warner Brothers	21881-2	1999	CD5	U.S.	1993	$4.00
Warner Brothers	CD-40574	7	CD5	Canada	1992	$10.00
Paisley Park	WPDP-6317	7	CD3	Japan	1992	$18.00/$5.00
Paisley Park	W-0147CD	7	CD5	U.K.	1992	$10.00
Warner Brothers	9 18824-2	7	CD5	U.S.	1992	$5.00
Warner Brothers	9 40574-2	7	CD5	U.S.	1992	$5.00
Paisley Park		7	CD5	U.S.	1992	$6.00
Paisley Park	PRO-CD-5581	7	CDJ	U.S.	1992	$8.00
Paisley Park	PRO-CD-5981	7	CDJ	U.S.	1992	$8.00
Paisley Park	920930-2	Alphabet St.	CD3	Germany	1988	$11.00
Paisley Park	10SW-35	Alphabet St.	CD3	Japan	1988	$15.00/$4.00
Paisley Park	W-7900CD	Alphabet St.	CD3	U.K.	1988	$11.00
Paisley Park	PRO-CD-3079	Alphabet St.	CDJ	U.S.	1988	$8.00
Warner Brothers	7599-21394-2	Arms of Orion	CD3	Germany	1989	$11.00
Warner Brothers	7599-21403-2	Arms of Orion	CD3	Germany	1989	$12.00
Warner Brothers	09P3-6208	Arms of Orion	CD3	Japan	1989	$18.00/$5.00
Warner Brothers	W-2757CD	Arms of Orion	CD3	U.K.	1989	$11.00
Warner Brothers	W-2757CDX	Arms of Orion	CD5	U.K.	1989	$12.00
Warner Brothers	PRO-CD-3787	Arms of Orion	CDJ	U.S.	1989	$7.00
Warner Brothers	9 21 272-2	Batdance	CD3	Germany	1989	$12.00
Warner Brothers	7599-21257-2	Batdance	CD5	Germany	1989	$12.00
Pioneer	09P3-6172	Batdance	CD3	Japan	1989	$18.00/$5.00
Warner Brothers	W-2924CD	Batdance	CD3	U.K.	1989	$12.00
Warner Brothers	W-2924CDX	Batdance	CD5	U.K.	1989	$13.00
Warner Brothers	9 21257-2	Batdance	CD5	U.S.	1989	$5.00
Warner Brothers	PRO-CD-3574	Batdance	CDJ	U.S.	1989	$7.00
		Beautiful Experience	CD5	Australia	1994	$12.00
		Controversy	CD5	U.K.		$10.00
		Controversy	CD5	U.K.		$10.00
	Second version.					
Paisley Park	9362-40213-2	Cream	CD5	Germany	1992	$12.00
Paisley Park	WPDP-6286	Cream	CD3	Japan	1991	$18.00/$5.00
WEA	W-0061CD	Cream	CD5	U.K.	1991	$12.00
Paisley Park	PRO-CD-4985	Cream	CDJ	U.S.	1991	$6.00
Paisley Park	9 40197-2	Cream	CD5	U.S.	1992	$5.00
Warner Brothers	9 18700-2	Damn U	CD5	U.S.	1992	$5.00
Paisley Park	PRO-CD-5890	Damn U	CDJ	U.S.	1992	$8.00
Paisley Park	9362-40323-2	Diamonds and Pearls	CD5	Germany	1991	$12.00
Paisley Park	WPDP-6290	Diamonds and Pearls	CD3	Japan	1991	$18.00/$5.00
Paisley Park	W-0075CDX	Diamonds and Pearls	CD5	U.K.	1991	$12.00
Paisley Park	PRO-CD-5148	Diamonds and Pearls	CDJ	U.S.	1991	$8.00
Warner Brothers		Dinner With Delores	CD5	U.K.	1996	$10.00
Warner Brothers	WPCR-440	Endorphinmachine	CDJ	Japan		$60.00
WEA	7599-21185-2	Erotic City	CD5	Germany	1990	$12.00
Warner Brothers	7599 21570-2	Future, The	CD5	Germany	1989	$12.00
Warner Brothers	PRO-CD-3597	Future, The	CDJ	U.S.	1989	$12.00
WEA	W-0056CD	Get Off	CD5	U.K.	1991	$12.00
Paisley Park	9 40138-2	Get Off	CD5	U.S.	1991	$5.00
Paisley Park	PRO-CD-4977	Get Off	CDJ	U.S.	1991	$7.00
Warner	12-40138	Gett Off	CD5	Canada	1994	$8.00
WEA	921019-2	Glam Slam	CD3	Germany	1988	$12.00
Pioneer	10P3-6007	Glam Slam	CD3	Japan	1988	$18.00/$5.00
WEA	W-7806CD	Glam Slam	CD3	U.K.	1988	$12.00
Paisley Park	PRO-CD-3181	Glam Slam	CDJ	U.S.	1988	$8.00
		Gold	CD5	U.K.	1995	$10.00
		Gold	CD5	U.K.	1995	$10.00
	Second version.					
Warner Brothers	PRO-CD-7941-R	Gold	CDJ	U.S.	1995	$7.00
Warner Brothers	17611	Hate U	CD5	U.S.	1995	$5.00
Warner Brothers		Hate U	CDJ	U.S.	1995	$6.00
Warner Brothers		Hate U	CDJ	U.S.	1995	$6.00
	Second version.					
Warner Brothers	PRO-CD-7793-R	Hate You	CDJ	U.S.	1995	$7.00
Paisley Park	921074-2	I Wish U Heaven	CD3	Germany	1988	$12.00
Paisley Park	10P3-6052	I Wish U Heaven	CD3	Japan	1988	$18.00/$5.00
Paisley Park	W-7745CD	I Wish U Heaven	CD3	U.K.	1988	$12.00
Paisley Park	PRO-CD-3242	I Wish U Heaven	CDJ	U.S.	1988	$8.00
Paisley Park	PRO-CD-2747	If I Was Your Girlfriend	CDJ	U.S.	1987	$8.00
Paisley Park	PRO-CD-5141	Insatiable	CDJ	U.S.	1991	$10.00
Warner Brothers	7599 2188-2	Kiss	CD5	Germany	1989	$10.00
Warner Brothers	7599 2188-2	Kiss	CD5	U.K.	1989	$10.00
Warner Brothers	PRO-CD-7000	Let It Go	CD5	Japan	1995	$20.00
Warner Brothers	7599 21187-2	Let's Go Crazy	CD5	Germany	1989	$10.00
Warner Brothers	7599 21187-2	Let's Go Crazy	CD5	U.K.	1989	$10.00
		Letitgo	CD5	Australia	1994	$10.00
Warner	12-18074	Letitgo	CD5	Canada	1994	$6.00
Warner	CD41745	Letitgo	CD5	Canada	1994	$8.00
NPG	PRO-CD-7000	Letitgo	CDJ	Japan	1994	$20.00
NPG		Letitgo	CD5	U.K.	1994	$10.00
Warner Brothers	41745	Letitgo	CD5	U.S.	1994	$5.00
NPG	9 41745-2	Letitgo	CD5	U.S.	1994	$6.00
NPG		Letitgo	CDJ	U.S.	1994	$7.00
NPG	PRO-CD-7000	Letitgo	CDJ	U.S.	1994	$7.00
	2 tracks.					
Warner Brothers	PRO-CD-7000	Letitgo	CDJ	U.S.	1994	$10.00
Warner Brothers	7599 21184-2	Little Red Corvette	CD5	Germany	1989	$10.00
Warner Brothers	7599 21184-2	Little Red Corvette	CD5	U.K.	1989	$10.00
Warner Brothers		Love Sign	CD5	U.K.	1994	$20.00
Warner Brothers		Love Sign	CDJ	U.S.	1994	$10.00
Paisley Park	9362-40419-2	Money Don't Matter	CD5	U.K.	1992	$10.00
Paisley Park	PRO-CD-5298	Money Don't Matter	CDJ	U.S.	1992	$7.00
Paisley Park	W-0162CD	Morning Papers, The	CD5	Germany	1992	$5.00
Paisley Park	1 8583-2	Morning Papers, The	CD5	U.S.	1992	$5.00
Paisley Park	PRO-CD-5985	Morning Papers, The	CDJ	U.S.	1992	$7.00
NPG		Most Beautiful Girl In the World	CD5	Australia	1994	$10.00
NPG		Most Beautiful Girl in the World	CD5	Germany	1994	$10.00
Bellmark	72514	Most Beautiful Girl in the World	CD5	U.S.	1994	$6.00
Bellmark	72516	Most Beautiful Girl in the World	CD5	U.S.	1994	$12.00
Bellmark		Most Beautiful Girl in the World	CDJ	U.S.	1994	$50.00
	Picture disc CD in 6"x12" folder.					
Paisley Park	CD-40700	My Name Is Prince	CD5	Canada	1992	$10.00
Paisley Park	9362-40704-2	My Name Is Prince	CD5	Germany	1992	$10.00
Paisley Park	9362-40709-2	My Name Is Prince	CD5	Germany	1992	$10.00
Paisley Park	WPDP-6309	My Name Is Prince	CD3	Japan	1992	$18.00/$5.00
Paisley Park	W-0132CD	My Name Is Prince	CD5	U.K.	1992	$10.00
Paisley Park	W-0142CD	My Name Is Prince	CD5	U.K.	1992	$10.00
Paisley Park	9 18707-2	My Name Is Prince	CD5	U.S.	1992	$5.00
Paisley Park	9 40700-2	My Name Is Prince	CD5	U.S.	1992	$5.00
Paisley Park	PRO-CD-5770	My Name Is Prince	CDJ	U.S.	1992	$7.00
Paisley Park	7599 21801-2	New Power Generation	CD5	Germany	1990	$10.00
Pioneer	WPDP-6259	New Power Generation	CD3	Japan	1990	$18.00/$5.00
WEA	W-9525CD	New Power Generation	CD5	U.K.	1990	$10.00
Paisley Park	PRO-CD-4515	New Power Generation	CDJ	U.S.	1990	$7.00
Paisley Park	PRO-CD-4578	New Power Generation	CDJ	U.S.	1990	$7.00
		Nothing Compares 2 U	CDJ	Spain	1993	$26.00
Paisley Park	9 18372-2	Nothing Compares 2 U	CD5	U.S.	1993	$5.00
Paisley Park	PRO-CD-5994	Nothing Compares 2 U	CDJ	U.S.	1993	$8.00
Warner Brothers	921330-2	Partyman	CD5	Germany	1989	$10.00
Warner Brothers	921370-2	Partyman	CD5	Germany	1989	$10.00
Warner Brothers	921341-2	Partyman	CD5	Germany	1989	$12.00
Pioneer	09P3-6179	Partyman	CD3	Japan	1989	$18.00/$5.00
Warner Brothers	W2814 CD	Partyman	CD5	U.K.	1989	$10.00
Warner Brothers	W2814 CDT	Partyman	CD5	U.K.	1989	$10.00
Warner Brothers	W2814 CDX	Partyman	CD5	U.K.	1989	$12.00
Warner Brothers	PRO-CD-3705	Partyman	CDJ	U.S.	1989	$7.00
		Peach	CD5	Germany	1993	$10.00
		Peach	CD5	Germany	1993	$10.00
	Second version.					
		Peach	CD5	U.K.		$10.00
		Peach	CD5	U.K.		$10.00
	Second version.					
Paisley Park	W-0210CD	Peach	CD5	U.K.	1993	$10.00
Warner Brothers	PRO-CD-5992	Peach	CDJ	U.S.	1993	$7.00
Paisley Park	PRO-CD-5993	Pink Cashmere	CDJ	U.S.		$7.00
Warner Brothers	18371-2	Pink Cashmere	CD5	U.S.	1993	$6.00
Warner Brothers	17903	Purple Medley	CD5	U.S.	1994	$5.00
Warner Brothers	43503	Purple Medley	CD5	U.S.	1994	$5.00
Warner Brothers		Purple Medley	CDJ	U.S.	1994	$8.00
Warner Brothers	PRO-CD-3704	Scandalous	CDJ	U.S.	1989	$7.00
Warner Brothers	9 21422-2	Scandalous Sex Suite	CD5	U.S.	1989	$5.00
Paisley Park	9362-40481-2	Sexy M.F.	CD5	Germany	1992	$10.00
Warner Brothers	WPDP-6305	Sexy M.F.	CD3	Japan	1992	$18.00/$5.00
Paisley Park	WPCP-4930CD	Sexy M.F.	CD5	Japan	1992	$16.00
Paisley Park	W-0123CD	Sexy M.F.	CD5	U.K.	1992	$10.00
NPG	72516	Sexy Staxaphone	CD5	U.S.	1994	$6.00
Warner Brothers	18012	Space	CD5	U.S.	1994	$5.00
Warner Brothers	41833	Space	CD5	U.S.	1994	$5.00
NPG	18012	Space	CD5	U.S.	1994	$6.00
Warner Brothers	PRO-CD-7241-R	Space	CDJ	U.S.	1994	$8.00
NPG		Super Hero	CDJ	U.S.	1994	$6.00
Denon	0060212NPG	The Beautiful Experience	CD5	Canada	1994	$15.00
Denon	0060155NPG	The Most Beautiful in the World	CD5	Canada	1994	$9.00
Paisley Park	7599 21598-2	Thieves in the Temple	CD5	Germany	1990	$10.00
WEA	WPDP-6240	Thieves in the Temple	CD3	Japan	1990	$18.00/$5.00
Paisley Park	9 21598-2	Thieves in the Temple	CD5	U.S.	1990	$5.00
Paisley Park	PRO-CD-4345	Thieves in the Temple	CDJ	U.S.	1990	$7.00
		Undertaker	CDJ	U.S.		$20.00
Paisley Park	7599 21186-2	When Doves Cry	CD5	Germany	1990	$10.00
Paisley Park	7599 21186-2	When Doves Cry	CD5	U.K.	1990	$10.00
Paisley Park	PRO-CD-5301	Willing And Able	CDJ	U.S.	1992	$8.00

Prince Markie Dee

Singles

Label	Catalog Number	Title	Type	Country	Year	Longbox Value / Value
		All My Love	CDJ	U.S.	1995	$3.00
Motown	860379	Crunch Time	CD5	U.S.	1995	$6.00

Label	Catalog Number	Title	Type	Country	Year	Longbox Value / Value
Columbia	CSK 74379	Trippin' Out	CDJ	U.S.	1992	$2.00
Columbia	44K 74865	Typical Reasons	CD5	U.S.	1993	$5.00

Princess Pang

Singles

Label	Catalog Number	Title	Type	Country	Year	Longbox Value / Value
		Find My Heart a Home	CDJ	U.S.		$2.00
		Trouble in Paradise	CDJ	U.S.		$2.00

Prine, John

Full Length

Label	Catalog Number	Title	Type	Country	Year	Longbox Value / Value
		Season's Greetings	DJ/Smplr	U.S.		$20.00

Sampler with photo cards.

Pritchard, Bill

Singles

Label	Catalog Number	Title	Type	Country	Year	Longbox Value / Value
SPV	9998-3	I'm in Love Forever	CD5	Germany	1992	$9.00
SPV	9954-3	In the Summer	CD5	Germany	1991	$9.00
SPV	8289-3	Number Five	CD5	Germany	1992	$9.00
Bias	BIAS-104CD	Tommy & Co.	CD5	Germany	1990	$9.00

Private Domain

Singles

Label	Catalog Number	Title	Type	Country	Year	Longbox Value / Value
		New Language	CDJ	U.S.		$2.00

Private Life

Singles

Label	Catalog Number	Title	Type	Country	Year	Longbox Value / Value
		Domino	CDJ	U.S.		$2.00
Warner Brothers	PRO-CD-3425	Last Heartbeat	CDJ	U.S.	1988	$2.00
Warner Brothers	PRO-CD-3278	Put Out the Fire	CDJ	U.S.	1988	$2.00
Warner Brothers	PRO-CD-4036	Touch Me	CDJ	U.S.	1990	$2.00

Pro Pain

Singles

Label	Catalog Number	Title	Type	Country	Year	Longbox Value / Value
Energy	PRO-2	Pound for Pound	CDJ	U.S.	1992	$2.00

Proclaimers

Full Length

Label	Catalog Number	Title	Type	Country	Year	Longbox Value / Value
Chrysalis		Hit the Highway	LTD/LP	U.S.	1994	$14.00

Stock CD with 5 track cassette sampler shrink wrapped together.

Label	Catalog Number	Title	Type	Country	Year	Longbox Value / Value
Chrysalis		Sunshine on Leith	LTD/LP	U.K.	1994	$15.00

25th Anniversary edition in 6"x11" longbox.

Singles

Label	Catalog Number	Title	Type	Country	Year	Longbox Value / Value
Chrysalis	CLAMCD-2	I'm Gonna Be	CD5	U.K.	1988	$8.00
Chrysalis	CLAMCD-4	I'm On My Way	CD5	U.K.	1989	$8.00
Chrysalis	DPRO-04555	I'm On My Way	CDJ	U.S.	1993	$3.00
Chrysalis	323622-2	King of the Road	CD5	Germany	1991	$8.00
Chrysalis	CLAMCD-5	King of the Road	CD5	U.K.	1991	$8.00
		Let's Get Married	CD5	U.K.		$10.00
		Let's Get Married	CD5	U.K.		$10.00

Second version.

Label	Catalog Number	Title	Type	Country	Year	Longbox Value / Value
Chrysalis	19803	Let's Get Married	CDJ	U.S.	1994	$3.00
Chrysalis	CHSCD-3219	Make My Heart Fly	CD5	U.K.	1991	$8.00
Chrysalis	CLAMCD-3	Sunshine on Leith	CD5	U.K.	1991	$8.00
		What Makes You Cry	CD5	U.K.		$10.00
		What Makes You Cry	CD5	U.K.		$10.00

Second version.

Procol Harum

Full Length

Label	Catalog Number	Title	Type	Country	Year	Longbox Value / Value
Mobile Fidelity	MFCD-823	A Salty Dog	LP/LB	U.S.†	1985	$25.00/$20.00
BBC Radio		BBC Classic Tracks	RS	U.S.	1992	$20.00

Airdate: 10/12/92.

Label	Catalog Number	Title	Type	Country	Year	Longbox Value / Value
Westwood One		BBC Classic Tracks	RS	U.S.	1993	$45.00

Airdate: 7/5/93.

Label	Catalog Number	Title	Type	Country	Year	Longbox Value / Value
Zoo	ZP17029-2	Chapter 1: Turning the Page	DJ/Smplr	U.S.	1991	$25.00
Zoo	72445-11011-2	Chapter 2: The Prodigal Stranger	DJ/LP	U.S.	1991	$25.00
Chrysalis		Chrysalis Years 1973-1977	LP/LB	U.S.		$18.00/$15.00
Zoo	ZP17044-2	Interview, The	DJ/Intvw	U.S.	1991	$10.00
DIR		King Biscuit Flour Hour	RS	U.S.	1988	$30.00

Airdate: 6/12/88.

Label	Catalog Number	Title	Type	Country	Year	Longbox Value / Value
DIR		King Biscuit Flour Hour	RS	U.S.	1991	$30.00

Airdate: 10/20/91.

Label	Catalog Number	Title	Type	Country	Year	Longbox Value / Value
DIR		King Biscuit Flour Hour	RS	U.S.	1994	$30.00

Airdate: 2/21/94.

Label	Catalog Number	Title	Type	Country	Year	Longbox Value / Value
DIR		King Biscuit Flour Hour	RS	U.S.	1994	$65.00

Airdate: 2/27/94.

Label	Catalog Number	Title	Type	Country	Year	Longbox Value / Value
DIR		King Biscuit Flour Hour	RS	U.S.	1996	$65.00

Airdate: 1/14/96.

Label	Catalog Number	Title	Type	Country	Year	Longbox Value / Value
		Shine on Brightly	LP	U.S.		$10.00

Singles

Label	Catalog Number	Title	Type	Country	Year	Longbox Value / Value
Zoo	ZP 17051	A Dream in Every Home	CDJ	U.S.	1991	$2.00
Zoo	ZP 17026	All Our Dreams Are Sold	CDJ	U.S.	1991	$2.00
Zoo	ZP 17041	Truth Won't Fade Away	CDJ	U.S.	1991	$2.00
Eastwest	2292-46872-2	White Shade of Pale	CD5	Germany	1989	$10.00

Prodigy

Singles

Label	Catalog Number	Title	Type	Country	Year	Longbox Value / Value
Intercord	825 921	Charly	CD5	Germany	1991	$8.00
XL	XLS-21CD	Charly	CD5	U.K.	1991	$8.00
Elektra	66411	Charly	CD5	U.S.	1992	$5.00
Intercord	825 932	Everybody in the Place	CD5	Germany	1991	$8.00
XL	XLS-26CD	Everybody in the Place	CD5	U.K.	1991	$8.00
XL	XLS-30CD	Fire	CD5	U.K.	1992	$8.00
Elektra	66370	Fire	CD5	U.S.	1992	$5.00
Warner Brothers	66370-2	Fire	CD5	U.S.	1996	$5.00
Warner Brothers	43843-2	Firestarter	CD5	U.S.	1996	$5.00
XL	XLS-35CD	Out of Space	CD5	U.K.	1991	$8.00
Elektra	66346-2	out Of Space	CD5	U.S.	1996	$6.00
Mute	7007	Voodoo People	CD5	U.S.	1995	$5.00
Elektra	66319	Wind It Up	CD5	U.S.	1993	$5.00

Professor Griff

Singles

Label	Catalog Number	Title	Type	Country	Year	Longbox Value / Value
Luke	465	Backdraft	CDJ	U.S.	1993	$2.00
Luke	4024	Jail Sale	CDJ	U.S.	1991	$2.00
BMG	663130	Pawns in the Game	CD5	Germany	1990	$8.00
Luke	4452	Verbal Intercourse	CDJ	U.S.	1991	$2.00

Professor Longhair

Full Length

Label	Catalog Number	Title	Type	Country	Year	Longbox Value / Value
Dancing Cat	DD-3006	Rock 'n Roll Gumbo	LP/LB	U.S.†	1985	$14.00/$8.00

Professor X

Singles

Label	Catalog Number	Title	Type	Country	Year	Longbox Value / Value
Polydor	CDP919	They Don't Know Jack	CDJ	U.S.	1993	$2.00

Program 2

Singles

Label	Catalog Number	Title	Type	Country	Year	Longbox Value / Value
Warner	12-41609	The Feeling	CD5	Canada	1994	$8.00
Sire	9 40879-2	Una	CD5	U.S.	1993	$5.00

Projection

Singles

Label	Catalog Number	Title	Type	Country	Year	Longbox Value / Value
		Heart & Soul	CDJ	U.S.		$2.00

Promise

Singles

Label	Catalog Number	Title	Type	Country	Year	Longbox Value / Value
Virgin	PRCD 2428	When in Rome	CDJ	U.S.	1988	$2.00

Promised Land

Singles

Label	Catalog Number	Title	Type	Country	Year	Longbox Value / Value
Epic	ESK 74260	Circle in a Square	CDJ	U.S.	1992	$2.00
ffrr	FCD-141	Something in the Air	CD5	U.K.	1990	$8.00

Prong

Full Length

Label	Catalog Number	Title	Type	Country	Year	Longbox Value / Value
Epic		Cleansing	LTD/LP	U.S.	1994	$16.00

Stock CD with live tour VHS video tape attached to jewelbox.

Label	Catalog Number	Title	Type	Country	Year	Longbox Value / Value
Epic	ESK 1951	Live At CBGB's	DJ/Smplr	U.S.	1990	$12.00

Singles

Label	Catalog Number	Title	Type	Country	Year	Longbox Value / Value
Epic		Broken Peices	CDJ	U.S.	1994	$3.00
Epic	ESK 2244	For Dear Life	CDJ	U.S.	1990	$3.00
Epic	ESK 2117	Lost and Found	CDJ	U.S.	1990	$2.00
Epic	ESK 4371	Prove You Wrong	CDJ	U.S.	1991	$3.00
Epic		Rude Awakening	CDJ	U.S.	1996	$3.00
		Snap Your Fingers	CD5	U.K.	1994	$10.00
Epic	ESK 4187	Unconditional	CDJ	U.S.		$2.00
Epic	ESCA-5642	Whose Fist Is This	CD3	Japan	1992	$15.00/$4.00
Epic	44K 74284	Whose Fist Is This	CD5	U.S.	1992	$5.00
Epic		Whose Fist is This	CDJ	U.S.	1992	$3.00

Propaganda

Singles

Label	Catalog Number	Title	Type	Country	Year	Longbox Value / Value
BMG	663100	Heaven Give Me Words	CD5	Germany	1990	$8.00
Virgin	VSCDT-1245	Heaven Give Me Words	CD5	U.K.	1990	$8.00
Charisma	PRCD 005	Heaven Give Me Words	CDJ	U.S.	1990	$2.00
Virgin	VJDP-110	How Much Love	CD3	Japan	1990	$13.00/$4.00
BMG	663518	Only One Word	CD5	Germany	1990	$8.00
Virgin	VJDP-131	Only One Word	CD3	Japan	1990	$13.00/$4.00
Virgin	VSCDT-1271	Only One Word	CD5	U.K.	1990	$8.00
Charisma	PRCD 009	Only One Word	CDJ	U.S.	1990	$2.00

Proper Grounds

Singles

Label	Catalog Number	Title	Type	Country	Year	Longbox Value / Value
Maverick	PRO-CD-6241	Backwards Mass	CDJ	U.S.	1993	$3.00
Maverick	9 40766-2	Jezebel	CD5	U.S.	1993	$5.00
Maverick	PRO-CD-5788	Mind Tempest	CDJ	U.S.	1993	$2.00

Prophecy

Singles

Label	Catalog Number	Title	Type	Country	Year	Longbox Value / Value
Visual	161851	Eyes, The	CD5	U.S.	1993	$5.00

Prophet

Singles

Label	Catalog Number	Title	Type	Country	Year	Longbox Value / Value
Megaforce	2197	Sound of a Breaking Heart	CDJ	U.S.	1988	$2.00

Proven Innocent

Singles

Label	Catalog Number	Title	Type	Country	Year	Longbox Value / Value
First Priority	4500	I'm Not the One	CDJ	U.S.	1992	$2.00

Pryor, Richard

Full Length

Label	Catalog Number	Title	Type	Country	Year	Longbox Value / Value
Columbia	VLD3376	Here and Now	LD	U.S.		$30.00

First pressing.

Label	Catalog Number	Title	Type	Country	Year	Longbox Value / Value
Columbia	VLD3376	Here and Now	LD	U.S.	1993	$30.00
Columbia	VLD3375	Live on the Sunset Strip	LD	U.S.	1983	$30.00
Vestron Video	VL3075	Smokin'	LD	U.S.	1985	$30.00

Pryor, Steve

Full Length

Label	Catalog Number	Title	Type	Country	Year	Longbox Value / Value
Zoo	11005	Steve Pryor Band	LP/LB	U.S.	1991	$14.00/$8.00

Singles

Label	Catalog Number	Title	Type	Country	Year	Longbox Value / Value
Zoo	ZD-17012	Spellbound	CDJ	U.S.	1991	$2.00

Psicom

Full Length

Label	Catalog Number	Title	Type	Country	Year	Longbox Value / Value
Triple X	CDPRO135	Psicom	DJ/LP	U.S.	1993	$20.00

Psyche

Singles

Label	Catalog Number	Title	Type	Country	Year	Longbox Value / Value
New Rose	NEW 99CD	Uncivilized	CD5	France		$8.00

Psychedelic Furs

Full Length

Label	Catalog Number	Title	Type	Country	Year	Longbox Value / Value
BBC Transcription		BBC Transcription Disc	RS		1992	$250.00
Columbia	CK-38261	Forever Now	LP/BP	U.S.†	1985	$14.00/$8.00
CBS	450256-2	Midnight to Midnight	LP	Germany		$15.00
Columbia	CK-39278	Mirror Moves	LP/BP	U.S.†	1984	$14.00/$8.00
Columbia	CSK 47303	World Outside	DJ/LP	U.S.	1991	$15.00

Singles

Label	Catalog Number	Title	Type	Country	Year	Longbox Value / Value
Columbia	651638-3	All That Money Wants	CD3	Germany	1988	$10.00
Columbia	651638-3	All That Money Wants	CD3	U.K.	1988	$10.00
Columbia	CDFURS-4	All That Money Wants	CD5	U.K.	1988	$10.00
Columbia	CSK 4193	Don't Be a Girl	CDJ	U.S.	1991	$2.00
Columbia	CDFURS-5	House	CD5	U.K.	1990	$10.00
Columbia	CSK 1944	House	CDJ	U.S.	1990	$2.00
Columbia	CSK 2739	Shock	CDJ	U.S.	1987	$2.00
Eastwest	YZ-587CD	Until She Comes	CD5	U.K.	1991	$8.00
Columbia	44K 73855	Until She Comes	CD5	U.S.	1991	$5.00
Columbia	CSK 4065	Until She Comes	CDJ	U.S.	1991	$2.00

Psychefunkapus

Singles

Label	Catalog Number	Title	Type	Country	Year	Longbox Value / Value
Atlantic	RPCD 4360-2	Surfin' on Jupiter	CDJ	U.S.	1991	$2.00
Atlantic	RPCD 3285-2	We Are the Young	CDJ	U.S.	1990	$2.00

Psychic TV

Singles

Label	Catalog Number	Title	Type	Country	Year	Longbox Value / Value
Sordid	SSCDV01	Listen Today	CDV	France	1987	$25.00

Psychopomps

Singles

Label	Catalog Number	Title	Type	Country	Year	Longbox Value / Value
Cleopatra	9537	In The Skin	CD5	U.S.	1994	$5.00

Public Enemy

Full Length

Label	Catalog Number	Title	Type	Country	Year	Longbox Value / Value
		Fight the Power Live	LD	U.S.		$50.00

Singles

Label	Catalog Number	Title	Type	Country	Year	Longbox Value / Value
Def Jam	655837-2	911 Is a Joke	CD5	U.K.	1990	$9.00
Def Jam	CSK 73309	911 Is a Joke	CDJ	U.S.	1990	$3.00
Def Jam	656018-3	Brothers Gonna Work It Out	CD3	Germany	1990	$9.00
Def Jam	656018-2	Brothers Gonna Work It Out	CD5	U.K.	1990	$9.00
Def Jam	CSK 73390	Brothers Gonna Work It Out	CDJ	U.S.	1990	$3.00
Def Jam	656385-2	Can't Do Nottin' for Ya Man	CD5	U.K.	1990	$9.00
Def Jam	44K 73612	Can't Do Nottin' for Ya Man	CD5	U.S.	1990	$5.00
Def Jam	657530-2	Can't Truss It	CD5	U.K.	1991	$9.00
Def Jam	73869	Can't Truss It	CD5	U.S.	1991	$5.00
Def Jam	CSK 73870	Can't Truss It	CDJ	U.S.	1991	$3.00
Def Jam	652833-3	Don't Believe the Hype	CD5	Germany	1988	$9.00
Def Jam	652833-2	Don't Believe the Hype	CD5	U.K.	1988	$9.00
RCA	ZD-42878	Fight the Power	CD5	Germany	1989	$9.00
Def jam		Give It Up	CD5	U.K.	1994	$10.00
Def jam		Give It Up	CD5	U.K.	1994	$10.00

Second version.

Label	Catalog Number	Title	Type	Country	Year	Longbox Value / Value
Def Jam		Give It Up	CDJ	U.S.	1994	$3.00
Def Jam	CSK 74488	Hazy Shade of Criminal	CDJ	U.S.	1992	$3.00
Sony	12EP-3070	Night of the Living Baseheads	CD3	Japan	1989	$15.00/$4.00
Def Jam	653046-2	Night of the Living Baseheads	CD5	U.K.	1988	$9.00
Def Jam	657864-2	Night Train	CD5	U.K.	1992	$9.00
Def Jam	44K 74254	Night Train	CD5	U.S.	1992	$5.00
Def Jam	CSK 74272	Night Train	CDJ	U.S.	1992	$3.00
Def Jam	657761-2	Shut 'Em Down	CD5	U.K.	1992	$9.00
Def Jam	774165	Shut 'Em Down	CD5	U.S.	1992	$5.00
Def Jam	CSK 4351	Shut 'Em Down	CDJ	U.S.	1992	$3.00
Def Jam	655476-3	Welcome to the Terror Dome	CD3	Germany	1992	$9.00
Def Jam	655476-2	Welcome to the Terror Dome	CD5	U.K.	1992	$9.00

Public Image Limited (Pil)

Full Length

Label	Catalog Number	Title	Type	Country	Year	Longbox Value / Value
Virgin	PRCD 3573	Don't Ask Me	DJ/Intvw	U.S.	1990	$8.00
Westwood One		In Concert-Nu Rock	RS	U.S.	1993	$50.00

Airdate: 4/26/93.

Label	Catalog Number	Title	Type	Country	Year	Longbox Value / Value
Virgin	PRCD 4383	What Is Metal	DJ/Smplr	U.S.	1992	$10.00

Singles

Label	Catalog Number	Title	Type	Country	Year	Longbox Value / Value
Virgin	PRCD 4551	Acid Drops	CDJ	U.S.	1992	$2.00
Columbia	10CY-8009	Body	CD3	Japan	1988	$15.00/$4.00
Rough Trade	604 3128 3	Cruel	CD5	Germany	1992	$10.00
Virgin	VSCDG 1390	Cruel	CD5	U.K.	1992	$10.00
BMG	162236	Disappointed	CD3	Germany	1989	$8.00
BMG	662236	Disappointed	CD5	Germany	1989	$8.00
Virgin	VSCD-1181	Disappointed	CD3	Japan	1989	$15.00/$4.00
Virgin	VSCDT-1231	Don't Ask Me	CD5	U.K.	1990	$10.00
		Happy	CDJ	U.S.		$3.00
Columbia	15CY-5013	Seattle	CD5	Japan	1987	$15.00
Virgin		That What Is Mental	CDJ	U.S.		$2.00
Virgin	CDF 14	This Is Not a Love Song	CD5	U.K.	1988	$10.00
Virgin	VJD-15555	Warrior	CD3	Japan	1989	$15.00/$4.00
Virgin	VSCDT-1195	Warrior	CD3	U.K.	1989	$10.00
BMG	162492	Warrior	CD3	U.K.	1989	$10.00
Virgin	PRCD 3031	Warrior	CDJ	U.S.	1989	$2.00

Public, Joe

Singles

Label	Catalog Number	Title	Type	Country	Year	Longbox Value / Value
Columbia	CSK 4793	Do You Every Night	CDJ	U.S.		$2.00
Columbia	CSK 74321	I Miss You	CDJ	U.S.		$2.00
Columbia	CSK 4428	Live and Learn	CDJ	U.S.		$2.00
Columbia	CSK 74812	This One's for You	CDJ	U.S.		$2.00

Pudgee

Singles

Label	Catalog Number	Title	Type	Country	Year	Longbox Value / Value
	PSSAD00184	Honey Don't Make Your World Stop	CDJ	U.S.	1995	$2.00

Puett, Tommy

Singles

Label	Catalog Number	Title	Type	Country	Year	Longbox Value / Value
		Kiss You All Over	CDJ	U.S.		$2.00

Puff Daddy

Singles

Label	Catalog Number	Title	Type	Country	Year	Longbox Value / Value
	79083	Can't Nobody Hold Me Down	CD5	U.S.	1996	$4.00

Pugh-Taylor Project

Full Length

Label	Catalog Number	Title	Type	Country	Year	Longbox Value / Value
Digital Music	CD-448	The Pugh-Taylor Project	LP/LB	U.S.†	1985	$14.00/$8.00

Pulp

Singles

Label	Catalog Number	Title	Type	Country	Year	Longbox Value / Value
Island	PRCD 6829-2	Babies	CDJ	U.S.	1995	$3.00
Island		Common People	CD5	U.K.	1995	$10.00
Island		Common People	CD5	U.K.	1995	$10.00

Second version.

Label	Catalog Number	Title	Type	Country	Year	Longbox Value / Value
Island	PRCD 7138-2	Common People	CDJ	U.S.	1995	$3.00
Island		Common People	CDJ	U.S.	1995	$3.00

Second version.

Label	Catalog Number	Title	Type	Country	Year	Longbox Value / Value
Island	PRCD 6833-2	Do You Remember the First Time	CDJ	U.S.	1995	$3.00
		Singles Box Set	CD5	Australia	1996	$55.00

6 CD set.

Label	Catalog Number	Title	Type	Country	Year	Longbox Value / Value
Island		Sisters	CD5	U.K.	1994	$10.00

Puppies

Singles

Label	Catalog Number	Title	Type	Country	Year	Longbox Value / Value
Epic	77724	Summer Night	CD5	U.S.	1994	$5.00

Pure

Singles

Label	Catalog Number	Title	Type	Country	Year	Longbox Value / Value
Reprise	PRO-CD-5947	Blast	CDJ	U.S.	1993	$2.00
Reprise	9 45003-2	Greedy	CD5	U.S.	1993	$5.00
Reprise	PRO-CD-6184	Spiritual Pollution	CDJ	U.S.	1992	$2.00

Pure Dee Funk

Singles

Label	Catalog Number	Title	Type	Country	Year	Longbox Value / Value
	9401	Warning	CD5	U.S.	1994	$5.00

Pure Prairie League

Full Length

Label	Catalog Number	Title	Type	Country	Year	Longbox Value / Value
RCA		If the Shoe Fits	LP/BP	U.S.		$14.00/$8.00
RCA		Live Takin' the Stage	LP/BP	U.S.		$14.00/$8.00

Singles

Label	Catalog Number	Title	Type	Country	Year	Longbox Value / Value
Rushmore		Momentos	CDJ	U.S.		$6.00

Pure Soul

Singles

Label	Catalog Number	Title	Type	Country	Year	Longbox Value / Value
	PRCD 6498-2	I Want You Back	CDJ	U.S.		$2.00
Atlantic	86108	I Want You Back	CD5	U.S.	1995	$5.00
	PRCD 6343-2	We Must Be in Love	CDJ	U.S.		$2.00

Purim, Flora

Full Length

Label	Catalog Number	Title	Type	Country	Year	Longbox Value / Value
Milestone	FCD-9095	Love Reborn	LP/LB	U.S.†	1985	$14.00/$8.00

Puro Latin Jazz

Singles

Label	Catalog Number	Title	Type	Country	Year	Longbox Value / Value
	130	Puro Latin Jazz	CD5	U.S.	1994	$5.00

Pursuit of Happiness

Singles

Label	Catalog Number	Title	Type	Country	Year	Longbox Value / Value
Mercury	CDP 840	Cigarette Dangles	CDJ	U.S.	1993	$2.00
Mercury	CDP 898	Pressing Lips	CDJ	U.S.	1993	$2.00
Chrysalis	POHCD-1	She's So Young	CD5	U.K.	1989	$8.00
Chrysalis	DPRO-23508	Two Girls in One	CDJ	U.S.	1990	$2.00

Pylon

Full Length

Label	Catalog Number	Title	Type	Country	Year	Longbox Value / Value
Sky		Sugarpop	DJ/Intvw	U.S.	1990	$5.00

Q

Singles

Label	Catalog Number	Title	Type	Country	Year	Longbox Value / Value
Polygram	877033-2	Moving Sensitive	CD5	Germany	1990	$8.00

Q - Feel

Singles

Label	Catalog Number	Title	Type	Country	Year	Longbox Value / Value
Jive	1221-2-JDJ	Dancing in Heaven	CDJ	U.S.		$2.00

Q-Beat

Singles

Label	Catalog Number	Title	Type	Country	Year	Longbox Value / Value
ZYX	6757-8	Mercedes Benz	CD5	Germany	1992	$6.00

Q-Crew

Singles

Label	Catalog Number	Title	Type	Country	Year	Longbox Value / Value
Chrysalis	323563-2	Gimmicks	CD5	Germany	1990	$8.00

Q-Tee

Singles

Label	Catalog Number	Title	Type	Country	Year	Longbox Value / Value
EMI	CDEM-179	Free the People	CD5	U.K.	1991	$8.00

Quad City DJ's

Singles

Label	Catalog Number	Title	Type	Country	Year	Longbox Value / Value
	PRCD 6624-2	C'mon & Ride It	CDJ	U.S.		$2.00

Quadrajets

Singles

Label	Catalog Number	Title	Type	Country	Year	Longbox Value / Value
Sympathy	362	When I Lay My Burden	CD5	U.S.	1994	$5.00

Quadrophonia

Singles

Label	Catalog Number	Title	Type	Country	Year	Longbox Value / Value
Columbia	657626-2	Find the Time	CD5	Germany	1992	$8.00
Columbia	657626-2	Find the Time	CD5	U.K.	1992	$8.00
BCM	20393	Paradise	CD5	Germany	1990	$8.00
Columbia	657685-2	Quadrophonia	CD5	Germany	1991	$8.00
Columbia	656768-2	Quadrophonia	CD5	U.K.	1991	$8.00
RCA	62232	Schizofrenia	CD5	U.S.	1992	$5.00

Quarterflash

Full Length

Label	Catalog Number	Title	Type	Country	Year	Longbox Value / Value
Geffen	4003-2	Quarterflash	LP/LB	U.S.†	1984	$14.00/$8.00
Geffen	4011-2	Take Another Picture	LP/LB	U.S.†	1984	$14.00/$8.00

Quatrero Musical

Full Length

Label	Catalog Number	Title	Type	Country	Year	Longbox Value / Value
Luna	LCDS-152	Sampler	DJ/Smplr	U.S.	1994	$5.00

Quatro, Suzi

Singles

Label	Catalog Number	Title	Type	Country	Year	Longbox Value / Value
Eastwest	247007-2	Baby, You're A Star	CD5	Germany	1989	$8.00
Bellaphon	130-07-595	Great Midnight	CD5	Germany	1991	$8.00
Bellaphon	130-07-605	Love Touch	CD5	Germany	1991	$8.00
EMI	TODP-2389	Wild One	CD3	Japan	1993	$12.00/$4.00

Quebec, Ike

Full Length

Label	Catalog Number	Title	Type	Country	Year	Longbox Value / Value
Mosaic	MD2-121	Complete Blue Note 45 Sessions	LTD/LP	U.S.		$25.00

2 CD set. Limited to 7500 copies.

Label	Catalog Number	Title	Type	Country	Year	Longbox Value / Value
Mosaic	MD2-107	Complete Blue Note Recordings of Ike Quebec and John Hardee	LP	U.S.		$45.00

3 CD Set.

Label	Catalog Number	Title	Type	Country	Year	Longbox Value / Value
Blue Note		Easy Living	LTD/LP	U.S.	1995	$19.00

Queen

Full Length

Label	Catalog Number	Title	Type	Country	Year	Longbox Value / Value
EMI		A Night At the Opera	LTD/LP	U.K.	1997	$35.00

Limited edition centennial CD edition housed in a slip case with a special 100 anniversary booklet.

Label	Catalog Number	Title	Type	Country	Year	Longbox Value / Value
EMI	SPCD-1524	A Sample of Magic	DJ/Smplr	Japan	1995	$300.00
BBC Radio		BBC Classic Tracks	RS	U.S.	1991	$45.00

Airdate: 8/19/91.

Label	Catalog Number	Title	Type	Country	Year	Longbox Value / Value
BBC Radio		BBC Classic Tracks	RS	U.S.	1992	$45.00

Airdate: 11/16/92.

Label	Catalog Number	Title	Type	Country	Year	Longbox Value / Value
Westwood One		BBC Classic Tracks	RS	U.S.	1994	$30.00

Airdate: 3/21/94.

Label	Catalog Number	Title	Type	Country	Year	Longbox Value / Value
Queen Prod	CDQTEL 0001	Box of Tricks	LTD/LP	U.K.	1992	$200.00

12" Remix CD, patch, pin, book, poster, T-shirt, in custum emobossed box.

Label	Catalog Number	Title	Type	Country	Year	Longbox Value / Value
Capitol	DPRO 79591	Classic Queen	DJ/Smplr	U.S.	1989	$50.00
EMI	QB1	Complete Works	LTD/LP	U.K.	1994	$60.00

2 CD set.

Label	Catalog Number	Title	Type	Country	Year	Longbox Value / Value
EMI	CD-DG1	Digital Master Sampler	DJ/Smplr	U.K.	1994	$60.00
Elektra	5E-513-2	Game	LP/LB	U.S.†	1983	$75.00/$70.00
Pioneer Artists	PA-82-026	Greatest Flix	LD	U.S.	1982	$25.00
Pioneer	PA-82-026	Greatest Flix	LD	U.S.	1990	$40.00
EMI	PCD-06070	Greatest History/Show Must Go On	DJ/Smplr	Japan	1995	$300.00
Elektra	5E-564-2	Greatest Hits	LP/LB	U.S.†	1981	$75.00/$70.00
EMI		Greatest Hits Vol. 1&2	LTD/LP	U.K.	1994	$40.00

2 CD set.

Label	Catalog Number	Title	Type	Country	Year	Longbox Value / Value
Westwood One		In Concert	RS	U.S.	1992	$120.00

2 CD set. With E.L.O., Airdate: 4/27/92.

Label	Catalog Number	Title	Type	Country	Year	Longbox Value / Value
Westwood One		In Concert	RS	U.S.	1993	$90.00

Airdate: 6/21/93.

Label	Catalog Number	Title	Type	Country	Year	Longbox Value / Value
Album Network		In the Studio (A Night at the Opera)	RS	U.S.	1989	$30.00

Airdate: 6/19/89.

Label	Catalog Number	Title	Type	Country	Year	Longbox Value / Value
Album Network		In the Studio (News of the World)	RS	U.S.	1990	$30.00
Airdate: 5/28/90.						
Album Network		In the Studio (The Game)	RS	U.S.	1994	$30.00
Airdate: 4/11/94.						
Parlophone	CDPCSD 115	Innuendo	LTD/LP	U.K.	1991	$30.00
CD in slipcase with calender.						
Capitol	CDP 7 46267 2	Kind of Magic	LP/LB	U.S.		$28.00/$23.00
DIR		King Biscuit Flour Hour	RS	U.S.	1988	$40.00
With Kansas, Airdate: 8/7/88.						
Hollywood	61104-2	Live at Wembly '86	LP/LB	U.S.	1992	$30.00/$23.00
2CD set in standard size double jewel box in long box.						
Polygram	080 510 1	Live in Budapest	LD	Germany	1987	$100.00
Polygram	080 5101	Live in Budapest	LD	U.K.	1987	$45.00
Pioneer Artists	PA-91-375	Live in Rio	LD	U.S.	1991	$40.00
EMI	TOCP-8700	Made in Heaven	LTD/LP	Japan	1995	$39.00
CD in slipcase and booklet.						
Hollywood	HR-62017-2	Made in Heaven	LTD/LP	U.S.	1995	$20.00
Limited edition with queen logos molded into the black tray.						
Pioneer	PA-91-348	Magic Years	LD	U.S.	1991	$100.00
Pioneer Artists	PA-90-348	Magic Years Trilogy	LD	U.S.	1991	$40.00
EMI	C21S-92357	Miracle	DJ/LP	U.K.	1989	$75.00
CD and cassette in box with press kit.						
Capitol	C21S-92357	Miracle	LP/LB	U.S.	1989	$15.00/$12.00
First pressing 3 color disc have white base color.						
Capitol	C21S-92357	Miracle	LP/LB	U.S.	1989	$15.00/$12.00
Subsequent pressings with 2 color printed disc with no white base color.						
Elektra	5E-112-2	News of the World	LP/LB	U.S.	1983	$70.00/$70.00
Westwood One		Off the Record	RS	U.S.	1992	$35.00
Airdate: 12/28/92.						
Westwood One		Off the Record	RS	U.S.	1992	$40.00
Airdate: 12/28/92.						
Westwood One		Off the Record	RS	U.S.	1992	$40.00
Airdate: 5/18/92.						
Westwood One		Off the Record	RS	U.S.	1993	$35.00
Airdate: 11/1/93.						
Westwood One		Off the Record	RS	U.S.	1993	$35.00
Airdate: 6/21/93.						
Westwood One		Off the Record	RS	U.S.	1993	$40.00
Airdate: 11/1/93.						
Westwood One		Off the Record	RS	U.S.	1993	$40.00
Airdate: 6/21/93.						
Hollywood	HR-61407-2	Queen Collection, The	LP	U.S.	1992	$35.00
3 CD Set.						
Hollywood	PRCD-8674-2	Queen Talks	DJ/Intvw	U.S.	1992	$18.00
Hollywood		Rocks Volume Box	DJ/Smplr	U.S.	1991	$250.00
4 CD "Rocks" volumes in custom drawer box.						
Hollywood	PRCD-8298-2	Rocks. Volume Four	DJ/Smplr	U.S.	1991	$15.00
Hollywood	PRCD-8263-2	Rocks. Volume One	DJ/Smplr	U.S.	1990	$20.00
Hollywood	PRCD-8297-2	Rocks. Volume Three	DJ/Smplr	U.S.	1991	$15.00
Hollywood	PRCD-8296-2	Rocks. Volume Two	DJ/Smplr	U.S.	1991	$15.00
Westwood One		Superstar Concert	RS	U.S.	1994	$100.00
2 CD set. Airdate: 4/4/94.						
Hollywood	PRCD-8674-2	Talks	DJ/Intvw	U.S.	1992	$30.00
Part of the Queen collection boxed set.						
EMI	SPCD-1543	Ultimate Collection, The	DJ/Smplr	Japan	1995	$300.00
EMI	QUEENBOX20	Ultimate Collection, The	LTD/LP	U.K.	1995	$675.00
20 CD picture disc set in framed wall mounted box.						
Media America		Up Close	RS	U.S.	1991	$50.00
2 CD set.						
Media America		Up Close	RS	U.S.	1992	$50.00
2 CD set						
Image	ID7551VE	We Will Rock You	LD	U.S.		$30.00
Sony	TOMW-7005	Works, The	8"LD	Japan	1984	$35.00
Sony	I-801	Works, The	8"LD	U.S.	1984	$35.00
Capitol/EMI	CDP 7 46016 2	Works, The	LP/LB	U.S.†	1984	$30.00/$25.00
Capitol/EMI	CDP 7 46016 2	Works, The	LP/LB	U.S.	1986	$30.00/$25.00

Singles

Label	Catalog Number	Title	Type	Country	Year	Longbox Value / Value
EMI	CDQUEEN 22	A Winter's Tale	CD5	U.K.	1995	$12.00
CD in Christmas card package.						
EMI	CDQUEEN 22	A Winter's Tale	CD5	U.K.	1995	$18.00
EMI	203051-3	Another One Bites the Dust	CD3	Germany	1989	$18.00
Parlophone	QUECD 8	Another One Bites the Dust	CD3	U.K.	1989	$18.00
EMI	203007-3	Bohemian Rhapsody	CD3	Germany	1989	$18.00
Toshiba	TODP-2345	Bohemian Rhapsody	CD3	Japan	1992	$18.00/$5.00
EMI	TOCP-7259	Bohemian Rhapsody	CD5	Japan	1992	$18.00
Parlophone	QUECD 3	Bohemian Rhapsody	CD3	U.K.	1989	$18.00
Parlophone	CDQUEEN20	Bohemian Rhapsody	CD5	U.K.	1991	$11.00
EMI	203421-3	Breakthru	CD3	Germany	1989	$18.00
Parlophone	QUECD 11	Breakthru	CD5	U.K.	1989	$12.00
Capitol	DPRO-79720	Breakthru	CDJ	U.S.	1989	$7.00
EMI	TODP-2251-62	CD Singles Box	CD3	Japan	1992	$100.00
12 CD3 boxed set with booklet.						
EMI	203062-3	Crazy Little Thing Called Love	CD3	Germany	1989	$18.00
Parlophone	QUECD 7	Crazy Little Thing Called Love	CD3	U.K.	1989	$18.00
EMI	SPCD 1796	Don't Stop Me Now	CDJ	France		$65.00
Parlophone	QUECD 5	First E.P.	CD3	U.K.	1989	$18.00
Hollywood		Hammer To Fall	CDJ	U.S.	1994	$13.00
EMI	204332-2	Headlong	CD5	Germany	1991	$11.00
EMI	TOCP-6801	Headlong	CD5	Japan	1991	$18.00
Parlophone	CDQUEEN-18	Headlong	CD5	U.K.	1991	$11.00
Hollywood	PRCD 8262-2	Headlong	CDJ	U.S.	1991	$7.00
EMI	DJ-DJUK1	Heaven for Everyone	CDJ	U.K.	1996	$25.00
Juke box edition.						
Hollywood		Heaven for Everyone	CDJ	U.S.	1995	$7.00
Hollywood	PRCD 8319-2	I Can't Live Without You	CDJ	U.S.	1991	$7.00
EMI	506-20 3360 3	I Want It All	CD3	Germany	1989	$18.00
Toshiba	XP10-2081	I Want It All	CD3	Japan	1989	$18.00/$5.00
Parlophone	CD QUEEN 10	I Want It All	CD5	U.K.	1989	$18.00
EMI	203053-3	I Want to Break Free	CD3	Germany	1989	$18.00
Parlophone	QUECD 11	I Want to Break Free	CD3	U.K.	1989	$18.00
Hollywood	HRCD020596	I Was Born to Love You	CDJ	Canada	1995	$50.00
EMI	204257-2	I'm Going Slightly Mad	CD5	Germany	1991	$11.00
Parlophone	CDQUEEN-17	I'm Going Slightly Mad	CD5	U.K.	1991	$11.00
EMI	204164-2	Innuendo	CD5	Germany	1991	$18.00
EMI	TODP-2209	Innuendo	CD3	Japan	1990	$18.00/$5.00
EMI	TOCP-6571	Innuendo	CD5	Japan	1991	$18.00
Parlophone	CD QUEEN 16	Innuendo	CD5	U.K.	1991	$18.00
Hollywood	PRCD 8319-2	Innuendo	CDJ	U.S.	1991	$18.00
EMI	552 20 3487 3	Invisible Man	CD3	Germany	1989	$18.00
Parlophone	QUECD 12	Invisible Man	CD3	U.K.	1989	$18.00
Parlophone	QUECD 2	Killer Queen	CD3	U.K.	1989	$18.00
EMI	203059-3	Kind of Magic	CD3	Germany	1989	$18.00
Parlophone	QUECD 12	Kind of Magic	CD3	U.K.	1989	$18.00
EMI	CDQUEEN24	Let Me Live	CD5	U.K.	1996	$18.00
EMI	CDQUEENS24	Let Me Live	CD5	U.K.	1996	$18.00
EMI	CDQUEENDJ 24	Let Me Live	CDJ	U.K.	1996	$15.00
Hollywood		Made in Heaven	CDJ	U.S.	1995	$18.00
Disc titled "Heaven For Everyone."						
EMI	522-20 3643 3	Miracle, The	CD3	Germany	1989	$18.00
Parlophone	QUEEN 15	Miracle, The	CD3	U.K.	1989	$18.00
Hollywood	PRCD 10196	One Year of Love	CDJ	U.S.	1992	$7.00
EMI	203052-3	Radio Ga Ga	CD3	Germany	1988	$18.00
Parlophone	QUECD 10	Radio Ga Ga	CD3	U.K.	1988	$18.00
EMI	552 20 3544 3	Scandal	CD3	Germany	1989	$18.00
EMI	CDQUEEN 14	Scandal	CD5	U.K.	1989	$18.00
Capitol	DPRO-79785	Scandal	CDJ	U.S.	1989	$9.00
EMI	203005-3	Seven Seas of Rhye	CD3	Germany	1989	$18.00
Parlophone	QUECD 1	Seven Seas of Rhye	CD3	U.K.	1989	$18.00
Parlophone	CD QUEEN 1991	Show Must Go on, The	CD5	U.K.	1991	$12.00
EMI	203008-3	Somebody to Love	CD3	Germany	1989	$18.00
Parlophone	QUECD 4	Somebody to Love	CD3	U.K.	1989	$18.00
Hollywood	PRCD 10193-2	Stone Cold Crazy	CDJ	U.S.	1992	$18.00
Hollywood	PRCD 8390-2	These Are the Days of Our Lives	CDJ	U.S.	1991	$7.00
Hollywood	PRCD 10061-2	These Are the Days of Our Lives	CDJ	U.S.	1991	$7.00
EMI		Too Much Love Will Kill You	CD5	U.K.	1995	$18.00
Second version.						
EMI	9286	Too Much Love Will Kill You	CD5	U.K.	1995	$30.00
CD and book in 7"x7" box.						
Hollywood	PRCD 105462	Too Much Love Will Kill You	CDJ	U.S.		$8.00
Hollywood		Too Much Love Will Kill You	CD5	U.S.	1995	$6.00
Hollywood		Too Much Love Will Kill You	CDJ	U.S.	1995	$7.00
EMI	203058-3	Under Pressure	CD3	Germany	1989	$18.00
Parlophone	QUECD 9	Under Pressure	CD3	U.K.	1989	$18.00
EMI	203061-3	We Are the Champions	CD3	Germany	1989	$18.00
		We Are the Champions	CD5	Germany	1994	$25.00
Recalled CD, plays "A Kind Of Magic" rather than correct track "Friends Will Be Friends."						
Parlophon	QUECD 6	We Are the Champions	CD3	U.K.	1989	$18.00
Parlophone	[illegible]	We Are the Champions	[illegible]	U.K.	1992	$18.00
EMI		We Are the Champions	CDV	U.K.	1996	$20.00
Hollywood	HR-65925-2	We Are the Champions	CD5	U.S.	1992	$5.00
Hollywood	PRCD-8347-2	We Are the Champions (With George Bush)	CDJ	U.S.	1991	$20.00
Hollywood	CD-66573-2	We Will Rock You & We Are the Champions	CD5	Canada	1991	$8.00
Hollywood	HB-66573-2	We Will Rock You & We Are the Champions	CD5	U.S.	1991	$5.00
EMI		You Don't Fool Me	CDJ	Holland	1995	$35.00
EMI		You Don't Fool Me	CD5	U.K.	1996	$18.00

Queen Latifah

Singles

Label	Catalog Number	Title	Type	Country	Year	Longbox Value / Value
Motown	4857	Black Hand Side	CD5	U.S.	1994	$5.00
Motown		Black Hand Side	CDJ	U.S.	1994	$2.00
Gee Street	GEECDS-27	Come Into My House	CD5	U.K.	1990	$8.00
	PRCD 9499-2	Elements I'm Among	CDJ	U.S.		$3.00
Gee Street	868803-2	Fly Girl	CD5	Germany	1991	$8.00
Eastwest	9031-74464-2	Fly Girl	CD5	Germany	1991	$8.00
Gee Street	GEECDS-34	Fly Girl	CD5	U.K.	1991	$8.00
Tommy Boy	502	Fly Girl	CD5	U.S.	1991	$2.00
Tommy Boy	995	Fly Girl	CDJ	U.S.	1991	$2.00
Tommy Boy	524	How Do I Love the	CD5	U.S.	1992	$4.00
Motown	4850	Just Another Day	CD5	U.S.	1994	$5.00
Gee Street	GEESCD-26	Mamma Gave Birth to Soul Children	CD5	U.K.	1990	$8.00
Sony	SRCS-5664	Nature of a Sista	CD3	Japan	1992	$13.00/$4.00
Motown	374631149	U.N.I.T.Y.	CDJ	U.S.	1993	$2.00

Queen Sarah Saturday Night

Singles

Label	Catalog Number	Title	Type	Country	Year	Longbox Value / Value
Chaos	5627	Seems	CDJ	U.S.	1994	$2.00

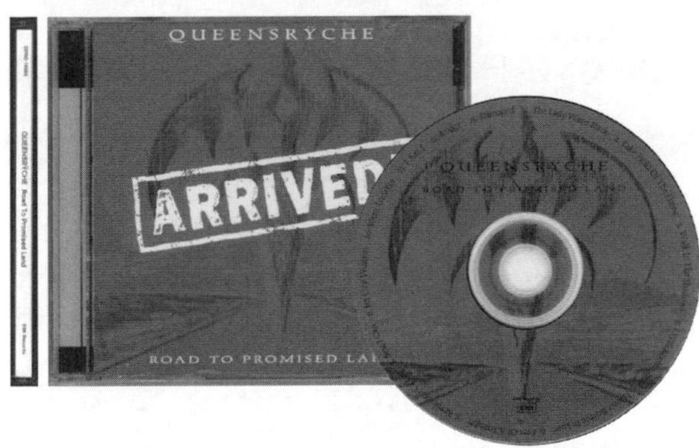

Queensryche – Road to the Promised Land (EMI DPRO-19985)

Queensryche

Full Length

Label	Catalog Number	Title	Type	Country	Year	Longbox Value / Value
EMI		Arrived: Road to the Promised Land	DJ/Smplr	U.S.	1995	$35.00
EMI	CDPRO-578	Building an Empire	DJ/Intvw	Canada	1992	$25.00
EMI		Disconected	DJ/Smplr	U.S.	1995	$20.00
EMI	TOCP-6274	Empire	LTD/LP	Japan	1990	$40.00
EMI	CDP-7-92806-2	Empire	DJ/LP	U.S.	1990	$55.00
EMI	DPRO 04686	Evolution Calling	DJ/Smplr	U.S.	1990	$20.00
EMI	DPRO 04760	Evolution Calling	DJ/Smplr	U.S.	1990	$20.00
EMI	E2-97048	Operation Live Crime	LTD/LP	U.S.	1991	$40.00
Boxed set with CD, VHS video, and booklet.						
EMI		Road to the Promised Land	DJ/Smplr	U.S.	1995	$30.00
EMI	DPRO-19985	Road to the Promised Land	DJ/Smplr	U.S.	1995	$50.00

Singles

Label	Catalog Number	Title	Type	Country	Year	Longbox Value / Value
EMI	204611-2	Another Rainy Night	CD5	Germany	1991	$18.00
EMI	DPRO 4808	Another Rainy Night	CDJ	U.S.	1991	$6.00
EMI		Anybody Listening?	CD5	U.S.	1991	$6.00
EMI	DPRO 04863	Anybody Listening?	CDJ	U.S.	1991	$6.00
EMI	TOCP-7035	Best I Can	CD5	Japan	1990	$17.00
EMI	CDMT-97	Best I Can	CD5	U.K.	1990	$18.00
EMI	DPRO 04674	Best I Can	CDJ	U.S.	1990	$7.00
Manhattan	DPRO 04049	Breaking the Silence	CDJ	U.S.	1988	$18.00
EMI		Bridge	CD5	U.K.	1995	$18.00

Label	Catalog Number	Title	Type	Country	Year	Longbox Value / Value
EMI		Bridge	CD5	U.K.	1995	$18.00
	Second version.					
EMI		Bridge	CDJ	U.S.	1995	$6.00
EMI	204032-2	Empire	CD5	Germany	1990	$18.00
EMI	CDMT-90	Empire	CD5	U.K.	1990	$18.00
EMI	DPRO 4640	Empire	CDJ	U.S.	1990	$7.00
EMI	203332-2	Eyes of a Stranger	CD5	Germany	1989	$18.00
EMI	CDMT65	Eyes of a Stranger	CD5	U.K.	1989	$18.00
EMI	CSDP100	I Am I	CDJ	Holland	1995	$30.00
EMI		I Am I	CDJ	U.K.	1995	$15.00
EMI		I Am I	CDJ	U.S.	1995	$6.00
EMI	DPRO 04344	I Don't Believe in Love	CDJ	U.S.	1989	$18.00
EMI	204469-2	Jet City Woman	CD5	Germany	1991	$18.00
EMI	CDMT-98	Jet City Woman	CD5	U.K.	1991	$18.00
EMI	DPRO 04756	Jet City Woman	CDJ	U.S.	1991	$7.00
EMI		Promised Land	CD5	U.K.		$18.00
EMI	CDMTLDJ-1081	Promised Land	CDJ	U.K.		$25.00
Columbia	CSK 5271	Real World	CDJ	U.S.	1993	$6.00
Columbia		Real World	CDJ	U.S.	1993	$6.00
	Second version.					
Manhattan	DPRO 04142	Revolution Calling	CDJ	U.S.	1988	$18.00
EMI		Silent Lucidity	CD5	Germany	1991	$18.00
EMI	CDMT-94	Silent Lucidity	CD5	U.K.	1991	$18.00
EMI	DPRO 4700	Silent Lucidity	CDJ	U.S.	1991	$7.00
EMI		Someone Else?	CDJ	U.S.	1995	$6.00

Quench

Singles

Label	Catalog Number	Title	Type	Country	Year	Longbox Value / Value
		Dreams	CD5	U.K.		$10.00
		Dreams	CD5	U.K.		$10.00
	Second version.					

Questionmark Asylum

Singles

Label	Catalog Number	Title	Type	Country	Year	Longbox Value / Value
RCA	64305	Hey Look Away	CD5	U.S.	1995	$5.00

Questionnaires

Singles

Label	Catalog Number	Title	Type	Country	Year	Longbox Value / Value
EMI	DPRO 4812	Killin' Kind	CDJ	U.S.	1991	$2.00
EMI	DPRO 4463	Window to the World	CDJ	U.S.	1989	$2.00

Quickland

Singles

Label	Catalog Number	Title	Type	Country	Year	Longbox Value / Value
	PRCD 6934-2	Landmine Spring	CDJ	U.S.		$2.00
Polydor	CDP 841	Dine Alone	CDJ	U.S.	1993	$2.00
Polydor	CDP 856	Fazer	CDJ	U.S.	1993	$2.00
Polydor	CDP 1054	Freezing Princess	CDJ	U.S.	1993	$2.00
Revelation		Omission	CD5	U.S.	1990	$5.00
Polydor	CDP 1069	Omission	CDJ	U.S.	1993	$3.00

Quiet Riot

Full Length

Label	Catalog Number	Title	Type	Country	Year	Longbox Value / Value
CBS	3541	By Thy Head	LD	U.S.	1990	$20.00
Pasha	ZK-39516	Condition Critical	LP/BP	U.S.†	1985	$14.00/$8.00
Pasha	ZK-38443	Mental Health	LP/BP	U.S.†	1984	$14.00/$8.00

Singles

Label	Catalog Number	Title	Type	Country	Year	Longbox Value / Value
Sony	10EP-3072	Joker	CD3	Japan	1989	$12.00/$4.00

Quindon

Singles

Label	Catalog Number	Title	Type	Country	Year	Longbox Value / Value
	DPRO 11087	It's You That's on My Mind	CDJ	U.S.		$2.00

Quireboys

Singles

Label	Catalog Number	Title	Type	Country	Year	Longbox Value / Value
		Brother Louie	CD5	U.K.		$10.00
		Brother Louie	CD5	U.K.		$10.00
	Second version.					

Quo

Singles

Label	Catalog Number	Title	Type	Country	Year	Longbox Value / Value
MJJ	6013	Huh What?	CDJ	U.S.	1994	$2.00

R.E.M.

Full Length

Label	Catalog Number	Title	Type	Country	Year	Longbox Value / Value
Warner Brothers		Alternative Radio Sampler	DJ/Smplr	U.K.	1993	$50.00
IRS	IRSD-seven	An AOR Radio Staple	DJ/Smplr	U.S.	1987	$70.00
Warner Brothers		Automatic for the People	LTD/LP	Australia	1995	$27.00
	Gold disc.					
Warner Brothers	9 45138-2	Automatic for the People	LP/LB	U.S.	1992	$18.00/$10.00
	Longbox only version with unique catalog number.					
Warner Brothers	2-45122	Automatic for the People	LTD/LP	U.S.	1992	$15.00
Warner Brothers	PCS-105	Berry, Buck, Mills, Stipe	DJ/Smplr	Japan	1992	$300.00
CBS	32DP-799	Dead Letter Office	LP	Japan	1991	$30.00
IRS	VICP-5132	Dead Letter Office	LP	Japan	1991	$30.00
CBS	32DP-842	Document	LP	Japan	1991	$30.00
IRS	VICP-5133	Document	LP	Japan	1991	$30.00
IRS	VDP-1426	Eponymous	LP	Japan	1991	$30.00
IRS	VICP-5134	Eponymous	LP	Japan	1991	$30.00
IRS	IRSD-5592	Fables of the Reconstruction	LP/LB	U.S.†	1985	$15.00/$9.00
Warner Brothers		Green	LTD/LP	Australia	1995	$27.00
	Gold disc.					
Warner Brothers	PRO-CD-3292	Green	DJ/LP	U.S.	1988	$40.00
	CD in clothbound digipak.					
Westwood One		In Concert	RS	U.S.	1993	$95.00
	2 CD set. Airdate: 3/29/93.					
Westwood One		In Concert	RS	U.S.	1994	$95.00
	2 CD set. Airdate: 10/10/94.					
Westwood One		In Concert	RS	U.S.	1995	$70.00
	2 CD set.					
Westwood One		In Concert	RS	U.S.	1995	$95.00
	2 CD set. Airdate: 7/17/95.					
Westwood One		In Concert	RS	U.S.	1996	$95.00
	2 CD set. Airdate: 2/12/96.					
Westwood One		In Concert-Nu Rock	RS	U.S.	1994	$95.00
	2 CD set. Airdate: 10/10/94.					
Westwood One		In Concert-Nu Rock	RS	U.S.	1996	$95.00
	2 CD set. Airdate: 1/1/96.					
Album Network		In the Studio (Document/Green)	RS	U.S.		$25.00
Album Network		In the Studio (Document/Green)	RS	U.S.		$40.00
Album Network		In the Studio (Out of Time)	RS	U.S.		$25.00
Album Network		In the Studio (Out Of Time)	RS	U.S.		$40.00
IRS		IRS Years - The Alternative Radio Sampler	DJ/Smplr	U.K.	1993	$125.00
Warner Brothers	PRO 2002-2	Les Irockuptibles	DJ/Smplr	France	1991	$90.00
CBS	32DP-533	Life's Rich Pageant	LP	Japan		$30.00
IRS	VICP-5131	Life's Rich Pageant	LP	Japan	1991	$30.00
IRS	CSCS-6083	Life's Rich Pageant	LP	Japan	1993	$30.00
Warner Brothers		Monster	LTD/LP	Australia	1994	$45.00
	Virgin Megastore edition with T-shirt.					
Warner Brothers		Monster	LTD/LP	Australia	1995	$27.00
	Gold disc.					
Warner Brothers	9 45783-2	Monster	LTD/LP	Germany	1994	$30.00
Warner Brothers		Monster	LTD/LP	U.S.	1994	$30.00
	CD in special binder. Limited to 40,000 copies.					
W#estwood One		Monster Radio	RS	U.S.	1995	$150.00
	4 CD set.					
IRS	CD-70604	Murmer	LP/LB	U.S.†	1984	$15.00/$9.00
Warner Brothers	PRO986	Music Between the Tours	DJ/Smplr	Germany	1995	$125.00
Warner Brothers	9 46321-2	New Adventures in Hi-Fi	LTD/LP	U.S.	1996	$32.00
	CD in book with 7"x7" outer sleeve.					
Westwood One		Off the Record	RS	U.S.	1992	$50.00
	Airdate: 11/16/92.					
Westwood One		Off the Record	RS	U.S.	1993	$45.00
	Airdate: 4/5/93.					
Westwood One		Off the Record	RS	U.S.	1995	$90.00
	2 CD set. Airdate: 5/1/95.					
Westwood One		On the Edge	RS	U.S.	1994	$45.00
	Airdate: 11/28/94.					
Warner Brothers		Out of Time	LTD/LP	Australia	1995	$27.00
	Gold disc.					
Warner Brothers		Out of Time	LTD/LP	U.K.	1995	$45.00
	CD and VHS video in box.					
Warner Brothers	26496-2	Out of Time	LP/LB	U.S.	1991	$20.00/$13.00
	One of the final U.S. releases packaged in a long box.					
Warner Brothers	26527-2	Out of Time	LTD/LP	U.S.	1991	$25.00
Warner Brothers	SAM1558	Pop Songs '89 To '95	DJ/Smplr	U.K.	1995	$100.00
IRS	CD-70044	Reckoning	LP/LB	U.S.†	1984	$15.00/$9.00
Warner Brothers	PRO-CD-6828	Sampler	DJ/Smplr	U.S.	1994	$7.00
Warner Brothers		Sampler From the Best of R.E.M.	DJ/Smplr	U.K.	1992	N/A
Warner	PRO-CD-3377	Should We Talk About the Weather	DJ/Intvw	U.S.	1988	$35.00
Warner Brothers	WPCP-4781-4	Singles Collection	LTD/LP	Japan	1995	$100.00
	4 CD boxed set.					
Warner Brothers		Songs That Are Live	DJ/Smplr	U.S.	1995	$18.00
		Special	RS	U.S.	1995	$175.00
	4 CD set. Airdate: 7/15/95.					
A&M	LV38403	Succumbs	LD	U.S.	1989	$30.00
	Analog audio.					
WEA	38254	This Film is On	LD	U.S.	1991	$30.00
WEA	38184	Tourfilm	LD	U.S.	1990	$30.00
Media America		Up Close	RS	U.S.	1989	$75.00
	2 CD set.					
Media America		Up Close	RS	U.S.	1991	$75.00
	2 CD set.					
Media America		Up Close	RS	U.S.	1992	$75.00
	2 CD set.					
Media America		Up Close	RS	U.S.	1995	$165.00
	3 CD set.					

Singles

Label	Catalog Number	Title	Type	Country	Year	Longbox Value / Value
Warner Brothers	17994	Bang and Blame	CD5	U.S.	1994	$5.00
Warner Brothers	41857	Bang and Blame	CD5	U.S.	1994	$5.00
Warner Brothers	PRO-CD-7271-R	Bang and Blame	CDJ	U.S.	1994	$7.00
Warner Brothers	PRO-CD-7455-R	Crush With Eyeliner	CDJ	U.S.	1994	$7.00
Warner Brothers	W0136CD	Drive	CD5	Germany	1992	$18.00
Warner Brothers	WPDP-6308	Drive	CD3	Japan	1992	$18.00/$5.00
Warner Brothers	9 18729-2	Drive	CD5	U.S.	1992	$4.00
Warner Brothers		Drive	CD5	U.S.	1992	$4.00
	Fourth version.					
Warner Brothers		Drive	CD5	U.S.	1992	$4.00
	Second version.					
Warner Brothers		Drive	CD5	U.S.	1992	$4.00
	Third version.					
Warner Brothers	PRO-CD-5700	Drive	CDJ	U.S.	1992	$7.00
Warner Brothers		E-Bow the Letter	CD5	U.K.	1996	$12.00
Warner Brothers	PRCD 358	E-Bow the Letter	CDJ	U.K.	1996	$22.00
Warner Brothers		E-Bow the Letter	CD5	U.S.	1996	$5.00
	Second version in "single-pack."					
Warner Brothers		E-Bow the Letter	CD5	U.S.	1996	$7.00
Warner Brothers		E-Bow the Letter	CDJ	U.S.	1996	$7.00
Warner Brothers	12-40989	Everybody Hurts	CD5	Canada	1994	$8.00
		Everybody Hurts	CD5	France	1994	$18.00
Warner Brothers	W0169	Everybody Hurts	CD5	U.K.	1993	$18.00
Warner Brothers		Everybody Hurts	CD5	U.K.	1993	$18.00
	Second version.					
Warner Brothers	9 40989-2	Everybody Hurts	CD5	U.S.	1993	$6.00
Warner Brothers		Everybody Hurts	CD5	U.S.	1993	$6.00
	Second version.					
Warner Brothers	PRO-CD-5900	Everybody Hurts	CDJ	U.S.	1993	$7.00
CBS	651320-2	Finest Worksong	CD5	U.K.	1987	$18.00
IRS	DIRM-161	Finest Worksong	CD5	U.K.	1987	$20.00
	Custom box packaging.					
Warner Brothers	PRO-CD-3716	Get Up	CDJ	U.S.	1988	$8.00
Warner Brothers		I Don't Sleep I Dream	CDJ	U.S.	1994	$7.00
Warner Brothers	PRO-CD-7894-R	I Took Your Name	CDJ	U.S.	1994	$7.00
		Ignoreland	CDJ	Spain	1992	$25.00
Warner Brothers	PRO-CD-5844	Ignoreland	CDJ	U.S.	1992	$7.00
IRS		It's the End of the World as We Know It	CDJ	U.K.	1987	$25.00
IRS	DIRMX 180	It's the End of the World as We Know It	CD5	U.K.	1992	$15.00
IRS	17476	It's the End of the World as We Know It	CDJ	U.S.	1987	$85.00
Warner Brothers	W0015CDX	Losing My Religion	CD5	Germany	1991	$18.00
Warner Brothers	W0015CDX	Losing My Religion	CD5	Germany	1991	$18.00
Warner Brothers	W-0015CD	Losing My Religion	CD5	U.K.	1991	$18.00
Warner Brothers	W0015CDX	Losing My Religion	CD5	U.K.	1991	$18.00
Warner Brothers	PRO-CD-4707	Losing My Religion	CDJ	U.S.	1991	$7.00
Warner Brothers	PRO-CD-4881	Losing My Religion	CDJ	U.S.	1991	$8.00
Warner Brothers	WPDP-6318	Man on the Moon	CD3	Japan	1993	$18.00/$5.00
		Man on the Moon	CD5	U.K.		$18.00
		Man on the Moon	CD5	U.K.		$18.00
	Second version.					
Warner Brothers	18642-2	Man on the Moon	CD5	U.S.	1992	$4.00
Warner Brothers		Man on the Moon	CD5	U.S.	1992	$4.00
	Second version.					
Warner Brothers	PRO-CD-5894	Man on the Moon	CDJ	U.S.	1992	$7.00
Warner Brothers	PRO-CDV-4460	Music From Tourfilm	DJ/CDV	U.S.	1990	$25.00
Warner Brothers	W0055CDX	Near Wild Heaven	CD5	Germany	1991	$18.00
		Near Wild Heaven	CD5	U.K.	1991	$18.00
Warner Brothers	PRO-CD-5058	Near Wild Heaven	CDJ	U.S.	1991	$7.00
IRS	DIRM-173	One I Love	CD5	U.K.	1987	$15.00
IRS	DIRMT-178	One I Love	CD5	U.K.	1987	$18.00
IRS	DIRM-X178	One I Love	CD5	U.K.	1991	$18.00
Pioneer	10P3-6078	Orange Crush	CD3	Japan	1988	$17.00/$6.00
Warner Brothers	W-2960CD	Orange Crush	CD3	U.K.	1988	$20.00
Warner Brothers	PRO-CD-3306	Orange Crush	CDJ	U.S.	1988	$18.00
Warner Brothers	PRO-CD-3357	Pop Song '89	CDJ	U.S.	1988	$8.00
Warner	12-40229	Radio Song	CD5	Canada	1994	$8.00

Label	Catalog Number	Title	Type	Country	Year	Longbox Value / Value
Warner Brothers	W0027CDX	Radio Song	CD5	Germany	1991	$18.00
Warner Brothers	W0027CDX	Radio Song	CD5	Germany	1991	$18.00
Warner Brothers	40229	Radio Song	CD5	U.S.	1991	$6.00
Warner Brothers	PRO-CD-4808	Radio Song	CDJ	U.S.	1991	$7.00
Warner Brothers	W0027 CDX	Shiny Happy People	CD5	Germany	1991	$18.00
Warner Brothers	W0027 CDX	Shiny Happy People	CD5	U.K.	1991	$18.00
Warner Brothers	PRO-CD-4888	Shiny Happy People	CDJ	U.S.	1991	$6.00
Warner Brothers		Sidewinder Sleeps Tonight	CD5	U.K.	1993	$18.00
Warner Brothers		Sidewinder Sleeps Tonight	CD5	U.K.	1993	$18.00
Warner Brothers		Sidewinder Sleeps Tonight	CD5	U.S.	1993	$5.00
Warner Brothers	PRO-CD-5903	Sidewinder Sleeps Tonight	CDJ	U.S.	1993	$7.00
WEA	W2833 CDX	Stand	CD3	Germany	1989	$13.00
WEA	W7577 CDX	Stand	CD3	Germany	1989	$20.00
	Leaf shaped package.					
Warner Brothers	2-27688	Stand	CD3	U.S.	1988	$20.00/$15.00
Warner Brothers	PRO-CD-3353	Stand	CDJ	U.S.	1988	$6.00
Warner Brothers		Star '69	CDJ	U.S.	1994	$7.00
Warner Brothers		Star '69	CDJ	U.S.	1994	$7.00
	CD in eco-pak.					
Warner	WPCR-260	Strange Currencies	CD5	Japan	1995	$21.00
Warner Brothers	17900	Strange Currencies	CD5	U.S.	1994	$5.00
Warner Brothers	PRO-CD-7510	Strange Currencies	CDJ	U.S.	1994	$7.00
Warner Brothers	PRO-CD-7510-R	Strange Currencies	CDJ	U.S.	1994	$7.00
Warner Brothers	PRO-CD-4826	Texarkana	CDJ	U.S.	1991	$7.00
Warner		Tongue	CD5	U.K.	1995	$11.00
Warner	SAM-1504	Tongue	CDJ	U.K.	1995	$20.00
Warner Brothers	PRO-CD-7875-R	Tongue	CDJ	U.S.	1994	$7.00
Warner Brothers	17737	Tounge	CD5	U.S.	1995	$5.00
Warner Brothers	PRO-CD-3446	Turn You Inside - Out	CDJ	U.S.	1988	$7.00
Warner		What's the Frequency Kenneth?	CD5	Australia	1994	$18.00
Warner	12-41760	What's the Frequency Kenneth?	CD5	Canada	1994	$8.00
Warner	12-18050	What's the Frequency Kenneth?	CD5	Canada	1994	$8.00
Warner Brothers	41760	What's the Frequency Kenneth?	CD5	U.S.	1994	$5.00
Warner Brothers	18050-2	What's the Frequency Kenneth?	CD5	U.S.	1994	$6.00
Warner Brothers		What's the Frequency Kenneth?	CDJ	U.S.	1994	$7.00

R.J.'s Latest Arrival

Singles

Label	Catalog Number	Title	Type	Country	Year	Longbox Value / Value
EMI	DPRO-04397	Rich Girls	CDJ	U.S.	1989	$2.00

Rabbitt, Eddie

Full Length

Label	Catalog Number	Title	Type	Country	Year	Longbox Value / Value
		Best Year of My Life	LP/LB	U.S.		$15.00/$9.00
		Country Star Tracks	RS	U.S.	1991	$15.00
	Airdate: 8/24/91.					
Masterpiece	CDCST-2	Country Store Collection	LP	U.K.		$15.00
		Radio Romance	LP/LB	U.S.		$15.00/$9.00
Capitol	CDP 790531-2	Step by Step	LP/LB	U.S.†	1984	$15.00/$9.00
Capitol	CDP 790531-2	Step by Step	LP/LB	U.S.	1984	$15.00/$9.00

Rabin, Trevor

Singles

Label	Catalog Number	Title	Type	Country	Year	Longbox Value / Value
Elektra	PR 8146-2	I Can't Look Away	CDJ	U.S.	1989	$2.00
Elektra	09P3-6034	Something to Hold on to	CD3	Japan	1989	$12.00/$4.00
Elektra	EKR-94CD	Something to Hold on to	CD3	U.K.	1989	$9.00
Elektra	PR 8086-2	Something to Hold on to	CDJ	U.S.	1989	$2.00
Elektra	PR 8123-2	Sorrow (Your Heart)	CDJ	U.S.	1989	$2.00

Radial Spangle

Singles

Label	Catalog Number	Title	Type	Country	Year	Longbox Value / Value
Beggars Banquet	BBQ 24CD	Birthday	CD5	U.K.		$8.00
Mint	MINT 7CD	Raze	CD5	U.K.	1993	$8.00

Radiators

Full Length

Label	Catalog Number	Title	Type	Country	Year	Longbox Value / Value
DIR		King Biscuit Flour Hour	RS	U.S.	1988	$30.00
	Airdate: 11/6/88.					
DIR		King Biscuit Flour Hour	RS	U.S.	1988	$30.00
	Airdate: 5/8/88.					
Epic	ESK 2809	Law of the Fish	DJ/Smplr	U.S.	1989	$15.00

Radio

Singles

Label	Catalog Number	Title	Type	Country	Year	Longbox Value / Value
Atlantic	95827	Groovin'	CD5	U.S.	1994	$5.00
Atlantic	95827	Groovin'	CD5	U.S.	1994	$5.00

Radio Active Cats

Full Length

Label	Catalog Number	Title	Type	Country	Year	Longbox Value / Value
Warner Brothers	9 26488-2-Dj	Radio Active Cats	DJ/LP	U.S.	1991	$9.00
	Picture disc.					

Singles

Label	Catalog Number	Title	Type	Country	Year	Longbox Value / Value
Warner Brothers	PRO-CD-5277	Bed of Roses	CDJ	U.S.	1992	$2.00
Warner Brothers	PRO-CD-4963	Shotgun Shack	CDJ	U.S.	1991	$2.00

Radio Heart

Singles

Label	Catalog Number	Title	Type	Country	Year	Longbox Value / Value
EMI	CDNBR-1	All Across the Nation	CD5	U.K.	1990	$8.00

Radiohead

Full Length

Label	Catalog Number	Title	Type	Country	Year	Longbox Value / Value
		Bends, The	LTD/LP	Australia	1995	$35.00
	2CD set.					
Westwood One		In Concert	RS	U.S.	1994	$80.00
	2 CD set. With Gin Blossoms, Airdate: 11/22/93.					
Westwood One		In Concert-Nu Rock	RS	U.S.	1993	$60.00
	Airdate: 11/22/93.					
Westwood One		In Concert-Nu Rock	RS	U.S.	1995	$60.00
	Airdate: 8/28/95.					
Westwood One		In Concert-Nu Rock	RS	U.S.	1996	$60.00
	Airdate: 1/29/96.					

Singles

Label	Catalog Number	Title	Type	Country	Year	Longbox Value / Value
		Anyone Can Play Guitar	CD5	Australia	1996	$12.00
Parlophone	CDR-6333	Anyone Can Play Guitar	CD5	U.K.	1993	$8.00
Capitol	DPRO-79773	Anyone Can Play Guitar	CDJ	U.S.	1993	$2.00
Parlophone	CDR-6078	Creep	CD5	U.K.	1992	$8.00
Capitol	DPRO-79684	Creep	CDJ	U.S.	1992	$2.00
Parlophone	CDR-6312	Drill	CD5	U.K.	1993	$8.00
EMI	58424	Fake Plastic Trees	CD5	U.K.	1995	$10.00
EMI		Fake Plastic Trees	CD5	U.K.	1995	$10.00
	Second version.					
EMI	CDR6411	Fake Plastic Trees	CDJ	U.K.	1995	$12.00
Capitol	DPRO-79567	Fake Plastic Trees	CDJ	U.S.	1995	$3.00
		High & Dry	CDJ	U.S.		$3.00
EMI	CDR6415	Just	CDJ	U.K.	1995	$12.00
	CORDJ6415	Just	CDJ	U.S.		$2.00
		My Iron Lung	CD5	Australia	1996	$12.00
EMI	E258274	My Iron Lung	CD5	Canada	1994	$13.00
Capitol	58274	My Iron Lung	CD5	U.S.	1994	$5.00
	CDR-DJ-6369	Stop Whispering	CDJ	U.K.		$10.00
Capitol	DPRO-79243	Stop Whispering	CDJ	U.S.	1993	$2.00

Raekwon, Chef

Singles

Label	Catalog Number	Title	Type	Country	Year	Longbox Value / Value
RCA	RDJ64372-2	Criminology	CDJ	U.S.		$2.00
RCA	RDJ64418-2	Ice Cream	CDJ	U.S.		$2.00

Rafferty, Gerry

Full Length

Label	Catalog Number	Title	Type	Country	Year	Longbox Value / Value
Polygram		North & South	LP/BP	U.S.		$12.00/$7.00

Singles

Label	Catalog Number	Title	Type	Country	Year	Longbox Value / Value
EMI	203750-2	Baker Street	CD5	Germany	1990	$8.00
EMI	CDEM-132	Baker Street	CD5	U.K.	1990	$8.00
A&M	PAMCD-350	Get Out of My Life Woman	CD5	U.K.	1992	$8.00
A&M	887751-2	Hearts Run Dry	CD5	Germany	1988	$8.00
A&M	PAMCD-998	I Could Be Wrong	CD5	U.K.	1992	$8.00
A&M	887415-2	Shipyard Town	CD5	Germany	1988	$8.00

Raffi

Full Length

Label	Catalog Number	Title	Type	Country	Year	Longbox Value / Value
A&M	LV38402	In Concert	LD	U.S.	1989	$25.00
A&M	LV38401	Young Children Concert	LD	U.S.	1989	$25.00

Rage

Singles

Label	Catalog Number	Title	Type	Country	Year	Longbox Value / Value
Noise	N-0426-3	Extended Power	CD5	Germany	1991	$8.00
Noise	VICP-15006	Extended Power	CD5	Japan	1991	$8.00
Noise	N-0169-3	Extended Power	CD5	U.K.	1991	$8.00
Noise	N-0136-3	Invisible Horizons	CD5	Germany	1989	$8.00

Rage Against The Machine

Singles

Label	Catalog Number	Title	Type	Country	Year	Longbox Value / Value
Epic		Bombtrack	CDJ	U.S.		$3.00
Epic	659258	Bullet in My Head	CD5	U.K.	1993	$10.00
Epic	EK-5063	Bullet in My Head	CDJ	U.S.	1993	$3.00
Epic	ESK 7775	Bulls on Parade	CDJ	U.K.		$15.00
Epic	ZSK 5503	Freedom	CDJ	U.S.	1994	$3.00
Epic	658492-2	Killing in the Name	CD5	U.K.	1993	$10.00
Epic	EK 4791	Killing in the Name	CDJ	U.S.	1993	$3.00

Ragged Jack

Singles

Label	Catalog Number	Title	Type	Country	Year	Longbox Value / Value
Island	CID-530	Get Radical	CD5	U.K.	1992	$8.00

Raging Slab

Full Length

Label	Catalog Number	Title	Type	Country	Year	Longbox Value / Value
Def American		A Taste o' Slab	DJ/Smplr	U.S.	1993	$6.00
Westwood One		In Concert	RS	U.S.	1994	$60.00
	2 CD set. With Jethro Tull, Airdate: 2/28/94.					
Westwood One		In Concert	RS	U.S.	1994	$75.00
	2 CD set with Jethro Tull. Airdate: 2/28/94.					

Singles

Label	Catalog Number	Title	Type	Country	Year	Longbox Value / Value
Def American	PRO-CD-6125	Anywhere But Here	CDJ	U.S.	1993	$2.00
		Bent For Silver	CDJ	U.S.		$2.00
RCA	9036-2-RDJ	Don't Dog Me	CDJ	U.S.	1989	$2.00
Def American	PRO-CD-6369	Take a Hold	CDJ	U.S.		$2.00
Def American	PRO-CD-6819	What Have You Done for Me Lately	CDJ	U.S.	1993	$2.00
Def American	PRO-CD-6659	What Have You Done for Me Lately	CDJ	U.S.	1993	$2.00

Raheem

Singles

Label	Catalog Number	Title	Type	Country	Year	Longbox Value / Value
A&M	CD 17674	Self Preservation	CDJ	U.S.	1988	$2.00
Life	79004	Short Shorts	CDJ	U.S.	1993	$2.00
A&M	CD 17674	Shotgun	CDJ	U.S.	1989	$2.00

Rahiem, Emanuel

Singles

Label	Catalog Number	Title	Type	Country	Year	Longbox Value / Value
Capitol	DPRO-79647	Spend a Little Time	CDJ	U.S.	1991	$3.00

Railway Children

Singles

Label	Catalog Number	Title	Type	Country	Year	Longbox Value / Value
Virgin	VJDP-116	Every Beat of the Heart	CD3	Japan	1990	$13.00/$4.00
Virgin	VSCD-1237	Every Beat of the Heart	CD3	U.K.	1990	$8.00
Virgin	VSCDT-1237	Every Beat of the Heart	CD5	U.K.	1990	$8.00
Virgin	PR 3358	Every Beat of the Heart	CDJ	U.S.	1990	$2.00
Virgin	VSCD-1070	In the Meantime	CD5	U.K.	1988	$8.00
Virgin	VSCDT-1255	Music Stop	CD5	U.K.	1990	$8.00
Virgin	PR 3606	Music Stop	CDJ	U.S.	1990	$2.00
Virgin	VSCD-1115	Over and Over	CD5	U.K.	1988	$8.00
Virgin	VSCDT-1289	So Right	CD5	U.K.	1990	$8.00
Virgin	VSCDT-1318	Something So Good	CD5	U.K.	1991	$8.00

Rain

Singles

Label	Catalog Number	Title	Type	Country	Year	Longbox Value / Value
Columbia	656732-2	Lemonstone Desired	CD5	U.K.	1991	$8.00
Columbia	657552-2	Lemonstone Desired	CD5	U.K.	1991	$8.00
Columbia	656981-2	Taste of Rain	CD5	U.K.	1991	$8.00
Columbia	52437	Taste of Rain	CD5	U.S.	1991	$5.00

Rain People

Singles

Label	Catalog Number	Title	Type	Country	Year	Longbox Value / Value
Epic	ESK 1475	Distance	CDJ	U.S.	1989	$2.00
Epic	654823-2	Little Bit of Time	CD5	U.K.	1989	$8.00

Rainbirds

Singles

Label	Catalog Number	Title	Type	Country	Year	Longbox Value / Value
Mercury	870275-2	Blueprint	CD5	Germany	1988	$8.00
Mercury	MERCD-264	Blueprint	CD5	U.K.	1988	$8.00
Mercury	870440-2	Boy on the Beach	CD5	Germany	1988	$8.00
Mercury	MERCD-274	Boy on the Beach	CD5	U.K.	1988	$8.00
Mercury	876337-2	Love Is A Better Word	CD5	Germany	1989	$8.00
Mercury	874662-3	Not Exactly	CD3	Germany	1989	$8.00
Mercury	874663-2	Not Exactly	CD5	Germany	1989	$8.00
Mercury	874004-3	Sea of Time	CD3	Germany	1989	$8.00
Mercury	874005-2	Sea of Time	CD5	Germany	1989	$8.00
Mercury	MERCD-287	Sea of Time	CD5	U.K.	1989	$8.00
Mercury	MERCD-344	Two Faces	CD5	U.K.	1991	$8.00

Rainbow

Full Length

Label	Catalog Number	Title	Type	Country	Year	Longbox Value / Value
Mercury	815305-2	Bent Out of Shape	LP/BP	U.S.	1984	$14.00/$8.00
Polydor	800018-2	Difficult to Cure	LP/BP	U.S.	1985	$14.00/$8.00
Pioneer	PA-83-052	Live Between the Lines	LD	U.S.	1985	$40.00
Polydor	800028-2	Straight Between the Eyes	LP/BP	U.S.	1984	$14.00/$8.00

Rainbow Girls

Singles

Label	Catalog Number	Title	Type	Country	Year	Longbox/Value
		Make Your Move for Love	CDJ	U.S.		$2.00

Raindogs

Singles

Label	Catalog Number	Title	Type	Country	Year	Longbox/Value
Atco	PRCD 4183-2	Baby Doll	CDJ	U.S.	1991	$2.00
Atco	PR 2971-2	I'm Not Scared	CDJ	U.S.	1989	$2.00
Atco	PRCD 3940-2	Let's Work Together	CDJ	U.S.	1991	$2.00
Atco	PRCD 3313-2	May Your Heart Keep Beauty	CDJ	U.S.	1990	$2.00
Atco	PRCD 3938-2	Some Fun	CDJ	U.S.	1991	$3.00

Rainmakers

Singles

Label	Catalog Number	Title	Type	Country	Year	Longbox/Value
Mercury	870 719-2	Downstream	CDV/BP	U.S.	1988	$14.00/$14.00
Mercury	870111-2	Small Circles	CD5	Germany	1988	$8.00
Mercury	MERCD-259	Small Circles	CD5	U.K.	1988	$8.00
Mercury	CDP 09	Small Circles	DJ/CD3	U.S.	1988	$5.00/$3.00
Mercury	MERCD-265	Snakedance	CD5	U.K.	1988	$8.00
Mercury	CDP 07	Snakedance	CDJ	U.S.	1987	$2.00
Mercury		Spend It on Love	CDJ	U.S.		$2.00

Raintree Crow

Singles

Label	Catalog Number	Title	Type	Country	Year	Longbox/Value
BMG	664071	Blackwater	CD5	Germany	1991	$8.00
Virgin	VSCDT-1340	Blackwater	CD5	U.K.	1991	$8.00

Raitt, Bonnie

Full Length

Label	Catalog Number	Title	Type	Country	Year	Longbox/Value
		1994 Interview	DJ/Intvw	Germany	1994	$35.00
Capitol		Airplay Sampler	DJ/Smplr	U.S.	1994	$15.00
Capitol		AOR Sampler	DJ/Smplr	U.S.	1994	$20.00
Capitol	DPRO-885	Bonnie Raitt	DJ/Smplr	Canada	1994	$45.00
Capitol	PCD 224	Eight Hot Slices	DJ/Smplr	Japan	1991	$100.00
	CD in Pizza box package.					
Capitol		Grammy Sampler	DJ/Smplr	U.S.	1994	$20.00
DIR		King Biscuit Flour Hour	RS	U.S.	1990	$40.00
	With Warren Zevon, Airdate: 3/19/90.					
DIR		King Biscuit Flour Hour	RS	U.S.	1992	$40.00
	With Paul Simon, Airdate: 3/15/92.					
DIR		King Biscuit Flour Hour	RS	U.S.	1994	$40.00
	With Paul Simon, Airdate: 4/24/94.					
DIR		King Biscuit Flour Hour	RS	U.S.	1995	$40.00
	With Paul Simon, Airdate: 5/21/95.					
EMI	SPCD-1199	Luck of the Draw	DJ/LP	Japan	1991	$45.00
	Advance issue.					
Capitol	CDP 596111	Luck of the Draw	LP	U.S.	1991	$14.00
	CD in jewel box.					
Capitol	CZ-96860	Luck of the Draw	LTD/LP	U.S.	1991	$20.00
Westwood One		Off the Record	RS	U.S.	1994	$30.00
	Airdate: 6/13/94.					
Westwood One		Off the Record	RS	U.S.	1994	$30.00
	Airdate: 6/13/94.					
Westwood One		Off the Record	RS	U.S.	1996	$30.00
	Airdate: 2/26/96.					
Capitol		Tour Sampler	DJ/Smplr	U.S.	1994	$15.00

Singles

Label	Catalog Number	Title	Type	Country	Year	Longbox/Value
Capitol	DPRO-79356	All at Once	CDJ	U.S.	1991	$3.00
A&M	CD17625	Baby Mine	CDJ	U.S.	1988	$3.00
Capitol	DPRO11167	Burning Down the House	CDJ	U.S.		$3.00
Capitol	CDCL-666	Good Man, Good Woman	CD5	U.K.	1992	$10.00
Capitol	DPRO-79336	Good Man, Good Woman	CDJ	U.S.	1989	$3.00
Capitol	203948-2	Have a Heart	CD5	Germany	1990	$10.00
Capitol	DPRO-79897	Have a Heart	CDJ	U.S.	1989	$3.00
Capitol	204585-2	I Can't Make You Love Me	CD5	Germany	1991	$10.00
Capitol	204606-2	I Can't Make You Love Me	CD5	Germany	1991	$14.00
Capitol	TODP-2315	I Can't Make You Love Me	CD3	Japan	1991	$12.00/$5.00
Capitol	CDCL-639	I Can't Make You Love Me	CD5	U.K.	1991	$10.00
Capitol	CDCLS-639	I Can't Make You Love Me	CD5	U.K.	1991	$14.00
Capitol	C2 15740	I Can't Make You Love Me	CD5	U.S.	1991	$5.00
Capitol	DPRO-79768	I Can't Make You Love Me	CDJ	U.S.	1991	$3.00
Chameleon	PRCD 072	I'm in the Mood	CDJ	U.S.	1989	$3.00
Capitol	DPRO-79348	Longing in Their Hearts	CDJ	U.S.	1994	$3.00
Capitol	DPRO-79127	Love Letter	CDJ	U.S.	1989	$3.00
Capitol	DPRO-79334	Love Sneakin' Up on You	CDJ	U.S.	1994	$3.00
Capitol	DPRO-79325	Love Sneakin' Up on You	CDJ	U.S.	1994	$7.00
Capitol	TODP-2279	Luck of the Draw	CD3	Japan	1991	$12.00/$5.00
Capitol	203345-2	Nick of Time	CD5	Germany	1989	$10.00
Capitol	CDCL-530	Nick of Time	CD5	U.K.	1989	$10.00
Capitol	DPRO-79721	Nick of Time	CDJ	U.S.	1989	$3.00
Capitol	204634-2	Not the Only One	CD5	Germany	1992	$10.00
Capitol	TODP-2366	Not the Only One	CD3	Japan	1989	$12.00/$5.00
Capitol	DPRO-79115	Not the Only One	CDJ	U.S.	1989	$3.00
Capitol		Slow Ride	CDJ	U.S.	1993	$6.00
Capitol	204362-2	Something to Talk About	CD5	Germany	1991	$10.00
Capitol	TODP-2315	Something to Talk About	CD3	Japan	19991	$12.00/$5.00
Capitol	CDCL-619	Something to Talk About	CD5	U.K.	1991	$10.00
Capitol	C2 15736	Something to Talk About	CD5	U.S.	1991	$5.00
Capitol	DPRO-79748	Something to Talk About	CDJ	U.S.	1991	$3.00
Capitol		Storm Warning	CDJ	U.S.	1994	$6.00
Capitol	CDCL-576	Thing Called Love	CD5	U.K.	1990	$8.00
Capitol	DPRO 79554	Thing Called Love	CDJ	U.S.	1989	$3.00
Arista	12803	You Got It	CD5	U.S.	1994	$5.00
Capitol	DPRO-79346	You Got It	CDJ	U.S.	1994	$6.00
Arista	ASCD 2795	You Got It	CDJ	U.S.	1995	$6.00

Rakim

Singles

Label	Catalog Number	Title	Type	Country	Year	Longbox/Value
MCA	MCA5P-2833	Heat It Up	CDJ	U.S.	1993	$2.00

Raleigh, Kevin

Singles

Label	Catalog Number	Title	Type	Country	Year	Longbox/Value
		Moonlight on Water	CDJ	U.S.		$2.00

Ralph & Red

Full Length

Label	Catalog Number	Title	Type	Country	Year	Longbox/Value
RCA	9757	Christmas With	LP/BP	U.S.		$12.00/$7.00

Ralph, Sheryl Lee

Singles

Label	Catalog Number	Title	Type	Country	Year	Longbox/Value
A&M	CD 17711	(I'm) Hurting Inside	CDJ	U.S.	1988	$2.00

Ram Jam

Singles

Label	Catalog Number	Title	Type	Country	Year	Longbox/Value
Epic	655430-3	Black Betty	CD3	Germany	1989	$8.00
Epic	654607-2	Black Betty	CD5	Germany	1989	$8.00
Epic	655430-2	Black Betty	CD5	U.K.	1989	$8.00
Epic	654607-2	Black Betty	CD5	U.K.	1989	$8.00
Epic	ESK-73195	Black Betty	CDJ	U.S.	1990	$2.00

Ramones

Full Length

Label	Catalog Number	Title	Type	Country	Year	Longbox/Value
Spin		Spin	RS	U.S.	1994	$35.00
	Airdate: 1/31/94.					
Radioactive	2658	Talkin' Mondo Bizarro	DJ/Intvw	U.S.	1993	$20.00

Singles

Label	Catalog Number	Title	Type	Country	Year	Longbox/Value
	RAR5P3402	I Don't Want to Grow Up	CDJ	U.S.		$6.00
Radioactive	2844	Journey to the Center of the Mind	CDJ	U.S.	1993	$7.00
Chrysalis	662489	Pet Sematary	CD5	Germany	1989	$10.00
Sire	PRO-CD-3569	Pet Sematary	CDJ	U.S.	1989	$3.00
		Poison Heart	CD5	U.K.	1992	$10.00
		Poison Heart	CD5	U.K.	1992	$10.00
	Second version.					
Radioactive	2343	Poison Heart	CDJ	U.S.	1992	$3.00
Radioactive	2896	Substitute	CDJ	U.S.	1993	$7.00
Radioactive	2584	Touring	CDJ	U.S.	1993	$3.00

Ramos, Kid

Full Length

Label	Catalog Number	Title	Type	Country	Year	Longbox/Value
		House of Blues	RS	U.S.	1996	$35.00
	2 CD set. Airdate: 3/17/96.					

Rancid

Singles

Label	Catalog Number	Title	Type	Country	Year	Longbox/Value
		Olympia	CDJ	U.S.		$2.00
Epitaph	86452	Roots Radical	CD5	U.S.	1994	$5.00
		Time Bomb	CDJ	U.S.		$2.00

Random Access

Singles

Label	Catalog Number	Title	Type	Country	Year	Longbox/Value
BMG	662930	Interceptor	CD5	Germany	1990	$8.00

Randy And The Gypsys

Singles

Label	Catalog Number	Title	Type	Country	Year	Longbox/Value
A&M	CD 17973	Love You Honey	CDJ	U.S.	1989	$2.00
Canyon	PCDY-10009	Perpetrators	CD3	Japan	1989	$13.00/$4.00
A&M	CD 17904	Perpetrators	CDJ	U.S.	1989	$2.00

Rankin, Louie

Singles

Label	Catalog Number	Title	Type	Country	Year	Longbox/Value
Mesa	76004	Typewriter	CD5	U.S.	1992	$4.00

Rankin, Roger

Singles

Label	Catalog Number	Title	Type	Country	Year	Longbox/Value
IRS	DIRM-166	So Excited	CD5	U.K.	1988	$8.00

Ranks, Shabba

Full Length

Label	Catalog Number	Title	Type	Country	Year	Longbox/Value
Epi	ESK 4786	X-tra Naked	DJ/LP	U.S.	1992	$12.00
	CD in digipak with condom.					

Singles

Label	Catalog Number	Title	Type	Country	Year	Longbox/Value
Atlas	1109	Family Affair	CDJ	U.S.	1993	$2.00
Epic	657347-2	Housecall	CD5	Germany	1991	$9.00
Epic	657347-2	Housecall	CD5	U.K.	1991	$9.00
Epic	49K 73929	Housecall	CD5	U.S.	1991	$5.00
Epic	ESK 74069	Jam, The	CDJ	U.S.	1991	$2.00
CBS	77819	Let's Get It On	CD5	U.S.	1994	$5.00
Epic	ESCA-5601	Mr. Loverman	CD3	Japan	1992	$12.00/$4.00
Epic	658251-2	Mr. Loverman	CD5	U.K.	1992	$9.00
Epic	49K-74248	Mr. Loverman	CD5	U.S.	1992	$5.00
Epic	ESK 74257	Mr. Loverman	CDJ	U.S.	1992	$2.00
Epic	ESK-74797	Muscle Grip	CDJ	U.S.	1992	$2.00
Epic		Ram Dancehall	CDJ	U.S.	1995	$6.00
Columbia	77677	Shine Eye Gal	CD5	U.S.	1995	$5.00
Epic	658772-2	Slow and Sexy	CD5	U.K.	1992	$9.00
Epic	49K-74742	Slow and Sexy	CD5	U.S.	1992	$5.00
Epic	ESK 4838	Slow and Sexy	CDJ	U.S.	1992	$2.00
Epic	ESK 74741	Slow and Sexy	CDJ	U.S.	1992	$2.00
Epic	656872-2	Trailor Load a Girls	CD5	U.K.	1991	$9.00
Epic	ESK-73808	Trailor Load a Girls	CDJ	U.S.	1991	$2.00
Epic	ESK-5114	What'cha Gonna Do?	CDJ	U.S.	1992	$2.00

Ranx, Skeeta

Singles

Label	Catalog Number	Title	Type	Country	Year	Longbox/Value
	20123	I Like	CD5	U.S.	1994	$5.00

Rapoon

Full Length

Label	Catalog Number	Title	Type	Country	Year	Longbox/Value
4AD		Raising Earthly Spirits	DJ/LP	U.S.	1993	$20.00

Rappin' 4-Tay

Singles

Label	Catalog Number	Title	Type	Country	Year	Longbox/Value
	DPRO10459	Ain't No Playa	CDJ	U.S.		$2.00
Capital	58331	I'll Be Around	CD5	U.S.	1994	$5.00
Capital	58267	Playaz Club	CD5	U.S.	1994	$5.00

Rappin' is Fundamental

Singles

Label	Catalog Number	Title	Type	Country	Year	Longbox/Value
A&M	390751-2	Rappin' Is Fundamental	CD5	Germany	1991	$8.00
A&M	AMCD-751	Rappin' Is Fundamental	CD5	U.K.	1991	$8.00
A&M	75021 7496 2	Rappin' Is Fundamental	CDJ	U.S.	1991	$2.00

Rare

Singles

Label	Catalog Number	Title	Type	Country	Year	Longbox/Value
SPV	8762-3	Set Me Free	CD5	Germany	1990	$8.00

Rare Earth

Singles

Label	Catalog Number	Title	Type	Country	Year	Longbox/Value
Koch	341 007	Livin' in a Different World	CD5	Germany	1991	$8.00
Motown	886594	Vintage Gold	CD3	Germany	1989	$9.00
Motown	ZD-41953	Vintage Gold	CD3	U.K.	1989	$9.00

Raspberries

Singles

Label	Catalog Number	Title	Type	Country	Year	Longbox/Value
Rhino	885850	Go All the Way	CD3	Germany	1990	$10.00

Rastine

Full Length

Label	Catalog Number	Title	Type	Country	Year	Longbox/Value
Zoo	11035	Afrodisiac	LP/LB	U.S.		$12.00/$7.00

Rat Cat

Singles

Label	Catalog Number	Title	Type	Country	Year	Longbox/Value
rooArt	RCTCD-1	Don't Go Now	CD5	U.K.	1991	$8.00
rooArt	868 573-2	Tingles	CDJ	U.S.	1990	$2.00

Ratpack

Singles

Label	Catalog Number	Title	Type	Country	Year	Longbox Value / Value
Big Giant	BGD-03	Changing Styles	CD5	U.K.	1992	$8.00

Ratt

Full Length

Label	Catalog Number	Title	Type	Country	Year	Longbox Value / Value
Atlantic		Detonator	LP/LB	U.S.		$12.00/$7.00
Pioneer	PA86-M043	Video, The	8"LD	U.S.	1985	$7.00
Pioneer	PA86-M043	Video, The	8"LD	U.S.	1985	$7.00

Singles

Label	Catalog Number	Title	Type	Country	Year	Longbox Value / Value
Atlantic	PRCD 3762-2	Givin' Yourself Away	CDJ	U.S.	1991	$3.00
Pioneer	09P3-6116	I Want a Woman	CD3	Japan	1989	$12.00/$4.00
Atlantic	PR 2635-2	I Want a Woman	CDJ	U.S.	1988	$3.00
Atlantic	AMDY-5027	Lovin' You is a Dirty Job	CD3	Japan	1990	$12.00/$4.00
Atlantic	PRCD 3495-2	Lovin' You is a Dirty Job	CDJ	U.S.	1990	$3.00
MCA	MVDM-2	Nobody Lies for Free	CD3	Japan	1991	$12.00/$4.00
Atlantic	PRCDE 3495-2	Nobody Lies for Free	CDJ	U.S.	1990	$3.00
Atlantic	AMDY-5038	Shame Shame Shame	CD3	Japan	1990	$12.00/$4.00
Atlantic	PRCD 3624-2	Shame Shame Shame	CDJ	U.S.	1990	$3.00
Atlantic	10P3-6026	Way Cool Jr.	CD3	Japan	1988	$12.00/$4.00
Atlantic	PR 2531-2	Way Cool Jr.	CDJ	U.S.	1988	$3.00

Rattlebone

Singles

Label	Catalog Number	Title	Type	Country	Year	Longbox Value / Value
Hollywood		Rattlebone	CDJ	U.S.	1995	$3.00
Hollywood	61405	X-Ray Eyes	CD5	U.S.	1990	$4.00

Rave Ups

Full Length

Label	Catalog Number	Title	Type	Country	Year	Longbox Value / Value
Epic	ESK 2010	A Chance Conversation	DJ/Intvw	U.S.	1990	$12.00
		Book of Your Regrets	DJ/LP	U.S.		$8.00
		Hamlet Meets John Doe	DJ/Smplr	U.S.		$6.00

Singles

Label	Catalog Number	Title	Type	Country	Year	Longbox Value / Value
Epic	ESK 1909	Respectfully King of Rain	CDJ	U.S.	1990	$3.00
Epic	ESK 2015	Respectfully King of Rain	CDJ	U.S.	1990	$3.00
Epic	ESK 2061	She Says (Come Around)	CDJ	U.S.	1990	$3.00

Raven

Full Length

Label	Catalog Number	Title	Type	Country	Year	Longbox Value / Value
Combat		Nothing Exceeds Like Excess	LP/LB	U.S.		$10.00/$6.00

Raw Fusion

Singles

Label	Catalog Number	Title	Type	Country	Year	Longbox Value / Value
Hollywood	66546	Throw Your Hands in the Air	CD5	U.S.	1991	$4.00

Raw Stylus

Full Length

Label	Catalog Number	Title	Type	Country	Year	Longbox Value / Value
	PRCD 4755-2	Six Cut Sampler	DJ/Smplr	U.S.		$6.00

Singles

Label	Catalog Number	Title	Type	Country	Year	Longbox Value / Value
	PRCD 74802	Believe in Me	CDJ	U.S.		$2.00

Raw Youth

Singles

Label	Catalog Number	Title	Type	Country	Year	Longbox Value / Value
RNA	90067	Tame Yourself	CDJ	U.S.	1991	$2.00

Rawls, Lou

Full Length

Label	Catalog Number	Title	Type	Country	Year	Longbox Value / Value
Image	ID7259VW	Lou Rawls Show, The	LD	U.S.		$30.00

Singles

Label	Catalog Number	Title	Type	Country	Year	Longbox Value / Value
Manhattan	DPRO-79700	A Lover's Question	CDJ	U.S.	1993	$2.00
EMI	203675-2	At Last	CD5	Germany	1990	$10.00
CBS	CDBLUE-7	At Last	CD5	U.K.	1990	$10.00
Blue Note	DPRO-79816	At Last	CDJ	U.S.	1990	$3.00
Blue Note	DPRO-79671	Don't Let Me Be Understood	CDJ	U.S.	1990	$3.00
EMI	203507-3	Fine Brown Flame	CD3	Germany	1990	$10.00
Blue Note	DPRO-79316	It's Supposed to Be Fun	CDJ	U.S.	1990	$3.00
EMI	TODP-2211	Love Me Tender	CD3	Japan	1990	$12.00/$4.00

Ray, James

Singles

Label	Catalog Number	Title	Type	Country	Year	Longbox Value / Value
Apt	MRAY-11CD	Dust Boat	CD5	U.K.	1989	$8.00
SPV	8670-3	Without Conscience	CD5	Germany	1990	$8.00
Apt	MRAY-101CD	Without Conscience	CD5	U.K.	1990	$8.00

Raye, Collin

Full Length

Label	Catalog Number	Title	Type	Country	Year	Longbox Value / Value
		'90s Country	RS	U.S.	1995	$35.00

Airdate: 7/29/95.

Label	Catalog Number	Title	Type	Country	Year	Longbox Value / Value
		Country Concert	RS	U.S.	1995	$55.00

2 CD set. Airdate: 8/27/95.

Label	Catalog Number	Title	Type	Country	Year	Longbox Value / Value
		Road, The	RS	U.S.	1995	$70.00

2 CD set. Airdate: 10/27/95.

Singles

Label	Catalog Number	Title	Type	Country	Year	Longbox Value / Value
Epic	ESK-74242	Every Second	CDJ	U.S.	1992	$2.00
Epic	ESK-77436	Little Rock	CDJ	U.S.	1994	$2.00

RBX

Singles

Label	Catalog Number	Title	Type	Country	Year	Longbox Value / Value
	PRO-CD-7764-R	A.W.O.L.	CDJ	U.S.		$2.00
Warner Brothers	17755	Rough is the Texture	CD5	U.S.	1995	$5.00

Rea, Chris

Full Length

Label	Catalog Number	Title	Type	Country	Year	Longbox Value / Value
Atco	PRCD 4147-2	Chris Rea Interview Summer 1991	DJ/Intvw	U.S.	1991	$8.00
Motown	6245	Dancing With the Stranger	LP/BP	U.S.	1988	$22.00/$18.00
Geffen	2 24276-Dj	Road to Hell, The	DJ/LP	U.S.	1989	$10.00

Singles

Label	Catalog Number	Title	Type	Country	Year	Longbox Value / Value
Eastwest	9031-73438-2	Auberge	CD5	Germany	1991	$10.00
Eastwest	9031-74255-2	Auberge	CD5	Germany	1991	$10.00
Eastwest	WMC5-391	Auberge	CD3	Japan	1991	$12.00/$4.00
Eastwest	YZ-555CD	Auberge	CD5	U.K.	1991	$10.00
Atco	PRCD 3839-2	Auberge	CDJ	U.S.	1991	$2.00
WEA	247238-2	Driving Home for Christmas	CD3	Germany	1988	$10.00
WEA	YZ-325CD	Driving Home for Christmas	CD3	U.K.	1988	$10.00
Atco		Fool If You Think It's Over	CDJ	U.S.		$6.00
Eastwest	9031-74231-2	Heaven	CD5	Germany	1991	$10.00
Eastwest	YZ-566CD	Heaven	CD5	U.K.	1991	$10.00
WEA	247549-2	I Can Hear Your Heartbeat	CD3	Germany	1988	$10.00
JVC	VDPS-1016	I Can Hear Your Heartbeat	CD3	Japan	1988	$12.00/$4.00
WEA	YZ-320CD	I Can Hear Your Heartbeat	CD3	U.K.	1988	$10.00
WEA	YZ-427	Josephine	CD5	U.K.	1989	$10.00
Magnet	CDMAG-314	Joys Of Christmas	CD5	U.K.	1990	$10.00
Eastwest	PECD 3839	Julia	CDJ	U.S.	1991	$3.00
Magnet	885888-2	Let's Dance	CD5	Germany	1988	$10.00
Magnet	CDMAG-299	Let's Dance	CD5	U.K.	1988	$10.00
Motown	PR 207MD	Let's Dance	CDJ	U.S.	1987	$10.00
Motown	PR207MD	Let's Dance	CDJ	U.S.	1988	$7.00
Eastwest	WMD5-4069	Looking for the Summer	CD3	Japan	1991	$12.00/$4.00
Eastwest	YZ-584CD	Looking for the Summer	CD5	U.K.	1991	$10.00
Eastwest	9031-74672-2	Looking for the Summer	CD5	U.K.	1991	$10.00
Atco	PRCD 3995-2	Looking for the Summer	CDJ	U.S.	1991	$2.00
Eastwest	AMCE-499	Nothing to Fear	CD3	Japan	1992	$12.00/$4.00
		Nothing to Fear	CD5	U.K.		$10.00
		Nothing to Fear	CD5	U.K.		$10.00

Second version.

Label	Catalog Number	Title	Type	Country	Year	Longbox Value / Value
Magnet	247787-2	On the Beach	CD3	Germany	1988	$10.00
Magnet	YZ-195CD	On the Beach	CD3	U.K.	1988	$10.00
Geffen	PRO-CD-3442	On the Beach	CDJ	U.S.	1988	$2.00
Magnet	887381-2	Que Sera	CD5	Germany	1989	$10.00
Magnet	CDMAG-318	Que Sera	CD5	U.K.	1989	$10.00
Magnet	246620-2	Road to Hell, The	CD3	Germany	1989	$10.00
Magnet	246583-2	Road to Hell, The	CD3	Germany	1989	$10.00
Magnet	YZ-431CD	Road to Hell, The	CD3	U.K.	1989	$10.00
Geffen	PRO-CD-3874	Road to Hell, The	CDJ	U.S.	1989	$2.00
		Soft Top, Hard Shoulder	CD5	U.K.		$10.00
		Soft Top, Hard Shoulder	CD5	U.K.		$10.00

Second version.

Label	Catalog Number	Title	Type	Country	Year	Longbox Value / Value
WEA	171046-2	Tell Me There's a Heaven	CD5	Germany	1990	$10.00
WEA	171047-2	Tell Me There's a Heaven	CD5	Germany	1990	$10.00
WEA	YZ-455CD	Tell Me There's a Heaven	CD5	U.K.	1990	$10.00
WEA	2292-46513-2	Tell What They Always Say	CD5	Germany	1990	$10.00
WEA	2292-46500-2	Tell What They Always Say	CD5	Germany	1990	$10.00
WEA	YZ-448CD	Tell What They Always Say	CD5	U.K.	1990	$10.00
Eastwest	YZ-468CD	Texas	CD5	U.K.	1990	$10.00
Geffen	PRO-CD-4110	Texas	CDJ	U.S.	1990	$2.00
		Too Much Pride	CD5	U.K.		$10.00
Eastwest	9031-75662-2	Winter Song	CD5	Germany	1992	$10.00
Eastwest	247137-2	Working on It	CD3	Germany	1992	$10.00
Warner Brothers	YZ-350CD	Working on It	CD5	U.K.	1988	$10.00
Geffen	PRO-CD-3404	Working on It	CDJ	U.S.	1988	$2.00

Reach

Singles

Label	Catalog Number	Title	Type	Country	Year	Longbox Value / Value
Eternal	YZ-601CD	Sooner or Later	CD5	U.K.	1991	$8.00
Eastwest	YZ-562CD	That's the Way Life Is	CD5	U.K.	1991	$8.00

Reader, Eddi

Singles

Label	Catalog Number	Title	Type	Country	Year	Longbox Value / Value
RCA	45018-2	What You Do When You've	CD5	U.K.	1992	$8.00

Reakwon

Singles

Label	Catalog Number	Title	Type	Country	Year	Longbox Value / Value
RCA	64426	Ice Cream	CD5	U.S.	1995	$5.00

Real Life

Singles

Label	Catalog Number	Title	Type	Country	Year	Longbox Value / Value
Curb	CD45 79014	God Tonight	CDJ	U.S.	1990	$2.00
Curb	026	Kiss the Ground	CDJ	U.S.	1990	$2.00
Intercord	827 720	Send Me an Angel	CD5	Germany	1988	$8.00
Curb	ZD-42962	Send Me an Angel	CD5	U.K.	1989	$8.00

Real McCoy

Singles

Label	Catalog Number	Title	Type	Country	Year	Longbox Value / Value
Arista	12724	Another Night	CD5	U.S.	1994	$5.00
Arista	12877	Automatic Lover	CD5	U.S.	1995	$5.00
Arista	ASCD 2834	Come & Get Your Love	CDJ	U.S.		$2.00
Arista	12809	Run Away	CD5	U.S.	1994	$5.00
Arista	ASCD 2964	Sleeping With an Angel	CDJ	U.S.		$2.00

Real People

Singles

Label	Catalog Number	Title	Type	Country	Year	Longbox Value / Value
Columbia	656612-2	Open Up Your Mind	CD5	U.K.	1990	$8.00
Columbia	656787-2	Truth	CD5	U.K.	1991	$8.00
Columbia	657698-2	Truth	CD5	U.K.	1992	$8.00
Sony	ESCA-5249	Window Plane	CD5	Japan	1992	$13.00

Real Seduction

Singles

Label	Catalog Number	Title	Type	Country	Year	Longbox Value / Value
Atlantic	PRCD 5191-2	Ain't Nothin Wrong	CDJ	U.S.	1993	$2.00

Real Thing

Singles

Label	Catalog Number	Title	Type	Country	Year	Longbox Value / Value
BMG	162068	Crime of Love	CD3	Germany	1989	$8.00
BMG	662068	Crime of Love	CD5	Germany	1989	$8.00
RCA	PD-42848	Crime of Love	CD5	U.K.	1989	$8.00

RealHot Jazz

Full Length

Label	Catalog Number	Title	Type	Country	Year	Longbox Value / Value
RealTime	RT-2002	(No name)	LP/LB	U.S.†	1985	$14.00/$8.00

Reality

Singles

Label	Catalog Number	Title	Type	Country	Year	Longbox Value / Value
Strictly Rhythm	12291	Wanna Get Busy	CD5	U.S.	1994	$5.00
Zyx	161	Yolanda	CD5	U.S.	1994	$5.00

Rebel Heels

Singles

Label	Catalog Number	Title	Type	Country	Year	Longbox Value / Value
		Break the Chain	CDJ	U.S.		$2.00
		Empty Love	CDJ	U.S.		$2.00
		In Hot Pursuit	CDJ	U.S.		$2.00

Rebel MC

Singles

Label	Catalog Number	Title	Type	Country	Year	Longbox Value / Value
Polygram	877285-2	Better World	CD5	Germany	1990	$8.00
Desire	WANCD-25	Better World	CD5	U.K.	1990	$8.00
Desire	WANCD-47	Black Meaning Good	CD5	U.K.	1991	$8.00
Polygram	879139-2	Culture	CD5	Germany	1990	$8.00
Desire	WANCD-38	Culture	CD5	U.K.	1990	$8.00
Polygram	877381-2	Rebel Music	CD5	Germany	1990	$8.00
Desire	WANCD-31	Rebel Music	CD5	U.K.	1990	$8.00
		Rebel Music	CDJ	U.S.	1990	$2.00
Desire	WANCD-44	Tribal Base	CD5	U.K.	1991	$8.00
Desire	WANCD-40	Wickedest Sound	CD5	U.K.	1991	$8.00

Rebel Pebbles

Singles

Label	Catalog Number	Title	Type	Country	Year	Longbox Value / Value
IRS	67054	Dream Lover	CDJ	U.S.	1991	$2.00
IRS	67063	How Do You Feel	CDJ	U.S.	1991	$2.00

Reckless Sleepers

Full Length

Label	Catalog Number	Title	Type	Country	Year	Longbox Value / Value
IRS		Big Boss Sounds	LP/LB	U.S.		$14.00/$8.00

Singles

Label	Catalog Number	Title	Type	Country	Year	Longbox Value / Value
IRS	17638	If We Never Meet Again	CDJ	U.S.	1988	$2.00

Label	Catalog Number	Title	Type	Country	Year	Longbox Value / Value
		Meet Jules Shears	CDJ	U.S.		$2.00

Recoil

Full Length

Label	Catalog Number	Title	Type	Country	Year	Longbox Value / Value
Sire		Bloodline	LP/LB	U.S.		$14.00/$8.00
Sire		Hydrology	LP/LB	U.S.		$14.00/$8.00

Singles

Label	Catalog Number	Title	Type	Country	Year	Longbox Value / Value
Mute	826 996	Faith Healer	CD5	Germany	1992	$8.00
Mute	CDMUTE-110	Faith Healer	CD5	U.K.	1992	$8.00
Sire	9 40345-2	Faith Healer	CD5	U.S.	1992	$4.00

Red

Singles

Label	Catalog Number	Title	Type	Country	Year	Longbox Value / Value
Forest	91353	Redder	CD5	U.S.	1993	$4.00

Red Box

Singles

Label	Catalog Number	Title	Type	Country	Year	Longbox Value / Value
WEA	YZ-531CD	Train	CD5	U.K.	1990	$8.00

Red Flag

Singles

Label	Catalog Number	Title	Type	Country	Year	Longbox Value / Value
Capitol	C2 13863	Machine	CD5	U.S.	1992	$3.00
		Russian Radio	CDJ	U.S.		$2.00

Red Hot Chili Peppers

Full Length

Label	Catalog Number	Title	Type	Country	Year	Longbox Value / Value
Warner Brothers	9 26681-2-Dj	Blood Sugar Sex Magik	DJ/LP	U.S.	1991	$20.00
Warner Brothers	PRO-CD-5170	Blood Sugar Sex Magik Sanitized	DJ/LP	U.S.	1991	$15.00
		Live From the Pit	RS	U.S.	1996	$65.00
2 CD set. Airdate: 5/26/96.						
Westwood One		Off the Record	RS	U.S.	1996	$25.00
Airdate: 2/5/96.						
Warner Brothers	9 45733-2-DJ	One Hot Minute	DJ/LP	U.S.	1995	$20.00
CD with multi-image jewel box cover.						
Warner Brothers		Plasma Shaft	LTD/LP	U.K.	1994	$35.00
2 CD set. CD of "Blood Sugar Sex.." plus extra disc of alternate tracks.						
EMI		Sock-Cess	DJ/Smplr	U.K.		$30.00
Media America		Up Close	RS	U.S.	1995	$40.00
EMI	DPRO-31492	Uplift Mofo Party Plan Sampler	DJ/Smplr	U.S.	1987	$20.00
Warner Brothers	RHCD1	What Promo Hits	DJ/Smplr	U.S.	1994	$18.00

Singles

Label	Catalog Number	Title	Type	Country	Year	Longbox Value / Value
Warner Brothers	PRO-CD-8018	Aeroplane	CDJ	U.S.	1995	$3.00
EMI	DPRO-04894	Behind the Sun	CDJ	U.S.	1992	$3.00
Warner Brothers	W-0126CDX	Breaking the Girl	CD5	U.K.	1992	$10.00
Warner Brothers		Breaking the Girl	CD5	U.S.	1991	$5.00
Warner Brothers	PRO-CD-5274	Breaking the Girl	CDJ	U.S.	1991	$2.00
WEA	CD-40261	Give It Away	CD5	Canada	1991	$10.00
WEA	9362-40206-2	Give It Away	CD5	Germany	1991	$10.00
Warner Brothers	WPCP-4750	Give It Away	CD5	Japan	1991	$15.00
		Give It Away	CD5	U.K.		$10.00
		Give It Away	CD5	U.K.		$10.00
Second version.						
Warner Brothers	40261-2	Give It Away	CD5	U.S.	1991	$5.00
Warner Brothers	PRO-CD-5042	Give It Away	CDJ	U.S.	1991	$6.00
Warner Brothers	PRO-CD-5048	Give It Away	CDJ	U.S.	1991	$6.00
EMI	203747-2	Higher Ground	CD5	Germany	1989	$10.00
EMI	CDMT-75	Higher Ground	CD5	U.K.	1989	$10.00
EMI	CDMT-88	Higher Ground	CD5	U.K.	1990	$10.00
EMI	DPRO 04389	Higher Ground	CDJ	U.S.	1989	$6.00
EMI	203476-3	Knock Me Down	CD3	Germany	1989	$10.00
EMI	CDMT-70	Knock Me Down	CD5	U.K.	1989	$10.00
EMI	DPRO 04380	Knock Me Down	CDJ	U.S.	1989	$3.00
Warner Brothers	PRO-CD-7807	My Friends	CDJ	U.S.	1995	$3.00
		Shallow Be Thy Game	CDJ	U.K.	1996	$10.00
EMI	DPRO-04513	Show Me Your Soul	CDJ	U.S.		$3.00
Warner Brothers	18401	Soul to Squeeze	CD5	U.S.	1993	$6.00
Warner Brothers	PRO-CD-6393	Soul to Squeeze	CDJ	U.S.	1993	$6.00
Warner Brothers	PRO-CD-5234	Suck My Kiss	CDJ	U.S.		$3.00
EMI	CDMT-85	Taste the Pain	CD5	U.K.	1990	$10.00
EMI	DPRO 07502	Taste the Pain	CDJ	U.S.	1989	$6.00
EMI	C2 50285	Taste the Pain	CD5	U.S.	1990	$5.00
EMI	DPRO 04507	Taste the Pain	CDJ	U.S.	1990	$6.00
Warner Brothers	W-0084CD	Under the Bridge	CD5	U.K.	1991	$10.00
Warner Brothers		Under the Bridge	CD5	U.K.	1991	$10.00
Second version.						
Warner Brothers	PRO-CD-5255	Under the Bridge	CDJ	U.S.	1991	$7.00
Warner Brothers	PRO-CD-7800	Warped	CDJ	U.S.	1995	$3.00

Red House

Singles

Label	Catalog Number	Title	Type	Country	Year	Longbox Value / Value
SBK	DPRO-05343	I Said a Prayer	CDJ	U.S.	1990	$2.00

Red House Painters

Full Length

Label	Catalog Number	Title	Type	Country	Year	Longbox Value / Value
4AD		Ocean Beach	DJ/LP	U.S.	1992	$15.00

Singles

Label	Catalog Number	Title	Type	Country	Year	Longbox Value / Value
4AD	CAD 2014	Down Colorful Hill	CD5	U.K.	1992	$9.00
4AD	45062	Down Colorful Hill	CD5	U.S.	1992	$5.00
4AD	PRO-CD-6108	Mistress	CDJ	U.S.	1992	$2.00
4AD	PRO-CD-7474	Summer Dress	CDJ	U.S.	1992	$3.00
4AD	PRO-CD-7800	Warped	CDJ	U.S.	1995	$3.00

Red Monster

Singles

Label	Catalog Number	Title	Type	Country	Year	Longbox Value / Value
Epic	ESDA-7017	Just Like Magic	CD3	Japan	1990	$12.00/$3.00

Red on Green

Full Length

Label	Catalog Number	Title	Type	Country	Year	Longbox Value / Value
		Gas Food Lodging	LP/LB	U.S.		$14.00/$10.00

Red Red Meat

Singles

Label	Catalog Number	Title	Type	Country	Year	Longbox Value / Value
Sub Pop	SUBPROCD 44	Chain Chain Chain	CDJ	U.S.		$3.00

Red Siren

Singles

Label	Catalog Number	Title	Type	Country	Year	Longbox Value / Value
Mercury	CDP 67	One Good Lover	CDJ	U.S.	1989	$2.00

Red Snaper

Singles

Label	Catalog Number	Title	Type	Country	Year	Longbox Value / Value
ZYX	6458-8	Keep It Up	CD5	Germany	1991	$6.00

Red Thunder

Singles

Label	Catalog Number	Title	Type	Country	Year	Longbox Value / Value
	1031	Red Thunder	CD5	U.S.	1994	$5.00

Redbelly

Singles

Label	Catalog Number	Title	Type	Country	Year	Longbox Value / Value
	PRCD 9213-2	Fire in the Hole	CDJ	U.S.	1995	$2.00
	PRCD 9400-2	Scraps	CDJ	U.S.	1995	$3.00

Redbone

Singles

Label	Catalog Number	Title	Type	Country	Year	Longbox Value / Value
Pioneer	PIFP1013	Witch Queen	CDV	Japan	1993	$20.00

Redd, Freddie

Full Length

Label	Catalog Number	Title	Type	Country	Year	Longbox Value / Value
Mosaic	MD2-124	Complete Blue Note Recordings	LP	U.S.		$30.00
2CD set.						

Redd, Jeff

Singles

Label	Catalog Number	Title	Type	Country	Year	Longbox Value / Value
Uptown	18214	I Found Lovin'	CDJ	U.S.	1989	$2.00
Uptown	1597	You Called & Told Me	CDJ	U.S.	1991	$2.00

Redd Kross

Singles

Label	Catalog Number	Title	Type	Country	Year	Longbox Value / Value
Atlantic	PRCD 3734-2	1976	CDJ	U.S.	1990	$2.00
Atlantic	PRCD 3565-2	Annie's Gone	CDJ	U.S.		$2.00
		Jimmy's Fantasy	CD5	Australia	1993	$10.00
		Jimmy's Fantasy	CD5	U.K.	1993	$8.00
		Lady in Front Row	CD5	Australia	1993	$10.00
		Lady in Front Row	CD5	U.K.	1993	$8.00
WEA	TWANG-14	Trance	CD5	U.K.	1992	$8.00
This Way Up	4228587452	Visionary	CD5	Canada	1994	$8.00

Redding, Otis

Full Length

Label	Catalog Number	Title	Type	Country	Year	Longbox Value / Value
Rhino		Definitive Otis Redding Sampler	DJ/Smplr	U.S.	1993	$25.00

Singles

Label	Catalog Number	Title	Type	Country	Year	Longbox Value / Value
WEA	786493-2	Dock of the Bay	CD3	Germany	1989	$10.00
Pioneer	10P3-6050	Dock of the Bay	CD3	Japan	1988	$12.00/$4.00
Atlantic	AMDY-5098	Dock of the Bay	CD3	Japan	1988	$12.00/$4.00
WEA	786493-2	Dock of the Bay	CD3	U.K.	1989	$10.00
WEA	786492-2	Satisfaction	CD3	Germany	1989	$10.00
WEA	786492-2	Satisfaction	CD3	U.K.	1989	$10.00

Reddington, Amanda

Singles

Label	Catalog Number	Title	Type	Country	Year	Longbox Value / Value
RCA	PD-429808	Fatal Attraction	CD5	U.K.	1989	$8.00

Redhead Kingpin & FBI

Singles

Label	Catalog Number	Title	Type	Country	Year	Longbox Value / Value
BMG	162427	Do the Right Thing	CD3	Germany	1989	$8.00
Virgin	TENCD-271	Do the Right Thing	CD3	U.K.	1989	$8.00
Virgin	TENCD-399	Do the Right Thing	CD3	U.K.	1992	$8.00
Virgin		Do the Right Thing	CDJ	U.S.	1989	$2.00
Virgin		Do the Right Thing	CDJ	U.S.	1989	$2.00
Second version.						
Virgin	TENCD-361	Get It Together	CD5	U.K.	1991	$8.00
Virgin	PR 3724	Get It Together	CDJ	U.S.	1991	$2.00
BMG	662636	I Want the Man	CD5	Germany	1989	$8.00
BMG	662639	I Want the Man	CD5	Germany	1989	$8.00
Virgin	TENCD-367	It's a Love Thang	CD5	U.K.	1991	$8.00
Virgin	PRCD 3952	It's a Love Thang	CDJ	U.S.	1991	$2.00
Virgin	2928	Look Who's Dancing	CDJ	U.S.	1989	$2.00
Virgin		Pump It Hottie	CDJ	U.S.		$2.00
BMG	885614	Superbad Superclick	CD5	Germany	1989	$8.00
Virgin	TENCD-286	Superbad Superclick	CD5	U.K.	1989	$8.00
Virgin	PRCD 3725	We Don't Have a Plan B	CDJ	U.S.	1990	$2.00
Virgin	TENCD-301	We Rock the Mic Tonight	CD5	U.K.	1990	$8.00
Virgin	PR 3725	We Rock the Mic Tonight	CDJ	U.S.	1990	$2.00

Redman

Singles

Label	Catalog Number	Title	Type	Country	Year	Longbox Value / Value
	PRCD 6910-2	Can't Wait	CDJ	U.S.	1995	$2.00
		How High	CDJ	U.S.	1995	$2.00

Redman and The Method Man

Singles

Label	Catalog Number	Title	Type	Country	Year	Longbox Value / Value
Polygram	579925	How High	CD5	U.S.	1995	$6.00

Rednex

Singles

Label	Catalog Number	Title	Type	Country	Year	Longbox Value / Value
Jive	46500	Cotton Eyed Joe	CD5	U.S.	1994	$5.00
Battery		Cotton Eyed Joe	CD5	U.S.	1995	$7.00
Battery		Cotton Eyed Joe	CDJ	U.S.	1995	$3.00

Reed, Dan Network

Full Length

Label	Catalog Number	Title	Type	Country	Year	Longbox Value / Value
Mercury		Excerpts From Slam	DJ/Smplr	U.S.		$5.00

Singles

Label	Catalog Number	Title	Type	Country	Year	Longbox Value / Value
Mercury	MERCD-352	Baby Now I	CD5	U.K.	1991	$9.00
Mercury	DRNCD-2	Come Back Baby	CD5	U.K.	1990	$9.00
Mercury	872275-2	Get to You	CD5	Germany	1988	$9.00
Mercury	MERCD-269	Get to You	CD5	U.K.	1988	$9.00
Mercury	870 730-2	Get to You	CDV/BP	U.S.	1988	$20.00/$20.00
Mercury	CDP 587	Long Way to Go	CDJ	U.S.	1991	$2.00
Mercury	DRNCD-5	Lover	CD5	U.K.	1990	$9.00
Mercury	CDP 117	Make It Easy	CDJ	U.S.	1989	$2.00
Mercury	868509-2	Mix It Up	CD5	Germany	1991	$9.00
Mercury	MERCD-345	Mix It Up	CD5	U.K.	1991	$9.00
Mercury	CDP 493	Mix It Up	CDJ	U.S.	1991	$2.00
Mercury	876989-2	Rainbow Child	CD5	Germany	1990	$9.00
Mercury	DRNCD-3	Rainbow Child	CD5	U.K.	1990	$9.00
Mercury	870183-2	Ritual	CD5	Germany	1988	$9.00
Mercury	DRNCD-4	Sardate 1990	CD5	U.K.	1990	$9.00
Mercury	876121-2	Tiger in a Dress	CD5	Germany	1989	$9.00
Mercury	DRNCD-1	Tiger in a Dress	CD5	U.K.	1989	$9.00
Mercury	CDP133	Tiger in a Dress	CDJ	U.S.	1989	$2.00

Reed, Lou

Full Length

Label	Catalog Number	Title	Type	Country	Year	Longbox Value / Value
Pioneer	PA-85-114	A Night With Lou Reed	LD	U.S.	1984	$35.00
Pioneer	PA-85-114	A Night With Lou Reed	LD	U.S.	1991	$35.00
Digital audio.						
Sire	PRO-CD-3358	A Rock & Roll Life	DJ/Smplr	U.S.	1989	$45.00
2 CD set.						
RCA		Berlin	LP/BP	U.S.		$15.00/$10.00
RCA		Between Thought and Expression	DJ/Smplr	Germany	1992	$35.00
RCA		Coney Island Baby	LP/BP	U.S.		$15.00/$10.00
Album Network		In the Studio (Rock 'n Roll Animal)	RS	U.S.	1989	$25.00
Airdate: 6/5/89.						

Reed, Lou – Selections from Between Thought and Expression (RCA RDJ 62284-2)

Label	Catalog Number	Title	Type	Country	Year	Longbox Value / Value
DIR		King Biscuit Flour Hour	RS	U.S.	1989	$40.00
	Airdate: 7/9/89.					
DIR		King Biscuit Flour Hour	RS	U.S.	1990	$30.00
	With Talking Heads, Airdate: 5/28/90.					
DIR		King Biscuit Flour Hour	RS	U.S.	1992	$40.00
	Airdate: 3/7/92.					
RCA		Legendary Hearts	LP/BP	U.S.		$14.00/$8.00
Sire	9 26662-2-PR	Magic and Loss	DJ/LP	U.S.	1991	$15.00
	Advance Issue.					
Sire		Magic and Loss	DJ/LP	U.S.	1992	$150.00
	Promo CD in metal case.					
WEA	38313	Magic and Loss	LD	U.S.	1992	$35.00
RCA		Mistrial	LP/BP	U.S.		$14.00/$8.00
RCA	4998	New Sensation	LP/BP	U.S.		$14.00/$8.00
RCA		Sally Can't Dance	LP/BP	U.S.		$14.00/$8.00
RCA	RDJ 62284-2	Selections From Between Thought and Expression	DJ/Smplr	U.S.	1992	$15.00
RCA	PCD1-4807	Transformer	LP/BP	U.S.†	1984	$15.00/$9.00
RCA	66000	Transformer	LTD/LP	U.S.	1995	$28.00
	Gold disc.					

Singles

Label	Catalog Number	Title	Type	Country	Year	Longbox Value / Value
Sire		Adventurer	CDJ	U.S.	1996	$3.00
Sire	PRO-CD-3510	Busload of Faith	CDJ	U.S.	1989	$3.00
Warner Brothers	921164-2	Dirty Boulavard	CD3	Germany	1988	$10.00
Warner Brothers	W-7547CD	Dirty Boulavard	CD3	U.K.	1988	$10.00
Sire	PRO-CD-3359	Dirty Boulavard	CDJ	U.S.	1988	$3.00
		Hooky Wooky	CDJ	U.K.		$15.00
Great Exp.	PIP CD023	Metal Machine Music	CD5	France		$15.00
Sire	PRO-CD-5454	Power and Glory	CDJ	U.S.	1992	$7.00
Sire	PRO-CD-3619	Romeo Had Juliette	CDJ	U.S.	1989	$3.00
		Tarbelly and Leatherfoot	CDJ	U.S.		$3.00
RCA	PD-49453	Walk on the Wild Side	CD3	Germany	1989	$10.00
RCA	PD-49453	Walk on the Wild Side	CD3	U.K.	1989	$10.00
RCA	8986-2-RH	Walk on the Wild Side	CD5	U.S.	1989	$10.00
	Juke box release.					
Sire	W-0090CD	What's Good	CD5	U.K.	1992	$10.00
Sire	PRO-CD-4988	What's Good	CDJ	U.S.	1992	$2.00
		Why Can't I Be Good	CD5	Australia	1993	$12.00

Reed, Lou and John Cale

Full Length

Label	Catalog Number	Title	Type	Country	Year	Longbox Value / Value
Sire/Warner Bros.	26205-2	Songs for Drella	LTD/LP	U.S.	1990	$13.00
Lumivision	LVD9225	Songs for Drella	LD	U.S.	1992	$30.00

Singles

Label	Catalog Number	Title	Type	Country	Year	Longbox Value / Value
WEA	921555-2	Nobody But You	CD5	Germany	1990	$9.00
Sire/Warner Bros.	PRO-CD-4056	Nobody But You	CDJ	U.S.	1990	$2.00

Reef

Singles

Label	Catalog Number	Title	Type	Country	Year	Longbox Value / Value
Epic	ESK 7610	Naked	CDJ	U.S.		$2.00

Reel 2 Real

Singles

Label	Catalog Number	Title	Type	Country	Year	Longbox Value / Value
Strictly Rhythm	12192	I Like to Move It	CD5	U.S.	1994	$5.00

Reese, Della

Full Length

Label	Catalog Number	Title	Type	Country	Year	Longbox Value / Value
RCA		Cha Cha Cha	LTD/LP	Germany	1994	$30.00

Reeves, Dianne

Full Length

Label	Catalog Number	Title	Type	Country	Year	Longbox Value / Value
EMI		Never Too Far	DJ/LP	U.S.	1989	$8.00

Singles

Label	Catalog Number	Title	Type	Country	Year	Longbox Value / Value
Blue Note	DPRO-79687	Afro Blue	CDJ	U.S.	1991	$3.00
EMI	CDMT-82	Never Too Far	CD5	U.K.	1990	$8.00
EMI	DPRO 04451	Never Too Far	CDJ	U.S.	1989	$2.00

Reeves, Martha

Singles

Label	Catalog Number	Title	Type	Country	Year	Longbox Value / Value
Motown	TMGCD 1418	Dancing in the Street	CD5	U.K.		$7.00
MCA	1445	Wild Night	CDJ	U.S.	1991	$2.00

Reeves, Ronna

Singles

Label	Catalog Number	Title	Type	Country	Year	Longbox Value / Value
River North Records	51416 4564 2	My Heart Wasn't in It	SCDJ	U.S.	1996	$15.00
	First U.S. made promotional shaped CD.					
Mercury	CDP 231	Sadly Mistaken	CDJ	U.S.	1990	$2.00
Mercury	CDP 778	We Can Hold Our Own	CDJ	U.S.	1992	$2.00

Reeves, Vic

Singles

Label	Catalog Number	Title	Type	Country	Year	Longbox Value / Value
		I'm A Believer	CD5	U.K.	1995	$10.00

Reflex

Singles

Label	Catalog Number	Title	Type	Country	Year	Longbox Value / Value
Capitol	DPRO 9122	Hurt	CDJ	U.S.	1983	$2.00

Refreshments

Singles

Label	Catalog Number	Title	Type	Country	Year	Longbox Value / Value
Mercury	CDP1544	Banditos	CDJ	U.S.		$2.00

Reggie Rough

Singles

Label	Catalog Number	Title	Type	Country	Year	Longbox Value / Value
	6211	Just Can't Take It	CD5	U.S.	1994	$5.00

Reggy O.

Singles

Label	Catalog Number	Title	Type	Country	Year	Longbox Value / Value
ZYX	7156	Let the Music Play	CD5	U.S.	1994	$5.00
Zyx	7553	Move My Body	CD5	U.S.	1994	$5.00

Regulators

Full Length

Label	Catalog Number	Title	Type	Country	Year	Longbox Value / Value
Polygram	511063-2	Regulators, The	LP/BP	U.S.		$12.00/$7.00

Rehenes, Los

Singles

Label	Catalog Number	Title	Type	Country	Year	Longbox Value / Value
	5314	Porque Estas Enamor	CD5	U.S.	1994	$5.00

Reid, Mike

Full Length

Label	Catalog Number	Title	Type	Country	Year	Longbox Value / Value
		Country Star Tracks	RS	U.S.	1991	$15.00
	Airdate: 9/14/91.					

Reid, Paul

Singles

Label	Catalog Number	Title	Type	Country	Year	Longbox Value / Value
CBS	659070-2	Diamond	CD5	U.K.	1993	$8.00
CBS	658152-2	Under the Love of God	CD5	U.K.	1993	$8.00

Reid, Terry

Full Length

Label	Catalog Number	Title	Type	Country	Year	Longbox Value / Value
Warner Brothers		Driver, The	LP/LB	U.S.		$14.00/$8.00

Singles

Label	Catalog Number	Title	Type	Country	Year	Longbox Value / Value
Warner Brothers	YZ-579CD	Fifth of July	CD5	U.K.	1991	$8.00
Warner Brothers	PRO-CD-5410	If You Let Her	CDJ	U.S.	1991	$2.00
Warner Brothers	YZ-620CD	Right to the End	CD5	U.K.	1991	$8.00
Warner Brothers	PRO-CD-5566	Whole of the Moon, The	CDJ	U.S.	1991	$2.00

Reilly, Bret

Singles

Label	Catalog Number	Title	Type	Country	Year	Longbox Value / Value
RCA	RDJ64326-2	Too Much of a Good Thing	CDJ	U.S.		$2.00

Reiner, Carl and Mel Brooks

Full Length

Label	Catalog Number	Title	Type	Country	Year	Longbox Value / Value
Rhino	PRCD 7056	Excerpts From the Complete 2,000 Year Old Man	DJ/Smplr	U.S.	1994	$25.00

Reinhardt, Djang

Singles

Label	Catalog Number	Title	Type	Country	Year	Longbox Value / Value
	41050	Gypsy Jazz	CD5	U.S.	1994	$5.00
	41050	Gypsy Jazz	CD5	U.S.	1994	$5.00

Rembrants

Full Length

Label	Catalog Number	Title	Type	Country	Year	Longbox Value / Value
Atlantic		Four Masterworks	DJ/Smplr	U.S.	1995	$7.00
Eastwest	61752-2	L.P.	DJ/LP	U.S.	1995	$16.00
	CD in album package.					
Atco	91412-2	Rembrants	DJ/LP	U.S.	1990	$12.00
	CD in cardboard picture frame.					

Singles

Label	Catalog Number	Title	Type	Country	Year	Longbox Value / Value
Atco	PRCD 3748-2	Burning Timber	CDJ	U.S.	1991	$2.00
Atco	PRCD 5068-2	Chase the Clouds Away	CDJ	U.S.	1993	$2.00
Atco	PRCD 5069-2	Chase the Clouds Away	CDJ	U.S.	1993	$2.00
Atco		Comin' Home	CDJ	U.S.	1995	$7.00
		Don't Hide Your Love	CD5	U.K.	1995	$10.00
Atlantic	PRCD 9421-2	Drowning In Your Tears	CDJ	U.S.	1995	$3.00
		I'll Be There For You	CD5	U.K.	1995	$10.00
Elektra	64428	I'll Be There For You	CD5	U.S.	1995	$6.00
Eastwest		I'll Be There For You	CDJ	U.S.	1995	$7.00
Atco	98504-2	Johnny Have You Seen Her	CD5	U.S.	1992	$5.00
Atco	PRCD-4728-2	Johnny Have You Seen Her	CDJ	U.S.	1992	$2.00
Atco	7567-96371-2	Just the Way It Is	CD5	Germany	1991	$9.00
Atco	B-8741CD	Just the Way It Is	CD5	U.K.	1991	$9.00
Atco	B-8840CD	Just the Way It Is	CD5	U.K.	1991	$9.00
Atco	PRCD 3532-2	Just the Way It Is	CDJ	U.S.	1990	$2.00
Atco	PRCD 4925-2	Maybe Tomorrow	CDJ	U.S.	1992	$2.00
Atco	7567-96278-2	Save Me	CD5	Germany	1991	$9.00
Atco	PRCD 3749-2	Save Me	CDJ	U.S.	1991	$2.00
Atco	7567-96333-2	Someone	CD5	Germany	1991	$9.00
Atco	PRCD 3498-2	Someone	CDJ	U.S.	1991	$2.00
Elektra	64384	This House Is not a Home	CD5	U.S.	1995	$5.00
Atco	PRCD 92792	This House Is not a Home	CDJ	U.S.	1995	$3.00

Remedy

Singles

Label	Catalog Number	Title	Type	Country	Year	Longbox Value / Value
Hollywood	PRCD 10316	Closer	CDJ	U.S.	1993	$2.00
Hollywood	PRCD 10353	Tiniest Grain of Sand	CDJ	U.S.	1993	$2.00

Ren & Stimpy

Full Length

Label	Catalog Number	Title	Type	Country	Year	Longbox Value / Value
Sony	LSK 5608	Little Crock o' Christmas	DJ/Smplr	U.S.	1993	$18.00
Sony	LXK 5473	Little Eediot	DJ/Smplr	U.S.	1993	$25.00
	2CD interview and sampler.					

Singles

Label	Catalog Number	Title	Type	Country	Year	Longbox Value / Value
Sony		Little Eediot	CD5	Australia	1994	$12.00

Rendon, Tony

Singles

Label	Catalog Number	Title	Type	Country	Year	Longbox Value / Value
Andrea Records	7030	Necesito Verte	CD5	U.S.	1994	$5.00

Rene & Angela

Full Length

Label	Catalog Number	Title	Type	Country	Year	Longbox Value / Value
Mercury	824607-2	Street Called Desire	LP/BP	U.S.†	1985	$14.00/$8.00

Renee, Nadine

Singles

Label	Catalog Number	Title	Type	Country	Year	Longbox Value / Value
	3007	Never Say No	CD5	U.S.	1994	$5.00

Renegade Soundwave

Singles

Label	Catalog Number	Title	Type	Country	Year	Longbox Value / Value
Mute	66589-2	Thunder	CD5	U.K.	1990	$8.00

Reno, Mike

Singles

Label	Catalog Number	Title	Type	Country	Year	Longbox Value / Value
Cypress	DPRO-17760	Whenever There's a Night	CDJ	U.S.	1989	$2.00

Rentals

Singles

Label	Catalog Number	Title	Type	Country	Year	Longbox Value / Value
	PRO-CD-7848	Friends of P.	CDJ	U.S.		$2.00

Label	Catalog Number	Title	Type	Country	Year	Longbox Value / Value
	PRO-CD-8058-R	Waiting	CDJ	U.S.		$2.00

Reo Speedwagon

Full Length

Label	Catalog Number	Title	Type	Country	Year	Longbox Value / Value
Epic	EK 45246	Earth, A Small Man, His Dog and a Chicken	DJ/LP	U.S.	1990	$14.00
		Advance issue.				
Epic	EK-36844	Hi Infidelity	LP/BP	U.S.†	1984	$14.00/$8.00
Album Network		In the Studio (Hi Fidelity)	RS	U.S.	1988	$25.00
		Airdate: 11/28/88.				
Album Network		In the Studio (Hi Fidelity)	RS	U.S.	1991	$20.00
		Airdate: 6/10/91.				
CBS	7061-80	Live	LD	U.S.	1983	$25.00
Media America		Up Close	RS	U.S.	1990	$30.00
		2 CD set.				
Epic	EK-39593	Wheels Are Turnin'	LP/LB	U.S.†	1985	$14.00/$8.00
Epic	EK-35082	You Can Tune a Piano, But You Can't Tuna Fish	LP/LB	U.S.†	1985	$14.00/$8.00

Singles

Label	Catalog Number	Title	Type	Country	Year	Longbox Value / Value
Epic	ESK 4186	All Heaven Broke Loose	CDJ	U.S.	1991	$2.00
Epic	ESK 73654	Halfway	CDJ	U.S.	1990	$2.00
Epic	108P-3029	Here With Me	CD3	Japan	1988	$12.00/$4.00
Epic	651646-2	Here With Me	CD5	U.K.	1988	$10.00
Epic	ESK 1139	Here With Me	CDJ	U.S.	1988	$2.00
Epic	ESK 2140	Live It Up	CDJ	U.S.	1990	$2.00
Epic	ESDA-7045	Love is a Rock	CD3	Japan	1990	$12.00/$4.00
Epic	ESK 73540	Love is a Rock	CDJ	U.S.	1990	$2.00
Epic	ESK 2270	You Won't See Me	CDJ	U.S.	1990	$2.00

Repercussions and Curtis Mayfield

Singles

Label	Catalog Number	Title	Type	Country	Year	Longbox Value / Value
Warner Brothers	PRO-CD-6771	Let's Do It Again	CDJ	U.S.	1994	$3.00

Replacements

Full Length

Label	Catalog Number	Title	Type	Country	Year	Longbox Value / Value
Sire	PRO-CD-4632	Don't Buy or Sell, It's Crap	DJ/Smplr	U.S.	1991	$25.00
Sire	PRO-CD-3633	Inconcerated	DJ/Smplr	U.S.	1989	$20.00

Singles

Label	Catalog Number	Title	Type	Country	Year	Longbox Value / Value
Sire	PRO-CD-3606	Achin' to Be	CDJ	U.S.	1989	$3.00
Sire	PRO-CD-3496	Back To Back	CDJ	U.S.	1989	$3.00
A&M	CD 17673	Cruella De Ville	CDJ	U.S.	1988	$3.00
Sire	PRO-CD-4574	Happy Town	CDJ	U.S.	1990	$3.00
Sire	PRO-CD-3419	I'll Be You	CDJ	U.S.	1989	$3.00
Sire	PRO-CD-4466	Merry Go Round	CDJ	U.S.	1990	$3.00
Sire	PRO-CD-4472	Someone to Take the Wheel	CDJ	U.S.	1990	$3.00
Sire	PRO-CD-4666	When It Began	CDJ	U.S.	1990	$3.00

Replicants

Singles

Label	Catalog Number	Title	Type	Country	Year	Longbox Value / Value
Zoo	ZP171912	Destination Unknown	CDJ	U.S.		$2.00

Republica

Singles

Label	Catalog Number	Title	Type	Country	Year	Longbox Value / Value
RCA	07863 64540-2	Ready to Go	CD5	U.S.	1996	$5.00
		Cool Disc.				
RCA		Ready to Go	CDJ	U.S.	1996	$3.00

Residents

Full Length

Label	Catalog Number	Title	Type	Country	Year	Longbox Value / Value
		Booger Breath	LP	U.S.		$10.00
Enigma		Cube-E in Holland	LP/LB	U.S.		$12.00/$7.00
BMG	76896-40006-2	Gingerbread Man	LP	U.S.	1995	$40.00
		CD-ROM				
Rykodisc		God in Three Persons	LP/LB	U.S.		$12.00/$7.00
		Uncle Willie's Highly Opinionated Guide to the Residents	Smplr	U.S.	1994	$23.00
		Book with sampler disc.				

Singles

Label	Catalog Number	Title	Type	Country	Year	Longbox Value / Value
Rykodisc	RCD3 1007	Holy Kiss of Flesh	CD3	U.S.		$6.00/$3.00

Restless Heart

Full Length

Label	Catalog Number	Title	Type	Country	Year	Longbox Value / Value
RCA	RDJ 62656-2	Big Iron Horses	DJ/Smplr	U.S.	1993	$5.00

Singles

Label	Catalog Number	Title	Type	Country	Year	Longbox Value / Value
RCA	RDJ-62389-2	Blame It on Love	CDJ	U.S.	1992	$2.00
RCA	RDJ-62150-2	Til I Loved You	CDJ	U.S.	1992	$2.00
RCA	RDJ-62334-2	When She Cries	CDJ	U.S.	1992	$2.00

Return to Forever

Full Length

Label	Catalog Number	Title	Type	Country	Year	Longbox Value / Value
Polygram	825206-2	Where Have I Known You Before	LP/LB	U.S.†	1985	$14.00/$8.00

Revenge

Singles

Label	Catalog Number	Title	Type	Country	Year	Longbox Value / Value
Factory	FACD-327	Gun World Porn	CD5	U.K.	1991	$10.00
Rough Trade	210 1315 3	Gun World Trade	CD5	Germany	1992	$10.00
Capitol	C2 15559 2	Pineapple Face	CD5	U.S.	1990	$3.00
Capitol	DPRO 79092	Pineapple Face	CDJ	U.S.	1990	$3.00
Factory	FACD-247	Seven Reasons	CD5	U.K.	1989	$10.00
Factory	COCY-7061	Slave	CD5	Japan	1990	$16.00
Factory	FACD-279	Slave	CD5	U.K.	1990	$10.00
Capitol	C2 15610 2	Slave	CDJ	U.S.	1990	$3.00

Reverend

Singles

Label	Catalog Number	Title	Type	Country	Year	Longbox Value / Value
Charisma	92149	Live	CD5	U.S.	1992	$5.00

Revolting Cocks

Singles

Label	Catalog Number	Title	Type	Country	Year	Longbox Value / Value
IRS	977 115	Beers, Steers, & Queers	CD5	Germany	1991	$8.00
Devotion	CDDVN-105	Beers, Steers, & Queers	CD5	U.K.	1991	$8.00
Wax Trax	WAX-9149CD	Beers, Steers, & Queers	CD5	U.K.	1991	$8.00
Wax Trax	9149	Beers, Steers, & Queers	CD5	U.S.	1991	$5.00
Teevee Tunes	8649	Beers, Steers & Queers	CD5	U.S.	1994	$5.00
Warner	12-41383	Crackin' Up	CD5	Canada	1994	$8.00
Warner Brothers	PRO-CD-6762	Crackin' Up	CDJ	U.S.	1994	$2.00
Warner Brothers	9 41088-2	Do Ya Think I'm Sexy	CD5	U.S.	1993	$6.00
Warner Brothers	PRO-CD-6517	Do Ya Think I'm Sexy	CDJ	U.S.	1993	$3.00
SPV	9167-3	Let's Get Physical	CD5	Germany	1990	$8.00
Wax Trax	WAX-9086CD	Let's Get Physical	CD5	U.K.	1990	$8.00
Wax Trax	9086	Let's Get Physical	CD5	U.S.	1990	$5.00
Teevee Tunes	8586	Let's Get Physical	CD5	U.S.	1994	$5.00
Teevee Tunes	7042	Stainless Steel	CD5	U.S.	1994	$5.00

Revolver

Singles

Label	Catalog Number	Title	Type	Country	Year	Longbox Value / Value
Hut	CD9	Crimson	CD5	U.S.	1991	$8.00

Rey

Singles

Label	Catalog Number	Title	Type	Country	Year	Longbox Value / Value
Chrysalis	DPRO-23648	Love Don't Come in a Minute	CDJ	U.S.	1990	$2.00

Reyne, James

Singles

Label	Catalog Number	Title	Type	Country	Year	Longbox Value / Value
		Fall of Rome	CDJ	U.S.		$2.00

Rhatigan, Suzanne

Full Length

Label	Catalog Number	Title	Type	Country	Year	Longbox Value / Value
Imago		To Hell With Love	DJ/LP	U.S.	1992	$45.00
		CD, Cassette, VHS video tape, press kit, in 12"x12" boxed set.				

Singles

Label	Catalog Number	Title	Type	Country	Year	Longbox Value / Value
Imago	28027	To Hell With Love	CDJ	U.S.	1992	$2.00
Imago	28035	To Hell With Love	CDJ	U.S.	1992	$2.00

Rhino Bucket

Singles

Label	Catalog Number	Title	Type	Country	Year	Longbox Value / Value
Reprise	PRO-CD5765	Beat to Death Like a Dog	CDJ	U.S.	1992	$2.00
Reprise	PRO-CD-4490	Blood on the Cross	CDJ	U.S.	1990	$2.00
Reprise	PRO-CD-4615	One Night Stand	CDJ	U.S.	1990	$2.00

Rhodes, Kim

Singles

Label	Catalog Number	Title	Type	Country	Year	Longbox Value / Value
	JR222012N1	I'm Not an Angel	CDJ	U.S.		$2.00

Rhodes, Lydia

Singles

Label	Catalog Number	Title	Type	Country	Year	Longbox Value / Value
MCA	DMCAT-1438	D.J. Give Me That Funky Bass	CD5	U.K.	1990	$8.00
		D.J. Give Me That Funky Bass	CDJ	U.S.	1990	$2.00

Rhodes, Sonny

Full Length

Label	Catalog Number	Title	Type	Country	Year	Longbox Value / Value
		House of Blues	RS	U.S.	1996	$40.00
		2 CD set. Airdate: 2/25/96.				

Rhyme Poetic Mafia

Singles

Label	Catalog Number	Title	Type	Country	Year	Longbox Value / Value
Giant	41031-2	Comin' Thru Your Neigborhood	CDJ	U.S.	1993	$6.00

Rhythm Corps

Singles

Label	Catalog Number	Title	Type	Country	Year	Longbox Value / Value
Pasha	1105	Common Ground	CDJ	U.S.	1988	$2.00
Pasha	2266	Satellites	CDJ	U.S.	1991	$2.00

Rhythm Method

Singles

Label	Catalog Number	Title	Type	Country	Year	Longbox Value / Value
Zyx	7404	Can You Give Me Love	CD5	U.S.	1994	$5.00

Rhythm Syndicate

Singles

Label	Catalog Number	Title	Type	Country	Year	Longbox Value / Value
Impact	2042	Blinded By You	CDJ	U.S.	1992	$2.00
SBK	TODP-2334	Hey Donna	CD3	Japan	1991	$13.00/$4.00
Impact	CDEM-213	Hey Donna	CD5	U.K.	1991	$9.00
EMI	745022-2	Hey Donna	CD5	U.K.	1991	$9.00
Impact	1579	Hey Donna	CDJ	U.S.	1991	$2.00
Impact	23151	I Wanna Make Love to You	CDJ	U.S.	1992	$2.00
EMI	745018-2	P.A.S.S.I.O.N.	CD5	Germany	1991	$9.00
EMI	745009-2	P.A.S.S.I.O.N.	CD5	Germany	1991	$9.00
EMI	745024-2	P.A.S.S.I.O.N.	CD5	Germany	1991	$9.00
EMI	TODP-2300	P.A.S.S.I.O.N.	CD3	Japan	1991	$13.00/$4.00
Impact	CDEM-2197	P.A.S.S.I.O.N.	CD5	U.K.	1991	$9.00
Impact	1416	P.A.S.S.I.O.N.	CDJ	U.S.	1991	$2.00

Rhythm Tribe

Full Length

Label	Catalog Number	Title	Type	Country	Year	Longbox Value / Value
Zoo	1101	Sol Moderno	LP/LB	U.S.		$12.00/$7.00

Singles

Label	Catalog Number	Title	Type	Country	Year	Longbox Value / Value
BMG	PD-49200	Gotta See Your Eyes	CD5	Germany	1991	$8.00
BMG	BVDP-35	Gotta See Your Eyes	CD3	Japan	1991	$13.00/$4.00
Zoo	ZP17001-2	Gotta See Your Eyes	CDJ	U.S.	1991	$2.00

Ricca

Singles

Label	Catalog Number	Title	Type	Country	Year	Longbox Value / Value
Epic	ESK 77216	Any Love	CDJ	U.S.	1993	$2.00

Rich, Buddy

Full Length

Label	Catalog Number	Title	Type	Country	Year	Longbox Value / Value
Pioneer	PA-85-132	Mr. Drum	LD	U.S.	1985	$30.00

Rich, Tony Project

Singles

Label	Catalog Number	Title	Type	Country	Year	Longbox Value / Value
LaFace	24116	Nobody Knows	CD5	U.S.	1995	$5.00
LaFace	LFPCD4115	Nobody Knows	CDJ	U.S.	1995	$2.00

Richard, Cliff

Full Length

Label	Catalog Number	Title	Type	Country	Year	Longbox Value / Value
EMI	46008	Give a Little Bit More	LP/LB	U.S.†	1984	$14.00/$8.00

Singles

Label	Catalog Number	Title	Type	Country	Year	Longbox Value / Value
EMI	203383-2	Best of Me	CD5	Germany	1989	$8.00
EMI	CDEM-92	Best of Me	CD5	U.K.	1989	$8.00
EMI	CDEM-155	From A Distance	CD5	U.K.	1990	$8.00
		Healing Love	CD5	U.K.		$10.00
		Healing Love	CD5	U.K.		$10.00
		Second version.				
		Human Work of Art	CD5	U.K.		$10.00
		Human Work of Art	CD5	U.K.		$10.00
		Second version.				
EMI	203477-3	I Just Don't Have the Heart	CD3	Germany	1989	$8.00
EMI	CDEM-101	I Just Don't Have the Heart	CD5	U.K.	1989	$8.00
		I Still Believe in You	CD5	U.K.		$10.00
		I Still Believe in You	CD5	U.K.		$10.00
		Second version.				
EMI	CDEM-105	Lean on Me	CD5	U.K.	1989	$8.00
EMI	203528-3	Lean on You	CD3	Germany	1989	$8.00
EMI	203026-2	Mistletoe and Wine	CD5	Germany	1988	$8.00
EMI	CDEM-78	Mistletoe and Wine	CD5	U.K.	1988	$8.00
EMI	CDEM-205	More to Life	CD5	U.K.	1991	$8.00
		Never Let Go	CD5	U.K.		$10.00
		Never Let Go	CD5	U.K.		$10.00
		Second version.				
		Peace in Our Time	CD5	U.K.		$10.00
		Peace in Our Time	CD5	U.K.		$10.00
		Second version.				
EMI	202201-2	Remember Me	CD5	Germany	1990	$8.00
EMI	CDEM-31	Remember Me	CD5	U.K.	1990	$8.00
EMI	CDXMAS-90	Saviour's Day	CD5	U.K.	1990	$8.00

Label	Catalog Number	Title	Type	Country	Year	Longbox Value / Value
EMI	204526-2	Scarlet Ribbon	CD5	Germany	1991	$8.00
EMI	204004-2	Silhouettes	CD5	Germany	1990	$8.00
EMI	CDEM-152	Silhouettes	CD5	U.K.	1990	$8.00
EMI	203709-2	Stronger Than That	CD5	Germany	1990	$8.00
EMI	CDEM-129	Stronger Than That	CD5	U.K.	1990	$8.00
EMI	CDEM-218	This New Year	CD5	U.K.	1992	$8.00
EMI	202342-2	Two Hearts	CD5	Germany	1988	$8.00
EMI	CDEM-42	Two Hearts	CD5	U.K.	1988	$8.00
EMI	204090-2	We Don't Talk Anymore	CD5	Germany	1990	$8.00
EMI	TOCP-6968	We Should Be Together	CD3	Japan	1991	$13.00/$4.00
EMI	CDXMAS-91	We Should Be Together	CD5	U.K.	1991	$8.00

Richard, Zachary

Full Length

Label	Catalog Number	Title	Type	Country	Year	Longbox Value / Value
A&M	31454 8003 2	Snake Bite Love	DJ/LP	U.S.	1992	$15.00
A&M		Snake Bite Love	DJ/LP	U.S.	1992	$15.00
	Second version.					

Singles

Label	Catalog Number	Title	Type	Country	Year	Longbox Value / Value
A&M	3458 8023	Come on, Sheila	CDJ	U.S.	1992	$2.00
A&M	31458 8195	One Kiss	CDJ	U.S.	1992	$2.00
A&M	75021 7513 2	Too Many Women	CDJ	U.S.	1990	$2.00
A&M	75021 8083 2	Who Stole My Monkey	CDJ	U.S.	1990	$2.00

Richards, Keith (and The Expensive Winos)

Full Length

Label	Catalog Number	Title	Type	Country	Year	Longbox Value / Value
Epic	AK 47898	Aranbee Pop Symphony Orchestra	LP/LB	U.S.		$50.00/$50.00
Virgin	VJCP-36032	Live at the Hollywood Palladium December 15, 1988	LTD/LP	Japan	1991	$90.00
	CD, VHS video, 2 booklets, and T-shirt in custom box.					
Virgin	50303-0	Live at the Hollywood Palladium December 15, 1988	LTD/LP	U.S.	1991	$40.00
	CD, VHS video, 2 booklets in custom numbered box.					
Album Network		On Tour	RS	U.S.	1993	$350.00
	Airdate: 2/13/93.					
		Rock & Roll Greats	RS	U.S.	1992	$70.00
	Airdate: 3/92.					
Virgin	2-9047C	Talk Is Cheap	LTD/LP	U.S.	1988	$35.00
	3-CD3s in can with booklet.					
Westwood One		Timothy White Sessions	RS	U.S.	1993	$225.00
	2 CD set. Airdate: 1/18/93.					
Media America		Up Close	RS	U.S.	1988	$140.00
	4 CD set.					
Media America		Up Close	RS	U.S.	1989	$140.00
	4 CD set.					
Media America		Up Close	RS	U.S.	1993	$140.00
	3 CD set.					

Singles

Label	Catalog Number	Title	Type	Country	Year	Longbox Value / Value
Virgin	DPRO 12770	999	CDJ	U.S.	1991	$7.00
Virgin		999 Live	CDJ	Canada	1989	$25.00
Virgin	K-RICH-1	Eileen	CDJ	U.K.	1992	$12.00
Virgin	DPRO-12770	Eileen	CDJ	U.S.	1992	$7.00
Virgin	665 622	Hate It When You Leave	CD5	Holland	1993	$12.00
Virgin	VJD-10204	Make No Mistake	CD3	Japan	1988	$18.00/$5.00
Virgin	VSCD-1179	Make No Mistake	CD3	U.K.	1988	$15.00
Virgin	PR CD 2633	Make No Mistake	CDJ	U.S.	1988	$10.00
Virgin	PRCD 2633	Struggle	CDJ	U.S.	1989	$7.00
Virgin	161690	Take It So Hard	CD3	Germany	1988	$12.00
Virgin	VSCD-1125	Take It So Hard	CD3	U.K.	1988	$12.00
Virgin	PRCD 2396	Take It So Hard	CDJ	U.S.	1988	$10.00
Virgin	91047-2	Talk Is Cheap	CD3	U.S.	1988	$3.00
Virgin	DPRO-12715	Wicked As It Seems	CDJ	U.S.	1992	$7.00
Virgin	PRCD 2557	You Don't Move Me	CDJ	U.S.	1988	$10.00

Richards, Nicki

Singles

Label	Catalog Number	Title	Type	Country	Year	Longbox Value / Value
Atlantic		Naked to the World	CDJ	U.S.		$2.00

Richie Family

Singles

Label	Catalog Number	Title	Type	Country	Year	Longbox Value / Value
Old Gold	OG-6505	Best Disco in Town	CD5	U.K.	1990	$9.00

Richie, Lionel

Full Length

Label	Catalog Number	Title	Type	Country	Year	Longbox Value / Value
Pioneer	PA-85-109	All Night Long	LD	U.S.	1985	$30.00
Pioneer	PA-85-109	All Night Long	LD	U.S.	1990	$40.00
	Digital audio.					
Motown	6059-MD	Can't Slow Down	LP/BP	U.S.†	1984	$14.00/$8.00
RCA	ZD-72388	Composer, The	LP	Germany		$15.00
Lorimar	LV394	Dancing on the Ceiling	LD	U.S.	1987	$30.00
Motown	6007-MD	Lionel Richie	LP/BP	U.S.†	1984	$14.00/$8.00
Warner Brothers	PRO986	Louder Than Words	DJ/Smplr	Germany	1995	$50.00
	CD in metal box.					
		Louder Than Words	DJ/LP	U.S.	1995	$8.00
		Louder Than Words	DJ/LP	U.S.	1995	$25.00
	CD in metal box.					
Mercury	314 532 240-2	Louder Than Words	DJ/LP	U.S.	1996	$25.00
Unistar		Weekly Specials, The	RS	U.S.	1992	$15.00
	Airdate: 7/17/92.					

Singles

Label	Catalog Number	Title	Type	Country	Year	Longbox Value / Value
Motown	R0M-113	All Night Long	CD3	Japan	1989	$12.00/$4.00
Motown	PODT-1003	Do It to Me	CD3	Japan	1992	$12.00/$4.00
Motown	TMGCD-1407	Do It to Me	CD5	U.K.	1992	$10.00
Motown	374634818	Do It to Me	CD5	U.S.	1992	$5.00
Motown	3746310532	Do It to Me	CDJ	U.S.	1992	$3.00
	CDP1578	Don't Wanna Lose	CDJ	U.S.	1996	$2.00
Motown	R10M-112	Hello	CD3	Japan	1989	$12.00/$4.00
Motown	860083-2	Love, Oh Love	CD5	Germany	1992	$10.00
Motown	PODT-1012	Love, Oh Love	CD3	Japan	1992	$12.00/$4.00
Motown	TMGCD-1413	Love, Oh Love	CD5	U.K.	1992	$10.00
Motown	PODM-1007	My Destiny	CD3	Japan	1992	$12.00/$4.00
Motown	TMGCD-1408	My Destiny	CD5	U.K.	1992	$10.00
Motown	374631057	My Destiny	CDJ	U.S.	1992	$3.00
Motown	R10M-114	Say You Say Me	CD3	Japan	1989	$12.00/$4.00
Aris	886084	Sela	CD5	Germany	1990	$10.00
Motown	LIOCD-4	Sela	CD5	U.K.	1990	$10.00
Motown	R10M-111	Truly	CD3	Japan	1989	$12.00/$4.00

Riddem Nation

Singles

Label	Catalog Number	Title	Type	Country	Year	Longbox Value / Value
Eclipse Music	64945-2	Reggae Christmas	SCDJ	U.S.	1996	$10.00
	Santa Clause shaped CD.					

Riddims Of A

Singles

Label	Catalog Number	Title	Type	Country	Year	Longbox Value / Value
Relativity	1234	Legend-Various	CD5	U.S.	1994	$5.00

Riddle, Nelson

Full Length

Label	Catalog Number	Title	Type	Country	Year	Longbox Value / Value
Verve	823760-2	Silver Collection	LP/LB	U.S.†	1985	$14.00/$8.00

Ride

Full Length

Label	Catalog Number	Title	Type	Country	Year	Longbox Value / Value
Sire		Carnival of Light	DJ/LP	U.S.	1994	$15.00
	Advance Issue.					
Sire	9 26836-2-DJ	Going Back Again	DJ/LP	U.S.	1992	$15.00
	Picture disc.					
Sire	PRO-CD-4961	Kaleidoscope	DJ/Smplr	U.S.	1992	$20.00
		Live	DJ/Smplr	France	1994	$25.00

Singles

Label	Catalog Number	Title	Type	Country	Year	Longbox Value / Value
Creation	CRESCD-072	Chelsea	CD5	France	1989	$10.00
Creation	CRESCD-087	Dreams Burn Down	CD5	U.K.	1990	$10.00
		How Does It Feel	CD5	U.K.	1994	$10.00
		How Does It Feel	CD5	U.K.	1994	$10.00
	Second version.					
		I Don't Know Where It Comes From	CD5	U.K.	1994	$10.00
Creation	CRESCD-123	Leave Them All Behind	CD5	U.K.	1992	$10.00
Sire	40332-2	Leave Them All Behind	CD5	U.S.	1992	$5.00
Sire	PRO-CD-5369	Leave Them All Behind	CDJ	U.S.	1992	$3.00
Creation	CRESCD-075	Like a Daydream	CD5	U.K.	1990	$10.00
Creation	CRESCD-072	Ride	CD5	U.K.	1990	$10.00
Sire	PRO-CD-4659	Taste	CDJ	U.S.	1990	$3.00
WEA	7599-26604-2	Today Forever	CD5	Germany	1991	$10.00
Sire	WPCP-4322	Today Forever	CD5	Japan	1991	$15.00
Creation	CRESCD-100	Today Forever	CD5	U.K.	1991	$10.00
Creation	CRESCD-150	Twisterella	CD5	U.K.	1991	$10.00
Sire	40448	Twisterella	CD5	U.S.	1992	$5.00
Sire	9 40055-2	Vapour Trail	CD5	U.S.	1990	$5.00
Sire	PRO-CD-4744	Vapour Trail	CDJ	U.S.	1991	$3.00

Ride Committee

Singles

Label	Catalog Number	Title	Type	Country	Year	Longbox Value / Value
Capitol	58305	Accident	CD5	U.S.	1995	$5.00
Capitol	58141	Love to Do It	CD5	U.S.	1994	$5.00

Ridgeley, Andrew

Singles

Label	Catalog Number	Title	Type	Country	Year	Longbox Value / Value
Columbia	655979-3	Red Dress	CD5	Germany	1990	$8.00
Epic	ESDA-7037	Red Dress	CD3	Japan	1990	$13.00/$4.00
Columbia	655979	Red Dress	CD3	U.K.	1990	$8.00
Columbia	CDAJR-2	Red Dress	CD5	U.K.	1990	$8.00
Columbia	CSK 73451	Red Dress	CDJ	U.S.	1990	$2.00
Columbia	655618-3	Shake	CD3	Germany	1990	$8.00
Epic	ESDA-7024	Shake	CD3	Japan		$13.00/$4.00
Epic	AJRC-1	Shake	CD5	U.K.	1990	$8.00
Columbia	CSK 73337	Shake	CDJ	U.S.	1990	$2.00

Ridgeway, Stan

Full Length

Label	Catalog Number	Title	Type	Country	Year	Longbox Value / Value
		Fly on the Wall	DJ/Intvw	U.S.		$6.00
		Mosquito	DJ/LP	U.S.		$8.00

Singles

Label	Catalog Number	Title	Type	Country	Year	Longbox Value / Value
IRS	EIRSCD-106	Calling Out to Carol	CD5	U.K.	1989	$8.00
EMI	244026-3	Goin' Southbound	CD3	Germany	1989	$8.00
Geffen	PRO-CD-3502	Goin' Southbound	CDJ	U.S.	1989	$2.00
IRS	204322-2	I Wanna Be a Boss	CD5	Germany	1991	$8.00
IRS	CDEIRS-166	I Wanna Be a Boss	CD5	U.K.	1991	$8.00
Geffen	PRO-CD-4283	I Wanna Be a Boss	CDJ	U.S.	1991	$2.00
EMI	241039-3	Lonely Town	CD3	Germany	1989	$8.00

Riff

Singles

Label	Catalog Number	Title	Type	Country	Year	Longbox Value / Value
SBK	DPRO-05420	Christmas Medley	CDJ	U.S.	1991	$2.00
SBK	DPRO-05418	Every Time My Heart Beats	CDJ	U.S.	1991	$2.00
		White Men Can't Jump	CDJ	U.S.	1993	$3.00

Right Said Fred

Singles

Label	Catalog Number	Title	Type	Country	Year	Longbox Value / Value
Intercord	825 937	Deeply Dippy	CD5	Germany	1992	$8.00
Tug	CDSNOG-3	Deeply Dippy	CD5	U.K.	1992	$8.00
Intercord	825 931	Don't Talk Just Kiss	CD5	Germany	1992	$8.00
Virgin	VJCP-14041	Don't Talk Just Kiss	CD5	Japan	1992	$15.00
Tug	CDSNOG-2	Don't Talk Just Kiss	CD5	U.K.	1992	$8.00
Charisma	96200	Don't Talk Just Kiss	CD5	U.S.	1992	$4.00
Charisma	VJDP-10191	I'm Too Sexy	CD3	Japan	1992	$13.00/$4.00
Tug	CDSNOG-4	Those Simple Things	CD5	U.K.	1992	$8.00

Righteous Brothers

Full Length

Label	Catalog Number	Title	Type	Country	Year	Longbox Value / Value
Verve	823 119-2	Greatest Hits	LP/BP	U.S.†	1984	$14.00/$8.00
Verve	879369-2	You've Lost That Lovin' Feeling	CD5	Germany	1990	$8.00
Verve	889809-2	You've Lost That Lovin' Feeling	CD5	Germany	1990	$8.00

Singles

Label	Catalog Number	Title	Type	Country	Year	Longbox Value / Value
Verve	PZCD-128	Just Once In My Life	CD5	U.K.	1991	$8.00
Verve	879103-2	Unchained Melody	CD5	Germany	1990	$8.00
Verve	PZCD-101	Unchained Melody	CD5	U.K.	1990	$8.00
Curb	76844	Unchained Melody	CD5	U.S.	1990	$5.00
Verve	PZCD-116	You've Lost That Lovin' Feeling	CD5	U.K.	1990	$8.00

Righteous Invasion of Truth

Full Length

Label	Catalog Number	Title	Type	Country	Year	Longbox Value / Value
		Carmen	DJ/LP	U.S.		$10.00

Riley, Cheryl Pepsii

Singles

Label	Catalog Number	Title	Type	Country	Year	Longbox Value / Value
Columbia	CSK 73955	Ain't No Way	CDJ	U.S.	1991	$2.00
Reprise	40903-2	Gimmie	CD5	U.S.	1993	$4.00
Reprise	40965-2	Guess I'm in Love	CD5	U.S.	1993	$4.00
Reprise	PRO-CD-6570	Guess I'm in Love	CDJ	U.S.	1993	$2.00
Columbia	CSK 73766	How Can You Hurt the One You Love	CDJ	U.S.	1991	$2.00
Columbia	653153-2	Thanks for My Child	CD5	U.K.	1989	$8.00

Riley, Jeannie C.

Singles

Label	Catalog Number	Title	Type	Country	Year	Longbox Value / Value
		Here's to the Cowboys	CDJ	U.S.		$2.00
MCA	20853	Sings the Gospel	CD5	U.S.	1994	$5.00

Riley, Melvin

Singles

Label	Catalog Number	Title	Type	Country	Year	Longbox Value / Value
		Who Is It	CDJ	U.S.		$2.00

Riley, Teddy

Singles

Label	Catalog Number	Title	Type	Country	Year	Longbox Value / Value
MCA	MCA5P-2697	Baby Be Mine	CDJ	U.S.	1992	$2.00

Label	Catalog Number	Title	Type	Country	Year	Longbox Value / Value
MCA	MSCTD-1611	Is It Good to You	CD5	U.K.	1992	$8.00
RCA	ZD-42946	My Fantasy	CD5	Germany	1989	$8.00
MCA	DMCAT-1353	My Fantasy	CD5	U.K.	1989	$8.00

Riley, Windsor

Singles

Label	Catalog Number	Title	Type	Country	Year	Longbox Value / Value
		Desert Animal	CDJ	U.S.		$2.00

Rimes, LeAnn

Full Length

Label	Catalog Number	Title	Type	Country	Year	Longbox Value / Value
Nor Va Jak		All That	LP	U.S.	1994	N/A

First CD recording.

Rio Bravo

Singles

Label	Catalog Number	Title	Type	Country	Year	Longbox Value / Value
Zyx	7565	Thank God I'm A C	CD5	U.S.	1994	$5.00

Riot

Full Length

Label	Catalog Number	Title	Type	Country	Year	Longbox Value / Value
CBS		Star Box	LTD/LP		1994	$25.00

Rippingtons

Full Length

Label	Catalog Number	Title	Type	Country	Year	Longbox Value / Value
Passport	VDJ-1153	Kilimanjaro	LP	Japan		$20.00
Passport	PJCD-88042	Kilimanjaro	LP/BP	U.S.		$16.00/$12.00
Passport	PJCD-88019	Moonlighting	LP	Germany		$12.00
Passport	PJCD-88019	Moonlighting	LP	U.K.		$12.00
Passport	PJCD-88019	Moonlighting	LP/BP	U.S.		$16.00/$12.00

Singles

Label	Catalog Number	Title	Type	Country	Year	Longbox Value / Value
GRP	9992	Indian Summer	CDJ	U.S.	1992	$2.00
GRP	9940	Welcome to the St. James Club	CDJ	U.S.	1990	$2.00

Rise Robots Rise

Singles

Label	Catalog Number	Title	Type	Country	Year	Longbox Value / Value
TVT	3212	All Sewn Up	CDJ	U.S.	1992	$2.00
TVT	3222	Bottle, The	CDJ	U.S.	1993	$2.00
TVT	3213	If I Only Knew	CDJ	U.S.	1992	$2.00
TVT	3211	Talk is Cheap	CDJ	U.S.	1991	$2.00

Rita Y Jose

Singles

Label	Catalog Number	Title	Type	Country	Year	Longbox Value / Value
Continental	1032	Con Tamborazo	CD5	U.S.	1994	$5.00

Ritenour, Lee

Full Length

Label	Catalog Number	Title	Type	Country	Year	Longbox Value / Value
Elektra	60024-2	Rio	LP/LB	U.S.†	1985	$14.00/$8.00
		Singles, The	8"LD	Japan		$35.00

Singles

Label	Catalog Number	Title	Type	Country	Year	Longbox Value / Value
GRP		Turn the Heat Up	CDJ	U.S.		$2.00
GRP	5110	Waiting in Vain	CDJ	U.S.	1993	$2.00
GRP	5116	Waiting in Vain	CDJ	U.S.	1993	$2.00

Rivas, Irene

Singles

Label	Catalog Number	Title	Type	Country	Year	Longbox Value / Value
Cema Latino	31827	Y Tropical Del Brav	CD5	U.S.	1994	$5.00

River Boys

Singles

Label	Catalog Number	Title	Type	Country	Year	Longbox Value / Value
WEA	9031-75745-2	Always Be Free	CD5	Germany	1991	$8.00
WEA	9031-75172-2	Flying Horses	CD5	Germany	1991	$8.00
WEA	9031-76540-2	House at the End of the Street	CD5	Germany	1991	$8.00

River City People

Singles

Label	Catalog Number	Title	Type	Country	Year	Longbox Value / Value
EMI	CDEM-145	California Dreaming	CD5	U.K.	1990	$8.00
EMI	204486-2	River City People	CD5	Germany	1991	$8.00
EMI	203561-3	Something Good to Say	CD3	Germany	1989	$8.00
EMI	CDEM-110	Something Good to Say	CD5	U.K.	1989	$8.00
EMI	CDEM-207	Special Way	CD5	U.K.	1991	$8.00
EMI	CDEMS 216	Standing in the Need of Love	CD5	U.K.	1991	$8.00
EMI	203726-2	Walking on Ice	CD5	Germany	1990	$8.00
EMI	CDEM-130	Walking on Ice	CD5	U.K.	1990	$8.00
EMI	203428-3	(What's Wrong With) Dreaming?	CD3	Germany	1990	$8.00
EMI	CDEM-95	(What's Wrong With) Dreaming?	CD5	U.K.	1990	$8.00
EMI	CDEM-156	(What's Wrong With) Dreaming?	CD5	U.K.	1990	$8.00
Capitol	DPRO 79929	(What's Wrong With) Dreaming?	CDJ	U.S.	1990	$2.00
Capitol	DPRO 79386	(What's Wrong With) Dreaming?	CDJ	U.S.	1990	$7.00
EMI	CDEM-176	When I Was Young	CD5	U.K.	1991	$8.00

River Ocean, (Feat, India)

Singles

Label	Catalog Number	Title	Type	Country	Year	Longbox Value / Value
		Love and Happiness	CD5	U.K.		$10.00
		Love and Happiness	CD5	U.K.		$10.00

Second version.

Riverdogs

Full Length

Label	Catalog Number	Title	Type	Country	Year	Longbox Value / Value
Epic	ZSK 2202	On Air	DJ/Smplr	U.S.	1990	$6.00
Epic	ZSK 2065	Special in Store Advance	DJ/LP	U.S.	1990	$7.00

Singles

Label	Catalog Number	Title	Type	Country	Year	Longbox Value / Value
Epic	ZSK 2055	I Believe	CDJ	U.S.	1990	$2.00
Epic		Toy Soldier	CDJ	U.S.	1990	$2.00

Rivers, Mavis

Full Length

Label	Catalog Number	Title	Type	Country	Year	Longbox Value / Value
Delos	D/CD 4002	It's a Good Day	LP/LB	U.S.†	1985	$14.00/$8.00

Rives, Carlos

Singles

Label	Catalog Number	Title	Type	Country	Year	Longbox Value / Value
Polygram	52176	La Tierra Del Olvido	CD5	U.S.	1995	$5.00

Roach, David

Full Length

Label	Catalog Number	Title	Type	Country	Year	Longbox Value / Value
Passport	PJCD-88005	Talking City	LP/BP	U.S.		$16.00/$12.00

Roach, Max

Full Length

Label	Catalog Number	Title	Type	Country	Year	Longbox Value / Value
Soul Note	SN-1109CD PSI	Easy Winners	LP/LB	U.S.†	1985	$14.00/$8.00
Soul Note	SN-1053CD PSI	In the Light	LP/LB	U.S.†	1985	$14.00/$8.00
Polygram	826456-2	Jazz in 3/4 Time	LP/BP	U.S.		$12.00/$7.00
Soul Note	SN-1103CD PSI	Scott Free	LP/LB	U.S.†	1985	$14.00/$8.00
Soul Note	SN-1093CD PSI	Survivors	LP/LB	U.S.†	1985	$14.00/$8.00

Roachford

Singles

Label	Catalog Number	Title	Type	Country	Year	Longbox Value / Value
Columbia	651611-3	Cuddly Toy	CD3	Germany	1988	$8.00
Columbia	CDROA-2	Cuddly Toy	CD5	U.K.	1988	$8.00
Columbia	CDROA-4	Cuddly Toy	CD5	U.K.	1988	$8.00
		Cuddly Toy	CDJ	U.S.	1988	$2.00
Columbia	654743-3	Family Man	CD3	Germany	1989	$8.00
Columbia	CDROA-1	Family Man	CD5	U.K.	1988	$8.00
Columbia	CDROA-5	Family Man	CD5	U.K.	1988	$8.00
		Family Man	CDJ	U.S.	1988	$2.00
Columbia	CDROA-3	Find Me Another Lover	CD5	U.K.	1988	$8.00
Columbia	656705-2	Get Ready	CD5	Germany	1989	$8.00
Columbia	656705-2	Get Ready	CD5	U.K.	1989	$8.00
Columbia	657368-2	Innocent Eyes	CD5	Germany	1991	$8.00
Columbia	657412-2	Innocent Eyes	CD5	U.K.	1991	$8.00
Columbia	653199-3	Kathleen	CD3	Germany	1989	$8.00
Columbia	655014-3	Kathleen	CD3	Germany	1989	$8.00
Columbia	ROAC-6	Kathleen	CD3	U.K.	1989	$8.00
Columbia	CDROA-6	Kathleen	CD3	U.K.	1989	$8.00
		Only to Be With You	CD5	U.K.		$10.00
		Only to Be With You	CD5	U.K.		$10.00

Second version.

Label	Catalog Number	Title	Type	Country	Year	Longbox Value / Value
Columbia	656966-2	Stone City	CD5	U.K.	1991	$8.00

Robb, Robbie

Singles

Label	Catalog Number	Title	Type	Country	Year	Longbox Value / Value
A&M	CD 17771	In Time	CDJ	U.S.	1989	$2.00

Robbins, Jarome

Full Length

Label	Catalog Number	Title	Type	Country	Year	Longbox Value / Value
		Broadway	DJ/Smplr	U.S.		$4.00

Roberts, Bruce

Singles

Label	Catalog Number	Title	Type	Country	Year	Longbox Value / Value
	PRCD 6577-2	Let Me Steal Your Heart	CDJ	U.S.		$6.00
	PRCD 6355-2	When Money's Gone	CDJ	U.S.		$6.00

Roberts, Joe

Singles

Label	Catalog Number	Title	Type	Country	Year	Longbox Value / Value
		Back in My Life/Losing You	CD5	U.K.		$10.00
		Back in My Life/Losing You	CD5	U.K.		$10.00

Second version.

Roberts, Juliet

Singles

Label	Catalog Number	Title	Type	Country	Year	Longbox Value / Value
Warner Brothers	40529-2	Free Love	CD5	U.S.	1992	$4.00
Reprise	41397-2	I Want You	CD5	U.S.	1994	$5.00
Reprise	PRO-CD-6796	I Want You	CDJ	U.S.	1994	$2.00
Reprise	PRO-CD-6893	I Want You	CDJ	U.S.	1994	$2.00

Roberts, Kane

Singles

Label	Catalog Number	Title	Type	Country	Year	Longbox Value / Value
DGC	PRO-CD-4219	Does Anybody Really Fall in	CDJ	U.S.		$2.00
		Twisted	CDJ	U.S.		$2.00

Robertson, Nick

Singles

Label	Catalog Number	Title	Type	Country	Year	Longbox Value / Value
Charism	PRCD 029	Show Me a Sign	CDJ	U.S.	1991	$2.00

Robertson, Robbie

Full Length

Label	Catalog Number	Title	Type	Country	Year	Longbox Value / Value
Geffen	PRO-CD-2877	Conversation for College Radio	DJ/Intvw	U.S.	1988	$8.00
Capitol		Music for Native Americans	DJ/LP	U.S.	1994	$12.00
Westwood One		Off the Record	RS	U.S.	1994	$25.00

Airdate: 10/24/94.

Label	Catalog Number	Title	Type	Country	Year	Longbox Value / Value
Geffen	GEFD 91102	Story About Storyville	DJ/Intvw	Canada	1991	$8.00
Media America		Up Close	RS	U.S.	1992	$30.00

2 CD set.

Singles

Label	Catalog Number	Title	Type	Country	Year	Longbox Value / Value
Atlas	1217	Bad Intentions	CDJ	U.S.	1994	$3.00
Geffen	PRO-CD-4415	Breakin' the Rules	CD5	U.S.	1992	$5.00
Geffen	PRO-CD-3158	Broken Arrow	CDJ	U.S.	1988	$3.00
A&M	CD 17661	Christmas Must Be Tonight	CDJ	U.S.	1988	$3.00
Geffen	GEF-46CD	Fallen Angel	CD3	U.K.	1988	$9.00
Geffen	PRO-CD-4357	Go Back To Your Woods	CDJ	U.S.		$3.00
Capitol	DPRO79467	Mahk Jcki	CDJ	U.S.		$3.00
Capitol	DPRO79442	Mahk Jcki	CDJ	U.S.		$3.00
Geffen	PRO-CD-4362	Shake This Town	CDJ	U.S.	1992	$3.00
Geffen	PRO-CD-2839	Showdown at Big Sky	CDJ	U.S.	1987	$3.00
		Somewhere Down the Crazy River	CDJ	U.S.		$3.00
Geffen	GFSTD-12	What About Now	CD5	U.K.	1991	$9.00
Geffen	PRO-CD-4312	What About Now	CDJ	U.S.	1991	$3.00

Robillard, Duke

Full Length

Label	Catalog Number	Title	Type	Country	Year	Longbox Value / Value
		House of Blues	RS	U.S.	1996	$40.00

2 CD set. Airdate: 1/28/96.

Robin, S.

Singles

Label	Catalog Number	Title	Type	Country	Year	Longbox Value / Value
Big Beat	95955	I Want to Thank You	CD5	U.S.	1994	$5.00
Big Beat	PRCD 5435-2	I Want to Thank You	CDJ	U.S.	1994	$2.00
Atlantic	PRCD 5180-2	Love for Love	CDJ	U.S.	1993	$2.00
Big Beat	PRCD 5240-2	Love for Love	CDJ	U.S.	1994	$2.00
Big Beat	5256	Quiet Storm	CDJ	U.S.		$7.00
Big Beat	10110	Show Me Love	CD5	U.S.	1993	$5.00
Big Beat	PRCD 5091-2	Show Me Love	CDJ	U.S.	1993	$2.00
Atlantic	95793	Show Me Love	CD5	U.S.	1994	$5.00
Big Beat	PRCD 5297-2	What I Do Best	CDJ	U.S.	1993	$2.00
Big Beat	PRCD 5345-2	What I Do Best	CD5	U.S.	1993	$2.00

Robinson, Smokey (and The Miracles)

Full Length

Label	Catalog Number	Title	Type	Country	Year	Longbox Value / Value
Motown	5349-MD	Being With You	LP/BP	U.S.		$14.00/$8.00
Motown	6071-MD	Compact Command Performance	LP/BP	U.S.†	1984	$14.00/$8.00
Motown	6268-MD	Love Smokey	LP/BP	U.S.		$14.00/$8.00
		Sixties Legends	RS	U.S.	1992	$15.00

2 CD set. Airdate: 5/29/92.

Label	Catalog Number	Title	Type	Country	Year	Longbox Value / Value
Motown	5134-MD	Smokey	LP/BP	U.S.		$14.00/$8.00
Motown	5418-MD	Special Occasion	LP/BP	U.S.		$14.00/$8.00

Singles

Label	Catalog Number	Title	Type	Country	Year	Longbox Value / Value
SBK	204612-3	Double Good Everything	CD5	Germany	1992	$10.00
SBK	CDSBK-33	Double Good Everything	CD5	U.K.	1992	$10.00
SBK	DPRO-05414	Double Good Everything	CDJ	U.S.	1992	$2.00
Motown	R10M-129	Everything You Touch	CD3	Japan	1989	$12.00/$4.00
Motown	PRD 90001	Everything You Touch	CDJ	U.S.	1989	$2.00
SBK	DPRO-05436	I Love Your Face	CDJ	U.S.	1992	$2.00
Motown	CD45 17806	(It's the) Same Old Love	CDJ	U.S.	1989	$2.00
Motown	ZD-41784	Love Don't Give No Reason	CD5	U.K.	1988	$10.00
SBK	DPRO-05414	Rewind	CDJ	U.S.		$2.00
Motown	CD45 128283	Take Me Through the Night	CDJ	U.S.		$2.00

Robotiko Rejekto

Singles

Label	Catalog Number	Title	Type	Country	Year	Longbox Value / Value
ZYX	6190-8	Confusion	CD5	Germany	1989	$6.00
ZYX	6197-8	Confusion	CD5	Germany	1989	$6.00
ZYX	8-5776	Rejekto	CD3	Germany	1988	$6.00
ZYX	6740-8	Technology	CD5	Germany	1992	$6.00
ZYX	6018-8	Umstruz	CD5	Germany	1988	$6.00

Rochelle

Singles

Label	Catalog Number	Title	Type	Country	Year	Longbox Value / Value
	1002	Praying for an Angel	CD5	U.S.	1994	$5.00

Roches

Singles

Label	Catalog Number	Title	Type	Country	Year	Longbox Value / Value
MCA	CD45 18036	Big Nuthin'	CDJ	U.S.	1989	$2.00
MCA	CD45 18102	Big Nuthin'	CDJ	U.S.	1989	$2.00
MCA	CD45 18230	Everyone is Good	CDJ	U.S.	1990	$2.00

Rock Aid Armenia

Full Length

Label	Catalog Number	Title	Type	Country	Year	Longbox Value / Value
LAR	AID CD001	Earthquake Album, The	LP	U.K.	1990	$15.00

Singles

Label	Catalog Number	Title	Type	Country	Year	Longbox Value / Value
LAR		Smoke on the Water	CDJ	Canada	1990	$25.00
LAR	ARMENCD-001	Smoke on the Water	CD5	U.K.	1990	$11.00

Rock And Hyde

Singles

Label	Catalog Number	Title	Type	Country	Year	Longbox Value / Value
		Dirty Water	CDJ	U.S.		

Rock City Angels

Full Length

Label	Catalog Number	Title	Type	Country	Year	Longbox Value / Value
Geffen	PRO-CD-3247	Young Man's Blues	DJ/Smplr	U.S.	1988	$5.00

Singles

Label	Catalog Number	Title	Type	Country	Year	Longbox Value / Value
Geffen	PRO-CD-3239	Deep Inside My Heart	CDJ	U.S.	1988	$2.00

Rock, Pete

Singles

Label	Catalog Number	Title	Type	Country	Year	Longbox Value / Value
Elektra	PRCD 8468-2	Creator, The	CDJ	U.S.	1991	$2.00
Elektra	66196	I Got a Love	CD5	U.S.	1994	$5.00
Elektra	PRCD 8712-2	Lots of Lovin'	CDJ	U.S.	1993	$2.00

Rock Therapy

Singles

Label	Catalog Number	Title	Type	Country	Year	Longbox Value / Value
		Reaching Out	CD5	U.K.	1996	$10.00

Rockapella

Singles

Label	Catalog Number	Title	Type	Country	Year	Longbox Value / Value
Elektra		Zombie Jamboree	CDJ	U.S.		$2.00

Rockers Revenge

Singles

Label	Catalog Number	Title	Type	Country	Year	Longbox Value / Value
Warlock	801	Wallking on Sunshine	CDJ	U.S.	1991	$2.00

Rocket From The Crypt

Singles

Label	Catalog Number	Title	Type	Country	Year	Longbox Value / Value
	PRCD 7944-2	Born in '69	CDJ	U.S.		$2.00
Interscope	PRCD 5198-2	Sturdy Wrists	CDJ	U.S.	1992	$2.00
	PRCD 6472-2	Young Livers	CDJ	U.S.		$2.00

Rockhead

Singles

Label	Catalog Number	Title	Type	Country	Year	Longbox Value / Value
Capitol	666	Bed of Roses	CDJ	Canada	1992	$6.00
Capitol		Chelsea Rose	CDJ	Canada	1994	$6.00

Rocky Hill

Singles

Label	Catalog Number	Title	Type	Country	Year	Longbox Value / Value
Virgin	PRCD 2183	I Won't Be Your Fool	CDJ	U.S.	1988	$2.00

Rocky V

Singles

Label	Catalog Number	Title	Type	Country	Year	Longbox Value / Value
		Go for It (Heart And Fire)	CDJ	U.S.		$2.00
EMI	204261-2	Thought You Were the One	CD5	Germany	1991	$8.00

Rodg

Singles

Label	Catalog Number	Title	Type	Country	Year	Longbox Value / Value
	5010	Always	CD5	U.S.	1994	$5.00

Rodgers, Jimmie

Singles

Label	Catalog Number	Title	Type	Country	Year	Longbox Value / Value
Aris	885851	Honeycomb	CD3	Germany	1990	$9.00

Rodgers, Paul

Full Length

Label	Catalog Number	Title	Type	Country	Year	Longbox Value / Value
Victory		A Tribute to Muddy Waters	LTD/LP	U.K.	1993	$25.00
	Limited 2CD set.					
Victory	SACD 679	A Tribute to Muddy Waters	DJ/LP	U.S.	1993	$30.00
	CD in digipak with numbered guitar pick.					
Westwood One		In Concert	RS	U.S.	1994	$40.00
	Airdate: 8/15/94.					
Westwood One		In Concert	RS	U.S.	1995	$65.00
	2 CD set. Airdate: 11/27/95.					
		Live At Electric Ladyland	RS	U.S.	1993	$40.00
	Airdate: 5/23/93.					
	CDS-206	Muddy Waters Blues	DJ/Smplr	Japan	1993	N/A
Westwood One		Off the Record	RS	U.S.	1993	$30.00
	Airdate: 10/11/93.					
Westwood One		Off the Record	RS	U.S.	1993	$30.00
	Airdate: 5/17/93.					
Westwood One		Superstar Concert	RS	U.S.	1994	$50.00
	2 CD set. Airdate: 1/24/94.					
Victory		Tour Sampler	DJ/Smplr	U.S.		$8.00

Singles

Label	Catalog Number	Title	Type	Country	Year	Longbox Value / Value
Victory	4228573672	Hendrix Set, The	CD5	Canada	1994	$8.00
Victory	383 480 014	Hendrix Set, The	CD5	U.S.	1993	$5.00
Victory	CDP 892	Hunter, The	CDJ	U.S.	1993	$3.00
Victory	CDP 951	Louisiana Blues	CDJ	U.S.	1993	$3.00

Rodney O & Joe

Singles

Label	Catalog Number	Title	Type	Country	Year	Longbox Value / Value
	89441	Insane Poetry	CD5	U.S.	1994	$5.00

Roger

Singles

Label	Catalog Number	Title	Type	Country	Year	Longbox Value / Value
Reprise	WPCP-4815	Everybody Get Up	CD5	Japan	1992	$12.00
Warner Brothers	40259	Everybody Get Up	CD5	U.S.	1992	$5.00
Warner Brothers	PRo-CD-5080	Everybody Get Up	CDJ	U.S.	1992	$2.00
WEA	920771-2	I Want to Be Your Man	CD5	Germany	1988	$8.00
WEA	W-8229CD	I Want to Be Your Man	CD5	U.K.	1988	$8.00
Reprise	PRO-CD-5203	Take Me Back	CDJ	U.S.	1991	$2.00
Reprise	PRO-CD-5059	You Should Be Mine	CDJ	U.S.	1991	$2.00

Rogers, Ce Ce

Singles

Label	Catalog Number	Title	Type	Country	Year	Longbox Value / Value
Atlantic	PRCD 4374-2	Never Give Up	CDJ	U.S.	1991	$2.00

Rogers, Jimmy

Full Length

Label	Catalog Number	Title	Type	Country	Year	Longbox Value / Value
		House of Blues	RS	U.S.	1995	$40.00
	2 CD set. Airdate: 5/26/95.					

Rogers, Kenny

Full Length

Label	Catalog Number	Title	Type	Country	Year	Longbox Value / Value
Reprise	9 25973-2	Christmas in America	LP/LB	U.S.	1989	$14.00/$8.00
RCA	PCD1-4697	Eyes That Sea in the Dark	LP/BP	U.S.†	1983	$14.00/$8.00
		Gambler, The	LP/LB	U.S.		$14.00/$8.00
EMI	CDP-46004	Greatest Hits	LP/LB	U.S.†	1984	$14.00/$8.00
RCA	PCD1-7023	Heart of the Matter	LP/BP	U.S.†	1985	$14.00/$8.00
		Kenny Rogers	LP/LB	U.S.		$14.00/$8.00
RCA	PCD1-5307	Once Upon a Christmas	LP/BP	U.S.†	1985	$14.00/$8.00
		We've Got Tonight	LP/LB	U.S.		$14.00/$8.00
RCA	PCD1-5335	What About Me	LP/BP	U.S.†	1985	$14.00/$8.00

Singles

Label	Catalog Number	Title	Type	Country	Year	Longbox Value / Value
		Crazy In Love	CDJ	U.S.		$2.00
Reprise	PRO-CD-3965	If I Knew Then What I Know Now	CDJ	U.S.	1989	$2.00
Reprise	PRo-CD-5159	If You Want to Find Love	CDJ	U.S.	1991	$2.00
Reprise	PRO-CD-3305	Planet Texas	CDJ	U.S.	1989	$2.00
WEA	9362-40028-2	Ruby Don't Take Your Love To Town	CD5	Germany	1991	$9.00
Reprise	PRO-CD-3653	Something Inside So Strong	CDJ	U.S.	1989	$2.00
WEA	7599-21803-2	What I Did for Love	CD5	Germany	1990	$9.00
WEA	W-9771CD	What I Did for Love	CD5	U.K.	1990	$9.00
WEA	W-7812CD	When You Put Your Heart in It	CD5	U.K.	1990	$9.00
		When You Put Your Heart in It	CDJ	U.S.	1990	$2.00

Rogers, Kenny Jr.

Full Length

Label	Catalog Number	Title	Type	Country	Year	Longbox Value / Value
Polygram	512337	Two Sides	LP/BP	U.S.		$14.00/$8.00

Singles

Label	Catalog Number	Title	Type	Country	Year	Longbox Value / Value
Polygram	CD 17876	Take Another Step Closer	CDJ	U.S.	1988	$2.00

Rogers, Kimm

Singles

Label	Catalog Number	Title	Type	Country	Year	Longbox Value / Value
		Right By You	CDJ	U.S.		$2.00
Island	PRCD 6713-2	Will Work for Food	CDJ	U.S.	1992	$2.00

Rogers, Lee

Singles

Label	Catalog Number	Title	Type	Country	Year	Longbox Value / Value
Pulse 8	CDLOSE-32	Love is the Most	CD5	U.K.	1992	$8.00

Rogers, Mark

Singles

Label	Catalog Number	Title	Type	Country	Year	Longbox Value / Value
BMG	662371	Let's Get Together	CD5	Germany	1989	$8.00

Rogers, Nile

Full Length

Label	Catalog Number	Title	Type	Country	Year	Longbox Value / Value
Warner Brothers	9 25290-2	B-Movie Matinee	LP/LB	U.S.†	1985	$14.00/$8.00

Rogers, Roy

Full Length

Label	Catalog Number	Title	Type	Country	Year	Longbox Value / Value
RCA	RDJ-61053-2	On Track...With Roy Rogers	DJ/Intvw	U.S.	1991	$15.00
RCA/Republic		Roy Rogers Deluxe Collector's Edition	LTD/LP	U.S.	1995	$80.00
	Tribute CD with 2 VHS tapes of "Golden Stallion" and "King Of Cowboys" and book in 12"x12"box.					

Rogers, Shorty

Full Length

Label	Catalog Number	Title	Type	Country	Year	Longbox Value / Value
Mosaic	MD4-125	Complete Atlantic and EMI Jazz	LP	U.S.		$60.00
	4 CD set.					

Rolling Stones – Desert Island Survival Kit (Abkco 1848-2 Promo)

Rolling Stones

Full Length

Label	Catalog Number	Title	Type	Country	Year	Longbox Value / Value
Abko		1963-1971 A Selection of No. 1 Singles	DJ/Smplr	U.S.	1994	$125.00
EMI	SPCD-1481	94/95 Voodoo Lounge Tour Souvenir	DJ/Smplr	Japan	1993	N/A
CBS	CSCS-5116	Another Side of Steel Wheels	LP	Japan	1990	$25.00
BBC Radio		BBC Classic Tracks	RS	U.S.	1991	$35.00
	Airdate: 12/30/91.					
BBC Radio		BBC Classic Tracks	RS	U.S.	1991	$50.00
	Airdate: 9/16/91.					
BBC Radio		BBC Classic Tracks	RS	U.S.	1992	$45.00
	Airdate: 7/6/92.					
Westwood One		BBC Classic Tracks	RS	U.S.	1993	$35.00
	Airdate: 3/15/93.					
Westwood One		BBC Classic Tracks	RS	U.S.	1993	$35.00
	Airdate: 6/28/93.					

Rolling Stones – Singles Collection: The London Years (Abko)

Label	Catalog Number	Title	Type	Country	Year	Longbox Value / Value
BBC Radio		BBC Classic Tracks	RS	U.S.	1994	$25.00
Airdate: 1/17/94.						
BBC Radio		BBC Classic Tracks	RS	U.S.	1994	$25.00
Airdate: 5/30/94.						
Westwood One		BBC Classic Tracks	RS	U.S.	1994	$35.00
Airdate: 10/3/94.						
Westwood One		BBC Classic Tracks	RS	U.S.	1995	$35.00
Airdate: 7/31/95.						
Virgin	39499	Black & Blue	LTD/LP	U.S.	1994	$18.00
Virgin	7243 4 83153 2 8	Coca Cola Presents Rolling Stones Vol. 1	DJ/Smplr	Mexico	1994	$40.00
Virgin	7243 4 83154 2 7	Coca Cola Presents Rolling Stones Vol. 2	DJ/Smplr	Mexico	1994	$40.00
Abkco	1848-2 Promo	Desert Island Survival Kit	DJ/Smplr	U.S.	1994	$40.00
Rolling Stones	CM 40500	Emotional Rescue	LP	U.S.	1993	$50.00
Minidisc.						
Virgin	7243-8-39591-2-6	Emotional Rescue	LTD/LP	U.S.	1993	$20.00
Virgin	7243-8-39503-2-4	Exile on Main Street	LTD/LP	U.S.	1994	$25.00
Rolling Stones		Flashpoint	LTD/LP	U.K.	1991	$40.00
CD of album plus bonus interview disc shrink-wrapped together.						
Rolling Stones	C2K 47880	Flashpoint + Collectibles	LTD/LP	U.S.	1991	$40.00
2CD in double digipak.						
Columbia	VLD3160	Gimmie Shelter	LD	U.S.	1984	$90.00
Virgin	7243-8-39498-3	Goats Head Soup	LTD/LP	U.S.	1994	$20.00
Media America		History of the Rolling Stones	RS	U.S.	1989	$600.00
20 CD set.						
Media America		History of the Rolling Stones	RS	U.S.	1994	$600.00
21 CD set.						
Album Network		In the Studio (Beggars Banquet)	RS	U.S.		$50.00
Album Network		In the Studio (Stripped)	RS	U.S.	1996	$50.00
Rolling Stones	SAMP-CD-1408	Interview 1990	DJ/Intvw	France	1990	$25.00
Rolling Stones	SAMP-CD-1408	Interview 1990	DJ/Intvw	U.K.	1990	$25.00
CBS	CSK 1910	Interview, The	DJ/Intvw	U.S.	1989	$35.00
Rolling Stones	CM 40493	It's Only Rock 'n Roll	LP	U.S.	1992	$50.00
Minidisc.						
Virgin	7243-8-39500-2-7	It's Only Rock 'n Roll	LTD/LP	U.S.	1994	$20.00
DIR		King Biscuit Flour Hour	RS	U.S.	1987	$80.00
Airdate: 9/27/87.						
DIR		King Biscuit Flour Hour	RS	U.S.	1988	$60.00
Airdate: 11/22/88.						
DIR		King Biscuit Flour Hour	RS	U.S.	1989	$60.00
Airdate: 9/4/89.						
DIR		King Biscuit Flour Hour	RS	U.S.	1990	$60.00
Airdate: 12/30/90.						
DIR		King Biscuit Flour Hour	RS	U.S.	1991	$60.00
Airdate: 12/29/91.						
DIR		King Biscuit Flour Hour	RS	U.S.	1992	$60.00
Airdate: 12/21/92.						
DIR		King Biscuit Flour Hour	RS	U.S.	1994	$60.00
Airdate: 3/14/94.						
DIR		King Biscuit Flour Hour	RS	U.S.	1995	$70.00
Airdate: 6/25/95.						
		Les Annees Stones	DJ/Smplr	France		$125.00
	12315	Let's Spend the Night Together	LD	U.S.		$90.00
Polygram Video	SACD 1004	Live at the Max	DJ/Smplr	U.S.	1994	$75.00
		Live at the Voodoo Lounge	RS	U.S.	1994	$500.00
6CD set. Airdate: 9/5/94.						
Columbia	C2K 40476	Love You Live	LP/LB	U.S.	1986	$35.00/$30.00
2 CD set.						
RCA	SSP RCD-2	Making of Symphonic Music of the Rolling Stones	DJ/RS	U.S.	1994	$18.00
Radio Ventures		Masters of Rock	RS	U.S.	1990	$80.00
Airdate: 9/26/90.						
Century 21 Programming		Nineteen Greatest Radio Hits	DJ/Smplr	U.S.	1991	$100.00
Westwood One		Off the Record	RS	U.S.	1994	$35.00
Airdate: 10/17/94.						
Westwood One		Off the Record	RS	U.S.	1994	$35.00
Airdate: 11/14/94.						
Westwood One		Off the Record	RS	U.S.	1995	$35.00
Airdate: 12/25/95.						
Westwood One		Off the Record	RS	U.S.	1995	$35.00
Airdate: 3/6/95.						
Westwood One		Off the Record	RS	U.S.	1995	$35.00
Airdate: 7/10/95.						
Rolling Stones	XDDP-93082	Pleasure of Pain	DJ/Smplr	Japan		$650.00
2 CD set.						
Rolling Stones	RSCD 1	Radio Sampler	DJ/Smplr	U.K.	1986	$80.00
Westwood One		Rarities on Compact Disc Volume 16	DJ/RS	U.S.	1993	$45.00
Westwood One		Rarities on Compact Disc Volume 20	DJ/RS	U.S.	1993	$45.00
Atco	90176-2	Rewind (1971-1984)	LP/BP	U.S.†	1984	$45.00/$40.00
Radio Today		Rock Stars	RS	U.S.	1990	$100.00
2 CD set. Airdate: 6/6/90.						
Nelson	12315	Rolling Stones	LD	U.S.	1983	$70.00
Global Satellite Network		Rolling Stones	RS	U.S.	1993	$150.00
2 CD set. Airdate: 5/24/93.						
Rolling Stones	SAMP-CD-1347	Say Ahh!	DJ/Smplr	U.K.	1990	$70.00
Rolling Stones	CSK 1827	Say Ahh!	DJ/Smplr	U.S.	1990	$70.00

Label	Catalog Number	Title	Type	Country	Year	Longbox Value / Value
EMI	SPCD-15250	Shine a Light	DJ/Smplr	Japan	1995	$300.00
ABKCO	121831	Singles Collection: The London Years	DJ/Smplr	U.S.	1989	$25.00
Rolling Stones	CM 40449	Some Girls	LP	U.S.	1992	$50.00
Minidisc.						
Virgin	7243-8-39505-2-2	Some Girls	LTD/LP	U.S.	1994	$20.00
CBS	CSCS-5115	Starbox	LP	Japan	1989	$40.00
		Steel Wheel	DJ/LP	U.K.	1989	$50.00
CD and press kit in custom box.						
Sony		Steel Wheels	DJ/Smplr	Japan	1989	$250.00
Rolling Stones	CSK 1952	Steel Wheels	DJ/LP	U.S.	1989	$100.00
Promo CD in metal case with correct track listing.						
Rolling Stones	CK 46009	Steel Wheels	LTD/LP	U.S.	1989	$70.00
CD in metal case with incorrect track listing.						
Columbia	CK 40488	Sticky Fingers	LP/LB	U.S.	1986	$15.00/$12.00
Rolling Stones	CM 40488	Sticky Fingers	LP	U.S.	1993	$50.00
Minidisc.						
Virgin	39504	Sticky Fingers	LTD/LP	U.S.	1994	$18.00
Virgin	7243-8-39504-2-3	Sticky Fingers	LTD/LP	U.S.	1994	$25.00
Atco	39113-2	Still Life	LP/BP	U.S.	1983	$75.00/$70.00
Rolling Stones	CSK 2498	Stones on CD: A RadioSampler	DJ/Smplr	U.S.	1986	$150.00
CBS	IVGD-22801	Stripped	DJ/Smplr	U.K.	1995	$200.00
2 CD set.						
		Superstar Concert	RS	U.S.	1995	$60.00
Westwood One		Superstars	RS	U.S.	1995	$225.00
2 CD set. Airdate: 6/25/95.						
Radio Today		Superstars	RS	U.S.	1996	$190.00
2 CD set. Airdate: 4/15/96.						
RCA	SSP CD-1	Symphonic Music of the Rolling Stones	DJ/Smplr	U.S.	1994	$18.00
Rolling Stones	CM 40502	Tatoo You	LP	U.S.	1992	$50.00
Minidisc.						
EMI		Tattoo You	LP	Japan	1983	$100.00
Virgin	7243-8-39502-2-5	Tattoo You	LTD/LP	U.S.	1994	$20.00
		Time on My Side	RS	U.S.	1993	$250.00
6 CD set. Airdate: 5/29/93.						
Columbia	CSK 4004	Too Great to Make You Wait	DJ/Smplr	U.S.	1991	$50.00
CD in jewel box.						
Columbia	CSK 4004	Too Great to Make You Wait	DJ/Smplr	U.S.	1991	$55.00
CD in paper sleeve.						
		Twenty-Fifth Anniversary Special	RS	U.S.	1989	$200.00
4 CD set. Airdate: 10/30/89.						
Media America		Up Close	RS	U.S.	1990	$80.00
2 CD set.						
Media America		Up Close	RS	U.S.	1991	$120.00
4 CD set.						
Media America		Up Close	RS	U.S.	1992	$80.00
2 CD set.						
Columbia		Urban Jungle Tour	DJ/Smplr	U.K.	1990	$60.00
Promo CD with press kit in custom box.						
Vestron	ML1016	Video Rewind	LD	U.S.	1984	$80.00
EMI		Voodoo Box	DJ/Smplr	Japan	1993	$400.00
CD and Bio in box.						
Virgin		Voodoo Lounge	DJ/LP	Australia	1993	$165.00
Promo package including CD, T-shirt, and press kit.						
Virgin		Voodoo Lounge	LTD/LP	Australia	1994	$40.00
Virgin Megastore issue with CD in numbered slipcase.						
Virgin	7243 8 39782 2 9	Voodoo Lounge	DJ/LP	U.S.	1994	$19.00
Virgin	DPRO-14158	Voodoo Lounge-A Sampler	DJ/Smplr	U.S.	1994	$40.00
		Voodoo Lounge Special	RS	U.S.	1995	$350.00
Airdate: 9/5/94.						
		Singles				
Columbia	656065-2	Almost Hear You Sigh	CD5	Germany	1989	$20.00
CBS	655981-3	Almost Hear You Sigh	CD3	Holland	1989	$20.00
Sony	CSDS-8120	Almost Hear You Sigh	CD3	Japan	1990	$20.00/$4.00
CBS		Almost Hear You Sigh	CD5	U.K.	1989	$20.00
CBS		Almost Hear You Sigh	CD5	U.K.	1989	$20.00
Gold colored CD.						
CBS	656065-2	Almost Hear You Sigh	CD5	U.K.	1990	$20.00
Columbia	CSK 73093	Almost Hear You Sigh	CDJ	U.S.	1989	$20.00
CBS		Angie	CD3	Holland		$20.00
		Black Limousine	CDJ	France		$75.00
		Black Limousine	CDJ	France	1996	$100.00
Polygram		Get Off My Cloud	CD5	U.K.	1994	$18.00
Sony	SRDS-8184	Highwire	CD3	Japan	1991	$18.00/$5.00
Columbia	656756-2	Highwire	CD5	U.K.	1991	$18.00
Columbia	CSK 73742	Highwire	CDJ	U.S.	1991	$7.00
Polygram		Honky Tonk Woman	CD5	U.K.	1994	$18.00
London	882 200-2	(I Can't Get no) Satisfaction	CD5	Germany	1990	$25.00
Virgin	VJDP-10243	I Go Wild	CD3	Japan	1995	$20.00/$5.00
Virgin	VJCP-15005	I Go Wild	CD5	Japan	1995	$23.00
Virgin	VSCDX 1539	I Go Wild	CD5	U.K.	1995	$11.00
Virgin	VSCDJ-1539	I Go Wild	CDJ	U.K.	1995	$30.00
Capital	38478	I Go Wild	CD5	U.S.	1994	$6.00
Virgin		I Go Wild	CDJ	U.S.	1994	$12.00
Polygram		It's All Over Now	CD5	U.K.	1994	$18.00
		Jump Back EP	CDJ	U.K.		$20.00
Polygram		Jumpin' Jack Flash	CD5	U.K.	1994	$18.00
Polygram		Last Time, The	CD5	U.K.	1994	$18.00
Virgin	38523	Like a Rolling Stone	CD5	U.S.	1995	$7.00
Virgin	DPRO-11044	Like a Rolling Stone	CDJ	U.S.	1995	$8.00
Polygram		Little Red Rooster	CD5	U.K.	1994	$18.00
Virgin		Love Is Strong	CD5	Australia	1994	$12.00
Virgin		Love Is Strong	CD5	Australia	1994	$12.00
Second version.						
Virgin		Love Is Strong	CD5	U.K.	1994	$12.00
Virgin		Love Is Strong	CD5	U.K.	1994	$18.00
Second version.						
Virgin		Love Is Strong	CD5	U.S.	1994	$6.00
Virgin	DPRO-14180	Love Is Strong	CDJ	U.S.	1994	$8.00
Virgin		Love Is Strong	CDJ	U.S.	1994	$8.00
Second version.						
CBS	3 655193	Mixed Emotions	CD3	Germany	1989	$18.00
Sony	10EP-3100	Mixed Emotions	CD3	Japan	1989	$18.00/$5.00
CBS	655193-2	Mixed Emotions	CD5	U.K.	1989	$18.00
Rolling Stones	CSK 1755	Mixed Emotions	CDJ	U.S.	1989	$18.00
Virgin	V238459	Out of Tears	CD5	Canada	1994	$10.00
Virgin	VSCD1524	Out of Tears	CD5	U.K.	1994	$18.00
Virgin	VSCDX1524	Out of Tears	CD5	U.K.	1994	$22.00
CD in tear-shaped folder.						
Virgin	38459	Out of Tears	CD5	U.S.	1994	$6.00
Virgin		Out of Tears	CDJ	U.S.	1994	$18.00
London	882144-2	Paint It Black	CD5	U.K.	1989	$25.00
Polygram		Paint It Black	CD5	U.K.	1994	$18.00
CBS	655422 3	Rock and a Hard Place	CD3	Germany	1989	$18.00
Sony	CSDS-8110	Rock and a Hard Place	CD3	Japan	1989	$18.00/$5.00
CBS	655448 2	Rock and a Hard Place	CD5	U.K.	1989	$18.00
CBS	655214 2	Rock and a Hard Place	CD5	U.K.	1989	$18.00
Columbia	CSK 73057	Rock and a Hard Place	CDJ	U.S.	1989	$15.00

Label	Catalog Number	Title	Type	Country	Year	Longbox Value / Value
Columbia	656892-2	Ruby Tuesday	CD5	Germany	1991	$18.00
Columbia	656892-5	Ruby Tuesday	CD5	U.K.	1991	$18.00
Columbia	656892-2	Ruby Tuesday	CD5	U.K.	1991	$18.00
Rolling Stones	656197-3	Sad Sad Sad	CD3	Germany	1990	$15.00
Polygram		Satisfaction	CD5	U.K.	1994	$18.00
Sony	657334 2	Sexdrive	CD5	Austria	1991	$18.00
CBS	657334-2	Sexdrive	CD5	Germany	1991	$15.00
Rolling Stones	SRCS-5532	Sexdrive	CD3	Japan	1991	$18.00/$5.00
Rolling Stones	CSK 73789	Sexdrive	CDJ	U.S.	1991	$7.00
Virgin		Sparks Will Fly	CDJ	U.S.	1994	$18.00
Columbia	655661-3	Terrifying	CD3	Germany	1989	$12.00
Columbia	655661-3	Terrifying	CD3	U.K.	1989	$12.00
Columbia	656122-2	Terrifying	CD5	U.K.	1989	$12.00
Columbia		Terrifying	CDJ	U.S.	1989	$20.00
London	PODD-1002	Time Is on My Side	CD3	Japan	1990	$18.00/$5.00
Virgin	DPRO11075	Wild Horses	CDJ	U.S.	1996	$6.00
Virgin		You Got Me Rocking	CD5	Australia	1994	$12.00
Virgin	VSCD1518	You Got Me Rocking	CD5	U.K.	1994	$18.00
Virgin	VSCDJ1518	You Got Me Rocking	CDJ	U.K.	1994	$18.00
Virgin	95808	You Got Me Rocking	CD5	U.S.	1994	$7.00
Virgin	V25H-38468	You Got Me Rocking	CD5	U.S.	1994	$7.00
Virgin		You Got Me Rocking	CDJ	U.S.	1994	$8.00
Virgin		You Got Me Rocking	CDJ	U.S.	1994	$8.00

Second version.

Rollins, Henry (Band)

Full Length

Label	Catalog Number	Title	Type	Country	Year	Longbox Value / Value
Imago	IM28024-2-DJ	End of Silence: Hammer of the Godz	DJ/Smplr	U.S.	1991	$20.00
Imago		Excerpts From Get in the Van	DJ/Smplr	U.S.	1994	$18.00
Image		Rollins Speaks	DJ/Intvw	U.S.	1992	$10.00

9 Tracks.

Label	Catalog Number	Title	Type	Country	Year	Longbox Value / Value
Image		Rollins Speaks	DJ/Intvw	U.S.	1992	$13.00

21 Tracks.

Label	Catalog Number	Title	Type	Country	Year	Longbox Value / Value
		Turned On: Live in Vienna Austria, 11/27/89	DJ/Smplr	U.S.		$30.00
Imago		Weight	DJ/LP	U.S.	1994	$12.00

Advance Issue.

Label	Catalog Number	Title	Type	Country	Year	Longbox Value / Value
Imago	IM 21047-2-DJ	Weight	DJ/LP	U.S.	1994	$20.00

CD in metal can.

Singles

Label	Catalog Number	Title	Type	Country	Year	Longbox Value / Value
Imago	25084	Disconnect	CD5	U.S.	1994	$6.00
Imago	28037	Do You Need a Friend	CDJ	U.S.	1992	$3.00
Imago	25072	Liar	CD5	U.S.	1994	$5.00
Imago	28075	Liar	CDJ	U.S.	1994	$3.00
Imago	28092	Liar	CDJ	U.S.	1994	$3.00
Imago	28017	Low Sell Option	CDJ	U.S.	1992	$3.00
Imago	250102	Tearing	CD5	U.K.	1992	$9.00
Imago	28026	Tearing	CDJ	U.S.	1992	$3.00

Rollins, Sonny

Full Length

Label	Catalog Number	Title	Type	Country	Year	Longbox Value / Value
Verve	815056-2	Brass/Trio	LP/LB	U.S.†	1985	$14.00/$8.00
Image	ID7174SO	Saxophone Colossus	LD	U.S.		$20.00
EMI		Sonny Rollins, Sonny Rollins Volume 2, Another I Couldn't Read	LTD/LP	U.K.	1994	$35.00

3 CD boxed set.

Label	Catalog Number	Title	Type	Country	Year	Longbox Value / Value
Milestone	FCD-9122	Sunny Days, Starry Nights	LP/LB	U.S.†	1985	$14.00/$8.00
Mobile	MFCD-801	Way Out West	LP/LB	U.S.†	1985	$14.00/$8.00

Romantics

Full Length

Label	Catalog Number	Title	Type	Country	Year	Longbox Value / Value
Nemp	ZK-38880	In Heat	LP/BP	U.S.†	1984	$14.00/$8.00
Nemp	ZK-340106	Rhythm Romance	LP/BP	U.S.†	1985	$14.00/$8.00

Singles

Label	Catalog Number	Title	Type	Country	Year	Longbox Value / Value
Columbia	651665-3	Talking In Your Sleep	CD3	U.K.	1988	$8.00

Romeo and

Singles

Label	Catalog Number	Title	Type	Country	Year	Longbox Value / Value
Elektra	PRCD 8695-2	For You I'll Do Anything	CDJ	U.S.	1993	$2.00

Romeo's Daughter

Singles

Label	Catalog Number	Title	Type	Country	Year	Longbox Value / Value
Alfa	10B3-4	Don't Break My Heart	CD3	Japan	1989	$13.00/$4.00
Jive		Don't Break My Heart	CDJ	U.S.	1988	$2.00
Jive	JIVECD-208	Heaven in Backseat	CD5	U.K.	1988	$8.00
Jive	1256-2-JDJ	Heaven in Backseat	CDJ	U.S.	1988	$2.00
Eastwest	247011-2	I Cry Myself to Sleep at Night	CD5	Germany	1989	$8.00
Jive	JIVECD-194	I Cry Myself to Sleep at Night	CD5	U.K.	1989	$8.00
Jive	1176-2-JDJ	I Cry Myself to Sleep at Night	CDJ	U.S.	1988	$2.00

Ronson, Mick

Full Length

Label	Catalog Number	Title	Type	Country	Year	Longbox Value / Value
Epic		A Mick Ronson Primier	DJ/Smplr	U.S.	1994	$15.00
Epic	ESK 6143	Heaven & Hull	DJ/Intvw	U.S.	1994	$10.00
Westwood One		Superstars: Mick Ronson Memorial Special	RS	U.S.	1994	$75.00

2 CD set. Airdate: 8/15/94.

Singles

Label	Catalog Number	Title	Type	Country	Year	Longbox Value / Value
		Don't Look Down	CD5	U.K.	1994	$10.00

Ronstadt, Linda

Full Length

Label	Catalog Number	Title	Type	Country	Year	Longbox Value / Value
Elektra	60185-2	Get Closer	LP/LB	U.S.†	1984	$14.00/$8.00
Asylum	106-2	Greatest Hits Vol. 1	LP/LB	U.S.†	1984	$14.00/$8.00
Asylum	516-2	Greatest Hits Vol. 1	LP/LB	U.S.†	1984	$14.00/$8.00
Capitol	CDP-46073	Heart Like a Wheel	LP/LB	U.S.†	1985	$14.00/$8.00
Image	IDML1012	In Concert	LD	U.S.		$30.00
Vestron	ML1012	In Concert	LD	U.S.	1984	$30.00
Elektra	960445-2	Linda Ronstadt	LP	Germany		$15.00
Elektra	60387-2	Lush Life	LP/LB	U.S.†	1985	$14.00/$8.00
Sony/Elektra		Sony Digital Masters Series	DJ/Smplr	U.S.		$35.00
Elektra	60260-2	What's New	LP/LB	U.S.†	1984	$14.00/$8.00

Singles

Label	Catalog Number	Title	Type	Country	Year	Longbox Value / Value
	DSP-1175	A Dream is a Wish Your Heart Makes	CDJ	Japan		$30.00
Elektra	PRCD 8904-2	A River for Him	CDJ	U.S.	1993	$2.00
Elektra	PR 8203-2	Adios	CDJ	U.S.	1989	$2.00
WEA	966651-2	All My Life	CD5	Germany	1990	$9.00
Pioneer	WPDP-6225	All My Life	CD3	Japan	1990	$12.00/$4.00
Elektra	EKR-105CD	All My Life	CD5	U.K.	1990	$9.00
Elektra	PR 8148	All My Life	CDJ	U.S.	1989	$2.00
Elektra	PR 8148-2	All My Life	CDJ	U.S.	1989	$2.00
		Blue Train	CDJ	U.S.		$3.00
WEA	966665-2	Don't Know Much	CD5	Germany	1989	$9.00
Pioneer	09P3-6196	Don't Know Much	CD3	Japan	1989	$12.00/$4.00
Elektra	EKR-101CD	Don't Know Much	CD5	U.K.	1989	$9.00
Elektra	PR 8118-2	Don't Know Much	CDJ	U.S.	1989	$2.00
MCA	MVDM-11	Dreams to Dream	CD3	Japan	1991	$12.00/$4.00
		Dreams to Dream	CDJ	U.S.		$7.00
Elektra	PRCD 8684-2	Entre Abismos	CDJ	U.S.	1992	$2.00
Elektra	PRCD 8626-2	Frenesi	CDJ	U.S.	1992	$2.00
Elektra	PRCD 8862-2	Heartbeat Accelerating	CDJ	U.S.	1993	$2.00
Elektra	PRCD 8905-2	Oh No, not My Baby	CDJ	U.S.	1993	$2.00
Elektra	PRCD 8550-2	Perfida	CDJ	U.S.	1992	$2.00
		Piel Canela	CDJ	Spain		$28.00
		Waiting, The	CDJ	U.S.		$3.00
Elektra	PR 9210-2	Waiting, The	CDJ	U.S.	1995	$3.00
Elektra	PR 8170-2	When Something is Wrong With My Baby	CDJ	U.S.	1989	$2.00
Elektra	EKR 177CD	Winter	CD5	U.K.	1993	$9.00

Ronstadt, Linda/Harris, Emmy Lou

Singles

Label	Catalog Number	Title	Type	Country	Year	Longbox Value / Value
		Feels Like Home	CDJ	U.S.		$3.00

Roots

Singles

Label	Catalog Number	Title	Type	Country	Year	Longbox Value / Value
Geffen	5176	Proceed II	CD5	U.S.	1995	$6.00

Ros, Edmundo

Full Length

Label	Catalog Number	Title	Type	Country	Year	Longbox Value / Value
London	810120-2	Latin Melodies	LP/LB	U.S.†	1985	$14.00/$8.00

Rose Chronicles

Singles

Label	Catalog Number	Title	Type	Country	Year	Longbox Value / Value
Nettwerk	W23077	Glide	CD5	Canada	1994	$8.00

Rose, Kennedy

Singles

Label	Catalog Number	Title	Type	Country	Year	Longbox Value / Value
IRS	PAND-013	Love Like This	CDJ	U.S.	1989	$7.00

Ross, Diana (and The Supremes)

Full Length

Label	Catalog Number	Title	Type	Country	Year	Longbox Value / Value
Warner	PCD-0538	30 Years of Music	DJ/Smplr	Japan		$150.00
Motown	MOTD-6105	All the Great Love Songs	LP/BP	U.S.		$14.00/$8.00
Motown	377463 6357-2/4	CD Sampler	DJ/Smplr	U.S.	1993	$10.00
Motown	6072-MD	Compact Command Performance	LP/BP	U.S.†	1984	$14.00/$8.00
Motown	6073-MD	Compact Command Performance	LP/BP	U.S.†	1984	$14.00/$8.00
Motown	5155-MD	Diana	LP/BP	U.S.		$14.00/$8.00
Pioneer	PA-84-070	Diana Ross in Concert	LD	U.S.	1984	$25.00
Motown	MOTD-8102	Diana + The Boss	LP/BP	U.S.		$14.00/$8.00
RCA	5422-2	Eaten Alive	LP/BP	U.S.		$14.00/$8.00
RCA	PCD1-5472	Eaten Alive	LP/BP	U.S.†	1985	$14.00/$8.00
Motown	MOTD-6072	Fourteen Greatest Hits	LP/BP	U.S.		$14.00/$8.00
Motown	MOTD-5313	Great Songs & Performances	LP/BP	U.S.		$14.00/$8.00
Motown	MOTD-237	Greatest Hits Vol. 1 & 2	LP/BP	U.S.		$14.00/$8.00
Motown	MOTD-5147	I Hear a Symphony	LP/BP	U.S.		$14.00/$8.00
Warner	PCD-232	If We Hold on Together Again	DJ/Smplr	Japan		$100.00
Motown	MOTD-8041	Join the Temptations + Together	LP/BP	U.S.		$18.00/$13.00
Motown	MOTD-5169	Live at Caesar's Palace	LP/BP	U.S.		$14.00/$8.00
Motown	MOTD-8121	Love Child + Supremes a Go-Go	LP/BP	U.S.		$18.00/$15.00
Motown	MOTD-8141	Merry Christmas + Someday at Christmas	LP/BP	U.S.		$18.00/$13.00
Motown	MOTD-5440	More Hits by the Supremes + Holland Dozier Holland	LP/BP	U.S.		$20.00/$18.00
RCA	6388-2	Red Hot Rhythm & Blues	LP/BP	U.S.		$14.00/$8.00
RCA	PCD1-4677	Ross	LP/BP	U.S.†	1984	$14.00/$8.00
		Sixties Legends	RS	U.S.	1992	$15.00

2 CD set. Airdate: 7/10/92.

Label	Catalog Number	Title	Type	Country	Year	Longbox Value / Value
Motown	MOTD-5371	Supremes Sing Motown	LP/BP	U.S.		$14.00/$8.00
RCA	PCD1-5009	Swept Away	LP/BP	U.S.†	1985	$14.00/$8.00
Motown	PCD-0538	Thirty Years of Music	DJ/Smplr	Japan		$120.00
Motown	MOTD-8126	Touch Me in the Morning + Baby It's Me	LP/BP	U.S.		$14.00/$8.00
Motown	MOTD-6073	Twenty Greatest Hits	LP/BP	U.S.		$14.00/$8.00
Motown	MOTD2-5382	Twenty-Fifth Anniversary	LP/BP	U.S.		$25.00/$20.00

2CD set.

Label	Catalog Number	Title	Type	Country	Year	Longbox Value / Value
EMI		Ultimate CD Sampler	DJ/Smplr	U.K.		$20.00
Pioneer	PA86-M048	Visions Of Diana	8"LD	U.S.	1985	$7.00
Motown	MOTD-5270	Where Did Our Love Go	LP/BP	U.S.		$14.00/$8.00

Singles

Label	Catalog Number	Title	Type	Country	Year	Longbox Value / Value
Motown	R10M-115	Ain't No Mountain High Enough	CD3	Japan	1989	$12.00/$4.00
EMI		Chain Reaction	CDJ	U.K.		$14.00
Motown	R10M-119	Endless Love	CD3	Japan	1989	$12.00/$4.00
EMI	204406-2	Force Behind the Power	CD5	Germany	1989	$10.00
EMI	CDEM-221	Force Behind the Power	CD5	U.K.	1989	$10.00
EMI		Gone	CDJ	U.K.		$10.00
EMI		Heart Don't Change	CDJ	U.K.		$14.00
Motown	ZD-43782	I'm Still Waiting	CD5	U.K.	1990	$10.00
	WMD5-4012	If We Hold on Together	CD3	Japan		$13.00/$4.00
MCA	MVDM-6	If We Hold on Together	CD3	Japan	1991	$12.00/$4.00
		If We Hold on Together	CD5	U.K.		$10.00
		If We Hold on Together	CD5	U.K.		$10.00

Second version.

Label	Catalog Number	Title	Type	Country	Year	Longbox Value / Value
Motown	860473	If You're Gonna Love Me Right	CD5	U.S.	1995	$5.00
		If You're Not Gonna Love Me Right	CDJ	U.S.		$2.00
Motown	ZD-42308	Love Hangover	CD5	Germany	1988	$10.00
Motown	ZD-42308	Love Hangover	CD5	U.K.	1988	$10.00
EMI	CDEM-73	Mr. Lee	CD5	U.K.	1988	$10.00
Warner Brothers	PRO-CD-4627	No Matter What You Do	CDJ	U.S.	1990	$2.00
Warner Brothers	9 21843-2	No Matter What You Do	CDJ	U.S.	1990	$2.00
EMI	203427-3	Paradise	CD5	Germany	1989	$10.00
EMI	CDEM-94	Paradise	CD5	U.K.	1989	$10.00
Motown	ZD-41955	Reach Out and Touch	CD3	U.K.	1989	$10.00
EMI		Take Me Higher	CDJ	U.K.		$14.00
Motown	860433	Take Me Higher	CD5	U.S.	1995	$5.00
EMI	TODP-2352	That's Why I Call You My Friend	CD3	Japan	1992	$12.00/$4.00
Motown	R10M-117	Theme From Mahogany	CD3	Japan	1989	$12.00/$4.00
EMI	203606-3	This House	CD3	Germany	1989	$10.00
EMI	CDEM-118	This House	CD5	U.K.	1989	$10.00
Motown	R10M-116	Touch Me in the Morning	CD3	Japan	1989	$12.00/$4.00
Motown	R10M-118	Upside Down	CD3	Japan	1989	$12.00/$4.00
Toshiba	TOCP-7526	When You Dream	CD3	Japan	1992	$15.00
EMI	205600-2	When You Tell Me That You Love Me	CD5	Germany	1991	$10.00
EMI	TODP-2363	When You Tell Me That You Love Me	CD3	Japan	1992	$12.00/$4.00
EMI	CDEM-217	When You Tell Me That You Love Me	CD5	U.K.	1991	$10.00
Motown	CD45 1648	When You Tell Me That You Love Me	CDJ	U.S.	1991	$2.00
Motown	886592	Where Did Our Love Go	CD3	Germany	1989	$10.00
Motown	ZD-41957	Where Did Our Love Go	CD3	U.K.	1989	$10.00
Motown	CD EM332	Why Do Fools Fall in Love	CD5	U.K.	1994	$10.00
Motown	XP10-2082	Workin' Overtime	CD3	Japan	1989	$12.00/$4.00
EMI	CDEM-91	Workin' Overtime	CD5	U.K.	1989	$10.00
Motown	CD45 17824	Workin' Overtime	CDJ	U.S.	1989	$2.00
Motown	374634812	You're Gonna Love It	CD5	U.S.	1991	$5.00
		Your Love	CD5	U.K.		$10.00
		Your Love	CD5	U.K.		$10.00

Second version.

Rossi, Francis

Singles

Label	Catalog Number	Title	Type	Country	Year	Longbox Value / Value
		This Summer	CD5	U.K.	1996	$10.00
		This Summer	CD5	U.K.	1996	$10.00

Second version.

Label	Catalog Number	Title	Type	Country	Year	Longbox Value / Value
		This Summer	CD5	U.K.	1996	$10.00

Third version.

Rossington-Collins Band

Full Length

Label	Catalog Number	Title	Type	Country	Year	Longbox Value / Value
MCA		Love Your Man	LP/LB	U.S.		$12.00/$7.00

With three bonus tracks.

Label	Catalog Number	Title	Type	Country	Year	Longbox Value / Value
MCA	MCAD 31323	This Is the Way	LP/LB	U.S.		$14.00/$8.00

Roth, David Lee

Full Length

Label	Catalog Number	Title	Type	Country	Year	Longbox Value / Value
Album Network		A Little Ain't Enough-World Premiere	DJ/RS	U.S.	1991	$15.00
Warner Brothers	2 6477-2-DJ	A Little Ain't Enough	DJ/LP	U.S.	1991	$15.00
		House of Blues	RS	U.S.	1994	$40.00

2 CD set. Airdate: 8/28/94.

Label	Catalog Number	Title	Type	Country	Year	Longbox Value / Value
Warner	PCS-130	Life's Just Rock 'N' Roll	DJ/Smplr	Japan	1994	$75.00
Westwood One		Off the Record	RS	U.S.	1994	$30.00

Airdate: 4/25/94.

Label	Catalog Number	Title	Type	Country	Year	Longbox Value / Value
Warner Brothers	43XD-2002	Skyscraper	LTD/LP	Japan	1988	$35.00

Gold disc.

Label	Catalog Number	Title	Type	Country	Year	Longbox Value / Value
Warner Brothers	9 25671-2-DJ	Skyscraper	DJ/LP	U.S.	1988	$10.00
Media America		Up Close	RS	U.S.	1988	$35.00

2 CD set.

Label	Catalog Number	Title	Type	Country	Year	Longbox Value / Value
Media America		Up Close	RS	U.S.	1994	$35.00

2 CD set.

Singles

Label	Catalog Number	Title	Type	Country	Year	Longbox Value / Value
WEA	W-7650CD	California Girls	CD5	U.K.	1988	$8.00
Warner Brothers	10P3-6028	Damn Good	CD3	Japan	1988	$13.00/$4.00
Warner Brothers	PRO-CD-3017	Damn Good	CDJ	U.S.	1988	$2.00
Warner Brothers		Damn Good/Knucklebones	CDJ	U.S.	1988	$7.00

2 promo CDs in shrink-wrapped set.

Label	Catalog Number	Title	Type	Country	Year	Longbox Value / Value
Warner Brothers	920863-2	Just Like Paradise	CD3	Germany	1988	$8.00
Atlantic	10SW-16	Just Like Paradise	CD3	Japan	1988	$13.00/$4.00
Warner Brothers	W-8119 CD	Just Like Paradise	CD3	U.K.	1988	$8.00
Warner Brothers	PRO-CD-2920	Just Like Paradise	CDJ	U.S.	1988	$2.00
Warner Brothers	PRO-CD-2956	Knucklebones	CDJ	U.S.	1988	$2.00
WEA	7599-21842-2	Lil Ain't Enough	CD5	Germany	1991	$8.00
Warner Brothers	PRO-CD-4672	Lil Ain't Enough	CDJ	U.S.	1991	$2.00
Warner Brothers		Night Life	CD5	U.K.	1994	$10.00

Second version.

Label	Catalog Number	Title	Type	Country	Year	Longbox Value / Value
Warner Brothers		Nightlife	CD5	U.K.	1994	$10.00
Warner Brothers	9362-40045-2	Sensible Shoes	CD5	Germany	1991	$8.00
Warner Brothers	W-0016CD	Sensible Shoes	CD5	U.K.	1991	$8.00
Warner Brothers	PRO-CD-4738	Sensible Shoes	CDJ	U.S.	1991	$2.00
Warner Brothers	PRO-CD-6744	She's My Machine	CDJ	U.S.	1994	$2.00
Warner Brothers	PRO-CD-2978	Skyscraper	CDJ	U.S.	1988	$2.00
Pioneer	10SW-5	Stand Up	CDJ	Japan	1988	$20.00
Warner Brothers	PRO-CD-2929	Stand Up	CDJ	U.S.	1988	$2.00
Warner Brothers	PRO-CD-4868	Tell the Truth	CDJ	U.S.	1991	$2.00

Roth, Kevin

Full Length

Label	Catalog Number	Title	Type	Country	Year	Longbox Value / Value
CBS	CK 48889	Daddy Sings	LP/LB	U.S.		$12.00/$7.00

Rothberg, Patti

Singles

Label	Catalog Number	Title	Type	Country	Year	Longbox Value / Value
	DPRO10450	Inside	CDJ	U.S.		$2.00

Rottin Raszkals

Singles

Label	Catalog Number	Title	Type	Country	Year	Longbox Value / Value
Motown	860367	Hey Alright	CD5	U.S.	1995	$6.00
Motown	860261	Ohh Yeah	CD5	U.S.	1994	$5.00

Roula

Singles

Label	Catalog Number	Title	Type	Country	Year	Longbox Value / Value
	1008	Lick It	CD5	U.S.	1994	$5.00

Rouse, Charlie

Full Length

Label	Catalog Number	Title	Type	Country	Year	Longbox Value / Value
Rykodisc	RCD 10053	Cinnamon Flower	LP/LB	U.S.		$12.00/$7.00

Roussos, Demis

Full Length

Label	Catalog Number	Title	Type	Country	Year	Longbox Value / Value
Mercury	800040-2	Demis	LP/BP	U.S.†	1983	$14.00/$8.00

Rowland

Singles

Label	Catalog Number	Title	Type	Country	Year	Longbox Value / Value
Mercury	ROWCD-1	Tonight	CD5	U.K.	1988	$8.00
Mercury	DEXCD-14	Walk Away	CD5	U.K.	1988	$8.00
Mercury	ROWCD-2	Young Man	CD5	U.K.	1988	$8.00

Roxanne

Singles

Label	Catalog Number	Title	Type	Country	Year	Longbox Value / Value
Select	8502	Ya Brother Does	CDJ	U.S.	1992	$2.00

Roxette

Full Length

Label	Catalog Number	Title	Type	Country	Year	Longbox Value / Value
McDonald's		Favorites From Crash! Boom! Bang!	LP	U.S.	1994	$8.00
Warner	PCD-0461	Hits After Hits: Special DJ Copy	DJ/Smplr	Japan	1994	$75.00
EMI		Look Sharp	LTD/LP	U.K.	1989	$30.00

Picture disc CD.

Label	Catalog Number	Title	Type	Country	Year	Longbox Value / Value
		Pearls of Passion	LP	Sweden	1986	$40.00
EMI	SPCD-1286	Singles Collection	DJ/Smplr	Japan		$80.00
EMI	SPCD-1280	Special DJ Copy	DJ/Smplr	Japan		$40.00

Singles

Label	Catalog Number	Title	Type	Country	Year	Longbox Value / Value
Capitol	880676-2	Almost Unreal	CD5	Germany	1993	$10.00
Toshiba	TODP-2415	Almost Unreal	CD3	Japan	1994	$12.00/$4.00
Capitol	CDEM-268	Almost Unreal	CD5	U.K.	1993	$10.00
Capitol	DPRO-79748	Almost Unreal	CDJ	U.S.	1993	$2.00
EMI	136434-2	Big L	CD5	Germany	1991	$10.00
Toshiba	TODP-2314	Big L	CD3	Japan	1991	$12.00/$4.00
EMI	136471-2	Church of Your Heart	CD5	Germany	1991	$10.00
EMI	CDEM-227	Church of Your Heart	CD5	U.K.	1991	$10.00
EMI	DPRO-04837	Church of Your Heart	CDJ	U.S.	1992	$2.00
EMI	CDEMS 324	Crash! Boom! Bang!	CD5	U.K.	1994	$10.00
EMI	CDEM 324	Crash! Boom! Bang!	CD5	U.K.	1994	$10.00
EMI	136379-2	Dangerous	CD5	Germany	1990	$10.00
EMI		Don't Bore Us	CDV	U.K.	1996	$12.00
EMI	136353-3	Dressed for Success	CD3	Germany	1989	$10.00
EMI	CDEM-96	Dressed For Success	CD5	U.K.	1989	$10.00
EMI	CDEM-162	Dressed For Success	CD5	U.K.	1989	$10.00
EMI	136404-2	Fading Like a Flower	CD5	Germany	1991	$10.00
Toshiba	TODP-2281	Fading Like a Flower	CD3	Japan	1991	$12.00/$4.00
EMI	CDEM-190	Fading Like a Flower	CD5	U.K.	1991	$10.00
EMI	DPRO-04755	Fading Like a Flower	CDJ	U.S.	1991	$2.00
EMI		Fingertips '93	CD5	Australia	1993	$15.00
		Fingertips '93	CD5	Australia	1994	$10.00
		Fireworks	CD5	Australia	1994	$10.00
EMI	TODP-2373	How Do You Do	CD3	Japan	1992	$12.00/$4.00
EMI	C2 56252	How Do You Do	CD5	U.S.	1992	$5.00
EMI	DPRO-04626	How Do You Do	CDJ	U.S.	1992	$2.00
EMI	136380-2	It Must Have Been Love	CD5	Germany	1990	$10.00
EMI	TOCP-6245	It Must Have Been Love	CD5	Japan	1990	$13.00
EMI	CDEM-141	It Must Have Been Love	CD5	U.K.	1990	$10.00
EMI	CDEM- 258	It Must Have Been Love	CD5	U.K.	1990	$10.00
EMI	136400-2	Joyride	CD5	Germany	1991	$10.00
EMI	CDEM-177	Joyride	CD5	U.K.	1991	$10.00
EMI	DPRO 04696	Joyride	CDJ	U.S.	1991	$2.00
EMI	DPRO 04724	Joyride	CDJ	U.S.	1991	$2.00
EMI		June Afternoon	CD5	Germany	1996	$12.00
EMI		June Afternoon	CD5	U.K.	1996	$10.00
EMI	136323-3	Listen to Your Heart	CD3	Germany	1989	$10.00
EMI	CDEM-108	Listen to Your Heart	CD5	U.K.	1989	$10.00
EMI	CDEM-149	Listen to Your Heart	CD5	U.K.	1990	$10.00
EMI	136350-3	Look, The	CD3	Germany	1989	$10.00
EMI	136333-2	Look, The	CD5	Germany	1989	$10.00
EMI	CDEM-87	Look, The	CD5	U.K.	1989	$10.00
EMI	TODP-2388	Queen of Rain	CD3	Japan	1993	$12.00/$4.00
		Queen of Rain	CD5	U.K.		$10.00
		Queen of Rain	CD5	U.K.		$10.00

Second version.

Label	Catalog Number	Title	Type	Country	Year	Longbox Value / Value
EMI		She Doesn't Live Here Anymore	CD5	Germany	1996	$12.00
EMI		Sleeping in My Car	CD5	U.K.	1994	$10.00
EMI		Sleeping in My Car	CD5	U.K.	1994	$10.00

Second version.

Label	Catalog Number	Title	Type	Country	Year	Longbox Value / Value
EMI	DPRO-19818	Sleeping in My Car	CDJ	U.S.	1994	$2.00
EMI	DPRO-04802	Spending My Time	CDJ	U.S.	1991	$2.00
		Vulnerable	CD5	U.K.	1995	$10.00
EMI	TOCD-8675	You Don't Understand Me	CD5	Japan	1995	$25.00

Roxx Gang

Singles

Label	Catalog Number	Title	Type	Country	Year	Longbox Value / Value
Virgin	VJD-10203	No Easy Way Out	CD3	Japan	1989	$12.00/$3.00
Virgin	PR 2661	No Easy Way Out	CDJ	U.S.	1988	$2.00
Virgin	PR 2862	Scratch My Back	CDJ	U.S.	1988	$2.00

Roxy Blue

Full Length

Label	Catalog Number	Title	Type	Country	Year	Longbox Value / Value
		In Concert	RS	U.S.	1992	$80.00

With Nirvana, Airdate: 10/1292.

Singles

Label	Catalog Number	Title	Type	Country	Year	Longbox Value / Value
Geffen	PRO-CD-4431	Luv on Me	CDJ	U.S.	1992	$2.00
Geffen	PRO-CD-4376	Rob in the Cradle	CDJ	U.S.	1992	$2.00
Geffen	PRO-CD-4377	Rob in the Cradle	CDJ	U.S.	1992	$2.00

Roxy Music

Full Length

Label	Catalog Number	Title	Type	Country	Year	Longbox Value / Value
Warner Brothers	23686-2	Avalon	LP/LB	U.S.†	1984	$14.00/$8.00
BBC Radio		BBC Classic Tracks	RS	U.S.	1991	$25.00

Airdate: 12/9/91.

Label	Catalog Number	Title	Type	Country	Year	Longbox Value / Value
BBC Radio		BBC Classic Tracks	RS	U.S.	1992	$20.00

Airdate: 8/10/92.

Label	Catalog Number	Title	Type	Country	Year	Longbox Value / Value
DIR		King Biscuit Flour Hour	RS	U.S.	1988	$30.00

Airdate: 2/7/88.

Label	Catalog Number	Title	Type	Country	Year	Longbox Value / Value
Pioneer Artists	PA-84-079	Roxy Music	LD	U.S.	1984	$25.00

Singles

Label	Catalog Number	Title	Type	Country	Year	Longbox Value / Value
Virgin	880986	Jealous Guy	CD3	Germany	1988	$10.00
BMG	880986	Jealous Guy	CD5	Germany	1988	$10.00
Virgin	CDT-8	Jealous Guy	CD3	U.K.	1988	$10.00
Virgin	CDF-8	Jealous Guy	CD5	U.K.	1988	$10.00
EG	663 704	Love is the Drug	CD5	U.K.	1990	$9.00

Royal, Billy Joe

Singles

Label	Catalog Number	Title	Type	Country	Year	Longbox Value / Value
Atlantic	PRCD 3431-2	A Ring Where a Ring Used to Be	CDJ	U.S.	1990	$2.00
Atlantic	PRCD 4641-2	Funny How Time Slips Away	CDJ	U.S.	1992	$2.00
Atlantic	PRCD 3694-2	If the Jukebox Took Teardrops	CDJ	U.S.	1990	$2.00
		Love Has no Right	CDJ	U.S.		$2.00
		Tell It Like It Is	CDJ	U.S.		$2.00
Atlantic	PR 2912-2	Til I Can't Take It Anymore	CDJ	U.S.	1989	$2.00

Royal Court of China

Singles

Label	Catalog Number	Title	Type	Country	Year	Longbox Value / Value
A&M	CD 17770	Geared & Primed	CDJ	U.S.	1989	$2.00
A&M	CD 17677	Half the Truth	CDJ	U.S.	1988	$2.00

Royal Crescent Mob

Singles

Label	Catalog Number	Title	Type	Country	Year	Longbox Value / Value
Sire	PRO-CD-3524	Hungry	CDJ	U.S.	1989	$3.00
Sire	PRO-CD-4681	Konk	CDJ	U.S.	1991	$2.00
Sire	PRO-CD-3710	Nana	CDJ	U.S.	1989	$2.00
Sire	9 40066-2	Time Bomb	CD5	U.S.	1991	$3.00

Royalty

Singles

Label	Catalog Number	Title	Type	Country	Year	Longbox Value / Value
Sire	PRO-CD-3484	Baby Gonna Shake	CDJ	U.S.	1989	$2.00

Rozalla

Singles

Label	Catalog Number	Title	Type	Country	Year	Longbox Value / Value
Pulse 8	665124	Are You Ready to Fly?	CD5	Germany	1992	$8.00
Pulse 8	AVCD-20001	Are You Ready to Fly?	CD5	Japan	1992	$12.00
Pulse 8	CDLOSE-21	Are You Ready to Fly?	CD5	U.K.	1992	$8.00
Epic	49K 74729	Are You Ready to Fly?	CD5	U.S.	1992	$5.00
Epic	ESK 74728	Are You Ready to Fly?	CDJ	U.S.	1992	$3.00
Pulse 8	664796	Everybody's Free	CD5	Germany	1991	$8.00
Avex Trax	AVDD-20025	Everybody's Free	CD3	Japan	1992	$12.00/$4.00
Pulse 8	CDLOSE-13	Everybody's Free	CD5	U.K.	1991	$8.00
Epic	49K 7444	Everybody's Free	CD5	U.S.	1992	$5.00
Epic	ESK 74388	Everybody's Free	CDJ	U.S.	1992	$3.00
Pulse 8	CDLOSE-15	Faith	CD5	U.K.	1991	$8.00
Epic	47887	Faith	CD5	U.S.	1991	$5.00
Epic	ESK 77286	I Love Music	CDJ	U.S.	1993	$3.00
Pulse 8	CDLOSE-29	In Four Choons Later	CD5	U.K.	1992	$8.00
Epic	49K 78023	Losing My Religon	CD5	U.S.	1995	$5.00
Pulse 8	7432110165	Love Breakdown	CD5	Germany	1992	$8.00
Pulse 8	CDLOSE-28	Love Breakdown	CD5	U.K.	1992	$8.00

Label	Catalog Number	Title	Type	Country	Year	Longbox Value / Value

RTZ

Label	Catalog Number	Title	Type	Country	Year	Longbox Value / Value
Full Length						
Giant	9 24422-2	Return to Zero	DJ/LP	U.S.	1991	$12.00
	CD and jewel box in slipcase.					
Singles						
Giant	PRO-CD-4859	Face the Music	CDJ	U.S.	1991	$2.00
Giant	W-0094CD	Until Your Love Comes Back Around	CD5	U.K.	1992	$9.00

Rubber Rodeo

Label	Catalog Number	Title	Type	Country	Year	Longbox Value / Value
Full Length						
Pioneer	PA-84-M016	Scenic Views	8"LD	U.S.	1984	$12.00

Ruby

Label	Catalog Number	Title	Type	Country	Year	Longbox Value / Value
Singles						
	42K78188	Paraffin	CD5	U.S.		$4.00
Pepsi Co.		Thank Heaven	CDJ	U.S.	1996	$3.00

Ruby Blue

Label	Catalog Number	Title	Type	Country	Year	Longbox Value / Value
Singles						
Fontana	RBCD-3	Can It Be	CD5	U.K.	1990	$8.00
Red Flame	RFSCD-63	I Feel Good Now	CD5	U.K.	1991	$8.00
Fontana	RBCD-2	Primitive Man	CD5	U.K.	1990	$8.00
Fontana	RBCD-1	Quiet Mind	CD5	U.K.	1990	$8.00

Rude Boys

Label	Catalog Number	Title	Type	Country	Year	Longbox Value / Value
Singles						
		Come on Let's Do This	CDJ	U.S.		$2.00
Atlantic	PRCD 4636-2	My Kinda Girl	CDJ	U.S.	1992	$2.00

Ruff, Michael

Label	Catalog Number	Title	Type	Country	Year	Longbox Value / Value
Singles						
NPE		That's Not Me	CDJ	U.S.	1988	$6.00

Ruff-N-Rugged

Label	Catalog Number	Title	Type	Country	Year	Longbox Value / Value
Singles						
	3007	Swing Sump'n Ruff	CD5	U.S.	1994	$5.00

Ruffin, Jimmy

Label	Catalog Number	Title	Type	Country	Year	Longbox Value / Value
Full Length						
Motown	5445	Sing Top Ten	LP/BP	U.S.		$12.00/$7.00

Ruffner, Mason

Label	Catalog Number	Title	Type	Country	Year	Longbox Value / Value
Full Length						
Columbia	CSK 40601	Gypsy Music	DJ/LP	U.S.	1987	$12.00
	Advance issue.					

Ruffnex Sound System

Label	Catalog Number	Title	Type	Country	Year	Longbox Value / Value
Singles						
Warner Brothers	43578	Stick by Me	CD5	U.S.	1995	$5.00

Rufinos, Los

Label	Catalog Number	Title	Type	Country	Year	Longbox Value / Value
Singles						
Continental	11452	Serie De Platino	CD5	U.S.	1994	$5.00

Rugburns

Label	Catalog Number	Title	Type	Country	Year	Longbox Value / Value
Singles						
	40204	Mommy I'm Sorry	CD5	U.S.	1994	$5.00
	DPRO 3005	War	CDJ	U.S.		$2.00

Ruin, C/Lunch, L

Label	Catalog Number	Title	Type	Country	Year	Longbox Value / Value
Singles						
Big Cat	26	Don't Fear the Reaper	CD5	U.S.	1994	$5.00

Rule, Bob

Label	Catalog Number	Title	Type	Country	Year	Longbox Value / Value
Singles						
Mercury	CDP 1187	She Gets too High	CDJ	U.S.	1994	$2.00

Rumblefish

Label	Catalog Number	Title	Type	Country	Year	Longbox Value / Value
Singles						
Eastwest	96181-2	Everything Electrical	CD5	U.S.	1992	$5.00
Eastwest	PRCD 4557-2	Everything Electrical	CDJ	U.S.	1992	$2.00

Run DMC

Label	Catalog Number	Title	Type	Country	Year	Longbox Value / Value
Singles						
Profile	977542	Down With the King	CD5	U.S.	1994	$5.00
Intercord	825 909	Faces	CD5	Germany	1991	$10.00
Profile	PROFCD-328	Faces	CD5	U.K.	1991	$10.00
Eastwest	257444-2	Ghostbusters	CD3	Germany	1989	$10.00
MCA	CD45 17929	Ghostbusters	CDJ	U.S.	1989	$2.00
Polygram	886335-2	Mary Mary	CD5	Germany	1988	$10.00
London	P13L-37003	Mary Mary	CD3	Japan	1988	$12.00/$4.00
London	P13L-40001	Mary Mary	CD3	Japan	1988	$12.00/$4.00
Profile	7400	Ooh, Whatcha Gonna Do	CDJ	U.S.	1993	$2.00
Polygram	886308-2	Run's House	CD5	Germany	1988	$10.00
London	LONCD-177	Run's House	CD5	U.K.	1988	$10.00
Profile	5202	Run's House	CDJ	U.S.	1988	$2.00
IRS	977 565	What's It All About	CD5	Germany	1990	$10.00
Profile	7315	What's It All About	CDJ	U.S.	1990	$2.00

Runaways

Label	Catalog Number	Title	Type	Country	Year	Longbox Value / Value
Full Length						
Mercury	PPD-3080	Queens of Noise	LP	Japan		$30.00
Collector's Pipeline	TCP 015CD	Queens of Noise	LP	U.S.	1994	$16.00
Mercury	PPD-3079	Runaways, The	LP	Japan	1986	$30.00
Collector's Pipeline	TCP 014CD	Runaways, The	LP	U.S.	1994	$16.00

Rundgren

Label	Catalog Number	Title	Type	Country	Year	Longbox Value / Value
Full Length						
		Difference, The	RS		1995 to present	$60.00
	2 CD radio show series with various artists of live material and intervies. Broadcasts about every week since 1995. Values per show average $60 but range from $30 to $100 depending on the artist.					
Warner Brothers	9 26478-2-Dj	2nd Wind	DJ/LP	U.S.	1991	$17.00
	Picture disc.					
Warner Brothers	9 26478-2	2nd Wind	LP/LB	U.S.	1991	$14.00/$8.00
Castle	CMC 3078 CD	Castle Masters Collection	LP	Germany	1992	$25.00
Album Network		In the Studio (Something/Anything)	RS	U.S.	1989	$25.00
	Airdate: 5/22/89.					
Album Network		In the Studio (Something/Anything)	RS	U.S.	1992	$25.00
	Airdate: 2/1/92.					
DIR		King Biscuit Flour Hour	RS	U.S.	1989	$40.00
	Airdate: 8/6/89.					
DIR		King Biscuit Flour Hour	RS	U.S.	1992	$40.00
	Airdate: 4/24/92.					
DIR		King Biscuit Flour Hour	RS	U.S.	1994	$50.00
	Airdate: 7/31/94.					
DIR		King Biscuit Flour Hour	RS	U.S.	1995	$25.00
DIR		King Biscuit Flour Hour	RS	U.S.	1995	$50.00
	Airdate: 8/27/95.					
Warner Brothers		Nearly Human	LP/LB	U.S.		$12.00/$7.00
Forward	71266	No World Order	DJ/LP	U.S.	1993	$10.00
Castle	TFO 3/2 3/1	Runt & Hermit of Mink Hollow	LP	France	1988	$25.00
	2 CD set.					
Philips	310690267-2	TR-I: No World Order	LP	U.S.	1994	$30.00
	CD+I version.					
Singles						
Castle	CD3-6	Bang the Drum All Day	CD3	U.K.	1988	$10.00
Warner Brothers	PRO-CD-3643	Can't Stop Running	CDJ	U.S.	1989	$3.00
Warner Brothers	PRO-CD-4551	Change Myself	CDJ	U.S.	1991	$3.00
		Day Job	CDJ	U.S.		$3.00
Forward	7005	Fascist Christ	CDJ	U.S.	1993	$3.00
Rhino	885852	I Saw the Light	CD3	Germany	1990	$9.00
Rhino	R373025	I Saw the Light	CD3	U.S.	1988	$6.00/$4.00
Forward		Individualist, The	CDJ	U.S.		$7.00
Canyon	PCDY-0018	No World Order	CD3	Japan	1993	$13.00/$4.00
Warner Brothers	PRO-CD-3632	Parallel Lines	CDJ	U.S.	1989	$3.00
Forward	7006	Property	CDJ	U.S.	1993	$3.00
Warner Brothers	PRO-CD-4553	Public Servant	CDJ	U.S.	1991	$3.00
Warner Brothers	PRO-CD-3538	Want of a Nail, The	CDJ	U.S.	1989	$3.00

Running Wild

Label	Catalog Number	Title	Type	Country	Year	Longbox Value / Value
Singles						
EMI	203552-2	Bad to the Bone	CD5	Germany	1989	$9.00
EMI	203555-2	Bad to the Bone	CD5	Germany	1989	$9.00
Victor	VICP-15007	Falling Away	CD5	Japan	1991	$13.00
Noise	VICP-15020	Lead or Gold	CD5	japan	1992	$13.00
EMI	204248-2	Little Big Horn	CD5	Germany	1991	$8.00
EMI	203652 2	Wild Animals	CD5	U.K.	1989	$9.00

Runrig

Label	Catalog Number	Title	Type	Country	Year	Longbox Value / Value
Full Length						
Chrysalis		Cutter and the Clean	LTD/LP	U.K.	1994	$25.00/$15.00
	25th Anniversary edition in 6"x11" longbox.					
Singles						
Chrysalis	CHSCD-3594	Capture the Heart	CD5	U.K.	1990	$8.00
		Greatest Flame	CD5	U.K.		$10.00
		Greatest Flame	CD5	U.K.		$10.00
	Second version.					
Chrysalis	323779-2	Hearthammer	CD5	Germany	1991	$8.00
Chrysalis	CHSCD-3754	Hearthammer	CD5	U.K.	1991	$8.00
Chrysalis	CHSCD-3404	News From Heaven	CD5	U.K.	1989	$8.00
Ario	885041	Protect and Survive	CD5	Germany	1988	$8.00
Chrysalis	CHSCD-3284	Protect and Survive	CD5	U.K.	1988	$8.00
Chrysalis	CHSCD-3952	Wonderful	CD5	U.K.	1993	$8.00

RuPaul

Label	Catalog Number	Title	Type	Country	Year	Longbox Value / Value
Full Length						
Tommy Boy		A Shade Shady	DJ/Smplr	U.S.		$8.00
Tommy Boy	854	Everything You Always Wanted to Know About Rupaul	DJ/Intvw	U.S.	1993	$15.00
Tommy Boy	565	Back To My Roots	CD5	U.S.	1993	$5.00
Singles						
Tommy Boy	7593	Little Drummer Boy	CD5	U.S.	1993	$5.00
Isba	IS12K-1052	Supermodel	CD5	Canada	1993	$7.00
Tommy Boy	542	Supermodel	CD5	U.S.	1993	$5.00

Rurales De N.L.

Label	Catalog Number	Title	Type	Country	Year	Longbox Value / Value
Singles						
Cema Latino	31829	Millonario De Amor	CD5	U.S.	1994	$5.00

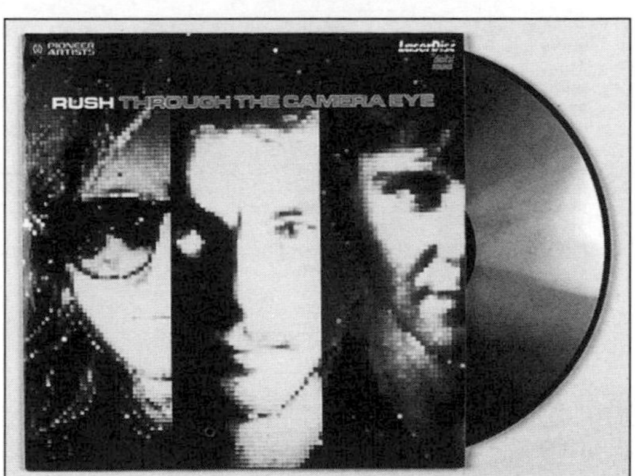

Rush – Through the Camera Eye (Pioneer PA-85-112)

Rush

Label	Catalog Number	Title	Type	Country	Year	Longbox Value / Value
Full Length						
Epic	258P-5166	2112	LP	Japan		$35.00
Epic	258P-5162	A Show of Hands	LP	Japan		$35.00
Polygram	080-575-1	A Show of Hands	LD	U.S.	1989	$45.00
Atlantic	ANK-1067	Counterparts	DJ/LP	Canada	1993	$40.00
	CD in press kit.					
Atlantic/Anthem	7567-82528-2	Counterparts	LTD/LP	Germany	1994	$35.00
	Etched jewel box.					
Epic	258P-5080	Exit...Stage Left	LP	Japan		$35.00
Pioneer	PA-83-035	Exit...Stage Left	LD	U.S.	1983	$50.00
Pioneer	PA-83-035	Exit...Stage Left	LD	U.S.	1990	$60.00
	Digital audio.					
Epic	258P-5167	Farewell To Kings	LP	Japan		$35.00
Epic	258P-5077	Grace Under Pressure	LP	Japan		$35.00
Mercury	818 476-2	Grace Under Pressure	LP/BP	U.S.†	1984	$14.00/$8.00
Polygram	080-103-1	Grace Under Pressure Tour	LD	U.S.	1988	$35.00
Epic	258P-5168	Hemisphere	LP	Japan		$35.00
Epic	258P-5079	Hold Your Fire	LP	Japan		$35.00
Album Network		In the Studio (Moving Pictures)	RS	U.S.	1989	$45.00
	Airdate: 1/2/89.					
Album Network		In the Studio (Moving Pictures)	RS	U.S.	1991	$40.00
	Airdate: 18/5/91.					
Album Network		In the Studio (Power Windows/Victor)	RS	U.S.	1996	$50.00
DIR		King Biscuit Flour Hour	RS	U.S.	1987	$100.00
	Airdate: 12/20//87.					

Rush – Power Windows (Epic 25 8P-5078)

Label	Catalog Number	Title	Type	Country	Year	Longbox Value / Value
DIR		King Biscuit Flour Hour	RS	U.S.	1990	$50.00
	Airdate: 12/10/90.					
DIR		King Biscuit Flour Hour	RS	U.S.	1991	$50.00
	Airdate: 3/11/91.					
DIR		King Biscuit Flour Hour	RS	U.S.	1993	$50.00
	Airdate: 11/29/93.					
DIR		King Biscuit Flour Hour	RS	U.S.	1995	$65.00
	Airdate: 1/15/95.					
Epic	258P-5076	Moving Pictures	LP	Japan		$35.00
Mercury	800048-2	Moving Pictures	LP/BP	U.S.†	1984	$14.00/$8.00
Westwood One		Off the Record	RS	U.S.	1992	$50.00
	Airdate: 6/29/92.					
Westwood One		Off the Record	RS	U.S.	1994	$50.00
	Airdate: 4/4/94.					
Epic	258P-5075	Permanent Waves	LP	Japan		$35.00
Epic	258P-5078	Power Windows	LP	Japan		$35.00
Mercury	826144-2	Power Windows	LP/BP	U.S.†	1985	$14.00/$8.00
Atlantic	7 82840-2	Presto	DJ/LP	U.S.	1989	$15.00
	With Promo Sticker.					
Atlantic	PRCD 3200-2	Profiled	DJ/Intvw	U.S.	1989	$40.00
Radio Today		Rock Stars	RS	U.S.	1989	$150.00
	2 CD set. Airdate: 12/24/89.					
Anthem	PR10	Roll the Bones Radio Special	DJ/RS	Canada	1992	$100.00
Epic	258P-5169	Signals	LP	Japan		$35.00
Mercury	810002-2	Signals	LP/BP	U.S.†	1983	$14.00/$8.00
Global Satellite Network		Spirit of Rush	RS	U.S.	1991	$250.00
	3 CD set. Airdate: 7/4/91.					
Atlantic	7567-82925-2	Test for Echo	DJ/LP	Germany	1996	$30.00
Pioneer	PA-85-112	Through the Camera Eye	LD	U.S.	1985	$50.00
Media America		Up Close	RS	U.S.	1990	$95.00
	2 CD set.					
Media America		Up Close	RS	U.S.	1991	$95.00
	2 CD set.					
Media America		Up Close	RS	U.S.	1994	$95.00
	3 CD set.					

Singles

Label	Catalog Number	Title	Type	Country	Year	Longbox Value / Value
Vertigo	080 084-2	Big Money, The	CDV	U.K.	1988	$45.00
Mercury	870 717-2	Big Money, The	CDV/BP	U.S.	1988	$45.00/$45.00
Atlantic	PRCD 4580-2	Bravado	CDJ	U.S.	1992	$13.00
Atlantic	PRCD 5431-2	Double Agent	CDJ	U.S.	1994	$6.00
Anthem	PRO8	Dreamline	CDJ	Canada	1991	$40.00
Atlantic	PRCD 4120-2	Dreamline	CDJ	U.S.	1991	$7.00
Atlantic	PRCD 8009	Driven	CDJ	U.S.	1997	$8.00
Atlantic	CD 7567-85874-2	Ghost of a Chance	CD5	France	1992	$12.00
Atlantic	PM-1119	Ghost of a Chance	CDJ	Germany	1991	$65.00
Atlantic	PRCD 4458-2	Ghost of a Chance	CDJ	U.S.	1991	$20.00
Atlantic	PRCD 82925-2	Half the World	CDJ	U.S.	1996	$15.00
Anthem	PRO1	Marathon	CDJ	Canada	1988	$120.00
Atlantic	PRCD 5430-2	Nobody's Hero	CDJ	U.S.	1994	$7.00
Atlantic	PRCD 5497-2	Nobody's Hero	CDJ	U.S.	1994	$7.00
Anthem	PRO5	Pass, The	CDJ	Canada	1989	$45.00
Anthem	PRO6	Pass, The	CDJ	Canada	1990	$45.00
Atlantic	PR 3165-2	Pass, The	CDJ	U.S.	1989	$15.00
Atlantic	PR 3175-2	Pass, The	CDJ	U.S.	1989	$15.00
Vertigo	8700108-2	Prime Mover	CD5	Germany	1987	$40.00
Anthem	PRO9	Roll the Bones	CDJ	Canada	1991	$30.00
Atlantic	7567-85929-2 LO	Roll the Bones	CD5	Germany	1992	$12.00
Atlantic	PM-1098	Roll the Bones	CDJ	Germany	1992	$65.00
Atlantic	7567-885901-2	Roll the Bones	CD5	U.K.	1992	$12.00
Atlantic	7567-885900-2	Roll the Bones	CD5	U.K.	1992	$15.00
	Image disc.					
Atlantic	PRCD 4260-2	Roll the Bones	CDJ	U.S.	1991	$50.00
Anthem	PRO-4	Show Don't Tell	CDJ	Canada	1989	$45.00
Anthem	PRO3	Show Don't Tell	CDJ	Canada	1989	$50.00
Atlantic	PR 3125-2	Show Don't Tell	CDJ	U.S.	1989	$6.00
Atlantic	PR 3082-2	Show Don't Tell	CDJ	U.S.	1989	$7.00
Atlantic	PRCD 5314-2	Stick It Out	CDJ	U.S.	1993	$7.00
Atlantic	PRCD 3331-2	Superconductor	CDJ	U.S.	1989	$28.00
Atlantic	PRCD 6853	Test for Echo	CDJ	U.S.	1996	$10.00
Atlantic		Test for Echo	CDJ	U.S.	1996	$10.00
	2 track version.					
Atlantic	PRCD 6885-2	Test For Echo	CDJ	U.S.	1996	$15.00
Vertigo	888 941-2	Time Stands Still	CD5	Germany	1987	$50.00
Mercury	CDP 05	Time Stands Still	CDJ	U.S.	1987	$7.00
Atlantic	PRCD 4126-2	Where's My Thing?	CDJ	U.S.	1991	$60.00

Rush, Donell

Singles

Label	Catalog Number	Title	Type	Country	Year	Longbox Value / Value
RCA	62482-2-RDJ	If Only I Knew	CDJ	U.S.	1993	$2.00
RCA	62421-2-RDJ	Symphony Heavies	CDJ	U.S.	1992	$2.00
RCA	62453-2-RDJ	Symphony Heavies	CDJ	U.S.	1992	$2.00

Rush, Jenifer

Singles

Label	Catalog Number	Title	Type	Country	Year	Longbox Value / Value
Epic	108EP-3042	Another Way	CD3	Japan	1988	$12.00/$4.00
CBS	655344-3	Higher Ground	CD3	Germany	1989	$9.00
CBS	655344-2	Higher Ground	CD5	U.K.	1989	$9.00
Columbia	653159-3	Keep the Fires Burning Bright	CD3	U.K.	1988	$9.00
Columbia	654695-3	Love Get Ready	CD3	Germany	1989	$9.00
Columbia	654575-3	Power of Love	CD3	Germany	1989	$9.00
Columbia	654575-3	Power of Love	CD3	U.K.	1989	$9.00
BMG	663807	We Are the Strong	CD5	Germany	1990	$9.00
Columbia	655615-3	Wings of Desire	CD3	Germany	1990	$9.00
Columbia	653043-3	You're My One and Only	CD3	Germany	1988	$9.00
Columbia	653043-2	You're My One and Only	CD5	U.K.	1988	$9.00

Rush, Otis

Full Length

Label	Catalog Number	Title	Type	Country	Year	Longbox Value / Value
		House Of Blues	RS	U.S.	1994	$40.00
	2 CD set. Airdate: 5/22/94.					

Russell, Brenda

Singles

Label	Catalog Number	Title	Type	Country	Year	Longbox Value / Value
A&M	S10Y-3050	Get Here	CD3	Japan	1988	$13.00/$4.00
A&M	CD 17612	Get Here	CDJ	U.S.	1988	$2.00
A&M	390306-2	Gravity	CD5	Germany	1989	$9.00
A&M	USACD-630	Gravity	CD5	U.K.	1989	$9.00
A&M	CD 17581	Gravity	CDJ	U.S.	1988	$2.00
EMI	DPRO-04585	In Over My Heart	CDJ	U.S.	1993	$2.00
A&M	AMCD-578	Kiss Me With the Wind	CD5	U.K.	1990	$9.00
A&M	S10Y-3022	Piano in the Dark	CD3	Japan	1988	$13.00/$4.00
A&M	USACD-623	Piano in the Dark	CD5	U.K.	1988	$9.00
A&M	75021 5274 2	Stop Running Away	CDJ	U.S.	1990	$2.00
A&M	75021 8907 2	Stop Running Away	CDJ	U.S.	1990	$2.00

Russell, George

Full Length

Label	Catalog Number	Title	Type	Country	Year	Longbox Value / Value
Soul Note	SN-1049CD PSI	American Time Spiral	LP/LB	U.S.†	1985	$14.00/$8.00

Russell, Leon

Full Length

Label	Catalog Number	Title	Type	Country	Year	Longbox Value / Value
Shelter		And the Shelter People	LP/BP	U.S.		$9.00/$6.00
Virgin		Anything Can Happen	LP/LB	U.S.		$12.00/$7.00
Shelter		Carney	LP/BP	U.S.		$9.00/$6.00
Shelter		Hank Wilson's Back	LP/BP	U.S.		$9.00/$6.00
Shelter		Leon Russell	LP/BP	U.S.		$9.00/$6.00
Shelter		Stop All That Jazz	LP/BP	U.S.		$9.00/$6.00
Shelter		Will o' the Wisp	LP/BP	U.S.		$9.00/$6.00

Singles

Label	Catalog Number	Title	Type	Country	Year	Longbox Value / Value
Virgin	PRCD 4470	Anything Can Happen	CDJ	U.S.	1992	$2.00
Virgin	PRCD 4475	Faces of the Children	CDJ	U.S.	1992	$7.00
Sony	SRDL-3584	I Feel the Echo	CD3	Japan	1992	$12.00/$4.00
Virgin	PRCD 4382	No Man's Land	CDJ	U.S.	1992	$2.00

Russell, Pee Wee

Singles

Label	Catalog Number	Title	Type	Country	Year	Longbox Value / Value
	41052	Clarinet Strut	CD5	U.S.	1994	$5.00

Rust

Singles

Label	Catalog Number	Title	Type	Country	Year	Longbox Value / Value
	PRCD 6462	Not Today	CDJ	U.S.		$2.00

Rusty

Singles

Label	Catalog Number	Title	Type	Country	Year	Longbox Value / Value
	PRCD 6452	Misogyny	CDJ	U.S.		$2.00
	2	Rusty	CD5	U.S.	1994	$5.00
	PRCD 6245-2	Wake Me	CDJ	U.S.		$2.00

Ruth Ruth

Singles

Label	Catalog Number	Title	Type	Country	Year	Longbox Value / Value
	PRO-CD-7698	Uninvited	CDJ	U.S.		$2.00
	PRO-CD-7963	Uptight	CDJ	U.S.		$2.00

Rutherford, Mike

Full Length

Label	Catalog Number	Title	Type	Country	Year	Longbox Value / Value
Atlantic		Acting Very Strange	LP/LB	U.S.		$14.00/$8.00
Passport	PBCD-9843	Small Creeps Day	LP/BP	U.S.		$18.00/$15.00

Rutherford, Paul

Singles

Label	Catalog Number	Title	Type	Country	Year	Longbox Value / Value
Aris	885153	Get Real	CD5	Germany	1989	$8.00
4th & B'way	BRCDP-113	Get Real	CD5	U.K.	1989	$8.00
BMG	162199	I Want Your Love	CD3	Germany	1989	$8.00
BMG	662199	I Want Your Love	CD5	Germany	1989	$8.00
4th & B'way	BRCDP-124	I Want Your Love	CD5	U.K.	1989	$8.00
BMG	662624	Oh World	CD5	Germany	1989	$8.00
4th & B'way	BRCDP-136	Oh World	CD5	U.K.	1989	$8.00
4th & B'way	CCD749	Oh World	CDJ	U.S.	1989	$2.00

Ryan, Barry

Singles

Label	Catalog Number	Title	Type	Country	Year	Longbox Value / Value
RCA	PD-43330	Barry Ryan	CD5	Germany	1989	$8.00
Polygram	867903-2	Eloise	CD5	Germany	1991	$8.00
RCA	PD-43990	Light In Your Heart	CD5	Germany	1989	$8.00

Ryan, Frank

Singles

Label	Catalog Number	Title	Type	Country	Year	Longbox Value / Value
EMI	147431-2	Fire In the Dark	CD5	Germany	1989	$8.00
Intercord	825 304	Wind & Fire	CD5	Germany	1991	$8.00
EMI	147395-2	You You	CD5	Germany	1989	$8.00

Ryan, Tim

Singles

Label	Catalog Number	Title	Type	Country	Year	Longbox Value / Value
Epic	ESK 73959	Seventh Direction	CDJ	U.S.	1991	$2.00

Ryder, Mitch

Singles

Label	Catalog Number	Title	Type	Country	Year	Longbox Value / Value
Rhino	71872	Devil With The Blue Dress	CD5	U.S.	1994	$5.00

Rypdal, Tim

Singles

Label	Catalog Number	Title	Type	Country	Year	Longbox Value / Value
ECM	1383	U.N.I.	CD5	Germany	1989	$8.00

Ryser, Jimmy

Singles

Label	Catalog Number	Title	Type	Country	Year	Longbox Value / Value
		Same Old Look	CDJ	U.S.		$2.00

S.O.S. Band

Singles

Label	Catalog Number	Title	Type	Country	Year	Longbox Value / Value
		Do You Love Me?	CDJ	U.S.		$2.00
Columbia	655527-3	I'm Still Missing Your Love	CD3	Germany	1989	$8.00
Columbia	654988-3	Just Be Good To Me	CD3	Germany	1990	$8.00
Columbia	655096-3	Just the Way You Like It	CD3	Germany	1990	$8.00
Columbia	653143-3	Official Bootleg	CD3	Germany	1989	$8.00
Tabu	ZSK 73089	Secret With	CDJ	U.S.	1989	$2.00
Columbia	390826-2	Sometimes I Wonder Why	CD5	Germany	1991	$8.00
Tabu	28965 1702	Sometimes I Wonder Why	CD5	U.S.	1991	$5.00

Label	Catalog Number	Title	Type	Country	Year	Longbox Value / Value
Tabu	ZSK 28965	Sometimes I Wonder Why	CDJ	U.S.	1991	$2.00
Columbia	654654-3	Take Your Time	CD3	Germany	1988	$8.00
Columbia	654654-3	Take Your Time	CD3	U.K.	1988	$8.00

S.O.U.L. S.Y.S.T.E.M.

Singles

Label	Catalog Number	Title	Type	Country	Year	Longbox Value / Value
Arista	12486	It's Gonna Be a Lovely Day	CD5	U.S.	1992	$4.00
Arista	ARCD-2487	It's Gonna Be a Lovely Day	CDJ	U.S.	1992	$2.00

S.W.V.

Singles

Label	Catalog Number	Title	Type	Country	Year	Longbox Value / Value
RCA	62823	Anything	CD5	U.S.	1994	$5.00

S'Express

Singles

Label	Catalog Number	Title	Type	Country	Year	Longbox Value / Value
Rhythm King	SEXY-02CD	Find 'Em, Fool 'Em, Forget 'Em	CD5	U.K.	1991	$8.00
Epic	658013-2	Find 'Em, Fool 'Em, Forget 'Em	CD5	U.K.	1992	$8.00
Rough Trade	CD1-35CD	Hey Music Lover	CD5	Germany	1989	$8.00
Rhythm King	LEFT-30CD	Hey Music Lover	CD5	U.K.	1989	$8.00
Capitol	DPRO 79551	Music Lover	CDJ	U.S.	1989	$2.00
Rhythm King	SEXY-1CD	Nothing to Lose	CD5	U.K.	1990	$8.00
Rhythm King	9 21789-2	Nothing to Lose	CD5	U.S.	19991	$5.00
Rhythm King	LEFT-28CD	Superfly Guy	CD5	U.K.	1988	$8.00
Rough Trade	CD1-66	Superfly Guy	CD5	U.K.	1988	$8.00
Rough Trade	CD1-44CD	Theme From S'Express	CD5	Germany	1989	$8.00
Rhythm King	LEFT-21CD	Theme From S'Express	CD5	U.K.	1990	$8.00
Capitol	C2 157175	Theme From S'Express	CD5	U.S.	1990	$5.00

Sa-Deuce

Singles

Label	Catalog Number	Title	Type	Country	Year	Longbox Value / Value
	PRCD 9296-2	Don't Waist My Time	CDJ	U.S.		$2.00

Sa-Fire

Singles

Label	Catalog Number	Title	Type	Country	Year	Longbox Value / Value
Polygram	874761-2	Gonna Make It	CD5	Germany	1988	$8.00
Mercury	MERCD-298	Gonna Make It	CD5	U.K.	1988	$8.00
Mercury	CDP 82	Gonna Make It	CDJ	U.S.	1988	$2.00
Phonogram	PPDS-23	I Will Survive	CD3	Japan	1990	$13.00/$4.00
		I Will Survive	CDJ	U.S.	1990	$2.00
Mercury	870 743-2	I've Been Told	CDV/ BP	U.S.	1988	$14.00/$14.00
Mercury	CDP 377	Made Up My Mind	CDJ	U.S.	1991	$2.00
Mercury	CDP 446	Taste the Base	CDJ	U.S.	1991	$2.00
Polygram	874508-3	Thinking of You	CD3	Germany	1989	$8.00
Polygram	874509-2	Thinking of You	CD5	Germany	1989	$8.00
Mercury	MERCD-283	Thinking of You	CD5	U.K.	1989	$8.00

Sabelle

Singles

Label	Catalog Number	Title	Type	Country	Year	Longbox Value / Value
Tommy Boy	TBXCD640	Where Did the Love Go	CD5	Canada	1994	$9.00
Tommy Boy	640	Where Did the Love Go	CD5	U.S.	1994	$5.00

Sacred Reich

Singles

Label	Catalog Number	Title	Type	Country	Year	Longbox Value / Value
Enigma	EPRO-317	31 Flavors	CDJ	U.S.	1990	$2.00
Hollywood	PRCD 66518-2	A Question	CDJ	U.S.	1991	$2.00
Enigma	EPRO-322	American Way, The	CDJ	U.S.	1990	$2.00
Enigma	EPRO-290	American Way, The	CDJ	U.S.	1990	$2.00
Hollywood	PRCD 10340-2	Free	CDJ	U.S.	1993	$2.00
Hollywood	PRCD 10347-2	I Never Said Goodbye	CDJ	U.S.	1993	$2.00
Hollywood	PRCD 10258-2	Independent	CDJ	U.S.	1991	$2.00

Sacred Spirits

Singles

Label	Catalog Number	Title	Type	Country	Year	Longbox Value / Value
Virgin	38501	Yeha Noha	CD5	U.S.	1995	$5.00

Sacrifice

Full Length

Label	Catalog Number	Title	Type	Country	Year	Longbox Value / Value
Warner Brothers	45235	Apocalypse Inside	LP/ LB	U.S.		$14.00/$8.00
Warner Brothers	26538	Soldiers of Misfortune	LP/ LB	U.S.		$14.00/$8.00

Sade – Interview Deluxe (Epic ESK 4877)

Sade

Full Length

Label	Catalog Number	Title	Type	Country	Year	Longbox Value / Value
Portrait	RK 39581	Diamond Life	LP/ LB	U.S.†	1985	$14.00/$8.00
Fox	7091-88	Diamond Life Video	8"LD	U.S.	1985	$14.00
Epic	ESK 4877	Interview Deluxe	DJ/ Intvw	U.S.	1992	$12.00

Singles

Label	Catalog Number	Title	Type	Country	Year	Longbox Value / Value
Epic	ESDA-7130	Feel No Pain	CD3	Japan	1993	$12.00/$4.00
Epic	ESCA-5700	Feel No Pain	CD5	Japan	1993	$14.00
Epic	658829-2	Feel No Pain	CD5	U.K.	1992	$9.00
Epic	658829-5	Feel No Pain	CD5	U.K.	1992	$9.00
Epic	ESDA-7121	Kiss of Life	CD3	Japan	1993	$12.00/$4.00
Epic	ESK 74848	Kiss of Life	CDJ	U.S.	1993	$2.00
Epic	651477-2	Love Is Stronger Than Pride	CD5	Germany	1988	$9.00
Epic	108P-3013	Love Is Stronger Than Pride	CD3	Japan	1988	$12.00/$4.00
Epic	CDSADE-1	Love Is Stronger Than Pride	CD5	U.K.	1988	$9.00
Epic	654684-3	Never as Good as the First	CD3	Japan	1989	$12.00/$4.00
Epic	ESDA-7112	No Ordinary Love	CD3	Japan	1992	$12.00/$4.00
Epic	658356-2	No Ordinary Love	CD5	U.K.	1992	$9.00
Epic	34K-74734	No Ordinary Love	CD5	U.S.	1992	$5.00
Epic	108P-3039	Nothing Can Come Between Us	CD3	Japan	1988	$12.00/$4.00
Epic	652921-3	Nothing Can Come Between Us	CD3	U.K.	1988	$9.00
Epic	CDSADE-3	Nothing Can Come Between Us	CD5	U.K.	1988	$9.00
		Nothing Can Come Between Us	CD5	U.S.	1988	$2.00
Epic	651617-2	Paradise	CD5	Germany	1988	$9.00
Epic	108P-3026	Paradise	CD3	Japan	1988	$12.00/$4.00
Epic	CDSADE-2	Paradise	CD5	U.K.	1988	$9.00
Epic	ESK 1143	Paradise	CDJ	U.S.	1988	$2.00
Epic	65403-3	Smooth Operator	CD3	Germany	1989	$9.00
Epic	65403-3	Smooth Operator	CD3	U.K.	1989	$9.00
Epic	653140-2	Turn Back on You	CD5	Germany	1989	$9.00
Epic	CDSADE-4	Turn Back on You	CD5	U.K.	1989	$9.00

Saffron

Singles

Label	Catalog Number	Title	Type	Country	Year	Longbox Value / Value
Reprise	9 40567-2	One Love	CD5	U.S.	1992	$5.00

Safire

Singles

Label	Catalog Number	Title	Type	Country	Year	Longbox Value / Value
Polygram	CDP 377	Made up My Mind	CDJ	U.S.	1991	$3.00

Saga

Full Length

Label	Catalog Number	Title	Type	Country	Year	Longbox Value / Value
Portrait	RK40145	Behaviour	LP/LB	U.S.†	1985	$14.00/$8.00
Portrait	RK38999	Heads or Tails	LP/LB	U.S.†	1984	$14.00/$8.00

Sagal, Katie

Singles

Label	Catalog Number	Title	Type	Country	Year	Longbox Value / Value
Virgin	[illegible]	[illegible] the Harvest	CDJ	U.S.	[illegible]	[illegible]

Sagat

Singles

Label	Catalog Number	Title	Type	Country	Year	Longbox Value / Value
Mxl	2014	Why It Is	CD5	U.S.	1994	$5.00

Sahm & Sons, Doug

Singles

Label	Catalog Number	Title	Type	Country	Year	Longbox Value / Value
Sire	PRO-CD-4735	You're Gonna Miss Me	CDJ	U.S.	1990	$2.00

Saigon Kick

Singles

Label	Catalog Number	Title	Type	Country	Year	Longbox Value / Value
Atlantic	PRCD 4644-2	All I Want	CDJ	U.S.	1992	$3.00
Atlantic	PRCD 5033-2	Feel the Same Way	CDJ	U.S.	1993	$3.00
Atlantic	PRCD 4834-2	Freedom	CDJ	U.S.	1992	$3.00
Atlantic	PRCD 4591-2	Hostile	CDJ	U.S.	1992	$3.00
Atlantic	PRCD 5287-2	I Love You	CDJ	U.S.	1993	$3.00
Atlantic	PRCD 5289-2	I Love You	CDJ	U.S.	1993	$3.00
Atlantic	A-7451CD	Love Is the Way	CD5	U.K.	1992	$9.00
Atlantic	PRCD 4645-2	Love Is the Way	CDJ	U.S.	1992	$3.00
Atlantic	PRCD 3766-2	New World	CDJ	U.S.	1991	$3.00
Atlantic	PRCD 3767	What You Say	CDJ	U.S.	1991	$3.00

Saint Etienne

Full Length

Label	Catalog Number	Title	Type	Country	Year	Longbox Value / Value
Warner Brothers	9 26793-2-Dj	Foxbase Alpha	DJ/LP	U.S.	1991	$18.00
Warner Brothers		Tiger Bay	DJ/LP	U.S.	1994	$15.00
Advance Issue.						
Warner Brothers	PRO-CD-5948	You're In A Bad Way	DJ/Intvw	U.S.	1993	$12.00

Singles

Label	Catalog Number	Title	Type	Country	Year	Longbox Value / Value
Warner Brothers	9 41591-2	Hug My Soul	CD5	U.S.	1994	$6.00
Heavenly	HVN-15CD	Join Our Club	CD5	U.K.	1992	$10.00
Heavenly	HVN-4CD	Kiss And Nake Up	CD5	U.K.	1990	$10.00
		Like A Motorway	CD5	U.K.	1994	$10.00
Warner Brothers	PRO-CD-6962	Like A Motorway	CDJ	U.S.	1994	$3.00
Heavenly	HVN-9CD	Nothing Can Stop Us	CD5	U.K.	1991	$10.00
Warner Brothers	9 40395-2	Nothing Can Stop Us	CD5	U.S.	1991	$5.00
Warner Brothers	PRO-CD-5337	Nothing Can Stop Us	CDJ	U.S.	1991	$3.00
Heavenly	HVN-12CD	Only Love Can Break Your Heart	CD5	U.K.	1991	$12.00
Warner Brothers	PRO-CD-5161	Only Love Can Break Your Heart	CDJ	U.S.	1991	$3.00
Warner Brothers	9 40910-2	Who Do You Think You Are	CD5	U.S.	1994	$5.00
Warner Brothers	PRO-CD-6265	Who Do You Think You Are	CDJ	U.S.	1994	$3.00
Heavenly	HVN-25CD	You're in a Bad Way	CD5	U.K.	1993	$10.00

Saint-Marie, Buffy

Full Length

Label	Catalog Number	Title	Type	Country	Year	Longbox Value / Value
Capitol	622	Interview	DJ/Intvw	Canada	1992	$10.00

Singles

Label	Catalog Number	Title	Type	Country	Year	Longbox Value / Value
Ensign	23816	Big Ones Get Away, The	CDJ	U.S.	1992	$2.00

Saints & Sinners

Singles

Label	Catalog Number	Title	Type	Country	Year	Longbox Value / Value
Savage	50020	Walk That Walk	CDJ	U.S.	1992	$6.00

Sakamoto, Ryuichi

Full Length

Label	Catalog Number	Title	Type	Country	Year	Longbox Value / Value
Midi	MDCZ-1097	Aile De Honneamise	LTD/LP	Japan		$40.00
Gold disc.						
Midi	MDCZ-1094	Coda	LTD/LP	Japan		$40.00
Gold disc.						
Midi	MDCZ-1095	Futurista	LTD/LP	Japan		$40.00
Gold disc.						
Midi	MDCZ-1046	Gruppo Musicale	LTD/LP	Japan		$40.00
Gold disc.						
Midi	MDCZ-1092	Left-Handed Dream	LTD/LP	Japan		$40.00
Gold disc.						
Midi	MDCZ-1096	Media Bahn	LTD/LP	Japan		$40.00
Gold disc.						
Midi	MDCZ-1091	Ongaku Zukan	LTD/LP	Japan		$40.00
Gold disc.						
Virgin	91002-2	Playing the Orchestra	LTD/LP	U.S.	1990	$40.00
CD+CD3 in shrine-style box.						
		Sweet Revenge	LTD/LP	Japan	1994	$45.00
CD in 12"x12" size package.						
Denon	CD-7137	Thousand Knives Of	LP/LB	U.S.†	1985	$14.00/$8.00

Singles

Label	Catalog Number	Title	Type	Country	Year	Longbox Value / Value
Midi	MID-507	Behind the Mask	CD5	Japan	1987	$18.00
Midi	MDC3-1071	Behind the Mask	CD5	Japan	1991	$15.00
Midi	MDC3-1073	Field Work	CD5	Japan	1991	$15.00
Virgin	VJCP-14037	Heartbeat	CD5	Japan	1992	$15.00
Midi	MDC3-1072	Image Sketch	CD5	Japan	1991	$15.00
Spin	ALCA-229	In the '90s	CD5	Japan	1991	$15.00
Virgin		Playing the Orchestra	CDJ	U.S.	1990	$6.00
Virgin	VJDP-10170	Sayonara	CD3	Japan	1991	$12.00/$5.00
Virgin	VJDP-14043	Tainai Kaiki 2	CD5	Japan	1992	$13.00
Virgin	VJCP-1417	We Love You	CD5	Japan	1992	$15.00

Label	Catalog Number	Title	Type	Country	Year	Longbox Value / Value
BMG	663138	You Do Me	CD5	Germany	1989	$10.00
Virgin	VJCP-1404	You Do Me	CD5	Japan	1989	$15.00
Virgin	PRCD 3227	You Do Me	CDJ	U.S.	1990	$6.00

Sakamoto, Ryuichi & Danceries

Full Length

Label	Catalog Number	Title	Type	Country	Year	Longbox Value / Value
Denon	CD-7045	The End Of Asia	LP/LB	U.S.†	1985	$14.00/$8.00

Salas, Stevie Colorcode

Full Length

Label	Catalog Number	Title	Type	Country	Year	Longbox Value / Value
	HI-5107	Electric Pow Wow	DJ/LP	Japan		$30.00

Advance issue.

Singles

Label	Catalog Number	Title	Type	Country	Year	Longbox Value / Value
		Harder They Come, The	CDJ	U.S.		$2.00
		Stand Up	CDJ	U.S.		$2.00

Salt, Veruca

Singles

Label	Catalog Number	Title	Type	Country	Year	Longbox Value / Value
		Victrola	CD5	U.K.	1995	$10.00
		Volcano Girls	CD5	U.K.	1997	$9.00
		Volcano Girls	CD5	U.K.	1997	$9.00

Second version.

Salt-N-Pepa

Singles

Label	Catalog Number	Title	Type	Country	Year	Longbox Value / Value
Motown	850347	Ain't Nothin' But a She Thing	CD5	U.S.	1995	$5.00
	PRCD 7041-2	Ain't Nuthin' But a She Thing	CDJ	U.S.		$2.00
Next Plateau	869311-2	Do You Want Me	CD5	Germany	1990	$9.00
Next Plateau	FCD-151	Do You Want Me	CD5	U.K.	1990	$9.00
Next Plateau	50137	Do You Want Me	CDJ	U.S.	1990	$2.00
Polygram	886907-2	Expression	CD5	Germany	1990	$9.00
London	POCD-1007	Expression	CD3	Japan	1990	$13.00/$4.00
London	POCD-1007	Expression	CD5	Japan	1990	$12.00
ffrr	FCD-127	Expression	CD5	U.K.	1990	$9.00
ffrr	FCD-182	Expression	CD5	U.K.	1992	$9.00
London	886409-2	Get Up Everybody	CD5	Germany	1988	$9.00
London	FFRCD-16	Get Up Everybody	CD5	U.K.	1988	$9.00
London	FFRCD-20	I Like It Like That	CD5	U.K.	1989	$9.00
Polygram	869059-2	Independent	CD5	Germany	1989	$9.00
Polygram	869481-2	Let's Talk About Sex	CD5	Germany	1991	$9.00
ffrr	FCD-162	Let's Talk About Sex	CD5	U.K.	1991	$9.00
ffrr	4228577152	None of Your Business	CD5	Canada	1994	$8.00
ffrr	4228577762	None of Your Business	CD5	Canada	1994	$8.00
	PRCD 6869-2	None of Your Business	CDJ	U.S.		$2.00
Polygram	857715	None of Your Business	CD5	U.S.	1994	$5.00
Polygram	857715	None of Your Business	CD5	U.S.	1994	$5.00
Polygram	886270-2	Push It	CD5	Germany	1988	$9.00
Polygram	886329-2	Shake Your Thing	CD5	Germany	1988	$9.00
London	P10L-40002	Shake Your Thing	CD3	Japan	1988	$13.00/$4.00
London	P13L-37005	Shake Your Thing	CD3	Japan	1988	$13.00/$4.00
London	FFRCD-11	Shake Your Thing	CD5	U.K.	1988	$9.00
Next Plateau	NPCD50077	Shake Your Thing	CDJ	U.S.	1988	$2.00
London	4228573152	Shoop	CD5	Canada	1994	$8.00
Polygram	857315	Shoop	CD5	U.S.	1993	$6.00
Next Plateau	NPCD50077	Shoop	CDJ	U.S.	1993	$2.00
Polygram	857315	Shoop	CD5	U.S.	1994	$5.00
Next Plateau	4228283612	Start Me Up	CD5	Canada	1992	$10.00
London	PODD-1025	Start Me Up	CD3	Japan	1992	$13.00/$4.00
ffrr	UKFCD-196	Start Me Up	CD5	U.K.	1992	$9.00
Next Plateau	NPCD752	Start Me Up	CDJ	U.S.	1992	$2.00
Next Plateau	NPCD50189	Start Me Up	CDJ	U.S.	1992	$2.00
Champion	CHAMPCD-51	Tramp	CD3	U.K.	1988	$9.00
London	P13L-59012	Twist And Shout	CD3	Japan	1989	$13.00/$4.00
London	1117	Whatta Man	CDJ	U.S.	1993	$3.00
Polygram	857391	Whatta Man	CD5	U.S.	1994	$5.00
Polygram	857391	Whatta Man	CD5	U.S.	1994	$5.00
Polygram	869599-2	You Showed Me	CD5	Germany	1991	$9.00
ffrr	PODD-1016	You Showed Me	CD3	Japan	1992	$13.00/$4.00
ffrr	FCD-174	You Showed Me	CD5	U.K.	1991	$9.00
Next Plateau	NPCD50165	You Showed Me	CDJ	U.S.	1992	$2.00

Salty Dog

Singles

Label	Catalog Number	Title	Type	Country	Year	Longbox Value / Value
Geffen		Come Along	CDJ	U.S.	1990	$2.00
Geffen	PRO-CD-4112	Lonesome Fool	CDJ	U.S.	1990	$2.00

Saluzzi, Dino

Singles

Label	Catalog Number	Title	Type	Country	Year	Longbox Value / Value
ECM	DINO2	Mojotoro	CDJ	U.S.	1992	$2.00

Sam Sneed/Danny Boy

Singles

Label	Catalog Number	Title	Type	Country	Year	Longbox Value / Value
Atlantic	95763	U Better Recognize	CD5	U.S.	1994	$5.00

Sam the Beast

Singles

Label	Catalog Number	Title	Type	Country	Year	Longbox Value / Value
Relativity	1241	Gucci Dance	CD5	U.S.	1994	$5.00

Sam the Sham and The Pharaohs

Singles

Label	Catalog Number	Title	Type	Country	Year	Longbox Value / Value
Polygram	889732-2	Wooly Bully	CD5	Germany	1990	$10.00

Samaniego, Enriq

Singles

Label	Catalog Number	Title	Type	Country	Year	Longbox Value / Value
	11421	Serie De Platino	CD5	U.S.	1994	$5.00

Samba Hell

Full Length

Label	Catalog Number	Title	Type	Country	Year	Longbox Value / Value
Independent		It	DJ/LP	U.S.	1991	$12.00

CD in box.

Sambora, Richie

Full Length

Label	Catalog Number	Title	Type	Country	Year	Longbox Value / Value
Mercury	CDP 515	Ballad of Youth Interview	DJ/Intvw	U.S.	1991	$15.00

CDJ and interview disc in longbox-style package.

Label	Catalog Number	Title	Type	Country	Year	Longbox Value / Value
Westwood One		In Concert	RS	U.S.	1992	$70.00

2 CD set. With Pearl Jam, Airdate: 9/28/92.

Label	Catalog Number	Title	Type	Country	Year	Longbox Value / Value
Mercury	510652-2	Stranger in This Town	LTD/LP	U.S.	1991	$15.00

2CD, chain in longbox-style package.

Singles

Label	Catalog Number	Title	Type	Country	Year	Longbox Value / Value
Mercury	PHDR-114	Answer	CD3	Japan	1992	$12.00/$4.00
Mercury	CDP 592	One Light Burning	CDJ	U.S.	1992	$2.00
Mercury	CDP 595	Stranger in This Town	CDJ	U.S.	1991	$2.00

Samian

Singles

Label	Catalog Number	Title	Type	Country	Year	Longbox Value / Value
	PRCD 5856-2	Stepson	CDJ	U.S.		$2.00

Sammy

Singles

Label	Catalog Number	Title	Type	Country	Year	Longbox Value / Value
	PRO-CD-4865	Neptune Ave.	CDJ	U.S.		$2.00

Sample, Joe

Full Length

Label	Catalog Number	Title	Type	Country	Year	Longbox Value / Value
Warner Brothers	PRO-CD-4712	Words & Music: Ashes to Ashes	DJ/Intvw	U.S.	1991	$5.00

Singles

Label	Catalog Number	Title	Type	Country	Year	Longbox Value / Value
	PRO-CD-4530	Born to Be Bad	CDJ	U.S.	1990	$6.00
Warner Brothers	PRO-CD-3783	Leading Me Back to You	CDJ	U.S.	1989	$2.00
		Road Less Traveled, The	CDJ	U.S.	1991	$2.00
Warner Brothers	PRO-CD-3949	Spellbound	CDJ	U.S.	1989	$2.00

Sample, Thisi

Singles

Label	Catalog Number	Title	Type	Country	Year	Longbox Value / Value
Elektra	PRCD 8750-2	Another Lie	CDj	U.S.	1993	$2.00

Samples

Singles

Label	Catalog Number	Title	Type	Country	Year	Longbox Value / Value
Arista	ASCD 2161	Waited Up	CDJ	U.S.	1991	$2.00

Sanborn, Dave

Full Length

Label	Catalog Number	Title	Type	Country	Year	Longbox Value / Value
Warner	25150-2	Straight to the Heart	LP/LB	U.S.†	1985	$14.00/$8.00
Pioneer Artists	PA-87-019	David Sanborn	LD	U.S.	1987	$30.00
Warner	3546-2	Voyeur	LP/LB	U.S.†	1985	$14.00/$8.00

Singles

Label	Catalog Number	Title	Type	Country	Year	Longbox Value / Value
Elektra	EKR-158CD	Bang Bang	CD5	U.K.	1992	$9.00
Elektra	PRCD 8599-2	Bang Bang	CDJ	U.S.	1992	$3.00
Elektra	PRCD 8683-2	Benny	CDJ	U.S.	1992	$3.00
Warner Brothers	PRO-CD-2880	Dream, The	CDJ	U.S.		$3.00
Warner Brothers		Everything Must Change	CDJ	U.S.		$6.00
Elektra/Asylum	64449	Everything Must Change	CD5	U.S.	1994	$5.00
Elektra	PRCD 8389-2	Hobbies	CDJ	U.S.	1991	$3.00
Reprise	PRO-CD-3521	Lesley Ann	CDJ	U.S.	1989	$3.00
Elektra	PRCD 9201	Masquerade	CDJ	U.S.	1995	$3.00
Reprise	PRO-CD-3122	Slam	CDJ	U.S.	1988	$3.00
Elektra	PRCD 8563-2	Snakes	CDJ	U.S.	1992	$3.00
		So Far Away	CDJ	U.S.		$3.00

Sanctuaty

Singles

Label	Catalog Number	Title	Type	Country	Year	Longbox Value / Value
Epic	ESK 2188	Into the Mirror	CDJ	U.S.	1990	$2.00

Sand Rubies

Singles

Label	Catalog Number	Title	Type	Country	Year	Longbox Value / Value
Atlas	CDP 832	Goodbye	CDJ	U.S.	1992	$2.00
Polygram	CDP 931	Guns in the Churchyard	CDJ	U.S.	1002	$2.00
Polygram	CDP 897	SantaMaria Street	CDJ	U.S.	1002	$2.00

Sandee

Singles

Label	Catalog Number	Title	Type	Country	Year	Longbox Value / Value
Columbia	CSK 73755	Love Desire	CDJ	U.S.	1991	$2.00

Sanderson, Richard

Singles

Label	Catalog Number	Title	Type	Country	Year	Longbox Value / Value
WEA	9031-72568-2	Anytime at All	CD5	Germany	1990	$8.00
WEA	171176-2	When the Night Comes	CD5	Germany	1990	$8.00

Sandler, Adam

Full Length

Label	Catalog Number	Title	Type	Country	Year	Longbox Value / Value
Warner Brothers	PRO-CD-6593	They're All Gonna Laugh at You	DJ/LP	U.S.	1993	$13.00

Singles

Label	Catalog Number	Title	Type	Country	Year	Longbox Value / Value
Warner Brothers	PRO-CD-8075-R	Bleeps	CDJ	U.S.	1995	$3.00
Warner Brothers	PRO-CD-6953	Buddy	CDJ	U.S.	1993	$3.00
Warner Brothers	PRO-CD-8176-R	Dip Doodle	CDJ	U.S.	1995	$3.00
Warner Brothers	18246	Lunchlady Land	CD5	U.S.	1994	$5.00
Warner Brothers	PRO-CD-6737	Lunchlady Land	CDJ	U.S.	1994	$3.00
Warner Brothers	PRO-CD-8088-R	Steve Polychronopolis	CDJ	U.S.	1995	$3.00
Warner Brothers	PRO-CD-6641	Thanksgiving Song, The	CDJ	U.S.	1993	$6.00

Sandler & Young

Singles

Label	Catalog Number	Title	Type	Country	Year	Longbox Value / Value
Ktel	3376	Sing Your Fav Love	CD5	U.S.	1994	$5.00

Sandmen

Singles

Label	Catalog Number	Title	Type	Country	Year	Longbox Value / Value
A&M	CD 17747	House in the Country	CDJ	U.S.	1988	$2.00
A&M	CD 17907	Say Yes	CDJ	U.S.	1989	$2.00
A&M	CD 17827	Western Blood	CDJ	U.S.	1989	$2.00

Sandoval, Arturo

Singles

Label	Catalog Number	Title	Type	Country	Year	Longbox Value / Value
GRP	5115	Dream Come True	CDJ	U.S.	1993	$6.00
Elektra	PRCD 8489-2	Mambo Caliente	CDJ	U.S.	1992	$2.00

Sandoval & Brib

Singles

Label	Catalog Number	Title	Type	Country	Year	Longbox Value / Value
	11422	Serie De Platino	CD5	U.S.	1994	$5.00

Sandra

Full Length

Label	Catalog Number	Title	Type	Country	Year	Longbox Value / Value
Virgin		Collector's Edition Box Set	LP	U.K.	1994	$48.00

3 CD Set.

Singles

Label	Catalog Number	Title	Type	Country	Year	Longbox Value / Value
Virgin	DINSD 114	Don't Be Aggressive	CD5	Germany	1992	$8.00
Virgin	665 401	I Need Love	CD5	Germany	1992	$8.00

Sandy

Singles

Label	Catalog Number	Title	Type	Country	Year	Longbox Value / Value
ZYX	7982-8	Bad Boy	CD5	U.S.	1995	$6.00

Santa Cecilla

Singles

Label	Catalog Number	Title	Type	Country	Year	Longbox Value / Value
	1416	El Fabuloso Grupo	CD5	U.S.	1994	$5.00

Santana

Full Length

Label	Catalog Number	Title	Type	Country	Year	Longbox Value / Value
CBS	CK-30130	Abraxas	LP/BP	U.S.†	1982	$14.00/$8.00
CBS	CK-39527	Beyond Appearences	LP/BP	U.S.†	1985	$14.00/$8.00
CBS	CK-33050	Greatest Hits	LP/BP	U.S.†	1985	$14.00/$8.00
		House of Blues	RS	U.S.	1993	$40.00

2 CD set. Airdate: 1/9/93.

Label	Catalog Number	Title	Type	Country	Year	Longbox Value / Value
		House of Blues	RS	U.S.	1995	$40.00

2 CD set. Airdate: 5/21/95.

Santana – Mother Earth Tour CD (Columbia CSK 2099)

Label	Catalog Number	Title	Type	Country	Year	Longbox Value / Value
Westwood One		In Concert	RS	U.S.	1993	$60.00
	2 CD set. Airdate: 4/12/93.					
Album Network		In the Studio (Abraxas)	RS	U.S.	1988	$25.00
	Airdate: 12/5/88.					
CBS	CK-35600	Inner Secrets	LP/BP	U.S.†	[illegible]	$14.00/$8.00
DIR		King Biscuit Flour Hour	RS	U.S.	1988	$30.00
	Airdate: 10/2/88.					
DIR		King Biscuit Flour Hour	RS	U.S.	1989	$30.00
	Airdate: 1/22/89.					
DIR		King Biscuit Flour Hour	RS	U.S.	1989	$30.00
	Airdate: 11/13/89.					
DIR		King Biscuit Flour Hour	RS	U.S.	1990	$30.00
	Airdate: 7/16/90.					
DIR		King Biscuit Flour Hour	RS	U.S.	1991	$30.00
	Airdate: 12/1/91.					
DIR		King Biscuit Flour Hour	RS	U.S.	1991	$30.00
	Airdate: 2/24/91.					
DIR		King Biscuit Flour Hour	RS	U.S.	1993	$40.00
	Airdate: 6/20/93.					
DIR		King Biscuit Flour Hour	RS	U.S.	1994	$40.00
	Airdate: 8/28/94.					
DIR		King Biscuit Flour Hour	RS	U.S.	1995	$40.00
	Airdate: 7/9/95.					
CBS		Lotus	DJ/Smplr	Japan		$100.00
	2 CD set.					
Columbia	CSK 2099	Mother Earth Tour CD	DJ/Smplr	U.S.	1990	$25.00
Westwood One		Off the Record	RS	U.S.	1992	$30.00
	Airdate: 9/14/92.					
Westwood One		Off the Record	RS	U.S.	1993	$30.00
	Airdate: 11/8/93.					
Westwood One		Off the Record	RS	U.S.	1994	$20.00
	Airdate: 11/21/94.					
Columbia		Santana	DJ/Smplr	U.S.	1995	$20.00
Columbia		Serpent, The	DJ/Smplr	U.S.		$15.00
CBS	CK-38122	Shango	LP/BP	U.S.†	1983	$14.00/$8.00
Sony		Starbox	LP	Japan	1989	$25.00
Sony		Starbox	LP	Japan	1993	$30.00
Westwood One		Superstar Concert	RS	U.S.	1992	$50.00
	2 CD set. Airdate: 6/21/92.					
Media America		Up Close	RS	U.S.	1988	$40.00
	2 CD set.					
Media America		Up Close	RS	U.S.	1990	$35.00
	2 CD set.					
Media America		Up Close	RS	U.S.	1992	$35.00
	2 CD set.					
Media America		Up Close	RS	U.S.	1994	$25.00
Columbia	CSK 1264	Viva Santana!	DJ/Smplr	U.S.	1988	$25.00
CBS	CK-37158	Zebop	LP/BP	U.S.†	1983	$14.00/$8.00

Singles

Label	Catalog Number	Title	Type	Country	Year	Longbox Value / Value
Columbia	CSK1011	Bella	CDJ	U.S.	1988	$3.00
CBS	654568-3	Black Magic Woman	CD3	Germany	1989	$10.00
CBS	654568-3	Black Magic Woman	CD3	U.K.	1989	$10.00
Polydor	CDP 1084	Esperando	CDJ	U.S.	1993	$3.00
Sony	10EP-3024	Europa	CD3	Japan	1988	$15.00/$4.00
CBS	656027-3	Gypsy Woman	CD3	Germany	1990	$10.00
CBS	656027-2	Gypsy Woman	CD5	U.K.	1990	$10.00
Columbia	CSK 73477	Gypsy Woman	CDJ	U.S.	1990	$3.00
Polydor	CDP 668	Right on	CDJ	U.S.	1992	$3.00
Polydor	CDP 724	We Don't Have to Wait	CDJ	U.S.	1992	$3.00

Santana Brothers

Full Length

Label	Catalog Number	Title	Type	Country	Year	Longbox Value / Value
Island	PRCD 6856-2	Sampler	DJ/Smplr	U.S.		$6.00

Singles

Label	Catalog Number	Title	Type	Country	Year	Longbox Value / Value
		Luz Amor Y Vide	CDJ	U.S.		$6.00

Santana, Julia

Singles

Label	Catalog Number	Title	Type	Country	Year	Longbox Value / Value
		Love Has a Name	CDJ	U.S.		$2.00

Saraya

Singles

Label	Catalog Number	Title	Type	Country	Year	Longbox Value / Value
Polygram		Back to the Bullet	CDJ	U.S.	1989	$2.00
Polygram	889293-2	Love Has Taken It's Toll	CD5	U.K.	1989	$8.00
Polydor	CDP 45	Love Has Taken It's Toll	CDJ	U.S.	1989	$2.00
Polydor	CDP 430	Seducer	CDJ	U.S.	1991	$2.00
SBK	DPRO-05321	Timeless Love	CDJ	U.S.	1989	$2.00

Sarde, Cliff

Full Length

Label	Catalog Number	Title	Type	Country	Year	Longbox Value / Value
Passport	PJCD-88034	Dreams out Loud	LP	U.K.		$12.00
Passport	PJCD-88034	Dreams out Loud	LP/BP	U.S.		$15.00/$12.00

Satchel

Full Length

Label	Catalog Number	Title	Type	Country	Year	Longbox Value / Value
Epic	ESK 6232	EDC	DJ/LP	U.S.	1994	$15.00

Singles

Label	Catalog Number	Title	Type	Country	Year	Longbox Value / Value
Epic	ESK 7018	Suffering	CDJ	U.S.		$2.00

Satellite of Undying Love

Singles

Label	Catalog Number	Title	Type	Country	Year	Longbox Value / Value
Virgin	VSCDG 1378	Endlessly	CD5	U.K.	1991	$8.00

Sativa Luvbox

Singles

Label	Catalog Number	Title	Type	Country	Year	Longbox Value / Value
Gasoline Ally	2767	U Got It All Wrong	CDJ	U.S.	1993	$2.00

Sator

Singles

Label	Catalog Number	Title	Type	Country	Year	Longbox Value / Value
WEA	9031-76521	We're Right	CD5	Germany	1992	$8.00

Satriani, Joe

Full Length

Label	Catalog Number	Title	Type	Country	Year	Longbox Value / Value
		House of Blues	RS	U.S.	1994	$35.00
	2 CD set. Airdate: 4/10/94.					
Westwood One		In Concert	RS	U.S.	1994	$60.00
	Airdate: 9/12/94.					
DIR		King Biscuit Flour Hour	RS	U.S.	1988	$40.00
	Airdate: 7/31/88.					
DIR		King Biscuit Flour Hour	RS	U.S.	1989	$40.00
	Airdate: 2/5/89.					
DIR		King Biscuit Flour Hour	RS	U.S.	1990	$40.00
	With ZZ Top, Airdate: 4/2/90.					
Relativity		Not Of This Earth	LP/BP	U.S.		$20.00/$20.00
	Original cover.					
Westwood One		Off the Record	RS	U.S.	1993	$35.00
	Airdate: 10/11/93.					
Westwood One		Off the Record	RS	U.S.	1993	$40.00
	Airdate: 10/11/93.					

Singles

Label	Catalog Number	Title	Type	Country	Year	Longbox Value / Value
Food For Thought	CD YUM 118	Big Bad Moon	CD3	France	1990	$10.00
IRS	977 118	Big Bad Moon	CD5	Germany	1990	$10.00
Relativity	CD YUM 118	Big Bad Moon	CD5	U.K.	1990	$10.00
Relativity	IRPROCD-0103	Big Bad Moon	CDJ	U.S.	1990	$7.00
Relativity		Friends	CDJ	U.S.	1992	$6.00
IRS	977 120	I Believe	CD5	U.K.	1992	$10.00
Relativity	88561-1038-2	I Believe	CD5	U.S.	1990	$5.00
Relativity	IRPROCD-0105	I Believe	CDJ	U.S.	1990	$6.00
Relativity	IRPROCD-0107	I Believe	CDJ	U.S.	1990	$6.00
		Look My Way	CDJ	U.K.		$12.00
Relativity	658953-2	Satch E.P.	CD5	U.K.	1993	$11.00
Relativity	RPROCD 0159	Summer Song	CDJ	U.S.	1992	$6.00
Relativity	88561-8193-2	Surfing With the Alien	CDJ/PD	U.S.	1987	$25.00

Saunders, Fernando

Full Length

Label	Catalog Number	Title	Type	Country	Year	Longbox Value / Value
		Biography	DJ/Smplr	U.S.		$6.00

Singles

Label	Catalog Number	Title	Type	Country	Year	Longbox Value / Value
A&M	31458 8139	Come a Little Closer	CDJ	U.S.	1993	$2.00

Saunders, Merle

Full Length

Label	Catalog Number	Title	Type	Country	Year	Longbox Value / Value
Summertone		Blues From the Rainforest: A Musical Suite	DJ/Smplr	U.S.	1990	$10.00
Sumertone		Live	DJ/Smplr	U.S.		$8.00

Singles

Label	Catalog Number	Title	Type	Country	Year	Longbox Value / Value
Summertone		Suger Free	CDJ	U.S.	1990	$7.00

Savage, Chantay

Singles

Label	Catalog Number	Title	Type	Country	Year	Longbox Value / Value
RCA	62787-2-RDJ	Don't Let It Go to Your Head	CDJ	U.S.	1994	$2.00
RCA	62824-2-RDJ	Give It to Ya	CDJ	U.S.	1994	$2.00
RCA	RDJ644832	I Will Survive	CDJ	U.S.		$2.00
RCA	62494-2-RDJ	If You Believe	CDJ	U.S.	1993	$2.00

Savannah

Singles

Label	Catalog Number	Title	Type	Country	Year	Longbox Value / Value
Cooltempo	COOLCD-211	Savannah	CD5	U.K.	1990	$8.00
BMG	663289	Soul Party	CD5	Germany	1990	$8.00

Savatage

Full Length

Label	Catalog Number	Title	Type	Country	Year	Longbox Value / Value
Atlantic		From the Dungeons to the Street	DJ/Smplr	U.S.	1989	$8.00

Singles

Label	Catalog Number	Title	Type	Country	Year	Longbox Value / Value
Atlantic	PRCD 6454-2	Dead Winter Dead	CDJ	U.S.	1993	$2.00
Atlantic	PRCD 66172	Doesn't Matter Anyway	CDJ	U.S.		$2.00
Atlantic	PRCD 5022-2	Edge ofThorns	CDJ	U.S.	1993	$2.00
Atlantic	PRCD 3220-2	Gutter Ballet	CDJ	U.S.	1989	$2.00
Atlantic	PRCD 5194-2	He Carves His Stone	CDJ	U.S.	1993	$7.00
Atlantic	PRCD 4453-2	Jesus Saves	CDJ	U.S.	1991	$2.00
Atlantic	PRCD 6615-2	Not What You See	CDJ	U.S.		$2.00
Atlantic	PRCD 4219-2	Sammy and Tex	CDJ	U.S.	1991	$2.00
Atlantic	PRCD 5264-2	Sleep	CDJ	U.S.		$2.00

Savoy

Singles

Label	Catalog Number	Title	Type	Country	Year	Longbox Value / Value
	PRO-CD-8077	Velvet	CDJ	U.S.		$2.00

Savoy Brown

Full Length

Label	Catalog Number	Title	Type	Country	Year	Longbox Value / Value
Deram		Getting to the Point	LP/LB	U.S.		$14.00/$8.00
Deram		Skin 'n Bone	LP/LB	U.S.		$14.00/$8.00
Relix		Slow Train	LP/LB	U.S.		$14.00/$8.00
Deram		Wire Fire	LP/LB	U.S.		$14.00/$8.00

Singles

Label	Catalog Number	Title	Type	Country	Year	Longbox Value / Value
Cresendo	PRO 8	Deep in My Heart	CD3	U.S.		$5.00
	520207	Getting to the Point	CD5	U.S.	1994	$5.00

Saw Doctors

Singles

Label	Catalog Number	Title	Type	Country	Year	Longbox Value / Value
		Wake Up Sleeping	CD5	U.K.		$10.00
		Wake Up Sleeping	CD5	U.K.		$10.00
	Second version.					

Sawada, Shungo & His Group

Full Length

Label	Catalog Number	Title	Type	Country	Year	Longbox Value / Value
Denon	CD-7208	Shungo	LP/LB	U.S.†	1985	$14.00/$8.00

Sawyer Brown

Full Length

Label	Catalog Number	Title	Type	Country	Year	Longbox Value / Value
		'90s Country	RS	U.S.	1995	$45.00
	Airdate: 8/12/95.					
		'90s Country	RS	U.S.	1996	$45.00
	Airdate: 2/10/96.					
		Outskirts of Town	RS	U.S.	1993	$25.00
Curb	CBRS-1	Radio Special	DJ/Intvw	U.S.	1993	$15.00

Singles

Label	Catalog Number	Title	Type	Country	Year	Longbox Value / Value
Curb	1031	All These Years	CDJ	U.S.	1992	$2.00
Capitol	DPRO 79422	It Wasn't His Child	CDJ	U.S.	1988	$2.00
Capitol	DPRO-79110	Somewhere in the Night	CDJ	U.S.		$2.00
Curb	1053	Thank God for You	CDJ	U.S.	1993	$2.00

Saxmachine

Singles

Label	Catalog Number	Title	Type	Country	Year	Longbox Value / Value
Capitol	C2 58177	Love is a Message	CD5	U.S.	1994	$5.00

Saxon

Full Length

Label	Catalog Number	Title	Type	Country	Year	Longbox Value / Value
BMG		Denim & Leather	LP	Canada		$12.00
		Greatest Hits Live	LP/BP	U.S.		$14.00/$8.00
Charisma	91672	Solid Ball of Rock	LP/LB	U.S.	1990	$14.00/$8.00

Singles

Label	Catalog Number	Title	Type	Country	Year	Longbox Value / Value
Virgin	665 529	Iron Wheels	CD5	Germany	1992	$8.00
BMG	664023	Requiem	CD5	Germany	1991	$8.00
Charisma	PRCD 038	Requiem	CDJ	U.S.	1990	$2.00
EMI	CDEM-43	Ride Like the Wind	CD5	U.K.	1988	$8.00
Virgin	DINISD-105	We Will Remember	CD5	U.K.	1991	$8.00

Sayer, Leo

Full Length

Label	Catalog Number	Title	Type	Country	Year	Longbox Value / Value
Chrysalis		Endless Flight	LTD/LP	U.K.	1994	$25.00/$15.00

25th Anniversary edition in 6"x11" longbox.

Label	Catalog Number	Title	Type	Country	Year	Longbox Value / Value
EMI	203910-2	Cool Touch	CD5	Germany	1990	$8.00
EMI	CDEM-147	Cool Touch	CD5	U.K.	1990	$8.00
EMI	204197-2	Rely on Me	CD5	Germany	1990	$8.00
Chrysalis	CDCHS-3926	When I Need You	CD5	U.K.	1993	$8.00

Scaggs, Boz

Full Length

Label	Catalog Number	Title	Type	Country	Year	Longbox Value / Value
CBS	CK-30796	Boz Scaggs & Band	LP/BP	U.S.		$14.00/$8.00
		Fly Like a Bird	DJ/Smplr	U.S.	1994	$12.00
Sony	XDDP 93013-4	He Is Back With His Other Roads	DJ/Smplr	Japan		$200.00

2CD set.

Label	Catalog Number	Title	Type	Country	Year	Longbox Value / Value
CBS	CK36841	Hits	LP/BP	U.S.†	1985	$14.00/$8.00
CBS	CK-30454	Moments	LP/BP	U.S.		$14.00/$8.00
CBS	CK-31384	My Time	LP/BP	U.S.		$14.00/$8.00
CBS	CK33920	Silk Degrees	LP/BP	U.S.†	1983	$14.00/$8.00
Columbia	CK-64420	Silk Degrees	LTD/LP	U.S.	1994	$25.00

Gold disc.

Label	Catalog Number	Title	Type	Country	Year	Longbox Value / Value
Columbia		Silk Degrees	LTD/LP	U.S.	1994	$28.00/$25.00

Gold disc. Last mastersound disc to employ longbox package.

Label	Catalog Number	Title	Type	Country	Year	Longbox Value / Value
Sony	SRCS-7906	Silk Degrees	LTD/LP	U.S.	1996	$35.00

20 bit mastering.

Label	Catalog Number	Title	Type	Country	Year	Longbox Value / Value
		Some Change	DJ/Smplr	U.S.		$5.00
Sony	25DP-5202	Star Box	LTD/LP	Japan	1988	$70.00

Singles

Label	Catalog Number	Title	Type	Country	Year	Longbox Value / Value
Sony	10EP-3042	Cool Running	CD3	Japan	1988	$12.00/$4.00
		Cool Running	CDJ	U.S.	1988	$2.00
	DPRO14234	Fly Like a Bird	CDJ	U.S.		$2.00
Columbia	651559-9	Heart of Mine	CD5	Germany	1988	$9.00
Sony	10EP-3035	Heart of Mine	CD3	Japan	1988	$12.00/$4.00
Columbia	651559-2	Heart of Mine	CD5	U.K.	1988	$9.00
Columbia		Heart of Mine	CDJ	U.S.	1988	$2.00
	DPRO-14163	I'll Be the One	CDJ	U.S.		$2.00
	DPRO142144	I'll Be the One	CDJ	U.S.		$2.00
Columbia	654560-3	Jo Jo	CD3	Germany	1988	$9.00
Virgin		Some Change	CDJ	Germany	1994	$15.00
Virgin	14139	Some Change	CDJ	U.S.	1994	$2.00
Sony	10EP-3020	We're All Alone	CD3	Japan	1988	$12.00/$4.00

Scandal

Full Length

Label	Catalog Number	Title	Type	Country	Year	Longbox Value / Value
CBS	CK-39173	Warrior, The	LP/BP	U.S.†	1984	$14.00/$8.00

Scarce

Singles

Label	Catalog Number	Title	Type	Country	Year	Longbox Value / Value
	1	Red Ep	CD5	U.S.	1994	$5.00

Scarface

Full Length

Label	Catalog Number	Title	Type	Country	Year	Longbox Value / Value
Rap-A-Lot		Untouchable, The	LTD/LP	U.S.	1997	$16.00

CD plus cassette sampler sold exclusively at Camelot Music.

Label	Catalog Number	Title	Type	Country	Year	Longbox Value / Value
Motown	60331	Among The Walking Dead	CD5	U.S.	1994	$5.00
Rap A Lot	7032	Now I Feel Ya	CDj	U.S.	1993	$2.00
Capital	38469	People Don't Believe	CD5	U.S.	1994	$5.00

Scarlet

Singles

Label	Catalog Number	Title	Type	Country	Year	Longbox Value / Value
	MJC35739PRO	Independent Love Songs	CDJ	U.S.		$2.00

Scarlett & Black

Full Length

Label	Catalog Number	Title	Type	Country	Year	Longbox Value / Value
Virgin	90647	Scarlett & Black	LP/LB	U.S.	1987	$12.00/$7.00

Singles

Label	Catalog Number	Title	Type	Country	Year	Longbox Value / Value
Virgin	PRCD 2329	Let Yourself Gogo	CDJ	U.S.	1988	$2.00
Virgin	VJD-12008	You Don't Know	CD3	Japan	1988	$13.00/$4.00
Virgin	PRCD 9405	You Don't Know	CDJ	U.S.	1987	$2.00

Scatman, John

Singles

Label	Catalog Number	Title	Type	Country	Year	Longbox Value / Value
RCA	64379	Scatman	CD5	U.S.	1995	$5.00

Scatterbrain

Full Length

Label	Catalog Number	Title	Type	Country	Year	Longbox Value / Value
		Herre Comes Trouble	LP/LB	U.S.		$18.00/$15.00

Singles

Label	Catalog Number	Title	Type	Country	Year	Longbox Value / Value
Elektra	PRCD 8459-2	Big Fun	CDj	U.S.	1991	$2.00

Schascle

Full Length

Label	Catalog Number	Title	Type	Country	Year	Longbox Value / Value
Reprise	9 26510-2-Dj	Haunted by Real Life	DJ/LP	U.S.	1991	$8.00

Picture disc CD with VHS video and press kit.

Label	Catalog Number	Title	Type	Country	Year	Longbox Value / Value
Reprise	9 26510-2-Dj	Schascle (Haunted by Real Life)	DJ/LP	U.S.	1991	$5.00

Picture disc.

Scheer

Singles

Label	Catalog Number	Title	Type	Country	Year	Longbox Value / Value
	PRO-CD-8150	Wish You Were Dead	CDJ	U.S.	1996	$2.00

Schell, Fenster

Singles

Label	Catalog Number	Title	Type	Country	Year	Longbox Value / Value
Atlantic	PRCD 3232-2	Love Hate Relationship	CDJ	U.S.	1990	$2.00
Atlantic	PRCD 3525-2	Whisper	CDJ	U.S.	1990	$2.00

Schenker, Michael Group

Full Length

Label	Catalog Number	Title	Type	Country	Year	Longbox Value / Value
		Built to Destroy	LP	U.S.		$15.00/$12.00
		M.S.G	LP/LB	U.S.		$15.00/$12.00

Schiedel, Thomas

Full Length

Label	Catalog Number	Title	Type	Country	Year	Longbox Value / Value
Blue Orchid	2002	All Alone	LP/BP	U.S.		$12.00/$7.00

Schilling, Peter

Singles

Label	Catalog Number	Title	Type	Country	Year	Longbox Value / Value
WEA	247971-2	Different Story, The	CD5	Germany	1989	$8.00
Pioneer	09P3-6155	Different Story, The	CD3	Japan	1989	$13.00/$4.00
WEA	YZ-411CD	Different Story, The	CD5	U.K.	1989	$8.00
Elektra	69307-2	Different Story, The	CD5	U.S.	1989	$4.00
Elektra	PR 8067-2	Different Story, The	CDJ	U.S.	1989	$2.00
WEA	2292-46927-2	Major Tom	CD5	Germany	1990	$8.00
WEA	9031-72618-2	Major Tom	CD5	Germany	1990	$8.00
Zyx	1222	Major Tom	CD5	U.S.	1994	$5.00
	1267	Sonne, Mond Und Ster	CD5	U.S.	1994	$5.00

Schmit, Timothy

Singles

Label	Catalog Number	Title	Type	Country	Year	Longbox Value / Value
MCA	1117	Something Sad	CDJ	U.S.	1990	$2.00
MCA	CD45 18332	Was It Just the Moonlight	CDJ	U.S.	1990	$2.00

Schmitt, Adam

Full Length

Label	Catalog Number	Title	Type	Country	Year	Longbox Value / Value
Reprise	PRO-CD-6181	Illiterature Sampler	DJ/Smplr	U.S.	1993	$5.00
Reprise	9 26551-2-Dj	World so Bright	DJ/LP	U.S.	1991	$5.00

Singles

Label	Catalog Number	Title	Type	Country	Year	Longbox Value / Value
Reprise	PRO-CD-4872	Can't Get You on My Mind	CDJ	U.S.	1991	$2.00
Reprise	PRO-CD-6646	Catching Up	CDJ	U.S.		$2.00
Reprise	PRO-CD-7469	Let It Be Me	CDJ	U.S.	1995	$3.00
Reprise	PRO-CD-6436	Waiting to Shine	CDJ	U.S.	1993	$2.00

Schneider, Fred

Singles

Label	Catalog Number	Title	Type	Country	Year	Longbox Value / Value
Reprise	PRO-CD-4875	Monster	CDJ	U.S.	1991	$2.00

Schneider, John

Full Length

Label	Catalog Number	Title	Type	Country	Year	Longbox Value / Value
MCA	MCAD-5668	A Memory Like You	LP/LB	U.S.	1986	$14.00/$8.00

Schnell, Fenster

Singles

Label	Catalog Number	Title	Type	Country	Year	Longbox Value / Value
Atlantic	PRCD 3232-2	Love Hate Relationship	CDJ	U.S.	1990	$2.00

Schnitt Act

Singles

Label	Catalog Number	Title	Type	Country	Year	Longbox Value / Value
Cheetah	9110	Rage	CDJ	U.S.		$3.00

Schon, Neal

Full Length

Label	Catalog Number	Title	Type	Country	Year	Longbox Value / Value
Westwood One		Off the Record	RS	U.S.	1995	$35.00

Airdate: 10/2/95.

Label	Catalog Number	Title	Type	Country	Year	Longbox Value / Value
Westwood One		Off the Record	RS	U.S.	1995	$35.00

Airdate: 5/15/95.

Singles

Label	Catalog Number	Title	Type	Country	Year	Longbox Value / Value
Columbia		I'll Cover You	CDJ	U.S.	1989	$2.00

Schonherz & Scott

Singles

Label	Catalog Number	Title	Type	Country	Year	Longbox Value / Value
		Wishing Well	CDJ	U.S.		$2.00

School of Fish

Full Length

Label	Catalog Number	Title	Type	Country	Year	Longbox Value / Value
Westwood One		In Concert	RS	U.S.	1993	$50.00

2 CD set. With Soul Asylum, Airdate: 6/21/93.

Label	Catalog Number	Title	Type	Country	Year	Longbox Value / Value
Capitol	DPRO-79795	Live In LA	DJ/Smplr	U.S.	1991	$15.00

Singles

Label	Catalog Number	Title	Type	Country	Year	Longbox Value / Value
Capitol	DPRO 79612	3 Strange Days	CDJ	U.S.	1991	$3.00
Capitol	C2-15675	3 Strange Days	CDJ	U.S.	1991	$7.00
Capitol	DPRO-79709	Everyday	CDJ	U.S.	1993	$3.00
Capitol	DPRO 79776	Greatest Living Englishman	CDJ	U.S.	1991	$3.00
Capitol	DPRO-79840	Jump off the World	CDJ	U.S.	1993	$3.00
Capitol	DPRO-79699	King of the Dollar	CDJ	U.S.	1993	$3.00
Capitol	C2 15959	Take Me Anywhere	CD5	Canada	1993	$6.00
Capitol	DPRO-79621	Take Me Anywhere	CDJ	U.S.	1993	$2.00
Capitol	DPRO 79713	Wrong	CDJ	U.S.	1991	$6.00

Schooly D

Singles

Label	Catalog Number	Title	Type	Country	Year	Longbox Value / Value
Ruffhouse	77265	Another Sign	CDJ	U.S.	1993	$2.00
Capitol	DPRO-79493	King of New York	CDJ	U.S.	1990	$2.00
Capitol	DPRO-79137	Original Gangster	CDJ	U.S.	1991	$2.00
Capitol	DPRO-79787	Where'd You Get That Funk	CDJ	U.S.	1991	$2.00

Schtum

Singles

Label	Catalog Number	Title	Type	Country	Year	Longbox Value / Value
	OSK 7326	Skydiver	CDJ	U.S.		$2.00

Schubert

Singles

Label	Catalog Number	Title	Type	Country	Year	Longbox Value / Value
	MADJ600142	Reflections of the Past	CDJ	U.S.		$2.00

Schuur, Diane

Singles

Label	Catalog Number	Title	Type	Country	Year	Longbox Value / Value
GRP	9943	Touch	CDJ	U.S.	1990	$2.00

Scialfa, Patti

Singles

Label	Catalog Number	Title	Type	Country	Year	Longbox Value / Value
Columbia	CSK 5236	As Long As I	CDJ	U.S.	1994	$2.00
Columbia	CSK 5500	Lucky Girl	CDJ	U.S.	1994	$7.00

Scofield, John

Full Length

Label	Catalog Number	Title	Type	Country	Year	Longbox Value / Value
Gramaphone	GRCD-8405	Electric Outlet	LP/LB	U.S.†	1985	$14.00/$8.00
Enja	403803	Out Like a Light	LP/LB	U.S.†	1985	$14.00/$8.00
Verve	SACD 1247	Selections From Quiet	DJ/Smplr	U.S.	1996	$12.00
Enja	311207	Shinola	LP/LB	U.S.†	1985	$14.00/$8.00

Scorn

Singles

Label	Catalog Number	Title	Type	Country	Year	Longbox Value / Value
Earache	MOSH-61CD	Lick Forever Dog	CD5	U.K.	1991	$8.00

Label	Catalog Number	Title	Type	Country	Year	Longbox Value / Value
Relativity	88561-1154	Lick Forever Dog	CDJ	U.S.	1992	$6.00

Scorpio Rising

Singles

Label	Catalog Number	Title	Type	Country	Year	Longbox Value / Value
Chapter 22	CHAPCD-71	Silver Surfer	CD5	U.K.	1992	$8.00
Chapter 22	CHAPCD-68	Welcome to Compact Saturnalia	CD5	U.K.	1992	$8.00

Scorpions – Can't Explain (EMI CDP 506 2 03597 3)

Scorpions

Full Length

Label	Catalog Number	Title	Type	Country	Year	Longbox Value / Value
Album Network		Album Network Special	RS	U.S.	1996	$80.00
2 CD set. Airdate: 6/30/96.						
EMI	793466-2	Best of Rockers & Ballads	LTD/LP	Germany	1989	$35.00
Picture disc version.						
Mercury	818 852-2	Blackout	LP/BP	U.S.†	1984	$14.00/$8.00
Pioneer	PA85-M023	First Sting	8"LD	U.S.	1985	$10.00
Foundations		FZ Interview	RS	U.S.	1993	$10.00
Scorpions interview with various artists music.						
Foundations		FZ Interview	RS	U.S.	1993	$20.00
EastWest		Live Bites	DJ/LP	U.S.		$15.00
Mercury	814 981-2	Love at First Sting	LP/BP	U.S.†	1984	$14.00/$8.00
EastWest		Pure Instinct	DJ/LP	Germany	1996	$30.00
Harvest	79 1590-2	Savage Amusement	LTD/LP	U.K.	1987	$30.00
Picture disc CD.						
EMI	797963-2	Scorpions	LTD/LP	Germany	1992	$40.00
3 CD boxed set.						
Electrola	CDP 519 158	Talk About…Still Loving You	DJ/Intvw	Germany	1992	$30.00
Polygram	080 615-1	To Russia	LD	U.S.	1989	$30.00
Media America		Up Close	RS	U.S.	1994	$30.00
Pioneer	PA-87-191	World Wide Live	LD	U.S.	1987	$20.00
Analog audio.						

Singles

Label	Catalog Number	Title	Type	Country	Year	Longbox Value / Value
Mercury		Alien Nation	CDJ	U.S.		$7.00
Mercury	CDP 981	Alien Nation	CDJ	U.S.	1994	$6.00
Mercury	CDP 982	Alien Nation	CDJ	U.S.	1994	$6.00
EMI	202784-2	Believe in Love	CD5	Germany	1987	$8.00
Mercury	870 735-2	Believe in Love	CDV/BP	U.S.	1988	$20.00/$20.00
Mercury	870 716-2	Big City Nights	CDV/BP	U.S.	1988	$20.00/$20.00
Vertigo	878787-2	Don't Believe Her	CD5	Germany	1990	$10.00
Vertigo	VERCD-52	Don't Believe Her	CD5	U.K.	1990	$10.00
Polygram	CDP 379	Don't Believe Her	CDJ	U.S.	1991	$6.00
		Edge of Time	CDJ	Holland		$15.00
Mercury	MCPRO-0016-2	Hit Between the Eyes	CDJ	U.S.	1994	$7.00
EMI	204046-2	Holiday	CD5	Germany	1990	$10.00
Mercury	CDP 208	Holiday	CDJ	U.S.	1990	$6.00
EMI	2 03597 3	I Can't Explain	CD3	Germany	1990	$10.00
Mercury	876 191-2	I Can't Explain	CD5	U.S.	1989	$5.00
Mercury	CDP 95	I Can't Explain	CDJ	U.S.	1989	$3.00
Mercury	CDP 145	I Can't Explain	CDJ	U.S.	1989	$3.00
Mercury		In Trance	CDJ	U.S.	1994	$6.00
EMI	20 3727 2	Is Anybody There	CD5	Germany	1989	$10.00
EMI	2 03057 2	Passion Rules the Game	CD5	Germany	1990	$10.00
Harvest	CDHAR-5242	Passion Rules the Game	CD5	U.K.	1989	$10.00
Toshiba	XP10-2014	Rhythm of Love	CD3	Japan	1988	$15.00/$4.00
Harvest	2 02405-2	Rhythm of Love	CD5	U.K.	1987	$8.00
Mercury	870 727-2	Rhythm of Love	CDV/BP	U.S.	1988	$20.00/$20.00
Vertigo	VERCD-60	Send Me an Angel	CD5	U.K.	1991	$10.00
Mercury	CDP 536	Send Me an Angel	CDJ	U.S.	1990	$6.00
EMI	204675-2	Still Loving You	CD5	Germany	1992	$10.00
Polygram	CDP 332	Tease Me, Please Me	CDJ	U.S.	1991	$7.00
		Under The Same Sun	CD5	U.K.		$10.00
Second version.						
Mercury	MERCD 395	Under the Same Sun	CD5	U.K.	1994	$10.00
Mercury	CDP 1110	Under the Same Sun	CDJ	U.S.	1994	$3.00
Mercury		Wild Child	CDJ	U.S.	1995	$6.00
Vertigo	866017-2	Winds of Change	CD5	Germany	1991	$10.00
Vertigo	868285-2	Winds of Change	CD5	Germany	1991	$10.00
Phonogram	PHDR-43	Winds of Change	CD3	Japan	1991	$15.00/$4.00
Vertigo	VERCD-54	Winds of Change	CD5	U.K.	1991	$10.00
Vertigo	VERCD-58	Winds of Change	CD5	U.K.	1991	$10.00
Mercury	CDP 423	Winds of Change	CDJ	U.S.	1991	$7.00
Phonogram		Woman	CD5	U.K.	1994	$11.00
Mercury	CDP 1080	Woman	CDJ	U.S.	1994	$3.00

Scott, Casey

Singles

Label	Catalog Number	Title	Type	Country	Year	Longbox Value / Value
Capitol	DPRO-79719	Seventh of November	CDJ	U.S.	1993	$2.00
Capitol	DPRO-79697	Sharp Metal Objects	CDJ	U.S.	1993	$6.00

Scott, Mike

Singles

Label	Catalog Number	Title	Type	Country	Year	Longbox Value / Value
	DPRO 10420	Bring 'Em on in	CDJ	U.S.		$3.00
		Building the City of Light	CD5	U.K.	1995	$10.00
		Building the City of Light	CD5	U.K.	1995	$10.00
Second version.						

Scott, Millie

Singles

Label	Catalog Number	Title	Type	Country	Year	Longbox Value / Value
		It's My Life	CDJ	U.S.		$2.00

Scott, Tom

Full Length

Label	Catalog Number	Title	Type	Country	Year	Longbox Value / Value
Elektra	60162-2	Desire	LP/LB	U.S.†	1985	$14.00/$8.00
Atlantic	80106-2	Target	LP/LB	U.S.†	1985	$14.00/$8.00

Singles

Label	Catalog Number	Title	Type	Country	Year	Longbox Value / Value
GRP	9957	If You're Not the One for Me	CDJ	U.S.	1991	$2.00

Scott, Tony

Full Length

Label	Catalog Number	Title	Type	Country	Year	Longbox Value / Value
Verve	817209-2	Music for Zen Meditation	LP/LB	U.S.†	1985	$14.00/$8.00

Singles

Label	Catalog Number	Title	Type	Country	Year	Longbox Value / Value
Eastwest	9031-74702-2	From Da Soul	CD5	Germany	1991	$8.00
Eastwest	9031-74702-2	From Da Soul	CD5	U.K.	1991	$8.00
BCM	20462	Gangster Boogie	CD5	Germany	1990	$8.00
Champion	CHAMPCD-249	Gangster Boogie	CD5	U.K.	1990	$8.00
BCM	20389	Get Into It	CD5	Germany	1990	$8.00
Champion	CHAMPCD-232	Get Into It	CD5	U.K.	1990	$8.00
Eastwest	9031-745614-2	Gimme Some Swing	CD5	U.K.	1991	$8.00
BCM	20503	Megamix	CD5	Germany	1991	$8.00
BCM	20236	That's How I'm Living	CD5	Germany	1989	$8.00

Scott-Heron, Gil

Singles

Label	Catalog Number	Title	Type	Country	Year	Longbox Value / Value
TVT	4311	Spirits Past	CDJ	U.S.	1993	$2.00

Scotti, Nick

Singles

Label	Catalog Number	Title	Type	Country	Year	Longbox Value / Value
Reprise	9 40711-2	Get Over	CD5	U.S.	1993	$5.00

Scratchmaster, Chuck T.

Singles

Label	Catalog Number	Title	Type	Country	Year	Longbox Value / Value
		[illegible] in Bli[illegible]	CDJ	U.S.		$2.00

Scream

Singles

Label	Catalog Number	Title	Type	Country	Year	Longbox Value / Value
Hollywood	PRCD 8515-2	Father, Mother, Son	CDJ	U.S.	1992	$2.00
Hollywood	PRCD 8444-2	I Believe in Me	CDJ	U.S.	1991	$2.00

Screamin' Cheetah Wheelies

Singles

Label	Catalog Number	Title	Type	Country	Year	Longbox Value / Value
Atlantic	PRCD 6677-2	Hello From Venus	CDJ	U.S.		$2.00
Atlantic	PRCD 5312-2	Let It Flow	CDJ	U.S.		$2.00

Screaming Jets

Singles

Label	Catalog Number	Title	Type	Country	Year	Longbox Value / Value
		Better	CD5	Australia	1991	$20.00
CD and video in box.						
rooArt	RARCD-7	Better	CD5	U.K.	1991	$7.00
Mercury	CDP 567	Better	CDJ	U.S.	1991	$2.00
roo Art	868 249	Blue Sashes	CD5	U.S.	1991	$5.00
roo Art	RARCD-6	C'mon	CD5	U.K.	1991	$7.00
roo Art	CDP 451	C'mon	CDJ	U.S.	1991	$2.00
rooArt	CDP 539	Stealth Live	CDJ	U.S.	1991	$3.00

Screaming Trees

Full Length

Label	Catalog Number	Title	Type	Country	Year	Longbox Value / Value
Epic		Canadian Tour '93	DJ/Smplr	Canada		$20.00
Westwood One		In Concert	RS	U.S.	1993	$50.00
Airdate: 3/29/93.						
Epic		Winter Songs Tour Tracks	DJ/Smplr	U.S.		$10.00

Singles

Label	Catalog Number	Title	Type	Country	Year	Longbox Value / Value
Epic	ESK 2296	Bed of Roses	CDJ	U.S.	1991	$2.00
Epic	ESK 5286	Butterfly	CDJ	U.S.	1993	$3.00
Epic	659179	Dollar Bill	CD5	Germany	1992	$8.00
Epic	ESK 4771	Dollar Bill	CDJ	U.S.	1993	$3.00
Epic	658237-2	Nearly Lost You	CD5	U.K.	1993	$8.00
Epic	ESK 4942	Nearly Lost You	CDJ	U.S.	1993	$3.00
Epic	ESK 4604	Nearly Lost You	CDJ	U.S.	1993	$7.00
Epic	ESK	Shadow of the Season	CDJ	U.S.	1993	$7.00
Epic	49K 73593 2	Something About Today	CD5	U.S.	1990	$5.00
Epic	ESK 3092	Something About Today	CDJ	U.S.	1991	$2.00

Screaming Tribesman

Singles

Label	Catalog Number	Title	Type	Country	Year	Longbox Value / Value
SPV	6812-3	I've Got a Feeling	CD5	Germany	1990	$8.00
Rykodisc	1006	I've Got a Feeling	CD3	U.S.	1990	$6.00/$4.00

Screeching Weas

Singles

Label	Catalog Number	Title	Type	Country	Year	Longbox Value / Value
Lookout Records	97	How to Make Enemies	CD5	U.S.	1994	$5.00

Screw Factor

Singles

Label	Catalog Number	Title	Type	Country	Year	Longbox Value / Value
MCA	DBRMD-10715	Eye	CD5	Canada	1993	$6.00
MCA		Eye	CD5	U.K.	1993	$8.00
MCA	10715	Eye	CD5	U.S.	1993	$5.00

Scritti Politti

Singles

Label	Catalog Number	Title	Type	Country	Year	Longbox Value / Value
Virgin	VJD-12024	Boom! There She Was	CD3	Japan	1988	$13.00/$4.00
Virgin	VSCD-1143	Boom! There She Was	CD5	U.K.	1988	$10.00
Warner Brothers	PRO-CD-2981	Boom! There She Was	CDJ	U.S.	1988	$2.00
Virgin	661579	First Boy in This Town	CD5	Germany	1988	$10.00
Virgin	VSCD-1082	First Boy in This Town	CD5	U.K.	1988	$10.00
Virgin	659823	Oh Patti	CD5	Germany	1989	$10.00
Virgin	VJD-12004	Oh Patti	CD3	Japan	1988	$12.00/$4.00
Virgin	CDEP-17	Oh Patti	CD5	U.K.	1989	$10.00
Warner Brothers	PRO-CD-3311	Oh Patti	CDJ	U.S.	1988	$2.00
Virgin	VJCP-14024	She's a Woman	CD5	Japan	1991	$15.00
Virgin	VCDT-1333	She's a Woman	CD5	U.K.	1991	$10.00
Virgin	VJCP-14029	Take Me in Your Arms	CD5	Japan	1991	$15.00
Virgin	CDT-34	Wood Bees	CD3	U.K.	1988	$10.00
Virgin	880990	Word Girl	CD3	Germany	1988	$10.00
Virgin	CDT-13	Word Girl	CD3	U.K.	1988	$10.00

Seal

Full Length

Label	Catalog Number	Title	Type	Country	Year	Longbox Value / Value
		Acoustic Sampler, The	DJ/Smplr	U.S.	1995	$28.00
		Acoustic Session, The	DJ/Smplr	U.S.	1994	$12.00
Westwood One		In Concert-Nu Rock	RS	U.S.	1995	$65.00
Airdate: 12/4/95.						

Singles

Label	Catalog Number	Title	Type	Country	Year	Longbox Value / Value
ZTT	9031-75028-2	Beginning	CD5	Germany	1991	$9.00
ZTT	9031-75030-2	Beginning	CD5	Germany	1991	$9.00
ZTT	WMC5-392	Beginning	CD5	Japan	1991	$12.00
ZTT	ZANG-21CD	Beginning	CD5	U.K.	1991	$9.00
ZTT	9 40200-2	Beginning	CD5	U.S.	1991	$5.00

Label	Catalog Number	Title	Type	Country	Year	Longbox Value / Value
Sire	PRO-CD-5043	Beginning	CDJ	U.S.	1991	$3.00
WEA	9031-73237-2	Crazy	CD5	Germany	1990	$9.00
ZTT	ZANG-8CD	Crazy	CD5	U.K.	1990	$9.00
Sire	9 41003-2	Crazy	CD5	U.S.	1990	$5.00
Sire	PRO-CD-4832	Crazy	CDJ	U.S.	1990	$3.00
Sire	PRO-CD-4879	Crazy	CDJ	U.S.	1990	$3.00
	PRO-CD-7939-R	Don't Cry	CDJ	U.S.		$3.00
ZTT	9031-74379-2	Future Love Paradise	CD5	Germany	1991	$9.00
ZTT	9031-74347-2	Future Love Paradise	CD5	Germany	1991	$9.00
ZTT	ZANG-11CD	Future Love Paradise	CD5	U.K.	1991	$9.00
	PRO-CD-7502-R	I'm Alive	CDJ	U.S.		$3.00
ZTT	9031-75754-2	Killer on the Lose	CD5	Germany	1991	$9.00
WEA	WMC5-467	Killer on the Lose	CD5	Japan	1991	$13.00
ZTT	5085	Killer on the Lose	CD5	U.S.	1991	$3.00
	PRO-CD-7190-R	Kiss From a Rose	CDJ	U.S.	1995	$6.00
ZTT	ZANG58CD-DJ	Newborn Friend	CD5	U.K.	1994	$12.00
Warner Brothers	18053	Newborn Friend	CD5	U.S.	1994	$6.00
	PRO-CD-7244-R	Newborn Friend	CDJ	U.S.	1995	$6.00
Warner	12-18138	Prayer for The Dying	CD5	Canada	1994	$6.00
ZTT	SAM 1357	Prayer for The Dying	CDJ	U.K.	1994	$12.00
Warner Brothers	18138	Prayer for The Dying	CD5	U.S.	1994	$6.00
Warner Brothers	PRO-CD-6958	Prayer for The Dying	CDJ	U.S.	1994	$3.00
Warner Brothers		Prayer for The Dying	CDJ	U.S.	1994	$3.00

Second version.

Label	Catalog Number	Title	Type	Country	Year	Longbox Value / Value
ZTT	9031-76550-2	Violet	CD5	Germany	1992	$9.00
ZTT	9031-76991--2	Violet	CD5	Germany	1992	$9.00
ZTT	ZANG-27CD	Violet	CD5	U.K.	1992	$9.00
ZTT	ZANG-27CDX	Violet	CD5	U.K.	1992	$9.00

Sealand Poets

Singles

Label	Catalog Number	Title	Type	Country	Year	Longbox Value / Value
Reprise	PRo-CD-6431	Shooting Star	CDJ	U.S.	1993	$2.00

Seals, Dan

Singles

Label	Catalog Number	Title	Type	Country	Year	Longbox Value / Value
Warner Brothers	PRO-CD-4984	Sweet Little Shoes	CDJ	U.S.	1991	$2.00

Searchers

Singles

Label	Catalog Number	Title	Type	Country	Year	Longbox Value / Value
Coconut	662033	Needles and Pins	CD3	Germany	1988	$9.00
Old Gold	OOG-6103	Needles and Pins	CD3	U.K.	1988	$9.00
BMG	662358	No Other Love	CD5	Germany	1988	$9.00

Sears, Dawn

Singles

Label	Catalog Number	Title	Type	Country	Year	Longbox Value / Value
		San Antone	CDJ	U.S.		$2.00

Searse, Marvin

Singles

Label	Catalog Number	Title	Type	Country	Year	Longbox Value / Value
Mercury	CDP 620	Show Me What You Got	CDJ	U.S.	1991	$2.00
Mercury	CDP 557	Tonight	CDJ	U.S.	1991	$2.00

Season to Risk

Singles

Label	Catalog Number	Title	Type	Country	Year	Longbox Value / Value
Red Decimal	74888	Mine Eyes	CDJ	U.S.	1993	$2.00
Columbia	CSK 5366	Snakes	CDJ	U.S.	1993	$2.00

Seaweed

Singles

Label	Catalog Number	Title	Type	Country	Year	Longbox Value / Value
Sub Pop	PRO 4	Bill	CDJ	U.S.	1992	$3.00
	PRCD 105202	Drug Free Zone	CDJ	U.S.		$2.00
	OSK 6648	Grow Your Own Way	CDJ	U.S.		$2.00
Sub Pop	SPCD-57/219	Measure	CD5	U.K.	1993	$9.00
Sub Pop	168	Measure	CD5	U.S.	1993	$5.00

Sebadoh

Singles

Label	Catalog Number	Title	Type	Country	Year	Longbox Value / Value
Sub Pop	284	Rebound	CD5	U.S.	1994	$5.00

Secada, Jon

Full Length

Label	Catalog Number	Title	Type	Country	Year	Longbox Value / Value
SBK	7243-8-56647-2-4	Secada	LTD/LP	U.S.	1997	$18.00

CD soundtrack plus bonus CD-single. Both discs packaged in tandam on a blister card. Available exclusively at Target Department Stores.

Singles

Label	Catalog Number	Title	Type	Country	Year	Longbox Value / Value
EMI	TODP-2398	Angel	CD3	Japan	1993	$15.00/$4.00
SBK	CDSBK-39	Angel	CD5	U.K.	1993	$9.00
Capitol	DPRO-79445	Angel	CDJ	U.S.	1992	$2.00
Columbia		Do You Believe In Me	CDJ	U.S.		$3.00
SBK	TOCP-7501	Do You Believe In Us	CD5	Japan	1992	$14.00
SBK	CDSBK-37	Do You Believe In Us	CD5	U.K.	1992	$9.00
Capitol	C2 19766	Do You Believe In Us	CD5	U.S.	1992	$5.00
		Do You Really Want Me	CD5	U.K.	1992	$10.00

Second version.

Label	Catalog Number	Title	Type	Country	Year	Longbox Value / Value
	PCDD-00004	If I Never Knew You	CD3	Japan		$13.00/$4.00
SBK	58166	If You Go	CDJ	U.S.	1994	$2.00
EMI	TODP-2350	Just Another Day	CD3	Japan	1992	$12.00/$4.00
SBK	CDSBK-35	Just Another Day	CD5	U.K.	1992	$9.00
Capitol	C2 19748	Just Another Day	CD5	U.S.	1992	$5.00
		Where Do I Go From You	CDJ	U.S.		$2.00

Secada, Jon & Shanice

Singles

Label	Catalog Number	Title	Type	Country	Year	Longbox Value / Value
Hollywood	PRCD-10527-2	If I Never Knew You	CDJ	U.S.	1995	$3.00

Second II None

Singles

Label	Catalog Number	Title	Type	Country	Year	Longbox Value / Value
		Let the Rhythm Take You	CDJ	U.S.		$2.00

Second Self

Full Length

Label	Catalog Number	Title	Type	Country	Year	Longbox Value / Value
EMI	DPRO 4518	Mood Rings	DJ/LP	U.S.	1990	$6.00

Singles

Label	Catalog Number	Title	Type	Country	Year	Longbox Value / Value
EMI	DPRO 4616	Lose Those Shadows	CDJ	U.S.	1990	$2.00

Secret Policman

Full Length

Label	Catalog Number	Title	Type	Country	Year	Longbox Value / Value
Pioneer Artists	PA-87-188	Private Part	LD	U.S.	1991	$35.00
Pioneer Artists	PA-87-188	The Secret Policeman's	LD	U.S.	1987	$35.00

Sedaka, Neil

Full Length

Label	Catalog Number	Title	Type	Country	Year	Longbox Value / Value
		In Italian	LTD/LP	Italy	1996	$50.00

2 CD set. All songs sung in Italian.

Label	Catalog Number	Title	Type	Country	Year	Longbox Value / Value
MCA	74-007	Neil Sedaka	LD	U.S.	1985	$30.00

Singles

Label	Catalog Number	Title	Type	Country	Year	Longbox Value / Value
Polydor	PZCD-188	Miracle Song	CD5	U.K.	1991	$9.00
Polydor	PZCD-201	You Turn Me On	CD5	U.K.	1991	$9.00

Seduction

Full Length

Label	Catalog Number	Title	Type	Country	Year	Longbox Value / Value
A&M	5280	Nothing Matters Without Love	LP/LB	U.S.		$14.00/$8.00

Singles

Label	Catalog Number	Title	Type	Country	Year	Longbox Value / Value
Canyon	PCDY-10019	Breakdown	CD3	Japan	1990	$13.00/$4.00
A&M	75021 8039 2	Breakdown	CDJ	U.S.	1990	$2.00
A&M	75021 8082 2	Could This Be Love	CDJ	U.S.	1989	$2.00
A&M	390502-2	Heartbreak	CD5	Germany	1990	$9.00
A&M	USACD-685	Heartbreak	CD5	U.K.	1990	$9.00
A&M	CD 17937	Heartbreak	CDJ	U.S.	1989	$2.00
A&M	CD 18020	Heartbreak	CDJ	U.S.	1989	$2.00
A&M	390489-2	Two to Make It Right	CD5	Germany	1990	$9.00
A&M	CD 17907	Two to Make It Right	CDJ	U.S.	1989	$2.00
A&M	390458-2	You Are My One True Love	CD5	Germany	1989	$9.00

See No Evil

Singles

Label	Catalog Number	Title	Type	Country	Year	Longbox Value / Value
Epic	ESK 2176	Scream Bloody Murder	CDJ	U.S.	1990	$2.00
Epic	ESK 2175	Witchdoctor	CDJ	U.S.	1990	$2.00

Seed

Singles

Label	Catalog Number	Title	Type	Country	Year	Longbox Value / Value
		Rapture	CDJ	U.S.		$2.00

Seger, Bob

Full Length

Label	Catalog Number	Title	Type	Country	Year	Longbox Value / Value
EMI	CDP-46060	Against the Wind	LP/LB	U.S.†	1985	$14.00/$8.00
EMI	CDP-46005	Distance, The	LP/LB	U.S.†	1984	$14.00/$8.00
		Fire Inside Special	RS	U.S.	1991	$35.00

Airdate: 8/26/91.

Label	Catalog Number	Title	Type	Country	Year	Longbox Value / Value
Capitol/Album Network		Fire Inside, The: World Premiere Broadcast	DJ/RS	U.S.	1991	$20.00
Capitol		Greatest Hits Sampler	DJ/Smplr	U.S.	1994	$10.00
		House Of Blues	RS	U.S.	1995	$40.00

2 CD set. Airdate: 1/15/95.

Label	Catalog Number	Title	Type	Country	Year	Longbox Value / Value
Album Network		In the Studio (Against the Wind)	RS	U.S.	1993	$25.00

Airdate: 1/25/93.

Label	Catalog Number	Title	Type	Country	Year	Longbox Value / Value
Album Network		In the Studio (Greatest Hits)	RS	U.S.		$50.00

2 CD set.

Label	Catalog Number	Title	Type	Country	Year	Longbox Value / Value
Album Network		In the Studio (Night Moves)	RS	U.S.	1991	$25.00

Airdate: 11/8/91.

Label	Catalog Number	Title	Type	Country	Year	Longbox Value / Value
Album Network		In the Studio (Stranger In Town)	RS	U.S.	1992	$25.00

Airdate: 9/21/92.

Label	Catalog Number	Title	Type	Country	Year	Longbox Value / Value
Capitol	DPRO-79227	Interview	DJ/Intvw	U.S.	1992	$15.00
EMI	CDP-46085	Live Bullet	LP/LB	U.S.†	1985	$14.00/$8.00
EMI	CDP-46075	Night Moves	LP/LB	U.S.†	1985	$14.00/$8.00
EMI	CDPB-46086	Nine Tonight	LP/LB	U.S.†	1985	$25.00/$23.00

2 CD set.

Label	Catalog Number	Title	Type	Country	Year	Longbox Value / Value
Westwood One		Off the Record	RS	U.S.	1995	$30.00

Airdate: 12/11/95.

Label	Catalog Number	Title	Type	Country	Year	Longbox Value / Value
Westwood One		Off the Record	RS	U.S.	1995	$30.00

Airdate: 7/3/95.

Label	Catalog Number	Title	Type	Country	Year	Longbox Value / Value
		Seger Story	RS	U.S.	1994	$50.00

2 CD set. Airdate: 11/14/94.

Label	Catalog Number	Title	Type	Country	Year	Longbox Value / Value
Capitol	DPRO-79622	Silver Seger Sampler	DJ/Smplr	U.S.	1993	$12.00
EMI	CDP-46074	Stranger in Town	LP/LB	U.S.†	1985	$14.00/$8.00
		Timothy White Sessions	RS	U.S.	1991	$80.00

2 CD set. Airdate: 12/22/91.

Label	Catalog Number	Title	Type	Country	Year	Longbox Value / Value
Media America		Up Close	RS	U.S.	1992	$35.00

2 CD set.

Label	Catalog Number	Title	Type	Country	Year	Longbox Value / Value
Media America		Up Close	RS	U.S.	1994	$50.00

2 CD set.

Singles

Label	Catalog Number	Title	Type	Country	Year	Longbox Value / Value
Capitol	204609-2	Fire Inside	CD5	Germany	1992	$10.00
Capitol	CDCL-648	Fire Inside	CD5	U.K.	1992	$10.00
Capitol	DPRO-79825	Fire Inside	CDJ	U.S.	1991	$3.00
Capitol	DPRO11179	I Wonder	CDJ	U.S.		$3.00
Capitol	DPRO79458	In Your Time	CDJ	U.S.		$3.00
Capitol	DPRO10283	Lock and Load	CDJ	U.S.		$3.00
Capitol	DPRO 79836	Real Love, The	CDJ	1991	1991	$3.00
Capitol	560-2044352	Real Love, The	CD5	Holand	1991	$10.00
Capitol	CDCL-628	Real Love, The	CD5	U.K.	1991	$10.00
Capitol	DPRO-79108	Take a Chance	CDJ	U.S.	1991	$3.00
Capitol		Turn the Page	CDJ	U.S.	1994	$7.00

Seiko

Singles

Label	Catalog Number	Title	Type	Country	Year	Longbox Value / Value
Epic	656475-2	All the Way to Heaven	CD5	U.K.	1990	$8.00
Epic	656083-3	Right Combination, The	CD3	Germany	1990	$8.00
Epic	656203-2	Right Combination, The	CD5	U.K.	1990	$8.00
Columbia		Right Combination, The	CDJ	U.S.	1990	$2.00
Columbia	CSK 73523	Who's That Boy	CDJ	U.S.	1990	$2.00

Selena

Singles

Label	Catalog Number	Title	Type	Country	Year	Longbox Value / Value
RCA	RCDJ68463-2	A Boy Like That	CDJ	U.S.	1995	$8.00
EMI Latin	DPRO-11947	Last Dance	CDJ	U.S.	1997	$10.00

From the original soundtrack "Selena."

Self

Singles

Label	Catalog Number	Title	Type	Country	Year	Longbox Value / Value
	SP17193-2	So Low	CDJ	U.S.		$2.00

Semi*Twang

Singles

Label	Catalog Number	Title	Type	Country	Year	Longbox Value / Value
		Salty Tears	CDJ	U.S.		$2.00

Semisonic

Singles

Label	Catalog Number	Title	Type	Country	Year	Longbox Value / Value
MCA	MCA5P3649	Down in Flames	CDJ	U.S.		$2.00

Senator Flux

Full Length

Label	Catalog Number	Title	Type	Country	Year	Longbox Value / Value
Roadrunner	9364	Criminal Special	LP/LB	U.S.		$12.00/$8.00

Sensation

Singles

Label	Catalog Number	Title	Type	Country	Year	Longbox Value / Value
CBS	77399	Beautiful Morning	CD5	U.S.	1994	$5.00

Senseless Things

Singles

Label	Catalog Number	Title	Type	Country	Year	Longbox Value / Value
EFA	CD-17157	Can't Do Anything	CD5	Germany	1990	$8.00
Decoy	DYS-17CD	Can't Do Anything	CD5	U.K.	1990	$8.00
Epic	ESCA-5599	Easy to Smile	CD5	Japan	1992	$14.00
Epic	657695-2	Easy to Smile	CD5	U.K.	1992	$8.00

Label	Catalog Number	Title	Type	Country	Year	Longbox Value / Value
Epic	656980-2	Everybody's Gone	CD5	U.K.	1991	$8.00
Epic	ESK 4415	Everybody's Gone	CDJ	U.S.	1993	$2.00
Epic	657449-2	Got It at the Delmar	CD5	U.K.	1991	$8.00
Epic	657926-2	Hold on Tight	CD5	U.K.	1992	$8.00
Epic	ESCA-5687	Homophobic Asshole	CD5	Japan	1992	$12.00
Epic	658833-2	Homophobic Asshole	CD5	U.K.	1992	$8.00
EFA	CD-17164	It's Too Late	CD5	Germany	1990	$8.00
Decoy	DYS-15CD	It's Too Late	CD5	U.K.	1990	$8.00
Epic	658940-2	Primary Instinct	CD5	U.K.	1993	$8.00

September String

Singles

Label	Catalog Number	Title	Type	Country	Year	Longbox Value / Value
Laserlight	12428	Simon & Garfunkel	CD5	U.S.	1994	$5.00

Sepultura

Full Length

Label	Catalog Number	Title	Type	Country	Year	Longbox Value / Value
Fems	APCY-6001	Chaos A.D.	LTD/LP	Japan		$35.00

CD in metal box.

Label	Catalog Number	Title	Type	Country	Year	Longbox Value / Value
New Rensc.	43	Morbid Visions	LP/LB	U.S.		$12.00/$8.00
Roadrunner		Roots of Sepultura, The	DJ/Smplr	U.S.	12996	$22.00

Singles

Label	Catalog Number	Title	Type	Country	Year	Longbox Value / Value
Intercord	826 236	Arise	CD5	Germany	1992	$9.00
Roadrunner	APCY-8081	Arise	CD5	Japan	1992	$15.00
		Dead Embrionic	CD5	U.K.	1994	$12.00
Columbia	77546	Refuse	CD5	U.S.	1994	$6.00
Epic		Refuse	CDJ	U.S.	1994	$3.00
		Slave New World	CD5	U.K.	1994	$10.00
		Slave New World	CD5	U.K.	1994	$10.00

Second version.

Label	Catalog Number	Title	Type	Country	Year	Longbox Value / Value
Roadrunner	2382	Territory	CD5	Germany	1993	$9.00
Epic	ESK 5442	Territory	CDJ	U.S.	1993	$2.00
Epic		Territory	CDJ	U.S.	1994	$3.00
Intercord	826 235	Under Seige	CD5	Germany	1991	$9.00
Pinnacle	RD-2424-3	Under Seige	CD5	U.K.	1991	$9.00

Serenes, The

Singles

Label	Catalog Number	Title	Type	Country	Year	Longbox Value / Value
RCA	74321 162792	Every Sunday	CD5	Germany	1993	$8.00

Sergio

Singles

Label	Catalog Number	Title	Type	Country	Year	Longbox Value / Value
	CRDJ155642	In And Out of Love	CDJ	U.S.		$2.00

Sermon, Erick

Singles

Label	Catalog Number	Title	Type	Country	Year	Longbox Value / Value
Polygram	577197	Bondigi	CD5	U.S.	1995	$5.00
Uptown	2681	Hittin' Switches	CDJ	U.S.	1993	$2.00
Def Jam	77140	Stay Real	CDJ	U.S.	1993	$2.00

Sesame Street Kids

Singles

Label	Catalog Number	Title	Type	Country	Year	Longbox Value / Value
Sony	SRDS-8191	Sesame Street Theme	CD3	Japan	1991	$13.00/$4.00

Setzer, Brian

Full Length

Label	Catalog Number	Title	Type	Country	Year	Longbox Value / Value
		Brian Setzer Orchestra	DJ/LP	U.S.		$20.00

Singles

Label	Catalog Number	Title	Type	Country	Year	Longbox Value / Value
	PRCD 6715	Hoodoo Voodoo Doll	CDJ	U.S.		$7.00
EMI	DPRO 04116	Rebelene	CDJ	U.S.	1988	$6.00
Manhattan	DPRO 04009	When the Sky Comes Tumbling Down	CDJ	U.S.	1988	$8.00

Sevelle, Taja

Singles

Label	Catalog Number	Title	Type	Country	Year	Longbox Value / Value
Paisley Park	PRO-CD-2812	Love Is Contagious	CDJ	U.S.		$2.00
Reprise	9 40172-2	Trouble Having You Near	CD5	U.S.	1991	$5.00
Reprise	PRO-CD-4921	Trouble Having You Near	CDJ	U.S.	1991	$2.00
WEA	W-8127CD	Wouldn't You Love to Love Me?	CD3	U.K.	1988	$8.00

Seven Day Diary

Singles

Label	Catalog Number	Title	Type	Country	Year	Longbox Value / Value
	PRO-CD-7984	He Can	CDJ	U.S.		$2.00
Warner	12-45753	Seven Day Diary	CD5	Canada	1994	$12.00

Seven Hundred Miles

Singles

Label	Catalog Number	Title	Type	Country	Year	Longbox Value / Value
		Are You Experienced?	CDJ	U.S.		$2.00
		Seven Hundred Miles	CDJ	U.S.		$7.00

Seven Mary Three

Full Length

Label	Catalog Number	Title	Type	Country	Year	Longbox Value / Value
Westwood One		In Concert	RS	U.S.	1996	$45.00

Airdate: 3/25/96.

Label	Catalog Number	Title	Type	Country	Year	Longbox Value / Value
Westwood One		In Concert Nu-Rock	RS	U.S.	1996	$45.00

Airdate 4/22/96.

Singles

Label	Catalog Number	Title	Type	Country	Year	Longbox Value / Value
Mammoth	PRCD6316-2	Cumbersome	CDJ	U.S.	1995	$3.00
Mammoth	PRCD6528-2	Cumbersome	CDJ	U.S.	1995	$3.00
		Water's Edge	CD5	U.K.	1996	$10.00
Mammoth	PRCD6588-2	Water's Edge	CDJ	U.S.	1995	$6.00

Seven Red Seven

Singles

Label	Catalog Number	Title	Type	Country	Year	Longbox Value / Value
Speed	105	Thinking of You	CD5	U.S.	1991	$4.00

Seven Seconds

Singles

Label	Catalog Number	Title	Type	Country	Year	Longbox Value / Value
Restless	223	I Can Sympathize	CDJ	U.S.	1989	$2.00

Seven Year Bitch

Singles

Label	Catalog Number	Title	Type	Country	Year	Longbox Value / Value
	PRCD 6650-2	History of My Future, The	CDJ	U.S.	1995	$2.00

Seventeen

Singles

Label	Catalog Number	Title	Type	Country	Year	Longbox Value / Value
		Let Loose	CD5	U.K.		$10.00
		Let Loose	CD5	U.K.		$10.00

Second version.

Severed Heads

Singles

Label	Catalog Number	Title	Type	Country	Year	Longbox Value / Value
Nettwerk	W2-3033	All Saints Day	CD5	Canada	1989	$7.00
Nettwerk	NET 004	Greater Reward	CD3	Germany		$8.00

Severinsen, Doc

Full Length

Label	Catalog Number	Title	Type	Country	Year	Longbox Value / Value
Passport	PJCD-88008	Doc Severinson & Xebron	LP	U.K.		$14.00
Passport	PJCD-88008	Doc Severinson & Xebron	LP/BP	U.S.		$16.00/$14.00

Singles

Label	Catalog Number	Title	Type	Country	Year	Longbox Value / Value
Amherst	CD DJ12	I Can't Get Started	CDJ	U.S.	1988	$3.00

Sex Club

Singles

Label	Catalog Number	Title	Type	Country	Year	Longbox Value / Value
FY	22	Big Dick Man	CD5	U.S.	1994	$4.00

Sex Pistols

Full Length

Label	Catalog Number	Title	Type	Country	Year	Longbox Value / Value
		We Have Come for Your Children	LP/LB	U.S.		$13.00/$8.00

Singles

Label	Catalog Number	Title	Type	Country	Year	Longbox Value / Value
Aris	880982	Anarchy in the U.K.	CD5	Germany	1988	$10.00
BMG	663261	Anarchy in the U.K.	CD5	Germany	1988	$10.00
Virgin	CDT-3	Anarchy in the U.K.	CD5	U.K.	1988	$10.00
Virgin	CDF-3	Anarchy in the U.K.	CD5	U.K.	1990	$10.00
BMG	663266	God Save the Queen	CD3	Germany	1990	$10.00
Virgin	CDT-37	God Save the Queen	CD3	U.K.	1988	$10.00
Virgin	CDF-37	God Save the Queen	CD3	U.K.	1990	$10.00
Virgin	VJCP-20005	Pretty Vacant	CD5	Japan	1993	$18.00
		Pretty Vacant	CD5	U.K.	1996	$10.00
		Pretty Vacant	CD5	U.K.	1996	$10.00

Second version.

Sextants

Singles

Label	Catalog Number	Title	Type	Country	Year	Longbox Value / Value
Imago	28036	I Don't Lie	CDJ	U.S.	1992	$7.00
Imago	28021	Sand Dollar World	CDJ	U.S.	1992	$2.00

Sexton, Charlie

Full Length

Label	Catalog Number	Title	Type	Country	Year	Longbox Value / Value
Westwood One		In Concert	RS	U.S.	1996	$45.00

Airdate: 3/11/96.

Singles

Label	Catalog Number	Title	Type	Country	Year	Longbox Value / Value
MCA	09P3-6134	Blowing Up Detroit	CD3	Japan	1989	$12.00/$4.00
MCA	874004	Don't Look Back	CD5	Germany	1989	$9.00
MCA	10P3-6091	Don't Look Back	CD3	Japan	1989	$12.00/$4.00
MCA	DMCA-1327	Don't Look Back	CD5	U.K.	1989	$9.00
MCA	17718-2	Don't Look Back	CDJ	U.S.	1989	$2.00
		Wishing Tree	CDJ	U.S.		$8.00

Sexx

Singles

Label	Catalog Number	Title	Type	Country	Year	Longbox Value / Value
Capitol	58439	Freak Freaky Remix	CD5	U.S.	1995	$5.00

Sha'Dasious

Singles

Label	Catalog Number	Title	Type	Country	Year	Longbox Value / Value
RCA	62472-2-RDJ	I'ma Put My Thing Down	CDJ	U.S.	1993	$2.00

Shades of Lace

Singles

Label	Catalog Number	Title	Type	Country	Year	Longbox Value / Value
		Come and Get It	CDJ	U.S.		$2.00
Wing	CDP 184	Smoovin' With	CDJ	U.S.	1990	$6.00

Shadow King

Singles

Label	Catalog Number	Title	Type	Country	Year	Longbox Value / Value
Atlantic	PRCD 4214-2	I Want You	CDJ	U.S.	1991	$2.00

Shadowcast

Singles

Label	Catalog Number	Title	Type	Country	Year	Longbox Value / Value
	U5P1009	Abyss, The	CDJ	U.S.	1995	$2.00

Shadowfax

Full Length

Label	Catalog Number	Title	Type	Country	Year	Longbox Value / Value
Private	2065	Odd Get Even, The	LP/LB	U.S.		$14.00/$8.00
Windham	WD-1029	Shadowdance	LP/LB	U.S.†	1985	$14.00/$8.00
Windham	WD-1022	Shadowfax	LP/LB	U.S.†	1985	$14.00/$8.00
Windham	WD-1038	The Dreams of Children	LP/LB	U.S.†	1985	$14.00/$8.00

Singles

Label	Catalog Number	Title	Type	Country	Year	Longbox Value / Value
Private		We Used to Laugh	CDJ	U.S.		$2.00

Shadowland

Full Length

Label	Catalog Number	Title	Type	Country	Year	Longbox Value / Value
Geffen	9 24826-2	Garden of Eden	DJ/LP	U.S.	1991	$15.00

CD in cardboard "Wheel" case.

Singles

Label	Catalog Number	Title	Type	Country	Year	Longbox Value / Value
Capitol	DPRO 79830	Garden of Eden	CDJ	U.S.	1991	$2.00
WEA	924273-2	Shadowland	CD5	Germany	1989	$8.00

Shadowy Men on a Shadowy Planet

Singles

Label	Catalog Number	Title	Type	Country	Year	Longbox Value / Value
		Sport Fishin' Accessories	CDJ	Canada		$12.00

Shadz Of Lingo

Singles

Label	Catalog Number	Title	Type	Country	Year	Longbox Value / Value
EMI	DPRO-04557	Mad Flavaz	CDJ	U.S.	1993	$2.00

Shaffer

Singles

Label	Catalog Number	Title	Type	Country	Year	Longbox Value / Value
Capitol	DPRO-79662	When the Radio Is On	CDJ	U.S.	1989	$3.00

Shaggy

Singles

Label	Catalog Number	Title	Type	Country	Year	Longbox Value / Value
Virgin	DPRO12727	Boombastic	CDJ	U.S.		$2.00
Virgin	38496	In the Summertime	CD5	U.S.	1995	$5.00
Virgin	72438921552	Nice & Lovely	CD5	Holland	1994	$8.00
Virgin	38420	Nice & Lovely	CD5	U.S.	1994	$5.00
Virgin	DPRO-14199	Nice & Lovely	CDJ	U.S.	1994	$2.00
Virgin	72438921902	Oh Carolina	CD5	Holland	1994	$8.00
Virgin		Train Is Coming, The	CDJ	U.S.		$2.00
Virgin	DPRO11092	Why You Treat Me So Bad	CDJ	U.S.		$2.00

Shai

Singles

Label	Catalog Number	Title	Type	Country	Year	Longbox Value / Value
MCA	MVCM-13001	Baby I'm Yours	CD3	Japan	1993	$13.00/$4.00
Gasoline Alley	2532	Baby I'm Yours	CDJ	U.S.	1993	$2.00
Gasoline Alley	GASP3466	Come With Me	CDJ	U.S.		$2.00
Gasoline Alley	54596	Comforter	CD5	U.S.	1993	$5.00
Gasoline Alley	2571	Comforter	CDJ	U.S.	1993	$2.00
Gasoline Alley	GASP3657	I Don't Want to Be Alone	CDJ	U.S.		$2.00
MCA	MVDM-35	If I Ever Fall in Love	CD3	Japan	1993	$13.00/$4.00
MCA	MCSTD-1727	If I Ever Fall in Love	CD5	U.K.	1992	$9.00
Gasoline Alley	54546	If I Ever Fall in Love	CD5	U.S.	1993	$5.00
Gasoline Alley	GAS2437	If I Ever Fall in Love	CDJ	U.S.	1993	$2.00
Gasoline Alley	54914	Place Where You Belong, The	CD5	U.S.	1994	$6.00
Gasoline Alley		Place Where You Belong, The	CDJ	U.S.	1994	$3.00
Gasoline Alley	2827	Together Forever	CDJ	U.S.	1993	$3.00
Gasoline Alley	2870	Yours	CDJ	U.S.	1993	$3.00

Shaka

Singles

Label	Catalog Number	Title	Type	Country	Year	Longbox Value/Value
Elektra/Asylum	66170	As-Salaam-Alaikum	CD5	U.S.	1994	$5.00
Arista	ASCD-2354	Steppin'	CDJ	U.S.	1991	$2.00

Shakatak

Full Length

Label	Catalog Number	Title	Type	Country	Year	Longbox Value/Value
Verve	SHAK 2	Perfect Sampler	DJ/Smplr	U.S.	1990	$12.00

Singles

Label	Catalog Number	Title	Type	Country	Year	Longbox Value/Value
Polydor	887425-2	Dr! Dr.!	CD5	Germany	1988	$8.00
Polydor	DTRCD-1	Dr! Dr.!	CD5	U.K.	1988	$8.00
Polygram	871001-2	Invitations	CD5	Germany	1988	$8.00
Polygram	887083-2	Mr. Manic & Sister Cool	CD5	Germany	1988	$8.00
Polygram	887083-2	Mr. Manic & Sister Cool	CD5	U.K.	1988	$8.00
Mercury	CDP 138	Mr. Manic & Sister Cool	CDJ	U.S.	1988	$2.00
Polydor	P10P-30010	Racing With the Wind	CD3	Japan	1988	$12.00/$4.00
Polydor	PODP-1038	Silent Eve	CD3	Japan	1991	$12.00/$4.00
Polygram	887700-2	Time of My Life	CD5	Germany	1988	$8.00
Polygram	887700-2	Time of My Life	CD5	U.K.	1988	$8.00
Polygram	889730-3	Turn the Music up	CD3	Germany	1988	$8.00
Polygram	889731-2	Turn the Music up	CD5	Germany	1988	$8.00
Polygram	PZCD-49	Turn the Music up	CD3	U.K.	1988	$8.00

Shakespeare's Sister

Singles

Label	Catalog Number	Title	Type	Country	Year	Longbox Value/Value
London	886356-2	Break My Heart	CD5	Germany	1989	$9.00
London	LONCD-200	Break My Heart	CD5	U.K.	1989	$9.00
ffrr	CDP 214	Break My Heart	CDJ	U.S.	1989	$2.00
ffrr	886893-2	Dirty Mind	CD5	Germany	1990	$9.00
ffrr	FCD-128	Dirty Mind	CD5	U.K.	1990	$9.00
ffrr	869199-2	Goodbye Cruel World	CD5	Germany	1992	$9.00
London	PODD-1021	Goodbye Cruel World	CD3	Japan	1992	$12.00/$4.00
ffrr	LONCD 309	Goodbye Cruel World	CD5	U.K.	1992	$9.00
Polydor	CDP 533	Goodbye Cruel World	CDJ	U.S.	1992	$12.00

Double-sided CD.

Label	Catalog Number	Title	Type	Country	Year	Longbox Value/Value
London	CDP 845	Hello	CDJ	U.S.	1992	$2.00
		Hello (Turn Your Radio on)	CD5	U.K.		$10.00
		Hello (Turn Your Radio on)	CD5	U.K.		$10.00

Second version.

Label	Catalog Number	Title	Type	Country	Year	Longbox Value/Value
	PODD-1021	I Don't Care	CD3	Japan		$13.00/$4.00
London	LONCD 318	I Don't Care	CD5	U.K.	1992	$9.00
London	869946	I Don't Care	CD5	U.S.	1992	$5.00
London	CDP 783	I Don't Care	CDJ	U.S.	1992	$2.00
London	CDP 795	I Don't Care	CDJ	U.S.	1992	$2.00
London	LONCD-337	My 16th Apology	CD5	U.K.	1993	$10.00
ffrr	886792-3	Run Silent	CD3	Germany	1989	$9.00
ffrr	886793-2	Run Silent	CD5	Germany	1989	$9.00
ffrr	FCD-119	Run Silent	CD5	U.K.	1989	$9.00
ffrr	SS1	Sacred Heart	CDJ	U.K.	1989	$15.00
Polydor	PODD-1019	Stay	CD3	Japan	1992	$12.00/$4.00
London	869 629	Stay	CD5	U.S.	1992	$5.00
London	869 731	Stay	CD5	U.S.	1992	$5.00
London	CDP 658	Stay	CDJ	U.S.	1992	$2.00
ffrr	886634-3	You're History	CD3	Germany	1989	$9.00
ffrr	886635-2	You're History	CD5	Germany	1989	$9.00
London	POOL-37017	You're History	CD3	Japan	1989	$12.00/$4.00
ffrr	FCD-112	You're History	CD5	U.K.	1989	$9.00
ffrr	CDP 110	You're History	CDJ	U.S.	1989	$2.00

Shakin' Stevens

Singles

Label	Catalog Number	Title	Type	Country	Year	Longbox Value/Value
Epic	SHAKYC-6	Feel the Need In Me	CD5	U.K.	1988	$8.00
Epic	SHAKYC-7	How Many Tears Can You Hide	CD5	U.K.	1988	$8.00
Epic	655603-2	I Might	CD5	Germany	1990	$8.00
Epic	SHAKYC-11	I Might	CD5	U.K.	1990	$8.00
Epic	657650-2	I'll Be Home for Christmas	CD5	Germany	1991	$8.00
Epic	654584-3	Jezebel	CD5	Germany	1989	$8.00
Epic	SHAKYC-9	Jezebel	CD5	U.K.	1989	$8.00
Epic	SHAKYC-10	Love Attack	CD5	U.K.	1989	$8.00
Epic	SHAKYC-14	My Cutie Cutie	CD5	U.K.	1990	$8.00
Epic	656193-3	Pink Champagne	CD3	U.K.	1990	$8.00
Epic	SHAKYC-13	Pink Champagne	CD5	U.K.	1990	$8.00
Epic	SHAKYC-8	True Love	CD5	U.K.	1988	$8.00
Epic	655946-3	Yes I Do	CD3	U.K.	1990	$8.00
Epic	SHAKYC-12	Yes I Do	CD5	U.K.	1990	$8.00

Shaking Family

Singles

Label	Catalog Number	Title	Type	Country	Year	Longbox Value/Value
Elektra	PRCD 8187-2	Hold On	CDJ	U.S.	1990	$2.00
Elektra	PR 8140-2	Tic Toc	CDJ	U.S.	1989	$2.00

Shaky

Singles

Label	Catalog Number	Title	Type	Country	Year	Longbox Value/Value
Epic	658436-2	Radio	CD5	U.K.	1992	$9.00
Epic	658436-5	Radio	CD5	U.K.	1992	$10.00

Shalamar

Full Length

Label	Catalog Number	Title	Type	Country	Year	Longbox Value/Value
Solar	28-2	Friends	LP/BP	U.S.†	1984	$14.00/$8.00
Solar	60385-2	Shango	LP/BP	U.S.†	1984	$14.00/$8.00

Singles

Label	Catalog Number	Title	Type	Country	Year	Longbox Value/Value
Epic	656263-3	Caution: This Love is Hot!	CD3	Germany	1990	$8.00
Epic	ESK 74518	Caution: This Love is Hot!	CDJ	U.S.	1990	$2.00
Epic	ESK 74531	Come Together	CDJ	U.S.	1991	$2.00
Epic		Wake Up	CDJ	U.S.	1990	$2.00

Shamen

Full Length

Label	Catalog Number	Title	Type	Country	Year	Longbox Value/Value
Epic	ESK 4283	En Tact	DJ/LP	U.S.	1991	$12.00

Singles

Label	Catalog Number	Title	Type	Country	Year	Longbox Value/Value
Columbia	COCY-5190	Boss Drum	CD5	Japan	1993	$10.00
		Boss Drum	CD5	U.K.		$10.00
		Boss Drum	CD5	U.K.		$10.00

Second version.

Label	Catalog Number	Title	Type	Country	Year	Longbox Value/Value
Columbia	78038	Destination Eschantan	CD5	U.S.	1995	$5.00
Epic	ESK 7303	Destination Eschanton	CDJ	U.S.		$2.00
Pinnacle	78-TP7CD	Ebeneezer Goode	CD5	U.K.	1992	$8.00
Pinnacle	FACE-1CD	Face	CD5	U.K.	1992	$8.00
Rough Trade	130-1125-3	Hyperreal	CD5	Germany	1991	$8.00
Columbia	COCY-5131	Hyperreal	CD5	Japan	1991	$8.00
Pinnacle	48TP-7CD	Hyperreal	CD5	U.K.	1991	$8.00
Ediesta	CALCCD-69	Jesus Loves Amerika	CD5	U.K.	1988	$8.00
Columbia	COCY-5180	L.S.I.	CD5	Japan	1992	$10.00
Pinnacle	68TP7CD	L.S.I.	CD5	U.K.	1992	$8.00
Epic	ESK 74437	L.S.I.	CDJ	U.S.	1992	$2.00
Epic	49K 74401	Love Sex Intelligence	CD5	U.S.	1992	$5.00
Epic	ESK 74437	Love Sex Intelligence	CDJ	U.S.	1992	$2.00
Pinnacle	46-TP7CD	Make It Mine	CD5	U.K.	1990	$8.00
Epic	ESK 4548	Make It Mine	CDJ	U.S.	1990	$2.00
Epic	ESK 74176	Make It Mine	CDJ	U.S.	1990	$2.00
Epic	ESK 74236	Make It Mine	CDJ	U.S.	1990	$2.00
Pinnacle	52-TP7CD	Move Any Mountain	CD5	U.K.	1991	$8.00
Pinnacle	30-TP7CD	Omega Amigo	CD5	U.K.	1989	$8.00
Columbia	COCY-5197	Phorever People	CD5	Japan	1993	$10.00
		Phorever People	CD5	U.K.		$10.00
		Phorever People	CD5	U.K.		$10.00

Second version.

Label	Catalog Number	Title	Type	Country	Year	Longbox Value/Value
Pinnacle	36-TP7CD	Pro-Gen	CD5	U.K.	1990	$8.00
		Show of Strength	CD5	U.K.		$10.00
		Show of Strength	CD5	U.K.		$10.00

Second version.

Label	Catalog Number	Title	Type	Country	Year	Longbox Value/Value
		Somewhere	CDJ	U.S.		$2.00

Shampoo

Full Length

Label	Catalog Number	Title	Type	Country	Year	Longbox Value/Value
Atlantic		We Are Shampoo	DJ/Smplr	U.S.	1995	$15.00

Singles

Label	Catalog Number	Title	Type	Country	Year	Longbox Value/Value
Atlantic		Delicious	CDJ	U.S.	1995	$3.00
Atlantic	87145	Trouble	CD5	U.S.	1995	$5.00
Atlantic		Trouble	CDJ	U.S.	1995	$3.00

Shanahan, Bernie

Singles

Label	Catalog Number	Title	Type	Country	Year	Longbox Value/Value
		Hard Luck & Heroes	CDJ	U.S.		$2.00

Shandling, Gary

Full Length

Label	Catalog Number	Title	Type	Country	Year	Longbox Value/Value
Paramount	LV2390	25th Anniversary	LD	U.S.	1986	$25.00

Shangri-Las

Singles

Label	Catalog Number	Title	Type	Country	Year	Longbox Value/Value
Charly	CDS-3	Remember	CD5	U.K.	1989	$10.00

Shanice

Singles

Label	Catalog Number	Title	Type	Country	Year	Longbox Value/Value
Arista	BVDA-55	Don't Wanna Love You	CD3	Japan	1990	$13.00/$4.00
Motown	PODT-1001	I Love Your Smile	CD3	Japan	1992	$13.00/$4.00
Motown	ZD-44908	I Love Your Smile	CD5	U.K.	1991	$8.00
Motown	TMGCD-1401	I Love Your Smile	CD5	U.K.	1992	$8.00
Motown	PODT-1004	I'm Cryin'	CD3	Japan	1992	$13.00/$4.00
Motown	PODT-1009	Lovin' You	CD3	Japan	1992	$13.00/$4.00
Motown	TMGCD-1409	Lovin' You	CD5	U.K.	1992	$8.00
Motown	374631056	Lovin' You	CDJ	U.S.	1992	$2.00
Giant	WPDP-6314	Saving Forever for You	CD3	Japan	1992	$13.00/$4.00
Giant	W-0148CD	Saving Forever for You	CD5	U.K.	1992	$8.00
Giant	PRO-CD-5745	Saving Forever for You	CDJ	U.S.	1992	$2.00
Motown	PODT-1006	Silent Prayer	CD3	Japan	1992	$13.00/$4.00
		Somewhere	CDJ	U.S.		$2.00

Shannon

Full Length

Label	Catalog Number	Title	Type	Country	Year	Longbox Value/Value
Mirage	90267-2	Do You Wanna Get Away	LP/LB	U.S.†	1985	$14.00/$8.00

Singles

Label	Catalog Number	Title	Type	Country	Year	Longbox Value/Value
Silvertone	ORECD-26	Are You Lovin' Me Too	CD5	U.K.	1991	$9.00
Old Gold	OG-6113	Runaway	CD3	U.K.	1989	$10.00
Silvertone	ORECD-24	Walk Away	CD5	U.K.	1991	$9.00
MCA	1453	Walk Away	CDJ	U.S.	1991	$2.00

Shante

Singles

Label	Catalog Number	Title	Type	Country	Year	Longbox Value/Value
Livin' Large	108	Dance To This	CDJ	U.S.	1992	$2.00

Shante, Roxanne

Singles

Label	Catalog Number	Title	Type	Country	Year	Longbox Value/Value
A&M	USACD-689	Go on Girl	CD5	U.K.	1990	$8.00
A&M	USACD-676	Independent Woman	CD5	U.K.	1990	$8.00
Reprise	PRO-CD-3928	Independent Woman	CDJ	U.S.	1989	$2.00
A&M	USACD-669	Live on Stage	CD5	U.K.	1990	$8.00
Reprise	PRO-CD-3663	Live on Stage	CDJ	U.S.	1989	$2.00

Shape Dance

Singles

Label	Catalog Number	Title	Type	Country	Year	Longbox Value/Value
Pikosso	874 00026	Popcorn	SCD5	Germany	1995	$18.00

"Popcorn Bucket" shaped CD.

Sharada House G

Singles

Label	Catalog Number	Title	Type	Country	Year	Longbox Value/Value
Zyx	7592	Keep It Up	CD5	U.S.	1994	$5.00

Shark Island

Full Length

Label	Catalog Number	Title	Type	Country	Year	Longbox Value/Value
Epic	ESK 1767	July 18, 1989 Bastille Day Alive at the Whiskey	DJ/Smplr	U.S.	1989	$17.00

Singles

Label	Catalog Number	Title	Type	Country	Year	Longbox Value/Value
Epic		Bad for Each Other	CDJ	U.S.		$3.00
Epic	ESK 1813	Paris Calling	CDJ	U.S.	1989	$3.00
Epic		Tied Up & Held Down	CDJ	U.S.		$3.00

Sharkey, Feargal

Singles

Label	Catalog Number	Title	Type	Country	Year	Longbox Value/Value
Virgin	VSCDT-1294	I've Got News For You	CD5	U.K.	1991	$8.00
Virgin	9339	If This Is Love	CDJ	U.S.	1988	$2.00
Virgin	CDEP-18	More Love	CD5	U.K.	1988	$8.00
Virgin	VSCD-1051	Out of My System	CD5	U.K.	1988	$8.00
Virgin	VSCDT-1349	Women and I	CD5	U.K.	1991	$8.00
Virgin	1349	Women and I	CDJ	U.S.	1991	$8.00
Virgin	CDT-36	You Little Thief	CD5	U.K.	1988	$8.00

Sharon, Lois

Full Length

Label	Catalog Number	Title	Type	Country	Year	Longbox Value/Value
A&M	540024	Great Big Hits	LP/LB	U.S.		$14.00/$8.00

Sharon, Lois & Bram

Full Length

Label	Catalog Number	Title	Type	Country	Year	Longbox Value/Value
A&M	LV38103	Living Room	LD	U.S.	1990	$25.00
A&M	LV38102	Sleep Over	LD	U.S.	1989	$25.00

Sharon S

Singles

Label	Catalog Number	Title	Type	Country	Year	Longbox Value/Value
Zyx	7610	Give Me Your Love	CD5	U.S.	1994	$5.00
ZYX	7149	Wonderful	CD5	U.S.	1994	$5.00

Sharp

Singles

Label	Catalog Number	Title	Type	Country	Year	Longbox Value / Value
Elektra	PR 8047-2	Playboy	CDJ	U.S.	1989	$2.00

Sharp, Becky

Singles

Label	Catalog Number	Title	Type	Country	Year	Longbox Value / Value
MCA	MCA5P3518	Beach Ball	CDJ	U.S.		$2.00

Sharples, Bob

Full Length

Label	Catalog Number	Title	Type	Country	Year	Longbox Value / Value
London	PPC-820176-2	America on the March	LP/BP	U.S.†	1985	$12.00/$7.00

Shaw, Artie

Singles

Label	Catalog Number	Title	Type	Country	Year	Longbox Value / Value
	41047	Irresistible Swing	CD5	U.S.	1994	$5.00

Shaw, Tommy

Full Length

Label	Catalog Number	Title	Type	Country	Year	Longbox Value / Value
A&M	CD-5020	Girls With Guns	LP/LB	U.S.†	1984	$14.00/$8.00
Polygram	395097-2	What If	LP	Germany		$20.00
A&M	D32Y-3028	What If	LP	Japan		$25.00
A&M	CD-5097	What If	LP/LB	U.S.		$18.00/$15.00

Shaw, Woody

Full Length

Label	Catalog Number	Title	Type	Country	Year	Longbox Value / Value
Mosaic	MD3-142	Complete CBS Recordings	LTD/LP	U.S.		$45.00

3 CD set. Limited to 7500 copies.

Shear, Jules

Full Length

Label	Catalog Number	Title	Type	Country	Year	Longbox Value / Value
Polydor	CDP 450	Great Puzzle, The	DJ/LP	U.S.	1991	$12.00
Island		Healing Bones	LP	U.S.	1994	$12.00

1st issue with misprinted order of booklet pages.

Label	Catalog Number	Title	Type	Country	Year	Longbox Value / Value
Polydor	SACD 443	Unplug This	DJ/Smplr	U.S.	1991	$12.00

Singles

Label	Catalog Number	Title	Type	Country	Year	Longbox Value / Value
Polydor	CDP 613	Sad Sound of the Wind	CDJ	U.S.	1992	$2.00
		Sun Ain't Gonna Shine Anymore	CDJ	U.S.		$2.00
Polydor	CDP 678	Trap Door, The	CDJ	U.S.	1992	$6.00
Polydor	CDP 677	We Were Only Making Love	CDJ	U.S.	1992	$2.00

Shearer, Harry

Full Length

Label	Catalog Number	Title	Type	Country	Year	Longbox Value / Value
Rhino	R2 71217	It Must Have Been Something I Said	LP	U.S.	1994	$18.00
Century Of Progress	PCR002	O.J. on Trial: That Endless Summer	LTD/LP	U.S.	1995	$18.00
Century Of Progress		O.J. on Trial: The Early Years	LTD/LP	U.S.	1995	$18.00

Singles

Label	Catalog Number	Title	Type	Country	Year	Longbox Value / Value
Rhino		Go to Russia (If U Want Free Speech)	CDJ	U.S.	1992	$2.00

Shearing, George

Full Length

Label	Catalog Number	Title	Type	Country	Year	Longbox Value / Value
Concord Jazz	CCD-4246	Live at the Cafe Carlyle	LP/LB	U.S.†	1985	$14.00/$8.00

Shearing, George & Stephane Grappelli

Full Length

Label	Catalog Number	Title	Type	Country	Year	Longbox Value / Value
Verve	821868-2	The Reunion	LP/LB	U.S.†	1985	$14.00/$8.00

Sheep On Drugs

Singles

Label	Catalog Number	Title	Type	Country	Year	Longbox Value / Value
		From A to H and Back Again	CD5	U.K.		$10.00
		From A to H and Back Again	CD5	U.K.		$10.00

Second version.

Label	Catalog Number	Title	Type	Country	Year	Longbox Value / Value
Smash	162 448 007	From A to H and Back Again	CD5	U.S.	1994	$5.00
Smash	162 880 007	Motorbike	CD5	U.S.	1993	$5.00
Smash	162 448 007	Track X	CD5	U.S.	1993	$5.00
Transglobal	TRAN08CD	TV USA	CD5	U.K.	1992	$9.00

Sheer Terror

Full Length

Label	Catalog Number	Title	Type	Country	Year	Longbox Value / Value
		Good Fer Nothin'	DJ/Smplr	U.S.	1995	$12.00

Sheila E.

Full Length

Label	Catalog Number	Title	Type	Country	Year	Longbox Value / Value
Warner Brothers	26255-2-Dj	Sex Symbol	DJ/LP	U.S.	1991	$23.00

CD in round can with custom booklet and miniature cymbal.

Singles

Label	Catalog Number	Title	Type	Country	Year	Longbox Value / Value
Warner Brothers	PRO-CD-4987	Cry Baby	CDJ	U.S.	1991	$2.00
Warner Brothers	9362-40089-2	Droppin' Like Flies	CD5	Germany	1991	$10.00
Warner Brothers	W-0038CD	Droppin' Like Flies	CD5	U.K.	1991	$10.00
Warner Brothers	9 21758-2	Droppin' Like Flies	CD5	U.S.	1991	$5.00
Warner Brothers	PRO-CD-4456	Droppin' Like Flies	CDJ	U.S.	1991	$2.00
Warner Brothers	PRO-CD-4869	Droppin' Like Flies	CDJ	U.S.	1991	$2.00
Warner Brothers	WPDP-6272	Sex Symbol	CD3	Japan	1991	$12.00/$4.00
Warner Brothers	W-0019CD	Sex Symbol	CD5	U.K.	1990	$10.00
Warner Brothers	PRO-CD-4651	Sex Symbol	CDJ	U.S.	1990	$2.00

Sheldon, Jack

Full Length

Label	Catalog Number	Title	Type	Country	Year	Longbox Value / Value
RealTime	RT-3003	Playin' It Straight	LP/LB	U.S.†	1985	$14.00/$8.00

Shelley, Pete

Full Length

Label	Catalog Number	Title	Type	Country	Year	Longbox Value / Value
Mercury		Heaven and the Sea	LP/BP	U.S.		$14.00/$8.00

Shellyan Orphan

Full Length

Label	Catalog Number	Title	Type	Country	Year	Longbox Value / Value
Columbia	CSK 4657	Waking Up Sampler	DJ/Smplr	U.S.	1992	$10.00

Shelter

Singles

Label	Catalog Number	Title	Type	Country	Year	Longbox Value / Value
		Here We Go	CDJ	U.S.		$2.00

Shenandoah

Full Length

Label	Catalog Number	Title	Type	Country	Year	Longbox Value / Value
		'90s Country	RS	U.S.	1995	$25.00

Airdate: 7/1/96.

Label	Catalog Number	Title	Type	Country	Year	Longbox Value / Value
		'90s Country	RS	U.S.	1996	$25.00

Airdate: 1/7/96.

Label	Catalog Number	Title	Type	Country	Year	Longbox Value / Value
RCA	66011-2-RDJ	Long Time Comin'	DJ/LP	U.S.	1992	$15.00

Singles

Label	Catalog Number	Title	Type	Country	Year	Longbox Value / Value
Columbia	CSK 73957	When You Were Mine	CDJ	U.S.	1991	$2.00

Shepard, Vonda

Singles

Label	Catalog Number	Title	Type	Country	Year	Longbox Value / Value
Reprise	PRO-CD-4017	Baby, Don't You Break My Heart Slow	CDJ	U.S.	1989	$2.00
Reprise	PRO-CD-3731	Don't Cry Ilene	CDJ	U.S.	1989	$2.00
Reprise	PRO-CD-4396	I Shy Away	CDJ	U.S.	1989	$2.00

Shepherd, Kenny Wayne

Full Length

Label	Catalog Number	Title	Type	Country	Year	Longbox Value / Value
Westwood One		In Concert	RS	U.S.	1996	$50.00

Airdate: 7/29/96.

Shepp, Archie

Full Length

Label	Catalog Number	Title	Type	Country	Year	Longbox Value / Value
Denon	CD-7264	Ballads for Trane	LP/LB	U.S.†	1985	$14.00/$8.00
Soul Note	SN-1102 CD PSI	Down Home New York	LP/LB	U.S.†	1985	$14.00/$8.00
Denon	CD-7262	On Green Dolphin Street	LP/LB	U.S.†	1985	$14.00/$8.00

Shepp, Archie & Dollar Brand

Full Length

Label	Catalog Number	Title	Type	Country	Year	Longbox Value / Value
Denon	CD-7008	Duet	LP/LB	U.S.†	1985	$14.00/$8.00

Sheppard, Andy

Full Length

Label	Catalog Number	Title	Type	Country	Year	Longbox Value / Value
Polygram	510344-2	In Co-Motion	LP/BP	U.S.		$12.00/$7.00

Sheppard, T.G.

Singles

Label	Catalog Number	Title	Type	Country	Year	Longbox Value / Value
Curb	DPRO 79566	Born in a High	CDJ	U.S.	1991	$2.00

Sheriff

Singles

Label	Catalog Number	Title	Type	Country	Year	Longbox Value / Value
EMI	885854-2	When I'm With You	CD5	Germany	1989	$8.00
		When I'm With You	CDJ	U.S.	1989	$2.00

Sherrick

Singles

Label	Catalog Number	Title	Type	Country	Year	Longbox Value / Value
		Baby I'm for Real	CDJ	U.S.		$2.00

Shew, Bobby & Chuck Findley

Full Length

Label	Catalog Number	Title	Type	Country	Year	Longbox Value / Value
Delos	D/CD 4003	Trumpets No End	LP/LB	U.S.†	1985	$14.00/$8.00

Shinas, Sofia

Singles

Label	Catalog Number	Title	Type	Country	Year	Longbox Value / Value
Warner Brothers	9 40534-2	Message, The	CD5	U.S.	1992	$5.00
Warner Brothers	PRO-CD-5805	Message, The	CDJ	U.S.	1992	$2.00
Warner Brothers	9 40795-2	One Last Kiss	CD5	U.S.	1992	$5.00
Warner Brothers	PRO-CD-5920	One Last Kiss	CDJ	U.S.	1992	$2.00
Warner Brothers	9 40924-2	State of Mind	CD5	U.S.	1992	$5.00

Shindell, Richard

Full Length

Label	Catalog Number	Title	Type	Country	Year	Longbox Value / Value
Shanachi		Live	DJ/Smplr	U.S.	1994	$18.00

Shinehead

Singles

Label	Catalog Number	Title	Type	Country	Year	Longbox Value / Value
Elektra	PR 8023-2	Chain Gang	CDJ	U.S.	1988	$2.00
Elektra	PRCD 8188-2	Family Affair	CDJ	U.S.	1990	$2.00
Elektra	PR 8061-2	Gimme No Crack	CDJ	U.S.	1989	$2.00
Elektra	PRCD 8716-2	Jamaican In New York	CDJ	U.S.	1993	$2.00
Elektra	PRCD 8238-2	Real Rock, The	CDJ	U.S.	1990	$2.00
Elektra	PRCD 8613-2	Try My Love	CDJ	U.S.	1992	$2.00

Shirelles

Singles

Label	Catalog Number	Title	Type	Country	Year	Longbox Value / Value
Aris	885855	Baby It's You	CD3	Germany	1990	$9.00
Aris	885854	Will You Love Me Tomorrow	CD3	Germany	1990	$9.00
Old Gold	OG-6105	Will You Love Me Tomorrow	CD3	U.K.	1988	$9.00

Shiro

Singles

Label	Catalog Number	Title	Type	Country	Year	Longbox Value / Value
		Tell Me (Would You)	CDJ	U.S.		$2.00

Shock

Singles

Label	Catalog Number	Title	Type	Country	Year	Longbox Value / Value
ZYX	6021-8	Talk About Love	CD5	Germany	1988	$6.00
		Talk About Love	CDJ	U.S.	1988	$2.00

Shocked, Michelle

Full Length

Label	Catalog Number	Title	Type	Country	Year	Longbox Value / Value
M.S. Fan Club		Kind Hearted Woman	LP	U.S.	1994	$18.00

Available only at concerts and fan club.

Singles

Label	Catalog Number	Title	Type	Country	Year	Longbox Value / Value
London	LONCD-193	Anchorage	CD5	U.K.	1988	$10.00
Mercury	CDP 680	Come a Long Way	CDJ	U.S.	1992	$7.00
Mercury	CDP 642	Jump Jim Crow	CDJ	U.S.	1992	$6.00
Mercury	CDP 223	Looks Like Mona Lisa	CDJ	U.S.	1989	$2.00
London	LONCD-251	My Little Sister	CD5	U.K.	1990	$10.00
Mercury	CDP 217	My Little Sister	CDJ	U.S.	1990	$2.00
London	876441-2	On the Greener Side	CD5	Germany	1989	$10.00
London	LONCD-245	On the Greener Side	CD5	U.K.	1989	$10.00
Polygram	CDP 142	On the Greener Side	CDJ	U.S.	1989	$7.00
Polygram	874156-3	When I Grow Up	CD3	Germany	1989	$9.00
Polygram	874157-2	When I Grow Up	CD5	Germany	1989	$9.00
London	LONCD-219	When I Grow Up	CD5	U.K.	1989	$9.00

Shomari

Singles

Label	Catalog Number	Title	Type	Country	Year	Longbox Value / Value
Mercury	CDP 672	If You Feel the Need	CDJ	U.S.	1992	$2.00
Mercury	CDP 781	Let It Be Me	CDJ	U.S.	1992	$2.00

Shonen Knife

Singles

Label	Catalog Number	Title	Type	Country	Year	Longbox Value / Value
Virgin	DPRO-14211	Quavers	CDJ	U.S.	1994	$3.00
Virgin	DPEO-14132	Tomato	CDJ	U.S.		$2.00
Virgin	DPRO-14132	Tomato Head	CDJ	U.S.	1994	$3.00

Shooting Gallery

Full Length

Label	Catalog Number	Title	Type	Country	Year	Longbox Value / Value
Mercury	SACD 479	Shooting Gallery	DJ/LP	U.S.	1992	$12.00

Singles

Label	Catalog Number	Title	Type	Country	Year	Longbox Value / Value
Mercury	CDP 648	House of Ecstasy	CDJ	U.S.	1992	$2.00
Mercury	CDP 713	Teenage Breakdown	CDJ	U.S.	1992	$2.00

Shooting Party

Singles

Label	Catalog Number	Title	Type	Country	Year	Longbox Value / Value
Mercury	CDP 644	Restless	CDJ	U.S.	1992	$2.00

Shooting Star

Full Length

Label	Catalog Number	Title	Type	Country	Year	Longbox Value / Value
		It's Not Over	DJ/LP	U.S.	1991	$7.00

Singles

Label	Catalog Number	Title	Type	Country	Year	Longbox Value / Value
JRS	803	Believe in Me	CDJ	U.S.	1991	$2.00
Enigma	EPRO 245	Christmas Together	CDJ	U.S.	1989	$2.00
Enigma	EPRO 262	Hollywood	CDJ	U.S.	1989	$2.00
V&R	0777	Rebel With a Cause	CDJ	U.S.	1991	$2.00
Enigma	EPRO 227	Touch Me	CDJ	U.S.	1989	$2.00

Shootz Groove

Full Length

Label	Catalog Number	Title	Type	Country	Year	Longbox Value / Value
		Five From J.I.V.E.	DJ/Smplr	U.S.		$10.00
		Jammin' in Vicious Environments	DJ/Smplr	U.S.		$12.00

Singles

Label	Catalog Number	Title	Type	Country	Year	Longbox Value / Value
Mercury	314582242	Respect	CD5	Canada	1994	$8.00

Shore, Pauly

Full Length

Label	Catalog Number	Title	Type	Country	Year	Longbox Value / Value
WTG	NSK 3093	Future of America, The	DJ/Smplr	U.S.	1991	$5.00

Shotgun Messiah

Singles

Label	Catalog Number	Title	Type	Country	Year	Longbox Value / Value
Relativity		Don't Care 'Bout Nothin'	CDJ	U.S.	1990	$2.00
Relativity	0148	Heartbreak Blvd	CDJ	U.S.	1991	$2.00
Relativity	EEPK-90938	I Want More	CD5	Canada	1992	$5.00
Relativity	1151-2	I Want More	CD5	U.S.	1992	$4.00
Relativity	88561-1021-2	Shout It Out	CDJ	U.S.	1990	$2.00

Shoveljerk

Singles

Label	Catalog Number	Title	Type	Country	Year	Longbox Value / Value
		Killing My Buzz	CDJ	U.S.		$2.00
		Swarm Warning	CDJ	U.S.		$7.00
		Unwind	CDJ	U.S.		$2.00

Showbiz & AG

Singles

Label	Catalog Number	Title	Type	Country	Year	Longbox Value / Value
London	CDP 792	Fat Pockets	CDJ	U.S.	1992	$2.00
Ffrr	120038	It's Time To Get Up	CD5	U.S.	1995	$6.00

Shramms

Singles

Label	Catalog Number	Title	Type	Country	Year	Longbox Value / Value
Matador	119	Heart Not Within	CD5	U.S.	1994	$5.00

Shriekback

Full Length

Label	Catalog Number	Title	Type	Country	Year	Longbox Value / Value
Island	90949	Go Bang!	LP/LB	U.S.	1988	$13.00/$7.00

Singles

Label	Catalog Number	Title	Type	Country	Year	Longbox Value / Value
World	15899	Bastard Son of Enoch, The	CDJ	U.S.	1992	$2.00
BMG	661740	Get Down Tonight	CD5	Germany	1988	$8.00
Island	PR 2407-2	Get Down Tonight	CDJ	U.S.	1988	$2.00
World	79609	Psycho Drift	CDJ	U.S.	1993	$2.00

Shudder To Think

Full Length

Label	Catalog Number	Title	Type	Country	Year	Longbox Value / Value
Epic	ESK 5691	Live	DJ/Smplr	U.S.		$10.00

Singles

Label	Catalog Number	Title	Type	Country	Year	Longbox Value / Value
		Hit Liqueur	CDJ	U.S.	1994	$3.00
Epic	ESK 6668	X	CDJ	U.S.		$2.00

Shug & Dap

Singles

Label	Catalog Number	Title	Type	Country	Year	Longbox Value / Value
Warner Brothers	17986	Another Man	CD5	U.S.	1994	$5.00
Warner Brothers	41681	Another Man	CD5	U.S.	1994	$5.00

Shuman, Mort

Singles

Label	Catalog Number	Title	Type	Country	Year	Longbox Value / Value
Atlantic	PRCD 4093-2	Promised Land	CDJ	U.S.	1991	$2.00

Shy England

Singles

Label	Catalog Number	Title	Type	Country	Year	Longbox Value / Value
		After the Love is Gone	CDJ	U.S.		$2.00
		Give It All You Got	CDJ	U.S.		$2.00

Shy Reptiles

Singles

Label	Catalog Number	Title	Type	Country	Year	Longbox Value / Value
Polygram	TILECD-2	High Desire	CD5	U.K.	1988	$8.00

Sibling Rivalry

Singles

Label	Catalog Number	Title	Type	Country	Year	Longbox Value / Value
Alternative Tenacles	153	In A Family Way	CD5	U.S.	1994	$5.00

Sick of It All

Singles

Label	Catalog Number	Title	Type	Country	Year	Longbox Value / Value
Motown	4848	Groove Thang	CD5	U.S.	1994	$5.00
		Maladjusted	CDJ	U.S.		$2.00
		Step Down	CDJ	U.S.		$2.00

Sidberry, Jane

Full Length

Label	Catalog Number	Title	Type	Country	Year	Longbox Value / Value
Reprise	9 25942-2	Bound by the Beauty	DJ/LP	U.S.	1989	$7.00

Picture disc.

Singles

Label	Catalog Number	Title	Type	Country	Year	Longbox Value / Value
Reprise	PRO-CD-3752	Bound by the Beauty	CDJ	U.S.	1989	$2.00
Reprise	PRO-CD-2954	Ingrid (and the Footman)	CDJ	U.S.	1988	$2.00
Reprise	W-0097CD	Life Is a Little Red Wagon	CD5	U.K.	1992	$8.00
Reprise	PRO-CD-3944	Life Is a Little Red Wagon	CDJ	U.S.	1989	$3.00
Warner Brothers	17742	Lovin' Cup	CD5	U.S.	1995	$5.00
Reprise	PRO-CD-6625	Temple	CDJ	U.S.	1993	$2.00

Sidewinders

Full Length

Label	Catalog Number	Title	Type	Country	Year	Longbox Value / Value
RCA	2700-2-RDj	Doesn't Anyone Believe	DJ/Smplr	U.S.	1990	$7.00

Singles

Label	Catalog Number	Title	Type	Country	Year	Longbox Value / Value
RCA	9035-2-RDj	Bad Bad Crazy Sun	CDJ	U.S.	1989	$2.00
RCA	2638-2-RDj	We Don't Do that Anymore	CDJ	U.S.	1990	$2.00
RCA	8968-2-RDj	What Am I Supposed to Do	CDJ	U.S.	1989	$2.00
		Witchdoctor	CDJ	U.S.		$2.00

Sidran, Ben

Full Length

Label	Catalog Number	Title	Type	Country	Year	Longbox Value / Value
Windham Hill	WH 17666	On the Cool Side	DJ/Smplr	U.S.	1988	$5.00

Singles

Label	Catalog Number	Title	Type	Country	Year	Longbox Value / Value
Windham Hill	WD 17666	Shine a Light on Me	CDJ	U.S.	1988	$6.00

Siegel, Dan

Singles

Label	Catalog Number	Title	Type	Country	Year	Longbox Value / Value
		Feelin' Happy	CDJ	U.S.		$2.00
CBS	CSK 1612	Hometown	CDJ	U.S.	1989	$2.00
CBS	CSK 1111	On the Road	CDJ	U.S.	1988	$2.00

Sierra

Full Length

Label	Catalog Number	Title	Type	Country	Year	Longbox Value / Value
		Devotion	DJ/LP	U.S.		$12.00

Siffre, Labi

Singles

Label	Catalog Number	Title	Type	Country	Year	Longbox Value / Value
China	CHICD-12	I Will Always Love You	CD5	U.K.	1989	$8.00
Polydor	CDP 143	I Will Always Love You	CDJ	U.S.	1989	$2.00
China	887833-2	Listen to the Voices	CD5	Germany	1988	$8.00
China	CHICD-9	Listen to the Voices	CD5	U.K.	1988	$8.00
China	WOKCD-2003	Most People Sleep Alone	CD5	U.K.	1991	$8.00
Polydor	CDP 100	Nothin's Gonna Change	CDJ	U.S.	1989	$2.00
China	889378-3	(Something Inside) So Strong	CD3	Germany	1989	$8.00
China	889379-2	(Something Inside) So Strong	CD3	Germany	1989	$8.00
Polydor	CDP 59	(Something Inside) So Strong	CDJ	U.S.	1989	$2.00

Sighs

Singles

Label	Catalog Number	Title	Type	Country	Year	Longbox Value / Value
Charisma	098	Think About Soul	CDJ	U.S.	1992	$2.00

Sigue Sigue Sputnik

Singles

Label	Catalog Number	Title	Type	Country	Year	Longbox Value / Value
Parlophone	CDSSS-4	Albinoni vs. Star Wars	CD5	U.K.	1989	$8.00
Parlophone	203291-2	Dancerama	CD5	Germany	1989	$8.00
Parlophone	CDSSS-5	Dancerama	CD5	U.K.	1989	$8.00
Parlophone	CDSSS-6	Rio Rocks	CD5	U.K.	1989	$8.00
Parlophone	203074-2	Success	CD5	Germany	1989	$8.00
Toshiba	XP10-2049	Success	CD3	Japan	1989	$12.00/$4.00
Parlophone	CDSSS-3	Success	CD5	U.K.	1989	$8.00

Silencers

Full Length

Label	Catalog Number	Title	Type	Country	Year	Longbox Value / Value
RCA	2852-2-RDj	Sampler	DJ/Smplr	U.S.	1991	$10.00

Singles

Label	Catalog Number	Title	Type	Country	Year	Longbox Value / Value
RCA	PD-42284	Answer Me	CD5	Germany	1988	$9.00
RCA	PD-42284	Answer Me	CD5	U.K.	1988	$9.00
RCA	PD-44316	Bulletproof Heart	CD5	Germany	1991	$9.00
RCA	PD-44316	Bulletproof Heart	CD5	U.K.	1991	$9.00
RCA	PD-41708	I See Red	CD5	U.K.	1988	$9.00
RCA		I See Red	CDJ	U.S.	1988	$2.00
RCA	PD-44418	I Want You	CD5	U.K.	1991	$9.00
RCA	RDJ 9160-2	Razor Blades of Love	CDJ	U.S.		$2.00
RCA	PD-42586	Real McCoy	CD5	Germany	1989	$9.00
RCA	PD-42586	Real McCoy	CD5	U.K.	1989	$9.00
RCA		Real McCoy	CDJ	U.S.	1988	$2.00
RCA	PD-42702	Scottish Rain	CD5	Germany	1989	$9.00
RCA	PD-42702	Scottish Rain	CD5	U.K.	1989	$9.00

Silent Rage

Singles

Label	Catalog Number	Title	Type	Country	Year	Longbox Value / Value
RCA	8979-2-RDj	Rebel With a Cause	CDJ	U.S.	1989	$2.00

Silent Running

Singles

Label	Catalog Number	Title	Type	Country	Year	Longbox Value / Value
		Deep in the Heart of Nowhere	CDJ	U.S.		$2.00

Silk

Singles

Label	Catalog Number	Title	Type	Country	Year	Longbox Value / Value
		Don't Rush	CDJ	U.S.		$2.00
Elektra	PRCD 8757-2	Girl U For Me	CDJ	U.S.	1993	$2.00
Elektra	PRCD 8637-2	Happy Days	CDJ	U.S.	1992	$2.00
Elektra	PRCD 8698-2	Happy Days	CDJ	U.S.	1992	$2.00
	PRCD 9356-2	Hooked on You	CDJ	U.S.		$2.00
	PRCD 9397-2	Hooked on You	CDJ	U.S.		$2.00
Elektra	64359	Hooked on You	CD5	U.S.	1995	$5.00
Elektra		Hooked on You	CDJ	U.S.	1995	$2.00
Jive	42263	I Can Go Deep	CD5	U.S.	1994	$5.00
Elektra	PRCD 8841-2	It Had to Be You	CDJ	U.S.	1993	$2.00

Silk, Garnett

Singles

Label	Catalog Number	Title	Type	Country	Year	Longbox Value / Value
Vp	1401	Nothing Can Divide U	CD5	U.S.	1994	$5.00

Silk Tyme Leather

Singles

Label	Catalog Number	Title	Type	Country	Year	Longbox Value / Value
Geffen	PRO-CD-4177	New Jack Thang	CDJ	U.S.	1990	$2.00

Silky Slim

Singles

Label	Catalog Number	Title	Type	Country	Year	Longbox Value / Value
Profile	7377	Sister Sister	CDJ	U.S.	1992	$2.00

Silos

Singles

Label	Catalog Number	Title	Type	Country	Year	Longbox Value / Value
RCA	2565-2-RDj	I'm Over You	CDJ	U.S.	1990	$2.00
RCA	2670-2-RDj	(We'll Go) out of Time	CDJ	U.S.	1990	$2.00

Silveira, Ricardo

Full Length

Label	Catalog Number	Title	Type	Country	Year	Longbox Value / Value
		Small World	DJ/Smplr	U.S.		$8.00

Silver, Horace

Full Length

Label	Catalog Number	Title	Type	Country	Year	Longbox Value / Value
Blue Note		Serenade to a Soul Sister	LTD/LP	U.S.	1995	$19.00

Silverchair

Full Length

Label	Catalog Number	Title	Type	Country	Year	Longbox Value / Value
Epic	SAMP3217	Live	DJ/Smplr	U.K.	1995	$25.00
Epic		Live	DJ/Smplr	U.S.	1995	$30.00

Multi-Image jewelbox cover.

Label	Catalog Number	Title	Type	Country	Year	Longbox Value / Value
		Live From the Pit	RS	U.S.	1996	$50.00

Airdate: 2/25/96.

Singles

Label	Catalog Number	Title	Type	Country	Year	Longbox Value / Value
		Israel's Son	CD5	Australia	1995	$12.00
Epic	ESK 7402	Israel's Son	CDJ	U.S.	1995	$6.00
Epic		Pure Massacre	CDJ	U.S.		$6.00
Epic		Tomorrow	CDJ	U.S.		$6.00
Epic	ESK 7137	Tomorrow	CDJ	U.S.	1995	$6.00

Silverfish

Singles

Label	Catalog Number	Title	Type	Country	Year	Longbox Value / Value
Creation	CRE SCD 113	Big Bad Baby Pig Squeal	CD5	U.K.	1991	$8.00
Chaos	42K 74923	Crazy	CD5	U.S.	1993	$5.00
Chaos		Crazy	CDJ	U.S.	1993	$2.00

Simken Heights

Singles

Label	Catalog Number	Title	Type	Country	Year	Longbox Value / Value
	6001	Smoke Box	CD5	U.S.	1994	$5.00

Label	Catalog Number	Title	Type	Country	Year	Longbox Value / Value
	6001	Smoke Box	CD5	U.S.	1994	$5.00

Simon and Garfunkel

Full Length

Label	Catalog Number	Title	Type	Country	Year	Longbox Value / Value
CBS	XACS-90022	A Hazy Shade of Winter-Special Sampler	DJ/Smplr	Japan	1994	$175.00
Sony	SRCS-7916	Bridge Over Troubled Water	LTD/LP	Japan	1996	$35.00
	20 bit mastering.					
CBS	CK-09914	Bridge Over Troubled Water	LP/BP	U.S.†	1985	$14.00/$8.00
CBS		Bridge Over Troubled Water	LTD/LP	U.S.	1992	$29.00/$25.00
	Gold disc version in special lonbox packaging.					
CBS	CK-64421	Bridge Over Troubled Water	LTD/LP	U.S.	1994	$25.00
	Gold disc.					
CBS	7133-80	Concert in the Park	LD	U.S.		$30.00
CBS	CK-31350	Greatest Hits	LP/BP	U.S.†	1985	$14.00/$8.00
Album Network		In the Studio (Bookends)	RS	U.S.	1990	$35.00
	Airdate: 4/16/90.					
CBS	CK-09914	Parsley, Sage, Rosemary & Thyme	LP/BP	U.S.†	1985	$14.00/$8.00
CBS/Fox	7133-80	Simon and Garfunkel	LD	U.S.	1983	$25.00
		Sixties Legends	RS	U.S.	1992	$15.00
	2 CD set. Airdate: 7/3/92.					
Sony	SRCS-7915	Sound of Silence	LTD/LP	Japan	1996	$35.00
	20 bit mastering.					

Singles

Label	Catalog Number	Title	Type	Country	Year	Longbox Value / Value
Columbia	657653-2	7 O'Clock News	CD5	U.K.	1992	$11.00
Columbia	657806-2	Boxer, The	CD5	U.K.	1992	$11.00
Columbia	655569-2	Bridge Over Troubled Water	CD5	U.K.	1990	$11.00

Simon, Carly

Full Length

Label	Catalog Number	Title	Type	Country	Year	Longbox Value / Value
Elektra	109-2	Best of	LP/LB	U.S.†	1984	$14.00/$8.00
Arista		Clouds in My Coffee 1965-1995	DJ/Smplr	U.S.		$18.00
Warner Brothers	23886-2	Hello, Big Man	LP/LB	U.S.†	1984	$14.00/$8.00
Epic	FK-39970	Spoiled Girl	LP/LB	U.S.†	1985	$14.00/$8.00

Singles

Label	Catalog Number	Title	Type	Country	Year	Longbox Value / Value
Arista		All I Want Is You	CDJ	U.S.		$3.00
Arista	BVDA-10	Better Not Tell Her	CD3	Japan	1990	$12.00/$4.00
Arista	ASCD 2083	Better Not Tell Her	CDJ	U.S.	1990	$3.00
Arista	ARISTCD-687	Coming Around Again	CD5	U.K.	1987	$10.00
Arista	ASCD 9525	Coming Around Again	CDJ	U.S.	1989	$3.00
Arista	162124	Let the River Run	CD3	Germany	1989	$8.00
Arista	662124	Let the River Run	CD5	Germany	1989	$8.00
Arista	162124	Let the River Run	CD3	U.K.	1989	$8.00
Arista	662124	Let the River Run	CD5	U.K.	1989	$8.00
Arista	ASCD 9793	Let the River Run	CDJ	U.S.	1988	$3.00
Arista	ASCD 2165	Life is Eternal	CDJ	U.S.	1991	$2.00
Qwest	PRCD 5356-2	Love of My Life	CDJ	U.S.	1992	$2.00
Arista	ASCD 9947	My Romance	CDJ	U.S.	1990	$3.00
Arista	ASCD 2940	Night Before Christmas, The	CDJ	U.S.		$3.00
Arista	885140	Nobody Does It Better	CD5	Germany	1989	$9.00
Arista	661807	Nobody Does It Better	CD5	U.K.	1989	$9.00
Arista	ASCD 2814	Tonight by the Sun	CDJ	U.S.	1995	$3.00
Angel	79219	Voulez-Vous Dancer	CDJ	U.S.	1993	$2.00
WEA	969338-2	You're So Vain	CD5	Germany	1989	$10.00
Elektra	7559-65551-2	You're So Vain	CD5	Gerrmany	1991	$10.00
WEA	969338-2	You're So Vain	CD5	U.K.	1989	$10.00
Elektra	EKR-123CD	You're So Vain	CD5	U.K.	1991	$10.00

Simon F

Singles

Label	Catalog Number	Title	Type	Country	Year	Longbox Value / Value
		American Dream	CDJ	U.S.		$2.00

Simon, Paul

Full Length

Label	Catalog Number	Title	Type	Country	Year	Longbox Value / Value
Warner Brothers	PRO-CD-6577	1964-1983 Boxed Set Sampler	DJ/Smplr	U.S.	1993	$15.00
WEA	38344	Born at the Right Time	LD	U.S.	1993	$35.00
Warner	WPCP-4421-23	Collection, The	LP	Japan	1991	$50.00
	3 CD Set.					
WEA	38277	Concert at the Park	LD	U.S.	1991	$35.00
Warner Brothers	PRO-CD-5220	Concert in Central Park Sampler	DJ/Smplr	U.S.	1991	$10.00
Warner Brothers	9 25447-2	Graceland	LP/LB	U.S.	1987	$19.00/$10.00
WEA	63813	Graceland African Concert	LD	U.S.	1991	$30.00
CBS	CK-35032	Greatest Hits	LP/BP	U.S.†	1985	$14.00/$8.00
Warner Brothers	23942-2	Hearts & Bones	LP/LB	U.S.†	1984	$14.00/$8.00
DIR		King Biscuit Flour Hour	RS	U.S.	1992	$40.00
	With Bonnie Raitt, Airdate: 3/15/92.					
DIR		King Biscuit Flour Hour	RS	U.S.	1994	$50.00
	With Bonnie Raitt, Airdate: 4/24/94.					
DIR		King Biscuit Flour Hour	RS	U.S.	1995	$40.00
	With Bonnie Raitt, Airdate: 5/21/95.					
Image	ID7673PA	Paul Simon	LD	U.S.	1993	$40.00
Pioneer	PA-81-001	Paul Simon	LD	U.S.	1986	$30.00
Pioneer	PA-81-001	Paul Simon	LD	U.S.	1992	$40.00
	Digital audio.					
Warner Brothers	9 26098-2-Dj	Rhythm of the Saints	DJ/LP	U.S.	1990	$20.00
	Promo CD in box wrapped with twine and miniature drum.					
Warner Brothers	9 26098-2-Dj	Rhythm of the Saints	DJ/LP	U.S.	1990	$20.00
	Second version Promo CD in box wrapped with twine and miniature bead.					
Media America		Up Close	RS	U.S.	1991	$40.00
	2 CD set.					

Singles

Label	Catalog Number	Title	Type	Country	Year	Longbox Value / Value
Warner Brothers	9362-40059-2	Born at the Right Time	CD5	Germany	1991	$10.00
Warner Brothers	W-0026CD	Born at the Right Time	CD5	U.K.	1991	$10.00
Warner Brothers	PRO-CD-4626	Born at the Right Time	CDJ	U.S.	1990	$3.00
Warner Brothers	PRO-CD-2659	Boy in the Bubble	CDJ	U.S.	1986	$6.00
Warner Brothers	921108-2	Mother and Child Reunion	CD3	Germany	1988	$10.00
Warner Brothers	W-7655CD	Mother and Child Reunion	CD3	U.K.	1988	$10.00
Warner Brothers	7599-21777-2	Obvious Child, The	CD5	Germany	1990	$10.00
Warner Brothers	W-9549CD	Obvious Child, The	CD5	U.K.	1990	$10.00
Warner Brothers	PRO-CD-4480	Obvious Child, The	CDJ	U.S.	1990	$3.00
Warner Brothers	7599-2187-2	Proof	CD5	Germany	1990	$10.00
Warner Brothers	W-0003CD	Proof	CD5	U.K.	1990	$10.00
Warner Brothers	PRO-CD-4604	Proof	CDJ	U.S.	1990	$3.00
Warner Brothers	PRO-CD-6427	Thelma	CDJ	U.S.		$3.00

Simone, Nina

Singles

Label	Catalog Number	Title	Type	Country	Year	Longbox Value / Value
Polygram	526702	After Hours	CD5	U.S.	1994	$5.00
Polygram	526702	After Hours	CD5	U.S.	1994	$5.00
ZYX	6157-8	My Baby Just Cares For Me	CD3	Germany		$6.00

Simple E

Singles

Label	Catalog Number	Title	Type	Country	Year	Longbox Value / Value
	FSCD0004	Play My Funk	CDJ	U.S.		$2.00

Simple Minds

Full Length

Label	Catalog Number	Title	Type	Country	Year	Longbox Value / Value
Warner	PCD-0557	81-95 DJ Copy	DJ/Smplr	Japan	1995	$150.00
Virgin	CDBRUCE 4	Amsterdam Ep, The	DJ/Smplr	U.K.	1989	$15.00
Westwood One		In Concert-Nu Rock	RS	U.S.	1995	$75.00
	2 CD set. Airdate: 10/23/95.					
Virgin	VOZCD 2052	Real Life	LTD/LP	U.K.	1991	$20.00
	2 CD set.					
A&M	75021 5352 2	Real Life	DJ/3CD	U.S.	1991	$25.00
	3 CD set.					
A&M	CD-4981	Sparkle in the Rain	LP/LB	U.S.†	1984	$14.00/$8.00
Virgin		Themes Vol. 1	LP	U.K.	1992	$25.00
	3 CD5 Set.					
Virgin		Themes Vol. 2	LP	U.K.	1992	$25.00
	3 CD5 Set.					
Virgin		Themes Vol. 3	LP	U.K.	1992	$25.00
	3 CD5 Set.					
Media America		Up Close	RS	U.S.	1995	$35.00

Singles

Label	Catalog Number	Title	Type	Country	Year	Longbox Value / Value
Virgin	SMXCD-6	Amsterdam Ep, The	CD5	U.K.	1989	$10.00
Virgin	SMXX-6	Amsterdam Ep, The	CD5	U.K.	1989	$10.00
A&M		And the Band Played On	CDJ	U.S.		$6.00
Virgin	SMXCD-3	Ballad of the Streets	CD5	Canada	1990	$10.00
BMG	161998	Belfast Child	CD3	Germany	1989	$10.00
BMG	661998	Belfast Child	CD5	Germany	1989	$10.00
Virgin	09P3-6143	Belfast Child	CD5	Japan	1989	$15.00
Virgin	SMXCD-3	Belfast Child	CD3	U.K.	1989	$10.00
Virgin	THEME 16	Belfast Child	CD5	U.K.	1990	$10.00
Virgin	880981	Don't You (Forget About Me)	CD5	Germany	1988	$10.00
Virgin	CDT-2	Don't You (Forget About Me)	CD5	U.K.	1988	$10.00
A&M	75021 2375-2	Don't You (Forget About Me)	CD5	U.S.	1988	$5.00
		Hypnotized	CD5	U.K.	1995	$10.00
		Hypnotized	CD5	U.K.	1995	$10.00
	Second version.					
A&M		Hypnotized	CDJ	U.S.		$6.00
Virgin	162495	Kick It In	CD3	Germany	1989	$10.00
Virgin	662495	Kick It In	CD5	Germany	1989	$10.00
Virgin	SMXCD-5	Kick It In	CD3	U.K.	1989	$10.00
Toshiba	VJDP-10153	Let There Be Love	CD3	Japan	1991	$12.00/$4.00
Virgin	VSCDT-1332	Let There Be Love	CD5	U.K.	1991	$10.00
A&M	75021 7532 2	Let There Be Love	CDJ	U.S.	1991	$3.00
		Love Song/Alive and Kicking	CD5	U.K.		$10.00
		Love Song/Alive and Kicking	CD5	U.K.		$10.00
	Second version.					
A&M	CD 17782	Mandella Day	CDJ	U.S.	1989	$3.00
BMG	664826	Real Life	CD5	Germany	1991	$10.00
Virgin	VSCDG 1382	Real Life	CD5	U.K.	1991	$10.00
BMG	664300	See the Lights	CD5	Germany	1991	$10.00
A&M	75021 7540 2	See the Lights	CDJ	U.S.	1991	$3.00
A&M	75021 7546 2	See the Lights	CDJ	U.S.	1991	$3.00
	DPRO 14231	She's a River	CDJ	U.S.		$2.00
Capital	38467	She's a River	CD5	U.S.	1994	$5.00
BMG	162887	Sign of the Times	CD3	Germany	1989	$10.00
BMG	662887	Sign of the Times	CD5	Germany	1989	$10.00
A&M	75021 7222 2	Stand by Love	CDJ	U.S.	1991	$3.00
A&M	CD 17824	Take a Step Back	CDJ	U.S.	1989	$3.00
Virgin	162240	This Is Your Land	CD3	Germany	1989	$10.00
Virgin	662240	This Is Your Land	CD5	Germany	1989	$10.00
Virgin	VJD-10202	This Is Your Land	CD3	Japan	1989	$12.00/$4.00
Virgin	SMXCD-4	This Is Your Land	CD3	U.K.	1989	$10.00
Virgin	CD BRUCE 2	This Is Your Land	CD5	U.K.	1989	$10.00
A&M	CD 17779	This Is Your Land	CDJ	U.S.	1989	$3.00

Simple Pleasure

Singles

Label	Catalog Number	Title	Type	Country	Year	Longbox Value / Value
Reprise	PRO-CD-6168	Givin' You All I've Got to Give	CDJ	U.S.	1992	$2.00

Simply Red

Full Length

Label	Catalog Number	Title	Type	Country	Year	Longbox Value / Value
WEA	SAM1140	Brit Awards	DJ/Smplr	U.K.	1994	$20.00
Eastwest	PRCD 4162-2	Simply the Hits	DJ/Smplr	U.S.	1991	$12.00
WEA	ASCD-107	Song Collection	DJ/Smplr	Japan		$120.00

Singles

Label	Catalog Number	Title	Type	Country	Year	Longbox Value / Value
WEA	YZ-161CD	Every Time We Say Goodbye	CD5	U.K.	1988	$10.00
Eastwest	EW001CD-DJ	Fairground	CDJ	U.K.		$14.00
		Fairground	CDJ	U.S.		$3.00
		Fairground	CDJ	U.S.		$3.00
	2 edits.					
		Fairground	CDJ	U.S.		$3.00
	4 edits.					
Elektra	64356	Fairground	CD5	U.S.	1995	$5.00
Elektra	64356	Fairground	CD5	U.S.	1995	$5.00
Eastwest	9031-76341-9	For Your Babies	CD5	Germany	1992	$10.00
Eastwest	WMD5-4095	For Your Babies	CD3	Japan	1992	$12.00/$4.00
Eastwest	YZ642CDX	For Your Babies	CD5	U.K.	1992	$13.00
	Image disc.					
Elektra	PRCD-4523-2	For Your Babies	CDJ	U.S.	1992	$2.00
WEA	YZ-172CD	I Won't Feel Sad	CD3	U.K.	1988	$10.00
WEA	246990-2	If You Don't Know Me by Now	CD3	Germany	1989	$10.00
WEA	09P3-6143	If You Don't Know Me by Now	CD3	Japan	1989	$13.00/$3.00
WEA	YZ-377CD	If You Don't Know Me by Now	CD3	U.K.	1989	$10.00
Elektra	667018 2	If You Don't Know Me by Now	CD5	U.S.	1989	$5.00
Elektra	PR 8079-2	If You Don't Know Me by Now	CDJ	U.S.	1989	$2.00
WEA	247164-2	It's Only Love	CD3	Germany	1989	$10.00
WEA	10P3-6110	It's Only Love	CD3	Japan	1989	$13.00/$3.00
WEA	YZ-349CD	It's Only Love	CD3	U.K.	1989	$10.00
Elektra	PR 8054-2	It's Only Love	CDJ	U.S.	1989	$2.00
Eastwest	AMCE-500	Montreaux	CD3	Japan	1992	$15.00
		Montreux	CD5	U.K.		$10.00
	Second version.					
	PRCD 9485-2	Never Never Love	CDJ	U.S.		$3.00
	PRCD 9424-2	Never Never Love	CDJ	U.S.		$3.00
WEA	2468215-2	New Flame	CD5	Germany	1992	$10.00
WEA	YZ-404CD	New Flame	CD5	U.K.	1992	$10.00
	PRCD 9429-2	Remembering the First Time	CDJ	U.S.		$3.00
	PRCD 4162-2	Simply the Hits	CDJ	U.S.		$3.00
Eastwest	WMD5-4079	Something Got Me Started	CD3	Japan	1991	$12.00/$4.00
Eastwest	YZ-614CD	Something Got Me Started	CD5	U.K.	1991	$10.00
Eastwest	PRCD 4168-2	Something Got Me Started	CDJ	U.S.	1991	$2.00
Eastwest	9031-75802-2	Stars	CD5	Germany	1993	$10.00
Eastwest	AMDE-5105	Stars	CD3	Japan	1993	$12.00/$4.00
Eastwest	YZ-626CD	Stars	CD5	U.K.	1993	$10.00
Eastwest	PRCD 4343	Stars	CDJ	U.S.	1993	$7.00
Eastwest	PRCD 4460	Stars	CDJ	U.S.	1993	$7.00
Eastwest	YZ-671CD	Thrill Me	CD5	U.K.	1992	$10.00
WEA	246603-2	You've Got It	CD3	Germany	1989	$10.00
WEA	YZ-424CD	You've Got It	CD3	U.K.	1989	$10.00

Label	Catalog Number	Title	Type	Country	Year	Longbox Value / Value
Elektra	66663	You've Got It	CD5	U.S.	1989	$5.00
Elektra	PRCD 8112-2	You've Got It	CDJ	U.S.	1989	$2.00

Simpson, Ray

Singles

Label	Catalog Number	Title	Type	Country	Year	Longbox Value / Value
Virgin	4455	Crazy Pictures	CDJ	U.S.	1992	$2.00

Simpsons

Singles

Label	Catalog Number	Title	Type	Country	Year	Longbox Value / Value
Geffen	GED-21637	Deep Deep Trouble	CD5	Germany	1991	$10.00
Geffen	GEF-88CD	Deep Deep Trouble	CD5	U.K.	1991	$10.00
Geffen	21633	Deep Deep Trouble	CD5	U.S.	1991	$5.00
Geffen	PRO-CD-4208	Deep Deep Trouble	CDJ	U.S.	1991	$3.00
Geffen	GED-21684	Do the Bartman	CD5	Germany	1990	$10.00
Geffen	GED-21685	Do the Bartman	CD5	Germany	1990	$10.00
Geffen	GEF-87CD	Do the Bartman	CD5	U.K.	1990	$10.00
Geffen	PRO-CD-4170	Do the Bartman	CDJ	U.S.	1990	$15.00
	CD in special sleeve with cartoon-motion book.					
Geffen	PRO-CD-4218	God Bless This Child	CDJ	U.S.	1991	$3.00

Sims, Kim

Singles

Label	Catalog Number	Title	Type	Country	Year	Longbox Value / Value
Atco	B-8528CD	A Little Bit More	CD5	U.K.	1992	$8.00
Atco	7567-96204-2	Take My Advice	CD5	Germany	1992	$8.00
Atco	B-8591CD	Take My Advice	CD5	U.K.	1992	$8.00
Atco	7567-96255-2	Too Blind to See It	CD5	Germany	1992	$8.00
Atco	AMDY-5072	Too Blind to See It	CD3	Japan	1992	$13.00/$4.00
Atco	B-8667CD	Too Blind to See It	CD5	U.K.	1992	$8.00

Sims, Kym

Singles

Label	Catalog Number	Title	Type	Country	Year	Longbox Value / Value
CRT	15545	I Must Be Free	CD5	U.S.	1995	$6.00

Sims, Zoot

Singles

Label	Catalog Number	Title	Type	Country	Year	Longbox Value / Value
Toshiba	TOCJ-5381	In Paris	CD5	Japan	1989	$12.00
Disq	8417	In Paris	CD5	U.S.	1989	$5.00

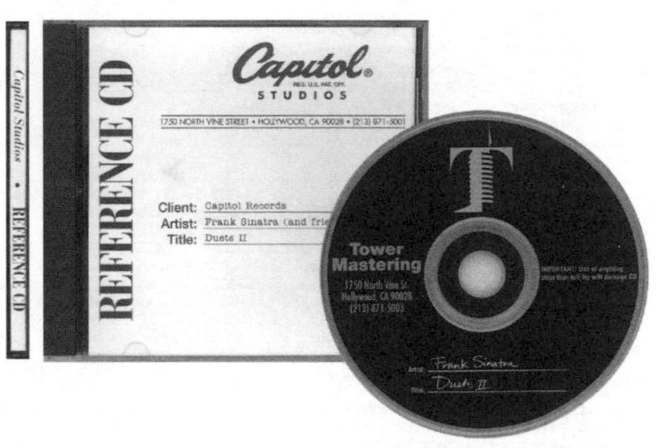

Sinatra, Frank – Duets II (Capitol Studios DPRO-79500)

Sinatra, Frank

Full Length

Label	Catalog Number	Title	Type	Country	Year	Longbox Value / Value
Capitol	DPRO 79375	Capitol Years, The	DJ/Smplr	U.S.	1990	$12.00
Capitol	C2-94777	Capitol Years, The	LTD/LP	U.S.	1990	$50.00
	3 disc set in clothbound digipak.					
Columbia	CSK 5224	Complete Frank Sinatra Sampler	DJ/Smplr	U.S.	1993	$15.00
Reprise		Complete Reprise Studio Recordings	LTD/LP	U.S.	1995	$450.00
	20 CD set in leatherette brass case. Limited to 20,000 copies.					
Reprise	FAS 80	Complete Reprise Studio Recordings Sampler	DJ/Smplr	U.S.	1995	$150.00
Capitol		Concepts	LTD/LP	U.S.	1994	$250.00
	16 CD set in wood box with booklet.					
DCC		Duets	LTD/LP	U.S.	1994	$30.00
	Gold disc numberd edition.					
Capitol Studios	DPRO-79500	Duets II	DJ/LP	U.S.	1996	$15.00
		Duets the Radio Special	RS	U.S.	1994	$60.00
	3 CD set.					
General Publishing Group	646846	Frank Sinatra: An American Legend	LP	U.S.	1995	$40.00
	CD in hardbound book by Nancy Sinatra.					
General Publishing Group	646846	Frank Sinatra: An American Legend	LP	U.S.	1995	$50.00
	CD and VHS Video in hardbound book by Nancy Sinatra.					
General Publishing Group	649694-2	Frank Sinatra: An American Legend	LP	U.S.	1995	$100.00
	5CD set in hardbound book with slipcase.					
EMI	CDP 486162	Frank Sinatra Collection, The	LP	Germany		$45.00
Qwest	925145-1	L.A. Is My Lady	LP	U.S.		$45.00
Reprise	43P2-0013	My Way	LTD/LP	Japan		$50.00
	Gold disc.					
MGM/UA	ML100648	Portrait	LD	U.S.	1986	$35.00
		Radio Show, The	RS	Germany		$125.00
	3 CD set.					
WEA	38196	Reprise Collection	LD	U.S.	1991	$80.00
Reprise	PRO-CD-4510	Selections From the Reprise Collection	DJ/Smplr	U.S.	1990	$12.00
Capitol	DPRO-11154	Sinatra's 80th Birthday Celebrity Tributes	DJ/Intvw	U.S.	1995	$12.00
		Sings the Select Johnny Mercer	LTD/LP	U.S.	1995	$22.00
WEA	38228	V.2 Reprise	LD	U.S.	1991	$80.00
WEA	38256	V.3 Reprise	LD	U.S.	1991	$80.00

Singles

Label	Catalog Number	Title	Type	Country	Year	Longbox Value / Value
		Black Novelty Hat	CDJ	U.S.	1995	$6.00
Reprise	PRO-CD-4753	Fly Me to the Moon	CDJ	U.S.	1990	$3.00
		I've Got a Crush On You	CD5	Australia	1993	$12.00
	With Barbara Streisand.					
Capitol	DPRO-79316	I've Got a Crush On You	CDJ	U.S.	1993	$3.00
	With Barbara Streisand.					
	DUETS-1	I've Got You Under My Skin	CDJ	U.K.	1993	$25.00
	With Barbara Streisand.					
Capitol	DPRO-79305	I've Got You Under My Skin	CDJ	U.S.	1993	$3.00
	With Bono.					
Reprise	PRO-CD-4653	It Was a Very Good Year	CDJ	U.S.	1990	$3.00
Reprise	PRO-CD-5937	It Was a Very Good Year	CDJ	U.S.	1992	$3.00
		My Way	CDJ	U.S.	1995	$6.00
Reprise	9 21882-2	New York New York	CD5	U.S.	1992	$5.00

Sinatra, Nancy

Singles

Label	Catalog Number	Title	Type	Country	Year	Longbox Value / Value
Cougar	CGRCD-401-P	Bone Dry	CDJ	U.S.	1995	$6.00
Cougar		Now I Have Everything	CDJ	U.S.	1995	$6.00
Eastwest	246874-2	These Boots	CD5	Germany	1989	$10.00

Sinbad

Singles

Label	Catalog Number	Title	Type	Country	Year	Longbox Value / Value
Wing	NSK 2781	I Ain't Lyin'	CDJ	U.S.	1990	$2.00

Singers Unlimited

Full Length

Label	Catalog Number	Title	Type	Country	Year	Longbox Value / Value
Verve	815671-2	A Capella	LP/LB	U.S.†	1985	$14.00/$8.00
Verve	821859-2	Christmas	LP/LB	U.S.†	1985	$14.00/$8.00
Verve	821858-2	Feeling Free	LP/LB	U.S.†	1985	$14.00/$8.00
Verve	817486-2	With Rob McConnell & Boss Brass	LP/LB	U.S.†	1985	$14.00/$8.00

Singing Dogs

Singles

Label	Catalog Number	Title	Type	Country	Year	Longbox Value / Value
RCA	64223	Jingle Bells	CD5	U.S.	1994	$5.00

Single Gun Theory

Singles

Label	Catalog Number	Title	Type	Country	Year	Longbox Value / Value
Capitol	58251	Fall	CD5	U.S.	1994	$5.00
Nettwerk	13850	Surrender	CD5	U.S.	1991	$5.00

Single Vision

Singles

Label	Catalog Number	Title	Type	Country	Year	Longbox Value / Value
	AMSAD007179	Felt	CDJ	U.S.		$3.00

Sinitta

Singles

Label	Catalog Number	Title	Type	Country	Year	Longbox Value / Value
Victor	VDPS-1011	Cross My Broken Heart	CD3	Japan	1988	$13.00/$4.00
Victor	VDPS-1004	G.T.O.	CD3	Japan	1988	$13.00/$4.00
Eastwest	171678-2	Hitchin' a Ride	CD5	Germany	1990	$8.00
Fanfare	CDFAN-24	Hitchin' a Ride	CD5	U.K.	1990	$8.00
Atlantic	PRCD 3288-2	Hitchin' a Ride	CDJ	U.S.	1990	$2.00
Eastwest	8 10959	I Don't Believe in Miracles	CD5	Germany	1990	$8.00
Fanfare	CDFAN-21	I Don't Believe in Miracles	CD5	U.K.	1990	$8.00
Eastwest	170821-2	Lay Me Down Easy	CD5	Germany	1990	$8.00
Fanfare	CDFAN-23	Lay Me Down Easy	CD5	U.K.	1990	$8.00
		Lay Me Down Easy	CDJ	U.S.	1990	$2.00
Fanfare	CDFAN-31	Love and Affection	CD5	U.K.	1990	$8.00
Eastwest	246629-2	Love on a Mountain Top	CD3	Germany	1989	$8.00
Eastwest	8 70001	Right Back Where We Started From	CD3	Germany	1989	$8.00
Eastwest	246910-2	Right Back Where We Started From	CD5	Germany	1989	$8.00
Fanfare	CDFAN-18	Right Back Where We Started From	CD5	U.K.	1989	$8.00
		Right Back Where We Started From	CDJ	U.S.		$2.00
Arista	74321-100322	Shame Shame Shame	CD5	U.K.	1992	$8.00
Victor	VDPS-1003	Toy Boy	CD3	Japan	1988	$13.00/$4.00

Siouxsie and The Banshees

Full Length

Label	Catalog Number	Title	Type	Country	Year	Longbox Value / Value
Geffen		Rapture Sampler	DJ/Smplr	U.K.		$12.00
Geffen	PRO-CD-4469	Sampler	DJ/Smplr	U.S.	1991	$8.00
Geffen		Songs Before the Rapture	DJ/Smplr	U.S.		$12.00
Geffen		Songs From Rapture	DJ/Smplr	U.S.		$8.00
Geffen	GEFCD-24387Dj	Superstition	DJ/LP	U.S.	1991	$18.00
	Promo CD in round mirror case.					

Singles

Label	Catalog Number	Title	Type	Country	Year	Longbox Value / Value
Geffen	PRO-CD-5567	Face to Face	CDJ	U.S.	1992	$2.00
Geffen	GEFDS 21702	Fear of the Unknown	CD5	U.K.	1991	$9.00
Geffen	PRO-CD-4306	Fear of the Unknown	CDJ	U.S.	1991	$2.00
Geffen	PRO-CD-4345	Fear of the Unknown	CDJ	U.S.	1991	$2.00
Geffen	9 21479-2	Fury Eyes	CD5	U.S.	1990	$5.00
Wonderland	SHECD-15	Killing Jar	CD5	U.K.	1988	$10.00
Wonderland	SHECD-19	Kiss Them for Me	CD5	U.K.	1991	$9.00
Geffen	PRO-CD-4260	Kiss Them for Me	CDJ	U.S.	1991	$2.00
Wonderland	SHECD-16	Last Beat of My Heart	CD5	U.K.	1988	$9.00
Geffen	PRO-CD-4708	Oh Baby	CDJ	U.S.		$3.00
Geffen	PRO-CD-4708	Oh Baby	CDJ	U.S.	1995	$3.00
Polygram	887642-2	Peek-a-Boo	CD5	Canada	1988	$9.00
Polygram	887642-2	Peek-a-Boo	CD5	Germany	1988	$9.00
Wonderland	SHECD-14	Peek-a-Boo	CD5	U.K.	1988	$9.00
Strange Frt	12	Peel Sessions	CD5	U.S.	1989	$5.00
Strange Frt	1SFPSCD-012	Peel Sessions	CD5	U.S.	1989	$8.00
Strange Frt	66	Peel Sessions 2	CD5	U.S.	1990	$5.00
Strange Frt	1SFPSCD-066	Peel Sessions 2	CD5	U.S.	1990	$8.00
Wonderland	SHECD-17	Standing There	CD5	U.K.	1989	$10.00
Geffen		Stargazer	CD5	U.K.	1995	$9.00
		Stargazer	CDJ	U.S.	1994	$6.00

Sir Mix-A-Lot

Singles

Label	Catalog Number	Title	Type	Country	Year	Longbox Value / Value
Polygram	864135-2	Baby Got Back	CD5	Germany	1992	$10.00
Polygram	DEFCD-20	Baby Got Back	CD5	U.K.	1992	$10.00
Def American	9 40233-2	Baby Got Back	CD5	U.S.	1992	$5.00
Def American	PRO-CD-5213	Baby Got Back	CDJ	U.S.	1992	$3.00
Def American	PRO-CD-5878	One Time's Got No Case	CD5	U.S.	1992	$2.00
Warner	12-41693	Ride	CD5	Canada	1994	$8.00
		Sleepin' Wit My Fork	CDJ	U.S.		$3.00
Def American	PRO-CD-5468	Swap Meet Louie	CD5	U.S.	1992	$2.00
Def American	9 40554-2	Swap Meet Louie	CD5	U.S.	1992	$5.00

Siren

Singles

Label	Catalog Number	Title	Type	Country	Year	Longbox Value / Value
Mercury	CDP 36	All Is Forgiven	CDJ	U.S.	1988	$2.00
Mercury	CDP 43	All Is Forgiven	CDJ	U.S.	1989	$2.00
Mercury		One Good Lover	CDJ	U.S.		$2.00

Siskin, Skew

Singles

Label	Catalog Number	Title	Type	Country	Year	Longbox Value / Value
Giant	PRO-CD-5536	If the Walls Could Talk	CDJ	U.S.	1992	$2.00

Sister Double Happiness

Full Length

Label	Catalog Number	Title	Type	Country	Year	Longbox Value / Value
Reprise	9 26657-2-Dj	Heart and Mind	DJ/LP	U.S.	1991	$12.00
	Picture disc.					

Label	Catalog Number	Title	Type	Country	Year	Longbox Value / Value
		Singles				
Columbia	CSK 4039	Frankie & Sue	CDJ	U.S.	1991	$2.00
Chaos	CSK 5083	Loving Arms	CDJ	U.S.	1993	$2.00

Smith, Erica

Label	Catalog Number	Title	Type	Country	Year	Longbox Value / Value
		Singles				
		Temptation Eyes	CDJ	U.S.		$2.00

Smith, G.E.

Label	Catalog Number	Title	Type	Country	Year	Longbox Value / Value
		Full Length				
Liberty	99955	Give a Little	DJ/LP	U.S.	1992	$10.00
		Singles				
Liberty	DPRO-79597	Fattenin' Frogs for Snakes	CDJ	U.S.	1992	$2.00
Liberty	DPRO-79716	Sloozy	CDJ	U.S.	1993	$2.00

Smith, Jimmy

Label	Catalog Number	Title	Type	Country	Year	Longbox Value / Value
		Full Length				
Verve	823308-2	Bashin'	LP/LB	U.S.†	1985	$14.00/$8.00
Elektra	60175-2	Off The Top	LP/LB	U.S.†	1985	$14.00/$8.00
Verve	81046-2	The Cat	LP/LB	U.S.†	1985	$14.00/$8.00
Verve	823309-2	Who's Afraid of Virginia Wolf?	LP/LB	U.S.†	1985	$14.00/$8.00

Smith, Jimmy & Wes Montgomery

Label	Catalog Number	Title	Type	Country	Year	Longbox Value / Value
		Full Length				
Verve	821577-2	Dynamic Duo	LP/LB	U.S.†	1985	$14.00/$8.00

Smith, Kendra

Label	Catalog Number	Title	Type	Country	Year	Longbox Value / Value
		Full Length				
		Five Ways of Disappearing	DJ/LP	U.S.		$15.00

Smith, Lonnie

Label	Catalog Number	Title	Type	Country	Year	Longbox Value / Value
		Full Length				
Blue Note		Think!	LTD/LP	U.S.	1995	$19.00

Smith, Mandy

Label	Catalog Number	Title	Type	Country	Year	Longbox Value / Value
		Singles				
		Victim of Pleasure	CDJ	U.S.		$2.00

Smith, Michael W.

Label	Catalog Number	Title	Type	Country	Year	Longbox Value / Value
		Full Length				
RCA	66348	Wonder Years, The	LP/LB	U.S.		$14.00/$8.00
		Singles				
Reunion	4301	For You	CDJ	U.S.	1991	$2.00
Geffen	GFSTD-28	I Will Be Here for You	CD5	U.K.	1992	$8.00
Geffen	PRO-CD-4452	Picture Perfect	CDJ	U.S.	1992	$2.00
Reunion	GED-21671	Place in This World	CD5	Germany	1991	$8.00
Reunion	RNSTD-1	Place in This World	CD5	U.K.	1991	$8.00
Reunion	62466	Somebody Love Me	CDJ	U.S.	1992	$2.00

Smith & Mighty

Label	Catalog Number	Title	Type	Country	Year	Longbox Value / Value
		Singles				
Three Stripes	SNMCD 5	Steppers Delight	CD5	U.K.	1992	$8.00

Smith, O.C.

Label	Catalog Number	Title	Type	Country	Year	Longbox Value / Value
		Singles				
Triune	629	Best Out of Me, The	CDJ	U.S.	1993	$2.00

Smith, Patti

Label	Catalog Number	Title	Type	Country	Year	Longbox Value / Value
		Full Length				
Arista	ASCD-9683	CD Sampler	DJ/Smplr	U.S.	1988	$35.00
Arista	ARCD 8453 2	Dream of Life	LP/LB	U.S.		$14.00/$8.00
Arista	ARCD-8166-2	Easter	LP/LB	U.S.		$14.00/$8.00
Arista	ARCD-8362-2	Horses	LP/LB	U.S.		$14.00/$8.00
Arista		Masters	LTD/LP	U.S.	1996	$62.00
6 CD set.						
Arista	ARCD-8161-2	Radio Ethiopia	LP/LB	U.S.		$14.00/$8.00
Arista		Selected Songs	DJ/Smplr	U.S.	1996	$25.00
Arista		Selected Songs	DJ/Smplr	U.S.	1996	$25.00
Arista		Video	DJ/Intvw	U.S.		$20.00
Arista	ARCD-8546-2	Wave	LP/LB	U.S.		$14.00/$8.00
		Singles				
Arista	A10D-115	Looking for You (I Was)	CD3	Japan	1989	$12.00/$4.00
Arista	ASCD 9762	Looking for You (I Was)	CDJ	U.S.	1988	$6.00
Arista	659877	People Have the Power	CD5	Germany	1988	$10.00
Arista	659877	People Have the Power	CD5	U.K.	1988	$10.00
Arista	ASCD 9689	People Have the Power	CDJ	U.S.	1988	$6.00
Arista		Summer Cannibals	CD5	U.K.	1996	$10.00

Smith, Wayne

Label	Catalog Number	Title	Type	Country	Year	Longbox Value / Value
		Singles				
Tommy Boy	609	Under Mi Teng	CDJ	U.S.	1993	$2.00

Smithereens

Label	Catalog Number	Title	Type	Country	Year	Longbox Value / Value
		Full Length				
Pioneer Artists	PA-90-333	10	LD	U.S.	1991	$30.00
	RMJ 66391-2	A Date With the Smithereens	DJ/LP	U.S.	1994	$14.00
Album Network		Album Network Special	RS	U.S.	1994	$100.00
		Beauty and Sadness	LP/LB	U.S.		$18.00/$15.00
Capitol	DPRO-79107	Blown to Smithereens	DJ/Smplr	U.S.	1991	$17.00
		In Concert	RS	U.S.	1992	$120.00
2 CD set. With Pearl Jam, Airdate: 4/13/92.						
Westwood One		In Concert	RS	U.S.	1994	$65.00
Airdate: 9/26/94.						
Restless		Live at the Ritz	DJ/Smplr	U.S.	1996	$15.00
Restless	72242-2	Live Tracks	DJ/Smplr	U.S.	1988	$10.00
		Singles				
EMI	203685-2	A Girl Like You	CD5	Germany	1990	$10.00
Enigma	ENVCD-15	A Girl Like You	CD5	U.K.	1990	$10.00
Enigma	EPRO 79777	A Girl Like You	CDJ	U.S.	1989	$3.00
EMI	203893-2	Blue Period	CD5	Germany	1990	$10.00
Enigma	ENVCD-21	Blue Period	CD5	U.K.	1990	$10.00
Capitol	DPRO 79051	Blue Period	CDJ	U.S.	1989	$3.00
Capitol	DPRO 79916	Blues Before and After	CDJ	U.S.	1989	$3.00
		Everything I Have Is Blue	CDJ	U.S.		$2.00
RCA		Everything I Have Is Blue	CDJ	U.S.	1994	$3.00
Capitol	DPRO-79267	Get a Hold of My Heart	CDJ	U.S.	1991	$3.00
Capitol	DPRO-79148	Girl in Room 12	CDJ	U.S.	1991	$3.00
EMI	21198082	Miles From Nowhere	CD5	Australia	1994	$10.00
RCA	62820-2-RDJ	Miles From Nowhere	CDJ	U.S.	1994	$3.00
Capitol	DPRO-79572	Rudolph the Red Nose Reindeer	CDJ	U.S.	1992	$3.00
RCA	62942-2	Time Won't Let Me	CD5	U.S.	1994	$6.00
Capitol	C2 15818	Too Much Passion	CD5	U.S.	1991	$5.00
Capitol	DPRO-79935	Too Much Passion	CDJ	U.S.	1991	$3.00
Capitol	DPRO-79933	Top of the Pops	CDJ	U.S.	1991	$3.00
Capitol	DPRO 79131	Yesterday Girl	CDJ	U.S.	1989	$3.00

Smiths

Label	Catalog Number	Title	Type	Country	Year	Longbox Value / Value
		Full Length				
		Handsome Devils	DJ/Smplr	France		$100.00
	VDP-5080	Hatefull of Hollow	DJ/Smplr	Japan		$100.00
Westwood One		In Concert-Nu Rock	RS	U.S.	1993	$50.00
Airdate: 9/27/93.						
Westwood One		In Concert-Nu Rock	RS	U.S.	1995	$50.00
Airdate: 9/25/95.						
Warner Brothers		Introspective	DJ/Smplr	U.S.		$30.00
Rough Trade	VICP-2001	Smiths	LP	Japan		$45.00
		Singles				
Rough Trade	RTT-194CD	Ask	CD5	U.K.	1988	$10.00
Rough Trade	CD1-94	Barbarism Begins at Home	CD5	Germany	1988	$10.00
Rough Trade	RTT-171CD	Barbarism Begins at Home	CD5	U.K.	1988	$10.00
Rough Trade	CD1-95	Boy With the Thorn in His Side	CD5	Germany	1988	$10.00
Rough Trade	RTT-191CD	Boy With the Thorn in His Side	CD5	U.K.	1988	$10.00
Rough Trade	CD1-96	Headmaster Ritual	CD5	Germany	1988	$40.00
		Headmaster Ritual	CD5	U.K.		$10.00
Rough Trade	RTT-215CD	Headmaster Ritual	CD5	U.K.	1988	$40.00
1st Pressing.						
Rough Trade	CD1-93	Heaven Knows I'm Miserable	CD5	Germany	1988	$10.00
Rough Trade	RTT-156CD	Heaven Knows I'm Miserable	CD5	U.K.	1988	$10.00
Rough Trade	RTT-200CD	Last Night I Dreamt That Somebody Loved Me	CD5	U.K.	1988	$10.00
Rough Trade	RTT-193CD	Panic	CD5	U.K.	1988	$10.00
Strange Frt	SFPSCD-055	Peel Sessions	CD5	U.S.	1989	$6.00
WEA	WMC5-532	This Charming Man	CD5	Japan	1992	$15.00
Warner Brothers	9 40583-2	This Charming Man	CD5	U.S.	1992	$4.00
Warner Brothers	9 40591-2	This Charming Man	CD5	U.S.	1992	$5.00
Rough Trade	RTT-146CD	What Difference Does It Make	CD5	U.K.	1988	$10.00
Rough Trade	RTT-166CD	William, It Was Really Nothing	CD5	U.K.	1988	$10.00

Smog

Label	Catalog Number	Title	Type	Country	Year	Longbox Value / Value
		Singles				
Drag City	41	Burning Kingdom	CD5	U.S.	1994	$5.00

Smokin' Mojo Filter

Label	Catalog Number	Title	Type	Country	Year	Longbox Value / Value
		Singles				
	CTPCD1	Come Together	CDJ	U.K.		$30.00

Smoking Pipes

Label	Catalog Number	Title	Type	Country	Year	Longbox Value / Value
		Singles				
	DPRO 79607	Need You Around	CDJ	U.S.		$2.00
	DPRO 10227	Rubella	CDJ	U.S.		$2.00

Smooth Ice

Label	Catalog Number	Title	Type	Country	Year	Longbox Value / Value
		Singles				
		Smooth But Def	CDJ	U.S.		$2.00

Smudge

Label	Catalog Number	Title	Type	Country	Year	Longbox Value / Value
		Singles				
Shock	8004	Don't Want to Be Grant McLennon	CD5	U.S.	1991	$4.00

Smyth, Patty

Label	Catalog Number	Title	Type	Country	Year	Longbox Value / Value
		Singles				
MCA	MCA5P-2638	I Should Be Laughing	CDJ	U.S.	1993	$3.00
MCA	25090	Look What Love Has Done	CD5	U.S.	1994	$5.00
MCA	MCSTD-1699	No Mistakes	CD5	U.K.	1992	$10.00
MCA	MCA5P-2423	No Mistakes	CDJ	U.S.	1992	$3.00
MCA	MCA5P-2641	Shine	CDJ	U.S.	1993	$3.00
MCA	MVDM-28	Sometimes Love Just Ain't Enough	CD3	Japan	1992	$12.00/$4.00
MCA	MCSTD-1692	Sometimes Love Just Ain't Enough	CD5	U.K.	1992	$10.00
MCA	54403	Sometimes Love Just Ain't Enough	CD5	U.S.	1992	$5.00
MCA	MCA5P-2235	Sometimes Love Just Ain't Enough	CDJ	U.S.	1992	$3.00

Snail

Label	Catalog Number	Title	Type	Country	Year	Longbox Value / Value
		Singles				
	9013	All Channels Are Open	CD5	U.S.	1994	$5.00

Snakes

Label	Catalog Number	Title	Type	Country	Year	Longbox Value / Value
		Singles				
Curb	10569	Pay Bo Diddley	CDJ	U.S.	1989	$2.00
Curb	10535	Walkaway	CDJ	U.S.	1989	$2.00

Snap

Label	Catalog Number	Title	Type	Country	Year	Longbox Value / Value
		Singles				
Arista	664678	Colour of Love	CD5	Germany	1991	$9.00
Arista	BVDP-53	Colour of Love	CD3	Japan	1992	$12.00/$4.00
Arista	664678	Colour of Love	CD5	U.K.	1991	$9.00
Arista	665186	Colour of Love	CD5	U.K.	1991	$9.00
Arista	ASCD 2404	Colour of Love	CDJ	U.S.	1993	$2.00
Arista	663596	Cult of Snap	CD5	Germany	1990	$9.00
Arista	663639	Cult of Snap	CD5	Germany	1990	$9.00
Arista	663596	Cult of Snap	CD5	U.K.	1990	$9.00
Arista	BVDP-72	Exterminate	CD3	Japan	1993	$12.00/$4.00
BMG	74321-10696-2	Exterminate	CD5	U.K.	1992	$9.00
Arista	07822-12545-2	Exterminate	CD5	U.S.	1992	$5.00
Arista	663831	Mary Had a Little Boy	CD5	Germany	1990	$9.00
Arista	663852	Mary Had a Little Boy	CD5	Germany	1990	$9.00
Arista	663831	Mary Had a Little Boy	CD5	U.K.	1990	$9.00
Arista	ASCD-2143	Mary Had a Little Boy	CDJ	U.S.	1990	$2.00
Arista	BVCP-9007	Megamix	CD5	Japan	1990	$13.00
Arista	664169	Megamix	CD5	U.K.	1990	$9.00
Arista	664169	Megamix	CD5	U.K.	1990	$9.00
Arista	663296	Ooops Up	CD5	Germany	1990	$9.00
Arista	663500	Ooops Up	CD5	Germany	1990	$9.00
Arista	663296	Ooops Up	CD5	U.K.	1990	$9.00
Arista	ASCD-2071	Ooops Up	CDJ	U.S.	1990	$2.00
Arista	ASCD-2092	Ooops Up	CDJ	U.S.	1990	$2.00
Arista	663133	Power	CD5	Germany	1990	$9.00
Arista	663107	Power	CD5	Germany	1990	$9.00
Arista	663133	Power	CD5	U.K.	1990	$9.00
Arista	665309	Rhythm is a Dancer	CD5	Germany	1992	$9.00
Arista	BVDP-64	Rhythm is a Dancer	CD3	Japan	1992	$12.00/$4.00
Arista	74321-102572	Rhythm is a Dancer	CD5	U.K.	1992	$9.00
		Welcome to Tomorrow	CDJ	U.S.		$2.00
Arista	12797	Welcome to Tomorrow	CD5	U.S.	1994	$5.00

Snider, Todd

Label	Catalog Number	Title	Type	Country	Year	Longbox Value / Value
		Full Length				
		Three Songs	DJ/Smplr	U.S.		$5.00
		Singles				
MCA	MCA5P3651	I Believe You	CDJ	U.S.		$2.00

Snipers

Label	Catalog Number	Title	Type	Country	Year	Longbox Value / Value
		Singles				
	1256	Fire	CD5	U.S.	1994	$5.00

Label	Catalog Number	Title	Type	Country	Year	Longbox Value / Value
Snitzer, Andy						
Full Length						
		Sampler	DJ/Smplr	U.S.		$5.00
Snog						
Singles						
Machinery	11-3	Corporate Slave	CD5	U.K.	1992	$8.00
Snoop Doggy Dog						
Singles						
	PRCD 5637	Doggy Dog World	CDJ	U.S.	1994	$3.00
		Murder Was the Case	CDJ	U.S.		$2.00
Snoopy						
Full Length						
Lightyear	LYD75059-2	Classiks on Toys	DJ/Smplr	U.S.	1995	$10.00
Snow						
Singles						
		Anything for You	CDJ	U.S.		$3.00
		Anything for You	CDJ	U.S.		$3.00
	Second version.					
Elektra/Asylum	66155	Anything for You	CD5	U.S.	1994	$5.00
Eastwest	PRCD 4971-2	Girl I've Been Hurt	CDJ	U.S.	1993	$2.00
Eastwest	PRCD 5001-2	Informer	CDJ	U.S.	1993	$2.00
Eastwest	PRCD 5162-2	Runaway	CDJ	U.S.	1993	$2.00
Snow, Phoebe						
Singles						
Pioneer	09P3-6146	If I Can Just Get Through the Night	CD3	Japan	1989	$12.00/$2.00
Elektra	EKR-91CD	If I Can Just Get Through the Night	CD3	U.K.	1989	$2.00
Elektra		If I Can Just Get Through the Night	CDJ	U.S.	1989	$2.00
Elektra	PR 8087-2	Something Real	CDJ	U.S.	1989	$2.00
Epic	ESK 73505	Speak to My Heart	CDJ	U.S.	1990	$2.00
So						
Singles						
Parlophone	202306-2	Are You Sure	CD5	Germany	1988	$8.00
Parlophone	CDR-6173	Are You Sure	CD5	U.K.	1988	$8.00
EMI	243	Are You Sure	CDJ	U.S.	1988	$2.00
Parlophone	CD S01	Breaking the Silence	CD5	U.K.	1988	$8.00
Parlophone	CDR-6182	Burning Bush	CD5	U.K.	1988	$8.00
EMI		Capitol Hill	CDJ	U.S.		$2.00
Parlophone	CDR-6200	Would You Die for Me	CD5	U.K.	1988	$8.00
Sobule, Jill						
Full Length						
MCA	257195-2	Things Are Different	LP	Germany		$20.00
MCA	WMC5-165	Things Are Different	LP	Japan		$25.00
MCA	DMCG-6102	Things Are Different	LP	U.K.		$20.00
MCA	MCAD-6375	Things Are Different	LP	U.S.		$15.00/$10.00
Singles						
	PRCD 6059-2	Good Person Inside	CDJ	U.S.		$2.00
S.	PRCD 6072-2	I Kissed a Girl	CDJ	U.S.		$2.00
SMCA	DMCAT-1431	Living Color	CD5	U.K.	1990	$8.00
SMCA		Living Color	CDJ	U.S.		$2.00
S.	PRCD 6299-2	Supermodel	CDJ	U.S.		$2.00
SMCA	DMCAT-1446	Too Cool to Fall in Love	CD5	U.K.	1990	$8.00
Social Distortion						
Full Length						
Westwood One		Off the Record	RS	U.S.	1992	$40.00
	With Pearl Jam, Airdate: 4/27/92.					
Restless	72251	Prison Bound	LP/LB	U.S.	1988	$15.00/$9.00
Singles						
	51021	1941	CD5	U.S.	1989	$5.00
Epic	ESK 4348	Bad Luck	CDJ	U.S.	1992	$3.00
Epic	ESK 2051	Ball and Chain	CDJ	U.S.	1990	$3.00
Epic	ESK 4689	Born to Lose	CDJ	U.S.	1992	$3.00
Epic	ESK 1969	Let It Be Me	CDJ	U.S.	1990	$3.00
Epic	ESK 2120	Ring of Fire	CDJ	U.S.	1990	$3.00
Epic	ESK 2198	Story of My	CDJ	U.S.	1990	$3.00
		When the Angel's Sing	CD5	U.K.	1997	$10.00
		When the Angel's Sing	CD5	U.K.	1997	$10.00
	Second version.					
Soft Cell						
Full Length						
Collector's Pipeline	TCP 019CD	Non-Stop Erotic Cabaret	LP	U.S.		$16.00
Singles						
Polygram	880743-2	Bedsitter	CD5	Germany	1990	$10.00
Polygram	818437-2	Down in the Subway	CD5	Germany	1990	$10.00
Polygram	875401-2	Memorabilia	CD5	Germany	1990	$10.00
Polygram	811139-2	Numbers	CD5	Germany	1990	$10.00
Mercury	868101-2	Say Hello Wave Goodbye	CD5	Germany	1990	$10.00
Mercury	868157-2	Say Hello Wave Goodbye	CD5	Germany	1990	$10.00
Rough Trade	608-5318-3	Say Hello Wave Goodbye	CD5	Germany	1991	$10.00
Mercury	SOFCD-1	Say Hello Wave Goodbye	CD5	U.K.	1990	$10.00
Mercury	SOFCP-1	Say Hello Wave Goodbye	CD5	U.K.	1990	$10.00
Polygram	878241-2	Singles Collection	CD5	Germany	1990	$12.00
Polygram	814249-2	Soul Inside	CD5	Germany	1990	$10.00
Polygram	888617-3	Tainted Love	CD3	Germany	1989	$10.00
Polygram	868315-2	Tainted Love	CD5	Germany	1990	$10.00
Polygram	868427-2	Tainted Love	CD5	Germany	1990	$10.00
Polygram	888647-2	Tainted Love	CD5	Germany	1990	$10.00
Polygram	875397-2	Torch	CD5	Germany	1990	$10.00
Polygram	875399-2	What	CD5	Germany	1990	$10.00
Polygram	812591-2	Where the Heart Is	CD5	Germany	1990	$10.00
Soho						
Singles						
Atco	96428-2	Freaky	CD5	U.S.	1990	$5.00
Atco	PR 3845-2	Freaky	CDJ	U.S.	1990	$2.00
Atco	PR 3920-2	Freaky	CDJ	U.S.	1990	$2.00
Tam Tam	SAV-108	Girl on a Motorbike	CD5	U.K.	1990	$8.00
Atlantic	7567-96428-2	Hippychick	CD5	Germany	1990	$8.00
Savage	CDSAV-106	Hippychick	CD5	U.K.	1990	$8.00
Atco	96428-2	Hippychick	CD5	U.S.	1990	$4.00
Atco	PRCD 3526-2	Hippychick	CDJ	U.S.	1990	$2.00
Savage	CDSZV-112	Love Generation	CD5	U.K.	1991	$8.00
Atco	PRCD 3653-2	Love Generation	CDJ	U.S.	1990	$2.00
Aris	885152	Message From my Baby	CD3	Germany	1988	$8.00
Virgin	HEDDCD-4	Message From my Baby	CD3	U.K.	1988	$8.00
Atco		Out of my Mind	CDJ	U.S.		$2.00
Atco	PR 4613-2	Ride	CDJ	U.S.	1992	$2.00
Virgin	HEDDCD-3	You Won't Hold Me Down	CD3	U.K.	1988	$8.00
Sol Invictus						
Full Length						
TURSA	0003 CD	Killing Tide, The	LTD/LP	U.K.	1991	$15.00
	CD in felt bag with postcard.					
Solo						
Singles						
A&M	587507	Heaven	CD5	U.S.	1995	$6.00
Solution A.D.						
Singles						
	PRCD 6653-2	Fearless	CDJ	U.S.		$2.00
Some, Belouis						
Singles						
		Let It Be With You	CDJ	U.S.		$2.00
Somerville, Jimmy						
Singles						
Polygram	850051	Heartbeat	CD5	U.S.	1994	$5.00
		Hurts So Good	CD5	U.K.	1995	$10.00
		Hurts So Good	CD5	U.K.	1995	$10.00
	Second version.					
London	LONCD 245	Read My Lips	CD5	U.K.	1990	$8.00
London	LONCD 281	To Love Somebody	CD5	U.K.	1990	$8.00
London	LONCD 249	You Make Me Feel	CD5	U.K.	1990	$8.00
Somethin' For The People						
Singles						
	PRO-CD-7833-R	You Want This Party Started	CDJ	U.S.		$2.00
Something Happens						
Singles						
Virgin	VSCDT-1246	Hello, Hello, Hello	CD5	U.K.	1990	$8.00
Charisma	PRCD 004	Hello, Hello, Hello	CDJ	U.S.	1990	$2.00
Charisma	097	Suffer It	CDJ	U.S.	1992	$2.00
Virgin	VSCDT-1269	What Now	CD5	U.K.	1990	$8.00
Virgin	VSCDX-1269	What Now	CD5	U.K.	1990	$10.00
Something Special						
Singles						
Epic	ESK 73306	I Wonder Who She's Lovin'	CDJ	U.S.	1990	$2.00
Epic	ESK 73487	U Can't Get Me Anytime	CDJ	U.S.	1990	$2.00
Son Huasteco						
Singles						
	1411	Viva Mexico	CD5	U.S.	1994	$5.00
Son Of Bazaak						
Singles						
		Change the Style	CDJ	U.S.		$2.00
Son of Slam						
Singles						
	1967	Trailer Park Politics	CD5	U.S.	1994	$5.00
Son Volt						
Singles						
	PRO-CD-7825	Drown	CDJ	U.S.		$2.00
	PRO-CD-8149	Loose String	CDJ	U.S.		$2.00
Sonia						
Singles						
IQ	ZD-44936	Be Young, Be Foolish, Be Happy	CD5	U.K.	1991	$8.00
IQ	664744	Be Young, Be Foolish, Be Happy	CD5	U.K.	1991	$8.00
Arista	74321-113462	Boogie Nights	CD5	U.K.	1992	$8.00
Chrysalis	662726	Can't Forget You	CD5	Germany	1989	$8.00
Chrysalis	CHSCD-3419	Can't Forget You	CD5	U.K.	1989	$8.00
Chrysalis	663175	Counting Every Minute	CD5	Germany	1990	$8.00
Chrysalis	CHSCD-3492	Counting Every Minute	CD5	U.K.	1990	$8.00
Chrysalis	323557-2	End of the World	CD5	Germany	1990	$8.00
Chrysalis	CHSCD-3557	End of the World	CD5	U.K.	1990	$8.00
Chrysalis	662924	Listen to Your Heart	CD5	Germany	1990	$8.00
Chrysalis	CHSCD-3465	Listen to Your Heart	CD5	U.K.	1990	$8.00
RCA	BVDP-52	Only Fools	CD3	Japan	1992	$13.00/$4.00
IQ	ZD-44614	Only Fools	CD5	U.K.	1991	$8.00
IQ	ZD-451522	You to Me Are Everything	CD5	U.K.	1992	$8.00
IQ	664937	You to Me Are Everything	CD5	U.K.	1992	$8.00
Chrysalis	162459	You'll Never Stop Me From Loving You	CD3	Germany	1989	$8.00
Chrysalis	662459	You'll Never Stop Me From Loving You	CD5	Germany	1989	$8.00
Chrysalis	XP10-2102	You'll Never Stop Me From Loving You	CD3	Japan	1989	$12.00/$4.00
Chrysalis	CHSCD-3385	You'll Never Stop Me From Loving You	CD5	U.K.	1989	$8.00
Sonia Dada						
Singles						
Capricorn	PRO 4037	Planes & Satelites	CDJ	U.S.		$3.00
Capricorn	PRO 1040	Screaming John	CDJ	U.S.		$3.00
Sonic Youth						
Full Length						
DGC	DGCD-24493	Dirty	LTD/LP	U.S.	1992	$20.00/$17.00
	Translucent orange tray with picture inside tray card.					
Pioneer Artists	PA-91-386	Goo That Lives On	LD	U.S.	1991	$30.00
Westwood One		In Concert-Nu Rock	RS	U.S.	1994	$50.00
	Airdate: 4/11/94.					
SST		Live	LP/BP	U.S.		$15.00/$10.00
		Screaming Fields of Sonic Love	DJ/Smplr	U.S.		$15.00
DGC	PRO-CD-4577	Screaming Fields of Sonic Love	DJ/Smplr	U.S.	1994	$20.00
SST		Sister	LP/BP	U.S.		$15.00/$10.00
Singles						
Geffen	GED 21735	100%	CD5	Germany	1992	$10.00
Geffen	MVCG-12002	100%	CD5	Japan	1992	$15.00
Geffen	DGCTD-11	100%	CD5	U.K.	1992	$10.00
Geffen	9 21735-2	100%	CD5	U.S.	1992	$5.00
Geffen	PRO-CD-4433	100%	CDJ	U.S.	1992	$6.00
DGC	PRO-CD-4638	Bull in the Heather	CD5	U.K.	1994	$10.00
Geffen	24511	Confusion is Sex	CD5	U.S.	1994	$5.00
Geffen	PRO-CD-4209	Dirty Boots	CDJ	U.S.	1991	$6.00
Geffen	9 21623-2	Disappearer	CD5	U.S.	1990	$5.00
Geffen	PRO-CD-4122	Disappearer	CDJ	U.S.	1990	$3.00
Efa	CD-79020	Kill Your Idols	CD5	Germany	1990	$10.00
Geffen	GEF-81CD	Kool Thing	CD5	U.K.	1990	$10.00
Geffen	PRO-CD-4123	Kool Thing	CDJ	U.S.	1990	$3.00
Geffen		Oz Tour Edition: Whore's Moaning	CD5	Australia	1993	$13.00
Geffen	DGCDM-21818	Sugar Kane	CD5	Canada	1993	$8.00
A&M	3458 8324 2	Superstar	CDJ	U.S.	1994	$7.00
	With one track by Bettie Serveert.					

Label	Catalog Number	Title	Type	Country	Year	Longbox Value / Value
Savage	RUFS 34CD	Teen Age Riot	CDJ	U.K.		$12.00
Geffen	GEFDM21783	Whore's Moaning	CDJ	Australia	1992	$15.00
Geffen	MVCG-13003	Youth Against Racism	CD3	Japan	1992	$12.00/$4.00
Geffen	GFSTD-26	Youth Against Racism	CD5	U.K.	1992	$10.00
Geffen	PRO-CD-4472	Youth Against Racism	CDJ	U.S.	1992	$6.00

Sonnier, Jo-el

Singles

Label	Catalog Number	Title	Type	Country	Year	Longbox Value / Value
		Baby Hold On	CDJ	U.S.		$2.00
Capitol	DPRO 79601	You May Change Your Mind	CDJ	U.S.	1991	$2.00

Sonny & Cher

Singles

Label	Catalog Number	Title	Type	Country	Year	Longbox Value / Value
WEA	786487-2	I Got You Babe	CD3	Germany	1989	$10.00
WEA	786487-2	I Got You Babe	CD3	U.K.	1989	$10.00

Sonora Veracruz

Singles

Label	Catalog Number	Title	Type	Country	Year	Longbox Value / Value
	1413	Salud Dinero Y Amor	CD5	U.S.	1994	$5.00

Sons Of Angels

Singles

Label	Catalog Number	Title	Type	Country	Year	Longbox Value / Value
Atlantic	AMDY-5018	Cowgirl	CD3	Japan	1990	$13.00/$3.00
		Cowgirl	CDJ	U.S.	1990	$2.00
Atlantic	PR 3521-2	Lonely Rose	CDJ	U.S.	1990	$2.00

Sons Of Soul

Singles

Label	Catalog Number	Title	Type	Country	Year	Longbox Value / Value
	CDPRO-RB-5001	Rainy Day	CDJ	U.S.	1995	$2.00

Sonz of a Loop Da Loop Era Scratchadelic Experience

Singles

Label	Catalog Number	Title	Type	Country	Year	Longbox Value / Value
Pyrotech	10093	Peace & Loveism	CD5	U.S.	1992	$5.00

Soraya

Singles

Label	Catalog Number	Title	Type	Country	Year	Longbox Value / Value
		Suddenly	CDJ	U.S.		$2.00

Sorted

Singles

Label	Catalog Number	Title	Type	Country	Year	Longbox Value / Value
PWL	234	Papa's Got A Brand New Pigbag	CD5	U.K.	1992	$8.00

Soul Asylum

Full Length

Label	Catalog Number	Title	Type	Country	Year	Longbox Value / Value
A&M	75021 8053 2	Horses They Rode in on...Plus Bonus Tracks	DJ/LP	U.S.	1989	$25.00
Westwood One		In Concert	RS	U.S.	1993	$50.00
	2 CD set.With School Of Fish, Airdate: 6/21/93.					
Westwood One		In Concert	RS	U.S.	1994	$60.00
	Airdate: 6/18/95.					
Westwood One		In Concert	RS	U.S.	1995	$60.00
	Airdate: 1/30/95.					
Westwood One		In Concert	RS	U.S.	1995	$60.00
	Airdate: 6/5/95.					
Westwood One		In Concert-Nu Rock	RS	U.S.	1994	$60.00
	Airdate: 5/9/94.					
Westwood One		In Concert-Nu Rock	RS	U.S.	1996	$45.00
Columbia	CDNK 918	Insomniac's Dream	DJ/Smplr	Canada	1993	$20.00
Media America		Up Close	RS	U.S.	1995	$30.00

Singles

Label	Catalog Number	Title	Type	Country	Year	Longbox Value / Value
		Black Gold	CD5	U.K.		$10.00
	Second version.					
CBS		Black Gold	CD5	U.K.	1993	$11.00
Columbia	CSK 4910	Black Gold	CDJ	U.S.	1993	$3.00
Columbia		Can't Even Tell	CDJ	U.S.	1995	$6.00
A&M	CD 17574	Cartoon	CDJ	U.S.	1988	$3.00
A&M	75021 7429 2	Easy Street	CDJ	U.S.	1989	$3.00
Columbia	CSK 7240	Just Life Anyone	CDJ	U.S.		$6.00
Columbia	CSK 7080	Misery	CDJ	U.S.		$6.00
Columbia	77960	Misery	CD5	U.S.	1995	$5.00
Columbia	77959	Misery	CD5	U.S.	1995	$6.00
Columbia	CSK 7080	Misery	CDJ	U.S.	1995	$10.00
		Promises Broken	CDJ	U.S.		$3.00
Columbia	CSK 7422	Promises Broken	CDJ	U.S.		$6.00
Columbia	44K 74947	Runaway Train	CD5	U.S.	1993	$6.00
Columbia	CSK 5016	Runaway Train	CDJ	U.S.	1993	$6.00
CBS	74947	Runaway Train	CD5	U.S.	1994	$5.00
		Somebody to Shove	CD5	U.K.		$10.00
		Somebody to Shove	CD5	U.K.		$10.00
	Second version.					
Columbia	PRO739	Somebody to Shove	CDJ	U.K.	1993	$14.00
Columbia	CSK 4730	Somebody to Shove	CDJ	U.S.	1993	$3.00
Columbia	CSK 4738	Somebody to Shove	CDJ	U.S.	1993	$3.00
A&M	75021 7498 2	Something out of Nothing	CDJ	U.S.	1991	$10.00
A&M	S10Y-3043	Sometime to Return	CD3	Japan	1988	$15.00/$3.00
A&M	75021 7423 2	Spinnin'	CDJ	U.S.	1990	$3.00
Columbia	CSK 5260	Summer of Drugs	CDJ	U.S.	1993	$3.00
Columbia	CSK 5274	Without a Trace	CDJ	U.S.	1993	$3.00

Soul Coughing

Singles

Label	Catalog Number	Title	Type	Country	Year	Longbox Value / Value
Warner Brothers	43582	Sugar Free Jazz	CD5	U.S.	1995	$5.00

Soul Family Sensation

Singles

Label	Catalog Number	Title	Type	Country	Year	Longbox Value / Value
Pinnacle	77TP7	Day You Went Away	CD5	U.K.	1992	$8.00

Soul For Real

Singles

Label	Catalog Number	Title	Type	Country	Year	Longbox Value / Value
MCA	54905	Candy Rain	CD5	U.S.	1994	$5.00
	UPT5P3335	Every Little Thing I Do	CDJ	U.S.		$2.00
	UPT5P3480	If You Want It	CDJ	U.S.		$2.00

Soul II Soul

Singles

Label	Catalog Number	Title	Type	Country	Year	Longbox Value / Value
Virgin	662374	Back to Life	CD3	Germany	1989	$9.00
Virgin	162374	Back to Life	CD3	Germany	1989	$9.00
Virgin	TENCD-265	Back to Life	CD3	U.K.	1989	$9.00
Virgin	663062	Dream a Little Dream	CD5	Germany	1990	$9.00
Virgin	VJDP-1407	Dream a Little Dream	CD5	Japan	1990	$13.00
Virgin	TENCD-300	Dream a Little Dream	CD5	U.K.	1990	$9.00
Virgin	PRCD 3344	Dream a Little Dream	CDJ	U.S.	1990	$2.00
Virgin	DREAM	Dream a Little Dream	CDJ	U.S.	1990	$2.00
Virgin	662867	Get a Life	CD5	Germany	1989	$8.00
Virgin	VJCP-1401	Get a Life	CD5	Japan	1990	$13.00
Virgin	TENCD-284	Get a Life	CD3	U.K.	1989	$8.00
Virgin	296481-2	Get a Life	CD5	U.S.	1990	$5.00
Virgin	PRCD 3256	Get a Life	CDJ	U.S.	1990	$2.00
Virgin	PRCD 3033	Jazzie's Groove	CDJ	U.S.	1989	$2.00
Virgin	TENDG-350	Joy	CD5	U.K.	1992	$9.00
Virgin	PRCD 4401	Joy	CDJ	U.S.	1992	$2.00
BMG	665048	Just Right	CD5	Germany	1992	$9.00
Virgin	TENDG-410	Just Right	CD5	U.K.	1992	$9.00
Virgin	162117	Keep on Movin'	CD3	Germany	1992	$9.00
Virgin	TENCD-263	Keep on Movin'	CD3	U.K.	1992	$9.00
Virgin	TENRCD-263	Keep on Movin'	CD5	U.K.	1992	$9.00
		Love Enough	CDJ	U.S.		$2.00
Virgin	VJCP-14018	Missing You	CD5	Japan	1991	$13.00
Virgin	TENCD-345	Missing You	CD5	U.K.	1990	$9.00
Virgin	PRCD 3600	Missing You	CDJ	U.S.	1990	$2.00
Tohiba	VJCP-14045	Move Me no Mountains	CD5	Japan	1992	$13.00
Virgin	TENG-400	Move Me no Mountains	CD5	U.K.	1992	$9.00
Virgin	PRCD 4628	Move Me no Mountains	CDJ	U.S.	1992	$2.00
Virgin	663428	People	CD5	Germany	1990	$9.00
Virgin	VJCP-1411	People	CD5	Japan	1990	$13.00
Virgin	PRCD 3470	People	CDJ	U.S.	1990	$2.00

Soul Kitchen

Singles

Label	Catalog Number	Title	Type	Country	Year	Longbox Value / Value
Giant	PRO-CD-5691	Rosie Jones	CDJ	U.S.	1992	$2.00

Sould Out International

Singles

Label	Catalog Number	Title	Type	Country	Year	Longbox Value / Value
Columbia	CSK 73926	Shine On	CDJ	U.S.	1991	$2.00

Souls Of Mischief

Singles

Label	Catalog Number	Title	Type	Country	Year	Longbox Value / Value
Jive	42256	Get The Girl	CD5	U.S.	1994	$5.00
Jive	42204-2-RDJ	Never no More	CDJ	U.S.	1994	$2.00

Soulsister

Singles

Label	Catalog Number	Title	Type	Country	Year	Longbox Value / Value
EMI	CDEM-133	Blame You	CD5	U.K.	1990	$8.00
		Blame You	CDJ	U.S.	1990	$2.00
EMI	119251-3	Like a Mountain	CD3	Germany	1989	$8.00
EMI	119312-2	Sweet Dreamer	CD5	Germany	1991	$8.00
EMI	119283-2	Through Before We Started	CD5	Germany	1990	$8.00
EMI	119239-2	Way to Your Heart, The	CD5	Germany	1989	$8.00
EMI	119239-2	Way to Your Heart, The	CD5	U.K.	1989	$8.00
EMI	119331-2	Way to Your Heart, The	CD5	U.S.	1989	$8.00
		Way to Your Heart, The	CDJ	U.S.	1989	$2.00
EMI	119311-2	Well Well Well	CD5	Germany	1991	$8.00
EMI	119311-2	Well Well Well	CD5	U.K.	1991	$8.00

Soultry

Singles

Label	Catalog Number	Title	Type	Country	Year	Longbox Value / Value
		Cash Money	CDJ	U.S.		$2.00
Motown	860474	Cash Money	CD5	U.S.	1995	$5.00
		I'll Get Mine	CDJ	U.S.		$2.00
Motown	860381	I'll Get Mine	CD5	U.S.	1995	$5.00
Motown	860474	Where Do Broken Hearts Belong	CD5	U.S.	1995	$5.00

Sound Barrier

Singles

Label	Catalog Number	Title	Type	Country	Year	Longbox Value / Value
Polygram	855671	Come and Get It	CD5	U.S.	1994	$5.00

Sound Factory

Singles

Label	Catalog Number	Title	Type	Country	Year	Longbox Value / Value
RCA	62569-2-RDJ	2 the Rhythm	CDJ	U.S.	1993	$2.00
RCA	62971-2	Come Take Control	CD5	U.S.	1994	$5.00
RCA	62839	Good Time	CD5	U.S.	1994	$5.00
Logic	62371-2	Understand This Groove	CD5	U.S.	1992	$5.00
Logic	62477-2-RDJ	Understand This Groove	CDJ	U.S.	1992	$2.00

Sound on Sound

Singles

Label	Catalog Number	Title	Type	Country	Year	Longbox Value / Value
Sire	9 40396-2	Time to Feel	CD5	U.S.	1992	$4.00

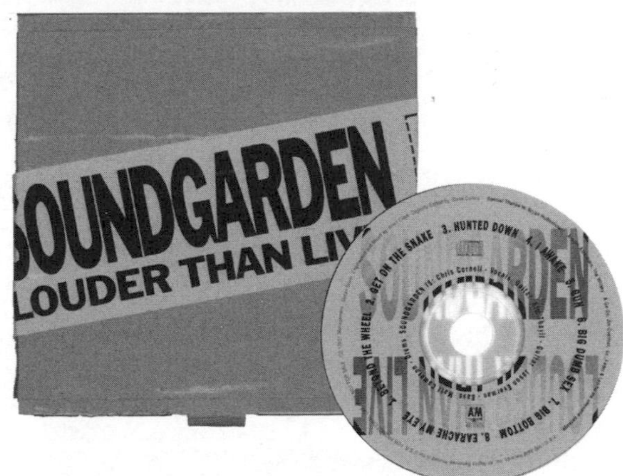

Soundgarden – Louder Than Live (A&M CD 17951) Special 1991 promotional sampler recorded live at the Whiskey in Los Angeles, California.

Soundgarden

Full Length

Label	Catalog Number	Title	Type	Country	Year	Longbox Value / Value
A&M	75021 54001 2	Badmotorfinger/Somms	LTD/LP	U.S.	1992	$45.00/$43.00
	2 CD set. CD of album plus bonus disc. With long box.					
A&M		Down on the Upside	LTD/LP	U.K.	1996	$35.00
	2 CD set.					
A&M	31454 8053--2	Foreshocks	DJ/Smplr	U.S.	1994	$75.00
Westwood One		In Concert	RS	U.S.	1995	$60.00
	Airdate: 7/3/95.					
A&M	AMSAD00223	Into the Upside	DJ/Intvw	U.S.	1996	$20.00

Soundgarden – Foreshocks (A&M 31454 8053 2)

Label	Catalog Number	Title	Type	Country	Year	Longbox Value / Value
A&M	CD 17951	Louder Than Live	DJ/Smplr	U.S.	1991	$40.00
	CD in a cardboard package wrapped with tape.					
A&M	CD 17843	Louder Than Love	DJ/LP	U.S.	1990	$45.00
	Picture disc.					
Westwood One		Off the Record	RS	U.S.	1994	$25.00
	Airdate: 11/7/94.					
Westwood One		Off the Record	RS	U.S.	1994	$25.00
	Airdate: 7/4/94.					
Westwood One		Spin Session	RS	U.S.	1996	$60.00
	2 CD set. Airdate: 8/5/96.					
A&M	31454 8056 2	Superinterview	DJ/Intw	U.S.	1994	$25.00
Media America		Up Close	RS	U.S.	1996	$30.00
		Singles				
A&M		Black Hole Sun	CD5	Germany	1994	$11.00
A&M		Black Hole Sun	CD5	Germany	1994	$11.00
	Second version.					
A&M		Black Hole Sun	CD5	U.K.	1994	$10.00
A&M		Black Hole Sun	CD5	U.K.	1994	$10.00
	Second version.					
A&M		Black Hole Sun	CDJ	U.S.	1994	$6.00
A&M	5805952	Day I Tried to Live, The	CDJ	U.K.	1994	$15.00
A&M		Day I Tried to Live, The	CDJ	U.S.	1994	$6.00
A&M		Fell on Black Days	CDJ	U.S.	1994	$6.00
A&M		Fell on Black Days	CDJ	U.S.	1994	$6.00
	Second version.					
SST	CD-16191	Flower	CD5	Germany	1989	$10.00
SST	SSTCD-231	Flower	CD5	U.K.	1989	$10.00
SST	SST-231	Flower	CD5	U.S.	1989	$6.00
A&M	CD 17811	Get on the Snake	CDJ	U.S.	1989	$3.00
A&M	CD 18029	Get on the Snake	CDJ	U.S.	1989	$3.00
A&M	AMCD-560	Hands All Over	CD5	U.K.	1990	$11.00
A&M	CD 17969	Hands All Over	CDJ	U.S.	1989	$3.00
A&M		Into the Void	CDJ	U.S.	1992	$15.00
A&M	75021 7284 2	Jesus Christ Pose	CDJ	U.S.	1994	$6.00
A&M	PCDY-10001	Loud Love	CD3	Japan	1989	$18.00/$5.00
A&M	AMCD-574	Loud Love	CD5	U.K.	1990	$11.00
A&M	CD 17893	Loud Love	CDJ	U.S.	1989	$3.00
A&M		My Wave	CD5	U.K.	1994	$10.00
		Outshined	CD5	U.K.		$10.00
		Outshined	CD5	U.K.		$10.00
	Second version.					
A&M	75021 7303-2	Outshined	CDJ	U.S.	1991	$3.00
A&M	75021 7309-2	Outshined	CDJ	U.S.	1991	$3.00
A&M	75021 7383-2	Outshined	CDJ	U.S.	1991	$3.00
		Pretty Noose	CDJ	U.S.		$3.00
A&M	AMCDP0029	Pretty Noose	CDJ	U.S.	1996	$7.00
A&M	AMCD 874	Rusty Cage	CD5	U.K.	1992	$10.00
A&M	75021 7334-2	Rusty Cage	CDJ	U.S.	1991	$7.00
A&M	75021 7342-2	Rusty Cage	CDJ	U.S.	1991	$7.00
A&M		Scenes From the Superunknown	CD5	U.S.	1995	$6.00
A&M	PCDY-1032	Spoonman	CD3	Japan	1994	$17.00/$5.00
A&M	5805392-DJ	Spoonman	CDJ	U.K.	1994	$15.00
A&M	31458 8248	Spoonman	CDJ	U.S.	1994	$7.00

Soundies

Full Length

Label	Catalog Number	Title	Type	Country	Year	Longbox Value / Value
Pioneer Artists	PA-90-330	Soundies	LD	U.S.	1990	$25.00

Sounds Of Blackness

Full Length

Label	Catalog Number	Title	Type	Country	Year	Longbox Value / Value
Perspective	31458 8064	Soul Holidays	DJ/Smplr	U.S.	1994	$10.00
		Singles				
Perspective	31458 8264	I Believe	CDJ	U.S.	1994	$2.00
Perspective	31458 8267	I Believe	CDJ	U.S.	1994	$2.00
Perspective	28968 1702	Optimistic	CDJ	U.S.	1991	$2.00

Sounds Of Life

Singles

Label	Catalog Number	Title	Type	Country	Year	Longbox Value / Value
	4503	Hush	CD5	U.S.	1994	$5.00

Soup Dragons

Full Length

Label	Catalog Number	Title	Type	Country	Year	Longbox Value / Value
Sire	PRO-CD-2965	Majestic Head?, The	DJ/Intvw	U.S.	1988	$7.00
		Singles				
Big Life	CDP 352	Backwards Dog	CDJ	U.S.	1990	$2.00
Big Life	BLRD-68	Divine Thing	CD5	U.K.	1992	$9.00
Polygram	867643-2	Electric Blues	CD5	Germany	1991	$9.00
Polygram	BLR D56	Electric Blues	CD5	U.K.	1991	$9.00
Polygram	877569-2	I'm Free	CD5	Germany	1990	$9.00
Big Life	RTV-9CD	I'm Free	CD5	U.K.	1990	$9.00
Big Life	877 843-2	I'm Free	CD5	U.S.	1990	$5.00
Big Life	CDP 308	I'm Free	CDJ	U.S.	1990	$2.00
Big Life	879141-2	Mother Universe	CD5	Germany	1990	$9.00
Big Life	RTV-8CD	Mother Universe	CD5	U.K.	1990	$9.00
Big Life	879141-2	Mother Universe	CD5	U.K.	1990	$9.00
Mercury	CDP 380	Mother Universe	CDJ	U.S.	1991	$2.00
		Pleasure	CD5	U.K.		$10.00
		Pleasure	CD5	U.K.		$10.00
	Second version.					
Mercury	CDP 721	Pleasure	CDJ	U.S.	1993	$2.00
Mercury	CDP 801	Running Wild	CDJ	U.S.	1992	$2.00

South Central Cartel

Singles

Label	Catalog Number	Title	Type	Country	Year	Longbox Value / Value
DJ West	77368	Gang Stories	CDJ	U.S.	1994	$2.00
Pump	19125	Papa Was A Rolling Stone	CDJ	U.S.	1992	$2.00
G.W.K.		U Gotta Deal With Dis	CDJ	U.S.	1991	$2.00

Souther, J.D.

Full Lengthq

Label	Catalog Number	Title	Type	Country	Year	Longbox Value / Value
		20 Songs	DJ/Smplr	U.S.	1994	$25.00

Southern Culture on the Skids

Singles

Label	Catalog Number	Title	Type	Country	Year	Longbox Value / Value
		Camel Walk	CDJ	U.S.		$2.00
		Soul City	CD5	U.K.	1996	$10.00

Southern Pacific

Full Length

Label	Catalog Number	Title	Type	Country	Year	Longbox Value / Value
Warner Brothers	PRO-CD-3374	6 Singles	DJ/Smplr	U.S.	1988	$6.00
		Singles				
Warner Brothers		All Is Lost	CDJ	U.S.		$2.00
Warner Brothers	PRO-CD-4015	I Go to Pieces	CDJ	U.S.	1990	$2.00
Warner Brothers	PRO-CD-4525	Memphis Queen	CDJ	U.S.	1990	$2.00
Warner Brothers	PRO-CD-3498	Never Givin' Up	CDJ	U.S.	1989	$2.00
Warner Brothers	PRO-CD-4342	Side Saddle	CDJ	U.S.	1989	$2.00

Southon, Sonny

Singles

Label	Catalog Number	Title	Type	Country	Year	Longbox Value / Value
		Another Day	CDJ	U.S.		$2.00
Siren	SRNCD-132	Don't Hold Back	CD5	U.K.	1991	$8.00
Toshiba	VJDP-136	Falling Through a Cloud	CD3	Japan	1990	$13.00/$4.00
Siren	SRNCD-128	Falling Through a Cloud	CD5	U.K.	1990	$8.00
Siren	SRNCD-135	I Don't Come Any Other Way	CD5	U.K.	1990	$8.00

Southside Johnny

Singles

Label	Catalog Number	Title	Type	Country	Year	Longbox Value / Value
RCA	PD-42844	Ain't That Peculiar	CD5	U.K.	1989	$10.00
A&M	CD 17637	Ain't That Peculiar	CDJ	U.S.	1988	$2.00
Impact	CDEM-224	Coming Back	CD5	U.K.	1992	$10.00
Impact	2123	Coming Back	CDJ	U.S.	1991	$2.00
Impact	2120	I've Been Working Hard	CDJ	U.S.	1991	$2.00
Impact	7455027-2	It's Been a Long Time	CD5	Germany	1991	$10.00
Impact	CDEM-211	It's Been a Long Time	CD5	U.K.	1991	$10.00
Impact	1688	It's Been a Long Time	CDJ	U.S.	1991	$2.00
Album Network	JUKEUP1	It's Been a Long Time	CDJ	U.S.	1991	$6.00
Cypress	YD 17705	Little Calcutta	CDJ	U.S.	1989	$2.00
RCA	PD-42618	On the Air Tonight	CD5	Germany	1989	$10.00
RCA	PD-42618	On the Air Tonight	CD5	U.K.	1989	$10.00
Cypress	YD 17820	Your Precious Love	CDJ	U.S.	1989	$2.00

Space Cowboys

Singles

Label	Catalog Number	Title	Type	Country	Year	Longbox Value / Value
Rough Trade	RTD 195 1383 3	You Got Me Goin'	CDJ	U.S.	1992	$2.00

Spacehog

Singles

Label	Catalog Number	Title	Type	Country	Year	Longbox Value / Value
	PRCD 9476	Hamsters of Rock	CDJ	U.S.		$3.00
Sire	EKR218CDX	In the Meantime	CD5	U.K.	1996	$12.00/$15.00
	3-D id picture disc and front sleeve.					
	PRCD 93142	In the Meantime	CDJ	U.S.		$3.00
	PRCD93132	Was It Likely?	CDJ	U.S.		$3.00

Spacemen 3

Singles

Label	Catalog Number	Title	Type	Country	Year	Longbox Value / Value
Fire	ZD-44328	Big City	CD3	Germany	1989	$8.00
Fire	BLAZE-41CD	Big City	CD3	U.K.	1989	$8.00
RCA	2801-2-RDJ	Big City	CDJ	U.S.	1991	$2.00
Fire	BLAZE-36CD	Hypnotize My Soul	CD3	U.K.	1989	$8.00
Fire	BLAZE-29CD	Revolution	CD3	U.K.	1989	$8.00

Spaghetti Surfers

Singles

Label	Catalog Number	Title	Type	Country	Year	Longbox Value / Value
Curb	CURBD1200	Misirlou	CDJ	U.S.		$6.00

Spagna

Full Length

Label	Catalog Number	Title	Type	Country	Year	Longbox Value / Value
		Siamo in Due	LTD/LP	Italy		$30.00

Spandau Ballet

Full Length

Label	Catalog Number	Title	Type	Country	Year	Longbox Value / Value
Vestron	LV1072	Spandau Ballet	LD	U.S.	1987	$30.00
Chrysalis		True	LTD/LP	U.K.	1994	$25.00/$15.00
	25th Anniversary edition in 6"x11" longbox.					
Chrysalis	VK-41403	True	LP/LB	U.S.†	1985	$14.00/$8.00
		Singles				
Columbia	654865-3	Be Free With Your Love	CD3	Germany	1989	$8.00
Columbia	SPANSC-4	Be Free With Your Love	CD5	U.K.	1989	$8.00
Columbia	SPANSC-6	Crashed Into Love	CD5	U.K.	1990	$8.00
Columbia	655455-3	Empty Space	CD3	Germany	1989	$8.00
Columbia	SPANSC-5	Empty Space	CD5	U.K.	1989	$8.00
Columbia	SPANSD-5	Empty Space	CD5	U.K.	1989	$8.00
Columbia	652959-3	Raw	CD3	Germany	1988	$8.00
Columbia	SPANSC-3	Raw	CD5	U.K.	1988	$8.00
Columbia	655577-3	Through the Barricades	CD3	Germany	1990	$8.00
Columbia	655577-2	Through the Barricades	CD5	Germany	1990	$8.00
Chrysalis	323793-2	True	CD5	Germany	1991	$8.00
Chrysalis	CHSCD-3793	True	CD5	U.K.	1991	$8.00

Spanic

Singles

Label	Catalog Number	Title	Type	Country	Year	Longbox Value / Value
ZYX	7386	Sister Golden Hair	CD5	U.S.	1994	$5.00

Spanish Fly

Singles

Label	Catalog Number	Title	Type	Country	Year	Longbox Value / Value
	PRO-CD-7988-R	Believe in Me	CDJ	U.S.		$2.00
	PRO-CD-7547-R	Crimson and Clover	CDJ	U.S.	1995	$2.00
Upstairs Records	108	Daddy's Home	CD5	U.S.	1994	$5.00
Warner Brothers	17876	Daddy's Home	CD5	U.S.	1994	$5.00
	PRO-CD-7619-R	Daddy's Home	CDJ	U.S.	1995	$2.00

Spann, Otis and Lightnin' Hopkins

Full Length

Label	Catalog Number	Title	Type	Country	Year	Longbox Value / Value
Mosaic	MD3-139	Complete Candid Recording of Otis Spann And Lightnin' Hopkins	LTD/LP	U.S.		$45.00
	3 CD set.					

Sparbanie, Keith

Singles

Label	Catalog Number	Title	Type	Country	Year	Longbox Value / Value
KDS	CD3101	Hard to Say No	DJ/CD3	U.S.	1989	$5.00

Spark

Singles

Label	Catalog Number	Title	Type	Country	Year	Longbox Value / Value
		Beat the Clock	CD5	Germany	1996	$10.00
		No. 1 In Heaven	CD5	Germany	1996	$13.00

Sparkle Horse

Singles

Label	Catalog Number	Title	Type	Country	Year	Longbox Value / Value
		Someday I Will Treat You Good	CDJ	U.S.		$2.00

Sparks

Singles

Label	Catalog Number	Title	Type	Country	Year	Longbox Value / Value
	59007	When Do I Get To	CD5	U.S.	1994	$5.00

Spazz

Singles

Label	Catalog Number	Title	Type	Country	Year	Longbox Value / Value
Selfless Records	36	Dwarf Jester Rising	CD5	U.S.	1994	$5.00

Spear of Destiny

Singles

Label	Catalog Number	Title	Type	Country	Year	Longbox Value / Value
Virgin	CDT 14	Never Take Me Alive	CD3	U.K.	1987	$8.00
Virgin	7 50119-6	Never Take Me Alive	CD5	U.K.	1987	$8.00

Spearhead

Full Length

Label	Catalog Number	Title	Type	Country	Year	Longbox Value / Value
		Live Radio Sessions	DJ/Smplr	U.S.		$5.00
		Live Radio Show, The	DJ/Smplr	U.S.		$8.00

Singles

Label	Catalog Number	Title	Type	Country	Year	Longbox Value / Value
Capital	58379	Hole in the Bucket	CD5	U.S.	1994	$5.00
Capitol	58379	Hole in the Bucket	CD5	U.S.	1995	$6.00
		Home	CDJ	U.S.		$3.00
Capital	58270	People in the Middle	CD5	U.S.	1994	$5.00
		Positive	CDJ	U.S.		$3.00
Capitol	48582	Positive	CD5	U.S.	1995	$5.00

Special EFX

Full Length

Label	Catalog Number	Title	Type	Country	Year	Longbox Value / Value
GRP	GRP D-9505	Special Effects	LP/LB	U.S.†	1985	$14.00/$8.00

Special Generation

Singles

Label	Catalog Number	Title	Type	Country	Year	Longbox Value / Value
		Love Me Just for Me	CDJ	U.S.		$2.00
Bust it	79499	Love Me Just for Me	CDJ	U.S.	1992	$2.00
Bust It	79690	Right One, The	CDJ	U.S.	1992	$2.00

Specials

Full Length

Label	Catalog Number	Title	Type	Country	Year	Longbox Value / Value
Chrysalis		Specials, The	LTD/LP	U.K.	1994	$15.00

25th Anniversary edition in 6"x11" longbox.

Spector, Phil

Full Length

Label	Catalog Number	Title	Type	Country	Year	Longbox Value / Value
ABKCO	28 XE-1	A Christmas Gift for You	LP	Japan	1986	$100.00
ABKCO	711831	Back to Mono (1958-1969)	DJ/Smplr	U.S.	1991	$15.00

Various artists.

Label	Catalog Number	Title	Type	Country	Year	Longbox Value / Value
	PHLP-5000X	Rare Masters	DJ/Smplr	Japan		$70.00

Singles

Label	Catalog Number	Title	Type	Country	Year	Longbox Value / Value
ABKCO	711832	A Christmas Gift for You	CDJ	U.S.	1991	$8.00

Speech

Singles

Label	Catalog Number	Title	Type	Country	Year	Longbox Value / Value
		Like Marvin Said	CDJ	U.S.		$2.00

Speedball Baby

Singles

Label	Catalog Number	Title	Type	Country	Year	Longbox Value / Value
Matador	18	Speedball Baby	CD5	U.S.	1994	$5.00

Spelvins

Singles

Label	Catalog Number	Title	Type	Country	Year	Longbox Value / Value
Zoo	ZD-17143	Don't You Love Me Anymore	CDJ	U.S.	1993	$2.00

Spence, Brian

Singles

Label	Catalog Number	Title	Type	Country	Year	Longbox Value / Value
Polydor	PZCD-12	Come Back Home	CD5	U.K.	1988	$8.00
		Come Back Home	CDJ	U.S.	1988	$2.00
Polydor	POCD-916	Reputation	CD5	U.K.	1988	$8.00
Chrysalis	662999	Traveling Man	CD5	Germany	1990	$8.00

Spence, Judson

Singles

Label	Catalog Number	Title	Type	Country	Year	Longbox Value / Value
Atlantic	PR 2477-2	Hot & Sweaty	CDJ	U.S.	1988	$2.00
Atlantic	AMDY-5080	I Can't Pretend	CD3	Japan	1992	$12.00/$4.00
Atlantic	A-8950CD	If You Don't Like It	CD3	U.K.	1989	$8.00
Pioneer	09P3-6114	Love Dies in Slow Motion	CD3	Japan	1989	$12.00/$4.00
		Love Dies in Slow Motion	CDJ	U.S.	1989	$2.00
Atlantic	10P3-6089	Yeah, Yeah, Yeah	CD3	Japan	1989	$12.00/$4.00
Atlantic	A-8999CD	Yeah, Yeah, Yeah	CD3	U.K.	1988	$8.00
		Yeah, Yeah, Yeah	CDJ	U.S.	1988	$2.00

Spencer Davis Group

Full Length

Label	Catalog Number	Title	Type	Country	Year	Longbox Value / Value
Capitol	CDP-91834-2	Best of	LP/LB	U.S.		$17.00/$14.00

Singles

Label	Catalog Number	Title	Type	Country	Year	Longbox Value / Value
Island	887179	Keep On Running	CD5	Germany	1991	$10.00
Island	CID-487	Keep On Running	CD5	U.K.	1991	$10.00

Spencer, J.

Singles

Label	Catalog Number	Title	Type	Country	Year	Longbox Value / Value
Mojazz	3746311442	Thinkin' About You	CDJ	U.S.	1993	$2.00
Motown	860362	U Should Be Mine	CD5	U.S.	1995	$5.00

Spencer, Tracie

Singles

Label	Catalog Number	Title	Type	Country	Year	Longbox Value / Value
EMI	203047-2	Imagine	CD5	Germany	1988	$8.00
Capitol	DPRO-79152	Love Me	CDJ	U.S.		$2.00
Capitol	TODP-2292	Make It Funky	CD3	Japan	1991	$13.00/$4.00
EMI	203998-2	Save Your Love	CD5	Germany	1990	$8.00
Capitol	DPRO-79179	Save Your Love	CDJ	U.S.	1990	$2.00
Capitol		Save Your Love	CDJ	U.S.	1990	$2.00

Second version.

Label	Catalog Number	Title	Type	Country	Year	Longbox Value / Value
EMI	202591-2	Symptoms of True Love	CD5	Germany	1988	$8.00
Toshiba	XP10-2018	Symptoms of True Love	CD3	Japan	1988	$13.00/$4.00
EMI	204228-2	This House	CD5	Germany	1991	$8.00
EMI	204229-2	This House	CD5	Germany	1991	$8.00
Toshiba	TODP-2270	This House	CD3	Japan	1991	$13.00/$4.00
Capitol	CDCL-612	This House	CD5	U.K.	1991	$8.00
Capitol	CDCL-621	This Time Make It Funny	CD5	U.K.	1991	$8.00

Spent Poets

Singles

Label	Catalog Number	Title	Type	Country	Year	Longbox Value / Value
Geffen	PRO-CD-4392	Dogtown	CDJ	U.S.	1992	$2.00

Spheeris, Chris

Singles

Label	Catalog Number	Title	Type	Country	Year	Longbox Value / Value
		Where the Angels Fly	CDJ	U.S.		$2.00

Spice 1

Singles

Label	Catalog Number	Title	Type	Country	Year	Longbox Value / Value
Jive	42040-2-JDJ	187 Proof	CDJ	U.S.	1991	$2.00
Jive	42057-2-JDJ	In My Neighborhood	CDJ	U.S.	1992	$2.00
Jive	42084-2-JDJ	Welcome to the Ghetto	CDJ	U.S.	1991	$2.00

Spice Girls

Singles

Label	Catalog Number	Title	Type	Country	Year	Longbox Value / Value
Virgin	38579-2	Wannabe	CD5	U.S.	1997	$5.00

Spin

Singles

Label	Catalog Number	Title	Type	Country	Year	Longbox Value / Value
Foundation	TFL 7CD	Scratches	CD5	U.K.	1990	$8.00

Spin Doctors

Full Length

Label	Catalog Number	Title	Type	Country	Year	Longbox Value / Value
Westwood One		In Concert	RS	U.S.	1993	$50.00

2 CD set. With Blind Melon, Airdate: 8/16/93

Label	Catalog Number	Title	Type	Country	Year	Longbox Value / Value
Westwood One		In Concert	RS	U.S.	1994	$40.00

2 CD set. Airdate: 3/14/94.

Label	Catalog Number	Title	Type	Country	Year	Longbox Value / Value
Westwood One		In Concert	RS	U.S.	1994	$50.00

Airdate: 8/29/95.

Label	Catalog Number	Title	Type	Country	Year	Longbox Value / Value
Westwood One		In Concert	RS	U.S.	1995	$50.00

Airdate: 1/30/95.

Label	Catalog Number	Title	Type	Country	Year	Longbox Value / Value
Westwood One		In Concert-Nu Rock	RS	U.S.	1994	$50.00

Airdate: 8/15/94.

Label	Catalog Number	Title	Type	Country	Year	Longbox Value / Value
Epic		Pocket Full of Kryptonite	DJ/LP	U.S.	1992	$22.00

CD in green bag with cassette and press kit.

Label	Catalog Number	Title	Type	Country	Year	Longbox Value / Value
Epic		Six Pack	DJ/Smplr	Canada	1994	$23.00
Media America		Up Close	RS	U.S.	1994	$40.00
Media America		Up Close	RS	U.S.	1996	$25.00
Epic	ZK 46981	Up for Grabs	LP/LB	U.S.	1991	$14.00/$8.00

Singles

Label	Catalog Number	Title	Type	Country	Year	Longbox Value / Value
Epic		Cleopatra's Cat	CD5	Germany	1994	$10.00
Epic	ESK 77525	Cleopatra's Cat	CDJ	U.S.	1994	$3.00
Epic	ESK 74910	How Could You Want Him	CDJ	U.S.		$3.00
Epic	659180	Jimmy Olsen Blues	CD5	Germany	1991	$10.00
Epic	659758	Jimmy Olsen Blues	CD5	Germany	1991	$10.00
Epic	ESK 4658	Jimmy Olsen Blues	CDJ	U.S.	1992	$3.00
Epic		Let Your Heart Go Too Fast	CDJ	U.S.	1994	$6.00
Epic	658489-2	Little Miss Can't Be Wrong	CD5	U.K.	1993	$10.00
Epic	ESK 4845	Little Miss Can't Be Wrong	CDJ	U.S.	1992	$3.00
Epic	ESK 6546	Mary Jane	CDJ	U.S.		$3.00
Epic	ESK 7715	She Used To Be Mine	CDJ	U.S.		$3.00
Epic	659145-2	Two Princes	CD5	Germany	1992	$10.00
Epic	ESK 74804	Two Princes	CDJ	U.S.	1992	$3.00
Epic	659683	What Time Is It?	CD5	Germany	1991	$10.00
Epic	ESK 5112	What Time Is It?	CDJ	U.S.		$3.00
Epic		You Let Your Heart Go too Far	CD5	U.K.	1994	$10.00
Epic	ESK 77600	You Let Your Heart Go too Far	CDJ	U.S.		$3.00
Epic		You Make Your Heart Go Too Fast	CD5	U.K.	1994	$10.00

Second version.

Spinal Tap

Full Length

Label	Catalog Number	Title	Type	Country	Year	Longbox Value / Value
		Break the Wind	8"LD	U.S.		$12.00

Singles

Label	Catalog Number	Title	Type	Country	Year	Longbox Value / Value
MCA	1624	Bitch School	CD5	U.K.	1992	$10.00
MCA	MCA5P-2169	Bitch School	CDJ	U.S.	1992	$3.00
MCA	MCA5P-2185	Majesty of Rock	CDJ	U.S.	1992	$3.00

Spinanes

Singles

Label	Catalog Number	Title	Type	Country	Year	Longbox Value / Value
Sub Pop	21	Noel, Jonah and Me	CDJ	U.S.		$3.00

Spinners

Singles

Label	Catalog Number	Title	Type	Country	Year	Longbox Value / Value
Atlantic	7567-86514-2	Working My Way Back To You	CD3	Germany	1989	$10.00
Atlantic	7567-86514-2	Working My Way Back To You	CD3	U.K.	1989	$10.00

Spirea X

Singles

Label	Catalog Number	Title	Type	Country	Year	Longbox Value / Value
4AD	BAD 1004CD	Chlorine Dream	CD5	U.K.	1991	$8.00
4AD	BAD 1006CD	Speed Reaction	CD5	U.K.	1991	$8.00
4AD	PRO-CD-5547	Speed Reaction	CDJ	U.S.	1991	$2.00

Spirit

Full Length

Label	Catalog Number	Title	Type	Country	Year	Longbox Value / Value
Crew		Chronicles	LP	Canada		$13.00
CBS		I've Got a Line On You	LP/LB	U.S.		$14.00/$8.00
Crew	22002	Nature's Way	DJ/Intvw	U.S.	1991	$13.00
IRS	82007	Rapture in the Chamber	LP/LB	U.S.	1989	$14.00/$8.00
Dolphin	22001	Tent of Miracles	LP/LB	U.S.	1990	$14.00/$8.00

Spirit Gum

Singles

Label	Catalog Number	Title	Type	Country	Year	Longbox Value / Value
		Climb out of Your Skull	CDJ	U.S.		$2.00

Spirit Of The West

Singles

Label	Catalog Number	Title	Type	Country	Year	Longbox Value / Value
Elektra	PRCD 8933-2	And If Venice Is Shaking	CDJ	U.S.	1994	$2.00

Spirits

Singles

Label	Catalog Number	Title	Type	Country	Year	Longbox Value / Value
MCA	54968	Don't Bring Me Down	CD5	U.S.	1994	$5.00

Spiritualized

Full Length

Label	Catalog Number	Title	Type	Country	Year	Longbox Value / Value
RCA		Lay Back in the Sun	DJ/Smplr	U.K.	1994	$15.00

Singles

Label	Catalog Number	Title	Type	Country	Year	Longbox Value / Value
RCA	62327-2-RDJ	I Want You	CDJ	U.S.	1992	$3.00
RCA	62327-2-RDJ	Run	CDJ	U.S.	1992	$3.00

Spiritualized Electronic Machine

Full Length

Label	Catalog Number	Title	Type	Country	Year	Longbox Value / Value
Arista		Pure Phase	LTD/LP	U.S.	1996	$22.00
	CD in plastic glow-box.					

Spit

Singles

Label	Catalog Number	Title	Type	Country	Year	Longbox Value / Value
	59	You Would If You Lo	CD5	U.S.	1994	$5.00

Splash

Singles

Label	Catalog Number	Title	Type	Country	Year	Longbox Value / Value
Grudge	4753	Dizzy Miss Lizzy	CDJ	U.S.	1989	$2.00
WEA	171600-2	I Need Rhythm	CD5	Germany	1990	$8.00
WEA	173038-2	I Need Rhythm	CD5	Germany	1990	$8.00
WEA	172125-2	I Need Rhythm	CD5	Germany	1990	$8.00
WEA	YZ-515CD	I Need Rhythm	CD5	U.K.	1990	$8.00
WEA	175530-2	Joy & Pain	CD5	Germany	1991	$8.00
WEA	173336-2	Set the Groove on Fire	CD5	Germany	1990	$8.00

Split Endz

Full Length

Label	Catalog Number	Title	Type	Country	Year	Longbox Value / Value
A&M	CD-4963	Conflicting Emotion	LP/LB	U.S.†	1984	$14.00/$8.00
Warner Brothers	23886-2	Hello Big Man	LP/LB	U.S.†	1984	$14.00/$8.00
A&M	CD-4822	True Colors	LP/LB	U.S.†	1984	$14.00/$8.00

Sponge

Full Length

Label	Catalog Number	Title	Type	Country	Year	Longbox Value / Value
Westwood One		In Concert	RS	U.S.	1995	$40.00
	Airdate: 7/31/95.					
Westwood One		In Concert	RS	U.S.	1996	$40.00
	Airdate: 2/26/96.					
Westwood One		In Concert-Nu Rock	RS	U.S.	1995	$40.00
	Airdate: 8/14/95.					
Westwood One		In Concert-Nu Rock	RS	U.S.	1996	$45.00
	Airdate: 5/6/96.					
		Wax Ecstatic	DJ/LP	U.S.	1995	$15.00
	Airdate: 8/14/95.					

Singles

Label	Catalog Number	Title	Type	Country	Year	Longbox Value / Value
	OSK 6941	Molly	CDJ	U.S.	1995	$2.00
	OSK 6257	Neenah Mensha	CDJ	U.S.	1995	$3.00
	OSK 6535	Plowed	CDJ	U.S.	1995	$3.00

Spooky Teeth

Full Length

Label	Catalog Number	Title	Type	Country	Year	Longbox Value / Value
Charisma		Mirror	LP	Germany		$10.00

Spoons

Singles

Label	Catalog Number	Title	Type	Country	Year	Longbox Value / Value
Anthem	PRO2	Waterline	CDJ	Canada		$15.00

Spot 109

Full Length

Label	Catalog Number	Title	Type	Country	Year	Longbox Value / Value
Frontier	34634	Promo For 10/22/91	DJ/LP	U.S.	1991	$14.00
	Also with tracks by This World Owes Me A Buzz.					

Spread Eagle

Full Length

Label	Catalog Number	Title	Type	Country	Year	Longbox Value / Value
		Sampler	DJ/Smplr	U.S.		$4.00

Singles

Label	Catalog Number	Title	Type	Country	Year	Longbox Value / Value
MCA	CD45 1077	Back on the Bitch	CDJ	U.S.	1990	$2.00
		Suzy Suicide	CDJ	U.S.		$2.00
		Switchblade	CDJ	U.S.		$2.00
	Second version.					

Springer, Dennis

Singles

Label	Catalog Number	Title	Type	Country	Year	Longbox Value / Value
Nasty Mix	NMJ 70310-2	Rio	CDJ	U.S.	1991	$2.00

Springfield, Dusty

Singles

Label	Catalog Number	Title	Type	Country	Year	Longbox Value / Value
Parlophone	204033-2	Arrested by You	CD5	Germany	1990	$8.00
Parlophone	CDR-6266	Arrested by You	CD5	U.K.	1990	$8.00
Polygram	888970-2	Don't Have to	CD5	Germany	1990	$8.00
EMI	203618-3	In Private	CD3	Germany	1989	$8.00
EMI	203669-3	In Private	CD5	Germany	1989	$8.00
Parlophone	CDR-6234	In Private	CD5	U.K.	1989	$8.00
Parlophone	203238-2	Nothing Has Been Proved	CD5	Germany	1989	$8.00
Toshiba	XP10-2086	Nothing Has Been Proved	CD3	Japan	1989	$13.00/$4.00
Parlophone	CDR-6207	Nothing Has Been Proved	CD5	U.K.	1989	$8.00
Enigma	EPRO-181	Nothing Has Been Proved	CDJ	U.S.	1989	$6.00
Parlophone	203845-2	Reputation	CD5	Germany	1990	$8.00
Parlophone	203901-2	Reputation	CD5	Germany	1990	$8.00
Parlophone	CDR-6253	Reputation	CD5	U.K.	1990	$8.00
Parlophone	CDR-6163	What Have I Done to Deserve This	CD5	U.K.	1990	$10.00

Springfield, Larry

Singles

Label	Catalog Number	Title	Type	Country	Year	Longbox Value / Value
Tabu	28965 1806	Stand by Woman	CDJ	U.S.	1992	$2.00

Springfield, Rick

Full Length

Label	Catalog Number	Title	Type	Country	Year	Longbox Value / Value
Pioneer	PA-86-155	Beat of the Live Drum	LD	U.S.	1986	$25.00
Mercury	824107-2	Beautiful Feelings	LP/BP	U.S.†	1985	$12.00/$7.00
RCA	PCD1-4660	Living in Oz	LP/BP	U.S.†	1984	$12.00/$7.00
Pioneer	PA-85-128	Platinum Videos	LD	U.S.	1985	$20.00
Pioneer	PA-85-128	Platinum Videos	LD	U.S.	1990	$20.00
	Digital audio.					
RCA	PD-84125	Success Hasn't Spoiled Me Yet	LP	Germany		$10.00
RCA	PD-84125	Success Hasn't Spoiled Me Yet	LP	U.K.		$10.00
RCA	PCD1-5370	Tao	LP/BP	U.S.†	1985	$12.00/$7.00
RCA	PCD1-3697	Working Class Dog	LP/BP	U.S.†	1985	$12.00/$7.00

Singles

Label	Catalog Number	Title	Type	Country	Year	Longbox Value / Value
RCA	R10D-1	Rock of Life	CD3	Japan	1988	$12.00/$4.00
RCA	PD-49606	Rock of Life	CD3	U.K.	1988	$9.00

Springhouse

Singles

Label	Catalog Number	Title	Type	Country	Year	Longbox Value / Value
Caroline	CAROL 1466	Eskimo	CD5	U.S.	1991	$5.00

Springsteen, Bruce

Full Length

Label	Catalog Number	Title	Type	Country	Year	Longbox Value / Value
Columbia	CDNK 677	1992 Sampler	DJ/Smplr	Canada	1992	$45.00
CBS	XDDP-93084	1992 Sampler	DJ/Smplr	Japan	1992	$150.00
	PLR-003	American Babylon	DJ/Intvw	U.K.	1995	$60.00
	Interview with Springsteen and Joe Grushecky.					
Columbia		Blood Brothers	LTD/LP	U.S.	1996	$20.00
	CD EP and VHS video in blister pak.					
Sony	SRCS-7908	Born in the U.S.A.	LTD/LP	Japan	1996	$35.00
	20 Bit mastering.					
CBS	CK-38653	Born in the U.S.A.	LP/BP	U.S.†	1983	$14.00/$8.00
Columbia	CK 38653	Born in the U.S.A.	DJ/LP	U.S.	1984	N/A
	First U.S.-made CD.					
Sony	SRCS-6679	Born to Run	LTD/LP	Japan	1992	$35.00
	Gold disc.					
Sony	SRCS-7907	Born to Run	LTD/LP	Japan	1996	$35.00
	20 Bit mastering.					
CBS	CK-33795	Born to Run	LP/BP	U.S.†	1983	$14.00/$8.00
Columbia	CK 52859	Born to Run	LP/LB	U.S.	1992	$28.00/$25.00
	First issue gold disc with tracking problem on "Born To Run."					
CBS	CK-35318	Darkness on the Edge of Town	LP/BP	U.S.†	1983	$14.00/$8.00
Sony		Future of Rock & Roll '70s To '80s, The	DJ/Smplr	Japan	1990	N/A
	2 CD set.					
Columbia	ACK 67060	Greatest Hits	DJ/LP	U.S.	1995	$50.00
CBS	CK-31903	Greetings From Asbury Park	LP/BP	U.S.†	1985	$14.00/$8.00
Columbia	471423 2	Human Touch	LTD/LP	U.K.	1992	$25.00
	Picture disc CD.					
CBS	XDDP 93084	Human Touch/Lucky Town	DJ/Smplr	Japan	1992	$150.00
CBS		In Concert: MTV Plugged	LP	U.K.	1993	$26.00
Columbia	C3K 40558	Live 1975-1985	LP	U.S.	1986	$45.00
	3 CD set in 12"x12" boxed set. configuration deleted in '92.					
Columbia	C3K 40558	Live 1975-85	LP	U.S.	1986	$55.00
	12"x12" box version.					
Columbia	471424-2	Lucky Town	LTD/LP	Germany	1992	$25.00
	Picture disc CD version.					
Columbia	471424 9	Lucky Town	LTD/LP	U.K.	1992	$25.00
	Picture disc CD.					
CBS	CK 38358	Nebraska	LP/BP	U.S.†	1983	$80.00/$80.00
	First pressing with extended version of "My Father's House."					
CBS	C2K-36854	River, The	LP/LB	U.S.†	1985	$22.00/$16.00
	2 CD set.					
CBS	SAMPCD 3066	Tom Joad	DJ/LP	Holland	1995	$40.00
CBS	460270 9	Tunnel of Love	LP/BP	Germany	1988	$20.00/$20.00
	Picture disc.					
CBS	30DP-900	Tunnel of Love	LTD/LP	Japan	1988	$35.00
	Picture disc CD.					
CBS	460270 9	Tunnel of Love	LP/BP	U.K.	1988	$20.00/$20.00
	Picture disc.					
Columbia	CSK 1046	Tunnel of Love Tour CD	DJ/Smplr	U.S.	1988	$35.00
Columbia	CSK 1108	Tunnel of Love Tour Cont.	DJ/Smplr	U.S.	1988	$45.00
CBS	CK-38653	Wild, Innocent & the E Street Shuffle	LP/BP	U.S.†	1983	$14.00/$8.00

Singles

Label	Catalog Number	Title	Type	Country	Year	Longbox Value / Value
Sony	SRDS-8231	57 Channels	CD3	Japan	1992	$18.00/$5.00
Sony	SRCS-5972	57 Channels	CD5	Japan	1992	$15.00
Columbia	658138 5	57 Channels	CD5	U.K.	1992	$15.00
Columbia	38K-74354	57 Channels	CD3	U.S.	1992	$6.00
Columbia	44K-74354	57 Channels	CD5	U.S.	1992	$6.00
Columbia	CSK 4599	57 Channels	CDJ	U.S.	1992	$7.00
Columbia	CSK 4670	57 Channels	CDJ	U.S.	1992	$7.00
Columbia	DISP 00159	57 Channels	CDJ	U.S.	1992	$7.00
CBS	SAMPCD1623	Better Days	CDJ	Germany	1992	$15.00
Columbia		Better Days	CD5	U.S.	1992	$6.00
Columbia	CSK 74274	Better Days	CDJ	U.S.	1992	$7.00
CBS	38K-4680	Born In the U.S.A.	CD3	U.S.	1987	$15.00/$9.00
CBS	BRUCE C2	Born to Run	CD5	U.K.	1988	$12.00
Columbia	CERK-44445	Chimes of Freedom	CD5	Canada	1988	$12.00
CBS	44K-44445	Chimes of Freedom	CD3	U.S.	1988	$14.00/$8.00
CBS	38K-07946	Cover Me	CD3	U.S.	1988	$7.00/$4.00
CBS	SAMPCD 3115	Deadman Walkin'	CDJ	Holland	1995	$20.00
CBS	SAMP-3142	Ghost of Tom Joad	CDJ	Holland	1995	$15.00
CBS	SAMPCD 3142	Ghost of Tom Joad	CDJ	Holland	1995	$19.00
Sony	SRCS-7891	Ghost of Tom Joad	CD5	Japan	1996	$35.00
Columbia	CSK 7626	Ghost of Tom Joad	CDJ	U.S.	1995	$7.00
CBS	657872-2	Human Touch	CD5	Germany	1992	$15.00
CBS	SAMP 1622	Human Touch	CD5	Germany	1992	$15.00
Sony	SRDS-8226	Human Touch	CD3	Japan	1992	$18.00/$5.00
Columbia	657872-5	Human Touch	CD5	U.K.	1992	$15.00
Columbia	CSK 74273	Human Touch	CDJ	U.S.	1992	$7.00
Sony	XDEP93043	Human Touch/Lucky Town	DJ/CD3	Japan	1992	$175.00
CBS		Hungry Heart	CD5	U.K.	1995	$11.00
CBS		If I Should Fall Behind	CD5	Holland	1993	$15.00
Sony	SRDS-8240	Leap of Faith	CD3	Japan	1992	$18.00/$5.00
		Leap of Faith	CD5	U.K.		$15.00
		Leap of Faith	CD5	U.K.		$15.00
	Second version.					
CBS	CSK 4703	Leap of Faith	CDJ	U.S.	1992	$8.00
CBS	659228 2	Lucky Town (Live)	CD5	U.K.	1993	$11.00
CBS		Murder Inc.	CDJ	U.K.	1995	$25.00
CBS	651442-2	One Step Up	CD3	Germany	1988	$15.00
Sony	10EP-3017	One Step Up	CD3	Japan	1988	$18.00/$5.00
CBS	651442-2	One Step Up	CD3	U.K.	1988	$15.00
Columbia	CSK 1031	One Step Up	CDJ	U.S.	1987	$50.00
Columbia	38K-7726	One Step Up	DJ/CD3	U.S.	1987	$70.00
CBS		Secret Garden	CD5	Australia	1995	$11.00
CBS		Secret Garden	CDJ	Brazil	1995	$50.00
CBS		Secret Garden	CD5	Canada	1995	$11.00
Sony	SRCS-7632	Secret Garden	CD5	Japan	1995	$20.00
CBS		Secret Garden	CD5	U.K.	1995	$11.00
CBS		Secret Garden	CD5	U.K.	1995	$11.00
	Second version.					
CBS		Secret Garden	CDJ	U.K.	1995	$25.00
Columbia		Secret Garden	CDJ	U.S.	1994	$7.00
Columbia	77854	Secret Garden	CD5	U.S.	1995	$6.00
CBS	652962-3	Spare Parts	CD3	Germany	1991	$15.00
CBS	15EP8010	Spare Parts	CD3	Japan	1988	$18.00/$5.00
CBS	BRUCE C4	Spare Parts	CD5	U.K.	1991	$30.00
CBS		Streets of Philadelphia	CD5	Australia	1994	$15.00
CBS		Streets of Philadelphia	CD5	U.K.	1994	$15.00
Columbia	CSK 5664	Streets of Philadelphia	CDJ	U.S.	1993	$7.00
CBS	77384	Streets of Philadelphia	CD5	U.S.	1994	$5.00
CBS	651641-3	Tougher Than the Rest	CD3	Germany	1988	$12.00
CBS	653192-3	Tougher Than the Rest	CD3	Germany	1989	$12.00
CBS	15EP8009	Tougher Than the Rest	CD3	Japan	1988	$18.00/$5.00
CBS	651641-3	Tougher Than the Rest	CD3	U.K.	1988	$12.00
CBS	BRUCE C3	Tougher Than the Rest	CD5	U.K.	1988	$15.00
CBS	10EP-3001	Tunnel of Love	CD3	Japan	1988	$18.00/$5.00
CBS	651295-2	Tunnel of Love	CD3	U.K.	1988	$15.00
CBS	15EP-8009	Tunnel of Love Express Volume 1	CD3	Japan	1988	$18.00/$5.00
CBS	15EP-8010	Tunnel of Love Express Volume 2	CD3	Japan	1988	$18.00/$5.00
		Viva Las Vega	CDJ	U.K.	1990	$60.00
	With "Its Now or Never" by Paul McCartney.					

Spudmasters

Full Length

Label	Catalog Number	Title	Type	Country	Year	Longbox Value / Value
	MASSCDD34	Stop the Madness	LTD/LP	U.K.	1994	$25.00

Spunkadelic

Singles

Label	Catalog Number	Title	Type	Country	Year	Longbox Value/Value
SBK	DPRO-05366	Boomerang	CDJ	U.S.	1990	$2.00
SBK	DPRO-05336	Take Me Like I Am	CDJ	U.S.	1990	$2.00

Spyro Gyra

Full Length

Label	Catalog Number	Title	Type	Country	Year	Longbox Value/Value
MCA	MCAD-5606	Alternating Currents	LP/LB	U.S.†	1985	$14.00/$8.00
MCA	MCAD-37148	Morning Dance	LP/LB	U.S.†	1985	$14.00/$8.00

Squeeze

Full Length

Label	Catalog Number	Title	Type	Country	Year	Longbox Value/Value
A&M	CD-3232	Argybargy	LP/LB	U.S.		$14.00/$8.00
A&M		Babylon and On	LP/LB	U.S.		$14.00/$8.00
A&M	CD-5161	Babylon and On	LP/LB	U.S.		$15.00/$8.00
A&M	CD-5080	Cosi Fan Tutti Frutti	LP/LB	U.S.		$15.00/$8.00
A&M		East Side Story	LP	U.K.		$13.00
A&M	CD-3253	East Side Story	LP/LB	U.S.		$15.00/$8.00
A&M		Frank	LP/LB	U.S.	1989	$14.00/$8.00
Westwood One		In Concert-Nu Rock	RS	U.S.	1994	$50.00
	2 CD set. With Counting Crows, Airdate: 4/25/94.					
DIR		King Biscuit Flour Hour	RS	U.S.	1988	$30.00
	With Crowded House, Airdate: 1/31/88.					
DIR		King Biscuit Flour Hour	RS	U.S.	1989	$30.00
	With Paul Carrack, Airdate: 12/18/89.					
Reprise	9 26644-2-Dj	Play	DJ/LP	U.S.	1991	$13.00
	Picture disc.					
Reprise	9 26644-2-Dj	Play	DJ/LP	U.S.	1991	$30.00
	Picture disc CD With flower pot and seeds					
		Ridiculous	DJ/LP	U.K.		$20.00
A&M	CD-4922	Singles 45's & Under	LP/LB	U.S.†	1984	$14.00/$8.00
A&M	LV38407	Squeeze Play	LP	U.S.	1980	$25.00
	Non-Digital.					
A&M	CD-3254	Sweets From a Stranger	LP/LB	U.S.		$14.00/$8.00

Singles

Label	Catalog Number	Title	Type	Country	Year	Longbox Value/Value
IRS	74004	Annie Get Your Gun	CD5	U.S.	1990	$5.00
IRS	022	Annie Get Your Gun	CDJ	U.S.	1990	$3.00
		Electric Trains	CD5	U.S.	1995	$10.00
		Electric Trains	CD5	U.S.	1995	$10.00
	Second version.					
A&M	31458 0447	Everything in the World	CD5	U.S.	1993	$5.00
A&M	31458 8179	Everything in the World	CDJ	U.S.	1993	$3.00
A&M	S12Y-3027	Footprints	CD3	Japan	1988	$15.00/$4.00
A&M	12371	Footprints	CD5	U.S.	1988	$5.00
		Heaven Knows	CD5	U.K.	1996	$10.00
		Heaven Knows	CD5	U.K.	1996	$10.00
	Second version.					
		Heaven Knows	CD5	U.K.	1996	$10.00
	Third version.					
A&M	CDEE-530	If It's Love	CD5	U.K.	1989	$9.00
A&M	AMCD-530	If It's Love	CD5	U.K.	1989	$9.00
A&M	CD 17884	If It's Love	CDJ	U.S.	1989	$3.00
A&M	CDEE-535	Love Circles	CD3	U.K.	1989	$9.00
A&M	21458 8230	Loving You Tonight	CDJ	U.S.	1993	$3.00
Reprise	9362-40247-2	Satisfied	CD5	U.K.	1991	$9.00
Reprise	PRO-CD-4930	Satisfied	CDJ	U.S.	1991	$3.00
Reprise	W-0054CD	Sunday Street	CD5	U.K.	1991	$9.00
Reprise	9362 40160	Sunday Street	CD5	U.K.	1991	$9.00
		Third Rail	CD5	U.K.		$10.00
		Third Rail	CD5	U.K.		$10.00
	Second version.					
		This Summer	CD5	U.K.	1995	$11.00
		This Summer	CD5	U.K.	1995	$11.00
	Second version.					
A&M	17490	Three from Babylon and On	DJ/CD3	U.S.	1987	$15.00

Squire, Billy

Full Length

Label	Catalog Number	Title	Type	Country	Year	Longbox Value/Value
Capitol	DPRO-79659	Angry	DJ/Smplr	U.S.	1993	$7.00
Chronicles		Anthology	DJ/Smplr	U.S.	1996	$30.00
	CD-ROM press kit.					
Capitol		Enough Is Enough	LP/LB	U.S.		$14.00/$8.00
Capitol	DPRO-79769	Hear, Then & Now	DJ/Smplr	U.S.	1989	$15.00
Album Network		In the Studio (Don't Say No)	RS	U.S.	1989	$20.00
	Airdate: 7/24/89.					
Album Network		In the Studio (Don't Say No)	RS	U.S.	1992	$20.00
	Airdate: 7/27/92.					
DIR		King Biscuit Flour Hour	RS	U.S.	1989	$40.00
	With Aerosmith, Airdate: 10/16/89.					
Mercury	CHRONIPK1	Reach for the Sky: Interactive Press Kit	DJ/CD-ROM	U.S.	1996	$35.00
	Multimedia CD-ROM press Kit.					

Singles

Label	Catalog Number	Title	Type	Country	Year	Longbox Value/Value
Capitol	DPRO-79750	Don't Let Me Go	CDJ	U.S.		$2.00
Capitol	DPRO-79635	Don't Say You Love Me	CDJ	U.S.	1989	$2.00
Capitol	C2 15746	Facts of Life	CD5	U.S.	1991	$5.00
Capitol	DPRO 79632	Facts of Life	CDJ	U.S.	1991	$2.00
Capitol	DPRO-79609	She Goes Down	CDJ	U.S.		$2.00

ST

Singles

Label	Catalog Number	Title	Type	Country	Year	Longbox Value/Value
		How Will I Laugh Tomorrow	CDJ	U.S.		$2.00

St. James, Noret

Singles

Label	Catalog Number	Title	Type	Country	Year	Longbox Value/Value
Next Plateau	1001	I'm Down	CDJ	U.S.	1993	$2.00

St. John, Blakey

Singles

Label	Catalog Number	Title	Type	Country	Year	Longbox Value/Value
		40 White Pearls	CDJ	U.S.		$2.00

St. Paul

Singles

Label	Catalog Number	Title	Type	Country	Year	Longbox Value/Value
Eastwest	786145-2	Down the Wire	CD5	Germany	1990	$8.00
		Every Heart Needs a Home	CDJ	U.S.		$2.00
		Stranger to Love	CDJ	U.S.		$2.00

St. Thomas

Singles

Label	Catalog Number	Title	Type	Country	Year	Longbox Value/Value
Tony Nicole	0001	I Hate	CDJ	U.S.	1992	$2.00

Stabbing Westward

Full Length

Label	Catalog Number	Title	Type	Country	Year	Longbox Value/Value
Columbia		Wither, Blister, Burn & Peel	DJ/LP	U.S.		$8.00

Singles

Label	Catalog Number	Title	Type	Country	Year	Longbox Value/Value
Columbia	CSK 6076	Lies	CDJ	U.S.		$2.00
Columbia	CSK 7098	Nothing	CDJ	U.S.		$2.00
Columbia	CSK 5515	Violent Moodswings	CDJ	U.S.		$2.00
Columbia	CSK 7388	What Do I Have to Do?	CDJ	U.S.		$2.00

Stace, Glen

Singles

Label	Catalog Number	Title	Type	Country	Year	Longbox Value/Value
		Three to Get Ready	CDJ	Canada		$8.00

Stacy Q

Singles

Label	Catalog Number	Title	Type	Country	Year	Longbox Value/Value
Pioneer	10SW-11	Don't Make a Fool of Yourself	CD3	Japan	1988	$12.00/$4.00
Atlantic	PR 2206-2	Don't Make a Fool of Yourself	CDJ	U.S.	1988	$2.00
Atlantic	PR 2518-2	Favorite Things	CDJ	U.S.	1988	$2.00
Pioneer	09P3-6149	Give You All My Love	CD3	Japan	1989	$12.00/$4.00
Atlantic	PR 2735-2	Give You All My Love	CDJ	U.S.	1989	$2.00
		Heartbeat	CDJ	U.S.		$2.00
Thump	1049	Two Hot For Love	CDJ	U.S.	1993	$2.00

Stage Dolls

Full Length

Label	Catalog Number	Title	Type	Country	Year	Longbox Value/Value
Polygram	849402	Stripped	LP/BP	U.S.		$12.00/$7.00

Singles

Label	Catalog Number	Title	Type	Country	Year	Longbox Value/Value
Chrysalis		Loraine	CDJ	U.S.	1988	$2.00
Polydor	889923-2	Love Cries	CD5	Germany	1990	$8.00
Polydor	PZCD-68	Love Cries	CD5	U.K.	1990	$8.00
Chrysalis	DPRO 23366	Love Cries	CDJ	U.S.	1988	$2.00
Polygram	CDP 625	Love Don't Bother Me	CDJ	U.S.	1988	$2.00
Polygram	PZCD-78	Still In Love	CD5	U.K.	1990	$8.00
Chyrsalis		Still In Love	CDJ	U.S.	1988	$2.00

Stairs

Full Length

Label	Catalog Number	Title	Type	Country	Year	Longbox Value/Value
Polygram	909215 0	Mexican R&B	LP/BP	U.S.		$10.00/$7.00

Singles

Label	Catalog Number	Title	Type	Country	Year	Longbox Value/Value
Stockholm	STOCDS532	Flying Machine	CD5	Sweden	1992	$8.00
London	CDP 745	Flying Machine	CDJ	U.S.	1992	$2.00

Stakka Bo

Singles

Label	Catalog Number	Title	Type	Country	Year	Longbox Value/Value
Polydor	CDP 1196	Here We Go	CDJ	U.S.	1993	$2.00

Stamey, Chris

Singles

Label	Catalog Number	Title	Type	Country	Year	Longbox Value/Value
Intercord	892 763	On the Radio	CD5	Germany	1992	$8.00

Stanley, Ralph

Full Length

Label	Catalog Number	Title	Type	Country	Year	Longbox Value/Value
Rebel		Ralph Stanley Box Sampler	DJ/Smplr	U.S.	1995	$12.00

Stansfield, Lisa

Full Length

Label	Catalog Number	Title	Type	Country	Year	Longbox Value/Value
Arista		Affection	DJ/LP	U.S.	1990	$15.00
	CD in cardboard suitcase.					

Singles

Label	Catalog Number	Title	Type	Country	Year	Longbox Value/Value
Arista	ASCD-2449	A Little More Love	CDJ	U.S.	1992	$3.00
Arista	BVDA-35	All Along	CD3	Japan	1990	$13.00/$4.00
Arista	662693	All Around the World	CD5	Germany	1989	$8.00
Arista	A10D-148	All Around the World	CD3	Japan	1990	$13.00/$4.00
Arista	662693	All Around the World	CD5	U.K.	1989	$8.00
Arista	66500	All Woman	CD5	U.K.	1991	$8.00
Arista	ASCD-2398	All Woman	CDJ	U.S.	1992	$3.00
Arista	BVDA-29	Change	CD3	Japan	1991	$13.00/$4.00
Arista	664820	Change	CD5	U.K.	1991	$8.00
Arista	12363	Change	CD5	U.S.	1991	$5.00
Arista	ASCD 2360	Change	CDJ	U.S.	1991	$2.00
Arista		In All the Right Places	CDJ	U.K.	1993	$10.00
Arista	ASCD-2685	In All the Right Places	CDJ	U.S.	1993	$3.00
Aris	884034	Live Together	CD3	Germany	1990	$8.00
BMG	662914	Live Together	CD5	Germany	1990	$8.00
BMG	662943	Live Together	CD5	Germany	1990	$8.00
Arista	662914	Live Together	CD5	U.K.	1990	$8.00
Arista	BVCA-9003	Real Woman	CD5	Japan	1992	$3.00
Arista	74321-12356-2	Someday	CD5	U.K.	1992	$8.00
Arista	662512	This Is the Right Time	CD5	Germany	1990	$8.00
Arista	BVDA-39	This Is the Right Time	CD3	Japan	1990	$13.00/$4.00
Arista	662512	This Is the Right Time	CD5	U.K.	1990	$8.00
Arista	ASCD 2069	This Is the Right Time	CDJ	U.S.	1990	$2.00
Arista	665113	Time To Make Mine	CD5	Germany	1992	$8.00
Arista	665113	Time To Make Mine	CD5	U.K.	1992	$8.00
Arista	663168	What Did I Do For You	CD5	Germany	1990	$8.00
Arista	BVCA-9001	What Did I Do For You	CD5	Japan	1990	$12.00
Arista	663168	What Did I Do For You	CD5	U.K.	1990	$8.00
Arista	BVDA-4	You Can't Deny It	CD3	Japan	1990	$13.00/$4.00
Arista	ASCD-2024	You Can't Deny It	CDJ	U.S.	1990	$3.00

Staples, Mavis

Singles

Label	Catalog Number	Title	Type	Country	Year	Longbox Value/Value
Paisley Park	PRO-CD-3506	20th Century Express	CDJ	U.S.	1989	$2.00
WEA	W-9728CD	Melody Cool	CD5	U.K.	1990	$8.00
Paisley Park	PRO-CD-4397	Melody Cool	CDJ	U.S.	1990	$2.00
Paisley Park	PRO-CD-3813	Time Waits For No One	CDJ	U.S.	1989	$2.00
Paisley Park	PRO-CD-5991	Voice, The	CDJ	U.S.	1993	$2.00

Star, Madame

Singles

Label	Catalog Number	Title	Type	Country	Year	Longbox Value/Value
Cold Chillin'	2020	Baby's Father	CD5	U.S.	1994	$5.00

Star Star

Singles

Label	Catalog Number	Title	Type	Country	Year	Longbox Value/Value
Roadrunner	061	Science Fiction Boy	CDJ	U.S.	1992	$2.00

Starclub

Singles

Label	Catalog Number	Title	Type	Country	Year	Longbox Value/Value
Island	PRCD 6755-2	Hard To Get	CDJ	U.S.	1992	$2.00
Island	PRCD 6767-2	Let Your Hair Down	CDJ	U.S.	1992	$2.00

Starland Vocal Band

Singles

Label	Catalog Number	Title	Type	Country	Year	Longbox Value/Value
Ktel	3278	Afternoon Delight	CD5	U.S.	1994	$5.00

Starlings

Singles

Label	Catalog Number	Title	Type	Country	Year	Longbox Value/Value
Anxious	ANXCD-699	Last One	CD5	U.K.	1991	$8.00
Anxious	ANXCD-700	Safe in Heaven Dead	CD5	U.K.	1991	$8.00
Atlantic	PRCD 4961-2	That's It	CDJ	U.S.		$2.00
Anxious	ANXCD-666	Try	CD5	U.K.	1991	$8.00

Starpoint

Label	Catalog Number	Title	Type	Country	Year	Longbox Value/Value
Full Length						
Elektra	60424-2	Restless	LP/LB	U.S.†	1985	$14.00/$8.00
Singles						
Elektra	PRCD 8155-2	I Want You - You Want Me	CDJ	U.S.	1990	$2.00
Elektra	PRCD 8185-2	Midnight Love	CDJ	U.S.	1990	$2.00
		Say You Will	CDJ	U.S.		$2.00
		Tough Act to Follow	CDJ	U.S.		$2.00

Starr, Brenda K.

Label	Catalog Number	Title	Type	Country	Year	Longbox Value/Value
Singles						
Pioneer	10SW-50	I Still Believe	CD3	Japan	1988	$12.00/$4.00
Epic	ESDA-7084	If You Could Read My Mind	CD3	Japan	1992	$12.00/$4.00
Epic	ESK 74035	If You Could Read My Mind	CDJ	U.S.	1991	$2.00
		What You Get Is What You See	CDJ	U.S.		$2.00
Pioneer	10P3-6015	What You See Is What You Get	CD3	Japan	1988	$12.00/$4.00

Starr, Edwin

Label	Catalog Number	Title	Type	Country	Year	Longbox Value/Value
Full Length						
Motown	5170	War & Peace	LP/BP	U.S.		$12.00/$7.00

Starr, Ringo

Label	Catalog Number	Title	Type	Country	Year	Longbox Value/Value
Full Length						
Private Issue	VRCD-0264	4-Starr Collection	DJ/Smplr	U.S.	1995	$45.00
Tour sampler issued for Discover Card's Private Issue credit card promotion.						
Rykodisc	RCD 10190	And His All Star Band	LTD/LP	U.S.	1990	$22.00/$15.00
2CD in slipcase with slicker and longbox.						
Right Stuff		Stop and Smell the Roses and Old Wave	DJ/Smplr	U.S.	1994	$75.00
Image	ID 7650HB	That'll Be the Day	LD	U.S.		$75.00
Media America		Up Close	RS	U.S.	1992	$145.00
2 CD set.						
Singles						
Right Stuff		Beaucoups of Blues	CDJ	U.S.		$15.00
Private Music	PDJ 81007	Don't Go Where the Road Don't Go	CDJ	U.S.	1992	$15.00
Rykodisc	RCD5 1019	It Ain't Easy	CD5	U.S.	1990	$5.00
Rykodisc	RCD 51019	Rocky Mountain Way	CDJ	U.S.	1990	$7.00
Private Music	665392	Weight of the World	CD5	Germany	1992	$12.00
Private Music	BVDP-58	Weight of the World	CD3	Japan	1992	$15.00/$5.00
Private Music	PDJ 81003	Weight of the World	CDJ	U.S.	1992	$12.00
Giant	PRO-CD-5153	You Never Know	CDJ	U.S.	1991	$10.00

Starr, Ringo and Buck Owens

Label	Catalog Number	Title	Type	Country	Year	Longbox Value/Value
Singles						
Capitol	DPRO-797650	Act Naturally	CDJ	U.S.	1989	$50.00

Starship

Label	Catalog Number	Title	Type	Country	Year	Longbox Value/Value
Full Length						
		House of Blues	RS	U.S.	1995	$100.00
2 CD set. Airdate: 6/2/95.						
Grunt	PCD1-5488	Knee Deep in the Hoopla	LP/BP	U.S.†	1985	$14.00/$8.00
Pioneer	CLD-86-001	Knee Deep in the Hoopla	LD	U.S.	1986	$20.00
BMG		Love Among the Cannibals	LP/LB	U.S.		$14.00/$8.00
Singles						
BMG	PD-49180	Good Hearts	CD5	Germany	1991	$9.00
RCA	BVDP-41	Good Hearts	CD3	Japan	1991	$12.00/$4.00
RCA	2796-2-RDj	Good Hearts	CDJ	U.S.	1991	$2.00
RCA	2847-2-RDj	Good Hearts	CDJ	U.S.	1991	$2.00
RCA	R10D-137	I Didn't Mean to Stay All Night	CD3	Japan	1989	$12.00/$5.00
RCA	9109-2-RDj	I Didn't Mean to Stay All Night	CDJ	U.S.	1989	$2.00
RCA	9195-2-RDj	I'll Be There	CDJ	U.S.	1989	$2.00
RCA	PD-49358	It's Not Enough	CD5	Germany	1989	$9.00
RCA	PD-49358	It's Not Enough	CD5	U.K.	1989	$9.00
Grunt	6478	It's Not Enough	CDJ	U.S.	1989	$2.00
Grunt	6478	It's Not Over	CDJ	U.S.		$2.00
RCA	PD-49451	Nothing's Gonna Stop Us Now	CD5	Germany	1989	$9.00
RCA	BVDP-50	Nothing's Gonna Stop Us Now	CD3	Japan	1991	$12.00/$4.00
RCA	PD-49451	Nothing's Gonna Stop Us Now	CD5	U.K.	1989	$9.00
RCA/NTSC	RCA 001	Nothing's Gonna Stop Us Now	DJ/CDV	U.S.	1987	$20.00
Pioneer	10P3-6087	Wild Again	CD3	Japan	1989	$13.00/$4.00
Elektra	EKR-88CD	Wild Again	CD5	U.K.	1989	$9.00
		Wild Again	CDJ	U.S.	1989	$2.00

Starz

Label	Catalog Number	Title	Type	Country	Year	Longbox Value/Value
Full Length						
Warner Brothers	26570	Attention Shoppers	LP/LB	U.S.		$14.00/$8.00
Warner Brothers	26571	Coliseum Rock	LP/LB	U.S.		$14.00/$8.00
Warner Brothers	26558	Starz	LP/LB	U.S.		$14.00/$8.00
Warner Brothers	26559	Violation	LP/LB	U.S.		$14.00/$8.00

State of Grace

Label	Catalog Number	Title	Type	Country	Year	Longbox Value/Value
Singles						
RCA	RDJ64459-2	Hello	CDJ	U.S.		$2.00

Staten, Keith

Label	Catalog Number	Title	Type	Country	Year	Longbox Value/Value
Singles						
		A Christmas Message	CDJ	U.S.		$2.00
Polydor	CDP 285	Miracles	CDJ	U.S.	1990	$2.00

Statler Brothers

Label	Catalog Number	Title	Type	Country	Year	Longbox Value/Value
Full Length						
		30th Anniversary	DJ/Intvw	U.S.	1994	$25.00
Mercury	818 652-2	Atlanta Blue	LP/BP	U.S.†	1984	$14.00/$8.00
Mercury	818 524-2	Best of, Vol. 1	LP/BP	U.S.†	1984	$14.00/$8.00
Mercury	818 528-2	Best of, Vol. 2	LP/BP	U.S.†	1984	$14.00/$8.00
Mercury	824 420-2	Partners in Rhyme	LP/BP	U.S.†	1985	$14.00/$8.00
Singles						
Polygram	518944	Lester'roadhog'mora	CD5	U.S.	1994	$5.00
Mercury	CDP 29	Let's Get Started if We're...	CDJ	U.S.	1988	$2.00
Mercury	CDP 580	Put it on the Card	CDJ	U.S.	1991	$2.00
Mercury	CDP 200	Walking Heartache in Disguise	CDJ	U.S.	1990	$2.00

Status Quo

Label	Catalog Number	Title	Type	Country	Year	Longbox Value/Value
Full Length						
Vertigo	WORK1CD	Thirsty Work Sampler	DJ/Smplr	U.K.		$12.00
Singles						
Vertigo	870226-2	Ain't Complaining	CD5	Germany	1988	$8.00
Vertigo	QUOCD-22	Ain't Complaining	CD5	U.K.	1988	$8.00
Vertigo	878323-2	Anniversary Waltz	CD5	Germany	1990	$8.00
Vertigo	QUOCD-28	Anniversary Waltz	CD5	U.K.	1990	$8.00
Vertigo	872307-2	Burning Bridges	CD5	Germany	1989	$8.00
Vertigo	QUOCD-25	Burning Bridges	CD5	U.K.	1989	$8.00
Vertigo	868931-2	Can't Give You More	CD5	Germany	1990	$8.00
Vertigo	868966-2	Can't Give You More	CD5	Germany	1990	$8.00
Vertigo	QUOCD-30	Can't Give You More	CD5	U.K.	1990	$8.00
		Come on You Reds	CD5	U.K.	1994	$10.00
Vertigo	888309-2	Dreamin'	CD5	Germany	1989	$8.00
Vertigo	888309-2	Dreamin'	CD5	U.K.	1989	$8.00
	SQ-RAD-1	Fun Fun Fun	CDJ	U.K.		$12.00
		Give Myself to Love	CD5	U.K.	1996	N/A
		I Didn't Mean It	CD5	Australia	1994	$10.00
		I Didn't Mean It	CD5	U.K.	1994	$10.00
		I Didn't Mean It	CD5	U.K.	1994	$10.00
Second version.						
		I Didn't Mean It	CD5	U.K.	1994	$10.00
Thirdversion.						
		I Didn't Mean It	CDJ	U.K.	1994	$12.00
Vertigo	888056-2	In the Army Now	CD5	Germany	1988	$8.00
Vertigo	888056-2	In the Army Now	CD5	U.K.	1988	$8.00
IMS	876527-2	Little Dreamer	CD5	Germany	1990	$8.00
Vertigo	QUOCD-27	Little Dreamer	CD5	U.K.	1990	$8.00
Vertigo	876393-2	Not at All	CD5	Germany	1989	$8.00
Vertigo	QUOCD-26	Not at All	CD5	U.K.	1989	$8.00
		Roadhouse Medley	CD5	U.K.		$10.00
		Roadhouse Medley	CD5	U.K.		$10.00
Second version.						
Vertigo	870592-2	Running All Over the World	CD5	Germany	1988	$8.00
Vertigo	QUOCD-1	Running All Over the World	CD5	U.K.	1988	$8.00
Vertigo	870389-2	Who Gets Love	CD5	Germany	1988	$8.00
Vertigo	QUOCD-23	Who Gets Love	CD5	U.K.	1988	$8.00

Staxx Of Joy

Label	Catalog Number	Title	Type	Country	Year	Longbox Value/Value
Singles						
Chaos	42K 77364	Joy	CD5	U.S.	1994	$5.00
Chaos	5634	Joy	CDJ	U.S.	1994	$2.00
CBS	773364	Love Joy	CD5	U.S.	1994	$5.00

Steady B

Label	Catalog Number	Title	Type	Country	Year	Longbox Value/Value
Singles						
		Girl's Gonna Getcha	CDJ	U.S.	1988	$2.00
Aris	886773	Going Steady	CD5	Germany	1990	$8.00
Jive	1456-2-JDj	Pay Me Baby	CDJ	U.S.	1991	$2.00

Stealin' Horses

Label	Catalog Number	Title	Type	Country	Year	Longbox Value/Value
Singles						
		Turnaround	CDJ	U.S.		$2.00

Steampacket

Label	Catalog Number	Title	Type	Country	Year	Longbox Value/Value
Full Length						
Charly		Steampacket	LP/BP	U.S.		$12.00/$7.00

Steel, Eric

Label	Catalog Number	Title	Type	Country	Year	Longbox Value/Value
Full Length						
Passport	PBCD-6059	Infectious	LP/BP	U.S.		$16.00/$12.00

Steel Pole Bathtub

Label	Catalog Number	Title	Type	Country	Year	Longbox Value/Value
Singles						
		Twist	CDJ	U.S.		$2.00

Steel Pulse

Label	Catalog Number	Title	Type	Country	Year	Longbox Value/Value
Singles						
MCA	54900	Bootstraps	CD5	U.S.	1994	$5.00
MCA	MCA5P-2551	Taxi Driver	CDJ	U.S.	1993	$2.00

Steele, Chrissy

Label	Catalog Number	Title	Type	Country	Year	Longbox Value/Value
Singles						
Chrysalis	DPRO-23729	Love You Till It Hurts	CDJ	U.S.	1991	$2.00
Chrysalis	23729	Love You Till It Hurts	CDJ	U.S.	1991	$3.00

Steele, Jevetta

Label	Catalog Number	Title	Type	Country	Year	Longbox Value/Value
Singles						
Great Jones	622	Calling You	CDJ	U.S.	1992	$2.00

Steele, Terry

Label	Catalog Number	Title	Type	Country	Year	Longbox Value/Value
Singles						
		If I Told You Once	CDJ	U.S.		$2.00
		Prisoner of Love	CDJ	U.S.		$2.00
SBK	DPRO-05380	Tonight's the Night	CDJ	U.S.	1991	$2.00

Steeleye Span

Label	Catalog Number	Title	Type	Country	Year	Longbox Value/Value
Full Length						
Chrysalis		All Around My Hat	LTD/LP	U.K.	1994	$25.00/$15.00
25th Anniversary edition in 6"x11" longbox.						

Steelheart

Label	Catalog Number	Title	Type	Country	Year	Longbox Value/Value
Singles						
MCA	WMD5-4031	Can't Stop Me Lovin' You	CD3	Japan	1990	$13.00/$4.00
		Can't Stop Me Lovin' You	CDJ	U.S.		$2.00
MCA	MCA5P-2322	Electric Love	CDJ	U.S.	1992	$2.00
Eastwest	9031-72676-2	I'll Never Let You Go	CD5	Germany	1990	$8.00
Pioneer	WMD5-4016	I'll Never Let You Go	CD3	Japan	1990	$13.00/$4.00
Pioneer	WMD5-4053	I'll Never Let You Go	CD3	Japan	1990	$13.00/$4.00
		I'll Never Let You Go	CDJ	U.S.		$2.00
MCA	MVDM-20	Mama Don't You Cry	CD3	Japan	1992	$13.00/$4.00
		Mama Don't You Cry	CDJ	U.S.		$2.00
MCA	MVDM-20	Sticky Side Up	CD3	Japan	1992	$13.00/$4.00
MCA	MCA5P-2269	Sticky Side Up	CDJ	U.S.	1992	$2.00

Steely Dan

Label	Catalog Number	Title	Type	Country	Year	Longbox Value/Value
Full Length						
MCA	MCAD-5570	A Decade of	LP/LB	U.S.†	1985	$14.00/$8.00
Giant		Alive in America	DJ/Smplr	U.S.	1995	$15.00
MCA	10981	Citizen Steely Dan 1972-1980	LP	U.S.	1993	$60.00
4 CD set with intro to "Rikki Don't Loose That Number" is missing.						
Album Network		In the Studio (Aja)	RS	U.S.	1990	$30.00
Airdate: 4/30/90.						
Album Network		In the Studio (Aja)	RS	U.S.	1992	$30.00
Airdate: 9/14/92.						
Album Network		In the Studio (Can't Buy a Thrill)	RS	U.S.	1989	$30.00
Airdate: 11/27/89.						
Album Network		In the Studio (Can't Buy a Thrill)	RS	U.S.	1992	$30.00
Airdate: 10/26/92.						
Westwood One		Off the Record	RS	U.S.	1994	$40.00
Airdate: 2/7/94.						
Westwood One		Off the Record	RS	U.S.	1995	$25.00
Airdate: 11/6/95.						
		Roaring of the Lamb	LP/BP	U.S.		$16.00/$12.00
Media America		Up Close	RS	U.S.		$75.00
3 CD set.						
Media America		Up Close	RS	U.S.	1995	$100.00
3 CD set.						
Success		You Go Where I Go	LP/LB	U.S.		$14.00/$8.00

Steen, Nikolaj

Singles

Label	Catalog Number	Title	Type	Country	Year	Longbox Value / Value
Imago	72787-2503	New Message, The	CD5	U.S.	1992	$4.00

Stegall, Keith

Full Length

Label	Catalog Number	Title	Type	Country	Year	Longbox Value / Value
Mercury		Passages	DJ/LP	U.S.	1996	$25.00

CD, cassette, VHS video and booklet in simulated "bound book" package.

Label	Catalog Number	Title	Type	Country	Year	Longbox Value / Value
		Passages	DJ/LP	U.S.		$18.00

CD, cassette, and VHS video in box.

Steinberg

Singles

Label	Catalog Number	Title	Type	Country	Year	Longbox Value / Value
Pikosso	743 213 213 82	Formula 1	SCD5	Germany	1995	$18.00

"Race Car" shaped CD.

Stems

Singles

Label	Catalog Number	Title	Type	Country	Year	Longbox Value / Value
A&M	CD 17837	At First Sight	CDJ	U.S.	1989	$2.00

Stephanie

Singles

Label	Catalog Number	Title	Type	Country	Year	Longbox Value / Value
Epic	NSK 3029	Winds of Change	CDJ	U.S.	1991	$2.00
CBS	656906-2	You Don't Die From Love	CD5	Germany	1991	$8.00

Stephens, Richie

Singles

Label	Catalog Number	Title	Type	Country	Year	Longbox Value / Value
Motown	374631098	Body Slam	CDJ	U.S.	1993	$2.00
Motown	374631127	Everytime You're There	CDJ	U.S.	1993	$2.00

Stephenson, Martin & Dantees

Singles

Label	Catalog Number	Title	Type	Country	Year	Longbox Value / Value
		Big Sky New Light	CD5	U.K.		$10.00
		Big Sky New Light	CD5	U.K.		$10.00

Second version.

Steppenwolf (John Kay)

Full Length

Label	Catalog Number	Title	Type	Country	Year	Longbox Value / Value
MCA	MCAD-1668	At Your Birthday Party	LP/LB	U.S.		$15.00/$10.00
Westwood One		BBC Classic Tracks	RS	U.S.	1994	$25.00

Airdate: 11/14/94.

Label	Catalog Number	Title	Type	Country	Year	Longbox Value / Value
Album Network		In the Studio (Besst Of)	RS	U.S.		$25.00
Album Network		In the Studio (Gold)	RS	U.S.	1993	$20.00

Airdate: 2/15/93.

Label	Catalog Number	Title	Type	Country	Year	Longbox Value / Value
ERA	5031-2	John Kay & Steppenwolf Sampler: Live At 25	DJ/Smplr	U.S.	1995	$18.00
MCA	MCAD-31178	Lone Steppenwolf	LP/LB	U.S.		$14.00/$10.00
MCA	MCAD-131328	Monster	LP/LB	U.S.		$15.00/$10.00
MCA	MCAD-37049	Sixteen Greatest Hits	LP/LB	U.S.		$15.00/$10.00
MCA	MCAD-31020	Steppenwolf	LP/LB	U.S.		$15.00/$10.00
MCA	MCAD-31021	Steppenwolf 2	LP/LB	U.S.		$15.00/$10.00
MCA	MCAD-1598	Steppenwolf 7	LP/LB	U.S.		$15.00/$10.00

Singles

Label	Catalog Number	Title	Type	Country	Year	Longbox Value / Value
BMG	MCD-17789	Born to Be Wild	CD5	Germany	1991	$10.00
IRS	IRSD 024	We Like It, We Love It	CDJ	U.S.	1990	$3.00

Steps Ahead

Full Length

Label	Catalog Number	Title	Type	Country	Year	Longbox Value / Value
Elektra	60168-2	Steps	LP/LB	U.S.†	1985	$14.00/$8.00

Stepz

Singles

Label	Catalog Number	Title	Type	Country	Year	Longbox Value / Value
Motown	4860	Hold Me Tight	CD5	U.S.	1994	$6.00

Stereo MC's

Singles

Label	Catalog Number	Title	Type	Country	Year	Longbox Value / Value
4th & B'way	BRCD-262	Connected	CD5	U.K.	1992	$8.00
	PRCD 6756-2	Connected	CDJ	U.S.		$2.00
4th & B'way	663665	Elevate My Mind	CD5	Germany	1990	$8.00
4th & B'way	BRCD-186	Elevate My Mind	CD5	U.K.	1990	$8.00
4th & B'way	BRCD-262	Elevate My Mind	CD5	U.K.	1990	$8.00
4th & B'way	519	Elevate My Mind	CDJ	U.S.	1990	$2.00
4th & B'way	BRCD-268	Ground Level	CD5	U.K.	1990	$8.00
BMG	664003	Lost in Music	CD5	Germany	1991	$8.00
4th & B'way	BRCD-198	Lost in Music	CD5	U.K.	1991	$8.00
4th & B'way	534	Lost in Music	CDJ	U.S.	1991	$2.00
4th & B'way	544	Lost In Music	CDJ	U.S.	1991	$2.00
4th & B'way	BRCD-266	Step It Up	CD5	U.K.	1992	$8.00
Gee Street	422 862 431	Step It Up	CD5	U.S.	1993	$5.00
Gee Street	PRCD 6772-2	Step It Up	CDJ	U.S.	1993	$2.00
Gee Street	444 026	What Is Soul?	CD5	U.S.	1990	$5.00

Stereolab

Full Length

Label	Catalog Number	Title	Type	Country	Year	Longbox Value / Value
		Music for Amorphous Body Study Center	LTD/LP	U.K.	1995	$35.00
Elektra	PRCD 8830-2	Jenny Ondioline	CDJ	U.S.	1993	$2.00
		Noise of Carpet	CDJ	U.S.		$2.00
Elektra	PRCD 9493-2	Noises	CDJ	U.S.		$6.00
		Ping Pong	CDJ	U.S.		$6.00
		Wow and Flutter	CDJ	U.S.		$6.00

Stern, Howard

Full Length

Label	Catalog Number	Title	Type	Country	Year	Longbox Value / Value
		Crucified by the FCC	LTD/LP	U.S.	1993	N/A

4 CD boxed set.

Stern, Leni

Full Length

Label	Catalog Number	Title	Type	Country	Year	Longbox Value / Value
Passport	VJD-1154	Next Day	LP	Japan		$20.00
Passport	PJCD-88035	Next Day	LP	U.K.		$12.00
Passport	PJCD-88035	Next Day	LP/BP	U.S.		$16.00/$12.00

Stetsasonic

Singles

Label	Catalog Number	Title	Type	Country	Year	Longbox Value / Value
Go Discs	GODCD-40	Africa	CD5	U.K.	1990	$8.00
BCM	20001	Talkin' All That Jazz	CD5	Germany	1988	$8.00
Tommy Boy	918	Talkin' All That Jazz	CDJ	U.S.	1988	$2.00

Stevens, Cat

Full Length

Label	Catalog Number	Title	Type	Country	Year	Longbox Value / Value
A&M	CD-3736	Footsteps in the Dark	LP/LB	U.S.†	1984	$14.00/$8.00
A&M	CD-4519	Greatest Hits	LP/LB	U.S.†	1984	$14.00/$8.00
A&M	CD-4280	Tea for the Tillerman	LP/LB	U.S.†	1984	$14.00/$8.00
Mobile Fidelity		Three	LTD/LP	U.S.	1996	$73.00

3 CD individually numbered set.

Singles

Label	Catalog Number	Title	Type	Country	Year	Longbox Value / Value
A&M	S12Y-3035	Morning Has Broken	CD3	Japan	1988	$12.00/$4.00

Stevens, Corey & Texas Flood

Singles

Label	Catalog Number	Title	Type	Country	Year	Longbox Value / Value
		Brothers, The	CDJ	U.S.		$2.00

Stevens, Jeff and The Bullets

Singles

Label	Catalog Number	Title	Type	Country	Year	Longbox Value / Value
		Johnny Lucky And Suzi 66	CDJ	U.S.		$2.00

Stevens, Ray

Full Length

Label	Catalog Number	Title	Type	Country	Year	Longbox Value / Value
Curb	CURBD-1058	Breakfast With...	DJ/Smplr	U.S.	1993	$5.00

CD in 12"x12" sleeve.

Label	Catalog Number	Title	Type	Country	Year	Longbox Value / Value
Curb	CURBD-1058	Breakfast With Ray Stevens	DJ/Smplr	U.S.	1993	$15.00

Singles

Label	Catalog Number	Title	Type	Country	Year	Longbox Value / Value
Old Gold	OG-6124	Misty	CD3	U.K.	1989	$9.00

Stevens, Steve and Atomic Playboys

Singles

Label	Catalog Number	Title	Type	Country	Year	Longbox Value / Value
Warner Brothers	PRO-CD-3778	Action	CDJ	U.S.	1989	$2.00
Warner Brothers	PRO-CD-3652	Atomic Playboys	CDJ	U.S.	1989	$2.00
Warner Brothers	PRO-CD-3744	Atomic Playboys	CDJ	U.S.	1989	$2.00

Stevie B

Full Length

Label	Catalog Number	Title	Type	Country	Year	Longbox Value / Value
		Love & Emotions & Other Greatest Hits	DJ/Smplr	U.S.		$4.00

Singles

Label	Catalog Number	Title	Type	Country	Year	Longbox Value / Value
Polydor	879597-2	Because I Love You	CD5	Germany	1991	$8.00
Polydor	PZCD-126	Because I Love You	CD5	U.K.	1991	$8.00
		Because I Love You	CDJ	U.S.	1991	$2.00
BCM	20507	Because You Love Me	CD5	Germany	1990	$8.00
Lefrak	62112	Forever More	CDJ	U.S.	1991	$2.00
Polydor	306030	I'll Be By Your Side	CD5	Germany	1991	$8.00
Polydor	PZCD-145	I'll Be By Your Side	CD5	U.K.	1991	$8.00
RCA	2758-2-RDJ	I'll Be By Your Side	CDJ	U.S.	1991	$2.00
BCM	20408	In Your Eyes	CD5	Germany	1990	$8.00
BCM	20465	Love & Emotion	CD5	Germany	1990	$8.00
RCA	2645-2-RDj	Love & Emotion	CDJ	U.S.	1990	$2.00
Toshiba	TODP-2307	Love Me For Life	CD3	Japan	1991	$12.00/$4.00
BCM	20402	Megamix	CD5	Germany	1990	$8.00
Epic	ESK 74359	Pump That Body	CDJ	U.S.	1992	$2.00
BCM	2003	Spring Love	CD5	Germany	1988	$8.00
RCA	2705-2-RDJ	Who's Lovin' You Tonight	CDJ	U.S.	1990	$2.00

Stewart, Al – Seemed Like A Good Idea At the Time (Acoustic Music Records)

Stewart, Al

Full Length

Label	Catalog Number	Title	Type	Country	Year	Longbox Value / Value
Westwood One		BBC Classic Tracks	RS	U.S.	1993	$10.00

Airdate: 11/15/93.

Label	Catalog Number	Title	Type	Country	Year	Longbox Value / Value
Album Network		In the Studio (Year of the Cat)	RS	U.S.	1988	$25.00

Airdate: 10/24/88.

Label	Catalog Number	Title	Type	Country	Year	Longbox Value / Value
Enigma		King of Portugal	LP/LB	U.S.	1988	$14.00/$8.00
Enigma	EPRO 123	King of Portugal + Interview	DJ/Intvw	U.S.	1988	$10.00
Mesa		Rhymes in Rooms	LP	Canada		$13.00
Acoustic Music Records		Seemed Like a Good Idea at the Time	LTD/LP	U.S.	1996	$50.00
Mobile Fidelity	MFCD-803	Year of the Cat	LP/LB	U.S.†	1984	$25.00/$20.00
Arista	ASCD-8229	Year of the Cat	LP/LB	U.S.†	1985	$14.00/$8.00

Singles

Label	Catalog Number	Title	Type	Country	Year	Longbox Value / Value
Enigma	ENVCD-4	King of Portugal	CD5	U.K.	1988	$8.00
Enigma		King of Portugal	CD3	U.S.		$6.00/$3.00
EMI	CDDEM-225	Year of the Cat	CD5	U.K.	1992	$8.00

Stewart, Dave

Full Length

Label	Catalog Number	Title	Type	Country	Year	Longbox Value / Value
Arista	ASCD-8626	Dave Stewart and the Spiritual Cowboys	LP/LB	U.S.	1990	$12.00/$7.00

Singles

Label	Catalog Number	Title	Type	Country	Year	Longbox Value / Value
Anxious	PD-44866	Crown of Madness	CD5	Germany	1991	$8.00
RCA	BVDP-48	Crown of Madness	CD3	Japan	1991	$12.00/$4.00
Anxious	PD-44866	Crown of Madness	CD5	U.K.	1991	$8.00
Arista	ASCD-2352	Crown of Madness	CDJ	U.S.	1991	$2.00
BMG	PD-44286	I'm on Fire	CD5	Germany	1990	$8.00
RCA	PD-43908	Jack Talking	CD5	Germany	1990	$8.00
RCA	PD-43908	Jack Talking	CD5	U.K.	1990	$8.00
Arista		Jealousy	CDJ	U.S.		$7.00
Anxious	ZD-45044	Jute City	CD5	U.K.	1991	$8.00
Arista	ASCD-2188	Lily Was Here	CDJ	U.S.	1988	$2.00
Arista	ASCD-2253	Lily Was Here	CDJ	U.S.	1991	$2.00
Arista	PD-44010	Love Shines	CD5	Germany	1990	$8.00
BMG	BVDP-16	Love Shines	CD3	Japan	1990	$12.00/$4.00
Arista	PD-44010	Love Shines	CD5	U.K.	1990	$8.00
Arista	ASCD-2113	Love Shines	CDJ	U.S.	1990	$2.00
Anxious	PD-45002	Out of Reach	CD5	Germany	1991	$8.00
Anxious	PD-45002	Out of Reach	CD5	U.K.	1991	$8.00
Arista	ASCD-2073	Party Town	CDJ	U.S.	1990	$2.00
BMG	PD-44824	Save Me	CD5	Germany	1991	$8.00
Rykodisc	PRO 9004	Subterranean Homesick	CDJ	U.S.		$2.00

Stewart, Jermaine

Singles

Label	Catalog Number	Title	Type	Country	Year	Longbox Value / Value
Virgin	661580	Don't Talk Dirty to Me	CD5	Germany	1988	$8.00

Label	Catalog Number	Title	Type	Country	Year	Longbox Value / Value
Siren	SRNCD-86	Don't Talk Dirty to Me	CD5	U.K.	1988	$8.00
BMG	663036	Every Woman Wants To	CD5	Germany	1990	$8.00
Virgin	TENCD-296	Every Woman Wants To	CD5	U.K.	1990	$8.00
Virgin	659878	Get Lucky	CD5	Germany	1988	$8.00
Siren	SRNCD-82	Get Lucky	CD5	U.K.	1988	$8.00
BMG	661999	Is It Really Love	CD5	Germany	1989	$8.00
Virgin	SAYCD-188	Say It Again	CD5	U.K.	1988	$8.00
Arista	ASCD-9668	Say It Again	CDJ	U.S.	1988	$2.00
Reprise	9 40635-2	Set Me Free	CD5	U.S.	1992	$5.00
BMG	662756	Tren Di Amor	CD5	Germany	1989	$8.00
Virgin	TENCD-292	Tren Di Amor	CD5	U.K.	1989	$8.00

Stewart, Mark

Singles

Label	Catalog Number	Title	Type	Country	Year	Longbox Value / Value
Mute	92	Hysteria	CD5	U.K.	1989	$8.00

Stewart, Poindexter

Singles

Label	Catalog Number	Title	Type	Country	Year	Longbox Value / Value
SST	SSTCD 299	College Rock	CD5	U.S.	1993	$5.00

Stewart, Rod

Full Length

Label	Catalog Number	Title	Type	Country	Year	Longbox Value / Value
BBC Radio		BBC Classic Tracks	RS	U.S.	1991	$20.00
	With the Faces, Airdate: 11/11/91.					
BBC Radio		BBC Classic Tracks	RS	U.S.	1991	$25.00
	Airdate: 2/4/91.					
BBC Radio		BBC Classic Tracks	RS	U.S.	1991	$25.00
	Airdate: 7/1/91.					
BBC Radio		BBC Classic Tracks	RS	U.S.	1992	$25.00
	Airdate: 11/9/92.					
BBC Radio		BBC Classic Tracks	RS	U.S.	1992	$25.00
	Airdate: 2/3/92.					
BBC Radio		BBC Classic Tracks	RS	U.S.	1992	$25.00
	Airdate: 7/13/92.					
Westwood One		BBC Classic Tracks	RS	U.S.	1993	$20.00
	Airdate: 11/15/93.					
Westwood One		BBC Classic Tracks	RS	U.S.	1993	$20.00
	Airdate: 6/14/93.					
Westwood One		BBC Classic Tracks	RS	U.S.	1993	$20.00
	Airdate: 8/23/93.					
BBC Radio		BBC Classic Tracks	RS	U.S.	1993	$25.00
	Airdate: 1/3/93.					
Westwood One		BBC Classic Tracks	RS	U.S.	1994	$20.00
	Airdate: 7/11/94.					
Westwood One		BBC Classic Tracks	RS	U.S.	1995	$20.00
	Airdate: 4/24/95.					
Warner Brothers	926034-2	Best of Rod Stewart, The	LP	France		$30.00
Eclipse	4861-2	Best of Rod Stewart, The	LTD/LP	U.S.	1996	$18.00
	CD in custom screen-printed square tin.					
Warner Brothers	23877-2	Body Wishes	LP/LB	U.S.†	1984	$14.00/$8.00
Warner Brothers	25095-2	Camouflage	LP/LB	U.S.†	1985	$14.00/$8.00
Mercury	822385-2	Every Picture Tells a Story	LP/BP	U.S.†	1985	$14.00/$8.00
Vertigo		Great Box	LTD/LP	Japan	1990	$65.00
	4CD set.					
Warner Brothers	03373-2	Greatest Hits	LP/LB	U.S.†	1984	$14.00/$8.00
		Have I Told You Lately	RS	U.S.		$30.00
	2 CD set.					
Nelson	121150	He's You	LD	U.S.	1983	$40.00
Album Network		In the Studio (Every Picture Tells a Story)	RS	U.S.	1988	$30.00
	Airdate: 7/25/88.					
Album Network		In the Studio (Every Picture Tells a Story)	RS	U.S.	1990	$25.00
	Airdate: 4/2/90.					
DIR		King Biscuit Flour Hour	RS	U.S.	1988	$35.00
	With Joe Walsh, Airdate: 7/26/88.					
DIR		King Biscuit Flour Hour	RS	U.S.	1989	$30.00
	Airdate: 7/16/89.					
DIR		King Biscuit Flour Hour	RS	U.S.	1990	$30.00
	Airdate: 12/18/90.					
DIR		King Biscuit Flour Hour	RS	U.S.	1990	$30.00
	Airdate: 2/12/90.					
DIR		King Biscuit Flour Hour	RS	U.S.	1990	$30.00
	Airdate: 8/27/90.					
DIR		King Biscuit Flour Hour	RS	U.S.	1991	$30.00
DIR		King Biscuit Flour Hour	RS	U.S.	1992	$30.00
	Airdate: 8/30/92.					
DIR		King Biscuit Flour Hour	RS	U.S.	1995	$20.00
	Airdate: 3/12/95.					
Radio Ventures		Masters of Rock	RS	U.S.	1989	$40.00
	Airdate: 11/13/89.					
Warner Brothers	9 25446-2	Rod Stewart	LP/LB	U.S.†	1986	$16.00/$12.00
Warner Brothers	9 25446-2	Rod Stewart	LP/LB	U.S.	1988	$16.00/$12.00
Lorimar	LV099	Rod Stewart in Concert	LD	U.S.	1987	$30.00
WEA	38255	Storyteller	LD	U.S.	1991	$30.00
Westwood One		Superstars	RS	U.S.	1993	$60.00
	2 CD set. Airdate: 11/14/93.					
Westwood One		Superstars	RS	U.S.	1994	$50.00
	2 CD set. Airdate: 5/30/94					
Westwood One		Superstars	RS	U.S.	1995	$60.00
	2 CD set. Airdate: 2/20/95.					
Media America		Up Close	RS	U.S.	1988	$35.00
	2 CD set.					
Warner Brothers	9 26300-2-Dj	Vagabond Heart	DJ/LP	U.S.	1991	$17.00
WEA	38300	Vagabond Heart Tour	LD	U.S.	1992	$35.00

Singles

Label	Catalog Number	Title	Type	Country	Year	Longbox Value / Value
WEA	PROP30	A Spanner In the Works	CDJ	U.K.		$15.00
Warner Brothers	W-0059CD	Broken Arrow	CD5	U.K.	1991	$10.00
Warner Brothers	PRO-CD-4864	Broken Arrow	CDJ	U.S.	1991	$3.00
WEA	921297-2	Crazy About Her	CD3	Germany	1989	$10.00
Warner Brothers	PRO-CD-3612	Crazy About Her	CDJ	U.S.	1988	$3.00
Warner Brothers	PRO-CD-3334	Crazy About Her	CDJ	U.S.	1989	$3.00
Warner Brothers	PRO-CD-6213	Cut Across Shortly	CDJ	U.S.	1993	$3.00
WEA	921448-2	Downtown Train	CD5	Germany	1989	$10.00
Pioneer	WPDP-6214	Downtown Train	CD3	Japan	1990	$15.00/$4.00
WEA	W-2647CD	Downtown Train	CD5	U.K.	1989	$10.00
Warner Brothers	PRO-CD-3836	Downtown Train	CDJ	U.S.	1989	$3.00
Warner Brothers	PRO-CD-3146	Dynamite	CDJ	U.S.	1988	$3.00
		Every Picture Tells a Story	CDJ	Spain	1993	$18.00
WEA	921031-2	Forever Young	CD3	Germany	1988	$10.00
Pioneer	10P3-6008	Forever Young	CD3	Japan	1988	$15.00/$4.00
WEA	W-7796CD	Forever Young	CD3	U.K.	1988	$10.00
Warner Brothers	PRO-CD-3169	Forever Young	CDJ	U.S.	1988	$3.00
Warner Brothers	WPDP-6327	Have I Told You Lately	CD3	Japan	1993	$15.00/$4.00
		Have I Told You Lately	CD5	U.K.		$10.00
		Have I Told You Lately	CD5	U.K.		$10.00
	Second version.					
Warner Brothers	PRO-CD-6161	Have I Told You Lately	CDJ	U.S.	1993	$3.00
		Having a Party	CDJ	Spain	1993	$18.00
Warner Brothers	PRO-CD-6360	Having a Party	CDJ	U.S.	1993	$2.00
Warner Brothers	PRO-CD-3902	I Don't Want to Talk About It	CDJ	U.S.	1989	$3.00
WEA	7599-21815-2	It Takes Two	CD5	Germany	1990	$10.00
Warner	W0310CD	Lady Luck	CD5	U.K.	1995	$11.00
Warner	W0310CDDJ	Lady Luck	CD5	U.K.	1995	$11.00
Warner		Lady Luck	CD5	U.K.	1995	$11.00
	Second version.					
Warner Brothers	PRO-CD-7624-R	Leave Virginia Alone	CDJ	U.S.	1995	$2.00
WEA	920949-2	Lost in You	CD3	Germany	1988	$10.00
Warner Brothers	10SW-23	Lost in You	CD3	Japan	1988	$15.00/$4.00
WEA	W-7927CD	Lost in You	CD3	U.K.	1988	$10.00
Warner Brothers	PRO-CD-3052	Lost in You	CDJ	U.S.	1988	$7.00
Polygram	888972-2	Maggie May	CD5	Germany	1990	$10.00
Warner Brothers	PRO-CD-4923	Moment of Glory	CDJ	U.S.	1991	$3.00
Warner Brothers	9362-40102-2	Motown Song, The	CD5	Germany	1991	$10.00
Warner Brothers	W0030CD	Motown Song, The	CD5	U.K.	1991	$10.00
Warner Brothers	PRO-CD-4857	Motown Song, The	CDJ	U.S.	1991	$3.00
Warner Brothers	PRO-CD-5061	Motown Song, The	CDJ	U.S.	1991	$3.00
WEA	921130-2	My Heart Can't Tell You No	CD3	Germany	1988	$10.00
WEA	W-27729CD	My Heart Can't Tell You No	CD3	U.K.	1988	$10.00
Warner Brothers	PRO-CD-3261	My Heart Can't Tell You No	CDJ	U.S.	1988	$3.00
		People Get Ready	CD5	U.K.		$10.00
		People Get Ready	CD5	U.K.		$10.00
	Second version.					
		Purple Heather	CD5	U.K.	1996	$10.00
Warner Brothers	W-0198CD	Reason to Believe	CD5	U.K.	1993	$10.00
Warner Brothers		Reason to Believe	CD5	U.K.	1993	$10.00
	Second version.					
Warner Brothers	9 18427-2	Reason to Believe	CD5	U.S.	1993	$5.00
Warner Brothers	PRO-CD-6354	Reason to Believe	CDJ	U.S.	1993	$3.00
Warner Brothers	PRO-CD-4831	Rebel Heart	CDJ	U.S.	1991	$3.00
WEA	9362-40036-2	Rhythm of My Heart	CD5	Germany	1991	$10.00
Warner Brothers	WPDP-6271	Rhythm of My Heart	CD3	Japan	1991	$15.00/$4.00
WEA	W-0017CD	Rhythm of My Heart	CD5	U.K.	1991	$10.00
Warner Brothers	PRO-CD-4742	Rhythm of My Heart	CDJ	U.S.	1991	$3.00
		Shotgun Wedding	CD5	U.K.		$10.00
		Shotgun Wedding	CD5	U.K.		$10.00
	Second version.					
Warner Brothers	PRO-CD-7602-R	This	CDJ	U.S.		$3.00
Warner Brothers	17854	This	CD5	U.S.	1995	$5.00
WEA	921405-2	This Old Heart of Mine	CD3	Germany	1989	$10.00
Warner Brothers	WPDP-6231	This Old Heart of Mine	CD3	Japan	1990	$15.00/$4.00
WEA	W-2686CD	This Old Heart of Mine	CD3	U.K.	1989	$10.00
Warner Brothers	PRO-CD-3837	This Old Heart of Mine	CDJ	U.S.	1989	$3.00
		Tom Traubert's Blues	CD5	U.K.		$10.00
	Second version.					
WEA	W-0144CD	Tom Traubert's Blues	CD5	U.K.	1992	$10.00
WEA	W-7629CD	Try a Little Tenderness	CD3	U.K.	1989	$10.00
Warner Brothers	PRO-CD-3145	Wild Horse, The	CDJ	U.S.	1988	$3.00
Mercury	MERCD-379	You Wear It Well	CD5	U.K.	1992	$10.00
WEA	9362-40450-2	Your Song	CD5	Germany	1992	$10.00
Warner Brothers	WPDP-6298	Your Song	CD3	Japan	1992	$15.00/$4.00
WEA	W-0104CD	Your Song	CD5	U.K.	1992	$10.00
Polydor	CDP 669	Your Song	CDJ	U.S.	1991	$6.00

Stiff Little Fingers

Singles

Label	Catalog Number	Title	Type	Country	Year	Longbox Value / Value
Essential	2035	Can't Believe in You	CDJ	U.K.	1994	$10.00
Kaz	CD6	No Sleep 'Til Belfast	CD5	U.K.	1988	$8.00

Stigers, Curtis

Singles

Label	Catalog Number	Title	Type	Country	Year	Longbox Value / Value
Arista	BVDA-31	I Wonder Why	CD3	Japan	1992	$12.00/$4.00
Arista	664716	I Wonder Why	CD5	U.K.	1992	$9.00
Arista	ASCD 2331	I Wonder Why	CDJ	U.S.	1991	$2.00
Arista	BVDA-52	Never Saw a Miracle	CD3	Japan	1992	$12.00/$4.00
		Never Saw a Miracle	CD5	U.K.		$10.00
		Never Saw a Miracle	CD5	U.K.		$10.00
	Second version.					
Arista	ASCD 2459	Never Saw a Miracle	CDJ	U.S.	1991	$2.00
Arista	BVDA-42	Sleeping With the Lights on	CD3	Japan	1992	$12.00/$4.00
Arista	74321-102302	Sleeping With the Lights on	CD5	U.K.	1992	$9.00
Arista	74321-102432	Sleeping With the Lights on	CD5	U.K.	1992	$9.00
Arista	ASCD 2430	Sleeping With the Lights on	CDJ	U.S.	1992	$2.00
Arista		Time Was	CDJ	U.S.		$3.00
Arista	BVDA-37	You're All That Matters	CD3	Japan	1992	$12.00/$4.00
Arista	ASCD-2391	You're All That Matters	CDJ	U.S.	1992	$2.00

Stigmata

Singles

Label	Catalog Number	Title	Type	Country	Year	Longbox Value / Value
		Going Up for Air	CDJ	Canada		$5.00

Stills, Stephen

Full Length

Label	Catalog Number	Title	Type	Country	Year	Longbox Value / Value
Atlantic	80177-2	Right by You	LP/LB	U.S.†	1985	$14.00/$8.00
		Superstars	RS	U.S.	1996	$90.00
	2 CD set. Airdate 3/18/96.					
Westwood One		Superstars	RS	U.S.	1996	$90.00
	2 CD set. Airdate: 3/18/96.					

Sting

Full Length

Label	Catalog Number	Title	Type	Country	Year	Longbox Value / Value
		A Self Portrait	RS	U.S.	1992	$35.00
A&M	PCCY-10281	Acoustic Live in New Castle, The Illustrated Lyrics	LTD/LP	Japan	1991	$60.00
	Limited live CD with book in 12"x12" box.					
Westwood One		BBC Classic Tracks	RS	U.S.	1995	$50.00
	Airdate: 11/6/95.					
A&M	DCI-3084	Best For D.J.	DJ/Smplr	Japan	1993	$225.00
A&M		Best of 1984 - 1994	LTD/LP	Japan	1994	$50.00
	2 CD set.					
A&M	CD-3750	Dream of the Blue Turtles	LP/LB	U.S.†	1985	$14.00/$8.00
Radio Ventures		Masters of Rock	RS	U.S.	1989	$40.00
	Airdate: 10/16/89.					
A&M		Nuggets From Fields of Gold	DJ/Smplr	U.S.	1993	$25.00
Westwood One		Off the Record	RS	U.S.	1992	$30.00
	Airdate: 5/11/92.					
Westwood One		Off the Record	RS	U.S.	1993	$25.00
	Airdate: 8/23/93.					
Westwood One		Off the Record	RS	U.S.	1993	$30.00
	Airdate: 3/22/93.					
Westwood One		Off the Record	RS	U.S.	1994	$25.00
	Airdate: 12/12/94.					
Westwood One		Off the Record	RS	U.S.	1994	$30.00
	Airdate: 2/14/94.					
Westwood One		On the Edge	RS	U.S.	1994	$30.00
	Airdate: 2/14/94.					

Label	Catalog Number	Title	Type	Country	Year	Longbox Value / Value
Radio Today		Self-Portrait	RS	U.S.		$50.00
A&M		Soul Cages Interview	DJ/Intvw	Canada	1991	$20.00
A&M		Soul Cages, The	DJ/LP	U.S.	1991	$60.00
	CD wrapped in linen cloth and twine.					
A&M	75021 6405 2	Soul Cages, The	LP/LB	U.S.	1991	$12.00/$7.00
	1st pressing packaged in longbox.					
A&M	CD 6405	Soul Cages, The	LP/JC	U.S.	1991	$15.00
A&M	DSP-112	Special 91 Compilation	DJ/Smplr	Japan	1991	$150.00
A&M	DSP-6	Special DJ Copy	DJ/Smplr	Japan	1992	N/A
		Sting	RS	U.S.	1996	$75.00
	3 CD set.					
Westwood One		Superstar Concert	RS	U.S.	1992	$70.00
	2 CD set. Airdate: 8/2/92.					
Westwood One		Superstar Concert	RS	U.S.	1994	$70.00
	2 CD set. Airdate: 6/27/94.					
Westwood One		Superstars	RS	U.S.	1995	$65.00
	Airdate: 4/3/95.					
A&M	540193-2	Ten Sumner's Tales	LTD/LP	Australia	1994	$35.00
	CD of album and bonus live CD in box.					
A&M	POCM-9005/6	Ten Sumner's Tales	LTD/LP	Japan	1994	$50.00
	CD of album and bonus live CD .					
A&M		Ten Sumner's Tales Interview	DJ/Intvw	U.S.	1993	$20.00
		Timothy White Sessions	RS	U.S.	1993	$90.00
	2 CD set. Airdate: 7/5/93.					
		Timothy White Sessions	RS	U.S.	1993	$100.00
	2 CD set. Airdate: 4/8/91.					
Media America		Up Close	RS	U.S.	1988	$50.00
	2 CD set.					
Media America		Up Close	RS	U.S.	1991	$50.00
	2 CD set.					
Media America		Up Close	RS	U.S.	1993	$95.00
	3 CD set.					
A&M	LV 38405	Videos Pt. 1 – Nothing Like the Sun	LD	U.S.	1989	$25.00
	Non-Digital.					
		Singles				
A&M	390614-2	All This Time	CD5	Germany	1990	$12.00
A&M	75021 7486 2	All This Time	CDJ	U.S.	1991	$3.00
A&M	CD 17529	Be Still My Beating Heart	CDJ	U.S.	1987	$3.00
A&M		Brought to My Senses	CD5	U.K.	1996	$12.00
A&M		Brought to My Senses	CD5	U.K.	1996	$12.00
	Second version.					
A&M	AMCD-911	Compact Hits	CD5	U.K.	1988	$12.00
A&M		Cowboy Song	CDJ	U.K.	1994	$12.00
A&M		Cowboy Song	CDJ	U.S.	1994	$7.00
A&M	PODM-1020	Demolition Man	CD3	Japan	1993	$18.00/$4.00
		Demolition Man	CD5	U.K.		$12.00
		Demolition Man	CD5	U.K.		$12.00
	Second version.					
A&M	31458 0465	Demolition Man	CDJ	U.S.	1993	$6.00
A&M	31458 8198	Demolition Man	CDJ	U.S.	1993	$6.00
A&M	390346-2	Englishman in New York	CD5	Germany	1988	$12.00
A&M	390562-2	Englishman in New York	CD5	Germany	1990	$12.00
A&M	S12Y-3025	Englishman in New York	CD3	Japan	1988	$18.00/$4.00
A&M	431	Englishman in New York	CD5	U.K.	1988	$12.00
A&M	AMCD-431	Englishman in New York	CD5	U.K.	1988	$12.00
A&M	AMCD-580	Englishman in New York	CD5	U.K.	1990	$20.00
A&M	31001	Englishman in New York	CD3	U.S.	1988	$12.00/$8.00
A&M	PODM-1013	Fields of Gold	CD3	Japan	1993	$18.00/$4.00
		Fields of Gold	CD5	U.K.		$12.00
		Fields of Gold	CD5	U.K.		$12.00
	Second version.					
A&M	31458 0259-2	Fields of Gold	CD5	U.S.	1993	$6.00
A&M	31458 8111	Fields of Gold	CDJ	U.S.	1993	$6.00
A&M	390307-2	Fragile	CD5	Germany	1988	$12.00
A&M	S10Y-3041	Fragile	CD3	Japan	1988	$18.00/$4.00
A&M	439	Fragile	CD5	U.K.	1988	$12.00
A&M	AMCD-439	Fragile	CD5	U.K.	1988	$12.00
A&M	PODM-1008	If I Ever Lose My Faith in You	CD3	Japan	1993	$18.00/$4.00
A&M	POCM-1022	If I Ever Lose My Faith in You	CD5	Japan	1993	$16.00
A&M		If I Ever Lose My Faith in You	CD5	U.K.	1993	$12.00
A&M		If I Ever Lose My Faith in You	CD5	U.K.	1993	$12.00
	Second version.					
A&M	31458 8091	If I Ever Lose My Faith in You	CDJ	U.S.	1993	$3.00
A&M	PCDY-10033	It's Probably Me	CD3	Japan	1992	$18.00/$4.00
A&M		It's Probably Me	CD5	U.K.	1992	$12.00
A&M		It's Probably Me	CD5	U.S.	1992	$5.00
A&M	75021 7391-2	It's Probably Me	CDJ	U.S.	1992	$3.00
A&M	PODM-1056	Let Your Soul Pilot	CD3	Japan		$13.00/$4.00
A&M		Live At T.G.I. Friday	CD5	U.K.	1996	$12.00
A&M	AMCDR-721	Mad About You	CD5	U.K.	1991	$12.00
A&M	75021 7294 2	Mad About You	CDJ	U.S.	1991	$6.00
A&M	75021 7499 2	Mad About You	CDJ	U.S.	1991	$6.00
A&M	31458-8138-2	Nothing 'Bout Me	CDJ	U.S.	1994	$6.00
A&M	S12Y-3010	Set Them Free	CD3	Japan	1988	$18.00/$4.00
A&M		Seven Days	CD5	Australia	1994	$12.00
		Seven Days	CD5	U.K.		$12.00
		Seven Days	CD5	U.K.		$12.00
	Second version.					
		Shape of My Heart	CD5	U.K.		$12.00
		Shape of My Heart	CD5	U.K.		$12.00
	Second version.					
A&M		Shape of My Heart	CD5	U.K.	1993	$12.00
A&M		Shape of My Heart	CD5	U.K.	1993	$12.00
	Second version.					
A&M		Shape of My Heart	CDJ	U.S.	1994	$7.00
A&M		She's So Good to Me	CD5	France	1994	$11.00
A&M	390759-2	Soul Cages, The	CD5	Germany	1991	$12.00
A&M	AMCD-759	Soul Cages, The	CD5	U.K.	1991	$12.00
A&M	75021 7530 2	Soul Cages, The	CDJ	U.S.	1991	$6.00
		Spirits in the Material World	CDJ	U.S.	1995	$6.00
A&M	390325-2	They Dance Alone	CD5	Germany	1988	$12.00
A&M	S10Y-3052	They Dance Alone	CD3	Japan	1988	$18.00/$4.00
A&M	AMCD-458	They Dance Alone	CD5	U.K.	1988	$12.00
A&M	CD 17613	They Dance Alone	CDJ	U.S.	1987	$6.00
A&M	D15Y-3197	We'll Be Together	CD5	Japan	1988	$15.00
A&M	AMCD-410	We'll Be Together	CD5	U.K.	1987	$12.00
A&M	PODM-1044	When We Dance	CD3	Japan		$13.00/$4.00
A&M		When We Dance	CD5	U.K.	1994	$12.00
A&M		When We Dance	CDJ	U.K.	1994	$12.00
A&M	80854	When We Dance	CD5	U.S.	1994	$5.00
A&M	31458 8345-2	When We Dance	CDJ	U.S.	1994	$7.00
A&M		When We Dance	CDJ	U.S.	1994	$7.00
	Second version.					
A&M	PCCY-10236	Why Should I Cry for You	CD3	Japan	1991	$18.00/$5.00
A&M	75021 2364 2	Why Should I Cry for You	CD5	U.S.	1991	$6.00
A&M	75021 7535 2	Why Should I Cry for You	CDJ	U.S.	1991	$6.00
A&M	75021 7547 2	Why Should I Cry for You	CDJ	U.S.	1991	$6.00
A&M		You Still Touch Me	CD5	Japan	1996	$18.00
A&M		You Still Touch Me	CD5	U.K.	1996	$12.00
A&M		You Still Touch Me	CD5	U.K.	1996	$12.00
	Second version.					
A&M		You Still Touch Me	CDJ	U.K.	1996	$12.00
A&M	AMCDP00207	You Still Touch Me	CDJ	U.S.		$3.00

Stitt, Sonny

Label	Catalog Number	Title	Type	Country	Year	Longbox Value / Value
		Full Length				
Denon	CD-7046	Moonlight in Vermont	LP/LB	U.S.†	1985	$14.00/$8.00

Stockman, Shawn

Label	Catalog Number	Title	Type	Country	Year	Longbox Value / Value
		Singles				
		Visions of Sunset	CDJ	U.S.		$2.00
Polydor	00129	Visions of Sunset	CDJ	U.S.	1995	$7.00

Stone, Doug

Label	Catalog Number	Title	Type	Country	Year	Longbox Value / Value
		Full Length				
		'90s Country	RS	U.S.	1995	$30.00
	Airdate: 8/26/95.					
		Country Special	RS	U.S.	1994	$40.00
	Airdate: 2/7/94.					
		Singles				
Epic	ESK 74259	Come in out of the Pain	CDJ	U.S.	1992	$2.00

Stone Fury

Label	Catalog Number	Title	Type	Country	Year	Longbox Value / Value
		Full Length				
MCA	25XD-1088	Best of	LP	Japan		$30.00
MCA	MCAD-42208	Best of	LP/LB	U.S.		$18.00/$15.00

Stone Roses

Label	Catalog Number	Title	Type	Country	Year	Longbox Value / Value
		Full Length				
Geffen		Complete Stone Roses, The	LTD/LP	Japan	1995	$35.00
	2CD set.					
		Complete, The	LTD/LP	Australia	1995	$28.00
	2 CD set.					
Jive		Stone Roses	LP/LB	U.S		$14.00/$8.00
	First pressing missing track "Fool's Gold."					
		Singles				
RCA	ZD-43600	Elephant Stone	CD5	Germany	1990	$9.00
Silvertone	ORECD-1	Elephant Stone	CD5	U.K.	1990	$9.00
RCA	ZD-43322	Fools Gold	CD5	Germany	1989	$9.00
Silvertone	ORECD-13	Fools Gold	CD5	U.K.	1989	$9.00
Silvertone	1315-2-JDj	Fools Gold	CDJ	U.S.	1990	$2.00
Silvertone	ORECD-40	I Am the Resurrection	CD5	U.K.	1992	$9.00
Silvertone	ALCB-392	I Wanna Be Adored	CD5	Japan	1991	$13.00
Silvertone	ORECD-31	I Wanna Be Adored	CD5	U.K.	1991	$9.00
Silvertone		I Wanna Be Adored	CDJ	U.S.	1991	$2.00
Jive		Love Spreads	CD5	U.K.		$12.00
Jive		Love Spreads	CDJ	U.S.		$6.00
RCA	886796	Made Of Stone	CD5	Germany	1990	$9.00
Silvertone	ORECD-2	Made Of Stone	CD5	U.K.	1990	$9.00
RCA	ZD-43686	One Love	CD5	Germany	1990	$9.00
Silvertone	ALCB-103	One Love	CD5	Japan	1990	$13.00
Silvertone	ORECD-17	One Love	CD5	U.K.	1990	$9.00
Silverton	1399	One Love	CD5	U.S.	1990	$5.00
Aris	884008	Sally Cinnamon	CD5	Germany	1990	$9.00
Alfa	ALCB-295	Sally Cinnamon	CD5	Japan	1990	$15.00
FM	REVXD-36	Sally Cinnamon	CD5	U.K.	1990	$9.00
RCA	ZD-42970	She Bangs the Drums	CD5	Germany	1989	$9.00
Alfa	09B3-46	She Bangs the Drums	CD3	Japan	1989	$12.00/$4.00
Silvertone	ORECD-6	She Bangs the Drums	CD5	U.K.	1989	$9.00
Silvertone	ORECD-37	So Young	CD5	U.K.	1989	$9.00
Silvertone	JDJ-421012	Standing Here	CD5	U.K.	1992	$9.00
Silvertone	42101	Standing Here	CDJ	U.S.	1992	$2.00
Geffen		Ten Storey Love Song	CD5	U.K.	1995	$10.00
Geffen	PRO-CD-4731	Ten Storey Love Song	CDJ	U.S.	1995	$6.00
Silvertone	ORECD-35	Waterfall	CD5	U.K.	1992	$9.00

Stone, Sharon

Label	Catalog Number	Title	Type	Country	Year	Longbox Value / Value
		Singles				
	FTR 38242	Wonderful	CD5	France	1994	$11.00

Stone, Steve

Label	Catalog Number	Title	Type	Country	Year	Longbox Value / Value
		Singles				
Epic	ESK 73484	Faces in the Rain	CDJ	U.S.	1990	$2.00
Epic	ESK 73638	Standing on the Edge	CDJ	U.S.	1990	$2.00

Stone Temple Pilots

Label	Catalog Number	Title	Type	Country	Year	Longbox Value / Value
		Full Length				
Westwood One		In Concert	RS	U.S.	1993	$50.00
	2 CD set. With Billy Idol, Airdate: 11/6/93.					
Westwood One		In Concert	RS	U.S.	1994	$70.00
	2 CD set. Airdate: 5/9/94.					
Westwood One		In Concert	RS	U.S.	1995	$50.00
	Airdate: 2/27/95.					
Westwood One		In Concert	RS	U.S.	1995	$50.00
	Airdate: 9/25/95.					
Westwood One		In Concert-Nu Rock	RS	U.S.	1995	$50.00
	Airdate: 2/13/95.					
Westwood One		In Concert-Nu Rock	RS	U.S.	1995	$65.00
	2 CD set with Faith No More. Airdate: 7/17/95.					
		Singles				
Atlantic	PRCD 6691-2	Big Bang Baby	CDJ	U.S.	1996	$6.00
Atlantic	PRCD 4973-2	Crackerman	CDJ	U.S.	1993	$8.00
Atlantic	PRCD 5328-2	Creep	CDJ	U.S.	1993	$7.00
Atlantic	PRCD 5339-2	Creep	CDJ	U.S.	1993	$7.00
Atlantic	PRCD 6223-2	Dancing Days	CDJ	U.S.	1995	$7.00
Atlantic	A7192CDX	Interstate Love Song	CDJ	U.K.	1994	$10.00
Atlantic		Interstate Love Song	CDJ	U.S.	1994	$7.00
Atlantic	PRCD 4982-2	Plush	CDJ	U.S.	1993	$7.00
Atlantic		Pretty Penny	CDJ	U.S.	1994	$6.00
Atlantic		Pretty Penny	CDJ	U.S.	1996	$7.00
		Sex Type Thing	CD5	U.K.		$10.00
		Sex Type Thing	CD5	U.K.		$10.00
	Second version.					
Atlantic	PRCD 4785-2	Sex Type Thing	CDJ	U.S.	1992	$7.00
Atlantic		Unglued	CDJ	U.S.	1994	$6.00
Atlantic		Vasoline	CD5	Australia	1994	$12.00
Atlantic		Vasoline	CD5	Germany	1994	$10.00
Atlantic		Vasoline	CD5	U.K.	1994	$10.00
Atlantic		Vasoline	CD5	U.K.	1994	$10.00
	Second version.					
Atlantic	PRCD 5672-2	Vasoline	CDJ	U.S.	1994	$7.00
	Vaseline label.					
Atlantic	PRCD 5672-2	Vasoline	CDJ	U.S.	1994	$8.00
	Picture disc version.					

Label	Catalog Number	Title	Type	Country	Year	Longbox Value / Value
Atlantic	PRCD 5672-2	Vasoline	CDJ	U.S.	1994	$10.00
Atlantic	PRCD 5141-2	Wicked Garden	CDJ	U.S.	1993	$7.00
Stories						
Full Length						
Buddah		About Us	LP/BP	U.S.		$12.00/$7.00
Story						
Full Length						
Elektra	PRCD 8785-2	Angel in the House, The	DJ/Smplr	U.S.	1993	$8.00
Singles						
Elektra	PRCD 8574-2	Grace in Gravity	CDJ	U.S.	1991	$2.00
Elektra	PRCD 8775-2	So Much Mine	CDJ	U.S.	1993	$2.00
Elektra	PRCD 8847-2	When Two and Two Are Five	CDJ	U.S.	1993	$2.00
Story, Liz						
Full Length						
Windham	WD-1023	Solid Colors	LP/LB	U.S.†	1985	$14.00/$8.00
Windham	WD-1034	Unaccountable Effect	LP/LB	U.S.†	1985	$14.00/$8.00
Stradlin, Izzy						
Full Length						
Westwood One		In Concert	RS	U.S.	1993	$60.00
2 CD set. Airdate: 7/7/93.						
Singles						
Geffen	GFSTD-25	Pressure Drop	CD5	U.K.	1992	$10.00
Geffen	GFSTD-33	Shuffle It All	CD5	U.K.	1992	$10.00
Geffen	PRO-CD-4464	Shuffle It All	CDJ	U.S.	1992	$3.00
Geffen	PRO-CD-4486	Somebody Knockin'	CDJ	U.S.	1992	$3.00
Geffen	PRO-CD-4509	Train Tracks	CDJ	U.S.	1992	$3.00
Strait, George						
Full Length						
		'90s Country	RS	U.S.	1995	$40.00
Airdate: 11/11/95.						
		'90s Country	RS	U.S.	1995	$40.00
Airdate: 4/8/95.						
MCA	40798	George Strait Live!	LD	U.S.	1991	$30.00
MCA	MCAD-5567	Greatest Hits	LP/LB	U.S.†	1985	$14.00/$8.00
	40798	Live	LD	U.S.		$30.00
MCA	MCAD-5605	Something Special	LP/LB	U.S.†	1985	$14.00/$8.00
MCA		Strait out of the Box Sampler	DJ/Smplr	U.S.	1995	$20.00
MCA	MCAC-10204	Tenth Anniversary Limited Edition	DJ/Smplr	U.S.	1991	$35.00
Picture CD in round wooden container with laser-etched lid.						
Singles						
MCA	DMCAT-1434	All My Ex's Live in Texas	CD5	U.K.	1990	$10.00
MCA	MCA5P-54180	Chill of an Early Fall, The	CDJ	U.S.	1991	$3.00
MCA	MCA5P-54379	Gone as a Girl Can Get	CDJ	U.S.	1992	$3.00
MCA	MCA5P-54563	Heartland	CDJ	U.S.	1992	$3.00
MCA	MCA5P-54478	I Cross My Heart	CDJ	U.S.	1992	$3.00
MCA	MCA5P-53969	I've Come to Expect It From You	CDJ	U.S.	1992	$3.00
MCA	CD45 4052	If I Know Me	CDJ	U.S.	1991	$3.00
MCA	CD45 3026	If I Know Me	CDJ	U.S.	1991	$7.00
MCA	CD45 79015	Love Without End, Amen	CDJ	U.S.	1990	$3.00
MCA	MCA5P-54819	Lovebug	CDJ	U.S.	1994	$3.00
MCA	CD45 53755	Overnight Success	CDJ	U.S.	1989	$3.00
MCA	MCA5P-54439	So Much Like My Dad	CDJ	U.S.	1992	$3.00
MCA	DMCAT-1447	Someone Had to Teach You	CD5	U.K.	1990	$10.00
Strait Jacket Fits						
Singles						
Arista	ASCD-2557	Cat Inna Can	CDJ	U.S.	1993	$2.00
Flying Nun	D11263	Done	CD5	Australia	1992	$8.00
Arista	ASCD-2639	If I Were You	CDJ	U.S.	1993	$2.00
Arista	ASCD-2244	Missing	CDJ	U.S.	1991	$7.00
Arista	ASCD-2256	Roller Ride	CDJ	U.S.	1991	$2.00
Stranglers						
Full Length						
		Rattus Norvegicus	LTD/LP	U.K.	1996	$30.00
2 CD set.						
Singles						
Epic	655656-3	96 Tears	CD3	Germany	1990	$8.00
Epic	TEARSC-1	96 Tears	CD5	U.K.	1990	$8.00
Epic	CDVICE-1	All Day and All of the Night	CD5	U.K.	1990	$8.00
Epic	655168-3	Always the Sun	CD3	Germany	1989	$8.00
Epic	656761-2	Golden Brown	CD5	U.K.	1991	$8.00
Liberty	CDEM-84	Grip '89	CD5	U.K.	1989	$8.00
		Lies & Deception	CD5	U.K.	1995	$10.00
		Lies & Deception	CD5	U.K.	1995	$10.00
Second version.						
Epic	656430-5	Live at Alexandria Palace	CD5	U.K.	1990	$8.00
Strange Frt	SFNTCD-020	Radio One Sessions	CD5	U.K.	1989	$8.00
Epic	ESK 2160	Someone Like You	CDJ	U.S.	1990	$2.00
Psycho	PSYCD-002	Sugar Bullets	CD5	U.K.	1992	$8.00
Epic	TEARSC-2	Sweet Smell of Success	CD5	U.K.	1990	$8.00
Epic	ESK 2067	Sweet Smell of Success	CDJ	U.S.	1990	$2.00
Straw, Sid						
Full Length						
		War and Peace	DJ/LP	U.S.		$8.00
Singles						
Virgin	VUSCD-6	Future '40s	CD3	U.K.	1989	$8.00
Virgin	PRCD 2788	Future '40s	CDJ	U.K.	1989	$2.00
Virgin	PRCD 3139	Heart of Darkness	CDJ	U.K.	1989	$2.00
	PRO4205A	Love and the Lack of It	CDJ	U.S.		$2.00
Virgin		Surprise	CDJ	U.S.	1989	$7.00
CD in spring loaded cardboard package.						
Virgin	VUSCD-16	Think Too Hard	CD3	U.K.	1990	$8.00
Virgin	PRCD 2932	Think Too Hard	CDJ	U.S.	1989	$2.00
Strawberry Zots						
Singles						
Continuum		And You (Drive Your Pretty Car)	CDJ	U.S.	1991	$2.00
Continuum		Give Me to the World on Time	CDJ	U.S.	1991	$2.00
Continuum	19105-2	Love Operation	CD5	U.S.	1991	$5.00
Continuum	19105-2	Love Operation	CD5	U.S.	1991	$5.00
Strawpeople						
Singles						
Pagan	8802542	Have a Little Faith	CD5	Austalia	1991	$8.00
Stray Cats						
Full Length						
EMI	91401	Best of	LP/LB	U.S.	1989	$14.00/$8.00
RCA	35812	Choo Choo Hot Fish	LP/LB	U.S.		$12.00/$7.00
DIR		King Biscuit Flour Hour	RS	U.S.	1989	$30.00
Airdate:4/30/89.						
	SPCD-1515	Special DJ Copy	DJ/Smplr	Japan	1995	$200.00
Pioneer	PA84-M008	Stray Cats	8"LD	U.S.	1984	$8.00
Pioneer Artists	PA-84-M008	Stray Cats	LD	U.S.	1984	$11.00
Singles						
EMI	203272-2	Bring It Back Again	CD5	Germany	1989	$9.00
EMI	CDMT-62	Bring It Back Again	CD5	U.K.	1989	$9.00
		Bring It Back Again	CDJ	U.S.	1989	$2.00
Pump	907047-2	Elvis on Velvet	CD5	U.K.	1992	$9.00
Great Pyramid	35884-2	Elvis on Velvet	CD5	U.S.	1992	$5.00
Great Pyramid	812	Elvis on Velvet	CDJ	U.S.	1992	$2.00
EMI	203523-3	Gene and Eddie	CD3	Germany	1989	$9.00
EMI	DPRO-4304	Gene and Eddie	CDJ	U.S.	1988	$6.00
EMI	203403-3	Gina	CD3	Germany	1989	$9.00
EMI	CDMT-67	Gina	CD5	U.K.	1989	$9.00
Streisand, Barbara						
Full Length						
CBS	CK-9557	A Christmas Album	LP/BP	U.S.†	1984	$14.00/$8.00
CBS	CK-08807	Album	LP/LB	U.S.		$14.00/$8.00
		Central Park	LD	U.S.		$30.00
CBS	MK-33452	Classical Barbra	LP/BP	U.S.†	1985	$14.00/$8.00
CBS	CK-39480	Emotion	LP/BP	U.S.†	1985	$14.00/$8.00
CBS	XPCD-417	Event of the Decade, The	DJ/Smplr	U.K.	1994	$60.00
2 CD set.						
CBS	CK-35679	Greatest Hits Vol. 2	LP/BP	U.S.†	1984	$14.00/$8.00
CBS	CK-36750	Guilty	LP/BP	U.S.†	1984	$14.00/$8.00
Pioneer Artists	PA-88-205	Hoping	LD	U.S.	1988	$25.00
CBS	7101-80	My Name is Barbra	LD	U.S.	1986	$20.00
CBS	3519-80	My Name is Barbra	LD	U.S.	1986	$20.00
Columbia	CK-40876	Nuts	LP/BP	U.S.†	1983	$80.00/$80.00
		One Voice	LD	U.S.		$30.00
Columbia	CSK-6120	Ordinary Miracle Tour CD	DJ/Smplr	U.S.	1994	$25.00
Columbia	CSK 4196	Selections From Just for the Record...	DJ/Smplr	U.S.	1991	$15.00
Columbia	CSK 4200	Selections From Just for the Record...	DJ/Smplr	U.S.	1991	$15.00
Sony	XDDP-93081	Special Selection	DJ/Smplr	Japan	1994	$250.00
2 CD set.						
Pioneer Artists	PA-87-204	Voice	LD	U.S.	1987	$35.00
CBS	CK-36258	Wet	LP/BP	U.S.†	1984	$14.00/$8.00
Singles						
Columbia	653011-3	All I Ask of You	CD3	Germany	1989	$9.00
Columbia	CPBARB-3	All I Ask of You	CD5	U.K.	1989	$9.00
Columbia	CDBARB-3	All I Ask of You	CD5	U.K.	1989	$9.00
Columbia	CSK 1258	All I Ask of You	CDJ	U.S.	1988	$3.00
Columbia	CSK 5288	Children Will Listen	CDJ	U.S.	1993	$3.00
CBS		Evergreen	CDJ	Spain	1994	$50.00
Columbia		Evergreen	CDJ	U.S.	1994	$7.00
		I've Got a Crush on You	CDJ	Germany	1994	$25.00
		I've Got a Crush on You	CD5	U.K.	1994	$9.00
		Music Of the Night, The	CDJ	U.S.		$3.00
Columbia	651379-2	Nuts	CD5	Germany	1988	$9.00
Columbia	651379-2	Nuts	CD5	U.K.	1988	$9.00
CBS		Ordinary Miracles	CD5	U.K.	1994	$10.00
Columbia	77534	Ordinary Miracles	CD5	U.S.	1994	$6.00
Sony	SRDS-8218	Places That Belong to You	CD3	Japan	1992	$16.00/$4.00
Columbia	657794-5	Places That Belong to You	CD5	U.K.	1992	$15.00
CBS	XPCD170	Prince of Tides	CD5	U.K.		$20.00
Columbia	CSK 73099	Someone I Used to Love	CDJ	U.S.		$3.00
Columbia	CSK 5580	Speak Low	CDJ	U.S.	1993	$3.00
Columbia	652979-3	Till I Loved You	CD3	Germany	1988	$9.00
Sony	10EP-3054	Till I Loved You	CD3	Japan	1988	$15.00/$4.00
Columbia	CDBARB-2	Till I Loved You	CD5	U.K.	1988	$9.00
Columbia	CSK 1312	Till I Loved You	CDJ	U.S.	1988	$2.00
Columbia	655334-3	We're Not Making Love Anymore	CD3	Germany	1989	$9.00
Columbia	CSDS-8112	We're Not Making Love Anymore	CD3	Japan	1989	$15.00/$4.00
Columbia	CDBARB-4	We're Not Making Love Anymore	CD5	U.K.	1989	$9.00
Columbia	CSK 1816	We're Not Making Love Anymore	CDJ	U.S.	1989	$2.00
CBS	659342-2	With One Look	CD5	U.K.		$12.00
Stress						
Full Length						
Reprise	9 26607-2Dj	Stress	DJ/LP	U.S.	1991	$15.00
CD in "mood" sensitive-material bound digipak.						
WEA	9031-72513-2	Beautiful People	CD5	Germany	1991	$8.00
Eternal	YZ-495CD	Beautiful People	CD5	U.K.	1991	$8.00
Reprise	PRO-CD-5112	Beautiful People	CDJ	U.S.	1990	$2.00
Eternal	YZ-550CD	Flowers in the Rain	CD5	U.K.	1991	$8.00
Reprise	PRO-CD-4722	Flowers in the Rain	CDJ	U.S.	1991	$2.00
Reprise	PRO-CD-4788	Flowers in the Rain	CDJ	U.S.	1991	$2.00
WEA	9031-74491-2	Rosechild	CD5	Germany	1991	$8.00
Eternal	YZ-583CD	Rosechild	CD5	U.K.	1991	$8.00
Reprise	PRO-CD-4992	Rosechild	CDJ	U.S.	1991	$2.00
Strip Mind						
Singles						
Sire	PRO-CD-6661	Censored Edits	CDJ	U.S.	1993	$7.00
Strummer, Joe						
Full Length						
Epic		Earthquake Weather	LP/LB	U.S.		$14.00/$8.00
		Earthquake Weather	LP/LB	U.S.		$18.00/$15.00
Singles						
Epic	STRUMC-1	Gangsterville	CD5	U.K.	1989	$8.00
Epic	STRUMC-2	Island Hopping	CD5	U.K.	1989	$8.00
Epic	ESK 1770	Shouting Street	CDJ	U.S.	1989	$3.00
Epic	TRASHC-1	Trash City	CD5	U.K.	1988	$8.00
Strunz & Farah						
Full Length						
Milestone	FCD-9123	Frontera	LP/LB	U.S.†	1985	$14.00/$8.00
Strut						
Full Length						
Tropical		Unlimited Acess	LP	U.S.		$15.00
Stryper						
Full Length						
Image	ID7917EN	In the Beginning	LD	U.S.	1988	$15.00
Image	ID7919EN	Live in Japan	LD	U.S.	1988	$15.00
Singles						
Virgin	661662	Always There for You	CD5	Germany	1988	$8.00
Enigma	10SR-20	Always There for You	CD3	Japan	1988	$13.00/$4.00
Enigma	ENVCD-1	Always There for You	CD5	U.K.	1988	$8.00
Enigma	03 75509	Always There for You	CD3	U.S.	1988	$7.00/$4.00
Enigma	EPRO 086	Always There for You	CDJ	U.S.	1988	$2.00
Enigma	10SR-41	I Believe in You	CD3	Japan	1988	$13.00/$4.00

Label	Catalog Number	Title	Type	Country	Year	Longbox Value / Value
Enigma	EPRO 125	I Believe in You	CDJ	U.S.	1988	$2.00
Enigma	10B3-9	Keep the Fire Burning	CD3	Japan	1989	$13.00/$4.00
Enigma	EPRO 154	Keep the Fire Burning	CDJ	U.S.	1989	$2.00
EMI	203978-2	Shining Star	CD5	Germany	1990	$8.00
Enigma	EPRO 304	Shining Star	CDJ	U.S.	1990	$2.00

Stuart, Marty

Singles

Label	Catalog Number	Title	Type	Country	Year	Longbox Value / Value
MCA	MCA5P-54253	Burning Me Down	CDJ	U.S.	1991	$3.00
MCA	MCA5P-54538	High on a Mountain Top	CDJ	U.S.	1992	$7.00
MCA	MCA5P-54568	Honky Tonk Crowd	CDJ	U.S.	1992	$3.00
MCA	MCA5P-54777	Kiss Me, I'm Gone	CDJ	U.S.	1992	$3.00
MCA	MCA5P-53975	Little Things	CDJ	U.S.	1990	$3.00
MCA	MCA5P-54405	This One's Gonna Hurt	CDJ	U.S.	1992	$3.00

Stuermer, Daryl

Full Length

Label	Catalog Number	Title	Type	Country	Year	Longbox Value / Value
Grp		Steppin' Out	LP/LB	U.S.		$14.00/$8.00

Stuttering John

Singles

Label	Catalog Number	Title	Type	Country	Year	Longbox Value / Value
Atlantic	PRCD 5579-2	I'll Talk My Way out of It	CDJ	U.S.	1994	$2.00
Atlantic	PRCD 5588-2	I'll Talk My Way out of It	CDJ	U.S.	1994	$2.00

Style Council

Full Length

Label	Catalog Number	Title	Type	Country	Year	Longbox Value / Value
Image	ID6360ME	Far East & Out	LD	U.S.		$20.00

Singles

Label	Catalog Number	Title	Type	Country	Year	Longbox Value / Value
Polydor	887255-2	Bird's and the B's	CD5	Germany	1988	$8.00
Polydor	TSCCD-102	Bird's and the B's	CD5	U.K.	1988	$8.00
Polydor	887255-2	Cafe Bleu	CD5	Germany	1988	$8.00
Polydor	TSCCD-101	Cafe Bleu	CD5	U.K.	1988	$8.00
Polydor	P13P-37004	How She Threw It All Away	CD3	Japan	1988	$13.00/$4.00
Polydor	P10P-30007	Life at a Top People's Health Farm	CD3	Japan	1988	$13.00/$4.00
Polydor		Life at a Top People's Health Farm	CDV	U.K.		$38.00
Polydor	TSCCD-105	Life at a Top People's Health Farm	CD5	U.K.	1988	$8.00
Polydor	LHSCD-1	Long Hot Summer	CD5	U.K.	1989	$8.00
Polydor	887256-2	Mick Talbot Is Agent 88	CD5	Germany	1988	$8.00
Polydor	TSCCD-103	Mick Talbot Is Agent 88	CD5	U.K.	1988	$8.00
Polydor		One, Two, Three	CDV	U.K.		$38.00
Polydor	PODP-40009	Promised Land	CD3	Japan	1989	$13.00/$4.00
Polydor	PODP-37009	Promised Land	CD3	Japan	1989	$13.00/$4.00
Polydor	TSCCD-17	Promised Land	CD5	U.K.	1989	$8.00
Polydor	P13P-30011	Spank	CD3	Japan	1988	$13.00/$4.00
Polydor	TSCCD-16	Summer Quartet	CD5	U.K.	1988	$8.00
Polydor	887174-2	Wanted	CD5	Germany	1988	$8.00
Polydor	P10P-30001	Wanted	CD3	Japan	1988	$13.00/$4.00
Polydor	TSCCD-14	Wanted	CD5	U.K.	1988	$8.00

Stylistics

Singles

Label	Catalog Number	Title	Type	Country	Year	Longbox Value / Value
Amherst	CD DJ 11	Always on My Mind	CDJ	U.S.	1991	$2.00
Amherst	CD DJ 10	Love Talk	CDJ	U.S.	1991	$2.00

Stylz

Singles

Label	Catalog Number	Title	Type	Country	Year	Longbox Value / Value
MCA	2703	Bounce	CDJ	U.S.	1993	$2.00

Styx

Full Length

Label	Catalog Number	Title	Type	Country	Year	Longbox Value / Value
RCA	PCD1-3597	Best of	LP/BP	U.S.†	1984	$12.00/$7.00
Pioneer	PA-84-086	Caught in the Act Live	LD	U.S.	1984	$30.00
Pioneer	PA-84-086	Caught in the Act Live	LD	U.S.	1990	$30.00

Digital audio.

Label	Catalog Number	Title	Type	Country	Year	Longbox Value / Value
A&M	CD-3223	Grand Illusion	LP/LB	U.S.†	1984	$14.00/$8.00
Album Network		In the Studio (Grand Illusion)	RS	U.S.	1989	$25.00

Airdate: 2/6/89.

Label	Catalog Number	Title	Type	Country	Year	Longbox Value / Value
Album Network		In the Studio (Grand Illusion)	RS	U.S.	1992	$25.00

Airdate: 7/6/92.

Label	Catalog Number	Title	Type	Country	Year	Longbox Value / Value
Album Network		In the Studio (Paradise Theater)	RS	U.S.	1991	$20.00

Airdate: 5/6/91.

Label	Catalog Number	Title	Type	Country	Year	Longbox Value / Value
Album Network		In the Studio (Pieces Of Eight)	RS	U.S.		$20.00
A&M	CD-3734	Kilroy Was Here	LP/LB	U.S.†	1984	$14.00/$8.00
DIR		King Biscuit Flour Hour	RS	U.S.	1991	$30.00

With The outfield, Airdate: 3/24/91.

Label	Catalog Number	Title	Type	Country	Year	Longbox Value / Value
A&M	CD-3719	Paradise Theater	LP/LB	U.S.†	1984	$14.00/$8.00
A&M	75021 7465 2	Radio Made Hits	DJ/Smplr	U.S.	1991	$20.00

Singles

Label	Catalog Number	Title	Type	Country	Year	Longbox Value / Value
A&M	S12Y-3034	Babe	CD3	Japan	1988	$15.00/$4.00
A&M	390340-2	Compact Hits	CD5	Germany	1988	$10.00
A&M	AMCD-904	Compact Hits	CD5	U.K.	1988	$10.00
A&M	75021 7511 2	Love at First Sight	CDJ	U.S.	1990	$2.00
A&M	75021 7428 2	Love Is the Ritual	CDJ	U.S.	1990	$2.00
A&M	AMCD-171	Show Me the Way	CD5	U.K.	1991	$9.00
A&M	75021 7438 2	Show Me the Way	CDJ	U.S.	1990	$2.00

Subdudes

Full Length

Label	Catalog Number	Title	Type	Country	Year	Longbox Value / Value
High Street	HD 96-03	Primitive Streak	DJ/LP	U.S.		$12.00

Singles

Label	Catalog Number	Title	Type	Country	Year	Longbox Value / Value
Atlantic	PR 2947-2	Any Cure	CDJ	U.S.	1989	$2.00
High Street	94-15	Why Can't I Forget About You	CDJ	U.S.	1994	$2.00

Subject To Change

Singles

Label	Catalog Number	Title	Type	Country	Year	Longbox Value / Value
Capitol	DPRO-79751	Your Life	CDJ	U.S.	1993	$2.00

Subjugator

Full Length

Label	Catalog Number	Title	Type	Country	Year	Longbox Value / Value
Iron Works Records	IW1056	Live	SCDJ	U.S.		$8.00

Sublime

Full Length

Label	Catalog Number	Title	Type	Country	Year	Longbox Value / Value
		Live Recordings	DJ/Smplr	U.S.	1996	$20.00

Fan club CD sampler.

Label	Catalog Number	Title	Type	Country	Year	Longbox Value / Value
Gasoline Alley	11413	Sublime	LTD/LP	U.S.	1996	$17.00

2 CD set.

Subliminal NY

Singles

Label	Catalog Number	Title	Type	Country	Year	Longbox Value / Value
Sire	PRO-CD-6535	Loungin'	CDJ	U.S.	1993	$2.00

Subway

Singles

Label	Catalog Number	Title	Type	Country	Year	Longbox Value / Value
Motown	860339	Fire	CD5	U.S.	1994	$5.00
Motown	860039	Fire	CD5	U.S.	1994	$5.00
Motown	860403	Get Da Money	CD5	U.S.	1995	$5.00

Suede

Singles

Label	Catalog Number	Title	Type	Country	Year	Longbox Value / Value
Columbia	CSK 5229	Animal Nitrate	CDJ	U.S.	1993	$2.00
		Dog Man Star	CDJ	U.S.		$6.00
		He's Dead	CDJ	France		$20.00
		New Generation	CDJ	U.S.		$6.00
		Saturday Night	CD5	Japan	1997	$20.00
Columbia	44K3213	Stay Together	CD5	Canada	1994	$8.00
		Wild Ones	CDJ	U.S.		$6.00

Suga

Singles

Label	Catalog Number	Title	Type	Country	Year	Longbox Value / Value
Polygram	577433	What's Up Star	CD5	U.S.	1995	$5.00

Sugar

Full Length

Label	Catalog Number	Title	Type	Country	Year	Longbox Value / Value
Rykodisc	RCD50260	Beaster	DJ/LP	U.S.	1993	$35.00

CD in binder with booklet and postcards.

Label	Catalog Number	Title	Type	Country	Year	Longbox Value / Value
Rykodisc		Besides	LTD/LP	U.S.	1995	$20.00

First pressing with bonus live CD.

Label	Catalog Number	Title	Type	Country	Year	Longbox Value / Value
Rykodisc	RCD10321	Besides	LTD/LP	U.S.	1995	$25.00
Rykodisc	RCD 90239	Copper Blue	DJ/LP	U.S.	1992	$30.00

CD in copper case with polaroid picture. Limited to 2,500 copies.

Label	Catalog Number	Title	Type	Country	Year	Longbox Value / Value
Rykodisc		File Under Easy Listening	DJ/Smplr	U.S.	1994	$18.00
Rykodisc	RCD 90300	File Under Easy Listening	LTD/LP	U.S.	1994	$25.00

CD in "file" package.

Label	Catalog Number	Title	Type	Country	Year	Longbox Value / Value
Rykodisc	VRCD 0239	Life Before Sugar/Copper Blue	DJ/Smplr	U.S.	1992	$50.00

2CD set- disc 1: Bob Mould Best Of..Disc 2: Copper Blue.

Singles

Label	Catalog Number	Title	Type	Country	Year	Longbox Value / Value
Rykodisc	RCD5 1030	A Good Idea	CD5	U.S.	1992	$5.00
Rykodisc	1039	Believe What You're	CD5	U.S.	1994	$5.00
Creation	CRESCD-126	Changes	CD5	U.K.	1992	$10.00
Rykodisc		Come Angel	CD5	U.S.	1992	$5.00
Rykodisc		Come Angel	CDJ	U.S.	1992	$3.00
Rykodisc	1040	Gee Angel	CD5	U.S.	1994	$5.00
Rykodisc	RCD5 1024	Helpless	CD5	U.S.	1992	$5.00
Rykodisc	CODY-194	If I Can't Change Your Mind	CD3	Japan	1993	$15.00/$5.00
Rykodisc	COCY-5188	If I Can't Change Your Mind	CD5	Japan	1993	$18.00
		If I Can't Change Your Mind	CD5	U.K.		$10.00
		If I Can't Change Your Mind	CD5	U.K.		$10.00

Second version.

Label	Catalog Number	Title	Type	Country	Year	Longbox Value / Value
Rykodisc	RCD5 1031	If I Can't Change Your Mind	CD5	U.S.	1992	$5.00
Rykodisc	RCD5 1032	If I Can't Change Your Mind	CD5	U.S.	1992	$5.00
Rykodisc		Your Favorite Thing	CDJ	U.S.	1994	$6.00

Sugar Blue

Full Length

Label	Catalog Number	Title	Type	Country	Year	Longbox Value / Value
		House of Blues	RS	U.S.	1995	$40.00

2 CD set. Airdate: 1/29/95.

Sugar Hill

Singles

Label	Catalog Number	Title	Type	Country	Year	Longbox Value / Value
	222	Boyz From Da Hill	CD5	U.S.	1994	$5.00

Sugar Ray

Singles

Label	Catalog Number	Title	Type	Country	Year	Longbox Value / Value
	PRCD 6338-2	10 Seconds Down	CDJ	U.S.		$2.00

Sugarbullet

Singles

Label	Catalog Number	Title	Type	Country	Year	Longbox Value / Value
Virgin	VCODT 1205	Rise	CD5	U.K.	1991	$8.00

Sugarcubes

Full Length

Label	Catalog Number	Title	Type	Country	Year	Longbox Value / Value
Elektra		Stick Around For Joy	LP/LB	U.S.		$14.00/$8.00

Singles

Label	Catalog Number	Title	Type	Country	Year	Longbox Value / Value
Rough Trade	CD1-86	Birthday	CD5	Germany	1988	$8.00
Columbia	10CY-8061	Birthday	CD3	Japan	1988	$12.00/$4.00
Pinnacle	7TP-7CD	Birthday	CD5	U.K.	1988	$8.00
Pinnacle	7TP-11CD	Birthday	CD5	U.K.	1988	$8.00
Elektra	66366-2	Birthday	CD5	U.S.	1988	$5.00
Elektra	PR 8002-2	Birthday	CDJ	U.S.	1988	$3.00
Rough Trade	CD1-89	Christmas Mix	CD5	Germany	1988	$8.00
Columbia	15CY-5021	Christmas Mix	CD5	Japan	1988	$13.00
Pinnacle	7TP-11CDL	Christmas Mix	CD5	U.K.	1988	$8.00
Pinnacle	7TP-9CD	Coldsweat	CD5	U.K.	1988	$8.00
Elektra	PR 8021-2	Coldsweat	CDJ	U.S.	1988	$3.00
Rough Trade	CD1-45	Dues	CD5	Germany	1988	$8.00
Pinnacle	7TP-10CD	Dues	CD5	U.K.	1988	$8.00
Rough Trade	230-1128-3	Hit	CD5	Germany	1992	$10.00
Elektra	PRCD 8492-2	Hit	CDJ	U.S.		$2.00
Rough Trade	CD1-240	Motorcrash	CD5	Germany	1988	$8.00
Elektra	6672	Motorcrash	CD3	U.S.	1988	$7.00/$4.00
Elektra	PR 8038-2	Motorcrash	CDJ	U.S.	1988	$3.00
Rough Trade	CD1-312	Planet	CD5	Germany	1990	$8.00
Columbia	15CY-5030	Planet	CD5	Japan	1990	$13.00
Pinnacle	7TP-32CDL	Planet	CD5	U.K.	1990	$8.00
Elektra	PR 8141-2	Planet	CDJ	U.S.	1989	$3.00
Columbia	CY-5026	Regina	CD5	Japan	1989	$13.00
Pinnacle	7TP-26CD	Regina	CD5	U.K.	1989	$8.00
Elektra	PR 8109-2	Regina	CDJ	U.S.	1989	$3.00
Pinnacle	102-TP7CD	Vitamin	CD5	U.K.	1992	$8.00
Elektra	66413-2	Vitamin	CD5	U.S.	1992	$5.00
Elektra	PRCD 8598-2	Vitamin	CDJ	U.S.	1992	$3.00
Rough Trade	130-1335-3	Walkabout	CD5	Germany	1992	$8.00
Columbia	COCY-5173	Walkabout	CD5	Japan	1992	$13.00
Pinnacle	7TP-72CD	Walkabout	CD5	U.K.	1992	$8.00
Elektra	PRCD 8557-2	Walkabout	CDJ	U.S.	1992	$3.00

Sugartooth

Singles

Label	Catalog Number	Title	Type	Country	Year	Longbox Value / Value
	PRO-CD-4614	Sold My Fortune	CDJ	U.S.		$2.00

Suggs

Singles

Label	Catalog Number	Title	Type	Country	Year	Longbox Value / Value
		I'm Only Sleeping	CD5	U.K.	1995	$11.00

Suicidal Tendencies

Full Length

Label	Catalog Number	Title	Type	Country	Year	Longbox Value / Value
Epic	ESK 5004	Busload Of Freaks	DJ/Smplr	U.S.	1993	$25.00

With Infectious Grooves.

Label	Catalog Number	Title	Type	Country	Year	Longbox Value / Value
Epic	ESK 2217	Lights...Camera...Conversation	DJ/Intvw	U.S.	1990	$15.00

Singles

Label	Catalog Number	Title	Type	Country	Year	Longbox Value / Value
Epic	ESK 2097	Alone	CDJ	U.S.	1990	$3.00
Epic	ESK 4653	Asleep At the Wheel	CDJ	U.S.	1992	$3.00
Epic		How Will I Laugh Tomorrow	CDJ	U.S.		$3.00
Epic	ESK 5147	I Saw Your Mommy	CDJ	U.S.	1993	$3.00

Label	Catalog Number	Title	Type	Country	Year	Longbox Value / Value
Epic		I Wouldn't Mind	CDJ	U.S.		$6.00
Epic	ESK 4870	I'll Hate You Better	CDJ	U.S.	1992	$3.00
Epic	ESK 5424	Institutionalized	CDJ	U.S.	1993	$6.00
Epic		Love vs. Loneliness	CDJ	U.S.	1994	$6.00
Epic	ESK 4011	Lovely	CDJ	U.S.	1991	$3.00
Epic	ESK 4736	Monopoly on Sorrow	CDJ	U.S.	1992	$3.00
Epic	ESK 2278	Send Me Your Money	CDJ	U.S.	1990	$6.00
Epic	ESK 6082	What You Need Is a Friend	CDJ	U.S.		$3.00

Sultans of Ping F.C.

Singles

Label	Catalog Number	Title	Type	Country	Year	Longbox Value / Value
Rhythm King	65887	U Talk 2 Much	CD5	U.K.	1992	$8.00

Summer, Donna

Full Length

Label	Catalog Number	Title	Type	Country	Year	Longbox Value / Value
Geffen	24040-2	Cats Without Claws	LP/LB	U.S.†	1984	$14.00/$8.00
Light	51416 4555 2	Christmas Spirit Radio	RS	U.S.	1995	$45.00
Geffen	GHS-2005-2	Donna Summer	LP/LB	U.S.†	1984	$14.00/$8.00
Pioneer	PA-84-083	Hot Summer Night	LD	U.S.	1984	$15.00
	Analog audio.					
Mercury	812 265-2	She Works Hard for the Money	LP/BP	U.S.†	1984	$14.00/$8.00
Casablanca	810011-2	Walk Away	LP/BP	U.S.†	1984	$14.00/$8.00

Singles

Label	Catalog Number	Title	Type	Country	Year	Longbox Value / Value
		Any Way at All	CDJ	U.S.		$3.00
WEA	9031-73309-2	Breakaway	CD5	Germany	1991	$10.00
Atlantic	PR 3003-2	Breakaway	CDJ	U.S.	1989	$2.00
Geffen	PRO CD 2804	Dinner With Gershwin	CDJ	U.S.		$2.00
WEA	257565-2	I Don't Wanna Get Hurt	CD3	Germany	1989	$10.00
Pioneer	09P3-6152	I Don't Wanna Get Hurt	CD3	Japan	1989	$12.00/$4.00
WEA	U-7567CD	I Don't Wanna Get Hurt	CD3	U.K.	1989	$10.00
WEA		I Feel Love	CDJ	U.K.	1995	$25.00
Polygram	874395-2	Love to Love You Baby	CD5	Germany	1989	$10.00
WEA	257493-2	Love's About to Change My Heart	CD3	Germany	1989	$10.00
WEA	09P3-6192	Love's About to Change My Heart	CD3	Japan	1989	$12.00/$4.00
WEA	U-7494CD	Love's About to Change My Heart	CD3	U.K.	1989	$10.00
WEA		Melody of Love	CDJ	U.K.	1995	$20.00
Polygram	85626	Melody of Love	CD5	U.S.	1994	$5.00
Polygram	85626	Melody of Love	CD5	U.S.	1994	$5.00
Polygram	856367	Melody of Love	CD5	U.S.	1994	$5.00
WEA	9031-73052-2	State of Independence	CD5	Germany	1990	$10.00
WEA	U-7857CD	State of Independence	CD5	U.K.	1990	$10.00
WEA	U-7957CD	State of Independence	CD5	U.K.	1990	$10.00
WEA	257778-2	This Time I Know It's for Real	CD3	Germany	1989	$10.00
Pioneer	09P3-6076	This Time I Know It's for Real	CD3	Japan	1989	$12.00/$4.00
WEA	U-7780CD	This Time I Know It's for Real	CD3	U.K.	1989	$10.00
		This Time I Know It's for Real	CDJ	U.S.	1989	$2.00
WEA	257360-2	When Love Takes You Over	CD3	Germany	1989	$10.00
WEA	U-7361CD	When Love Takes You Over	CD3	U.K.	1989	$10.00
WEA	9031-75433-2	When Loves Cries	CD5	Germany	1991	$10.00
WEA	WMD5-4081	When Loves Cries	CD3	Japan	1991	$12.00/$4.00
Atlantic	PRCD 4092-2	When Loves Cries	CDJ	U.S.	1991	$2.00
Atlantic	PRCD 4163-2	When Loves Cries	CDJ	U.S.	1991	$2.00
Atlantic	PRCD 4311-2	Work That Magic	CDJ	U.S.	1991	$2.00

Summer, Henry Lee

Full Length

Label	Catalog Number	Title	Type	Country	Year	Longbox Value / Value
Epic		H.L.S. (Advance Issue)	DJ/LP	U.S.		$10.00

Singles

Label	Catalog Number	Title	Type	Country	Year	Longbox Value / Value
Sony	10EP-3096	Don't Leave	CD3	Japan	1989	$12.00/$5.00
Epic		Don't Leave	CDJ	U.S.	1989	$2.00
Epic		Hands on the Radio	CDJ	U.S.		$2.00
Epic	655018-2	Hey Baby	CD5	U.K.	1989	$9.00
Epic		Hey Baby	CDJ	U.S.	1989	$2.00
Epic	651484-2	I Wish I Had a Girl	CD5	U.K.	1988	$9.00
Epic	657320-2	Till Somebody Loves You	CD5	Germany	1992	$9.00
Epic	ESK 4216	Turn It Up	CDJ	U.S.	1991	$2.00

Summers, Andy

Full Length

Label	Catalog Number	Title	Type	Country	Year	Longbox Value / Value
A&M	CD-5011	Bewitched	LP/LB	U.S.†	1984	$14.00/$8.00
Private Music		Charming Snakes	LP/LB	U.S.		$14.00/$8.00
Private Music		Golden Wire, The	LP/LB	U.S.		$14.00/$8.00
Private Music		Mysterious Barricades	LP/LB	U.S.		$14.00/$8.00
Private Music		World Gone Strange	LP/LB	U.S.		$14.00/$8.00

Summers, Bill

Singles

Label	Catalog Number	Title	Type	Country	Year	Longbox Value / Value
Zyx	2096	Straight to the Ban	CD5	U.S.	1994	$5.00

Sun 60

Singles

Label	Catalog Number	Title	Type	Country	Year	Longbox Value / Value
Epic	ESK 7139	C'mon Kiss Me	CDJ	U.S.		$2.00
Epic	ESK 5186	Hold On	CDJ	U.S.	1993	$2.00
Epic	ESK 77243	Hold On	CDJ	U.S.	1994	$2.00
Epic	ESK 4937	Mary Xmas	CDJ	U.S.	1993	$2.00
Epic	ESK 4566	Middle of My Life	CDJ	U.S.	1992	$2.00
Epic	ESK 5344	Never Seen God	CDJ	U.S.	1993	$2.00
Epic	ESK 4347	Out of My Head	CDJ	U.S.	1992	$2.00
Epic	ESK 4603	Responsible	CDJ	U.S.	1992	$2.00

Sundays

Full Length

Label	Catalog Number	Title	Type	Country	Year	Longbox Value / Value
		Black Sessions	DJ/Smplr	France	1992	$30.00

Singles

Label	Catalog Number	Title	Type	Country	Year	Longbox Value / Value
Rough Trade	RTT-218CD	Can't Be Sure	CD3	U.K.	1989	$9.00
Geffen	PRO-CD-4168	Can't Be Sure	CDJ	U.S.	1990	$2.00
DGC	PRO-CD-4168	Can't Be Sure	CDJ	U.S.	1990	$6.00
Parlophone	724388022125	Goodbye	CD5	U.K.	1992	$9.00
Geffen	PRO-CD-3998	Here's Where the Story Ends	CDJ	U.S.	1990	$2.00
Geffen	PRO-CD-4456	Love	CDJ	U.S.	1992	$2.00
Geffen	PRO-CD-4460	Love	CDJ	U.S.	1992	$2.00
Geffen	PRO-CD-4503	Wild Horses	CDJ	U.S.	1992	$2.00

Sunni

Singles

Label	Catalog Number	Title	Type	Country	Year	Longbox Value / Value
		Why Did My Baby Get Over Me	CDJ	U.S.		$2.00

Sunny Day Real Estate

Full Length

Label	Catalog Number	Title	Type	Country	Year	Longbox Value / Value
Sub Pop		Sunny Day Real Estate	DJ/LP	U.S.	1994	$15.00

Singles

Label	Catalog Number	Title	Type	Country	Year	Longbox Value / Value
		Seven	CDJ	U.S.		$3.00
		T.B.A.	CDJ	U.S.	1994	$3.00

Sunscreem

Singles

Label	Catalog Number	Title	Type	Country	Year	Longbox Value / Value
		Broken English	CD5	U.K.	1993	$10.00
		Broken English	CD5	U.K.	1993	$10.00
	Second version.					
Epic	ESDA-7128	Love U More	CD3	Japan	1993	$13.00/$4.00
Epic	ESCA-5693	Love U More	CD5	Japan	1993	$14.00
Epic	658172-2	Love U More	CD5	U.K.	1992	$8.00
Columbia	44K 74807	Love U More	CD5	U.S.	1992	$2.00
Columbia	657801-2	Pressure	CD5	U.K.	1992	$8.00
Columbia	44K 74916	Pressure	CD5	U.S.	1993	$5.00
Columbia	CSK 5069	Pressure	CDJ	U.S.	1993	$2.00
		Pressure Us	CD5	U.K.	1993	$10.00
	Second version.					
Columbia	657450-2	Walk On	CD5	U.K.	1991	$8.00

Sunshot

Full Length

Label	Catalog Number	Title	Type	Country	Year	Longbox Value / Value
Pipeline	PIPE CD003	Caught in the Act of Enjoying Ourselves	LP	U.S.	1994	$16.00

Super 8

Full Length

Label	Catalog Number	Title	Type	Country	Year	Longbox Value / Value
	PRCD 2014-2	Super 8	DJ/LP	U.S.		$8.00

Singles

Label	Catalog Number	Title	Type	Country	Year	Longbox Value / Value
		King of the World	CDJ	U.S.		$2.00

Super Cat

Singles

Label	Catalog Number	Title	Type	Country	Year	Longbox Value / Value
Columbia	44K 74449	Dem No Worry Me	CD5	U.S.	1993	$5.00
Columbia	CSK 74720	Dem No Worry Me	CDJ	U.S.	1993	$2.00
Columbia	44K 74855	Dolly My Baby	CD5	U.S.	1993	$5.00
Columbia	CSK 4957	Dolly My Baby	CDJ	U.S.	1993	$2.00
Columbia	CSK 74391	Ghetto Red Hot	CDJ	U.S.	1992	$6.00
Columbia	CSK 6933	Girlstown	CDJ	U.S.		$2.00
Columbia	44K 77751	Girlstown	CD5	U.S.	1995	$5.00
Columbia	78083	Girlstown	CD5	U.S.	1995	$5.00
Columbia	44K 77648	Scalp Dem	CD5	U.S.	1994	$5.00
CBS	77648	Scalp Dem	CD5	U.S.	1994	$5.00

Super Deluxe

Singles

Label	Catalog Number	Title	Type	Country	Year	Longbox Value / Value
		She Came On	CDJ	U.S.		$2.00

Super Lover Cee and Casanova

Singles

Label	Catalog Number	Title	Type	Country	Year	Longbox Value / Value
Elektra	PR 8058-2	I Gotta Good Thing	CDJ	U.S.	1988	$2.00

Super Star

Full Length

Label	Catalog Number	Title	Type	Country	Year	Longbox Value / Value
		Super Star	DJ/LP	U.S.		$8.00

Superchunk

Singles

Label	Catalog Number	Title	Type	Country	Year	Longbox Value / Value
Mercury	69	Driveway to Driveway	CD5	U.S.	1994	$5.00
		Hyper Enough	CDJ	U.S.		$2.00
Merge	02	Mower	CD5	Canada	1992	$7.00
Merge	034	Mower	CD5	Canada	1992	$7.00
		Yeah, It's Beautiful Here, Too	CDJ	U.S.		$2.00

Superdrag

Singles

Label	Catalog Number	Title	Type	Country	Year	Longbox Value / Value
		Sucked Out	CDJ	U.S.		$2.00

Supergrass

Singles

Label	Catalog Number	Title	Type	Country	Year	Longbox Value / Value
		Alright	CD5	U.K.	1995	$10.00
	CDR6396	Caught By the Fuzz	CD5	U.K.		$8.00

Superiors

Singles

Label	Catalog Number	Title	Type	Country	Year	Longbox Value / Value
		Perfect Timing	CDJ	U.S.		$2.00
Columbia	CSK 73210	Temptation	CDJ	U.S.	1990	$2.00

Supernatural

Singles

Label	Catalog Number	Title	Type	Country	Year	Longbox Value / Value
Elektra	66083	Buddah Blessed It	CD5	U.S.	1995	$5.00

Supernova

Singles

Label	Catalog Number	Title	Type	Country	Year	Longbox Value / Value
		Vitamins	CDJ	U.S.		$2.00

Supersax

Full Length

Label	Catalog Number	Title	Type	Country	Year	Longbox Value / Value
Verve	821867-2	Chasin' the Bird	LP/LB	U.S.†	1985	$14.00/$8.00

Supersport 2000

Singles

Label	Catalog Number	Title	Type	Country	Year	Longbox Value / Value
	95786	Pinkslip	CD5	U.S.	1994	$5.00

Supersuckers

Singles

Label	Catalog Number	Title	Type	Country	Year	Longbox Value / Value
SubPop	SP249B	400 Bucks	CD5	Canada	1994	$9.00
		Born With a Tail	CDJ	U.S.		$2.00

Supertramp

Full Length

Label	Catalog Number	Title	Type	Country	Year	Longbox Value / Value
BBC Radio		BBC Classic Tracks	RS	U.S.	1991	$20.00
	Airdate: 10/21/91.					
BBC Radio		BBC Classic Tracks	RS	U.S.	1991	$20.00
	Airdate: 4/20/92.					
BBC Radio		BBC Classic Tracks	RS	U.S.	1991	$20.00
	Airdate: 5/6/91.					
BBC Radio		BBC Classic Tracks	RS	U.S.	1992	$20.00
	Airdate: 12/28/92.					
A&M	CD-3708	Breakfast in Bed	LP/LB	U.S.†	1984	$14.00/$8.00
Pioneer	PA86-M040	Brother Were You Bound	8"LD	U.S.	1986	$10.00
Pioneer	PA86-M040	Brother Were You Bound	8"LD	U.S.	1990	$10.00
	Digital audio.					
A&M	CD-3647	Crime of the Century	LP/LB	U.S.†	1984	$14.00/$8.00
A&M	CD-33732	Famous Last Words	LP/LB	U.S.†	1984	$14.00/$8.00
Westwood One		In Concert	RS	U.S.	1992	$50.00
	Airdate: 3/30/92.					
Album Network		In the Studio (Breakfast in America)	RS	U.S.	1990	$30.00
	Airdate: 6/25/90.					
Album Network		In the Studio (Crime of the Century)	RS	U.S.	1990	$30.00
	Airdate: 2/5/90.					
Album Network		In the Studio (Crime of the Century)	RS	U.S.	1992	$30.00
	Airdate: 11/16/92.					
A&M		Indelibly Stamped	LP	Germany		$18.00

Label	Catalog Number	Title	Type	Country	Year	Longbox Value / Value
Westwood One		Superstars	RS	U.S.	1993	$50.00

2 CD set. Airdate: 7/12/93.

Label	Catalog Number	Title	Type	Country	Year	Longbox Value / Value
Westwood One		Superstars	RS	U.S.	1994	$40.00

2 CD set. Airdate: 10/31/94.

Label	Catalog Number	Title	Type	Country	Year	Longbox Value / Value
Westwood One		Superstars	RS	U.S.	1995	$40.00

2 CD set. Airdate: 9/18/95.

Singles

Label	Catalog Number	Title	Type	Country	Year	Longbox Value / Value
A&M	390349-2	Compact Hits	CD5	Germany	1988	$10.00
A&M	AMCD-914	Compact Hits	CD5	U.K.	1988	$10.00

Supreme Love Gods

Singles

Label	Catalog Number	Title	Type	Country	Year	Longbox Value / Value
Def American	PRO-CD-5946	Fire	CDJ	U.S.	1993	$2.00
Pinnacle	53TP7CD	Righteous	CD5	U.K.	1991	$8.00

Surf MC's

Singles

Label	Catalog Number	Title	Type	Country	Year	Longbox Value / Value
		Surf or Die	CDJ	U.S.		$2.00

Surface

Singles

Label	Catalog Number	Title	Type	Country	Year	Longbox Value / Value
Sony	SRDS-8188	All I Want Is You	CD3	Japan	1991	$13.00/$4.00
Columbia	CSK 73684	All I Want Is You	CDJ	U.S.	1991	$2.00
Columbia		Can We Spend Some Time	CDJ	U.S.		$2.00
Columbia	CSK 74071	Christmas Time Is Here	CDj	U.S.	1991	$2.00
Columbia		Closer Than Friends	CDJ	U.S.		$2.00
Columbia	656476-2	First Time, The	CD5	U.K.	1990	$8.00
Columbia	CSK 73502	First Time, The	CDJ	U.S.	1990	$2.00
Columbia	653009-3	I Missed	CD3	Germany	1988	$8.00
Columbia		I Missed	CDJ	U.S.	1988	$2.00
Columbia	CSK 73643	Never Gonna Let You Down	CDJ	U.S.	1991	$2.00
Sony	CSDS-8111	Shower Me With Your Love	CD3	Japan	1989	$13.00/$4.00
Columbia	655245-2	Shower Me With Your Love	CD5	U.K.	1989	$8.00
Columbia	CSK 3964	You're the One	CDJ	U.S.	1991	$2.00

Surfing Brides

Singles

Label	Catalog Number	Title	Type	Country	Year	Longbox Value / Value
		Diceman	CDJ	U.S.		$2.00

Surgery

Singles

Label	Catalog Number	Title	Type	Country	Year	Longbox Value / Value
Atlantic	PRCD 5521-2	D-Nice	CDJ	U.S.	1994	$2.00

Surman, John

Full Length

Label	Catalog Number	Title	Type	Country	Year	Longbox Value / Value
ECM	825407-2	Withholding Pattern	LP/LB	U.S.†	1985	$14.00/$8.00

Survivor

Full Length

Label	Catalog Number	Title	Type	Country	Year	Longbox Value / Value
Intercord	832 315	Caught in the Game	LP	Germany		$25.00
Scotti Brothers	D32Y-0101	Caught in the Game	LP	Japan		$30.00
Scotti Brothers	ZK-38062	Eye of the Tiger	LP/BP	U.S.†	1985	$14.00/$8.00
Scotti Brothers	ZK-39578	Vital Signs	LP/BP	U.S.†	1985	$14.00/$8.00

Singles

Label	Catalog Number	Title	Type	Country	Year	Longbox Value / Value
Scotti Brothers	ZSK 1406	Across the Mile	CDJ	U.S.	1988	$2.00
Scotti Brothers	ZSK 73037	Desperate Dreams	CDJ	U.S.	1989	$2.00
Intercord	827 335	Didn't Know It Was Love	CD5	Germany	1988	$9.00
Canyon	S10Y-1022	Didn't Know It Was Love	CD3	Japan	1988	$12.00/$4.00
Scotti Brothers	ZSK 1292	Didn't Know It Was Love	CDJ	U.S.	1988	$2.00
Canyon	S12Y-1005	Eye of the Tiger	CD3	Japan	1988	$12.00/$4.00
Scotti Brothers		Eye of the Tiger	CDJ	U.S.	1988	$3.00

Susquehanna Hat Company

Singles

Label	Catalog Number	Title	Type	Country	Year	Longbox Value / Value
Giant	PRO-CD-4631	Too Much Joy	CDJ	U.S.	1988	$2.00

Sutton, Shane

Singles

Label	Catalog Number	Title	Type	Country	Year	Longbox Value / Value
		With You All the Way	CDJ	U.S.		$2.00

Swallow, Steve

Singles

Label	Catalog Number	Title	Type	Country	Year	Longbox Value / Value
ECM	SWALLOW 2	Belles	CDJ	U.S.	1992	$3.00

Swamp Dogg

Singles

Label	Catalog Number	Title	Type	Country	Year	Longbox Value / Value
Volt	34	She's Built to Kill	CD5	U.S.	1991	$2.00

Swamp Terrorists

Singles

Label	Catalog Number	Title	Type	Country	Year	Longbox Value / Value
Noise	3612 4484	Nightmare	CD5	U.S.	1991	$5.00

Swans

Singles

Label	Catalog Number	Title	Type	Country	Year	Longbox Value / Value
MCA	DMCAT-1347	Can't Find My Way Home	CD5	U.K.	1989	$8.00
Invisible	36	Celebrity Lifestyle	CD5	U.S.	1994	$5.00
Product	PROD-23CD	Love Will Tear Us Apart	CD5	U.K.	1988	$8.00
MCA	DMCAT-1332	Saved	CD5	U.K.	1989	$8.00
Uni	CD45-17836	Saved	CDJ	U.S.	1989	$2.00

Swayze, Patrick

Singles

Label	Catalog Number	Title	Type	Country	Year	Longbox Value / Value
RCA	162438	Raising Heaven	CD3	Germany	1989	$8.00
RCA	662438	Raising Heaven	CD5	Germany	1989	$8.00
RCA		Raising Heaven	CD3	Japan	1989	$13.00/$4.00
RCA	PD-49566	She's Like the Wind	CD5	U.K.	1991	$8.00

Sweat, Keith

Singles

Label	Catalog Number	Title	Type	Country	Year	Longbox Value / Value
Elektra	PR 8034-2	Don't Stop Your Love	CDJ	U.S.	1988	$2.00
Elektra	PRCD 8617-2	Dream Team	CDJ	U.S.	1992	$2.00
Elektra	66190	Get Up on It	CD5	U.S.	1994	$5.00
Elektra	PRCD 61550	Get Up on It	CDJ	U.S.	1994	$13.00
Elektra/Asylum	66235	How Do You Like It	CD5	U.S.	1994	$5.00
Elektra	PRCD 8913-2	How Do You Like It?	CDJ	U.S.	1994	$2.00
Elektra	966764-2	I Want Her	CD5	Germany	1988	$9.00
Elektra	10SW-8	I Want Her	CD3	Japan	1988	$12.00/$4.00
Elektra	6648-2	I Want to Love You Down	CDJ	U.S.	1992	$2.00
Elektra	WMD5-4064	I'll Give All My Love to You	CD3	Japan	1991	$12.00/$4.00
Elektra	EKR-120CD	I'll Give All My Love to You	CD5	U.K.	1991	$8.00
Elektra	PRCD 8268-2	I'll Give All My Love to You	CDJ	U.S.	1990	$2.00
Elektra	7559-66454-2	Keep It Comin'	CD5	Germany	1992	$8.00
Elektra	WMD5-4083	Keep It Comin'	CD3	Japan	1991	$12.00/$4.00
Elektra	EKR-104CD	Keep It Comin'	CD5	U.K.	1992	$8.00
Elektra	PRCD 8493-2	Keep It Comin'	CDJ	U.S.	1991	$2.00
Elektra	10P3-6030	Make It Last Forever	CD3	Japan	1988	$12.00/$4.00
Elektra	PRCD 8013-2	Make It Last Forever	CDJ	U.S.	1988	$2.00
Elektra	PRCD 8107-2	Make It Last Forever	CDJ	U.S.	1990	$2.00
Elektra	966618-2	Make You Sweat	CD3	Germany	1990	$8.00
Elektra	966630-2	Make You Sweat	CD3	Germany	1990	$8.00
Elektra	WPDP-6229	Make You Sweat	CD3	Japan	1990	$12.00/$4.00
Elektra	EKR-113CD	Make You Sweat	CD3	U.K.	1990	$8.00
Elektra	EKR-96CD	Make You Sweat	CD3	U.K.	1990	$8.00
Elektra	PRCD 8107-2	Make You Sweat	CDJ	U.S.	1990	$2.00
Elektra	WPDP-6258	Merry Go Round	CD3	Japan	1990	$12.00/$4.00
Elektra		Merry Go Round	CDJ	U.S.	1990	$2.00
Elektra		Merry Go Round	CDJ	U.S.	1990	$2.00

Second version.

Label	Catalog Number	Title	Type	Country	Year	Longbox Value / Value
Elektra	65982-2	Nobody	CD5	U.S.	1996	$5.00
Elektra	966767	Something Just Ain't Right	CD3	Germany	1987	$9.00
Elektra	10SW-38	Something Just Ain't Right	CD3	Japan	1988	$12.00/$4.00
Elektra	EKR-72CD	Something Just Ain't Right	CD3	U.K.	1988	$8.00
Elektra	PR 2218-2	Something Just Ain't Right	CDJ	U.S.	1987	$2.00
Elektra	WMDS-4094	Why Me, Baby?	CD3	Japan	1992	$12.00/$4.00
Elektra	PRCD 8529-2	Why Me, Baby?	CDJ	U.S.	1991	$2.00
Elektra	PRCD 8569-2	Why Me, Baby?	CDJ	U.S.	1991	$2.00
Elektra	WMC5-417	Your Love	CD5	Japan	1991	$14.00
Elektra	PRCD 8376-2	Your Love	CDJ	U.S.	1990	$2.00
Elektra	PRCD 8321-2	Your Love Part I & II	CDJ	U.S.	1990	$2.00
Elektra	PRCD 8360-2	Your Love Part I & II	CDJ	U.S.	1990	$2.00

Sweeney, Michelle

Singles

Label	Catalog Number	Title	Type	Country	Year	Longbox Value / Value
Atlantic	95859-2	This Time	CD5	U.S.	1994	$5.00

Sweet

Full Length

Label	Catalog Number	Title	Type	Country	Year	Longbox Value / Value
Zoo		16.66% Extra Fun	LTD/LP	Australia	1995	$35.00

CD in slipcase with extra booklet

Label	Catalog Number	Title	Type	Country	Year	Longbox Value / Value
Collector's Pipeline	TCP 005CD	Level Headed	LP	U.S.	1992	$16.00

Sweet F.A.

Full Length

Label	Catalog Number	Title	Type	Country	Year	Longbox Value / Value
MCA	MCAD-6400	Stick to Your Guns	DJ/LP	U.S.	1990	$15.00

CD and Cassette in round tin.

Label	Catalog Number	Title	Type	Country	Year	Longbox Value / Value
Charisma	086	Liquid Emotion	CDJ	U.S.	1991	$2.00
MCA		Prince of the City	CDJ	U.S.		$2.00
MCA	CD45-18484	Rhythm of Action	CDJ	U.S.	1990	$2.00
Charisma	066	Temptation	CDJ	U.S.	1991	$2.00

Sweet, Matthew

Full Length

Label	Catalog Number	Title	Type	Country	Year	Longbox Value / Value
Zoo	74321-26205-2	100% Fun	LTD/LP	Germany	1995	$25.00
Zoo	ZMJ11081-2	100% Fun	DJ/LP	U.S.	1994	$18.00
Zoo		100% Fun	LTD/LP	U.S.	1995	$30.00

2 Bonus tracks.

Label	Catalog Number	Title	Type	Country	Year	Longbox Value / Value
Zoo	61422-31130-2	Blue Sky On Mars	LTD/LP	U.S.	1997	$18.00

CD album plus bonus CD-single. Available exclusively at Best Buy stores.

Label	Catalog Number	Title	Type	Country	Year	Longbox Value / Value
Zoo	61422-31130-2	Blue Sky On Mars	LTD/LP	U.S.	1997	$18.00

CD album plus bonus CD-single. Available exclusively at Circuit City stores.

Label	Catalog Number	Title	Type	Country	Year	Longbox Value / Value
Zoo	ZP17098-2	Goodfriend: Another Take on Girlfriend	DJ/Smplr	U.S.	1992	$25.00
Westwood One		In Concert	RS	U.S.	1995	$60.00

Airdate: 10/9/95.

Label	Catalog Number	Title	Type	Country	Year	Longbox Value / Value
Westwood One		In Concert-Nu Rock	RS	U.S.	1994	$70.00

Airdate: 3/28/94.

Label	Catalog Number	Title	Type	Country	Year	Longbox Value / Value
Westwood One		In Concert-Nu Rock	RS	U.S.	1995	$60.00

Airdate: 7/31/95.

Label	Catalog Number	Title	Type	Country	Year	Longbox Value / Value
Zoo		Sweet 'n Low	DJ/Smplr	U.S.		$18.00
Media America		Up Close	RS	U.S.	1995	$25.00

Singles

Label	Catalog Number	Title	Type	Country	Year	Longbox Value / Value
Zoo	ZP 17035	Divine Intervention	CDJ	U.S.	1991	$3.00
A&M	CD 17847	Easy	CDJ	U.S.	1989	$3.00
RCA	PD-49120	Girlfriend	CD5	U.K.	1991	$10.00
Zoo	72445-14042-2	Girlfriend	CD5	U.S.	1991	$5.00
Zoo	72445-1414-2	Girlfriend	CDJ	U.S.	1991	$7.00
Zoo	74321-106902	I've Been Waiting	CD5	U.K.	1992	$10.00
Zoo	ZP 17070	I've Been Waiting	CDJ	U.S.	1992	$10.00
Zoo	ZP14206-2	Sick of Myself	CDJ	U.S.	1994	$7.00
Zoo		Sick of Myself	CDJ	U.S.	1994	$8.00
Zoo		Son of Altered Beast	CD5	U.K.	1994	$10.00
Zoo		Superbaby	CDJ	U.S.		$3.00
Zoo		Sweet in Low	CDJ	U.S.	1994	$8.00
Zoo	ZP 17145	Time Capsule	CDJ	U.S.	1993	$3.00
RCA	BVDP-84	Ugly Truth	CD3	Japan	1993	$12.00/$4.00
Zoo		Ugly Truth	CDJ	U.S.	1993	$7.00
A&M	CD 17706	Vertigo	CDJ	U.S.	1989	$3.00
Zoo		We're the Same	CDJ	U.S.	1994	$8.00
A&M	CD 17801	When I Feel Again	CDJ	U.S.	1989	$3.00

Sweet N LO

Singles

Label	Catalog Number	Title	Type	Country	Year	Longbox Value / Value
Third Stone	5309	Directified	CDJ	U.S.	1993	$2.00

Sweet Obsession

Singles

Label	Catalog Number	Title	Type	Country	Year	Longbox Value / Value
Epic	ESK 73750	Elevator	CDJ	U.S.	1991	$2.00
Atco	AMDY-5033	Each & Every Time	CD3	Japan	1990	$13.00/$4.00
Atco		Each & Every Time	CDJ	U.S.	1990	$2.00
Atco	7567-96422-2	If Wishes Come True	CD5	Germany	1990	$8.00
Atco	1990-5029	If Wishes Come True	CD3	Japan	1990	$13.00/$4.00
Atco	B-8905CD	If Wishes Come True	CD5	U.K.	1990	$8.00
Atco	PRCD 3361-2	If Wishes Come True	CDJ	U.S.	1990	$2.00
Atco	AMDY-5016	Love Child	CD3	Japan	1990	$13.00/$4.00
Atco	B-8983CD	Love Child	CD5	U.K.	1990	$8.00
Atco	PRCD 3242-2	Love Child	CDJ	U.S.	1990	$2.00
Atco		Never Let You Go	CDJ	U.S.		$2.00
Atco		One Good Man	CDJ	U.S.		$2.00
Atco	09P3-6137	Sincerely Yours	CD3	Japan	1989	$13.00/$4.00

Sweet Water

Singles

Label	Catalog Number	Title	Type	Country	Year	Longbox Value / Value
Atlantic	PRCD 5023-2	Crawl	CDJ	U.S.	1993	$2.00
Atlantic	PRCD 5024-2	Everything Will Be Alright	CDJ	U.S.	1993	$2.00
Atlantic	PRCD 5165-2	Head Down	CDJ	U.S.	1993	$2.00
Atlantic	PRCD 4790-2	Road Lies	CDJ	U.S.	1993	$7.00
		Superstar	CDJ	U.S.		$2.00

Sweethearts of the Rodeo

Full Length

Label	Catalog Number	Title	Type	Country	Year	Longbox Value / Value
Columbia	CSK 45373	Buffalo Zone	DJ/Smplr	U.S.	1990	$8.00
Columbia	CSK 2823	Their Greatest Hits On Compact Disc	DJ/Smplr	U.S.		$8.00

Singles

Label	Catalog Number	Title	Type	Country	Year	Longbox Value / Value
Columbia	CSK 73360	Como Se Dice	CDJ	U.S.	1990	$2.00
Columbia	CSK 74064	Devil And Your Deep Blue Eyes	CDJ	U.S.	1991	$2.00

Label	Catalog Number	Title	Type	Country	Year	Longbox Value / Value
Columbia	CSK 73360	Hard Headed Man	CDJ	U.S.	1990	$2.00
Columbia	CSK 1509	If I Never See Midnight Again	CDJ	U.S.	1989	$2.00

Swell

Singles

Label	Catalog Number	Title	Type	Country	Year	Longbox Value / Value
Wea	CDW45787	Here It Is	CD5	Canada	1994	$14.00
Def American	PRO-CD-5917	Room to Think	CDJ	U.S.	1993	$2.00

Swervedriver

Singles

Label	Catalog Number	Title	Type	Country	Year	Longbox Value / Value
Creation	CRESCD 136	Duel	CD5	U.K.	1993	$9.00
A&M	31458 8207	Duel	CDJ	U.S.	1993	$2.00
A&M	31458 8232	Last Train to Satansville	CDJ	U.S.	1993	$2.00
A&M	75021 7279-2	Rave Down	CDJ	U.S.	1991	$2.00
A&M	31458 2402	Reel to Reel	CD5	U.S.	1991	$5.00
Creation	CRESCD 102	Sandblast	CD5	U.K.	1991	$9.00
A&M	31458 7302-2	Son of Mustang	CDJ	U.S.	1991	$2.00

Swift

Singles

Label	Catalog Number	Title	Type	Country	Year	Longbox Value / Value
	1	Ruff Shitt	CD5	U.S.	1994	$5.00

Swing Out Sister

Full Length

Label	Catalog Number	Title	Type	Country	Year	Longbox Value / Value
PMV	080 197-9	And Why Not	8"LD	U.S.	1987	$6.00

Singles

Label	Catalog Number	Title	Type	Country	Year	Longbox Value / Value
Fontana	PHDR-102	Am I the Same Girl	CD3	Japan	1992	$13.00/$4.00
Fontana	SWICD-9	Am I the Same Girl	CD5	U.K.	1992	$8.00
		Breakout	CDJ	U.K.		$8.00
Fontana	PHDR-120	Circulate	CD3	Japan	1992	$13.00/$4.00
Fontana	SWICD-8	Forever Blue	CD5	U.K.	1989	$15.00

CD in piano shaped package.

Label	Catalog Number	Title	Type	Country	Year	Longbox Value / Value
Fontana	SWICD11	La La La Means	CD5	U.K.	1994	$10.00
Fontana	SWIDD11	La La La Means	CD5	U.K.	1994	$10.00
Fontana	856199	La La La Means	CD5	U.S.	1994	$5.00
Polygram	856199	La La La Means	CD5	U.S.	1994	$5.00
Fontana	PHDR-111	Not Gonna Change	CD3	Japan	1992	$13.00/$4.00
Fontana	SWICD-10	Not Gonna Change	CD5	U.K.	1992	$8.00
Fontana	866855	Not Gonna Change	CD5	U.S.	1992	$4.00
Fontana	PPDS-10	Waiting Game	CD3	Japan	1989	$13.00/$4.00
Fontana	CDP 61	Waiting Game	CDJ	U.S.	1989	$3.00
Fontana	874795-2	Where in the World	CD5	Germany	1989	$8.00
Fontana	SWICD-7	Where in the World	CD5	U.K.	1989	$8.00
Fontana	874229-2	You on My Mind	CD5	Germany	1989	$8.00
Fontana	874228-3	You on My Mind	CD5	Germany	1989	$8.00
Fontana	PPDS-2	You on My Mind	CD3	Japan	1989	$13.00/$4.00
Fontana	SOCDS 1	You on My Mind	CD5	U.K.	1989	$8.00
Fontana	CDP 112	You on My Mind	CDJ	U.S.	1989	$3.00

Swinging Steaks

Singles

Label	Catalog Number	Title	Type	Country	Year	Longbox Value / Value
Capricorn	6690	Circlin'	CDJ	U.S.	1993	$2.00

Sybil

Singles

Label	Catalog Number	Title	Type	Country	Year	Longbox Value / Value
Champion	CHAMPCD-225	All Through the Night	CD5	U.K.	1989	$8.00
PWL	PWCD-265	Beyond Your Wildest Dreams	CD5	U.K.	1993	$8.00
Next Plateau	1006	Beyond Your Wildest Dreams	CDJ	U.S.	1993	$2.00
Bellaphon	130-07-303	Can't Wait on Tomorrow	CD5	Germany	1988	$8.00
PWL	PWCD-53	Crazy for You	CD5	U.K.	1990	$8.00
		Crazy for You	CDJ	U.S.	1990	$2.00
Bellaphon	130-07-343	Don't Make Me Over	CD5	Germany	1989	$8.00
Polygram	873451-2	Don't Make Me Over	CD5	Germany	1989	$8.00
Columbia	CY-5028	Don't Make Me Over	CD3	Japan	1989	$13.00/$3.00
Champion	CHAMPCD-213	Don't Make Me Over	CD5	U.K.	1989	$8.00
Next Plateau	911	Love I Lost, The	CDJ	U.S.	1993	$2.00
PWL	PWCD-65	Make It Easy on Me	CD5	U.K.	1990	$8.00
Polygram	873883-2	Walk on By	CD5	Germany	1990	$8.00
PWL	PWCD-48	Walk on By	CD5	U.K.	1990	$8.00
Next Plateau	422 857 065	You're the Love of My Life	CD5	U.S.	1993	$5.00

Sykes

Full Length

Label	Catalog Number	Title	Type	Country	Year	Longbox Value / Value
	SACA-54	If You Ever Need Love	LP	Japan		$45.00

Singles

Label	Catalog Number	Title	Type	Country	Year	Longbox Value / Value
		Don't Say Goodbye	CDJ	U.S.		$2.00

Sylvers, Foster

Singles

Label	Catalog Number	Title	Type	Country	Year	Longbox Value / Value
A&M	CD 17988	I'll Do It	CDJ	U.S.	1990	$2.00

Sylvers, Leon

Singles

Label	Catalog Number	Title	Type	Country	Year	Longbox Value / Value
Motown	18131	Safe and Sound	CDJ	U.S.	1989	$2.00

Sylvia

Full Length

Label	Catalog Number	Title	Type	Country	Year	Longbox Value / Value
RCA	PCD1-4312	Just Sylvia	LP/BP	U.S.†	1984	$14.00/$8.00
RCA	PCD1-5413	One Step Closer	LP/BP	U.S.†	1985	$14.00/$8.00
RCA	PCD1-4672	Snapshot	LP/BP	U.S.†	1984	$14.00/$8.00
RCA	PCD1-4960	Surprise	LP/BP	U.S.†	1985	$14.00/$8.00

Sylvian, David

Singles

Label	Catalog Number	Title	Type	Country	Year	Longbox Value / Value
Venture	2-90904	Plight	CD5	U.K.	1988	$8.00

Sylvian, David & Robert Fripp

Full Length

Label	Catalog Number	Title	Type	Country	Year	Longbox Value / Value
		Damage	LTD/LP	Australia	1994	$25.00
Virgin	V239905	Damage	LTD/LP	Canada	1994	$19.00
Virgin		Damage	DJ/Smplr	U.K.	1994	$8.00
		God's Monkey Retropective	DJ/Smplr	Australia	1994	$35.00
Virgin		God's Monkey Retropective	DJ/Smplr	U.S.	1994	$15.00

Singles

Label	Catalog Number	Title	Type	Country	Year	Longbox Value / Value
Virgin	DPRO-14125	Darshan	CDJ	U.S.	1994	$2.00
		Jean the Birdman	CD5	U.K.		$10.00
		Jean the Birdman	CD5	U.K.		$10.00

Second version.

Symone, Raven

Singles

Label	Catalog Number	Title	Type	Country	Year	Longbox Value / Value
MCA	2853	Raven Is the Flavor	CDJ	U.S.	1993	$2.00
MCA	2636	That's What Little Girls Are Made Of	CDJ	U.S.	1993	$2.00

Synergy

Full Length

Label	Catalog Number	Title	Type	Country	Year	Longbox Value / Value
Passport	PBCD-6005	Audion	LP	U.K.		$12.00
Passport	PBCD-6005	Audion	LP/BP	U.S.		$16.00/$12.00
Passport	PBCD-6000	Cords	LP/BP	U.S.		$16.00/$12.00
Passport	PBCD-6001	Electric Realizations	LP	U.K.		$12.00
Passport	PBCD-6001	Electric Realizations	LP/BP	U.S.		$16.00/$12.00
Passport	PBCD-6003	Games	LP	U.K.		$12.00
Passport	PBCD-6003	Games	LP/BP	U.S.		$16.00/$12.00
Passport	PBCD-6002	Sequencer	LP/BP	U.S.		$16.00/$12.00

System

Singles

Label	Catalog Number	Title	Type	Country	Year	Longbox Value / Value
Pioneer	10SW-65	Coming to America	CD3	Japan	1988	$12.00/$3.00
Atco	PR 2352-2	Coming to America	CDJ	U.S.	1988	$2.00
Atco	PR 2712-2	Midnight Special	CDJ	U.S.	1989	$2.00

T 99

Singles

Label	Catalog Number	Title	Type	Country	Year	Longbox Value / Value
Columbia	CSK 74486	Anathesia	CDJ	U.S.	1992	$2.00
Columbia	CSK 74468	Let Me Go	CDJ	U.S.	1992	$2.00
Columbia	657975	Maximzor	CD5	Germany	1992	$8.00
Columbia	44K 74316	Maximzor	CD5	U.S.	1992	$5.00

T.C.F. Crew

Singles

Label	Catalog Number	Title	Type	Country	Year	Longbox Value / Value
Cold Chillin'	6019	I Ain't the One	CDJ	U.S.	1993	$2.00

T.N.G.

Singles

Label	Catalog Number	Title	Type	Country	Year	Longbox Value / Value
Reprise	PRO-CD-5684	Sweet Okole	CDJ	U.S.	1992	$2.00

T.N.N.

Singles

Label	Catalog Number	Title	Type	Country	Year	Longbox Value / Value
	1266	Ayayay Cielito	CD5	U.S.	1994	$5.00

T.N.T.

Full Length

Label	Catalog Number	Title	Type	Country	Year	Longbox Value / Value
Atlantic		Realized Fantasies	LP/LB	U.S.		$14.00/$8.00

Singles

Label	Catalog Number	Title	Type	Country	Year	Longbox Value / Value
		All Night	CDJ	U.S.		$2.00
Atlantic	AMDY-5074	Downhill Racer	CD3	Japan	1992	$13.00/$4.00
Mercury	PPDS-3	Intuition	CD3	Japan	1989	$13.00/$4.00
Mercury	CDP 72	Intuition	CDJ	U.S.	1989	$2.00
Atlantic	PRCD 4663-2	Rain	CDJ	U.S.	1992	$2.00
Mercury	CDP 37	Tonight I'm Falling	CDJ	U.S.	1989	$2.00

T. Rex

Full Length

Label	Catalog Number	Title	Type	Country	Year	Longbox Value / Value
		25th Anniversary Sampler	DJ/Smplr	Japan		$100.00
Teichiku	28DN-125	Christmas Box	LTD/LP	Japan		$30.00
Castle		Peel Sessions	LP	Germany		$12.00
Techiku	CD8-12-1	Special Sampler	DJ/Smplr	Japan		$100.00
Techiku	CD-30402	Super Sampler	DJ/Smplr	Japan		$100.00
Relativity		T.Rex Sampler	DJ/Smplr	U.S.	1991	$18.00

Singles

Label	Catalog Number	Title	Type	Country	Year	Longbox Value / Value
	PIFP1010	20th Century Boy	CDV	Japan	1993	$20.00
Marc	00DP-1001	Best	CD3	Japan	1991	$12.00/$4.00
Marc	MARCD-10	Get It On '87	CD5	U.K.	1987	$10.00
Eastwest	246879-2	Hot Love	CD3	Germany	1989	$10.00
BMG	661865	Megarex	CD5	Germany	1988	$10.00
Old Gold	OG-6134	Solid Gold	CD3	U.K.	1989	$10.00
Old Gold	OG-6130	Telegram Sam	CD3	U.K.	1989	$10.00

T Ride

Singles

Label	Catalog Number	Title	Type	Country	Year	Longbox Value / Value
Hollywood	PRCD 8553-2	Backdoor Romeo	CDJ	U.S.	1992	$2.00
Hollywood	PRCD 10208-2	Hit Squad	CDJ	U.S.	1989	$2.00
Hollywood	PRCD 10213-2	I Hunger	CDJ	U.S.	1992	$2.00
Hollywood	PRCD 10208-2	Zombies From Hell	CDJ	U.S.	1989	$2.00

T'Pau

Full Length

Label	Catalog Number	Title	Type	Country	Year	Longbox Value / Value
		Secret Garden	DJ/LP	Japan		$40.00

Different Sleeve than standard release.

Singles

Label	Catalog Number	Title	Type	Country	Year	Longbox Value / Value
Virgin	659576	China in Your Hand	CD5	Germany	1987	$8.00
Virgin	SRNCD-64	China in Your Hand	CD5	U.K.	1987	$8.00
Virgin	661575	I Will Be With You	CD5	Germany	1988	$8.00
Virgin	SRNCD-87	I Will Be With You	CD5	U.K.	1988	$8.00
Virgin	162153	Only a Heartbeat	CD3	Germany	1988	$8.00
Siren	VJDP-10183	Only a Heartbeat	CD3	Japan	1991	$13.00/$4.00
Virgin	SRNCD-107	Only a Heartbeat	CD3	U.K.	1988	$8.00
Charisma	PRCD 041	Only a Heartbeat	CDJ	U.S.	1991	$2.00
Siren	SRNCD-100	Road to Your Dream	CD3	U.K.	1988	$8.00
Virgin	661748	Secret Garden	CD5	Germany	1988	$8.00
Virgin	VJD-12028	Secret Garden	CD3	Japan	1988	$12.00/$4.00
Siren	SRNCD-93	Secret Garden	CD5	U.K.	1988	$8.00
Siren	SRNCD-80	Sex Talk	CD5	U.K.	1988	$8.00
Virgin	659733	Valentine	CD5	Germany	1988	$8.00
Virgin	VJD-12005	Valentine	CD3	Japan	1988	$13.00/$4.00
Siren	SRNCD-69	Valentine	CD5	U.K.	1988	$8.00
Siren	VALEG-1	Valentine	CD5	U.K.	1993	$8.00
Virgin	664556	Walk on Air	CD5	Germany	1991	$8.00
Virgin	664249	Whenever You Need Me	CD5	Germany	1991	$8.00
Siren	SRNCD-140	Whenever You Need Me	CD5	U.K.	1991	$8.00
Charisma	PRCD 057	Whenever You Need Me	CDJ	U.S.	1991	$2.00

T-Boz

Singles

Label	Catalog Number	Title	Type	Country	Year	Longbox Value / Value
	35091-2	Touch Myself	CD5	U.S.	1996	$5.00

Ta Mara and The Seen

Singles

Label	Catalog Number	Title	Type	Country	Year	Longbox Value / Value
A&M	CD 17556	Blueberry Gossip	CDJ	U.S.	1988	$2.00

Tab Two

Singles

Label	Catalog Number	Title	Type	Country	Year	Longbox Value / Value
		No Flagman Ahead	CDJ	U.S.		$2.00

Tackhead

Singles

Label	Catalog Number	Title	Type	Country	Year	Longbox Value / Value
SBK	CDSBK 7014	Dangerous Sex	CD5	U.K.	1990	$8.00

Taco

Full Length

Label	Catalog Number	Title	Type	Country	Year	Longbox Value / Value
RCA	PCD1-4818	After Eight	LP/BP	U.S.		$12.00/$7.00
RCA	PCD1-4818	After Eight	LP/BP	U.S.†	1984	$12.00/$7.00

Tacuma, Jamaaladeen

Label	Catalog Number	Title	Type	Country	Year	Longbox Value/Value
Full Length						
Gramaphone	GRCD-8308	Renaissance Man	LP/LB	U.S.†	1985	$14.00/$8.00
Gramaphone	GRCD-8301	Showstopper	LP/LB	U.S.†	1985	$14.00/$8.00

Tad

Label	Catalog Number	Title	Type	Country	Year	Longbox Value/Value
Full Length						
Gianr		Inhaler	DJ/LP	U.S.	1993	$10.00
Advance issue.						
Singles						
Efa	CD-08121	Jack Pepsi	CD5	Germany	1991	$8.00
Sub Pop	SPCD7/121	Jack Pepsi	CD5	U.K.	1991	$8.00
Sub Pop	99	Jack Pepsi	CD5	U.S.	1991	$5.00
Giant	PRO-CD-6458	Leafy Incline	CDJ	U.S.	1994	$2.00
Sub Pop	SPCD-62/229	Salem	CD5	U.K.	1993	$8.00
Sub Pop	182	Salem	CD5	U.S.	1993	$5.00

Taff, Russ

Label	Catalog Number	Title	Type	Country	Year	Longbox Value/Value
Singles						
A&M	CD 17900	Winds of Change	CDJ	U.S.	1989	$2.00

Tag

Label	Catalog Number	Title	Type	Country	Year	Longbox Value/Value
Singles						
Scotti Brothers	ZSK 75302	Love and Money	CDJ	U.S.	1991	$6.00

Tag Team

Label	Catalog Number	Title	Type	Country	Year	Longbox Value/Value
Singles						
		Funky Situation	CDJ	U.S.		$2.00
Life	033	Here It Is, Bam!	CDJ	U.S.	1994	$2.00
		U Go Girl	CDJ	U.S.	1993	$2.00
	79010	Whoomp (remixes)	CD5	U.S.	1994	$5.00
Life	9516	Whoomp (Si Lo Es)	CDJ	U.S.	1993	$7.00
Atlas	79001	Whoomp (There It Is)	CD5	U.S.	1993	$5.00
Atlas	1095	Whoomp (There It Is)	CDJ	U.S.	1993	$3.00
Life	001	Whoomp (There It Is)	CDJ	U.S.	1993	$3.00
Life	002	Whoomp (There It Is)	CDJ	U.S.	1993	$3.00
	79001	Whoomps (There It Is)	CD5	U.S.	1994	$5.00

Tah, Geggy

Label	Catalog Number	Title	Type	Country	Year	Longbox Value/Value
Full Length						
Warner Brothers	PRO-CD-6758-A	Geggy Tah	DJ/LP	U.S.		$10.00

Take Six

Label	Catalog Number	Title	Type	Country	Year	Longbox Value/Value
Singles						
Reprise	18064	All I Need	CD5	U.S.	1994	$5.00
Warner Brothers	18064	All I Need	CD5	U.S.	1994	$5.00
Reprise	PRO-CD-5204	God Rest Ye Merry Gentlemen	CDJ	U.S.	1991	$2.00
Reprise	PRO-CD-3342	Gold Mine	CDJ	U.S.	1988	$2.00
Reprise	PRO-CD-4789	I Believe	CDJ	U.S.	1990	$2.00
Pioneer	WPDP-6247	I-L-O-V-E-U	CD3	Japan	1990	$12.00/$4.00
Reprise	PRO-CD-4392	I-L-O-V-E-U	CDJ	U.S.	1990	$2.00
Pioneer	WPDP-6301	So Much to Say	CD3	Japan	1992	$12.00/$4.00
Reprise	PRO-CD-3468	Spread Love	CDJ	U.S.	1988	$2.00
Reprise		Where Do the Children Play?	CDJ	U.S.	1995	$2.00
Reprise	PRO-CD-7172	You Can Never Ask Too Much	CDJ	U.S.	1995	$2.00

Take That

Label	Catalog Number	Title	Type	Country	Year	Longbox Value/Value
Full Length						
	TAKE26	Greatest Hits Sampler	DJ/Smplr	U.K.		$25.00
Singles						
RCA	62639-2-RDJ	A Million Love Songs	CDJ	U.S.	1993	$3.00
		Babe	CD6	U.K.		$10.00
		Babe	CD5	U.K.		$10.00
Second version.						
		Every Guy	CD5	Australia		$10.00
		Everything Changes	CD5	U.K.		$10.00
		Everything Changes	CD5	U.K.		$10.00
Second version.						
		Love Ain't Here Anymore	CD5	U.K.	1994	$10.00
		Pray	CD5	Australia		$10.00
		Pray	CD5	U.K.		$10.00
		Pray	CD5	U.K.		$10.00
Second version.						
		Relight That Fire	CD5	U.K.		$10.00
		Relight That Fire	CD5	U.K.		$10.00
Second version.						

Talk Talk

Label	Catalog Number	Title	Type	Country	Year	Longbox Value/Value
Full Length						
EMI	Talk 90	Selections From Natural History	DJ/Smplr	U.K.		$10.00
Manhattan	04144	Spirit of Eden	DJ/Smplr	U.S.	1988	$8.00
Singles						
Polydor	TALKD1	After the Flood	CD5	U.K.	1991	$15.00
CD in 12"x12" box to also hold 2 more CD5s.						
Polydor	TALK 1	After the Flood	CD5	U.K.	1991	$30.00
EMI	202896-2	I Believe in You	CD5	Germany	1988	$9.00
Parolphone	CDR-6189	I Believe in You	CD5	U.K.	1988	$9.00
EMI	203849-2	It's My Life	CD5	Germany	1990	$9.00
Parolphone	CDR-6254	It's My Life	CD5	U.K.	1990	$9.00
Polydor	867 923-2	Laughing Stock Collection	CD5	U.K.	1991	$35.00
3CD set in 12"x12" box.						
EMI	204335-2	Life's What You Make It	CD5	Germany	1990	$9.00
Parolphone	CDR-6264	Life's What You Make It	CD5	U.K.	1990	$9.00
Parlophone	CDR-6282	Living in Another World	CD5	U.K.	1991	$9.00
EMI	204018-2	Such a Shame	CD5	Germany	1990	$9.00
Parolphone	CDR-6276	Such a Shame	CD5	U.K.	1990	$9.00

Talking Heads

Label	Catalog Number	Title	Type	Country	Year	Longbox Value/Value
Full Length						
Sire	6076-2	Fear of Music	LP/LB	U.S.†	1984	$14.00/$8.00
Album Network		In the Studio (Best of)	RS	U.S.		$20.00
Album Network		In the Studio (Talking Heads)	RS	U.S.	1990	$30.00
Airdate: 6/18/90.						
DIR		King Biscuit Flour Hour	RS	U.S.	1990	$30.00
With Lou Reed, Airdate: 5/28/90.						
Sire	25305-2	Little Creatures	LP/LB	U.S.†	1985	$14.00/$8.00
Sire	6095-2	Remain in Light	LP/LB	U.S.†	1984	$14.00/$8.00
Sire	23883-2	Speaking in Tongues	LP/LB	U.S.†	1984	$14.00/$8.00
Warner Brothers		Special	DJ/Smplr	Japan		N/A
Sire	25121-2	Stop Making Sense	LP/LB	U.S.†	1984	$18.00/$14.00
First Issue.						
Sire	25186-2	Stop Making Sense	LP/LB	U.S.†	1985	$14.00/$8.00
Singles						
EMI	202822-2	Blind	CD5	Germany	1988	$10.00
EMI	CDEM-68	Blind	CD5	U.K.	1988	$10.00
Sire	PRO-CD-3022	Blind	CDJ	U.S.	1988	$3.00
Toshiba	XP10-2005	Flowers	CD3	Japan	1988	$12.00/$4.00
EMI	CDEM-53	Flowers	CD5	U.K.	1988	$10.00
EMI	TODP-2378	Lifetime Piling Up	CD3	Japan	1992	$12.00/$4.00
		Lifetime Piling Up	CD5	U.K.		$10.00
		Lifetime Piling Up	CD5	U.K.		$10.00
Second version.						
Sire	PRO-CD-5151	Lifetime Piling Up	CDJ	U.S.	1992	$3.00
WEA	921135-2	Love Goes to a Building on Fire	CD3	Germany	1989	$10.00
WEA	921135-2	Love Goes to a Building on Fire	CD3	U.K.	1989	$10.00
Sire	PRO-CD-2947	Nothing But Flowers	CDJ	U.S.	1988	$3.00
EMI	CDEM 1	Radio Head	CD5	U.K.	1987	$10.00
Sire	PRO-CD-5335	Sex and Violins	CDJ	U.S.	1991	$3.00

Tall Tales & True

Label	Catalog Number	Title	Type	Country	Year	Longbox Value/Value
Singles						
rooArt	RART-2CD	Heart	CD5	U.K.	1990	$8.00
rooArt	CDP 207	Trust	CDJ	U.S.	1990	$2.00

Tam Tam

Label	Catalog Number	Title	Type	Country	Year	Longbox Value/Value
Singles						
ZYX	6279-8	Be Yourself	CD5	Germany	1990	$6.00
Island	PRCD 6679-2	Do the Tam Tam	CDJ	U.S.	1991	$2.00

Tami Show

Label	Catalog Number	Title	Type	Country	Year	Longbox Value/Value
Singles						
Scotti Brothers	78022	Let's Do It Again	CD5	U.S.	1995	$5.00
RCA	2694-2-RDJ	Truth, The	CDJ	U.S.	1991	$2.00

Tangerine Dream

Label	Catalog Number	Title	Type	Country	Year	Longbox Value/Value
Full Length						
HMR	HMIXD-29	Flashpoint	LP	U.K.		$18.00
Private Music		Optical Race	DJ/Smplr	U.S.		$15.00
Private Music		Sampler	DJ/Smplr	U.S.	1994	$22.00
Virgin		Tangents 1973 - 1983 Box Set Sampler	DJ/Smplr	U.S.	1995	$25.00
Singles						
BMG	662892	Alexander Square	CD5	Germany	1989	$10.00
Private Music	2042-2	Cat Scan	CDJ	U.S.	1988	$6.00
Private Music	663 747	Oranges Don't Dance	CD5	U.K.	1990	$45.00
Miramar	2803	Rockoon	CD5	U.S.	1992	$5.00

Tangier

Label	Catalog Number	Title	Type	Country	Year	Longbox Value/Value
Singles						
Atco		On the Line	CDJ	U.S.		$2.00
Atco	PR 2887-2	Southbound Train	CDJ	U.S.	1988	$3.00
Atco	PRCD 3779-2	Stranded	CDJ	U.S.	1991	$2.00

Tara, T.J.

Label	Catalog Number	Title	Type	Country	Year	Longbox Value/Value
Singles						
SBK	DPRO-05400	Feel So Good	CDJ	U.S.	1991	$2.00

Tarz-lo

Label	Catalog Number	Title	Type	Country	Year	Longbox Value/Value
Singles						
Insomniac	CDS-702	Crazy Eyes	CDJ	U.S.	1989	$2.00

Tashan

Label	Catalog Number	Title	Type	Country	Year	Longbox Value/Value
Singles						
Chaos	77072	Love Is Forever	CDJ	U.S.	1993	$2.00
Chaos	77242	Love Is Forever	CDJ	U.S.	1993	$2.00

Tashian, Daniel

Label	Catalog Number	Title	Type	Country	Year	Longbox Value/Value
Singles						
		Where Have You Gone	CDJ	U.S.		$2.00

Tate, Danny

Label	Catalog Number	Title	Type	Country	Year	Longbox Value/Value
Full Length						
		Sampler	DJ/Smplr	U.S.	1994	$8.00
Singles						
Charisma	096	How Much	CDJ	U.S.	1992	$2.00
Charisma	0975	Lead Me to the Water	CDJ	U.S.	1992	$2.00

Tate, Terry

Label	Catalog Number	Title	Type	Country	Year	Longbox Value/Value
Singles						
Atlantic	PR 2938-2	Babies Having Babies	CDJ	U.S.	1989	$2.00

Tatjana

Label	Catalog Number	Title	Type	Country	Year	Longbox Value/Value
Singles						
		Santa Maria	CDJ	U.S.		$2.00

Tattoo Rodeo

Label	Catalog Number	Title	Type	Country	Year	Longbox Value/Value
Singles						
Atlantic	PRCD 3888-2	Been Your Fool	CDJ	U.S.	1991	$2.00
Atlantic		Everybody Wants What She's Got	CDJ	U.S.		$2.00
Atlantic	PRCD 4234-2	Let Me Be the One	CDJ	U.S.	1991	$2.00

Tatum, Art

Label	Catalog Number	Title	Type	Country	Year	Longbox Value/Value
Singles						
	41049	Fine Art & Dandy	CD5	U.S.	1994	$5.00

Taylor, Andy

Label	Catalog Number	Title	Type	Country	Year	Longbox Value/Value
Singles						
A&M	AMCD-596	Lola	CD5	U.K.	1990	$8.00
A&M	AMCD-710	Stone Cold Sober	CD5	U.K.	1990	$8.00

Taylor, Art

Label	Catalog Number	Title	Type	Country	Year	Longbox Value/Value
Full Length						
Blue Note	CDP-84047	A.T.'s Delights	LP/LB	U.S.	1988	$20.00/$15.00

Taylor, Cecil

Label	Catalog Number	Title	Type	Country	Year	Longbox Value/Value
Full Length						
Mosaic	MD3-127	Complete Candid Recording	LTD/LP	U.S.		$60.00
4 CD set. Limited to 7500 copies.						
Free Music Production		In Berlin '88	LTD/LP	Germany	1989	$400.00
11 CD boxed set.						

Taylor, Gary

Label	Catalog Number	Title	Type	Country	Year	Longbox Value/Value
Singles						
Virgin	PRCD 2372	Tease Me	CDJ	U.S.	1988	$2.00

Taylor, J.T.

Label	Catalog Number	Title	Type	Country	Year	Longbox Value/Value
Singles						
MCA	2026	Heart to Heart	CDJ	U.S.	1991	$2.00

Taylor, James

Label	Catalog Number	Title	Type	Country	Year	Longbox Value/Value
Full Length						
CBS	241089-2	Classic Songs	LP	Germany		$30.00
CBS	CK-37009	Dad Loves His Work	LP/BP	U.S.†	1984	$14.00/$8.00
Columbia	CSK 5329	Five Live	DJ/Smplr	U.S.	1993	$12.00
CBS	CK-36058	Flag	LP/BP	U.S.†	1985	$14.00/$8.00

Label	Catalog Number	Title	Type	Country	Year	Longbox Value / Value
CBS	7023-80	In Concert	LD	U.S.	1983	$35.00
	XCDS-93170	James Collectors	DJ/Smplr	Japan		$200.00
CBS	CK-34811	JT	LP/BP	U.S.†	1984	$14.00/$8.00
Columbia	53787	JT	LP/LB	U.S.	1993	$28.00/$25.00

Gold disc.

Label	Catalog Number	Title	Type	Country	Year	Longbox Value / Value
Columbia	CSK 5342	Selections From James Taylor (Live)	DJ/Smplr	U.S.	1993	$20.00
Warner Brothers	1843-2	Sweet Baby James	LP/LB	U.S.†	1985	$14.00/$8.00
Columbia	CDNK 702	View From the Inside - A Radio Special	DJ/Smplr	Canada		$30.00

Singles

Label	Catalog Number	Title	Type	Country	Year	Longbox Value / Value
Columbia		All I Want Is Forever	CDJ	U.S.		$3.00
Columbia	CSK 4183	Copperline	CDJ	U.S.	1991	$3.00
Columbia		Eight Days a Week	CDJ	U.S.		$3.00
Columbia	CSK 4499	Everybody Loves to Cha Cha	CDJ	U.S.	1992	$3.00
Columbia	CSK 4338	(I've Got To) Stop Thinking About That	CDJ	U.S.	1991	$3.00
Columbia	CSK 4746	Like Everyone She Knows	CDJ	U.S.	1992	$3.00
Columbia		Master of the Game	CDJ	U.S.		$3.00
Columbia	651204-2	Never Die Young	CD5	U.K.	1988	$10.00
Columbia	CSK 2906	Never Die Young	CDJ	U.S.	1988	$3.00
Columbia	CSK 5464	Secret o' Life	CDJ	U.S.		$3.00
Eastwest	257362-2	Sister Rosa	CD3	Germany	1989	$10.00
Pioneer	WMD5-4002	Sister Rosa	CD3	Japan	1989	$12.00/$4.00
Columbia		Sister Rosa	CDJ	U.S.	1988	$3.00
Columbia	CSK 5672	Your Smiling Face	CDJ	U.S.	1994	$3.00

Taylor, Jobeth

Singles

Label	Catalog Number	Title	Type	Country	Year	Longbox Value / Value
Interscope	PRCD 3859-2	If This Isn't Love	CDJ	U.S.	1991	$2.00

Taylor, Johnny

Singles

Label	Catalog Number	Title	Type	Country	Year	Longbox Value / Value
Malaco	2178	Crazy Over You	CDJ	U.S.	1992	$2.00
Malaco	2197	Lady Soul	CDJ	U.S.	1992	$2.00

Taylor, Jude

Singles

Label	Catalog Number	Title	Type	Country	Year	Longbox Value / Value
Mardi Gras	5011	Best of Zydeco	CD5	U.S.	1994	$5.00

Taylor, Lisa

Singles

Label	Catalog Number	Title	Type	Country	Year	Longbox Value / Value
Giant	PRO-CD-5099	Secrets of the Heart	CDJ	U.S.	1992	$2.00

Taylor, Roger

Singles

Label	Catalog Number	Title	Type	Country	Year	Longbox Value / Value
		Foreign Sand	CD5	U.K.	1994	$10.00
EMI		Nazis	CDJ	U.K.		$20.00
		Nazis	CD5	U.K.	1994	$10.00

Taylor, S.

Singles

Label	Catalog Number	Title	Type	Country	Year	Longbox Value / Value
Rhino	74447	Holiday Affair	CD5	U.S.	1994	$5.00
Rhino	74447	I've Got Some Press	CD5	U.S.	1994	$5.00

TBTBT

Singles

Label	Catalog Number	Title	Type	Country	Year	Longbox Value / Value
Cold Chillin'	6358	One Track Mind	CDJ	U.S.	1993	$2.00
Cold Chillin'	6452	One Track Mind	CDJ	U.S.	1993	$2.00

TC 1993

Singles

Label	Catalog Number	Title	Type	Country	Year	Longbox Value / Value
		Harmony	CD5	U.K.		$10.00
		Harmony	CD5	U.K.		$10.00

Second version.

TDC

Singles

Label	Catalog Number	Title	Type	Country	Year	Longbox Value / Value
Mercury	CDP 347	Keep Groovin'	CDJ	U.S.	1990	$2.00

Tea Party

Full Length

Label	Catalog Number	Title	Type	Country	Year	Longbox Value / Value
Capitol	DPRO-748	Splender Soils	DJ/Smplr	Canada		$10.00
		Splendor Spoils Sampler	DJ/Smplr	Canada		$15.00

Singles

Label	Catalog Number	Title	Type	Country	Year	Longbox Value / Value
		A Certain Slant of Light	CD5	Australia		$10.00
		A Certain Slant of Light	CDJ	Canada		$7.00
		Midsummer Day	CDJ	Canada		$6.00
Chrysalis	DPRO-19805	River, The	CDj	U.S.	1993	$2.00
		Save Me	CDJ	Canada		$6.00
Capitol	DPRO-801	Save Me	CDJ	Canada		$8.00

Teardrop

Singles

Label	Catalog Number	Title	Type	Country	Year	Longbox Value / Value
	1000	3 Strikes You're Out	CD5	U.S.	1994	$5.00

Teardrop Explorers

Singles

Label	Catalog Number	Title	Type	Country	Year	Longbox Value / Value
Fontana	DROCD 1	Serious Danger	CD5	U.K.	1990	$8.00

Tears For Fears

Full Length

Label	Catalog Number	Title	Type	Country	Year	Longbox Value / Value
	SND-10	And 4 Years Passed	DJ/Intvw	Japan		$100.00
Mercury	811039-2	Hurting, The	LP/BP	U.S.†	1984	$14.00/$8.00
Image	ID6359ME	In My Mind's Eye	LD	U.S.		$25.00
Album Network		In the Studio (Songs From the Big Chair)	RS	U.S.	1989	$20.00

Airdate: 4/10/89.

Label	Catalog Number	Title	Type	Country	Year	Longbox Value / Value
Phonogram		Interview	DJ/Intvw	U.K.	1994	$35.00
Epic	67383	Raoul and the Kings of Spain	LTD/LP	U.S.	1995	$25.00

CD in simulated cigar box.

Label	Catalog Number	Title	Type	Country	Year	Longbox Value / Value
		Songs From the Big Chair	DJ/Smplr	U.K.		$10.00
Mercury	824300-2	Songs From the Big Chair	LP/BP	U.S.†	1985	$14.00/$8.00
Pioneer	PA85-M020	Tears For Fears	8" LD	U.S.	1985	$10.00
Pioneer	PA-86-147	Tears For Fears	LD	U.S.	1986	$30.00
Pioneer	PA85-M020	Tears For Fears	8" LD	U.S.	1990	$10.00
Polygram	PCD 192	Tears Laid Low	DJ/Smplr	Canada	1992	$75.00

Singles

Label	Catalog Number	Title	Type	Country	Year	Longbox Value / Value
Polygram	876895-2	Advice for Young of Heart	CD5	Canada	1990	$10.00
Polygram	876895-2	Advice for Young of Heart	CD5	Germany	1990	$10.00
Fontana	IDCD-14	Advice for Young of Heart	CD5	U.K.	1990	$10.00
Fontana	875 145-2	Advice for Young of Heart	CD5	U.S.	1990	$5.00
Fontana	CDP 206	Advice for Young of Heart	CDJ	U.S.	1990	$2.00
		Break It Down	CDJ	France	1993	$35.00

CD in oversized sleeve.

Label	Catalog Number	Title	Type	Country	Year	Longbox Value / Value
Fontana	PHDR-125	Break It Down	CD3	Japan	1993	$13.00/$3.00
Mercury	862 331	Break It Down	CD5	U.S.	1993	$5.00
Mercury	CDP 953	Break It Down	CDJ	U.S.	1993	$2.00
		Break It Down Again	CD5	U.K.		$10.00
		Break It Down Again	CD5	U.K.		$10.00

Second version.

Label	Catalog Number	Title	Type	Country	Year	Longbox Value / Value
Fontana	COLD-1	Cold	CDJ	U.K.		$15.00
Fontana		Elemental	CDJ	U.K.	1994	$40.00

CDJ of "Break It Down," photo and bio in custom bag.

Label	Catalog Number	Title	Type	Country	Year	Longbox Value / Value
Fontana	858 499-2	Elemental	CD5	U.S.	1994	$5.00
Fontana	CDP1158	Elemental	CDJ	U.S.	1994	$3.00
Mercury	870 745-2	Everybody Wants to Rule the World	CDV/BP	U.S.	1988	$20.00/$20.00
Phonogram	080 033-2	Everybody Wants to Rule the World	DJ/CDV	U.S.	1988	$20.00
		Falling Down	CDJ	U.S.		$3.00
Fontana	IDECD-15	Famous Last Words	CD5	U.K.	1990	$10.00
		God's Mistake	CD5	U.K.	1995	$10.00
		God's Mistake	CD5	U.K.	1995	$10.00

Second version.

Label	Catalog Number	Title	Type	Country	Year	Longbox Value / Value
		God's Mistake	CD5	U.K.	1995	$11.00
		God's Mistake	CDJ	U.S.		$3.00
Epic	78064	God's Mistake	CD5	U.S.	1995	$5.00
Epic	ESK 7283	God's Mistake	CDJ	U.S.	1995	$3.00
Fontana		Goodnight Song	CDJ	U.K.	1993	$13.00
Fontana	CDP1032	Goodnight Song	CDJ	U.S.	1993	$3.00
Fontana	866429-2	Laid So Low	CD5	Germany	1992	$10.00
Fontana	IDECD-17	Laid So Low	CD5	U.K.	1992	$10.00
Fontana	CDP 639	Laid So Low	CDJ	U.S.	1992	$3.00
Mercury	TFF-CJ-1	Raoul	CDJ	U.K.	1995	$20.00

Withdrawn CD single never released by the Mercury label.

Label	Catalog Number	Title	Type	Country	Year	Longbox Value / Value
Epic	ESK 7717	Secrets	CDJ	U.S.	1995	$3.00
Polygram	874711-2	Sowing the Seeds of Love	CD5	Canada	1989	$10.00
Polygram	874992-3	Sowing the Seeds of Love	CD3	Germany	1989	$10.00
Polygram	874993-3	Sowing the Seeds of Love	CD3	Germany	1989	$10.00
Polygram	874711-2	Sowing the Seeds of Love	CD5	Germany	1989	$10.00
Fontana	PPDS-13	Sowing the Seeds of Love	CD3	Japan	1989	$13.00/$3.00
Fontana	IDCDL-12	Sowing the Seeds of Love	CD3	U.K.	1989	$10.00
Fontana	IDCD-12	Sowing the Seeds of Love	CD5	U.K.	1989	$10.00
		Sowing the Seeds of Love	CDJ	U.S.	1988	$3.00
		Tears Roll Down	CDJ	France		$25.00

CDJ and vinyl 7" record in 7"x7" sleeve.

Label	Catalog Number	Title	Type	Country	Year	Longbox Value / Value
Fontana	PHDR-54	Tears Roll Down	CD3	Japan	1992	$13.00/$3.00
Polygram	876249-2	Woman in Chains	CD5	Canada	1989	$10.00
Polygram	876434-3	Woman in Chains	CD3	Germany	1989	$10.00
Polygram	876435-2	Woman in Chains	CD5	Germany	1989	$10.00
Fontana	IDSUN-13	Woman in Chains	CD5	U.K.	1989	$10.00
Fontana	IDECD-16	Woman in Chains	CD5	U.K.	1992	$10.00
Fontana	876 249-2	Woman in Chains	CD5	U.S.	1989	$5.00
Fontana	CDP 163	Woman in Chains	CDJ	U.S.	1989	$3.00

Technotronic

Singles

Label	Catalog Number	Title	Type	Country	Year	Longbox Value / Value
BCM	20400	Get Up	CD5	Germany	1990	$8.00
Alfa	ALDB-27	Get Up	CD3	Japan	1990	$12.00/$4.00
Alfa	ALDB-28	Get Up	CD3	Japan	1990	$12.00/$4.00
Swanyard	CDSYR-8	Get Up	CD5	U.K.	1990	$8.00
BCM	20475	Megamix	CD5	Germany	1990	$8.00
Swanyard	CDSYR-17	Megamix	CD5	U.K.	1990	$8.00
CBS	657647-2	Money Makes the World Go Round	CD5	Germany	1992	$8.00
CBS	658049-2	Money Makes the World Go Round	CD5	U.K.	1992	$8.00
Capital	58359	Move It	CD5	U.S.	1994	$5.00
CBS	656837-2	Move That Body	CD5	Germany	1991	$8.00
BCM	24308	Pump Up the Jam	CD5	Germany	1989	$8.00
Alfa	ALDB-14	Pump Up the Jam	CD3	Japan	1990	$12.00/$4.00
Chrysalis	DPRO-19701	Pump Up the Jam	CDJ	U.S.	1989	$3.00
BCM	20495	Rockin' Over the Beat	CD5	Germany	1990	$8.00
Swanyard	CDSYR-14	Rockin' Over the Beat	CD5	U.K.	1990	$8.00
EMI	DPRO-05360	Rockin' Over the Beat	CDJ	U.S.	1990	$2.00
BCM	20420	This Beat Is Technotronic	CD5	Germany	1990	$8.00
Alfa	ALDB-57	This Beat Is Technotronic	CD3	Japan	1990	$12.00/$3.00
Swanyard	CDSYR-9	This Beat Is Technotronic	CD5	U.K.	1990	$8.00
EMI	DPRO-05341	This Beat Is Technotronic	CDJ	U.S.	1990	$2.00
Swanyard	CDSYD-9	Turn It Up	CD5	U.K.	1990	$8.00
CBD	657331-2	Work	CD5	U.K.	1991	$8.00

Teenage Fanclub

Full Length

Label	Catalog Number	Title	Type	Country	Year	Longbox Value / Value
		God Knows It's True	LP/LB	U.S.		$13.00/$8.00
		Grand Prix	LTD/LP	Austrailia	1995	$28.00

2 CD set.

Singles

Label	Catalog Number	Title	Type	Country	Year	Longbox Value / Value
Creation	CRESCD-111	Concept	CD5	U.K.	1991	$8.00
Geffen	PRO-CD-4370	Concept	CDJ	U.S.	1991	$3.00
Geffen	PRO-CD-4619	Escher	CDJ	U.S.	1994	$3.00
Paperhouse	PAPER-003CD	Everything Flows	CD5	U.K.	1991	$8.00
Epic	ESK 5598	Fallin'	CDJ	U.S.	1994	$3.00
Geffen	PRO-CD-4575	Hang On	CDJ	U.S.	1993	$3.00
		Mellow Doubt	CD5	U.K.	1995	$10.00
		Mellow Doubt	CD5	U.K.	1995	$10.00

Second version.

Label	Catalog Number	Title	Type	Country	Year	Longbox Value / Value
Strange Frt	SFPSCD-081	Peel Sessions	CD5	U.K.	1992	$8.00
Creation	977 965	Starsign	CD5	Germany	1991	$8.00
Creation	CRESCD-105	Starsign	CD5	U.K.	1991	$8.00
Geffen	PRO-CD-4333	Starsign	CDJ	U.S.	1991	$3.00
Creation	828 917	What You Do to Me	CD5	Germany	1992	$8.00
Geffen	MVCG-17004	What You Do to Me	CD3	Japan	1992	$13.00/$4.00
Creation	CRESCD-115	What You Do to Me	CD5	U.K.	1992	$8.00
Geffen	PRO-CD-4420	What You Do to Me	CDJ	U.S.	1992	$3.00
Geffen	PRO-CD-4417	What You Do to Me	CDJ	U.S.	1992	$3.00
Geffen	PRO-CD-4420	What You Do to Me	CDJ	U.S.	1992	$3.00

Teknoe

Singles

Label	Catalog Number	Title	Type	Country	Year	Longbox Value / Value
A&M	75021 7318-2	I Wanna Be Like Mike	CDJ	U.S.	1991	$7.00

Television

Singles

Label	Catalog Number	Title	Type	Country	Year	Longbox Value / Value
Capitol	DPRO-79452	Call Mr. Lee	CDJ	U.S.	1992	$2.00
Capitol	DPRO-79557	In World	CDJ	U.S.	1992	$2.00

Tell Me Tell Me

Singles

Label	Catalog Number	Title	Type	Country	Year	Longbox Value / Value
		Whisper to Me	CDJ	U.S.		$2.00

Temerarios, Los

Singles

Label	Catalog Number	Title	Type	Country	Year	Longbox Value / Value
Afg Sigma Records	7001	Lobo Disco Mix	CD5	U.S.	1994	$5.00

Temple of the Dog

Singles

Label	Catalog Number	Title	Type	Country	Year	Longbox Value / Value
A&M	AMCD-0091	Hunger Strike	CD5	U.K.	1992	$11.00
A&M	75021 7538 2	Hunger Strike	CDJ	U.S.	1991	$7.00
A&M	75021 7530-2	Say Hello 2 Heaven	CDJ	U.S.	1991	$3.00

Tempo, Nino

Label	Catalog Number	Title	Type	Country	Year	Longbox Value / Value
		Singles				
Atlantic	PRCD 3979-2	Darn That Dream	CDJ	U.S.	1990	$2.00
		This Masquerade	CDJ	U.S.		$2.00
		You Are So Beautiful	CDJ	U.S.		$2.00

Temptations

Label	Catalog Number	Title	Type	Country	Year	Longbox Value / Value
		Full Length				
Motown	1016	Jones'	CD	U.S.	1992	$3.00
Motown	1628	Jones'	CD	U.S.	1992	$3.00
Motown		Motown Collector	DJ/Smplr	France	1994	$15.00
		Sixties Legends	RS	U.S.	1992	$15.00
	2 CD set. Airdate: 6/27/92.					
Motown	6246-MD	Solid Rock	LP/BP	U.S.		$12.00/$7.00
Image	ID64176FR	Temptations and The Four Tops	LD	U.S.		$20.00
Motown	6246-MD	Together Again	LP/BP	U.S.		$12.00/$7.00
		Singles				
RCA	ZD-43006	All I Want From You	CD5	Germany	1989	$10.00
RCA	ZD-43234	All I Want From You	CD5	U.K.	1989	$10.00
Motown	TMGCD-1405	Get Ready	CD5	U.K.	1992	$10.00
MCA	CD45 1050	Get Ready 1990	CDJ	U.S.	1990	$2.00
Motown	TMGCD-1403	Jones'	CD5	U.K.	1992	$10.00
Epic	657676-2	My Girl	CD5	Germany	1992	$10.00
Epic	ESDA-7088	My Girl	CD3	Japan	1992	$12.00/$4.00
Epic	657676-2	My Girl	CD5	U.K.	1992	$10.00
Epic	ESK 74108	My Girl	CDJ	U.S.	1992	$3.00
GRP	9953	Shake Your Paw	CDJ	U.S.	1990	$2.00
RCA	ZD-43456	Soul to Soul	CD5	Germany	1990	$10.00
Motown	R10M-127	Special	CD3	Japan	1989	$12.00/$4.00

Ten C.C.

Label	Catalog Number	Title	Type	Country	Year	Longbox Value / Value
		Singles				
Polygram	888964-3	I'm Not in Love	CD3	Germany	1989	$8.00
Polygram	888964-2	I'm Not in Love	CD5	Germany	1989	$8.00
Polygram	888964-3	I'm Not in Love	CD3	U.K.	1989	$8.00
Polydor	PODP-1072	Welcome to My Paradise	CD3	Japan	1993	$12.00/$4.00
Polydor	PODP-1053	Woman in Love	CD3	Japan	1992	$12.00/$4.00
Polygram	PZCD-196	Woman in Love	CD5	U.K.	1992	$8.00

Ten City

Label	Catalog Number	Title	Type	Country	Year	Longbox Value / Value
		Singles				
Atlantic	A-8916CD	Devotion	CD3	U.K.	1989	$8.00
Columbia	CSK 77104	Fantasy	CDJ	U.S.	1993	$2.00
Eastwest	PRCD 4669-2	My Peace Of Heaven	CDJ	U.S.	1992	$2.00
Eastwest	7567-96147-2	Only Time Will Tell	CD5	Germany	1992	$8.00
Eastwest	A-8516CD	Only Time Will Tell	CD5	U.K.	1992	$8.00
Eastwest	PRCD 4853-2	Only Time Will Tell	CDJ	U.S.	1992	$2.00
WEA	786460-2	That's the Way Love Is	CD3	Germany	1989	$8.00
Pioneer	09P3-6160	That's the Way Love Is	CD3	Japan	1989	$15.00/$4.00
		That's the Way Love Is	CDJ	U.S.	1989	$2.00
Altlantic	7657-87806-2	Whatever Makes You Happy	CD5	Gemany	1990	$8.00
Altlantic	A-7819CD	Whatever Makes You Happy	CD5	U.K.	1990	$8.00
		Whatever Makes You Happy	CDJ	U.S.	1989	$2.00
Altlantic	A-8864CD	Where Do We Go	CD3	U.K.	1989	$8.00
Altlantic	7567-86326-2	Where Do We Go	CD3	U.K.	1989	$8.00

Ten Inch Men

Label	Catalog Number	Title	Type	Country	Year	Longbox Value / Value
		Singles				
Victory	CDP 912	Crazy Daydream	CDJ	U.S.	1993	$2.00

Ten Tray

Label	Catalog Number	Title	Type	Country	Year	Longbox Value / Value
		Full Length				
Polygram	510107	Realm of Darkness	LP/BP	U.S.		$12.00/$7.00
		Singles				
Smash	629	I Convey!	CDJ	U.S.	1992	$2.00

Ten Years After

Label	Catalog Number	Title	Type	Country	Year	Longbox Value / Value
		Full Length				
Chrysalis		About Time	LP/LB	U.S.		$14.00/$8.00
		Alvin Lee & Company	LP/LB	U.S.		$14.00/$8.00
EMI		Cicklewood, Watt, A Space In Time	LTD/LP	U.K.	1994	$35.00
	3 CD boxed set.					
Album Network		In the Studio (Ten Years After)	RS	U.S.	1990	$20.00
	Airdate: 9/25/89.					
DIR		King Biscuit Flour Hour	RS	U.S.	1988	$30.00
	With Edgar Winter, Airdate: 6/19/88.					
Chrysalis		SSSH	LTD/LP	U.K.	1994	$25.00/$15.00
	25th Anniversary edition in 6"x11" longbox.					
		Singles				
Chrysalis	DPRO-23447	Highway of Love	CDJ	U.S.	1989	$2.00
Chrysalis	DPRO-23413	Let's Shake It Up	CDJ	U.S.	1989	$2.00

Tennille, Toni

Label	Catalog Number	Title	Type	Country	Year	Longbox Value / Value
		Full Length				
Atco	90162-2	More Than You Know	LP/LB	U.S.†	1985	$12.00/$7.00

Terminal Power

Label	Catalog Number	Title	Type	Country	Year	Longbox Value / Value
		Full Length				
RCA	66069	Run Silent Run Deep	LP/LB	U.S.		$14.00/$8.00

Terminata

Label	Catalog Number	Title	Type	Country	Year	Longbox Value / Value
		Singles				
Cold Chillin'	2030	Grt Bizi/Sex	CD5	U.S.	1994	$5.00

Terminator X

Label	Catalog Number	Title	Type	Country	Year	Longbox Value / Value
		Singles				
Columbia	CSK 73759	Homey Don't Play Dat	CDJ	U.S.	1991	$2.00
Columbia	CSK 73894	Juvenile Delinquent	CDJ	U.S.	1991	$2.00

Terrell

Label	Catalog Number	Title	Type	Country	Year	Longbox Value / Value
		Full Length				
Giant	9 24400-2-Dj	On the Wings of Dirty Angels	DJ/LP	U.S.	1990	$8.00
	Picture disc.					
Reprise		Piece of Time, The Official Bootleg	DJ/Smplr	U.S.		$15.00
		Singles				
Giant	PRO-CD-4404	Shotgun Ground	CDJ	U.S.	1990	$2.00
Giant	PRO-CD-4413	Soul of Pirates	CDJ	U.S.	1990	$7.00

Terri & Monica

Label	Catalog Number	Title	Type	Country	Year	Longbox Value / Value
		Singles				
Epic	ESK 5688	Intentions	CDJ	U.S.	1994	$2.00
Epic	ESK 5375	Uh Huh Vibe	CDJ	U.S.	1993	$2.00
Epic	ESK 77110	Uh Huh Vibe	CDJ	U.S.	1993	$2.00

Terror Fabulous

Label	Catalog Number	Title	Type	Country	Year	Longbox Value / Value
		Singles				
Warner	32-98260	Action	CD5	Canada	1994	$6.00
		Action	CDJ	U.S.		$2.00
Atlantic	95807	Yaga Yaga	CD5	U.S.	1994	$5.00

Terrorvision

Label	Catalog Number	Title	Type	Country	Year	Longbox Value / Value
		Full Length				
	FRIEND-1	How To Make Friends	DJ/Smplr	U.K.	1994	$14.00
		Singles				
Total Vegas	CDVEGASS7	Middleman	CD5	U.K.	1994	$10.00
Total Vegas	CDVEGAS7	Middleman	CD5	U.K.	1994	$10.00
		My House	CD5	U.K.		$10.00
		My House	CD5	U.K.		$10.00
	Second version.					
		New Policy One	CD5	U.K.		$10.00
		New Policy One	CD5	U.K.		$10.00
	Second version.					
		Oblivion	CD5	U.K.		$10.00
		Oblivion	CD5	U.K.		$10.00
	Second version.					
Total Vegas	CDVEGS1	Thrive	CD5	U.K.	1992	$10.00

Terry, Tony

Label	Catalog Number	Title	Type	Country	Year	Longbox Value / Value
		Singles				
Epic	ESK 74119	Everlasting Love	CDJ	U.S.	1991	$2.00
Epic	CDTONY-3	Forever Yours	CD5	U.K.	1988	$8.00
Epic	ESK 1136	Forever Yours	CDJ	U.S.	1987	$2.00
Epic	655021-2	Forget the Girl	CD5	U.K.	1989	$8.00
Epic	ESK 73619	Head over Heels	CDJ	U.S.	1990	$2.00
Epic	657645-2	With You	CD5	U.K.	1991	$8.00
Epic	ESK 73713	With You	CDJ	U.S.	1991	$2.00

Tesh, John

Label	Catalog Number	Title	Type	Country	Year	Longbox Value / Value
		Full Length				
		Discovery	DJ/LP	U.S.		$8.00
GTSP	314533707-2	Home For the Holidays	LTD/LP	U.S.	1996	$15.00
	Distributed exclusively at Macy's Department Stores.					
Private Music		Tour De France	DJ/Smplr	U.S.		$4.00
		Singles				
GT	3-4492-2	Concetta	CDJ	U.S.	1992	$2.00
Private Music		That Ole Demon Meaness	CDJ	U.S.	1988	$2.00
Private Music		You Are Here	CDJ	U.S.	1988	$2.00
Cypress	CD 17886	You Break It	CDJ	U.S.	1989	$2.00

Tesla

Label	Catalog Number	Title	Type	Country	Year	Longbox Value / Value
		Full Length				
Geffen	PRO-CD-4411	Electric, Acoustic and Psychotic	DJ/Smplr	U.S.	1992	$25.00
Geffen	MVCZ-8	Five Man Acoustical Jam	LTD/LP	Japan	1990	$30.00
	10"x10" outer package with lobby cards.					
Geffen	MVCG-63	Psychotic Supper	LTD/LP	Japan	1991	$30.00
	Bonus track and outer slipcase.					
Geffen		Time's Makin' Changes	DJ/LP	U.S.		$8.00
		Singles				
Geffen	GED-21672	Call It What You Will	CD5	Germany	1991	$10.00
Geffen	PRO-CD-4348	Call It What You Will	CDJ	U.S.	1991	$3.00
Geffen	PRO-CD-4351	Call It What You Will	CDJ	U.S.	1991	$3.00
Geffen	GFSTD-13	Edison's Medicine	CD5	U.K.	1991	$10.00
Geffen	PRO-CD-4310	Edison's Medicine	CDJ	U.S.	1991	$3.00
Geffen	PRO-CD-3406	Heaven's Trail (No Way Out)	CDJ	U.S.	1988	$3.00
Geffen	921494-2	Love Song	CD5	Germany	1990	$10.00
Geffen	GEF-74CD	Love Song	CD5	U.K.	1989	$10.00
Geffen	PRO-CD-3648	Love Song	CDJ	U.S.	1989	$3.00
Geffen	PRO CD 4211	Paradise	CDJ	U.S.	1991	$3.00
Geffen		Signs	CD5	Germany	1991	$10.00
Geffen	GFSTD-3	Signs	CD5	U.K.	1991	$10.00
Geffen	PRO-CD-4178	Signs	CDJ	U.S.	1990	$6.00
Geffen	PRO-CD-4425	Song & Emotion	CDJ	U.S.	1991	$7.00
Geffen	PRO-CD-4450	Stir It Up	CDJ	U.S.	1991	$3.00
Geffen	PRO-CD-3886	Way It Is, The	CDJ	U.S.	1990	$3.00
Geffen	PRO-CD-4380	What You Give	CDJ	U.S.	1991	$3.00

Testament

Label	Catalog Number	Title	Type	Country	Year	Longbox Value / Value
		Singles				
Atlantic		Dog Faced Gods	CDJ	U.S.		$6.00
Atlantic	PRCD 4553-2	Electric Crown	CDJ	U.S.	1992	$2.00
Atlantic	PRCD 3286-2	Greenhouse Effect	CDJ	U.S.	1989	$2.00
Atlantic		Low	CDJ	U.S.		$3.00
Atlantic	PRCD 34726-2	Return to Serenity	CDJ	U.S.		$2.00

Texas

Label	Catalog Number	Title	Type	Country	Year	Longbox Value / Value
		Full Length				
Warner Brothers	PRO-CD-68111	Decade	DJ/LP	U.S.	1994	$18.00
	2 CD set.					
Mercury		Decade	DJ/Smplr	U.S.	1994	$20.00
	2 CD set					
Mercury		In-Store Play	DJ/Smplr	U.S.	1994	$10.00
Mercury		Live From the Rocks Road	DJ/Smplr	U.S.	1994	$15.00
Mercury		On Tour	DJ/Smplr	U.S.	1994	$30.00
	Disc 1 is a 6 track live sampler with Texas. Disc 2 is John Mellencamp Live.					
		Singles				
Mercury	TEXCD7	Alone With You	CD5	U.K.	1991	$8.00
Mercury	874983-2	Everyday Now	CD5	Canada	1989	$8.00
Mercury	876029-2	Everyday Now	CD5	Germany	1989	$8.00
Mercury	TEXCD-3	Everyday Now	CD5	U.K.	1989	$8.00
Mercury	CDP 139	Everyday Now	CDJ	U.S.	1989	$3.00
Mercury	CDP 1165	Fade Away	CDJ	U.S.	1994	$3.00
Mercury	874480-3	I Don't Want a Lover	CD3	Germany	1989	$8.00
Mercury	872351-5	I Don't Want a Lover	CD5	Germany	1989	$8.00
Phonogram	PPDS-6	I Don't Want a Lover	CD3	Japan	1989	$12.00/$4.00
Mercury	TEXCD-1	I Don't Want a Lover	CD5	U.K.	1989	$8.00
Mercury	CDP 60	I Don't Want a Lover	CDJ	U.S.	1989	$3.00
Mercury	CDP 549	In My Heart	CDJ	U.S.	1991	$3.00
Mercury	TEXCD-4	Prayer for You	CD5	U.K.	1989	$8.00
Mercury	TEXCDR-4	Prayer for You	CD5	U.K.	1989	$8.00
Mercury		So Called Friend	CDJ	U.S.	1994	$3.00
Mercury	874378-2	Thrill Has Gone	CD3	Germany	1989	$8.00
Mercury	874379-2	Thrill Has Gone	CD5	Germany	1989	$8.00
Mercury	TEXCD 8	Tired of Being Alone	CD5	U.K.	1991	$8.00
Mercury	TEXDJ 8	Tired of Being Alone	CDJ	U.K.	1991	$10.00
Mercury	868213-2	Why Believe in You	CD5	Germany	1991	$8.00
Phonogram	PHDR-39	Why Believe in You	CD3	Japan	1991	$12.00/$4.00
Mercury	866 165	Why Believe in You	CD5	U.S.	1991	$5.00
Mercury	CDP 632	Why Believe in You	CDJ	U.S.	1991	$3.00
Mercury	CDP 607	Why Believe in You	CDJ	U.S.	1991	$6.00

Texas Tornados

Label	Catalog Number	Title	Type	Country	Year	Longbox Value / Value
		Singles				
Reprise	PRO-CD-4527	A Man Can Cry	CDJ	U.S.	1990	$2.00
Reprise	PRO-CD-5029	Is Anybody Goin' To San Antone	CDJ	U.S.	1991	$2.00

Label	Catalog Number	Title	Type	Country	Year	Longbox/Value
Reprise	PRO-CD-4309	Who Were You Thinkin' Of	CDJ	U.S.	1990	$2.00

Tha Dog Pound

Singles

Label	Catalog Number	Title	Type	Country	Year	Longbox/Value
		Let's Play House	CDJ	U.S.		$2.00
		New York, New York	CDJ	U.S.		$2.00
		Respect	CDJ	U.S.		$2.00

Tharp, Twila

Full Length

Label	Catalog Number	Title	Type	Country	Year	Longbox/Value
WEA	40161	Catherine Wheel	LD	U.S.	1992	$40.00

That Dog

Singles

Label	Catalog Number	Title	Type	Country	Year	Longbox/Value
DGC	PRO-CD-4747	He's Kissing Christian	CDJ	U.S.		$2.00
DGC	PRO-CD-4663	He's Kissing Christian	CDJ	U.S.		$2.00

That Petrol Emotion

Full Length

Label	Catalog Number	Title	Type	Country	Year	Longbox/Value
Virgin		Exploded View	DJ/Smplr	U.S.		$15.00
Virgin	VSCDT-1242	Abandon	CD5	U.K.	1990	$9.00
Virgin	CDEP-13	Genius Move	CD5	U.K.	1987	$9.00
Virgin	VSCD-1159	Groove Check	CD3	U.K.	1989	$9.00
Virgin	PR 2469	Groove Check	CDJ	U.S.	1988	$2.00
Virgin	VSCDT-1290	Hey Venus	CD5	U.K.	1990	$9.00
Virgin	PRCD 3211	Hey Venus	CDJ	U.S.	1989	$2.00
Strange Frt	SFPMACD-205	Peel Sessions	CD5	U.K.	1989	$9.00
Virgin	VSCDT-1261	Sensitize	CD5	U.K.	1990	$9.00
Virgin	PRCD 3316	Sensitize	CDJ	U.S.	1990	$2.00
Virgin	VSCDT-1312	Tingle	CD5	U.K.	1990	$9.00

The The

Full Length

Label	Catalog Number	Title	Type	Country	Year	Longbox/Value
Epic		A Little Hanky Panky	DJ/Smplr	U.S.	1995	$10.00
Epic	ESK 1867	Alive	DJ/Intvw	U.S.	1989	$20.00
Epic	XPCD 222	Dusk	DJ/Smplr	U.K.	1992	$20.00
Epic		Dusk	LTD/LP	U.S.	1994	$18.00
CD with bonus "Live In N.Y." cassette						
Epic	XPCD561	Hanky Panky	DJ/Smplr	U.K.	1995	$15.00
Epic		Hanky Panky	DJ/LP	U.S.	1995	$20.00
2 CD set in wooden box.						
Epic	ESK 5300	Live in New York	DJ/Smplr	U.S.	1993	$18.00
Epic		Vs. Hank	DJ/Smplr	U.S.	1995	$20.00
Epic	ESK 1958	Vs. the World	DJ/Smplr	U.S.		$25.00

Singles

Label	Catalog Number	Title	Type	Country	Year	Longbox/Value
Epic	CDEMU-10	Armageddon Days Are Here Again	CD5	U.K.	1989	$10.00
Epic	EMUC-10	Armageddon Days Are Here Again	CD5	U.K.	1989	$10.00
Epic	654578-3	Beat(en) Generation	CD5	Germany	1989	$10.00
Epic	CBEMU-9	Beat(en) Generation	CD3	U.K.	1989	$10.00
Epic	CPEMU-9	Beat(en) Generation	CD5	U.K.	1989	$10.00
Some Bizar	SBZCD-016	Cold Spell Ahead	CD5	U.K.	1992	$10.00
		Dogs of Lust	CD5	U.K.		$10.00
		Dogs of Lust	CD5	U.K.		$10.00
Second version.						
Epic	ESK 4836	Dogs of Lust	CDJ	U.S.		$3.00
CBS	654971-3	Gravitate to Me	CD3	Germany	1989	$10.00
Epic	CDEMU-9	Gravitate to Me	CD5	U.K.	1989	$10.00
Epic		I Saw the Light	CDJ	U.S.	1995	$7.00
		Jealous of Youth	CDJ	France	1990	$20.00
Epic	49K 73151	Jealous of Youth	CD5	U.S	1990	$5.00
		Love Is Stronger Than Death	CD5	U.K.		$10.00
		Love Is Stronger Than Death	CD5	U.K.		$10.00
Second version.						
Epic	ESK 5108	Love Is Stronger Than Death	CDJ	U.S.		$3.00
Epic	ESCA-5278	Shades of Blue	CD5	Japan	1991	$18.00
Epic	655796-2	Shades of Blue	CD5	U.K.	1991	$10.00
Columbia	47410-2	Shades of Blue	CD5	U.S.	1991	$5.00
Epic	ESCA-5757	Slow Emotion Replay	CD5	Japan	1993	$18.00
Epic	659077	Slow Emotion Replay	CD5	U.K.	1993	$10.00
Epic	ESK 5218	Slow Emotion Replay	CDJ	U.S.	1993	$3.00
		Slow Motion Replay	CD5	U.K.		$10.00
		Slow Motion Replay	CD5	U.K.		$10.00
Second version.						
Epic	ESK 6141	That Was the Day	CDJ	U.S.	1993	$3.00

Thelonious Monster

Singles

Label	Catalog Number	Title	Type	Country	Year	Longbox/Value
Capitol	DPRO-79392	Blood Is Thicker Than Water	CDJ	U.S.	1992	$2.00
Capitol	DPRO-79590	Body & Soul	CDJ	U.S.	1992	$2.00

Then Jericho

Singles

Label	Catalog Number	Title	Type	Country	Year	Longbox/Value
Polygram	886389-2	Big Area	CD5	Germany	1989	$8.00
London	LONCD-204	Big Area	CD5	U.K.	1989	$8.00
		Let Her Fall	CDJ	U.S.		$2.00
London	LONCD-156	Muscle Deep	CD5	U.K.	1988	$8.00
London	LONCD-131	Prairie Rose	CD5	U.K.	1988	$8.00
Polygram	886725-2	Sugar Box	CD5	Germany	1989	$8.00
London	LONCD 235	Sugar Box	CD5	U.K.	1989	$8.00
Polygram	886560-3	What Does It Take	CD3	Germany	1989	$8.00
Polygram	886561-2	What Does It Take	CD5	Germany	1989	$8.00
London	POOL-40012	What Does It Take	CD3	Japan	1989	$12.00/$4.00
London	LONCD-223	What Does It Take	CD5	U.K.	1989	$8.00

Theory

Singles

Label	Catalog Number	Title	Type	Country	Year	Longbox/Value
Columbia	CSK 5453	Why Do Fools Fall in Love	CDJ	U.S.	1993	$2.00

Therapy

Full Length

Label	Catalog Number	Title	Type	Country	Year	Longbox/Value
A&M		Infernal Life	DJ/LP	U.S.		$8.00
A&M	AMSAD00068	Misery	DJ/Smplr	U.S.		$8.00

Singles

Label	Catalog Number	Title	Type	Country	Year	Longbox/Value
A&M	31458 0196-4/2	Die Laughing	CDJ	U.S.	1994	$2.00
A&M	AMCDP00135	Loose	CDJ	U.S.		$2.00
A&M	31458 8086	Nausea	CDJ	U.S.	1992	$2.00
A&M	31458 8124	Perversonality	CDJ	U.S.	1993	$2.00
A&M	31458 8206	Screamager	CDJ	U.S.	1993	$2.00
A&M	AMCD 0097	Teethgrinder	CD5	U.K.	1992	$9.00

Thermadore

Singles

Label	Catalog Number	Title	Type	Country	Year	Longbox/Value
		Amerasian	CDJ	U.S.		$2.00

They Eat Their Own

Singles

Label	Catalog Number	Title	Type	Country	Year	Longbox/Value
Relativity	IRPROCD-0115	Like a Drug	CDJ	U.S.	1990	$2.00

They Might Be Giants

Full Length

Label	Catalog Number	Title	Type	Country	Year	Longbox/Value
		John Henry	LTD/LP	Australia	1995	$35.00
2 CD set.						
Bar/Non	EPRO 138	"Lincoln" Sampler, The	DJ/Smplr	U.S.	1990	$3.00
Image	ID7920EN	Videos 1986-1989, The	8"LD	U.S.	1989	$8.00

Singles

Label	Catalog Number	Title	Type	Country	Year	Longbox/Value
		Aka Driver	CDJ	U.S.		$3.00
Elektra	EKR-124CD	Ana Ng	CD5	U.K.	1991	$10.00
Elektra	EKR-104CD	Birdhouse in Your Soul	CD5	U.K.	1991	$10.00
Elektra	PR 8136-2	Birdhouse in Your Soul	CDJ	U.S.	1991	$2.00
Elektra	EKR-115CD	Don't Let's Start	CD5	U.K.	1990	$10.00
Elektra	EKR-145CD	Guitar	CD5	U.K.	1992	$10.00
Elektra	66394-2	Guitar	CD5	U.S.	1992	$5.00
Elektra	PRCD 8606-2	Guitar	CDJ	U.S.	1992	$2.00
Restless	009	Hey Mr. D.J.	CDJ	U.S.	1991	$2.00
Elektra	PRCD 8573-2	I Palindrome!	CDJ	U.S.	1992	$2.00
Elektra	66425-2	I Palindrome!	CDJ	U.S.	1992	$7.00
Elektra	EKR-110CD	Istanbul (Not Constantinople)	CD5	U.K.	1990	$10.00
Elektra	66631-2	Istanbul (Not Constantinople)	CD5	U.S.	1990	$5.00
Elektra	PR8182-2	Istanbul (Not Constantinople)	CDJ	U.S.	1990	$2.00
Bar/Non	EPRO 190	Purple Toupee	CDJ	U.S.	1989	$2.00
		Sleeping in the Flowers	CDJ	U.S.		$3.00
		Snail Shell	CDJ	U.S.	1994	$2.00
Elektra	7559-66450-2	Statue Got Me High	CD5	Germany	1992	$10.00
Rough Trade	604-3130-3	Statue Got Me High	CD5	Germany	1992	$10.00
Elektra	EKR-141CD	Statue Got Me High	CD5	U.K.	1992	$10.00
Elektra	PRCD 8523-2	Statue Got Me High	CDJ	U.S.	1992	$2.00
Elektra	PR 8166-2	Twisting	CDJ	U.S.	1990	$2.00

Thiele, Bob

Singles

Label	Catalog Number	Title	Type	Country	Year	Longbox/Value
Red Baron	5617	Addams Family Theme, The	CDJ	U.S.	1994	$3.00

Thielemans, Toots

Full Length

Label	Catalog Number	Title	Type	Country	Year	Longbox/Value
Verve	825086-2	The Silver Collection	LP/LB	U.S.†	1985	$14.00/$8.00

Thieves

Singles

Label	Catalog Number	Title	Type	Country	Year	Longbox/Value
Capitol	DPRO-79491	Everything But My Heart	CDJ	U.S.	1989	$2.00
Nursery	NYSCD-11	Through the Door	CD5	U.K.	1992	$8.00

Thin Lizzy

Full Length

Label	Catalog Number	Title	Type	Country	Year	Longbox/Value
BBC Radio		BBC Classic Tracks	RS	U.S.	1991	$25.00
Airdate: 8/5/91.						
BBC Radio		BBC Classic Tracks	RS	U.S.	1992	$25.00
Airdate: 8/24/92.						
BBC Radio		BBC Classic Tracks	RS	U.S.	1993	$15.00
Airdate: 4/5/93.						
Warner Brothers	45172	Black Rose	LP/LB	U.S.		$14.00/$8.00
Warner Brothers	45173	Chinatown	LP/LB	U.S.		$14.00/$8.00
Vertigo	PCHR-3113/46	Great Box	LP	Japan	1990	$80.00
4 CD set.						
DIR		King Biscuit Flour Hour	RS	U.S.	1988	$50.00
With Aerosmith, Airdate: 9/4/88.						
Warner Brothers	45176	Life Live	LP/LB	U.S.		$14.00/$8.00
Warner Brothers	45174	Renegade	LP/LB	U.S.		$14.00/$8.00
Vertigo		Rockers	LTD/LP	U.K.	1995	$35.00
Warner Brothers	45175	Thunder & Lightning	LP/LB	U.S.		$14.00/$8.00
		Wild One	DJ/Smplr	U.K.	1996	$40.00

Singles

Label	Catalog Number	Title	Type	Country	Year	Longbox/Value
Vertigo	LIZCD-15	Boys Are Back in Town	CD5	U.K.	1991	$10.00
Vertigo	LIZ CD 14	Dedication	CD5	U.K.	1991	$10.00
Mercury	CDP 409	Dedication	CDJ	U.S.	1991	$7.00

Think Out Loud

Singles

Label	Catalog Number	Title	Type	Country	Year	Longbox/Value
A&m	S10Y-3005	After All This Time	CD3	Japan	1988	$12.00/$3.00
A&M	CD 17534	After All This Time	CDJ	U.S.	1988	$2.00

Think Three

Singles

Label	Catalog Number	Title	Type	Country	Year	Longbox/Value
Caroline	2	Abbreviated	CDJ	U.S.	1991	$2.00
Caroline	3	Rattlesnake	CDJ	U.S.	1992	$2.00

Third Bass

Full Length

Label	Catalog Number	Title	Type	Country	Year	Longbox/Value
Def Jam	CSK 1919	Cactus Album Sampler, The	DJ/Smplr	U.S.	1989	$8.00
CBS	655830-2	Brooklyn Queens	CD5	U.K.	1990	$8.00
Def Jam	CSK 73328	Brooklyn Queens	CDJ	U.S.	1990	$2.00
CBS	655398-3	Gas Face, The	CD3	Germany	1989	$8.00
Def Jam	655627-2	Gas Face, The	CD5	U.K.	1990	$8.00
Def Jam	CSK 73046	Gas Face, The	CDJ	U.S.	1989	$2.00
Def Jam	CSK 73728	Pop Goes the Weasel	CDJ	U.S.	1990	$2.00

Third Eye

Singles

Label	Catalog Number	Title	Type	Country	Year	Longbox/Value
Regular	D 10211	Real Thing, The	CD5	Australia	1990	$8.00

Third World

Full Length

Label	Catalog Number	Title	Type	Country	Year	Longbox/Value
CBS	CK-39877	Sense of Purpose	LP/BP	U.S.†	1985	$14.00/$8.00

Singles

Label	Catalog Number	Title	Type	Country	Year	Longbox/Value
Mercury	CDP 706	Committed	CDJ	U.S.	1992	$2.00
Mercury	CDP 54	Forbidden Love	CDJ	U.S.	1989	$2.00
Mercury	CDP 97	It's the Same Old Song	CDJ	U.S.	1989	$2.00
Mercury	CDP 157	Love Will Always Be There	CDJ	U.S.	1989	$2.00
Mercury	CDP 830	Mi Legal	CDJ	U.S.	1993	$2.00

Thirteen Engines

Full Length

Label	Catalog Number	Title	Type	Country	Year	Longbox/Value
Capitol		Ignition	DJ/Smplr	Canada		$10.00

Singles

Label	Catalog Number	Title	Type	Country	Year	Longbox/Value
Capitol		Bread in the Bones	CDJ	Canada		$5.00
Capitol		Golden Age, The	CDJ	Canada		$5.00
Capitol		More	CDJ	Canada		$5.00
		Slow	CDJ	U.S.		$2.00
Capitol		Smoke & Ashes	CDJ	Canada		$5.00

Thirty-Aught-Six

Singles

Label	Catalog Number	Title	Type	Country	Year	Longbox/Value
		Adamantine	CDJ	U.S.		$2.00

Thirty-Eight Special

Full Length

Label	Catalog Number	Title	Type	Country	Year	Longbox/Value
Westwood One		BBC Classic Tracks	RS	U.S.	1994	$20.00
Airdate: 10/24/94.						
Album Network		In the Studio (Southern Boys)	RS	U.S.		$15.00
		Live From Electric Ladyland	RS	U.S.	1991	$30.00
Airdate: 8/12/91.						
A&M	CD-4888	Special Forces	LP/LB	U.S.†	1984	$14.00/$8.00
A&M	CD5115	Strength in Numbers	LP/LB	U.S.†	1985	$14.00/$8.00
CD in Digipak.						
A&M	CD-4971	Tour De Force	LP/LB	U.S.†	1984	$14.00/$8.00
Media America		Up Close	RS	U.S.	1989	$30.00
2 CD set.						
Media America		Up Close	RS	U.S.	1991	$30.00
2 CD set.						
Pioneer	PA-85-119	Wild Eyed & Live	LD	U.S.	1985	$30.00
Pioneer	PA-85-119	Wild Eyed & Live	LD	U.S.	1990	$30.00
Digital audio.						
A&M	CD-4835	Wild Eyed Southern Boys	LP/LB	U.S.†	1984	$14.00/$8.00

Singles

Label	Catalog Number	Title	Type	Country	Year	Longbox/Value
A&M	CD 17759	Coming Down Tonight	CDJ	U.S.	1989	$2.00
A&M	S12Y-3015	Like No Other Night	CD3	Japan	1988	$12.00/$4.00
A&M	CD 17378	Like No Other Night	CDJ	U.S.	1986	$15.00
A&M	CD 17623	Rock & Roll Strategy	CDJ	U.S.	1988	$2.00
A&M	390423-3	Second Chance	CD3	Germany	1988	$9.00
A&M	S9Y-13108	Second Chance	CD3	Japan	1988	$12.00/$4.00
A&M	CD 17671	Second Chance	CDJ	U.S.	1988	$2.00
Charisma	PRCD 070	Signs of Love	CDJ	U.S.	1992	$2.00
Charisma	VJDP-10164	Sound of Your Voice, The	CD3	Japan	1991	$12.00/$4.00
Charisma	PRCD 046	Sound of Your Voice, The	CDJ	U.S.	1991	$2.00

This Mortal Coil

Full Length

Label	Catalog Number	Title	Type	Country	Year	Longbox/Value
	CDP 490	Blood	DJ/Smplr	Canada	1994	$30.00
4AD	PRO-CD-5876	CD Sampler	DJ/Smplr	U.S.	1993	$20.00

This Perfect Day

Singles

Label	Catalog Number	Title	Type	Country	Year	Longbox/Value
Snap	SNAPC 1	In the Mood	CD5	U.K.	1992	$8.00
Snap	1001	This Friendship is Ours	CD5	U.K.	1992	$8.00

This Picture

Singles

Label	Catalog Number	Title	Type	Country	Year	Longbox/Value
RCA	62177-2-RDJ	Breathe Deeply	CDJ	U.S.	1991	$2.00
Dedicated	THISP-002CD	Great Tree	CD5	U.K.	1991	$8.00
Dedicated	74321146372	Highrise	CD5	U.K.	1993	$8.00
Dedicated	THISP-001CD	Naked Rain	CD5	U.K.	1991	$8.00
RCA	62052-2-RDJ	Naked Rain	CDJ	U.S.	1991	$2.00
RCA	621261-2-RDJ	Step Up	CDJ	U.S.	1991	$6.00
Dedicated	ZD-44306	Stronger Than Life	CD5	U.K.	1991	$8.00
Motown	ZD-43984	With You I Can	CD5	U.K.	1990	$8.00

This World Owes Me a Buzz

Full Length

Label	Catalog Number	Title	Type	Country	Year	Longbox/Value
Frontier	34634	Promo for 10/22/91	DJ/LP	U.S.	1991	$14.00
Also with tracks by Spot 109.						

Thomas

Singles

Label	Catalog Number	Title	Type	Country	Year	Longbox/Value
Zyx	7486	Can You Feel The Love	CD5	U.S.	1994	$5.00

Thomas, BJ

Singles

Label	Catalog Number	Title	Type	Country	Year	Longbox/Value
Reprise	PRO-CD-3668	Don't Leave Love	CDJ	U.S.	1989	$2.00
Reprise	PRO-CD-3883	Midnight Minute	CDJ	U.S.	1989	$2.00

Thomas, Chris

Singles

Label	Catalog Number	Title	Type	Country	Year	Longbox/Value
Sire	PRO-CD-4029	Wanna Die with a Smile On My Face	CDJ	U.S.	1990	$2.00

Thomas, Earl

Singles

Label	Catalog Number	Title	Type	Country	Year	Longbox/Value
Bizarre Strght	90112	I Won't Be Around	CDJ	U.S.	1991	$2.00

Thomas, Kenny

Full Length

Label	Catalog Number	Title	Type	Country	Year	Longbox/Value
Chrysalis		Voices	LTD/LP	U.K.	1994	$25.00/$15.00
25th Anniversary edition in 6"x11" longbox.						

Thomas, Lillo

Singles

Label	Catalog Number	Title	Type	Country	Year	Longbox/Value
THG	865	Out There Doing Wrong	CDJ	U.S.	1993	$2.00

Thomas, Mickey

Singles

Label	Catalog Number	Title	Type	Country	Year	Longbox/Value
Columbia	CSK 1452	Sing	CDJ	U.S.	1989	$2.00

Thomas, Rufus

Full Length

Label	Catalog Number	Title	Type	Country	Year	Longbox/Value
		House of Blues	RS	U.S.	1996	$40.00
2 CD set. Airdate: 1/7/96.						

Thompson, Hank and His Brazos Valley Boys

Full Length

Label	Catalog Number	Title	Type	Country	Year	Longbox/Value
Bear Family		1946-1964	LTD/LP	Germany	1996	$150.00
12 CD set.						

Thompson, Jeff

Singles

Label	Catalog Number	Title	Type	Country	Year	Longbox/Value
Arista	ASCD-2201	Greatest Man I Never Knew, The	CDJ	U.S.	1991	$2.00

Thompson, Michael Band

Singles

Label	Catalog Number	Title	Type	Country	Year	Longbox/Value
Geffen	PRO-CD-3473	Can't Miss	CDJ	U.S.	1989	$2.00
Geffen	PRO-CD-3601	Give Love a Chance	CDJ	U.S.	1989	$2.00

Thompson, Richard

Full Length

Label	Catalog Number	Title	Type	Country	Year	Longbox/Value
Polygram	825421-2	Across a Crowded Room	LP/BP	U.S.†	1985	$14.00/$8.00
Capitol	DPRO-79346	Easy There Steady Now	DJ/Smplr	U.S.	1994	$10.00
Rykodisc		Live at Crawley	DJ/Smplr	U.K.	1994	$30.00
Available through mail order only. Limited to 2000 copies.						
Pioneer Artists	PA-86-151	Richard Thompson	LD	U.S.	1986	$30.00
	CDAS107	Selections From You? Me? Us?	DJ/Smplr	U.K.		$18.00
Capitol	DPRO-11214	Selections From You? Me? Us?	DJ/Smplr	U.S.		$14.00
Rykodisc	VRCD-5303	Watching the Dark	DJ/Smplr	U.S.	1993	$15.00

Singles

Label	Catalog Number	Title	Type	Country	Year	Longbox/Value
	CDCL-DJ-769	Dark Over My Heart	CDJ	U.K.		$12.00
		I Can't Wake Up	CDJ	U.S.	1994	$3.00
Rykodisc		I Can't Wake Up to Save My Life	CDJ	U.S.		$6.00
Capitol	C2 15728 2	I Feel So Good	CD5	U.S.	1991	$5.00
Capitol	CDCL 617	I Feel So Good	CD5	U.K.	1991	$10.00
Capitol	DPRO 79730	I Feel So Good	CDJ	U.S.	1991	$2.00
Capitol	CDCL-638	Read About Love	CD5	U.K.	1991	$10.00
Capitol	C2 15805	Read About Love	CD5	U.S.	1991	$5.00
Capitol	CDCL-550	Reckless	CD5	U.K.	1989	$10.00
Capitol	DPRO-79388	Turning of the Tide	CDJ	U.S.	1988	$2.00

Thompson, Richard and Linda Thompson

Full Length

Label	Catalog Number	Title	Type	Country	Year	Longbox/Value
Rykodisc	HNCD 81303	Shoot Out the Lights	LTD/LP	U.S.	1995	$24.00
20 bit master gold CD.						

Thompson Twins

Full Length

Label	Catalog Number	Title	Type	Country	Year	Longbox/Value
		Close to the Bone	LP/LB	U.S.		$13.00/$8.00
Arista	ARCD-8200	Into the Gap	LP/LB	U.S.†	1984	$14.00/$8.00
Pioneer	SM068-0138	Into the Gap Live	LD	U.S.†	1987	$35.00
Warner Brothers	9 26631-2-Dj	Queer	DJ/LP	U.S.	1991	$10.00
Arista	ARCD-8202	Side Kicks	LP/LB	U.S.†	1984	$14.00/$8.00
Pineer	SM058-3051	Single Vision	LD	U.S.†	1987	$35.00

Singles

Label	Catalog Number	Title	Type	Country	Year	Longbox/Value
Warner Brothers	PRO-CD-3901	Bombers in the Sky	CDJ	U.S.	1991	$2.00
Warner Brothers	9362-40190-2	Come Inside	CD5	Germany	1991	$9.00
Warner Brothers	W-0058CD	Come Inside	CD5	U.K.	1991	$9.00
Warner Brothers	PRO-CD-3941	Come Inside	CDJ	U.S.	1991	$3.00
Arista	162050	Doctor! Doctor!	CD3	Germany	1989	$9.00
Arista	162050	Doctor! Doctor!	CD3	U.K.	1989	$9.00
Arista	TWINSCD-12	Get That Love	CD5	U.K.	1988	$9.00
Arista	ASCD-9577	Get That Love	CDJ	U.S.	1988	$2.00
Warner Brothers	PRO-CD-5207	Groove on	CDJ	U.S.	1991	$2.00
Arista	885121	In the Name of Love	CD5	Germany	1988	$9.00
Arista	661808	In the Name of Love	CD5	U.K.	1988	$9.00
Arista	TWINSCD-13	Long Goodbye	CD5	U.K.	1988	$9.00
Arista	ASCD-9600	Long Goodbye	CDJ	U.S.	1987	$2.00
Warner Brothers	W-0124CD	Play With Me	CD5	U.K.	1992	$9.00
Warner Brothers	40607-2	Play With Me	CD5	U.S.	1992	$5.00
Warner Brothers	W-0080	Saint	CD5	U.K.	1992	$9.00
WEA	921335-2	Sugar Daddy	CD5	Germany	1989	$9.00
WEA	966355-2	Sugar Daddy	CD5	Germany	1989	$9.00
Pioneer	09P3-6188	Sugar Daddy	CD3	Japan	1989	$12.00/$4.00
WEA	W-2819CD	Sugar Daddy	CD3	U.K.	1989	$9.00
Warner Brothers	9 21320 2	Sugar Daddy	CD5	U.S.	1989	$5.00
Warner Brothers	PRO-CD-3677	Sugar Daddy	CDJ	U.S.	1989	$2.00
Warner Brothers	PRO-CD-3901	Sugar Daddy	CDJ	U.S.	1990	$2.00

Thorn

Singles

Label	Catalog Number	Title	Type	Country	Year	Longbox/Value
Roadracer	2354	Pacing	CD5	U.S.	1994	$5.00

Thorney, Tim

Full Length

Label	Catalog Number	Title	Type	Country	Year	Longbox/Value
		Some Other Time	DJ/LP	Canada		$6.00

Thorogood, George

Full Length

Label	Catalog Number	Title	Type	Country	Year	Longbox/Value
		Anthology, The Collection	LTD/LP	Australia	1996	$35.00
2 CD set.						
Capitol	CDP-46083	Bad to the Bone	LP/LB	U.S.†	1985	$14.00/$8.00
Westwood One		BBC Classic Tracks	RS	U.S.	1994	$20.00
Airdate: 6/27/94.						
EMI	DPRO-4715	Bone-A-Fide Badness	DJ/Smplr	U.S.	1990	$20.00
		House of Blues	RS	U.S.	1993	$45.00
2 CD set. Airdate: 11/14/93.						
Westwood One		In Concert	RS	U.S.	1994	$50.00
2 CD set. Airdate: 3/28/94						
Album Network		In the Studio (Move It on Over)	RS	U.S.		$20.00
DIR		King Biscuit Flour Hour	RS	U.S.	1988	$35.00
Airdate: 4/17/88.						
DIR		King Biscuit Flour Hour	RS	U.S.	1989	$35.00
Airdate: 3/12/89.						
DIR		King Biscuit Flour Hour	RS	U.S.	1990	$35.00
Airdate: 9/3/90.						
DIR		King Biscuit Flour Hour	RS	U.S.	1991	$35.00
With Blues Traveler, Airdate: 4/7/91.						
DIR		King Biscuit Flour Hour	RS	U.S.	1992	$35.00
Airdate: 9/20/92.						
DIR		King Biscuit Flour Hour	RS	U.S.	1993	$35.00
Airdate: 6/21/93.						
DIR		King Biscuit Flour Hour	RS	U.S.	1994	$35.00
Airdate: 5/9/94.						
		Live From Electric Ladyland	RS	U.S.	1993	$35.00
Airdate: 7-93.						
Capitol	CDP-46084	Maverick	LP/LB	U.S.†	1985	$14.00/$8.00
Westwood One		Off the Record	RS	U.S.	1993	$30.00
Airdate: 8/30/93.						
Westwood One		Off the Record	RS	U.S.	1994	$20.00
Airdate: 5/2/94.						
Westwood One		Off the Record	RS	U.S.	1994	$30.00
Airdate: 1/30/94.						
Westwood One		Superstar Concert	RS	U.S.	1992	$40.00
2 CD set. With Little Feat, Airdate: 11/22/92						
Westwood One		Superstars	RS	U.S.	1995	$40.00
2 CD set. Airdate: 8/14/95.						
Media America		Up Close	RS	U.S.	1992	$40.00
2 CD set.						

Singles

Label	Catalog Number	Title	Type	Country	Year	Longbox/Value
EMI	DPRO-04880	Bad to the Bone	CDJ	U.S.	1992	$3.00
Capitol	DPRO 4780	Boogie People	CDJ	U.S.	1991	$3.00
EMI	DPRO-04533	Get A Haircut	CDJ	U.S.	1993	$3.00
EMI	DPRO-08710	Gone Dead Train	CDJ	U.S.	1993	$3.00
EMI	DPRO 04754	Hello Little Girl	CDJ	U.S.	1991	$3.00
EMI	DPRO-04584	Howlin' For My Baby	CDJ	U.S.	1990	$3.00
EMI	DPRO 4697	If You Don't Start Drinking...	CDJ	U.S.	1991	$3.00
EMI	DPRO-19842	Killer Bluze	CDJ	U.S.	1991	$3.00
Capitol	DPRO-19989	Let's Work Together	CDJ	U.S.		$3.00
EMI	DPRO 04650	Louie to Frisco	CDJ	U.S.	1990	$3.00
EMI	DPRO 4736	Oklahoma Sweetheart	CDJ	U.S.	1990	$3.00
EMI	DPRO 04030	Treat Her Right	CDJ	U.S.	1988	$3.00
EMI	DPRO 79235	You Talk Too Much	CDJ	U.S.		$3.00

Thousand Yard Stare

Singles

Label	Catalog Number	Title	Type	Country	Year	Longbox Value/Value
Polydor	CDP 850	0-0 A.E.T.	CDJ	U.S.	1993	$6.00
Polydor	CDP 799	Buttermouth	CDJ	U.S.	1992	$6.00
Polydor	CDP 799	Comeuppance	CDJ	U.S.	1992	$6.00
Aardvark	AARDC 010	Spindrift	CD5	U.K.	1992	$8.00
		Version of Me	CD5	U.K.		$10.00
		Version of Me	CD5	U.K.		$10.00

Second version.

Thrashing Doves

Singles

Label	Catalog Number	Title	Type	Country	Year	Longbox Value/Value
A&M	CDEE-497	Angel Visit	CD3	U.K.	1989	$8.00
A&M	CD 17704	Angel Visit	CDJ	U.K.	1989	$2.00
A&M	CDEE-523	Another Deadly Sunset	CD3	U.K.	1989	$8.00
A&M	CDEE-511	Lorelei	CD3	U.K.	1989	$8.00
A&M	CDEE-479	Reprobate's Hymn	CD3	U.K.	1989	$8.00
Axiom	6763	Try Some Ammonia	CDJ	U.S.	1993	$2.00

Three Amazing Colossal Men

Singles

Label	Catalog Number	Title	Type	Country	Year	Longbox Value/Value
Siren	SRNCD 126	Superlovexperience	CD5	U.K.	1990	$8.00

Three Day Wheely

Singles

Label	Catalog Number	Title	Type	Country	Year	Longbox Value/Value
	DPRO 70876	Mud	CDJ	U.S.		$2.00

Three Dog Night

Full Length

Label	Catalog Number	Title	Type	Country	Year	Longbox Value/Value
MCA		Harmony	LP/LB	U.S.		$14.00/$8.00
MCA	MCAD31047	It Ain't Easy	LP/LB	U.S.		$14.00/$8.00
MCA		One	LP/LB	U.S.		$14.00/$8.00
MCA	MCAD-31045	Suitable for Framing	LP/LB	U.S.		$14.00/$8.00
MCA	MCAD-31045	Three Dog Night	LP/LB	U.S.		$14.00/$8.00

Singles

Label	Catalog Number	Title	Type	Country	Year	Longbox Value/Value
Pioneer	PIFP-1029	One	CDV	Japan		$45.00

Three Hypnotics

Singles

Label	Catalog Number	Title	Type	Country	Year	Longbox Value/Value
Situation	SIT 67	Half Man Half Boy	CD5	U.K.	1990	$9.00
American	6863	Heavy Liquid	CDJ	U.S.	1994	$2.00
Situation	SIT 82	Shakedown	CD5	U.K.	1994	$9.00
Beggars Banquet	61079	Soul, Glitter & Sin	CD5	U.S.	1991	$5.00

Three Merry Windows

Singles

Label	Catalog Number	Title	Type	Country	Year	Longbox Value/Value
		Black Halo	CDJ	U.S.		$2.00

Three Pound Thrill

Singles

Label	Catalog Number	Title	Type	Country	Year	Longbox Value/Value
Epic	ESK 7601	Diana	CDJ	U.S.		$2.00

Three Shades Of Brown

Singles

Label	Catalog Number	Title	Type	Country	Year	Longbox Value/Value
Interscope	PRCD 4463-2	Nasty Bass	CDJ	U.S.	1992	$2.00

Three Sixties

Singles

Label	Catalog Number	Title	Type	Country	Year	Longbox Value/Value
		Step Outside	CDJ	U.S.		$2.00
		Texas	CDJ	U.S.		$7.00

Three Times Dope

Singles

Label	Catalog Number	Title	Type	Country	Year	Longbox Value/Value
City Beat	CBE-758CD	Mr. Sandman	CD5	U.K.	1990	$8.00
		Words	CDJ	U.S.		$2.00

Thrill Kill Kult

Singles

Label	Catalog Number	Title	Type	Country	Year	Longbox Value/Value
Interscope	PRCD 5267-2	Blue Buddha	CDJ	U.S.	1993	$2.00
Interscope	PRCD 4621-2	Sex on Wheelz	CDJ	U.S.	1993	$2.00

Throbs

Singles

Label	Catalog Number	Title	Type	Country	Year	Longbox Value/Value
DGC	DGCTD-1	Come Down Sister	CD5	U.K.	1991	$8.00
DGC	PRO-CD-4196	Come Down Sister	CD5	U.S.	1991	$2.00
DGC	PRO-CD-4228	Sweet Addiction	CDJ	U.S.	1991	$2.00

Throwing Muses

Full Length

Label	Catalog Number	Title	Type	Country	Year	Longbox Value/Value
Sire	9 26489-2-Dj	Real Ramona, The	DJ/LP	U.S.	1991	$15.00
Sire	PRO-CD-5650	Red Heaven	DJ/Smplr	U.S.	1992	$13.00
		University	LTD/LP	Australia	1996	$35.00

Limited edition CD housed in a slip case with postcards.

Label	Catalog Number	Title	Type	Country	Year	Longbox Value/Value
4AD	CADD 5002 CD	University	LTD/LP	U.K.		$25.00

CD in red slipcase with postcards.

Label	Catalog Number	Title	Type	Country	Year	Longbox Value/Value
Sire	PRO-CD-5832	Various Tracks	DJ/Smplr	U.S.	1992	$8.00

Singles

Label	Catalog Number	Title	Type	Country	Year	Longbox Value/Value
Sire		Big Yellow Ugly Gun	CDJ	U.S.		$6.00
4AD	BAD-1101CD	Country Backwards	CD5	U.K.	1990	$8.00
Sire	9 21833-2	Country Backwards	CD5	U.S.	1991	$5.00
4AD	BAD-903CD	Dizzy	CD5	U.K.	1989	$9.00
Sire	PRO-CD-3618	Dizzy	CDJ	U.S.	1989	$2.00
Sire	PRO-CD-5653	Firepile	CDJ	U.S.	1992	$3.00
4AD	520 3121 3	Not Too Soon	CD5	Germany	1991	$9.00
4AD	BAD-1015CD	Not Too Soon	CD5	U.K.	1991	$9.00
Sire	9 40135-2	Not Too Soon	CD5	U.S.	1991	$5.00
Sire		Snakeface	CDJ	U.S.		$6.00

Thug Life

Singles

Label	Catalog Number	Title	Type	Country	Year	Longbox Value/Value
		How Long Will They Mourn	CDJ	U.S.		$2.00
		It Don't Stop	CDJ	U.S.		$2.00

Thum, Pam

Full Length

Label	Catalog Number	Title	Type	Country	Year	Longbox Value/Value
Benson		Pam Thum	DJ/LP	U.S.	1993	$15.00

CD in press kit package.

Thunder

Full Length

Label	Catalog Number	Title	Type	Country	Year	Longbox Value/Value
EMI	THUNDER-1	CD Sampler	DJ/Smplr	U.K.		$15.00

Singles

Label	Catalog Number	Title	Type	Country	Year	Longbox Value/Value
EMI	CDEM-137	Backstreet Symphony	CD5	U.K.	1990	$8.00
EMI	TOCP-7654	Better Man	CD3	Japan	1993	$13.00/$4.00
EMI	203868-2	Dirty Love	CD5	Germany	1990	$8.00
EMI	TOCP-6802	Dirty Love	CD5	Japan	1991	$13.00
EMI	CDEM-126	Dirty Love	CD5	U.K.	1990	$8.00
Geffen	PRO-CD-4454	Does It Feel Like Love	CDJ	U.S.	1992	$2.00
EMI	TOCP-7502	Everybody Wants Her	CD5	Japan	1992	$13.00
EMI	203953-2	Gimme Some Lovin'	CD5	Germany	1990	$8.00
EMI	CDEM-148	Gimme Some Lovin'	CD5	U.K.	1990	$8.00
EMI	CDEM-175	Love Walked In	CD5	U.K.	1991	$8.00
Geffen		Love Walked In	CDJ	U.S.	1991	$2.00
EMI	TOCP-7349	Low Life in High Places	CD5	Japan	1992	$13.00
EMI	CDEM-111	She's So Fine	CD5	U.K.	1989	$8.00
EMI	CDEM-158	She's So Fine	CD5	U.K.	1990	$8.00
Geffen		She's So Fine	CDJ	U.S.	1989	$2.00
Geffen	PRO-CD-4292	Until My Dying Day	CDJ	U.S.	1991	$2.00

Thunder, Shelly

Singles

Label	Catalog Number	Title	Type	Country	Year	Longbox Value/Value
Mango	7830	Break Up	CDJ	U.S.	1989	$2.00

Thunderbuck Ram

Full Length

Label	Catalog Number	Title	Type	Country	Year	Longbox Value/Value
		Long Time No See	LP	U.K.	1994	$23.00

Tiffany

Full Length

Label	Catalog Number	Title	Type	Country	Year	Longbox Value/Value
	5CS-11	New Inside And More	DJ/Smplr	Japan		$30.00
MCA	43XD-2008	Tiffany	LTD/LP	Japan	1988	$35.00

Gold disc.

Singles

Label	Catalog Number	Title	Type	Country	Year	Longbox Value/Value
Eastwest	257689-2	All This Time	CD5	Germany	1989	$9.00
Pioneer	10P3-6070	All This Time	CD3	Japan	1989	$13.00/$4.00
MCA	TIFF-6	All This Time	CD3	U.K.	1989	$9.00
MCA		All This Time	CDJ	U.S.	1988	$2.00
Eastwest	258004-2	Could've Been	CD3	Germany	1989	$9.00
Pioneer	10SW-20	Could've Been	CD3	Japan	1988	$13.00/$4.00
MCA	DTIFF-2	Could've Been	CD5	U.K.	1988	$9.00
MCA		Could've Been	CDJ	U.S.	1988	$2.00
Pioneer	10SW-56	Feelings of Forever	CD3	Japan	1988	$13.00/$4.00
MCA	DTIFF-4	Feelings of Forever	CD3	U.K.	1988	$9.00
MCA		Feelings of Forever	CDJ	U.S.	1988	$2.00
MCA	CD45 1191	Here in My Heart	CDJ	U.S.	1990	$2.00
Pioneer	09P3-6162	Hold an Old Friends' Hand	CD3	Japan	1989	$13.00/$4.00
MCA	DTIFF-7	Hold an Old Friends' Hand	CD5	U.K.	1989	$9.00
MCA	CD45 17786	Hold an Old Friends' Hand	CDJ	U.S.	1988	$2.00
MCA	CD45 18402	I Always Thought I'd See You Again	CDJ	U.S.	1990	$2.00
Eastwest	258024-2	I Saw Him Standing There	CD3	Germany	1988	$9.00
Pioneer	10SW-19	I Saw Him Standing There	CD3	Japan	1988	$13.00/$4.00
MCA	DTIFF-3	I Saw Him Standing There	CD3	U.K.	1988	$9.00
Pioneer	10SW-14	I Think We're Alone Now	CD3	Japan	1988	$13.00/$4.00
MCA	DMCA-1211	I Think We're Alone Now	CD5	U.K.	1988	$9.00
	MVDM-45	If Love Is Blind	CD3	Japan		$13.00/$4.00
		If Love Is Blind	CDJ	Japan	1994	$15.00
MCA	CD45 17977	It's Not the Lover	CDJ	U.S.	1988	$2.00
Eastwest	9031-72811-2	New Inside	CD5	Germany	1990	$9.00
Pioneer	WMD5-4038	New Inside	CD3	Japan	1990	$13.00/$4.00
MCA	CD45 1106	New Inside	CDJ	U.S.	1990	$2.00
MCA	CD45 1136	New Inside	CDJ	U.S.	1990	$2.00
Pioneer	10P3-6122	Oh Jackie	CD3	Japan	1989	$13.00/$4.00
Eastwest	820967	Radio Romance	CD3	Germany	1988	$9.00
Pioneer	10P3-6035	Radio Romance	CD3	Japan	1988	$13.00/$4.00
MCA	DTIFF-5	Radio Romance	CD3	U.K.	1988	$9.00
MCA	CD45 17794	Radio Romance	CDJ	U.S.	1988	$2.00

Tiger

Singles

Label	Catalog Number	Title	Type	Country	Year	Longbox Value/Value
Chaos	5301	Nobody Move	CDJ	U.S.	1993	$2.00
Chaos	42KL 74944	Who Planned It	CD5	U.S.	1993	$5.00

Tikaram, Tanita

Singles

Label	Catalog Number	Title	Type	Country	Year	Longbox Value/Value
WEA	247221-3	Cathedral Song	CD3	Germany	1989	$9.00
WEA	YZ-331CD	Cathedral Song	CD3	U.K.	1989	$9.00
Reprise	PRO-CD-3418	Cathedral Song	CDJ	U.S.	1988	$2.00
WEA	247820-2	Good Tradition	CD3	Germany	1988	$9.00
Pioneer	10P3-6099	Good Tradition	CD3	Japan	1989	$13.00/$4.00
WEA	YZ-196CD	Good Tradition	CD3	U.K.	1988	$9.00
Reprise	PRO-CD-3416	Good Tradition	CDJ	U.S.	1988	$2.00
WEA	9031-73919-2	I Love the Heaven's Solo	CD5	Germany	1991	$9.00
WEA	YZ-569CD	I Love the Heaven's Solo	CD5	U.K.	1991	$9.00
WEA	9031-71161	Little Sister Leaving Town	CD5	Germany	1990	$9.00
Pioneer	WMD5-4018	Little Sister Leaving Town	CD3	Japan	1990	$13.00/$4.00
WEA	YZ-459CD	Little Sister Leaving Town	CD5	U.K.	1990	$9.00
WEA	9031-73403-2	Only the Ones We Love	CD5	Germany	1991	$9.00
Eastwest	WMD5-4058	Only the Ones We Love	CD3	Japan	1991	$13.00/$4.00
WEA	YZ-558CD	Only the Ones We Love	CD5	U.K.	1991	$9.00
Reprise	PRO-CD-4686	Only the Ones We Love	CDJ	U.S.	1991	$2.00
WEA	9031-71533-2	Thursday's Child	CD5	Germany	1990	$9.00
WEA	YZ-481CD	Thursday's Child	CD5	U.K.	1990	$9.00
WEA	247560-2	Twist in My Sobriety	CD3	Germany	1988	$9.00
Eastwest	09P3-6144	Twist in My Sobriety	CD3	Japan	1989	$13.00/$4.00
WEA	YZ-321CD	Twist in My Sobriety	CD3	U.K.	1988	$9.00
Reprise	PRO-CD-3417	Twist in My Sobriety	CDJ	U.S.	1988	$2.00
WEA	SAM 543	Valentine Heart	CDJ	U.K.	1988	$15.00
WEA	246489-2	We Almost Got It Together	CD5	Germany	1990	$9.00
Pioneer	WMD5-4014	We Almost Got It Together	CD3	Japan	1990	$13.00/$4.00
WEA	YZ-443CD	We Almost Got It Together	CD5	U.K.	1990	$9.00
Reprise	PRO-CD-3888	We Almost Got It Together	CDJ	U.S.	1990	$2.00
WEA	247058-2	World Outside Your Window	CD3	Germany	1989	$9.00
WEA	YZ-363CD	World Outside Your Window	CD3	U.K.	1989	$9.00
Eastwest	9031-76503-2	You Make the Whole World Cry	CD5	Germany	1992	$9.00

Til Tuesday

Full Length

Label	Catalog Number	Title	Type	Country	Year	Longbox Value/Value
Epic	EK-39458	Voices Carry	LP/LB	U.S.†	1985	$14.00/$8.00

Singles

Label	Catalog Number	Title	Type	Country	Year	Longbox Value/Value
Epic	108P-3033	(Believed You Were) Lucky	CD3	Japan	1988	$13.00/$4.00
Epic	653064-2	(Believed You Were) Lucky	CD5	U.K.	1988	$9.00
Epic	ESK 1298	(Believed You Were) Lucky	CDJ	U.S.	1988	$2.00
Epic	654592-3	R.I.P. in Heaven	CD3	Germany	1989	$9.00
Epic	ESK 1501	R.I.P. in Heaven	CDJ	U.S.	1988	$2.00

Tillis, Mel

Singles

Label	Catalog Number	Title	Type	Country	Year	Longbox Value/Value
Radio	001	City Lights	CDJ	U.S.		$3.00
	1504	Ultimate	CD5	U.S.	1994	$5.00

Tillis, Pam

Full Length

Label	Catalog Number	Title	Type	Country	Year	Longbox Value/Value
		'90s Country	RS	U.S.	1995	$40.00

Airdate: 6/17/95.

Label	Catalog Number	Title	Type	Country	Year	Longbox/Value
		'90s Country	RS	U.S.	1996	$40.00
Airdate: 1/14/96.						
Arista	ASCD-2130	CD Sampler	DJ/Smplr	U.S.	1990	$15.00
		Singles				
Arista	ASCD-2208	Blue Rose Is	CDJ	U.S.	1992	$2.00
Arista	ASCD-2606	Do You Know Where Your Man Is	CDJ	U.S.	1993	$2.00
Arista	ASCD-2203	One of These Things	CDJ	U.S.	1991	$2.00

Timbuk Three

Singles

Label	Catalog Number	Title	Type	Country	Year	Longbox/Value
Sony	12EP-8005	Easy	CD3	Japan	1988	$13.00/$4.00
CBS	651447-2	Easy	CD5	U.K.	1988	$9.00
IRS	CD45 17549	Easy	CDJ	U.S.	1988	$2.00
Sony	VDPS-1045	National Holiday	CD3	Japan	1989	$13.00/$4.00
IRS	014	National Holiday	CDJ	U.S.	1989	$2.00
EMI	241046-2	Standard White Jesus	CD5	Germany	1990	$10.00
IRS	67070	Sunshine	CDJ	U.S.	1991	$2.00

Time

Full Length

Label	Catalog Number	Title	Type	Country	Year	Longbox/Value
Warner Brothers	25109-2	Ice Cream Castles	LP/LB	U.S.†	1985	$14.00/$8.00
Paisley Park	27490-2-DJ	Pandemonium	DJ/LP	U.S.	1989	$25.00
Clothbound digipak with digital clock on face.						
Paisley Park	PRO-CD-4378	Words and Music - Reunion Show	DJ/Intvw	U.S.	1990	$5.00
		Singles				
Paisley Park	9 21588-2	Chocolate	CD5	U.S.	1990	$5.00
Paisley Park	PRO-CD-4500	Chocolate	CDJ	U.S.	1990	$2.00
Reprise	921722-2	Jerk Out	CD5	Germany	1990	$9.00
Reprise	W-9750CD	Jerk Out	CD5	U.K.	1990	$9.00
Paisley Park	9 321701-2	Jerk Out	CD5	U.S.	1990	$5.00
Paisley Park	PRO-CD-4347	Jerk Out	CDJ	U.S.	1990	$2.00
Warner Brothers	PRO-CD-4587	Shake!	CDJ	U.S.	1990	$2.00
Warner Brothers	PRO-CD-4544	Shake!	CDJ	U.S.	1990	$2.00

Time Frequency

Singles

Label	Catalog Number	Title	Type	Country	Year	Longbox/Value
		Power Zone	CD5	U.K.		$10.00
		Power Zone	CD5	U.K.		$10.00
Second version.						
		Real Love	CD5	U.K.		$10.00
		Real Love	CD5	U.K.		$10.00
Second version.						
		Such a Phantasy	CD5	U.K.		$10.00
		Such a Phantasy	CD5	U.K.		$10.00
Second version.						

Time Gallery

Singles

Label	Catalog Number	Title	Type	Country	Year	Longbox/Value
Atlantic	PR 2652-2	Taking the Best	CDJ	U.S.	1989	$2.00
Atlantid		Valerie	CDJ	U.S.		$2.00

Time Lords

Singles

Label	Catalog Number	Title	Type	Country	Year	Longbox/Value
TVT	4024	Doctorin' the Tardis	CD3	U.S.	1988	$6.00/$4.00

Times Three

Singles

Label	Catalog Number	Title	Type	Country	Year	Longbox/Value
Solar	4578	Typical Relationship	CDJ	U.S.	1992	$2.00

Times Two

Singles

Label	Catalog Number	Title	Type	Country	Year	Longbox/Value
Pioneer	10P3-6006	Cecilia	CD3	Japan	1988	$13.00/$4.00
Reprise	PRO-CD-3131	Cecilia	CDJ	U.S.	1988	$2.00
EMI	204088-2	Set Me Free	CD5	Germany	1990	$8.00
Pioneer	10SW-3	Strange But True	CD3	Japan	1988	$13.00/$4.00
Reprise	PRO-CD-2940	Strange But True	CDJ	U.S.	1988	$2.00

Timmy T

Singles

Label	Catalog Number	Title	Type	Country	Year	Longbox/Value
Quality	19117	Cry a Million Tears	CDJ	U.S.	1992	$2.00

Tin Machine

Full Length

Label	Catalog Number	Title	Type	Country	Year	Longbox/Value
EMI		Tin Machine	DJ/LP	U.S.		$40.00
CD, cassette, and press kit in custom box.						
EMI		Tin Machine	LP/LB	U.S.	1989	$12.00/$7.00
Victory		Tin Machine II	LP	U.S.	1991	$8.00
Victory	314 511 575-2	Tin Machine II	LTD/LP	U.S.	1991	$16.00
		Singles				
Victory	VICP-15012	Baby Universal	CD5	Japan	1991	$14.00
Victory	CDP 588	Baby Universal	CDJ	U.S.	1991	$7.00
EMI	4375	Heaven's in Here	CDJ	U.S.	1989	$6.00
EMI	CDMT-63	Live '89	CD5	U.K.	1989	$10.00
EMI	TOCP-5998	Maggie's Farm	CD5	Japan	1989	$14.00
EMI	CDMT-73	Maggie's Farm	CD5	U.K.	1989	$10.00
Polygram	869574-2	One Shot	CD5	Germany	1992	$10.00
Victory	VIDP-33	One Shot	CD3	Japan	1991	$12.00/$4.00
Victory	CDP-522	One Shot	CDJ	U.S.	1991	$6.00
EMI	203547-3	Prisoner of Love	CD3	Germany	1989	$10.00
EMI	203547-2	Prisoner of Love	CD5	Germany	1989	$10.00
EMI	CDMT-76	Prisoner of Love	CD5	U.K.	1990	$10.00
EMI	DPRO 04424	Prisoner of Love	CDJ	U.S.	1990	$8.00
Victory	VICP-15014	Radio Sessions	CD5	Japan	1992	$14.00
EMI	203415-2	Under the God	CD5	Germany	1989	$10.00
EMI-USA	CDMT 68	Under the God	CD5	U.K.	1989	$10.00
EMI	DPRO 4283	Under the God	CDJ	U.S.	1989	$7.00
London	LONCD 305	You Belong in Rock & Roll	CD5	U.K.	1991	$10.00

Tin Man

Singles

Label	Catalog Number	Title	Type	Country	Year	Longbox/Value
Full Frequency	120044	18 Strings	CD5	U.S.	1994	$5.00
ffrr	4228578062	18 Strings	CD5	Canada	1994	$8.00

Tina and The B-Side Movement

Singles

Label	Catalog Number	Title	Type	Country	Year	Longbox/Value
		Run To Stay	CDJ	U.S.		$2.00

Tindersticks

Full Length

Label	Catalog Number	Title	Type	Country	Year	Longbox/Value
		Tindersticks	LTD/LP	U.K.	1995	$35.00
2CD set.						
		Singles				
Bar None		This Way Up	CD5	U.K.	1993	$8.00
		Traveling Light	CD5	U.K.	1995	$10.00

Tippin, Aaron

Singles

Label	Catalog Number	Title	Type	Country	Year	Longbox/Value
RCA	62520-2-RDJ	Working Man's Phd	CDJ	U.S.	1993	$2.00

Tisdale, Wayman

Singles

Label	Catalog Number	Title	Type	Country	Year	Longbox/Value
Motown	860354	Circumstance	CD5	U.S.	1995	$6.00

Titiyo

Singles

Label	Catalog Number	Title	Type	Country	Year	Longbox/Value
Arista	662722	After the Rain	CD5	Germany	1990	$9.00
Arista	662722	After the Rain	CD5	U.K.	1990	$9.00
Arista	663212	Flowers	CD5	U.K.	1990	$9.00
Arista	662733	My Body Says Yes	CD5	Germany	1991	$9.00
Arista	662733	My Body Says Yes	CD5	U.K.	1991	$9.00
Arista	ASCD-2224	My Body Says Yes	CDJ	U.S.	1991	$2.00

Tjader, Cal

Full Length

Label	Catalog Number	Title	Type	Country	Year	Longbox/Value
Concord Picante	CCD-4113	La Onda Va Bien	LP/LB	U.S.†	1985	$14.00/$8.00
Verve	815058-2	Sona Libre	LP/LB	U.S.†	1985	$14.00/$8.00

Tjader, Cal & Carmen McRae

Full Length

Label	Catalog Number	Title	Type	Country	Year	Longbox/Value
Concord Jazz	CCD-4189	Heat Wave	LP/LB	U.S.†	1985	$14.00/$8.00

Tjader, Cal & Charlie Bird

Full Length

Label	Catalog Number	Title	Type	Country	Year	Longbox/Value
Fantasy	FCD-9453	Tambu	LP/LB	U.S.†	1985	$14.00/$8.00

TKA

Singles

Label	Catalog Number	Title	Type	Country	Year	Longbox/Value
Intercord	825 7998	Crash	CD5	Germany	1990	$8.00
Warner Brothers	PRO-CD-4511	Crash	CDJ	U.S.	1990	$2.00
Tommy Boy	963	Crash	CDJ	U.S.	1990	$7.00
Sony	12EP-8027	Don't Be Afraid	CD3	Japan	1989	$13.00/$4.00
Sony	CSDS-8152	I Won't Give Up on You	CD3	Japan	1990	$13.00/$4.00
Warner Brothers	PRO-CD-4369	I Won't Give Up on You	CDJ	U.S.	1990	$2.00
Tommy Boy	954	I Won't Give Up on You	CDJ	U.S.	1990	$7.00

TLC

Singles

Label	Catalog Number	Title	Type	Country	Year	Longbox/Value
Arista	665265	Ain't 2 Proud 2 Beg	CD5	U.K.	1992	$8.00
LaFace	LFPCD-4008	Ain't 2 Proud 2 Beg	CDJ	U.S.	1992	$2.00
LaFace	LFPCD-4009	Ain't 2 Proud 2 Beg	CDJ	U.S.	1992	$2.00
Arista	BVDA-43	Baby-Baby-Baby	CD3	Japan	1992	$13.00/$4.00
LaFace	74321-111292	Baby-Baby-Baby	CD5	U.K.	1992	$8.00
	LFCD-4028	Baby-Baby-Baby	CDJ	U.S.	1992	$2.00
Arista	24088	Creep	CD5	U.S.	1994	$5.00
Epic	ESK 77059	Get It Up	CDJ	U.S.	1992	$2.00
LaFace	BVDA-57	Hat 2 Da Back	CD3	Japan	1993	$13.00/$4.00
LaFace	24046	Hat 2 Da Back	CD5	U.S.	1993	$5.00
LaFace	LFCD-4043	Hat 2 Da Back	CDJ	U.S.	1993	$2.00
Leface	LPCD 4119	On You	CDJ	U.S.		$2.00
Arista	24099	Red Light Special	CD5	U.S.	1994	$5.00
LaFace	LFPCD-4097	Red Light Special	CDJ	U.S.	1995	$2.00
LaFace	LFPCD-4107	Waterfalls	CDJ	U.S.	1995	$2.00
LaFace	LFPCD-4109	Waterfalls	CDJ	U.S.	1995	$2.00
Arista	BVDA-51	What About Your Friends	CD3	Japan	1992	$13.00/$4.00
Arista	74321-11817-2	What About Your Friends	CD5	U.K.	1992	$8.00
LaFace	24033	What About Your Friends	CD5	U.S.	1992	$5.00
LaFace	4025	What About Your Friends	CDJ	U.S.	1992	$2.00

To Be Continued

Singles

Label	Catalog Number	Title	Type	Country	Year	Longbox/Value
Eastwest	PRCD 5044-2	Free to Be	CDJ	U.S.	1993	$2.00

Toad The Wet Sprocket

Full Length

Label	Catalog Number	Title	Type	Country	Year	Longbox/Value
Columbia		Acoustic Dance Party	DJ/Smplr	U.S.	1995	$18.00
Columbia	CK-45326	Bread and Circus	LP/LB	U.S.	1988	$15.00/$10.00
Columbia	CSK 6058	Fall Down	DJ/Smplr	U.S.	1994	$15.00
Columbia	CSK 4509	Five Live	DJ/Smplr	U.S.	1992	$15.00
Westwood One		In Concert	RS	U.S.	1995	$45.00
Airdate: 9/25/95.						
Westwood One		In Concert-Nu Rock	RS	U.S.	1996	$45.00
Airdate: 2/26/96.						
Columbia		R&R #3	DJ/Smplr	U.S.	1994	$15.00
Media America		Up Close	RS	U.S.	1995	$25.00
		Singles				
Columbia	658331-2	All I Want	CD5	U.K.	1992	$10.00
Columbia	38K 74355	All I Want	CD5	U.S.	1992	$5.00
Columbia	CSK 4359	All I Want	CDJ	U.S.	1992	$3.00
Columbia	CSK 7663	Brothers	CDJ	U.S.		$3.00
Columbia	CSK 1960	Come Back Down	CDJ	U.S.	1990	$3.00
CBS		Crowing	CD5	U.K.	1995	$10.00
Columbia	6603682	Fall Down	CD5	U.K.	1994	$10.00
Columbia	6603650	Fall Down	CD5	U.K.	1994	$10.00
Sony	XDCS-93144	Fly From Heaven	CD5	Japan	1995	$50.00
Columbia	77858	Fly From Heaven	CD5	U.S.	1994	$5.00
Columbia	CSK 6500	Fly From Heaven	CDJ	U.S.	1994	$3.00
Columbia		Good Intentions	CDJ	U.S.		$3.00
Columbia	CSK 4262	Hold Her Down	CDJ	U.S.	1991	$3.00
Columbia	CSK 2059	I Will Not Take These Things For Granted	CDJ	U.S.	1993	$3.00
Columbia	CSK 4145	Is It for Me	CDJ	U.S.	1991	$3.00
Columbia	CSK 2059	Jam	CDJ	U.S.	1990	$3.00
Columbia	CSK 6127	Rock 'n Roll Party All Night	CDJ	U.S.		$3.00
CBS	77727	Something's Always Wrong	CD5	U.S.	1994	$5.00
Columbia	44K 77639	Something's Always Wrong	CD5	U.S.	1994	$6.00
Columbia	CSK 6289	Something's Always Wrong	CDJ	U.S.	1994	$3.00
Columbia	CSK 7181	Stupid	CDJ	U.S.		$3.00
Columbia	CSK 4683	Walk on the Ocean	CDJ	U.S.	1993	$3.00

Toadies

Singles

Label	Catalog Number	Title	Type	Country	Year	Longbox/Value
		Away	CDJ	U.S.		$3.00

Tobin, Karen

Singles

Label	Catalog Number	Title	Type	Country	Year	Longbox/Value
Atlantic	PRCD 4003-2	Carolina Smokey Moon	CDJ	U.S.	1991	$2.00

Today

Full Length

Label	Catalog Number	Title	Type	Country	Year	Longbox/Value
Motown	6309-MD	New Formula, The	LP/BP	U.S.		$12.00/$7.00
		Singles				
Motown	1102	I Got the Feeling	CDJ	U.S.	1990	$2.00

Label	Catalog Number	Title	Type	Country	Year	Longbox/Value / Value
Toenut						
Singles						
		Seizure	CDJ	U.S.		$2.00
Togashi, Masahiko						
Full Length						
Denon	CD-7281	Breath	LP/LB	U.S.†	1985	$14.00/$8.00
Tokens						
Singles						
RCA	62955	Lion Sleeps Tonight	CD5	U.S.	1994	$5.00
Toll						
Singles						
		Johnathan Toledo	CDJ	U.S.		$2.00
Tom, David & Geoffrey Gordon						
Full Length						
ECM	823642-2	Best Laid Plans	LP/LB	U.S.†	1985	$14.00/$8.00
Tom Tom Club						
Singles						
Sire	PRO-CD-3662	Call of the Wild	CDJ	U.S.	1989	$2.00
Sire	PRO-CD-3494	Suboceana	CDJ	U.S.	1989	$2.00
Sire	9 40444-2	Sunshine & Ecstasy	CD5	U.S.	1992	$5.00
Sire	PRO-CD-5438	Sunshine & Ecstasy	CDJ	U.S.	1992	$2.00
Sire	9 40600 2	You Sexy Thing	CD5	U.S.	1992	$5.00
Sire	PRO-CD-5672	You Sexy Thing	CDJ	U.S.	1992	$3.00
Tomlin, Lily						
Full Length						
Image	ID5258LO	Lily Tomlin Special, Vol. 1, The	LD	U.S.		$20.00
Tomlinson, Michael						
Singles						
Cypress	YD 17815	Gettin' Gone	CDJ	U.S.	1989	$2.00
Tommye						
Singles						
	1020	My Mind	CD5	U.S.	1994	$5.00
	1020	My Mind	CD5	U.S.	1994	$5.00
Tone Loc						
Singles						
4th & B'way	BRCD-237	All Through the Night	CD5	U.K.	1991	$9.00
Delicious Vinyl	422 866 105	All Through the Night	CD5	U.S.	1991	$5.00
Delicious Vinyl	6684	All Through the Night	CDJ	U.S.	1991	$2.00
Hollywood	PRCD-10176	Cool Hand Loc	CDJ	U.S.		$2.00
BMG	662193	Funky Cold Medina	CD3	Germany	1989	$9.00
BMG	162193	Funky Cold Medina	CD3	Germany	1989	$9.00
Delicious Vinyl	PO9D-31003	Funky Cold Medina	CD3	Japan	1989	$12.00/$4.00
Hollywood	PRCD5199	Hit the Coast	CDJ	U.S.		$2.00
BMG	662476	I Got It Goin'	CD5	Germany	1989	$9.00
4th & B'way	BRCD-140	I Got It Goin'	CD5	U.K.	1989	$9.00
Delicious Vinyl	106	I Got It Goin'	CDJ	U.S.	1989	$2.00
4th & B'way	BRCD-129	On Fire	CD5	U.K.	1989	$9.00
BMG	662476	Wild Thing	CD5	Germany	1989	$9.00
BMG	162476	Wild Thing	CD5	Germany	1989	$9.00
Delicious Vinyl	PO9D-31002	Wild Thing	CD3	Japan	1989	$12.00/$4.00
4th & B'way	BRCD-121	Wild Thing	CD5	U.K.	1989	$9.00
Delicious Vinyl	102	Wild Thing	CDJ	U.S.	1988	$2.00
Tones on Tail						
Full Length						
		Night Music	LP	U.S.		$18.00
Tonio K						
Singles						
A&M	S10Y-3020	Stay	CD3	Japan	1988	$12.00/$4.00
A&M	CD 17548	Stay	CDJ	U.S.	1988	$2.00
A&M		Stay	DJ/CD3	U.S.	1988	$4.00
Tonnage						
Singles						
CBS	66821	A Compilation	CD5	U.S.	1994	$5.00
Tonto Tonto						
Singles						
Victory	0001	Mirror	CDJ	U.S.	1993	$2.00
Tony D.						
Singles						
4th & B'way		E.F.F.E.C.T.	CDJ	U.S.		$2.00
Tony! Toni! Tone!						
Singles						
Wing	CDP 1003	Anniversary	CDJ	U.S.	1993	$2.00
Polydor	PODP-1007	Blues	CD3	Japan	1990	$12.00/$4.00
Polygram	PZCD-81	Blues	CD5	U.K.	1990	$8.00
Wing	WINCD-8	Blues	CD5	U.K.	1990	$8.00
Wing	870 732-2	Born To Know	CDV/BP	U.S.	1988	$14.00/$14.00
Wing	CDP 359	Coolin' at Christmas	CDJ	U.S.	1990	$2.00
IMS	879079-2	Feels Good	CD5	Germany	1990	$8.00
Wing	WINCD-9	Feels Good	CD5	U.K.	1990	$8.00
Polygram	CDP 267	Feels Good	CDJ	U.S.	1990	$6.00
Wing	CDP 267	Feels Good	CDJ	U.S.	1990	$7.00
Wing	CDP 96	For the Love of You	CDJ	U.S.	1989	$2.00
MCA	1563	House Party II	CDJ	U.S.	1991	$2.00
Wing	WINCD-10	It Never Rains	CD5	U.K.	1991	$8.00
Wing	CDP 1123	Lay Your Head On My Pillow	CDJ	U.S.	1994	$2.00
Wing	CDP 1205	Leavin'	CDJ	U.S.	1994	$2.00
Polydor	P10P-30018	Little Walter	CD3	Japan	1988	$13.00/$4.00
Wing	870 733-2	Little Walter	CDV/BP	U.S.	1988	$14.00/$14.00
Polygram	877425-2	Oakland Stroke	CD5	Germany	1990	$8.00
Wing	WINCD-7	Oakland Stroke	CD5	U.K.	1990	$8.00
Wing	CDP 396	Whatever You Want	CDJ	U.S.	1991	$2.00
Too Down						
Singles						
IRS	6713	You Got It Going On	CDJ	U.S.	1993	$2.00
Too Much Joy						
Singles						
Giant	PRO-CD-4650	Crush Story	CDJ	U.S.	1990	$2.00
Giant	PRO-CD-6021	In Perpetuity	CDJ	U.S.	1992	$2.00
Giant	PRO-CD-4914	Long Haired Guys From England	CDJ	U.S.	1991	$2.00
Giant	PRO-CD-4631	Susquehanna Hat Company	CDJ	U.S.	1991	$2.00

Label	Catalog Number	Title	Type	Country	Year	Longbox/Value / Value
Giant	PRO-CD-4352	That's a Lie	CDJ	U.S.	1990	$2.00
Too Short						
Singles						
Jive	JDJ423702	Gettin' It	CDJ	U.S.		$2.00
Jive	42068-2-RDJ	I Want to Be Free	CDJ	U.S.	1992	$2.00
Jive	42152-2-RDJ	I'm a Prayer	CDJ	U.S.	1993	$2.00
BMG	ZD-44120	In the Ghetto	CD5	U.K.	1990	$8.00
Jive	1397-2-RDJ	In the Ghetto	CDJ	U.S.	1990	$2.00
Jive	42072-2-RDJ	In the Trunk	CDJ	U.S.	1992	$2.00
Jive	JDJ-42234	Parlayin'	CDJ	U.S.	1994	$3.00
Jive	1429-2-JDj	Short But Funky	CDJ	U.S.	1991	$2.00
Tooks, Darryl						
Full Length						
		Moods	DJ/Smplr	U.S.		$4.00
Singles						
SBK	DPRO-05320	What About Me?	CDJ	U.S.	1989	$2.00
Tool						
Full Length						
Zoo/Blockbuser Music		Aenima	LTD/LP	U.S.	1996	$30.00
2 CD set. Bonus 3 track CD with purchase of CD album. Exclusive to Blockbuster Music.						
Zoo		In-Store Play Sampler	DJ/Smplr	U.S.	1993	$10.00
Singles						
Zoo	ZD-17148	Prison Sex	CDJ	U.S.	1994	$3.00
Zoo		Sober	CD5	U.K.	1994	$10.00
Zoo	72445-11027	Sweet	CD5	U.S.	1992	$5.00
Top						
Singles						
Island	PRCD 6709-2	Easy	CDJ	U.S.	1992	$2.00
Island	PRCD 6702-2	Number One Dominator	CDJ	U.S.	1991	$2.00
Top Choice Clique						
Singles						
A&M	31458 8136	I Think to Myself	CDJ	U.S.	1993	$2.00
Top Quality						
Singles						
RCA	62644-2-RDJ	Magnum Opus	CDJ	U.S.	1993	$3.00
Tora Tora						
Singles						
A&M	75021 7380-2	Amnesia	CDJ	U.S.	1992	$2.00
A&M	31458 8024	Dead Man's Hand	CDJ	U.S.	1992	$2.00
A&M	75021 7394	Faith Healer	CDJ	U.S.	1992	$2.00
A&M	CD 17905	Guilty	CDJ	U.S.	1989	$2.00
A&M	CD 17983	Phantom Rider	CDJ	U.S.	1989	$2.00
A&M	75021 7394-2	Phantom Rider	CDJ	U.S.	1993	$2.00
A&M	S9Y-13113	Walkin' Shoes	CD3	Japan	1989	$12.00/$3.00
A&M	CD 17756	Walkin' Shoes	CDJ	U.S.	1989	$2.00
A&M	75021 7380	Wild America	CDJ	U.S.	1992	$3.00
Torme, Mel						
Full Length						
		Collection	DJ/Smplr	U.S.	1995	$18.00
Verve	823 248-2	Duke Ellington & Count Basie Songbooks	LP/BP	U.S.†	1984	$12.00/$7.00
Verve	823248-2	Duke Ellington & Count Basie Songbooks	LP/LB	U.S.†	1985	$14.00/$8.00
Discovision		Mel Torme and Della Reese In Concert	LD			$30.00
Rhino		Mel Torme Collection (1942-1985) Sampler	DJ/Smplr	U.S.	1996	$18.00
Verve	821 581-2	Swing Shubert Alley	LP/BP	U.S.†	1984	$12.00/$7.00
Verve	821581-2	Swings Shubert Alley	LP/LB	U.S.†	1985	$14.00/$8.00
Torme, Mel and Della Reese						
Full Length						
MCA	74-009	Mel Torme and Della Reese In Concert	LD	U.S.	1985	$25.00/$35.00
Torme, Mel & George Shearing						
Full Length						
Concord Jazz	CCD-4248	An Evening at Charlie's	LP/LB	U.S.†	1985	$14.00/$8.00
Torne, David						
Singles						
Windham Hill	90-12	Voodoo Chile	CDJ	U.S.	1990	$2.00
Torres, Liz						
Singles						
Jive	JIVECD-249	If U Keep It Up	CD5	U.K.	1990	$8.00
		If U Keep It Up	CDJ	U.S.		$2.00
Total						
Singles						
		Kissin' You	CDJ	U.S.		$2.00
	BBPCD9050	No One Else	CDJ	U.S.		$2.00
	BBPCD9042	No One Else	CDJ	U.S.		$2.00
Total Devastation						
Singles						
Arista	12625	Many Clouds Of Smoke	CDJ	U.S.	1993	$2.00
PGA	ASCD-2710	Wonderful World Of Skins	CDJ	U.S.	1994	$10.00
Total Eclipse						
Singles						
Tabu	28965 1816	Fire in the Rain	CDJ	U.S.	1992	$2.00
Tabu	31458 8036	Time's a Changin'	CDJ	U.S.	1992	$2.00
Total Look And The Style						
Singles						
Columbia	CSK 74341	Room 252	CDJ	U.S.	1992	$2.00
Toto						
Full Length						
Sony	XDP-93054	Hits on Hits	DJ/Smplr	Japan		$150.00
CBS	CK-38962	Isolation	LP/BP	U.S.†	1985	$14.00/$8.00
Sony	XDCS-93192	Recall	DJ/Smplr	Japan	1995	$150.00
CBS		Starbox	LTD/LP	Japan	1988	$40.00
CBS	SAMP-CD-2924	Tambu Sampler	DJ/Smplr	Australia		$25.00
Sony	SRCS-7917	Toto IV	LTD/LP	Japan	1996	$35.00
20 bit mastering.						
CBS	CK-37728	Toto IV	LP/BP	U.S.†	1983	$14.00/$8.00
Columbia	CK-37728	Toto IV	LP/LB	U.S.	1993	$28.00/$25.00
Gold disc.						
CBS	CK-64423	Toto IV	LTD/LP	U.S.	1994	$25.00
Gold disc.						
CBS	CK-36913	Turn Back	LP/BP	U.S.†	1983	$14.00/$8.00

Label	Catalog Number	Title	Type	Country	Year	Longbox Value / Value

Singles

Label	Catalog Number	Title	Type	Country	Year	Longbox Value / Value
Columbia	657611-2	Africa	CD5	Germany	1990	$9.00
CBS/Sony	10EP-3022	Africa	CD3	Japan	1988	$12.00/$4.00
Columbia	656298-2	Africa	CD5	U.K.	1990	$9.00
CBS/Sony	CSDS-8162	Can You Hear What I'm Saying	CD3	Japan	1990	$12.00/$4.00
Columbia	656298-2	Can You Hear What I'm Saying	CD5	U.K.	1990	$8.00
Columbia	CSK 73488	Can You Hear What I'm Saying	CDJ	U.S.	1990	$2.00
		Don't Chain My Heart	CDJ	Canada		$6.00
Epic	SMC 359 000	Hold the Line	CDJ	France	1996	$40.00
Columbia	656066-3	Love Has the Power	CD3	Germany	1990	$8.00
Columbia	656210-3	Only You	CD3	Germany	1992	$8.00
CBS/Sony	SRDS-8237	Only You	CD3	Japan	1992	$12.00/$4.00
CBS/Sony	XDDS93045	Only You	DJ/CD3	Japan	1992	$70.00
Sony	XDCS-93194	Other End of Time	CD5	Japan		$50.00
Columbia		Out Of Love	CDJ	U.S.		$2.00
Columbia	654569-3	Pamela	CD3	Germany	1989	$8.00
Columbia	651607-2	Pamela	CD5	Germany	1989	$8.00
CBS/Sony	10EP-3009	Pamela	CD3	Japan	1988	$12.00/$4.00
Columbia	654569-3	Pamela	CD3	U.K.	1989	$8.00
Columbia	651607-2	Pamela	CD5	U.K.	1989	$8.00
Columbia		Pamela	CDJ	U.S.	1988	$2.00
CBS/Sony	10EP-3023	Rosanna	CD3	Japan	1988	$12.00/$4.00
CBS		Selections From Tabu	CDJ	U.K.	1996	$25.00
Columbia		Stay Away	CDJ	U.S.		$2.00
Columbia	651411-2	Stop Lovin' You	CD5	Germany	1988	$8.00
CBS/Sony	10EP 3036	Stop Lovin' You	CD3	Japan	1988	$12.00/$4.00
Columbia	651411-2	Stop Lovin' You	CD5	U.K.	1988	$8.00
Relativity	0212	Two Hearts	CDJ	U.S.		$2.00

Toups, Wayne & Zydecajun

Singles

Label	Catalog Number	Title	Type	Country	Year	Longbox Value / Value
Mercury	CDP 394	Fish Out Of Water	CDJ	U.S.	1991	$2.00

Toure, Ali Farka

Singles

Label	Catalog Number	Title	Type	Country	Year	Longbox Value / Value
Hannibal	1381	Ai Du	CDJ	U.S.	1994	$3.00
Hannibal	1381	Ai Du	CDJ	U.S.	1994	$3.00

Toure Kunda

Full Length

Label	Catalog Number	Title	Type	Country	Year	Longbox Value / Value
		1983/1984	LP/LB	U.S.		$15.00/$12.00

Tovey, Frank

Singles

Label	Catalog Number	Title	Type	Country	Year	Longbox Value / Value
Mute	CD 121	Liberty Tree, The	CD5	U.K.	1991	$2.00

Tower of Power

Full Length

Label	Catalog Number	Title	Type	Country	Year	Longbox Value / Value
Sheffield	CD-17	Direct	LP/BP	U.S.†	1985	$14.00/$8.00

Singles

Label	Catalog Number	Title	Type	Country	Year	Longbox Value / Value
Epic	ESK 4025	Mr. Toad's Wild Ride	CDJ	U.S.	1991	$2.00
Epic	ESK 5372	Please Come Back	CDJ	U.S.	1993	$2.00

Towner, Ralph

Singles

Label	Catalog Number	Title	Type	Country	Year	Longbox Value / Value
ECM	TOWN 2	Magic Pouch	CDJ	U.S.	1992	$3.00

Townsell, Lidell

Singles

Label	Catalog Number	Title	Type	Country	Year	Longbox Value / Value
Mercury	CDP 716	Get With You	CDJ	U.S.	1992	$2.00
Mercury	CDP 645	Nu Nu	CDJ	U.S.	1992	$2.00
Mercury	CDP 682	Nu Nu	CDJ	U.S.	1992	$2.00

Townsend, Pete

Full Length

Label	Catalog Number	Title	Type	Country	Year	Longbox Value / Value
Atlantic	32100-2	Empty Glass	LP/LB	U.S.†	1985	$14.00/$8.00
Atlantic	PRCD 5161	Interview	DJ/Intvw	U.S.	1993	$15.00
Atlantic		Iron Man, The	LP/LB	U.S.		$14.00/$8.00
DIR		King Biscuit Flour Hour	RS	U.S.	1988	$40.00
	With Roger Daltrey, Airdate: 12/18/88.					
DIR		King Biscuit Flour Hour	RS	U.S.	1989	$50.00
	Airdate: 8/14/89.					
Polygram		Live	DJ/Smplr	U.S.	1993	$5.00
Polygram	310690054-2 DEMO	Live	DJ/CD+I	U.S.	1993	$35.00
Westwood One		Off the Record	RS	U.S.	1992	$40.00
	Airdate: 4/4/94.					
Westwood One		Off the Record	RS	U.S.	1993	$30.00
	Airdate: 9/20/93.					
Westwood One		Off the Record	RS	U.S.	1995	$20.00
	Airdate: 5/29/95.					
Westwood One		Off the Record	RS	U.S.	1996	$20.00
	Airdate: 1/29/96.					
		One on One	RS	U.S.	1993	$60.00
	Airdate: 4/19/93.					
WEA		Pete Townsend Interview	DJ/Intvw	Canada	1989	$35.00
Polygram	90054-2 DEMO	Pete Townsend Live	DJ/Smplr	U.S.	1992	$50.00
	CD + 1 disc.					
Atlantic	PRCD 5103-2	Psychoderelict	DJ/LP	U.S.	1993	$35.00
	2 picture disc CDs, with and without dialogue.					
Atlantic		Psychoderelict	DJ/LP	U.S.	1993	$125.00
	2 CD boxed set with PAL video and press kit.					
Media America		Up Close	RS	U.S.	1989	$60.00
	2 CD set.					
Media America		Up Close	RS	U.S.	1990	$60.00
Media America		Up Close	RS	U.S.	1993	$65.00
	3 CD set.					
Media America		Up Close	RS	U.S.	1996	$50.00
	2 CD set.					
Rykodisc	RCD-90246	Who Came First	LTD/LP	U.S.	1992	$25.00
	CD with extra booklet in slipcase.					

Singles

Label	Catalog Number	Title	Type	Country	Year	Longbox Value / Value
Virgin	162385	A Friend is a Friend	CD3	Germany	1989	$10.00
Virgin	662385	A Friend is a Friend	CD5	Germany	1989	$10.00
Virgin	VSCD-1198	A Friend is a Friend	CD3	U.K.	1989	$10.00
Atlantic	PR 2781-2	A Friend is a Friend	CDJ	U.S.	1989	$3.00
		English Boy	CD5	U.K.		$10.00
		English Boy	CD5	U.K.		$10.00
	Second version.					
Atlantic	A7370CD1	English Boy	CD5	U.K.	1993	$10.00
Atlantic		English Boy	CD5	U.K.	1993	$10.00
	Second version.					
Atlantic	PRCD 5102-2	English Boy	CDJ	U.S.	1993	$3.00
Atlantic	PR 2974-2	Fire	CDJ	U.S.	1989	$3.00

Toy Matinee

Full Length

Label	Catalog Number	Title	Type	Country	Year	Longbox Value / Value
Reprise	9 26235-2	Toy Matinee	DJ/LP	U.S.	1990	$8.00

Picture disc.

Singles

Label	Catalog Number	Title	Type	Country	Year	Longbox Value / Value
Reprise	PRO-CD-4589	Ballad of Jenny Ledge	CDJ	U.S.	1990	$2.00
Reprise	PRO-CD-4331	Last Plane Out	CDJ	U.S.	1990	$2.00

Tractors

Singles

Label	Catalog Number	Title	Type	Country	Year	Longbox Value / Value
Arista	12771	Santa Claus Boogie	CD5	U.S.	1994	$5.00

Traffic

Full Length

Label	Catalog Number	Title	Type	Country	Year	Longbox Value / Value
Virgin	CDVDJ2727	Far From Home	DJ/Smplr	U.K.	1994	$30.00
		House of Blues	RS	U.S.	1994	$40.00
	2 CD set. Airdate: 9/4/94.					
Westwood One		In Concert	RS	U.S.	1992	$70.00
	2 CD set. Airdate: 7/6/92					
Westwood One		In Concert	RS	U.S.	1993	$30.00
	Airdate: 7/19/93.					
Westwood One		In Concert	RS	U.S.	1993	$70.00
	2 CD set. Airdate: 7/19/93.					
Album Network		In the Studio (Best of)	RS	U.S.		$20.00
Album Network		In the Studio (Mr. Fantasy)	RS	U.S.	1994	$25.00
	Airdate: 11/26/90.					
Westwood One		Off the Record	RS	U.S.	1993	$30.00
	Airdate: 7/19/93.					
Westwood One		Off the Record	RS	U.S.	1994	$30.00
	Airdate: 5/9/94.					
Westwood One		Superstars	RS	U.S.	1994	$40.00
	2 CD set. With Steve Winwood, Airdate: 6/13/94					
Island	PR 2300-2	Traffic Control	DJ/Smplr	U.S.	1988	$40.00
Island	PR 2158-2	Traffic Report	DJ/Smplr	U.S.	1987	$45.00

Singles

Label	Catalog Number	Title	Type	Country	Year	Longbox Value / Value
Virgin		Here Comes a Man	CD5	U.K.	1994	$10.00
Virgin	DPRO-14133	Here Comes a Man	CDJ	U.S.	1994	$3.00
		Nowhere Is Their Freedom	CDJ	Spain	1996	$25.00
Virgin		Nowhere Is Their Freedom	CDJ	U.S.	1994	$3.00
Virgin	DPRO-14208	Some Kinda Woman	CDJ	U.S.	1994	$3.00

Tragically Hip

Full Length

Label	Catalog Number	Title	Type	Country	Year	Longbox Value / Value
MCA	9474	Greatest Hits	DJ/Smplr	Canada		$50.00

Singles

Label	Catalog Number	Title	Type	Country	Year	Longbox Value / Value
		Ahead by a Century	CDJ	U.S.		$3.00
MCA	2616	At the Hundredth Meridian	CDJ	U.S.	1993	$2.00
MCA		Blow At High Dough	CDJ	U.S.		$2.00
MCA	30238	Courage	CD5	Germany	1993	$8.00
MCA	2499	Courage	CDJ	U.S.	1992	$7.00
MCA		Gift Shop	CDJ	U.S.		$6.00
MCA	MCSTD-1565	Little Bones	CD5	U.K.	1991	$10.00
		Locked in the Trunk of a Car	CDJ	Canada		$15.00
MCA	MCSTD-1733	Locked in the Trunk of a Car	CD5	U.K.	1993	$10.00
	PRCD-6152	Nautical Disaster	CDJ	U.S.	1995	$2.00
MCA	CD45 18105	New Orleans is Sinking	CDJ	U.S.	1989	$2.00
MCA	DMCAT-1363	Small Town Bring Down	CD5	U.K.	1989	$10.00
MCA		Small Town Bring Down	CDJ	U.S.	1989	$2.00
	PRCD-6148	So Hard Done By	CDJ	U.S.	1995	$2.00
MCA	CD45 1270	Three Pistols	CDJ	U.S.	1991	$2.00
		Twist My Hip	CDJ	Canada		$20.00

Trans-Global Underground

Singles

Label	Catalog Number	Title	Type	Country	Year	Longbox Value / Value
CBS	77682	Temple Head	CD5	U.S.	1994	$5.00

Transmission

Singles

Label	Catalog Number	Title	Type	Country	Year	Longbox Value / Value
	9403	U Got Me Burnin	CD5	U.S.	1994	$5.00

Transvision Vamp

Singles

Label	Catalog Number	Title	Type	Country	Year	Longbox Value / Value
MCA	25784-2	Baby I Don't Care	CD5	Germany	1989	$10.00
Pioneer	09P3-6170	Baby I Don't Care	CD3	Japan	1989	$12.00/$4.00
MCA	DTVVT-6	Baby I Don't Care	CD5	U.K.	1989	$10.00
MCA	CD45 17985	Baby I Don't Care	CDJ	U.S.	1989	$6.00
MCA	DTVVT-9	Born To Be Sold	CD5	U.K.	1989	$10.00
MCA	MCD-17556	(I Just Wanna) B With U	CD5	Germany	1991	$10.00
MCA	MVDM-4	(I Just Wanna) B With U	CD3	Japan	1991	$12.00/$4.00
MCA	DTVVT-10	(I Just Wanna) B With U	CD5	U.K.	1991	$10.00
MCA	54113	(I Just Wanna) B With U	CD5	U.S.	1991	$5.00
MCA	CD45 1586	(I Just Wanna) B With U	CDJ	U.S.	1991	$2.00
MCA	CD45 1673	(I Just Wanna) B With U	CDJ	U.S.	1991	$2.00
MCA	257852-2	I Want Your Love	CD5	Germany	1988	$10.00
MCA	10P3-6083	I Want Your Love	CD3	Japan	1988	$12.00/$4.00
MCA	DTVV-3	I Want Your Love	CD3	U.K.	1988	$10.00
Uni	CD45 18003	I Want Your Love	CDJ	U.S.	1989	$2.00
MCA	DTVVT 11	If Looks Could Kill	CD5	U.K.	1991	$10.00
MCA	T1	If Looks Could Kill	CDJ	U.K.	1991	$8.00
MCA	2030	If Looks Could Kill	CDJ	U.S.	1991	$2.00
Eastwest	257450-2	Landslide of Love	CD3	Germany	1989	$10.00
MCA	09P3-6198	Landslide of Love	CD3	Japan	1989	$12.00/$4.00
MCA	DTVVT-8	Landslide of Love	CD5	U.K.	1989	$10.00
MCA	257510-2	Only One	CD3	Germany	1989	$10.00
MCA	DTVVT-7	Only One	CD5	U.K.	1989	$10.00
MCA	DTVV-4	Revolution Baby	CD3	U.K.	1988	$10.00
MCA	DTVV-5	Sister Moon	CD3	U.K.	1988	$10.00
WEA	257724-2	Tell That Girl to Shut Up	CD5	Germany	1988	$10.00
Pioneer	10P3-6036	Tell That Girl to Shut Up	CD3	Japan	1988	$12.00/$4.00
MCA	DTVVT-2	Tell That Girl to Shut Up	CD5	U.K.	1988	$10.00
MCA		Tell That Girl to Shut Up	CDJ	U.S.	1988	$2.00

Trash Can Sinatras

Singles

Label	Catalog Number	Title	Type	Country	Year	Longbox Value / Value
Polygram	CDP 895	Blood Rush	CDJ	U.S.	1993	$2.00
Go Discs	GODCD-46	Circling the Circumference	CD5	U.K.	1990	$8.00
Go Discs	GODCD 98	Hay Fever	CD5	U.K.	1993	$8.00
Go Discs	876075-2	Obscurity Knocks	CD5	Germany	1990	$8.00
Go Discs	GODCD-34	Obscurity Knocks	CD5	U.K.	1990	$8.00
London	CDp 392	Obscurity Knocks	CDJ	U.S.	1991	$2.00
Go Discs	GODCD-41	Only Tongue Can Tell	CD5	U.K.	1990	$8.00

Traveling Wilburys

Full Length

Label	Catalog Number	Title	Type	Country	Year	Longbox Value / Value
		Classic CD (Vol. 1)	RS	U.S.	1990	$150.00
	2 CD set. Airdate: 7/30/90.					
Album Network		In the Studio (Vol. 1)	RS	U.S.	1990	$30.00
	Airdate: 3/26/90.					
Wilbury	9 25796-2	Vol. 1	DJ/LP	U.S.	1988	$25.00
	Picture disc.					

Label	Catalog Number	Title	Type	Country	Year	Longbox Value / Value
Wilbury	9 26324-2-Dj	Vol. 3	DJ/LP	U.S.	1990	$20.00

Singles

Label	Catalog Number	Title	Type	Country	Year	Longbox Value / Value
Wilbury	2-27637	End of the Line	CD3	Germany	1988	$10.00
Pioneer	10P3-6096	End of the Line	CD3	Japan	1988	$18.00/$5.00
Wilbury	W-7637CD	End of the Line	CD3	U.K.	1988	$10.00
Warner Brothers	PRO-CD-3364	End of the Line	CDJ	U.S.	1988	$8.00
Wilbury	921081-2	Handle With Care	CD3	Germany	1988	$12.00
WARNER	W7732CD 921081-2	Handle With Care	CD3	Germany	1988	$25.00
Warner Brothers	10P3-6073	Handle With Care	CD3	Japan	1988	$18.00/$5.00
Wilbury	W-7732CD	Handle With Care	CD3	U.K.	1988	$12.00
Warner Brothers	921081-2	Handle With Care	CD3	U.S.	1988	$18.00/$12.00
Warner Brothers	PRO-CD-3258	Handle With Care	CDJ	U.S.	1988	$12.00
WEA	921265-2	Heading For the Light	CD3	Germany	1989	$10.00
Wilbury	9362-40011-2	Inside Out	CD5	Germany	1991	$10.00
Wilbury	PRO-CD-4652	Inside Out	CDJ	U.S.	1991	$6.00
Warner Brothers	PRO-CD-3337	Last Night	CDJ	U.S.	1988	$8.00
WEA	919575-2	Nobody's Child	CD3	Germany	1990	$10.00
Pioneer	WPDP-6241	Nobody's Child	CD3	Japan	1990	$18.00/$5.00
WEA	W-9773CD	Nobody's Child	CD3	U.K.	1990	$10.00
Wilbury	7559-21799-2	She's My Baby	CD5	Germany	1990	$8.00
Pioneer	WPDP-6251	She's My Baby	CD3	Japan	1990	$18.00/$5.00
Warner Brothers	PRO-CD-4518	She's My Baby	CDJ	U.S.	1990	$8.00
Wilbury	9362-40044-2	Wilbury Twist	CD5	Germany	1991	$10.00
Wilbury	W-0018CD	Wilbury Twist	CD5	U.K.	1991	$10.00
Warner Brothers	PRO-CD-4652	Wilbury Twist	CDJ	U.S.	1991	$8.00

Travers, Pat

Full Length

Label	Catalog Number	Title	Type	Country	Year	Longbox Value / Value
Pioneer	PA-85-104	Just Another Killer Day	LD	U.S.	1985	$40.00

Travis, Harold

Singles

Label	Catalog Number	Title	Type	Country	Year	Longbox Value / Value
MCA	2709	Where Did Our Love Go	CDJ	U.S.	1993	$2.00

Travis, Randy

Full Length

Label	Catalog Number	Title	Type	Country	Year	Longbox Value / Value
		'90s Country	RS	U.S.	1995	$45.00

Airdate: 11/25/95.

Label	Catalog Number	Title	Type	Country	Year	Longbox Value / Value
		'90s Country	RS	U.S.	1995	$45.00

Airdate: 4/29/95.

Label	Catalog Number	Title	Type	Country	Year	Longbox Value / Value
Heartland	HD 3045	Best of Randy Travis, The	LP	U.S		$20.00

2 CD set.

Label	Catalog Number	Title	Type	Country	Year	Longbox Value / Value
WEA	38257	Forever	LD	U.S.	1991	$25.00
Warner Brothers	PRO-CD-5675	He Opened the Door (Greatest Hits)	DJ/LP	U.S.	1992	$60.00

2CD in "barn" package, with standee. Limited to 1500 copies.

Label	Catalog Number	Title	Type	Country	Year	Longbox Value / Value
Warner Brothers	PRO-CD-6363	Straight Talk With..	DJ/Intvw	U.S.	1993	$20.00

Singles

Label	Catalog Number	Title	Type	Country	Year	Longbox Value / Value
Warner Brothers	PRO-CD-4429	A Few Ole Country Boys	CDJ	U.S.	1990	$3.00
Warner Brothers	PRO-CD-6813	Before You Kill Us All	CDJ	U.S.		$3.00
Warner Brothers	PRO-CD-5185	Better Class of Losers	CDJ	U.S.	1991	$3.00
Warner Brothers	PRO-CD-6346	Cowboy Boogie	CDJ	U.S.	1993	$3.00
Warner Brothers	W-7804CD	Deeper Than the Holler	CD3	U.K.	1988	$10.00
Warner Brothers	W-8384CD	Forever And Ever Amen	CD3	U.K.	1988	$10.00
Warner Brothers	PRO-CD-4598	Heroes & Friends	CDJ	U.S.	1990	$3.00
Warner Brothers	2-27833	Honky Tonk Moon	CD3	U.S.	1988	$8.00/$4.00
Warner Brothers	PRO-CD-3167	Honky Tonk Moon	CDJ	U.S.	1988	$3.00
Warner Brothers	PRO-CD-4605	How Do I Wrap My Heart for Christmas	CDJ	U.S.	1988	$3.00
Warner Brothers	PRO-CD-3072	I Told You So	CDJ	U.S.	1988	$3.00
Warner Brothers	PRO-CD-5405	I'd Surrender	CDJ	U.S.	1991	$3.00
Warner Brothers	W-2841CD	It's Just a Matter of Time	CD5	U.K.	1989	$10.00
Warner Brothers	PRO-CD-3660	It's Just a Matter of Time	CDJ	U.S.	1989	$3.00
Warner Brothers	PRO-CD-3712	It's Just a Matter of Time	CDJ	U.S.	1989	$3.00
Warner Brothers	PRO-CD-5762	Look Heart, No Hands	CDJ	U.S.	1992	$3.00
Warner Brothers	PRO-CD-2904	Too Gone Too Long	CDJ	U.S.	1987	$3.00
Warner Brothers	PRO-CD-6678	Wind in the Fire	CDJ	U.S.	1993	$3.00

Travolta, John

Singles

Label	Catalog Number	Title	Type	Country	Year	Longbox Value / Value
Polygram	PZCD-136	Grease	CD5	U.K.	1991	$10.00

With Olivia Newton-John.

Label	Catalog Number	Title	Type	Country	Year	Longbox Value / Value
Polygram	879411-2	You're the One That I Want	CD5	Germany	1991	$10.00

With Olivia Newton-John.

Tre'+6

Singles

Label	Catalog Number	Title	Type	Country	Year	Longbox Value / Value
	DDS1003	Life is Crazy	CD5	U.S.	1995	$5.00

Treat

Singles

Label	Catalog Number	Title	Type	Country	Year	Longbox Value / Value
Da Bomb	1119	Shut Your Punk Ass Up	CDJ	U.S.	1994	$2.00

Treat Her Right

Singles

Label	Catalog Number	Title	Type	Country	Year	Longbox Value / Value
RCA	9000-2-RDj	Junk Yard	CDJ	U.S.	1989	$2.00
RCA	9040-2-RDj	Marie	CDJ	U.S.	1989	$2.00
RCA	8928-2-RDj	Picture of the Future	CDJ	U.S.	1989	$2.00

Tremendos Gavil

Singles

Label	Catalog Number	Title	Type	Country	Year	Longbox Value / Value
	5315	12 Exitos	CD5	U.S.	1994	$5.00

Trendz Of Culture

Singles

Label	Catalog Number	Title	Type	Country	Year	Longbox Value / Value
Motown	860472	Make A Move	CD5	U.S.	1995	$5.00

Tresvant, Ralph

Singles

Label	Catalog Number	Title	Type	Country	Year	Longbox Value / Value
Perspective	31458 1714	Money Can't Buy You Love	CDJ	U.S.	1992	$2.00
Perspective	31458 8021	Money Can't Buy You Love	CDJ	U.S.	1992	$2.00
MCA	54148	Rated R	CD5	U.S.	1991	$5.00
MCA	7567-72993-2	Sensitivity	CD5	Germany	1991	$8.00
MCA	WMD5-4045	Sensitivity	CD3	Japan	1990	$13.00/$4.00
MCA	DMCAT-1462	Sensitivity	CD5	U.K.	1991	$8.00
MCA	53933	Sensitivity	CD5	U.S.	1990	$5.00
MCA	CD45 1097	Sensitivity	CDJ	U.S.	1990	$2.00
MCA	MCSTD-1521	Stone Cold Gentleman	CD5	U.K.	1991	$10.00
MCA	1310	Stone Cold Gentleman	CDJ	U.S.	1991	$2.00
MCA	1340	Stone Cold Gentleman	CDJ	U.S.	1991	$2.00
MCA	2877	Who's the Mac	CDJ	U.S.	1993	$2.00
MCA	1561	Yo, Baby, Yo	CDJ	U.S.	1993	$2.00

Trevino, Rick

Full Length

Label	Catalog Number	Title	Type	Country	Year	Longbox Value / Value
Columbia	CSK 77373	Honky Tonk Crowd	DJ/Intvw	U.S.	1993	$12.00
		Looking for Light	DJ/Intvw	U.S.	1995	$20.00

Singles

Label	Catalog Number	Title	Type	Country	Year	Longbox Value / Value
Sony	CSK 10335	Honky Tonk Crowd	CDJ	U.S.	1993	$2.00

Tri Atma

Singles

Label	Catalog Number	Title	Type	Country	Year	Longbox Value / Value
		Yummy Moon	CDJ	U.S.		$2.00

Tribal Global Underground

Singles

Label	Catalog Number	Title	Type	Country	Year	Longbox Value / Value
Columbia	77862	Temple Head	CD5	U.S.	1994	$5.00

Tribe

Singles

Label	Catalog Number	Title	Type	Country	Year	Longbox Value / Value
Warner Brothers	PRO-CD-5370	Here at the Home	CDJ	U.S.	1991	$2.00
Slash	PRO-CD-6227	Red Rover	CDJ	U.S.	1993	$2.00
Slash	PRO-CD-66607	Supercollider	CDJ	U.S.	1993	$2.00

Tribe 8

Singles

Label	Catalog Number	Title	Type	Country	Year	Longbox Value / Value
Altern. Tenacles	156	Fist City	CD5	U.S.	1994	$5.00

Tribe After Tribe

Singles

Label	Catalog Number	Title	Type	Country	Year	Longbox Value / Value
Megaforce	961	Ice Blelow	CDJ	U.S.	1993	$2.00

Tribe Called Quest

Singles

Label	Catalog Number	Title	Type	Country	Year	Longbox Value / Value
Jive	42197	Electric Relaxation	CD5	U.S.	1994	$5.00

Tricky

Singles

Label	Catalog Number	Title	Type	Country	Year	Longbox Value / Value
4th & B'way	162-440 590	Aftermath	CD5	U.S.	1993	$5.00
4th & Broadway	440590	Aftermath	CD5	U.S.	1994	$5.00
		Ponderosa	CDJ	U.S.	1996	$2.00

Triffids

Singles

Label	Catalog Number	Title	Type	Country	Year	Longbox Value / Value
Island	CID-424	Bury Me in Deep Love	CD5	U.K.	1989	$8.00
Island		Bury Me in Deep Love	DJ/CD3	U.K.	1989	$10.00
Island	CID-413	Falling Over You	CD5	U.K.	1989	$8.00
Island	CID-420	Goodbye Little Boy	CD5	U.K.	1989	$8.00
Island	CIDX-350	Trick of the Light	CD5	U.K.	1988	$8.00

Trilobites

Singles

Label	Catalog Number	Title	Type	Country	Year	Longbox Value / Value
rooArt	CDP 212	New Head	CDJ	U.S.	1989	$2.00

Trilogy

Singles

Label	Catalog Number	Title	Type	Country	Year	Longbox Value / Value
Atco	PRCD 4695-2	Good Time	CDJ	U.S.	1992	$2.00
Atco	PRCD 3680-2	Love Me Forever or Love Me Not	CDJ	U.S.	1990	$2.00

Trinere

Singles

Label	Catalog Number	Title	Type	Country	Year	Longbox Value / Value
Luke	PRCD 39202-2	Games	CDJ	U.S.	1991	$2.00
Luke	PRCD 4215-2	It's the Music	CDJ	U.S.	1991	$2.00
Pandisc	094	Rockin' to the Rhythm	CDJ	U.S.	1993	$2.00

Trio

Singles

Label	Catalog Number	Title	Type	Country	Year	Longbox Value / Value
Warner Brothers	PRO-CD-2735	Telling Me Lies	CDJ	U.S.		$2.00

Trio Tariacuri

Singles

Label	Catalog Number	Title	Type	Country	Year	Longbox Value / Value
	1419	Exitos De Oro Del	CD5	U.S.	1994	$5.00

Trip

Singles

Label	Catalog Number	Title	Type	Country	Year	Longbox Value / Value
South Side	MIKHA CD1	Border, The	CD5	U.K.	1990	$8.00
MCA	1583	Chill Out Jack	CDJ	U.S.	1991	$2.00

Trip Dis

Singles

Label	Catalog Number	Title	Type	Country	Year	Longbox Value / Value
	72020	Dip	CD5	U.S.	1994	$5.00
	72020	Drip	CD5	U.S.	1994	$5.00

Trip Shakespeare

Singles

Label	Catalog Number	Title	Type	Country	Year	Longbox Value / Value
A&M	75021 7283 2	Bachelorette	CDJ	U.S.	1991	$2.00
A&M	CD 18024	Crane, The	CDJ	U.S.	1990	$7.00
A&M	75021 8017 2	Gone, Gone, Gone,	CDJ	U.S.	1990	$2.00
A&M	887 847-2	Pearle	CD5	U.S.	1990	$4.00
A&M	75021 8100 2	Pearle	CDJ	U.S.	1990	$2.00
Black Hole	89248	Volt	CD5	U.K.	1992	$8.00
A&M	75021 7311-2	Your Mouth	CDJ	U.S.	1991	$2.00

Triple M

Singles

Label	Catalog Number	Title	Type	Country	Year	Longbox Value / Value
A&M	75021 7287 2	Prisoner of Passion	CDJ	U.S.	1991	$2.00

Triple3fastaction

Singles

Label	Catalog Number	Title	Type	Country	Year	Longbox Value / Value
		R3W3DUP	CDJ	U.S.		$2.00

Triplets

Singles

Label	Catalog Number	Title	Type	Country	Year	Longbox Value / Value
Mercury	PHDR-41	Dancing in the Shadow	CD3	Japan	1991	$12.00/$3.00
Mercury	CDP 576	Light a Candle	CDJ	U.S.	1991	$2.00
Polygram	868719-2	Sunrise	CD5	Germany	1991	$8.00
Mercury	PHDR-32	Sunrise	CD3	Japan	1991	$12.00/$3.00
Mercury	CDP 460	Sunrise	CDJ	U.S.	1991	$2.00
Mercury	868271-2	You Don't Have to Go Home Tonight	CD5	Germany	1991	$8.00
Mercury	MERCD-342	You Don't Have to Go Home Tonight	CD5	U.K.	1991	$8.00
Mercury	CDP 390	You Don't Have to Go Home Tonight	CDJ	U.S.	1991	$2.00

Tripmaster Monkey

Singles

Label	Catalog Number	Title	Type	Country	Year	Longbox Value / Value
		Faster Than Dwight	CD5	U.S.	1993	$4.00

Tripping Daisy

Full Length

Label	Catalog Number	Title	Type	Country	Year	Longbox Value / Value
Westwood One		In Concert-Nu Rock	RS	U.S.	1995	$45.00

Airdate: 12/4/95.

Singles

Label	Catalog Number	Title	Type	Country	Year	Longbox Value / Value
Island	PRCD 5004-2	Blown Away	CDJ	U.S.	1993	$2.00
		I Got a Girl	CDJ	U.S.		$2.00
Island	PRCD 5001-2	My Umbrella	CDJ	U.S.	1993	$2.00

Label	Catalog Number	Title	Type	Country	Year	Longbox Value / Value
		Piranha	CDJ	U.S.		$2.00
		Trip Along	CDJ	U.S.		$2.00
		Live	CDJ	U.S.	1994	$3.00

Trique-Dik-Slik

Singles

Label	Catalog Number	Title	Type	Country	Year	Longbox Value / Value
MCA		Euphoria	CD5	U.S.	1993	$5.00
MCA	2824	Euphoria	CDJ	U.S.	1993	$2.00

Tritt, Travis

Full Length

Label	Catalog Number	Title	Type	Country	Year	Longbox Value / Value
		'90s Country	RS	U.S.	1995	$30.00
Airdate: 27/8/95.						
		'90s Country	RS	U.S.	1996	$30.00
Airdate: 2/24/96.						
		Restless Kind	LTD/LP	U.S.	1996	$20.00
CD and bonus cassette-single. Sold exclusively at Blockbuster Music stores.						
Warner Brothers	PRO-CD-4726	Straight Talk	DJ/Intvw	U.S.	1991	$30.00
Warner Brothers	PRO-CD-4816	Straight Talk With Travis Tritt	DJ/Smplr	U.S.	1991	$15.00
Unistar		Travis Tritt Story	RS	U.S.	1993	$30.00
Airdate: 6/18/93.						

Singles

Label	Catalog Number	Title	Type	Country	Year	Longbox Value / Value
Warner Brothers	PRO-CD-5857	Can I Trust You With My Heart	CDJ	U.S.	1992	$3.00
Warner Brothers	PRO-CD-3511	Country Club	CDJ	U.S.	1989	$3.00
Warner Brothers		Here's a Quarter	CDJ	U.S.		$3.00
Warner Brothers	PRO-CD-6238	Looking Out for Number One	CDJ	U.S.	1992	$3.00
Warner Brothers	PRO-CD-5660	Lord Have Mercy	CDJ	U.S.	1992	$3.00
Warner Brothers	PRO-CD-5409	Nothing Short of Dying	CDJ	U.S.	1992	$3.00
Warner Brothers		Put Some Drive in Your Country	CDJ	U.S.		$3.00
Warner Brothers	PRO-CD-5122	Whiskey Ain't Workin'	CDJ	U.S.	1991	$3.00
Warner Brothers	PRO-CD-5767	Winter Wonderland	CDJ	U.S.	1992	$7.00
Warner Brothers	PRO-CD-6562	Worth Every Mile	CDJ	U.S.	1993	$3.00

Triumph – Long Time Gone (MCA CD45-17425)

Triumph

Full Length

Label	Catalog Number	Title	Type	Country	Year	Longbox Value / Value
Emperor	ID7771EM	A Night of... Triumph	LD	U.S.	1990	$30.00
MCA	MCAD-5543	Allied Forces	LP/LB	U.S.†	1985	$14.00/$8.00
Album Network		In the Studio (Allied Forces)	RS	U.S.		$20.00
Album Network		In the Studio (Just a Game/Allied Forces)	RS	U.S.		$20.00
MCA	MCAD-31118	Just a Game	LP/LB	U.S.	1986	$12.00/$8.00
DIR		King Biscuit Flour Hour	RS	U.S.	1993	$30.00
Airdate: 1/28/93.						
MCA	MCAD-31069	Never Surrender	LP/LB	U.S.	1986	$12.00/$8.00
MCA	MCAD-1453	Progressions of Power	LP/LB	U.S.	1987	$14.00/$8.00
MCA	MCAD-5786	Sport of Kings	LP/LB	U.S.	1986	$12.00/$8.00
MCA	MCAD-5537	Thunder Seven	LP/LB	U.S.†	1985	$14.00/$8.00
MCA	MCAD-5537	Thunder Seven	LP/LB	U.S.	1986	$12.00/$8.00

Singles

Label	Catalog Number	Title	Type	Country	Year	Longbox Value / Value
Victory	CDP 834	Child of the City	CDJ	U.S.	1992	$2.00
MCA	CD45-17425	Long Time Gone	CDJ	U.S.	1989	$7.00
		Somewhere Tonight	CDJ	Canada	1992	$5.00

Trixter

Singles

Label	Catalog Number	Title	Type	Country	Year	Longbox Value / Value
MCA	MCSTD-1553	Give It to Me Good	CD5	U.K.	1991	$9.00
Mechanic	18393	Give It to Me Good	CDJ	U.S.	1990	$2.00
Mechanic	CD45 18244	Line Of Fire	CDJ	U.S.	1990	$2.00
MCA	CD45 1098	One in a Million	CDJ	U.S.	1990	$2.00
MCA	2309	Road of a Thousand Dreams	CDJ	U.S.	1992	$2.00

Troccoli, Kathy

Singles

Label	Catalog Number	Title	Type	Country	Year	Longbox Value / Value
Reunion	4422	Can't Get You out of My Head	CDJ	U.S.	1992	$2.00
Reunion	4371	Everything Changes	CDJ	U.S.	1992	$2.00
Reunion	4381	Everything Changes	CDJ	U.S.	1992	$2.00
RCA	64216	If I'm Not in Love	CD5	U.S.	1994	$5.00
Reunion	62784	Tell Me Where It Hurts	CDJ	U.S.	1994	$2.00
Reunion	4336	You've Got a Way	CDJ	U.S.	1991	$2.00
Reunion	4410	You've Got a Way	CDJ	U.S.	1991	$2.00

Troggs

Singles

Label	Catalog Number	Title	Type	Country	Year	Longbox Value / Value
Intercord	825 327	Don't You Know	CD5	Germany	1992	$9.00
Intercord	825 767	Wild Thing	CD5	Germany	1992	$10.00
Fontana	TFCD-689	Wild Thing	CD5	U.K.	1991	$10.00
Fontana	TFCD 717	With a Girl Like You	CD5	U.K.	1991	$10.00

Troop

Singles

Label	Catalog Number	Title	Type	Country	Year	Longbox Value / Value
		All I Do is Think Of You	CDJ	U.S.		$2.00
		I Will Always Love You	CDJ	U.S.		$2.00
		My Heart	CDJ	U.S.		$2.00
Atlantic	PRCD 4723	Sweet November	CDJ	U.S.		$2.00
WEA	A-7810CD	That's My Attitude	CD5	U.K.	1990	$8.00

Tropea, John

Full Length

Label	Catalog Number	Title	Type	Country	Year	Longbox Value / Value
Digital Music	CD-453	Hushed Intensity	LP/LB	U.S.†	1985	$14.00/$8.00

Tropicalismio A

Singles

Label	Catalog Number	Title	Type	Country	Year	Longbox Value / Value
Andrea Records	3512	Con Sabor Apache	CD5	U.S.	1994	$5.00

Trouble

Full Length

Label	Catalog Number	Title	Type	Country	Year	Longbox Value / Value
Def American	PRO-CD-5599	Manic Frustration	DJ/LP	U.S.	1992	$14.00
Def American	26484	Psalm 9	LP/LB	U.S.		$14.00/$8.00
Def American	26485	Skull, The	LP/LB	U.S.		$14.00/$8.00

Singles

Label	Catalog Number	Title	Type	Country	Year	Longbox Value / Value
Def American	PRO-CD-5538	Memories Garden	CDJ	U.S.	1992	$2.00
Def American	PRO-CD-4101	Misery Shows, The	CDJ	U.S.	1990	$6.00
Def American	PRO-CD-5525	'Scuse Me	CDJ	U.S.	1992	$2.00
Def American	PRO-CD-5792	'Scuse Me	CDJ	U.S.	1992	$2.00

Trouble Tribe

Singles

Label	Catalog Number	Title	Type	Country	Year	Longbox Value / Value
		Tattoo	CDJ	U.S.		$2.00

Troup

Full Length

Label	Catalog Number	Title	Type	Country	Year	Longbox Value / Value
		Whatever It Takes	DJ/Smplr	U.S.		$8.00

Trower, Robin

Full Length

Label	Catalog Number	Title	Type	Country	Year	Longbox Value / Value
Passport		Beyond the Mist	LP	Canada		$15.00
Chrysalis		Bridge of Sighs	LTD/LP	U.K.	1994	$15.00
25th Anniversary edition in 6"x11" longbox.						
Chrysalis	VK-41057	Bridge of Sighs	LP/LB	U.S.†	1994	$14.00/$8.00
Atlantic		In the Line of Fire	LP/LB	U.S.		$14.00/$8.00
Album Network		In the Studio (Bridge o Sighs)	RS	U.S.	1990	$20.00
Airdate: 4/9/90.						
Album Network		In the Studio (Bridge of Sighs)	RS	U.S.	1993	$20.00
Airdate: 2/22/93.						
DIR		King Biscuit Flour Hour	RS	U.S.	1988	$30.00
With Johnny Winter, Airdate: 7/17/88.						

Singles

Label	Catalog Number	Title	Type	Country	Year	Longbox Value / Value
Atlantic	PRCD 3172-2	Turn the Volume Up	CDJ	U.S.	1990	$2.00

Tru

Singles

Label	Catalog Number	Title	Type	Country	Year	Longbox Value / Value
	53261-2	I Always Feel Like	CD5	U.S.	1997	$5.00

Truck Stop Love

Singles

Label	Catalog Number	Title	Type	Country	Year	Longbox Value / Value
Scotti Brothers	72392 75427	River Mountain	CD5	U.S.	1993	$5.00

Trudell, John

Singles

Label	Catalog Number	Title	Type	Country	Year	Longbox Value / Value
Rykodisc	0256	Rant 'n Roll	CDJ	U.S.	1993	$2.00
Rykodisc	0286	That Love	CDJ	U.S.	1994	$2.00

Truth

Singles

Label	Catalog Number	Title	Type	Country	Year	Longbox Value / Value
IRS	L3317776	Throwing It All Away	CDJ	U.S.	1989	$2.00
IRS		Weapons of Love	CDJ	U.S.		$2.00

Truth Be Known

Singles

Label	Catalog Number	Title	Type	Country	Year	Longbox Value / Value
Sisapa	76707	War	CDJ	U.S.	1990	$2.00

Truth Inc.

Singles

Label	Catalog Number	Title	Type	Country	Year	Longbox Value / Value
Interscope	PRCD 4571-2	Can I Get With You Tonight	CDJ	U.S.	1992	$2.00

Trynin, Jennifer

Singles

Label	Catalog Number	Title	Type	Country	Year	Longbox Value / Value
		1 Year Down	CDJ	U.S.		$2.00
		All This Could Be Yours	CDJ	U.S.		$2.00

TSOL

Singles

Label	Catalog Number	Title	Type	Country	Year	Longbox Value / Value
Enigma	EPRO-271	Hell on Earth	CDJ	U.S.	1990	$2.00

Tubes

Full Length

Label	Catalog Number	Title	Type	Country	Year	Longbox Value / Value
Mobile Fidelity	MFCD-822	Tubes, The	LP/LB	U.S.†	1985	$27.00/$25.00
Mobile Fidelity	MFCD-822	Tubes, The	LP/LB	U.S.	1987	$27.00/$25.00
Pioneer Artists	PA-82-012	Tubes Video	LD	U.S.	1982	$30.00

Tuck & Patti

Singles

Label	Catalog Number	Title	Type	Country	Year	Longbox Value / Value
Windham Hill	WD 17934	Castles Made of Sand	CDJ	U.S.	1989	$2.00
		Learning How to Fly	CDJ	U.S.	1994	$3.00
Windham Hill	WD 17818	Love Warriors	CDJ	U.S.	1989	$2.00
Windham Hill		Takes My Breath Away	CDJ	U.S.		$2.00
Windham Hill	WD 17633	Time After Time	CDJ	U.S.	1988	$2.00

Tucker, Tanya

Full Length

Label	Catalog Number	Title	Type	Country	Year	Longbox Value / Value
		'90s Country	RS	U.S.	1995	$30.00
Airdate: 12/16/95.						
		'90s Country	RS	U.S.	1995	$30.00
Airdate: 5/27/95.						
		Fire to Fire	DJ/Invw	U.S.	1995	$25.00
Capitol	C2-89048	Soon	LP/LB	U.S.	1993	$15.00
Pioneer Artists	PA-92-443	Tanya Tucker	LD	U.S.	1992	$25.00

Singles

Label	Catalog Number	Title	Type	Country	Year	Longbox Value / Value
Liberty	DPRO-79600	It's a Little Too Late	CDJ	U.S.	1992	$2.00
Capitol	DPRO 79955	Walking Shoes	CDJ	U.S.	1990	$2.00

Tuesday Blue

Singles

Label	Catalog Number	Title	Type	Country	Year	Longbox Value / Value
		Love Me Simple	CDJ	U.S.		$2.00

Tuff

Singles

Label	Catalog Number	Title	Type	Country	Year	Longbox Value / Value
Atlantic	PRCD 4042-2	I Hate Kissing You Goodbye	CDJ	U.S.	1991	$2.00

Tukka Voots

Singles

Label	Catalog Number	Title	Type	Country	Year	Longbox Value / Value
EMi	DPRO-79326	Riddim	CDJ	U.S.		$2.00

Tumbleweed

Singles

Label	Catalog Number	Title	Type	Country	Year	Longbox Value / Value
Waterfront	DAMP 17S	Fish out of Water	CDJ	U.S.	1992	$6.00
	CD in spiralbound book.					

Tung Twista

Singles

Label	Catalog Number	Title	Type	Country	Year	Longbox Value / Value
Zoo	ZD-17092	Ratatattat	CDJ	U.S.	1992	$2.00

Turner, Ruby

Singles

Label	Catalog Number	Title	Type	Country	Year	Longbox Value / Value
Jive	RTSCD-6	Baby I Need Your Loving	CD5	U.K.	1989	$8.00
Jive	RTSCD-1	I'd Rather Go Blind	CD5	U.K.	1989	$8.00
Jive	RTSCD-2	I'm in Love	CD5	U.K.	1989	$8.00
Jive		It's a Crying Shame	CDJ	U.S.		$2.00
Jive	ZD-43248	It's Gonna Be Alright	CD5	Germany	1989	$8.00
Jive	RTSCD-7	It's Gonna Be Alright	CD5	U.K.	1989	$8.00
Jive		It's Gonna Be Alright	CDJ	U.K.	1989	$2.00
Jive	RTSCD-8	Paradise	CD5	U.K.	1990	$8.00
Jive		Paradise	CDJ	U.K.	1990	$2.00
Jive	JIVECD-285	Rumors	CD5	U.K.	1991	$8.00
Jive	RTSCD-4	Signed Sealed Delivered	CD5	U.K.	1988	$8.00
		Stay With Me Baby	CD5	U.K.		$10.00
		Stay With Me Baby	CD5	U.K.		$10.00
	Second version.					
Jive	JIVECD-278	Vibe Is Right	CD5	U.K.	1991	$8.00
Jive	RTSCD-5	What Becomes of the Broken Hearted	CD5	U.K.	1988	$8.00

Turner, Tina

Full Length

Label	Catalog Number	Title	Type	Country	Year	Longbox Value / Value
Warner	PCD-32	Best 15 Tracks 1984-1987	DJ/Smplr	Japan	1988	$100.00
Capitol		Collected Works	DJ/Smplr	U.S.	1994	$15.00
Capitol	CDP 7 93129 2	Foreign Affair	LTD/LP	U.S.	1989	$25.00
	CD in passport-style book.					
McDonald's		Greatest Hits	LP	U.S.	1994	$8.00
Virgin	DPRO-11544	Hanes Collector's Edition	DJ/Smplr	U.S.	1996	$10.00
Polygram	080 349-1	Live In Rio	LD	U.S.	1988	$25.00
Capitol	DPRO 79777	Play This In-Store	DJ/Smplr	U.S.	1993	$15.00
Capitol	CDP-46041	Private Dancer	LP/LB	U.S.†	1985	$14.00/$8.00
EMI		Private Dancer Live	LTD/LP	U.K.	1994	$35.00
	CD and Video (PAL).					
Pioneer	PA85-M017	Private Dancer Tour	8"LD	U.S.	1984	$10.00
Capitol	DPRO-79011	Simply the Best	DJ/LP	U.S.	1991	$25.00
	2CD picture disc set in special tandem digipak.					
Capitol	DPRO 79330	Tearing Us Apart	DJ/Smplr	U.S.	1988	$5.00
Capitol		Tina Live	DJ/Smplr	U.S.	1988	$10.00

Singles

Label	Catalog Number	Title	Type	Country	Year	Longbox Value / Value
Capitol	CDCL-484	Addicted to Love	CD5	U.K.	1988	$10.00
Capitol	204075-2	Be Tender With Me Baby	CD5	Germany	1990	$10.00
Capitol	CDCL-593	Be Tender With Me Baby	CD5	U.K.	1990	$10.00
EMI	203498-3	Best, The	CD3	Germany	1989	$10.00
EMI	XP10-2105	Best, The	CD3	Japan	1989	$15.00/$4.00
Capitol	CDCL-543	Best, The	CD5	U.K.	1989	$10.00
Capitol	DPRO 79709	Best, The	CDJ	U.S.	1989	$3.00
EMI	203858-2	Foreign Affair	CD5	Germany	1989	$10.00
EMI	203903-2	Foreign Affair	CD5	Germany	1989	$10.00
EMI		Goldeneye	CDJ	U.K.	1995	$18.00
Virgin	38524	Goldeneye	CD5	U.S.	1995	$5.00
Virgin		Goldeneye	CDJ	U.S.	1995	$7.00
		I Don't Wanna Fight	CD5	U.K.		$10.00
	Second version.					
Capitol	DPRO-79272	I Don't Wanna Fight	CDJ	U.S.	1989	$3.00
Virgin	DPRO-12775	I Don't Wanna Fight	CDJ	U.S.	1993	$3.00
Virgin	DPRO-12807	I Don't Wanna Fight	CDJ	U.S.	1994	$3.00
Capitol	203565-2	I Don't Wanna Lose Your Love	CD5	Germany	1989	$10.00
Capitol	CDCL-553	I Don't Wanna Lose Your Love	CD5	U.K.	1989	$10.00
Capitol	CDCL-584	Look Me in the Heart	CD5	U.K.	1990	$10.00
Capitol	DPRO 79918	Look Me in the Heart	CDJ	U.S.	1989	$3.00
Capitol	204618-2	Love Thing	CD5	Germany	1992	$10.00
Capitol	CDCL-644	Love Thing	CD5	U.K.	1992	$10.00
Capitol	DPRO-79947	Love Thing	CDJ	U.S.	1992	$3.00
EMI		Missing You	CDJ	U.K.	1996	$18.00
Capitol	202474-2	Nutbush City Limits	CD5	Germany	1988	$10.00
Capitol	204518-2	Nutbush City Limits	CD5	Germany	1991	$10.00
Capitol	202474-2	Nutbush City Limits	CD5	U.K.	1988	$10.00
Capitol	CDCL-630	Nutbush City Limits	CD5	U.K.	1991	$10.00
		On Silent Wings	CDJ	U.K.	1995	$15.00
		On Silent Wings	CDJ	U.K.	1996	$10.00
		On Silent Wings	CDJ	U.K.	1996	$10.00
	Second version.					
Virgin	38434	Proud Mary	CD5	U.S.	1994	$6.00
Virgin	DPRO-14149	Proud Mary	CDJ	U.S.	1994	$6.00
Pioneer	PIFP 1025	River Deep	CDV	Japan	1988	$35.00
EMI	203567-3	Steamy Windows	CD3	Germany	1989	$10.00
EMI	203567-2	Steamy Windows	CD5	Germany	1989	$10.00
EMI	203693-2	Steamy Windows	CD5	Germany	1990	$10.00
Capitol	CDCL-560	Steamy Windows	CD5	U.K.	1990	$10.00
Capitol	DPRO 79825	Steamy Windows	CDJ	U.S.	1989	$3.00
Capitol	DPRO 79907	Steamy Windows	CDJ	U.S.	1989	$3.00
EMI	203180-2	Tonight	CD5	Germany	1988	$10.00
EMI	654683-3	Two People	CD3	Germany	1989	$10.00
Capitol	DPRO 79770	Undercover Agent for the Blues	CDJ	U.S.	1989	$3.00
Capitol	204581-2	Way of the World	CD5	Germany	1991	$10.00
Capitol	CDCL-637	Way of the World	CD5	U.K.	1991	$10.00
Capitol	DPRO-79116	Way of the World	CDJ	U.S.	1991	$3.00
Pioneer		What You Get	DJ/CDV	U.S.	1987	$35.00
EMI		Whatever You Want	CDJ	Holland	1996	$18.00
EMI		Whatever You Want	CDJ	U.K.	1996	$18.00
EMI		Why Must We Wait Until Tonight?	CDJ	Spain	1996	$40.00
		Why Must We Wait Until Tonight?	CD5	U.K.		$10.00
	Second version.					
Capitol	CDRS 6366	Why Must We Wait Until Tonight	CD5	U.K.	1994	$13.00
	CD in box.					
Virgin	DPRO-12812	Why Must We Wait Until Tonight	CDJ	U.S.	1994	$3.00

Turrentine, Stanley

Full Length

Label	Catalog Number	Title	Type	Country	Year	Longbox Value / Value
Blue Note		Joyride & Blue Hour	LTD/LP	U.S.	1995	$19.00
Fantasy	FCD-9465	Pieces of Dreams	LP/LB	U.S.†	1985	$14.00/$8.00

Turtle Island String Quartet

Singles

Label	Catalog Number	Title	Type	Country	Year	Longbox Value / Value
Windam Hill	90-10	Crossroads	CDJ	U.S.	1990	$2.00

Turtles

Full Length

Label	Catalog Number	Title	Type	Country	Year	Longbox Value / Value
Rhino	RNCD-5160	Greatest Hits	LP/LB	U.S.†	1984	$14.00/$8.00
Rhino	885857	Happy Together	CD3	Germany	1988	$10.00
Rhino	R3 73017	Happy Together	CD3	U.S.	1988	$7.00/$4.00
Rhino	71873	Love Songs	CD5	U.S.	1994	$5.00

Twain, Shania

Singles

Label	Catalog Number	Title	Type	Country	Year	Longbox Value / Value
Polygram	856449	Any Man of Mine	CD5	U.S.	1995	$6.00
Polygram	522886	Woman In Me	CD5	U.S.	1994	$5.00

Twenty 4 Seven

Singles

Label	Catalog Number	Title	Type	Country	Year	Longbox Value / Value
ZYX	66006R-8	Slave To the Music	CD5	U.S.	1995	$7.00

Twenty Ninth Street Sax Quartet

Full Length

Label	Catalog Number	Title	Type	Country	Year	Longbox Value / Value
Polygram	848415	Underground	LP/BP	U.S.		$12.00/$7.00

Twenty One

Singles

Label	Catalog Number	Title	Type	Country	Year	Longbox Value / Value
		Knee Deep	CDJ	U.S.		$2.00
		Walking	CDJ	U.S.		$2.00

Twenty-Two Brides

Singles

Label	Catalog Number	Title	Type	Country	Year	Longbox Value / Value
		Lullaby	CDJ	U.S.		$2.00

Twilley, Dwight Band

Full Length

Label	Catalog Number	Title	Type	Country	Year	Longbox Value / Value
DCC		Rock Yourself	LP	U.S.		$8.00

Twinz

Singles

Label	Catalog Number	Title	Type	Country	Year	Longbox Value / Value
		Jump Ta This	CDJ	U.S.		$2.00
Polygram	579385	Round & Round	CD5	U.S.	1995	$6.00

Twisted Sister

Full Length

Label	Catalog Number	Title	Type	Country	Year	Longbox Value / Value
Pioneer	PA-84-093	Stay Hungry	LD	U.S.	1984	$25.00
Atlantic	80156-2	Stay Hungry	LP/LB	U.S.†	1985	$14.00/$8.00

Twister Alley

Singles

Label	Catalog Number	Title	Type	Country	Year	Longbox Value / Value
Mercury	CDP 955	Dance	CDJ	U.S.	1993	$2.00

Twitty, Conway

Full Length

Label	Catalog Number	Title	Type	Country	Year	Longbox Value / Value
MCA	2860	Best Friend a Song Ever Had, The	DJ/Intvw	U.S.	1993	$20.00

Singles

Label	Catalog Number	Title	Type	Country	Year	Longbox Value / Value
	120	Away Too Long	CD5	U.S.	1994	$5.00
MCA	54766	Don't It Make You Lonely	CDJ	U.S.	1993	$2.00
MCA	CD45 79000	Fit to Be Tied	CDJ	U.S.	1990	$2.00
MCA	54077	One Bridge I Didn't Burn	CDJ	U.S.	1990	$2.00
MCA	54186	She's Got a Man on Her Mind	CDJ	U.S.	1991	$2.00
MCA	54281	Who Did They Think He Was	CDJ	U.S.	1991	$2.00

Twitty, Conway & Loretta Lynn

Full Length

Label	Catalog Number	Title	Type	Country	Year	Longbox Value / Value
Warner Sound Exchange		22 Legendary Hits	LTD/LP	U.S.	1995	$17.00

Two Bit Thief

Singles

Label	Catalog Number	Title	Type	Country	Year	Longbox Value / Value
Combat	0906	Broken Hearts	CDJ	U.S.	1990	$2.00

Two Deep

Singles

Label	Catalog Number	Title	Type	Country	Year	Longbox Value / Value
Cold Chillin'	4021	I Didn't Do My Homework	CDJ	U.S.	1990	$2.00
Atomic	WNRCD-821	Life Party	CD5	U.K.	1991	$8.00

Two Die For

Singles

Label	Catalog Number	Title	Type	Country	Year	Longbox Value / Value
		You Got What It Takes	CDJ	U.S.		$2.00

Two In A Room

Singles

Label	Catalog Number	Title	Type	Country	Year	Longbox Value / Value
Cutting Records	332	Ahora (Now)	CD5	U.S.	1994	$5.00
		She's Got Me Going Crazy	CDJ	U.S.		$2.00
		What Do You Want	CDJ	U.S.		$2.00

Two Kings in a Cipher

Singles

Label	Catalog Number	Title	Type	Country	Year	Longbox Value / Value
		Movin' On 'Em	CDJ	U.S.		$2.00

Two Live Crew

Singles

Label	Catalog Number	Title	Type	Country	Year	Longbox Value / Value
BMG	663626	Banned in the U.S.A.	CD5	Germany	1990	$8.00
Atlantic		Banned in the U.S.A.	CD5	U.S.	1990	$4.00
Atlantic	PRCD 3483-2	Banned in the U.S.A.	CDJ	U.S.	1990	$3.00
Atlantic	PRCD 3486-2	Banned in the U.S.A.	CDJ	U.S.	1990	$3.00
BMG	663075	C'mon Babe	CD5	Germany	1990	$8.00
Luke	PRCD 3898-2	Hangin' With the Boys	CDJ	U.S.	1991	$3.00
BMG	663923	Mama Juanita	CD5	Germany	1990	$8.00
BMG	662734	Me So Horny	CD5	Germany	1990	$8.00
Efa	CD-04264	We Want Some Pussy	CD5	Germany	1988	$8.00
Efa	CD-04272	We Want Some Pussy	CD5	Germany	1988	$8.00
WTG	654798-2	Yakety Yak	CD5	U.K.	1989	$8.00

Two Lost Suns

Singles

Label	Catalog Number	Title	Type	Country	Year	Longbox Value / Value
		I Can't Wait	CD5	U.S.		$5.00
		Rainbow Me	CD5	U.S.		$2.00

Two New

Singles

Label	Catalog Number	Title	Type	Country	Year	Longbox Value / Value
		This is Ponderous	CDJ	U.S.		$2.00

Two Serious

Singles

Label	Catalog Number	Title	Type	Country	Year	Longbox Value / Value
		You're so Fine	CDJ	U.S.		$2.00

Two Third

Singles

Label	Catalog Number	Title	Type	Country	Year	Longbox Value / Value
		Hear Me Calling	CD5	U.K.		$10.00
		Hear Me Calling	CD5	U.K.		$10.00
	Second version.					

Two Unlimited

Singles

Label	Catalog Number	Title	Type	Country	Year	Longbox Value / Value
		Do What's Good for Me	CDJ	U.S.	1992	$2.00

Label	Catalog Number	Title	Type	Country	Year	Longbox Value / Value
Mercury	PHDR-51	Get Ready for This	CD3	Japan	1992	$12.00/$3.00
PWL	PWCD-206	Get Ready for This	CD5	U.K.	1991	$8.00
Critique	15490	Get Ready for This	CD5	U.S.	1991	$4.00
Critique	15535	Get Ready for This	CD5	U.S.	1994	$5.00
Mercury	PHDR-122	Magic Friend	CD3	Japan	1992	$12.00/$3.00
PWL	PWCD-240	Magic Friend	CD5	U.K.	1992	$8.00
		Magic Friend	CDJ	U.S.	1992	$2.00
Mercury	PHCR-8024	No Limit	CD5	Japan	1993	$12.00
PWL	PWCD-256	No Limit	CD5	U.K.	1992	$8.00
Critique	15499	No Limit	CD5	U.S.	1992	$5.00
Critique	15520	Sim Limites	CD5	U.S.	1994	$5.00
ZYX	6735-8	Twilight Zone	CD5	Germany	1992	$6.00
Mercury	PHDR-103	Twilight Zone	CD3	Japan	1992	$12.00/$3.00
PWL	PWCD-211	Twilight Zone	CD5	U.K.	1992	$8.00
Critique	15486	Twilight Zone	CD5	U.S.	1992	$4.00
PWL	PWCD-228	Workaholic	CD5	U.K.	1992	$8.00

Tyketto

Singles

Label	Catalog Number	Title	Type	Country	Year	Longbox Value / Value
DGC	DGCTD-2	Forever Young	CD5	U.K.	1991	$8.00
DGC	PRO-CD-4207	Forever Young	CDJ	U.S.	1991	$2.00

Tyler, Boonie

Full Length

Label	Catalog Number	Title	Type	Country	Year	Longbox Value / Value
CBS	CK-38710	Faster Than the Speed of Light	LP/BP	U.S.†	1984	$14.00/$8.00

Singles

Label	Catalog Number	Title	Type	Country	Year	Longbox Value / Value
BMG	664991	Against the Wind	CD5	Germany	1991	$8.00
Columbia	CDBEST-1	Best, The	CD5	U.K.	1988	$8.00
BMG	664751	Bitterblue	CD5	Germany	1991	$8.00
BMG	663748	Breakout	CD5	Germany	1990	$8.00
Columbia	651516-2	Hide Your Heart	CD5	Germany	1988	$8.00
Columbia	651516-2	Hide Your Heart	CD5	U.K.	1988	$8.00
Columbia	CSK 1279	Hide Your Heart	CDJ	U.S.	1988	$2.00
Total	657711-2	Holding out for a Hero	CD5	Germany	1991	$8.00
Total	CDTYLER-10	Holding out for a Hero	CD5	U.K.	1991	$8.00
Old Gold	OG-6138	It's a Heartache	CD3	U.K.	1989	$10.00
Columbia	TYLERC-3	Notes From America	CD5	U.K.	1989	$8.00
Columbia	CSK 1366	Save Up All Your Tears	CDJ	U.S.	1988	$2.00
Columbia	655167-3	Total Eclipse of the Heart	CD3	Germany	1989	$8.00
Hansa	665211	Where Were You	CD5	Germany	1992	$8.00
Hansa	665211	Where Were You	CD5	U.K.	1992	$8.00

Tyner, McCoy

Full Length

Label	Catalog Number	Title	Type	Country	Year	Longbox Value / Value
Blue Note		Expansions	LTD/LP	U.S.	1995	$19.00
Milestone	FCD-9067	Fly With The Wind	LP/LB	U.S.†	1985	$14.00/$8.00

Singles

Label	Catalog Number	Title	Type	Country	Year	Longbox Value / Value
Verve	777	Turning Point	CDJ	U.S.	1992	$2.00

Type O Negative

Full Length

Label	Catalog Number	Title	Type	Country	Year	Longbox Value / Value
Attic	RR90032	Bloody Kisses	LTD/LP	Canada	1994	$25.00
		Bloody Kisses	LTD/LP	U.S.	1994	$18.00

CD in digipak with VHS video. .

Tyrrel Corp.

Singles

Label	Catalog Number	Title	Type	Country	Year	Longbox Value / Value
Cooltempo	FLYRCD 3	Six O'Clock	CD5	U.K.	1991	$8.00

Tyson, Moses

Singles

Label	Catalog Number	Title	Type	Country	Year	Longbox Value / Value
Curb	050	Deck of Cards	CDJ	U.S.		$2.00

Tyzik, Jeff

Full Length

Label	Catalog Number	Title	Type	Country	Year	Longbox Value / Value
Mercury	821605-2	Jammin' in Manhattan	LP/BP	U.S.†	1984	$14.00/$8.00
Mercury	827272-2	Smile	LP/BP	U.S.†	1985	$14.00/$8.00

U 96

Singles

Label	Catalog Number	Title	Type	Country	Year	Longbox Value / Value
Cohiba	22102	Das Boot	CDJ	U.S.	1992	$3.00

U.K. Bassheads

Singles

Label	Catalog Number	Title	Type	Country	Year	Longbox Value / Value
Capitol	C2 15829	Is There Anybody Out There	CD5	U.S.	1991	$5.00

U.K.G.

Singles

Label	Catalog Number	Title	Type	Country	Year	Longbox Value / Value
Jive	42121-2-RDJ	Use Me	CDJ	U.S.	1993	$2.00

U.N.V.

Singles

Label	Catalog Number	Title	Type	Country	Year	Longbox Value / Value
Maverick		Close Tonight	CDJ	U.S.	1993	$2.00
Maverick	9 18564-2	Something's Goin' On	CD5	U.S.	1993	$5.00
Maverick	PRO-CD-6071	Something's Goin' On	CDJ	U.S.	1993	$2.00
Maverick	PRO-CD-6162	Something's Goin' On	CDJ	U.S.	1993	$2.00
Maverick	PRO-CD-6340	Something's Goin' On	CDJ	U.S.	1993	$2.00
Maverick	PRO-CD-6501	Straight From the Heart	CDJ	U.S.	1993	$2.00

U Roy

Full Length

Label	Catalog Number	Title	Type	Country	Year	Longbox Value / Value
Caroline		Collector's Edition	LTD/ LP	U.K.	1994	$40.00

3 CD picture disc boxed set.

U.S.A. for Africa

Full Length

Label	Catalog Number	Title	Type	Country	Year	Longbox Value / Value
Pioneer	PA-85-M025	We Are the World	8"LD	U.S.	1985	$30.00
Polygram	824822-2	We Are the World	LP/ BP	U.S.†	1985	$15.00/$10.00

U-Krew

Singles

Label	Catalog Number	Title	Type	Country	Year	Longbox Value / Value
EMI	203882-2	If U Were Mine	CD5	U.K.	1990	$8.00
Enigma		If U Were Mine	CDJ	U.S.	1990	$2.00
Enigma	EPRO 291	Let Me Be Your Lover	CDJ	U.S.	1990	$2.00
Enigma		Ugly	CDJ	U.S.	1990	$2.00

U-Mynd

Singles

Label	Catalog Number	Title	Type	Country	Year	Longbox Value / Value
Luke	478	Prove My Love	CDJ	U.S.	1994	$2.00
Luke	472	Stop Look & Listen	CDJ	U.S.	1994	$2.00

U2

Full Length

Label	Catalog Number	Title	Type	Country	Year	Longbox Value / Value
Album Network		Album Network Special	RS	U.S.	1993	$150.00
		2 CD set. Airdate: 12/24/93.				
BBC Radio		BBC Classic Tracks	RS	U.S.	1991	$45.00
		Airdate: 6/3/91.				
BBC Radio		BBC Classic Tracks	RS	U.S.	1992	$45.00
		Airdate: 6/1/92.				
BBC Radio		BBC Classic Tracks	RS	U.S.	1993	$45.00
		Airdate: 3/1/93.				
Westwood One		BBC Classic Tracks	RS	U.S.	1993	$50.00
		Airdate: 12/13/93.				
Westwood One		BBC Classic Tracks	RS	U.S.	1994	$50.00
		Airdate: 5/16/94.				
Island	90040-2	Boy	LP/ LB	U.S.†	1985	$16.00/$12.00
		Digipak version.				
Island	U-2V 7	Excerpts From Rattle and Hum	DJ/ Smplr	U.S.	1989	$30.00
Island	PR 2677-2	God Part II	DJ/ Smplr	U.S.	1989	$40.00
Album Network		In the Studio (Achtung Baby)	RS	U.S.		$50.00
Album Network		In the Studio (Rattle and Hum)	RS	U.S.		$50.00
Island		Joshua Tree	DJ/ LP	U.K.		$125.00
		CD, cassette, and pres kit in custom box.				
		Live From Dublin	RS	U.S.	1993	$350.00
		3 CD set. Airdate: 9/4/93. Distributed to about 65 college radio stations.				
Polygram		Melon	DJ/ Smplr	U.K.	1994	$35.00
		"Propoganda" fan club issue remix CD.				
Island	90092-2	October	LP/ LB	U.S.†	1985	$16.00/$12.00
		Digipak version.				
Island		Previously	DJ/ Smplr	U.S.	1997	$35.00
Paramount	LV132228	Rattle and Hum	LD	U.S.	1989	$25.00
Polystar	HI-4001	Special Collection	DJ/ Smplr	Japan	1987	N/A
Island	PHR-8713	Stay	CD	Japan	1993	$20.00
Westwood One		Superstars	RS	U.S.	1994	$150.00
		2 CD set. Airdate: 11/28/94.				
		Transmit	RS	U.S.		$60.00
Island	90127-2	Under Blood Red Skies	LP/ LB	U.S.†	1986	$16.00/$12.00
		Digipak version.				
Island	90067-2	War	LP/ LB	U.S.†	1984	$14.00/$8.00
Unistar		Weekly Specials, The	RS	U.S.	1992	$50.00
		Airdate: 9/4/92.				
Westwood One		Zoo TV: Recorded Live In Sidney Australia	RS	U.S.	1994	$100.00
		2 CD set. Airdate: 5/9/94.				
		Zoo TV Special	RS	U.S.	1992	$80.00
		2 CD set.				
		Zooradio	RS	U.S.	1993	$120.00
		2 CD set. Airdate: 8/21/93.				
Island	518047-2	Zooropa	LP	Australia	1994	$27.00
		2 CD set in slipcase.				
Island		Zooropa	LP	U.S.	1992	$13.00
		Digitrak version.				
Westwood One		Zooropa	RS	U.S.	1993	$80.00
		2 CD set.				

Singles

Label	Catalog Number	Title	Type	Country	Year	Longbox Value / Value
Island	162406-2	All I Want Is You	CD3	Germany	1990	$12.00
Island	662406-2	All I Want Is You	CD5	Germany	1990	$20.00
Polystar	P09D-31005	All I Want Is You	CD3	Japan	1990	$25.00/$5.00
Island	P19D-10037	All I Want Is You	CD5	Japan	1990	$15.00
Island	CIDP-422	All I Want Is You	CD5	U.K.	1990	$20.00
Island	PR 2770-2	All I Want Is You	CDJ	U.S.	1990	$15.00
Island	3CID-96590	Angel of Harlem	CD5	Canada	1989	$20.00
Aris	885250-2	Angel of Harlem	CD3	Germany	1989	$20.00
Island	661920-2	Angel of Harlem	CD5	Germany	1989	$20.00
Polystar	P10D-30007	Angel of Harlem	CD3	Japan	1989	$18.00/$5.00
Island	P18D-20085	Angel of Harlem	CD5	Japan	1989	$12.00
Island	CIDP-402	Angel of Harlem	CD5	U.K.	1989	$20.00
Island	PR 2559-2	Angel of Harlem	CDJ	U.S.	1989	$20.00
Island	661670-2	Desire	CD5	Germany	1989	$12.00
Island	P10D-30006	Desire	CD3	Japan	1989	$18.00/$5.00
Island	P18D-20082	Desire	CD5	Japan	1989	$16.00
Island	CIDP-400	Desire	CD5	U.K.	1989	$12.00
Island	PR 2500-2	Desire	CDJ	U.S.	1988	$50.00
Island	PR 2500-2	Desire	CDJ	U.S.	1989	$25.00
Island		Discotheque	CD5	U.K.	1997	$10.00
Island		Discotheque	CD5	U.K.	1997	$10.00
		Second version.				
Island	854774-2	Discotheque	CD5	U.S.	1997	$4.00
Island	854789-2	Discotheque	CD5	U.S.	1997	$7.00
Island		Discotheque	CDJ	U.S.	1997	$8.00
Island	PHCR-12701	Even Better Than the Real Thing	CD5	Japan	1992	$15.00
		Even Better Than the Real Thing	CD5	U.K.	1992	$20.00
Island	86428-2	Even Better Than the Real Thing	CD5	U.S.	1992	$5.00
Island	866977-2	Even Better Than the Real Thing	CD5	U.S.	1992	$5.00
sland	PRCD 6723-2	Even Better Than the Real Thing	CDJ	U.S.	1992	$7.00
Island	PSDD-1102	Fly, The	CD3	Japan	1991	$18.00/$5.00
Island	PSCD-1182	Fly, The	CD5	Japan	1991	$15.00
Island	CID-500	Fly, The	CD5	U.K.	1991	$20.00
Island	PRCD 6680-2	Fly, The	CDJ	U.S.	1991	$7.00
Atlantic		Hold Me, Thrill Me, Kiss Me	CDJ	Germany	1995	$30.00
Atlantic		Hold Me, Thrill Me, Kiss Me	CD5	U.K.	1995	$14.00
Atlantic	87131-2	Hold Me, Thrill Me, Kiss Me	CD5	U.S.	1995	$6.00
Atlantic	2-87125	Hold Me, Thrill Me, Kiss Me	CD5	U.S.	1995	$20.00
		CD with comic book. Sold exclusively at WalMart.				
Island		Hold Me, Thrill Me, Kiss Me	CDJ	U.S.	1995	$14.00
Island		Hold Me, Thrill Me, Kiss Me	CDJ	U.S.	1995	$14.00
		Second version.				
Island	659152-2	I Still Haven't Found What I'm Looking For	CD5	Germany	1988	$12.00
Island	664987-2	I Still Haven't Found What I'm Looking For	CD5	Germany	1991	$20.00
Island	CIDP328	I Still Haven't Found What I'm Looking For	CD5	U.K.	1988	$12.00
Island		In the Name of the Father	CD5	U.K.	1994	$20.00
Island		In the Name of the Father	CDJ	U.S.	1994	$7.00
Island	422-878-389-2	Island Treasures	CD5	U.S.	1991	$6.00
Island	LEMCD1	Lemon	CDJ	U.K.	1993	$18.00
Island	PRCD 6800-2	Lemon	CDJ	U.S.	1993	$15.00
Island		Live, The	CD5	U.K.	1993	$20.00
Island	WG 659871	Missing Tracks	CD5	Germany	1988	$20.00
Island	WG 659871	Missing Tracks	CD5	U.K.	1988	$20.00
Island		Mysterious Ways	CDJ	Australia	1991	$25.00
Island	664930	Mysterious Ways	CD5	Germany	1991	$20.00
Island	CID 509	Mysterious Ways	CD5	U.K.	1991	$13.00
Island	PRCD 6698-2	Mysterious Ways	CDJ	U.S.	1991	$7.00
Island	PRCD 6701-2	Mysterious Ways	CDJ	U.S.	1991	$7.00
Island	664973	New Year's Day	CD5	Germany	1991	$20.00
Island	NUMCD1	Numb	CDJ	U.K.	1994	$20.00
Island	PRCD 6785-2	Numb	CDJ	U.S.	1994	$15.00
		Perfecto mix.				
Island	665164	One	CD5	Germany	1992	$14.00
Island	PHCR-8701	One	CD5	Japan	1992	$15.00
Island	CID-515	One	CD5	U.K.	1992	$14.00
Island	866533	One	CD5	U.S.	1992	$5.00
Island	PRCD 6806-2	One	CDJ	U.S.	1992	$7.00
Island	664975	Pride	CD5	Austria	1991	$20.00
Island		Staring At the Sun	CD5	U.K.	1997	$10.00

Label	Catalog Number	Title	Type	Country	Year	Longbox Value/Value
Island		Staring At the Sun	CD5	U.K.	1997	$10.00
	Second version.					
sland		Stay	CD5	U.K.	1993	$20.00
Island	CID 578	Stay	CDJ	U.K.	1993	$15.00
Island	422-858 097-2	Stay	CD5	U.S.	1993	$7.00
Island	PRCD 6806-2	Stay	CDJ	U.S.	1993	$7.00
Polygram	858097	Stay	CD5	U.S.	1994	$5.00
Island	664971	Sunday Bloody Sunday	CD5	Germany	1991	$20.00
Island		Swing, The	CD5	U.K.	1993	$20.00
Island	664974	Unforgettable Fire	CD5	Germany	1991	$20.00
Island	PSDD-1103	Until the End of the World	CD3	Japan	1991	$25.00/$5.00
lIsland	PRCD 6704-2	Until the End of the World	CDJ	U.S.	1991	$7.00
Island	162200	When Love Comes to Town	CD3	Germany	1989	$12.00
Island	662200-2	When Love Comes to Town	CD5	Germany	1989	$14.00
Polystar	P09D-31001	When Love Comes to Town	CD3	Japan	1989	$25.00/$5.00
Island	P19D-10019	When Love Comes to Town	CD5	Japan	1989	$15.00
Island	CIDP-411	When Love Comes to Town	CD5	U.K.	1989	$14.00
Island	PR 2659-2	When Love Comes to Town	CDJ	U.S.	1989	$7.00
Island	659382-2	Where the Streets Have No Name	CD5	Germany	1988	$15.00
Island	CIDP-340	Where the Streets Have No Name	CD5	U.K.	1988	$15.00
Island	PR 2104-2	Where the Streets Have No Name	CDJ	U.S.	1988	$40.00
Island	PHCR-8706	Who's Gonna Ride Your Wild Horses	CD5	Japan	1992	$15.00
		Who's Gonna Ride Your Wild Horses	CD5	U.K.		$20.00
		Who's Gonna Ride Your Wild Horses	CD5	U.K.		$20.00
	Second version.					
Island	864521	Who's Gonna Ride Your Wild Horses	CD5	U.S.	1992	$5.00
Island	PRCD 6744-2	Who's Gonna Ride Your Wild Horses	CDJ	U.S.	1992	$7.00
Island	658922-2	With or Without You	CD5	Germany	1988	$20.00
Island	CIDP-319	With or Without You	CD5	U.K.	1988	$12.00
Island/NTSC		With or Without You	CDV	U.K.	1988	$125.00
	Withdrawn disc.					
Island/NTSC	IS 319	With or Without You	DJ/CDV	U.S.	1988	$200.00
Island	422 878 389-2	With or Without You	CD5	U.S.	1990	$20.00
Island	PRCD 6792-2	Zooropa	CDJ	U.S.	1993	$8.00

UB40

Full Length

Label	Catalog Number	Title	Type	Country	Year	Longbox Value/Value
Virgin		Best of	DJ/Smplr	U.S.	1995	$15.00
A&M	LV38404	CCCP-The Video Mix	LD	U.S.	1989	$30.00
Westwood One		In Concert	RS	U.S.	1993	$45.00
	Airdate: 7/19/93.					
Virgin	UBCDJ 94	Reggae Music	DJ/Smplr	U.K.	1994	$20.00
	With calender.					
Unistar		Weekly Specials, The	RS	U.S.	1991	$15.00
	Airdate: 7/5/91.					

Singles

Label	Catalog Number	Title	Type	Country	Year	Longbox Value/Value
Virgin	661569	Breakfast in Bed	CD5	Germany	1988	$10.00
Virgin	VJD-10006	Breakfast in Bed	CD3	Japan	1988	$12.00/$4.00
Virgin	DEPX-29	Breakfast in Bed	CD5	U.K.	1988	$10.00
A&M	CD 17595	Breakfast in Bed	CDJ	U.S.	1988	$3.00
A&M	CD 17648	Breakfast in Bed	CDJ	U.S.	1988	$3.00
		Bring Me Your Cup	CD5	U.K.		$10.00
		Bring Me Your Cup	CD5	U.K.		$10.00
	Second version.					
Virgin	DPRO-14126	C'est La Vie	CDJ	U.S.		$3.00
Virgin	VJDP-10206	Can't Help Falling in Love	CD3	Japan	1993	$12.00/$4.00
Virgin	DEPX-31	Come Out to Play	CD3	U.K.	1988	$10.00
Virgin	PRCD 4202	Groovin'	CDJ	U.S.	1989	$2.00
Virgin	DEPX-34	Here I Am (Come and Take Me)	CD3	U.K.	1990	$10.00
Virgin	PRCD 3038	Here I Am (Come and Take Me)	CDJ	U.S.	1989	$3.00
Virgin	PRCD 3671	Here I Am (Come and Take Me)	CDJ	U.S.	1989	$3.00
Virgin	DEPX 41	Higher Ground	CD5	U.K.	1993	$10.00
Virgin	C2 38405	Higher Ground	CD5	U.S.	1993	$5.00
Virgin	DPRO-12811	Higher Ground	CDJ	U.S.	1993	$7.00
Virgin	662768	Homely Girl	CD5	Germany	1989	$10.00
Virgin	DEPX-33	Homely Girl	CD3	U.K.	1989	$10.00
Virgin	DEPX-32	I Would Lie for You	CD3	U.K.	1989	$10.00
Virgin	DEPCD-32	I Would Lie for You	CD5	U.K.	1989	$10.00
Virgin	663085	Kingston	CD5	Germany	1990	$10.00
Virgin	DEPTX-35	Kingston	CD5	U.K.	1990	$10.00
Virgin	PRCD 3317	Kingston	CDJ	U.S.	1989	$3.00
Virgin	38526	Kingston Town	CD5	U.S.	1995	$5.00
A&M	CD 17619	Red Red Wine	CDJ	U.S.	1990	$3.00
BMG	663538	Way You Do the Things You Do	CD5	Germany	1991	$10.00
Virgin	DEPXT-38	Way You Do the Things You Do	CD5	U.K.	1991	$10.00
Virgin	PRCD 3262	Way You Do the Things You Do	CDJ	U.S.	1989	$3.00
Virgin	DEPXT-36	Wear You to the Ball	CD5	U.K.	1990	$10.00
Virgin	PRCD 3607	Wear You to the Ball	CDJ	U.S.	1989	$3.00
Virgin	661704	Where Did I Go Wrong	CD5	Germany	1988	$10.00
Virgin	DEPX-30	Where Did I Go Wrong	CD5	U.K.	1988	$10.00
Virgin	PRCD 17703	Where Did I Go Wrong	CDJ	U.S.	1989	$3.00

UDO

Full Length

Label	Catalog Number	Title	Type	Country	Year	Longbox Value/Value
RCA		Faceless World	LP/BP	U.S.		$12.00/$7.00

UFO

Full Length

Label	Catalog Number	Title	Type	Country	Year	Longbox Value/Value
Metal Blade		Ain't Misbehaving	LP/LB	U.S.		$12.00/$7.00
Chrysalis		Strangers in the Night	LTD/LP	U.K.	1994	$15.00
	25th Anniversary edition in 6"x11" longbox.					

Singles

Label	Catalog Number	Title	Type	Country	Year	Longbox Value/Value
Metal Blade	157	Between a Rock and a Hard Place	CDJ	U.S.	1989	$2.00

Ugly Kid Joe

Full Length

Label	Catalog Number	Title	Type	Country	Year	Longbox Value/Value
Westwood One		In Concert	RS	U.S.	1993	$40.00
	Airdate: 6/7/93.					

Singles

Label	Catalog Number	Title	Type	Country	Year	Longbox Value/Value
Stardog	CDP 789	Busy Bee	CDJ	U.S.	1993	$3.00
Mercury		Cat's in the Cradle	CD5	U.K.	1992	$10.00
Stardog	CDP 813	Cat's in the Cradle	CDJ	U.S.	1992	$3.00
Stardog		Cat's in the Cradle	CDJ	U.S.	1992	$3.00
Stardog	PHDR-113	Everything About You	CD3	Japan	1992	$12.00/$4.00
Mercury	MERCD-367	Everything About You	CD5	U.K.	1992	$10.00
Stardog	CDP 584	Everything About You	CDJ	U.S.	1991	$3.00
Stardog	CDP 788	Goddamn Devil	CDJ	U.S.	1992	$3.00
Stardog	CDP 640	Madman	CDJ	U.S.	1992	$3.00
Mercury	MERCD-374	Neighbor	CD5	U.K.	1992	$10.00
Stardog		Neighbor	CDJ	U.S.	1992	$3.00
Stardog	CDP 566	So Damn Good	CDJ	U.S.	1992	$3.00
Stardog	CDP 566	Sweet Loaf	CDJ	U.S.	1992	$3.00

Uk Apachi W

Singles

Label	Catalog Number	Title	Type	Country	Year	Longbox Value/Value
Moonshine Music	88411	Original Nutta	CD5	U.S.	1994	$5.00

Ultimate Kaos

Singles

Label	Catalog Number	Title	Type	Country	Year	Longbox Value/Value
Motown	860395	Some Girls	CD5	U.S.	1995	$5.00

Ultimate Kiss

Singles

Label	Catalog Number	Title	Type	Country	Year	Longbox Value/Value
		Some Girls	CDJ	U.S.		$2.00

Ultra Bide

Singles

Label	Catalog Number	Title	Type	Country	Year	Longbox Value/Value
AlternateTenacles	158	Ultra Bide	CD5	U.S.	1994	$5.00

Ultra Nate

Singles

Label	Catalog Number	Title	Type	Country	Year	Longbox Value/Value
Warner Brothers	41415	How Long	CD5	U.S.	1994	$5.00
Warner Brothers	9 40007-2	Is It Love	CD5	U.S.	1991	$5.00
Warner Brothers	9 40955-2	Joy	CD5	U.S.	1993	$5.00
Warner Brothers	PRO-CD-6312	Joy	CDJ	U.S.	1993	$2.00
Warner Brothers	9 41207-2	Show Me	CD5	U.S.	1993	$5.00
Warner Brothers	PRO-CD-6601	Show Me	CDJ	U.S.	1993	$2.00
Warner Brothers	41207	Show Me Remix	CD5	U.S.	1994	$5.00

Ultra Vivid Scene

Singles

Label	Catalog Number	Title	Type	Country	Year	Longbox Value/Value
4AD	BAD3003	Blood and Thunder	CD5	U.K.	1993	$8.00
Chaos	4826	Blood and Thunder	CDJ	U.S.	1992	$2.00
Chaos	74841	Blood and Thunder	CDJ	U.S.	1993	$2.00
4AD	806	She Screamed	CD5	U.K.	1988	$8.00
Columbia	44K 73534	Special One	CD5	U.S.	1990	$5.00
4AD	BAD3004	Staring at the Sun	CD5	U.K.	1993	$8.00

Ultramagnetic M.C.s

Singles

Label	Catalog Number	Title	Type	Country	Year	Longbox Value/Value
Mercury	CDP 605	Make It Happen	CDJ	U.S.	1991	$6.00

Ultramarine

Singles

Label	Catalog Number	Title	Type	Country	Year	Longbox Value/Value
Sire	PRO-CD-6526	Happy Land	CDJ	U.S.	1993	$2.00

Ultravox

Full Length

Label	Catalog Number	Title	Type	Country	Year	Longbox Value/Value
Chrysalis	VK-41490	Collection, The	LP/LB	U.S.†	1985	$14.00/$8.00
Chrysalis		Vienna	LTD/LP	U.K.	1994	$25.00/$15.00
	25th Anniversary edition in 6"x11" longbox.					
Chrysalis	VK-41296	Vienna	LP/LB	U.S.†	1985	$14.00/$8.00

Singles

Label	Catalog Number	Title	Type	Country	Year	Longbox Value/Value
		Vienna	CD5	U.K.		$10.00
		Vienna	CD5	U.K.		$10.00
	Second version.					

Uncanny Alliance

Singles

Label	Catalog Number	Title	Type	Country	Year	Longbox Value/Value
A&M	31458 8077	I Got My Education	CDJ	U.S.	1992	$2.00
A&M	31458 8209	I'm Beautiful Dammit!	CDJ	U.S.	1993	$2.00

Uncle Green

Singles

Label	Catalog Number	Title	Type	Country	Year	Longbox Value/Value
Atlantic	PRCD 4495-2	I Know All About You	CDJ	U.S.	1992	$2.00

Uncle Tupelo

Full Length

Label	Catalog Number	Title	Type	Country	Year	Longbox Value/Value
Sire	PRO-CD-6727	Long Cut, The	DJ/Smplr	U.S.		$20.00
Reprise		Long Cut, The	DJ/Smplr	U.S.	1994	$8.00
Sire	PRO-CD-6546	Give Back the Key to My Heart	CDJ	U.S.	1993	$2.00

Under The Noise

Singles

Label	Catalog Number	Title	Type	Country	Year	Longbox Value/Value
	13	Future Automatic	CD5	U.S.	1994	$5.00

Underneath What

Singles

Label	Catalog Number	Title	Type	Country	Year	Longbox Value/Value
Atco	PR 3222-2	Firebomb Telecom	CDJ	U.S.	1989	$2.00
WEA	YZ-456CD	Their Heads Exploded	CD5	U.K.	1990	$8.00

Undertones

Full Length

Label	Catalog Number	Title	Type	Country	Year	Longbox Value/Value
Rykodisc		Best of the Undertones	DJ/Smplr	U.S.	1994	$25.00

Singles

Label	Catalog Number	Title	Type	Country	Year	Longbox Value/Value
Strange Fruit	016	Peel Sessions	CD5	U.K.	1989	$10.00

Underworld

Singles

Label	Catalog Number	Title	Type	Country	Year	Longbox Value/Value
Sire	PRO-CD-3823	Change in the Weather	CDJ	U.S.	1989	$2.00
TeeVee Records	8722	Cowgirl	CD5	U.S.	1994	$5.00
TeeVee Tunes	8722	Cowgirl	CD5	U.S.	1994	$5.00
	8722-2	Dirty Epic	CD5	U.S.	1996	$5.00
Sire	PRO-CD-3084	Glory! Glory! Glory!	CDJ	U.S.	1988	$2.00
	8748-2	Pearl's Gate	CD5	U.S.	1997	$9.00
Sire	PRO-CD-3191	Show Some Emotion	CDJ	U.S.	1988	$2.00
WEA	921284-2	Stand Up	CD3	Germany	1989	$8.00
WEA	W-2854CD	Stand Up	CD3	U.K.	1989	$8.00
Sire	PRO-CD-3639	Stand Up	CDJ	U.S.	1989	$2.00
Sire	PRO-CD-2942	Underneath the Radar	CDJ	U.S.	1988	$2.00

Union

Singles

Label	Catalog Number	Title	Type	Country	Year	Longbox Value/Value
Jive	JIVECD-309	You Are the No.1	CD5	U.K.	1992	$8.00

Unity 2

Singles

Label	Catalog Number	Title	Type	Country	Year	Longbox Value/Value
WEA	W-7968CD	Shirlee	CD5	U.K.	1990	$8.00
Warner Brothers	PRO-CD-3818	Shirlee	CDJ	U.S.	1989	$2.00

Universe

Full Length

Label	Catalog Number	Title	Type	Country	Year	Longbox Value/Value
Zoo	11008	Universe	LP/LB	U.S.		$9.00/$6.00

Unrest

Full Length

Label	Catalog Number	Title	Type	Country	Year	Longbox Value/Value
4AD	PRO-CD-6787	Cath Carroll	DJ/Smplr	U.S.	1993	$12.00
4AD	45401-2	Perfect Teeth	DJ/LP	U.S.	1994	$12.00

Singles

Label	Catalog Number	Title	Type	Country	Year	Longbox Value/Value
4AD	PRO-CD-6535	Make Out Club	CDJ	U.S.	1993	$3.00

Unsane

Singles

Label	Catalog Number	Title	Type	Country	Year	Longbox Value/Value
Matador	74	Peel Sessions	CD5	U.S.	1994	$5.00

Untouchables

Singles

Label	Catalog Number	Title	Type	Country	Year	Longbox Value / Value
Enigma	EPRO-095	Under the Boardwalk	CDJ	U.S.	1988	$3.00

UNV

Singles

Label	Catalog Number	Title	Type	Country	Year	Longbox Value / Value
Warner Brothers	17743	What's It Like	CD5	U.S.	1995	$5.00

Ups & Downs

Singles

Label	Catalog Number	Title	Type	Country	Year	Longbox Value / Value
Nettwerk	6312	Rash	CD5	U.S.	1991	$5.00

Uptown Horns

Full Length

Label	Catalog Number	Title	Type	Country	Year	Longbox Value / Value
Collector's Pipeline	TCP 017CD	Uptown Horns Revue	LP	U.S.		$16.00

Urban Dance Squad

Full Length

Label	Catalog Number	Title	Type	Country	Year	Longbox Value / Value
Arista	ASCD-2150	Hollywood Live	DJ/Smplr	U.S.	1990	$15.00
Arista	ASCD-2150	Live	DJ/Smplr	U.S.	1990	$25.00

Singles

Label	Catalog Number	Title	Type	Country	Year	Longbox Value / Value
Ariola	664632	Bureaucrat of Flaccostreet	CD5	U.K.	1992	$9.00
Arista	ASCD 2354	Bureaucrat of Flaccostreet	CDJ	U.S.	1991	$3.00
Arista	ASCD 2360	Clashing Perspectives	CDJ	U.S.	1991	$6.00
Ariola	663180	Deeper Shade of Soul	CD5	Germany	1990	$10.00
Ariola	663180	Deeper Shade of Soul	CD5	U.K.	1990	$10.00
Arista		Deeper Shade of Soul	CDJ	U.S.	1990	$7.00
Ariola	663661	No Kid	CD5	U.K.	1990	$9.00
Arista	ASCD 2395	Routine	CDJ	U.S.	1992	$3.00

Urban Soul

Singles

Label	Catalog Number	Title	Type	Country	Year	Longbox Value / Value
Chrysalis	DPRO-23712	Alright	CDJ	U.S.	1991	$2.00

Urban Species

Singles

Label	Catalog Number	Title	Type	Country	Year	Longbox Value / Value
		Brother	CD5	U.K.		$10.00
		Brother	CD5	U.K.		$10.00
Second version.						

Ure, Midge

Singles

Label	Catalog Number	Title	Type	Country	Year	Longbox Value / Value
RCA	62033-2-RDJ	Cold, Cold Heart	CDJ	U.S.	1991	$3.00

Urge Overkill

Full Length

Label	Catalog Number	Title	Type	Country	Year	Longbox Value / Value
		Exit the Dragon	LTD/LP	Austraila	1995	$28.00
2 CD set.						
		Stay Tuned 1988-1991	DJ/Smplr	U.S.	1995	$12.00
	UOSAMP	Urge Overkill Story, The	DJ/Smplr	U.S.	1993	$12.00

Singles

Label	Catalog Number	Title	Type	Country	Year	Longbox Value / Value
Geffen	PRO-CD-4626	Bottle of Fur	CDJ	U.S.	1994	$3.00
		Break, The	CDJ	U.S.		$3.00
Geffen		Girl You'll Be a Woman Soon	CDJ	U.S.		$6.00
		Girl You'll Be a Woman Soon	CDJ	U.S.	1995	$3.00
Geffen	PRO-CD-4527	Positive Bleeding	CDJ	U.S.	1993	$3.00
Geffen	PRO CD 4527	Sister Havana	CDJ	U.S.	1994	$3.00

Urgent

Singles

Label	Catalog Number	Title	Type	Country	Year	Longbox Value / Value
		I Can't Take It No More	CDJ	U.S.		$2.00

Uriah Heep

Full Length

Label	Catalog Number	Title	Type	Country	Year	Longbox Value / Value
Enigma		Raging Silence	LP/LB	U.S.		$14.00/$8.00

Singles

Label	Catalog Number	Title	Type	Country	Year	Longbox Value / Value
BMG	653007	Lady in Black	CD5	Germany	1989	$10.00

Us3

Singles

Label	Catalog Number	Title	Type	Country	Year	Longbox Value / Value
Blue Note	58053	Cantaloop	CD5	U.S.	1994	$5.00
Capital	58083	Cantaloop	CD5	U.S.	1994	$5.00
Blue Note	DPRO-79774	Cantaloop	CDJ	U.S.	1994	$6.00
		I Got It Goin' Up	CD5	U.K.		$10.00
		I Got It Goin' Up	CD5	U.K.		$10.00
Second version.						
RCA		Manhattan	SCD5	Germany	1996	$35.00
Statue Of Liberty shaped disc.						
EMI	80764	Yukka Yoot's Riddim	CD5	Holland	1993	$10.00
Blue Note	DPRO-79326	Yukka Yoot's Riddim	CDJ	U.S.	1994	$6.00

Usher

Singles

Label	Catalog Number	Title	Type	Country	Year	Longbox Value / Value
LaFace	24052	Call Me a Mack	CDJ	U.S.	1993	$2.00
		Comin' for Christmas	CDJ	U.S.		$2.00
Arista	24095	Think of You	CD5	U.S.	1994	$5.00

Utah Saints

Singles

Label	Catalog Number	Title	Type	Country	Year	Longbox Value / Value
London	8571452	Believe in Me	CD5	Canada	1994	$8.00
		I Want You	CD5	U.K.		$10.00
		I Want You	CD5	U.K.		$10.00
Second version.						
Polygram	CDP 815	I Want You	CDJ	U.S.	1992	$2.00
ffrr	FCD-187	Something Good	CD5	U.K.	1992	$8.00
Polygram	CDP 811	Something Good	CDJ	U.S.	1992	$2.00
London	857 103	What Can You Do for Me	CD5	U.S.	1993	$5.00
London	CDP 871	What Can You Do for Me	CDJ	U.S.	1993	$2.00

Utopia

Full Length

Label	Catalog Number	Title	Type	Country	Year	Longbox Value / Value
Passport	PBCD 6029	Oblivion	LP	U.S.	1983	$100.00
Passport	PBCD 6029	Oblivion	LP/LB	U.S.†	1984	$55.00/$50.00
Rhino		Oops! Wrong Planet	LP/LB	U.S.		$14.00/$8.00
Castle	TFO 9/1 & 9/2	Oops! Wrong Planet & Adventures In Utopia	LP	France	1988	$40.00
2 CD set.						
Passport	PBCD 6044	POV	LP	U.S.	1985	$60.00
Passport	PBCD 6044	POV	LP/LB	U.S.†	1985	$55.00/$50.00
		Ra	LP	U.K.		$15.00
		Redux '92 Live in Japan	LP	U.S.		$10.00
Rhino		Swing to the Right	LP/LB	U.S.		$14.00/$8.00
Passport	PBCD 6053	Trivia	LP	U.S.	1986	$100.00
Passport	PBCD 6053	Trivia	LP/LB	U.S.	1986	$55.00/$50.00

V

Singles

Label	Catalog Number	Title	Type	Country	Year	Longbox Value / Value
Capitol	C2 15938	Washed Away	CD5	U.S.	1991	$5.00

Vai, Steve

Singles

Label	Catalog Number	Title	Type	Country	Year	Longbox Value / Value
Relativity	IRPROCD-0110	Audience is Listening	CDJ	U.S.	1990	$6.00
Relativity	IRPROCD-0117	For the Love of God	CDJ	U.S.	1991	$7.00
Relativity	0219	In My Dreams	CDJ	U.S.	1993	$2.00
Interscope	PRCD 4075-2	Reaper, The	CDJ	U.S.	1991	$6.00
Interscope	PRCD 4271-2	Reaper, The	CDJ	U.S.	1991	$12.00
Picturedisc CD.						

Vain

Full Length

Label	Catalog Number	Title	Type	Country	Year	Longbox Value / Value
		No Respect	DJ/LP	U.S.	1988	$12.00
CD in press kit.						

Singles

Label	Catalog Number	Title	Type	Country	Year	Longbox Value / Value
Island		1000 Degrees	CDJ	U.S.	1988	$3.00
Island	CIDX-432	Beat the Bullet	CD5	U.K.	1989	$7.00
Island	PR 2793-2	Beat the Bullet	CDJ	U.S.	1989	$3.00
Island	PR-3111-2	Who's Watching You	CDJ	U.S.	1988	$6.00

Valdy

Full Length

Label	Catalog Number	Title	Type	Country	Year	Longbox Value / Value
		Double Solitaire	DJ/Intvw	Canada		$10.00

Vale

Singles

Label	Catalog Number	Title	Type	Country	Year	Longbox Value / Value
Atlantic	PRCD 4662-2	Love Plus Love	CDJ	U.S.	1992	$2.00
Atlantic	PRCD 4529-2	Remember	CDJ	U.S.	1992	$2.00
Atlantic	PRCD 4917-2	Waiting in the Wings	CDJ	U.S.	1992	$2.00
Atlantic	PRCD 4833-2	Waiting in the Wings	CDJ	U.S.	1992	$2.00

Vale, Jerry

Singles

Label	Catalog Number	Title	Type	Country	Year	Longbox Value / Value
CBS	66906	Love Me the Way I Like	CD5	U.S.	1994	$5.00

Valentin, Dave

Full Length

Label	Catalog Number	Title	Type	Country	Year	Longbox Value / Value
GRP	D-9508	Kalahari	LP/LB	U.S.†	1985	$14.00/$8.00

Valentine

Full Length

Label	Catalog Number	Title	Type	Country	Year	Longbox Value / Value
Giant	9 24404-2-Dj	Valentine	DJ/LP	U.S.	1991	$8.00
Picture disc.						

Singles

Label	Catalog Number	Title	Type	Country	Year	Longbox Value / Value
Giant		No Way	CDJ	U.S.	1991	$2.00
Giant		Runnin' on Luck Again	CDJ	U.S.	1991	$2.00

Valentine, Cindy

Singles

Label	Catalog Number	Title	Type	Country	Year	Longbox Value / Value
		Pick up the Pieces	CDJ	U.S.		$2.00

Valentine Saloon

Full Length

Label	Catalog Number	Title	Type	Country	Year	Longbox Value / Value
Collector's Pipeline	PIPE CD 001	Super Duper	LP	U.S.	1992	$16.00
Collector's Pipeline	DBAWCD001	Under My Skin E.P.	LP	U.S.	1992	$16.00

Vallejo, Orlando

Singles

Label	Catalog Number	Title	Type	Country	Year	Longbox Value / Value
	11453	Serie De Platino	CD5	U.S.	1994	$5.00

Vamp

Singles

Label	Catalog Number	Title	Type	Country	Year	Longbox Value / Value
Atlantic	PR 3063-2	Heartbreak, Heartache	CDJ	U.S.	1989	$2.00

Van Gogh's Daughter

Full Length

Label	Catalog Number	Title	Type	Country	Year	Longbox Value / Value
Hollywood		Shove	DJ/LP	U.S.	1995	$15.00

Van Halen

Full Length

Label	Catalog Number	Title	Type	Country	Year	Longbox Value / Value
Warner Brothers	23985-2	1984	LP/LB	U.S.†	1984	$14.00/$8.00
Warner Brothers	2-46332-DJ	Best Of	DJ/LP	U.S.	1996	$35.00
CD in silver foil digipak and black slip case.						
Warner Brothers	3677-2	Diver Down	LP/LB	U.S.†	1984	$14.00/$8.00
Warner Brothers	PRO-CD-7368	Don't Tell Me (What Love Can Do)	DJ/Smplr	U.S.	1996	$6.00
Warner Brothers		For Unlawful Carnal Knowledge	LTD/LP	U.K.	1995	$45.00
CD and video in box.						
Warner Brothers	9 26594-2	For Unlawful Carnal Knowledge	LP/LB	U.S.	1991	$15.00/$10.00
First pressing with phone numbers listed in chalk board photo in booklet.						
Album Network		In the Studio (For Unlawful Carnal Knowledge)	RS	U.S.	1991	$25.00
Airdate: 12/20/91.						
Album Network		In the Studio (OU812)	RS	U.S.	1988	$25.00
Airdate: 12/26/88.						
Warner Brothers		Live: Right Here, Right Now.	LTD/LP	Japan	1993	$37.00
3 CD set.						
Warner Brothers	9 45198-2-Dj	Live: Right Here, Right Now.	DJ/LP	U.S.	1993	$30.00
2 CD set.						
Westwood One		Off the Record	RS	U.S.	1994	$40.00
Airdate: 1/17/94.						
Westwood One		Off the Record	RS	U.S.	1995	$30.00
Airdate: 3/27/95.						
Westwood One		Off the Record	RS	U.S.	1995	$30.00
Airdate: 8/28/95.						
Warner Brothers	PRO-CD-6154	Selections From: Right Here, Right Now	DJ/Smplr	U.S.	1993	$12.00
Westwood One		Standing on top of the World	RS	U.S.	1993	$60.00
3 CD set. Airdate: 8/16/93.						
Westwood One		Superstar Concert	RS	U.S.	1993	$50.00
2 CD set. Airdate: 5/31/93.						
Westwood One		Superstar Concert	RS	U.S.	1994	$50.00
2 CD set. Airdate: 3/7/94.						
Westwood One		Superstars	RS	U.S.	1995	$65.00
2 CD set. Airdate: 3/6/95.						
Westwood One		Superstars	RS	U.S.	1995	$65.00
2 CD set. Airdate: 8/1/94.						
Media America		Up Close	RS	U.S.	1995	$75.00
3 CD set.						
Warner Brothers	3075-2	Van Halen	LP/LB	U.S.†	1985	$14.00/$8.00
WEA	38290	Van Halen Live: Right Here, Right Now	LD	U.S.	1993	$35.00

Singles

Label	Catalog Number	Title	Type	Country	Year	Longbox Value / Value
Warner Brothers	W0302CDX	Amsterdam	CD5	U.K.	1995	$12.00
CD in round tin.						
Warner Brothers		Amsterdam	CDJ	U.S.	1995	$7.00

Label	Catalog Number	Title	Type	Country	Year	Longbox Value / Value
Warner Brothers	10SW-53	Black & Blue	CD3	Japan	1988	$18.00/$5.00
Warner Brothers	PRO-CD-3085	Black & Blue	CDJ	U.S.	1988	$3.00
Warner Brothers	17909	Can't Stop Lovin' You	CD5	U.S.	1994	$5.00
Warner Brothers	PRO-CD-7470-R	Can't Stop Lovin' You	CDJ	U.S.	1995	$7.00
Warner Brothers	PRO-CD-7368	Don't Tell Me	CDJ	U.S.	1995	$7.00
Warner Brothers	PRO-CD-6158	Dreams	CDJ	U.S.	1993	$3.00
Warner Brothers	PRO-CD-7784-R	Feelin'	CDJ	U.S.	1995	$6.00
Warner Brothers	921177-2	Feels so Good	CD3	Germany	1989	$10.00
Warner Brothers	W-7565CD	Feels so Good	CD3	U.K.	1989	$10.00
Warner Brothers	PRO-CD-3279	Feels so Good	CDJ	U.S.	1988	$3.00
Warner Brothers	PRO-CD-3422	Feels so Good	CDJ	U.S.	1988	$3.00
Pioneer	10P3-6095	Finish What Ya Started	CD5	Japan	1989	$15.00
Warner Brothers	PRO-CD-3240	Finish What Ya Started	CDJ	U.S.	1988	$3.00
Warner Brothers	PRO-CD-8200-R	Human Beings	CDJ	U.S.		$6.00
		Jump	CD5	U.K.		$10.00
	Second version.					
Warner Brothers	9362-40771-2	Jump	CD5	U.K.	1993	$12.00
Warner Brothers	PRO-CD-7681	Not Enough	CDJ	U.S.		$6.00
Warner Brothers	PRO-CD-7838-R	Not Enough	CDJ	U.S.		$6.00
Warner Brothers	PRO-CD-7664-R	Not Enough	CDJ	U.S.	1995	$7.00
Warner Brothers	9362-40126-2	Poundcake	CD5	Germany	1991	$10.00
Warner Brothers	WPDP-6283	Poundcake	CD3	Japan	1991	$18.00/$5.00
Warner Brothers	W-0045CD	Poundcake	CD5	U.K.	1991	$10.00
Warner Brothers	PRO-CD-4884	Poundcake	CDJ	U.S.	1991	$3.00
Warner Brothers	PRO-CD-5150	Right Now	CDJ	U.S.	1991	$3.00
Warner Brothers	PRO-CD-4922	Runaround	CDJ	U.S.	1991	$7.00
Warner Brothers	W-0066CD	Top of the World	CD5	U.K.	1991	$10.00
Warner Brothers	PRO-CD-5027	Top of the World	CDJ	U.S.	1991	$3.00
Warner Brothers	17909	Van Halen	CD5	U.S.	1994	$5.00
Warner Brothers	921007-2	When It's Love	CD5	Germany	1988	$10.00
Warner Brothers	W-7816CD	When It's Love	CD5	U.K.	1988	$10.00
Warner Brothers	PRO-CD-3142	When It's Love	CDJ	U.S.	1988	$3.00
Warner Brothers	PRO-CD-5961	Won't Get Fooled Again	CDJ	U.S.	1993	$3.00

Van Hook, Lament

Singles

Label	Catalog Number	Title	Type	Country	Year	Value
		You Were My 911	CDJ	U.S.		$2.00

Van Shelton, Ricky

Full Length

Label	Catalog Number	Title	Type	Country	Year	Value
Image	ID7944CB	To Be Continued	LD	U.S.		$20.00

Singles

Label	Catalog Number	Title	Type	Country	Year	Value
Columbia	CSK 77130	A Couple of Good Years Left	CDJ	U.S.	1993	$3.00
Columbia	CSK 74104	After the Lights Go Out	CDJ	U.S.	1991	$2.00

Van Tieghem, David

Full Length

Label	Catalog Number	Title	Type	Country	Year	Value
Private	2015	Safety In Numbers	LP/LB	U.S.		$14.00/$8.00

Van Zant, Johnny

Full Length

Label	Catalog Number	Title	Type	Country	Year	Value
Atlantic		Brickyard Road	LP/LB	U.S.		$14.00/$8.00

Singles

Label	Catalog Number	Title	Type	Country	Year	Value
Atlantic	PRCD 3383-2	Brickyard Road	CDJ	U.S.	1990	$2.00
Atlantic	PRCD 3568-2	Hearts Are Gonna Roll	CDJ	U.S.	1990	$2.00
Atlantic	PRCD 3714-2	Love is Not Enough	CDJ	U.S.	1990	$2.00

Vandross & Carey

Singles

Label	Catalog Number	Title	Type	Country	Year	Value
Epic	660702 2	Endless Love	CD5	Germany	1994	$15.00
Columbia	44K-77637	Endless Love	CD5	U.S.	1994	$6.00

Vandross, Luther

Full Length

Label	Catalog Number	Title	Type	Country	Year	Value
Epic	ESM 5068	1993 Commemorative NARM Mini-Disc Sampler	LP	U.S.	1993	$25.00
	Minidisc.					
Epic	EK-39196	Busy Body	LP/LB	U.S.†	1984	$14.00/$8.00
Epic	ESM 5068	Commemorative 1993 Sampler	DJ/Smplr	U.S.	1993	$20.00
	Minidisc.					
Epic	EK-39882	Night I Fell In Love	LP/LB	U.S.†	1985	$14.00/$8.00

Singles

Label	Catalog Number	Title	Type	Country	Year	Value
CBS	7735	Always and Forever	CD5	U.S.	1994	$5.00
Epic	LUTHC-8	Any Love	CD3	U.K.	1988	$9.00
Epic	CDLUTH-8	Any Love	CD5	U.K.	1988	$9.00
Epic	CDLUTH-11	Any Love	CD5	U.K.	1989	$9.00
Epic	ESK 1290	Any Love	CDJ	U.S.	1988	$2.00
Perspective	587400-2	Best Things in Life Are Free	CD5	Germany	1992	$9.00
Perspective	PERD-7400	Best Things in Life Are Free	CD5	U.K.	1992	$9.00
A&M	75021 7406 2	Best Things in Life Are Free	CD5	U.S.	1992	$2.00
Epic	CDLUTH-10	Come Back	CD5	U.K.	1989	$9.00
Epic	657399-5	Don't Want to be a Fool	CD5	U.K.	1991	$9.00
Epic	ESK 73879	Don't Want to be a Fool	CDJ	U.S.	1991	$2.00
Epic	ESK 4139	Don't Want to be a Fool	CDJ	U.S.	1991	$2.00
Epic	CDLUTH-5	Give Me the Reason	CD5	U.K.	1988	$9.00
CBS	77755	Going in Circles	CD5	U.S.	1994	$5.00
Epic	ESK 74738	Heart of a Hero	CDJ	U.S.	1993	$2.00
Epic	ESK 74996	Heaven Knows	CDJ	U.S.	1993	$2.00
Epic	CDLUTH-13	Here and Now	CD5	U.K.	1989	$9.00
Epic	CDLUTH-6	I Gave It Up	CD5	U.K.	1988	$9.00
Epic	CSK 2740	I Really Didn't Mean It	CDJ	U.S.	1987	$2.00
Epic	ESK 74945	Little Miracles	CDJ	U.S.		$2.00
Epic		Love Won't Let Me Wait	CDJ	U.S.		$2.00
Atlantic	PRCD 96247-2	May Christmas Bring You Happiness	CD5	U.S.	1991	$5.00
Atlantic	PRCD 4279-2	May Christmas Bring You Happiness	CDJ	U.S.	1991	$2.00
Epic	CDLUTH-12	Never Too Much	CD5	U.K.	1989	$9.00
Epic	656822-2	Power of Love/Love Power	CD5	Germany	1991	$9.00
Epic	656962-2	Power of Love/Love Power	CD5	Germany	1991	$9.00
Epic	656822-2	Power of Love/Love Power	CD5	U.K.	1991	$9.00
Epic	ESK 73778	Power of Love/Love Power	CDJ	U.S.	1991	$2.00
Epic	ESK 73779	Power of Love/Love Power	CDJ	U.S.	1991	$2.00
Epic	ESK 74049	Rush, The	CDJ	U.S.	1991	$2.00
Epic	654517-3	She Won't Talk to Me	CD3	Germany	1989	$9.00
Epic	CDLUTH-9	She Won't Talk to Me	CD5	U.K.	1989	$9.00
Epic		She Won't Talk to Me	CDJ	U.S.		$2.00
Epic	ESK 74226	Sometimes It's Only Love	CDJ	U.S.	1991	$2.00
Epic	CDLUTH-7	There's Nothing Better Than Love	CD5	U.K.	1988	$9.00
Epic	CDLUTH-14	Treat Her Right	CD5	U.K.	1990	$9.00
Epic	ESK 73258	Treat Her Right	CDJ	U.S.	1990	$2.00

Vangelis

Full Length

Label	Catalog Number	Title	Type	Country	Year	Value
Polygram	813653-2	China	LP/BP	U.S.†	1984	$14.00/$8.00
Polygram	825245-2	Mask, The	LP/BP	U.S.†	1985	$14.00/$8.00
Polygram	8123 396-2	Soil Festivities	LP/BP	U.S.†	1984	$14.00/$8.00

Singles

Label	Catalog Number	Title	Type	Country	Year	Value
Polydor	889969-2	Chariots of Fire	CD5	Germany	1989	$10.00

Label	Catalog Number	Title	Type	Country	Year	Longbox Value / Value
Eastwest	YZ-704CD	Conquest of Paradise	CD5	U.K.	1992	$10.00
Atlantic	PRCD 3908-2	Good To See You	CDJ	U.S.	1990	$2.00
Chacra	036	In London	CDJ	Canada	1992	$7.00
Eastwest	YZ736CD	Twenty-Eighth Parallel	CD5	Germany	1993	$10.00
Arista	661767	Will of the Wild	CD5	Germany	1988	$10.00
Arista	661767	Will of the Wild	CD5	U.K.	1988	$10.00

Vanilla Ice

Singles

Label	Catalog Number	Title	Type	Country	Year	Value
SBK	DPRO-05413	Cool as Ice	CDJ	U.S.	1991	$2.00
SBK	204268-2	I Love You	CD5	Germany	1991	$4.00
SBK	CDSBK-22	I Love You	CD5	U.K.	1991	$4.00
SBK	204122-2	Ice Ice Baby	CD5	Germany	1991	$5.00
SBK	CDSBK 18	Ice Ice Baby	CD5	U.K.	1991	$5.00
SBK	204192-2	Play That Funky Music	CD5	Germany	1990	$4.00
SBK	TODP-2248	Play That Funky Music	CD3	Japan	1991	$12.00/$3.00
SBK	CDSBK-20	Play That Funky Music	CD5	U.K.	1991	$4.00
SBK	204194-2	Play That Funky Music, Vol.1	CD5	Germany	1990	$4.00
SBK	204193-2	Play That Funky Music, Vol.2	CD5	Germany	1990	$4.00
SBK	204531-2	Road To Riches	CD5	Germany	1991	$4.00
SBK	TODP-2316	Rollin' In My 5.0	CD3	Japan	1991	$12.00/$3.00
SBK	CDSBK-27	Rollin' In My 5.0	CD5	U.K.	1991	$4.00
SBK	DPRO-05393	Rollin' In My 5.0	CDJ	U.S.	1991	$2.00
SBK	204418-2	Satisfaction	CD5	Germany	1991	$4.00
SBK	204419-2	Satisfaction	CD5	Germany	1991	$4.00
SBK	TODP-2283	Satisfaction	CD3	Japan	1991	$15.00/$3.00
SBK	CDSBK-29	Satisfaction	CD5	U.K.	1991	$4.00

Vanity Kills

Singles

Label	Catalog Number	Title	Type	Country	Year	Value
Hollywood	PRCD 8395-2	Holiday of Passion	CDJ	U.S.	1991	$2.00

Vannelli, Gino

Full Length

Label	Catalog Number	Title	Type	Country	Year	Value
Arista	ARCD-8186	Nightwalker	LP/LB	U.S.†	1984	$14.00/$8.00

Singles

Label	Catalog Number	Title	Type	Country	Year	Value
Vie	4300	If I Should Lose This Love	CDJ	U.S.		$2.00

Varga

Singles

Label	Catalog Number	Title	Type	Country	Year	Value
Zoo	14122	Greed	CD5	U.S.	1994	$5.00

Vargas, Wilfrido

Singles

Label	Catalog Number	Title	Type	Country	Year	Value
The Rodven Latino	3178	Con La Plata Baila	CD5	U.S.	1994	$5.00

Various

Singles

Label	Catalog Number	Title	Type	Country	Year	Value
		Gimme Shelter	CD5	U.K.		$10.00
		Gimme Shelter	CD5	U.K.		$10.00
	Second version.					

Vasik Casandra

Singles

Label	Catalog Number	Title	Type	Country	Year	Value
		Sadly Mistaken	CDJ	Canada		$6.00

Vasquez, Junior

Singles

Label	Catalog Number	Title	Type	Country	Year	Value
Capital	58145	Get Your Hands Off	CD5	U.S.	1994	$5.00

Vath, Sven

Singles

Label	Catalog Number	Title	Type	Country	Year	Value
Warner Brothers	9 41054-2	L'Esperanza	CD5	U.S.	1993	$5.00
Warner Brothers	PRO-CD-6554	L'Esperanza	CDJ	U.S.	1993	$2.00
Warner Brothers	9 41403-2	Ritual of Life	CD5	U.S.	1993	$5.00

Vaughan Brothers

Full Length

Label	Catalog Number	Title	Type	Country	Year	Value
DIR		King Biscuit Flour Hour	RS	U.S.	1991	$70.00
	With Blues Traveler, Airdate: 4/28/91.					
CBS	ZSK 2169	Vaughan Brothers, The	DJ/LP	U.S.	1990	$25.00

Singles

Label	Catalog Number	Title	Type	Country	Year	Value
Epic	ESK 73673	Good Texan	CDJ	U.S.	1990	$7.00
Epic	ESK 2250	Telephone Song	CDJ	U.S.	1990	$7.00
CBS	656352-3	Tic Tock	CD3	Germany	1990	$11.00
Epic	ESK 2207	Tic Tock	CDJ	U.S.	1990	$7.00
Epic	ESK 73576	Tic Tock	CDJ	U.S.	1990	$7.00

Vaughan, Jimmy

Full Length

Label	Catalog Number	Title	Type	Country	Year	Value
		House of Blues	RS	U.S.	1996	$40.00
	2 CD set. Airdate: 1/14/96.					

Singles

Label	Catalog Number	Title	Type	Country	Year	Value
Epic	ESK 6000	Boom-Bapa-Boom	CDJ	U.S.	1990	$6.00
Epic	ESK 6186	Sweet Soul Vibe	CDJ	U.S.		$6.00

Vaughan, Stevie Ray

Full Length

Label	Catalog Number	Title	Type	Country	Year	Value
Epic	EK-39304	Couldn't Stand the Weather	LP/BP	U.S.†	1984	$14.00/$8.00
CBS	EK-39304	Couldn't Stand the Weather	LP/LB	U.S.	1993	$28.00/$25.00
	Gold disc.					
CBS	EK-66425	Couldn't Stand the Weather	LTD/LP	U.S.	1994	$25.00
	Gold disc.					
CBS	ESK 1901	Fire Meets Fury	DJ/Smplr	U.S.	1989	$35.00
CBS/Fender	ESK 1901	Fire Meets Fury	DJ/Smplr	U.S.	1989	$50.00
	Fender guitar cover.					
Media America		His Own Words	RS	U.S.	1995	$85.00
	2 CD set.					
		House of Blues	RS	U.S.	1993	$40.00
	Airdate: 10/3/93.					
Epic	ESK 4822	In the Beginning	DJ/LP	U.S.	1992	$20.00
Album Network		In the Studio (Best of)	RS	U.S.		$85.00
	2 CD set.					
Epic	ESK 4418	Interchords	DJ/Intvw	U.S.	1992	$20.00
DIR		King Biscuit Flour Hour	RS	U.S.	1988	$40.00
	Airdate: 11/8/92.					
DIR		King Biscuit Flour Hour	RS	U.S.	1989	$70.00
	Airdate: 1/15/89.					
DIR		King Biscuit Flour Hour	RS	U.S.	1990	$70.00
	Airdate: 11/4/90.					
DIR		King Biscuit Flour Hour	RS	U.S.	1990	$70.00
	Airdate: 4/23/90.					
DIR		King Biscuit Flour Hour	RS	U.S.	1991	$50.00
	Airdate: 1/5/91.					
DIR		King Biscuit Flour Hour	RS	U.S.	1992	$50.00
	Airdate: 11/8/92.					

Label	Catalog Number	Title	Type	Country	Year	Longbox Value / Value
DIR		King Biscuit Flour Hour	RS	U.S.	1992	$60.00
Airdate: 1/5/92.						
DIR		King Biscuit Flour Hour	RS	U.S.	1994	$50.00
Airdate: 10/2/94.						
Epic	ESK 2221	October 3, 1954 - August 27, 1990	DJ/Smplr	U.S.	1990	$35.00
		Rock 'n Roll Greats	RS	U.S.	1992	$60.00
Airdate: 3/92.						
Radio Today		Rock Stars	RS	U.S.	1990	$80.00
2 CD set. Airdate: 3/12/90.						
Epic	ESK 4252	Sky Is Crying, The	DJ/LP	U.S.	1991	$20.00
Advance Issue.						
Epic	EK-40036	Soul To Soul	LP/BP	U.S.†	1985	$14.00/$8.00
Westwood One		Superstars	RS	U.S.	1993	$85.00
2 CD set. Airdate: 4/19/93.						
Westwood One		Superstars	RS	U.S.	1995	$65.00
2 CD set. Airdate: 7/31/95.						
Epic	EK-38734	Texas Flood	LP/BP	U.S.†	1984	$14.00/$8.00
Westwood One		Timothy White Sessions	RS	U.S.	1996	$150.00
2 CD set. Airdate: 8/26/96.						
Media America		Up Close	RS	U.S.	1991	$80.00
2 CD set.						
Media America		Up Close	RS	U.S.	1992	$80.00
2 CD set.						

Singles

Label	Catalog Number	Title	Type	Country	Year	Longbox Value / Value
Epic	ESK 1638	Crossfire	CDJ	U.S.	1989	$6.00
Epic	ESK 1887	Crossfire	CDJ	U.S.	1989	$6.00
Epic	ESK 1732	Crossfire	CDJ	U.S.	1989	$6.00
Epic		Empty Arms	CDJ	U.S.	1992	$6.00
Epic	ESK 1931	House is Rockin', The	CDJ	U.S.	1989	$6.00
		House is Rockin', The	CDJ	U.S.	1995	$8.00
Epic	ESK 4435	Little Wing	CDJ	U.S.	1992	$10.00
Epic	ESK 1930	Riviera Paradise	CDJ	U.S.	1989	$10.00
From Fire Meets Fury.						
Epic	ESK 4846	Shake for Me	CDJ	U.S.	1992	$6.00
Epic	ESK 4181	Sky is Crying	CDJ	U.S.	1991	$6.00
Epic		Wall of Denial	CDJ	U.S.		$6.00

Vaughn, Sarah

Full Length

Label	Catalog Number	Title	Type	Country	Year	Longbox Value / Value
CBS	MK-37277	Gershwin Live!	LP/LB	U.S.†	1985	$14.00/$8.00
Emarcy	824057-2	No Count Sarah	LP/LB	U.S.†	1985	$14.00/$8.00
Emarcy	814641-2	Sarah Vaughn	LP/LB	U.S.†	1985	$14.00/$8.00
Mercury	814587-2	Sassy Swings Again	LP/LB	U.S.†	1985	$14.00/$8.00
Emarcy	824864-2	The Rodgers & Hart Songbook	LP/LB	U.S.†	1985	$14.00/$8.00

Vaughn, Sarah & Billy Eckstine

Full Length

Label	Catalog Number	Title	Type	Country	Year	Longbox Value / Value
Verve	822526-2	Irving Berlin Songbook	LP/LB	U.S.†	1985	$14.00/$8.00

Vega, Suzanne

Full Length

Label	Catalog Number	Title	Type	Country	Year	Longbox Value / Value
A&M	31454 0026 2	99.9°F	LTD/LP	U.S.	1992	$18.00
A&M	397 088-2	Compact Disc Collection, The	LTD/LP	U.K.	1990	$45.00
3 CD boxed set with hologram cover.						
A&M	75021/3933/2	Days of Open Hand	LTD/LP	U.S.	1988	$22.00
Hologram digipak.						
A&M	397 088-2	Limited Edtion Compact Disc Set	LP	Germany	1990	$45.00
3 CD Set.						

Singles

Label	Catalog Number	Title	Type	Country	Year	Longbox Value / Value
A&M	PODM-1005	99.9°F	CD3	Japan	1992	$15.00/$4.00
A&M	AMOD-0005	99.9°F	CD5	U.K.	1992	$10.00
A&M	31458 8052	99.9°F	CDJ	U.S.	1992	$3.00
A&M	390526-2	Blood Makes Noise	CD5	Germany	1992	$10.00
A&M	PODM-1002	Blood Makes Noise	CD3	Japan	1992	$15.00/$4.00
A&M	AMCD-0112	Blood Makes Noise	CD5	U.K.	1992	$10.00
A&M	AMCDH-559	Blood Makes Noise	CD5	U.K.	1992	$10.00
A&M	31458 8018 2	Blood Makes Noise	CDJ	U.S.	1992	$3.00
A&M	CD 18015	Book of Dreams	CDJ	U.S.	1990	$3.00
A&M	AMCDP00188	Caramel	CDJ	U.S.		$3.00
A&M	390347-2	Compact Hits	CD5	Germany	1988	$10.00
A&M	AMCD-912	Compact Hits	CD5	U.K.	1988	$10.00
A&M	31458 8103 2	Fat Man and Dancing Girl	CDJ	U.S.	1992	$3.00
A&M	390303-2	Gypsy	CD5	Germany	1989	$10.00
A&M	31458 8140	In Liverpool	CDJ	U.S.	1993	$3.00
		Long Voyage, The	CDJ	U.S.		$7.00
A&M	S12Y-3026	Luka	CD3	Japan	1988	$15.00/$4.00
A&M	D15Y-3196	Luka	CD5	Japan	1988	$15.00
A&M	31003	Luka	CD3	U.S.	1988	$7.00/$4.00
A&M	390583-2	Men in War	CD5	Germany	1990	$10.00
A&M	AMCD-584	Men in War	CD5	U.K.	1990	$10.00
A&M	S12Y-3013	Solitude Standing	CD3	Japan	1988	$15.00/$4.00
A&M	VEGCD-3	Solitude Standing	CD5	U.K.	1988	$10.00
A&M	390550-2	Tired Of Sleeping	CD5	Germany	1990	$10.00
A&M	AMCD-565	Tired Of Sleeping	CD5	U.K.	1990	$10.00
A&M	75021 7479 2	Tom's Diner	CDJ	U.S.	1990	$3.00
A&M	PODM-1014	When Heroes Go Down	CD3	Japan	1993	$15.00/$4.00
		When Heroes Go Down	CD5	U.K.		$10.00
		When Heroes Go Down	CD5	U.K.		$10.00
Second version.						
A&M	31458 8093 2	When Heroes Go Down	CDJ	U.S.	1993	$3.00

Vegas

Singles

Label	Catalog Number	Title	Type	Country	Year	Longbox Value / Value
RCA	74321-112465	She	CD5	U.K.	1992	$8.00

Velasquez, Nesto

Singles

Label	Catalog Number	Title	Type	Country	Year	Longbox Value / Value
Uptown	2413	Personality	CDJ	U.S.	1992	$2.00

Veldt

Singles

Label	Catalog Number	Title	Type	Country	Year	Longbox Value / Value
Stardog	CDP 771	CCCP	CDJ	U.S.	1992	$2.00
Stardog	CDP 1083	Soul in a Jar	CDJ	U.S.	1992	$6.00

Velez, Martha

Singles

Label	Catalog Number	Title	Type	Country	Year	Longbox Value / Value
Sire	PRO-CD-3762	Shake Some Action	CDJ	U.S.		$2.00

Velocity Girl

Full Length

Label	Catalog Number	Title	Type	Country	Year	Longbox Value / Value
Sub Pop		Simpatico	DJ/LP	U.S.	1994	$15.00

Singles

Label	Catalog Number	Title	Type	Country	Year	Longbox Value / Value
Sub Pop	13	Audrey's Eyes	CDJ	U.S.	1993	$3.00
Sub Pop	6	My Forgotten Favorite	CDJ	U.S.	1993	$6.00
		Nothing	CDJ	U.S.		$2.00
SubPop	SP257B	Sorry Again	CD5	Canada	1994	$9.00
Sub Pop	SP257b	Sorry Again	CD5	U.S.	1994	$6.00

Velvet Crush

Singles

Label	Catalog Number	Title	Type	Country	Year	Longbox Value / Value
		Hold Me Up	CD5	U.K.	1994	$10.00
Creation	CDERCD 122	Post Greatness, The	CDJ	U.S.	1992	$10.00

Velvet Underground

Full Length

Label	Catalog Number	Title	Type	Country	Year	Longbox Value / Value
Reprise	9 45434-2	Live MCMXCIII	LTD/LP	U.S.	1993	$25.00
CD in oversied digipak.						
Rhino	R2 72563	Loaded (Fully Loaded Edition)	LTD/LP	U.S.	1997	$23.00
2 CD set with "tornado" multi-Image cover and slip case.						
Reprise		Peels & See Slowly	DJ/Smplr	U.S.	1995	$25.00
WEA		Ride Into the Sun	DJ/Smplr	Germany	1995	$70.00

Singles

Label	Catalog Number	Title	Type	Country	Year	Longbox Value / Value
Sire	PRO-CD-6623	Sweet Jane	CDJ	U.S.	1993	$3.00
		White Light White Heat	CDJ	Spain	1993	$20.00

Vengeance

Singles

Label	Catalog Number	Title	Type	Country	Year	Longbox Value / Value
		Hard Rock	CDJ	U.S.		$2.00

Venice

Singles

Label	Catalog Number	Title	Type	Country	Year	Longbox Value / Value
		All My Life	CDJ	U.S.		$2.00
		People Laugh	CDJ	U.S.		$2.00

Ventures

Singles

Label	Catalog Number	Title	Type	Country	Year	Longbox Value / Value
Manhattan	TODP-2319	Memories of Love	CD3	Japan	1991	$12.00/$4.00
Inside Out	TODP-2112	Try It	CD3	Japan	1989	$12.00/$4.00
Aris	885861	Walk Don't Run	CD3	Germany	1990	$8.00
Rhino	R3 73020	Walk Don't Run	CD3	U.S.	1988	$6.00/$4.00
Eric	401	Walk Don't Run	CD5	U.S.	1992	$5.00

Venus Beads

Singles

Label	Catalog Number	Title	Type	Country	Year	Longbox Value / Value
Emergo	037	Moon is Red	CDJ	U.S.	1991	$2.00

Verlane, Tom

Singles

Label	Catalog Number	Title	Type	Country	Year	Longbox Value / Value
Fontana	VLACD 5	Shimmer	CD5	U.K.	1989	$8.00

Veronica

Singles

Label	Catalog Number	Title	Type	Country	Year	Longbox Value / Value
		Without Love	CDJ	U.S.		$2.00

Vertical Hold

Singles

Label	Catalog Number	Title	Type	Country	Year	Longbox Value / Value
A&M	31458 8053	A.S.A.P.	CDJ	U.S.	1993	$2.00
A&M	31458 8217	A.S.A.P.	CDJ	U.S.	1993	$2.00
A&M	31458 8195	Matter of Time	CDJ	U.S.	1993	$2.00
A&M	31458 8083	Seems You're Much Too Busy	CDJ	U.S.	1993	$2.00
A&M	31458 8087	Seems You're Much Too Busy	CDJ	U.S.	1993	$6.00

Veruca Salt

Singles

Label	Catalog Number	Title	Type	Country	Year	Longbox Value / Value
		Number One Blind	CDJ	U.S.		$3.00
		Number One Blind	CDJ	U.S.		$2.00
		Seether	CD5	U.K.	1994	$9.00

Verve

Singles

Label	Catalog Number	Title	Type	Country	Year	Longbox Value / Value
		Blue	CDJ	U.S.		$7.00
Hut	21	Gravity Grave	CD5	U.K.	1992	$8.00
Vernon Yard	12790	Slide Away	CDJ	U.S.	1993	$3.00

Verve Pipe

Full Length

Label	Catalog Number	Title	Type	Country	Year	Longbox Value / Value
RCA	RADV66809-2	Villains	DJ/LP	U.S.		$10.00

Singles

Label	Catalog Number	Title	Type	Country	Year	Longbox Value / Value
RCA	RDJ64497-2	Photograph	CDJ	U.S.		$3.00

Vicious

Singles

Label	Catalog Number	Title	Type	Country	Year	Longbox Value / Value
CBS	57857	Destination Brooklyn	CD5	U.S.	1994	$5.00

Vicious Rumors

Singles

Label	Catalog Number	Title	Type	Country	Year	Longbox Value / Value
		Don't Wait For Me	CDJ	U.S.		$2.00
		Raise Your Hands	CDJ	U.S.		$2.00

Victor

Singles

Label	Catalog Number	Title	Type	Country	Year	Longbox Value / Value
Anthem	PRCD 6686	I Am the Spirit	CD5	U.S.	1996	$15.00

Vienna

Singles

Label	Catalog Number	Title	Type	Country	Year	Longbox Value / Value
Cutting	TODP-2358	I Should Have Known	CD3	Japan	1992	$12.00/$4.00
Warner Brothers	PRO-CD-2795	Talking With the Heart	CDJ	U.S.	1987	$2.00

Vierra, Christine

Singles

Label	Catalog Number	Title	Type	Country	Year	Longbox Value / Value
Warner Brothers	PRO-CD-3225	You Can Float on My Boat	CDJ	U.S.	1988	$2.00

Vigard, Kristen

Full Length

Label	Catalog Number	Title	Type	Country	Year	Longbox Value / Value
Private	2066	Kristen Vigard	LP/LB	U.S.		$14.00/$8.00

Vigilantes Of Love

Singles

Label	Catalog Number	Title	Type	Country	Year	Longbox Value / Value
		Blister Soul	CDJ	U.S.		$2.00
		Tempest	CDJ	U.S.		$2.00

Village People

Singles

Label	Catalog Number	Title	Type	Country	Year	Longbox Value / Value
	520225	Live & Sleazy	CD5	U.S.	1994	$5.00
BCM	20299	Megamix Medley	CD5	Germany	1989	$9.00
Groove	GMCS-9CD	Megamix Medley	CD5	U.K.	1989	$9.00
Casablanca	PSDW-1014	YMCA	CD3	Japan	1990	$15.00/$5.00
Old Gold	OG-6510	YMCA	CD5	U.K.	1990	$10.00

Vinton, Bobby

Singles

Label	Catalog Number	Title	Type	Country	Year	Longbox Value / Value
Epic	650524-2	Blue Velvet	CD5	U.K.	1990	$10.00
Curb	1014	I Know What It Is to Be Young	CDJ	U.S.	1992	$3.00
Epic	656467-2	Roses Are Red	CD5	U.K.	1990	$10.00
Curb	DPRO-76751	What Did You Do With Your Old	CDJ	U.S.	1990	$2.00

Label	Catalog Number	Title	Type	Country	Year	Longbox Value / Value
Violence						
Singles						
		World in a World	CDJ	U.S.		$2.00
Violent Femmes						
Full Length						
		In Concert-Nu Rock	RS	U.S.	1994	$70.00
	Airdate: 9/26/94.					
Slash	9 26476-2-Dj	Why Do Birds Sing	DJ/LP	U.S.	1991	$15.00
Singles						
Slash	LASCD-29	American Music	CD5	U.K.	1991	$10.00
Slash	PRO-CD-4770	American Music	CDJ	U.S.	1991	$3.00
		Breakin' Up	CDJ	U.S.		$3.00
Elektra	PRCD 8925-2	Breakin' Up	CDJ	U.S.	1994	$3.00
Slash	PRO-CD-6483	I Held Her in My Arms	CDJ	U.S.	1993	$3.00
Warner	22-66186	Machine	CD5	Canada	1994	$8.00
Elektra/Asylum	66186	Machine	CD5	U.S.	1994	$5.00
Elektra	66186-2	Machine	CD5	U.S.	1994	$6.00
Elektra	PRO-CD-9036	Machine	CDJ	U.S.	1994	$6.00
Warner Brothers	PRO-CD-3444	Nightmares	CDJ	U.S.	1989	$3.00
Violet Hour						
Singles						
Epic		Falling	CDJ	U.S.	1991	$3.00
Visage						
Singles						
Polydor	887 586	Fade to Grey	CD5	Germany		$8.00
Vision Quest						
Singles						
	2012	Soul Clique	CD5	U.S.	1994	$5.00
Vital Signs						
Singles						
A&M	CD 17702	Boys and Girls Are Doing It	CDJ	U.S.	1989	$2.00
Vix, Valeria						
Singles						
ZYX	8078-8	Viciosa	CD5	U.S.	1996	$6.00
Vixen						
Full Length						
EMI USA	TOCP-6137	Rev It Up	LTD/LP	Japan	1990	$25.00
	Picture disc CD.					
EMI	CDP-7-92923-2	Rev It Up	DJ/LP	U.S.	1990	$40.00
	2 copies of the CD in custom rubber tire.					
EMI	746991-0	Vixen	LTD/LP	U.K.	1988	$25.00
	Picture disc CD.					
Singles						
EMI		Cryin'	CDJ	U.S.		$2.00
Capitol	DPRO 04099	Edge of a Broken Heart	CDJ	U.S.	1988	$7.00
EMI	DPRO 04541	How Much Love	CDJ	U.S.	1990	$8.00
	Digipak with flashing lights.					
EMI	DPRO 04657	Love Is a Killer	CDJ	U.S.	1990	$2.00
EMI	DPRO 04268	Love Made Me	CDJ	U.S.	1989	$2.00
EMI		Start Your Engines	CDJ	U.S.	1990	$2.00
Vogt, Sarah						
Singles						
		Chains	DJ/CD3	U.S.		$4.00
Voice Farm						
Singles						
Morgan Creek	0001	Free Love	CDJ	U.S.	1991	$2.00
Morgan Creek	0006	Hey Freethinker	CDJ	U.S.	1991	$2.00
Morgan Creek	0014	Seeing is Believing	CDJ	U.S.	1991	$2.00
Voice of the Beehive						
Singles						
London	CDP 609	Adonis Blue	CDJ	U.S.	1991	$3.00
		Angel Come Down	CD5	U.K.	1995	$11.00
London	886280-2	Don't Call Me Baby	CD5	Germany	1988	$8.00
London	LONCD-175	Don't Call Me Baby	CD5	U.K.	1988	$8.00
London	886334-2	I Say Nothing	CD5	Germany	1988	$8.00
London	LONCD-190	I Say Nothing	CD5	U.K.	1988	$8.00
London	869527 2	I Think I Love You	CD5	U.K.	1991	$13.00
	CD In Heart shaped sleeve.					
London	P13L-37006	I Walk the Earth	CD3	Japan	1988	$13.00/$4.00
London	LONCD-169	I Walk the Earth	CD5	U.K.	1988	$8.00
London	LONCD-206	I Walk the Earth	CD5	U.K.	1988	$8.00
London	P10L-40003	Let It Bee	CD3	Japan	1988	$13.00/$4.00
London	LONCD-209	Man in the Moon	CD5	U.K.	1989	$8.00
London	CDP 513	Monsters and Angels	CDJ	U.S.	1991	$3.00
London	PODD-1015	Perfect Place	CD3	Japan	1992	$13.00/$4.00
London	CDP 534	Perfect Place	CDJ	U.S.	1991	$3.00
Strange Fruit	SFNTCD-017	Radio 1 Sessions	CD5	U.K.	1989	$9.00
		Scary Kisses	CDJ	U.S.		$3.00
Voice Of The City						
Singles						
Scotti Brothers	72392	Stand and Be Proud	CDJ	U.S.	1992	$3.00
Voices						
Singles						
Zoo	ZD-17108	Cloudy With a Chance of Tears	CDJ	U.S.	1993	$2.00
Zoo	ZD-17097	My Mama Didn't Raise a Fool	CDJ	U.S.	1992	$2.00
Zoo	ZD-17078	Yeah Yeah Yeah	CDJ	U.S.	1992	$2.00
Voivod						
Full Length						
Mechanic	2000	Angel Rat Sampler	DJ/Smplr	U.S.	1991	$8.00
Mechanic		Outer Limits	DJ/LP	U.S.		$10.00
	CD with 3-D cover and glasses.					
Singles						
MCA	CD45-17979	Astronomy Domine	CDJ	U.S.	1989	$3.00
MCA	2822	Fix My Heart	CDJ	U.S.	1993	$3.00
MCA	CD45-18196	Into My Hypercube	CDJ	U.S.	1989	$3.00
MCA	2668	Lost Machine, The	CDJ	U.S.	1993	$3.00
MCA	2926	Nile Song, The	CDJ	U.S.	1994	$3.00
Vollenweider, Andreas						
Full Length						
CBS	MK-37793	Behind The Gardens-Behind The Wall-Under The Tree	LP/LB	U.S.†	1985	$14.00/$8.00
CBS	MK-37827	Caverna Magica	LP/LB	U.S.†	1985	$14.00/$8.00
CBS	MK-39963	White Winds	LP/LB	U.S.†	1985	$14.00/$8.00
Singles						
Columbia	CSK 1507	Dancing With the Lion	CDJ	U.S.	1989	$2.00
Columbia	CSK 1629	Dancing With the Lion	CDJ	U.S.	1989	$2.00
Volume 10						
Singles						
Immortal	62633	Pistol-Grip Pump	CDJ	U.S.	1993	$2.00
Von Groove						
Singles						
Chrysalis	DPRO-05482	Metal Radio EP	CDJ	U.S.	1992	$6.00
Voodoo Glowing Skulls						
Singles						
		Fat Randy	CDJ	U.S.		$3.00
	18	Who Is, This Is?	CD5	U.S.	1994	$5.00
Voodoo Queens						
Singles						
		F Is For Fame	CD5	U.K.	1994	$18.00
Voodoo X						
Singles						
CBS	654873	Voodoo Queen	CD3	Germany	1989	$8.00
Voyce						
Singles						
Atco	PRCD 4735-2	Here We Are	CDJ	U.S.	1992	$2.00
Atco	PRCD 4020-2	Within My Heart	CDJ	U.S.	1991	$2.00
Voyceboxing						
Singles						
GRP	9961	Pain	CDJ	U.S.	1991	$2.00
Voyou						
Singles						
EMI	2 03 660 2	Ten Commandments, The	CD5	Germany	1989	$8.00
Vybe						
Singles						
Polygram	854363	Warm Summer Dayze	CD5	U.S.	1995	$5.00
W.A.S.P.						
Singles						
Restless	72104-2	Animal (F**K Like a Beast)	CD5	U.S.	1987	$10.00
Capitol	TOCP-7190	Chainsaw Charlie	CD3	Japan	1992	$12.00/$4.00
Parlophone	CDR 6308	Chainsaw Charlie	CD5	U.K.	1992	$10.00
	7"x7" package.					
Capitol	203486-2	Forever Free	CD5	Germany	1989	$9.00
Capitol	CDCL-546	Forever Free	CD5	U.K.	1989	$9.00
Capitol	DPRO 79707	Forever Free	CDJ	U.S.	1989	$7.00
Capitol	DPRO-79331	Hold on to My Heart	CDJ	U.S.	1993	$3.00
EMI	TOCP-7335	Idol	CD5	Japan	1992	$12.00
Music For Nations	CD12KUT 109	Live Animal (F**K Like a Beast)	CD5	U.K.	1988	$10.00
Restless	72235-2	Live Animal (F**K Like a Beast)	CD5	U.S.	1987	$10.00
Capitol	203239-2	Mean Man	CD5	Germany	1989	$9.00
Capitol	CDCL-521	Mean Man	CD5	U.K.	1989	$9.00
Capitol	CDCL 534	Real Me	CD5	U.K.	1990	$20.00
Capitol	203368-3	Real Me, The	CD3	Germany	1990	$9.00
Capitol	CDCL 534	Real Me, The	CD5	U.K.	1990	$9.00
Capitol	DPRO 79507	Real Me, The	CDJ	U.S.	1989	$3.00
Capitol	80927	Sunset & Babylon	CD5	U.K.	1993	$9.00
W, Kristine						
Singles						
Atlantic	95899	Feel What You Want	CD5	U.S.	1994	$5.00
Wag Ya Tail						
Singles						
PWL	238	Xpand Ya Mind	CDJ	U.S.	1992	$2.00
Wagner, Jack						
Singles						
		It's My Baby Too	CDJ	U.S.	1993	$2.00
Wagoneers						
Singles						
A&M	390333-2	I Wanna Know Her Again	CD5	Germany	1988	$8.00
A&M	AMCD-454	I Wanna Know Her Again	CD5	U.K.	1988	$8.00
A&M	CD 17565	I Wanna Know Her Again	CDJ	U.S.	1988	$2.00
A&M	CD 17816	Sit a Little Bit Closer	CDJ	U.S.	1989	$2.00
A&M	CD 17916	Test of Time	CDJ	U.S.	1989	$2.00
Wailers Band						
Singles						
Atlantic	PR 2743-2	Irie	CDJ	U.S.	1989	$2.00
Tabu	28965 1701 2	My Friend	CDJ	U.S.	1991	$2.00
Wailing Soul						
Singles						
Chaos	4647	All Over the World	CDJ	U.S.	1992	$2.00
Chaos	74763	If I Were You	CDJ	U.S.	1992	$2.00
Chaos	4619	Shark Attack	CDJ	U.S.	1992	$6.00
Chaos	5107	Sweet Black Angel	CDJ	U.S.	1993	$2.00
Chaos	77175	Wild Wild Life	CDJ	U.S.	1993	$2.00
Wainwright, Loudon III						
Singles						
Charisma	12764	People in Love	CDJ	U.S.	1992	$2.00
Waite, John						
Full Length						
		Bone Machine	DJ/Intvw	U.S.		$5.00
EMI	CDP 746167	Mask of Smiles	LP	U.K.		$25.00
Capitol	CDP-46078	No Brakes	LP/LB	U.S.†	1985	$14.00/$8.00
Singles						
Epic	656516-3	Deal for Life	CD3	Germany	1990	$9.00
Epic	656516-3	Deal for Life	CD5	U.K.	1990	$9.00
Imago	25091	How Did I Get By	CD5	U.S.	1994	$5.00
Imago	28065	In Dreams	CDJ	U.S.	1993	$2.00
Chrysalis	CDCHS-3938	Missing You	CD5	U.K.	1993	$9.00
EMI	DPRO 79054	These Times Are Hard for Lovers	CDJ	U.S.	1987	$2.00
Waits, Tom						
Full Length						
Islnad		Bone Machine: Operator's Manual	DJ/Intvw	U.S.	1993	$25.00

Singles

Label	Catalog Number	Title	Type	Country	Year	Longbox Value / Value
		Downtown Train	CDJ	Spain		$25.00
Island	CID-537	Going Out West	CD5	U.K.	1992	$8.00
Island	PRCD 6727-2	Going Out West	CDJ	U.S.	1992	$2.00
Elektra	EKR-162CD	Heart Attack and Vine	CD5	U.K.	1993	$8.00
Island	PRCD 6748-2	I Don't Wanna Grow Up	CDJ	U.S.	1992	$2.00
Elektra	PRCD 6821-2	I'll Shoot the Moon	CDJ	U.S.		$2.00

Wakeland

Singles

Label	Catalog Number	Title	Type	Country	Year	Longbox Value / Value
		Falling Again	CDJ	U.S.		$2.00
		Half of You	CDJ	U.S.		$2.00

Wakeling, Dave

Singles

Label	Catalog Number	Title	Type	Country	Year	Longbox Value / Value
IRS	1991	I Want More	CDJ	U.S.	1991	$2.00

Wakeman, Rick

Full Length

Label	Catalog Number	Title	Type	Country	Year	Longbox Value / Value
	JSP-0001	Special Sampler	DJ/Smplr	Japan		$50.00
Griffin	GCDRW-156-2	Wakeman With Wakeman: Official Live Bootleg, The	LTD/LP	U.S.	1995	$120.00
	CD in wood piano package.					

Waldman, Wendy

Full Length

Label	Catalog Number	Title	Type	Country	Year	Longbox Value / Value
Cypress	112	Letters Home	DJ/Smplr	U.S.	1987	$8.00

Waldron, Mal

Label	Catalog Number	Title	Type	Country	Year	Longbox Value / Value
Soul Note	121 198	Our Colline's A Treasure	CD5	Italy	1991	$10.00

Walk This Way

Singles

Label	Catalog Number	Title	Type	Country	Year	Longbox Value / Value
		In My Room	CDJ	U.S.		$2.00

Walkabouts

Singles

Label	Catalog Number	Title	Type	Country	Year	Longbox Value / Value
Sub Pop	150	Dead Man Rise	CD5	U.S.		$5.00
Sub pop	80	Jack Candy	CD5	Germany	1992	$10.00

Walker, Chris

Singles

Label	Catalog Number	Title	Type	Country	Year	Longbox Value / Value
Pendulum	8427	Giving You All My Love	CDJ	U.S.	1991	$2.00
Pendulum	8576	No Place Like Love	CDJ	U.S.	1992	$2.00
Pendulum	8520	Take Time	CDJ	U.S.	1991	$2.00

Walker, Clay

Full Length

Label	Catalog Number	Title	Type	Country	Year	Longbox Value / Value
Giant		Hypnotize	LTD/LP	U.S.	1995	$25.00
	CD in "belt buckle" package.					
Giant	2-2460-A	Hypnotize the Moon	DJ/LP	U.S.	1995	$30.00
	CD in belt buckle package.					
		Make a Living	RS	U.S.	1994	$20.00

Walker, Jerry Jeff

Singles

Label	Catalog Number	Title	Type	Country	Year	Longbox Value / Value
Rykodisc	RCD5 1020	Nolan Ryan	CD5	U.S.	1990	$3.00

Walker, Scott

Full Length

Label	Catalog Number	Title	Type	Country	Year	Longbox Value / Value
		Tilt	DJ/Intvw	U.K.	1995	$60.00

Singles

Label	Catalog Number	Title	Type	Country	Year	Longbox Value / Value
		Patriot & Cockfighter	CDJ	U.K.	1995	$14.00
		Tilt & Farmer	CDj	U.K.	1995	$14.00

Walker, T-Bone

Full Length

Label	Catalog Number	Title	Type	Country	Year	Longbox Value / Value
Mosaic	MD6-130	Complete Recordings	LTD/LP	U.S.		$90.00
	6 CD set. Limited to 7500 copies.					

Walking Wounded

Singles

Label	Catalog Number	Title	Type	Country	Year	Longbox Value / Value
Chameleon	PRCD 67	Raging Winds of Time	CDJ	U.S.	1989	$2.00

Wall, Michael

Singles

Label	Catalog Number	Title	Type	Country	Year	Longbox Value / Value
	1111	Love Song	CD5	U.S.	1994	$5.00

Wall Of Voodoo

Full Length

Label	Catalog Number	Title	Type	Country	Year	Longbox Value / Value
IRS	IRSD-42140	Ugly Americans	LP/LB	U.S.		$18.00/$14.00

Wall, Wendy

Singles

Label	Catalog Number	Title	Type	Country	Year	Longbox Value / Value
SBK	DPRO-05329	Dig That Crazy Beat	CDJ	U.S.	1990	$2.00
SBK	DPRO-05308	Real Love	CDJ	U.S.	1989	$2.00

Wallace, Bennie & Chick Corea

Full Length

Label	Catalog Number	Title	Type	Country	Year	Longbox Value / Value
Enja	311233	Bennie Wallace Trio & Chick Corea	LP/LB	U.S.†	1985	$14.00/$8.00

Wallace, Kate

Full Length

Label	Catalog Number	Title	Type	Country	Year	Longbox Value / Value
Honest Entertainment		Kate Wallace	DJ/Smplr	U.S.	1995	$15.00
	Enhanced CD.					

Wallace, Sippie

Singles

Label	Catalog Number	Title	Type	Country	Year	Longbox Value / Value
	41043	Mighty Tight Woman	CD5	U.S.	1994	$5.00

Waller, Robert James

Singles

Label	Catalog Number	Title	Type	Country	Year	Longbox Value / Value
Atlantic	PRCD 5184-2	Madison County Waltz	CDJ	U.S.		$2.00

Wallflowers

Singles

Label	Catalog Number	Title	Type	Country	Year	Longbox Value / Value
		6th Avenue Heartache	CDJ	U.S.		$2.00
Virgin	PRCD 12690	Ashes to Ashes	CDJ	U.S.	1992	$2.00
Virgin	PRCD 12763	Be Your Own Girl	CDJ	U.S.	1992	$2.00

Wallington, George

Full Length

Label	Catalog Number	Title	Type	Country	Year	Longbox Value / Value
Savoy Records	CY-78994	Jazz at Hotchkiss	LTD/LP	U.S.	1995	$20.00
	CD in miniature repica of original LP sleeve.					

Walsh, Joe

Full Length

Label	Catalog Number	Title	Type	Country	Year	Longbox Value / Value
Westwood One		BBC Classic Tracks	RS	U.S.	1994	$20.00
	Airdate: 7/18/94.					
Warner Brothers	25281-2	Confessor	LP/LB	U.S.†	1985	$14.00/$8.00
Warner Brothers		Got Any Gum?	LP/LB	U.S.		$15.00/$10.00
		House of Blues	RS	U.S.	1995	$35.00
	Airdate: 2/12/95.					
Westwood One		In Concert	RS	U.S.	1994	$30.00
	Airdate: 8/1/94.					
Album Network		In the Studio (Smoker You Drink)	RS	U.S.	1991	$25.00
	Airdate: 9/2/91.					
DIR		King Biscuit Flour Hour	RS	U.S.	1988	$35.00
	With Rod Stewart, Airdate: 7/26/88.					
DIR		King Biscuit Flour Hour	RS	U.S.	1991	$35.00
	Airdate: 11/10/91.					
DIR		King Biscuit Flour Hour	RS	U.S.	1992	$35.00
	Airdate: 12/14/92.					
DIR		King Biscuit Flour Hour	RS	U.S.	1993	$35.00
	Airdate: 11/1/93.					
MCA	MCAD 5869	Smoker You Drink The Player The Get/You Can't Argue With A Sick Mind	LP/LB	U.S.†	1986	$22.00/$18.00
Westwood One		Superstar Concert	RS	U.S.	1992	$40.00
	2 CD set. Airdate: 8/16/92.					
Westwood One		Superstars	RS	U.S.	1992	$50.00
	2 CD set. Airdate: 8/16/92.					
Westwood One		Superstars	RS	U.S.	1993	$50.00
	2 CD set. Airdate: 6/7/93.					

Singles

Label	Catalog Number	Title	Type	Country	Year	Longbox Value / Value
Epic	ZSK 4092	All of a Sudden	CDJ	U.S.	1991	$3.00
Epic	ZSK 4804	Fairbanks Alaska	CDJ	U.S.	1992	$3.00
Fox	62683-2	Honey Don't	CDJ	U.S.	[illegible]	[illegible]
Epic	ZSK 4202	Look at Us Now	CDJ	U.S.	1991	$3.00
Epic	ZSK 3070	Ordinary Average Guy	CDJ	U.S.	1991	$3.00
Epic	ZSK 4680	Vote for Me	CDJ	U.S.	1992	$3.00

Walsh, Mike

Singles

Label	Catalog Number	Title	Type	Country	Year	Longbox Value / Value
Imago	72787	Had It, Done It, Did That	CDJ	U.S.	1993	$2.00

Walter & Scotty

Singles

Label	Catalog Number	Title	Type	Country	Year	Longbox Value / Value
Capitol	DPRO-79785	Sticks & Stones	CDJ	U.S.	1993	$2.00

Walters, Jamie

Singles

Label	Catalog Number	Title	Type	Country	Year	Longbox Value / Value
		Perfect World	CDJ	U.S.		$2.00
		Why	CDJ	U.S.		$2.00

Waltons

Full Length

Label	Catalog Number	Title	Type	Country	Year	Longbox Value / Value
		Naked Rain, The	DJ/Smplr	Canada		$20.00

Singles

Label	Catalog Number	Title	Type	Country	Year	Longbox Value / Value
Wea	CD96143	Simple Brain	CD5	Canada	1994	$10.00

Wanderlust

Singles

Label	Catalog Number	Title	Type	Country	Year	Longbox Value / Value
RCA	RDJ64434-2	Before We Fade	CDJ	U.S.	1995	$3.00
RCA	RDJ64325-2	I Walked	CDJ	U.S.	1995	$3.00

Wang Chung

Full Length

Label	Catalog Number	Title	Type	Country	Year	Longbox Value / Value
Geffen	4004-2	Points On the Curve	LP/LB	U.S.†	1985	$14.00/$8.00

Singles

Label	Catalog Number	Title	Type	Country	Year	Longbox Value / Value
Geffen	GEF-65CD	Dancehall Days	CD3	U.K.	1989	$8.00
Geffen	921254-2	Praying to a New God	CD3	Germany	1989	$8.00
Geffen	09P3-6140	Praying to a New God	CD3	Japan	1989	$13.00/$4.00
Geffen	GEF-54CD	Praying to a New God	CD3	U.K.	1989	$8.00
Geffen	PRO-CD-3501	Praying to a New God	CDJ	U.S.	1989	$3.00

War

Full Length

Label	Catalog Number	Title	Type	Country	Year	Longbox Value / Value
Rhino		Collector's Edition	DJ/Smplr	U.S.	1992	$80.00
	8 CD set. Eight albums in box with "War" embossed on cover.					

Singles

Label	Catalog Number	Title	Type	Country	Year	Longbox Value / Value
Avenue	7014	Don't Let No One Get You Down	CDJ	U.S.	1992	$2.00
Avenue	90132	Don't Let No One Get You Down	CDJ	U.S.	1992	$2.00
Avenue Records	PRCD 7070	Peace Sign	CDJ	U.S.	1994	$7.00

War Babies

Singles

Label	Catalog Number	Title	Type	Country	Year	Longbox Value / Value
Columbia	CSK 4654	Cry Yourself to Sleep	CDJ	U.S.	1992	$2.00
Columbia	CSK 4185	Hang Me Up	CDJ	U.S.	1991	$2.00

Ward, Anita

Singles

Label	Catalog Number	Title	Type	Country	Year	Longbox Value / Value
		Ring My Bell	CD5	U.K.		$8.00

Ward, Bill

Singles

Label	Catalog Number	Title	Type	Country	Year	Longbox Value / Value
Chameleon	77	Snakes And Ladders	CDJ	U.S.	1992	$2.00

Warfield, Justin

Singles

Label	Catalog Number	Title	Type	Country	Year	Longbox Value / Value
Qwest	PRCD 5945	K Sera Sera	CDJ	U.S.	1993	$2.00

Wargasm

Singles

Label	Catalog Number	Title	Type	Country	Year	Longbox Value / Value
	36	Fireball	CD5	U.S.	1994	$5.00

Warhol, Andy

Full Length

Label	Catalog Number	Title	Type	Country	Year	Longbox Value / Value
		Andy Warhol Museum	Smplr	U.S.	1994	$25.00
	Picture book and CD sampler.					

Warhol Babies

Singles

Label	Catalog Number	Title	Type	Country	Year	Longbox Value / Value
Columbia	CSK 4654	Cry Yourself To Sleep	CDJ	U.S.	1992	$2.00
Columbia	CSK 4185	Hang Me Up	CDJ	U.S.	1991	$2.00

Wariner, Steve

Full Length

Label	Catalog Number	Title	Type	Country	Year	Longbox Value / Value
		Gotta Drive	DJ/Intvw	U.S.	1993	$20.00
Arista	2638	Gotta Drive	DJ/Intvw	U.S.	1993	$25.00
	Interviewed by Garth Brooks.					
MCA	CD33 3022	MCA Radio Special	DJ/RS	U.S.	1990	$8.00
MCA	CD45 53733	Domino Theory, The	CDJ	U.S.	1990	$2.00

Label	Catalog Number	Title	Type	Country	Year	Longbox Value / Value
MCA	CD45 1164	On Christmas Morning	CDJ	U.S.	1990	$2.00

Warlock

Full Length

Label	Catalog Number	Title	Type	Country	Year	Longbox Value / Value
Image	ID7773EM	Live From London	LD	U.S.		$20.00
Mercury		True as Steel	LP/LB	U.S.		$14.00/$8.00

Warner

Singles

Label	Catalog Number	Title	Type	Country	Year	Longbox Value / Value
CBS	655602 3	Pump Up Das Bier	CD3	Germany	1989	$8.00

Warnes, Jennifer

Singles

Label	Catalog Number	Title	Type	Country	Year	Longbox Value / Value
Cypress	37581	First We Take Manhattan	CD3	U.S.	1988	$6.00/$4.00
Cypress		First We Take Manhattan	CDJ	U.S.	1988	$2.00

Warpipes

Singles

Label	Catalog Number	Title	Type	Country	Year	Longbox Value / Value
Artful	AB 7224	Back A Ma Buick	CDJ	U.S.	1991	$2.00

Warrant

Full Length

Label	Catalog Number	Title	Type	Country	Year	Longbox Value / Value
Sony	XDDP-93062	Hits	DJ/Smplr	Japan		$35.00

Singles

Label	Catalog Number	Title	Type	Country	Year	Longbox Value / Value
Sony	CSDS-8114	Big Talk	CD3	Japan	1989	$12.00/$4.00
Columbia	CSK 1839	Big Talk	CDJ	U.S.	1989	$2.00
Columbia	CSK 4818	Bitter Pill, The	CDJ	U.S.	1992	$2.00
Columbia	CSK 73598	Blind Faith	CDJ	U.S.	1991	$2.00
Columbia	656258-3	Cherry Pie	CD3	Germany	1990	$8.00
Columbia	486563-2	Cherry Pie	CD5	Germany	1996	$11.00
Sony	CSDS-8170	Cherry Pie	CD3	Japan	1990	$12.00/$4.00
Columbia	656686-5	Cherry Pie	CD5	U.K.	1990	$10.00
Columbia	CSK 73510	Cherry Pie	CDJ	U.S.	1990	$2.00
Columbia		Dog Eat Dog	CDJ	U.S.		$2.00
Columbia	CSK 1602	Down Boys	CDJ	U.S.	1989	$2.00
		Followed	CDJ	U.S.		$2.00
Columbia	HEAVNC-1	Heaven	CD5	U.K.	1989	$8.00
Columbia	CSK 4829	Hole in My Wall, The	CDJ	U.S.	1992	$2.00
Columbia	CSK 73597	I Saw Red	CDJ	U.S.	1990	$2.00
Columbia	CSK 4701	Inside Out	CDJ	U.S.	1992	$2.00
Sony	SRDS-8235	Machine Gun	CD3	Japan	1992	$12.00/$4.00
Columbia	CSK 4685	Machine Gun	CDJ	U.S.	1991	$2.00
Sony	CSDS-8123	Sometimes She Cries	CD3	Japan	1990	$12.00/$4.00
Columbia	CSK 73095	Sometimes She Cries	CDJ	U.S.	1990	$2.00
		Stronger Now	CDJ	U.S.		$2.00
Sony	CSDS8179	Uncle Tom's Cabin	CD3	Japan	1991	$12.00/$4.00
Columbia	CSK 73644	Uncle Tom's Cabin	CDJ	U.S.	1991	$2.00
Sony	SRDS-8227	We Will Rock You	CD3	Japan	1992	$12.00/$4.00
Columbia	CSK 74207	We Will Rock You	CDJ	U.S.	1992	$2.00

Warrior

Full Length

Label	Catalog Number	Title	Type	Country	Year	Longbox Value / Value
Warner Brothers	26531	Fighting for the Earth	LP/LB	U.S.		$14.00/$8.00

Warrior Soul

Full Length

Label	Catalog Number	Title	Type	Country	Year	Longbox Value / Value
DGC	2-24285-Dj	Last Decade Dead Century	DJ/LP	U.S.	1990	$15.00
DGC	PRO-CD-4153	Superpower Dreamland	DJ/Intvw	U.S.	1990	$12.00

Singles

Label	Catalog Number	Title	Type	Country	Year	Longbox Value / Value
Geffen	DGCT-10	Hero	CD5	U.K.	1992	$10.00
DGC	PRO-CD-4457	Love Destruction	CDJ	U.S.	1992	$3.00
DGC	PRO-CD-4472	Shock Um Down	CDJ	U.S.	1992	$3.00
DGC	PRO-CD-4242	Wasteland, The	CDJ	U.S.	1991	$3.00
DGC		We Cry Out	CDJ	U.S.	1990	$3.00

Warwick, Dionne

Full Length

Label	Catalog Number	Title	Type	Country	Year	Longbox Value / Value
		A Taste of Brazil Sampler	DJ/Smplr	U.S.		$8.00
Arista	ARCD-8262	Finder of Lost Love	LP/LB	U.S.†	1985	$14.00/$8.00
Arista	ARCD-8006	Heartbreaker	LP/LB	U.S.†	1984	$14.00/$8.00
Disky	DCD 5403	Here Where This Love	LTD/LP	Germany	1994	$22.00
CD in box.						
Disky	DCD 5499	Valley Of Dolls	LTD/LP	Germany	1994	$22.00
CD in box.						

Singles

Label	Catalog Number	Title	Type	Country	Year	Longbox Value / Value
Hit Avenue	FHDG-1003	Alfie	CD3	Japan	1991	$13.00/$4.00
Old Gold	OG-6140	Anyone Who Had a Heart	CD3	U.K.	1989	$9.00
Arista	162055	Heartbreaker	CD3	Germany	1989	$9.00
Arista	162055	Heartbreaker	CD3	U.K.	1989	$9.00
Arista	ASCD-9940	I Don't Need Another	CDJ	U.S.	1989	$2.00
Arista	ASCD-9567	Love Power	CDJ	U.S.	1987	$2.00
Arista	BVDA-50	Sunny Weather Lover	CD3	Japan	1993	$12.00/$4.00
Arista	ASCD-2477	Sunny Weather Lover	CDJ	U.S.	1993	$2.00
Arista	A10D-146	Take Good Care of You and Me	CD3	Japan	1989	$12.00/$4.00
Arista	662894	Take Good Care of You and Me	CD5	U.K.	1989	$9.00
Arista	ASCD-9901	Take Good Care of You and Me	CDJ	U.S.	1989	$2.00
Arista	663101	Walk Away	CD5	U.K.	1989	$9.00

Was (Not Was)

Singles

Label	Catalog Number	Title	Type	Country	Year	Longbox Value / Value
Fontana	870518-2	Anything Can Happen	CD5	Canada	1989	$10.00
Fontana	WASCD-5	Anything Can Happen	CD5	U.K.	1988	$9.00
Fontana	WASCD-6	Anything Can Happen	CD5	U.K.	1989	$9.00
Chrysalis	DPRO-43365	Anything Can Happen	CDJ	U.S.	1989	$3.00
Fontana	SFSPC-9	Boy's Gone Crazy	CD5	U.K.	1989	$9.00
Fontana	875977-2	How the Heart Behaves	CD5	Germany	1990	$9.00
Fontana	WASCD-8	How the Heart Behaves	CD5	U.K.	1990	$9.00
Fontana	WASCD-9	I Feel Better Than James Brown	CD5	U.K.	1990	$9.00
Fontana	WASCD-10	Listen Like Thieves	CD5	U.K.	1992	$9.00
Fontana	WASCD-4	Out Come the Freaks	CD5	U.K.	1988	$9.00
Fontana	WASCD-7	Papa Was a Rollin' Stone	CD5	U.K.	1990	$9.00
Chrysalis	DPRO-23584	Papa Was a Rollin' Stone	CDJ	U.S.	1990	$3.00
Fontana	WASCD-11	Shake Your Head	CD5	U.K.	1992	$9.00
Fontana	WASCD-12	Somewhere in America	CD5	U.K.	1992	$9.00
Fontana	870091-2	Spy in the House of Love	CD5	Germany	1988	$9.00
Fontana	WASCD-2	Spy in the House of Love	CD5	U.K.	1988	$9.00
Fontana	88809-2	Walk the Dinosaur	CD5	Germany	1988	$9.00
Fontana	88809-2	Walk the Dinosaur	CD5	U.K.	1988	$9.00

Wash, Martha

Singles

Label	Catalog Number	Title	Type	Country	Year	Longbox Value / Value
RCA	62367-2-RDJ	Carry On	CD5	U.S.	1992	$5.00
RCA	62434-2-RDJ	Give It to You	CDJ	U.S.	1992	$2.00
RCA	62461-2-RDJ	Give It to You	CDJ	U.S.	1992	$2.00
RCA	62525-2-RDJ	Now That You're Gone	CDJ	U.S.	1993	$2.00
RCA	62542-2-RDJ	Runaround	CD5	U.S.	1992	$5.00

Washington, Dinah

Full Length

Label	Catalog Number	Title	Type	Country	Year	Longbox Value / Value
Emarcy	814639-2	Dinah Jams	LP/LB	U.S.†	1985	$14.00/$8.00
Emarcy	818930-2	Fats Waller Songbook	LP/LB	U.S.†	1985	$14.00/$8.00
Mercury	818815-2	What a Difference a Day Makes	LP/LB	U.S.†	1985	$14.00/$8.00

Washington, Grover, Jr.

Full Length

Label	Catalog Number	Title	Type	Country	Year	Longbox Value / Value
Elektra	562-2	Come Morning	LP/LB	U.S.†	1985	$14.00/$8.00
Elektra	60318-2	Inside Moves	LP/LB	U.S.†	1985	$14.00/$8.00
Elektra	182-2	Paradise	LP/LB	U.S.†	1985	$14.00/$8.00
Elektra	60215-2	The Best Is Yet to Come	LP/LB	U.S.†	1985	$14.00/$8.00
Warner Brothers	43P2-0010	Winelight	LTD/LP	Japan	1988	$45.00
Gold disc.						
Elektra	305-2	Winelight	LP/LB	U.S.†	1985	$14.00/$8.00

Singles

Label	Catalog Number	Title	Type	Country	Year	Longbox Value / Value
Columbia	CSK 730404	Jamaica	CDJ	U.S.	1989	$2.00
WEA	969340-2	Just the Two of Us	CD3	Germany	1989	$8.00
WEA	969340-2	Just the Two of Us	CD3	U.K.	1989	$8.00
Columbia	CSK 4524	Love Like This	CDJ	U.S.	1992	$2.00
Columbia	CSK 73234	Sacred King of Love	CDJ	U.S.	1990	$2.00
Columbia	CSK 4724	Take Five	CDJ	U.S.	1992	$2.00

Washington, Keith

Full Length

Label	Catalog Number	Title	Type	Country	Year	Longbox Value / Value
QWest/Warner Bros.	9 26528-2-Dj	Make Time for Love	DJ/LP	U.S.	1991	$10.00
Picture disc.						

Singles

Label	Catalog Number	Title	Type	Country	Year	Longbox Value / Value
QWest/Warner Bros.	PRO-CD-4877	Are You Still In Love With Me	CDJ	U.S.	1991	$2.00
Warner Brothers	9362-40125-2	Kissing You	CD5	Germany	1991	$8.00
Warner Brothers	W-0041CD	Kissing You	CD5	U.K.	1991	$8.00
QWest/Warner Bros.	PRO-CD-6429	Stay in My Corner	CDJ	U.S.	1993	$2.00

Washington Squares

Singles

Label	Catalog Number	Title	Type	Country	Year	Longbox Value / Value
Gold Castle	DPRO 79514	Everybody Knows	CDJ	U.S.	1989	$2.00

Washington, Walter Wolfman

Singles

Label	Catalog Number	Title	Type	Country	Year	Longbox Value / Value
Pointblank	WOLF 1	Ain't No Love in the Heart	CDJ	U.S.	1991	$2.00

Wasserman, Rob

Singles

Label	Catalog Number	Title	Type	Country	Year	Longbox Value / Value
		White-Wheeled Limousine	CDJ	U.S.		$2.00

Wasted Time

Singles

Label	Catalog Number	Title	Type	Country	Year	Longbox Value / Value
		Brown-Eyed Girl	CDJ	U.S.		$2.00

Watanabe, Kazumi

Full Length

Label	Catalog Number	Title	Type	Country	Year	Longbox Value / Value
Pioneer	SM037-3479	Kazumi Watanabe	LD	U.S.	1987	$30.00
Denon	CD-7135	Kylyn	LP/LB	U.S.†	1985	$14.00/$8.00
Denon	CD-7017	Lonesome Cat	LP/LB	U.S.†	1985	$14.00/$8.00
Gramaphone	18-8506-2	Mobo Club	LP/LB	U.S.†	1985	$14.00/$8.00
Gramaphone	GRCD-8406	Mobo II	LP/LB	U.S.†	1985	$14.00/$8.00
Am Gramm		Mobo Splash	LP/LB	U.S.		$14.00/$8.00
Am Gramm		Spice of Life	LP/LB	U.S.		$14.00/$8.00
Am Gramm		Spice of Life Too	LP/LB	U.S.		$14.00/$8.00
Denon	CD-7136	To Chi Ka	LP/LB	U.S.†	1985	$14.00/$8.00

Watanabe, Sado

Full Length

Label	Catalog Number	Title	Type	Country	Year	Longbox Value / Value
Elektra	43XD-2010	Fill up the Light	LTD/LP	Japan	1988	$45.00
Gold disc.						
Elektra	60297-2	Fill up the Night	LP/LB	U.S.†	1985	$14.00/$8.00
Elektra	43P2-0015	Selected	LTD/LP	Japan	1988	$45.00
Gold disc.						

Singles

Label	Catalog Number	Title	Type	Country	Year	Longbox Value / Value
Pioneer	09P3-6200	Any Other Fool	CD3	Japan	1989	$13.00/$4.00
		Any Other Fool	CDJ	U.S.	1988	$2.00
Pioneer	10SW-42	Manhattan Paulista	CD3	Japan	1988	$13.00/$4.00
Pioneer	09P3-6158	Only in My Mind	CD3	Japan	1989	$13.00/$4.00
Pioneer	WPDP-6276	Only Love	CD3	Japan	1991	$13.00/$4.00

Watchmen

Full Length

Label	Catalog Number	Title	Type	Country	Year	Longbox Value / Value
		Interview	DJ/Intvw	U.S.	1993	$15.00

Water Walk

Singles

Label	Catalog Number	Title	Type	Country	Year	Longbox Value / Value
IRS	67033	Never Leaving Eden Again	CDJ	U.S.	1990	$2.00

Waterboys

Full Length

Label	Catalog Number	Title	Type	Country	Year	Longbox Value / Value
EMI		Best Of the Waterboys	LTD/LP	U.K.	1997	$35.00
Limited edition centennial CD edition housed in a slip case with a special 100 anniversary booklet.						
Geffen	PRO-CD-4522	Dream Harder	DJ/Intvw	U.S.	1993	$10.00
Geffen	PRO-CD-4522	Mike Scott Dream Harder Interview	DJ/Intvw	U.S.		$10.00
Chrysalis	DPRO 23719	Mike Scott Interview, The	DJ/Intvw	U.S.	1991	$10.00
Chrysalis		This is the Sea	LTD/LP	U.K.	1994	$25.00/$15.00
25th Anniversary edition in 6"x11" longbox.						

Singles

Label	Catalog Number	Title	Type	Country	Year	Longbox Value / Value
BMG	662345	And a Bang on the Ear	CD5	Germany	1989	$10.00
Ensign	ENYCD-624	And a Bang on the Ear	CD5	U.K.	1989	$10.00
Chrysalis	DPRO-23377	And a Bang on the Ear	CDJ	U.S.	1989	$2.00
BMG	885286	Fisherman's Blues	CD5	Germany	1989	$10.00
Ensign	ENYCD-621	Fisherman's Blues	CD5	U.K.	1989	$10.00
Ensign	ENYCD-645	Fisherman's Blues	CD5	U.K.	1991	$10.00
Geffen	21824	Glastonbury Song	CDJ	U.S.	1993	$2.00
EMI	323611-2	How Long Will I Love You	CD5	Germany	1990	$10.00
EMI	323778-2	Man in Love	CD5	Germany	1991	$10.00
Geffen	PRO-CD-4544	Preparing to Fly	CDJ	U.S.	1993	$2.00
Geffen	21807	Return of Pan	CD5	Germany	1993	$10.00
Geffen	MVCG-13006	Return of Pan	CD3	Japan	1993	$12.00/$4.00
Geffen	GFSTD 42	Return of Pan	CD5	U.K.	1993	$10.00
Geffen	PRO-CD-4518	Return of Pan	CDJ	U.S.	1993	$7.00
Geffen	PRO-CD-4518	Return of Pan	CDJ	U.S.	1993	$8.00
Ensign	ENYCD-642	Whole of the Moon	CD5	U.K.	1991	$10.00
Chrysalis	DPRO-23716	Whole of the Moon	CDJ	U.S.	1991	$6.00

Waterdog

Singles

Label	Catalog Number	Title	Type	Country	Year	Longbox Value / Value
		My Life	CDJ	U.S.		$2.00

Waterfront

Singles

Label	Catalog Number	Title	Type	Country	Year	Longbox Value / Value
Polydor	WONCD-3	Broken Arrow	CD5	U.K.	1989	$8.00
Polygram	889540-3	Cry	CD3	Germany	1989	$8.00
Polygram	889541-2	Cry	CD5	Germany	1989	$8.00
Polydor	WONCD-1	Cry	CD5	U.K.	1989	$8.00
Polydor	CDP 38	Cry	CDJ	U.S.	1988	$2.00
Polydor		Cry	CDJ	U.S.	1988	$2.00
Second version.						
Polydor	WONCD-5	Move On	CD5	U.K.	1989	$8.00
Polydor		Move On	CDJ	U.S.	1988	$2.00
Polygram	889092-3	Nature of Love	CD3	Germany	1989	$8.00
Polygram	889093-2	Nature of Love	CD5	Germany	1989	$8.00
Polygram	WONCD-2	Nature of Love	CD5	U.K.	1989	$8.00
Polydor	CDP 94	Nature of Love	CDJ	U.S.	1988	$2.00

Waterlilies

Singles

Label	Catalog Number	Title	Type	Country	Year	Longbox Value / Value
Warner Brothers	41879	Never Got Enough	CD5	U.S.	1994	$5.00
Warner	12-41612	Tempted	CD5	Canada	1994	$8.00
Warner Brothers	9 41612-2	Tempted	CD5	U.S.	1994	$5.00

Waters, Crystal

Full Length

Label	Catalog Number	Title	Type	Country	Year	Longbox Value / Value
		Storyteller	DJ/Smplr	U.S.		$12.00
Mercury	858711	100% Pure Love	CD5	U.S.	1994	$5.00
Polygram	858711	100% Pure Love	CD5	U.S.	1994	$5.00
Epic	658437-2	Gypsy Woman	CD5	Germany	1992	$8.00
A&M	AMCD-772	Gypsy Woman	CD5	U.K.	1991	$8.00
A&M	868397-2	Gypsy Woman	CD5	U.K.	1991	$8.00
Mercury	868209	Gypsy Woman	CD5	U.S.	1991	$5.00
Mercury	CDP 449	Gypsy Woman	CDJ	U.S.	1991	$2.00
Mercury	PHDR-30	Ladaddy Ladada	CD3	Japan	1991	$12.00/$3.00
A&M	868849-2	Makin' Happy	CD5	Germany	1991	$8.00
A&M	AMCD-790	Makin' Happy	CD5	U.K.	1991	$8.00
Mercury	CDP 538	Makin' Happy	CDJ	U.S.	1991	$2.00
A&M	AMCD-843	Megamix	CD5	U.K.	1992	$8.00
Polygram	578943-2	Say If You Feel Alright	CD5	U.S.	1997	$3.50

Waters, Kim

Singles

Label	Catalog Number	Title	Type	Country	Year	Longbox Value / Value
		Hello Stranger	CDJ	U.S.		$2.00
		Just Be My Lady	CDJ	U.S.		$2.00
Warlock	7074	Sweet and Saxy	CDJ	U.S.		$2.00

Waters, Muddy

Full Length

Label	Catalog Number	Title	Type	Country	Year	Longbox Value / Value
		House of Blues	RS	U.S.	1994	$40.00
2 CD set. Airdate: 4/3/94.						

Singles

Label	Catalog Number	Title	Type	Country	Year	Longbox Value / Value
Sony	651637-3	Mannish Boy	CD3	Germany	1988	$10.00
Columbia	CK-53196	Amused to Death	LP/LB	U.S.	1993	$28.00/$25.00
Gold disc.						

Waters, Roger

Full Length

Label	Catalog Number	Title	Type	Country	Year	Longbox Value / Value
Columbia	CK-64426	Amused to Death	LTD/LP	U.S.	1994	$25.00
Gold disc.						
Mecury	CDP 318	Live in Berlin	DJ/Smplr	U.S.	1990	$6.00
Westwood One		Off the Record	RS	U.S.	1992	$30.00
Airdate: 10/12/92.						
Westwood One		Off the Record	RS	U.S.	1992	$35.00
Airdate: 10/12/92.						
CBS	CK 39290	Pros & Cons of Hitchhiking	LP/PD	U.S.†	1984	$14.00/$8.00
Westwood One		Superstars	RS	U.S.	1995	$100.00
2 CD set. Airdate: 6/12/95.						
Media America		Up Close	RS	U.S.	1993	$60.00
2 CD set.						
Columbia	CSK 2126	Wall, Berlin, The	DJ/Smplr	U.S.	1990	$35.00
Mercury		Wall, The	DJ/LP	U.S.	1990	$80.00
2CD live album, video and tour book in large box.						

Singles

Label	Catalog Number	Title	Type	Country	Year	Longbox Value / Value
Mercury	878185-2	Another Brick in the Wall	CD5	Germany	1990	$10.00
Mercury	MERCD-332	Another Brick in the Wall	CD5	U.K.	1990	$10.00
Mercury	CDP 342	Another Brick in the Wall	CDJ	U.S.	1990	$25.00
CD in foam brick.						
Columbia	CSK 4830	Bravery of Being Out of Range	CDJ	U.S.	1992	$6.00
Mercury	CDP 349	Hey You	CDJ	U.S.	1990	$6.00
		Pieces From the Wall	CDJ	U.K.	1990	$12.00
Mercury		Pieces From the Wall	CDJ	U.S.	1990	$6.00
	27LP132	Radio Kaos	8" LD	Japan		$45.00
EMI	201824-2	Radio Waves	CD5	Germany	1987	$10.00
EMI	CDEM-6	Radio Waves	CD5	U.K.	1987	$10.00
Columbia	CSK 4941	Three Wishes	CDJ	U.S.	1992	$7.00
Polygram	878549-2	Tide Is Turning	CD5	Germany	1990	$10.00
EMI	CDEM-37	Tide Is Turning	CD5	U.K.	1990	$10.00
Mercury	MERCD-336	Tide Is Turning	CD5	U.K.	1990	$10.00
Mercury	CDP 367	Tide Is Turning	CDJ	U.S.	1990	$6.00
Columbia	658139	What God Wants	CD5	Germany	1992	$10.00
Columbia		What God Wants	CD5	U.K.	1992	$13.00
Columbia	44K 74363	What God Wants	CD5	U.S.	1992	$5.00
Columbia	CSK 4607	What God Wants	CDJ	U.S.	1992	$7.00

Watford, Michael

Singles

Label	Catalog Number	Title	Type	Country	Year	Longbox Value / Value
Eastwest	PRCD 5474-2	So Into You	CDJ	U.S.	1994	$2.00

Watkins, Derek

Singles

Label	Catalog Number	Title	Type	Country	Year	Longbox Value / Value
		He Man	CDJ	U.S.		$2.00

Watkins, Mitch

Singles

Label	Catalog Number	Title	Type	Country	Year	Longbox Value / Value
		Underneath It All	CDJ	U.S.		$2.00

Watley, Jody

Full Length

Label	Catalog Number	Title	Type	Country	Year	Longbox Value / Value
Unistar		Jody Watley Story, The	RS	U.S.	1992	$10.00
Airdate: 3/27/92.						

Singles

Label	Catalog Number	Title	Type	Country	Year	Longbox Value / Value
Eastwest	257416-2	Everything	CD3	Germany	1989	$8.00
MCA	DMCAT-1382	Everything	CD5	U.K.	1989	$8.00
MCA	DMCAT-1395	Everything	CD5	U.K.	1990	$8.00
MCA	257536-2	Friends	CD3	Germany	1989	$8.00
Pioneer	09P3-6168	Friends	CD3	Japan	1989	$13.00/$4.00
MCA	DMCAT-1352	Friends	CD5	U.K.	1989	$8.00
MCA	MVDM-7	I Want You	CD3	Japan	1991	$13.00/$4.00
MCA	CD45 51634	I Want You	CDJ	U.S.	1991	$2.00
MCA	1634	I Want You	CDJ	U.S.	1991	$2.00
MCA	2064	I Want You	CDJ	U.S.	1991	$2.00
MCA	MVDM-17	I'm the One You Need	CD3	Japan	1992	$13.00/$4.00
MCA	MCA5P 4382	I'm the One You Need	CD5	U.S.	1990	$5.00
MCA	2049	I'm the One You Need	CDJ	U.S.	1990	$2.00
MCA	2162	I'm the One You Need	CDJ	U.S.	1990	$2.00
MCA	2163	I'm the One You Need	CDJ	U.S.	1990	$2.00
MCA	MVDM-26	It All Began With You	CD3	Japan	1992	$13.00/$4.00
MCA	MCA5P 2226	It All Began With You	CD5	U.S.	1992	$4.00
MCA	10SW-43	Most of All	CD3	Japan	1988	$13.00/$4.00
MCA		Most of All	CDJ	U.S.	1988	$2.00
MCA	DMCAT-1410	Precious Love	CD5	U.K.	1990	$8.00
MCA	CD45 18114	Precious Love	CDJ	U.S.	1989	$2.00
MCA	257632-2	Real Love	CD3	Germany	1989	$8.00
MCA	09P3-6108	Real Love	CD3	Japan	1989	$13.00/$4.00
MCA	DMCAT-1324	Real Love	CD5	U.K.	1989	$8.00
MCA	CD45 17790	Real Love	CDJ	U.S.	1989	$2.00
MCA	10SW-32	Some Kind of Lover	CD3	Japan	1988	$13.00/$4.00
MCA	2925	When A Man Loves a Woman	CDJ	U.S.	1993	$2.00
MCA	2975	When A Man Loves a Woman	CDJ	U.S.	1994	$2.00
MCA	2925	You Love Keeps Working on Me	CDJ	U.S.	1993	$2.00

Watson, Gene

Singles

Label	Catalog Number	Title	Type	Country	Year	Longbox Value / Value
Step One	SOR 468	Snake the House	CDJ	U.S.	1993	$2.00
		This Country's Bigger Than Texas	CDJ	U.S.		$2.00

Watson, Johnny

Singles

Label	Catalog Number	Title	Type	Country	Year	Longbox Value / Value
Bellmark Records	72515	Bow Wow	CD5	U.S.	1994	$5.00
Belmark Records	72533	Heal Me Up	CD5	U.S.	[illegible]	[illegible]

Watson, Kno

Singles

Label	Catalog Number	Title	Type	Country	Year	Longbox Value / Value
		Bring It On	CDJ	U.S.		$2.00

Watson, Wayne

Singles

Label	Catalog Number	Title	Type	Country	Year	Longbox Value / Value
		When God's People Pray	CDJ	U.S.		$2.00

Watt, Mike

Full Length

Label	Catalog Number	Title	Type	Country	Year	Longbox Value / Value
Columbia	CK 66464	Ball-Hog or Tug-Boat	LTD/LP	U.S.	1995	$16.00
CD in 6"x12" folder.						

Singles

Label	Catalog Number	Title	Type	Country	Year	Longbox Value / Value
Columbia	CSK 7028	Big Train	CDJ	U.S.	1995	$3.00
Columbia	CSK 7117	Piss-Bottle Man	CDJ	U.S.	1995	$3.00

Watts, Charlie

Full Length

Label	Catalog Number	Title	Type	Country	Year	Longbox Value / Value
Continuum		Warm & Tender	DJ/LP	U.S.	1993	$12.00
Advance issue in plastic sleeve.						

Singles

Label	Catalog Number	Title	Type	Country	Year	Longbox Value / Value
Continuum	13310	I'll Be Around	CDJ	U.S.	1994	$7.00
Continuum	12201	Loverman	CDJ	U.S.	1992	$7.00
Continuum		Practising	CDJ	U.S.		$7.00

Watts, Ernie And Gamalon

Singles

Label	Catalog Number	Title	Type	Country	Year	Longbox Value / Value
		Lift Off	CDJ	U.S.		$2.00

Wawanee

Singles

Label	Catalog Number	Title	Type	Country	Year	Longbox Value / Value
		Sugar Free	CDJ	U.S.		$2.00

Way Moves

Singles

Label	Catalog Number	Title	Type	Country	Year	Longbox Value / Value
Chameleon	75	One More Kiss	CDJ	U.S.	1990	$2.00
Chameleon	90	Revel	CDJ	U.S.	1990	$2.00

WC and the Mad Circle

Singles

Label	Catalog Number	Title	Type	Country	Year	Longbox Value / Value
Polygram		One, The	CDJ	U.S.	1995	$2.00
Polygram	850298	West Up!	CDJ	U.S.	1995	$2.00

We All Fall Down

Singles

Label	Catalog Number	Title	Type	Country	Year	Longbox Value / Value
	10	Fairy Tales	CD5	U.S.	1994	$5.00
	10	Fairy Tales	CD5	U.S.	1994	$5.00

Weapon of Choice

Full Length

Label	Catalog Number	Title	Type	Country	Year	Longbox Value / Value
	BSK 7758	Highperspice Sampler	DJ/Smplr	U.S.		$6.00

Weather Report

Full Length

Label	Catalog Number	Title	Type	Country	Year	Longbox Value / Value
Columbia	CK-39142	Domino Theory	LP/LB	U.S.		$14.00/$8.00
CBS	39147	Domino Theory	LP/LB	U.S.†	1985	$14.00/$8.00
CBS	CK-34418	Heavy Weather	LP/LB	U.S.†	1985	$14.00/$8.00
Legacy	CK-57185	Heavy Weather	LP/LB	U.S.	1993	$28.00/$25.00
Gold disc.						
Legacy	CK-64427	Heavy Weather	LTD/LP	U.S.	1994	$25.00
Gold disc.						
CBS	CK-32494	Mysterious Traveller	LP/LB	U.S.†	1985	$14.00/$8.00
CBS	CK-36793	Night Passage	LP/LB	U.S.†	1985	$14.00/$8.00
		Spiral	8"LD	U.S.		$10.00
CBS	CK-39908	Sportin' Life	LP/LB	U.S.†	1985	$14.00/$8.00
Sony	SRCS6907	Starbox	LTD/LP	Japan	1993	$30.00

Weathermen

Singles

Label	Catalog Number	Title	Type	Country	Year	Longbox Value / Value
		Bang!	CD3	Germany		$8.00

Weathers, Barbara

Singles

Label	Catalog Number	Title	Type	Country	Year	Longbox Value / Value
		Master Key, The	CDJ	U.S.		$2.00
		My Only Love	CDJ	U.S.		$2.00

Weaver, Jason

Singles

Label	Catalog Number	Title	Type	Country	Year	Longbox Value / Value
Motown	860349	I Can't Stand the Pain	CD5	U.S.	1995	$5.00
Motown	860349	I Can't Stand the Pain	CD5	U.S.	1995	$5.00
Motown	374631076	I Wanna Be Where You Are	CDJ	U.S.	1992	$2.00
		Love Ambition	CDJ	U.S.		$2.00

Weavers

Full Length

Label	Catalog Number	Title	Type	Country	Year	Longbox Value/Value
Vanguard	706	Wasn't That a Time	DJ/Smplr	U.S.	1993	$12.00

Webb, Jimmy

Singles

Label	Catalog Number	Title	Type	Country	Year	Longbox Value/Value
CBS	66654	Angel Heart	CD5	U.S.	1994	$5.00
Elektra	PRCD 8798-2	Too Young to Die	CDJ	U.S.	1993	$2.00

Webber, Andrew Lloyd

Full Length

Label	Catalog Number	Title	Type	Country	Year	Longbox Value/Value
Polydor	SACD646	Premiere Collection Encore	DJ/Smplr	U.S.	1992	$20.00
Polydor	SACD 646	Premiere Collection Oncore	DJ/Smplr	U.S.	1993	$25.00

Webster, Ben

Full Length

Label	Catalog Number	Title	Type	Country	Year	Longbox Value/Value
Polygram	814410-2	Big Ben Time	LP/BP	U.S.		$12.00/$7.00
Philips	814410-2	Big Ben Time	LP/LB	U.S.†	1985	$14.00/$8.00

Wedding Present

Singles

Label	Catalog Number	Title	Type	Country	Year	Longbox Value/Value
Island	CID-585	Yeah Yeah Yeah	CD5	U.K.	1994	$10.00

Weddings, Parties, Anything

Singles

Label	Catalog Number	Title	Type	Country	Year	Longbox Value/Value
		Island Of Humor	CD5	Australia		$10.00

Wee Papa Girl Rappers

Singles

Label	Catalog Number	Title	Type	Country	Year	Longbox Value/Value
Jive	1362-2JDJ	Bump, The	CDJ	U.S.	1990	$2.00

Ween

Singles

Label	Catalog Number	Title	Type	Country	Year	Longbox Value/Value
Elektra	PRCD 8670-2	Little Birdy	CDJ	U.S.	1992	$2.00

Weezer

Singles

Label	Catalog Number	Title	Type	Country	Year	Longbox Value/Value
Columbia		Buddy Holly	CDJ	U.S.	1995	$6.00
CBS		Say It Ain't So	CD5	U.K.	1995	$10.00
Columbia		Say it Ain't So	CD5	U.K.	1995	$11.00
Geffen	PRO-CD-4742	Say It Ain't So	CDJ	U.S.	1994	$7.00
Columbia		Undone	CDJ	U.S.	1995	$6.00

Weisberg, Tim

Singles

Label	Catalog Number	Title	Type	Country	Year	Longbox Value/Value
Cypress	YD 17791	Outrageous Temptations	CDJ	U.S.	1989	$2.00

Welch, Bob

Full Length

Label	Catalog Number	Title	Type	Country	Year	Longbox Value/Value
Cema		French Kiss	LP/LB	U.S.		$14.00/$8.00

Welch, Kevin

Singles

Label	Catalog Number	Title	Type	Country	Year	Longbox Value/Value
Warner Brothers	PRO-CD-3347	Stay November	CDJ	U.S.		$2.00

Welk, Lawrence

Full Length

Label	Catalog Number	Title	Type	Country	Year	Longbox Value/Value
EMI		World's Greatest Polka Hits	LP	U.K.	1986	$50.00

Plays the Sex Pistols' "Rock And Roll Swindle"

Weller, Paul

Full Length

Label	Catalog Number	Title	Type	Country	Year	Longbox Value/Value
		A Conversation With Paul Weller	DJ/Intvw	U.S.	1995	$15.00
		Conversation With	DJ/Intvw	U.S.		$15.00
		Peacock Suit	DJ/Smplr	U.K.		$25.00
	PWRT 1	Peacock Suit Repeated	DJ/Smplr	U.K.		$60.00
		Stanley Road	LTD/LP	U.K.	1995	$30.00
2 CD set.						
		Wild Wood	DJ/LP	U.K.	1994	$18.00
Advance issue.						
Polygram	CDP 1216	Wild Wood	DJ/LP	U.S.	1994	$20.00
2 CD set.						

Singles

Label	Catalog Number	Title	Type	Country	Year	Longbox Value/Value
Go Discs	869927-2	Above the Clouds	CD5	Germany	1992	$8.00
Go Discs	GODCD-91	Above the Clouds	CD5	U.K.	1992	$8.00
London	CDP 861	Above the Clouds	CDJ	U.S.	1993	$2.00
		Bull-Rush	CDJ	U.S.		$8.00
		Changingman, The	CD5	U.K.	1995	$10.00
Polygram		Changingman, The	CDJ	U.S.	1994	$6.00
Canyon	PCDY-00098	Into Tomorrow	CD3	Japan	1991	$13.00/$4.00
		Into Tomorrow	CDJ	U.S.		$12.00
Polygram		Out of the Sinking	CDJ	U.K.	1994	$10.00
Go Discs		Out of the Sinking	CD5	U.K.	1996	$10.00
Polygram		Sexy Sadie & Wild Wood	CDJ	France	1994	$35.00
Go Discs!	8572032	Sunflower	CD5	Canada	1994	$8.00
		Sunflower	CDJ	Japan	1994	$15.00
Polygram	CDP 1219	Sunflower	CDJ	U.S.	1994	$2.00
Go Discs	869837-2	Uh Huh Oh Yes	CD5	Germany	1992	$8.00
Go Discs	GODCD-86	Uh Huh Oh Yes	CD5	U.K.	1992	$8.00
London	CDP 764	Uh Huh Oh Yes	CDJ	U.S.	1992	$2.00
Polygram		Visportished	CDJ	U.K.	1994	$35.00

Weller, Peter

Singles

Label	Catalog Number	Title	Type	Country	Year	Longbox Value/Value
	DSP-1019	Sunflower	CDJ	Japan		$35.00

Wells

Singles

Label	Catalog Number	Title	Type	Country	Year	Longbox Value/Value
MCA	54810	Out of Control	CD5	U.S.	1994	$5.00

Wells, Junior

Full Length

Label	Catalog Number	Title	Type	Country	Year	Longbox Value/Value
		House of Blues	RS	U.S.	1995	$40.00
2 CD set. Airdate: 4/23/95.						
		House of Blues	RS	U.S.	1995	$75.00
2 CD set. Airdate: 10/13/95.						

Wells, Mary

Full Length

Label	Catalog Number	Title	Type	Country	Year	Longbox Value/Value
Motown	5420-MD	One Who Really Loves	LP/BP	U.S.		$12.00/$7.00

Wells, Peter

Full Length

Label	Catalog Number	Title	Type	Country	Year	Longbox Value/Value
Zoo	11004	Everything You Like	LP/LB	U.S.		$12.00/$7.00

Singles

Label	Catalog Number	Title	Type	Country	Year	Longbox Value/Value
Zoo	ZP 17007	Between the Saddle and the Ground	CDJ	U.S.	1991	$2.00

Wendy & Lisa

Singles

Label	Catalog Number	Title	Type	Country	Year	Longbox Value/Value
Virgin	VSCD-1156	Are You My Baby	CD3	U.K.	1989	$9.00
Virgin	VSCDX-1337	Are You My Baby	CD5	U.K.	1991	$9.00
Columbia	CSK 1459	Are You My Baby	CDJ	U.S.	1989	$2.00
Geffen	PRO-CD-4480	Closing of the Year	CDJ	U.S.	1992	$2.00
Columbia	CSK 2914	Honeymoon Express	CDJ	U.S.	1988	$2.00
Virgin	162118	Lolly & Lolly	CD3	Germany	1989	$9.00
Virgin	662118	Lolly & Lolly	CD5	Germany	1989	$9.00
Virgin	VSCD-1175	Lolly & Lolly	CD3	U.K.	1989	$9.00
Virgin	663718	Rainbow Lake	CD5	Germany	1990	$9.00
Virgin	VSCDT-1280	Rainbow Lake	CD5	U.K.	1990	$9.00
Virgin	162434	Satisfaction	CD3	Germany	1989	$9.00
Virgin	VSCD-1194	Satisfaction	CD3	U.K.	1989	$9.00
Virgin	CDEP-16	Sideshow	CD5	U.K.	1988	$9.00
Virgin	663412	Strung Out	CD5	Germany	1990	$9.00
Virgin	VJCP-1410	Strung Out	CD3	Japan	1990	$12.00/$4.00
Virgin	VSCDT-1272	Strung Out	CD5	U.K.	1990	$9.00
Virgin	PRCD 3473	Strung Out	CDJ	U.S.	1990	$2.00
Virgin	162832	Waterfall '89	CD3	Germany	1989	$9.00
Virgin	VSCD-1223	Waterfall '89	CD3	U.K.	1989	$9.00
Virgin	PRCD 3635	Why Wait For Heaven	CDJ	U.S.	1990	$2.00

Wendy's

Singles

Label	Catalog Number	Title	Type	Country	Year	Longbox Value/Value
Eastwest	PRCD 4115-2	Sun's Going to Shine for Me Soon	CDJ	U.S.	1990	$2.00

Werner, Susan

Singles

Label	Catalog Number	Title	Type	Country	Year	Longbox Value/Value
		Introducing	CDJ	U.S.		$3.00

West Coast Rap All-Stars

Singles

Label	Catalog Number	Title	Type	Country	Year	Longbox Value/Value
Warner Brothers	9 21725-2	We're All in the Same Gang	CD5	Japan	1990	$4.00

West End Girls

Singles

Label	Catalog Number	Title	Type	Country	Year	Longbox Value/Value
A&M	030491	Not Like Kissing You	CDJ	Canada	1991	$3.00

West, Leslie

Full Length

Label	Catalog Number	Title	Type	Country	Year	Longbox Value/Value
IRS		Alligator	LP/LB	U.S.		$12.00/$7.00
Passport	PBCD-6061	Theme	LP/BP	U.S.		$17.00/$13.00

West Winds

Singles

Label	Catalog Number	Title	Type	Country	Year	Longbox Value/Value
Eclipse Music	CMM 026-2	Jazzy Christmas	SCDJ	U.S.	1996	$10.00
Snow man shaped CD.						

West World

Singles

Label	Catalog Number	Title	Type	Country	Year	Longbox Value/Value
MCA	CD45 1596	Do No Wrong	CDJ	U.S.	1991	$2.00

Westerberg, Paul

Full Length

Label	Catalog Number	Title	Type	Country	Year	Longbox Value/Value
Sire	45335-2	14 Songs	LTD/LP	U.S.	1993	$25.00
CD in book.						
Sire	PRO-CD-8110-A	Eventually	DJ/LP	U.S.		$12.00
CD in book.						

Singles

Label	Catalog Number	Title	Type	Country	Year	Longbox Value/Value
Epic	ESK 4479	Dyslexic Heart	CDJ	U.S.	1992	$3.00
Sire		Knockin' On Mine	CDJ	U.S.	1994	$7.00
		Love Untold	CD5	Germany	1996	$12.00
		Love Untold	CDJ	U.S.		$2.00
Sire	PRO-CD-6433	Runaway Wind	CDJ	U.S.	1993	$3.00
Sire	PRO-CD-6231	Silver Naked Ladies	CDJ	U.S.	1993	$3.00
		World Class Fad	CD5	U.K.		$10.00
		World Class Fad	CD5	U.K.		$10.00
Second version.						
Sire	W0209CD	World Class Fad	CD5	U.K.	1993	$10.00
Sire	PRO-CD-6229	World Class Fad	CDJ	U.S.	1993	$6.00

Weston, Randy

Full Length

Label	Catalog Number	Title	Type	Country	Year	Longbox Value/Value
Antillies	002	Discussions of the Spirits of Our Ancestors	DJ/Intvw	U.S.	1992	$10.00

Westworld

Singles

Label	Catalog Number	Title	Type	Country	Year	Longbox Value/Value
MCA	1596	Do No Wrong	CDJ	U.S.	1991	$2.00

Wet Wet Wet

Singles

Label	Catalog Number	Title	Type	Country	Year	Longbox Value/Value
Mercury	87005-2	Angel Eyes	CD5	Germany	1988	$8.00
Mercury	JWLCD-6	Angel Eyes	CD5	U.K.	1988	$8.00
IMS	876543-2	Broke Away	CD5	Germany	1990	$8.00
Mercury	JWLCD-10	Broke Away	CD5	U.K.	1990	$8.00
Mercury	JWLPD-10	Broke Away	CD5	U.K.	1990	$8.00
		Cold Cold Heart	CD5	U.K.		$10.00
		Cold Cold Heart	CD5	U.K.		$10.00
Second version.						
		Don't Want to Forgive Me Now	CDJ	U.S.		$2.00
		Goodnight Girl	CD5	Australia	1992	$8.00
Mercury		Goodnight Girl	CDJ	U.S.		$6.00
Polygram	856244	Goodnight Girl	CD5	U.S.	1994	$5.00
Polygram	856244	Goodnight Girl	CD5	U.S.	1994	$5.00
Mercury	876971-2	Hold Back the River	CD5	Germany	1990	$8.00
Mercury	JWLCD-11	Hold Back the River	CD5	U.K.	1990	$8.00
Mercury	4228560902	Love Is All Around	CD5	Canada	1994	$8.00
		Love Is All Around	CD5	U.K.		$10.00
		Love Is All Around	CD5	U.K.		$10.00
Second version.						
Polygram	856194	Love Is All Around	CD5	U.S.	1994	$5.00
Precious	868969-2	Make It Tonight	CD5	Germany	1991	$8.00
Mercury	PHDR-48	Make It Tonight	CD3	Japan	1991	$12.00/$4.00
Precious	JWLCD-15	Make It Tonight	CD5	U.K.	1991	$8.00
Precious	JWLCD-18	More Than Love	CD5	U.K.	1991	$8.00
Precious	875885-2	Stay With Me Heartache	CD5	Germany	1990	$8.00
Precious	JWLCD-13	Stay With Me Heartache	CD5	U.K.	1990	$8.00
Precious	870563-2	Sweet Little Mystery	CD5	Germany	1989	$8.00
Precious	876210-3	Sweet Sensation	CD3	Germany	1989	$8.00
Precious	876211-2	Sweet Sensation	CD5	Germany	1989	$8.00
Precious	JWLCD-9	Sweet Sensation	CD3	U.K.	1989	$8.00
Precious	870227-2	Temptation	CD5	Germany	1988	$8.00
Precious	JWLCD-7	Temptation	CD5	U.K.	1988	$8.00
		Wishing I Was Lucky	CDJ	U.S.	1988	$2.00

Whale

Singles

Label	Catalog Number	Title	Type	Country	Year	Longbox/Value
Atlantic	98281	Hobo Humpin'	CD5	U.S.	1994	$5.00
Atlantic	98281	Hobo Humpin'	CD5	U.S.	1995	$6.00
Warner	32-98281	Hobo Humpin' Slobo Babe	CD5	Canada	1994	$6.00
Wea	CD92412	Hobo Humpin' Slobo Babe	CD5	Canada	1994	$8.00
Eastwest	98281-2	Hobo Humpin' Slobo Babe	CD5	U.S.	1994	$5.00
Eastwest	PRCD 5596-2	Hobo Humpin' Slobo Babe	CDJ	U.S.	1994	$2.00
		Kickin'	CDJ	U.S.		$2.00
		Pray For Me	CDJ	U.S.		$2.00
Virgin	38504	Pray For Me	CD5	U.S.	1995	$5.00

Whalum, Kirk

Singles

Label	Catalog Number	Title	Type	Country	Year	Longbox/Value
Columbia	CSK 5251	Language of Life	CDJ	U.S.	1993	$2.00
Columbia	CSK 4964	Love Is a Losing Game	CDJ	U.S.	1993	$2.00

Wham!

Full Length

Label	Catalog Number	Title	Type	Country	Year	Longbox/Value
CBS	CK-38911	Fantastic	LP/BP	U.S.†	1985	$12.00/$7.00
CBS	CK-39595	Make It Big	LP/BP	U.S.†	1985	$12.00/$7.00
Fox	3048-88	Video, The	8"LD	U.S.	1985	$6.00
CBS/Fox	7142-80	Wham! In China	LD	U.S.	1987	$30.00

Singles

Label	Catalog Number	Title	Type	Country	Year	Longbox/Value
Epic	655216	I'm Your Man	CD3	Germany	1989	$10.00
	CD in greeting card.					
Epic	653185	Last Christmas	CD3	Germany	1988	$6.00
	ESFU-7004	Last Christmas	CDV	Japan		$30.00
Epic	108P-3057	Last Christmas	CD3	Japan	1988	$12.00/$3.00
CBS	654915-3	Wake Me Up Before You Go Go	CD3	Germany	1989	$5.00
CBS	654915-3	Wake Me Up Before You Go Go	CD3	U.K.	1989	$5.00
CBS	651668-3	Young Guns	CD3	Germany	1988	$5.00

Wheeler, Caron

Singles

Label	Catalog Number	Title	Type	Country	Year	Longbox/Value
RCA	PD-44536	Blue	CD5	Germany	1991	$8.00
RCA	BVDP-39	Blue	CD3	Japan	1991	$13.00/$4.00
EMI	DPRO 14695	Blue	CDJ	U.S.	1991	$2.00
RCA	PD-44260	Don't Quit	CD5	Germany	1991	$8.00
RCA	PD-44260	Don't Quit	CD5	U.K.	1991	$8.00
Capitol	DPRO-79193	Estate Sale	CDJ	U.S.	1990	$2.00
Perpective	PERD-7407	I Adore You	CD5	U.K.	1992	$8.00
Perspective	31458 8016	I Adore You	CDJ	U.S.	1992	$2.00
EMI	DPRO-04651	In Our Love	CDJ	U.S.	1992	$2.00
RCA	PD-43940	Livin' in the Light	CD5	Germany	1990	$8.00
RCA	BVDP-22	Livin' in the Light	CD3	Japan	1990	$13.00/$4.00
RCA	PD-43940	Livin' in the Light	CD5	U.K.	1990	$8.00
EMI	DPRO 4519	Livin' in the Light	CDJ	U.S.	1990	$2.00
EMI	DPRO 4684	Livin' in the Light	CDJ	U.S.	1990	$2.00
EMI	DPRO 4710	Massive	CDJ	U.S.	1990	$2.00
RCA	PD-43720	UK Remix	CD5	U.K.	1990	$8.00

Wheeler, Cheryl

Singles

Label	Catalog Number	Title	Type	Country	Year	Longbox/Value
Capitol	DPRO 79193	Estate State	CDJ	U.S.	1990	$2.00

When In Rome

Singles

Label	Catalog Number	Title	Type	Country	Year	Longbox/Value
Virgin	TENCD-277	Heaven Knows	CD5	U.K.	1989	$8.00
Virgin	PRCD 2599	Heaven Knows	CDJ	U.S.	1988	$2.00
Virgin	161823	Promise, The	CD3	Germany	1989	$8.00
Virgin	VJD 12002	Promise, The	CD3	Japan	1988	$13.00/$4.00
Virgin	TENCD-244	Promise, The	CD3	U.K.	1989	$8.00
Virgin		Promise, The	CD5	U.S.	1988	$2.00
Virgin	TENCD-267	Sight of Your Tears	CD3	U.K.	1989	$8.00
Virgin		Sight of Your Tears	CDJ	U.S.	1989	$2.00

Whigfield

Singles

Label	Catalog Number	Title	Type	Country	Year	Longbox/Value
		Another Day	CDJ	U.S.		$2.00
		Saturday Night	CDJ	U.S.		$2.00

Whipkey, Kim

Singles

Label	Catalog Number	Title	Type	Country	Year	Longbox/Value
	5650	Can't You See	CD5	U.S.	1994	$5.00

Whipping Boy

Singles

Label	Catalog Number	Title	Type	Country	Year	Longbox/Value
Columbia	CSK 7611	Twinkle	CDJ	U.S.		$2.00

Whirling Dervishes

Singles

Label	Catalog Number	Title	Type	Country	Year	Longbox/Value
		Grinch	CDJ	U.S.		$2.00
Continuum Records	12421	You're A Mean One	CD5	U.S.	1994	$5.00

Whiskey Train

Full Length

Label	Catalog Number	Title	Type	Country	Year	Longbox/Value
Masque Music	MSQ 1630	Whiskey Train	LTD/LP	U.S.	1993	$15.00
	Shaped CD.					

Whispers

Full Length

Label	Catalog Number	Title	Type	Country	Year	Longbox/Value
CBS	75305	Happy Holidays	LP/LB	U.S.		$14.00/$8.00
CBS	75303	Just Gets Better	LP/LB	U.S.		$14.00/$8.00
Solar	60356-2	So Good	LP/BP	U.S.†	1985	$14.00/$8.00

Singles

Label	Catalog Number	Title	Type	Country	Year	Longbox/Value
Solar	74510	Give It to Me	CDJ	U.S.	1990	$2.00
		Heaven	CDJ	U.S.		$2.00
Capitol	DPRO-79175	Innocent	CDJ	U.S.	1990	$2.00
Capitol	DPRO 79339	My Heart Your Heart	CDJ	U.S.	1990	$2.00

Whistle

Singles

Label	Catalog Number	Title	Type	Country	Year	Longbox/Value
Select	004	Bad Habit	CDJ	U.S.	1990	$2.00
Select	8494	I Am	CDJ	U.S.	1992	$2.00

White, Barry

Full Length

Label	Catalog Number	Title	Type	Country	Year	Longbox/Value
Mercury	SACD 602	Selections From Just for You	DJ/Smplr	U.S.	1993	$15.00

Singles

Label	Catalog Number	Title	Type	Country	Year	Longbox/Value
Priority Records	53686	Beware	CD5	U.S.	1994	$5.00
A&M Records	81027	Come on	CD5	U.S.	1994	$5.00
A&M	81027	Come on	CD5	U.S.	1995	$6.00
A&M	75021 7322 2	Dark and Lovely	CDJ	U.S.	1991	$2.00
A&M	75021 7327 2	Dark and Lovely	CDJ	U.S.	1991	$2.00
A&M	CDEE-670	Follow That & See	CD5	U.K.	1989	$8.00
A&M	75021 8093 2	Good Night My Love	CDJ	U.S.	1989	$2.00
A&M	USACD-682	I Wanna Do It Good to Ya	CD5	U.K.	1990	$8.00
A&M	CD 17996	I Wanna Do It Good to Ya	CDJ	U.S.	1989	$2.00
A&M	CD 18009	I Wanna Do It Good to Ya	CDJ	U.S.	1989	$2.00
A&M	PCDY-10003	L.A. My Kinda Place	CD3	Japan	1989	$13.00/$4.00
		Practice What You Preach	CDJ	U.S.		$6.00
A&M Records	80891	Practice What You Preach	CD5	U.S.	1994	$5.00
A&M	AMCD-833	Put Me in Your Mix	CD5	U.K.	1991	$8.00
A&M	75021 7288 2	Put Me in Your Mix	CDJ	U.S.	1991	$2.00
Priority Records	53685	Sheet Music	CD5	U.S.	1994	$5.00
A&M	CD 17879	Super Lover	CDJ	U.S.	1989	$2.00
A&M	75021 8077 2	When Will I See You Again	CDJ	U.S.	1989	$2.00
A&M	874391-2	You're the First, the Last	CD5	Germany	1989	$8.00

White Boy Worry

Singles

Label	Catalog Number	Title	Type	Country	Year	Longbox/Value
Axis	008	Survive	CD5	U.S.	1990	$4.00

White, J.J.

Singles

Label	Catalog Number	Title	Type	Country	Year	Longbox/Value
Curb	063	Crush, The	CDJ	U.S.	1991	$2.00

White Kaps

Singles

Label	Catalog Number	Title	Type	Country	Year	Longbox/Value
	604	Cannonball Man	CD5	U.S.	1994	$5.00

White, Karyn

Full Length

Label	Catalog Number	Title	Type	Country	Year	Longbox/Value
Warner Brothers	9 26320-2-Dj	Ritual of Love	DJ/LP	U.S.	1991	$8.00
	Picture disc.					
Warner Brothers	PRO-CD-5131	Ritual of Love. Words & Music	DJ/Intvw	U.S.	1991	$8.00
Unistar		Story of	RS	U.S.	1991	$15.00
	Airdate: 10/11/91.					

Singles

Label	Catalog Number	Title	Type	Country	Year	Longbox/Value
Warner Brothers	18007	Can I Stay With You	CD5	U.S.	1994	$5.00
Warner Brothers	9 40566-2	Do Unto Me	CD5	U.S.	1991	$5.00
Warner Brothers	PRO-CD-5250	Do Unto Me	CDJ	U.S.	1991	$2.00
Warner Brothers	12-41615	Hungah	CD5	Canada	1994	$8.00
Warner Brothers	9 41615-2	Hungah	CD5	U.S.	1994	$5.00
Warner Brothers	9362-40180-2	Romantic	CD5	Germany	1991	$8.00
Warner Brothers	WPDP-6269	Romantic	CD3	Japan	1991	$12.00/$4.00
Warner Brothers	WPCP-4573	Romantic	CD5	Japan	1991	$15.00
Warner Brothers	W-0028CD	Romantic	CD5	U.K.	1991	$8.00
Warner Brothers	9 40069-2	Romantic	CD5	U.S.	1991	$5.00
Warner Brothers	PRO-CD-4800	Romantic	CDJ	U.S.	1991	$2.00
Warner Brothers	PRO-CD-4800	Romantic	CDJ	U.S.	1991	$10.00
	CDJ with VHS video In box.					
Warner Brothers	921293-2	Secret Rendezvous	CD3	Germany	1989	$8.00
Warner Brothers	921293-2	Secret Rendezvous	CD5	Germany	1989	$8.00
Warner Brothers	W-7562CD	Secret Rendezvous	CD3	U.K.	1989	$8.00
Warner Brothers	W-2855CD	Secret Rendezvous	CD3	U.K.	1989	$8.00
Warner Brothers	PRO-CD-3436	Secret Rendezvous	CDJ	U.S.	1988	$2.00
Warner Brothers	PRO-CD-3402	Slow Down	CDJ	U.S.	1989	$2.00
Warner Brothers		Super Lover	CDJ	U.S.		$2.00
Pioneer	09P3-6142	Superwoman	CD3	Japan	1989	$12.00/$4.00
Warner Brothers	W-2920CD	Superwoman	CD3	U.K.	1989	$8.00
Warner Brothers	PRO-CD-3375	Superwoman	CDJ	U.S.	1988	$2.00
Warner Brothers	921025-2	That's the Way	CD3	Germany	1989	$8.00
Warner Brothers	PRO-CD-5081	Walkin' the Dog	CDJ	U.S.	1991	$2.00
Warner Brothers	WPDP-6289	Way I Feel About You	CD3	Japan	1991	$12.00/$4.00
Warner Brothers	PRO-CD-5135	Way I Feel About You	CDJ	U.S.	1991	$2.00
Warner Brothers	9 40256-2	Way I Feel About You	CDJ	U.S.	1991	$7.00
Warner Brothers	10P3-6097	Way You Love Me, The	CD3	Japan	1989	$12.00/$4.00
Warner Brothers	W 2681CD	Way You Love Me, The	CD3	U.K.	1989	$4.00

White, Lari

Full Length

Label	Catalog Number	Title	Type	Country	Year	Longbox/Value
RCA	ADV66117	White on White	DJ/LP	U.S.	1993	$11.00
		Wishes	DJ/LP	U.S.	1994	$11.00
	Advance issue.					

White Lion

Singles

Label	Catalog Number	Title	Type	Country	Year	Longbox/Value
Atlantic		Broken Heart	CDJ	U.S.		$2.00
Atlantic	PR 3060-2	Cry for Freedom	CDJ	U.S.	1989	$2.00
Atlantic	A-7727CD	Lights and Thunder	CD5	U.K.	1991	$8.00
Atlantic	786396-2	Little Fighter	CD3	Germany	1989	$8.00
Atlantic	PR 2778-2	Little Fighter	CDJ	U.S.	1988	$2.00
Atlantic	7567-86033-2	Love Don't Come Easy	CD5	Germany	1991	$8.00
Atlantic	AMDY-5044	Love Don't Come Easy	CD3	Japan	1991	$12.00/$4.00
Atlantic	A-7672CD	Love Don't Come Easy	CD5	U.K.	1991	$8.00
Atlantic	PRCD 3786-2	Love Don't Come Easy	CDJ	U.S.	1991	$2.00
Atlantic	A-8836CD	Radar Love	CD3	U.K.	1989	$8.00
Atlantic		Radar Love	CDJ	U.S.	1990	$2.00
Atlantic	VDP-15001	Wait	CD5	Japan	1988	$13.00
Atlantic	A-9063CD	Wait	CD3	U.K.	1988	$8.00
Atlantic	PR 2461-2	When the Children Cry	CDJ	U.S.	1988	$2.00

White, Maurice

Full Length

Label	Catalog Number	Title	Type	Country	Year	Longbox/Value
CBS	CK-39883	Maurice White	LP/BP	U.S.†	1985	$14.00/$8.00

White Trash

Singles

Label	Catalog Number	Title	Type	Country	Year	Longbox/Value
Elektra	PRCD 8365-2	Apple Pie	CDJ	U.S.	1991	$3.00
Elektra	PRCD 8507-2	Crawl, The	CDJ	U.S.	1991	$3.00
Elektra	66257-2	Minor Happiness	CD5	U.S.	1993	$5.00

White Zombie

Full Length

Label	Catalog Number	Title	Type	Country	Year	Longbox/Value
Global Satellite Network		Live From the Pit	RS	U.S.	1995	$60.00
	2 CD set. Airdate: 11/26/95.					
Geffen	GEFD-A-24976	Presents Supersexy Swingin' Sounds	DJ/LP	U.S.	1996	$10.00

Singles

Label	Catalog Number	Title	Type	Country	Year	Longbox/Value
		Black Single	CDJ	U.S.		$3.00
Geffen	PRO-CD-4601	Black Sunshine	CDJ	U.S.	1992	$3.00
Geffen	PRO-CD-4435	Black Sunshine	CDJ	U.S.	1992	$6.00
Geffen		Electric Head	CDJ	U.S.	1994	$6.00
Geffen	PRO-CD-4589	I Am Hell	CDJ	U.S.	1993	$6.00
	With Beavis And Butthead.					
Geffen		More Human Than Human	CDJ	U.S.	1994	$6.00
Geffen		More Human Than Human	CDJ	U.S.	1994	$6.00
	Second version.					
Geffen	9 21817-2	Night Crawlers	CD5	U.S.	1992	$5.00
Geffen	21817	Nightcrawlers	CD5	U.S.	1994	$5.00
Geffen		Real Solution No. 9	CD5	Australia	1996	$12.00

Label	Catalog Number	Title	Type	Country	Year	Longbox Value / Value
Geffen		Super Charger Heaven	CDJ	U.S.	1994	$6.00
Geffen	PRO-CD-4188	Thunder Kiss	CDJ	U.S.	1992	$3.00
Geffen	PRO-CD-4587	Thunder Kiss	CDJ	U.S.	1992	$3.00

Whitehead Brothers

Singles

Label	Catalog Number	Title	Type	Country	Year	Longbox Value / Value
Motown	860257	Forget I Was A G	CD5	U.S.	1994	$5.00
Motown	860279	Sex On The Beach	CD5	U.S.	1994	$5.00

Whiteheart

Full Length

Label	Catalog Number	Title	Type	Country	Year	Longbox Value / Value
Curb		Inside	DJ/LP	U.S.	1995	$20.00
CD album, CD radio show and VHS video in custom printed wood box.						

Whitesnake

Full Length

Label	Catalog Number	Title	Type	Country	Year	Longbox Value / Value
EMI		1987	LTD/LP	U.K.	1997	$35.00
Limited edition centennial CD edition housed in a slip case with a special 100 anniversary booklet.						
EMI		1987, Slide It In, Slip of the Tongue	LTD/LP	U.K.	1994	$35.00
3 CD boxed set.						
Pioneer	PA91-350	Four Play	8"LD	U.S.	1983	$10.00
Radio Ventures		Masters of Rock	RS	U.S.	1989	$30.00
Airdate: 2/4/89.						
Radio Ventures		Masters of Rock	RS	U.S.	1990	$30.00
Airdate: 1/22/90.						
TDK	25055	Ready & Willing	DJ/Smplr	Japan		$40.00
Geffen	2 24249-Dj	Slip of the Tounge	DJ/LP	U.S.	1989	$35.00
Custom digipak with red plastic seal.						
Geffen	PRO-CD-3846	Snake Bites	DJ/Smplr	U.S.	1990	$20.00

Singles

Label	Catalog Number	Title	Type	Country	Year	Longbox Value / Value
Geffen	PRO-CD-2844	Crying in the Rain	CDJ	U.S.	1988	$3.00
EMI	203704-2	Deeper the Love, The	CD5	Germany	1990	$10.00
Sony	CSDS-8122	Deeper the Love, The	CD3	Japan	1990	$12.00/$4.00
EMI	CDEM-128	Deeper the Love, The	CD5	U.K.	1990	$10.00
Geffen	PRO-CD-3887	Deeper the Love, The	CDJ	U.S.	1988	$3.00
EMI	203635-3	Fool for Your Loving	CD3	Germany	1989	$10.00
Sony	CSDS-8113	Fool for Your Loving	CD3	Japan	1989	$12.00/$4.00
Geffen	PRO-CD-3808	Fool for Your Loving	CDJ	U.S.	1989	$3.00
Geffen	PRO-CD-3817	Fool for Your Loving	CDJ	U.S.	1989	$3.00
Geffen	PRO-CD-3828	Fool for Your Loving	CDJ	U.S.	1989	$3.00
Sony	10EP-3007	Give Me All Your Love	CD3	Japan	1988	$12.00/$4.00
EMI	CDEM-23	Give Me All Your Love	CD5	U.K.	1988	$10.00
Geffen	PRO-CD-2932	Give Me All Your Love	CDJ	U.S.	1987	$3.00
EMI	201787-2	Is This Love	CD5	Germany	1988	$10.00
EMI	CDEM-3	Is This Love	CD5	U.K.	1988	$10.00
EMI	CD EM329	Is This Love	CD5	U.K.	1994	$10.00
EMI		Is This Love	CD5	U.K.	1994	$10.00
EMI	CDEM-DJ-290	Is This Love	CDJ	U.K.	1994	$12.00
Lists release date as 7/25/94.						
EMI	CDEM-DJ-290	Is This Love	CDJ	U.K.	1994	$15.00
Lists release date as 7/20/94.						
EMI	203987-2	Now You're Gone	CD5	Germany	1990	$10.00
EMI	CDEM-150	Now You're Gone	CD5	U.K.	1990	$10.00
Geffen	PRO-CD-3917	Now You're Gone	CDJ	U.S.	1989	$3.00
Geffen	PRO-CD-2669	Still of the Night	CDJ	U.S.	1987	$3.00

Whitey, Don

Singles

Label	Catalog Number	Title	Type	Country	Year	Longbox Value / Value
Jive	42305	Artical	CD5	U.S.	1995	$5.00

Whitfield, Mark

Singles

Label	Catalog Number	Title	Type	Country	Year	Longbox Value / Value
		Marksman, The	CDJ	U.S.		$2.00

Whitley, Chris

Full Length

Label	Catalog Number	Title	Type	Country	Year	Longbox Value / Value
		In Concert	RS	U.S.	1992	$50.00
2 CD set. With Jeff Healy, Airdate: 6/8/92.						
		In the Foreground Radio Special	DJ/Intvw	Canada		$20.00

Singles

Label	Catalog Number	Title	Type	Country	Year	Longbox Value / Value
Columbia	657506-2	Big Sky Country	CD5	U.K.	1992	$8.00
Columbia	CSK 4135	Big Sky Country	CDJ	U.S.	1991	$2.00
		Din	CDJ	U.S.		$2.00
		Kick the Stones	CDJ	Canada		$8.00
Columbia	CSK 4057	Living With the Law	CDJ	U.S.	1991	$2.00
Columbia	CSK 6997	O God My Heart Is Ready	CDJ	U.S.		$2.00
Columbia	CSK 4340	Poison Girl	CDJ	U.S.		$2.00

Whitley, Keith

Full Length

Label	Catalog Number	Title	Type	Country	Year	Longbox Value / Value
BNA		Keith Whitley: The Singles	DJ/Smplr	U.S.	1995	$20.00
		Tribute	DJ/Intvw	U.S.	1994	$25.00
BNA		Wherever You Are Tonight	DJ/LP	U.S.	1995	$25.00
2 CD set.						
BNA		Wherever You Are Tonight	LTD/LP	U.S.	1995	$25.00
2 CD set.						

Whitman, Slim

Full Length

Label	Catalog Number	Title	Type	Country	Year	Longbox Value / Value
Warner Sound Exchange		22 Legendary Hits	LTD/LP	U.S.	1995	$17.00
Warner Sound Exchange		Songs You Love to Hear Him Sing	LTD/LP	U.S.	1995	$17.00

Whittaker, Roger

Full Length

Label	Catalog Number	Title	Type	Country	Year	Longbox Value / Value
RCA	5166	Best of	LP/LB	U.S.		$12.00/$7.00
RCA	2933	Christmas Album	LP/LB	U.S.		$12.00/$7.00
RCA	4743	Greatest Hits	LP/LB	U.S.		$12.00/$7.00
RCA	0855	Last Farewell	LP/LB	U.S.		$12.00/$7.00
RCA	4321	Wind Beneath My Wings	LP/LB	U.S.		$12.00/$7.00

Who, The

Full Length

Label	Catalog Number	Title	Type	Country	Year	Longbox Value / Value
MCA		30 Years Of Maximum R&B	DJ/Smplr	U.K.	1994	$50.00
2CD sampler.						
MCA	MCA3P-2592	30th Anniversary Sampler	DJ/Smplr	U.S.	1993	$25.00
BBC Radio		BBC Classic Tracks	RS	U.S.	1991	$30.00
Airdate: 10/14/91.						
BBC Radio		BBC Classic Tracks	RS	U.S.	1991	$30.00
Airdate: 3/4/91.						
BBC Radio		BBC Classic Tracks	RS	U.S.	1991	$30.00
Airdate: 5/11/91.						
BBC Radio		BBC Classic Tracks	RS	U.S.	1992	$30.00
Airdate: 2/24/91.						
Westwood One		BBC Classic Tracks	RS	U.S.	1993	$35.00
Airdate: 10/17/93.						
Westwood One		BBC Classic Tracks	RS	U.S.	1993	$35.00
Airdate: 10/30/93.						
Westwood One		BBC Classic Tracks	RS	U.S.	1993	$35.00
Airdate: 10/4/93.						
Westwood One		BBC Classic Tracks	RS	U.S.	1993	$35.00
Airdate: 4/12/93.						
BBC Radio		BBC Classic Tracks	RS	U.S.	1994	$20.00
Airdate: 1/10/94.						
Westwood One		BBC Classic Tracks	RS	U.S.	1994	$35.00
Airdate: 1/10/94.						
MCA	CD33-17721	Bet You Just Can't Pick One	DJ/Smplr	U.S.	1990	$30.00
MCA	MCAD-37002	By Numbers	LP/LB	U.S.†	1985	$14.00/$8.00
		Classic CD (Who's Next)	RS	U.S.	1990	$50.00
2 CD set. Airdate: 6/25/90.						
MCA	WHO-BOX-2	Extracts From 30 Years Maximum R&B	DJ/Smplr	U.K.	1994	$20.00
Pink disc.						
MCA	WHO-BOX-2	Extracts From 30 Years Maximun R&B	DJ/Smplr	U.K.	1994	$15.00
Red, white and blue disc.						
Warner Brothers	3516-2	Face Dances	LP/LB	U.S.†	1984	$25.00/$23.00
Warner Brothers	3516-2	Face Dances	LP/LB	U.S.	1986	$25.00/$23.00
		Fourth Of July Special	RS	U.S.	1990	$100.00
2 CD set.						
Album Network		In the Studio (Live at Leeds)	RS	U.S.		$35.00
Album Network		In the Studio (Maximum R&B)	RS	U.S.		$60.00
2 CD set.						
Album Network		In the Studio (Tommy)	RS	U.S.		$75.00
2 CD set.						
Album Network		In the Studio (Who's Next)	RS	U.S.		$35.00
Warner Brothers	9 23731-2	It's Hard	LP/LB	U.S.†	1984	$25.00/$23.00
Warner Brothers	9 23731-2	It's Hard	LP/LB	U.S.	1986	$25.00/$23.00
MCA	CD45-18258	Join Together	DJ/Smplr	U.S.	1990	$18.00
DIR		King Biscuit Flour Hour	RS	U.S.	1987	$60.00
Airdate: 9/13/87.						
DIR		King Biscuit Flour Hour	RS	U.S.	1988	$50.00
Airdate: 7/10/88.						
MCA	MCAD-37000	Live at Leeds	LP/LB	U.S.†	1985	$14.00/$8.00
MCA	MCAD-11230	Live at Leeds	LTD/LP	U.S.	1995	$35.00
		Maximum R&B	RS	U.S.	1995	$90.00
4 CD set. Airdate: 7/4/95.						
MCA	WHO-BOX-1	Maximum R&B Sampler	DJ/Smplr	U.K.	1994	$30.00
MCA	MCAD-37001	Meaty, Beaty, Big & Bouncy	LP/LB	U.S.†	1985	$14.00/$8.00
Virgin	CDV-2179	My Generation	LP	U.K.		$20.00
Westwood One		Off the Record	RS	U.S.	1995	$20.00
Airdate: 2/27/95.						
Westwood One		Off the Record	RS	U.S.	1995	$20.00
Airdate: 9/4/95.						
MCA	MCAD-37001	Quadrophenia	LP/LB	U.S.†	1985	$22.00/$16.00
CBS/Fox	6234-80	Rocks America	LD	U.S.	1983	$80.00
CBS/Fox	C6234	Rocks America	LD	U.S.	1989	$80.00
Westwood One		Superstar Concert	RS	U.S.	1992	$60.00
Airdate: 4/26/922 CD set.						
MCA	MCA3P-3082	Thirty Years Of Maximum R&B Sampler	DJ/Smplr	U.S.	1994	$25.00
MCA	MCAD2-10005	Tommy	LP/LB	U.S.		$22.00/$17.00
2 CD set.						
MCA	MCAD2-10005	Tommy	LP/LB	U.S.†	1985	$22.00/$17.00
2 CD set.						
		Tommy: 25th Anniversary Special	RS	U.S.	1993	$70.00
2 CD set. Airdate: 3/18/93.						
Media America		Up Close	RS	U.S.	1989	$75.00
2 CD set.						
Media America		Up Close	RS	U.S.	1990	$80.00
2 CD set.						
Media America		Up Close	RS	U.S.	1994	$65.00
3 CD set.						
MCA	MCAD-37003	Who Are You	LP/LB	U.S.†	1985	$14.00/$8.00
Polygram	080 345-9	Who's Better, Who's Best	LD	U.S.	1988	$50.00
MCA	MCAD-8018	Who's Last	LP/LB	U.S.†	1985	$17.00/$15.00
MCA	MCAD-37217	Who's Next	LP/LB	U.S.†	1985	$14.00/$8.00
		Who's Next Classic	RS	U.S.		$120.00
3 CD set.						

Singles

Label	Catalog Number	Title	Type	Country	Year	Longbox Value / Value
Virgin	663156	Join Together	CD5	Germany	1989	$12.00
Virgin	VSCDT 1259	Join Together	CD5	U.K.	1990	$12.00
MCA	18258	Join Together	CDJ	U.S.	1990	$7.00
		My Generation	CDJ	Spain	1996	$30.00
MCA		My Generation	CD5	U.K.	1996	$12.00
MCA	MCAD-37303	My Generation	CD3	U.S.	1988	$10.00/$5.00
Polydor	CDP 586	Saturday Night's Alright	CDJ	U.S.	1991	$7.00
Polydor	POCD-907	This Is My Generation	CD5	U.K.	1987	$12.00
Polygram	887576-2	Won't Get Fooled Again	CD5	Germany	1989	$12.00
Polydor	POCD-917	Won't Get Fooled Again	CD5	U.K.	1989	$12.00

Who Needs Pants

Singles

Label	Catalog Number	Title	Type	Country	Year	Longbox Value / Value
Capital	30589	When You've Got Nic	CD5	U.S.	1994	$5.00

Whodini

Singles

Label	Catalog Number	Title	Type	Country	Year	Longbox Value / Value
Arista	ASCD-9628	Be Yourself	CDJ	U.S.	1987	$2.00
MCA	CD45 1267	Freaks	CDJ	U.S.	1991	$2.00
MCA	CD45 1457	Judy	CDJ	U.S.	1991	$2.00
Jive	JIVECD-144	Rock You Again	CD5	U.K.	1988	$8.00
MCA	CD45 1585	Smilin' Faces	CDJ	U.S.	1991	$2.00

Whooliganz

Singles

Label	Catalog Number	Title	Type	Country	Year	Longbox Value / Value
Tommy Boy	579	Put Your Handz Up	CDJ	U.S.	1993	$2.00

Why Store

Singles

Label	Catalog Number	Title	Type	Country	Year	Longbox Value / Value
		Lack of Water	CDJ	U.S.		$2.00

Widespread Panic

Full Length

Label	Catalog Number	Title	Type	Country	Year	Longbox Value / Value
		Special Advance Club Sampler	DJ/Smplr	U.S.	1993	$5.00

Singles

Label	Catalog Number	Title	Type	Country	Year	Longbox Value / Value
Capricorn	5096	Makes Sense to Me	CDJ	U.S.	1991	$2.00
Capricorn	6628	Postcard	CDJ	U.S.	1993	$2.00
Capricorn	4946	Walkin'	CDJ	U.S.	1993	$2.00

Widowmaker

Full Length

Label	Catalog Number	Title	Type	Country	Year	Longbox Value / Value
		Blood & Bullets	LP	U.S.		$10.00
RCA	74301	Widowmaker	LP/BP	U.S.	1992	$12.00/$7.00

Singles

Label	Catalog Number	Title	Type	Country	Year	Longbox Value / Value
Esquire	74340	Widowmaker	CDJ	U.S.	1992	$2.00

Wiedlin, Jane

Singles

Label	Catalog Number	Title	Type	Country	Year	Longbox Value/Value
EMI	DPRO 14669	Guardian Angel	CDJ	U.S.	1990	$2.00
EMI	202934-2	Inside a Dream	CD5	Germany	1988	$8.00
EMI	CDMT-55	Inside a Dream	CD5	U.K.	1988	$8.00
EMI		Inside a Dream	CDJ	U.S.	1988	$2.00
EMI	202574-2	Rush Hour	CD3	Germany	1988	$8.00
Toshiba	XP10-2012	Rush Hour	CD3	Japan	1989	$13.00/$4.00
EMI	CDMT-36	Rush Hour	CD5	U.K.	1988	$8.00
EMI	DPRO 4017	Rush Hour	CDJ	U.S.	1988	$2.00
EMI	TODP-2177	World on Fire	CD3	Japan	1990	$13.00/$4.00
EMI	E2-56191	World on Fire	CD5	U.S.	1988	$108.00
"Matchbook" package.						
EMI	DPRO 4575	World on Fire	CDJ	U.S.	1990	$3.00

Wigfield

Singles

Label	Catalog Number	Title	Type	Country	Year	Longbox Value/Value
Elektra/Asyklum	77080	Saturday Night	CD5	U.S.	1994	$5.00

Wiggins, John & Audrey

Singles

Label	Catalog Number	Title	Type	Country	Year	Longbox Value/Value
Mercury	CDP 1174	Falling Out Of Love	CD5	U.S.	1994	$20.00
CD in leatherbound book.						

Wilco

Singles

Label	Catalog Number	Title	Type	Country	Year	Longbox Value/Value
		I Must Be High	CDJ	U.S.		$2.00

Wilcox, David

Full Length

Label	Catalog Number	Title	Type	Country	Year	Longbox Value/Value
		Live	DJ/Smplr	U.S.		$25.00
CD in guitar shaped package.						
A&M	750217241 2	(Mostly) Live - Authorized Bootleg	DJ/Smplr	U.S.	1991	$6.00

Singles

Label	Catalog Number	Title	Type	Country	Year	Longbox Value/Value
		Bless the World	CDJ	Canada		$5.00
		Ecstacy	CDJ	Canada		$5.00
A&M	CD 18007	Eye of the Hurricane	CDJ	U.S.	1989	$2.00
A&M	31458 8263	It's the Same Old Song	CDJ	U.S.	1994	$2.00
A&M	31458 8250	New World	CDJ	U.S.	1994	$2.00
A&M	75021 7298-2	She's Just Dancing	CDJ	U.S.	1991	$2.00

Wild

Singles

Label	Catalog Number	Title	Type	Country	Year	Longbox Value/Value
Columbia	CSK 1176	Hurricane	CDJ	U.S.	1988	$2.00

Wild Colonials

Full Length

Label	Catalog Number	Title	Type	Country	Year	Longbox Value/Value
DGC	PRO-CD4621	Fruit of Life	DJ/Smplr	U.S.	1994	$10.00
CD in "menu" type package.						
Geffen	PRO-CD-4621	Fruit of Life	DJ/Smplr	U.S.	1994	$20.00

Wild Flowers

Singles

Label	Catalog Number	Title	Type	Country	Year	Longbox Value/Value
Slash	PRO-CD-3993	Feeling's Gone, The	CDJ	U.S.	1990	$2.00

Wild Planet

Singles

Label	Catalog Number	Title	Type	Country	Year	Longbox Value/Value
Imago	25067	Love So Strong	CD5	U.S.	1994	$5.00

Wild River Apples

Singles

Label	Catalog Number	Title	Type	Country	Year	Longbox Value/Value
Chrysalis	CHSCD 3000	I Can't Wait for Heaven	CD5	U.K.	1991	$8.00

Wild Seeds

Full Length

Label	Catalog Number	Title	Type	Country	Year	Longbox Value/Value
Passport	PBCD-6060	Mud Lies & Shame	LP/BP	U.S.		$16.00/$12.00

Wild Swans

Full Length

Label	Catalog Number	Title	Type	Country	Year	Longbox Value/Value
Sire	PRO-CD-3062	Music & Talk From Liverpool	DJ/Intvw	U.S.	1988	$12.00

Singles

Label	Catalog Number	Title	Type	Country	Year	Longbox Value/Value
Sire	PRO-CD-2964	Young Manhood	CDJ	U.S.		$2.00

Wild Weekend

Singles

Label	Catalog Number	Title	Type	Country	Year	Longbox Value/Value
Parlophone	CDR 6228	Ignition	CD5	U.K.	1990	$8.00

Wilde, Danny

Singles

Label	Catalog Number	Title	Type	Country	Year	Longbox Value/Value
Geffen	PRO-CD-3665	The Stuff That Dreams Are Made of	CDJ	U.S.	1989	$2.00
Geffen	PRO-CD-2891	Time Runs Wild	CDJ	U.S.		$2.00
Cypress	YD 17806	Time Runs Wild	CDJ	U.S.	1989	$2.00

Wilde, Eugene

Singles

Label	Catalog Number	Title	Type	Country	Year	Longbox Value/Value
MCA	CD45 17944	Ain't Nobody's Business	CDJ	U.S.	1989	$2.00
MCA	2184	How About Tonight	CDJ	U.S.	1992	$2.00
MCA	2340	Special Feelings	CDJ	U.S.	1992	$2.00

Wilde, Kim

Full Length

Label	Catalog Number	Title	Type	Country	Year	Longbox Value/Value
EMI		Kim Wilde, Catch as Catch Can, Select	LTD/LP	U.K.	1994	$35.00
3 CD boxed set.						
MCA	MVCM-558	Now And Forever	LTD/LP	Japan	1994	$35.00

Singles

Label	Catalog Number	Title	Type	Country	Year	Longbox Value/Value
Eastwest	257245-2	Can't Get Enough	CD5	Germany	1990	$8.00
MCA	WMD5-4037	Can't Get Enough	CD3	Japan	1990	$12.00/$4.00
WEA	257696-2	Four Letter World	CD3	Germany	1989	$8.00
MCA	10P3-6107	Four Letter World	CD3	Japan	1989	$12.00/$4.00
MCA	DKIM-10	Four Letter World	CD5	U.K.	1988	$8.00
MCA	257999-2	Hey Mr. Heartache	CD5	Germany	1988	$8.00
MCA	DKIM-7	Hey Mr. Heartache	CD5	U.K.	1988	$8.00
MCA	54737	If I Can't Have You	CD5	U.S.	1993	$5.00
		In My Life	CD5	U.K.		$10.00
		In My Life	CD5	U.K.		$10.00
Second version.						
MCA	KIMXD 19	In My Life	CD5	U.K.	1993	$8.00
MCA	257274-2	It's Here	CD5	Germany	1990	$8.00
MCA	WMD5-4024	It's Here	CD3	Japan	1990	$12.00/$4.00
MCA	DKIMT-12	It's Here	CD5	U.K.	1990	$8.00
MCA	JCD-27	Live Is Holy	DJ/CD3	Japan	1993	$25.00
		Love in a Natural Way	CDJ	U.K.		$18.00
MCA	DKIMT-11	Love in a Natural Way	CD5	U.K.	1989	$8.00
MCA	MVDM-21	Love Is Holy	CD3	Japan	1992	$12.00/$4.00
MCA	MCD-18636	Love Is Holy	DJ/CD3	Japan	1992	$35.00
MCA	KIMT-15	Love Is Holy	CD5	U.K.	1992	$8.00
MCA	MVDM-29	Million Miles Away	CD3	Japan	1992	$12.00/$4.00
WEA	257820-2	Never Trust a Stranger	CD3	Germany	1988	$8.00
Pioneer	10P3-6082	Never Trust a Stranger	CD3	Japan	1988	$12.00/$4.00
MCA	DKIM-9	Never Trust a Stranger	CD5	U.K.	1988	$8.00
		Share	CDJ	France		$25.00
MCA	DKIMT-13	Time	CD5	U.K.	1990	$8.00
Eastwest	9031-72856-2	World in a Perfect World	CD5	Germany	1990	$8.00
MCA	2557881-2	You Came	CD5	Germany	1988	$8.00
MCA	10P3-6024	You Came	CD3	Japan	1988	$12.00/$4.00
MCA	DKIM-8	You Came	CD5	U.K.	1988	$8.00
MCA	CD45 17596	You Came	CDJ	U.S.	1988	$3.00

Wilder, Joe

Full Length

Label	Catalog Number	Title	Type	Country	Year	Longbox Value/Value
Savoy Records	CY-78988	Wilder 'n Wilder	LTD/LP	U.S.	1995	$20.00
CD in miniature repica of original LP sleeve.						

Wilder, Matthew

Full Length

Label	Catalog Number	Title	Type	Country	Year	Longbox Value/Value
Private	ZZK-39112	I Don't Speak the Language	LP/BP	U.S.†	1984	$14.00/$8.00

Wilder, Webb

Singles

Label	Catalog Number	Title	Type	Country	Year	Longbox Value/Value
Island	CID-458	Cold Front	CD5	U.K.	1990	$8.00
Island	PR 2835-2	Cold Front	CDJ	U.S.	1989	$2.00
Island	PRCD 3162-2	Hittin' Where It Hurts	CDJ	U.S.	1990	$2.00
Island	CID-454	Human Cannonball	CD5	U.K.	1990	$8.00
Praxis	17066	Sittin' Pretty	CDJ	U.S.	1991	$2.00
Zoo	ZP 17025	Tough It Out	CDJ	U.S.	1991	$2.00

Wildflowers

Singles

Label	Catalog Number	Title	Type	Country	Year	Longbox Value/Value
Slash	PRO-CD-3993	Feeling's Gone, The	CDJ	U.S.	1990	$2.00

Wildhearts

Full Length

Label	Catalog Number	Title	Type	Country	Year	Longbox Value/Value
		Fishing for Luckies	LTD/LP	U.K.	1996	$25.00
WEA	PROP21	P.H.U.Q.	DJ/Smplr	U.K.	1995	$14.00
WEA	SAM1574	P.H.U.Q. Sampler	DJ/Smplr	U.K.	1995	$12.00
WEA	YZ923CDX	I Wanna Go	CD5	U.K.	1995	$9.00

Wildside

Singles

Label	Catalog Number	Title	Type	Country	Year	Longbox Value/Value
Capitol	DPRO-79233	Hang on Lucy	CDJ	U.S.	1992	$2.00
Capitol	DPRO-79360	How Many Lies	CDJ	U.S.	1992	$2.00

Wiley, Ken

Full Length

Label	Catalog Number	Title	Type	Country	Year	Longbox Value/Value
Passport	PJCD-88020	Visage	LP	U.K.		$12.00
Passport	PJCD-88020	Visage	LP/BP	U.S.		$12.00/$7.00

Will and The Bushman

Full Length

Label	Catalog Number	Title	Type	Country	Year	Longbox Value/Value
SBK	DPRO-05328	Suck on This	DJ/Smplr	U.S.	1990	$4.00

Singles

Label	Catalog Number	Title	Type	Country	Year	Longbox Value/Value
SBK	DPRO-05313	Blow Me Up	CDJ	U.S.	1989	$2.00
SBK	DPRO-05333	Book of Love	CDJ	U.S.	1990	$2.00

Will and The Kill

Singles

Label	Catalog Number	Title	Type	Country	Year	Longbox Value/Value
Pioneer	10SW-13	Heart of Steel	CD3	Japan	1988	$13.00/$4.00
		Heart of Steel	CDJ	U.S.		$2.00

Will To Power

Singles

Label	Catalog Number	Title	Type	Country	Year	Longbox Value/Value
Epic	653183-3	Baby, I Love Your Way	CD3	Germany	1988	$8.00
Epic	653094-2	Baby, I Love Your Way	CD5	U.K.	1988	$8.00
Epic	656600-5	Boogie Nights	CD5	Germany	1991	$8.00
Epic	ESK 73670	Boogie Nights	CDJ	U.S.	1991	$2.00
Epic	654651-3	Fading Away	CD3	Germany	1989	$8.00
Epic	654651-2	Fading Away	CD5	Germany	1989	$8.00
Epic	656537-3	I'm Not in Love	CD5	Germany	1990	$8.00
Epic	ESK 73636	I'm Not in Love	CDJ	U.S.	1990	$2.00

Willi One Blood

Singles

Label	Catalog Number	Title	Type	Country	Year	Longbox Value/Value
RCA	64270	Whiney, Whiney	CD5	U.S.	1994	$5.00

Williams, Alyson

Singles

Label	Catalog Number	Title	Type	Country	Year	Longbox Value/Value
		All Cried Out!	CD5	U.K.		$10.00
		All Cried Out!	CD5	U.K.		$10.00
Second version.						
OBR	74224	Can't Have My Man	CDJ	U.S.	1992	$2.00
OBR	74493	Everybody Knew But Me	CDJ	U.S.	1992	$2.00
Def Jam	655143-2	I Need Your Lovin'	CD5	U.K.	1989	$8.00
OBR	73097	I Need Your Lovin'	CDJ	U.S.	1989	$2.00
CBS	655456-3	I Second That Emotion	CD3	Germany	1989	$8.00
Def Jam	655456-2	I Second That Emotion	CD5	U.K.	1989	$8.00
Columbia	CSK 74171	Just My Luck	CDJ	U.S.	1992	$2.00
CBS	654898-3	My Love is so Raw	CD3	Germany	1989	$8.00
Def Jam	654898-2	My Love is so Raw	CD5	U.K.	1989	$8.00
Def Jam		Not on the Outside	CDJ	U.S.		$2.00
Def Jam	CSK 4189	She's Not Your Fool	CDJ	U.S.	1991	$2.00
Def Jam	CSK 73725	She's Not Your Fool	CDJ	U.S.	1991	$2.00
CBS	654656-3	Sleep Talk	CD3	Germany	1989	$8.00
Def Jam	654656-2	Sleep Talk	CD5	U.K.	1989	$8.00
Def Jam	1436	Sleep Talk	CDJ	U.S.	1989	$2.00

Williams, Andy

Full Length

Label	Catalog Number	Title	Type	Country	Year	Longbox Value/Value
CBS	CK-40169	Merry Christmas	LP/BP	U.S.†	1985	$14.00/$8.00

Singles

Label	Catalog Number	Title	Type	Country	Year	Longbox Value/Value
CBS	655220-2	Can't Take My	CD5	Germany	1990	$8.00

Williams Brothers

Full Length

Label	Catalog Number	Title	Type	Country	Year	Longbox Value/Value
Warner Brothers	9 26503-2-Dj	Williams Brothers, The	DJ/LP	U.S.	1991	$6.00
Picture disc.						

Singles

Label	Catalog Number	Title	Type	Country	Year	Longbox Value/Value
Warner Brothers	PRO-CD-4791	Can't Cry Hard Enough	CDJ	U.S.	1991	$2.00

Williams, Christopher

Singles

Label	Catalog Number	Title	Type	Country	Year	Longbox Value/Value
Uptown	2415	All I See	CDJ	U.S.	1992	$2.00
Uptown	2765	Come With Me	CDJ	U.S.	1993	$2.00
Uptown	54613	Every Little Thing I Do	CD5	U.S.	1993	$5.00
Uptown	2600	Every Little Thing I Do	CDJ	U.S.	1993	$2.00

Label	Catalog Number	Title	Type	Country	Year	Longbox Value / Value
Uptown	2655	Every Little Thing I Do	CDJ	U.S.	1993	$2.00
Giant	PRO-CD-4644	I'm Dreamin'	CDJ	U.S.	1991	$2.00
Geffen	PRO-CD-3479	One Girl	CDJ	U.S.	1989	$2.00
		Promises, Promises	CDJ	U.S.		$2.00
Geffen	PRO-CD-3544	Talk to Myself	CDJ	U.S.	1991	$2.00
Geffen	PRO-CD-3674	Talk to Myself	CDJ	U.S.	1991	$2.00

Williams, Dar

Singles

Label	Catalog Number	Title	Type	Country	Year	Longbox Value / Value
Razor & Tie	RTS 718	Christmas & the Pagans, The	CDJ	U.S.		$7.00

Williams, Deniece

Singles

Label	Catalog Number	Title	Type	Country	Year	Longbox Value / Value
MCA	CD45 18028	Every Moment	CDJ	U.S.	1989	$2.00
Columbia	653061-2	I Can't Wait	CD5	U.K.	1988	$8.00
		I Can't Wait	CDJ	U.S.	1988	$2.00
Columbia	654563-3	Let's Hear It for the Boys	CD3	Germany	1989	$8.00

Williams, Don

Full Length

Label	Catalog Number	Title	Type	Country	Year	Longbox Value / Value
Capitol	CCT 48034-2	Traces	LP/LB	U.S.		$15.00/$9.00

Williams, Freedom

Singles

Label	Catalog Number	Title	Type	Country	Year	Longbox Value / Value
Columbia	44K 74943	Voice of Freedom	CD5	U.S.	1993	$5.00
Columbia	CSK 5172	Voice of Freedom	CDJ	U.S.	1993	$2.00

Williams, Geoffrey

Singles

Label	Catalog Number	Title	Type	Country	Year	Longbox Value / Value
WEA	786270-3	Blue	CD5	Germany	1989	$8.00
Atlantic	A-7962CD	Blue	CD5	U.K.	1989	$8.00
Atlantic	PR 3152-2	Blue	CDJ	U.S.	1990	$2.00
Polygram	889087-2	Cinderella	CD5	Germany	1989	$8.00
Giant	9 40554-2	Deliver Me Up	CD5	U.S.	1992	$5.00
EMI	CDEM-228	It's Not a Love Thing	CD5	U.K.	1992	$8.00
Giant	PRO-CD-5282	It's Not a Love Thing	CDJ	U.S.	1992	$2.00
Giant	PRO-CD-5350	It's Not a Love Thing	CDJ	U.S.	1992	$2.00
WEA	786392-2	Lipstick	CD3	Germany	1989	$8.00
EMI	CDEM-245	Summer Breeze	CD5	U.K.	1992	$8.00
Polygram	871948-3	There Is a Need in Me	CD3	Germany	1989	$8.00
Polygram	871949-5	There Is a Need in Me	CD5	Germany	1989	$8.00
Polydor	POCD-906	There Is a Need in Me	CD5	U.K.	1988	$8.00

Williams, Hank

Full Length

Label	Catalog Number	Title	Type	Country	Year	Longbox Value / Value
Warner Sound Exchange		40 Legendary Hits	LTD/LP	U.S.	1995	$30.00
2 CD set.						
Mercury		Collector's Edition, The	LTD/LP	U.S.	1995	$100.00
8CD album set in box. Sold exclusively through Tower Records.						

Williams, Hank Jr.

Full Length

Label	Catalog Number	Title	Type	Country	Year	Longbox Value / Value
		American Country	RS	U.S.	1990	$50.00
3 CD set. Airdate: 5/28/90.						
Curb	PRO-CD-5814	Bocephus Box Sampler	DJ/Smplr	U.S.	1992	$15.00
Warner Brothers	25267-2	Five-O	LP/LB	U.S.†	1984	$14.00/$8.00
Polygram	811903-2	Greatest Hits	LP/BP	U.S.		$14.00/$8.00
Warner Brothers	2-60193	Greatest Hits Vol.1	LP/LB	U.S.†	1984	$14.00/$8.00
Warner Brothers	25328-2	Greatest Hits Vol.2	LP/LB	U.S.†	1985	$14.00/$8.00
Warner Brothers		Hank	DJ/Smplr	U.S.		$25.00
Pacific Arts	PAV12530	Hank Williams Jr.	LD	U.S.	1986	$40.00
Warner Brothers	PRO-CD-4825	Pure Hank Radio Special	DJ/RS	U.S.	1991	$22.00

Singles

Label	Catalog Number	Title	Type	Country	Year	Longbox Value / Value
Capricorn	5426	A Little Less Talk	CDJ	U.S.	1992	$3.00
Warner Brothers	PRO-CD-3904	Ain't Nobody's Business	CDJ	U.S.	1990	$3.00
Curb	5434	Come on Over to the Country	CDJ	U.S.	1992	$3.00
Curb	6173	Diamond Mine	CDJ	U.S.	1993	$3.00
Curb	5895	Everything Comes Down to Money and Love	CDJ	U.S.	1993	$3.00
Curb	5980	Everything Comes Down to Money and Love	CDJ	U.S.	1993	$3.00
Curb	77723	Family Tradition	CD5	U.S.	1994	$5.00
Warner Brothers	PRO-CD-3574	Finders Are Keepers	CDJ	U.S.	1989	$3.00
Curb	77725	Habits Old & New	CD5	U.S.	1994	$5.00
Curb	77728	High Notes	CD5	U.S.	1994	$5.00
Curb	5296	Hotel Whiskey	CDJ	U.S.	1993	$3.00
Warner Brothers	PRO-CD-4606	I Mean I Love You	CDJ	U.S.	1990	$3.00
Warner Brothers	PRO-CD-4794	If It Will It Will	CDJ	U.S.	1991	$3.00
Curb	5613	Lyin' Jukebox	CDJ	U.S.	1992	$3.00
Curb	77730d	Man of Steel	CD5	U.S.	1994	$5.00
Warner Brothers	PRO-CD-4063	Man to Man	CDJ	U.S.	1990	$3.00
Warner Brothers	PRO-CD-5109	Monday Night Football Boogie	CDJ	U.S.	1991	$3.00
Curb	77721	One Night Stands	CD5	U.S.	1994	$5.00
Curb	77727	Pressure Is On	CD5	U.S.	1994	$5.00
Curb	77726	Rowdy	CD5	U.S.	1994	$5.00
Curb	77729	Strong Stuff	CD5	U.S.	1994	$5.00
Curb	77722	The New South	CD5	U.S.	1994	$5.00
Warner Brothers		There's a Tear in My Beer	CDJ	U.S.		$3.00
	77724	Whiskey Bent & Hell Bound	CD5	U.S.	1994	$5.00
Warner Brothers	PRO-CD-3179	You're Gonna Be a Sorry Man	CDJ	U.S.	1988	$3.00

Williams, Jane Kelly

Singles

Label	Catalog Number	Title	Type	Country	Year	Longbox Value / Value
		Breaking Into the Past	CDJ	U.S.		$2.00

Williams, Joe

Full Length

Label	Catalog Number	Title	Type	Country	Year	Longbox Value / Value
Delos	D/CD 4001	Nothin' but The Blues	LP/LB	U.S.†	1985	$14.00/$8.00

Williams, John

Singles

Label	Catalog Number	Title	Type	Country	Year	Longbox Value / Value
MCA	CD45 18122	Born on the Fourth of July	CDJ	U.S.	1989	$2.00
Warner Brothers	PRO-CD-3560	Raiders March	CDJ	U.S.	1989	$2.00

Williams, Lenny

Singles

Label	Catalog Number	Title	Type	Country	Year	Longbox Value / Value
Crush	ONE-6903	Givin' Up on Love	CD5	U.K.	1989	$7.00
Crush	663-8	Givin' Up on Love	CDJ	U.S.	1988	$2.00
ZYX	6396-8	Gotta Otta Luv	CD5	Germany	1990	$6.00
		Gotta Otta Luv	CDJ	U.S.		$2.00

Williams, Lucinda

Singles

Label	Catalog Number	Title	Type	Country	Year	Longbox Value / Value
Chameleon	8669	Hot Blood	CDJ	U.S.	1992	$2.00
Rough Trade	ROUGH US 66CD	Passionate Kisses	CD5	U.K.	1987	$8.00
Chameleon	8630	Six Blocks Away	CDJ	U.S.	1992	$2.00
Chameleon		Something About	CDJ	U.S.		$7.00

Williams, Robin

Full Length

Label	Catalog Number	Title	Type	Country	Year	Longbox Value / Value
Vestron	VL3147	In Concert	LD	U.S.	1987	$40.00

Williams, Tene

Singles

Label	Catalog Number	Title	Type	Country	Year	Longbox Value / Value
Pendulum	8817	Just a Matter of Time	CDJ	U.S.	1993	$2.00

Williams, Vanessa

Full Length

Label	Catalog Number	Title	Type	Country	Year	Longbox Value / Value
Wing	CDP 476	Quiet Zone, The	DJ/Smplr	U.S.	1991	$5.00

Singles

Label	Catalog Number	Title	Type	Country	Year	Longbox Value / Value
Polygram	64001	Colors Of the Wind	CD5	U.S.	1995	$6.00
Wing	CDP 579	Comfort Zone, The	CDJ	U.S.	1991	$3.00
Wing	CDP 583	Comfort Zone, The	CDJ	U.S.	1991	$3.00
London	POOL-400112	Darling	CD3	Japan	1989	$13.00/$4.00
Polygram	889230-3	Dreamin'	CD3	Germany	1989	$8.00
Polygram	8892301-2	Dreamin'	CD5	Germany	1989	$8.00
Polygram	871749-2	Dreamin'	CD3	U.K.	1989	$8.00
Polydor	865843-2	Just for Tonight	CD5	Germany	1992	$8.00
Polydor	PODP-1056	Just for Tonight	CD3	Japan	1992	$13.00/$4.00
Polydor	PZCD-213	Just for Tonight	CD5	U.K.	1992	$8.00
Polydor	CDP 673	Just for Tonight	CDJ	U.S.	1992	$2.00
Giant	WPDP-6326	Love Is	CD3	Japan	1993	$13.00/$4.00
		Open Your Eyes You Can Fly	CDJ	U.S.		$3.00
Polygram	887660-2	Right Stuff, The	CD5	Germany	1988	$8.00
Wing	CDP 14	Right Stuff, The	CDJ	U.S.	1988	$3.00
Wing	870 733-2	Right Stuff, The	CDV/BP	U.S.	1988	$20.00/$17.00
Polydor	867747-2	Running Back To You	CD5	Germany	1991	$8.00
Polydor	PODP-1028	Running Back To You	CD3	Japan	1991	$12.00/$4.00
Polydor	PZCD-172	Running Back To You	CD5	U.K.	1991	$8.00
Wing	867519	Running Back To You	CD5	U.S.	1991	$5.00
Wing	CDP 434	Running Back To You	CDJ	U.S.	1991	$6.00
Polydor	PODP-1046	Save the Best For Last	CD3	Japan	1992	$12.00/$4.00
Polydor	PZCD-192	Save the Best For Last	CD5	U.K.	1991	$9.00
Polydor	CDP 593	Save the Best For Last	CDJ	U.S.	1991	$3.00
Polygram	85112	Sweetest Days	CD5	U.S.	1994	$5.00
Polygram	85111	Sweetest Days	CD5	U.S.	1994	$5.00
Polygram	856770	Way That You Love	CD5	U.S.	1994	$5.00
Polygram	856770	Way That You Love, The	CD5	U.S.	1995	$6.00
Polydor	PZCD-236	Work	CD5	U.K.	1992	$8.00
Wing	863544	Work	CD5	U.S.	1991	$3.00
Mercury	CDP 759	Work To Do	CDJ	U.S.		$2.00
		You Can't Run	CDJ	U.S.		$3.00
Polygram	852224	You Can't Run	CD5	U.S.	1995	$6.00
Polygram		You R Loved	CDJ	U.S.	1994	$8.00

Williams, Vesta

Full Length

Label	Catalog Number	Title	Type	Country	Year	Longbox Value / Value
A&M	75021 7236	Special	DJ/LP	U.S.	1991	$19.00
CD in ribbon tied digipak.						

Singles

Label	Catalog Number	Title	Type	Country	Year	Longbox Value / Value
A&M	CD 17669	4U	CDJ	U.S.	1991	$3.00
A&M	31458 8181	Always	CDJ	U.S.	1993	$2.00
Breakout	USACD-680	Congratulations	CD5	U.K.	1989	$8.00
A&M	CD 17764	Congratulations	CDJ	U.S.	1988	$2.00
A&M	75021 7289 2	Do Ya	CDJ	U.S.	1991	$3.00
A&M		How You Feel	CDJ	U.S.		$2.00
A&M	75021 7221 2	Special	CDJ	U.S.	1991	$2.00
A&M	CD 17630	Sweet Sweet Love	CDJ	U.S.	1988	$2.00

Williams, Victoria

Singles

Label	Catalog Number	Title	Type	Country	Year	Longbox Value / Value
		Nature's Way	CDJ	U.S.		$3.00
		Selections From Loose	CDJ	U.S.		$3.00
Rough Trade	PC10	Tarbelly and Featherfoot	CD5	U.K.	1990	$8.00
		You R Loved	CDJ	U.S.		$3.00

Williams, Wendy O

Full Length

Label	Catalog Number	Title	Type	Country	Year	Longbox Value / Value
		Wendy O Williams	LP/LB	U.S.		$15.00/$10.00

Willis, Allee

Full Length

Label	Catalog Number	Title	Type	Country	Year	Longbox Value / Value
Virgin		Hits	DJ/Smplr	U.S.		$20.00

Willis, Bruce

Singles

Label	Catalog Number	Title	Type	Country	Year	Longbox Value / Value
Motown	ZD-41654	Comin' Right Up	CD5	U.K.	1989	$8.00
Motown	ZD-43170	Save the Last Dance for Me	CD5	Germany	1989	$8.00
Motown	R10M-128	Save the Last Dance for Me	CD3	Japan	1989	$12.00/$3.00
Motown	ZD-43170	Save the Last Dance for Me	CD5	U.K.	1989	$8.00
Motown	CD45 17993	Save the Last Dance for Me	CDJ	U.S.	1989	$2.00
RCA	ZD-43453	Turn It Up	CD5	Germany	1990	$8.00

Willis, Kelly

Full Length

Label	Catalog Number	Title	Type	Country	Year	Longbox Value / Value
A&M		Fading Fast	DJ/Smplr	U.S.	1996	$15.00

Singles

Label	Catalog Number	Title	Type	Country	Year	Longbox Value / Value
		Drive South	CDJ	U.S.		$2.00
MCA	54198	Heart That Love Forgot, The	CDJ	u.S.	1991	$2.00
MCA	54251	Settle for Love	CDJ	u.S.	1991	$2.00

Willson-Piper, Marty

Singles

Label	Catalog Number	Title	Type	Country	Year	Longbox Value / Value
Rykodisc	1025	Luscious Ghost	CD3	U.S.		$6.00/$3.00

Wilson, Brian

Full Length

Label	Catalog Number	Title	Type	Country	Year	Longbox Value / Value
Sire	PRO-CD-3176	Brian Wilson	DJ/LP	U.S.	1988	$16.00
Picture disc.						
Sire	PRO-CD-3176	Brian Wilson	DJ/LP	U.S.	1988	$30.00
Picture disc CD in clothbound digipak package.						
MCA		I Just Wasn't Made for These Times	DJ/Intvw	U.S.	1995	$15.00
Interview and music.						
MCA		I Just Wasn't Made for These Times	DJ/Intvw	U.S.	1995	$15.00
Interview only.						
		Still I Dream of You	DJ/Smplr	Japan	1994	$120.00
CD in hardbound photobook.						
Sire	PRO-CD-3248	Words & Music From Brian Wilson	DJ/Intvw	U.S.	1988	$18.00

Singles

Label	Catalog Number	Title	Type	Country	Year	Longbox Value / Value
MCA		Do It Again	CDJ	Sweden	1996	$12.00
		Fantasy Is Reality	CDJ	U.S.		$12.00
Sire	921032-2	Love & Mercy	CD3	Germany	1988	$10.00
Sire	W-7814CD	Love & Mercy	CD3	U.K.	1988	$10.00
Warner Brothers		Love & Mercy	CDJ	U.S.		$7.00

Label	Catalog Number	Title	Type	Country	Year	Longbox Value / Value
Sire	PRO-CD-3168	Love & Mercy	CDJ	U.S.	1988	$6.00
Sire	PRO-CD-3303	Melt Away	CDJ	U.S.	1988	$6.00
Sire	W-7787CD	Night Time	CD3	U.K.	1988	$10.00
Sire	PRO-CD-3200	Night Time	CDJ	U.S.	1988	$6.00

Wilson, Brian and Van Dyke Parks

Full Length

Label	Catalog Number	Title	Type	Country	Year	Longbox Value / Value
Warner Brohers	2-45427-A	Orange Create Art	DJ/LP	U.S.	1995	$15.00

Wilson, Cassandra

Singles

Label	Catalog Number	Title	Type	Country	Year	Longbox Value / Value
		My Corner of the Sky	CDJ	U.S.	1992	$2.00

Wilson, Charlie

Singles

Label	Catalog Number	Title	Type	Country	Year	Longbox Value / Value
MCA	2224	Sprung on Me	CDJ	U.S.	1992	$2.00
MCA	2170	You Turn My Life Around	CDJ	U.S.	1992	$2.00

Wilson, Danny

Full Length

Label	Catalog Number	Title	Type	Country	Year	Longbox Value / Value
Virgin	91255	Bebop Motop	LP/LB	U.S.		$14.00/$8.00
Virgin	90596	Meet Danny Wilson	LP/LB	U.S.		$14.00/$8.00

Singles

Label	Catalog Number	Title	Type	Country	Year	Longbox Value / Value
Virgin	VSCD-1095	Davy	CD5	U.K.	1988	$8.00
Virgin	CDEP-12	Girl I Used To Know	CD5	U.K.	1988	$8.00
Virgin	VJD-10214	I Can't Wait	CD3	Japan	1989	$12.00/$3.00
Virgin	VSCD-1226	I Can't Wait	CD3	U.K.	1989	$8.00
Virgin	VSCDX-1226	I Can't Wait	CD5	U.K.	1989	$8.00
Virgin	662640	If Everything You Said Is True	CD5	Germany	1989	$8.00
Virgin	PRCD 2777	If Everything You Said Was True	CDJ	U.S.	1989	$2.00
Virgin	VJD-10222	If Everything You Said Is True	CD3	Japan	1989	$12.00/$3.00
Virgin	661302	Mary's Prayer	CD5	Germany	1988	$8.00
Virgin	VSCD-934	Mary's Prayer	CD5	U.K.	1988	$8.00
Virgin	VSCD-1203	Never Gonna Be the Same	CD5	U.K.	1989	$8.00
Virgin	162418	Second Summer of Love	CD3	Germany	1989	$8.00
Virgin	662418	Second Summer of Love	CD5	Germany	1989	$8.00
Virgin	VSCD-1186	Second Summer of Love	CD3	U.K.	1989	$8.00

Wilson, Jackie

Full Length

Label	Catalog Number	Title	Type	Country	Year	Longbox Value / Value
Epic	EGK-38623	Jackie Wilson Story	LP/LB	U.S.†	1984	$14.00/$8.00

Singles

Label	Catalog Number	Title	Type	Country	Year	Longbox Value / Value
Rhino	71850	Higher & Higher	CD5	U.S.	1994	$5.00

Wilson, Kim

Full Length

Label	Catalog Number	Title	Type	Country	Year	Longbox Value / Value
		House of Blues	RS	U.S.	1994	$40.00

2 CD set. Airdate: 8/21/94.

Wilson, Lesette

Singles

Label	Catalog Number	Title	Type	Country	Year	Longbox Value / Value
Atlantic	PRCD 5143-2	Unfinished Business	CDJ	U.S.	1993	$2.00

Wilson, Nancy

Full Length

Label	Catalog Number	Title	Type	Country	Year	Longbox Value / Value
Image	ID7515VW	At Carnegie Hall	LD	U.S.		$25.00
Denon	CD-7188	Godsend	LP/BP	U.S.†	1984	$14.00/$8.00
Denon	CD-7061	I'll Be a Song	LP/BP	U.S.†	1985	$14.00/$8.00
Denon	CD-7597	Keep You Satisfied	LP/BP	U.S.†	1985	$14.00/$8.00
Denon	CD-7556	Yaksa	LP/BP	U.S.†	1985	$14.00/$8.00

Singles

Label	Catalog Number	Title	Type	Country	Year	Longbox Value / Value
		All for Love	CDJ	U.S.		$2.00
Columbia	CSK 73353	Don't Ask My Neighbors	CDJ	U.S.	1990	$2.00
		Epilogue	CD3	Japan		$12.00/$4.00
Epic	3265	Epilogue	CD3	Japan	1991	$12.00/$4.00
Columbia	CSK 1973	Heaven's Hand	CDJ	U.S.	1990	$2.00
Columbia		Quiet Fire	CDJ	U.S.		$2.00
Sony	108H-3047	Still Enough Love	CD3	Japan	1988	$12.00/$4.00

Wilson Phillips

Full Length

Label	Catalog Number	Title	Type	Country	Year	Longbox Value / Value
EMI	SPCD-1259	Shadows & Lights	DJ/Smplr	Japan		$50.00
EMI		Special DJ Copy	DJ/Smplr	Japan		$50.00

Singles

Label	Catalog Number	Title	Type	Country	Year	Longbox Value / Value
SBK	204416-2	Dream Is Still Alive, The	CD5	Germany	1991	$8.00
Toshiba	TODP-2301	Dream Is Still Alive, The	CD3	Japan	1991	$12.00/$4.00
SBK	CDSBK-31	Dream Is Still Alive, The	CD5	U.K.	1991	$8.00
SBK	DPRO-05391	Dream Is Still Alive, The	CDJ	U.S.	1991	$2.00
SBK	DPRO-19770	Flesh and Blood	CD5	U.S.	1992	$4.00
SBK	TODP-2371	Give It Up	CD3	Japan	1992	$12.00/$4.00
SBK	CDSBK-36	Give It Up	CD5	U.K.	1992	$8.00
SBK	DPRO-19763	Give It Up	CD5	U.S.	1992	$4.00
SBK	203831-2	Hold on	CD5	Germany	1990	$8.00
SBK	CDSBK-6	Hold on	CD5	U.K.	1990	$8.00
SBK	DPRO-05334	Hold on	CDJ	U.S.	1990	$3.00
SBK	204103-2	Impulsive	CD5	Germany	1990	$8.00
SBK	204240-2	Impulsive	CD5	Germany	1991	$8.00
SBK	CDSBK-16	Impulsive	CD5	U.K.	1990	$8.00
SBK	DPRO-05359	Impulsive	CDJ	U.S.	1990	$2.00
SBK	203942-2	Release Me	CD5	Germany	1990	$8.00
SBK	TODP-2196	Release Me	CD3	Japan	1990	$12.00/$4.00
SBK	CDSBK-11	Release Me	CD5	U.K.	1990	$8.00
SBK	DPRO-05342	Release Me	CDJ	U.S.	1990	$6.00
SBK	DPRO-05449	You Won't See Me Cry	CDJ	U.S.	1992	$2.00
SBK	204264-2	You're in Love	CD5	Germany	1991	$8.00
SBK	TODP-2269	You're in Love	CD3	Japan	1991	$12.00/$4.00
SBK	TOCP-6666	You're in Love	CD5	Japan	1991	$12.00
SBK	CDSBK-25	You're in Love	CD5	U.K.	1991	$8.00
SBK	DPRO-04729	You're in Love	CDJ	U.S.	1991	$10.00

Wilson-James, Victoria

Singles

Label	Catalog Number	Title	Type	Country	Year	Longbox Value / Value
Epic	ESK 73873	Bright Lights	CDJ	U.S.	1991	$2.00
Epic	ESK 73981	One World	CDJ	U.S.	1991	$2.00
Epic	ESK 73707	Through	CDJ	U.S.	1991	$2.00

Wilson-Piper, Marty

Singles

Label	Catalog Number	Title	Type	Country	Year	Longbox Value / Value
Rykodisc	RCD5-1025	Luscious Ghost	CD5	U.S.	1992	$5.00
Rykodisc	RCD 0114	Questions Without Answers	CDJ	U.S.	1992	$3.00
Rykodisc	RCD 31002	She's King	CD3	U.S.	1988	$6.00/$3.00

Winans

Singles

Label	Catalog Number	Title	Type	Country	Year	Longbox Value / Value
Qwest	6692	Extra Mile, The	CDJ	U.S.	1993	$2.00
Warner Brothers	17756	Heart & Soul	CD5	U.S.	1995	$5.00
Warner Brothers	PRO-CD-3953	It's True	CDJ	U.S.	1990	$2.00
Qwest	6249	Payday	CDJ	U.S.	1993	$2.00
Warner Brothers	PRO-CD-4457	When You Cry	CDJ	U.S.	1990	$2.00

Winans, Bebe and Cece

Singles

Label	Catalog Number	Title	Type	Country	Year	Longbox Value / Value
EMI	204511-2	Addicted to Love	CD5	Germany	1991	$8.00
Capitol	C2 15732	Addicted to Love	CD5	U.S.	1991	$5.00
Capitol	DPRO-79751	Addicted to Love	CDJ	U.S.	1991	$2.00
Capitol	DPRO-79402	Blood, The	CDJ	U.S.	1991	$2.00
EMI	203548-3	Celebrate New Life	CD3	Germany	1989	$8.00
Capitol	CDCL-551	Celebrate New Life	CD5	U.K.	1989	$8.00
Capitol	DPRO-79323	Depend on You	CDJ	U.S.	1991	$2.00
EMI	204584-2	I'll Take You There	CD5	Germany	1992	$8.00
Capitol	C2 15760	I'll Take You There	CD5	U.S.	1992	$5.00
Capitol	DPRO-79873	I'll Take You There	CDJ	U.S.	1992	$3.00
Capitol	DPRO-79126	It's OK	CDJ	U.S.	1992	$2.00
Capitol	DPRO-79288	Jingle Bell	CDJ	U.S.	1993	$2.00
Capitol	DPRO-79565	Lost Without You	CDJ	U.S.	1989	$2.00
Capitol		Meantime	CDJ	U.S.		$2.00
Capitol	DPRO-79912	Silent Night	CDJ	U.S.	1991	$2.00

Winans, Vickie

Singles

Label	Catalog Number	Title	Type	Country	Year	Longbox Value / Value
MCA	2014	Don't Throw Your Life Away	CDJ	U.S.	1993	$2.00

Winbush, Angela

Singles

Label	Catalog Number	Title	Type	Country	Year	Longbox Value / Value
Mercury	870 700-2	Angel	CDV/BP	U.S.	1988	$14.00/$14.00
Elektra	PRCD 8968-2	Inner City Blues	CDJ	U.S.	1994	$2.00
Mercury	CDP 121	It's the Real Thing	CDJ	U.S.	1989	$2.00
Mercury	CDP 248	Lay Your Troubles on Me	CDJ	U.S.	1990	$2.00
Mercury	CDP 181	No More Tears	CDJ	U.S.	1989	$2.00
Mercury	CDP 305	Please Bring Your Love Back	CDJ	U.S.	1990	$2.00
		Treat U Rite	CDJ	U.S.		$2.00

Windows

Singles

Label	Catalog Number	Title	Type	Country	Year	Longbox Value / Value
Cypress	YD 17813	New Sneakers	CDJ	U.S.	1989	$2.00

Winger

Singles

Label	Catalog Number	Title	Type	Country	Year	Longbox Value / Value
Atlantic	PRCD 5063-2	Blind Revolution	CDJ	U.S.	1993	$3.00
Atlantic	AMDY-5026	Can't Get Enough	CD3	Japan	1990	$12.00/$4.00
Atlantic	A-7884CD	Can't Get Enough	CD5	U.K.	1990	$8.00
Atlantic	PRCD 3393-2	Can't Get Enough	CDJ	U.S.	1990	$3.00
Atlantic	PRCD 5061-2	Down Incognito	CDJ	U.S.	1994	$2.00
Atlantic	A-7773CD	Easy Come Easy Go	CD3	Japan	1991	$12.00/$4.00
Atlantic	PRCD 3690-2	Easy Come Easy Go	CDJ	U.S.	1990	$6.00
Atlantic	PR 2644-2	Headed for a Heartbreak	CDJ	U.S.	1988	$3.00
Atlantic	PR 2655-2	Headed for a Heartbreak	CDJ	U.S.	1988	$3.00
Atlantic	PR 2803-2	Hungry	CDJ	U.S.	1989	$3.00
Atlantic		Madalaine	CDJ	U.S.		$3.00
Atlantic		Madalaine	CDJ	U.S.		$3.00

Second version.

Label	Catalog Number	Title	Type	Country	Year	Longbox Value / Value
Atlantic	7567-86102-2	Miles Away	CD5	Germany	1990	$8.00
Atlantic	AMDY-5036	Miles Away	CD3	Japan	1990	$12.00/$4.00
Atlantic	A-7802CD	Miles Away	CD5	U.K.	1990	$8.00
Atlantic		Miles Away	CDJ	U.S.	1990	$3.00
Atlantic		Seventeen	CDJ	U.S.	1988	$3.00

Winston, George

Full Length

Label	Catalog Number	Title	Type	Country	Year	Longbox Value / Value
Windham	WD-1012	Autumn	LP/LB	U.S.†	1985	$14.00/$8.00
Windham	WD-1025	December	LP/LB	U.S.†	1985	$14.00/$8.00
Windham	WD-1019	Winter Into Spring	LP/LB	U.S.†	1985	$14.00/$8.00

Winter, Edgar

Full Length

Label	Catalog Number	Title	Type	Country	Year	Longbox Value / Value
Album Network		In the Studio (They Only Come out at Night)	RS	U.S.	1989	$25.00

Airdate: 2/20/89.

Label	Catalog Number	Title	Type	Country	Year	Longbox Value / Value
Album Network		In the Studio (They Only Come out at Night)	RS	U.S.	1991	$20.00

Airdate: 9/23/91.

Label	Catalog Number	Title	Type	Country	Year	Longbox Value / Value
DIR		King Biscuit Flour Hour	RS	U.S.	1988	$30.00

With Ten Years After, Airdate: 6/19/88.

Label	Catalog Number	Title	Type	Country	Year	Longbox Value / Value
DIR		King Biscuit Flour Hour	RS	U.S.	1990	$30.00

With Johnny Winter, Airdate: 2/19/90.

Label	Catalog Number	Title	Type	Country	Year	Longbox Value / Value
DIR		King Biscuit Flour Hour	RS	U.S.	1991	$30.00

With Johnny Winter, Airdate: 4/21/91.

Label	Catalog Number	Title	Type	Country	Year	Longbox Value / Value
Rhino		Mission Earth	LP/LB	U.S.		$14.00/$8.00

Singles

Label	Catalog Number	Title	Type	Country	Year	Longbox Value / Value
Rhino	90021	Cry Out	CDJ	U.S.	1989	$6.00
Rhino	PRO2 90021	Cry Out	CDJ	U.S.	1990	$2.00

Winter Hours

Singles

Label	Catalog Number	Title	Type	Country	Year	Longbox Value / Value
Chrysalis	DPRO-23487	Roadside Flowers	CDJ	U.S.	1989	$2.00

Winter, Johnny

Full Length

Label	Catalog Number	Title	Type	Country	Year	Longbox Value / Value
DIR		King Biscuit Flour Hour	RS	U.S.	1988	$30.00

With Robin Trower, Airdate: 7/17/88.

Label	Catalog Number	Title	Type	Country	Year	Longbox Value / Value
DIR		King Biscuit Flour Hour	RS	U.S.	1990	$30.00

With Edgar Winter, Airdate: 2/19/90.

Label	Catalog Number	Title	Type	Country	Year	Longbox Value / Value
DIR		King Biscuit Flour Hour	RS	U.S.	1991	$30.00

With Edgar Winter, Airdate: 4/21/91.

Label	Catalog Number	Title	Type	Country	Year	Longbox Value / Value
Pioneer	PA-85-121	Live	LD	U.S.	1990	$30.00
		Texas Tornado	LP/BP	U.S.		$14.00/$8.00

Singles

Label	Catalog Number	Title	Type	Country	Year	Longbox Value / Value
Charisma	PRCD 052	Illustrated Man	CDJ	U.S.	1991	$2.00
Pioneer	PIFP-1025	Johnny B. Goode	CDV	Japan		$45.00
Charisma	12722	Johnny Guitar	CDJ	U.S.	1992	$2.00
Charisma	PRCD 069	Life Is Hard	CDJ	U.S.	1991	$2.00

Winter, Joy

Singles

Label	Catalog Number	Title	Type	Country	Year	Longbox Value / Value
Epic	ESK 2115	In Time You'll See	CDJ	U.S.	1990	$2.00
Epic	ESK 73324	In Time You'll See	CDJ	U.S.	1990	$2.00

Winwood, Steve

Full Length

Label	Catalog Number	Title	Type	Country	Year	Longbox Value / Value
BBC Radio		BBC Classic Tracks	RS	U.S.	1991	$20.00

Airdate: 10/28/91.

Label	Catalog Number	Title	Type	Country	Year	Longbox Value / Value
BBC Radio		BBC Classic Tracks	RS	U.S.	1992	$20.00

Airdate: 10/1/92.

Label	Catalog Number	Title	Type	Country	Year	Longbox Value / Value
Westwood One		BBC Classic Tracks	RS	U.S.	1992	$20.00

Airdate: 7/19/92.

Label	Catalog Number	Title	Type	Country	Year	Longbox Value / Value
Westwood One		BBC Classic Tracks	RS	U.S.	1993	$20.00
Airdate: 7/12/93.						
Westwood One		BBC Classic Tracks	RS	U.S.	1994	$20.00
Airdate: 1/24/94.						
Westwood One		BBC Classic Tracks	RS	U.S.	1995	$20.00
Airdate: 8/14/95.						
Island		Finer Things Sampler, The	DJ/Smplr	U.S.	1995	$25.00
CD sampler in press kit folder.						
Island	PRCD 6842-2	Highlights From the Finer Things Boxed Set	DJ/Smplr	U.S.	1995	$25.00
Westwood One		In Concert	RS	U.S.	1993	$35.00
Airdate: 7/19/93.						
Westwood One		In Concert	RS	U.S.	1993	$40.00
2 CD set. Airdate: 7/19/93.						
Westwood One		Off the Record	RS	U.S.	1995	$20.00
Airdate: 1/20/95.						
Westwood One		Off the Record	RS	U.S.	1995	$20.00
Airdate: 5/8/95.						
Virgin	PRCD STEVE	Refugees	DJ/LP	U.S.	1990	$18.00
CD in fabric pouch.						
Westwood One		Superstars	RS	U.S.	1994	$40.00
2 CD set. With Traffic, Airdate: 6/13/94						
Media America		Up Close	RS	U.S.	1989	$40.00
4 CD set.						
Media America		Up Close	RS	U.S.	1990	$40.00
4 CD set.						

Singles

Label	Catalog Number	Title	Type	Country	Year	Longbox Value / Value
		Another Deal Goes Down	CDJ	U.S.		$3.00
Virgin	661685	Don't You Know What the Night Can Do	CD5	Germany	1988	$10.00
Virgin	VJD-10007	Don't You Know What the Night Can Do	CD3	Japan	1988	$12.00/$4.00
Virgin	VSCD-1107	Don't You Know What the Night Can Do	CD5	U.K.	1988	$10.00
Virgin	PR 2427	Don't You Know What the Night Can Do	CD5	U.S.	1988	$3.00
Virgin	VJD-10210	Hearts on Fire	CD3	Japan	1988	$12.00/$4.00
Virgin	PR 2637	Hearts on Fire	CDJ	U.S.	1988	$3.00
Virgin	P15D-37002	Higher Love	CD3	Japan	1988	$12.00/$4.00
Virgin	VJD-12035	Holding On	CD3	Japan	1988	$12.00/$4.00
Virgin	VSCD-1135	Holding On	CD3	U.K.	1988	$10.00
Virgin		Holding On	CDJ	U.S.	1988	$3.00
Virgin	663917	I Will Be Here	CD5	Germany	1990	$10.00
Virgin	VJCP-14020	I Will Be Here	CD5	Japan	1990	$15.00
Virgin	PRCD 3763	I Will Be Here	CDJ	U.S.	1990	$3.00
Virgin	663798	One and Only Man	CD5	Germany	1990	$8.00
Virgin	VJDP-132	One and Only Man	CD3	Japan	1990	$12.00/$4.00
Virgin	VJCP-1412	One and Only Man	CD5	Japan	1990	$15.00
Virgin	VSCDT-1299	One and Only Man	CD5	U.K.	1990	$8.00
Virgin	PRCD 3517	One and Only Man	CDJ	U.S.	1990	$3.00
		Reach for the Light	CDJ	U.S.		$3.00
Virgin	661534	Roll With It	CD5	Germany	1988	$10.00
Virgin	VJD-12011	Roll With It	CD3	Japan	1988	$12.00/$4.00
Virgin	2-99326	Roll With It	CD3	U.K.	1988	$10.00
Virgin	VSCD-1085	Roll With It	CD5	U.K.	1988	$10.00
Virgin	2-99326	Roll With It	CD3	U.S.	1988	$6.00/$3.00
Virgin	PRCD 9326	Roll With It	CDJ	U.S.	1988	$3.00
Island	PRCD 2792	Time Is Running Out	CDJ	U.S.		$3.00
Polydor	P15D-37003	Valerie	CD3	Japan	1988	$12.00/$4.00

Wire

Singles

Label	Catalog Number	Title	Type	Country	Year	Longbox Value / Value
Mute	8351	Drill in Every City	CDJ	U.S.	1991	$2.00
Mute	CDMUTE-87	Eardrum Buzz	CD5	U.K.	1989	$8.00
Enigma	7 75520-3	Eardrum Buzz	CD3	U.S.	1989	$6.00/$3.00
Enigma	EPRO 166	Eardrum Buzz	CDJ	U.S.	1989	$2.00
Intercord	826 915	In Vivo	CD3	Germany	1989	$8.00
IRS	977 298	In Vivo	CD5	Germany	1989	$8.00
Mute	CDMUTE-98	In Vivo	CD3	U.K.	1989	$8.00
Mute	CDMUTE-67	Kidney Bingos	CD3	U.K.	1988	$8.00
Enigma	7 75553 2	Life in the Manscape	CD5	U.S.	1990	$4.00
Enigma	EPRO 285	Life in the Manscape	CDJ	U.S.	1990	$2.00
Enigma	EPRO 301	Life in the Manscape	CDJ	U.S.	1990	$2.00
Mute	977 284	Silkskin Paws	CD5	Germany	1988	$8.00
Mute	CDMUTE-84	Silkskin Paws	CD3	U.K	1988	$8.00
Restless	7 72299-3	Silkskin Paws	CD3	U.S.	1988	$7.00/$4.00

Wire Train

Singles

Label	Catalog Number	Title	Type	Country	Year	Longbox Value / Value
MCA	2304	Crashing Back to Work	CDJ	U.S.	1992	$2.00
MCA	DMCAT-1457	Should She Cry	CD5	U.K.	1990	$8.00
MCA	CD 18470	Should She Cry	CDJ	U.S.	1990	$2.00
MCA	CD 1108	Spin	CDJ	U.S.	1990	$2.00
MCA	DMCAT-1682	Stone Me	CD5	U.K.	1992	$8.00
MCA	2202	Stone Me	CDJ	U.S.	1992	$2.00
MCA	2244	Stone Me	CDJ	U.S.	1992	$2.00

Wisanggeni, Tjahjo

Full Length

Label	Catalog Number	Title	Type	Country	Year	Longbox Value / Value
Azra	ETR 102	From the Other Side	LTD/LP	U.S.	1991	$15.00

Wiseblood

Singles

Label	Catalog Number	Title	Type	Country	Year	Longbox Value / Value
Big Cat	30	Pedal to The Metal	CD5	U.S.	1994	$5.00

Wishbone Ash

Full Length

Label	Catalog Number	Title	Type	Country	Year	Longbox Value / Value
Griffin		BBC Live in Concert	LTD/LP	U.S.		$30.00
CD and Book.						
IRS		Here to Hear	LP/LB	U.S.		$14.00/$8.00

Singles

Label	Catalog Number	Title	Type	Country	Year	Longbox Value / Value
IRS	006	Keeper of the Light	CDJ	U.S.	1989	$2.00

Withers, Bill

Full Length

Label	Catalog Number	Title	Type	Country	Year	Longbox Value / Value
CBS	CK-39887	Watching You Watching Me	LP/BP	U.S.†	1985	$14.00/$8.00

Witness

Singles

Label	Catalog Number	Title	Type	Country	Year	Longbox Value / Value
Lectium	272	Go Right Ahead	CDJ	U.S.	1990	$2.00
A&M	AMCD-756	House Called Love	CD5	U.K.	1991	$8.00
A&M	AMCD-760	Light at the End of the Tunnel	CD5	U.K.	1991	$8.00
A&M	AMCD-776	Loverman	CD5	U.K.	1991	$8.00
Lectium	230	Old Landmark	CDJ	U.S.	1990	$2.00
Strange Frt	SFPMACD-206	Peel Sessions	CD5	U.K.	1990	$8.00

Wobble, Jah

Singles

Label	Catalog Number	Title	Type	Country	Year	Longbox Value / Value
Oval	102CD	Erzulie	CD5	U.K.	1991	$8.00
Island	854053	Sun Does Rise	CD5	U.S.	1994	$5.00
Island	PRCD 6832-2	Sun Does Rise	CDJ	U.S.	1994	$2.00
Oval	103CD	Visions of You	CD5	Germany	1992	$8.00
Atlantic	PRCD 4462-2	Visions of You	CDJ	U.S.	1991	$2.00

Wolf, Michael

Singles

Label	Catalog Number	Title	Type	Country	Year	Longbox Value / Value
Columbia	CSK 5397	Soul Sauce	CDJ	U.S.		$2.00

Wolf, Peter

Full Length

Label	Catalog Number	Title	Type	Country	Year	Longbox Value / Value
		House Of Blues	RS	U.S.	1994	$40.00
2 CD set. Airdate: 6/26/94.						
EMI	CDP 7 46046	Lights Out	LP/LB	U.S.		$15.00/$9.00
EMI	CDP 7 46046	Lights Out	LP/LB	U.S.†	1985	$15.00/$9.00
Radio Today		Rock Stars	RS	U.S.	1990	$30.00
2 CD set. Airdate: 4/29/90						

Singles

Label	Catalog Number	Title	Type	Country	Year	Longbox Value / Value
MCA	WMD5-4023	99 Worlds	CD3	Japan	1990	$12.00/$4.00
MCA	CD45 18188	99 Worlds	CDJ	U.S.	1990	$2.00
Album Network		99 Worlds	CDJ	U.S.	1990	$10.00
MCA	CD45 18383	When Women Are Lonely	CDJ	U.S.	1990	$2.00

Wolff, Kate

Full Length

Label	Catalog Number	Title	Type	Country	Year	Longbox Value / Value
	CDC 00494	California Gold	LP	Japan		$25.00
Kaleidosc	K-15	Close to You	LP/LB	U.S.		$14.00/$8.00
Kaleidosc	K-36	Evening in Austin	LP/LB	U.S.		$14.00/$8.00
Kaleidosc	K-13000	Give Yourself to Love	LP/LB	U.S.		$14.00/$8.00
Kaleidosc	K-3001	Gold in California	LP/LB	U.S.		$14.00/$8.00
Kaleidosc	K-24	Poet's Heart	LP/LB	U.S.		$14.00/$8.00
Kaleidosc	K-30	Safe at Anchor	LP/LB	U.S.		$14.00/$8.00
Kaleidosc	K-30	Wind Blows Wild	LP/LB	U.S.		$14.00/$8.00

Wolfgang Press

Singles

Label	Catalog Number	Title	Type	Country	Year	Longbox Value / Value
4AD	9 40547-2	A Girl Like You	CD5	U.S.	1992	$5.00
4AD	PRO-CD-5415	A Girl Like You	CDJ	U.S.	1992	$3.00
4AD		Christianity	CDJ	U.S.		$6.00
4AD		Going South	CDJ	U.S.		$6.00
4AD		Going South	CDJ	U.S.		$6.00
Second version.						
Warner Brothers	41883	Going South	CD5	U.S.	1994	$5.00
4AD	PRO-CD-5753	Mama Told Me Not to Come	CDJ	U.S.	1992	$3.00
4AD	1003	Time	CD5	U.K.	1991	$10.00

Wolfsbane

Full Length

Label	Catalog Number	Title	Type	Country	Year	Longbox Value / Value
Def American		Live Fast, Die Fast	DJ/Smplr	U.S.		$4.00

Singles

Label	Catalog Number	Title	Type	Country	Year	Longbox Value / Value
Def American	DEFAC-14	After Midnight	CD5	U.K.	1992	$8.00
Def American	DEFAC-11	Ezy	CD5	U.K.	1991	$8.00
Def American	DEFAC-3	I Like It Hot	CD5	U.K.	1989	$8.00
Def American	PRO-CD-3583	I Like It Hot	CDJ	U.S.	1989	$2.00
Def American	886383-2	Loco	CD5	Germany	1989	$8.00
Def American	DEFAC-2	Shakin'	CD5	U.K.	1989	$8.00

Wolvz

Singles

Label	Catalog Number	Title	Type	Country	Year	Longbox Value / Value
		She's Lookin' Pretty	CDJ	U.S.		$2.00

Womack & Womack

Singles

Label	Catalog Number	Title	Type	Country	Year	Longbox Value / Value
Milan	BM-620	Alimony	CD5	U.K.	1992	$8.00
BMG	162059	Celebrate the World	CD3	Germany	1989	$8.00
BMG	662059	Celebrate the World	CD5	Germany	1989	$8.00
4th & B'way	BRCD-125	Celebrate the World	CD5	U.K.	1989	$8.00
		Conscious of My Conscience	CDJ	U.S.		$2.00
4th & B'way	BRCD-132	I Am Love	CD5	U.K.	1989	$8.00
BMG	661912	Life's Just a Ballgame	CD5	Germany	1988	$8.00
4th & B'way	BRCD-116	Life's Just a Ballgame	CD5	U.K.	1988	$8.00
BMG	662471	MPB	CD5	Germany	1989	$8.00
4th & B'way	BRCD-138	MPB	CD5	U.K.	1989	$8.00
BMG	664457	My Dear	CD5	Germany	1991	$8.00
Warner Brothers	PRO-CD-6099	Passion & Pain	CDJ	U.S.	1993	$2.00
BMG	661542	Teardrops	CD5	Germany	1988	$8.00
Aris	885065	Teardrops	CD5	Germany	1988	$8.00
4th & B'way	BRCP-101	Teardrops	CD5	U.K.	1988	$8.00
		Teardrops	CDJ	U.S.	1988	$2.00
		Teardrops	CDJ	U.S.	1988	$2.00
Second version.						
BMG	664032	Uptown	CD5	Germany	1991	$8.00
BMG	664487	Uptown	CD5	Germany	1991	$8.00

Womak, Bobby

Full Length

Label	Catalog Number	Title	Type	Country	Year	Longbox Value / Value
CBS	75317	Save the Children	LP/LB	U.S.		$14.00/$8.00

Singles

Label	Catalog Number	Title	Type	Country	Year	Longbox Value / Value
Charly	CDS-10	Lookin' for Love	CD5	U.K.	1989	$8.00
Slolar	74600	Priorities	CDJ	U.S.	1990	$2.00
		Save the Children	CDJ	U.S.		$2.00

Wonder, Stevie

Full Length

Label	Catalog Number	Title	Type	Country	Year	Longbox Value / Value
		Conversation Peace	DJ/LP	U.S.		$30.00
Boxed set with CD, VHS video and rice paper prints in box.						
Motown		Keep Our Love Alive	DJ/LP	U.S.	1990	$60.00
CD, VHS video, pin and pouch in large presentation box.						
Motown	AMCD040595	Sampler	DJ/Smplr	Canada		$25.00
		Sixties Legends	RS	U.S.	1992	$15.00
2 CD set. Airdate: 8/22/92.						
Motown	5183-MD	Uptight	LP/BP	U.S.		$14.00/$8.00
Motown		Woman in Red	LP/BP	U.S.†	1985	$14.00/$8.00
		Wonder Piece	DJ/Smplr	Canada		$30.00

Singles

Label	Catalog Number	Title	Type	Country	Year	Longbox Value / Value
		For Your Love	CDJ	U.S.		$8.00
Motown	860291	For Your Love	CD5	U.S.	1994	$5.00
Motown	ZD-42856	Free	CD5	Germany	1989	$9.00
Motown	ZD-42856	Free	CD5	U.K.	1989	$9.00
Motown	ZD-44910	Fun Day	CD5	Germany	1991	$9.00
Motown	BVDM-15	Fun Day	CD3	Japan	1991	$12.00/$4.00
Motown	ZD-44958	Fun Day	CD5	U.K.	1991	$9.00
Motown	1649	Fun Day	CDJ	U.S.	1991	$3.00
Motown	ZD-44270	Gotta Have You	CD5	Germany	1991	$9.00
Motown	1145	Gotta Have You	CDJ	U.S.	1991	$3.00
Motown	1593	Gotta Have You	CDJ	U.S.	1991	$3.00
Motown	R10M-109	I Just Called to Say I Love You	CD3	Japan	1989	$12.00/$4.00
Motown	ZD-44014	Keep Our Love Alive	CD5	Germany	1990	$9.00
Motown	BVDM-4	Keep Our Love Alive	CD3	Japan	1990	$12.00/$4.00

Label	Catalog Number	Title	Type	Country	Year	Longbox Value / Value
Motown	ZD-44014	Keep Our Love Alive	CD5	U.K.	1990	$9.00
Motown	18241	Keep Our Love Alive	CDJ	U.S.	1990	$3.00
Motown	ZD-42260	My Eyes Don't Cry	CD5	Germany	1988	$9.00
Motown	R10M-101	My Eyes Don't Cry	CD3	Japan	1988	$12.00/$4.00
Motown	ZD-42260	My Eyes Don't Cry	CD5	U.K.	1988	$9.00
Motown	17658	My Eyes Don't Cry	CDJ	U.S.	1988	$3.00
Motown	R10M-110	Part Time Lovers	CD3	Japan	1989	$12.00/$4.00
Motown	R10M-108	Sir Duke	CD3	Japan	1989	$12.00/$4.00
Motown	PR211MD	Skeletons	DJ/CD3	U.S.	1987	$15.00
Motown	R10M-105	Superstition	CD3	Japan	1989	$12.00/$4.00
Motown	1007	These Three Words	CDJ	U.S.	1991	$3.00
		Tomorrow Robins Will Sing	CDJ	U.S.		$8.00
		Treat Myself	CDJ	U.S.		$3.00
Motown	ZD-41959	Uptown	CD3	U.K.	1989	$9.00
Motown	R10M-106	You Are the Sunshine of My Life	CD3	Japan	1989	$12.00/$4.00
Motown	R10M-107	You Haven't Done Nothing	CD3	Japan	1989	$12.00/$4.00
Motown	R10M-1	You Will Know	CD3	Japan	1988	$12.00/$4.00
Motown	ZD-41724	You Will Know	CD5	U.K.	1988	$8.00
Motown	PR222MD	You Will Know	DJ/CD3	U.S.	1987	$15.00

Wonderstuff

Label	Catalog Number	Title	Type	Country	Year	Longbox Value / Value
		Full Length				
Polygram	SACD 166	Deliverance Tour 1990, The	DJ/Smplr	U.S.	1990	$15.00
	With the Mission U.K..					
	IDIOT1	Idiot 1 Sampler	DJ/Smplr	U.K.	1995	$13.00
	IDIOT2	Idiot 2 Sampler	DJ/Smplr	U.K.	1995	$13.00
		Live In Manchester	LTD/LP	U.K.	1995	$24.00
	Special digipak version.					
Polydor	CDP 518	Never Loved Elvis/The Greatest Hits and More...	DJ/Smplr	Canada	1991	$60.00
	2 CD set.					
		Resurrection for the Modern Idiot	LTD/LP	U.S.	1994	$34.00
	2CD version					
		Singles				
Polydor	CDP 234	Cartoon Boyfriend	CDJ	U.S.	1990	$6.00
Far Out	GONCD-12	Caught in My Shadow	CD5	U.K.	1991	$10.00
Polydor	CDP 476	Caught in My Shadow	CD5	U.S.	1991	$4.00
Far Out	GONCD-10	Circlesquare	CD5	U.K.	1990	$10.00
Polydor	GONCD-7	Don't Let Me Down, Gently	CD5	U.K.	1989	$10.00
Polydor		Don't Let Me Down, Gently	CDJ	U.K.	1989	$10.00
Polydor	CDP 137	Don't Let Me Down, Gently	CDJ	U.S.	1989	$6.00
Polydor		Full of Life	CD5	U.K.	1990	$10.00
Polydor		Full of Life	CD5	U.K.	1990	$10.00
	Second version.					
Polydor	CDP 1081	Full of Life	CDJ	U.S.	1990	$6.00
Polydor	GONCD-3	Give, Give, Give Me More More More	CD5	U.K.	1988	$10.00
Far Out	GONCD-8	Golden Green	CD5	U.K.	1989	$10.00
Far Out	GONCD-5	It's Yer Money I'm After Baby	CD5	U.K.	1988	$10.00
Polydor	CDP 517	Mission Drive And Give	CDJ	U.S.	1991	$6.00
Polydor	CDP 1017	On the Ropes	CDJ	U.S.	1993	$6.00
Far Out	879769-2	Size of a Cow	CD5	Germany	1991	$10.00
Polydor	POCP-1104	Size of a Cow	CD5	Japan	1991	$15.00
Far Out	GONCD-11	Size of a Cow	CD5	U.K.	1991	$10.00
Polydor	CDP 562	Size of a Cow	CDJ	U.S.	1991	$6.00
Far Out	GONCD-13	Sleep Alone	CD5	U.K.	1991	$10.00
		Unbearable	CD5	U.K.	1994	$10.00
		Unbearable	CD5	U.K.	1994	$10.00
	Second version.					
Far Out	GONCD-14	Welcome to the Cheap Seats	CD5	U.K.	1992	$10.00
Polydor	CDP 631	Welcome to the Cheap Seats	CDJ	U.S.	1991	$6.00
Far Out	GONCD-6	Who Wants to Be Disco King	CD5	U.K.	1989	$10.00
Far Out	GONCD-4	Wish Away	CD5	U.K.	1988	$10.00

Wood, Brenton

Label	Catalog Number	Title	Type	Country	Year	Longbox Value / Value
		Singles				
Beckwood	51492	That's the Deal	CDJ	U.S.	1992	$2.00

Wood, D.D.

Label	Catalog Number	Title	Type	Country	Year	Longbox Value / Value
		Singles				
Hollywood		Louie Cooper	CDJ	U.S.	1991	$3.00
Hollywood	PRCD 10274-2	Louie Cooper	CDJ	U.S.	1993	$2.00

Wood, Lauren

Label	Catalog Number	Title	Type	Country	Year	Longbox Value / Value
		Singles				
EMI	DPRO-04587	Fallen	CDJ	U.S.	1990	$2.00

Wood, Ronnie (& Hothouse Flowers)

Label	Catalog Number	Title	Type	Country	Year	Longbox Value / Value
		Full Length				
		Live At Electric Ladyland	RS	U.S.	1992	$80.00
	Airdate: 11/2/92.					
Continuum		Slide On "Live"	DJ/LP	U.S.	1993	$15.00
		Singles				
Continuum		Always Wanted More	CDJ	U.S.	1992	$6.00
Continuum		Josephine	CDJ	U.S.	1992	$6.00
Continuum	12211-2	Like It	CDJ	U.S.	1992	$6.00
Continuum	12211-2	Like it	CDJ	U.S.	1994	$8.00
		Show Me	CD5	Australia	1992	$12.00
Continuum	12210-2	Show Me	CD5	U.S.	1992	$6.00
Continuum	12210-2	Show Me	CDJ	U.S.	1992	$80.00
	CD in custom digipak with lithograph #1. Limited to 600 copies.					
Continuum	12210-2	Show Me	CDJ	U.S.	1992	$80.00
	CD in custom digipak with lithograph #2. Limited to 600 copies.					
Continuum	12210-2	Show Me	CDJ	U.S.	1992	$80.00
	CD in custom digipak with lithograph #3. Limited to 600 copies.					
Continuum	12210-2	Show Me	CDJ	U.S.	1992	$80.00
	CD in custom digipak with lithograph #4. Limited to 600 copies.					
		Somebody Else Might	CD5	Australia	1993	$12.00
Continuum		Somebody Else Might	CD5	U.K.	1993	$10.00
Continuum	12309-2	Stay With Me	CDJ	U.S.	1993	$7.00

Woods, Phil

Label	Catalog Number	Title	Type	Country	Year	Longbox Value / Value
		Full Length				
Image	ID7276VW	In Concert With Joe Sudler's Swing Machine	LD	U.S.		$25.00

Woods, Phil & Chris Swansen

Label	Catalog Number	Title	Type	Country	Year	Longbox Value / Value
		Full Length				
Rykodisc	RCD-1007	Piper at the Gates of Dawn	LP/LB	U.S.†	1985	$14.00/$8.00

Wooten Brothers

Label	Catalog Number	Title	Type	Country	Year	Longbox Value / Value
		Singles				
		Friendz	CDJ	U.S.		$2.00
	Second version.					
A&M	75021 7421 2	Friendz	CDJ	U.S.	1990	$2.00
A&M	31458 8148	Happy	CDJ	U.S.	1993	$2.00

Wop Bop Torledo

Label	Catalog Number	Title	Type	Country	Year	Longbox Value / Value
		Singles				
BMG	162566	Beat Bomb	CD3	Germany	1989	$8.00
BMG	662566	Beat Bomb	CD5	Germany	1989	$8.00
Virgin	TENCX-276	Beat Bomb	CD5	U.K.	1990	$8.00
		Beat Bomb	CDJ	U.S.	1989	$2.00
BMG	662762	Jungle Fever	CD5	Germany	1990	$8.00
Virgin	TENCD-293	Jungle Fever	CD3	U.K.	1990	$8.00
Charisma	PRCD 010	Jungle Fever	CDJ	U.S.	1990	$2.00
Virgin	TENCD-363	Kissaway	CD5	U.K.	1991	$8.00
Virgin	TENCD-313	Take Me With You	CD5	U.K.	1990	$8.00

Wopat, Tom

Label	Catalog Number	Title	Type	Country	Year	Longbox Value / Value
		Full Length				
		Country Star Tracks	RS	U.S.	1991	$15.00
	Airdate: 9/7/91.					

Worl-A-Girl

Label	Catalog Number	Title	Type	Country	Year	Longbox Value / Value
		Singles				
CBS	77412	No Gunshot	CD5	U.S.	1994	$5.00
Chaos	ESK 77413	No Gunshot	CDJ	U.S.	1994	$2.00

World Class Wreckin' Cru

Label	Catalog Number	Title	Type	Country	Year	Longbox Value / Value
		Singles				
World Class	1710	Lights Are Out, The	CD5	U.S.	1990	$4.00

World Party – Goodbye Jumbo (Chrysalis CD25CR13)

World Party

Label	Catalog Number	Title	Type	Country	Year	Longbox Value / Value
		Full Length				
Chrysalis		Bang!	DJ/Smplr	U.K.	1993	$10.00
	CD sampler in pres kit with photos.					
Chrysalis	CD25CR13	Goodbye Jumbo	LTD/LP	U.K.	1994	$25.00/$15.00
	25th Anniversary edition in 6"x11" longbox.					
Chrysalis	DPRO-21654	Goodbye Jumbo	DJ/LP	U.S.	1990	$14.00
Chrysalis	DPRO-04716	History of the World	DJ/Smplr	U.S.	1993	$20.00
		Singles				
		Give It All Away	CD5	U.K.		$10.00
		Give It All Away	CD5	U.K.		$10.00
	Second version.					
Chrysalis	DPRO-04526	Give It All Away	CDJ	U.S.	1993	$2.00
Chrysalis	DPRO-04575	Hollywood	CDJ	U.S.	1993	$2.00
		Is It Like Today?	CD5	U.K.		$10.00
		Is It Like Today?	CD5	U.K.		$10.00
	Second version.					
BMG	663069	Message in the Box	CD5	Germany	1990	$10.00
Ensign	ENYCD-631	Message in the Box	CD5	U.K.	1990	$10.00
Chrysalis	DPRO-23507	Message in the Box	CDJ	U.S.	1990	$2.00
Aris	880482	Ship of Fools	CD5	Germany	1987	$10.00
Ensign	SCD-1	Ship of Fools	CD5	U.K.	1987	$10.00
Ensign	EYNCD-643	Thank You World	CD5	U.K.	1991	$10.00
Mercury	MERCD-341	Two For Joy	CD5	U.K.	1991	$10.00
EMI	323582-2	Way Down Now	CD5	Germany	1990	$10.00
EMI	253582-2	Way Down Now	CD5	Germany	1990	$10.00
Ensign	ENYCD-634	Way Down Now	CD5	U.K.	1990	$10.00
Chrysalis	23522	Way Down Now	CDJ	U.S.	1990	$2.00

World Saxophone Quartet

Label	Catalog Number	Title	Type	Country	Year	Longbox Value / Value
		Full Length				
Black Saint	BSR-0056CD PSI	Revue	LP/LB	U.S.†	1985	$14.00/$8.00

Worrell, Bernie

Label	Catalog Number	Title	Type	Country	Year	Longbox Value / Value
		Singles				
Gramavision	R2 74450	BW Jam	CD5	U.S.	1991	$4.00

Wrathchild America

Label	Catalog Number	Title	Type	Country	Year	Longbox Value / Value
		Singles				
Atlantic	PRCD 3737-2	3-D	CDJ	U.S.	1991	$2.00

Wreckx-N-Effect

Label	Catalog Number	Title	Type	Country	Year	Longbox Value / Value
		Singles				
MCA	2541	Knock n Boots	CD5	U.S.	1993	$2.00
MCA	C2 54583	Knock n Boots	CD5	U.S.	1993	$4.00
MCA	54662	My Cutie	CD5	U.S.	1993	$5.00
MCA	MCA5P-2680	My Cutie	CDJ	U.S.	1993	$2.00
MCA	MCA5P-2735	My Cutie	CDJ	U.S.	1993	$2.00
MCA	MCSTD-1725	Rump Shaker	CD5	U.K.	1992	$10.00
MCA	2990	Rump Shaker	CDJ	U.S.	1994	$2.00
MCA	54532	Wreckx Shop	CD5	U.S.	1994	$5.00
MCA	2454	Wreckx Shop	CDJ	U.S.	1994	$2.00

Wrens

Label	Catalog Number	Title	Type	Country	Year	Longbox Value / Value
		Singles				
		Rest Your Head	CDJ	U.S.		$2.00

Wright, Gary

Label	Catalog Number	Title	Type	Country	Year	Longbox Value / Value
		Full Length				
Album Network		In the Studio (Dream Weaver)	RS	U.S.	1989	$25.00
	Airdate: 5/8/89.					

Label	Catalog Number	Title	Type	Country	Year	Longbox Value / Value
Album Network		In the Studio (Dream Weaver)	RS	U.S.	1992	$20.00
Airdate: 7/20/92.						
Cypress	YL0111	Who I Am	DJ/Intvw	U.S.	1988	$8.00
A&M	YD-17585	Who I Am	DJ/Smplr	U.S.	1988	$20.00
		Singles				
Warner Brothers	W-0118CD	Dream Weaver	CD5	U.K.	1992	$10.00
Reprise	PRO-CD-5305	Dream Weaver	CDJ	U.S.	1991	$3.00
Cypress	YD 17617	It Ain't Right	CDJ	U.S.	1988	$3.00
Cypress	YD 17584	Who I Am	CDJ	U.S.	1988	$3.00

Wright, Michelle

Singles

Label	Catalog Number	Title	Type	Country	Year	Longbox Value / Value
Arista	ASCD-2208	All You Really Wanna Do	CDJ	U.S.	1991	$2.00
		New Kind of Love	CDJ	U.S.		$2.00
Arista	ASCD-2444	One Time Around	CDJ	U.S.	1992	$2.00
Arista	ASCD-2406	Take It Like a Man	CDJ	U.S.	1992	$2.00
		Woman's Intuition	CDJ	U.S.		$2.00

Wright, Steven

Full Length

Label	Catalog Number	Title	Type	Country	Year	Longbox Value / Value
Vestron	3146	Steven Wright	LD	U.S.	1987	$35.00

Wu-Tang Clan

Singles

Label	Catalog Number	Title	Type	Country	Year	Longbox Value / Value
Loud	62766	C.R.E.A.M.	CDJ	U.S.	1994	$2.00
RCA	62890-2	Can It Be So	CD5	U.S.	1994	$5.00
RCA	62648	Method Man	CDJ	U.S.	1993	$2.00
RCA	62747	Method Man	CDJ	U.S.	1993	$2.00
RCA	62530	Protect Ya Neck	CDJ	U.S.	1993	$2.00

WWF Superstars

Singles

Label	Catalog Number	Title	Type	Country	Year	Longbox Value / Value
Arista	74321 12488-2	Slam Jam	CD5	U.K.	1992	$9.00

Wyatt, Robert

Singles

Label	Catalog Number	Title	Type	Country	Year	Longbox Value / Value
Voiceprint	VP108CD	A Short Break	CD5	U.K.	1992	$8.00

Wyman, Bill

Full Length

Label	Catalog Number	Title	Type	Country	Year	Longbox Value / Value
Polystar	HI-5176	Let's Get Stoned With the Silent Stone	LTD/LP	Japan		$150.00
Passport	PBCD-6047	Willie and the Poorboys	LP/BP	U.S.		$16.00/$14.00
		Singles				
Victor	VIDP-46	Stuff	CD3	Japan	1992	$12.00/$4.00

Wynette, Tammy

Full Length

Label	Catalog Number	Title	Type	Country	Year	Longbox Value / Value
Epic		Selected Album Thangs	DJ/Smplr	U.S.		$8.00
Vestron Video	M1061	Tammy Wynette	LD	U.S.	1986	$30.00
		Singles				
Epic	ESK 73579	I'm Turning You Loose	CDJ	U.S.	1990	$2.00

Wynn, Steve

Singles

Label	Catalog Number	Title	Type	Country	Year	Longbox Value / Value
Rhino	PRO2 90042	Carolyn	CDJ	U.S.	1990	$2.00
RNA	74427	Kerosene Man	CDJ	U.S.	1991	$2.00
Rhino	PRO2 90125	Tuesday	CDJ	U.S.	1992	$2.00

X

Full Length

Label	Catalog Number	Title	Type	Country	Year	Longbox Value / Value
Westwood One		In Concert-Nu Rock	RS	U.S.	1994	$60.00
Airdate: 1/31/94.						
CBS/Fox	6200-80	The Unheard Music	LD	U.S.	1989	$25.00
		Singles				
Big Life	861 821	Country at War	CD5	U.S.	1993	$4.00
		New Life	CDJ	U.S.		$7.00
		Wild Thing	CDJ	U.S.		$3.00

X-Clan

Full Length

Label	Catalog Number	Title	Type	Country	Year	Longbox Value / Value
Polygram	CDP 2099	Limited Edition Sampler	DJ/Smplr	U.S.		$7.00
		Singles				
Polydor	CDP 582	Fire & Ice	CDJ	U.S.	1991	$2.00
		Funkin' Lesson	CDJ	U.S.		$2.00
Polydor	CDP 689	Xodus	CDJ	U.S.	1992	$2.00

X-Statik

Singles

Label	Catalog Number	Title	Type	Country	Year	Longbox Value / Value
Instinct	4104	Rapture	CD5	U.S.	1993	$4.00

Xavier

Singles

Label	Catalog Number	Title	Type	Country	Year	Longbox Value / Value
		Saturday Song	CDJ	U.S.		$2.00
Atlantic	98107	Saturday Song	CD5	U.S.	1995	$5.00

XC-NN

Singles

Label	Catalog Number	Title	Type	Country	Year	Longbox Value / Value
		Lifted	CDJ	U.S.		$2.00

Xotique

Singles

Label	Catalog Number	Title	Type	Country	Year	Longbox Value / Value
		First Time, The	CDJ	U.S.		$2.00

Xscape

Singles

Label	Catalog Number	Title	Type	Country	Year	Longbox Value / Value
Columbia	CSK 7858	Can't Hang	CDJ	U.S.		$2.00
Columbia	CSK 7314	Do You Wan't To	CDJ	U.S.		$2.00
Columbia	77920	Feels Do Good	CD5	U.S.	1995	$6.00
Columbia		Feels So Good	CDJ	U.S.		$2.00
Columbia	CSK 77119	Just Kickin'	CDJ	U.S.		$2.00
Columbia	CSK 77438	Love on My Mind	CDJ	U.S.		$2.00
Columbia	CSK 5569	Tonight	CDJ	U.S.		$2.00
Columbia	CSK 5667	Understanding	CDJ	U.S.		$2.00
Columbia	CSK 577335	Understanding	CDJ	U.S.		$2.00
Columbia	CSK 7367	Who Can I Run To	CDJ	U.S.		$2.00
Columbia	78056	Who Can I Run To	CD5	U.S.	1995	$5.00

XTC

Full Length

Label	Catalog Number	Title	Type	Country	Year	Longbox Value / Value
		Fossil Fuel 1977-1992	LTD/LP	U.S.		$33.00
2 CD set.						
		Gribouilage	DJ/Smplr	France	1993	$50.00
Geffen	PRO-CD-4398	NAC Sampler	DJ/Smplr	U.S.	1992	$5.00
Virgin		Oranges & Lemons	LTD/LP	U.K.	1989	$20.00
3 CD3s in box.						
Geffen	PRO-CD-4897	Radios in Motion…A History of XTC	DJ/Smplr	U.S.	1992	$10.00
Geffen	GEFD24417DJ	Rag & Bone Buffet	DJ/LP	U.S.	1990	$14.00
Geffen	PRO-CD-4396	This Is Not the New Album	DJ/Smplr	U.S.	1992	$5.00
		Singles				
Geffen	21813	Ballad of Peter Pan	CD5	U.S.	1994	$5.00
Virgin	VJCP-14044	Ballad of Peter Pumpkinhead	CD5	Japan	1992	$15.00
Virgin	VSCDT 1415	Ballad of Peter Pumpkinhead	CD5	U.K.	1992	$10.00
Geffen	9 21813-2	Ballad of Peter Pumpkinhead	CD5	U.S.	1992	$5.00
Geffen	PRO-CD-4394	Ballad of Peter Pumpkinhead	CDJ	U.S.	1992	$3.00
Geffen	PRO-CD-4407	Ballad of Peter Pumpkinhead	CDJ	U.S.	1992	$3.00
Virgin	CDEP-3	Dear God	CD5	U.K.	1988	$10.00
Geffen	PRO-CD-4447	Dear Madam Barnum	CDJ	U.S.	1992	$2.00
Virgin	VJDP-10187	Disappointed	CD3	Japan	1992	$12.00/$4.00
Virgin	VSCDG-1404	Disappointed	CD5	U.K.	1992	$10.00
Geffen	PRO-CD-4447	Dream Madman Barnum	CDJ	U.S.	1992	$3.00
Geffen	PRO-CD-4251	Extrovert	CDJ	U.S.	1990	$6.00
Virgin	VJD-15552	King for the Day	CD5	Japan	1989	$15.00
Virgin	VSCD-1177	King for the Day	CD3	U.K.	1989	$10.00
Geffen	21236	King for the Day	CD5	U.S.	1989	$5.00
Geffen	PRO-CD-3522	King for the Day	CDJ	U.S.	1989	$3.00
Virgin	VSCD-1201	Loving	CD3	U.K.	1989	$10.00
Virgin	662021	Mayor of Simpleton	CD5	Germany	1989	$10.00
Virgin	VJD-12034	Mayor of Simpleton	CD3	Japan	1989	$12.00/$4.00
Virgin	VSCD-1158	Mayor of Simpleton	CD3	U.K.	1989	$10.00
Geffen	9 27552-2	Mayor of Simpleton	CD3	U.S.	1988	$6.00/$4.00
Virgin	PRCD 3408	Mayor of Simpleton	CDJ	U.S.	1989	$3.00
Geffen	PRO-CD-4398	My Bird Performs	CDJ	U.S.	1992	$3.00
Virgin	885271	Oranges and Lemons	CD3	Germany	1989	$10.00
Virgin	CDVT 2581	Oranges and Lemons	CD3	U.K.	1989	$10.00
Geffen	PRO-CD-4251	Rag & Bone Buffet	CDJ	U.S.	1990	$3.00
Virgin	CDT-9	Senses Working Overtime	CD3	U.K.	1988	$10.00

Xtra Large

Singles

Label	Catalog Number	Title	Type	Country	Year	Longbox Value / Value
Giant	PRO-CD-5681	Hooker	CDJ	U.S.	1992	$2.00

Xtra Watt

Singles

Label	Catalog Number	Title	Type	Country	Year	Longbox Value / Value
		I Love Christmas	CDJ	U.S.		$2.00

Xymox

Singles

Label	Catalog Number	Title	Type	Country	Year	Longbox Value / Value
Wing	867 321-2	At the End of the Day	CDJ	U.S.	1991	$2.00
Polygram	CDP 123	Imagination	CDJ	U.S.	1989	$2.00
Wing	WINCD-5	Obsesion	CD5	U.K.	1989	$10.00
Polydor	PZCD-146	Phoenix of My Heart	CD5	U.K.	1991	$10.00
Wing	CDP 868	Phoenix of My Heart	CDJ	U.S.	1991	$2.00
		Reaching Out	CD5	U.K.	1993	$2.00
Mercury	CDP 520	Wonderland	CDJ	U.S.	1991	$2.00

XYZ

Singles

Label	Catalog Number	Title	Type	Country	Year	Longbox Value / Value
Enigma	EPRO 238	Inside Out	CDJ	U.S.	1989	$2.00
Enigma	EPRO 263	What Keeps Me Loving You	CDJ	U.S.	1990	$2.00

Y.T. Style

Singles

Label	Catalog Number	Title	Type	Country	Year	Longbox Value / Value
Third Stone	5288	You'll Never Find Another	CDJ	U.S.		$8.00

Y&T

Full Length

Label	Catalog Number	Title	Type	Country	Year	Longbox Value / Value
		Contagious	LP	U.S.		$10.00
A&M	CD-5007	In Rock We Trust	LP/LB	U.S.†	1985	$14.00/$8.00
A&M	395076-2	Open Fire	LP	Germany		$15.00
Geffen	9 2-24283-Dj	Ten	DJ/LP	U.S.	1990	$10.00
Geffen	9 2-24283-2	Ten	LP/LB	U.S.	1990	$12.00/$7.00
Metal Blade	26572	Yesterday & Today Live	LP/LB	U.S.		$14.00/$8.00
		Singles				
Geffen	PRO-CD-4134	Don't Be Afraid of the Dark	CDJ	U.S.	1990	$3.00
Geffen	PRO-CD-4106	Don't Be Afraid of the Dark	CDJ	U.S.	1990	$3.00

Ya Kid K

Singles

Label	Catalog Number	Title	Type	Country	Year	Longbox Value / Value
EMI	204375-2	Awsome	CD5	Germany	1991	$8.00
EMI	204376-2	Awsome	CD5	Germany	1991	$8.00
EMI	TODP-2282	Awsome	CD3	Japan	1991	$12.00/$3.00
SBK	CDSBK-26	Awsome	CD5	U.K.	1991	$8.00
SBK	DPRO-05384	Awsome	CDJ	U.S.	1991	$2.00

Ya'll So Stupid

Singles

Label	Catalog Number	Title	Type	Country	Year	Longbox Value / Value
Rowdy	5000	85 South	CDJ	U.S.	1992	$2.00

Yaggfu Front

Singles

Label	Catalog Number	Title	Type	Country	Year	Longbox Value / Value
Mercury	CDP 1018	Busted Loop	CDJ	U.S.	1993	$2.00

Yaki-Da

Singles

Label	Catalog Number	Title	Type	Country	Year	Longbox Value / Value
	PRCD-6954-2	I Saw You Dancing	CDJ	U.S.	1995	$2.00

Yamashita, Stomu

Full Length

Label	Catalog Number	Title	Type	Country	Year	Longbox Value / Value
Kuckuck	CD-072	Sea and Sky	LP/LB	U.S.†	1985	$14.00/$8.00

Yamashita, Yosuke

Full Length

Label	Catalog Number	Title	Type	Country	Year	Longbox Value / Value
Enja	311228	Banslikana	LP/LB	U.S.†	1985	$14.00/$8.00

Yanai, Kate

Singles

Label	Catalog Number	Title	Type	Country	Year	Longbox Value / Value
WEA	9031-75190	Bacardi Feeling	CD5	Germany	1991	$8.00

Yankovic, Weird Al

Singles

Label	Catalog Number	Title	Type	Country	Year	Longbox Value / Value
Scotti Brothers	SBDJ 75378-2	Bedrock Anthem	CDJ	U.S.	1993	$6.00
Canyon	S10Y-1008	Fat	CD3	Japan	1988	$12.00/$4.00
Attic	CD446	Headline News	CD5	Canada	1994	$9.00
Scotti Brothers	78011	Headline News	CD5	U.S.	1994	$5.00
Scotti Brothers	78011	Headline News	CD5	U.S.	1994	$6.00
Rock 'n' Roll	1776	Isle Thing	CDJ	U.S.	1989	$2.00
Scotti Brothers	SBDJ 75378-2	Jurassic Park	CDJ	U.S.	1993	$6.00
Canyon	S10Y-1017	Lasagna	CD3	Japan	1988	$12.00/$4.00
Scotti Brothers	ZSK 1723	Money for Nothing	CDJ	U.S.	1989	$2.00
Scotti Brothers	75314	Smells Like Nirvana	CDJ	U.S.	1992	$6.00
Canyon	PCDY-00009	UHF	CD3	Japan	1989	$12.00/$4.00
Scotti Brothers	ZSK 1706	UHF	CDJ	U.S.	1989	$2.00
Scotti Brothers	75346	White Stuff, The	CDJ	U.S.	1992	$2.00

Label	Catalog Number	Title	Type	Country	Year	Longbox Value / Value
Yanni						
		Full Length				
Private Music	PDJ-81017-2	Special Radio Edits	DJ/Smplr	U.S.	1994	$15.00
		Singles				
Private	01005810192	Aria	CD5	Canada	1994	$8.00
Private Music		Aria	CDJ	U.S.		$2.00
Private Music	81019	Aria	CD5	U.S.	1994	$5.00
Private Music	81002	Nice to Meet You	CDJ	U.S.	1992	$2.00
Private Music		Paths on the Water	CDJ	U.S.		$2.00
Private Music	2084	Swept Away	CDJ	U.S.	1990	$2.00
Yarbrough, Glen						
		Singles				
Laserlight	12429	I Think of You	CD5	U.S.	1994	$5.00
Yarbrough & Peoples						
		Singles				
Uni	1578	You Dropped a Bomb on Me	CD5	Canada	1992	$6.00
Yardbirds						
		Full Length				
BBC Radio		BBC Classic Tracks	RS	U.S.	1991	$30.00
	Airdate: 9/23/91.					
BBC Radio		BBC Classic Tracks	RS	U.S.	1992	$30.00
	Airdate: 9/21/92.					
Westwood One		BBC Classic Tracks	RS	U.S.	1993	$30.00
	Airdate: 9/13/93.					
Westwood One		BBC Classic Tracks	RS	U.S.	1994	$30.00
	Airdate: 12/12/94.					
	Y12-53	Special Digest	DJ/Smplr	Japan		N/A
		Singles				
Old Gold	OG-6118	For Your Love	CD3	U.K.	1989	$10.00
Charly	CDS-4	For Your Love	CD5	U.K.	1989	$10.00
		Happenings Ten Years Time Ago	CD5	U.K.		$8.00
Yasmin						
		Singles				
Geffen	GFSTD-14	Sacrifice	CD5	U.K.	1991	$8.00
Geffen	PRO-CD-4231	Stop That Scene	CDJ	U.S.	1991	$2.00
Geffen	PRO-CD-4245	Wanna Dance	CDJ	U.S.	1991	$2.00
Yates, Lori						
		Singles				
CBS	CSK 1583	Promises, Promises	CDJ	U.S.	1989	$2.00
Yaz						
		Singles				
Intercord	825 757	Fine Time	CD5	Germany	1989	$8.00
Intercord	825 579	Fine Time	CD5	Germany	1989	$8.00
Big Life	BLR-6CD	Fine Time	CD5	U.K.	1989	$8.00
		Have Mercy	CD5	U.K.		$10.00
		Have Mercy	CD5	U.K.		$10.00
	Second version.					
Polydor	PZCD-198	One True Woman	CD5	U.K.	1992	$8.00
Intercord	810 744	Only Way Is Up, The	CD5	Germany	1988	$8.00
Intercord	810 749	Only Way Is Up, The	CD5	Germany	1989	$8.00
Intercord	810 773	Only Way Is Up, The	CD5	Germany	1989	$8.00
Toshiba	XP10-2042	Only Way Is Up, The	CD3	Japan	1988	$12.00/$4.00
Big Life	BLR-4CD	Only Way Is Up, The	CD5	U.K.	1988	$8.00
Intercord	825 751	Stand Up for Your Rights	CD5	Germany	1988	$8.00
Toshiba	XP10-2075	Stand Up for Your Rights	CD3	Japan	1989	$12.00/$4.00
Big Life	BLR 5MCD	Stand Up for Your Rights	CD3	U.K.	1988	$8.00
Big Life	BLR-5CD	Stand Up for Your Rights	CD5	U.K.	1988	$8.00
Elektra	PR 8063-2	Stand Up for Your Rights	CDJ	U.S.	1988	$2.00
Intercord	877 265	Treat Me Good	CD5	Germany	1990	$8.00
Toshiba	TODP-2208	Treat Me Good	CD3	Japan	1990	$12.00/$4.00
Big Life	BLR-24CD	Treat Me Good	CD5	U.K.	1990	$8.00
Big Life	CDP 293	Treat Me Good	CDJ	U.S.	1990	$2.00
Big Life	825 762	Where Has All the Love Gone	CD5	Germany	1989	$8.00
Big Life	BLR-8CD	Where Has All the Love Gone	CD5	U.K.	1989	$8.00
Yearwood, Trisha						
		Full Length				
		'90s Country	RS	U.S.	1995	$40.00
	Airdate: 12/21/95.					
		'90s Country	RS	U.S.	1995	$40.00
	Airdate: 4/15/95.					
		Country Concert	RS	U.S.	1993	$55.00
	Airdate: 6/14/93.					
		Everybody Knows	LTD/LP	U.S.	1996	$20.00
	CD and bonus cassette interview. Sold exclusively at Blockbuster Music stores.					
	1CD-64	In-Store Promotion Sampler	DJ/Smplr	Japan		$45.00
		Sweetest Gift	RS	U.S.	1994	$40.00
	3 CD set. Airdate: 12/12/94.					
		Singles				
MCA	54172	Like We Never Had a Broken Heart	CDJ	U.S.	1991	$2.00
MCA	MCSTD-1576	She's In Love With the Boy	CD5	U.K.	1991	$8.00
MCA	54734	Song Remembers When, The	CDJ	U.S.	1993	$2.00
MCA	54270	That's What I Like About You	CDJ	U.S.	1991	$2.00
		Walkaway Joe	CD5	U.K.		$10.00
		Walkaway Joe	CD5	U.K.		$10.00
	Second version.					
MCA	54362	Woman Before Me, The	CDJ	U.S.	1991	$2.00
MCA	54414	Wrong Side of Memphis	CDJ	U.S.	1992	$2.00
MCA	54600	You Say You Will	CDJ	U.S.	1992	$2.00
Yello						
		Full Length				
Polygram		Do It	LTD/CD5	U.K.	1994	$15.00
		Singles				
Polygram	874928-3	Blazing Saddles	CD3	Germany	1989	$10.00
Polygram	874929-2	Blazing Saddles	CD5	Germany	1989	$10.00
Polygram	YUELCD-4	Blazing Saddles	CD5	U.K.	1989	$10.00
Polygram	888311-2	Call It Love	CD5	Germany	1988	$10.00
Vertigo	888 311-2	Call It Love	CD5	U.K.	1988	$10.00
		CD Singles Collection, The	CD5	U.K.		$45.00
Smash	010	Drive Driven	CDJ	U.S.	1993	$3.00
Polygram	884877-2	Goldrush	CD5	Germany	1988	$10.00
4th & Broadway	440604	How How	CD5	U.S.	1994	$5.00
Mercury	MERCD-376	Jungle Bill	CD5	U.K.	1992	$10.00
Smash	003	Jungle Bill	CDJ	U.S.	1993	$3.00
Polygram	822262-2	Live At the Roxy '83	CD5	Germany	1989	$10.00
Polygram	822262-2	Live At the Roxy '83	CD5	U.K.	1989	$10.00
Polygram	872748-3	Of Course I'm Leaving	CD3	Germany	1989	$10.00
Polygram	872745-2	Of Course I'm Leaving	CD5	Germany	1989	$10.00
Polygram	872947-2	Of Course I'm Leaving	CD5	Germany	1989	$10.00
Polygram	YELCD-3	Of Course I'm Leaving	CD5	U.K.	1989	$10.00
Polygram	YELCD-3B	Of Course I'm Leaving	CD5	U.K.	1989	$10.00
Polygram	YELCD-32	Of Course I'm Leaving	CD5	U.K.	1989	$10.00
Mercury	888 908-2	Oh Yeah!	CD5	Germany	1987	$10.00
Mercury	888 908-2	Oh Yeah!	CD5	U.K.	1987	$10.00
Mercury	870615-2	Race, The	CD5	Canada	1988	$10.00
Polygram	870330-2	Race, The	CD5	Germany	1988	$10.00
Mercury	YELCD 1	Race, The	CD5	U.K.	1988	$10.00
Mercury	MERCD-382	Race, The	CD5	U.K.	1992	$10.00
Mercury	CDP 113	Race, The	CDJ	U.S.	1989	$7.00
Polygram	888746-2	Rhythm Divine	CD5	Germany	1988	$10.00
Polygram	868341-2	Rubberband Man	CD5	Germany	1991	$10.00
Polygram	872367-2	Tied Up	CD5	Germany	1988	$10.00
Mercury	YELCD-2	Tied Up	CD5	U.K.	1988	$10.00
Yellow Jackets						
		Full Length				
MCA	CD33-17344	Discovery and Four Corners Sampler	DJ/Smplr	U.S.	1987	$20.00
	Also with 4 tracks by Larry Carlton.					
		Singles				
		Geraldine	CDJ	U.S.	1989	$2.00
		Local Heroes	CDJ	U.S.		$2.00
Yen						
		Singles				
IRS	EIRSCD-136	Talk to Me	CD5	U.K.	1990	$8.00
IRS	027	Talk to Me	CDJ	U.S.	1990	$2.00

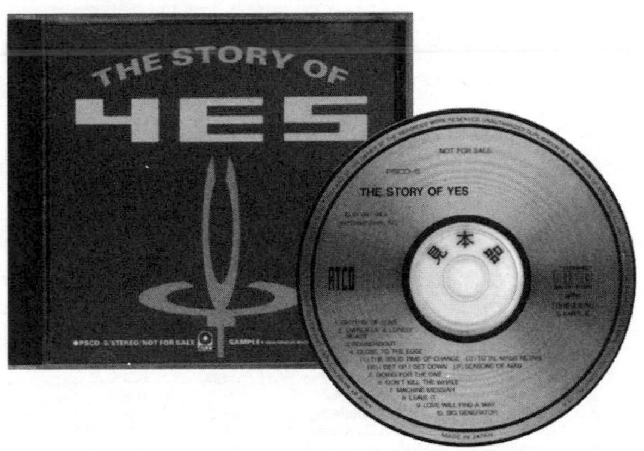

Yes – Story Of Yes (Warner/Pioneer PSCD-5)

Label	Catalog Number	Title	Type	Country	Year	Longbox Value / Value
Yes						
		Full Length				
Atco	90125-2	90125-2	LP/LB	U.S.†	1983	$14.00/$8.00
Herald	HER PRO 1	An Evening of Yes Music Plus	DJ/Smplr	U.S.	1994	$35.00
	Sampler in cardboard sleeve with large color press kit.					
Herald	HER PRO 1	An Evening of Yes Music Plus	DJ/Smplr	U.S.	1994	$20.00
Atlantic	19320-2	Classic Yes	LP/LB	U.S.		$14.00/$8.00
	Nonremastered version.					
Atlantic	19133-2	Closer to the Edge	LP/LB	U.S.		$14.00/$8.00
	Nonremastered version.					
Global Satellite Network		Closer to the Edge	RS	U.S.	1991	$100.00
	3 CD set. Airdate: 5/31/91.					
Atlantic	16019-2	Drama	LP/LB	U.S.		$14.00/$8.00
	Nonremastered version.					
Atlantic	19132-2	Fragile	LP/LB	U.S.		$14.00/$8.00
	Nonremastered version.					
Atlantic		Fragile	LTD/LP	U.S.	1994	$30.00
	First Issue missing reprise in "We have Heaven."					
Atlantic	19106-2	Going for the One	LP/LB	U.S.		$14.00/$8.00
	Nonremastered version.					
Album Network		In the Studio (90125)	RS	U.S.	1989	$30.00
	Airdate: 9/18/89.					
Album Network		In the Studio (Close To the Edge)	RS	U.S.	1991	$30.00
	Airdate: 8/26/91.					
Album Network		In the Studio (Fragile)	RS	U.S.	1989	$30.00
	Airdate: 4/17/89.					
Album Network		In the Studio (Fragile)	RS	U.S.	1992	$30.00
	Airdate: 1/13/92.					
Album Network		In the Studio (Yes Album)	RS	U.S.	1988	$30.00
	Airdate: 7/18/88					
DIR		King Biscuit Flour Hour	RS	U.S.	1988	$40.00
	Airdate: 3/6/88.					
DIR		King Biscuit Flour Hour	RS	U.S.	1989	$80.00
	Airdate: 6/18 - 6/25/89.					
DIR		King Biscuit Flour Hour	RS	U.S.	1991	$40.00
	Airdate: 8/18/91.					
DIR		King Biscuit Flour Hour	RS	U.S.	1993	$100.00
	2 CD set. Airdate: 3/28/93					
Atlantic	19135-2	Relayer	LP/LB	U.S.		$14.00/$8.00
	Nonremastered version.					
Warner	ASCD-26	Special Digest	DJ/Smplr	Japan	1991	$200.00
Warner	PSCD-5	Story of Yes, The	DJ/Smplr	Japan	1987	$250.00
Westwood One		Superstar Concert	RS	U.S.	1993	$70.00
	2 CD set. Airdate: 7/19/92					
RCA Victor	09026-61971-2	Symphonic Music Of Yes	DJ/Smplr	U.S.	1993	$45.00
	CD with deleted "Yes" logo. Replaced with plain "yes" titles-work.					
Atlantic	908-2	Tales From Topographic Oceans	LP/LB	U.S.		$14.00/$8.00
	Nonremastered version.					
Atlantic	8273-2	Time and a Word	LP/LB	U.S.		$14.00/$8.00
	Nonremastered version.					
Herald	PRO 2	Time and a Word	DJ/Smplr	U.S.	1994	$15.00
Media America		Up Close	RS	U.S.	1991	$110.00
	4 CD set.					
Media America		Up Close	RS	U.S.	1992	$80.00
Media America		Up Close	RS	U.S.	1994	$80.00
	3 CD set.					
Atlantic	8243-2	Yes	LP/LB	U.S.		$14.00/$8.00
	Nonremastered version.					

Label	Catalog Number	Title	Type	Country	Year	Longbox Value / Value
Atlantic	19131-2	Yes Album	LP/LB	U.S.		$14.00/$8.00
	Nonremastered version.					
WEA	50181-6	Yes: Greatest Video Hits	LD	U.S.	1992	$30.00
Atlantic	100-2	Yes Songs	LP/LB	U.S.		$14.00/$8.00
	Nonremastered version.					
Vid-America	7033	Yes Songs	LD	U.S.	1985	$30.00
Westwood One		Yes Story Special, The	RS	U.S.	1994	$80.00
	3 CD set. Airdate: 5/30/94.					
Atco		Yes Years	DJ/LP	U.S.	1991	$45.00
	4 CD set in double jewel case package.					
WEA	50250	Yes Years	LD	U.S.	1992	$35.00
Atco	PRCD 4009-2	Yes Years Sampler	DJ/Smplr	U.S.	1991	$15.00
Atco	PRCD 4009-2	Yes Years Sampler	DJ/Smplr	U.S.	1991	$30.00
	6"x6" simulated "boxed set" box.					
Atlantic	19134-2	Yesterdays	LP/LB	U.S.		$14.00/$8.00
	Nonremastered version.					

Singles

Label	Catalog Number	Title	Type	Country	Year	Longbox Value / Value
Victory	CDP 1178	Calling, The	CDJ	U.S.	1994	$6.00
Arista	ASCD-2344	I Would Have Waited Forever	CDJ	U.S.	1991	$7.00
Arista	ASCD-2218	Lift Me Up	CDJ	U.S.	1991	$7.00
Arista	ASCD-2248	Lift Me Up	CDJ	U.S.	1991	$7.00
Atco	PR 2088-2	Love Will Find a Way	CDJ	U.S.	1987	$7.00
Atco	PRCD 4008-2	Make It Easy	CDJ	U.S.	1991	$7.00
Atlantic	7567-96292-2	Owner of a Lonely Heart	CD5	Germany	1991	$10.00
Atco	PR 2089-2	Rhythm of Love	CDJ	U.S.	1987	$8.00
Arista	664 553	Saving My Heart	CD5	U.K.	1991	$10.00
Arista	ASCD 2263	Saving My Heart	CDJ	U.S.	1991	$7.00
		State of Play	CDJ	U.S.	1994	$6.00
		Walls	CDJ	U.S.	1994	$6.00

YG's

Singles

Label	Catalog Number	Title	Type	Country	Year	Longbox Value / Value
Reprise	9 45480-2	Street Nigga	CD5	U.S.	1993	$4.00

Ygmgeez

Singles

Label	Catalog Number	Title	Type	Country	Year	Longbox Value / Value
	1870	Streets of Compton	CD5	U.S.	1994	$5.00

Yindi, Yothu

Singles

Label	Catalog Number	Title	Type	Country	Year	Longbox Value / Value
		Dots on the Shell	CD5	Australia	1994	$10.00

YMO

Full Length

Label	Catalog Number	Title	Type	Country	Year	Longbox Value / Value
	H12-20	Special Sampler	DJ/Smplr	Japan		$100.00

Singles

Label	Catalog Number	Title	Type	Country	Year	Longbox Value / Value
Internal	LIECD 2	Reconstructions	CD5	U.K.	1992	$8.00

Yo La Tengo

Singles

Label	Catalog Number	Title	Type	Country	Year	Longbox Value / Value
Matador	5276	Big Day Coming	CDJ	U.S.		$2.00
Matador	5402	From a Motel 6	CDJ	U.S.		$2.00
Matador	139	Tom Courtenay	CD5	U.S.	1994	$5.00
Matador	139	Tom Courtenay	CD5	U.S.	1995	$6.00

Yo Yo

Singles

Label	Catalog Number	Title	Type	Country	Year	Longbox Value / Value
Eastwest	PRCD 4038-2	Ain't Nobody Better	CDJ	U.S.	1991	$2.00
Eastwest	PRCD 5138-2-2	Bonnie & Clyde Theme, The	CDJ	U.S.	1993	$2.00
Eastwest	PRCD 4619-2	Home Girl Don't Play Dat	CDJ	U.S.	1992	$2.00
Eastwest	PRCD 5018-2	IB Win' Wit My Crewin'	CDJ	U.S.	1993	$2.00

Yoakam, Dwight

Full Length

Label	Catalog Number	Title	Type	Country	Year	Longbox Value / Value
		'90s Country	RS	U.S.	1995	$25.00
	Airdate: 12/21/95.					
		Country Edge	RS	U.S.	1995	$30.00
	Airdate: 5/20/95.					
Reprise		If There Was Another Way Sampler	DJ/Smplr	U.S.	1993	$8.00

Singles

Label	Catalog Number	Title	Type	Country	Year	Longbox Value / Value
Reprise	PRO-CD-6282	A Thousand Miles From Nowhere	CDJ	U.S.	1993	$3.00
Reprise	PRO-CD-6028	Ain't That Lonely Yet	CDJ	U.S.	1993	$3.00
Reprise		Fast as You	CD5	U.K.	1994	$10.00
Reprise	PRO-CD-6519	Fast as You	CDJ	U.S.	1994	$3.00
Reprise	PRO-CD-5041	It Only Hurts When I Cry	CDJ	U.S.	1990	$3.00
Warner Brothers	17734	Nothing	CD5	U.S.	1995	$5.00
Reprise	PRO-CD-4885	Nothing's Changed Here	CDJ	U.S.	1990	$3.00
Reprise	PRO-CD-6932	Pocket of a Clown	CDJ	U.S.		$3.00
Reprise	PRO-CD-5545	Send a Message to My Heart	CDJ	U.S.	1990	$3.00
Epic	ESK 74753	Suspicious Minds	CD5	U.K.	1993	$10.00
Reprise	PRO-CD-5273	Takes a Lot to Rock You	CDJ	U.S.	1990	$3.00
Reprise	PRO-CD-4623	Takes a Lot to Rock You	CDJ	U.S.	1990	$7.00
Reprise	W-0133CD	Things We Said Today	CD5	U.K.	1992	$12.00
Reprise	PRO-CD-6057	Thousand Miles From Nowhere	CDJ	U.S.		$3.00
Arista	ASCD-2249	Truckin'	CDJ	U.S.	1991	$3.00
Reprise	PRO-CD-6756	Try Not to Be so Pretty	CDJ	U.S.	1994	$3.00
		Turn It On, Turn It Up	CDJ	U.S.		$3.00
Reprise	PRO-CD-4684	You're the One	CDJ	U.S.	1990	$3.00

Yoakam, Dwight and Buck Owens

Singles

Label	Catalog Number	Title	Type	Country	Year	Longbox Value / Value
		Streets of Bakersfield	CDJ	U.S.		$7.00

Yothu Tindi

Singles

Label	Catalog Number	Title	Type	Country	Year	Longbox Value / Value
Hollywood	66358-2	Djapana	CD5	U.S.	1992	$5.00
Hollywood	66358-2	Treaty	CD5	U.S.	1992	$5.00
Hollywood	PRCD 8508-2	Treaty	CDJ	U.S.	1992	$2.00

You Am I

Singles

Label	Catalog Number	Title	Type	Country	Year	Longbox Value / Value
Restless	727891	Berlin Chair	CD5	U.S.	1994	$5.00

Young Black Teenagers

Singles

Label	Catalog Number	Title	Type	Country	Year	Longbox Value / Value
MCA	CD45 18416	Nobody Knows Kelli	CDJ	U.S.	1990	$2.00
Soul	2634	Roll With the Flavor	CDJ	U.S.	1993	$2.00
MCA	MCSTD-1527	To My Donna	CD5	U.K.	1991	$8.00
Soul	1292	To My Donna	CDJ	U.S.	1991	$2.00

Young Dubliners

Singles

Label	Catalog Number	Title	Type	Country	Year	Longbox Value / Value
		Wash My Hands	CDJ	U.S.		$2.00

Young Gods

Full Length

Label	Catalog Number	Title	Type	Country	Year	Longbox Value / Value
Pias	29	L'eau Rouge	LP/LB	U.S.		$14.00/$8.00
Pias	241	Live Sky Tour	LP/LB	U.S.		$14.00/$8.00
Pias	188	Play Kurt Weill	LP/LB	U.S.		$14.00/$8.00
Interscope	PRCD 6708	Retrospective	DJ/Smplr	U.S.		$15.00
Pias	201	T.V. Sky	LP/LB	U.S.		$14.00/$8.00
Wax Trax	7135	Young Gods	LP/LB	U.S.		$14.00/$8.00

Singles

Label	Catalog Number	Title	Type	Country	Year	Longbox Value / Value
		Kissing the Sun	CDJ	U.S.		$2.00
Play It Again	101	L'Amour	CD3	Germany		$8.00

Young, James

Full Length

Label	Catalog Number	Title	Type	Country	Year	Longbox Value / Value
Passport	PBCD-6051	City Slicker	LP/BP	U.S.		$16.00/$13.00

Young, James Group

Singles

Label	Catalog Number	Title	Type	Country	Year	Longbox Value / Value
		Heaven in Your Heart	CDJ	U.S.		$2.00
		Heaven in Your Heart	CDJ	U.S.		$3.00

Young, Jesse Col

Singles

Label	Catalog Number	Title	Type	Country	Year	Longbox Value / Value
	1036	Desire	CD5	U.S.	1994	$5.00

Young, Larry

Full Length

Label	Catalog Number	Title	Type	Country	Year	Longbox Value / Value
Mosaic	MD6-137	Complete Blue Note Recording	LTD/LP	U.S.		$72.00
	6 CD set. Limited to 7500 copies.					
Blue Note		Unity	LTD/LP	U.S.	1995	$19.00

Young, Lester

Full Length

Label	Catalog Number	Title	Type	Country	Year	Longbox Value / Value
Savoy Records	CY-78817	Blue Lester	LTD/LP	U.S.	1996	$20.00
	CD in miniature replica of original LP sleeve.					

Young M.C.

Full Length

Label	Catalog Number	Title	Type	Country	Year	Longbox Value / Value
Capitol	DPRO 79882	Brainstorm	DJ/LP	U.S.	1991	$18.00
	Picture disc CD in die-cut digipak.					

Singles

Label	Catalog Number	Title	Type	Country	Year	Longbox Value / Value
BMG	662477	Bust a Move	CD5	Germany	1989	$9.00
Polydor	P09D-31008	Bust a Move	CD3	Japan	1989	$12.00/$4.00
BMG	663053	I Come Off	CD5	Germany	1990	$9.00
Delicious Vinyl	3192	I Come Off	CDJ	U.S.	1990	$2.00
Delicious Vinyl	6644	Pick up the Pace	CDJ	U.S.	1990	$2.00
Polydor	PSDD-1001	Principal's Office	CD3	Japan	1990	$12.00/$4.00
4th & B'way	BRCD-161	Principal's Office	CD5	U.K.	1989	$9.00
Delicious Vinyl	3068	Principal's Office	CDJ	U.S.	1989	$2.00
Capitol	C25S-15750	That's the Way Love Goes	CD5	Canada	1991	$10.00
EMI	204423-2	That's the Way Love Goes	CD5	Germany	1991	$9.00
EMI	2045352	That's the Way Love Goes	CD5	Germany	1991	$9.00
Capitol	CDCL-623	That's the Way Love Goes	CD5	U.K.	1991	$9.00
Capitol	DPRO 79819	That's the Way Love Goes	CDJ	U.S.	1991	$2.00
Capitol	DPRO 79754	What's the Flavor?	CDJ	U.S.	1993	$2.00

Young, Neil (and Crazy Horse)

Full Length

Label	Catalog Number	Title	Type	Country	Year	Longbox Value / Value
Reprise	9 26746-2	Arc Weld	LP/LB	U.S.	1991	$35.00/$30.00
	3 CD Set.					
Warner Brothers	925271-2	Best of	LP	Germany		$23.00
Warner Brothers	925271-2	Best of	LP	U.K.		$23.00
WEA		Broken Arrow	DJ/LP	U.K.	1996	$25.00
Reprise	9 46291 (#1)	Broken Arrow	DJ/LP	U.S.	1996	$25.00
	Advance pressing with an extended version of the track "Loose Change."					
Reprise		Complex Sessions, The	DJ/Smplr	U.S.	1995	$15.00
Vapor	46178	Dead Man (Movie Soundtrack)	LTD/LP	U.S.	1996	$30.00
Reprise	20P2-2651	Eldorado	LP	Japan	1989	$25.00
Geffen	9 4013-2	Everybody's Rockin'	LP/LB	U.S.		$25.00/$23.00
Geffen	9 4013-2	Everybody's Rockin'	LP/LB	U.S.†	1983	$25.00/$23.00
Warner Brothers	SAC3110	For the Turntables	DJ/Smplr	U.K.	1994	$45.00
Reprise	9 25899-2	Freedom	DJ/Smplr	U.S.	1990	$30.00
	Picture disc edition.					
Reprise	9 2277-2	Harvest	LP/LB	U.S.†	1984	$14.00/$8.00
Reprise		Harvest/Harvest Moon	LTD/LP	Australia	1994	$45.00
	Gold disc.					
Vid-America	LL7077	In Berlin	LD	U.S.	1985	$80.00
Album Network		In the Studio (Harvest)	RS	U.S.	1989	$30.00
	Airdate: 2/27/89.					
Album Network		In the Studio (Ragged Glory)	RS	U.S.		$35.00
Album Network		In the Studio (Ragged Glory)	RS	U.S.		$50.00
Geffen	9 24109-2	Landing on Water	LP/LB	U.S.	1986	$20.00/$18.00
Geffen	9 24154-2	Life	LP/LB	U.S.	1987	$25.00/$23.00
Geffen	NYCD 1	Lucky Thirteen Album Sampler	DJ/Smplr	U.K.	1993	$15.00
Reprise		Mirrorball	LP	U.S.	1995	$16.00
	Record club version with CD in jewel box rather than card sleeve.					
Reprise	9 45934-2	Mirrorball	LP	U.S.	1995	$25.00
	CD in jewel box.					
Reprise	PRO 808	Needle and the Damage Done, The	DJ/Smplr	Germany	1993	$35.00
WEA	38273-6	Neil Young & Crazy Horse	LD	U.S.	1991	$35.00
WEA	38354	Neil Young: Unplugged	LD	U.S.	1993	$30.00
Westwood One		Off the Record	RS	U.S.	1993	$80.00
	2 CD set. Airdate: 1/11/93					
Westwood One		Off the Record	RS	U.S.	1994	$35.00
	Airdate: 10/10/94.					
Westwood One		Off the Record	RS	U.S.	1994	$40.00
	Airdate: 4/18/94.					
Westwood One		Off the Record	RS	U.S.	1996	$35.00
	Airdate: 1/1/96.					
On the Radio		Rarities On Compact Disc	DJ/RS	U.S.	1994	$30.00
	Vol. 17.					
CBS	465012-2	Serenade	LP	Germany		$23.00
Reprise	PRO-CD-7136	Sleep With Angels	DJ/LP	U.S.	1994	$15.00
Pioneer	PA-85-131	Solo Trans.	LD	U.S.	1985	$30.00
Westwood One		Superstars	RS	U.S.	1995	$90.00
	2 CD set. Airdate: 7/10/95.					
Westwood One		Superstars	RS	U.S.	1996	$90.00
	2 CD set. Airdate: 1/22/96.					

Singles

Label	Catalog Number	Title	Type	Country	Year	Longbox Value / Value
Columbia	CSK 5493	All Along the Watchtower	CDJ	U.S.		$3.00
Reprise	PRO-CD-5232	Arc, The Single	CDJ	U.S.	1991	$7.00
Warner Brothers		Big Time	CD5	Germany	1996	$12.00
Reprise		Change Your Mind	CDJ	U.S.	1994	$6.00
Reprise	PRO-CD-3952	Crime in the City	CDJ	U.S.	1990	$6.00
Reprise		Downtown	CDJ	Germany	1995	$40.00
Reprise		Downtown	CDJ	U.S.	1995	$6.00
Reprise	9362-40675-2	Harvest Moon	CD5	Germany	1992	$10.00
Reprise	9362-40781-2	Harvest Moon	CD5	Germany	1992	$10.00
Reprise	9 18685-2	Harvest Moon	CD5	U.S.	1992	$4.00
Reprise	PRO-CD-5811	Harvest Moon	CDJ	U.S.	1992	$6.00

Label	Catalog Number	Title	Type	Country	Year	Longbox Value / Value
Geffen	PRO-CD-2796	Inca Queen	CDJ	U.S.	1986	$10.00
Reprise	PRO-CD-6292	Long May You Run	CDJ	U.S.	1993	$7.00
Reprise	PRO-CD-4669	Love To Burn	CDJ	U.S.	1991	$6.00
Reprise	CD-21759	Mansion on the Hill	CD5	Canada	1991	$10.00
Warner	12-21759	Mansion on the Hill	CD5	Canada	1994	$8.00
Reprise	921759-2	Mansion on the Hill	CD5	Germany	1990	$10.00
Reprise	9 21759-2	Mansion on the Hill	CD5	U.S.	1990	$5.00
Reprise	PRO-CD-4448	Mansion on the Hill	CDJ	U.S.	1990	$10.00
Warner Brothers		Merkinball	CD5	U.K.	1995	$10.00
Reprise	PRO-CD-6294	Mr. Soul	CDJ	U.S.	1993	$6.00
Reprise		Needle & the Damage	CDJ	Germany	1993	$10.00
Reprise	PRO 808	Needle & the Damage	CDJ	U.K.	1993	$25.00
Reprise	PRO-CD-6319	Needle & the Damage	CDJ	U.S.	1993	$3.00
Reprise	PRO-CD-3864	No More	CDJ	U.S.	1989	$8.00
Reprise	PRO-CD-4576	Over and Over	CDJ	U.S.	1990	$6.00
Reprise		Over and Over	CDJ	U.S.	1994	$6.00
		Philadelphia	CD5	U.K.	1994	$10.00
Reprise		Piece of Crap	CD5	U.K.	1994	$10.00
Reprise		Piece of Crap	CDJ	U.S.	1994	$6.00
Reprise		Prime of Life	CDJ	U.S.	1994	$6.00
		Prime of Life	CDJ	U.S.	1995	$6.00
Reprise	921-388-2	Rockin' the Free World	CD5	Germany	1989	$10.00
Reprise	W-2776CD	Rockin' the Free World	CD5	U.K.	1989	$10.00
Reprise	PRO-CD-3729	Rockin' the Free World	CDJ	U.S.	1989	$7.00
Warner Brothers		Sleeps With Angels	CD5	U.K.	1994	$10.00
Reprise		Sleeps With Angels	CDJ	U.S.	1994	$6.00
Reprise	921-464-2	Someday	CD5	Germany	1990	$10.00
Reprise	PRO-CD-3073	Ten Men Workin'	CDJ	U.S.	1988	$7.00
Reprise	PRO-CD-3091	This Note's For You	CDJ	U.S.	1988	$25.00
Reprise		Throw Your Head Down	CDJ	Spain	1996	$45.00
Reprise	PRO-CD-5960	Unknown Legend	CDJ	U.S.	1993	$7.00
Warner Brothers	PRO 808	Unplugged	CDJ	Germany	1993	$20.00
	D3P-1108	Until You Come Back to Me	CDJ	Japan		$35.00
Reprise	PRO-CD-5864	War of Man	CDJ	U.S.	1993	$6.00

Young, Paul

Full Length

Label	Catalog Number	Title	Type	Country	Year	Longbox Value / Value
CBS	CK-38976	No Parlez	LP/BP	U.S.†	1985	$14.00/$8.00
CBS	CK-39957	Secret of Association	LP/BP	U.S.†	1985	$14.00/$8.00
		Selections from Time to Time	DJ/Smplr	Canada		$20.00

Singles

Label	Catalog Number	Title	Type	Country	Year	Longbox Value / Value
Columbia	657411-2	Don't Dream It's Over	CD5	Germany	1991	$9.00
Columbia	657411-2	Don't Dream It's Over	CD5	U.K.	1991	$9.00
Columbia	656312-3	Heaven Can Wait	CD5	Germany	1990	$9.00
Columbia	YOUNGC-6	Heaven Can Wait	CD5	U.K.	1990	$9.00
Columbia	YOUNGD-6	Heaven Can Wait	CD5	U.K.	1990	$10.00
Columbia	CSK 73557	Heaven Can Wait	CDJ	U.S.	1990	$2.00
		Hope in a Hopeless World	CD5	U.K.		$10.00
		Hope in a Hopeless World	CD5	U.K.		$10.00

Second version.

Label	Catalog Number	Title	Type	Country	Year	Longbox Value / Value
		It Will Be You	CD5	U.K.		$10.00
		It Will Be You	CD5	U.K.		$10.00

Second version.

Label	Catalog Number	Title	Type	Country	Year	Longbox Value / Value
		Now I Know What Made Otis Blue	CD5	U.K.		$10.00
		Now I Know What Made Otis Blue	CD5	U.K.		$10.00

Second version.

Label	Catalog Number	Title	Type	Country	Year	Longbox Value / Value
Columbia	656100-3	Oh Girl	CD3	Germany	1990	$9.00
Sony	EDA-7043	Oh Girl	CD3	Japan	1990	$12.00/$4.00
Columbia	YOUNGC-5	Oh Girl	CD5	U.K.	1990	$9.00
Columbia	YOUNGD-5	Oh Girl	CD5	U.K.	1990	$10.00
Columbia	CSK 73377	Oh Girl	CDJ	U.S.	1990	$2.00
Columbia	656800 3	Softly Whispering I Love You	CD5	Germany	1990	$0.00
Epic	ESDA-7019	Softly Whispering I Love You	CD3	Japan	1990	$12.00/$4.00
Columbia	YOUNGC-4	Softly Whispering I Love You	CD5	U.K.	1990	$9.00
Columbia	YOUNGD-4	Softly Whispering I Love You	CD5	U.K.	1990	$10.00
Columbia	CSK 2282	Softly Whispering I Love You	CDJ	U.S.	1991	$2.00
MCA	CD45-2106	What Becomes Of the Broken Hearted	CDJ	U.S.	1992	$3.00

Young, Steve

Singles

Label	Catalog Number	Title	Type	Country	Year	Longbox Value / Value
	41060	Honky Tonk Man	CD5	U.S.	1994	$5.00

Young, Trey

Singles

Label	Catalog Number	Title	Type	Country	Year	Longbox Value / Value
	001	Chevy on Thangs	CD5	U.S.	1994	$5.00

Youngblood, Sydney

Singles

Label	Catalog Number	Title	Type	Country	Year	Longbox Value / Value
Circa	YRCD 43	I'd Rather Go Blind	CD5	U.K.	1990	$8.00

Yours Truely

Singles

Label	Catalog Number	Title	Type	Country	Year	Longbox Value / Value
Motown	1421	Come and Get It	CDJ	U.S.	1991	$2.00

Youssou N'dour

Singles

Label	Catalog Number	Title	Type	Country	Year	Longbox Value / Value
CBS	77711	Undecided	CD5	U.S.	1994	$5.00

Yulara

Full Length

Label	Catalog Number	Title	Type	Country	Year	Longbox Value / Value
		All Is One	DJ/LP	U.S.		$10.00

Z'Looke

Singles

Label	Catalog Number	Title	Type	Country	Year	Longbox Value / Value
Orpheus	74125	I Can't Stop Thinkin'	CDJ	U.S.	1991	$2.00

Zadora, Pia

Singles

Label	Catalog Number	Title	Type	Country	Year	Longbox Value / Value
Epic	653123-3	Dance out of My Head	CD3	Germany	1988	$8.00
Epic	653123-3	Dance out of My Head	CD3	U.K.	1988	$8.00
CBS	ZSK 3075	Heartbeat of Love	CDJ	U.S.	1989	$2.00
CBS	ZSK 1928	Heartbeat of Love	CDJ	U.S.	1989	$2.00
CBS	ZSK 73392	If You Were Mine	CDJ	U.S.	1989	$2.00

Zamfir

Full Length

Label	Catalog Number	Title	Type	Country	Year	Longbox Value / Value
Time Warner Sound Exchange		20 Popular Favorites	LP	U.S.	1995	$16.00
Warner Sound Exchange		20 Popular Favorites	LTD/LP	U.S.	1995	$17.00

Zan

Singles

Label	Catalog Number	Title	Type	Country	Year	Longbox Value / Value
Warner Brothers	PRO-CD-3684	House You	CDJ	U.S.	1989	$2.00

Zander, Robin

Singles

Label	Catalog Number	Title	Type	Country	Year	Longbox Value / Value
Interscope	PRCD 5012-2	I've Always Got You	CDJ	U.S.	1993	$2.00
Interscope	PRCD 5013-2	I've Always Got You	CDJ	U.S.	1993	$2.00
lInterscope	PRCD 5253-2	Show Me Heaven	CDJ	U.S.	1993	$2.00

Zap Mama

Singles

Label	Catalog Number	Title	Type	Country	Year	Longbox Value / Value
Luaka Bop	9 41002	Bottom	CD5	U.S.	1993	$5.00
Luaka Bop	PRO-CD-6111	Bottom	CDJ	U.S.	1993	$2.00

Zapp

Singles

Label	Catalog Number	Title	Type	Country	Year	Longbox Value / Value
Warner Brothers	PRO-CD-3684	Fire	CDJ	U.S.	1989	$2.00
Warner Brothers	PRO-CD-3951	Fire	CDJ	U.S.	1989	$2.00
Reprise	PRO-CD-3814	I Play the Talk Box	CDJ	U.S.	1989	$2.00
Reprise	PRO-CD-3656	Ooh Baby Baby	CDJ	U.S.	1989	$2.00

Zapp & Roger

Singles

Label	Catalog Number	Title	Type	Country	Year	Longbox Value / Value
Warner Brothers	PRO-CD-6722	Computer Love	CDJ	U.S.	1993	$2.00
Warner Brothers	18251-2	Computer Love	CDJ	U.S.	1993	$7.00
Warner Brothers	18251	Computer Love	CD5	U.S.	1994	$5.00
Warner Brothers	18251	Computer Love	CD5	U.S.	1994	$5.00
Warner Brothers	9 40982-2	Mega Medley	CD5	U.S.	1993	$5.00
Warner Brothers	PRO-CD-6370	Mega Medley	CDJ	U.S.	1993	$2.00
Warner Brothers	PRO-CD-6596	Slow & Easy	CDJ	U.S.	1993	$2.00

Zappa, Dweezil

Full Length

Label	Catalog Number	Title	Type	Country	Year	Longbox Value / Value
Rykodisc	RCD 10057	Havin' A Bad Day	LP/LB	U.S.		$15.00/$12.00

Singles

Label	Catalog Number	Title	Type	Country	Year	Longbox Value / Value
IRS	977 121	Stayin' Alive	CD5	Germany	1991	$10.00

Zappa, Frank – In-Store Play CD, The (Rykodisc VRCD 0501)

Zappa, Frank

Full Length

Label	Catalog Number	Title	Type	Country	Year	Longbox Value / Value
Rykodisc	RCD-10093	Absolutely Free	LP/LB	U.S.		$15.00/$9.00
Rykodisc	RCD 80519	Apostrophe (')	LTD/LP	U.S.	1995	$24.00

20 bit master gold CD.

Label	Catalog Number	Title	Type	Country	Year	Longbox Value / Value
Rykodisc	RCD-40025	Apostrophe/Overnite Sensation	LP/LB	U.S.		$15.00/$9.00
Rykodisc	70372-2	Beat the Boots #2	LTD/LP	U.S.		$150.00

10 CD set.

Label	Catalog Number	Title	Type	Country	Year	Longbox Value / Value
Rykodisc	RCD-10097	Bongo Fury	LP/LB	U.S.		$15.00/$9.00
Rykodisc	RCD-40096	Broadway the Hardway	LP/LB	U.S.		$15.00/$9.00
Rykodisc	RCD-40164	Chunga's Revenge	LP/LB	U.S.		$15.00/$9.00
Rykodisc	RCD-10063	Cruising With Ruben & the Jets	LP/LB	U.S.		$15.00/$9.00
Rykodisc		Ditties and Beer	DJ/Smplr	U.K.	1996	$45.00
EMI	CDP-746188-2	Does Humor Belong In Music	LP	Germany		$23.00
		Dr. Demento	RS	U.S.	1994	$150.00

Airdate: 1/2/94.

Label	Catalog Number	Title	Type	Country	Year	Longbox Value / Value
Rykodisc	RCD-40167	Filmore East '71	LP/LB	U.S.		$15.00/$9.00
Rykodisc	RCD-10026	Grand Wazoo	LP/LB	U.S.		$15.00/$9.00
Rykodisc	RCD-10079/80	Guitar	LP/LB	U.S.		$30.00/$20.00

2CD.

Label	Catalog Number	Title	Type	Country	Year	Longbox Value / Value
Rykodisc	RCD-10066	Hot Rats	LP/LB	U.S.		$15.00/$9.00
Rykodisc	RCDG-10066	Hot Rats	LP/LP	U.S.		$30.00/$25.00

Gold disc CD.

Label	Catalog Number	Title	Type	Country	Year	Longbox Value / Value
Rykodisc	VRCD 0501	In-Store Play CD, The	DJ/Smplr	U.S.	1995	$50.00
EMI	CDP-790078-2	Jazz From Hell	LP	Germany		$23.00
Rykodisc	RCD-10030	Jazz From Hell	LP/LB	U.S.		$15.00/$9.00
Rykodisc	RCD-10060/61	Joe's Garage	LP/LB	U.S.		$30.00/$20.00

2CD.

Label	Catalog Number	Title	Type	Country	Year	Longbox Value / Value
EMI	CDP-790087-2	Joes Garage	LP	Germany		$35.00

2 CD set.

Label	Catalog Number	Title	Type	Country	Year	Longbox Value / Value
Rykodisc	RCD-10060/61	Joes Garage	LP/LB	U.S.		$30.00/$25.00

2 CD set.

Label	Catalog Number	Title	Type	Country	Year	Longbox Value / Value
Rykodisc	RCD-40161	Just Another Band From L.A.	LP/LB	U.S.		$15.00/$9.00
Rykodisc	VRCD-0502	Kill Ugly Radio	DJ/Smplr	U.S.	1995	$25.00
Rykodisc	VRCD-0503	Kill Ugly Radio Some More	DJ/Smplr	U.S.	1995	$25.00
Rykodisc		Kill Ugly Radio Some More	DJ/LP	U.S.	1996	$25.00

Debut CD of album in box titled "35 years of Golden Smog."

Label	Catalog Number	Title	Type	Country	Year	Longbox Value / Value
EMI	CDP-790074-2	Man From Utopia	LP	Germany		$23.00
Rykodisc	RCD-10023	Meets Mother of Prevention	LP/LB	U.S.		$15.00/$9.00
EMI	CDP-790078-2	Meets Mothers of Prevention	LP	Germany		$23.00
Rykodisc	RYKODISC-ZAP-1	No Commercial Potential	DJ/Smplr	U.K.	1996	$150.00
Rykodisc	RCD-10095	One Size Fits All	LP/LB	U.S.		$15.00/$9.00
Rykodisc	RCD 80521	One Size Fits All	LTD/LP	U.S.	1995	$24.00

20 bit master gold CD.

Label	Catalog Number	Title	Type	Country	Year	Longbox Value / Value
EMI	CDP-790076-2	Sheik Yerbouti	LP	Germany		$23.00
Rykodisc	RCD-40162	Sheik Yerbouti	LP/LB	U.S.		$15.00/$9.00
Rykodisc	RCD-10028/29	Shut Up 'n Play Guitar	LP/LB	U.S.		$30.00/$20.00

2CD.

Label	Catalog Number	Title	Type	Country	Year	Longbox Value / Value
		Specialized Digital Audio Gratification	DJ/Smplr	Austria		$65.00
	DC1-7026	Strictly Commercial	DJ/Smplr	Japan	1995	$150.00
Rykodisc	VRCD 10500	Strictly Commercial: The Best Of FZ	DJ/Smplr	U.S.	1995	$20.00
EMI	CDP-790080-2	Them or Us	LP	Germany		$23.00
Rykodisc	RCD-40027	Them or Us	LP/LB	U.S.		$15.00/$9.00

Label	Catalog Number	Title	Type	Country	Year	Longbox Value / Value
EMI	CDP-790081-2	Thing-Fish	LP	Germany		$23.00
Rykodisc	RCD-10020/21	Thing-Fish	LP/LB	U.S.		$30.00/$20.00
	2CD.					
EMI	CDP-790077-2	Tinsel Town Rebellion	LP	Germany		$23.00
Rykodisc	RCD-40162	Tinsel Town Rebellion	LP/LB	U.S.		$15.00/$9.00
Rykodisc	RCD-10064/65	Uncle Meat	LP/LB	U.S.		$30.00/$20.00
	2CD.					
Rykodisc	RCD-10094	Wakajawaka	LP/LB	U.S.		$15.00/$9.00
Rykodisc	RCD-40024	We're Only in/Lumpy Gravy	LP/LB	U.S.		$15.00/$9.00
Rykodisc	RCD-40163	Weasels Ripped My Flesh	LP/LB	U.S.		$15.00/$9.00
Rykodisc	RCD-40165	You Are What You Is	LP/LB	U.S.		$15.00/$9.00
Rykodisc	RCD-10081/82	You Can't Do That on Radio Anymore	LP/LB	U.S.		$30.00/$20.00
	2CD.					
Rykodisc	PRO 9003	You Can't Do That on Radio Anymore	DJ/Smplr	U.S.	1990	$30.00
	Jewelbox version.					
Rykodisc	PRO 9003	You Can't Do That on Radio Anymore	DJ/Smplr	U.S.	1990	$50.00
	Digipak version.					
Rykodisc	FZCDTOSA	You Can't Do That on Radio Anymore	LTD/LP	U.S.	1992	$45.00
	4 CDs in painted wood box.					
Rykodisc	RCDPRO 9003	You Can't Do That on Radio Anymore	DJ/Smplr	U.S.	1994	$28.00
	Green jewelbox version.					
Rykodisc	RCD-10083/84	You Can't Do That on Stage Anymore 2	LP/LB	U.S.		$30.00/$20.00
	2CD.					
Rykodisc	RCD-10085/86	You Can't Do That on Stage Anymore 3	LP/LB	U.S.		$30.00/$20.00
	2CD.					
Rykodisc	RCD-10087/88	You Can't Do That on Stage Anymore 4	LP/LB	U.S.		$30.00/$20.00
	2CD.					
Rykodisc	RCD-10089/90	You Can't Do That on Stage Anymore 5	LP/LB	U.S.		$30.00/$20.00
	2CD.					
Rykodisc	RCD-10091/92	You Can't Do That on Stage Anymore 6	LP/LB	U.S.		$30.00/$20.00
2CD						
Rykodisc	RCD-10022	Zappa & The London Symphony Orchestra	LP/LB	U.S.		$15.00/$9.00
Rykodisc	RCD-40160	Zoot Allures	LP/LB	U.S.		$15.00/$9.00
		Singles				
		Bobby Brown	CD5	U.K.	1995	$10.00
Zappa	828 510	Bobby Brown Goes Down	CD5	Germany	1991	$10.00
Rykodisc	1012	Montana	CD3	U.S.		$8.00/$5.00
Rykodisc	1001	Peaches En Regalia	CD3	U.S.		$8.00/$5.00
Rykodisc	1010	Sexual Harassment	CD3	U.S.		$8.00/$5.00
Zappa	977 101	Stairway to Heaven	CD5	U.K.	1991	$10.00
Rykodisc	1011	Zombie Wolf	CD3	U.S.		$8.00/$5.00

Zappa's Universe

Singles

Label	Catalog Number	Title	Type	Country	Year	Longbox Value / Value
Verve	726	Choice Morsels	CDJ	U.S.	1993	$7.00

Zazou, Hector

Singles

Label	Catalog Number	Title	Type	Country	Year	Longbox Value / Value
Crammed	08-012269-17	I'll Strangle You	CD5	Germany	1992	$8.00

Zebra

Full Length

Label	Catalog Number	Title	Type	Country	Year	Longbox Value / Value
Atlantic	80159-2	No Tellin' Lies	LP/LB	U.S.†	1985	$14.00/$8.00

Zereno

Singles

Label	Catalog Number	Title	Type	Country	Year	Longbox Value / Value
Cema Latino	31493	Nacio Un Amor	CD5	U.S.	1994	$5.00

Zevon, Warren

Full Length

Label	Catalog Number	Title	Type	Country	Year	Longbox Value / Value
Album Network		In the Studio (Excitable)	RS	U.S.	1990	$20.00
	Airdate: 4/23/90.					
DIR		King Biscuit Flour Hour	RS	U.S.	1990	$40.00
	With Bonnie Raitt, Airdate: 3/19/90.					
DIR		King Biscuit Flour Hour	RS	U.S.	1993	$50.00
	With John Lennon, Airdate: 2/14/93.					
DIR		King Biscuit Flour Hour	RS	U.S.	1994	$80.00
	With John Lennon. Airdate: 9/4/94.					
DIR		King Biscuit Flour Hour	RS	U.S.	1995	$80.00
	With John Lennon. Airdate: 8/20/95.					
Giant	2-24496	Learning to Flinch	LTD/LP	U.S.	1993	$25.00
	Felt-bound digipak.					
		Singles				
Giant	PRO-CD-5017	Finishing Touches	CDJ	U.S.	1991	$3.00
Virgin	CDEP-2	Leave My Monkey Alone	CD5	U.K.	1988	$9.00
Virgin	PRCD 2216	Reconsider Me	CDJ	U.S.	1987	$7.00
Virgin	PRCD2216	Reconsider Me	CDJ	U.S.	1987	$20.00
Giant	PRO-CD-7483	Rottweiler Blues	CDJ	U.S.	1995	$3.00
Virgin	PRCD 2987	Run Straight Down	CDJ	U.S.	1989	$3.00
Giant	PRO-CD-5171	Searchin' for a Heart	CDJ	U.S.	1991	$3.00
Virgin	PRCD 2033	Setimental Hygiene	CDJ	U.S.	1987	$3.00
Virgin	VUSCD-9	Splendid Isolation	CD3	U.K.	1990	$9.00
Virgin	PRCD 3157	Splendid Isolation	CDJ	U.S.	1989	$3.00
Virgin		Transverse City	CDJ	U.K.	1994	$15.00

Zhane

Singles

Label	Catalog Number	Title	Type	Country	Year	Longbox Value / Value
Motown	374631141	Groove Thang	CDJ	U.S.	1993	$2.00
Motown	4848	Groove Thang	CD5	U.S.	1994	$5.00
Jive	42268	Shame	CD5	U.S.	1994	$5.00
Motown	4862	Vibe	CD5	U.S.	1994	$5.00

Zhigge

Singles

Label	Catalog Number	Title	Type	Country	Year	Longbox Value / Value
Polydor	CDP 671	Toss It Up	CDJ	U.S.	1992	$2.00

Zion Train

Singles

Label	Catalog Number	Title	Type	Country	Year	Longbox Value / Value
Atlantic	85706	Mesa Blue Moon	CD5	U.S.	1995	$5.00

Zippers

Singles

Label	Catalog Number	Title	Type	Country	Year	Longbox Value / Value
		Top Shelf	CDJ	U.S.		$2.00

Zodiac Mindwarp

Full Length

Label	Catalog Number	Title	Type	Country	Year	Longbox Value / Value
		Tattooed Beat Messiah	DJ/LP	U.S.		$8.00
		Singles				
IRS	977 723	Elvis Died for You	CD5	Germany	1991	$8.00
Musidisc	10873-2	Elvis Died for You	CD5	U.K.	1991	$8.00
Musidisc	10922-2	Meanstreak	CD5	U.K.	1992	$8.00
Mercury	ZOCD-3	Planet Girl	CD5	U.K.	1988	$8.00

Zoe

Full Length

Label	Catalog Number	Title	Type	Country	Year	Longbox Value / Value
Polygram	513036-2	Scarlet Red & Blue	LP/BP	U.S.		$12.00/$7.00

Zombies

Singles

Label	Catalog Number	Title	Type	Country	Year	Longbox Value / Value
RCA	PD-43672	Lula Lula	CD5	Germany	1990	$8.00
RCA	PD-43428	New World	CD5	Germany	1990	$8.00

Zonjic, Alexander

Singles

Label	Catalog Number	Title	Type	Country	Year	Longbox Value / Value
Reprise	PRO-CD-6589	Memphis Underground	CDJ	U.S.	1993	$2.00

Zoo

Full Length

Label	Catalog Number	Title	Type	Country	Year	Longbox Value / Value
Westwood One		In Concert	RS	U.S.	1992	$50.00
	Airdate: 12/7/92.					
Capricorn		Shakin' the Cage	LP/LB	U.S.		$14.00/$8.00
		Singles				
Capricorn	5892	How Does It Feel	CDJ	U.S.	1992	$2.00
Capricorn	5620	Reach Out	CDJ	U.S.	1992	$2.00
Capricorn	5892	Shakin' the Cage	CDJ	U.S.	1992	$2.00
Capricorn	5436	Shakin' the Cage	CDJ	U.S.	1992	$7.00

Zot

Full Length

Label	Catalog Number	Title	Type	Country	Year	Longbox Value / Value
Elektra	60380-2	Zot	LP/LB	U.S.†	1985	$14.00/$8.00

Zuccero

Singles

Label	Catalog Number	Title	Type	Country	Year	Longbox Value / Value
A&M	AMCDP00166	No More Regrets	CDJ	U.S.		$2.00
London	864825-2	Come Back Again	CD5	U.K.	1993	$8.00
Polydor	PODP-1045	Diamante	CD3	Japan	1992	$12.00/$4.00
London	LONCD-313	Diamante	CD5	U.K.	1992	$8.00
Polygram	877467-2	Madre Dolcissima	CD5	Germany	1990	$8.00
London	LONCD 262	Mama	CD5	U.K.	1990	$8.00
London	LONCD-294	Senza Una Donna	CD5	U.K.	1991	$8.00
London	CDP 527	Senza Una Donna	CDJ	U.S.	1991	$2.00
London	867283-2	Wonderful World	CD5	Germany	1991	$8.00
London	LONCD-300	Wonderful World	CD5	U.K.	1991	$8.00

Zucchero and Luciano Pavarotti

Singles

Label	Catalog Number	Title	Type	Country	Year	Longbox Value / Value
		Miserere	CD5	U.K.		$10.00

ZuZu's Petals

Singles

Label	Catalog Number	Title	Type	Country	Year	Longbox Value / Value
Twin One	2384	Cinderella's Daydream	CD5	U.K.	1993	$8.00
		How Long	CD5	U.K.	1992	$8.00

Zydeco, Buckwheat

Singles

Label	Catalog Number	Title	Type	Country	Year	Longbox Value / Value
Charisma	094	Cry To Me	CDJ	U.S.	1992	$2.00
Island		Cry To Me	CDJ	U.S.		$2.00
Island	CID-398	Down Dallas Alley	CD5	U.K.	1989	$8.00
Island	PRCD 6626-2	Hey Good Lookin'	CDJ	U.S.	1990	$2.00
Charisma	079	Hey Joe	CDJ	U.S.	1992	$2.00
Island	CID-412	Make Change	CD5	U.K.	1989	$8.00
Island	PR 2146-2	My Lil' Girl	CDJ	U.S.	1987	$2.00
Island	885281	Why Does Love Hurt So Bad	CD5	Germany	1989	$8.00
Island	CID-386	Why Does Love Hurt So Bad	CD5	U.K.	1989	$8.00

ZZ Top

Full Length

Label	Catalog Number	Title	Type	Country	Year	Longbox Value / Value
Warner Brothers	PRO-CD-2875	A Taste of the ZZ Top Six Pack	DJ/Smplr	U.S.	1987	$20.00
RCA	RJC 66317-2	Antenna	DJ/LP	U.S.	1994	$14.00
	Advance promo in sleeve.					
RCA	62732-2SP	Antenna	DJ/Smplr	U.S.	1994	$8.00
RCA	RDJ 62732-2	Antenna	DJ/Smplr	U.S.	1994	$35.00
	Brass layered disc in leather-bound digipak.					
Warner Brothers	3273-2	Best Of	LP/LB	U.S.†	1984	$14.00/$8.00
Warner Brothers	2-3361	Deguello	LP/LB	U.S.†	1984	$14.00/$8.00
Warner Brothers	23774-2	Eliminator	LP/LB	U.S.†	1984	$14.00/$8.00
Album Network		In the Studio (Eliminator)	RS	U.S.		$25.00
Album Network		In the Studio (Greatest Hits)	RS	U.S.	1992	$25.00
	Airdate: 4/13/92.					
Album Network		In the Studio (Greatest Hits)	RS	U.S.	1992	$25.00
	Airdate: 4/20/92.					
DIR		King Biscuit Flour Hour	RS	U.S.	1990	$40.00
	With Joe Satriani, Airdate: 4/2/90.					
Media America		Memorial Day Blues Blast Bar-B-Q	RS	U.S.	1991	$50.00
	3 CD set.					
Westwood One		Off the Record	RS	U.S.	1992	$40.00
	Airdate: 4/20/92.					
Westwood One		Off the Record	RS	U.S.	1994	$30.00
	Airdate: 3/28/94.					
Westwood One		Off the Record	RS	U.S.	1996	$25.00
	Airdate: 2/5/96.					
Warner Brothers	26458-2-Dj	Recycler	DJ/LP	U.S.	1990	$30.00
	CD in metal-bound digipak.					
Warner Brothers	26265-2	Recycler	LP/LB	U.S.	1990	$14.00/$8.00
Warner Brothers	26458-2	Recycler	LTD/LP	U.S.	1990	$30.00
	CD in metal-bound digipak.					
Album Network		Recycler/World Premiere Broadcast	DJ/RS	U.S.	1990	$20.00
RCA		Rhythmeen	LTD/LP	U.S.	1996	$18.00
	CD and bonus cassette-single. Sold exclusively at Blockbuster Music stores.					
WEA	38299	ZZ Top: Greatest Hits	LD	U.S.	1992	$30.00
		Singles				
		Breakaway	CD5	U.K.	1994	$10.00
RCA		Breakaway	CDJ	U.S.	1994	$3.00
Warner Brothers	9362-40147-2	Burger Man	CD5	Germany	1991	$10.00
Warner Brothers	PRO-CD-4938	Burger Man	CDJ	U.S.	1992	$6.00
Warner Brothers	PRO-CD-4494	Concrete and Steel	CDJ	U.S.	1990	$7.00
Warner Brothers	PRO-CD-4719	Decision or Collision	CDJ	U.S.	1990	$3.00
Warner Brothers	921561-2	Doubleback	CD5	Germany	1990	$10.00
Warner Brothers	WPDP-6239	Doubleback	CD3	Japan	1990	$15.00/$4.00
Warner Brothers	W-9812CD	Doubleback	CD5	U.K.	1990	$10.00
Warner Brothers	PRO-CD-4074	Doubleback	CDJ	U.S.	1990	$3.00
WEA		Gimme All Your Lovin'	CDJ	Germany	1994	$25.00
RCA	RDJ 62845-2	Girl in a T-Shirt	CDJ	U.S.	1994	$7.00

Label	Catalog Number	Title	Type	Country	Year	Longbox Value / Value
Warner Brothers	CD-21840	Give It Up	CD5	Canada	1991	$10.00
Warner Brothers	7599-21810-2	Give It Up	CD5	Germany	1990	$10.00
Warner Brothers	W-9509CD	Give It Up	CD5	U.K.	1991	$10.00
Warner Brothers	PRO-CD-4584	Give It Up	CDJ	U.S.	1990	$3.00
Warner Brothers	9 21840-2	Give It Up	CD5	U.S.	1991	$5.00
Warner Brothers	9362-40018-2	My Head's in Mississippi	CD5	Germany	1991	$10.00
Warner Brothers	W-0009CD	My Head's in Mississippi	CD5	U.K.	1991	$10.00
Warner Brothers	PRO-CD-4777	My Head's in Mississippi	CDJ	U.S.	1990	$3.00
		Pincushion	CDJ	France	1994	$13.00
		Pincushion	CD5	U.K.		$10.00
	Second version.					
		Pincushion	CD5	U.K.	1994	$12.00
	ZZ-001	Pincushion	CDJ	U.K.	1994	$10.00
RCA	62741-2	Pincushion	CDJ	U.S.	1994	$3.00
		Pretty Vacant	CD5	U.K.	1996	$10.00
Warner Brothers		Rough Boys	CD5	U.K.	1993	$11.00
Warner Brothers	WO 111CDX	Rough Boys	CD5	U.K.	1993	$11.00
	Second version.					
		She's Just Killing Me	CD5	U.K.	1996	$10.00
Warner Brothers	9362-40430-2	Viva Las Vegas	CD5	U.K.	1992	$10.00
Warner Brothers	W 0098 CD	Viva Las Vegas	CD5	U.K.	1992	$15.00
Warner Brothers	PRO-CD-5483	Viva Las Vegas	CDJ	U.S.	1992	$3.00
Warner Brothers		Viva Las Vegas	CDJ	U.S.	1992	$3.00
	Second version.					
		What's Up With That	CD5	U.K.	1996	$1.00

Label Catalog Number Title Type Country Year Longbox Value / Value

CD Soundtracks

Label	Catalog Number	Title	Type	Country	Year	Longbox Value / Value
Walt Disney Pictures		101 Dalmations	DJ/Smplr	U.S.	1996	$35.00
CD-ROM press kit.						
Walt Disney Records	60382-7	101 Dalmations Picture Disc CD	CD5	U.S.	1997	$5.00
Cool Disc™ CD. Sold only at Kmart department stores.						
Capitol	CDP-46079	13 Original Themes	LP/LB	U.S.†	1985	$14.00/$8.00
Columbia	MK-45439	2001 A Space Odyssey	LP/LB	U.S.		$18.00/$15.00
Rhino		2001 Space Odyssey	LTD/LP	U.S.	1996	$18.00
Limited edition CD in slip case.						
Polygram	820244-2	3 Guys Naked From The Waist Down	LP/LB	U.S.†	1985	$14.00/$8.00
RCA	RCD1-3891	42nd Street	LP/LB	U.S.†	1985	$14.00/$8.00
Philips	310690252-2	7th Guest, The	LTD/LP	U.S.	1995	$45.00
CD+I limited edition with bonus soundtrack CD.						
Casablanca	826306-2	A Chorus Line	LP/LB	U.S.†	1985	$14.00/$8.00
Soundscreen	SL5147-2	A Fish Called Wanda	LP	U.S.	1988	$20.00
		A Time Of Destiny	LP	U.S.		$15.00
Silva Screen	FILMCD-1004	A to Z of British TV Themes	LP/BP	U.S.		$10.00/$7.00
EMI	CDP-746159-2	A View to a Kill	LP	U.K.		$20.00
EMI	CDP-90621-2	Absolute Beginners	LP/LB	U.S.		$20.00/$15.00
		Ace Ventura: When Nature Calls	DJ/LP	U.S.	1996	$50.00
Rare promotional CD with score only.						
Capitol	C21-98172-2	Addams Family	LP/LB	U.S.		$18.00/$15.00
Warner Brothers	25826-2	Adventures of Baron Munchausen	LP/LB	U.S.		$12.00/$7.00
Elektra	60952-2	Adventures of Ford Fairlane	LP/LB	U.S.		$14.00/$10.00
Varese Sarabande	5418	Adventures of Huckleberry Finn	LP/LB	U.S.		$18.00/$15.00
London		Adventures of Pinocchio: I1 Colosso	SCDJ	U.S.	1996	$15.00
Pinocchio Shaped CD.						
Facet	FCD-8104	Adventures of Robin Hood	LP/LB	U.S.		$14.00/$9.00
Varase	VCD-47202	Adventures of Robin Hood	LP/LB	U.S.†	1985	$14.00/$8.00
Varese Sarabande	VSD-5359	Adventures of the Great Mouse Detective, The	LP/LB	U.S.	1992	$18.00/$15.00
Varese Sarabande	VSD-5274	After Dark My Sweet	LP/LB	U.S.		$14.00/$9.00
Atlantic	80152-2	Against All Odds	LP/LB	U.S.†	1985	$14.00/$8.00
Interscope	92342	Air Up There, The	LP	U.S.		$15.00
Galaxis	GLX-9035	Airwolf – The Wonder Weapon	LP	Germany		$25.00
Disney		Aladdin	LTD/LP	Japan	1994	$50.00
Picture Disc CD with plastic figures housed in box.						
Disney	CD 026	Aladdin	LP/LB	U.S.	1993	$15.00/$8.00
Original pressing with censored lyrics.						
Walt Disney	CD026	Aladdin	LTD/LP	U.S.	1993	$90.00
Boxed set with CD, 2 VHS tapes and book.						
Disney	60013-2	Aladdin	LTD/LP	U.S.	1993	$40.00
Picture disc CD with previously unreleased track. Housed in box with lenticular and certificate.						
Sony	SRDS-8254	Aladdin – A Whole New World	CD3	Japan	1993	$13.00/$5.00
CBS	44K 74751	Aladdin – A Whole New World	CD5	U.S.	1992	$5.00
Tristar	80947	Alamo	LP	U.S.		$15.00
Curb	D21K-77276-2	All Dogs Go To Heaven	LP/LB	U.S.		$15.00/$13.00
Varese Sarabande	VSD-5307	Almost an Angel	LP/LB	U.S.		$14.00/$9.00
Fantasy	FCD-1791	Amadeus	LP/LB	U.S.†	1985	$25.00/$18.00
2 CD set.						
Hannibal	HNCD-9301	Amarcord	LP/LB	U.S.		$14.00/$9.00
Varese	VCD-47285	Amazing Grace And Chuck	LP/LB	U.S.		$15.00/$12.00
Virgin	V21S-86289	American Me	LP/LB	U.S.		$15.00/$13.00
Atlantic	82530-2	Amongst Friends	LP/LB	U.S.		$15.00/$13.00
Southern X	SCCD-1015	Anastasia	LP/LB	U.S.		$14.00/$9.00
Sandy Hook	2024	Anchors Aweigh	LP/LB	U.S.		$15.00/$13.00
Columbia	COCC-9682	Anne of Green Gables	LTD/LP	Japan		$28.00
CBS	CK 34712	Annie	LP/LB	U.S.†	1985	$14.00/$8.00
1977 version						
CBS	CK 34712	Annie	LP/LB	U.S.†	1985	$14.00/$8.00
1982 version						
Varese Sarabande	VSD-5285	Anthony Adverse	LP/LB	U.S.		$14.00/$9.00
DRG	12597	Apartment Zero	LP/LB	U.S.		$14.00/$9.00
Edel	5407	Apocalypse	LP/LB	U.S.		$15.00/$13.00
MCA		Apollo 13	LTD/LP	Australia	1995	$35.00
2 CD set.						
MCA		Apollo 13	DJ/LP	U.S.	1996	$80.00
Rare promotional CD with score only.						
Hollywood	60974-2	Arachnophobia	LP/LB	U.S.	1990	$12.00/$7.00
Live interactive		Arival: CD-ROM Adventure Sampler	DJ/Smplr	U.S.	1996	$7.00
CD-ROM sampler.						
Varese Sarabande	VSD-5352	Article 99	LP/LB	U.S.		$14.00/$9.00
Intrada	7018	Astronomers	LP/BP	U.S.		$14.00/$9.00
A&M	CD-316	Aurthur 2 on the Rocks	LP/LB	U.S.		$12.00/$7.00
Reprise	26466-2	Awakenings	LP/LB	U.S.		$18.00/$15.00
Polygram	821593-2	Baby	LP/LB	U.S.†	1985	$14.00/$8.00
mainstream	603	Baby the Rain Must Fall	LP/BP	U.S.		$11.00/$7.00
Varese	VCD-47281	Back to School/Pee-Wee's Big Adventure	LP/LB	U.S.		$15.00/$12.00
Virgin	CDVDJ	Backbeat	DJ/LP	U.S.	1994	$150.00
CD, CDJ, Cassette, VHS video, booklets,pin, poster and drum sticks in box.						
Virgin	14148	Backbeat Original Score Edits	DJ/Smplr	U.S.	1994	$15.00
Mango	CCD-9860	Bad Influence	LP/LB	U.S.		$15.00/$13.00
Walt Disney Records	60380-7	Bambi Picture Disc CD	CD5	U.S.	1997	$5.00
Cool Disc™ CD. Sold only at Kmart department stores.						
Walt Disney Records	CD-009	Bambi: Story and Songs	LP	U.S.	1988	$35.00
Label X	LXCD-3	Band of Angels	LP/LB	U.S.		$15.00/$13.00
Silva Screen	FILMCD-1001	Bandolero	LP/BP	U.S.		$10.00/$7.00
Masterworks	61684	Barry Lyndon	LP/LB	U.S.		$18.00/$15.00
Varese Sarabande	VSD-5202	Bat-21	LP/LB	U.S.		$14.00/$9.00
Atlantic	82759-2	Batman Forever	LTD/LP	U.S.	1995	$16.00
CD with limited edition card.						
RCA	3573-2-R	Batman Theme: Neal Hefti	LP	U.S.	1989	$20.00
MCA	MCAD-6225	Batteries Not Included	LP/LB	U.S.		$14.00/$9.00
Southern X	SCCD-5005	Battle of Neretva	LP/LB	U.S.		$14.00/$9.00
Intrada	7019	Beastmaster 2	LP/BP	U.S.		$14.00/$9.00
Atlantic	80154-2	Beat Street	LP/LB	U.S.†	1985	$14.00/$8.00
Disney	PCCD-1009	Beauty and the Beast	LTD/LP	Japan	1994	$60.00
Picture Disc CD with plastic figures housed in box.						
Disney		Beauty and the Beast	LP/LB	U.S.	1990	$14.00/$8.00
First pressing with incorrect track listing.						
Walt Disney	1514	Beauty and the Beast	LTD/LP	U.S.	1992	$80.00
VHS Video, CD soundtrack and book in box.						
Walt Disney	60861-7	Beauty and the Beast: The Broadway Musical	LTD/LP	U.S.	1994	$25.00
Limited picture disc edition made exclusively for Musicland stores. Limited to 50,000 copies.						
Capitol	CDP 99896-2	Bebe's Kids	LP/LB	U.S.		$14.00/$9.00
Varese Sarabande	5479	Being Human	LP/LB	U.S.		$18.00/$15.00
Silva Scrn	43	Ben Hur	LP	U.S.		$15.00
MCA	55XD-512/3	Benny Goodman Story	LP	Japan		$30.00
EMI	0777-7-98560-2	Best of James Bond 30th	LTD/LP	U.S.	1992	$30.00/$25.00
2 CD set.						
Edel	5401	Best of the Best 2	LP/LB	U.S.		$18.00/$15.00
		Best Soundtracks in Show Business	DJ/Smplr	U.S.		$10.00
RCA	68313-2	Beverly Hillbillies	LP/LB	U.S.		$14.00/$14.00
MCA	MCAD-5553	Beverly Hills Cop	LP/LB	U.S.†	1985	$14.00/$8.00
MCA	MCAD-6207	Beverly Hills Cop 2	LP/LB	U.S.		$15.00/$12.00
Capitol	CDP-92055	Beyond the Fringe	LP/LB	U.S.		$15.00/$12.00
Motown	6062-MD	Big Chill, The	LP/LB	U.S.†	1985	$14.00/$8.00
Realistic	51-5003	Big Screen Sound	DJ/Smplr	U.S.†	1984	$20.00
Enigma	D21S-73227	Big Trouble in Little Trouble	LP/LB	U.S.		$18.00/$15.00
Interscope	PRCD 3914-2	Bill & Ted's Bogus Journey	DJ/Smplr	U.S.	1991	$15.00
Atlantic	91292-2	Black Rain	LP/LB	U.S.		$18.00/$15.00
Varese Serabande	VSD-5349	Black Rose	LP/LB	U.S.		$15.00/$13.00
Off World Music	OFW-9301	Blade Runner	LTD/LP			N/A
Rhino	RNCD-70705	Blind Date	LP/LB	U.S.		$15.00/$13.00
Legacy	LLMCD-3007	Blood Brothers	LP	U.K.		$18.00
Columbia	CD-70285	Blow-Up	LP	Germany		$18.00
Silvia	SCCD-1018	Blue Lagoon	LP	U.K.		$20.00
Varese Serabande	VSD-5448	Body Bags	LP/LB	U.S.		$15.00/$13.00
Fifth Continent		Body Heat	LP/LB	U.S.	1989	$45.00/$30.00
RCA	66141-2	Body Of Evidence	LP/LB	U.S.		$18.00/$15.00
Varese Sarabande	VSD-5337	Body Parts	LP/LB	U.S.		$18.00/$15.00
Arista	169292	Bodyguard, The	LTD/LP	U.S.	1993	$22.00
Picture CD in box.						
		Bonfires of the Vanities	LP	U.S.		$15.00
		Book of Love	LP	U.S.		$15.00
Warner	24535-2	Bopha!	LP	U.S.		$18.00/$15.00
Varese Sarabande	SRS 2001	Boys From Brazil, The	LTD/LP	U.S.		$20.00
A&M	CD-5045	Breakfast Club, The	LP/LB	U.S.†	1985	$14.00/$8.00
Mercury	821919-2	Breakin'	LP/LB	U.S.†	1985	$14.00/$8.00
Polygram	813696-2	Breakin' 2: Electric Boogaloo	LP/LB	U.S.†	1985	$14.00/$8.00
Mobile Fidelity	790	Brideshead Revisited	LP/LB	U.S.		$18.00/$15.00
Malpaso	9 45949-2	Bridges of Madison County	DJ/LP	U.S.	1995	$20.00
CD in digipak						
Warner Brothers		Bridges of Madison County Sampler	DJ/Smplr	U.S.	1995	$5.00
Warner Brothersq	256888-2	Bright Lights Big City	LP/LB	U.S.		$18.00/$15.00
		Browning Version, The	LP	U.S.		$15.00
Warner Brothers	9 26494-2-Dj	Bugs Bunny on Broadway	DJ/LP	U.S.	1990	$25.00
Picturedisc CD.						
Capitol	90586	Bull Durham	LP/LB	U.S.		$15.00/$12.00
Varese Sarabande	9201.10	Burbs, The	LTD/LP	U.S.	1992	$20.00
Limited to 2500 copies.						
Philips	310690145-2	Burn Cycle	LTD/LP	U.S.	1995	$45.00
CD+I limited edition with bonus soundtrack CD.						
Columbia	CK-44317	Caddyshack 2	LP/LB	U.S.		$15.00/$12.00
Columbia	CK 57317	Calender Girl	LP/LB	U.S.		$17.00/$15.00
CBS	CK-32602	Camelot	LP/LB	U.S.†	1985	$14.00/$8.00
Capitol	91248	Can-Can	LP/LB	U.S.		$15.00/$12.00
Facet	FCD-8103	Captain From Castle	LP/LB	U.S.		$14.00/$12.00
Preamble	PRCD-1778	Cardinal	LP/LB	U.S.		$15.00/$13.00
Warner Bros	9 26027-2	Carl Stalling Project	LP/LB	U.S.	1990	$50.00/$50.00
Picture disc version randomly distributed in long box						
Polygram	817247-2	Carmen	LP/LB	U.S.†	1985	$14.00/$8.00
RCA	1681	Carmen Jones	LP/LB	U.S.		$13.00/$10.00
Capitol	CDP-746635-2	Carousel	LP/LB	U.S.		$15.00/$12.00
		Casablanca	LP	U.S.		$15.00
MCA	MCAD-1498	Cat People	LP	U.S.		$20.00
EMI	746192-8	Cats	LP	Germany		$20.00
Polydor	575 427-2	Cats	SCD5	Germany	1996	$30.00
Shaped CD single from German performance.						
Geffen	0312-2	Cats (Complete, Broadway)	LP/LB	U.S.		$25.00/$17.00
2 CD set.						
Geffen	2026-2	Cats (Highlights, Broadway)	LP/LB	U.S.		$13.00/$8.00
Geffen	2017-2	Cats (London, Complete)	LP/LB	U.S.		$25.00/$17.00
2 CD set.						
Geffen	2017-2	Cats (Original, Complete)	LP/LB	U.S.		$25.00/$17.00
2 CD set.						
RCA	2755-2	Charade	LP/LB	U.S.		$15.00/$13.00
Polygram	800020-2	Chariots of Fire	LP/LB	U.S.†	1985	$14.00/$8.00
Varese Sarabande	VCL 8903.1	Cherry 2000	LTD/LP	U.S.	1989	$20.00
RCA	PCD2-5340	Chess: The Musical on Record	LP/LB	U.S.†	1985	$14.00/$8.00
Warner Bros	26529-2	China Cry	LP/LB	U.S.		$16.00/$15.00
Polygram	826306-2	Chorus Line the Movie	LP	Germany		$20.00
London	417848-2	Cinema Classics	LP/LB	U.S.		$13.00/$10.00
Elektra	PRCD 8260-2	Civil War–Sampler	DJ/Smplr	U.S.		$10.00
Varese Sarebande	VSD-5303	Class Action	LP/LB	U.S.		$18.00/$15.00
Warner	2-2573	Clockwork Orange	LP/LB	U.S.†	1985	$14.00/$8.00
	DPRO79654	Clueless Sampler	DJ/Smplr	U.S.		$6.00
MCA	MCA5P-3060	Coach Theme	CDJ	U.S.	1995	$7.00
Polygram	827041-2	Cocoon	LP/LB	U.S.†	1985	$14.00/$8.00
Varese Sarebande	VSD-5211	Cocoon 2 – The Return	LP/LB	U.S.		$18.00/$15.00
Varese Sarebande	VSD-5231	Cold Feet	LP/LB	U.S.		$18.00/$15.00
Varese Sarebande	VSD-5306	Come See the Paradise	LP/LB	U.S.		$18.00/$15.00
Atco	90958-2	Coming to America	LP/LB	U.S.		$18.00/$15.00
CBS	CK-03550	Company	LP/LB	U.S.†	1985	$14.00/$8.00
Milan	35630-2	Consenting Adults	LP/LB	U.S.		$17.00/$15.00
Geffen	GEFD-2462	Cotton Club	LP/LB	U.S.		$18.00/$15.00
Windham	WD-1039	Country	LP/LB	U.S.†	1985	$14.00/$8.00
20th Century Fox		Courage Under Fire: International Multimedia Press Kit	DJ/Smplr	U.S.	1990	$20.00
CD-ROM press kit.						
Virgin	2517	Courier	LP	U.K.	1988	$25.00
Atlantic	90954-2	Courier	LP/LB	U.S.		$18.00/$15.00
Varese Sarebande	VSD-5210	Criminal Law	LP/LB	U.S.		$18.00/$15.00
Varese Sarebande	VSD-5201	Crossing Delancy	LP/LB	U.S.		$18.00/$15.00
Varese Sarebande	VSD-5326	Crossing the Line	LP/LB	U.S.		$18.00/$15.00
Hollywood	PRCD 62047-2 DGO1	Crow, The: City of Angels	DJ/LP	U.S.	1996	$27.00
Hollywood	MH620742 DGO1	Crow, The: City of Angels	LTD/LP	U.S.	1996	$27.00
2 CD set in digipack and cardboard sleeve.						
DRG	12602	Cyrano De Bergerac	LP/LB	U.S.		$18.00/$15.00
Varese Sarebande	VCD-70461	D.O.A.	LP/LB	U.S.		$18.00/$15.00
MCA	MCAD-6359	Dad	LP/LB	U.S.		$18.00/$15.00
Columbia	MK-42565	Dancers	LP/LB	U.S.		$18.00/$15.00
Epic	ESK 2248	Dances With Wolves Sampler	DJ/Smplr	U.S.	1990	$8.00
Geffen		Days of Thunder	LP/LB	U.S.	1989	$15.00/$12.00
CBS		Dead Man Walking	CD5	Germany	1996	$12.00
Columbia		Dead Man Walking	LP/LB	U.S.	1996	$15.00
RCA	7722-2	Deceivers	LP/LB	U.S.		$18.00/$15.00
Capitol	CDP 90205	Decline of Western Civilization Part II: The Metal Years	LP/LB	U.S.	1988	$18.00/$14.00
CBS	75330	Deep Cover	LP/LB	U.S.		$12.00/$7.00
		Defending Your Life With Every Breath	LP	U.S.		$15.00
Varese Sarebande	VSD-5447	Demolition Man (Score)	LP/LB	U.S.		$18.00/$15.00

Label	Catalog Number	Title	Type	Country	Year	Longbox Value / Value
Giant	25415-2	Dennis the Mennice (Score)	LP	U.S.		$15.00
		Desperado	DJ/Smplr	U.S.		$7.00
Varese Sarebande	VSD-5284	Desperate Hours	LP/LB	U.S.		$18.00/$15.00
Warner Brothers		Dick Tracy	DJ/LP	U.S.	1989	$5.00
Angel	7243 5 55567 2 1	Dig	LTD/LP	U.S.	1996	$18.00
	2 CD set.					
Walt Disney	60848-2	Dinosaurs: Big Songs	LP	U.S.	1992	$25.00
		Dirty Dancing Live–Sampler	DJ/Smplr	U.S.	1989	$5.00
Walt Disney Records	60810	Disney Afternoon	LP	U.S.	1990	$16.00
Walt Disney	PCCW-00031	Disney Classic Story: 101 Dalmations	LTD/LP	U.S.	1991	$32.00
Walt Disney	PCCW-00026	Disney Classic Story: Alice In Wonderland	LTD/LP	Japan	1991	$32.00
Walt Disney	PCCW-00032	Disney Classic Story: Bambi	LTD/LP	Japan	1991	$32.00
Walt Disney	PCCW-00027	Disney Classic Story: Cinderella	LTD/LP	Japan	1991	$32.00
Walt Disney	PCCW-00023	Disney Classic Story: Dumbo	LTD/LP	Japan	1991	$32.00
Walt Disney	PCCW-00029	Disney Classic Story: Lady and the Tramp	LTD/LP	Japan	1991	$32.00
Walt Disney	PCCW-00030	Disney Classic Story: Peter Pan	LTD/LP	Japan	1991	$32.00
Walt Disney	PCCW-00033	Disney Classic Story: Pinocchio	LTD/LP	Japan	1991	$32.00
Walt Disney	PCCW-00028	Disney Classic Story: Sleeping Beauty	LTD/LP	Japan	1991	$32.00
Walt Disney	PCCW-00025	Disney Classic Story: Snow White	LTD/LP	Japan	1991	$32.00
Walt Disney	PCCW-00022	Disney Classic Story: Three Little Pigs	LTD/LP	Japan	1991	$32.00
Walt Disney	PCCW-00024	Disney Classic Story: Winnie the Pooh	LTD/LP	Japan	1991	$32.00
Walt Disney	PCCD-00135	Disney: My First Disney CD	LTD/LP	Japan	1995	$50.00
	CD in large Mickey Mouse shaped case.					
Tin Pan	823274-2	Disorderlies	LP/LB	U.S.		$18.00/$15.00
RCA/Milan	CD-061	Diva	LP/LB	U.S.†	1985	$14.00/$8.00
Metro	CDX MMI-4	Doctor Who–Variations On A Theme	SCD5	U.K.	1990	$95.00
	World's first shaped CD: square shaped.					
		Double Vie	LP	U.S.		$15.00
Capitol	C21-90968	Down By Law	LP/LB	U.S.		$18.00/$15.00
Intrada	7043	Dr. Giggles	LP/LB	U.S.		$25.00/$20.00
Geffen	2007-2	Dreamgirls	LP/LB	U.S.†	1985	$14.00/$8.00
Novus	3077-2	Drugstore Cowboy	LP/LB	U.S.		$15.00/$12.00

Dumb And Dumber Radio Special – (BMG RJC 66572-2) Radio interview disc.

Label	Catalog Number	Title	Type	Country	Year	Longbox Value / Value
BMG	RJC 66572-2	Dumb and Dumber Radio Special	DJ/Smplr	U.S.	1995	$15.00
Collector's Pipeline	TCP 013CD	Dune	LP	U.S.		$20.00
Polygram	823770-2	Dune	LP/LB	U.S.†	1985	$20.00/$20.00
MCA	MCAD-37264	E.T. The Extra-Terrestrial	LP/LB	U.S.†	1985	$14.00/$8.00
Scotti	ZK-38929	Eddie & The Cruisers	LP/LB	U.S.†	1985	$14.00/$8.00
Scotti Brothers	75238	Eddie & The Cruisers Live In	LP/LB	U.S.		$12.00/$8.00
Varese Sarebande	VSD-5258	Egyptian	LP/LB	U.S.		$18.00/$15.00
Varese Sarebande	VSD-5277	Eiger Sanction	LP/LB	U.S.		$18.00/$15.00
		Eight Seconds Soundtrack (Country Edge)	RS	U.S.	1995	$20.00
	Airdate: 1/15/94.					
Varese Sarebande	VSD-5253	Enemies-A Love Story	LP/LB	U.S.		$18.00/$15.00
Varese Sarebande	VCD-47249	Enemy Mine	LP/LB	U.S.		$18.00/$15.00
Varase	VCD-47224	Escape From New York	LP/LB	U.S.†	1985	$14.00/$8.00
MCA	MCAD2-11007	Evita	LP/LB	U.S.†	1985	$20.00/$18.00
	2 CD set.					
Milan	35650-2	Extreme Justice	LP/LB	U.S.		$18.00/$15.00
Varese Sarabande	VCL 9101.9	Eye of the Needle/Last Embrace	LTD/LP	U.S.	1991	$20.00
	Limited to 1000 copies.					
Point	269821	Fabulous Film Themes	LP/LB	U.S.		$12.00/$8.00
Mercury	512004-2	Falling From Grace	LP	U.S.		$15.00
RSO	80034-2	Fame	LP/LB	U.S.†	1985	$14.00/$8.00
Disney	CD-001	Fantasia	LP/LB	U.S.		$25.00/$18.00
	2 CD set					
Walt Disney		Fantasia	LTD/LP	U.S.	1991	$40.00
	VHS Video, CD soundtrack and lithograph in box.					
Pioneer	PR-CD1	Fantasia, Selections From…	DJ/Smplr	U.S.	1990	$50.00
Walt Disney		Fantasmic	LP	U.S.	1994	$18.00
Polygram	821943-2	Fantasticks	LP/LB	U.S.†	1985	$14.00/$8.00
		Faraway, So Close	CD5	U.K.	1994	$10.00
Atlantic	81809-2	Fatal Beauty	LP/LB	U.S.		$13.00/$10.00
Margaritaville	524 309	Fear and Loathing in Las Vegas	LTD/LP	U.S.	1996	$16.00
	Multi-Image cover.					
Silva Scrn	4004	Fellini/Rota	LP/LB	U.S.		$13.00/$10.00
Capital	CDP-46091	Fiddler on the Roof	LP/LB	U.S.†	1985	$14.00/$8.00
Varese Sarebande	VSD-5292	Field	LP/LB	U.S.		$18.00/$15.00
Silva Scrn	FILMCD-17	Fifty Years of Classic Horror Films	LP/LB	U.S.		$13.00/$10.00
Varese Sarebande	VSD-47236	Films of John Wayne	LP/LB	U.S.		$18.00/$15.00
Varese Sarebande	VSD-47264	Films of John Wayne 2	LP/LB	U.S.		$18.00/$15.00
Varese Sarebande	VCD-47354	Five Corners	LP/LB	U.S.		$18.00/$15.00
Casablanca	811492-2	Flashdance	LP/LB	U.S.†	1985	$14.00/$8.00
Varese Sarabande	BCL 6002	Flesh & Blood	LTD/LP	U.S.	1992	$20.00
	Limited to 1500 copies.					
Varese Sarebande	VSD-5460	Flesh & Bone	LP/LB	U.S.		$18.00/$15.00
Varese Sarebande	VCD-47267	Fog, The	LP/LB	U.S.		$18.00/$15.00
RCA	RCD2-7128	Follies	LP/LB	U.S.†	1985	$14.00/$8.00
CBS	CK-39242	Footloose	LP/LB	U.S.†	1985	$14.00/$8.00
		Four Weddings and a Funeral	DJ/LP	U.S.	1994	$30.00
	CD and VHS video in box.					
Epic	EK 53194	Frankie's House	LP/LB	U.S.		$19.00/$16.00
Elektra	60782-2	Frantic	LP/LB	U.S.		$18.00/$15.00
Warner Brothers	26726	Freddy's Dead	LP/LB	U.S.		$12.00/$8.00
EMI	791110-2	From Russia With Love	LP	Germany		$20.00
CBS	CK-03220	Funny Girl	LP/LB	U.S.†	1985	$14.00/$8.00
Sandy Hook	2009	Gang's All Here	LP/LB	U.S.		$18.00/$15.00

Label	Catalog Number	Title	Type	Country	Year	Longbox Value / Value
Mute	61029-2	Garden	LP/LB	U.S.		$18.00/$15.00
MGM/UA		Gettysburg	LTD/LP	U.S.	1995	$90.00
	CD and VHS in box with book, map and simulated civil war bullet.					
Milan	MLDJ-003-2	Gettysburg: Highlights From More Songs And Music	DJ/Smplr	U.S.	1994	$8.00
Varese Sarebande	VSD-5259	Ghost Story	LP/LB	U.S.		$18.00/$15.00
MCA	MCAD—6306	Ghostbuster 2	LP/LB	U.S.		$18.00/$15.00
Arista	ARCD-8246	Ghostbusters	LP/LB	U.S.†	1985	$14.00/$8.00
Polydor		Girl on a Motorcycle	DJ/LP	U.S.	1994	$10.00
Mercury	824510-2	Girls Just Want to Have Fun	LP/LB	U.S.†	1985	$14.00/$8.00
Varese Sarebande	VSD-5470	Golden Gate	LP/LB	U.S.		$18.00/$15.00
EMI	791111-2	Goldfinger	LP	Germany		$20.00
RCA	9676-2	Gone With the Wind	LP/LB	U.S.		$18.00/$15.00
MCA	MCAD-39063	Gone With the Wind	LP/LB	U.S.	1986	$15.00/$9.00
Arista	11013-2	Good Son, The	LP	U.S.		$12.00
Disney		Goofy Movie	LP	U.S.	1994	$15.00
Epic	EK-40067	Goonies	LP/LB	U.S.		$14.00/$8.00
Epic	EK-40067	Goonies, The	LP/LB	U.S.†	1985	$14.00/$8.00
Auvidis	A-6128	Gospel Caravan	LP	U.S.		$8.00
		Grace of My Heart	DJ/Smplr	U.S.	1996	$12.00
		Grace of My Heart	LP	U.S.	1996	$50.00
	Rare first pressing with Joni Mitchell track.					
RCA	61115-2	Grand Canyon	LP/LB	U.S.		$18.00/$15.00
Polydor		Grease: Megamix	DJ/Smplr	U.S.	1996	$12.00
London	PPC-820040-2	Great Film Themes	LP/LB	U.S.†	1985	$14.00/$8.00
Varese Sarebande	VSD-5336	Greatest Films of John Carpenter 2	LP/LB	U.S.		$18.00/$15.00
Varese Sarebande	VSD-5290	Grifters	LP/LB	U.S.		$18.00/$15.00
Disney	CD-0017	Gumby	LP/LB	U.S.	1989	$20.00/$17.00
Tristar	80950	Guns of Navarone	LP/LB	U.S.		$18.00/$15.00
MCA	MCAD-6228	Hairspray	LP/LB	U.S.	1988	$22.00/$20.00
Virgin	86206	Hamlet	LP/LB	U.S.		$18.00/$15.00
DRG	6110	Handful of Dust	LP/LB	U.S.		$18.00/$15.00
Luke	91663-2	Hangin' With the Homeboys	LP/LB	U.S.		$12.00/$8.00
MCA	MCAD-6190	Hannah and Her Sisters	LP/LB	U.S.		$18.00/$15.00
RCA	PCD1-4935	Hard to Hold	LP/LB	U.S.†	1985	$14.00/$8.00
Varese Sarebande	VSD-5315	Hard Way	LP/LB	U.S.		$18.00/$15.00
Polygram	510323-2	Harley Davidson & the Marlboro Man	LP/BP	U.S.		$16.00/$15.00
Columbia	CK-40670	Hearts of Fire	LP/LB	U.S.		$18.00/$15.00
Capitol	80328	Heights	LP/LB	U.S.		$18.00/$15.00
RCA	1030-2	Helen Morgan Story	LP/LB	U.S.		$12.00/$8.00
Cenidisc	CDC-1001	Hellraiser	LP/LB	U.S.		$15.00/$12.00
		Hellraiser III	DJ/Smplr	U.S.	1992	$5.00
Label "X"	LXCD-1	Hemingway's Adventure of a Young Man	LP/LB	U.S.†	1985	$14.00/$8.00
Cenidisc	CDJ-1007	Hero & the Terror	LP/LB	U.S.		$15.00/$12.00
Varese Sarebande	VCD-47349	Hidden	LP/LB	U.S.		$18.00/$15.00
		Higher Learning	DJ/Smplr	U.K.	1995	$20.00
Pro Art	524	Hitchcock – Master of Mayhem	LP/LB	U.S.		$18.00/$15.00
Arista	ARCD-11001	Hoffa	LP/LB	U.S.		$18.00/$15.00
Virgin	91241-2	Homeboy	LP/LB	U.S.		$18.00/$15.00
Intrada	7030	Honey I Blew Up the Kids	LP/LB	U.S.		$18.00/$15.00
K-Tel	1663	Hooked on Themes	LP/LB	U.S.		$18.00/$15.00
Varese Sarebande	VSD-5336	Hot Shots	LP/LB	U.S.		$18.00/$15.00
Virgin	39219	House of Spirits	LP/LB	U.S.		$18.00/$15.00
Silver Wave	801	How the West Was Lost	LP	U.S.	1993	$10.00
Walt Disney Records	60893-2	Hunchback of Notre Dame	LP	U.S.	1996	$18.00
	Limited Edition Picture Disc					
Walt Disney Records	60893-7	Hunchback of Notre Dame	LTD/LP	U.S.	1996	$15.00
	CD soundtrack and cassette sampler on blister card.					
Walt Disney Records	60894-2	Hunchback of Notre Dame Sing Along	LP	U.S.	1996	$10.00
	CD with book					
CBS/Fox	LUCY001	I Love Lucy/The Honeymooners	DJ/LP	U.S.	1990	$100.00
	Picture disc.					
Polygram	827336-2	I Remember Mama	LP/LB	U.S.†	1985	$14.00/$8.00
Varese Sarebande	VSD-5474	I'll Do Anything	LP/LB	U.S.		$18.00/$15.00
capitol	55097	In Custody	LP/LB	U.S.		$18.00/$15.00
Columbia	CK-57307	In the Line of Fire	LP/LB	U.S.		$18.00/$15.00
Island	PRCD 6822-2	In the Name of the Father	DJ/Smplr	U.S.	1993	$15.00
Capitol	C2-96830-2	Indian Runner	LP/LB	U.S.		$18.00/$15.00
Capitol	C2-96830-2	Indian Runner	LP/LB	U.S.		$18.00/$15.00
Polygram	821592-2	Indiana Jones	LP/LB	U.S.†	1985	$14.00/$8.00
Walt Disney Records	CD-015	Indiana Jones And the Last Crusade: Story of	LP	U.S.	1989	$25.00
Milan	35613-2	Inner Circle	LP/LB	U.S.		$13.00/$10.00
		Inner City Blues	DJ/Smplr	U.S.	1996	$30.00
	CD and VHS video in box.					
Milan	35663-2	Intersection	LP/LB	U.S.		$13.00/$10.00
Epic	EK-45006	Iron Eagle II	LP/LB	U.S.		$13.00/$10.00
Tristar	80951	Is Paris Burning	LP/LB	U.S.		$13.00/$10.00
Varese Sarabande	BCL 6001	Jagged Edge	LTD/LP	U.S.	1992	$20.00
	Limited to 1500 copies.					
Capitol	46079	James Bond: Thirteen Original 007 Themes	LP/LB	U.S.		$18.00/$15.00
Columbia	MK-42307	Jarre By Jarre	LP/LB	U.S.		$13.00/$10.00
Edel	5405	Jason Goes to Hell	LP/LB	U.S.		$18.00/$15.00
TVT	3004	Jeanne la Pucelle	LP/LB	U.S.		$18.00/$15.00
RCA	60422-2-RCDJ	Jekyll & Hyde, Selections From	DJ/Smplr	U.S.	1991	$5.00
RCA	66120	Jennifer 8	LP/LB	U.S.		$18.00/$15.00
Atlantic	PRCD 5980	Jerky Boys Soundtrack Sampler	DJ/Smplr	U.S.	1995	$6.00
Polygram	820207-2	Jerry's Girls	LP/LB	U.S.†	1985	$14.00/$8.00
		JFK	LP	U.S.		$15.00
Atlantic	81837-2	Johnny B Goode	LP/LB	U.S.		$18.00/$15.00
Varese Sarebande	VSD-5377	Johnny Guitar	LP/LB	U.S.		$18.00/$15.00
CBS	CK-32550	Jonathan Livingston Seagull	LP/LB	U.S.†	1985	$14.00/$8.00
	XPCD677	Judge Dredd	DJ/Smplr	U.K.	1995	$20.00
Mercury	830545-2	Jumpin' Jack Flash	LP/LB	U.S.		$18.00/$15.00
Walt Disney Pictures		Jungle 2 Jungle: Multimedia CD-ROM Press Kit	LP	U.S.	1997	$40.00
	CD-ROM press kit.					
Virgin	V2-86273-2	Kafka	LP/LB	U.S.		$18.00/$15.00
Preamble	PRCD-1777	Kentuckian	LP/LB	U.S.		$13.00/$10.00
RCA	RCD1-2160	King & I, The	LP/LB	U.S.†	1985	$14.00/$8.00
South Cross	901	King Kong	LP/LB	U.S.†	1985	$14.00/$8.00
Sony	52424	King of Kings	LP/LB	U.S.		$13.00/$10.00
Varese	VSD-5425	King of the Hill	LP/LB	U.S.		$18.00/$15.00
Varase	VCD-47203	King's Row	LP/LB	U.S.†	1985	$14.00/$8.00
Columbia	CK-46196	Kiss Me Kate	LP/LB	U.S.		$18.00/$15.00
Milan	35632-2	Knight Moves	LP/LB	U.S.		$18.00/$15.00
Columbia	MK-35873	Kramer vs. Kramer	LP/LB	U.S.		$18.00/$15.00
Warner	25295-2	Krush Groove	LP/LB	U.S.†	1985	$14.00/$8.00
RCA	RCD1-4824	La Cage aux Folles	LP/LB	U.S.†	1985	$14.00/$8.00
Varese	VSD-5387	Last Butterfly	LP/LB	U.S.		$18.00/$15.00
Silva Scrn	FILMCD-36	Lawrence of Arabia	LP/LB	U.S.		$18.00/$15.00
MCA	2582	Leap of Faith	DJ/Smplr	U.S.	1992	$8.00
		Leaving Las Vegas	DJ/Smplr	U.S.	1995	$8.00
Varese	VSD-5495	Leprechaun 2	LP/LB	U.S.		$18.00/$15.00
RCA	PD-70033	Les Unes Les Autres	LP/LB	U.S.		$12.00/$8.00
Columbia	CK 44042	Less Than Zero	LP	U.S.	1989	$15.00/$11.00
Virgin	86272-2	Let Him Have It	LP	U.S.		$15.00
Hollywood	61523-2	Life With Mikey	LP	U.S.		$15.00

Label	Catalog Number	Title	Type	Country	Year	Longbox Value / Value
Varese	VSD-5320	Lifeforce	LP/LB	U.S.		$20.00/$18.00
Arista	ASCD-8670	Lily Was Here	LP/LB	U.S.	1989	$17.00/$15.00
Walt Disney	PCCD-00117	Lion King	LTD/LP	Japan	1994	$65.00
	Picture disc CD in box with figurines.					
Walt Disney	608682-2	Lion King: Rhythm of the Pride Lands	LP	U.S.	1995	$30.00/$28.00
	CD-ROM. Limited to 3,500 copies					
Walt Disney	60871-2	Lion King: Rhythm of the Pride Lands	LP	U.S.	1995	$30.00/$28.00
	CD-ROM. Limited to10,000 copies					
Walt Disney	60858-2	Lion King, The	LTD/LP	U.S.	1994	$55.00
	Picture disc version.					
Varese Sarabande	VCD-47282	Lionheart 1	LP/LB	U.S.		$18.00/$15.00
Varese Sarabande	VCD-47288	Lionheart 2	LP/LB	U.S.		$18.00/$15.00
Walt Disney Records	60841-2	Little Mermaid, The	LP/BP	U.S.	1989	$20.00/$18.00
RCA	RCD1-5090	Little Night Music, A	LP/LB	U.S.†	1985	$14.00/$8.00
Mercury	44639	Little Odessa	LP	U.S.		$15.00
EMI	790629-2	Live and Let Die	LP	Germany		$20.00
Silva Scrn	FILMCD-20	Long Good Friday	LP/LB	U.S.		$18.00/$15.00
Varese	VSD-5304	Long Walk Home	LP/LB	U.S.		$18.00/$15.00
		Lost Horizon	LP	U.S.		$15.00
Milan	35661	Love In the Cinema	LP/LB	U.S.		$18.00/$15.00
Varese Sarabande	VSD-5372	Luingini Incident	LP/LB	U.S.		$18.00/$15.00
Varese Sarabande	VSD-5405	Lust For Life	LP/LB	U.S.		$18.00/$15.00
Varese Sarabande	VCD-47262	Mad Max 2: Road Warrior	LP/LB	U.S.		$25.00/$25.00
Varese Sarabande	VSD-5204	Madame Sousatzka	LP/LB	U.S.		$18.00/$15.00
		Madela	DJ/LP	U.S.	1996	$15.00
Curb	77275-2	Major League	LP/LB	U.S.		$18.00/$15.00
Warner Bros	45157-2	Malcom X	LP/LB	U.S.		$25.00/$10.00
	Longbox version.					
Warner Brothers	PRO-CD-5943	Malcom X	DJ/Smplr	U.S.	1993	$15.00
Varase	VCD-47217	Man From Snowy River, The	LP/LB	U.S.†	1985	$14.00/$8.00
Silva Scrn	712	Man From U.N.C.L.E. and Other Cult Classics	LP/LB	U.S.		$18.00/$15.00
Varese	VSD-5369	Man Trouble	LP/LB	U.S.		$18.00/$15.00
EMI	790619-2	Man With the Golden Gun	LP	Germany		$20.00
Delicious	92196-2	Marked For Death	LP/LB	U.S.		$18.00/$15.00
RCA	6618-2	Maurice	LP/LB	U.S.		$12.00/$10.00
MGM/UA		Meet Me in St. Louis	LTD/LP	U.S.	1995	$30.00
	CD and VHS video in box.					
Varese	VSD-5355	Memoirs of the Invisible Man	LP/LB	U.S.		$18.00/$15.00
RCA	6658-2	Merchant Ivory: 25th Anniversary	LP/LB	U.S.		$12.00/$10.00
Motown	6364-2	Meteor Man	LP	U.S.		$15.00
CBS	CK-39526	Metropolis	LP/LB	U.S.†	1985	$14.00/$8.00
Casablanca	824206-2	Midnight Express	LP/LB	U.S.†	1985	$14.00/$8.00
Saban		Mighty Morphin Power Rangers: Excerpts From the White Album	DJ/Smplr	U.S.	1995	$10.00

Mighty Morphin Power Rangers TV Theme & Soundbites – (Atlantic PRCD 6019)

Label	Catalog Number	Title	Type	Country	Year	Longbox Value / Value
Atlantic	PRCD 6019	Mighty Morphin Power Rangers TV Theme & Soundbites	DJ/Smplr	U.S.	1994	$20.00
		Miss Saigon – Selections From	DJ/Smplr	U.S.	1988	$5.00
Island		Mission Impossible: Theme From	CD5	U.K.	1996	$10.00
Island		Mission Impossible: Theme From	CDJ	U.K.	1996	$15.00
Island		Mission Impossible: Theme From	CD5	U.S.	1996	$5.00
	CD in card sleeve.					
Island		Mission Impossible: Theme From	CD5	U.S.	1996	$6.00
	CD in jewel box.					
Island	PRCD 7180-2	Mission Impossible: Theme From	CDJ	U.S.	1996	$12.00
Island	PRCD 7180-2	Mission Impossible: Theme From	CDJ	U.S.	1996	$125.00
	CDJ in plastic brief case with t-shirt and camera.					
Island	842598-2	Mississippi Burning	LP/LB	U.S.		$18.00/$15.00
Varese	VSD-5334	Mobsters	LP/LB	U.S.		$18.00/$15.00
Varese	5334	Mobsters	LP/LB	U.S.	1991	$14.00/$8.00
Spelling Films		Moll Flanders: Multimedia Press Kit	DJ/Smplr	U.S.	1996	$15.00
	CD-ROM press kit.					
MCA	MCAD-6214	Moonlighting	LP/LB	U.S.	1987	$15.00/$8.00
EMI	790620-2	Moonraker	LP	Germany		$20.00
TVT	6110	Mortal Kombat	DJ/LP	U.S.	1995	$25.00
	CD in box with poster and magazine.					
Polygram	843013-2	Mountains of the Moon	LP/BP	U.S.		$15.00/$15.00
Varese	VSD-5299	Mr. Destiny	LP/LB	U.S.		$18.00/$15.00
Novus	3100	Mr. & Mrs. Bridge	LP/LB	U.S.	1990	$17.00/$15.00
Giant	24479-2	Mr. Saturday Night	LP/LB	U.S.		$15.00/$13.00
Zoom	30017-2	Muppet Christmas Carol	LP/LB	U.S.		$18.00/$15.00
BMG KIDZ	ZMDJ 38017-2	Muppets – It Feels Like Christmas	CDJ	U.S.	1992	$3.00
Varese	VSD-5248	Music Box	LP/LB	U.S.		$13.00/$10.00
Disney	03MSO8900	Musical Clasics	DJ/Smplr	U.S.	1994	$15.00
Walt Disney	03MSO8900	Musical Classics Sampler	DJ/Smplr	U.S.	1994	$25.00
CBS	CK-2015d	My Fair Lady	LP/LB	U.S.†	1985	$14.00/$8.00
CBS	66128	My Fair Lady	LTD/LP	U.S.	1994	$25.00
	Gold disc CD.					
DRG	12604	My Father's Glory	LP/LB	U.S.		$13.00/$10.00
Varese	VSD-5244	My Left Foot	LP/LB	U.S.		$18.00/$15.00
Polygram	837798-2	My Stepmother is an Alien	LP/LB	U.S.		$18.00/$15.00
Best Buy		Myst Gift Pack	LTD/LP	U.S.	1996	$25.00
	CD soundtrack, calender, CD-ROM hint book, novel, mouse pad and T-shirt.					
	PRCD 5899-2	Natural Born Killers Sampler	DJ/Smplr	U.S.	1995	$5.00
Varese	VSD-5438	Needful Things	LP/LB	U.S.		$18.00/$15.00
		New Age	LP	U.S.		$15.00
Capital	CDP-46090	New York, New York	LP/LB	U.S.†	1985	$14.00/$8.00
Intrada	6004	Night Crossing	LP/LB	U.S.		$18.00/$15.00
Varese Sarabande	VSD-5363	Nightmare Cafe	LP/LB	U.S.		$18.00/$15.00

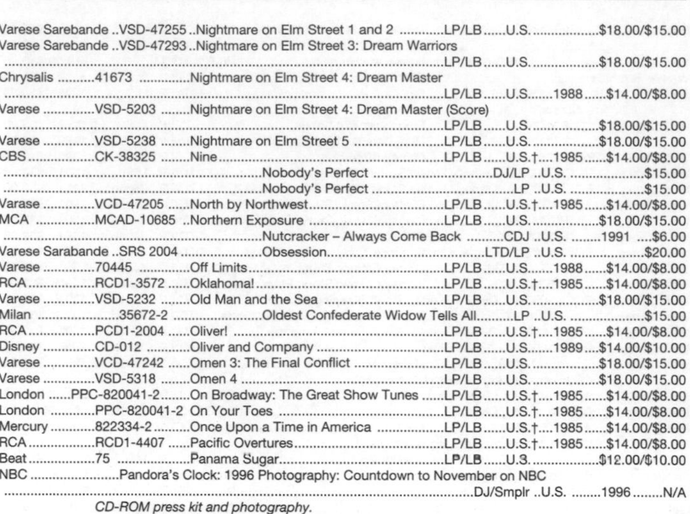

Label	Catalog Number	Title	Type	Country	Year	Longbox Value / Value
Varese Sarabande	VSD-47255	Nightmare on Elm Street 1 and 2	LP/LB	U.S.		$18.00/$15.00
Varese Sarabande	VSD-47293	Nightmare on Elm Street 3: Dream Warriors	LP/LB	U.S.		$18.00/$15.00
Chrysalis	41673	Nightmare on Elm Street 4: Dream Master	LP/LB	U.S.	1988	$14.00/$8.00
Varese	VSD-5203	Nightmare on Elm Street 4: Dream Master (Score)	LP/LB	U.S.		$18.00/$15.00
Varese	VSD-5238	Nightmare on Elm Street 5	LP/LB	U.S.		$18.00/$15.00
CBS	CK-38325	Nine	LP/LB	U.S.†	1985	$14.00/$8.00
		Nobody's Perfect	DJ/LP	U.S.		$15.00
		Nobody's Perfect	LP	U.S.		$15.00
Varase	VCD-47205	North by Northwest	LP/LB	U.S.†	1985	$14.00/$8.00
MCA	MCAD-10685	Northern Exposure	LP/LB	U.S.		$18.00/$15.00
		Nutcracker – Always Come Back	CDJ	U.S.	1991	$6.00
Varese Sarabande	SRS 2004	Obsession	LTD/LP	U.S.		$20.00
Varese	70445	Off Limits	LP/LB	U.S.	1988	$14.00/$8.00
RCA	RCD1-3572	Oklahoma!	LP/LB	U.S.†	1985	$14.00/$8.00
Varese	VSD-5232	Old Man and the Sea	LP/LB	U.S.		$18.00/$15.00
Milan	35672-2	Oldest Confederate Widow Tells All	LP	U.S.		$15.00
RCA	PCD1-2004	Oliver!	LP/LB	U.S.†	1985	$14.00/$8.00
Disney	CD-012	Oliver and Company	LP/LB	U.S.	1989	$14.00/$10.00
Varese	VCD-47242	Omen 3: The Final Conflict	LP/LB	U.S.		$18.00/$15.00
Varese	VSD-5318	Omen 4	LP/LB	U.S.		$18.00/$15.00
London	PPC-820041-2	On Broadway: The Great Show Tunes	LP/LB	U.S.†	1985	$14.00/$8.00
London	PPC-820041-2	On Your Toes	LP/LB	U.S.†	1985	$14.00/$8.00
Mercury	822334-2	Once Upon a Time in America	LP/LB	U.S.†	1985	$14.00/$8.00
RCA	RCD1-4407	Pacific Overtures	LP/LB	U.S.†	1985	$14.00/$8.00
Beat	75	Panama Sugar	LP/LB	U.S.		$12.00/$10.00
NBC		Pandora's Clock: 1996 Photography: Countdown to November on NBC	DJ/Smplr	U.S.	1996	N/A
	CD-ROM press kit and photography.					
Nonesuch	79186-2	Patty Hearst	LP/LB	U.S.		$18.00/$15.00

PCU – (Fox Records)

Label	Catalog Number	Title	Type	Country	Year	Longbox Value / Value
Fox Records		PCU	DJ/LP	U.S.	1994	$10.00
Arista	ARCD-8278	Perfect	LP/LB	U.S.†	1985	$14.00/$8.00
Columbia		Permanent Record	LP/LB	U.S.	1988	$25.00/$22.00
Southern Cross	SCCD-1011	Peter the Great	LP/LB	U.S.		$18.00/$15.00
Polydor		Phantom of the Opera	SCD5	Germany	1996	$30.00
	"Phantom mask" shaped CD single from German performance.					
CBS	SAMP 2164	Philadelphia	DJ/LP	U.K.	1993	$65.00
CBS	XPCD373	Philadelphia: Highlights From	DJ/Smplr	U.K.	1993	$25.00
Sire	9 26624-3-Dj	Pimps, Players & Private Eyes	DJ/LP	U.S.	1991	$25.00
	Picturedisc CD.					
Warner Bros	25922-2	Pink Cadillac	LP/LB	U.S.		$18.00/$15.00
RCA	66319-2	Pink Panther: Son of	LP/LB	U.S.		$18.00/$15.00
		Plains, Trains and Automobiles	LP/LB	U.S.		$15.00/$13.00
Walt Disney	60874-7	Pocahontas	LTD/LP	U.S.	1995	$20.00
	Picture disc CD.					
Disney Records		Pocahontas: Academy Package	DJ/LP	U.S.	1996	$50.00
	CD single, cassette single, full length "Pocahontas" CD and two lyric books in folder.					
Tristar	80958	Porgy and Bess	LP/LB	U.S.		$18.00/$15.00
Arista		Preacher's Wife	LTD/LP	U.S.	1997	$16.00
	Multi-Image CD with CD travel case in blister pack. Available at WalMart.					
Arista	18951-2	Preacher's Wife, The	LTD/LP	U.S.	1996	$16.00
	Multi-Image cover.					
Varese	VSD-5207	Prince and the Pauper	LP/LB	U.S.		$18.00/$15.00
Varese	VCD-47310	Prince of Darkness	LP/LB	U.S.		$18.00/$15.00

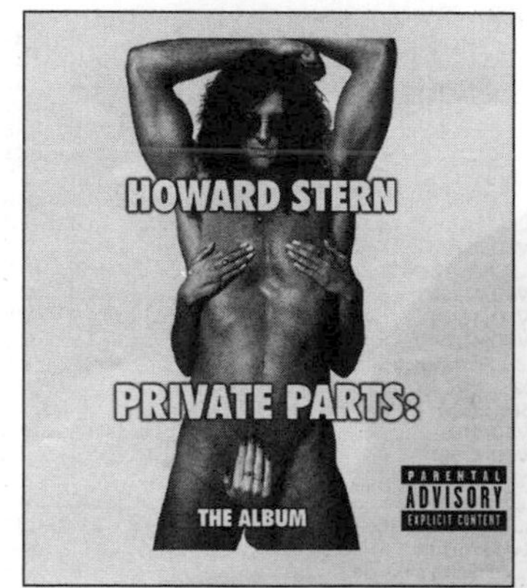

Stern, Howard – Private Parts (Warner Brothers)

Label	Catalog Number	Title	Type	Country	Year	Longbox Value / Value
Warner Brothers		Private Parts	DJ/LP	U.S.	1997	$85.00
	"Nude" cover. Limited to 2,000 copies.					

Label	Catalog Number	Title	Type	Country	Year	Longbox Value / Value
Warner Brothers	9 46477-2	Private Parts	LTD/LP	U.S.	1997	$18.00
		"Choking Chicken" cover.				
Warner Brothers	9 46477-2	Private Parts	LTD/LP	U.S.	1997	$18.00
		"Fire specs" cover.				
Warner Brothers	9 46477-2	Private Parts	LTD/LP	U.S.	1997	$18.00
		"King Kong" cover.				
Varese Sarabande	VSD-5252	Psycho 2	LP/LB	U.S.		$18.00/$15.00
MCA		Pulp Fiction	LTD/LP	Australia	1994	$35.00
		2 CD set.				
MCA		Pulp Fiction: Royale With Cheese	DJ/Intvw	U.S.	1995	$10.00
		Punch Line	LP	U.S.		$15.00
Varese Sarabande	VSD-5330	Pure Luck	LP/LB	U.S.		$18.00/$15.00
		Quicksilver	LP	U.S.		$15.00
		Raffle	LP	U.S.		$15.00
Varese Sarabande	VCL 9101.7	Raggedy Man	LTD/LP	U.S.	1991	$20.00
Silva Scrn	FILMCD-33	Raggedy Rawney	LP/LB	U.S.		$18.00/$15.00
Polydor	P33P-50033	Raiders of the Lost Ark	LP	Japan	1985	$28.00
Polydor	821583-2	Raiders of the Lost Ark	LP	U.K.	1985	$18.00
Polygram	821583-2	Raiders of the Lost Ark	LP/LB	U.S.†	1985	$14.00/$8.00
Polydor	821583-2	Raiders of the Lost Ark	LP/LB	U.S.	1987	$18.00/$15.00
Milan	35621-2	Raising Cain	LP/LB	U.S.		$18.00/$15.00
		Rambling Rose	LP	U.S.		$15.00
		Rampage	LP/LB	U.S.		$16.00/$14.00
Rap	3101	Rap to Rock	LP/LB	U.S.		$12.00/$10.00
Southern Cross	904	Razor's Edge	LP/LB	U.S.†	1985	$14.00/$8.00
Varese Sarabande	VSD-5450	Real McCoy	LP/LB	U.S.		$18.00/$15.00
Atlantic	90989-2	Red Heat	LP/LB	U.S.		$18.00/$15.00
Varese Sarabande	VSD-5230	Red Scorpion	LP/LB	U.S.		$18.00/$15.00
Varese Sarabande	VCL 9001.6	Red Sonja/Bloodline	LTD/LP	U.S.	1990	$20.00
		Limited to 1000 copies.				
MCA	CD33-1256/57	Reel Music Sampler From	DJ/Smplr	U.S.	1991	$25.00
		2 CD set in metal "film can."				
Imago	21046-2	Ref, The	LP	U.S.		$15.00
Disney Records	60613-2	Rescuers Down Under, The	LP	U.S.	1991	$40.00
Capitol	94244	Return of the Scorpion	LP/LB	U.S.		$18.00/$15.00
Rhino	70480-2	Return to the Forbidden Planet	LP/LB	U.S.		$18.00/$15.00
RCA	PCD1-5032	Rhinestone	LP/LB	U.S.†	1985	$14.00/$8.00
Varese Sarabande	VSD-5344	Riccochet	LP/LB	U.S.		$18.00/$15.00
Varese Sarabande	VSD-5423	Rich Man Poor Man	LP/LB	U.S.		$18.00/$15.00
HMR & Lace	124017	Ride, The	LP	U.S.		$15.00
Polydor	823125-2	Rink	LP/LB	U.S.		$18.00/$15.00
Polygram	823125-2	Rink	LP/LB	U.S.†	1985	$14.00/$8.00
Arista	11003-2	Rising Sun	LP	U.S.		$15.00
Varese Sarabande	SRS 2009	Rivers, The	LTD/LP	U.S.		$20.00
Varese Sarabande	VSD-5295	Robe	LP/LB	U.S.		$18.00/$15.00
Milan	35662-2	Robin Hood: Men in Tights	LP/LB	U.S.		$18.00/$15.00
Capital	CDP-46081	Rocky	LP/LB	U.S.†	1985	$14.00/$8.00
Capitol	95613-2	Rocky 5	LP/LB	U.S.		$18.00/$15.00
Pacific	RHBXCD1	Rocky Horror Picture Show	LTD/LP	U.K.	1987	$40.00
		3 CD boxed set.				
		Rocky Horror Picture Show	LTD/LP	U.K.	1991	$30.00
		Picture disc CD.				
Capital	CDP-46082	Rocky II	LP/LB	U.S.†	1985	$14.00/$8.00
Silva Scrn	FILMCD-5000	Romeo & Juliet	LP/LB	U.S.		$15.00/$12.00
Cinedisc	CDC-1004	Rosary Murders	LP/LB	U.S.		$15.00/$12.00
Varese Sarabande	VCL 9001.5	Rose Tattoo, The	LTD/LP	U.S.	1990	$20.00
		Limited to 1000 copies.				
Atlantic	16010-2	Rose, The	LP/LB	U.S.†	1985	$14.00/$8.00
Polygram	822747-2 PSI	Rota, Nino: 14 Movie Themes	LP/LB	U.S.†	1985	$14.00/$8.00
Warner Bros	26709-2	Rover Dangerfield	LP/LB	U.S.		$15.00/$12.00
Varase	VCD-47221	Runaway	LP/LB	U.S.†	1985	$14.00/$8.00
MCA	MCAD-31053	Running Scared	LP/LB	U.S.		$15.00
Varese	VSD-5444	Saint of Fort	LP/LB	U.S.		$18.00/$15.00
Polygram	800068-2GH	Saturday Night Feaver	LP/BP		1987	$25.00/$20.00
		2 CD set				
RSO	800068-2GH	Saturday Night Fever	LP/LB	U.S.†	1985	$28.00/$20.00
		2 CD set				
WTG	PSK 1678	Say Anything	DJ/Smplr	U.S.		$30.00
MCA		Schindler's List	LTD/LP	U.S.	1994	$70.00
		2 VHS video tapes , Picture disc CD soundtrack and book in box.				
Giant	24476-2	School Ties	LP	U.S.		$15.00
A&M	CD-3921	Scrooged	LP/LB	U.S.		$15.00/$13.00
		Scrooged–Sampler	DJ/Smplr	U.S.	1988	$5.00
Milan	35695	Second Best	LP/LB	U.S.		$18.00/$15.00
Varese	VCD-47231	Secret of N.I.M.H.	LP/LB	U.S.		$18.00/$15.00
EMI Latin	8 55535 2 3	Selena	LTD/LP	U.S.	1997	$18.00
		CD soundtrack plus bonus picture disc CD-single. Both discs packaged in tandam on a blister card. Available exclusively at Target Department Stores.				
Warner Brothers		Selections From Evita	DJ/Smplr	U.S.	1996	$25.00
Cinedisc	CDC-1006	Seventh Sign	LP/LB	U.S.		$15.00/$12.00
Varese	VCD-47256	Seventh Voyage of Sinbad	LP/LB	U.S.		$18.00/$15.00
Atlantic	91298-2	Sex, Lies, & Videotape	LP/LB	U.S.		$18.00/$15.00
Milan	35609-2	Shattered	LP/LB	U.S.		$18.00/$15.00
MCA	MCAD-6281	She's Out of Control	LP/LB	U.S.		$18.00/$15.00
Milan	61145-2	Shining Through	LP/LB	U.S.		$18.00/$15.00
Varese	VSD-5247	Shocker	LP/LB	U.S.		$18.00/$15.00
		Shocker	DJ/Smplr	U.S.	1989	$5.00
Imago	21014-2	Short Cuts	LP/LB	U.S.		$16.00/$15.00
Milan	35608-2	Shout	LP/LB	U.S.		$17.00/$15.00
Collossal	XCD-1005	Show of Force	LP/LB	U.S.		$18.00/$15.00
Columbia	MK-45436	Showboat	LP/LB	U.S.		$18.00/$15.00
New Line Cinema/DTS		Showest 1994	DJ/Smplr	U.S.	1994	$50.00
Columbia	MK-46198	Silk Stockings	LP/LB	U.S.		$18.00/$15.00
Southern Cross	903	Sisters	LP/LB	U.S.†	1985	$14.00/$8.00
Varese	VSD-5376	Sketch Artist	LP/LB	U.S.		$18.00/$15.00
Virgin	88064	Sliver	LP	U.S.		$15.00
		Smoke	DJ/Smplr	U.S.	1995	$12.00
Walt Disney	PCCD-00110	Snow White	LTD/LP	Japan	1994	$50.00
		Picture disc CD in box with figurines.				
RCA	8455-2-R	Snow White	LP	U.S.	1988	$30.00
Walt Disney	CD-004	Snow White and the Seven Dwarfs	LP	U.S.	1989	$25.00
Walt Disney	60999-2	Snow White and the Seven Dwarfs	LTD/LP	U.S.	1993	$35.00
		Picture disc CD in box with lenticular.				
Varese	5322	Soap Dish	LP/LB	U.S.	1991	$14.00/$8.00
MCA	MCAD-5154	Somewhere in Time	LP/LB	U.S.†	1985	$14.00/$8.00
Southern Cross	902	Sophie's Choice	LP/LB	U.S.†	1985	$18.00/$15.00
A&M	CD-3903	Soul Man	LP/LB	U.S.		$18.00/$15.00
Varese	VSD-5297	Sound and Fury	LP/LB	U.S.		$18.00/$15.00
RCA	2005-2	Sound of Music, The	LP/LB	U.S.		$15.00/$8.00
RCA	PCD1-2005	Sound of Music, The	LP/LB	U.S.†	1985	$14.00/$8.00
Columbia	MK-42205	South Pacific	LP/LB	U.S.		$18.00/$15.00
Cartoon Network	SGCTC1CD	Space Ghost Coast to Coast	DJ/Smplr	U.S.	1994	$20.00
Epic	EK 66384	Specialist, The	LP	U.S.		$15.00
Varese Sarabande	VCD-47226	Spellbound	LP/LB	U.S.		$18.00/$15.00
Varese Sarabande	VSD-5255	Stanley & Iris	LP/LB	U.S.		$18.00/$15.00
Capital	CDP-46089	Star Trek III: The Search for Spock	LP/LB	U.S.†	1985	$14.00/$8.00
Paramount		Star Trek – The Astral Symphony	DJ/LP	U.S.	1991	$50.00

Label	Catalog Number	Title	Type	Country	Year	Longbox Value / Value
GRP Crescendo	GNPD-8006	Star Trek: The Cage	LP/LB	U.S.		$18.00/$15.00
Columbia	MK-36334	Star Trek: The Motion Picture	LP/LB	U.S.		$18.00/$15.00
Label X	LXCD-704	Star Trek TV Scores 2	LP/LB	U.S.		$18.00/$15.00
RSO	800096-2	Star Wars	LP/LB	U.S.†	1985	$30.00/$28.00
		2 CD set.				
RSO	800096-2	Star Wars	LP/LB	U.S.	1987	$30.00/$28.00
		2 CD set.				
RCA Victor	RCDJ-68795-2	Star Wars: A New Hope	DJ/Smplr	U.S.	1997	$45.00
RCA Victor	09026-68746-2	Star Wars: A New Hope	LTD/LP	U.S.	1997	$40.00
		2 CD set with 3-D•ld printing on discs housed in bound book with foil embossed slip case.				
BMG/Pepsi	74321 455952	Star Wars: A New Hope - Main Title	SCD5	Holland	1996	N/A
		"Mellenium Falcon" shaped CD. Pepsi-Holland promotional release.				
High Bridge	1-56511-114-1	Star Wars and The Empire Strikes Back: The Complete Original Radio Dramas	LTD/LP	U.S.	1993	$125.00
		Audio book. 12 CD set.				
Warner Brothers Audio Video	2-523474	Star Wars: Dark Empire, The Collector's Edition	LTD/LP	U.S.	1995	$75.00
		Audio book. 4 CD Picturedisc set.				
RCA Victor	09026-68747-2	Star Wars: Empire Strikes Back	LTD/LP	U.S.	1997	$40.00
		2 CD set with 3-D•ld printing on discs housed in bound book with foil embossed slip case.				
Polygram	825298-2	Star Wars: Empire Strikes Back, The	LP/LB	U.S.†	1985	$14.00/$8.00
Varase	VCD-47204	Star Wars: Empire Strikes Back, The: Music From The Film	LP/LB	U.S.†	1985	$14.00/$8.00
RSO	811767-2GH	Star Wars: Return of the Jedi	LP/LB	U.S.†	1985	$14.00/$8.00
RCA Victor	68748-2	Star Wars: Return of the Jedi	LTD/LP	U.S.	1997	$40.00
		2 CD set with 3-D•ld printing on discs housed in bound book with foil embossed slip case.				
RCA	RCD1-4748	Star Wars: Return of the Jedi: Music From The Film	LP/LB	U.S.†	1985	$14.00/$8.00
HighBridge	56511-165-6	Star Wars: The Complete Trilogy Collector's Limited Edition	LTD/LP	U.S.	1996	$200.00
		15 CD set in special collectors box. Limited to 7,500 copies.				
Verase	VCD-47201	Star Wars Trilogy	LP/LB	U.S.†	1985	$14.00/$8.00
Fox Film Scores	07822-11012-2	Star Wars Trilogy	LP	U.S.	1993	$40.00
		4CD set. First pressing without "The Original Soundtrack Anthology" not printed on front of the box.				
BDD	0-553-45540-0	Star Wars: We Don't Do Weddings	LP	U.S.	1995	$15.00
		Audio book.				
Verase	VCD-47220	Starman	LP/LB	U.S.†	1985	$14.00/$8.00
Varese Sarabande	VCL 9101.8	Stars 'n Bars	LTD/LP	U.S.	1991	$20.00
		Limited to 1000 copies.				
RSO	813269-2GH	Staying Alive	LP/LB	U.S.†	1985	$25.00/$20.00
		2 CD set.				
Sire	2-25186	Stop Making Sense	LP/LB	U.S.†	1985	$14.00/$8.00
Atlantic	90962-2	Stormy Monday	LP/LB	U.S.		$18.00/$15.00
Enigma	73308	Straight to Hell	LP/LB	U.S.		$18.00/$15.00
Fox	XPCD2015	Strange Days	DJ/Smplr	U.K.	1996	$18.00
20th Century Fox		Strange Days	DJ/Smplr	U.S.	1995	$20.00
		CD-ROM.				
Signature	47486	Subterraneans	LP/LB	U.S.		$12.00/$10.00
IBR	CDIBR-9012	Sugar Babies	LP/LB	U.S.		$12.00/$10.00
RCA	RCD1-5042	Sunday in the Park With George	LP/LB	U.S.†	1985	$14.00/$8.00
RCA	RCD1-7017	Sunset Boulevard	LP/LB	U.S.		$18.00/$15.00
Varase	VCD-47218	Supergirl	LP/LB	U.S.†	1985	$14.00/$8.00
Varese	47312	Surrender	LP/LB	U.S.	1987	$14.00/$8.00
RCA	RCD1-5033	Sweeney Todd	LP/LB	U.S.†	1985	$14.00/$8.00
Saban		Sweet Valley High Sampler	DJSmplr		1995	$15.00
Varese Sarabande	VSD-5312	Switch	LP/LB	U.S.		$18.00/$15.00
Varese Sarabande	VSD-5215	Talk Radio	LP/LB	U.S.		$17.00/$15.00
Walt Disney	606867-7	Tall Tale: The Unbelievable Adventures of Pecos Bill	LP	U.S.	1995	$18.00
		Limited to 35,000 copies				
Epic	45084	Tap	LP/LB	U.S.		$18.00/$15.00
Polygram	820210-2	Tap Dance	LP/LB	U.S.†	1985	$14.00/$8.00
Arista	ARCD10-8179	Taxi Driver	LP/LB	U.S.		$18.00/$15.00
Capitol	CDP-46062	Teachers	LP/LB	U.S.†	1985	$20.00/$18.00
Capital	CDP-46062	Teachers	LP/LB	U.S.	1987	$20.00/$18.00
SBK	K2-91066-2	Teenage Mutant Ninja Turtles	LP/LB	U.S.		$18.00/$15.00
MCA	1037	Teenage Mutant Ninja Turtles:	CDJ	U.S.	1990	$3.00
SBK	DPRO-05352	Teenage Mutant Ninja Turtles	DJ/Smplr	U.S.	1990	$5.00
Pioneer	PICD-1001A	Tenchi the Movie	LTD/LP	U.S.	1996	$16.00
		Picture disc CD in digipak				
Capitol	C21-91185-3	Tequila Sunrise	LP/LB	U.S.		$16.00/$15.00
Capital	CDP-46076	Terms of Endearment	LP/LB	U.S.†	1985	$14.00/$8.00
Sandy Hook	2012	Thank Your Lucky Stars	LP/LB	U.S.		$12.00/$10.00
Epic		That Thing You Do!	LTD/LP	U.S.	1996	$18.00
		CD with exclusive bonus booklet. Available only through Best Buy stores.				
Columbia	57136	Themes By Hollywood's Great Composers 2	LP/LB	U.S.		$12.00/$10.00
Enigma	73367	They Live	LP/LB	U.S.		$18.00/$15.00
Casablanca	822942-2	Thief of Hearts	LP/LB	U.S.†	1985	$14.00/$8.00
Geffen	PRO-CD-4255	Thirty Something	DJ/Smplr	U.S.	1991	$5.00
Nouveau	1060	This Boy's Life	LP/LB	U.S.		$12.00/$10.00
Radiola	1161	Those Fabulous Busby Berkley Musicals	LP/LB	U.S.		$12.00/$10.00
Varese Sarabande	SRS 2013	Those Secrets	LTD/LP	U.S.	1992	$20.00
		Limited to 1500 copies.				
Varese	VSD-5219	Three Fugitives	LP/LB	U.S.		$18.00/$15.00
Hollywood	61040-2	Three Men and a Little Lady	LP/LB	U.S.		$15.00/$15.00
Jimco	JIMC-89144	Thunderbirds	LTD/LP	Japan	1992	$32.00
		CD in box with plastic models.				
Jimco	JIDM-29004/9	Thunderbirds Are Go	LTD/LP	Japan	1992	$60.00
		6 CD3 set.				
Jive	3095-2	Tie Me Up Tie Me Down	LP/LB	U.S.		$18.00/$15.00
MCA	MCAD-10721	Tom & Jerry the Movie	LP	U.S.		$15.00
RCA	RDJ 61874	Tommy	DJ/Smplr	U.S.	1993	$12.00
		Tommy	LTD/LP	U.S.	1993	$35.00
		CD sampler in hard-bound book.				
Warner Brothers		Tommy Boy: Sing Along With Chris Farley & David Spade	DJ/Smplr	U.S.	1995	$15.00
RCA		Tommy – Pinball Wizard	CDJ	U.S.	1993	$7.00
Immediate	47893	Tonite Let's All Make Love	LP/LB	U.S.		$12.00/$10.00
Hollywood/Disney Records		Toy Story: Academy Package	DJ/LP	U.S.	1996	$50.00
		CD single, full length "Toy Story" CD and lyric book in folder.				
Mattel	16628	Toy Story Computer Cars CD-ROM	LTD/LP	U.S.	1996	$15.00
		CD-ROM picture disc sampler and Hot Wheels car,				
Walt Disney	HFS-CD-ROM	Toy Story: Multimedia CD-ROM Press Kit	DJ/Smplr	U.S.	1995	$100.00
		CD-ROM.				
Walt Disney Records	60347-7	Toy Story Picture Disc CD	CD5	U.S.	1996	$6.00
		Sold only at KMart stores.				
Sire	45013-2	Tresspass	LP	U.S.		$15.00
		Censored version.				
Sire	45220-2	Tresspass (Score)	LP	U.S.		$15.00
Varese	VSD-254	Triumph of the Spirit	LP/LB	U.S.		$18.00/$15.00
Intrada	7048	Trusting Beatrice	LP/LB	U.S.		$12.00/$10.00
A&M	CD-3917	Tucker: The Man And His Dream	LP/LB	U.S.		$18.00/$15.00
RCA	RCD1-4327	Turned-On Broadway	LP/LB	U.S.†	1985	$14.00/$8.00
IRS	IRSCD-6270	Twenty-One Jump Street	LP/LB	U.S.		$15.00/$10.00
Varese	VCD-47233	Twilight Zone: Best of Volume 2	LP/LB	U.S.		$18.00/$15.00
Warner Brothers	9 26316-2-DJ	Twin Peaks	DJ/LP	U.S.	1990	$50.00
		Picture disc CD.				
Mute	47893	Tyranny of the Beat	LP/LB	U.S.		$12.00/$10.00
Enigma	CDE 73276	Under Cover	LP/LB	U.S.	1987	$15.00/$14.00

Label	Catalog Number	Title	Type	Country	Year	Longbox Value / Value
Varese Sarabande	SRS 2011	Under the Volcano	LTD/LP	U.S.	1992	$20.00
	Limited to 1500 copies.					
United Artists		United Artists Fall/Winter Releases	DJ/Smplr	U.S.	1995	$30.00
	CD-ROM press kit in folder					
Columbia	MK-45442	Unsinkable Molly Brown	LP/LB	U.S.		$18.00/$15.00
Dancing Cat	CD-3007	Velveteen Rabbit, The	LP/LB	U.S.†	1985	$14.00/$8.00
Varese Sarabande	VCL 9001.4	Vibes	LTD/LP	U.S.	1990	$20.00
RCA		Victory at Sea	LP	U.S.		$15.00
Geffen	24063-2	Vision Quest	LP/LB	U.S.†	1985	$14.00/$8.00
Saban		VR5	DJ/Smplr	U.S.	1995	$20.00
	CD soundtrack, 2 VHS video, and press kit.					
Arista	ASCD 2945	Waiting to Exhale	DJ/Smplr	U.S.	1995	$6.00
Varese	VSD-70440	Wall Street	LP/LB	U.S.		$18.00/$15.00
CBS		War of the Worlds	DJ/Smplr	U.K.	1995	$16.00
Columbia	X FILE CD	War of the Worlds – The New Files	DJ/Smplr	U.S.	1995	$20.00
A&M	CD-3151	Warriors	LP/LB	U.S.		$18.00/$15.00
CBS	CK-32801	Way We Were, The	LP/LB	U.S.†	1985	$14.00/$8.00
MCA	MCAD-10986	We're Back	LP	U.S.		$15.00
Varese Sarabande	9201.12	We're No Angels	LTD/LP	U.S.	1992	$20.00
	Limited to 1500 copies.					
Sony	SRCS-6683	West Side Story	LP	Japan	1993	$35.00
	Gold disc					
Columbia	CK-53152	West Side Story	LTD/LP	U.S.	1993	$30.00/$20.00
	Gold disc					
RCA Victor	68473-2	West Side Story: Songs of West Side Story	LTD/LP	U.S.	1996	$18.00
	CD soundtrack plus bonus CD-single. Both discs packaged in tandam on a blister card. Available exclusively at Target Department Stores.					
MGM/UA		White Christmas	LTD/LP	U.S.	1994	$40.00
	CD and VHS video in box.					
EMI	DPRO-04883	White Men Can't Jump	DJ/Smplr	U.S.	1992	$15.00
Atlantic	81273-2	White Nights	LP/LB	U.S.†	1985	$14.00/$8.00
Disney	CD-010	Who Framed Roger Rabbit	LP/LB	U.S.	1988	$25.00/$25.00
Disney	CD-013	Who Framed Roger Rabbit	LP/LB	U.S.	1989	$25.00/$25.00
Varese Sarabande	SRS 2002	Wild Geese, The	LTD/LP	U.S.		$20.00
Capitol	C21-89098	Wild Palms	LP/LB	U.S.		$16.00/$15.00
Virgin	90939-2	Willow	LP/LB	U.S.		$25.00/$20.00
Walt Disney Records	CD-008	Willow: Story of	LP	U.S.	1988	$25.00
Varese Sarebande	VSD-5237	Wired	LP/LB	U.S.		$18.00/$15.00
Varese Sarebande	VSD-5209	With Honors	LP/LB	U.S.		$18.00/$15.00
Varase	VCD-47227	Witness	LP/LB	U.S.†	1985	$14.00/$8.00
Turner/MGM		Wizard of Oz in Concert	LTD/LP	U.S.	1995	$80.00
	CD soundtrack,video tape of concert, theatrical video, and script in box.					
Motown	6108-MD	Woman in Red, The	LP/LB	U.S.†	1985	$14.00/$8.00
20th Century Fox		X-Files Soundbites	DJ/Smplr	U.S.	1996	$12.00
20th Century Fox Home Video		X-Files: The Truth is Out There	DJ/LP	U.S.	1996	$45.00
	Warner Brothers CD soundtrack and the first two VHS video X-Files episodes in white box with press kit.					
Warner Brothers		X-Files Theme	CD5	U.K.	1996	$10.00
Warner Brothers	PRO-CD-8151-R	X-Files Theme	CDJ	U.S.	1996	$6.00
Varase	VCD-47222	Year of Living Dangerously, The	LP/LB	U.S.†	1985	$14.00/$8.00
Milan	35610-2	Year of the Gun	LP/LB	U.S.		$18.00/$15.00
A&M	CD-3929	Young Einstein	LP/LB	U.S.		$25.00/$25.00
Varese Sarebande	VSD-5403	Young Lions	LP/LB	U.S.		$18.00/$15.00
Varese Sarebande	VSD-5456	Younger & Younger	LP/LB	U.S.		$18.00/$15.00
Sony	52417	Zabrinski Point	LP/LB	U.S.		$12.00/$10.00
Varese Sarebande	VSD-70442	Zelly and Me	LP/LB	U.S.		$18.00/$15.00

Label Catalog Number Title Type Country Year Longbox Value / Value

Series CDs

Label	Title	Type	Country	Year	Value
	Adventures in Music	DJ/Smplr	U.S.		$5.00–$10.00
	Monthly sampler series featuring new and upcoming releases.				
	Album Rock Tune Up	DJ/Smplr	U.S.		$4.00–$6.00
	Monthly sampler series featuring new and upcoming releases.				
	America's Musicmakers CD's	RS	U.S.		$8.00–$12.00
	1 CD, 10 artists per show with music and interviews series.				
	American Country Countdown	RS	U.S.	1992 - Present	$15.00–$20.00
	4 CD , various artist country music countdown show series.				
	American Gold	RS	U.S.	1992 - Present	$25.00–$40.00
	4 CD, 60's and 70's various artist music & interviews series.				
	American Gold With Dick Bartley	RS	U.S.		$10.00–$13.00
	4 CD, various artist music and interviews series.				
ABC Radio Network	American Top 40	RS	U.S.	7/1/89 - Present	$10.00–$20.00
	4CD/Various artist countdown show series.				
	Art Of Mix	DJ/Smplr	U.S.		$20.00–$30.00
	Dance remix series.				
	Ask the Stars	RS	U.S.		$12.00–$15.00
	1 CD, various artist interview show series.				
Atlantic	Atlantic Releases	DJ/Smplr	U.S.	1995 to present	$4.00–$10.00
	Monthly sampler series featuring new and upcoming releases.				
	Backtrack U.S.A.	RS	U.S.	1995	$40.00
	2 CD 2 hour music and interview series.				
Westwood One	Beatle Years	RS	U.S.	3/30/92 to Present	$30.00–$35.00
	1 CD, weekly show covering the history of the Beatles series.				
	Big Back Yard, The	RS	Australia	1992	$5.00–$7.00
	Alternative music radio show series.				
	Blender	LP	U.S.	1995 to Present	$10.00–$15.00
	Interactive Entertainment Magazine on CD-ROM. (add 15% to value if disc is accompanied by its 8.5 inch x11 inch longbox.				
Album Network	CD Top 40 Tune Up	DJ/Smplr	U.S.		$4.00–$10.00
	1 CD new music sampler series.				
Album Network	CD Tune Up In-Store Play	DJ/Smplr	U.S.		$4.00–$10.00
Album Network	CD Tune Up In-Store Play	DJ/Smplr	U.S.		$10.00–$20.00
	2 various artists CD set. Bonus disc full length CD album of featured artist.				
Album Network	CD Tune Up Next 40 Album Network	DJ/Smplr	U.S.		$5.00–$10.00
	1 CD new music sampler series.				
Century 21	Century 21 Programming Gold Disc Series	DJ/Smplr	U.S.		$8.00–$15.00
Remastered various artist tracks.					
	Certain Damage	DJ/Smplr	U.S.		$4.00–$8.00
	Monthly sampler series featuring new and upcoming releases.				

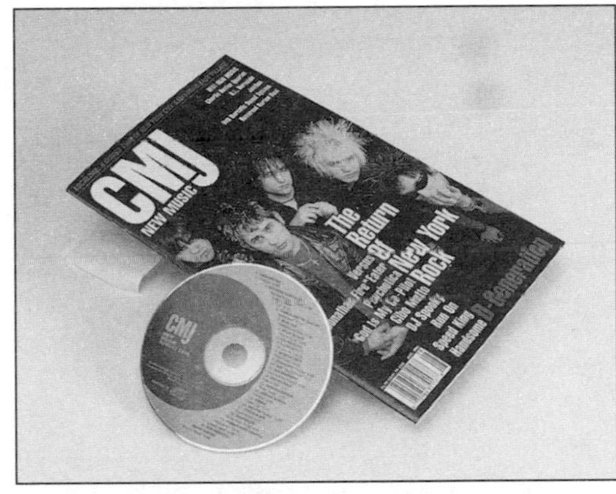

CMJ New Music Monthly January 1996 CMJ Monthly magazine containing exclusive CD sampler.

Label	Title	Type	Country	Year	Value
CMJ	CMJ New Music Monthly	LP	U.S.	1995 to Present	$5.00–$10.00
	Monthly Magazine with CD sampler. Add 15% to value if disc comes with original magazine.				
CMJ	CMJ New Releases	DJ/Smplr	U.S.	1994 to Present	$5.00–$10.00
Citibank Visa	Coffehouse Sessions	RS	U.S.	1994	$8.00–$10.00
	Countdown America	RS	U.S.		$10.00–$15.00
	3 CD set. various artists countdown show series.				
Olympia Broadcasting	Country Calendar	RS	U.S.		$10.00–$15.00
	1CD, country music & interviews.				
	Country Edge	RS	U.S.	1994 to Present	$15.00–$35.00
	1 CD, country artist music and interview radio program series.				
	Country Edge	RS	U.S.	1995 to present	$15.00–$35.00
	1 CD, various country artist music and interview yndicated radio program.				
	David Sanborn Show	RS	U.S.		$20.00–$30.00
	2 CD, various artist jazz show series.				
Unistar	Dick Clark's Rock 'n Roll Remember	RS	U.S.	1991	$25.00–$30.00
	4 CD, arious artist music and interview show series.				
	Digizine	LP	U.S.	1995 to Present	$10.00–$15.00
	Quarterly Interactive Entertainment Magazine on CD-ROM Add 15% to value if disc is accompanied by its 8.5 inch x 11 inch longbox.				
	Disconet CD Mix Service	DJ/Smplr	U.S.		$20.00–$30.00
	Remixed various artist dance tracks.				
DIR	Don Kirshner's 35th Anniversary of Rock	RS	U.S.		$20.00–$30.00
	3 CD, Oldies music & interviews series.				
	Double Threats	RS	U.S.	11/25/93	$30.00
	1CD, various country music & interviews.				
	Eight Seconds (Country's Cutting Edge)	RS	U.S.	1/15/94	$10.00
	1CD, country soundtrack primiere.				
Atlantic	Elektra Releases	DJ/Smplr	U.S.	1995 to Present	$4.00–$10.00
	Monthly sampler series featuring new and upcoming releases.				
Album Network	Expando CD Tune Up	DJ/Smplr	U.S.		$4.00–$6.00
	Fast Track	RS	U.S.		$20.00–$25.00
	2 CD, music & interview series.				
Radio Today	Flashback	RS	U.S.		$5.00–$10.00
	2 CD, various artist show featuring music and soundbites from the 60's and 70's.				
Global Satellite Network	FMBQ	RS	U.S.		$50.00
	1 CD, Music and interviews with many tracks exclusive to this show.				
DSP	For Rockers Only	RS	U.S.		$5.00–$10.00
	1 CD, 5 shows (10 min each) per disc.				
	Future Hits	RS	U.S.		$18.00–$20.00
	1 CD, various artist with about 10 artists per disc.				
	Future Hits	RS	U.S.	1995	$10.00
	1 Hour music and interview series.				
	Great Country Fathers	RS	U.S.		$16.00
	1 CD, various country artists hosted by Ricky Scaggs.				
	Headsets	RS	U.S.		$10.00
	2 CD, hosted by Jim Ladd featuring music with a particular theme series.				
Hello CD Of the Month	Hello	LP	U.S.	1994-Present	$5.00
	Monthly subscription CD.				
TM Century	Hit Disc	DJ/Smplr	U.S.		$8.00–$10.00
	Radio sampler series.				
Album Network	Hitmakers	DJ/Smplr	U.S.	1989 to present	$4.00–$6.00
	Monthly sampler series featuring new and upcoming releases.				
Album Network	Hitmakers Top 40	DJ/Smplr	U.S.		$4.00–$6.00
	Monthly sampler series featuring new and upcoming releases.				
	Hot Tracks	DJ/Smplr	U.S.		$20.00–$30.00
	Monthly sampler series featuring new and upcoming releases.				
	Huh	LP	U.S.	1994 to present	$5.00
	Monthly Magazine with CD sampler. Add 15% to value if disc comes with original magazine.				
Atlantic	Island Releases	DJ/Smplr	U.S.	1995 to present	$4.00–$10.00
	Monthly sampler series featuring new and upcoming releases.				
2 Way Media	Launch	LP	U.S.	1995	$8.00–$12.00
	BI-Monthly entertainment CD-ROM.				
Leak	Leak CD Magazine	LP	U.S.	1996	$5.00–$8.00
	Monthly Magazine with CD sampler. Add 15% to value if disc comes with original magazine.				
DIR	Live Cuts	RS	U.S.		$10.00–$15.00
	1CD, weekly various artists show.				
ABC Radio Network	"Live Show, The"	RS	U.S.		$8.00–$15.00
	1 CD, various artists show featuring all live tracks.				
Media America	Media America Specials: at the Core	RS	U.S.	1989	$12.00–$20.00
	1 CD, music & interview series.				
Metatec	Multimedia World Live	LP	U.S.	1996 To Present	$5.00–$10.00
	CD-ROM magazine containing, video clips reviews, interviews, game previews and utility software.				
	Music Week Music Week	DJ/Smplr	U.K.		$10.00–$15.00
	Nascar Country	RS	U.S.	1993	$15.00–$20.00
	2 CD, various country music & interview series.				
Westwood One	New Gold on CD	RS	U.S.		$8.00–$10.00
	1 CD, 18-20 cuts, golden oldies series.				
	New Power Source	DJ/Smplr	U.S.		$8.00–$10.00
	Monthly sampler series featuring new and upcoming releases.				
	Nineties Ladies	RS	U.S.	9/2/93	$12.00–$20.00
	1CD/1Hr/Various country artist music & interviews				
	NRG Mixxx	DJ/Smplr	U.S.		$20.00–$30.00
	Remix CD series.				
Westwood One	On the Edge	RS	U.S.	1994 to present	$25.00–$35.00
	1CD one hour music & interview series featuring various alternative artists.				
	On Tour	RS	U.S.	1996 to Present	$40.00–$50.00
	Various alternative artist live concert series radio show. One hour one CD.				
	Out of Order	RS	U.S.	1994-95	$20.00–$25.00
	2 CD, alternative music show series.				

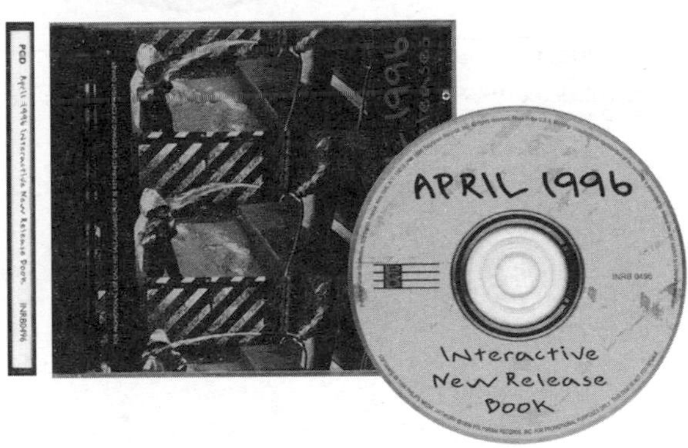

PGD April 1996 New Release Book – (Polygram INRB0496) CD-ROM release book.

Label	Title	Type	Country	Year	Value
Polygram	PGD Interactive New Release Book	DJ/Smplr	U.S.	1995 to Present	$5.00–$10.00
	Monthly promotional CD-ROM listing upcoming CD releases from Polygram Group Distribution.				
	Polygram Classics & Jazz	DJ/Smplr	U.S.		$5.00–$7.00
	Monthly sampler series featuring new and upcoming releases.				
Promo only	Promo Only	DJ/Smplr	U.S.		$20.00–$25.00
	Remix CD series.				
	Ralph Emery Show	RS	U.S.		$12.00–$20.00
	1 CD, various country artist music & interview show series.				
	Rarities	RS	U.S.		$30.00–$40.00
	1 CD, various artist show series featuring all rare tracks.				
	Razormaid	DJ/Smplr	U.S.		$20.00–$30.00
	Remix CD series.				
	Reelin' In the Years	RS	U.S.		$15.00–$20.00
	2 CD, music & interviews series.				
	Rhythm Based	RS	U.S.		$5.00–$10.00
	1 CD, various R&B artists music and interview series.				
ABC	Rick Dee's Weekly Top 40	RS	U.S.		$5.00–$10.00
	4 CD, weekly countdown show series.				
Album Network	Rock 40	DJ/Smplr	U.S.		$4.00–$6.00
	Monthly sampler series featuring new and upcoming releases.				
	Rock Over London	RS	U.S.		$12.00–$15.00
	1 CD, top 10 countdown show series.				
	Rock Trends	RS	U.S.		$10.00–$15.00
	2 CD, music & interview series.				
	Sixties Legends	RS	U.S.		$25.00–$35.00
	2 CD, music & interview Summer 1992 Series.				
	Solid Gold Country	RS	U.S.		$20.00–$25.00
	5 CD, various artist music & interview.				
Unistar	Solid Gold Scrapbook	RS	U.S.	7/29 to 8/2/92	$25.00–$35.00
	5 CD, various artist music & interview series.				
	Soul of the Sixties	RS	U.S.	5-25-92 - Present	$10.00–$15.00
	2 CD, various artist music & interview series.				

Label	Title	Type	Country	Year	Value
....	Sounds of Sinatra *2 CD, weekly show devoted soley to Frank Sinatra.*	RS	U.S.	2/13/94 to 6/26/94	$50.00–$70.00
....	Spin Radio *1 CD, various alternative artist music and interview show series.*	RS	U.S.		$15.00–$25.00
....	Star Tracks Country *1 CD, various artist show, hosted by a particular country artist series.*	RS	U.S.		$10.00–$15.00
....	Stars Are Out in Georgia *3 CD, country artist show hosted by Trisha Yearwood.*	RS	U.S.		$15.00–$25.00
....	TDK New Music Report *1 CD, demo versions and acoustic cuts from various artists series.*	RS	U.S.		$25.00
....	This Is Only a Test *Remix CD dance series.*	DJ/Smplr	U.S.		$20.00–$30.00
....	Top Hits U.S.A. *Various artist countdown show series.*	RS	U.S.		$15.00–$15.00
....	Top Thirty Hit List *3 CD, various artist countdown show series.*	RS	U.S.		$10.00–$15.00
....	U.K. Chart Attack *1CD countdown show series.*	RS	U.S.		$5.00–$10.00
....	Ultra Hot Razor Compilation *Remix CD series.*	DJ/Smplr	U.S.		$30.00–$45.00
Album Network	Unsigned Bands – Tune Up *Monthly sampler series featuring new and upcoming releases.*	DJ/Smplr	U.S.		$4.00–$6.00
....	Various Artists *Monthly sampler series featuring new and upcoming releases.*	RS		12/5 To 1/2/93	$8.00–$15.00
....	Vault, The *1 CD one hour music & interview series featuring various alternative artists.*	RS	U.S.	1995 to present	$25.00–$35.00
Verve	Verve Releases *Monthly sampler series featuring new and upcoming releases.*		U.S.	1995 to present	$4.00–$10.00
....	Weekly Country Music Countdown *3 CD, various artist countdown show series.*	RS	U.S.		$10.00–$15.00
....	Your Goodtime Oldies Magazine *3 CD, various artist music & interview show series.*	RS	U.S.		$10.00–$15.00

ZOOM – (Pioneer) Promotional 8" laser disc magazine.

Label	Title	Type	Country	Year	Value
Pioneer	Zoom Laser Video Magazine *8" LD magazine series.*	LD	U.S.	1991 to present	$8.00–$20.00

Theatrical Laserdiscs

Label	Catalog Number	Title	Type	Country	Year	Value
Paramount	LV2374	16 Days of Glory	LD	U.S.	1986	$40.00
Columbia	VLD30204	"1776"	LD	U.S.	1985	$30.00
Psedition	PSE92-23	"1776"	LD	U.S.	1992	$80.00
Letterbox version.						
Discovision	16-014	1941	LD	U.S.	1980	$40.00
MCA	16-014	1941	LD	U.S.	1982	$30.00
MCA	16014	1941	LD	U.S.	1982	$50.00
Image	ID6750ME	1969	LD	U.S.		$30.00
Image	ID6236IV	1984	LD	U.S.		$80.00
Columbia	30717	1986	LD	U.S.	1987	$10.00
Walt Disney	15AS	20,000 Leagues Under the Sea	LD	U.S.	1985	$30.00
Walt Disney	15AS	20,000 Leagues Under the Sea	LD	U.S.	1987	$30.00
CAV version.						
Criterion	CC1160L	2001	LD	U.S.	1989	$125.00
CAV version.						
Criterion	CC1235L	2001	LD	U.S.	1990	$60.00
CLV version.						
MGM/UA	ML100002	2001 Space Odyssy	LD	U.S.	1983	$40.00
Paramount	LV8803	3 Days of the Condor	LD	U.S.	1982	$30.00
Vestron Video	VL5192	3 Men and a Cradle	LD	U.S.	1987	$35.00
Columbia	30444	3:10 to Yuma	LD	U.S.	1985	$30.00
CBS/Fox	6680-80	400 Blows, The	LD	U.S.	1986	$35.00
Paramount	LV1139	48 Hours	LD	U.S.	1983	$30.00
Columbia	90166	5,000 Fingers of Dr. T, The	LD	U.S.	1991	$30.00
CBS/Fox	6118-80	8 Million Ways to Die	LD	U.S.	1986	$35.00
Republic	[illegible]	3 & 1/2 Ninjas	LD	U.S.	1991	$30.00
Columbia	09876	976-Evil	LD	U.S.	1990	$20.00
Magnetic Video		99 and 44/100% Dead	LD	U.S.†	1984	$30.00
Image	ID7054TU	A Damsel in Distress	LD	U.S.		$30.00
Columbia	32004	A Dandy in Aspic	LD	U.S.	1991	$20.00
MGM/UA	ML100064	A Day at the Races	LD	U.S.		$25.00
Columbia	30723	A Fine Mess	LD	U.S.	1987	$40.00
Image	ID7351MG	A Fistful of Dynamite	LD	U.S.	1971	$120.00
Image	ID7987MF	A Gathering of Men	LD	U.S.	1989	$15.00
Image	ID7015TU	A Girl in Every Port	LD	U.S.	1952	$30.00
Columbia	59116	A Girl to Kill For	LD	U.S.	1990	$30.00
Image	ID5300PA	A Great Wall	LD	U.S.		$30.00
Maljack Prod.	MP1064D	A Hard Day's Night	LD	U.S.	1984	$80.00
Image	ID6758FL	A Killing Affair	LD	U.S.		$15.00
Columbia	32000	A Night to Remember	LD	U.S.	1989	$30.00
Lumivision	LVD9207	A Paper Wedding	LD	U.S.	1992	$25.00
Image	ID7808FR	A Raisin in the Sun	LD	U.S.		$30.00
Columbia	90256	A Sinful Life	LD	U.S.	1990	$30.00
Image	ID7756AX	A Special Day	LD	U.S.		$30.00
Image	I-6001	A Star Is Born	LD	U.S.		$30.00
Walt Disney	PILA 1351	A Star Is Born: Donald	LD	Japan	1995	$90.00
Walt Disney	PILA 1294	A Star Is Born: Mickey	LD	Japan	1995	$90.00
Walt Disney	523AS	A Tale of Two Chipmunks	LD	U.S.	1987	$40.00
Image	ID8099RG	A Town Like Alice	LD	U.S.		$30.00
CBS	4730	A View To a Kill	LD	U.S.	1985	$15.00
Lumivision	LVD9101	A Walk in the Sun	LD	U.S.	1991	$25.00
Image	ID7958PA	A Walk Through the 20th Century With Bill Moyers	LD	U.S.		$20.00
Image	ID8126AC	A Woman Obsessed	LD	U.S.		$30.00
Image	ID7190ME	A World Apart	LD	U.S.		$30.00
Discovision	22-008	Abbott And Costello Meet Frankenstein	LD	U.S.	1979	$175.00
Image	ID6902VE	Abominable Dr. Phibes/Doctor Phibes Rises Again	LD	U.S.		$40.00
Columbia	30735	About Last Night	LD	U.S.	1992	$25.00
Republic	LV20010	Abraham Lincoln	LD	U.S.	1991	$30.00
Columbia	VLD1015	Absence of Malice	LD	U.S.	1983	$30.00
Walt Disney	28AS	Absent-Minded Professor	LD	U.S.	1983	$25.00
Non-remastered version.						
		Absolute Beginners	LD	U.S.		$35.00
Image	ID6124TW	Absolution	LD	U.S.		$30.00
CBS	1561-85	Abyss, The	LD	U.S.	1990	$30.00
Image	ID7549VE	Academy Award Winners Animated Short Films	LD	U.S.		$30.00
Discovision		Acrobats of God	LD	U.S.	1979	$20.00
Image		Adam Ant Vol. 1	LD	U.S.		$40.00
Criterion	CC1147L	Adam's Rib	LD	U.S.	1989	$40.00
Lumivision	LVD9216	Addams Family V. 1	LD	U.S.	1992	$30.00
Lumivision	LVD9217	Addams Family V. 2	LD	U.S.	1992	$30.00
Lumivision	LVD9218	Addams Family V. 3	LD	U.S.	1992	$30.00
Lumivision	LVD9260	Addams Family V. 4	LD	U.S.	1993	$30.00
Lumivision	LVD9261	Addams Family V. 5	LD	U.S.	1993	$30.00
Lumivision	LVD9262	Addams Family V. 6	LD	U.S.	1993	$30.00
U.S. Magna	SSLM-3011	Adventure Kid Volume 1	LP	U.S.	1995	$25.00
Japanese anime CD-ROM.						
U.S. Magna	SSLM-3012	Adventure Kid Volume 2	LP	U.S.	1995	$25.00
Japanese anime CD-ROM.						
Columbia	50146	Adventure of Milo & Otis	LD	U.S.	1990	$30.00
Walt Disney	595	Adventures in Babysitting	LD	U.S.	1988	$20.00
Republic	LV20032	Adventures in Dinosaurs	LD	U.S.	1992	18
Columbia	50156	Adventures of Baron Munchausen	LD	U.S.		$30.00
Image	IDVL5056	Adventures of Buckaroo Banzai	LD	U.S.		$90.00
Republic	LV25001	Adventures of Captain Marvel, The	LD	U.S.	1989	$40.00
Discovision	D61-506	Adventures of Chip 'n Dale	LD	U.S.	1979	$40.00
Pacific Arts	12020	Adventures of Mark Twain	LD	U.S.	1987	$40.00
Criterion	CC1166L	Adventures of Robin Hood	LD	U.S.	1989	$65.00
CAV version.						
Criterion	CC1215L	Adventures of Robin Hood	LD	U.S.	1990	$50.00
CLV version.						
CBS	7776-80	Adventures of Sherlock Holmes	LD	U.S.	1989	$40.00
Columbia	30983	Adventures of the Galaxy Rangers	LD	U.S.	1989	$20.00
Vestron Video	CL1508	Adventures of the Little Prince	LD	U.S.	1985	$30.00
CBS	8014-80	Adventures of Tom Sawyer	LD	U.S.	1990	$25.00
Columbia	32008	Affair in Trinidad	LD	U.S.	1983	$100.00
Magnetic Video	2025-80	African Queen	LD	U.S.†	1982	$20.00
CBS	2025-80	African Queen	LD	U.S.	1982	$20.00
Magnetic Video	2025-80	African Queen	LD	U.S.	1982	$20.00
CBS	5901	African Queen	LTD/LD	U.S.	1993	$70.00
Boxed set with LD and book						
Image		African Screams	LD	U.S.		$100.00
Image	ID8237IV	After Dark My Sweet	LD	U.S.		$40.00
Columbia	30077	Against All Odds	LD	U.S.	1992	$30.00
Image		Agatha Christie: Alibi/Lady	LD	U.S.		$30.00
Image	ID7474PA	Agatha Christie: Ambassador's Boot/The Man In the Mist	LD	U.S.		$30.00
Image	ID7463PA	Agatha Christie: Crackler, The/The Affair Of the Pink Pearl	LD	U.S.		$30.00
Image		Agatha Christie: House/King	LD	U.S.		$30.00
Image	ID8284PA	Agatha Christie: Murder by the Book	LD	U.S.		$30.00
Image	ID7473PA	Agatha Christie: Sunningdale Mystery/Clergyman's Daughter	LD	U.S.		$30.00
Image	ID7475PA	Agatha Christie: Unbreakable Alibi/Case of the Missing Lady	LD	U.S.		$30.00
Columbia	30563	Agnes of God	LD	U.S.	1992	$30.00
Magnetic Video		Agony and the Ecstasy	LD	U.S.†	1984	$30.00
CBS	1007-80	Agony and the Ecstasy	LD	U.S.	1989	$60.00
Image	ID7619IV	Air America	LD	U.S.		$20.00
Paramount	LV1489	Airplane 2	LD	U.S.	1983	$55.00
Discovision	10-010	Airport '77	LD	U.S.	1979	$40.00
Image	ID 5118	Airport '77	LD	U.S.	1987	$30.00
CID	SFO-781098	Airwolf	LD	Japan		$125.00
CID	SFO-781098	Airwolf: Flight Into Danger	LD	Japan		$125.00
CID	SFO-781098	Airwolf: Mission Airwolf	LD	Japan		$125.00
Disney	1662 CS	Aladdin	LD	U.S.	1994	$50.00
CAV version.						
Disney	1662 AS	Aladdin	LD	U.S.	1994	$30.00
CLV version.						
Columbia	VLD30561	Alamo Bay	LD	U.S.	1986	$40.00
MGM/UA	ML101813	Alamo, The	LD	U.S.	1990	$40.00
Image	ID8110AC	Alexa	LD	U.S.		$30.00
Discovision		Ali Vs. Folley And Williams	LD	U.S.	1979	$40.00
Disney	36AS	Alice in Wonderland	LD	U.S.	1983	$40.00
Disney	036AS	Alice in Wonderland	LD	U.S.	1987	$40.00
Walt Disney	36CS	Alice in Wonderland	LD	U.S.	[illegible]	[illegible]
CAV version.						
CBS		Alien	LD	Japan	1986	$100.00
CBS		Alien	LD	U.K.	1987	$30.00
PAL Format						
Magnetic Video	1090-80	Alien	LD	U.S.	1981	$50.00
2 Discs.						
Magnetic Video		Alien	LD	U.S.†	1983	$40.00
CBS	1090-80	Alien	LD	U.S.	1987	$30.00
2 Discs.						
CBS	1090-85	Alien	LD	U.S.	1989	$30.00
CBS		Alien	LD	U.S.	1992	$120.00
4 CD boxed set.						
Image	ID6150ME	Alien From L.A.	LD	U.S.		$20.00
Fox		Alien (Giger's Version)	LD	Swiss	1987	$180.00
CBS	1585-80	Alien Nation	LD	U.S.	1989	$25.00
Image	ID7662PR	Alienator	LD	U.S.		$30.00
CBS		Aliens	LD	Japan	1987	$100.00
CBS	1504-80	Aliens	LD	U.S.	1987	$20.00
CBS	C12504	Aliens	LD	U.S.	1989	$20.00
CBS	1504-85	Aliens	LD	U.S.	1991	$150.00
4 CD boxed set.						
Lumivision	LVD9213	Aliens, Dragons, Monsters & Me	LD	U.S.	1992	$25.00
CBS	1076-80	All About Eve	LD	U.S.	1989	$25.00
MGM/UA	ML101868	All Dogs Go to Heaven	LD	U.S.	1989	$25.00
CLV version.						
Columbia	50856	All in the Family 20th Anniversary	LD	U.S.	1991	$30.00
HBO	2715	All of Me	LD	U.S.	1986	$30.00
MGM/UA	ML1048	All Star Swing Festival	LD	U.S.		$20.00
Criterion	V1042L	All That Bach	LD	U.S.	1991	$40.00
Magnetic Video		All That Jazz	LD	U.S.†	1981	$25.00
CBS	1095-80	All That Jazz	LD	U.S.	1985	$45.00
CBS	1095-80	All That Jazz	LD	U.S.	1989	$40.00
Columbia	30588	All the Kings Men	LD	U.S.	1993	$40.00
CBS	1299-80	All the Right Moves	LD	U.S.	1984	$35.00
		Allegheny Uprising	LD	U.S.		$80.00
Image	ID8181MN	Almost	LD	U.S.		$30.00
Live Entertainment		Almost Blue	LD	U.S.	1994	$175.00
Image	ID7476PA	Alsino and the Condor	LD	U.S.		$40.00
Pacific Arts	PAV12626	Alsino and the Condor	LD	U.S.	1986	$40.00
Vestron Video	VL5161	Always	LD	U.S.	1986	$35.00
Saul Zaentz	LV1791	Amadeus	LD	U.S.	1987	$45.00
Pioneer	PSE-95-70	Amadeus	LTD/LD	U.S.	1995	$160.00
LD boxed set with 2 CD soundtrack and book.						
		Amazing Grace	LD	U.S.		$75.00
HBO	TV0029	Amazing Grace & Chuck	LD	U.S.	1988	$35.00
Columbia	30726	Ambushers, The	LD	U.S.	1987	$30.00
Lorimar	LV386	American Anthem	LD	U.S.	1986	$40.00
	0773-L	American Blue Note	LD	U.S.		$30.00
Columbia	92376	American Blue Note	LD	U.S.	1992	$30.00
Image	ID7850ME	American Boyfriends	LD	U.S.	1989	$15.00
		American Cowboy Collection	LD	U.S.		$45.00
Image	ID7600VK	American Eagle	LD	U.S.		$30.00
Image	ID5342PA	American Friend	LD	U.S.		$20.00
Paramount	LV8989	American Gigolo	LD	U.S.	1985	$30.00
		American Gothic	LD	U.S.		$35.00
Discovision	16-001	American Graffiti	LD	U.S.	1981	$35.00
MGM/UA	ML100006	American in Paris, An	LD	U.S.	1983	$40.00
		American Indian Collection	LD	U.S.		$45.00
Image	ID5161	American Ninja 2	LD	U.S.		$20.00
Cannon Video	31108	American Ninja III	LD	U.S.	1989	$30.00
Cannon Video	32022	American Ninja IV	LD	U.S.	1991	$30.00
		American Patchwork	LD	U.S.		$45.00
Image	ID7131VK	American Roulette	LD	U.S.		$30.00
Cannon Video	32009	American Samurai	LD	U.S.	1993	$30.00
		American Tiger	LD	U.S.		$30.00
Discovision		Amish, The	LD	U.S.	1979	$40.00
Republic	LV20066	Amityville 1992: It's About Time	LD	U.S.	1992	$30.00
Vestron	VL 5034	Amityville 3D	LD	U.S.	1984	$45.00
Republic	LV20065	Amityville: A New Generation	LD	U.S.		$35.00
		Amityville Curse	LD	U.S.		$20.00
Vestron Video	VL4022	Amityville Horror	LD	U.S.	1983	$35.00
Vestron	VL 4022	Amityville Horror, The	LD	U.S.	1979	$70.00
Nelson	17095	Amityville II	LD	U.S.	1983	$35.00
MCA	40536	An American Tail	LD	U.S.	1987	$70.00
CAV version.						
MCA	41067	An American Tail: Fievel Goes West	LD	U.S.		$25.00
MCA	41250	An American Tail: Fievel Goes West	LD	U.S.		$25.00
MCA	40546	An American Tale	LD	U.S.	1987	$50.00
CLV version.						
MCA	40017	An American Werewolf in London	LD	U.S.		$35.00
Vestron	ID5239VE	An American Werewolf in London	LD	U.S.	1985	$35.00
Magnetic Video		An Unmarried Woman	LD	U.S.†	1984	$30.00
Columbia	30701	Anatomy of a Murder	LD	U.S.	1992	$30.00
MGM/UA	ML100309	Anchors Away	LD	U.S.	1988	$30.00
Vestron Video	VL3002	And God Created Woman	LD	U.S.	1983	$35.00

Label	Catalog Number	Title	Type	Country	Year	Value
Columbia	VLD1020	And Justice for All	LD	U.S.	1983	$30.00
Columbia	VLD1025	Anderson Tapes, The	LD	U.S.	1983	$30.00
Columbia	90246	Andy and the Airwave Ranger	LD	U.S.	1990	$15.00
		Andy Warhol's Frankenstein	LD	U.S.		$120.00
Republic	LV20107	Angel and Badman	LD	U.S.	1990	$30.00
Republic	LV20068	Angel and Badman: 45th Anniversary	LD	U.S.	1992	$35.00
Image	ID7269NE	Angel and the Badman	LD	U.S.		$20.00
Image	ID6127IV	Angel Heart	LD	U.S.		$20.00
Image	ID6092NW	Angel III: The Final Chapter	LD	U.S.		$20.00
Vestron Video	VL4009	Angel of H.E.A.T.	LD	U.S.	1983	$30.00
Columbia	VLD1026	Angelo My Love	LD	U.S.	1984	$30.00
Columbia	VLD30688	Angels Over Broadway	LD	U.S.	1986	$30.00
CBS	4588-80	Angels With Dirty Faces	LD	U.S.	1985	$35.00
CBS/Fox	5145-80	Anguish	LD	U.S.	1988	$35.00
Discovision	22-005	Animal Crackers	LD	U.S.	1979	$40.00
Vestron Video	VL4418	Animal Farm	LD	U.S.	1986	$35.00
Discovision	16-007	Animal House	LD	U.S.	1979	$40.00
Discovision	16-007	Animal House	LD	U.S.	1981	$40.00
Paramount	LV60754-6	Animated Adventures of Gene Roddenberry's Star Trek	LTD/LD	U.S.	1990	$150.00
	6 LD boxed set.					
Paramount	LV60754-6	Animated Adventures of Gene Roddenberry's Star Trek	LTD/LD	U.S.	1994	$150.00
	6 LD boxed set.					
Lumivision	LVD9257	Animation Celebration	LD	U.S.	1993	$25.00
Image	ID7591VK	Anna Karenina	LD	U.S.		$30.00
Walt Disney	650 AS	Anne of Avonlea	LD	U.S.	1990	$40.00
Walt Disney	642 AS	Anne of Green Gables	LD	U.S.	1990	$40.00
Columbia		Annie	LD	U.S.		$30.00
	Analog Audio					
Columbia	30127	Annie	LD	U.S.	1990	$30.00
MGM	ML 100251	Annie Hall	LD	U.S.		$35.00
Magnetic Video		Annie Hall	LD	U.S.†	1982	$20.00
CBS/Fox	4518-80	Annie Hall	LD	U.S.	1985	$30.00
Criterion	CC1231L	Annie Hall	LD	U.S.	1990	$50.00
	CLV version.					
Paramount	LV32386	Another 48 Hours	LD	U.S.	1990	$35.00
Republic	LV20120	Another Chance	LD	U.S.	1991	$30.00
Nelson	75585	Another County	LD	U.S.	1985	$70.00
Image	ID6502OR	Another Woman	LD	U.S.		$30.00
Columbia	70666	Another You	LD	U.S.	1991	$30.00
Image	ID7931PR	Any Man's Death	LD	U.S.		$30.00
Paramount	LV2306	Apocalypse Now	LD	U.S.	1981	$25.00
Paramount	LV2306	Apocalypse Now	LD	U.S.	1989	$35.00
Image Entertainment	ID5119	Appaloosa	LD	U.S.	1987	$35.00
		Appaloosa, The	LD	U.S.		$35.00
Live Entertainment	LD60486	Appointment Fear	LD	U.S.	1993	$25.00
		Aquarius	LD	Japan	1987	$100.00
		Arabian Nights	LD	U.S.		$50.00
Discovision		Archeological Dating/The Big Deal	LD	U.S.	1979	$40.00
Columbia	59356	Arena	LD	U.S.	1991	$30.00
		Argetno, Dario – World Of Horror	LD	U.S.		$120.00
Columbia	30724	Armed and Dangerous	LD	U.S.	1993	$25.00
Columbia	30758	Armed Response	LD	U.S.	1993	$25.00
Nelson	902296	Around the World In 80 Days	LD	U.S.	1989	$35.00
CBS/Fox	4603-80	Arsenic & Old Lace	LD	U.S.	1984	$30.00
Discovision		Art Conservator	LD	U.S.	1979	$40.00
Image	ID6474PA	Arthur C. Clarke's Mysterious World Vol. 1	LD	U.S.		$30.00
Image	ID6538PA	Arthur C. Clarke's Mysterious World Vol. 2	LD	U.S.		$30.00
Image	ID6539PA	Arthur C. Clarke's Mysterious World Vol.3	LD	U.S.		$30.00
Image	ID8037PA	Arthur C. Clarke's World Of Strange Powers Vol. 1	LD	U.S.		$30.00
Image	ID8038PA	Arthur C. Clarke's World Of Strange Powers Vol. 2	LD	U.S.		$30.00
Image	ID8039PA	Arthur C. Clarke's World Of Strange Powers Vol. 3	LD	U.S.		$30.00
Image	ID8040PA	Arthur C. Clarke's World Of Strange Powers Vol. 4	LD	U.S.		$30.00
Criterion	CC1226L	Asphalt Jungle	LD	U.S.	1988	$40.00
Image	ID7225HB	Assassin, The	LD	U.S.		$30.00
Republic	LV27022	Assassination of Trotsky	LD	U.S.	1991	$30.00
Walt Disney	860AS	Asterx	LD	U.S.	1990	$30.00
Walt Disney	861AS	Asterx and Cleopatra	LD	U.S.	1990	$30.00
CID	SF2201700	Astro Boy (Limited Edition)	LTD/LD	Japan	1993	$1300.00
	7 LD boxed set.					
Image	ID7999PA	Astronomers	LD	U.S.		$110.00
Image	IDVL5170	At Close Range	LD	U.S.	1986	$80.00
Discovision	D61-505	At Home With Donald Duck	LD	U.S.	1979	$90.00
		At Sword's Point	LD	U.S.		$30.00
Paramount	LV1460	Atlantic City	LD	U.S.	1982	$30.00
Magnetic Video		Autumn Sonata	LD	U.S.	1982	$20.00
CBS	9021-80	Autumn Sonata	LD	U.S.	1985	$30.00
HBO	LD90673	AV. Carmeola! A Film by Carlos Saura	LD	U.S.	1993	$35.00
Columbia	70546	Avalon	LD	U.S.	1991	$25.00
Image	ID5066	Avenging Force	LD	U.S.		$30.00
Columbia	50566	Awakenings	LD	U.S.	1991	$30.00
Columbia	30625-1	Awful Truth, The	LD	U.S.	1986	$30.00
Nelson	75075	B.C. Holiday Happenings	LD	U.S.	1984	$40.00
Image	ID7809IV	Babar the Movie	LD	U.S.		$20.00
Discovision		Baboons of Gombe	LD	U.S.	1979	$40.00
CBS	4744	Baby Boom	LD	U.S.	1988	$25.00
Live Entertainment	LD69939	Baby Girl Scott	LD	U.S.	1993	$35.00
Walt Disney	269AS	Baby: Secret of the Lost Legend	LD	U.S.	1987	$30.00
		Baby, the Rain Must Fall	LD	U.S.		$50.00
HBO	TVL3388	Babysitter, The	LD	U.S.	1988	$30.00
Image	ID6837TU	Bachelor and the Bobby Soxer	LD	U.S.		$85.00
		Bachelor Mother	LD	U.S.		$40.00
CBS	1440-80	Bachelor Party	LD	U.S.	1985	$40.00
		Back From Eternity	LD	U.S.		$35.00
Image	ID7858ME	Back Stab	LD	U.S.		$30.00
		Back to Bataan	LD	U.S.		$50.00
HBO	TVL2988	Back to School	LD	U.S.	1987	$35.00
Paramount	31980	Back to the Beach	LD	U.S.	1988	$35.00
MCA	41056	Back to the Future	LD	U.S.	1991	$35.00
Image	ID6931VK	Backfire	LD	U.S.		$30.00
Image	ID6847HB	Bad Boys	LD	U.S.		$30.00
Image	ID7060TU	Bad Company	LD	U.S.		$15.00
CBS/Fox	1659-80	Bad Dreams	LD	U.S.	1988	$35.00
Columbia	59236	Bad Influence	LD	U.S.	1990	$30.00
Columbia	77046	Bad Jim	LD	U.S.	1990	$30.00
Live Entertainment	LD69948	Bad Lieutenant	LD	U.S.	1993	$35.00
Paramount	LV8863	Bad News Bears	LD	U.S.	1982	$35.00
Image	ID7720MN	Bad Taste	LD	U.S.		$80.00
		Bagunca	LD	U.S.		$40.00
Image	ID7980MF	Balcony, The	LD	U.S.		$35.00
Nelson	30275	Ball of Fire	LD	U.S.	1985	$35.00
Nelson	20625	Ballad of Gregorio Cortez	LD	U.S.	1984	$35.00
		Ballet Ruse	LD	U.S.		$20.00
Walt Disney	942 CS	Bambi	LD	U.S.	1990	$50.00
	CAV version.					
Walt Disney	942 AS	Bambi	LD	U.S.	1990	$30.00

Label	Catalog Number	Title	Type	Country	Year	Value
	CLV version.					
CBS	4555-80	Bananas	LD	U.S.	1983	$40.00
Columbia	30709	Band of the Hand	LD	U.S.	1986	$30.00
MGM/UA	ML100113	Bandwagon, The	LD	U.S.	1987	$35.00
Paramount	LV8732	Bang The Drum Slowly	LD	U.S.	1985	$30.00
Image	ID7138VV	Banker, The	LD	U.S.		$30.00
Paramount	LV6812	Barbarella	LD	U.S.	1985	$30.00
J2	J2-6035	Barbarosa	LD	U.S.	1990	$25.00
Nelson	30285	Barbary Coast	LD	U.S.	1985	$35.00
Paramount	LV9027	Barefoot in The Park	LD	U.S.	1983	$30.00
Warner	11178	Barry Linden	LD	U.S.	1987	$40.00
Image	ID6844CO	Bartleby	LD	U.S.		$30.00
Image	ID7953RH	Baseball's Greatest Hits	LD	U.S.		$20.00
		Basket Case 2	LD	U.S.		$35.00
Discovision		Basketball With Bill Foster & Gail Goodrich	LD	U.S.	1979	$40.00
Image	ID6388ME	Bat 21	LD	U.S.		$30.00
Image	ID757804PK	Bat Whispers, The	LD	U.S.		$30.00
CBS	1470-80	Batman – The Movie	LD	U.S.	1990	$30.00
Image	ID6786AX	Battle of Algiers	LD	U.S.		$30.00
		Battle of Britain	LD	U.S.		$150.00
Republic	LV20225	Battleship Potemkin	LD	U.S.	1991	18
Discovision	19-007	Battlestar Galactica	LD	U.S.	1979	$40.00
MCA	19-007	Battlestar Galactica	LD	U.S.	1982	$80.00
CIC	SF0781310	Battlestar Galactica: Conquest of Earth	LD	Japan		$100.00
Discovision	19-007	Battlestar Galactica: Mission Galactica	LD	U.S.	1980	$60.00
MCA	19-007	Battlestar Galactica: Mission Galactica	LD	U.S.	1985	$40.00
Lumivision	LVD9252	Baxter	LD	U.S.	1993	$25.00
HBO	TVL3349	Beach Blanket Bingo	LD	U.S.	1988	$30.00
Paramount	LV2314	Beach Girls, The	LD	U.S.	1983	$30.00
Walt Disney	797AS	Beaches	LD	U.S.	1989	$30.00
	Distributed by Pioneer.					
Image	ID6223RC	Beany and Cecil	LD	U.S.		$30.00
Columbia	70216	Bear, The	LD	U.S.	1990	$35.00
Republic	LV20230	Beast Master II: Through the Portal Of Time	LD	U.S.	1992	$30.00
Vestron	VL5047	Beat Street	LD	U.S.	1984	$35.00
		Beat, The	LD	U.S.		$35.00
Image	ID6020RC	Beat the Devil	LD	U.S.		$30.00
Image Entertainment	IG-5006	Beatlemania	LD	U.S.	1985	$35.00
Walt Disney	PILA-1232	Beauty and the Beast	LTD/LD	Japan	1993	$170.00
	3 LD boxed set containing the LBX film plus the "Work In Progress" along with a "Making Of..." Book.					
CBS/Fox	6395-80	Beauty and the Beast	LD	U.S.	1984	$25.00
Walt Disney	1325 CS	Beauty and the Beast	LD	U.S.	1994	$70.00
	CAV version.					
Walt Disney	1325 AS	Beauty and the Beast	LD	U.S.	1994	$35.00
	CLV version.					
Republic	LV20242	Beauty and the Beast: Episode 1 & 2	LD	U.S.	1992	$25.00
Republic	LV20236	Beauty and the Beast: Episode 3 & 4	LD	U.S.	1992	$25.00
Republic	LV20237	Beauty and the Beast: Episode 5& 6	LD	U.S.	1992	$25.00
Republic	LV20245	Beauty and the Beast: Though Lovers Be Lost	LD	U.S.	1991	$25.00
Walt Disney	1591 CS	Beauty and the Beast: Work In Progress	LD	U.S.	1992	$70.00
Image	ID 6199MP	Becket	LD	U.S.	1964	$50.00
CBS/Fox	1120-80	Bedazzled	LD	U.S.	1990	$45.00
Walt Disney	16AS	Bedknobs and Broomsticks	LD	U.S.	1983	$25.00
	Non-remastered version.					
Image		Bedlam	LD	U.S.		$80.00
Vestron Video	VL5209	Bedroom Window	LD	U.S.	1987	$35.00
		Beetle Bailey – Camp Swampy	LD	U.S.		$25.00
Walt Disney		Behind the Scenes At Walt Disney Studios	LD	Japan		N/A
CBS	7026-80	Being There	LD	U.S.	1983	$30.00
HBO	TVL0034	Believers, The	LD	U.S.	1988	$35.00
Image	ID6109RC	Bell, Book and Candle	LD	U.S.		$30.00
Image	ID7286IV	Bellboy, The	LD	U.S.		$30.00
MGM/UA	ML100063	Bells Are Ringing	LD	U.S.	1986	$40.00
Image	ID6231RE	Bells of St. Mary's	LD	U.S.		$30.00
	8003	Belly of An Architect	LD	U.S.		$20.00
Image	I5052	Ben	LD	U.S.	1986	$90.00
MGM/UA		Ben Hur	LD	Japan	1986	$200.00
	3 disc boxed set.					
MGM/UA		Ben Hur	LD	U.S.	1984	$30.00
MGM/UA		Ben Hur	LD	U.S.	1988	$30.00
Disney	939AS	Ben & Me	LD	U.S.	1989	$30.00
Lumivision	LVD9313	Beneath the 12-Mile	LD	U.S.	1993	$25.00
CBS	1013-80	Beneath the Planet of the Apes	LD	U.S.		$100.00
Magnetic Video		Beneath the Planet of the Apes	LD	U.S.†	1984	$100.00
Disney	594 AS	Benji the Hunted	LD	U.S.	1987	$35.00
Disney	594LV	Benji the Hunted	LD	U.S.	1988	$35.00
Nelson	75085	Berenstein Bears	LD	U.S.	1984	$35.00
Cannon	31072	Berlin Blues	LD	U.S.	1990	$30.00
Columbia	91926	Berlin Conspiracy, The	LD	U.S.	1992	$30.00
Image	ID7057TU	Berlin Express	LD	U.S.		$30.00
Lumivision	LVD9102	Best Boy	LD	U.S.	1991	$35.00
Paramount	LV1587	Best Defense	LD	U.S.	1985	$30.00
Discovision	17-008	Best Little Whorehouse in Texas	LD	U.S.	1983	$35.00
Image	ID6596VS	Best of Ray Bradbury Theater Vol. 1	LD	U.S.		$35.00
Image	ID7128FI	Best of Ray Bradbury Theater Vol. 1	LD	U.S.		$35.00
Image	ID7122FL	Best of Ray Bradbury Theater Vol. 2	LD	U.S.		$35.00
Image		Best of Roger Rabit, The	LD	U.S.	1996	$80.00
	1st pressing released February 1996, recalled March 1996 because of questionalble scenes.					
Image	ID7511SO	Best of the Best	LD	U.S.		$30.00
Image	ID6730RH	Best of the Cutting Edge	LD	U.S.		$30.00
Republic	LV27019	Best of the Little Rascals	LD	U.S.	1989	$25.00
Nelson	13075	Best of Times	LD	U.S.	1986	$35.00
Paramount	LV12538	Best Spike Jones - I	LD	U.S.	1987	$25.00
Paramount	12539LV	Best Spike Jones - II	LD	U.S.	1987	$25.00
Nelson	30315	Best Years of Our Lives	LD	U.S.	1985	$40.00
Discovision		Better Tennis in Thirty Minutes	LD	U.S.	1979	$40.00
Republic	LV27065	Betty Boop 60th Anniversary	LD	U.S.	1990	$25.00
Republic	LV20266	Betty Boop 60th Anniversary Vol. II	LD	U.S.	1991	$25.00
Columbia	50486	Beulah Land	LD	U.S.	1990	$30.00
Image	ID7847ME	Beverly Hills Brats	LD	U.S.		$30.00
Paramount	LV1134	Beverly Hills Cop	LD	U.S.	1985	$30.00
Paramount	LV1860	Beverly Hills Cop II	LD	U.S.	1988	$35.00
Republic	LV27067	Beware My Lovely	LD	U.S.	1992	$30.00
Columbia	25564	Beyond the Door III	LD	U.S.	1991	$30.00
Image	ID7315IV	Beyond the Stars	LD	U.S.		$30.00
Magnetic Video		Bible, The	LD	U.S.†	1984	$30.00
CBS	1020-85	Bible, The	LD	U.S.	1991	$70.00
	Letterbox version.					
CBS	1658-80	Big	LD	U.S.	1989	$25.00
Image	ID7706MN	Big Bad John	LD	U.S.		$30.00
Columbia	31026	Big Blue	LD	U.S.	1989	$120.00
Walt Disney	650AS	Big Business	LD	U.S.	1989	$30.00
Criterion	CC1233L	Big Chill	LD	U.S.	1991	$50.00
Columbia	VLD2018	Big Chill	LD	U.S.	1992	$35.00
Vestron Video	VL3137	Big City Comedy	LD	U.S.	1986	$30.00
HBO	TVL0052	Big Easy	LD	U.S.	1988	$25.00
Image	ID6384RC	Big Heat	LD	U.S.		$120.00

Label	Catalog Number	Title	Type	Country	Year	Value
7149-85		Big Jake	LD	U.S.		$25.00
Columbia	90946	Big Man	LD	U.S.	1992	$30.00
Columbia	50266	Big Picture, The	LD	U.S.	1990	$30.00
CBS/Fox	7052-80	Big Red One, The	LD	U.S.	1987	$35.00
CBS/Fox	4532-80	Big Sleep, The	LD	U.S.	1984	$35.00
Image		Big Steal, The	LD	U.S.		$40.00
CBS	1502-80	Big Trouble In Little China	LD	U.S.	1987	$20.00
	P&S version.					
Image	ID5209VE	Big Town, The	LD	U.S.		$30.00
Columbia	10627	Big Trouble	LD	U.S.	1992	$30.00
Image	ID8641PR	Bikini Island	LD	U.S.		$30.00
Interscope	PRCD 3914-2	Bill & Ted's Bogus Journey	DJ/Smplr	U.S.	1991	$5.00
Nelson		Bill & Ted's Excellant Adventure	LD	U.S.	1989	$60.00
Vestron Video	VL3140	Billy Crystal	LD	U.S.	1986	$35.00
Columbia	70726	Bingo	LD	U.S.	1992	$30.00
Discovision	16-0	Bingo Long Traveling All-Stars and Motor Kings	LD	U.S.	1979	$40.00
Discovision	20-001	Bionic Woman, The	LD	U.S.	1979	$40.00
Image	ID6593VC	Bird With the Crystal Plumage, The	LD	U.S.		$80.00
Discovision	11-007	Birds, The	LD	U.S.	1979	$40.00
Columbia	30457	Birdy	LD	U.S.	1992	$30.00
Lumivision	LVD9028	Birth of a Nation	LD	U.S.	1991	$25.00
Republic	LV20308	Birth of a Nation	LD	U.S.	1991	$25.00
Nelson	30305	Bishop's Wife, The	LD	U.S.	1985	$50.00
Columbia	VLD2008	Bite the Bullet	LD	U.S.	1984	$30.00
		Black Caesar	LD	U.S.		$80.00
		Black Cat	LD	U.S.		$55.00
Walt Disney	11AS	Black Hole, The	LD	U.S.	1985	$50.00
Image	I5057	Black Moon Rising	LD	U.S.	1986	$25.00
Criterion	CC1138L	Black Narcissus	LD	U.S.	1988	$50.00
Criterion	CC1172L	Black Orpheus	LD	U.S.	1989	$50.00
Republic	LV20314	Black Pirate, The	LD	U.S.	1991	$30.00
		Black Room, The	LD	U.S.		$100.00
CBS	4503-80	Black Stallion	LD	U.S.		$30.00
Magnetic Video		Black Stallion	LD	U.S.	1982	$30.00
Magnetic Video		Black Stallion	LD	U.S.†	1982	$30.00
CBS	4712-80	Black Stallion Returns	LD	U.S.	1983	$30.00
Paramount	LV8855-2	Black Sunday	LD	U.S.	1983	$36.00
		Black Sunday/Black Sabbath	LD	U.S.		$80.00
CBS	5033-80	Black Widow	LD	U.S.	1987	$30.00
Image	ID7072TU	Blackbeard the Pirate	LD	U.S.		$30.00
Image	ID7721MN	Blackout	LD	U.S.		$30.00
HBO	TVL3242	Blacula	LD	U.S.	1988	$110.00
Nelson	13805	Blade Runner	LD	U.S.	1983	$40.00
Criterion	CC1169L	Blade Runner	LD	U.S.	1989	$50.00
Criterion	CC1120L	Blade Runner	LD	U.S.	1989	$90.00
	CAV version.					
Image	ID7853ME	Blades	LD	U.S.	1988	$15.00
Vestron	VL 5040	Blame It on Rio	LD	U.S.		$40.00
Vestron Video	VL5040	Blame It on Rio	LD	U.S.	1984	$35.00
Disney	915AS	Blaze	LD	U.S.	1990	$30.00
	Distributed by Pioneer.					
Columbia	30822	Blind Date	LD	U.S.	1992	$30.00
Columbia	70256	Blind Fury	LD	U.S.	1990	$30.00
Nelson	90237LV	Blindside	LD	U.S.	1988	$30.00
Criterion	CC1165L	Blob, The	LD	U.S.	1989	$50.00
Warner Home Video	LRP-009	Blockbuster Highlights	DJ/LD	Japan		$100.00
	Film clips of various home video releases including the Beatles' "Yellow Submarine."					
Image		Blood and Sand	LD	U.S.		$40.00
Republic	LV20341	Blood and Sand	LD	U.S.	1991	$40.00
Columbia	90996	Blood & Concrete	LD	U.S.	1992	$30.00
		Blood Feast	LD	U.S.		$100.00
Columbia	59146	Blood Games	LD	U.S.	1990	$30.00
J2	J2-6034	Blood Money	LD	U.S.	1989	$25.00
Republic	LV20004	Blood of the Gun	LD	U.S.	1990	$25.00
Nelson	7738	Blood Red	LD	U.S.	1990	$35.00
Nelson	77406	Blood Relations	LD	U.S.	1990	$85.00
Image	ID7822MN	Blood Salvage	LD	U.S.		$30.00
Columbia	50276	Bloodhounds of Broadway	LD	U.S.	1990	$20.00
Full Moon	LV83124	BLOODLUST: SUBSPECIES III	LD	U.S.	1994	$35.00
		Bloodmoon	LD	U.S.		$20.00
Image	ID7522VE	Bloody Mama	LD	U.S.		$30.00
Image	IDVL4023	Blow Out	LD	U.S.		$35.00
Criterion	CC1148L	Blow-Up	LD	U.S.	1988	$80.00
Republic	LV20346	Blowing Wild	LD	U.S.	1993	$30.00
Vestron Video	VL4023	Blowout	LD	U.S.	1983	$35.00
Paramount	LV1648	Blue City	LD	U.S.	1986	$30.00
Discovision	10-017	Blue Collar	LD	U.S.	1979	$40.00
Image Entertainment	ID5120	Blue Collar	LD	U.S.	1987	$35.00
		Blue Desert	LD	U.S.		$26.00
Magnetic Video		Blue Hawaii	LD	U.S.†	1982	$50.00
CBS	2001	Blue Hawaii	LD	U.S.	1985	$30.00
Columbia	VLD2990	Blue Lagoon	LD	U.S.	1993	$30.00
Magnetic Video		Blue Max, The	LD	U.S.†	1984	$30.00
CBS	1062-80	Blue Max, The	LD	U.S.	1989	$70.00
Lumivision	LVD9214	Blue Planet	LD	U.S.	1993	$25.00
Image Entertainment	I-5055	Blue Steel/Man From Utah	LD	U.S.	1986	$35.00
Columbia	350496	Blue & the Grey	LD	U.S.	1990	$50.00
Columbia	VLD2991	Blue Thunder	LD	U.S.	1992	$20.00
Lorimar	LV399	Blue Velvet	LD	U.S.	1987	$40.00
Discovision	16-020	Blues Brothers, The	LD	U.S.	1980	$40.00
Discovision	16-020	Blues Brothers, The	LD	U.S.	1981	$35.00
Columbia	VLD2293	Boat, The	LD	U.S.	1992	$30.00
Image	ID6022RC	Bob & Carol & Ted & Alice	LD	U.S.		$30.00
Columbia	90756	Body Chemistry	LD	U.S.	1990	$30.00
Columbia		Body Double	LD	U.S.		$20.00
	Non-remastered version.					
Columbia	30411	Body Double	LD	U.S.	1992	$20.00
		Body Moves	LD	U.S.		$25.00
		Body Music	LD	U.S.		$20.00
Image	ID6235RE	Body & Soul	LD	U.S.		$80.00
Image	ID7846ME	Boggy Creek II	LD	U.S.		$15.00
		Bohemian Girl	LD	U.S.		$60.00
Discovision		Bolero	LD	U.S.	1979	$40.00
Image	IG-5009	Bolero	LD	U.S.	1985	$30.00
Paramount	LV1158	Bon Voyage, Charlie Brown	LD	U.S.	1983	$30.00
Image	ID7708MN	Boogyman, The	LD	U.S.		$40.00
Columbia	75146	Book of Love	LD	U.S.	1991	$30.00
		Boost, The	LD	U.S.		$20.00
Image	ID6841CO	Boris Godunov	LD	U.S.		$30.00
Image	ID6166RC	Born Free	LD	U.S.		$30.00
Image	ID7088TU	Born to Be Bad	LD	U.S.		$25.00
Columbia	30143	Born Yesterday	LD	U.S.	1988	$30.00
Cannon	32108	Borrower, The	LD	U.S.	1992	$30.00
Vestron	VL5067	Bostonians	LD	U.S.	1985	$35.00
Image	ID6512MG	Bound For Glory	LD	U.S.		$45.00
Image	IDVL5044	Bounty, The	LD	U.S.	1984	$80.00
Republic	LV20420	Bounty Tracker	LD	U.S.	1993	$35.00

Label	Catalog Number	Title	Type	Country	Year	Value
Image	ID7251VE	Boxcar Bertha	LD	U.S.		$85.00
Image	ID28170	Boxing Helena	LTD/LD	U.S.	1996	$100.00
	Autographed LD boxed set with CD Soundtrack.					
CBS	7121-80	Boy Named Charlie Brown	LD	U.S.	1984	$30.00
Lorimar	LV351	Boy Who Could Fly	LD	U.S.	1987	$40.00
CBS/Fox	6393-80	Boy Who Left Home, The	LD	U.S.	1984	$35.00
CBS	9002-80	Boys From Brazil, The	LD	U.S.	1982	$30.00
Magnetic Video		Boys From Brazil, The	LD	U.S.†	1984	$30.00
CBS	C7017	Boys in the Band	LD	U.S.	1989	$30.00
		Boys Next Door, The	LD	U.S.		$35.00
Vid-America	VL7017	Boys of Summer, The	LD	U.S.	1986	$30.00
Columbia	50816	Boyz N the Hood	LD	U.S.	1992	$30.00
Criterion	CC11289L	Boyz N the Hood	LD	U.S.	1992	$50.00
		Bozo the Clown – Ding Dong	LD	U.S.		$25.00
		Bozo the Clown – Wowie Kazowie	LD	U.S.		$25.00
Vid-America	7021	Brady's Escape	LD	U.S.	1985	$35.00
		Brain From Planet Arous	LD	U.S.		$50.00
		Brain, The	LD	U.S.		$30.00
MGM/UA	ML100314	Brainstorm	LD	U.S.		$35.00
MGM/UA	ML102235	Brainstorm	LD	U.S.	1991	$35.00
MGM/UA	ML100199	Brass Target	LD	U.S.	1984	$35.00
Nelson	19405	Breaker Morant	LD	U.S.	1984	$40.00
Live Entertainment	LD51018	Breaker Morant	LD	U.S.	1992	$35.00
Lorimar	LV6505	Breakfast at Tiffany's	LD	U.S.		$30.00
		Breakfast at Tiffany's	LTD/LD	U.S.	1994	$70.00
	Boxed Set					
Image	ID6514MG	Breakheart Pass	LD	U.S.		$30.00
CBS	1081-80	Breaking Away	LD	U.S.	1984	$30.00
		Breaking Point	LD	U.S.		$25.00
Image	ID6298RC	Breakout	LD	U.S.		$30.00
Vestron	VL5017	Breathless	LD	U.S.	1983	$35.00
Image	ID6108RC	Brian's Song	LD	U.S.		$80.00
		Bride of Frankenstein	LD	Japan	1986	$120.00
Discovision	23-003	Bride of Frankenstein	LD	U.S.	1979	$40.00
Image	ID7610IV	Bride of Re-Animator	LD	U.S.		$125.00
Columbia	30569	Bride, The	LD	U.S.	1986	$30.00
Columbia	VLD2010	Bridge Over River Kwai	LD	U.S.	1992	$20.00
Paramount	5906	Bridges at Toko-Ri, The	LD	U.S.	1988	$110.00
MGM/UA	ML100040	Brigadoon	LD	U.S.	1983	$35.00
Lorimar	LV344	Bring on the Night	LD	U.S.	1986	$40.00
CBS	1654-80	Broadcast News	LD	U.S.	1988	$20.00
Image	IDVL5041	Broadway Danny Rose	LD	U.S.	1984	$50.00
Republic	LV20444	Broken Blossoms	LD	U.S.	1991	$30.00
		Brood	LD	U.S.		$55.00
Republic	LV20400	Brothers in Arms	LD	U.S.	1991	$30.00
CBS	1098-80	Brubaker	LD	U.S.	1985	$40.00
Image	ID7161SO	Brute Man, The	LD	U.S.		$95.00
	95003	Bubble Gum Crisis Universe	LTD/LD	U.S.	1995	240
Discovision	22-007	Buck Private	LD	U.S.	1979	$40.00
Discovision	13-002	Buck Rogers in the 25th Century	LD	U.S.	1981	$75.00
J2	J2-6045	Bud and Lou	LD	U.S.	1990	$30.00
Columbia	30801	Buddy Holly Story	LD	U.S.	1988	$30.00
Image	ID7432IN	Buffet Froid	LD	U.S.		$30.00
		Bugsy Malone	LD	U.S.		$30.00
Paramount	LV8898	Bugsy Malone	LD	U.S.	1985	$30.00
		Bullet in the Head	LD	U.S.		$100.00
Columbia	60932	Bulletproof	LD	U.S.	1989	$30.00
Republic	LV20245	Bullfighter and the Lady, The	LD	U.S.	1991	$25.00
Columbia	77156	Bullseye	LD	U.S.	1991	$30.00
		Buried Alive	LD	U.S.		$30.00
Nelson	902146	Burke & Wills	LD	U.S.	1987	$35.00
Image	ID7326VV	Burndown	LD	U.S.		$30.00
J2	J2-6039	Burning Rage	LD	U.S.	1990	$30.00
Image	ID6461VE	Burning Secret	LD	U.S.		$30.00
Columbia	VLD30537	Burns, George & Gracie Allen Vol. 1	LD	U.S.	1986	$40.00
Magnetic Video		Bus Stop	LD	U.S.†	1984	$30.00
CBS	1031-80	Bus Stop	LD	U.S.	1985	$30.00
Image	ID7815HB	Buster	LD	U.S.	1988	$15.00
Discovision		Bustin' Loose	LD	U.S.		$40.00
MCA	16-026	Bustin' Loose	LD	U.S.	1985	$30.00
CBS	1061-80	Butch and Cassidy	LD	U.S.	1985	$30.00
Magnetic Video		Butch Cassidy and the Sundance Kid	LD	U.S.†	1981	$30.00
Magnetic Video		Butch Cassidy and the Sundance Kid	LD	U.S.†	1984	$30.00
Vestron Video	VL6007	Butterfly	LD	U.S.	1983	$45.00
Image	ID7815HB	By Dawn's Early Light	LD	U.S.	1990	$20.00
Columbia	30150	Bye Bye Birdie	LD	U.S.	1985	$40.00
Psedition	PSE91-10	Bye Bye Birdie	LD	U.S.	1991	$50.00
Image	I5044	C.H.U.D.	LD	U.S.	1986	$15.00
Image	ID 6554VE	C.H.U.D. II	LD	U.S.	1988	$15.00
Disney	251AS	Cab Calloway	LD	U.S.	1985	$35.00
CBS	7035-80	Cabaret	LD	U.S.	1983	$25.00
Republic	LV20480	Cabinet of Dr. Caligari, The	LD	U.S.	1991	$30.00
Columbia	VLD3011	Cactus Flower	LD	U.S.	1984	$30.00
Warner Home Video	2005LV	Caddy Shack	LD	U.S.	1983	$25.00
Republic	LV20482	Cadence	LD	U.S.	1991	$30.00
Republic	LV20485	Cafe Romeo	LD	U.S.	1992	$30.00
Image	ID7348OR	Cage	LD	U.S.		$30.00
Columbia	77036	Caged Fury	LD	U.S.	1990	$30.00
Image	ID7216VK	Caged in Paradiso	LD	U.S.		$30.00
Columbia	30425	Caine Mutiny, The	LD	U.S.	1992	$20.00
		California Casanova	LD	U.S.		$25.00
Columbia	VLD3010	California Suite	LD	U.S.	1985	$100.00
Vestron Video	PL5032	Caligula	LD	U.S.	1984	$40.00
Paramount	LV40150	Call To Glory	LD	U.S.	1985	$30.00
Warner Home Video	11084LV	Camelot	LD	U.S.	1984	$30.00
Paramount	1867	Campus Man	LD	U.S.	1988	$35.00
CBS	C1016	Can Can	LD	U.S.	1989	$30.00
Paramount	LV12764	Can She Bake A Cherry Pie?	LD	U.S.	1992	$35.00
Disney	597AS	Can't Buy Me Love	LD	U.S.	1988	$30.00
Image	IDVL6001	Cannonball Run	LD	U.S.		$30.00
Image	ID 8507WB	Cantebury Tales, The	LD	U.S.		$20.00
CBS	9007-80	Capricorn 1	LD	U.S.		$110.00
Magnetic Video		Capricorn 1	LD	U.S.	1982	$110.00
		Captain Scarlet & the Mysterons Vol. 1	LD	Japan		$135.00
		Captain Scarlet & the Mysterons Vol. 2	LD	Japan		$135.00
		Captain Scarlet & the Mysterons Vol. 3	LD	Japan		$135.00
		Captain Scarlet & the Mysterons Vol. 4	LD	Japan		$135.00
Discovision	16-003	Car Wash	LD	U.S.	1979	$40.00
Image	ID7258CV	Caravaggio	LD	U.S.		$30.00
Nelson	16095	Carbon Copy	LD	U.S.	1983	$40.00
Vestron Video	VL2017	Carlin at Carnegie	LD	U.S.	1984	$30.00
Vestron Video	VL3061	Carlin on Campus	LD	U.S.	1985	$30.00
MGM/UA	ML100859	Carlyle	LD	U.S.	1986	$35.00
Image	ID5069	Carmen	LD	U.S.		$30.00
Columbia	30487	Carmen	LD	U.S.	1987	$30.00
Columbia	1048-85	Carmen Jones	LD	U.S.		$30.00
Image	ID6838CO	Carmen: Poem of Dances	LD	U.S.		$30.00

Label	Catalog Number	Title	Type	Country	Year	Value
Magnetic Video		Carnal Knowledge	LD	U.S.	1982	$20.00
Magnetic Video		Carnal Knowledge	LD	U.S.†	1984	$30.00
CBS/Fox	4003-80	Carnal Knowledge	LD	U.S.	1985	$45.00
Nelson	20306	Carnal Knowledge	LD	U.S.	1989	$35.00
Criterion	CC1275L	Carnal Knowledge	LD	U.S.	1991	$50.00
Image	ID7767VA	Carnival of Souls	LD	U.S.		$80.00
Republic	LV21817	Caroline?	LD	U.S.	1992	$30.00
Republic	LV20532	Carpenter	LD	U.S.	1991	$25.00
CBS	4512-80	Carrie	LD	U.S.	1981	$20.00
Magnetic Video		Carrie	LD	U.S.	1981	$25.00
Criterion	CC1278L	Carrie	LD	U.S.	1992	$90.00
	CAV version. Distributed by Pioneer.					
Walt Disney		Cartoon Classics: Here's Donald/Here's Goofy	LD	U.S.	1988	$25.00
Disney		Cartoon Classics Limited Gold Daisy	LD	Japan	1984	$150.00
Disney	SFO68-1072	Cartoon Classics Limited Gold Edition Mickey Mouse	LD	Japan	1984	$200.00
Disney		Cartoon Classics Limited Gold From Pluto With Love	LD	Japan	1984	$150.00
Disney		Cartoon Classics Limited Gold Mini Mouse	LD	Japan	1984	$150.00
Disney	868AS	Cartoon Classics: Micki & Minnie	LD	U.S.	1988	$35.00
Disney		Cartoon Classics Vol. 3: Scary Tales	LD	U.S.		$80.00
Disney		Cartoon Classics Vol. 4: Animal Tales	LD	U.S.		$80.00
Republic	LV27106	Cartoonies Featuring Gaby	LD	U.S.	1991	$25.00
CBS	4514-2	Casablanca	LD	U.S.	1982	$20.00
MGM/UA	ML101264	Casablanca	LD	U.S.	1989	$25.00
Criterion	CC1179L	Casablanca	LD	U.S.	1989	$100.00
	CAV version.					
Criterion	CC1287L	Casablanca	LD	U.S.	1992	$50.00
	CLV version.					
		Casanova's Night Out	LD	U.S.		$30.00
Columbia	30630	Casino Royale	LD	U.S.	1992	$30.00
Magnetic Video		Cassandra Crossing	LD	U.S.†	1984	$30.00
Columbia	50186	Casualties of War	LD	U.S.	1990	$30.00
MGM/UA	ML100060	Cat on a Hot Tin Roof	LD	U.S.	1983	$26.00
Vestron Video	VL4213	Cat on a Hot Tin Roof	LD	U.S.	1985	$30.00
MCA		Cat People	LD	Japan	1985	$70.00
MCA		Cat People	LD	U.K.	1983	$40.00
	PAL					
MCA		Cat People	LD	U.S.	1982	$30.00
Image	I6005	Cat People (1934)	LD	U.S.	1986	$25.00
Image	ID7427VV	Catch Me If You Can	LD	U.S.		$15.00
Paramount	LV6924	Catch-22	LD	U.S.	1983	$30.00
Walt Disney	781AS	Cattle Queen	LD	U.S.	1985	$30.00
Columbia	VLD30529	Cave Girl	LD	U.S.	1985	$30.00
Walt Disney		Celebrate With Disney	LD	Japan	1995	$70.00
		Celler Dweller	LD	U.S.		$30.00
		Center of the Web	LD	U.S.		$35.00
Image Entertainment	I-5040	Certain Fury	LD	U.S.	1985	$35.00
Nelson	90035	Chain Reaction, The	LD	U.S.	1985	$35.00
Image	ID7529VE	Chained Heat	LD	U.S.		$30.00
Pioneer		Challenge to Hi-Fi Picture	DJ/LD	U.S.		$40.00
	Test disc					
Republic	LV20617	Champion	LD	U.S.	1992	$50.00
Image	7744J2	Champions Forever	LD	U.S.		$30.00
Discovision		Champions Never Quit	LD	U.S.	1979	$40.00
Nelson	20865	Champions, The	LD	U.S.	1984	$35.00
Image	ID6621TS	Chances Are	LD	U.S.		$30.00
Vestron Video	VL6006	Changeling, The	LD	U.S.	1983	$35.00
Columbia	3040	Chapter Two	LD	U.S.	1985	$35.00
CBS	4602-80	Charge of the Light	LD	U.S.	1984	$20.00
Warner Home Video	20004LV	Chariots of Fire	LD	U.S.	1983	$35.00
CBS	1714-80	Charlie Chan	LD	U.S.	1989	$50.00
Image	ID6047ME	Charlie Chaplin Lost and Found	LD	U.S.		$30.00
Image	ID6048ME	Charlie Chaplin Lost and Found	LD	U.S.		$30.00
Image	ID6049ME	Charlie Chaplin Lost and Found II	LD	U.S.		$30.00
Image	ID6052ME	Charlie Chaplin Lost and Found III	LD	U.S.		$30.00
Image	ID6050ME	Charlie Chaplin Lost and Found: The Mutual 1	LD	U.S.		$30.00
Image	ID6051ME	Charlie Chaplin Lost And Found: The Mutual II	LD	U.S.		$30.00
Republic	LV27118	Charlie Chaplin Vol. 1	LD	U.S.	1991	$35.00
Republic	LV27119	Charlie Chaplin Vol. 2	LD	U.S.	1991	$35.00
Republic	LV27120	Charlie Chaplin Vol. 3	LD	U.S.	1991	$35.00
Paramount	LV8099	Charlotte's Web	LD	U.S.	1985	$30.00
CBS	8020-80	Charly	LD	U.S.	1982	$30.00
Columbia		Chase, The	LD	U.S.	1986	$40.00
Psedition	PSE91-17	Chase, The	LD	U.S.	1991	$40.00
		Check and Double Check	LD	U.S.		$50.00
Discovision		Cheech & Chong	LD	U.S.	1981	$40.00
Disney	912AS	Cheetah	LD	U.S.	1990	$35.00
Image	ID6242OR	Cherry 2000	LD	U.S.	1987	$40.00
Image	ID7616IV	Chicago Joe and the Showgirl	LD	U.S.		$30.00
Sony Video	J0067DL	Chico Hamilton	LD	U.S.	1986	$30.00
Image	ID7145VE	Children in the Crossfire	LD	U.S.		$15.00
Paramount	LV1839	Children of a Lessor God	LD	U.S.	1987	$40.00
Nelson	40395	Children of the Corn	LD	U.S.	1984	$40.00
Image	ID5208VE	China Girl	LD	U.S.		$30.00
Columbia	30159	China Syndrome	LD	U.S.		$20.00
	Analog audio					
RCA/Columbia	VLD3060	China Syndrome	LD	U.S.	1981	$40.00
Columbia	30159	China Syndrome	LD	U.S.	1991	$30.00
Paramount	LV8674	Chinatown	LD	U.S.	1982	$40.00
Walt Disney	618AS	Chip 'n Dale Rescue Rangers	LD	U.S.	1989	$25.00
Image	ID5262LO	Chipmunk Adventure, The	LD	U.S.		$25.00
CBS/Fox	4557-80	Chitty Chitty Bang Bang	LD	U.S.	1983	$45.00
Image	ID7201VV	Chocolate War	LD	U.S.		$30.00
Discovision	12-011	Choirboys, The	LD		1979	$40.00
Image	I5045	Choose Me	LD	U.S.	1986	$30.00
Nelson	21835	Chorus Line: The Movie	LD	U.S.	1986	$30.00
Columbia		Christine	LD	U.S.		$30.00
	First pressing					
Columbia	VLD3065	Christine	LD	U.S.	1993	$30.00
		Christmas With Flicka	LD	U.S.		$25.00
		Christopher Strong	LD	U.S.		$30.00
WEA	50255	Chroma	LD	U.S.	1992	$30.00
Image	ID7464PA	Ciao! Manhattan	LD	U.S.		$30.00
Walt Disney	410 CS	Cinderella	LD	U.S.	1988	$60.00
	CAV version.					
Walt Disney	410 AS	Cinderella	LD	U.S.	1988	$20.00
	CLV version.					
Walt Disney	410	Cinderella	LD	U.S.	1995	$30.00
Walt Disney	4964	Cinderella	LTD/LD	U.S.	1995	$100.00
	3 LD boxed set.					
Walt Disney	PILA-1125	Cinderella – A Commemoration of LaserDisc Release	LTD/LD	Japan	1992	$150.00
	CAV LD, book, framed lithograph, and metal plate housed in 12"x12" box.					
		Cinema Paradiso	LD	U.S.		$200.00
Columbia	90516	Circuitry Man	LD	U.S.	1991	$30.00
Image		Circus of Horror/Baron Blood	LD	U.S.		$60.00
Image	1-6002	Citizen Kane	LD	U.S.		$100.00
	Commentary track.					
Criterion	CC1115L	Citizen Kane	LD	U.S.	1987	$50.00
Criterion	CC101L	Citizen Kane	LD	U.S.	1987	$100.00
	CAV version.					
Criterion	CC1285L	Citizen Kane	LD	U.S.	1992	$40.00
Nelson	75266	City Slickers	LD	U.S.	1991	$30.00
ABC		City, The	DJ/Smplr	U.S.		$25.00
	CD-ROM					
PBS	LPBS306	Civil War, The	LTD/LD	U.S.	1991	$200.00
	6 LD boxed set.					
Image	ID5353ME	Clair's Knee	LD	U.S.		$30.00
CBS	6795-80	Clan of the Cave Bear	LD	U.S.	1986	$40.00
MGM/UA	ML100074	Clash of the Titans	LD	U.S.	1983	$35.00
Vestron	VL5026	Class	LD	U.S.	1984	$35.00
Vestron	VL5022	Class of 1984	LD	U.S.	1983	$80.00
Vestron	VL5021	Class Reunion	LD	U.S.	1983	$80.00
CBS	1143-80	Cleopatra	LD	U.S.	1991	$75.00
RCA/Columbia	LD52236	Cliffhanger	LD	U.S.	1993	$30.00
RCA/Columbia	LD52236WS	Cliffhanger	LD	U.S.	1993	$30.00
Image	ID5321VV	Climb, The	LD	U.S.		$30.00
Republic	LV20694	Cloak and Dagger	LD	U.S.	1992	$30.00
Warner Home Video	1031LV	Clockwork Orange	LD	U.S.	1984	$35.00
Warner	1031LV	Clockwork Orange	LD	U.S.	1984	$25.00
	P&S version.					
Columbia	VLD3095	Close Encounters of the Third Kind	LD	U.S.		$30.00
	First pressing					
Criterion	CC1241L	Close Encounters of the Third Kind	LD	U.S.	1990	124
Columbia	VLD3095	Close Encounters of the Third Kind	LD	U.S.	1992	$30.00
Criterion	CC1242L	Close Encounters of the Third Kind	LD	U.S.	1992	$60.00
		Closer, The	LD	U.S.		$30.00
Columbia	59106	Clown House	LD	U.S.	1990	$30.00
Image	ID8051PR	Club Extinction	LD	U.S.		$30.00
Paramount	LV1840	Clue	LD	U.S.	1986	$30.00
Discovision	15-005	Coal Miner's Daughter	LD	U.S.	1980	$40.00
Discovision		Coal Miner's Daughter	LD	U.S.	1981	$30.00
		Coast to Coast	LD	U.S.		$30.00
Vestron	VL5099	Coca-Cola Kid	LD	U.S.	1985	$45.00
Disney	606AS	Cocktail	LD	U.S.	1989	$30.00
	Distributed by Pioneer.					
CBS/Fox	1476-80	Cocoon	LD	U.S.	1986	$35.00
CBS	C1476	Cocoon	LD	U.S.	1989	$25.00
CBS	1710-80	Cocoon: The Return	LD	U.S.	1989	$30.00
CBS	4734-80	Code Name Emerald	LD	U.S.	1986	$35.00
HBO	TVL2985	Code of Silence	LD	U.S.	1987	112
		Coffy	LD	U.S.		$50.00
Nelson	77276	Cohen & Tate	LD	U.S.	1989	$35.00
Image	ID7347IV	Cold Feet	LD	U.S.		$30.00
Image	ID7379HB	Cold Front	LD	U.S.		$15.00
		Collector	LD	U.S.		$80.00
Republic	LV20724	College	LD	U.S.	1991	$25.00
Image	ID7481PA	Colonel Red	LD	U.S.		$30.00
Pioneer		Color Bar Test Disc	DJ/LD	U.S.		$100.00
CBS/Fox	3518-80	Color Me Barbra	LD	U.S.	1986	$25.00
Disney	513AS	Color of Money	LD	U.S.	1987	$45.00
Columbia	30997	Columbia Pictures	LD	U.S.	1989	$20.00
Image		Comedy of Terrors/Oblong Box	LD	U.S.		$50.00
Paramount	LV12532	Comedy Theater 2	LD	U.S.	1987	$30.00
Paramount	LV12534	Comedy Theater IV	LD	U.S.	1987	$30.00
Paramount	LV12531	Comedy Theater V	LD	U.S.	1987	$30.00
Vestron Video	VL3120	Comedy Videos	LD	U.S.	1985	$35.00
CBS	4516-80	Coming Home	LD	U.S.	1983	$35.00
CBS	C1484	Commando	LD	U.S.	1989	$25.00
Vestron Video	VL5092	Company of Wolves, The	LD	U.S.	1985	$35.00
Columbia	VLD3100	Competition, The	LD	U.S.	1983	$40.00
Paramount	LV1928	Compromising Positions	LD	U.S.	1985	$30.00
		Computer Magic	LD	U.S.		$35.00
Paramount	LV8721	Conformist, The	LD	U.S.	1984	$30.00
Image	ID7675NL	Contempt	LD	U.S.		$30.00
MCA	40020	Continental Divide	LD	U.S.	1984	$110.00
		Conversation	LD	U.S.		$120.00
Columbia	59016	Cool Blue	LD	U.S.	1990	$30.00
MGM/UA	ML100317	Cool Cats	LD	U.S.	1984	$35.00
Warner Home Video	11037	Cool Hand Luke	LD	U.S.	1990	$40.00
Image	ID74180OR	Cooley High	LD	U.S.	1975	$40.00
Republic	LV20742	Copacabana	LD	U.S.	1993	$25.00
Discovision		Coral Divers of Corsica	LD	U.S.	1979	$40.00
Image		Cornered	LD	U.S.		$40.00
LIghting Video	LL9900	Corsican Brothers, The	LD	U.S.	1985	$90.00
Discovision		Cortege of Eagles	LD	U.S.	1979	$40.00
Nelson	17145	Cotton Club	LD	U.S.	1985	$40.00
		Count Yorga, Vampire/Cry of the Banshee	LD	U.S.		$80.00
Disney	241AS	Country	LD	U.S.	1985	$35.00
Columbia	59166	Courage Mountain	LD	U.S.	1990	$30.00
Paramount	LV5512	Court Jester	LD	U.S.	1984	$30.00
Republic	LV20770	Court Martial of Billy Mitchell	LD	U.S.	1989	$25.00
Image	ID6782AX	Cousin Cousine	LD	U.S.		$30.00
Image	ID6010OR	Coutch Trio	LD	U.S.		$30.00
Columbia	90416	Cover Girl	LD	U.S.	1991	$30.00
Image	ID8279IV	Cover-Up	LD	U.S.		$30.00
Discovision	D61-507	Coyote's Lament	LD	U.S.	1979	$40.00
Discovision		CPR/Choking	LD	U.S.	1979	$40.00
		Crack Up	LD	U.S.		$40.00
Cannon	31135	Crackhouse	LD	U.S.	1990	$30.00
Image	ID5113	Crawling Eye	LD	U.S.		$150.00
		Crawling Hand	LD	U.S.		32
Nelson	76846	Crazy Moon	LD	U.S.	1988	$35.00
Image	ID7962PA	Creation of the Universe	LD	U.S.		$30.00
Image	ID6872HB	Creator	LD	U.S.		$30.00
Image	ID5076	Creature	LD	U.S.		$50.00
		Creeping Flesh	LD	U.S.		$70.00
Full Moon	LV13003	Creepozoids	LD	U.S.	1993	$35.00
Image	INW5185	Creepshow II	LD	U.S.	1987	$75.00
		Crime Story	LD	U.S.		$75.00
Image	ID7361OR	Crimes and Misdemeanors	LD	U.S.		$75.00
		Crimes of the Heart	LD	U.S.		$40.00
Image Entertainment	I-5026	Crimes Passion	LD	U.S.	1986	$35.00
Paramount	LV1879	Critical Condition	LD	U.S.	1987	$30.00
Columbia	32666	Critters	LD	U.S.	1987	$25.00
Columbia	62773	Critters II	LD	U.S.	1989	$30.00
Paramount	LV1890	Crocodile Dundee	LD	U.S.	1987	$30.00
Columbia	30639	Cromwell	LD	U.S.	1987	$30.00
Nelson	40205	Cross Country	LD	U.S.	1984	$35.00
Image	ID6889TU	Cross Fire	LD	U.S.		$30.00
Nelson	77436	Cross Fire	LD	U.S.	1989	$80.00
Republic	LV20794	Crossing, The	LD	U.S.	1992	$30.00
Columbia	59226	Crossing the Line	LD	U.S.	1990	$30.00

Label	Catalog Number	Title	Type	Country	Year	Value
Columbia	30665	Crossroads	LD	U.S.	1986	$50.00
Live Entertainment	LD61405	Cry From Mountain	LD	U.S.	1992	$25.00
Lumivision	LVD8911	Crystal Vista	LD	U.S.	1989	$25.00
Warner Home Video	11331LV	Cujo	LD	U.S.	1984	$40.00
Columbia	59326	Curse III: Blood Sacrifce	LD	U.S.	1991	$30.00
Image Entertainment	I606	Curse of the Cat People	LD	U.S.	1986	$60.00
		Curse of the Demon	LD	U.S.		$100.00
Republic	LV20773	Cutting Class	LD	U.S.	1991	$25.00
U.S. Magna	SSLM-3013	Cyber City Oedo 808, Data 1	LP	U.S.	1995	$25.00
	CD-ROM with comic book.					
U.S. Magna	SSLM-3019	Cybernetics Guardian	LP	U.S.		$25.00
	Japanese anime CD-ROM.					
Cannon	31030	Cyborg	LD	U.S.	1989	$30.00
Vidmark	LDCVM5729	Cyborg Cop	LD	U.S.	1994	$35.00
Lumivision	LVD9015	Cycling Experience	LD	U.S.	1990	$25.00
Columbia	30792	Cyclone	LD	U.S.	1987	$30.00
Image	ID7115NE	Cyrano De Bergerac	LD	U.S.		$30.00
Republic	LV20822	Cyrano De Bergerac	LD	U.S.	1992	$35.00
Paramount	LV1810	D.A.R.Y.L.	LD	U.S.	1985	$30.00
Disney	698AS	D.O.A.	LD	U.S.	1988	$30.00
Image	ID6111VV	DA	LD	U.S.		$30.00
Columbia	90236	Daddy's Boys	LD	U.S.	1990	$30.00
Warner Brothers	11324LV	Daffy Duck's Movie: Fantastic Island	LD	U.S.	1983	$30.00
	Original pressing					
Republic	LV20830	Dakota	LD	U.S.	1992	$35.00
CBS	1087-80	Damien II the Omen	LD	U.S.	1990	$45.00
Image	ID6877RC	Damn the Defiant!	LD	U.S.		$50.00
Image		Damsel in Distress	LD	U.S.		$40.00
Vestron	VL5137	Dance With a Stranger	LD	U.S.	1986	$75.00
		Dances With Wolves	LTD/LD	Japan	1993	$125.00
	Boxed set with CD Soundtrack an book.					
Image	ID2814OR	Dances With Wolves	LTD/LD	U.S.	1994	$100.00
	Boxed set with CD soundtrack, book, prints.					
Walt Disney	38AS	Darby O'Gill	LD	U.S.	1983	$40.00
Nelson	90286	Dark Age	LD	U.S.	1988	$35.00
Columbia	91016	Dark Backward	LD	U.S.	1992	$30.00
Image	ID6850HB	Dark Crystal, The	LD	U.S.		$20.00
Image	ID7257CV	Dark Habits	LD	U.S.		$30.00
Live Entertainment	LD69028	Dark Horse	LD	U.S.	1992	$35.00
		Dark River – A Father's Revenge	LD	U.S.		$30.00
		Dark Side of the Moon	LD	U.S.		$40.00
Republic	LV20212	Darkest Africa	LD	U.S.	1992	$50.00
Nelson	20116	Darling	LD	U.S.	1989	$35.00
Image	ID6586HB	Date With an Angel	LD	U.S.		$30.00
MGM/UA	ML101450	Date With Judy, A	LD	U.S.	1990	$35.00
CBS	1380-80	David and Bathsheba	LD	U.S.	1991	$35.00
Columbia	30761	David and Lisa	LD	U.S.	1987	$30.00
		Davy Crockett and River Pirates	LD	U.S.		$80.00
Image	ID6683HB	Dawn of the Dead	LD	U.S.		$80.00
Republic	LV25831	Dawn of the Dead	LD	U.S.	1993	$35.00
Nelson	13755	Day After, The	LD	U.S.	1984	$45.00
Image	I5048	Day of the Dead	LD	U.S.	1986	$150.00
CBS	4004-80	Day of the Dolphin	LD	U.S.	1982	$30.00
Magnetic Video		Day of the Dolphin	LD	U.S.†	1982	$25.00
Magnetic Video		Day of the Dolphin	LD	U.S.†	1984	$30.00
Discovision	11-004	Day of the Jackyl	LD	U.S.	1979	$40.00
Image	ID7638JO	Day of the Triffids	LD	U.S.	1962	$130.00
CBS	1011-80	Day the Earth Stood Still	LD	U.S.	1988	$35.00
Fox	8739-80	Day the Earth Stood Still	LTD/LD	U.S.	1995	$200.00
	Boxed set with book and gold CD Soundtrack. Limited to 2500.					
Full Moon	LV13003	Day Time Ended, The	LD	U.S.	1993	$35.00
Paramount	LV8942	Days of Heaven	LD	U.S.	1983	$30.00
Paramount	LV8679-2	Days of the Locust	LD	U.S.	1983	$40.00
Nelson	30385	Dead End	LD	U.S.	1985	$35.00
Image	ID6000NW	Dead Heat	LD	U.S.		$30.00
Image	ID6873HB	Dead Man Out	LD	U.S.		$30.00
Discovision	16-028	Dead Men Don't Wear Plaid	LD	U.S.	1982	$50.00
MCA	16-028	Dead Men Don't Wear Plaid	LD	U.S.	1984	$50.00
Image	ID6853HB	Dead of Night	LD	U.S.		$110.00
CBS	5147-80	Dead of Winter	LD	U.S.	1987	$30.00
Disney	947AS	Dead Poets Society	LD	U.S.	1990	$30.00
	Distributed by Pioneer.					
Columbia	50641	Dead Reckoning	LD	U.S.	1988	$30.00
Columbia	91206	Dead Space	LD	U.S.	1992	$30.00
Image	ID6135VE	Dead, The	LD	U.S.	1987	$30.00
Paramount	LV1646	Dead Zone	LD	U.S.	1984	$30.00
Columbia	30879	Deadly Illusion	LD	U.S.	1992	$30.00
Image	ID6661VE	Deadly Possesion	LD	U.S.		$15.00
Image	ID15MN	Deadtime Stories	LD	U.S.		$40.00
	35326ABCDE	Dean, James: 35th Anniversary Collection	LD	U.S.		$150.00
Image	ID5306PA	Dean, James – Story	LD	U.S.	1957	$30.00
Image	ID5203NW	Death Before Dishonor	LD	U.S.		$30.00
CBS	1125-80	Death Hunt	LD	U.S.	1983	$80.00
Lorimar	LV380	Death of a Salesman	LD	U.S.	1987	$40.00
		Death of a Scoundrel	LD	U.S.		$30.00
Image	ID6919HB	Death on the Nile	LD	U.S.		$80.00
Image	ID7954RH	Death Valley Days	LD	U.S.		$30.00
Nelson	19555	Death Watch	LD	U.S.	1984	$35.00
Paramount	LV8774	Death Wish	LD	U.S.	1982	$30.00
Vestron	VL5017	Death Wish	LD	U.S.	1983	$35.00
Image	IDVL4017	Death Wish II	LD	U.S.	1982	$25.00
Vestron Video	VL5048	Deathstalker	LD	U.S.	1985	$50.00
Image	ID6522VE	Deathstalker 2	LD	U.S.		$50.00
Image	ID6523VE	Deathstalker 3: Warriors From Hell	LD	U.S.		$50.00
Republic	LV20981	Deceptions	LD	U.S.	1991	$30.00
Image	ID6046ME	Decline of Western Civilization	LD	U.S.		$100.00
Republic	LV25216	Decoration Day	LD	U.S.	1992	$30.00
Columbia	VLD3120	Deep, The	LD	U.S.	1984	$50.00
Psedition	PSE91-01	Deep, The	LD	U.S.	1991	$50.00
Image	ID6346IV	Deepstar Six	LD	U.S.	1988	$40.00
Nelson	76896	Defense Of the Realm	LD	U.S.	1987	$35.00
Lorimar	LV025	Deja Vu	LD	U.S.	1987	$40.00
Discovision		Deliverance	LD	U.S.	1978	$40.00
Discovision		Deliverance	LD	U.S.	1981	$30.00
Image	I-5049	Delta Force	LD	U.S.	1986	$30.00
Columbia	90786	Delusion	LD	U.S.	1991	$30.00
U.S. Magna	SSLM-3028	Demon City Shinjuku	LP	U.S.		$25.00
	Japanese anime CD-ROM.					
		Demons	LD	U.S.		$30.00
Image	ID67565FR	Demonstone	LD	U.S.		$30.00
Republic	LV20989	Denial	LD	U.S.	1991	$30.00
Columbia	30689	Desert Bloom	LD	U.S.	1986	$30.00
Magnetic Video		Desert Fox, The	LD	U.S.†	1984	$30.00
CBS	1014-80	Desert Fox, The	LD	U.S.	1989	$95.00
Vestron	VL5120	Desert Hearts	LD	U.S.	1987	$35.00
Image		Desk Set	LD	U.S.		$40.00
Republic	LV20999	Desperadoes Of The West	LD	U.S.	1992	$40.00
HBO	TVL2991	Desperately Seeking Susan	LD	U.S.	1985	$35.00
Image	ID5110	Destination Moon	LD	U.S.		$180.00
Lumivision	LVD9025	Destination Universe	LD	U.S.	1991	$25.00
U.S. Magna	SSLM-3031	Detonator Orgun, Part 1	LP	U.S.		$25.00
	Japanese anime CD-ROM.					
U.S. Magna	SSLM-3032	Detonator Orgun, Part 2	LP	U.S.		$25.00
	Japanese anime CD-ROM.					
U.S. Magna	SSLM-3033	Detonator Orgun, Part 3	LP	U.S.		$25.00
	Japanese anime CD-ROM.					
Image	ID7644NE	Detour	LD	U.S.		$30.00
Nelson	60515	Devil in Daniel Weds	LD	U.S.	1985	$35.00
Republic	LV21012	Devil's Daughter	LD	U.S.	1992	$30.00
		Devil's Rain	LD	U.S.		$120.00
Columbia	30548	Diamond Head	LD	U.S.	1987	$30.00
Image	ID7604	Diamond Run	LD	U.S.		$30.00
CBS	4605-80	Diamonds Are for	LD	U.S.	1983	$35.00
		Diary of a Chambermaid	LD	U.S.		$50.00
Discovision		Diary of a Mad Housewife	LD	U.S.	1979	$35.00
Magnetic Video		Diary of Anne Frank	LD	U.S.†	1984	$30.00
CBS	1074-80	Diary Of Anne Frank	LD	U.S.	1990	$60.00
Vestron Video	VL3006	Dick Cavett's Hocus Pocus	LD	U.S.	1983	$35.00
Vestron Video	ML1028	Dick Clark Best of Bandstand	LD	U.S.	1986	$30.00
CBS	C1666	Die Hard	LD	U.S.	1989	$40.00
Image	ID7524VE	Dillinger	LD	U.S.		$30.00
MGM/UA	ML100533	Dinner at Eight	LD	U.S.	1985	$35.00
Lumivision	LVD9243	Dinosaur!	LD	U.S.	1993	$70.00
Lumivision	LVD9003	Dinosaurs	LD	U.S.	1990	$25.00
Image	ID7013TU	Diplomats	LD	U.S.		$30.00
Nelson	901086	Dirt Bike Kid	LD	U.S.	1986	$35.00
Image	ID6248VE	Dirty Dancing Live In Concert	LD	U.S.		$30.00
MGM/UA	ML100008	Dirty Dozen	LD	U.S.	1984	$30.00
Magnetic Video		Dirty Marry, Crazy Larry	LD	U.S.†	1984	$30.00
Magnetic Video		Dirty Marry, Crazy Larry	LD	U.S.†	1984	$30.00
	Bilingual version.					
Image	ID5352ME	Discreet Charm of the Bourgeoise	LD	U.S.		$30.00
Walt Disney	224AS	Disney Christmas Gift	LD	U.S.	1984	$50.00
	First Issue.					
Walt Disney	224AS	Disney Christmas Gift	LD	U.S.	1990	$50.00
		Disney Dream Music 1933–1938	LD	U.S.		$100.00
Walt Disney	167AS	Disney's Best of 1931–1948	LD	U.S.	1983	$60.00
Walt Disney	951AS	Disorganized Crime	LD	U.S.	1989	$30.00
Republic	LV21035	Distant Drums	LD	U.S.	1992	$25.00
Image	ID7221IV	Distant Voices, Still Lives	LD	U.S.		$30.00
Image	ID8238IV	Disturbed	LD	U.S.		$30.00
MGM/UA	ML100183	Diva	LD	U.S.	1983	$75.00
Image	ID8635PR	Divine Enforcer	LD	U.S.		$30.00
Columbia	90736	Do or Die	LD	U.S.	1992	$30.00
	SHLY51	Document of the Dead: George A. Remero's Zombie World	LD	Japan	1995	$85.00
CBS	4625-80	Dodge City	LD	U.S.	1984	$35.00
Nelson	E30405	Dodsworth	LD	U.S.	1985	$35.00
Image	ID6469MG	Dogs of War, The	LD	U.S.		$30.00
Lumivision	LVD9022	Dollar	LD	U.S.	1990	$35.00
Image	ID5178	Dolls	LD	U.S.		$30.00
Vidmark	LDCVM5475	Dolly Dearest	LD	U.S.	1992	$35.00
U.S. Magna	SSLM-3022	Dominion Tank Police, Volume 1	LP	U.S.		$25.00
	Japanese anime CD-ROM.					
U.S. Magna	SSLM-3023	Dominion Tank Police, Volume 2	LP	U.S.		$25.00
	Japanese anime CD-ROM.					
Paramount	LV8704	Don't Look Now	LD	U.S.	1983	$90.00
Image	ID7302VA	Don't Mess With My Sister	LD	U.S.		$15.00
WHV/HBO	90218	Don't Tell Her It's Me	LD	U.S.	1992	$30.00
WHV/HBO	90637	Don't Tell Mom the Babysitter's Dead	LD	U.S.	1992	$30.00
Image	ID7121FL	Dona Flor and Her Two Husbands	LD	U.S.		$30.00
Image	ID7251CV	Dona Herlinda and Her Son	LD	U.S.		$30.00
Walt Disney		Donald Duck	LD	Japan	1996	$220.00
	3 LD Box set.					
Walt Disney		Donald Duck Shorts	LD	Japan	1995	$75.00
		Donovan's Brain	LD	U.S.		$80.00
Paramount	LV6220	Donovan's Reef	LD	U.S.		$25.00
Image	ID7466PA	Doonesbury Special	LD	U.S.	1984	$20.00
Image	ID6373J2	Dorf on Golf	LD	U.S.		$30.00
Columbia	59686	Double Impact	LD	U.S.	1992	$30.00
Columbia	91526	Double Trouble	LD	U.S.	1992	$30.00
Image	ID7477PA	Down Among the "Z" Men	LD	U.S.		$30.00
Disney	473AS	Down and Out in Beverly Hills	LD	U.S.	1987	$30.00
	Distributed by Pioneer.					
Columbia	59096	Down the Drain	LD	U.S.	1990	$30.00
Psedition	PSE91-02	Down to Earth	LD	U.S.	1991	$50.00
Paramount	LV6910	Downhill Racer	LD	U.S.	1982	$30.00
Magnetic Video		Dr. Doolittle	LD	U.S.†	1984	$30.00
Magnetic Video		Dr. Doolittle	LD	U.S.†	1984	$30.00
	Bilingual version.					
Image	ID7483PA	Dr. Ducks Super Secret All-Purpose Sauce	LD	U.S.		$30.00
Republic	LV21068	Dr. Jekyll and Mr. Hyde	LD	U.S.	1991	$30.00
Warner		Dr. No	LD	Germany	1983	$60.00
Fox		Dr. No	LD	Japan	1983	$60.00
CBS	4525-80	Dr. No	LD	U.S.	1983	$20.00
CBS	4525-80	Dr. No	LD	U.S.	1987	$20.00
MGM/UA		Dr. No	LD	U.S.	1988	$20.00
Critereon	CC1234L	Dr. No	LD	U.S.	1991	$200.00
	CAV version.					
Criterion	CC1292L	Dr. No	LD	U.S.	1992	$40.00
MGM/UA	ML100176	Dr. Seuss Video Festival	LD	U.S.	1984	$35.00
Columbia		Dr. Strangelove	LD	U.S.		$30.00
	First issue.					
Criterion		Dr. Strangelove	LD	U.S.		$100.00
	First presing with supplementary material					
RCA/Columbia	VLD3134	Dr. Strangelove	LD	U.S.	1984	$35.00
Columbia	VLD3134	Dr. Strangelove	LD	U.S.	1992	$30.00
Discovision	23-001	Dracula	LD	U.S.	1979	$40.00
Disney		Dragonslayer	LD	U.S.		$50.00
Paramount	LV1367	Dragonslayer	LD	U.S.	1982	$30.00
Lumivision	LVD9019	Dream Is Alive	LD	U.S.	1991	$25.00
Criterion	CC1001L	Dream Machine Vol. 1	LD	U.S.	1987	$50.00
Criterion	CC1012L	Dream Machine Vol. 2	LD	U.S.	1989	$50.00
Criterion	CC10047L	Dream Machine Vol. 3	LD	U.S.	1991	$50.00
Image	ID6678HB	Dreamscape	LD	U.S.		$30.00
Paramount	LV27155	Dressed to Kill	LD	U.S.		$30.00
Vestron Video	VL4050	Dressed to Kill	LD	U.S.	1983	$35.00
Republic	LV27155	Dressed to Kill/S. Holmes	LD	U.S.	1990	$30.00
Columbia	30111	Dresser	LD	U.S.	1984	$30.00
Lumivision	LVD9232	Dressmaker, The	LD	U.S.	1993	$35.00
Columbia	91236	Driving Me Crazy	LD	U.S.	1992	$30.00
Image	ID7354IV	Drugstore Cowboy	LD	U.S.		$30.00
Image	ID7676NI	Drums	LD	U.S.		$40.00
CBS	1382-80	Drums Along the Mohawk	LD	U.S.	1990	$30.00

Label	Catalog Number	Title	Type	Country	Year	Value
CBS/Fox	4768-80	Dry White Season	LD	U.S.	1990	$35.00
Walt Disney	706AS	DTV: Rhythm & Blues	LD	U.S.	1984	$30.00
Walt Disney	1071AS	Ducktails	LD	U.S.	1990	$30.00
Walt Disney	616AS	Ducktails: Accidental Adventures of Seafaring Sailors	LD	U.S.	1989	$30.00
Image	ID6125IV	Dudes	LD	U.S.		$30.00
Discovision		Duel	LD	U.S.	1979	$40.00
		Duel of Hearts	LD	U.S.		$40.00
Paramount	LV8975	Duelists, The	LD	U.S.	1984	$30.00
WEA	73830	Duke Bluebeard's Castle	LD	U.S.	1993	$40.00
Walt Disney	24AS	Dumbo	LD	U.S.	1982	$30.00
	First issue.					
Walt Disney	24AS	Dumbo	LD	U.S.	1989	$35.00
Walt Disney	24C	Dumbo	LD	U.S.	1995	$40.00
	CAV version.					
Vestron Video	VL3012	Dunder Klumpen	LD	U.S.	1983	$50.00
MCA	40161	Dune	LD	U.S.	1985	$40.00
Columbia	91476	Dune Warriors	LD	U.S.	1992	$30.00
Lighting Video	LL9907	Dungeon Master, The	LD	U.S.	1985	$35.00
Pioneer	PILF2301	E.R. Box 1	LTD/LD	Japan	1996	$250.00
	3 LD boxed set.					
MCA	42734-6	E.T. The Extra-Terrestrial	LTD/LD	U.S.	1996	$150.00
	4 LD boxed set with CD soundtrack and booklet. Limited to 8000 copies.					
Image	ID7482PA	Eagle Has Landed	LD	U.S.		$30.00
Image	ID6864HB	Eagle, The	LD	U.S.		$30.00
Columbia	30760	Early Frost	LD	U.S.	1987	$30.00
Lumivision	LVD9110	Earth Dance	LD	U.S.	1991	$25.00
Lumivision	LVD9009	Earth Dreaming	LD	U.S.	1990	$25.00
Image		Earth Girls Are Easy	LD	U.S.		$40.00
Image	ID6042RC	Earth vs. the Flying Saucers	LD	U.S.		$30.00
Discovision	10-002	Earthquake	LD	U.S.	1979	$40.00
	CAV version.					
MGM/UA	ML100256	Easter Parade	LD	U.S.	1988	$35.00
Image	ID7421VE	Easterbunny Is Coming to Town	LD	U.S.		$30.00
Image	ID7048TU	Easy Living	LD	U.S.		$30.00
Vestron Video	VL5029	Easy Money	LD	U.S.	1984	$35.00
RCA/Columbia	VLD3140	Easy Rider	LD	U.S.	1983	$50.00
Image	ID7140FR	Easy Wheels	LD	U.S.		$30.00
Columbia	50246	Eat A Bowl of Tea	LD	U.S.	1990	$30.00
		Echo Park	LD	U.S.		$30.00
Image	ID8141AC	Echos of Paradise	LD	U.S.		$30.00
Discovision		Ecology: Barry Commoner's View	LD	U.S.	1979	$40.00
Psedition	PSE91-03	Eddie Duchan Story, The	LD	U.S.	1991	$50.00
		Eddie Macon's Run	LD	U.S.		$30.00
Nelson	20665	Eddie & the Cruisers	LD	U.S.	1984	$35.00
Image	ID6955IV	Eddie & the Cruisers II: Eddie Lives	LD	U.S.		$25.00
Image	ID6760VV	Edge Of Sanity	LD	U.S.		$30.00
Columbia		Educating Rita	LD	U.S.		$35.00
	First issue					
RCA/Columbia	VLD3142	Educating Rita	LD	U.S.	1984	$35.00
Columbia	VLD3142	Educating Rita	LD	U.S.	1992	$35.00
Lumivision	LVD9027	Egg	LD	U.S.	1991	$25.00
Discovision		Eiger Sanction	LD	U.S.	1979	$40.00
Criterion	CC1177L	Eight One-Half	LD	U.S.	1989	$60.00
Columbia	09946	Eighty Four Charlie Mopic	LD	U.S.	1990	$30.00
Image	ID5345PA	El Amor Brujo (Love, the Magician	LD	U.S.		$30.00
Vestron	VL3014	El Cid	LD	U.S.	1983	$100.00
Image	ID6410MG	Electra Glide in Blue	LD	U.S.		$30.00
MGM/UA	ML100580	Electric Boogaloo	LD	U.S.	1985	$35.00
Discovision	10-025	Electric Horseman	LD	U.S.	1981	$40.00
Nelson	76095	Eleni	LD	U.S.	1986	$35.00
Paramount	LV1347	Elephant Man	LD	U.S.	1985	$40.00
J2	J2-6030	Elephant Man	LD	U.S.	1990	$30.00
Magnetic Video		Eleven Harrowhouse	LD	U.S.†	1984	$30.00
Image	ID6820MD	Elm Street: The Making Of A Nightmare	LD	U.S.	1988	$50.00
CBS	4582-80	Elmer Gantry	LD	U.S.	1985	$30.00
Lumivision	LVD8908	Elvira Madigan	LD	U.S.	1989	$25.00
Image	ID6289NW	Elvira: Mistress of the Dark	LD	U.S.		$45.00
Nelson	21795	Emerald Forest	LD	U.S.	1985	$35.00
Image	ID6648VV	Emissary	LD	U.S.		$30.00
Columbia	VLD3146	Emmanuelle	LD	U.S.		$30.00
Image	ID6282SO	Emperor and the Nightengale	LD	U.S.		$30.00
	MGLS95007	Encyclopedia of Horror, The	LTD/LD	Japan	1996	$350.00
	4LD boxed set.					
CBS	4607-80	End, The	LD	U.S.	1984	$100.00
Image	ID8235IV	Endless Decent	LD	U.S.		$30.00
MCA	40018	Endless Love	LD	U.S.	1983	$40.00
Image	ID7658HB	Endless Night	LD	U.S.		$30.00
Image	ID5437PA	Endless Summer	LD	U.S.		$30.00
Pacific Arts	PAV12530	Endless Summer	LD	U.S.	1984	$40.00
CBS	1492-80	Enemy Mine	LD	U.S.	1986	$25.00
Republic	LV21173	Enforcer, The	LD	U.S.	1990	$25.00
Image	ID7136VK	Enormous Changes	LD	U.S.		$30.00
Image	ID8152AT	Enrapture	LD	U.S.		$30.00
	1006LV	Enter the Dragon	LD	U.S.		$30.00
Image	ID7514SO	Entertaining the Troops	LD	U.S.		$30.00
		Equus	LD	U.S.		$70.00
		Eraserhead	LD	U.S.		$50.00
Image	ID7411OR	Erik the Viking	LD	U.S.		$40.00
Walt Disney	953AS	Ernest Saves Christmas	LD	U.S.	1989	$25.00
	Distributed by Pioneer.					
Image	ID7293PO	Erotic Adventures of Pinocchio	LD	U.S.		$25.00
Image	ID6927IV	Errand Boy, The	LD	U.S.		$30.00
Paramount	LV1256	Escape From Alcatraz	LD	U.S.	1982	$50.00
Nelson	16025	Escape From New York	LD	U.S.	1983	$35.00
Image	ID8433SO	Escape From Safehaven	LD	U.S.		$30.00
Walt Disney	13AS	Escape From Witch Mountain	LD	U.S.	1982	$30.00
	First issue					
		Eternal Evil	LD	U.S.		$35.00
Image	ID6843CO	Eugene Onegin	LD	U.S.		$30.00
Nelson	7753	Eve of Destruction	LD	U.S.	1991	$35.00
Image		Every Girl Should Get Married	LD	U.S.		$40.00
Image	ID7755OR	Everybody Wins	LD	U.S.		$30.00
CBS	4598-80	Everything You Always Wanted To Know About Sex	LD	U.S.	1983	$30.00
Vestron Video	V9961	Everytime We Say Goodbye	LD	U.S.	1987	$35.00
Vestron	VL5212	Evil Dead 2	LD	U.S.	1987	$110.00
Columbia	30407	Evil That Men Do	LD	U.S.	1985	$30.00
Image	ID6918HB	Evil Under the Sun	LD	U.S.		$40.00
Sony Video	J0030DL	Evolutionary Spiral 8	LD	U.S.	1986	$17.00
MGM/UA	ML101425	Ewoks: The Battle For Endor	LD	U.S.	1990	$40.00
CBS	4544-80	Exodus	LD	U.S.	1984	$35.00
Magnetic Video		Exorcist	LD	Japan	1981	$60.00
Warner Home Video	100LV	Exorcist	LD	U.S.	1983	$30.00
Warner Home Video		Exorcist	LD	U.S.	1985	$30.00
Warner Home Video		Exorcist	LD	U.S.	1988	$30.00
Paramount	LV1676	Explorers	LD	U.S.	1985	$30.00
Image	ID8159FL	Exquisite Corpses	LD	U.S.		$30.00

Label	Catalog Number	Title	Type	Country	Year	Value
Nelson	20026	Exterminator	LD	U.S.	1989	$35.00
Image	ID6128IV	Extreme Prejudice	LD	U.S.		$30.00
Columbia	91986	Extreme Winter	LD	U.S.	1991	$30.00
Vidmark	LDCVM5305	Eye of the Demon	LD	U.S.	1994	$35.00
Live Entertainment	LD51502	Eye of the Tiger	LD	U.S.	1992	$35.00
Image	ID7429IN	Eyes Hear, The Ear Sees, The	LD	U.S.		$30.00
Vestron	VL5205	Eyes of Fire	LD	U.S.	1987	$30.00
Columbia	VLD3149	Eyes of Laura Mars	LD	U.S.	1992	$30.00
Image	ID7429IN	Eyes Without a Face	LD	U.S.		$30.00
Magnetic Video		Eyewitness	LD	U.S.†	1984	$30.00
CBS	1116-80	Eyewitness	LD	U.S.	1988	$35.00
Image	ID6413MG	F.I.S.T.	LD	U.S.	1978	$30.00
HBO	TVL3769	F/X	LD	U.S.	1987	$30.00
Image	ID7353IV	Fabulous Baker Boys, The	LD	U.S.		$30.00
Republic	LV21236	Fabulous Dorsey's, The	LD	U.S.	1990	$25.00
		Fabulous Fleischer	LD	U.S.		$35.00
		Faerie Tale Theatre: Tale of the Frog Prince	LD	U.S.		$30.00
Columbia	VLD3152	Fail Safe	LD	U.S.	1992	$100.00
Vidmark	LDCVM5372	Fair Game	LD	U.S.	1993	$25.00
Vidmark	LDCVM5649	Faith	LD	U.S.	1993	$25.00
Vestron Video	VL5073	Falcon and the Snowman	LD	U.S.	1985	$75.00
Paramount	LV1628	Falling in Love	LD	U.S.	1985	$30.00
Image	ID7667PR	False Identity	LD	U.S.		$30.00
Columbia	70236	Family Business	LD	U.S.	1990	$30.00
Vidmark	LDCVM5441	Family Matter, A	LD	U.S.	1993	$25.00
Discovision	11-005	Family Plot	LD	U.S.	1979	$30.00
Paramount	LV1469	Fan, The	LD	U.S.	1985	$30.00
		Fangoria Video Magazine1	LD	U.S.		$30.00
Nelson	21755	Fanny & Alexander	LD	U.S.	1984	$35.00
Walt Disney	1132 AS	Fantasia	LD	U.S.	1991	$30.00
Walt Disney	1236CS	Fantasia	LTD/CAV	U.S.	1991	$70.00
	4LD boxed set with lithograph and booklet.					
Magnetic Video		Fantastic Voyage	LD	U.S.†	1984	$30.00
CBS/Fox	1002-80	Fantastic Voyage	LD	U.S.	1990	$45.00
		Fantasy Film Worlds of George Pal	LD	Japan	1986	$100.00
Image	INW5197	Fantasy Film Worlds of George Pal	LD	U.S.	1988	$80.00
Image	ID6649VE	Far From Home	LD	U.S.		$30.00
Nelson	77256	Far North	LD	U.S.	1989	$35.00
Columbia	90626	Far Out Man	LD	U.S.	1990	$30.00
3M		Farewell to Arms	LD	U.S.		$40.00
Columbia		Fast Forward	LD	U.S.	1985	$30.00
Columbia	91046	Fast Getaway	LD	U.S.	1991	$30.00
Discovision	16-029	Fast Time	LD	U.S.	1983	$35.00
Paramount	1762	Fatal Attraction	LD	U.S.	1988	$35.00
Image	ID7856ME	Fatal Mission	LD	U.S.		$30.00
Columbia		Fatal Vision	LD	U.S.	1993	$30.00
Image	ID7388CS	Father	LD	U.S.		$30.00
Michael Agee	LVA-1012	Father's Little Dividend	LD	U.S.	1990	$25.00
Image	ID8176VA	Felix the Cat: An Hour Of Fun	LD	U.S.		$30.00
Discovision		Fellini's Casanova	LD	Japan	1979	140
		Female Impersonator Pageant	LD	U.S.		$30.00
Republic	LV21295	Femme Fatale	LD	U.S.	1991	$30.00
Image	ID7843ME	Ferocious Female Freedom Fighter	LD	U.S.		$30.00
Paramount	LV1890	Ferris Bueller's Day Off	LD	U.S.	1987	$30.00
CBS/Fox	4524-80	Fiddler on the Roof	LD	U.S.	1982	$45.00
		Field of Dreams	LD	U.S.		$35.00
	Letterbox version.					
		Field of Dreams	LD	U.S.		$30.00
	P&S version.					
Image	ID6954OR	Field of Honor	LD	U.S.		$30.00
Live Entertainment	LD68965	Field, The	LD	U.S.	1992	$35.00
Republic	LV27210	Fiend Without a Face	LD	U.S.	1991	$25.00
Image	ID8223PA	Fifteen Years of MacNeil-Lehrer	LD	U.S.		$30.00
Columbia	77266	Fifth Monkey	LD	U.S.	1991	$30.00
Cannon	32072	Fifty Fifty	LD	U.S.	1993	$35.00
Image	ID5068	Fifty-Two Pick-Up	LD	U.S.		$30.00
Cannon	31138	Fight for Us	LD	U.S.	1990	$30.00
Columbia	59276	Final Alliance	LD	U.S.	1990	$30.00
CBS	1115-80	Final Conflict	LD	U.S.	1990	$35.00
Image	ID5238VE	Final Countdown, The	LD	U.S.	1980	$85.00
Walt Disney	1063AS	Fire Birds	LD	U.S.	1990	$30.00
	Distributed by Pioneer.					
Columbia	30184	Fire & Ice	LD	U.S.	1986	$30.00
Nelson	76826	Fire & Ice	LD	U.S.	1988	$35.00
Image	ID5137	Firewalker	LD	U.S.		$30.00
		First Blood	LD	Japan	1989	$70.00
		First Blood	LD	U.K.	1985	$50.00
HBO	1573	First Blood	LD	U.S.	1985	$35.00
Image	ID8060IV	First Blood	LD	U.S.	1989	$30.00
Paramount	LV1744	First Born	LD	U.S.	1987	$30.00
Lumivision	LVD9006	First Ladies	LD	U.S.	1990	$30.00
Psedition	PSE91-11	First Men in the Moon	LD	U.S.	1991	$50.00
Paramount	LV1408	First Monday in October	LD	U.S.	1982	$30.00
Nelson	7779-6	First Power	LD	U.S.	1990	$35.00
CBS	4752-80	Fish Called Wanda	LD	U.S.	1989	$25.00
Columbia	70616	Fisher King	LD	U.S.	1992	$30.00
Criterion	CC1288L	Fisher King	LD	U.S.	1992	$100.00
Image	ID7168SO	Fisherman and His Wife, The	LD	U.S.		$30.00
Image	ID6812IV	Fist Fighter	LD	U.S.		$30.00
CBS	4556-80	Fistful of Dollars	LD	U.S.	1985	$35.00
Image	ID6773TU	Five Came Back	LD	U.S.		$30.00
Criterion	CC1196L	Five Easy Pieces	LD	U.S.	1990	$50.00
Vestron	VL5072	Flamingo Kid, The	LD	U.S.	1984	$25.00
Discovision	13000	Flash Gordon	LD	U.S.	1981	$30.00
		Flashdance	LD	Japan	1983	$60.00
Paramount	LV1454	Flashdance	LD	U.S.	1983	$60.00
Republic	LV21336	Flat Top	LD	U.S.	1993	$25.00
Columbia	50386	Flatliners	LD	U.S.	1991	$30.00
Image	ID5247VE	Flesh + Blood	LD	U.S.	1985	$20.00
		Flesh for Frankenstein	LD	Japan		$200.00
		Flesh Gordon	LD	U.S.		$80.00
Walt Disney	499AS	Flight of the Navigator	LD	U.S.	1987	$30.00
	Distributed by Pioneer.					
Magnetic Video		Flight of the Phoenix	LD	U.S.†	1984	$30.00
CBS	1221-80	Flight of the Phoenix	LD	U.S.	1985	$30.00
Image	ID7104VK	Flight, The	LD	U.S.		$30.00
Vidmark	LDCVM5686	Flirting	LD	U.S.	1993	$35.00
Criterion	CC1183L	Floating Weeds	LD	U.S.	1989	$50.00
		Flowers in the Attic	LD	U.S.		$35.00
CBS/Fox	1586-80	Fly II, The	LD	U.S.	1990	$60.00
CBS	1503-80	Fly, The	LD	U.S.	1987	$60.00
CBS	C 1503	Fly, The	LD	U.S.	1989	$60.00
CBS/Fox	1715-80	Fly, The (1958)	LD	U.S.	1989	$50.00
Vestron Video	VL2009	Flying Deuces	LD	U.S.	1983	$35.00
		Flying Deuces, Laurel and Hardy	LD	U.S.		$60.00
Vid-America	934	Flying Leathernecks	LD	U.S.	1986	$30.00
Republic	LV21389	Flying Tigers	LD	U.S.	1992	$25.00

Label	Catalog Number	Title	Type	Country	Year	Value
Magnetic Video		Fog, The	LD	U.S.†	1982	$30.00
CBS/Fox	4067-80	Fog, The	LD	U.S.	1982	$40.00
Magnetic Video		Fog, The	LD	U.S.†	1984	$30.00
Nelson	20036	Fog, The	LD	U.S.	1989	$35.00
		Food of the Gods, Part 2	LD	U.S.		$40.00
Image	ID7335KN	Foolish Wives	LD	U.S.		$30.00
Columbia	91186	Fools of Fortune	LD	U.S.	1991	$30.00
Paramount	LV1589	Footloose	LD	U.S.	1984	$30.00
Image	ID85338PA	Footsteps of Giants	LD	U.S.		$30.00
MGM/UA	ML10226	For A Few Dollars More	LD	U.S.		$30.00
CBS	4675-80	For A Few Dollars More	LD	U.S.	1984	$30.00
Criterion	CC1019L	For All Mankind	LD	U.S.	1989	$100.00
	CAV version.					
Criterion	CC1018L	For All Mankind	LD	U.S.	1989	$50.00
	CLV version.					
CBS	4568-80	For Your Eyes Only	LD	U.S.	1983	$20.00
Columbia	77106	Forbidden Dance, The	LD	U.S.	1990	$20.00
Criterion	CC1130L	Forbidden Games	LD	U.S.	1988	$40.00
MGM/UA	ML100041	Forbidden Planet	LD	U.S.	1983	$40.00
Criterion	CC1153L	Forbidden Planet	LD	U.S.	1989	$100.00
		Forbidden Sun	LD	U.S.		$20.00
		Forbidden World	LD	U.S.		$40.00
Republic	LV21362	Force of Evil	LD	U.S.	1990	$80.00
Vestron	VL4051	Force Ten From Navarone	LD	U.S.	1983	$30.00
Discovision		Forgive and Forget/Thank You Thank You	LD	U.S.	1979	$20.00
Vid-America	703	Fort Apache	LD	U.S.	1986	$30.00
Vestron Video	VL6000	Fort Apache, The Bronx	LD	U.S.	1983	$35.00
MGM/UA	ML102145	Fortune Cookie, The	LD	U.S.		$30.00
Vestron	VL1044	Forty-Five to Eighty-Five America and the World Since WWII	LD	U.S.		$30.00
Vestron	VL1046	Forty-Five to Eighty-Five America and the World Since WWII	LD	U.S.		$30.00
Vestron	VL1047	Forty-Five to Eighty-Five America and the World Since WWII	LD	U.S.		$30.00
Criterion	CC1240L	Forty-Ninth Parallel	LD	U.S.	1990	$40.00
CBS	4502	Forty-Second Street	LD	U.S.	1983	$25.00
Paramount	LV1116	Foul Play	LD	U.S.	1985	$30.00
Image	ID7678NL	Four Fathers, The	LD	U.S.		$30.00
CBS	6680-80	Four Hundred Blows, The	LD	U.S.		$35.00
Discovision		Four Seasons	LD	U.S.		$40.00
MCA	16-025	Four Seasons, The	LD	U.S.	1985	$30.00
Image	ID5357ME	Fourth Man, The	LD	U.S.		$70.00
Image	ID7601VV	Fourth War, The	LD	U.S.		$30.00
Republic	LV21818	Foxfire	LD	U.S.	1992	$30.00
Image	ID6848HB	Frances	LD	U.S.		$30.00
Discovision	22-003	Francis the Talking Mule	LD	U.S.	1979	$40.00
		Frank Capra: AFI Awards	LD	U.S.		32
Image	ID7743SG	Frankenhooker	LD	U.S.		$70.00
Discovision		Frankenstein	LD	U.S.	1979	$40.00
		Frankenstein and the Monster	LD	Japan		$80.00
MGM/UA	ML100843	Freaks	LD	U.S.	1986	$35.00
	SS058-6019	Free Fall	LD	U.S.		$30.00
Live Entertainment	LD62610	Free Ride	LD	U.S.	1993	$25.00
Image	ID5303PA	Freedom Beat	LD	U.S.		$30.00
Magnetic Video		French Connection, The	LD	U.S.†	1981	$25.00
Magnetic Video		French Connection, The	LD	U.S.†	1984	$30.00
Magnetic Video		French Connection, The	LD	U.S.†	1984	$30.00
	Bilingual version.					
CBS/Fox	1009-80	French Connection, The	LD	U.S.	1985	$35.00
CBS	1009	French Connection, The	LD	U.S.	1989	$30.00
CBS	4586	French Lieutentant's Women	LD	U.S.	1982	$30.00
Discovision	11-006	Frenzy	LD	U.S.	1979	$40.00
Columbia	31027	Fresh Horses	LD	U.S.	1989	$30.00
Columbia	70296	Freshman	LD	U.S.	1991	$30.00
Paramount	LV1395	Friday the 13th	LD	U.S.	1985	$30.00
Paramount	LV1457	Friday the 13th Part 2	LD	U.S.	1985	$30.00
Paramount	LV1539	Friday the 13th Part 3	LD	U.S.	1983	$30.00
Paramount	LV1765	Friday the 13th Part 4	LD	U.S.	1984	$30.00
Paramount	LV1823	Friday the 13th Part 5	LD	U.S.	1983	$30.00
Paramount	LV31982	Friday the 13th Part 6	LD	U.S.	1987	$30.00
CBS	7318	Friendly Persuasion	LD	U.S.	1989	$30.00
Image	ID7019TU	Friends and Lovers	LD	U.S.		$30.00
Image	ID7193FR	Friends, Lovers and Lunatics	LD	U.S.		$30.00
Columbia		Fright Night	LD	U.S.		$30.00
	First issue.					
Columbia	30562	Fright Night	LD	U.S.	1993	$30.00
Image	ID6813IV	Fright Night II	LD	U.S.	1988	16
Vestron	VL5117	From Beyond	LD	U.S.	1987	$30.00
Columbia	30762	From Here to Eternity	LD	U.S.	1993	$30.00
	First issue					
Image	ID7852ME	From Hollywood to Deadwood	LD	U.S.	1989	$15.00
Walt Disney	261AS	From Pluto With Love	LD	U.S.	1985	$30.00
Fox		From Russia With Love	LD	Japan	1983	$80.00
CBS	4566	From Russia With Love	LD	U.S.	1983	$20.00
CBS	4566	From Russia With Love	LD	U.S.	1987	$20.00
MGM/UA	4566	From Russia With Love	LD	U.S.	1988	$20.00
Criterion	CC1266L	From Russia With Love	LD	U.S.	1990	$200.00
	CAV version.					
Criterion	CC1290L	From Russia With Love	LD	U.S.	1992	$40.00
Image	ID6945TU	From the Earth to the Moon	LD	U.S.		$30.00
Image	ID5155	From the Hip	LD	U.S.		$30.00
Image	ID7250IV	From the Life of the Marionette	LD	U.S.		$30.00
Image	ID6019RC	Front, The	LD	U.S.	1976	$75.00
Image	ID8326IV	Frosty the Snow Man/Little Drummer Boy	LD	U.S.		$35.00
Image	ID7956PA	Frugal Gormet/Colonial Christmas With Friends	LD	U.S.		$15.00
Image	ID7179SO	Fugitive Samurai	LD	U.S.		$80.00
Image	ID6997TU	Fugitive, The Vol. 1	LD	U.S.		$35.00
Image		Fugitive, The Vol. 2	LD	U.S.		$35.00
Image		Fugitive, The Vol. 3	LD	U.S.		$35.00
Image		Fugitive, The Vol. 4	LD	U.S.		$35.00
Image		Fugitive, The Vol. 5	LD	U.S.		$35.00
Image	ID6552RC	Fuller Brush Man	LD	U.S.		$30.00
Walt Disney		Fun and Fancy Free	LD	Japan		N/A
Paramount	LV5608	Funny Face	LD	U.S.	1985	$30.00
Pioneer	SF070-5296	Funny Girl	LD	Japan		$100.00
Columbia		Funny Girl	LD	U.S.		
First issue						
Columbia	30191	Funny Girl	LD	U.S.	1992	$30.00
Columbia	30685	Funny Lady	LD	U.S.	1986	$30.00
Psedition	PSE91-12	Funny Lady	LD	U.S.	1991	$50.00
WEA	16001	Funny: The Movie	LD	U.S.	1992	$40.00
CBS/Fox	4618-80	Funny Thing Happened	LD	U.S.	1984	$35.00
Image	ID5401ME	Further Adventures of Tennessee Buck	LD	U.S.		$30.00
CBS/Fox	FY572-24MA	Fury, The	LD	Japan	1983	$20.00
Magnetic Video		Fury, The	LD	U.S.†	1984	$30.00
Image	ID8417IV	G.I. Joe: Arise Serpentor, Arise!	LD	U.S.		$25.00
Republic	LV21455	G-Men Vs. The Black Dragon	LD	U.S.	1990	$45.00

Label	Catalog Number	Title	Type	Country	Year	Value
Image	ID3347SY	Gadget Trips	LTD/LD	U.S.	1996	$120.00
	LD boxed set with soundtrack CD and CR-ROM game.					
MCA	13-007	Galaxina	LD	U.S.	1982	$30.00
Nelson	40156	Galaxy of Terror	LD	U.S.	1989	$35.00
Paramount	LV1504	Gallipoli	LD	U.S.	1982	$30.00
Paramount	LV8678	Gambler	LD	U.S.	1982	$30.00
Image	ID7998FL	Game, The	LD	U.S.		$30.00
Image	ID5260LO	Garden Of the Finzi-Continis	LD	U.S.		$80.00
CBS/Fox	3731-80	Gardens of Stone	LD	U.S.		$35.00
Vestron Video	WL5502	Gas Pump Girls	LD	U.S.	1983	$30.00
MGM/UA	ML100473	Gaslight	LD	U.S.	1985	$35.00
Vestron	VL5208	Gate, The	LD	U.S.	1987	$40.00
Discovision		Gene Littler's Golf	LD	U.S.	1979	$40.00
Republic	LV 21476	General, The	LD	U.S.	1991	$35.00
Discovision		Genocide/The World at War	LD	U.S.		$40.00
U.S. Magna	SSLM-3025	Genocyber, Volume 1	LP	U.S.		$25.00
	Japanese anime CD-ROM.					
U.S. Magna	SSLM-3026	Genocyber, Volume 2	LP	U.S.		$25.00
	Japanese anime CD-ROM.					
U.S. Magna	SSLM-3027	Genocyber, Volume 3	LP	U.S.		$25.00
	Japanese anime CD-ROM.					
CBS	4527	Gentleman Jim	LD	U.S.	1985	$30.00
CBS	1019	Gentlemen Prefer Blondes	LD	U.S.	1988	$30.00
Magnetic Video		Gentlemen Prefer Blonds	LD	U.S.†	1984	$30.00
Columbia	90846	Genuine Risk	LD	U.S.	1991	$30.00
Image	ID6351RC	Georgy Girl	LD	U.S.		$30.00
Image	ID7196VV	Getting It Right	LD	U.S.		$30.00
Image	ID2419TU	Gettysburg	LTD/LD	U.S.	1995	$160.00
	3LD/1CD boxed set with book, photos, map and civil war bullet					
Columbia	VLD3161	Ghandi	LD	U.S.	1984	$30.00
Psedition	PSE91-01	Ghandi	LD	U.S.	1991	$50.00
CBS	1385	Ghost and Mrs. Muir	LD	U.S.	1990	$40.00
Nelson	902096	Ghost Fever	LD	U.S.	1987	$35.00
MCA	11-0113	Ghost Story	LD	U.S.	1982	$150.00
Columbia	30580-2	Ghostbusters	LD	U.S.		$20.00
Columbia	30413	Ghostbusters	LD	U.S.		$25.00
	P&S version. First issue.					
RCA/Columbia	30413	Ghostbusters	LD	U.S.	1985	$35.00
RCA/Columbia	30580-2	Ghostbusters	LD	U.S.	1986	$50.00
Criterion	CC1182L	Ghostbusters	LD	U.S.	1987	$50.00
	CLV version.					
Criterion	CC1181L	Ghostbusters	LD	U.S.	1989	$100.00
	CAV version.					
Columbia	30413	Ghostbusters	LD	U.S.	1992	$30.00
	LBX. Digital Audio.					
Columbia	50166	Ghostbusters II	LD	U.S.	1989	$30.00
Columbia/Tri Star	79076	Ghostbusters II	LD	U.S.	1994	$35.00
Image	ID7582CE	Ghostbusters: The Revenge of Prime Evil	LD	U.S.		$20.00
Columbia	59516	Ghosts Can't Do It	LD	U.S.	1990	$30.00
Columbia	30470	Gidget	LD	U.S.	1985	$30.00
MGM/UA	ML100050	Gigi	LD	U.S.		$25.00
Columbia	30194	Gilda	LD	U.S.	1988	$30.00
		Girl in a Swing	LD	U.S.		$30.00
Image	ID7375IV	Girlfriend From Hell	LD	U.S.		$30.00
CBS	1448	Give My Regards to Broadstreet	LD	U.S.	1986	$50.00
Image	ID7396HO	Glamour Through Your Lens	LD	U.S.		$30.00
Image	ID6592VC	Glen and Randa	LD	U.S.		$30.00
Columbia	VLD3160	Gloria	LD	U.S.	1985	$30.00
Columbia	70286	Glory	LD	U.S.	1990	$30.00
Vestron	VL5000	Go Tell the Spartans	LD	U.S.	1983	$30.00
Columbia	30728	Goddess	LD	U.S.	1987	$30.00
Paramount	LV8049	Godfather	LD	U.S.	1985	$40.00
		Godfather 1901–1959, The Epic	LD	Japan		$200.00
Paramount	LV12959-7	Godfather Collector's Edition, The	LTD/LD	U.S.	1991	$150.00
	7 LD set.					
Paramount	LV8459-2	Godfather Part II	LD	U.S.	1985	$40.00
Paramount	LV8459-1	Godfather Part II	LD	U.S.	1989	$45.00
Paramount	LV15147-7	Godfather Trilogy	LTD/LD	U.S.	1992	$160.00
	7 LD set.					
Columbia	10316	Gods Must Be Crazy 2, The	LD	U.S.	1990	$40.00
CBS	1450	Gods Must Be Crazy, The	LD	U.S.	1987	$50.00
Vestron Video	VL3010	Godzilla	LD	U.S.	1983	$35.00
Image	I-5042	Godzilla 1985	LD	U.S.	1985	$40.00
		Godzilla vs. King Ghidora	LD	Japan		$100.00
HBO		Godzilla vs. (PPK) Biollante	LD	U.S.	1993	$175.00
TLL2434		Godzilla vs. Queen Mothra	LD	Japan	1992	230
Image	ID6923OR	Godzilla vs. Smog Monster/Monster From a Prehistoric Planet	LD	U.S.		$30.00
Paramount	LV1133	Goin' South	LD	U.S.	1983	$30.00
MCA	40012	Going Beserk	LD	U.S.	1984	$30.00
Discovision		Going My Way	LD	U.S.	1979	$40.00
Image	ID7132VK	Going Undercover	LD	U.S.		$30.00
Republic	LV27110	Gold Rush, The	LD	U.S.	1992	$25.00
Magnetic Video		Golden Age of College Football	LD	U.S.†	1982	$25.00
MGM/UA		Golden Age of Looney Tunes Vol. 1	LD	U.S.		$135.00
Image	ID6265RC	Golden Boy	LD	U.S.		$30.00
Paramount	LV1930	Golden Child	LD	U.S.	1987	$30.00
Nelson	30225	Golden Seal, The	LD	U.S.	1984	$20.00
Columbia	30199	Golden Voyage of Sinbad	LD	U.S.	1986	$45.00
Psedition	PSE91-20	Golden Voyage of Sinbad	LD	U.S.	1991	$60.00
Warner		Goldfinger	LD	Germany	1985	$60.00
MGM/UA		Goldfinger	LD	Japan	1983	$60.00
CBS/Fox	4595-80	Goldfinger	LD	U.S.	1983	$35.00
CBS		Goldfinger	LD	U.S.	1987	$20.00
MGM/UA		Goldfinger	LD	U.S.	1988	$20.00
Criterion	CC1267L	Goldfinger	LD	U.S.	1991	$300.00
	CAV version.					
Criterion	CC1291L	Goldfinger	LD	U.S.	1992	$40.00
	CLV version.					
CBS	6368	Goldilocks and the 3 Bears	LD	U.S.	1985	$20.00
MGM/UA	ML100284	Gone With the Wind	LD	U.S.	1985	$50.00
Vestron Video	VL6002	Good Guys Wear Black	LD	U.S.	1983	$35.00
Image	ID5180	Good Morning Babylon	LD	U.S.		$30.00
Disney	66006AS	Good Morning Vietnam	LD	U.S.	1988	$39.00
	Distributed by Pioneer.					
Disney	610AS	Good Mother	LD	U.S.	1989	$35.00
MGM/UA	ML100877	Good News	LD	U.S.	1989	$35.00
Image	ID8376HA	Good, the Bad and Huckleberry Hound	LD	U.S.		$30.00
Paramount	LV6826	Goodbye, Columbus	LD	U.S.	1983	$30.00
MGM/UA	ML100069	Goodbye Girl	LD	U.S.		$30.00
MGM/UA	ML100617	Goodbye Mr. Chips	LD	U.S.	1991	$35.00
Vestron	VL5000	Goodbye New York	LD	U.S.	1983	$30.00
Nelson	20705	Goodbye People	LD	U.S.	1986	$35.00
		Gorgon	LD	U.S.		$110.00
Image	ID7242NE	Gorilla, The	LD	U.S.		$100.00
Image	IDVL5035	Gorky Park	LD	U.S.	1983	$50.00
		Gospel According To St. Matthew	LD	U.S.		$50.00

Label	Catalog Number	Title	Type	Country	Year	Value
Vestron	VL5215	Gothic	LD	U.S.	1987	$95.00
Republic	LV21580	Government Agents vs. Phantom Legion	LD	U.S.	1992	$35.00
CBS	4006	Graduate	LD	U.S.	1982	$25.00
Magnetic Video		Graduate, The	LD	U.S.†	1982	$30.00
Nelson	20176	Graduate, The	LD	U.S.	1983	$25.00
Magnetic Video		Graduate, The	LD	U.S.†	1984	$30.00
Criterion	CC1168L	Graduate, The	LD	U.S.	1987	$100.00
Criterion	CC1115L	Graduate, The	LD	U.S.	1989	$50.00
	CLV version.					
MGM/UA	ML100069	Grand Hotel	LD	U.S.		$30.00
MGM/UA	ML100564	Grand Hotel	LD	U.S.	1985	$35.00
Criterion	CC1114L	Grand Illusion	LD	U.S.	1988	$50.00
Republic	LV21586	Grass is Greener, The	LD	U.S.	1993	$35.00
Image	ID7766SG	Grave Secrets	LD	U.S.		$30.00
Image	ID5176	Graveyard Shift	LD	U.S.		$30.00
Discovision		Gray Lady Down	LD	U.S.	1979	$40.00
Paramount		Grease	LD	Japan	1987	$80.00
Paramount		Grease	LD	U.S.	1981	$30.00
Paramount	LV1108	Grease	LD	U.S.	1985	$30.00
Paramount		Grease 2	LD	Japan	1988	$80.00
Paramount	LV1193	Grease 2	LD	U.S.	1983	$35.00
CBS	4558	Great Escape	LD	U.S.	1983	$40.00
Criterion	CC1273L	Great Escape	LD	U.S.	1992	$90.00
Walt Disney	1062AS	Great Expectations	LD	U.S.	1990	$35.00
	Distributed by Pioneer.					
Paramount	LV8569	Great Gatsby	LD	U.S.	1982	$36.00
Disney	1360CS	Great Mouse Detective, The	LD	U.S.	1992	$50.00
	CAV version.					
Disney	1360AS	Great Mouse Detective, The	LD	U.S.	1992	$35.00
	CLV version.					
CBS/Fox	9035-80	Great Muppet Caper	LD	U.S.	1983	$35.00
Criterion	ABC-CP-1	Great Quake Of '89	LD	U.S.	1990	$50.00
WEA	38319	Great Rock 'n Roll Swindle	LD	U.S.	1993	$35.00
CBS	4531	Great Train Robbery	LD	U.S.	1982	$30.00
Discovision		Great Waldo Pepper	LD	U.S.	1979	$40.00
Vestron	VL2005	Greatest Adventure, The	LD	U.S.	1983	$30.00
		Greatest Adventures, The	LD	Japan	1983	$80.00
Paramount	LV6617-2	Greatest Show on Earth, The	LD	U.S.		$30.00
MGM/UA	ML102245	Greatest Story Ever Told	LD	U.S.	1992	$50.00
Discovision		Greek Cooking With Theonie Baklava/Orange Sweets	LD	U.S.	1979	$40.00
Discovision	10-011	Greek Tycoon, The	LD	U.S.	1979	$40.00
J2	J2-6038	Green Ice	LD	U.S.	1990	$30.00
Vestron	VL2032	Green Peace	LD	U.S.	1986	$30.00
Paramount	11388LV	Gremlins	LD	U.S.		$30.00
Image	I5035	Grey Fox	LD	U.S.	1985	$35.00
WHV/HBO	90545	Grifters, The	LD	U.S.	1991	$30.00
Walt Disney	961	Gross Anatamy	LD	U.S.	1990	$35.00
Columbia	30687	Guess Who's Coming to Dinner	LD	U.S.	1987	$30.00
Republic	LV21645	Guest Wife	LD	U.S.	1992	$30.00
Vestron Video	VL2011	Gulliver's Travels	LD	U.S.	1983	$35.00
Republic	LV21650	Gulliver's Travels	LD	U.S.	1990	$100.00
Michael Agee	LVA1003	Gulliver's Travels	LD	U.S.	1990	$100.00
Columbia	30687	Gun Fury	LD	U.S.	1987	$30.00
Paramount	LV6218	Gunfight at the O.K. Corral	LD	U.S.	1983	$30.00
CBS/Fox	1213-80	Gunfighter, The	LD	U.S.	1990	$35.00
Paramount	LV1751	Gung Ho	LD	U.S.	1986	$30.00
Vid-America	911	Gunga Din	LD	U.S.	1985	$100.00
Image	ID6458NW	Gunrunner, The	LD	U.S.		$30.00
Columbia	90716	Guns	LD	U.S.	1991	$30.00
Walt Disney	29AS	Gus	LD	U.S.		$50.00
CBS/Fox	7039-80	Guys & Dolls	LD	U.S.	1984	$40.00
CBS	C7039	Guys & Dolls	LD	U.S.	1989	$30.00
U.S. Magna	SSLM-3029	Hades Project Zeorymer, Volume 1	LP	U.S.		$25.00
	Japanese anime CD-ROM.					
U.S. Magna	SSLM-3030	Hades Project Zeorymer, Volume 2	LP	U.S.		$25.00
	Japanese anime CD-ROM.					
Image	ID7532VE	Hail Mary	LD	U.S.		$30.00
Columbia	32822	Hairspray	LD	U.S.	1989	$30.00
		Haley's Comet	LD	Japan	1986	$100.00
Nelson	13286	Half Moon Street	LD	U.S.	1987	$35.00

Halloween – (Image I-5033)

Label	Catalog Number	Title	Type	Country	Year	Value
Image	I-5033	Halloween	LD	U.S.	1985	$30.00
MCA	11-019	Halloween 2	LD	U.S.	1983	$120.00
MCA		Halloween 3	LD	U.S.		$75.00
CBS/Fox	2100-80	Halloween 4	LD	U.S.	1989	$50.00
CBS/Fox	2425-80	Halloween 5	LD	U.S.	1990	$50.00
Walt Disney	1072AS	Halloween Cartoon Classics	LD	U.S.	1990	$30.00
	Distributed by Pioneer.					
Paramount	LV12569-2	Hamlet	LD	U.S.	1948	$30.00
Image	ID6393NW	Hammer: The Best of Sledge Hammer	LD	U.S.		$40.00
		Handmaid's Tale	LD	U.S.		$30.00
CBS	4628	Hang 'Em High	LD	U.S.	1983	$30.00
Image	ID8618WV	Hanger 18	LD	U.S.		$40.00
Columbia	91076	Hangfire	LD	U.S.	1991	$15.00
Columbia	75176	Hangin' With the	LD	U.S.	1992	$30.00
Columbia	LVD33171	Hanky Panky	LD	U.S.	1983	$30.00
Image	ID8157HA	Hanna-Barbera Christmas Disc	LD	U.S.		$30.00

Halloween II – (MCA 11-019)

Halloween IV – (CBS/Fox 2100-80)

Halloween V – (CBS/Fox 2425-80)

Label	Catalog Number	Title	Type	Country	Year	Value
		Hannah and Her Sisters	LD	U.S.		$50.00
Image	ID6170RC	Hanover Street	LD	U.S.	1979	$50.00
Nelson	30445	Hans Christian Andersen	LD	U.S.	1985	$35.00
CBS	6409	Hansel & Gretel	LD	U.S.	1984	$30.00
Columbia	50296	Hanussen	LD	U.S.	1990	$30.00
Warner Home Video	PILA-35041	Happy Birthday 007: 25 Years of James Bond	LD	Japan	1987	$100.00
Columbia	VLD3175	Happy Birthday to Me	LD	U.S.	1982	$80.00
Vestron Video	VL5503	Happy Hooker	LD	U.S.	1982	$40.00
MCA	28-009	Happy Hooker Goes to Hollywood	LD	U.S.	1982	$40.00
Live Entertainment	LD62790	Happy Hour	LD	U.S.	1993	$25.00
Image	ID6803IV	Happy Together	LD	U.S.		$30.00
Columbia	30366	Hard Bodies	LD	U.S.	1985	$30.00
Columbia	30706	Hard Bodies II	LD	U.S.	1987	$30.00
		Hard Boiled	LD	U.S.		$80.00
J2	J2-6037	Hard County	LD	U.S.	1990	$30.00
Criterion	CC1113L	Hard Day's Night	LD	U.S.	1987	$80.00
	CAV version.					
Criterion	CC1175L	Hard Day's Night	LD	U.S.	1989	$50.00
Columbia	VDL3177	Hardcore	LD	U.S.	1984	$30.00
Criterion	CC1282L	Harder They Come	LD	U.S.	1992	$50.00
		Hardware	LD	U.S.		$50.00
Discovision	19-008	Hardy Boys: Mystery of the Haunted House	LD	U.S.	1979	$100.00
Vestron	LV5201	Harlem	LD	U.S.	1987	$30.00
Paramount	LV8042	Harold and Maude	LD	U.S.	1982	$30.00
Vestron Video	VL5037	Harry and Son	LD	U.S.	1984	$35.00
Nelson	25015	Hartman, Mary Vol. II	LD	U.S.	1985	$35.00
Paramount	LV6629-2	Hatari	LD	U.S.	1983	$36.00
HBO	TVL3911	Haunted Honeymoon	LD	U.S.	1987	$35.00

Label	Catalog Number	Title	Type	Country	Year	Value
		Haunted Palace/Curse of the Crimson Altar	LD	U.S.		$50.00
Paramount	LV68340-2	Haunting of Sarah Hardy, The	LD	U.S.	1991	$36.00
MGM/UA	ML100903	Haunting, The	LD	U.S.	1986	$35.00
Image	ID6925IV	Hawk the Slayer	LD	U.S.		$40.00
		Hawks & Sparrows	LD	U.S.		$50.00
RCA/Columbia	VLD3181	He Man and the Masters of the Universe	LD	U.S.	1984	$25.00
Columbia	VLD3181	He Man and the Masters of the Universe	LD	U.S.	1993	$20.00
Columbia	30320	He Man and the Masters of the Universe Vol. 2	LD	U.S.	1985	$20.00
Columbia	30702	Head	LD	U.S.	1986	$50.00
Columbia	75026	Heart Condition	LD	U.S.	1990	$30.00
CBS	1300	Heart Like a Wheel	LD	U.S.	1984	$35.00
Vestron Video	VL4024	Heartaches	LD	U.S.	1983	$35.00
Disney	609AS	Heartbreak Hotel	LD	U.S.	1989	$30.00
Image	ID5075	Heartbreak Kid	LD	U.S.		$75.00
Paramount	LV1688	Heartburn	LD	U.S.	1987	$30.00
Paramount	LV2250	Hearts and Minds	LD	U.S.	1983	$30.00
Republic	LV21713	Hearts of the World	LD	U.S.	1991	$25.00
Paramount	LV112584	Heat	LD	U.S.	1987	$40.00
Image		Heathers	LD	U.S.		$40.00
Live Entertainment	LD69026	Heaven and Earth	LD	U.S.	1992	$35.00
Paramount	LV1109	Heaven Can Wait	LD	U.S.	1982	$30.00
MCA	A-4	Heaven Can Wait	LD	U.S.	1985	$25.00
CBS	1771	Heaven Can Wait	LD	U.S.	1990	$25.00
Image	ID7652HB	Heaven Help Us	LD	U.S.		$30.00
Columbia	90646	Heaven Is a Playground	LD	U.S.	1992	$30.00
90646		Heaven Is My Playground	LD	U.S.	1991	$15.00
CBS	1731	Heidi/Poor Little Rich Girl	LD	U.S.	1989	$25.00
Republic	LV23015	Height of the Cyclone	LD	U.S.	1991	$25.00
		Hell Is For Heroes	LD	U.S.		$80.00
Image	ID7593VK	Hellgate	LD	U.S.	1989	$15.00
Columbia	30495	Hellhole	LD	U.S.	1985	$20.00
Image	ID2299AI	Hellmaster	LD	U.S.		$35.00
Disney	656LV	Hello Again	LD	U.S.	1988	$35.00
Magnetic Video		Hello Dolly	LD	U.S.	1981	$30.00
Magnetic Video		Hello Dolly	LD	U.S.†	1982	$30.00
CBS/Fox	1001-80	Hello Dolly	LD	U.S.	1985	$45.00
		Hellraiser	LD	U.S.		$20.00
Lumivision	LVD9536	Hellraiser	LTD/LD	U.S.	1996	$150.00
	LD set with original shooting script in "signed" box. limited to 2500 copies.					
Lumivision	LVD9536	Hellraiser	LTD/LD	U.S.	1996	$100.00
	LD set with original shooting script in "unsigned" box. limited to 2500 copies.					
Criterion	C2004L	Help!	LD	U.S.	1987	$90.00
Criterion	2004L	Help!	LD	U.S.	1987	$40.00
Walt Disney	42AS	Herbie Rides Again	LD	U.S.	1983	$40.00
Image	ID7295VA	Hercules	LD	U.S.		$75.00
MGM/UA	ML100319	Hercules	LD	U.S.	1984	$75.00
Image	ID7296VA	Hercules Unchained	LD	U.S.		$90.00
Nelson	20745	Hercules Unchained	LD	U.S.	1985	$90.00
Columbia	30015	Here Comes Mr. Jordan	LD	U.S.	1988	$80.00
Vestron Video	VL3004	Here It Is, Burlesque	LD	U.S.	1983	$35.00
Discovision		Heroes	LD	U.S.	1979	$40.00
Image	ID6686OR	Hey Babu Riba	LD	U.S.		$30.00
Disney	806AS	Hey Cinderella	LD	U.S.	1983	$30.00
WHV/HBO	90558	Hidden Agenda	LD	U.S.	1992	$30.00
Criterion	CC1111L	Hidden Fortress	LD	U.S.	1987	$90.00
Image	ID5206ME	Hidden, The	LD	U.S.		$30.00
Image	ID5334PA	High and Low	LD	U.S.		$30.00
CBS	1107	High Anxiety	LD	U.S.	1984	$100.00
Magnetic Video		High Anxiety	LD	U.S.†	1984	$100.00
Image	ID7198VV	High Frequency	LD	U.S.		$30.00
Criterion	CC1173L	High Noon	LD	U.S.	1987	$50.00
Republic	LV25532	High Noon: 40th Anniversary	LD	U.S.	1992	$60.00
Discovision		High Plains Drifter	LD	U.S.	1979	$40.00
Warner Home Video	11309LV	High Road to China	LD	U.S.	1983	$30.00
Republic	LV21808	High School Confidential	LD	U.S.	1992	$30.00
Nelson	77146	High Season	LD	U.S.	1988	$35.00
CBS/Fox	4629-80	High Sierra	LD	U.S.	1983	$35.00
MGM/UA	ML100292	High Society	LD	U.S.	1985	$35.00
Image	ID6476ME	High Spirits	LD	U.S.		$30.00
Nelson	77226	High Tide	LD	U.S.	1988	$35.00
Nelson	40345	Highest Honor	LD	U.S.	1985	$35.00
Image	ID6679HB	Highlander	LD	U.S.		$20.00
Nelson	40365	Highpoint	LD	U.S.	1985	$35.00
		Hills Have Eyes, The	LD	U.S.		$50.00
CBS	1350-80	Himself (Bill Cosby)	LD	U.S.	1985	$35.00
Discovision		Hindenberg	LD	U.S.	1979	$40.00
Lighting Video	LL9905	History Is Made at Night	LD	U.S.	1986	$35.00
		History of Rockets	LD	Japan	1983	$80.00
CBS		History of the World Part 1	LD	U.S.		$35.00
Columbia	09926	Hit List	LD	U.S.	1989	$30.00
Nelson	75995	Hit, The	LD	U.S.	1985	$35.00
MGM/UA	ML100441	Hit the Deck	LD	U.S.		$30.00
HBO	TVL3756	Hitcher	LD	U.S.	1988	$30.00
Image	ID5263LO	Hitchicker Vol. 1	LD	U.S.		$30.00
Image	ID5264LO	Hitchicker Vol. 2	LD	U.S.		$30.00
Image	ID5208LO	Hitchicker Vol. 3	LD	U.S.		$30.00
Image	ID5205LO	Hitchicker Vol. 4	LD	U.S.		$30.00
Cannon	32045	Hitman, The	LD	U.S.	1992	$30.00
		Hocus Pocus	LD	U.S.		$30.00
Cannon	31022	Holcroft Covenant	LD	U.S.	1989	$30.00
Columbia	30784	Holiday	LD	U.S.	1987	$30.00
Image	ID6777TU	Holiday Affair	LD	U.S.		$30.00
Image	ID7355IV	Hollywood Hot Tubs II	LD	U.S.		$30.00
Lumivision	LVD9011	Hollywood Mavericks	LD	U.S.	1990	$35.00
Image	ID6311CO	Hollywood On Trial	LD	U.S.		$30.00
Columbia	VLD30432	Hollywood Out-Takes & Rare Footage	LD	U.S.	1985	$30.00
Image	ID5167	Hollywood Shuffle	LD	U.S.		$50.00
Image	ID7714MN	Hollywood Vice Squad	LD	U.S.		$30.00
CBS	1012	Hombre	LD	U.S.	1990	$30.00
	Letterbox version.					
Image	ID7540VE	Home Movies	LD	U.S.		$30.00
Republic	LV21845	Home of the Brave	LD	U.S.	1993	$30.00
Image	ID6817IV	Homeboy	LD	U.S.		$30.00
MCA	16-030	Homework	LD	U.S.	1983	$30.00
Columbia	91446	Homicide	LD	U.S.	1992	$30.00
Walt Disney	909	Honey I Shrunk the Kids	LD	U.S.	1990	$30.00
	Distributed by Pioneer.					
		Honeymoon Killers	LD	U.S.		$80.00
HBO		Hoosiers	LD	U.S.	1988	$25.00
Nelson	77136	Hope and Glory	LD	U.S.	1988	$35.00
Republic	LV21866	Hoppity Goes to Town	LD	U.S.	1990	$25.00
Nelson	001046	Hopscotch	LD	U.S.	1989	$35.00
Image	ID7559NL	Horror Planet	LD	U.S.		$80.00
Image	ID8392KN	Horse Thief	LD	U.S.		$30.00
Criterion	CC1171L	Horse's Mouth	LD	U.S.	1989	$40.00
Republic	LV21872	Horseplayer	LD	U.S.	1992	$30.00
Nelson	19045	Hostage Tower	LD	U.S.	1984	$35.00
Image	ID7220IV	Hostile Takeover	LD	U.S.		$30.00
Paramount	32082	Hot Pursuit	LD	U.S.	1988	$35.00
RCA	VLD3180	Hot Stuff	LD	U.S.	1984	$25.00
	First issue					
RCA	VLD3180	Hot Stuff	LD	U.S.	1992	$25.00
Nelson	7721LV	Hotel Colonial	LD	U.S.	1984	$35.00
Vestron Video	VL5042	Hotel New Hampshire	LD	U.S.	1984	$80.00
Image	ID6763VV	Hotel Terminus: The Life and Times of Klaus Barbie	LD	U.S.		$30.00
		Hound of the Baskerville	LD	U.S.	1989	$50.00
Image	I-5058	House	LD	U.S.	1986	$35.00
Discovision		House Calls	LD	U.S.	1979	$40.00
MCA	16-006	House Calls	LD	U.S.	1982	$30.00
Image	INW5184	House II	LD	U.S.		$30.00
Image	ID6588HB	House of Games	LD	U.S.		$30.00
Columbia	77226	House of Usher	LD	U.S.	1991	$30.00
Image	ID6921HB	House on Carroll Street	LD	U.S.		$30.00
CBS	2179	House on Haunted Hill	LD	U.S.	1989	$110.00
Vestron Video	VL4059	House on Sorority Row	LD	U.S.	1984	$80.00
Columbia	75036	House Party	LD	U.S.	1990	$30.00
Paramount		Houseboat	LD	U.S.	1987	$30.00
Lumivision	LVD9268	Householder, The	LD	U.S.	1993	$35.00
CBS	1728	How I Got Into College	LD	U.S.	1990	$15.00
Image	ID7167SO	How the Leopard Got His Spots	LD	U.S.		$30.00
Disney	259AS	How the West: 1933–1960	LD	U.S.	1985	$30.00
MGM/UA	ML100356	How the West Was Won	LD	U.S.		$30.00
		How the West Was Won 1933–60	LD	U.S.		$80.00
Magnetic Video		How to Marry a Millionaire	LD	U.S.†	1984	$30.00
CBS	1023	How to Marry a Millionaire	LD	U.S.	1988	$25.00
Discovision		How to Stop Smoking	LD	U.S.	1979	$10.00
Republic	LV205871	Howling II: Your Sister Is a Werewolf	LD	U.S.	1993	$45.00
Nelson	16155	Howling, The	LD	U.S.	1983	$50.00
Image	ID6815IV	Howling V: The Rebirth	LD	U.S.		$40.00
Image	ID8109IV	Howling VI: The Freaks	LD	U.S.		$40.00
Disney	760AS	Hubleys: Cosmic Eye	LD	U.S.	1990	$30.00
Paramount	LV6630	Hud	LD	U.S.	1983	$30.00
Columbia	70596	Hudson Hawk	LD	U.S.	1991	$30.00
Cannon	32031	Human Shield	LD	U.S.	1993	$30.00
Image	I-5034	Hunchback of Notre Dame	LD	U.S.	1985	$80.00
Republic	LV21933	Hunchback of Notre Dame	LD	U.S.	1991	$30.00
MGM/UA	ML100281	Hunger, The	LD	U.S.		$25.00
Columbia	60813LV	Hunk	LD	U.S.	1987	$30.00
Paramount	LV1192	Hunter	LD	U.S.	1985	$100.00
Nelson	75656	Hunter's Blood	LD	U.S.	1987	$35.00
Nelson	30455	Hurricane, The	LD	U.S.	1986	$50.00
Magnetic Video		Hustler, The	LD	U.S.†	1984	$150.00
CBS	1006	Hustler, The	LD	U.S.	1990	$150.00
Image	ID8622WV	Hustling	LD	U.S.		$25.00
Discovision		Hyena Story, The	LD	U.S.	1979	$40.00
Image	ID7710MN	Hysterical	LD	U.S.		$30.00
Columbia	31001A	I Am the Law	LD	U.S.	1989	$25.00
Criterion	CTC1000L	I Love Lucy	LD	U.S.	1992	$50.00
CBS	2324	I Love Lucy Vol. 1	LD	U.S.	1990	$35.00
CBS	2325	I Love Lucy Vol. 2	LD	U.S.	1990	$35.00
CBS	2429	I Love Lucy Vol. 3	LD	U.S.	1990	$35.00
CBS	2430	I Love Lucy Vol. 4	LD	U.S.	1990	$35.00
Image	ID7225MN	I Love N.Y.	LD	U.S.		$30.00
Columbia	70306	I Love You to Death	LD	U.S.	1990	$30.00
Image	ID7232MN	I Madman	LD	U.S.		$30.00
Image	ID7157SO	I Married a Centerfold	LD	U.S.		$30.00
Lighting Video	LL9904	I Married a Witch	LD	U.S.	1986	$60.00
Image	ID7018TU	I Married a Woman	LD	U.S.		$30.00
Republic	LV23239	I Posed For Playboy	LD	U.S.	1992	$30.00
Image	ID6795CS	I Spit on Your Grave	LD	U.S.		$80.00
Wizard	ZL016	I Spit on Your Grave	LD	U.S.	1984	$80.00
		I Walked With a Zombie	LD	U.S.		$80.00
Warner Home Video	35006	I Wanna Hold Your Hand	LD	U.S.	1989	$25.00
Nelson	902166	I Was a Teenage Zombie	LD	U.S.	1988	$35.00
Paramount	LV1295	I'm Dancing as Fast	LD	U.S.	1985	$30.00
Image	ID7731FL	I'm the One You're Looking For	LD	U.S.		$30.00
Republic	LV22078	I've Always Loved You	LD	U.S.	1991	$25.00
Nelson	90234	I've Heard the Mermaids Sing	LD	U.S.	1988	$35.00
MGM/UA	ML100427	Ice Pirates, The	LD	U.S.	1984	$45.00
MGM/UA	ML100610	Idiot's Delight	LD	U.S.	1992	$35.00
MGM/UA	ML100370	Idol Maker, The	LD	U.S.	1984	$35.00
Paramount	LV6838	If...	LD	U.S.	1984	$30.00
Discovision	21-003	If I Had a Million	LD	U.S.	1979	$40.00
Discovision		If You Can Walk/Listen To the Mountains	LD	U.S.	1979	$40.00
Vestron Video	VL5014	If You Could See...	LD	U.S.	1985	$35.00
Criterion	CC1224L	Ikiru	LD	U.S.	1990	$50.00
Image	ID6795CS	Il Bidone	LD	U.S.		$100.00
Columbia	50196	Immediate Family	LD	U.S.	1990	$30.00
Columbia	59216	Immortalizer, The	LD	U.S.	1990	$30.00
	8001	Impromptu	LD	U.S.		$25.00
Vestron	LV5011	Improper Channels	LD	U.S.	1983	$50.00
Vestron	LV5066	Impulse	LD	U.S.	1985	$30.00
Columbia	VLD3108	In Cold Blood	LD	U.S.	1983	$100.00
Republic	LV6418-2	In Harm's Way	LD	U.S.		$30.00
MGM/UA	ML101788	In Her Majesty's Secret Service	LD	U.S.		$40.00
CBS	1761	In Like Flint	LD	U.S.	1990	$25.00
Image	ID6998TU	In Name Only	LD	U.S.		$30.00
Image	ID7050TU	In Person	LD	U.S.		$15.00
Discovision		In Pursuit of Number One	LD	U.S.	1979	$40.00
Republic	LV21990	In the Cold of Night	LD	U.S.	1991	$30.00
Columbia	77306	In the Heat of Passion	LD	U.S.	1992	$30.00
Image	ID5221LO	In the Mood	LD	U.S.		$30.00
CBS	1290	Incident	LD	U.S.	1990	$25.00
Pioneer	PA-87-186	Incident at Channel Q	LD	U.S.	1984	$35.00
Pioneer Artists	PA-87-186	Incident at Channel Q	LD	U.S.	1987	$35.00
Image	ID6421NW	Incredible Hulk Returns, The	LD	U.S.	1988	$95.00
Discovision	23-004	Incredible Shrinking Man	LD	U.S.	1979	$40.00
Discovision	16-023	Incredible Shrinking Woman	LD	U.S.	1981	$40.00
MCA	16-023	Incredible Shrinking Woman	LD	U.S.	1985	$40.00
Vestron Video	VL4016	Incubus	LD	U.S.	1983	$90.00
Paramount	LV1643-2	Indiana Jones	LD	U.S.	1986	$50.00
Image	ID7854ME	Indio	LD	U.S.		$30.00
		Informer	LD	U.S.		$30.00
CBS	4651	Inherit the Wind	LD	U.S.	1985	$40.00
Columbia	59076	Inner Sanctum	LD	U.S.	1991	$30.00
J2	J2-6036	Inside Moves	LD	U.S.	1989	$30.00
Image	ID7680NL	Inside the Third Reich	LD	U.S.		$30.00
Image	ID5143q	Insignificance	LD	U.S.		$40.00
CBS	8036	Intermezzo	LD	U.S.	1986	$35.00
Image	ID6376VE	Into the Fire	LD	U.S.		$30.00
Republic	LV22002	Intolerance	LD	U.S.	1991	$25.00
Image	ID7592VK	Intrigue	LD	U.S.		$30.00
Image	I-5064	Invaders From Mars	LD	U.S.		$50.00
Criterion	CC1108L	Invasion of the Body Snatchers	LD	U.S.	1989	$80.00

Label	Catalog Number	Title	Type	Country	Year	Value
	CAV version.					
Criterion	CC1174L	Invasion of the Body Snatchers	LD	U.S.	1989	$45.00
	CLV version.					
Republic	LV22018	Invasion of the Body Snatchers	LD	U.S.	1992	$40.00
U.S. Magna	SSLM-3018	Ira: Zeiram the Animation, Volume 1	LP	U.S.		$25.00
	Japanese anime CD-ROM.					
U.S. Magna	SSLM-3020	Ira: Zeiram the Animation, Volume 2	LP	U.S.		$25.00
	Japanese anime CD-ROM.					
Image	ID7478VK	Irezumi (Spirit Of Tattoo)	LD	U.S.		$30.00
CBS/Fox	6160-80	Iron Eagle	LD	U.S.	1987	$25.00
Image	ID6288IV	Iron Eagle II	LD	U.S.		$25.00
Republic	LV22025	Iron Mask, The	LD	U.S.	1991	$25.00
Image	ID6345IV	Iron Triangle, The	LD	U.S.		$30.00
Image	ID8353TU	Ironclads	LD	U.S.		$30.00
Vestron Video	VL5057	Irreconcilable Differences	LD	U.S.	1985	$45.00
Columbia	60849	Ishtar	LD	U.S.	1987	$30.00
	MS162-22LD	Island Breeze	LD	U.S.		$30.00
Image	ID5122	Island, The	LD	U.S.	1987	$35.00
		Isle of the Dead	LD	U.S.		$50.00
Image	ID7823MN	Istanbul	LD	U.S.		$30.00
Paramount	LV1421	It Came F/Holly W	LD	U.S.	1983	$30.00
RCA/Columbia	30491	It Came From Beneath The Sea	LD	U.S.	1986	$35.00
Columbia	30491	It Came From Beneath the Sea	LD	U.S.	1993	$30.00
Columbia	59676	It Couldn't Happen Here	LD	U.S.	1992	$30.00
Columbia	30382	It Happened One Night	LD	U.S.	1992	$30.00
Columbia		It Should Happen to You	LD	U.S.		$40.00
Image	ID 5088	It's a Gift	LD	U.S.	1987	$100.00
CBS	4534	It's a Mad Mad World	LD	U.S.	1983	$15.00
Criterion	CC1112L	It's a Wonderful Life	LD	U.S.	1987	$90.00
	CAV version.					
Republic	LV22060	It's a Wonderful Life	LD	U.S.	1989	$35.00
Republic	LV22062	It's a Wonderful Life: 45th	LD	U.S.	1991	$40.00
Columbia	VLD3190	It's My Turn	LD	U.S.	1985	$30.00
Image	ID7698CO	Ivan the Terreble	LD	U.S.		$30.00
Image	ID8354TU	Ivory Hunters	LD	U.S.		$30.00
Image	ID7125VK	Izzy & Moe	LD	U.S.		$20.00
Image	ID7202VV	J. Edgar Hoover	LD	U.S.		$30.00
Lumivision	LVD9007	J.F. Kennedy: A Celebration	LD	U.S.	1990	$25.00
CBS	6369	Jack & the Beanstock	LD	U.S.	1984	$30.00
Image	ID8239IV	Jacob's Ladder	LD	U.S.		$30.00
Columbia	30591	Jagged Edge	LD	U.S.	1986	$30.00
Psedition	PSE91-05	Jagged Edge	LD	U.S.	1991	65
MGM/UA	ML100011	Jailhouse Rock	LD	U.S.		$30.00
Image	ID7207VV	Jakarta	LD	U.S.		$30.00
Image	I5060	Jake Speed	LD	U.S.	1986	$35.00
Republic	LV22102	James Brothers of Missouri	LD	U.S.	1992	$40.00
Discovision		Jane Goodall: The World of Animal Behavior	LD	U.S.	1979	$40.00
CBS	4759	January Man, The	LD	U.S.	1990	$40.00
Columbia	9VLD3191	Jason and the Argonauts	LD	U.S.	1992	$30.00
Criterion	CC1303L	Jason and the Argonauts	LD	U.S.	1992	$100.00
Discovision		Jaws	LD	U.S.	1979	$40.00
	CAV					
Discovision		Jaws	LD	U.S.	1981	$40.00
	CLV					
Discovision	12-010	Jaws 2	LD	U.S.	1979	$40.00
MCA	42583	Jaws: Limited Edition Signature Collection	LTD/LD	U.S.	1995	$160.00
	4 LD boxed set with book and CD soundtrack.					
Columbia	30975	Jayce and the Wheeled Warriors	LD	U.S.	1989	$30.00
		Jazz Life	LD	U.S.		$40.00
Paramount	LV2305	Jazz Singer, The	LD	U.S.	1982	$20.00
Discovision	16-015	Jerk, The	LD	U.S.	1981	$30.00
MCA	16-015	Jerk, The	LD	U.S.	1985	$30.00
CBS	1485	Jesse James	LD	U.S.	1990	$35.00
Republic	LV22113	Jesse James Rides Again	LD	U.S.	1992	$40.00
Discovision		Jesus Christ Superstar	LD	U.S.	1979	$40.00
MCA	17-002	Jesus Christ Superstar	LD	U.S.	1985	$35.00
Image	ID8381HA	Jetsons, The Vol. 2	LD	U.S.		$30.00
CBS	1491	Jewel of the Nile	LD	U.S.	1986	$20.00
CBS	4626	Jezebel	LD	U.S.	1985	$35.00
Columbia	90536	Jezebel's Kiss	LD	U.S.	1990	$30.00
Warner	35574	JFK	LTD/4LD	U.S.	1993	$145.00
	4 CD boxed set.					
Image	ID7497HB	Jigsaw Man, The	LD	U.S.		$30.00
Walt Disney	747AS	Jiminy Cricket's Christmas	LD	U.S.	1990	$30.00
Columbia	30683	Jo Jo Dancer	LD	U.S.	1986	$30.00
Vid-America	889	Joan of Arc	LD	U.S.	1985	$30.00
Vestron Video	LL6005	Joe	LD	U.S.	1983	$80.00
Discovision		Joe Jidd	LD	U.S.	1979	$40.00
Image	ID6149OR	Johnny B. Good	LD	U.S.		$30.00
Republic	LV22124	Johnny Come Lately	LD	U.S.	1992	$35.00
Image	ID5275ME	Johnny Got His Gun	LD	U.S.		$35.00
Image	ID6117RE	Johnny Guitar	LD	U.S.		$95.00
Image	ID7313IV	Johnny Handsome	LD	U.S.		$30.00
Image	ID6610HA	Johnny Quest Vol. 1	LD	U.S.		$30.00
Image	ID6610HA	Johnny Quest Vol. 2	LD	U.S.		$30.00
Columbia	30766	Jolson Sings Again	LD	U.S.		$30.00
	First issue					
RCA/Columbia	30766	Jolson Sings Again	LD	U.S.	1987	$35.00
Columbia	30766	Jolson Sings Again	LD	U.S.	1993	$35.00
Columbia	30686	Jolson Story	LD	U.S.	1993	$30.00
Criterion	CC1207L	Jour De Fete	LD	U.S.	1991	$50.00
Image	ID6403TU	Journey Into Fear	LD	U.S.		$80.00
Walt Disney	400AS	Journey of Natty	LD	U.S.	1987	$40.00
CBS	1248-80	Journey to the Center of the Earth	LD	U.S.	1991	$25.00
CBS	1248-85	Journey to the Center of the Earth	LD	U.S.	1991	$35.00
	Letterbox version.					
Image	ID7491HB	Journey to the Seventh Planet/The Angry Red Planet	LD	U.S.		$150.00
Image	ID7531VE	Joysticks	LD	U.S.		$30.00
Image	ID6641RC	Jubal	LD	U.S.		$30.00
Columbia	62774	Judgement in Berlin	LD	U.S.	1989	$30.00
Republic	LV22136	Judith of Bethulia	LD	U.S.	1991	$25.00
Image		Judy's Favorites				
CBS	6679	Jules and Jim	LD	U.S.	1986	$25.00
Magnetic Video		Julia	LD	U.S.†	1984	$30.00
CBS	1091	Julia	LD	U.S.	1990	$35.00
CBS/Fox	5034-80	Julia and Julia	LD	U.S.	1988	$40.00
Image	ID6259RE	Julius Caesar	LD	U.S.		$80.00
Nelson	13255	Jungle Book	LD	U.S.	1984	$35.00
Walt Disney	1122CS	Jungle Book, The	LD	U.S.		$75.00
	CAV version.					
Walt Disney	1122AS	Jungle Book, The	LD	U.S.		$55.00
	CLV version.					
Lumivision	LVD8914	Just a Gigolo	LD	U.S.	1990	$40.00
		Just Heroes	LD	U.S.		$80.00
Columbia	30493	Just One of the Guys	LD	U.S.	1985	$30.00
Image	ID5231NW	Kandyland	LD	U.S.		$30.00
Columbia	30406	Karate Kid	LD	U.S.		$40.00
Columbia	30717	Karate Kid II	LD	U.S.		$40.00
Columbia	50176	Karate Kid III	LD	U.S.	1990	$40.00
Cannon	31151	Keaton's Cop	LD	U.S.	1990	$30.00
Paramount	LV1563	Keep	LD	U.S.	1984	$30.00
Nelson	902006	Keeping Track	LD	U.S.	1987	$35.00
MGM/UA	ML100168	Kelly's Heroes	LD	U.S.		$30.00
Image	ID6985TU	Kentucky Kernels	LD	U.S.		$30.00
CBS/Fox	4594-80	Key Largo	LD	U.S.	1983	$35.00
Columbia	32006	Key, The	LD	U.S.	1989	$30.00
Image	ID7713MN	KGB, The Secret War	LD	U.S.		$30.00
Image	ID8244IV	Kid	LD	U.S.		$30.00
Nelson	30475	Kid From Brooklyn	LD	U.S.	1986	$35.00
Discovision	D18-506	Kidnapped	LD	U.S.	1979	$40.00
MGM/UA	ML100205	Kids From Fame	LD	U.S.	1984	$35.00
Discovision	D61-504	Kids is Kids	LD	U.S.	1979	$40.00
Image	ID7869ME	Kill Crazy	LD	U.S.		$30.00
Columbia	59096	Kill Reflex	LD	U.S.	1990	$30.00
Nelson	77656	Kill Slade	LD	U.S.	1989	$35.00
Image	ID6251ME	Killer Clowns From Outerspace	LD	U.S.		$30.00
Image	ID6412MG	Killer Elite	LD	U.S.		$40.00
Discovision		Killer Instinct	LD	U.S.	1979	$40.00
Vidmark	LDCVM5609	Killer Instinct	LD	U.S.	1993	$25.00
Nelson	77696	Killing Floor, The	LD	U.S.	1989	$35.00
Criterion	CC1164L	Killing, The	LD	U.S.	1988	$40.00
Image	ID6876HB	Kind Hearts and Coronets/The Captain's Paradise	LD	U.S.		$30.00
Vestron Video	LV5210	Kindred	LD	U.S.	1987	$35.00
Magnetic Video		King and I, The	LD	U.S.†	1981	$25.00
Magnetic Video		King and I, The	LD	U.S.†	1984	$30.00
CBS/Fox	1004-80	King and I, The	LD	U.S.	1985	$35.00
CBS	1004	King and I, The	LD	U.S.	1991	$60.00
	Letterbox version.					
Paramount	LV1284	King David	LD	U.S.	1985	$30.00
Paramount	LV8872-2	King Kong	LD	U.S.	1983	$36.00
Image	ID6003	King Kong	LD	U.S.	1985	$100.00
	Special edition with comentary track					
Criterion	CC102L	King Kong	LD	U.S.	1987	$75.00
Criterion	CC1116L	King Kong	LD	U.S.	1987	$40.00
Image	ID5154	King Kong Lives	LD	U.S.		$80.00
		King Kong/Son of Kong	LD	U.S.		$100.00
Image	ID5335PA	King: Montgomery to Memphis	LD	U.S.		$30.00
Columbia	VLD3192	King of Comedy	LD	U.S.	1993	$30.00
Criterion	CC1225L	King of Hearts	LD	U.S.	1990	$50.00
Criterion	CC1295L	King of Kings	LD	U.S.	1992	$50.00
Image	ID7612IV	King of New York	LD	U.S.		$30.00
Paramount	LV8868	King of the Gypsies	LD	U.S.	1985	$30.00
Republic	LV27322	King of the Rocketmen	LD	U.S.	1992	$40.00
Republic	LV22199	King of the Texas Rangers	LD	U.S.	1992	$40.00
Cannon	31036	Kinjite Forbidden Subjects	LD	U.S.	1989	$30.00
Columbia	91906	Kiss Me a Killer	LD	U.S.	1992	$30.00
MGM/UA	ML100307	Kiss Me Kate	LD	U.S.		$30.00
Nelson	90001-6	Kiss of the Spider Woman	LD	U.S.	1986	$50.00
Image	ID6394TS	Kiss, The	LD	U.S.		$100.00
Republic	LV22205	Kiss Tomorrow Goodbye	LD	U.S.	1990	$25.00
		Kloss Novabeam 100	LD	U.S.		$30.00
Republic	LV22200	Knight Moves	LD	U.S.	1993	$25.00
MGM/UA	ML100399	Knights of the Round Table	LD	U.S.	1988	$35.00
Columbia	30029	Knock on Any Door	LD	U.S.	1984	$30.00
Grolier	GEP85-010	Knowledgedisc	LD	U.S.	1985	$90.00
Republic	LV28210	Koko the Clown Cartoon	LD	U.S.	1991	$25.00
Image	ID5304PA	Koyaanisqatsi	LD	U.S.		$180.00
Pacific Arts	PAV12539	Koyaanisqatsi	LD	U.S.	1985	$180.00
RCA/Columbia	VLD3205	Kramer vs. Kramer	LD	U.S.	1982	$35.00
Columbia	30030	Kramer vs. Kramer	LD	U.S.	1984	$30.00
	Digital audio					
Columbia	30030	Kramer vs. Kramer	LD	U.S.	1992	$30.00
Columbia	90976	Krays, The	LD	U.S.	1991	$30.00
	Letterbox version.					
Republic	LV22210	Kriemhilde's Revenge	LD	U.S.	1991	$25.00
RCA/Columbia	VLD3207	Krull	LD	U.S.	1984	$40.00
Columbia	VLD3207	Krull	LD	U.S.	1993	$30.00
Criterion	CC1237L	Kwaindan	LD	U.S.	1990	$60.00
Image	ID6624IV	L.A. Bounty	LD	U.S.		$30.00
Image	ID8246IV	L.A. Story	LD	U.S.		$30.00
Criterion	CC1162L	L'Avventura	LD	U.S.	1989	$120.00
Columbia	30854	La Bamba	LD	U.S.	1988	$30.00
U.S. Magna	SSLM-3005	La Blue Girl, Volume 1	LP	U.S.		$30.00
	Japanese anime CD-ROM.					
U.S. Magna	SSLM-3006	La Blue Girl, Volume 2	LP	U.S.		$30.00
	Japanese anime CD-ROM.					
U.S. Magna	SSLM-3034	La Blue Girl, Volume 3	LP	U.S.		$30.00
	Japanese anime CD-ROM.					
U.S. Magna	SSLM-3035	La Blue Girl, Volume 4	LP	U.S.		$30.00
	Japanese anime CD-ROM.					
Image	IG-5004	La Cage	LD	U.S.	1985	$30.00
CBS/Fox	4506-80	La Cage Aux Folles	LD	U.S.	1984	$35.00
Columbia	30645	La Cage Aux Folles 3	LD	U.S.	1986	$30.00
Image	ID6262RE	La Dolce Vita	LD	U.S.		$30.00
Image	ID6952OOR	La Lectrice (The Reader)	LD	U.S.		$30.00
Criterion		La Strada	LD	U.S.	1988	$40.00
Nelson	76666	Labyrinth	LD	U.S.	1987	$50.00
Criterion	CC1222L	Lacemaker	LD	U.S.	1990	$50.00
Image	ID5099	Ladies in Alaska	LD	U.S.		$30.00
Walt Disney		Lady and the Tramp	LD	Japan		$100.00
Walt Disney	582AS	Lady and the Tramp	LD	U.S.	1987	$250.00
	CAV version.					
Walt Disney	582CS	Lady and the Tramp	LD	U.S.	1987	$200.00
	CLV version.					
Image	ID 6179IV	Lady Beware	LD	U.S.	1988	$40.00
MGM/UA	ML100184	Lady Chatterley's Lover	LD	U.S.	1983	$35.00
Lightning	LL929	Lady Chatterley's Lover	LD	U.S.	1986	$40.00
Columbia	30451	Lady From Shanghai	LD	U.S.	1993	$30.00
Warner Home Video	11464	Lady Hawke	LD	U.S.	1985	$30.00
Columbia	32035	Lady In Question, The	LD	U.S.	1989	$30.00
Image	ID6018	Lady In White	LD	U.S.		$30.00
Paramount	LV1705	Lady Jane	LD	U.S.	1986	$40.00
Image	ID7273IV	Lady Sings the Blues	LD	U.S.		$30.00
Image	ID6103ME	Lady Vanishes, The	LD	U.S.		$15.00
Criterion		Lady Vanishes, The	LD	U.S.	1989	$40.00
		Lair of the White Worm	LD	U.S.		$90.00
Republic	22262	Lake Consequence	LD	U.S.	1993	$35.00
Nelson	11105	Lamaze Method	LD	U.S.	1984	$30.00
Cannon	31193	Lambada	LD	U.S.	1990	$25.00
MCA	40864	Land Before Time	LD	U.S.	1989	$25.00
MCA	40924	Land Before Time	LD	U.S.	1989	$35.00
Republic	LV22271	Landslide	LD	U.S.	1992	$25.00

Lady Beware – (Image ID6179IV)

Label	Catalog Number	Title	Type	Country	Year	Value
Full Moon	LV13008	Laserblast	LD	U.S.	1993	$35.00
Warner Home Video	11372LV	Lassiter	LD	U.S.	1984	$35.00
Columbia	VLD3252	Last Detail, The	LD	U.S.	1984	$30.00
Nelson	7715LV	Last Emperor	LD	U.S.	1988	$70.00
Columbia	90636	Last Exit to Brooklyn	LD	U.S.	1990	$80.00
Vestron	LV5096	Last House on the Left	LD	U.S.	1986	$180.00
Columbia	30922	Last Hurrah	LD	U.S.	1988	$30.00
Discovision		Last Married Couple in America	LD	U.S.	1980	$40.00
Image	ID7289RF	Last of the Blue Devils	LD	U.S.		$30.00
Live	LD01007	Last of the Mohicans	LD	U.S.	1992	$35.00
		Last of the Red Hot Lovers	LD	U.S.		$40.00
Paramount	LV8094	Last of the Red Hot Lovers	LD	U.S.	1983	$30.00
Columbia	50426	Last Picture Show	LD	U.S.	1991	$30.00
Discovision		Last Remake of Beau Geste	LD	U.S.	1979	$40.00
Vestron Video	5177	Last Resort	LD	U.S.	1987	$35.00
CBS	4757	Last Rites	LD	U.S.	1990	$30.00
CBS/Fox	4507-80	Last Tango in Paris	LD	U.S.	1983	$40.00
Criterion	CC1232L	Last Tango in Paris	LD	U.S.	1991	$70.00
MGM/UA	ML101773	Last Tango in Paris	LD	U.S.	1992	$40.00
J2	J2-6032	Last Unicorn	LD	U.S.	1990	$30.00
Image	ID7513SO	Last Warrior	LD	U.S.		$30.00
Image	ID8218PR	Lauderdale	LD	U.S.		$30.00
CBS	1094	Laura	LD	U.S.	1990	$40.00
Image	ID6866HB	Lavender Hill Mob/The Man in the White Suit	LD	U.S.		$30.00
Image	ID7399CV	Law of Desire	LD	U.S.		$30.00
Columbia/Tri Star	75896	Lawnmower Man	LD	U.S.	1992	$40.00
		Lawrence of Arabia	LD	Japan	1985	$50.00
Columbia	VLD3250	Lawrence of Arabia	LD	U.S.	1984	$30.00
Columbia		Lawrence of Arabia	LD	U.S.	1988	$30.00
Columbia	50136	Lawrence of Arabia	LD	U.S.	1992	$30.00
	Letterbox version.					
Lumivision	LVD9253	Lé Boucher	LD	U.S.	1993	$25.00
Image	ID6151PA	Lé Grand Chemin (The Grand Highway)	LD	U.S.		$30.00
Live Entertainment	LD51044V	Leader of the Band	LD	U.S.	1993	$25.00
Image	ID7298VA	Leathal Woman	LD	U.S.		$30.00
Columbia	75016	Leatherface: Texas Chainsaw Massacre III	LD	U.S.	1990	$30.00
CBS	1465	Legend of Hell House	LD	U.S.	1990	$30.00
U.S. Magna	SSLM-3017	Legend of Lemnear	LP	U.S.		$30.00
	Japanese anime CD-ROM.					
Image	ID8043SP	Legend of Love (Bolshoi At the Bolshoi)	LD	U.S.		$30.00
Image	ID6284SO	Legend of Sleepy Hollow	LD	U.S.		$30.00
Vidmark	LDCVM5740	Legends of The West	LD	U.S.	1993	$35.00
Columbia	59246	Legion of Iron	LD	U.S.	1992	$30.00
Image	ID7973RC	Lemon Drop Kid	LD	U.S.		$90.00
Image	ID7372HB	Lemon Sisters, The	LD	U.S.	1990	$15.00
CBS	4563	Lenny	LD	U.S.	1983	$30.00
Columbia	30896	Leonard Part VI	LD	U.S.	1988	$30.00
		Leopard Man, The	LD	U.S.		$60.00
Lumivision	LVD9228	Les Bitches	LD	U.S.	1992	$25.00
Polygram	080647-1	Les Miserables	LD	U.S.	1989	$35.00
CBS	1268	Les Miserables (1935)	LD	U.S.	1986	$40.00
CBS	1649	Less Than Zero	LD	U.S.	1988	$30.00
Magnetic Video		Let It Be	LD	U.S.†	1981	$250.00
HBO	TVL9953	Let's Get Harry	LD	U.S.	1988	$30.00
		Let's Talk About Sex	LD	U.S.		$40.00
Republic	LV22330	Letter From an Unknown Woman	LD	U.S.	1992	$25.00
CBS	4684	Letter, The	LD	U.S.	1987	$35.00
CBS	1667	License to Drive	LD	U.S.	1989	$30.00
CBS	4755	License to Kill	LD	U.S.	1990	$15.00
Image	ID8413OR	Life and Nothing But	LD	U.S.		$30.00
Republic	LV22349	Life Is Sweet	LD	U.S.	1992	$25.00
CBS/Fox	1393-80	Lifeboat	LD	U.S.	1990	$40.00
Vestron Video	VL5097	Lifeforce	LD	U.S.	1985	$35.00
		Lift, The	LD	U.S.		$30.00
Vestron Video	IDV5200	Light of Day	LD	U.S.	1987	$35.00
		Light Years	LD	U.S.		$40.00
Image	ID5287TS	Like Father Like Son	LD	U.S.		$30.00
Vestron Video	V5159	Lily in Love	LD	U.S.	1986	$35.00
Image	ID7309VV	Limit Up	LD	U.S.		$30.00
Magnetic Video		Lion in Winter, The	LD	U.S.†	1984	$30.00
Nelson	20575	Lion of Winter, The	LD	U.S.	1985	$30.00
Discovision		Lions of the Serengeti	LD	U.S.	1979	$40.00
Paramount	LV8882	Lipstick	LD	U.S.	1983	$30.00
Image	ID5078	Liquid Sky	LD	U.S.		$150.00
Columbia	10326	Listen to Me	LD	U.S.	1990	$30.00
Magnetic Video		Little Big Man	LD	U.S.†	1984	$30.00
Paramount	LV1301	Little Darlings	LD	U.S.	1982	$30.00
Nelson	30505	Little Foxes	LD	U.S.	1985	$50.00
Image	ID7527VE	Little Girl Who Lives Down the Lane	LD	U.S.		$30.00
Walt Disney	913CS	Little Mermaid, The	LD	U.S.	1990	$200.00
	CAV version.					
Walt Disney	913AS	Little Mermaid, The	LD	U.S.	1990	$150.00
	CLV version.					
		Little Night Music	LD	U.S.		$70.00
Columbia	65000	Little Nikita	LD	U.S.	1989	$30.00
Paramount	LV8017	Little Prince, The	LD	U.S.	1983	$30.00
Nelson	76916	Little Sweetheart	LD	U.S.	1990	$35.00
Columbia	VLD30560	Little Treasure	LD	U.S.	1986	$30.00
Columbia	90526	Little Vegas	LD	U.S.	1991	$30.00
Lumivision	LVD8907	Little Vera	LD	U.S.	1989	$25.00
Discovision	32-001	Littler's, Gene Golf	LD	U.S.	1979	$40.00
CBS	4633	Live and Let Die	LD	U.S.	1984	$25.00
MGM/UA	ML101418	Live and Let Die	LD	U.S.	1991	$40.00
Discovision		Lives of a Bengal Lancer	LD	U.S.	1979	$40.00
CBS	5277	Living Daylights	LD	U.S.	1988	$15.00
Columbia	30662	Living Free	LD	U.S.	1986	$30.00
Image	ID7376IV	Lobster Man From Mars	LD	U.S.		$30.00
	11307	Local Hero	LD	U.S.		$30.00
MGM/UA	ML100082	Logan's Run	LD	U.S.	1984	$35.00
Criterion	1213L	Lola Monte's	LD	U.S.	1956	$100.00
Image	ID6913RH	Lone Ranger, Vol. 1	LD	U.S.	1989	$25.00
Image	ID7500RH	Lone Ranger, Vol. 2	LD	U.S.	1989	$25.00
Image		Lone Ranger, Vol. 3	LD	U.S.	1989	$25.00
Image		Lone Ranger, Vol. 4	LD	U.S.	1989	$25.00
Image		Lone Ranger, Vol. 5	LD	U.S.	1989	$25.00
Vestron Video	VL5019	Lone Wolf McQuade	LD	U.S.	1983	$40.00
Discovision	12-008	Lonely Are the Brave	LD	U.S.	1979	$50.00
MCA	40014	Lonely Guy	LD	U.S.	1984	$40.00
Republic	LV25548	Long Days Journey Into Night	LD	U.S.	1992	$25.00
Lighting Video	LL9907	Long Voyage Home	LD	U.S.	1985	$75.00
Image	ID8245IV	Long Walk Home	LD	U.S.		$30.00
Magnetic Video		Longest Day, The	LD	U.S.†	1984	$30.00
CBS	1021	Longest Day, The	LD	U.S.	1989	$30.00
Vidmark	LDCVM5233	Longest Drive	LD	U.S.	1992	$25.00
Paramount	LV8708	Longest Yard	LD	U.S.	1985	$30.00
Columbia	70186	Look Who's Talking	LD	U.S.	1990	$25.00
Columbia/Tri Star	79106	Look Who's Talking	LD	U.S.	1994	$35.00
Columbia	70556	Look Who's Talking Too	LD	U.S.	1991	$25.00
Discovision	P10-520	Looking for Mr. Goodbar	LD	U.S.	1979	$85.00
Paramount	LV8874-2	Looking for Mr. Goodbar	LD	U.S.	1983	$100.00
Columbia	70196	Loose Cannons	LD	U.S.	1990	$30.00
Nelson	7746-6	Lord of the Flies	LD	U.S.	1990	$35.00
Paramount	LV1433	Lords of Discipline, The	LD	U.S.	1983	$55.00
Columbia	30479	Lords of Flatbush	LD	U.S.		$70.00
Discovision		Loretta	LD	U.S.	1980	$40.00
MCA	74-004	Loretta	LD	U.S.	1985	$25.00
Nelson	20615	Losin' It	LD	U.S.	1984	$35.00
Pioneer	30763	Lost Horizon	LD	U.S.		$35.00
Psedition	PSE91-25	Lost Horizon	LD	U.S.	1992	$55.00
Pioneer		Lost in Space Volume 1	LD	Japan	1995	$300.00
	4 LD boxed set.					
Pioneer		Lost in Space Volume 2	LD	Japan	1995	$510.00
	8 LD boxed set.					
Pioneer		Lost in Space Volume 3	LD	Japan	1996	$510.00
	8 LD boxed set.					
Pioneer	PILF 2185	Lost in Space Volume 4	LD	Japan	1996	$400.00
	6 LD boxed set.					
Pioneer	PILF2130	Lost in Space Volume 5	LD	Japan	1996	$450.00
	7 LD boxed set.					
Image	ID7983MF	Lost Man's River	LD	U.S.		$30.00
Republic	LV22448	Lost Moment	LD	U.S.	1992	$35.00
		Lost Patrol	LD	U.S.		$50.00
Image	ID6790ML	Lost Pharoh: The Search for Akhenaten	LD	U.S.		$30.00
Discovision		Lost Weekend	LD	U.S.	1979	$40.00
Lumivision	LVD9019	Lost World, The	LD	U.S.	1991	$25.00
Discovision		Louis vs. Conn	LD	U.S.	1979	$40.00
		Lourve Tour, Paris	LD	Japan		$70.00
CBS	8038	Love Among the Ruins	LD	U.S.	1990	$35.00
Vestron Video	VL4052	Love at First Bite	LD	U.S.	1983	$50.00
Nelson	77166	Love at Stake	LD	U.S.	1989	$35.00
Walt Disney	12AS	Love Bug	LD	U.S.	1982	$20.00
Walt Disney	12AS	Love Bug	LD	U.S.	1993	$35.00
WHV/HBO	90771	Love Crimes (Unrated Version)	LD	U.S.	1992	$30.00
CBS	4585	Love & Death	LD	U.S.	1983	$30.00
Criterion	V1024L	Love Godesses	LD	U.S.	1990	$50.00
Image	ID6234RE	Love Happy	LD	U.S.		$65.00
CBS	1039	Love is a Many Splendored	LD	U.S.	1987	$30.00
Image	ID7533VE	Love Letters	LD	U.S.		$30.00
Republic	LV22473	Love Lies & Murder	LD	U.S.	1993	$25.00
MGM/UA	ML100755	Love Me or Leave Me	LD	U.S.	1989	$40.00
Discovision	P10-523	Love Story	LD	U.S.	1979	$20.00
Paramount	LV8006	Love Story	LD	U.S.	1983	$30.00
Columbia	70206	Loverboy	LD	U.S.	1989	$20.00
Republic	LVD22485	Lower Level	LD	U.S.	1992	$30.00
Disney	850AS	Lucky Luke Vol. 1: Daisy Town	LD	U.S.	1990	$30.00
Disney	851AS	Lucky Luke Vol. 2: Ballad of Dalton	LD	U.S.	1990	$30.00
Columbia	32827	Lucky Stiff	LD	U.S.	1989	$20.00
Republic	LV22495	Lucy and Desi Before the Laughter	LD	U.S.	1993	$30.00
U.S. Magna	SSLM-3024	Lum-Beautiful Dreamer	LP	U.S.		$25.00
	Japanese anime CD-ROM.					
Image	ID7660HB	Lust for a Vampire/Die Monster, Die!	LD	U.S.		$70.00
		Lust in the Dust	LD	U.S.		$100.00
		Lusty Men	LD	U.S.		$30.00
Discovision		Luther	LD	U.S.	1979	$40.00
		M	LD	U.S.		$50.00
Magnetic Video		M*A*S*H	LD	U.S.†	1984	$30.00
Discovision	22-022	Ma & Pa Kettle	LD	U.S.	1979	$40.00
		Macao	LD	U.S.		$65.00
Paramount	LV1937	Macaroni	LD	U.S.	1986	$40.00
Discovision		MacArthur	LD	U.S.	1979	$40.00
Image	ID7471PA	MacArthur's Children	LD	U.S.		$30.00
Columbia	306088RE	Macbeth	LD	U.S.		$30.00
Republic	LV25551	Macbeth: 45th Anniversary	LD	U.S.	1992	$50.00
Columbia	77006	Mack the Knife	LD	U.S.	1990	$30.00
Republic	LV22516	Mad at the Moon	LD	U.S.	1993	$30.00
Vestron	LV4030	Mad Max	LD	U.S.	1983	$20.00
		Mad Miss Manton	LD	U.S.		$30.00
Republic	LV22518	Madame Bovary	LD	U.S.	1992	$40.00
Discovision	22-022	Made in Milan	LD	U.S.	1979	$40.00
Nelson	90244LV	Made in U.S.A.	LD	U.S.	1988	$40.00
Image	ID8148OR	Madhouse	LD	U.S.		$30.00
		Madmoiselle Fifi	LD	U.S.		$30.00
Nelson	150150	Magic	LD	U.S.	1983	$75.00
Image	ID6233RE	Magic Christian, The	LD	U.S.		$30.00
Republic	LV22548	Magic Christian, The	LD	U.S.	1991	$25.00
Paramount	LV2351-2	Magic Flute	LD	U.S.	1986	$40.00
Discovision		Magic Moments	LD	U.S.		$40.00
Vestron	LV3011	Magic Pony	LD	U.S.	1983	$30.00
Discovision		Magic Rolling Board/Skateboard Safety	LD	U.S.	1979	$40.00
Republic	LV22556	Magic Town	LD	U.S.	1992	$35.00
Image	ID6197MP	Magical Mystery Tour	LD	U.S.		$100.00
		Magician	LD	U.S.		$70.00
CBS	4553	Magnificent Seven	LD	U.S.	1983	$15.00
MGM/UA	ML101563	Magnificent Seven	LD	U.S.	1991	$40.00
Paramount	LV2320A	Magoo in Sherwood	LD	U.S.	1983	$30.00

Label	Catalog Number	Title	Type	Country	Year	Value
Paramount	LV8835	Mahogany	LD	U.S.	1983	$30.00
Image	ID8108ME	Maid, The	LD	U.S.		$30.00
Image	ID6180IV	Maid to October	LD	U.S.		$30.00
Republic	LV25552	Majorie Morningstar	LD	U.S.	1992	$25.00
HBO	TVL0016	Making Mr. Right	LD	U.S.	1988	$50.00
Fox	PIMF-1002	Making of Die Hard With a Vengence	8" LD	Japan	1995	$30.00
Image	ID6822MD	Making of Invaders From Mars	LD	U.S.	1985	$50.00
Paramount	LV83049	Making of Raiders	LD	U.S.	1983	$30.00
		Making of Robocop	LD	Japan	1988	$90.00
Magnetic Video		Making of Star Wars/SP FX: The Empire Strikes Back	LD	U.S.	1981	$200.00
Magnetic Video		Making of Star Wars/SP FX: The Empire Strikes Back	LD	U.S.†	1981	$150.00
CBS/Fox	1052-80	Making of Star Wars/SP FX: The Empire Strikes Back	LD	U.S.	1981	$200.00
		Making of Superman	LD	Japan	1983	$150.00
Discovision		Making of the Torah, The	LD	U.S.	1979	$40.00
Image	ID7159SO	Malarek	LD	U.S.		$30.00
Vestron Video	VL5183	Malcolm	LD	U.S.	1987	$35.00
Image	ID5169	Malone	LD	U.S.	1987	$25.00
CBS/Fox	4530-80	Maltese Falcon	LD	U.S.	1983	$35.00
Discovision		Mamouth Mountain Adventure	LD	U.S.	1979	$40.00
Columbia	VLD3332	Man for All Seasons	LD	U.S.	1992	$30.00
CBS	1233	Man From Snowy River	LD	U.S.	1984	$25.00
Nelson	77116	Man in Love	LD	U.S.	1988	$35.00
Columbia	75116	Man Inside, The	LD	U.S.	1991	$15.00
Image	ID7537VE	Man of Flowers	LD	U.S.		$30.00
CBS	4575	Man of LaMancha	LD	U.S.	1987	$40.00
Image	ID7682NL	Man Who Could Work Miracles	LD	U.S.		$30.00
Columbia	VLD3333	Man Who Fell to Earth	LD	U.S.	1983	$40.00
Image	ID7462FP	Man Who Knew Too Much (1934)	LD	U.S.		$50.00
Columbia	VLD3334	Man Who Loved Women	LD	U.S.	1992	$30.00
Paramount	LV6114	Man Who Shot Liberty Valance	LD	U.S.	1983	$30.00
CBS	7434	Man Who Would Be King	LD	U.S.	1990	$65.00
MGM/UA	ML101419	Man With the Golden Gun	LD	U.S.		$15.00
MGA/UA	4606	Man With the Golden Gun	LD	U.S.	1983	$15.00
Paramount	LV8771-2	Mandingo	LD	U.S.	1983	$40.00
MGM/UA	ML102242	Manhattan	LD	U.S.		$25.00
MGM/UA	ML100469	Manhattan	LD	U.S.	1985	$35.00
Republic	LV22635	Manhunt in the African Jungle	LD	U.S.	1992	$40.00
Republic	LV22637	Manhunt of Mystery Island	LD	U.S.	1992	$40.00
Lorimar	LV411	Manhunter	LD	U.S.	1987	$40.00
Image	ID8090IV	Maniac Cop 2	LD	U.S.		$20.00
Nelson	900546	Manitou, The	LD	U.S.	1989	$35.00
Image	ID5149	Mannequin	LD	U.S.		$50.00
Walt Disney	25AS	Many Adventures of Winnie the Pooh	LD	U.S.	1982	$30.00
HBO		Map of Human Heart	LD	U.S.	1993	$175.00
Paramount	LV8789	Marathon Man	LD	U.S.	1982	$36.00
		March of the Wooden Soldiers	LD	U.S.		$125.00
Discovision		Marciano vs. Wolcott and More	LD	U.S.	1979	$40.00
Discovision		Marcus-Nelson Murders	LD	U.S.	1979	$40.00
Image	ID7969PS	Marilyn Diaries	LD	U.S.		$30.00
		Marilyn Monroe	LD	Japan	1987	$90.00
		Marilyn Monroe: Photos 1926–62	LD	Japan	1988	$90.00
Image		Mark of Zorro, The	LD	U.S.		$40.00
Republic	LV22686	Mark of Zorro, The	LD	U.S.	1991	$40.00
Image	ID7383VK	Marked for Murder	LD	U.S.		$30.00
Nelson	13446	Marlene	LD	U.S.	1987	$35.00
		Married to the Mob	LD	U.S.		$40.00
Image	ID7613IV	Martians Go Home	LD	U.S.		$30.00
CBS	4634	Marty	LD	U.S.	1986	$30.00
Image	ID6662VE	Marx Brothers: In a Nutshell	LD	U.S.		$30.00
Disney		Mary Poppins	LD	Japan		$50.00
Disney	23AS	Mary Poppins	LD	U.S.	1983	$30.00
Disney	23AS	Mary Poppins	LD	U.S.	1990	$30.00
Image		Mask	LD	U.S.		$40.00
Pioneer	PILF1384	Mask, The: Animated Series	LTD/LD	Japan	1996	$180.00
	3 LD boxed set.					
Columbia	77236	Masque of the Red Death	LD	U.S.	1991	$50.00
Image	ID5246VE	Masque of the Red Death/Premature Burial	LD	U.S.		$80.00
CBS	4749	Masquerade	LD	U.S.	1988	$20.00
Columbia	90926	Masters of Menace	LD	U.S.	1991	$30.00
Image	ID7252CV	Matador	LD	U.S.		$30.00
Image		Matewan	LD	U.S.		$40.00
Discovision	64-010	Math That Counts	LD	U.S.	1979	$40.00
Image	ID7342KN	Matter of the Heart	LD	U.S.		$30.00
Image	ID7683NL	Mausoleum	LD	U.S.		$40.00
CBS	1236	Max Dugan Returns	LD	U.S.	1984	$25.00
Lorimar	LV367	Max Headroom	LD	U.S.	1987	$90.00
Lorimar	LV395	Maximum Overdrive	LD	U.S.	1987	$30.00
Image	ID7265NW	Maximum Security	LD	U.S.		$30.00
Image	ID7873ME	May Wine	LD	U.S.		$30.00
O.P.A.	OPA-37-603	Maze Mania	LD	U.S.	1983	$30.00
Image	ID7525VE	McVicar	LD	U.S.		$30.00
Columbia	50236	Me and Him	LD	U.S.	1990	$30.00

Meatballs – (Vestron VL 6009)

Label	Catalog Number	Title	Type	Country	Year	Value
Vestron	VL6009	Meatballs	LD	U.S.	1983	$60.00
Columbia	3045	Meatballs II	LD	U.S.	1985	$30.00
Michael Agee	LVA1005	Meet John Doe	LD	U.S.	1990	$100.00
MGM/UA	ML100005	Meet Me in St. Louis	LD	U.S.	1984	$35.00
Image	ID7859ME	Meet the Hollowheads	LD	U.S.		$30.00
Live Entertainment	LD68955	Megaville	LD	U.S.	1992	$35.00
Nelson	75555	Mein Kempf	LD	U.S.	1985	$35.00
Walt Disney		Melody Time	LD	Japan	1986	N/A
Discovision	10-031	Melvin & Howard	LD	U.S.		$40.00
MCA	10-031	Melvin & Howard	LD	U.S.	1985	$40.00
Nelson	77676	Memorial Valley Massacre	LD	U.S.	1989	$35.00
CBS	4754-80	Memories of Me	LD	U.S.		$30.00
Image	ID8651PR	Memories of Murder	LD	U.S.		$30.00

Men at Work – (Epic 59466)

Label	Catalog Number	Title	Type	Country	Year	Value
Columbia	59466	Men at Work	LD	U.S.	1990	$40.00
Columbia	90546	Men of Respect	LD	U.S.	1991	$30.00
	Letterbox version.					
Republic	LV22710	Men, The	LD	U.S.	1992	$35.00
Image	ID6044ME	Mercenary Fighters	LD	U.S.		$30.00
Image	ID6292ME	Messenger of Death	LD	U.S.		$30.00
MCA	40045	Metalstorm	LD	U.S.	1984	$30.00
Vestron Video	VL5090	Metropolis	LD	U.S.	1985	$100.00
Columbia	75156	Metropolitan	LD	U.S.	1991	$40.00
MGM/UA		MGM/UA HomeVideo Laserdisc Sampler	DJ/LD	U.S.	1990	$25.00
MGM/UA	ML102880	MGM/UA HomeVideo Laserdisc Sampler	DJ/LD	U.S.	1993	$25.00
		Miami Vice	LD	U.S.		$40.00
Disney	69AS	Mickey/Donald Vol. 1	LD	U.S.	1982	$50.00
Disney	70AS	Mickey/Donald Vol. 2	LD	U.S.	1982	$50.00
Walt Disney	34AS	Mickey/Donald Vol. 3	LD	U.S.	1983	$30.00
Walt Disney	1997 CS	Mickey Mouse the Black And White Years	LD	U.S.		$100.00
Walt Disney	798 AS	Mickey & the Gang	LD	U.S.	1989	$30.00
Walt Disney	459AS	Mickey's Christmas	LD	U.S.	1990	$25.00
Walt Disney		Mickey's Jungle	LD	Japan	1995	$70.00
Walt Disney		Mickey's Summer Madness	LD	Japan	1995	$70.00
RCA/Columbia	30456	Micki and Maude	LD	U.S.	1985	$35.00
Columbia	30456	Micki and Maude	LD	U.S.	1993	$30.00
Image	ID7163SO	Midnight	LD	U.S.		$15.00
Criterion	CC1270L	Midnight Cowboy	LD	U.S.	1992	$90.00
RCA/Columbia	VLD3275	Midnight Express	LD	U.S.	1985	$40.00
Columbia	VLD3275	Midnight Express	LD	U.S.	1992	$50.00
Discovision	12-003	Midway	LD	U.S.	1979	$40.00
Image	ID7008TU	Mighty Joe Young	LD	U.S.		$85.00
Image	I5032	Mighty Joe Young	LD	U.S.	1986	$85.00
CBS	4761	Mighty Quinn	LD	U.S.	1990	$30.00
CBS	4579	Mildred Pierce	LD	U.S.	1985	$35.00
Image	ID5356ME	Milky Way, The	LD	U.S.		$30.00
Michael Agee	LVA-1014	Milky Way, The	LD	U.S.	1990	$30.00
Image	ID7223IV	Millennium	LD	U.S.		$40.00
HBO	TVL0045	Million Dollar Mystery	LD	U.S.	1988	$35.00
Image	ID6915RH	Milton Berle's Mad World of Comedy	LD	U.S.		$30.00
Image	ID7723MN	Mindfield	LD	U.S.		$30.00
Image	ID7290RF	Mingus	LD	U.S.		$30.00
Image	ID57844ME	Ministry of Vengence	LD	U.S.		$30.00
Nelson	55005	Minor Miracle	LD	U.S.	1984	$35.00
Image	ID6912HB	Miracle Mile	LD	U.S.		$30.00
CBS	1072	Miracle on 34th St.	LD	U.S.	1987	24
Image	ID8001HB	Miracles	LD	U.S.		$30.00
Image	ID7494HB	Mirror Crack'd	LD	U.S.		$30.00
CBS	1459	Mischief	LD	U.S.	1985	$35.00
Nelson	7777	Misery	LD	U.S.	1991	$35.00
Image	ID6808HB	Miss Firecraker	LD	U.S.		$30.00
Image	ID7172SO	Miss Right	LD	U.S.		$30.00
Image	ID6638RC	Miss Sadie Thompson	LD	U.S.		$30.00
MCA	10-034	Missing	LD	U.S.	1982	$35.00
MGM/UA	ML100557	Missing in Action	LD	U.S.	1985	$35.00
Pioneer	PILF2311	Mission Impossible: First Season Volume 1	LTD/LD	Japan	1996	$500.00
	7 LD boxed set.					
Image	ID7304VV	Mission Manila	LD	U.S.		$30.00
Republic	LV22775	Mission of Justice	LD	U.S.	1993	$25.00
		Mississippi Burning	LD	U.S.		$50.00
Image	ID8033SG	Mob Story	LD	U.S.	1990	$15.00
Image	ID7197VV	Mob War	LD	U.S.		$30.00
CBS/Fox	4635-80	Moby Dick	LD	U.S.	1984	$35.00
Image	ID8429SO	Modern Love	LD	U.S.		$30.00
Nelson	77126	Moderns, The	LD	U.S.	1989	$35.00
Discovision		Moebus Flip, The	LD	U.S.	1979	$40.00
Columbia	59256	Mom	LD	U.S.	1991	$30.00
Paramount	LV1263	Mommie Dearest	LD	U.S.	1985	$36.00
Criterion	CC1205L	Mon Oncle	LD	U.S.	1990	$50.00
Image	ID6846HB	Mona Lisa	LD	U.S.		$80.00
Image	IG5001	Mondo Cane	LD	U.S.	1985	$100.00
CBS	5140	Monkey Business	LD	U.S.	1988	$30.00
		Monkey Shine	LD	U.S.		$40.00
		Monster Club, The	LD	U.S.		$30.00
Columbia	90186	Monster High	LD	U.S.	1990	$30.00
Paramount	LV12543	Monty Python 1	LD	U.S.	1987	$30.00
Paramount	LV12544	Monty Python 2	LD	U.S.	1987	$30.00
Paramount	12545	Monty Python 3	LD	U.S.	1988	$30.00
Paramount	12560	Monty Python 4	LD	U.S.	1988	$30.00
RCA/Columbia	VLD3337	Monty Python Holy Grail	LD	U.S.	1983	$25.00
Image	ID7668IV	Moon 44	LD	U.S.		$30.00
Magnetic Video		Moon Is Blue	LD	U.S.†	1981	$25.00

Label	Catalog Number	Title	Type	Country	Year	Value
MCA	10-035	Moonlighting	LD	U.S.	1983	$30.00
CBS	4636	Moonraker	LD	U.S.	1983	$15.00
Republic	LV22790	Moonrise	LD	U.S.	1992	$70.00
MGM/UA	ML101135	Moonstruck	LD	U.S.	1988	$35.00
Image	ID6520MT	Moontapes: Autumn Whispers	LD	U.S.		$30.00
Image	ID6243MT	Moontapes: Tranquility	LD	U.S.		$30.00
Image	ID6752SG	Moontrap	LD	U.S.	1989	$40.00
Disney		More Sports Goofy Volume 6	LD	U.S.		$55.00
Columbia	90606	More the Merrier	LD	U.S.	1991	$30.00
Image	ID8008HB	Morgan: A Suitable Case For Treatment	LD	U.S.		$30.00
Image	ID7684NL	Morgan and the Pirate	LD	U.S.		$30.00
HBO	TVL0025	Morgan Stewart's Coming Home	LD	U.S.	1988	$40.00
Image	ID5140	Morning After	LD	U.S.		$30.00
Image	ID 5123	Morocco	LD	U.S.	1987	$30.00
Columbia	50746	Mortal Thoughts	LD	U.S.	1991	$30.00
Columbia	09346	Mortuary Academy	LD	U.S.	1991	$30.00
RCA/Columbia	30309	Moscow on the Hudson	LD	U.S.	1985	$35.00
Columbia	30309	Moscow on the Hudson	LD	U.S.	1992	$30.00
MGM/UA	ML100302	Motown 25	LD	U.S.	1986	$40.00
Columbia	VLD3340	Mountain Men	LD	U.S.	1983	$30.00
Image	ID7374IV	Mountains of the Moon	LD	U.S.		$30.00
Discovision		Moussaka/Baked Spaghetti	LD	U.S.	1979	$40.00
Image	ID8163IV	Mowgli's Brothers/Rikki-Tikki-Tavi/The White Seal	LD	U.S.		$40.00
Image	ID6405TU	Mr. and Mrs. Smith	LD	U.S.		$30.00
Image	ID6450TU	Mr. Blandlings Builds His Dream House	LD	U.S.		$50.00
Criterion	CC1119L	Mr. Hulot's Holiday	LD	U.S.	1988	$60.00
Columbia	30997	Mr. Magoo	LD	U.S.		$25.00
Paramount	LV2320	Mr. Magoo Christmas Carol	LD	U.S.	1982	$50.00
		Mr. Magoo In Sherwood Forest	LD	U.S.		$30.00
Vestron	LV5025	Mr. Mom	LD	U.S.	1984	$30.00
Image	ID6249VV	Mr. North	LD	U.S.		$30.00
Republic	LV22822	Mr. Robinson Crusoe	LD	U.S.	1991	$30.00
RCA/Columbia	30064	Mr. Smith Goes to Washington	LD	U.S.	1985	$40.00
Columbia	30064	Mr. Smith Goes to Washington	LD	U.S.	1993	$40.00
Image	ID6329RO	Mrs. 45	LD	U.S.		$30.00
		Mummy's Boys	LD	U.S.		$40.00
Magnetic Video	9001	Muppet Movie	LD	U.S.†	1981	$20.00
CBS	9001	Muppet Movie	LD	U.S.	1985	$20.00
CBS	6731	Muppets Take Manhattan	LD	U.S.	1985	$75.00
RCA/Columbia	VLD3348	Murder by Death	LD	U.S.	1984	$35.00
Columbia	LD3348	Murder by Death	LD	U.S.	1993	$30.00
Magnetic Video		Murder by Decree	LD	U.S.†	1982	$50.00
CBS	4059	Murder By Decree	LD	U.S.	1985	$30.00
Image	ID7707MN	Murder by Numbers	LD	U.S.		$15.00
Paramount	LV8790-2	Murder on the Orient Express	LD	U.S.	1985	$75.00
Nelson	77346	Murder One	LD	U.S.	1989	$35.00
Image	ID7285CM	Murder Weapon	LD	U.S.		$30.00
Image	ID9502OR	Murmer of the Heart	LD	U.S.		$30.00
Image	ID5062	Murphy's Law	LD	U.S.		$30.00
RCA/Columbia	30649	Murphy's Romance	LD	U.S.	1986	$35.00
Columbia	30649	Murphy's Romance	LD	U.S.	1993	$30.00
HBO	TVL9945	Muscle Beach Party	LD	U.S.	1988	$30.00
Image	ID7362IV	Music Box	LD	U.S.		$30.00
Warner Home Video	11473LV	Music Man	LD	U.S.	1986	$30.00
Image	ID9503OR	Music Teacher	LD	U.S.		$30.00
Vestron	LV5062	Mutant	LD	U.S.	1985	$30.00
Vestron Video	VL5103	Mutilator	LD	U.S.	1985	$35.00
MGM/UA	ML100450	Mutiny on the Bounty	LD	U.S.	1985	$40.00
Lorimar	LV385	My Beautiful Launde	LD	U.S.	1987	$40.00
Image	ID7879PK	My Best Girl	LD	U.S.		$30.00
Vestron Video	VL5185	My Chauffeur	LD	U.S.	1986	$35.00
CBS	1398	My Darling Clementine	LD	U.S.	1990	$30.00
Columbia	32821	My Demon Lover	LD	U.S.	1987	$30.00
Image	ID5307PA	My Dinner With Andre	LD	U.S.		$30.00
Pacific Arts	PAV12532	My Dinner With Andre	LD	U.S.	1986	$40.00
CBS/Fox	7038-80	My Fair Lady	LD	U.S.	1984	$25.00
Fox Video	0107-85	My Fair Lady	LTD/LD	U.S.	1994	$150.00
	4 LD boxed set with book, prints, 6 frames of 70 mm film, and CD Soundtrack.					
Image	ID6882NE	My Favorite Brunette	LD	U.S.		$30.00
Image	ID7037TU	My Favorite Spy	LD	U.S.		$30.00
Paramount	12651	My Life as a Dog	LD	U.S.	1988	$40.00
Image	ID7127FL	My Little Girl	LD	U.S.		$30.00
Image	ID7119FL	My Mom's A Werewolf	LD	U.S.		$30.00
CBS/Fox	3519-80	My Name is Barbara	LD	U.S.	1986	$25.00
Image	ID7187ME	My New Partner	LD	U.S.		$30.00
Walt Disney	360 AS	My Science Project	LD	U.S.	1986	$50.00
	Distributed by Pioneer.					
Psedition	PSE91-13	My Sister Eileen	LD	U.S.	1992	$50.00
Columbia	31028	My Stepmother is an Alien	LD	U.S.	1989	$30.00
Columbia	70326	My Wonderful Life	LD	U.S.	1990	$30.00
Columbia	VLD3349	Mysterious Island	LD	U.S.	1984	$30.00
Psedition	PSE91-26	Mysterious Island	LD	U.S.	1992	$90.00
	VMD82-001	Mystery Disc: Murder, Anyone?	LD	U.S.		$15.00
Vidmax	V-MD-82-001	Mystery Disc Vol. 1	LD	U.S.	1982	$30.00
Image	IDVL4486	Mystery of Picasso, The	LD	U.S.		$30.00
Image	ID8066VX	MysteryDisc	LD	U.S.	1983	$15.00
	VMD83-002	MysteryDisc: Many Roads to Murder	LD	U.S.		$15.00
Image	ID6398VV	Mystic Pizza	LD	U.S.	1988	$50.00
CBS	3841	Nadine	LD	U.S.	1988	$35.00
Criterion	CC1184L	Naked Kiss, The	LD	U.S.	1989	$45.00
Nelson	13426	Name of the Rose	LD	U.S.	1987	$35.00
		Narrow Margin (1952)	LD	U.S.		$100.00
Paramount	LV8821-2	Nashville	LD	U.S.	1983	$36.00
Columbia	09646	Nasty Hero	LD	U.S.	1990	$30.00
Paramount	LV1549	Nate and Hayes	LD	U.S.	1984	$60.00
		National Gallery of Art	LD	U.S.		$60.00
Vestron Video	VL9963	Native Son	LD	U.S.	1987	$40.00
Columbia	30380	Natural, The	LD	U.S.	1985	$30.00
Psedition	PSE91-24	Natural, The	LD	U.S.	1991	$50.00
Image	ID8220PA	Nature: Hawaii Island of the Fire Goddess	LD	U.S.		$30.00
Image	ID8221PA	Nature: Rain Forest	LD	U.S.		$30.00
Image	ID7959PA	Nature: Volcano Watchers, The	LD	U.S.		$30.00
Columbia	VLD3352	Neighbors	LD	U.S.	1992	$30.00
MGM/UA	ML100012	Network	LD	U.S.	1983	$35.00
		Never a Dull Moment	LD	U.S.		$30.00
Disney	182AS	Never Cry Wolf	LD	U.S.	1984	$40.00
Warner	11337LV	Never Say Never Again	LD	U.S.	1984	$40.00
Nelson	900466	Never Too Young to Die	LD	U.S.	1987	$35.00
Columbia	65008	New Adventures of Pippie Longstocking	LD	U.S.	1989	$30.00
Disney	617AS	New Adventures of Winnie the Pooh Vol. 1	LD	U.S.	1989	$30.00
Columbia	30409	New Kids, The	LD	U.S.	1985	$20.00
Walt Disney	952AS	New Stories	LD	U.S.	1990	$50.00
Nelson	75225	New Three Stooges, The	LD	U.S.	1985	$40.00
Paramount	LV12780	New Year's Day...Time to Move On	LD	U.S.	1985	$35.00
MGM	ML101321	New York, New York	LD	U.S.		$30.00
CBS	4596	New York, New York	LD	U.S.	1985	$15.00
Nelson	90025	News Front	LD	U.S.	1985	$35.00

Label	Catalog Number	Title	Type	Country	Year	Value
Discovision		NFL Films: Catch It If You Can	LD	U.S.	1979	$40.00
Discovision		NFL Films: The Gamebreakers	LD	U.S.	1979	$40.00
Discovision		NFL Films: The Runners	LD	U.S.	1979	$40.00
Discovision		NFL Films: They Call It Pro Football	LD	U.S.	1979	$40.00
Discovision		NFL Films: Trial and Triumphs	LD	U.S.	1979	$40.00
Discovision		NFL FIlms: Young Old and Bold	LD	U.S.	1979	$40.00
CBS	5138	Niagara	LD	U.S.	1988	$35.00
Columbia	VLD3355	Nice Dreams	LD	U.S.	1983	$35.00
Columbia	30072	Nicholas & Alexandria	LD	U.S.	1986	$30.00
Psedition	PSE91-21	Nicholas & Alexandria	LD	U.S.	1991	$50.00
		Night Angel	LD	U.S.		$30.00
Criterion	CC1131L	Night at the Opera	LD	U.S.	1988	$80.00
	CAV version.					
Criterion	CC1131L	Night at the Opera	LD	U.S.	1990	$40.00
	CLV version.					
Image	ID7158SO	Night Caller From Outer Space	LD	U.S.		$80.00
		Night Gallery	LD	Japan		$130.00
CBS/Fox	3855-80	Night in The Life of Jimmy Reardon	LD	U.S.	1988	$40.00
90196		Night Life	LD	U.S.		$25.00
HBO	TVL9959	Night of the Creeps	LD	U.S.	1988	$90.00
Republic	LV23015	Night of the Cyclone	LD	U.S.	1991	$30.00
Republic	LV23019	Night of the Demons	LD	U.S.	1989	$25.00
Image	ID7595VK	Night of the Fox	LD	U.S.		$30.00
Columbia	30430	Night of the Generals	LD	U.S.	1985	$30.00
Image	I-6000	Night of the Living Dead	LD	U.S.	1986	$35.00
Republic	LV27460	Night of the Living Dead	LD	U.S.	1990	$35.00
Columbia	77176	Night of the Living Dead	LD	U.S.	1991	$85.00
Elite		Night of the Living Dead	LTD/LD	U.S.	1995	$90.00
Image	ID7848ME	Night of the Sharks	LD	U.S.		$30.00
Vidmark	LDCVM5425	Night of the Warrior	LD	U.S.	1993	$25.00
Image	I5025	Night Patrol	LD	U.S.	1986	$35.00
Nelson	150250	Night Porter, The	LD	U.S.	1982	$50.00
HBO	LD90942	Night We Never Met	LD	U.S.	1994	$175.00
		Nightcomers	LD	U.S.		$40.00
MCA	12-021	Nighthawks	LD	U.S.	1985	$35.00
CBS	6392	Nightingale	LD	U.S.	1984	$25.00
Columbia	90196	Nightlife	LD	U.S.	1991	$30.00
Touchstone	27874 CS	Nightmare Before Christmas, The	LTD/LD	U.S.	1994	$120.00
	First pressing with bonus shorts.					
Image	I 5036	Nightmare on Elm Street	LD	U.S.	1985	$35.00
Elite	EE3733	Nightmare on Elm Street	LTD/LD	U.S.	1996	$90.00
Image	I 5047	Nightmare on Elm Street Part 2	LD	U.S.	1986	$35.00
Image	ID5053	Nightmare on Elm Street Part 3	LD	U.S.		$35.00
Image	ID6218ME	Nightmare on Elm Street Part 4	LD	U.S.		$30.00
Image	ID7189ME	Nightmare on Elm Street Part 5	LD	U.S.		$30.00
	SMo58-3066	Nightsongs	LD	U.S.		$30.00
		Nightwish	LD	U.S.		$40.00
Magnetic Video		Nine to Five	LD	U.S.†	1981	$25.00
CBS	1099	Nine to Five	LD	U.S.	1985	$20.00
Columbia	30648	Ninja Turf	LD	U.S.	1986	$30.00
Image	ID8221PA	Ninotchka	LD	U.S.		$30.00
MGM/UA	ML100115	Ninth Configuration, The	LD	U.S.		$80.00
Columbia	90206	No Holds Barred	LD	U.S.	1989	$30.00
Columbia	30791	No Mercy	LD	U.S.	1987	$30.00
CBS	7065	No Nukes	LD	U.S.	1983	$25.00
Cannon	32035	No Place to Hide	LD	U.S.	1993	$30.00
Columbia	90856	No Secrets	LD	U.S.	1991	$15.00
Columbia	70429	No Small Affair	LD	U.S.	1993	$30.00
HBO	TVL0051	No Way Out	LD	U.S.	1988	$30.00
Image	ID7855ME	Nobody's Perfect	LD	U.S.		$40.00
Discovision		Nobody's Victim	LD	U.S.	1979	$40.00
Image	ID7040TU	Nocturnal	LD	U.S.		$30.00
CBS	1082	Norma Rae	LD	U.S.	1984	$25.00
MGM/UA	ML100104	North by Northwest	LD	U.S.	1984	$30.00
Criterion	CC1145L	North by Northwest	LD	U.S.	1989	$125.00
	CAV version.					
Criterion	CC1226L	North by Northwest	LD	U.S.	1989	$50.00
	CLV version.					
Paramount	LV8773	North Dallas Forty	LD	U.S.	1985	$30.00
CBS	1212	North to Alaska	LD	U.S.	1990	$20.00
Republic	LV23029	Nosferatu	LD	U.S.	1991	$60.00
HBO	TVL9960	Nothing in Common	LD	U.S.	1988	$35.00
Lumivision		Nothing Sacred	LD	U.S.		$50.00
CBS/Fox	8011-80	Notorious	LD	U.S.	1981	$30.00
Magnetic Video		Notorious	LD	U.S.†	1982	$25.00
Criterion	CC1203L	Notorious	LD	U.S.	1990	$90.00
	CAV version.					
Criterion	CC1204L	Notorious	LD	U.S.	1990	$50.00
	CLV version.					
Image	ID6535VE	Nova: All American Bear	LD	U.S.		$30.00
Image	ID6072VE	Nova: Ancient Animal Olympians	LD	U.S.		$30.00
Image	ID8412VE	Nova: Ancient Treasures of the Deep	LD	U.S.		$30.00
Image	ID8411VE	Nova: Baby Talk	LD	U.S.		$30.00
Image	ID6658VE	Nova: Cities of Coral	LD	U.S.		$30.00
Image	ID8410VE	Nova: Disguises of War	LD	U.S.		$30.00
Image	ID7105VE	Nova: Echoes of War	LD	U.S.		$30.00
Image	ID5211VE	Nova: Einstein	LD	U.S.		$30.00
Image	ID6194VE	Nova: Hitler's Secret Weapon	LD	U.S.		$30.00
Image	ID6192VE	Nova: Secret of the Sexes	LD	U.S.		$30.00
Image	ID6193VE	Nova: Whale Watch	LD	U.S.		$30.00
Image	ID7106VE	Nova: Yellowstone's Burning Question	LD	U.S.		$30.00
MCA	11021	Now and Forever	LD	U.S.	1983	$30.00
CBS/Fox	4572-80	Now Voyager	LD	U.S.	1985	$35.00
Image	ID7485PA	Nudo Di Donna (Portrait Of A Woman Nude)	LD	U.S.		$30.00
Image	ID7241SP	Nutcracker	LD	U.S.		$30.00
Paramount	LV6712	Nutty Professor	LD	U.S.	1984	$60.00
Republic	LV23027	Nyoka and the Tigerman	LD	U.S.	1992	$40.00
Republic	LV25258	O Pioneers!	LD	U.S.	1992	$30.00
Image	ID7139NS	Obsessed	LD	U.S.		$30.00
Psedition	PSE91-18	Obsession	LD	U.S.	1991	$50.00
Live Entertainment	LD69011	Obsessive Love	LD	U.S.	1992	$35.00
Image	ID7185SO	Occult Experience	LD	U.S.		$30.00
Vidmark	LDCVM4901	Oceans of Fire	LD	U.S.	1993	$35.00
Image	ID6045ME	Octagon, The	LD	U.S.		$30.00
Image	ID6253CO	October	LD	U.S.		$30.00
Discovision		Octopus, Octopus	LD	U.S.	1979	$40.00
CBS	4715	Octopussy	LD	U.S.	1983	$15.00
Paramount	LV8026	Odd Couple	LD	U.S.	1983	$30.00
Paramount	12575	Odd Man Out	LD	U.S.	1988	$40.00
Cannon	32048	Oddball Hall	LD	U.S.	1992	$30.00
Columbia	30317	Odessa File	LD	U.S.	1993	$30.00
CBS	1657	Off Limits	LD	U.S.	1989	$30.00
Disney	455AS	Offbeat	LD	U.S.	1987	$35.00
Disney	258AS	Officer and a Duck	LD	U.S.	1985	$35.00
Paramount	LV1467-2	Officer and a Gentleman	LD	U.S.	1983	$40.00
Pacific Arts	PAV12630	Official Story	LD	U.S.	1986	$40.00
Live Entertainment	LD51136	Offspring, The	LD	U.S.	1992	$25.00

Label	Catalog Number	Title	Type	Country	Year	Value
CBS/Fox	7020-80	Oklahoma	LD	U.S.	1984	$25.00
CBS	7020	Oklahoma	LD	U.S.	1990	$25.00
CBS/Fox	7020-85	Oklahoma	LD	U.S.	1990	$35.00
Nelson	20086	Old Boyfriends	LD	U.S.	1989	$35.00
Columbia	50206	Old Gringo	LD	U.S.	1990	$30.00
	Letterbox version.					
Disney	37AS	Old Yeller	LD	U.S.	1983	$35.00
Columbia	VLD30526	Oliver!	LD	U.S.	1985	$30.00
Psedition	PSE91-27	Oliver!	LD	U.S.	1991	$50.00
Paramount	12571	Oliver Twist	LD	U.S.	1988	$35.00
Magnetic Video		Omen II, The	LD	U.S.†	1984	$30.00
Magnetic Video		Omen III, The	LD	U.S.†	1984	$30.00
Magnetic Video		Omen, The	LD	U.S.†	1982	$25.00
CBS/Fox	1079-80	Omen, The	LD	U.S.	1982	$35.00
CBS	1079	Omen, The	LD	U.S.	1989	$20.00
Image	ID6978TU	On Dangerous Ground	LD	U.S.		$40.00
CBS	9073	On Golden Pond	LD	U.S.	1982	$50.00
J2	J2-6031	On Golden Pond	LD	U.S.	1992	$30.00
Columbia	30354	On the Waterfront	LD	U.S.	1993	$30.00
Discovision	D61-503	On Vacation With Mickey Mouse and Friends	LD	U.S.	1979	$40.00
		Once A Thief	LD	U.S.		$80.00
Vestron	LV5115	Once Bitten	LD	U.S.	1986	$30.00
		Once Upon a Honeymoon	LD	U.S.		$40.00
Paramount	LV6830-2	Once Upon Time West	LD	U.S.	1985	$40.00
Discovision		One, and Only, Genuine Original Family Band	LD	U.S.	1979	$40.00
Vidmark	LDCVM5785	One Crazy Night	LD	U.S.	1993	$35.00
Saul Zaentz		One Flew Over the Cuckoo's Nest	LD	U.S.	1988	$40.00
RCA/Columbia	VLD3360	One From the Heart	LD	U.S.	1983	$35.00
Image	ID7727J2	One Hundred Years: Visual History of the Dodgers	LD	U.S.	1990	$15.00
Image	ID7512SO	One Man Out	LD	U.S.		$30.00
		One Million B.C.	LD	U.S.		$120.00
Columbia	30703	One More Saturday Night	LD	U.S.	1986	$20.00
Columbia	90426	One Night of Love	LD	U.S.	1991	$30.00
Walt Disney	30AS	One & Only	LD	U.S.	1982	$40.00
Republic	LV23060	One Touch of Venus	LD	U.S.	1992	$25.00
Image	ID7349MG	One, Two, Three	LD	U.S.		$30.00
Paramount	LV6537-2	One-Eyed Jacks	LD	U.S.	1990	$40.00
Nelson	20346	Onion Field	LD	U.S.	1989	$35.00
Republic	LV23062	Only the Valiant	LD	U.S.	1990	$25.00
RCA/Columbia	VLD3362	Only When I Laugh	LD	U.S.	1983	$35.00
Image	ID6089RE	Operation Petticoat	LD	U.S.		$80.00
Image	ID7420VK	Opponent, The	LD	U.S.		$30.00
Paramount	LV8935	Orca, The Killer Whale	LD	U.S.	1982	$30.00
Paramount	LV8964	Ordinary People	LD	U.S.	1985	$36.00
Pioneer	1992	Oriental Dreams	DJ/LD	U.S.		$30.00
Republic	LV23078	Orphans of the Storm	LD	U.S.	1991	$25.00
Columbia	50976	Oscar's Greatest Moments	LD	U.S.	1992	$35.00
Image	ID7492HB	Osterman Weekend, The	LD	U.S.		$30.00
Image	ID5152	Othello	LD	U.S.		$30.00
Pioneer	PA-83-054	Othello	LD	U.S.	1984	$30.00
MGM/UA	ML100351	Other Side of Nashville	LD	U.S.	1984	$35.00
Discovision		Other Side of the Mountain	LD	U.S.	1979	$40.00
Image	ID7507DS	Our Daily Bread	LD	U.S.		$30.00
Image	ID6863HB	Our Hospitality	LD	U.S.		$30.00
CBS	1131	Our Man Flint	LD	U.S.	1990	$30.00
MCA	40350	Out of Africa	LD	U.S.	1986	$40.00
Columbia	30722	Out of Bounds	LD	U.S.	1987	$35.00
Image	ID7664PR	Out of Sight Out of Mind	LD	U.S.		$30.00
Columbia	09896	Out of the Dark	LD	U.S.	1989	$30.00
Image		Out of the Past	LD	U.S.		$40.00
Image	ID8240IV	Out of the Rain	LD	U.S.		$30.00
Image	ID7338KN	Outlaw	LD	U.S.		$30.00
Walt Disney	569AS	Outrageous Fortune	LD	U.S.	1988	$30.00
	Distributed by Pioneer.					
CBS	4746	Overboard	LD	U.S.	1988	$25.00
		Owl and the Pussycat	LD	U.S.		$80.00
CBS/Fox	1652-80	Ox-Bow Incident, The	LD	U.S.	1990	$40.00
Image	I5059	P.O.W. The Escape	LD	U.S.	1986	$30.00
Image	ID7332VE	Paint It Black	LD	U.S.		$30.00
Paramount	LV6933-2	Paint Your Wagon	LD	U.S.	1983	$36.00
Republic	LV25038	Painted Stallion	LD	U.S.	1990	$40.00
Image	ID6165PA	Painting With Light	LD	U.S.		$30.00
Columbia	30798	Pal Joey	LD	U.S.		$20.00
Columbia	91306	Pale Start	LD	U.S.	1992	$30.00
Image	ID8286IV	Palermo Connection, The	LD	U.S.		$30.00
Magnetic Video		Panic in Needle Park	LD	U.S.†	1984	$30.00
Republic	LV23138	Panther Girl of the Congo	LD	U.S.	1992	$40.00
Magnetic Video		Paper Chase, The	LD	U.S.†	1984	$30.00
CBS	1046	Paper Chase, The	LD	U.S.	1990	$35.00
Paramount	LV8465	Paper Moon	LD	U.S.	1982	$25.00
Image	ID6660VE	Paperhouse	LD	U.S.		$30.00
CBS	7090	Papillon	LD	U.S.	1984	$40.00
Image	ID 5116	Paradise Alley	LD	U.S.	1987	$70.00
Nelson	30125	Pardon Mon Affaire	LD	U.S.	1984	$35.00
Disney	107AS	Parent Trap	LD	U.S.	1985	$35.00
CBS	1457	Paris, Texas	LD	U.S.	1990	$40.00
Image	ID8521ME	Paris Trout	LD	U.S.		$30.00
MCA	37-608	Party Games	LD	U.S.	1984	$50.00
Image	ID8432SO	Party Line	LD	U.S.		$30.00
Columbia	30485	Passage to India	LD	U.S.	1993	$30.00
Image	ID6225VV	Passion of Beatrice	LD	U.S.		$30.00
Columbia	92816	Past Midnight	LD	U.S.		$30.00
	MP046-U	Pastel Color	LD	U.S.		$20.00
Columbia	91466	Pastime	LD	U.S.	1992	$30.00
Paramount	LV1401	Paternity	LD	U.S.	1982	$30.00
Criterion	CC1157L	Paths of Glory	LD	U.S.	1989	$50.00
Magnetic Video		Patton	LD	U.S.†	1982	$30.00
CBS	1005-80	Patton	LD	U.S.	1989	$30.00
CBS/Fox	1005-85	Patton	LD	U.S.	1989	$60.00
Image	ID7188ME	Pauline at the Beach	LD	U.S.		$30.00
Image	ID6261RE	Pawnbroker	LD	U.S.		$70.00
Image	ID8523ME	Payoff	LD	U.S.		$30.00
Image	ID6992TU	Peach O'Reno	LD	U.S.		$15.00
Rebo Associates	21692	Pearlstein/Draws Model	LD	U.S.	1986	$70.00
Republic	LV23152	Peck's Bad Boy	LD	U.S.	1991	$30.00
Image	ID6283SO	Pecos Bill	LD	U.S.		$30.00
		Pee-Wee's Big Adventure	LD	U.S.		$90.00
Image	ID7233ME	Pee-Wee's Playhouse Christmas Special	LD	U.S.	1988	$90.00
Image	ID6304ME	Pee-Wee's Playhouse Fun-O-Rama	LD	U.S.	1986	$90.00
Image	ID6366ME	Pee-Wee's Playhouse Potpourri	LD	U.S.	1986	$90.00
CBS	3800	Peggy Sue Got Married	LD	U.S.	1989	$25.00
		Penguin Pool Murder	LD	U.S.		$30.00
MGM/UA	ML100191	Pennies From Heaven	LD	U.S.	1989	$35.00
Republic	LV23173	Penny Serenade	LD	U.S.	1990	$30.00
Columbia	30494	Perfect	LD	U.S.	1985	$30.00
Image	ID7488 HB	Perfect Witness	LD	U.S.		$30.00
Vestron Video	VL5071	Perils of Gwendoline	LD	U.S.	1985	$35.00

Label	Catalog Number	Title	Type	Country	Year	Value
Republic	LV23156	Perils of the Darkest Jungle	LD	U.S.	1992	$40.00
		Personal Best	LD	Japan	1986	$200.00
Vestron Video	VL5221	Personal Services	LD	U.S.	1987	$35.00
Walt Disney	010 AS	Pete's Dragon	LD	U.S.		$75.00
Image	ID6914RH	Peter Gunn: The Coolest Private Eye Ever! Vol. 1	LD	U.S.		$30.00
Walt Disney		Peter Pan	LD	Japan		$60.00
Walt Disney	960 CS	Peter Pan	LD	U.S.	1990	$80.00
	CAV version.					
Walt Disney	960 AS	Peter Pan	LD	U.S.	1990	$50.00
	CLV version.					
Magnetic Video		Phantasm	LD	U.S.†	1982	$50.00
CBS	4066	Phantasm	LD	U.S.	1985	$25.00
Nelson	20056	Phantasm	LD	U.S.	1989	$25.00
Image	ID3071SU	Phantasm	LTD/LD	U.S.	1995	$200.00
	LD boxed set with gold CD soundtrack.					
MCA	40839	Phantasm II	LD	U.S.	1989	$40.00
Image	ID7195FR	Phantom of the Mall	LD	U.S.		$30.00
Columbia	77016	Phantom of the Opera	LD	U.S.	1990	$150.00
CBS	1473	Phantom of the Paradise	LD	U.S.	1988	$20.00
		Phanton of Crestwood	LD	U.S.		$30.00
Paramount	LV8470	Phase IV	LD	U.S.	1984	$50.00
MGM/UA	ML100059	Philadelphia Experiment, The	LD	U.S.		$30.00
MGM/UA	ML100059	Philadelphia Story	LD	U.S.	1987	$35.00
Image	ID6537VE	Physical Evidence	LD	U.S.		$30.00
CBS/Fox	1529-80	Pickup Artist	LD	U.S.	1988	$40.00
Psedition	PSE91-28	Picnic	LD	U.S.	1992	$50.00
MGM/UA	ML100566	Picture of Dorian Gray	LD	U.S.	1985	$35.00
Image	ID7455IN	Pierrot Lé Fou	LD	U.S.		$30.00
		Pin	LD	U.S.		$60.00
CBS/Fox	4509-80	Pink Panther	LD	U.S.	1982	$35.00
CBS	4564	Pink Panther Strikes	LD	U.S.	1985	$15.00
CBS	6390	Pinocchio	LD	U.S.	1984	$20.00
Walt Disney	239AS	Pinocchio	LD	U.S.	1986	$20.00
Walt Disney	239CS	Pinocchio	LD	U.S.	1987	$30.00
	CAV version.					
Walt Disney	239AS	Pinocchio	LD	U.S.	1993	$30.00
Walt Disney	239CS	Pinocchio	LTD/LD	U.S.	1993	$90.00
	CAV LD Boxed set with "Making Of…" LD, CD Soundtrack and book.					
		Pippin	LD	U.S.		$125.00
Nelson	13895	Piranha II: The Spawning	LD	U.S.	1984	$90.00
Republic	LV23217	Pitfall	LD	U.S.	1991	$25.00
CBS/Fox	6836-80	Places in The Heart	LD	U.S.	1985	$30.00
Image	I5070	Plan 9 From Outer Space	LD	U.S.	1958	$40.00
Pioneer	PILF-2069	Planet of the Apes	LD	Japan	1995	$325.00
4 LD boxed set.						
Magnetic Video	1054	Planet of the Apes	LD	U.S.	1982	$50.00
Magnetic Video		Planet of the Apes	LD	U.S.†	1984	$50.00
CBS	1054	Planet of the Apes	LD	U.S.	1990	$75.00
	Letterbox version.					
HBO	TVL0040	Platoon	LD	U.S.	1988	$25.00
Pioneer	PSE-95-58	Platoon	LTD/LD	U.S.	1994	$135.00
Image	ID6356ME	Platoon Leader	LD	U.S.		$30.00
Paramount	LV8112	Play It Again Sam	LD	U.S.	1982	$90.00
MCA	12-024	Play Misty for Me	LD	U.S.	1985	$40.00
Nelson	902366	Playing Away	LD	U.S.	1989	$35.00
Republic	LV26470	Playroom	LD	U.S.	1991	$30.00
Paramount	LV8046	Plaza Suite	LD	U.S.	1984	$30.00
Image	ID7498HB	Plenty	LD	U.S.		$30.00
Buena Vista	145AS	Pluto	LD	U.S.	1984	$40.00
Lumivision	LVD9222	Plymptoons, The	LD	U.S.	1992	$25.00
Image	ID5240VE	Point, The	LD	U.S.		$150.00
Image	IG-5007	Police	LD	U.S.	1985	$30.00
Paramount	LV60630	Police Squad, Help	LD	U.S.	1985	$40.00
Paramount	LV60630-02	Police Squad, More	LD	U.S.	1985	$40.00
Image	ID7729PK	Pollyanna	LD	U.S.		$40.00
Live Entertainment	LD69946	Poor Little Rich Girl	LD	U.S.	1994	$35.00
Image	ID7508DS	Pop Goes the Comic	LD	U.S.		$30.00
Columbia	91256	Popcorn	LD	U.S.	1991	$30.00
Image	ID6473MG	Pope of Greenwich Village	LD	U.S	1984	$20.00
Paramount	LV1171	Popeye	LD	U.S.	1985	$30.00
Republic	LV27554	Popeye the Sailor Cartoons	LD	U.S.	1991	$25.00
Image	ID6513MG	Pork Chop Hill	LD	U.S.	1959	$100.00
CBS	1149	Porky's	LD	U.S.	1983	$40.00

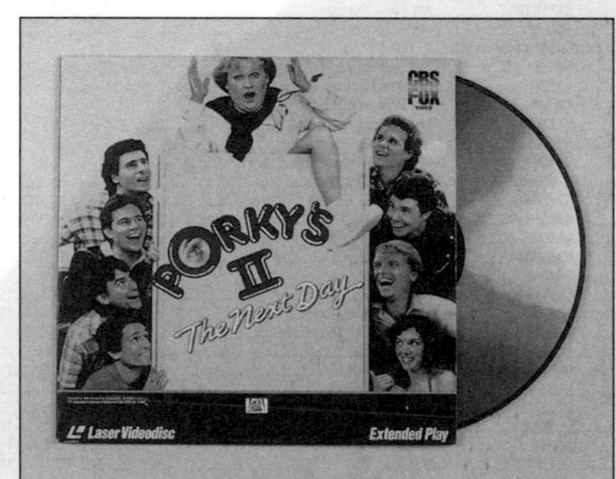

Porky's II The Next Day – (CBS Fox 1294-80)

Label	Catalog Number	Title	Type	Country	Year	Value
CBS Fox	1294-80	Porky's II The Next Day	LD	U.S.	1984	$40.00
CBS	1463	Porky's Revenge	LD	U.S.	1985	$30.00
Magnetic Video		Poseidon Adventure, The	LD	U.S.†	1984	$30.00
Columbia	50556	Postcards From the Edge	LD	U.S.	1991	$30.00
CBS/Fox	7077-80	Postman Always Rings Twice	LD	U.S.	1983	$35.00
Lorimar	LV401	Power	LD	U.S.	1986	$40.00
Nelson	7780	Prancer	LD	U.S.	1990	$35.00
Image	ID7526VE	Pray TV	LD	U.S.		$30.00
Image	ID2056AC	Prayer of the Rollerboys	LD	U.S.		$25.00
CBS	1515-80	Predator	LD	U.S.	1988	$35.00
Paramount	LV8940	Pretty Baby	LD	U.S.	1983	$30.00
Paramount	LV1858	Pretty in Pink	LD	U.S.	1986	$30.00
Republic	LV23220	Priceless Beauty	LD	U.S.	1989	$30.00
Image	ID5520VV	Prick up Your Ears	LD	U.S.		$30.00

Label	Catalog Number	Title	Type	Country	Year	Value
CBS	7145	Pride of the Yankees	LD	U.S.	1983	$20.00
Image	ID8136AC	Prince of Bel-Air	LD	U.S.		$30.00
Columbia	32828	Prince of Pennsylvania	LD	U.S.	1987	$30.00
Criterion		Prince of Tides	LD	U.S.	1993	$100.00
		Original cover and uncut commentary Track				
Nelson	30575	Princess and the Pirate	LD	U.S.	1985	$35.00
Nelson	7709	Princess Bride, The	LD	U.S.	1988	$50.00
Criterion	CC1140L	Princess Bride, The	LD	U.S.	1989	$80.00
		CAV version.				
Criterion	CC1194L	Princess Bride, The	LD	U.S.	1989	$40.00
		CLV version.				
Image	ID8306FR	Princess in Exile	LD	U.S.		$30.00
CBS	6397	Princess & the Pea	LD	U.S.	1984	$20.00
Image	ID5270NW	Prison	LD	U.S.		$30.00
Image	ID6201MP	Prisoner, The #1: Arrival	LD	U.S.		12
Image	ID6210MP	Prisoner, The #10: It's Your Funeral	LD	U.S.		18
Image	ID6211MP	Prisoner, The #11: Checkmate	LD	U.S.		18
Image	ID6212MP	Prisoner, The #12: Living In Harmony	LD	U.S.		18
Image	ID6213MP	Prisoner, The #13: Change of Mind	LD	U.S.		18
Image	ID6214MP	Prisoner, The #14: Hammer Into Anvil	LD	U.S.		18
Image	ID6215MP	Prisoner, The #15: The Girl Who Was Death	LD	U.S.		18
Image	ID6216MP	Prisoner, The #16: Once Upon a Time	LD	U.S.		18
Image	ID6217MP	Prisoner, The #17: Fallout	LD	U.S.		$35.00
Image	ID6202MP	Prisoner, The #2: The Chimes of Big Ben	LD	U.S.		18
Image	ID6203MP	Prisoner, The #3: A, B & C	LD	U.S.		18
Image	ID6204MP	Prisoner, The #4: Free for All	LD	U.S.		18
Image	ID6205MP	Prisoner, The #5: The Schizoid Man	LD	U.S.		18
Image	ID6206MP	Prisoner, The #6: the General	LD	U.S.		18
Image	ID6207MP	Prisoner, The #7: Many Happy Returns	LD	U.S.		18
Image	ID6208MP	Prisoner, The #8: Dance of the Dead	LD	U.S.		18
Image	ID6209MP	Prisoner, The #9: Do Not Forsake Me Darling	LD	U.S.		18
		Prisoners of the Lost Universe	LD	U.S.		$30.00

Prisoner of the Lost Universe

Label	Catalog Number	Title	Type	Country	Year	Value
Vestron	VL5001	Private Eyes	LD	U.S.	1982	$40.00
Republic	LV23239	Private Hell 36	LD	U.S.	1992	$25.00
MCA	16-027	Private Lessons	LD	U.S.	1982	$35.00
Nelson	31005	Private Life of Henry VIII	LD	U.S.	1986	$35.00
Columbia	30539	Private Resort	LD	U.S.	1985	$30.00
Vestron	LV5106	Prizzi's Honor	LD	U.S.	1985	$40.00
Live Entertainment	LD65810	Prodigal, The	LD	U.S.	1992	$25.00
Magnetic Video		Producers, The	LD	U.S.†	1982	$25.00
Magnetic Video		Producers, The	LD	U.S.†	1984	$30.00
CBS/Fox	4058-80	Producers, The	LD	U.S.	1985	$30.00
Nelson	20516	Producers, The	LD	U.S.	1988	$35.00
Criterion	CC1136L	Producers, The	LD	U.S.	1989	$40.00
Psedition	PSE91-14	Professionals	LD	U.S.	1991	$70.00
Columbia	30390	Professionals	LD	U.S.	1992	$30.00
Discovision	12-022	Prom Night	LD	U.S.	1981	$75.00
MCA	12-022	Prom Night	LD	U.S.	1985	$75.00
Image	ID7364IV	Prom Night III: The Last Kiss	LD	U.S.		$35.00
Live Entertainment	LD69010	Prom Night IV, Deliver Us From Evil	LD	U.S.	1992	$35.00
Republic	LV23312	Promised a Miracle	LD	U.S.	1993	$25.00
Live Entertainment	LD90114	Prototype	LD	U.S.	1993	$35.00
Image		Psych-Out/Wild in the Streets	LD	U.S.		$40.00
Discovision	11-003	Psycho	LD	U.S.	1979	$40.00
MCA	40008	Psycho	LD	U.S.	1983	$35.00
MCA	11-003	Psycho	LD	U.S.	1984	$40.00
CBS	4589	Public Enemy	LD	U.S.	1987	$20.00
Columbia	65004	Pulse	LD	U.S.	1989	$30.00
Columbia	75106	Pump Up the Jam	LD	U.S.	1991	$30.00
Image	ID6224RC	Pumping Iron	LD	U.S.		$40.00
Vestron	LV5093	Pumping Iron Vol. 2	LD	U.S.	1985	$15.00
Columbia	35010	Punchline	LD	U.S.	1989	65
Image	ID7607IV	Punisher, The	LD	U.S.		$30.00
Image	ID6122IV	Puppetoon Movie, The	LD	U.S.		$30.00
Image	ID6565NS	Purgatory	LD	U.S.		$30.00
Image	IDVL 5068	Purple Rose of Cairo, The	LD	U.S.	1985	$25.00
Vestron Video	VL5068	Purple Rose of Cairo, The	LD	U.S.	1985	$35.00
Republic	LV23326	Pursued	LD	U.S.	1992	$50.00
Image	ID7543VE	Pursuit of D.B. Cooper, The	LD	U.S.	1981	$30.00
Criterion	CC1133L	Pygmalion	LD	U.S.	1988	$40.00
Image	ID6595VC	Quackser Fortune Has a Cousin in the Bronx	LD	U.S.		$30.00
Columbia	VLD3368	Quadrophenia	LD	U.S.	1984	$70.00
		Quality Street	LD	U.S.		$30.00
Image		Quartermas II	LD	U.S.		$100.00
Image	ID7337KN	Queen Kelly	LD	U.S.	1929	$40.00
		Queen of Blood/Planet Of	LD	U.S.		$70.00
Image	ID6720IV	Queen's Logic	LD	U.S.		$30.00
CBS	1148	Quest for Fire	LD	U.S.	1987	$35.00
Columbia	59256	Quest for the Mighty Sword	LD	U.S.	1990	$30.00
Columbia	30644	Quicksilver	LD	U.S.	1992	$30.00
Columbia	32768	Quiet Cool	LD	U.S.	1987	$30.00
CBS	3042	Quiet Earth, The	LD	U.S.	1989	$35.00
Republic	LV23361	Quiet Man	LD	U.S.	1992	$50.00
Live Entertainment	LD65886	Quiet Thunder	LD	U.S.	1993	$25.00
Nelson	13085	R.A.D.	LD	U.S.	1986	$35.00
Nelson	900036	Rabbit Test	LD	U.S.	1989	$35.00
Image	ID7842ME	Rabid Grannies	LD	U.S.		$30.00

Label	Catalog Number	Title	Type	Country	Year	Value
Paramount	LV8850	Race for Your Life Charlie Brown	LD	U.S.	1982	$30.00
Paramount	LV1668	Racing With the Moon	LD	U.S.	1984	$30.00
		Racket, The	LD	U.S.		$30.00
Republic	LV25043	Radar Men From the Moon	LD	U.S.	1992	$25.00
HBO	TVL0014	Radio Days	LD	U.S.	1988	$80.00
WHV/HBO	90531	Rage in Harlem	LD	U.S.	1992	$30.00
CBS	4523	Raging Bull	LD	U.S.	1983	$15.00
Criterion	CC1230L	Raging Bull	LD	U.S.	1990	$125.00
Criterion	CC1238L	Raging Bull	LD	U.S.	1990	$60.00
Paramount	LV1486-2	Ragtime	LD	U.S.	1982	$40.00
Paramount	LV1376-2	Raiders of the Lost Ark	LD	U.S.	1984	$45.00
Discovision	18-002	Railway Children, The	LD	U.S.	1979	NA
Columbia	90986	Rain Killer, The	LD	U.S.	1991	$30.00
Vestron Video	VL1510	Rainbow Brite	LD	U.S.	1985	$15.00
Image	ID6664VE	Rainbow, The	LD	U.S.		$30.00
Magnetic Video		Raise the Titanic	LD	U.S.†	1981	$40.00
Magnetic Video		Raise the Titanic	LD	U.S.†	1984	$35.00
CBS	5191	Raising Arizona	LD	U.S.	1987	$15.00
HBO	3002	Rambo: First Blood Part II	LD	U.K.	1986	$60.00
		PAL format.				
HBO	3002	Rambo: First Blood Part II	LD	U.S.	1986	$30.00
Image	ID6119IV	Rambo: First Blood Part II	LD	U.S.	1989	$30.00
Image	ID6120IV	Rambo: First Blood Part III	LD	U.S.	1989	$30.00
CBS	3732	Ran	LD	U.S.	1982	$40.00
Pioneer		Ran - Green Legend Ran	LTD/LD	U.S.	1995	$70.00
		LD in box with booklet, cards , and t-shirt.				
		Rancho Notorious	LD	U.S.		$60.00
Columbia	75396	Rapture	LD	U.S.	1992	$30.00
HBO	2651	Raquel	LD	U.S.	1951	$30.00
Nelson	13245	Rascal Dazzle	LD	U.S.	1985	$40.00
Criterion	CC1149L	Rashmon	LD	U.S.	1989	$50.00
Image	IDVL 4021	Raven, The	LD	U.S.	1963	$100.00
HBO	22345	Raw Deal	LD	U.S.	1988	$30.00
Columbia	30410	Razor's Edge, The	LD	U.S.	1993	$30.00
Image	IDVL5114D	Re-Animator	LD	U.S.		$30.00
Image	ID7317VK	Real Bullets	LD	U.S.		$30.00
RCA/Columbia	30568	Real Genius	LD	U.S.	1986	$55.00
Columbia	30568	Real Genius	LD	U.S.	1992	$55.00
CBS	4743	Real Men	LD	U.S.	1988	$20.00
Image	ID7597VK	Reason to Die	LD	U.S.		$30.00
Criterion	CC1998L	Rebecca	LD	U.S.	1990	$125.00
		CAV version.				
Criterion	CC1999L	Rebecca	LD	U.S.	1990	$70.00
		CLV version.				
CBS	1702	Rebecca of Sunnybrook	LD	U.S.	1989	$20.00
Vestron Video	VL5184	Rebel	LD	U.S.	1987	$35.00
		Rebel Storm	LD	U.S.		$30.00
Warner Home Video	1011LV	Rebel Without a Cause	LD	U.S.	1984	$45.00
MGM/UA	ML100421	Reckless	LD	U.S.	1984	$35.00
U.S. Magna	SSLM-3002	Record of Lodoss War 1	LP	U.S.		$25.00
		Japanese anime CD-ROM.				
U.S. Magna	SSLM-3002	Record of Lodoss War 2	LP	U.S.		$25.00
		Japanese anime CD-ROM.				
U.S. Magna	SSLM-3003	Record of Lodoss War 3	LP	U.S.		$25.00
		Japanese anime CD-ROM.				
U.S. Magna	SSLM-3004	Record of Lodoss War 4	LP	U.S.		$25.00
		Japanese anime CD-ROM.				
Vestron Video	VL5179	Recruits	LD	U.S.	1987	$40.00
Criterion	CC2000L	Red Balloon/White Mane	LD	U.S.	1988	$30.00
Criterion	CC1239L	Red Beard	LD	U.S.	1991	$70.00
Image	ID7932PR	Red Blooded American Girl	LD	U.S.		$30.00
Nelson	901536	Red Headed Stranger	LD	U.S.	1987	$35.00
Image	ID6244IV	Red Heat	LD	U.S.		$30.00
Republic	LV23406	Red Menace, The	LD	U.S.	1991	$30.00
Republic	25566	Red Pony, The 45th Anniversary	LD	U.S.	1993	$35.00
CBS	4656	Red River	LD	U.S.	1985	$30.00
MGM/UA	ML101724	Red River	LD	U.S.	1990	$40.00
Image	ID6693SG	Red Scorpion	LD	U.S.		$30.00
Republic	LV23407	Red Shoe Diaries	LD	U.S.	1992	$25.00
Republic	LV23381	Red Shoe Diaries 2	LD	U.S.	1993	$25.00
Paramount	LV12572	Red Shoes	LD	U.S.	1984	$30.00
Paramount	LV1331-2	Reds	LD	U.S.	1983	$40.00
Image	I-5083	Reform School Girls	LD	U.S.		$30.00
Image	ID7535VE	Reincarnation of Peter Proud	LD	U.S.		$30.00
Image	ID7181SO	Rejuvenator, The	LD	U.S.	1988	$60.00
Columbia	90496	Relentless	LD	U.S.	1990	$30.00
Columbia	91226	Relentless II: Dead On	LD	U.S.	1992	$30.00
HBO	TVL3676	Remo Williams	LD	U.S.	1988	$25.00
Image	ID7389CS	Rendez-Vous	LD	U.S.		$30.00
Image	ID7378IV	Repossessed	LD	U.S.		$30.00
Republic	LV23387	Republic Pictures Story	LD	U.S.	1992	$25.00
Walt Disney	869AS	Rescue, The	LD	U.S.	1989	$36.00
Walt Disney	1142 CS	Rescuers Down Under, The	LD	U.S.	1991	$45.00
		CAV version.				
Walt Disney	1142 AS	Rescuers Down Under, The	LD	U.S.	1991	$30.00
		CLV version.				
Walt Disney	1399 CS	Rescuers, The	LD	U.S.	1977	$45.00
		CAV version.				
Walt Disney	1399 AS	Rescuers, The	LD	U.S.	1977	$30.00
		CLV version.				
Image	ID8309FR	Restless Breed, The	LD	U.S.		$30.00
Image	ID7704MN	Return of Captain Invincible	LD	U.S.		$30.00
CBS	1328	Return of Frank James	LD	U.S.	1990	$30.00
Nelson	13045	Return of Martin Guerre	LD	U.S.	1984	$35.00
Image	ID6851HB	Return of the Living Dead	LD	U.S.		$95.00
Magnetic Video		Return of the Pink Panther	LD	U.S.	1981	$80.00
Magnetic Video		Return of the Pink Panther	LD	U.S.†	1983	$80.00
CBS	9031-80	Return of the Pink Panther	LD	U.S.	1985	$80.00
J2	J2-6064	Return of the Pink Panther	LD	U.S.	1992	$80.00
Columbia	90176	Return of the Swamp Thing	LD	U.S.	1989	$50.00
		Return of the Vampire	LD	U.S.		$80.00
Pioneer		Return of Ultraman Memorial Boxed set	LTD/LD	Japan	1995	$600.00
		6LD boxed set				
Columbia	920205	Return to Blue Lagoon	LD	U.S.	1992	$30.00
Walt Disney	341AS	Return to Oz	LD	U.S.	1986	$40.00
Walt Disney	699	Return to Snowy River	LD	U.S.	1988	$25.00
		Distributed by Pioneer.				
Image	ID8308FR	Reunion	LD	U.S.	1988	$15.00
Columbia	50216	Revenge	LD	U.S.	1990	$30.00
		Letterbox version.				
CBS/Fox	1439-80	Revenge of The Nerds	LD	U.S.	1985	$40.00
CBS/Fox	1514-80	Revenge of The Nerds II	LD	U.S.	1988	$40.00
CBS	4610	Revenge of the Pink Panther	LD	U.S.	1983	$30.00
MGM/UA	ML100111	Rich and Famous	LD	U.S.	1984	$35.00
Image	ID7407NE	Rich And Strange	LD	U.S.		$30.00
Columbia	91546	Rich Girl	LD	U.S.	1991	$30.00
MGM/UA	ML102666	Rich, Young and Pretty	LD	U.S.	1993	$45.00

Label	Catalog Number	Title	Type	Country	Year	Value
		Rick's Your Place for Fantasy	LD	U.S.		$30.00
WHV/HBO	90683	Ricochet	LD	U.S.	1992	$30.00
Image	ID6616HA	Ricochet Rabbit	LD	U.S.		$30.00
Nelson	7681LV	Riders of the Storm	LD	U.S.	1988	$35.00
Image	ID7813HB	Riding the Edge	LD	U.S.		$30.00
CBS	4750	Rikky & Pete	LD	U.S.	1989	$30.00
Lumivision	LVD9206	Rikyu	LD	U.S.	1992	$35.00
Republic	LV23457	Rio Grande	LD	U.S.	1993	$25.00
CBS	7016	Rio Lobo	LD	U.S.	1990	$30.00
Image	ID7687NL	Rise of Catherine the Great	LD	U.S.		$30.00
Warner	11323LV	Risky Business	LD	U.S.	1983	$35.00
Cannon	31128	River of Death	LD	U.S.	1990	$30.00
CBS/Fox	5139-80	River of No Return	LD	U.S.	1988	$35.00
Criterion	CC1176L	River, The	LD	U.S.	1989	$45.00
Nelson	76906	River's Edge	LD	U.S.	1987	$35.00
Warner	11181LV	Road Warrior	LD	U.S.	1983	$30.00
CBS	1022	Robe, The	LD	U.S.	1989	$25.00
	Letterbox version.					
Vestron Video	VL3151	Robert Klein	LD	U.S.	1987	$30.00
Walt Disney	1189 AS	Robin Hood	LD	U.S.	1990	$30.00
Walt Disney	1189 CS	Robin Hood	LD	U.S.	1990	$40.00
	CAV version.					
Psedition	PSE91-22	Robin & Marian	LD	U.S.	1991	$80.00
Republic	LV25045	Robinson Crusoe of Clipper	LD	U.S.	1990	$25.00
Discovision		Robinson vs. Graiano and LaMotta	LD	U.S.	1979	$40.00
		Robocop	LD	Japan	1988	$50.00
	Subtitled					
Image		Robocop	LD	U.S.	1988	$30.00
Columbia	59366	Robot Jox	LD	U.S.	1991	$30.00
		Rocco & Hid Brothers	LD	U.S.		$100.00
MGM/UA	ML100728	Rock And Rule	LD	U.S.		$30.00
Image	ID8243IV	Rock 'n Roll High School Forever	LD	U.S.		$40.00
Lumivision	LVD9202	Rocketship Reel	LD	U.S.	1992	$35.00
Image	ID5109	Rocketship X-M	LD	U.S.		$150.00
Cannon	31146	Rockula	LD	U.S.	1990	$30.00
CBS	4546	Rocky	LD	U.S.	1982	$35.00
CBS	4564	Rocky II	LD	U.S.	1982	$35.00
CBS	4708	Rocky III	LD	U.S.	1983	$35.00
CBS/Fox	4735-80	Rocky IV	LD	U.S.	1986	$35.00
Vestron	VL 3013	Rodan	LD	U.S.	1983	$30.00
Discovision		Rollercoaster	LD	U.S.	1979	$40.00
	SM0583098	Rolling in the Sky/Snow Birds	LD	U.S.		$30.00
Image	ID6904VE	Rolling Thunder	LD	U.S.		$30.00
Discovision		Romagnolias' Table: Abruzzi	LD	U.S.	1979	$40.00
Discovision		Romagnolias' Table: Made In Milan	LD	U.S.	1979	$40.00
Discovision		Romagnolias' Table: Roman Family	LD	U.S.	1979	$40.00
Paramount	LV6204	Roman Holiday	LD	U.S.	1983	$30.00
Image	ID7479PA	Romance With a Double Bass	LD	U.S.		$40.00
CBS	1358	Romancing the Stone	LD	U.S.	1984	$20.00
Image	ID6839CO	Romeo and Juliet	LD	U.S.		$30.00
Paramount	LV6809-2	Romeo and Juliet	LD	U.S.	1982	$36.00
Image	ID7217VK	Romero	LD	U.S.		$30.00
Vid-America	936	Room Service	LD	U.S.	1985	$30.00
CBS	6915	Room With a View	LD	U.S.	1987	$20.00
Discovision		Rooster Cogburn	LD	U.S.	1979	$40.00
Image	ID5117	Rooster Cogburn	LD	U.S.	1987	$25.00
Cannon	31142	Rose Garden	LD	U.S.	1990	$30.00
CBS	1092	Rose, The	LD	U.S.	1982	$20.00
Magnetic Video		Rose, The	LD	U.S.†	1982	$30.00
Magnetic Video		Rose, The	LD	U.S.†	1984	$30.00
Paramount	LV6831-2	Rosemary's Baby	LD	U.S.	1985	$36.00
Image	ID 5183	Rosmary Murders, The	LD	U.S.	1987	$30.00
Paramount	LV1213	Rough Cut	LD	U.S.	1982	$30.00
U.S. Magna	SSLM-3016	Roujin Z	LP	U.S.		$25.00
	Japanese anime CD-ROM.					
Columbia	30853	Roxanne	LD	U.S.	1992	$30.00
Magnetic Video		Royal Flash	LD	U.S.†	1984	$30.00
Image	ID7114HB	Rude Awakening	LD	U.S.		$30.00
Image	ID8204CE	Rude Dog & Dweebs	LD	U.S.	1989	$15.00
Image	ID7267IV	Rudolph the Red-Nosed Raindeer	LD	U.S.		$30.00
Discovision		Ruggles of Red Gap	LD	U.S.	1979	$40.00
Criterion	CC1150L	Rule of the Game, The	LD	U.S.	1989	$90.00
Image		Rulling Class	LD	U.S.		$50.00
MCA	40056	Rumble Fish	LD	U.S.	1984	$70.00
CBS	6391	Rumpelstiltskin	LD	U.S.	1984	$20.00
Columbia	30469	Runaway	LD	U.S.	1985	$30.00
MGM	ML100867	Runaway Train	LD	U.S.	1985	$60.00
Walt Disney	183AS	Running Brave	LD	U.S.	1984	$35.00
CBS/Fox	3503-80	Running Out of Luck	LD	U.S.	1986	$100.00
Columbia	09936	Rush Week	LD	U.S.	1991	$20.00
CBS	4573	Russians are Coming	LD	U.S.	1984	$20.00
Paramount	LV1781	Rustler's Rhaphsody	LD	U.S.	1985	$30.00
Walt Disney	485AS	Ruthless People	LD	U.S.	1987	$35.00
	Distributed by Pioneer.					
Image	ID7672PA	Rutles, The	LD	U.S.		$30.00
Republic	LV23826	S-O-S Coast Guard	LD	U.S.	1990	$25.00
Criterion	CC1117L	Sabotage	LD	U.S.	1987	$40.00
Image	ID5343PA	Sacrifice, The	LD	U.S.		$30.00
Image	ID7336KN	Sadie Thompson	LD	U.S.		$30.00
Columbia	30098	Sahara	LD	U.S.	1988	$30.00
Image	ID5274ME	Saigon Commandos	LD	U.S.		$30.00
Image	ID6761VV	Salaam Bombay	LD	U.S.		$30.00
Warner Home Video	31001LV	Salsa	LD	U.S.	1988	$35.00
Criterion	VP1005L	Salt of the Earth	LD	U.S.	1988	$40.00
Vestron	LV5167	Salvador	LD	U.S.1986$55.00		
Image	ID5124	Same Time Next Year	LD	U.S.	1987	$50.00
Image	ID5216LO	Sammy and Rosie Get Laid	LD	U.S.		$30.00
MGM/UA	ML100474	Samson and Delilah	LD	U.S.		$30.00
Paramount	LV6726-2	Samson and Delilah	LD	U.S.	1983	$36.00
Image	ID6565NS	San Francisco	LD	U.S.		$30.00
MGM/UA	ML100474	San Francisco	LD	U.S.	1985	$35.00
CBS	1029-85	Sand and Pebbles	LD	U.S.		$30.00
Magnetic Video		Sand and Pebbles	LD	U.S.†	1984	$30.00
Image	ID6087RE	Sands Of Iwo Jima	LD	U.S.		$90.00
Image	ID7268IV	Santa Claus Is Coming to Town	LD	U.S.		$30.00
Image	I5054	Santa Claus: The Movie	LD	U.S.	1986	$35.00
		Santa Fe Trail	LD	U.S.		$80.00
Republic	LV23561	Santa Sangre	LD	U.S.	1991	$25.00
		Saps at Sea/Oliver the Eighth	LD	U.S.		$80.00
Republic	LV21821	Sarah Plain and Tall	LD	U.S.	1992	$25.00
Discovision		Satin Stich/Chains	LD	U.S.	1979	$20.00
CBS	1655	Satisfaction	LD	U.S.	1988	$20.00
Discovision		Saturday Night Fever	LD	U.S.	1979	$40.00
Paramount	LV1113	Saturday Night Fever	LD	U.S.	1985	$30.00
CBS	9004	Saturn III	LD	U.S.	1981	$30.00
Magnetic Video		Saturn III	LD	U.S.†	1981	$25.00
Magnetic Video		Saturn III	LD	U.S.†	1982	$25.00
Magnetic Video		Saturn III	LD	U.S.†	1984	$30.00
Criterion		Satyricon	LD	U.S.	1988	$125.00
		Saueeze	LD	U.S.		$30.00
Columbia	90706	Savage Beach	LD	U.S.	1990	$25.00
Nelson	20585	Savannah Smiles	LD	U.S.	1983	$35.00
Paramount	LV8479	Save the Tiger	LD	U.S.	1982	$30.00
Nelson	21805	Saving Grace	LD	U.S.	1986	$35.00
Nelson	60305	Sawdust & Tinsel	LD	U.S.	1984	$40.00
Image	ID7468PA	Say Amen, Somebody	LD	U.S.		$30.00
CBS	1701	Say Anything	LD	U.S.	1990	$20.00
Columbia	30629	Say Yes	LD	U.S.	1986	$30.00
Vestron Video	VL5036	Scandalous	LD	U.S.	1984	$35.00
Nelson	20805	Scanners	LD	U.S.	1983	$50.00
Republic	LV23598	Scanners III: The Takeover	LD	U.S.	1992	$35.00
Criterion	CC1132L	Scaramouche	LD	U.S.	1989	$90.00
	CAV version.					
Criterion	CC1193L	Scaramouche	LD	U.S.	1989	$40.00
	CLV version.					
Image	ID7204VV	Scarecrows	LD	U.S.		$30.00
Republic	LV27710	Scared Stiff	LD	U.S.	1991	$30.00
Image	ID7688NL	Scarlet Pimpernel	LD	U.S.		$30.00
Image	ID7828HB	Scars of Dracula/Horror of Frankenstien	LD	U.S.		$60.00
Disney		Scary Tales	LD	U.S.		$50.00
	AE1119	Scavengers	LD	U.S.		$15.00
MCA	42132	Schindler's List	LTD/LD	U.S.	1994	$135.00
	LD with picture disc CD Booklet and Schindler's List novel . Limited to 10,000 copies.					
Columbia	65006	School Daze	LD	U.S.	1989	$40.00
Image	ID6615HA	Scoobie Doo	LD	U.S.		$30.00
Columbia	30814	Scorpion	LD	U.S.	1987	$30.00
		Scream Blackula Scream	LD	Japan		$80.00
Paramount	LV2368	Scream Great I	LD	U.S.	1986	$30.00
Paramount	LV2378	Scream Great II	LD	U.S.	1987	$30.00
Paramount	LV2368	Scream Greats Volume I	LD	U.S.	1986	$60.00
Paramount	LV2378	Scream Greats Volume II	LD	U.S.		$60.00
Columbia	30578	Screen Test	LD	U.S.	1986	$30.00
CBS/Fox	7126-80	Scrooge	LD	U.S.	1984	$35.00
CBS/Fox	4696-80	Seahawk, The	LD	U.S.	1985	$35.00
Image	ID7045TU	Second Chance	LD	U.S.		$30.00
Republic	LV23583	Second Chorus	LD	U.S.	1990	$30.00
Image	ID7499HB	Secret Admirer	LD	U.S.		$30.00
Criterion	CC1118L	Secret Agent	LD	U.S.	1987	$35.00
Republic	LV21822	Secret Garden, The	LD	U.S.	1992	$25.00
Nelson	30625	Secret Life of Walter Mitty	LD	U.S.	1985	$80.00
MGM/UA	ML100211	Secret of Nimh	LD	U.S.	1983	$35.00
		See No Evil	LD	U.S.		$40.00
Columbia	70226	See No Evil, Hear No Evil	LD	U.S.	1990	$30.00
Columbia	VLD5545	Seems Like Old Times	LD	U.S.		$30.00
	First Issue					
RCA/Columbia	VLD5545	Seems Like Old Times	LD	U.S.	1985	$35.00
Columbia	VLD5545	Seems Like Old Times	LD	U.S.	1993	$40.00
Image	ID6561ME	Self Defense	LD	U.S.		$30.00
CBS	4517	Semi-Tough	LD	U.S.	1982	$20.00
Paramount	LV1537	Sender	LD	U.S.	1983	$30.00
Discovision		Sentinel: The West Face	LD	U.S.	1979	$40.00
Republic	LV23617	Separate But Equal	LD	U.S.	1991	$40.00
Discovision		Seraphic Dialog	LD	U.S.	1979	$40.00
Paramount	LV1191	Serial	LD	U.S.	1985	$30.00
Image	ID8059PR	Serpent of Death, The	LD	U.S.		$30.00
Paramount	LV8689	Serpico	LD	U.S.	1982	$40.00
Image		Set Up, The	LD	U.S.		$50.00
Paramount	LV6313	Seven Days in May	LD	U.S.	1984	$40.00
Image	ID6390ME	Seven Hours to Judgement	LD	U.S.		$30.00
Discovision		Seven Percent Solution	LD	U.S.	1979	$40.00
Criterion	CC1167L	Seven Samurai	LD	U.S.	1989	$125.00
	CAV version.					
Criterion	CC1236L	Seven Samurai	LD	U.S.	1990	$60.00
	CLV version.					
Magnetic Video		Seven Year Itch	LD	U.S.†	1984	$30.00
CBS	1043	Seven Year Itch	LD	U.S.	1988	$25.00
Criterion	CC1110L	Seventh Seal	LD	U.S.	1990	$80.00
	CAV version.					
Criterion	CC1212L	Seventh Seal	LD	U.S.	1990	$50.00
	CLV version.					
Image	I 6007	Seventh Victim	LD	U.S.	1986	$80.00
Columbia	30114	Seventh Voyage of Sinbad	LD	U.S.	1985	$30.00
Psedition	PSE91-29	Seventh Voyage of Sinbad	LD	U.S.	1992	$70.00
Columbia	90486	Sex, Lies and Video Tape	LD	U.S.	1990	$30.00
Criterion	CC1217L	Sex, Lies and Video Tape	LD	U.S.	1990	$125.00
Image	ID-5030	Sexy Shorts	LD	U.S.		$30.00
Image Entertainment	I-5030	Sexy Shorts	LD	U.S.	1986	$30.00
		SFX Museum Vol. 2: Motion Control	LD	Japan	1985	$100.00
Discovision	17-004	Sgt. Pepper's Lonely Hearts Club Band	LD	U.S.	1979	$40.00
MCA	17-004	Sgt. Pepper's Lonely Hearts Club Band	LD	U.S.	1985	$25.00
Republic	LV23469	Shadow Hunter	LD	U.S.	1993	$25.00
Image	ID7318VK	Shadows In the Storm	LD	U.S.		$30.00
Image	ID6943HB	Shag: The Movie	LD	U.S.		$30.00
Nelson	30845	Shaker Run	LD	U.S.	1986	$35.00
Republic	LV27732	Shame	LD	U.S.	1991	$30.00
RCA/Columbia	30528	Shampoo	LD	U.S.	1985	$35.00
Criterion	CC11272L	Shampoo	LD	U.S.	1991	$50.00
Columbia	30528	Shampoo	LD	U.S.	1992	$30.00
Paramount	LV6522	Shane	LD	U.S.	1982	$30.00
Image	ID7981MF	Shanghai Gesture	LD	U.S.		$80.00
Vestron Video	ML5141	Shanghai Surprise	LD	U.S.	1987	$35.00
Image	ID7369OR	She Devil	LD	U.S.		$30.00
Vid-America	933	She Wore a Yellow Ribbon	LD	U.S.	1986	$30.00
Columbia	10306	She's Out of Control	LD	U.S.	1989	$35.00
Columbia	30404	Sheena	LD	U.S.	1985	$30.00
Discovision		Shenandoah	LD	U.S.	1980	$40.00
Image	ID 5125	Shenandoah	LD	U.S.	1987	$35.00
Paramount	LV27725	Sherlock Holmes and the Secret Weapon	LD	U.S.		$55.00
		Sherlock Holmes Dressed to Kill	LD	U.S.		$55.00
		Sherlock Holmes Terror by Night	LD	U.S.		$55.00
Columbia	30542	Ship of Fools	LD	U.S.	1986	$30.00
Criterion	CC1189L	Shock Corridor	LD	U.S.	1989	$45.00
Image	ID7390SG	Shock Troop	LD	U.S.		$30.00
Paramount	LV1423	Shogun	LD	U.S.	1982	$100.00
Discovision	12-023	Shogun Assasin	LD	U.S.	1980	$40.00
	CAV version.					
MCA	12-023	Shogun Assasin	LD	U.S.	1985	$30.00
Criterion	CC1143L	Shoot the Piano Player	LD	U.S.	1988	$45.00
Walt Disney	697	Shoot to Kill	LD	U.S.	1988	$35.00
	Distributed by Pioneer.					
Paramount	LV8904	Shootist	LD	U.S.	1983	$30.00
Image	ID6169RC	Shop on Main Street	LD	U.S.		$30.00
CBS/Fox	3724-80	Short Circuit	LD	U.S.	1987	$35.00
CBS	C3724	Short Circuit	LD	U.S.	1989	$35.00

Label	Catalog Number	Title	Type	Country	Year	Value
Image	ID7618IV	Short Time	LD	U.S.		$30.00
Image	ID7528VE	Shout at the Devil	LD	U.S.		$30.00
Criterion	CC1144L	Show Boat	LD	U.S.	1989	$125.00
CAV version.						
Criterion	CC1191L	Show Boat	LD	U.S.	1989	$50.00
CLV version.						
MGM/UA	ML100167	Showboat	LD	U.S.	1988	$35.00
Image	ID8088ME	Shrimp on the Barbie, The	LD	U.S.		$30.00
Nelson	7782	Sibling Rivalry	LD	U.S.	1991	$35.00
Nelson	13096	Sid and Nancy	LD	U.S.	1987	$80.00
Columbia	70336	Side Out	LD	U.S.	1990	$30.00
Republic	LV23685	Siegfried	LD	U.S.	1991	$25.00
Image	ID7219IV	Signs of Life	LD	U.S.		$30.00
Image	ID7872ME	Silence Like Glass	LD	U.S.		$30.00
Orion	ID7434OR	Silence of the Lambs	LD	U.S.	1991	$35.00
First pressing in "laserdisc" digipak						
Lumivision	LVD9246	Silent Enemy	LD	U.S.	1993	$35.00
CBS	1437	Silent Movie	LD	U.S.	1985	$50.00
Image	ID6909IV	Silent Night, Deadly Night	LD	U.S.		$80.00
Image	ID6816IV	Silent Night, Deadly Night 3: Better Watch Out	LD	U.S.		$70.00
Image	ID7615IV	Silent Night, Deadly Night 4: Initiation	LD	U.S.		$70.00
Image	ID6908IV	Silent Night, Deadly Night Part 2	LD	U.S.		$70.00
Vestron Video	VL5007	Silent Partner, The	LD	U.S.	1983	$55.00
RCA/Columbia	VLD5549	Silent Rage	LD	U.S.	1983	$35.00
Columbia	VLD5549	Silent Rage	LD	U.S.	1992	$30.00
Discovision		Silent Safari	LD	U.S.	1979	$40.00
Image	ID7839SR	Silk Road: An Ancient World o Adventure Vol. 4	LD	U.S.		$30.00
Image	ID7836SR	Silk Road: An Ancient World of Adventure Vol. 1	LD	U.S.		$30.00
Image	ID7837SR	Silk Road: An Ancient World of Adventure Vol. 2	LD	U.S.		$30.00
Image	ID7838SR	Silk Road: An Ancient World of Adventure Vol. 3	LD	U.S.		$30.00
Image	ID7840SR	Silk Road: An Ancient World of Adventure Vol. 5	LD	U.S.		$30.00
Image	ID7841SR	Silk Road: An Ancient World of Adventure Vol. 6	LD	U.S.		$30.00
Nelson	13775	Silkwood	LD	U.S.	1984	$40.00
Walt Disney	365AS	Silly Symphony	LD	U.S.	1986	$25.00
Paramount	LV1827	Silver Bullet	LD	U.S.	1986	$30.00
Magnetic Video		Silver Streak	LD	U.S.†	1984	$30.00
RCA/Columbia	30567-2	Silverado	LD	U.S.	1986	$40.00
Criterion	CC1229L	Silverado	LD	U.S.	1990	$60.00
CLV version.						
Criterion	CC1228L	Silverado	LD	U.S.	1991	$100.00
CAV version.						
Columbia	30567-2	Silverado	LD	U.S.	1992	$30.00
CBS	1080	Silverstreak	LD	U.S.	1984	$25.00
Columbia	VLD5550	Sinbad and the Eye of the Tiger	LD	U.S.	1993	$30.00
Cannon	31130	Sinbad of the Seven Seas	LD	U.S.	1990	$30.00
Image	ID6406TU	Sinbad the Sailor	LD	U.S.		$30.00
Columbia	30771	Sincerely Charlot	LD	U.S.	1987	$30.00
MGM/UA	ML100185	Singin' in the Rain	LD	U.S.	1983	$30.00
Criterion	CC1210L	Singin' in the Rain	LD	U.S.	1989	$40.00
Criterion	CC1152L	Singin' in the Rain	LD	U.S.	1989	$90.00
CAV version.						
Image	ID5296PA	Singing Whale, The	LD	U.S.		$30.00
Discovision		Singing Whale, The	LD	U.S.	1979	$40.00
Image		Sirocco	LD	U.S.		$90.00
		Sisterhood, The	LD	U.S.		$30.00
		Sisters	LD	Japan		$120.00
Discovision		Six Million Dollar Man: Secret of Bigfoot	LD	U.S.	1979	$100.00
Discovision	19-003	Six Million Dollar Man, The Cyborg	LD	U.S.	1979	$100.00
Columbia	VLD3377	Six Weeks	LD	U.S.	1983	$30.00
Image	ID7135VK	Sizzle Beach U.S.A.	LD	U.S.		$30.00
Nelson	77446	Skeleton Coast	LD	U.S.	1989	$35.00
Columbia	59086	Ski Patrol	LD	U.S.	1990	$30.00
Discovision		Ski Racer	LD	U.S.	1979	$40.00
Magnetic Video		Sky Riders	LD	U.S.†	1984	$30.00
Image	ID7094TU	Sky's the Limit	LD	U.S.		$30.00
Image	ID7486PA	Skyline	LD	U.S.		$30.00
		Slammer Girls	LD	U.S.		$40.00
Discovision	16-004	Slap Shot	LD	U.S.	1979	$40.00
MCA	16-004	Slap Shot	LD	U.S.	1985	$25.00
CAV version.						
MCA	16004	Slap Shot	LD	U.S.	1991	$40.00
Discovision		Slaughterhouse Five	LD	U.S.	1979	$40.00
Image	ID 5092	Slaughterhouse Five	LD	U.S.	1987	$30.00
Full Moon	LV13004	Slave Girls From Beyond Infinity	LD	U.S.	1993	$35.00
CBS/Fox	4522-80	Sleeper	LD	U.S.	1983	$35.00
Walt Disney	476AS	Sleeping Beauty	LD	U.S.	1987	$200.00
Walt Disney	476CS	Sleeping Beauty	LD/CAV	U.S.	1987	$250.00
Image	ID7279SP	Sleeping Beauty, The	LD	U.S.		$30.00
CBS	6371	Sleeping Beauty, The	LD	U.S.	1984	$20.00
Image	ID7218VK	Sleeping Car, The	LD	U.S.		$30.00
Discovision		Sleeping Sharks of Yucatan	LD	U.S.	1979	$40.00
Nelson	77686	Sleepwalk	LD	U.S.	1989	$35.00
Nelson	77586	Sleepway Camp 3	LD	U.S.	1989	$25.00
Image	I-5072	Sleuth	LD	U.S.		$30.00
Discovision		Slipper and the Rose	LD	U.S.	1979	$40.00
		Slipstream	LD	U.S.		$40.00
RCA/Columbia	30486	Slugger's Wife	LD	U.S.	1985	$35.00
Columbia	30486	Slugger's Wife	LD	U.S.	1993	$30.00
Nelson Entertainment	76886	Slumber Party Massacre 2	LD	U.S.	1987	$35.00
Image	ID7543VE	Smash Palace	LD	U.S.		$30.00
Discovision		Smile of the Walrus	LD	U.S.	1979	$40.00
Criterion	CC1251L	Smiles of a Summer Night	LD	U.S.	1990	$50.00
Columbia	59036	Smokescreen	LD	U.S.	1990	$30.00
Discovision	12-004	Smokey and the Bandit	LD	U.S.	1979	$40.00
MCA	12004	Smokey and the Bandit	LD	U.S.	1985	$30.00
Discovision		Smokey and the Bandit 2	LD	U.S.	1980	$40.00
MCA	40013	Smokey and the Bandit 3	LD	U.S.	1984	$50.00
Discovision		Smoking: How to Stop	LD	U.S.	1979	$40.00
Vestron Video	VL5143	Smooth Talk	LD	U.S.	1986	$35.00
Vestron	CL2509	Smurfs and the Magic Flute, The	LD	U.S.	1984	$15.00
Image	ID7845ME	Snake Eater	LD	U.S.		$30.00
CBS/Fox	7125-80	Snoopy, Come Home	LD	U.S.	1985	$35.00
Nelson	76926	Snow Motion	LD	U.S.	1988	$30.00
CBS/Fox	6394-80	Snow White	LD	U.S.	1984	$30.00
Walt Disney	2921 CS	Snow White	LTD/LD	U.S.	1994	$100.00
3 LD set in box with book and lithographs.						
Republic	LV23787	Society	LD	U.S.	1992	$30.00
Discovision	D61-506	Solar System/The Universe	LD	U.S.	1979	$40.00
Image	ID5350ME	Soldier of Orange	LD	U.S.		$40.00
Columbia	30408	Soldier's Story	LD	U.S.	1992	$30.00
MGM/UA	ML100376	Soldier's Tale	LD	U.S.	1984	$35.00
Republic	LV23795	Soldier's Tale	LD	U.S.	1992	$25.00
Paramount	LV1118	Some Kind of Hero	LD	U.S.	1982	$30.00
MGM/UA	ML103848	Some Like It Hot	LD	U.S.		$30.00
CBS	4577	Some Like It Hot	LD	U.S.	1982	$30.00
Criterion	CC1286L	Some Like It Hot	LD	U.S.	1992	$60.00
Image Entertainment	15041	Someone Behind the Door	LD	U.S.	1986	$35.00
RCA/Columbia	30877	Someone to Watch Over Me	LD	U.S.	1988	$100.00
Columbia	30877	Someone to Watch Over Me	LD	U.S.	1992	$100.00
Image	ID7712MN	Something Special	LD	U.S.		$30.00
Michael Agee	LVA	Something to Sing About	LD	U.S.	1990	$25.00
Walt Disney	166AS	Something Wicked This Way Comes	LD	U.S.	1983	$50.00
HBO	TVL0001	Something Wild	LD	U.S.	1987	$30.00
		Son of Monte Cristo	LD	U.S.		$65.00
Image	ID6709RC	Son of Paleface	LD	U.S.		$30.00
Republic	LV23810	Son of the Morningstar	LD	U.S.	1991	$25.00
Republic	LV23809	Son of The Sheik	LD	U.S.	1991	$30.00
Republic	LV25046	Son of Zorro	LD	U.S.	1992	$25.00
CBS	1034	Song of Bernadette	LD	U.S.	1990	$25.00
Walt Disney	PILF-1096	Song of the South	LD	Japan		$90.00
Columbia	30546	Song to Remember	LD	U.S.	1985	$30.00
Columbia	30427	Songwriter	LD	U.S.	1985	$30.00
CBS	9076	Sophie's Choice	LD	U.S.	1983	$30.00
Image	ID6371J2	Sophisticated Ladies	LD	U.S.		$30.00
Full Moon	LV13006	Sorority Babes in the Slimeball Bowl-A-Rama	LD	U.S.	1993	$35.00
Image	ID5100	Soul Man	LD	U.S.		$30.00
Magnetic Video		Sound of Music	LD	U.S.†	1982	$25.00
CBS/Fox	1051-80	Sound of Music	LD	U.S.	1982	$40.00
CBS/Fox	1051-80	Sound of Music	LD	U.S.	1987	$40.00
CBS/Fox	C1561	Sound of Music	LD	U.S.	1989	$40.00
Fox Video	4267-85	Sound of Music	LTD/LD	U.S.	1994	$130.00
3 LD boxed set with "gold" edition CD soundtrack and movie script.						
Image	ID5295PA	Sound of the Dolphin	LD	U.S.		$30.00
Discovision		Sound of the Dolphin	LD	U.S.	1979	$40.00
Paramount	LV2324	Sounder	LD	U.S.	1984	$30.00
Republic	LV23830	South of Reno	LD	U.S.	1991	$30.00
CBS	7045	South Pacific	LD	U.S.	1984	$20.00
CBS	7045	South Pacific	LD	U.S.	1984	$25.00
Letterbox version.						
J2	J2-6050	Space 1999 Collector's Edition	LD	U.S.	1990	$30.00
Image	ID77821V	Space 1999 Vol. 1	LD	U.S.		$40.00
Image	ID7790J2	Space 1999 Vol. 10	LD	U.S.		$20.00
Image	ID7791J2	Space 1999 Vol. 11	LD	U.S.		$20.00
Image	ID7792J2	Space 1999 Vol. 12	LD	U.S.		$20.00
Image	ID7793J2	Space 1999 Vol. 13	LD	U.S.		$20.00
Image	ID7794J2	Space 1999 Vol. 14	LD	U.S.		$20.00
Image	ID7795J2	Space 1999 Vol. 15	LD	U.S.		$20.00
Image	ID7796J2	Space 1999 Vol. 16	LD	U.S.		$20.00
Image	ID7797J2	Space 1999 Vol. 17	LD	U.S.		$20.00
Image	ID7798J2	Space 1999 Vol. 18	LD	U.S.		$20.00
Image	ID7799J2	Space 1999 Vol. 19	LD	U.S.		$20.00
Image	ID7781J2	Space 1999 Vol. 2	LD	U.S.		$20.00
Image	ID7800J2	Space 1999 Vol. 20	LD	U.S.		$20.00
Image	ID7801J2	Space 1999 Vol. 21	LD	U.S.		$20.00
Image	ID7802J2	Space 1999 Vol. 22	LD	U.S.		$20.00
Image	ID7803J2	Space 1999 Vol. 23	LD	U.S.		$20.00
Image	ID7783IV	Space 1999 Vol. 3	LD	U.S.		$20.00
Image	ID7784J2	Space 1999 Vol. 4	LD	U.S.		$20.00
Image	ID7785J2	Space 1999 Vol. 5	LD	U.S.		$20.00
Image	ID7786J2	Space 1999 Vol. 6	LD	U.S.		$20.00
Image	ID7787J2	Space 1999 Vol. 7	LD	U.S.		$20.00
Image	ID7788J2	Space 1999 Vol. 8	LD	U.S.		$20.00
Image	ID7789J2	Space 1999 Vol. 9	LD	U.S.		$20.00
Pioneer		Space Archive: Apollo 17	LD	U.S.	1983	$100.00
Pioneer		Space Archive: Encounters	LD	U.S.	1987	$100.00
Pioneer		Space Archive: Greetings From Earth	LD	U.S.	1985	$100.00
Pioneer		Space Archive: Mars & Beyond	LD	U.S.	1985	$100.00
Pioneer		Space Archive: Shuttle Downlink	LD	U.S.	1984	$100.00
Pioneer		Space Archive: Shuttle Mission	LD	U.S.	1983	$100.00
Pioneer		Space Archive: Space Shuttle	LD	U.S.	1983	$100.00
Vestron Video	V-5174	Space Camp	LD	U.S.	1986	$35.00
VideoVision		Space Disc Volume 1- Voyager	LD	U.S.	1982	$80.00
VideoVision		Space Disc Volume 2-Apollo 17	LD	U.S.	1982	$80.00
VideoVision		Space Disc Volume 3-Space Shuttle	LD	U.S.	1982	$80.00
VideoVision		Space Disc Volume 4-The Sun	LD	U.S.	1982	$80.00
VideoVision		Space Disc Volume 5-Astronomy	LD	Japan	1987	$100.00
VideoVision		Space Disc Volume 5-Astronomy	LD	U.S.	1982	$80.00
VideoVision		Space Disc Volume 6-Earth Science	LD	U.S.	1982	$80.00
Image	ID8042PA	Space: Frontiers and Beyond	LD	U.S.		$30.00
Columbia	VLD3381	Space Hunter: Adventures in the Forbidden Zone	LD	U.S.		$20.00
Columbia	VLD23665	Space Hunters	LD	U.S.	1984	$30.00
MGM/UA	ML101179	Spaceballs	LD	U.S.	1988	$25.00
Walt Disney	1064AS	Spaced Invaders	LD	U.S.	1990	$40.00
		Spacewatch	LD	Japan	1984	$100.00
		Spacewatch Volume II	LD	Japan	1986	$100.00
		Spanish Main	LD	U.S.		$30.00
Image	ID7702CO	Spartacus	LD	U.S.		$30.00
Criterion	CC1298L	Spartacus	LD	U.S.	1992	$125.00
Image Entertainment	IG-5005	Spectreman Vol. 1	LD	U.S.	1985	$30.00
Columbia	59696	Spellcaster	LD	U.S.	1992	$30.00

Spider-Man

Label	Catalog Number	Title	Type	Country	Year	Value
Prism	ID7763PR	Spider-Man	LD	U.S.	1990	$30.00
Discovision		Spinach Pie/Dolmathes	LD	U.S.	1979	$20.00
Columbia	91266	Spirit of '76	LD	U.S.	1992	$30.00
Image	ID8183SG	Spirit of the Eagle	LD	U.S.		$30.00

Label	Catalog Number	Title	Type	Country	Year	Value
Walt Disney	213AS	Splash	LD	U.S.	1984	$35.00
	Distributed by Pioneer.					
Image	ID7867ME	Spontaneous Combustion	LD	U.S.		$30.00
Walt Disney	165AS	Sport Goofy	LD	U.S.	1983	$35.00
Walt Disney	168AS	Sport Goofy #6	LD	U.S.	1983	$35.00
Columbia	VLD3378	Spring Break	LD	U.S.	1984	$30.00
CBS	1742-80	Springtime in the Rockies/Song	LD	U.S.	1990	$30.00
Image	ID7689NL	Spy in Black	LD	U.S.		$30.00
CBS	4638	Spy Who Loved Me	LD	U.S.	1983	$15.00
HBO	0053	Squeeze, The	LD	U.S.	1988	$35.00
RCA/Columbia	VLD30559	St. Elmo's Fire	LD	U.S.	1986	$80.00
Columbia	VLD30559	St. Elmo's Fire	LD	U.S.	1992	$80.00
Magnetic Video		St. Valentine's Day Massacre	LD	U.S.†	1984	$30.00
Nelson	90227	Stacking	LD	U.S.	1988	$35.00
Walt Disney	596	Stakeout	LD	U.S.	1988	$30.00
	Distributed by Pioneer.					
Paramount	LV5816	Stalag 17	LD	U.S.	1983	$40.00
Image	ID6934VK	Stalking Danger	LD	U.S.		$15.00
RCA/Columbia	30736	Stand by Me	LD	U.S.	1987	$35.00
Columbia	30736	Stand by Me	LD	U.S.	1992	$30.00
CBS	1295	Star Chamber, The	LD	U.S.	1989	$20.00
Image	I6001	Star is Born (1937)	LD	U.S.	1986	$100.00
Vidmark	LDCVM4502	Star Slammer: The Escape	LD	U.S.	1993	$35.00
Nelson	90015	Star Struck	LD	U.S.	1984	$50.00
Paramount	LV60040-81	Star Trek 1 (6/8)	LD	U.S.	1985	$30.00
Paramount	LV60040-90	Star Trek 10 (22/24)	LD	U.S.	1985	$30.00
Paramount	LV60040 00	Star Trek 11 (23/25)	LD	U.S.	1985	$30.00
Paramount	LV60040-92	Star Trek 12 (26/27)	LD	U.S.	1985	$30.00
Paramount	LV60040-93	Star Trek 13 (20/28)	LD	U.S.	1985	$30.00
Paramount	LV60040-94	Star Trek 14 (29/34)	LD	U.S.	1985	$30.00
Paramount	LV60040-96	Star Trek 16 (38/39)	LD	U.S.	1986	$30.00
Paramount	LV60040-97	Star Trek 17 (30/35)	LD	U.S.	1986	$30.00
Paramount	LV60040-98	Star Trek 18 (31/41)	LD	U.S.	1986	$30.00
Paramount	LV60040-99	Star Trek 19 (32/44)	LD	U.S.	1986	$30.00
Paramount	LV60040-82	Star Trek 2 (2/7)	LD	U.S.	1985	$30.00
Paramount	LV60040-100	Star Trek 20 (40/47)	LD	U.S.	1986	$30.00
Paramount	LV60040-101	Star Trek 21 (36/42)	LD	U.S.	1986	$30.00
Paramount	LV60040-102	Star Trek 22 (46/49)	LD	U.S.	1986	$30.00
Paramount	LV60040-103	Star Trek 23 (48/45)	LD	U.S.	1986	$30.00
Paramount	LV60040-104	Star Trek 24 (51/52)	LD	U.S.	1986	$30.00
Paramount	LV60040-105	Star Trek 25 (50/54)	LD	U.S.	1986	$30.00
Paramount	LV12954-7WS	Star Trek 25th Anniversary–The Movies	LTD/LD	U.S.	1991	$500.00
	7 LD boxed set.					
Paramount	LV60040-109	Star Trek 29 (59/58)	LD	U.S.	1987	$30.00
Paramount	LV60040-83	Star Trek 30 (5/4)	LD	U.S.	1985	$30.00
Paramount	LV60040-110	Star Trek 30 (60/62)	LD	U.S.	1987	$30.00
Paramount	LV60040-111	Star Trek 31 (56/66)	LD	U.S.	1987	$30.00
Paramount	LV60040-84	Star Trek 4 (10/12)	LD	U.S.	1985	$30.00
Paramount	LV60040-85	Star Trek 5 (11/3)	LD	U.S.	1985	$30.00
Paramount	LV60040-86	Star Trek 6 (13/9)	LD	U.S.	1985	$30.00
Paramount	LV60040-87	Star Trek 7 (17/14)	LD	U.S.	1985	$30.00
Paramount	LV60040-88	Star Trek 8 (18/19)	LD	U.S.	1985	$30.00
Paramount	LV60040-89	Star Trek 9 (21/15)	LD	U.S.	1985	$30.00
Paramount		Star Trek Cage	LD	U.S.	1986	$30.00
Pioneer	PILF3231	Star Trek: Deep Space Nine First Season Volume 1	LTD/LD	Japan	1996	$400.00
	6 LD boxed set.					
Paramount	LV1180	Star Trek II	LD	U.S.	1982	$30.00
Paramount	LV1621	Star Trek III	LD	U.S.	1985	$30.00
Paramount	LV1797	Star Trek IV: The Voyage Home	LD	U.S.	1987	$40.00
Paramount	LV8858-2A	Star Trek (Longer Version)	LD	U.S.	1983	$40.00
Paramount	LV8858	Star Trek, Motion Picture	LD	U.S.	1985	$30.00
Paramount	45276	Star Trek Movie Voyage	LTD/LD	U.S.	1995	$250.00
	Seven Movie Set in custom box					
Paramount	LV60040106	Star Trek – The Cage	LD	U.S.		$25.00
Pioneer	LV15340-3	Star Trek: The Captain's Collection	LTD/LD	U.S.	1996	$100.00
	3 LD set with limited edition Skybox® uncut trading card sheet.					
Paramount	LV60041	Star Trek The Menagerie Part 1 & 2	LD	U.S.	1984	$30.00
Paramount	LV15341-3	Star Trek the Next Generation: The Q Continuum	LTD/LD	U.S.	1996	$100.00
	3 LD boxed set.					
CBS		Star Wars	LD	France	1985	$60.00
CBS		Star Wars	LD	Germany	1985	$60.00
Magnetic Video		Star Wars	LD	Japan	1983	$40.00
CBS		Star Wars	LD	Japan	1986	$40.00
CBS	USF1481196	Star Wars	LD	Japan	1986	$50.00
	CAV version.					
CBS		Star Wars	LD	U.K.	1984	$60.00
CBS	1130-85	Star Wars	LD	U.S.	1982	$25.00
	CAV version.					
CBS	1130-80	Star Wars	LD	U.S.	1985	$35.00
CBS	1130-80	Star Wars	LD	U.S.	1989	$25.00
CBS	1130-85	Star Wars	LD	U.S.	1989	$35.00
	CAV version.					
CBS	USF1481242	Star Wars: Empire Strikes Back	LD	Japan		$50.00
	CAV version					
CBS	1425-80	Star Wars: Empire Strikes Back	LD	U.S.	1984	$30.00
CBS	1425-84	Star Wars: Empire Strikes Back	LD	U.S.	1985	$35.00
	CAV version.					
CBS	1425-85	Star Wars: Empire Strikes Back	LD	U.S.	1990	$30.00
	Letterbox version.					
Fox		Star Wars: From Star Wars to Jedi	LD	Japan		$350.00
CBS	USF1481343	Star Wars: Return of the Jedi	LD	Japan		$50.00
	CAV version.					
CBS	1478-80	Star Wars: Return of the Jedi	LD	U.S.	1985	$20.00
CBS	1478-85	Star Wars: Return of the Jedi	LD	U.S.	1985	$35.00
	Letterbox version.					
Fox Video	9693-84	Star Wars Trilogy, The	LD	U.S.	1994	$250.00
	9 LD Boxed set with book					
Paramount	LV2347	Starchaser	LD	U.S.	1986	$30.00
CBS	4554	Starduct Memories	LD	U.S.	1983	$20.00
Republic	LV23900	Starlight Hotel	LD	U.S.	1992	$25.00
Columbia	30412	Starman	LD	U.S.	1985	$30.00
Psedition	PSE91-09	Starman	LD	U.S.	1991	$50.00
Columbia	65005	Stars & Bars	LD	U.S.	1989	$30.00
Paramount	LV1239	Starting Over	LD	U.S.	1985	$30.00
Image	ID5332PA	State of the Art of Computer Animation	LD	U.S.		$30.00
Image	ID7203VV	Static	LD	U.S.		$30.00
Vestron	LV1049	Statue of Liberty	LD	U.S.	1986	$30.00
Nelson	77666	Stay Awake	LD	U.S.	1989	$35.00
Paramount	LV1302	Staying Alive	LD	U.S.	1984	$30.00
Image	ID6567HB	Steal the Sky	LD	U.S.		$30.00
Image	ID6457VV	Stealing Heaven	LD	U.S.		$40.00
Image		Steamboat Bill Jr.	LD	U.S.		$40.00
		Steel and Lace	LD	U.S.		$30.00
Image	ID5214VE	Steel Dawn	LD	U.S.		$30.00
Columbia	70246	Steel Magnolias	LD	U.S.	1990	$30.00

Label	Catalog Number	Title	Type	Country	Year	Value
Image	ID5266LO	Steep and Deep	LD	U.S.		$30.00
Walt Disney	995AS	Stella	LD	U.S.	1990	$30.00
Nelson	30665	Stella Dallas	LD	U.S.	1985	$35.00
Nelson	75676	Stepfather	LD	U.S.	1987	$40.00
Paramount	LV6904	Sterile Cuckoo	LD	U.S.	1985	$30.00
Columbia	30769	Stewardess School	LD	U.S.	1987	$30.00
CBS	4711	Still of the Night	LD	U.S.	1984	$20.00
Paramount	LV2315	Still Smoking	LD	U.S.	1983	$30.00
MCA	11-017	Sting II	LD	U.S.	1983	$30.00
Discovision	11-001	Sting, The	LD	U.S.	1979	$40.00
MCA	11-001	Sting, The	LD	U.S.	1985	$25.00
Image	ID7583IV	Stingray: Incredible Voyage of Stingray	LD	U.S.		$30.00
Image	ID7584IV	Stingray: Invaders From the Deep	LD	U.S.		$30.00
RCA/Columbia	VLD3380	Stir Crazy	LD	U.S.	1982	$35.00
Columbia	VLD3380	Stir Crazy	LD	U.S.	1993	$30.00
Columbia	50726	Stone Cold	LD	U.S.	1991	$30.00
CBS	1168	Stormy Weather	LD	U.S.	1989	$20.00
MGM/UA	ML100202	Story of O	LD	U.S.	1983	$35.00
Image	ID6780TU	Story of Vernon and Irene Castle	LD	U.S.		$30.00
Columbia	32771	Stranded	LD	U.S.	1988	$30.00
Republic	LV23925	Strange Affair of Uncle Harry, The	LD	U.S.	1991	$30.00
Columbia	30355	Stranger and the Gunfighter	LD	U.S.	1985	$30.00
Image	ID7036TU	Stranger on the Third Floor	LD	U.S.		$30.00
CBS	6896	Stranger Than Paradise	LD	U.S.	1896	$30.00
Columbia	90896	Strapless	LD	U.S.	1990	$30.00
Paramount	LV25426	Strategic Air Command	LD	U.S.	1987	$30.00
CBS	8005	Straw Dogs	LD	U.S.	1983	$30.00
		Streamers	LD	U.S.		$100.00
Image	ID7722MN	Street Asylum	LD	U.S.		$30.00
Columbia	77196	Street Hunter	LD	U.S.	1990	$30.00
Cannon	32117	Street Knight	LD	U.S.	1993	$25.00
Image	ID5157	Street Smart	LD	U.S.		$30.00
CBS	4571	Streetcar Named Desire, A	LD	U.S.	1983	$30.00
Warner Home Video	34019	Streetcar Named Desire, A	LD	U.S.	1987	$30.00
		Streets of Fire	LD	U.S.		$30.00
Vestron Video	VL5199	Streets of Gold	LD	U.S.	1987	$35.00
Image	ID8678WV	Streets of San Francisco Vol. 1	LD	U.S.		$35.00
		Streetwise	LD	U.S.		$50.00
Image	ID7226HB	Strepfather II: Make Room For Dady	LD	U.S.		$30.00
MGM/UA	ML102197	Strike Up the Band	LD	U.S.		$30.00
MGM/UA	ML100565	Strike Up The Band	LD	U.S.	1985	$35.00
RCA/Columbia	VLD5557	Stripes	LD	U.S.	1983	$20.00
Columbia	VLD5557	Stripes	LD	U.S.	1992	$20.00
Paramount	LV85037	Strong Kids, Safe Kids	LD	U.S.	1985	$25.00
Paramount	LV1476	Student Bodies	LD	U.S.	1982	$30.00
Image	ID7849ME	Stuff Stephanie In the Incinerator	LD	U.S.		$20.00
CBS	1110	Stuntman, The	LD	U.S.		$35.00
MCA	40085	Stuntman, The	LD	U.S.		$35.00
CBS/Fox	6969-80	Subway	LD	U.S.	1987	$35.00
Image	ID7917EN	Success Is the Best Revenge	LD	U.S.	1985	$15.00
Vestron	LV5117	Sudden Death	LD	U.S.	1986	$30.00
Columbia	CLD5560	Suddenly Last Summer	LD	U.S.	1992	$30.00
Nelson	75666	Summer Camp Nightmare	LD	U.S.	1987	$35.00
Nelson	17045	Summer Lovers	LD	U.S.	1983	$35.00
Paramount	LV1785	Summer Rental	LD	U.S.	1986	$30.00
Paramount	1518	Summer School	LD	U.S.	1988	$35.00
Criterion	CC1284L	Sunday Bloody Sunday	LD	U.S.	1992	$50.00
Image	ID6133TS	Sunset	LD	U.S.		$30.00
Paramount	LV4927	Sunset Boulevard	LD	U.S.	1984	$30.00
		Superfight: Hagler vs. Leonard	LD	U.S.		$20.00
Image	I-5024	Supergirl	LD	U.S.	1985	65
		Superman (Animated)	LD	U.S.		$80.00
Warner Home Video	11120LV	Superman II	LD	U.S.	1983	$30.00
Walt Disney	1069AS	Superted Vol. 1	LD	U.S.	1990	$30.00
Walt Disney	1070AS	Superted Vol. 2	LD	U.S.	1990	$30.00
Pioneer		Supertuner	DJ/LD	U.S.		$100.00
Nelson	21785	Sure Thing	LD	U.S.	1985	$35.00
Columbia	VLD3382	Survivors, The	LD	U.S.	1984	$30.00
Image	ID6946TU	Susan Slept Here	LD	U.S.		$30.00
Image	ID6404TU	Suspicion!	LD	U.S.		$50.00
Nelson	16055	Swamp Thing	LD	U.S.	1983	$60.00
Image	ID7283SP	Swan Lake	LD	U.S.		$30.00
Image	ID7711MN	Sweat Country	LD	U.S.		$25.00
Image	ID7605IV	Sweetie	LD	U.S.		$30.00
Columbia	VLD5568	Swept Away	LD	U.S.	1983	$60.00
CBS/Fox	1110-80	Swimmer, The	LD	U.S.	1974	$50.00
Discovision	32-003	Swimming: Breast Stroke and Butterfly	LD	U.S.	1979	$40.00
Discovision	32-002	Swimming: Freestyle and Back Stroke	LD	U.S.	1979	$40.00
Image	ID6529VE	Swimwear Illustrated	LD	U.S.		$30.00
Criterion	CC1106L	Swingtime	LD	U.S.	1988	$75.00
	CAV version.					
Criterion	CC1200L	Swingtime	LD	U.S.	1990	$40.00
	CLV version.					
Walt Disney	53AS	Swiss Family Robinson	LD	U.S.	1983	$25.00
WHV/HBO	90550	Switch	LD	U.S.	1992	$30.00
Walt Disney	229AS	Sword and the Stone	LD	U.S.		$35.00
	First issue					
Walt Disney	229AS	Sword and the Stone	LD	U.S.	1986	$40.00
MCA	13-010	Sword & the Scorecer	LD	U.S.	1983	$35.00
Republic	LV24021	Swordsman, The	LD	U.S.	1993	$30.00
Columbia	VLD30476	Sylvester	LD	U.S.	1985	$30.00
		Sylvia Scarlett	LD	U.S.		$25.00
Lorimar	LV412	T.V.'s Greatest Hits	LD	U.S.	1987	$40.00
CBS	7043	Table for Five	LD	U.S.	1983	$20.00
Republic	LV24245	Tabor the Great	LD	U.S.	1992	$25.00
Image	IDVL5180	Tai-Pan	LD	U.S.	1987	$40.00
Image	ID7663PR	Tailspin	LD	U.S.		$30.00
	MP-020U	Takanaka World	LD	U.S.		$25.00
Sony		Take Five	DJ/LD	U.S.	1991	
Magnetic Video		Take the Money And Run	LD	U.S.†	1982	$25.00
CBS/Fox	8007-80	Take The Money and Run	LD	U.S.	1985	$25.00
Image	ID6281SO	Tale of Jeremy Fisher/The Tale of Peter Rabit	LD	U.S.		$30.00
Image	ID6807HB	Tales From the Crypt Vol.1	LD	U.S.		$30.00
Image	ID6906IV	Tales From the Dark Side Vol. 1	LD	U.S.		$30.00
Image	ID6940IV	Tales From the Dark Side Vol. 2	LD	U.S.		$30.00
Image	ID6941IV	Tales From the Dark Side Vol. 3	LD	U.S.		$30.00
Image	ID6942IV	Tales From the Dark Side Vol. 4	LD	U.S.		$30.00
Columbia	30780	Talk of the Town	LD	U.S.	1987	$30.00
Columbia	90886	Tall Guy	LD	U.S.	1991	$30.00
Image	ID6544TU	Tall in the Saddle	LD	U.S.		$50.00
Columbia	30110	Taming of the Shrew	LD	U.S.	1984	$30.00
Psedition	PSE91-30	Taming of the Shrew	LD	U.S.	1992	$50.00
Republic	LV24050	Tampopo	LD	U.S.	1989	$25.00
Image	ID6623TS	Tap	LD	U.S.		$30.00
Image	ID6516PA	Tape Heads	LD	U.S.		$30.00
Magnetic Video		Taps	LD	U.S.†	1984	$30.00
RCA/Columbia	VLD5920	Taxi Driver	LD	U.S.	1983	$35.00

Label	Catalog Number	Title	Type	Country	Year	Value
Criterion	CC1218L	Taxi Driver	LD	U.S.	1990	$100.00
	CAV version.					
Criterion	CC1218L	Taxi Driver	LD	U.S.	1990	$50.00
	CLV version.					
Columbia	VLD5920	Taxi Driver	LD	U.S.	1992	$30.00
Lumivision	LVD8903	Taxing Woman, A	LD	U.S.	1989	$40.00
CBS	4728	Teachers	LD	U.S	1985	$50.00
Paramount	LV2350	Teen Wolf	LD	U.S.	1985	$40.00
Image	ID7519IV	Teenage Mutant Ninja Turtles	LD	U.S.	1990	$15.00
Image	ID7609IV	Teenage Mutant Ninja Turtles: The Movie	LD	U.S.	1990	$20.00
Image	ID6448IV	Teenage Mutant Ninja Turtles Vol. 1	LD	U.S.	1990	$15.00
Image	ID6325IV	Teenage Mutant Ninja Turtles Vol. 2	LD	U.S.	1990	$15.00
Image	ID6416IV	Teenage Mutant Ninja Turtles Vol. 3	LD	U.S.	1990	$15.00
Image	ID7643IV	Teenage Mutant Ninja Turtles Vol. 4	LD	U.S.	1990	$15.00
Image		Ten From Your Show of Shows	LD	U.S.		$40.00
Cannon	31134	Ten Little Indians	LD	U.S.	1990	$25.00
		Ten Rollington Place	LD	U.S.		$80.00
Columbia	31000	Ten Wanted Men	LD	U.S.	1989	$30.00
HBO	1640	Tender Mercies	LD	U.S.	1985	$25.00
Cannon	32049	Terminal Bliss	LD	U.S.	1992	$30.00
Image	ID6637NW	Terminal Force	LD	U.S.		$15.00
Live	LD48864-4WS	Terminator 2	LTD/LD	U.S.	1991	$120.00
	Boxed set with CAV LD and booklet					
Pioneer	PSE-82997-6WS3	Terminator 2: T2-SE Pioneer	LD	U.S.	1993	$150.00
	3 LD first Pressing with silver "T2" logo.					
Pioneer		Terminator 2: T2-SE Promotional Trailer	DJ/8"LD	U.S.	1991	$50.00
Pioneer	VSD-001	Terminator 2: Teaser & Trailer	DJ/CDV	U.S.	1991	$100.00
Image	ID8316HD	Terminator, The	LD	U.S.		$35.00
HBO	2535	Terminator, The	LD	U.S.	1985	$35.00
Paramount	LV1407-2	Terms of Endearment	LD	U.S.	1984	$40.00
Republic	LV27820	Terror by Night	LD	U.S.	1990	$25.00
CBS	1665	Terror Train	LD	U.S.	1988	$50.00
Columbia		Tess	LD	U.S.	1982	$30.00
Columbia	VLD5945	Tess	LD	U.S.	1985	$30.00
Paramount	LV1739	Testament	LD	U.S.	1984	$30.00
Walt Disney	142AS	Tex	LD	U.S.	1983	$35.00
Vestron	ZL034	Texas Chainsaw Massacre	LD	U.S.	1983	$30.00
75016		Texas Chainsaw Massacre 3: Leatherface	LD	U.S.		$30.00
HBO		Texas Cheerleader Scandal	LD	U.S.	1994	$175.00
Nelson	7778	Texasville	LD	U.S.	1991	$35.00
Nelson	31075	That Hamilton Woman	LD	U.S.	1985	$50.00
Criterion	CC1223L	That Obscure Object	LD	U.S.	1990	$50.00
Image	ID7870ME	That Summer of White Roses	LD	U.S.	1990	$20.00
Republic	LV24115	That Touch of Mink	LD	U.S.	1993	$25.00
Paramount	LV1954	That Was Then, This Is Now	LD	U.S.	1986	$30.00
MGM/UA	ML10007	That's Entertainment	LD	U.S.	1983	$35.00
MGM/UA	ML100007	That's Entertainment	LD	U.S.	1987	$40.00
MGM/UA	ML103059	That's Entertainment	LTD/LD	U.S.	1994	$100.00
Vestron Video	LV5203	That's Life	LD	U.S.	1987	$35.00
Image	ID7052TU	That's Right You're Wrong	LD	U.S.	1990	$30.00
Image	ID5259LO	That's Singing	LD	U.S.	1990	$30.00
Image	ID6408MG	Theater of Blood	LD	U.S.		$150.00
Criterion	CC1012L	Theatre of Imagination	LD	U.S.	1989	$40.00
CBS	1086	There's No Business	LD	U.S.	1989	$20.00
Nelson	30685	These Three	LD	U.S.	1985	$35.00
Vestron	LV5005	They All Laughed	LD	U.S.	1983	$30.00
MGM/UA	ML102473	They Died With Their Boots On	LD	U.S.	1992	$40.00
Nelson	30695	They Got Me Covered	LD	U.S.	1986	$35.00
		They Live	LD	Japan		$80.00
	Letterbox version.					

They Live – (MCA 40843)

Label	Catalog Number	Title	Type	Country	Year	Value
MCA	40843	They Live	LD	U.S.	1989	$45.00
Image	ID6979TU	They Live by Night	LD	U.S.		$90.00
Image	ID7567NE	They Made Me a Criminal	LD	U.S.	1990	$30.00
Magnetic Video		They Shoot Horses, Don't They?	LD	U.S.†	1982	$30.00
CBS	8004	They Shoot Horses, Don't They?	LD	U.S.	1985	$40.00
Fox Video	0835685	They Shoot Horses, Don't They?	LTD/LD	U.S.	1996	$130.00
	LD set and CD in box. Limited to 2,500 copies.					
		They Won't Believe Me	LD	U.S.		$40.00
Image	ID6468MG	Thief	LD	U.S.		$30.00
Nelson	31085	Thief of Bagdad	LD	U.S.	1985	$50.00
Image	ID6860HB	Thief of Bagdad	LD	U.S.	1990	$30.00
Paramount	LV1660	Thief of Hearts	LD	U.S.	1985	$30.00
Image	ID6568HB	Thin Blue Line, The	LD	U.S.	1990	$30.00
Paramount	LV32843	Thing Called Love	LD	U.S.	1994	$35.00
Vid-America	994	Thing, The (Original)	LD	U.S.	1985	$30.00
RCA/Columbia	VLD5948	Things Are Tough All Over	LD	U.S.	1983	$35.00
Columbia	VLD5948	Things Are Tough All Over	LD	U.S.	1993	$30.00
Columbia	35011	Things Change	LD	U.S.	1989	$30.00
		Things to Come	LD	Japan	1986	$200.00
Image	ID7851ME	Think Big	LD	U.S.	1990	$30.00
Criterion	CC1105L	Third Man, The	LD	U.S.	1989	$40.00
Columbia	70316	Third Solution	LD	U.S.	1990	$15.00
Criterion	CC1103L	Thirty-Nine Steps	LD	U.S.	1989	$40.00
Image	ID 5126	This Gun's for Hire	LD	U.S.	1987	$30.00
Nelson	20185	This Is Spinal Tap	LD	U.S.	1984	$60.00
		This Land Is Mine	LD	U.S.		$30.00
Discovision		Thoroughly Modern Millie	LD	U.S.	1979	$40.00
CBS	1033	Those Magnificent Men in Their Flying Machines	LD	U.S.	1986	$30.00
HBO	TVL0007	Three Amigos	LD	U.S.	1987	$35.00
Criterion	CC1248L	Three by Scorsese	LD	U.S.	1991	$50.00
		Three Caballeros	LD	Japan		$65.00
Walt Disney	091CS	Three Caballeros	LD	U.S.	1989	$40.00
	CAV Version					
Discovision	P11-510	Three Days of the Condor	LD	U.S.	1979	$40.00
Psedition	PSE91-15	Three for the Show	LD	U.S.	1991	$40.00
Walt Disney	950AS	Three Fugitives	LD	U.S.	1990	$30.00
	Distributed by Pioneer.					
	VL5192	Three Men and a Cradle	LD	U.S.	1990	$30.00
Image	ID7047TU	Three Musketeers (1935)	LD	U.S.		$50.00
Columbia	VLD5947	Three Stooges Vol. 1	LD	U.S.	1992	$50.00
Image	ID 6717RC	Three Stooges Vol. 10	LD	U.S.		$35.00
Image	ID 6618RC	Three Stooges Vol. 11	LD	U.S.		$35.00
Columbia	30235	Three Stooges Vol. 2	LD	U.S.	1985	$50.00
Columbia	90766	Three Stooges Vol. 26 & 28	LD	U.S.	1990	$50.00
Columbia	90776	Three Stooges Vol. 27 & 29	LD	U.S.	1990	$50.00
Image	ID 6371RC	Three Stooges Vol. 3	LD	U.S.		$50.00
Image	ID 6301RC	Three Stooges Vol. 4	LD	U.S.		$50.00
Image	ID 6385RC	Three Stooges Vol. 5	LD	U.S.		$50.00
Image	ID 6489RC	Three Stooges Vol. 7	LD	U.S.		$50.00
Image	ID 6639RC	Three Stooges Vol. 8	LD	U.S.		$50.00
Image	ID 6716RC	Three Stooges Vol. 9	LD	U.S.		$50.00
Psedition	PSE91-31	Three Worlds of Gulliver	LD	U.S.	1992	$50.00
Criterion	CC1139L	Three-Penny Opera	LD	U.S.	1988	$40.00
		Throw Momma From the Train	LD	U.S.		$30.00
CBS	6396	Thumbelina	LD	U.S.	1984	$25.00
Columbia	90596	Thunder and the Mud	LD	U.S.	1990	$30.00
CBS	4611	Thunderball	LD	U.S.	1983	
Image	ID6555IV	Thunderbirds: Countdown to Disaster	LD	U.S.		$60.00
Image	ID6499IV	Thunderbirds: In Outerspace	LD	U.S.		$60.00
CBS	4547	Thunderbolt and Lightfoot	LD	U.S.	1985	$15.00
Image	ID7208SG	Thunderground	LD	U.S.		$30.00
Image	ID7133VK	Thursday's Game	LD	U.S.		$30.00
Lucasfilm		THX Laser Disc Sampler	DJ/LD	U.S.	1991	$200.00
Columbia	90906	Tie Me Up! Tie Me Down	LD	U.S.	1990	$30.00
Image	ID7155SO	Tiger Warsaw	LD	U.S.		$30.00
Vidmark	LDCVM5701	Tigress	LD	U.S.	1993	$35.00
Vestron Video	LV3005	Till Marriage Do Us Part	LD	U.S.	1982	$35.00
Republic	LV24212	Tillie's Punctured Romance	LD	U.S.	1991	$25.00
Paramount	LV2310	Time Bandits	LD	U.S.	1982	$30.00
Nelson	77366	Time Guardian	LD	U.S.	1990	$35.00
MGM/UA	ML100152	Time Machine	LD	U.S.	1984	$35.00
Nelson	75706	Time of Destiny	LD	U.S.	1989	$35.00
Columbia	50306	Time of the Gypsies	LD	U.S.	1990	$30.00
Image	ID8383HA	Timeless Tales From Hallmark Vol. 2	LD	U.S.		$30.00
Image	ID5346PA	Timerider	LD	U.S.		$30.00
Pacific Arts	PAV12528	Timerider	LD	U.S.	1985	$40.00
Walt Disney	571AS	Tin Men	LD	U.S.	1988	$35.00
CBS	1336	To Be or Not To Be	LD	U.S.	1984	$30.00
Paramount	LV6308	To Catch a Thief	LD	U.S.	1982	$30.00
		To Die For	LD	U.S.		$75.00
Columbia	91166	To Die Standing	LD	U.S.	1991	$30.00
Discovision		To Kill a Mockingbird	LD	U.S.	1979	$40.00
Columbia	50286	To Kill a Priest	LD	U.S.	1990	$30.00
Vestron Video	LV5123	To Live and Die in L.A.	LD	U.S.	1986	$75.00
Nelson	902116	Toby McTeague	LD	U.S.	1987	$35.00
Columbia	32007	Tokyo Joe	LD	U.S.	1989	$60.00
MGM/UA	ML102219	Tom and Jerry Classics	LD	U.S.	1991	$35.00
MGM/UA	ML100019	Tom and Jerry Volume 1	LD	U.S.	1983	$25.00
MGM/UA	ML100146	Tom and Jerry Volume 2	LD	U.S.	1984	$35.00
Image	ID7011IV	Tom, Dick and Harry	LD	U.S.		$30.00
MGM/UA	ML100019	Tom & Jerry Cartoon Festival Vol. 1	LD	U.S.		$30.00
MGM/UA	ML100146	Tom & Jerry Cartoon Festival Vol. 2	LD	U.S.		$30.00
Magnetic Video		Tom Jones	LD	U.S.†	1982	$25.00
Discovision		Tom Sawyer	LD	U.S.	1979	$40.00
		Tomb of Ligeia, The	LD	U.S.		$80.00
Republic	LV24184	Tomcat	LD	U.S.	1993	$25.00
RCA/Columbia	VLD5951	Tommy	LD	U.S.	1983	$35.00
Columbia	VLD5951	Tommy	LD	U.S.	1993	$40.00
		Tony Rose	LD	U.S.		$40.00
		Too Many Girls	LD	U.S.		$30.00
Columbia	90826	Too Much Sun	LD	U.S.	1991	$30.00
RCA/Columbia	VLD5955	Tootsie	LD	U.S.	1984	$35.00
Columbia	VLD5955	Tootsie	LD	U.S.	1992	$30.00
Criterion	CC1264L	Tootsie	LD	U.S.	1992	$80.00
Paramount	LV1692	Top Gun	LD	U.S.	1987	$30.00
Vid-America	LL929	Top Hat	LD	U.S.	1985	$30.00
Paramount	LV1567	Top Secret	LD	U.S.	1985	$25.00
		Topper	LD	U.S.		$80.00
CBS	1017	Tora! Tora! Tora!	LD	U.S.	1982	$20.00
Magnetic Video		Tora! Tora! Tora!	LD	U.S.†	1982	$30.00
Columbia	32829	Torch Song Trilogy	LD	U.S.	1989	$30.00
Nelson	75905	Torchlight	LD	U.S.	1985	$35.00
Image	ID7617HB	Torrents of Spring	LD	U.S.		$30.00
Republic	LV24265	Total Exposure	LD	U.S.	1991	$30.00
Discovision		Total Fitness in Thirty Minutes A Week	LD	U.S.		$40.00
Image	ID7779IV	Total Recall	LD	U.S.		$30.00
		Touch & Go	LD	U.S.		$30.00
Discovision		Touch of Love	LD	U.S.		$40.00
MCA	30-001	Touch of Love	LD	U.S.	1985	$30.00
Walt Disney	511AS	Tough Guys	LD	U.S.	1987	$35.00
		Tough Guys Don't Dance	LD	U.S.		$30.00
Image	ID5250NW	Tour of Duty	LD	U.S.		$20.00
Image	ID6093NW	Tour of Duty II: Bravo Company	LD	U.S.		$20.00
Image	ID6755NW	Tour of Duty: The Hill	LD	U.S.		$20.00
Full Moon	LV13002	Tourist Trap	LD	U.S.	1993	$25.00
CBS	C1071	Towering Inferno, The	LD	U.S.	1989	$25.00
		Town With a Party	LD	U.S.		$65.00
Image	ID7552VE	Toxic Avenger, The	LD	U.S.		$90.00
Vestron Video	LL9953	Toxic Avenger, The	LD	U.S.	1987	$50.00
Image	IG-5016	Toy Soldier	LD	U.S.	1985	$25.00
Columbia	70626	Toy Soldier	LD	U.S.	1991	$25.00
Disney	8847	Toy Story	LD	U.S.	1996	$30.00
	CLV version.					
Disney	8847CS	Toy Story	LTD/LD	U.S.	1996	$125.00
	4 LD boxed set in box with book and lenticular.					
RCA/Columbia	VLD5975	Toy, The	LD	U.S.	1983	$35.00
Columbia	VLD5975	Toy, The	LD	U.S.	1993	$30.00
Paramount	LV1551	Trading Places	LD	U.S.	1984	$30.00
Image	ID8280IV	Tragedy of Flight 103: The Inside Story	LD	U.S.		$45.00
Discovision		Tragedy of the Red Salmon	LD	U.S.	1979	$40.00
CBS	4710	Trail of the Pink Panther	LD	U.S.	1983	$15.00
Vestron	LV5086	Trancers	LD	U.S.	1985	$30.00
		Transformations	LD	U.S.		$30.00
Image	ID8166IV	Transformers: Five Faces Of Darkness	LD	U.S.		$20.00

Label	Catalog Number	Title	Type	Country	Year	Value
Republic	LV27860	Trapper County War	LD	U.S.	1991	$30.00
Image	ID8346TU	Treasure Island	LD	U.S.		$30.00
CBS	4639	Treasure of Sierra Madre	LD	U.S.	1983	$20.00
CBS/Fox	1517-80	Tree Grows in Brooklyn, A	LD	U.S.	1990	$50.00
MCA	40957	Tremors	LD	U.S.	1990	$25.00
VL6003		Tribute	LD	U.S.		$20.00
Nelson	13415	Trip to Bountiful	LD	U.S.	1986	$50.00
Columbia	90746	Tripwire	LD	U.S.	1990	$30.00
Columbia	59066	Triumph of the Spirit	LD	U.S.	1990	$30.00
Walt Disney	122AS	Tron	LD	U.S.	1982	$50.00
Columbia	10296	Troop of Beverly Hills	LD	U.S.	1989	$30.00
Nelson	901096	Trouble in Mind	LD	U.S.	1986	$35.00
RCA/Columbia	30250	Trouble With Angels, The	LD	U.S.	1985	$35.00
Columbia	30250	Trouble With Angels, The	LD	U.S.	1992	$30.00
Columbia	35012	True Believers	LD	U.S.	1989	$30.00
Image	ID6515FR	True Blood	LD	U.S.		$20.00
MGM/UA	ML100145	True Confessions	LD	U.S.	1983	$35.00
Paramount	LV6833-2	True Grit	LD	U.S.	1983	$36.00
Image	ID8252HB	True in Tomorrow	LD	U.S.		$20.00
MGM/UA	ML101763	True Love	LD	U.S.		$20.00
Republic	LV24205	Trust	LD	U.S.	1992	$25.00
Vidmark	LDCVM5395	Truth or Die	LD	U.S.	1993	$35.00
Republic	PA-24206	Tumbleweeds	LD	U.S.	1991	$25.00
Criterion	CC1170L	Tunes of Glory	LD	U.S.	1989	$40.00
Image	ID6564VE	Tunnel, The	LD	U.S.		$30.00
Cannon	31156	Turn of the Screw	LD	U.S.	1990	$25.00
Walt Disney	911AS	Turner and Hooch	LD	U.S.	1990	$25.00
	Distributed by Pioneer.					
Magnetic Video		Turning Point	LD	U.S.†	1984	$30.00
Vestron	LV5173	Turtle Diary	LD	U.S.	1986	$30.00
Image	ID7824MN	Tusks	LD	U.S.		$30.00
Criterion	CC1127L	Twelve Angry Men	LD	U.S.	1988	$40.00
Image	I-5073	Twelve Chairs	LD	U.S.		$30.00
		Twelve O'Clock High	LD	U.S.		$150.00
Psedition	PSE91-07	Twenty Million Miles From Earth	LD	U.S.	1991	$35.00
MS182-22BT		Twenty-Four Heures Du Mans	LD	U.S.		$25.00
Columbia	91106	Twenty-One	LD	U.S.	1992	$30.00
Nelson	7745-80	Twice Dead	LD	U.S.	1989	$35.00
Vestron Video	VL5119	Twice in a Lifetime	LD	U.S.	1986	$35.00
		Twilight Zone Vol. 1	LD	Japan		$60.00
		Twilight Zone Vol. 10	LD	Japan		$60.00
		Twilight Zone Vol. 11	LD	Japan		$60.00
		Twilight Zone Vol. 2	LD	Japan		$60.00
		Twilight Zone Vol. 3	LD	Japan		$60.00
		Twilight Zone Vol. 4	LD	Japan		$60.00
		Twilight Zone Vol. 5	LD	Japan		$60.00
		Twilight Zone Vol. 6	LD	Japan		$60.00
		Twilight Zone Vol. 7	LD	Japan		$60.00
		Twilight Zone Vol. 8	LD	Japan		$60.00
		Twilight Zone Vol. 9	LD	Japan		$60.00
CBS	7653	Twilight's Last Gleaming	LD	U.S.	1989	$25.00
U.S. Magna	SSLM-3036	Twin Angels, Volume 1	LP	U.S.		$30.00
	Japanese anime CD-ROM.					
U.S. Magna	SSLM-3037	Twin Angels, Volume 2	LP	U.S.		$30.00
	Japanese anime CD-ROM.					
MCA	40066	Twist of Fate	LD	U.S.	1984	$35.00
Image	ID7606IV	Twisted Obsession	LD	U.S.		$20.00
Image	ID7108VE	Twister	LD	U.S.		$30.00
		Two Evil Eyes	LD	U.S.		$50.00
Columbia	60966	Two Moon Junction	LD	U.S.	1989	$30.00
CBS	1339	Two of a Kind	LD	U.S.	1984	$25.00
Image	ID6644RC	Two Road Together	LD	U.S.		$30.00
Pioneer		UFO Box Set Vol. 1	LTD/LD	Japan		$250.00
	4 LD boxed set.					
Pioneer		UFO Box Set Vol. 2	LTD/LD	Japan		$250.00
	4 LD boxed set.					
Pioneer		UFO Box Set Vol. 3	LTD/LD	Japan		$250.00
	4 LD boxed set.					
Pioneer		UFO Box Set Vol. 4	LTD/LD	Japan		$250.00
	4 LD boxed set.					
Image	ID7246TY	UFO Vol. 1	LD	U.S.		$120.00
Image	ID7247TY	UFO Vol. 2	LD	U.S.		$120.00
Image	ID7247TY	UFO Vol. 3	LD	U.S.		$120.00
Image	ID7249TY	UFO Vol. 4	LD	U.S.		$120.00
Image	ID9501OR	UHF	LD	U.S.		$20.00
Columbia	91486	Unborn, The	LD	U.S.	1991	$15.00
Columbia	91986	Uncaged, The	LD	U.S.	1991	$30.00
Paramount	LV1657	Uncommon Valor	LD	U.S.	1984	$30.00
Image	ID6559NW	Under Boardwalk	LD	U.S.		$20.00
Image	ID8171VA	Under Capricorn	LD	U.S.		$20.00
Vestron	VL5033	Under Fire	LD	U.S.	1984	$50.00
Nelson	77706	Under the Baltimore Clock	LD	U.S.	1990	$35.00
Image	ID8430SO	Underground Terror	LD	U.S.		$30.00
Republic	LV25050	Undersea Kingdom	LD	U.S.	1990	$25.00
		Understudy, The	LD	U.S.		$30.00
CBS	1340	Unfaithfully Yours	LD	U.S.	1984	$35.00
		Unholy	LD	U.S.		$30.00
Image	ID6086NS	Univited, The	LD	U.S.		$15.00
		Unnamable	LD	U.S.		$50.00
Image	ID8426SO	Unremarkable Life	LD	U.S.		$15.00
Nelson	77496	Unsettled Land	LD	U.S.	1989	$35.00
MGM/UA	ML100578	Unsinkable Molly Brown, The	LD	U.S.		$20.00
Image	ID5297PA	Unsinkable Sea Otter	LD	U.S.		$30.00
Discovision		Unsinkable Sea Otter	LD	U.S.	1979	$40.00
Paramount	LV8966	Up in Smoke	LD	U.S.	1985	$30.00
Vestron	LV5043	Up the Creek	LD	U.S.	1984	$30.00
Image	ID6625IV	Up Your Alley	LD	U.S.		$20.00
Paramount	LV1285	Urban Cowboy	LD	U.S.	1985	$36.00
U.S. Magna	SSLM-3008	Urotsukidoji III, Volume 2	LP	U.S.		$25.00
	Japanese anime CD-ROM.					
U.S. Magna	SSLM-3009	Urotsukidoji III, Volume 3	LP	U.S.		$25.00
	Japanese anime CD-ROM.					
U.S. Magna	SSLM-3010	Urotsukidoji III, Volume 4	LP	U.S.		$25.00
	Japanese anime CD-ROM.					
U.S. Magna	SSLM-3007	Urotsukidoji III, Volume I	LP	U.S.		$25.00
	Japanese anime CD-ROM.					
U.S. Magna	CD9050	Urotsukidoji: Legend Of the Overfiend	LP	U.S.		$30.00
	Japanese anime CD-ROM.					
	R0034	Urotsukidoji: Perfect Collection	LTD/LD	Japan	1994	$120.00
	3 LD set.					
U.S. Magna	EE1024	Urotsukidoji: Perfect Collection	LP	U.S.		$70.00
	Japanese anime CD-ROM.					
		Urotsukidoji: Perfect Collection	LTD/LD	U.S.	1994	$100.00
	3 LD set.					
Columbia	VLD6000	Used Cars	LD	U.S.	1984	$30.00
Vestron Video	VL5059	Utilities	LD	U.S.	1985	$35.00
Warner Pioneer	NJL-11433	V, (T.V. Series) Vol. 1	LD	Japan	1987	$425.00
	5 LD boxed set.					
Warner Pioneer	NJL-11576	V (T.V. Series) Vol. 2	LTD/LD	Japan	1987	$350.00
Vestron Video	VL5175	Valet Girls	LD	U.S.	1987	$35.00
Vestron Video	VL5016	Valley Girls	LD	U.S.	1983	$35.00
		Vamp	LD	U.S.		$80.00
CBS	1028	Vanishing Point	LD	U.S.	1990	$40.00
Discovision		VD: The Hidden Epidemic	LD	U.S.	1979	$40.00
		Velvet Vampire	LD	U.S.		$30.00
Image	ID7102VK	Vengeance	LD	U.S.		$20.00
Criterion	CC1134L	Vengeance Is Mine	LD	U.S.	1988	$90.00
U.S. Magna	SSLM-3021	Venus Wars, The	LP	U.S.		$25.00
	Japanese anime CD-ROM.					
CBS	1188	Verdict, The	LD	U.S.	1983	$30.00
Nelson	77316	Vern Miller	LD	U.S.	1989	$30.00
Nelson	20155	Vice Squad	LD	U.S.	1983	$35.00
Columbia	35007	Vice Versa	LD	U.S.	1988	$20.00
MGM/UA	ML100151	Victor/Victoria	LD	U.S.		$20.00
Nelson	75725	Victory at Sea Vol. 1-3	LD	U.S.	1985	$50.00
Nelson	75755	Victory at Sea Vol. 10-12	LD	U.S.	1985	$50.00
Nelson	75765	Victory at Sea Vol. 13-15	LD	U.S.	1985	$50.00
Nelson	75775	Victory at Sea Vol. 16-18	LD	U.S.	1985	$50.00
Nelson	75785	Victory at Sea Vol. 19-21	LD	U.S.	1985	$50.00
Nelson	75795	Victory at Sea Vol. 22-24	LD	U.S.	1985	$50.00
Nelson	75805	Victory at Sea Vol. 25-26	LD	U.S.	1985	$50.00
Nelson	75735	Victory at Sea Vol. 4-6	LD	U.S.	1985	$50.00
Nelson	75745	Victory at Sea Vol. 7-9	LD	U.S.	1985	$50.00
MCA	11-018	Videodrome	LD	U.S.	1983	$120.00
Columbia	59196	Vietnam Texas	LD	U.S.	1990	$30.00
Nelson	76345	Vietnam War Vol. 1	LD	U.S.	1985	$50.00
Nelson	76355	Vietnam War Vol. 2	LD	U.S.	1985	$50.00
Nelson	76365	Vietnam War Vol. 3	LD	U.S.	1985	$50.00
Nelson	76375	Vietnam War Vol. 4	LD	U.S.	1985	$50.00
Nelson	76385	Vietnam War Vol. 5	LD	U.S.	1985	$50.00
Nelson	76395	Vietnam War Vol. 6	LD	U.S.	1985	$50.00
Image	ID6798CS	Vincent, Francois, Paul and the Others	LD	U.S.		$30.00
8002		Vincent & Theo	LD	U.S.		$20.00
		Vineyard, The	LD	U.S.		$40.00
Psedition	PSE91-16	Violent Men	LD	U.S.	1992	$50.00
Columbia	30690	Violets Are Blue	LD	U.S.	1986	$30.00
Columbia	77206	Virgin High	LD	U.S.	1991	$30.00
Image	ID6930VK	Visitors, The	LD	U.S.	1990	$15.00
CBS	1352	Viva Sapata	LD	U.S.	1989	$90.00
Discovision		Volcano/San Andreas Fault	LD	U.S.	1979	$40.00
Image	I5051	Voltron Castle of Lions	LD	U.S.	1986	$40.00
Image Entertainment	I5050	Voltron, Planet Doom	LD	U.S.	1986	$40.00
HBO	TVL2983	Volunteers	LD	U.S.	1988	$30.00
Magnetic Video		Von Ryan's Express	LD	U.S.†	1984	$30.00
Magnetic Video		Voyage to the Bottom of the Sea	LD	U.S.†	1984	$50.00
Pioneer	PILF1996	Voyage to the Bottom of the Sea Volume 1	LD	Japan	1995	$250.00
	4 LD boxed set.					
Pioneer	PILF1997	Voyage to the Bottom of the Sea Volume 2	LD	Japan	1995	$250.00
	4 LD boxed set.					
Pioneer		Voyage to the Bottom of the Sea Volume 3	LD	Japan	1995	$250.00
	4 LD boxed set.					
Pioneer	PILF 2123	Voyage to the Bottom of the Sea Volume 4	LD	Japan	1996	$250.00
	4 LD boxed set.					
Pioneer	PILF 2205	Voyage to the Bottom of the Sea Volume 5	LD	Japan	1996	$350.00
	5 LD boxed set.					
Pioneer	PILF2207	Voyage to the Bottom of the Sea Volume 7	LTD/LD	Japan	1996	$250.00
	3 LD boxed set.					
Image	ID6551RC	Wackiest Ship in the Army	LD	U.S.		$40.00
Image	ID7530VE	Wacko	LD	U.S.		$20.00
Image	ID7001TU	Wagon Master	LD	U.S.		$30.00
Columbia	59286	Waiting for the Light	LD	U.S.	1991	$30.00
Republic	LV25586	Wake of the Red	LD	U.S.	1993	$25.00
		Walking on Air	LD	U.S.		$30.00
Lightning	LL950	Walking Tall	LD	U.S.	1985	$50.00
Lighting Video	LL9911	Walking Tall Final Chapter	LD	U.S.	1985	$50.00
Lighting Video	LL9910	Walking Tall Part 2	LD	U.S.	1985	$50.00
CBS		Wall Street	LD	U.S.	1988	$15.00
Walt Disney	92AS	Walt Disney Christmas	LD	U.S.	1984	$40.00
Walt Disney	394AS	Walt Disney Mini Classics	LD	U.S.	1988	$30.00
Walt Disney	394AS	Walt Disney Mini Classics	LD	U.S.	1988	$40.00

Wanted Dead Or Alive – (Image ID-5201)

Label	Catalog Number	Title	Type	Country	Year	Value
Image	ID5201	Wanted Dead or Alive	LD	U.S.	1987	$50.00
Paramount	LV5626-2	War And Peace	LD	U.S.	1985	$40.00
CBS/Fox	4714-80	War Games	LD	U.S.	1983	$35.00
Image	ID6645RC	War Is Over	LD	U.S.		$20.00
		War Lover	LD	U.S.		$100.00
Paramount	LV5303	War of the Worlds	LD	U.S.	1982	$20.00
	CLV version.					
Image	ID7113HB	War Party	LD	U.S.		$30.00
Image	ID6932VK	Warlords	LD	U.S.		$30.00
Image	ID7118FL	Warm Nights on a Slow Moving Train	LD	U.S.		$20.00
Columbia	90676	Warm Summer Rain	LD	U.S.	1990	$30.00
Vestron	LV5060	Warrior and the Sorceress	LD	U.S.	1985	$30.00
Image	ID7541VE	Warrior Queen	LD	U.S.		$20.00

Label	Catalog Number	Title	Type	Country	Year	Value
Paramount	LV1122	Warriors, The	LD	U.S.	1985	$30.00
Image	ID77382IV	Watchers, The	LD	U.S.		$20.00
Promo		Waterfall Display	LD	U.S.	1986	191
Columbia	30463	Watermelon Man	LD	U.S.	1985	$30.00
Nelson	40185	Wavelength	LD	U.S.	1984	$35.00
Image	ID6293VE	Waxworks	LD	U.S.		$20.00
Discovision		Way Home, The	LD	U.S.	1979	$40.00
	SF070-5279	Way We Were, The	LD	Japan		$100.00
Columbia	VLD6040	Way We Were, The	LD	U.S.	1984	$30.00
Psedition	PSE91-19	Way We Were, The	LD	U.S.	1991	$50.00
Image	ID6264RC	We All Loved Each Other So Much	LD	U.S.		$30.00
Image	ID7965PA	We Shall Overcome	LD	U.S.		$20.00
Lumivision	LVD8902	We the Living	LD	U.S.	1989	$25.00
Nelson	77376	We Think of the World of You	LD	U.S.	1989	$35.00
Paramount	LV5414	We're No Angels	LD	U.S.	1984	$30.00
Columbia	90506	Wedding Band	LD	U.S.	1990	$30.00
Image	ID6576HB	Weeds	LD	U.S.		$30.00
Image	ID6818IV	Weekend At Bernie's	LD	U.S.	1989	$25.00
Vestron Video	VL5045	Weekend Pass	LD	U.S.	1985	$35.00
Image	ID6732RH	Weird Cartoons Vols. 1 & 2	LD	U.S.		$30.00
Image	ID7214VE	Welcome Home	LD	U.S.		$30.00
Image	ID7224IV	Welcome to Spring Break	LD	U.S.		$20.00
Magnetic Video		West Side Story	LD	U.S.†	1982	$30.00
Polyram	072 206-1	West Side Story	LD	U.S.	1988	$30.00
Criterion	CC1178L	West Side Story	LD	U.S.	1989	$125.00
	CAV version.					
Criterion	CC1192L	West Side Story	LD	U.S.	1989	$70.00
	CLV version.					
Nelson	30755	Westerner	LD	U.S.	1985	$35.00
Nelson	22475	Whales of August, The	LD	U.S.	1988	$35.00
Nelson	8258	What Comes Around	LD	U.S.	1987	$35.00
Image	ID7256CV	What Have I Done to Deserve This	LD	U.S.		$30.00
Discovision		What Makes Rain?/Storms	LD	U.S.	1979	$40.00
Vestron Video	VL5088	Wheels of Fire	LD	U.S.	1985	$35.00
Columbia	VLD6050	When a Stranger Calls	LD	U.S.	1983	$30.00
Nelson	77326	When Harry Met Sally	LD	U.S.	1989	$35.00
Paramount	LV 5106	When World's Collide	LD	U.S.		$40.00
Paramount	LV5106	When World's Collide	LD	U.S.	1982	$30.00
Walt Disney	997AS	Where the Heart Is	LD	U.S.	1990	$30.00
Discovision		Which Way Is Up?	LD	U.S.	1979	$80.00
MCA	A-5	Which Way Is Up?	LD	U.S.	1985	$100.00
Image	ID7012TU	While the City Sleeps	LD	U.S.		$95.00
Image	ID8210IV	Whispers	LD	U.S.		$20.00
Nelson	7665	Whistle Blower, The	LD	U.S.	1987	$35.00
Paramount	LV6104	White Christmas	LD	U.S.	1986	$40.00
Vestron	LV1025	White City	LD	U.S.	1985	$30.00
Paramount	LV8724	White Dawn, The	LD	U.S.	1984	$30.00
CBS	4642	White Heat	LD	U.S.	1987	$35.00
CBS/Fox	4642-80	White Heat	LD	U.S.	1987	$35.00
Image	ID6643RC	White Line Fever	LD	U.S.		$30.00
Nelson	77246	White Mischief	LD	U.S.	1989	$10.00
RCA/Columbia	30611	White Nights	LD	U.S.	1986	$40.00
Psedition	PSE91-08	White Nights	LD	U.S.	1991	$70.00
Columbia	30858	White Water Summer	LD	U.S.	1988	$30.00
Image	ID7571ME	Who Am I?	LD	U.S.		$30.00
Walt Disney	940CS	Who Framed Roger Rabbit	LD	U.S.	1990	$40.00
	CAV version. Distributed by Pioneer.					
Walt Disney	940AS	Who Framed Roger Rabbit	LD	U.S.	1990	$30.00
	CLV version. Distributed by Pioneer.					
Walt Disney	PILF2249	Who Framed Roger Rabbit Special Edition	LTD/LD	Japan	1996	$90.00
Discovision		Who Is God, Where Is God	LD	U.S.	1979	$40.00
Image	ID6470MG	Who'll Stop the Rain	LD	U.S.		$50.00
Image	ID6556TS	Who's Harry Crumb	LD	U.S.		$30.00
RCA/Columbia	VLD6060	Wholly Moses	LD	U.S.	1983	$35.00
Columbia	VLD6060	Wholly Moses	LD	U.S.	1993	$30.00
Columbia	59316	Why Me?	LD	U.S.	1990	$30.00
Discovision		Wild Dogs of Africa	LD	U.S.	1979	$40.00
CBS/Fox	7691-80	Wild Geese, The	LD	U.S.	1989	$50.00
RCA/Columbia	30623	Wild One, The	LD	U.S.	1986	$35.00
Columbia	30623	Wild One, The	LD	U.S.	1993	$30.00
Columbia	59576	Wild Orchid	LD	U.S.	1990	$30.00
Columbia	59126	Wild Zone	LD	U.S.	1990	$30.00
Image	I5053	Willard	LD	U.S.	1986	$80.00
Columbia	30936	Willow	LD	U.S.	1989	$30.00
Paramount	LV2851-2	Wings	LD	U.S.	1985	$40.00
		Wings of Desire	LD	U.S.		$30.00
Nelson	13276	Winner Takes All	LD	U.S.	1987	$35.00
Walt Disney	226AS	Winnie and Friends	LD	U.S.	1984	$30.00
Walt Disney	598AS	Winnie the Pooh	LD	U.S.	1987	$30.00
Walt Disney	521AS	Winnie the Pooh and Tigger Too	LD	U.S.	1987	$30.00
Nelson	20566	Winter Kills	LD	U.S.	1990	$35.00
Nelson	77266	Winter People	LD	U.S.	1990	$35.00
Discovision		Winterwings	LD	U.S.	1979	$40.00
Image	ID5284LO	Wired	LD	U.S.		$15.00
Image	ID6273FR	Wish You Were Here	LD	U.S.		$30.00
Image	ID7709MN	Witchboard	LD	U.S.		$30.00
Image	ID8129AC	Witchcraft	LD	U.S.		$30.00
Image	ID7703MN	Witchtrap	LD	U.S.		$30.00
Image	ID6131ME	With Nail and I	LD	U.S.		$30.00
Paramount	LV1738	Witness	LD	U.S.	1986	$30.00
CBS	4665	Witness For the Prosecution	LD	U.S.	1985	$35.00
Vidmark	LDCVM5804	Wiz Kid, The	LD	U.S.	1993	$35.00
Discovision	17-005	Wiz, The	LD	U.S.		$40.00
MCA	17-005	Wiz, The	LD	U.S.	1985	$35.00
MGM/UA	ML100001	Wizard of Oz	LD	U.S.	1983	$20.00
Paramount	LV2322	Wizard of Oz	LD	U.S.	1984	$20.00
Criterion	UCC1159L	Wizard of Oz	LD	U.S.	1989	$50.00
Paramount	LV2322	Wizard of Oz (Animated)	LD	U.S.	1984	$40.00
CBS/Fox	1342-80	Wizards	LD	U.S.	1989	$35.00
Discovision		Woman at Work	LD	U.S.	1979	$40.00
Republic	LV24622	Woman, Her Men & Her Futon	LD	U.S.	1992	$30.00
Paramount	LV27950	Woman in Green/S. Holmes	LD	U.S.	1990	$30.00
Image		Woman in Love	LD	U.S.		$40.00
Vestron	LV5055	Woman in Red	LD	U.S.	1985	$30.00
Columbia	30708	Woman of Distinction	LD	U.S.	1987	$30.00
MGM/UA	ML100093	Woman of the Year	LD	U.S.	1988	$35.00
Image	ID6951OR	Woman on the Edge of a Nervous Breakdown	LD	U.S.		$60.00
MGM/UA	ML100506	Woman, The	LD	U.S.		$30.00
Image	ID7147VE	Wonderland	LD	U.S.		$30.00
MCA	61-008	Woody Woodpecker	LD	U.S.	1983	$45.00
CBS	1709	Working Girl	LD	U.S.	1990	$35.00
Discovision		World at War: Bonzai	LD	U.S.	1979	$40.00
Discovision		World at War: Genocide	LD	U.S.	1979	$40.00
Discovision		World at War: Morning D-Day	LD	U.S.	1979	$40.00
Discovision		World at War: The Bomb	LD	U.S.	1979	$40.00
		World Gone Wild	LD	U.S.		$30.00
Discovision		World of Abbott and Costello	LD	U.S.	1979	$90.00
Columbia	30367	World of d-Base	LD	U.S.	1985	8
		World on a Silver Platter	DJ/LD	U.S.	1982	$100.00
CBS/Fox	1700-80	Worth Winning	LD	U.S.	1990	$40.00
Image	ID5232VE	Wraith, The	LD	U.S.		$20.00
		Wrestlmania	LD	U.S.		$30.00
Columbia	91056	Write to Kill	LD	U.S.	1991	$30.00
		Wrong Guys	LD	U.S.		$30.00
Image	ID6381RC	Wrong Is Right	LD	U.S.		$30.00
Warner Home Video	11155	Wrong Man, The	LD	U.S.	1990	$25.00
Image	ID7657HB	Wuthering Heights	LD	U.S.		$90.00
Nelson	30795	Wuthering Heights	LD	U.S.	1985	$90.00
		X From Outer Space/Yongary Monster	LD	U.S.		$40.00
Warner	PILF2118	X-Files First Season Volume 1	LTD/LD	Japan	1995	$400.00
	6 LD boxed set					
Warner	PILF2119	X-Files First Season Volume 2	LTD/LD	Japan	1995	$400.00
	6 LD boxed set					
Warner	PILF2119	X-Files Second SeasonVolume 1	LTD/LD	Japan	1996	$450.00
	7LD boxed set					
Discovision		Xanadu	LD	U.S.	1981	$40.00
CBS	4513	Yankee Doodle Dandy	LD	U.S.	1983	$35.00
Magnetic Video		Yankee Doodle Dandy	LD	U.S.†	1983	$35.00
Columbia	91456	Year of the Gun	LD	U.S.	1991	$30.00
Image	ID5284LO	Year of the Quiet Sun	LD	U.S.		$15.00
MGM/UA	ML102870	Yellow Rolls Royce	LD	U.S.	1993	$40.00
Warner	NJL-99655	Yellow Submarine	LD	Japan	1987	$95.00
MGM/UA	ML101170	Yellow Submarine	LD	U.S.	1983	$150.00
Image	IDVL5024	Yellowbeard	LD	U.S.	1983	$50.00
CBS	4724	Yentel	LD	U.S.	1984	$25.00
MGM/UA	ML100208	Yes, Giorgio	LD	U.S.	1983	$35.00
Image	ID7470PA	Yesterday's Witness	LD	U.S.		$20.00
Image	ID815HA	Yogi's First Christmas	LD	U.S.		$30.00
Criterion	CC1211L	Yojimbo	LD	U.S.	1990	$50.00
Columbia	VLD6070	Yor: The Hunter of the Futer	LD	U.S.	1984	$30.00
Criterion	CC1011L	You Can't Get There From Here	LD	U.S.	1990	$40.00
Columbia/Tri Star	79216	You Can't Take It	LD	U.S.	1994	$40.00
CBS	4526	You Only Live Twice	LD	U.S.	1984	$20.00
Columbia	30401	You Were Never Lovelier	LD	U.S.	1985	$30.00
Columbia	30401	You Were Never Lovelier	LD	U.S.	1993	$30.00
		You'll Find Out	LD	U.S.		$40.00
Columbia	30265	You'll Never Get Rich	LD	U.S.	1985	$30.00
Vestron Video	VL5012	Young Doctor's in Love	LD	U.S.	1983	$35.00
CBS	1103	Young Frankenstein	LD	U.S.	1983	$30.00
CBS	1057	Young Lions, The	LD	U.S.	1990	$30.00
CBS	1420	Young Mr. Lincoln	LD	U.S.	1990	$30.00
Paramount	LV1670	Young Sherlock Holmes	LD	U.S.	1986	$30.00
Image	ID6989TU	Young Stranger	LD	U.S.		$30.00
Columbia	VLD6100	Z	LD	U.S.	1983	$40.00
Image	ID8276IV	Zandalee	LD	U.S.		$20.00
Nelson	16045	Zapped	LD	U.S.	1983	$50.00
Nelson	77756	Zapped Again	LD	U.S.	1990	$45.00
CBS	1208	Zardos	LD	U.S.	1990	$35.00
Columbia	65003	Zelly & Me	LD	U.S.	1989	$30.00
Emotion	BELL-745	Zombie (Dawn of the Dead) Perfect Collection	LTD/LD	Japan	1995	$300.00
	4 LD boxed set.					
		Zombie Island Massacre`	LD	Japan		$150.00
Republic	LV25052	Zombies of the Stratosphere	LD	U.S.	1992	$85.00
Image	ID7964	Zora is My Name!	LD	U.S.		$30.00
Republic	LV24770	Zorro Rides Again	LD	U.S.	1992	$40.00
Republic	LV25054	Zorro's Black Whip	LD	U.S.	1990	$25.00
Republic	LV25055	Zorro's Fighting Legion	LD	U.S.	1990	$40.00
Criterion	CC1154L	Zulu	LD	U.S.	1989	$60.00
Image	ID5173	Zulu Dawn	LD	U.S.		$20.00

Various Artists

Label	Catalog Number	Title	Type	Country	Year	Value
		#1 Country Special	RS	U.S.	1995	$20.00
		3 CD set. Airdate: 5/30/95.				
Sony		1/4 Notes	DJ/Smplr	U.S.	1995	$15.00
		Minidisc.				
K-Tel		101 Greatest Country Hits	LTD/LP	U.S.	1995	$90.00
		10 CD set in slipcase.				
MTV Networks		120 Minutes: Left Of the Dial	RS	U.S.	1992	$15.00
		18 Original Hits By 18 Unoriginal Artists	DJ/Smplr	U.S.	1995	$18.00
		2 CD set.				
Warner Brothers		1988 Summer Olympics Sampler	DJ/Smplr	U.S.	1988	$10.00
Atlantic		1990 Year In Review	DJ/Smplr	U.S.	1990	$5.00
Arbitron		1993 Radio Mercury Awards	DJ/Intvw	U.S.	1993	$8.00
Audio Publisher Ass.		1994 Audio Publisher's Association Sampler	DJ/Smplr	U.S.	1994	$4.00
Columbia		1994 Columbia Records Grammy Nominees	DJ/Smplr	U.S.	1994	$12.00
Warner Brothers		1994 Limited Edition Warner/Reprise Sampler	DJ/Smplr	U.S.		$15.00
		2 CD set.				
MCA	MCA3P-2988	1994 MCA NARM Compilation	DJ/Smplr	U.S.	1994	$25.00
Westwood One		1994 New Faces Of Country Music	RS	U.S.	1994	$40.00
		3 CD set. Airdate: 5/28/94.				
		1995 Country Music Review	RS	U.S.	1995	$50.00
		3 CD set. Airdate: 12/31/95.				
Razor & Tie		1995 Sampler	DJ/Smplr	U.S.	1995	$15.00
WDC		1997	DJ/Smplr	U.S.	1997	$5.00
Chrysalis		20 Years of Chrysalis Music	DJ/Smplr	U.S.	1995	$20.00
		2 CD set.				
RCA		24 Karat Gold Sampler	DJ/Smplr	U.S.	1995	$40.00
Chrysalis		25 Years of Chrysalis Music	DJ/Smplr	U.S.	1995	$30.00
		3 CD set				
Rykodisc	RCD3-1009	3 Inches of the World	CD3	U.S.	1998	$5.00
Nimbus Manufacturing		3-D ID: Looking Into the Next Dimension	DJ/Smplr	U.S.	1996	$50.00
		4 CD set of 3D hologram printed discs.				
Warner Sound Exchange		40 Legendary Vocal Hits of the '60s	LTD/LP	U.S.	1995	$30.00
		2 CD Set				
Verve	314 525 609-1	'40s Mercury Sessions: Blues Boogie & Bop	LTD/LP	U.S.	1995	$120.00
		7 CD set in simulated "old-time radio" package.				
4AD		4AD Collection	DJ/Smplr	Canada	1990	$150.00
		4 CD boxed set.				
		'90s Country: Christmas '95	RS	U.S.	1995	$20.00
		Airdate: 12/23/95.				
Warner Brothers	PRO-CD-3300	91 x 5th Anniversary Sampler	DJ/Smplr	U.S.	1988	$12.00
		911 CD1	DJ/Smplr	U.S.		$30.00
		A 4AD Retail Sampler	DJ/Smplr	U.S.	1995	$25.00
		A British Invasion: 25th Aniversary Celebration	RS	U.S.	1995	$150.00
		10 CD set.				
Capitol	DPRO-79437	A Country Christmas Tapastry	DJ/Smplr	U.S.	1990	$15.00
Nettwerk		A Decade of Nettwerk	LTD/LP	U.S.	1995	$60.00
		5 disc enhanced CD set in box.				
Musician	MST 9101	A Little on the CD Side	DJ/Smplr	U.S.	1990	$5.00
Musician	MST 9110	A Little on the CD Side Vol. 10	DJ/Smplr	U.S.	1992	$5.00
Musician	MST 9111	A Little on the CD Side Vol. 11	DJ/Smplr	U.S.	1993	$5.00
Musician	MST 9112	A Little on the CD Side Vol. 12	DJ/Smplr	U.S.	1993	$5.00
Musician	MST 9113	A Little on the CD Side Vol. 13	DJ/Smplr	U.S.	1994	$5.00
Musician	MST 9102	A Little on the CD Side Vol. 2	DJ/Smplr	U.S.	1990	$5.00
Musician	MST 9103	A Little on the CD Side Vol. 3	DJ/Smplr	U.S.	1990	$5.00
Musician	MST 9104	A Little on the CD Side Vol. 4	DJ/Smplr	U.S.	1991	$5.00
Musician	MST 9105	A Little on the CD Side Vol. 5	DJ/Smplr	U.S.	1991	$5.00
Musician	MST 9106	A Little on the CD Side Vol. 6	DJ/Smplr	U.S.	1991	$5.00
Musician	MST 9107	A Little on the CD Side Vol. 7	DJ/Smplr	U.S.	1991	$5.00
Musician	MST 9108	A Little on the CD Side Vol. 8	DJ/Smplr	U.S.	1992	$5.00
Musician	MST 9109	A Little on the CD Side Vol. 9	DJ/Smplr	U.S.	1992	$5.00
Warner Brothers	PRO-CD-2866	A Little Taste	DJ/Smplr	U.S.		$15.00
		CD3 Sampler				
Geffen		A Musical History of the Decade	DJ/Smplr	U.S.	1990	$80.00
		4 CD bosed set				
Warner Brothers	PRO 15027	A New Dimension	DJ/Smplr	U.S.	1991	$25.00
		CD+G				
Putumayo		A Putumayo World Music Sampler	DJ/Smplr	U.S.	1996	$8.00
Putumayo		A Putumayo World Music Sampler	DJ/Smplr	U.S.	1997	$8.00
Restless	PRO002	A Restless World	DJ/Smplr	U.S.	1991	$8.00
Columbia	CSK 2890	A Sneak Peak	DJ/Smplr	U.S.	1988	$10.00
		2 CD set.				
Rhino/Borders	R2 72212	A Soulful Christmas	LTD/LP	U.S.	1995	$15.00
Ear Candy	1001	A Taste of Ear Candy	DJ/Smplr	U.S.	1991	$8.00
		A Taste of Tradition	DJ/Smplr	U.S.		$8.00
TVT	1905-2P	A Tasty Sampling From Four New Volumes Of Television's Greatest Hits	DJ/Smplr	U.S.	1996	$15.00
DMP	CD 1751	A Touch of DMP	DJ/CD3	U.S.	1987	$10.00
Putumayo		A Toure Kunda, Dalom Kids/Splash and World Instrumental Sampler	DJ/Smplr	U.S.	1996	$18.00
Caras	SAMCD 50	A Tribute to Sam Sniderman	DJ/Smplr	Canada	1988	$60.00
Epic	ESK 1974	A Wake-Up Call for the '90s	DJ/Smplr	U.S.	1990	$5.00
A&M	CD 17413	A Year Ago We Hadn't Heard of Them Either	DJ/Smplr	U.S.	1986	$10.00
A&M		A&M 25th: The Singles Collection	DJ/Smplr	Japan		$45.00
A&M	75021 7358-2	A&M Gospel	DJ/Smplr	U.S.	1992	$5.00
A&M	CD 17607	A&M Jazz Heritage Sampler	DJ/Smplr	U.S.	1988	$8.00
A&M	CD 17767	A&M Jazz Series Sampler 1989	DJ/Smplr	U.S.	1989	$10.00
A&M		A&M Music Week '94	DJ/Smplr	Canada	1994	$10.00
		A&M Night Play	DJ/Smplr	U.S.	1988	$5.00
A&M	CD 17543	A&M Presents CD3	DJ/Smplr	U.S.	1987	$50.00
		CD3 with 3"x11" booklet, adapter,CD3 holder				
A&M	31458 8047	A&M Records Sampler	DJ/Smplr	U.S.	1993	$8.00
A&M	CD 8330	A&M Summer Spectacular	DJ/Smplr	U.S.		$8.00
Sony		Abbey Road Distributors	DJ/Smplr	U.S.	1992	$5.00
		AC/DC Sampler, The	DJ/Smplr	U.S.		$4.00
KOME Radio		Acoustic Aid	Smplr	U.S.	1992	$15.00
Acoustic Music		Acoustic Music Sampler	DJ/Smplr	U.S.	1996	$10.00
		Act On Impulse	DJ/Smplr	U.S.		$8.00
Arista	Spring 1996	Aimee 3	DJ/Smplr	U.S.	1996	$8.00
		Ain't Nuthin' But a Sampler	DJ/Smplr	U.S.	1995	$6.00
CMJ		Aiwa New Music Awards	RS	U.S.	1990	$18.00
EMI		Aladdin Records Story, The	LTD/LP	U.S.	1994	$30.00
Album Network		Album Network Special: Earth Day	RS	U.S.	1995	$35.00
		2 CD set. 4/23/95.				
Alia		Alias With A Bullet	DJ/Smplr	U.S.		$10.00
		All Access	RS	U.S.	1993	$90.00
		3 CD set.				
Warner Brothers	PRO-CD-4960	All Roads Lead to Burbank	DJ/Smplr	U.S.	1991	$12.00
4AD	FNAC	All Virgos Are Mad	DJ/Smplr	France	1995	$35.00
4AD		All Virgos Are Mad	DJ/Smplr	U.S.		$13.00
		All-American All-Stars	RS	U.S.	1995	$30.00
		3 CD set. Airdate: 7/4/95.				
Fruit Of the Loom		All-Star Collection	LTD/LP	U.S.	1996	$15.00
		Available via mail-order only.				
Virgin		Allee Willis Hits	DJ/Smplr	U.S.		$10.00
Alliance		Alliance	DJ/Smplr	U.S.	1995	$35.00
		3 CD set.				
A&M	75021 8052	Almost Free CD	DJ/Smplr	U.S.	1990	$10.00
Alternative	001	Alternative Distribution Alliance Sampler '93	DJ/Smplr	U.S.	1993	$5.00
Alternative		Alternative Distribution Alliance Sampler '94	DJ/Smplr	U.S.	1994	$5.00
Hollywood	PRCD 61449-2	Alternative NRG	DJ/Smplr	U.S.	1994	$12.00
AP		Alternative Press Nine	DJ/Smplr	U.S.	1994	$10.00
Arista	ASCD-2111	Alternative States	DJ/Smplr	U.S.	1990	$12.00
Warner Sound Exchange		Amazing Grace	LTD/LP	U.S.	1995	$17.00
Caroline		Ambient – Collector's Edition	LTD/LP	U.K.	1994	$40.00
		3 CD picture disc boxed set. Featuring the albums Edgar Froese "Aqua", Ashra "Blackouts", Klaus Schulze "Timewind".				
Rhino		American Comedy Box	DJ/Smplr	U.S.	1995	$20.00
Elektra	PRCD 8379-2	American Explorer Series	DJ/Smplr	U.S.	1991	$5.00
CBS	CSK 1831	American Originals Selected Cuts Vol. 2	DJ/Smplr	U.S.	1990	$5.00
ABC Networks		American Top 40: 20th Aniversary Commemorative CD	DJ/Smplr	U.S.		$35.00
		Americans on the Beeb	RS	U.S.	1994	$20.00/$25.00
		Airdate 7/4/94				
Warner Brothers	PRO-CD-5764	Ampcrushers	DJ/Smplr	U.S.	1992	$10.00
Arista	ASCD-2058	Ample Samples	DJ/Smplr	U.S.	1990	$5.00
Warner/Sony	PR CD 8724	An American Reunion	DJ/Smplr	U.S.	1993	$70.00
Epic	ESK 4892	An Epic Christmas	DJ/Smplr	U.S.	1992	$5.00
Epic	ESK 5294	An Epic Tour De Force	DJ/Smplr	U.S.	1993	$10.00
Windham	WD-1026	An Evening With Windham Hill Live	LP/LB	U.S.†	1985	$14.00/$8.00
MCA	MCA3P-3015	An MCA Nashville Sampler	DJ/Smplr	U.S.	1994	$50.00
Geffen	PRO-CD-4199	And Music for All	DJ/Smplr	U.S.	1991	$10.00
Angel/EMI	DPRO 79044	Angel Fall/Winter '91 Highlights	DJ/Smplr	U.S.	1991	$10.00
		Angels in the Architecture	LP/LB	U.S.		$13.00/$10.00
Alternative Press		AP Ninth Anniversary Sampler	DJ/Smplr	U.S.	1994	$4.00
EMI	CD APPS 1	Apple E.P., The	Smplr	U.K.	1991	$12.00
		CD in Apple shaped sleeve				
EMI/Apple	SPCD 1219	Apple Phase 1	DJ/Smplr	Japan	1992	$500.00
EMI/Apple		Apple Phase 2	DJ/Smplr	Japan	1992	$500.00
Epic	ESK 53437	Are You Ready to Dance	DJ/Smplr	U.S.	1993	$5.00
Argh!!!	001	Argh!!! It's a Loud Rock CD	DJ/Smplr	U.S.	1990	$5.00
Argh!!!	002	Argh!!! It's a Loud Rock CD	DJ/Smplr	U.S.	1990	$5.00
Argh!!!	003	Argh!!! It's a Loud Rock CD	DJ/Smplr	U.S.	1991	$5.00
Argh!!!	004	Argh!!! It's a Loud Rock CD	DJ/Smplr	U.S.	1991	$5.00
Argh!!!	005	Argh!!! It's a Loud Rock CD	DJ/Smplr	U.S.	1993	$5.00
Arista	ASCD-2644	Arista Alternative	DJ/Smplr	U.S.	1993	$5.00
Arista	ASCD-2641	Arista Brand High Performance Country	DJ/Smplr	U.S.	1993	$10.00
Arista	ASCD-9635	Arista From La Room	DJ/Smplr	U.S.		$5.00
Arista		Arista Nashville 5th Anniversary Sampler	DJ/Smplr	U.S.	1995	$40.00
		4 CD set.				
Arista	ASCD-9756	Arista Top 40 From Coast To Coast	DJ/Smplr	U.S.	1988	$5.00
Arista	ASCD-2111	Arista's New Music Sampler	DJ/Smplr	U.S.	1990	$4.00
Arista	ARCD-8268	Arista's Perfect 10	LP/BP	U.S.	1985	$14.00/$8.00
Arista	ARCD-8308	Arista's Perfect 10 Rides Again	LP/BP	U.S.	1985	$14.00/$8.00
Arista		Arista's Six Pack of Hits	DJ/Smplr	U.S.		$5.00
Geffen	PRO-CD-4637	Armed and Dangerous, Packing Hits	DJ/Smplr	U.S.	1994	$10.00
		Around the World	DJ/Smplr	U.S.		$5.00
WTH	002	Artifacts World Talent Hunt 2	DJ/Smplr	U.S.	1991	$5.00
WEA		Artist Breaker	DJ/Smplr	U.S.	1990	$8.00
Virgin	662 764	Artists United for Nature	CD5	Germany	1987	$8.00
Warner Sound Exchange		As Time Goes By	LTD/LP	U.S.	1995	$30.00
		2 CD Set				
ASCAP		ASCAP Christmas Sampler	DJ/Smplr	U.S.	1993	$120.00
		Picture CD in Christmas card with mailing envelope.				
Geffen	PRO-CD-4557	Astro Sheen	DJ/Smplr	U.S.	1993	$10.00
Atco	PRCD 3970-2	Atco Hits Spring 91	DJ/Smplr	U.S.	1991	$5.00
Atlantic	PRCD 4233-2	Atlantic & Atco Remasters Series Sampler One	DJ/Smplr	U.S.	1991	$10.00
Atlantic	PRCD 4300-2	Atlantic & Atco Remasters Series Sampler Two	DJ/Smplr	U.S.	1991	$10.00
Atlantic		Atlantic Hook Sampler	DJ/Smplr	U.S.	1995	$15.00
Atlantic		Atlantic Jazz legends Sampler	DJ/Smplr	U.S.		$12.00
Atlantic		Atlantic Jazz Sampler	DJ/Smplr	U.S.		$6.00
Atlantic	PRCD 5338-2	Atlantic's Hits for the Holidays	DJ/Smplr	U.S.		$18.00
		2 CD set.				
Atlantic	PR 2566-2	Atlantic's Year in Review	DJ/Smplr	U.S.	1988	$10.00
Atlantic	PR 3129-2	Atlantic's Year in Review	DJ/Smplr	U.S.	1989	$10.00
Atlantic	PRCD 5338-2	Atlantic's Year in Review	DJ/Smplr	U.S.	1993	$10.00
Atlantic	PRCD 6338-2	Atlantic's Year in Review	DJ/Smplr	U.S.	1996	$15.00
Elektra		Attack of the 50-Foot Ear Infection	DJ/Smplr	U.S.	1995	$15.00
Chrysalis		Audio Buffet	DJ/Smplr	U.S.		$6.00
Chrysalis		Audio Buffet #2	DJ/Smplr	U.S.		$5.00
GRP	CSIG 000173	Audio CD3 Sampler, The	CD3	U.S.	1989	$15.00
Polygram	SACD 419	Aural Fixations	DJ/Smplr	U.S.	1991	$10.00
		Back To School	DJ/Smplr	U.S.		$5.00
Atlantic		Back To School Survival Kit	DJ/Smplr	U.S.	1995	$15.00
MCA	MCA3P-2619	Bait: Alluring Sounds From MCA	DJ/Smplr	U.S.	1993	$6.00
Max	NS10CD	Ballantine's Mix	SCDJ	Germany	1996	$35.00
		Rum bottle shaped CD.				
Polydor	CDP 88	Bands You've Never Seen on Hee Haw	DJ/Smplr	U.S.	1989	$5.00
Alternative Tent.	VIRUS 112	Bat Is Back, The	DJ/Smplr	U.S.	1992	$10.00
Westwood One		BBC Classic Tracks	RS	U.S.	1990	$20.00
		Airdate: 12/17/90.				
Westwood One		BBC Classic Tracks	RS	U.S.	1990	$20.00
		Airdate: 12/30/90.				
Westwood One		BBC Classic Tracks: '60s American	RS	U.S.	1996	$20.00
		Airdate: 1/22/96.				
Westwood One		BBC Classic Tracks: '70s Rock	RS	U.S.	1995	$20.00
		Airdate: 5/212/95.				
Westwood One		BBC Classic Tracks: '70s Rock	RS	U.S.	1996	$20.00
		Airdate: 3/18/96				
Westwood One		BBC Classic Tracks: All-Time Classics	RS	U.S.	1996	$30.00
		Airdate: 1/8/96.				
Westwood One		BBC Classic Tracks: American Rock	RS	U.S.	1995	$20.00
		Airdate: 12/11/95.				
Westwood One		BBC Classic Tracks: Americans on the Beeb	RS	U.S.	1994	$20.00
		Airdate: 7/4/94.				
Westwood One		BBC Classic Tracks: Anthems	RS	U.S.	1996	$20.00
		Airdate: 1/15/96.				

Label	Catalog Number	Title	Type	Country	Year	Value
Westwood One		BBC Classic Tracks: Art Rock	RS	U.S.	1995	$20.00
		Airdate: 5/15/95.				
Westwood One		BBC Classic Tracks: Beatle Covers	RS	U.S.	1995	$20.00
		Airdate: 9/4/95.				
Westwood One		BBC Classic Tracks: Beatle Covers	RS	U.S.	1996	$20.00
		Airdate: 3/4/96.				
Westwood One		BBC Classic Tracks: Blues Rock	RS	U.S.	1994	$35.00
		Airdate: 11/28/94.				
Westwood One		BBC Classic Tracks: Body Parts	RS	U.S.	1996	$35.00
		Airdate: 2/26/96.				
Westwood One		BBC Classic Tracks: British Bands of the Early Seventies	RS	U.S.	1994	$35.00
		Airdate: 6/13/94.				
Westwood One		BBC Classic Tracks: British Folk Rock	RS	U.S.	1995	$35.00
		Airdate: 1/9/95.				
Westwood One		BBC Classic Tracks: British Invasion	RS	U.S.	1994	$35.00
		Airdate: 2/21/94.				
Westwood One		BBC Classic Tracks: British Invasion	RS	U.S.	1996	$35.00
		Airdate: 3/25/96.				
Westwood One		BBC Classic Tracks: British Rock	RS	U.S.	1995	$20.00
		Airdate: 10/2/95.				
Westwood One		BBC Classic Tracks: Canadian Rock	RS	U.S.	1995	$25.00
		Airdate: 2/27/95.				
Westwood One		BBC Classic Tracks: Classic Cover Tunes	RS	U.S.	1994	$30.00
		Airdate: 3/7/94.				
Westwood One		BBC Classic Tracks: Classic Cover Tunes	RS	U.S.	1995	$30.00
		Airdate: 2/20/95.				
Westwood One		BBC Classic Tracks: Classic Singer/Songwriters	RS	U.S.	1995	$20.00
		Airdate: 1/30/95.				
Westwood One		BBC Classic Tracks: Covers	RS	U.S.	1996	$20.00
		Airdate: 4/29/96				
Westwood One		BBC Classic Tracks: Duets	RS	U.S.	1995	$25.00
		Airdate: 10/16/95.				
Westwood One		BBC Classic Tracks: Folk Rock	RS	U.S.	1994	$30.00
		Airdate: 3/28/94.				
Westwood One		BBC Classic Tracks: Folk Rock	RS	U.S.	1995	$30.00
		Airdate: 5/29/95.				
Westwood One		BBC Classic Tracks: From the Heart	RS	U.S.	1996	$20.00
		Airdate: 2/12/96.				
Westwood One		BBC Classic Tracks: Gone But Not Forgotten	RS	U.S.	1995	$30.00
		Airdate: 12/4/95.				
Westwood One		BBC Classic Tracks: Guitar Heroes	RS	U.S.	1994	$35.00
		Airdate: 8/29/94.				
Westwood One		BBC Classic Tracks: Guitar Heroes	RS	U.S.	1995	$35.00
		Airdate: 4/17/95.				
Westwood One		BBC Classic Tracks: Guitar Players	RS	U.S.	1995	$30.00
		Airdate: 3/27/95.				
Westwood One		BBC Classic Tracks: Hard Rock	RS	U.S.	1995	$20.00
		Airdate: 6/5/95.				
Westwood One		BBC Classic Tracks: Hard Rock	RS	U.S.	1995	$20.00
		Airdate: 7/24/95.				
Westwood One		BBC Classic Tracks: Monterey Pop Festival	RS	U.S.	1995	$25.00
		Airdate: 6/19/95.				
Westwood One		BBC Classic Tracks: One-Hit Wonders	RS	U.S.	1994	$25.00
		Airdate: 12/26/94.				
Westwood One		BBC Classic Tracks: One-Hit Wonders	RS	U.S.	1995	$25.00
		Airdate: 11/13/95.				
Westwood One		BBC Classic Tracks: Places	RS	U.S.	1996	$20.00
		Airdate: 4/22/96				
Westwood One		BBC Classic Tracks: Politics	RS	U.S.	1995	$20.00
		Airdate: 8/28/95.				
Westwood One		BBC Classic Tracks: Prince's Trust 1987	RS	U.S.	1996	$20.00
		Airdate: 2/5/96.				
Westwood One		BBC Classic Tracks: Psychedelia	RS	U.S.	1994	$20.00
		Airdate: 5/23/94.				
Westwood One		BBC Classic Tracks: Reggae	RS	U.S.	1995	$25.00
		Airdate: 4/10/95.				
Westwood One		BBC Classic Tracks: Rock Ballads	RS	U.S.	1995	$20.00
		Airdate: 9/25/95.				
Westwood One		BBC Classic Tracks: Rock 'n Roll Tribute	RS	U.S.	1996	$25.00
		Airdate: 1/1/96.				
Westwood One		BBC Classic Tracks: Rock Vocalists	RS	U.S.	1995	$20.00
		Airdate: 1/16/95				
Westwood One		BBC Classic Tracks: San Francisco Bands	RS	U.S.	1995	$20.00
		Airdate: 8/7/95.				
Westwood One		BBC Classic Tracks: Siblings	RS	U.S.	1996	$20.00
		Airdate: 1/29/96.				
Westwood One		BBC Classic Tracks: Songwriting Classics	RS	U.S.	1994	$20.00
		Airdate: 10/10/94.				
Westwood One		BBC Classic Tracks: Strictly British	RS	U.S.	1995	$20.00
		Airdate: 12/25/95.				
Westwood One		BBC Classic Tracks: Summer Of Love	RS	U.S.	1995	$20.00
		Airdate: 7/17/95.				
Westwood One		BBC Classic Tracks: Summer of Love '67	RS	U.S.	1992	$20.00
		Airdate: 6/15/92.				
Westwood One		BBC Classic Tracks: The Sixties	RS	U.S.	1995	$20.00
		Airdate: 11/27/95.				
Westwood One		BBC Classic Tracks: Trios	RS	U.S.	1995	$20.00
		Airdate: 9/18/95.				
Westwood One		BBC Classic Tracks: U.K. (Early '70s)	RS	U.S.	1994	$20.00
		Airdate: 10/31/94.				
Westwood One		BBC Classic Tracks: U.K. (Early '70s)	RS	U.S.	1994	$20.00
		Airdate: 4/25/94.				
Westwood One		BBC Classic Tracks: U.K. (Early '70s)	RS	U.S.	1995	$20.00
		Airdate: 7/10/95.				
Westwood One		BBC Classic Tracks: Where Are They Now?	RS	U.S.	1995	$20.00
		Airdate: 6/12/95.				
Westwood One		BBC Classic Tracks: Women in Rock	RS	U.S.	1995	$20.00
		Airdate: 3/13/95.				
Westwood One		BBC Classic Tracks: Woodstock	RS	U.S.	1994	$20.00
		Airdate: 8/15/94.				
Westwood One		BBC Classic Tracks: Yardbirds Alumni	RS	U.S.	1995	$25.00
		Airdate: 8/21/95.				
BBC Transcription		BBC Transcription Disc	RS			$150.00
		Music and interview.				
Epic	ESK 47492	Beat Is Hot…The Competition Is Not	DJ/Smplr	U.S.	1991	$5.00
Polygram	SACD 632	Bedrock vs. Jellystone	DJ/Smplr	U.S.	1993	$12.00
CDI-PRO	260	Best of '93 Classic Hits	DJ/Smplr	U.S.		$30.00
		Special compressed CD+I sampler. About 3 hours of music.				
Delta	11073	Best of American Black Bands	LP/BP	U.S.		$10.00/$6.00
		Best of Big Bands	DJ/Smplr	U.S.		$5.00
Philips	818651-2	Best of British Traditional Jazz	LP/LB	U.S.†	1985	$14.00/$8.00
Rhino	PRO2 90050	Best of Comic Relief '90 Sampler	DJ/Smplr	U.S.	1990	$6.00
Polygram	SACD 072	Best of Dick James Music	DJ/Smplr	U.S.	1988	$125.00
		Contains exclusive Beatles tracks.				
Passport	PBCD-6902	Best of Music and Rhythm	LP/BP	U.S.		$15.00/$12.00
Pilz	449950-2	Best of the '60s: 1960	LTD/LP	U.S.	1995	$13.00
		Picture disc CD.				

Best Of Dick James Music (Polygram SACD 072) U.S. 1988 promotional CD sampler. Contains the first appearance of the *Beatles Please Please Me, Ask Me Why and Don't Bother Me* in digitally remastered stereo.

Label	Catalog Number	Title	Type	Country	Year	Value
Pilz	449951-2	Best of the '60s: 1961	LTD/LP	U.S.	1995	$13.00
		Picture disc CD.				
Pilz	449952-2	Best of the '60s: 1962	LTD/LP	U.S.	1995	$13.00
		Picture disc CD.				
Pilz	449953-2	Best of the '60s: 1963	LTD/LP	U.S.	1995	$13.00
		Picture disc CD.				
Pilz	449954-2	Best of the '60s: 1964	LTD/LP	U.S.	1995	$13.00
		Picture disc CD.				
Pilz	449955-2	Best of the '60s: 1965	LTD/LP	U.S.	1995	$13.00
		Picture disc CD.				
Pilz	449956-2	Best of the '60s: 1966	LTD/LP	U.S.	1995	$13.00
		Picture disc CD.				
Pilz	449957-2	Best of the '60s: 1967	LTD/LP	U.S.	1995	$13.00
		Picture disc CD.				
Pilz	449958-2	Best of the '60s: 1968	LTD/LP	U.S.	1995	$13.00
		Picture disc CD.				
Pilz	449959-2	Best of the '60s: 1969	LTD/LP	U.S.	1995	$13.00
		Picture disc CD.				
Wolf Records/Bayside Distributing	120.999 CD	Best of the Blues	DJ/Smplr	U.S.	1995	$18.00
BMG	66345-2-RDJ	Best of the Fest, The	DJ/Smplr	U.S.	1993	$8.00
Varta		Best of Varta Musikpreis	SCDJ	Germany	1995	$30.00
		Battery-shaped CD. Limited to 5,000 copies.				
Warner Brothers	PRO-CD-3980	Best of WEA '89	DJ/Smplr	U.S.	1990	$15.00
		Warner Bros. country hits performed by WEA employees				
Rhino		Billboard Hits Sampler	DJ/Smplr	U.S.	1995	$15.00
		Birthday CD Card #1	CD3	Japan	1994	$10.00
		CD3 with birthday card.				
		Birthday CD Card #2	CD3	Japan	1994	$10.00
		CD3 with birthday card.				
		Bizarre/Straight Sampler	DJ/Smplr	U.S.		$5.00
Wax Trax		Black Box	LTD/LP	U.S.	1994	$65.00
		3 CD set in metal box with cards.				
Right Stuff		Black In the Past	DJ/Smplr	U.S.	1996	$10.00
Warner Brothers	PRO-CD-6105	Black Light Special	DJ/Smplr	U.S.	1993	$8.00
Polygram	SACD 694	Black Music Is Infinite	DJ/Smplr	U.S.	1993	$8.00
Capitol	DPRO-79731	Black Music Month 1991	DJ/Smplr	U.S.	1991	$8.00
MCA	ASCD 2281	Black Music Month 1992	DJ/Smplr	U.S.	1992	$8.00
Mercury	SACD 685	Black Music Month 1993	DJ/Smplr	U.S.	1993	$8.00
CBS	CSK 1146	Blink, It's a Hit	DJ/Smplr	U.S.	1988	$5.00
Blue Note		Blue Note Connoisseur Sampler	DJ/Smplr	U.S.	1995	$25.00
Pioneer	PA-85-143	Blues Alive	LD	U.S.	1985	$20.00
Pioneer	PA-85-143	Blues Alive	LD	U.S.	1990	$30.00
		Digital Audio.				
Capitol		Blues Collection	DJ/Smplr	U.S.	1995	$20.00
Rhino	PRO2 90128	Blues Master Sampler	DJ/Smplr	U.S.	1992	$10.00
Rhino	PRO2 90128	Blues Master Sampler	DJ/Smplr	U.S.	1992	$10.00
		CD in 7" x 7" box version.				
BMG		BMG Entertainment: Ten Years Young	DJ/Smplr	U.S.	1997	$10.00
		Enhanced CD.				
BMG		BMG Salutes Sound Wherehouse	DJ/Smplr	U.S.		$8.00
		2 CD set.				
BMG		BMG U.S. Latin: 1995 NARM Convention	DJ/Smplr	U.S.	1995	$18.00
BMI		BMI 50th Anniversary	DJ/Smplr	U.S.	1990	$80.00
		3 CD set packaged in jewel boxes with book.				
BMI		BMI 50th Anniversary	DJ/Smplr	U.S.	1990	$80.00
		3 CD set packaged in sleeves with book.				
Bose		Bose: Adventures In Surround	DJ/CDV	U.S.		$40.00
Unistar		Bountry Six Pack	RS	U.S.	1991	$50.00
		3 CD set. Airsate: 12/91.				
Sire	PRO-CD-4442	Boy Howdy & Sire Launch the Next British Invasion	DJ/Smplr	U.S.	1990	$15.00
BMG	74321 34406 2	BP Electronic Shopping Entertainment	SCD5	Germany	1996	$20.00
		"BP Shield" shaped CD single.				
		Breaking the Silence	DJ/Smplr	U.S.		$12.00
		Bride Of Post Modern, The	DJ/Smplr	U.S.	1988	$5.00
Era	5023-2	Brill Building Sound	DJ/Smplr	U.S.	1994	$15.00
Cema	DPRO-79939	Brilliant New Music	DJ/Smplr	U.S.	1991	$8.00
EMI	CDBEAT1	British Beat Before the Beatles	DJ/Smplr	U.K.	1994	$18.00
		British Blues From Blue Horizon	DJ/Smplr	France		$30.00
Buddah	BB-1	Buddah Box, The	DJ/Smplr	U.S.	1995	$18.00
Burger King/Pikosso		Burger King Beats Volume 1	SCD5	Germany	1995	$25.00
		"Whopper" shaped disc.				
Burger King/Pikosso		Burger King Beats Volume 2	SCD5	Germany	1995	$25.00
		Burger & Fries shaped disc.				
Burger King/Pikosso		Burger King Beats Volume 3	SCD5	Germany	1995	$25.00
		"Coca-cola" shaped disc.				
DGC	PRO-CD-4474	Burning Leaves	DJ/Smplr	U.S.	1992	$10.00
Epic	ESK 5004	Busload of Freaks	DJ/Smplr	U.S.	1993	$30.00
Rhino		But Seriously: The American Comedy Box Sampler	DJ/Smplr	U.S.	1995	$15.00
Columbia	CSK 1926	Bzz	DJ/Smplr	U.S.	1989	$5.00
CBS	A 21426	Canada Dry '80s Encore	DJ/Smplr	U.S.	1989	$18.00
Capitol	DPRO-79471	Capitol 50th Anniversary Collectors' Series	DJ/Smplr	U.S.	1992	$40.00
Capitol	DPRO-79385	Capitol Christmas Sampler	DJ/Smplr	U.S.	1990	$20.00
Capitol	DPRO-79346	Capitol Collector's Series	DJ/Smplr	U.S.		$20.00
Capitol		Capitol Hit Parade	DJ/Smplr	U.S.	1987	$8.00

Label	Catalog Number	Title	Type	Country	Year	Value
Capitol	DPRO-79242	Capitol Records 1942–1992 Fiftieth Anniversary	DJ/Smplr	U.S.	1992	$100.00
		8CD boxed set.				
Decca		Capitol Sings Sampler	DJ/Smplr	U.S.		$15.00
Capitol	DPRO 79461	Capitol Tasty Tower Treats	DJ/Smplr	U.S.	1991	$35.00
		Custom pie box with picture CD of pie filling and menu.				
Capitol	DPRO-79968	Capitol's Leaning Tower of Pizza	DJ/Smplr	U.S.	1991	$35.00
		Custom pizza box with picture CD of pizza and menu.				
Capitol	DPRO-79842	Capitol's Perfect Pitch	DJ/Smplr	U.S.	1991	$18.00
Virgin	PRCD 4244	Captive Sampler	DJ/Smplr	U.S.	1991	$10.00
Caroline		Caroline Distribution Fall 1993	DJ/Smplr	U.S.	1993	$5.00
Casablanca		Casablanca Story, The	DJ/Smplr	U.S.	1994	$10.00
A&M	CD 17715	Case of the Slipped Disc	DJ/Smplr	U.S.	1989	$8.00
Image	ID6190VE	Casey Kasem's Rock 'n Roll Goldmine	LD	U.S.		$30.00
Image	ID6191VE	Casey Kasem's Rock 'n Roll Goldmine	LD	U.S.		$30.00
		Digital Audio.				
Capitol	DPRO-79387	Catalogue, The	DJ/Smplr	U.S.		$20.00
		Catalyst – Music Refined	DJ/Smplr	U.S.		$15.00
Pioneer	PA-85-142	Catch a Rising Star	LD	U.S.	1985	$15.00
		Catch Up	DJ/Smplr	Japan		$25.00
Rhino		Category, The	DJ/Smplr	U.S.		$12.00
		CD in envelope with wax seal.				
Attic		Caught In the Attic	DJ/Smplr	Canada		$25.00
		3 CD set.				
Geffen	PRO-CD-4602	Caution: Explosive In-Store Play	DJ/Smplr	U.S.	1994	$15.00
Collision Arts	7059	CBGB's 20th Anniversary Sampler	DJ/Smplr	U.S.	1994	$12.00
CBS	ASK 1734	CBS Records Compact Disc Demonstration	DJ/Smplr	U.S.	1983	$50.00
Columbia	CSK 2861	CBS Sampler	DJ/Smplr	U.S.		$5.00
Capitol	DPRO-79570	CD Hits Sampler	DJ/Smplr	U.S.	1989	$5.00
CD Plus	CDPRO 890	CD Plus/Blue Note	DJ/Smplr	U.S.	1994	$40.00
CD Review	CDR0395D	CD Review – March 1995	DJ/Smplr	U.S.	1995	$10.00
DMI		CD Sampler 1	DJ/Smplr	U.S.	1995	$10.00
		Image-disc CD and Cassette in box.				
Vee-Jay	NVX2-002	CD Sampler 4/93 - 7/93	DJ/Smplr	U.S.	1993	$12.00
Chameleon	A ORC D1	CD Sampler One	DJ/Smplr	U.S.	1990	$5.00
Magnavox	MAG 002	CD Single Demonstration Disc	DJ/CDV	U.S.	1987	$40.00
MCA	ASCD 2497	Celebrate the Seasons	DJ/Smplr	U.S.	1992	$10.00
Decca		Celtic Heartbeat Collection	DJ/Smplr	U.S.		$15.00
CMJ	CMJ-CD-76	Certain Damage 76 Volume 1 & 2	DJ/Smplr	U.S.	1996	$25.00
		2 CD set. First production CD in "Laserfile" package.				
MCA	MCA3P-2731	Chameleon Caravan Tour	DJ/Smplr	U.S.	1993	$12.00
Chameleon	A ORC D2	Chameleon Colors	DJ/Smplr	U.S.	1990	$10.00
Charisma	PRCD 002	Charisma	DJ/Smplr	U.S.	1990	$5.00
		Chart Attack	RS	U.K.		$20.00
		1 hour various artist music and interview CD.				
WEA	C101	Check It Out	DJ/Smplr	U.S.	1991	$5.00
Chess		Chess History Sampler	DJ/Smplr	U.S.		$15.00
Savant	1003	Chicago Nineteen '92	DJ/Smplr	U.S.	1992	$8.00
Disc Art	80132	Children's Favorite Lullaby & Nursery Rhymes	SCD5	U.S.	1996	$10.00
		Teddy Bear shaped CD				
Disney	30CC-1631	Children's Favorites Vol. 1	LP	Japan		$25.00
Disney	30CC-1632	Children's Favorites Vol. 2	LP	Japan		$25.00
Disc Art	80152	Children's Sing Alongs	SCD5	U.S.	1996	$10.00
		School bus shaped CD				
Disc Art	80142	Children's Sing and Play Songs	SCD5	U.S.	1996	$10.00
		Stuffed Doll shaped CD				
Dennis Maxim		Chill Out With the Class of '97	DJ/Smplr	U.S.	1997	$5.00
		CD sampler free with premiere issue of Maxim magazine.				
MCA	18469	CHR Sampler	DJ/Smplr	U.S.		$5.00
MCA	18338	CHR Sampler	DJ/Smplr	U.S.	1990	$5.00
		Christmas CHR Sampler	DJ/Smplr	U.S.		$10.00
Eclipse Music	CMM 022-2	Christmas Concerto	SCDJ	U.S.	1996	$10.00
		Angel shaped CD.				
Polygram	SACD 739	Chronicles Sampler Volume 2	DJ/Smplr	U.S.	1993	$20.00
Polygram	SACD 551	Chronicles Vol. 1	DJ/Smplr	U.S.	1992	$5.00
Polygram	SACD 739	Chronicles Vol. 2	DJ/Smplr	U.S.	1993	$5.00
Chrysalis	DPRO-21738	Chrysalis "No Shit" Hard Rock Sampler	DJ/Smplr	U.S.	1989	$5.00
Chrysler		Chrysler Audio System	DJ/Smplr	U.S.	1991	$20.00
CHR		Cinema Sampler	DJ/Smplr	U.S.		$5.00
Cinram, Inc.		Cinram CD Sampler	DJ/Smplr	U.S.	1995	$8.00
Zoo	11026	Cio Mondo	LP/LB	U.S.		$7.00
Time Life		Civil War Music Collector's Edition	LP	U.S.	1994	$45.00
		3 CD Boxed set				
Warner Brothers	PRO-CD-6155	Class of '93	DJ/Smplr	U.S.	1993	$12.00
Warner Brothers		Class of '94	DJ/Smplr	U.S.	1994	$12.00
		2 CD set				
CDI-PRO	9951/52/53	Classic Hits	DJ/Smplr	U.S.		$75.00
		3 CD set. CD+I sampler.				
Chronicles	314 515 913-2	Classic Rock Box	LTD/LP	U.S.	1992	$70.00
		4 CD in simulated portable CD player package.				
Myriad		Club Indee	DJ/Smplr	U.S.	1995	$10.00
		CD-ROM				
Virgin	PRCD 3073	CMJ Prisoner	DJ/Smplr	U.S.	1989	$8.00
Capricorn	PRO-CD-5972	Cobra Records Story	DJ/Smplr	U.S.	1993	$8.00
Columbia/Epic	CSK 3052	Coca-Cola Pop Music Volume 1	DJ/CD3	U.S.	1991	$8.00
Columbia/Epic	CSK 3053	Coca-Cola Pop Music Volume 2	DJ/CD3	U.S.	1991	$8.00
Columbia/Epic	CSK 3054	Coca-Cola Pop Music Volume 3	DJ/CD3	U.S.	1991	$8.00
Columbia/Epic	CSK 3055	Coca-Cola Pop Music Volume 4	DJ/CD3	U.S.	1991	$8.00
Warner Brothers	PRO-CD-5508	Coca-Cola Volume 1	Smplr	U.S.	1992	$5.00
Warner Brothers	PRO-CD-5509	Coca-Cola Volume 2	Smplr	U.S.	1992	$5.00
Warner Brothers	PRO-CD-5510	Coca-Cola Volume 3	Smplr	U.S.	1992	$5.00
		Cocktails at 5	DJ/Smplr	U.S.	1994	$12.00
Arista	ASCD-9712	Color These #1	LP/BP	U.S.	1988	$14.00/$8.00
Columbia	CSK 5356	Columbia Adult Contemporary Sampler	DJ/Smplr	U.S.	1993	$8.00
Columbia	6791	Columbia Jazz: Limited Edition	DJ/Smplr	U.S.	1996	$18.00
		CD in box with press kit.				
Def Jam	CSK 1360	Columbia Street Sounds	DJ/Smplr	U.S.	1988	$5.00
		Common Ground	DJ/Smplr	U.K.		$60.00
		CD boxed set with extra interview disc, postcards, and photos.				
World/Epic		Common Ground	DJ/Smplr	U.S.	1995	$15.00
Westwood One		Common Thread: Songs of the Eagles	RS	U.S.	1993	$50.00
		3 CD set. Airdate: 10/16/93.				
Clarity	CCD-1010	Compact Disc Sampler	DJ/Smplr	U.S.	1995	$18.00
		Compact Disc Xpress	DJ/Smplr	U.S.	1993	$5.00
Mercury	824642-2	Compact Disco	LP/BP	U.S.	1985	$14.00/$8.00
DADC	CSG 000028	Compact Discovery	DJ/CD3	U.S.	1987	$18.00
DADC	CISG 000031	Compact Discovery	DJ/CD3	U.S.	1987	$18.00
DADC	CISG 000029	Compact Discovery	DJ/CD3	U.S.	1987	$18.00
Mosaic	MD4-109	Complete Edmund Hall/James P. Johnson/Sidney De Paris/Vic Dickenson Blue Note Sessions	LTD/LP	U.S.		$60.00
		4 CD set.				
Mosaic	MD4-150	Complete Master Jazz Piano	LTD/LP	U.S.		$60.00
		4 CD set.				
Blue Note		Connoisseur Series	DJ/Smplr	U.S.		$15.00
Attic	ACDP 1395	Contact! All-Star Collection	DJ/Smplr	Canada	1994	$35.00
ABC Radio		Continuous History of Rock and Roll	RS	U.S.	1989	$500.00
		50 CD set. Airdate: 10/1/89.				
ABC Radio		Continuous History of Rock and Roll	RS	U.S.	1995	$650.00
		50 CD set.				
Geffen	PRO-CD-4555	Convention Sampler	DJ/Smplr	U.S.	1993	$10.00
Philips	310690007-2	Cool Oldies Jukebox	LP	U.S.	1991	$25.00
		CD+I. First pressing with deleted Janis Ian track "Society's Child".				
		Cotton Patch Blues	DJ/Smplr	U.S.		$10.00
Curb		Country 90	DJ/Smplr	U.S.		$5.00
		Country Aids Awareness	DJ/Intvw	U.S.	1993	$10.00
Polygram	848999	Country Christmas	LP/BP	U.S.		$12.00/$7.00
Westwood One		Country Concert	RS	U.S.	1994	$25.00
		Airdate: 6/13/94.				
Westwood One		Country Concert	RS	U.S.	1994	$25.00
		Airdate: 6/4/94				
Westwood One		Country Concert	RS	U.S.	1994	$25.00
		Airdate: 6/6/94.				
Westwood One		Country Concert	RS	U.S.	1994	$25.00
		Airdate: 8/1/94.				
Global Satellite Network		Country Dance Party	RS	U.S.	1994	$25.00
		3 CD set. Airdate: 5/28/94.				
		Country Edge: Beatles And Nascar Tribute	RS	U.S.	1995	$20.00
		Airdate: 4/1/95.				
		Country Edge: Cutting Edge Christmas	RS	U.S.	1995	$20.00
		Airdate: 12/23/95.				
Sam Goody/Musicland		Country Heart	LTD/LP	U.S.	1996	$8.00
Mercury		Country Music Then and Now	LTD/LP	U.S.	1994	$50.00
		3 CD set. "As seen on TV" boxed set.				
		Country Salutes Lonesome Dove	RS	U.S.		$20.00
		Various country artists hosted by Clint Black.				
Unistar		Country Six Pack	RS	U.S.	1993	$35.00
		/3CD/Country music & interviews. Airdate: 7/4/93.				
		Country Special: Country's Top Vocalists	RS	U.S.	1995	$50.00
		3 CD set. Airdate: 11/25/95.				
MCA/Blockbuster Music	MCA3P-3719	Country's Hottest Faces Volume 1	LTD/LP	U.S.	1996	$18.00
		Sold exclusively at Blockbuster Music stores.				
MCA/Blockbuster Music	MCA3P-3839	Country's Hottest Faces Volume 2	LTD/LP	U.S.	1996	$18.00
		Sold exclusively at Blockbuster Music stores.				
		Country's Top Vocalists	RS	U.S.	1993	$40.00
		2 CD set. Airdate: 5/29/93.				
RCA	9701-2-RDJ	Cow Cow Boogie VIII	DJ/Smplr	U.S.	1989	$5.00
		Crazy Horse	RS	U.S.	1994	$40.00
		2 CD set. Airdate: 5/16/94.				
Rodven	CDP-303	Creando Una Nueva Era De Exitos	DJ/Smplr	U.S.	1994	$15.00
Sheffield Lab	CD-CRM	Creme de la Creme	LP/LB	U.S.†	1985	$14.00/$8.00
CRT		CRT Custom Products Sampler	DJ/Smplr	U.S.	1994	$5.00
Elektra	PRCD 8839-2	Crunchy Goodness	DJ/Smplr	U.S.	1993	$8.00
Cruz		Cruz Fall '93 Sampler	DJ/Smplr	U.S.	1993	$5.00
Cuba		Cuba: Let's Shape Together	SCD5	Germany	1996	$8.00
		Shaped CD.				
Curb		Curb Country '88	DJ/Smplr	U.S.		$5.00
Curb	041	Curb Country '91	DJ/Smplr	U.S.	1991	$5.00
Curb	051	Curb Country '91	DJ/Smplr	U.S.	1991	$5.00
		Cuts	DJ/Smplr	Japan		$25.00
Rhino		D.I.Y.	DJ/Smplr	U.S.	1994	$15.00
Warner Brothers		Damn Critics Damn Right	DJ/Smplr	U.S.	1996	$18.00
Max	NS09CD	Dance Factory 2 by Winston Fun Time	SCDJ	Germany	1996	$35.00
		Cigarette box shaped CD.				
Pandisc	002	Dance Sampler	DJ/Smplr	U.S.		$5.00
Pow Wow	7425	Dancehall Superhits	DJ/Smplr	U.S.	1992	$5.00
Capitol	MNE1	Dave's Dedicated Decades	DJ/Smplr	U.S.	1987	N/A
Westwood One		Dawn of the Deacade	RS	U.S.		$50.00
		3 CD set.				
DCC	GZS-PRO-1	DCC 24 Karat Gold Disc Sampler	DJ/Smplr	U.S.	1993	$100.00
Arista	ARCD-8669	Deadicated	DJ/LP	U.S.	1991	$25.00
		CD in special 10"x10" sleeve with large booklet.				
Nettwerk	W2-3010	Decadance	LTD/LP	U.S.	1995	$60.00
		5 CD set.				
Sony/Billboard	A 23565	Decade of Music	DJ/Smplr	U.S.	1992	$25.00
Elektra	8149-2	Decadent Music	DJ/Smplr	U.S.	1990	$5.00
Decca		Decca Musical History	DJ/Smplr	U.S.	1995	$15.00
RCA	2460-2-RDJ	Dedicated: An Introduction	DJ/Smplr	U.S.	1990	$8.00
Rondor	DCPJ-054	Deep Cuts	DJ/Smplr	U.S.	1996	$20.00
Rhino		Deep in the Grooves	DJ/Smplr	U.S.	1995	$30.00
		CD in bound promotional book				
Rhino		Deep in the Grooves	DJ/Smplr	U.S.	1995	$18.00
		CD in cardboard sleeve				
Def Jam		Def 7/93	DJ/Smplr	U.S.	1993	$8.00
Image	ID7943CD	Def Jam Classics Vols. 1& 2	LD	U.S.		$20.00
Def Jam		Def Jam Sampler	DJ/Smplr	U.S.		$5.00
Denon	TD 9027	Denon PCM Digital	DJ/CD3	U.S.	1987	$7.00
		Desert Storm	RS	U.S.	1991	$75.00
		4 CD set.				
Details		Details Music	LP	U.S.	1995	$6.00
Image	IDML1028	Dick Clark's VBest Of Bandstand	LD	U.S.		$30.00
Rhino	PRCD 7196	Didn't It Blow Your Mind: Soul Hits From the Seventies	DJ/Smplr	U.S.	1995	$15.00
Rhino	PRCD 7196	Didn't It Blow Your Mind: Soul Hits of the '70s Vol. 6-10	DJ/Smplr	U.S.	1991	$9.00
Warner Brothers/Sony	PRO-CD-2294	Digital Discovery	DJ/Smplr	U.S.	1985	$30.00
Elektra	9 60303-2	Digital Domain A Demonstration	LP	U.S.†	1983	$16.00
Sony	001-004	Digital Masterpiece Collection	DJ/Smplr	U.S.	1991	$40.00
		4 CD set.				
		Digital Memories	DJ/Smplr	U.S.		$8.00
Epic	ESK 5438	Dining Hall Classics	DJ/Smplr	U.S.	1993	$8.00
Polydor	SACD 417	Disc of Revelations	DJ/Smplr	U.S.	1991	$5.00
Rhino		Disco Sucks	DJ/Smplr	U.S.	1995	$12.00
		Discover Hits Post Modern	DJ/Smplr	U.S.		$5.00
		Discoverer Sampler	DJ/Smplr	U.S.		$5.00
AEC One Stop Group		Discoveries 18	DJ/Smplr	U.S.	1997	$10.00
Sony	ESK 4137	Discovery	DJ/Smplr	U.S.	1991	$8.00
Disney	CD-002	Disney Collection Vol. 1	LP/LB	Canada	1989	$15.00/$9.00
Disney	CD-003	Disney Collection Vol. 2	LP/LB	U.S.	1989	$15.00/$9.00
Disney	CD-005	Disney Presents a Family	LP/LB	U.S.		$15.00/$9.00
Disney Records	60915-7	Disney's Music From the Park	LTD/LP	U.S.	1996	$18.00
		Picture disc CD.				
Disney	30CC-1311	Disneyworld Official Album	LP	Japan		$25.00
Legacy	JSK 7679	Do Your Homework: The Whole World Is Listening	DJ/Smplr	U.S.	1995	$15.00
A&M	831	Do Yourself A Favor	DJ/Smplr	U.S.	1987	$5.00
Doctor	Dream115	Doctor Dream Records Sampler	DJ/Smplr	U.S.	1992	$5.00
Virgin	PRCD BOILER	Dodgy Boilers	DJ/Smplr	U.S.	1991	$5.00
CCM	58002	Don't It Sound Good: The Great Atlantic Vocal Groups	LP	U.S.	1995	$25.00
		2 CD set.				
Innovative	71066	Dream Code	LP/BP	U.S.		$12.00/$7.00

Label	Catalog Number	Title	Type	Country	Year	Value
		Dreaming Out Loud	DJ/Smplr	U.S.	1994	$25.00
	CD in box with pillow.					
Columbia	CSK 4897	Dreamland	DJ/Smplr	U.S.	1992	$5.00
Delicious Vinyl	PRO2211-2	DV Pro CD Sampler	DJ/Smplr	U.S.	1997	$8.00
Columbia	CSK 2920	E/P/A's New Year's Resolution	DJ/Smplr	U.S.	1988	$5.00
Polydor	SACD 161	Ear This	DJ/Smplr	U.S.	1990	$5.00
Polygram	SACD 162	Ear This. Alternative Sampler Vol. 1	DJ/Smplr	U.S.	1990	$5.00
Polygram	SACD 448	Earnog	DJ/Smplr	U.S.	1991	$5.00
Geffen	PRO-CD-4335	Earphoria	DJ/Smplr	U.S.	1991	$5.00
		Earth Has Music For Those Who Listen	DJ/Smplr	U.S.		$6.00
		Earth Music	LTD/LP	Australia	1994	$25.00
Life Aid Armenia	Aid CD001	Earthquake Album, The	LTD/LP	U.S.	1990	$30.00
Motown	3746310732	East Coast Family 1 4 all 4 1	DJ/Smplr	U.S.	1992	$5.00
Rondor	ECD 50008	East Memphis Music The Hits	DJ/Smplr	U.S.	1990	$45.00
	4 CD set and booklet in plastic "longbox-size" sleeve.					
Eastwest		Eastwest Story	DJ/Smplr	U.K.	1995	$35.00
Murcury/Polydor		Eat Me	DJ/Smplr	Canada	1995	$40.00
	2 CD set. Includes rare version of Tears For Fears song "Falling Down".					
DADC	DADA 1	Edison CD Sampler, The	DJ/Smplr	Austria	1987	N/A
DADC	ECDS-1	Edison CD Sampler, The	DJ/Smplr	U.S.	1984	N/A
Polygram Music & Publishing Group		Eighteen Original Hits By Eighteen Unoriginal Artists	DJ/Smplr	U.S.	1995	$30.00
Elektra	PRCD 8110-2	Elektra Entertainment of the '90s	DJ/Smplr	U.S.	1989	$8.00
Elektra	PR 8445-2	Elektra Music of Champions	DJ/Smplr	U.S.	1991	$8.00
		Elwood's New Years Bash At the House Of Blues	RS	U.S.	1996	$40.00
	2 CD set. Airdate: 1/1/96					
EMI	DPRO 04528	EMI – Energy Milestones Imagination	DJ/Smplr	U.S.	1990	$5.00
EMI	DPRO-79857	EMI Latin	DJ/Smplr	U.S.	1993	$5.00
EMI	DPRO-04888	EMI Legends of Rock 'n Roll	DJ/Smplr	U.S.		$10.00
EMI	DPRO 04611	EMI – New Visions	DJ/Smplr	U.S.	1990	$5.00
EMI Music Publishing	EMP-16 to EMP-45	EMI Professional Compact Disc Library	DJ/Smplr	U.S.	1993	$250.00
	35 CD boxed sets with 7 spiral bound books.					
A&M	31450384 2	Empire Records the Soundtrack	DJ/LP	U.S.	1995	$18.00
	CD in jewel box in prited bag.					
Time Warner Sound Exchange		Enchanted Woodwind, The	LP	U.S.	1995	$16.00
Atlantic		Encomium	DJ/LP	U.S.	1995	$15.00
A&M		Enhanced CD Sampler	DJ/Smplr	U.S.	1996	$27.00
	Enhanced CD.					
Enigma	EPRO 202	Enigma Summer Grand Slam	DJ/Smplr	U.S.	1989	$6.00
Epitaph	QDCA 93059	Epitaph: This Is Epitaph	DJ/Smplr	Japan		$125.00
Polygram	8526	Essence of Christmas	LP/BP	U.S.		$12.00/$7.00
		Essential Blues	DJ/Smplr	U.S.		$6.00
		Essential Gospel	DJ/Smplr	U.S.		$6.00
Polygram	CDP 518	Even Better Than the Real Thing	DJ/Smplr	U.S.	1992	$8.00
Polyram	823 490-2	Every Man Has a Woman	LP/BP	U.S.	1984	$14.00/$8.00
Spartacus	CDPRO 001	Exitos	DJ/Smplr	U.S.	1996	$12.00
Radioactive		Exposed	DJ/Smplr	U.S.	1995	$8.00
Philips	080 017-2	Eyes of the Wind	DJ/CDV	U.S.	1987	$40.00
Island	PRCD 6638-2	F*ck Dance, This Is Art	DJ/Smplr	U.S.	1990	$8.00
Challenge	CHR 70020	Face the Challenge in Music Vol. 1	DJ/Smplr	U.S.	1995	$15.00
		Face the Music	DJ/Smplr	U.S.		$18.00
	2 CD set.					
Columbia		Facts About Black History	DJ/Smplr	U.S.		$5.00
Rhino/R.N.A	90057	Facts About R.N.A.	DJ/Smplr	U.S.	1990	$5.00
Polygram	SACD 749	Fall From Grace	DJ/Smplr	U.S.	1993	$8.00
		Fall of America	DJ/Smplr	U.S.		$6.00
Nastymix	PRO 1	Fall Radio Compilation	DJ/Smplr	U.S.	1990	$5.00
ffrr	SACD 045	Fall Trip '93	DJ/Smplr	U.S.	1993	$5.00
Disney	PCCD-00018	Family Christmas	LTD/LP	Japan		$35.00
		Family Harmony Sampler	DJ/Smplr	U.S.		$15.00
A&M		Faster A&M Kill	DJ/Smplr	U.S.		$6.00
	2 CD set.					
Harper Collins		Ferrington Guitars	LTD/LP	U.S.	1992	$175.00
	CD with autographed book in limited edition guitar case.					
Spartacus	SDM22307	Fiesta Cubana	DJ/Smplr	U.S.	1996	$12.00
Max	NS 15CD	Fiesta Delapierre	SCDJ	Germany	1996	$20.00
	Wine bottle and glasses shaped CD.					
Global Satellite Network		Fifty Great American Rock Albums	RS	U.S.	7/4/92	$80.00
	6 CD set.					
Figdish		Figdish Sampler	DJ/Smplr	U.S.	1995	$15.00
Right Stuff	DPRO-10907	Filet 'O Soul	DJ/Smplr	U.S.	1996	$18.00
	Picture disc CD of steak in wrapped styrofoam plate.					
BMG	RDJ 61144-2	First Note in Black Music	DJ/Smplr	U.S.	1992	$28.00
	3 CD set.					
Varta		Fit am Start mit Blue Dynamic Volume 1	SCDJ	Germany	1995	$30.00
	Automotive battery-shaped CD. Limited to 5,000 copies.					
Arista	ASCD-9755	Fit to be Tied	DJ/Smplr	U.S.	1988	$8.00
Pioneer		Five	DJ/Smplr	U.S.		$8.00
Curb	023	Five Easy Pieces	DJ/Smplr	U.S.	1990	$5.00
Red Eye		Five Years in the Future	DJ/Smplr	U.S.	1991	$8.00
		Flash Forward	DJ/Smplr	U.S.		$5.00
U.S. Postal Service		Folk Heroes: Stamp Folio	LTD/LP	U.S.	1996	$12.00
	CD sampler with stamps and booklet in cardboard sleeve.					
Image	ID7774EM	Follies in Concert	LD	U.S.	1985	$40.00
Warner Brothers	PRO-CD-3503	Follow Our Trax	DJ/Smplr	U.S.	1989	$8.00
Warner Brothers	PRO-CD-3650	Follow Our Trax Volume II	DJ/Smplr	U.S.	1989	$8.00
Warner Brothers	PRO-CD-3831	Follow Our Trax Volume III	DJ/Smplr	U.S.	1989	$8.00
Warner Brothers	PRO-CD-4018	Follow Our Trax Volume IV	DJ/Smplr	U.S.	1989	$8.00
Reprise	PRO-CD-6344	Follow Our Trax Volume IX	DJ/Smplr	U.S.	1993	$5.00
Warner Brothers	PRO-CD-4555	Follow Our Trax Volume V	DJ/Smplr	U.S.	1990	$8.00
Warner Brothers	PRO-CD-4634	Follow Our Trax Volume VI	DJ/Smplr	U.S.	1991	$8.00
Reprise	PRO-CD-5067	Follow Our Trax Volume VII	DJ/Smplr	U.S.	1991	$8.00
Reprise	PRO-CD-5348	Follow Our Trax Volume VIII	DJ/Smplr	U.S.	1992	$8.00
		For Lovers Only	DJ/Smplr	U.S.		$5.00
Galaxy	389602	For You, With Love	SCD5	Germany	1996	$13.00
Arista	ASCD-2553	Forplay	DJ/Smplr	U.S.	1993	$8.00
Rhino	PRCD 7058	Forward: A New Direction From Rhino	DJ/Smplr	U.S.	1994	$8.00
Fossil/Sony Music Special Products	A 26396	Fossil Time Warp	DJ/Smplr	U.S.	1995	$20.00
	Free with Fossil watch					
Concrete	8801	Foundations Forum '88	DJ/Smplr	U.S.	1988	$15.00
	2 CD set					
Concrete		Foundations Forum '88	DJ/Smplr	U.S.	1994	$35.00
	4 CD set.					
Concrete		Foundations Forum '89	DJ/Smplr	U.S.	1989	$15.00
	2 CD set					
Concrete		Foundations Forum '90	DJ/Smplr	U.S.	1990	$15.00
	2 CD set					
Concrete		Foundations Forum '91	DJ/Smplr	U.S.	1991	$15.00
	2 CD set					
Concrete		Foundations Forum '92	DJ/Smplr	U.S.	1992	$15.00
	2 CD set					
Concrete		Foundations Forum '93	DJ/Smplr	U.S.	1993	$15.00
	2 CD set					
Coca Cola	CC101-2	Fountain Favorites	LP	U.S.	1994	$20.00
		Four of Hearts	RS	U.S.	1994	$55.00
	2 CD set. Airdate: 2/7/94.					
		Four of Hearts Valentine Special	RS	U.S.		$12.00
	2 CD set. Top 40 artist valentine tribute.					
Mercury	856800	Freedom	CD5	U.S.	1995	$5.00
Rhino	PRCD 7224	Fresh Out Da Crates: Spring 1997 Releases	DJ/Smplr	U.S.	1997	$10.00
		Fresh Produce	DJ/Smplr	U.S.		$6.00
Warner Brothers	PRO-CD-2776	From Hendrix to Replacements	DJ/Smplr	U.S.		$8.00
MCA	CD33 3026	From the Hip	DJ/Smplr	U.S.	1990	$5.00
Warner Brothers	ESK 7441	Fuck the Rules	DJ/Smplr	U.S.	1995	$8.00
ffrr	CDP1262	Full Frequency Range Recordings Sample Disc	DJ/Smplr	U.S.	1996	$20.00
	ImageDisc.					
Warner Brothers	PRO-CD-4883	Full House	DJ/Smplr	U.S.	1991	$8.00
MCA	ASCD 2397	Fully Amped	DJ/Smplr	U.S.	1992	$8.00
		Fundamental Hymnal, The	DJ/Smplr	U.S.		$5.00
		Fundamental Hymnal, The	LP/LB	U.S.		$13.00/$10.00
Chronicles		Funk on Fire	DJ/Smplr	U.S.	1995	$12.00
		Funkology/Love Jams	DJ/Smplr	U.S.		$7.00
		Funky Stuff	DJ/Smplr	U.S.		$7.00
Time Warner Sound Exchange		Gabriel's Golden Harp	LTD/LP	U.S.	1995	$17.00
BMG	RDJ 66415-2	Galaxy of Stars	DJ/Smplr	U.S.	1994	$5.00
Disc Art	80112	German Beer Drinking Songs	SCD5	U.S.	1996	$10.00
	Beer Stein shaped CD					
Milan	MLDJ-003-2	Gettysburg: Highlights From	DJ/Smplr	U.S.	1994	$5.00
	Blue sleeve					
Milan	MLDJ-003-2	Gettysburg: Highlights From	DJ/Smplr	U.S.	1994	$5.00
	white sleeve					
		Gigantic Recording Corp. Vol 1	DJ/Smplr	U.S.		$7.00
		Gigantic Recording Corp. Vol 2	DJ/Smplr	U.S.		$7.00
Virgin	PRCD PEACE	Give Peace a Chance	DJ/Smplr	U.S.	1991	$12.00
WEA	DGM91	Give Us Liberty and Darn Good Music	DJ/Smplr	U.S.	1991	$15.00
		Glastonbury '95	RS	U.S.	1995	$250.00
	9 CD set. Airdate: 7/4/95.					
		Glastonbury Festival	RS	U.S.	1996	$145.00
	3 CD set. Airdate: 7/7/96.					
MBI	1993	Global Dance Showcase	DJ/Smplr	U.S.	1993	$5.00
Global Voyage	331	Global Voyage	DJ/Smplr	U.S.		$5.00
GNP		GNP Crescendo: 40th Anniversary Sampler 1954-1994	DJ/Smplr	U.S.	1994	$15.00
MCA	1547	GNU Music	DJ/Smplr	U.S.	1991	$5.00
Time Warner Sound Exchange		God Bless the U.S.A.	LTD/LP	U.S.	1995	$17.00
		Going for the Gold	RS	U.S.	1994	$20.00
	2 CD set. Airdate: 2/21/94. Country artist music and interview show.					
		Going Mobile	RS	U.S.	1996	$20.00
	Airdate: 4/1/96.					
RCA	5962-2-RDj	Golden Country Oldies	DJ/Smplr	U.S.	1987	$15.00
General Mills/EMI	72438-19195-2-1	Golden Grahams: Golden Jams	LTD/LP	U.S.	1996	$8.00
Rhino	R2 71007	Golden Throats – More Celebrity Rock Oddities	LP/LB	U.S.	1991	$17.00/$15.00
Major Flash	MF107	Goldmine 1992 Music Sampler	DJ/Smplr	U.S.	1992	$5.00
A&M	CD 17524	Good Records Don't Know...	DJ/Smplr	U.S.	1988	$5.00
		Goodman Groove	DJ/Smplr	U.S.		$70.00
	3 CD set.					
		Goya...A Life in a Song	DJ/Smplr	U.S.		$5.00
Gramavision		Gramavision 10th Anniversary Sampler	LTD/LP	U.S.	1993	$20.00/$18.00
Columbia	CSK 5034	Grammy Music	DJ/Smplr	U.S.	1993	$10.00
Sony	CSM 5029	Grammy Music	DJ/Smplr	U.S.	1993	$10.00
	Minidisc sampler					
Grand Royal		Grand Royal Mixed Drink	DJ/Smplr	U.S.		$15.00
Grand Royal		Grand Royal Mixed Drink #2	DJ/Smplr	U.S.	1995	$15.00
Westwood One		Great Groups	RS	U.S.	1994	$25.00
	3 CD set. Airdate: 6/27/94.					
		Great Sounds	DJ/Smplr	U.S.		$10.00
EMI	SPCD 1524126	Greatest 3 Campaign Sampler	DJ/Smplr	Japan	1995	$1,000.00
	3 CD boxed set including the following Japanese promotional Samplers: Queen - A Sample Of Magic, Rolling Stones - Shine A Light, Paul McCartney - Paul Is Cool.					
EMI	SPCD 1472	Greatest 3, The	DJ/Smplr	Japan	1994	$400.00
	Sampler with two songs each from the Beatles, Rolling Stones, and Queen					
Image	ML1032	Greenpeace: Non-Toxic Video Hits	LD	U.S.		$10.00
Gridlock		Gridlock 10	DJ/Smplr	U.S.		$10.00
GRP	WD-1026	GRP – All Stars Live In Japan	LP/LB	U.S.†	1985	$14.00/$8.00
Guerilla	13901	Guerilla Artists Singles '93	DJ/Smplr	U.S.	1993	$5.00
Warner Brothers		Guide: November/December 1994, The	DJ/Smplr	U.S.	1994	$25.00
Media America		Guitar Heroes	RS	U.S.	1996	$150.00
	3 CD set.					
Global Satellite Network		Guitar Legends	RS	U.S.		$175.00
	3 CD set.					
Guitar Player		Guitar Player: Legends of Guitar Vol. 1	Smplr	U.S.	1993	$15.00
Guitar Player		Guitar Player: Legends of Guitar Vol. 2	Smplr	U.S.	1993	$15.00
Warner Brothers	26828-2	Guitars That Ruled the World	LP/LB	U.S.		$14.00/$8.00
Gyroscope	001	Gyroscope Label Sampler	DJ/Smplr	U.S.	1993	$10.00
A&M	31454 8035 2	H.O.R.D.E. Festival 1993 Sampler	DJ/Smplr	U.S.	1993	$15.00
A&M	31454 8104 2	H.O.R.D.E. Festival 1994 Sampler	DJ/Smplr	U.S.	1994	$15.00
A&M	0008644-03	H.O.R.D.E. Festival 1995 Sampler	DJ/Smplr	U.S.	1995	$15.00
Philips	310691071-2	H.O.R.D.E. Festival CD-ROM, The	DJ/Smplr	U.S.	1996	$75.00
	2 CD-ROM set in large box with press kit and t-shirt.					
Time/Warner Sound Exchange	227769	Halarious Hits Of the '50s	LP	U.S.	1996	$30.00
	2 CD set.					
		Hampton Roads..	DJ/Smplr	U.S.	1988	$5.00
Hamstein		Hamstein Catalog Sampler	DJ/Smplr	U.S.	1993	$55.00
	6 CD set.					

Happy Holidays – (Sub Pop SP 1995B)

Label	Catalog Number	Title	Type	Country	Year	Value
Sub Pop	SP 1995B	Happy Holidays	DJ/Smplr	U.S.	1995	$15.00

Label	Catalog Number	Title	Type	Country	Year	Value
MCA	18100	Happy Holidays From MCA	DJ/Smplr	U.S.	1989	$5.00
Hard Report	1	Hard Attack Compact Disc Sampler	DJ/Smplr	U.S.	1987	$10.00
		Hard Attack Vol. 4	DJ/Smplr	U.S.		$5.00
MCA	1509	Hard Grooves 1	DJ/Smplr	U.S.	1991	$5.00
		Hard Hitters – Metal Sampler #2	DJ/Smplr	U.S.		$5.00
		Hard Rock	Japan	DJ/Smplr		$20.00
		Hard Workin' Country	RS	U.S.	1994	$45.00
		3 CD set. Airdate: 9/5/94.				
Right Stuff	72438-36448-2-7	Harley Davidson Country Road Songs	LTD/LP	U.S.	1996	$35.00
		2 CD set in leather wallet.				
Right Stuff		Harley Davidson: Road Songs	LTD/LP	U.S.	1995	$32.00
		2 CD set in black wallet package.				
Rhino		Have a Nice Day: Super Hits of the Seventies	DJ/Smplr	U.S.	1992	$20.00
		CD in digpak with denim sleeve and "smile" pack				
Reference	RR-S3CD	HDCD Sampler	DJ/Smplr	U.S.	1992	$15.00
Polydor		Head Tripp	DJ/Smplr	U.S.	1995	$15.00
		2 CD set. disc one is a CD-ROM sampler.				
Polydor	816054-2	Hear the Light	LP/BP	U.S.	1985	$14.00/$8.00
Polydor	816055-2	"Hear the Light, Vol. 2"	LP/BP	U.S.	1985	$14.00/$8.00
Sony	CSK 7767	Heavy Hitters	DJ/Smplr	U.S.	1996	$15.00
Arista	ASCD 2534	Heavy Metal Arista Style	DJ/Smplr	U.S.	1993	$15.00
		2 CD set				
Warner Brothers	PRO-CD-5787	Heck on Wheels	DJ/Smplr	U.S.	1992	$10.00
Warner Brothers	PRO-CD-6457	Heck on Wheels Vol. 3	DJ/Smplr	U.S.	1993	$10.00
Warner Brothers	PRO-CD-6807	Heck on Wheels Vol. 4	DJ/Smplr	U.S.	1994	$10.00
		Hello My Name Is...	DJ/Smplr	U.S.		$6.00
Capitol	DPRO-79692	Herd This	DJ/Smplr	U.S.	1991	$5.00
Rykodisc	Ryko 00099	Here It Is, The Music	DJ/Smplr	U.S.	1988	$5.00
		Heroes & Legends	RS	U.S.	1994	$45.00
		3 CD set. Airdate: 10/3/94.				
Razor & Tie		Heroes of Rock And Roll	LP	U.S.	1995	$30.00
		2CD set				
Columbia	CSK 45240	Highwayman 2	DJ/LP	U.S.	1990	$15.00
		Hillbilly Fever Sampler	DJ/Smplr	U.S.	1995	$20.00
Time Warner Sound Exchange		Hillbilly Heaven	LTD/LP	U.S.	1995	$17.00
Trojan		History of Trojan Records 1968–1972	LTD/LP	U.S.	1995	$30.00
		2 CD set.				
Trojan		History of Trojan Records 1972–1995	LTD/LP	U.S.	1995	$30.00
		2 CD set.				
CBS	CSK 1598	Hitchhiker College Radio Hour	DJ/Smplr	U.S.	1989	$5.00
Columbia	CSK 3033	Hitchhiker Radio Saga 3	DJ/Smplr	U.S.	1991	$5.00
Columbia		Hitchhiker Sampler	LP/LB	U.S.		$13.00/$10.00
Columbia	ASK 1560	Hitchhiker Sampler Vol. 1	DJ/Smplr	U.S.	1989	$5.00
Hits	5017900	Hits Ain't Nuthin' But A NARM Thing	DJ/Smplr	U.S.		$5.00
Atlantic		Hits for the Holidays	DJ/Smplr	U.S.	1993	$15.00
		2 CD set				
RCA	RJC66285-2	Hits From the Big Dog	DJ/Smplr	U.S.	1993	$8.00
Hits	HT005	Hits Night of the Living Post Modern	DJ/Smplr	U.S.		$5.00
		Hits Sampler Volume 3	DJ/Smplr	U.S.		$5.00
		Hits Songs of Post Modern	DJ/Smplr	U.S.		$5.00
Columbia	CSK 5221	Hits You Might Have Missed	DJ/Smplr	U.S.	1993	$10.00
On the Radio		Hittsville U.S.A.	RS	U.S.	1993	$40.00
		6 CD set. Airdate: 11/93.				
Epic		Holiday In-Store Sampler '95	DJ/Smplr	U.S.	1995	$15.00
Hollywood	PRCD 10239-2	Hollywood	DJ/Smplr	U.S.	1992	$8.00
Hollywood	PRCD 10138-2	Hollywood Alternative Sampler	DJ/Smplr	U.S.	1992	$8.00
Capitol	DPRO 79215	Hollywood And Vinyl	DJ/Smplr	U.S.	1987	$5.00
Rhino	PRCD 7141	Hollywood's Most Precious Jewels	DJ/Smplr	U.S.	1995	$25.00
		CD in "jewelry box" package				
Epic	ESK 7665	Home Alive: The Art of Self Defense	DJ/Smplr	U.S.	1995	$15.00
Pioneer	PA86-M032	Hot Rock Videos: Volume 1	"8""LD	U.S.	1984	$7.00
Pioneer	PA86-M045	Hot Rock Videos: Volume 2	"8""LD	U.S.	1985	$7.00
PGD	SACD 589	Hot Stocking Stuffers	DJ/Smplr	U.S.	1992	$5.00
Mercury	SACD 841	Hot Stuff	DJ/Smplr	U.S.	1994	$10.00
Mercury	SACD 841	Hot Stuff Vol. Two	DJ/Smplr	U.S.	1994	$15.00
HDH		Hot Wax	DJ/Smplr	U.S.	1990	$10.00
		Hottest Stars Of '93 (Country's Cutting Edge)	RS	U.S.	1994	$10.00
		Airdate: 1/1/94.				
		House of Blues	RS	U.S.	1993	$30.00
		2 CD set. Airdate: 10/17/93.				
		House of Blues	RS	U.S.	1994	$40.00
		2 CD set. Airdate: 11/27/94.				
		House of Blues	RS	U.S.	1994	$35.00
		2 CD set. Airdate: 5/8/94.				
		House of Blues	RS	U.S.	1994	$30.00
		2 CD set. Airdate: 6/5/94.				
		House of Blues	RS	U.S.	1994	$50.00
		2 CD set. Airdate: 9/18/94.				
		House of Blues	RS	U.S.	1995	$50.00
		2 CD set. 2/3/95.				
		House of Blues	RS	U.S.	1995	$55.00
		2 CD set. Airdate: 10/13/95.				
		House of Blues	RS	U.S.	1995	$50.00
		2 CD set. Airdate: 10/27/95.				
		House of Blues	RS	U.S.	1995	$40.00
		2 CD set. Airdate: 11/24/95.				
		House of Blues	RS	U.S.	1995	$45.00
		2 CD set. Airdate: 12/15/95.				
		House of Blues	RS	U.S.	1995	$30.00
		2 CD set. Airdate: 2/24/95				
		House of Blues	RS	U.S.	1995	$40.00
		2 CD set. Airdate: 3/10/95.				
		House of Blues	RS	U.S.	1995	$80.00
		2 CD set. Airdate: 3/31/95.				
		House of Blues	RS	U.S.	1995	$40.00
		2 CD set. Airdate: 4/28/95.				
		House of Blues	RS	U.S.	1995	$50.00
		2 CD set. Airdate: 5/12/95.				
		House of Blues	RS	U.S.	1995	$35.00
		2 CD set. Airdate: 5/14/95.				
		House of Blues	RS	U.S.	1995	$55.00
		2 CD set. Airdate: 6/23/95.				
		House of Blues	RS	U.S.	1995	$40.00
		2 CD set. Airdate: 6/30/95.				
		House of Blues	RS	U.S.	1995	$35.00
		2 CD set. Airdate: 8/4/95.				
		House of Blues	RS	U.S.	1995	$45.00
		Airdate: 10/27/95.				
		House of Blues	RS	U.S.	1995	$45.00
		Airdate: 2/17/95.				
		House of Blues	RS	U.S.	1995	$45.00
		Airdate: 6/5/95.				
		House of Blues	RS	U.S.	1996	$40.00
		2 CD set. Airdate: 7/12/96.				
		House of Blues	RS	U.S.	1996	$40.00
		2 CD set. Airdate: 7/19/96.				
		House of Blues	RS	U.S.	1996	$40.00
		2 CD set. Airdate: 7/5/96.				
		House of Blues	RS	U.S.	1996	$50.00
		Airdate: 2/2/96.				
		House of Blues	RS	U.S.	1996	$45.00
		Airdate: 4/5/96.				
		House of Blues: 1994 Top Ten	RS	U.S.	1995	$50.00
		2 CD set. Airdate: 1/1/95.				
		House of Blues: 1995 Top Ten	RS	U.S.	1996	$50.00
		2 CD set. Airdate: 1/1/96.				
		House of Blues: Alligator Records	RS	U.S.	1996	$40.00
		2 CD set. Airdate: 4/7/96.				
		House of Blues: America	RS	U.S.	1995	$40.00
		2 CD set. Airdate: 7/2/95.				
		House of Blues: American Music	RS	U.S.	1994	$40.00
		2 CD set. Airdate: 7/3/94.				
		House of Blues: Austin Texas	RS	U.S.	1994	$40.00
		2 CD set. Airdate: 10/23/94.				
		House of Blues: Blues the Next Generation	RS	U.S.	1995	$30.00
		2 CD set. Airdate: 10/1/95.				
		House of Blues: Blues Valentine	RS	U.S.	1996	$30.00
		2 CD set. Airdate: 2/11/96.				
		House of Blues: California Blues	RS	U.S.	1994	$20.00
		2 CD set. Airdate: 5/1/94.				
		House of Blues: Capitol Records Concert	RS	U.S.	1995	$45.00
		2 CD set. Airdate: 9/1/95.				
		House of Blues: Chicago Blues	RS	U.S.	1994	$40.00
		2 CD set. Airdate: 12/4/94				
		House of Blues: Christmas	RS	U.S.	1995	$40.00
		2 CD set. Airdate: 12/24/95.				
		House of Blues: Easter	RS	U.S.	1995	$35.00
		2 CD set. Airdate: 4/16/95.				
		House of Blues: Elwood's New Years Bash	RS	U.S.	1996	$35.00
		2 CD set. Airdate: 1/1/96.				
		House of Blues: Elwood's Top Songs Of '93	RS	U.S.	1993	$35.00
		2 CD set. Airdate: 1/2/93.				
		House of Blues: Excello Records	RS	U.S.	1996	$35.00
		2 CD set. Airdate: 3/8/96.				
		House of Blues: Grammy Awards	RS	U.S.	1995	$35.00
		2 CD set. Airdate: 2/26/95.				
		House of Blues: Guest	RS	U.S.	1994	$25.00
		2 CD set. Airdate: 10/30/94.				
		House of Blues: Guitars	RS	U.S.	1995	$40.00
		2 CD set. Airdate: 11/17/95.				
		House of Blues: Halloween	RS	U.S.	1995	$40.00
		2 CD set. Airdate: 10/29/95.				
		House of Blues: History of New Orleans	RS	U.S.	1994	$40.00
		2 CD set. Airdate: 1/20/94.				
		House of Blues: Internet & Bobby Parker	RS	U.S.	1995	$40.00
		2 CD set. Airdate: 12/17/95.				
		House of Blues: Jump Blues	RS	U.S.	1994	$40.00
		2 CD set. Airdate: 2/14/94.				
		House of Blues: King of the Blues	RS	U.S.	1995	$40.00
		2 CD set. Airdate: 6/17/95.				
		House of Blues: Mardi Gras	RS	U.S.	1996	$40.00
		2 CD set. Airdate: 2/16/96.				
		House of Blues: New Orleans	RS	U.S.	1995	$40.00
		2 CD set. Airdate: 10/15/95.				
		House of Blues: Peter Green Project	RS	U.S.	1995	$40.00
		2 CD set. Airdate: 8/6/95.				
		House of Blues: Piano Blues	RS	U.S.	1994	$40.00
		2 CD set. Airdate: 8/7/94.				
		House of Blues: Radio Hour Second Anniversary	RS	U.S.	1995	$40.00
		2 CD set. Airdate: 8/27/95.				
		House of Blues: Rhino's Blues Fest	RS	U.S.	1996	$40.00
		2 CD set. Airdate: 1/14/96.				
		House of Blues: San Francisco	RS	U.S.	1995	$40.00
		2 CD set. Airdate: 4/2/95.				
		House of Blues: Slide Guitar	RS	U.S.	1993	$40.00
		2 CD set. Airdate: 11/28/93.				
		House of Blues: St. Louis Blues	RS	U.S.	1995	$40.00
		2 CD set. Airdate: 6/18/95.				
		House of Blues: Upton Horns	RS	U.S.	1994	$40.00
		2 CD set. Airdate: 7/10/94.				
		House of Blues: W.C. Handy Awards	RS	U.S.	1995	$40.00
		2 CD set. Airdate: 4/30/95.				
		House of Blues: W.C. Handy Awards	RS	U.S.	1995	$40.00
		2 CD set. Airdate: 6/9/95.				
		House of Blues: Zydeco Night	RS	U.S.	1995	$40.00
		2 CD set. Airdate: 12/15/95.				
MCA	2044	House Party II Dance Sampler	DJ/Smplr	U.S.	1991	$8.00
MCA	2045	House Party II Quiet Storm Sampler	DJ/Smplr	U.S.	1991	$8.00
MCA	2043	House Party II Rap Sampler	DJ/Smplr	U.S.	1991	$8.00
Time Warner Sound Exchange		How Great Thou Art	LTD/LP	U.S.	1995	$17.00
Elektra	PR 8282-2	How Our World Floats	DJ/Smplr	U.S.	1990	$5.00
Rhino	PRO2 90045	I Guess We Didn't Save The LP	DJ/Smplr	U.S.	1990	$45.00
		3CD set in 12"x12" vinyl album sleeve.				
Seed		I Lick You Because I Love You	DJ/Smplr	U.S.	1993	$5.00
IRS		I'm With the Band – Confessions of An IRS Groupie	DJ/Smplr	U.S.		$5.00
		Ichioshi-Kun	DJ/Smplr	Japan		$25.00
Island	NMS '89	If This Were A Radio...	DJ/Smplr	U.S.	1989	$10.00
		2 CD set				
A&M	CD 17456	If You Know All This Music...	DJ/Smplr	U.S.	1987	$10.00
Windham Hill	WD 17639	Imaginary Roads	DJ/Smplr	U.S.	1988	$10.00
Westwood One		In Concert	RS	U.S.	1992	$50.00
		2 CD set. Airdate: 11/23/92.				
Westwood One		In Concert	RS	U.S.	1992	$50.00
		2 CD set. Airdate: 8/17/92.				
Westwood One		In Concert	RS	U.S.	1993	$80.00
		2 CD set. Airdate: 10/11/93.				
Westwood One		In Concert	RS	U.S.	1993	$55.00
		2 CD set. Airdate: 9/27/93.				
Westwood One		In Concert	RS	U.S.	1995	$50.00
		2 CD set. 3/27/95.				
Westwood One		In Concert: Best of 1994	RS	U.S.	1995	$40.00
		2 CD set. Airdate: 1/2/95.				
Westwood One		In Concert: Best of 1995	RS	U.S.	1995	$40.00
		2 CD set. Airdate: 12/18/95.				
Westwood One		In Concert: Best of In Concert '92	RS	U.S.	1993	$50.00
		4 CD set. Airdate: 1/4/93.				
Westwood One		In Concert: Best of In Concert '93	RS	U.S.	1993	$50.00
		2 CD set. Airdate: 12/20/93.				
Westwood One		In Concert: Grammy Award Edition	RS	U.S.	1994	$45.00
		2 CD set. Airdate: 2/14/94				
Westwood One		In Concert – Nu Rock	RS	U.S.	1995	$70.00
		2 CD set. 1/16/95				

Label	Catalog Number	Title	Type	Country	Year	Value
Westwood One		In Concert – Nu Rock	RS	U.S.	1995	$50.00
	2 CD set. 6/19/95.					
Westwood One		In Concert – Nu Rock	RS	U.S.	1996	$60.00
	2 CD set. Airdate 3/25/96.					
Westwood One		In Concert – Nu Rock	RS	U.S.	1996	$60.00
	2 CD set. Airdate 4/8/96.					
Westwood One		In Concert – Nu Rock: Acoustic	RS	U.S.	1995	$50.00
	2 CD set. Airdate: 4/24/95.					
Westwood One		In Concert – Nu Rock: Acoustic Holiday Special	RS	U.S.	1994	$55.00
	2 CD set. Airdate: 12/19/94.					
Westwood One		In Concert – Nu Rock: Acoustic Special	RS	U.S.	1994	$55.00
	4 CD set. Airdate: 2/28/94.					
Westwood One		In Concert – Nu Rock: Barely Acoustic	RS	U.S.	1996	$60.00
	2 CD set. Airdate: 3/25/96.					
Westwood One		In Concert – Nu Rock: Best Of Nu-Rock '93	RS	U.S.	1993	$45.00
	2 CD set. Airdate: 12/20/93.					
Westwood One		In Concert – Nu Rock: Semi-Acoustic Part 1	RS	U.S.	1995	$40.00
	2 CD set. Airdate: 4/24/95.					
Westwood One		In Concert – Nu Rock: Semi-Acoustic Part 2	RS	U.S.	1995	$40.00
	2 CD set. Airdate: 5/8/95.					
CBS	ASK 1503	In Your Ear: The CBS Records CD3 Sampler Vol. 1	DJ/CD3	U.S.	1989	$10.00
CBS	ASK 1543	In Your Ear: The CBS Records CD3 Sampler Vol. 2	DJ/CD3	U.S.	1989	$10.00
Rhino		In Your Face: History of Funk	DJ/Smplr	U.S.		$15.00
Arista		In-Store Fall '90	DJ/Smplr	U.S.		$5.00
		Incredible Song of Swag	DJ/Smplr	U.S.		$6.00
Independent		Independent: Blue Collage	DJ/Smplr	U.S.	1993	$4.00
Independent		Independent Power 1	DJ/Smplr	U.S.	1994	$4.00
Independent		Independent Power 2	DJ/Smplr	U.S.	1994	$4.00
KAO		Independent Presentation	DJ/Smplr	U.S.	1995	$18.00
Independent		Independent: Red Collage	DJ/Smplr	U.S.	1993	$4.00
		Inner City Blues	DJ/Smplr	U.S.		$6.00
New Alliance		Innings and Quarters	DJ/Smplr	U.S.	1992	$5.00
Universal Dist		Inside Tracks	DJ/Smplr	U.S.	1992	$5.00
Northwood	22412	Inspired Artists	DJ/Smplr	U.S.	1996	$15.00
Interscope	ISR S8-91	Interscope 1991 National Sales Meeting Sampler	DJ/Smplr	U.S.	1991	$10.00
Interscope	PRCD 585-2	Interscope Sampler	DJ/Smplr	U.S.	1995	$8.00
IRS	MILES	IRS No Speak Compilation	DJ/Smplr	U.S.	1988	$6.00
		Island Sampler Vol. 1	DJ/Smplr	U.S.		$5.00
		Island Sampler Vol. 2	DJ/Smplr	U.S.		$5.00
Island		Island Summer Sampler	DJ/Smplr	U.S.	1995	$12.00
Island		Island Treasures	DJ/Smplr	U.S.		$20.00
	4 CD set					
Capitol	72438-19193-2-3	It Stands for All	LTD/LP	U.S.	1996	$15.00
	Sold exclusively at Target Department Stores.					
Polygram		It's a Beautiful Thing	DJ/LP	U.S.	1991	$20.00
	CD set in cardboard flower package					
Polydor	CDP 186	It's a Beautiful Time	DJ/Smplr	U.S.	1990	$15.00
	2 CD set					
Disney	PCCW-00036	It's a Small World	CD5	Japan	1991	$18.00
PGD	SACD 536	It's an Alternative Thing	DJ/Smplr	U.S.	1992	$8.00
BMG	RDJ 66337-2	It's BMG Time	DJ/Smplr	U.S.	1993	$15.00
	2 CD set					
Virgin	PRCD 3950	It's Kozmik	DJ/Smplr	U.S.	1991	$8.00
Mercury	CDP 217	January 1991 Mercury New Releases	DJ/Smplr	U.S.	1991	$5.00
Columbia	CSK 4419	January Blizzard Blitz of Hits	DJ/Smplr	U.S.	1992	$8.00

Jazz Collection, The – (Dove/RCA DPC1-1309)

Label	Catalog Number	Title	Type	Country	Year	Value
Dove/RCA	DPC1-1309	Jazz Collection, The	LTD/LP	U.S.	1996	$13.00
Polygram	819344-2	Jazz Like You've Never Heard It Before	LP/LB	U.S.†	1985	$14.00/$8.00
U.S. Postal Service		Jazz Musicians: Stamp Folio	LTD/LP	U.S.	1996	$12.00
	CD sampler with stamps and booklet in cardboard sleeve.					
Denon		Jazz On Denon	DJ/Smplr	U.S.	1987	$5.00
CDI-PRO	438	Jazz Vocal Blend	DJ/Smplr	U.S.		$25.00
	CD+I sampler.					
Pioneer		Jazziz Vol. 1	DJ/Smplr	U.S.		$5.00
Novus		Jazzzpizzaz	DJ/Smplr	U.S.	1991	$5.00
Capricorn	PRO-CD-5973	Jewel/Paula Records Story	DJ/Smplr	U.S.	1993	$5.00
Warner Brothers		Jimi Hendrix Tribute	DJ/LP	U.S.	1993	$70.00
	CD-R version.					
CBS	CK-40166	Jingle Bell Jazz	LP/LB	U.S.†	1985	$14.00/$8.00
Time Life		Jingle Bells	DJ/Smplr	U.S.	1993	$20.00
Dutch East India Trading		John Peel Sessions, The	DJ/Smplr	U.S.	1991	$8.00
Huh/Joop!		Joop!	DJ/Smplr	U.S.	1995	$15.00
		Journey Continues	DJ/Smplr	U.S.		$10.00
	2 CD set					
Columbia	CSK 45294	Jubilation	DJ/Smplr	U.S.	1989	$5.00
Immortal	5455	Judgement Night	DJ/Smplr	U.S.	1993	$5.00
Immortal	5472	Judgement Night Street Legal Vers	DJ/Smplr	U.S.	1993	$5.00
CDI-PRO	6658	Jukebox	DJ/Smplr	U.S.		$25.00
	CD+I sampler.					
A&M		June 1996	DJ/Smplr	U.S.	1996	$25.00
	With unreleased Styx track "While There's Still Time" deleted from their Greatest Hits II CD.					
Americ disc, Inc.		Juno Awards 1991 Official Collection	DJ/Smplr	Canada	1991	$30.00
	2 CD set.					
Americ disc, Inc.		Juno Awards 1992 Official Collection	DJ/Smplr	Canada	1992	$30.00
	2 CD set.					
Rhino	PRCD 7055	Just Can't Get Enough: New Wave Hits Of the 80's	DJ/Smplr	U.S.	1994	$20.00

Label	Catalog Number	Title	Type	Country	Year	Value
Sparrow		Just Listen	DJ/Smplr	U.S.	1991	$5.00
PLG	SACD 566	Just Listen	DJ/Smplr	U.S.	1992	$8.00
K-Tel		K-Tel Sampler	DJ/Smplr	U.S.	1997	$10.00
		Kansas City	DJ/Smplr	U.S.		$6.00
DGC	PRO-CD-4401	KDGC	DJ/Smplr	U.S.	1992	$8.00
RCA/Kellog's	DPC1-1301	Kellogg's Mega Music Mix	DJ/Smplr	U.S.	1996	$15.00
Kenwood		Kenwood Stage 3 Home Theater Controller	DJ/Smplr	U.S.	1996	$15.00
	CD-ROM sampler in press kit.					
A&M	849 347	Key Notes	DJ/Smplr	U.S.	1991	$8.00
Geffen	PRO-CD-4400	KGEF	DJ/Smplr	U.S.	1992	$8.00
DIR		King Biscuit Flower Hour	RS	U.S.	1987	$50.00
	Airdate: 12/27/87.					
DIR		King Biscuit Flower Hour	RS	U.S.	1988	$30.00
	Airdate: 12/25/88.					
DIR		King Biscuit Flower Hour	RS	U.S.	1988	$20.00
	Airdate: 5/29/88.					
DIR		King Biscuit Flower Hour	RS	U.S.	1989	$30.00
	2 CD set. Airdate: 11/27/89					
DIR		King Biscuit Flower Hour	RS	U.S.	1989	$40.00
	2 CD set. Airdate: 3/26/89					
DIR		King Biscuit Flower Hour	RS	U.S.	1989	$30.00
	Airdate: 1/29/89.					
DIR		King Biscuit Flower Hour	RS	U.S.	1989	$30.00
	Airdate: 12/25/89					
DIR		King Biscuit Flower Hour	RS	U.S.	1990	$30.00
	Airdate: 10/1/90.					
DIR		King Biscuit Flower Hour	RS	U.S.	1991	$30.00
	Airdate: 3/31/91.					
DIR		King Biscuit Flower Hour	RS	U.S.	1994	$35.00
	Airdate: 1/30/94.					
DIR		King Biscuit Flower Hour	RS	U.S.	1994	$35.00
	Airdate: 11/20/94					
DIR		King Biscuit Flower Hour	RS	U.S.	1996	$35.00
	Airdate: 1/21/96.					
King Biscuit	KBJC 01	King Biscuit Flower Hour Sampler	DJ/Smplr	U.S.	1996	$15.00
Polygram		Kiss My Ass	DJ/LP	Australia	1994	$35.00
Polygram		Kiss My Ass	LTD/LP	Australia	1994	$25.00
	Gold disc version.					
Phonogram		Kiss My Ass	DJ/LP	France	1994	$45.00
Mercury		Kiss My Ass	DJ/LP	U.S.	1994	$15.00
Denon	CDKKSF-01-5	KKSF Sampler For AIDS Relief 3	LTD/LP	U.S.	1993	$25.00/$22.00
Max	NS 16CD	Kodak Fun	SCDJ	Germany	1996	$35.00
	Camera shaped CD.					
KROQ		KROQ Calender 1995	DJ/Smplr	U.S.		$7.00
L'Oreal/Westwood One		L'Oreal Studio Line Live!	DJ/Smplr	U.S.	1995	$20.00
		Labor Day Rock Special	RS	U.S.	1995	$65.00
	2 CD set. Airdate: 9/4/95.					
Polygram	ASCD 34	Ladies and Gentlemen, Elvis Has Left the Building	DJ/Smplr	U.S.	1988	$10.00
LaFace	4038	Laface Is the Place	DJ/Smplr	U.S.	1992	$5.00

LaserActive – (Pioneer/Private Music PJC-Pinr2-2)

Label	Catalog Number	Title	Type	Country	Year	Value
Pioneer/Private Music	PJC-Pinr2-2	LaserActive	DJ/Smplr	U.S.	1994	$15.00
Time Warner Sound Exchange		Late Night Piano for Lovers	LTD/LP	U.S.	1995	$17.00
Invisible	012	Lean Juicy Pork	DJ/Smplr	Canada		$15.00
Warner Brothers	Pro-CD-Lee	Lee Herchberg: The Sound Of Music	DJ/Smplr	U.S.	1997	N/A
Sony	CSK 4037	Legacy: Music For the Next Generation	DJ/Smplr	U.S.	1991	$6.00
MCA	MCA3P-2771	Legacy, the True & Untamed	DJ/Smplr	U.S.	1993	$25.00
	3 CD set.					
Legacy		Legacy's Rhythm & Soul	DJ/Smplr	U.S.		$5.00
		Legends	DJ/Smplr	U.S.		$40.00
Image	ID7626HB	Legends of Rock 'n Roll	LD	U.S.		$30.00
Warner Brothers	DMC 1-1100	Legends of Rock 'n Roll	LTD/LP	U.S.	1993	$30.00
	CD in box with booklet & stamps, sponsered by the U.S. Postal Service.					
Imago		Let Go of My Ears	DJ/Smplr	U.S.		$10.00
Max	NS 14CD	Levis Summer Mix	SCD5	Germany	1996	$30.00
	"Levis' pants' pocket" shaped CD single.					
Rhino	PRCD 7138	Library of Congress Presents: Historic Presidential Speeches (1909–1993) Sampler	DJ/Smplr	U.S.	1995	$20.00
Lieber & Stoller		Lieber & Stoller Music Publishing	DJ/Smplr	U.S.	1995	$220.00
	5 CD set plus sixth disc of Elvis Presley tracks.					
Lieber & Stoller		Lieber & Stoller: The '60s, '70s and '80s	DJ/Smplr	U.S.		$40.00
Lieber & Stoller		Lieber & Stoller: The Fifties	DJ/Smplr	U.S.		$40.00
Lieber & Stoller		Lieber & Stoller Volume 1 and 2	DJ/Smplr	U.S.	1993	$100.00
	2 CD set.					
BMG	662558	Life Aid Armenia – What's Going On	CD5	Germany		$10.00
Capitol	DPRO-79264	Lighten Up	DJ/Smplr	U.S.	1992	$10.00
4AD	LILIPUT 1/2	Liliput	DJ/Smplr	U.S.	1992	$150.00
	2 CD sampler set in large book.					
Mercury	SACD 439	Lindbergh's Baby	DJ/Smplr	U.S.	1991	$10.00
Chrysalis	23512	Listen to the Nineties	DJ/Smplr	U.S.	1990	$8.00
Columbia	CSK 4460	Listen to Your History	DJ/Smplr	U.S.	1992	$5.00
Capitol	DPRO 79373	Listen Up!	DJ/Smplr	U.S.	1990	$5.00
Rhino		Little Bit of Gold	DJ/CD3	U.S.		$10.00
WXPN Radio		Live at the World Cafe Vol. 1	LTD/LP	U.S.	1995	$18.00
Media America		Live at Virgin	RS	U.S.	1994	$20.00
	2 CD set.					
Media America		Live Classics From the Cutting Edge	RS	U.S.	1993	$30.00
	4 CD set.					

Label	Catalog Number	Title	Type	Country	Year	Value
Media America		Live Classics From the Cutting Edge II	RS	U.S.		$30.00
		4 CD set. Airdate: 5/28/94.				
KSCA Radio		Live From the Music Hall Volume 1	LTD/LP	U.S.	1995	$30.00
		Available only through Virgin Megastores.				
KSCA Radio		Live From the Music Hall Volume 2	LTD/LP	U.S.	1996	$20.00
		Available only through Virgin Megastores.				
		Live From the Pit	RS	U.S.	1996	$50.00
		2 CD set. Airdate: 6/30/96.				
Atlantic		Live From Woodstock '94	DJ/Smplr	U.S.	1994	$20.00
Westwood One		Live in the U.S.A.	RS	U.S.		$30.00
		2 CD set.				
Warner Brothers	PRO-CD-4926	Lollapalooza	DJ/Smplr	U.S.	1991	$10.00
Warner Brothers	PRO-CD-5500	Lollapalooza '92	DJ/Smplr	U.S.	1992	$10.00
Epic	ESK 5256	Lollapalooza '93	DJ/Smplr	U.S.	1993	$10.00
Elektra	PRCD 9021-2	Lollapalooza '94	DJ/Smplr	U.S.	1994	$10.00
		Loose Cannon Comedy Classics Sampler	DJ/Smplr	U.S.	1995	$12.00
Warner	1647	Loose Interpretations of the Originals	DJ/Smplr	U.S.	1993	$10.00
Time/Warner Sound Exchange	237362	Lost Hits of the '60s	LP	U.S.	1996	$30.00
		2 CD set.				
Time Warner Sound Exchange		Lost Hits of the '60s: 40 Solid Gold AM Radio Classics	LTD/LP	U.S.	1996	$25.00
		2 CD set.				
Music & Media	50/90	Loud & Proud	DJ/Smplr	U.S.	1990	$8.00
Alias		Love Is Like a Poke in the Eye With a Sharp Stick	DJ/Smplr	U.S.		$8.00
Mercury	SACD 767	Mad Tidings	DJ/Smplr	U.S.	1993	$8.00
Westwood One		Made in America	RS	U.S.	1991	$60.00
		12 CD set.				
Creative Wonders	15090-0	Madeline European Adventures	LTD/LP	U.S.	1996	$40.00
		CD-ROM, plush doll and toothbrush/cup set in custom package.				
Capitol	CDPRO 339	Magic Behind the Music, The	DJ/Smplr	Canada	1990	$30.00
Walt Disney		Magic Behind the Music, The	LTD/LP	U.S.	1995	$150.00
		4 CD picture disc set in 12 "x12" linen-bound box. Autographed by Alan Menken and Tim Rice. Limited to 2500 copies.				
Charisma	GAV 1	Magnetic Attraction	DJ/Smplr	U.S.	1991	$5.00
Warner Brothers		Making History: WEA's 15th Anniversary	DJ/Smplr	U.S.	1986	$65.00
		4 CD boxed set.				
Malaco	1144	Malaco Sampler	DJ/Smplr	U.S.	1988	$5.00
Rhino		Mardi 'Till You Drop	DJ/Smplr	U.S.	1994	$12.00
Tree Int.	TP 0003	Masters Box, The	DJ/Smplr	U.S.	1993	$35.00
		3 CD boxed set.				
Rhino		Masters of the Old School	DJ/Smplr	U.S.		$12.00
Columbia	CSK 4407/8/9	Mastersound Limited Edition Commemorative Discs	DJ/Smplr	U.S.	1992	$300.00
		3 CD set. 20-SBM albums in special 10th Anniversary slip case. Discs include B.Joel's-52nd St., B. Springsteen-Born To Run.				
Columbia	CSK 4757	Mastersound Sampler	DJ/Smplr	U.S.	1992	$60.00/$35.00
Legacy		Mastersound Sampler	DJ/Smplr	U.S.	1995	$35.00
Columbia	CSK 5033	Mastersound Sampler (Stereo Review 35th Anniversary Sampler)	DJ/Smplr	U.S.	1992	$25.00
		Gold CD in gold tray				
Legacy	CSK 5033	Mastersound Sampler (Stereo Review 35th Anniversary Sampler)	DJ/Smplr	U.S.	1992	$70.00/$35.00
		Gold CD in white tray, in custom longbox				
Capitol	DPRO-790232	Maxi Mega Mobile Master Massive	DJ/Smplr	U.S.	1987	$25.00
Navarre		May All Your Wishes Be Safe Priced	DJ/Smplr	U.S.		$8.00
MCA	MCA3P-2988	MCA 1994 NARM Sampler	DJ/Smplr	U.S.	1994	$4.00
MCA	MCA3P-3327	MCA 1995 NARM Sampler	DJ/Smplr	U.S.	1995	$18.00
MCA	17691	MCA Black/Urban CD Sampler	DJ/Smplr	U.S.	1988	$10.00
MCA	17690	MCA CHR CD Sampler	DJ/Smplr	U.S.	1988	$5.00
MCA	18053	MCA CHR CD Sampler	DJ/Smplr	U.S.	1989	$5.00
MCA	17529	MCA Instore Play Sampler	DJ/Smplr	U.S.		$5.00
MCA	17296	MCA Radio Golden Oldies Vol.1	DJ/Smplr	U.S.	1992	$8.00
MCA	172405	MCA Radio Golden Oldies Vol.2	DJ/Smplr	U.S.	1992	$8.00
MCA		MCA Sixling Summer Rock Sampler	DJ/Smplr	U.S.		$5.00
Sony		MD Sampler, The	DJ/Smplr	U.S.	1993	$15.00
		Red label minidisc, in minidisc jewelbox with extra coupon booklet.				
		Means to an End of Joy Division	DJ/LP	U.S.		$8.00
Rykodisc	0001	Medium Rare	DJ/Smplr	U.S.	1993	$15.00
Megaforce	G14	Megaforce	DJ/Smplr	U.S.	1992	$8.00
Mercury	824116	Mercury 40th Anniversary	LP/BP	U.S.		$14.00/$8.00
Mercury	824116-2	Mercury 40th Anniversary	LP/LB	U.S.†	1985	$14.00/$8.00
Mercury	CDP 133	Mercury Menu	DJ/Smplr	U.S.	1989	$15.00
Mercury		Mercury Nashville Gold Vol. 1	DJ/Smplr	U.S.		$8.00
Mercury		Mercury Nashville Gold Vol. 2	DJ/Smplr	U.S.		$8.00
Mercury		Mercury Nashville Gold Vol. 3	DJ/Smplr	U.S.		$8.00
		Merry little X-mas	DJ/Smplr	U.S.		$7.00
RCD	METALCD 1	Metal CD	Smplr	U.K.	1992	$15.00
		Metal Detector	DJ/Smplr	U.S.	1989	$10.00
		Metal Years, The	DJ/Smplr	U.S.		$5.00
		Metropolitan Recording Corporation Metropolitan	DJ/Smplr	U.S.		$5.00
RCA		Mexican Rock	DJ/Smplr	U.S.	1994	$15.00
		2 CD set				
Sony		Michael Schulhof Christmas Gift 1991: Joy to the World	DJ/Smplr	U.S.	1991	$75.00
		2 CD commemorative set in black digipack with gold feather on front.				
Sony		Michael Schulhof Christmas Gift 1992	DJ/Smplr	U.S.	1994	$100.00
		2 CD set in large 6"x12" package with prints.				
Sony	MS0016/MS0017	Michael Schulhof Christmas Gift 1994	DJ/Smplr	U.S.	1994	$100.00
		2 CD set in large fold out book package with art prints.				
Sony	MS0010/MS0011	Michael Schulhof Christmas Sampler 1993: Create Change	DJ/Smplr	U.S.	1993	$100.00
		2 CD set in "chinese puzzle" package.				
Westwood One		Mick Ronson Memorial Concert (Superstars)	RS	U.S.	1994	$80.00
		2 CD set. Airdate 8/15/94.				
Disney	PCCW-00037	Mickey Mouse March	CD5	Japan	1991	$18.00
Jobet		Million Performance Songs	DJ/Smplr	U.S.	1994	$40.00
		4 CD set.				
Sony		Minidisc Sampler, The	DJ/Smplr	U.S.	1992	$25.00
		Black label minidisc in cardboard sleeve.				
Sony		Minidisc Sampler, The	DJ/Smplr	U.S.	1994	$50.00
		Blue label in actual-size minidisc player box.				
Sony		Minidisc Sampler, The	DJ/Smplr	U.S.	1994	$18.00
		Blue label in minidisc jewelbox.				
EMI		Minit Records Story, The	LTD/LP	U.S.	1994	$30.00
Pioneer	PA-84-M014	Minor Detail	8"LD	U.S.	1984	$14.00
Arista	ASCD 9775	Miracle on 57th Street	DJ/Smplr	U.S.	1988	$5.00
Miramar	MPCD 4101	Miramar Collection: One	DJ/Smplr	U.S.	1995	$15.00
Capitol	DPRO-79487	Mixed Up!	DJ/Smplr	U.S.	1992	$8.00
Warner Brothers		Mo's Songs				$250.00
		6 CD various artists set with exclusive track "Mo" by George Harrison.				
Sony/Global Satallite Network		Modern Rock Live Vol. One	DJ/Smplr	U.S.	1996	$35.00
		2 CD set.				
		Mojo Working	DJ/Smplr	U.K.	1995	$80.00
Geffen	PRO-CD-4501	Mondo Supreme	DJ/Smplr	U.S.	1993	$8.00
RCA	3152-2-RDj	Money Is Not the Answer	DJ/Smplr	U.S.	1991	$5.00
Rhino		Monterey International Pop Festival Box Set Sampler	DJ/Intvw	U.S.	1992	$25.00
Radio Express		Monterey Pop	RS	U.S.	1988	$350.00
		9 CD set.				
Criterion	CC1164	Monterey Pop	LD	U.S.	1989	$50.00
		Monterey Pop: Limited Edition	LTD/LP	Germany	1989	N/A
		6 CD set.				
EMI	PCD-0640	Monthly Power Picks 1995	DJ/Smplr	U.S.	1995	$50.00
Capitol	DPRO-79166	Mood Indigo	DJ/Smplr	U.S.	1990	$5.00
CBS		More New Stuff	DJ/Smplr	U.S.		$5.00
Rhino	75777	More Nuggets	DJ/Smplr	U.S.	1987	$10.00
		Mother & Child	DJ/Smplr	U.S.	1995	$6.00
		Mother & Child	DJ/Smplr	U.S.	1995	$6.00
		Second version.				
Eclipse	4863-2	Motown Love Songs	LTD/LP	U.S.	1996	$18.00
		CD in custom screen-printed square tin.				
Motown	37463-1338-2	Motown Sound, The	DJ/Smplr	U.S.	1996	$35.00
Motown	90004	Motown Spring 1990 Rock and Roll Convention	DJ/Smplr	U.S.	1990	$6.00
Pioneer	PA-86-173	Motown Time Capsule	LD	U.S.	1986	$20.00
Pioneer	PA-86-168	Motown's Mustang	LD	U.S.	1986	$20.00
Pioneer	PA-86-168	Motown's Mustang	LD	U.S.	1989	$25.00
		Digital audio.				
MPL	MPLCD1-3	MPL's Treasury of Songs: The Rock 'n Roll Classics	DJ/Smplr	U.S.	1994	$40.00
		2 CD set				
MPL	MPLCZD	MPL's Treasury of Songs: The Standards	DJ/Smplr	U.S.	1994	$45.00
		2 CD set				
Premiere		MTV 1992 Video Music Awards	RS	U.S.		$100.00
		3 CD set.				
Vestron	V-1043	MTV Closet Classics	LD	U.S.	1986	$20.00
Sony	A2 23344/45/46	MTV Replay	DJ/Smplr	U.S.	1992	$20.00
		2CD Set				
MTV		MTV Video Music Awards	DJ/Smplr	U.S.	1990	$25.00
		CD in 5"x6" fold-open package.				
MTV	PRO CD II	MTV Video Music Awards	DJ/Smplr	U.S.	1991	$25.00
		Murphy, Michael Martin/Southern Sampler	DJ/Smplr	U.S.		$5.00
		Muscle	DJ/Smplr	U.S.		$5.00
Eclipse Music	CMM 025-2	Music Box Collection	SCDJ	U.S.	1996	$10.00
		Christmas music box shaped CD.				
		Music Culture Common Sense	DJ/Smplr	U.S.		$7.00
Columbia	CSK 05969	Music First Vol. 1	DJ/Smplr	U.S.	1994	$5.00
Columbia		Music First Vol. 2	DJ/Smplr	U.S.	1995	$5.00
Columbia		Music First Vol. 3	DJ/Smplr	U.S.	1995	$5.00
Columbia		Music First Vol. 4	DJ/Smplr	U.S.	1996	$5.00
		Music for "Disc" Riminating L.I.S.T.E.N.E.R.S.	DJ/Smplr	U.S.		$5.00
		Music for Night People	DJ/Smplr	U.S.	1996	$5.00
		Music for Starving Millions	DJ/Smplr	U.S.		$5.00
Atlantic	PRCD 4763-2	Music for the Rest Of Us	DJ/Smplr	U.S.	1991	$15.00
Wndm Hll	WD-7777	Music for the Season	DJ/Smplr	U.S.	1991	$10.00
A&M	75021 7247-2	Music From a Quiet Perspective	DJ/Smplr	U.S.	1991	$8.00
		Music From Woodstock, NY	DJ/Smplr	Japan		$45.00
Capitol		Music Journalism Awards	DJ/Smplr	U.S.	1996	$15.00
Details	MM691	Music Matters	Smplr	U.S.	1991	$8.00
Details Magazine		Music Matters	DJ/Smplr	U.S.	1995	$9.00
Muic & Media	41	Music Monitor IV	DJ/Smplr	U.S.	1991	$8.00
Radioactive	1575	Music Most People Wouldn't Touch	DJ/Smplr	U.S.	1991	$5.00
Disney	60957-2	Music of Disney	LP	U.S.	1992	$50.00
		4 CD set.				
Atlantic		Music So Good It Must Be Atlantic	DJ/Smplr	U.S.		$5.00
MCA	9204	Music That Hits a Nirv Ana Whole Lot More	DJ/Smplr	Canada	1992	$12.00
Dali	8668	Music That Lasts a Lifetime	DJ/Smplr	U.S.	1992	$5.00
EMI	DPRO-79679	Music That Travels the World	DJ/Smplr	U.S.	1991	$50.00
		2CD and 2cass in miniature suitcase				
RCA	RJC 66967-2	Music to Floss Your Ears With	DJ/Smplr	U.S.	1996	$4.50/$8.00
		Music to Keep You Up All Night	DJ/Smplr	U.S.		$5.00
Reprise		Music to Light Your Pilot By	DJ/Smplr	U.S.	1995	$8.00
Music Week	1	Music Week	DJ/Smplr	U.K.	1988	$5.00
Columbia	CSK 6846	N.I.B. Collectors CD	DJ/Smplr	U.S.	1995	$10.00
Narada	Z00048ND	Narada 1994	DJ/Smplr	U.S.	1994	$15.00
Narada	ND33 1686	Narada Contemporary Christmas Classics	DJ/Smplr	U.S.	1991	$8.00
Sony	CDP-10170	NARM 1993	DJ/Smplr	U.S.	1993	$5.00
Sony	CDP-10186	NARM 1993	DJ/Smplr	U.S.	1993	$5.00
Epic	ESK 5026	NARM Sampler	DJ/Smplr	U.S.	1993	$6.00
Capitol	DPRO-79359	Nashville New Release	DJ/Smplr	U.S.		$12.00
Laservideo		Nashville Rock	DJ/Smplr	U.S.	1987	$25.00
		National Public Radio	DJ/Smplr	U.S.	1991	$20.00
		2 CD set				
Columbia		Nativity in Black: NIB Collector's CD	DJ/Smplr	U.S.	1995	$10.00
Navarre	971	Navarre Corporation Spring Narm 1997	DJ/Smplr	U.S.	1997	$8.00
Mercury	314 534 322-2	NBA At 50	LTD/LP	U.S.	1997	$20.00
		CD in hardbound slip case with extra booklet.				
MCA	MCAD-10786	NBA Jam Session	DJ/LP	U.S.	1993	$50.00
		Picture CD in Basketball-skinned folder with booklet and numbered hologram identification sticker. Limited to 1500 copies.				
James&Astor/GZ	JA 1-30	NBC Olympic Music Library	DJ/Smplr	C.S.F.R.	1992	N/A
		30 CD set.				
Razor & Tie		Near Legends And Soon-To-Be Household Names	DJ/Smplr	U.S.	1992	$10.00
Nettwerk		Nettwerk Box Set Sampler	DJ/Smplr	U.S.	1995	$20.00
Spin	093	New Alternative, The	DJ/Smplr	U.S.	1993	$8.00
		New Artists for the New Year	DJ/Smplr	U.S.		$5.00
Columbia	CSK 2230	New Edge Muzik	DJ/Smplr	U.S.	1990	$5.00
		New Faces	RS	U.S.	1995	$30.00
		3 CD set. Airdate: 5/1/95.				
		New Faces of Country	RS	U.S.	1994	$50.00
		3 CD set. Airdate: 5/28/94.				
		New Rock: Acoustic Special	RS	U.S.		$60.00
		4 CD set.				
Columbia	CSK 1209	New Stuff	DJ/Smplr	U.S.		$5.00
Rhino		New Wave of Hits	DJ/Smplr	U.S.	1994	$20.00
IRS	0001	Night of the Guitar-Live!	DJ/Smplr	U.S.	1989	$12.00
Nimbus		Nimbus Picture Disc Sampler 1988	DJ/Smplr	U.S.	1988	$8.00
		Nipper Trax	DJ/Smplr	U.S.		$5.00
RCA	RDJ 62722-2	Nipper's Holiday Favorites II	DJ/Smplr	U.S.	1993	$20.00
Arista		No Alternative	LP	U.S.	1993	$14.00/$8.00
		First pressing with defective Bob Mould track.				
4AD	PRO-CD-7300	No Balls	DJ/Smplr	U.S.		$15.00
		No Boundries	DJ/Smplr	U.S.		$5.00
SBK	DPRO-05397	No Flies Here!	DJ/Smplr	U.S.	1991	$5.00
IRS	187	No Speak	DJ/Smplr	U.S.	1987	$5.00
North Sound	22392	North Sound Sampler	DJ/Smplr	U.S.	1996	$18.00
Decca		Not Fade Away: Remembering Buddy Holly	DJ/Smplr	U.S.	1995	$15.00
		Not Your Average Christmas	DJ/Smplr	U.S.		$10.00
A&M	CD17715	Now How Much Would You Pay	DJ/Smplr	U.S.	1989	$8.00
CBS	ASK 1980	Number One Country Hits of the '80s	DJ/Smplr	U.S.	1993	$35.00
		5 CD set.				
Westwood One		Number One Goodtime Oldies	RS	U.S.	1991	$50.00
		12 CD set.				

Label	Catalog Number	Title	Type	Country	Year	Value
Eclipse Music	CMM 023-2	Nutcracker: Highlights From	SCDJ	U.S.	1996	$10.00
	Nutcracker shaped CD.					
		NWOBHM Special Sampler	DJ/Smplr	Japan		$25.00
Westwood One		Off the Record	RS	U.S.	1995	$25.00
	2 CD set. Airdate: 9/11/95.					
Westwood One		Off the Record	RS	U.S.	1995	$25.00
	Airdate: 10/16/95.					
Westwood One		Off the Record	RS	U.S.	1995	$30.00
	Airdate: 10/16/95.					
Westwood One		Off the Record	RS	U.S.	1995	$25.00
	Airdate: 10/23/95					
Westwood One		Off the Record	RS	U.S.	1995	$25.00
	Airdate: 10/30/95					
Westwood One		Off the Record	RS	U.S.	1995	$20.00
	Airdate: 10/9/95					
Westwood One		Off the Record	RS	U.S.	1995	$25.00
	Airdate: 11/13/95.					
Westwood One		Off the Record	RS	U.S.	1995	$25.00
	Airdate: 11/20/95.					
Westwood One		Off the Record	RS	U.S.	1995	$25.00
	Airdate: 11/27/95.					
Westwood One		Off the Record	RS	U.S.	1995	$25.00
	Airdate: 11/27/95.					
Westwood One		Off the Record	RS	U.S.	1995	$30.00
	Airdate: 12/11/95.					
Westwood One		Off the Record	RS	U.S.	1995	$25.00
	Airdate: 12/18/95.					
Westwood One		Off the Record	RS	U.S.	1995	$40.00
	Airdate: 5/15/95.					
Westwood One		Off the Record	RS	U.S.	1995	$25.00
	Airdate: 5/22/95.					
Westwood One		Off the Record	RS	U.S.	1995	$20.00
	Airdate: 6/12/95.					
Westwood One		Off the Record	RS	U.S.	1995	$25.00
	Airdate: 6/19/95.					
Westwood One		Off the Record	RS	U.S.	1995	$35.00
	Airdate: 6/26/95.					
Westwood One		Off the Record	RS	U.S.	1995	$25.00
	Airdate: 7/17/95					
Westwood One		Off the Record	RS	U.S.	1995	$20.00
	Airdate: 7/3/95					
Westwood One		Off the Record	RS	U.S.	1995	$25.00
	Airdate: 7/31/95.					
Westwood One		Off the Record	RS	U.S.	1995	$20.00
	Airdate: 8/14/95					
Westwood One		Off the Record	RS	U.S.	1995	$20.00
	Airdate: 8/21/95.					
Westwood One		Off the Record	RS	U.S.	1995	$25.00
	Airdate: 8/7/95.					
Westwood One		Off the Record	RS	U.S.	1995	$20.00
	Airdate: 9/11/95.					
Westwood One		Off the Record	RS	U.S.	1996	$25.00
	Airdate: 1/1/96					
Westwood One		Off the Record	RS	U.S.	1996	$25.00
	Airdate: 1/2/96.					
Westwood One		Off the Record	RS	U.S.	1996	$30.00
	Airdate: 1/8/96.					
Westwood One		Off the Record	RS	U.S.	1996	$25.00
	Airdate: 2/12/96.					
Westwood One		Off the Record	RS	U.S.	1996	$20.00
	Airdate: 2/19/96.					
Westwood One		Off the Record	RS	U.S.	1996	$20.00
	Airdate: 3/16/96.					
Westwood One		Off the Record	RS	U.S.	1996	$25.00
	Airdate: 3/18/06.					
Westwood One		Off the Record	RS	U.S.	1996	$25.00
	Airdate: 3/25/96.					
Westwood One		Off the Record	RS	U.S.	1996	$25.00
	Airdate: 4/1/96.					
Westwood One		Off the Record	RS	U.S.	1996	$20.00
	Airdate: 5/9/96					
Westwood One		Off the Record	RS	U.S.	1996	$20.00
	Airdate: 8/26/96.					
Westwood One		Off the Record: Best of '95	RS	U.S.	1995	$30.00
	Airdate: 12/25/95.					
Westwood One		Off the Record: L.A. Rock	RS	U.S.	1995	$20.00
	Airdate: 11/13/95.					
Westwood One		Off the Record: L.A. Rock	RS	U.S.	1995	$20.00
	Airdate: 8/7/95.					
Westwood One		Off the Record: Rock & Roll for Amnesty	RS	U.S.	1992	$20.00
	Airdate: 12/7/92.					
Legacy/Okeh	ESK 5037	Okeh Rhythm & Blues Story Sampler 1949–1957	DJ/Smplr	U.S.	1994	$20.00
	CD and 7" record in folder.					
		On Stage Live	RS	U.S.	1995	$80.00
	3 CD set.					
Westwood One		On the Edge: 1994 Rewind	RS	U.S.	1994	$30.00
	Airdate: 12/26/94.					
Westwood One		On the Edge: Acoustic	RS	U.S.	1993	$30.00
	Airdate: 12/20/93.					
Westwood One		On the Edge: Best In-Studio	RS	U.S.	1995	$30.00
	Airdate: 12/25/95.					
Westwood One		On the Edge: Best of 1994 In-Studio	RS	U.S.	1994	$30.00
	Airdate: 12/19/94.					
Caroline		On the Nineties	DJ/Smplr	U.S.	1990	$8.00
		On The Radio: Born in the U.S.A.	RS	U.S.	1990	$100.00
	12 CD set. Airdate: 7/4/90.					
		On Tour	RS	U.S.	1996	$40.00
	Airdate: 7/14/96.					
		On Tour	RS	U.S.	1996	$40.00
	Airdate: 7/21/96.					
WNNX		One Life	LP	U.S.	1992	$25.00
Polygram	SACD 467	One Small Step For Mankind	DJ/Smplr	U.S.	1992	$8.00
Opal/Warner Bros.	PRO-CD-3175	Opal: Assembly 1	DJ/Smplr	U.S.	1988	$15.00
Epic	ESK 4097	Operation Rock & Roll	DJ/Smplr	U.S.	1991	$15.00
Pioneer	ME003-U	Oriental Dreams	LD	U.S.†	1982	$40.00
Savoy Records	REX-0003	Original V Mix	DJ/Smplr	U.S.	1996	$30.00
	First "cool disc" CD.					
Media America		Other Side of Love, The	RS	U.S.	1990	$35.00
	2 CD set.					
EMI	DPRO 04236	Other Sides	DJ/Smplr	U.S.	1989	$5.00
Relativity	OR 7	Ouch	DJ/Smplr	U.S.	1991	$5.00
		Our Music Is Life's Soundtrack	DJ/Smplr	U.S.		$7.00
		Out of Order	RS	U.S.	1994	$20.00
	2 CD set. Airdate: 5/14/94.					
Demon	FIEND CD67	Out of Our Idiot	LP	U.K.	1987	$25.00
Rykodisc	RCD-20003	Out of the Blue	LP/LB	U.S.	1985	$14.00/$8.00

Label	Catalog Number	Title	Type	Country	Year	Value
Panasonic	BSD P012/794	Panasonic Power Hits	DJ/Smplr	U.S.	1994	$8.00
Virgin	DPRO12762	Pants Off, Into the Hot Tub	DJ/Smplr	U.S.	1993	$8.00
RCA	0912	Parliment Platinum Collection	DJ/Smplr	U.S.	1990	$10.00
Warner Brothers	PRO-CD-6550	Particle Theory	DJ/Smplr	U.S.	1993	$5.00
Galaxy	3896062	Party Time	SCD5	Germany	1996	$13.00
Rhino	90138	Passion, The Difference, The Secret Policeman's Concert	DJ/Smplr	U.S.		$8.00
A&M		Pave the Earth	DJ/Smplr	U.S.		$8.00
PGD Distribution		PGD NARM '93 Orlando	DJ/Smplr	U.S.	1993	$35.00
	8 CD set in wallet.					
		PGD Pack	DJ/Smplr	U.S.	1995	$20.00
	9 CD set in wallet.					
Polygram	SACD 437	PGD PResents Great Sounds	DJ/Smplr	U.S.	1991	$8.00
Polygram	SACD-435	PGD Presents Sound Savers	DJ/Smplr	U.S.	1991	$8.00
Polygram	SACD-516	PGD Presents Sound Savers Vol. 2	DJ/Smplr	U.S.	1992	$8.00
Polygram	SACD-640	PGD Presents Sound Savers Vol. 3	DJ/Smplr	U.S.	1993	$12.00
Polygram		PGD Presents Sound Savers Vol. 4	DJ/Smplr	U.S.	1993	$12.00
Polygram		PGD Presents Sound Savers Vol. 5	DJ/Smplr	U.S.	1993	$12.00
Polygram	SACD 466	PGD Salutes Black History Month	DJ/Smplr	U.S.	1992	$8.00
Phase 4		Phase 4 Experience	DJ/Smplr	U.S.		$8.00
Rhino	PRCD 7071	Phat Trax	DJ/Smplr	U.S.	1994	$15.00
	CD in oversized digipak with booklet.					
Capitol	DPRO 79891	Phi Beta Capitol	DJ/Smplr	U.S.	1991	$5.00
Restless	029	Phi Beta Restless	DJ/Smplr	U.S.	1993	$5.00
Arista	ASCD 2234	Picked to Click	DJ/Smplr	U.S.	1991	$5.00
Atlantic	PRCD 6576-2	Picks For '96	DJ/Smplr	U.S.	1996	$15.00
		Picture Music	LD	U.S.		$50.00
		Pinnacle Independent News	DJ/Smplr	U.S.	1995	$18.00
	2 CD set.					
Pioneer	PA-82-S1	Pioneer Artists/Video Music Sampler Disc	LD	U.S.	1982	$30.00
Pioneer	PA-82-S1	Pioneer Music Video Sampler	DJ/LD	U.S.	1981	$100.00
Westwood One		Pirate Radio USA	RS	U.S.		$100.00
	12 CD set.					
Max	NS 13CD	Pizza World Mix	SCD5	Germany	1996	$20.00
	Pizza slice shaped CD					
Tommy Boy	1076	Planet Rap	DJ/Smplr	U.S.	1993	$5.00
Chanel	417	Platinum Collection, The	DJ/Smplr	U.S.	1994	$25.00
Polygram	CDP 185	Play	DJ/Smplr	U.S.	1990	$5.00
Columbia		Play Hits and They Will Buy	DJ/Smplr	U.S.		$8.00
Columbia		Play Hits and They Will Buy	DJ/Smplr	U.S.		$8.00
	Second version.					
Columbia	CSK 7637	Play Hits and They Will Buy	DJ/Smplr	U.S.	1996	$15.00
Elektra	2213	Play This	DJ/Smplr	U.S.		$5.00
Epic	ESK 2142	Play This Now	DJ/Smplr	U.S.	1990	$5.00
Passport	PJCD-88014	Players	LP/BP	U.S.		$17.00/$12.00
Buddah	BSD-0001	Pleasure From the Buddha Group	DJ/Smplr	U.S.		$15.00
Charisma	PRCD 026	Point Blank	DJ/Smplr	U.S.	1991	$5.00
		Point Blank Doggone Blues Sampler	DJ/Smplr	U.S.		$8.00
Pointblank	091	Point Blank Exclusive Interview	DJ/Smplr	U.S.	1992	$5.00
Polygram	SACD 062	Polygram Compact Discoverer	DJ/Smplr	U.S.	1987	$15.00
Polygram		Polygram Special Markets	DJ/Smplr	U.S.	1996	$18.00
	CD with hardbound book in box.					
Polygram	SACD 20	Polygram's 1988 All-Star Lineup	DJ/Smplr	U.S.	1988	$5.00
Polygram	SACD 065	Polygram's Winter Slammin' CD Jammin' Sampler	DJ/Smplr	U.S.	1988	$5.00
MCA	1510	Pop Grooves 1	DJ/Smplr	U.S.	1991	$5.00
Magnavox		Pop Sampler	DJ/8"LD	U.S.	1987	$25.00
		Portrait Records Sampler	DJ/Smplr	U.S.		$5.00
Rykodisc		Post Groundhog's Day Spectacular	DJ/Smplr	U.S.	1991	$5.00
Epic	ESK 1963	Power Move	DJ/Smplr	U.S.	1990	$5.00
DGC	PRO-CD-4427	Power of Positive Listening	DJ/Smplr	U.S.	1992	$5.00
Geffen		Power Surge	DJ/Smplr	U.S.		$20.00
	2 CD set					
Geffen		Power Surge 2	DJ/Smplr	U.S.		$25.00
	2 CD set					
PPI	0901-2	PPI Entertainment Group Sampler	DJ/Smplr	U.S.	1993	$5.00
Time Warner Sound Exchange		Precious Memories	LTD/LP	U.S.	1995	$17.00
Grooves	1651	Premiere Volume	DJ/Smplr	U.S.	1994	$5.00
World Disc Music	CD101P	Previews	DJ/Smplr	U.S.	1996	$15.00
Fox	7114-88	Prime Cuts: Jazz and Beyond	DJ/8" LD	U.S.	1985	$8.00
Private Music	PDJ-81023-2	Private Music: Headed in a New Direction	DJ/Smplr	U.S.	1995	$15.00
Warner	CDP 0294	Promo Invendavel	DJ/Smplr	Brazil	1994	$25.00
		Promo Pack	DJ/CD3	U.S.		$15.00
Warner	CDP0294	Promocional Invendavel	DJ/Smplr	Brazil	1993	$35.00
Proxima		Proxima Sampler	DJ/Smplr	U.S.		$8.00
BBC		Psychedelia	RS	U.S.	1994	$25.00
	Airdate: 5/23/94.					
Warner New Media		Psychedelica	DJ/Smplr	U.S.	1988	$75.00
	CD+G sampler.					
BMG	93	Pulse Sampler	DJ/Smplr	U.S.	1993	$8.00
Putumayo		Putumayo Presents: Dougie MacLean Collection/Laura Love Collection	DJ/Smplr	U.S.	1995	$20.00
Q/EMI		Q Sweet Sixteen	DJ/Smplr	U.K.	1992	$20.00
Mercury	SACD 362	Quiet Cuts	DJ/Smplr	U.S.	1991	$8.00
		Quiet Rhythms	DJ/Smplr	U.S.		$5.00
Rhino		R&B Box: Thirty Years Of Rhythm &	DJ/Smplr	U.S.	1994	$15.00
Racer Records	100	Racer Radio 1	DJ/Smplr	U.S.	1992	$15.00
Kubaney	K-1055-2	Radio & Musica '97	DJ/Smplr	U.S.	1997	$8.00
		Radio & Retail's Best Friend Vol. 1	DJ/Smplr	U.S.		$5.00
		Radio & Retail's Best Friend Vol. 2	DJ/Smplr	U.S.		$5.00
Radioactive	1574	Radioactive: Do Not Touch	DJ/Smplr	U.S.	1991	$8.00
DADC	001	Radioactive Mix of Art	DJ/Smplr	U.S.		$5.00
Radioactive	2382	Radioactive: No Safe Haven	DJ/Smplr	U.S.	1992	$8.00
Radium	055	Radium Hits	DJ/Smplr	U.S.	1992	$8.00
		Rah Rah Sis Boom Swag	DJ/Smplr	U.S.		$8.00
		RAINN Sampler	DJ/Smplr	U.S.		$12.00
Avenue	PRO2901	Rap Declares War	DJ/Smplr	U.S.	1992	$8.00
Westwood One		Rarities on Compact Disc Vol. 13	RS	U.S.	1992	$30.00
Westwood One		Rarities on Compact Disc Vol. 15	RS	U.S.	1992	$30.00
Westwood One		Rarities on Compact Disc Vol. 4	RS	U.S.	1992	$35.00
Westwood One		Rarities on Compact Disc Vol. 5	RS	U.S.	1992	$35.00
Westwood One		Rarities on Compact Disc Vol. 6	RS	U.S.	1992	$35.00
Westwood One		Rarities on Compact Disc Vol. 8	RS	U.S.	1990	$40.00
Westwood One		Rarities on Compact Disc Vol. 9	RS	U.S.	1990	$30.00
Meat	003	Raw M.E.A.T. 3	DJ/Smplr	Canada	1992	$8.00
Razzor & Tie		Razor & Tie's Near Legends & Soon to Be Household Names	DJ/Smplr	U.S.	1993	$10.00
RCA	6864-2-RDJ	RCA Nashville 60 Years 1928–1988	DJ/Smplr	U.S.	1988	$30.00
	3 CD set.					
RCA Victor	09026-60894-2	RCA Victor Dolby Surround Sampler	DJ/Smplr	U.S.	1991	$7.00
RCA	66335	RCA's Slammin' Hip Hop	DJ/Smplr	U.S.	1993	$5.00
		Reading Festival	RS	U.S.	1996	$80.00
	3 CD set. Airdate: 3/30/96.					
Westwood One		Reading Festival Special	RS	U.S.	1996	$95.00
	3 CD set. Airdate: 3/30/96					
		Recall '95	RS	U.S.	1996	$50.00
	3 CD set. Airdate: 1/1/96.					
Mobile Fidelity	UDCD-542	Red Hot & Blue	LTD/LP	U.S.		$30.00/$25.00

Label	Catalog Number	Title	Type	Country	Year	Value
Mercury Nashville	314-522-639-2	Red Hot Country	DJ/LP	U.S.	1994	$25.00
		CD in plastic tire with booklet.				
Red Light	68372-2	Red Light Records Music Sampler	DJ/Smplr	U.S.	1994	$10.00
		Red, White & Blue	RS	U.S.	1993	$100.00
		Airdate: 6/28/93.				
Caroline		Reggae – Collector's Edition	LTD/LP	U.K.	1994	$40.00
		3 CD picture disc boxed set. Featuring the albums U Roy "Dread In Babylon," Gladiators "Dreadlocks The Time Is Now" Culture "Too Long In Slavery."				
MCA	2472	Reggae Sunsplash Live	DJ/Smplr	U.S.	1992	$8.00
Relativity	88561 1054	Relativity Hear and Now	DJ/Smplr	U.S.	1991	$8.00
Relativity		Relativity, In-Effect, Combat	DJ/Smplr	U.S.		$15.00
		3 CD set.				
Atlantic	PRCD 6012-2	Remasterpieces	DJ/Smplr	U.S.	1995	$20.00
Reprise	PRO-CD-7968	Reprise Seasonal Sampler	DJ/Smplr	U.S.	1995	$10.00
		Requiem For the Americas	LP/LB	U.S.		$13.00/$10.00
Rhino	R21S-70199	Rerun Rock: Alternative TV Theme Songs	LP/LB	U.S.		$15.00/$10.00
Restless	27	Restless 1993 New Artist Sampler	DJ/Smplr	U.S.	1993	$8.00
		Retro Show	RS	U.S.	1995	$40.00
		3 CD set.				
Columbia	CSK 5513	Return of Sampler Clause	DJ/Smplr	U.S.	1993	$8.00
Epic	ESK 2228	Return of...Twisting Your Knobs...Epic	DJ/Smplr	U.S.	1990	$8.00
Hits	HT-007	Revenge of Post Modern	DJ/Smplr	U.S.	1990	$8.00
Rhino	PRCD 7072	Rhino's Famous Sweet 16	DJ/Smplr	U.S.	1994	$35.00
		2 CD in candy box.				
Rhino/Atlantic	PRO2 98120	Rhino/Atlantic Remasters	DJ/Smplr	U.S.	1992	$40.00
		2 CD sampler in leather wallet.				
Rhino/Atlantic	PRO2 90127	Rhino/Atlantic Remasters	DJ/Smplr	U.S.	1993	$20.00
		Rhythm, Country & Blues (Country's Cutting Edge)	RS	U.S.	1994	$10.00
		Airdate: 1/15/94				
		Rhythm of Black Lifestyle	DJ/Smplr	U.S.		$8.00
Laface		Rhythm of the Games	DJ/Smplr	U.S.	1996	$15.00
		Rhythm Stick	DJ/Smplr	U.S.	1989	$18.00
		Ribbed Ticklers	DJ/Smplr	U.S.		$15.00
		Richard Blades Flashback Sampler	DJ/Smplr	U.S.	1995	$15.00
		Road Ahead, The	DJ/Smplr	U.S.		$8.00
		Road, The	RS	U.S.	1995	$40.00
		2 CD set. Airdate: 2/10/95.				
		Road, The	RS	U.S.	1995	$60.00
		2 CD set. Airdate: 3/31/95.				
		Road, The	RS	U.S.	1995	$45.00
		2 CD set. Airdate: 4/14/95				
		Road, The	RS	U.S.	1995	$60.00
		2 CD set. Airdate: 6/30/95.				
		Road, The	RS	U.S.	1995	$30.00
		Airdate: 9/1/95.				
		Road, The: Christmas Show	RS	U.S.	1995	$50.00
		2 CD set. Airdate: 12/22/95.				
Roadrunner	063	Roadrunner Records	DJ/Smplr	U.S.	1992	$8.00
Pioneer	MS009	Rock Adventure	LD	U.S.†	1985	$25.00
Global Satellite Network		Rock and Roll Greats	RS	U.S.	1992	$100.00
		3 CD set. Airdate: 5/1/92				
		Rock and Roll Hall Of Fame 1989	DJ/Smplr	U.S.		$45.00
Warner Comm.		Rock and Roll Hall Of Fame 1990	DJ/Smplr	U.S.	1990	$45.00
		Rock and Roll Hall Of Fame 1991	DJ/Smplr	U.S.	1991	$45.00
		Rock and Roll Hall Of Fame 1992	DJ/Smplr	U.S.	1992	$45.00
		Rock and Roll Hall Of Fame 1993	DJ/Smplr	U.S.	1993	$45.00
		Rock and Roll Hall Of Fame 1994	DJ/Smplr	U.S.	1994	$45.00
		Rock and Roll Hall Of Fame 1995	DJ/Smplr	U.S.	1995	$45.00
		Rock and Roll Hall Of Fame 1996	DJ/Smplr	U.S.	1996	$45.00
Polygram	080551-1	Rock and Roll Meltdown	LD	U.S.	1989	$20.00
Pioneer	PA-87-190	Rock and Roll the Early Days	LD	U.S.	1984	$20.00
Pioneer	PA-87-190	Rock and Roll the Early Days	LD	U.S.	1990	$20.00
		Digital audio.				
Global Satellite Network		Rock and the Enviroment	RS	U.S.	1992	$50.00
		3 CD set. Airdate: 4/1/92.				
Album Network		Rock and the Environment	RS	U.S.	1995	$75.00
		2 CD set. Airdate: 4/23/95.				
Legacy	CSK-04925	Rock Artifacts	DJ/Smplr	U.S.	1993	$10.00
Rock Core		Rock: At the Core	RS	U.S.		$50.00
		3 CD set.				
RCD	RCD4	Rock CD Volume 4	Smplr	U.K.	1992	$15.00
Media America		Rock From the Inside: The Beginnings	RS	U.S.	1989	$40.00
		3 CD set.				
Rhino	PRCD 7043	Rock Instrumental Classics Sampler	DJ/Smplr	U.S.	1994	$20.00
Time-Life	2RNR-4489	Rock 'n Roll Era, The	LP	U.S.	1995	$30.00
Warner New Media/Sega		Rock Paintings/Hot Hits: Adventurous New Music Sampler	LTD/LP	U.S.	1992	$40.00
		Free promotional CD given away with purchase of Sega CD in 1992.				
		Rock Summer Sampler	DJ/Smplr	U.S.		$8.00
		Rock the Environment	RS	U.S.	1994	$50.00
		2 CD set. Airdate: 1/94.				
Warner Brothers	PRO-CD-5721	Rock the Vote	DJ/Smplr	U.S.	1992	$15.00
Polygram	SACD 076	Rock 'Til You Drop	DJ/Smplr	U.S.	1988	$5.00
R.A.D.D.		Rockers Against Drunk Driving	DJ/Smplr	U.S.	1987	$20.00
Rock Hard	SAMPCD 1674	Rockin' the Cradle	DJ/Smplr	U.K.	1992	$30.00
		Rollercoaster	DJ/Smplr	U.S.		$4.00
Rolling Stn	RS-MD1	Rolling Stone: Turn It Up!	DJ/Smplr	U.S.	1994	$15.00
		Minidisc sampler given away with Rolling Stone magazine.				
Rondor	MSPJ 032	Rondor Music International Music Sampler	DJ/Smplr	U.S.	1996	$220.00
		10 CD set in large binder with song information.				
rooArt	SACD 145	rooArt Presents	DJ/Smplr	U.S.	1990	$4.00
Polygram	SACD 536	Roots, Rap & Reggae	DJ/Smplr	U.S.	1992	$5.00
Rounder	1	Rounder CD 45	DJ/Smplr	U.S.		$5.00
Capitol	DPRO 79416	Route 91	DJ/Smplr	U.S.		$5.00
Capitol	DPRO 79416	Route 91	DJ/Smplr	U.S.		$15.00
		CD in Jewelbox housed in "roadmap" folder package				
		Royalty of British Rock	RS	U.S.	1991	$150.00
		12 CD set. Airdate: 7/1/91.				
Elektra	PRCD 8247-2	Rubaiyat Plunderphonics	DJ/Smplr	U.S.	1991	$20.00
Elektra	PRCD 8208-2	Rubaiyat-Elektra's 40th Anniversary	DJ/Smplr	U.S.	1990	$55.00
		2CDof covers and 2CD of Originals in box.				
Elektra	PRCD 8216-2	Rubaiyat-Selections From...	DJ/Smplr	U.S.	1990	$12.00
Capitol		Rumble & Scratch	DJ/Smplr	U.S.	1995	$10.00
Rykodisc		Ryko	DJ/Smplr	Japan	1994	$25.00
Rykodisc		Rykodisc Reggae Sampler	DJ/Smplr	U.S.	1991	$5.00
Island	987	Sampler #1	DJ/Smplr	U.S.	1987	$10.00
Image	ID6374SO	San Francisco Blues Festival	LD	U.S.		$30.00
MCA	MCA11348A	Saturday Morning (Cartoon Theme Songs)	DJ/LP	U.S.	1995	$10.00
Savoy Records	TDCL-91156	Savoy Jazz Special Sampler	DJ/Smplr	U.S.	1996	$25.00
SBK	DPRO-05310	SBK The Artists, The Songs	DJ/Smplr	U.S.		$5.00
Eclipse Music	CMM 012-2	Scary Halloween	SCDJ	U.S.	1996	$10.00
		Pumpkin shaped CD.				
Eclipse Music	CMM 019-2	Scary Sounds From the Haunted House	SCDJ	U.S.	1996	$10.00
		Haunted House shaped CD.				
Capricorn	PRO-CD-5422	Scepter Records Story	DJ/Smplr	U.S.	1992	$10.00
Rhino		School House Rock Sampler	DJ/Smplr	U.S.	1996	$12.00
Creative Wonders	25080-8	Schoolhouse Rock: America Rock	LTD/LP	U.S.	1996	$40.00
		CD-ROM, VHS video and t-shirt in custom package.				
Creative Wonders		Schoolhouse Rock: Gift Box	LTD/LP	U.S.	1995	$40.00
		CD-ROM, VHS video and sweatshirt in large square box.				
Screen Tracks	901	Screen Tracks Sampler	DJ/Smplr	U.S.	1994	$8.00
		CD+G sampler.				
Island		Seasons Greeting	DJ/Smplr	U.S.		$12.00
CBS	CK-40170	Seasons Greetings From Nashville	LP/BP	U.S.†	1985	$12.00/$7.00
Giant/Warner Bros.	PRO-CD-5037	Selected Tracks From the NY Rock and Soul Review	DJ/Smplr	U.S.	1991	$10.00
NBK		Selections From NBK	DJ/Smplr	U.S.		$10.00
Rykodisc		September Songs	DJ/Smplr	U.S.	1990	$5.00
		Serious R&B	DJ/Smplr	U.S.		$8.00
Creative Wonders	09601-7	Sesame Street: Get Set to Learn!	LTD/LP	U.S.	1996	$40.00
		CD-ROM, plush doll and mug in custom package.				
Creative Wonders		Sesame Street: Gift Box	LTD/LP	U.S.	1995	$40.00
		CD-ROM, VHS video and sweatshirt in large square box.				
Disney Music Publishing		Seven Summits Music & Seven Peaks Music	DJ/Smplr	U.S.	1995	$25.00
Time Warner Sound Exchange		Seventies Feelings	LP	U.S.	1995	$16.00
NME		Sgt. Pepper Knew My Father	DJ/LP	U.S.	1988	$80.00
Pikosso		Shape Rave Volume 1	SCDJ	Germany	1995	$25.00
		Saw-blade shaped CD.				
Pikosso	743 213 112 82	Shape Rave Volume 2	SCDJ	Germany	1995	$25.00
		Saw-blade shaped CD.				
Mercury	SACD 337	Shecky and Jackie's Greatest Hits	DJ/Smplr	U.S.	1991	$6.00
Mercury	SACD 478	Shecky and Jackie's Greatest Hits Vol. II	DJ/Smplr	U.S.	1992	$6.00
Mercury	SACD 659	Shecky and Jackie's Greatest Hits Vol. III	DJ/Smplr	U.S.	1993	$5.00
Mercury	SACD 039	Shecky & Jackie Break Out the Hits	DJ/Smplr	U.S.	1994	$6.00
Mercury	SACD 1000	Shecky & Jackie's Hits Feeding Frenzy	DJ/Smplr	U.S.	1995	$6.00
Putumayo	M115-2	Shelter	DJ/Smplr	U.S.	1995	$10.00
FonoVisa	PROCD 393	Silverado/Banda Rayo	DJ/Smplr	Canada	1995	$10.00
Silvertone	JSAM-9-2	Silvertone Records Sampler 96	DJ/Smplr	U.S.	1996	$15.00
Sin-Drome	SD-2093	Sin-Drome Collection Vol. 2	DJ/Smplr	U.S.	1994	$8.00
Virgin	PRCD 2018	Singles Scene	DJ/Smplr	U.S.		$5.00
Atlantic	PR 2424-2	Sinitta/Troop/Christine Day	CDJ	U.S.	1988	$7.00
Sire/Warner Bros.	PRO-CD-5906	Sire's Lucky 13 for '93	DJ/Smplr	U.S.	1993	$5.00
Westwood One		Sixties at the Beeb	RS	U.S.	1990	$300.00
		6 CD set. Airdate: 7/24/90.				
Westwood One		Sixties (On the Radio), The	RS	U.S.	1990	$100.00
		12 CD set. Airdate:6/14/90.				
Rhino		Sixties Rock Classic Vol. 1	LP	U.S.	1994	$13.00
		Sizzling Summer Rock Sampler	DJ/Smplr	U.S.		$5.00
MCA	MCAD-11192	Skynyrd's Frynds	LTD/LP	U.S.	1994	$15.00
		CD in box with patch.				
Warner Brothers	PRO-CD-7393	Slayer, Biohazard, Machine Head Tour Sampler	DJ/Smplr	U.S.	1994	$15.00
CEMA/Cystal Pepsi	S21-17499	Slipped Disc	DJ/Smplr	Canada	1993	$15.00
Best New Music	1001	Smart Music for Smart People	DJ/Smplr	U.S.	1988	$5.00
Smith & Alster		Smith & Alster Christmas 1996 Sampler	DJ/Smplr	U.S.	1996	$10.00
Rhino		Smooth Grooves	DJ/Smplr	U.S.		$8.00
EPA	ASK 2848	Soft Soul	DJ/Smplr	U.S.	1987	$5.00
A&M	31458037-2	Some Music Makes Me Dizzy	DJ/Smplr	U.S.	1992	$8.00
		Son of CD Hits Sampler	DJ/Smplr	U.S.		$5.00
Virgin	PRCD 2019	Son of Singles Scene	DJ/Smplr	U.S.	1987	$5.00
Rhino	R2 71451	Songs From the Old West	LTD/LP	U.S.	1993	$70.00
		4 CD set. Limited edition in leather 12"x12" digipak.				
Rhino		Songs From the Old West Sampler	DJ/Smplr	U.S.	1993	$10.00
Rykodisc	Ryko PRO 9001	Songs From the Sacred Napkin	DJ/Smplr	U.S.	1990	$5.00
Bomr.	31-7502	Songs of New York: East Side, West Side, All Around the Town	LP/LB	U.S.	1985	$20.00/$15.00
		2 CD set.				
Epic	ESK 5536	Sony Music Fall Feast Sampler	DJ/Smplr	U.S.	1993	$8.00
Rhino	PRO2 90080	Soul Hits of the '70s	DJ/Smplr	U.S.	1991	$9.00
Rhino		Soul Hits of the '70s Vol. 6-10	DJ/Smplr	U.S.	1991	$9.00
Westwood One		Soul of the Sixties	RS	U.S.	1989	$80.00
		10 CD set.				
Rhino		Soul Train 20th Anniversary	LP	U.S.	1994	$45.00
		3 CD First pressing in felt-bound 6"x12" package				
Atlanta Olympic Committee		Sound of the Games, The	LTD/LP	U.S.	1996	$100.00
		5 CD set in acrylic case with large booklet and slipcase. Artwork by Michel Delacroix. Made available only through mail order or at the Olympic games in Atlatnta, GA.				
PGD	SACD 435	Sound Savers	DJ/Smplr	U.S.	1991	$10.00
PGD	SACD 640	Sound Savers 3	DJ/Smplr	U.S.	1993	$10.00
PGD	SACD 746	Sound Savers Volume 4	DJ/Smplr	U.S.	1993	$25.00
Enigma	EPRO 216	Sound & Vision Vol. 1	DJ/Smplr	U.S.	1989	$5.00
Enigma		Sound & Vision Vol. 2	DJ/Smplr	U.S.		$5.00
WEA	PRO-CD-3623	Sounds By Light	DJ/Smplr	U.S.	1989	$5.00
Scotti Brothers	SBDJ 75442 2	Sounds From the Street	DJ/Smplr	U.S.	1994	$5.00
EMI Manufacturing	1P400001	Sounds of Our Times: The Ballad of EMI	DJ/Smplr	U.S.	1997	$10.00
Enigma	EPRO-192	Sounds of Success	DJ/Smplr	U.S.	1989	$5.00
Sun	SP10122	Sounds of the Holidays	LP	U.S.	1996	$8.00
		Availble exclusively at Sun Super Saving Centers.				
Durkee/Cema	S21-18590	Sounds of the Season	DJ/Smplr	U.S.	1995	$20.00
Geffen	PRO-CDD-4476	Spawn	DJ/Smplr	U.S.	1995	$8.00
		Special	RS	U.S.	1995	$65.00
		With Bruce Springsteen, R.E.M. and Eric Clapton. Airdate: 9/4/95.				
Columbia		Special CD Sampler-2	DJ/Smplr	U.S.		$5.00
Specialty Records		Specialty Story, The	DJ/Smplr	U.S.		$15.00
Atlantic		Spew	DJ/Smplr	U.S.	1995	$8.00
Atlantic		Spew+	DJ/Smplr	U.S.	1995	$8.00
		Enhanced CD				
Atlantic	82844-2	Spew	LP	U.S.	1995	$15.00
		Enhanced CD				
Atlantic		Spew 2	DJ/Smplr	U.S.	1995	$8.00
Atlantic		Spew 3	DJ/Smplr	U.S.	1995	$8.00
Atlantic		Spew 4	DJ/Smplr	U.S.	1995	$8.00
Atlantic		Spew 5	DJ/Smplr	U.S.	1995	$8.00
Atlantic		Spew 6	DJ/Smplr	U.S.	1995	$8.00
Atlantic		Spew 7	DJ/Smplr	U.S.	1996	$8.00
Atlantic		Spew 8	DJ/Smplr	U.S.	1996	$8.00
Atlantic		Spew v. Spew	DJ/Smplr	U.S.	1995	$10.00
Spin Magazine		Spin This 7	DJ/Smplr	U.S.	1996	$18.00
Fontana	SACD 556	Spin/Fontana Tour Sampler	DJ/Smplr	U.S.	1992	$8.00
		Spirit of '73	DJ/Smplr	U.S.	1995	$12.00
Virgin	PRCD 2795	Spirit of the Forest	DJ/Smplr	U.S.	1989	$5.00
EMI	DPRO-04728	Spirit of the Music	DJ/Smplr	U.S.	1991	$5.00
Geffen	PRO-CD-4507	Splunge	DJ/Smplr	U.S.	1991	$8.00
		Spotlight On	DJ/Smplr	U.S.		$12.00
		Spotlight on Part 2	DJ/Smplr	U.S.		$12.00
Navarre	Vol 2 No 3	Spread the Bytes	DJ/Smplr	U.S.	1997	$15.00
		CD-ROM sampler.				
		Spread the Jam	DJ/Smplr	U.S.	1994	$30.00
		4 CD set.				
Polygram	SACD 099	Spring Break	DJ/Smplr	U.S.	1989	$5.00
Atlantic	PRCD 5021-2	Spring Breakers '93	DJ/Smplr	U.S.	1993	$18.00
		2 CD set				
Liberty	DPRO-79028	Spring Fever Sampler	DJ/Smplr	U.S.	1994	$5.00

Label	Catalog Number	Title	Type	Country	Year	Value
		Spring Into Summer	DJ/Smplr	U.S.		$5.00
SST		SST Godhead Storedude/Dudess In Store Play Device Vol. 10	DJ/Smplr	U.S.	1989	$8.00
SST		SST Godhead Storedude/Dudess In Store Play Device Vol. 8	DJ/CD3	U.S.	1989	$8.00
Disc Art	80102	St. Patrick's Day Favorites	SCD5	U.S.	1996	$10.00
	Clover shaped CD.					
Arista	07822-18822-2	Star of Wonder	LP	U.S.	1996	$18.00
	First pressing contianing foil stars in the spine of the jewel box.					
Stax	SVSCD-68712	Stax Soul Singles Volume 2	DJ/Smplr	U.S.	1993	$20.00
Rykodisc	00056	Steal This Disc	Smplr	U.S.	1987	$5.00
Rykodisc	00076	Steal This Disc Vol. 2	Smplr	U.S.	1988	$5.00
Virgin	PR 2228	Stick It In	DJ/Smplr	U.S.		$10.00
	2 CD set.					
Epic	ESK 5398	Stick It In	DJ/Smplr	U.S.	1993	$10.00
EMCI		Stolar Tracks Vol. 1	Smplr	U.S.	1992	$4.00
Stolar		Stolar Tracks Vol. 2	DJ/Smplr	U.S.	1993	$10.00
Reprise		Stone Free: A Tribute to Jimi Hendrix Interview	DJ/Intvw	U.S.	1993	$15.00
Fiction		Stranger Than Fiction	DJ/Smplr	U.K.		$125.00
K-Tel	6079-2	Street Flava Sampler	DJ/Smplr	U.S.	1995	$15.00
Guitar World	PRO-CD-4568	Strung Out	DJ/Smplr	U.S.	1993	$8.00
Caroline		Stuck on Caroline	DJ/Smplr	U.S.		$10.00
Showrom		Studio Directory	DJ/Smplr	U.S.	1996	$10.00
	Enhancd CD					
Sub Pop/Sega		Sub Pop Sampler	DJ/Smplr	U.S.	1995	$25.00
	Given away free with purchase of Sega's Saturn CD video game player.					
Geffen	PRO-CD-4250	Submerge Yourself in Sound	DJ/Smplr	U.S.	1990	$10.00
Geffen	PRO-CD-4399	Submerge Yourself in Sound	DJ/Smplr	U.S.	1992	$10.00
EMI		Sue Records Story	LTD/LP	U.S.	1994	$60.00
	4CD boxed set.					
Curb		Summer 90	DJ/Smplr	U.S.		$5.00
		Summer Country Concert	RS	U.S.	1996	$40.00
	2 CD set. Airdate: 7/1/96.					
Unistar		Summer Encore	RS	U.S.	1991	$20.00
	Airdate: 9/1/91.					
Atlantic	PRCD 4689-2	Summer Madness	DJ/Smplr	U.S.		$8.00
Delicious Vinyl	5228	Summer Madness '93	DJ/Smplr	U.S>	1993	$8.00
		Summer Sampler	DJ/Smplr	U.S.		$5.00
Capitol	DPRO-79328	Summer Spectacular 1990	DJ/Smplr	U.S.	1990	$5.00
Global Satellite Network		Summertime Blues	RS	U.S.	1994	$35.00
	3 CD set.					
Sundazed		Sundazed Sampler	DJ/Smplr	U.S.	1994	$15.00
Warner New Media	WNM CDV+G PRO #2	Super CD System, The	DJ/Smplr	U.S.	1995	$250.00
	CD+Graphics and laser video (CD+G and CDV combination) disc.					
BMG		Super Snax	DJ/Smplr	U.S.	1996	$8.00
Pioneer	WEA/P-SCD-1	Super Stars/Super CD	DJ/Smplr	U.S.	1989	$15.00
Capitol	DPRO 79203	Superfly Sampler	DJ/Smplr	U.S.	1990	$5.00
		Superstar Concert Series-Farm Aid V	RS	U.S.	1992	$80.00
	2 CD set. Airdate:5/10/92.					
Westwood One		Superstars	RS	U.S.	1994	$45.00
	2 CD set. Airdate: 10/3/94.					
Westwood One		Superstars	RS	U.S.	1995	$80.00
	2 CD set. Airdate: 5/29/95.					
Westwood One		Superstars	RS	U.S.	1995	$65.00
	2 CD set. Airdate: 8/21/95.					
Westwood One		Superstars: Best Of 1995	RS	U.S.	1995	$40.00
	2 CD set. Airdate: 12/25/95.					
Westwood One		Superstars: Best Of Superstars '92	RS	U.S.	1993	$50.00
	6 CD set. Airdate: 1/3/93.					
Westwood One		Superstars: Best Of Superstars '94	RS	U.S.	1994	$50.00
	2 CD set. Airdate: 12/26/94.					
Westwood One		Superstars: Live in the U.S.A.	RS	U.S.	1993	$65.00
	2 CD set. Airdate: 6/28/93.					
Westwood One		Superstars: Rock & Roll Hall Of Fame	RS	U.S.	1993	$50.00
	2 CD set. Airdate: 1/17/93.					
Westwood One		Superstars: Rock & Roll Hall Of Fame	RS	U.S.	1995	$45.00
	2 CD set. Airdate: 8/28/95.					
Westwood One		Superstars: Salute Blues Guitarists	RS	U.S.	1994	$50.00
	2 CD set. Airdate: 8/29/94.					
Westwood One		Superstars: Southern Rock Special	RS	U.S.	1995	$40.00
	2 CD set. Airdate: 5/15/95.					
Dolby	51-1128	Surround Music Sampler Volume Two	LP	U.S.		$10.00
		Swag American Style	DJ/Smplr	U.S.		$8.00
Time Warner Sound Exchange		Sweet Hour of Prayer	LTD/LP	U.S.	1995	$17.00
Chaos	5731	Sweet Relief	DJ/Smplr	U.S.	1993	$8.00
Parlophone/Q Magazine		Sweet Sixteen	Smplr	U.K.	1993	$5.00
Rhino		Sweet Sixteen Sampler	DJ/Smplr	U.S.	1994	$20.00
	2 CD set picture disc set in candy box.					
London	PPC-820044-2	Swingtime	LP/LB	U.S.†	1985	$14.00/$8.00
Swingtime		Swingtime Records Story Sampler	DJ/Smplr	U.S.		$8.00
CBS		Tabu Nights	DJ/Smplr	Japan		$25.00
Epic	ASK 1468	Take a Hit	DJ/Smplr	U.S.	1989	$6.00
Sony		Take Five	LD	U.S.	1990	$25.00
Walt Disney	60863-7	Take My Hand	LP	U.S.	1995	$17.00
Atlantic		Tapestry Revisited: A Tribute to Carole King	DJ/Smplr	U.S.	1995	$12.00
Azra	NFSD 615	Tasty Delights For the Connoisseur	LTD/LP	U.S.	1991	$18.00
	CD in candy box.					
Azra	NFSD 615	Tasty Delights For the Connoisseur	LTD/LP	U.S.	1991	$18.00
	CD in menu package.					
Geffen	PRO-CD-4404	Taylor/The Album Some People Call "Time Out II"	DJ/Smplr	U.S.	1992	$10.00
Caroline	CARTDK01	TDK Mailrock	DJ/Smplr	U.S.		$8.00
CCM	58002	Teen Idols: For a Moment	LP	U.S.	1995	$16.00
Teldarc	CD-502S	Teldarc's Decade of Digital 1978–1988 (Winter C.E.S. 1988)	DJ/CD3	U.S.	1988	$25.00
U.S. Postal Service		Tennessee: Stamp Folio	LTD/LP	U.S.	1996	$12.00
	CD sampler with stamps and booklet in cardboard sleeve.					
		Thanksgiving Blues	RS	U.S.	1995	$75.00
	3 CD set. Airdate: 11/26/95.					
Image	ID5074	That Was Rock	LD	U.S.		$15.00
A&M	CD-6600	That's The Way I Feel Now: A Tribute to Thelonious Monk	LP/LB	U.S.†	1985	$14.00/$8.00
Mobile	MFCD-813	The Blues...A Real Summit Meeting	LP/LB	U.S.†	1985	$14.00/$8.00
Disney	CD-007	Theme Park CD	LP/LB	U.S.		$15.00/$9.00
Uni		Then and Now	DJ/Smplr	U.S.	1988	$10.00
Mobile Fidelity	MFCD GS-1	Then Sing My Soul	DJ/Smplr	U.S.	1993	$15.00
		These People Are Nuts	DJ/Smplr	U.S.		$4.00
A&M	AMSAD00137	Things I Do in Denver When Dead	DJ/Smplr	U.S.	1996	$8.00
BMG	PROMO 126	Think Big Get A Head	DJ/Smplr	Australia	1991	$15.00
Epic	ESK 47492	This Beat Is Hot	DJ/Smplr	U.S.	1991	$8.00
Landmark	0101	This Is Independent Distribution Vol. I	DJ/Smplr	U.S.		$8.00
A&M	CD 17946	This Is Not the Age of Aquarius	DJ/Smplr	U.S.	1989	$6.00
	CD in jewelbox and Back sleeve.					
A&M	CD 17946	This Is Not the Age of Aquarius	DJ/Smplr	U.S.	1989	$10.00
	CD in oversized paper sleeve.					
A&M	31458 8033	This Music Knows What Month It Is	DJ/Smplr	U.S.	1993	$8.00
		This Thing Just Might Work	DJ/Smplr	U.S.	1995	$18.00
Rykodisc	1009	Three-Inchers of the World	CD3	U.S.		$5.00
DGC	PRO-CD-4230	Time Out	DJ/Smplr	U.S.	1990	$5.00

Label	Catalog Number	Title	Type	Country	Year	Value
Columbia	CSK 4294	Tis the Sampler	DJ/Smplr	U.S.	1991	$10.00
		Today's Leading Ladies	RS	U.S.	1994	$30.00
	2 CD set. Airdate: 6/27/94.					
Mute		Tonal Evidence	DJ/Smplr	U.K.		$30.00
DIR		Top 25 Albums of All Time	RS	U.S.	1989	$60.00
	6 CD set.					
EMI	CDP 7 91714 2	Top Hits, Formel Enis-Brandneu	LTD/LP	Germany	1990	$20.00
	Picture disc CD.					
EMI	SPCD-1519	Top of the U.K.	DJ/Smplr	Japan	1995	$50.00
Polygram Group Distribution		Total Entertainment From PGD	DJ/Smplr	U.S.	1993	$50.00
Capitol	DPRO 79465	Touching	DJ/Smplr	U.S.	1990	$5.00
Capitol	DPRO 79364	Tower Trip, The	DJ/Smplr	U.S.		$5.00
Warner/Reprise	PRO-CD-5798	Trademark of Quality	DJ/Smplr	U.S.	1992	$20.00
Warner/Reprise	PRO-CD-6579	Trademark of Quality	DJ/Smplr	U.S.	1993	$20.00
Capitol		Train Tunes	DJ/Smplr	U.S.	1992	$25.00
MCA	33-3024	Tree Hits on MCA	DJ/Smplr	U.S.	1991	$15.00
	2 CD set					
CBS	C4K 1416	Tree International: CBS Records 1958-1988	DJ/Smplr	U.S.	1988	$35.00
	4 CD set.					
ECM		Tribute	DJ/Smplr	U.S.		$5.00
Enigma	EPRO-300	Tune Master-CD Viewer	DJ/Smplr	U.S.	1989	$15.00
	Picture CD in "viewmaster" package					
Island	PRCD 6683-2	Tunes From the Missing Channel	DJ/Smplr	U.S.	1991	$5.00
A&M	31458 8008	Turn It Down	DJ/Smplr	U.S.	1992	$5.00
Disney	PCD-00078	Twelve Day of Christmas	LTD/LP	Japan		$35.00
		Twenty-Five Years of Rolling Stone Magazine	RS	U.S.		$100.00
	10 CD set. Airdate: 5/25/92 to 8/3/92					
DCC	GZS-PRO-1	Twenty-Four Karat Gold Disc Sampler	DJ/Smplr	U.S.	1993	$65.00
	Gold disc					
		Twisted Willie	DJ/LP	U.S.	1996	$10.00
Time Warner Sound Exchange		Two Dozen Roses	LTD/LP	U.S.	1995	$17.00
BBC		U.K. Early '70s	RS	U.S.	1994	$20.00
	Airdate: 4/25/94.					
Capitol	DPRO-11181	Ultra-Lounge	DJ/Smplr	U.S.	1996	$22.00
	cardboard sleeve.					
Capitol	DPRO-11166	Ultra-Lounge	DJ/Smplr	U.S.	1996	$30.00
	Leopard-skin digipak.					
Capitol		Ultra-Lounge	LTD/LP	U.S.	1996	$25.00
	Leopard-skin digipak.					
Justice	0004	Under Construction	DJ/Smplr	U.S.	1992	$8.00
Uni	MCA3P-2632	Uni Distribution NARM 1993 Sampler	DJ/Smplr	U.S.	1993	$4.00
MCA	17692	Uni/Motown CD Sampler	DJ/Smplr	U.S.	1988	$5.00
Warner/MTV	PCS-117	Unplugged Triangle	DJ/Smplr	Japan	1993	$150.00
	3 tracks from Eric Clapton, Rod Stewart, Neil Young					
MCA	MCA3P-3015	Untamed and True	DJ/Smplr	U.S.	1994	$12.00
Media America		Up-Close – Deadicated	RS	U.S.	1991	$45.00
	2 CD set.					
Uptown	2695	Uptown Sound Sampler, The	DJ/Smplr	U.S.	1993	$5.00
Capitol	DPRO-79874	Various Artists	DJ/Smplr	U.S.		$5.00
Virgin	2525	Various Artists	DJ/Smplr	U.S.	1988	$5.00
Capitol	DPRO-79108	Various Artists	DJ/Smplr	U.S.	1990	$5.00
Capitol		Various Artists 7" Versions	DJ/Smplr	U.S.		$5.00
Varta		Varta Musikpreis '96: Dance Power	SCDJ	Germany	1996	$50.00
	First hologram shaped CD. Limited to 10,000 copies.					
Varta		Varta Musikpreis '96: Rock Power	SCDJ	Germany	1996	$50.00
	First hologram shaped CD. Limited to 10,000 copies.					
Warner Brothers		VH-1: E2 CD	LP	U.S.	1992	$10.00
		Vibe-Rater	DJ/Smplr	U.S.		$8.00
Pioneer	PA85-M017	Video a Go-Go: Volume 2	8" LD	U.S.	1985	$7.00
Pioneer		Video Music Disc Sampler	LD	U.S.		$25.00
Virgin	PRCD 2336	Virgin Black Music Month Sampler	DJ/Smplr	U.S.	1986	$5.00
Virgin	PRCD 2634	Virgin Goes Buck Wild	DJ/Smplr	U.S.	1991	$8.00
Virgin	PRCD 2086	Virgin Music Around the World	DJ/Smplr	U.S.	1987	$8.00
Virgin	PRCD 3114	Virgin Nineteen Ninety	DJ/Smplr	U.S.	1990	$8.00
Virgin	PRCD 2546	Virgin Singles Sampler	DJ/Smplr	U.S.	1988	$8.00
Virgin	PRCD 1288	Virgin Versions	DJ/Smplr	U.S.	1988	$8.00
Virgin		Virgin's 21st Anniversary Sampler	DJ/Smplr	U.K.	1994	$15.00
A&M	31458 7358	Volume Head	DJ/Smplr	U.S.	1992	$8.00
Walt Disney Records	03MS24400	Walt Disney Records Spring 96	DJ/Smplr	U.S.	1996	$15.00
Def American		Wanna Be Indie But We Got Too Much $ Sampler	DJ/Smplr	U.S.	1992	$8.00
Warner Brothers		Warner Archives	DJ/Smplr	U.S.	1993	$15.00

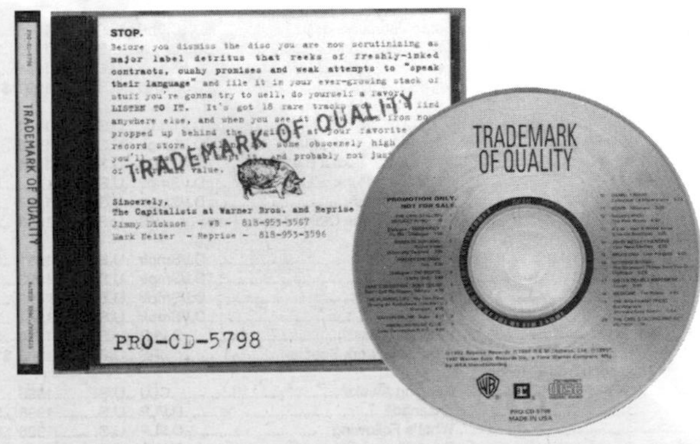

Trademark Of Quality – (Warner Brothers/Reprise PRO-CD-5798)

Label	Catalog Number	Title	Type	Country	Year	Value
Warner Brothers	PRO-CD3764	Warner Bros. Jazz Fall Classics	DJ/Smplr	U.S.	1989	$8.00
Warner Brothers		Warner Brothers	DJ/LP	U.S.	1991	N/A
	36CD set in binder.					
Warner Brothers	PRO-CD-3764	Warner Brothers Jazz Fall Classics	DJ/Smplr	U.S.	1989	$5.00
Warner Brothers		Warner Brothers Presents Loss Leaders Revisited	DJ/Smplr	U.S.		$10.00
Warner Music Group		Warner in Celebration	DJ/Smplr	U.S.	1994	$50.00
	2 CD in blue book-type package.					
Warner Music Group		Warner in Celebration	DJ/Smplr	U.S.	1994	$50.00
	2 CD in red book-type package.					
Warner/Reprise	PRO-CD-5072	Warner Reprise Christmas	DJ/Smplr	U.S.	1991	$10.00
Warner/Reprise	PRO-CD-5859	Warner Reprise Christmas 1992	DJ/Smplr	U.S.	1992	$20.00
Warner Brothers	PRO-CD-4675	Warner Reprise Hits of the '90s	DJ/Smplr	U.S.	1991	$10.00
Warner	PRO-V-5023	Warner Reprise Laserdisc Sampler	DJ/8"LD	U.S.	1992	$50.00
	Picture disc LD.					
Warner	9 38307-6	Warner Reprise Laserdisc Sampler Vol. 2	DJ/8"LD	U.S.	1992	$20.00
Warner Brothers	PRO-CD-3979	Warner Reprise Lost In the '80s	DJ/Smplr	U.S.	1990	$5.00

Label	Catalog Number	Title	Type	Country	Year	Value
Warner Brothers	PRO-CD-6493	Warner Reprise Presents Hearing is Believing	DJ/Smplr	U.S.	1993	$10.00
Mercury	SACD 103	Watch Our Moves	DJ/Smplr	U.S.	1989	$5.00
Wax Trax		Wax Trax Records: The First 13 Years	DJ/Smplr	U.S.	1994	$25.00
Luke	475	We Bring You Joy	DJ/Smplr	U.S.	1993	$5.00
Elektra	PRCD 8809-2	We're In Your Hands	DJ/Smplr	U.S.	1993	$8.00
Polydor	SACD 377	We're Ready	DJ/Smplr	U.S.	1991	$8.00
Mercury	SACD 375	We're Two Planets Over	DJ/Smplr	U.S.	1991	$5.00
Columbia	CSK 4697	Weird Nightmare	DJ/Smplr	U.S.	1992	$5.00
Rykodisc	9002	Welcome to Our World	DJ/Smplr	U.S.	1990	$5.00
Westwood One		Westwood One Concerts Volume 1	DJ/Smplr	U.S.	1993	$50.00
Westwood One		Westwood One Concerts Volume 2	DJ/Smplr	U.S.	1996	$50.00
		What's New	DJ/Smplr	U.S.		$5.00
Disney	PCCW-00019	White Christmas	CD5	Japan	1991	$18.00
Doctor Dream	9158	White Christmas Album	DJ/Smplr	U.S.	1991	$5.00
MCA		White Cliffs of Dover, The	LP	U.S.	1995	$20.00
	2 CD set.					
White Cloud	110010	White Cloud Sampler 1	DJ/Smplr	U.S.	1995	$18.00
Sparrow	SGD WNTR 90	White Hot Winter	DJ/Smplr	U.S.	1990	$5.00
Columbia	CSK 1214	White's Radio	DJ/Smplr	U.S.	1988	$5.00
Windham Hill	WD 17748	Windham Hill Radio Sampler Vol. 1	DJ/Smplr	U.S.	1989	$10.00
Windham	WD-1024	Windham Hill Sampler '82	LP/LB	U.S.†	1985	$14.00/$8.00
Windham	WD-1035	Windham Hill Sampler '84	LP/LB	U.S.†	1985	$14.00/$8.00
Windswept Pacific		Windswept Pacific Song Sampler	DJ/Smplr	U.S.	1992	$50.00
	10 CD set.					
Wing	SACD 357	Wing Christmas	DJ/Smplr	U.S.	1990	$8.00
Columbia	CSK 2921	Winter Heat	DJ/Smplr	U.S.	1988	$5.00
Eastest	PRCD 4391-2	Winter Hits	DJ/Smplr	U.S.	1992	$5.00
		Winter Slamin' Jamin'	DJ/Smplr	U.S.		$5.00
Warner Brothers	PRO-CD-3328	Winter Wonderland	DJ/Smplr	U.S.		$25.00
Sony	A 18403	Winter Wonderland	LP	U.S.	1992	$18.00
Geffen	PRO-CD-4542	Wipe Out	DJ/Smplr	U.S.	1993	$15.00
Geffen	PRO-CD-4542	Wipe Out	DJ/Smplr	U.S.	1993	$5.00
	Distributed in CD cleaning kit					
Gospel Music Association		With One Voice	DJ/Smplr	U.S.	1996	$15.00
	Multi-Image cover.					
EPA		With Our Compliments	DJ/Smplr	U.S.		$5.00
Rykodisc		With These Hands: Music & Interview Session	DJ/Smplr	U.S.	1996	$35.00
WMG		WMG, Inc. Quality Sampler	DJ/Smplr	U.S.	1996	$6.00
Atlantic	400-2	Woodstock	LP/LB	U.S.		$26.00/$22.00
	2 CD set.					
MFSL	MFCD-816	Woodstock	LP	U.S.†	1985	$80.00
	4 CD set.					
Atlantic		Woodstock	LP	U.S.	1994	$50.00
	3 CD first pressing with limited edition computer demo disc					
Time Warner		Woodstock 25th Anniversary CD-ROM	DJ/Smplr	U.S.	1994	$375.00
	2 CD-ROM in large, custom wood box with presskit and T-shirt.					
		Woodstock Anniversary Special	RS	U.S.	1994	$75.00
	3 CD set.					
		Woodstock Best of the Rest	RS	U.S.	1994	$175.00
	4 CD set.					
A&M		Woodstock Box Set Sampler	DJ/Smplr	U.S.	1994	$20.00
		Woodstock Minutes	RS	U.S.	1989	$70.00
	5 CD set					
		Woodstock Minutes	RS	U.S.	1994	$150.00
	6 CD set. Airdates: 7/3/94 to 8/7/94.					
		Woodstock Minutes	RS	U.S.	1994	$30.00
	Various artists music and interview show. Airdate: 7/13/94					
		Woodstock Radio Show	RS	U.S.	1994	$75.00
	4 CD set.					
		Woodstock Re-visited	RS	U.S.	1994	$40.00
	3 CD set.					
Global Satellite Network		Woodstock Revisited: Summer of '69	RS	U.S.	1994	$40.00
	4 CD set. Airdate: 7/3/94.					
		Woodstock Revisited: Where Are They Now?	RS	U.S.	1989	$70.00
	3 CD set.					
		Woodstock Revisited: Where Are They Now?	RS	U.S.	1994	$70.00
	3 CD set.					
		Woodstock Road	RS	U.S.	1994	$75.00
	3 CD set.					
		Woodstock Rock Blocks	RS	U.S.	1994	$75.00
	5 CD set. Airdate: 8/8/94.					
		Woodstock: Spotlight On A Generation	RS	U.S.	1989	$70.00
	5 CD set.					
Hollywood		Working Class Hero – A Tribute to John Lennon	DJ/LP	U.S.	1995	$13.00
Hollywood		Working Class Hero – A Tribute to John Lennon	DJ/Smplr	U.S.	1995	$10.00
ECM	WM2	World	DJ/Smplr	U.S.	1991	$5.00
		World Music	RS	U.S.	1991	$125.00
	2 CD set. Airdate: 9/2/91.					
Columbia	CSK 4171	Would U Like 2 Touch My Sampler	DJ/Smplr	U.S.	1991	$5.00
Musicland		Xtreme Music Sampler	DJ/Smplr	U.S.	1996	$6.00
	06044	Yakety Yak Take It Back	CD5	U.S.	1991	$5.00
Geffen		Year of the Punk	DJ/Smplr	U.S.		$12.00
Virgin	PR 1016	Young Virgins	DJ/Smplr	U.S.	1987	$5.00
Westwood One		Your Goodtime Oldies Theme Party	RS	U.S.	1993	$50.00
	12 CD set.					
Blue Note	DPRO 79345	Yule Struttin'	DJ/Smplr	U.S.	1991	$10.00
Rhino		Yule Train	DJ/Smplr	U.S.	1993	$15.00
Zoo	72445	Zoo Rave	DJ/Smplr	U.S.	1992	$8.00
Zoo Ent	ZP 17009	Zoology	DJ/Smplr	U.S.	1991	$5.00
		Peace at Last	DJ/LP	U.S.	1996	$15.00
Album Network		Album Network Special	RS	U.S.	1996	$120.00
	2 CD set. Airdate 4/7/96.					
A&M	AMSAD 00107	Keeping Awake	CDJ	U.S.	1996	$3.00
		Ensanada	DJ/LP	U.S.	1996	$15.00
		What's Following	DJ/LP	U.S.	1996	$15.00
		Plantation	DJ/LP	U.S.	1996	$15.00
		Twilight	DJ/LP	U.S.	1996	$15.00
		Book Of	DJ/LP	U.S.	1996	$15.00

Miscellaneous

Label	Catalog Number	Title	Type	Country	Year	Value
ABC Television		1995–1996 Fall Programming	DJ/Smplr	U.S.	1995	$50.00
		2 CD-ROM Set.				
NBC		1996 Photography: It's Must See on NBC	DJ/Smplr	U.S.	1996	N/A
		CD-ROM press kit and photography.				
NBC		1996 Photography: Monster May on NBC	DJ/Smplr	U.S.	1996	N/A
		CD-ROM press kit and photography.				
Warner Media Services		38th Annual Grammy Program Book CD-ROM, The	DJ/Smplr	U.S.	1996	$25.00
		CD-ROM				
Sound Source		Adventures of Batman & Robin	LP	U.S.	1994	$25.00
		CD-ROM comic book.				
Pioneer		All There is to Know About Laserdisc, Foresight, Synthesized Surround Processor	DJ/LD	U.S.	1984	$100.00
U.S. Magna Corps	VMAHG01	Anime Hyperguide Volume 1: Project A-ko	LTD/LP	U.S.	1996	$25.00
		Limited edition picture disc CD-ROM.				
Inverse Ink	1	Aquaman: War of the Water Worlds	LTD/LP	U.S.	1996	$10.00
		CD-ROM comic book in folder.				
Inverse Ink	1	Batman: Partners in Peril	LTD/LP	U.S.	1996	$10.00
		CD-ROM comic book in folder.				
Inverse Ink	1	Bobby's World: One Clump or Two?	LTD/LP	U.S.	1996	$10.00
		CD-ROM comic book in folder.				
Buena Vista Television		Buena Vista Television 1995 Fall Programming Multimedia CD-ROM	DJ/Smplr	U.S.	1995	$65.00
		2 CD-ROM set.				
Philips		CD+I Demonstration Disc	DJ/Smplr	U.S.	1992	$30.00
		Promotional CD+I.				
CD-I International		CD-I World Volume 1	DJ/Smplr	U.S.	1992	$20.00
		Promotional CD+I.				
CEMA		CEMA Home Theater 1996 Press Kit	DJ/Smplr	U.S.	1996	$15.00
		CD-ROM press kit.				
Pioneer		Checking Dolby Surround	DJ/LD	Japan		$100.00
Charles S. Anderson	100/76	CSA Archive CD-ROM	LTD/LP	U.S.	1995	$100.00
		CD-ROM in round embossed tin with enamel pin.				
Pioneer		Digital Sound Demo Disc	DJ/LD	U.S.		$70.00
Philips		Digital Video Demo Disc	DJ/Smplr	U.S.	1993	$10.00
		CD+I				
CD+I World		Digital Video Free Demo Disc	DJ/Smplr	U.K.	1994	$20.00
		CD+I				
DMI		DMI Image Disc	DJ/Smplr	U.S.	1995	$10.00
		Promotional Image disc, promoting technology				
Sound Source		Exo Squad	LP	U.S.	1994	$25.00
		CD-ROM comic book.				
Pioneer		F2 Test Disc	DJ/LD	U.S.		$100.00
Toy Biz	48250	Fantastic Four	LP	U.S.	1995	$10.00
		CD-ROM comic book.				
Malibu		Feex #1	LP	U.S.	1995	$12.00
		CD-ROM comic Book				
Pioneer		Frank's Big Decision	DJ/8"LD	U.S.		$10.00
Malibu		Hard Case #1	LP	U.S.	1995	$12.00
		CD-ROM comic Book				
Toy Biz		Iron Man	LP	U.S.	1995	$10.00
		CD-ROM comic book.				
Pioneer	USP-001	Laserdisc: What is it/How Does it Work	DJ/LD	U.S.	1981	$200.00
Discovision		Leonard Nemoy Demonstrates the Magnavision Videodisc Player	DJ/LD	U.S.	1981	$180.00
Kid Rhino		Mad: Bytes It!	LTD/LP	U.S.	1996	$10.00
		CD sampler and America Online software distributed free with October 1996 Mad Magazine.				
Magnavox		Magnivox Retail Demonstration Disc	DJ/LD	U.S.	1980	$150.00
Soft Key	PLM5AE-BI	Mask: The Original	LP	U.S.	1994	$10.00
		CD-ROM comic book.				
Discovision		MCA Consumer Demonstration Disc	DJ/LD	U.S.	1978	$180.00
	SM078-3105	Mercedes Benz: 100 Years	LD	U.S.		$30.00
Discovision	64-013	Money in the Marketplace and Choosing What to Buy	LD	U.S.	1979	$40.00
Metatec		Nautilus CD	LP	U.S.	1995	$25.00
		CD-ROM with promo of never-released John Lennon CD-ROM.				
Sega		Night Trap	LP	U.S.	1995	$40.00
		Original Sega CD CD-ROM.				
IBM		OS/2 Warp	SCD5	Germany	1995	$20.00
		Television setshaped disc. CD-ROM sampler				
Paramount	LV 26349	Paramount Pictures Promotional Sampler Laserdisc	LD	U.S.	1992	$35.00
Pioneer	HEDP-92002U	Pioneer Home Theater	LD	U.S.	1992	$50.00
Pioneer	PA-89-01	Pioneer: Laser Optics II	DJ/LD	U.S.	1989	$25.00
Pioneer		Pioneer Presents High Fidelity for Humans	DJ/LD	U.S.		$100.00
Pioneer		Player Operating Instructions	DJ/LD	U.S.		$100.00
Malibu		Prime #1	LP	U.S.	1995	$12.00
		CD-ROM comic Book				
RCA/Columbia		RCA/Columbia Demo Disc	DJ/LD	U.S.	1991	$30.00
Irwin	30672	Reboot Action Figure: Bob	LP	Canada	1996	$12.00
		Action figure with 5-color off-set printed CD-ROM game.				
Irwin	30671	Reboot Action Figure: Dot	LP	Canada	1996	$12.00
		Action figure with 5-color off-set printed CD-ROM game.				
Irwin	30670	Reboot Action Figure: Enzo	LP	Canada	1996	$12.00
		Action figure with 5-color off-set printed CD-ROM game.				
Irwin	30676	Reboot Action Figure: Frisket	LP	Canada	1996	$12.00
		Action figure with 5-color off-set printed CD-ROM game.				
Irwin	30674	Reboot Action Figure: Hack	LP	Canada	1996	$15.00
		Action figure with 5-color off-set printed CD-ROM game.				
Irwin	30673	Reboot Action Figure: Megabyte	LP	Canada	1996	$12.00
		Action figure with 5-color off-set printed CD-ROM game.				
Irwin	30675	Reboot Action Figure: Slash	LP	Canada	1996	$15.00
		Action figure with 5-color off-set printed CD-ROM game.				
Inverse Ink		Reflux.01	LTD/LP	U.S.	1995	$12.00
		CD-ROM comic book.				
Inverse Ink		Reflux.02	LTD/LP	U.S.	1996	$12.00
		CD-ROM comic book.				
Republic Pictures		Republic Pictures Home Video Catalog: Volume 2	LP	U.S.	1996	$15.00
		CD-ROM				
Scotch		Scotch Videodisc	DJ/LD	U.S.		$100.00
		Sears Catalog (1981)	LD	U.S.	1981	$250.00
		Multimedia catalog for Sears Department Store.				
CBS		Season Line-Up	DJ/Smplr	U.S.	1995	$45.00
		CD-ROM sampler.				
Sega		Sega Proven Family Fun	DJ/Smplr	U.S.	1996	N/A
		Cool Disc™ CD-ROM sampler.				
Sega		Sega Virtua Fighter PC	DJ/Smplr	U.S.	1996	N/A
		Cool Disc™ CD-ROM sampler.				
Toy Biz	48271T	Silver Surfer	LTD/LP	U.S.	1996	$15.00
		CD-ROM with Silver Surfer action figure.				
Toy Biz		Spider Man	LP	U.S.	1995	$10.00
		CD-ROM comic book.				
Sound Source	SWWNEUDS09	Star Trek: Deep Space Nine CD-ROM Entertainment Utility	LTD/LP	U.S.	1996	$35.00
		CD-ROM screen utility. Numbered limited edition.				
Interplay	XD-ICD-200-0	Star Trek: Judgement Rites	LTD/LP	U.S.	1995	$60.00
		2 CD-ROM set in numbered box, with VHS video and pin.				
Spectrum Halobyte		Star Trek Next Generation: Final Unity	LTD/LP	U.S.	1995	$60.00
		Limited edition CD-ROM game in numbered plastic box box, with pin.				
Playmates	16004	Star Trek: Star Fleet Academy – Cadet Geordi LaForge	LP	U.S.	1996	$9.00
		CD-ROM with Star Trek action figure.				
Playmates	16001	Star Trek: Star Fleet Academy – Cadet Jean Luc Picard	LP	U.S.	1996	$9.00
		CD-ROM with Star Trek action figure.				
Playmates	16002	Star Trek: Star Fleet Academy – Cadet William Riker	LP	U.S.	1996	$9.00
		CD-ROM with Star Trek action figure.				
Playmates	16005	Star Trek: Star Fleet Academy – Cadet Worf	LP	U.S.	1996	$9.00
		CD-ROM with Star Trek action figure.				
Sound Source	SWWNCLSW04	Star Wars Trilogy CD-ROM Entertainment Utility	LTD/LP	U.S.	1995	$35.00
		CD-ROM screen utility. Numbered limited edition.				
Inverse Ink	1	Superboy: Spies From Outer Space	LTD/LP	U.S.	1996	$10.00
		CD-ROM comic book in folder.				
Inverse Ink	1	Superman: The Mysterious Mr. Mist	LTD/LP	U.S.	1996	$10.00
		CD-ROM comic book in folder.				
Sound Source	SWWNEUTM01	T2 CD-ROM Entertainment Utility	LTD/LP	U.S.	1996	$35.00
		CD-ROM screen utility. Numbered limited edition.				
TDK	CDK 0100	TDK's Ultimate Guide to Recording From CDs	Smplr	U.S.	1991	$10.00
Inverse Ink	1	Tick, The: The Tick v. The Uncommon Cold	LTD/LP	U.S.	1996	$10.00
		CD-ROM comic book in folder.				
Pioneer		Tune Up Audio/Video	DJ/LD	Japan		$100.00
Applewood Books	357	Walt Disney's Story of Clarabelle Cow	LTD/LP	U.S.	1996	$40.00
		Picture CD with reproduction of the1930s Disneyana book in slip case. Limited to 2,500 copies.				
Applewood Books	355	Walt Disney's Story of Dippy the Goof	LTD/LP	U.S.	1996	$40.00
		Picture CD with reproduction of the1930s Disneyana book in slip case. Limited to 2,500 copies.				
Applewood Books	354	Walt Disney's Story of Donald Duck	LTD/LP	U.S.	1996	$40.00
		Picture CD with reproduction of the1930s Disneyana book in slip case. Limited to 2,500 copies.				
Applewood Books	352	Walt Disney's Story of Mickey Mouse	LTD/LP	U.S.	1996	$40.00
		Picture CD with reproduction of the1930s Disneyana book in slip case. Limited to 2,500 copies.				
Applewood Books	353	Walt Disney's Story of Minnie Mouse	LTD/LP	U.S.	1996	$40.00
		Picture CD with reproduction of the1930s Disneyana book in slip case. Limited to 2,500 copies.				
Applewood Books	356	Walt Disney's Story of Pluto the Pup	LTD/LP	U.S.	1996	$40.00
		Picture CD with reproduction of the1930s Disneyana book in slip case. Limited to 2,500 copies.				
Toy Biz	48230	X-Men	LP	U.S.	1995	$10.00
		CD-ROM comic book.				
Toy Biz	48272T	X-Men	LTD/LP	U.S.	1996	$15.00
		CD-ROM with X-Men figure.				
ZDNet		ZDNet	DJ/Smplr	U.S.	1996	$25.00
		CD-ROM 3-D•ld disc.				

Endnotes

[1]Japan and Germany were the locations of the only CD manufacturing plants in the world from 1982 to 1984. A few titles were made for Columbia and RCA by the first two U.S. pressing plants — Digital Audio Disc Corporation and Laservideo (now Disc Manufacturing, Inc.) in 1984 and 1985. Most CDs however, were still imported up until 1986.

[2]Today U.S. labels occasionally purchase discs from England, Germany, or Japan if needed to fill the demand for a particular title. This was the case for the release of Guns 'N Roses albums *Use Your Illusion I and II* in 1991. Because the initial demand for the album was so great, many consumers found that their disc was pressed in Germany rather than the DADC plant in Indiana where most of these discs were manufactured. These CDs however, are not "first issues" and generally hold no more value than their domestic counterpart.

[3]These discs usually start out on the secondary market valued at their current retail price.

[4]Theoretically, first issues are a subset of first pressings because first issues were the first pressing of many currently available titles.

[5]The track listing of this disc is identical to the track listing for the 1988 U.S. CDV of the same title, less the video track.

[6]Do not confuse the CD-single CD5 with the promotional CD-single CDJ. Both are 5" CD-single formats but distributed to different markets.

[7]At this time premium discs have no other designation in the listing other than LP or LTD/ LP.

[8]A blister card is a component of the blister pack. Blister packs are outer packages for the CD having the same dimensions as the long box. Blister packs however, are clear plastic clamshells encasing the jewel box. Often a panel is placed on the front face of the blister pack for graphical purposes. This card is called a blister card.

[9]The white box printed on back containing a series of different sized vertical lines and numbers.

[10]CD-ROM press kits are also becoming cross-collectibles with traditional paper press kit collectors, hence expanding their collectible base and increasing their demand.

[11]Those are just the imports we have been able to find out about.

[12]A U.S. CD having a wholesale price of $11 and selling for $15 allows less room to invest in special packaging than does a comparable Japanese title that wholesales for $15 to $16 and sells for $28. Larger profit margins for both the manufacturer and the retailer mean more resources can be used to create special editions. What's more, sources have told the *CCDPG* that the cost of making a CD in Japan is about the same as it is in the United States.

[13]This cloud of illegality has also enhanced mystique to import CD-singles adding to their collectibility.

[14]"Parallels" are foreign CDs available having a similar U.S version. For our purposes parallels are analogous to gray market goods.

[15]Thanks to Wes Oishi from Sound Source in Los Angeles for his assistance with this section.

[16]The CDV's video format is the same as the traditional 12" laser disc format (not digital video) which is why this video information can only be played on a laser disc player and not on a CD player equipped to play digital video.

[17]The metal reflective layer is in fact aluminum common to most compact discs. CDVs should therefore not be considered "gold discs" i.e. disc's whose reflective layer is made from 24K gold.

[18]This is why CD+G discs can play in a normal CD player without any effect to sound quality.

[19]DVD uses the MPEG-2 format.

[20]Do not confuse "test discs" or "acetate masters" which carry over from the vinyl LP world. By nature of the manufacturing process of vinyl LPs, test discs were necessary to determine the quality of the cutting tool, master disc, etc. In the CD world these considerations are irrelevant. Every master and CD is tested electronically before and during the manufacturing process. There is no need to make a special run to test every stamper disc or master disc. Disc testing is most often done in the label printing process. Usually the first few discs that run though the printing press are checked for print quality. That is why an unprinted disc which is currently termed a "test pressing" in the collectors' world is not really a test pressing. Rather it is simply a disc that has not gone through the label printing process. If disc testing is done, usually an entire press run is made rather than just one disc.

[21]"Acetate masters" is another term derived from the days of vinyl misapplied to CDRs and not used in the CD industry. The CD industry uses glass masters, stamper discs, etc., not an acetate master.

[22]If you see a Tori Amos Y Kan't Tori Read European limited edition for sale, it is a pirated CDR.

[23]Usually a set of instructions on how and why to skip track one is included.

[24]The computer data is actually on track zero of the CD.

[25]Zoo claims that the this technology was developed independently of Justice. Verna, Paul. "Hidden Track Exposes Conflict," *Billboard*, 16 April 1994.

[26]Verna, Paul. "Texas Indie Sues Sony/Philips Over Patents," *Billboard*, 13 January 1996.
[27]This starting point is opposite to that of a traditional vinyl record.
[28]The booklets must be thick enough to press booklet's cover up against the inside of the jewel box lid.
[29]Day, ReBecca. "Where's the Rot?" *Stereo Review*. April 1989.p, 23.
[30]Cellitti, David Robert. "Collecting DiscoVision." *Perfect Vision*. p.103.
[31]McGouldrick, Stephen. *Laser 4*. p.1
[32]Now Pioneer Video Manufacturing, Inc.
[33]One interesting point of contention within DiscoVision was the infighting between MCA and IBM over the production of adult titles on laser disc. It was shortly after this dispute that IBM decided to pull out of the partnership.
[34]Pioneer purchased the entire interest in DiscoVision but for the patents accumulated over the years
[35]I wonder how much of the laser disc market is subsidized by the compact disc market since Pioneer received significant revenue from the sale of CDs.
[36]These patents are the sole assets of the company.
[37]The following chapter provided courtesy of the Recording Industry Association of America.
[38]Courtesy the Recording Industry Association of America.
[39]The United States is applying pressure to countries like Japan to adhere to international treaties that protect all recordings made after 1946. Much of America's modern culture evolved from the music of the 50s and 60s, and much of that music is subject to piracy.
[40]As we discussed before, "acetate" is an improper designation for a CDR.
[41]This section courtesy the Recording Industry Association of America.
[42]McClure, Steve. "The Sony Perspective." *Billboard*, 26 Sept. 1992 p. CD-10.
[43]Much of the information in this section was graciously provided by Marc Finer of Communication Research, Inc., former Products Communications Manager for Sony Electronics.
[44]Nakajima, H. and T. Doi, J. Fukuda and A. Iga. *The Sony Book of Digital Audio Technology*. Summit, PA: Tab Books Inc., 1983. pp. 8-9.
[45]Ibid. at p.124.
[46]Sony did not purchase CBS Records and their catalog of music until 1987.
[47]Miller, Trudi. "CD's Launch The Hidden History." *Billboard*, 26 Sept. 1992 p. CD-6.
[48]Laservideo is now Disc Manufacturing, Inc.
[49]These codes were made for use on all audio formats, thus if used for vinyl LPs, the last character designation would always be A since vinyl is an analog music carrier.
[50]The labels therefore, had no legal recourse against retailers selling used CDs from a copyright theory.
[51]In fact the Garth Brooks CD *In Pieces* was not distributed to stores that were suspected of selling used CDs.
[52]The survey was commissioned by the National Association of Recording Merchandisers and Sound Data Inc., conducted by George Fine Surveys, Inc. The survey was conducted during July and August 1993 via telephone to 1,200 consumers age 12 and older.
[53]Holland, Bill, "Class Action Suit Claiming Price Fixing Filed Against Major Labels" *Billboard*, July 20, 1996.
[54]Chris Robinson and George Silvey v. EMI Music Distribution et. al. L-10462.
[55]A practice whereby CDs are sold at or below wholesale to entice consumers to visit the store in hopes of not only buying the CD but maybe a new CD player as well.
[56]Ibid.
[57]Ibid.
[58]Digital Distribution d/b/a/ Compact Disc Warehouse v. CEMA et al., 95-3596.
[59]Apparently this tactic was made to force MTV to pay royalties for the videos the labels supply them, and which MTV currently receives free.
[60]Jewel box is the term for the three piece plastic case that houses your CD. The jewel case comprises a base, a tray that secures into the base and which the CD fits onto, and a lid that hingedly attaches to the base.
[61]Ironically, the digipak returned years later and has become the number one packaging alternative to the jewel box. Over 300 million CDs since 1985 have been packaged in the digipak cardboard packaging.
[62]There is a question whether this 23 million pounds is accurate, but to opponents of the long box it hardly seemed to matter.
[63]An important consideration when you need to produce hundreds of thousands, if not millions of discs.
[64]This category was not introduced separately until 1994.
[65]Some used CD stores have become very selective in what CDs they take, usually buying only your most popular discs and refusing the rest. If you run into a dealer like this, demand much more for each disc that he or she is initially willing to offer.
[66]However, with such a new collectible, it is as of yet impossible to distinguish a definite value of a first issue with an original jewel box and a first issue without an original jewel box.
[67]Including compact disc, laser disc, minidisc, CD-ROM, etc.

Phone: (410) 356-4567
FAX: (410) 356-4693
11459 Cronhill Drive
Suite O
Owings Mills, MD 21117
U.S.A.
music machine
Rock Specialist
SEE OUR Full PAGE ADS in EVERY ISSUE OF Goldmine
WE STOCK FULL LENGTH CD'S & MAXI-CD'S FROM AROUND THE WORLD!!
US + UK PROMOS!!
HARD to FIND Imports!! JAPAN • GERMANY • U.K.
BOX SETS + ltd. special packs!!
WE ALSO CARRY NEW + OLD VINYL!
LP'S, 12" + 7"
Worldwide Mail Order
SPECIAL ORDERS + WANT LISTS TAKEN!

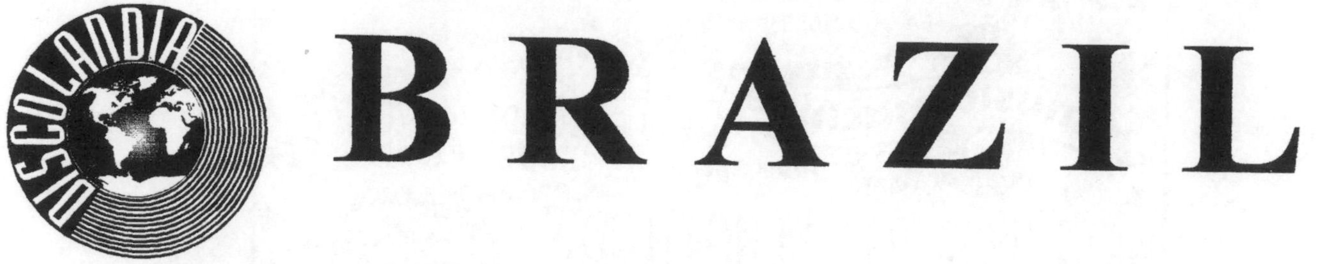
DISCOLANDIA
BRAZIL